YEARBOOK OF THE
UNITED NATIONS
1984

Volume 38

YEARBOOK
OF THE
UNITED
NATIONS
1984

Volume 38

Department of Public Information
United Nations, New York

COPYRIGHT © 1988 UNITED NATIONS

ISSN: 0082-8521

ISBN: 92-1-100398-9

s/o

UNITED NATIONS PUBLICATION

SALES NO. E.87.I.1

09000

Foreword

FROM the day the United Nations came into being, it has had to face diverse issues arising from massive changes in human affairs. As this transition has generated new demands and expectations, global concerns have vastly multiplied. These range from banishing the spectre of a nuclear holocaust to reducing poverty, eradicating racial discrimination and promoting the rights of the disadvantaged such as women and children, the handicapped and the elderly. Added to them have been emergencies of various kinds: some man-made like armed conflicts, others the result of natural disasters including famine and drought. On all these questions, the United Nations is the central instrument through which States can jointly devise the appropriate policies or courses of action.

Decisions made at the United Nations are often inadequately reported in the world press. It is understandable, therefore, that only those professionally involved are well acquainted with the working of the world Organization. Far removed from the headlines is the quiet drama, the unsung heroism infusing the enterprise of the United Nations in far-flung lands. Unarmed, a blue-bereted soldier dies while trying to keep apart warring parties in a country not his own; a tree is planted to hold back the encroaching desert; a shelter is built for refugees to provide against the coming monsoon; and a malnourished child receives the food vital to her very existence. This is the human face of plans and programmes launched by the world body.

I commend the *Yearbook of the United Nations* to everyone who wishes to study how, in a particular year, nations addressed the complex problems confronting them. The tale is told without embellishment; the record is of success as well as stalemate but it has to be judged on a continuous basis. At any rate, the direction of the effort—towards a world with steadily less fear, misery and violence and greater order, justice, respect for human rights and compassion—is beyond question.

Javier PÉREZ DE CUÉLLAR
Secretary-General

Contents

Part One: *United Nations*

POLITICAL AND SECURITY QUESTIONS

ECONOMIC AND SOCIAL QUESTIONS

TRUSTEESHIP AND DECOLONIZATION

LEGAL QUESTIONS

ADMINISTRATIVE AND BUDGETARY QUESTIONS

Part Two: *Intergovernmental organizations related to the United Nations*

Appendices

Indexes

About the 1984 edition of the *Yearbook*

The 1984 *YEARBOOK OF THE UNITED NATIONS* has been designed as a reference tool for use not only by diplomats and other officials but also by writers, researchers, journalists, librarians and students, in fact all who might need readily available information on a particular activity of the United Nations system.

The *Yearbook* covers, during a calendar year, the main activities of the United Nations (Part One) and those of each related organization in the United Nations system (Part Two).

The 1984 edition is subject-oriented like previous editions. Part One (United Nations), containing 50 chapters, is divided into five major sections: political and security questions, economic and social questions, trusteeship and decolonization, legal questions, and administrative and budgetary questions.

Each chapter is divided into a hierarchy of topics, with each level having a heading of distinctive appearance. The assignment of headings implies no editorial judgement about the relative importance of a topic.

Structure and scope of articles

Presented under each topical heading is a summary of pertinent United Nations activities, including those of intergovernmental and expert bodies, major reports, Secretariat activities, and the views of States in written communications. The 1984 edition also gives the position of those States explaining their votes in the principal organs of the Organization. Such explanations are generally given when a recorded vote was taken. At the end of each chapter or subchapter is a list of references, linked by numerical indicators to the text. These references indicate document symbols, previous *Yearbook* volumes supplying additional information, and previous resolutions and/or decisions by the principal United Nations organs. The *Yearbook* covers the following:

Activities of United Nations bodies. All resolutions, decisions and other major activities of the principal organs and, where applicable, those of subsidiary bodies, including sub-commissions and sub-committees, are either reproduced or summarized in the respective articles. The texts of all resolutions and decisions adopted by the General Assembly, the Security Council, the Economic and Social Council and the Trusteeship Council, with information on their adoption, are reproduced under the relevant topic. Where provisions of other resolutions and decisions of those bodies are mentioned, the full text can be found by using the INDEX OF RESOLUTIONS AND DECISIONS at the end of this volume.

Major reports. Most 1984 reports of the Secretary-General on which a United Nations body took action during the year, along with selected reports from other United Nations sources such as seminars and working groups, are summarized briefly under the relevant topic(s). The document symbols of all reports cited in an article appear in the references.

Secretariat activities. The operational activities of the United Nations for development and humanitarian assistance are described under the relevant topics. For all major activities financed outside the United Nations regular budget, information is given on contributions by individual countries and on expenditures. Financial data are generally obtained from the audited accounts prepared for each fund, and cover the 1984 calendar year unless otherwise specified.

Views of States. Each written communication sent to the United Nations by a Member State and circulated separately as a document of a principal organ has been summarized under the most relevant topic.

All substantive debates in the Security Council have been analysed by *Yearbook* editors, and their main points can be found under the pertinent topic(s). Users wishing details on the position of individual States in the principal organs of the United Nations or any of their main/sessional committees should refer to the meeting numbers to be found at the end of the summaries of procedural action following all resolution/decision texts.

Related intergovernmental organizations. Part Two of the *Yearbook* describes the 1984 activities of each specialized agency and the International Atomic Energy Agency, based on information prepared by them. Included are data on budgets, contributions by member States, and principal officials.

Texts

The *Yearbook* reproduces the texts of all resolutions and substantive decisions adopted in 1984 by the General Assembly, the Security Council, the Economic and Social Council and the Trusteeship Council. These texts, together with the title (if any) of the resolution/decision, are followed by the procedural details giving: date of adoption, meeting number and vote totals (in favour-against-abstaining); information on their approval by a sessional or subsidiary body prior to final adoption, with document symbols of drafts, approved amendments and committee reports; and a list of sponsors. Also given are the document symbols of any financial implications and all relevant meeting numbers of the principal organs and the General Assembly's Main Committees. Details of any recorded or roll-call vote on the resolution/decision as a whole also follow the text.

Terminology

Formal titles of bodies, organizational units, conventions, declarations and officials are given in full on first mention in an article or sequence of articles. They are also used in resolution/decision texts, and in the SUBJECT INDEX under the key word of the title.

Short titles may be used in subsequent references. They employ key words, usually not capitalized, from the formal title, such as "Committee on colonial countries" for "Special Committee on the Situation with regard to the Implementation of the Declaration on the Granting of Independence to Colonial Countries and Peoples". Capital letters are used when the only difference between full and short title is the omission of a term such as "*Ad Hoc*", "International", "Special" or "United Nations" ("Committee against *Apartheid*", for "Special Committee against *Apartheid*"). These short titles have no official standing.

How to find information in the *Yearbook*

The 1984 edition has been designed to enable the user to locate information on United Nations activities in a number of ways.

By subject: Broad subjects may be located in the table of contents on pages vi-xii. Each chapter opens with an introduction highlighting the main developments. Where a main topic is subdivided, shorter introductions may precede subchapters. Cross-references give chapters for related information. The SUBJECT INDEX may be used to locate individual topics and specific references to the bodies dealing with each.

By body: Although the *Yearbook* is oriented by subject rather than by body, surveys of the work of many bodies appear under the topic of their main concern. For the principal organs, APPENDIX IV gives the 1984 agenda for each session. The members, officers, and date and place of sessions of each body are given in APPENDIX III. The SUBJECT INDEX lists bodies by the key word(s) of their formal title: "*Apartheid*, Special Committee against".

By resolution and decision number: A numerical list of all resolutions and substantive decisions adopted in 1984 by the principal organs, with page numbers for their text, appears in the final pages of this volume.

Each resolution/decision text appears in an article together with the circumstances of its adoption. Summaries of relevant provisions of other resolutions or decisions may also be added where applicable.

Other information: The annual report of the Secretary-General on the work of the Organization in 1984 is reproduced, beginning on page 3. A list of Member States, with their dates of admission to the United Nations, comprises APPENDIX I. The Charter of the United Nations, including the Statute of the International Court of Justice, is in APPENDIX II. An INDEX OF NAMES follows the SUBJECT INDEX.

ABBREVIATIONS COMMONLY USED IN THE *YEARBOOK*

AALCC	Asian-African Legal Consultative Committee
ACABQ	Advisory Committee on Administrative and Budgetary Questions
ACC	Administrative Committee on Co-ordination
ACPAQ	Advisory Committee on Post Adjustment Questions
ADB	African Development Bank
AMS	Administrative Management Service
ANC	African National Congress of South Africa
APDC	Asian and Pacific Development Centre
ASEAN	Association of South-East Asian Nations
BIS	Bank for International Settlements
CCAQ	Consultative Committee on Administrative Questions
CCIR	International Radio Consultative Committee (ITU)
CCISUA	Committee for Independent Staff Unions and Associations of the United Nations System
CCITT	International Telegraph and Telephone Consultative Committee
CCOP/ SOPAC	Committee for Co-ordination of Joint Prospecting for Mineral Resources in South Pacific Offshore Areas
CCSQ	Consultative Committee on Substantive Questions
CDP	Committee for Development Planning
CEDAW	Committee on the Elimination of Discrimination against Women
CELADE	Latin American Demographic Centre
CERD	Committee on the Elimination of Racial Discrimination
CFA	Committee on Food Aid Policies and Programmes
CILSS	Permanent Inter-State Committee on Drought Control in the Sahel
CMEA	Council for Mutual Economic Assistance
CNR	Committee on Natural Resources
COPAC	Joint Committee for the Promotion of Aid to Co-operatives
COPUOS	Committee on the Peaceful Uses of Outer Space
CPC	Committee for Programme and Co-ordination
CSDHA	Centre for Social Development and Humanitarian Affairs (DIESA)
DAC	Development Assistance Committee (OECD)
DIEC	Development and International Economic Co-operation
DIESA	Department of International Economic and Social Affairs
DIS	Development Information System (ISU)
DPI	Department of Public Information
DTA	Democratic Turnhalle Alliance (Namibia)
DTCD	Department of Technical Co-operation for Development
EC	European Community
ECA	Economic Commission for Africa
ECDC	economic co-operation among developing countries
ECE	Economic Commission for Europe
ECLAC	Economic Commission for Latin America and the Caribbean
ECOWAS	Economic Community of West African States
ECWA	Economic Commission for Western Asia
EEC	European Economic Community
ESA	European Space Agency
ESC	Economic and Social Council
ESCAP	Economic and Social Commission for Asia and the Pacific
EURATOM	European Atomic Energy Community
FADINAP	Fertilizer Advisory, Development and Information Network for Asia and the Pacific
FALPRO	Special Programme on Trade Facilitation
FAO	Food and Agriculture Organization of the United Nations
FICSA	Federation of International Civil Servants' Associations
FRETILIN	Frente Revolucionária de Timor Leste Independente
GA	General Assembly
GATT	General Agreement on Tariffs and Trade
GCO	Greeting Card Operation (UNICEF)
GDP	gross domestic product
GDPS	Global Data-Processing System (WMO)
GEMS	Global Environmental Monitoring System (UNEP)
GNP	gross national product
GOS	Global Observing System (WMO)
GSP	generalized system of preferences
GSTP	global system of trade preferences
GTS	Global Telecommunication System (WMO)
IAEA	International Atomic Energy Agency
IBI	Intergovernmental Bureau of Informatics
ICAO	International Civil Aviation Organization
ICARA	International Conference on Assistance to Refugees in Africa
ICCROM	International Centre for the Study of the Preservation and the Restoration of Cultural Property

ICITO	Interim Commission for the International Trade Organization
ICJ	International Court of Justice
ICRC	International Committee of the Red Cross
ICRP	International Commission on Radiological Protection
ICSC	International Civil Service Commission
IDA	International Development Association
IDB	Industrial Development Board (UNIDO)
IDDA	Industrial Development Decade for Africa
IEFR	International Emergency Food Reserve
IFAD	International Fund for Agricultural Development
IFC	International Finance Corporation
ILC	International Law Commission
ILMAC	Israel-Lebanon Mixed Armistice Commission
ILO	International Labour Organisation
ILPES	Latin American Institute for Economic and Social Planning
IMF	International Monetary Fund
IMO	International Maritime Organization
INCB	International Narcotics Control Board
INFOTERRA	International Referral System for Sources of Environmental Information (UNEP)
INRES	Information Referral System for TCDC
INSTRAW	International Research and Training Institute for the Advancement of Women
INTIB	Industrial and Technological Information Bank (UNIDO)
IOC	International Oceanographic Commission
IPC	International Pepper Community
IPCS	International Programme on Chemical Safety
IPDC	International Programme for Development of Communication (UNESCO)
IPF	indicative planning figure (UNDP)
IRPTC	International Register of Potentially Toxic Chemicals (UNEP)
ISIP	Integrated Systems Improvement Project (UNDP)
ISU	Information Systems Unit (DIESA)
ITC	International Trade Centre (UNCTAD/GATT)
ITO	International Trade Organization
ITU	International Telecommunication Union
IUCN	International Union for Conservation of Nature and Natural Resources
IYDP	International Year of Disabled Persons
IYC	International Year of the Child
IYY	International Youth Year
JAG	Joint Advisory Group on the International Trade Centre
JIU	Joint Inspection Unit
JUNIC	Joint United Nations Information Committee
LDC	least developed country
MFA	Multifibre Arrangement (Arrangement Regarding Trade in Textiles) (GATT)
MULPOC	Multinational Programming and Operational Centre (ECA)
NATO	North Atlantic Treaty Organization
NEA	Nuclear Energy Agency (OECD)
NGO	non-governmental organization
NPT	Treaty on the Non-Proliferation of Nuclear Weapons
NRSE	new and renewable sources of energy
NSGT	Non-Self-Governing Territory
NUSS	Nuclear Safety Standards (IAEA)
OAPEC	Organization of Arab Petroleum Exporting Countries
OAS	Organization of American States
OAU	Organization of African Unity
ODA	official development assistance
OECD	Organisation for Economic Co-operation and Development
OPEC	Organization of Petroleum Exporting Countries
PAC	Pan Africanist Congress of Azania
PADIS	Pan-African Documentation and Information System
PANS	Procedure for Air Navigation Services (ICAO)
PCT	Patent Co-operation Treaty (WIPO)
PHC	primary health care
PLO	Palestine Liberation Organization
POLISARIO	Frente Popular para la Liberación de Saguia el-Hamra y de Río de Oro
POPIN	Population Information Network
PPBB	Programme Planning and Budgeting Board
SADCC	Southern African Development Co-ordination Conference
SALT	strategic arms limitation talks
SC	Security Council
SDR	special drawing right
S-G	Secretary-General
SIDFA	Senior Industrial Development Field Adviser (UNIDO)

SIS	Special Industrial Services (UNIDO)
SNA	United Nations System of National Accounts
SNPA	Substantial New Programme of Action for the 1980s for the Least Developed Countries
SOLAS	International Convention for the Safety of Life at Sea (IMO)
SPC	Special Political Committee
START	strategic arms reduction talks
SWAPO	South West Africa People's Organization (Namibia)
TC	Trusteeship Council
TCDC	technical co-operation among developing countries
TCP	Technical Co-operation Programme (FAO)
TDB	Trade and Development Board (UNCTAD)
TIR	*transport international routier* (international road transport) (ECE)
TNC	transnational corporation
UN	United Nations
UNCDF	United Nations Capital Development Fund
UNCHS	United Nations Centre for Human Settlements (Habitat)
UNCITRAL	United Nations Commission on International Trade Law
UNCIVPOL	United Nations civilian police (UNFICYP)
UNCTAD	United Nations Conference on Trade and Development
UNDOF	United Nations Disengagement Observer Force (Golan Heights)
UNDP	United Nations Development Programme
UNDRO	Office of the United Nations Disaster Relief Co-ordinator
UNEF	United Nations Emergency Force
UNEOTF	United Nations Emergency Operation Trust Fund
UNEP	United Nations Environment Programme
UNESCO	United Nations Educational, Scientific and Cultural Organization
UNFDAC	United Nations Fund for Drug Abuse Control
UNFICYP	United Nations Peace-keeping Force in Cyprus
UNFPA	United Nations Fund for Population Activities
UNFSSTD	United Nations Financing System for Science and Technology for Development
UNHCR	United Nations High Commissioner for Refugees
UNIC	United Nations Information Centre
UNICEF	United Nations Children's Fund

UNIDF	United Nations Industrial Development Fund (UNIDO)
UNIDIR	United Nations Institute for Disarmament Research
UNIDO	United Nations Industrial Development Organization
UNIDROIT	International Institute for the Unification of Private Law
UNIFIL	United Nations Interim Force in Lebanon
UNIPAC	UNICEF Packing and Assembly Centre
UNISPACE-82	Second United Nations Conference on the Exploration and Peaceful Uses of Outer Space
UNITAR	United Nations Institute for Training and Research
UNRFNRE	United Nations Revolving Fund for Natural Resources Exploration
UNRISD	United Nations Research Institute for Social Development
UNRWA	United Nations Relief and Works Agency for Palestine Refugees in the Near East
UNSCEAR	United Nations Scientific Committee on the Effects of Atomic Radiation
UNSDRI	United Nations Social Defence Research Institute
UNSO	United Nations Sudano-Sahelian Office
UNTAG	United Nations Transition Assistance Group
UNTSO	United Nations Truce Supervision Organization (Israel and neighbouring States)
UNU	United Nations University
UNV	United Nations Volunteers
UPU	Universal Postal Union
WAPA	weighted average of post adjustments
WARC	World Administrative Radio Conference
WCIP	World Climate Impact Studies Programme
WFC	World Food Council
WFP	World Food Programme
WFS	World Fertility Survey
WHO	World Health Organization
WIPO	World Intellectual Property Organization
WMO	World Meteorological Organization
WTO	World Tourism Organization
WWW	World Weather Watch (WMO)
YUN	*Yearbook of the United Nations*

EXPLANATORY NOTE ON DOCUMENTS

References at the end of each article in Part One of this volume give the symbols of the main documents issued in 1984 on the topic, arranged in the order in which they are referred to in the text. The following is a guide to the principal document symbols:

A/- refers to documents of the General Assembly, numbered in separate series by session. Thus, A/39/- refers to documents issued for consideration at the thirty-ninth session, beginning with A/39/1. Documents of special and emergency special sessions are identified as A/S- and A/ES-, followed by the session number.

A/C.- refers to documents of six of the Assembly's Main Committees, e.g. A/C.1/- is a document of the First Committee, A/C.6/-, a document of the Sixth Committee. The symbol for documents of the seventh Main Committee, the Special Political Committee, is A/SPC/-. A/BUR/- refers to documents of the General Committee. A/AC.- documents are those of the Assembly's *ad hoc* bodies and A/CN.-, of its commissions; e.g. A/AC.105/- identifies documents of the Assembly's Committee on the Peaceful Uses of Outer Space, A/CN.4/-, of its International Law Commission. Assembly resolutions and decisions since the thirty-first (1976) session have been identified by two Arabic numerals: the first indicates the session of adoption; the second, the sequential number in the series. Resolutions are numbered consecutively from 1 at each session. Decisions of regular sessions are numbered consecutively, from 301 for those concerned with elections and appointments, and from 401 for all other decisions. Decisions of special and emergency special sessions are numbered consecutively, from 11 for those concerned with elections and appointments, and from 21 for all other decisions.

E/- refers to documents of the Economic and Social Council, numbered in separate series by year. Thus, E/1984/- refers to documents issued for consideration by the Council at its 1984 sessions, beginning with E/1984/1. E/AC.-, E/C.- and E/CN.-, followed by identifying numbers, refer to documents of the Council's subsidiary *ad hoc* bodies, committees and commissions. For example, E/C.1/-, E/C.2/- and E/C.3/- refer to documents of the Council's sessional committees, namely, the First (Economic), Second (Social) and Third (Programme and Co-ordination) Committees, respectively; E/CN.5/- refers to documents of the Council's Commission for Social Development, E/CN.7/-, to documents of its Committee on Natural Resources. E/ICEF/- documents are those of the United Nations Children's Fund (UNICEF). Symbols for the Council's resolutions and decisions, since 1978, consist of two Arabic numerals: the first indicates the year of adoption and the second, the sequential number in the series. There are two series: one for resolutions, beginning with 1 (resolution 1984/1); and one for decisions, beginning, since 1983, with 101 (decision 1984/101).

S/- refers to documents of the Security Council. Its resolutions are identified by consecutive numbers followed by the year of adoption in parentheses, beginning with resolution 1 (1946).

T/- refers to documents of the Trusteeship Council. Its resolutions are numbered consecutively, with the session at which they were adopted indicated by Roman numerals, e.g. resolution 2177(LI) of the fifty-first session. The Council's decisions are not numbered.

ST/-, followed by symbols representing the issuing department or office, refers to documents of the United Nations Secretariat.

Documents of certain bodies bear special series symbols, including the following:

ACC/-	Administrative Committee on Co-ordination
CD/-	Conference on Disarmament
CERD/-	International Convention on the Elimination of All Forms of Racial Discrimination
DC/-	Disarmament Commission
DP/-	United Nations Development Programme
HS/-	Commission on Human Settlements
ID/-	United Nations Industrial Development Organization
ITC/-	International Trade Centre
LOS/PCN/-	Preparatory Commission for the International Sea-Bed Authority and for the International Tribunal for the Law of the Sea
TD/-	United Nations Conference on Trade and Development
UNEP/-	United Nations Environment Programme
UNITAR/-	United Nations Institute for Training and Research

Many documents of the regional commissions bear special symbol series. These are sometimes preceded by the following:

E/CEPAL/-	Economic Commission for Latin America and the Caribbean
E/CN.14/-, E/ECA/-	Economic Commission for Africa
E/ECE/-	Economic Commission for Europe
E/ECWA/-	Economic Commission for Western Asia
E/ESCAP/-	Economic and Social Commission for Asia and the Pacific

"L" in a symbol refers to documents of limited distribution, such as draft resolutions; "CONF." to documents of a conference; "INF." to those of general information. Summary records are designated by "SR.", verbatim records by "PV.", each followed by the meeting number.

United Nations sales publications each carry a sales number with the following components separated by periods: a capital letter indicating the language(s) of the publication; two Arabic numerals indicating the year; a Roman numeral indicating the subject category; a capital letter indicating a subdivision of the category, if any; and an Arabic numeral(s) indicating the number of the publication within the category. Examples: E.84.V.7; E/F/R.84.II.E.8; E.84.IX.3.

PART ONE

United Nations

Report of the Secretary-General on the work of the Organization

Following is the text of the report of the Secretary-General on the work of the Organization, submitted to the General Assembly and dated 5 September 1984. [1]

After nearly three years as Secretary-General of the United Nations, I am more convinced than ever of the need to preserve and strengthen the Organization as a centre for harmonizing the actions of nations. I also believe that an extended and tolerable future for all humanity ultimately depends upon our success in making the purposes and principles of the Charter of the United Nations the basis of the day-to-day relations of Governments and peoples. On the eve of our fortieth anniversary, in this, my third, report on the work of the Organization I intend to examine the basic premises of our activity in the United Nations which is the practical embodiment of the concept of multilateralism.

The original intent of the United Nations was to provide a framework in which Governments of differing persuasions could, in their wisdom, work out solutions to international problems and, if necessary, together take action to put those solutions into effect rather than engaging in conflict. As the Preamble to the Charter puts it, the main purpose was, and is, "to unite our strength to maintain international peace and security". The basic assumption was that all nations had a vital common interest in peace and in an orderly and equitable world and would be prepared to co-operate to achieve it.

Unfortunately the history of post-war international relations has so far shown that the common interest in peace and security has tended to assert itself only when things have reached a dangerously critical stage. Until that stage short-term national interest and opportunism tend to override the common interest. We are still very far from general acceptance of the principles of the Charter as rules to be lived by at all times by all Governments in their international relations.

In these circumstances, it is paradoxical that while contemporary realities have strengthened the need for the use of multilateral means for dealing with our problems and enlarged the scope for growth and development through multilateralism, there is an increasing questioning of the rules, instruments and modalities of multilateral co-operation. There is also, on occasion, an apparent reluctance to make the effort required to use international organizations effectively.

The past year has been a time of great-Power tension accentuated by a lack of progress in disarmament and arms limitation which has heightened fears of nuclear confrontation; of violence or threatened violence in several parts of the world; of continued economic difficulties in spite of a recovery in certain developed countries, and a deterioration in the situation of many developing countries; of drought and famine in several regions; and of a tendency to side-step major problems in a way which is likely in the long run to increase frustration and bitterness. Virtually nothing that has happened has shown that these problems can be solved effectively by purely bilateral or unilateral efforts.

Why has there been a retreat from internationalism and multilateralism at a time when actual developments both in relation to world peace and to the world economy would seem to demand their strengthening? We need to consider this question carefully if we are to make our institution work better. I hope very much that political scientists and intellectuals the world over, as well as political leaders and diplomats, will ponder this essential problem on the occasion of the fortieth anniversary of the United Nations.

* * *

After the Second World War there was admittedly a certain over-confidence in the capacity of international institutions, born of a desperate desire to build a new and better world. It then seemed possible to establish, as a first priority, a system for maintaining international peace and security under the provisions of the Charter. If such a system could become effective, the main obstacle to disarmament and arms limitation, the insecurity of nations, would be removed, and the rule of law rather than the rule of force would at last begin to come into its own on the international level. With these co-operative achievements a world community would have come into being, capable of directing its affairs by reason and enlightened self-interest. The system would include equitable economic institutions and steady progress in social justice and human rights.

What has happened to that majestic vision? It was soon clouded by the differences of the major Powers. The advent of atomic weapons brought with it a new doctrine of security based on nuclear deterrence, a doctrine which was not taken account of when the Charter was drafted. Moreover, the world turned out to be a more complex, far less orderly place than had been hoped at San Francisco. The problems of post-war international peace and security were less clear-cut and less susceptible to the kind of international action envisaged in the Charter. The forces of nationalism and fears for national security, far from abating after the Second World War, were soon very much on the increase. The international community's inability to solve many of its problems, whether political or economic, even when it could agree in principle on what the solution should be, gave rise to a process of side-stepping the United Nations and recourse to other measures—force, unilateral action or confronting military alliances—which weakened reliance on the Organization.

* * *

In looking back, however, it would be a grave mistake to underestimate, or simply take for granted, what has been achieved and what is now being done by the United Nations system. During a period of revolutionary change it has accomplished a great deal for the betterment of the human condition.

The United Nations has played a decisive role in the process of decolonization which has brought independence to hundreds of millions of people. The Security Council has throughout its existence considered many of the difficult problems of conflict in the world and on a large number of occasions has come up with a basic formula on which their solution might be based. It has also taken numerous actions to limit and control conflict. Peacekeeping operations have successfully controlled violence in a number of critical areas. Nor should we forget that, although there have been a number of regional conflicts, their escalation into global conflict has been avoided. Even on the most difficult question of disarmament and arms limitation a number of agreements have in fact been reached.

The United Nations Development Programme, together with the specialized agencies, has come to represent a vital source of economic and technical assistance for developing countries. The United Nations Children's Fund has brought life and hope to millions of children and mothers and is the leading influence in furthering technological communication advances that can bring a virtual survival revolution for children in Asia, Africa and Latin America. The specialized agencies have, in their various fields of activity, made major contributions to the alleviation of global problems.

The United Nations has provided authoritative definitions of the fundamental rights and freedoms which all human beings should enjoy. It is responsible

for the development of the Convention on the Law of the Sea which provides a broadly accepted new régime for the oceans. In the past 40 years more has been done by the United Nations in codifying international law than in all the previous years of history together. Millions of refugees have gained protection and assistance through United Nations instruments and agencies; international humanitarian activity and concern have been mobilized on an unprecedented scale; guidelines have been established to deal with many of the most critical problems of our time, and the Governments and peoples of the world have been sensitized to their importance through the great international conferences and programmes which the United Nations has sponsored, the most recent of which was the International Conference on Population held in August this year.

All of these accomplishments required a multilateral structure of co-operation. Moreover, in some situations the United Nations, or the Secretary-General, remains essential to communication between the parties. I think, for example, of Cyprus, over which at this moment I am engaged in a new effort to find a just solution; of Afghanistan, the Iran/Iraq war and South-East Asia. The critical value of peace-making and peace-keeping efforts would be instantly evident if they were to cease. It is essential, in considering our problems, to remember the positive side of the United Nations account and to keep in perspective politically-motivated criticism.

However, for all of the accomplishments of the past decades, and they have been major, the fact of the matter is that the three main elements of a stable international order—an accepted system of maintaining international peace and security; disarmament and arms limitation; and the progressive development of a just and effective system of international economic relations—have yet to take hold as they should.

In dealing with the most vital problems of the widest concern, we often witness heated rhetoric rather than a reasoned co-operative approach. In such an atmosphere, which extends far beyond the Organization, the United Nations, which should be used to provide constructive solutions, provides a convenient target of criticism.

* * *

The United Nations reflects in a unique way the aspirations and frustrations of many nations and groups all over the world. One of its great merits is that all nations—including the weak, the oppressed and the victims of injustice—can get a hearing and have a platform even in the face of the hard realities of power. A just cause, however frustrated or disregarded, can find a voice in the United Nations.

This is not always a well-liked attribute of the Organization, but it is an essential one.

What needs to be studied in the light of experience is whether present practices in the United Nations are in all instances best suited to promote concrete and just solutions and strengthen confidence in an Organization the essence of which is its universality. If confrontations in the deliberative organs are carried too far, either by one side or the other, they destroy the possibility of a consensus which could form the basis for practical action. I am totally in sympathy with the pursuit of just aspirations, however great the difficulties. But for the good of all, as well as of the United Nations itself, we should assess very carefully the most effective and correct method of using the Organization. The United Nations is a willing and patient horse, but it should not be ridden to a standstill without thought of the consequences.

We should beware of blurring the separate and specific functions of the main organs and specialized agencies by treating them as interchangeable platforms for pursuing the same political aims. Issues must be dealt with primarily on their own merits and in their own context. Otherwise the fever of one or two issues can pervade the entire body politic of the United Nations.

The non-implementation of resolutions, as well as their proliferation, has tended to downgrade the seriousness with which Governments and the public take the decisions of the United Nations. Very often the only outcome of such a process is to ask the Secretary-General to make yet another report to the next session, thus perpetuating a stalemate which, to be resolved, requires governmental and intergovernmental action. This process, and the almost automatic repetition of some agenda items and debates, is expensive and time-consuming both in terms of meetings and documentation, as well as often being ineffective in terms of practical results. I believe that such tendencies have been debilitating to the efforts of the Organization in the cause of peace and economic co-operation. I hope that Member States, even during the forthcoming session of the General Assembly, will give serious thought to the best way of doing business.

* * *

Two years ago in my first annual report I made a series of suggestions as to how the Charter system of international peace and security might be made to work better. Although the Security Council has devoted many hours of thoughtful consultations to these and related ideas, concrete results are still needed for which the impetus must come from the highest political levels. I feel that the realization of the full potential of the United Nations depends upon a willingness to take active steps to experiment with new approaches.

In recent years the collective capacity and influence of the Security Council have been insufficiently tested. There are important issues where the members of the Council, including the permanent members, hold substantially similar views. And yet other factors not directly related to these problems inhibit the Council from exerting collective influence as envisaged in the Charter.

The same consideration applies to peace-keeping. We are often urged to strengthen the peace-keeping capacity of the United Nations, the implication being that this is a matter that can be handled without regard to the political relations of Member States and particularly of members of the Security Council. A number of lessons have been learned recently about the nature of peace-keeping, but it is essential to emphasize the fundamental issue. Peace-keeping is an expression of international political consensus and will. If that consensus or will is weak, uncertain, divided or indecisive, peace-keeping operations will be correspondingly weakened. There are occasions when the differences among members of the Security Council even make it impossible to take any peace-keeping action at all. The strongest peace-keeping operation would be one which had the unreserved support, political, diplomatic and financial, of *all* the Members of the United Nations and even the actual participation of the permanent members of the Security Council under the mandate of the Council. This may be unrealistic at present, but it is also the political truth which indeed applies across the whole range of the activities of the Organization.

I give the example of peace-keeping to demonstrate the process by which internationalism becomes discredited in the public mind. Peace-keeping is one of the more successful innovations of the United Nations. But when this technique cannot be used in a situation which obviously requires it, because the members of the Security Council are divided on the matter, the public generally concludes that there is something wrong with the United Nations and with the concept of internationalism. This conclusion is, of course, easier than analysing the conflicting positions and motives of Governments which are the real cause of the impasse and of the failure of the United Nations to act or to respond.

I do not have any simple solutions to offer to this problem. Obviously a radical improvement in the international political climate would make a profound difference, but we cannot rely on miracles. In the mean time we could perhaps work on a few ideas for improving the situation, on the assumption that our common and agreed objective is human survival in reasonably decent conditions.

I myself have put forward some ideas and suggestions on a number of issues—about Lebanon, for example, and the Middle East problem—but the reactions so far have been mixed. I notice that there is a tendency at present in the direction of bilateral or unilateral action, or no action at all. And yet bilateral or unilateral approaches do not seem to be noticeably effective in most cases. Nor is this surprising, for by their very nature many of the disputes that we face around the globe require the building of a wide consensus if solutions are to hold.

I suggest that we review the current tendency in relation to specific situations. I very much hope, for instance, that we shall see real—and long overdue—progress in proceeding to the independence of Namibia on the basis of the United Nations plan. I also hope that in the coming months we shall see the full and concrete co-operation and positive action which are needed to ensure the success of the untiring efforts which the Contadora Group is making for peace in Central America.

In many disputes accusations and counter-accusations are freely traded over a situation which, to most people, is mystifying and complex. What harm would be done if United Nations teams were dispatched to clarify and certify what the real facts are? Surely such clarification of the situation by objective observers might help to reduce international tension and strengthen other efforts. Let us ask ourselves what useful steps can be taken in a given situation rather than starting by thinking of all the extraneous reasons why they *cannot* be taken.

Most of all we need to reaffirm the Charter concept that threats to international peace and security, from whatever source or in whatever region of the world, override ideological or other differences between States and entail an obligation on all States to agree and co-operate. Under the terms of the Charter some situations clearly require immediate consideration and action by the Security Council regardless of political disagreements. Surely one such situation is when a national frontier is violated and the State concerned calls for United Nations action.

*   *   *

There must of course be a substantial improvement in the international climate if there is to be meaningful progress in the limitation and reduction of arms. This is a field in which it is essential to utilize the full potential of multilateral *and* bilateral negotiations, both to improve mutual understanding of the reasoning behind military postures and negotiating positions and to reach substantive, balanced arms regulation and disarmament agreements. During the past year there has been little sign of movement in this direction, and the arms race has continued to burgeon both qualitatively and quantitatively.

It is only realistic to recognize that nuclear disarmament will depend primarily on agreement among the nations having nuclear weapons, espe-

cially, and beginning with, the two most powerful. It is equally true, however, that success or failure in the reduction of nuclear weapons can have a most important bearing on the future of the entire international community. To approach nuclear disarmament exclusively as a factor in the relations of the nuclear Powers and their allies is to do injustice to the broad and grave responsibility that the possession of nuclear weapons carries with it. It is also unfortunate and, I believe, unnecessary to allow the course of disarmament negotiations on the whole range of issues in the multilateral forums to be largely governed by tension stemming from other causes. The fact is that progress on the issues included in the agenda of the General Assembly and its subsidiary bodies, and especially on those currently before the Conference on Disarmament, could help to restore confidence and improve the critical bilateral relationship on which the international political climate so heavily depends.

It is especially valuable in times of tension that a multilateral structure is available within which nations, despite their differences, can come together for dialogue and serious negotiations, whether in the General Assembly, the Security Council or the Geneva Conference on Disarmament. In fact, the possibility exists in that Conference for nuclear and non-nuclear countries to work together towards agreement on such vital subjects as measures to avoid nuclear war, the prohibition of nuclear-weapon tests, the prevention of an arms race in outer space, and the complete prohibition and destruction of chemical weapons. If, instead, the Conference is used mainly for the public presentation of rigid positions and rhetorical exchanges, the potential of this broadly representative negotiating forum will be largely wasted. I urge all concerned—East, West, non-aligned and neutral alike—to recognize that the need for disarmament measures—both nuclear and conventional—is too compelling to allow this to happen.

*   *   *

Let me turn to another aspect, namely, multilateral co-operation through the United Nations in the economic and social spheres. We are here in the presence of a slightly different set of political realities and in a predominantly North-South dimension. Global economic relations have changed significantly since the immediate post-war years when most international economic institutions began their work. There has been growing frustration among the developing countries, a large international constituency which has looked upon the institutions of multilateral economic co-operation established after the Second World War as insufficiently responsive to the needs of those countries. This perception has been strengthened in light of the serious economic difficulties which have affected them in the 1970s and early 1980s. Their attempts in the United Nations, through an essentially political process, to obtain changes in that system have not had the desired results, as shown by the failure to launch global negotiations. It is in a way comprehensible that some developed countries, whose influence in those institutions has been paramount, should find this shift difficult to accept and should tend to favour retaining the existing institutional structures and decision-making machinery as they are.

It is easy to criticize United Nations economic institutions because such institutions often fall short of their high aims. Conflicting national interests in a time of flux and change make such a falling short virtually inevitable. Nevertheless, multilateral co-operation has already achieved much, most of it taken for granted as soon as it is achieved. In an economically interdependent world where the growth and stability of the North is intertwined with accelerated development of the South, it is hard to see how international economic problems can be solved, except through intensified multilateral co-operation. Despite the difficulties involved in such co-operation, it is short-sighted to turn away from the concept of multilateralism and the institutions which embody it.

There is a distinction to be made between United Nations operational activities in the field of development at the national level where much is being achieved, and activities at the *global* level, in trade, money and finance, for example, where there is a high degree of frustration.

The support provided by the United Nations system for development, excluding the World Bank, now amounts to over $2 billion a year. High priority is given to the low-income countries with particular attention to the problems of the poorest of the poor. In a period of restricted resources, continuous efforts are being made to ensure more effective operational co-operation within the United Nations system.

It should be mentioned that in the domain of "global" issues, the "achievements" of the Organization cannot be measured simply in terms of the number of treaties and agreements negotiated and signed. Of course, there have been many of these. But many of the contributions of the United Nations are in less tangible forms: for example, the extent to which the United Nations has succeeded in raising global consciousness on key issues, the critical situation in Africa being a case in point, or in shaping the framework of international debates on major problems. For instance, I have consistently stressed the importance of finding solutions to the acute debt problem that go beyond the short term and that take into account the need to ensure growth in the export earnings of developing countries. It is, similarly, in no small measure due to the discussions on the International Development Strategy that the world community today gives a high priority to the cause of development which, in its simplest form, must be understood to mean the raising of the living standards of the vast majority of mankind in this interdependent world, and in a manner that benefits the global economy as a whole.

This aspect of the work of the United Nations has recently met with some doubts and criticisms. These need to be faced. Where substantive issues are raised, they need to be adequately debated, and misunderstandings dispelled. Otherwise, the normal functioning of important organs of the United Nations will be impaired. One of these, for example, relates to the complex issue of the relative roles accorded in United Nations discussions to Governments and to the private sector.

Another matter frequently raised is the extent to which issues that are essentially economic and technical are politicized in the United Nations. I have mentioned one aspect of this problem earlier in this report. There is another aspect. In the present world few issues in human affairs can be regarded as completely unpolitical. Nevertheless, the extent to which economic issues are politicized in the United Nations should also be understood as a reflection of the frustrations which developing countries feel in their long attempt to reshape their economic destiny. The absence of global policy-makers—i.e., politics in the best sense—to meet this need is also a factor in this frustration. There is an additional factor: many Governments feel that only when economic issues are politicized will they attract the attention of the highest level of decision makers. And many economic issues are so complex that only decisions at the highest levels can make any significant impact in the current situation.

The difficulties which the community of nations experiences in strengthening economic co-operation in the United Nations stem from a number of causes. A new consensus on economic issues in the light of world economic and political realities has not yet emerged. There is disagreement on the cause of the trouble as well as on what to do about it. Ideological differences on economic problems further complicate the issue. But the absence of a consensus, which will take time to emerge, need not prevent progress in critical areas.

These are not difficulties which can be ignored or willed away. The world is not just one country or one point of view. If we are serious about the future, this is the context in which we need to seek practical solutions to both short-term and long-term problems. Patience, perception and persistence are more relevant to this search than relentless criticism whether from one side or another.

Human solidarity demands these qualities. If we do not address current economic problems seriously and urgently, we will not be able to confine them to the economic sphere alone. In our world of growing economic interdependence, impoverished people faced perpetually with a variety of overwhelming economic and social crises constitute not only a challenge to international conscience, but a threat to international stability as well.

*   *   *

Respect for human rights and fundamental freedoms is one of the basic principles of the United Nations. A human rights philosophy based on the concept of an international rule of law pervades the Charter, the Universal Declaration of Human Rights and the codifying instruments adopted by the United Nations since its establishment. These instruments are the yardstick for measuring regard or disregard for human rights.

In this area, too, we constantly encounter trenchant criticism. I welcome such criticism in the hope that it will spur everyone, including the critics, on to a more serious assessment of the importance—and the difficulty—of reducing injustice in an unjust world, of promoting development in a world divided between rich and poor, and of instilling the virtues of mercy and compassion into people many of whom are fighting—or believe they are fighting—for their lives.

I spend much of my time, sometimes with encouraging results, on human rights and humanitarian problems, which I regard as uniquely important. Despite the existence of definitive norms developed within the United Nations, perceptions differ greatly. One person's freedom fighter is another person's terrorist; one's champion of human rights is another's subversive; one's plaintiff is another's criminal. The reality is that many are dispossessed, many confined, many tortured and many starve. This is the world we have to deal with.

In the field of human rights, gross violations, such as the system of *apartheid*, are obviously the first priority for the Organization. In addition, it is my concern to help individuals whose human rights may have been violated. In particular, I seek to facilitate the release of those who may have been imprisoned or sentenced for political reasons. The criteria for judging such efforts must be whether they advance the cause of human rights and not whether they serve the political interest of one side or another.

The primary responsibility in this important matter rests, of course, with Governments which have entered into firm commitments towards each other and towards their peoples to respect inter-

nationally recognized standards proclaimed by the United Nations. We must try to create the conditions which will encourage all Governments to ensure respect of human rights in accordance with those standards. At the same time, we should examine existing United Nations practices and consider ways and means to make them more effective in dealing with gross violations of human rights wherever they occur.

The question of human rights is closely linked with the humanitarian activities of the United Nations. It seems to be a general rule that in times of recession or other difficulties, the weakest developing countries suffer the most, and the weakest groups in those countries are the most vulnerable of all.

In such cases, multilateral action through the United Nations is essential to alleviate the plight of the victims—action parallel to and co-ordinated with the remarkable work of non-governmental agencies. Various institutions within the United Nations system, including the Office of the United Nations High Commissioner for Refugees, the United Nations Relief and Works Agency for Palestine Refugees in the Near East, the United Nations Children's Fund and the Office of the United Nations Disaster Relief Co-ordinator, as well as the specialized agencies, have done much in this field.

During the past year, the United Nations has focused attention on two major problems. In December 1983, I launched an appeal for help to the many African countries which were facing the worst drought in the twentieth century. The Second International Conference on Assistance to Refugees in Africa in July of this year was another manifestation of multilateral co-operation in dealing with urgent social and humanitarian problems.

It is essential that we learn from our experience to approach future humanitarian problems in a coherent manner which takes account of all their elements. We must develop better means of alleviating and preventing crises. We must improve our capacity to provide humanitarian assistance quickly. In order to establish an early warning system, I have requested the heads of the various agencies of the United Nations as well as those of my field offices to inform me, on an urgent basis, of any situation which in their view could give rise to a major humanitarian crisis. Such a system should enable the United Nations to react to cases of emergency more adequately and speedily. The problems are enormous, but I believe that the level of public and governmental consciousness of the need to provide assistance in great humanitarian tragedies is growing. It is a fundamental responsibility of the international community to come to the aid of its least fortunate and most afflicted members.

The growing problem of narcotic drugs has become a major international anxiety, not least because of its effect on the future of children and young people. It has become more and more evident that international and multilateral efforts provide the best hope for arresting and reducing the traffic in and use of drugs, which have such appalling effect on both individuals and the societies in which they live. The institutions of the United Nations system, in co-operation with Governments and other groups concerned with the problem, are actively working to deal with it. Greater effort is needed, however, and, for my part, I have taken steps to improve the co-ordination within the United Nations system of this vital activity.

Finally I wish to mention the steady increase in various forms of politically motivated violence, including hijacking, kidnapping, car-bombing and assassination. Our society is in some sectors becoming an armed camp. Order, civility and even public life are under serious threat in many parts of the world. As usual, the toll of innocent victims is appalling. It is not enough to deplore or condemn or try to control such acts of violence. Attention has also to be focused on ways of dealing with the root causes of these phenomena.

* * *

The machinery of international co-operation must be serviced by an efficient and solid secretariat. One of my priorities is to improve the efficient functioning of the Secretariat, so that I may be able to satisfy Member States that all necessary human and other resources—but not more than is needed—are available and are being effectively used. To this end, last year I asked some of my senior colleagues to advise me on measures that could be taken to improve the administration and functioning of the Secretariat. On the basis of their advice, I have now decided on a number of actions designed either to increase efficiency or reduce costs, or both. For example, I have directed that there shall be a temporary suspension of recruitment. I shall report on these matters to the General Assembly in greater detail shortly. I very much hope that the Assembly will be mindful, in the resolutions it adopts, of my objectives.

The success of any programme for administrative improvement requires the active co-operation not only of all the members of the Secretariat but also of the Member States themselves. To this end I intend to ascertain the views of the membership on a number of approaches which I believe could with advantage be explored.

The General Assembly will be called upon to consider this year a number of issues of personnel policy including, in particular, those concerning salaries and other conditions of service of the staff. Different points of view inevitably will arise, and indeed have already been expressed to me, on the adequacy of these conditions of service. I am sure that Member States will recognize that the achievement of the highest standards of competence and integrity called for by the Charter requires corresponding and appropriate conditions of service.

The current system of salaries, allowances and pensions extends far beyond the United Nations itself. It affects all the agencies which, with the United Nations, participate in what has come to be known as the "common system". The General Assembly has repeatedly stressed the need to preserve and promote that linkage, without which the recruitment and administration of staff for the many participating organizations would be a chaotic exercise. The common system is also one in which a number of organs—notably the International Civil Service Commission and the Joint Staff Pension Board—have a regulatory role to play. I am confident that the discussion in the Assembly on these issues will take these facts into account.

* * *

In considering the purpose and necessity of multilateralism, we should not forget that national interest generally stands first in the priorities of Governments. There is also, however, a growing sense of the *international* interest, the common good of humanity, and the preservation and wise stewardship of the world's resources for the benefit of future generations. That is why there is a widespread commitment to the United Nations and a general interest in making the Organization work better. Quite naturally different Governments or groups of Governments have different ideas about the work of the United Nations and wish it to work on *their* terms. To make the United Nations work better, what is needed, above all, is a determined and persistent effort to strike a balance between national and international interest.

In conclusion, therefore, I wish to repeat my call for a multilateral and rational approach to the problems of international peace and development. I believe that this is what the peoples of the United Nations really desire in spite of all the difficulties and irritations encountered by Governments in trying to make a multilateral system work. It is widely understood that without such a system we shall run unacceptable risks and that it is therefore irresponsible to weaken the multilateral approach. Without the safety net which multilateral organization provides, the world would certainly be a much more dangerous and disorderly place.

In the United Nations we have now had nearly 40 years of experience, 40 years of change, and, for all the conflict of our time, 40 years without a global war. Let us look back at the road we have travelled, distil the experience and set out again refreshed and with a new determination. The purposes for which the United Nations was set up are essential for the future of our planet. The vision expressed in the Charter remains, and we should rally to it.

Javier PÉREZ DE CUÉLLAR
Secretary-General

**Report of the Secretary-General on
the work of the Organization**
At its 94th plenary meeting, on 11 December 1984, the General Assembly took note of the report of the Secretary-General on the work of the Organization.

General Assembly decision 39/413
Adopted without vote

Oral proposal by President; agenda item 10.
Meeting number. GA 39th session: plenary 94.

REFERENCE

(1)A/39/1.

Political and security questions

Disarmament

Little progress was made in 1984 in disarmament or arms limitation, despite the continuing arms race absorbing more than $800 billion in estimated global military expenditures for the year.

The General Assembly, at its 1984 regular session, decided to convene an International Conference on the Relationship between Disarmament and Development, with a view to examining the implications of the continuing military expenditures for the international economic and social situation, and recommending remedial measures. The Assembly, acting on the recommendations of the First Committee, also adopted 62 other resolutions on disarmament and related international security questions, many of which reflected competing approaches to substantive issues. While most resolutions dealt with arms control and disarmament measures, the Assembly also adopted the statute of the United Nations Institute for Disarmament Research and requested the Secretary-General to prepare new studies—one on nuclear deterrence and the other on the climatic effects of nuclear war.

The Conference on Disarmament, the main intergovernmental negotiating body known until 1984 as the Committee on Disarmament, and the United Nations Disarmament Commission, a deliberative body composed of all United Nations Member States, continued to discuss much the same issues as in previous years. Outside the United Nations framework, the USSR and the United States announced, in November, their intention to hold bilateral negotiations early in 1985.

Topics related to this chapter. Peaceful uses of outer space. International peace and security: implementation of the 1970 Declaration. Arms race and environment.

PUBLICATIONS

Disarmament: A Periodic Review by the United Nations, vol. VII: No. 1, Sales No. E.84.IX.1; No. 2, Sales No. E.84.IX.2; No. 3, Sales No. E.84.IX.4. *The United Nations Disarmament Yearbook*, vol. 9, *1984*, Sales No. E.85.IX.4.

General aspects of disarmament

The Secretary-General, in his 1984 annual report to the General Assembly on the work of the United Nations (p. 3), emphasized that it was essential to use the full potential of multilateral and bilateral negotiations to improve mutual understanding and reach substantive, balanced arms regulation and disarmament agreements. Addressing the Assembly on 12 December, he stressed that nuclear hostilities would be suicidal; a nuclear war could never remain limited and a conflict of hours or minutes would render meaningless the entire work of civilization.

Communications. In 1984, the Secretary-General received a large number of communications calling for arms control and disarmament, some being submitted under a variety of related agenda items (see p. 21).

By a letter dated 29 March,[1] France transmitted on behalf of the 10 States members of the European Economic Community (EEC) the declarations adopted on 27 March by the EEC Ministers for Foreign Affairs, in which they expressed their support of arms control and disarmament negotiations and of the Stockholm Conference on Confidence- and Security-building Measures and Disarmament in Europe. Similar support for such negotiations was expressed in the Declaration on East-West Relations and Arms Control, issued at the London Economic Summit (7-9 June) and transmitted by the United Kingdom on 12 June.[2]

In a Joint Declaration issued on 22 May,[3] the heads of State or Government of Argentina, Greece, India, Mexico, Sweden and the United Republic of Tanzania urged efforts to reduce and eliminate the risk of war between nations.

In the final communiqué of the Meeting of Ministers for Foreign Affairs and Heads of Delegation of Non-Aligned Countries to the 1984 session of the General Assembly (New York, 1-5 October), transmitted by India on 8 October,[4] the participants asserted that international peace and security could be ensured only through general and complete disarmament, expressed concern over the escalation of tension in Europe and the growing stockpiling and introduction of new weapon systems, and called on the major Powers to undertake arms control and disarmament negotiations.

By a letter of 5 December,[5] the German Democratic Republic transmitted a communiqué adopted by the Committee of Foreign Ministers of the States Parties to the Warsaw Treaty of Friendship, Co-operation and Mutual Assistance (Berlin, 3 and 4 December), welcoming the November announcement on the holding of USSR–United States negotiations on nuclear and space weapons (see p. 24), expressing their readiness to negotiate agreements based on equality and equal security, and supporting a wide range of disarmament measures.

The United Kingdom, by a letter dated 21 December,[6] transmitted a communiqué by the North Atlantic Council Foreign Ministers (Brussels, Belgium, 13 and 14 December), stating, among other things, that none of their weapons would ever be used except in response to attack.

Other appeals for peace and disarmament were from: the National Conference of Delegates of the Polish United Workers' Party (Warsaw, 18 March);[7] the Interaction Council, comprising 26 former heads of Government (Brioni, Yugoslavia, 24-26 May);[8] the National Seminar on Peace and Disarmament (Lomé, Togo, 6-9 August),[9] recommending, among other things, the establishment at Lomé of a regional institute for research on peace and disarmament; and the Conference of Veteran Organizations on Security, Disarmament and Co-operation in Europe (Belgrade, Yugoslavia, 18-20 October).[10]

Some communications submitted under the item on general and complete disarmament also dealt with the Assembly's annual review of its 1970 Declaration on the Strengthening of International Security (see p. 114).

Proposed comprehensive programme

No agreement was reached in 1984 in the Conference on Disarmament[11] towards a comprehensive programme of disarmament. The programme was first envisaged in paragraph 109 of the Final Document[12] of the Tenth Special Session of the General Assembly in 1978—the first such session devoted to disarmament—and had been considered annually since 1980 by the Committee on Disarmament (as the Conference was formerly known) without success. In December 1983,[13] the Assembly had urged the Conference to renew its work on elaborating the programme, and to

submit a progress report in 1984 and a draft programme not later than 1986. In December 1984, the Assembly again urged that the draft be completed in 1986 (resolution 39/148 I).

Consideration by the Conference on Disarmament. The *Ad Hoc* Committee on the Comprehensive Programme of Disarmament, re-established by the Conference on 28 February 1984, held two meetings between 10 and 24 July under the chairmanship of Alfonso García Robles (Mexico). It agreed that current circumstances were not conducive to resolving outstanding issues and that it would not be fruitful, therefore, to pursue work at the Conference's 1984 session. The Committee expressed the hope that maximum efforts would be made to ensure that early in 1985 the circumstances would permit the resumption and conclusion of work on the programme.

The *Ad Hoc* Committee's report was adopted by the Conference on 23 August as part of its report to the Assembly.

GENERAL ASSEMBLY ACTION

On the recommendation of the First Committee, the General Assembly, on 17 December 1984, adopted resolution 39/148 I without vote.

Comprehensive programme of disarmament
The General Assembly,

Recalling that, in paragraph 109 of the Final Document of the Tenth Special Session of the General Assembly, the Assembly called for the elaboration of a comprehensive programme of disarmament encompassing all measures thought to be advisable in order to ensure that the goal of general and complete disarmament under effective international control becomes a reality in a world in which international peace and security prevail and in which the new international economic order is strengthened and consolidated,

Recalling also its resolution 38/183 K of 20 December 1983, in which it urged the Conference on Disarmament, as soon as it considered that the circumstances were propitious for that purpose, to renew its work on the elaboration of the comprehensive programme of disarmament previously requested, to submit to the General Assembly at its thirty-ninth session a progress report on the matter and to submit to the Assembly not later than at its forty-first session a complete draft of such a programme,

Having examined the progress report of the *Ad Hoc* Committee on the Comprehensive Programme of Disarmament, which is an integral part of the report of the Conference on Disarmament on its 1984 session,

Noting that in its report the *Ad Hoc* Committee stated that it was agreed that circumstances were not conducive to making progress towards the resolution of outstanding issues and expressed the hope that maximum efforts would be exerted to ensure that early the following year the circumstances would be such as to permit the resumption of the work on the elaboration of the programme and its successful conclusion,

1. *Regrets* that during the 1984 session of the Conference on Disarmament it was not possible to renew the work on the elaboration of the comprehensive programme of disarmament;

2. *Urges* that all efforts be made so that the Conference on Disarmament may resume its work on the elaboration of the comprehensive programme of disarmament early in its 1985 session with a view to submitting to the General Assembly at its forty-first session a complete draft of such a programme;

3. *Requests* the Conference on Disarmament to report to the General Assembly at its fortieth session on the progress of its work.

General Assembly resolution 39/148 I

17 December 1984   Meeting 102   Adopted without vote

Approved by First Committee (A/39/749) without vote, 19 November (meeting 41); 12-nation draft (A/C.1/39/L.31); agenda item 59 *(i)*.
Sponsors: Algeria, Argentina, Bangladesh, Ecuador, Indonesia, Mexico, Pakistan, Sri Lanka, Sweden, Uruguay, Venezuela, Yugoslavia.
Meeting numbers. GA 39th session: 1st Committee 3-37, 41, 42; plenary 102.

In explanation of position, Belgium said it had agreed to the consensus despite the contradiction it saw between the last preambular paragraph and paragraph 2; it doubted whether circumstances would change so quickly that any useful purpose could be served by a speedy resumption of the activities of the Conference.

Conference on Disarmament

The Conference on Disarmament, the main multilateral negotiating body and formerly known as the Committee on Disarmament, was renamed and its status changed at the beginning of its 1984 session, pursuant to a 1982 General Assembly resolution[14] evolving from proposals considered at the Assembly's second (1982) special session devoted to disarmament.[15] Accordingly, the position of Chairman was redesignated as President and the subsidiary bodies as committees.

The Secretary-General, in his 1984 annual report to the General Assembly on the work of the United Nations (p. 3), urged that full use be made of the Conference's potential as the broadly representative negotiating forum, and that it not be used for the public presentation of rigid positions and rhetorical exchanges.

Expressing disappointment over the lack of concrete agreements in the Conference in 1984 on any disarmament issues, the Assembly, in December, called on it to concentrate on substantive negotiations on priority issues (resolution 39/148 N) and reaffirmed the right of all States not members of that body to participate in its work (resolution 39/148 L).

Activities of the Conference. The Conference met in 1984 at Geneva from 7 February to 27 April and from 12 June to 31 August.[11] Holding 49 formal and 50 informal plenary meetings, it considered—in addition to the proposed comprehensive programme of disarmament (see p. 12)—a nuclear-test ban, cessation of the nuclear-arms race and nuclear disarmament, prevention of nuclear war, chemical weapons, prevention of an arms race in outer space, security assurances to non-nuclear-weapon States, and radiological weapons. Details on developments on these questions during the year can be found elsewhere in this chapter.

The Conference re-established, on 28 February, *ad hoc* bodies on chemical weapons, security assurances to non-nuclear-weapon States, and the comprehensive programme of disarmament; and, on 17 April, an *ad hoc* committee on radiological weapons. On 8 March, the Conference decided, in the light of its new nomenclature, to designate each subsidiary body dealing with a specific agenda item as an *"ad hoc* committee"; the decision involved no financial or structural implications, nor change in the Conference's working procedures or rules of procedure, and it was to have no bearing on the views of members on the substance of matters under consideration.

As regards its membership, the Conference, which had agreed in principle to an increase by not more than four States,[16] decided to continue consultations with a view to taking a decision and reporting to the General Assembly in 1985. The Conference also held three informal meetings on the question of its improved and effective functioning, focusing on a working paper—prepared by an informal group of seven members—incorporating various proposals. It was understood that consideration of the matter would continue in 1985.

In a letter of 17 May to the Secretary-General,[17] Iraq, a non-member of the Conference, protested that Iran had prevented it from exercising the right of reply in the Conference in April.

GENERAL ASSEMBLY ACTION

On the recommendation of the First Committee, the General Assembly, on 17 December 1984, adopted two resolutions on the work of the Conference on Disarmament: one on its report (39/148 N) and the other on participation in its work by non-members (39/148 L).

The Assembly adopted resolution 39/148 N by recorded vote.

Report of the Conference on Disarmament
The General Assembly,
Recalling its resolutions 34/83 B of 11 December 1979, 35/152 J of 12 December 1980, 36/92 F of 9 December 1981, 37/78 G of 9 December 1982 and 38/183 I of 20 December 1983,
Recalling also the Final Document of the Tenth Special Session of the General Assembly, the first special

session devoted to disarmament, and the Concluding Document of the Twelfth Special Session of the General Assembly, the second special session devoted to disarmament,

Having considered the report of the Conference on Disarmament,

Convinced that the Conference on Disarmament, as the single multilateral negotiating body on disarmament, should play the central role in substantive negotiations on priority questions of disarmament and on the implementation of the Programme of Action set forth in section III of the Final Document of the Tenth Special Session,

Reaffirming that the establishment of *ad hoc* committees offers the best available machinery for the conduct of multilateral negotiations on items of the agenda of the Conference on Disarmament and contributes to the strengthening of the negotiating role of the Conference,

Deploring the fact that, despite the repeated requests of the General Assembly and the expressed wish of the great majority of members of the Conference on Disarmament, the establishment of an *ad hoc* committee on the cessation of the nuclear-arms race and on nuclear disarmament was once again prevented during the 1984 session of the Conference,

Deploring also the fact that the Conference on Disarmament has not been enabled to set up *ad hoc* committees under item 1 of its agenda, entitled "Nuclear-test ban", on the cessation of the nuclear-arms race and nuclear disarmament, on the prevention of nuclear war and on the prevention of an arms race in outer space,

1. *Expresses its deep concern and disappointment* that the Conference on Disarmament has not been enabled, this year either, to reach concrete agreements on any disarmament issues to which the United Nations has assigned greatest priority and urgency and which have been under consideration for a number of years;

2. *Calls upon* the Conference on Disarmament to intensify its work, to further its mandate more earnestly through negotiations and to adopt concrete measures on the specific priority issues of disarmament on its agenda, in particular those relating to nuclear disarmament;

3. *Once again urges* the Conference on Disarmament to continue or to undertake, during its 1985 session, substantive negotiations on the priority questions of disarmament on its agenda, in accordance with the provisions of the Final Document of the Tenth Special Session of the General Assembly and other relevant resolutions of the Assembly on those questions;

4. *Calls upon* the Conference on Disarmament to provide the existing *ad hoc* committees with appropriate negotiating mandates and to establish, as a matter of urgency, the *ad hoc* committees under item 1 of its agenda, entitled "Nuclear-test ban", on the cessation of the nuclear-arms race and nuclear disarmament, on the prevention of nuclear war and on the prevention of an arms race in outer space;

5. *Urges* the Conference on Disarmament to undertake, without further delay, negotiations with a view to elaborating a draft treaty on a nuclear-weapon-test ban;

6. *Also urges* the Conference on Disarmament to intensify its work on the elaboration of a draft convention on the prohibition of the development, production and stockpiling of all chemical weapons and on their destruction and to submit the preliminary draft of such

a convention to the General Assembly at its fortieth session;

7. *Once again calls upon* the Conference on Disarmament to organize its work in such a way as to concentrate most of its attention and time on substantive negotiations on priority issues of disarmament;

8. *Calls upon* the members of the Conference on Disarmament that have opposed the negotiations on substantive issues of disarmament to enable the Conference, by adopting a positive stand, to fulfil effectively the mandate that the international community has entrusted to it in the field of negotiations on disarmament;

9. *Requests* the Conference on Disarmament to submit a report on its work to the General Assembly at its fortieth session;

10. *Decides* to include in the provisional agenda of its fortieth session the item entitled "Report of the Conference on Disarmament".

General Assembly resolution 39/148 N

17 December 1984   Meeting 102   123-1-21 (recorded vote)

Approved by First Committee (A/39/749) by recorded vote (113-1-19), 19 November (meeting 41); 27-nation draft (A/C.1/39/L.56); agenda item 59 (b).

Sponsors: Algeria, Argentina, Bangladesh, Bolivia, Brazil, Burma, Colombia, Cuba, Ecuador, Egypt, Ethiopia, India, Indonesia, Iran, Madagascar, Mexico, Nigeria, Pakistan, Peru, Romania, Sri Lanka, Sudan, Sweden, Uruguay, Venezuela, Yugoslavia, Zaire.

Meeting numbers. GA 39th session: 1st Committee 3-36, 40-42; plenary 102.

Recorded vote in Assembly as follows:

In favour: Afghanistan, Algeria, Angola, Antigua and Barbuda, Argentina, Austria, Bahamas, Bahrain, Bangladesh, Barbados, Benin, Bhutan, Bolivia, Botswana, Brazil, Brunei Darussalam, Bulgaria, Burkina Faso, Burma, Burundi, Byelorussian SSR, Cape Verde, Central African Republic, Chad, Chile, China, Colombia, Congo, Costa Rica, Cuba, Cyprus, Czechoslovakia, Democratic Kampuchea, Democratic Yemen, Djibouti, Dominican Republic, Ecuador, Egypt, El Salvador, Equatorial Guinea, Ethiopia, Fiji, Finland, Gabon, Gambia, German Democratic Republic, Ghana, Guatemala, Guinea, Guyana, Haiti, Honduras, Hungary, India, Indonesia, Iran, Iraq, Ireland, Ivory Coast, Jamaica, Jordan, Kenya, Kuwait, Lao People's Democratic Republic, Lebanon, Lesotho, Liberia, Libyan Arab Jamahiriya, Madagascar, Malaysia, Maldives, Mali, Malta, Mauritania, Mauritius, Mexico, Mongolia, Morocco, Mozambique, Nicaragua, Niger, Nigeria, Oman, Pakistan, Panama, Paraguay, Peru, Philippines, Poland, Qatar, Romania, Rwanda, Saint Lucia, Saint Vincent and the Grenadines, Sao Tome and Principe, Saudi Arabia, Senegal, Seychelles, Sierra Leone, Singapore, Somalia, Sri Lanka, Sudan, Suriname, Sweden, Syrian Arab Republic, Thailand, Togo, Trinidad and Tobago, Tunisia, Uganda, Ukrainian SSR, USSR, United Arab Emirates, United Republic of Tanzania, Uruguay, Venezuela, Viet Nam, Yemen, Yugoslavia, Zaire, Zambia, Zimbabwe.

Against: United States.

Abstaining: Australia, Belgium, Cameroon, Canada, Denmark, France, Germany, Federal Republic of, Greece, Iceland, Israel, Italy, Japan, Luxembourg, Nepal,[a] Netherlands, New Zealand, Norway, Portugal, Spain, Turkey, United Kingdom.

[a]Later advised the Secretariat it had intended to vote in favour.

In explanation of vote, the United States asserted that, in recent years, the authors of drafts on the topic had increasingly sought to reflect an extreme view of what the Conference on Disarmament could and should attempt to accomplish and, by inference, castigated members holding other views.

The Netherlands felt the text failed to take into account the consensus character of the Conference, took sides in the discussions in that body, especially as regards its subsidiary bodies and their mandates, and over-emphasized the negative aspects of its work. France found it unfitting for the Assembly to call on the Conference to act on the mandates of its subsidiary bodies. Similarly,

Belgium regarded the draft as giving instructions to the Conference and as conveying the impression that complex and subtle problems could be solved through setting up and mandating working groups. Australia objected to the call for a nuclear-weapon-test ban, a goal far more limited in scope than its aim of banning all nuclear tests.

The Assembly adopted resolution 39/148 L by recorded vote.

Implementation of the recommendations and decisions of the tenth special session

The General Assembly,

Recalling paragraph 28 of the Final Document of the Tenth Special Session of the General Assembly, in which it affirmed that all the peoples of the world had a vital interest in the success of disarmament negotiations, that, consequently, all States had the duty to contribute to efforts in the field of disarmament and that all States had the right to participate in disarmament negotiations,

Recalling its resolution 38/183 F of 20 December 1983, in which it called upon the Governments of all States to contribute substantially, *inter alia*, to halting and reversing the arms race, particularly in the nuclear field, and thus to reducing the danger of nuclear war,

Taking note of the fact that at the 1984 session of the Conference on Disarmament, twenty-one States not members of the Conference participated in its work,

1. *Reaffirms* the right of all States not members of the Conference on Disarmament to participate in the work of the plenary meetings of the Conference on substantive questions;

2. *Requests* the States members of the Conference on Disarmament not to misuse the rules of procedure of the Conference so as to prevent States not members from participating in the work of the plenary meetings of the Conference.

General Assembly resolution 39/148 L

17 December 1984   Meeting 102   120-0-18 (recorded vote)

Approved by First Committee (A/39/749) by recorded vote (107-0-21), 20 November (meeting 43); draft by Iraq (A/C.1/39/L.47); agenda item 59 *(g)*.

Meeting numbers. GA 39th session: 1st Committee 3-36, 40, 43; plenary 102.

Recorded vote in Assembly as follows:

In favour: Afghanistan, Algeria, Angola, Antigua and Barbuda, Argentina, Australia, Bahamas, Bahrain, Bangladesh, Barbados, Benin, Bhutan, Bolivia, Botswana, Brazil, Bulgaria, Burkina Faso, Burundi, Byelorussian SSR, Cameroon, Cape Verde, Central African Republic, Chad, Chile, China, Colombia, Congo, Costa Rica, Cuba, Czechoslovakia, Democratic Yemen, Denmark, Djibouti, Dominican Republic, Ecuador, Egypt, El Salvador, Equatorial Guinea, Fiji, Finland, France, Gabon, Gambia, German Democratic Republic, Ghana, Greece, Guatemala, Guinea, Guyana, Haiti, Honduras, Hungary, Iceland, Iraq, Ireland, Ivory Coast, Jamaica, Japan, Jordan, Kenya, Kuwait, Lao People's Democratic Republic, Lebanon, Lesotho, Libyan Arab Jamahiriya, Madagascar, Malawi, Malaysia, Maldives, Mali, Malta, Mauritania, Mauritius, Mexico, Mongolia, Morocco, Mozambique, Nepal,ᵃ Nicaragua, Niger, Norway, Oman, Panama, Paraguay, Peru, Philippines, Poland, Portugal, Qatar, Romania, Rwanda, Saint Lucia, Saint Vincent and the Grenadines, Sao Tome and Principe, Saudi Arabia, Senegal, Sierra Leone, Somalia, Spain, Sri Lanka, Sudan, Suriname, Syrian Arab Republic, Togo, Trinidad and Tobago, Tunisia, Turkey, Uganda, Ukrainian SSR, USSR, United Arab Emirates, United Republic of Tanzania, Uruguay, Venezuela, Viet Nam, Yemen, Yugoslavia, Zaire, Zambia, Zimbabwe.

Against: None.

Abstaining: Austria, Belgium, Canada, Ethiopia, Germany, Federal Republic of, India, Iran, Israel, Italy, Liberia, Luxembourg, Netherlands, New Zealand, Nigeria, Pakistan, Sweden, United Kingdom, United States.

ᵃLater advised the Secretariat it had intended to abstain.

Introducing the draft, Iraq said the proposal did not aim at changing the Conference's rules of procedure, but at making it possible for non-members to contribute to its work.

Italy, New Zealand, Sweden and the United Kingdom, although sympathetic to the idea put forward, objected to the Assembly's attempting to alter the rules of procedure of the independent Conference or their application. The United States felt that paragraph 1 failed to make it clear that non-members participated in the Conference in accordance with those rules. France expressed the reservation that paragraph 2 could be interpreted as inviting the Conference to ignore the rules relating to decision-making.

In 1984, the Assembly adopted a number of other resolutions concerning the Conference on Disarmament. It called on the Conference to take up specific topics, such as: a comprehensive programme of disarmament (39/148 I), the nuclear-arms race and nuclear disarmament (39/148 C, D, K, O, P), prohibiting nuclear weapons (39/63 H), a comprehensive nuclear-test-ban treaty (39/53), banning nuclear-weapon tests (39/60), banning the neutron weapon (39/148 E), strengthening the security of non-nuclear-weapon States (39/57, 39/58), new types of weapons of mass destruction (39/62), chemical weapons (39/65 A-C), and the arms race in outer space (39/59).

Disarmament Commission

Disarmament Commission activities. The Disarmament Commission, composed of all United Nations Member States, held its 1984 session in New York, holding nine plenary meetings between 7 May and 1 June.[18] It also met on 3 and 5 December to organize its work and elect officers for 1985.

Its agenda included items on aspects of the arms race, particularly the nuclear-arms race; reduction of military budgets and expenditures; South Africa's nuclear capability; guidelines for confidence-building measures; and the relationship between disarmament and development. Details on the Commission's discussion of these questions can be found elsewhere in this chapter.

The Commission established a Committee of the Whole, which in turn established a contact group to deal with the item on aspects of the arms race; in addition, a working group was set up for each of the other four substantive items on the agenda. None of them, however, was able to conclude its work in 1984; they recommended that the Commission either further pursue its efforts to reach agreement, or refer the questions concerned to the General Assembly's 1984 session.

GENERAL ASSEMBLY ACTION

On 17 December 1984, the General Assembly, on the recommendation of the First Committee, adopted resolution 39/148 R without vote.

Report of the Disarmament Commission

The General Assembly,

Having considered the report of the Disarmament Commission,

Emphasizing again the importance of an effective follow-up to the relevant recommendations and decisions contained in the Final Document of the Tenth Special Session of the General Assembly, the first special session devoted to disarmament,

Taking into account the relevant sections of the Concluding Document of the Twelfth Special Session of the General Assembly, the second special session devoted to disarmament,

Considering the important role that the Disarmament Commission has played and the significant contribution that it has made in examining and submitting recommendations on various problems in the field of disarmament and in the promotion of the implementation of the relevant decisions of the tenth special session,

Desirous of strengthening the effectiveness of the Disarmament Commission as the deliberative body in the field of disarmament,

Recalling its resolutions 33/71 H of 14 December 1978, 34/83 H of 11 December 1979, 35/152 F of 12 December 1980, 36/92 B of 9 December 1981, 37/78 H of 9 December 1982 and 38/183 E of 20 December 1983,

1. *Takes note* of the report of the Disarmament Commission;

2. *Notes* that the Disarmament Commission has yet to conclude its consideration of some items on its agenda;

3. *Requests* the Disarmament Commission to continue its work in accordance with its mandate, as set forth in paragraph 118 of the Final Document of the Tenth Special Session of the General Assembly, and with paragraph 3 of resolution 37/78 H, and to that end to make every effort to achieve specific recommendations, at its 1985 substantive session, on the outstanding items on its agenda, taking into account the relevant resolutions of the General Assembly as well as the results of its 1984 substantive session;

4. *Requests* the Disarmament Commission to meet for a period not exceeding four weeks during 1985 and to submit a substantive report, containing specific recommendations on the items inscribed on its agenda, to the General Assembly at its fortieth session;

5. *Requests* the Secretary-General to transmit to the Disarmament Commission the report of the Conference on Disarmament, together with all the official records of the thirty-ninth session of the General Assembly relating to disarmament matters, and to render all assistance that the Commission may require for implementing the present resolution;

6. *Decides* to include in the provisional agenda of its fortieth session the item entitled "Report of the Disarmament Commission".

General Assembly resolution 39/148 R

17 December 1984   Meeting 102   Adopted without vote

Approved by First Committee (A/39/749) without vote, 19 November (meeting 41); 13-nation draft (A/C.1/39/L.70); agenda item 59 *(a)*.

Sponsors: Argentina, Bahamas, Byelorussian SSR, German Democratic Republic, Germany, Federal Republic of, Ghana, Greece, Liberia, Nepal, Pakistan, Romania, Sudan, Uruguay.

Meeting numbers. GA 39th session: 1st Committee 3-36, 41; plenary 102.

In another 17 December resolution (39/148 O) on implementing the recommendations of the 1978 special session on disarmament, the Assembly called on the Commission to intensify and improve its work with a view to making recommendations on specific items on its agenda. In addition, the Assembly instructed the Commission on certain topics, among them: implementation of the Declaration of the 1980s as the Second Disarmament Decade (39/148 Q), South Africa's nuclear capability (39/61 B), the naval arms race (39/151 I), confidence-building measures (39/63 E), and a review of the United Nations role in disarmament (39/151 G).

Special sessions of the General Assembly on disarmament

Implementation of recommendations adopted at two special sessions of the General Assembly devoted to disarmament—its first in 1978[19] and its second in 1982[15]—continued to be monitored in 1984, leading to the Assembly adopting 29 resolutions and one decision relating to those recommendations.

Implementation of the recommendations of the 1978 special session

In 1984, the General Assembly adopted 18 resolutions and one decision on implementation of recommendations it had adopted in 1978 at its tenth special session—the first such session devoted to disarmament. They dealt with unilateral nuclear disarmament measures (39/148 A), bilateral nuclear-arms negotiations (39/148 B, G), cessation of the nuclear-arms race and nuclear disarmament (39/148 C, K), non-use of nuclear weapons and prevention of nuclear war (39/148 D), prohibiting the nuclear neutron weapon (39/148 E), nuclear-war prevention (39/148 F, P), the statute of the United Nations Institute for Disarmament Research (39/148 H), a comprehensive programme of disarmament (39/148 I), Disarmament Week (39/148 J), implementation of the recommendations and decisions of the tenth special session (39/148 L, O), international co-operation for disarmament (39/148 M), the work of the Conference on Disarmament (39/148 N) and the Disarmament Commission (39/148 R), and review of the Declaration of the 1980s as the Second Disarmament Decade (39/148 Q). The decision (39/423) dealt with the work of the Advisory Board on Disarmament Studies.

GENERAL ASSEMBLY ACTION

On 17 December 1984, the General Assembly, on the recommendation of the First Committee, adopted resolution 39/148 O by recorded vote.

Implementation of the recommendations and decisions of the tenth special session

The General Assembly,

Having reviewed the implementation of the recommendations and decisions adopted by the General Assembly at its tenth special session, the first special session devoted to disarmament, as well as the Concluding Document of the Twelfth Special Session of the General Assembly, the second special session devoted to disarmament,

Recalling its resolutions S-10/2 of 30 June 1978, 34/83 C of 11 December 1979, 35/46 of 3 December 1980, 35/152 E of 12 December 1980, 36/92 M of 9 December 1981, 37/78 F of 9 December 1982, 38/183 H of 20 December 1983 and its decision S-12/24 of 10 July 1982,

Deeply concerned that no concrete results regarding the implementation of the recommendations and decisions of the tenth special session have been realized in the course of more than six years since that session, that in the mean time the arms race, particularly in its nuclear aspect, has gained in intensity, that there has been further deployment of nuclear weapons in some parts of the world, that the absence of constructive dialogue among the nuclear-weapon States has reached unprecedented levels, that annual global military expenditures are approaching the staggering figure of $1,000 billion, that mankind is faced with a real danger of spreading the arms race into outer space, that urgent measures to prevent nuclear war and for disarmament have not been adopted and that continued colonial domination and foreign occupation, open threats, pressures and military intervention against independent States and violations of the fundamental principles of the Charter of the United Nations have taken place, posing the most serious threat to international peace and security,

Expressing serious concern that even the limited negotiations on arms reduction and disarmament which were already under way have been stalled,

Convinced that the renewed escalation of the nuclear-arms race, in both the quantitative and qualitative dimensions, as well as reliance on nuclear deterrence and on the use of nuclear weapons, has heightened the risk of the outbreak of nuclear war and led to greater insecurity and instability in international relations,

Further convinced that international peace and security can only be ensured through general and complete disarmament under effective international control and that one of the most urgent tasks is to halt and reverse the arms race and to undertake concrete measures of disarmament, particularly nuclear disarmament, and that, in this respect, the nuclear-weapon States and other militarily significant States have the primary responsibility,

Noting with great concern that no real progress in disarmament negotiations has been achieved for several years, which has rendered the current international situation even more dangerous and insecure, and that negotiations on disarmament issues are lagging far behind the rapid technological development in the field of armaments and the relentless growth of military arsenals, particularly nuclear arsenals,

Considering that it is more than ever imperative in the present circumstances to give a new impetus to negotiations in good faith on disarmament, in particular nuclear disarmament, at all levels and to achieve genuine progress in the immediate future, and that all States should refrain from any actions which have or may have negative effects on the outcome of disarmament negotiations,

Convinced that the success of disarmament negotiations, in which all the people of the world have a vital interest, can be achieved through the active participation of Member States in such negotiations, contributing thereby to the maintenance of international peace and security,

Reaffirming that the United Nations has a central role and primary responsibility in the sphere of disarmament,

Stressing that the Final Document of the Tenth Special Session of the General Assembly, which was unanimously and categorically reaffirmed by all Member States at the twelfth special session as the comprehensive basis for efforts towards halting and reversing the arms race, retains all its validity and that the objectives and measures contained therein still represent one of the most important and urgent goals to be achieved,

1. *Expresses its grave concern* over the acceleration and intensification of the arms race, particularly the nuclear-arms race, as well as the continued, very serious deterioration of relations in the world, and the intensification of focal points of aggression and hotbeds of tension in different regions of the world, which threaten international peace and security and increase the danger of nuclear war;

2. *Calls upon* all States, in particular nuclear-weapon States and other militarily significant States, to take urgent measures in order to put an end to the serious aggravation of the international situation, to promote international security on the basis of disarmament, to halt and reverse the arms race and to launch a process of genuine disarmament;

3. *Invites* all States, particularly nuclear-weapon States and especially those among them which possess the most important nuclear arsenals, to take urgent measures with a view to implementing the recommendations and decisions contained in the Final Document of the Tenth Special Session of the General Assembly, as well as to fulfilling the priority tasks set forth in the Programme of Action contained in section III of the Final Document;

4. *Calls upon* great Powers to undertake genuine negotiations in a constructive and accommodating spirit and taking into account the interest of the entire international community in order to halt the arms race, particularly the nuclear-arms race, and to achieve disarmament;

5. *Calls upon* the Conference on Disarmament to concentrate its work on the substantive and priority items on its agenda, to proceed to negotiations on the cessation of the nuclear-arms race and nuclear disarmament, on the prevention of nuclear war as well as the prevention of an arms race in outer space without further delay and to elaborate drafts of treaties on a nuclear-weapon-test ban and on a complete and effective prohibition of the development, production and stockpiling of all chemical weapons and on their destruction;

6. *Calls upon* the Disarmament Commission to intensify its work in accordance with its mandate and to continue improving its work with a view to making concrete recommendations on specific items on its agenda;

7. *Invites* all States engaged in disarmament and arms limitation negotiations outside the framework of the United Nations to keep the General Assembly and the Conference on Disarmament informed on the status and/or results of such negotiations, in conformity with the relevant provisions of the Final Document of the Tenth Special Session;

8. *Decides* to include in the provisional agenda of its fortieth session the item entitled "Implementation of the recommendations and decisions of the tenth special session".

General Assembly resolution 39/148 O

17 December 1984   Meeting 102   127-11-7 (recorded vote)

Approved by First Committee (A/39/749) by recorded vote (111-11-9), 21 November (meeting 46); 29-nation draft (A/C.1/39/L.58/Rev.1); agenda item 59 *(g)*.
Sponsors: Algeria, Argentina, Bahamas, Bangladesh, Bolivia, Burma, Colombia, Cuba, Ecuador, Egypt, Ethiopia, German Democratic Republic, Ghana, India, Indonesia, Iran, Madagascar, Nigeria, Pakistan, Peru, Romania, Sri Lanka, Sudan, Tunisia, Uruguay, Venezuela, Viet Nam, Yugoslavia, Zaire.
Meeting numbers. GA 39th session: 1st Committee 3-37, 43, 46; plenary 102.

Recorded vote in Assembly as follows:

In favour: Afghanistan, Algeria, Angola, Antigua and Barbuda, Argentina, Austria, Bahamas, Bahrain, Bangladesh, Barbados, Benin, Bhutan, Bolivia, Botswana, Brazil, Brunei Darussalam, Bulgaria, Burkina Faso, Burma, Burundi, Byelorussian SSR, Cameroon,[a] Cape Verde, Central African Republic, Chad, Chile, China, Colombia, Congo, Costa Rica, Cuba, Cyprus, Czechoslovakia, Democratic Kampuchea, Democratic Yemen, Denmark, Djibouti, Dominican Republic, Ecuador, Egypt, El Salvador, Equatorial Guinea, Ethiopia, Fiji, Finland, Gabon, Gambia, German Democratic Republic, Ghana, Greece, Guatemala, Guinea, Guyana, Haiti, Honduras, Hungary, India, Indonesia, Iran, Iraq, Ireland, Ivory Coast, Jamaica, Jordan, Kenya, Kuwait, Lao People's Democratic Republic, Lebanon, Lesotho, Liberia, Libyan Arab Jamahiriya, Madagascar, Malawi, Malaysia, Maldives, Mali, Malta, Mauritania, Mauritius, Mexico, Mongolia, Morocco, Mozambique, Nepal, Nicaragua, Niger, Nigeria, Oman, Pakistan, Panama, Paraguay, Peru, Philippines, Poland, Qatar, Romania, Rwanda, Saint Lucia, Sao Tome and Principe, Saudi Arabia, Senegal, Seychelles, Sierra Leone, Singapore, Somalia, Sri Lanka, Sudan, Suriname, Sweden, Syrian Arab Republic, Thailand, Togo, Trinidad and Tobago, Tunisia, Uganda, Ukrainian SSR, USSR, United Arab Emirates, United Republic of Tanzania, Uruguay, Venezuela, Viet Nam, Yemen, Yugoslavia, Zaire, Zambia, Zimbabwe.

Against: Belgium, Canada, France, Germany, Federal Republic of, Israel, Italy, Luxembourg, Netherlands, Portugal, Turkey, United States.

Abstaining: Australia, Iceland, Japan, New Zealand, Norway, Spain, United Kingdom.

[a]Later advised the Secretariat it had intended to abstain.

The revised text resulted from consultations among the sponsors on two drafts—one by the German Democratic Republic[20] and one by the 28 other States. By the former draft, on the obligation of States to contribute to effective disarmament negotiations, which was not pressed to a vote, the Assembly would have called for the holding of negotiations in the spirit of the 1978 Final Document,[12] for avoiding actions which might have negative effects on such talks and for preserving existing arms limitation and disarmament agreements.

Prior to acting on the draft that became resolution 39/148 O, the Assembly adopted the fifth preambular paragraph by a recorded vote of 117 to 19. The same paragraph had been approved in the First Committee by a recorded vote—requested by the United Kingdom—of 100 to 19, with 3 abstentions.

Three of the States which voted against the paragraph explained their position on that paragraph and the text as a whole. The United States said that, while in sympathy with various aspects of the text, it found certain language provocative

and insensitive to the views of others. The United Kingdom asserted that the sponsors had failed to negotiate on the language used in the text and expressed, instead, their own partisan opinions. Australia considered that the preambular paragraph contained an unacceptable attack on the concept of deterrence, which it considered as the only current guarantor of global security; further, the call for a nuclear-weapon-test ban reflected a more limited concept than that which it favoured.

Implementation of the recommendations of the 1982 special session

In 1984, the General Assembly adopted 11 resolutions on implementation of the recommendations of its 1982 special session on disarmament. They were on: the World Disarmament Campaign (39/63 A, D, J), the United Nations fellowships programme on disarmament (39/63 B), a nuclear-arms freeze (39/63 C), confidence-building measures (39/63 E), regional disarmament (39/63 F), a nuclear-weapons freeze (39/63 G), a convention against nuclear weapons (39/63 H), convening the Assembly's third special session on disarmament (39/63 I), and disarmament and international security (39/63 K).

Third special session

GENERAL ASSEMBLY ACTION

On the recommendation of the First Committee, the General Assembly, on 12 December 1984, adopted resolution 39/63 I without vote.

Convening of the third special session of the General Assembly devoted to disarmament

The General Assembly,

Bearing in mind the decision adopted at its twelfth special session, the second special session devoted to disarmament, concerning the convening of the third special session devoted to disarmament,

Recalling its resolution 38/73 I of 15 December 1983 in which it decided that the third special session devoted to disarmament should be held not later than 1988,

Desiring to contribute to the furthering and broadening of positive processes initiated through the laying down of the foundations of an international disarmament strategy at its tenth special session, the first special session devoted to disarmament,

Decides to set, at its fortieth session, the date of the third special session of the General Assembly devoted to disarmament and to establish the Preparatory Committee for the third special session.

General Assembly resolution 39/63 I

12 December 1984   Meeting 97   Adopted without vote

Approved by First Committee (A/39/750) without vote, 19 November (meeting 41); 27-nation draft (A/C.1/39/L.57); agenda item 60.
Sponsors: Algeria, Argentina, Bangladesh, Bolivia, Colombia, Cuba, Ecuador, Egypt, Ethiopia, Ghana, India, Indonesia, Iran, Madagascar, Mexico, Nigeria, Pakistan, Peru, Romania, Sri Lanka, Sudan, Tunisia, Uruguay, Venezuela, Viet Nam, Yugoslavia, Zaire.
Meeting numbers. GA 39th session: 1st Committee 3-36, 38, 41; plenary 97.

Implementation of the 1979 Declaration on co-operation for disarmament

As in previous years, the General Assembly, in 1984, again called for implementation of its 1979 Declaration on International Co-operation for Disarmament.[21]

GENERAL ASSEMBLY ACTION

On 17 December, the Assembly, on the recommendation of the First Committee, adopted resolution 39/148 M by recorded vote.

International co-operation for disarmament

The General Assembly,

Stressing again the urgent need for an active and sustained effort to intensify the implementation of the recommendations and decisions unanimously adopted at its tenth special session, the first special session devoted to disarmament, as contained in the Final Document of that session and confirmed in the Concluding Document of the Twelfth Special Session of the General Assembly, the second special session devoted to disarmament,

Recalling the Declaration on International Co-operation for Disarmament of 11 December 1979 and General Assembly resolutions 36/92 D of 9 December 1981, 37/78 B of 9 December 1982 and 38/183 F of 20 December 1983,

Stressing the vital importance of eliminating the danger of a nuclear war, halting the arms race and attaining disarmament, particularly in the nuclear field, for the preservation of peace and the strengthening of international security,

Deeply concerned over the continued nuclear-arms race and the initiation of a new, quantitatively and qualitatively more dangerous round of that race, which has an immediate negative impact on the development of the international situation and international relations,

Bearing in mind the vital interest of all States in the adoption of concrete effective disarmament measures, which would release considerable financial and material resources to be used for the economic and social development of all States, in particular developing countries,

Considering the increased activity of peace and anti-war movements against the arms race and for disarmament,

Convinced of the need to strengthen constructive international co-operation based on the political goodwill of States for successful negotiations on disarmament, in accordance with the Final Document of the Tenth Special Session,

Emphasizing the duty of States to co-operate for the preservation of international peace and security, in accordance with the Charter of the United Nations, as confirmed in the Declaration on Principles of International Law concerning Friendly Relations and Co-operation among States in accordance with the Charter of the United Nations, of 24 October 1970, the obligation to co-operate actively and constructively for the attainment of the aims of disarmament being an indispensable part of that duty,

Stressing that, within the framework of international co-operation for the attainment of the aims of disarmament, it is necessary to avert nuclear war by means of gradual limitation and reduction of nuclear armaments up to a complete liquidation of all their kinds on the basis of the principle of equal security,

Expressing the conviction that concrete manifestations of political goodwill, including unilateral measures, such as an obligation not to make first use of nuclear weapons, improve conditions for resolving disarmament issues in a spirit of co-operation among States,

Stressing that proposals, relatively simple in their execution and at the same time effective, and agreements aimed at eliminating the use or the threat of use of force, be it on a world-wide or regional scale, contribute considerably to that end,

Bearing in mind that the United Nations bears primary responsibility and plays a central role in unifying efforts to maintain and to develop active co-operation among States in order to resolve the issues of disarmament,

1. *Calls upon* all States, in implementing the Final Document of the Tenth Special Session of the General Assembly, to make active use of the principles and ideas contained in the Declaration on International Co-operation for Disarmament by actively participating in disarmament negotiations, with a view to achieving concrete results, and by conducting them on the basis of the principles of reciprocity, equality, undiminished security and the non-use of force in international relations, and to refrain at the same time from developing new channels of the arms race;

2. *Stresses* the importance of strengthening the effectiveness of the United Nations in fulfilling its responsibility for maintaining international peace and security in accordance with the Charter of the United Nations;

3. *Emphasizes* the necessity of refraining from war propaganda, in particular nuclear war—global or limited—and from the elaboration and dissemination of any doctrines and concepts endangering international peace and justifying the unleashing of nuclear war, which lead to deterioration of the international situation and to further intensification of the arms race and which are also detrimental to the generally recognized necessity of international co-operation for disarmament;

4. *Declares* that the use of force in international relations as well as in attempts to prevent the full implementation of the Declaration on the Granting of Independence to Colonial Countries and Peoples is a phenomenon incompatible with the ideas of international co-operation for disarmament;

5. *Expresses the firm conviction* that, for effective international co-operation for the attainment of the aims of disarmament, it is inevitable that the policy of States, primarily of those which dispose of nuclear weapons, be directed to averting a nuclear war;

6. *Appeals* to States which are members of military groupings to promote, on the basis of the Final Document of the Tenth Special Session, in the spirit of international co-operation for disarmament, the gradual mutual limitation of military activities of these groupings, thus creating conditions for their dissolution;

7. *Calls upon* all Member States to cultivate and disseminate, particularly in connection with the World Disarmament Campaign, launched by the General Assembly at its twelfth special session, the ideas of international co-operation for disarmament, in particular through their educational systems, mass media and cultural policies;

8.   *Calls upon* the United Nations Educational, Scientific and Cultural Organization to continue to consider, in order further to mobilize world public opinion on behalf of disarmament, measures aimed at strengthening the ideas of international co-operation for disarmament through research, education, information, communication and culture;

9.   *Calls upon* the Governments of all States to contribute substantially, while observing the principle of undiminished security, to halting and reversing the arms race, particularly in the nuclear field, and thus to reducing the danger of nuclear war.

General Assembly resolution 39/148 M

17 December 1984   Meeting 102   109-19-7 (recorded vote)

Approved by First Committee (A/39/749) by recorded vote (99-19-8), 20 November (meeting 43); 21-nation draft (A/C.1/39/L.53); agenda item 59.

Sponsors: Afghanistan, Angola, Benin, Congo, Cuba, Czechoslovakia, Democratic Yemen, Ethiopia, German Democratic Republic, Guinea, Guyana, Hungary, Indonesia, Lao People's Democratic Republic, Madagascar, Mongolia, Mozambique, Poland, Syrian Arab Republic, Ukrainian SSR, Viet Nam.

Meeting numbers. GA 39th session: 1st Committee 3-37, 43; plenary 102.

Recorded vote in Assembly as follows:

In favour: Afghanistan, Algeria, Angola, Antigua and Barbuda, Argentina, Bahrain, Bangladesh, Barbados, Benin, Bhutan, Botswana, Brazil,[a] Bulgaria, Burkina Faso, Burundi, Byelorussian SSR, Cameroon, Cape Verde, Central African Republic, Chad, Chile, Colombia, Congo, Costa Rica, Cuba, Cyprus, Czechoslovakia, Democratic Yemen, Djibouti, Dominican Republic, Ecuador, Egypt, El Salvador, Equatorial Guinea, Ethiopia, Fiji, Gabon, Gambia, German Democratic Republic, Ghana, Guatemala, Guinea, Guyana, Haiti, Honduras, Hungary, India, Indonesia, Iran, Iraq, Ivory Coast, Jordan, Kenya, Kuwait, Lao People's Democratic Republic, Lebanon, Lesotho, Liberia, Libyan Arab Jamahiriya, Madagascar, Malawi, Malaysia, Maldives, Mali, Mauritania, Mauritius, Mexico, Mongolia, Mozambique, Nepal, Nicaragua, Niger, Nigeria, Oman, Pakistan, Panama, Peru, Poland, Qatar, Romania, Rwanda, Saint Lucia, Saint Vincent and the Grenadines, Sao Tome and Principe, Saudi Arabia, Seychelles, Sierra Leone, Somalia, Sri Lanka, Sudan, Suriname, Syrian Arab Republic, Thailand, Togo, Trinidad and Tobago, Tunisia, Uganda, Ukrainian SSR, USSR, United Arab Emirates, United Republic of Tanzania, Uruguay, Venezuela, Viet Nam, Yemen, Yugoslavia, Zaire, Zambia, Zimbabwe.

Against: Australia, Belgium, Canada, Denmark, France, Germany, Federal Republic of, Iceland, Israel, Italy, Japan, Luxembourg, Netherlands, New Zealand, Norway, Portugal, Spain, Turkey, United Kingdom, United States.

Abstaining: Austria, Bahamas, Finland, Greece, Ireland, Paraguay, Sweden.

[a]Later advised the Secretariat it had intended to abstain.

In explanation of vote, Oman stated that its agreement with the principle set forth in the text should not be taken as approval of some of the paragraphs or in connection with the cold war between the major Powers.

Implementation of the 1980 Declaration on the Second Disarmament Decade

In 1984, the General Assembly called for a review, in 1985, of the implementation of its Declaration of the 1980s as the Second Disarmament Decade.[22]

GENERAL ASSEMBLY ACTION

Acting on the recommendation of the First Committee, the Assembly, on 17 December 1984, adopted resolution 39/148 Q without vote.

Review of the Declaration of the 1980s as the Second Disarmament Decade

The General Assembly,

Recalling its resolution 35/46 of 3 December 1980, by which it adopted the Declaration of the 1980s as the Second Disarmament Decade,

Expressing its concern that the purposes and objectives of the Decade are far from being realized,

Alarmed at the continued escalation of the arms race, particularly the nuclear-arms race,

Also alarmed at the recent findings of the possible consequences of a nuclear war under present circumstances, as documented by competent scientists,

Deeply concerned at the continued dissipation of ever-increasing human and material resources on the arms race,

Expressing its anguish that no negotiations are taking place on the crucial issue of nuclear weapons,

Convinced of the urgent necessity for the resumption of negotiations, both bilaterally between the Government of the Union of Soviet Socialist Republics and the Government of the United States of America and multilaterally by the Conference on Disarmament,

1.   *Decides* to undertake at its fortieth session, in 1985, a review and appraisal of the implementation of the Declaration of the 1980s as the Second Disarmament Decade;

2.   *Requests* the Disarmament Commission at its 1985 session to make a preliminary assessment of the implementation of the Declaration, as well as suggestions to ensure progress, and to submit a report to the General Assembly at its fortieth session;

3.   *Calls upon* the Disarmament Commission to include in its assessment any relevant matters which, in the view of any Member State, require such review;

4.   *Requests* Member States to submit to the Secretary-General their views and suggestions;

5.   *Requests* the Secretary-General to give all necessary assistance to the Disarmament Commission in implementing the present resolution.

General Assembly resolution 39/148 Q

17 December 1984   Meeting 102   Adopted without vote

Approved by First Committee (A/39/749) without vote, 19 November (meeting 42); 10-nation draft (A/C.1/39/L.65); agenda item 59.

Sponsors: Algeria, Argentina, Bangladesh, India, Indonesia, Nigeria, Pakistan, Romania, Tunisia, Yugoslavia.

Meeting numbers. GA 39th session: 1st Committee 3-36, 39, 42; plenary 102.

In explanation of position on the final preambular paragraph, the USSR called attention to its frequently expressed position with regard to the need for the resumption of negotiations. Believing that bilateral negotiations between the USSR and the United States held the best hope under current circumstances for progress in nuclear disarmament, the United Kingdom questioned the usefulness of the reference in that paragraph to multilateral negotiations.

Disarmament negotiations

The importance of disarmament negotiations was emphasized in a number of 1984 General Assembly resolutions, among them 39/148 M on implementing the 1979 Declaration on International Co-operation for Disarmament, 39/148 N on the work of the Conference on Disarmament, 39/148 O on implementing the recommendations of its 1978 disarmament special session, and 39/155 on implementing the 1970 Declaration on the Strengthening of International Security.

Areas of ongoing or proposed negotiations, covered elsewhere in this chapter, concerned nuclear-war prevention (39/148 P) and nuclear disarmament (39/148 C, K), security of non-nuclear-weapon States (39/57, 39/58), and negotiations for a treaty or a convention against: nuclear-weapon tests (39/52, 39/60), the arms race in outer space (39/59), the use or threat of use of nuclear weapons (39/63 H), chemical and bacteriological weapons (39/65 A-C), the neutron weapon (39/148 E), the naval arms race (39/151 I) and radiological weapons (39/151 J).

REFERENCES

(1)A/39/161-S/16456. (2)A/39/305. (3)A/39/277-S/16587. (4)A/39/560-S/16773. (5)A/39/763-S/16849. (6)A/40/57. (7)A/39/162 & Corr.1. (8)A/39/314. (9)A/39/529. (10)A/39/810. (11)A/39/27. (12)YUN 1978, p. 39, GA res. S-10/2, 30 June 1978. (13)YUN 1983, p. 12, GA res. 38/183 K, 20 Dec. 1983. (14)YUN 1982, p. 150, GA res. 37/99 K, 13 Dec. 1982. (15)*Ibid.*, p. 11. (16)YUN 1983, p. 13. (17)A/39/264. (18)A/39/42. (19)YUN 1978, p. 17. (20)A/C.1/39/L.9. (21)YUN 1979, p. 86, GA res. 34/88, 11 Dec. 1979. (22)YUN 1980, p. 102, GA res. 35/46, annex, 3 Dec. 1980.

Nuclear weapons

Nuclear disarmament

The General Assembly in 1984 adopted 26 resolutions dealing with nuclear questions, including one on a new subject—the climatic effects of nuclear war, also known as nuclear winter.

As in the past, the Assembly called on States to pursue nuclear disarmament and nuclear-war prevention through efforts including negotiations aimed at freezing or banning such weapons, prohibiting nuclear-weapon tests or banning the use of fissionable material for weapons purposes. It continued to support the call for nuclear non-proliferation through the establishment of nuclear-weapon-free zones, and called for the strengthening of the security of non-nuclear-weapon States.

Communications. In the course of the year, the Secretary-General received a number of communications containing calls for various nuclear disarmament measures, including, in particular, resumption of the USSR–United States negotiations (see also p. 24). Several letters dealt with the deployment of medium-range nuclear missiles in Europe.

On 9 January,(1) Mongolia transmitted two statements of 7 December 1983 pointing out that the deployment of United States medium-range nuclear missiles, which it described as first-strike weapons, had disrupted the Geneva talks on the limitation of that type of weapon and had launched a new round of the arms race.

By a letter dated 9 April,(2) Romania transmitted an appeal of 24 March by its Grand National Assembly addressed to the Supreme Soviet of the USSR, the United States Congress and parliaments of European countries and Canada, calling on them to diminish international tension and halt the nuclear-arms race; in particular, it appealed to the two major nuclear Powers to resume nuclear disarmament negotiations, and to the others to work towards halting the emplacement of United States medium-range nuclear missiles in Europe and the application of the nuclear countermeasures announced by the USSR. The call was repeated by the Romanian Communist Party—an extract of whose report was transmitted on 29 November(3)—along with its support for establishing nuclear-weapon-free zones in the Balkans and in north and central Europe, and for preventing militarization of outer space.

Hungary, by a letter of 24 April,(4) transmitted an appeal by a meeting of the States members of the Warsaw Treaty of Friendship, Co-operation and Mutual Assistance (Budapest, 19 and 20 April) to those of the North Atlantic Treaty Organization (NATO) to co-operate in terminating the deployment of new medium-range nuclear missiles, withdrawing those already placed and realizing various disarmament measures in Europe.

In a Declaration issued on 22 May,(5) the heads of State or Government of Argentina, Greece, India, Mexico, Sweden and the United Republic of Tanzania urged China, France, the USSR, the United Kingdom and the United States to halt all testing, production and deployment of nuclear weapons and their delivery systems as a necessary first step, to be followed immediately by substantial reductions in nuclear forces. The Declaration also called for a halt in the nuclear-arms race to allow for renewed talks on nuclear disarmament.

The Declaration was endorsed by Peru, which, in its note verbale of 7 June,(6) considered as particularly important the appeal to the five States for a substantial reduction in nuclear forces. It was also supported by the USSR which, on 1 June,(7) stated that its proposals for reducing nuclear confrontation could be translated into action as soon as the United States removed its obstacles to their discussion. By a letter of 14 June,(8) the United Kingdom, also supporting the Declaration, stated that nuclear deterrence had contributed to peace in Europe and called for USSR–United States negotiations on balanced reductions.

Letters dealing with nuclear disarmament were also submitted in connection with the Assembly's annual review of its 1970 Declaration on strengthening international security (see p. 114).

In November, the USSR and the United States announced that they would enter into new negotiations aimed at reaching mutually acceptable agreements on a whole range of questions concerning nuclear and outer-space arms. The meeting was scheduled for early January 1985.

Activities of the Conference on Disarmament. Questions relating to nuclear-arms limitation and disarmament were discussed—again without tangible results—by the Conference on Disarmament[9] in 1984.

Consensus could not be reached either in the contact group, which had been set up to discuss how the Conference should proceed on the topic, or in the Conference itself, where proposals for the mandate of an *ad hoc* committee had been submitted, respectively, by a group of eight socialist States members of the Conference and by the group of 21 (the non-aligned and neutral States within the Conference—Algeria, Argentina, Brazil, Burma, Cuba, Egypt, Ethiopia, India, Indonesia, Iran, Kenya, Mexico, Morocco, Nigeria, Pakistan, Peru, Sri Lanka, Sweden, Venezuela, Yugoslavia, Zaire). The socialist group envisaged such a committee to begin elaborating practical measures for the cessation of the arms race and nuclear disarmament, while the group of 21 suggested that the proposed body should recommend to the Conference the best ways to initiate multilateral negotiations of agreements. A group of Western States asserted that they were not convinced of the need for such an *ad hoc* committee.

Disarmament Commission activities. As in 1983, the Disarmament Commission[10] considered in 1984, under a two-tiered agenda item, various aspects of the nuclear-arms race and nuclear disarmament in order to expedite negotiations aimed at effectively eliminating the danger of nuclear war; and a general approach to negotiations on nuclear and conventional disarmament in accordance with priorities established by the General Assembly in 1978 at its first special session devoted to disarmament.[11]

Following the Commission's decision that both aspects of the agenda item should be dealt with in the Committee of the Whole, the Committee established a contact group, which held 12 meetings between 10 and 31 May under the leadership of the Commission Chairman. In addition to a compilation of proposals considered by the Commission in 1983,[12] the contact group had before it seven working papers submitted, respectively, by China, the German Democratic Republic, Mexico, Romania and the USSR, as well as by a group of socialist States and a group of Western and other States. Again unable to agree on a set of recommendations on the agenda item, the group submitted an updated compilation for 1984—which was subsequently annexed to the Commission's report—and recommended continued consideration of the topic.

On 17 December 1984, the General Assembly, on the recommendation of the First Committee, adopted resolution 39/148 C by recorded vote.

Nuclear weapons in all aspects

The General Assembly,

Recalling that at its twelfth special session, the second special session devoted to disarmament, it expressed its profound preoccupation over the danger of war, in particular nuclear war, the prevention of which remains the most acute and urgent task of the present day,

Reaffirming that nuclear weapons pose the most serious threat to mankind and its survival and that it is therefore essential to proceed with nuclear disarmament and the complete elimination of nuclear weapons,

Reaffirming also that all nuclear-weapon States, in particular those which possess the most important nuclear arsenals, bear a special responsibility for the fulfilment of the task of achieving the goals of nuclear disarmament,

Stressing again that existing arsenals of nuclear weapons alone are more than sufficient to destroy all life on Earth, and bearing in mind the devastating results which nuclear war would have on belligerents and non-belligerents alike,

Recalling that at its tenth special session, the first special session devoted to disarmament, it decided that effective measures of nuclear disarmament and the prevention of nuclear war had the highest priority and that it was essential to halt and reverse the nuclear-arms race in all its aspects in order to avert the danger of war involving nuclear weapons,

Stressing that any expectation of winning a nuclear war is senseless and that such a war would inevitably lead to the destruction of nations, to enormous devastation and to catastrophic consequences for civilization and life itself on Earth,

Recalling further that, in its resolution 35/152 B of 12 December 1980, it noted with alarm the increased risk of a nuclear catastrophe associated both with the intensification of the nuclear-arms race and with the adoption of the new doctrines of limited or partial use of nuclear weapons, which are incompatible with its resolution 110(II) of 3 November 1947, entitled "Measures to be taken against propaganda and the inciters of a new war", and which give rise to illusions of the admissibility and acceptability of a nuclear conflict,

Noting with alarm that to the doctrine of a limited nuclear war was later added the concept of a protracted nuclear war and that these dangerous doctrines lead to a new twist in the spiral of the arms race, which may seriously hamper the reaching of agreement on nuclear disarmament,

Gravely concerned about the renewed escalation of the nuclear-arms race, in both its quantitative and qualitative dimensions, as well as reliance on the doctrine of nuclear deterrence, which in fact are heightening the risk of the outbreak of nuclear war and lead to increased tensions and instability in international relations,

Taking note of the relevant deliberations of the Disarmament Commission in 1984 with regard to item 4 of its agenda, as contained in its report,

Stressing the urgent need for the cessation of the development and deployment of new types and systems of nuclear weapons as a step on the road to nuclear disarmament,

Stressing again that priority in disarmament negotiations should be given to nuclear weapons, and referring to paragraphs 49 and 54 of the Final Document of the Tenth Special Session of the General Assembly,[13]

Recalling its relevant resolutions on this subject,

Welcoming the Joint Declaration issued on 22 May 1984 by the heads of State or Government of Argentina, Greece, India, Mexico, Sweden and the United Republic of Tanzania, as well as the positive response this Declaration has met with in many States,

Noting that the Conference on Disarmament, at its 1984 session, discussed the question of the cessation of the nuclear-arms race and nuclear disarmament and, in particular, the establishment of an *ad hoc* committee for negotiations on that question,

Regretting, however, that the Conference on Disarmament was prevented from reaching agreement on the establishment of an *ad hoc* committee for the purpose of undertaking multilateral negotiations on the question of the cessation of the nuclear-arms race and nuclear disarmament,

Considering that efforts will continue to be made in order to enable the Conference on Disarmament to fulfil its negotiating role with regard to the cessation of the nuclear-arms race and nuclear disarmament, and that for this purpose all members of the Conference on Disarmament should display a constructive approach to such negotiations, bearing in mind the high priority they have accorded to this question in the Final Document of the Tenth Special Session,

Convinced that the Conference on Disarmament is the most suitable forum for the preparation and conduct of negotiations on nuclear disarmament,

1. *Calls upon* the Conference on Disarmament to proceed without delay to negotiations on the cessation of the nuclear-arms race and nuclear disarmament and especially to begin the elaboration of practical measures for the cessation of the nuclear-arms race and for nuclear disarmament in accordance with paragraph 50 of the Final Document of the Tenth Special Session of the General Assembly, including a nuclear-disarmament programme, and to establish for this purpose an *ad hoc* committee;

2. *Decides* to include in the provisional agenda of its fortieth session the item entitled "Cessation of the nuclear-arms race and nuclear disarmament: report of the Conference on Disarmament".

General Assembly resolution 39/148 C

17 December 1984   Meeting 102   102-19-13 (recorded vote)

Approved by First Committee (A/39/749) by recorded vote (96-19-12), 20 November (meeting 44); 16-nation draft (A/C.1/39/L.8); agenda item 59 *(e)*.

Sponsors: Afghanistan, Angola, Bulgaria, Byelorussian SSR, Cuba, Czechoslovakia, German Democratic Republic, Hungary, Lao People's Democratic Republic, Mongolia, Poland, Romania, Ukrainian SSR, USSR, Viet Nam, Zimbabwe.

Meeting numbers. GA 39th session: 1st Committee 3-36, 44; plenary 102.

Recorded vote in Assembly as follows:

In favour: Afghanistan, Algeria, Angola, Antigua and Barbuda, Argentina, Austria, Bahrain, Bangladesh, Barbados, Benin, Bhutan, Bolivia, Botswana, Brazil, Brunei Darussalam, Bulgaria, Burkina Faso, Burma, Burundi, Byelorussian SSR, Cameroon, Cape Verde, Chile, Colombia, Congo, Costa Rica, Cuba, Cyprus, Czechoslovakia, Democratic Yemen, Djibouti, Ecuador, Egypt, El Salvador, Ethiopia, Fiji, Finland, Gabon, German Democratic Republic, Ghana, Greece, Guinea, Guyana, Haiti, Hungary, India, Indonesia, Iran, Iraq, Jordan, Kenya, Kuwait, Lao People's Democratic Republic, Lebanon, Lesotho, Liberia, Libyan Arab Jamahiriya, Madagascar, Malawi, Malaysia, Maldives, Mali, Mauritania, Mauritius, Mexico, Mongolia, Morocco, Mozambique, Nepal, Nicaragua, Nigeria, Oman, Pakistan, Panama, Peru, Poland, Qatar, Romania, Saint Lucia, Saint Vincent and the Grenadines, Seychelles, Sierra Leone, Singapore, Somalia, Sri Lanka, Sudan, Suriname, Syrian Arab Republic, Thailand, Togo, Trinidad and Tobago, Tunisia, Uganda, Ukrainian SSR, USSR, United Arab Emirates, United Republic of Tanzania, Venezuela, Viet Nam, Yemen, Yugoslavia, Zambia.

Against: Australia, Belgium, Canada, Denmark, France, Germany, Federal Republic of, Iceland, Israel, Italy, Japan, Luxembourg, Netherlands, New Zealand, Norway, Portugal, Spain, Turkey, United Kingdom, United States.

Abstaining: Bahamas, Chad, Dominican Republic, Gambia, Honduras, Ireland, Ivory Coast, Niger, Paraguay, Senegal, Sweden, Uruguay, Zaire.

In explanation of vote, Austria and Finland said they supported the thrust of the draft, despite reservations on certain formulations in the preamble; Finland had reservations, in particular, about the sixth to ninth preambular paragraphs. Similarly, Bangladesh agreed with the text's underlying spirit, despite what it saw as one-sided or contradictory positions; its vote did not imply endorsement of any negotiating position of the principal contenders.

Also on 17 December, the Assembly, on the recommendation of the First Committee, adopted resolution 39/148 K by recorded vote.

Cessation of the nuclear-arms race and nuclear disarmament

The General Assembly,

Recalling that, in paragraph 11 of the Final Document of the Tenth Special Session of the General Assembly, the Assembly stated that the nuclear-arms race, far from contributing to the strengthening of the security of all States, on the contrary weakens it and increases the danger of the outbreak of a nuclear war and that existing arsenals of nuclear weapons are more than sufficient to destroy all life on Earth,

Recalling also that, in paragraph 47 of the Final Document, the Assembly expressed the belief that nuclear weapons pose the greatest danger to mankind and to the survival of civilization, that it is essential to halt and reverse the nuclear-arms race in all its aspects in order to avert the danger of war involving nuclear weapons, and that the ultimate goal in this context is the complete elimination of nuclear weapons,

Noting that, in the Political Declaration adopted at the Seventh Conference of Heads of State or Government of Non-Aligned Countries, held at New Delhi from 7 to 12 March 1983, it was declared that the renewed escalation of the nuclear-arms race, both in its quantitative and qualitative dimensions, as well as reliance on doctrines of nuclear deterrence, had heightened the risk of the outbreak of nuclear war and led to greater insecurity and instability in international relations, and that it was also stated that nuclear weapons were more than weapons of war, that such weapons were instruments of mass annihilation,

Believing that all nations have a vital interest in negotiations on nuclear disarmament because the existence of nuclear weapons in the arsenals of a handful of States and the quantitative and qualitative development of such weapons directly and fundamentally jeopardize the vital security interests of both nuclear- and non-nuclear-weapon States alike,

Considering that it is necessary to halt all testing, production and deployment of nuclear weapons and their delivery systems as a first step in the process which should lead to the achievement of substantial reductions in nuclear forces, and welcoming in this context the Joint Declaration issued on 22 May 1984 by the heads of State or Government of Argentina, Greece, India, Mexico, Sweden and the United Republic of Tanzania,

Convinced of the urgent need to take constructive action towards halting and reversing the nuclear-arms race,

1. *Believes* that efforts should be intensified with a view to initiating, as a matter of the highest priority, multilateral negotiations in accordance with the provisions of paragraph 50 of the Final Document of the Tenth Special Session of the General Assembly;

2. *Requests* the Conference on Disarmament to establish an *ad hoc* committee at the beginning of its 1985 session to elaborate on paragraph 50 of the Final Document and to submit recommendations to the Conference as to how it could best initiate multilateral negotiations of agreements, with adequate measures of verification, in appropriate stages for:

(*a*) Cessation of the qualitative improvement and development of nuclear-weapon systems;

(*b*) Cessation of the production of all types of nuclear weapons and their means of delivery, and of the production of fissionable material for weapons purposes;

(*c*) Substantial reduction of existing nuclear weapons with a view to their ultimate elimination;

3. *Requests* the Conference on Disarmament to report to the General Assembly at its fortieth session on its consideration of this subject;

4. *Decides* to include in the provisional agenda of its fortieth session the item entitled "Cessation of the nuclear-arms race and nuclear disarmament".

General Assembly resolution 39/148 K

17 December 1984   Meeting 102   124-13-9 (recorded vote)

Approved by First Committee (A/39/749) by recorded vote (115-13-7), 20 November (meeting 44); 8-nation draft (A/C.1/39/L.43); agenda item 59 (*e*).

Sponsors: Argentina, Bangladesh, Greece, India, Indonesia, Mexico, Romania, Sweden.

Meeting numbers. GA 39th session: 1st Committee 3-36, 44; plenary 102.

Recorded vote in Assembly as follows:

In favour: Afghanistan, Algeria, Angola, Antigua and Barbuda, Argentina, Austria, Bahrain, Bangladesh, Barbados, Benin, Bhutan, Bolivia, Botswana, Brazil, Brunei Darussalam, Bulgaria, Burkina Faso, Burma, Burundi, Byelorussian SSR, Cameroon, Cape Verde, Central African Republic, Chad, Chile, China, Colombia, Congo, Costa Rica, Cuba, Cyprus, Czechoslovakia, Democratic Kampuchea, Democratic Yemen, Djibouti, Dominican Republic, Ecuador, Egypt, El Salvador, Equatorial Guinea, Ethiopia, Fiji, Finland, Gabon, Gambia, German Democratic Republic, Ghana, Greece, Guatemala, Guinea, Guyana, Haiti, Honduras, Hungary, India, Indonesia, Iran, Iraq, Ireland, Ivory Coast, Jamaica, Jordan, Kenya, Kuwait, Lao People's Democratic Republic, Lebanon, Lesotho, Liberia, Libyan Arab Jamahiriya, Madagascar, Malawi, Malaysia, Maldives, Mali, Malta, Mauritania, Mauritius, Mexico, Mongolia, Morocco, Mozambique, Nepal, Nicaragua, Niger, Nigeria, Oman, Pakistan, Panama, Peru, Philippines, Poland, Qatar, Romania, Rwanda, Saint Vincent and the Grenadines, Sao Tome and Principe, Saudi Arabia, Senegal, Seychelles, Sierra Leone, Singapore, Somalia, Sri Lanka, Sudan, Suriname, Sweden, Syrian Arab Republic, Thailand, Togo, Trinidad and Tobago, Tunisia, Uganda, Ukrainian SSR, USSR, United Arab Emirates, United Republic of Tanzania, Uruguay, Venezuela, Viet Nam, Yemen, Yugoslavia, Zaire, Zambia, Zimbabwe.

Against: Belgium, Canada, France, Germany, Federal Republic of, Iceland, Italy, Luxembourg, Netherlands, Norway, Portugal, Turkey, United Kingdom, United States.

Abstaining: Australia, Bahamas, Denmark, Israel, Japan, New Zealand, Paraguay, Saint Lucia, Spain.

The Netherlands found the draft unbalanced, in that it did not mention the need for bilateral negotiations between the two major nuclear-weapon States, while proposing unrealistically, in its view, multilateral negotiations in the Conference. Also pointing to the lack of reference to bilateral negotiations, Australia regretted that the draft attacked the concept of deterrence which it considered as the only guarantor of global security currently available. Japan said it had difficulty accepting some of the preambular paragraphs, particularly those referring to a moratorium and doctrines of nuclear deterrence.

Brazil, which saw the aspirations of the international community embodied in the draft, stressed that the role of the Conference on Disarmament was to facilitate negotiations and not to interfere with negotiating processes outside its own framework. The German Democratic Republic said that obstructing the multilateral negotiating process on nuclear disarmament was contrary to the 1978 Final Document.[13] The USSR said it was the fault of the United States that the multilateral negotiations had not begun.

USSR–United States negotiations

At the end of 1984, the SALT II Treaty—Treaty between the United States of America and the Union of Soviet Socialist Republics on the Limitation of Strategic Offensive Arms, concluded in 1979 at Vienna, Austria—had not entered into force, although each party had agreed to adhere to its substantive provisions as long as the other reciprocated. No bilateral negotiations on nuclear-weapons questions took place in 1984, but the two parties announced on 22 November their agreement to enter into new negotiations on the subject in 1985.

A number of the 1984 communications received by the Secretary-General concerning nuclear disarmament referred specifically to the bilateral negotiations (see p. 21).

GENERAL ASSEMBLY ACTION

On 17 December, the General Assembly adopted two resolutions (39/148 B and G), as recommended by the First Committee, dealing with the bilateral nuclear-arms negotiations.

It adopted resolution 39/148 B by recorded vote.

Bilateral nuclear-arms negotiations

The General Assembly,

Recalling its resolution 38/183 P of 20 December 1983,

Deeply regretting that the bilateral nuclear-arms negotiations at Geneva between the Union of Soviet Socialist Republics and the United States of America are not continuing,

Firmly convinced that an early agreement in those disrupted negotiations, in accordance with the principle of undiminished security at the lowest possible level of armaments and military forces, would be of crucial importance for the strengthening of international peace and security,

Deeply concerned that the absence of negotiations has impeded efforts to strengthen international peace and security and to achieve progress towards disarmament,

Convinced that, through negotiations pursued in a spirit of flexibility and responsibility for the security interests of all States, it is possible to reach agreement,

1. *Urges* the Government of the Union of Soviet Socialist Republics and the Government of the United States of America to resume, without delay or pre-conditions, bilateral nuclear-arms negotiations in order to achieve positive results in accordance with the security interests of all States and the universal desire for progress towards disarmament;

2. *Calls upon* the Government of the Union of Soviet Socialist Republics and the Government of the United States of America to spare no effort in seeking the attainment of the final objective of the negotiations;

3. *Invites* the Governments of the two States mentioned above to work actively towards the enhancement of mutual trust in order to create an atmosphere more conducive to disarmament agreements;

4. *Expresses its firmest possible encouragement and support* to efforts to resume negotiations and bring them to a successful conclusion.

General Assembly resolution 39/148 B

17 December 1984   Meeting 102   98-16-24 (recorded vote)

Approved by First Committee (A/39/749) by recorded vote (86-17-24), 20 November (meeting 44); 12-nation draft (A/C.1/39/L.5); agenda item 59 *(k)*.
Sponsors: Belgium, Canada, France, Germany, Federal Republic of, Italy, Japan, Netherlands, Norway, Portugal, Rwanda, Turkey, United Kingdom.
Meeting numbers. GA 39th session: 1st Committee 3-36, 44; plenary 102.

Recorded vote in Assembly as follows:

In favour: Antigua and Barbuda, Australia, Austria, Bahrain, Bangladesh, Belgium, Bolivia, Botswana, Brazil, Brunei Darussalam, Burundi, Cameroon, Canada, Chad, Chile, China, Colombia, Costa Rica, Democratic Kampuchea, Denmark, Djibouti, Dominican Republic, Ecuador, Egypt, El Salvador, Equatorial Guinea, Fiji, Finland, France, Gabon, Gambia, Germany, Federal Republic of, Ghana, Guinea, Guyana, Haiti, Honduras, Iceland, Indonesia, Iran, Iraq, Ireland, Israel, Italy, Ivory Coast, Jamaica, Japan, Jordan, Kenya, Kuwait, Lebanon, Lesotho, Liberia, Luxembourg, Malawi, Malaysia, Maldives, Mali, Mauritania, Morocco, Nepal, Netherlands, New Zealand, Niger, Nigeria, Norway, Oman, Pakistan, Panama, Paraguay, Peru, Philippines, Portugal, Qatar, Saint Lucia, Saint Vincent and the Grenadines, Senegal, Seychelles, Sierra Leone, Singapore, Somalia, Spain, Sri Lanka, Sudan, Sweden, Thailand, Togo, Trinidad and Tobago, Tunisia, Turkey, United Arab Emirates, United Kingdom, United Republic of Tanzania, United States, Uruguay, Yemen, Zaire, Zambia.

Against: Afghanistan, Angola, Bulgaria, Byelorussian SSR, Cuba, Czechoslovakia, Democratic Yemen, German Democratic Republic, Hungary, Lao People's Democratic Republic, Mongolia, Poland, Syrian Arab Republic, Ukrainian SSR, USSR, Viet Nam.

Abstaining: Algeria, Argentina, Bahamas, Barbados, Benin, Bhutan, Burkina Faso, Burma, Cape Verde, Congo, Cyprus, Ethiopia, Greece, India, Madagascar, Mauritius, Mexico, Mozambique, Nicaragua, Sao Tome and Principe, Suriname, Uganda, Venezuela, Yugoslavia.

In explanation of vote, the USSR said it was not prepared to engage in talks while it was the target of new missiles stationed in Europe and when presented with an ultimatum as the text essentially did; it asked the United States to remove the obstacles it had placed in the way of such negotiations. The United States, reiterating its regret that the USSR had walked out of the negotiations, said it was ready to resume talks without pre-conditions; it felt the text was simple and effective and prescribed no pre-conditions or set of procedures for the commencement of negotiations or the negotiations themselves.

Czechoslovakia and Yugoslavia viewed the text as one-sided and lacking in real incentive or common basis for the resumption of negotiations.

Cuba felt it attempted to justify the actions that had led to the breaking off of the bilateral negotiations; Cuba could not accept the so-called appeal for the resumption of negotiations without pre-conditions. Mexico considered more effective the procedures detailed in a draft which it had co-sponsored (see resolution 39/148 G below).

China asserted that the two Powers should first cease deploying new nuclear missiles and agree on substantial reductions of nuclear weapons.

Bangladesh, Finland, Nigeria and Pakistan said their votes expressed a position of principle, without endorsing any particular negotiating approach or taking a stand on substantive issues. Nigeria, however, regretted the impression created that the talks were undertaken when convenient and interrupted at will. While finding some parts of the text one-sided and contradictory, Bangladesh felt the underlying spirit of the text conformed with the common aspiration of humanity. Sri Lanka could not identify itself with some of the language and restrictive scope of the text, and said it could not endorse any particular reason for the interruption of talks or negotiating approach. Indonesia felt that, given the current situation, the words "without pre-conditions" in paragraph 1 would not be conducive to attaining the objectives being pursued, and Greece added that it would have voted in favour of the draft if it had not been for that expression. Tunisia appreciated that the resumption of negotiations required conditions acceptable to both parties and due recognition of their urgent security needs.

The Assembly adopted resolution 39/148 G by recorded vote.

Bilateral nuclear-arms negotiations

The General Assembly,

Recalling that at its tenth special session, the first special session devoted to disarmament, it approved by consensus a Declaration, contained in section II of the Final Document of the Tenth Special Session, in paragraph 27 of which, *inter alia*, it proclaimed that, in order effectively to discharge the central role and primary responsibility in the sphere of disarmament which belong to the United Nations in accordance with its Charter, the United Nations should be kept appropriately informed of all steps in this field, whether unilateral, bilateral, regional or multilateral, without prejudice to the progress of negotiations,

Recalling also that at its twelfth special session, the second special session devoted to disarmament, Member States reiterated their solemn commitment to implement the Final Document of the Tenth Special Session, the validity of which received their unanimous and categorical reaffirmation,

Regretting the interruption of the two series of bilateral nuclear-arms negotiations begun on 30 November 1981 and 29 June 1982, respectively, between the Union of Soviet Socialist Republics and the United States of America,

Deploring that, prior to such interruption, it had already become evident that the negotiations were not producing the desired results,

Bearing in mind that the General Assembly on several occasions has requested the major nuclear-weapon States to proclaim a freeze embracing, *inter alia*, a ban on all further deployment of nuclear weapons and their delivery vehicles,

1. *Requests* the Government of the Union of Soviet Socialist Republics and the Government of the United States of America to inform the General Assembly, before the closure of its thirty-ninth session, of the reasons for the interruption of their negotiations, the present situation and the prospects for their resumption;

2. *Urges again* the Governments of the two States mentioned above to examine immediately, as a way out of the present impasse, the possibility of combining into a single forum the two series of negotiations which they had been carrying out and of broadening their scope so as to embrace also the "tactical" or "battlefield" nuclear weapons;

3. *Invites* those Governments to consider the advisability of conducting henceforward their bilateral negotiations in a subsidiary body of the Conference on Disarmament whose membership could be limited to themselves, a possibility which was expressly contemplated when article 25 of the rules of procedure of the Committee—now the Conference—on Disarmament was approved;

4. *Reiterates once more its request* to the two negotiating parties that they bear constantly in mind that not only their national interests but also the vital interests of all the peoples of the world are at stake in this question;

5. *Decides* to include in the provisional agenda of its fortieth session the item entitled "Bilateral nuclear-arms negotiations".

General Assembly resolution 39/148 G

17 December 1984   Meeting 102   100-12-26 (recorded vote)

Approved by First Committee (A/39/749) by recorded vote (93-11-22), 26 November (meeting 48); 3-nation draft (A/C.1/39/L.26/Rev.1); agenda item 59 *(k)*.

Sponsors: Mexico, Sweden, Yugoslavia.

Meeting numbers. GA 39th session: 1st Committee 3-36, 40, 48; plenary 102.

Recorded vote in Assembly as follows:

In favour: Afghanistan, Algeria, Angola, Antigua and Barbuda, Argentina, Austria, Bahrain, Bangladesh, Benin, Bhutan, Bolivia, Botswana, Brunei Darussalam, Burkina Faso, Burma, Burundi, Cameroon, Cape Verde, Chad, Chile, China, Costa Rica, Cuba, Cyprus, Democratic Kampuchea, Democratic Yemen, Djibouti, Dominican Republic, Ecuador, Egypt, El Salvador, Equatorial Guinea, Ethiopia, Fiji, Finland, Ghana, Greece, Guatemala, Guinea, Guyana, Honduras, India, Indonesia, Iran, Ireland, Ivory Coast, Jamaica, Jordan, Kenya, Kuwait, Lao People's Democratic Republic, Lebanon, Lesotho, Liberia, Libyan Arab Jamahiriya, Madagascar, Malaysia, Maldives, Mali, Malta, Mauritania, Mauritius, Mexico, Morocco, Nepal, Nicaragua, Nigeria, Oman, Pakistan, Panama, Paraguay, Peru, Qatar, Saint Lucia, Saint Vincent and the Grenadines, Senegal, Seychelles, Sierra Leone, Singapore, Somalia, Sri Lanka, Sudan, Suriname, Sweden, Syrian Arab Republic, Thailand, Togo, Trinidad and Tobago, Tunisia, Uganda, United Arab Emirates, United Republic of Tanzania, Uruguay, Venezuela, Viet Nam, Yemen, Yugoslavia, Zaire, Zambia, Zimbabwe.

Against: Belgium, Canada, France, Germany, Federal Republic of, Israel, Italy, Luxembourg, Netherlands, Portugal, Turkey, United Kingdom, United States.

Abstaining: Australia, Bahamas, Barbados, Brazil, Bulgaria, Byelorussian SSR, Colombia, Czechoslovakia, Denmark, Gabon, Gambia, German Democratic Republic, Haiti, Hungary, Iceland, Japan, Malawi, Mongolia, New Zealand, Niger, Norway, Philippines, Poland, Spain, Ukrainian SSR, USSR.

Introducing the draft, Mexico said the text contained new elements, in the last preambular paragraph and in paragraphs 1 and 3, in addition to some of the language used in a December 1983 Assembly resolution on the topic.[14]

The United States said the text lacked an objective approach; it disagreed that the previous negotiations, prior to interruption, were not producing desired results, rejected the call for a nuclear freeze, asserted that the States concerned must be allowed flexibility in their negotiating process, and stated that negotiations on such delicate and complex matters vital to security required a degree of confidentiality. In a similar vein, Italy said the text contained concepts and language that contradicted some of its basic positions; it could not accept the freeze proposal or the assessment of the interrupted negotiations. The USSR sympathized with the sponsors' motives, and said it could have supported a number of provisions of the text, particularly the appeal for a freeze proclamation. Bangladesh asked the parties involved to keep in mind the vital interests of all humanity. Supporting the text, Pakistan said it was not partial to any negotiating approach.

Unilateral nuclear disarmament measures

Study by expert group. The Group of Governmental Experts on Unilateral Nuclear Disarmament Measures—experts from Austria, Egypt, Mexico and Pakistan, appointed by the Secretary-General in pursuance of a December 1983 General Assembly resolution[15]—held three sessions in 1984 (Geneva, 13-17 February, 30 April–7 May; New York, 27-31 August) and submitted its study on the topic to the Secretary-General, who forwarded it to the Assembly in October.[16]

The Group concluded that the dynamics of the arms race could be traced to a series of unilateral and reciprocal decisions taken by States in the name of national security, and that its de-escalation and reversal could, therefore, be facilitated by unilateral initiatives of States aimed at reducing the level of international tension, creating an atmosphere of mutual trust and confidence and improving the environment for arms control and disarmament negotiations. It listed four priority areas for unilateral measures with a view to promoting and complementing disarmament negotiations: a nuclear-test ban; nuclear-war prevention, including the non-first-use of nuclear weapons and a nuclear freeze; security guarantees to non-nuclear-weapon States; and prevention of an arms race in outer space.

GENERAL ASSEMBLY ACTION

On the recommendation of the First Committee, the General Assembly, on 17 December 1984, adopted resolution 39/148 A by recorded vote.

Unilateral nuclear disarmament measures

The General Assembly,

Recalling its resolution 38/183 J of 20 December 1983, in which it requested the Secretary-General to prepare, with the assistance of qualified governmental experts and applying the methods customary in these cases, a report on ways and means that seemed advisable for stimulating the adoption of unilateral nuclear disarmament measures which, without prejudice to the security of States, would come to promote and complement bilateral and multilateral negotiations in this sphere,

Recalling also the concrete proposal submitted to the Disarmament Commission at its 1983 session to the effect that the preparation of a study on unilateral measures would be at present of particular value in view of the impasse existing in both the bilateral and the multilateral negotiations,

Recalling further the conclusion of the General Assembly at its tenth special session, to the effect that unilateral measures of arms limitation or reduction could contribute to limiting the arms race,

Having examined the report of the Secretary-General transmitting the study prepared by the Group of Governmental Experts on Unilateral Nuclear Disarmament Measures,

1. *Takes note with satisfaction* of the study on unilateral nuclear disarmament measures;*

2. *Expresses its appreciation* to the Secretary-General and to the Group of Governmental Experts on Unilateral Nuclear Disarmament Measures that assisted him in the preparation of the study;

3. *Takes note* of the conclusions of the study and trusts that they may encourage nuclear-weapon States to take the steps necessary to promote and orient adequately disarmament negotiations;

4. *Requests* the Secretary-General to arrange for the reproduction of the report as a United Nations publication and, making full use of all the facilities of the Department of Public Information of the Secretariat, to publicize the report in as many languages as is considered desirable and practicable.

---

*The study was subsequently issued under the title *Unilateral Nuclear Disarmament Measures* (Sales No. E.85.IX.2).

General Assembly resolution 39/148 A

17 December 1984   Meeting 102   126-1-13 (recorded vote)

Approved by First Committee (A/39/749) by recorded vote (118-1-13), 20 November (meeting 44); 6-nation draft (A/C.1/39/L.4); agenda item 59 (h).
Sponsors: Austria, Ecuador, Egypt, Mexico, Pakistan, Sweden.
Meeting numbers. GA 39th session: 1st Committee 3-37, 44; plenary 102.

Recorded vote in Assembly as follows:

In favour: Afghanistan, Algeria, Angola, Antigua and Barbuda, Argentina, Australia, Austria, Bahamas, Bahrain, Bangladesh, Barbados, Benin, Bhutan, Bolivia, Botswana, Brazil, Brunei Darussalam, Bulgaria, Burkina Faso, Burma, Burundi, Byelorussian SSR, Cameroon, Cape Verde, Chad, Chile, China, Colombia, Congo, Costa Rica, Cuba, Cyprus, Czechoslovakia, Democratic Kampuchea, Democratic Yemen, Denmark, Djibouti, Dominican Republic, Ecuador, Egypt, El Salvador, Equatorial Guinea, Ethiopia, Fiji, Finland, Gabon, Gambia, German Democratic Republic, Ghana, Greece, Guinea, Guyana, Haiti, Honduras, Hungary, Iceland, India, Indonesia, Iran, Iraq, Ireland, Ivory Coast, Jamaica, Jordan, Kenya, Kuwait, Lao People's Democratic Republic, Lebanon, Lesotho, Liberia, Libyan Arab Jamahiriya, Madagascar, Malawi, Malaysia, Maldives, Mali, Malta, Mauritania, Mauritius, Mexico, Mongolia, Morocco, Mozambique, Nepal, Nicaragua, Niger, Nigeria, Norway, Oman, Pakistan, Panama, Paraguay, Peru, Philippines, Poland, Qatar, Romania, Saint Lucia, Saint Vincent and the Grenadines, Sao Tome and Principe, Senegal, Seychelles, Sierra Leone, Singapore, Spain, Sri Lanka, Sudan, Suriname, Sweden, Syrian Arab Republic, Thailand, Togo, Trinidad and Tobago, Tunisia, Uganda, Ukrainian SSR, USSR, United Arab Emirates, United Republic of Tanzania, Uruguay, Venezuela, Viet Nam, Yemen, Yugoslavia, Zaire, Zambia.
Against: United States.
Abstaining: Belgium, Canada, France, Germany, Federal Republic of, Israel, Italy, Japan, Luxembourg, Netherlands, New Zealand, Portugal, Turkey, United Kingdom.

In explanation of vote, the Federal Republic of Germany said the report lacked political objectivity and created the notion that unilateral initia-tives did not require mutual trust; it objected to the unqualified condemnation of the doctrine of nuclear deterrence and also regretted that one of the earliest endeavours at unilateral disarmament—its contractual undertaking of 1954 not to produce nuclear, biological and chemical weapons—had not been given the attention it deserved. The United Kingdom said the report showed a distinct bias in handling information and put forward opinions which were at best partial and at worst actively discriminatory; it expressed concern at what it felt was the increasing politicization of studies conducted by United Nations expert groups, and asserted that it was not acceptable for a single political group to use a United Nations study in order to endorse its own interests.

Denmark saw the report as a point of departure for further deliberations, but stressed that its vote did not signify its support for all its parts. The USSR said the study took a generally constructive approach, but failed to reflect the numerous steps it had unilaterally initiated in order to create favourable conditions for arms control and disarmament negotiations. The USSR disagreed with the experts' view that it shared with the United States a responsibility for the current stalemate; reproduction of the study should not involve any additional financial expenditure.

Prevention of nuclear war

Little progress was made in 1984 in the Conference on Disarmament on the issue of nuclear-war prevention, and the General Assembly, in December, again requested it to negotiate with a view to agreeing on practical measures to that end (resolution 39/148 P). No action was taken on a second proposal made in the Assembly, on prevention of war in the nuclear age.

Consideration by the Conference on Disarmament. In 1984, the Conference on Disarmament[9] took up the prevention of nuclear war, including all related matters, as a separate agenda item from the question of the cessation of the nuclear-arms race and nuclear disarmament, in accordance with a December 1983 General Assembly request[17] that the Conference establish a subsidiary body to negotiate on reaching agreement on measures for preventing nuclear war.

A contact group, set up to consider establishing a subsidiary body, considered proposals submitted to that effect by a group of socialist States[18] and by the group of 21.[19] The latter's proposal—that an *ad hoc* committee should consider initially all existing and future proposals relating to the item, including appropriate and practical measures for preventing nuclear war—was supported by the socialist States and China, although they regarded it as a minimum mandate.

The Western delegations, however, could not support the proposal nor suggest any amendment to make it acceptable to them. Therefore, no consensus was reached on the question of a subsidiary body.

GENERAL ASSEMBLY ACTION

While the General Assembly adopted, in 1984, a resolution on nuclear-war prevention, a second draft on the topic was withdrawn by the sponsors (see p. 29).

On the recommendation of the First Committee, the Assembly, on 17 December, adopted resolution 39/148 P by recorded vote.

Prevention of nuclear war

The General Assembly,

Alarmed by the threat to the survival of mankind posed by the existence of nuclear weapons and the continuing nuclear-arms race,

Deeply concerned by an increased danger of nuclear war as a result of the intensification of the nuclear-arms race and the serious deterioration of the international situation,

Conscious that removal of the threat of nuclear war is the most acute and urgent task of the present day,

Reiterating that it is the shared responsibility of all Member States to save succeeding generations from the scourge of another world war, which would inevitably be a nuclear war,

Recalling the provisions of paragraphs 47 to 50 and 56 to 58 of the Final Document of the Tenth Special Session of the General Assembly regarding the procedures designed to secure the avoidance of nuclear war,

Recalling also that at the Seventh Conference of Heads of State or Government of Non-Aligned Countries, held at New Delhi from 7 to 12 March 1983, it was stated that nuclear weapons are more than weapons of war, they are instruments of mass annihilation,

Recalling further its resolutions 36/81 B of 9 December 1981 and 37/78 I of 9 December 1982 and, in particular, its resolution 38/183 G of 20 December 1983, in which it requested the Conference on Disarmament to undertake, as a matter of the highest priority, negotiations with a view to achieving agreement on appropriate and practical measures for the prevention of nuclear war,

Having considered the report of the Conference on Disarmament on its 1984 session,

Noting with grave concern that the Conference on Disarmament was once again unable to start negotiations on the question during its 1984 session,

Taking into account the deliberations on this item at its thirty-ninth session,

Convinced that the prevention of nuclear war and the reduction of the risk of nuclear war are matters of the highest priority and of vital interest to all peoples of the world,

Also convinced that the prevention of nuclear war is a problem too important to be left to the nuclear-weapon States alone,

1. *Notes with regret* that despite the fact that the Conference on Disarmament has discussed the question of the prevention of nuclear war for two years, it has been unable even to establish a subsidiary body to consider appropriate and practical measures to prevent it;

2. *Again requests* the Conference on Disarmament to undertake, as a matter of the highest priority, negotiations with a view to achieving agreement on appropriate and practical measures for the prevention of nuclear war and to establish for that purpose an *ad hoc* committee on the subject at the beginning of its 1985 session;

3. *Expresses its conviction* that, in view of the urgency of this matter and the inadequacy or insufficiency of existing measures, it is necessary to devise suitable steps to expedite effective action for the prevention of nuclear war;

4. *Requests* the Secretary-General to prepare a report on steps to that effect which should be completed in time to be transmitted to the Conference on Disarmament in April 1985 and submitted to the General Assembly at its fortieth session;

5. *Invites* all Governments to submit to the Secretary-General, not later than 1 February 1985, their views on steps to expedite effective action on the question of the prevention of nuclear war so that they might be taken into account in the preparation of the above-mentioned report;

6. *Decides* to include in the provisional agenda of its fortieth session the item entitled "Prevention of nuclear war".

General Assembly resolution 39/148 P

17 December 1984   Meeting 102   128-6-12 (recorded vote)

Approved by First Committee (A/39/749) by recorded vote (116-5-13), 26 November (meeting 48); 19-nation draft (A/C.1/39/L.64); agenda item 59 *(f)*.

Sponsors: Algeria, Argentina, Bangladesh, Brazil, Colombia, Congo, Ecuador, Egypt, German Democratic Republic, India, Indonesia, Mexico, Nigeria, Pakistan, Romania, Sudan, Uruguay, Venezuela, Yugoslavia.

Meeting numbers. GA 39th session: 1st Committee 3-37, 48; plenary 102.

Recorded vote in Assembly as follows:

In favour: Afghanistan, Algeria, Angola, Antigua and Barbuda, Argentina, Australia, Austria, Bahamas, Bahrain, Bangladesh, Barbados, Benin, Bhutan, Bolivia, Botswana, Brazil, Brunei Darussalam, Bulgaria, Burkina Faso, Burma, Burundi, Byelorussian SSR, Cameroon, Cape Verde, Central African Republic, Chad, Chile, China, Colombia, Congo, Costa Rica, Cuba, Cyprus, Czechoslovakia, Democratic Kampuchea, Democratic Yemen, Djibouti, Dominican Republic, Ecuador, Egypt, El Salvador, Equatorial Guinea, Ethiopia, Fiji, Finland, Gabon, Gambia, German Democratic Republic, Ghana, Greece, Guatemala, Guinea, Guyana, Haiti, Honduras, Hungary, India, Indonesia, Iran, Iraq, Ireland, Ivory Coast, Jamaica, Jordan, Kenya, Kuwait, Lao People's Democratic Republic, Lebanon, Lesotho, Liberia, Libyan Arab Jamahiriya, Madagascar, Malawi, Malaysia, Maldives, Mali, Malta, Mauritania, Mauritius, Mexico, Mongolia, Morocco, Mozambique, Nepal, Nicaragua, Niger, Nigeria, Oman, Pakistan, Panama, Paraguay, Peru, Philippines, Poland, Qatar, Romania, Rwanda, Saint Lucia, Saint Vincent and the Grenadines, Sao Tome and Principe, Saudi Arabia, Senegal, Seychelles, Sierra Leone, Singapore, Somalia, Sri Lanka, Sudan, Suriname, Sweden, Syrian Arab Republic, Thailand, Togo, Trinidad and Tobago, Tunisia, Uganda, Ukrainian SSR, USSR, United Arab Emirates, United Republic of Tanzania, Uruguay, Venezuela, Viet Nam, Yemen, Yugoslavia, Zaire, Zambia, Zimbabwe.

Against: Belgium, France, Germany, Federal Republic of, Italy, United Kingdom, United States.

Abstaining: Canada, Denmark, Iceland, Israel, Japan, Luxembourg, Netherlands, New Zealand, Norway, Portugal, Spain, Turkey.

Introducing the text, Argentina explained that the envisaged report should not be a compilation of responses but, rather, provide an overview of the question of nuclear-war prevention, making use of the comments from Governments and containing the ideas the Secretary-General had developed on the question.

In explanation of vote, the Byelorussian SSR appealed to all those eager to see immediate and effective steps taken for nuclear-war prevention to support the text. France felt that the terms of the draft went beyond what was desirable as regards the range and objectives of the discussions; it was premature to contemplate negotiations on agreement on practical measures, before an in-depth discussion identified what could actually be done within the Conference on Disarmament.

Several delegations also spoke on a nine-nation draft on "Prevention of nuclear war, including all related matters: prevention of war in the nuclear age",[20] which, at the sponsors' request, was not acted on.

The draft—proposed by Australia, Canada, Denmark, the Federal Republic of Germany, Italy, Japan, Norway, Turkey and the United Kingdom—would have had the Assembly: reaffirm the urgency of reducing and removing the threat of nuclear war and eliminating the threat of all armed conflict as the ultimate goal of the international community; declare that a nuclear war could not be won and that a conventional war might involve the risk of escalating to nuclear war; urge all States never to use force except in exercising their right of individual or collective self-defence; reject doctrines and policies aimed at achieving military superiority; and call on the USSR and the United States especially to agree on reducing to the lowest possible level their strategic and intermediate-range nuclear weapons.

Argentina, India, Mexico and Yugoslavia subsequently submitted a series of amendments[21] affecting most of the nine-nation draft and shifting its emphasis clearly to the nuclear aspects of the question.

Stating that the sponsors had decided not to press their draft to a vote, the Federal Republic of Germany said a minority of delegations had drawn a distorted picture of the draft—largely based on the language of the United Nations Charter—as advocating or legitimizing the use of nuclear weapons. It stressed that the Western security policy helped to remove the menace of war in all its forms, while many of the criticisms voiced against it suggested that conventional attacks were a legitimate part of international life and should be exempt from defensive action. The sponsors had no intention of splitting the group of non-aligned countries, in which the draft had aroused particular interest as well as internal controversy; it regretted that the amendments had been submitted in spite of a formal undertaking by leaders of that group not to take such action.

Several States expressed satisfaction at the draft's withdrawal. In the opinion of India—the current Chairman of the group of non-aligned countries—the draft represented a radical departure from the approach the international commu-

nity had adopted, such as in the 1978 Final Document,[13] on nuclear-war prevention; it was unrealistic to expect the Assembly to endorse the partisan view of a group of countries belonging to a particular military alliance. In addition, India felt that treating nuclear war as an extension of war in general, and lumping all wars together, represented a dangerous over-simplification or a wilful disregard of contemporary realities; not attending to the immediate need to prevent nuclear war, it said, could deny humanity a chance to work towards eliminating all wars. Stating that no commitment had been made in meetings of the group on non-submission of amendments, Mexico viewed the draft as an attempt surreptitiously to obtain amendments to what had been adopted in the 1978 Final Document. Argentina added that some elements in the draft ran counter to the fundamental positions of the non-aligned countries and legitimized the doctrine of nuclear deterrence. Brazil believed the draft sought to justify policies and practices contrary to the Charter and the Final Document. Cuba and Czechoslovakia stressed that the most urgent task was to prevent the outbreak of nuclear war.

Australia, a sponsor, regretted the withdrawal of the proposal, both on the substantive grounds that it affirmed fundamental principles embodied in the Charter concerning the refusal to accept war, and for the procedural reason that the amendments—which, if accepted, would have destroyed the thrust of the original text—had been put forward after a similar draft resolution on nuclear-war prevention (see p. 28) had been approved. It rejected any suggestion that the draft had departed from, or had quoted selectively, the Final Document, and stressed that the text had unequivocally reaffirmed the importance of nuclear disarmament.

Climatic consequences of a nuclear war

Two draft texts were presented to the General Assembly in 1984 on the climatic consequences of a nuclear war—sometimes referred to as nuclear winter—with the Assembly, in December, adopting a text proposed by eight non-aligned countries.

GENERAL ASSEMBLY ACTION

On 17 December 1984, the Assembly, on the recommendation of the First Committee, adopted resolution 39/148 F by recorded vote.

Climatic effects of nuclear war: nuclear winter
The General Assembly,
Recalling that, in the Final Document of the Tenth Special Session of the General Assembly, after referring specifically to "the threat to the very survival of mankind" posed by the existence of nuclear weapons, it declared, in paragraph 18, that removing the threat of a world

war—a nuclear war—is the most acute and urgent task of the present day,

Noting that, in spite of recent scientific endeavours, the environmental and other climatic consequences of a nuclear war still pose a major challenge to science,

Noting that, as a result of recent atmospheric and biological studies, there have been new findings which indicate that in addition to blast, heat and radiation, nuclear war, even on a limited scale, would produce smoke, soot and dust of sufficient magnitude as to trigger an arctic nuclear winter which may transform the Earth into a darkened, frozen planet where conditions would be conducive to mass extinction,

Recognizing that the prospect of nuclear winter poses an unprecedented peril to all nations, even those far removed from the nuclear explosions, which would add immeasurably to the previously known dangers of nuclear war,

Conscious of the urgent need to continue and develop scientific studies to increase the knowledge and understanding of the various elements and consequences on climate, including nuclear winter,

1. *Requests* the Secretary-General to compile and distribute as a document of the United Nations appropriate excerpts of all national and international scientific studies on the climatic effects of nuclear war, including nuclear winter, published so far or which may be published before 31 July 1985;

2. *Urges* all States and intergovernmental organizations, as well as non-governmental organizations, through their intermediary, to transmit to the Secretary-General, prior to the above-mentioned date, the relevant material in their possession which may be useful for the above purpose;

3. *Recommends* that the above-mentioned document be examined at the fortieth session of the General Assembly in connection with the item dealing with the prevention of a nuclear war.

General Assembly resolution 39/148 F

17 December 1984   Meeting 102   130-0-11 (recorded vote)

Approved by First Committee (A/39/749) by recorded vote (123-0-10), 27 November (meeting 49); 8-nation draft (A/C.1/39/L.22/Rev.1); agenda item 59 (f).

Sponsors: Bangladesh, India, Mexico, Pakistan, Romania, Sweden, Uruguay, Yugoslavia.

Meeting numbers. GA 39th session: 1st Committee 3-37, 49; plenary 102.

Recorded vote in Assembly as follows:

In favour: Afghanistan, Algeria, Angola, Antigua and Barbuda, Argentina, Australia, Austria, Bahamas, Bahrain, Bangladesh, Barbados, Benin, Bhutan, Bolivia, Botswana, Brazil, Brunei Darussalam, Bulgaria, Burkina Faso, Burma, Burundi, Byelorussian SSR, Cameroon, Canada, Cape Verde, Chad, Chile, China, Congo, Costa Rica, Cuba, Cyprus, Czechoslovakia, Democratic Yemen, Denmark, Djibouti, Dominican Republic, Ecuador, Egypt, El Salvador, Equatorial Guinea, Ethiopia, Fiji, Finland, Gabon, Gambia, German Democratic Republic, Ghana, Greece, Guatemala, Guinea, Guyana, Haiti, Honduras, Hungary, Iceland, India, Indonesia, Iran, Iraq, Ireland, Ivory Coast, Jamaica, Japan, Jordan, Kenya, Kuwait, Lao People's Democratic Republic, Lebanon, Lesotho, Liberia, Libyan Arab Jamahiriya, Madagascar, Malawi, Malaysia, Maldives, Mali, Malta, Mauritania, Mauritius, Mexico, Mongolia, Morocco, Mozambique, Nepal, New Zealand, Nicaragua, Niger, Nigeria, Norway, Oman, Pakistan, Panama, Paraguay, Peru, Philippines, Poland, Portugal, Qatar, Romania, Saint Lucia, Saint Vincent and the Grenadines, Sao Tome and Principe, Senegal, Seychelles, Sierra Leone, Singapore, Somalia, Spain, Sri Lanka, Sudan, Sweden, Syrian Arab Republic, Thailand, Togo, Trinidad and Tobago, Tunisia, Uganda, Ukrainian SSR, USSR, United Arab Emirates, United Republic of Tanzania, Uruguay, Venezuela, Viet Nam, Yemen, Yugoslavia, Zaire, Zambia, Zimbabwe.

Against: None.

Abstaining: Belgium, Colombia, France, Germany, Federal Republic of, Israel, Italy, Luxembourg, Netherlands, Turkey, United Kingdom, United States.

A second text on the topic—sponsored by Belgium, Canada, the Federal Republic of Germany and Japan, entitled "Studies on climatic effects of nuclear war including a possibility of nuclear winter"[22]—was not acted on at the request of the sponsors. By that draft, the Assembly would have invited Member States to submit to the Secretary-General any reports or studies on large-scale climatic effects of a nuclear conflict, clarifying underlying hypotheses as well as methods of analysis employed therein, and requested him to provide the Assembly in 1985 with an annotated list of those studies.

Mexico, in introducing the draft that became resolution 39/148 F, stated that the specialized studies carried out on the subject were not so numerous and that their sources—Australia, Canada, Sweden (where studies had been initiated in 1980), the USSR, the United Kingdom and the United States—were relatively few, well-known and accessible.

Prior to acting on the draft as a whole, the First Committee rejected, by recorded votes, two oral amendments proposed by Canada, the first—to replace the third preambular paragraph by "Bearing in mind that some recent scientific studies have concluded that a nuclear war could trigger large-scale climatic consequences, leading in the worst analysis to what is sometimes termed a nuclear winter"— by 63 votes to 24, with 31 abstentions, and the second—to have the document in question compiled and distributed "within existing resources"—by 56 votes to 27, with 35 abstentions. In proposing the amendments, Canada had asserted that the draft should deal with all possible climatic effects and not focus exclusively on one possibility, especially at the current stage of research.

In explanation of vote, Canada regretted that its efforts towards a consensus text had been in vain; despite its continuing reservations about certain passages in the eight-nation draft, it cast an affirmative vote because it believed the question should be studied at the United Nations.

Japan, which supported both the text as a whole and the proposed amendments, had reservations about the manner in which the concept had been presented in some parts, as well as the financial aspects; instead of sounding alarmist and giving the impression that nuclear winter was a proven scientific fact, it would have been more advisable for the Assembly to take an unbiased position, while making it clear that, nuclear winter or not, nuclear war should be prevented. Similarly, Belgium felt that the fourth preambular paragraph confused hypothesis with proven theory. Also feeling that the language prejudged the results of continuing scientific studies on the topic, the United Kingdom regretted that the draft's sponsors had been unable to agree to relatively small changes; it expected the resolution to have no additional financial implications.

Proposed convention against nuclear weapons

In 1984, the Conference on Disarmament,[9] which could not agree on a subsidiary body on nuclear disarmament, was unable to negotiate on an international convention prohibiting the use or threat of use of nuclear weapons, the draft text of which had been provided by the General Assembly in December 1983.[23]

In December 1984, the Assembly again called on the Conference to undertake work on such a convention (39/63 H) as well as on an international instrument on the non-first-use of nuclear weapons (39/148 D).

Another proposal entitled "Prohibition of use of nuclear weapons",[24] submitted by Nigeria but not put to a vote at its request, would have had the Assembly convene in 1985, as part of the activities marking the fortieth anniversary of the United Nations, a plenipotentiary conference to adopt a legal instrument prohibiting the use of nuclear weapons.

GENERAL ASSEMBLY ACTION

On 12 December 1984, the Assembly, on the recommendation of the First Committee, adopted resolution 39/63 H by recorded vote.

Convention on the Prohibition of the Use of Nuclear Weapons

The General Assembly,

Alarmed by the threat to the survival of mankind and to the life-sustaining system posed by nuclear weapons and by their use, inherent in concepts of deterrence,

Conscious of an increased danger of nuclear war as a result of the intensification of the nuclear-arms race and the serious deterioration of the international situation,

Convinced that nuclear disarmament is essential for the prevention of nuclear war and for the strengthening of international peace and security,

Further convinced that a prohibition of the use or threat of use of nuclear weapons would be a step towards the complete elimination of nuclear weapons leading to general and complete disarmament under strict and effective international control,

Recalling that, in paragraph 58 of the Final Document of the Tenth Special Session of the General Assembly, it is stated that all States should actively participate in efforts to bring about conditions in international relations among States in which a code of peaceful conduct of nations in international affairs could be agreed upon and which would preclude the use or threat of use of nuclear weapons,

Reaffirming that the use of nuclear weapons would be a violation of the Charter of the United Nations and a crime against humanity, as declared in its resolutions 1653(XVI) of 24 November 1961, 33/71 B of 14 December 1978, 34/83 G of 11 December 1979, 35/152 D of 12 December 1980 and 36/92 I of 9 December 1981,

Noting with regret that the Conference on Disarmament, during its session in 1984, was not able to undertake negotiations with a view to achieving agreement on an international convention prohibiting the use or threat of use of nuclear weapons under any circumstances, taking as a basis the text annexed to General Assembly resolution 38/73 G of 15 December 1983,

1. *Reiterates its request* to the Conference on Disarmament to commence negotiations, as a matter of priority, in order to achieve agreement on an international convention prohibiting the use or threat of use of nuclear weapons under any circumstances, taking as a basis the text of the draft Convention on the Prohibition of the Use of Nuclear Weapons annexed to the present resolution;

2. *Further requests* the Conference on Disarmament to report to the General Assembly at its fortieth session on the results of those negotiations.

ANNEX
Draft Convention on the Prohibition of the Use of Nuclear Weapons

The States Parties to this Convention,

Alarmed by the threat to the very survival of mankind posed by the existence of nuclear weapons,

Convinced that any use of nuclear weapons constitutes a violation of the Charter of the United Nations and a crime against humanity,

Convinced that this Convention would be a step towards the complete elimination of nuclear weapons leading to general and complete disarmament under strict and effective international control,

Determined to continue negotiations for the achievement of this goal,

Have agreed as follows:

Article 1

The States Parties to this Convention solemnly undertake not to use or threaten to use nuclear weapons under any circumstances.

Article 2

This Convention shall be of unlimited duration.

Article 3

1. This Convention shall be open to all States for signature. Any State which does not sign the Convention before its entry into force in accordance with paragraph 3 of this article may accede to it at any time.

2. This Convention shall be subject to ratification by signatory States. Instruments of ratification or accession shall be deposited with the Secretary-General of the United Nations.

3. This Convention shall enter into force on the deposit of instruments of ratification by twenty-five Governments, including the Governments of the five nuclear-weapon States, in accordance with paragraph 2 of this article.

4. For States whose instruments of ratification or accession are deposited after the entry into force of this Convention, it shall enter into force on the date of the deposit of their instruments of ratification or accession.

5. The depositary shall promptly inform all signatory and acceding States of the date of each signature, the date of deposit of each instrument of ratification or accession and the date of the entry into force of this Convention, as well as of the receipt of other notices.

6. This Convention shall be registered by the depositary in accordance with Article 102 of the Charter of the United Nations.

Article 4

This Convention, of which the Arabic, Chinese, English, French, Russian and Spanish texts are equally authentic, shall be deposited with the Secretary-General of the United Nations, who shall send duly certified copies thereof to the Governments of the signatory and acceding States.

IN WITNESS WHEREOF, the undersigned, being duly authorized thereto by their respective Governments, have signed this Convention, opened for signature at _____ on the _____ day of _____ one thousand nine hundred and _____.

General Assembly resolution 39/63 H

12 December 1984　　　　Meeting 97　　　　128-17-5 (recorded vote)

Approved by First Committee (A/39/750) by recorded vote (113-17-5), 21 November (meeting 45); 14-nation draft (A/C.1/39/L.50); agenda item 60 *(f)*.
Sponsors: Algeria, Argentina, Bahamas, Bangladesh, Bhutan, Ecuador, Egypt, Ethiopia, India, Indonesia, Madagascar, Romania, Viet Nam, Yugoslavia.
Meeting numbers. GA 39th session: 1st Committee 3-36, 40, 45; plenary 97.

Recorded vote in Assembly as follows:

In favour: Afghanistan, Algeria, Angola, Antigua and Barbuda, Argentina, Bahamas, Bahrain, Bangladesh, Barbados, Belize, Benin, Bhutan, Bolivia, Botswana, Brazil, Brunei Darussalam, Bulgaria, Burkina Faso, Burma, Burundi, Byelorussian SSR, Cameroon, Cape Verde, Central African Republic, Chad, Chile, China, Colombia, Comoros, Congo, Costa Rica, Cuba, Cyprus, Czechoslovakia, Democratic Kampuchea, Democratic Yemen, Djibouti, Dominica, Dominican Republic, Ecuador, Egypt, El Salvador, Equatorial Guinea, Ethiopia, Fiji, Finland, Gabon, German Democratic Republic, Ghana, Guatemala, Guinea, Guinea-Bissau, Guyana, Haiti, Honduras, Hungary, India, Indonesia, Iran, Iraq, Ivory Coast, Jamaica, Jordan, Kenya, Kuwait, Lao People's Democratic Republic, Lebanon, Lesotho, Liberia, Libyan Arab Jamahiriya, Madagascar, Malawi, Malaysia, Maldives, Mali, Malta, Mauritania, Mauritius, Mexico, Mongolia, Morocco, Mozambique, Nepal, Nicaragua, Niger, Nigeria, Oman, Pakistan, Panama, Papua New Guinea, Paraguay, Peru, Poland, Qatar, Romania, Rwanda, Saint Lucia, Samoa, Sao Tome and Principe, Saudi Arabia, Senegal, Seychelles, Sierra Leone, Singapore, Somalia, Sri Lanka, Sudan, Suriname, Sweden, Syrian Arab Republic, Thailand, Togo, Trinidad and Tobago, Tunisia, Uganda, Ukrainian SSR, USSR, United Arab Emirates, United Republic of Tanzania, Uruguay, Vanuatu, Venezuela, Viet Nam, Yemen, Yugoslavia, Zaire, Zambia, Zimbabwe.
Against: Australia, Belgium, Canada, Denmark, France, Germany, Federal Republic of, Iceland, Italy, Luxembourg, Netherlands, New Zealand, Norway, Portugal, Spain, Turkey, United Kingdom, United States.
Abstaining: Austria, Greece, Ireland, Israel, Japan.

Cameroon said its affirmative vote did not necessarily mean endorsement of the procedures and approaches recommended in the draft. Mongolia held that an international convention prohibiting the use of nuclear weapons would help strengthen mutual confidence and trust, and thus help create conditions favourable for adopting practical measures of nuclear disarmament. The Byelorussian SSR and Hungary also spoke in support of the text.

On 17 December, acting on the recommendation of the First Committee, the General Assembly adopted resolution 39/148 D by recorded vote.

Non-use of nuclear weapons and prevention of nuclear war

The General Assembly,

Alarmed by the threat to the survival of mankind posed by the existence of nuclear weapons and the continuing arms race, in particular in the nuclear field,

Recalling that, in accordance with the Final Document of the Tenth Special Session of the General Assembly, the first special session devoted to disarmament, effective measures of nuclear disarmament and the prevention of nuclear war have the highest priority,

Recalling also that this commitment was reaffirmed by the General Assembly at its twelfth special session, the second special session devoted to disarmament,

Bearing in mind its relevant resolutions on this subject,

Reaffirming that the most effective guarantee against the danger of nuclear war and the use of nuclear weapons is nuclear disarmament and the complete elimination of nuclear weapons,

Recalling that, in paragraph 58 of the Final Document of the Tenth Special Session, it is stated that all States should actively participate in efforts to bring about conditions in international relations among States in which a code of peaceful conduct of nations in international affairs could be agreed upon and which would preclude the use or threat of use of nuclear weapons,

Reaffirming also that the nuclear-weapon States have the primary responsibility for nuclear disarmament and for undertaking measures aimed at preventing the outbreak of nuclear war, *inter alia*, by establishing corresponding norms regulating relations between them,

Convinced that the renunciation of the first use of nuclear weapons is a most important and urgent measure for the prevention of nuclear war, and taking note of the broad, positive international reaction to the concept of non-first-use of nuclear weapons, including the appeal contained in the Final Communiqué adopted at the Meeting of Ministers for Foreign Affairs and Heads of Delegation of the Non-Aligned Countries to the thirty-ninth session of the General Assembly, held in New York from 1 to 5 October 1984,

1. *Considers* that the solemn declarations by two nuclear-weapon States made or reiterated at the twelfth special session of the General Assembly, concerning their respective obligations not to be the first to use nuclear weapons, offer an important avenue to decrease the danger of nuclear war;

2. *Expresses the hope* that those nuclear-weapon States that have not yet done so would consider making similar declarations with respect to not being the first to use nuclear weapons;

3. *Requests* the Conference on Disarmament to consider under its relevant agenda item, *inter alia*, the elaboration of an international instrument of a legally binding character laying down the obligation not to be the first to use nuclear weapons;

4. *Decides* to include in the provisional agenda of its fortieth session the item entitled "Non-use of nuclear weapons and prevention of nuclear war".

General Assembly resolution 39/148 D

17 December 1984　　　　Meeting 102　　　　101-19-17 (recorded vote)

Approved by First Committee (A/39/749) by recorded vote (95-19-15), 21 November (meeting 45); 4-nation draft (A/C.1/39/L.12), orally revised; agenda item 59.
Sponsors: Cuba, German Democratic Republic, Hungary, Romania.
Meeting numbers. GA 39th session: 1st Committee 3-36, 45; plenary 102.

Recorded vote in Assembly as follows:

In favour: Afghanistan, Algeria, Angola, Antigua and Barbuda, Argentina, Bahrain, Bangladesh, Barbados, Benin, Bhutan, Bolivia, Botswana, Bulgaria, Burkina Faso, Burundi, Byelorussian SSR, Cameroon, Cape Verde, Chad, Congo, Cuba, Cyprus, Czechoslovakia, Democratic Yemen, Djibouti, Ecuador, Egypt, El Salvador, Equatorial Guinea, Ethiopia, Fiji, Finland, Gabon, Gambia, German Democratic Republic, Ghana, Greece, Guinea, Guyana, Hungary, India, Indonesia, Iran, Iraq, Ireland, Jordan, Kenya, Kuwait, Lao People's Democratic Republic, Lebanon, Lesotho, Liberia, Libyan Arab Jamahiriya, Madagascar, Malawi, Malaysia, Maldives, Mali, Mauritania, Mauritius, Mexico, Mongolia, Morocco, Mozambique, Nepal, Nicaragua, Niger, Nigeria, Oman, Pakistan, Panama, Peru, Poland, Qatar, Romania, Saint Vincent and the Grenadines, Sao Tome and Principe, Senegal, Seychelles, Sierra Leone, Somalia, Sri Lanka, Sudan, Suriname, Sweden, Syrian Arab Republic, Thailand, Togo, Trinidad and Tobago, Tunisia,

Uganda, Ukrainian SSR, USSR, United Arab Emirates, United Republic of Tanzania, Venezuela, Viet Nam, Yemen, Yugoslavia, Zambia, Zimbabwe.

Against: Australia, Belgium, Canada, Denmark, France, Germany, Federal Republic of, Iceland, Israel, Italy, Japan, Luxembourg, Netherlands, New Zealand, Norway, Portugal, Spain, Turkey, United Kingdom, United States.

Abstaining: Austria, Bahamas, Brazil, Burma, Chile, China, Colombia, Costa Rica, Dominican Republic, Haiti, Honduras, Jamaica, Paraguay, Philippines, Saint Lucia, Uruguay, Zaire.

Introducing the draft on behalf of the sponsors, the German Democratic Republic recalled that China and the USSR had already pledged not to be the first to use nuclear weapons, and expressed the hope that the other nuclear-weapon Powers would act likewise.

In explanation of vote, the Federal Republic of Germany stated that the call for a non-first-use commitment emanating from the USSR had to be viewed in the context of the East-West relationship where Western Europe was confronted by the vast military superiority of the USSR and its allies. Moreover, it felt that the nuclear non-first-use concept provided no incentives to deal with existing nuclear arsenals and preserved them at their current level, and weakened the interdiction of force and condemnation of all wars as contained in the United Nations Charter. Norway, though supporting efforts to reduce dependence on nuclear weapons, viewed the draft as being directed at NATO's defensive strategy.

Brazil thought that the prevention of nuclear war was not served by the non-first-use concept, which implied legitimizing the ulterior use of such weapons. Colombia said the concept should also include conventional weapons.

Argentina, the Byelorussian SSR, Czechoslovakia, Finland, India, Indonesia, Ireland, Liberia, Mongolia, Sweden and the USSR saw in the draft a valid course of action, pending the achievement of nuclear disarmament. Argentina added, however, that the total elimination of nuclear weapons was the ultimate solution, and India likewise stressed the need to forswear the use or threat of use of such weapons under all circumstances. Indonesia also emphasized that all use of nuclear weapons must be proscribed, but felt that the last preambular paragraph did not fully reflect the complexities of the issue involved. Finland reaffirmed its declared policy that nuclear weapons should never be used.

Ireland expressed reservations about paragraph 3, regarding the activity foreseen for the Conference as impractical under the existing circumstances. Sweden felt that the establishment of a rough parity in conventional forces at a lower level would facilitate such commitments; a firm commitment to that effect, made through an international instrument of legally binding character dealing solely with the issue and promoting concrete measures for implementing effective non-first-use policies, would contribute to preventing nuclear warfare. Liberia stressed that there must be com-

mitments by States, because mere declarations could be reversed by any party. The USSR, which had made the declaration, said similar action by other nuclear-weapon States would amount to a general refusal to use nuclear weapons. Czechoslovakia said claims about the so-called military superiority of the socialist States served only to build a smoke-screen around the plans of the Western countries for what was called a limited nuclear war. The Byelorussian SSR and Mongolia expressed their support for all efforts aimed at outlawing the use of nuclear weapons.

Proposed negotiations on the neutron weapon

For the fourth consecutive year, the General Assembly, in 1984, requested the Conference on Disarmament to start without delay negotiations aimed at concluding a convention prohibiting the development, production, stockpiling, deployment and use of nuclear neutron weapons, also known as enhanced radiation weapons.

GENERAL ASSEMBLY ACTION

On 17 December, the Assembly, on the recommendation of the First Committee, adopted resolution 39/148 E by recorded vote.

Prohibition of the nuclear neutron weapon
The General Assembly,

Recalling paragraph 50 of the Final Document of the Tenth Special Session of the General Assembly, in which it is stated that the achievement of nuclear disarmament will require urgent negotiation of agreements, *inter alia,* for the cessation of the qualitative improvement and development of nuclear-weapon systems, which is especially emphasized in paragraph 50 *(a)* of that Document,

Recalling also that in paragraph 50 of the Final Document it is also underlined that in the course of negotiations consideration can be given to mutual and agreed limitation or prohibition, without prejudice to the security of any State, of any types of nuclear armaments,

Stressing that the development and production of the nuclear neutron weapon is a dangerous consequence of the continuing qualitative arms race in the field of nuclear weapons, especially through the qualitative improvement and development of new nuclear warheads by enhancing specific characteristics of nuclear weapons,

Reaffirming its relevant resolutions on the prohibition of the nuclear neutron weapon,

Sharing the world-wide concern expressed by Member States, as well as by non-governmental organizations, about the continued and expanded production and introduction of the nuclear neutron weapon in military arsenals, which escalates the nuclear-arms race and significantly lowers the threshold of nuclear war,

Aware of the inhuman effects of that weapon, which constitutes a grave threat, particularly to the unprotected civilian population,

Noting the consideration by the Conference on Disarmament at its 1984 session of issues connected with the cessation of the nuclear-arms race and nuclear disarmament as well as the prohibition of the nuclear neutron weapon,

Regretting that the Conference on Disarmament was prevented from reaching agreement on the commencement of negotiations on the cessation of the nuclear-arms race and nuclear disarmament, including the prohibition of the nuclear neutron weapon in an appropriate organizational framework,

1. *Reaffirms its request* to the Conference on Disarmament to start without delay negotiations within an appropriate organizational framework, with a view to concluding a convention on the prohibition of the development, production, stockpiling, deployment and use of nuclear neutron weapons as an organic element of negotiations, as envisaged in paragraph 50 of the Final Document of the Tenth Special Session of the General Assembly;

2. *Requests* the Secretary-General to transmit to the Conference on Disarmament all documents relating to the consideration of this question by the General Assembly at its thirty-ninth session;

3. *Requests* the Conference on Disarmament to submit a report on this question to the General Assembly at its fortieth session;

4. *Decides* to include in the provisional agenda of its fortieth session the item entitled "Prohibition of the nuclear neutron weapon".

General Assembly resolution 39/148 E

17 December 1984   Meeting 102   71-11-53 (recorded vote)

Approved by First Committee (A/39/749) by recorded vote (61-11-51), 20 November (meeting 44); 19-nation draft (A/C.1/39/L.20); agenda item 59 *(d)*.

Sponsors: Afghanistan, Angola, Bulgaria, Byelorussian SSR, Cuba, Czechoslovakia, Democratic Yemen, Ethiopia, German Democratic Republic, Hungary, Lao People's Democratic Republic, Mongolia, Mozambique, Poland, Romania, Syrian Arab Republic, Ukrainian SSR, Viet Nam, Zimbabwe.

Meeting numbers. GA 39th session: 1st Committee 3-36, 44; plenary 102.

Recorded vote in Assembly as follows:

In favour: Afghanistan, Algeria, Angola, Antigua and Barbuda, Bahrain, Barbados, Benin, Botswana, Bulgaria, Burkina Faso, Burundi, Byelorussian SSR, Cameroon, Congo, Cuba, Cyprus, Czechoslovakia, Democratic Yemen, Ethiopia, Fiji, Finland, Gabon, Gambia, German Democratic Republic, Ghana, Guinea, Guyana, Hungary, India, Indonesia, Iran, Iraq, Jordan, Kenya, Lao People's Democratic Republic, Lesotho, Libyan Arab Jamahiriya, Madagascar, Malawi, Malaysia, Mali, Mauritania, Mauritius, Mexico, Mongolia, Mozambique, Nicaragua, Niger, Nigeria, Panama, Poland, Qatar, Romania, Saint Vincent and the Grenadines, Seychelles, Sierra Leone, Suriname, Syrian Arab Republic, Togo, Trinidad and Tobago, Tunisia, Uganda, Ukrainian SSR, USSR, United Arab Emirates, United Republic of Tanzania, Viet Nam, Yemen, Yugoslavia, Zambia, Zimbabwe.

Against: Belgium, Canada, France, Germany, Federal Republic of, Israel, Italy, Japan, Portugal, Turkey, United Kingdom, United States.

Abstaining: Argentina, Australia, Austria, Bahamas, Bangladesh, Bhutan, Bolivia, Brazil, Brunei Darussalam, Burma, Chad, Chile, China, Colombia, Costa Rica, Denmark, Djibouti, Dominican Republic, Ecuador, Egypt, El Salvador, Equatorial Guinea, Greece, Haiti, Honduras, Iceland, Ireland, Ivory Coast, Liberia, Luxembourg, Maldives, Morocco, Nepal, Netherlands, New Zealand, Norway, Oman, Pakistan, Paraguay, Peru, Philippines, Saint Lucia, Senegal, Singapore, Somalia, Spain, Sri Lanka, Sudan, Sweden, Thailand, Uruguay, Venezuela, Zaire.

Introducing the draft on behalf of the sponsors, the German Democratic Republic said the nuclear neutron weapon, which it considered as a prototype of a third generation of nuclear weapons being developed, lowered the nuclear threshold and served to give material form to aggressive nuclear doctrines.

In explanation of vote, Bangladesh, Brazil, Egypt, Oman, Pakistan and the Sudan said all nuclear weapons, without singling out one specific type, should be prohibited; Ireland believed like-

wise, although it considered the neutron weapon to be a particularly destabilizing nuclear device. Australia did not believe the neutron weapon could be the subject of a separate disarmament treaty because of the difficulty of verification. Denmark reiterated its stance that, while it opposed the production of the neutron weapon and would not accept it on its territory, it saw the draft as an attempt to split the Western allies in an important area of defence policy.

Proposed nuclear-weapon freeze

In December 1984, the General Assembly adopted three resolutions (39/63 C and G, 39/151 D) calling for a freeze on nuclear armaments. A number of States explained in single statements their positions on these texts (see p. 31).

In November, the Secretary-General submitted to the Assembly, in accordance with a December 1983 resolution,[25] a note[26] containing information received from the USSR regarding its views on the freeze.

GENERAL ASSEMBLY ACTION

On the recommendation of the First Committee, the Assembly, on 12 December 1984, adopted resolution 39/63 C by recorded vote.

Nuclear-arms freeze

The General Assembly,

Recalling that in the Final Document of the Tenth Special Session of the General Assembly, the first special session devoted to disarmament, adopted in 1978 and unanimously and categorically reaffirmed in 1982 during the twelfth special session of the General Assembly, the second special session devoted to disarmament, the Assembly expressed deep concern over the threat to the very survival of mankind posed by the existence of nuclear weapons and the continuing arms race,

Recalling also that, on those occasions, it pointed out that existing arsenals of nuclear weapons are more than sufficient to destroy all life on earth and stressed that mankind is therefore confronted with a choice: halt the arms race and proceed to disarmament, or face annihilation,

Noting that the conditions prevailing today are a source of even more serious concern than those existing in 1978 because of several factors, such as the deterioration of the international situation, the increase in the accuracy, speed and destructive power of nuclear weapons, the promotion of illusory doctrines of "limited" or "winnable" nuclear war and the many false alarms which have occurred owing to accidental reasons,

Noting also that at the Seventh Conference of Heads of State or Government of Non-Aligned Countries, held at New Delhi from 7 to 12 March 1983, it was declared that the renewed escalation in the nuclear-arms race, both in its quantitative and qualitative dimensions, as well as reliance on doctrines of nuclear deterrence, had heightened the risk of the outbreak of nuclear war and led to greater insecurity and instability in international relations,

Bearing in mind that in their Joint Declaration, issued on 22 May 1984, the Heads of State or Government of six States Members of the United Nations, coming from five different continents, urged the nuclear-weapon States as a necessary first step to halt all testing, production and deployment of nuclear weapons and their delivery systems,

Believing that it is a matter of the utmost urgency to stop any further increase in the awesome arsenals of the two major nuclear-weapon States, which already have ample retaliatory power and a frightening overkill capacity,

Believing also that it is equally urgent to initiate or resume negotiations for the substantial reduction and qualitative limitation of nuclear arms,

Considering that a nuclear-arms freeze, while not an end in itself, would constitute the most effective first step for the achievement of the above-mentioned two objectives, since it would encourage the initiation or resumption of negotiations and prevent the continued increase and qualitative improvement of existing nuclear weaponry during the period when the negotiations would take place,

Firmly convinced that at present the conditions are most propitious for such a freeze, since the Union of Soviet Socialist Republics and the United States of America are now equivalent in nuclear military power and it seems evident that there exists between them an overall rough parity,

Conscious that the application of the systems of surveillance, verification and control already agreed upon in some previous cases would be sufficient to provide a reasonable guarantee of faithful compliance with the undertakings derived from the freeze,

Convinced that it would be to the benefit of all other States possessing nuclear weapons to follow the example of the two major nuclear-weapon States,

1. *Urges once more* the Union of Soviet Socialist Republics and the United States of America, as the two major nuclear-weapon States, to proclaim, either through simultaneous unilateral declarations or through a joint declaration, an immediate nuclear-arms freeze, which would be a first step towards the comprehensive programme of disarmament and whose structure and scope would be the following:

(a) It would embrace:
(i) A comprehensive test ban of nuclear weapons and of their delivery vehicles;
(ii) The complete cessation of the manufacture of nuclear weapons and of their delivery vehicles;
(iii) A ban on all further deployment of nuclear weapons and of their delivery vehicles;
(iv) The complete cessation of the production of fissionable material for weapons purposes;

(b) It would be subject to appropriate measures and procedures of verification, such as those which have already been agreed by the parties in the case of the SALT I and SALT II treaties, and those agreed upon in principle by them during the preparatory trilateral negotiations on the comprehensive test ban held at Geneva;

(c) It would be of an initial five-year duration, subject to prolongation when other nuclear-weapon States join in such a freeze, as the General Assembly urges them to do;

2. *Notes with satisfaction* that the Union of Soviet Socialist Republics has already submitted the report requested by the General Assembly in its resolution 38/73 E of 15 December 1983;

3. *Hopes* that the other major nuclear-weapon State will find it possible to comply also with the request of the General Assembly before the closure of its thirty-ninth session;

4. *Decides* to include in the provisional agenda of its fortieth session an item entitled "Implementation of General Assembly resolution 39/63 C on a nuclear-arms freeze".

General Assembly resolution 39/63 C

12 December 1984   Meeting 97   129-12-8 (recorded vote)

Approved by First Committee (A/39/750) by recorded vote (111-12-7), 20 November (meeting 44); 6-nation draft (A/C.1/39/L.32); agenda item 60 *(e)*.

Sponsors: Indonesia, Mexico, Pakistan, Romania, Sweden, Uruguay.

Meeting numbers. GA 39th session: 1st Committee 3-36, 40, 44; plenary 97.

Recorded vote in Assembly as follows:

In favour: Afghanistan, Algeria, Angola, Antigua and Barbuda, Argentina, Australia, Austria, Bahrain, Bangladesh, Barbados, Belize, Benin, Bhutan, Bolivia, Botswana, Brazil, Brunei Darussalam, Bulgaria, Burkina Faso, Burma, Burundi, Byelorussian SSR, Cameroon, Cape Verde, Central African Republic, Chad, Chile, Colombia, Comoros, Congo, Costa Rica, Cuba, Cyprus, Czechoslovakia, Democratic Yemen, Denmark, Djibouti, Dominica, Dominican Republic, Ecuador, Egypt, El Salvador, Equatorial Guinea, Ethiopia, Fiji, Finland, Gabon, German Democratic Republic, Ghana, Greece, Guatemala, Guinea, Guinea-Bissau, Guyana, Haiti, Honduras, Hungary, India, Indonesia, Iran, Iraq, Ireland, Ivory Coast, Jamaica, Jordan, Kenya, Kuwait, Lao People's Democratic Republic, Lebanon, Lesotho, Liberia, Libyan Arab Jamahiriya, Madagascar, Malawi, Malaysia, Maldives, Mali, Malta, Mauritania, Mauritius, Mexico, Mongolia, Morocco, Mozambique, Nepal, Nicaragua, Niger, Nigeria, Oman, Pakistan, Panama, Papua New Guinea, Paraguay, Peru, Poland, Qatar, Romania, Rwanda, Samoa, Sao Tome and Principe, Saudi Arabia, Senegal, Seychelles, Sierra Leone, Singapore, Somalia, Sri Lanka, Sudan, Suriname, Sweden, Syrian Arab Republic, Thailand, Togo, Trinidad and Tobago, Tunisia, Uganda, Ukrainian SSR, USSR, United Arab Emirates, United Republic of Tanzania, Uruguay, Vanuatu, Venezuela, Viet Nam, Yemen, Yugoslavia, Zaire, Zambia, Zimbabwe.

Against: Belgium, Canada, France, Germany, Federal Republic of, Israel, Italy, Japan, Luxembourg, Portugal, Turkey, United Kingdom, United States.

Abstaining: Bahamas, China, Iceland, Netherlands, New Zealand, Norway, Saint Lucia, Spain.

Explaining its vote, the Netherlands said the military imbalance prevailing in Europe—contrary to the draft's assertion—had to be brought down to the lowest possible level of parity before a freeze could be considered; rather than a declaratory freeze, bilateral negotiations should resume immediately without pre-conditions. Norway regretted that the draft failed to stress requirements such as verification and negotiated agreement among the parties concerned; it had reservations on those paragraphs questioning the defensive strategy of the alliance to which it belonged and endorsing one-sidedly the policies of one nuclear Power concerning a freeze.

Australia said it voted for the first time for a nuclear freeze proposal to express support for the broad aspirations to that end; as a first step, it favoured a mutual and verifiable freeze of nuclear-weapon testing, production and development, to be followed by negotiations on reductions. The USSR said that, given the current approximate parity in nuclear and conventional capabilities, an agreement on freezing and reducing levels of nuclear weapons would harm no one's security.

The Netherlands felt the other two texts on the topic (see p. 36) fell further short of the standards it used to measure the draft that became resolution 39/63 C. Guyana believed that resolution fully covered the objectives of the other two proposals, and voted accordingly in order to avoid duplication and unnecessary proliferation of resolutions.

On the recommendation of the First Committee, the Assembly, on 12 December, adopted resolution 39/63 G by recorded vote.

Freeze on nuclear weapons

The General Assembly,

Recalling its resolutions 37/100 A of 13 December 1982 and 38/73 B of 15 December 1983 concerning a freeze on nuclear weapons,

Convinced that in this nuclear age lasting world peace can be based only on the attainment of the goal of general and complete disarmament under effective international control,

Further convinced that the highest priority objectives in the field of disarmament have to be nuclear disarmament and the elimination of all weapons of mass destruction,

Recognizing the urgent need to halt the arms race, particularly in nuclear weapons,

Recognizing further the urgent need for a negotiated reduction of nuclear-weapon stockpiles leading to their complete elimination,

Noting with deep concern that nuclear-weapon States have not so far taken any action in response to the call made in resolutions 37/100 A and 38/73 B,

1. *Once again calls upon* all nuclear-weapon States to agree to a freeze on nuclear weapons, which would, *inter alia*, provide for a simultaneous total stoppage of any further production of nuclear weapons and a complete cut-off in the production of fissionable material for weapons purposes;

2. *Decides* to include in the provisional agenda of its fortieth session the item entitled "Freeze on nuclear weapons".

General Assembly resolution 39/63 G

12 December 1984   Meeting 97   127-11-11 (recorded vote)

Approved by First Committee (A/39/750) by recorded vote (110-12-9), 20 November (meeting 44); draft by India (A/C.1/39/L.49); agenda item 60 *(b)*.

Meeting numbers. GA 39th session: 1st Committee 3-36, 40, 44; plenary 97.

Recorded vote in Assembly as follows:

In favour: Afghanistan, Algeria, Angola, Antigua and Barbuda, Argentina, Austria, Bahrain, Bangladesh, Barbados, Belize, Benin, Bhutan, Bolivia, Botswana, Brazil, Brunei Darussalam, Bulgaria, Burkina Faso, Burma, Burundi, Byelorussian SSR, Cameroon, Cape Verde, Central African Republic, Chad, Chile, Colombia, Comoros, Congo, Costa Rica, Cuba, Cyprus, Czechoslovakia, Democratic Yemen, Denmark, Djibouti, Dominica, Dominican Republic, Ecuador, Egypt, El Salvador, Equatorial Guinea, Ethiopia, Fiji, Finland, Gabon, German Democratic Republic, Ghana, Greece, Guatemala, Guinea, Guinea-Bissau, Haiti, Honduras, Hungary, India, Indonesia, Iran, Iraq, Ireland, Ivory Coast, Jordan, Kenya, Kuwait, Lao People's Democratic Republic, Lebanon, Lesotho, Liberia, Libyan Arab Jamahiriya, Madagascar, Malawi, Malaysia, Maldives, Mali, Malta, Mauritania, Mauritius, Mexico, Mongolia, Morocco, Mozambique, Nepal, Nicaragua, Niger, Nigeria, Oman, Pakistan, Panama, Papua New Guinea, Paraguay, Peru, Philippines, Poland, Qatar, Romania, Rwanda, Samoa, Sao Tome and Principe, Saudi Arabia, Senegal, Seychelles, Sierra Leone, Singapore, Somalia, Sri Lanka, Sudan, Suriname, Sweden, Syrian Arab Republic, Thailand, Togo, Trinidad and Tobago, Tunisia, Uganda, Ukrainian SSR, USSR, United Arab Emirates, United Republic of Tanzania, Uruguay, Vanuatu, Venezuela, Viet Nam, Yemen, Yugoslavia, Zaire, Zambia, Zimbabwe.

Against: Belgium, Canada, France, Germany, Federal Republic of, Italy, Luxembourg, Netherlands, Portugal, Turkey, United Kingdom, United States.

Abstaining: Australia, Bahamas, China, Guyana, Iceland, Israel,[a] Japan, New Zealand, Norway, Saint Lucia, Spain.

[a]Later advised the Secretariat it had intended to vote in favour.

Introducing the text, India said a freeze would be simple, direct and immediately enforceable, as compared to the meagre and always uncertain outcome of the protracted negotiations on nuclear-arms reduction.

Norway felt that the text, while calling for an agreement among the parties concerned, failed to deal explicitly with the need for adequate verification. The USSR interpreted the last preambular paragraph as referring to those nuclear-weapon States that not only had failed to respond to the call for a freeze, but had even spoken against it.

On 17 December, the Assembly, on the recommendation of the First Committee, adopted resolution 39/151 D by recorded vote.

Nuclear-weapon freeze

The General Assembly,

Expressing its deep alarm over the continuation and intensification of the nuclear-arms race, which seriously increases the threat of nuclear war,

Conscious of the fact that further buildup and improvement of nuclear weapons is not only dangerous but senseless,

Taking into account the great responsibility of nuclear-weapon States for the preservation of universal peace and the prevention of nuclear war,

Recalling its previous resolutions calling for a nuclear-weapon freeze both in quantitative and in qualitative terms,

Recalling also that on several occasions it has expressed the firm conviction that at present the conditions are most propitious for such a freeze,

Noting the wide support for the Joint Declaration of the Heads of State or Government of six States Members of the United Nations, issued on 22 May 1984, which contained an appeal to the nuclear-weapon States to halt testing, production and deployment of nuclear weapons and their means of delivery,

Deeply regretting that some nuclear Powers have not responded positively to its relevant appeals or to appeals and proposals by other States made repeatedly during the last two years,

Convinced that a nuclear-weapon freeze would raise the level of trust among States, ease international tension and create a favourable atmosphere for drastic reductions of nuclear arsenals,

Convinced also that striving for such reductions on the basis of equal security up to the complete elimination of nuclear weapons should become a binding norm of conduct for the nuclear-weapon States,

1. *Reaffirms its appeal* to all nuclear-weapon States to freeze, from a specific date, their nuclear arsenals on a global scale and under appropriate verification, as provided for in its resolution 38/76 of 15 December 1983;

2. *Urges once again* the Union of Soviet Socialist Republics and the United States of America, which possess the largest nuclear arsenals, to freeze, in the first place and simultaneously, their nuclear weapons on a bilateral basis by way of example to the other nuclear-weapon States;

3. *Strongly believes* that all the other nuclear-weapon States should subsequently and as soon as possible freeze their nuclear weapons;

4. *Stresses* the urgent need to intensify efforts aimed at the speedy achievement of agreements on substantial limitations on and radical reductions of nuclear weapons, with a view to their complete elimination as the ultimate goal.

General Assembly resolution 39/151 D

17 December 1984   Meeting 102   104-18-18 (recorded vote)

Approved by First Committee (A/39/755) by recorded vote (95-18-13), 20 November (meeting 44); 10-nation draft (A/C.1/39/L.25); agenda item 65.
Sponsors: Angola, Bulgaria, Byelorussian SSR, Czechoslovakia, German Democratic Republic, Hungary, Mongolia, Poland, Ukrainian SSR, USSR.
Meeting numbers. GA 39th session: 1st Committee 3-36, 40, 44; plenary 102.

Recorded vote in Assembly as follows:

In favour: Afghanistan, Algeria, Angola, Antigua and Barbuda, Argentina, Austria, Bahrain, Bangladesh, Barbados, Benin, Bhutan, Bolivia, Botswana, Brazil, Brunei Darussalam, Bulgaria, Burkina Faso, Burma, Burundi, Byelorussian SSR, Cameroon, Cape Verde, Central African Republic, Chile, Colombia, Congo, Cuba, Cyprus, Czechoslovakia, Democratic Yemen, Djibouti, Ecuador, Egypt, Equatorial Guinea, Ethiopia, Fiji, Finland, Gabon, German Democratic Republic, Ghana, Greece, Guinea, Hungary, India, Indonesia, Iran, Iraq, Ireland, Jordan, Kenya, Kuwait, Lao People's Democratic Republic, Lebanon, Lesotho, Libyan Arab Jamahiriya, Madagascar, Malawi, Malaysia, Maldives, Mali, Mauritania, Mauritius, Mexico, Mongolia, Morocco, Mozambique, Nepal, Nicaragua, Niger, Nigeria, Oman, Pakistan, Panama, Papua New Guinea, Peru, Poland, Qatar, Romania, Saint Vincent and the Grenadines, Samoa, Saudi Arabia, Seychelles, Sierra Leone, Singapore, Somalia, Sri Lanka, Sudan, Suriname, Syrian Arab Republic, Thailand, Togo, Trinidad and Tobago, Tunisia, Uganda, Ukrainian SSR, USSR, United Arab Emirates, United Republic of Tanzania, Venezuela, Viet Nam, Yemen, Yugoslavia, Zambia, Zimbabwe.
Against: Belgium, Canada, Denmark, France, Germany, Federal Republic of, Iceland, Israel, Italy, Japan, Luxembourg, Netherlands, New Zealand, Norway, Portugal, Spain, Turkey, United Kingdom, United States.
Abstaining: Australia, Bahamas, Chad, China, Costa Rica,[a] Dominican Republic, El Salvador, Guatemala, Guyana, Haiti, Honduras, Ivory Coast, Paraguay, Rwanda, Saint Lucia, Sweden, Uruguay, Zaire.
[a] Later advised the Secretariat it had intended to vote in favour.

Explaining its vote, Norway said the text contained no important substantive improvements on the previous year's resolution.[27] Indonesia, supporting the thrust of the draft, emphasized that the importance of a freeze, as only a means to an end, should be judged in conjunction with the provisions in paragraph 4.

A number of States explained in single statements their positions on the three texts which became resolutions 39/63 C and G, and 39/151 D.

Belgium, France, the Federal Republic of Germany and the United States asserted that, given the current military situation, freeze proposals were tantamount to unilateral disarmament and to expecting the Western European countries to acquiesce in a codification of the USSR superiority and to live with that threat for an indefinite period. The Netherlands also spoke of the existing military imbalance in Europe, and Canada stated that all arms-control agreements must enhance mutual security, which could not be achieved if current imbalances were locked in. The Federal Republic of Germany noted that, according to paragraph 29 of the 1978 Final Document,[13] a freeze decision should not be taken independently from underlying security situations and force relationships.

The Federal Republic of Germany and the United States feared that a freeze would diminish incentives for the USSR to negotiate seriously on nuclear-arms reduction. Among those rejecting a declaratory freeze, Canada and the Netherlands stressed the importance of resumption, without pre-conditions and delay, of bilateral negotiations on nuclear disarmament. France added that such negotiations must begin with defining and establishing a satisfactory balance, and Canada asserted that they should take into account the legitimate security interests of both sides and provide for adequate verification measures. The Federal Republic of Germany agreed that the verification issue was consistently underemphasized in the drafts. The United States also argued that the verification of some aspects of a freeze would require measures beyond national technical means; it therefore believed that the time required for negotiating a freeze and its verification would be better spent negotiating deep reductions. For Canada, the texts did not deal with the potentially destabilizing problem of peaceful nuclear explosions. Australia stressed the requirement for mutuality and balance, and called for resumption of negotiations on the intermediate-range nuclear forces.

Nigeria supported the three texts in the belief that only a freeze could create the most desirable basis for progress in nuclear disarmament negotiations. Pakistan voted similarly, asserting that it was not partial to any negotiating approach and that it only wanted a thaw in the prevailing situation.

The German Democratic Republic asserted that a nuclear-weapons freeze and reduction were complementary. Czechoslovakia felt that the Western countries' allegation of an imbalance of forces in Europe was an excuse for bringing more of their armaments into the region. For Hungary, a freeze, though not an end in itself, could contribute to making the international situation more propitious to negotiating reduction and elimination of nuclear weapons.

Nuclear non-proliferation

Among the efforts made in 1984 to prevent the spread of nuclear weapons, the preparatory process began at Geneva for the Third Review Conference of the Parties to the 1968 Treaty on the Non-Proliferation of Nuclear Weapons (NPT).[28] The International Atomic Energy Agency (IAEA), for its part, continued its efforts concerning nuclear safeguards, particularly in relation to NPT (see PART II, Chapter I). In resolution 39/12, the Assembly urged States to ensure the effectiveness of IAEA's safeguards system.

The Assembly adopted a number of resolutions relating to nuclear-weapon-free zones, including one on extending the work of an expert group on such zones (resolution 39/151 B).

Nuclear-weapon-free zones

The establishment of nuclear-weapon-free zones in various parts of the world continued to be considered in 1984 by the Disarmament Commission, the Conference on Disarmament and the General Assembly. In addition to the establishment of zones in Africa, the Middle East and South Asia, references were made in debates to informal proposals for zones in the Balkans, northern and central Europe and the South Pacific region.

By a letter of 15 March 1984[29] to the Secretary-General, Bangladesh transmitted the resolutions and final declaration adopted by the Fourteenth Islamic Conference of Foreign Ministers (Dhaka, 6-11 December 1983). The meeting supported the establishment of nuclear-weapon-free zones in Africa, the Middle East and South Asia, and condemned the nuclear collaboration between Israel and South Africa.

Group of Experts

The 21-member Group of Governmental Experts on Nuclear-Weapon-Free Zones, set up in 1983[30] in accordance with a 1982 General Assembly resolution[31] to review and supplement a 1975 expert study,[32] held two further sessions in 1984—its third (27 February–9 March) and fourth (25-29 June).

On 29 June, the Chairman of the Group, Klaus Törnudd (Finland), informed the Secretary-General that the Group had been unable to reach agreement on the study in time for its submission to the Assembly's session. The letter, with a request that consideration be given to extending the deadline, was annexed to the Secretary-General's report to the Assembly.[33]

GENERAL ASSEMBLY ACTION

On 17 December 1984, the General Assembly, on the recommendation of the First Committee, adopted resolution 39/151 B by recorded vote.

Study of the question of nuclear-weapon-free zones in all its aspects

The General Assembly,

Recalling its resolution 37/99 F of 13 December 1982, in which it decided that a study should be undertaken to review and supplement the *Comprehensive study of the question of nuclear-weapon-free zones in all its aspects* in the light of information and experience accumulated since 1975,

Recalling also that it requested the Secretary-General, with the assistance of an *ad hoc* group of qualified governmental experts, to carry out the study and to submit it to the General Assembly at its thirty-ninth session,

Recalling further its resolution 38/188 I of 20 December 1983, in which it requested the Secretary-General to transmit to the Group of Governmental Experts on Nuclear-Weapon-Free Zones for its consideration and analysis all the relevant documents submitted to the General Assembly at its thirty-eighth session, as well as

the records of the debate on the question of nuclear-weapon-free zones,

1. *Takes note* of the report of the Secretary-General, to which is annexed a letter from the Chairman of the Group of Governmental Experts on Nuclear-Weapon-Free Zones, informing the Secretary-General that the Group has not been able to conclude the study within the time available and that the experts consider that the work could be completed if the time period of the study were extended;

2. *Requests* the Secretary-General to continue the study and to submit the report to the General Assembly at its fortieth session;

3. *Requests* the Secretary-General to transmit to the Group of Governmental Experts for its consideration and analysis all the relevant documents submitted to the General Assembly at its thirty-ninth session, as well as the records of the debate on the question of nuclear-weapon-free zones.

General Assembly resolution 39/151 B

17 December 1984   Meeting 102   143-0-2 (recorded vote)

Approved by First Committee (A/39/755) by recorded vote (135-0-2), 19 November (meeting 41); 2-nation draft (A/C.1/39/L.13); agenda item 65 (a).

Sponsors: Finland, Romania.

Financial implications. ACABQ, A/39/7/Add.10; 5th Committee, A/39/795; S-G, A/C.1/39/L.73, A/C.5/39/56.

Meeting numbers. GA 39th session: 1st Committee 3-36, 41; 5th Committee 43; plenary 102.

Recorded vote in Assembly as follows:

In favour: Afghanistan, Algeria, Angola, Antigua and Barbuda, Argentina, Australia, Austria, Bahamas, Bahrain, Bangladesh, Barbados, Belgium, Benin, Bhutan, Bolivia, Botswana, Brunei Darussalam, Bulgaria, Burkina Faso, Burma, Burundi, Byelorussian SSR, Cameroon, Canada, Cape Verde, Central African Republic, Chad, Chile, China, Colombia, Congo, Costa Rica, Cuba, Cyprus, Czechoslovakia, Democratic Kampuchea, Democratic Yemen, Denmark, Djibouti, Dominican Republic, Ecuador, Egypt, El Salvador, Equatorial Guinea, Ethiopia, Fiji, Finland, France, Gabon, German Democratic Republic, Germany, Federal Republic of, Ghana, Greece, Guatemala, Guinea, Guyana, Haiti, Honduras, Hungary, Iceland, Indonesia, Iran, Iraq, Ireland, Israel, Italy, Ivory Coast, Jamaica, Japan, Jordan, Kenya, Kuwait, Lao People's Democratic Republic, Lebanon, Lesotho, Libyan Arab Jamahiriya, Luxembourg, Madagascar, Malawi, Malaysia, Maldives, Mali, Malta, Mauritania, Mauritius, Mexico, Mongolia, Morocco, Mozambique, Nepal, Netherlands, New Zealand, Nicaragua, Niger, Nigeria, Norway, Oman, Pakistan, Panama, Papua New Guinea, Paraguay, Peru, Philippines, Poland, Portugal, Qatar, Romania, Rwanda, Saint Lucia, Saint Vincent and the Grenadines, Samoa, Sao Tome and Principe, Saudi Arabia, Senegal, Seychelles, Sierra Leone, Singapore, Somalia, Spain, Sri Lanka, Sudan, Suriname, Sweden, Syrian Arab Republic, Thailand, Togo, Trinidad and Tobago, Tunisia, Turkey, Uganda, Ukrainian SSR, USSR, United Arab Emirates, United Kingdom, United Republic of Tanzania, Uruguay, Venezuela, Viet Nam, Yemen, Yugoslavia, Zaire, Zambia, Zimbabwe.

Against: None.

Abstaining: India, United States.

Introducing the draft, Finland said the Group—which had examined five consecutive drafts in four sessions totalling six weeks—was unable even to begin examining the analytical part of the study because it had been held up by slow progress on those chapters intended to summarize facts and describe historical developments. It felt the Group, which believed it could complete the study if its mandate was extended, deserved that chance, adding that none of the experts had intended to detract from the agreed principles and other conclusions reached in the 1975 study, which had retained its value.

Explaining their votes, Cameroon and the United Kingdom emphasized that the extension of the Group's work should be seen as exceptional, while the United States objected to the draft's financial implications. The United Kingdom added that, as with all studies covering a contentious issue, the methodology adopted by the Group should allow for opinions to be given adequate and balanced expression in a consensus report. Egypt attached importance to the completion of the study which, it felt, would make available valuable information for establishing nuclear-weapon-free zones. India said that, although the text was concerned with a purely procedural matter, it could not support the underlying approach that viewed the establishing of such zones as a realistically viable way to cope with the menace of an unchecked escalation of the nuclear-arms race.

While delegations explained in the General Assembly their votes on individual resolutions on the proposed zones, Chile explained its affirmative vote on all of them, saying that it understood, as the fundamental condition for their establishment, the political and legal will of the nuclear Powers in terms of undertaking verifiable commitments and fully respecting the status of those areas.

Africa

Since the Declaration on the Denuclearization of Africa[34] was adopted in 1964 by the Organization of African Unity (OAU), the question of its implementation had been on the General Assembly's agenda. In addition to a resolution on implementation of that Declaration (39/61 A), the Assembly, in 1984 as in previous years, adopted a text on the nuclear capability of South Africa (39/61 B).

Throughout 1984, South Africa's military and nuclear relations with other States were kept under consideration by various other United Nations bodies (see p. 139).

Nuclear weapons and South Africa

Disarmament Commission activities. As in previous years, the Disarmament Commission[10] established in 1984 a working group (Working Group II) to consider, in pursuance of a December 1983 General Assembly request,[35] the question of South Africa's nuclear capability.

The Group, chaired by Davidson L. Hepburn (Bahamas), held 11 meetings and additional informal consultations between 11 and 30 May, using a text submitted in 1983 by Mauritius on behalf of the African States members of the Commission as a basis for discussion and taking into account another 1983 working paper by the Federal Republic of Germany. In the absence of consensus, the Group agreed to annex to its report a working paper produced as a result of its 1984 discussion, and recommended that the Commission refer the question to the Assembly later in the year.

Reports by the Secretary-General. By a February 1984 note to the Security Council,[36] the Secretary-General drew the Council's attention to two December 1983 Assembly resolutions—one on the implementation of the 1964 OAU Declaration,[37] and the other on South Africa's nuclear capability.[35] By the latter, the Assembly had requested the Council to prevent South Africa from acquiring arms or arms technology or enjoying nuclear collaboration. In September, the Secretary-General submitted a report to the Assembly on South Africa's nuclear capability,[38] stating that he had followed closely South Africa's nuclear activities; at the same time, he drew the Assembly's attention to a report prepared by the United Nations Institute for Disarmament Research (UNIDIR).[39]

UNIDIR report. The UNIDIR report on South Africa's nuclear capability[39]—prepared, in pursuance of a December 1983 Assembly request,[37] in co-operation with the Secretariat's Department for Disarmament Affairs and in consultation with OAU—covered developments since the Secretary-General's 1980 report on South Africa's plan and capability in the nuclear field.[40] It found, among other things, that: uranium production in South Africa and Namibia had increased by about 50 per cent in the period from 1978 to 1982; a pilot enrichment plant had been in operation for 8 to 10 years; the first reactor of a nuclear power plant started operations in March 1984 and a second was expected to be completed later that year; research and development on fuel technology to enable South Africa to manufacture its own nuclear fuel was in progress; a decision had been taken to establish a new nuclear research centre; new legislation had been enacted with a view to strengthening the control and management of its nuclear programme; South Africa had stated its readiness to resume discussions with IAEA on safeguards in respect of its semi-commercial enrichment plant, but not its pilot enrichment plant; and South Africa continued to have a technical capability to manufacture nuclear weapons.

GENERAL ASSEMBLY ACTION

On the recommendation of the First Committee, the General Assembly, on 12 December 1984, adopted resolution 39/61 A by recorded vote.

Implementation of the Declaration

The General Assembly,

Bearing in mind the Declaration on the Denuclearization of Africa adopted by the Assembly of Heads of State and Government of the Organization of African Unity at its first ordinary session, held at Cairo from 17 to 21 July 1964,

Recalling resolution 1652(XVI) of 24 November 1961, its earliest on the subject, as well as its resolutions 2033(XX) of 3 December 1965, 31/69 of 10 December

1976, 32/81 of 12 December 1977, 33/63 of 14 December 1978, 34/76 A of 11 December 1979, 35/146 B of 12 December 1980, 36/86 B of 9 December 1981, 37/74 A of 9 December 1982 and 38/181 A of 20 December 1983, in which it called upon all States to consider and respect the continent of Africa and its surrounding areas as a nuclear-weapon-free zone,

Recalling that in its resolution 33/63 it vigorously condemned any overt or covert attempt by South Africa to introduce nuclear weapons into the continent of Africa and demanded that South Africa refrain forthwith from conducting any nuclear explosion in the continent of Africa or elsewhere,

Taking note of the report of the United Nations Institute for Disarmament Research entitled "South Africa's nuclear capability", undertaken in co-operation with the Department for Disarmament Affairs of the Secretariat and in consultation with the Organization of African Unity, as well as the report of the Disarmament Commission,

Expressing regret that, despite the threat South Africa's nuclear capability constitutes to international peace and security, in particular to the realization of the objective of the Declaration on the Denuclearization of Africa, the Disarmament Commission has, once again, in 1984, failed to reach a consensus on this important item on its agenda,

1. *Strongly renews its call* upon all States to consider and respect the continent of Africa and its surrounding areas as a nuclear-weapon-free zone;

2. *Reaffirms* that the implementation of the Declaration on the Denuclearization of Africa adopted by the Assembly of Heads of State and Government of the Organization of African Unity would be an important measure to prevent the proliferation of nuclear weapons and to promote international peace and security;

3. *Expresses once again its grave alarm* at South Africa's possession and continued development of nuclear-weapon capability;

4. *Condemns* South Africa's continued pursuit of a nuclear capability and all forms of nuclear collaboration by any State, corporation, institution or individual with the racist régime that enable it to frustrate the objective of the Declaration which seeks to keep Africa free from nuclear weapons;

5. *Calls upon* all States, corporations, institutions and individuals to desist from further collaboration with the racist régime that may enable it to frustrate the objective of the Declaration on the Denuclearization of Africa;

6. *Demands once again* that the racist régime of South Africa refrain from manufacturing, testing, deploying, transporting, storing, using or threatening to use nuclear weapons;

7. *Appeals* to all States that have the means to do so to monitor South Africa's research on, and development and production of nuclear weapons, and to publicize any information in that regard;

8. *Demands once again* that South Africa submit forthwith all its nuclear installations and facilities to inspection by the International Atomic Energy Agency;

9. *Requests* the Secretary-General to render all necessary assistance that the Organization of African Unity may seek towards the implementation of its solemn Declaration on the Denuclearization of Africa;

10. *Decides* to include in the provisional agenda of its fortieth session the item entitled "Implementation of the Declaration on the Denuclearization of Africa".

General Assembly resolution 39/61 A

12 December 1984   Meeting 97   147-0-5 (recorded vote)

Approved by First Committee (A/39/747) by recorded vote (132-0-5), 21 November (meeting 45); draft by Cameroon, for African Group (A/C.1/39/L.44); agenda item 57 (a).

Meeting numbers. GA 39th session: 1st Committee 3-36, 40, 45, 46; plenary 97.

Recorded vote in Assembly as follows:

In favour: Afghanistan, Albania, Algeria, Angola, Antigua and Barbuda, Argentina, Australia, Austria, Bahamas, Bahrain, Bangladesh, Barbados, Belize, Benin, Bhutan, Bolivia, Botswana, Brazil, Brunei Darussalam, Bulgaria, Burkina Faso, Burma, Burundi, Byelorussian SSR, Cameroon, Canada, Cape Verde, Central African Republic, Chad, Chile, China, Colombia, Comoros, Congo, Costa Rica, Cuba, Cyprus, Czechoslovakia, Democratic Kampuchea, Democratic Yemen, Denmark, Djibouti, Dominica, Dominican Republic, Ecuador, Egypt, El Salvador, Equatorial Guinea, Ethiopia, Fiji, Finland, Gabon, German Democratic Republic, Germany, Federal Republic of, Ghana, Greece, Guatemala, Guinea, Guinea-Bissau, Guyana, Haiti, Honduras, Hungary, Iceland, India, Indonesia, Iran, Iraq, Ireland, Italy, Ivory Coast, Jamaica, Japan, Jordan, Kenya, Kuwait, Lao People's Democratic Republic, Lebanon, Lesotho, Liberia, Libyan Arab Jamahiriya, Luxembourg, Madagascar, Malawi, Malaysia, Maldives, Mali, Malta, Mauritania, Mauritius, Mexico, Mongolia, Morocco, Mozambique, Nepal, Netherlands, New Zealand, Nicaragua, Niger, Nigeria, Norway, Oman, Pakistan, Panama, Papua New Guinea, Paraguay, Peru, Philippines, Poland, Portugal, Qatar, Romania, Rwanda, Saint Lucia, Samoa, Sao Tome and Principe, Saudi Arabia, Senegal, Seychelles, Sierra Leone, Singapore, Somalia, Spain, Sri Lanka, Sudan, Suriname, Sweden, Syrian Arab Republic, Thailand, Togo, Trinidad and Tobago, Tunisia, Turkey, Uganda, Ukrainian SSR, USSR, United Arab Emirates, United Republic of Tanzania, Uruguay, Vanuatu, Venezuela, Viet Nam, Yemen, Yugoslavia, Zaire, Zambia, Zimbabwe.

Against: None.

Abstaining: Belgium, France, Israel, United Kingdom, United States.

In explanation of vote, Canada expressed a reservation concerning the assertion in the last preambular paragraph, believing that it fell within the purview of the Security Council. Belgium found the assertion in paragraph 3 to be unproven and the language in paragraph 4 to be ambiguous. Similarly, Japan did not fully agree with some assertions, which, it felt, lacked conclusive evidence. Sweden, speaking also on behalf of Denmark, Finland, Iceland and Norway, voiced reservations about paragraph 7. The Netherlands, though unable to support all ideas in the text, supported the call on South Africa to submit its nuclear installations to IAEA inspection.

The Federal Republic of Germany supported the objectives of the draft, although it continued to have doubts about some aspects, notably "surrounding areas" in connection with the confines of the envisaged zone, to which it gave the strictest possible interpretation. Recalling its concerns about the requirements for nuclear-weapon-free zones in general, Brazil stated that it did not object to a consensus on the text, as particular situations of the region in question warranted special regard.

Also on 12 December, the Assembly, on the recommendation of the First Committee, adopted resolution 39/61 B by recorded vote.

Nuclear capability of South Africa

The General Assembly,

Recalling its resolutions 34/76 B of 11 December 1979, 35/146 A of 12 December 1980, 36/86 A of 9 December 1981, 37/74 B of 9 December 1982 and 38/181 B of 20 December 1983,

Bearing in mind the Declaration on the Denuclearization of Africa adopted by the Assembly of Heads of State and Government of the Organization of African Unity at its first ordinary session, held at Cairo from 17 to 21 July 1964,

Recalling that, in paragraph 12 of the Final Document of the Tenth Special Session of the General Assembly, it noted that the accumulation of armaments and the acquisition of armaments technology by the racist régimes, as well as their possible acquisition of nuclear weapons, presented a challenging and increasingly dangerous obstacle to a world community faced with the urgent need to disarm,

Recalling also that in its resolution 33/63 of 14 December 1978, it vigorously condemned any overt or covert attempt by South Africa to introduce nuclear weapons into the continent of Africa and demanded that South Africa refrain forthwith from conducting any nuclear explosion in the continent or elsewhere,

Taking note of resolution GC(XXVIII)/RES/423 on South Africa's nuclear capabilities, adopted on 27 September 1984 by the General Conference of the International Atomic Energy Agency during its twenty-eighth regular session,

Taking note of the report of the United Nations Institute for Disarmament Research, entitled "South Africa's nuclear capability", undertaken in co-operation with the Department for Disarmament Affairs and in consultation with the Organization of African Unity,

Expressing regret that, despite the threat South Africa's nuclear capability constitutes to international peace and security, in particular to the realization of the objective of the Declaration on the Denuclearization of Africa, the Disarmament Commission has, once again, in 1984, failed to reach a consensus on this important item on its agenda,

Gravely concerned that South Africa, in flagrant violation of the principles of international law and the relevant provisions of the Charter of the United Nations, has continued its acts of aggression and subversion against the peoples and the independent States of southern Africa,

Strongly condemning the continued military occupation by South African troops of parts of the territory of Angola in violation of its national sovereignty, independence and territorial integrity, and urging the immediate and unconditional withdrawal of South African troops from Angolan soil,

Expressing its grave disappointment that, despite repeated appeals by the international community, certain Western States and Israel have continued to collaborate with the racist régime of South Africa in the military and nuclear fields and that some of the same Western States have, by a ready recourse to the use of the veto, consistently frustrated every effort in the Security Council to deal decisively with the question of South Africa,

Recalling its decision taken at the tenth special session that the Security Council should take appropriate effective steps to prevent the frustration of the implementation of the decision of the Organization of African Unity for the denuclearization of Africa,

Stressing the need to preserve peace and security in Africa by ensuring that the continent is a nuclear-weapon-free zone,

1. *Condemns* the massive buildup of South Africa's military machine, in particular, its frenzied acquisition of nuclear-weapon capability for repressive and aggressive purposes and as an instrument of blackmail;

2. *Expresses its full support* for the African States faced with the danger of South Africa's nuclear capability;

3. *Reaffirms* that the racist régime's acquisition of nuclear-weapon capability constitutes a very grave danger to international peace and security and, in particular, jeopardizes the security of African States and increases the danger of the proliferation of nuclear weapons;

4. *Condemns* all forms of nuclear collaboration by any State, corporation, institution or individual with the racist régime of South Africa, in particular the decision by some Member States to grant licences to several corporations in their territories to provide equipment, technical and maintenance services for nuclear installations in South Africa;

5. *Demands* that South Africa and all other foreign interests put an immediate end to the exploration and exploitation of uranium resources in Namibia;

6. *Calls upon* all States, corporations, institutions and individuals to terminate forthwith all forms of military and nuclear collaboration with the racist régime;

7. *Requests* the Disarmament Commission to consider as a matter of priority during its session in 1985 South Africa's nuclear capability, taking into account, *inter alia*, the findings of the report of the United Nations Institute for Disarmament Research on South Africa's nuclear capability;

8. *Requests* the Security Council, for the purposes of disarmament and to fulfil its obligations and responsibility, to take enforcement measures to prevent any racist régimes from acquiring arms or arms technology;

9. *Further requests* the Security Council to conclude expeditiously its consideration of the recommendations of its Committee established by resolution 421(1977) concerning the question of South Africa, with a view to blocking the existing loopholes in the arms embargo, so as to render it more effective and prohibiting, in particular, all forms of co-operation and collaboration with the racist régime of South Africa in the nuclear field;

10. *Demands once again* that South Africa submit forthwith all its nuclear installations and facilities to inspection by the International Atomic Energy Agency;

11. *Requests* the Secretary-General to follow very closely South Africa's evolution in the nuclear field and to report thereon to the General Assembly at its fortieth session.

General Assembly resolution 39/61 B

12 December 1984   Meeting 97   137-4-11 (recorded vote)

Approved by First Committee (A/39/747) by recorded vote (123-4-11), 21 November (meeting 45); draft by Cameroon, for African Group (A/C.1/39/L.51), orally revised; agenda item 57 *(b)*.

Meeting numbers. GA 39th session: 1st Committee 3-36, 40, 45, 46; plenary 97.

Recorded vote in Assembly as follows:

In favour: Afghanistan, Albania, Algeria, Angola, Antigua and Barbuda, Argentina, Austria, Bahamas, Bahrain, Bangladesh, Barbados, Belize, Benin, Bhutan, Bolivia, Botswana, Brazil, Brunei Darussalam, Bulgaria, Burkina Faso, Burma, Burundi, Byelorussian SSR, Cameroon, Cape Verde, Central African Republic, Chad, Chile, China, Colombia, Comoros, Congo, Costa Rica, Cuba, Cyprus, Czechoslovakia, Democratic Kampuchea, Democratic Yemen, Denmark, Djibouti, Dominica, Dominican Republic, Ecuador, Egypt, El Salvador, Equatorial Guinea, Ethiopia, Fiji, Finland, Gabon, German Democratic Republic, Ghana, Greece, Guatemala, Guinea, Guinea-Bissau, Guyana, Haiti, Honduras, Hungary, Iceland, India, Indonesia, Iran, Iraq, Ireland, Ivory Coast, Jamaica, Jordan, Kenya, Kuwait, Lao People's Democratic Republic, Lebanon, Lesotho, Liberia, Libyan Arab Jamahiriya, Madagascar, Malaysia, Maldives, Mali, Malta, Mauritania, Mauritius, Mexico, Mongolia, Morocco, Mozambique, Nepal, Nicaragua, Niger, Nigeria, Norway, Oman, Pakistan, Panama, Papua New Guinea, Paraguay, Peru, Philippines, Poland, Qatar, Romania, Rwanda, Saint Lucia, Samoa, Sao Tome and Principe,

Saudi Arabia, Senegal, Seychelles, Sierra Leone, Singapore, Somalia, Spain, Sri Lanka, Sudan, Suriname, Sweden, Syrian Arab Republic, Thailand, Togo, Trinidad and Tobago, Tunisia, Turkey, Uganda, Ukrainian SSR, USSR, United Arab Emirates, United Republic of Tanzania, Uruguay, Vanuatu, Venezuela, Viet Nam, Yemen, Yugoslavia, Zaire, Zambia, Zimbabwe.
Against: France, Israel, United Kingdom, United States.
Abstaining: Australia, Belgium, Canada, Germany, Federal Republic of, Italy, Japan, Luxembourg, Malawi, Netherlands, New Zealand, Portugal.

In explanation of vote, several delegations expressed reservations on a number of paragraphs, while supporting the general objectives of the text. Belgium and the Netherlands objected to prohibiting all forms of collaboration with South Africa in the nuclear field. Ecuador disagreed with what it felt was selective language such as in paragraphs 1 and 6. Australia objected to condemning a specific State and expressed misgivings about the call on the Security Council to take actions beyond its constitutional powers. While not agreeing with the formulation of the request to the Council in paragraph 8, the Netherlands supported strengthening the arms embargo against South Africa.

Cuba asserted that the main obstacle to implementing the 1964 Declaration was the nuclear collaboration of certain Western States and Israel with South Africa. Sharing that view, the USSR added that Africa's efforts to create a nuclear-weapon-free zone on its continent, which the USSR supported, must have no effect on generally acknowledged norms of international law, including the principle of free navigation on the high seas. The Ukrainian SSR stressed the urgency of condemning all forms of co-operation with South Africa, particularly military and nuclear.

In explanation of vote on both texts (resolutions 39/61 A and B above), France and Sweden, speaking for the Nordic group, voiced reservations over formulations that, in their view, disregarded the division of competence between the Security Council and the General Assembly.

The Nordic countries, as well as Ireland, deplored the singling out of countries for condemnation. France and Ireland objected to the failure to distinguish between co-operation in or use of nuclear energy for peaceful and weapons purposes. The United Kingdom also believed it wrong to try to limit, in individual cases for political reasons, the right to peaceful uses of nuclear energy. Sharing those views, the United States added that, while it supported efforts for a denuclearized Africa, it could not accept as a fact the nuclear capability of South Africa, as stated in the draft on the Declaration.

Albania stated that its affirmative votes were in keeping with its support for the cause of the African peoples against the racist régime of South Africa, but did not change its position of principle on the issue of nuclear-weapon-free zones.

The question of nuclear weapons and South Africa was also dealt with by the Assembly in reso-

lutions 39/72 A, on comprehensive sanctions against the *apartheid* régime and support to the liberation struggle in South Africa; 39/72 C, on relations between Israel and South Africa; 39/72 G, on concerted international action for the elimination of *apartheid;* and 39/155, on review of the implementation of the Declaration on the Strengthening of International Security. The Assembly also condemned military and nuclear collaboration with South Africa in resolutions 39/42, 39/50 A and 39/72 C.

Latin America

Since the signature and ratification of Additional Protocol II of the Treaty for the Prohibition of Nuclear Weapons in Latin America (Treaty of Tlatelolco) by five nuclear-weapon States by 1979,[41] only one item concerning that Treaty remained on the General Assembly's agenda: the signature and ratification of Additional Protocol I concerning the application of the Treaty to Latin American territories for which extraregional States had *de jure* or *de facto* responsibility, such as the colonial Powers.

GENERAL ASSEMBLY ACTION

On the recommendation of the First Committee, the General Assembly, on 12 December 1984, adopted resolution 39/51 by recorded vote.

Implementation of General Assembly resolution 38/61 concerning the signature and ratification of Additional Protocol I of the Treaty for the Prohibition of Nuclear Weapons in Latin America (Treaty of Tlatelolco)

The General Assembly,

Recalling its resolutions 2286(XXII) of 5 December 1967, 3262(XXIX) of 9 December 1974, 3473(XXX) of 11 December 1975, 32/76 of 12 December 1977, S-10/2 of 30 June 1978, 33/58 of 14 December 1978, 34/71 of 11 December 1979, 35/143 of 12 December 1980, 36/83 of 9 December 1981, 37/71 of 9 December 1982 and 38/61 of 15 December 1983 concerning the signature and ratification of Additional Protocol I of the Treaty for the Prohibition of Nuclear Weapons in Latin America (Treaty of Tlatelolco),

Taking into account that within the zone of application of that Treaty, to which twenty-three sovereign States are already parties, there are some territories which, in spite of not being sovereign political entities, are nevertheless in a position to receive the benefits deriving from the Treaty through its Additional Protocol I, to which the four States that *de jure* or *de facto* are internationally responsible for those territories may become parties,

Recalling that three of those States—the United Kingdom of Great Britain and Northern Ireland, the Kingdom of the Netherlands and the United States of America—became parties to Additional Protocol I in 1969, 1971 and 1981, respectively,

1. *Deplores* that the signature of Additional Protocol I by France, which took place on 2 March 1979, has

not yet been followed by the corresponding ratification, notwithstanding the time already elapsed and the pressing invitations which the General Assembly has addressed to it;

2. *Once more urges* France not to delay any further such ratification, which has been requested so many times and which appears all the more advisable, since France is the only one of the four States to which the Protocol is open that is not yet party to it;

3. *Decides* to include in the provisional agenda of its fortieth session an item entitled "Implementation of General Assembly resolution 39/51 concerning the signature and ratification of Additional Protocol I of the Treaty for the Prohibition of Nuclear Weapons in Latin America (Treaty of Tlatelolco)".

General Assembly resolution 39/51

12 December 1984   Meeting 97   139-0-8 (recorded vote)

Approved by First Committee (A/39/735) by recorded vote (129-0-9), 21 November (meeting 45); 20-nation draft (A/C.1/39/L.14); agenda item 45.

Sponsors: Bahamas, Barbados, Bolivia, Colombia, Costa Rica, Dominican Republic, Ecuador, El Salvador, Guatemala, Haiti, Honduras, Jamaica, Mexico, Nicaragua, Panama, Paraguay, Peru, Suriname, Trinidad and Tobago, Uruguay.

Meeting numbers. GA 39th session: 1st Committee 3-36, 45, 46; plenary 97.

Recorded vote in Assembly as follows:

In favour: Afghanistan, Algeria, Angola, Antigua and Barbuda, Australia, Austria, Bahamas, Bahrain, Bangladesh, Barbados, Belgium, Benin, Bhutan, Bolivia, Botswana, Brazil, Brunei Darussalam, Bulgaria, Burkina Faso, Burma, Burundi, Byelorussian SSR, Cameroon, Canada, Central African Republic, Chad, Chile, China, Colombia, Comoros, Congo, Costa Rica, Cyprus, Czechoslovakia, Democratic Kampuchea, Democratic Yemen, Denmark, Dominican Republic, Ecuador, Egypt, El Salvador, Equatorial Guinea, Ethiopia, Fiji, Finland, Gabon, German Democratic Republic, Germany, Federal Republic of, Ghana, Greece, Guatemala, Guinea, Guinea-Bissau, Honduras, Hungary, Iceland, India, Indonesia, Iran, Iraq, Ireland, Israel, Italy, Jamaica, Japan, Jordan, Kenya, Kuwait, Lao People's Democratic Republic, Lebanon, Lesotho, Liberia, Libyan Arab Jamahiriya, Luxembourg, Madagascar, Malaysia, Maldives, Malta, Mauritania, Mauritius, Mexico, Mongolia, Morocco, Mozambique, Nepal, Netherlands, New Zealand, Nicaragua, Niger, Nigeria, Norway, Oman, Pakistan, Panama, Papua New Guinea, Paraguay, Peru, Philippines, Poland, Portugal, Qatar, Romania, Rwanda,[a] Saint Lucia, Samoa, Sao Tome and Principe, Saudi Arabia, Senegal, Seychelles, Sierra Leone, Singapore, Somalia, Spain, Sri Lanka, Sudan, Suriname, Sweden, Syrian Arab Republic, Thailand, Togo, Trinidad and Tobago, Tunisia, Turkey, Uganda, Ukrainian SSR, USSR, United Arab Emirates, United Kingdom, United Republic of Tanzania, United States, Uruguay, Vanuatu, Venezuela, Viet Nam, Yemen, Yugoslavia, Zaire, Zambia, Zimbabwe.

Against: None.

Abstaining: Argentina, Belize, Cuba, France, Guyana, Ivory Coast, Malawi, Mali.

[a]Later advised the Secretariat it had intended to abstain.

In explanation of vote, France and the United States expressed regret that only one country continued to be singled out in the text, while there were countries in the region in question which had not ratified or adhered to the Treaty.

Cuba said it could not unilaterally renounce the right to possess weapons as long as a nuclear Power in its area continued to pursue what it called a hostile and aggressive policy towards Cuba and continued to maintain a military base on its territory.

Middle East

The Secretary-General, in a September 1984 report[42] submitted to the General Assembly in response to its December 1983 request,[43] expressed the view that, since the establishment of a nuclear-weapon-free zone in the Middle East would contribute to improving the situation in the area, further efforts should be made to that end.

On 12 December 1984, the Assembly, on the recommendation of the First Committee, adopted resolution 39/54 without vote.

Establishment of a nuclear-weapon-free zone in the region of the Middle East

The General Assembly,

Recalling its resolutions 3263(XXIX) of 9 December 1974, 3474(XXX) of 11 December 1975, 31/71 of 10 December 1976, 32/82 of 12 December 1977, 33/64 of 14 December 1978, 34/77 of 11 December 1979, 35/147 of 12 December 1980, 36/87 of 9 December 1981, 37/75 of 9 December 1982 and 38/64 of 15 December 1983 on the establishment of a nuclear-weapon-free zone in the region of the Middle East,

Recalling also the recommendations for the establishment of such a zone in the Middle East consistent with paragraphs 60 to 63, in particular paragraph 63 (*d*), of the Final Document of the Tenth Special Session of the General Assembly,

Emphasizing the basic provisions of the above-mentioned resolutions, which call upon all parties directly concerned to consider taking the practical and urgent steps required for the implementation of the proposal to establish a nuclear-weapon-free zone in the region of the Middle East and, pending and during the establishment of such a zone, to declare solemnly that they will refrain, on a reciprocal basis, from producing, acquiring or in any other way possessing nuclear weapons and nuclear explosive devices and from permitting the stationing of nuclear weapons on their territory by any third party, to agree to place all their nuclear facilities under International Atomic Energy Agency safeguards and to declare their support for the establishment of the zone and deposit such declarations with the Security Council for consideration, as appropriate,

Reaffirming the inalienable right of all States to acquire and develop nuclear energy for peaceful purposes,

Emphasizing further the need for appropriate measures on the question of the prohibition of military attacks on nuclear facilities,

Bearing in mind the consensus reached by the General Assembly at its thirty-fifth session that the establishment of a nuclear-weapon-free zone in the region of the Middle East would greatly enhance international peace and security,

Desirous to build on that consensus so that substantial progress can be made towards establishing a nuclear-weapon-free zone in the region of the Middle East,

Emphasizing the essential role of the United Nations in the establishment of a nuclear-weapon-free zone in the region of the Middle East,

Taking note of the report of the Secretary-General,

1. *Urges* all parties directly concerned to consider seriously taking the practical and urgent steps required for the implementation of the proposal to establish a nuclear-weapon-free zone in the region of the Middle East in accordance with the relevant resolutions of the General Assembly and, as a means of promoting this objective, invites the countries concerned to adhere to the Treaty on the Non-Proliferation of Nuclear Weapons;

2. *Calls upon* all countries of the region that have not done so, pending the establishment of the zone, to agree

to place all their nuclear activities under International Atomic Energy Agency safeguards;

3. *Invites* those countries, pending the establishment of a nuclear-weapon-free zone in the region of the Middle East, to declare their support for establishing such a zone, consistent with the relevant paragraph of the Final Document of the Tenth Special Session of the General Assembly, and to deposit those declarations with the Security Council;

4. *Further invites* those countries, pending the establishment of the zone, not to develop, produce, test or otherwise acquire nuclear weapons or permit the stationing on their territories, or territories under their control, of nuclear weapons or nuclear explosive devices;

5. *Invites* the nuclear-weapon States and all other States to render their assistance in the establishment of the zone and at the same time to refrain from any action that runs counter to both the letter and spirit of the present resolution;

6. *Requests* the Secretary-General to seek the views of all concerned parties regarding the establishment of a nuclear-weapon-free zone in the region of the Middle East;

7. *Requests* the Secretary-General to submit a report to the General Assembly at its fortieth session on the implementation of the present resolution;

8. *Decides* to include in the provisional agenda of its fortieth session the item entitled "Establishment of a nuclear-weapon-free zone in the region of the Middle East".

General Assembly resolution 39/54

12 December 1984   Meeting 97   Adopted without vote

Approved by First Committee (A/39/738) without vote, 19 November (meeting 41); draft by Egypt (A/C.1/39/L.54); agenda item 48.
Meeting numbers. GA 39th session: 1st Committee 3-36, 40-42, 45; plenary 97.

Introducing the draft, Egypt pointed out that the 1984 text had two new elements added to the 1983 Assembly resolution on the subject:[43] emphasis on the United Nations role in establishing the zone, and a request to the Secretary-General to seek the views of all concerned.

In explanation of position, Argentina and India stated that their going along with the consensus was without prejudice to their stance concerning NPT[28] and the application of the IAEA safeguards. Israel reiterated the reservations it had made in the past: among other things, with the Treaty of Tlatelolco serving as a model, the initiative for the zone's establishment should originate with the States in the region, and the consultations for reaching that aim should be carried out directly among them; also the draft omitted to mention the negotiating process, without which the proposed arrangement was unlikely to come about. Iraq asserted that the Treaty of Tlatelolco was not relevant to the Middle East, where the situation was different; existing nuclear-weapons stockpiles in the Middle East obstructed the creation of the proposed zone, and Israel needed to accede to NPT and subject its nuclear installations to IAEA safeguards. Brazil stated that it did not object to

consensus on the draft because the particular situation of the Middle East region warranted special regard for its specific characteristics.

Zambia dissociated itself from paragraph 1 as it was not a party to NPT.

Israeli nuclear armament

In an August 1984 report to the General Assembly,[44] the Secretary-General recalled that the Assembly, by a December 1983 resolution,[45] had requested him to continue following closely Israel's nuclear activities and the nuclear and military collaboration between Israel and South Africa. He reported that he had received no new information in that regard and had nothing to add to his previous reports on the subject (see also p. 150).

By a letter of 12 July to the Secretary-General,[46] Israel expressed support for international arrangements aimed at ensuring the inviolability of nuclear facilities dedicated to peaceful purposes; it had no policy of attacking such facilities (see also p. 280).

GENERAL ASSEMBLY ACTION

On 17 December 1984, the General Assembly, on the recommendation of the First Committee, adopted resolution 39/147 by recorded vote.

Israeli nuclear armament

The General Assembly,

Recalling its previous resolutions on Israeli nuclear armament,

Recalling resolution 38/64 of 15 December 1983, in which, *inter alia*, it called upon all countries of the Middle East, pending the establishment of a nuclear-weapon-free zone in the Middle East, to agree to place all their nuclear activities under International Atomic Energy Agency safeguards, and invited those countries also, pending the establishment of a nuclear-weapon-free zone in the region, to declare their support for establishing such a zone and to deposit those declarations with the Security Council,

Considering that the Israeli statements contained in a letter dated 12 July 1984 continue to disregard the safeguards system of the International Atomic Energy Agency,

Recalling further Security Council resolution 487(1981) of 19 June 1981 in which, *inter alia*, the Council called upon Israel urgently to place its nuclear facilities under International Atomic Energy Agency safeguards,

Noting with concern Israel's persistent refusal to commit itself not to manufacture or acquire nuclear weapons, despite repeated calls by the General Assembly, the Security Council and the International Atomic Energy Agency, and to place its nuclear facilities under Agency safeguards,

Conscious of the grave consequences which endanger international peace and security as a result of Israel's development and acquisition of nuclear weapons and Israel's collaboration with South Africa to develop nuclear weapons and their delivery systems,

Recalling its repeated condemnation of nuclear collaboration between Israel and South Africa,

Taking note of the report of the Secretary-General on Israeli nuclear armament,

1. *Condemns* Israel's continued refusal to implement Security Council resolution 487(1981), unanimously adopted by the Council on 19 June 1981, and its refusal to renounce any possession of nuclear weapons;

2. *Requests* the Security Council to take urgent and effective measures to ensure that Israel complies with the resolution and places all its nuclear facilities under International Atomic Energy Agency safeguards;

3. *Requests again* the Security Council to investigate Israel's nuclear activities and the collaboration of other States, parties and institutions in these activities;

4. *Reiterates its request* to the International Atomic Energy Agency to suspend any scientific co-operation with Israel which could contribute to Israel's nuclear capabilities;

5. *Reiterates further* its condemnation of the Israeli threat, in violation of the Charter of the United Nations, to repeat its armed attack on peaceful facilities in Iraq and in other countries;

6. *Reaffirms* its condemnation of the continuing nuclear collaboration between Israel and South Africa;

7. *Requests* the United Nations Institute for Disarmament Research, in co-operation with the Department for Disarmament Affairs of the Secretariat and in consultation with the League of Arab States and the Organization of African Unity, to prepare a report providing data and other relevant information relating to Israeli nuclear armament and further nuclear developments taking into account, *inter alia*, the report of the Secretary-General on Israeli nuclear armament, and to submit it to the General Assembly at its fortieth session;

8. *Requests* the Secretary-General to provide the necessary support to the United Nations Institute for Disarmament Research to enable it to carry out the task entrusted to it under the present resolution and for the Institute to submit a report to the General Assembly at its fortieth session;

9. *Decides* to include in the provisional agenda of its fortieth session the item entitled "Israeli nuclear armament".

General Assembly resolution 39/147

17 December 1984   Meeting 102   94-2-44 (recorded vote)

Approved by First Committee (A/39/743) by recorded vote (85-2-36), 4 December (meeting 58); 24-nation draft (A/C.1/39/L.45/Rev.1); agenda item 53.

Sponsors: Afghanistan, Algeria, Bahrain, Bangladesh, Democratic Yemen, Djibouti, Iraq, Jordan, Kuwait, Lebanon, Libyan Arab Jamahiriya, Malaysia, Mali, Mauritania, Morocco, Oman, Qatar, Saudi Arabia, Somalia, Sudan, Syrian Arab Republic, Tunisia, United Arab Emirates, Yemen.

Financial implications. 5th Committee, A/39/806; S-G, A/C.1/39/L.84, A/C.5/39/74.

Meeting numbers. GA 39th session: 1st Committee 3-36, 38, 56, 58; 5th Committee 44; plenary 102.

Recorded vote in Assembly as follows:

In favour: Afghanistan, Albania, Algeria, Angola, Argentina, Bahrain, Bangladesh, Barbados, Benin, Bhutan, Botswana, Brazil, Brunei Darussalam, Bulgaria, Burkina Faso, Burundi, Byelorussian SSR, Cameroon, Cape Verde, Chad, China, Congo, Cuba, Cyprus, Czechoslovakia, Democratic Kampuchea, Democratic Yemen, Djibouti, Egypt, Equatorial Guinea, Ethiopia, Gabon, Gambia, German Democratic Republic, Ghana, Greece, Guinea, Guyana, Hungary, India, Indonesia, Iran, Iraq, Jordan, Kenya, Kuwait, Lao People's Democratic Republic, Lebanon, Lesotho, Libyan Arab Jamahiriya, Madagascar, Malaysia, Maldives, Mali, Malta, Mauritania, Mauritius, Mexico, Mongolia, Morocco, Mozambique, Nicaragua, Niger, Nigeria, Oman, Pakistan, Peru, Philippines, Poland, Qatar, Romania, Sao Tome and Principe, Senegal, Seychelles, Sierra Leone, Sri Lanka, Sudan, Suriname, Syrian Arab Republic, Thailand, Togo, Trinidad and Tobago, Tunisia, Turkey, Uganda, Ukrainian SSR, USSR, United Arab Emirates, United Republic of Tanzania, Venezuela, Viet Nam, Yemen, Yugoslavia, Zambia.

Against: Israel, United States.

Abstaining: Antigua and Barbuda, Australia, Austria, Bahamas, Belgium, Bolivia, Burma, Canada, Chile, Colombia, Costa Rica, Denmark, Dominican Republic, Ecuador, El Salvador, Fiji, Finland, France, Germany, Federal Republic of, Haiti, Honduras, Iceland, Ireland, Italy, Ivory Coast, Jamaica, Japan, Liberia, Luxembourg, Malawi, Nepal, Netherlands, New Zealand, Norway, Panama, Paraguay, Portugal, Saint Lucia, Saint Vincent and the Grenadines, Spain, Sweden, United Kingdom, Uruguay, Zaire.

The Assembly, before adopting the text as a whole, adopted, by separate recorded votes, paragraph 3 by 78 to 23, with 27 abstentions, and paragraph 4 by 70 to 26, with 32 abstentions. The First Committee had likewise approved those paragraphs: paragraph 3 by 73 to 23, with 18 abstentions, and paragraph 4 by 68 to 26, with 23 abstentions.

Introducing the draft, Iraq stated that a 1981 expert group report[47] had established that Israel had the technical capability to manufacture nuclear weapons, and there was increasing evidence of the growth of Israel's nuclear military capability and of related collaboration with South Africa.

Explaining its vote, Israel stated that the current text, like its predecessors, discriminated against Israel by singling it out for investigation on a matter in which many other Member States found themselves in the same position; many of the sponsors, including some Arab States, either were not parties to NPT or had not fulfilled their NPT obligations. Further, the draft represented interference by the General Assembly in the affairs of IAEA, involving the Agency in a political matter beyond its mandate and incompatible with its statute. An additional biased element in the text, Israel added, was the request to the Assembly to spend more of the limited United Nations resources on another report and UNIDIR to perform a task serving the political ends of Arab States. The United States shared Israel's views as regards the text's discriminatory condemnation and the implications of the request in paragraph 4, and questioned the need for a new report.

Among those voting in favour of the draft as a whole, Ghana said it was aware of the military and nuclear collaboration between Israel and South Africa. Argentina expressed reservations concerning paragraphs 3 and 4, saying that it could not agree to calling for suspension of scientific co-operation. Similarly, the Philippines abstained on paragraph 4 because the IAEA statute contained specific provisions pertaining to the suspension of scientific co-operation with any member country. Greece abstained in the vote on the paragraph, objecting also to expelling Member States from the United Nations system. Both Cuba, whose positive vote did not affect its position regarding NPT, and the USSR, which supported the thrust of the text, had serious misgivings about paragraph 8, which, they felt, might suggest a departure from the voluntary financing of UNIDIR activities.

The question of Israeli nuclear armament was also taken up in Assembly resolution 39/14, on armed Israeli aggression against Iraqi nuclear installations.

South Asia

In an October 1984 report to the General Assembly,[48] the Secretary-General stated that he had been in contact with the States of South Asia with regard to a December 1983 Assembly request[49] that he render assistance required to promote a nuclear-weapon-free zone in that region, but there had been no request by those States for his assistance. In the course of those contacts, a view had been expressed that he should continue to be available for that purpose.

GENERAL ASSEMBLY ACTION

On 12 December 1984, the General Assembly, on the recommendation of the First Committee, adopted resolution 39/55 by recorded vote.

Establishment of a nuclear-weapon-free zone in South Asia

The General Assembly,

Recalling its resolutions 3265 B (XXIX) of 9 December 1974, 3476 B (XXX) of 11 December 1975, 31/73 of 10 December 1976, 32/83 of 12 December 1977, 33/65 of 14 December 1978, 34/78 of 11 December 1979, 35/148 of 12 December 1980, 36/88 of 9 December 1981, 37/76 of 9 December 1982 and 38/65 of 15 December 1983 concerning the establishment of a nuclear-weapon-free zone in South Asia,

Reiterating its conviction that the establishment of nuclear-weapon-free zones in various regions of the world is one of the measures which can contribute most effectively to the objectives of non-proliferation of nuclear weapons and general and complete disarmament,

Believing that the establishment of a nuclear-weapon-free zone in South Asia, as in other regions, will strengthen the security of the States of the region against the use or threat of use of nuclear weapons,

Noting the declarations issued at the highest level by Governments of South Asian States reaffirming their undertaking not to acquire or manufacture nuclear weapons and to devote their nuclear programmes exclusively to the economic and social advancement of their peoples,

Recalling that in the above-mentioned resolutions it called upon the States of the South Asian region, and such other neighbouring non-nuclear-weapon States as might be interested, to make all possible efforts to establish a nuclear-weapon-free zone in South Asia and to refrain, in the mean time, from any action contrary to this objective,

Further recalling that, in its resolution 3265 B (XXIX), it requested the Secretary-General to convene a meeting for the purpose of the consultations mentioned therein and to render such assistance as might be required to promote the efforts for the establishment of a nuclear-weapon-free zone in South Asia,

Bearing in mind the provisions of paragraphs 60 to 63 of the Final Document of the Tenth Special Session of the General Assembly regarding the establishment of nuclear-weapon-free zones, including in the region of South Asia,

Taking note of the report of the Secretary-General,

1. *Reaffirms* its endorsement, in principle, of the concept of a nuclear-weapon-free zone in South Asia;

2. *Urges once again* the States of South Asia, and such other neighbouring non-nuclear-weapon States as may be interested, to continue to make all possible efforts to establish a nuclear-weapon-free zone in South Asia and to refrain, in the mean time, from any action contrary to this objective;

3. *Calls upon* those nuclear-weapon States that have not done so to respond positively to this proposal and to extend the necessary co-operation in the efforts to establish a nuclear-weapon-free zone in South Asia;

4. *Requests* the Secretary-General to render such assistance as may be required to promote the efforts for the establishment of a nuclear-weapon-free zone in South Asia and to report on the subject to the General Assembly at its fortieth session;

5. *Decides* to include in the provisional agenda of its fortieth session the item entitled "Establishment of a nuclear-weapon-free zone in South Asia".

General Assembly resolution 39/55

12 December 1984   Meeting 97   100-3-42 (recorded vote)

Approved by First Committee (A/39/739) by recorded vote (90-2-43), 21 November (meeting 45); draft by Pakistan (A/C.1/39/L.6); agenda item 49.

Meeting numbers. GA 39th session: 1st Committee 3-36, 45, 46; plenary 97.

Recorded vote in Assembly as follows:

In favour: Antigua and Barbuda, Australia, Bahrain, Bangladesh, Barbados, Belgium, Bolivia, Botswana, Brunei Darussalam, Burundi, Cameroon, Canada, Central African Republic, Chad, Chile, China, Colombia, Comoros, Costa Rica, Democratic Kampuchea, Djibouti, Dominican Republic, Ecuador, Egypt, El Salvador, Equatorial Guinea, Finland, Gabon, Germany, Federal Republic of, Ghana, Greece, Guatemala, Guinea, Guinea-Bissau, Guyana, Haiti, Honduras, Iran, Iraq, Ireland, Ivory Coast, Jamaica, Japan, Jordan, Kenya, Kuwait, Lebanon, Lesotho, Liberia, Libyan Arab Jamahiriya, Luxembourg, Malawi, Malaysia, Maldives, Mali, Malta, Mauritania, Mexico, Morocco, Nepal, Netherlands, New Zealand, Niger, Nigeria, Oman, Pakistan, Panama, Papua New Guinea, Paraguay, Peru, Philippines, Portugal, Qatar, Romania, Rwanda, Saint Lucia, Samoa, Saudi Arabia, Senegal, Sierra Leone, Singapore, Somalia, Spain, Sri Lanka, Sudan, Thailand, Togo, Trinidad and Tobago, Tunisia, Turkey, Uganda, United Arab Emirates, United Republic of Tanzania, United States, Uruguay, Venezuela, Yemen, Zaire, Zambia, Zimbabwe.

Against: Bhutan, India, Mauritius.

Abstaining: Afghanistan, Algeria, Angola, Argentina, Austria, Bahamas, Belize, Benin, Brazil, Bulgaria, Burkina Faso, Burma, Byelorussian SSR, Cape Verde, Congo, Cuba, Cyprus, Czechoslovakia, Democratic Yemen, Denmark, Ethiopia, Fiji, France, German Democratic Republic, Hungary, Iceland, Indonesia, Israel, Italy, Lao People's Democratic Republic, Madagascar, Mongolia, Mozambique, Nicaragua, Norway, Poland, Sweden, Ukrainian SSR, USSR, United Kingdom, Viet Nam, Yugoslavia.

In explanation of vote, India said it had consistently rejected the proposal for reasons explained in the past; the countries of South Asia did not have a consensus on setting up such a zone, and the annual consideration of such a draft introduced discord to the process of regional co-operation.

Those explaining their affirmative votes or abstentions all expressed support for the establishment of nuclear-weapon-free zones, with some listing requirements for their success. Unanimity on the issue based on close consultations among the countries of the region was stressed by Bangladesh,

Brazil, Indonesia, Japan and Sri Lanka. Sweden observed that the resolution did not enjoy unanimous regional support. For Bangladesh, consensus on the delimitation of the zone was important, and, for Sri Lanka, full recognition of the characteristics of the zone. Indonesia and Japan stressed that the initiatives for such a zone should emanate from the countries of the region, as did the United States which listed as other requirements: arrangements for adequate verification of compliance; non-disturbance of existing security arrangements; and unimpeded exercise of rights recognized under international law.

Brazil said the text did not reflect adequately its concerns regarding the requirements for establishing such a zone, among them a commitment by the nuclear-weapon States to respect the zone's status and to refrain from interfering in the negotiating process. Ghana felt all regions should be encouraged to establish nuclear-weapon-free zones, while Australia, which supported one in the South Pacific region, stated that its abstention in the First Committee should not be taken to imply any lack of support for the concept.

Preparations for the 1985 Review Conference on NPT

After the entry into force on 5 March 1970 of the Treaty on the Non-Proliferation of Nuclear Weapons,[28] two quinquennial review conferences were held—in 1975 and 1980—and a third was scheduled for 1985.

The preparatory process for the third review conference of the parties to NPT was initiated in 1984, with a Preparatory Committee holding two sessions at Geneva.

Sixty-two States parties participating in the first session (2-6 April), under the chairmanship of Ryukichi Imai (Japan), and 57 States parties attending the second session (1-11 October), under the chairmanship of Milos Vejvoda (Czechoslovakia), discussed questions relating to the holding of the Conference, among them, financing, agenda, rules of procedure, final document(s) and background documentation.

The third and final session of the Preparatory Committee was to be held in 1985.

Cessation of nuclear-weapon tests

In 1984, in contrast to the two preceding years, the Conference on Disarmament was unable even to agree on the establishment of a subsidiary body to consider the cessation of nuclear-weapon tests; in December, the General Assembly adopted three resolutions calling on the Conference to negotiate on a test-ban treaty (39/52, 39/53 and 39/60).

By a letter dated 9 July to the Secretary-General,[50] the Permanent Commission for the South Pacific (Chile, Colombia, Ecuador, Peru) transmitted its declaration protesting against the resumption by France, in May, of nuclear explosions on Mururoa Atoll as being detrimental to the interests of the States members of the South-East Pacific Maritime System.

Negotiations for a treaty against nuclear-weapon tests

In 1984, the Conference on Disarmament,[9] which had been asked again by the General Assembly in December 1983[51] to initiate immediately negotiations on a nuclear-weapon test-ban treaty, discussed, but did not reach consensus on, the mandate of an *ad hoc* subsidiary body on the topic. Proposals submitted included one each by Mexico,[52] a group of socialist States,[53] and seven Western countries and Japan,[54] and two by the Group of 21—in March[55] and in July.[56] A majority of members, including the socialist States and the Group of 21, maintained that the Conference should revise the mandate of the subsidiary body so as to enable it actually to negotiate a treaty, while others, mainly Western members, felt the work entrusted to it in the previous sessions,[57] covering issues relating to verification and compliance, had not been completed.

On the question of nuclear tests, Sweden submitted a working paper[58] containing information from the Swedish Defence Research Institute to the effect that 1,469 nuclear explosions were believed to have been carried out between 1945 and 1983, with an annual average in recent years of 51 explosions, or almost one test a week. Sweden appealed to the Conference to make 1984 the year of the comprehensive test-ban treaty.

Verification

Activities of the Conference on Disarmament. Japan submitted to the Conference on Disarmament[9] in 1984 a working paper[59] based on a step-by-step approach to a comprehensive test ban, by which underground nuclear-test explosions of a yield currently considered technically verifiable multinationally would be taken as a threshold, and an agreement would be reached on banning test explosions of a yield above that threshold; thereafter, the threshold would be lowered as the verification capability was improved. Other working papers submitted in 1984 included one by Australia,[60] in which it proposed principles for the verification of a comprehensive nuclear-test-ban treaty, and another by the Federal Republic of Germany[61] on aspects of modern developments in seismic-event recording techniques.

Expert group. In 1984, the *Ad Hoc* Group of Scientific Experts to Consider International Co-operative Measures to Detect and Identify Seismic Events, with a representative of the World

Meteorological Organization (WMO) participating, held its seventeenth[62] and eighteenth[63] sessions (Geneva, 27 February–9 March and 30 July–10 August) under the chairmanship of Ola Dahlman (Sweden).

In addition to the Group's progress report on each session, the Conference took note of the Group's third report[64] on recent developments in seismograph data processing, containing a number of recommendations for further studies concerning the establishment of a global seismic monitoring system under a future nuclear-test-ban treaty, and a paper[65] containing an overview of the procedures for a technical test of seismic data using the WMO Global Telecommunication System, to be conducted later in 1984.

Some Western and other delegations supported the continuation of the Group's efforts, while others, including the USSR, felt the Group could not continue its work in a vacuum and that its future work should be related to a negotiating process on a nuclear-test ban.

GENERAL ASSEMBLY ACTION

On 12 December 1984, the General Assembly adopted three resolutions on the cessation of nuclear tests (39/52, 39/53 and 39/60), all on the recommendation of the First Committee.

The Assembly adopted resolution 39/60 by recorded vote.

Implementation of General Assembly resolution 38/72 on the immediate cessation and prohibition of nuclear-weapon tests

The General Assembly,

Deeply concerned over the intensification of the nuclear-arms race and the growing threat of nuclear war,

Recalling that over the past thirty years the need for cessation and prohibition of nuclear-weapon testing has been in the focus of attention of the General Assembly,

Reaffirming its conviction that the conclusion of a multilateral treaty on the prohibition of nuclear-weapon tests by all States would constitute an indispensable element for the success of efforts to halt and reverse the nuclear-arms race and the qualitative improvement of nuclear weapons, and to prevent the expansion of existing nuclear arsenals and the spread of nuclear weapons to additional countries,

Stressing once again that the elaboration of such a treaty is the task of the highest priority and should not be made dependent on the attainment of any other measure in the field of disarmament,

Deeply deploring that the Conference on Disarmament has to date been prevented from carrying out negotiations with a view to reaching agreement on such a treaty,

Recalling its previous resolutions on this subject,

1. *Resolutely urges* all States, and especially all nuclear-weapon States, to exert maximum efforts and exercise political will for the elaboration and conclusion, without any delay, of a multilateral treaty on the prohibition of nuclear-weapon tests by all States;

2. *Urges* the Conference on Disarmament to proceed promptly to negotiations with a view to elaborating such a treaty as a matter of the highest priority, taking into account all existing proposals and future initiatives, and, for that purpose, to establish an *ad hoc* committee with a negotiating mandate;

3. *Decides* to include in the provisional agenda of its fortieth session an item entitled "Implementation of General Assembly resolution 39/60 on the immediate cessation and prohibition of nuclear-weapon tests".

General Assembly resolution 39/60

12 December 1984　　Meeting 97　　123-2-24 (recorded vote)

Approved by First Committee (A/39/746) by recorded vote (109-2-24), 26 November (meeting 47); 13-nation draft (A/C.1/39/L.18); agenda item 56.

Sponsors: Afghanistan, Angola, Bulgaria, Byelorussian SSR, Czechoslovakia, German Democratic Republic, Hungary, Lao People's Democratic Republic, Mongolia, Poland, Ukrainian SSR, USSR, Viet Nam.

Meeting numbers. GA 39th session: 1st Committee 3-37, 47, 48; plenary 97.

Recorded vote in Assembly as follows:

In favour: Afghanistan, Algeria, Angola, Antigua and Barbuda, Argentina, Austria, Bahrain, Bangladesh, Barbados, Belize, Benin, Bhutan, Bolivia, Botswana, Brazil, Brunei Darussalam, Bulgaria, Burkina Faso, Burma, Burundi, Byelorussian SSR, Cameroon, Cape Verde, Central African Republic, Chad, Chile, Colombia, Comoros, Congo, Costa Rica, Cuba, Cyprus, Czechoslovakia, Democratic Yemen, Djibouti, Dominica, Dominican Republic, Ecuador, Egypt, El Salvador, Equatorial Guinea, Ethiopia, Fiji, Finland, Gabon, German Democratic Republic, Ghana, Greece, Guatemala, Guinea, Guinea-Bissau, Guyana, Honduras, Hungary, India, Indonesia, Iran, Iraq, Ireland, Jamaica, Jordan, Kenya, Kuwait, Lao People's Democratic Republic, Lebanon, Lesotho, Liberia, Libyan Arab Jamahiriya, Madagascar, Malawi, Malaysia, Maldives, Mali, Mauritania, Mauritius, Mexico, Mongolia, Morocco, Mozambique, Nepal, Nicaragua, Niger, Nigeria, Oman, Pakistan, Panama, Papua New Guinea, Paraguay, Peru, Philippines, Poland, Qatar, Romania, Rwanda, Sao Tome and Principe, Saudi Arabia, Senegal, Seychelles, Sierra Leone, Singapore, Somalia, Sri Lanka, Sudan, Suriname, Sweden, Syrian Arab Republic, Thailand, Togo, Trinidad and Tobago, Tunisia, Uganda, Ukrainian SSR, USSR, United Arab Emirates, United Republic of Tanzania, Uruguay, Vanuatu, Venezuela, Viet Nam, Yemen, Yugoslavia, Zambia, Zimbabwe.

Against: United Kingdom, United States.

Abstaining: Australia, Bahamas, Belgium, Canada, China, Denmark, France, Germany, Federal Republic of, Haiti, Iceland, Israel, Italy, Ivory Coast, Japan, Luxembourg, Netherlands, New Zealand, Norway, Portugal, Saint Lucia, Samoa, Spain, Turkey, Zaire.

In explanation of vote, Australia, New Zealand and Samoa, supporting a ban covering all nuclear explosive testing, objected to a treaty prohibiting nuclear-weapon tests only; they also found difficulty with other aspects of the text, in particular its failure to deal with the verification question. Similarly, Fiji and Ireland did not accept that a ban should be limited to nuclear-weapon tests. The United Kingdom also saw no possibility of successful negotiation on a comprehensive test ban unless the issue of nuclear explosions for peaceful purposes was adequately dealt with.

Zambia stressed the need for a political decision and an end to what it felt was unproductive discussion on verification.

On 12 December, the Assembly also adopted resolution 39/52 by recorded vote.

Cessation of all test explosions of nuclear weapons

The General Assembly,

Bearing in mind that the complete cessation of nuclear-weapon tests, which has been examined for more than twenty-five years and on which the General Assembly has adopted nearly fifty resolutions, is a basic objective of the United Nations in the sphere of disarmament, to the attainment of which it has repeatedly assigned the highest priority,

Stressing that on seven different occasions it has condemned such tests in the strongest terms and that, since 1974, it has stated its conviction that the continuance of nuclear-weapon testing will intensify the arms race, thus increasing the danger of nuclear war,

Convinced that the existing means of verification are adequate to ensure compliance with a nuclear-test ban and that the alleged absence of such means of verification is nothing but an excuse for further development and refinement of nuclear weapons,

Reiterating the assertion made in several previous resolutions that, whatever may be the differences on the question of verification, there is no valid reason for delaying the conclusion of an agreement on a comprehensive test ban,

Recalling that since 1972 the Secretary-General has declared that all the technical and scientific aspects of the problem have been so fully explored that only a political decision is now necessary in order to achieve final agreement, that when the existing means of verification are taken into account it is difficult to understand further delay in achieving agreement on an underground-test ban, and that the potential risks of continuing underground nuclear-weapon tests would far outweigh any possible risks from ending such tests,

Bearing in mind that the three nuclear-weapon States which act as depositaries of the Treaty Banning Nuclear Weapon Tests in the Atmosphere, in Outer Space and under Water in the report they submitted on 30 July 1980 to the Committee on Disarmament, after four years of trilateral negotiations, stated, *inter alia*, that they were "mindful of the great value for all mankind that the prohibition of all nuclear-weapon-test explosions in all environments will have" as well as "conscious of the important responsibility placed upon them to find solutions to the remaining problems", adding furthermore that they were determined to exert their best efforts and necessary will and persistence "to bring the negotiations to an early and successful conclusion",

Taking into account that the same three nuclear-weapon States undertook twenty years ago, in the above-mentioned Treaty, to seek the achievement of the discontinuance of all test explosions of nuclear weapons for all time and that such an undertaking was explicitly reiterated in 1968 in the preamble to the Treaty on the Non-Proliferation of Nuclear Weapons, article VI of which further embodies their solemn and legally binding commitment to take effective measures relating to cessation of the nuclear-arms race at an early date and to nuclear disarmament,

Bearing in mind the growing negative influence that the total lack of compliance with those undertakings had on both the first and the second Review Conferences of the Parties to the Treaty on the Non-Proliferation of Nuclear Weapons, held at Geneva from 5 to 30 May 1975 and from 11 August to 7 September 1980, respectively,

Convinced that the maintenance of such a situation would not augur well for the third review conference of that Treaty, which is to take place from 22 April to 3 May 1985, and even for the future of the Treaty itself,

Deploring that, due to the persistent obstruction of a very small number of its members, the Conference on Disarmament has been unable to initiate multilateral negotiation of a treaty for the prohibition of all nuclear-weapon tests, as it was specifically requested to do in General Assembly resolution 38/62 of 15 December 1983,

Noting that the Conference on Disarmament has already received various concrete proposals on this question, including a complete draft for the eventual text of the treaty as a whole,

1. *Reiterates*, for the eighth time, its strongest condemnation of all nuclear-weapon tests;

2. *Reiterates also once again its grave concern* that nuclear-weapon testing continues unabated, against the wishes of the overwhelming majority of Member States;

3. *Reaffirms its conviction* that a treaty to achieve the prohibition of all nuclear-test explosions by all States for all time is a matter of the highest priority;

4. *Reaffirms also its conviction* that such a treaty would constitute a contribution of the utmost importance to the cessation of the nuclear-arms race and an indispensable element for the success of the Treaty on the Non-Proliferation of Nuclear Weapons, since it is only through the fulfilment of the obligations under the Treaty that its three depositary Powers may expect all other parties to comply likewise with their respective obligations;

5. *Urges once more* the three depositary Powers of the Treaty Banning Nuclear Weapon Tests in the Atmosphere, in Outer Space and under Water and of the Treaty on the Non-Proliferation of Nuclear Weapons to abide strictly by their undertakings to seek to achieve the early discontinuance of all test explosions of nuclear weapons for all time and to expedite negotiations to this end;

6. *Urges also* all States that have not yet done so to adhere to the Treaty Banning Nuclear Weapon Tests in the Atmosphere, in Outer Space and under Water and, meanwhile, to refrain from testing in the environments covered by that Treaty;

7. *Reiterates its appeal* to all States members of the Conference on Disarmament to initiate immediately the multilateral negotiation of a treaty for the prohibition of all nuclear-weapon tests and to exert their best endeavours in order that the Conference may transmit to the General Assembly at its fortieth session the complete draft of such a treaty;

8. *Calls upon* the States depositaries of the Treaty Banning Nuclear Weapon Tests in the Atmosphere, in Outer Space and under Water and the Treaty on the Non-Proliferation of Nuclear Weapons, by virtue of their special responsibilities under those two Treaties and as a provisional measure, to bring to a halt without delay all nuclear-test explosions, either through a trilaterally agreed moratorium or through three unilateral moratoria;

9. *Decides* to include in the provisional agenda of its fortieth session the item entitled "Cessation of all test explosions of nuclear weapons".

General Assembly resolution 39/52

12 December 1984   Meeting 97   122-3-23 (recorded vote)

Approved by First Committee (A/39/736) by recorded vote (111-2-24), 26 November (meeting 47); 11-nation draft (A/C.1/39/L.33); agenda item 46.
Sponsors: Bangladesh, Ecuador, Indonesia, Kenya, Mexico, Pakistan, Sri Lanka, Sweden, Uruguay, Venezuela, Yugoslavia.
Meeting numbers. GA 39th session: 1st Committee 3-36, 38, 47, 48; plenary 97.

Recorded vote in Assembly as follows:

In favour: Afghanistan, Algeria, Angola, Antigua and Barbuda, Argentina, Austria, Bahrain, Bangladesh, Barbados, Belize, Benin, Bhutan, Bolivia, Botswana, Brunei Darussalam, Bulgaria, Burkina Faso, Burundi, Byelorussian SSR, Cameroon, Cape Verde, Central African Republic, Chad, Chile, Colombia, Comoros, Congo, Costa Rica, Cuba, Cyprus, Czechoslovakia, Democratic Yemen, Djibouti, Dominican Republic, Ecuador, Egypt, El Salvador, Equatorial Guinea, Ethiopia, Fiji, Finland, Gabon, German Democratic Republic, Ghana, Greece, Guatemala, Guinea, Guinea-Bissau, Guyana, Honduras, Hungary, Indonesia, Iran, Iraq, Ireland, Ivory Coast, Jamaica, Jordan, Kenya, Kuwait, Lao People's Democratic Republic, Lebanon, Lesotho, Liberia, Libyan Arab Jamahiriya, Madagascar, Malawi, Malaysia, Maldives, Mali, Malta, Mauritania, Mauritius, Mexico, Mongolia, Morocco, Mozambique, Nepal, Nicaragua, Niger, Nigeria, Oman, Pakistan, Panama, Papua New Guinea, Paraguay, Peru, Philippines, Poland, Qatar, Romania, Rwanda, Sao Tome and Principe, Saudi Arabia, Senegal, Seychelles, Sierra Leone, Singapore, Somalia, Sri Lanka, Sudan, Suriname, Sweden, Syrian Arab Republic, Thailand, Togo, Trinidad and Tobago, Tunisia, Uganda, Ukrainian SSR, USSR, United Arab Emirates, United Republic of Tanzania, Uruguay, Vanuatu, Venezuela, Viet Nam, Yemen, Yugoslavia, Zaire, Zambia, Zimbabwe.

Against: France,[a] United Kingdom, United States.

Abstaining: Australia, Bahamas, Belgium, Brazil, Burma, Canada, China, Denmark, Germany, Federal Republic of, Iceland, India, Israel, Italy, Japan, Luxembourg, Netherlands, New Zealand, Norway, Portugal, Saint Lucia, Samoa, Spain, Turkey.

[a]Later advised the Secretariat it had intended to abstain.

Introducing the draft, Mexico said it drew attention, among other things, to the adequacy of existing verification measures and to the discrepancy between the statements and the recent attitude of two of the nuclear-weapon States depositaries of the 1963 Treaty Banning Nuclear Weapon Tests in the Atmosphere, in Outer Space and under Water,[66] also known as the partial test-ban Treaty.

Australia, New Zealand and Samoa could not endorse the banning of nuclear-weapon tests only or a moratorium on testing by just three nuclear-weapon States; Fiji and Ireland also felt that a future treaty should embrace all nuclear-test explosions. India regarded as important an immediate suspension of testing by all nuclear-weapon States. Australia felt it inappropriate in the current situation to suggest resumption of the trilateral negotiations, and the United Kingdom could not accept the proposed moratorium, or the failure to address how nuclear explosions for peaceful purposes should be dealt with in a comprehensive test ban. Samoa found the verification aspects of the text unsatisfactory, as did Belgium, which questioned why those which regarded that problem as completely resolved had not supported the approach proposed by Japan[59] in the Conference on Disarmament (see p. 47). Further, Belgium considered the fifth preambular paragraph to be irrelevant, contending that the Secretary-General did not possess the scientific expertise to state an opinion on that subject.

Ireland disagreed that a comprehensive test ban was indispensable to the success of NPT,[28] and Brazil and India abstained because of the linkage in the text between a ban and NPT. Sharing those reservations, New Zealand saw in the formulation of the appeal to the Conference on Disarmament an indication that the draft's sponsors saw little prospect of practical progress.

Argentina, Bulgaria, Czechoslovakia, the USSR and Zambia endorsed the thrust of the draft, with Bulgaria, Czechoslovakia and the USSR agreeing specifically with the text's proposed moratorium.

Argentina, Chile and Zambia also had reservations about the references to NPT in the text.

Also on 12 December, the Assembly adopted resolution 39/53 by recorded vote.

Urgent need for a comprehensive nuclear-test-ban treaty

The General Assembly,

Convinced of the urgent need for a comprehensive nuclear-test-ban treaty capable of attracting the widest possible international support and adherence,

Reaffirming its conviction that an end to all nuclear testing by all States in all environments for all time would be a major step towards ending the qualitative improvement, development and proliferation of nuclear weapons, a means of relieving the deep apprehension concerning the harmful consequences of radioactive contamination for the health of present and future generations and a measure of the utmost importance in bringing the nuclear-arms race to an end,

Recalling that the parties to the Treaty Banning Nuclear Weapon Tests in the Atmosphere, in Outer Space and under Water undertook not to carry out any nuclear-weapon-test explosion, or any other nuclear explosion, in the environments covered by that Treaty, and that in that Treaty the parties expressed their determination to continue negotiations to achieve the discontinuance of all test explosions of nuclear weapons for all time,

Recalling also that the parties to the Treaty on the Non-Proliferation of Nuclear Weapons recalled the determination expressed by the parties to the Treaty Banning Nuclear Weapon Tests in the Atmosphere, in Outer Space and under Water in its preamble to seek to achieve the discontinuance of all test explosions of nuclear weapons for all time and to continue negotiations to this end, declaring their intention to achieve at the earliest possible date the cessation of the nuclear-arms race and to undertake effective measures in the direction of nuclear disarmament,

Recalling further its previous resolutions on this subject,

Taking into account that part of the report of the Conference on Disarmament concerning consideration of the item entitled "Nuclear-test ban" during its session in 1984,

Also taking into account relevant proposals and initiatives put forward in the Conference on Disarmament during its session in 1984,

Expressing its profound regret that, in spite of strenuous efforts, the Conference on Disarmament was unable to reach agreement on the re-establishment at its session in 1984 of an *Ad Hoc* Committee under item 1 of its agenda, entitled "Nuclear-test ban",

Recognizing the important role of the Conference on Disarmament in the negotiation of a comprehensive nuclear-test-ban treaty,

Recognizing the importance to such a treaty of the work on a global seismic detection network, assigned by the Conference on Disarmament to the *Ad Hoc* Group of Scientific Experts to Consider International Co-operative Measures to Detect and Identify Seismic Events,

Recalling paragraph 31 of the Final Document of the Tenth Special Session of the General Assembly, relating to verification of disarmament and arms control agreements, which stated that the form and modalities of the verification to be provided for in any specific agreement depend on, and should be determined by, the purposes, scope and nature of the agreement,

1. *Reiterates its profound concern* that, despite the express wishes of the majority of Member States, nuclear testing continues;

2. *Reaffirms its conviction* that a treaty to achieve the prohibition of all nuclear-test explosions by all States in all environments for all time is a matter of greatest importance;

3. *Expresses the conviction* that such a treaty would constitute a vital element for the success of efforts to halt and reverse the nuclear-arms race and the qualitative improvement of nuclear weapons, and to prevent the expansion of existing nuclear arsenals and the spread of nuclear weapons to additional countries;

4. *Urges* the Conference on Disarmament to establish at the beginning of its session in 1985 an *Ad Hoc* Committee under item 1 of its agenda, entitled "Nuclear-test ban" and

(a) To resume immediately its substantive work relating to a comprehensive test ban, including the issue of scope as well as those of verification and compliance, with a view to the negotiation of a treaty on the subject;

(b) Taking into account the work previously performed by and the results of the technical test being conducted by the *Ad Hoc* Group of Scientific Experts to Consider International Co-operative Measures to Detect and Identify Seismic Events, to take steps for the establishment as soon as possible of an international seismic monitoring network:

(i) to monitor nuclear explosions;

(ii) to determine the capabilities of such a network for monitoring compliance with a comprehensive nuclear-test-ban treaty;

(c) To initiate detailed investigation of other measures to monitor and verify compliance with such a treaty, including an international network to monitor atmospheric radioactivity;

5. *Urges* all members of the Conference on Disarmament, in particular the nuclear-weapon States, to co-operate within the Conference in fulfilling these tasks;

6. *Calls upon* the Conference on Disarmament to report on progress to the General Assembly at its fortieth session;

7. *Decides* to include in the provisional agenda of its fortieth session the item entitled "Urgent need for a comprehensive nuclear-test-ban treaty".

General Assembly resolution 39/53

12 December 1984   Meeting 97   124-0-24 (recorded vote)

Approved by First Committee (A/39/737) by recorded vote (109-0-26), 26 November (meeting 47); 25-nation draft (A/C.1/39/L.71); agenda item 47.

Sponsors: Australia, Bahamas, Brunei Darussalam, Canada, Denmark, Fiji, Finland, Iceland, Ireland, Japan, Kenya, Netherlands, New Zealand, Norway, Papua New Guinea, Philippines, Portugal, Samoa, Sierra Leone, Singapore, Solomon Islands, Spain, Sweden, Thailand, Vanuatu.

Meeting numbers. GA 39th session: 1st Committee 3-36, 40, 47, 48; plenary 97.

Recorded vote in Assembly as follows:

In favour: Algeria, Antigua and Barbuda, Australia, Austria, Bahamas, Bahrain, Bangladesh, Barbados, Belgium, Belize, Benin, Bhutan, Bolivia, Botswana, Brazil, Brunei Darussalam, Burkina Faso, Burma, Burundi, Cameroon, Canada, Cape Verde, Central African Republic, Chad, Chile, Colombia, Comoros, Costa Rica, Cyprus, Democratic Kampuchea, Denmark, Djibouti, Dominican Republic, Ecuador, Egypt, El Salvador, Equatorial Guinea, Ethiopia, Fiji, Finland, Gabon, Germany, Federal Republic of, Ghana, Greece, Guatemala, Guinea, Guinea-Bissau, Guyana, Haiti, Honduras, Iceland, Indonesia, Iran, Iraq, Ireland, Israel, Italy, Ivory Coast, Jamaica, Japan, Jordan, Kenya, Kuwait, Lebanon, Lesotho, Liberia, Libyan Arab Jamahiriya, Luxembourg, Madagascar, Malawi, Malaysia, Maldives, Mali, Malta, Mauritania, Mauritius, Morocco, Nepal, Netherlands, New Zealand, Niger, Nigeria, Norway, Oman, Pakistan, Papua New Guinea, Paraguay, Peru, Philippines, Portugal, Qatar, Romania, Rwanda, Saint Lucia, Samoa, Sao Tome and Principe, Saudi Arabia, Senegal, Seychelles, Sierra Leone, Singapore, Somalia, Spain, Sri Lanka, Sudan, Suriname, Sweden, Syrian Arab Republic, Thailand, Togo, Trinidad and Tobago, Tunisia, Turkey, Uganda, United Arab Emirates, United Republic of Tanzania, Uruguay, Vanuatu, Venezuela, Yemen, Yugoslavia, Zaire, Zambia, Zimbabwe.

Against: None.

Abstaining: Afghanistan, Angola, Argentina, Bulgaria, Byelorussian SSR, China, Congo, Cuba, Czechoslovakia, France, German Democratic Republic, Hungary, India, Lao People's Democratic Republic, Mexico, Mongolia, Mozambique, Nicaragua, Poland, Ukrainian SSR, USSR, United Kingdom, United States, Viet Nam.

Prior to adopting the text as a whole, the Assembly adopted paragraph 4 by a recorded vote of 80 to 19, with 41 abstentions. The First Committee had approved that paragraph by a recorded vote, requested by the USSR, of 71 to 18, with 35 abstentions.

Introducing the draft, Australia said paragraph 4 listed the practical steps required to remove the remaining obstacles to a treaty; it was disturbed that the proposals calling for immediate negotiations tended to cover nuclear-weapon tests only, rather than all nuclear tests.

In explanation of vote, the USSR held that the paragraph might be used by the United States and others to block talks on drafting a treaty; that paragraph, it asserted, was aimed at perpetuating an abnormal situation where a verification system was proposed when negotiations were blocked. Similarly, the Byelorussian SSR, the German Democratic Republic and Poland felt the paragraph over-emphasized the verification issue in disregard of the majority view that the technical prerequisites for verification already existed and the details should be settled in the negotiating process.

Argentina and Mexico, while agreeing with many elements of the text, could not accept its failure to appeal to all members of the Conference on Disarmament to initiate the negotiation of a treaty immediately. The Ukrainian SSR felt the proposed mandate would make the subsidiary body counter-productive. Cuba viewed paragraph 4 as promoting paralysis. India viewed the draft as seeking to modify the well-defined objective of a treaty aimed at complete cessation of the testing of nuclear weapons by all States in all environments for all time. For Poland, the eighth preambular paragraph suggested blaming the impasse on all members of the Conference.

Bulgaria said the text allowed for a continuation of testing by those blocking work on the question, over-emphasized the verification issue and put in a wrong perspective the work of the seismic expert group. Czechoslovakia also believed the importance of technical aspects of verification had been over-emphasized.

Chile, Ecuador, Sri Lanka and Yugoslavia abstained on paragraph 4 but supported the text as a whole, because of the importance they attached to negotiating a substantive agreement. Sri Lanka and Yugoslavia doubted the practicability of implementing paragraph 4 *(b)* and *(c)*, with the latter adding that the Conference on Disarmament was not the body within whose framework an international seismic monitoring network should be established. Chile added that academic debates on verification and other matters should not be allowed to block speedy achievement of a final agreement.

The United Kingdom and the United States, which voted for paragraph 4, stressed that verification and other problems relating to security considerations had to be resolved before negotiations could hold any prospect of being productive; while committed to achieving a comprehensive test ban, the United States did not agree that the issue was as urgent as reducing the existing arsenals of weapons.

Belgium, Brazil and Zambia, voting affirmatively in both votes, appreciated the intention of the sponsors, although Zambia regretted the mention of NPT. Belgium particularly favoured paragraph 4 as setting forth the kind of scientific and technical work necessary for credible international verification.

Expressing the hope that the Conference on Disarmament would agree at its 1985 session to initiate negotiations, Nigeria said its affirmative vote on the text did not indicate an endorsement of paragraph 4.

Speaking on all three resolutions on a nuclear-test ban, France reiterated that a test ban should be part of an effective nuclear disarmament process, as stated in paragraph 51 of the 1978 Final Document;[13] therefore, it could not associate itself with measures to reduce nuclear weapons or participate in drawing up a test-ban treaty until the two major nuclear Powers, through reductions, made it possible for France to limit its own nuclear capabilities, including its testing.

Fissionable material for weapons purposes

As in previous years, the General Assembly discussed in 1984, under the agenda item on general and complete disarmament, the question of prohibiting the production of fissionable material for weapons purposes.

GENERAL ASSEMBLY ACTION

On 17 December, the Assembly, on the recommendation of the First Committee, adopted resolution 39/151 H by recorded vote.

Prohibition of the production of fissionable material for weapons purposes

The General Assembly,

Recalling its resolutions 33/91 H of 16 December 1978, 34/87 D of 11 December 1979, 35/156 H of 12 December 1980, 36/97 G of 9 December 1981, 37/99 E of 13 December 1982 and 38/188 E of 20 December 1983, in which it requested the Committee on Disarmament, at an appropriate stage of the implementation of the Programme of Action set forth in section III of the Final Document of the Tenth Special Session of the General Assembly, and of its work on the item entitled "Nuclear weapons in all aspects", to consider urgently the question of adequately verified cessation and prohibition of fissionable material for nuclear weapons and other nuclear explosive devices and to keep the Assembly informed of the progress of that consideration,

Noting that the agenda of the Conference on Disarmament for 1984 included the item entitled "Nuclear weapons in all aspects" and that the Conference's programme of work for both parts of its session held in 1984 contained the item entitled "Cessation of the nuclear arms race and nuclear disarmament",

Recalling the proposals and statements made in the Conference on Disarmament on those items,

Considering that the cessation of production of fissionable material for weapons purposes and the progressive conversion and transfer of stocks to peaceful uses would be a significant step towards halting and reversing the nuclear arms race,

Considering that the prohibition of the production of fissionable material for nuclear weapons and other explosive devices also would be an important measure in facilitating the prevention of the proliferation of nuclear weapons and explosive devices,

Requests the Conference on Disarmament, at an appropriate stage of its work on the item entitled "Nuclear weapons in all aspects", to pursue its consideration of the question of adequately verified cessation and prohibition of the production of fissionable material for nuclear weapons and other nuclear explosive devices and to keep the General Assembly informed of the progress of that consideration.

General Assembly resolution 39/151 H

17 December 1984   Meeting 102   140-0-8 (recorded vote)

Approved by First Committee (A/39/755) by recorded vote (125-1-9), 20 November (meeting 44); 19-nation draft (A/C.1/39/L.42); agenda item 65 *(f)*.

Sponsors: Australia, Austria, Bahamas, Bangladesh, Canada, Denmark, Finland, Greece, Indonesia, Ireland, Japan, Netherlands, New Zealand, Norway, Philippines, Romania, Singapore, Sweden, Uruguay.

Meeting numbers. GA 39th session: 1st Committee 3-36, 44; plenary 102.

Recorded vote in Assembly as follows:

In favour: Afghanistan, Algeria, Angola, Antigua and Barbuda, Australia, Austria, Bahamas, Bahrain, Bangladesh, Barbados, Belgium, Benin, Bhutan, Bolivia, Botswana, Brunei Darussalam, Bulgaria, Burkina Faso, Burma, Burundi, Byelorussian SSR, Cameroon, Canada, Cape Verde, Central African Republic, Chad, Chile, Colombia, Congo, Costa Rica, Cuba, Cyprus, Czechoslovakia, Democratic Kampuchea, Democratic Yemen, Denmark, Djibouti, Dominican Republic, Ecuador, Egypt, El Salvador, Equatorial Guinea, Ethiopia, Fiji, Finland, Gabon, German Democratic Republic, Germany, Federal Republic of, Ghana, Greece, Guatemala, Guinea, Guinea-Bissau, Guyana, Haiti, Honduras, Hungary, Iceland, Indonesia, Iran, Iraq, Ireland, Israel, Italy, Ivory Coast, Jamaica, Japan, Kenya, Kuwait, Lao People's Democratic Republic, Lebanon, Lesotho, Liberia, Libyan Arab Jamahiriya, Luxembourg, Madagascar, Malawi, Malaysia, Maldives, Mali, Malta, Mauritania, Mauritius, Mexico, Mongolia, Morocco, Nepal, Netherlands, New Zealand, Nicaragua, Niger, Nigeria, Norway, Oman, Pakistan, Panama, Papua New Guinea, Paraguay, Peru, Philippines, Poland, Portugal, Qatar, Romania, Rwanda, Saint Lucia, Saint Vincent and the Grenadines, Samoa, Sao Tome and Principe, Saudi Arabia, Senegal, Seychelles, Sierra Leone, Singapore, Somalia,

Spain, Sri Lanka, Sudan, Suriname, Sweden, Syrian Arab Republic, Thailand, Togo, Trinidad and Tobago, Tunisia, Turkey, Uganda, Ukrainian SSR, USSR, United Arab Emirates, United Republic of Tanzania, Uruguay, Venezuela, Viet Nam, Yemen, Yugoslavia, Zaire, Zambia, Zimbabwe.

Against: None.

Abstaining: Argentina, Brazil, China, France, India, Mozambique, United Kingdom, United States.

Explaining its vote, India considered the approach partial and inconsistent with the goals set out in the 1978 Final Document;[13] it remained convinced of the need for a simultaneous stoppage of the production of nuclear weapons and of all fissionable material for weapons purposes, adding that all States would then have no reason not to accept the same system of equitable and non-discriminatory safeguards on all their nuclear facilities.

The USSR said the question should be regarded as a step towards a nuclear-weapons freeze and nuclear disarmament; it understood the word "work" in the text to mean practical negotiations.

The Assembly's call for stopping the production of fissionable material for weapons purposes was also contained in resolutions 39/63 C and G, on a nuclear-weapons freeze, and 39/148 K, on cessation of the nuclear-arms race and nuclear disarmament.

Strengthening the security of non-nuclear-weapon States

The General Assembly, in two 1984 resolutions (39/57 and 39/58), again called for negotiations leading to conclusion of international arrangements to assure non-nuclear-weapon States against the use or threat of use of nuclear weapons—arrangements also known as negative security assurances.

Consideration by the Conference on Disarmament. In 1984, the Conference on Disarmament[9] again considered an agenda item on negative security assurances, from 26 to 30 March and from 23 to 27 July. Discussion also took place in an *ad hoc* subsidiary body, set up in 1979 and re-established on 28 February 1984. That body, subsequently designated as an *Ad Hoc* Committee, held 11 meetings between 16 July and 15 August under the chairmanship of Borislav Konstantinov (Bulgaria).

In a joint statement submitted to the Conference in June,[67] the Group of 21 expressed regret that negotiations on the topic had reached an impasse because several nuclear-weapon States refused to revise their existing unilateral declarations; the Group urged those States to allow the *Ad Hoc* Committee to elaborate a common formula acceptable to all, to be included in an international instrument as previously called for. Among other documents submitted were one by the USSR on "Not to use nuclear weapons under any circumstances against non-nuclear countries, in whose

territory there are no such weapons"[68] and another by a group of socialist countries.[18]

In its conclusions and recommendations, the *Ad Hoc* Committee reaffirmed the need for effective security guarantees to non-nuclear-weapon States and stated that agreement could not be reached due to specific difficulties relating to differing perceptions of security interests and the complexity of the issues. It recommended to the Conference that ways should be explored to overcome the difficulties, that an *ad hoc* committee be re-established in 1985 and that consultations take place to determine the most appropriate course of action.

GENERAL ASSEMBLY ACTION

In December 1984, the General Assembly, on the recommendation of the First Committee, adopted two resolutions on negative security assurances.

On 12 December, it adopted resolution 39/57 by recorded vote.

Conclusion of an international convention on the strengthening of the security of non-nuclear-weapon States against the use or threat of use of nuclear weapons

The General Assembly,

Convinced of the need to take effective measures for the strengthening of the security of States and prompted by the desire shared by all nations to eliminate war and prevent nuclear conflagration,

Taking into account the principle of non-use of force or threat of force enshrined in the Charter of the United Nations and reaffirmed in a number of United Nations declarations and resolutions,

Considering that, until nuclear disarmament is achieved on a universal basis, it is imperative for the international community to develop effective measures to ensure the security of non-nuclear-weapon States against the use or threat of use of nuclear weapons from any quarter,

Recognizing that effective measures to assure non-nuclear-weapon States against the use or threat of use of nuclear weapons can constitute a positive contribution to the prevention of the spread of such weapons,

Noting with satisfaction the determination of non-nuclear-weapon States in various parts of the world to prevent nuclear weapons from being introduced into their territories and to ensure the complete absence of such weapons in their respective regions, including through the establishment of nuclear-weapon-free zones on the basis of arrangements freely arrived at among the States of the region concerned, and being anxious to encourage and contribute to the attainment of this objective,

Concerned at the continuing escalation of the arms race, in particular the nuclear-arms race having entered a qualitatively new stage, and the possibility of the use or threat of use of nuclear weapons and the danger of nuclear war,

Desirous of promoting the implementation of paragraph 59 of the Final Document of the Tenth Special Session of the General Assembly, the first special session devoted to disarmament, in which it urged the nuclear-weapon States to pursue efforts to conclude, as appropriate, effective arrangements to assure non-nuclear-weapon States against the use or threat of use of nuclear weapons,

Recalling its numerous resolutions on this subject as well as the relevant part of the special report of the Committee on Disarmament, submitted to the General Assembly at its twelfth special session, the second special session devoted to disarmament,

Noting that the Conference on Disarmament considered in 1984 the item entitled "Effective international arrangements to assure non-nuclear-weapon States against the use or threat of use of nuclear weapons" and the work done by its *Ad Hoc* Committee on this item, as reflected in the report of the Conference on Disarmament,

Recalling the proposals submitted on this subject to the General Assembly and in the Conference on Disarmament, including the drafts of an international convention, and the widespread international support for the conclusion of such a convention,

Wishing to promote an early and successful completion of the negotiations in the Conference on Disarmament aimed at the elaboration of a convention on the item,

Further noting that the idea of interim arrangements as a first step towards the conclusion of such a convention has also been considered in the Conference on Disarmament,

Welcoming once again the solemn declaration made by some nuclear-weapon States concerning non-first-use of nuclear weapons, and convinced that, if all nuclear-weapon States were to assume obligations not to be the first to use nuclear weapons, that would be tantamount, in practice, to banning the use of nuclear weapons against all States, including all non-nuclear-weapon States,

Considering that, in the search for a solution to the problem of security assurances, priority should be given to the legitimate security concerns of the non-nuclear-weapon States which, by virtue of their forgoing the nuclear option and of not allowing nuclear weapons to be stationed on their territories, have every right to expect to be most effectively guaranteed against the use or threat of use of nuclear weapons,

Being aware that unconditional guarantees by all nuclear-weapon States not to use or threaten to use nuclear weapons under any circumstances against the non-nuclear-weapon States having no nuclear weapons on their territories should constitute an integral element of a mandatory system of norms regulating the relations between the nuclear-weapon States, which bear the primary responsibility for preventing a nuclear war, thus sparing mankind from its devastating consequences,

1. *Reaffirms once again* the urgent need to reach agreement on effective international arrangements to assure non-nuclear-weapon States against the use or threat of use of nuclear weapons;

2. *Notes with satisfaction* that in the Conference on Disarmament there was once again no objection, in principle, to the idea of an international convention on this subject, although the difficulties involved were also pointed out;

3. *Expresses its regret* that specific difficulties related to differing perceptions of security interests of some

nuclear-weapon States and non-nuclear-weapon States have once again prevented the Conference on Disarmament from making substantive progress towards the achievement of an agreement;

4. *Considers* that the Conference on Disarmament should continue to explore ways and means of overcoming the difficulties encountered in the negotiations to reach an appropriate agreement on effective international arrangements to assure non-nuclear-weapon States against the use or threat of use of nuclear weapons;

5. *Requests* the Conference on Disarmament to continue the negotiations, as recommended in the report on its 1984 session, with a view to concluding an international instrument of a legally binding character to assure non-nuclear-weapon States against the use or threat of use of nuclear weapons;

6. *Decides* to include in the provisional agenda of its fortieth session the item entitled "Conclusion of an international convention on the strengthening of the security of non-nuclear-weapon States against the use or threat of use of nuclear weapons".

General Assembly resolution 39/57

12 December 1984   Meeting 97   104-19-20 (recorded vote)

Approved by First Committee (A/39/741) by recorded vote (88-19-16), 21 November (meeting 45); 10-nation draft (A/C.1/39/L.21); agenda item 51.

Sponsors: Afghanistan, Angola, Bulgaria, Byelorussian SSR, Czechoslovakia, Democratic Yemen, Ethiopia, Mongolia, USSR, Viet Nam.

Meeting numbers. GA 39th session: 1st Committee 3-36, 45; plenary 97.

Recorded vote in Assembly as follows:

In favour: Afghanistan, Algeria, Angola, Antigua and Barbuda, Bahrain, Bangladesh, Barbados, Belize, Benin, Bolivia, Botswana, Bulgaria, Burkina Faso, Burundi, Byelorussian SSR, Cameroon, Cape Verde, Central African Republic, Chad, Chile, Comoros, Congo, Costa Rica, Cuba, Cyprus, Czechoslovakia, Democratic Yemen, Djibouti, Ecuador, Egypt, El Salvador, Equatorial Guinea, Ethiopia, Fiji, Finland, Gabon, German Democratic Republic, Ghana, Greece, Guatemala, Guinea, Guinea-Bissau, Guyana, Hungary, Indonesia, Iran, Iraq, Jordan, Kenya, Kuwait, Lao People's Democratic Republic, Lebanon, Lesotho, Liberia, Libyan Arab Jamahiriya, Madagascar, Malawi, Maldives, Mali, Malta, Mauritania, Mauritius, Mexico, Mongolia, Morocco, Mozambique, Nepal, Nicaragua, Niger, Nigeria, Oman, Pakistan, Panama, Papua New Guinea, Peru, Poland, Qatar, Romania, Rwanda, Saudi Arabia, Senegal, Seychelles, Sierra Leone, Somalia, Sri Lanka, Sudan, Suriname, Syrian Arab Republic, Thailand, Togo, Trinidad and Tobago, Tunisia, Uganda, Ukrainian SSR, USSR, United Arab Emirates, United Republic of Tanzania, Vanuatu, Venezuela, Viet Nam, Yemen, Yugoslavia, Zambia, Zimbabwe.

Against: Australia, Belgium, Canada, Denmark, France, Germany, Federal Republic of, Iceland, Israel, Italy, Japan, Luxembourg, Netherlands, New Zealand, Norway, Portugal, Spain, Turkey, United Kingdom, United States.

Abstaining: Argentina, Austria, Bahamas, Brazil, Burma, China, Colombia, Dominica, Dominican Republic, Honduras, India, Ireland, Ivory Coast, Malaysia, Paraguay, Saint Lucia, Samoa, Sweden, Uruguay, Zaire.

Explaining its vote, the Federal Republic of Germany said the call emanating from the USSR for a nuclear non-first-use commitment was directed against the security of Western States which had pledged non-use of weapons except in the case of armed attack; further, that concept provided no incentives to deal with existing nuclear arsenals and preserved them at their current level. It added that the text made no reference to conventional wars, whereas the United Nations Charter condemned all wars; declaratory policy needed confirmation through verifiable action. Japan considered the text lacking in objectivity and balance and failing to refer to a common approach acceptable to all.

Expressing opposition to all wars, Colombia said it would have welcomed the draft if the non-first-use concept also covered conventional weapons. For Ireland, the text did not take into account the possibility of different approaches to achieving international arrangements; by clearly favouring a convention, the text implied further obligations for non-nuclear-weapon States, a requirement which it believed was inappropriate in the case of States already party to NPT. Sweden expressed similar reservations.

Indonesia, although agreeing with the general thrust of the text, would have abstained, had a separate vote been taken, on the final preambular paragraph. While believing that the declarations need not be identical, Liberia said it was more interested in commitments than in declarations, because the latter could be abrogated by any one party.

Argentina, Brazil and India explained their abstentions on the same grounds as on the draft which became resolution 39/58 (see p. 56), as did Chile and the German Democratic Republic which voted in favour.

Also on 12 December, the Assembly adopted resolution 39/58 by recorded vote.

Conclusion of effective international arrangements to assure non-nuclear-weapon States against the use or threat of use of nuclear weapons

The General Assembly,

Bearing in mind the need to allay the legitimate concern of the States of the world with regard to ensuring lasting security for their peoples,

Convinced that nuclear weapons pose the greatest threat to mankind and to the survival of civilization,

Deeply concerned at the continuing escalation of the arms race, in particular the nuclear-arms race, and the possibility of the use or threat of use of nuclear weapons,

Convinced that nuclear disarmament and the complete elimination of nuclear weapons are essential to remove the danger of nuclear war,

Taking into account the principle of the non-use of force or threat of force enshrined in the Charter of the United Nations,

Deeply concerned about the possibility of the use or threat of use of nuclear weapons,

Recognizing that the independence, territorial integrity and sovereignty of non-nuclear-weapon States need to be safeguarded against the use or threat of use of force, including the use or threat of use of nuclear weapons,

Considering that, until nuclear disarmament is achieved on a universal basis, it is imperative for the international community to develop effective measures to ensure the security of non-nuclear-weapon States against the use or threat of use of nuclear weapons from any quarter,

Recognizing that effective measures to assure the non-nuclear-weapon States against the use or threat of use of nuclear weapons can constitute a positive contribution to the prevention of the spread of nuclear weapons,

Recalling its resolutions 3261 G (XXIX) of 9 December 1974 and 31/189 C of 21 December 1976,

Bearing in mind paragraph 59 of the Final Document of the Tenth Special Session of the General Assembly, in which it urged the nuclear-weapon States to pursue efforts to conclude, as appropriate, effective arrangements to assure non-nuclear-weapon States against the use or threat of use of nuclear weapons,

Desirous of promoting the implementation of the relevant provisions of the Final Document of the Tenth Special Session,

Recalling its resolutions 33/72 B of 14 December 1978, 34/85 of 11 December 1979, 35/155 of 12 December 1980, 36/95 of 9 December 1981, 37/81 of 9 December 1982 and 38/68 of 15 December 1983,

Further recalling paragraph 12 of the Declaration of the 1980s as the Second Disarmament Decade, contained in the annex to its resolution 35/46 of 3 December 1980, which states, *inter alia,* that all efforts should be exerted by the Committee on Disarmament urgently to negotiate with a view to reaching agreement on effective international arrangements to assure non-nuclear-weapon States against the use or threat of use of nuclear weapons,

Noting the in-depth negotiations undertaken in the Conference on Disarmament and its *Ad Hoc* Committee on Effective International Arrangements to Assure Non-Nuclear-Weapon States against the Use or Threat of Use of Nuclear Weapons, with a view to reaching agreement on this item,

Noting the proposals submitted under that item in the Conference on Disarmament, including the drafts of an international convention,

Taking note of the decision of the Seventh Conference of Heads of State or Government of Non-Aligned Countries, held at New Delhi from 7 to 12 March 1983, as well as the relevant recommendations of the Organization of the Islamic Conference reiterated in the final declaration of the Fourteenth Islamic Conference of Foreign Ministers, held at Dhaka from 6 to 11 December 1983, calling upon the Committee on Disarmament to reach an urgent agreement on an international convention to assure non-nuclear-weapon States against the use or threat of use of nuclear weapons,

Further noting the support expressed in the Conference on Disarmament and in the General Assembly for the elaboration of an international convention to assure non-nuclear-weapon States against the use or threat of use of nuclear weapons, as well as the difficulties pointed out in evolving a common approach acceptable to all,

1. *Reaffirms* the urgent need to reach agreement on effective international arrangements to assure non-nuclear-weapon States against the use or threat of use of nuclear weapons;

2. *Notes with satisfaction* that in the Conference on Disarmament there is no objection, in principle, to the idea of an international convention to assure non-nuclear-weapon States against the use or threat of use of nuclear weapons, although the difficulties as regards evolving a common approach acceptable to all have also been pointed out;

3. *Appeals* to all States, especially the nuclear-weapon States, to demonstrate the political will necessary to reach agreement on a common approach and, in particular, on a common formula which could be included in an international instrument of a legally binding character;

4. *Recommends* that further intensive efforts should be devoted to the search for such a common approach or common formula and that the various alternative approaches, including in particular those considered in the Conference on Disarmament, should be further explored in order to overcome the difficulties;

5. *Recommends* that the Conference on Disarmament should actively continue negotiations with a view to reaching early agreement and concluding effective international arrangements to assure non-nuclear-weapon States against the use or threat of use of nuclear weapons, taking into account the widespread support for the conclusion of an international convention and giving consideration to any other proposals designed to secure the same objective;

6. *Decides* to include in the provisional agenda of its fortieth session the item entitled "Conclusion of effective international arrangements to assure non-nuclear-weapon States against the use or threat of use of nuclear weapons".

General Assembly resolution 39/58

12 December 1984   Meeting 97   146-0-4 (recorded vote)

Approved by First Committee (A/39/742) by recorded vote (129-0-5), 21 November (meeting 45); draft by Pakistan (A/C.1/39/L.7); agenda item 52.

Meeting numbers. GA 39th session: 1st Committee 3-36, 45; plenary 97.

Recorded vote in Assembly as follows:

In favour: Afghanistan, Algeria, Angola, Antigua and Barbuda, Australia, Austria, Bahamas, Bahrain, Bangladesh, Barbados, Belgium, Belize, Benin, Bolivia, Botswana, Brunei Darussalam, Bulgaria, Burkina Faso, Burma, Burundi, Byelorussian SSR, Cameroon, Canada, Cape Verde, Central African Republic, Chad, Chile, China, Colombia, Comoros, Congo, Costa Rica, Cuba, Cyprus, Czechoslovakia, Democratic Kampuchea, Democratic Yemen, Denmark, Djibouti, Dominica, Dominican Republic, Ecuador, Egypt, El Salvador, Equatorial Guinea, Ethiopia, Fiji, Finland, France, Gabon, German Democratic Republic, Germany, Federal Republic of, Ghana, Greece, Guatemala, Guinea, Guinea-Bissau, Guyana, Haiti, Honduras, Hungary, Iceland, Indonesia, Iran, Iraq, Ireland, Israel, Italy, Ivory Coast, Jamaica, Japan, Jordan, Kenya, Kuwait, Lao People's Democratic Republic, Lebanon, Lesotho, Liberia, Libyan Arab Jamahiriya, Luxembourg, Madagascar, Malawi, Malaysia, Maldives, Mali, Malta, Mauritania, Mauritius, Mexico, Mongolia, Morocco, Mozambique, Nepal, Netherlands, New Zealand, Nicaragua, Niger, Nigeria, Norway, Oman, Pakistan, Panama, Papua New Guinea, Paraguay, Peru, Philippines, Poland, Portugal, Qatar, Romania, Rwanda, Saint Lucia, Samoa, Sao Tome and Principe, Saudi Arabia, Senegal, Seychelles, Sierra Leone, Singapore, Somalia, Spain, Sri Lanka, Sudan, Suriname, Sweden, Syrian Arab Republic, Thailand, Togo, Trinidad and Tobago, Tunisia, Turkey, Uganda, Ukrainian SSR, USSR, United Arab Emirates, United Kingdom, United Republic of Tanzania, Uruguay, Vanuatu, Venezuela, Viet Nam, Yemen, Yugoslavia, Zaire, Zambia, Zimbabwe.

Against: None.

Abstaining: Argentina, Brazil, India, United States.

Introducing the draft, Pakistan asserted that unilateral declarations could not be considered an acceptable substitute for an international agreement of a binding character.

In explanation of vote, Brazil stated that the subject continued to be approached from the narrow point of view of the security perceptions of the nuclear Powers; such a parochial view of reality presupposed a recognition of the legitimacy of the exclusive possession of nuclear weapons by the current nuclear Powers which, with one exception, had attached qualifications to their unilateral declarations; it stood by the Group of 21 statement, according to which no progress on the question could be achieved as long as the nuclear-weapon Powers maintained

their attitudes and policies. Argentina and India said the most credible security guarantees were the complete elimination of nuclear weapons. Argentina said declarations, which were, with a single exception, difficult to understand with regard to the scope of applicability, amounted to lack of assurances, because they were unverifiable. India added that as long as the nuclear-weapon States possessed such arsenals and predicated their security policies on their use, there was little point in the non-nuclear-weapon States seeking security assurances from them.

The German Democratic Republic stressed the urgency of concluding international arrangements, saying that, in their absence, some argued for the permissibility of using nuclear weapons. Czechoslovakia said the possibility of the use of nuclear weapons played a role in Western strategic plans; it emphasized that it favoured measures designed to decrease international tension. While considering the text to be relatively balanced and objective, Japan had some reservations as regards its reference to a specific modality for assurances which, Japan felt, prejudged the work of the Conference on Disarmament. Despite reservations about the idea of an international convention, Sweden supported the text because it also gave consideration to other proposals aimed at effective negative security assurances. Chile supported proposals that gave effective content to the obligation of nuclear-weapon States towards those that had rejected the nuclear option.

REFERENCES

(1)A/39/76. (2)A/39/175. (3)A/39/720. (4)A/39/209-S/16504. (5)A/39/277-S/16587. (6)A/39/296-S/16619. (7)A/39/285-S/16600. (8)A/39/311-S/16629. (9)A/39/27. (10)A/39/42. (11)YUN 1978, p. 17. (12)YUN 1983, p. 20. (13)YUN 1978, p. 39, GA res. S-10/2, 30 June 1978. (14)YUN 1983, p. 23, GA res. 38/183 N, 20 Dec. 1983. (15)*Ibid.*, p. 27, GA res. 38/183 J, 20 Dec. 1983. (16)A/39/516. (17)YUN 1983, p. 30, GA res. 38/183 G, 20 Dec. 1983. (18)CD/484. (19)CD/515. (20)A/C.1/39/L.40/Rev.1. (21)A/C.1/39/L.80. (22)A/C.1/39/L.69/Rev.1. (23)YUN 1983, p. 34, GA res. 38/73 G, annex, 15 Dec. 1983. (24)A/C.1/39/L.66. (25)YUN 1983, p. 32, GA res. 38/73 E, 15 Dec. 1983. (26)A/39/623. (27)YUN 1983, p. 33, GA res. 38/76, 15 Dec. 1983. (28)YUN 1968, p. 17, GA res. 2373(XXII), annex, 12 June 1968. (29)A/39/133-S/16417. (30)YUN 1983, p. 37. (31)YUN 1982, p. 64, GA res. 37/99 F, 13 Dec. 1982. (32)*Comprehensive study of the question of nuclear-weapon-free zones in all its aspects*, Sales No. E.76.I.7. (33)A/39/400. (34)YUN 1964, p. 69. (35)YUN 1983, p. 40, GA res. 38/181 B, 20 Dec. 1983. (36)S/16324. (37)YUN 1983, p. 38, GA res. 38/181 A, 20 Dec. 1983. (38)A/39/466. (39)A/39/470. (40)YUN 1980, p. 45. (41)YUN 1979, p. 46. (42)A/39/472. (43)YUN 1983, p. 43, GA res. 38/64, 15 Dec. 1983. (44)A/39/435. (45)YUN 1983, p. 44, GA res. 38/69, 15 Dec. 1983. (46)A/39/349. (47)YUN 1981, p. 51. (48)A/39/434. (49)YUN 1983, p. 45, GA res. 38/65, 15 Dec. 1983. (50)A/39/343. (51)YUN 1983, p. 49, GA res. 38/62, 15 Dec. 1983. (52)CD/438. (53)CD/522. (54)CD/521. (55)CD/492. (56)CD/520. (57)YUN 1983, p. 48. (58)CD/430. (59)CD/524. (60)CD/531. (61)CD/491. (62)CD/449. (63)CD/535. (64)CD/448 & Add.1. (65)CD/534. (66)YUN 1963, p. 137. (67)CD/513. (68)CD/444.

Other weapons of mass destruction

Chemical and biological warfare

In 1984, fundamental disagreements persisted on a number of issues relating to an envisaged convention banning chemical and biological weapons, and the General Assembly adopted three resolutions (39/65 A-C) in December, all urging the Conference on Disarmament to intensify its negotiations on such a convention.

A Group of Consultant Experts submitted to the Assembly a finalized report on procedures for investigating violations of the 1925 Geneva Protocol for the Prohibition of the Use in War of Asphyxiating, Poisonous or Other Gases, and of Bacteriological Methods of Warfare. In resolution 39/65 D, the Assembly agreed to the holding, in 1986, of a second conference to review the implementation of the 1971 Convention on the Prohibition of the Development, Production and Stockpiling of Bacteriological (Biological) and Toxin Weapons and on Their Destruction.

Implementation of the 1925 Protocol

Report of the Secretary-General. In an October 1984 report to the General Assembly,[1] the Secretary-General transmitted, in an annex, the final report by the Group of Consultant Experts which, in pursuance of a 1982 Assembly resolution,[2] had devised procedures for investigating possible violation of the 1925 Geneva Protocol—which prohibits the use in war of asphyxiating, poisonous or other gases and of all analogous liquids, materials or devices, as well as of bacteriological methods of warfare. Also annexed to the report were the replies of three additional Governments (Canada, Portugal, Spain) to his 1983 request[3] for the names of qualified experts and laboratories whose services would be available at short notice to investigate alleged uses of chemical weapons.

The Group—experts from Austria, Ecuador, Egypt, France, Sweden and the United States, acting in their personal capacities—held two sessions in 1984 (Geneva, 24 April–4 May; New York, 13-24 August), as in 1983. In addition to reviewing and modifying its previous report[3] in the light of developments, the Group concentrated, among other things, on the systematic organization and assembly of the documentation relevant to identifying signs and symptoms associated with the use of chemical agents. It also focused on procedures related to security, logistic support and transportation, and included in its report a new section dealing with administrative support for implementing and updating the procedures.

Some of the scientific literature and other relevant data available to the Group were organized in three appendices to its report, covering both general and specific references concerning health aspects of potential chemical and biological warfare agents and lists of some such agents. Included among seven other appendices were: an illustrative list of items required for an investigation; a questionnaire for interviews; and model clauses for inclusion in letters—relating to security, logistic support, transportation and laboratory analysis—to be exchanged between the United Nations and States involved in the conduct of an investigation.

GENERAL ASSEMBLY ACTION

On 12 December 1984, the General Assembly, on the recommendation of the First Committee, adopted resolution 39/65 E by recorded vote.

Chemical and bacteriological (biological) weapons

The General Assembly,

Recalling its resolution 37/98 D of 13 December 1982, and particularly paragraph 7, in which it requested the Secretary-General, with the assistance of qualified consultant experts, to devise procedures for the investigation of information concerning activities that may constitute a violation of the Protocol for the Prohibition of the Use in War of Asphyxiating, Poisonous or Other Gases, and of Bacteriological Methods of Warfare, signed at Geneva on 17 June 1925, or of the relevant rules of customary international law and to assemble and organize systematically documentation relating to the identification of signs and symptoms associated with the use of agents covered by the 1925 Geneva Protocol,

Recognizing that the use of such agents in war is universally condemned,

Underlining the importance of impartially and rapidly ascertaining, through an appropriate international procedure as provided for in resolution 37/98 D, facts that may constitute a violation of the provisions of the Geneva Protocol or of the relevant rules of customary international law,

Recalling its resolution 38/187 C of 20 December 1983, in which it took note of the report of the Secretary-General submitted pursuant to paragraph 7 of resolution 37/98 D and requested him to complete during 1984, with the assistance of the Group of Consultant Experts established by him, the task entrusted to him under the terms of paragraph 7 of resolution 37/98 D, and to report to the General Assembly at its thirty-ninth session,

1. *Takes note* of the report by the Secretary-General, to which is annexed the report of the Group of Consultant Experts established by him concerning the implementation of the provisions of paragraph 7 of resolution 37/98 D and of resolution 38/187 C;

2. *Notes with satisfaction* that, with the submission of the report of the Group of Consultant Experts, the provisions for the implementation of resolution 37/98 D are completed.

General Assembly resolution 39/65 E

12 December 1984   Meeting 97   87-18-30 (recorded vote)

Approved by First Committee (A/39/754) by recorded vote (83-17-30), 21 November (meeting 46); 13-nation draft (A/C.1/39/L.60); agenda item 64.

Sponsors: Australia, Belgium, Canada, Colombia, Costa Rica, Ecuador, France, Netherlands, New Zealand, Norway, Sweden, United Kingdom, Uruguay.
Meeting numbers. GA 39th session: 1st Committee 3-36, 39, 46; plenary 97.

Recorded vote in Assembly as follows:

In favour: Australia, Austria, Bangladesh, Barbados, Belgium, Bhutan, Bolivia, Botswana, Brunei Darussalam, Burundi, Cameroon, Canada, Central African Republic, Chad, China, Colombia, Costa Rica, Democratic Kampuchea, Denmark, Djibouti, Dominica, Dominican Republic, Ecuador, Egypt, Equatorial Guinea, Fiji, France, Gabon, Germany, Federal Republic of, Ghana, Greece, Guinea, Guinea-Bissau, Guyana, Haiti, Honduras, Indonesia, Ireland, Italy, Ivory Coast, Jamaica, Japan, Kenya, Liberia, Luxembourg, Malawi, Malaysia, Maldives, Mali, Malta, Mauritania, Mauritius, Morocco, Nepal, Netherlands, New Zealand, Niger, Nigeria, Norway, Pakistan, Panama, Papua New Guinea, Paraguay, Peru, Philippines, Portugal, Romania, Rwanda, Samoa, Sao Tome and Principe, Senegal, Sierra Leone, Singapore, Somalia, Spain, Sudan, Suriname, Sweden, Thailand, Togo, Trinidad and Tobago, Tunisia, Turkey, United Kingdom, United States, Uruguay, Zambia.

Against: Afghanistan, Bulgaria, Byelorussian SSR, Cuba, Czechoslovakia, Democratic Yemen, German Democratic Republic, Hungary, India, Lao People's Democratic Republic, Libyan Arab Jamahiriya, Mongolia, Mozambique, Poland, Syrian Arab Republic, Ukrainian SSR, USSR, Viet Nam.

Abstaining: Algeria, Argentina, Bahamas, Bahrain, Benin, Brazil, Burkina Faso, Burma, Cape Verde, Chile, Cyprus, Ethiopia, Finland, Iran,[a] Iraq, Jordan, Kuwait, Madagascar, Mexico, Nicaragua, Oman, Qatar, Saudi Arabia, Sri Lanka, Uganda, United Republic of Tanzania, Venezuela, Yemen, Yugoslavia, Zimbabwe.

[a]Later advised the Secretariat it had intended to vote in favour.

Indonesia, joined by many others explaining their votes, asserted that the early elaboration of a comprehensive convention in the Conference on Disarmament would provide the most effective guarantee of non-use of the weapons in question (see also p. 59). Poland, speaking on behalf of the Eastern European States and Mongolia, stressed that no action should be taken which could complicate the process of drafting a convention; it was joined by Brazil, Chile and the Lao People's Democratic Republic in stating that the draft constituted an attempt to undermine and illegally revise the 1925 Geneva Protocol by a United Nations resolution with the participation of non-parties to the instrument, in violation of the 1969 Vienna Convention on the Law of Treaties.[4] The USSR added that the text attempted to impose on the Secretary-General what it considered illegal functions which he could not appropriately carry out under the United Nations Charter. Cuba and Viet Nam pointed out that they had consistently opposed drafts of the kind in question.

Finland held that the lack of verification provisions in the Geneva Protocol must be corrected in the future ban on chemical weapons, either by parties to the Protocol or in the context of negotiations in the Conference on Disarmament. Yugoslavia felt that an effective system of verification should aim at building confidence and promoting co-operation among signatories through universal, not selective, application.

On the other hand, Belgium said the draft attempted to organize the vigilance of the international community with regard to the Protocol and customary international law. Bangladesh said it supported the draft for the same reason it had voted in favour of those on prohibiting chemical weapons (see p. 60).

Second Review Conference of the parties to the biological weapons Convention

In 1984, the General Assembly agreed to the holding in 1986 of a second Review Conference of the Parties to the 1971 Convention on the Prohibition of the Development, Production and Stockpiling of Bacteriological (Biological) and Toxin Weapons and on Their Destruction.[5] The first Review Conference, held in 1980,[6] had decided that a second would be held at Geneva sometime between 1985 and 1990, at the request of a majority of parties to the Convention. At the end of 1984, 100 States were parties to that instrument.

GENERAL ASSEMBLY ACTION

During the First Committee's discussion of the topic, Norway informed the Committee that, through a note dated 20 July to the depositary Governments, it had proposed the holding of a second review conference in 1986 and that, as of 29 October 1984, 58 of the 100 States parties to the Convention had supported the proposal; an informal meeting of the States parties (New York, 6 November) had recommended that the preparatory committee of the review conference hold one session in April/May 1986.

On 12 December 1984, the General Assembly, on the recommendation of the First Committee, adopted resolution 39/65 D without vote.

Review Conference of the Parties to the Convention on the Prohibition of the Development, Production and Stockpiling of Bacteriological (Biological) and Toxin Weapons and on Their Destruction

The General Assembly,

Recalling its resolution 2826(XXVI) of 16 December 1971 in which it commended the Convention on the Prohibition of the Development, Production and Stockpiling of Bacteriological (Biological) and Toxin Weapons and on Their Destruction, and expressed the hope for the widest possible adherence to the Convention,

Noting that, in accordance with the provisions of article XII of the Convention, the first Review Conference of the Parties to the Convention on the Prohibition of the Development, Production and Stockpiling of Bacteriological (Biological) and Toxin Weapons and on Their Destruction was held at Geneva from 3 to 21 March 1980,

Bearing in mind that the Review Conference decided, in its Final Declaration, that a second Review Conference should be held at Geneva at the request of a majority of States parties not earlier than 1985 and, in any case, not later than 1990,

Recalling its resolution 35/144 A of 12 December 1980, in which it welcomed the Final Declaration of the Review Conference of the Parties to the Convention,

1. *Notes* that, at the request of a majority of States parties to the Convention on the Prohibition of the Development, Production and Stockpiling of Bacteriological (Biological) and Toxin Weapons and on Their Destruction, a second Review Conference of the Parties

to the Convention will be held in 1986, and that, following appropriate consultations, a preparatory committee is to be established prior to the holding of the Review Conference;

2. *Requests* the Secretary-General to render the necessary assistance and to provide such services, including summary records, as may be required for the second Review Conference and its preparation.

General Assembly resolution 39/65 D

12 December 1984   Meeting 97   Adopted without vote

Approved by First Committee (A/39/754) without vote, 19 November (meeting 41); 48-nation draft (A/C.1/39/L.27); agenda item 64.

Sponsors: Argentina, Australia, Austria, Bangladesh, Belgium, Bolivia, Canada, Chile, Colombia, Costa Rica, Czechoslovakia, Denmark, Ecuador, France, Finland, German Democratic Republic, Germany, Federal Republic of, Greece, Hungary, Iceland, India, Ireland, Italy, Jamaica, Mexico, Netherlands, New Zealand, Niger, Nigeria, Norway, Pakistan, Philippines, Poland, Romania, Rwanda, Senegal, Singapore, Spain, Sweden, Thailand, Togo, Tunisia, Turkey, USSR, United Kingdom, United States, Uruguay, Yugoslavia.

Meeting numbers. GA 39th session: 1st Committee 3-36, 41; plenary 97.

Draft convention on chemical weapons

Activities of the Conference on Disarmament. Negotiations on a convention banning chemical weapons continued in 1984 in the Conference on Disarmament,[7] which considered the question from 12 to 16 March and from 9 to 13 July.

In addition to the report of the *Ad Hoc* Working Group on Chemical Weapons (16 January–6 February 1984),[8] which met as agreed by the Committee on Disarmament—the predecessor to the Conference—in 1983,[9] the Conference received a large number of proposals during the year.

China put forward its proposals on major elements of a future chemical weapons convention,[10] in which it asserted, among other things, that the countries possessing such weapons should first destroy the most toxic and dangerous in their arsenals.

The Federal Republic of Germany submitted three papers—prohibition of transfer and permitted transfers,[11] ban on use and the right of withdrawal in a future convention[12] and verification of destruction.[13] It asserted that all technological prerequisites existed for verifying the destruction and that only a continuous monitoring system could guarantee effective verification.

France, in its proposal on eliminating stocks and production facilities,[14] suggested that States parties to a convention should complete such endeavours within 10 years of the convention's entry into force; international on-site inspection would verify the destruction process.

Iran put forward proposals on the general provisions of a convention,[15] in which the use of chemical weapons would constitute a war crime.

The Netherlands proposal on size and structure of a chemical disarmament inspectorate[16] concluded that a future international inspectorate would be relatively limited in size.

A group of socialist States submitted two documents—improved effectiveness of the work of the Conference on Disarmament in prohibiting chemical weapons,[17] containing suggestions for formulating the text of a convention; and the organization and functioning of a consultative committee,[18] for ensuring adherence to the convention.

The United Kingdom submitted two documents. One, on a chemical weapons convention: verification and compliance—the challenge element,[19] dealt with initiating investigation, in addition to mandatory routine on-site inspection, following a challenge, in order to maintain confidence in a convention. A second, on verification of non-production of chemical weapons,[20] dealt with identification of compounds that should be subject to declarations and monitoring, and proposed a classification of compounds according to risk in terms of biological hazard and of threat to the convention.

The United States submitted a text of a draft convention,[21] which included a verification proposal based on what were termed open-invitation inspections, by which States parties would enter into a mutual obligation to open for international inspection on short notice all their military, government-owned or -controlled facilities. Subsequently, the United States submitted a working paper on a declaration and interim monitoring of stockpiles.[22]

Yugoslavia's proposal on national verification measures[23] dealt with co-operation between a consultative committee, an international team of experts and a national authority.

Before the beginning of the 1984 session, Sweden submitted two documents, on the verification of the destruction of stockpiles[24] and the prohibition of military preparations for use of chemical weapons.[25] Denmark,[26] Finland[27] and Norway[28]—which were not members of the Conference—also submitted documents dealing with verification aspects.

Also before the Conference was a 23 February letter from Czechoslovakia, transmitting a proposal made in January by the member States of the Warsaw Treaty Organization to those of NATO on the convening of a meeting in 1984 to exchange views on freeing Europe of chemical weapons.[29]

The Conference re-established on 28 February a subsidiary body, subsequently designated as the *Ad Hoc* Committee on Chemical Weapons, to elaborate and negotiate a convention. Under the chairmanship of Rolf Ekéus (Sweden), the Committee held 22 meetings between 29 February and 28 August; in addition, the Chairman held a number of informal consultations.

The Committee set up three working groups to deal with specific spheres of the convention: Working Group A, on scope and definitions; Working

Group B, on elimination of stocks and facilities; and Working Group C, on compliance. The issues of the prohibition of use of chemical weapons and the structure of the convention were dealt with directly by the Committee Chairman with the assistance of a number of delegations.

The report of the *Ad Hoc* Committee—later incorporated into the Conference's report to the General Assembly[7]—contained three annexes. Annex I reflected the results of preliminary drafting on some provisions of the future convention, based on the results achieved in the Working Groups and the Chairman's proposals. Annex II contained the reports of the Chairmen of the three Working Groups. Annex III contained the texts of the draft convention proposed by the United States,[21] the working paper by the socialist States on the consultative committee[18] and a 1982 USSR proposal on the basic provisions of a convention.[30]

The preliminary structure of the convention, as contained in Annex I of the *Ad Hoc* Committee's report, consisted of: a preamble; general provisions on scope; definitions and criteria; declarations; measures on chemical weapons; measures on production facilities; permitted activities; national implementation measures; consultative committee; consultations, co-operation and fact-finding; assistance; economic and technological development; relation to other international agreements; amendments; duration, withdrawal; signature, ratification, entry into force; languages; and annexes and other documents. It was understood that the texts reproduced in the annex did not contain all positions or reflect all proposals regarding the placement of provisions; in the texts, differing views appeared within brackets in cases where alternative formulations were suggested.

The Conference on Disarmament adopted the recommendations of the *Ad Hoc* Committee that further negotiation and drafting of a convention should be based on the contents of annexes I and II, together with other relevant current and future documents of the Conference. It also agreed that the Committee resume its work between 14 January and 1 February 1985 and deal with, among other things, the issues of permitted activities and verification on challenge; that the Committee be re-established at the beginning of the 1985 session of the Conference; and that a decision be taken in the first part of that session on inter-sessional work, so that the period between September 1985 and January 1986 would be more fully utilized for negotiations.

GENERAL ASSEMBLY ACTION

In 1984, the General Assembly, acting on the recommendation of the First Committee, adopted three resolutions on the prohibition of chemical and bacteriological (biological) weapons, in each of which it urged the Conference on Disarmament

to speed up its negotiations on a multilateral convention to that end.

On 12 December, the Assembly adopted resolution 39/65 A by recorded vote.

Chemical and bacteriological (biological) weapons

The General Assembly,

Reaffirming the urgent necessity of strict observance by all States of the principles and objectives of the Protocol for the Prohibition of the Use in War of Asphyxiating, Poisonous or Other Gases, and of Bacteriological Methods of Warfare, signed at Geneva on 17 June 1925, and of the adherence by all States to the Convention on the Prohibition of the Development, Production and Stockpiling of Bacteriological (Biological) and Toxin Weapons and on Their Destruction, signed in London, Moscow and Washington on 10 April 1972,

Noting that it has been reported that such weapons have been used,

Noting also international efforts under way to strengthen relevant international prohibitions, including efforts to develop appropriate fact-finding mechanisms,

Rededicating its efforts to protect mankind from chemical and biological warfare,

1. *Calls* for strict observance of existing international obligations regarding prohibitions on chemical and biological weapons and condemns actions that contravene them;

2. *Welcomes* the ongoing efforts to ensure the most effective prohibitions possible on chemical and biological weapons;

3. *Urges* the Conference on Disarmament to accelerate its negotiations on a multilateral convention on the complete and effective prohibition of the development, production and stockpiling of chemical weapons and on their destruction.

General Assembly resolution 39/65 A

12 December 1984   Meeting 97   118-16-14 (recorded vote)

Approved by First Committee (A/39/754) by recorded vote (99-14-13), 21 November (meeting 46); 17-nation draft (A/C.1/39/L.10/Rev.1); agenda item 64.

Sponsors: Australia, Belgium, Canada, Colombia, Costa Rica, Denmark, Ecuador, Italy, Japan, Kenya, Netherlands, Norway, Sierra Leone, Sweden, United Kingdom, United States, Uruguay.

Meeting numbers. GA 39th session: 1st Committee 3-36, 46; plenary 97.

Recorded vote in Assembly as follows:

In favour: Antigua and Barbuda, Argentina, Australia, Austria, Bahamas,[a] Bahrain, Bangladesh, Barbados, Belgium, Belize, Bhutan, Bolivia, Botswana, Brazil, Brunei Darussalam, Burma, Burundi, Cameroon, Canada, Central African Republic, Chad, Chile, China, Colombia, Comoros, Costa Rica, Democratic Kampuchea, Denmark, Djibouti, Dominica, Dominican Republic, Ecuador, Egypt, El Salvador, Equatorial Guinea, Fiji, Finland, France, Gabon, Germany, Federal Republic of, Ghana, Greece, Guatemala, Guinea, Guinea-Bissau, Guyana, Haiti, Honduras, Iceland, Indonesia, Iran, Iraq, Ireland, Italy, Ivory Coast, Jamaica, Japan, Jordan, Kenya, Kuwait, Lebanon, Lesotho, Liberia, Luxembourg, Malawi, Malaysia, Maldives, Mali, Malta, Mauritania, Mauritius, Morocco, Nepal, Netherlands, New Zealand, Niger, Nigeria, Norway, Oman, Pakistan, Panama, Papua New Guinea, Paraguay, Peru, Philippines, Portugal, Qatar, Rwanda, Saint Lucia, Samoa, Sao Tome and Principe, Saudi Arabia, Senegal, Sierra Leone, Singapore, Somalia, Spain, Sri Lanka, Sudan, Suriname, Thailand, Togo, Trinidad and Tobago, Tunisia, Turkey, Uganda, United Arab Emirates, United Kingdom, United Republic of Tanzania, United States, Uruguay, Vanuatu, Venezuela, Yemen, Zaire, Zambia, Zimbabwe.

Against: Afghanistan, Bulgaria, Byelorussian SSR, Cuba, Czechoslovakia, Democratic Yemen, German Democratic Republic, Hungary, Lao People's Democratic Republic, Libyan Arab Jamahiriya, Mongolia, Mozambique, Poland, Ukrainian SSR, USSR, Viet Nam.

Abstaining: Algeria, Angola, Benin, Burkina Faso, Cape Verde, Congo, Cyprus, Ethiopia, India, Madagascar, Mexico, Nicaragua, Romania, Yugoslavia.

[a]Later advised the Secretariat it had intended to abstain.

A number of delegations explained their votes. Cuba said the composition of fact-finding mechanisms—mentioned in the text and being promoted by some in the Conference on Disarmament—discriminated against the non-aligned countries; further, it believed the text tried to conceal, by referring to chemical warfare, the need for an explicit prohibition of the use of chemical weapons. Viet Nam felt the text aimed at whitewashing the chemical warfare conducted in that country by the United States and at covering the production of new kinds of chemical weapons, such as binary weapons. The USSR considered the draft an example of the policy of confrontation. The Lao People's Democratic Republic felt the convention being considered in the Conference on Disarmament would offer the most effective guarantee of the non-use of chemical weapons.

Yugoslavia saw the text as a continuation of an action it had not supported in previous years. Brazil understood that the mention of efforts to strengthen relevant international prohibitions referred specifically to the ongoing Conference negotiations on a convention, which was expected to reinforce the 1925 Geneva Protocol. Similarly, Indonesia supported the kind of comprehensive convention that was being elaborated.

On 12 December, the General Assembly adopted resolution 39/65 B by recorded vote.

Prohibition of chemical and bacteriological weapons

The General Assembly,

Recalling paragraph 75 of the Final Document of the Tenth Special Session of the General Assembly, which states that the complete and effective prohibition of the development, production and stockpiling of all chemical weapons and their destruction represents one of the most urgent measures of disarmament,

Referring to the unanimous and categorical reaffirmation by all Member States at the twelfth special session of the General Assembly of the validity of the Final Document of the Tenth Special Session,

Convinced of the need for the earliest conclusion of a convention on the prohibition of the development, production and stockpiling of all chemical weapons and on their destruction, which would significantly contribute to general and complete disarmament under effective international control,

Recalling its resolutions 36/96 B of 9 December 1981, 37/98 A of 13 December 1982 and 38/187 A of 20 December 1983,

Expressing profound concern at the intended production and deployment of binary chemical weapons,

Taking into consideration the decision by the Conference on Disarmament on the mandate for the *Ad Hoc* Committee on Chemical Weapons, as well as the work of this Committee during the session of the Conference in 1984,

Deeming it desirable for States to refrain from taking any action that could delay or further complicate negotiations and to display a constructive approach to such negotiations and the political will to reach an early agreement on the chemical weapons convention,

Aware that the qualitative improvement and development of chemical weapons complicate ongoing negotiations on the prohibition of chemical weapons,

Taking note of proposals on the creation of chemical-weapon-free zones aimed at facilitating the complete prohibition of chemical weapons,

1. *Reaffirms* the necessity of the speediest elaboration and conclusion of a convention on the prohibition of the development, production and stockpiling of all chemical weapons and on their destruction;

2. *Appeals* to all States to facilitate in every possible way the conclusion of such a convention;

3. *Urges* the Conference on Disarmament to intensify the negotiations in the *Ad Hoc* Committee on Chemical Weapons with a view to achieving accord on a chemical weapons convention at the earliest possible date and, for this purpose, to proceed immediately to drafting such a convention for submission to the General Assembly at its fortieth session;

4. *Reaffirms its call* to all States to conduct serious negotiations in good faith and to refrain from any action that could impede negotiations on the prohibition of chemical weapons and specifically to refrain from the production and deployment of binary and other new types of chemical weapons, as well as from stationing chemical weapons on the territory of other States.

General Assembly resolution 39/65 B

12 December 1984　　　　Meeting 97　　　　84-1-62 (recorded vote)

Approved by First Committee (A/39/754) by recorded vote (75-1-51), 21 November (meeting 46); 13-nation draft (A/C.1/39/L.15); agenda item 64.

Sponsors: Afghanistan, Angola, Bulgaria, Byelorussian SSR, Czechoslovakia, German Democratic Republic, Hungary, Lao People's Democratic Republic, Mongolia, Poland, Ukrainian SSR, USSR, Viet Nam.

Meeting numbers. GA 39th session: 1st Committee 3-36, 39, 46; plenary 97.

Recorded vote in Assembly as follows:

In favour: Afghanistan, Algeria, Angola, Antigua and Barbuda, Bahrain, Bangladesh, Barbados, Belize, Benin, Bhutan, Bolivia, Botswana, Bulgaria, Burkina Faso, Burundi, Byelorussian SSR, Cameroon, Central African Republic, Comoros, Congo, Cuba, Cyprus, Czechoslovakia, Democratic Yemen, Ecuador, Egypt, Equatorial Guinea, Ethiopia, Fiji, German Democratic Republic, Ghana, Guinea, Guyana, Hungary, Indonesia, Iran, Iraq, Jordan, Kenya, Kuwait, Lao People's Democratic Republic, Lebanon, Lesotho, Libyan Arab Jamahiriya, Madagascar, Malawi, Malaysia, Maldives, Mali, Mauritania, Mauritius, Mexico, Mongolia, Mozambique, Nicaragua, Nigeria, Oman, Pakistan, Panama, Papua New Guinea, Peru, Poland, Qatar, Romania, Saudi Arabia, Senegal, Sierra Leone, Somalia, Syrian Arab Republic, Thailand, Togo, Trinidad and Tobago, Tunisia, Uganda, Ukrainian SSR, USSR, United Arab Emirates, United Republic of Tanzania, Vanuatu, Viet Nam, Yemen, Yugoslavia, Zambia, Zimbabwe.

Against: United States.

Abstaining: Argentina, Australia, Austria, Bahamas, Belgium, Brazil, Brunei Darussalam, Burma, Canada, Cape Verde, Chad, Chile, China, Colombia, Costa Rica, Democratic Kampuchea, Denmark, Djibouti, Dominica, Dominican Republic, El Salvador, Finland, France, Gabon, Germany, Federal Republic of, Greece, Guatemala, Guinea-Bissau, Haiti, Honduras, Iceland, India, Ireland, Italy, Ivory Coast, Jamaica, Japan, Liberia, Luxembourg, Morocco, Nepal, Netherlands, New Zealand, Niger, Norway, Paraguay, Philippines, Portugal, Rwanda, Saint Lucia, Samoa, Singapore, Spain, Sri Lanka, Sudan, Suriname, Sweden, Turkey, United Kingdom, Uruguay, Venezuela, Zaire.

Explaining its vote, Belgium said it shared the principles contained in paragraphs 1 and 3 but did not approve paragraph 4, which, in its view, made a pernicious distinction between bad chemical binary weapons which the United States was contemplating and good ones which the USSR was supposed to be producing. Brazil objected to the mention of chemical-weapon-free zones and the singling out of specific types of chemical weapons as matters of special concern. Sharing that view,

Australia added that the text made no mention of including a ban on use in the scope of a future convention. Along the same vein, the Netherlands felt that the USSR had failed to match the restraint it believed the United States had shown on chemical weapons. Democratic Kampuchea abstained because one of the sponsors of the text, it asserted, had used such weapons in its territory.

On 12 December, the General Assembly adopted resolution 39/65 C without vote.

Chemical and bacteriological (biological) weapons

The General Assembly,

Recalling its previous resolutions relating to the complete and effective prohibition of the development, production and stockpiling of all chemical weapons and to their destruction,

Reaffirming the urgent necessity of strict observance by all States of the principles and objectives of the Protocol for the Prohibition of the Use in War of Asphyxiating, Poisonous or Other Gases, and of Bacteriological Methods of Warfare, signed at Geneva on 17 June 1925, and of the adherence by all States to the Convention on the Prohibition of the Development, Production and Stockpiling of Bacteriological (Biological) and Toxin Weapons and on Their Destruction, signed in London, Moscow and Washington on 10 April 1972,

Having considered the report of the Conference on Disarmament, which incorporates, *inter alia*, the report of its *Ad Hoc* Committee on Chemical Weapons,

Considering it necessary that all efforts be exerted for the continuation and successful conclusion of negotiations on the prohibition of the development, production and stockpiling of all chemical weapons and on their destruction,

1. *Takes note* of the work of the Conference on Disarmament during its session in 1984 regarding the prohibition of chemical weapons and, in particular, appreciates the work of its *Ad Hoc* Committee on Chemical Weapons on that question and the progress achieved therein;

2. *Expresses its regret and concern* that an agreement on the complete and effective prohibition of the development, production and stockpiling of all chemical weapons and on their destruction has not yet been elaborated;

3. *Urges again* the Conference on Disarmament, as a matter of high priority, to intensify, during its session in 1985, the negotiations on such a convention and to reinforce further its efforts, *inter alia*, by increasing the time during the year that the Conference on Disarmament devotes to such negotiations, taking into account all existing proposals and future initiatives, with a view to the final elaboration of a convention at the earliest possible date, and to re-establish its *Ad Hoc* Committee on Chemical Weapons for this purpose with the 1984 mandate;

4. *Requests* the Conference on Disarmament to report to the General Assembly at its fortieth session on the results of its negotiations.

General Assembly resolution 39/65 C

12 December 1984   Meeting 97   Adopted without vote

Approved by First Committee (A/39/754) without vote, 21 November (meeting 46); 19-nation draft (A/C.1/39/L.24); agenda item 64.

Sponsors: Argentina, Australia, Belgium, Canada, German Democratic Republic, Germany, Federal Republic of, Indonesia, Ireland, Japan, Kenya, Mongolia, Netherlands, Norway, Poland, Rwanda, Spain, Ukrainian SSR, Uruguay, Viet Nam.

Meeting numbers. GA 39th session: 1st Committee 3-36, 39, 46; plenary 97.

In explanation of position, the Netherlands noted that the text, by virtue of its consensus character, underlined the general agreement on the need to work for a ban on chemical weapons. For Brazil, the text was entirely satisfactory.

In a statement on all the drafts on chemical weapons, Finland stressed the importance of strict adherence to the 1925 Protocol until an agreement was reached on a comprehensive ban and said that the Protocol's lack of credible assurances concerning verification must be corrected in a future ban on chemical weapons.

Bangladesh supported resolutions 39/65 A and C despite what it felt were certain one-sided and contradictory positions contained in them, because it believed their underlying spirit conformed with mankind's common desire to promote negotiations on the prohibition of chemical weapons; its vote did not imply endorsement of any negotiating position of the principal contenders.

Alleged uses of chemical and bacteriological (biological) weapons

In 1984, the Secretary-General received communications from several States concerning the alleged use of chemical weapons (see Chapter VII of this section).

On 21 February,[31] the United States presented information on the alleged use of chemical and toxin weapons in Afghanistan and South-East Asia, updating a report submitted in 1983,[32] asserting, among other things, that there appeared to be a diminution of attacks in Afghanistan, and a decrease in the lethality of attacks in Democratic Kampuchea and the Lao People's Democratic Republic; at the same time, it claimed that evidence existed of continuing use in those two countries of an as yet unidentified, non-lethal agent or agents.

New weapons of mass destruction, including radiological weapons

In December 1984, the General Assembly requested the Conference on Disarmament to intensify its negotiations leading to a draft agreement banning the development and manufacture of new types of weapons of mass destruction and new systems of such weapons (39/62) and to continue considering the question of radiological weapons with a view to concluding its work promptly on reaching agreement on a convention prohibiting them (39/151 J).

Consideration by the Conference on Disarmament. The Conference on Disarmament[7] considered the item "New types of weapons of mass destruction and new systems of such weapons;

radiological weapons" from 2 to 6 April and from 30 July to 3 August 1984. A contact group was set up at the beginning of the first part of the session to consider the establishment of a subsidiary body on the question.

In a memorandum of 17 February,[33] a group of socialist countries members of the Conference proposed such a body to draft, with the assistance of qualified governmental experts, a comprehensive agreement on banning the development and manufacture of new types of weapons of mass destruction and new systems of such weapons, and possible agreements on particular types of such weapons, as well as to deal with questions relating to radiological weapons.

Some other delegations continued to maintain that agreements to ban potential new weapons of mass destruction should be negotiated only on a case-by-case basis as those weapons might be identified, and pointed out that none had been identified.

On 17 April, the *Ad Hoc* Committee on Radiological Weapons was established with a view to reaching agreement on a convention prohibiting the development, production, stockpiling and use of such weapons. The Committee held 11 meetings from 15 June to 10 August, under the chairmanship of Milos Vejvoda (Czechoslovakia), who also held a number of informal consultations. As in previous years, it continued examining questions relating to "traditional" radiological weapons subject-matter and those relating to prohibition of attacks against nuclear facilities, without setting up two subsidiary bodies to deal with those questions or prejudging the relationship between them. Working papers were submitted in 1984 by the Federal Republic of Germany, Sweden and the United Kingdom; the Committee Chairman also presented a working paper in August, reflecting some of the proposals made by delegations during the session.

On 12 July, the *Ad Hoc* Committee adopted a work programme, by which it decided to discuss—without prejudging the final positions of delegations as regards the link between the two aspects of the issue—problems such as definitions, scope, peaceful uses, cessation of the nuclear-arms race and nuclear disarmament, and compliance and verification.

The Committee concluded that its discussions had contributed to a better understanding of the issues, as well as to a further search for their solution. Because the Committee's mandate had not been fulfilled, it recommended that the Conference on Disarmament re-establish the *Ad Hoc* Committee at the beginning of its 1985 session. On 23 August, the Conference adopted the Committee's report as part of its own report to the General Assembly.

GENERAL ASSEMBLY ACTION

In 1984, the General Assembly, on the recommendation of the First Committee, adopted two resolutions aimed at banning new weapons of mass destruction.

On 12 December, it adopted resolution 39/62 by recorded vote.

Prohibition of the development and manufacture of new types of weapons of mass destruction and new systems of such weapons

The General Assembly,

Recalling its resolutions 3479(XXX) of 11 December 1975, 31/74 of 10 December 1976, 32/84 A of 12 December 1977, 33/66 B of 14 December 1978, 34/79 of 11 December 1979, 35/149 of 12 December 1980, 36/89 of 9 December 1981, 37/77 A of 9 December 1982 and 38/182 of 20 December 1983 concerning the prohibition of new types of weapons of mass destruction,

Bearing in mind the provisions of paragraph 39 of the Final Document of the Tenth Special Session of the General Assembly, according to which qualitative and quantitative disarmament measures are both important for halting the arms race and efforts to that end must include negotiations on the limitation and cessation of the qualitative improvement of armaments, especially weapons of mass destruction, and the development of new means of warfare,

Recalling the decision contained in paragraph 77 of the Final Document to the effect that, in order to help prevent a qualitative arms race and so that scientific and technological achievements might ultimately be used solely for peaceful purposes, effective measures should be taken to prevent the emergence of new types of weapons of mass destruction based on new scientific principles and achievements, and that efforts aiming at the prohibition of such new types and new systems of weapons of mass destruction should be appropriately pursued,

Expressing once again its firm belief, in the light of the decisions adopted at the tenth special session, in the importance of concluding an agreement or agreements to prevent the use of scientific and technological progress for the development of new types of weapons of mass destruction and new systems of such weapons,

Noting that in the course of its session in 1984 the Conference on Disarmament considered the item entitled "New types of weapons of mass destruction and new systems of such weapons; radiological weapons",

Convinced that all ways and means should be utilized to prevent the development and manufacture of new types of weapons of mass destruction and new systems of such weapons,

Taking into consideration the report of the Conference on Disarmament relating to this question,

1. *Requests* the Conference on Disarmament, in the light of its existing priorities, to intensify negotiations, with the assistance of qualified governmental experts, with a view to preparing a draft comprehensive agreement on the prohibition of the development and manufacture of new types of weapons of mass destruction and new systems of such weapons, and to draft possible agreements on particular types of such weapons;

2. *Once again urges* all States to refrain from any action which could adversely affect the talks aimed at work-

ing out an agreement or agreements to prevent the emergence of new types of weapons of mass destruction and new systems of such weapons;

3. *Calls upon* the States permanent members of the Security Council as well as upon other militarily significant States to make declarations, identical in substance, concerning the refusal to create new types of weapons of mass destruction and new systems of such weapons, as a first step towards the conclusion of a comprehensive agreement on this subject, bearing in mind that such declarations would be approved thereafter by a decision of the Security Council;

4. *Calls again upon* all States to undertake efforts to ensure that ultimately scientific and technological achievements may be used solely for peaceful purposes;

5. *Requests* the Secretary-General to transmit to the Conference on Disarmament all documents relating to the consideration of this item by the General Assembly at its thirty-ninth session;

6. *Requests* the Conference on Disarmament to submit a report on the results achieved to the General Assembly for consideration at its fortieth session;

7. *Decides* to include in the provisional agenda of its fortieth session the item entitled "Prohibition of the development and manufacture of new types of weapons of mass destruction and new systems of such weapons: report of the Conference on Disarmament".

General Assembly resolution 39/62

12 December 1984   Meeting 97   125-1-23 (recorded vote)

Approved by First Committee (A/39/748) by recorded vote (111-1-24), 20 November (meeting 43); 26-nation draft (A/C.1/39/L.63); agenda item 58.

Sponsors: Afghanistan, Angola, Benin, Bulgaria, Burkina Faso, Burundi, Byelorussian SSR, Congo, Cuba, Czechoslovakia, Democratic Yemen, Ethiopia, German Democratic Republic, Guinea, Hungary, Lao People's Democratic Republic, Libyan Arab Jamahiriya, Mongolia, Mozambique, Poland, Romania, Syrian Arab Republic, Ukrainian SSR, USSR, Viet Nam, Zimbabwe.

Meeting numbers. GA 39th session: 1st Committee 3-36, 39, 43; plenary 97.

Recorded vote in Assembly as follows:

In favour: Afghanistan, Algeria, Angola, Antigua and Barbuda, Argentina, Bahamas, Bahrain, Bangladesh, Barbados, Belize, Benin, Bhutan, Bolivia, Botswana, Brazil, Brunei Darussalam, Bulgaria, Burkina Faso, Burma, Burundi, Byelorussian SSR, Cameroon, Cape Verde, Central African Republic, Chad, Chile, Colombia, Comoros, Congo, Costa Rica, Cuba, Cyprus, Czechoslovakia, Democratic Yemen, Djibouti, Dominica, Dominican Republic, Ecuador, Egypt, El Salvador, Equatorial Guinea, Ethiopia, Fiji, Finland, Gabon, German Democratic Republic, Ghana, Guatemala, Guinea, Guinea-Bissau, Guyana, Haiti, Honduras, Hungary, India, Indonesia, Iran, Iraq, Ivory Coast, Jordan, Kenya, Kuwait, Lao People's Democratic Republic, Lebanon, Lesotho, Liberia, Libyan Arab Jamahiriya, Madagascar, Malawi, Malaysia, Maldives, Mali, Malta, Mauritania, Mauritius, Mexico, Mongolia, Morocco, Mozambique, Nepal, Nicaragua, Niger, Nigeria, Oman, Pakistan, Panama, Papua New Guinea, Paraguay, Peru, Philippines, Poland, Qatar, Romania, Rwanda, Saint Lucia, Samoa, Sao Tome and Principe, Saudi Arabia, Senegal, Seychelles, Sierra Leone, Singapore, Somalia, Sri Lanka, Sudan, Suriname, Syrian Arab Republic, Thailand, Togo, Trinidad and Tobago, Tunisia, Uganda, Ukrainian SSR, USSR, United Arab Emirates, United Republic of Tanzania, Uruguay, Vanuatu, Venezuela, Viet Nam, Yemen, Yugoslavia, Zaire, Zambia, Zimbabwe.

Against: United States.

Abstaining: Australia, Austria, Belgium, Canada, China, Denmark, France, Germany, Federal Republic of, Greece, Iceland, Ireland, Israel, Italy, Japan, Luxembourg, Netherlands, New Zealand, Norway, Portugal, Spain, Sweden, Turkey, United Kingdom.

In explanation of vote, Ireland, speaking on behalf of the 10 States members of the European Community, asserted that there should be a prohibition of any new weapons of mass destruction if and when they could be identified; a single blanket prohibition of the type proposed would

risk undermining progress in research and development without necessarily helping prevent the emergence of new types of weapons; the approach contained in the text did not reflect the difficulty of establishing the precise delimitations of civilian and military research or the growing interaction between them. Australia shared that view. Sweden also questioned the value of a general prohibition, while supporting efforts to ensure peaceful uses of new major scientific discoveries; it noted with satisfaction that the Conference on Disarmament was requested to draft possible agreements on prohibiting particular weapon types.

On 17 December, the General Assembly adopted resolution 39/151 J without vote.

Prohibition of the development, production, stockpiling and use of radiological weapons

The General Assembly,

Recalling its resolution 38/188 D of 20 December 1983,

1. *Takes note* of that part of the report of the Conference on Disarmament that deals with the question of radiological weapons, in particular the report of the *Ad Hoc* Committee on Radiological Weapons and its recommendation that, in view of the fact that the Committee's mandate was not fulfilled, the Conference on Disarmament should re-establish the *Ad Hoc* Committee on Radiological Weapons at the beginning of its 1985 session;

2. *Requests* the Conference on Disarmament to continue its negotiations on the subject with a view to a prompt conclusion of its work, taking into account all proposals presented to the Conference to this end, the result of which should be submitted to the General Assembly at its fortieth session;

3. *Requests* the Secretary-General to transmit to the Conference on Disarmament all relevant documents relating to the discussion of all aspects of the issue by the General Assembly at its thirty-ninth session;

4. *Decides* to include in the provisional agenda of its fortieth session the item entitled "Prohibition of the development, production, stockpiling and use of radiological weapons".

General Assembly resolution 39/151 J

17 December 1984   Meeting 102   Adopted without vote

Approved by First Committee (A/39/755) without vote, 19 November (meeting 41); 4-nation draft (A/C.1/39/L.68); agenda item 65 (e).

Sponsors: Czechoslovakia, Germany, Federal Republic of, Japan, Sweden.

Meeting numbers. GA 39th session: 1st Committee 3-37, 41; plenary 102.

REFERENCES

(1)A/39/488. (2)YUN 1982, p. 94, GA res. 37/98 D, 13 Dec. 1982. (3)YUN 1983, p. 58. (4)YUN 1969, p. 734. (5)YUN 1971, p. 19, GA res. 2826(XXVI), annex, 16 Dec. 1971. (6)YUN 1980, p. 70. (7)A/39/27. (8)CD/429. (9)YUN 1983, p. 60. (10)CD/443. (11)CD/439. (12)CD/496. (13)CD/518. (14)CD/494. (15)CD/483. (16)CD/445. (17)CD/435. (18)CD/532. (19)CD/431. (20)CD/514. (21)CD/500. (22)CD/516. (23)CD/482. (24)CD/425. (25)CD/426. (26)CD/537. (27)CD/505. (28)CD/508 & CD/509. (29)CD/437. (30)YUN 1982, p. 98. (31)A/39/113. (32)YUN 1983, p. 62. (33)CD/434.

Conventional weapons

Conventional arms and armed forces absorbed four fifths of the almost $800 billion spent in 1983 on military activities, according to a study on conventional disarmament, completed in 1984 by an expert group; in resolution 39/151 C, the General Assembly invited States to comment on the study.

The Assembly again invited States to submit their views on holding negotiations on limiting and reducing naval armaments (resolution 39/151 I). A group of governmental experts held two sessions during the year to try to prepare a study on the naval arms race, naval forces and naval arms systems. The Assembly called for wider adherence to the 1980 Convention on Prohibitions or Restrictions on the Use of Certain Conventional Weapons Which May Be Deemed to Be Excessively Injurious or to Have Indiscriminate Effects, and its three Protocols[1] (resolution 39/56).

Study by Group of Experts

In August 1984, the Secretary-General submitted to the General Assembly a study, carried out by a group of experts, on all aspects of the conventional arms race and on disarmament relating to conventional weapons and armed forces.[2] The Secretary-General noted that the study constituted the first effort at a comprehensive consideration of the subject as a whole, that over 20 million people had died in some 150 armed conflicts since the end of the Second World War, and that additional efforts were needed for effective conventional disarmament measures, in addition to those for nuclear disarmament.

As approved by the Assembly in 1980,[3] work on the study began when its guidelines were finalized by the Disarmament Commission in 1982.[4] The Group of Experts on All Aspects of the Conventional Arms Race and on Disarmament relating to Conventional Weapons and Armed Forces—experts from 23 countries, appointed by the Secretary-General in accordance with a 1981 Assembly request[5]—held a total of seven sessions between July 1982 and June 1984, including two in 1984 (New York, 23 January–3 February, 11-23 June), under the chairmanship of Skjold G. Mellbin (Denmark), and adopted its report on the study by consensus on 23 June.

The study sought to identify practical approaches to, and realistic measures for, limiting and reducing conventional weapons and armed forces, with a view to achieving general and complete disarmament under effective international control. It consisted of four parts—an introduction and chapters on: the nature, causes and effects of the conventional arms race; principles, approaches and measures relevant to conventional disarmament; and conclusions and recommendations. Annexed were guidelines for the study and working papers submitted to the Disarmament Commission by China, Denmark, the German Democratic Republic and India.

The Group stated that the current conventional arms race was closely related to the political tensions and differences between East and West and to confrontations elsewhere, including situations arising from foreign occupation, colonial domination, denial of the right of peoples to self-determination, racism and intervention. Citing information from various sources, the Group noted, among other things, that: conventional arms and armed forces absorbed four fifths of the almost $800 billion spent in 1983 on military activities, the global arms trade had progressively expanded (in constant 1981 prices) from $20.3 billion in 1972 to $34.3 billion in 1982, and during 1978-1982 the USSR and the United States accounted for about a third each of total world arms exports of major weapons. The massive consumption of resources for potentially destructive purposes, the Group concluded, ran counter to the objectives of promoting social progress and better standards of life.

While the Group, in view of the breadth and political sensitivity of the matter, did not make specific proposals, it pointed to certain topics which, depending on particular circumstances, could be pursued in consultations and negotiations, among them: restricting/reducing specified categories of major weapons, the number of military personnel, deployments of different types of armed forces, and military budgets and expenditure; qualitative restrictions on armaments, and qualitative/quantitative limitations on arms transfers; and measures concerned with the peaceful uses of outer space, weapons having indiscriminate effects, confidence-building measures, and reversal or curtailment of foreign military activities.

The Group felt that efforts by the USSR and the United States to improve their mutual relationship would facilitate practical steps of conventional arms limitation and disarmament; at the same time, all States should explore ways of contributing to conventional disarmament.

Given the complexity of the subject, the Group was unable to deal in depth with all the elements set out in the guidelines for the study agreed on by the Disarmament Commission, among them, factual account of all aspects of the conventional arms race, the international transfer of conventional weapons, and the impact of emerging technologies on the arms race. Further, there remained a need for thorough consideration of future developments in the conventional arms race and their impact on international security, and of approaches to negotiating agreements.

On 17 December 1984, the General Assembly, on the recommendation of the First Committee, adopted resolution 39/151 C without vote.

Study on conventional disarmament

The General Assembly,

Recalling its previous resolutions in which, *inter alia,* it approved the carrying out of a study on all aspects of the conventional arms race and on disarmament relating to conventional weapons and armed forces, to be undertaken by the Secretary-General with the assistance of a group of qualified experts appointed by him on a balanced geographical basis,

Recalling the discussions at the 1981 and 1982 substantive sessions of the Disarmament Commission on the general approach to the study, its structure and scope, which resulted in the establishment of agreed guidelines for the study,

Recalling also its resolution 38/188 A of 20 December 1983, by which it took note of the status report of the Secretary-General and requested him to continue the study and to submit the final report to the General Assembly at its thirty-ninth session,

Having examined the report of the Secretary-General containing the study,

1. *Takes note with satisfaction* of the study on all aspects of the conventional arms race and on disarmament relating to conventional weapons and armed forces,* prepared by the Secretary-General;

2. *Expresses its appreciation* to the Secretary-General and to the Group of Experts on All Aspects of the Conventional Arms Race and on Disarmament relating to Conventional Weapons and Armed Forces who assisted him in the preparation of the study;

3. *Draws the attention* of all the Member States to the study and its conclusions;

4. *Invites* all Member States to inform the Secretary-General, no later than 31 May 1985, of their views regarding the study;

5. *Requests* the Secretary-General to make the necessary arrangements for the reproduction of the study as a United Nations publication and to give it the widest possible distribution;

6. *Requests* the Secretary-General to prepare a report for the General Assembly at its fortieth session containing the views of Member States received regarding the study.

---

*The study was subsequently issued with the title *Study on Conventional Disarmament* (Sales No. E.85.IX.1).

General Assembly resolution 39/151 C

17 December 1984   Meeting 102   Adopted without vote

Approved by First Committee (A/39/755) by recorded vote (129-0-6), 19 November (meeting 42); draft by Denmark (A/C.1/39/L.16), orally revised; agenda item 65 *(c).*
Meeting numbers. GA 39th session: 1st Committee 3-37, 42; plenary 102.

Explaining its position in the First Committee, China felt that the study failed to emphasize the special responsibilities of the two super-Powers and that its recommendations were not sufficiently specific. The Federal Republic of Germany would have preferred a more detailed analysis of the causes of the world-wide accumulation of conventional weapons. It disagreed that there were no feasible means of reversing the trend, and felt that the conclusions had not been drawn from earlier studies or proposals concerning the steady growth in arms transfer; it recalled a proposal it had made at the beginning of the 1984 Assembly session—that the Assembly should establish a register to provide the international community with data on the extent and flow of the weapons trade.

Ratification of the 1980 Convention and Protocols

In a September report,[6] the Secretary-General, as depositary of the Convention on Prohibitions or Restrictions on the Use of Certain Conventional Weapons Which May Be Deemed to Be Excessively Injurious or to Have Indiscriminate Effects, and its three Protocols,[1] informed the General Assembly of the status of ratification as at 31 August 1984.

The Convention and Protocols, which entered into force in December 1983,[7] provided new rules to protect military personnel, civilians and civilian objects from injury or attack by means of incendiary weapons, land-mines, booby traps and other devices, as well as fragments that cannot be easily detected in the human body by X-rays.

As at 31 December 1984, there were 24 States parties to the Convention, India having ratified it during the year.[8] Those States had also accepted the three Protocols dealing with non-detectable fragments; mines, booby traps and other devices; and incendiary weapons.

On 12 December 1984, the General Assembly, on the recommendation of the First Committee, adopted resolution 39/56 without vote.

Convention on Prohibitions or Restrictions on the Use of Certain Conventional Weapons Which May Be Deemed to Be Excessively Injurious or to Have Indiscriminate Effects

The General Assembly,

Recalling its resolutions 32/152 of 19 December 1977, 35/153 of 12 December 1980, 36/93 of 9 December 1981, 37/79 of 9 December 1982 and 38/66 of 15 December 1983,

Recalling with satisfaction the adoption, on 10 October 1980, of the Convention on Prohibitions or Restrictions on the Use of Certain Conventional Weapons Which May Be Deemed to Be Excessively Injurious or to Have Indiscriminate Effects, together with the Protocol on Non-Detectable Fragments (Protocol I), the Protocol on Prohibitions or Restrictions on the Use of Mines, Booby Traps and Other Devices (Protocol II) and the Protocol on Prohibitions or Restrictions on the Use of Incendiary Weapons (Protocol III),

Reaffirming its conviction that general agreement on the prohibition or restriction of use of specific conventional weapons would significantly reduce the suffering of civilian populations and of combatants,

Taking note with satisfaction of the report of the Secretary-General,

1. *Notes with satisfaction* that an increasing number of States have either signed, ratified, accepted or acceded to the Convention on Prohibitions or Restrictions on the Use of Certain Conventional Weapons Which May Be Deemed to Be Excessively Injurious or to Have Indiscriminate Effects, which was opened for signature in New York on 10 April 1981;

2. *Further notes with satisfaction* that, consequent upon the fulfilment of the conditions set out in article 5 of the Convention, the Convention and the three Protocols annexed thereto entered into force on 2 December 1983;

3. *Urges* all States that have not yet done so to exert their best endeavours to become parties to the Convention and the Protocols annexed thereto as early as possible, so as ultimately to obtain universality of adherence;

4. *Notes* that, under article 8 of the Convention, conferences may be convened to consider amendments to the Convention or any of the annexed Protocols, to consider additional protocols relating to other categories of conventional weapons not covered by the existing annexed Protocols, or to review the scope and operation of the Convention and the Protocols annexed thereto and to consider any proposal for amendments to the Convention or to the existing Protocols and any proposals for additional protocols relating to other categories of conventional weapons not covered by the existing Protocols;

5. *Requests* the Secretary-General as depositary of the Convention and its three annexed Protocols to inform the General Assembly from time to time of the state of adherence to the Convention and its Protocols;

6. *Decides* to include in the provisional agenda of its fortieth session the item entitled "Convention on Prohibitions or Restrictions on the Use of Certain Conventional Weapons Which May Be Deemed to Be Excessively Injurious or to Have Indiscriminate Effects".

General Assembly resolution 39/56

12 December 1984   Meeting 97   Adopted without vote

Approved by First Committee (A/39/740) without vote, 19 November (meeting 41); 18-nation draft (A/C.1/39/L.52); agenda item 50.

Sponsors: Austria, Belgium, Cuba, Denmark, Ecuador, Finland, France, German Democratic Republic, Greece, Ireland, Italy, Netherlands, New Zealand, Nigeria, Norway, Sweden, United Kingdom, Yugoslavia.

Meeting numbers. GA 39th session: 1st Committee 3-36, 39, 41; plenary 97.

Naval armaments

In 1984, the General Assembly again invited Member States to submit their views on holding negotiations on limiting and reducing naval armaments (resolution 39/151 I). A group of governmental experts, appointed by the Secretary-General in accordance with a December 1983 Assembly request,[9] held two sessions in an effort to prepare a comprehensive study—for submission to the Assembly in 1985—on the naval arms race, naval forces and naval arms systems.

Experts' study

Early in 1984, the Secretary-General appointed a Group of Governmental Experts to Carry Out a Comprehensive Study on the Naval Arms Race, Naval Forces and Naval Arms Systems, composed of experts from China, France, Gabon, Indonesia, the Netherlands, Peru and Sweden.

The Group held two sessions in 1984, under the chairmanship of Ali Alatas (Indonesia). At its first session (New York, 9-13 April), the Group agreed on an outline for the draft study, a division of the task of preparing contributions and a timetable for action; at its second session (Geneva, 15-26 October), it considered the first draft of the report and discussed its future work. Two further sessions were scheduled for 1985.

Proposed negotiations

In a September 1984 report, with a later corrigendum,[10] the Secretary-General transmitted to the General Assembly the replies received from 11 Member States, in response to its December 1983 request[11] for views concerning the holding of negotiations on limiting and reducing naval armaments.

GENERAL ASSEMBLY ACTION

Acting on the recommendation of the First Committee, the General Assembly, on 17 December 1984, adopted resolution 39/151 I by recorded vote.

Curbing the naval arms race: limitation and reduction of naval armaments and extension of confidence-building measures to seas and oceans

The General Assembly,

Recalling its resolution 38/188 F of 20 December 1983,

Convinced that all channels of the arms race, in particular the nuclear-arms race, should be effectively covered by the efforts to halt and reverse it,

Disturbed by the growing threat to peace, international security and global stability posed by the continuing escalation of the naval arms race,

Alarmed by the ever more frequent use of naval fleets or other naval formations for demonstrations or use of force and as an instrument to exert pressure against sovereign States, especially developing countries, to interfere in their internal affairs, to commit acts of armed aggression and intervention and to preserve the remnants of the colonial system,

Aware that the growing presence of naval fleets and the intensification of the naval activities of some States in conflict areas or far from their own shores increase tensions in these regions and could adversely affect the security of the international sea lanes through these areas and the exploitation of maritime resources,

Firmly convinced that the undertaking of urgent steps to curb military confrontation at sea would be a significant contribution to preventing war, especially nuclear war, and to strengthening peace and international security,

Aware of the numerous initiatives and concrete proposals to undertake effective measures aimed at limiting naval activities, limiting and reducing naval armaments and extending confidence-building measures to seas and oceans,

Stressing once again the importance of relevant measures of a regional character, such as the implementation of the Declaration of the Indian Ocean as a Zone of Peace, and the transformation of the Mediterranean into a zone of peace, security and co-operation,

Reaffirming once again that seas and oceans, being of vital importance to mankind, should be used exclusively for peaceful purposes,

Taking note of the report of the Secretary-General, containing the replies of Member States, including a major naval Power, on the modalities for negotiations, as well as various specific ideas and new proposals for joint measures on curbing the naval arms race and naval activities,

Noting with satisfaction that the prevailing view expressed in these replies strongly favours an early commencement of negotiations aimed at curbing the naval arms race and naval activities, strengthening confidence and security at sea and reducing naval armaments,

1. *Appeals once again* to all Member States, in particular the major naval Powers, to refrain from enlarging their naval activities in areas of conflict or tensions, or far from their own shores;

2. *Reaffirms* its recognition of the urgent need to start negotiations with the participation of the major naval Powers, the nuclear-weapon States in particular, and other interested States on the limitation of naval activities, the limitation and reduction of naval armaments and the extension of confidence-building measures to seas and oceans, especially to areas with the busiest international sea lanes or to regions where the probability of conflict situations is high;

3. *Invites* Member States, particularly the major naval Powers, to consider the possibility of holding direct consultations, bilateral and/or multilateral, with a view to preparing the opening at an early date of such negotiations;

4. *Also invites* Member States, especially those that have not yet done so, to communicate to the Secretary-General not later than April 1985 their views concerning the modalities for holding the negotiations referred to above;

5. *Requests* the Disarmament Commission to consider this question and to report to the General Assembly at its fortieth session;

6. *Decides* to include in the provisional agenda of its fortieth session the item entitled "Curbing the naval arms race: limitation and reduction of naval armaments and extension of confidence-building measures to seas and oceans".

General Assembly resolution 39/151 I

17 December 1984   Meeting 102   70-19-53 (recorded vote)

Approved by First Committee (A/39/755) by recorded vote (68-20-45), 20 November (meeting 43); 8-nation draft (A/C.1/39/L.55); agenda item 65 *(g)*.

Sponsors: Bulgaria, Democratic Yemen, German Democratic Republic, Lao People's Democratic Republic, Libyan Arab Jamahiriya, Poland, Syrian Arab Republic, Viet Nam.

Meeting numbers. GA 39th session: 1st Committee 3-36, 40, 43; plenary 102.

Recorded vote in Assembly as follows:

In favour: Afghanistan, Algeria, Angola, Antigua and Barbuda, Argentina, Bahrain, Benin, Botswana, Bulgaria, Burkina Faso, Burundi, Byelorussian SSR, Cameroon, Central African Republic, Chile, Colombia, Congo, Cuba, Cyprus, Czechoslovakia, Democratic Yemen, Equatorial Guinea, Ethiopia, German Democratic Republic, Ghana, Guinea, Guyana, Hungary, Iran, Iraq, Jamaica, Jordan, Kenya, Kuwait, Lao People's Democratic Republic, Lesotho, Libyan Arab Jamahiriya, Madagascar, Malawi, Mali, Malta, Mauritania, Mexico, Mongolia, Mozambique, Nicaragua, Nigeria, Panama, Poland, Qatar, Romania, Saint Vincent and the Grenadines, Saudi Arabia, Seychelles, Sierra Leone, Syrian Arab Republic, Togo, Trinidad and Tobago, Tunisia, Uganda, Ukrainian SSR, USSR, United Arab Emirates, United Republic of Tanzania, Venezuela, Viet Nam, Yemen, Yugoslavia, Zambia, Zimbabwe.

Against: Australia, Belgium, Canada, Denmark, France, Germany, Federal Republic of, Iceland, Israel, Italy, Japan, Luxembourg, Netherlands, New Zealand, Norway, Portugal, Spain, Turkey, United Kingdom, United States.

Abstaining: Austria, Bahamas, Bangladesh, Barbados, Bhutan, Bolivia, Brazil, Brunei Darussalam, Burma, Chad, China, Costa Rica, Democratic Kampuchea, Djibouti, Dominican Republic, Ecuador, Egypt, El Salvador, Fiji, Finland, Greece, Guatemala, Guinea-Bissau, Haiti, Honduras, India, Indonesia, Ireland, Ivory Coast, Liberia, Malaysia, Maldives, Mauritius, Morocco, Niger, Oman, Pakistan, Paraguay, Peru, Philippines, Rwanda, Saint Lucia, Samoa, Senegal, Singapore, Somalia, Sri Lanka, Sudan, Suriname, Sweden, Thailand, Uruguay, Zaire.

Introducing the draft, Bulgaria stated that the sponsors had incorporated the suggestion put forward by one State in its reply to the Secretary-General, and supported by a number of others, to request the Disarmament Commission to consider the matter. They believed that the Commission would provide for the broadest possible involvement of all interested States in preparing for future negotiations, and that its deliberations should in no way be linked to or prejudiced by specific documents or concepts.

Explaining its vote, the Netherlands stated that the deadline for submitting views did not allow Member States to benefit from the ongoing study by naval experts (see p. 67), that the scope of the views requested under the draft was so delineated as to prejudge the results of that study, and that it would set a bad precedent to adopt recommendations encouraging States to ignore those studies previously agreed on by the Assembly; while in favour, in principle, of negotiations on aspects of naval armaments, it felt that the measures indicated in paragraphs 1 and 2 of the draft would be incompatible with the existing geographical disparities affecting the major naval Powers and would run counter to their legitimate interests concerning security and commerce; and the preamble contained partisan notions which cast doubt on the sincerity of the sponsors' desire to achieve results in the negotiations.

Oman stressed that its position was to remain apart from the cold war, and spoke of the imbalance of some paragraphs in the text. Indonesia felt that the Disarmament Commission's consideration should be deferred until the study was submitted. Yugoslavia shared that view.

The USSR considered it timely to entrust the matter to the Disarmament Commission, adding that discussion in the Commission and a continuation of research supplemented each other. Asserting that the draft would make possible a substantive analysis of the subject by providing material for the group of experts to consider, Argentina said that naval armaments, especially in their nuclear aspects, required urgent consideration in a multilateral forum.

REFERENCES

[1]YUN 1980, p. 76. [2]A/39/348. [3]YUN 1980, p. 115, GA res. 35/156 A, 12 Dec. 1980. [4]YUN 1982, p. 113. [5]YUN

1981, p. 88, GA res. 36/97 A, 9 Dec. 1981. (6)A/39/471. (7)YUN 1983, p. 66. (8)*Multilateral Treaties Deposited with the Secretary-General: Status as at 31 December 1984* (ST/LEG/SER.E/3), Sales No. E.85.V.4. (9)YUN 1983, p. 68, GA res. 38/188 G, 20 Dec. 1983. (10)A/39/419 & Corr.1. (11)YUN 1983, p. 67, GA res. 38/188 F, 20 Dec. 1983.

Other aspects of disarmament and related matters

The General Assembly decided in 1984 to convene an International Conference on the Relationship between Disarmament and Development to examine the issue comprehensively and consider measures for releasing additional resources, through disarmament, for development purposes. It also called on the Security Council to consider—and initiate procedures for halting—the arms race as the international community observed in 1985 the fortieth anniversary of the United Nations.

The Disarmament Commission, at its 1984 session, could not agree on the governing principles on reducing military budgets and expenditures, nor could it finalize guidelines for appropriate types of confidence-building measures. In the mean time, the Group of Experts on the Reduction of Military Budgets continued refining the standardized reporting instrument, and the Assembly gave an additional year to the Group of Governmental Experts on Military Research and Development to complete a comprehensive study on that topic.

In connection with its consideration of preventing an arms race in outer space, the Assembly took up in 1984 a new agenda item on using outer space exclusively for the benefit of mankind. The Assembly again addressed questions of regional disarmament, as well as proposals on convening a Conference on the Indian Ocean and a World Disarmament Conference.

In September, the first conference to review the implementation of the 1976 Convention on the Prohibition of Military or Any Other Hostile Use of Environmental Modification Techniques found that the instrument had proven its effectiveness.

The World Disarmament Campaign entered its third year of implementation under United Nations auspices, and the Organization's disarmament fellowship programme continued to provide training.

The Assembly adopted the statute of the United Nations Institute for Disarmament Research. Under the United Nations disarmament studies programme, studies were concluded or in progress during the year; new ones were also authorized by the Assembly.

Military budgets and expenditures

For the fourth consecutive year, the Disarmament Commission was unable to arrive at a consensus on the principles that should govern efforts to freeze and reduce military expenditures. Meanwhile, the Group of Experts on the Reduction of Military Budgets continued refining the standardized reporting instrument, with a view to submitting its final report to the General Assembly in 1985.

Disarmament Commission consideration. As in previous years, the Disarmament Commission, at its May/June 1984 session,(1) considered two aspects of the reduction of military budgets: harmonization of views on their gradual, agreed reduction and the reallocation to economic and social development of resources thus saved; and examination and identification of ways to achieve verifiable agreements to freeze, reduce or otherwise restrain military expenditures in a balanced manner.

Romania transmitted to the Commission Chairman, on 11 May, a March proposal by the States members of the Warsaw Treaty Organization addressed to those of NATO concerning negotiations on freezing and reducing military expenditures.(2)

An informal open-ended working group (Working Group I), re-established by the Commission to consider the question, held nine meetings between 11 and 25 May under the chairmanship of Ion Diaconu (Romania).

The Group based its deliberations on a working paper submitted by the Group's Chairman in 1983,(3) as well as on those submitted during the previous sessions of the Commission by Australia, Belgium, Canada, France, Italy, Japan, the Netherlands and the United Kingdom;(3) by Bulgaria, Czechoslovakia, the German Democratic Republic, Hungary and Poland;(3) by Romania and Sweden;(4) and by India.(5)

Differences in views continued to persist, particularly with regard to transparency, comparability, verification and reporting of military expenditures. The Chairman of the Working Group prepared a working paper towards the end of the session, containing a synopsis of the texts—and stages of agreement—on the principles and the texts of amendments proposed by some members; the working paper was annexed to the Group's report to the Commission.

On 1 June, the Disarmament Commission adopted by consensus the Working Group's report, in which it was suggested, among other things, that the Commission should continue in 1985 considering proposals and ideas on the topic, with a view to identifying and elaborating the principles which should govern further actions of States on freezing and reducing military expenditures.

GENERAL ASSEMBLY ACTION

As recommended by the First Committee, the General Assembly, on 12 December 1984, adopted without vote resolution 39/64 A, under the item on reduction of military budgets.

The General Assembly,

Deeply concerned about the ever-spiralling arms race and growing military expenditures, which constitute a heavy burden for the economies of all nations and have extremely harmful effects on world peace and security,

Reaffirming once again the provisions of the Final Document of the Tenth Special Session of the General Assembly, the first special session devoted to disarmament, according to which the gradual reduction of military budgets on a mutually agreed basis, for example, in absolute figures or in terms of percentage, particularly by nuclear-weapon States and other militarily significant States, would contribute to curbing the arms race and would increase the possibilities for the reallocation of resources now being used for military purposes to economic and social development, particularly for the benefit of the developing countries,

Convinced that the freezing and reduction of military budgets would have favourable consequences on the world economic and financial situation and might facilitate efforts made to increase international assistance for the developing countries,

Recalling that at its twelfth special session, the second special session devoted to disarmament, all Member States unanimously and categorically reaffirmed the validity of the Final Document of the Tenth Special Session, as well as their solemn commitment to it,

Recalling also that, in the Declaration of the 1980s as the Second United Nations Disarmament Decade, it is provided that during this period renewed efforts should be made to reach agreement on the reduction of military expenditures and the reallocation of resources thus saved to economic and social development, especially for the benefit of developing countries,

Recalling further the provisions of its resolution 34/83 F of 11 December 1979, reaffirmed in its resolutions 35/142 A of 12 December 1980, 36/82 A of 9 December 1981, 37/95 A of 13 December 1982 and 38/184 A of 20 December 1983, in which it considered that a new impetus should be given to the endeavours to achieve agreements to freeze, reduce or otherwise restrain, in a balanced manner, military expenditure, including adequate measures of verification satisfactory to all parties concerned,

Aware of the various proposals submitted by Member States and of the activities carried out so far within the framework of the United Nations in the field of the reduction of military budgets,

Convinced that identification and elaboration of the principles which should govern further actions of States in freezing and reducing military budgets could contribute to harmonizing the views of States and create confidence among them conducive to achieving international agreements in the reduction of military budgets,

Considering that the identification and elaboration of the principles which should govern further actions of States in freezing and reducing military budgets and the other current activities within the framework of the United Nations related to the question of the reduction of military budgets should be regarded as having the fundamental objective of reaching international agreements on the reduction of military expenditures,

Taking note of the report of the Disarmament Commission on the work accomplished during its session in 1984 on the question of the reduction of military budgets,

1. *Declares once again its conviction* that it is possible to achieve international agreements on the reduction of military budgets without prejudice to the right of all States to undiminished security, self-defence and sovereignty;

2. *Reaffirms* that the human and material resources released through the reduction of military expenditures could be reallocated to economic and social development, particularly for the benefit of the developing countries;

3. *Calls upon* all Member States, in particular the most heavily armed States, to reinforce their readiness to co-operate in a constructive manner with a view to reaching agreements to freeze, reduce or otherwise restrain military expenditures;

4. *Appeals* to all States, in particular to the most heavily armed States, pending the conclusion of agreements on the reduction of military expenditures, to exercise self-restraint in their military expenditures with a view to reallocating the funds thus saved to economic and social development, particularly for the benefit of developing countries;

5. *Requests* the Disarmament Commission to continue, at its 1985 substantive session, the consideration of the item entitled "Reduction of military budgets" on the basis of the relevant working paper annexed to its report, as well as other proposals and ideas on the subject-matter, with a view to finalizing the identification and elaboration of the principles which should govern further actions of States in the field of freezing and reduction of military expenditures, keeping in mind the possibility of embodying such principles in a suitable document at an appropriate stage;

6. *Decides* to include in the provisional agenda of its fortieth session the item entitled "Reduction of military budgets".

General Assembly resolution 39/64 A

12 December 1984   Meeting 97   Adopted without vote

Approved by First Committee (A/39/751) without vote, 19 November (meeting 42); 15-nation draft (A/C.1/39/L.19); agenda item 61 *(a)*.
Sponsors: Austria, Bangladesh, Colombia, Costa Rica, Indonesia, Ireland, Malta, Nigeria, Peru, Romania, Rwanda, Senegal, Sudan, Sweden, Uruguay.
Meeting numbers. GA 39th session: 1st Committee 3-36, 42; plenary 97.

While going along with the consensus action on the text, a number of States explained their positions.

Argentina and Brazil asserted that those States which were militarily the most powerful and responsible for the highest military expenditures should take the initiative in reducing military budgets. For similar reasons, India would have abstained, had a vote been taken.

Belgium, although supporting a number of ideas contained in the text, felt that it failed to attach due importance to comparability and verification, which it said were essential in efforts to reduce military budgets. The United Kingdom said systematic reporting of those budgets, not principles alone, could help strengthen international confidence by contributing to greater transparency in military matters. France also joined in the consensus despite certain reservations, in order to acknowledge that Romania, by co-sponsoring the drafts which became resolutions 39/64 A and B (see below), subscribed to paragraphs 2 and 3 of the latter text referring to the need for the broadest possible participation of States in the standardized reporting system.

Also in 1984, the General Assembly, in agreeing to hold an International Conference on the Relationship between Disarmament and Development (resolution 39/160), decided that the Conference should examine, among other things, the implications of the level and magnitude of the continuing military expenditures for the international economic and social situation (see p. 83).

Reporting procedures

Report of the Group of Experts. The Group of Experts on the Reduction of Military Budgets—experts from Indonesia, Italy, Nigeria, Peru, Romania, Sweden and the United States, appointed in 1983 by the Secretary-General in pursuance of a 1982 General Assembly request[6]—held two sessions in 1984 (New York, 6-17 February and 9-20 July) under the chairmanship of Hans Christian Cars (Sweden).

In its second progress report,[7] following one submitted in 1983,[8] on the construction of price indices and purchasing-power parities for military expenditures as a means of allowing comparisons and thus facilitating relevant negotiations, the Group stated that it had requested and received data on military expenditures and prices from 7 (Australia, Austria, Finland, Norway, Sweden, United Kingdom, United States) of the 10 countries (the remaining three being Canada, Federal Republic of Germany, Italy) which had earlier volunteered to participate in the exercise. At the time of submitting the report in July, the Group was analysing and evaluating the data, with the actual computations to follow, with the assistance of the United Nations Statistical Office. In two 1985 sessions, the Group planned to evaluate the results of those computations in relation to other available means of comparison, and to draft its final report for submission to the Assembly.

GENERAL ASSEMBLY ACTION

In addition to the progress report prepared by the Group of Experts, the Secretary-General submitted to the Assembly in October 1984, with later addenda, an annual report on military expenditures in standardized form reported by 23 States.[9] A majority of the responding States had used the standard reporting instrument, consisting of a matrix designed to show how much each force group (such as land, naval and air forces) spent in each resource category (such as personnel, procurement and operations).

On 12 December 1984, the Assembly, on the recommendation of the First Committee, adopted by recorded vote resolution 39/64 B, under the item on reduction of military budgets.

The General Assembly,

Deeply concerned about the arms race and present tendencies to increase further the rate of growth of military expenditures, the deplorable waste of human and economic resources and the potentially harmful effects on world peace and security,

Considering that a gradual reduction of military expenditures on a mutually agreed basis would be a measure that would contribute to curbing the arms race and would increase the possibilities of reallocating resources now being used for military purposes to economic and social development, particularly for the benefit of the developing countries,

Convinced that such reductions could and should be carried out on a mutually agreed basis without detriment to the national security of any country,

Reaffirming its conviction that provisions for defining, reporting, comparing and verifying military expenditures will have to be basic elements of any international agreement to reduce such expenditures,

Recalling that an international system for the standardized reporting of military expenditures has been introduced in pursuance of General Assembly resolution 35/142 B of 12 December 1980, and that annual reports on military expenditures are now being received from a number of Member States,

Considering that a wider participation in the reporting system of States from different geographic regions and representing different budgeting systems would promote its further refinement and would, by contributing to greater openness in military matters, increase confidence between States,

Noting, in this connection, the proposal to convene an international conference on military expenditures,

Recalling its resolution 37/95 B of 13 December 1982, in which it requested the Secretary-General, with the assistance of a group of qualified experts and with the voluntary co-operation of States, to undertake the task of constructing price indices and purchasing-power parities for the military expenditures of participating States,

Emphasizing that the above-mentioned activities and initiatives, as well as other ongoing activities within the United Nations related to the reduction of military budgets, have the objective of facilitating future negotiations aimed at the conclusion of international agreements on the reduction of military expenditures,

1. *Takes note with appreciation* of the report of the Secretary-General containing the replies received in 1984 from Member States in the framework of the above-mentioned reporting system;

2. *Stresses* the need to increase the number of reporting States with a view to the broadest possible participation from different geographic regions and representing different budgeting systems;

3. *Reiterates its recommendation* that all Member States should report annually, by 30 April, to the Secretary-General, using the reporting instrument, their military expenditures for the latest fiscal year for which data are available;

4.   *Also takes note with appreciation* of the progress report of the Secretary-General on the ongoing exercise undertaken in pursuance of resolution 37/95 B, and which will result in a final report to the General Assembly at its fortieth session;

5.   *Requests* the Secretary-General to provide the Group of Experts on the Reduction of Military Budgets with the necessary assistance and Secretariat services;

6.   *Decides* to include in the provisional agenda of its fortieth session the item entitled "Reduction of military budgets".

General Assembly resolution 39/64 B

12 December 1984   Meeting 97   114-16-7 (recorded vote)

Approved by First Committee (A/39/751) by recorded vote (100-14-7), 19 November (meeting 42); 21-nation draft (A/C.1/39/L.28); agenda item 61 *(b)*.

Sponsors: Australia, Austria, Bangladesh, Belgium, Canada, Colombia, Costa Rica, Denmark, Finland, France, Germany, Federal Republic of, Ireland, Italy, Malta, Mexico, New Zealand, Norway, Romania, Sudan, Sweden, Uruguay.

Meeting numbers. GA 39th session: 1st Committee 3-36, 38, 42; plenary 97.

Recorded vote in Assembly as follows:

In favour: Antigua and Barbuda, Argentina, Australia, Austria, Bangladesh, Barbados, Belgium, Belize, Benin, Bhutan, Bolivia, Botswana, Brunei Darussalam, Burundi, Cameroon, Canada, Cape Verde, Central African Republic, Chad, Chile, Colombia, Costa Rica, Cyprus, Democratic Kampuchea, Denmark, Djibouti, Dominica, Dominican Republic, Ecuador, Egypt, El Salvador, Equatorial Guinea, Fiji, Finland, France, Gabon, Germany, Federal Republic of, Ghana, Greece, Guatemala, Guinea, Guinea-Bissau, Guyana, Haiti, Honduras, Iceland, Indonesia, Iran,[a] Iraq, Ireland, Italy, Ivory Coast, Jamaica, Japan, Jordan, Kenya, Lebanon, Lesotho, Liberia, Luxembourg, Malawi, Malaysia, Maldives, Mali, Malta, Mauritania, Mauritius, Mexico, Morocco, Nepal, Netherlands, New Zealand, Niger, Nigeria, Norway, Pakistan, Panama, Papua New Guinea, Paraguay, Peru, Philippines, Portugal, Romania, Rwanda, Saint Lucia, Samoa, Sao Tome and Principe, Saudi Arabia, Senegal, Seychelles, Sierra Leone, Singapore, Somalia, Spain, Sri Lanka, Sudan, Suriname, Sweden, Thailand, Togo, Trinidad and Tobago, Tunisia, Turkey, Uganda, United Arab Emirates, United Kingdom, United States, Uruguay, Vanuatu, Venezuela, Yemen, Yugoslavia, Zaire, Zimbabwe.

Against: Afghanistan, Bulgaria, Byelorussian SSR, Congo, Cuba, Czechoslovakia, German Democratic Republic, Hungary, Israel,[b] Lao People's Democratic Republic, Mongolia, Mozambique, Poland, Ukrainian SSR, USSR, Viet Nam.

Abstaining: Bahamas, Brazil, Burma, China, India, United Republic of Tanzania, Zambia.

[a]Later advised the Secretariat it had intended not to participate in the vote.

[b]Later advised the Secretariat it had intended to vote in favour.

In explanation of vote, the USSR asserted that the questions of reporting machinery and comparability of military expenses, as well as the proposal for an international conference on military expenditures, were an attempt by some States to shirk from actually reducing military expenditure and to distract attention from the growth in their own military budgets.

Brazil said the text failed to stress the special responsibilities borne by the nuclear-weapon States which, it asserted, should be the first to reduce military budgets. Sharing that view, India added that, in the absence of political will on the part of the major Powers, exercises such as those endorsed in the text merely distracted attention from nuclear disarmament, to which it attached utmost importance.

Argentina, in spite of its affirmative vote, expressed misgivings about the effectiveness of the reporting exercise with only a small number of States participating. The United Kingdom—welcoming the text's emphasis on wider participation in the reporting system and expressing regret that no party to the Warsaw Treaty Organi-

zation had participated in the exercise—said that balanced, verifiable agreements to restrain and reduce military expenditures would be difficult to reach without a generally accepted procedure for comparing such expenditures.

Information on military capabilities

Pursuant to a December 1983 General Assembly resolution,[10] the Secretary-General submitted in September 1984 a report[11] containing the views of seven States on measures to facilitate objective information on military capabilities.

The Advisory Board on Disarmament Studies (see p. 91), responding also to the 1983 Assembly request[10] through the Secretary-General,[12] recommended that UNIDIR (see p. 92), in cooperation with the Stockholm International Peace Research Institute (SIPRI), might consider further the modalities of studying such measures, particularly as they related to nuclear-weapon and other militarily significant States.

Study on military research and development

The Group of Governmental Experts on Military Research and Development, established by the Secretary-General in 1983[13] in pursuance of a 1982 General Assembly request,[14] held three sessions in 1984 (New York, 13-24 February, 4-15 June and 27-31 August).

The Group—experts from Argentina, China, Czechoslovakia, Egypt, France, the German Democratic Republic, Ghana, India, Japan, Peru, Sweden, the USSR, the United Kingdom and the United States—was to complete, for the Assembly's 1984 session, a comprehensive study on the scope, role and direction of the military use of research and development, the mechanisms involved, its role in the arms race, and its impact on arms limitation and disarmament, with a view to preventing a qualitative arms race and to ensuring that scientific and technological achievements might ultimately be used solely for peaceful purposes.

On 5 November, the Group's Chairman, Rolf Björnerstedt (Sweden), informed the Secretary-General that, while the Group had made substantial progress in preparing its report, certain issues remained to be resolved; an extension of the Group's mandate could enable it to resolve those issues and to submit its final report at the Assembly's 1985 session. This request was annexed to the Secretary-General's report to the Assembly.[15]

GENERAL ASSEMBLY ACTION

On 17 December 1984, the General Assembly, on the recommendation of the First Committee, adopted resolution 39/151 F by recorded vote.

Military research and development

The General Assembly,

Recalling its resolution 37/99 J of 13 December 1982 in which the Secretary-General was requested to carry out, with the assistance of qualified governmental experts, a comprehensive study of the military use of research and development,

1. *Takes note* of the report of the Secretary-General to which is annexed a letter from the Chairman of the Group of Governmental Experts on Military Research and Development informing the Secretary-General that, although substantial progress has been made in the preparation of the report, certain issues remain to be resolved, and that after consultations among the experts an extension of the time period of the study is requested in order to enable the Group to resolve these issues and to submit its final report in time for the fortieth session of the General Assembly;

2. *Requests* the Secretary-General to continue the study, bearing in mind the savings that might be made from the existing budgetary appropriations, and to submit the final report to the General Assembly at its fortieth session.

General Assembly resolution 39/151 F

17 December 1984   Meeting 102   141-1-5 (recorded vote)

Approved by First Committee (A/39/755) by recorded vote (133-1-4), 19 November (meeting 41); draft by Sweden (A/C.1/39/L.38); agenda item 65 *(b)*.

Financial implications. ACABQ, A/39/7/Add.10; 5th Committee, A/39/795; S-G, A/C.1/39/L.76, A/C.5/39/57.

Meeting numbers. GA 39th session: 1st Committee 3-37, 41; 5th Committee 43; plenary 102.

Recorded vote in Assembly as follows:

In favour: Afghanistan, Algeria, Angola, Antigua and Barbuda, Argentina, Australia, Austria, Bahamas, Bahrain, Bangladesh, Barbados, Benin, Bhutan, Bolivia, Botswana, Brazil, Brunei Darussalam, Bulgaria, Burkina Faso, Burma, Burundi, Byelorussian SSR, Cameroon, Canada, Cape Verde, Central African Republic, Chad, Chile, China, Colombia, Congo, Costa Rica, Cuba, Cyprus, Czechoslovakia, Democratic Kampuchea, Democratic Yemen, Denmark, Djibouti, Dominican Republic, Ecuador, Egypt, El Salvador, Equatorial Guinea, Ethiopia, Fiji, Finland, France, Gabon, German Democratic Republic, Ghana, Greece, Guatemala, Guinea, Guinea-Bissau, Guyana, Haiti, Honduras, Hungary, Iceland, India, Indonesia, Iran, Iraq, Ireland, Israel, Italy, Ivory Coast, Jamaica, Japan, Jordan, Kenya, Kuwait, Lao People's Democratic Republic, Lebanon, Lesotho, Liberia, Libyan Arab Jamahiriya, Madagascar, Malawi, Malaysia, Maldives, Mali, Malta, Mauritania, Mauritius, Mexico, Mongolia, Morocco, Nepal, New Zealand, Nicaragua, Niger, Nigeria, Norway, Oman, Pakistan, Panama, Papua New Guinea, Paraguay, Peru, Philippines, Poland, Portugal, Qatar, Romania, Rwanda, Saint Lucia, Saint Vincent and the Grenadines, Samoa, Sao Tome and Principe, Saudi Arabia, Senegal, Seychelles, Sierra Leone, Singapore, Somalia, Spain, Sri Lanka, Sudan, Suriname, Sweden, Syrian Arab Republic, Thailand, Togo, Trinidad and Tobago, Tunisia, Uganda, Ukrainian SSR, USSR, United Arab Emirates, United Kingdom, United Republic of Tanzania, Uruguay, Venezuela, Viet Nam, Yemen, Yugoslavia, Zaire, Zambia, Zimbabwe.

Against: United States.

Abstaining: Belgium, Germany, Federal Republic of, Luxembourg, Netherlands, Turkey.

Introducing the text, Sweden pointed out that what was envisaged in 1985 was not a review of the entire draft report, but an effort to resolve certain differences of opinion.

In explanation of vote, the United States said it approved the substance of the draft, but not its financial implications; it would have liked the text to contain language to keep within existing resources the cost of extending the time allotted to the study. Although the United Kingdom shared that view, it supported the draft because of the importance it attached to both the study and its suc-

cessful completion; it was disappointed, however, that the Group had failed to complete its work within the allocated time, and urged the experts to be flexible and not insist that their own or their Governments' views be included in their entirety. Cameroon felt that the extension of the Group's mandate should be seen as exceptional.

Review Conference on the Convention to prohibit the hostile use of environmental modification techniques

In September 1984, the first Review Conference of the Parties to the Convention on the Prohibition of Military or Any Other Hostile Use of Environmental Modification Techniques,[16] often referred to as the ENMOD Convention, met to examine the effectiveness of that instrument, which had been in force since October 1978. Article II of the Convention defined environmental modification techniques as those for changing the dynamics, composition or structure of the earth or of outer space through the deliberate manipulation of natural processes.

During 1984, Australia, Brazil, the Democratic People's Republic of Korea, New Zealand and Sweden became parties to the Convention, bringing the total, as at 31 December, to 47 States.[17]

Work of the Preparatory Committee. In 1982, the General Assembly[18] had noted that the Secretary-General, as depositary of the Convention and according to its article VIII, intended to convene the Review Conference at the earliest practicable time after 5 October 1983, when the instrument would have been in force for five years. Following consultations, it was agreed that a Preparatory Committee, open to all States parties, would convene at Geneva on 30 April 1984.

The Preparatory Committee met at Geneva from 30 April to 2 May, with 31 States parties participating, set the Conference's date and venue and recommended a provisional agenda for it.

Review Conference. The Review Conference, held at Geneva from 10 to 20 September 1984, was attended by 35 of the 45 States parties at that time, four signatories, four observer States and two non-governmental organizations, as well as representatives of UNEP and WMO. It elected Keijo Korhonen (Finland) as its President.

In its Final Declaration,[19] adopted by consensus on 20 September, the Review Conference stressed that the six years since the Convention's entry into force had demonstrated its effectiveness; it noted with satisfaction that no State party had found it necessary to invoke the provisions of article V dealing with international complaints and verification procedures. It also decided that a second Review Conference might be held at Geneva at the request of a majority of States parties not earlier than 1989; if no such meeting took place before 1994, the depositary would be requested to solicit the views of all States parties on its convening.

Related action. UNIDIR, together with SIPRI and in co-operation with UNEP, organized at Geneva, from 24 to 27 April 1984, a symposium on environmental warfare, where special attention was paid to the ENMOD Convention.

GENERAL ASSEMBLY ACTION

On 17 December 1984, the General Assembly, on the recommendation of the First Committee, adopted resolution 39/151 A by recorded vote.

Review Conference of the Parties to the Convention on the Prohibition of Military or Any Other Hostile Use of Environmental Modification Techniques

The General Assembly,

Recalling its resolution 31/72 of 10 December 1976, in which it referred the Convention on the Prohibition of Military or Any Other Hostile Use of Environmental Modification Techniques to all States for their consideration, signature and ratification and expressed its hope for the widest possible adherence to the Convention,

Recalling that the States parties to the Convention met at Geneva from 10 to 20 September 1984 to review the operation of the Convention, with a view to ensuring that its purposes and provisions were being realized,

Noting with satisfaction that in its Final Declaration the Review Conference of the Parties to the Convention on the Prohibition of Military or Any Other Hostile Use of Environmental Modification Techniques concluded that the obligations assumed under the Convention had been faithfully observed by the States parties,

Noting also that the Review Conference found the Convention and its objectives to be of continuing importance and that it was in the common interest of mankind to maintain its effectiveness in prohibiting the use of environmental modification techniques as a means of war,

Noting, in this context, that the Review Conference recognized the need to keep under continuing review and examination the provisions of paragraph 1 of article I of the Convention, in order to assure their continued effectiveness,

Noting that the Review Conference affirmed its belief that universal adherence to the Convention would enhance international peace and security,

Noting furthermore that the States parties to the Convention reaffirmed their strong support for the Convention, their continued dedication to its principles and objectives and their commitment to implement effectively its provisions,

1. *Takes note* of the positive assessment by the Review Conference of the Parties to the Convention on the Prohibition of Military or Any Other Hostile Use of Environmental Modification Techniques of the effectiveness of the Convention since its entry into force, as reflected in its Final Declaration;

2. *Calls upon* all States to refrain from military or any other hostile use of environmental modification techniques;

3. *Reiterates its hope* for the widest possible adherence to the Convention.

General Assembly resolution 39/151 A

17 December 1984   Meeting 102   136-0-4 (recorded vote)

Approved by First Committee (A/39/755) by recorded vote (129-0-2), 19 November (meeting 41); 10-nation draft (A/C.1/39/L.11); agenda item 65.

Sponsors: Byelorussian SSR, Czechoslovakia, Finland, Hungary, India, Norway, Ukrainian SSR, USSR, United Kingdom, United States.

Meeting numbers. GA 39th session: 1st Committee 3-36, 41; plenary 102.

Recorded vote in Assembly as follows:

In favour: Afghanistan, Angola, Antigua and Barbuda, Argentina, Australia, Austria, Bahamas, Bahrain, Bangladesh, Barbados, Belgium, Benin, Bhutan, Bolivia, Botswana, Brazil, Brunei Darussalam, Bulgaria, Burkina Faso, Burma, Burundi, Byelorussian SSR, Cameroon, Canada, Cape Verde, Central African Republic, Chad, Chile, Colombia, Congo, Costa Rica, Cuba, Cyprus, Czechoslovakia, Democratic Kampuchea, Democratic Yemen, Denmark, Djibouti, Dominican Republic, Ecuador, Egypt, El Salvador, Equatorial Guinea, Ethiopia, Fiji, Finland, Gabon, German Democratic Republic, Germany, Federal Republic of, Ghana, Greece, Guatemala, Guinea, Guyana, Haiti, Honduras, Hungary, Iceland, India, Indonesia, Iran, Iraq, Ireland, Israel, Italy, Ivory Coast, Jamaica, Japan, Jordan, Kenya, Kuwait, Lao People's Democratic Republic, Lebanon, Lesotho, Libyan Arab Jamahiriya, Luxembourg, Madagascar, Malawi, Malaysia, Maldives, Mali, Malta, Mauritania, Mauritius, Mongolia, Morocco, Nepal, Netherlands, New Zealand, Nicaragua, Niger, Nigeria, Norway, Papua New Guinea, Peru, Philippines, Poland, Portugal, Qatar, Romania, Rwanda, Saint Lucia, Saint Vincent and the Grenadines, Samoa, Sao Tome and Principe, Saudi Arabia, Senegal, Seychelles, Sierra Leone, Singapore, Somalia, Spain, Sri Lanka, Sudan, Suriname, Sweden, Syrian Arab Republic, Thailand, Togo, Trinidad and Tobago, Tunisia, Turkey, Uganda, Ukrainian SSR, USSR, United Arab Emirates, United Kingdom, United Republic of Tanzania, United States, Uruguay, Viet Nam, Yemen, Yugoslavia, Zaire, Zambia, Zimbabwe.

Against: None.

Abstaining: Mexico, Mozambique, Panama, Venezuela.

In explanation of vote, Mexico, recalling that it had voted against the 1976 Assembly resolution—referring the ENMOD Convention to States for their consideration, signature and ratification—said its abstention on what it considered to be a procedural draft did not imply any changes from its previous position; it found article I of the Convention unacceptable, which, in its view, was tantamount to legitimizing the use of environmental modification techniques so long as they had no widespread, long-lasting or severe effects.

Argentina, which also saw the text as procedural, continued to believe that the Convention would be fully operative only after its scope had been expanded; it regretted that the Review Conference had not put into motion machinery that could have led to the revision of article I.

Arms race in outer space

In 1984, the Conference on Disarmament continued to discuss, but was unable to agree on, the mandate of a proposed subsidiary body concerned with preventing an arms race in outer space. The militarization of outer space was also considered by the Committee on the Peaceful Uses of Outer Space. Of four draft resolutions before the General Assembly, only one was voted on and adopted (resolution 39/59).

Consideration by the Conference on Disarmament. The Conference on Disarmament[20] considered the item on preventing an arms race in outer space from 19 to 23 March and from 16 to 20 July 1984. A contact group—established, as in 1983, and meeting under the President of the

Conference—again failed to reach a consensus on an appropriate mandate for an *ad hoc* subsidiary body on the question; it considered various proposals, including those submitted by the Group of 21 non-aligned countries,[21] a group of socialist States[22] and a number of Western countries.[23]

The Group of 21 continued to maintain that the mandate should spell out the ultimate objective of reaching an agreement or agreements, as appropriate, to prevent an arms race in all its aspects in outer space, as specifically requested by the General Assembly in 1983.[24] A number of Western countries held that a subsidiary body should, in the first instance, identify relevant issues through substantive examination. The socialist countries felt that the Western proposal to study issues, without a mandate to negotiate, was being advanced in order to avoid negotiations on the question.

The USSR, by a letter of 20 March,[25] submitted to the Conference the text of a draft treaty—on prohibiting the use of force in outer space and from space against the Earth—which it had proposed to the Assembly in 1983.[26]

Many delegations expressed concern over the plans for developing new types of weapons systems in outer space in the name of defensive weapons, and urged the Conference to concentrate on urgent negotiations rather than spend time on what they felt were superficial issues.

The Conference reported to the Assembly that, in view of the absence of a consensus on a mandate for an *ad hoc* committee, no progress was achieved on the item.

Consideration by the Committee on outer space. Pursuant to a December 1983 General Assembly request,[27] the Committee on the Peaceful Uses of Outer Space (Vienna, 12-21 June)[28] (see next chapter) discussed as a priority matter questions relating to the militarization of outer space. As in 1983, divergent views were expressed on the competence of the Committee, as against that of the Conference on Disarmament, in addressing arms control issues. Some asserted that the Assembly, by its 1983 resolution,[27] had given the Committee a clear mandate to consider the issue, while others felt that mandate was a serious mistake. Some others believed that the Committee could make a concrete contribution by supporting negotiations carried out in other forums, while making sure that such involvement would not diminish the Committee's role in promoting co-operation in the peaceful uses of outer space. Some proposed that the Committee set up an informal working group for preliminary examination of related questions, while others envisaged a similar body in the Conference on Disarmament to negotiate an agreement or agreements on preventing an arms race in all its aspects in outer space.

On 14 December, the Assembly, in resolution 39/96, again requested the Committee on outer space to consider as a priority matter ways for maintaining outer space for peaceful purposes and to report to the Assembly in 1985.

GENERAL ASSEMBLY ACTION

In addition to an agenda item on the report of the Conference on Disarmament[20] as it related to preventing an arms race in outer space, the General Assembly took up in 1984 a new item proposed by the USSR, on the use of outer space exclusively for peaceful purposes for the benefit of mankind.

In submitting that request by a letter of 27 September to the Secretary-General,[29] the USSR declared that no attack weapons of any kind—conventional, nuclear, laser, particle beam or any other—should be deployed in outer space, whether on manned or unmanned systems, and that any such systems already created should be destroyed. The United Nations, it added, should call for early elaboration through negotiation of reliably verifiable agreements on a bilateral and multilateral basis. A draft resolution was annexed to the letter (see p. 76).

The USSR also transmitted to the Secretary-General three related communications: on 4 July, it submitted a 29 June statement addressed to the United States,[30] proposing negotiations on preventing the militarization of outer space; on 30 July, it submitted the text of a 27 July TASS news agency statement charging that the United States had avoided the USSR's proposal;[31] and on 4 September,[32] it transmitted the text of replies by K. U. Chernenko, General Secretary of the Central Committee of the Communist Party, to questions from the newspaper *Pravda*. He proposed, among other things, a reciprocal moratorium with the United States on the testing and deployment of strike space systems and the simultaneous commencement of talks.

By a letter of 14 November to the Secretary-General,[33] the German Democratic Republic transmitted an appeal from the States participating in the Intercosmos programme on outer space—Bulgaria, Cuba, Czechoslovakia, the German Democratic Republic, Hungary, Mongolia, Poland, the USSR and Viet Nam—(Berlin, October) stating that the United States plan to create new systems of space weapons added to the danger of nuclear catastrophe, and that the United Nations should adopt immediate measures to ensure the peaceful uses of outer space.

Four draft resolutions were introduced in the Assembly's First Committee, each with a different emphasis. Three of them—submitted, respectively, by the USSR, China and a group of Western countries—were not put to a vote, at the request of the sponsors concerned, to facilitate adoption of a single text on the question. All the texts, with the exception of the USSR draft, were entitled "Prevention of an arms race in outer space".

The USSR draft,[34] with the same title as the new agenda item, "Use of outer space exclusively for peaceful purposes for the benefit of mankind", would have had the Assembly call on all States, particularly those with major space capabilities: to prohibit for all time the use of force in outer space and from space against the Earth, as well as from the Earth against objects in outer space, and to ban and eliminate space attack systems, including space-based anti-satellite and anti-ballistic missile systems; and to negotiate verifiable bilateral and multilateral agreements. The USSR said that verification would be made easier if only for the reason that its proposal called for a complete ban on developing such systems and for eliminating the few that had already been developed.

In December, the Assembly, on an oral proposal by its President, adopted without vote decision 39/415, taking note of the report of the First Committee[35] on its consideration of the USSR-proposed agenda item.

Use of outer space exclusively for peaceful purposes for the benefit of mankind

At its 97th plenary meeting, on 12 December 1984, the General Assembly took note of the report of the First Committee.

General Assembly decision 39/415
                                                  Adopted without vote

Oral proposal by President; agenda item 142.
Meeting numbers. GA 39th session: 1st Committee 3-36; plenary 97.

The draft proposed by China[36] would have had the Assembly request the Conference on Disarmament to establish, at its 1985 session, an *ad hoc* committee to negotiate an agreement or agreements to prevent an arms race in outer space, and urge the USSR and the United States to start serious bilateral negotiations for that purpose. China stressed that bilateral and multilateral talks were complementary and mutually reinforcing, and that talks between the USSR and the United States could not substitute for multilateral negotiations.

The proposal by Belgium, Canada, the Federal Republic of Germany, Italy, Japan, the Netherlands and the United Kingdom[37] would have had the Assembly reiterate that the Conference had the primary role in negotiating multilateral agreements on using space for peaceful purposes; urge the Conference to give that question priority in 1985 and agree on the establishment of an *ad hoc* committee and on its mandate; and call on the USSR and the United States to seek with priority

mutually acceptable negotiating approaches for effective and verifiable agreements to strengthen international security. On behalf of the sponsors, Italy said the bilateral and multilateral processes were complementary and essential, and that the Conference itself should agree by consensus on a mandate which it deemed to be most appropriate for a helpful and prompt start on the substantive work.

The General Assembly acted on a fourth draft, which was twice revised and sponsored by 17 nations.

On 12 December 1984, the Assembly, on the recommendation of the First Committee, adopted resolution 39/59 by recorded vote.

Prevention of an arms race in outer space
The General Assembly,

Inspired by the great prospects opening up before mankind as a result of man's entry into outer space,

Recognizing the common interest of all mankind in the exploration and use of outer space for peaceful purposes,

Reaffirming that the exploration and use of outer space, including the Moon and other celestial bodies, shall be carried out for the benefit and in the interest of all countries, irrespective of their degree of economic or scientific development, and shall be the province of all mankind,

Reaffirming further the will of all States that the exploration and use of outer space, including the Moon and other celestial bodies, shall be for peaceful purposes,

Recalling that the States parties to the Treaty on Principles Governing the Activities of States in the Exploration and Use of Outer Space, including the Moon and Other Celestial Bodies, have undertaken, in article III, to carry on activities in the exploration and use of outer space, including the Moon and other celestial bodies, in accordance with international law and the Charter of the United Nations, in the interest of maintaining international peace and security and promoting international co-operation and understanding,

Reaffirming, in particular, article IV of the above-mentioned Treaty, which stipulates that States parties to the Treaty undertake not to place in orbit around the earth any objects carrying nuclear weapons or any other kinds of weapons of mass destruction, install such weapons on celestial bodies or station such weapons in outer space in any other manner,

Reaffirming also paragraph 80 of the Final Document of the Tenth Special Session of the General Assembly, in which it is stated that, in order to prevent an arms race in outer space, further measures should be taken and appropriate international negotiations held in accordance with the spirit of the Treaty,

Recalling its resolutions 36/97 C and 36/99 of 9 December 1981, as well as resolutions 37/83 of 9 December 1982, 37/99 D of 13 December 1982, and 38/70 of 15 December 1983,

Gravely concerned at the danger posed to all mankind by an arms race in outer space, in particular the impending danger of exacerbating the current state of insecurity by developments that could further undermine international peace and security,

Mindful of the widespread interest expressed by Member States in the course of the negotiations on and following the adoption of the above-mentioned Treaty in ensuring that the exploration and use of outer space should be for peaceful purposes, and taking note of proposals submitted to the General Assembly at its tenth special session, and at its regular sessions and to the Conference on Disarmament,

Noting the grave concern expressed by the Second United Nations Conference on the Exploration and Peaceful Uses of Outer Space over the extension of an arms race into outer space and the recommendations made to the competent organs of the United Nations, in particular the General Assembly, and also to the Committee on Disarmament,

Convinced that further measures are needed for the prevention of an arms race in outer space,

Recognizing that, in the context of multilateral negotiations for preventing an arms race in outer space, bilateral negotiations between the Union of Soviet Socialist Republics and the United States of America could make a significant contribution to such an objective, in accordance with paragraph 27 of the Final Document of the Tenth Special Session,

Deeply regretting that bilateral negotiations between the Union of Soviet Socialist Republics and the United States of America on the prevention of an arms race in outer space have not taken place,

Taking note of the report of the Conference on Disarmament relating to this question,

Aware of the various proposals submitted by Member States to the Conference on Disarmament, particularly concerning the establishment of an *ad hoc* committee on the prevention of an arms race in outer space and its draft mandate, which had been considered extensively by a contact group and through informal consultations and by formal and informal meetings of the Conference on Disarmament,

Expressing its deep concern and disappointment that, although there was no objection, in principle, to the establishment without delay of such an *ad hoc* committee, the Conference on Disarmament has not thus far been enabled to reach agreement on a mandate for the *ad hoc* committee during its 1984 session,

1. *Recalls* the obligation of all States to refrain from the threat or use of force in their space activities;

2. *Reaffirms* that general and complete disarmament under effective international control warrants that outer space shall be used exclusively for peaceful purposes and that it shall not become an arena for an arms race;

3. *Emphasizes* that further measures with appropriate and effective provisions for verification to prevent an arms race in outer space should be adopted by the international community;

4. *Calls upon* all States, in particular those with major space capabilities, to contribute actively to the objective of the peaceful use of outer space and to take immediate measures to prevent an arms race in outer space in the interest of maintaining international peace and security and promoting international co-operation and understanding;

5. *Reiterates* that the Conference on Disarmament, as the single multilateral disarmament negotiating forum, has the primary role in the negotiation of a multilateral agreement or agreements, as appropriate, on the prevention of an arms race in outer space in all its aspects;

6. *Requests* the Conference on Disarmament to consider as a matter of priority the question of preventing an arms race in outer space;

7. *Also requests* the Conference on Disarmament to intensify its consideration of the question of the prevention of an arms race in outer space in all its aspects, taking into account all relevant proposals, including those submitted at the thirty-ninth session of the General Assembly;

8. *Further requests* the Conference on Disarmament to establish an *ad hoc* committee at the beginning of its session in 1985, with a view to undertaking negotiations for the conclusion of an agreement or agreements, as appropriate, to prevent an arms race in outer space in all its aspects;

9. *Urges* the Union of Soviet Socialist Republics and the United States of America to initiate immediately and in a constructive spirit negotiations aimed at preventing an arms race in outer space and to advise the Conference on Disarmament regularly of the progress of their bilateral negotiations so as to facilitate its work;

10. *Requests* the Conference on Disarmament to report on its consideration of this subject to the General Assembly at its fortieth session;

11. *Requests* the Secretary-General to transmit to the Conference on Disarmament all documents relating to the consideration of this subject by the General Assembly at its thirty-ninth session;

12. *Decides* to include in the provisional agenda of its fortieth session the item entitled "Prevention of an arms race in outer space".

General Assembly resolution 39/59

12 December 1984   Meeting 97   150-0-1 (recorded vote)

Approved by First Committee (A/39/744) by recorded vote (127-0-1), 27 November (meeting 49); 17-nation draft (A/C.1/39/L.37/Rev.2); agenda item 54.

Sponsors: Austria, Bangladesh, China, German Democratic Republic, Hungary, India, Indonesia, Ireland, Maldives, Mexico, Pakistan, Romania, Sri Lanka, Sudan, Sweden, Yugoslavia.

Meeting numbers. GA 39th session: 1st Committee 3-36, 38, 39, 47, 49; plenary 97.

Recorded vote in Assembly as follows:

In favour: Afghanistan, Algeria, Angola, Antigua and Barbuda, Argentina, Australia, Austria, Bahamas, Bahrain, Bangladesh, Barbados, Belgium, Belize, Benin, Bhutan, Bolivia, Botswana, Brazil, Brunei Darussalam, Bulgaria, Burkina Faso, Burma, Burundi, Byelorussian SSR, Cameroon, Canada, Cape Verde, Central African Republic, Chad, Chile, China, Colombia, Comoros, Congo, Costa Rica, Cuba, Cyprus, Czechoslovakia, Democratic Kampuchea, Democratic Yemen, Denmark, Djibouti, Dominica, Dominican Republic, Ecuador, Egypt, El Salvador, Equatorial Guinea, Ethiopia, Fiji, Finland, France, Gabon, German Democratic Republic, Germany, Federal Republic of, Ghana, Greece, Guatemala, Guinea, Guinea-Bissau, Guyana, Haiti, Honduras, Hungary, Iceland, India, Indonesia, Iran, Iraq, Ireland, Israel, Italy, Ivory Coast, Jamaica, Japan, Jordan, Kenya, Kuwait, Lao People's Democratic Republic, Lebanon, Lesotho, Liberia, Libyan Arab Jamahiriya, Luxembourg, Madagascar, Malawi, Malaysia, Maldives, Mali, Malta, Mauritania, Mauritius, Mexico, Mongolia, Morocco, Mozambique, Nepal, Netherlands, New Zealand, Nicaragua, Niger, Nigeria, Norway, Oman, Pakistan, Panama, Papua New Guinea, Paraguay, Peru, Philippines, Poland, Portugal, Qatar, Romania, Rwanda, Saint Lucia, Samoa, Sao Tome and Principe, Saudi Arabia, Senegal, Seychelles, Sierra Leone, Singapore, Somalia, Spain, Sri Lanka, Sudan, Suriname, Sweden, Syrian Arab Republic, Thailand, Togo, Trinidad and Tobago, Tunisia, Turkey, Uganda, Ukrainian SSR, USSR, United Arab Emirates, United Kingdom, United Republic of Tanzania, Uruguay, Vanuatu, Venezuela, Viet Nam, Yemen, Yugoslavia, Zaire, Zambia, Zimbabwe.

Against: None.

Abstaining: United States.

Action on the text in the Assembly followed the adoption of paragraph 8 by a recorded vote of 138 to 1, with 10 abstentions. The First Committee had also taken a recorded vote on that paragraph, approving it by 114 to 1, with 11 abstentions.

Several States explained their votes in the Committee.

The United States, voting against the paragraph and abstaining on the text as a whole, said it could not agree to the Assembly's instructing the Conference on Disarmament on the detailed conduct of its affairs and taking sides between competing mandates for a subsidiary body.

Italy, speaking also on behalf of Belgium, the Federal Republic of Germany, Japan, Luxembourg, the Netherlands, Portugal, Turkey and the United Kingdom, stated that, while they supported the text as a whole, they abstained in the vote on paragraph 8 because it prejudged the outcome of discussions taking place in the Conference.

France, agreeing that the Assembly should not make explicit recommendations to the Conference on the way it should organize its work, did not consider the provisions in paragraph 8 as a formal proposal for the mandate of the subsidiary body; paragraphs 8 and 9 gave a balanced and realistic reflection of the responsibilities of the Conference as well as those of the Powers with major space capabilities.

The USSR, which voted in favour of the paragraph, welcomed the text as taking account of its position. Australia expressed support for all peaceful uses of outer space as well as other uses which contributed to the preservation of peace and security.

In other 1984 resolutions, the Assembly expressed concern over the danger of the arms race extending into outer space (39/148 J), and urged all States that had not done so to adhere to the Treaty Banning Nuclear Weapon Tests in the Atmosphere, in Outer Space and under Water (39/52).

Regional disarmament

The General Assembly's 1984 consideration of regional disarmament measures focused on implementing its 1971 Declaration of the Indian Ocean as a Zone of Peace[38] and on the possibility of establishing a zone of peace in South-East Asia.

Report of the Secretary-General. In connection with the Assembly's 1984 consideration of regional disarmament, the Secretary-General, in a September report[39] submitted in response to a December 1983 Assembly request,[40] informed the Assembly of the related activities carried out by the Secretariat, in particular the Department for Disarmament Affairs, and by UNIDIR.

GENERAL ASSEMBLY ACTION

Acting on the recommendation of the First Committee, the General Assembly, on 12 December 1984, adopted resolution 39/63 F without vote.

Regional disarmament

The General Assembly,

Recalling its resolutions 37/100 F of 13 December 1982 and 38/73 J of 15 December 1983 on regional disarmament,

Taking note of the report of the Secretary-General,

1. *Requests* the Secretary-General to submit a further report to the General Assembly at its forty-second session on the implementation of resolutions 37/100 F and 38/73 J;

2. *Decides* to include in the provisional agenda of its forty-second session the item entitled "Regional disarmament: report of the Secretary-General".

General Assembly resolution 39/63 F

12 December 1984   Meeting 97   Adopted without vote

Approved by First Committee (A/39/750) without vote, 19 November (meeting 41); 34-nation draft (A/C.1/39/L.48); agenda item 60 *(h)*.

Sponsors: Austria, Bahamas, Bangladesh, Belgium, Bulgaria, Canada, Costa Rica, Czechoslovakia, Denmark, Ecuador, Egypt, Finland, France, Germany, Federal Republic of, Greece, Guatemala, Ireland, Italy, Liberia, Netherlands, Norway, Pakistan, Peru, Poland, Portugal, Romania, Singapore, Spain, Sudan, Sweden, Turkey, United Kingdom, Uruguay, Zaire.

Meeting numbers. GA 39th session: 1st Committee 3-36, 39, 41; plenary 97.

Introducing the draft on behalf of the sponsors, Belgium stated that since the item did not seem to need any new momentum from the Assembly and in order to avoid the ritual adoption of a resolution on the subject every year, the text proposed that the topic be discussed further at the 1987 session.

In explanation of position, the USSR asserted that studies on the question of a so-called disarmament fund (see p. 83) should not be included among regional disarmament measures, as had happened in the Secretary-General's report.[39] India stated that it would have abstained had the draft been put to a vote, adding that there could not be a piecemeal approach to disarmament in geographical terms and that only a global approach with generally accepted principles, priorities and objectives could have a chance of succeeding.

Zones of peace

Indian Ocean

The *Ad Hoc* Committee on the Indian Ocean continued, but did not complete in 1984, its preparatory work for the convening, at Colombo, Sri Lanka, in 1985, of a Conference on the Indian Ocean, as had been requested by the General Assembly in 1983.[41] The Assembly, in December 1984, called for the holding of the Conference in the first half of 1986 and requested the Committee to complete its preparations in 1985 (resolution 39/149).

Activities of the Committee on the Indian Ocean. The *Ad Hoc* Committee on the Indian Ocean, established by the General Assembly in 1972[42] to study practical measures for achieving the objectives of the 1971 Declaration of the Indian Ocean as a Zone of Peace,[38] held three sessions in 1984 in New York—12 to 23 March, 9 to 20 July and 20 to 31 August—with an additional meeting on 21 November to adopt its annual report to the Assembly,[43] containing a draft resolution for the Assembly's consideration. Thirty-two formal meetings were held in addition to a number of informal ones, as the Committee continued efforts to harmonize views on the convening of a Conference on the Indian Ocean—as first decided by the Assembly in 1979[44] as a necessary step for implementing the Declaration.

Membership of the *Ad Hoc* Committee rose to 48, with the appointment of Uganda by the Assembly President on 26 July 1984.[45]

At its first session of the year, the *Ad Hoc* Committee agreed to a suggestion by the Chairman to devote equal time to organizational work, including the provisional agenda for the Conference and consideration of appropriate arrangements for any international agreement that might ultimately be reached on maintaining the Indian Ocean as a zone of peace, and to substantive issues related to the zone of peace.

At its July session, the Committee accepted a formulation, reached by its Chairman through consultations, that decisions in matters affecting the Indian Ocean would be taken by consensus, it being understood that consensus meant the absence of any formal objection by a delegation against taking a decision. The formulation was meant to guide the Committee's work, but not to be taken as a precedent applicable to other discussions and negotiations.

Among documents submitted to the Committee in 1984 was one, introduced in March by Sri Lanka on behalf of the non-aligned members of the Committee, on a draft framework of the provisional agenda for the Conference.[46] In July, the Committee received draft provisional rules of procedure of the proposed Conference,[47] prepared by the Secretariat at the Committee's request. The USSR presented, on 10 July,[48] an April 1984 letter from its Minister for Foreign Affairs to the Secretary-General, on limiting and reducing naval activities and armaments (see p. 67), including those in the Indian Ocean.

Two different approaches continued to be advocated in the Committee. Most delegations, mainly non-aligned and Eastern European States, were of the opinion that the Committee should proceed without delay to prepare for the Conference with the aim of holding it in the first half of 1985. The Western States, however, emphasized the need for harmonizing views on substantive issues related to the proposed zone of peace and for improving the political and security climate in the region before contemplating the convening of the Conference.

On 31 August, the Committee adopted by consensus parts I and II of its report to the General Assembly, but was not able to agree on part III, containing a draft resolution to be recommended to the Assembly for adoption. As the result of an informal open-ended drafting group meeting to elaborate the text, the Committee adopted that part of the report by consensus on 21 November.

The draft resolution, which was later adopted by the Assembly (see below), differed in a number of ways from a draft text submitted to the Committee in August by Sri Lanka on behalf of the non-aligned members of the Committee.[49] By that text, the Assembly would have, among other things: decided to open the proposed Conference in the first half of 1985; requested the *Ad Hoc* Committee to hold sessions totalling 10 weeks in early 1985, including one session outside New York, to complete the preparatory work; and requested the Secretary-General to set up a Conference secretariat headed by a secretary-general.

Related action. In an October 1984 communiqué,[50] the Meeting of Ministers for Foreign Affairs and Heads of Delegation of Non-Aligned Countries (New York, 1-5 October) expressed concern over the continuous escalation of great-Power military presence in the Indian Ocean area, and reaffirmed their determination to ensure that the Conference be held during 1985. It also expressed satisfaction over initiatives by the President of Madagascar in suggesting the convening of a summit conference on the Indian Ocean at Tananarive.

GENERAL ASSEMBLY ACTION

On 17 December 1984, the General Assembly adopted without vote resolution 39/149, the draft of which had been recommended by the *Ad Hoc* Committee on the Indian Ocean and approved by the First Committee.

Implementation of the Declaration of the Indian Ocean as a Zone of Peace

The General Assembly,

Recalling the Declaration of the Indian Ocean as a Zone of Peace, contained in its resolution 2832(XXVI) of 16 December 1971, and recalling also its resolutions 2992(XXVII) of 15 December 1972, 3080(XXVIII) of 6 December 1973, 3259 A (XXIX) of 9 December 1974, 3468(XXX) of 11 December 1975, 31/88 of 14 December 1976, 32/86 of 12 December 1977, S-10/2 of 30 June 1978, 33/68 of 14 December 1978, 34/80 A and B of 11 December 1979, 35/150 of 12 December 1980, 36/90 of 9 December 1981, 37/96 of 13 December 1982 and 38/185 of 20 December 1983, and other relevant resolutions,

Recalling further the report of the Meeting of the Littoral and Hinterland States of the Indian Ocean,

Reaffirming its conviction that concrete action for the achievement of the objectives of the Declaration of the Indian Ocean as a Zone of Peace would be a substantial contribution to the strengthening of international peace and security,

Recalling its decision, taken at its thirty-fourth session in resolution 34/80 B, to convene a Conference on the Indian Ocean at Colombo during 1981,

Recalling also its decision to make every effort, in consideration of the political and security climate in the Indian Ocean area and progress made in the harmonization of views, to finalize, in accordance with its normal methods of work, all preparations for the Conference, including the dates for its convening,

Recalling further its decision, taken at its thirty-eighth session in resolution 38/185, concerning the convening of the Conference in the first half of 1985,

Recalling the exchange of views in the *Ad Hoc* Committee on the Indian Ocean in 1984,

Noting the exchange of views on the adverse political and security climate in the region,

Noting further the various documents before the *Ad Hoc* Committee,

Convinced that the continued military presence of the great Powers in the Indian Ocean area, conceived in the context of their confrontation, gives urgency to the need to take practical steps for the early achievement of the objectives of the Declaration of the Indian Ocean as a Zone of Peace,

Considering that any other foreign military presence in the area, whenever it is contrary to the objectives of the Declaration of the Indian Ocean as a Zone of Peace and the purposes and principles of the Charter of the United Nations, gives greater urgency to the need to take practical steps towards the early achievement of the objectives of the Declaration,

Considering also that the creation of a zone of peace in the Indian Ocean requires the active participation of and full co-operation among the littoral and hinterland States, the permanent members of the Security Council and the major maritime users to ensure conditions of peace and security based on the purposes and principles of the Charter, as well as on the general principles of international law,

Considering further that the creation of a zone of peace requires co-operation and agreement among the States of the region to ensure conditions of peace and security within the area, as envisaged in the Declaration of the Indian Ocean as a Zone of Peace, and respect for the independence, sovereignty and territorial integrity of the littoral and hinterland States,

Calling for the renewal of genuinely constructive efforts through the exercise of the political will necessary for the achievement of the objectives of the Declaration of the Indian Ocean as a Zone of Peace,

Deeply concerned at the danger posed by the grave and ominous developments in the area and the resulting sharp deterioration of peace, security and stability which particularly seriously affect the littoral and hinterland States, as well as international peace and security,

Convinced that the continued deterioration of the political and security climate in the Indian Ocean area is an important consideration bearing on the question of the urgent convening of the Conference and that the easing of tension in the area would enhance the prospect of success being achieved by the Conference,

1. *Takes note* of the report of the *Ad Hoc* Committee on the Indian Ocean and the exchange of views in the Committee;

2. *Emphasizes* its decision to convene the Conference on the Indian Ocean at Colombo as a necessary step for the implementation of the Declaration of the Indian Ocean as a Zone of Peace, adopted in 1971;

3. *Takes note* of the progress made by the *Ad Hoc* Committee during 1984;

4. *Requests* the *Ad Hoc* Committee, taking into account the political and security climate in the region, to complete preparatory work relating to the Conference on the Indian Ocean, in 1985, in order to enable the opening of the Conference at Colombo thereafter at the earliest date in the first half of 1986 to be decided by the Committee in consultation with the host country;

5. *Decides* that preparatory work would comprise organizational matters and substantive issues, including the provisional agenda for the Conference, rules of procedure, participation, stages of conference, level of representation, documentation, consideration of appropriate arrangements for any international agreements that may ultimately be reached for the maintenance of the Indian Ocean as a zone of peace and the preparation of the draft final document of the Conference;

6. *Requests* the *Ad Hoc* Committee at the same time to seek the necessary harmonization of views on remaining relevant issues;

7. *Requests* the Chairman of the *Ad Hoc* Committee to consult the Secretary-General, at the appropriate time, on the establishment of a secretariat for the Conference;

8. *Renews* the mandate of the *Ad Hoc* Committee as defined in the relevant resolutions, and requests the Committee to intensify its work with regard to the implementation of its mandate;

9. *Requests* the *Ad Hoc* Committee to hold three further preparatory sessions in 1985 of a duration of two weeks each, with the possibility of holding a fourth session to be considered as required;

10. *Requests* the Chairman of the *Ad Hoc* Committee to continue his consultations on the participation in the work of the Committee by States Members of the United Nations which are not members of the Committee, with the aim of resolving this matter at the earliest possible date;

11. *Requests* the *Ad Hoc* Committee to submit to the General Assembly at its fortieth session a full report on the implementation of the present resolution;

12. *Requests* the Secretary-General to continue to render all necessary assistance to the *Ad Hoc* Committee, including the provision of summary records, in recognition of its preparatory function.

General Assembly resolution 39/149

17 December 1984   Meeting 102   Adopted without vote

Approved by First Committee (A/39/752) without vote, 28 November (meeting 51); draft by Committee on Indian Ocean (A/39/29); agenda item 62.
Financial implications. 5th Committee, A/39/801/Rev.1; S-G, A/C.1/39/L.81, A/C.5/39/67.
Meeting numbers. GA 39th session: 1st Committee 3-36, 47, 51; 5th Committee 41; plenary 102.

A number of delegations, in explanation of position, expressed regret over the renewed postponement of the proposed Conference, with many stressing its importance towards implementing the 1971 Declaration. Indonesia said the draft resolution did not reflect its basic position; it was not satisfied with the inordinate delay in the convening of the Conference. Expressing hope that postponement would not become an annual ritual, Democratic Yemen said that, unless genuine efforts were made, the Committee would still face obstacles created by the Western countries and would not complete preparatory work. Similarly, Bulgaria stated that the *Ad Hoc* Committee's inability to set a date was due to lack of readiness and political will on the part of a minority of its members. Madagascar was disillusioned that, in order to achieve consensus, the *Ad Hoc* Committee had been forced to make a fourth postponement; it added that harmonization of views on substantive questions, while important, should not be placed above the security needs of the States of the region.

The German Democratic Republic said that some elements in the text practically set preconditions and did not contribute to the Conference preparatory work and the establishment of the zone of peace. India regretted that attempts were being made not only to delay implementing the Declaration, which spelt out the nature and scope of the Conference, but also to portray the concept of the zone as a purely regional disarmament measure; it called for restoring a proper sense of direction in the Committee's work.

Pakistan, which felt the draft showed some progress over that of the preceding year, believed that a partial approach dealing only with foreign military presence was unlikely to realize the peace-zone objective; the regional States themselves needed to enter into arrangements, including those for renouncing nuclear weapons; it considered the preparation of a draft final document as an essential prerequisite for the convening of the Conference.

The USSR recalled its proposal that coastal States of the Indian Ocean should declare that they would refrain from worsening the situation in the area, without awaiting the convening of the Conference.

South-East Asia

In resolution 39/5 of 30 October 1984 on the situation in Kampuchea, the General Assembly again urged the South-East Asia countries to renew their efforts to establish a zone of peace, freedom and neutrality in the region (see Chapter VII of this section).

Confidence-building measures

Disarmament Commission consideration. In pursuance of a December 1983 General Assembly resolution,[51] the Disarmament Commission[1] established Working Group III on 7 May 1984 to elaborate guidelines for appropriate types of confidence-building measures and for their global or regional implementation. The Group held 11 meetings between 11 and 30 May, as well

as informal consultations, under the chairmanship of Henning Wegener (Federal Republic of Germany). In addition to the related documents from 1983,[52] it had before it four new working papers—those submitted by Finland, the Federal Republic of Germany and a group of socialist countries (Bulgaria, Byelorussian SSR, Czechoslovakia, German Democratic Republic, Hungary, Mongolia, Poland, Ukrainian SSR, USSR), and the Chairman's composite draft of guidelines for confidence-building measures.

In summarizing its work, the Working Group stated that, while the guidelines could not be finalized, its extensive debate had been useful. In its recommendations, which were approved by the Committee of the Whole on 31 May, the Group recommended that the Assembly urge States to consider the widest possible use of confidence-building measures in their international relations, and decide, at its 1984 session, on a format to conclude work on the guidelines as early as possible.

GENERAL ASSEMBLY ACTION

On the recommendation of the First Committee, the General Assembly, on 12 December 1984, adopted resolution 39/63 E without vote.

Consideration of guidelines for confidence-building measures

The General Assembly,

Recalling its resolution 38/73 A of 15 December 1983 on confidence-building measures,

Taking note of the views expressed and the useful work accomplished during the 1983 and 1984 sessions of the Disarmament Commission,

Aware of the heightened importance of confidence-building measures as well as of measures of disarmament in the present international situation,

Expressing its regret that, notwithstanding the progress already achieved, the guidelines for appropriate types of confidence-building measures and for the implementation of such measures on a global or regional level could not be elaborated fully within the allotted time frame,

1. *Reiterates its invitation* to all States to encourage and assist all efforts designed to explore further the ways in which confidence-building measures can strengthen peace and security and promote disarmament;

2. *Urges* all States to consider the widest possible use of confidence-building measures in their international relations, taking into account the views expressed during the work of the Disarmament Commission;

3. *Requests* the Disarmament Commission, at its 1986 session, to continue and conclude its consideration of the item "Elaboration of guidelines for appropriate types of confidence-building measures and for the implementation of such measures on a global or regional level";

4. *Further requests* the Disarmament Commission to submit to the General Assembly at its forty-first session a report containing such guidelines;

5. *Decides* to include in the provisional agenda of its fortieth session the item entitled "Consideration of guidelines for confidence-building measures".

General Assembly resolution 39/63 E

12 December 1984   Meeting 97   Adopted without vote

Approved by First Committee (A/39/750) without vote, 21 November (meeting 46); 39-nation draft (A/C.1/39/L.36); agenda item 60 *(a)*.
Sponsors: Austria, Bahamas, Bangladesh, Belgium, Bolivia, Cameroon, Canada, Chile, Congo, Denmark, Ecuador, Egypt, Finland, France, Germany, Federal Republic of, Ghana, Greece, Ireland, Italy, Japan, Liberia, Mali, Mauritania, Netherlands, New Zealand, Norway, Pakistan, Peru, Philippines, Romania, Rwanda, Spain, Sudan, Sweden, Turkey, United Kingdom, United States, Uruguay, Zaire.
Meeting numbers. GA 39th session: 1st Committee 3-36, 46; plenary 97.

In explanation of position, the USSR expressed concern that the subject had been exploited to create illusions that confidence could be created by building up armaments, if accompanied by openness; it added that confidence-building measures should be determined for each individual case in the light of specific circumstances. India could not support placing confidence-building measures on the same footing as disarmament measures, as in the third preambular paragraph. The Byelorussian SSR regretted that the text did not reflect that confidence-building measures could not replace those for disarmament and that they needed to be buttressed by practical steps.

In another 1984 disarmament resolution (39/151 I), the Assembly reaffirmed the need to extend confidence-building measures to seas and oceans.

Disarmament and international security

Concerned over the deterioration in world affairs, the General Assembly, in 1984, called on the Security Council to hold meetings on the escalating arms race (resolution 39/63 K).

Study on concepts of security. Pursuant to a December 1983 Assembly resolution,[53] the Secretary-General established in early 1984 the Group of Governmental Experts to Carry Out a Comprehensive Study of Concepts of Security. The study was to focus on security policies emphasizing co-operative efforts and mutual understanding between States, with a view to developing proposals for policies aimed at preventing the arms race, building confidence in relations between States, enhancing the possibility of reaching agreements on arms limitation and disarmament and promoting political and economic security.

The Group—13 experts from Algeria, Argentina, Australia, China, the German Democratic Republic, India, the Philippines, Romania, Sweden, Uganda, the USSR, Venezuela and Yugoslavia—which held one session in 1984 from 23 to 27 July, under the chairmanship of Anders Ferm (Sweden), adopted an outline and requested the Secretariat to prepare a first draft of the study. Three further sessions were scheduled in 1985 to enable the Secretary-General to submit the final report to the Assembly's 1985 session.

Related action. In October 1984,[50] the non-aligned countries (see p. 79) asserted that the escalating arms race, the rise in international tensions and the absence of constructive dialogue among the nuclear-weapon States had reached unprecedented levels; they declared that international peace and security could be ensured only through general and complete disarmament, particularly nuclear disarmament under effective international control.

GENERAL ASSEMBLY ACTION

On the recommendation of the First Committee, the General Assembly, on 12 December 1984, adopted resolution 39/63 K by recorded vote.

Disarmament and international security

The General Assembly,

Gravely concerned over the sharp deterioration in world affairs characterized by the continued recourse to the use of force, in violation of the Charter of the United Nations, and the escalation of the arms race, particularly in new and more destructive nuclear weapons, adding to their quantity and quality,

Concerned also over the vast expenditure, amounting to many billions of dollars, in escalation of the arms race while millions are dying from famine this year,

Bearing in mind that under Article 26 of the Charter the Security Council shall be responsible for formulating plans for the establishment of a system for the regulation of armaments,

Considering that in these circumstances, coinciding as they do with the fortieth anniversary of the United Nations, the international community must cross the threshold and take a historical decision to bring the arms race, particularly the nuclear-arms race, to a halt before it is too late,

1. *Calls upon* the Security Council to hold a series of meetings devoted to the consideration of the escalating arms race—particularly the nuclear-arms race—with a view to initiating due procedures, in accordance with the Charter of the United Nations, for bringing it to a halt;

2. *Requests* the Secretary-General to report thereon to the General Assembly at its fortieth session.

General Assembly resolution 39/63 K

12 December 1984   Meeting 97   128-0-19 (recorded vote)

Approved by First Committee (A/39/750) by recorded vote (99-0-22), 26 November (meeting 48); draft by Cyprus (A/C.1/39/L.67/Rev.2); agenda item 60 *(g)*.
Meeting numbers. GA 39th session: 1st Committee 3-37, 48; plenary 97.
Recorded vote in Assembly as follows:

In favour: Afghanistan, Algeria, Angola, Antigua and Barbuda, Argentina, Australia, Bahamas, Bahrain, Bangladesh, Barbados, Belize, Benin, Bhutan, Bolivia, Botswana, Brazil, Brunei Darussalam, Bulgaria, Burkina Faso, Burma, Burundi, Byelorussian SSR, Cameroon, Cape Verde, Central African Republic, Chad, Chile, China, Colombia, Comoros, Congo, Costa Rica, Cuba, Cyprus, Czechoslovakia, Democratic Yemen, Djibouti, Dominica, Dominican Republic, Ecuador, Egypt, El Salvador, Equatorial Guinea, Ethiopia, Fiji, Gabon, German Democratic Republic, Ghana, Greece, Guatemala, Guinea, Guinea-Bissau, Guyana, Haiti, Honduras, Hungary, India, Indonesia, Iran,[a] Iraq, Ireland, Ivory Coast, Jamaica, Jordan, Kenya, Kuwait, Lao People's Democratic Republic, Lebanon, Lesotho, Liberia, Libyan Arab Jamahiriya, Madagascar, Malawi, Malaysia, Maldives, Mali, Mauritania, Mauritius, Mexico, Mongolia, Morocco, Mozambique, Nepal, New Zealand, Nicaragua, Niger, Nigeria, Oman, Pakistan, Panama, Papua New Guinea, Paraguay, Peru, Philippines, Poland, Qatar, Romania, Saint Lucia, Samoa, Sao Tome and Principe, Saudi Arabia, Senegal, Seychelles, Sierra Leone, Singapore,

Somalia, Sri Lanka, Sudan, Suriname, Syrian Arab Republic, Thailand, Togo, Trinidad and Tobago, Tunisia, Uganda, Ukrainian SSR, USSR, United Arab Emirates, United Republic of Tanzania, Uruguay, Vanuatu, Venezuela, Viet Nam, Yemen, Yugoslavia, Zaire, Zambia, Zimbabwe.

Against: None.

Abstaining: Austria, Belgium, Canada, Denmark, Finland, France, Germany, Federal Republic of, Iceland, Italy, Japan, Luxembourg, Netherlands, Norway, Portugal, Rwanda, Spain, Sweden, United Kingdom, United States.

[a]Later advised the Secretariat it had intended not to participate in the vote.

In related action, the Assembly, in resolution 39/155 on implementing its 1970 Declaration on strengthening international security, called for general and complete disarmament under effective international control and, among other things, reiterated its call to the great Powers to abandon policies of confrontation which gave rise to tension and mistrust and to negotiate in good faith, taking into account the interests of the entire international community (see p. 116).

The question of disarmament and international security was also taken up by the Assembly in other 1984 disarmament resolutions, among them 39/59 and 39/148 M and O, and in decision 39/423.

Disarmament and development

In 1984, the General Assembly decided to hold at a future date an International Conference on the Relationship between Disarmament and Development (resolution 39/160) and set the venue for the Preparatory Committee (decision 39/424).

Disarmament Commission consideration. In 1984, the Disarmament Commission[1] took up consideration of proposals concerning the relationship between disarmament and development—an item added to its agenda in pursuance of a December 1983 General Assembly request.[54]

Working Group IV, established by the Commission on 7 May to deal with the topic, held nine meetings between 11 and 30 May under the chairmanship of Uddhav Deo Bhatt (Nepal), who also conducted informal consultations. The Working Group considered a proposal by France for an international conference, as well as replies received by the Secretary-General from 29 Member States—with six additional States replying after the Commission's session[55]—in response to the Assembly's 1983 invitation[54] for views and proposals concerning the relationship between disarmament and development.

Although members in the Working Group agreed that the world economy, and the economies of the developing countries in particular, would benefit from international action that took into account the close relationship between disarmament and development, opinions differed as to the specific structure and content of the recommendation the Commission might make to the Assembly.

Several members wanted the Commission to recommend that the Assembly decide in 1984 to convene an international conference under the auspices of the United Nations, preceded by thorough preparations. They envisioned the purpose of the conference as being to: conduct a comprehensive review of the relationship; examine the impact of continuing military expenditures on the world economy and the international economic and social situation; and consider ways of channelling a significant part of the resources for military purposes to socio-economic development, particularly of the developing countries.

Another group of countries, however, asserted that the holding of a special conference, which had nothing to do with disarmament measures, would not only be inappropriate, but might be used by the opponents of disarmament as a screen to conceal their unwillingness to take real steps for arms limitation. They proposed that the Commission recommend that the Assembly appeal to the Conference on Disarmament, as the sole multilateral disarmament negotiating body, to accelerate elaborating international agreements on all items of its agenda, and appeal to all Member States to take account of the importance of ensuring that the resources released as a result of implementing disarmament measures would be used to promote the well-being of all peoples and to improve economic conditions in the developing countries.

The Working Group concluded that the Commission should recommend continued efforts to enable the Assembly to reach, at its 1984 session, a broad measure of agreement on the topic.

International disarmament fund for development. In May 1984, UNIDIR submitted to the General Assembly, through the Secretary-General, a report on an investigation, carried out in response to a 1982 Assembly request,[56] of the modalities of an international disarmament fund for development.[57]

Intended to be more limited and specific in scope than the 1981 study by the Group of Governmental Experts on the Relationship between Disarmament and Development,[58] the UNIDIR study focused on the political, administrative and financial aspects of such a fund. The report concluded that the establishment of a fund was a desirable and tangible way of recognizing the link between disarmament and development and starting the process of transferring the resources to development. It recommended that the fund be established phase by phase, but only if assured of adequate resources from the beginning.

GENERAL ASSEMBLY ACTION

In separate actions taken in December 1984, the General Assembly decided to convene a Conference and selected the venue of its Preparatory Committee.

On 17 December, the Assembly, acting on the recommendation of the First Committee, adopted resolution 39/160 without vote.

Relationship between disarmament and development

The General Assembly,

Recalling its resolution 38/71 B, of 15 December 1983,

Recalling the provisions of the Final Document of the Tenth Special Session of the General Assembly, concerning the relationship between disarmament and development,

Considering:

(a) That world-wide military spending has acquired a staggering magnitude and the global trend continues to be towards a faster rate of annual increase in these expenditures,

(b) That this situation stands in dramatic contrast to the sombre state of the global economy and has serious implications for the economic prospects of the world, particularly those of the developing countries,

(c) That the world economy, particularly that of developing countries, would benefit from appropriate international action that took into account the close relationship of disarmament and development,

Also considering that in view of the importance and urgency of giving international consideration and practical expression to that relationship, the time has come for a comprehensive discussion of the subject at a high political level,

Taking note of the report adopted by the Disarmament Commission at the end of its 1984 session,

Taking note, in particular, of the recommendation contained in the report of the Disarmament Commission according to which efforts should be continued to enable the General Assembly to reach, at its thirty-ninth session, a broad measure of agreement on the subject, taking into account the views expressed in the report,

1. *Decides* to convene an International Conference on the Relationship between Disarmament and Development, which should be preceded by thorough preparation and should take decisions by consensus;

2. *Also decides* that the purposes of the Conference should be:

(a) To review the relationship between disarmament and development in all its aspects and dimensions with a view to reaching appropriate conclusions;

(b) To undertake an examination of the implications of the level and magnitude of the continuing military expenditures, in particular those of nuclear-weapon States and other militarily important States, for the world economy and international economic and social situation, particularly for the developing countries, and to make recommendations for remedial measures;

(c) To consider ways and means of releasing additional resources, through disarmament measures, for development purposes, in particular in favour of developing countries;

3. *Further decides* to set up a Preparatory Committee for the International Conference on the Relationship between Disarmament and Development composed of fifty-four members, which should formulate and submit, by consensus, to the General Assembly at its fortieth session, recommendations as to the provisional agenda, procedure, place, date and duration of the Conference.

General Assembly resolution 39/160

17 December 1984   Meeting 102   Adopted without vote

Approved by First Committee (A/39/745) without vote, 21 November (meeting 46); 34-nation draft (A/C.1/39/L.72/Rev.1); agenda item 55.

Sponsors: Bahamas, Bangladesh, Burkina Faso, Cameroon, Colombia, Djibouti, Ecuador, Egypt, France, Gabon, Ghana, Greece, India, Indonesia, Ivory Coast, Kenya, Liberia, Mali, Mauritania, Mexico, Nepal, Niger, Norway, Pakistan, Senegal, Sri Lanka, Sudan, Sweden, Trinidad and Tobago, Tunisia, Uruguay, Venezuela, Yugoslavia, Zaire.

Financial implications. ACABQ, A/39/7/Add.10; 5th Committee, A/39/795; S-G, A/C.1/39/L.79, A/C.5/39/60.

Meeting numbers. GA 39th session: 1st Committee 3-36, 40, 46; 5th Committee 43; plenary 102.

Introducing the text on behalf of the sponsors, France said the topic could be discussed only in an essentially political conference; it felt that the Preparatory Committee's projected membership of 54—corresponding to that of the Economic and Social Council—would allow for satisfactory representation of the various regional groups.

The United Kingdom believed that the conference should focus on the general relationship between disarmament and development, and on the underlying international and regional security situations which led States to spend scarce resources on defence; currently, it would be inappropriate for such a forum to discuss reallocation of resources. It saw no automatic link between the process of disarmament, the reallocation of resources that might result from such a process and the provision of development aid; it believed that any relationship between disarmament and development should be considered in a more complex triangular relationship that included security.

Argentina, questioning the advisability of changes made during efforts to achieve a generally accepted draft, was concerned about what it saw as a growing trend to impose the consensus rule on all disarmament-related decisions. Brazil expressed similar reservations, adding that the growing trend promoted by the super-Powers and their allies, towards institutionalizing the consensus rule in multilateral decision-making, was tantamount to extending the veto power to all occasions.

The Assembly adopted, on an oral proposal by its President, decision 39/424 without vote.

Venue of the Preparatory Committee for the International Conference on the Relationship between Disarmament and Development

At its 102nd plenary meeting, on 17 December 1984, the General Assembly decided that the preferred venue of the Preparatory Committee for the International Conference on the Relationship between Disarmament and Development should be Geneva, provided that that would not entail any additional expenditure for the United Nations.

General Assembly decision 39/424

Adopted without vote

Oral proposal by President; agenda item 55.

In follow-up action to resolution 39/160 on 18 December, the Assembly agreed to the President's oral suggestion that he should appoint the Preparatory Committee's members.

Parties and signatories to disarmament agreements

In September 1984, the Secretary-General submitted to the General Assembly his annual report on the status of multilateral disarmament agreements,[59] based on information received from the States depositaries of those agreements. Listing the parties to and signatories of agreements as at 31 July 1984, the report also contained similar information on the Convention on the Prohibition of Military or Any Other Hostile Use of Environmental Modification Techniques (see p. 73), the Agreement Governing the Activities of States on the Moon and Other Celestial Bodies (see p. 106), and the Convention on Prohibitions or Restrictions on the Use of Certain Conventional Weapons Which May Be Deemed to Be Excessively Injurious or to Have Indiscriminate Effects (see p. 66), of which the Secretary-General was the depositary.

As at 31 December 1984, the following numbers of States had become parties to the agreements covered in the Secretary-General's report (listed in chronological order, with the years in which they were initially signed or opened for signature in parentheses):[60]

(Geneva) Protocol for the Prohibition of the Use in War of Asphyxiating, Poisonous or Other Gases, and of Bacteriological Methods of Warfare (1925): 105 parties

The Antarctic Treaty (1959): 32 parties

Treaty Banning Nuclear Weapons Tests in the Atmosphere, in Outer Space and under Water (1963): 111 parties

Treaty on Principles Governing the Activities of States in the Exploration and Use of Outer Space, including the Moon and Other Celestial Bodies (1967):[61] 84 parties

Treaty for the Prohibition of Nuclear Weapons in Latin America (1967): 31 parties

Treaty on the Non-Proliferation of Nuclear Weapons (1968):[62] 125 parties

Treaty on the Prohibition of the Emplacement of Nuclear Weapons and Other Weapons of Mass Destruction on the Sea-Bed and the Ocean Floor and in the Subsoil Thereof (1971):[63] 74 parties

Convention on the Prohibition of the Development, Production and Stockpiling of Bacteriological (Biological) and Toxin Weapons and on Their Destruction (1972):[64] 100 parties (see also p. 58)

Convention on the Prohibition of Military or Any Other Hostile Use of Environmental Modification Techniques (1977):[16] 47 parties

Agreement Governing the Activities of States on the Moon and Other Celestial Bodies (1979):[65] 5 parties

Convention on Prohibitions or Restrictions on the Use of Certain Conventional Weapons Which May Be Deemed to Be Excessively Injurious or to Have Indiscriminate Effects (1981): 24 parties

Proposed World Disarmament Conference

The idea of a world disarmament conference, first endorsed by the General Assembly in 1965,[66] was again discussed in 1984, as it had been every year since 1971. No further progress was made towards its convening, as the basic positions of nuclear-weapon States remained largely unchanged.

***Ad Hoc* Committee activities.** The 40-member *Ad Hoc* Committee on the World Disarmament Conference held two sessions in New York in 1984: four meetings each between 2 and 5 April and between 2 and 6 July. Its 1984 annual report[67] to the Assembly contained the updated views of the five nuclear-weapon States regarding the holding of such a conference. The Committee, which had been discussing the question since it first met in 1974,[68] also informed the Assembly that, through its Chairman, it had maintained close contact with those States so as to remain currently informed of their attitudes.

According to the report, the USSR continued to support the convening of a conference, rejected what it saw as attempts by some nuclear-weapon States to justify their unconstructive attitudes by allusions to the unfavourable international situation, and called for a decision on specific preparatory measures.

China expressed its readiness to support the holding of a conference if the majority of Member States favoured such an opportunity to discuss how the two super-Powers should take the lead in drastically cutting their armaments.

France, noting the absence of consensus on the question, said it had no objection to the *Ad Hoc* Committee's considering spacing its meetings in view of the persistent impasse. The United Kingdom maintained that, in the current international climate, no useful purpose would be served by preparing for a conference; it also doubted the usefulness of further Committee meetings, and considered it inappropriate for that body to undertake any substantive work. The United States continued to believe it premature to convene a conference, in view of the insufficient political agreement on fundamental disarmament issues, and that an unsuccessful conference would impede future efforts towards concrete and verifiable measures; it also stated that serious consideration should be given to whether or not future meetings of the Committee were warranted.

The *Ad Hoc* Committee reiterated its previous conclusions: that the idea of a world disarmament conference had wide support, though with varying degrees of emphasis and differences regarding conditions and aspects related to its convening, including the deteriorating international situation; and that no consensus on convening a conference under current conditions had been reached among the nuclear-weapon States, whose participation was widely deemed essential. It suggested that the Assembly might review the Committee's mandate and request it to maintain close contact with the nuclear-weapon and all other States and to consider any comments and observations which might be made to the Committee.

GENERAL ASSEMBLY ACTION

On the recommendation of the First Committee, the General Assembly, on 17 December 1984, adopted resolution 39/150 without vote.

World Disarmament Conference

The General Assembly,

Recalling its resolutions 2833(XXVI) of 16 December 1971, 2930(XXVII) of 29 November 1972, 3183(XXVIII) of 18 December 1973, 3260(XXIX) of 9 December 1974, 3469(XXX) of 11 December 1975, 31/190 of 21 December 1976, 32/89 of 12 December 1977, 33/69 of 14 December 1978, 34/81 of 11 December 1979, 35/151 of 12 December 1980, 36/91 of 9 December 1981, 37/97 of 13 December 1982 and 38/186 of 20 December 1983,

Reiterating its conviction that all the peoples of the world have a vital interest in the success of disarmament negotiations and that all States should be in a position to contribute to the adoption of measures for the achievement of this goal,

Stressing anew its conviction that a world disarmament conference, adequately prepared and convened at an appropriate time, could provide the realization of such an aim and that the co-operation of all nuclear-weapon Powers would considerably facilitate its attainment,

Taking note of the report of the *Ad Hoc* Committee on the World Disarmament Conference,

Recalling that, in paragraph 122 of the Final Document of the Tenth Special Session of the General Assembly, it decided that, at the earliest appropriate time, a world disarmament conference should be convened with universal participation and with adequate preparation,

Recalling also that, in paragraph 23 of the Declaration of the 1980s as the Second Disarmament Decade, contained in the annex to its resolution 35/46 of 3 December 1980, the General Assembly considered it pertinent also to recall that in paragraph 122 of the Final Document of the Tenth Special Session it had stated that at the earliest appropriate time a world disarmament conference should be convened with universal participation and with adequate preparation,

1. *Notes with satisfaction* that, in paragraph 14 of its report to the General Assembly, the *Ad Hoc* Committee on the World Disarmament Conference stated, *inter alia,* the following:

"Having regard for the important requirements of the world disarmament conference to be convened at the earliest appropriate time, with universal participation and with adequate preparation, the General Assembly should take up the question at its thirty-ninth session for further consideration, bearing in mind the relevant provisions of resolution 36/91, adopted by consensus, in particular paragraph 1 of that resolution, and resolution 38/186, also adopted by consensus";

2. *Renews* the mandate of the *Ad Hoc* Committee;

3. *Requests* the *Ad Hoc* Committee to continue to maintain close contact with the representatives of the nuclear-weapon States in order to remain currently informed of their positions, as well as with all other States, and to consider any relevant comments and observations which might be made to the Committee, especially bearing in mind paragraph 122 of the Final Document of the Tenth Special Session of the General Assembly;

4. *Requests* the *Ad Hoc* Committee to report to the General Assembly at its fortieth session;

5. *Decides* to include in the provisional agenda of its fortieth session the item entitled "World Disarmament Conference".

General Assembly resolution 39/150

17 December 1984   Meeting 102   Adopted without vote

Approved by First Committee (A/39/753) without vote, 19 November (meeting 41); 5-nation draft (A/C.1/39/L.23); agenda item 63.
Sponsors: Burundi, Peru, Poland, Spain, Sri Lanka.
Financial implications. ACABQ, A/39/7/Add.10; 5th Committee, A/39/795; S-G, A/C.1/39/L.74, A/C.5/39/59.
Meeting numbers. GA 39th session: 1st Committee 3-37, 41; 5th Committee 43; plenary 102.

In explanation of position, the United States repeated its position, as set out in the *Ad Hoc* Committee's report,[67] and wondered whether the funding for the Committee might not be better put to other uses.

Public information

In 1984, the World Disarmament Campaign, aimed at generating public understanding and support for the disarmament objectives of the United Nations, entered its third year of implementation. By resolution 39/63 J, the General Assembly provided for the Campaign's regional implementation. The second United Nations Pledging Conference for the World Disarmament Campaign was held in New York during Disarmament Week, and the Assembly, in resolution 39/63 D, decided to hold a third conference in 1985. In resolution 39/63 A, the Assembly called for wider publicity of its work on disarmament, and in resolution 39/148 J stressed the mass media's role in publicizing Disarmament Week.

World Disarmament Campaign

As the World Disarmament Campaign—launched by the General Assembly on 7 June 1982, at the start of its second special session devoted to disarmament[69]—entered its third year of implementation in 1984, diversified activities were carried out for informing, educating and generating public understanding and support for the disarmament objectives of the United Nations.

The Committee for Programme and Co-ordination, at its 1984 session,[70] discussed questions relating to the activities of the United Nations Department of Disarmament Affairs in implementing the Campaign.

Reports of the Secretary-General. In an October 1984 report,[71] submitted in response to a December 1983 Assembly request,[72] the

Secretary-General discussed various 1984 activities for promoting the Campaign's objectives, including publication of United Nations information materials; interpersonal communication, seminars and training; special events; a publicity programme; and the roles played by United Nations information centres and other field offices. Activities of relevant agencies and organizations in the United Nations system were also discussed.

The Department for Disarmament Affairs organized or participated in a number of conferences and seminars, among them a regional conference for the World Disarmament Campaign (Leningrad, USSR, 11-15 June) and a national seminar on peace and disarmament (Lomé, Togo, 6-9 August).[73]

In another October report,[12] submitted in pursuance of a 1982 Assembly request,[74] the Secretary-General observed that, as agreed in 1983,[75] the Advisory Board on Disarmament Studies (see p. 91) and representatives of non-governmental organizations discussed, in September, implementation of the Campaign.

GENERAL ASSEMBLY ACTION

The General Assembly, in 1984, adopted three resolutions on the World Disarmament Campaign—two concerning activities and one dealing with the Campaign's financial aspects.

On 12 December, on the recommendation of the First Committee, it adopted resolution 39/63 A by recorded vote.

World Disarmament Campaign: actions and activities

The General Assembly,

Aware of the growing public concern at the dangers of the arms race, particularly the nuclear-arms race, and its negative social and economic consequences,

Noting with satisfaction the successful implementation of the World Disarmament Campaign, launched by the General Assembly at its twelfth special session, the second special session devoted to disarmament, and its positive impact on the mobilization on a large scale of world public opinion on behalf of peace and disarmament,

Recalling its resolutions 36/92 J of 9 December 1981, 37/100 H of 13 December 1982 and 38/73 F of 15 December 1983, as well as the report of the Secretary-General on world-wide action for collecting signatures in support of measures to prevent nuclear war, to curb the arms race and for disarmament,

Welcoming the voluntary contributions made to the World Disarmament Campaign Voluntary Trust Fund to carry out the objectives of the Campaign,

Taking into account the report of the Secretary-General on the progress in the implementation of the programme of activities of the World Disarmament Campaign during 1984 and on the activities contemplated for 1985,

Convinced that the United Nations system, Member States, with respect for their sovereign rights, and other bodies, in particular non-governmental organizations, all have their role to play in achieving the objectives of the Campaign,

Taking into account the great number of various activities carried out within the framework of the Campaign, including actions for collecting signatures in support of measures to prevent nuclear war, to curb the arms race and for disarmament,

1. *Reaffirms* the usefulness of further carrying out actions and activities which are an important manifestation of the will of world public opinion and contribute effectively to the achievement of the objectives of the World Disarmament Campaign and thus to the creation of a favourable climate for making progress in the field of disarmament with a view to achieving the goal of general and complete disarmament under effective international control;

2. *Urges* the Governments of all States, especially the nuclear-weapon States and other militarily significant States, in formulating their policies in the field of disarmament, to take into account the main demands of the mass peace and disarmament movements, in particular, with regard to the prevention of nuclear war and curbing the nuclear-arms race;

3. *Reaffirms* the importance of carrying out the World Disarmament Campaign in accordance with the priorities in the field of disarmament established in the Final Document of the Tenth Special Session of the General Assembly, the first special session devoted to disarmament, taking into account that the adoption of effective measures for nuclear disarmament and prevention of nuclear war has the highest priority;

4. *Invites once again* Member States to co-operate with the United Nations to ensure a better flow of accurate information with regard to the various aspects of disarmament as well as actions and activities of the world public in support of peace and disarmament, and to avoid dissemination of false and tendentious information;

5. *Requests* the Secretary-General, in implementing the programme of activities of the World Disarmament Campaign, to give wider publicity to the work of the General Assembly in the field of disarmament, paying due attention, in particular, to the proposals of Member States and the action taken thereon;

6. *Also requests* the Secretary-General to report annually to the General Assembly on the implementation of the provisions of the present resolution.

General Assembly resolution 39/63 A

12 December 1984   Meeting 97   117-0-31 (recorded vote)

Approved by First Committee (A/39/750) by recorded vote (96-0-34), 19 November (meeting 41); 7-nation draft (A/C.1/39/L.17); agenda item 60 (d).

Sponsors: Bulgaria, Byelorussian SSR, German Democratic Republic, Mongolia, Romania, Ukrainian SSR, Viet Nam.

Meeting numbers. GA 39th session: 1st Committee 3-36, 40, 41; plenary 97.

Recorded vote in Assembly as follows:

In favour: Afghanistan, Algeria, Angola, Antigua and Barbuda, Argentina, Australia, Bahrain, Bangladesh, Barbados, Belize, Benin, Bhutan, Bolivia, Botswana, Brunei Darussalam, Bulgaria, Burkina Faso, Burundi, Byelorussian SSR, Cameroon, Cape Verde, Central African Republic, Chad, China, Colombia, Comoros, Congo, Costa Rica, Cuba, Cyprus, Czechoslovakia, Democratic Yemen, Djibouti, Dominica, Dominican Republic, Ecuador, Egypt, El Salvador, Equatorial Guinea, Ethiopia, Fiji, Gabon, German Democratic Republic, Ghana, Guinea, Guinea-Bissau, Guyana, Honduras, Hungary, India, Indonesia, Iran, Iraq, Ivory Coast, Jamaica, Jordan, Kenya, Kuwait, Lao People's Democratic Republic, Lebanon, Lesotho, Liberia, Libyan Arab Jamahiriya, Madagascar, Malawi, Malaysia, Maldives, Mali, Malta, Mauritania, Mauritius, Mexico, Mongolia, Morocco, Mozambique, Nepal, Nicaragua, Niger, Nigeria, Pakistan, Panama, Papua New Guinea, Peru, Philippines, Poland, Qatar, Romania, Rwanda, Saint Lucia, Samoa, Sao Tome and Principe, Saudi Arabia, Senegal, Seychelles, Sierra Leone, Somalia, Sri Lanka, Sudan, Suriname, Syrian Arab Republic, Thailand, Togo, Trinidad and

Tobago, Tunisia, Uganda, Ukrainian SSR, USSR, United Arab Emirates, United Republic of Tanzania, Vanuatu, Venezuela, Viet Nam, Yemen, Yugoslavia, Zaire, Zambia, Zimbabwe.
Against: None.
Abstaining: Austria, Bahamas, Belgium, Brazil, Burma, Canada, Chile, Democratic Kampuchea, Denmark, Finland, France, Germany, Federal Republic of, Greece, Guatemala, Haiti, Iceland, Ireland, Italy, Japan, Luxembourg, Netherlands, New Zealand, Norway, Paraguay, Portugal, Spain, Sweden, Turkey, United Kingdom, United States, Uruguay.

In explanation of vote, several States objected to the wording of paragraph 4. The United Kingdom could not support what it said appeared to be censorship of a free exchange of ideas. Sharing that view, Belgium added that its democratic tradition made it impossible for it to condemn ideas. Similarly, the United States said it believed in free and unhindered dissemination of information, and it was up to recipients to decide what was true or false.

Liberia, while supporting the text, also had reservations over questioning the credibility of information provided by Member States. Japan regarded the overall tone of the draft as more alarmist and emotional than the versions of previous years.

On 12 December 1984, the General Assembly, acting on the recommendation of the First Committee, adopted resolution 39/63 J without vote.

World Disarmament Campaign

The General Assembly,

Recalling that, in paragraph 15 of the Final Document of the Tenth Special Session of the General Assembly, the first special session devoted to disarmament, it declared that it was essential that not only Governments but also the peoples of the world recognize and understand the dangers in the present situation and stressed that in order that an international conscience might develop and that world public opinion might exercise a positive influence, the United Nations should increase the dissemination of information on the armaments race and disarmament with the full co-operation of Member States,

Recalling with satisfaction that the World Disarmament Campaign, whose first three fundamental objectives are to inform, to educate and to create understanding and public support for the objectives of the United Nations in the field of arms limitation and disarmament, was solemnly launched by unanimous decision of the General Assembly on 7 June 1982 at the opening meeting of the Assembly's twelfth special session, the second special session devoted to disarmament,

Recalling also its resolutions 37/100 I of 13 December 1982 and 38/73 D of 15 December 1983 on the implementation of the Campaign,

Taking fully into account the objectives, contents, modalities and financial implications of the Campaign defined by the General Assembly at its twelfth special session,

Reaffirming its conviction that the Campaign should be carried out under the auspices of the United Nations in all parts of the world in a balanced, positive and objective manner and that the universality of the Campaign should be guaranteed by the co-operation and par-

ticipation of all States and the widest possible diffusion of information relating to it,

Recognizing that, with a view to strengthening the objective of universality and giving the Campaign the confidence and continuity necessary to ensure its maximum effectiveness, there may be a need for arrangements at the regional level, making it possible to develop initiatives, discuss concepts and take specific action in order to promote the objectives of the Campaign with the participation of the countries of the region concerned,

Recalling its resolution 37/100 F of 13 December 1982 on regional disarmament,

Having examined the reports of the Secretary-General of 12 September 1984 on regional disarmament and of 3 October 1984 on the World Disarmament Campaign,

Taking note of the Lomé Peace Message, adopted by the National Seminar on Peace and Disarmament, held from 6 to 9 August 1984,

Convinced that the implementation of the recommendations contained in the aforementioned Peace Message would contribute significantly to the effective promotion of the objectives of the Campaign,

Desiring to make the best possible use of the contributions that have been or may be made by Member States in the form of local or non-convertible currency and also of other types of material assistance in the countries or regions concerned, in order to attain the objectives of the Campaign in specific countries or regions,

Emphasizing the need for maximum economy and maximum results in the administration of the Campaign,

Recognizing the potential beneficial effects in terms of results, efficiency and economy in the use of field offices to carry out all regional or local activities in the context of the programme of activities of the Campaign,

Reaffirming that the United Nations should furnish the informational material and should in general co-ordinate the implementation of the Campaign and that the Department of Disarmament Affairs of the Secretariat should supervise and centralize such co-ordination,

Aware of the specific needs of developing countries with regard to programmes of information, research and training in the fields of arms limitation and disarmament,

1. *Requests* the Secretary-General to provide assistance to such Member States in the regions concerned as may request it with a view to establishing regional and institutional arrangements for the implementation of the World Disarmament Campaign, on the basis of existing resources and of voluntary contributions which Member States may make to that end;

2. *Requests* the Secretary-General to report to the General Assembly at its fortieth session on the implementation of the present resolution.

General Assembly resolution 39/63 J

12 December 1984   Meeting 97   Adopted without vote

Approved by First Committee (A/39/750) without vote, 21 November (meeting 46); 18-nation draft (A/C.1/39/L.59), orally revised; agenda item 60 *(d)*.
Sponsors: Angola, Botswana, Burundi, Cameroon, Central African Republic, Chad, Congo, Djibouti, Guinea, Liberia, Mali, Mozambique, Niger, Senegal, Singapore, Thailand, Togo, Uganda.
Meeting numbers. GA 39th session: 1st Committee 3-36, 39, 46; plenary 97.

Although joining in the consensus, the Federal Republic of Germany cautioned that regional preferences, if introduced on too broad a scale into the World Disarmament Campaign, might cause the Secretariat to lose overall planning competence for the Campaign and jeopardize the principles of universality. The USSR understood that paragraph 1 would be implemented exclusively on the basis of existing resources and voluntary contributions.

In related action, the Assembly called on Member States to disseminate, in connection with the Campaign, the ideas of international co-operation for disarmament (resolution 39/148 M).

Financing

Report of the Secretary-General. In his October 1984 report to the Assembly,[71] the Secretary-General stated that successful implementation of the World Disarmament Campaign depended in part on the active and material support of Member States, especially contributions to the Campaign's Voluntary Trust Fund. He reported that, as at August 1984, 35 countries had made pledges to the Fund, totalling approximately $3.4 million, most of it in non-convertible currencies.

Pledges. The Second United Nations Pledging Conference for the World Disarmament Campaign, with 63 delegations participating, was convened at United Nations Headquarters on United Nations Day, 24 October, which also marked the opening day of Disarmament Week.

Either during the Conference or at other times in the course of the year, the following pledges were made: Australia ($A 50,000), Austria ($10,000), Cameroon (800,000 CFA francs), Canada ($Can 100,000), China (40,000 yuan renminbi), Hungary (100,000 forint), Indonesia ($5,000), Ireland (5,000 Irish pounds), Kuwait ($10,000), Lao People's Democratic Republic ($500), Mexico ($5,000), New Zealand ($10,000), Norway ($15,000), Pakistan (100,000 rupees), Sweden (180,000 kronor) and Yugoslavia ($5,000).

At the closing of the Conference, its President announced that 14 new pledges totalling $209,192 had been made at the Conference, in addition to written intentions to contribute.

GENERAL ASSEMBLY ACTION

Acting on the recommendation of the First Committee, the General Assembly, on 12 December 1984, adopted resolution 39/63 D by recorded vote.

World Disarmament Campaign

The General Assembly,

Recalling that in paragraph 15 of the Final Document of the Tenth Special Session of the General Assembly, the first special session devoted to disarmament, it declared that it was essential that not only Governments but also the peoples of the world recognize and under-

stand the dangers in the present situation and stressed the importance of mobilizing world public opinion on behalf of disarmament,

Recalling also its resolutions 35/152 I of 12 December 1980, 36/92 C of 9 December 1981, 37/100 I of 13 December 1982 and 38/73 D of 15 December 1983, as well as the reports of the Secretary-General of 17 September 1981, 11 June 1982, 3 November 1982 and 30 August 1983,

Having examined the report of the Secretary-General of 3 October 1984 on the implementation of the programme of activities of the World Disarmament Campaign during 1984 and the activities contemplated for 1985, as well as its main financial aspects,

Having also examined the part of the report of the Secretary-General of 4 October 1984 dealing with the activities of the Advisory Board on Disarmament Studies relating to the implementation of the World Disarmament Campaign, as well as the Final Act of the 1984 United Nations Pledging Conference for the Campaign, held on 24 October 1984,

1. *Commends* the manner in which, as described in the above-mentioned reports, the World Disarmament Campaign has been geared by the Secretary-General in order to guarantee "the widest possible dissemination of information and unimpeded access for all sectors of the public to a broad range of information and opinions on questions of arms limitation and disarmament and the dangers relating to all aspects of the arms race and war, in particular nuclear war";

2. *Recalls* that, as was also agreed by consensus at the twelfth special session of the General Assembly, the second special session devoted to disarmament, it is likewise an essential requisite for the universality of the World Disarmament Campaign that it receive "the co-operation and participation of all States";

3. *Endorses* the statement made by the Secretary-General on the occasion of the 1984 United Nations Pledging Conference for the World Disarmament Campaign to the effect that such co-operation implies that adequate funds be made available and that consequently the criterion of universality also applies to pledges, since a campaign without world-wide participation and funding will have difficulty in reflecting this principle in its implementation;

4. *Regrets* that most of the States which have the largest military expenditures have not so far made any financial contribution to the World Disarmament Campaign;

5. *Decides* that at its fortieth session there should be a third United Nations Pledging Conference for the World Disarmament Campaign, and expresses the hope that on that occasion all those Member States that have not yet announced any voluntary contribution may do so;

6. *Reiterates its recommendation* that the voluntary contributions made by Member States to the World Disarmament Campaign Voluntary Trust Fund should not be earmarked for specific activities inasmuch as it is most desirable that the Secretary-General enjoy full freedom to take the decisions he deems fit within the framework of the Campaign previously approved by the General Assembly and in exercise of the powers vested in him in connection with the Campaign;

7. *Requests* the Secretary-General to give permanent character to his instructions to the United Nations in-

formation centres and regional commissions to give wide publicity to the World Disarmament Campaign and, whenever necessary, to adapt, as far as possible, United Nations information materials to local languages;

8. *Also requests* the Secretary-General to submit to the General Assembly at its fortieth session a report covering both the implementation of the programme of activities of the World Disarmament Campaign by the United Nations system during 1985 and the programme of activities contemplated by the system for 1986;

9. *Decides* to include in the provisional agenda of its fortieth session the item entitled "World Disarmament Campaign".

General Assembly resolution 39/63 D

12 December 1984   Meeting 97   139-0-12 (recorded vote)

Approved by First Committee (A/39/750) by recorded vote (124-0-12), 19 November (meeting 41); 10-nation draft (A/C.1/39/L.35); agenda item 60 *(d)*.
Sponsors: Bangladesh, Egypt, Indonesia, Mexico, Pakistan, Romania, Sri Lanka, Sweden, Venezuela, Yugoslavia.
Meeting numbers. GA 39th session: 1st Committee 3-37, 41; plenary 97.

Recorded vote in Assembly as follows:

In favour: Afghanistan, Algeria, Angola, Antigua and Barbuda, Argentina, Australia, Austria, Bahrain, Bangladesh, Barbados, Belize, Benin, Bhutan, Bolivia, Botswana, Brazil, Brunei Darussalam, Bulgaria, Burkina Faso, Burma, Burundi, Byelorussian SSR, Cameroon, Canada, Cape Verde, Central African Republic, Chad, Chile, China, Colombia, Comoros, Congo, Costa Rica, Cuba, Cyprus, Czechoslovakia, Democratic Kampuchea, Democratic Yemen, Denmark, Djibouti, Dominica, Dominican Republic, Ecuador, Egypt, El Salvador, Equatorial Guinea, Ethiopia, Fiji, Finland, Gabon, German Democratic Republic, Ghana, Greece, Guatemala, Guinea, Guinea-Bissau, Guyana, Haiti, Honduras, Hungary, Iceland, India, Indonesia, Iran, Iraq, Ireland, Ivory Coast, Jamaica, Japan, Jordan, Kenya, Kuwait, Lao People's Democratic Republic, Lebanon, Lesotho, Liberia, Libyan Arab Jamahiriya, Madagascar, Malawi, Malaysia, Maldives, Mali, Malta, Mauritania, Mauritius, Mexico, Mongolia, Morocco, Mozambique, Nepal, New Zealand, Nicaragua, Niger, Nigeria, Norway, Oman, Pakistan, Panama, Papua New Guinea, Paraguay, Peru, Philippines, Poland, Portugal, Qatar, Romania, Saint Lucia, Samoa, Sao Tome and Principe, Saudi Arabia, Senegal, Seychelles, Sierra Leone, Singapore, Somalia, Spain, Sri Lanka, Sudan, Suriname, Sweden, Syrian Arab Republic, Thailand, Togo, Trinidad and Tobago, Tunisia, Uganda, Ukrainian SSR, USSR, United Arab Emirates, United Republic of Tanzania, Uruguay, Vanuatu, Venezuela, Viet Nam, Yemen, Yugoslavia, Zaire, Zambia, Zimbabwe.
Against: None.
Abstaining: Bahamas, Belgium, France, Germany, Federal Republic of, Israel, Italy, Luxembourg, Netherlands, Rwanda, Turkey, United Kingdom, United States.

Five Western countries explained their abstentions. France could not support the draft because of paragraph 4; it felt its efforts to disseminate disarmament information as well as its contribution to the budget of UNIDIR represented a sizeable contribution to the Campaign. Similarly, the United Kingdom noted that the Campaign was funded from regular United Nations resources, to which it annually contributed; further, it devoted substantial sums of money to its own disarmament information activities. Recalling that the Campaign was meant to be funded by voluntary contributions, the United States said it could not accept criticism of those who had not contributed. The Federal Republic of Germany added that, contrary to the implication of paragraph 3, the Campaign was to be conducted only if it encompassed all regions of the world without discrimination and if unimpeded access was accorded to the whole spectrum of information available on disarmament matters. Sharing that view, the Netherlands said the draft unduly emphasized the financial aspects of the Campaign, whose success

depended essentially on an unqualified free flow of information everywhere.

Disarmament Week (24-30 October)

Disarmament Week—proclaimed by the General Assembly in 1978[76] to start on United Nations Day, 24 October—was marked on that day in 1984 at United Nations Headquarters at a special meeting of the Assembly's First Committee, where statements were made by the Assembly President, the Secretary-General and representatives of regional groups.

In his message, the President decried the outlay of huge military expenditures at the expense of development needs, emphasized that the fast pace at which the trade and transfer of conventional weapons had been taking place merited serious attention, and advocated the complete prohibition of the development, production and stockpiling of all chemical weapons and their destruction.

The Secretary-General stressed the importance of international confidence in facilitating real progress in arms limitation and reduction. He called attention to military expenditures, estimated to reach $1 trillion in 1985—a sum that could otherwise benefit humanity, particularly the vast number of people living in conditions of scandalous underdevelopment. He emphasized that the long impasse in arms negotiations had to be broken and called for the opening of successful negotiations on nuclear weapons—the gravest threat to world security.

In October, the Secretary-General submitted to the Assembly in an annual report[77] the replies received from 18 Governments and from several United Nations bodies concerning activities in connection with Disarmament Week 1983. A number of international non-governmental organizations (NGOs) also supplied information.

On 25 October, the annual Disarmament Week NGO Forum, sponsored by the Department for Disarmament Affairs and the Department of Public Information, took place in New York. On the same day, an NGO Forum was held at Geneva for the first time—with Olof Palme, Prime Minister of Sweden, as key speaker.

GENERAL ASSEMBLY ACTION

On 17 December 1984, the General Assembly, acting on the First Committee's recommendation, adopted resolution 39/148 J by recorded vote.

Disarmament Week

The General Assembly,

Gravely concerned over the escalating arms race, especially the nuclear-arms race, which represents a serious threat to the very existence of mankind,

Stressing the vital importance of eliminating the threat of a nuclear war, ending the nuclear-arms race and bringing about disarmament for the maintenance of world peace,

Emphasizing anew the urgent need for and the importance of wide and continued mobilization of world public opinion in support of halting and reversing the arms race, especially the nuclear-arms race, in all its aspects,

Mindful of the world-wide mass anti-war and anti-nuclear movement,

Recognizing the important role of the mass media in mobilizing world public opinion in support of disarmament,

Noting with satisfaction the broad and active support by Governments and international and national organizations of the decision taken by the General Assembly at its tenth special session, the first special session devoted to disarmament, regarding the proclamation of the week starting 24 October, the day of the foundation of the United Nations, as a week devoted to fostering the objectives of disarmament,

Recalling the recommendations concerning the World Disarmament Campaign contained in annex V to the Concluding Document of the Twelfth Special Session of the General Assembly, the second special session devoted to disarmament, in particular the recommendation that Disarmament Week should continue to be widely observed,

Recalling also its resolutions 33/71 D of 14 December 1978, 34/83 I of 11 December 1979, 37/78 D of 9 December 1982 and 38/183 L of 20 December 1983,

1. *Takes note with satisfaction* of the report of the Secretary-General on the follow-up measures undertaken by governmental and non-governmental organizations in holding Disarmament Week;

2. *Expresses its appreciation* to all States and international and national governmental and non-governmental organizations for their energetic support of and active participation in Disarmament Week;

3. *Expresses serious concern* over the continued escalation of the arms race, especially the nuclear-arms race, and the imminent danger of its extension into outer space which gravely jeopardizes international peace and security and increases the danger of outbreak of a nuclear war;

4. *Stresses* the important role of the mass media in acquainting the world public with the aims of Disarmament Week and measures undertaken within its framework;

5. *Recommends* to all States that they observe Disarmament Week in 1985 in close connection with the celebrations of the fortieth anniversary of the foundation of the United Nations and the International Youth Year, as well as with other commemorative dates;

6. *Invites* all States, in carrying out appropriate measures at the local level on the occasion of Disarmament Week, to take into account the elements of the model programme for Disarmament Week, prepared by the Secretary-General;

7. *Invites* the relevant specialized agencies and the International Atomic Energy Agency to intensify activities, within their areas of competence, to disseminate information on the consequences of the arms race, especially the nuclear-arms race, and requests them to inform the Secretary-General accordingly;

8. *Also invites* international non-governmental organizations to take an active part in Disarmament Week and to inform the Secretary-General of the activities undertaken;

9. *Further invites* the Secretary-General to use the United Nations mass media as widely as possible to promote better understanding among the world public of disarmament problems and the objectives of Disarmament Week;

10. *Requests* Governments to continue, in accordance with General Assembly resolution 33/71 D, to inform the Secretary-General of activities undertaken to promote the objectives of Disarmament Week;

11. *Requests* the Secretary-General, in accordance with paragraph 4 of resolution 33/71 D, to submit to the General Assembly at its fortieth session a report on the implementation of the provisions of the present resolution.

General Assembly resolution 39/148 J

17 December 1984   Meeting 102   124-0-19 (recorded vote)

Approved by First Committee (A/39/749) by recorded vote (110-0-20), 19 November (meeting 41); 12-nation draft (A/C.1/39/L.39), orally revised; agenda item 59 (j).

Sponsors: Afghanistan, Angola, Bulgaria, Byelorussian SSR, Cuba, Czechoslovakia, German Democratic Republic, Lao People's Democratic Republic, Mongolia, Mozambique, Ukrainian SSR, Viet Nam.

Meeting numbers. GA 39th session: 1st Committee 3-37, 41; plenary 102.

Recorded vote in Assembly as follows:

In favour: Afghanistan, Algeria, Angola, Antigua and Barbuda, Argentina, Austria, Bahamas, Bahrain, Bangladesh, Barbados, Benin, Bhutan, Bolivia, Botswana, Brazil, Brunei Darussalam, Bulgaria, Burkina Faso, Burma, Burundi, Byelorussian SSR, Cameroon, Cape Verde, Central African Republic, Chad, Chile, Colombia, Congo, Costa Rica, Cuba, Cyprus, Czechoslovakia, Democratic Yemen, Djibouti, Dominican Republic, Ecuador, Egypt, El Salvador, Equatorial Guinea, Ethiopia, Fiji, Finland, Gabon, Gambia, German Democratic Republic, Ghana, Greece, Guatemala, Guinea, Guyana, Haiti, Honduras, Hungary, India, Indonesia, Iran, Iraq, Ireland, Jamaica, Japan, Jordan, Kenya, Kuwait, Lao People's Democratic Republic, Lebanon, Lesotho, Liberia, Libyan Arab Jamahiriya, Madagascar, Malawi, Malaysia, Maldives, Mali, Malta, Mauritania, Mauritius, Mexico, Mongolia, Morocco, Mozambique, Nepal, Nicaragua, Niger, Nigeria, Pakistan, Panama, Peru, Philippines, Poland, Portugal, Qatar, Romania, Rwanda, Saint Lucia, Saint Vincent and the Grenadines, Sao Tome and Principe, Saudi Arabia, Senegal, Seychelles, Sierra Leone, Somalia, Spain, Sri Lanka, Sudan, Suriname, Sweden, Syrian Arab Republic, Thailand, Togo, Trinidad and Tobago, Tunisia, Uganda, Ukrainian SSR, USSR, United Arab Emirates, United Republic of Tanzania, Uruguay, Venezuela, Viet Nam, Yemen, Yugoslavia, Zaire, Zambia, Zimbabwe.

Against: None.

Abstaining: Australia, Belgium, Canada, China, Denmark, France, Germany, Federal Republic of, Iceland, Israel, Italy, Ivory Coast, Luxembourg, Netherlands, New Zealand, Norway, Paraguay, Turkey, United Kingdom, United States.

In explanation of vote, Japan expressed reservations about what it regarded as alarmist overtones in the language used in the text. Australia felt it included inappropriate language concerning activities of IAEA and other specialized bodies. France felt that paragraph 7 called for activities diverting the agencies and IAEA from their proper fields of action.

Disarmament research

The General Assembly in 1984 approved, by resolution 39/148 H, the statute of the United Nations Institute for Disarmament Research, as prepared and revised by the Advisory Board on Disarmament Studies, acting as the Institute's Board of Trustees.

Two new disarmament studies were initiated by the Assembly in 1984.

Advisory Board on Disarmament Studies

The Advisory Board on Disarmament Studies, established in 1978 to advise the Secretary-General on various aspects of studies on disarmament and arms limitation,[78] held its tenth and eleventh sessions in 1984 (30 April–4 May, 10-14 September) under the chairmanship of Hadj Benabdelkader Azzout (Algeria).[12] The Board considered the United Nations studies on disarmament as well as implementation of the World Disarmament Campaign (see p. 86), and discussed the current disarmament situation. It also examined, in its capacity as the UNIDIR Board of Trustees, the UNIDIR work programme and draft statute (see p. 93).

The Board recommended, among other things, that the Assembly mandate a small group of governmental experts to carry out a study on the implications of deterrence (see below). It also agreed on the usefulness of inviting specialists to address the Board, considered a UNIDIR study on conditions and possibilities for negotiating reductions in nuclear weapons, and recommended further study of the question of information on military capabilities (see p. 72).

Disarmament studies

The General Assembly initiated two new disarmament studies in 1984—one, on deterrence and the other on the climatic effects of nuclear war (see p. 29). In addition, four studies were in progress, on nuclear-weapon-free zones, military research and development, concepts of security and the naval arms race.

The year saw the conclusion of two studies called for in previous years by the Assembly—one on unilateral nuclear disarmament measures, and the other on conventional disarmament.

Information on these studies can be found under the related subject headings in this chapter.

Study on deterrence

In 1984, the Advisory Board proposed that a group of governmental experts be asked to carry out a study on the implications of deterrence, which would cover the differing views and their supporting arguments, without attempting to arrive at joint conclusions and recommendations, thus permitting readers to draw their own conclusions.[12] The Board also suggested that UNIDIR could be involved in a consultative capacity.

GENERAL ASSEMBLY ACTION

In December 1984, the General Assembly, on the recommendation of the First Committee, adopted decision 39/423 by recorded vote.

Study on deterrence and its implications for disarmament and the arms race, negotiated arms reductions and international security and other related matters

At its 102nd plenary meeting, on 17 December 1984, the General Assembly, on the recommendation of the First Committee:

(a) Requested the Secretary-General to prepare a study under the title: "Deterrence: its implications for disarmament and the arms race, negotiated arms reductions and international security and other related matters", as recommended by the Advisory Board on Disarmament Studies in paragraph 6 of the report of the Secretary-General, to carry out the study in accordance with the recommendations of the Advisory Board in paragraphs 6 and 7 of the same document, and to submit the final report to the General Assembly at its forty-first session;

(b) Requested those Member States that wished to submit their views on the subject to communicate them to the Secretary-General not later than 1 April 1985.

General Assembly decision 39/423

17 December 1984   Meeting 102   145-1 (recorded vote)

Approved by First Committee (A/39/749) by recorded vote (128-1), 21 November (meeting 46); 8-nation draft (A/C.1/39/L.62), orally revised; agenda item 59.
Sponsors: Algeria, Argentina, Germany, Federal Republic of, India, Mexico, Romania, Sri Lanka, Yugoslavia.
Financial implications. ACABQ, A/39/7/Add.10; 5th Committee, A/39/795; S-G, A/C.1/39/L.77, A/C.5/39/58.
Meeting numbers. GA 39th session: 1st Committee 3-36, 40, 46; 5th Committee 43; plenary 102.

Recorded vote in Assembly as follows:

In favour: Afghanistan, Algeria, Angola, Antigua and Barbuda, Argentina, Australia, Austria, Bahamas, Bahrain, Bangladesh, Barbados, Belgium, Benin, Bhutan, Bolivia, Botswana, Brazil, Brunei Darussalam, Bulgaria, Burkina Faso, Burma, Burundi, Byelorussian SSR, Cameroon, Canada, Cape Verde, Central African Republic, Chad, Chile, China, Colombia, Congo, Costa Rica, Cuba, Cyprus, Czechoslovakia, Democratic Kampuchea, Democratic Yemen, Denmark, Djibouti, Dominican Republic, Ecuador, Egypt, El Salvador, Equatorial Guinea, Ethiopia, Fiji, Finland, France, Gabon, Gambia, German Democratic Republic, Germany, Federal Republic of, Ghana, Greece, Guatemala, Guinea, Guyana, Haiti, Honduras, Hungary, Iceland, India, Indonesia, Iran, Iraq, Ireland, Israel, Italy, Ivory Coast, Jamaica, Japan, Jordan, Kenya, Kuwait, Lao People's Democratic Republic, Lebanon, Lesotho, Liberia, Libyan Arab Jamahiriya, Luxembourg, Madagascar, Malawi, Malaysia, Maldives, Mali, Malta, Mauritania, Mauritius, Mexico, Mongolia, Morocco, Mozambique, Nepal, Netherlands, New Zealand, Nicaragua, Niger, Nigeria, Norway, Oman, Pakistan, Panama, Paraguay, Peru, Philippines, Poland, Portugal, Qatar, Romania, Rwanda, Saint Lucia, Saint Vincent and the Grenadines, Sao Tome and Principe, Saudi Arabia, Senegal, Seychelles, Sierra Leone, Singapore, Somalia, Spain, Sri Lanka, Sudan, Suriname, Sweden, Syrian Arab Republic, Thailand, Togo, Trinidad and Tobago, Tunisia, Turkey, Uganda, Ukrainian SSR, USSR, United Arab Emirates, United Kingdom, United Republic of Tanzania, Uruguay, Venezuela, Viet Nam, Yemen, Yugoslavia, Zaire, Zambia, Zimbabwe.
Against: United States.

The United States said that, although it considered the topic important, it was obliged to vote against the text because of its commitment to seeing no real growth in the United Nations budget.

The USSR felt the proposed study would reveal why deterrence was being used as an excuse for escalating the arms race; however, the expenditure envisaged should be reviewed with the aim of reducing it substantially.

UN Institute for Disarmament Research

Activities of the Institute. The Director of UNIDIR, in an October 1984 report,[79] stated that two reports requested by the Assembly—on establishing an international disarmament fund for development[57] (see p. 83), and South Africa's nuclear capability[80] (see p. 39)—had been completed and submitted to the Assembly. In the period covered by the report, September 1983 to August 1984, UNIDIR had also completed a number of research projects, while strengthening its scientific capacity. The Director informed the Assembly that UNIDIR, in order to succeed, had to have its statute approved and the material conditions for work assured.

Activities of the Board of Trustees. In 1984, the Advisory Board on Disarmament Studies,[12] in its capacity as Board of Trustees of UNIDIR, submitted to the Assembly a revised draft statute of the Institute.

In December 1983, the Assembly had returned the draft statute to the Board,[81] requesting clarification of provisions that it considered were vague about financial and other arrangements for the Institute. The Advisory Committee on Administrative and Budgetary Questions (ACABQ), which had advised the Assembly on the matter, observed that the vagueness resulted from an attempt to make the statute cover both the UNIDIR financing on a voluntary basis and the possibility of an Assembly decision to fund certain expenditures from the United Nations regular budget.

The Board also approved the report of the Director on the work of UNIDIR (see above),[79] approved the 1985 UNIDIR programme of 12 research projects, and adopted proposed budget estimates for 1985, recommending that one third be allocated from the United Nations regular budget.

GENERAL ASSEMBLY CONSIDERATION

ACABQ recommended in a November report to the Assembly[82] that—in order to implement the principle of mixed financing—article VII of the draft statute be changed so that the actual amount of a subvention from the United Nations regular budget to meet the cost of the Director and his staff would not exceed an amount equivalent to one half of the assured income of UNIDIR from voluntary sources in respect of the year for which a subvention was being requested. ACABQ also suggested amendments in articles III and VIII of the draft statute, so as to avoid the artificial formulation of two separate budgets for UNIDIR.

Further, ACABQ recommended against either a grant or an advance from the United Nations regular budget, saying that the autonomous nature of the Institute and the requirement that voluntary contributions should form its principal source of financing could best be preserved if the sums necessary to eliminate the deficit were set aside from future voluntary income.

GENERAL ASSEMBLY ACTION

On 27 November 1984, the Assembly's Fifth (Administrative and Budgetary) Committee, to which the First Committee had earlier referred the draft statute for consideration, endorsed the ACABQ comments and recommendations by 79 votes to 10, with 8 abstentions; endorsement of article VII as amended was by a recorded vote of 75 to 17, with 5 abstentions.

On 17 December, the General Assembly, acting on the recommendation of the First Committee, adopted resolution 39/148 H by recorded vote.

United Nations Institute for Disarmament Research

The General Assembly,

Considering the role of disarmament research as a means to promote disarmament measures,

Recalling its resolution 37/99 K, section IV, of 13 December 1982,

1. *Takes note* of annex II to the report of the Secretary-General of 4 October 1984;

2. *Approves* the statute of the United Nations Institute for Disarmament Research, annexed to the present resolution;

3. *Takes note* of the report of the Director of the United Nations Institute for Disarmament Research;

4. *Renews the invitations* to Governments to consider making voluntary contributions to the Institute;

5. *Requests* the Secretary-General to continue to give the Institute administrative and other support;

6. *Invites* the Director of the Institute to report annually to the General Assembly on the activities carried out by the Institute.

ANNEX
Statute of the United Nations Institute
for Disarmament Research

Article I

Purposes

The United Nations Institute for Disarmament Research (hereinafter referred to as "the Institute") is an autonomous institution within the framework of the United Nations, established by the General Assembly for the purpose of undertaking independent research on disarmament and related problems, particularly international security issues, and working in close relationship with the Department for Disarmament Affairs of the Secretariat.

Article II

Functions

1. The Institute shall work on the basis of the provisions of the Final Document of the Tenth Special Session of the General Assembly, the first special session devoted to disarmament.

2. The work of the Institute shall aim at:

(a) Providing the international community with more diversified and complete data on problems relating to international security, the armaments race and disarmament in all fields, particularly in the nuclear field, so as to facilitate progress, through negotiations, towards greater security for all States and towards the economic and social development of all peoples;

(b) Promoting informed participation by all States in disarmament efforts;

(c) Assisting ongoing negotiations on disarmament and continuing efforts to ensure greater international security at a progressively lower level of armaments, particularly nuclear armaments, by means of objective and factual studies and analyses;

(d) Carrying out more in-depth, forward-looking and long-term research on disarmament, so as to provide a general insight into the problems involved, and stimulating new initiatives for new negotiations.

3. The Institute shall take into account the relevant recommendations of the General Assembly and shall be organized in such a manner as to ensure participation on an equitable political and geographical basis.

Article III

Board of Trustees

1. The Institute and its work shall be governed by a Board of Trustees (hereinafter referred to as "the Board"). The Advisory Board on Disarmament Studies, referred to in General Assembly resolution 37/99 K, section III, with the Director of the Institute (hereinafter referred to as "the Director") as an *ex officio* member, shall function as the Board.

2. The Board shall:

(a) Establish principles and directives to govern the activities and operation of the Institute;

(b) Consider and adopt the annual work programme and the proposed annual budget estimates;

(c) Recommend, if it considers necessary, a subvention from the regular budget of the United Nations in accordance with articles VII and VIII of this statute;

(d) Review the financial situation of the Institute and make appropriate recommendations with a view to ensuring the effectiveness of its operations and their continuity;

(e) Take such other decisions as are deemed necessary for the effective functioning of the Institute;

(f) Undertake the other functions specified in this statute.

3. The Board shall meet at least once a year.

4. Organs of the United Nations, specialized agencies and the International Atomic Energy Agency may be represented as appropriate at meetings of the Board upon invitation.

Article IV

The Director and the staff

1. The Director shall be appointed by the Secretary-General of the United Nations, after consultations with the Board.

2. The Director shall have overall responsibility for the organization, direction and administration of the Institute, in accordance with general directives formulated by the Board, and shall, *inter alia:*

(a) Prepare and submit the draft work programme of the Institute to the Board;

(b) Prepare and submit a proposed annual budget to the Board in accordance with articles VII and VIII of this statute;

(c) Execute the work programme and make the expenditure authorized in the approved budget;

(d) Appoint and direct the staff of the Institute;

(e) Set up *ad hoc* consultative bodies as may be necessary;

(f) Negotiate arrangements with Governments and international as well as national, public and private agencies with a view to offering and receiving services related to the activities of the Institute;

(g) Accept, subject to the provisions of article VII, paragraph 4, below, voluntary contributions to the Institute;

(h) Co-ordinate the work of the Institute with that of other international and national programmes in similar fields;

(i) Report to the Board, as appropriate, on the Institute's activities and the execution of its work programmes;

(j) Submit to the General Assembly reports approved by the Board.

3. The staff of the Institute shall be appointed by the Director under letters of appointment signed by him in the name of the Secretary-General and limited to service with the Institute. The staff shall be responsible to the Director in the exercise of their functions.

4. The terms and conditions of service of the Director and the staff shall be those provided in the Staff Regulations and Rules of the United Nations, subject to such arrangements for special rules or terms of appointment as may be proposed by the Director and approved by the Secretary-General.

5. The Director and the staff of the Institute shall not seek or receive instructions from any Government or from any authority external to the United Nations. They shall refrain from any action which might reflect on their position as international officials responsible only to the Organization.

6. The Director and the staff of the Institute are officials of the United Nations and are therefore covered by Article 105 of the Charter of the United Nations and by other international agreements and United Nations resolutions defining the status of such officials.

Article V

Senior fellows, consultants and correspondents

1. The Director may designate each year, with the approval of the Board and for a period not longer than one year at a time, qualified persons to serve as senior fellows of the Institute. Such persons, who may be invited to participate as lecturers or research scholars, shall be selected on the basis of outstanding contributions they have made in fields germane to the work of the Institute. They may receive honorariums and be paid travel expenses.

2. The Director may also arrange for the services of consultants for the purpose of contributing to the analysis and planning of the activities of the Institute or for special assignments in connection with the Institute's programmes. Such consultants shall be engaged in accordance with policies established by the Secretary-General.

3. The Director may appoint correspondents in countries or regions to assist in maintaining contacts with national or regional institutions and in carrying out or advising on studies and research.

Article VI

Co-operation with other bodies

1. In addition to the close co-operation with the Department for Disarmament Affairs required by article I of this statute, the Institute shall develop arrangements for active co-operation with the specialized agencies and other organizations, programmes and institutions of the United Nations system.

2. The Institute may also develop arrangements for co-operation with other organizations and institutions active in the field of disarmament research which may be of assistance in the performance of the Institute's functions.

Article VII

Finance

1. Voluntary contributions from States and public and private organizations shall form the principal source of financing of the Institute.

2. A subvention towards meeting the costs of the Director and the staff of the Institute may be provided from the regular budget of the United Nations. The actual amount of any subvention shall be determined in accordance with article VIII of this statute; it may be less than, but shall not exceed, an amount equivalent to one half of the assured income of the Institute from voluntary sources in respect of the year for which a subvention is being requested. The assured income shall be that which has already been received or which has been pledged in writing by the time the level of any subvention is being considered.

3. Specific activities which the General Assembly may request the Institute to add to its regular work programme shall be paid for from the regular budget of the United Nations in amounts to be determined at the time the activities are requested.

4. The Director may accept voluntary contributions to the Institute that are unrestricted or that are designated for the implementation of an activity approved by the Board. Other voluntary contributions may be accepted only with the approval of the Board, which shall take into account the comments of the Secretary-General of the United Nations.

5. Voluntary contributions to the Institute shall be kept in a special account to be established by the Secretary-General in accordance with the Financial Regulations and Rules of the United Nations.

6. The special account of the Institute shall be held and administered solely for the purposes of the Institute. The Controller of the United Nations shall perform all necessary financial and accounting functions for the Institute, including the custody of its funds, and shall prepare and certify the annual accounts of the Institute.

7. The Financial Regulations and Rules of the United Nations and the financial policies established by the Secretary-General shall apply to the financial operations of the Institute. Funds of the Institute shall be subject to audit by the United Nations Board of Auditors.

Article VIII

Budget

1. The proposed annual budget of the Institute shall be based on the proposed draft work programme of the Institute. It shall be prepared by the Director in consultation with the Department for Disarmament Affairs and the Office of Financial Services of the Secretariat.

2. The proposed annual budget, together with the comments and recommendations thereon of the Advisory Committee on Administrative and Budgetary Questions, shall be submitted to the Board for action in accordance with article III, paragraphs 2 _(b)_ and _(c)_ of this statute.

3. A recommendation by the Board, under article III, paragraph 2 _(c)_, for a subvention from the regular budget of the United Nations shall be transmitted by the Secretary-General to the General Assembly for approval.

Article IX

Administrative and other support

The Secretary-General of the United Nations shall provide the Institute with appropriate administrative and other support in accordance with the Financial Regulations and Rules of the United Nations. The Institute shall reimburse the United Nations for the costs of such support, as determined by the Controller of the United Nations after consultation with the Director.

Article X

Location

The Institute shall have its seat at Geneva.

Article XI

Status

The Institute, being part of the United Nations, enjoys the status, privileges and immunities provided in Articles 104 and 105 of the Charter of the United Nations and other relevant international agreements and United Nations resolutions relating to the status, privileges and immunities of the Organization.

Article XII

Amendments

Amendments to this statute may be made by the General Assembly.

General Assembly resolution 39/148 H

17 December 1984   Meeting 102   141-1-3 (recorded vote)

Approved by First Committee (A/39/749) by recorded vote (108-1-2), 3 December (meeting 56); 25-nation draft (A/C.1/39/L.30/Rev.1); agenda item 59 _(II)._

Sponsors: Algeria, Australia, Bahamas, Bangladesh, Cameroon, China, Costa Rica, Cyprus, Ecuador, Egypt, Finland, France, Greece, India, Liberia, Nigeria, Norway, Pakistan, Romania, Senegal, Sri Lanka, Togo, Tunisia, Uruguay, Yugoslavia.

Financial implications. ACABQ, A/39/7/Add.8; 5th Committee, A/39/807; Secretariat, A/C.1/39/L.82, A/C.5/39/76; S-G, A/C.5/39/33.

Meeting numbers. GA 39th session: 1st Committee 3-36, 44, 56; 5th Committee 34, 44; plenary 102.

Recorded vote in Assembly as follows:

In favour: Afghanistan, Algeria, Angola, Antigua and Barbuda, Argentina, Australia, Austria, Bahamas, Bahrain, Bangladesh, Barbados, Belgium, Benin, Bhutan, Bolivia, Botswana, Brazil, Brunei Darussalam, Bulgaria, Burkina Faso, Burma, Burundi, Byelorussian SSR, Cameroon, Canada, Cape Verde, Chad, Chile, China, Colombia, Congo, Costa Rica, Cuba, Cyprus, Czechoslovakia, Democratic Kampuchea, Democratic Yemen, Denmark, Djibouti, Dominican Republic, Ecuador, Egypt, El Salvador, Equatorial Guinea, Ethiopia, Fiji, Finland, France, Gabon, Gambia, German Democratic Republic, Germany, Federal Republic of, Ghana, Greece, Guatemala, Guinea, Guyana, Honduras, Hungary, Iceland, India, Indonesia, Iran, Iraq, Ireland, Italy, Ivory Coast, Jamaica, Jordan, Kenya, Kuwait, Lao People's Democratic Republic, Lebanon, Lesotho, Liberia, Libyan Arab Jamahiriya, Luxembourg, Madagascar, Malawi, Malaysia, Maldives, Mali, Malta, Mauritania, Mauritius, Mexico, Mongolia, Morocco, Mozambique, Nepal, Netherlands, New Zealand, Nicaragua, Niger, Nigeria, Norway, Oman, Pakistan, Panama, Paraguay, Peru, Philippines, Poland, Portugal, Qatar, Romania, Rwanda, Saint Lucia, Saint Vincent and the Grenadines, Sao Tome and Principe, Saudi Arabia, Senegal, Seychelles, Sierra Leone, Singapore, Somalia, Spain, Sri Lanka, Sudan, Suriname, Sweden, Syrian Arab Republic, Thailand, Togo, Trinidad and Tobago, Tunisia, Turkey, Uganda, Ukrainian SSR, USSR, United Arab Emirates, United Kingdom, United Republic of Tanzania, Uruguay, Venezuela, Viet Nam, Yemen, Yugoslavia, Zaire, Zambia, Zimbabwe.

Against: United States.

Abstaining: Haiti, Israel, Japan.

The Assembly adopted paragraph 2 of the resolution by a recorded vote of 114 to 3 (Japan, United Kingdom, United States), with 20 abstentions. The First Committee, at the request of the USSR, had similarly approved that paragraph by 88 votes to 3 (Japan, United Kingdom and United States), with 18 abstentions.

In explanation of vote, the United States objected to the mixed funding of UNIDIR, saying that such a system contradicted the 1982 Assembly decision that the activities should be funded voluntarily.[74] Sharing that view, the United Kingdom believed that the estimated voluntary contributions should be adequate to finance all activities, and urged that programmes be tempered by economic realities. The USSR, abstaining on paragraph 2, could not agree with the provisions of articles III, VII and VIII of the statute; a dual system of financing might create a dangerous precedent, one which might lead to considerable inflation in the United Nations regular budget. Japan also expressed concern over the financial implications for the United Nations. The Federal Republic of Germany, which abstained in the vote on paragraph 2 because of what it said were the statute's financial ambiguities, and the United Kingdom none the less welcomed the fact that approval of the statute put the Institute's work on a legally sound footing.

The Assembly, by resolution 39/147, requested UNIDIR to prepare a report on Israeli nuclear armament.

UN fellowship programme

The Secretary-General reported to the General Assembly in October[83] that the 1984 United Nations programme of fellowships on disarmament had started at Geneva during the June-August session of the Conference on Disarmament and was scheduled to end in New York towards the end of the 1984 regular session of the Assembly. Twenty-five fellows from as many States participated in the programme, which consisted of lectures, seminars, research, observation of the Conference on Disarmament and the Assembly's First Committee, and a visit to IAEA at Vienna. The 1984 programme also included study visits, at the invitation of the respective Governments, to the Federal Republic of Germany, Japan, Romania, Sweden and the United States.

The Secretary-General noted that the programme, established by the Assembly in 1978 at its first special session on disarmament[76] to promote expertise in disarmament, especially in developing countries, had trained some 130 government officials from 77 countries in its six years of existence.

GENERAL ASSEMBLY ACTION

On 12 December 1984, the General Assembly, acting on the recommendation of the First Committee, adopted resolution 39/63 B without vote.

United Nations programme of fellowships on disarmament

The General Assembly,

Recalling its decision, contained in paragraph 108 of the Final Document of the Tenth Special Session of the General Assembly, the first special session devoted to disarmament, to establish a programme of fellowships on disarmament, as well as its decisions contained in annex IV to the Concluding Document of the Twelfth Special Session of the General Assembly, the second special session devoted to disarmament, in which it, *inter alia,* decided to continue the programme and to increase the number of fellowships from twenty to twenty-five as from 1983,

Noting with satisfaction that the programme has already trained one hundred and thirty public officials from seventy-seven countries, most of whom are now in positions of responsibility in the field of disarmament affairs within their Governments or permanent missions to the United Nations, or representing their Governments at international disarmament meetings,

Recognizing the fact that the programme of studies and activities as outlined in the report of the Secretary-General on the United Nations programme of fellowships on disarmament has continued to expand and intensify,

Believing that existing facilities within the Secretariat for implementing the programme of fellowships can be further utilized to promote expertise in disarmament,

1. *Takes note with satisfaction* of the report of the Secretary-General;

2. *Expresses its appreciation* to the Governments of the Federal Republic of Germany, Japan, Romania, Sweden and the United States of America for inviting fellows to their countries in 1984 to study selected activities in the field of disarmament, thereby contributing to the fulfilment of the overall objectives of the programme;

3. *Requests* the Secretary-General:

(a) To devise a system of evaluating the research papers prepared by the fellows with a view to identifying those that are outstanding;

(b) To publish such papers in an annual issue of an appropriate publication to be devoted to the programme of fellowships on disarmament;

(c) To submit proposals for further utilization of the existing capacity within the Department for Disarmament Affairs for training in the field of disarmament;

4. *Also requests* the Secretary-General to report to the General Assembly at its fortieth session on the operations of the programme and the implementation of the present resolution.

General Assembly resolution 39/63 B

12 December 1984   Meeting 97   Adopted without vote

Approved by First Committee (A/39/750) without vote, 19 November (meeting 41); 28-nation draft (A/C.1/39/L.29); agenda item 60 (c).

Sponsors: Algeria, Australia, Bahamas, Bangladesh, Cameroon, Ecuador, France, Greece, India, Indonesia, Kenya, Liberia, Mali, New Zealand, Niger, Nigeria, Philippines, Senegal, Sri Lanka, Sudan, Togo, Tunisia, Uganda, Uruguay, Venezuela, Yugoslavia, Zaire, Zambia.

Meeting numbers. GA 39th session: 1st Committee 3-36, 39, 41; plenary 97.

Organizational aspects

The Secretary-General, pursuant to a December 1983 General Assembly resolution,[84] submitted to the Assembly in October 1984[85] information received from a number of specialized agencies and other United Nations bodies on activities carried out, within their areas of competence, in contributing to arms limitation and disarmament.

The Administrative Committee on Coordination, in its annual overview report for 1983/84,[86] noted that the United Nations system was strengthening its co-operation regarding disarmament-related activities through the Consultative Committee on Substantive Questions (Programme Matters).

GENERAL ASSEMBLY ACTION

On 17 December 1984, the General Assembly adopted two resolutions—39/151 E and G—on organizational aspects of disarmament, as recommended by the First Committee.

The Assembly adopted resolution 39/151 E by recorded vote.

Contribution of the specialized agencies and other organizations and programmes of the United Nations system to the cause of arms limitation and disarmament

The General Assembly,

Recalling its resolution 38/188 J of 20 December 1983,

Reaffirming that the United Nations, in accordance with its Charter, has a central role and primary responsibility in the sphere of disarmament and should, accordingly, play a more active role in this field,

Reaffirming also the role of the Conference on Disarmament as the single multilateral negotiating body,

Stressing again the close relationship between matters concerning international security and disarmament, and the interest in close co-operation between the units in the Secretariat dealing with them,

Convinced that all possible avenues should be effectively utilized for the cause of preventing war, in particular nuclear war, and achieving disarmament,

Reaffirming further the close link existing between disarmament and development,

Convinced that disarmament would contribute to the effective economic and social development of all States, in particular developing countries, by contributing to reducing the economic disparities between developed and developing countries and establishing the new international economic order on the basis of justice, equality and co-operation, and towards solving other global problems,

Convinced also that there is a close relationship between the development of international co-operation in various fields, such as trade, economic development, exploration and use of outer space, environmental protection, health and the prevention of war, in particular nuclear war, and the achievement of arms limitation and disarmament,

Taking note of various activities carried out by the specialized agencies and other organizations and programmes of the United Nations system in pursu-

ance of its resolution 38/188 J as reflected in the note by the Secretary-General,

Noting also the wide range of activities carried out by the specialized agencies and other organizations and programmes of the United Nations system in the framework of the World Disarmament Campaign and in observance of Disarmament Week, reflected in relevant reports of the Secretary-General,

Taking note of the report of the Committee for Programme and Co-ordination on the work of its twenty-fourth session,

1. *Reaffirms* its invitation to the specialized agencies and other organizations and programmes of the United Nations system to broaden further their contribution, within their areas of competence, to the cause of arms limitation and disarmament;

2. *Recommends* that, at periodic meetings of the Secretary-General with the executive heads of the specialized agencies mentioned in paragraph 4 of its resolution 38/188 J, consideration should be given to the elaboration of a plan of co-ordination of the activities of the specialized agencies in the field of disarmament;

3. *Requests* the Secretary-General to submit to the General Assembly at its forty-first session a report on the implementation of the present resolution, including information on relevant activities carried out by the specialized agencies and other organizations and programmes of the United Nations system;

4. *Decides* to include in the provisional agenda of its forty-first session the item entitled "Contribution of the specialized agencies and other organizations and programmes of the United Nations system to the cause of arms limitation and disarmament: report of the Secretary-General".

General Assembly resolution 39/151 E

17 December 1984   Meeting 102   109-18-14 (recorded vote)

Approved by First Committee (A/39/755) by recorded vote (98-17-16), 20 November (meeting 43); 4-nation draft (A/C.1/39/L.34/Rev.1); agenda item 65 (h).

Sponsors: Byelorussian SSR, Cuba, Czechoslovakia, German Democratic Republic.

Meeting numbers. GA 39th session: 1st Committee 3-37, 43; plenary 102.

Recorded vote in Assembly as follows:

In favour: Afghanistan, Algeria, Angola, Antigua and Barbuda, Argentina, Bahrain, Bangladesh, Benin, Bhutan, Bolivia, Botswana, Brunei Darussalam, Bulgaria, Burkina Faso, Burundi, Byelorussian SSR, Cameroon, Cape Verde, Central African Republic, Chad, Chile, Colombia, Congo, Costa Rica, Cuba, Cyprus, Czechoslovakia, Democratic Yemen, Dominican Republic, Ecuador, Egypt, El Salvador, Equatorial Guinea, Ethiopia, Fiji, Gabon, German Democratic Republic, Ghana, Guatemala, Guinea, Guyana, Haiti, Honduras, Hungary, India, Indonesia, Iran, Iraq, Ivory Coast, Jordan, Kenya, Kuwait, Lao People's Democratic Republic, Lebanon, Lesotho, Libyan Arab Jamahiriya, Madagascar, Malawi, Malaysia, Maldives, Mali, Mauritania, Mauritius, Mexico, Mongolia, Morocco, Mozambique, Nepal, Nicaragua, Niger, Nigeria, Oman, Pakistan, Panama, Papua New Guinea, Paraguay, Peru, Philippines, Poland, Qatar, Romania, Rwanda, Saint Lucia, Saint Vincent and the Grenadines, Samoa, Sao Tome and Principe, Senegal, Seychelles, Sierra Leone, Sudan, Suriname, Syrian Arab Republic, Thailand, Togo, Trinidad and Tobago, Tunisia, Uganda, Ukrainian SSR, USSR, United Arab Emirates, United Republic of Tanzania, Uruguay, Venezuela, Viet Nam, Yemen, Yugoslavia, Zaire, Zambia, Zimbabwe.

Against: Australia, Belgium, Canada, France, Germany, Federal Republic of, Iceland, Israel, Italy, Japan, Luxembourg, Netherlands, New Zealand, Norway, Portugal, Saudi Arabia,[a] Turkey, United Kingdom, United States.

Abstaining: Austria, Bahamas, Barbados, Brazil, China, Denmark, Djibouti, Finland, Greece, Ireland, Liberia, Somalia, Spain, Sweden.

[a]Later advised the Secretariat it had intended to abstain.

In explanation of vote, the United States said that many United Nations agencies had been politicized and had had to neglect their real missions in order to deal with disarmament issues, in which they had no experience or competence. Speaking on behalf of the 10 member States of the European Community, Ireland said they could not support the dilution of the central role of the Department for Disarmament Affairs in co-ordinating disarmament activities within the United Nations system and conducting liaison with governmental and other bodies; they feared that the text would seriously affect the autonomy of the specialized agencies under their respective mandates and that paragraph 2, if implemented, would detract from the Secretary-General's ability to pursue his co-ordinating role in disarmament.

Sweden, while supporting concrete, case-by-case initiatives in the specialized agencies, felt that unqualified recommendations to such bodies to extend their activities to political issues could hamper support for, and work in, those bodies.

On the other hand, the USSR asserted that the specialized agencies would benefit from concrete recommendations with respect to the arms race, arms limitation and disarmament; it expected the appropriate ones to examine their disarmament-related activities during meetings of their executive bodies.

On 17 December, the Assembly adopted, without vote, resolution 39/151 G, as recommended by the First Committee.

Review of the role of the United Nations in the field of disarmament

The General Assembly,

Bearing in mind that the primary purpose of the United Nations is to maintain international peace and security,

Reaffirming its conviction that genuine and lasting peace can only be created through the effective implementation of the security system provided for in the Charter of the United Nations and the speedy and substantial reduction of arms and armed forces, by international agreement and mutual example, leading ultimately to general and complete disarmament under effective international control,

Deeply concerned that the arms race has continued unabated and that world military expenditures are increasing,

Conscious of the need to utilize resources spent on the arms race for constructive development purposes, particularly in the developing countries,

Reaffirming its conviction that the process of disarmament affects the vital security interests of all States and that all States must be actively concerned with and contribute to that process,

Reaffirming further that the United Nations, in accordance with its Charter, has a central role and primary responsibility in the field of disarmament,

Regretting that, especially in recent years, no substantive progress has been made in the field of disarmament,

Recognizing the urgent need for meaningful measures to prevent any erosion of the security of States and initiate the long overdue process of real disarmament, particularly in the nuclear field,

Recognizing further the need for the United Nations, in discharging its central role and primary responsibility in the field of disarmament, to play a more active role in that field in accordance with its primary purpose under the Charter to maintain international peace and security,

Recalling its resolution 31/90 of 14 December 1976 by which it, *inter alia*, decided to keep the question of the strengthening of the role of the United Nations in the field of disarmament under continued review,

1. *Invites* all States to communicate to the Secretary-General, not later than 15 April 1985, their views and suggestions on ways and means by which the United Nations can more effectively exercise its central role and primary responsibility in the field of disarmament;

2. *Requests* the Secretary-General to transmit those views and suggestions to the Disarmament Commission before the convening of its substantive session in 1985;

3. *Requests* the Disarmament Commission, at its substantive session in 1985, to carry out as a matter of priority a comprehensive review of the role of the United Nations in the field of disarmament, taking into account, *inter alia*, the views and suggestions of Member States on the subject;

4. *Requests further* the Disarmament Commission to submit its report on the subject, including findings, recommendations and proposals, as appropriate, to the General Assembly at its fortieth session;

5. *Decides* to include in the provisional agenda of its fortieth session an item entitled "Review of the role of the United Nations in the field of disarmament: report of the Disarmament Commission".

General Assembly resolution 39/151 G

17 December 1984   Meeting 102   Adopted without vote

Approved by First Committee (A/39/755) without vote, 20 November (meeting 43); 22-nation draft (A/C.1/39/L.41); agenda item 65.

Sponsors: Bahamas, Burundi, Cameroon, Cape Verde, Central African Republic, Chad, Congo, Djibouti, Equatorial Guinea, Gabon, Germany, Federal Republic of, Guinea, Guyana, Kenya, Liberia, Madagascar, Mali, Niger, Singapore, Togo, Uganda, Zaire.

Meeting numbers. GA 39th session: 1st Committee 3-36, 40, 43; plenary 102.

In explanation of position, the United States expressing hope that Member States would use the proposed mechanism to make serious suggestions on how the United Nations might more usefully contribute to disarmament, pointed to the danger of passing numerous, often wordy and contradictory resolutions, and hoped that the current text would begin a move in the correct direction. Argentina expressed doubts about the effectiveness of the procedure outlined in the text, especially the request in paragraph 3 to the Disarmament Commission, with its already heavy agenda, to conduct a comprehensive review of so vast and complex a subject as the United Nations role in disarmament; it also disagreed with the penultimate preambular paragraph for the implication that the United Nations was responsible for the lack of success of disarmament efforts.

REFERENCES

(1)A/39/42. (2)A/CN.10/64. (3)YUN 1983, p. 70. (4)YUN 1981, p. 90. (5)YUN 1982, p. 115. (6)YUN 1982, p. 119, GA res. 37/95 B, 13 Dec. 1982. (7)A/39/399. (8)YUN 1983, p. 71. (9)A/39/521 & Corr.1,2 & Add.1,2. (10)YUN 1983, p. 80, GA res. 38/188 C, 20 Dec. 1983. (11)A/39/436. (12)A/39/549. (13)YUN 1983, p. 86. (14)YUN 1982, p. 135, GA res. 37/99 J, 13 Dec. 1982. (15)A/39/525. (16)YUN 1976, p. 45, GA res. 31/72, annex, 10 Dec. 1976. (17)*Multilateral Treaties Deposited with the Secretary-General: Status as at 31 December 1984* (ST/LEG/SER.E/3), Sales No. E.85.V.4. (18)YUN 1982, p. 121, GA res. 37/99 I, 13 Dec. 1982. (19)A/C.1/39/5. (20)A/39/27. (21)CD/329/Rev.2. (22)CD/529. (23)CD/527. (24)YUN 1983, p. 74, GA res. 38/70, 15 Dec. 1983. (25)CD/476. (26)YUN 1983, p. 74. (27)*Ibid.*, p. 100, GA res. 38/80, 15 Dec. 1983. (28)A/39/20. (29)A/39/243. (30)A/39/335. (31)A/39/369. (32)A/39/467. (33)A/39/666. (34)A/C.1/39/L.1. (35)A/39/760. (36)A/C.1/39/L.3. (37)A/C.1/39/L.61. (38)YUN 1971, p. 34, GA res. 2832(XXVI), 16 Dec. 1971. (39)A/39/485. (40)YUN 1983, p. 76, GA res. 38/73 J, 15 Dec. 1983. (41)*Ibid.*, p. 77, GA res. 38/185, 20 Dec. 1983. (42)YUN 1972, p. 29, GA res. 2992(XXVII), 15 Dec. 1972. (43)A/39/29. (44)YUN 1979, p. 67, GA res. 34/80 B, 11 Dec. 1979. (45)A/38/828. (46)A/AC.159/L.60. (47)A/AC.159/L.61. (48)A/AC.159/L.62. (49)A/AC.159/L.63. (50)A/39/560-S/16773. (51)YUN 1983, p. 79, GA res. 38/73 A, 15 Dec. 1983. (52)*Ibid.*, p. 79. (53)*Ibid.*, p. 83, GA res. 38/188 H, 20 Dec. 1983. (54)*Ibid.*, p. 85, GA res. 38/71 B, 15 Dec. 1983. (55)A/CN.10/57 & Add.1-16. (56)YUN 1982, p. 145, GA res. 37/84, 9 Dec. 1982. (57)*Establishment of an International Disarmament Fund for Development* (A/39/229), Sales No. GV.E.84.0.2. (58)YUN 1981, p. 96. (59)A/39/454. (60)*The United Nations Disarmament Yearbook*, vol. 9, *1984*, Sales No. E.85.IX.4. (61)YUN 1966, p. 41, GA res. 2222(XXI), annex, 19 Dec. 1966. (62)YUN 1968, p. 17, GA res. 2373(XXII), annex, 12 June 1968. (63)YUN 1970, p. 18, GA res. 2660(XXV), annex, 7 Dec. 1970. (64)YUN 1971, p. 19, GA res. 2826(XXVI), annex, 16 Dec. 1971. (65)YUN 1979, p. 111, GA res. 34/68, annex, 5 Dec. 1979. (66)YUN 1965, p. 62, GA res. 2030(XX), 29 Nov. 1965. (67)A/39/28. (68)YUN 1974, p. 52. (69)YUN 1982, p. 31. (70)A/39/38 & Corr.1,2 & Add.1. (71)A/39/492. (72)YUN 1983, p. 88, GA res. 38/73 D, 15 Dec. 1983. (73)A/39/529. (74)YUN 1982, p. 150, GA res. 37/99 K, 13 Dec. 1982. (75)YUN 1983, p. 88. (76)YUN 1978, p. 39, GA res. S-10/2, 30 June 1978. (77)A/39/493. (78)YUN 1978, p. 109. (79)A/39/553. (80)A/39/470. (81)YUN 1983, p. 92, GA dec. 38/447, 20 Dec. 1983. (82)A/39/7/Add.8. (83)A/39/567. (84)YUN 1983, p. 94, GA res. 38/188 J, 20 Dec. 1983. (85)A/39/544. (86)E/1984/66.

Chapter II

Peaceful uses of outer space

The Agreement Governing the Activities of States on the Moon and Other Celestial Bodies, adopted by the General Assembly in 1979, entered into force in July 1984 following its ratification by a fifth State. In December, the Assembly adopted resolution 39/96 by which it invited States that had not become parties to international outer space treaties to do so. It endorsed the United Nations Programme on Space Applications for 1985 and emphasized the importance of implementing the recommendations of the Second (1982) United Nations Conference on the Exploration and Peaceful Uses of Outer Space (UNISPACE-82). It urged all States, in particular those with major space capabilities, to prevent an arms race in outer space.

The Assembly's 1984 actions were based mainly on the work of the Committee on the Peaceful Uses of Outer Space (Committee on outer space) (twenty-seventh session, Vienna, Austria, 12-21 June) and that of the Committee's two sub-committees—the Legal Sub-Committee and the Scientific and Technical Sub-Committee.

Topics related to this chapter. Disarmament: arms race in outer space. Other administrative and management questions: communications satellite. International Telecommunication Union.

Science, technology and law

Space science and technology

The Scientific and Technical Sub-Committee of the Committee on outer space held its twenty-first session in New York from 13 to 24 February 1984.[1] The Sub-Committee continued to stress the necessity of co-ordination in outer space activities among United Nations organizations. It reiterated that the General Assembly, in 1983,[2] had emphasized the urgency of implementing the recommendations of UNISPACE-82.[3] It also continued to consider remote sensing of the Earth by satellites and the use of nuclear power sources in outer space, examined some aspects of the geostationary orbit, and called attention to the progress made in developing various programmes related to space transportation systems. The Sub-Committee's report was reviewed by the Committee on outer space at its June session.[4]

UN Programme on Space Applications

During 1984, as part of the United Nations Programme on Space Applications, fellowships were awarded, training courses, workshops and technical meetings were given and technical advisory services were provided.[5]

Two one-year fellowships in microwave technology were offered by Austria at the Technical University Graz. Ten fellowships, each for six years, were offered by the USSR for studies in geodesy, cartography, aerial photography and photogeodesy at the Moscow Engineering Institute for Geodesy, Cartography and Air Photography. Three one-year fellowships were offered by the European Space Agency (ESA) at the European Space Research and Technology Centre, Noordwijk, Netherlands; the European Space Research Institute, Frascati, Italy; and the European Space Operations Centre, Darmstadt, Federal Republic of Germany. Negotiations were concluded with Brazil on fellowships in remote sensing technology at the Instituto de Pesquisas Espaciais, São José dos Campos, São Paulo, Brazil.

Two international training courses were given. The ninth United Nations/Food and Agriculture Organization of the United Nations (FAO) international training course, held with Italy's co-operation (Rome, 10-28 September), focused on the applications of remote sensing to aquaculture and inland fisheries. The course was attended by 20 participants and two observers from 21 countries. It consisted of lectures, case-studies, workshops and practical exercises. Participants received instruction on the practical applications of airborne and satellite remote sensing techniques for mapping of water bodies.

The third United Nations international training course on remote sensing applications to forestry (Moscow, 21 May–9 June) was attended by 24 participants from 24 countries who were technical personnel responsible for their countries' forestry programmes. Expert instruction was provided by FAO, the German Democratic Republic and the USSR. Presentations focused on general aspects of earth resources study; basic principles of space engineering; earth observation systems and methods; characteristics and analysis of images of the environment; applications of air and space images for inventory and evaluation of forest resources; long-term forecast of structures of forests; and methods of thematic forest maps compilation.

Seeking greater co-operation in space science and technology among developed and developing countries, the Programme, in collaboration with the Committee on Space Research and the United Nations Educational, Scientific and Cultural Organization, sponsored two workshops (Graz, Austria, 25-30 June) focusing on satellite remote sensing of interest to developing countries and on promoting space research in those countries.

In 1982,[6] the General Assembly had endorsed the recommendations of UNISPACE-82 that an international space information service be established to direct Member States to data banks and other information sources. In carrying out that mandate, an international meeting of experts on remote sensing information systems (Feldafing and Oberpfaffenhofen, Federal Republic of Germany, 7-11 May 1984) was attended by 56 participants from 24 countries and 11 international organizations, including United Nations specialized agencies. Basic elements of a remote sensing information system were reviewed. Other analysis was of the global status of such systems, emphasizing their specializations, capabilities, accessibility and future directions.

Requests for technical advisory services were received from 47 Member States and, subsequently, consultancy missions were carried out in Colombia, Costa Rica, Ecuador and Mexico.

The United Nations Expert on Space Applications reported in January 1984 on requests for technical advisory services in basic space sciences, remote sensing, meteorology and communications from countries in the Economic Commission for Africa (ECA) region;[7] the Economic Commission for Europe (ECE) and Economic Commission for Western Asia (ECWA) regions;[8] the Economic Commission for Latin America (ECLA) region;[9] and the Economic and Social Commission for Asia and the Pacific (ESCAP) region.[10] A total of 45 countries had responded to a request from the Secretariat for a list of their specific needs; of those, 17 were in the ECA region, 6 in the ECE and ECWA regions, 15 in the ECLA region and 7 in the ESCAP region.

In addition, a regional meeting of experts on space science and technology (Jakarta, Indonesia, 23-25 May)[11] brought together individuals responsible for shaping their countries' national/regional policy in space science and technology. Participants expressed concern about the cost of equipment for ground receiving stations and processing and interpretation facilities, the rising cost of satellite data and personnel training. The meeting recommended the establishment of a regional information system for space-related fields and the organization of a regional workshop to set operational and compatible norms and codes for the system.

Voluntary contributions in cash and kind to the Programme were received in 1984 from Austria, Brazil, Cameroon, Chile, China, Cyprus, the Dominican Republic, France, Pakistan and Sweden. The subject of voluntary contributions was dealt with in a September report by the Secretary-General[12] on implementing the recommendations of UNISPACE-82 (see below).

At its June 1984 session, the Committee on outer space endorsed the 1985 Programme as proposed by the Expert and recommended by the Sub-Committee. In December, the General Assembly in resolution 39/96 also endorsed it. Among the activities planned for 1985 were fellowship programmes for in-depth training, technical advisory services to Member States, workshops and training courses, the promotion of greater co-operation in space science and technology, and implementation of recommendations on remote sensing information systems—including the publication of a directory on space information and data services.

Co-ordination in the UN system

The Scientific and Technical Sub-Committee[1] noted the progress achieved in co-ordinating programmes on space activities among organizations within the United Nations system, and continued to stress the need for effective consultations to avoid duplication of activities. The Committee on outer space[4] noted the participation in its work and that of its Sub-Committee by United Nations bodies, the specialized agencies and other international organizations, and expressed appreciation to the Sub-Committee for continuing to stress the necessity of effective consultations and co-ordination.

The sixth Inter-Agency Meeting on Outer Space Activities, convened by the Administrative Committee on Co-ordination (ACC) (Geneva, 1-3 October),[13] felt that existing co-ordination machinery was satisfactory and that there were no major questions to be addressed by ACC. It discussed a draft report of the Secretary-General to the Sub-Committee on co-ordination of outer space activities for 1985, 1986 and future years, which was subsequently submitted to the Committee on outer space in November 1984.[14] The report listed United Nations organizations and specialized agencies participating in outer space activities, which included remote sensing, communications, meteorology, maritime communications and air navigation. The activities planned ranged from education and training programmes through fellowships, training workshops and summer schools, to expert services and survey missions. The Meeting recommended to ACC that the next such Meeting be held in the latter part of 1985.

Implementation of the recommendations of the 1982 Conference on outer space

The Scientific and Technical Sub-Committee[1] noted that the General Assembly in 1983[2] had expressed appreciation to Governments which had made voluntary contributions towards carrying out the recommendations of UNISPACE-82.[3] However, since such contributions were not an assured funding source, the Sub-Committee recommended to the Committee on outer space that it request the Assembly to increase the allocation of funds to the Secretariat's Outer Space Affairs Division from the United Nations regular budget.

Pursuant to a 1983 General Assembly request,[2] the Secretary-General submitted a report in September 1984 on implementation of the recommendations of UNISPACE-82.[12] He had drawn Member States' attention to the newly mandated and expanded activities of the Programme on Space Applications and asked for their views on making voluntary contributions to carry out the recommendations; as at 10 August, replies had been received from Belgium, Burkina Faso, Cuba, Hungary, Saint Vincent and the Grenadines, and Uganda.

The Sub-Committee requested the Secretariat to invite Member States to submit their views on future projects which would implement the recommendations of UNISPACE-82. The Committee on outer space[4] appealed to Member States to reply promptly, in time for the 1985 session of the Sub-Committee. Some delegations agreed with the suggestion about increased funding for the Outer Space Affairs Division. The view was also put forward that the mechanisms of regional co-operation should be studied.

Three groups of experts considered assistance to countries on remote sensing, educational satellites and closer spacing of satellites. The Group of Experts on remote sensing (New York, 21-24 February 1984)[15] proposed the establishment of a regularly updated catalogue on satellite remote sensing applications, an archive for remote sensing data and centres to advise developing countries on processing, application, distribution and verification of the data, and the organization of courses about advances in remote sensing.

The Group of Experts on closer spacing of satellites in the geostationary orbit (Geneva, 20-23 March)[16] took up the geostationary orbit, the radio frequency spectrum, satellite spacing, co-ordinating the geostationary orbit, and economic and organizational factors. It found that closer spacing of satellites in orbit was feasible, but that there was no simple solution to the problem of meeting the needs of all countries in an equitable fashion. Further studies of the long-term possibilities for relieving the pressure on the geostationary orbit by use of other geosynchronous orbits

should consider particularly the orbital perturbations and consequent station-keeping requirements in such orbits as well as the advances in spacecraft technology that might be required.

The Group of Experts on direct broadcasting satellites for education (Vienna, 12-15 June)[17] discussed broadcasting satellites, earth stations, programming, and regional and international co-operation. It concluded that, while the use of satellites for educational purposes was technologically feasible, it was not currently economical for most countries. It said that research contributing to reductions in cost should be encouraged.

Remote sensing of the Earth by satellites

The Scientific and Technical Sub-Committee[1] continued to consider remote sensing of the Earth by satellites. Regarding a list of remote sensing applications,[18] which the Secretariat had been compiling, the Sub-Committee reaffirmed that updating of the list should be continued and that more Member States should provide information. The Sub-Committee also reaffirmed that remote sensing from outer space should be carried out with the greatest possible international co-operation, and again emphasized the urgency of providing assistance in the matter to developing countries. It pointed out that FAO, in following up the recommendations of UNISPACE-82, had expanded its remote sensing training activities in co-operation with its members and other United Nations organizations.

The Committee on outer space[4] took note of the importance of the compatibility and complementarity of remote sensing systems; of the importance of continuity of data availability in a form compatible with current systems, given the investments made by many countries in ground stations, processing equipment, software, etc.; and of the importance of non-discriminatory and free-of-charge access to information from weather satellites.

Nuclear power sources and safety in spacecraft

The use of nuclear devices as sources of power for spacecraft was considered in 1984 by the Scientific and Technical Sub-Committee.[1] It adopted the report of its Working Group on the subject which it annexed to its report.

The Group (fourth session, New York, 13-17 February) reviewed working papers by Canada, Pakistan and Sweden. It reaffirmed the conclusions it had presented previously, particularly in 1983.[19] Some delegations stated that there was a need to establish international criteria on the design and operation of nuclear power sources in outer space. Some declared that space vehicles carrying nuclear reactors in orbit should be used only in orbits with lifetimes of at least 300 years after reactor shut-down, which would be called a nuclear-safe orbit. Space systems carrying reactors with lifetimes of fewer than 300 years after shut-down should include provisions for disposal of power sources by retrieval or reboosting to a higher, nuclear-safe orbit. To be nuclear safe, other delegations felt that orbits with lifetimes of at least 500 or 600 years would be more reasonable and that the disposal system should be highly reliable. Monitoring releases of radioactive material and notification in cases of malfunction also were discussed.

The Group recommended that the Secretary-General be requested to invite Member States to submit their views on radiological risks and environmental impact, safety and reliability, information and emergency planning.

The Committee on outer space[4] endorsed the Sub-Committee's recommendation that the item be kept as a priority on its agenda for its 1985 session and that the Working Group continue its work at that session.

Space transportation

Progress made in space transportation systems was considered by the Scientific and Technical Sub-Committee,[1] which particularly noted activities by China, India, Japan, the USSR, the United States and ESA. The Committee on outer space[4] endorsed a decision by the Sub-Committee that it continue to consider space transportation systems in 1985.

Technical aspects of the geostationary orbit

Preparatory work by the International Telecommunication Union (ITU) to establish scientific and technical criteria for the World Administrative Radio Conference (WARC) to be held in 1985 and 1988 on the use of the geostationary orbit—in which satellites for communications and other purposes maintain a position approximately 36,000 kilometres above specific points on the Equator—was noted by the Scientific and Technical Sub-Committee.[1] The Sub-Committee recommended that it continue in 1985 to consider the subject and reiterated its request that the study of the physical nature and technical aspects of the geostationary orbit be updated as required.

That decision was endorsed by the Committee on outer space in June.[4]

GENERAL ASSEMBLY ACTION

For General Assembly action on space science and technology, see resolution 39/96 below.

Space law

The Legal Sub-Committee of the Committee on outer space held its twenty-third session at Geneva from 19 March to 6 April 1984.[20] It considered three substantive items: the legal implications of remote sensing of the Earth from space, with the aim of formulating draft principles; the possibility of supplementing the norms of international law relevant to the use of nuclear power sources in outer space; and matters relating to the definition and delimitation of outer space and to the character and utilization of the geostationary orbit.

In June,[4] the Committee on outer space considered the Sub-Committee's work and recommended that it continue to consider the substantive items in 1985.

Legal aspects of remote sensing from satellites

A working group re-established on 19 March 1984 by the Legal Sub-Committee continued considering until 4 April the legal implications of remote sensing of the Earth from space, with the aim of formulating draft principles. The group reviewed the 17 draft principles as they appeared at the end of the Sub-Committee's 1983 session,[21] and then decided for the second consecutive year to concentrate on principles XI to XV. Those principles concerned State responsibility (XI), access to data by a State whose territory was being sensed (XII), notification to the United Nations of planned sensing activities (XIII), consultation with sensed States (XIV), and the need for prior approval by a sensed State before data on its natural resources could be disseminated by a sensing State (XV). The group devoted most of its time to principles XI, XII and XV. Working papers were submitted by Chile on four of the draft principles, by France on 15 of them, and by Romania on two.

While discussions were not conclusive, the group recommended that work on the draft principles should continue on a priority basis at the Sub-Committee's next session. The draft principles as they appeared at the end of the group's session were set out in an annex to the Sub-Committee's report.

The Committee on outer space in June[4] expressed concern at the lack of progress achieved by the Sub-Committee and emphasized the importance of completing the draft principles. The Committee recommended that the item be treated as a priority at the Sub-Committee's 1985 session.

Legal aspects of nuclear power sources in spacecraft

The Legal Sub-Committee re-established on 19 March 1984 a working group to consider supplementing the norms of international law relevant to the use of nuclear power sources in outer space; the group met between that date and 4 April.[20]

Working papers by the Federal Republic of Germany and Sweden and joint working papers by Canada/China/Sweden and Canada/China/the Netherlands/Sweden were submitted to the group and appended to the Sub-Committee's report. The Federal Republic of Germany's paper offered a proposal on repeated and updated notification of the re-entry into the Earth's atmosphere of a nuclear-powered satellite following malfunction. The other papers concerned safety provisions related to the use of nuclear power sources in outer space.

In the Committee on outer space, some delegations felt that the item should be recognized as a priority and that the time allocated to it in the Sub-Committee be increased. Those delegations also stated that, to make further progress, the Sub-Committee should be given a mandate to draft a set of principles governing the use of nuclear power sources in outer space. Other delegations saw no need to change the basis on which the Sub-Committee had been treating the issue. The Committee recommended that the Sub-Committee continue to consider the question in 1985.[4]

Legal aspects of the geostationary orbit and definition of outer space

On 19 March 1984,[20] the Legal Sub-Committee established a working group to consider the definition and/or delimitation of outer space, including questions relating to the geostationary orbit. The group, which met from 19 March to 6 April, had before it a working paper by the USSR outlining an approach to the delimitation of airspace and outer space and a joint working paper by Colombia, Ecuador, Indonesia and Kenya containing draft general principles governing the geostationary orbit.

Some delegations stated that a definition and delimitation of outer space was urgent. They suggested that a multilateral agreement be concluded, setting a specific altitude as the upper limit of airspace. Two fundamental questions had to be resolved—first, whether outer space should be viewed as beginning where airspace should be regarded as ending, and second, at what altitude airspace should be regarded as ending. Some delegations expressed support for the USSR paper which envisaged setting the boundary between airspace and outer space at an altitude not exceeding 110 kilometres above sea-level. Others declared that a definition and delimitation was premature. They maintained that there was no current scientific basis for placing a boundary between airspace and outer space at any particular altitude; that development and application of the law of outer space had proceeded satisfactorily without such a definition; and that it would be undesirable to adopt an arbitrary boundary which could create

difficulties and impede the development of space technology.

With respect to the geostationary orbit, some delegations said that the United Nations should establish appropriate general principles and ITU should be responsible for technical arrangements. Some of them emphasized that the geostationary orbit lay on the equatorial plane and that the equatorial countries had special rights and responsibilities in relation to segments of the orbit superjacent to their territories; others disagreed.

The view was put forward that the following principles should underlie the legal régime of the geostationary orbit: the relevant provisions of the 1966 Treaty on Principles Governing the Activities of States in the Exploration and Use of Outer Space, including the Moon and Other Celestial Bodies[22] would apply; the orbit could not be the subject of national appropriation; placing of a geostationary satellite in outer space did not vest a State with any property rights to its stationing position; equitable access to the orbit by different States or groups of States should be ensured; the needs of developing States should be considered; and States should co-operate within ITU in placing geostationary satellites.

Other delegations stated that a legal régime for the geostationary orbit was not necessary. They declared that ITU was currently considering the question of access and equitable use, and that WARC in 1985 and 1988 would review it. They said that the working group should not conclude its discussions until those conferences had been held.

The Committee on outer space[4] recommended that the Sub-Committee continue considering the definition and delimitation of outer space and the geostationary orbit in 1985.

GENERAL ASSEMBLY ACTION

On 14 December 1984, the General Assembly, on the recommendation of the Special Political Committee, adopted by consensus resolution 39/96.

International co-operation in the peaceful uses of outer space

The General Assembly,

Recalling its resolution 38/80 of 15 December 1983,

Deeply convinced of the common interest of mankind in promoting the exploration and use of outer space for peaceful purposes and in continuing efforts to extend to all States the benefits derived therefrom, and of the importance of international co-operation in this field, for which the United Nations should continue to provide a focal point,

Reaffirming the importance of international co-operation in developing the rule of law for the advancement and preservation of the exploration and peaceful uses of outer space,

Gravely concerned at the extension of an arms race into outer space,

Recognizing that all States, in particular those with major space capabilities, should contribute actively to the goal of preventing an arms race in outer space as an essential condition for the promotion of international co-operation in the exploration and uses of outer space for peaceful purposes,

Aware of the need to increase the benefits of space technology and its applications and to contribute to an orderly growth of space activities favourable to the socio-economic advancement of mankind, in particular the peoples of developing countries,

Taking note of the progress achieved in the further development of peaceful space exploration and application as well as in various national and co-operative space projects, which contribute to international co-operation in this field,

Taking note also of the report of the Secretary-General on the implementation of the recommendations of the Second United Nations Conference on the Exploration and Peaceful Uses of Outer Space,

Having considered the report of the Committee on the Peaceful Uses of Outer Space on the work of its twenty-seventh session,

1. *Endorses* the report of the Committee on the Peaceful Uses of Outer Space;

2. *Invites* States that have not yet become parties to the international treaties governing the use of outer space* to give consideration to ratifying or acceding to those treaties;

3. *Notes* that the Legal Sub-Committee of the Committee on the Peaceful Uses of Outer Space at its twenty-third session:

(a) Continued, on a priority basis, its detailed consideration of the legal implications of remote sensing of the Earth from space, with the aim of formulating draft principles relating to remote sensing;

(b) Continued its consideration of the possibility of supplementing the norms of international law relevant to the use of nuclear power sources in outer space through its working group;

(c) Established a working group to consider, on a priority basis, matters relating to the definition and delimitation of outer space and to the character and utilization of the geostationary orbit, including the elaboration of general principles to govern the rational and equitable use of the geostationary orbit, a limited natural resource;

4. *Decides* that the Legal Sub-Committee at its twenty-fourth session should, in its working groups, continue:

(a) Its detailed consideration of the legal implications of remote sensing of the Earth from space, with the aim of formulating draft principles relating to remote sensing;

(b) Its consideration of the possibility of supplementing the norms of international law relevant to the use of nuclear power sources in outer space;

(c) Its consideration of matters relating to the definition and delimitation of outer space and to the character and utilization of the geostationary orbit, including consideration of ways and means to ensure the rational and equitable use of the geostationary orbit without prejudice to the role of the International Telecommunication Union;

5. *Notes* that the Scientific and Technical Sub-Committee of the Committee on the Peaceful Uses of Outer Space at its twenty-first session continued:

(a) Its consideration of the following items on a priority basis:

(i) United Nations Programme on Space Applications and the co-ordination of space activities within the United Nations system;

(ii) Implementation of the recommendations of the Second United Nations Conference on the Exploration and Peaceful Uses of Outer Space;

(iii) Questions relating to remote sensing of the Earth by satellites;

(iv) Use of nuclear power sources in outer space;

(b) Its consideration of the following items:

(i) Questions relating to space transportation systems and their implications for future activities in space;

(ii) Examination of the physical nature and technical attributes of the geostationary orbit;

6. *Endorses* the recommendation of the Committee on the Peaceful Uses of Outer Space that the Scientific and Technical Sub-Committee at its twenty-second session should:

(a) Consider the following items on a priority basis:

(i) United Nations Programme on Space Applications and the co-ordination of space activities within the United Nations system;

(ii) Implementation of the recommendations of the Second United Nations Conference on the Exploration and Peaceful Uses of Outer Space; and, in this context, it is particularly urgent to implement the following recommendations:

a. All countries should have the opportunity to use the techniques resulting from medical studies in space;

b. Data banks at the national and regional levels should be strengthened and expanded and an international space information service should be established to function as a centre of co-ordination;

c. The United Nations should support the creation of adequate training centres at the regional level, linked, whenever possible, to institutions implementing space programmes; necessary funding for the development of such centres should be made available through financial institutions;

(iii) Questions relating to remote sensing of the Earth by satellites;

(iv) Use of nuclear power sources in outer space;

(b) Consider the following items:

(i) Questions relating to space transportation systems and their implications for future activities in space;

(ii) Examination of the physical nature and technical attributes of the geostationary orbit;

7. *Endorses further* the recommendation of the Committee on the Peaceful Uses of Outer Space that, during the twenty-second session of the Scientific and Technical Sub-Committee, the Working Group on the Use of Nuclear Power Sources in Outer Space should be reconvened to conduct additional work on the basis of the report of the Working Group on the work of its fourth session;

8. *Endorses* the United Nations Programme on Space Applications for 1985, as proposed to the Committee on the Peaceful Uses of Outer Space by the Expert on Space Applications;

9. *Emphasizes* the urgency and importance of implementing fully the recommendations of the Second United Nations Conference on the Exploration and Peaceful Uses of Outer Space as early as possible;

10. *Reaffirms* its approval of the recommendation of the Conference regarding the establishment and strengthening of regional mechanisms of co-operation and their promotion and creation through the United Nations system;

11. *Expresses its appreciation* to all Governments that made or expressed their intention to make contributions towards carrying out the recommendations of the Conference;

12. *Invites* all Governments to take effective action for the implementation of the recommendations of the Conference;

13. *Urges* all States, in particular those with major space capabilities, to contribute actively to the goal of preventing an arms race in outer space as an essential condition for the promotion of international co-operation in the exploration and uses of outer space for peaceful purposes;

14. *Takes note* of the views expressed during the twenty-seventh session of the Committee on the Peaceful Uses of Outer Space and during the thirty-ninth session of the General Assembly concerning questions relating to the militarization of outer space;

15. *Requests* the Committee on the Peaceful Uses of Outer Space to consider, as a matter of priority, ways and means for maintaining outer space for peaceful purposes and to report thereon to the General Assembly at its fortieth session;

16. *Takes note* of the fact that work on the following three study projects proposed by the Second United Nations Conference on the Exploration and Peaceful Uses of Outer Space has reached an advanced stage and that the final reports will be submitted to the Scientific and Technical Sub-Committee at its twenty-second session:

(a) Assistance to countries in studying their remote-sensing needs and assessing appropriate systems for meeting such needs (United Nations, United Nations Environment Programme, United Nations Development Programme and Food and Agriculture Organization of the United Nations);

(b) The feasibility of using direct broadcasting satellites for educational purposes and of internationally or regionally owned space segments (United Nations, United Nations Educational, Scientific and Cultural Organization and International Telecommunication Union);

(c) The feasibility of obtaining closer spacing of satellites in the geostationary orbit and their satisfactory coexistence, including a closer examination of techno-economic implications, particularly for developing countries, in order to ensure the most effective utilization of this orbit in the interest of all countries (United Nations, International Telecommunication Union and other organizations);

17. *Affirms* that the interference that satellite systems to be newly established may cause to systems already registered with the International Telecommunication Union shall not exceed the limits specified in the relevant provision of the International Telecommunication Union Radio Regulations applicable to space services;

18. *Requests* all organs, organizations and bodies of the United Nations system and other intergovernmental organizations working in the field of outer space or on space-related matters to co-operate in the implementation of the recommendations of the Conference;

19. *Requests* the Secretary-General to report to the General Assembly at its fortieth session on the implementation of the recommendations of the Conference;

20. *Requests* the specialized agencies and other international organizations to continue and, where appropriate, enhance their co-operation with the Committee on the Peaceful Uses of Outer Space and to provide it with progress reports on their work relating to the peaceful uses of outer space;

21. *Requests* the Committee on the Peaceful Uses of Outer Space to continue its work, in accordance with the present resolution, to consider, as appropriate, new projects in outer space activities and to submit a report to the General Assembly at its fortieth session, including its views on which subjects should be studied in the future.

---

*Treaty on Principles Governing the Activities of States in the Exploration and Use of Outer Space, including the Moon and Other Celestial Bodies (resolution 2222(XXI), annex); Agreement on the Rescue of Astronauts, the Return of Astronauts and the Return of Objects Launched into Outer Space (resolution 2345(XXII), annex); Convention on International Liability for Damage Caused by Space Objects (resolution 2777(XXVI), annex); Convention on Registration of Objects Launched into Outer Space (resolution 3235(XXIX), annex); Agreement Governing the Activities of States on the Moon and Other Celestial Bodies (resolution 34/68, annex).

General Assembly resolution 39/96

14 December 1984   Meeting 100   Adopted by consensus

Approved by SPC (A/39/713) by consensus, 6 December (meeting 49); draft by Austria, for SPC working group (A/SPC/39/L.33); agenda item 72.
Meeting numbers. GA 39th session: SPC 39-45, 47, 49; plenary 100.

Following approval of the resolution, Colombia, Egypt (on behalf of the Group of 77), France, the USSR, the United Kingdom and the United States said they had joined in the consensus to strengthen the work of the Committee on outer space and its sub-committees; however, they felt that the text did not take into account their various concerns.

The German Democratic Republic and Mexico voiced concern about the growing militarization of outer space.

Agreement concerning the Moon and other celestial bodies

The Agreement Governing the Activities of States on the Moon and Other Celestial Bodies, adopted by the General Assembly in 1979,[(23)] entered into force on 11 July 1984, the thirtieth day following the day of deposit of the fifth instrument of ratification—by Austria on 11 June.[(24)] The Agreement had previously been ratified by Chile, the Philippines and Uruguay in 1981 and by the Netherlands in 1983. Other States which had signed but had not ratified the Agreement were France, Guatemala, Morocco and Romania (1980), Peru (1981) and India (1982).

Among other things, the 21-article Agreement stressed that the Moon should be used for peaceful purposes, provided for the establishment of an international régime for the exploitation of the Moon's resources, regarded as the common heritage of mankind, and prohibited its use for any form of military activity.

REFERENCES

[1]A/AC.105/336. [2]YUN 1983, p. 100, GA res. 38/80, 15 Dec. 1983. [3]YUN 1982, p. 162. [4]A/39/20. [5]A/AC.105/348. [6]YUN 1982, p. 163, GA res. 37/90, 10 Dec. 1982. [7]A/AC.105/L.141. [8]A/AC.105/L.142. [9]A/AC.105/L.143. [10]A/AC.105/L.144. [11]A/AC.105/346. [12]A/39/515. [13]ACC/1984/PG/8. [14]A/AC.105/342. [15]A/AC.105/339/Rev.1. [16]A/AC.105/340/Rev.1. [17]A/AC.105/341/Rev.1. [18]A/AC.105/297/Add.1-4. [19]YUN 1983, p. 98. [20]A/AC.105/337. [21]YUN 1983, p. 99. [22]YUN 1966, p. 41, GA res. 2222(XXI), annex, 19 Dec. 1966. [23]YUN 1979, p. 111, GA res. 34/68, annex, 5 Dec. 1979. [24]*Multilateral Treaties Deposited with the Secretary-General: Status as at 31 December 1984* (ST/LEG/SER.E/3), Sales No. E.85.V.4.

Launchings of functional spacecraft

During 1984, four countries and an intergovernmental organization provided information to the United Nations on the launching of objects into orbit or beyond, in accordance with a 1961 General Assembly resolution[1] and the Convention on Registration of Objects Launched into Outer Space.[2]

Twenty-three notifications of objects launched during 1984 and the latter part of 1983 were received in 1984 and distributed as United Nations documents.[3]

Information was submitted by the Federal Republic of Germany on 1 launching, by Japan on 2, by the USSR on 87, by the United States on 30 and by ESA on 3.

As at 31 December 1984, there were 32 States parties to the Convention on Registration.[4]

REFERENCES

[1]YUN 1961, p. 35, GA res. 1721 B (XVI), 20 Dec. 1961. [2]YUN 1974, p. 63, GA res. 3235(XXIX), annex, 12 Nov. 1974. [3]ST/SG/SER.E/95-108, 110-118. [4]*Multilateral Treaties Deposited with the Secretary-General: Status as at 31 December 1984* (ST/LEG/SER.E/3), Sales No. E.85.V.4.

Chapter III

Law of the sea

The United Nations Convention on the Law of the Sea was widely recognized as a significant contribution to the progressive development of international law and one of the most outstanding achievements of the United Nations, the Secretary-General stated in 1984. Adopted in 1982, it established rules governing virtually all uses of the oceans, including navigation, fisheries, mineral resource development and scientific research.

Signatories to the Convention rose to 159 during 1984, while the number of ratifications increased to 14.

The Preparatory Commission, charged with setting up the two main organs under the Convention—the International Sea-Bed Authority and the International Tribunal for the Law of the Sea—continued its work with meetings at Kingston, Jamaica, and at Geneva.

By resolution 39/73, adopted in December, the General Assembly called on States to safeguard the Convention's unified character and to desist from undermining or defeating its purpose. The Assembly also called on States that had not done so to consider ratifying the Convention.

Topics related to this chapter. Disarmament: naval armaments. Transport: maritime transport. Natural resources: marine resources. Food: fisheries management and development. Environment: marine ecosystems. International Court of Justice: continental shelf delimitation (Libyan Arab Jamahiriya and Tunisia, Libyan Arab Jamahiriya and Malta); maritime boundary delimitation (Canada and the United States).

UN Convention on the Law of the Sea

Signatures and ratifications

The number of signatories to the United Nations Convention on the Law of the Sea totalled 159 as at 9 December 1984,[1] when the period for signature closed. The Third United Nations Conference on the Law of the Sea had adopted the Convention in April 1982,[2] with the General Assembly welcoming that action in December 1982.[3]

Signatories in 1984 were: Argentina, Belgium, Bolivia, Botswana, Brunei Darussalam, Central African Republic, Comoros, El Salvador, Equatorial Guinea, European Economic Community, Guinea, Italy, Lebanon, Libyan Arab Jama-

hiriya, Liechtenstein, Luxembourg, Malawi, Nicaragua, Niue, Qatar, Saint Christopher and Nevis, Samoa, Saudi Arabia, South Africa, Spain, Swaziland and Switzerland.

The number of ratifications to the Convention—which was to enter into force 12 months after receipt of the sixtieth instrument of ratification or accession—increased during 1984 to 14 with the addition of Cuba, the Gambia, the Ivory Coast, the Philippines and Senegal.

A letter from India to the Secretary-General of 8 October[4] forwarded the final communiqué of the Meeting of Ministers for Foreign Affairs and Heads of Delegation of Non-Aligned Countries (New York, 1-5 October). They reiterated their support for the Convention and reaffirmed that sea-bed resources could only be lawfully explored and exploited in accordance with it; reiterated their opposition to any mini-convention or other parallel régime inconsistent with the Convention and declared that any such arrangement would be illegal; and encouraged those who had not done so to sign and ratify the Convention.

Developments relating to the Convention

The Secretary-General, pursuant to a December 1983 General Assembly resolution,[5] submitted a report in November 1984[6] on developments relating to the Convention and on the implementation of the 1983 resolution. He stated that it had been widely recognized as one of the international community's most important achievements. Though not in force, the Convention was having a stabilizing effect on the law of the sea through the rationalization of different uses of the oceans and the reconciliation of States' competing interests. It was also having an impact on the attitudes of States towards marine affairs at national and international levels. Nationally, new trends in State practice were developing as States adjusted their policies and legislation to the new legal order for the oceans; at the same time, international organizations concerned with marine affairs were assessing the Convention's impact on their activities.

The report was divided into two parts: the first part contained an overview of the Convention's effect on State practice and on international organizations, and information on other law of the sea developments; the second provided information on the activities of the Office of the Special Representative of the Secretary-General for the Law of the Sea (see p. 111).

Most States were adopting national policy and legislation consistent with the Convention, but current State practice with regard to marine affairs was far from integrated. The predominant approach had been a sectoral one; that is, policies tended to relate to such marine sectors as fisheries, oil and gas, or shipping and transport, independently of each other. Inter-sectoral relationships—for example, those between marine and non-marine sectors—were rarely addressed.

The Convention provided a foundation for an integrated national approach to marine-related activities, the Secretary-General pointed out.

Trends in national policy compatible with the Convention were developing in regard to a number of issues. One such trend concerned the question of the nature and breadth of maritime zones under national jurisdiction. The Convention allowed for a territorial sea of up to 12 nautical miles, a further 12 miles of contiguous zone and an exclusive economic zone of 200 miles. Eighty-three States had established a claim to a territorial sea of 12 miles in breadth, while 24 had claimed breadths beyond 12 miles; 60 countries had established exclusive economic zones of up to 200 miles.

Currently, 21 countries had fisheries zones extending up to 200 miles. The essential distinction between an exclusive economic zone and a fisheries zone lay in the extent of jurisdiction retained by the coastal State and the resources over which that jurisdiction might be exercised. Under the Convention, the exclusive economic zone covered all living and non-living resources; fisheries zones pertained only to living resources or to certain species of them.

A few States—France, the Federal Republic of Germany, Japan, the USSR, the United Kingdom and the United States—had enacted legislation on the international sea-bed. The legality of such legislation had been challenged in international forums by other States.

The need for orderly regulation of ocean space could best be demonstrated by noting the international conflicts directly related to the question of the uses of the sea. Among them were the mining of the Red Sea; the questions of the Strait of Hormuz and of the Beagle Channel; the Canada/United States disputes over Georges Bank, the Beaufort Sea and the North-West Passage; the Nicaragua/United States dispute regarding the mining of Nicaraguan waters; the Solomon Islands/United States dispute over fishing rights; the Canada/France dispute over the Saint Pierre and Miquelon Isles; the Colombia/Venezuela dispute over the Gulf of Venezuela; and the China/Philippines/Viet Nam dispute over the Spratly and Paracels archipelagoes. (For further information on these topics, refer to the SUBJECT INDEX.)

Several international organizations examined the impact of the Convention on their activities. They included the International Maritime Organization (IMO), the International Civil Aviation Organization, the Intergovernmental Oceanographic Commission of the United Nations Educational, Scientific and Cultural Organization, the World Meteorological Organization, the United Nations Environment Programme (UNEP), the International Hydrographic Organization and the United Nations Division of Narcotic Drugs.

The Secretary-General's report also reviewed developments in such matters covered by the Convention as peaceful uses of the sea-bed, maritime law, environmental law, legislative developments under UNEP programmes, fisheries management, marine scientific co-operation and rescue at sea, as well as development of regional and subregional co-operation. Several meetings were held in 1984 on these matters.

The United Nations Conference on Conditions for Registration of Ships (Geneva, 16 July–3 August) considered an international agreement concerning conditions under which vessels should be accepted on national shipping registers (see ECONOMIC AND SOCIAL QUESTIONS, Chapter V).

The Joint Maritime Commission of the International Labour Office (Geneva, September) took up aspects of labour law related to seafearers (see PART TWO, Chapter II).

The IMO Marine Environment Protection Committee (London, September) adopted amendments to the 1973 International Convention for the Prevention of Pollution from Ships,[7] as modified by the 1978 Protocol thereto.[8] An international conference convened by IMO (London, April/May) adopted two protocols to amend the 1969 International Convention on Civil Liability for Oil Pollution Damage[9] and the 1971 International Convention on the Establishment of an International Fund for Compensation for Oil Pollution Damage[10] (see PART TWO, Chapter XIV).

The Eighth Consultative Meeting of Contracting Parties to the 1975 Convention on the Prevention of Marine Pollution by Dumping of Wastes and Other Matter (London, February) took action on the report of the Scientific Group on Dumping, including establishing criteria for the allocation of substances in annexes I and II of the Convention and guidelines for the application of annex III.

In its annual overview report for 1983/84,[11] the Administrative Committee on Co-ordination declared that the Convention had provided new opportunities for co-operation. The foremost considerations in that respect should be adoption of a unified approach to law of the sea matters and a uniform interpretation and application of the Convention. The complexity of the Convention underscored the importance of maintaining close contact among international organizations and the possibility that regular consultations might be required.

GENERAL ASSEMBLY ACTION

For General Assembly action with regard to the Convention, see resolution 39/73 below.

Preparatory Commission

The Preparatory Commission for the International Sea-Bed Authority and for the International Tribunal for the Law of the Sea met twice during 1984.[6] It held its second session at Kingston from 19 March to 13 April, with 88 members and 14 observers attending; and a meeting at Geneva from 13 August to 5 September, when 93 members and 16 observers were present.

Priority was given to adopting rules for the registration of pioneer investors. Three principal issues were addressed: those relating to conflicts arising from the overlapping of areas claimed; the nature of the group of technical experts to assist the Commission in examining applications; and the confidentiality of data and information. The first reading of the draft rules for the registration of pioneer investors and on confidentiality of data and information was completed, and several rules were provisionally adopted.

Applications for registration as pioneer investors had been received from France, India, Japan and the USSR. The Commission decided that, following the adoption of the rules for registration, it would register the first group of applicants at its third session in 1985.

During its Geneva meeting, the Commission was informed that an intergovernmental agreement regarding sea-bed matters had been concluded on 3 August 1984 among eight Governments: Belgium, France, Federal Republic of Germany, Italy, Japan, Netherlands, United Kingdom, United States. The Commission was assured that the agreement aimed at avoiding conflicts due to overlapping claims and that it was fully compatible with the Convention. In response, the Group of 77 developing countries and the Group of Eastern European States reiterated their opposition to instruments based on national legislation and reciprocal agreements purporting to regulate sea-bed activities; they asserted that the carrying out of such activities outside the Convention was illegal. The

Chairman announced that an understanding had been reached on a procedure and timetable for conflict resolution for the first group of applicants.

At its Kingston session, the Commission discussed the establishment of the Authority, including its staffing. It concluded that the Authority should be cost-effective with a lean staffing structure; the Secretariat was asked to prepare a working paper on the subject. Working papers prepared for the session covered draft rules for the registration of pioneer investors and the confidentiality of data; proposed amendments to the registration rules; draft rules of procedure for the Authority's Assembly; and a proposal by Belgium, France, the Federal Republic of Germany, Italy, Japan and the United Kingdom on draft work programmes for the four Special Commissions.

Special Commissions

The Commission's four Special Commissions considered the work allotted to them. Special Commission 1, charged with studying the possible adverse effect of sea-bed mining on developing land-based producer States, had begun to examine relevant data. Special Commission 2 on the Enterprise, the operational arm of the Authority, examined measures necessary to bring the Enterprise into operation. Special Commission 3, mandated to draft regulations for sea-bed mining, took up a first set of regulations dealing with the application for approval of plans of work. Special Commission 4 prepared recommendations regarding establishment of the International Tribunal for the Law of the Sea.

Developing land-based producer States

Special Commission 1 held seven meetings during the Preparatory Commission's Kingston session. In studying the problems of developing land-based producer States, the Chairman of Special Commission 1 said in a statement to the plenary Commission,[12] it was necessary to know which minerals would be produced from the sea-bed; how minerals from that new source would affect existing land-based sources; what those effects would be; the problems that developing States would encounter in connection with them; and what might be done to minimize those problems. Special Commission 1 considered whether it should deal with each of the 50 or so minerals contained in sea-bed polymetallic nodules or limit itself to the minerals which appeared to be economically exploitable; it agreed that it should concentrate on copper, nickel, cobalt and manganese, while keeping in view trends regarding the other minerals. It had before it a Secretariat background paper which presented an overview of the topic along with possible approaches to it and pertinent statistics.

The Enterprise

Special Commission 2 was mandated to take all necessary measures for the early operation of the Enterprise, which was to carry out sea-bed activities, as well as the transport, processing and marketing of recovered minerals. The Chairman of Special Commission 2 informed the Preparatory Commission[13] that its discussions had made clear that current economic indicators called for a pragmatic approach to planning for the Enterprise's early operation. Two points were emphasized: first, though all operational options should be studied, a joint venture appeared to be the most feasible; second, initial operations might mature quickly under favourable conditions. Special Commission 2, which held seven meetings during the Preparatory Commission's Kingston session, requested the Secretariat to prepare studies on a charter for the Enterprise and on a model joint venture.

Sea-bed mining code

Special Commission 3, mandated to prepare rules, regulations and procedures for the exploration and exploitation of the international sea-bed "Area" (the sea-bed beyond national jurisdiction), held eight meetings during the Preparatory Commission's Kingston session. Addressing that body, the Chairman of Special Commission 3 said[14] that it had adopted a work programme under which the use of terms and the rules, regulations and procedures for prospecting, exploration and exploitation, and the scope of their applicability, would be elaborated. The subject of partnerships or consortia was discussed, particularly whether it was necessary to establish objective criteria for assessing their nationality or the control exercised over them, or to leave these matters to the sponsoring State or States.

International Tribunal

Special Commission 4, which met seven times during the Preparatory Commission's Kingston session, was mandated to prepare recommendations for the establishment of the International Tribunal for the Law of the Sea to be submitted to a meeting of States parties. Speaking to the Preparatory Commission, the Chairman of Special Commission 4 said[15] that it had discussed the composition of the Tribunal and its Chambers, the different officials and the precedence that would be applied in the Tribunal and the Sea-Bed Disputes Chamber, and the manner of selecting Chamber members. The access of entities other than States to the Tribunal and to the Chamber and the question of advisory opinions also were examined. The Secretariat was requested to prepare draft procedural rules for the Tribunal, using the Rules of the International Court of Justice as a guide.

The site for the permanent seat of the Tribunal in the Federal Republic of Germany was inspected in September (see below).

GENERAL ASSEMBLY ACTION

For General Assembly action concerning the work of the Preparatory Commission, see resolution 39/73 below.

Functions of the Secretary-General

Office of the Special Representative

The Office of the Special Representative of the Secretary-General was responsible for executing the central programme on law of the sea affairs and was the core office of the Organization for the law of the sea.[6]

Under its mandate to assist States in the Convention's application, the Office acted as the repository for charts and co-ordinates establishing baselines and limits of maritime zones. The Office was engaged in rationalizing the various scales of charts and different methods used for the drawing of baselines and listing of co-ordinates.

The legislative history of the Convention's provisions had been collated and analysed to provide the negotiating background to the text of the Convention; the analyses would be an aid to interpreting the treaty provisions and to its implementation by Governments in national policy and legislation.

The reference library, which was begun at an early point in the Conference, continued to be updated. A selected bibliography on the law of the sea, the first volume in the series "Law of the Sea Studies" under the publication programme, was submitted for printing; it was to be supplemented or revised annually. A comprehensive collection of national legislation on marine affairs, organized by country and subject area, had been supplemented and analysed and extracts were circulated to delegations in the *Law of the Sea Bulletin*.

Work also continued on obtaining, extracting and evaluating materials on other aspects of State practice in the implementation of the Convention. Among the materials were bilateral or regional arrangements, declarations made when signing or ratifying the Convention, statements made in the records of the Conference or Sea-Bed Committee, and records of other intergovernmental meetings relevant to the Convention. A computerized data storage system was also being set up.

United Nations agencies and bodies co-operated in collecting materials for the preparation of annotations to the Convention.

Requests for information, advice and assistance from the Office grew perceptibly in 1984, the main users being Governments, government agencies, intergovernmental organizations and academic institutions. For example, the Office responded to inquiries on the implications of signing or ratifying the Convention. Moreover, the Office had been requested to give advice on updating, supplementing or modifying national maritime legislation to ensure its conformity with the Convention.

The development of the fellowship programme centred on that set up in 1980 in honour of the late Hamilton Shirley Amerasinghe of Sri Lanka,[16] who had served as Chairman of the Sea-Bed Committee and then as President of the Conference. Voluntary contributions received indicated that one fellowship each year, beginning in 1985, could be awarded.

Publications in 1984 included the *Law of the Sea Bulletin*, which covered developments related to the Convention.

The Special Representative and a Secretariat team visited the Federal Republic of Germany from 11 to 14 September to discuss a site proposed at Hamburg for the permanent seat of the International Tribunal for the Law of the Sea.

GENERAL ASSEMBLY ACTION

For the Assembly's action concerning the Secretary-General's functions, see resolution 39/73 below.

Pioneer investors

The Secretary-General submitted a report to the Preparatory Commission in February 1984,[17] summarizing polymetallic nodule pre-production activities. The report covered the exploration phase (information needs, prospecting, determination of the area for exploration) and matters to be considered in a work plan (a definition of reserves, the development of the mining system, processing systems, plant siting, environment protection).

In notes dated 14 February,[18] 22 August[19] and 23 August 1984,[20] the Secretary-General informed the Commission that applications for registration as pioneer investors had been received from India, Japan and France, respectively.

GENERAL ASSEMBLY ACTION

On 13 December 1984, the General Assembly adopted by recorded vote resolution 39/73.

Law of the sea
The General Assembly,

Recalling its resolutions 37/66 of 3 December 1982 and 38/59 A of 14 December 1983, regarding the Third United Nations Conference on the Law of the Sea,

Taking note of the increasing and overwhelming support for the United Nations Convention on the Law of the Sea, as evidenced, *inter alia*, by the one hundred and

fifty-nine signatures and fourteen ratifications as at the closing of the Convention for signature,

Seriously concerned at any attempt to undermine the Convention and the related resolutions of the Third United Nations Conference on the Law of the Sea,

Recognizing that, as stated in the third preambular paragraph of the Convention, the problems of ocean space are closely interrelated and need to be considered as a whole,

Convinced that it is important to safeguard the unified character of the Convention and related resolutions adopted therewith and to refrain from any action to apply their provisions selectively, in a manner inconsistent with their object and purpose,

Noting the increasing needs of countries, especially developing countries, for information, advice and assistance in the implementation of the Convention and in their developmental process for the full realization of the benefits of the comprehensive legal régime established by the Convention, as also recognized by the Economic and Social Council in its resolution 1983/48 of 28 July 1983,

Noting also that the Preparatory Commission for the International Sea-Bed Authority and for the International Tribunal for the Law of the Sea has decided to hold its third regular session at Kingston from 11 March to 4 April 1985 and its summer meeting in 1985 at Geneva, Kingston or New York as it may decide,

Taking note also of activities carried out in 1984 under the major programme on marine affairs, set forth in chapter 25 of the medium-term plan for the period 1984-1989, in accordance with the report of the Secretary-General as approved in General Assembly resolution 38/59 A,

Recalling its approval of the financing of the expenses of the Preparatory Commission from the regular budget of the United Nations,

Taking special note of the report of the Secretary-General prepared in response to paragraph 8 of General Assembly resolution 38/59 A,

1. *Recalls* the historic significance of the United Nations Convention on the Law of the Sea as an important contribution to the maintenance of peace, justice and progress for all peoples of the world;

2. *Expresses its satisfaction* at the large number of signatures affixed to the Convention as well as at the number of ratifications deposited with the Secretary-General;

3. *Calls upon* all States that have not done so to consider ratifying or acceding to the Convention at the earliest possible date to allow the effective entry into force of the new legal régime for the uses of the sea and its resources;

4. *Calls upon* all States to safeguard the unified character of the Convention and related resolutions adopted therewith;

5. *Calls upon* States to desist from taking actions which undermine the Convention or defeat its object and purpose;

6. *Expresses its appreciation* for the effective execution by the Secretary-General of the central programme in law of the sea affairs under chapter 25 of the medium-term plan for the period 1984-1989;

7. *Further expresses its appreciation* for the report of the Secretary-General in response to General Assembly resolution 38/59 A and requests the Secretary-General to continue the activities outlined therein, special em-

phasis being placed on the work of the Preparatory Commission for the International Sea-Bed Authority and for the International Tribunal for the Law of the Sea, including the implementation of resolution II of the Third United Nations Conference on the Law of the Sea;

8. *Approves* the programme of meetings of the Preparatory Commission for 1985;

9. *Calls upon* the Secretary-General to continue to assist States in the implementation of the Convention and in the development of a consistent and uniform approach to the new legal régime thereunder, as well as in their national, subregional and regional efforts towards the full realization of the benefits therefrom and invites the agencies and bodies within the United Nations system to co-operate and lend assistance in these endeavours;

10. *Requests* the Secretary-General to report to the General Assembly at its fortieth session on developments relating to the Convention and on the implementation of the present resolution;

11. *Decides* to include in the provisional agenda of its fortieth session the item entitled "Law of the sea".

General Assembly resolution 39/73

13 December 1984   Meeting 99   138-2-5 (recorded vote)

37-nation draft (A/39/L.35 & Add.1); agenda item 34.

Sponsors: Algeria, Angola, Antigua and Barbuda, Bahamas, Barbados, Cameroon, Chile, Colombia, Costa Rica, Dominica, Fiji, Guinea-Bissau, Honduras, India, Indonesia, Ivory Coast, Jamaica, Kenya, Kuwait, Madagascar, Malawi, Malta, Mauritania, Nigeria, Oman, Philippines, Saint Lucia, Sierra Leone, Singapore, Sri Lanka, Sudan, Suriname, Trinidad and Tobago, Tunisia, Uganda, United Republic of Tanzania, Uruguay.

Financial implications. 5th Committee, A/39/821; S-G, A/C.5/39/73 & Corr.1.

Meeting numbers. GA 39th session: 5th Committee 47; plenary 99.

Recorded vote in Assembly as follows:

In favour: Afghanistan, Algeria, Angola, Argentina, Australia, Austria, Bahamas, Bahrain, Bangladesh, Barbados, Belgium, Belize, Benin, Bhutan, Bolivia, Botswana, Brazil, Brunei Darussalam, Bulgaria, Burkina Faso, Burma, Burundi, Byelorussian SSR, Cameroon, Canada, Cape Verde, Central African Republic, Chad, Chile, China, Colombia, Congo, Costa Rica, Cuba, Cyprus, Czechoslovakia, Democratic Kampuchea, Democratic Yemen, Denmark, Djibouti, Dominican Republic, Egypt, El Salvador, Equatorial Guinea, Ethiopia, Fiji, Finland, France, Gabon, German Democratic Republic, Ghana, Greece, Guinea, Guyana, Haiti, Honduras, Hungary, Iceland, India, Indonesia, Iran, Iraq, Ireland, Italy, Ivory Coast, Jamaica, Japan, Jordan, Kenya, Kuwait, Lao People's Democratic Republic, Lebanon, Lesotho, Liberia, Libyan Arab Jamahiriya, Luxembourg, Madagascar, Malawi, Malaysia, Maldives, Mali, Malta, Mauritania, Mauritius, Mexico, Mongolia, Morocco, Mozambique, Nepal, Netherlands, New Zealand, Nicaragua, Niger, Nigeria, Norway, Oman, Pakistan, Panama, Papua New Guinea, Paraguay, Philippines, Poland, Portugal, Qatar, Romania, Rwanda, Saint Lucia, Saint Vincent and the Grenadines, Samoa, Sao Tome and Principe, Saudi Arabia, Senegal, Seychelles, Sierra Leone, Singapore, Solomon Islands, Somalia, Spain, Sri

Lanka, Sudan, Suriname, Sweden, Thailand, Togo, Trinidad and Tobago, Tunisia, Uganda, Ukrainian SSR, USSR, United Arab Emirates, United Republic of Tanzania, Uruguay, Vanuatu, Viet Nam, Yemen, Yugoslavia, Zaire, Zambia.

Against: Turkey, United States.

Abstaining: Germany, Federal Republic of, Israel, Peru, United Kingdom, Venezuela.

The United States recalled that it had not signed the Convention because part XI governed exploration and exploitation of sea-bed resources in the area beyond national jurisdiction, which ran contrary to its policy; it would continue withholding its *pro rata* share of the United Nations annual assessment for the regular budget pertaining to the Preparatory Commission and earmarked for part XI.

Several others which had not signed the Convention explained their abstentions. The Federal Republic of Germany felt that it would have to be modified substantially to establish a generally acceptable sea-bed mining régime. Israel held that the Convention contained provisions introduced for political considerations extraneous to the law of the sea. Peru noted that differences between its Constitution and the Convention's provisions made it impossible for it to subscribe to the Convention. The United Kingdom pointed out that, since it had not signed, it must be clear that there were many aspects of the resolution which it could not support.

Japan regretted that there had been criticism of the eight-nation provisional understanding on sea-bed matters concluded in August (see above).

REFERENCES

[1]*Multilateral Treaties Deposited with the Secretary-General: Status as at 31 December 1984* (ST/LEG/SER.E/3), Sales No. E.85.V.4. [2]YUN 1982, p. 178. [3]*Ibid.*, p. 180, GA res. 37/66, 3 Dec. 1982. [4]A/39/560-S/16773. [5]YUN 1983, p. 107, GA res. 38/59 A, 14 Dec. 1983. [6]A/39/647 . & Corr.1 & Add.1. [7]YUN 1973, p. 964. [8]YUN 1978, p. 1161. [9]YUN 1969, p. 940. [10]YUN 1971, p. 755. [11]E/1984/66. [12]LOS/PCN/L.2. [13]LOS/PCN/L.5. [14]LOS/PCN/L.3. [15]LOS/PCN/L.4. [16]YUN 1980, p. 159, GA res. 35/116, 10 Dec. 1980. [17]LOS/PCN/L.1. [18]LOS/PCN/32. [19]LOS/PCN/50. [20]LOS/PCN/51.

Chapter IV

International peace and security

International peace and security and ways to strengthen it continued to be a major concern of the United Nations in 1984.

In November, the Assembly adopted the Declaration on the Right of Peoples to Peace (resolution 39/11) and, in December, it urged further action to implement its 1978 Declaration on the Preparation of Societies for Life in Peace (39/157).

The Assembly called for measures to prevent further deterioration of the international situation (39/155). It recommended that the Security Council give priority consideration to strengthening collective security (39/154) and encouraged the Council to intensify its efforts to prevent international conflict (39/156). The Assembly expressed regret that the *Ad Hoc* Committee on implementing the collective security provisions of the Charter of the United Nations had not been constituted (39/158) and renewed the mandate of the Special Committee on Peace-keeping Operations (39/97). Further preparations were made for the International Year of Peace (1986) and an appeal made for contributions to the Voluntary Fund (39/10).

Acting on a new item on State terrorism, the Assembly demanded that no State take action aimed at military intervention and occupation, forcible change in or undermining of the socio-political system of States, destabilization and overthrow of their Governments (39/159).

The Secretary-General, in his annual report to the Assembly (p. 3), declared that most of all a reaffirmation was needed of the Charter concept that threats to peace overrode ideological or other differences and required that all States agree and co-operate. He emphasized that peace-keeping was an expression of international political will and, if that will were weak, uncertain, divided or indecisive, peace-keeping operations would be correspondingly weakened.

Maintaining international peace and security was also a main topic considered by the Special Committee on the Charter (see LEGAL QUESTIONS, Chapter IV).

Topics related to this chapter. Disarmament. Human rights: human rights and international security. Legal aspects of international political relations: peaceful settlement of disputes between States; good-neighbourliness between States; non-use of force in international relations; draft Code of Offences against peace and security. International organizations and international law: strengthening the role of the United Nations.

Declarations on international peace and security

Implementation of the 1970 Declaration on international security

Following its yearly review of the implementation of the 1970 Declaration on the Strengthening of International Security,[1] the General Assembly, in December 1984, adopted resolution 39/155 in which it called on States, particularly the permanent members of the Security Council, to take a number of actions aimed at preventing the further deterioration of the international situation.

Communications. In relation to the review of the implementation of the Declaration, letters were received from Member States throughout 1984.

On 12 June,[2] Hungary forwarded an appeal by the States parties to the 1955 Warsaw Treaty of Friendship, Co-operation and Mutual Assistance to the member States of the North Atlantic Treaty Organization concerning the joint consideration of the proposal presented by the Warsaw Treaty States in their 1983 declaration[3] and the possibility of concluding a treaty on the mutual renunciation of the use of armed force and the maintenance of peaceful relations.

Czechoslovakia and Poland, in a letter of 15 October,[4] transmitted a joint statement signed at Warsaw following a meeting of their Foreign Ministers (6 and 7 September) in which they declared it necessary for States to cease interfering in the internal affairs of others, to resume negotiations aimed at ending the arms race, to give up attempts to undermine the realities shaped in Europe after the Second World War and to return to friendly, mutually beneficial co-operation. An extract from a 19 November report of the Central Committee of the Romanian Communist Party, concerning the international situation, was transmitted by Romania on 29 November;[5] it stated the conviction that peoples could change the course of events, avert world war and nuclear catastrophe and impose disarmament and world peace. The German Democratic Republic, in a letter of 5 December,[6] transmitted a communiqué on a meeting of the Committee of Foreign Ministers of the Warsaw Treaty States (Berlin, 3 and 4 December), expressing concern at the persistence of dangerous tensions in Europe and the world and declaring that international relations must be guided back to détente.

The USSR forwarded a number of communications on the subject of United States foreign policy. Four letters contained statements by the General Secretary of the Central Committee of the Communist Party: one of 26 January[7] transmitted the replies by Y. V. Andropov to questions from *Pravda* (USSR), published on 25 January, while letters of 10 April[8] and 4 September[9] gave the replies of K. U. Chernenko to the same newspaper which were issued on 9 April and 2 September respectively. Mr. Chernenko's replies to questions from *The Washington Post* dated 17 October were transmitted in a letter of 22 October.[10] A 15 August statement by TASS on the United States President's informal radio remarks was forwarded in a letter of 16 August.[11]

On 2 March,[12] Mongolia stated that China was continuing to put forward pre-conditions for the normalization of its relations with the USSR; among them was a matter entirely within the competence of Mongolia—a demand, which Mongolia rejected, for the withdrawal from Mongolia of USSR military units.

On 8 October,[13] India forwarded the final communiqué adopted by the Meeting of Ministers for Foreign Affairs and Heads of Delegation of Non-Aligned Countries (New York, 1-5 October), which noted with concern that policies of intervention and interference and the threat or use of force were continuing to be pursued against many countries, with dangerous consequences for peace and security.

Other 1984 letters received under this subject heading dealt with general or nuclear disarmament (see Chapter I of this section) or specific situations, such as: Afghanistan, Central America, China–Viet Nam dispute, Ethiopia-Somalia, Iran-Iraq, Lao People's Democratic Republic–Thailand, and international security of the Mediterranean countries (see SUBJECT INDEX).

GENERAL ASSEMBLY ACTION

On 17 December 1984, on the recommendation of the First Committee, the General Assembly adopted by recorded vote resolution 39/155.

Implementation of the Declaration on the Strengthening of International Security

The General Assembly,

Having considered the item entitled "Review of the implementation of the Declaration on the Strengthening of International Security",

Noting with concern that the provisions of the Declaration on the Strengthening of International Security have not been fully implemented,

Noting further with concern that the United Nations system of collective security has not been used effectively,

Recalling the duty of States not to intervene in the internal or external affairs of any State, in accordance with the purposes and principles of the Charter of the United Nations,

Recalling the provisions of the Declaration on Principles of International Law concerning Friendly Relations and Co-operation among States in accordance with the Charter of the United Nations,

Noting the provisions of the Declaration on the Inadmissibility of Intervention and Interference in the Internal Affairs of States,

Recalling the Manila Declaration on the Peaceful Settlement of International Disputes,

Alarmed by increasing tensions in international relations and the heightened confrontations that characterize the relations between the great Powers, accompanied by the policy of competition for spheres of influence, domination and exploitation in more and more parts of the world, the escalation to new levels of the arms race, particularly in nuclear weapons and the danger of its extension into outer space, all of which pose a grave threat to global peace and security,

Profoundly disturbed by the increasing recourse to the use or threat of use of force, military intervention and interference, aggression and foreign occupation, by the aggravation of existing crises in the world and the outbreak of new ones, by the continued infringement of the independence, sovereignty and territorial integrity of countries, by the denial of the right to self-determination of peoples under colonial and foreign occupation and by attempts to characterize erroneously the struggles of peoples for independence and human dignity as falling within the context of East-West confrontation, thus denying them the right to self-determination, to decide their own destiny and realize their legitimate aspirations, by the persistence of colonialism, racism and *apartheid* supported by the growing use of military force, by the intensification and expansion of the scope and frequency of manoeuvres and other military activities conceived within the context of big-Power confrontation and used as means of pressure, threat and destabilization, and by the lack of solutions to the world economic crisis in which the deeper underlying problems of a structural nature have been compounded by cyclical factors and which has further aggravated the inequalities and injustices in international economic relations,

Aware of the increasing interdependence among nations and of the fact that in the present-day world there is no alternative to a policy of peaceful coexistence, détente and co-operation among States on the basis of equality, irrespective of their economic or military power, political and social systems or size and geographic location,

Stressing the need for the main organs of the United Nations responsible for the maintenance of peace and security, particularly the Security Council, to contribute more effectively to the promotion of international peace and security by seeking solutions to unresolved problems and crises in the world,

Bearing in mind that the year 1985 will mark four decades since the United Nations was established on the conclusion of the Second World War, which had brought untold sorrow to mankind, and should provide an occasion to review the performance of the United Nations system over the past four decades with a view to enhancing its role and effectiveness towards the achievement of peace, security, justice and development,

Urging all States to take effective measures during the year of the fortieth anniversary of the United Nations to contribute towards the amelioration of international political and economic relations in the interest of lasting world peace and the progress of mankind,

Noting that the year 1985 will also mark the fifteenth anniversary of the adoption of the Declaration on the Strengthening of International Security,

1. *Reaffirms* the validity of the Declaration on the Strengthening of International Security and calls upon all States to contribute effectively to its implementation;

2. *Urges once again* all States to abide strictly, in their international relations, by their commitment to the Charter of the United Nations and, to this end:

(a) To refrain from the use or threat of use of force, intervention, interference, aggression, foreign occupation and colonial domination or measures of political and economic coercion which violate the sovereignty, territorial integrity, independence and security of other States as well as the permanent sovereignty of peoples over their natural resources;

(b) To refrain from supporting or encouraging any such act for any reason whatsoever and to reject and refuse recognition of situations brought about by any such act;

3. *Calls upon* all States, in particular the nuclear-weapon States and other militarily significant States, to take immediate steps aimed at:

(a) Promoting and using effectively the system of collective security as envisaged in the Charter;

(b) Halting effectively the arms race and achieving general and complete disarmament under effective international control and, to this end, to start serious, meaningful and effective negotiations with a view to implementing the recommendations and decisions contained in the Final Document of the Tenth Special Session of the General Assembly, and to fulfilling the priority tasks listed in its Programme of Action set forth in section III of the Final Document;

4. *Invites* all States, in particular the major military Powers and States members of military alliances, to refrain, especially in critical situations and in crisis areas, from actions, including military activities and manoeuvres, conceived within the context of big-Power confrontation and used as a means of pressure on, threat to and destabilization of other States and regions;

5. *Urges* all States, in particular the permanent members of the Security Council, to take all necessary measures to prevent the further deterioration of the international situation and, to this end:

(a) To seek, through more effective utilization of the means provided for in the Charter, the peaceful settlement of disputes and the elimination of the focal points of crisis and tension which constitute a threat to international peace and security;

(b) To proceed without delay to a global consideration of ways and means for bringing about a revival of the world economy and for the restructuring of international economic relations within the framework of the global negotiations with a view to establishing the new international economic order;

(c) To accelerate the economic development of developing countries, particularly the least developed ones;

(d) To implement urgently measures agreed upon to ameliorate the critical economic situation in Africa which is the result, *inter alia*, of persistent inclement climatic factors;

6. *Calls upon* all States, particularly the members of the Security Council, to take appropriate and effective measures to promote the fulfilment of the objective of the denuclearization of Africa in order to avert the serious danger which the nuclear capability of South Africa constitutes to the African States, in particular the front-line States, as well as to international peace and security;

7. *Emphasizes* the role that the United Nations has in the maintenance of peace and security and in economic and social development and progress for the benefit of all mankind;

8. *Reiterates* that the current deterioration of the international situation requires an effective Security Council and, to that end, emphasizes the need to examine mechanisms and working methods on a continued basis in order to enhance the authority and enforcement capacity of the Council, in accordance with the Charter;

9. *Emphasizes* that the Security Council should consider holding periodic meetings in specific cases to consider and review outstanding problems and crises, thus enabling the Council to play a more active role in preventing conflicts;

10. *Reiterates* the need for the Security Council, in particular its permanent members, to ensure the effective implementation of its decisions in compliance with the relevant provisions of the Charter;

11. *Considers* that respect for and promotion of human rights and fundamental freedoms in their civil, political, economic, social and cultural aspects, on the one hand, and the strengthening of international peace and security, on the other, mutually reinforce each other;

12. *Reaffirms* the legitimacy of the struggle of peoples under colonial domination, foreign occupation or racist régimes and their inalienable right to self-determination and independence, and urges Member States to increase their support for and solidarity with them and their national liberation movements and to take urgent and effective measures for the speedy completion of the implementation of the Declaration on the Granting of Independence to Colonial Countries and Peoples and for the final elimination of colonialism, racism and *apartheid;*

13. *Welcomes* the continuation of the process within the framework of the Conference on Security and Co-operation in Europe and expresses the hope that the Stockholm Conference on Confidence- and Security-building Measures and Disarmament in Europe, the continent with the greatest concentration of armaments and military forces, will achieve significant and positive results;

14. *Reiterates its call* upon great Powers to abandon policies of confrontation which have hitherto given rise to tension and mistrust and to engage without any further delay in genuine and constructive negotiations in good

faith, taking into account the interests of the entire international community;

15. *Reaffirms* that the democratization of international relations is an imperative necessity enabling, under the conditions of interdependence, the full development and independence of all States as well as the attainment of genuine security, peace and cooperation in the world, and stresses its firm belief that the United Nations offers the best framework for the promotion of these goals;

16. *Invites* Member States to submit their views on the question of the implementation of the Declaration on the Strengthening of International Security, and requests the Secretary-General to submit a report to the General Assembly at its fortieth session on the basis of the replies received;

17. *Decides* to include in the provisional agenda of its fortieth session the item entitled "Review of the implementation of the Declaration on the Strengthening of International Security".

General Assembly resolution 39/155

17 December 1984   Meeting 102   137-0-11 (recorded vote)

Approved by First Committee (A/39/758) by recorded vote (120-0-11), 7 December (meeting 62); 24-nation draft (A/C.1/39/L.87); agenda item 68 *(a)*.

Sponsors: Algeria, Bahamas, Bangladesh, Congo, Cyprus, Egypt, Ethiopia, Ghana, Guyana, India, Indonesia, Madagascar, Mali, Nigeria, Pakistan, Senegal, Sierra Leone, Sri Lanka, Sudan, Tunisia, Uganda, Uruguay, Yugoslavia, Zambia.

Meeting numbers. GA 39th session: 1st Committee 56-62; plenary 102.

Recorded vote in Assembly as follows:

In favour: Afghanistan, Algeria, Angola, Antigua and Barbuda, Argentina, Australia, Austria, Bahamas, Bahrain, Bangladesh, Barbados, Benin, Bhutan, Bolivia, Botswana, Brazil, Brunei Darussalam, Bulgaria, Burkina Faso, Burma, Burundi, Byelorussian SSR, Cameroon, Cape Verde, Central African Republic, Chad, Chile, China, Colombia, Congo, Costa Rica, Cuba, Cyprus, Czechoslovakia, Democratic Kampuchea, Democratic Yemen, Denmark, Djibouti, Dominican Republic, Ecuador, Egypt, El Salvador, Equatorial Guinea, Ethiopia, Fiji, Finland, France, Gabon, German Democratic Republic, Ghana, Greece, Guatemala, Guinea, Guinea-Bissau, Guyana, Haiti, Honduras, Hungary, Iceland, India, Indonesia, Iran, Iraq, Ireland, Ivory Coast, Jamaica, Jordan, Kenya, Kuwait, Lao People's Democratic Republic, Lebanon, Lesotho, Liberia, Libyan Arab Jamahiriya, Madagascar, Malawi, Malaysia, Maldives, Mali, Malta, Mauritania, Mauritius, Mexico, Mongolia, Morocco, Mozambique, Nepal, Netherlands, New Zealand, Nicaragua, Niger, Nigeria, Norway, Oman, Pakistan, Panama, Papua New Guinea, Paraguay, Peru, Philippines, Poland, Qatar, Romania, Rwanda, Saint Lucia, Saint Vincent and the Grenadines, Samoa, Sao Tome and Principe, Saudi Arabia, Senegal, Seychelles, Sierra Leone, Singapore, Somalia, Spain, Sri Lanka, Sudan, Suriname, Sweden, Syrian Arab Republic, Thailand, Togo, Trinidad and Tobago, Tunisia, Uganda, Ukrainian SSR, USSR, United Arab Emirates, United Republic of Tanzania, Uruguay, Venezuela, Viet Nam, Yemen, Yugoslavia, Zaire, Zambia, Zimbabwe.

Against: None.

Abstaining: Belgium, Canada, Germany, Federal Republic of, Israel, Italy, Japan, Luxembourg, Portugal, Turkey, United Kingdom, United States.

Implementation of the 1978 Declaration on societies and peace

The Secretary-General, pursuant to a 1981 General Assembly resolution,[14] submitted in October 1984 a report with a later addendum[15] on the implementation of the 1978 Declaration on the Preparation of Societies for Life in Peace.[16] A total of 20 countries and 15 United Nations organizations had responded to his request for information. The Secretary-General pointed out that several specific measures were proposed in the replies which, if endorsed by the Assembly, might be undertaken by the United

Nations prior to a further review of the Declaration's implementation. Among them were the legal and political codification of the concept of the right to life in peace, a report on ways to counter the danger of nuclear war, and a report by a panel of peace research experts.

GENERAL ASSEMBLY ACTION

On 17 December, following the recommendation of the First Committee, the General Assembly adopted by recorded vote resolution 39/157.

Implementation of the Declaration on the Preparation of Societies for Life in Peace

The General Assembly,

Recalling its Declaration on the Preparation of Societies for Life in Peace, contained in resolution 33/73 of 15 December 1978,

Recalling also its resolution 36/104 of 9 December 1981, in which, *inter alia,* it reaffirmed the lasting importance of the preparation of societies for life in peace as part of all constructive efforts to shape relations among States and to strengthen international peace and security, and recognized the paramount value of positive moulding of human consciousness for the fulfilment of the purposes and principles of the Charter of the United Nations,

Noting that the year 1985 will mark the twenty-fifth anniversary of the adoption of the historic Declaration on the Granting of Independence to Colonial Countries and Peoples and the fifteenth anniversary of the adoption of the Declaration on Principles of International Law concerning Friendly Relations and Cooperation among States in accordance with the Charter of the United Nations and the Declaration on the Strengthening of International Security,

Taking into consideration that the General Assembly declared 1986 to be the International Year of Peace, which will be solemnly proclaimed on 24 October 1985 and linked with the fortieth anniversary of the United Nations,

Aware of and concerned over the current state of international relations, which calls for renewed efforts to promote confidence and create lasting guarantees for a propitious climate of international relations,

Reiterating that the peoples of the United Nations are determined to contribute their genuine share of efforts towards international peace and understanding,

Noting the important role and historic responsibility of Governments, heads of State or Government as well as other statesmen, politicians, diplomats and civic leaders for the maintenance and strengthening of international peace and security,

Expressing its satisfaction that notwithstanding the unfavourable trends in international relations, there is specific evidence of some progress, although insufficient, in both national and international efforts towards the preparation of societies for life in peace, notably in the activities of the United Nations and the specialized agencies concerned as well as other governmental and non-governmental organizations,

Taking note with appreciation of the report of the Secretary-General prepared in accordance with General Assembly resolution 36/104,

1. *Solemnly reaffirms* the lasting validity of the purposes and principles enshrined in the Declaration on the Preparation of Societies for Life in Peace, based on the Charter of the United Nations;

2. *Invites* all Governments, the United Nations and the concerned organizations of its system, other international as well as national organizations, both governmental and non-governmental, to incorporate active promotion of the ideas of the preparation of societies for life in peace in their programmes, including those concerning the observances of the International Year of Peace, 1986;

3. *Reaffirms* the determination of the peoples of the United Nations to establish lasting conditions of world peace, international understanding and mutually beneficial co-operation;

4. *Recognizes* the role and great historic responsibility of Governments, heads of State or Government as well as other statesmen, politicians, diplomats and civic leaders for the establishment, maintenance and strengthening of a just and durable peace for present and future generations;

5. *Solemnly invites* all States to further intensify their efforts towards the implementation of the Declaration on the Preparation of Societies for Life in Peace by strictly adhering to the principles enshrined in the Declaration and by taking all necessary steps towards that end at the national and international levels;

6. *Reiterates its appeal* for concerted action on the part of Governments, the United Nations and the specialized agencies, as well as other interested international and national organizations, both governmental and non-governmental, to give tangible effect to the supreme importance of and need for establishing, maintaining and strengthening a just and durable peace for present and future generations;

7. *Requests* the Secretary-General to consider convening in 1986, within the programme of the International Year of Peace, a panel of peace research experts to consider, in a comprehensive manner, questions pertaining to the implementation of the Declaration;

8. *Further requests* the Secretary-General to continue following the progress made in the implementation of the Declaration on all planes and in the light of the observances of the International Year of Peace, and to submit a report thereon to the General Assembly not later than at its forty-second session.

General Assembly resolution 39/157

17 December 1984   Meeting 102   119-0-28 (recorded vote)

Approved by First Committee (A/39/758) by recorded vote (105-0-24), 7 December (meeting 62); 25-nation draft (A/C.1/39/L.89); agenda item 68 *(b)*.

Sponsors: Afghanistan, Algeria, Benin, Bulgaria, Cameroon, Congo, Costa Rica, Czechoslovakia, Ecuador, German Democratic Republic, Ghana, Hungary, Indonesia, Madagascar, Mauritius, Mongolia, Panama, Peru, Philippines, Poland, Syrian Arab Republic, Tunisia, Uruguay, Viet Nam, Yugoslavia.

Meeting numbers: GA 39th session: 1st Committee 56-62; plenary 102.

Recorded vote in Assembly as follows:

In favour: Afghanistan, Algeria, Angola, Antigua and Barbuda, Argentina, Bahrain, Bangladesh, Barbados, Benin, Bhutan, Bolivia, Botswana, Brunei Darussalam, Bulgaria, Burkina Faso, Burma, Burundi, Byelorussian SSR, Cameroon, Cape Verde, Central African Republic, Chad, Chile, China, Colombia, Congo, Costa Rica, Cuba, Cyprus, Czechoslovakia, Democratic Kampuchea, Democratic Yemen, Djibouti, Dominican Republic, Ecuador, Egypt, El Salvador, Equatorial Guinea, Ethiopia, Fiji, Gabon, German Democratic Republic, Ghana, Greece, Guatemala, Guinea, Guinea-Bissau, Guyana, Haiti, Honduras, Hungary, India, Indonesia, Iran, Iraq, Ivory Coast, Jordan, Kenya, Kuwait, Lao

People's Democratic Republic, Lebanon, Lesotho, Liberia, Libyan Arab Jamahiriya, Madagascar, Malawi, Malaysia, Maldives, Mali, Malta, Mauritania, Mauritius, Mexico, Mongolia, Morocco, Mozambique, Nepal, Nicaragua, Niger, Nigeria, Oman, Pakistan, Panama, Papua New Guinea, Paraguay, Peru, Philippines, Poland, Qatar, Romania, Rwanda, Sao Tome and Principe, Saudi Arabia, Senegal, Seychelles, Sierra Leone, Singapore, Somalia, Sri Lanka, Sudan, Suriname, Syrian Arab Republic, Thailand, Togo, Trinidad and Tobago, Tunisia, Uganda, Ukrainian SSR, USSR, United Arab Emirates, United Republic of Tanzania, Uruguay, Venezuela, Viet Nam, Yemen, Yugoslavia, Zaire, Zambia, Zimbabwe.

Against: None.

Abstaining: Australia, Austria, Bahamas, Belgium, Brazil, Canada, Denmark, Finland, France, Germany, Federal Republic of, Iceland, Ireland, Israel, Italy, Japan, Luxembourg, Netherlands, New Zealand, Norway, Portugal, Saint Lucia, Saint Vincent and the Grenadines, Samoa, Spain, Sweden, Turkey, United Kingdom, United States.

Brazil said it abstained because it felt the text condoned State promotion of ideological directions which might curtail the rights of private organizations; given the fact that few Member States had replied to the Secretary-General's request, only a short procedural text on the question was justified. Supporting these views, the Federal Republic of Germany regretted the absence of any meaningful reference to the concept of human rights, while the Netherlands declared that the notion pertaining to the positive moulding of human consciousness could prejudice the exercise of individual freedom.

Declaration on the Right of Peoples to Peace

In a letter of 11 July,[(17)] Mongolia requested the inclusion in the agenda of the 1984 General Assembly session of an item on the right of peoples to peace. Annexed to the letter were an explanatory memorandum, which stated that adoption by the Assembly of an appropriate document would make a substantial contribution to the support of the peoples' struggle to achieve a peaceful life, and a draft declaration, which was the basis for a resolution adopted by the Assembly.

GENERAL ASSEMBLY ACTION

On 12 November, the Assembly adopted by recorded vote resolution 39/11.

Declaration on the Right of Peoples to Peace

The General Assembly,

Having considered the item entitled "Right of peoples to peace",

Convinced that a proclamation of the right of peoples to peace would contribute to the efforts aimed at the strengthening of international peace and security,

1. *Approves* the Declaration on the Right of Peoples to Peace, the text of which is annexed to the present resolution;

2. *Requests* the Secretary-General to ensure the widest dissemination of the Declaration to States, intergovernmental and non-governmental organizations as well as other appropriate organizations.

ANNEX
Declaration on the Right of Peoples to Peace
The General Assembly,

Reaffirming that the principal aim of the United Nations is the maintenance of international peace and security,

Bearing in mind the fundamental principles of international law set forth in the Charter of the United Nations,

Expressing the will and the aspirations of all peoples to eradicate war from the life of mankind and, above all, to avert a world-wide nuclear catastrophe,

Convinced that life without war serves as the primary international prerequisite for the material well-being, development and progress of countries, and for the full implementation of the rights and fundamental human freedoms proclaimed by the United Nations,

Aware that in the nuclear age the establishment of a lasting peace on Earth represents the primary condition for the preservation of human civilization and the survival of mankind,

Recognizing that the maintenance of a peaceful life for peoples is the sacred duty of each State,

1. *Solemnly proclaims* that the peoples of our planet have a sacred right to peace;

2. *Solemnly declares* that the preservation of the right of peoples to peace and the promotion of its implementation constitute a fundamental obligation of each State;

3. *Emphasizes* that ensuring the exercise of the right of peoples to peace demands that the policies of States be directed towards the elimination of the threat of war, particularly nuclear war, the renunciation of the use of force in international relations and the settlement of international disputes by peaceful means on the basis of the Charter of the United Nations;

4. *Appeals* to all States and international organizations to do their utmost to assist in implementing the right of peoples to peace through the adoption of appropriate measures at both the national and the international level.

General Assembly resolution 39/11

12 November 1984   Meeting 57   92-0-34 (recorded vote)

8-nation draft (A/39/L.14), orally revised; agenda item 138.

Sponsors: Bulgaria, Cuba, Equatorial Guinea, German Democratic Republic, Lao People's Democratic Republic, Libyan Arab Jamahiriya, Mongolia, Nicaragua.

Recorded vote in Assembly as follows:

In favour: Afghanistan, Algeria, Argentina, Bahamas, Bahrain, Bangladesh, Belize, Benin, Bolivia, Botswana, Brazil, Bulgaria, Burkina Faso, Burma, Burundi, Byelorussian SSR, Central African Republic, Chile, China, Colombia, Congo, Cuba, Cyprus, Czechoslovakia, Democratic Yemen, Djibouti, Dominican Republic, Ecuador, Egypt, El Salvador, Equatorial Guinea, Ethiopia, German Democratic Republic, Ghana, Guatemala, Guinea, Guyana, Haiti, Honduras, Hungary, India, Indonesia, Iraq, Ivory Coast, Jordan, Kenya, Kuwait, Lao People's Democratic Republic, Lebanon, Liberia, Libyan Arab Jamahiriya, Madagascar, Maldives, Mali, Mauritania, Mauritius, Mexico, Mongolia, Mozambique, Nepal, Nicaragua, Nigeria, Oman, Pakistan, Panama, Peru, Poland, Qatar, Romania, Rwanda, Sao Tome and Principe, Seychelles, Sierra Leone, Sri Lanka, Sudan, Suriname, Syrian Arab Republic, Thailand, Togo, Tunisia, Uganda, Ukrainian SSR, USSR, United Arab Emirates, United Republic of Tanzania, Uruguay, Venezuela, Viet Nam, Yemen, Yugoslavia, Zaire, Zambia.

Against: None.

Abstaining: Australia, Austria, Belgium, Brunei Darussalam, Cameroon, Canada, Cape Verde, Denmark, Finland, France, Gabon, Germany, Federal Republic of, Greece, Grenada, Guinea-Bissau, Iceland, Ireland, Italy, Japan, Luxembourg, Malawi, Netherlands, New Zealand, Niger, Norway, Philippines, Portugal, Saint Christopher and Nevis, Senegal, Spain, Sweden, Turkey, United Kingdom, United States.

Ireland, speaking for the 10 members of the European Community, explained that their abstention was because there was no agreed legal basis for the assertions in the Declaration and because

they questioned how the text could be reconciled with the right to self-defence and would relate to human rights and fundamental freedoms. The Philippines stated that the Declaration merited greater thought, more careful study and more balanced formulation.

Albania said it had not participated in the vote since it believed the draft did not deal with the main aspects of the problem and did not mention the two imperialist super-Powers, the USSR and the United States, whose rivalry for hegemony was detrimental to peace and security.

REFERENCES

[1]YUN 1970, p. 105, GA res. 2734(XXV), 16 Dec. 1970. [2]A/39/300-S/16617. [3]YUN 1983, p. 110. [4]A/C.1/39/3. [5]A/39/720. [6]A/39/763-S/16849. [7]A/39/91. [8]A/39/178. [9]A/39/467. [10]A/39/597. [11]A/39/409-S/16705. [12]A/39/122. [13]A/39/560-S/16773. [14]YUN 1981, p. 150, GA res. 36/104, 9 Dec. 1981. [15]A/39/143 & Add.1. [16]YUN 1978, p. 165, GA res. 33/73, 15 Dec. 1978. [17]A/39/141.

Implementation of the security provisions of the UN Charter

The Secretary-General, in response to a December 1983 General Assembly resolution,[1] reported in a September 1984 note with a later addendum[2] that eight Governments had replied to his request for their views on implementing the collective security provisions of the Charter of the United Nations. The Assembly had requested that their views be transmitted to the *Ad Hoc* Committee which was to have been established under the 1983 resolution. However, the Secretary-General said, the Committee had not been formed because of differing opinions regarding the distribution of its seats.

GENERAL ASSEMBLY ACTION

On 17 December 1984, on the recommendation of the First Committee, the General Assembly adopted by recorded vote resolution 39/158.

Implementation of the collective security provisions of the Charter of the United Nations for the maintenance of international peace and security
The General Assembly,

Recalling its resolutions 37/119 of 16 December 1982 and 38/191 of 20 December 1983 on the implementation of the collective security provisions of the Charter of the United Nations for the maintenance of international peace and security,

Reaffirming that the primary function of the United Nations, in particular through the Security Council, is the maintenance of international peace and security,

Stressing that the purposes of the United Nations can be achieved only under conditions in which States comply fully with their obligations assumed under the Charter,

Alarmed over the growing tendency of States to resort to the use of force, intervention and interference in the internal affairs of other States, thus ignoring the Charter and the Declaration on Principles of International Law concerning Friendly Relations and Co-operation among States in accordance with the Charter of the United Nations,

Concerned that the Security Council has not always been able to take decisive action for the maintenance of international peace and for resolving international problems,

Recognizing that fundamental approaches to genuine security include, *inter alia*, the strengthening of the Charter system of collective security,

Conscious of the important role with which the Security Council is entrusted in enhancing the collective security provisions of the Charter for the promotion of peace and security in the world in accordance with the Charter,

Regretting that the provisions of the Charter relating to collective security measures have not been fully implemented,

Taking into account, in this connection, the reports of the Secretary-General on the work of the Organization to the General Assembly at its thirty-seventh, thirty-eighth and thirty-ninth sessions,

Also taking into account the note by the President of the Security Council dated 12 September 1983,

Recalling the Political Declaration adopted by the Seventh Conference of Heads of State or Government of Non-Aligned Countries, held at New Delhi from 7 to 12 March 1983,

Also recalling the views of the Governments of the five Nordic countries on the strengthening of the United Nations,

Taking note of the note by the Secretary-General on the implementation of the collective security provisions of the Charter of the United Nations for the maintenance of international peace and security,

Having considered the item entitled "Implementation of the collective security provisions of the Charter of the United Nations for the maintenance of international peace and security",

1. *Regrets* that the *Ad Hoc* Committee on the Implementation of the Collective Security Provisions of the Charter of the United Nations which the General Assembly decided to establish by its resolution 38/191 has not been constituted;

2. *Requests* the President of the General Assembly, as a matter of urgency, to undertake consultations with the regional groups to appoint fifty-four Member States to constitute the membership of the *Ad Hoc* Committee on the basis of equitable geographical representation and including the permanent members of the Security Council;

3. *Requests* the Secretary-General urgently to invite those Member States that have not yet done so to communicate to him not later than 30 April 1985 their views and comments on the matter and to transmit those views and comments to the *Ad Hoc* Committee as soon as possible;

4. *Requests* the *Ad Hoc* Committee, in considering the matter, to take due account of the views and comments of Member States, including their recommendations, and to submit a progress report to the Security Council for its consideration and comments and to the General Assembly at its fortieth session, and a final report to the Assembly at its forty-first session;

5. *Decides* to include in the provisional agenda of its fortieth session the item entitled "Implementation of the collective security provisions of the Charter of the United Nations for the maintenance of international peace and security".

General Assembly resolution 39/158

17 December 1984   Meeting 102   108-22-13 (recorded vote)

Approved by First Committee (A/39/759) by recorded vote (93-22-14), 7 December (meeting 62); 10-nation draft (A/C.1/39/L.86/Rev.1); agenda item 69.
Sponsors: Algeria, Cameroon, Ghana, Indonesia, Jamaica, Mali, Sierra Leone, Trinidad and Tobago, Uruguay, Zambia.
Financial implications. 5th Committee, A/39/786; S-G, A/C.1/39/L.93, A/C.5/39/82.
Meeting numbers. GA 39th session: 1st Committee 56-62; 5th Committee 45; plenary 102.

Recorded vote in Assembly as follows:

In favour: Algeria, Angola, Antigua and Barbuda, Argentina, Australia, Bahamas, Bahrain, Bangladesh, Barbados, Benin, Bhutan, Bolivia, Botswana, Brazil, Brunei Darussalam, Burkina Faso, Burma, Burundi, Cameroon, Cape Verde, Central African Republic, Chad, Chile, China, Colombia, Congo, Costa Rica, Democratic Kampuchea, Djibouti, Dominican Republic, Ecuador, Egypt, El Salvador, Equatorial Guinea, Ethiopia, Fiji, Gabon, Ghana, Greece, Guatemala, Guinea, Guinea-Bissau, Guyana, Haiti, Honduras, India, Indonesia, Iran, Iraq, Ivory Coast, Jamaica, Jordan, Kenya, Kuwait, Lebanon, Lesotho, Liberia, Libyan Arab Jamahiriya, Madagascar, Malawi, Malaysia, Maldives, Mali, Mauritania, Mexico, Morocco, Mozambique, Nepal, Nicaragua, Niger, Nigeria, Oman, Pakistan, Panama, Papua New Guinea, Paraguay, Peru, Philippines, Qatar, Romania, Rwanda, Saint Lucia, Saint Vincent and the Grenadines, Samoa, Sao Tome and Principe, Saudi Arabia, Senegal, Seychelles, Sierra Leone, Singapore, Somalia, Sri Lanka, Sudan, Suriname, Thailand, Togo, Trinidad and Tobago, Tunisia, Uganda, United Arab Emirates, United Republic of Tanzania, Uruguay, Venezuela, Yemen, Yugoslavia, Zaire, Zambia, Zimbabwe.
Against: Afghanistan, Belgium, Bulgaria, Byelorussian SSR, Cuba, Czechoslovakia, France, German Democratic Republic, Germany, Federal Republic of, Hungary, Italy, Lao People's Democratic Republic, Luxembourg, Mongolia, Netherlands, Poland, Portugal, Turkey, Ukrainian SSR, USSR, United Kingdom, United States.
Abstaining: Austria, Canada, Denmark, Finland, Iceland, Ireland, Israel, Japan, New Zealand, Norway, Spain, Sweden, Viet Nam.

Cuba and France explained their negative votes, declaring that the proposed *Ad Hoc* Committee would duplicate and encroach upon the mandate of the Special Committee on the Charter of the United Nations and on the Strengthening of the Role of the Organization.

On the other hand, Australia said it supported all efforts to enhance the collective security provisions of the Charter.

Albania stated that it had not participated in the vote because of its reservations on some formulations in the draft and because the draft did not reveal the causes of world insecurity—the super-Powers, other imperialist Powers and reactionary forces.

Strengthening international security

The President of the Security Council issued a note in September 1984[3] and recalled a 1983 note[4] on Council discussions to enhance its effectiveness in maintaining international peace and security (see p. 372).

GENERAL ASSEMBLY ACTION

In December 1984, the General Assembly, having considered the 1983 and 1984 notes by the Council President, adopted two resolutions on strengthening international security. Both actions were taken following the recommendation of the First Committee.

On 17 December, the Assembly adopted resolution 39/154 without vote.

Review of the implementation of the Declaration on the Strengthening of International Security
The General Assembly,

Recalling its resolution 38/73 H of 15 December 1983,

Profoundly concerned over the situation of the international community today in circumstances of tensions and conflicts long continuing between nations, denoting a marked decline in the respect for the Charter of the United Nations and the basic elements of international law,

Gravely concerned over the increasing manifestations of various forms of international terrorism,

Considering that the main organ of the United Nations which under the Charter has the essential characteristic of rendering effective its decisions is the Security Council,

Bearing in mind that the notes by the President of the Security Council dated 12 September 1983 and 28 September 1984, although referring to the subject of collective security, indicate no concrete steps taken or to be taken to implement the relevant provisions of the Charter,

Taking due account of the need that, on the occasion of the fortieth anniversary of the United Nations, specific endeavours should be devoted by the international community to enhance the effectiveness of the United Nations required by the Charter,

1. *Recommends* that the Security Council give priority consideration to the need for strengthening the system of collective security provided for in the Charter of the United Nations;

2. *Requests* the Secretary-General to report thereon to the General Assembly at its fortieth session.

General Assembly resolution 39/154

17 December 1984   Meeting 102   Adopted without vote

Approved by First Committee (A/39/758) without vote, 7 December (meeting 62); draft by Cyprus (A/C.1/39/L.85/Rev.1), orally revised; agenda item 68 *(a)*.
Meeting numbers. GA 39th session: 1st Committee 56-62; plenary 102.

While it did not wish to prevent adoption of the draft by consensus, the Netherlands felt that nothing should be done to diminish the Security Council's responsibilities under the Charter for maintaining international peace and security. Turkey stated that it would not have participated if the draft had been put to a vote.

Also on 17 December, the Assembly adopted resolution 39/156 without vote.

Strengthening of international security: common security
The General Assembly,

Recognizing the common interest of all nations in promoting an effective approach to security, which will seek the common security of all nations,

Firmly believing that the mind of man can prevail over the weapons of war,

1. *Notes with appreciation* the relevant information on the consultations in the Security Council, provided by the President of the Council in his notes dated 12 September 1983 and 28 September 1984;

2. *Welcomes* the important considerations contained therein;

3. *Reaffirms*, in particular, as the prerequisite for peace, the need for strict compliance by all Member States with the purposes and principles of the Charter of the United Nations, and with the Charter itself, as well as the obligation of States to accept and carry out the decisions of the Security Council;

4. *Expresses its awareness* of the respective functions and specific powers of the Security Council and the other principal organs of the United Nations;

5. *Welcomes* the serious, comprehensive discussions that have already taken place;

6. *Takes note*, in particular, of the concentration of discussion on specific aspects of the work of the Security Council, as well as of the prevailing collegial efforts to advance ideas with best prospects for producing agreement;

7. *Stresses* the primary responsibility of the Security Council, acting on behalf of the international community, in the collective maintenance of peace and security;

8. *Encourages* the Security Council, subject to its own priorities, to intensify its efforts in the prevention of international conflict and the peaceful settlement of disputes by envisaging, if possible, a more systematic series of meetings under the agreed five main aspects mentioned in paragraph 2 of the note of the President of the Council dated 12 September 1983;

9. *Welcomes* further information from the Security Council on the progress achieved, at periodic intervals, as deemed appropriate.

General Assembly resolution 39/156

17 December 1984   Meeting 102   Adopted without vote

Approved by First Committee (A/39/758) without vote, 7 December (meeting 62); 7-nation draft (A/C.1/39/L.88/Rev.1), orally revised; agenda item 68 *(a)*.
Sponsors: Bahamas, Ecuador, Ghana, Malta, Sierra Leone, Singapore, Uruguay.
Meeting numbers. GA 39th session: 1st Committee 56-62; plenary 102.

REFERENCES

[1]YUN 1983, p. 113, GA res. 38/191, 20 Dec. 1983. [2]A/39/144 & Add.1. [3]S/16760. [4]YUN 1983, p. 389.

State terrorism

Taking up the question of terrorism under a new agenda item, the General Assembly, in 1984, condemned policies and practices of terrorism in relations between States.

Communications. An item on the inadmissibility of the policy of State terrorism and any actions by States aimed at undermining the socio-political system in other sovereign States was included in the agenda of the General Assembly at its 1984 session at the request of the USSR. In making that request, in a 27 September letter,[1] the USSR proposed that the Assembly condemn action aimed at forcibly changing or undermining the socio-political system of sovereign States, and destabilizing and overthrowing their legitimate

Governments, and demand that States refrain from initiating, or terminate any ongoing, military action to such end. A draft resolution which became the basis for a resolution adopted by the Assembly was annexed to the letter.

The Assembly also had before it the text of a Declaration on International Terrorism—issued at the London Economic Summit (7-9 June 1984)—as transmitted by the United Kingdom in a letter of 12 June.[2] The participating heads of State and Government noted with concern, among other things, the ease with which terrorists operated as well as the increasing involvement of States and Governments in acts of terrorism, including the abuse of diplomatic immunity; they expressed their resolve to combat terrorism by every possible means.

GENERAL ASSEMBLY ACTION

On 17 December 1984, the General Assembly, on the recommendation of the First Committee, adopted resolution 39/159 by recorded vote.

Inadmissibility of the policy of State terrorism and any actions by States aimed at undermining the socio-political system in other sovereign States

The General Assembly,

Reaffirming the obligation of all States to refrain in their international relations from the threat or use of force against the sovereignty, territorial integrity and political independence of any State, as well as the inalienable right of all peoples to determine their own form of government and to choose their own economic, political and social system free from outside intervention, subversion, coercion and constraint of any kind whatsoever,

Expressing its profound concern that State terrorism has lately been practised ever more frequently in relations between States and that military and other actions are being taken against the sovereignty and political independence of States and the self-determination of peoples,

Noting that all this seriously endangers the independent existence of States and the possibility of ensuring peaceful relations and mutual trust between them and leads to a sharp exacerbation of tensions and a growing threat of war,

Reaffirming the inalienable right of all peoples freely to determine their own destiny and the course of their development,

Convinced that the interests of maintaining peace require that relations between States, regardless of ideologies, should be based on strict observance of the Charter of the United Nations, as well as on generally recognized principles and norms of international relations, *inter alia*, renunciation of the threat or use of force against the territorial integrity or political independence of any State, non-intervention and non-interference in the internal and external affairs of States, permanent sovereignty of States and peoples over their natural resources and self-determination and independence of peoples under colonial domination, foreign occupation or racist régimes,

Categorically rejecting all concepts, doctrines or ideologies intended to justify actions of States aimed at undermining the socio-political system of other States,

1. *Resolutely condemns* policies and practices of terrorism in relations between States as a method of dealing with other States and peoples;

2. *Demands* that all States take no actions aimed at military intervention and occupation, forcible change in or undermining of the socio-political system of States, destabilization and overthrow of their Governments and, in particular, initiate no military action to that end under any pretext whatsoever and cease forthwith any such action already in progress;

3. *Urges* all States to respect and strictly observe, in accordance with the Charter of the United Nations, the sovereignty and political independence of States and the right of peoples to self-determination, as well as their right freely, without outside interference and intervention, to choose their socio-political system and to pursue their political, economic, social and cultural development.

General Assembly resolution 39/159

17 December 1984   Meeting 102   117-0-30 (recorded vote)

Approved by First Committee (A/39/761) by recorded vote (101-0-29), 7 December (meeting 62); draft by USSR (A/C.1/39/L.2/Rev.2); agenda item 143.
Meeting numbers. GA 39th session: 1st Committee 57-62; plenary 102.

Recorded vote in Assembly as follows:

In favour: Afghanistan, Algeria, Angola, Antigua and Barbuda, Argentina, Bahamas, Bahrain, Bangladesh, Barbados, Benin, Bhutan, Bolivia, Botswana, Brunei Darussalam, Bulgaria, Burkina Faso, Burma, Burundi, Byelorussian SSR, Cameroon, Cape Verde, Central African Republic, Chad, China, Congo, Costa Rica, Cuba, Cyprus, Czechoslovakia, Democratic Kampuchea, Democratic Yemen, Djibouti, Dominican Republic, Ecuador, Egypt, El Salvador, Equatorial Guinea, Ethiopia, Fiji, Gabon, German Democratic Republic, Ghana, Greece, Guatemala, Guinea, Guinea-Bissau, Guyana, Haiti, Hungary, India, Indonesia, Iran, Iraq, Ivory Coast, Jamaica, Jordan, Kenya, Kuwait, Lao People's Democratic Republic, Lebanon, Lesotho, Liberia, Libyan Arab Jamahiriya, Madagascar, Malaysia, Maldives, Mali, Malta, Mauritania, Mexico, Mongolia, Morocco, Mozambique, Nepal, Nicaragua, Niger, Nigeria, Oman, Pakistan, Panama, Papua New Guinea, Peru, Philippines, Poland, Qatar, Romania, Rwanda, Saint Lucia, Saint Vincent and the Grenadines, Samoa, Sao Tome and Principe, Saudi Arabia, Senegal, Seychelles, Sierra Leone, Singapore, Somalia, Sri Lanka, Sudan, Suriname, Syrian Arab Republic, Thailand, Togo, Trinidad and Tobago, Tunisia, Uganda, Ukrainian SSR, USSR, United Arab Emirates, United Republic of Tanzania, Uruguay, Viet Nam, Yemen, Yugoslavia, Zaire, Zambia, Zimbabwe.

Against: None.

Abstaining: Australia, Austria, Belgium, Brazil, Canada, Chile, Colombia, Denmark, Finland, France, Germany, Federal Republic of, Honduras, Iceland, Ireland, Israel, Italy, Japan, Luxembourg, Malawi, Netherlands, New Zealand, Norway, Paraguay, Portugal, Spain, Sweden, Turkey, United Kingdom, United States, Venezuela.

The text was twice revised by the sponsor, taking into account amendments proposed, and later withdrawn, by two groups—one[3] by Belgium, Canada, Denmark, the Federal Republic of Germany, Italy, Japan, the Netherlands and the United Kingdom, and the other[4] by the Bahamas, Cameroon, Costa Rica, Jamaica, Kenya, Malaysia, Papua New Guinea, Singapore, and Trinidad and Tobago.

The text as adopted incorporated such proposals by the first group as inserting the first preambular paragraph, and replacing "State terrorism" with "policies and practices of terrorism in relations between States". Proposals by the second group, also reflected in the final text, concerned deleting from the end of the sixth preambular paragraph "in contradiction to the United Nations Charter and the Declaration on Principles of International Law concerning Friendly Relations and Co-operation among States", and inserting in paragraph 2 "military intervention and occupation".

Many delegations speaking in explanation of vote said the concept of State terrorism had not yet been clearly defined. Norway said no satisfactory attempt had been made to define it in the text, while Sweden was convinced that the principles laid down in the United Nations Charter excluded any practices that might be understood by the concept. Similarly, Finland said a political solution could not be reached in the absence of a legal framework within which to work.

Colombia felt the text should have condemned all violent actions regardless of the political characteristics of either victim or perpetrator. Turkey said the question of terrorism should be dealt with as a whole, while the text covered only one aspect of the phenomenon; Senegal agreed, adding that it also had reservations about the appropriateness of the First Committee considering the question, which lacked clear definition. Greece voted in favour because it saw improvements in the revised draft, despite the legally unresolved problem of definition. Ghana supported the text on the understanding that the concept would be further refined.

Chile abstained, saying that the presentation and treatment of the question showed that the Assembly was faced with a political rather than a technical and legal exercise, involving elements of confrontation between the nuclear Powers and their alliances. Sharing that view, Brazil rejected what it termed the constant attempts at utilizing the United Nations as an arena for rivalry and confrontation between the two main military alliances. Guyana said that the Assembly's consideration of State terrorism was timely.

Pakistan voted positively, despite a number of shortcomings it saw in the draft, and on the understanding that all forms of foreign interference in the affairs of States were condemned and prohibited. Democratic Kampuchea expressed particular support for the principles expressed in the first preambular paragraph and in paragraph 2; it questioned, however, whether the text's sponsor was sincere in its belief or was trying to force the international community to accept its military intervention and that of its allies as a *fait accompli*. In a similar vein, China, voting in favour despite reservations about the ambiguity of the phrase State terrorism, hoped the sponsor would set an example by matching words with deeds.

Cuba said that, despite objections by others to including, in a draft on State terrorism, reference to States' permanent sovereignty over their natural resources or the right to choose their socio-political

system on the pretext that they were not contained in the Charter, those concepts, as well as prohibition of terrorism as State policy, were contained in the 1981 Declaration on the Inadmissibility of Intervention and Interference in the Internal Affairs of States.[5]

REFERENCES

[1]A/39/244. [2]A/39/306. [3]A/C.1/39/L.91/Rev.1. [4]A/C.1/39/L.92. [5]YUN 1981, p. 147, GA res. 36/103, annex, 9 Dec. 1981.

Review of peace-keeping operations

The Special Committee on Peace-keeping Operations, established by the General Assembly in 1965,[1] did not meet in 1984. United Nations peace-keeping forces continued to operate in Cyprus and Lebanon and on the Golan Heights between Israel and the Syrian Arab Republic (see Chapters VIII and IX of this section).

GENERAL ASSEMBLY ACTION

On 14 December 1984, on the recommendation of the Special Political Committee, the General Assembly adopted without vote resolution 39/97.

Comprehensive review of the whole question of peace-keeping operations in all their aspects
The General Assembly,

Recalling its resolutions 2006(XIX) of 18 February 1965, 2053 A (XX) of 15 December 1965, 2249(S-V) of 23 May 1967, 2308(XXII) of 13 December 1967, 2451(XXIII) of 19 December 1968, 2670(XXV) of 8 December 1970, 2835(XXVI) of 17 December 1971, 2965(XXVII) of 13 December 1972, 3091(XXVIII) of 7 December 1973, 3239(XXIX) of 29 November 1974, 3457(XXX) of 10 December 1975, 31/105 of 15 December 1976, 32/106 of 15 December 1977, 33/114 of 18 December 1978, 34/53 of 23 November 1979, 35/121 of 11 December 1980, 36/37 of 18 November 1981, 37/93 of 10 December 1982 and 38/81 of 15 December 1983,

Awaiting the issuance of the report of the Special Committee on Peace-keeping Operations to the General Assembly at its fortieth session,

1. *Reaffirms and renews* the mandate given to the Special Committee on Peace-keeping Operations by the relevant resolutions of the General Assembly;

2. *Decides* to include in the provisional agenda of its fortieth session the item entitled "Comprehensive review of the whole question of peace-keeping operations in all their aspects".

General Assembly resolution 39/97

14 December 1984   Meeting 100   Adopted without vote

Approved by SPC (A/39/610) without vote, 19 October (meeting 8); draft by Chairman (A/SPC/39/L.5), following informal consultations; agenda item 73.
Meeting numbers. GA 39th session: SPC 5-8; plenary 100.

REFERENCE
[1]YUN 1964, p. 59, GA res. 2006(XIX), 18 Feb. 1965.

International Year of Peace (1986)

The Secretary-General, responding to a December 1983 General Assembly request,[1] submitted a report in September 1984 with a later addendum on preparations for the International Year of Peace (1986).[2] As at 30 October, 26 States had made proposals regarding the Year and two had pledged contributions. The Secretary-General opened a trust fund of voluntary contributions for the Year with the first pledge of $2,000 from Costa Rica. He noted that consultations had been held with the heads of 23 United Nations organizations and that the Consultative Committee on Substantive Questions (Geneva, 26-30 March) had discussed the participation of those organizations in the programme of the Year. Three briefings were organized for non-governmental organizations in New York, Geneva and Vienna, and a list of the organizations that had expressed interest in the activities of the Year was annexed to the Secretary-General's report. Among the proposed activities were joint research, debates, statements, seminars, publications, television and radio programmes, contests, and the issuance of commemorative stamps and a peace medal.

Also annexed to the report was a draft information programme for the Year which was to include pamphlets, a film, radio specials, a conference of non-governmental organizations, and in-depth briefings on the themes of international peace and security and peace-keeping and peace-making.

GENERAL ASSEMBLY ACTION

On 8 November 1984, the General Assembly adopted without vote resolution 39/10.

International Year of Peace

The General Assembly,

Recalling its resolution 37/16 of 16 November 1982, in which it declared 1986 to be the International Year of Peace,

Recalling also its resolution 38/56 of 7 December 1983 concerning the preparations and the draft programme for the International Year of Peace,

Aware that peace constitutes one of the principal aspirations of mankind and that the attainment and preservation of peace is a universal responsibility,

Mindful of the paramount objective of the United Nations as enunciated in the Charter, namely, to save succeeding generations from the scourge of war, which twice in our lifetime has brought untold sorrow to mankind,

Recognizing that the foundation of international peace and security can and must be strengthened within the framework of the United Nations and that this requires a strong commitment by Member States,

Recognizing also that the fortieth anniversary of the United Nations, at which time the International Year of Peace will be proclaimed, constitutes a unique opportunity for Member States to reaffirm their commitment to the purposes and principles of the Charter of the United Nations,

1. *Takes note with satisfaction* of the implementation of resolution 38/56, as reflected in the report of the Secretary-General, and of the updated version of the draft programme for the International Year of Peace contained therein;

2. *Invites* all States, United Nations organs, inter-governmental and non-governmental organizations, educational, scientific, cultural and research organizations and the communication media to make an even greater contribution to promote international peace and security on the basis of the Charter of the United Nations;

3. *Appeals* to Member States to submit proposals on specific activities which can be carried out by the United Nations, as well as those that they decide to execute at the national level, including the establishment of national co-ordination committees or other machinery for the observance of the International Year of Peace;

4. *Welcomes* the establishment of the Voluntary Fund for the Programme of the International Year of Peace and invites all States and interested organizations to contribute to the Fund;

5. *Decides* to convene a pledging conference during the first quarter of 1985 so that all Member States which have not yet announced their voluntary contributions may have an opportunity to do so;

6. *Emphasizes* the importance of the co-ordination and co-operation established between the preparations for the International Year of Peace and the World Disarmament Campaign, the International Youth Year, the United Nations Decade for Women and the celebration of the fortieth anniversary of the United Nations;

7. *Requests* the Secretary-General to report to the General Assembly at its fortieth session on the contribution of the regional seminars devoted to promoting the objectives of the International Year of Peace, to be organized during 1985;

8. *Also requests* the Secretary-General to report to the General Assembly at its fortieth session on the final version of the draft programme of the International Year of Peace, on any new observations made to him and on the arrangements for financing the programme;

9. *Decides* to include in the provisional agenda of its fortieth session the item entitled "International Year of Peace".

General Assembly resolution 39/10

8 November 1984   Meeting 54   Adopted without vote

43-nation draft (A/39/L.9/Rev.1 and Rev.1/Add.1); agenda item 32.

Sponsors: Argentina, Australia, Bahamas, Bangladesh, Bolivia, Chile, China, Colombia, Costa Rica, Cyprus, Dominican Republic, Ecuador, Egypt, El Salvador, Equatorial Guinea, Guatemala, Haiti, Honduras, India, Lebanon, Nepal, New Zealand, Nicaragua, Nigeria, Pakistan, Panama, Papua New Guinea, Peru, Philippines, Poland, Romania, Saint Lucia, Senegal, Singapore, Somalia, Sri Lanka, Swaziland, Thailand, Togo, Trinidad and Tobago, Uruguay, Venezuela, Zambia.

The Assembly, in resolution 39/157, requested the Secretary-General to consider convening within the programme of the Year an expert panel to examine implementation of the Declaration on the Preparation of Societies for Life in Peace, and to submit a report on its implementation to the Assembly no later than 1987.

REFERENCES

[1]YUN 1983, p. 117, GA res. 38/56, 7 Dec. 1983. [2]A/39/500 & Add.1.

Chapter V

Africa

In 1984, the United Nations considered a number of political questions concerning Africa and continued to focus on ways to abolish the *apartheid* policies of South Africa (see below, under "South Africa and *apartheid*").

The Security Council, the General Assembly, the Special Committee against *Apartheid*, the United Nations Council for Namibia, the Special Committee on the Situation with regard to the Implementation of the Declaration on the Granting of Independence to Colonial Countries and Peoples (Committee on colonial countries), the Commission on Human Rights, and the Commission on Transnational Corporations were the main bodies concerned with *apartheid* and the related matter of South Africa's relations with neighbouring countries. Regarding those relations, they condemned South Africa's aggression against and occupation of Angola, which South Africa had invaded and bombed in early January. The Security Council condemned South Africa for its premeditated and unprovoked bombing and for its use of Namibia for launching attacks against Angola, demanded that it withdraw, requested States to assist Angola in its self-defence, and reaffirmed that Angola was due appropriate compensation. In December, the Assembly condemned South Africa for its aggression and its economic blockade against Lesotho. Earlier, Lesotho and South Africa had informed the Secretary-General about their respective positions in regard to a proposed non-aggression pact. As for Mozambique, it notified the United Nations in March that it had signed a non-aggression agreement with South Africa.

Chad and the Libyan Arab Jamahiriya continued to disagree over who represented the Government of Chad, while the Sudan complained about aggression by the Jamahiriya, which it denied. The Council considered the Sudan's complaint in March.

Ethiopia and Somalia disputed the cause of military activity in two areas in Somalia. Somalia alleged that Ethiopian forces were in its territory, but Ethiopia denied that it was involved in the area, where, it said, Somalia was confronting resistance from local opposition.

The Assembly reaffirmed the sovereignty of the Comoros over the Indian Ocean island of Mayotte, appealed for increased contributions to the United Nations Educational and Training Programme for Southern Africa which provided scholarships for students from that region, and called for continued co-operation with OAU.

Topics related to this chapter. Disarmament: nuclear-weapon-free zones—Africa. Mediterranean: Libyan Arab Jamahiriya–United States dispute. Transnational corporations. Regional economic and social activities: Africa. Environment: environment and *apartheid*. Human rights: human rights violations—South Africa and Namibia. Women: women under *apartheid*. Refugees: Africa. Namibia.

South Africa and *apartheid*

In 1984, various United Nations bodies took action on ways to end *apartheid*—the system of laws imposed by South Africa to enforce racial separation. Those bodies were particularly alarmed about South Africa's "new constitution", which went into effect in September. Under the constitution, the black majority continued to be excluded from Parliament. Three chambers of Parliament were created—for whites, for "coloureds" (South Africa's term for those of mixed race) and for the people of Asian origin. Whites would dominate the Government, owing to their numbers in the Parliament and to the legislative powers of their parliamentary body.

The Security Council adopted two resolutions dealing with the new constitution and its consequences. By resolution 554(1984) of 17 August, the Council declared the constitution null and void. Following protests against the new Government, the Council, by resolution 556(1984) of 23 October, condemned the continued massacres of the oppressed people of South Africa, as well as the arbitrary arrest and detention of leaders and activists of mass organizations. The General Assembly, in resolution 39/2 of 28 September, also rejected the new constitution and declared that the wave of violence and killing of demonstrators that followed was the consequence of its imposition.

As it had done since South Africa adopted its *apartheid* system, the Assembly repeatedly condemned that Government and called for an end to those policies, including brutal oppression, repression, bantustanization, violence and armed force against the black people and their forced removal from their homes. On 13 December, the Assembly adopted seven resolutions on the issue. By resolution 39/72 A, it urged the Security Council to consider, under Chapter VII of the Charter of the United Nations, comprehensive and mandatory sanctions against South Africa, in particular, to halt military and nuclear co-operation with the régime, to impose an oil embargo, to reinforce the arms embargo, and to prohibit financial loans to and new investments in South Africa. The Assembly condemned collaboration with South Africa by Governments, in particular by certain Western States and Israel, reiterated that the South African liberation movements recognized by the Organization of African Unity (OAU) were the authentic representatives of the people of South Africa and called for assistance to them, and reaffirmed the legitimacy of the armed struggle by the oppressed people.

The Assembly, in resolution 39/72 B, approved the future programme of work of the Special Committee against *Apartheid*, the main Secretariat body dealing with *apartheid* matters, as recommended by the Committee. In resolution 39/72 C, the Assembly condemned the collaboration between Israel and South Africa and demanded that Israel terminate all such collaboration, particularly in the military and nuclear fields. Further drafting work on the proposed International Convention against *Apartheid* in Sports was called for in resolution 39/72 D. In resolution 39/72 E, the Assembly called on the Secretariat, Governments, information media, non-governmental organizations and individuals to promote public action in support of the struggle against *apartheid*. It called for contributions to the United Nations Trust Fund for South Africa in resolution 39/72 F. In resolution 39/72 G, the Assembly demanded that South Africa release political prisoners and appealed to States to take measures to increase pressure on South Africa, such as cessation of investments in and loans to South Africa, an end to the promotion of trade with it, cessation of military and police co-operation, and an end to nuclear collaboration.

The Security Council took action in resolution 558(1984) adopted in December to strengthen the mandatory arms embargo against South Africa by requesting States not to import arms, ammunition and military vehicles made there.

In regard to political prisoners, the Council, having been alerted that the South African authorities had rejected an appeal against the death sentence imposed on Malesela Benjamin Maloise, a member of the African National Congress of South Africa (ANC), by resolution 547(1984) of 13 January, called on the authorities to commute the death sentence.

The United Nations continued to take action to limit activities of transnational corporations (TNCs) operating in South Africa. The Commission on TNCs was the main body following those activities and, having received the Commission's report, the Economic and Social Council commended those that had terminated investments in South Africa and those Governments which were attempting to end activities of their TNCs there. The Council decided to begin preparations in 1984 for public hearings on TNC activities in South Africa and Namibia.

Other bodies which considered various aspects of *apartheid* were the Commission on Human Rights, the Council for Namibia, the Committee on colonial countries, the Committee on the Elimination of Racial Discrimination, the United Nations Conference on Trade and Development and the *Ad Hoc* Committee on the Drafting of an International Convention against *Apartheid* in Sports. The United Nations Environment Programme considered the impact of South Africa's *apartheid* and bantustan policies on the environment (see ECONOMIC AND SOCIAL QUESTIONS, Chapter XVI).

General aspects

Activities of the Committee against *Apartheid*. The Special Committee against *Apartheid*, in its annual report to the General Assembly and the Security Council adopted unanimously on 17 October,[1] reviewed developments in South Africa since its previous report,[2] described its work in promoting the international campaign against *apartheid*, and made recommendations for further action. Following is a summary of the Committee's work and related developments; fuller information can be found under the relevant subject headings throughout this chapter.

During the year, the South African Government continued its bantustan policy by forcing millions of blacks to live in certain designated areas. It also imposed a new constitution, which provided limited political rights for coloureds—those of mixed-race descent—and Asians but excluded the indigenous African majority, comprising over 70 per cent of the population, from any political rights. At the same time, the Committee stated, South Africa announced some sham "reforms" or "changes" in *apartheid* with a view to diverting world attention and dividing the black people. Although South Africa signed security agreements with Mozambique and Swaziland, it continued its aggressive acts against other countries of the region but failed to halt the armed struggle of ANC. Stating that propaganda about the peaceful intentions of South Africa or its willingness to make positive changes inside the country was contrary to reality, the Committee called for more decisive action against South Africa, for efforts to dissuade its allies from collaboration with it, and for assistance to the national liberation movements and to front-line States.

The resistance to *apartheid* was demonstrated in various ways—by strikes by black workers, particularly in the mining, metal and automobile industries; school boycotts by hundreds of thousands of black students; and mass actions by community organizations against community councils and against increases in rent and electricity charges. The Government reacted by detaining, torturing or intimidating political leaders, including leaders of the United Democratic Front, the Azanian People's Organization, the Natal Indian Congress and the Southern Africa Catholic Bishops' Conference. During the year, political arrests and detentions increased, and police banned meetings, raided offices of black organizations, confiscated documents and attacked students at protest meetings and demonstrations. South Africa continued to apply its system of "pass laws", which limited the movement of blacks outside their assigned areas. Blacks arrested for violations of those laws in 1984 numbered 163,000.

The Committee continued to draw the attention of the international community to the situation in southern Africa resulting from South Africa's policies—not only *apartheid* but also its aggression against neighbouring States. It repeatedly urged the Security Council to take effective measures, including mandatory sanctions under Chapter VII of the Charter, to force South Africa to end those policies. It noted that the *apartheid* régime had been encouraged to undertake those acts by the protection afforded by major Western Powers, first of all by the United States. Those countries continued to support and collaborate with the régime in military, economic, sports and other areas, and to invest in and provide loans to South Africa. Reiterating its past recommendations for comprehensive mandatory sanctions against the régime, the Committee mentioned, in particular, the cessation of all military and nuclear co-operation, an oil embargo, the termination of trade with and investments in South Africa, and a sports and cultural boycott. It urged the United Nations and other international organizations to refrain from relations with that country, and called on the General Assembly to condemn again all collaboration with South Africa by Governments, TNCs and institutions.

In encouraging the widest possible international action against *apartheid* in pursuance of Assembly resolutions, the Committee paid particular attention to promoting public action by trade unions, youth and students, and other organizations engaged in the struggle against *apartheid*. It recommended that the Assembly appeal to the international community to act against the régime and

its collaborators, commend organizations for their actions against *apartheid*, appeal to Governments and organizations to support anti-*apartheid* movements, and ensure the necessary resources for the Committee to expand its campaign against *apartheid*. It also gave special attention to the plight of women and children under *apartheid*.

Another area of special concern—the collaboration between Israel and South Africa—was the subject of a special report,[3] issued as an addendum to the Committee's annual report to the Assembly.

The Committee believed that the developments of the past year had further confirmed that South Africa had no intention of abandoning *apartheid*. Recalling that the Assembly had recognized the right of the oppressed people of South Africa and their national liberation movement to resort to all means at their disposal, including armed struggle, the Committee welcomed the growing support of the armed struggle by ANC and other organizations and undertook to publicize its progress. In view of this, it recommended that the Assembly reaffirm the legitimacy of the armed struggle, hold the South African Government responsible for any violence and conflict, and urge Governments and organizations to support the oppressed people and their liberation movements—ANC and the Pan Africanist Congress of Azania (PAC)—in their just struggle.

Communications. During the year, the Secretary-General received a number of communications regarding the *apartheid* policies of South Africa. The Chairman of the Committee against *Apartheid* also forwarded several texts which were issued as General Assembly and Security Council documents; some contained declarations adopted by international conferences organized by the Committee under its 1984 work programme (see p. 173).

Two communiqués, issued at the Conference on Southern Africa (Arusha, United Republic of Tanzania, 4 and 5 September), were forwarded on 3 October.[4] The Conference was organized by the Socialist International Committee on Southern Africa and the Socialist Group of the European Parliament and was attended also by representatives of the front-line States, ANC and the South West Africa People's Organization (SWAPO) of Namibia. The parties condemned South Africa's occupation of Angola, called for withdrawal of its troops, rejected the United States policy of "constructive engagement" towards South Africa, called for comprehensive, binding international sanctions against that country and pledged to support ANC.

In a statement adopted on 16 March,[5] the Committee against *Apartheid*, pointing out that South Africa was imposing a new racist constitution to dispossess the African majority, affirmed that the international community had a duty to impose comprehensive and mandatory sanctions and that it must demand the release of political prisoners. It also condemned collaboration with the régime and called for increased assistance to the liberation movements, the front-line States and Lesotho.

Similar calls were made in communications from other bodies throughout the year. These included: the final communiqué and resolutions of the Fourth Islamic Summit Conference (Casablanca, 16-19 January), transmitted by Morocco on 13 March;[6] resolutions of the Fourteenth Islamic Conference of Foreign Ministers (Dhaka, 6-11 December 1983), forwarded by Bangladesh on 15 March;[7] resolutions of the fortieth ordinary session of the Council of Ministers of OAU (Addis Ababa, Ethiopia, 27 February–5 March), forwarded by the Upper Volta on 18 April;[8] the final communiqué of the Meeting of Ministers for Foreign Affairs and Heads of Delegation of Non-Aligned Countries (New York, 1-5 October), transmitted by India on 8 October;[9] and resolutions of the seventy-second Inter-Parliamentary Conference (Geneva, 29 September), forwarded by the Sudan on 16 October.[10]

GENERAL ASSEMBLY ACTION

On 13 December, the General Assembly dealt with the broad aspects of the situation in South Africa in adopting resolution 39/72 A by recorded vote.

Comprehensive sanctions against the *apartheid* régime and support to the liberation struggle in South Africa

The General Assembly,

Recalling and reaffirming its resolution 38/39 of 5 December 1983,

Recalling its many resolutions and those of the Security Council calling upon the authorities in South Africa to abandon *apartheid*, dismantle bantustans, end repression of the black majority and all other opponents of *apartheid* and seek a peaceful, just and lasting solution in accordance with the principles of the Charter of the United Nations and the Universal Declaration of Human Rights,

Having considered the report of the Special Committee against *Apartheid,*

Taking note of the declarations adopted at the following conferences organized or co-sponsored by the Special Committee:

(a) Latin American Regional Conference for Action against *Apartheid*, held at Caracas from 16 to 18 September 1983,

(b) Inter-faith Colloquium on *Apartheid*, held in London from 5 to 8 March 1984,

(c) North American Regional Conference for Action against *Apartheid*, held at United Nations Headquarters from 18 to 21 June 1984,

(d) Conference of Arab Solidarity with the Struggle for Liberation in Southern Africa, held at Tunis from 7 to 9 August 1984,

(e) Seminar on the Legal Status of the *Apartheid* Régime and Other Legal Aspects of the Struggle against *Apartheid*, held at Lagos from 13 to 16 August 1984,

Condemning the recent further escalation of ruthless repression by the Pretoria régime, including the use of the armed forces against the oppressed people, resulting in the killing and wounding of hundreds of people and the arrest of thousands of opponents of *apartheid*,

Further condemning the imposition by the racist régime of South Africa of the so-called "new constitution", rejected by the great majority of the population, in defiance of General Assembly resolution 38/11 of 15 November 1983 and Security Council resolutions 554(1984) of 17 August 1984 and 556(1984) of 23 October 1984,

Gravely concerned over the threat to international peace and security, and repeated breaches of the peace and acts of aggression, caused by the policies and actions of the racist régime in South Africa,

Reaffirming that *apartheid* is a crime against humanity and a threat to international peace and security,

Reaffirming the legitimacy of the struggle of the oppressed people of South Africa waged by all means at their disposal, including armed struggle, for the exercise of their right to self-determination and for the establishment of a society in which all the people of South Africa as a whole, irrespective of race, colour or creed, will enjoy equal and full political and other rights and participate freely in the determination of their destiny,

Commending the growing unity, courage and heroism of the oppressed people of South Africa in resisting *apartheid* and in their struggle for the establishment of a non-racial society in a united South Africa and the opposition to the "new constitution",

Taking note of the heightening and sustained militant struggle waged by the people of South Africa in the political, labour, student and other fields, and the role played by the national liberation movements in intensifying the struggle, particularly the stepping-up of the armed struggle,

Strongly convinced that peace and stability in southern Africa require the total eradication of *apartheid* and the exercise of the right of self-determination by all the people of South Africa, irrespective of race, colour, sex or creed,

Gravely concerned over the attempts of the Pretoria régime to establish hegemony over southern Africa, and the encouragement given to it by certain Western States,

Deploring the action of certain Governments in Western Europe which received the Prime Minister of the Pretoria régime in May and June 1984 and thereby assisted its efforts to break out of its isolation,

Reaffirming that the elimination of *apartheid* constitutes a major objective of the United Nations,

Considering that all the organizations in the United Nations system have a duty to make a maximum contribution, within their mandates, to the international campaign against *apartheid*,

Highly commending the work of the Special Committee against *Apartheid* in combating the manoeuvres of the Pretoria régime and its collaborators, in informing world opinion of the situation in southern Africa and in encouraging the widest support to the struggle for liberation in South Africa,

Recalling that the racist régime of South Africa has consistently defied the relevant resolutions of the General Assembly and the Security Council, and violated its obligations under the Charter of the United Nations,

Considering that, in the light of General Assembly resolutions 38/11 of 15 November 1983 and 39/2 of 28 September 1984 and Security Council resolutions 554(1984) and 556(1984), no recognition can be accorded to the so-called "new constitution" of 1984,

Reaffirming its conviction that comprehensive and mandatory sanctions imposed by the Security Council under Chapter VII of the Charter, universally applied, are the most appropriate and effective means by which the international community can assist the legitimate struggle of the oppressed people of South Africa and discharge its responsibilities for the maintenance of international peace and security,

Deploring the attitude of those Western permanent members of the Security Council that have so far prevented the Council from adopting comprehensive sanctions against South Africa under Chapter VII of the Charter,

Considering that opposition by certain Western States to sanctions or other effective action against the Pretoria régime has encouraged it to defy the United Nations, escalate violence and repression against the oppressed people in South Africa and commit acts of aggression and destabilization against independent African States,

Recognizing the urgent need for the termination of military, nuclear, economic and technological collaboration with the racist régime of South Africa, as well as the cessation of sports, cultural and other relations with South Africa,

Recognizing that the policies and actions of certain Western Powers and Israel are the main obstacles which have frustrated international efforts for the elimination of *apartheid*,

Deploring, in particular, the actions of those States, in particular the Western States and Israel, which have continued and increased their political, economic and other collaboration with the Pretoria régime,

Gravely concerned that the racist régime of South Africa has continued, despite the mandatory arms embargo instituted by the Security Council in resolution 418(1977) of 4 November 1977, to obtain military equipment and ammunition, as well as technology and know-how, to develop its armaments industry and to acquire nuclear-weapon capability,

Expressing alarm at the growing violation of the arms embargo as well as the continued nuclear collaboration by some Western States and Israel with the *apartheid* régime,

Convinced of the urgent need to ensure the effective implementation of embargoes imposed or policies declared by most oil-producing and oil-exporting countries with regard to the supply of their oil and oil products to South Africa and to secure a mandatory oil embargo against South Africa under Chapter VII of the Charter,

Gravely concerned over the activities of those transnational corporations that continue to collaborate with the *apartheid* régime and of those financial institutions that have continued to provide loans and credits to South Africa and over the failure of the States concerned to take effective action to prevent such collaboration,

Condemning, in particular, the actions of those transnational corporations that continue, through their collaboration with the racist régime of South Africa, to enhance its military and nuclear capabilities,

Expressing great appreciation to intergovernmental and non-governmental organizations, in particular anti-*apartheid* and solidarity movements, trade unions and religious bodies, as well as city and other local authorities, that have contributed to the international campaign against *apartheid*,

Commending athletes, entertainers and others who have demonstrated solidarity with the oppressed people of South Africa by complying with the boycotts of South Africa,

1. *Endorses* the annual report of the Special Committee against *Apartheid;*

2. *Commends* the declarations of conferences organized or co-sponsored by the Special Committee to the attention of all Governments and organizations;

3. *Strongly condemns* the *apartheid* régime of South Africa for its continued brutal oppression, repression and violence, including the recent use of the armed forces against the black people, its illegal occupation of Namibia and its repeated acts of aggression, subversion and terrorism against independent African States;

4. *Condemns* the policy of "bantustanization" and the so-called "new constitution" designed to dispossess the African majority of its inalienable rights and to deprive it of citizenship, as well as the continuing forced removals of black people;

5. *Again declares* that only the total eradication of *apartheid* and the establishment of a non-racial democratic society based on majority rule, through the full and free exercise of adult suffrage by all the people in a united and non-fragmented South Africa, can lead to a just and lasting solution of the explosive situation in South Africa;

6. *Proclaims* that the United Nations and the international community have a special responsibility towards the oppressed people of South Africa, their liberation movements and all those engaged in the legitimate struggle for the elimination of *apartheid* and the establishment of a non-racial democratic society ensuring human rights and fundamental freedoms for all the people of the country, irrespective of race, colour, sex or creed;

7. *Demands* that all troops of the racist régime of South Africa be immediately and unconditionally withdrawn from Angola, that an end be put to the illegal occupation of Namibia and that South Africa respect fully the independence, sovereignty and territorial integrity of independent African States;

8. *Further demands* that the racist régime of South Africa pay full compensation to Angola, Lesotho and other independent African States for the damage to life and property caused by its acts of aggression;

9. *Declares* that the situation in South Africa constitutes a grave threat to international peace and security and that the racist régime of South Africa is guilty of acts of aggression, breaches of the peace and constant violations of the provisions of the Charter of the United Nations;

10. *Urges* the Security Council to consider urgently measures to ensure the total exclusion of the racist régime of South Africa from the United Nations and its family of organizations;

11. *Again requests* the Security Council to give special attention to action, under Chapter VII of the Charter, against South Africa and, in particular:

(a) To consider comprehensive and mandatory sanctions against the racist régime of South Africa, with priority for measures to ensure the total cessation of all military and nuclear co-operation with the racist régime of

South Africa and to institute a mandatory oil embargo against South Africa;

(b) To monitor effectively and reinforce the mandatory arms embargo against South Africa;

(c) To prohibit all co-operation with South Africa in the military and nuclear fields by Governments, corporations, institutions and individuals;

(d) To prohibit imports of any military equipment or components from South Africa;

(e) To prevent any co-operation or association with South Africa by any military alliances;

(f) To impose an effective embargo on the supply of oil and oil products to South Africa and on all assistance to the oil industry in South Africa;

(g) To prohibit financial loans to and new investments in South Africa, as well as all promotion of trade with South Africa;

12. *Requests* all States to refrain from any action that would provide to or imply legitimacy for the Pretoria régime;

13. *Condemns* all collaboration with the Pretoria régime by Governments, transnational corporations and institutions;

14. *Condemns* the policies of certain Western States and Israel and of their transnational corporations and financial institutions that have increased political, economic, military and nuclear collaboration with the racist minority régime of South Africa despite repeated appeals by the General Assembly;

15. *Rejects and denounces* any alliance or co-operation with the Pretoria régime on grounds of strategic or any other interests;

16. *Appeals* to all States to respect and support the aspirations of the people of South Africa to attain freedom and independence, and to contribute to peace and international co-operation;

17. *Calls upon* all Governments that have not yet done so:

(a) To terminate all military and nuclear collaboration with South Africa and to take all necessary measures for preventing corporations and enterprises under their jurisdiction from any such collaboration;

(b) To take effective legislative and other measures to ensure the implementation of an oil embargo against South Africa and to take action against corporations and tanker companies involved in the illicit supply of oil to South Africa;

(c) To accede to or ratify the International Convention on the Suppression and Punishment of the Crime of *Apartheid;*

(d) To support sports, cultural, academic, consumer and other boycotts of South Africa;

18. *Again proclaims* that the South African liberation movements recognized by the Organization of African Unity are the authentic representatives of the people of South Africa in their just struggle for national liberation;

19. *Recognizes* the right of the oppressed people and their national liberation movements to resort to all the means at their disposal in their resistance to the illegitimate racist minority régime of South Africa;

20. *Reaffirms,* in particular, the legitimacy of the armed struggle by the oppressed people of South Africa and their national liberation movements, and holds the Pretoria régime responsible for any violence and conflict;

21. *Reaffirms* that freedom-fighters of South Africa should be treated as prisoners of war in accordance with Additional Protocol I to the Geneva Conventions of 12 August 1949;

22. *Strongly supports* the movement against conscription into the armed forces of the racist régime of South Africa;

23. *Invites* all Governments and organizations to assist, in consultation with the liberation movements, persons genuinely compelled to leave South Africa because of their objection on the ground of conscience to serving in the military or police force of the *apartheid* régime;

24. *Urges* all Governments and organizations to provide maximal moral, political and material assistance to the South African liberation movements recognized by the Organization of African Unity, namely, the African National Congress of South Africa and the Pan Africanist Congress of Azania, and all those struggling for freedom in South Africa in uncompromising opposition to *apartheid;*

25. *Decides* to continue the authorization of adequate financial provision in the regular budget of the United Nations to enable the South African liberation movements recognized by the Organization of African Unity, namely, the African National Congress of South Africa and the Pan Africanist Congress of Azania, to maintain offices in New York in order to participate effectively in the deliberations of the Special Committee against *Apartheid* and other appropriate bodies;

26. *Calls upon* the international community and all countries to render concrete support and assistance to the front-line and other neighbouring States in the region to enable them to provide adequate security for refugees and to continue to resist the mounting aggression, subversion and economic pressure of the Pretoria régime;

27. *Calls upon* all specialized agencies and other organizations of the United Nations system, as well as other international organizations that have not yet done so, to exclude the Pretoria régime forthwith;

28. *Urgently calls upon* the International Monetary Fund to terminate credits or other assistance to the racist minority régime of South Africa;

29. *Again requests* the International Atomic Energy Agency to refrain from extending to South Africa any facilities which may assist it in its nuclear plans;

30. *Recommends* that, in connection with the observance of the International Youth Year in 1985, Governments and organizations give special attention to the role of youth and students in the struggle against *apartheid* and effectively observe the anniversary of the Soweto uprising on 16 June 1985;

31. *Commends* those Member States that have continued to take a firm position in the struggle against *apartheid* and for the action undertaken in support of the liberation movements in southern Africa;

32. *Further commends* the anti-*apartheid* and solidarity movements, religious bodies, trade unions, youth and student organizations and other groups engaged in campaigns for the isolation of the *apartheid* régime and for assistance to the South African liberation movements recognized by the Organization of African Unity;

33. *Requests and authorizes* the Special Committee against *Apartheid* to intensify its activities for the total isolation of the racist régime of South Africa, for promoting comprehensive and mandatory sanctions against South Africa and for mobilizing public opinion and encouraging public action against collaboration with South Africa.

General Assembly resolution 39/72 A

13 December 1984   Meeting 99   123-15-15 (recorded vote)

36-nation draft (A/39/L.28 and Add.1), orally revised; agenda item 31.

Sponsors: Afghanistan, Algeria, Angola, Benin, Burkina Faso, Burundi, Byelorussian SSR, Cape Verde, Congo, Cuba, Czechoslovakia, Democratic Yemen, Equatorial Guinea, Ethiopia, Gambia, German Democratic Republic, Ghana, Guinea, Hungary, Iran, Kenya, Lao People's Democratic Republic, Libyan Arab Jamahiriya, Malaysia, Mongolia, Morocco, Nigeria, Qatar, Sierra Leone, Syrian Arab Republic, Tunisia, Uganda, Ukrainian SSR, United Republic of Tanzania, Viet Nam, Zimbabwe.

Financial implications. 5th Committee, A/39/787; SG, A/C.5/39/75.

Meeting numbers. GA 39th session: 5th Committee 45; plenary 13, 66-71, 98, 99.

Recorded vote in Assembly as follows:

In favour: Afghanistan, Albania, Algeria, Angola, Argentina, Bahrain, Bangladesh, Barbados, Belize, Benin, Bhutan, Bolivia, Brazil, Brunei Darussalam, Bulgaria, Burkina Faso, Burma, Burundi, Byelorussian SSR, Cameroon, Cape Verde, Central African Republic, Chad, China, Colombia, Comoros, Congo, Costa Rica, Cuba, Cyprus, Czechoslovakia, Democratic Kampuchea, Democratic Yemen, Djibouti, Dominica, Dominican Republic, Ecuador, Egypt, El Salvador, Equatorial Guinea, Ethiopia, Gabon, Gambia, German Democratic Republic, Ghana, Grenada, Guatemala, Guinea, Guinea-Bissau, Guyana, Haiti, Honduras, Hungary, India, Indonesia, Iran, Iraq, Jamaica, Jordan, Kenya, Kuwait, Lao People's Democratic Republic, Lebanon, Liberia, Libyan Arab Jamahiriya, Madagascar, Malaysia, Maldives, Mali, Malta, Mauritania, Mauritius, Mexico, Mongolia, Morocco, Mozambique, Nepal, Nicaragua, Niger, Nigeria, Oman, Pakistan, Panama, Papua New Guinea, Peru, Philippines, Poland, Qatar, Romania, Rwanda, Saint Christopher and Nevis, Saint Lucia, Sao Tome and Principe, Saudi Arabia, Senegal, Seychelles, Sierra Leone, Singapore, Solomon Islands, Somalia, Sri Lanka, Sudan, Suriname, Syrian Arab Republic, Thailand, Togo, Trinidad and Tobago, Tunisia, Turkey, Uganda, Ukrainian SSR, USSR, United Arab Emirates, United Republic of Tanzania, Uruguay, Vanuatu, Venezuela, Viet Nam, Yemen, Yugoslavia, Zaire, Zambia, Zimbabwe.

Against: Belgium, Canada, Denmark, France, Germany, Federal Republic of, Iceland, Ireland, Italy, Japan, Luxembourg, Netherlands, Norway, Portugal, United Kingdom, United States.

Abstaining: Australia, Austria, Bahamas, Botswana, Fiji, Finland, Greece, Ivory Coast, Lesotho, Malawi, New Zealand, Saint Vincent and the Grenadines, Samoa, Spain, Sweden.

Prior to acting on the draft resolutions on the question of *apartheid*, the Assembly adopted, by a recorded vote of 81 to 33, with 18 abstentions, a motion by Iran that the item be considered as an important question under Article 18 of the Charter and that all draft resolutions and amendments relating thereto should require a two-thirds majority for adoption.

With regard to the text that became resolution 39/72 A, separate recorded votes, by request of the United States, were taken on a preambular paragraph and two operative paragraphs. All three were rejected.

By the preambular paragraph, the Assembly would have expressed grave anxiety at the increased collaboration by the United States with South Africa in pursuance of its policy of "constructive engagement", which had encouraged the régime to defy the United Nations and the international community, entrench *apartheid*, intensify repression and escalate aggression against African States; the vote was 57 to 54, with 31 abstentions. The operative paragraphs would have had the Assembly strongly condemn the United States constructive engagement policy (the vote was 59 to 57, with 26 abstentions) and appeal to Governments and organizations to persuade the United States and others concerned to desist from their policies of collaboration with the *apartheid* régime and to co-operate in international action for the elimination of *apartheid* (62 to 47, with 29 abstentions).

In explanation of vote, many speakers expressed general reservations about the series of seven resolutions on *apartheid*, which are set out below, as well as specific objections to particular resolutions.

Speaking about the resolutions in general, many States objected to what they described as arbitrary or unfair naming of specific Member States in connection with relations with South Africa. Among those expressing such reservations were Australia, Austria, Barbados, Belgium, Ecuador, Finland, speaking for the five Nordic countries, the Federal Republic of Germany, Honduras, Ireland, speaking for the 10 member countries of the European Community (EC), Malawi, the Netherlands, New Zealand, Panama, Portugal, Sri Lanka, Togo, Turkey and the United Kingdom. Barbados opposed selective name-calling on the grounds that it tended to exacerbate a situation rather than to conciliate. Similarly, the Federal Republic of Germany said that was why it supported amendments aimed at deleting the names of countries in resolutions. Israel believed that its being singled out again for specific condemnation in connection with the *apartheid* question was based on patent falsehoods.

Taking a different approach, Iran said that, when it observed a change by the United States towards the South African indigenous population, it would propose deleting all phrases condemning the United States for its co-operation with South Africa.

A group of countries—Australia, Austria, Finland for the five Nordic countries, Ireland for the EC members, the Netherlands, New Zealand and Portugal—expressed reservations about the endorsement of the use of armed struggle to achieve a solution. Finland affirmed that the United Nations had above all the obligation to encourage peaceful solutions to international problems.

Some countries were opposed to isolating South Africa completely. Belgium believed that a widespread boycott would have effects contrary to those being sought by the international community and that the maintenance of channels of communication with South Africa was necessary in order to bring pressure that would lead to a peaceful dismantling of *apartheid* structures. Similarly, Ireland (for the EC members) considered that to cut off all relations would be counter-productive to the Assembly's objective—the total eradication of *apartheid*. Portugal did not believe that completely isolating South Africa could bring about the fundamental changes that the United Nations was seeking. The Netherlands agreed, and added that it had a two-track policy aimed at increasing the political and economic pressure on South Africa while using existing channels of communication to encourage peaceful change. In the view of the United Kingdom, the most effective way to help dismantle *apartheid* was not through isolation, comprehensive sanctions or other measures which would entrench South Africa's stance and have serious consequences for neighbouring countries, but through dialogue and communication.

Several countries had reservations about the Assembly's request that the Security Council consider mandatory sanctions. Austria believed that the Assembly should respect the prerogatives of the Council with regard to coercive measures and therefore could not support provisions which might be understood as an obligation to curtail relations with South Africa. Similarly, Finland (for the Nordic countries) said that, because of their strict adherence to the Charter, they reserved their position with regard to formulations which failed to take into account that only the Council could adopt decisions binding on Member States. The United States was opposed to destroying the tools for building a future for black South Africans through a policy of economic sanctions that would deprive them of the wages, skills and organizational base needed in their quest for justice.

Botswana, Lesotho and Mozambique said they were not in a position to support the imposition of economic sanctions against South Africa.

Ireland said it would favour imposing a series of graduated sanctions such as a mandatory oil embargo and a ban on foreign investment, but added that they would have to be imposed by the Council, which alone had the power to adopt mandatory sanctions on behalf of the international community.

In regard to the recommendations that South Africa be excluded from the United Nations, Australia, Finland, for the Nordic countries, and Ireland stressed that they upheld the principle of universal membership in the United Nations.

Australia, Finland (for the Nordic countries) and the Netherlands did not support the proclamation of the national liberation movements as the authentic representative of the South African people.

In addition to those reservations applying to the seven resolutions in general, States brought up objections to specific provisions in resolution 39/72 A.

Austria, Burma, Finland, Japan, Peru and Sri Lanka were opposed to singling out particular countries for condemnation. A group of States expressed reservations about the language of the text, describing it as inappropriate, unbalanced, biased or intemperate. The Bahamas, Barbados, Burma, Ecuador, New Zealand, Turkey and the United Kingdom made such comments. The Bahamas said the text had several conflicting elements and selective naming of States detracted from its efficacy because of its lack of balance. Ecuador said it did not agree with certain selective paragraphs

which were worded inappropriately and would not bring about a solution to the problem; it preferred instead an approach that would bring about an understanding rather than heightening existing tensions. Turkey had reservations on specific references to Western countries mentioned individually and as a group.

Finland, Ireland and Peru objected to any endorsement, directly or indirectly, of armed struggle. In regard to the proposal for sanctions against South Africa, Ireland and the Netherlands said they did not favour a total severance of contacts. Ireland said total isolation would only have the effect of abandoning black South Africans still further to the whim of the South African authorities, who, without the international community's reprobation, would be even freer from restraints on their treatment of the black majority, and the outside world would have increased difficulty in continuing to monitor the situation. The Netherlands feared that total isolation and comprehensive sanctions would gravely exacerbate existing tensions and inflict suffering on the people of South Africa and neighbouring States, but it believed that the selective, mandatory sanctions mentioned in paragraph 11 pointed the way to possible future collective action against South Africa. Ireland also supported many of the specific measures in that paragraph.

Finland and Ireland supported universal membership in the United Nations and therefore objected to the Assembly's recommending that South Africa be excluded from the Organization. Finland said that paragraphs 10, 11 and 27 were contradictory to that principle and not in accordance with the provisions of the Charter on the mandate of the Security Council.

Malawi said it had abstained in the vote due to historical and geographical factors over which it had no control, and it appealed to South Africa to establish constructive dialogue with its black majority. Japan said its negative vote was because it opposed paragraphs 10, 14, 17 to 20 and 27 to 29.

In addition to resolution 39/72 A, the Assembly adopted six other resolutions on specific measures to eliminate *apartheid*. It endorsed the work programme of the Special Committee against *Apartheid* (39/72 B), dealt with relations between Israel and South Africa (39/72 C) and the drafting of an International Convention against *Apartheid* in Sports (39/72 D), and called for information activities to inform world public opinion about *apartheid* (39/72 E). The Assembly appealed for increased contributions to the United Nations Trust Fund for South Africa (39/72 F) and recommended action for the Security Council, States and organizations to take to eliminate *apartheid* (39/72 G).

In related action, the Assembly, in resolutions 39/2 and 39/17, rejected South Africa's new constitution and its policy of bantustanization.

In accordance with an Assembly decision that those having a special interest in the *apartheid* policies of South Africa should be heard, the Special Political Committee, on 5 and 6 November, heard statements by 18 representatives of non-governmental organizations who had submitted written requests to speak.[11] They were:

Philip Oke, Christian Peace Conference; Beatrice von Roemer, International Confederation of Free Trade Unions; Jeanne Woods, National Anti-Imperialist Movement in Solidarity with African Liberation; Vera Michelson, Capital District Coalition against *Apartheid* and Racism; Arnold Braithwaite, United States Peace Council; Gay J. McDougall, Southern Africa Project of the Lawyers' Committee for Civil Rights Under Law; Kwame Ture, All African People's Revolutionary Party; Quentin Smith, African Heritage; Paul Wee, Lutheran World Federation; Stephanie Urdang, American Committee on Africa; Bojana Jordan, American–South African People's Friendship Association; Julie Nalibov, Revolution in Africa Action Committee; Frank Dexter Brown, National Association of Black Journalists; Yvonne Ismail, Southern Africa Task Force of the People's Organization for Progress; Paula Finn, Art against *Apartheid;* Richard Harvey, International Association of Democratic Lawyers; Adrien K. Wing, National Conference of Black Lawyers; Vicki Erenstein, National Lawyers Guild.

The Special Political Committee reported the hearings to the Assembly on 16 November;[12] subsequently, the Assembly, on an oral proposal of its President, adopted decision 39/407 without vote.

Policies of *apartheid* of the Government of South Africa

At its 66th plenary meeting, on 20 November 1984, the General Assembly took note of the report of the Special Political Committee.

General Assembly decision 39/407

Adopted without vote

Oral proposal by President; agenda item 31.
Meeting numbers. GA 39th session: SPC 2, 17, 20, 22, 24; plenary 66.

International action to eliminate *apartheid*

In its annual report to the Assembly,[1] the Special Committee against *Apartheid*, while expressing concern at the actions of those Powers which continued collaboration with South Africa (see p. 135), noted progress in international action against *apartheid* and called for further action in that regard.

The Committee commended the African, non-aligned and socialist States for their continued firm position in the struggle against *apartheid* and in support of the liberation movements in southern Africa. It also commended the important role played by the Movement of Non-Aligned Countries, OAU, the League of Arab States, the Organization of the Islamic Conference and other intergovernmental organizations in this regard, and expressed appreciation to other States for such action. Special mention was made of the decision by the new Government of New Zealand to close the South African Consulate there and to support the boycott of *apartheid* sport.

The Committee noted with satisfaction that, especially in countries where the Government collaborated with South Africa, public opposition to *apartheid* was reflected in action by state and local authorities. In the United States, legislation for divestment from South Africa had been enacted or introduced in about 25 states. A number of cities—including New York, Washington, D.C., and Philadelphia—had taken such positions. Over 100 local authorities in the United Kingdom had taken action against *apartheid*, while the Greater London Council had declared itself an anti-*apartheid* zone. Commending the cities of Leeds and Sheffield in the United Kingdom for anti-*apartheid* stands, the Committee continued to encourage similar actions in other countries.

It commended the international trade union movement for taking new steps in solidarity with the black workers of South Africa and the independent trade unions there. It had encouraged action by religious organizations and leaders and was gratified by the response. Regarding relations with the Catholic Church, the Committee noted the disappointment expressed by black clergymen in South Africa at the granting of an audience by Pope John Paul II to the Prime Minister of South Africa, but welcomed a special message given by the Pope to the Chairman of the Committee.

GENERAL ASSEMBLY ACTION

On 13 December, the General Assembly adopted resolution 39/72 G by recorded vote.

Concerted international action for the elimination of *apartheid*

The General Assembly,

Alarmed by the aggravation of the situation in South Africa caused by the policy of *apartheid*,

Convinced that the root-cause of the grave situation in southern Africa is the policy of *apartheid*,

Noting with grave concern that in order to perpetuate *apartheid* in South Africa the authorities there have committed acts of aggression and breaches of the peace,

Convinced that only the total eradication of *apartheid* and the establishment of majority rule on the basis of the free and fair exercise of universal adult suffrage can lead to a peaceful and lasting solution in South Africa,

Noting that the so-called reforms in South Africa, including the so-called "new constitution", have the effect of further entrenching the *apartheid* system and further dividing the people of South Africa,

Recognizing that the bantustan policy will deprive the majority of the people of their citizenship and make them foreigners in their own country,

Recognizing the responsibility of the United Nations and the international community to take all necessary action for the eradication of *apartheid*, and in particular the need for increased and effective pressure on the South African authorities as a peaceful means of achieving the abolition of *apartheid*,

Convinced of the vital importance of the strict observance of Security Council resolution 418(1977) of 4 November 1977, by which the Council instituted a mandatory arms embargo against South Africa, and the need to make it fully effective,

Commending the decisions of oil-exporting countries that have declared it their policy not to sell oil to South Africa,

Considering that measures to ensure effective implementation of such embargoes through international co-operation are essential and urgent,

Noting with concern that, through a combination of military and economic pressures, in violation of international law, the authorities of South Africa have sought to destabilize the neighbouring States,

Considering that contacts between *apartheid* South Africa and its neighbouring States, necessitated by geography, colonial legacy and other reasons, should not be used by other States as a pretext for legitimizing the *apartheid* system or justifying attempts to break the international isolation of that system,

Convinced that the efforts to entrench *apartheid* by force will continue to lead to ever-increasing resistance by the oppressed people by all possible means and increased tension and conflict that will have far-reaching consequences for southern Africa and the world,

Convinced that policies of active and direct collaboration with the *apartheid* régime, instead of respect for the genuine representatives of the great majority of the people, will encourage its repression and aggression against neighbouring States and defiance of the United Nations,

Expressing its full support for the legitimate aspiration of African States and peoples, and of the Organization of African Unity, for the total liberation of the continent of Africa from colonialism and racism,

1. *Strongly condemns* the policy of *apartheid* which deprives the majority of the South African population of their citizenship, fundamental freedoms and human rights;

2. *Condemns* the recent killings, arbitrary arrests and the detention of members of mass organizations for opposing the *apartheid* system and the so-called "new constitution";

3. *Further condemns* the overt and the covert aggressive actions of South Africa directed at the destabilization of neighbouring States, and those aimed against refugees from South Africa and Namibia;

4. *Demands* that the authorities of South Africa:

(a) Release without conditions Nelson Mandela and all other political prisoners, detainees and restrictees;

(b) Abrogate discriminatory laws and lift bans on organizations, news media and individuals opposing *apartheid*;

(c) Grant freedom of association and full trade union rights to all workers of South Africa;

(d) Dismantle the bantustan structures;

(e) Immediately withdraw its troops from southern Angola and end the destabilization of front-line and other States;

5. *Urges* the Security Council to consider without delay the adoption of effective mandatory sanctions against South Africa;

6. *Further urges* the Security Council to take steps for the strict implementation of the mandatory arms embargo instituted by it in resolution 418(1977) and, within this context, to secure an end to military and nuclear co-operation with South Africa and the import of military equipment or supplies from South Africa;

7. *Appeals* to all States that have not yet done so, pending mandatory sanctions by the Security Council, to consider national legislative or other appropriate measures to increase the pressure on the *apartheid* régime of South Africa, such as:

(a) Cessation of further investments in, and financial loans to, South Africa;

(b) An end to all promotion of trade with South Africa;

(c) Cessation of all forms of military, police or intelligence co-operation with the authorities of South Africa;

(d) An end to nuclear collaboration with South Africa;

8. *Appeals* to all States, organizations and institutions:

(a) To increase humanitarian, legal, educational and other assistance to the victims of *apartheid;*

(b) To increase support for the liberation movements recognized by the Organization of African Unity and to all those struggling against *apartheid* and for a non-racial, democratic society;

(c) To increase assistance to the front-line States and the Southern African Development Co-ordination Conference in order to increase their economic strength and independence from South Africa;

9. *Appeals* to all Governments and organizations to take appropriate action for the cessation of all academic, cultural, scientific and sport relations that would support the *apartheid* régime of South Africa as well as relations with individuals, institutions and other bodies endorsing or based on *apartheid* and also appeals for further strengthening of contacts with those opposed to *apartheid;*

10. *Reaffirms* the legitimacy of the struggle of the oppressed people of South Africa for the total eradication of *apartheid* and for the establishment of a non-racial, democratic society in which all the people, irrespective of race, colour or creed, enjoy human rights and fundamental freedoms;

11. *Pays tribute to and expresses solidarity with* organizations and individuals struggling against *apartheid* and for a non-racial, democratic society in accordance with the principles of the Universal Declaration of Human Rights.

General Assembly resolution 39/72 G

13 December 1984   Meeting 99   146-2-6 (recorded vote)

22-nation draft (A/39/L.36 and Add.1); agenda item 31.
Sponsors: Australia, Congo, Denmark, Finland, Ghana, Greece, Guinea, Iceland, Ireland, Jamaica, Malaysia, Mauritania, New Zealand, Nicaragua, Nigeria, Norway, Sweden, Trinidad and Tobago, United Republic of Tanzania, Viet Nam, Zambia, Zimbabwe.
Meeting numbers. GA 39th session: plenary 13, 66-71, 98, 99.

Recorded vote in Assembly as follows:

In favour: Afghanistan, Albania, Algeria, Angola, Argentina, Australia, Austria, Bahamas, Bahrain, Bangladesh, Barbados, Belize, Benin, Bhutan, Bolivia, Botswana, Brazil, Brunei Darussalam, Bulgaria, Burkina Faso, Burma, Burundi, Byelorussian SSR, Cameroon, Canada, Cape Verde, Central African Republic,

Chad, Chile, China, Colombia, Comoros, Congo, Costa Rica, Cuba, Cyprus, Czechoslovakia, Democratic Kampuchea, Democratic Yemen, Denmark, Djibouti, Dominica, Dominican Republic, Ecuador, Egypt, El Salvador, Equatorial Guinea, Ethiopia, Fiji, Finland, Gabon, Gambia, German Democratic Republic, Ghana, Greece, Grenada, Guatemala, Guinea, Guinea-Bissau, Guyana, Haiti, Honduras, Hungary, Iceland, India, Indonesia, Iran, Iraq, Ireland, Ivory Coast, Jamaica, Japan, Jordan, Kenya, Kuwait, Lao People's Democratic Republic, Lebanon, Lesotho, Liberia, Libyan Arab Jamahiriya, Madagascar, Malaysia, Maldives, Mali, Malta, Mauritania, Mauritius, Mexico, Mongolia, Morocco, Mozambique, Nepal, Netherlands, New Zealand, Nicaragua, Niger, Nigeria, Norway, Oman, Pakistan, Panama, Papua New Guinea, Peru, Philippines, Poland, Portugal, Qatar, Romania, Rwanda, Saint Christopher and Nevis, Saint Lucia, Saint Vincent and the Grenadines, Samoa, Sao Tome and Principe, Saudi Arabia, Senegal, Seychelles, Sierra Leone, Singapore, Solomon Islands, Somalia, Spain, Sri Lanka, Sudan, Suriname, Sweden, Syrian Arab Republic, Thailand, Togo, Trinidad and Tobago, Tunisia, Turkey, Uganda, Ukrainian SSR, USSR, United Arab Emirates, United Republic of Tanzania, Uruguay, Vanuatu, Venezuela, Viet Nam, Yemen, Yugoslavia, Zaire, Zambia, Zimbabwe.

Against: United Kingdom, United States.

Abstaining: Belgium, France, Germany, Federal Republic of, Italy, Luxembourg, Malawi.

In explanation of vote, several countries expressed reservations about the language of the text which they found discriminatory. Austria, Belgium, Italy and Portugal brought up such objections. Italy and Portugal mentioned paragraphs 5, 7 and 9 in particular, with Italy adding that it supported the goals of the resolution nevertheless. In regard to paragraph 9, Canada did not favour the complete isolation of South Africa and did not interpret that paragraph to endorse the termination of all contacts.

Canada, Japan and the Netherlands also expressed reservations on paragraph 7. Canada said that it did not lend funds to South Africa and was terminating official promotion of trade with it, but those measures did not prevent, by law, Canadians from pursuing trade in peaceful goods or pursuing investment opportunities there. Japan said the paragraph contained an element whose implementation it could not ensure. The Netherlands said it would welcome a mandatory decision by the Security Council to restrict investments in South Africa, but in the sphere of national action it did not wish to prejudge the outcome of its consultations with employer organizations and trade unions to consider in what way investments by Dutch companies in South Africa could be influenced as effectively as possible. The Netherlands shared the view that South Africa must be denied any military nuclear capability but, rather than an appeal to cease all nuclear co-operation, it would have preferred a call on South Africa to accede to the Treaty on the Non-Proliferation of Nuclear Weapons[13] or to accept full-scale safeguards on all its nuclear installations.

Regarding paragraph 8, Canada and Japan said they did not support armed struggle as a means to effect change. They also expressed reservations on paragraph 5: Canada recognized the Security Council's right under the Charter to decide on sanctions, but questioned which new forms might currently be relevant or effective; in Japan's view, the paragraph went beyond the allocation of responsibilities provided for in the Charter.

Malawi said its abstention was because of historical and geographical reasons beyond its control.

Relations with South Africa

At its 1984 session, the General Assembly continued to call for ending relations between South Africa and other countries, particularly military, nuclear, economic, sports and cultural ties. In addition to the Assembly's calls for ending the various relationships to isolate South Africa and force it to abandon *apartheid*, a number of other United Nations bodies urged similar measures.

Activities of the Committee against *Apartheid*. The Special Committee against *Apartheid*[1] felt that South Africa was able to defy the United Nations and give the appearance of strength only because of the collusion and support of the United States, certain other Western Powers and Israel, as well as a number of TNCs and financial institutions. The Committee was distressed at the persistence of certain major Western Powers in increasing collaboration with South Africa and their resistance against the imposition of sanctions against it under Chapter VII of the Charter—the only effective peaceful means available to the international community to eliminate *apartheid*.

It condemned the May/June 1984 visits of the South African Prime Minister to Portugal, Switzerland, the United Kingdom, the Federal Republic of Germany, Belgium, France, Austria, Italy and the Vatican, and commended local demonstrations against the visits and France for refusing to receive the Prime Minister officially. At a Committee meeting on 12 June, the Chairman said that, during those visits, the Prime Minister sought respectability, investments and arms. His trip had been accompanied by propaganda that the régime had become peaceful because it had signed some agreements with neighbouring States and had adopted a new constitution. Those agreements had little moral or legal validity, according to the Chairman, and the constitution was a plot to entrench *apartheid* and exclude the African majority from all rights. The visits were also condemned by other bodies (see p. 138).

When the Committee learned that South Africa would take part in an international air show at Santiago, Chile, correspondence was exchanged between the Committee and Chile, with the Committee expressing the view that the facilities provided to South Africa were contrary to the spirit of the 1977 mandatory arms embargo imposed by the Security Council.[14] Chile's position was that no United Nations resolution had been violated because it was only following a widespread international practice.

The Chairman also wrote to Belgium and the United States expressing concern that South African representatives had been invited to the twentieth International Symposium on Applied Military Psychology, held in Belgium from 25 to 29 June and organized by the United States Office of Naval Research. The Chairman said that the invitation represented another instance of collaboration with the military establishment of South Africa by countries which professed to abide by the arms embargo. The Committee was subsequently informed that the invitation to South Africa had been withdrawn.

The Committee expressed its regret at the policies and actions of the Governments which found common interests with South Africa and encouraged it in the pursuit of its crimes against Africa and humanity. The United States, in particular, had opposed international action to deal effectively with the aggression of the régime, the Committee said, and had welcomed and encouraged its manoeuvres to entrench racism and to resort to more aggression. The United States had begun to use the régime as an instrument to secure its own interests, as exemplified by the espousal of the linkage between the withdrawal of Cuban forces from Angola and the implementation of the 1978 United Nations plan[15] for the independence of Namibia (see TRUSTEESHIP AND DECOLONIZATION, Chapter III). Furthermore, it had shown hostility towards the national liberation movements of South Africa and Namibia and had resisted any action against the *apartheid* régime.

The Committee expressed particular distress at the attitude of the current United States Administration, which viewed South Africa as an ally and espoused "constructive engagement" with the régime in pursuit of its own global strategic interests.

In addition, the Committee expressed regret at the attitude of the United Kingdom which, while dissociating itself from some aspects of United States policy, continued to collaborate with South Africa. It deplored the attitudes of several other Western Powers and it condemned the blatant collaboration by Israel with South Africa (see p. 150). The Committee drew attention to the growing collaboration between South Africa and the local authorities in Taiwan, as well as its links with Chile. The Committee expressed the hope that Governments and peoples of the world would exert their influence to persuade the United States and others to desist from their policies and co-operate in international action for the elimination of *apartheid*.

The Committee emphasized that the propaganda about the so-called peaceful intentions of the régime must be condemned, and that claims by any Power that its strategic interests required an alliance or understanding with the régime must be rejected.

Activities of the Council for Namibia. In response to the December 1983 request of the General Assembly that it monitor the political, economic, military and cultural boycott of South Africa,[16] the United Nations Council for Namibia, in its annual report to the Assembly,[17] reported on contacts between Member States and South Africa. The Council based its findings on the work of its Standing Committee II, which issued a report in May 1984[18] on such contacts since the adoption of a 1982 Assembly resolution calling on States to terminate all dealings with South Africa.[19]

In particular, the Council noted that a number of States continued to maintain political and consular relations with South Africa and to be its major trading partners, despite numerous United Nations resolutions requesting them to isolate that country. The Council concluded that certain Western and other States, including France, Israel, Switzerland, the United Kingdom and the United States, as well as the local authorities in Taiwan, continued to increase their collaboration with South Africa. This collaboration, together with the policy of open support for South Africa adopted by the United States, contributed to the survival of the *apartheid* policies of the régime, its illegal occupation of Namibia and its aggression against African States. Most States which had had political and diplomatic relations with South Africa prior to the adoption of the 1981[20] and subsequent resolutions calling on States to isolate it totally had made little or no effort to discontinue those relations. A small number of those States, however, had taken measures to terminate contacts.

It was clear to the Council that, while an overwhelming majority of States had boycotted South Africa, the support accorded to the régime by certain States not only militated against those genuine efforts, but encouraged it to step up its *apartheid* policies and entrench its occupation of Namibia.

The Council listed the 37 States maintaining diplomatic and/or consular relations with South Africa, and the 35 countries with South African diplomatic and/or consular missions in their territory in 1983. In addition, the Council reported on the changes during 1984 in other contacts. It noted that some Member States had established contacts with the bantustans, established by South Africa but not recognized by the United Nations and most of its Member States.

In regard to South Africa's relationship with intergovernmental organizations, the Council reported that the régime continued to be represented in the International Bank for Reconstruction and Development, the International Monetary Fund (IMF) (see p. 150) and the International Atomic Energy Agency (IAEA), and at meetings of the European Economic Community (EEC) and the European Atomic Energy Commission.

At the conclusion of its extraordinary plenary meetings held from 21 to 25 May (Bangkok, Thailand), the Council adopted the Bangkok Declaration and Programme of Action on Namibia in which it again condemned South Africa for its *apartheid* policies and other violations of human rights, and demanded an end to those policies. Rejecting propaganda perpetuated by South Africa and its allies, the Council stated that a relaxation of international action against *apartheid* was not possible as long as the régime continued to pursue that policy and sought to establish hegemony in the region. The Council deplored the continued assistance rendered to South Africa by the major Western countries and Israel in the political, economic, military and nuclear fields, called for an immediate end to such assistance, and appealed to the international community to isolate South Africa completely. In particular, the Council rejected the policy of so-called constructive engagement of the United States, which it said had encouraged South Africa to intensify its repression of the peoples of South Africa and Namibia.

The Council decided to consult with Governments, non-governmental organizations and other groups, with a view to intensifying pressure on South Africa as well as those States supporting it. In that regard, the Council deemed it important to maintain contacts with those Member States which had not complied with United Nations resolutions, with a view to convincing them to comply, to cease all collaboration with South Africa and to exert pressure on that Government in order to expedite Namibia's independence.

Action by the Commission on Human Rights. The Commission on Human Rights, in a 28 February resolution on human rights violations in southern Africa,[(21)] condemned the increased assistance rendered by the major Western countries and Israel to South Africa in the political, economic, financial and particularly the military fields, demanded that such assistance be terminated immediately and stated that it constituted a hostile action against the people of South Africa, Namibia and the neighbouring States.

In a report of 10 July, the Sub-Commission on Prevention of Discrimination and Protection of Minorities informed the Commission of the adverse consequences for the enjoyment of human rights of assistance given to South Africa (see ECONOMIC AND SOCIAL QUESTIONS, Chapter XVIII).

Action by the Committee on colonial countries. The Committee on colonial countries, in a decision of 20 August,[(22)] condemned the continued military, economic and intelligence collaboration between South Africa and certain Western and other States, particularly the United States and Israel, and called for such collaboration to be terminated; it particularly rejected the "constructive engagement" pursued by the United States.

GENERAL ASSEMBLY ACTION

The General Assembly, in numerous related resolutions, rejected South Africa's *apartheid* policies and called for an end to contacts with that country.

In resolution 39/17, it condemned the policy of those Western States, Israel and others whose political, economic, military, nuclear, strategic, cultural and sports relations with South Africa encouraged it to persist in suppressing the aspirations of the people to self-determination and independence. In resolution 39/50 A, the Assembly condemned the increased assistance by the same States and stated that it was a hostile act against the people of Namibia and the front-line States since it would strengthen South Africa's military power. By resolution 39/50 D, the Assembly decided to expose the collusion of certain States with the régime.

The Assembly, condemning collaboration with South Africa in resolution 39/72 A, requested States to refrain from any action that would imply or recognize legitimacy of the Pretoria régime, and condemned the policies of certain Western States and Israel and of their corporations that had increased collaboration; furthermore, it denounced any alliance with the régime on grounds of strategic or other interests. All collaboration was again condemned in resolution 39/91, and States were called on to end such ties.

By resolution 39/42, the Assembly condemned those Western States and others, as well as TNCs, which continued their investments in, and supply of arms and oil and nuclear technology to, South Africa. Calling on States to end collaboration in the political, diplomatic, economic, trade, military and nuclear fields and to refrain from entering into other relations, it requested them to end all assistance to South Africa and to isolate it totally. Such collaboration was also condemned in resolution 39/15, on the grounds that it encouraged the persistent oppression of the southern African peoples and denial of their human rights; the Assembly reaffirmed that those giving assistance to the régime became accomplices to racial discrimination, colonialism and *apartheid*, as well as in the aggression against the liberation movements and neighbouring States.

In resolution 39/72 G, the Assembly appealed to Governments and organizations to cease academic, cultural, scientific and sports relations that would support the régime, as well as relations with individuals and bodies endorsing *apartheid*, and appealed for further contacts with *apartheid* opponents. The international community, in resolution 39/16, was called on to give priority to programmes for combating *apartheid* and to intensify efforts to assist victims of racial discrimination and *apartheid*, especially in South Africa and Namibia and in occupied territories. The status of the International Convention on the Suppression and Punishment of the Crime of *Apartheid* was the subject of resolution 39/19.

Communications. In 1984, several States sent letters to the Secretary-General concerning relations with South Africa.

In connection with the Cyprus question (see p. 240), Cyprus and Turkey exchanged letters on relations between Cyprus and South Africa. On 24 January,[23] Turkey forwarded a letter from Nail Atalay, described as the "representative of the Turkish Republic of Northern Cyprus", who said that an official from the South African Embassy in Athens had indeed visited southern Cyprus on 17 October 1983, despite denials by the Greek Cypriot administration.[24] Cyprus responded on 12 March,[25] stating that those allegations were false and malicious and charging that Turkey was following neo-*apartheid* policies by its partitionist designs against Cyprus. On 16 April,[26] Mr. Atalay rejected those accusations.

On 6 January,[27] Iran referred to a 1983 letter from Iraq[24] regarding the alleged diplomatic relations between Iran and South Africa. Iran said it had broken off those relations immediately after the 1979 Islamic Revolution and, in order to protect its property during the process of liquidation, had established an interests section in the Swiss Embassy in Johannesburg.

India forwarded two texts—on 6 June,[28] it transmitted a communiqué adopted that day by the Co-ordinating Bureau of the Movement of Non-Aligned Countries, and on 18 June[29] transmitted a letter from Alfred Nzo, Secretary-General of ANC. Both Mr. Nzo and the Movement condemned the official visits by South Africa's Prime Minister to several Western European countries (see p. 135).

A 2 July letter[30] from the United Kingdom to the Chairman of the Committee against *Apartheid* referred to a recent Rugby Football Union tour to South Africa (see p. 165) and to claims that it did not fully support the arms embargo against South Africa (see p. 142).

Sanctions and boycotts

Activities of the Committee against *Apartheid*. The Special Committee against *Apartheid*[1] reiterated its call for comprehensive and mandatory sanctions against South Africa as a means to isolate the *apartheid* régime. The inability of the international community to take peaceful measures, such as sanctions, had obliged the national liberation movement of South Africa to give up its adherence to non-violence and resort to armed struggle, the Committee said. It recommended that the Assembly request the Security Council to consider the situation in southern Africa and institute sanctions under Chapter VII of the United Nations Charter and, pending such action, suggested that States adopt an embargo on military and nuclear co-operation, terminate economic relations, establish an oil embargo, ban foreign investment in South Africa, and prevent transnational corporations from operating there (see p. 146). In addition, the Committee urged States, organizations and individuals to establish sports (see p. 165) and other boycotts of that country.

On 13 February, the Committee heard statements on efforts to establish a cultural boycott. Participants pointed out that many entertainers, in a gesture of solidarity with the oppressed people of South Africa, had rejected lucrative offers to perform there. The Committee reported that since it had published in October 1983 the first register of entertainers who had performed in South Africa since 1981, the number of foreign performers there had declined. Of those who had toured South Africa since the register was issued, most were from the United Kingdom and the United States. A second register was published in 1984. Anti-*apartheid* groups, trade unions, local authorities, cultural personalities and others stepped up efforts to persuade those who had performed in South Africa not to perform there again and to encourage others to join the cultural boycott.

Activities of the Council for Namibia. The Council for Namibia[17] reported that, during the previous year, the call for world action in support of the cultural and social boycott of South Africa was reiterated in many international forums and by anti-*apartheid* movements. Despite that action and numerous General Assembly resolutions calling for an end to sports, cultural and social contacts with South Africa, such contacts continued to increase.

The United States policy of "constructive engagement" had encouraged its entertainment promoters to collaborate with South Africa, the Council said. South Africa had created Sun City, an entertainment complex in Bophuthatswana, a declared bantustan, to lure foreigners by paying high fees for entertainers and by claiming that *apartheid* was not practised at the complex. Between January 1981 and September 1983, more than 200 individuals or groups performed in South Africa. Of those, 86 were from the United States and 50 from the United Kingdom. Other individuals were from Argentina, Australia, Austria, Belgium, Canada, Denmark, the Federal Republic of Germany, Greece, Ireland, Israel, Italy, Japan, the Netherlands and Spain, as well as from Puerto

Rico and the Republic of Korea. Available information indicated that educational and scientific contacts between South Africa and other countries continued. Nevertheless, there were signs that the international campaign to isolate South Africa was having an effect—some planned sports events had to be cancelled and some entertainers declined offers to perform there. Since the foundation by many well-known personalities on 14 September 1983 of an organization, co-chaired by Arthur Ashe and Harry Belafonte, entitled "Artists and Athletes against *Apartheid*", a campaign was under way to seek the support of some 15,000 United States entertainers and sports figures and to dissuade them from performing in South Africa until *apartheid* was dismantled.

The Council predicted that, without decisive action by the international community to isolate South Africa, the result would be catastrophic violence. It believed that the Security Council should impose comprehensive mandatory sanctions without delay because such action was the only effective means to ensure South Africa's compliance with United Nations resolutions. Such action had been thwarted by three permanent members—France, the United Kingdom and the United States; they were urged to bring their policies into accord with the wish of the international community.

In its Bangkok Declaration and Programme of Action on Namibia, the Council for Namibia urged all States, pending the imposition of such sanctions, unilaterally and collectively to adopt measures against South Africa and commended those Governments which had already done so. In addition to action by the Security Council, the Council for Namibia said that Governments and organizations must play a more active role in bringing pressure to bear on South Africa, particularly by adopting sanctions. The Council also urged trade unions to act, including organizing an embargo on all shipments to and from South Africa, as well as on transport and communication with that country.

Action by the Committee on colonial countries. The Committee on colonial countries also called for sanctions against South Africa. On 20 August,[22] it recommended that the Security Council respond to the overwhelming demand of the international community by imposing forthwith comprehensive mandatory sanctions; and on 21 August,[31] condemned those Western States and all others which continued their contacts with South Africa, calling on States to terminate all collaboration or to refrain from entering into new relations.

Action by the Commission on Human Rights. The Commission on Human Rights, on 12 March,[32] also called for mandatory economic sanctions and appealed to Security Council members to support such proposals. On 28 Febru-

ary,[21] it called on States, specialized agencies and organizations to intensify their campaign to mobilize public opinion for the enforcement of sanctions against South Africa.

Action by the Committee on the Elimination of Racial Discrimination. In similar action on 20 August,[33] the Committee on the Elimination of Racial Discrimination appealed to States which had not done so to suspend all relations with South Africa.

GENERAL ASSEMBLY ACTION

Numerous calls for sanctions and boycotts against South Africa were made by the General Assembly in 1984.

In resolution 39/72 G, it urged the Security Council to consider without delay the adoption of effective mandatory sanctions, and, pending such action, appealed to States to consider national legislative or other measures to increase the pressure on the *apartheid* régime; Governments and organizations were urged to cease academic, cultural, scientific and sports relations with the régime as well as relations with individuals, institutions and other bodies endorsing *apartheid*, and to strengthen contacts with opponents of *apartheid*. Again calling for Council sanctions, as well as sports, cultural, academic, consumer and other boycotts by States, the Assembly, in resolution 39/72 A, also urged the Council to consider excluding South Africa from United Nations organizations.

The Council was requested, in resolution 39/2, to take all necessary measures, in accordance with the United Nations Charter, to avert the aggravation of tension and conflict in South Africa and the region. Specific sanctions by the Council were also called for in resolution 39/15. By resolution 39/42, the Assembly again requested States to take legislative, administrative and other measures to isolate South Africa totally.

In resolution 39/50 A, comprehensive mandatory sanctions under the Charter were again declared to be the only effective measures to ensure South Africa's compliance with United Nations resolutions. The Council for Namibia was requested to continue monitoring the boycott and relations with South Africa, and States were requested to co-operate with the Council in fulfilling that function. The Assembly, in resolution 39/50 B, expressed dismay that the Security Council had been prevented by its three Western permanent members from adopting effective measures against South Africa and considered that sanctions would ensure its compliance with United Nations decisions.

Military and nuclear relations

Activities of the Committee against *Apartheid*. The Special Committee against *Apartheid* continued following developments concerning military and nuclear collaboration with South Africa.[1] In March 1984, South Africa announced its largest-ever increase in military spending, the Committee reported. Defence spending went up by 21.4 per cent reaching a record level of 2,086 million pounds sterling, police spending went up by 44 per cent to 437 million pounds, and secret service expenditure rose by 25 per cent to 46 million pounds. According to the International Institute for Strategic Studies in London, South Africa supported an army of 82,400 men, up from 50,500 in 1976. Among its areas of expansion, the South African Defence Force (SADF) reported an air force base currently under construction at Trichardt near the Zimbabwe border, the recently completed airfield in the Transvaal and Natal provinces and plans to establish a ship building industry for naval vessels. SADF was already building strike craft with missiles. In addition, it was developing new weapons such as air-to-air missiles and weapons for use at night.

According to studies referred to in the Committee's report, South Africa had increased its reliance on a wide range of more and more sophisticated equipment while expanding its dependence on imports of foreign military component equipment and technology, despite the Security Council's mandatory arms embargo (see p. 142).[14] During 1981-1983, the United States had authorized 29 separate exports to South Africa of commodities on the munitions list worth $28.3 million. Evidence indicated that corporations in other nations had maintained contacts with South Africa's arms industry and that they continued to provide it with valuable military technology. For instance, in March 1984, British customs officials arrested four South Africans for illegal arms procurement for their Government. There were numerous clandestine arms deals between South Africa and some Western corporations that went unnoticed, according to the Committee. South Africa was seeking to sell its arms abroad, and it reportedly produced 143 types of ammunition. In March, its arms manufacturer participated in the international air show Fida '84, held at Santiago, at which it displayed Kukri missiles.

South Africa held its largest military manœuvres since the Second World War from 24 August to 22 September. More than 4,000 vehicles and 11,000 troops participated along with aircraft.

In addition to certain Western countries, Israel played an important role in building South Africa's military (see p. 150), which the Committee described in an addendum[3] to its annual report.

Activities of the Council for Namibia. Collaboration with South Africa in the military and nuclear fields was also considered by the Council for Namibia[17] and its Standing Committee II.[18]

The Council said South Africa had been able to acquire all the armaments it needed from certain Western and other States, which continued to ignore the mandatory arms embargo imposed against South Africa by the Security Council in 1977.[14] Clandestine transfers of arms were carried out from an undetermined number of countries. Currently, South Africa had the largest and most modern military arsenal on the continent. The State-owned Armaments Development and Production Corporation was one of the country's largest industrial groups with assets of about $1.2 billion, but South Africa still relied on considerable imports of technology and machinery as well as the acquisition of production licences.

For many years, South African arms manufacturers had developed contacts with many Western States, Israel and the local authorities in Taiwan. Various ways to circumvent the embargo had been devised, primarily the sale of "civilian" equipment with military applications. Many Western firms had established local subsidiaries in South Africa which were not subject to the embargo. The current United States Administration had relaxed previous restrictions on the sale of certain equipment to the South African military and police; for example, it permitted the sale of light planes, sophisticated artillery shells, cannon barrels and military trucks. Eleven British arms-producing concerns were active in South Africa. In addition, some 300 British mercenaries were serving in SADF. Other mercenaries had been recruited from Australia and New Zealand. Israel was another important source for South Africa's arms, having supplied missile boats, ship-to-ship missiles and small arms. The industrial firms of the Federal Republic of Germany also supplied arms for Pretoria, including parts for tanks and reconnaissance systems, and Spain reportedly supplied small arms and ammunition.

The Council said the development of the nuclear potential of South Africa, a near-nuclear State, had been considerably accelerated by the collaboration extended by certain Western and other States, including the United States, the United Kingdom, France, Israel and the Netherlands. This collaboration had included assistance in the extraction and processing of Namibian uranium, the supply of nuclear equipment, transfers of technology, provision of training and exchange of scientists. South Africa had reportedly obtained from Switzerland, through United States brokers, supplies for its Koeberg nuclear power station near Cape Town; Switzerland, however, informed the Council that it complied with the arms embargo. The uranium was manufactured into fuel rods by the French. France, the United States and other Western countries had participated in constructing South Africa's first nuclear reactor at Koeberg, which became operational in March 1984, and plans were reportedly drawn up for a second reactor to be built by French industrialists, which France denied. South Africa had recruited British nuclear scientists and technicians for the development of its nuclear power industry. In 1984, Israel and South Africa were reported to have established a committee to work out the terms of a long-term agreement under which South Africa would be supplied with technology for nuclear armaments.

In its Bangkok Declaration and Programme of Action on Namibia, the Council denounced South Africa for its military buildup in Namibia and for its acquisition of nuclear weapons capability. It condemned the collusion by Western and other States, particularly the United States and Israel, with South Africa in the nuclear field. The Council called on States to refrain from supplying the régime, directly or indirectly, with installations that might enable it to produce nuclear materials, reactors or military equipment. Also condemned was the military collaboration, including arms traffic, of certain States with South Africa. The Council expressed concern at the possible existence of military and security agreements between South Africa and certain countries in other regions, and considered that such arrangements would violate the arms embargo. It reiterated its request to the Federal Republic of Germany, the Netherlands and the United Kingdom, which operated the Urenco uranium-enrichment plant in South Africa, to have Namibian uranium specifically excluded from the Treaty of Almelo, which regulated Urenco's activities. The Council, calling on the Security Council to prevent the acquisition by South Africa of nuclear weapons and to ensure the cessation of collaboration with South Africa in the nuclear field, urged States, corporations, institutions and individuals to cease such collaboration.

Action by the Commission on Human Rights. On 28 February,[21] the Commission on Human Rights also condemned the continuing nuclear collaboration of certain Western States, Israel and others with South Africa and urged them to cease supplying nuclear equipment and technology. Governments were urged to end all technological assistance in the manufacture of arms and military supplies in South Africa and Namibia, and in particular to cease all nuclear collaboration with South Africa.

Action by the Committee on colonial countries. On 20 August,[22] the Committee on colonial countries condemned the military collaboration between South Africa and certain Western and other States, and expressed its concern at their continued nuclear collaboration, which it considered to be a violation of the 1977 Security Council arms embargo[14] as well as a threat to international peace and security. The acquisition of a nuclear weapons capability by South Africa added another dimension to a grave situation, and the Committee accordingly called for all such collaboration to be terminated forthwith. It recommended that the Council consider adopting further measures to widen the scope of its arms embargo in order to make it more effective and comprehensive.

Again condemning any military collaboration, particularly by the United States and Israel, and calling for strict compliance with the arms embargo, the Committee, by a decision of 21 August,[34] deplored the fact that South Africa engaged in military activities and maintained military installations in Namibia in violation of the United Nations Charter. In that connection, the Committee condemned the co-operation of certain Western and other States with South Africa in supplying it with military equipment and technology, including nuclear equipment and technology capable of being utilized for military purposes. It called for an end to all such co-operation.

GENERAL ASSEMBLY ACTION

The General Assembly joined the other United Nations bodies in calling for an end to military and nuclear relations with South Africa.

In resolution 39/72 A, it requested the Security Council to give special attention to action under Chapter VII of the Charter, including comprehensive mandatory sanctions, with priority for measures to ensure the total cessation of all military and nuclear co-operation; Governments that had not done so were called on to terminate such collaboration and to prevent corporations and enterprises under their jurisdiction from so doing. In addition, IAEA was called on to refrain from extending to South Africa any facilities which might assist its nuclear plans. By resolution 39/72 G, the Assembly appealed to States, pending Council sanctions, to consider national legislative or other measures to increase the pressure on South Africa, such as cessation of all military, police or intelligence co-operation and an end to nuclear collaboration.

The Council was again requested to consider mandatory sanctions in resolution 39/15, particularly the prohibition of technological assistance or collaboration in the manufacture of arms and military supplies in South Africa, and the cessation of all nuclear collaboration.

The Assembly, in resolution 39/50 A on Namibia, condemned the continuing military and nuclear collaboration of certain Western States and Israel with South Africa, in violation of the arms embargo, and called for immediate cessation. It expressed concern at the acquisition of nuclear weapons capability by South Africa and stated that such acquisition constituted a threat to peace and security in Africa. The Assembly condemned the collusion between South Africa, Israel and certain Western States, particularly the United States, in the nuclear field and called on France and all other States to refrain from supplying South Africa with installations that might enable it to produce nuclear materials, reactors or military equipment. Similar condemnations and calls were made in resolution 39/42. In resolution 39/61 B, the Assembly urged the Security Council to prohibit all forms of nuclear co-operation with South Africa and demanded that South Africa submit its nuclear installations and facilities to inspection by IAEA. The Assembly took related action in resolution 39/155 on implementing its 1970 Declaration on strengthening international security. It called on States, particularly the members of the Council, to promote the objective of the denuclearization of Africa in order to avert the serious danger posed by the nuclear capability of South Africa to the African States, in particular the front-line States, as well as to international peace and security.

By decision 39/412 on the military activities of colonial Powers, the Assembly considered that the acquisition of nuclear weapons capability by South Africa constituted a further effort to intimidate States in the region while also posing a threat to all mankind. According to the decision, the continuing military and nuclear assistance rendered to South Africa by certain Western and other States belied their stated opposition to the racist practice of South Africa and made them willing partners of its policies. The Assembly condemned nuclear co-operation and called for an end to it, in particular a halt to the supply of equipment, technology, nuclear materials and related training, which increased South Africa's nuclear capability.

In related action (resolutions 39/61 A and B), the Assembly called for disarmament efforts in Africa.

Arms embargo

Activities of the Committee against *Apartheid.* The Special Committee against *Apartheid*[1] held hearings on 3 April on the implementation of the arms embargo imposed against South Africa by the Security Council in 1977.[14] Statements were made by Stephen Cary, Chairman of the Board of Directors of the American Friends Services Committee; Jean Sindab, Executive Director of the Washington Office on Africa; Richard Knight of the American Committee on Africa; and Abdul S. Minty, Director of the World Campaign against Military and Nuclear Collaboration with South Africa. They condemned the military and nuclear collaboration of certain States and multinational corporations with South Africa, and observed that materials provided by the United States, France, the Federal Repub-

lic of Germany and Israel had enabled South Africa to develop its nuclear capability to the extent that it had become capable of exploding a nuclear device. According to them, the current United States Administration's policy of constructive engagement had led to a significant relaxation of the arms embargo and contributed to the arming of *apartheid*. They called for the strengthening of the mandatory arms embargo against South Africa.

Secretariat report. The Secretariat, in a February report to the Commission on Transnational Corporations,[35] described measures adopted by home countries with regard to the operations of TNCs in South Africa and Namibia (see p. 146), including national measures to limit the sale and shipment or the manufacture of arms and related *matériel*. Such measures had been adopted by Belgium, Canada, Denmark, Finland, the Federal Republic of Germany, Israel, Italy, the Netherlands, Norway, Spain, Sweden, the United Kingdom and the United States. Those steps included: observing a voluntary embargo on the provision of arms to South Africa; taking court action to ensure that the mandatory arms embargo was enforced; adopting legislation prohibiting the sale, transfer or provision to South Africa of arms and related *matériel;* denying licences for manufacturing and maintaining arms for South Africa; and denying permission for the export of arms or spare parts to that country.

Action by the Council for Namibia. The Council for Namibia, in its Bangkok Declaration and Programme of Action on Namibia,[17] called on the Security Council to tighten the arms embargo against South Africa and to ensure strict compliance by all States. In that connection, the Security Council was called on to implement urgently the recommendations contained in the 1980 report[36] of its Committee established by resolution 421(1977)[37] concerning the question of South Africa. That Committee had been created to study ways to make the arms embargo more effective.

Action by the Committee on colonial countries. The Committee on colonial countries, on 20 August,[22] also recommended that the Council consider adopting urgently further measures to widen the scope of the arms embargo.

Communication. In a letter of 2 July to the Chairman of the Special Committee against *Apartheid*,[30] the United Kingdom denied claims made at a meeting of the Committee that it did not fully support the arms embargo against South Africa.

GENERAL ASSEMBLY ACTION

On numerous occasions in 1984, the General Assembly reiterated its call for reinforcing the arms embargo.

In resolution 39/72 A, it again requested the Security Council to give special attention to action, under Chapter VII of the Charter, against South Africa, including: prohibiting all co-operation with South Africa in the military and nuclear fields by Governments, corporations, institutions and individuals; prohibiting imports of any military equipment or components from it; and preventing co-operation or association with it by any military alliances. The Assembly, in resolution 39/72 G, urged the Council to take steps for strict implementation of the arms embargo and to secure an end to military and nuclear co-operation with South Africa and the import of military equipment or supplies from it.

Resolution 39/17 included a demand for the immediate application of the embargo by all countries and more particularly by those that maintained military and nuclear co-operation with the régime and continued to supply it with related *matériel*.

In resolution 39/50 A, the Assembly called on the Council to tighten the arms embargo, to ensure compliance by all States, and to implement urgently the recommendations contained in the 1980 report of the Council's Committee.[36]

By resolution 39/61 B, the Assembly requested the Council, for disarmament purposes and to fulfil its responsibility, to take enforcement measures to prevent any racist régimes from acquiring arms or arms technology and again requested the Council to conclude its consideration of the Committee's recommendations with a view to making the arms embargo more effective.

SECURITY COUNCIL ACTION

On 13 December 1984, the Security Council, in resolution 558(1984) adopted unanimously, also took action on the 1977 arms embargo against South Africa.[14]

The Security Council,

Recalling its resolution 418(1977), in which it decided upon a mandatory arms embargo against South Africa,

Recalling its resolution 421(1977), by which it entrusted a Committee consisting of all its members with the task of, among other things, studying ways and means by which the mandatory arms embargo could be made more effective against South Africa and to make recommendations to the Council,

Taking note of the Committee's report to the Security Council contained in document S/14179 of 19 September 1980,

Recognizing that South Africa's intensified efforts to build up its capacity to manufacture armaments undermines the effectiveness of the mandatory arms embargo against South Africa,

Considering that no State should contribute to South Africa's arms-production capability by purchasing arms manufactured in South Africa,

1. *Reaffirms* its resolution 418(1977) and stresses the continuing need for the strict application of all its provisions;

2. *Requests* all States to refrain from importing arms, ammunition of all types and military vehicles produced in South Africa;

3. *Requests* all States, including States not Members of the United Nations, to act strictly in accordance with the provisions of the present resolution;

4. *Requests* the Secretary-General to report to the Security Council Committee established by resolution 421(1977) concerning the question of South Africa on the progress of the implementation of the present resolution before 31 December 1985.

Security Council resolution 558(1984)

13 December 1984   Meeting 2564   Adopted unanimously

Draft by Committee established by resolution 421(1977) (S/16860).

Before the debate began, the Council invited South Africa, at its request, to participate in the discussion without the right to vote.

South Africa said that it was ironic that the Council intended to extend the arms embargo, because the development of South Africa's armament industry traced its origin to the embargo imposed in 1977. As a result, South Africa had created an efficient industry—providing employment for thousands of all races, colours and creeds—for manufacturing arms of all types necessary for its self-defence, and was able to participate internationally in exporting arms. Apparently, certain arms-exporting nations felt threatened by the competition, it said. South Africa would not be deterred by any attempt by the Council to prevent it from exercising its fundamental responsibility, namely, self-defence.

Pakistan, Chairman of the Council's Committee, hoped that adopting resolution 558(1984) would be the prelude to the Council's consideration of the Committee's 1980 recommendations,[36] which it felt were vital for enforcing the arms embargo. The Committee's functions had been restricted to compiling data and obtaining information on breaches of the embargo, relying on information gleaned from the international media and from contacts with non-governmental agencies and organizations. If the Committee were to fulfil its mandate, it would need to be revitalized by meaningful Council action in regard to the 1980 recommendations, provision of adequate resources to enable the Committee to monitor the embargo, and willingness by the Council members to strengthen it.

India also urged action on the Committee's recommendations and was joined by the USSR in stating that they would have preferred stronger Council action. In India's view, the Council's request to States to refrain from importing arms, ammunition and military vehicles produced in South Africa should have included "related material of all types". The USSR stressed that it was important to supplement the embargo in order to ensure compliance by eliminating loopholes; however, it added, such measures were not enough and it supported the African countries' long-standing demand for sanctions under Chapter VII of the Charter.

Remarking that it had taken the initiative in the Council's Committee to extend the embargo by banning imports of South African arms, the Netherlands pointed out that, since establishment of the arms embargo, South Africa had built up its own manufacturing capacity and become self-sufficient in military equipment.

The United Kingdom said that, in principle, it opposed trade sanctions because they were difficult to enforce, would lead to a hardening of views and tended to harm the poorest and most vulnerable; by adopting a non-mandatory resolution directed against importers, the Council had pursued a realistic course.

Economic relations

Activities of the Committee against *Apartheid*. The Special Committee against *Apartheid*[1] stated that over the previous year, economic collaboration by some Western and other countries with South Africa had increased. Israel's economic relations with South Africa, which covered all aspects of bilateral relations, were also examined by the Committee (see p. 150).

In 1984, South Africa had a favourable trade balance, with exports increasing by 28 per cent in terms of value. Real gross national product increased by 5 per cent due to an improvement in terms of trade. As in previous years, South Africa's major trading partners were Western Europe, Japan and North America. In 1984, the Federal Republic of Germany overtook the United States as the major exporter to South Africa, followed by Japan, the United Kingdom, Italy, France, the Netherlands, Belgium/Luxembourg, Switzerland, Sweden and Canada. The major importers of South African goods, in descending order, were the United States, Japan, the Federal Republic of Germany, the United Kingdom, France, Italy, Belgium/Luxembourg, Canada, the Netherlands, Switzerland and Sweden.

Trade missions from several countries continued to visit South Africa. Thirteen British trade missions visited in 1984 to promote their products. Portugal increased its exchange of visits. In Denmark, on the other hand, the Parliament, in May, called on the Government to require from all import companies annual statements on coal imports from South Africa and to inform oil companies and shipowners that it was against Danish policy to transport oil to South Africa. Although Japan did not allow direct Japanese investment in South Africa, trade between them increased.

South African mineral sales increased by 17 per cent in 1984 over the previous year, and mineral sales made up 84 per cent of export revenues. Gold, constituting approximately 50 per cent of South Africa's exports, continued to be marketed through financial institutions in Switzerland (40 to 50 per cent of the total), the United Kingdom (20 per cent) and the Federal Republic of Germany, Hong Kong, Japan and the United States. Agricultural exports were irregular as a result of a severe drought which continued through 1984.

Activities of the Council for Namibia. The Council for Namibia[17] also described economic contacts with South Africa, basing its findings on the report of its Standing Committee II.[18] It stated that most of South Africa's trade, investment, loans, transfer of technology and expertise were channelled through TNCs based in the United States, Western Europe and Japan. Some 400 United States companies had subsidiaries in South Africa, and an additional 6,000 United States firms did business there through agency networks. Corporations of France and the Federal Republic of Germany had at least as many subsidiaries there, and British companies with operations numbered 650. In all, some 2,000 TNCs operated in South Africa, supported by externally owned banks and insurance companies.

The Council, in its Bangkok Declaration and Programme of Action on Namibia, urged States, pending the imposition of comprehensive mandatory sanctions by the Security Council, unilaterally and collectively, to adopt economic measures against South Africa as called for by the General Assembly, and commended those Governments that had done so.

Action by the Commission on Human Rights. The Commission on Human Rights, on 28 February,[21] condemned the activities of foreign economic interests operating in Namibia which were exploiting the Territory's resources and demanded that TNCs refrain from any new investment or activities in Namibia by ending their co-operation with South Africa. The Commission urged Governments that had not done so to take legislative, administrative or other measures, in respect of their nationals and the bodies corporate under their jurisdiction that owned and operated enterprises in South Africa and Namibia, with a view to ending their trading, manufacturing and investing activities there.

GENERAL ASSEMBLY ACTION

The General Assembly, in resolution 39/72 G, appealed to States that had not done so, pending mandatory sanctions by the Security Council, to consider national legislative or other appropriate measures to increase the pressure on South Africa through various measures, including an end to all promotion of trade with it.

In resolution 39/42, the Assembly again called on States to discontinue all economic, financial and trade relations with South Africa and to refrain from entering into any relations with it which might lend support to its continued illegal occupation of Namibia.

Oil embargo

According to the Council for Namibia,[17] South Africa imported about three quarters of its oil requirements at an annual cost of $4 billion, despite an oil embargo called for by the Special Committee against *Apartheid*[38] and implemented by members of the Organization of Petroleum Exporting Countries and other oil exporters. Two New York trading companies handled much of the oil that South Africa bought secretly.

The Secretariat, reporting to the Commission on TNCs on responsibilities of home countries with respect to TNCs operating in South Africa and Namibia,[35] said that, despite the Assembly's repeated call for an oil embargo, no home country had prohibited or restricted the sale, supply or shipment of petroleum and petroleum products to South Africa, as far as was known.

The Committee on colonial countries, on 21 August,[31] called on those oil-producing and oil-exporting countries that had not done so to take measures against oil companies so as to terminate the supply of crude oil and petroleum products to South Africa.

GENERAL ASSEMBLY ACTION

The General Assembly took action on an oil embargo in several resolutions.

In resolution 39/72 A, it again requested the Security Council to consider action, under Chapter VII of the Charter, against South Africa, including comprehensive mandatory sanctions, with priority to instituting a mandatory oil embargo, and imposing an embargo on the supply of oil and oil products to South Africa and on all assistance to the oil industry there. Governments were urged to ensure the implementation of an embargo and to take action against corporations and tanker companies involved in supplying oil to South Africa.

A similar request to the Council was made in resolution 39/15, which included the Assembly's request for an embargo on the supply of petroleum, petroleum products and other strategic goods to South Africa.

By resolution 39/42, the Assembly called on those oil-producing and oil-exporting countries that had not done so to take measures against the oil companies concerned so as to terminate the supply of crude oil and petroleum products to South Africa.

In resolution 39/50 C on the work programme of the Council for Namibia, the Assembly decided that the Council should contact the management of corporations, tanker companies and other shipping interests involved in the illicit transportation and/or supply of petroleum and petroleum products to South Africa and Namibia.

Foreign investments and loans

According to the Special Committee against *Apartheid*,[1] international financial markets in 1984 provided South Africa with $195 million in syndicated credits and $633 million in bonds. As of January 1984, the total liabilities of South African banks equalled $11 billion, approximately 14 billion rand, showing an increase of 40 per cent over 1981. At the same time, South Africa's assets in foreign banks overseas totalled $2.1 billion. Several factors made Western financial markets attractive for South African companies to seek loans, including the reluctance of most Western Governments to discourage South Africa's access to their markets, high interest rates in South Africa, and the willingness of North American and Western European banks to continue business as usual with South Africa. Loans by United States banks alone to the South African private sector increased to $4.2 billion in 1984 from $1 billion in 1980.

Western European and North American TNCs and South African companies licensed to assemble and sell overseas products increased their activities in 1984 to capture a larger share of the South African market. The falling rate of exchange for the South African rand, coupled with a 15 per cent return on investment, had attracted many United States–based companies to invest in South Africa. Patents, blueprints, new technology, management skills and personnel training continued to be provided to South African firms by their parent companies overseas.

Meanwhile, anti-*apartheid* movements in the United States and Western Europe gained ground in promoting disinvestment actions by universities, states and municipalities, and further measures were reported in 1984.

The Council for Namibia[17] also reviewed foreign investments in and loans to South Africa and provided figures on South Africa's trade with its major partners in 1981 and 1982. The South African economy continued to profit not only from extensive international trade links but also from foreign investments in and bank loans to South Africa, which, until the current recession, accounted for about one third of the growth of the country's gross domestic product.

As at 31 August 1984, there were some 2,000 TNCs operating in South Africa, supported by externally owned banks and insurance companies. Foreign investment, with its financial resources and modern technology, had set up production facilities in some of the most critical areas of South Africa's economy. The Council noted the advantages of the South African system for foreign investors: the absence of labour supply problems, the low cost of labour under the *apartheid* system, the restriction of trade unions, and the political system of white domination and privilege enforced through organized repression.

The Secretariat in February[35] described measures taken by home countries of TNCs to reduce foreign investment, loans, trade and technical assistance to South Africa and Namibia, as repeatedly requested by the General Assembly (see below). The Commission on Human Rights, on 28 February,[21] requested all specialized agencies, particularly IMF and the World Bank (see p. 150), to refrain from granting any type of loans to South Africa.

GENERAL ASSEMBLY ACTION

The General Assembly, in resolution 39/72 A on sanctions against South Africa, again called on the Security Council to give special attention to such action, including prohibiting financial loans to, new investments in and all promotion of trade with South Africa. In resolution 39/15, the Assembly again requested the Council to consider mandatory sanctions under the Charter, including prohibiting loans and investments. Resolution 39/72 G included the Assembly's appeal to States, pending mandatory sanctions by the Council, to consider national legislative or other measures to increase pressure on South Africa, including cessation of further investments and financial loans.

The Assembly took related action in resolution 39/42, calling on States to terminate investments in Namibia or loans to South Africa and to refrain from agreements or measures to promote trade or other economic relations with the régime.

Transnational corporations

In January 1984, the Secretary-General, as requested by the Economic and Social Council in July 1983,[39] reported to the Commission on Transnational Corporations on TNC activities and measures by Governments to prohibit investments in South Africa and Namibia.[40] According to that report, South Africa's foreign liabilities continued to increase in the early 1980s, mostly through loans, showing an increase of 27.5 per cent in 1981 over the previous year, with direct investment increasing by 21 per cent and non-direct investment by 32 per cent. Despite further pressures on TNCs to disinvest in South Africa, the country continued to attract more capital, at least in the case of TNCs based in the United Kingdom and the Federal Republic of Germany. In the same period, the stock of investment of TNCs based in the United States declined after consecutive increases up to 1981. In the case of Namibia, direct investment by TNCs was declining as a result of political uncertainty. There were instances of TNCs reducing their investments in South Africa in 1982-

1983, but those divestments were generally explained by commercial rather than political factors. Overall, TNC involvement in South Africa had increased, especially through indirect investment.

In 1984, Western European and North American-based TNCs increased their activities in South Africa, according to the Special Committee against *Apartheid*.[1] The Council for Namibia[17] estimated that some 2,000 TNCs were currently operating in South Africa. It reported that most trade, foreign investment and loans, and transfer of technology and expertise were channelled through TNCs based in the United States, Western Europe and Japan. Some 400 United States companies had subsidiary operations in South Africa, and another 6,000 United States firms did business there through agency networks. Corporations of the Federal Republic of Germany and France had at least as many subsidiaries, and British companies with operations in South Africa numbered at least 650.

In response to a July 1983 Economic and Social Council decision,[41] the Secretariat reported in February[35] to the Commission on TNCs on measures adopted by home countries with regard to TNC operations in South Africa and Namibia in violation of relevant United Nations actions. The report, updated in March, was based partly on information supplied by countries and partly on information collected from official sources. The Secretariat reported that two codes of conduct had been adopted for companies operating in South Africa: in 1977, EEC adopted a voluntary code for companies with subsidiaries, branches or representation in South Africa; and in 1978, Canada issued a voluntary code concerning employment practices of Canadian companies operating in South Africa. Those codes made recommendations on minimum wages for South African workers, equal pay for equal work, training programmes and working conditions.

Canada, Denmark, France, the Federal Republic of Germany, Japan, the Netherlands, Norway, Sweden and the United States were those countries reported to have adopted various measures at the national and local levels to restrict TNC investment in, trade with and the provision of loans and technical assistance to South Africa. Canada, for example, said that in 1977 it had terminated programmes which encouraged or promoted trade with or investment in South Africa. That same year, Denmark and Norway withdrew official support for credits and guarantees in respect of their exports to South Africa, and the Federal Republic of Germany had limited investment guarantees and export credits available to its TNCs operating there. Similarly, in 1979, the Netherlands withdrew government support for export credits or investment guarantees for its companies. France said that it was discouraging its companies from operating in Namibia. Japan reported that its laws and regulations expressly prohibited direct investment by Japanese companies in South Africa and Namibia, and Sweden enacted a law prohibiting new investments by Swedish companies and individuals. In 1983, the United States passed a law to withhold support of IMF loans to and the use of IMF facilities by South Africa (see p. 150) so long as it continued to pursue *apartheid*. In addition to the United States Government's discouraging new investments in Namibia, a number of 1982 and 1983 state and municipal actions prohibited or terminated the investment of their funds in companies operating in South Africa.

In their communications to the United Nations, Australia, Denmark, Finland, Ireland, New Zealand, Norway, Pakistan, Spain, Uganda and the USSR indicated that they did not have corporations doing business in Namibia.

The Secretariat concluded that the measures taken so far by home countries to regulate private capital flows to and other business transactions with South Africa by TNCs had been limited. Those measures covered mostly the withdrawal of official guarantees or support for credits to companies investing in or trading with South Africa, and the termination of official export or trade promotion with it. This was apparently due to the fact that most home-country Governments considered themselves under no legal obligation, with the exception of the mandatory arms embargo of 1977, or they lacked the requisite jurisdiction to influence the activities of subsidiaries and affiliates operating under South African law. However, the adoption of measures not related to the arms embargo indicated that the home countries accepted some responsibilities for TNC activities within their national jurisdiction and having operations in South Africa.

The Secretariat report noted that resolutions adopted by the General Assembly and the Economic and Social Council calling for the cessation of TNC activities were generally opposed by the home countries. This matter was under consideration by the Commission on TNCs, the body charged with elaborating a code of conduct on TNCs (see ECONOMIC AND SOCIAL QUESTIONS, Chapter VII). Under the draft code, TNCs would be called on to comply strictly with obligations resulting from Security Council decisions and to respect those resulting from all relevant United Nations resolutions, to refrain from operations supporting South Africa, and to engage in activities to eliminate racial discrimination and *apartheid*. With regard to investment in Namibia, TNCs would be called on to comply with obligations resulting from Security Council

resolution 283(1970),[42] by which States were urged to ensure that companies under their ownership or control ceased all dealings with commercial or industrial enterprises or concessions in Namibia.

The Commission on TNCs, at its April 1984 session,[43] discussed and took note of the Secretariat's report.

As in previous years, the Commission on Human Rights took action on TNC activity in southern Africa (see also ECONOMIC AND SOCIAL QUESTIONS, Chapter XVIII). On 28 February,[21] it called on Governments to take measures, in respect of their nationals and bodies corporate under their jurisdiction that owned and operated enterprises in South Africa and Namibia, with a view to stopping their trading, manufacturing and investing activities there. It also called on States parties to the 1973 International Convention on the Suppression and Punishment of the Crime of *Apartheid*[44] to express their views on the extent and nature of the responsibility of TNCs for the continued existence of the *apartheid* system. Also on 28 February,[45] it again urged States to ratify or accede to that Convention, in particular those which had jurisdiction over TNCs operating in South Africa and Namibia, and without whose co-operation such operations could not be halted. In addition, the Commission requested the Group of Three members of the Commission set up under the Convention to continue examining the responsibility of TNCs for the existence of the *apartheid* system.

A Special Rapporteur of the Sub-Commission on Prevention of Discrimination and Protection of Minorities, in a July report[46] to the Commission on the adverse consequences for the enjoyment of human rights of political, military, economic and other assistance to South Africa, listed banks, firms and other organizations which gave assistance to South Africa (see ECONOMIC AND SOCIAL QUESTIONS, Chapter XVIII). The list had been updated annually since 1980. On 28 August,[47] the Sub-Commission invited the Rapporteur to continue to update the list and welcomed the Commission's recommendation on government measures.

ECONOMIC AND SOCIAL COUNCIL ACTION

On 25 July, the Economic and Social Council, acting on the recommendation of its First (Economic) Committee, adopted two resolutions on TNC activities in South Africa and Namibia.

Resolution 1984/53 was adopted by roll-call vote.

Activities of transnational corporations in South Africa and Namibia and collaboration of such corporations with the racist minority régime in South Africa

The Economic and Social Council,

Recalling General Assembly resolutions 3201(S-VI) and 3202(S-VI) of 1 May 1974, containing the Declaration and the Programme of Action on the Establishment of a New International Economic Order, 3281(XXIX) of

12 December 1974, containing the Charter of Economic Rights and Duties of States, and 3362(S-VII) of 16 September 1975 on development and international economic co-operation,

Recalling also General Assembly resolutions 38/36 of 1 December 1983 on the question of Namibia, and 38/39 D on sanctions against South Africa, 38/39 G on military and nuclear collaboration with South Africa, 38/39 I on investments in South Africa and 38/39 J on an oil embargo against South Africa, all of 5 December 1983,

Recalling further General Assembly resolution 38/50 of 7 December 1983 on activities of foreign economic and other interests which are impeding the implementation of the Declaration on the Granting of Independence to Colonial Countries and Peoples in Namibia and in all other Territories under colonial domination and efforts to eliminate colonialism, *apartheid* and racial discrimination in southern Africa,

Reaffirming its previous resolutions on the activities of transnational corporations in southern Africa and the collaboration of such corporations with the racist minority régime in South Africa,

Having considered the report of the Secretary-General on the activities of transnational corporations and measures being taken by Governments to prohibit investments in South Africa and Namibia and the report of the Secretariat on the responsibilities of home countries with respect to the transnational corporations operating in South Africa and Namibia in violation of the relevant resolutions and decisions of the United Nations, prepared pursuant to Economic and Social Council resolution 1983/74 and decision 1983/182, both of 29 July 1983,

Considering that the persistent operations of transnational corporations in Namibia in contravention of various United Nations resolutions continue to reinforce the illegal occupation of Namibia by South Africa and to pose a serious threat to the future political and economic independence of Namibia,

Considering also that the role of transnational corporations in the strategic sectors, including the military and nuclear sectors, of the South African economy has persisted in violation of United Nations resolutions,

Considering further that the continued collaboration of transnational corporations with the racist minority régime in South Africa has caused widespread concern in recent years among national and local legislators, non-governmental organizations, trade unions, academic institutions and numerous other groups,

Affirming the need for action at the international level by intergovernmental organizations in order to complement national measures,

1. *Takes note with satisfaction* of the report of the Secretary-General on the activities of transnational corporations and measures being taken by Governments to prohibit investments in South Africa and Namibia and the report of the Secretariat on the responsibilities of home countries with respect to the transnational corporations operating in South Africa and Namibia in violation of the relevant resolutions and decisions of the United Nations, prepared pursuant to Economic and Social Council resolution 1983/74 and decision 1983/182;

2. *Commends* those groups, bodies and institutions that have exerted pressure on transnational corporations to terminate their investments in South Africa and other forms of collaboration with the racist minority régime, and calls upon such organizations to intensify their efforts in those areas;

3. *Welcomes* as a positive step the policies of Governments directed towards bringing to an end the activities of their transnational corporations in southern Africa;

4. *Condemns* the racist minority régime in South Africa for its perpetuation of the inhuman system of *apartheid* and the illegal occupation of Namibia;

5. *Condemns* those transnational corporations which collaborate with the racist minority régime in South Africa, and calls upon all transnational corporations to respect the various United Nations resolutions concerning southern Africa;

6. *Calls upon* all home countries of transnational corporations to take effective measures to terminate the collaboration of their transnational corporations with the racist minority régime in South Africa, to prevent further new investments and reinvestments and to bring about an immediate withdrawal of all existing investments in South Africa and Namibia;

7. *Calls upon* all countries concerned to re-examine their relations with the transnational corporations operating in their territories which collaborate with the racist minority régime in South Africa;

8. *Calls upon* all anti-*apartheid* movements, religious institutions and bodies, trade unions, universities and other institutions which are shareholders of transnational corporations operating in South Africa and Namibia to contribute to the efforts of the international community to eradicate *apartheid* by withdrawing their shareholdings in such transnational corporations;

9. *Urges* all transnational corporations to comply fully with the relevant United Nations resolutions by terminating all further investments in South Africa and Namibia and by ending their collaboration with the racist minority régime;

10. *Further calls upon* all States Members of the United Nations and all transnational corporations operating in South Africa and Namibia to co-operate with the Secretary-General and the Commission on Transnational Corporations in organizing public hearings on the activities of transnational corporations in South Africa and Namibia;

11. *Reaffirms* Security Council resolution 301(1971) of 20 October 1971, in which the Council called upon States to abstain from entering into economic relations with South Africa in respect of Namibia and declared that rights, titles or contracts granted to individuals or corporations by South Africa after the termination of the mandate were not subject to protection or espousal by their States against the claims of a future lawful Government of Namibia;

12. *Reaffirms* that the code of conduct on transnational corporations should include effective measures against the collaboration of transnational corporations with the racist minority régime in southern Africa;

13. *Requests* the Secretary-General:

(a) To intensify the useful work of the Secretariat in the collection and dissemination of information on the activities of all transnational corporations in southern Africa;

(b) To make arrangements for the organization of public hearings, to be conducted by the Commission on Transnational Corporations, with the assistance of the United Nations Centre on Transnational Corporations, on the activities of transnational corporations in South Africa and Namibia, in accordance with the modalities and procedures to be prescribed by the Commission at its eleventh session;

(c) To report to the Commission at its eleventh session on the measures taken in pursuance of the present resolution;

(d) To prepare an updated report on the activities of transnational corporations in South Africa and Namibia, including an annex containing a list of all transnational corporations operating in South Africa and Namibia, to be submitted to the Commission at its eleventh session;

(e) To bring up to date for the eleventh session of the Commission the report of the Secretariat on the responsibilities of home countries with respect to the transnational corporations operating in South Africa and Namibia in violation of the relevant resolutions and decisions of the United Nations.

Economic and Social Council resolution 1984/53

25 July 1984   Meeting 48   26-3-11 (roll-call vote)

Approved by First Committee (E/1984/141) by roll-call vote (17-3-11), 17 July (meeting 10); draft by Commission on TNCs (E/1984/18); agenda item 10.

Roll-call vote in Council as follows:

In favour: Algeria, Argentina, Benin, Brazil, Bulgaria, China, Congo, Djibouti, German Democratic Republic, Guyana, Indonesia, Malaysia, Pakistan, Papua New Guinea, Poland, Qatar, Romania, Rwanda, Saint Lucia, Saudi Arabia, Somalia, Tunisia, Uganda, USSR, Yugoslavia, Zaire.
Against: Germany, Federal Republic of, United Kingdom, United States.
Abstaining: Austria, Canada, Finland, France, Greece, Japan, Luxembourg, Netherlands, New Zealand, Portugal, Sweden.

In explanation of vote, Canada said it could not support a text that gave the impression that the mere presence of TNCs in South Africa constituted collaboration with a racist régime, and because the text implied a certain extraterritorial application of law in Africa to the subsidiaries of external countries; furthermore, it felt that paragraph 13 *(e)* was too specific and believed that TNC activities could have a beneficial effect on peaceful development in South Africa.

Poland, speaking also on behalf of Bulgaria, the Byelorussian SSR, Czechoslovakia, the German Democratic Republic, Hungary, Mongolia, the Ukrainian SSR and the USSR, said the Western Powers' support to the South African régime encouraged its aggressive attitude and strengthened it as a bastion of colonialism on the African continent; the harm done to the South African majority through TNC activities, amounting to billions of dollars, should be compensated by South Africa and its supporters.

Resolution 1984/52, concerning further preparations for public hearings on TNC activities to be held by the Commission in 1985, was also adopted by roll-call vote.

Organization of public hearings on the activities of transnational corporations in South Africa and Namibia

The Economic and Social Council,

Recalling its resolutions on the activities of transnational corporations in southern Africa, in particular resolution 1981/86 of 2 November 1981, in which it called for the organization of public hearings on the activities of transnational corporations in South Africa and Namibia, and its resolution 1983/75 of 29 July 1983,

1. *Decides* that the *Ad Hoc* Committee on the Preparations for the Public Hearings on the Activities of Transnational Corporations in South Africa and Namibia shall commence its work no later than 1 August 1984, and requests it to report on the modalities and subjects of the hearings to the Commission on Transnational Corporations at its eleventh session;

2. *Calls upon* the regional groups that have not yet done so to nominate their representatives to the *Ad Hoc* Committee.

Economic and Social Council resolution 1984/52

25 July 1984   Meeting 48   23-0-14 (roll-call vote)

Approved by First Committee (E/1984/141) by roll-call vote (13-0-15), 17 July (meeting 10); draft by Commission on TNCs (E/1984/18); agenda item 10.

Roll-call vote in Council as follows:

In favour: Algeria, Benin, Brazil, Bulgaria, China, Congo, Djibouti, German Democratic Republic, Guyana, Indonesia, Malaysia, Pakistan, Poland, Qatar, Romania, Rwanda, Saint Lucia, Saudi Arabia, Tunisia, Uganda, USSR, Yugoslavia, Zaire.
Against: None.
Abstaining: Austria, Canada, Finland, France, Germany, Federal Republic of, Greece, Japan, Luxembourg, Netherlands, New Zealand, Portugal, Sweden, United Kingdom, United States.

The *Ad Hoc* Committee on the Preparations for the Public Hearings on the Activities of TNCs in South Africa and Namibia held its first two meetings in New York on 31 July,[48] at which it elected a Chairman and adopted an agenda. The Committee requested the United Nations Centre on TNCs to draft guidelines on the organization of the hearings and rules of procedure to be used in conducting them. It also requested the Centre to submit a list of persons and institutions to be invited. In response, the Centre drew up suggestions for guidelines relating to the objectives and purpose of the hearings, the topics to be addressed and organizational questions.[49] The Committee met again on 25 September and requested revisions to the draft guidelines.

GENERAL ASSEMBLY ACTION

The General Assembly, in resolution 39/72 A, condemned the policies of certain Western States and Israel and of their TNCs that had increased collaboration with South Africa despite repeated appeals by the Assembly. It took similar action in resolution 39/42, condemning those States and TNCs which continued their investments in, and supply of armaments and oil and nuclear technology to, South Africa, thus buttressing it and aggravating the threat to world peace. The Secretary-General was requested to undertake a campaign to inform world public opinion of the facts concerning the pillaging of natural resources in colonial Territories and the exploitation of their indigenous populations by foreign monopolies and, in respect of Namibia, the support they rendered to South Africa.

In resolution 39/15, the Assembly invited the Special Rapporteur of the Sub-Commission on discrimination and minorities to update the list of TNCs, banks and other organizations assisting South Africa, and called on the Governments of countries where they were based to put a stop to their trading, manufacturing and investing activities in South Africa and Namibia.

IMF relations with South Africa

In 1984, several United Nations bodies reiterated their appeals to United Nations specialized agencies, particularly the International Monetary Fund, to reject South Africa's requests for loans.

The Committee on colonial countries took such action in two decisions. On 20 August,[22] it noted with concern the continued assistance provided to the régime by certain international organizations, as exemplified by the granting of a loan of $1.1 billion in 1982 by IMF.[50] The Committee said that such assistance only served to augment the military capability of the Pretoria régime, thus enabling it to continue its suppression of the oppressed majority in South Africa while subsidizing its illegal occupation of Namibia and, at the same time, encouraging the régime to commit aggression against neighbouring States (see p. 177). The Committee reiterated its call on IMF to terminate co-operation with and assistance to the régime and urged all IMF States members to take appropriate action towards that end. The Committee called on all other international organizations to respect the United Nations position on Namibia and to refrain from any co-operation with South Africa.

On 22 August,[51] the Committee expressed regret that, notwithstanding repeated assurances by the World Bank that it had terminated business relations with South Africa, the Bank and IMF continued to maintain links with South Africa, as exemplified by its membership in both agencies. The Committee condemned the collaboration between IMF and South Africa, in disregard of General Assembly resolutions, particularly the 1982 loan, and called on IMF to rescind the loan, to put an end to such collaboration and not to grant any new loans. It commended those non-governmental organizations which informed public opinion and mobilized it against IMF assistance to South Africa, and called on them to reinforce those efforts.

The Council for Namibia, in its Bangkok Declaration and Programme of Action on Namibia,[17] also noted with concern the continued assistance provided to South Africa by certain specialized agencies and other United Nations organizations, for example the 1982 IMF loan. The Council agreed with the Committee that such assistance only served to allow Pretoria to continue those policies mentioned by the Committee. The Council also called on IMF to terminate co-operation with the régime.

In a resolution of 28 February,[21] the Commission on Human Rights also urgently requested all specialized agencies, particularly IMF and the World Bank, to refrain from granting any type of loans to South Africa.

GENERAL ASSEMBLY ACTION

The General Assembly, in resolution 39/50 A, called on all specialized agencies, in particular IMF, to terminate all collaboration with and assistance to South Africa, since such assistance served to augment its military capability thus enabling it not only to continue its repression in Namibia and South Africa, but also to commit aggression against neighbouring States. The Assembly took similar action in resolution 39/72 A, calling on IMF to terminate credits or other assistance to South Africa.

In resolution 39/43, it regretted that, notwithstanding the assurances of the World Bank that it had terminated business relations with South Africa, the Bank and IMF continued to maintain links with South Africa, as exemplified by its membership in both agencies, which, the Assembly stated, should end all links with the régime. Condemning the collaboration between IMF and South Africa, particularly the 1982 loan, the Assembly called on IMF to rescind the loan, to end such collaboration and not to grant any new loans. It commended those non-governmental organizations which helped inform public opinion and mobilize it against IMF assistance to South Africa, and called for renewed efforts in this respect. The Assembly reiterated its proposal, under the Agreement between the United Nations and IMF, for the inclusion in the agenda of the IMF Board of Governors of an item on the relationship between IMF and South Africa as well as its proposal that the relevant United Nations organs should participate in the Board's meetings at which the item was discussed, and urged IMF to discuss its relationship with South Africa at its annual meeting.

Israel-South Africa relations

On 17 October, the Special Committee against *Apartheid* unanimously adopted a report on recent developments concerning relations between Israel and South Africa,[3] which it submitted to the General Assembly and the Security Council as an addendum to its 1984 annual report,[1] in accordance with a December 1983 request by the Assembly.[52] The Committee stated that despite the denials of Israel, it continued to collaborate with South Africa as well as with the bantustans, resulting in serious consequences for peace and security in southern Africa. The Committee expressed its regret at the unwillingness of certain Western

States to recognize the dangers of the collusion between Israel and South Africa and the encouragement they extended to Israel to continue its defiance of the United Nations. Urging the international community to persuade Israel to disengage from its collaboration, the Committee recommended that the United Nations intensify efforts to publicize this collaboration and take action under the United Nations Charter to end it.

The Committee said there had been increasing awareness of the collaboration between the two countries and their close links with the United States, which provided protection to both of them. Despite the unwillingness of certain Western States to consider the serious developments arising from the relations between Israel and South Africa, public opinion in the West was becoming more aware of, and concerned over, the situation.

The main aspect of their collaboration was in the military and nuclear fields. According to a study cited by the Committee, Israel supplied military technology and strategic advice and equipped the South African armed forces; in addition, it served as a conduit to smuggle arms to South Africa. Israel was also assisting South Africa in providing it with nuclear technology, while South Africa was helping to finance the research and development of Israel's Levi aircraft, expected to begin production in 1990. Both States were reported to have established an inter-ministerial committee to work out a long-term agreement under which Israel would supply South Africa with technology for nuclear armaments.

The South African Trade Mission at Tel Aviv announced that South Africa's exports to Israel had risen by 138 per cent from 1981 to 1982, largely because of the growth in the export of base metals and other mineral products. Imports from Israel remained stable in 1982, but over the previous decade had increased sevenfold. Machinery, electrical equipment and parts had become South Africa's largest category of imports from Israel, accounting for 35 per cent of the total from that country.

As for economic relations, South African investment in Israel reached $15 million a year in both 1982 and 1983. South Africa continued to make direct investments in Israel; in accordance with various agreements between the two countries, South African citizens could invest in certain projects, including industrial projects, tourism and hotels, industrial infrastructural developments, commercial centres and community services, film production and the purchase of shares in existing Israeli companies for the purpose of financing production expansion, construction projects, oil exploration and agricultural projects. Koor Industries, Israel's largest industrial conglomerate, had a number of South African interests. South Africa

and Israel also co-operated in tourism, the scientific field, sports and cultural exchanges.

Despite its denials, Israel was one of the few countries which maintained contacts on all levels with the bantustans, homelands established by South Africa for blacks, the Committee reported. For example, Israel had been involved in agricultural projects and the development of a television service in Bophuthatswana. A delegation led by "Prime Minister" Chief George Matanzima of Transkei visited Israel in March 1984, accompanied by, among others, Ntutuzeli Lujabe, "Minister for Foreign Affairs", and Major-General Martin Ngceba, "Commissioner of the Transkei Civil Defence Force". Chief Matanzima said that, as a result of the visit, many Israeli industrialists had decided to invest large sums of money in the construction of industries in Transkei. Israel continued to collaborate with the bantustans in military and police affairs; for example, it was helping to plan a pilots' school in Bophuthatswana and was assisting in establishing an intelligence network and air force in Ciskei. The "Deputy Defence Minister" of Ciskei said Ciskei was buying "about six" new aircraft, made in the United States, from Israel. The Israeli Ambassador to Pretoria acknowledged that there were a number of Israeli firms operating in the bantustans. Israeli interests in Ciskei were reported to include the construction of two hospitals, aviation contracts to supply aircraft and train pilots, construction of factories, provision of agricultural training and expertise, and supply of computer systems.

GENERAL ASSEMBLY ACTION

On 13 December, the General Assembly adopted resolution 39/72 C by recorded vote.

Relations between Israel and South Africa

The General Assembly,

Reaffirming its resolutions on relations between Israel and South Africa,

Having considered the special report of the Special Committee against *Apartheid* on recent developments concerning relations between Israel and South Africa,

Taking note of the declaration and resolutions of the Conference of Arab Solidarity with the Struggle for Liberation in Southern Africa, held at Tunis from 7 to 9 August 1984,

Reiterating that the increasing collaboration by Israel with the racist régime of South Africa, especially in the military and nuclear fields, in defiance of resolutions of the General Assembly and the Security Council is a serious hindrance to international action for the eradication of *apartheid*, an encouragement to the racist régime of South Africa to persist in its criminal policy of *apartheid* and a hostile act against the oppressed people of South Africa and the entire African continent and constitutes a threat to international peace and security,

1. *Commends* the Special Committee against *Apartheid* for publicizing the growing relations between Israel and South Africa and promoting public awareness

of the grave dangers of the alliance between Israel and South Africa;

2. *Again strongly condemns* the continuing and increasing collaboration of Israel with the racist régime of South Africa, especially in the military and nuclear fields;

3. *Demands* that Israel desist from and terminate all forms of collaboration with South Africa forthwith, particularly in the military and nuclear fields, and abide scrupulously by the relevant resolutions of the General Assembly and the Security Council;

4. *Calls upon* all Governments and organizations to exert their influence to persuade Israel to desist from such collaboration and abide by the resolutions of the General Assembly;

5. *Requests* the Special Committee to continue to publicize, as widely as possible, information on the relations between Israel and South Africa;

6. *Requests* the Secretary-General to render, through the Department of Public Information and the Centre against *Apartheid* of the Secretariat, all possible assistance to the Special Committee in disseminating information relating to the collaboration between Israel and South Africa;

7. *Further requests* the Special Committee to keep the matter under constant review and to report to the General Assembly and the Security Council as appropriate.

General Assembly resolution 39/72 C

13 December 1984   Meeting 99   108-19-25 (recorded vote)

40-nation draft (A/39/L.30 and Add.1); agenda item 31.

Sponsors: Afghanistan, Algeria, Angola, Benin, Burkina Faso, Burundi, Byelorussian SSR, Cape Verde, Cuba, Czechoslovakia, Democratic Yemen, Equatorial Guinea, Gambia, German Democratic Republic, Ghana, Guinea, Hungary, India, Iran, Iraq, Kenya, Lao People's Democratic Republic, Libyan Arab Jamahiriya, Madagascar, Malaysia, Mauritania, Mongolia, Morocco, Mozambique, Nigeria, Qatar, Sao Tome and Principe, Sierra Leone, Syrian Arab Republic, Tunisia, Uganda, Ukrainian SSR, United Republic of Tanzania, Viet Nam, Zimbabwe.

Financial implications. 5th Committee, A/39/787; S-G, A/C.5/39/75.

Meeting numbers. GA 39th session: 5th Committee 45; plenary 13, 66-71, 98, 99.

Recorded vote in Assembly as follows:

In favour: Afghanistan, Albania, Algeria, Angola, Argentina, Bahamas, Bahrain, Bangladesh, Benin, Bhutan, Bolivia, Botswana, Brazil, Brunei Darussalam, Bulgaria, Burkina Faso, Burma, Burundi, Byelorussian SSR, Cameroon, Cape Verde, Central African Republic, Chad, China, Comoros, Congo, Cuba, Cyprus, Czechoslovakia, Democratic Kampuchea, Democratic Yemen, Djibouti, Ecuador, Egypt, Equatorial Guinea, Ethiopia, Gabon, Gambia, German Democratic Republic, Ghana, Greece, Guinea, Guinea-Bissau, Guyana, Hungary, India, Indonesia, Iran, Iraq, Jordan, Kenya, Kuwait, Lao People's Democratic Republic, Lebanon, Lesotho, Libyan Arab Jamahiriya, Madagascar, Malaysia, Maldives, Mali, Malta, Mauritania, Mauritius, Mexico, Mongolia, Morocco, Mozambique, Nepal, Nicaragua, Niger, Nigeria, Oman, Pakistan, Papua New Guinea, Peru, Philippines, Poland, Qatar, Romania, Rwanda, Sao Tome and Principe, Saudi Arabia, Senegal, Seychelles, Sierra Leone, Singapore, Solomon Islands, Somalia, Sri Lanka, Sudan, Suriname, Syrian Arab Republic, Thailand, Togo, Tunisia, Turkey, Uganda, Ukrainian SSR, USSR, United Arab Emirates, United Republic of Tanzania, Vanuatu, Venezuela, Viet Nam, Yemen, Yugoslavia, Zambia, Zimbabwe.

Against: Australia, Austria, Belgium, Canada, Denmark, Finland, France, Germany, Federal Republic of, Iceland, Ireland, Israel, Italy, Luxembourg, Netherlands, New Zealand, Norway, Sweden, United Kingdom, United States.

Abstaining: Barbados, Belize, Colombia, Costa Rica, Dominica, Dominican Republic, El Salvador, Fiji, Grenada, Guatemala, Haiti, Honduras, Ivory Coast, Jamaica, Japan, Liberia, Malawi, Panama, Portugal, Saint Christopher and Nevis, Saint Lucia, Saint Vincent and the Grenadines, Samoa, Spain, Uruguay.

At the request of the United States, the Assembly took a separate vote on a preambular paragraph of the draft, by which the Assembly would have expressed grave concern over the policy of the United States which, by its strategic co-operation with Israel and its "constructive engagement" with South Africa, had strengthened the Israel–South

Africa alliance. The paragraph was rejected when it failed, in a recorded vote of 65 to 55, with 17 abstentions, to obtain the necessary two-thirds majority (see p. 131).

In explanation of vote, Israel, affirming that it unequivocally rejected racism, said that the resolution's sponsors had put forward unsubstantiated allegations based on speculative press reports and previous one-sided resolutions, seeking to divert attention from the real problems of *apartheid* and thus undermining the purpose of the debate and subverting the genuine concern for the victims of racial prejudice; a single and impartial standard should be set and applied with regard to the struggle against racism in all its manifestations. Israel had again been singled out as the only country for condemnation based on patent falsehoods.

A number of countries objected to the arbitrary or selective singling out of a Member State. Australia, Austria, Bermuda, Burma, Finland, for the five Nordic countries, Ireland, Malawi, Panama, Peru and the United Kingdom made such comments. Finland said such action made it difficult to maintain the international consensus in the struggle against *apartheid*. In the view of the Bahamas, the lack of balance in the text was not constructive in obtaining its goals. Australia found the language extravagant. Ecuador said it was inappropriate and would have preferred an attempt to bring about an understanding rather than heightening tensions.

The Assembly also took action on Israel–South Africa relations in other resolutions. By resolution 39/17, the Assembly denounced the collusion between them and expressed support for the 1983 Declaration of the International Conference on the Alliance between South Africa and Israel.[53] In resolution 39/146 A on the Middle East situation, it condemned their continuing and increasing collaboration, especially in the economic, military and nuclear fields.

Situation in South Africa

Activities of the Committee against *Apartheid*. The Special Committee against *Apartheid*,[1] describing the current political situation in South Africa, drew particular attention to and condemned the so-called constitutional reforms in that country (see p. 157). The Committee said South Africa had accelerated implementation of the policy of bantustanization, its process of confining black people's homes to certain areas, allegedly on a tribal basis. As part of that process, it applied even more stringently the "pass laws", which regulated the movement of blacks in South Africa, and intensified forced population removals. Africans arrested for offences under the pass laws in

1984 numbered 163,000, approximately 21,000 more than in 1983. According to official 1984 figures, 22,936 Africans were forcibly removed, mostly to "homelands". There was a marked acceleration in forced removals after the referendum on the "new constitution" in November 1983. From 1960 to 1982, over 3.5 million people were removed forcibly, and about 1.7 million others were scheduled for removal. In December, South Africa stated its intention to declare Kwa Ndebele "independent". It was to be the fifth homeland to achieve that status from among 10 homelands. No State had recognized any of those entities. In South Africa's terminology, Bophuthatswana, Ciskei, Kwa Ndebele, Transkei and Venda were "independent states" while Lebowa, Gazankulu, Ka Ngwane, Qwa Qwa and Kwa Zulu were "national states".

On 7 July during an audience at the Vatican,[54] Pope John Paul II addressed a message to the Chairman of the Committee against *Apartheid*, stating that the local Catholic Church had expressed its protest at the displacement of vast numbers of South African citizens to the places of residence assigned to them by the Government and that a joint ecumenical initiative had been taken by the Southern Africa Catholic Bishops' Conference and the South African Council of Churches to draw the public's attention to that situation. The message was transmitted by a letter of 9 July from the Chairman to the Secretary-General. In South Africa, Archbishop Denis Hurley, Bishop Desmond Tutu and Allan Boesak, President of the World Alliance of Reformed Churches, were among church leaders who spoke out against the removals.

According to studies presented at the Second Carnegie Inquiry into Poverty and Development in South Africa (April 1984), one third of African children under 14 years of age were underweight and stunted, their death rate from malnutrition was 31 times higher than that for white children, and the magnitude of poverty and hunger in bantustans and African townships was appalling.

The situation of black workers, who were paid much less than white workers, deteriorated, and legislative and other measures further repressed them and their trade unions. Retrenchments, dismissals, higher rail fares and higher bread prices adversely affected mostly black workers. Their living standards declined by 4.1 per cent from 1982 to 1983, according to a labour economist at the University of Cape Town. The Labour Relations Amendment Act, passed in June 1984 to impose further controls over industrial relations and labour agreements between trade unions and management, required that all collective bargaining agreements, to be enforceable, be submitted to the Department of Manpower. The Aliens and Immigration Law Amendment Bill, introduced in

March, was intended to control the influx of black workers and impose penalties on companies which employed aliens, which included the 9 million Africans who lost their citizenship when their homelands were declared independent. Black workers on strike were harassed, intimidated, detained or tried; nevertheless they continued to strengthen their unions. According to official figures for 1984, 426 strikes occurred involving African workers. These actions were mainly concerned with wage demands, working conditions, disciplinary measures and other trade union matters. Some 167,948 African, 4,697 coloured, 1,713 Asian and 6 white workers were involved in strikes, particularly in the mining, metal and automobile industries.

The armed and underground struggle against *apartheid* continued and freedom fighters took actions against military, economic and other institutions. Among the targets attacked were petrol tanks, railway tankers and lines, a police warehouse, government offices, electricity plants, offices of homelands, a bank and a gold mine. ANC claimed responsibility for most of the attacks.

In protest against the unequal education policy and other practices, black students in substantial numbers boycotted their classes. Church opposition to *apartheid* also grew as religious leaders, inside and outside South Africa, opposed the forced removals of blacks.

Action by the Commission on Human Rights and its subsidiary bodies. Among the actions it took on 28 February 1984 on human rights violations in South Africa and Namibia, the Commission on Human Rights expressed its abhorrence of the system of *apartheid* and indignation at the forced population removals and the alarming increase in the number of prosecutions under the homelands policy laws.[55] The Commission condemned South Africa for its military attacks and economic and political pressures against neighbouring States, the activities of TNCs and other foreign economic interests operating in South Africa and Namibia, and the increased assistance to South Africa by the major Western countries and Israel. It urged States to accede to the 1973 International Convention on the Suppression and Punishment of the Crime of *Apartheid*.[44]

The Group of Three established under that Convention dealt with, among other things, the question of TNCs operating in South Africa within the context of the crime of *apartheid*.

The Commission's *Ad Hoc* Working Group of Experts on southern Africa reported on a wide variety of aspects of the situation in South Africa.

The Sub-Commission on Prevention of Discrimination and Protection of Minorities on 30 August[56] reaffirmed that *apartheid* was an international crime and that the *apartheid* régime was both illegitimate and contrary to the 1948 Univer-

sal Declaration of Human Rights.[57] It repudiated South Africa's efforts to entrench white rule
through such means as the so-called new constitution and elections held in August, and condemned the mass arrests of political activists, workers and students that preceded and followed those
elections.

(For further details, see ECONOMIC AND SOCIAL
QUESTIONS, Chapter XVIII, under "South Africa
and Namibia".)

GENERAL ASSEMBLY ACTION

The General Assembly, in resolution 39/19, also
expressed appreciation of the role of the Group of
Three in analysing the periodic reports of States
and in publicizing the experience gained in the international struggle against *apartheid.*

In resolution 39/72 A, it condemned South
Africa for its continued oppression, repression and
violence, including the recent use of the armed
forces against the black people, its "bantustanization" policy, the "new constitution" designed to
dispossess the African majority, and the forced
removals of black people. It again declared that
only the total eradication of *apartheid* and the establishment of a non-racial democratic society
based on majority rule could lead to a just solution in South Africa. The Assembly proclaimed
that the United Nations and the international
community had a special responsibility towards the
oppressed people, their liberation movements and
those engaged in the struggle to eliminate *apartheid.* It declared that the situation in South Africa
constituted a grave threat to international peace
and security and that the régime was guilty of aggression, breaches of the peace and violations of
the United Nations Charter. It expressed support
for the movement against conscription into the
South African armed forces.

The Assembly, in resolution 39/2, rejected the
new constitution and reiterated that only the eradication of *apartheid* and the establishment of a democratic society could lead to a just and lasting solution of the South Africa situation.

The Assembly took related action in resolution
39/17, condemning bantustanization and reiterating support for the oppressed people of South
Africa in its just and legitimate struggle against
the régime.

SECURITY COUNCIL ACTION

In resolution 556(1984) of 23 October, by which
it condemned the massacres of the oppressed people and expressed concern over the treatment of
demonstrators, the Security Council demanded:
the dismantling of the bantustan structures and
the cessation of the relocation of the indigenous
African people; the abrogation of the bans and re-
strictions·on political organizations, individuals

and news media opposed to *apartheid;* and the
unimpeded return of exiles.

Political prisoners and other detained persons

Activities of the Committee against *Apartheid.*
The Special Committee against *Apartheid* continued
to pay attention to the repression of opponents of
apartheid and to the campaign for the release of political prisoners. In its 1984 report,[1] the Committee
said it had intensified its promotion of the campaign for the release of Nelson Mandela and all
other political prisoners in South Africa, and for
an end to all repression against the opponents of
apartheid. At a meeting on 12 June, the Chairman
of the Committee remarked that it had been 20 years
since Mr. Mandela and other leaders were sentenced
to life imprisonment for their opposition to *apartheid.*

On 24 February, the Committee learned of the
sentencing of Albertina Sisulu, former executive
member of the banned Federation of South African Women and one of the three presidents of the
United Democratic Front, to four years in prison
for singing freedom songs and supporting ANC at
funerals of ANC members and trade union activists in April and June 1983. Mrs. Sisulu, 66
years old, was the wife of an imprisoned ANC
leader and the mother of five children. She had
been banned for over 18 years and detained and
imprisoned several times. Three other members
of the Sisulu family were detained in August. The
Chairman denounced, in a statement of 29 February, the sentencing of Mrs. Sisulu. He said that
the sentence was passed at a time when the international community was observing the Year of the
Women of South Africa. The Committee noted
that six members of PAC were the longest-serving
political prisoners on Robben Island and the
Chairman called for their release.

During the preceding year, the Committee said,
South Africa intensified repression as opposition
to its policies mounted, particularly in protest of
the "new constitution". It arrested, detained, tortured, tried or banned opponents of *apartheid,* including freedom fighters, trade union leaders,
church and community activists, students and
journalists. It imposed more restrictions on legal
organizations and those active in them. Police
banned meetings, raided offices of black organizations, confiscated documents and attacked students during protest meetings and demonstrations.
According to official reports, 339 persons were detained in 1984 under the Internal Security Act. A
South African press report said that, as of 15
February, there were 336 Africans, 5 coloureds and
2 Asians serving sentences for crimes against the
security of the State. In March, for similar crimes,
36 Namibians were serving sentences in South
African prisons.

Among those arrested were leading members of the United Democratic Front and the Natal Indian Congress because of their opposition to the new constitution. Also arrested were most of the executive board of the Alexandra Youth Congress and the Alexandra Commuters' Committee, about 11 persons, as well as the General Secretary of the Food and Beverage Workers' Union. In Ciskei, police detained the Reverend Smangaliso Mkhatshwa, Secretary-General of the Southern Africa Catholic Bishops' Conference. In February, 20 African schoolchildren were arrested in the Atteridgeville township after clashes between police and students, which resulted in the death of a teenager. There were at least four deaths in prison under unclear circumstances. As disclosed in Parliament on 24 February, there had been complaints of assault from detainees held under the Internal Security Act.

On 1 February, 12 persons were under banning orders. In July, there were 134 listed persons who could not be quoted. For external propaganda reasons, the régime had shifted its policy from banning people to banning meetings.

The Committee reported that several persons were convicted of high treason over the year, and in some cases the court equated ANC membership with treason. Others received heavy sentences for possessing banned literature. Those who refused to testify for the State also received jail sentences. Many others were tried for alleged public violence, intimidation and holding illegal meetings, or for having quoted banned persons.

The Chairman of the Committee, in a letter of 20 September to the President of the Security Council,[58] said the Committee was anxious about the safety of six South African leaders who had sought refuge in the British Consulate in Durban—Archie Gumede, M. J. Naidoo, George Sewpershad, Mewa Ramgobin, Billy Nair and Paul Joseph—all leaders of the United Democratic Front and the Natal Indian Congress, and five of whom had been detained for opposing the new constitution; the Committee said the international community had an obligation to protect the six and all other opponents of *apartheid*.

On 19 November, the Chairman issued an appeal to Governments and organizations to condemn the wave of killings and repression by the South African authorities. He said the authorities had deployed military forces against African townships. Official reports said that at least 165 people, mostly blacks, had been killed, hundreds wounded and thousands arrested.

Action by the Council for Namibia. The Council for Namibia, in its Bangkok Declaration and Programme of Action,[17] reaffirmed that the liberation struggle in Namibia was a conflict of international character in terms of Additional Protocol I of 1977 to the 1949 Geneva Conventions,[59] and therefore demanded that South Africa apply those Conventions. In particular, it demanded that all captured freedom fighters, pending their release, be accorded prisoner-of-war status as called for by the Geneva Convention relative to the Treatment of Prisoners of War and Additional Protocol thereto. Furthermore, it demanded the immediate and unconditional release of all Namibian political prisoners held in South Africa and Namibia.

Action by the Commission on Human Rights and its subsidiary bodies. The Commission on Human Rights, on 28 February,[55] expressed indignation at the scale and variety of human rights violations in South Africa and the homelands (for further details, see ECONOMIC AND SOCIAL QUESTIONS, Chapter XVIII), in particular the increase in the number of sentences passed and executions which had taken place, the torture of political activists during interrogation, the ill-treatment of captured freedom fighters and other detainees, and the deaths of detainees in prisons under suspicious circumstances. The Commission called for the release of all political prisoners, especially those who had been incarcerated for long terms, including life imprisonment. It renewed its request to South Africa to allow the *Ad Hoc* Working Group of Experts on southern Africa to make on-the-spot investigations of prison conditions and the treatment of prisoners. On the same date,[60] the Commission, reiterating that request, expressed indignation at South Africa's ill-treatment of Namibian detainees and captured freedom fighters.

The Sub-Commission on Prevention of Discrimination and Protection of Minorities, on 30 August,[56] condemned the mass arrests of political activists, workers and students occurring around the time of the elections for segregated houses of South Africa's Parliament. It demanded the immediate release of all political prisoners, including all persons subjected to banning, house arrest and banishment, and of those arrested for opposition to the elections.

Communication. In a letter of 24 August to the Secretary-General,[61] India forwarded a statement issued on 22 August on behalf of the Movement of Non-Aligned Countries, deploring the recent raids and arrests in South Africa which it linked to the protest against the elections in South Africa scheduled for 22 and 28 August to establish segregated chambers for coloured people and people of Asian origin; India said the raids and arrests of a number of leaders of the non-white communities were intended to intimidate the local population into submission and passivity, and it called on the people of South Africa to oppose the elections.

SECURITY COUNCIL ACTION

The Security Council, in resolution 556(1984) adopted in October at the time of many demonstrations against the legislative system under the new constitution (see p. 157), demanded the unconditional release of all political prisoners and detainees, and condemned the arbitrary arrest and detention of leaders and activists of mass organizations.

GENERAL ASSEMBLY ACTION

The General Assembly also took action in regard to political prisoners and detainees.

In resolution 39/72 A, it reaffirmed that freedom fighters of South Africa should be treated as prisoners of war in accordance with Additional Protocol I to the 1949 Geneva Conventions.[59] The Assembly, in resolution 39/72 G, condemned the recent killings, arbitrary arrests and detention of members of mass organizations for opposing the *apartheid* system and the new constitution. It demanded that the South African authorities release without conditions Nelson Mandela and all other political prisoners, detainees and restrictees. By resolution 39/2, it condemned the continued massacre of the oppressed people, as well as the arbitrary arrest and detention of leaders and activists of mass organizations and demanded their immediate and unconditional release. Resolution 39/17 also included the Assembly's condemnation of the arbitrary arrests of the leaders and activists of mass organizations.

In resolution 39/50 A on Namibia, the Assembly demanded that South Africa immediately release all Namibian political prisoners, including all those imprisoned or detained under the internal security laws, martial law or other arbitrary measures, whether such Namibians had been charged or tried or were being held without charge in Namibia or South Africa. It demanded that South Africa account for all "disappeared" Namibians and release any who were still alive. It declared that South Africa would be liable to compensate the victims, their families and the future lawful Government of an independent Namibia for the losses. The Assembly declared that the liberation struggle in Namibia was a conflict of an international character in terms of Additional Protocol I to the 1949 Geneva Conventions and, in that regard, demanded that the Conventions and Protocol be applied by South Africa, in particular that all captured freedom fighters be accorded prisoner-of-war status.

In resolution 39/17, the Assembly demanded the immediate and unconditional release of all persons detained or imprisoned as a result of their struggle for self-determination and independence, full respect for their fundamental individual rights and compliance with article 5 of the Universal Declaration of Human Rights,[57] under which no one was to be subjected to torture or to cruel, inhuman or degrading treatment.

Sentencing of an ANC member

By a letter of 10 January 1984,[62] Togo, as Chairman of the African Group, requested the President of the Security Council to convene an urgent meeting to consider the question of the death sentence passed by the Supreme Court of South Africa against Malesela Benjamin Maloise, a member of the African National Congress of South Africa. South Africa, referring to that request in a letter to the Secretary-General of 11 January,[63] said it constituted unwarranted interference in South Africa's domestic affairs. It added that the facts of the case, which it outlined, related to the common law crime of murder, and pointed out that the death sentence could not be carried out without the authority of the Minister of Justice.

SECURITY COUNCIL ACTION

The Council met to consider the request on 13 January and unanimously adopted resolution 547(1984).

The Security Council,
Having considered the question of the death sentence passed on 6 June 1983 in South Africa on Mr. Malesela Benjamin Maloise,
Recalling its resolutions 503(1982), 525(1982) and 533(1983),
Gravely concerned over the current decision of the South African authorities to reject an appeal against the death sentence imposed upon Mr. Maloise,
Conscious that carrying out the death sentence will further aggravate the situation in South Africa,
1. *Calls upon* the South African authorities to commute the death sentence imposed upon Mr. Maloise;
2. *Urges* all States and organizations to use their influence and to take urgent measures, in accordance with the Charter of the United Nations, the resolutions of the Security Council and relevant international instruments, to save the life of Mr. Malesela Benjamin Maloise.

Security Council resolution 547(1984)
13 January 1984   Meeting 2512   Adopted unanimously
Draft prepared in consultations among Council members (S/16275).

Following the death sentence imposed on Mr. Maloise and the Security Council action, organizations and individuals throughout the world demonstrated their solidarity with political prisoners. In London, a vigil was held outside the South African Embassy to mark the fifth anniversary of the death of Solomon Mahlangu, a freedom fighter, and to campaign for clemency for Mr. Maloise. Also, Southern Africa—The Imprisoned Society and Amnesty International appealed for clemency for him.[1]

Communications. Several communications were sent to the Secretary-General concerning the death sentence. On 21 January,[64] Brazil said that, in accordance with the recommendations of resolution 547(1984), it had informed South Africa through diplomatic channels of its support for the appeal of the international community for the commutation of the death sentence imposed on Mr. Maloise. The Lao People's Democratic Republic, on 25 January,[65] forwarded a message of the same date from its Vice-President of the Council of Ministers and Minister for Foreign Affairs, stating that the arrogant attitude of South Africa towards the United Nations and the international community was again demonstrated by the death sentence and the decision of the South African judicial authorities to reject an appeal against that judgement; the effective way to deal with that attitude was to apply comprehensive and mandatory sanctions against South Africa. In regard to the Council's recommendation that States use their influence to save Mr. Maloise's life, Thailand, on 25 January,[66] forwarded a message of the same date from its Foreign Minister, stating that Thailand was constrained in its action since it had no diplomatic relations with South Africa.

South African "constitution"

In 1984, both the Security Council and the General Assembly adopted resolutions dealing with South Africa's "new constitution" and the demonstrations which followed protesting the legislative system set up under it. In August (resolution 554(1984)), the Council declared the constitution null and void. In September, the Assembly (resolution 39/2) also rejected it and condemned the continued massacre of the oppressed people of South Africa, as well as the arbitrary arrest and detention of leaders and activists of mass organizations. That condemnation was echoed by the Council in October (resolution 556(1984)).

Activities of the Committee against *Apartheid*. In 1984, the Special Committee against *Apartheid* repeatedly condemned the constitutional "reforms" in South Africa which it said were designed to perpetuate the *apartheid* régime and destroy the unity of the people.[1] In various statements, the Chairman rejected the "new constitution" of South Africa, adopted in September 1983,[67] as another step to dispossess the African majority, to divide the oppressed people and to consolidate racist domination. He pointed out that in South Africa the overwhelming majority of "coloured" people (South Africa's term for those of mixed race) and people of Asian origin had boycotted the fraudulent elections, held in August 1984, to the racially segregated chambers of Parliament. In a statement of 28 August, the Chairman commended the coloured and Indian communities for their boycott.

Under the constitution, the black majority was still excluded from Parliament. The three chambers of Parliament—for whites, for coloureds and for Asians—had 178, 85 and 45 members, respectively. Whites would dominate owing to their numbers and to the legislative powers of their parliamentary body. According to the Committee, the constitution entrenched white domination, attempted to divide the black people, gave illusory power to coloureds and Asians, and created a potentially dictatorial (white) executive by entrenching one-party domination and conferring extraordinary powers on the President.

Black people showed their opposition by peaceful demonstrations in August and September, which were met with violence by the authorities. Scores of people were shot dead and hundreds injured, including children. Hundreds were detained, including leaders of opposition groups. Six leaders of the United Democratic Front and the Natal Indian Congress sought refuge in the British Consulate in Durban on 13 September (see p. 155).

The Committee regretted that the United States had described the plan as a step in the right direction. It noted the courageous resistance by the black people against the new constitution and the overwhelming election boycott by the coloureds and Asians, thus demonstrating their unity in the struggle for a non-racial democratic society.

Citing the Security Council's August resolution (554(1984)) rejecting the constitution (see p. 160), the Committee stated that any régime established thereby was without legitimacy. It added that no Government could maintain normal relations with such a régime and no international organization could regard it as representing a member State; the régime should be expelled forthwith from the United Nations and its agencies. The Committee recommended that the Assembly call on all States and organizations to act in accordance with the Council's resolution and refrain from action implying the legitimacy of the racist régime. It also recommended that the Assembly call on specialized agencies and other associated institutions to take note of resolution 554(1984) and refrain from any relations with the régime. In that regard, it recommended that IMF, the World Bank and IAEA, as well as other international organizations and institutions, be urged to take urgent action.

SECURITY COUNCIL ACTION (August)

On 8 August,[68] Algeria, on behalf of the Group of African States, requested the President of the Council to convene an urgent meeting to consider the so-called constitutional reforms in South Africa.

At four meetings held on 16 and 17 August, Afghanistan, Algeria, Argentina, Benin, the Congo, Cuba, Czechoslovakia, Guyana, Indonesia, Kenya, Kuwait, Mongolia, Nigeria, Qatar, South Africa, Sri Lanka, the Syrian Arab Republic, Thailand, Togo, Trinidad and Tobago, and Yugoslavia were invited, at their request, to participate in the Council's discussion without the right to vote. Certain individuals were also invited to participate, under rule 39[a] of the Council's provisional rules of procedure.

On 15 August,[69] Burkina Faso, Egypt and Zimbabwe asked that Mfanafuthi J. Makatini, the ANC representative to the United Nations, be invited, and, by a separate letter of that date,[70] that Ahmed Gora Ebrahim, chief representative of PAC, also be heard. Those three States made a similar request on 17 August[71] for Lesaoana Makhanda, representative of PAC. At their request, the Acting Chairman of the Special Committee against *Apartheid* and the Chairman of the Committee on colonial countries were also invited to speak.

Addressing the Council, South Africa said the debate concerned its internal constitutional arrangements and thus should not be a subject for the Council to consider. According to South Africa, a substantial percentage of its black peoples had, years earlier, opted for political independence, and four independent black States had been created, whether or not the world chose to recognize them. The time had come to include the coloured and Asian peoples in the decision-making process in a meaningful way. Their case needed to be approached differently, owing to the different historical and cultural circumstances. Designed to do away with confrontational politics, the new constitutional system would emphasize consensus. Whatever actions the Council took, they would be irrelevant and South Africa rejected them.

During the debate, most speakers described South Africa's constitutional changes as manœuvres or ploys to camouflage its true intent of maintaining the whites' domination of the Government. Algeria, speaking for the African Group, China, Czechoslovakia, India, Indonesia, Kuwait, Malta, Mongolia, Nicaragua, Nigeria, Pakistan, Qatar, the Syrian Arab Republic, the Ukrainian SSR, Yugoslavia and Zimbabwe made such statements. For example, Indonesia said the changes proposed by Pretoria represented nothing more than a refinement of bantustanization dressed up in quasi-legal form, which would lead to increased strife and division within South Africa and the region. According to Malta, the new constitution would establish separate chambers for some groups, thus extending the franchise based on racially separate roles to two minority groups (coloureds and Asians), while ensuring the whites'

governmental control and excluding the indigenous African population, or 72 per cent of the population, on the grounds that a different constitutional path had been provided for them within the homeland system. Yugoslavia said that the constitutional plan, based on the *apartheid* system and bantustanization, was an attempt to give an illusion of change, but was aimed at prolonging and consolidating oppression and exploitation of the black population, which was deprived of its basic rights.

Algeria, for the African Group, Benin, the Congo, Cuba, Egypt and India believed that South Africa's plan was part of its propaganda campaign to gain international acceptance and to reverse the trend to isolate it politically. Benin said that campaign was launched to pass off the constitutional proposals as reforms, and it was up to the Council to reject the sham, which merely institutionalized *apartheid*, and to impress on South Africa that only the eradication of *apartheid* and the establishment of a democratic society could lead to a lasting solution. In Cuba's view, the new constitution, the United States support for Pretoria, the South African Prime Minister's tour of Western Europe (see p. 135), and the efforts of the Western press to depict the changes as true reform were all components of the campaign to make Pretoria's policies palatable to the public opinion of Europe and the United States. India said the elections were a façade intended to mislead world public opinion, with the objective of diluting opposition to *apartheid* abroad and reducing the pressure for political isolation and economic disinvestment.

Many countries—Argentina, Benin, China, Czechoslovakia, India, Malta, Nicaragua, Nigeria, Pakistan, Peru, Qatar, Togo, Trinidad and Tobago, and the Ukrainian SSR—said the real aim of the constitutional changes was to entrench *apartheid* or racism. Peru, for example, said the so-called reforms had been designed to perfect the racist apparatus in its illegality.

Argentina, Benin, Burkina Faso, China, Czechoslovakia, Kuwait, Mongolia, Nicaragua, Pakistan, the Syrian Arab Republic, Thailand, Trinidad and Tobago, the Ukrainian SSR, the USSR and Zimbabwe said the South African plan was intended to divide the unity of the oppressed people. The intent, Pakistan said, was to drive a wedge between the different races of South Africa which had presented a united front against *apartheid*, and to end South Africa's ostracization by the international community, but such deceptive reforms would not weaken the anti-*apartheid* movement.

---

[a]Rule 39 of the Council's provisional rules of procedure states: "The Security Council may invite members of the Secretariat or other persons, whom it considers competent for the purpose, to supply it with information or to give other assistance in examining matters within its competence".

Among those expressing concern about the denial of citizenship or political rights for the black majority were Algeria, for the African Group, Argentina, Benin, Burkina Faso, France, Guyana, Indonesia, Kuwait, Malta, the Netherlands, Nicaragua, Nigeria, Qatar, the Syrian Arab Republic, Thailand, Togo, the Ukrainian SSR, the USSR, the United Kingdom and Zimbabwe. Nigeria said the races were being ranked in a new tricameral system that arbitrarily nominated the whites as the master race, the coloureds as second class, Indians and Asians as third class, and implicitly named a fourth class, thus denationalizing the indigenous populations by not only divesting them of civil and political rights but also creating a landless alien people. Thailand believed that the constitutional proposals would worsen the status and impair further the fundamental rights of the indigenous African majority, and that they constituted another act of repression against that majority. Under the new system, Togo said, black South Africans would be totally excluded from the Government, and the policy of bantustanization was aimed at controlling the blacks while denying them South African nationality. The United States condemned the constitution, as it deplored all constitutions of Governments that did not feature democratic elections in which all adult citizens might participate under conditions of free speech, access to the media, free assembly, majority rule and protection of minority rights.

Those countries which noted that governmental control would remain in the hands of the white minority were Algeria, for the African Group, Burkina Faso, China, Cuba, Indonesia, Malta, Mongolia, the Netherlands, Nicaragua, Qatar, the Syrian Arab Republic, Trinidad and Tobago, and Zimbabwe. Burkina Faso said the major goal of the new constitution was to perpetuate the domination of the white minority and, in order to do that, the Government was trying to break the unity of the oppressed majority by instigating internal conflicts and by killing politically the indigenous Africans.

Argentina, Pakistan, Trinidad and Tobago, and Zimbabwe believed that the South African proposals were aimed at pursuing or justifying bantustanization. In Argentina's opinion, the constitutional proposals would consolidate that system, which was designed to deprive the majority still further of its inalienable rights and citizenship. Under the bantustan system, Trinidad and Tobago said, the African majority would be converted into tribal minority groups, fragmented, separated from their families, relegated to eking out an existence in the infertile areas and labouring under appalling conditions and inferior wages; thus black South Africans were relegated to the status of migrant workers in their own land.

Others, including Benin, Togo, Trinidad and Tobago, and Yugoslavia, noted that the new constitution, by giving limited political rights to coloureds and persons of Asian origin, made them eligible for conscription in the South African army.

Guyana and India believed that the co-operation of certain States had encouraged South Africa to pursue its policies—a view shared by Czechoslovakia, Nicaragua, Nigeria, the Syrian Arab Republic, the Ukrainian SSR and the USSR, which specifically mentioned the United States policy of constructive engagement with South Africa. According to Czechoslovakia, the factor enabling Pretoria to carry out the *apartheid* system, with its aggressive consequences for other countries, was the political, diplomatic, military and economic co-operation by the United States and Israel. In Guyana's view, what had helped South Africa sustain *apartheid* was its conviction that its strategic and economic value would prevent its Western friends from taking action which would help make difficult the survival of *apartheid*. Nicaragua said South Africa was able to perpetuate its racist régime and commit aggression against neighbouring States because of the protection it enjoyed from the policy of constructive engagement. Similarly, the USSR stated that the Pretoria régime could not behave so arrogantly without the support of its Western allies—the same countries which were blocking mandatory sanctions against South Africa. Qatar urged the Council to take action against the South African constitution because the Government would continue to challenge the will of the international community unless convinced that the States on whose political support it relied had finally decided to take a stand on the side of justice and to join the majority of the international community in United Nations resolutions on *apartheid*.

In regard to Council action, Algeria, for the African Group, Benin, the Congo, Cuba, Czechoslovakia, Egypt, Guyana, Indonesia, Kuwait, Nicaragua, Nigeria, Pakistan, Qatar, Sri Lanka, Togo, and Trinidad and Tobago called on the Council to reject the constitution as null and void. Speaking for the African Group, Algeria said it called for such action since the constitution left the structures of *apartheid* intact and institutionalized the exclusion of 24 million blacks from their fatherland. The Congo said the purpose of the debate was to call on the Council to shoulder its responsibilities by using all the resources conferred on it by the Charter when international peace and security were threatened; it hoped the Council would take appropriate countermeasures that would strip any legitimacy from the manœuvres of the régime. Egypt stated that the Council's consideration had demonstrated its insistence that the constitutional amendments be rejected, thereby upholding the international community's opposition to racist policies.

Zimbabwe hoped that the Council's message would be the result of a consensus decision so that Pretoria would be served notice that the international community was unanimous in condemning the new constitution and the sham elections leading to its implementation. Sri Lanka also expected a common response from the Council, demanding that South Africa abandon its constitutional changes and introduce such reforms as would confer on all citizens, without distinction, the dignity and rights they deserved.

Nigeria, the Syrian Arab Republic and the Ukrainian SSR believed that the Council should adopt comprehensive and mandatory sanctions against South Africa in order to compel it to dismantle *apartheid*. The Syrian Arab Republic said the Council should adopt such measures to isolate South Africa. The Ukrainian SSR supported the initiative of the African Group, requesting the Council to reject the constitution, as an expression of the will of the international community, as well as effective measures to eradicate *apartheid*, including mandatory sanctions. China believed that the Council should take all necessary measures to mobilize the international community to support the struggle of the oppressed people for racial equality. Mongolia hoped that the Council would take all necessary measures to force the régime to comply with United Nations decisions and to renounce its repressive policies. Similarly, the Netherlands expressed support for initiatives in the Council which would increase the pressure on South Africa to embark on a process of meaningful reforms towards that goal.

The objective of the United Nations should be the elimination of *apartheid*, according to Argentina, Benin, Burkina Faso, Guyana, the Ukrainian SSR and Yugoslavia. Indonesia said the constitutional changes would only lead to more resistance on the part of the oppressed and consequent violence in South Africa.

The Acting Chairman of the Special Committee against *Apartheid* affirmed the Committee's rejection of South Africa's attempt to impose a constitutional fraud on the oppressed people because it was not founded on the people's sovereignty. The Chairman of the Committee on colonial countries said that, by rejecting the constitution, the Council would leave the South African authorities no doubt that only the eradication of *apartheid* and the establishment of a non-racial democratic society in a unified South Africa could lead to a just and lasting solution to the explosive situation facing that country. Also appealing to the Council to reject the new constitution, Mr. Makatini of ANC said that such a move would support the democratic mass organizations inside South Africa

which had called for a boycott of pseudo-elections due to take place in September; the boycott movement was co-ordinated by the United Democratic Front, which had been formed a year earlier and comprised 600 organizations opposing the constitution and repressive legislation. Also denouncing the constitution as a fraud, Mr. Makhanda of PAC stated that the inherent racial foundation of the constitution invalidated the argument that the system under the new version would eventually transform itself into an instrument of democratic government based on respect for the individual.

On 17 August, the Council adopted resolution 554(1984).

The Security Council,

Recalling its resolution 473(1980) and General Assembly resolution 38/11 of 15 November 1983, as well as other relevant United Nations resolutions calling upon the authorities in South Africa to abandon *apartheid*, end oppression and repression of the black majority and seek a peaceful, just and lasting solution in accordance with the principles of the Charter of the United Nations and the Universal Declaration of Human Rights,

Convinced that the so-called "new constitution" endorsed on 2 November 1983 by the exclusively white electorate in South Africa would continue the process of denationalization of the indigenous African majority, depriving it of all fundamental rights, and further entrench *apartheid*, transforming South Africa into a country for "whites only",

Aware that the inclusion in the "new constitution" of the so-called "coloured" people and people of Asian origin is aimed at dividing the unity of the oppressed people of South Africa and fomenting internal conflict,

Noting with grave concern that one of the objectives of the so-called "constitution" of the racist régime is to make the "coloured" people and people of Asian origin in South Africa eligible for conscription into the armed forces of the *apartheid* régime for further internal repression and aggressive acts against independent African States,

Welcoming the massive united resistance of the oppressed people of South Africa against these "constitutional" manœuvres,

Reaffirming the legitimacy of the struggle of the oppressed people of South Africa for the elimination of *apartheid* and for the establishment of a society in which all the people of South Africa as a whole, irrespective of race, colour, sex or creed, will enjoy equal and full political and other rights and participate freely in the determination of their destiny,

Firmly convinced that the so-called "elections" to be organized by the Pretoria régime in the current month of August for the "coloured" people and people of Asian origin and the implementation of this "new constitution" will inevitably aggravate tension in South Africa and in southern Africa as a whole,

1. *Declares* that the so-called "new constitution" is contrary to the principles of the Charter of the United Nations, that the results of the referendum of 2 November 1983 are of no validity whatsoever and that the enforcement of the "new constitution" will further aggra-

vate the already explosive situation prevailing inside *apartheid* South Africa;

2. *Strongly rejects and declares as null and void* the so-called "new constitution" and the "elections" to be organized in the current month of August for the "coloured" people and people of Asian origin as well as all insidious manœuvres by the racist minority régime of South Africa further to entrench white minority rule and *apartheid*;

3. *Further rejects* any so-called "negotiated settlement" based on bantustan structures or on the so-called "new constitution";

4. *Solemnly declares* that only the total eradication of *apartheid* and the establishment of a non-racial democratic society based on majority rule, through the full and free exercise of universal adult suffrage by all the people in a united and unfragmented South Africa, can lead to a just and lasting solution of the explosive situation in South Africa;

5. *Urges* all Governments and organizations not to accord recognition to the results of the so-called "elections" and to take appropriate action, in co-operation with the United Nations and the Organization of African Unity and in accordance with the present resolution, to assist the oppressed people of South Africa in their legitimate struggle for a non-racial, democratic society;

6. *Requests* the Secretary-General to report to the Security Council on the implementation of the present resolution;

7. *Decides* to remain seized of the matter.

Security Council resolution 554(1984)

17 August 1984   Meeting 2551   13-0-2

8-nation draft (S/16700).

Sponsors: Burkina Faso, Egypt, India, Malta, Nicaragua, Pakistan, Peru, Zimbabwe. *Meeting numbers.* SC 2548-2551.

Vote in Council as follows:

In favour: Burkina Faso, China, Egypt, France, India, Malta, Netherlands, Nicaragua, Pakistan, Peru, Ukrainian SSR, USSR, Zimbabwe. *Against:* None. *Abstaining:* United Kingdom, United States.

Speaking in explanation of vote, France and the United States expressed reservations about the competence of the Security Council to deal with the matter of South Africa's constitution. In addition, France and the United Kingdom had reservations about some of the language of the resolution, with France mentioning paragraphs 1 and 2. The United Kingdom and the United States believed that the Council's action would not be helpful because an opportunity currently existed for facilitating the process of positive change. According to the United Kingdom, only the people of South Africa could determine their future and it was not for outsiders to prescribe solutions or to determine the validity or otherwise of internal arrangements. The United States did not endorse the constitutional developments, but hoped that the change was a first step towards the goal of equal rights; for that reason, it did not agree with the basic tenets on which the resolution was based.

GENERAL ASSEMBLY ACTION (September)

In a letter of 26 September to the President of the General Assembly,[72] Botswana, on behalf of the African Group, requested that the Assembly consider the situation in South Africa as a matter of urgency, if possible not later than 28 September.

The Assembly, on that day, considered a 37-nation draft resolution introduced by Botswana, which said that it was generally acknowledged that the current explosion of violence in South Africa was a direct consequence of the imposition of a racist "constitution" on its people, even though the Government had a different explanation for it.

In a letter of 28 September to the Secretary-General,[73] South Africa said it took exception to the Assembly's consideration of this matter and rejected the draft as unwarranted interference in South Africa's internal affairs. It was seeking to come to terms with the complexities and realities of the region and the challenges posed by its diversity, particularly the problems of a population composed altogether of minorities—of white people, brown people, people of Asian origin and various black peoples; of Christians, Hindus, Muslims and pagans; of first-world and third-world peoples. The Government would not be diverted from its responsibility for the safety and well-being of all South African citizens by the irresponsible activities of the Assembly, and it would continue to promote orderly and evolutionary change for the benefit of all South Africa's peoples, regardless of any resolutions the Assembly might adopt.

After considering the matter on 28 September, the Assembly adopted resolution 39/2 by recorded vote.

Situation in South Africa

The General Assembly,

Recalling its resolution 38/11 of 15 November 1983 and Security Council resolution 554(1984) of 17 August 1984, which declared the so-called "new constitution" a further entrenchment of *apartheid*,

Recalling in particular that Security Council resolution 554(1984) rejected the so-called "new constitution" and declared it null and void,

Also recalling that the said resolutions warned that the imposition of the so-called "new constitution" by the racist régime in South Africa would "further aggravate the already explosive situation prevailing inside *apartheid* South Africa",

Further recalling its various resolutions and those of the Security Council calling upon the authorities in South Africa to abandon *apartheid*, to end oppression and repression of the black majority and to seek a peaceful, just and lasting solution in accordance with the principles of the Charter of the United Nations and the Universal Declaration of Human Rights,

Aware that the majority of the oppressed people of South Africa have decisively rejected the so-called "new constitution" and that the recent demonstrations, strikes and mass uprisings inside *apartheid* South Africa by the oppressed people directly emanate from the imposition of the so-called "new constitution",

Commending the united resistance of the oppressed people of South Africa against the imposition of the so-called "new constitution" and recognizing the legitimacy of their struggle to eliminate *apartheid* and establish a society based on majority rule with equal participation by all the people of South Africa, irrespective of race, colour or creed,

Alarmed by the aggravation of the situation in South Africa, in particular the wanton killing and the maiming of defenceless demonstrators and workers on strike as well as the imposition of virtual martial law conditions intended to facilitate the brutal repression of the black population,

Deeply concerned over the wave of new arbitrary arrests and detention of leaders and activists of mass organizations inside the country, as well as the closure of several schools and universities,

Convinced that South Africa's continued defiance of United Nations resolutions and its imposition of the rejected so-called "new constitution" will inevitably lead to further escalation of the already explosive situation in South Africa and will have far-reaching consequences for southern Africa and the world,

1. *Reiterates its rejection* of the so-called "new constitution" as null and void;

2. *Declares* that the current wave of violence and killing of defenceless demonstrators and striking workers is the direct consequence of the imposition of the so-called "new constitution" by the South African racist régime;

3. *Condemns* the South African racist régime for defying relevant resolutions of the United Nations and persisting with the further entrenchment of *apartheid*, a system declared a crime against humanity and a threat to international peace and security;

4. *Further condemns* the continued massacre of the oppressed people, as well as the arbitrary arrest and detention of leaders and activists of mass organizations, and demands their immediate and unconditional release;

5. *Rejects* any so-called "negotiated settlement" based on bantustan structures or on the so-called "new constitution";

6. *Reaffirms* that only the total eradication of *apartheid* and the establishment of a non-racial democratic society based on majority rule, through the full and free exercise of adult suffrage by all the people in a united and unfragmented South Africa, can lead to a just and lasting solution of the explosive situation in South Africa;

7. *Urges* all Governments and organizations to take appropriate action, in co-operation with the United Nations and the Organization of African Unity and in accordance with the present resolution, to assist the oppressed people of South Africa in their legitimate struggle for national liberation;

8. *Requests* the Security Council, as a matter of urgency, to consider the serious situation in South Africa emanating from the imposition of the so-called "new constitution" and to take all necessary measures, in accordance with the Charter of the United Nations, to avert the further aggravation of tension and conflict in South Africa and in southern Africa as a whole.

General Assembly resolution 39/2

28 September 1984   Meeting 13   133-0-2 (recorded vote)

37-nation draft (A/39/L.2 and Add.1); agenda item 31.

Sponsors: Algeria, Angola, Benin, Botswana, Burundi, Cameroon, Cape Verde, Central African Republic, Chad, Congo, Djibouti, Egypt, Equatorial Guinea, Ethiopia, Gabon, Ghana, Guinea, Guinea-Bissau, Kenya, Liberia, Libyan Arab Jamahiriya, Madagascar, Mali, Mauritania, Morocco, Mozambique, Niger, Nigeria, Rwanda, Senegal, Sudan, Togo, Tunisia, Uganda, United Republic of Tanzania, Zambia, Zimbabwe.

Recorded vote in Assembly as follows:

In favour: Afghanistan, Albania, Algeria, Angola, Argentina, Australia, Austria, Bahamas, Bahrain, Bangladesh, Barbados, Belgium, Benin, Bhutan, Bolivia,

Botswana, Brazil, Brunei Darussalam, Bulgaria, Burma, Burundi, Byelorussian SSR, Cameroon, Canada, Cape Verde, Central African Republic, Chad, China, Colombia, Comoros, Congo, Costa Rica, Cuba, Cyprus, Czechoslovakia, Democratic Kampuchea, Democratic Yemen, Denmark, Djibouti, Egypt, El Salvador, Ethiopia, Fiji, Finland, France, Gabon, Gambia, German Democratic Republic, Germany, Federal Republic of, Ghana, Greece, Grenada, Guinea, Guinea-Bissau, Guyana, Honduras, Hungary, Iceland, India, Indonesia, Iran, Iraq, Ireland, Italy, Ivory Coast, Japan, Jordan, Kenya, Kuwait, Lao People's Democratic Republic, Lesotho, Libyan Arab Jamahiriya, Luxembourg, Madagascar, Malawi, Malaysia, Maldives, Mali, Mauritania, Mauritius, Mexico, Mongolia, Morocco, Mozambique, Netherlands, New Zealand, Nicaragua, Niger, Nigeria, Norway, Oman, Pakistan, Papua New Guinea, Peru, Philippines, Poland, Portugal, Romania, Rwanda, Sao Tome and Principe, Saudi Arabia, Senegal, Seychelles, Sierra Leone, Singapore, Solomon Islands, Somalia, Spain, Sri Lanka, Sudan, Suriname, Swaziland, Sweden, Syrian Arab Republic, Thailand, Togo, Trinidad and Tobago, Tunisia, Turkey, Uganda, Ukrainian SSR, USSR, United Arab Emirates, United Republic of Tanzania, Uruguay, Vanuatu, Venezuela, Viet Nam, Yemen, Yugoslavia, Zaire, Zambia, Zimbabwe.

Against: None.

Abstaining: United Kingdom, United States.

In explanation of vote, Canada, France, the Federal Republic of Germany, Italy, the United Kingdom and the United States objected to some of the language of the resolution. Canada had legal and policy reservations, particularly over the latter part of paragraph 3. France's objections concerned terms used in the second preambular paragraph and in paragraphs 1 and 3, but it voted in favour of the text in order to make clear its condemnation of the brutal repression in the recent uprisings. The Federal Republic of Germany also objected to paragraphs 1 and 3. Italy expressed reservations on paragraph 3 and on some of the other wording, particularly in the seventh preambular paragraph and paragraphs 4 and 7. The United Kingdom regretted that the language of the resolution, notably where it referred to "wanton killing", "virtual martial law", "continued massacre", and "a crime against humanity and a threat to international peace and security", distorted an already grave state of affairs; nor could it endorse the implicit preference for armed struggle over peaceful solutions. The United States said that its revulsion of the injustice of *apartheid* did not authorize the Assembly to indulge in rhetoric that could only exacerbate an already violent situation; for this reason, it opposed language such as that in paragraph 3.

Belgium, the Federal Republic of Germany, Italy, the Netherlands, the United Kingdom and the United States questioned the Assembly's competence to declare a constitution of a Member State null and void. Belgium expressed reservations on the formulation of certain provisions which did not take into account the competence of the Assembly and that of the Security Council. The Federal Republic of Germany said the constitution could not be rejected by the Assembly for juridical reasons alone, since it could not pronounce itself on questions reserved by the United Nations Charter for the Council. The Netherlands said it was not for the Organization to pass judgement on the legal validity of a Member State's constitution, nor could the Assembly endorse a call for national liberation because the situation in South Africa was not a colonial one.

Mentioning its reservations on some elements, Japan regretted that the resolution was adopted before all States were given a chance to express their positions in the general debate; on a matter such as this, efforts should have been made for a consensus resolution so as to ensure that it would exert pressure on the South African authorities.

Swaziland had reservations on certain prescriptions designed to solve the situation inside South Africa, and it opposed the use of violence because Swaziland's geographical position and economic vulnerability would cause it to suffer a heavy burden. While stating that the text was the embodiment of the world's opposition to racial discrimination, Malawi reiterated its belief in the policy of dialogue as a means of solving disputes, affirmed that it did not advocate public condemnations as solutions for problems of that region, and appealed to the South African authorities to create a political atmosphere that would promote peace, security and stability and would allow political participation by all South Africans as equals.

SECURITY COUNCIL ACTION (October)

By a letter of 17 October to the President of the Security Council,[74] Ethiopia, on behalf of the African Group, requested the Council to consider what it said was the serious situation in South Africa emanating from imposition of the so-called new constitution and to take all necessary measures in accordance with the Charter to avert the further aggravation of tension and conflict in South Africa and in southern Africa as a whole. The Council considered the matter on 23 October.

Ethiopia and South Africa, at their request, were invited to participate in the Council's discussion without the right to vote. Certain individuals were also invited to participate under rule 39[b] of the Council's provisional rules of procedure. On 23 October,[75] Burkina Faso, Egypt and Zimbabwe requested that such an invitation be extended to Bishop Desmond Tutu, Secretary-General of the South African Council of Churches and 1984 Nobel Peace Laureate. The Chairman of the Special Committee against *Apartheid* was similarly invited, at his request.

South Africa said the Council had again been convened to consider, in violation of the Charter, matters which fell solely within the sphere of South Africa's domestic affairs. Again rejecting any Council decision concerning those affairs, South Africa said it would continue to promote orderly and evolutionary change for the benefit of all its peoples. There was no desire in the United Nations to evaluate the socio-economic and political developments and progress in South Africa fairly and objectively. The current meeting had been called for the purpose of enhancing anti–South African sentiment; those efforts would fail because South Africa's achievements would increasingly receive international recognition. If the United Nations continued on its current course, South Africa would be forced to withdraw its contribution towards peace in southern Africa, and the neighbouring States would suffer as a result.

Speaking for the African Group, Ethiopia said that the draft resolution before the Council contained modest measures that were the minimum demanded by the exigencies of the situation and that could help defuse the current tension; because *apartheid* remained a threat to international peace and security, the Council was duty-bound to take every measure commensurate with its responsibilities under the Charter and to remain seized of the situation in South Africa. According to India, the Council's resolution rejecting South Africa's constitution (554(1984)) had fortified the resolve of the oppressed people to resist Pretoria's attempts to entrench *apartheid;* it was a testimony to the courage and wisdom of the vast majority of South Africans that the elections were boycotted on a massive scale and that so many of them had risen in protest rather than yield to injustice.

The Chairman of the Committee against *Apartheid* said that behind the propaganda about changes, in orchestration with some Western Powers and interests, the régime had been trying to dispossess and denationalize the African majority through bantustanization; it had understood the attitudes of major Western Powers as a licence for repression.

Bishop Tutu, who described the current unrest and protests in South Africa, appealed to the Council to urge the South African authorities to negotiate with the authentic representatives of all sections of the South African community so that freedom could come for all with the least possible violence.

On 23 October, the Council adopted resolution 556(1984).

The Security Council,

Recalling its resolution 554(1984) and General Assembly resolutions 38/11 of 15 November 1983 and 39/2 of 28 September 1984, which declared the so-called "new constitution" contrary to the principles of the Charter of the United Nations,

Reaffirming the provisions of the Universal Declaration of Human Rights, particularly article 21, para-

[b]See footnote a on p. 158.

graphs 1 and 3, which recognize, *inter alia*, the right of everyone to take part in the Government of his country, directly or through freely chosen representatives, and the will of the people as the basis of the authority of Government,

Alarmed by the aggravation of the situation in South Africa, in particular the wanton killing and the maiming of defenceless demonstrators and workers on strike as well as the imposition of virtual martial-law conditions intended to facilitate the brutal repression of the black population,

Gravely concerned at the continuing arbitrary arrests and detentions without trial of leaders and activists of mass organizations inside the country as well as the closure of several schools and universities,

Commending the massive united resistance of the oppressed people of South Africa, including the strike by hundreds of thousands of black students, to the imposition of the so-called "new constitution",

Commending also the Asian and coloured communities in South Africa for their large-scale boycott of the recent "elections" which constituted a clear rejection of the so-called "new constitution",

Reaffirming the legitimacy of the struggle of the oppressed people of South Africa for the full exercise of the right to self-determination and the establishment of a non-racial democratic society in an unfragmented South Africa,

Convinced that racist South Africa's defiance of world public opinion and the imposition of the rejected so-called "new constitution" will inevitably lead to further escalation of the explosive situation and will have far-reaching consequences for southern Africa and the world,

1. *Reiterates* its condemnation of the *apartheid* policy of the South African régime and South Africa's continued defiance of the resolutions of the United Nations and designs further to entrench *apartheid*, a system characterized as a crime against humanity;

2. *Further condemns* the continued massacres of the oppressed people, as well as the arbitrary arrest and detention of leaders and activists of mass organizations;

3. *Demands* the immediate cessation of the massacres and the prompt and unconditional release of all political prisoners and detainees;

4. *Reaffirms* that only the total eradication of *apartheid* and the establishment of a non-racial, democratic society based on majority rule, through the full and free exercise of adult suffrage by all the people in a united and unfragmented South Africa, can lead to a just, equitable and lasting solution of the situation in South Africa;

5. *Urges* all Governments and organizations to take appropriate action, in co-operation with the United Nations and the Organization of African Unity and in accordance with the present resolution, to assist the oppressed people of South Africa in their legitimate struggle for the full exercise of the right to self-determination;

6. *Demands* the immediate eradication of *apartheid* as the necessary step towards the full exercise of the right to self-determination in an unfragmented South Africa, and to this end demands:

(a) The dismantling of the bantustan structures as well as the cessation of uprooting, relocation and denationalization of the indigenous African people;

(b) The abrogation of the bans and restrictions on political organizations, parties, individuals and news media opposed to *apartheid;*

(c) The unimpeded return of all the exiles;

7. *Requests* the Secretary-General to report to the Security Council on the implementation of the present resolution;

8. *Decides* to remain seized of the matter.

Security Council resolution 556(1984)

23 October 1984   Meeting 2560   14-0-1

8-nation draft (S/16791).

Sponsors: Burkina Faso, Egypt, India, Malta, Nicaragua, Pakistan, Peru, Zimbabwe.

Vote in Council as follows:

In favour: Burkina Faso, China, Egypt, France, India, Malta, Netherlands, Nicaragua, Pakistan, Peru, Ukrainian SSR, USSR, United Kingdom, Zimbabwe.

Against: None.

Abstaining: United States.

In explanation of vote, the Netherlands, the United Kingdom and the United States expressed reservations about the language in the resolution. The United Kingdom voted for the text because it did not believe the problems of South Africa could or should be resolved by repression, by the denial of civil and political rights or by violence, but it regretted, and regarded as counter-productive, the exaggerated language in several parts of the resolution, including the term "massacre", to describe the situation; it regarded the expression "crime against humanity" as one of abhorrence rather than a technical legal description and it did not interpret any part of the resolution as falling within the terms of Chapter VII of the Charter. The United States said that some excesses of language prevented it from joining the Council's affirmative vote, although it supported the demands for equal rights, majority rule and respect for minority rights for all South African citizens, as well as equal opportunity, freedom, self-government and self-determination for all citizens of all countries.

France and the Netherlands had particular problems with paragraph 1. The Netherlands mentioned the implicit reference therein to the International Convention on the Suppression and Punishment of the Crime of *Apartheid*,[44] while France's reservations were in regard to certain terms in the first preambular paragraph and in paragraph 1, particularly concerning the description of *apartheid* as a "crime against humanity".

The Netherlands and the United Kingdom considered that it was not within the competence of the Council to pass judgement on the validity of a Member State's constitution.

Communications. The Secretary-General received several letters in 1984 concerning South Africa's new constitution.

On 3 July,[76] India forwarded a letter sent to the chief representative of ANC (Asian Mission) stationed at New Delhi by the Indian Minister for External Affairs. Stating that the elections for the new legislature of 22 August appeared to be a façade to mislead world public opinion, the Minister said India urged all the people of South Africa, and especially those of Indian origin, to take no part in the so-called election and to maintain unity in the struggle against *apartheid* and racism.

On behalf of the 10 States members of EEC, Ireland, on 13 September,[77] transmitted the text of a declaration on South Africa adopted on 11 September at the Ministerial Meeting on European Political Co-operation. While expressing concern that the frustration of black South Africans at their deliberate exclusion from South Africa's political life and at the lack of political means to express their grievances had led to the recent violence, EEC stated that those negative developments were in contrast to more positive developments in relations between South Africa and its neighbours. Responding to the EEC text on 20 September,[78] South Africa affirmed that the events were its internal affair and in no way the concern of any outside authority, and that there were elements who would not allow the democratic process to proceed unhindered so the Government had had no alternative but to take preventive action to protect lives and property.

On 8 October,[9] India forwarded the final communiqué adopted by the Meeting of Ministers for Foreign Affairs and Heads of Delegation of Non-Aligned Countries to the General Assembly's 1984 session, affirming that the rejection of the constitutional changes by the so-called coloureds and people of Asian origin during the recent elections, as well as by the Security Council in resolution 554(1984), demonstrated solidarity with the black majority in its struggle against *apartheid;* they believed that the current demonstrations were the result of the régime's imposition of the illegal new constitution.

Apartheid in sports

On 3 April 1984, the Special Committee against *Apartheid* held a hearing on the sports boycott against South Africa.[1] Statements were made by Paul Stephenson, Chairman of the British Black Standing Conference against *Apartheid* Sport; Sam Ramsamy, Chairman of the South African Non-Racial Olympic Committee; and Abdul S. Minty, on behalf of the British Anti-*Apartheid* Movement. In addition to urging Governments and sports organizations to discourage sports contacts with South Africa, the participants referred in particular to the planned May/June tour of South Africa by the English Rugby Football Union, which

would violate United Nations resolutions, the Gleneagles Agreement of Commonwealth States and the Code of Conduct adopted by the Commonwealth Games Federation in 1982. Despite protests from anti-*apartheid* movements, political parties, church members and trade unions, the tour went ahead.

The Committee heard statements by African sports leaders on 12 June, which laid the basis for an intensified campaign against collaboration with *apartheid* sports.

The United Kingdom referred to the Committee's June discussions in a 2 July letter to its Chairman, with a copy to the Secretary-General.[30] The United Kingdom said that its position was misrepresented by allegations that the tour had been facilitated by its covert support of *apartheid* in sports; the tour had been carried out by the English Rugby Football Union, a private body not answerable to the British Government, which had made every effort to dissuade it from proceeding.

In 1984, the Committee continued to publish its semi-annual register of sports contacts with South Africa, listing sports exchanges—including the names and countries of participants—covering the periods 1 July–31 December 1983 and 1 January–30 June 1984. The registers indicated that there had been progress towards the international isolation of South African sport, although improvement had been slow in professional sports as several sportsmen and women were lured to that country by large financial rewards. Overseas-based TNCs in South Africa and South African companies contributed significant amounts of money to sponsor international sporting events there. South Africa was barred from participating in international sports, both amateur and professional, in over 80 per cent of the world, but collaboration with *apartheid* sports continued in a few countries.

According to the Committee, South Africa and its supporters continued trying to persuade the international community that racial discrimination in sports no longer existed in South Africa; however, no international sports body which had excluded that country from membership had reversed its decision. The International Golfers' Association informed the South African Professional Golfers' Association that it would not allow South African participation in the 1984 World Cup Tournament. Most Governments, except the United Kingdom and the United States, continued to deny visas to South African sports personalities and banned them from participating in international events if they represented South Africa.

The Committee reported on sports contacts with South Africa. In January, Australia, in conformity with its policy on sporting contacts with South Africa, refused visas to representatives of the South African Rugby Board. As for the United Kingdom, it granted citizenship in May 1984 to Zola Budd, a record-breaking South African runner, and she consequently became a member of the British Olympic team for the 1984 Olympic Games.

The Prime Minister elect of New Zealand, David Lange, issued a statement[79] on 20 July in regard to New Zealand's bid to host the 1990 Commonwealth Games, affirming that the Labour Government would stand by the country's obligations under the Gleneagles Agreement, not allowing sports teams from South Africa to compete in New Zealand.

In October, Argentina addressed two letters to the Chairman of the Committee about Argentina's opposition to the planned visit of Argentine rugby players to South Africa.[80] In the first, it stated that the players were making a private trip and did not represent any official Argentine body. The Government had tried to persuade the players to give up the plan, but it could not prevent travel by its citizens; the Argentine Rugby Union had endorsed the Government's action. By the second letter, Argentina said it would deny visas to South Africans requesting entry into Argentina to engage in sports events; it had requested its Secretariat of State for Sports to ban a South African boxing referee from Argentina, and his visa was cancelled; and the Government had cancelled the permits of stay of a group of South Africans who took part in rugby matches.

The Council for Namibia[17] agreed that many Governments and organizations had reaffirmed their commitment to boycott *apartheid* sports, but some sports bodies and administrators continued their contacts with South Africa under the pretext of separation of sports and politics. It said that from September 1980 to December 1983, sportsmen and women from the United Kingdom and the United States had participated in larger numbers and in more categories than individuals of any other nationality. Individuals from Australia, Belgium, France, the Federal Republic of Germany, Ireland, Israel, Spain and Switzerland had also competed in South Africa. For the first time a rugby team from Namibia toured South America and matches were held against teams from Chile and Uruguay, who were joined by some Argentine players.

Draft convention

The *Ad Hoc* Committee on the Drafting of an International Convention against *Apartheid* in Sports, established by the General Assembly in 1976,[81] submitted a report[82] adopted on 15 October 1984 to the Assembly, in accordance with a December 1983 request.[83] Having concluded work on the remaining 5 of the 22 articles, the 24-member Committee submitted the draft Convention to the Assembly in an annex to its report and expressed the hope that the Convention could be finalized in 1985.

In order to complete its work, the Committee sent a delegation to the Ivory Coast from 15 to 20 March to hold consultations with the President and the Secretary-General of the Supreme Council for Sport in Africa. The Council said it had recommended that African countries give support to the new amendments to the draft Convention proposed by the Committee. During 1984, Jamaica and the German Democratic Republic suggested alternative amendments. The Jamaican proposal did not alter the main thrust of the Chairman's 1983 proposed amendments,[84] but, as the German Democratic Republic's proposal would have the effect of removing from the Convention any element of the "third-party principle", the Committee decided to send a delegation to Eastern European States for consultations with sports officials to seek a compromise solution. Under that principle, which had been the main focus of negotiations on the draft for the previous four years, States parties to the Convention would be required to boycott countries that allowed the participation of their sportsmen, sportswomen and teams with South Africa in the same manner that South Africa would be boycotted.

The mission visited the German Democratic Republic and the USSR from 7 to 15 September.[85] Officals of those two countries expressed reservations about the possible application of the third-party principle and emphasized the need for a convention which would be widely adhered to. The Chairman of the Committee explained that a compromise was being sought that would be flexible enough to meet the objectives of African States, who supported the principle, without endangering the interests of international sports. The Committee intended to invite Member States to comment on the proposals. It recommended that the Assembly extend the Committee's mandate for another year with a view to submitting the draft Convention in 1985, request the Secretary-General to circulate the draft and proposed amendments to Member States to solicit their views, and authorize the Committee to continue its consultations in order to finalize the draft Convention and to secure wider support.

Under the Committee's proposal on the third-party principle, States parties would prohibit entry into their countries for participation in sports activities of sports bodies and sportsmen and women who had participated in sports competitions in a country practising *apartheid*, and would take steps to prevent the participation of such sports bodies and individuals in international sports competitions. In the case of Governments violating the provisions of the Convention, States parties would take appropriate action, including exclusion of the countries concerned from international sport competition if necessary. An international commission would be set up to monitor implementation of those provisions and make recommendations on possible action by States parties. In addition, the commission would examine complaints of States parties concerning breaches of the Convention by other parties. Under an alternative proposal, States parties would take all necessary action to ensure that their nationals refrained from participating in all sports events which included individuals or teams from a country practising *apartheid*.

GENERAL ASSEMBLY ACTION

On 13 December, the General Assembly adopted resolution 39/72 D by recorded vote.

Apartheid in sports

The General Assembly,

Having considered the report of the *Ad Hoc* Committee on the Drafting of an International Convention against *Apartheid* in Sports,

1. *Authorizes* the *Ad Hoc* Committee on the Drafting of an International Convention against *Apartheid* in Sports to continue consultations, as required, with representatives of Governments and organizations concerned and experts on *apartheid;*

2. *Requests* the Secretary-General to send the text of the revised draft of the International Convention against *Apartheid* in Sports and the amendments thereto to all Member States for their comments and views, to be submitted by 31 March 1985, so that the *Ad Hoc* Committee may take them into account in preparing the final text;

3. *Requests* the *Ad Hoc* Committee to continue its work with a view to submitting the draft Convention to the General Assembly at its fortieth session.

General Assembly resolution 39/72 D

13 December 1984   Meeting 99   148-0-6 (recorded vote)

57-nation draft (A/39/L.31 and Add.1), amended by Barbados (A/39/L.41); agenda item 31.

Sponsors: Afghanistan, Algeria, Angola, Barbados, Benin, Botswana, Burkina Faso, Burundi, Byelorussian SSR, Cameroon, Cape Verde, Congo, Cuba, Czechoslovakia, Democratic Yemen, Djibouti, Equatorial Guinea, Ethiopia, Gambia, German Democratic Republic, Ghana, Guinea, Hungary, India, Indonesia, Iran, Jamaica, Kenya, Lesotho, Libyan Arab Jamahiriya, Madagascar, Malaysia, Mali, Mauritania, Mongolia, Morocco, Mozambique, Nepal, Nicaragua, Niger, Nigeria, Qatar, Rwanda, Sao Tome and Principe, Senegal, Sierra Leone, Syrian Arab Republic, Togo, Trinidad and Tobago, Tunisia, Uganda, Ukrainian SSR, United Republic of Tanzania, Viet Nam, Yugoslavia, Zambia, Zimbabwe.

Financial implications. 5th Committee, A/39/787; S-G, A/C.5/39/75.

Meeting numbers. GA 39th session: 5th Committee 45; plenary 66-71, 98, 99.

Recorded vote in Assembly as follows:

In favour: Afghanistan, Albania, Algeria, Angola, Argentina, Australia, Austria, Bahamas, Bahrain, Bangladesh, Barbados, Belgium, Belize, Benin, Bhutan, Bolivia, Botswana, Brazil, Brunei Darussalam, Bulgaria, Burkina Faso, Burma, Burundi, Byelorussian SSR, Cameroon, Canada, Cape Verde, Central African Republic, Chad, Chile, China, Colombia, Comoros, Congo, Costa Rica, Cuba, Cyprus, Czechoslovakia, Democratic Kampuchea, Democratic Yemen, Djibouti, Dominica, Dominican Republic, Ecuador, Egypt, El Salvador, Equatorial Guinea, Ethiopia, Fiji, Finland, France, Gabon, Gambia, German Democratic Republic, Ghana, Greece, Grenada, Guatemala, Guinea, Guinea-Bissau, Guyana, Haiti, Honduras, Hungary, India, Indonesia, Iran, Iraq, Ireland, Italy, Ivory Coast, Jamaica, Japan, Jordan, Kenya, Kuwait, Lao People's Democratic Republic, Lebanon, Lesotho, Liberia, Libyan Arab Jamahiriya, Luxembourg, Madagascar, Malawi, Malaysia, Maldives, Mali, Malta, Mauritania, Mauritius, Mexico, Mongolia, Morocco, Mozambique, Nepal, New Zealand, Nicaragua, Niger, Nigeria, Norway, Oman, Pakistan, Panama, Papua New Guinea, Peru, Philippines, Poland, Portugal, Qatar, Romania, Rwanda, Saint Christopher and Nevis, Saint Lucia, Saint Vincent and the Grenadines, Samoa, Sao Tome and Principe, Saudi Arabia, Senegal, Seychelles, Sierra Leone, Singapore, Solomon Islands, Somalia, Spain, Sri Lanka, Sudan, Suriname, Sweden, Syrian Arab Republic, Thailand, Togo, Trinidad and Tobago, Tunisia, Turkey, Uganda, Ukrainian SSR, USSR, United Arab Emirates, United Republic of Tanzania, Uruguay, Vanuatu, Venezuela, Viet Nam, Yemen, Yugoslavia, Zaire, Zambia, Zimbabwe.

Against: None.

Abstaining: Denmark, Germany, Federal Republic of, Iceland, Netherlands, United Kingdom, United States.

Prior to the vote on the text as a whole, the Assembly adopted, by a recorded vote of 147 to 1, with 5 abstentions, an amendment by Barbados, which added paragraph 2 of the adopted text.

In explanation of vote, France, Ireland, speaking for the EC members, the Netherlands and New Zealand expressed support for eliminating *apartheid* from international sports, but added that currently they could not pass judgement on a draft convention.

France voted for the resolution but reserved its position on the contents of any future draft convention. Ireland pointed out that in the EC countries sport was organized on a private basis, but they would continue to discourage sporting contacts involving racial discrimination. Speaking for itself, Ireland hoped that the terms of the proposed Convention would not give it legal or constitutional problems, a position shared by New Zealand, which said it discouraged its sports people from contacts with South Africa until *apartheid* was abolished.

The Netherlands said it had certain visa requirements for South Africans as a means to restrict their participation in sporting events in the Netherlands, but it could not accept some provisions of the proposed Convention because they were incompatible with certain of its constitutionally guaranteed freedoms.

In related action (resolution 39/72 A), the Assembly called on Governments that had not done so to support boycotts of South Africa, including sports boycotts.

Aid programmes and inter-agency co-operation

The United Nations continued to provide aid to victims of *apartheid* in 1984. Such aid was provided either through national liberation movements or directly to South African refugees or to individuals for educational and training purposes.

National liberation movements

Various United Nations specialized agencies and other related bodies continued to provide assistance to peoples of colonial countries and their national liberation movements. Those organizations described their assistance in a report which the Secretary-General submitted to the General Assembly (see TRUSTEESHIP AND DECOLONIZATION, Chapter I).

UNDP report and action. The Administrator of the United Nations Development Programme (UNDP), in a March 1985 report to the Governing Council,[86] described UNDP's 1984 assistance programmes to national liberation movements of southern Africa recognized by OAU. Assistance was again extended to three movements: SWAPO of Namibia, and ANC and PAC of South Africa. The assistance continued to focus on the priority areas of promoting professional skills and manpower development through formal education and practical training, and promoting self-reliance in the movements in their respective countries of asylum in such vital areas as food production, public health services and vocational trades. The assistance was aimed at helping the movements to develop the skills necessary for eventually assuming civic responsibility and gainful employment.

In 1984, UNDP staff conducted monitoring visits to all national liberation movement projects in Angola, the United Republic of Tanzania and Zambia to evaluate the programmes and follow up on earlier recommendations. After consultations with the respective executing agencies, proposals were made for improving the quality and timeliness of programme delivery.

Two related developments took place in 1984 that significantly affected the flow of UNDP assistance to the movements. The first was the signing on 16 March of the Nkomati Accord between Mozambique and South Africa (see p. 184), and the second was the revelation that South Africa had signed an identical agreement in 1983 with Swaziland. Under the Nkomati Accord, both parties agreed not to allow their territories to be used as a base or passage by another State, foreign forces, organizations or individuals preparing to attack the other. In particular, they would forbid and prevent training centres, places of shelter, accommodation and transit for those with such intent. As a result of the Accord, a large number of South African civilians who had sought asylum in Mozambique and Swaziland under the aegis of ANC were compelled to leave those countries. A massive relocation began, with most ANC followers moving north to the United Republic of Tanzania, which had allocated land to ANC with a view to enabling it to establish and develop long-term, self-sufficient settlements at Mazimbu and Dakawa. Those settlements were soon overcrowded and health and educational services were strained, requiring more assistance than originally anticipated.

During 1984, four more projects were approved and begun, bringing the total to 17. Three were completed, leaving 14 by the end of the year. Of the 17 projects, 15 were financed from the UNDP indicative planning figure for national liberation movements and the other 2 from the Trust Fund for Assistance to Colonial Countries and Peoples. The total UNDP contribution was $2,930,133 for the year. As in 1983, most UNDP assistance was for education, mainly at primary and secondary levels, with smaller contributions for health and agricultural production. All the 11 educational projects, valued at $2,061,746, were executed by the United Nations Educational, Scientific and Cultural Organization. Two health projects, valued at $504,511, were executed by the World Health Organization. The agricultural project, for which $195,350 was spent, was carried out by the Food and Agriculture Organization of the United Nations.

In view of the fact that a tendency had developed over the years for each movement to create its own system and infrastructure of primary and secondary education, most projects were movement-specific. Projects valued at $1,014,115 were directed towards ANC, $548,949 to PAC, and $882,617 to SWAPO.

The UNDP Governing Council, on 29 June,[87] took note with appreciation of the Administrator's efforts to improve assistance to the national liberation movements recognized by OAU and requested him to continue assisting them as flexibly as possible within the context of the UNDP mandate. He was also requested to follow through with initiatives aimed at improving the design, implementation and monitoring of assistance projects, to ensure timely delivery of inputs to approved projects, and to continue reporting to the Council.

UNIDO action. The Fourth General Conference of the United Nations Industrial Development Organization (UNIDO) (Vienna, Austria, August) adopted a resolution[88] on 19 August, requesting UNIDO to strengthen its technical assistance to the national liberation movements in southern Africa recognized by OAU. It appealed to member States and international organizations to provide increased resources for UNIDO activities within its mandate on all aspects of economic planning in an independent Namibia, in accordance with a 1982 General Assembly resolution.[89] It also appealed to member States, the United Nations system and organizations to provide assistance, through those national liberation movements, for the social and economic development of the oppressed majority of southern Africa. The UNIDO Executive Director was requested to report in 1985 to the Industrial Development Board and the UNIDO General Conference on progress in providing technical assistance to those movements.

UNCTAD action. The Trade and Development Board of the United Nations Conference on Trade and Development (UNCTAD), by a resolution of 21 September,[90] requested the UNCTAD Secretary-General to implement UNCTAD resolution 147(VI) of July 1983,[91] calling on him to undertake, in consultation with OAU, a survey of the economic and social conditions of the oppressed people of South Africa, and urging the UNDP Administrator to provide adequate resources to the UNCTAD secretariat for that purpose. The appeal to UNDP was repeated in the Board's 1984 resolution and the UNCTAD Secretary-General was to report on its implementation in 1985.

Activities of the Committee against *Apartheid*. The Special Committee against *Apartheid*[1] repeatedly appealed for more assistance to the oppressed people of South Africa and the South African liberation movements recognized by OAU, emphasizing the need for all possible political, moral, humanitarian, educational, material and other assistance. It expressed appreciation to those who had contributed such assistance. The Committee maintained contact with other United Nations agencies and non-governmental organizations concerned with assistance to victims of *apartheid*.

On 6 April, the Committee, at a meeting to mark the twenty-fifth anniversary of PAC, called on the international community to extend assistance to the oppressed people of South Africa.

Among its recommendations to the General Assembly, the Committee suggested the continued authorization of funds from the regular United Nations budget to enable the South African liberation movements recognized by OAU (ANC and PAC) to maintain their offices in New York.

ECONOMIC AND SOCIAL COUNCIL ACTION

In July (resolution 1984/55), the Economic and Social Council recommended that a separate item on assistance to national liberation movements recognized by OAU be included in the agenda of high-level meetings of the OAU General Secretariat and the secretariats of the United Nations and other organizations within the United Nations system, with a view to ensuring the best use of available resources for assistance to the peoples of the colonial Territories. The Council noted with satisfaction the arrangements by several specialized agencies and United Nations institutions which enabled representatives of those movements to participate as observers in proceedings concerning their respective countries, and called on those international institutions which had not done so to follow that example and make the necessary arrangements, including defraying the participation costs of those representatives.

A similar recommendation was made by the Committee on colonial countries in a resolution of 22 August.[51]

GENERAL ASSEMBLY ACTION

In numerous 1984 resolutions, the General Assembly took action related to assistance for national liberation movements.

In resolution 39/17, the Assembly called for a substantial increase in assistance given by States, United Nations organs, specialized agencies and non-governmental organizations to the victims of racism, racial discrimination and *apartheid* through their national liberation movements recognized by OAU. Similarly, in resolution 39/72 G, it appealed for increased support for those movements and to all those struggling against *apartheid* and for a non-racial, democratic society. By resolution 39/8, the Assembly urged United Nations organizations to expand their co-operation with OAU and, through it, their assistance to the liberation movements.

Resolution 39/72 A included the Assembly's appeal to Governments and organizations to provide maximal moral, political and material assistance to ANC and PAC and all struggling for freedom in South Africa in opposition to *apartheid*. By that text, the Assembly decided to continue the authorization of adequate financial provision in the United Nations regular budget to enable those movements to maintain New York offices in order to participate in appropriate deliberations. In resolution 39/15, it again appealed for the extension of all possible co-operation to the liberation movements.

By resolution 39/43, the Assembly echoed the action taken by the Economic and Social Council in resolution 1984/55 (see above), without, however, specifying that the participation costs of liberation movement representatives should be defrayed by the organization concerned.

In resolution 39/76 on the observer status of national liberation movements recognized by OAU and/or the League of Arab States, the Assembly called on the States concerned to accord to the delegations of those movements, which were accorded observer status by international organizations, the facilities, privileges and immunities necessary for performing their functions.

UN Trust Fund for South Africa

The United Nations Trust Fund for South Africa, established by the General Assembly in 1965[92] to provide voluntary assistance to persons persecuted under discriminatory legislation in South Africa and Namibia, made five grants totalling $1,925,000 in 1984, according to an October report by the Secretary-General.[93] By that report, the Secretary-General submitted the report of the Fund's Committee of Trustees. The Fund received $1,726,396 in contributions during 1984 (see table, p. 170) and a further $481,648 was pledged for that year. The total income since the Fund's inception, including interest, was

$19,946,983 and the total amount of grants was $19,586,670 as at 30 September, leaving a balance of $360,313. In December, the Assembly appealed for increased contributions to the Fund.

CONTRIBUTIONS TO THE UN TRUST FUND FOR SOUTH AFRICA, 1984
(as at 31 December 1984, in US dollar equivalent)

Country	Amount
Australia	55,902
Austria	37,200
Barbados	1,000
Bulgaria	2,000
Canada	20,161
China	30,000
Cyprus	196
Democratic Yemen	1,500
Denmark	239,831
Finland	97,431
France	50,600
Germany, Federal Republic of	64,328
Greece	4,500
Hungary	2,500
Iceland	2,000
India	4,000
Indonesia	3,000
Ireland	46,370
Italy	7,794
Japan	20,000
Kuwait	4,000
Malaysia	1,000
Netherlands	118,644
New Zealand	5,314
Norway	457,044
Pakistan	3,000
Sweden	313,000
Togo	172
Trinidad and Tobago	1,250
Tunisia	2,060
Turkey	7,007
United States	85,750
Venezuela	2,000
Zambia	5,040
Zimbabwe	30,802
Total	1,726,396

SOURCE: Accounts for the 12-month period of the biennium 1984-1985 ended 31 December 1984—schedules of individual trust funds.

GENERAL ASSEMBLY ACTION

On 13 December, the General Assembly adopted resolution 39/72 F without vote.

United Nations Trust Fund for South Africa
The General Assembly,

Having considered the report of the Secretary-General on the United Nations Trust Fund for South Africa, to which is annexed the report of the Committee of Trustees of the United Nations Trust Fund for South Africa,

Gravely concerned at the continued and increased repression against opponents of *apartheid* and racial discrimination in South Africa and the institution of numerous trials under arbitrary security legislation, as well as continued repression in Namibia,

Reaffirming that increased humanitarian assistance by the international community to those persecuted under repressive and discriminatory legislation in South Africa and Namibia is appropriate and essential,

Recognizing that increased contributions to the Trust Fund and to the voluntary agencies concerned are necessary to enable them to meet the increased needs for humanitarian and legal assistance,

1. *Commends* the Secretary-General and the Committee of Trustees of the United Nations Trust Fund for South Africa for their efforts to promote humanitarian and legal assistance to persons persecuted under repressive and discriminatory legislation in South Africa and Namibia, as well as assistance to their families and to refugees from South Africa;

2. *Expresses its appreciation* to the Governments, organizations and individuals that have contributed to the Trust Fund and to the voluntary agencies engaged in rendering humanitarian and legal assistance to the victims of *apartheid* and racial discrimination;

3. *Appeals* for generous and increased contributions to the Trust Fund;

4. *Also appeals* for direct contributions to the voluntary agencies engaged in assistance to the victims of *apartheid* and racial discrimination in South Africa and Namibia.

General Assembly resolution 39/72 F

13 December 1984   Meeting 99   Adopted without vote

50-nation draft (A/39/L.33 and Add.1); agenda item 31.
Sponsors: Algeria, Angola, Australia, Austria, Canada, Cape Verde, China, Congo, Democratic Yemen, Denmark, Egypt, Finland, France, Gambia, Germany, Federal Republic of, Greece, Guinea, Guyana, Iceland, India, Indonesia, Ireland, Italy, Japan, Kenya, Lesotho, Madagascar, Malaysia, Malta, Morocco, Mozambique, Nepal, Netherlands, Nicaragua, Nigeria, Norway, Pakistan, Qatar, Sierra Leone, Sri Lanka, Sweden, Syrian Arab Republic, Togo, Trinidad and Tobago, Tunisia, Turkey, United Republic of Tanzania, Venezuela, Yugoslavia, Zambia.
Meeting numbers. GA 39th session: plenary 66-71, 98, 99.

Other UN assistance

The United Nations Educational and Training Programme for Southern Africa (see p. 190) also provided educational and training assistance to South Africans, as described by the Secretary-General in an October 1984 report.[94] During the 1983/84 school year, it granted scholarships to 777 South Africans, as compared with 613 the year before. Of the 777 scholarships, 378 were new awards and the remaining 399 were extensions of previous grants.

GENERAL ASSEMBLY ACTION

In resolution 39/109, the General Assembly called for further assistance to student refugees in southern Africa.

Other aspects

Among other activities to promote the international campaign against *apartheid*, the United Nations, and especially the Special Committee against *Apartheid*, promoted the dissemination of information to inform the public world-wide. Non-governmental organizations were encouraged to participate in this effort, and special meetings, missions and observances were held to promote the campaign. The Committee drew up its work plan, which was approved by the General Assembly in December.

Public information

The Special Committee against *Apartheid* continued to encourage the widest possible international action against *apartheid*, paying particular attention to promoting public action by trade unions, youth and students, and all other organizations engaged in the struggle against *apartheid*.[(1)] The Committee also participated in meetings organized by various organizations (see p. 173). It gave financial and other assistance to several conferences which it helped to organize. In its recommendations to the General Assembly, the Committee said it was essential to give attention to efforts to inform Governments and world public opinion of the serious implications of the offensive of the Pretoria régime against the people of South Africa and Namibia, and the front-line States, in collusion with powerful external interests.

The Committee continued to welcome and encourage the mobilization of world public opinion against *apartheid*, and action by trade unions, religious bodies and leaders, and organizations of students, youth, women and other segments of the population. It expressed satisfaction with the progress in such mobilization during the year.

The Committee noted the increasing participation of artists in the campaign against *apartheid*. Many artists contributed works to the Art contre/against *Apartheid* exhibit, supported by the Committee. "Artists and Athletes against *Apartheid*", a United States organization assisted by the Committee, received the support of many entertainers and athletes in the United States. The Committee encouraged similar activities by artists and intellectuals in other countries.

The Committee attached importance to promoting public opinion against the crimes of the Pretoria régime—which it described as blackmail of independent African States, attempts at denationalization of the indigenous African majority, forced removals of the African people from their land and homes, and repression, torture and killing of patriots—as well as against the collusion of major Western Powers and vested interests with that régime. The demonstrations in European countries against the visit of the Prime Minister of South Africa (see p. 135) showed, according to the Committee, that when the people were informed of the facts, they would not fail to respond in support of the oppressed people and the United Nations. The Committee stated that world public opinion should be encouraged to demand that there be no collaboration with the régime, and that all relevant United Nations resolutions be implemented. Governments and public organizations should be encouraged to persuade the collaborators with *apartheid* to desist from that course. For these reasons, the Committee recommended that the General Assembly commend the anti-*apartheid* movements and other organizations concerned for actions against *apartheid*, appeal to Governments and organizations to support the anti-*apartheid* movements, and ensure necessary resources to enable the Committee to expand its activities to promote the campaign.

As for its own programme of work, the Committee recommended that activities be organized to pay tribute to the national liberation movement of South Africa, and its leaders and martyrs, in conjunction with the observance of the fortieth anniversary of the United Nations in 1985. The Committee planned to co-operate with OAU in promoting such activities, and suggested they be co-ordinated with tributes to all martyrs in the struggle for the emancipation of Africa.

India, by a letter of 20 March to the Secretary-General,[(95)] forwarded the final declaration of the Conference of the Ministers of Information of Non-Aligned Countries (Jakarta, Indonesia, 26-30 January), which included a statement on the international campaign against *apartheid*. Affirming their support for educating public opinion, the Ministers called on member Governments to encourage the information and mass media in their countries to contribute to the campaign.

ECONOMIC AND SOCIAL COUNCIL ACTION

The Economic and Social Council, in resolution 1984/55 of 25 July, requested United Nations organizations, in accordance with United Nations resolutions on *apartheid*, to intensify support for the oppressed people of South Africa and to take such measures as would isolate the régime and mobilize world public opinion against *apartheid*.

GENERAL ASSEMBLY ACTION

On 13 December, the General Assembly adopted resolution 39/72 E by recorded vote.

Public information and public action against *apartheid*

The General Assembly,

Recognizing the inescapable moral challenge posed by the inhuman system of *apartheid* in South Africa,

Reaffirming its solidarity with the just struggle of the South African people for the elimination of *apartheid* and the exercise of the right of self-determination by the people of South Africa as a whole, irrespective of race, colour or creed,

Recognizing the important role of public information and public involvement in international efforts for the elimination of *apartheid*,

Aware of the enormous resources devoted by the *apartheid* régime and its collaborators for nefarious propaganda to confuse and divert public opinion,

Considering that the United Nations should intensify efforts to inform world public opinion of the inhumanity of *apartheid*, the just struggle of the oppressed people of South Africa and the action by the international community for the elimination of *apartheid*,

Recognizing the importance of contributions by Governments, non-governmental organizations, information media and individuals towards such efforts,

Welcoming and commending the relevant activities of many trade unions, religious bodies and other non-governmental organizations, as well as writers, artists, athletes and other individuals committed to freedom and human dignity,

1. *Encourages* the Special Committee against *Apartheid* and the Centre against *Apartheid* of the Secretariat to intensify their activities designed to inform world public opinion of the situation in South Africa, and to promote public action in support of the just struggle of the oppressed people and the objectives of the United Nations;

2. *Invites* the Secretary-General to take all appropriate steps to ensure full co-operation by the Department of Public Information of the Secretariat, the United Nations Educational, Scientific and Cultural Organization and all United Nations offices and agencies with the Special Committee and the Centre against *Apartheid;*

3. *Calls upon* the Department of Public Information to ensure the widest dissemination of information on atrocities and crimes committed by the *apartheid* régime;

4. *Appeals* to all Governments, information media, non-governmental organizations and individuals to lend their co-operation to the United Nations in disseminating information against *apartheid;*

5. *Also appeals* to all Governments, information media, non-governmental organizations and individuals to intensify further the international campaign for the release of Nelson Mandela and all South African political prisoners and detainees;

6. *Appeals* to all Governments to contribute generously to the Trust Fund for Publicity against *Apartheid* and to information activities of non-governmental organizations engaged in programmes against *apartheid;*

7. *Launches an appeal* to all information media, intellectuals and other public leaders to contribute to efforts to arouse the conscience of the world against *apartheid;*

8. *Requests* the Special Committee to submit to the General Assembly at its fortieth session a special report on further action to intensify efforts to inform world public opinion and encourage wider public action in support of the just struggle of the oppressed people of South Africa.

General Assembly resolution 39/72 E

13 December 1984   Meeting 99   152-0-2 (recorded vote)

55-nation draft (A/39/L.32 and Add.1); agenda item 31.

Sponsors: Afghanistan, Algeria, Angola, Benin, Botswana, Burkina Faso, Burundi, Byelorussian SSR, Cameroon, Cape Verde, Congo, Cuba, Czechoslovakia, Democratic Yemen, Djibouti, Equatorial Guinea, Ethiopia, Gambia, German Democratic Republic, Ghana, Guinea, Hungary, India, Indonesia,. Iran, Kenya, Lesotho, Libyan Arab Jamahiriya, Madagascar, Malaysia, Mali, Mauritania, Mongolia, Morocco, Mozambique, Nepal, Nicaragua, Niger, Nigeria, Qatar, Rwanda, Sao Tome and Principe, Senegal, Sierra Leone, Syrian Arab Republic, Togo, Trinidad and Tobago, Tunisia, Uganda, Ukrainian SSR, United Republic of Tanzania, Viet Nam, Yugoslavia, Zambia, Zimbabwe.

Financial implications. 5th Committee, A/39/787; S-G, A/C.5/39/75.

Meeting numbers. GA 39th session: 5th Committee 45; plenary 66-71, 98, 99.

Recorded vote in Assembly as follows:

In favour: Afghanistan, Albania, Algeria, Angola, Argentina, Australia, Austria, Bahamas, Bahrain, Bangladesh, Barbados, Belgium, Belize, Benin, Bhutan, Bolivia, Botswana, Brazil, Brunei Darussalam, Bulgaria, Burkina Faso, Burma, Burundi, Byelorussian SSR, Cameroon, Canada, Cape Verde, Central African Republic, Chad, Chile, China, Colombia, Comoros, Congo, Costa Rica, Cuba, Cyprus, Czechoslovakia, Democratic Kampuchea, Democratic Yemen, Denmark, Djibouti, Dominica, Dominican Republic, Ecuador, Egypt, El Salvador, Equatorial Guinea, Ethiopia, Fiji, Finland, France, Gabon, Gambia, German Democratic Republic, Germany, Federal Republic of, Ghana, Greece, Grenada, Guatemala, Guinea, Guinea-Bissau, Guyana, Haiti, Honduras, Hungary, Iceland, India, Indonesia, Iran, Iraq, Ireland, Italy, Ivory Coast, Jamaica, Japan, Jordan, Kenya, Kuwait, Lao People's Democratic Republic, Lebanon, Lesotho, Liberia, Libyan Arab Jamahiriya, Luxembourg, Madagascar, Malawi, Malaysia, Maldives, Mali, Malta, Mauritania, Mauritius, Mexico, Mongolia, Morocco, Mozambique, Nepal,

Netherlands, New Zealand, Nicaragua, Niger, Nigeria, Norway, Oman, Pakistan, Panama, Papua New Guinea, Peru, Philippines, Poland, Portugal, Qatar, Romania, Rwanda, Saint Christopher and Nevis, Saint Lucia, Saint Vincent and the Grenadines, Samoa, Sao Tome and Principe, Saudi Arabia, Senegal, Seychelles, Sierra Leone, Singapore, Solomon Islands, Somalia, Spain, Sri Lanka, Sudan, Suriname, Sweden, Syrian Arab Republic, Thailand, Togo, Trinidad and Tobago, Tunisia, Turkey, Uganda, Ukrainian SSR, USSR, United Arab Emirates, United Republic of Tanzania, Uruguay, Vanuatu, Venezuela, Viet Nam, Yemen, Yugoslavia, Zaire, Zambia, Zimbabwe.

Against: None.

Abstaining: United Kingdom, United States.

In resolution 39/72 A, the Assembly commended the anti-*apartheid* and solidarity movements, religious bodies, trade unions, youth and student organizations and other groups engaged in campaigns for the isolation of the *apartheid* régime and for assistance to South African liberation movements recognized by OAU.

Non-governmental organizations

The United Nations, and especially the Special Committee against *Apartheid*, continued in 1984 to encourage non-governmental organizations (NGOs) to promote the campaign against *apartheid*.[1]

The International Conference for the Independence of Namibia and the Eradication of *Apartheid* (Geneva, 2-5 July) was attended by anti-*apartheid* and solidarity organizations from many countries, liberation movements of South Africa and Namibia, and representatives of United Nations Member States based in Geneva. It was organized by the NGO Sub-Committee on Racism, Racial Discrimination, *Apartheid* and Decolonization in co-operation with the Special Committee against *Apartheid* and the United Nations Council for Namibia. The Conference adopted two Declarations, one on *apartheid* in South Africa and the other on Namibia. The Declaration on South Africa condemned those Western countries which collaborated with South Africa, especially those Governments and leaders who had received the Prime Minister of South Africa during his trip to Western Europe (see p. 135).

Among its activities, the Special Committee participated in a number of conferences, seminars and meetings organized by various international and national NGOs. The Chairman sent several messages to conferences and other events. On several occasions, the Committee gave financial and other assistance to conferences which it helped organize.

Following its mission to London on 9 and 10 January to participate in the ceremony for the proclamation of the Declaration of the Greater London Council designating Greater London as an anti-*apartheid* zone, the Committee delegation met with members of the British Anti-*Apartheid* Movement and was received by the Mayor and Councillors of the borough of Camden, which had changed the name of the street where the Movement's office was located to "Mandela Street", in honour of Nelson Mandela, the ANC leader imprisoned in South Africa for over 20 years. The delegation also held meetings with leaders of British organizations active against *apartheid* and with Commonwealth officials and the High Commissioners of front-line States.

The Committee assisted at a press conference on 2 March organized by the British Anti-*Apartheid* Movement in London and held consultations with the General Secretary of the National Union of Seamen who was head of the Maritime Unions against *Apartheid*. In April, the Chairman addressed student groups in Cambridge, Massachusetts, and Stanford University, California, and had a series of meetings with a number of anti-*apartheid* groups in the New York area. During his visit to Paris from 21 to 23 May, he had consultations with the three main French anti-*apartheid* organizations.

While attending the twenty-fifth anniversary conference of the British Anti-*Apartheid* Movement in June, the Chairman held consultations with Archbishop Trevor Huddleston and Bob Hughes, Member of Parliament, President and Chairman, respectively, of the Movement. He also held consultations with anti-*apartheid* movements from Australia, Austria, Belgium, Denmark, Finland, Ireland, the Netherlands, Norway, Spain, Switzerland and the United States, as well as other British groups. On his mission to Rome from 6 to 8 July, the Chairman held consultations with leaders of Italian anti-*apartheid* groups.

At a meeting on 30 November, the Committee heard a statement by Walter Fauntroy, delegate of the District of Columbia in the United States House of Representatives, who informed the meeting about action of North American organizations and leaders against *apartheid*, and referred in particular to the Free South Africa Movement, which was seeking the release of leaders of non-violent protests. At the same meeting, the Committee consulted with J. N. Scholten, Chairman of the Association of West European Parliamentarians for Action against *Apartheid*, who said that the increased level of action within South Africa must be supported by action from outside, particularly by the imposition of economic sanctions against South Africa (see p. 144), and he looked forward to closer ties between United States congressmen and West European parliamentarians for joint action against *apartheid*.

Representatives of 18 anti-*apartheid* and solidarity groups from Australia, the Nordic countries, the United States and Western Europe met in London on 25 and 26 June and adopted a statement[96] saying that South Africa's "agreement" with some African countries had been extracted as a result of military aggression and destabiliza-tion (see p. 177), and that there was no significant internal change in South Africa despite the so-called reform constitution (see p. 157). The participants pledged to focus on the total isolation of South Africa, the immediate independence of Namibia and support for the front-line States.

GENERAL ASSEMBLY ACTION

In resolution 39/72 E, the General Assembly appealed to NGOs, among others, to co-operate with the United Nations in disseminating information against *apartheid*, and to intensify the international campaign for the release of Nelson Mandela and all South African political prisoners and detainees.

Meetings, missions and observances

As in previous years, the Special Committee against *Apartheid* organized or co-sponsored in 1984 a number of meetings, missions and observances to promote the international campaign against *apartheid*.[1] It devoted attention to the dissemination of information on the situation in South Africa, and in southern Africa as a whole, and to the encouragement of public action all over the world on various aspects of the campaign and by various segments of the population. It considered that those efforts should be intensified.

Meetings. The Committee participated in the International Hearings on South African Aggression against Neighbouring States (Oslo, Norway, 22-24 March) (see p. 179).

The North American Regional Conference for Action against *Apartheid*[97] (United Nations Headquarters, 18-21 June) was attended by Governments, the chairmen of relevant United Nations bodies, specialized agencies, the Non-Aligned Movement, OAU, representatives of the southern African liberation movements (ANC, PAC and SWAPO), the Palestine Liberation Organization (PLO) and a number of representatives of religious, trade union, student, anti-*apartheid* and other organizations from Canada and the United States. The participants unanimously adopted a Declaration,[98] in which they noted that the South African régime was intensifying repression internally and conducting a campaign to create the illusion of change in South Africa externally, and that the new constitutional changes were designed to entrench *apartheid*. The Conference stressed that the United States policy of "constructive engagement" and the continuing support given to South Africa by Canada and certain Western countries was largely responsible for helping to maintain *apartheid* rule and for the escalation of South African destruction against neighbouring States. Convinced that isolating the régime and cutting off international support would quicken the arrival of peace and freedom for all the people of southern Africa, the Conference adopted a programme of action on ways for Governments, organizations and individuals to help end collaboration with South Africa.

The Conference of Arab Solidarity with the Struggle for Liberation in Southern Africa was organized by the Committee in co-operation with the League of Arab States (Tunis, Tunisia, 7-9 August).[99] It also was attended by representatives of Arab States, front-line States, United Nations bodies, OAU, ANC, PAC, SWAPO and PLO and other governmental and non-governmental organizations. In the Declaration, adopted by acclamation,[100] the Conference pledged increased support in the struggle for liberation in southern Africa, and total solidarity with Africa in the effort for the emancipation from colonialist and racist oppression. It considered that the continued opposition by the Western permanent members of the Security Council to comprehensive and mandatory sanctions against South Africa had permitted the continuation of its crimes. The Conference condemned the close alliance which had developed between the racist régimes in Pretoria and Tel Aviv in their hostility to genuine freedom of African and Arab peoples. Recognizing the importance of intensifying the dissemination of information in Arab countries on the situation in southern Africa, it requested the League of Arab States and Arab Governments and organizations to take steps toward this end.

The Inter-Faith Colloquium on *Apartheid* (London, 5-8 March)—the first-ever gathering of representatives from the major world religions convened to draw up a common stand against *apartheid*—was organized by Archbishop Trevor Huddleston, in co-operation with the Committee.[101] It was attended by theologians and representatives from the Buddhist, Christian, Hindu, Jewish, Muslim and Sikh faiths. In their unanimously adopted Declaration, the participants made recommendations for their particular religious communities, including: developing information and education about the effects of *apartheid*, as well as spiritual and theological reflection on its implications; support for those struggling in South Africa and Namibia for self-determination and for political freedom; support for the policy of isolating the *apartheid* régime by boycotts in trade, finance, cultural and sporting activities, tourism, emigration and other areas; opposition to the supply of military and nuclear resources to the *apartheid* régime; support for the rights to property, including equitable land distribution and respect for places of worship; and continued prayer and meditation with and for those victimized by *apartheid*.

An International NGO Conference for the Independence of Namibia and the Eradication of *Apartheid* was also held (Geneva, 2-5 July) (see p. 172).

The Seminar on the Legal Status of the *Apartheid* Régime in South Africa and Other Legal Aspects of the Struggle against *Apartheid* (Lagos, 13-16 August) was organized by the Committee in co-operation with Nigeria.[102] The participants examined the international and national legal implications of the situation in South Africa as a result of its *apartheid* policies, particularly the legal status of the régime under international law, and the need to develop strategies for concerted legal and political action against it. The Seminar was attended by international jurists, social scientists, international, regional and national legal bodies, anti-*apartheid* movements and other relevant organizations, as well as United Nations bodies; and other intergovernmental organizations and liberation movements of South Africa and Namibia. In its Declaration,[103] the Seminar recognized that recent developments in southern Africa made it imperative for the international community to understand the need for action through the application of international law to a situation which constituted a serious threat to international peace and security. The Seminar found that there was a strong body of law to support the international campaign for the eradication of *apartheid* and colonialism in South Africa and to provide support for the primary instrument of change, the national liberation movement of the people of South Africa. The régime—which deprived the majority of its people of elementary rights, left them without citizenship and subjected them to racial discrimination—lacked fundamental legitimacy because of its racist and minority foundations. In the view of the Seminar, a United Nations Member State which was in a situation of illegitimacy could be expelled from the Organization. Moreover, a State which had persistently violated the United Nations Charter and which had been expelled would still be answerable to the international community as provided for in Article 2 of the Charter.

In its annual report to the General Assembly issued in September,[1] the Committee recommended that the Assembly commend the declarations of the conferences it had organized or co-sponsored during the previous year to the attention of Governments, organizations and individuals.

Missions. In 1984, the Committee sent a number of missions and held consultations with Governments as part of its activities in the campaign against *apartheid*.

The Chairman of the Committee met on 4 April with the Prime Minister of Sweden, who assured him that Sweden would provide all appropriate assistance to those engaged in the legitimate struggle against *apartheid* and to the front-line States. Also in April, during a mission to the United Kingdom, he met with the Secretary of State for Foreign and Commonwealth Affairs and conveyed to him the Committee's view that *apartheid* was the root cause of the problems in southern Africa. In May, he travelled to Washington, D.C., and had discussions on the situation in southern Africa with the Assistant Secretary of State for African Affairs. During his visit to Paris from 21 to 23 May, the Chairman met with the Minister for External Relations of France, who pledged his Government's co-operation in the struggle against *apartheid*.

The Chairman undertook a mission to Rome and to the Vatican on 6 and 7 July. He met with the Director-General for Political Affairs in the Italian Ministry of Foreign Affairs. On 7 July, he was received in audience by Pope John Paul II, who presented him with a special message.[54] From 28 to 30 August, he visited India for consultations with the Prime Minister, current Chairman of the Movement of Non-Aligned Countries, and other officials.

From 30 October to 6 November, the Chairman visited Norway, Sweden, Denmark and the Netherlands for further discussions with governmental leaders on international action against *apartheid* in the light of recent developments in South Africa. He emphasized that Western countries were in a position to make the most significant contribution to the eradication of *apartheid*.

The Committee held consultations with various government officials, including the Minister for External Affairs of France on 9 October; Walter Fauntroy, delegate of the District of Columbia in the United States House of Representatives, on 30 November; and J. N. Scholten, Chairman of the Association of West European Parliamentarians for Action against *Apartheid*, also on 30 November.

The Committee organized and sent a delegation of women leaders to Japan, Australia, New Zealand, Singapore, Thailand and India from 24 August to 19 September to promote wider awareness of the plight of women and children under *apartheid* and of the need for increased assistance to them. The delegation was led by Naome Nhiwatiwa, Deputy Minister of Information, Posts and Telecommunications of Zimbabwe. In each country, the delegation met with officials of the Ministry of Foreign Affairs, had discussions with NGOs and met with members of the news media.

Observances. As part of its activities, the Committee organized or was represented at several special observances in 1984.

As in previous years, it held solemn meetings in observance of the International Day for the Elimination of Racial Discrimination (21 March),

the International Day of Solidarity with the Struggling People of South Africa (16 June), the International Day of Solidarity with the Struggle of Women of South Africa and Namibia (9 August), and the Day of Solidarity with South African Political Prisoners (11 October).

In connection with the Day for eliminating racial discrimination, the Committee issued a statement[104] noting with satisfaction the actions taken by many cities in support of the oppressed peoples of southern Africa. The Committee appealed to all cities to take appropriate action against *apartheid* and urged citizens to promote such action through such measures as ceasing purchase of goods originating from South Africa and Namibia; withdrawing investments in companies owned by or operating in South Africa; discouraging transnational corporations and financial institutions from investing in, or making loans to, South Africa; and withholding city facilities from any sporting or cultural event involving South Africans and Namibians, or sportsmen or entertainers who had toured South Africa and were included in the Committee's registers (see p. 165).

At its meeting on 6 January, the Committee issued a statement endorsing the observance of 1984 as the Year of the Women of South Africa, called for by ANC. In that statement, the Committee expressed the hope that the observance of the Year would lead to wider support and solidarity with the oppressed women of South Africa and Namibia and their national liberation movements. It also urged Governments, organizations and media to undertake concrete programmes for that purpose. In related action, the Committee held a solemn meeting on 17 April on the occasion of the thirtieth anniversary of the founding of the Federation of South African Women. Drawing attention to the particular oppression inflicted on black women under the *apartheid* system, the participants emphasized that black women had been the worst sufferers under the pass laws, the bantustan policy, the forced uprooting of millions of African people, and numerous laws enforcing racial discrimination. They explained that black women constituted most of the domestic workers who were denied trade union rights and were subjected to exploitation. Women and children, they added, had been victims of raids by the South African armed forces against refugees in neighbouring countries. (See also ECONOMIC AND SOCIAL QUESTIONS, Chapter XIX.)

In addition, the United Nations Council for Namibia held a special meeting on 25 May in observance of Africa Liberation Day and the Week of Solidarity with the Peoples of Namibia and All Other Colonial Territories, as well as those in South Africa, Fighting for Freedom, Independence and Human Rights. The Committee against

Apartheid and the Committee on colonial countries participated in that meeting (see TRUSTEESHIP AND DECOLONIZATION, Chapter I).

GENERAL ASSEMBLY ACTION

In resolution 39/72 A, the General Assembly commended the declarations of conferences organized or co-sponsored by the Special Committee against *Apartheid* to the attention of all Governments and organizations.

Work programme of the Committee against *Apartheid*

In the light of the current situation in South Africa, the Special Committee against *Apartheid*, recognizing the need for greater action under United Nations auspices towards the total isolation of the Pretoria régime and support to the national liberation struggle of the South African people, pledged to strengthen its activities, with the assistance of the Secretariat's Centre against *Apartheid*.[(1)] The Committee said it would need to expand its activities as regards: consultations with Governments and organizations; dissemination of information; promotion of public campaigns for the boycott of South Africa, for support of the liberation struggle, for the unconditional release of South African political prisoners, against collaboration with the Pretoria régime, and on other aspects of mobilization against *apartheid;* and encouragement of artists, writers, sportspersons, religious leaders and others to contribute to the campaign against *apartheid*. Towards that end, it intended to organize, co-sponsor or support several conferences or seminars, and to give greater support for public campaigns. It planned to publicize the struggle of the oppressed people against *apartheid* and for liberation, and the activities of liberation movements recognized by OAU. In that connection, it intended to co-operate with ANC in observing on 26 June 1985 the thirtieth anniversary of the adoption of the Freedom Charter of South Africa.

For its special projects in 1985, the Committee recommended that the General Assembly make an allocation of $400,000, and it appealed for increased voluntary contributions to the Trust Fund for Publicity against *Apartheid* and for the special projects. The Committee recognized the need to expand the work of the Centre against *Apartheid* to meet the increased requirements of the Committee and the international campaign against *apartheid*, and it planned to consult with the Secretary-General on the most effective arrangements.

GENERAL ASSEMBLY ACTION

On 13 December, the General Assembly adopted resolution 39/72 B by recorded vote.

Programme of work of the Special Committee against *Apartheid*

The General Assembly,

Having considered the report of the Special Committee against *Apartheid,*

1. *Commends* the Special Committee against *Apartheid* for its vigorous efforts to promote concerted international action in support of the legitimate aspirations of the oppressed people of South Africa and in implementation of relevant United Nations resolutions;

2. *Expresses great appreciation* for the work of the Centre against *Apartheid* of the Secretariat in assisting the Special Committee;

3. *Endorses* the recommendations in the report of the Special Committee relating to its programme of work and activities to promote the international campaign against *apartheid;*

4. *Authorizes* the Special Committee to organize or co-sponsor conferences, seminars or other events, to send missions to Governments, organizations and conferences and to assist campaigns against *apartheid* as it may deem necessary in the discharge of its responsibilities, within the financial resources allocated under the present resolution, and requests the Secretary-General to provide the necessary staff and services for such activities;

5. *Decides* to make a special allocation of $400,000 to the Special Committee for 1985 from the regular budget of the United Nations for the cost of special projects to be decided upon by the Committee in order to promote the international campaign against *apartheid;*

6. *Again requests* Governments and organizations to make voluntary contributions or provide other assistance for the special projects of the Special Committee and to make generous contributions to the Trust Fund for Publicity against *Apartheid;*

7. *Requests* the Secretary-General to provide the Centre against *Apartheid* with all the necessary resources to enable it effectively to discharge its responsibilities in assisting the Special Committee.

General Assembly resolution 39/72 B

13 December 1984   Meeting 99   152-2 (recorded vote)

55-nation draft (A/39/L.29 and Add.1); agenda item 31.

Sponsors: Afghanistan, Algeria, Angola, Barbados, Benin, Botswana, Burkina Faso, Burundi, Byelorussian SSR, Cameroon, Cape Verde, Congo, Cuba, Czechoslovakia, Democratic Yemen, Djibouti, Equatorial Guinea, Ethiopia, Gambia, German Democratic Republic, Ghana, Guinea, Hungary, India, Indonesia, Iran, Iraq, Kenya, Lesotho, Libyan Arab Jamahiriya, Malaysia, Mali, Mauritania, Mongolia, Morocco, Mozambique, Nepal, Nicaragua, Niger, Nigeria, Qatar, Rwanda, Sao Tome and Principe, Senegal, Sierra Leone, Syrian Arab Republic, Togo, Trinidad and Tobago, Tunisia, Uganda, Ukrainian SSR, United Republic of Tanzania, Viet Nam, Zambia, Zimbabwe.

Financial implications. 5th Committee, A/39/787; S-G, A/C.5/39/75.

Meeting numbers. GA 39th session: 5th Committee 45; plenary 66-71, 98, 99.

Recorded vote in Assembly as follows:

In favour: Afghanistan, Albania, Algeria, Angola, Argentina, Australia, Austria, Bahamas, Bahrain, Bangladesh, Barbados, Belgium, Belize, Benin, Bhutan, Bolivia, Botswana, Brazil, Brunei Darussalam, Bulgaria, Burkina Faso, Burma, Burundi, Byelorussian SSR, Cameroon, Canada, Cape Verde, Central African Republic, Chad, Chile, China, Colombia, Comoros, Congo, Costa Rica, Cuba, Cyprus, Czechoslovakia, Democratic Kampuchea, Democratic Yemen, Denmark, Djibouti, Dominica, Dominican Republic, Ecuador, Egypt, El Salvador, Equatorial Guinea, Ethiopia, Fiji, Finland, France, Gabon, Gambia, German Democratic Republic, Germany, Federal Republic of, Ghana, Greece, Grenada, Guatemala, Guinea, Guinea-Bissau, Guyana, Haiti, Honduras, Hungary, Iceland, India, Indonesia, Iran, Iraq, Ireland, Italy, Ivory Coast, Jamaica, Japan, Jordan, Kenya, Kuwait, Lao People's Democratic Republic, Lebanon, Lesotho, Liberia, Libyan Arab Jamahiriya, Luxembourg, Madagascar, Malawi, Malaysia, Maldives, Mali, Malta, Mauritania, Mauritius, Mexico, Mongolia, Morocco, Mozambique, Nepal, Netherlands, New Zealand, Nicaragua, Niger, Nigeria, Norway, Oman, Pakistan, Panama, Papua New Guinea, Peru, Philippines, Poland, Portugal, Qatar, Romania,

Rwanda, Saint Christopher and Nevis, Saint Lucia, Saint Vincent and the Grenadines, Samoa, Sao Tome and Principe, Saudi Arabia, Senegal, Seychelles, Sierra Leone, Singapore, Solomon Islands, Somalia, Spain, Sri Lanka, Sudan, Suriname, Sweden, Syrian Arab Republic, Thailand, Togo, Trinidad and Tobago, Tunisia, Turkey, Uganda, Ukrainian SSR, USSR, United Arab Emirates, United Republic of Tanzania, Uruguay, Vanuatu, Venezuela, Viet Nam, Yemen, Yugoslavia, Zaire, Zambia, Zimbabwe.

Against: United Kingdom, United States.

In explanation of vote, a number of States expressed reservations about the resolution and the Committee's report.[1]

Belgium, the Federal Republic of Germany, Italy, Japan, the Netherlands and New Zealand did not agree with all the conclusions and recommendations made by the Committee.

The Federal Republic of Germany and the United Kingdom expressed concern over the report's balance. The former hoped that the Committee would display a more equitable position towards it and other Western States in its publications. Terming the report slanted and in several places seriously misrepresenting its position, the United Kingdom objected to the Committee's tendentious attacks on Member States.

The Federal Republic of Germany, Japan and the Netherlands expressed concern over the financial implications of the resolution. Japan was concerned about paragraphs 4 and 5, which it felt gave the Committee an excessively wide margin of discretion, and hoped that it would manage its budget efficiently and report back on how it spent the $400,000. In the view of the Netherlands, the means for implementing the work programme should be found within regular budget resources.

In related action in resolution 39/72 A, the Assembly endorsed the annual report of the Special Committee. By resolution 39/72 C, it requested the Committee to continue publicizing information on the relations between Israel and South Africa, to keep the matter under review and to report to the Assembly and the Security Council as appropriate; the Secretary-General was requested to assist the Committee in disseminating information on the collaboration between those States. The Assembly, in resolution 39/72 E, encouraged the Committee and the Centre against *Apartheid* to intensify their activities designed to inform world public opinion of the South Africa situation, and promote public action in support of the struggle of the oppressed people and the United Nations objectives.

REFERENCES
[1]A/39/22. [2]YUN 1983, p. 120. [3]A/39/22/Add.1. [4]A/39/557. [5]A/39/137-S/16401. [6]A/39/131-S/16414 & Corr.1. [7]A/39/133-S/16417. [8]A/39/207. [9]A/39/560-S/16773. [10]A/39/590 & Corr.1. [11]A/SPC/39/L.3 & Add.1-18. [12]A/39/669. [13]YUN 1968, p. 17, GA res. 2373(XXII), annex, 12 June 1968. [14]YUN 1977, p. 161, SC res. 418(1977), 4 Nov. 1977. [15]YUN 1978, p. 915, SC res. 435(1978), 29 Sep. 1978. [16]YUN 1983, p. 1061, GA res. 38/36 A, 1 Dec. 1983. [17]A/39/24. [18]A/AC.131/120. [19]YUN 1982, p. 1300, GA res. 37/233 A, 20 Dec. 1982. [20]YUN 1981, p. 1153, GA res. ES-8/2, 14 Sep. 1981. [21]E/1984/14 (res. 1984/6). [22]A/39/23 (A/AC.109/794). [23]A/39/85-S/16290. [24]YUN 1983, p. 129. [25]A/39/129-S/16406. [26]A/39/183-S/16484. [27]A/39/69. [28]A/39/294-S/16605 & Corr.1. [29]A/39/315-S/16634. [30]A/39/336. [31]A/39/23 (A/AC.109/795). [32]E/1984/14 (res. 1984/40). [33]A/39/18 (dec. 1(XXX)). [34]A/39/23 (A/AC.109/796). [35]E/C.10/1984/19 & Add.1. [36]YUN 1980, p. 200. [37]YUN 1977, p. 162, SC res. 421(1977), 9 Dec. 1977. [38]YUN 1983, p. 139. [39]*Ibid.*, p. 144, ESC res. 1983/74, 29 July 1983. [40]E/C.10/1984/10. [41]YUN 1983, p. 610, ESC dec. 1983/182, 29 July 1983. [42]YUN 1970, p. 753, SC res. 283(1970), 29 July 1970. [43]E/1984/18. [44]YUN 1973, p. 103, GA res. 3068(XXVIII), annex, 30 Nov. 1973. [45]E/1984/14 (res. 1984/7). [46]E/CN.4/Sub.2/1984/8 & Add.1,2. [47]E/CN.4/1985/3 (res. 1984/4). [48]E/AC.69/2. [49]E/AC.69/3. [50]YUN 1982, p. 287. [51]A/39/23 (A/AC.109/797). [52]YUN 1983, p. 148, GA res. 38/39 F, 5 Dec. 1983. [53]*Ibid.*, p. 147. [54]A/39/346-S/16669. [55]E/1984/14 (res. 1984/5). [56]E/CN.4/1985/3 (res. 1984/34). [57]YUN 1948-49, p. 535, GA res. 217 A (III), 10 Dec. 1948. [58]S/16752. [59]YUN 1977, p. 706. [60]E/1984/14 (res. 1984/4). [61]A/39/425-S/16711. [62]S/16265. [63]S/16271. [64]S/16283. [65]A/39/86-S/16292. [66]A/39/90-S/16298. [67]YUN 1983, p. 154. [68]S/16692. [69]S/16698. [70]S/16699. [71]S/16704. [72]A/39/523. [73]A/39/531. [74]S/16786. [75]S/16794. [76]A/39/338-S/16659. [77]A/39/487-S/16741. [78]A/39/514-S/16755. [79]A/AC.115/L.612. [80]A/AC.115/L.619. [81]YUN 1976, p. 136, GA res. 31/6 F, 9 Nov. 1976. [82]A/39/36. [83]YUN 1983, p. 158, GA res. 38/39 K, 5 Dec. 1983. [84]*Ibid.*, p. 158. [85]A/AC.192/2. [86]DP/1985/17. [87]E/1984/20 (dec. 84/11). [88]ID/CONF.5/46 & Corr.1 (res. 15). [89]YUN 1982, p. 1314, GA res. 37/233 E, 20 Dec. 1982. [90]A/39/15, vol. II (res. 304(XXIX)). [91]YUN 1983, p. 160. [92]YUN 1965, p. 115, GA res. 2054 B (XX), 15 Dec. 1965. [93]A/39/605. [94]A/39/351. [95]A/39/139-S/16430. [96]A/AC.115/L.613. [97]A/AC.115/L.614. [98]A/39/370-S/16686. [99]A/AC.115/L.615 & Corr.1. [100]A/39/450-S/16726. [101]A/AC.115/L.605. [102]A/AC.115/L.616. [103]A/39/423-S/16709 & Corr.1. [104]A/AC.115/L.606.

South Africa and the front-line States of southern Africa

In 1984, several United Nations bodies expressed concern over South Africa's relations with its neighbours. Those countries—Angola, Botswana, Mozambique, the United Republic of Tanzania, Zambia and Zimbabwe—were known as the front-line States. The General Assembly, the Special Committee against *Apartheid*, the Commission on Human Rights and the United Nations Council for Namibia were the main bodies taking such action.

The situation between Angola and South Africa deteriorated in early 1984; in January Angola complained to the Security Council that South African troops had moved further into its territory during a bombing attack. The Council responded in resolution 546(1984), demanding that South Africa unconditionally withdraw its occupation forces from Angola. The Assembly also called for the withdrawal of South African troops. The Committee against *Apartheid* reported that most of those forces were withdrawn during 1984.

Relations between Mozambique and South Africa took a new direction. The two countries informed the Secretary-General that they had reached a security agreement in March, known as the Nkomati Accord, by which they agreed not to allow their territories to be used for launching acts of aggression against each other.

In an exchange of letters, Lesotho and South Africa mentioned that they might arrive at some kind of security arrangement.

The Committee against *Apartheid* condemned South Africa's aggression against the front-line States and said the régime was pressuring them to sign non-aggression accords.

Activities of the Committee against *Apartheid*. The Special Committee against *Apartheid*, in its annual report to the General Assembly,[1] condemned South Africa's actions against the front-line States and expressed concern about the security of the region of southern Africa as a whole.

In a statement issued on 3 January 1984, the Acting Chairman condemned, on behalf of the Committee, the escalation of aggression by South Africa against Angola (see p. 180) since December 1983.[2] He said that unless urgent action was taken by the international community, there was danger of escalation of South Africa's aggression all over the region. He urged Governments and organizations to demonstrate their solidarity with Angola and press for comprehensive sanctions against South Africa (see p. 138).

On 16 March 1984,[3] the Committee adopted a statement on developments in South Africa and southern Africa as a whole. It reaffirmed that the primary cause of tension and conflict in the region was the *apartheid* policy, and that tension would remain unless *apartheid* was eliminated and the people of South Africa as a whole were enabled to establish a non-racial democratic State. It added that South Africa's expressions of willingness to accept non-intervention in neighbouring States—after causing enormous damage to their economies through aggression, destabilization and terrorism—required vigilance by the international community. The Committee urged the community to condemn the actions of Governments, transnational corporations and other interests which, through collaboration with South Africa, encouraged it in its racist, repressive and aggressive policies.

Among its conclusions,[1] the Committee stated that after a series of acts of aggression, massive destabilization, terrorism and economic blackmail against neighbouring States, the Pretoria régime had proceeded, with the support and encouragement of certain Western States, to pressure front-line States to enter into security agreements with it. It had sought recognition as a regional power with a view to acquiring hegemony over southern

Africa in return for serving the interests of major Western Powers. South Africa's offensive, encouraged by the United States policy of "constructive engagement", was accompanied by propaganda that its pressure against neighbouring States to sign agreements reflected a desire to seek peaceful solutions. An unpublicized accord by South Africa with Swaziland, followed by an understanding with Angola (the Lusaka Understanding of February 1984, which provided for the withdrawal of South African forces from Angola) and a non-aggression agreement with Mozambique (the Nkomati Accord of 16 March), had failed to halt the armed struggle of the opposition.

Following the accord with Angola and after a long delay, South Africa withdrew its forces but left behind some 60 soldiers. In addition it continued to support the forces of the Uniao Nacional para a Independência Total de Angola (UNITA) opposed to the Angolan Government. Despite the Nkomati Accord, Mozambique claimed that South African agents continued to supply the National Resistance Movement with arms and ammunition. Reports indicated that just before the signing of the Accord, South Africa had resupplied the Movement with war *matériel*.

The Committee believed that the South African régime constituted a greater menace than ever to international peace and security. Its agreements were directed against the legitimate struggle of internationally recognized national liberation movements and were intended to provide legitimacy to the Pretoria régime and help it establish a southern African "constellation of States" under its hegemony. Despite the agreements, South Africa continued to occupy Angolan territory and to subvert neighbouring States. It had increased its military budget by 21.4 per cent for 1984-1985 and was expanding military bases near its borders. It staged its biggest military manoeuvres in September 1984. South Africa was able to take such steps because of its confidence in protection by Western Powers against international action, the Committee concluded.

The Committee urged the international community to show concern for the States which had been subjected to aggression and destabilization, and it considered it essential for the United Nations to promote assistance to all front-line States and Lesotho so that they could overcome their economic, security and other problems. It called for urgent action to defend the States which were currently under pressure by Pretoria to sign "security agreements". It urged the General Assembly to demand that the United States and the United Kingdom, in particular, take action to oblige South Africa to end its illegal pressure against neighbouring States. Noting that the difficulties of the front-line States had created certain problems for the national liberation movement of South Africa, the Committee urged the international community to assist the movement to overcome the difficulties caused by the vulnerability of neighbouring States to South Africa's pressure. It recommended that the Assembly urge all States and organizations to provide maximum moral, political and material assistance to the front-line States and Lesotho, to the liberation movements of South Africa and to all those struggling for freedom in that country in opposition to *apartheid*.

The Committee participated in the International Hearings on South African Aggression against Neighbouring States (Oslo, Norway, 22-24 March), which were conducted by a panel of more than 20 prominent persons presided over by the former Minister for Foreign Affairs of Denmark. Statements were made by the Foreign Minister of Norway, Bishop Desmond Tutu and representatives of the front-line States and Lesotho. The panel adopted a declaration calling for greater efforts to increase the effectiveness of the arms embargo against South Africa, strengthen efforts to obtain binding international sanctions against it, increase assistance to the front-line States and the liberation movements in South Africa and Namibia, exercise more control to isolate South Africa, and strengthen diplomatic, political and economic pressure on it with a view to preventing it from carrying out aggression against neighbouring States.

Action by the Committee on colonial countries. The Committee on colonial countries also took action on South Africa's aggression against neighbouring States.

In a decision of 20 August,[4] the Committee condemned the repeated aggression by South African armed forces against neighbouring States and its use of Namibian territory to launch such attacks, which had resulted in the loss of innocent lives and the destruction of property. It called on Member States to extend all possible assistance to those States so that they might better defend their territorial integrity. On 21 August,[5] the Committee, citing South Africa's continued illegal occupation of Namibia, said that in its escalating war against the people of Namibia and their national liberation movement, SWAPO, South Africa had committed armed aggression against the neighbouring African countries, particularly Angola, causing extensive loss of human lives and destruction of the economic infrastructure.

Action by the Commission on Human Rights. In two 28 February resolutions on the violation of human rights in southern Africa, the Commission on Human Rights also condemned South Africa's aggression (see ECONOMIC AND SOCIAL QUESTIONS, Chapter XVIII). It condemned South Africa for its military attacks and its economic and political pressures againt neighbouring States and

demanded the immediate cessation of the aggression.[6] The Commission rejected all policies which encouraged South Africa to intensify its repression of the people of South Africa and Namibia and escalate its acts of aggression against the neighbouring States; and demanded that South Africa cease forthwith its aggression aimed at undermining the economies and destabilizing the political institutions of neighbouring States.[7]

Action by the Council for Namibia. The United Nations Council for Namibia, at extraordinary plenary meetings (Bangkok, Thailand, 21-25 May), adopted the Bangkok Declaration and Programme of Action on Namibia, which it included in its annual report to the General Assembly.[8] In the Declaration, the Council condemned the use of Namibia by South Africa as a staging ground for armed aggression against neighbouring States, in order to intimidate them and to prevent them from supporting the struggle of Namibian and South African peoples for independence. The Council stated that support of the front-line States continued to be important to bring independence to Namibia. It deemed it imperative that the international community increase, as a matter of urgency, financial, material, military and political support to the front-line States to enable them to resolve their own economic difficulties, which were largely a consequence of South Africa's policies, and to defend themselves better against South Africa's attempts to destabilize them.

The Programme called on States to give maximum support, including military assistance, to the front-line States so that they could strengthen their economies and repel South Africa's aggression. The Council called on organizations to extend all possible assistance to those States, and urged Governments, agencies and organizations, to support the Southern African Development Co-ordination Conference, of which the States were members, to reduce their dependence on South Africa.

Communications. During 1984, several bodies adopted declarations which dealt with relations between South Africa and its neighbours.

On 2 March,[9] France forwarded the declaration adopted on 28 February at the EEC Ministerial Meeting on European Political Co-operation. On southern Africa, the 10 EEC States welcomed the initiatives aimed at ending the conflicts in the region—the February Lusaka agreement on military disengagement in southern Angola and the understanding between South Africa and Mozambique. They called on all concerned to seize the opportunity to implement the plan for Namibia's independence outlined by the Security Council in resolution 435(1978).[10]

The OAU Council of Ministers (Addis Ababa, Ethiopia, 27 February–5 March) adopted a series of resolutions,[11] including one on the situation in southern Africa. The Council condemned South Africa for its destabilizing policy against neighbouring countries and particularly the recruitment, training and financing of armed bandits and mercenaries directed against States in the region, as well as the military occupation of Angola, and demanded the withdrawal of the South African army; the Council also condemned South Africa's raids against Lesotho and Mozambique.

The Front-line States' Summit Meeting (Arusha, United Republic of Tanzania, 29 April) adopted a final communiqué.[12] In regard to the understanding between Angola and South Africa, the heads of State and Government hoped that South Africa would honour its commitment to withdraw its troops from Angola, which they believed would be an opportunity for the implementation of Security Council resolution 435(1978). As for South Africa's agreement with Mozambique, they hoped that South Africa would honour its commitment to cease destabilizing Mozambique through the use of armed bandits, and expressed appreciation of its support for ANC in the struggle against *apartheid*.

The Fourth Islamic Summit (Casablanca, 16-19 January)[13] confirmed its support for the struggle of the peoples of South Africa and Namibia for liberation through all means and condemned the aggression by South Africa against front-line States and demanded the withdrawal of South African troops from Angola.

In the final communique of the Foreign Ministers and Heads of Delegation of Non-Aligned Countries (New York, 1-5 October)[14] the participants condemned the aggression, economic pressure and acts of terrorism and sabotage launched by South Africa against independent African countries, and demanded the withdrawal of South African troops from Angola.

GENERAL ASSEMBLY ACTION

The General Assembly, on numerous occasions in 1984, condemned South Africa's aggression against neighbouring countries.

In resolution 39/72 A, it condemned the régime for its repeated acts of aggression, subversion and terrorism against independent African States. It demanded that all South African troops be immediately and unconditionally withdrawn from Angola and that South Africa respect the independence, sovereignty and territorial integrity of independent African States. The international community and all countries were called on to render concrete support and assistance to the front-line and other neighbouring States in the region to enable them to provide adequate security for refugees and to resist the mounting aggression, subversion and economic pressure of South Africa.

The Assembly, in resolution 39/72 G, condemned the overt and covert aggressive actions of South Africa directed at the destabilization of neighbouring States,

and demanded that South Africa immediately withdraw its troops from southern Angola and end the destabilization of front-line and other States.

In resolution 39/50 A on Namibia, the Assembly reaffirmed its conviction that support of the front-line States for the Namibian cause continued to be an important factor in the efforts to bring independence to the Territory. It urged the international community to increase financial, material, military and political support to those States so as to enable them to resolve their own economic difficulties, which were largely a consequence of South Africa's policies of aggression and subversion, and to defend themselves. The Assembly again condemned South Africa for using Namibia as a staging ground to launch acts of subversion, destabilization and aggression against neighbouring States.

By resolution 39/17, the Assembly condemned the establishment and use of armed terrorist groups by South Africa with a view to pitting them against the national liberation movements and destabilizing the legitimate Governments of southern Africa. The Assembly reaffirmed its solidarity with the independent African countries and national liberation movements that were victims of aggression and destabilization by South Africa, and called on the international community to support those countries so that they could strengthen their defence capacity, defend their sovereignty and territorial integrity, and rebuild and develop. Stating that the practice of using mercenaries against sovereign States and national liberation movements constituted a criminal act, the Assembly called on Governments to ban the recruitment, financing and training of mercenaries in their territories and the transit of mercenaries through them, and to prohibit their nationals from serving as such.

In resolution 39/43, the Assembly urged United Nations organizations to extend material assistance to the front-line States in order to enable them to support the struggle of the Namibian people for independence and to resist the violation of their territorial integrity by South African armed forces directly or, as in Angola and Mozambique, through puppet traitor groups.

The Assembly, in resolution 39/8, reiterated its appreciation to the Secretary-General for organizing and mobilizing special programmes of economic assistance for African States, in particular for the front-line States and others in the region, to help them cope with the situation caused by South Africa's aggression.

Angola-South Africa armed incidents and South African occupation of Angola

On 1 January 1984, Angola, in a letter to the President of the Security Council,[15] requested an urgent Council meeting in the face of what it said was the worsening military situation created by the South

African army's movement further north into Angolan territory and the combat occurring between military units of the two countries in localities more than 200 kilometres from the Namibian border.

The Council took action that month, demanding that South Africa withdraw immediately from Angola and cease all violations against its territory.

SECURITY COUNCIL ACTION

In response to Angola's request,[15] the Security Council held three meetings from 4 to 6 January. Algeria, Angola, Ethiopia, Mozambique, Nigeria, South Africa, the Syrian Arab Republic, Togo, the United Republic of Tanzania, Viet Nam, Yugoslavia and Zambia were invited, at their request, to participate in the discussion without vote.

Addressing the Council, Angola said that just two weeks earlier South Africa had offered a "disengagement" of its troops in Angola to begin on 31 January 1984,[16] but, before Angola could begin to study that offer, South Africa had fortified its military positions inside Angolan territory, where they had been in illegal occupation since 1981, and had moved further into Angolan territory—200 kilometres north of the Namibian border. The aggression, including bombing, strafing, rocket attacks, artillery shelling and mine detonations, disproved South Africa's claim that its troops would operate only against Namibian freedom fighters. Sophisticated military arms were available to South Africa through direct and indirect military assistance, in contravention of the Council's embargo on arms sales, by Pretoria's Western friends. South Africa's moves, which began in 1975 and ranged from airspace violations to wholesale slaughter, were aimed at installing a puppet administration in areas under its military occupation. Despite the continuing operations, Angola was willing to test South Africa's offer and had reaffirmed its own offer of 31 December 1983[16] to accept a 30-day truce beginning 1 February 1984, if SWAPO agreed and if South Africa withdrew from Angola and promised to initiate the United Nations plan for Namibia's independence.[10]

South Africa said that its operations in southern Angola had one objective—protecting Namibia's inhabitants from SWAPO terrorist attacks launched from Angola. It was that State's support in providing facilities and arms to SWAPO that had led to the current situation. As it had stated before, South Africa would not sit idly by while SWAPO operated with impunity from the safety of Angolan territory. The cross-border activities were aimed at eradicating SWAPO bases in Angola; if Angolan forces continued to give military support to SWAPO or interfere with South Africa's operations against it, then they must bear responsibility for the consequences. South Africa denied that

its forces had committed atrocities against the civilian population of Angola. It reiterated its 1983 offer[16] to begin a disengagement on 31 January 1984 of its forces in Angola, on the understanding that this would be reciprocated by Angola assuring that its own forces, SWAPO and the Cuban forces in Angola would not exploit the situation by threatening the security of Namibia. In regard to the Namibia situation, South Africa remained prepared to begin implementing Security Council resolution 435(1978)[10] upon resolution of the problem of Cuban forces in Angola.

Almost all speakers remarked that Angola was bringing its complaint about South African aggression to the Council only two weeks after the Council had condemned such action and demanded that South Africa withdraw.[17] Peru recalled that South Africa had violated Angola's sovereignty and territorial integrity ever since its independence.

Mozambique, the Syrian Arab Republic, the Ukrainian SSR, the USSR, the United Republic of Tanzania and Viet Nam believed that through such aggressive acts, South Africa was attempting to gain control of southern Africa. According to the USSR, South Africa, expecting impunity, intended to eliminate the progressive régime in Angola and perpetuate racist colonial systems in the region. The Ukrainian SSR spoke similarly, stating that South Africa sought to safeguard *apartheid* and maintain colonial systems in southern Africa. Nicaragua believed that the latest offensive was aimed at destabilizing neighbouring States and South Africa was attempting to do so by giving support to the counter-revolutionary forces in Angola, financed and trained by South Africa and its allies; the leadership of the Angolan counter-revolution was based in South Africa and its operations depended on Pretoria and a great Power.

Mozambique, the Syrian Arab Republic, the Ukrainian SSR, the USSR and Zambia stated that South Africa was aided in its aggressive acts by certain Western States, and some of those speakers singled out the United States. The Syrian Arab Republic, for example, said that South Africa, thanks to the military power it had gained and to the protection it enjoyed from some Western States, in particular the United States, had arrogated to itself the right to invade other African States. Viet Nam stated that South Africa could act with impunity due to the support and encouragement proffered by international imperialism, particularly by a powerful permanent member of the Council.

France and the Netherlands believed that the cause of the escalation of military operations was the result of South Africa's continued presence in Namibia and its refusal to implement the United Nations plan on Namibian independence.[10]

A number of countries—including China, France, India, Nicaragua, the United Republic of Tanzania and Yugoslavia—affirmed that South Africa had used pretexts to justify its occupation of Angola. In China's view, South Africa's pretext of protecting the Namibian people from SWAPO attacks was a complete reversal of right and wrong since the South African occupation of Namibia was in itself illegal. The United Republic of Tanzania remarked that South Africa was attempting to link its withdrawal from Angolan territory to the question of Cuban troops there, as it had attempted to link Namibia's independence to the same issue. Togo, speaking for the African Group, urged the Council to reject "linkage". According to Yugoslavia, the solution to the problem of southern Africa could not remain hostage to the political manoeuvres and delays by South Africa or to its proposals aimed at postponing the solution. Zimbabwe stated that the Council had already rejected South Africa's attempt to justify its aggression by the need to protect the people of Namibia against SWAPO freedom fighters. Concerning South Africa's statement on its security needs, Egypt said that it was not South Africa but Angola that needed to have its security protected against aggression, particularly since South Africa was exploiting its military superiority.

In regard to South Africa's offer to disengage its forces from Angola during a 30-day cease-fire,[16] Algeria, Mozambique, the Netherlands and Viet Nam questioned South Africa's sincerity in the light of its current actions against that country, describing the offer either as a smoke-screen to conceal its real intentions or a mockery. The Netherlands hoped that the truce proposed by Angola on 31 December 1983 would meet with more success. France, India and Pakistan also expressed support for the the Angolan proposal for a cease-fire. France requested South Africa not to miss the opportunity of reaching peaceful settlement in southern Africa; to make this peace initiative possible, South Africa should immediately halt its military operation. Describing the proposal as positive and constructive, India noted that the Secretary-General was in direct touch with the parties concerned and looked forward to hearing the outcome of his consultations. Pakistan said that Angola's positive response to South Africa's offer should create an opportunity for the Secretary-General to ascertain whether South Africa was genuinely interested in peace in the region and willing to co-operate in the United Nations plan for Namibian independence.

A number of countries made specific recommendations for Council action. In addition to urging it to condemn South Africa's aggression, many called for a halt in its military operations and an unconditional withdrawal of its troops from Angola. Algeria, Egypt, India, Nicaragua, Peru, Togo, for the African Group, the USSR, the United Republic of Tanzania, Viet Nam, Yugoslavia and Zimbabwe called for such action. Algeria, Nicaragua, the USSR, the United Republic of Tanzania and Zambia said that the Council should demand compensation from South Africa for the damage caused in Angola. In this regard, Ethiopia, Mozambique, the USSR and Zambia remarked that many innocent lives, including civilians and refugees, had been lost during the South African operations, and extensive damage was done to Angola's economic infrastructure. Both Ethiopia and Viet Nam called for assistance to Angola to help it overcome problems resulting from the aggression. Ethiopia urged Governments to increase material and financial support to the front-line countries, in particular to Angola. Among those calling for compensation for the loss of life and destruction of property, Zambia said that as a result of South Africa's aggression, 2,000 Angolan refugees had fled to Zambia over the previous fortnight.

Many countries called on the Council to take measures under Chapter VII of the United Nations Charter if South Africa failed to comply with its demands. Algeria, China, Egypt, India, Mozambique, Pakistan, the Syrian Arab Republic, the USSR, the United Republic of Tanzania, Viet Nam, Yugoslavia, Zambia and Zimbabwe made such recommendations. Algeria said the Council's actions had not had a deterrent effect; therefore the Council should invoke Chapter VII which was designed to impose respect for the law. In Mozambique's view, the Council had a choice to make between encouraging South Africa to flout the Charter or taking measures to force it to respect international law through the imposition of sanctions. Malta hoped that the Council would devise more appropriate means to negotiate stumbling-blocks and to encourage further dialogue and progress, relying on the efforts of the Secretary-General in the pursuit of United Nations objectives for southern Africa.

The Upper Volta, Yugoslavia and Zimbabwe urged the Council to take a unanimous decision on the problem. The Upper Volta said that the Council must act with firmness in demanding implementation of its resolutions. Previous Council resolutions had raised questions concerning that body's effectiveness, according to Algeria, Ethiopia, Pakistan, the Syrian Arab Republic, the United Republic of Tanzania and the Upper Volta.

On 6 January, the Council adopted resolution 546(1984).

The Security Council,
Having considered the statement of the Permanent Representative of Angola to the United Nations,

Recalling its resolutions 387(1976), 418(1977), 428(1978), 447(1979), 454(1979), 475(1980) and 545(1983),

Gravely concerned at the renewed escalation of unprovoked bombing and persistent acts of aggression, including the continued military occupation, committed by the racist régime of South Africa in violation of the sovereignty, airspace and territorial integrity of Angola,

Grieved at the tragic and mounting loss of human life and concerned about the damage and destruction of property resulting from those escalated bombing and other military attacks against and occupation of the territory of Angola by South Africa,

Indignant at the continued military occupation of parts of the territory of Angola by South Africa in contravention of the Charter of the United Nations and relevant Security Council resolutions,

Conscious of the need to take effective steps for the prevention and removal of threats to international peace and security posed by South Africa's military attacks,

1. *Strongly condemns* South Africa for its renewed, intensified, premeditated and unprovoked bombing, as well as the continuing occupation of parts of the territory of Angola, which constitute a flagrant violation of the sovereignty and territorial integrity of that country and endanger seriously international peace and security;

2. *Further strongly condemns* South Africa for its utilization of the international Territory of Namibia as a springboard for perpetrating the armed attacks as well as sustaining its occupation of parts of the territory of Angola;

3. *Demands* that South Africa should cease immediately all bombing and other acts of aggression and unconditionally withdraw forthwith all its military forces occupying Angolan territory as well as undertake scrupulously to respect the sovereignty, airspace, territorial integrity and independence of Angola;

4. *Calls upon* all States to implement fully the arms embargo imposed against South Africa in Security Council resolution 418(1977);

5. *Reaffirms* the right of Angola, in accordance with the relevant provisions of the Charter of the United Nations and, in particular, Article 51, to take all the measures necessary to defend and safeguard its sovereignty, territorial integrity and independence;

6. *Renews* its request to Member States to extend all necessary assistance to Angola, in order that Angola may defend itself against the escalating military attacks by South Africa as well as the continuing occupation of parts of Angola by South Africa;

7. *Reaffirms further* that Angola is entitled to prompt and adequate compensation for the damage to life and property consequent upon these acts of aggression and the continuing occupation of parts of its territory by the South African military forces;

8. *Decides* to meet again in the event of non-compliance by South Africa with the present resolution in order to consider the adoption of more effective measures in accordance with appropriate provisions of the Charter;

9. *Requests* the Secretary-General to monitor the implementation of the present resolution and report to the Security Council thereon not later than 10 January 1984;

10. *Decides* to remain seized of the matter.

Security Council resolution 546(1984)

6 January 1984	Meeting 2511	13-0-2

13-nation draft (S/16247/Rev.1).

Sponsors: Angola, Egypt, India, Malta, Mozambique, Nicaragua, Nigeria, Pakistan, Peru, United Republic of Tanzania, Upper Volta, Zambia, Zimbabwe.
Meeting numbers. SC 2509-2511.
Vote in Council as follows:
In favour: China, Egypt, France, India, Malta, Netherlands, Nicaragua, Pakistan, Peru, Ukrainian SSR, USSR, Upper Volta, Zimbabwe.
Against: None.
Abstaining: United Kingdom, United States.

In explanation of vote, the United Kingdom said that, while it condemned South Africa's military action in Angola, it could not accept the extreme language of the resolution, in particular in the last preambular paragraph and in paragraph 1, and it questioned whether such language could serve any useful purpose; it also objected to paragraph 6, which might be taken as an invitation to widen the conflict, the third preambular paragraph and paragraph 8, and mentioned that the text did not reflect the latest diplomatic offers.

The United States, which deplored the South African military activity in Angola and welcomed the proposals for disengagement and a 30-day ceasefire, was concerned that the resolution focused on conflict, recrimination and condemnation rather than on the exploration of opportunities for peaceful reconciliation.

The Netherlands said that its positive vote did not mean it was considering measures for the implementation of paragraph 6.

Report of the Secretary-General. As requested by the Security Council, the Secretary-General reported on 10 January on the implementation of resolution 546(1984).[18] He said he had requested Angola and South Africa to provide all pertinent information on implementation of the resolution.

South Africa replied that it would continue to act against terrorist organizations that sought to determine the future of Namibia through violence; it accepted that its position could entail confrontation with the whole world. With regard to the demand that it withdraw from Angola, the Defence Minister of South Africa, in a statement on 8 January, said the South African security forces had reached their goal with the pre-emptive operations against SWAPO in southern Angola and withdrawal had commenced. South Africa hoped that Angola would cease protecting and supporting terrorist actions against Namibia. The Minister stated that South Africa remained prepared to negotiate with Angola. Angola informed the Secretary-General that there had been no fundamental change in the military situation in Angola and no signs of withdrawal of South African forces, which continued to conduct operations and to occupy parts of southern Angola. The Secretary-General said he would continue to monitor the situation closely.

Communications. In a letter of 24 January to the Council President,[19] Angola listed what it said was the number of South African battalions in southern Angola and stated that, from 15 to 17 January, South African forces had violated Angola's airspace about five times by reconnaissance flights. Israel addressed a letter to the Council President on 13 January,[20] stating that on 5 January, in the course of the debate on the situation in southern Angola, the Syrian Arab Republic had maligned Israel by injecting irrelevant unwarranted references to Israel.

The Secretary-General also received letters concerning the situation in Angola.

On 3 January,[21] Jamaica transmitted a 30 December 1983 statement by its Deputy Prime Minister and Minister for Foreign Affairs stating that South Africa's aggressive acts against Angola resulted from Pretoria's determination to maintain its illegal hold on Namibia and from its policy that other Governments in the region should be kept in a constant state of weakness and fear; the first step to rectifying the problems of the region would be to achieve independence for Namibia. By a letter of 5 January,[22] the USSR forwarded a TASS statement of that date describing the recent actions by South Africa against Angola and saying they were linked to the increased aggressiveness of international, and primarily United States, imperialism; TASS welcomed Angola's December 1983 proposals.[16]

On 9 January,[23] Guinea-Bissau forwarded a telex from its head of State, on behalf also of Angola, Cape Verde, Mozambique and Sao Tome and Principe, stating their belief that the United Nations, and the Security Council in particular, must take action under the Charter to establish the responsibility of South Africa for the situation in southern Africa and to ensure assistance to Angola.

The issue of the presence of South African forces in Angola, in particular how it affected the implementation of the United Nations plan for Namibia's independence, was also brought up by Angola and Cuba in a joint letter of 20 March, by South Africa on 26 March, and by Angola on 17 November (see TRUSTEESHIP AND DECOLONIZATION, Chapter III).

Action by the Commission on Human Rights. The Commission on Human Rights, on 28 February, demanded that South Africa immediately end aggression against neighbouring countries and withdraw its armed forces from Angola.[24] It also condemned South Africa for its persistent acts of subversion and aggression against Angola, including the occupation of a part of its territory, and called on South Africa to cease all acts of aggression against and withdraw all its troops from that country.[7]

Lesotho-South Africa dispute

Lesotho and South Africa transmitted to the Secretary-General letters exchanged between them in 1984 on security concerns.

On 15 August,[25] Lesotho forwarded a message it had sent on 10 August in response to a South African proposal that the two countries enter into a non-aggression pact. While reaffirming its readiness to adhere to the principles of sovereign equality, territorial inviolability and the obligation of every State to prevent its territory from being used for aggression against another, Lesotho said that the two positions were still far apart. It affirmed that it would continue to refrain from interfering directly in the internal affairs of other States.

In reply, South Africa, in a message of 28 August transmitted on 7 September,[26] said the facts did not support Lesotho's claim to uphold those principles. In view of Lesotho's failure to meet South Africa's security concerns, South Africa found it difficult to proceed with a feasibility study on the highlands water project, which it said was vulnerable to acts of violence by subversive elements. South Africa remained determined to ensure that its security interests were not jeopardized.

Lesotho, in a 31 August message transmitted on 14 September,[27] said the Government was in the process of consulting its people about the South African proposal for a formal security agreement. The study on the water project, a Lesotho project, had progressed uninterrupted, evidence that it was not vulnerable to violence; urging South Africa not to withdraw its participation in the study, Lesotho affirmed that it had no intentions nor means of jeopardizing the security interests of South Africa and it was determined to live in peace with it.

The United Kingdom, in a letter to the Secretary-General of 2 July,[28] rejected certain statements made in the Special Committee against *Apartheid* concerning its policy, including an allegation that it was attempting to coerce Lesotho into signing an agreement with South Africa.

GENERAL ASSEMBLY ACTION

The General Assembly, in resolution 39/17, condemned South Africa for its acts of destabilization, armed aggression against and economic blockade of Lesotho and urged the international community to extend maximum assistance to that country to enable it to fulfil its international humanitarian obligations towards refugees and to use its influence on South Africa to desist from its terrorist acts against Lesotho. In resolution 39/72 A, the Assembly demanded that South Africa fully compensate Lesotho and other African States for the damage to life and property caused by its acts of aggression. The Assembly called for special economic assistance to Lesotho in resolution 39/183.

Mozambique-South Africa accord

Mozambique, by a letter of 30 March to the Secretary-General,[29] forwarded the Agreement on Non-Aggression and Good Neighbourliness signed by the heads of State of Mozambique and South Africa on 16 March at Nkomati. By the Nkomati Accord, the two countries agreed not to allow their respective territories to be used to launch acts of aggression against the other and not to use the territory of third States for aggression against the other. They agreed to set up a joint security commission to monitor the Accord's application.

On 11 April,[30] South Africa forwarded to the Secretary-General the address given by its Prime Minister at the signing of the Nkomati Accord. He said the Accord demonstrated that States with different socio-economic and political systems could live together in peace and work together in the pursuit of common interests; South Africa looked forward to a new era of co-operation and peaceful coexistence between the two countries. Mozambique addressed a letter to the Secretary-General on 25 April,[31] transmitting excerpts of a speech by its President on 5 April. He stated that the Accord ensured the defence of Mozambique's borders and formed part of the general movement of the coastal States to transform the Indian Ocean into an area free from military bases and nuclear weapons (see p. 78).

REFERENCES

[1]A/39/22. [2]YUN 1983, p. 173. [3]A/39/137-S/16401. [4]A/39/23 (A/AC.109/794). [5]*Ibid.* (A/AC.109/796). [6]E/1984/14 (res. 1984/5). [7]*Ibid.* (res. 1984/6). [8]A/39/24. [9]A/39/123-S/16389. [10]YUN 1978, p. 915, SC res. 435(1978), 29 Sep. 1978. [11]A/39/207. [12]A/AC.115/L.611. [13]A/39/131-S/16414 & Corr.1. [14]A/39/560-S/16773. [15]S/16244. [16]YUN 1983, p. 174. [17]*Ibid.*, p. 177, SC res. 545(1983), 20 Dec. 1983. [18]S/16266. [19]S/16287. [20]S/16277. [21]A/39/62-S/16248. [22]A/39/65-S/16254. [23]S/16267. [24]E/1984/14 (res. 1984/4). [25]S/16703. [26]S/16737. [27]S/16746. [28]A/39/336. [29]A/39/159-S/16451. [30]A/39/179-S/16477. [31]A/39/213-S/16506.

Questions involving the Libyan Arab Jamahiriya

In 1984, Chad and the Libyan Arab Jamahiriya addressed letters to the President of the Security Council concerning their continuing territorial dispute. The Council met at the Sudan's request to consider its complaint of aggression by the Jamahiriya, which the Jamahiriya denied. The Council took no action on a draft resolution on the subject.

For other questions concerning the Libyan Arab Jamahiriya, see p. 253 and LEGAL QUESTIONS, Chapter I.

Chad–Libyan Arab Jamahiriya dispute

By a letter of 31 January to the Security Council President,[1] the Libyan Arab Jamahiriya transmitted a statement issued in Paris by what it described as the legitimate Government of Chad. The statement said that France, which had intensified its military operations in Chad, should expect an appropriate reaction from the citizens of Chad, that it would bear responsibility for a deterioration of the military situation, and that the legitimate Government of Chad had appealed to the Jamahiriya to stand by the forces of national liberation.

Chad responded on 3 February,[2] stating that the legitimate Government of Chad was headed by Hissein Habré and that French forces were in Chad to help it defend itself against the aggression of the Jamahiriya, which continued to occupy Chadian territory.

India forwarded to the Secretary-General on 8 October[3] the final communiqué adopted by the Meeting of Ministers for Foreign Affairs and Heads of Delegation of Non-Aligned Countries to the General Assembly (New York, 1-5 October). The Meeting expressed satisfaction at the decision on the withdrawal of foreign troops from Chad and called on all members of the Non-Aligned Movement to assist that country to complete the task of reconciliation and national reconstruction.

Libyan Arab Jamahiriya–Sudan dispute

The Sudan, by a letter of 17 March to the Secretary-General,[4] transmitted a letter of the same date from its Foreign Minister, stating that the Libyan Arab Jamahiriya had committed aggression against Sudanese territory, threatening its security and violating the United Nations Charter and international law; the Jamahiriya had bombed Omdurman on 16 March, killing five Sudanese citizens and destroying four buildings. In a letter of 18 March to the Security Council President,[5] the Sudan requested the Council to meet to consider that aggression.

The Libyan Arab Jamahiriya denied the allegations in a letter of 19 March to the Secretary-General.[6] It said the Sudan had been experiencing continuous revolutions and disturbances for a number of years and it was trying to find external justifications through empty accusations against neighbouring States; furthermore, the Sudan's accusation was in preparation for military aggression against the Jamahiriya with the co-operation of imperialist Powers.

SECURITY COUNCIL CONSIDERATION

The Security Council considered the Sudan's complaint at two meetings on 27 March.

Meeting numbers. SC 2520, 2521.

At their request, Benin, Chad, Indonesia, the Libyan Arab Jamahiriya, Nigeria, Oman, the Sudan and Zaire were invited to participate in the discussion without the right to vote.

Addressing the Council, the Sudan described the damage done by the 16 March bombing attack and said it was clear that the bomber took off from a military base at Kufra in the southeastern part of the Libyan Arab Jamahiriya. The unprovoked act was not only a flagrant act of aggression against civilian targets in the most densely populated city in the Sudan, but was also another of a series of acts of aggression and interference in its internal affairs. Another such act was a speech by the head of State of the Jamahiriya on 2 March when he said that he supported the revolution in south Sudan to liberate the rest of the country. Over the past few years, the Sudan had been subjected to attacks by the Jamahiriya because of its wish to impose its hegemony on the Sudan. The Council should condemn the aggression, call on the Jamahiriya to desist from such acts and persuade it to respect the Sudan's territorial integrity.

The Libyan Arab Jamahiriya said the matter was rooted in the Sudan's internal situation, which had experienced 18 or more attempted *coups d'état* since 1969. The current civil war was the result of violations of agreements on national conciliation in the south, and the political problems were reflected in the adverse economic situation resulting from mismanagement. Because of its indebtedness, the Sudan had become a protectorate of the United States and was making charges against the Jamahiriya to obtain American assistance. The President of the Sudan had also made public statements that he intended to get rid of the Jamahiriya's head of State. The Sudan had to justify United States intervention and the dispatch of that country's AWACS surveillance aircraft to the Sudan. Recent Western press reports raised the possibility that the Sudan had launched the raid on its own people in an attempt to obtain United States aid. Denying the Sudan's allegations and stating there was no evidence to support them, the Jamahiriya said the real culprit was the United States, against which it had brought a complaint before the Council on 22 March (see p. 253).

Benin, the USSR and the Upper Volta said there was a lack of evidence to support the Sudan's allegations. Benin, Nicaragua and the USSR believed that the real cause of the incident could be traced to international imperialism. According to Benin, everything seemed to indicate that the incident was a plot hatched by imperialism against the Jamahiriya, and an international campaign of defamation was being carried out against that country. Nicaragua said it knew from experience the capacity of imperialism to provoke conflicts in neighbouring countries whenever it considered its political or security interests threatened. The USSR stated that the forces of imperialism were ready to utilize any pretext in order to flex their

military muscles and impose their will on young non-aligned States; it added that the United States had sent reconnaissance aircraft to the region for espionage operations against the Jamahiriya.

On the other hand, Chad, Egypt, the Netherlands, Oman and the United States said that the evidence supported the Sudan's claims or that the Libyan Arab Jamahiriya was responsible for the air raid. Indonesia and Oman expressed support for the Sudan. Chad and the United States said the attack was further evidence of the Jamahiriya's plans for regional expansion, and Chad added that the attack was an act of State terrorism. According to Chad, the Jamahiriya's head of State had made known his plans for expansion and hegemony against neighbouring countries; although he had failed in his attempts to merge his country with certain neighbouring States, including Chad, Egypt, the Sudan and Tunisia, that did not discourage him. The United States pointed out that the Jamahiriyan leader had affirmed that his Government was allied with the popular revolution in southern Sudan; he had threatened war on fronts all over the world and had used tactics of assassination and violence as well as subversion in Africa.

France, the United Kingdom and the Upper Volta condemned the act of violence without blaming any particular party. The Upper Volta felt more information was needed to clarify the situation, as did France, which added that such an act could affect peace and stability in a friendly country, which it hoped would be able to overcome its difficulties free from external interference. Similarly, Indonesia regretted that regional conflicts, such as those in north Africa, were increasingly being drawn into the cast of East-West rivalry, further complicating their solution.

The Netherlands defended the Sudan's right to self-defence when confronted with aggression. Egypt agreed and reaffirmed its support for the Sudan under their mutual defence pact, stressing that the stability and security of both States were intimately linked.

The USSR believed that the best approach to the current debate was through a regional mechanism; Nigeria urged the use of OAU.

Some countries called on the Council to take action, while others believed that it should refrain from premature judgements. Chad, Egypt and Oman called on the Council to take appropriate measures to uphold the principles of the United Nations and international law. Oman, for example, said the Council must act to put an end to intervention in the Sudan's internal affairs, since further acts would bring about a regional war. Chad, Egypt, the Netherlands, the United States and Zaire also said the Council should demand an end to such aggression and intervention. In addition, Zaire said that African Governments had the right and the duty to unite their forces to guarantee the security of the States of the region against such acts in violation of the OAU principles of the inviolability of the borders inherited from colonial times and non-interference in the internal affairs of other States.

Taking the opposite view, Nigeria, the United Kingdom and the Upper Volta urged the Council to refrain from a premature decision or called for quiet diplomacy as a means of conciliation. Appealing to the international community not to exacerbate tension by further magnifying the differences that had given rise to it, Nigeria said it was ready to be of any assistance in the search for a peaceful resolution of the current misunderstanding. Similarly, the United Kingdom said it had sought to encourage an exchange of views between the two countries through quiet diplomacy and through the offices of the Council President. In the circumstances, the Upper Volta said, the Council should refrain from any hasty decision and should denounce foreign intervention that might inflame passions; it appealed to the two parties involved not to insist on a Council decision but to allow the Council simply to consider the matter.

At the conclusion of the Council's meetings, the President announced that the next meeting to consider the complaint would be scheduled in consultation with the Council members; no further meetings on the item were held in 1984. On 30 March,[7] Egypt and the Sudan submitted a draft resolution by which the Council would have affirmed that the unprovoked air attack against the Sudan constituted a flagrant violation of the sovereignty and territorial integrity of a Member State, and would have condemned the indiscriminate bombardment of civilian targets in Omdurman.

REFERENCES

[1]S/16303. [2]S/16308. [3]A/39/560-S/16773. [4]S/16419.
[5]S/16420. [6]S/16421. [7]S/16455.

Ethiopia-Somalia dispute

In 1984, Ethiopia and Somalia addressed letters to the Secretary-General concerning actions by forces in Somali territory.

Somalia, by a letter of 5 January,[1] forwarded two resolutions adopted by the Fourteenth Islamic Conference of Foreign Ministers (Dhaka, Bangladesh, 6-11 December 1983). The Conference, in a resolution on Ethiopia's occupation of two areas of Somalia's territory, condemned Ethiopian armed aggression against Somalia and called on Ethiopia to withdraw its forces from the two oc-

cupied areas. In a resolution on the problem of the Horn of Africa, the Conference reiterated its rejection of the presence of foreign forces in the region and called for their immediate withdrawal. The two resolutions were also submitted by Bangladesh on 15 March[2] along with all the other resolutions and a final communiqué adopted by the Conference.

Rejecting Somalia's allegations, Ethiopia, on 16 January,[3] said Somalia was attempting to cover up its internal unrest and added that the two areas under dispute were regions held by forces in Somalia opposed to the current Government there.

Referring to Ethiopia's letter, Somalia, on 30 January,[4] said that Ethiopia, by attempting to shift responsibility to phantom forces in Somalia, had implicitly admitted that two areas in Somali territory were currently under Ethiopian occupation; Somalia was willing to have the facts verified, provided that Ethiopia would permit an independent fact-finding mission to visit the occupied settlements.

On 24 January,[5] Somalia forwarded a resolution adopted by the Fourth Islamic Summit Conference (Casablanca, Morocco, 16-19 January) in which the Conference expressed concern over the continuing occupation by Ethiopia of two areas of Somali territory and called on Ethiopia to withdraw immediately and unconditionally. That text was also included in a document forwarded by Morocco on 13 March[6] containing the final communiqué and resolutions of the Conference.

Somalia, on 30 May,[7] complained of an Ethiopian air attack against densely populated civilian centres of Somalia on 24, 25 and 28 May, causing considerable loss of life and property damage. Referring to that complaint on 5 June,[8] Ethiopia transmitted a press statement issued by its Ministry of Foreign Affairs, rejecting the allegations as unfounded and stating that they were calculated to help Somalia procure arms in purusit of its expansionist policies.

REFERENCES

[1]A/39/66. [2]A/39/133-S/16417. [3]A/39/78. [4]A/39/93.
[5]A/39/84. [6]A/39/131-S/16414 & Corr.1. [7]A/39/280.
[8]A/39/291.

Comorian island of Mayotte

Report of the Secretary-General. As requested by the General Assembly in November 1983,[1] the Secretary-General submitted a report in September 1984[2] on the question of the Comorian island of Mayotte, submitting the information received from the Comoros, France and OAU in response to his request for pertinent information.

The Comoros said there had been little change in the situation, despite many high-level contacts between the Comorian and French Governments. In spite of France's repeatedly proclaimed willingness to seek without delay a just solution to the problem within the framework of Franco-Comorian friendship, it had not put forward any specific proposals. The Comoros added that, on the contrary, owing to the lax administration maintained on Mayotte, there had been a deterioration of the situation, which, unless halted, was likely to place the solution of the problem in serious jeopardy. Stating its intention to pursue diplomatic efforts aimed at recovering the Comorian island of Mayotte, the Comoros said it would like the United Nations to give a new impetus to its legitimate demands by taking action along the lines of the resolutions which the Assembly had previously adopted on the subject.

France replied that the atmosphere of trust between it and the Comoros was conducive to the continuation of a constructive dialogue between them, with the aim of finding a solution to the Mayotte problem that was acceptable to all. France intended to continue to develop and increase economic, social and cultural contacts in order to foster closer relations between the islands of the archipelago.

According to OAU, there had been little change in the situation, despite the many high-level contacts between the two Governments and the direct talks that had been held between the heads of State of France and the Comoros. The Comorian Government was actively pursuing diplomatic steps to recover Mayotte, it added.

Communications. On 15 March,[3] Bangladesh transmitted to the Secretary-General resolutions adopted by the Fourteenth Islamic Conference of Foreign Ministers (Dhaka, 6-11 December 1983). In a resolution on Mayotte, the Conference reaffirmed the unity and territorial integrity of the Comoros and its sovereignty over Mayotte, invited France to open negotiations with the Comoros to secure the rapid restoration of Mayotte to the Comoros, called on members of the Organization of the Islamic Conference to exert their influence on France to accelerate the negotiations, and invited the organization's Secretary-General to contact France to inform it of the organization's concern. By a letter of 13 March,[4] Morocco forwarded resolutions adopted by the Fourth Islamic Summit Conference (Casablanca, 16-19 January) including one on Mayotte, by which the Conference reaffirmed the stand taken by the Islamic Foreign Ministers.

On 8 October,[5] India forwarded the final communiqué of the Meeting of Ministers for Foreign Affairs and Heads of Delegation of Non-Aligned Countries to the General Assembly. The communiqué included a statement on Mayotte, in which the non-aligned countries reaffirmed that it was an integral part of the Comoros and called on France to end its occupation.

GENERAL ASSEMBLY ACTION

On 11 December, the General Assembly adopted resolution 39/48 by recorded vote.

Question of the Comorian island of Mayotte
The General Assembly,

Recalling its resolutions 1514(XV) of 14 December 1960, containing the Declaration on the Granting of Independence to Colonial Countries and Peoples, and 2621(XXV) of 12 October 1970, containing the programme of action for the full implementation of the Declaration,

Recalling also its previous resolutions, in particular resolutions 3161(XXVIII) of 14 December 1973, 3291(XXIX) of 13 December 1974, 31/4 of 21 October 1976, 32/7 of 1 November 1977, 34/69 of 6 December 1979, 35/43 of 28 November 1980, 36/105 of 10 December 1981, 37/65 of 3 December 1982 and 38/13 of 21 November 1983, in which it, *inter alia*, affirmed the unity and territorial integrity of the Comoros,

Recalling, in particular, its resolution 3385(XXX) of 12 November 1975 on the admission of the Comoros to membership in the United Nations, in which it reaffirmed the necessity of respecting the unity and territorial integrity of the Comoro Archipelago, composed of the islands of Anjouan, Grande-Comore, Mayotte, and Mohéli,

Recalling further that, in accordance with the agreements between the Comoros and France, signed on 15 June 1973, concerning the accession of the Comoros to independence, the results of the referendum of 22 December 1974 were to be considered on a global basis and not island by island,

Convinced that a just and lasting solution to the question of Mayotte is to be found in respect for the sovereignty, unity and territorial integrity of the Comoro Archipelago,

Convinced further that a speedy solution of the problem is essential for the preservation of the peace and security which prevail in the region,

Bearing in mind the wish expressed by the President of the French Republic to seek actively a just solution to that problem,

Taking note of the repeated wish of the Government of the Comoros to initiate as soon as possible a frank and serious dialogue with the French Government with a view to accelerating the return of the Comorian island of Mayotte to the Islamic Federal Republic of the Comoros,

Taking note of the report of the Secretary-General,

Bearing in mind the decisions of the Organization of African Unity, the Movement of Non-Aligned Countries and the Organization of the Islamic Conference concerning this question,

1. *Reaffirms* the sovereignty of the Islamic Federal Republic of the Comoros over the island of Mayotte;

2. *Invites* the Government of France to honour the commitments entered into prior to the referendum on the self-determination of the Comoro Archipelago of 22 December 1974 concerning respect for the unity and territorial integrity of the Comoros;

3. *Calls* for the translation into practice of the wish expressed by the President of the French Republic to seek actively a just solution to the question of Mayotte;

4. *Urges* the Government of France to open the negotiations with the Government of the Comoros with a view to ensuring the effective and prompt return of the island of Mayotte to the Comoros;

5. *Requests* the Secretary-General of the United Nations to follow developments concerning this question, in conjunction with the Secretary-General of the Organization of African Unity, and to report thereon to the General Assembly at its fortieth session;

6. *Decides* to include in the provisional agenda of its fortieth session the item entitled "Question of the Comorian island of Mayotte".

General Assembly resolution 39/48

11 December 1984   Meeting 94   122-1-21 (recorded vote)

32-nation draft (A/39/L.42); agenda item 27.
Sponsors: Algeria, Bahamas, Benin, Botswana, Comoros, Congo, Cuba, Ethiopia, Gambia, Ghana, Guinea-Bissau, Guyana, Haiti, Kenya, Lesotho, Libyan Arab Jamahiriya, Mauritania, Mauritius, Morocco, Nigeria, Oman, Qatar, Senegal, Sierra Leone, Somalia, Sudan, Swaziland, Uganda, United Arab Emirates, United Republic of Tanzania, Yemen, Zambia.

Recorded vote in Assembly as follows:

In favour: Afghanistan, Albania, Algeria, Angola, Argentina, Bahamas, Bahrain, Bangladesh, Barbados, Belize, Benin, Bolivia, Botswana, Brazil, Brunei Darussalam, Bulgaria, Burkina Faso, Burma, Burundi, Byelorussian SSR, Cameroon, Cape Verde, Central African Republic, Chad, Chile, China, Colombia, Comoros, Congo, Costa Rica, Cuba, Czechoslovakia, Democratic Kampuchea, Democratic Yemen, Djibouti, Ecuador, Egypt, Equatorial Guinea, Ethiopia, Fiji, Finland, Gabon, German Democratic Republic, Ghana, Guatemala, Guinea, Guyana, Haiti, Honduras, Hungary, India, Indonesia, Iran, Iraq, Ivory Coast, Jamaica, Jordan, Kenya, Kuwait, Lao People's Democratic Republic, Lesotho, Liberia, Libyan Arab Jamahiriya, Madagascar, Malawi, Malaysia, Maldives, Mali, Malta, Mauritania, Mauritius, Mexico, Mongolia, Morocco, Mozambique, Nepal, Nicaragua, Niger, Nigeria, Oman, Pakistan, Panama, Papua New Guinea, Paraguay, Peru, Philippines, Poland, Qatar, Romania, Rwanda, Saint Lucia, Sao Tome and Principe, Saudi Arabia, Senegal, Sierra Leone, Singapore, Somalia, Sri Lanka, Sudan, Suriname, Swaziland, Sweden, Syrian Arab Republic, Thailand, Togo, Trinidad and Tobago, Tunisia, Turkey, Uganda, Ukrainian SSR, USSR, United Arab Emirates, United Republic of Tanzania, Uruguay, Vanuatu, Venezuela, Viet Nam, Yemen, Yugoslavia, Zaire, Zambia, Zimbabwe.

Against: France.

Abstaining: Australia, Austria, Belgium, Canada, Cyprus, Denmark, Germany, Federal Republic of, Greece, Iceland, Ireland, Israel, Italy, Japan, Luxembourg, Netherlands, New Zealand, Norway, Portugal, Spain, United Kingdom, United States.

The Comoros said Mayotte shared the same language, culture and religion as the other islands of the Comoros and should have been granted independence by France at the time the Comoros became independent in 1973. The solution to the problem was not to be found in the repeated referendums that had been declared illegal by the international community, but in sincere dialogue and agreement between France and the Comoros, in accordance with the resolutions of international organizations.

France regretted that the question of Mayotte was again before the Assembly. Although it opposed the resolution, particularly paragraph 1, it hoped that a solution could be found and believed that the text rightly recalled France's expression of will for a lasting solution. France would continue to develop all economic, social and cultural bonds between Mayotte and the Comoros in order to promote a *rapprochement* among the islands of the archipelago.

The Assembly took related action in resolution 39/17, in which it noted the contacts between the Comoros and France in the search for a solution to the problem of the integration of Mayotte in the Comoros, in accordance with OAU and United Nations resolutions. In resolution 39/193, the Assembly called for special economic assistance to the Comoros.

REFERENCES
[1]YUN 1983, p. 188, GA res. 38/13, 21 Nov. 1983. [2]A/39/518. [3]A/39/133-S/16417. [4]A/39/131-S/16414 & Corr.1. [5]A/39/560-S/16773.

Malagasy islands question

For the fourth successive year, the General Assembly in 1984 did not debate the question of the Malagasy islands of Glorieuses, Juan de Nova, Europa and Bassas da India, but decided to include the item in its provisional agenda for the following year. This question, pertaining to islands north and west of Madagascar, had been on the Assembly's agenda each year since 1979, when the Assembly invited France to negotiate with Madagascar on the reintegration of the islands with Madagascar,[1] a position it reaffirmed in 1980.[2]

The Meeting of Ministers for Foreign Affairs and Heads of Delegation of Non-Aligned Countries to the Assembly (New York, 1-5 October) adopted a final communiqué which included a statement on the islands. The communiqué was transmitted to the Secretary-General by India on 8 October.[3] Concerning the Malagasy islands in the Mozambique Channel and the Indian Ocean, the non-aligned countries called on the two parties to pursue their talks with a view to resolving the issue in conformity with the United Nations Charter.

GENERAL ASSEMBLY ACTION

On 3 December, the Chairman of the Special Political Committee informed that body that he had held consultations with interested delegations, particularly those of France and Madagascar. Since talks between the two authorities were in progress, and in order to take into account a meeting held in Paris on 13 and 14 September during which their senior officials had exchanged views, it had been requested that consideration of the question be postponed until the 1985 General Assembly session.

Acting on the recommendation of the Special Political Committee, the Assembly adopted decision 39/421 without vote.

Question of the Malagasy islands of Glorieuses, Juan de Nova, Europa and Bassas da India

At its 100th plenary meeting, on 14 December 1984, the General Assembly, on the recommendation of the

Special Political Committee, decided to include in the provisional agenda of its fortieth session the item entitled "Question of the Malagasy islands of Glorieuses, Juan de Nova, Europa and Bassas da India".

General Assembly decision 39/421

Adopted without vote

Approved by SPC (A/39/717/Rev.1) without vote, 3 December (meeting 46); oral proposal by Chairman; agenda item 78.
Meeting numbers. GA 39th session: SPC 46; plenary 100.

REFERENCES

[1]YUN 1979, p. 270, GA res. 34/91, 12 Dec. 1979. [2]YUN 1980, p. 262, GA res. 35/123, 11 Dec. 1980. [3]A/39/560-S/16773.

UN Educational and Training Programme for Southern Africa

The United Nations Educational and Training Programme for Southern Africa granted scholarships to 896 persons in 1983/84. The Programme was financed from the Trust Fund made up of voluntary contributions by States, organizations and individuals; also offers of scholarships for training in their own countries were received from 23 States. The Secretary-General described the activities of the Programme in a report covering the period from 1 October 1983 to 30 September 1984.[1] During that period, 410 new awards were granted and 486 awards were extended. Of the total, 777 South Africans received grants (see p. 170), 70 scholarships were granted to Zimbabweans and 49 to Namibians (see TRUSTEESHIP AND DECOLONIZATION, Chapter III). The awards were granted for a wide variety of professional, commercial and technical training, in addition to university studies. Those receiving scholarships attended programmes in the following regions: Africa (446 students), North America (317), Asia (102), Europe (28) and Latin America and the Caribbean (3).

Noting inflation rates and rising scholarship costs, the Secretary-General said that the 1984 contributions and pledges totalling $3,303,064 as at 30 September 1984 represented, in real terms, a significant decrease in resources over the previous year. In view of the increasing demand for educational opportunities by the people of South Africa and Namibia and the rapidly increasing costs of higher education and training, the Secretary-General appealed for greater financial and other support to the Programme.

Financial contributions

In 1984, 34 States contributed $3,276,925 to the Programme (see table following), as compared to $3,791,427 in 1983.

CONTRIBUTIONS TO THE UN EDUCATIONAL AND TRAINING PROGRAMME FOR SOUTHERN AFRICA, 1984

(as at 31 December 1984; in US dollars)

Country	1984 payment
Australia	83,853
Austria	37,200
Bahamas	1,000
Barbados	500
Burma	1,000
Canada	268,391
Cyprus	196
Denmark	287,797
Finland	106,289
France	79,310
Germany, Federal Republic of	64,328
Greece	9,000
India	4,000
Indonesia	3,000
Ireland	23,898
Italy	20,785
Japan	200,000
Kenya	1,151
Kuwait	1,000
Malaysia	1,000
Netherlands	67,797
New Zealand	10,627
Norway	718,259
Republic of Korea	5,000
Sweden	125,200
Switzerland	59,195
Togo	343
Trinidad and Tobago	1,250
Tunisia	824
Turkey	(894)
United Kingdom	68,826
United States	1,000,000
Venezuela	10,000
Zambia	16,800
Total	3,276,925

NOTE: Figure in parentheses indicates a loss due to changes in exchange rates.

SOURCE: Accounts for the 12-month period of the biennium 1984-1985 ended 31 December 1984—schedules of individual trust funds.

GENERAL ASSEMBLY ACTION

On 5 December, the General Assembly, on the recommendation of the Fourth Committee, adopted resolution 39/44 without vote.

United Nations Educational and Training Programme for Southern Africa

The General Assembly,

Recalling its resolutions on the United Nations Educational and Training Programme for Southern Africa, in particular resolution 38/52 of 7 December 1983,

Having considered the report of the Secretary-General, containing an account of the work of the Advisory Committee on the United Nations Educational and Training Programme for Southern Africa and the operation of the Programme for the period from 1 October 1983 to 30 September 1984,

Recognizing the valuable assistance rendered by the Programme to the peoples of South Africa and Namibia,

Strongly convinced that the continuation and expansion of the Programme is essential in order to meet the increasing demand for educational and training opportunities by the peoples of South Africa and Namibia,

Fully recognizing the need to provide educational opportunities and counselling to student refugees in a wide variety of professional, cultural, technical and linguistic disciplines, particularly in the areas of development and international co-operation,

1. *Endorses* the report of the Secretary-General on the United Nations Educational and Training Programme for Southern Africa;

2. *Commends* the Secretary-General and the Advisory Committee on the United Nations Educational and Training Programme for Southern Africa for their continued efforts to promote generous contributions to the Programme and to enhance co-operation with governmental, intergovernmental and non-governmental scholarship agencies;

3. *Expresses its appreciation* to all those who have supported the Programme by providing contributions, scholarships or places in their educational institutions;

4. *Notes with concern* that, owing to inflation and rising scholarship costs, contributions and pledges have declined, in real terms, in 1984 from the corresponding figure in 1983;

5. *Appeals* to all States, institutions, organizations and individuals to offer greater financial and other support to the Programme in order to ensure its continuation and expansion.

General Assembly resolution 39/44

5 December 1984   Meeting 87   Adopted without vote

Approved by Fourth Committee (A/39/677) without objection, 12 November (meeting 18); 33-nation draft (A/C.4/39/L.5); agenda item 106.
Sponsors: Australia, Bangladesh, Brazil, Canada, Colombia, Denmark, Egypt, Finland, France, Germany, Federal Republic of, Iceland, India, Indonesia, Ireland, Italy, Japan, Kenya, Lesotho, Liberia, Netherlands, Nigeria, Norway, Romania, Sweden, Trinidad and Tobago, Tunisia, Turkey, United Republic of Tanzania, United Kingdom, United States, Venezuela, Zambia, Zimbabwe.
Meeting numbers. GA 39th session: 4th Committee 12-18; plenary 87.

REFERENCE

[1]A/39/351.

Co-operation between OAU and the UN system

The United Nations and the Organization of African Unity (OAU) continued to co-operate in various political and economic areas during 1984, as the General Assembly had urged in 1983.[1] In a report of 12 September 1984 to the Assembly,[2] the Secretary-General gave details on co-operation between the two organizations.

The Secretary-General met with his OAU counterpart on several occasions to discuss matters of mutual concern. At the invitation of the respective States, the Secretary-General visited eight African countries of the Sahel region, which was severely affected by drought in January and February (see ECONOMIC AND SOCIAL QUESTIONS, Chapter III), to gain first-hand knowledge of the economic and social situation there. A message on the current economic crisis in Africa was delivered, on his behalf, to a meeting of the OAU Council of Ministers in February/March. Areas of co-operation between the two organizations had been agreed upon at an April 1983 meeting of the secretariats of OAU and United Nations organizations.[3]

The Secretary-General addressed the OAU Assembly of Heads of State and Government (Addis Ababa, November). Reviewing Africa's main problems including the emergency situation and the drought, he called on the international community to increase its assistance to the affected African countries. In regard to southern Africa, he emphasized that South Africa's *apartheid* policy was at the centre of the violence and conflicts in the region. Concerning Namibia, he said that South Africa's insistence on the linkage of the issue with the presence of Cuban troops in Angola still made it impossible to proceed with the United Nations plan for Namibia's independence[4] (see TRUSTEESHIP AND DECOLONIZATION, Chapter III). On the question of refugees in Africa, the Secretary-General stated that the United Nations organizations would continue to do all possible to help implement the Programme of Action adopted by the 1984 Second International Conference on Assistance to Refugees in Africa (see ECONOMIC AND SOCIAL QUESTIONS, Chapter XXI).

The Secretary-General received several letters in 1984 by which countries forwarded statements or resolutions adopted by OAU. On 18 April,[5] the Upper Volta transmitted the resolutions adopted at the fortieth ordinary session of the OAU Council of Ministers. The resolutions dealt with such subjects as the critical economic situation in Africa, support for the victims of natural disasters in Mozambique and Swaziland, Namibia, the situation in southern Africa, refugees in Africa, and a programme for the Industrial Development Decade for Africa (see relevant chapters). On behalf of the Chairman of OAU, the United Republic of Tanzania on 21 November[6] forwarded a report on Western Sahara adopted at the 1984 OAU Assembly of Heads of State and Government (see TRUSTEESHIP AND DECOLONIZATION, Chapter IV). On 6 December,[7] the United Republic of Tanzania transmitted a letter of 28 November from its President, in his capacity as OAU Chairman, endorsing the Secretary-General's call for an international conference, to be held under United Nations auspices, to consider united action on the famine and hunger afflicting most of Africa. Those areas were affected by severe drought as well as economic regression caused by other factors (see ECONOMIC AND SOCIAL QUESTIONS, Chapter III).

In a letter to the Secretary-General on 25 May,[8] Egypt forwarded a message from its President on the occasion of Africa Day, stating that Egypt's participation in celebrating that Day, the anniversary of the signing of the OAU Charter, with the other OAU members emphasized its close relationship with African solidarity and its determination to preserve the cohesion and effectiveness of OAU through the principles laid down 21 years earlier.

On 8 November, the General Assembly adopted resolution 39/8 without vote.

Co-operation between the United Nations and the Organization of African Unity

The General Assembly,

Having considered the report of the Secretary-General on co-operation between the United Nations and the Organization of African Unity,

Recalling its previous resolutions on the promotion of co-operation between the United Nations and the Organization of African Unity and the practical measures taken for their implementation, in particular resolution 38/5 of 28 October 1983,

Taking note of the resolutions, decisions and declarations adopted by the Organization of African Unity on the promotion of co-operation between the United Nations and the Organization of African Unity,

Noting with satisfaction the continued co-operation between the United Nations and the Organization of African Unity in areas of common interest,

Gravely concerned about the serious and deteriorating economic situation in Africa, in particular the effects of the prolonged drought, desertification and the adverse effects of the international economic environment on the African States,

Deeply conscious of the special needs of the independent African States, particularly with regard to the consolidation of their national independence, their endeavours towards social and economic betterment and the adverse impact on their economies of the current international economic situation,

Recalling in this connection the Lagos Plan of Action for the Implementation of the Monrovia Strategy for the Economic Development of Africa, adopted by the Assembly of Heads of State and Government of the Organization of African Unity at its second extraordinary session, held at Lagos on 28 and 29 April 1980,

Recalling also the Special Memorandum on Africa's Economic and Social Crisis adopted by the Conference of Ministers of the Economic Commission for Africa at its tenth meeting and by the Commission at its nineteenth session, held at Addis Ababa from 24 to 28 May 1984,

Recognizing the need for closer co-operation between the Organization of African Unity and all specialized organs, organizations and bodies of the United Nations system in realizing the goals and objectives set forth in the Lagos Plan of Action,

Noting with appreciation the timely initiative of the Secretary-General to alert the international community about the rapidly deteriorating economic and social conditions in Africa, his personal involvement and the measures he has taken to assist the international community to respond to the situation,

Deeply concerned at the gravity of the situation of the refugees in Africa and their increasing needs for international assistance as well as at the heavy social, economic and security burden imposed on African countries of asylum,

Having considered the report of the Secretary-General on the Second International Conference on Assistance to Refugees in Africa, held at Geneva from 9 to 11 July 1984 and the report on arrangements for follow-up action to the Conference,

Gravely concerned also at the need for special economic and emergency assistance programmes for African States affected by serious economic problems, in particular problems of displaced persons, resulting from natural or other disasters, to enable them to pursue effective economic development,

Gravely concerned further at the deteriorating situation in southern Africa arising from the continued domination of the peoples of the area by the minority racist régime of South Africa and conscious of the need to provide increased assistance to the peoples of the region and to their liberation movements in their struggle against colonialism, racial discrimination and *apartheid,*

Conscious of its responsibilities to provide economic, material and humanitarian assistance to independent States in southern Africa to help them to cope with the situation caused by the acts of aggression committed against their territories by the *apartheid* régime of South Africa,

Recognizing the importance of taking effective steps to provide the widest possible dissemination of information relating to the liberation struggle of the peoples of southern Africa,

Recognizing the important role which the various information units and departments of the United Nations system can play in disseminating information to bring about a greater awareness of the social and economic problems and needs of African States and their regional and subregional institutions,

Aware of the need for continuous liaison, exchange of information at the secretariat level and technical co-operation on such matters as training and research between the Organization of African Unity and the United Nations,

1. *Takes note* of the report of the Secretary-General on co-operation between the United Nations and the Organization of African Unity and commends his efforts to strengthen such co-operation as well as his updated report on the critical economic situation in Africa;

2. *Notes with appreciation* the increasing participation of the Organization of African Unity in the work of the United Nations and the specialized agencies and its constructive contribution to that work;

3. *Commends* the continued efforts of the Organization of African Unity to promote multilateral co-operation among African States and to find solutions to African problems of vital importance to the international community and notes with satisfaction the increased collaboration of various organizations of the United Nations system in support of those efforts;

4. *Reiterates* the determination of the United Nations, in co-operation with the Organization of African Unity, to intensify its efforts to eliminate colonialism, racial discrimination and *apartheid* in southern Africa;

5. *Reaffirms* its willingness to co-operate fully with the Organization of African Unity and its organs in the implementation of the relevant resolutions and decisions of that organization;

6. *Calls upon* the competent organizations and bodies of the United Nations system to continue to give urgent consideration to the various recommendations and proposals contained in the conclusions of the joint meetings of organizations of the United Nations system and the Organization of African Unity, with the objective of enhancing co-operation between them;

7. *Calls upon* the competent United Nations organs, the specialized agencies and other organizations of the

United Nations system to continue to ensure that their personnel and recruitment policies provide for the just and equitable representation of Africa at all levels at their respective headquarters and in their regional and field operations;

8. *Requests* the Secretary-General, in consultation with the Secretary-General of the Organization of African Unity, to arrange the date and venue in Africa for the next meeting between representatives of the General Secretariat of that organization and the secretariats of the United Nations and other organizations of the United Nations system, taking into account paragraph 10 of General Assembly resolution 38/5;

9. *Recognizes* the importance of continued close association by the United Nations and the specialized agencies with the efforts of the Organization of African Unity to promote social and economic development and to advance intra-African co-operation in that vital field;

10. *Reaffirms* the determination of the United Nations to work closely with the Organization of African Unity towards the establishment of the new international economic order in accordance with the resolutions adopted by the General Assembly and, in that regard, to take full account of the Lagos Plan of Action for the Implementation of the Monrovia Strategy for the Economic Development of Africa in the implementation of the International Development Strategy for the Third United Nations Development Decade;

11. *Expresses its appreciation* to the Secretary-General for the timely initiative he has taken to alert the international community to the critical economic and social situation in Africa and welcomes the measures he has taken to facilitate international co-operation and co-ordination to assist Africa;

12. *Reiterates its appreciation* to the Secretary-General for his efforts, on behalf of the international community, to organize and mobilize special programmes of economic assistance for African States experiencing grave economic difficulties, in particular for the front-line States and other independent States of southern Africa, to help them to cope with the situation caused by the acts of aggression committed against their territories by the *apartheid* régime of South Africa;

13. *Expresses its appreciation* to the World Bank, the United Nations Development Programme and other concerned international financial institutions for their response to the critical economic situation in Africa as well as their assistance in the organization of round-table and donor conferences in favour of the least-developed countries of Africa, as well as those requiring special programmes of economic assistance, in response to resolutions of the General Assembly;

14. *Expresses its appreciation also* to donor countries, the European Economic Community and other intergovernmental organizations for their participation in the round-table and consultative groups and for their response to the emergency food situation in Africa;

15. *Calls upon* all Member States, regional and international organizations and organizations of the United Nations system to participate actively in measures to deal with the current economic crisis in Africa as well as in the implementation of those special programmes of economic assistance;

16. *Calls upon* the international community to provide generous assistance on a long-term basis to all African States affected by the economic crisis, particularly

those suffering calamities such as drought and flood, and expresses its appreciation to the Office of the United Nations Disaster Relief Co-ordinator, the World Food Programme, the Food and Agriculture Organization of the United Nations, the World Health Organization and the United Nations Children's Fund for the assistance they have so far rendered to the African States that have suffered those calamities;

17. *Requests* the Secretary-General to keep the Organization of African Unity informed periodically of the response of the international community to those special programmes of economic assistance and to co-ordinate efforts with all similar programmes initiated by that organization;

18. *Also requests* the Secretary-General and the organizations of the United Nations system to ensure that adequate facilities continue to be made available for the provision of technical assistance to the General Secretariat of the Organization of African Unity, as required;

19. *Further requests* the Secretary-General to continue to take the necessary measures to strengthen co-operation at the political, economic, cultural and administrative levels between the United Nations and the Organization of African Unity in accordance with the relevant resolutions of the General Assembly, particularly with regard to the provision of assistance to the victims of colonialism and *apartheid* in southern Africa, and in this connection draws once again the attention of the international community to the need to contribute to the Assistance Fund for the Struggle against Colonialism and *Apartheid* established by the Organization of African Unity;

20. *Calls upon* all Member States and organizations of the United Nations system to increase their assistance to the African States affected by serious economic problems, in particular problems of displaced persons, resulting from natural or other disasters, by mobilizing special programmes of economic and emergency assistance;

21. *Urges* all Member States and regional and international organizations, in particular those of the United Nations system, and non-governmental organizations to continue their support of African refugee programmes and to provide material and economic assistance to help host countries to cope with the heavy burden imposed on their limited resources and weak infrastructures;

22. *Expresses its appreciation* to the Secretary-General of the United Nations, the Secretary-General of the Organization of African Unity, the United Nations High Commissioner for Refugees and the Administrator of the United Nations Development Programme for their commendable efforts in organizing the Second International Conference on Assistance to Refugees in Africa;

23. *Invites* Member States and regional and international organizations, in particular those of the United Nations system, and non-governmental organizations to contribute generously and effectively to the implementation of the Declaration and Programme of Action of the Second International Conference on Assistance to Refugees in Africa;

24. *Requests* the Secretary-General to draw the attention of the specialized agencies and other organizations of the United Nations system to the need to give increasingly wide publicity to all matters relating to the social and economic development of Africa, in particular to the critical economic situation facing African countries;

25. *Calls upon* United Nations organs—in particular the Security Council, the Economic and Social Council, the Special Committee on the Situation with regard to the Implementation of the Declaration on the Granting of Independence to Colonial Countries and Peoples, the Special Committee against *Apartheid* and the United Nations Council for Namibia—to continue to associate closely the Organization of African Unity with all their work concerning Africa;

26. *Urges* the specialized agencies and other organizations concerned within the United Nations system to continue and to expand their co-operation with the Organization of African Unity and, through it, their assistance to the liberation movements recognized by that organization;

27. *Invites* the Secretary-General to continue his commendable efforts in alerting and sensitizing the international community to the plight of African countries, in mobilizing additional assistance to Africa and in co-ordinating the activities of the United Nations system in Africa, monitoring the situation and presenting periodic reports thereon;

28. *Requests* the Secretary-General to report to the General Assembly at its fortieth session on the implementation of the present resolution and on the development of co-operation between the Organization of African Unity and the organizations concerned within the United Nations system.

General Assembly resolution 39/8

8 November 1984   Meeting 54   Adopted without vote

50-nation draft (A/39/L.12 and Add.1); agenda item 22.

Sponsors: Algeria, Angola, Benin, Botswana, Burkina Faso, Burundi, Cameroon, Cape Verde, Central African Republic, Chad, Comoros, Congo, Djibouti, Egypt, Equatorial Guinea, Ethiopia, Gabon, Gambia, Ghana, Guinea, Guinea-Bissau, Ivory Coast, Kenya, Lesotho, Liberia, Libyan Arab Jamahiriya, Madagascar, Malawi, Mali, Mauritania, Mauritius, Morocco, Mozambique, Niger, Nigeria, Rwanda, Sao Tome and Principe, Senegal, Seychelles, Sierra Leone, Somalia, Sudan, Swaziland, Togo, Tunisia, Uganda, United Republic of Tanzania, Zaire, Zambia, Zimbabwe.

Co-operation between the United Nations and OAU was dealt with in numerous other 1984 Assembly resolutions.

In resolution 39/40, the Assembly welcomed the OAU efforts to promote a solution to the question of Western Sahara in accordance with resolutions and decisions of OAU and the United Nations. Reaffirming the United Nations determination to co-operate with a view to implementing the OAU decisions, the Assembly invited the OAU Secretary-General to keep the United Nations Secretary-General informed of the progress achieved in implementing them.

The Assembly, in resolution 39/43, expressed its appreciation to those United Nations organizations which had co-operated with the United Nations and OAU in implementing the 1960 Declaration on the Granting of Independence to Colonial Countries and Peoples[9] and other relevant United Nations resolutions, and urged all United Nations bodies to accelerate implementation of the relevant provisions of those resolutions. The Assembly reiterated its recommendation that United Nations organizations

should initiate or broaden contacts and co-operation with the colonial peoples and their national liberation movements directly or through OAU. It recommended that future high-level meetings between the secretariats of OAU, the United Nations and United Nations organizations should discuss assistance to national liberation movements recognized by OAU, with a view to ensuring the best use of available resources for assistance to the peoples of the colonial Territories. The Assembly urged those organizations to formulate, with the co-operation of OAU where appropriate, proposals for implementing United Nations decisions on decolonization, in particular specific programmes of assistance to the peoples of colonial Territories and their national liberation movements.

In resolution 39/61 A, the Assembly reaffirmed that implementation of the 1964 OAU Declaration on the Denuclearization of Africa[10] would be an important measure to prevent the proliferation of nuclear weapons, and it requested the Secretary-General to render assistance that OAU might seek to implement the Declaration.

In regard to the Industrial Development Decade for Africa, proclaimed in 1980,[11] the Assembly, in resolution 39/233, welcomed the efforts that UNIDO was deploying in order to assist African countries and intergovernmental organizations in defining national and subregional programmes for the Decade and in order to maintain co-ordination with OAU, the Economic Commission for Africa and other international organizations.

ECONOMIC AND SOCIAL COUNCIL ACTION

In action similar to that of the Assembly on implementing the 1960 Declaration on colonial countries,[9] the Economic and Social Council, in resolution 1984/55, expressed appreciation to those United Nations organizations which had co-operated with the United Nations and OAU in implementing the Declaration and relevant United Nations resolutions, and urged them to accelerate their implementation. Those organizations were requested to give increased assistance to the people of Namibia, in consultation with OAU and the United Nations Council for Namibia. The Council urged United Nations organizations to formulate, with the co-operation of OAU, proposals for implementing United Nations decisions.

REFERENCES

[1]YUN 1983, p. 192, GA res. 38/5, 28 Oct. 1983. [2]A/39/427. [3]YUN 1983, p. 191. [4]YUN 1978, p. 915, SC res. 435(1978), 29 Sep. 1978. [5]A/39/207. [6]A/39/680. [7]A/39/797-S/16854. [8]A/39/276. [9]YUN 1960, p. 49, GA res. 1514(XV), 14 Dec. 1960. [10]YUN 1964, p. 69. [11]YUN 1980, p. 662, GA res. 35/66 B, 5 Dec. 1980.

Chapter VI

Americas

Both the Security Council and the General Assembly considered the situation in Central America during 1984. The Assembly looked at the question as a whole, while the Council addressed specific disputes between countries.

The Council met in February, March/April, September and November at Nicaragua's request regarding allegations of aggression against it. In April, a draft resolution on the mining of Nicaragua's ports was not adopted owing to the negative vote of a permanent Council member, the United States.

In October, the Assembly, by resolution 39/4, urged the five Central American Governments—Costa Rica, El Salvador, Guatemala, Honduras and Nicaragua—to speed up their consultations with the Contadora Group—Colombia, Mexico, Panama and Venezuela—and to bring about the early signing of the Contadora Act on Peace and Co-operation in Central America, a legal instrument designed to bring about a negotiated solution to the problems of the region. The Assembly also called on all States, especially those with ties to and interests in the region, to respect fully the Contadora Act and the commitments undertaken by them by acceding to its Additional Protocol. In his annual report to the Assembly on the work of the Organization (p. 3), the Secretary-General stressed the need for full co-operation with the Contadora Group to ensure the success of its efforts.

Topics related to this chapter. Disarmament: nuclear-weapon-free zones—Latin America. Regional economic and social activities: Latin America. Human rights violations: Latin America. Refugees and displaced persons: Americas. Other colonial Territories: Falkland Islands (Malvinas) question. International Court of Justice: military and paramilitary activities in and against Nicaragua.

Central America situation

Communications. The bulk of the 1984 communications addressed to the Secretary-General on the Central America situation concerned the Contadora Group's activities, either communiqués from that Group or comments on those communiqués and proposals by the Central American States. The meetings of the Contadora Group and those held jointly with the Central American countries were held at Panama City; the communications relating to such meetings were transmitted by Panama. Other 1984 communications dealt with disputes between Nicaragua and several States (see below, under the relevant subject heading).

On 9 January,[1] after a meeting of the Group's Foreign Ministers with their Central American counterparts on 7 and 8 January, a communiqué was forwarded pointing out that, in the one-year period that had elapsed since the Group initiated the regional peace-making process, it had met 12 times, including five times with the Central American Foreign Ministers. Appended to the communiqué was a joint declaration on measures to be taken immediately by Costa Rica, El Salvador, Guatemala, Honduras and Nicaragua relating to security questions, political matters, and economic and social co-operation. To prepare studies, legal drafts and recommendations on these questions, three working commissions were to be created, with each commission to present its findings to a joint meeting of Foreign Ministers by 30 April.

Honduras, on 23 January,[2] sent a letter containing the names of the members it had appointed to the working commissions, and pointed out that the commissions were the result of a September 1983 Honduran initiative.

Following the inauguration of the working commissions on 31 January in Panama, a press communiqué was transmitted on 2 February[3] listing the persons attending the inauguration ceremony. On 6 March,[4] Panama forwarded a communiqué issued at the conclusion of a meeting of the Contadora Group's Foreign Ministers on 27 and 28 February. That communiqué pointed out that a detailed report on the work of the commissions had been received. Meanwhile, on 9 February,[5] Costa Rica and Panama transmitted a 6 February joint communiqué issued on the occasion of a visit to Panama by the President of Costa Rica. The Presidents of the two countries agreed that the development of the frontier zone between them could be a model of friendly co-operation which would put into practice the objectives of harmonious development between Central American States, as proposed by the Contadora Group.

The Foreign Ministers met again in Panama on 8 April and, by a communiqué transmitted on 11

April,[6] they noted that the situation in the region was showing signs of serious deterioration—activities of irregular forces had been stepped up with assistance from the territories of neighbouring countries with the aim of destabilizing Governments in the area, operations such as the mining of ports were being carried out and foreign troops and advisers were increasingly present. They therefore considered it essential for countries with links in the region to demonstrate the support they had expressed for the Contadora Group. In assessing the progress made by the working commissions, they noted that obstacles remained, stemming in some cases from attitudes that were not always flexible and effectively geared to negotiation.

By a letter of 29 April,[7] Costa Rica, El Salvador and Honduras transmitted a 25 April joint declaration by their Foreign Ministers on the Central America situation, the Contadora process and the forthcoming joint Contadora/Central American ministerial meeting of 30 April (see below). They invited the Inter-American Commission of Human Rights to visit their countries before and during electoral periods, to report on freedom of information, propaganda, assembly, demonstration, movement and transit, and on the exercise of political rights. They called on Nicaragua to abandon its obstructive attitude to the Contadora Group's working commissions, stating that Nicaragua had, that day, again displayed such an attitude by asserting that it would continue to arm itself, maintaining that its problems were with the United States and not its neighbours. Moreover, the communiqué said, Nicaragua had rejected the document on principles and commitments to be accepted by the Central American States in the political sphere, thus thwarting one of the main political objectives—democratization.

After the sixth joint meeting between the Foreign Ministers of the Contadora Group and those of Central America on 30 April and 1 May, an information bulletin was issued[8] on the conclusions of the working commissions. In the Political Affairs Commission, agreement was reached on items relating to a policy of détente and there was consensus on establishing or improving institutions on which representative and pluralistic democracy was based. The Security Affairs Commission agreed on legal principles relating to security, on specific confidence-building measures, and on the prohibition of the installation of military bases and of any other form of foreign military intervention. There was consensus on preventing the use of territory by irregular forces for action against neighbouring countries and preventing destabilizing operations, sabotage amd terrorism. There was broad agreement that foreign advisers should be withdrawn. Basic criteria were identified for determining levels of military development of the Central American countries. The Commission for Economic and Social Questions formulated recommendations covering integration, intra-zonal trade and technical co-operation, investment and finance, labour questions and health. Studies would continue to try to ensure joint handling of the refugee situation. The joint meeting warned that the progress achieved nevertheless contrasted with the increase in violence, military escalation, the arms buildup and the foreign military presence in the area. The Central American Ministers reaffirmed their belief that the negotiation process promoted by the Contadora Group represented the genuine regional alternative for the resolution of conflicts.

In a 21 June note[9] to the Security Council, the Secretary-General stated that on 15 June representatives of the Contadora Group had handed him a communication sent to the heads of State of the five Central American countries on 9 June, by which the Group had transmitted a draft comprehensive agreement known as the Contadora Act on Peace and Co-operation in Central America; a copy of the communication was annexed to the note. The Secretary-General believed that the diplomatic process had entered a decisive phase in which the most determined support of the international community was more than ever necessary. He also considered that every encouragement should be given to the decision announced by Nicaragua and the United States to initiate a dialogue designed to reduce tension in the area (see p. 209). The draft Contadora Act contained legal commitments, general and specific recommendations, aspects relating to a verification and control commission, and formulae for settling disputes. An additional protocol would be open for signature by other States of the international community having interests in the region and through which they would undertake to respect the commitments made by the signatories to the Act.

In a letter of 25 June,[10] Honduras transmitted an official declaration of 22 June by which its Government accepted the Contadora Act as a basic text for the negotiation of a treaty to preserve peace and co-operation in Central America.

From 24 to 28 August the Deputy Foreign Ministers of the Contadora Group and their counterparts and representatives of the Central American countries met at the Group's initiative to ascertain the views of the Central American Governments on the Act. In an information bulletin issued after the meeting,[11] the participants stated that the suggestions made would enable the Contadora Group to identify the next stages in their efforts.

A seventh joint meeting of the respective Foreign Ministers was held on 7 September and a communiqué was issued, together with a communication from the Contadora Group's Foreign Ministers to the heads of State of the five Central American countries concerning a new version of the draft Contadora Act.[12] The communication stated that the revised version again highlighted the principal role of the Central American Governments in the peaceful settlement of disputes and in overcoming regional problems. The signing of the Act should provide the basis for security and coexistence governed by mutual respect which was essential for guaranteeing the area's political and economic stability. In the light of the persistent threat to peace, the Governments of the region must expedite the process of assuming the legal commitments contained in the Act. Similarly, it was imperative for others with interests in the region to respect the right of self-determination of the Central American peoples and demonstrate unequivocal support for political negotiation in place of force.

A letter of 19 September[13] from Honduras contained an 18 September official declaration on its willingness to assume the responsibilities resulting from the negotiation process with a view to signing the revised draft Act.

Nicaragua's acceptance of the revised text was contained in a 21 September letter[14] from the Co-ordinator of its Governing Junta of National Reconstruction, who explained that Nicaragua was willing to accept the Act in its entirety because of the serious increase of military threats by the United States.

On 4 October,[15] Costa Rica transmitted a letter it had sent to the Foreign Ministers of the Contadora Group stating that it intended to sign the revised Act; none the less it felt that the proposed verification and control system should be improved and reiterated its view that the system should be mandatory and binding. Also, essential power for the *Ad Hoc* Committee (see p. 199) regarding the democratization process was not given for it to investigate *in situ;* the possibility of verification and control *in loco* should be accorded to political and refugee matters.

A letter of 8 October[16] transmitted a Honduran invitation to the Foreign Ministers of the Central American countries to attend a meeting of co-ordination on 19 October at Tegucigalpa, Honduras. On 12 October,[17] Honduras stated that it had, on 10 October, submitted its comments on the draft Act to the Contadora Group members and Central American countries.

Nicaragua, on 16 October,[18] transmitted a communication of the previous day to the Presidents of the Contadora Group countries reiterating that it accepted the revised Act entirely and was prepared to sign it immediately, without modification. Concern was expressed over the Honduran proposal to convene a meeting of Central American Foreign Ministers, since the Act should not be subject to further negotiations for substantive amendments or modifications and meetings without the Contadora Group would adversely affect the Group's peace efforts. Given the obstacles created by some Central American Governments to immediate signing of the revised Act, the Group should convene a high-level meeting of the Central American and Contadora countries to promote the willingness and the political decisions necessary for the unequivocal acceptance of the Act, which would pave the way for peace in Central America.

Honduras, on 22 October,[19] sent the joint communiqué of the discussions held on 19 and 20 October at Tegucigalpa between the Foreign Ministers of Costa Rica, El Salvador and Honduras and the Deputy Foreign Minister of Guatemala, who expressed their views on the revised Act, harmonized into a single text the observations made and expressed regret at Nicaragua's non-attendance. Honduras stated that it did not share Nicaragua's opinion that the meeting was intended to exclude the Contadora Group. By a letter of 30 October,[20] Costa Rica, El Salvador and Honduras forwarded their consolidated comments on the revised Act, covering such matters as implementation mechanisms, establishment of an interim *ad hoc* disarmament group between the date of the signing and the date of the entry into force of the Act, verification and control machinery for security matters, regulation of military manoeuvres, entry into force of obligations regarding foreign military bases, the fate of irregular forces, displaced persons, final provisions and the question of the Additional Protocol. Referring to the joint comments, Nicaragua, in a declaration transmitted on 1 November,[21] saw them as substantive changes seriously affecting the nature of the agreements reached by consensus after nearly two years of difficult negotiations. The attempt to reopen the debate was endangering the process of negotiation itself. The comments of the three Governments reflected the observations of the United States and formed part of its policy of changing the nature of the Act and of preventing its signature. On 15 November,[22] Nicaragua reiterated that the amendments reflected United States observations and attached an article from *The Washington Post* on how the United States reputedly blocked the Contadora Act.

On 6 November,[23] Costa Rica stated that Nicaragua was again trying to confuse public opinion by describing the position of the three States as obstructionist or linked to interests of another country. Costa Rica had no difficulty in accepting the letter and spirit of the revised Act, but found it difficult to subscribe to a document that was not verifiable. On 8 November,[24] El Salvador also rejected Nicaragua's views, stating that the proposals did not constitute substantive changes, nor did they destroy the consensus, and did not reopen debate on questions on which agreement existed; Nicaragua, claiming it favoured negotiations, was obstructing the remaining stage. Likewise Honduras, on 23 November,[25] felt Nicaragua was trying to justify its attempt to break up the Contadora negotiations; the comments of the three Governments were in line with the setting of 15 October as the deadline for views on the revised Act.

Communiqués from the Movement of Non-Aligned Countries relating wholly or in part to the situation in Central America were also sent to the Secretary-General during the year, as were communications from other intergovernmental bodies. On 15 March,[26] India forwarded a communiqué adopted by the Movement's Co-ordinating Bureau, commending the efforts of the Contadora Group and calling for an immediate end to all foreign military activities on Central American territories and coasts. Concern was also expressed over the new escalation of hostile acts against Nicaragua and the deterioration of the situation in El Salvador due to continuing foreign intervention.

On 29 March,[27] France on behalf of the 10 States members of the European Economic Community transmitted the declarations adopted by the Community Foreign Ministers on 27 March in which they expressed the hope that the Contadora Group's efforts could contribute to reducing tension and to progress towards peace, respect for independence, the establishment of pluralistic democracy and the solution of the economic and social problems of the countries concerned.

On 1 October,[28] Costa Rica transmitted the joint communiqué of a ministerial meeting (San José, Costa Rica, 28 and 29 September) attended by the Foreign Ministers of the European Community and its member States, Portugal and Spain, and the States of Central America and of the Contadora Group. A united view was expressed that regional problems could not be solved by armed force, but only by political solutions springing from the region itself. The revised draft Contadora Act was seen as fundamental to the negotiating process and they agreed on the necessity for a commitment to the implementation of any such agreement by all States in the region and all other countries which had interests there, and on the necessity for the verification and control of that implementation. The Ministers of the European Community and of Central America

declared themselves ready to start discussions as soon as possible with a view to negotiating an interregional framework co-operation agreement.

On 16 October,[29] the Sudan circulated resolutions adopted by the Seventy-second Inter-Parliamentary Conference, held at Geneva on 29 September. A unanimously adopted resolution on the Central America crisis urged all Central American States to solve their problems themselves, free from any foreign interference, and expressed support for the Contadora Group's negotiations, particularly the Contadora peace treaty expected to be signed in October.

On 25 October,[30] Venezuela transmitted an agreement adopted by the Chamber of Deputies of the Venezuelan Congress on 17 October, welcoming the initiative taken by the President of El Salvador to establish a dialogue, begun two days earlier, with the representatives of the revolutionary fronts of that country.

A letter to the President of the General Assembly from Costa Rica of 3 October[31] referred to a 2 October statement to the Assembly by the Lao People's Democratic Republic. Costa Rica said it was surprised, since it had no army, that in that statement the speaker had urged the overthrow of Costa Rica's military dictatorship.

Report of the Secretary-General (October). Responding to 1983 requests by the Security Council[32] and the General Assembly,[33] the Secretary-General on 9 October 1984 submitted a report on the Central America situation.[34] Annexed to the report was the revised version of the proposed Contadora Act on Peace and Co-operation in Central America. The Contadora Foreign Ministers had told the Secretary-General that they had delivered the document to their Central American counterparts on 7 September,[12] with 15 October fixed as a deadline for them to make their views known on the matter. He noted that to date Costa Rica,[15] Honduras[13] and Nicaragua[14] had transmitted their comments on the revised Act to the Council and/or the Assembly.

The Secretary-General expressed satisfaction with regard to the contribution made by the Contadora Group in giving momentum to the negotiations among the Central American countries and finding formulae which would enable the causes of regional tension to be eliminated. He said the Group's efforts were especially important in view of the persistent gravity of the situation.

He noted that the Security Council had met three times during the year to consider complaints by Nicaragua but had not adopted a resolution (see below). With regard to the southern area of Nicaragua bordering Costa Rica, he said it should be noted that a Commission for Supervision and Prevention had been set up under the auspices of the Contadora Group which appeared to have facilitated a reduction in the frontier incidents involving the two countries.

The Secretary-General recalled that the International Court of Justice had indicated certain provisional measures regarding the Nicaragua versus United States case (see LEGAL QUESTIONS, Chapter I) and the Court's Order had been transmitted to the Council. He stated that as a result of a visit to Managua by the United States Secretary of State, a two-way dialogue had been initiated since the end of May between the two States with, to date, six meetings held under the auspices of Mexico. Both sides had welcomed the fact that the talks had entered their substantive stage.

The Secretary-General said he had followed attentively the electoral process which had taken place recently in El Salvador and the steps taken by its President with a view to the country's political stabilization. The fact that a political segment abstained from participating in the elections, as well as the continuation of armed conflict, made it difficult to bring about a broad, effective and lasting political reconciliation. To date, the efforts to bring about a dialogue between the Government and the Frente Democrático Revolucionario–Frente Farabundo Martí para la Liberación Nacional (FDR-FMLN), including those sponsored by foreign Governments, had not met with the success hoped for.

He found it encouraging that electoral processes were being conducted in Guatemala and Nicaragua. In the latter, negotiations had been proceeding in order to achieve the broadest possible participation in the election and he hoped the holding of the election would promote a genuine process of democratization.

The upheaval in Central America was still causing a flood of refugees, the Secretary-General observed. According to host-country figures, the number of refugees in the area was estimated at 350,000, of whom 104,900 as at the end of September were receiving assistance from the United Nations High Commissioner for Refugees.

The Secretary-General appealed to the countries of the region to pursue their efforts to negotiate a comprehensive solution to their problems under the auspices of the Contadora Group.

The revised version of the Contadora Act consisted of a preamble; general commitments and commitments with regard to political, security and economic and social matters; commitments on execution and follow-up; final provisions regarding the entry into force of the Act and dispute settlement procedures; an annex on agreed definitions of military terms; and an Additional Protocol open for other Governments to sign regarding co-operation and support for the Act. The general commitments section laid down principles by which the parties would abide, while the political matters section covered commitments regarding regional détente and confidence-building,

national reconciliation, human rights, and electoral processes and parliamentary co-operation. The section on security matters encompassed commitments regarding military manoeuvres, armaments, foreign military bases, foreign military advisers, traffic in arms, prohibition of support for irregular forces, terrorism, subversion or sabotage, and direct communications systems. The commitments with regard to economic and social affairs covered those matters and refugees. Those on execution and follow-up dealt with *Ad Hoc* Committees for commitments concerning political and refugee matters and economic and social matters; and a Verification and Control Commission for Security Matters.

By a letter of 23 October,[35] the Contadora Group's representatives transmitted a joint communiqué issued after a meeting of the Group's Foreign Ministers at Madrid, Spain, on 17 October, underscoring the importance of the submission of the revised Act to the Security Council President and the Secretary-General and expressing their approval of the latter's positive report. The Ministers noted that the Governments of the region had expressed their readiness to sign the Act as soon as possible, and said their comments would be useful in concluding the current stage of the process; they agreed that it was appropriate to incorporate those comments in order to lend greater precision to the statements without modifying the balance achieved in the document.

GENERAL ASSEMBLY ACTION

On 26 October 1984, the General Assembly adopted resolution 39/4 by consensus.

The situation in Central America: threats to international peace and security and peace initiatives

The General Assembly,

Recalling Security Council resolution 530(1983) of 19 May 1983, in which the Council encouraged the efforts of the Contadora Group and appealed urgently to all interested States in and outside the region to co-operate fully with the Group, through a frank and constructive dialogue, so as to achieve solutions to the differences between them,

Recalling General Assembly resolution 38/10 of 11 November 1983, in which the Assembly, *inter alia*, expressed its firmest support for the Contadora Group and urged it to persevere in its efforts, which enjoy the effective support of the international community and the forthright co-operation of the countries in and outside the region,

Noting with satisfaction the results of the efforts made by the Contadora Group, in particular the Contadora Act on Peace and Co-operation in Central America of 7 September 1984,

Considering that the Contadora Act is the result of an intense process of consultations and negotiations between the Governments of Costa Rica, El Salvador, Guatemala, Honduras and Nicaragua, promoted by the Contadora Group,

Also considering that the Contadora Act is a major step in bringing to fruition the negotiation process in that it lays the foundations for détente, lasting peace and the promotion of economic and social development in the region,

Taking note of the report submitted by the Secretary-General in pursuance of General Assembly resolution 38/10,

1. *Urges* each of the five Central American Governments to speed up its consultations with the Contadora Group with the aim of bringing to a conclusion the negotiation process with the early signing of the Contadora Act on Peace and Co-operation in Central America, thereby facilitating full compliance with the commitments provided for in the Act and the entry into force of the various mechanisms for implementation and follow-up;

2. *Also urges* all States, in particular those with ties to and interests in the region, to respect fully the purposes and principles of the Contadora Act and the commitments undertaken by virtue of their accession to its Additional Protocol;

3. *Requests* the Secretary-General, in accordance with Security Council resolution 530(1983), to report at regular intervals to the Council on developments in the situation and the implementation of that resolution;

4. *Requests* the Secretary-General to submit to the General Assembly, by 15 December 1984 at the latest, a report on progress made in the implementation of the present resolution;

5. *Decides* to include in the provisional agenda of its fortieth session the item entitled "The situation in Central America: threats to international peace and security and peace initiatives".

General Assembly resolution 39/4

26 October 1984   Meeting 39   Adopted by consensus

4-nation draft (A/39/L.6); agenda item 25.
Sponsors: Colombia, Mexico, Panama, Venezuela.
Meeting numbers. GA 39th session: plenary 35-39.

As a result of consultations, Nicaragua did not press to a vote a draft[36] which would have had the Assembly reaffirm Nicaragua's right to sovereignty and independence—to be respected and not endangered by military or paramilitary activities—and call for the unconditional and immediate cessation of the threats and hostile acts against it.

On 18 December, the Assembly, by decision 39/456 on the suspension of its thirty-ninth (1984) session, decided to include the item on the Central America situation among the items to be considered at the resumed session at a date to be announced.

Report of the Secretary-General (December). On 15 December,[37] the Secretary-General submitted a further report in accordance with Assembly resolution 39/4. He had written to each Foreign Minister of the Contadora Group requesting information on the negotiating process for transmission to the Assembly and had received a communication on 13 December reporting on the Group's peace efforts since 26 October. Annexed to the Secretary-General's report were: a report of 13 November from the Group's Ministers to the General Assembly of the Organization of American States (OAS), which met from 12 to 17 November; a resolution adopted by the OAS Assembly supporting the Contadora efforts; and a joint communiqué of 14 November issued by the Contadora Ministers at the OAS Assembly.

The communiqué said that the Contadora Ministers had met that day to consider the observations made at Tegucigalpa by Costa Rica, El Salvador and Honduras on the revised Act.[20] They had agreed that some contained useful ideas and were in keeping with the aim of improving the text but, in their current form, the observations could upset the balance achieved. There was, therefore, a need to intensify the negotiation process to produce the final text of an agreement preserving the spirit of the Act. The Contadora Ministers held consultations in Brazil (where the OAS Assembly was meeting) with each of the five Central American Governments individually and, in the light of these, indicated there was a possibility of incorporating some of the Tegucigalpa observations, it being understood that any such changes would not reopen discussion on commitments previously accepted by all the parties. The Contadora Foreign Ministers again underscored the importance of a clear expression of political will on the part of States directly involved in the search for viable agreements and also drew attention to the need for a constructive attitude on the part of Governments with links to the region so that negotiations could be speedily concluded. They expressed concern at the current situation in Central America and stated that a solution based on force was wrong.

In the report from the Group's Ministers to the OAS Assembly, it was pointed out that the consultations with the Central American Governments in Brazil reflected the possibility of leading negotiations towards a final agreement.

By its resolution, the OAS Assembly urged all the Central American Governments to manifest their will for peace and to intensify consultations among themselves and with the Contadora Group in order to conclude the negotiations by prompt signature of the Act. It exhorted all States, particularly those having interests in the region, to facilitate the Act's signature, to respect commitments that might be agreed on and to adhere to the Additional Protocol.

Nicaragua situation

Costa Rica-Nicaragua dispute and armed incidents

Costa Rica and Nicaragua continued to accuse each other of aggressive acts at various times throughout the year and a number of communications were addressed to the President of the Security Council regarding the situation between the two States. For the most part, the communications contained letters exchanged between the respective Foreign Ministers or Deputies.

Communications. On 19 March,[38] Nicaragua transmitted a 16 March note from Nicaragua to the United States Secretary of State protesting that, on 14 March, a group of United States mercenaries had entered Nicaragua from Costa Rica initiating action leading to the death of an eight-year-old child and the wounding of others aged five and seven years, nine months and others not identified.

Nicaragua, on 3 May,[39] transmitted a Foreign Ministry communiqué of 25 April, and a letter dated 28 April and two of 30 April addressed to Costa Rica from Nicaragua. The communiqué concerned Nicaraguan efforts to repatriate Sandinist People's Army reservists said to have been abducted to Costa Rica by United States Central Intelligence Agency (CIA) mercenaries. It denounced Costa Rica's lack of co-operation and demanded the immediate return of those abducted. The 28 April letter referred to a mercenary invasion from Costa Rica, stating that its Deputy Minister of the Interior was collaborating with CIA-backed counter-revolutionary elements launching such attacks. It also named 15 Nicaraguans it said were remaining in Costa Rica as a result of threats. The 30 April letters concerned a reported concentration of mercenary forces in Costa Rican border territory, with incursions into Nicaragua and resulting casualties, said to coincide with CIA-directed attacks from Honduras.

By a letter of 4 May,[40] Nicaragua transmitted a number of documents said to have been provided by concerned Costa Rican citizens regarding the use of that territory by the CIA and involvement of Costa Rican Government officials in such activities. Nicaragua said that the documents confirmed its assertions about the use of Costa Rican territory in carrying out the undeclared war which the United States was waging against Nicaragua through undercover operations. Costa Rica in the preceding few days had accused Nicaragua of attacks by its armed forces; those attacks were actually self-inflicted attacks and CIA provocations aimed at inducing Costa Rica to serve as a springboard for military aggression, a role Nicaragua had in the past attributed to Honduras. Costa Rica, on 9 May,[41] transmitted a note of 8 May sent to Nicaragua, protesting the contents of its letter of 4 May, which Costa Rica said echoed the campaign of disinformation waged by Nicaragua against Costa Rica and reflected an attitude of hostility.

A further letter of 4 May[42] from Nicaragua transmitted a protest it had sent to Costa Rica on 3 May, stating that the Costa Rican rural guard had that day staged an attack on itself in complic-

ity with United States plans; that incident and others were aimed at a further deterioration in relations between Costa Rica and Nicaragua, and coincided with the United States Congress debate on continuing assistance to Somozan mercenaries. Responding on 10 May,[43] Costa Rica transmitted two notes of 9 May sent to Nicaragua. Costa Rica, protesting the act of aggression on its frontier post, said it had been established that the attack was carried out by members of the Sandinist People's Army.

Responding to Nicaragua's charges of 3 May[39] and 4 May,[40], [42] Costa Rica, on 8 May,[44] said that they were untrue, since persecuted Nicaraguans of various ideological tendencies were seeking political asylum in Costa Rica. Annexed was a 30 April letter to Nicaragua stating that Costa Rica did not permit military activities to be conducted from its territory to the detriment of Nicaragua. Since Democratic Revolutionary Alliance forces, fighting against the Nicaraguan Government, controlled a broad area on the Nicaraguan bank of the San Juan River, it was unnecessary for them to use Costa Rican territory as a starting-point for their war movements. The charges against the Deputy Minister of the Interior and other officials were also rejected. Regarding the 15 Nicaraguans said to be in Costa Rican territory, whom Nicaragua had asked to be returned, with the exception of one who had requested political asylum and one handed over to the Nicaraguan Embassy on 29 April, they were not on Costa Rican territory.

On 4 May,[45] Costa Rica transmitted a 2 May note from Costa Rica to the Contadora Group alleging a new attack by the Sandinist Air Force on 29 April on Costa Rican territory, said to be the most serious incident of the past two years, confirming that Nicaragua had hardened its position towards Costa Rica. The Contadora Group was asked to dispatch an observer mission to investigate the attack.

On 8 May,[46] Nicaragua transmitted a note of 7 May sent to Costa Rica complaining that some 80 to 100 mercenaries had that day attacked a Nicaraguan frontier post and had murdered four civilians, including two children aged four and seven. At 500 metres from where the counter-revolutionaries penetrated was a post of the Costa Rican rural guard, giving further evidence of passivity towards acts of aggression committed from Costa Rica, since it was impossible for the mercenaries to pass through without being seen. Nicaragua urged Costa Rica to resume control over its frontier area and prevent such criminal acts.

On 21 May,[47] Costa Rica and Nicaragua submitted to the Secretary-General a joint declaration signed by their Foreign Ministers at Panama City on 15 May. In the covering letter, they stated that the agreement confirmed their desire for peace and was a worthy outcome of efforts being made by the

Contadora Group. The declaration covered the creation of a Commission for Supervision and Prevention as part of the efforts to end tension and incidents in the frontier zone and to promote a climate of confidence between the two countries. The Commission was to consist of a high-level representative and an alternate from both States and a representative from each of the Contadora Group countries to be involved in mediation. Its principal function was to be on-site inspection and verification of facts that might give rise to tension or frontier incidents, with both States undertaking to correct situations giving rise to an investigation. The Commission was to be installed in the Peñas Blancas frontier post on 26 May.

On 3 October,[48] Costa Rica addressed a letter to the President of the General Assembly stating that the Nicaraguan head of State, in his 2 October statement to the Assembly, had questioned Costa Rica's desire not to become involved in military conflicts. Since the two States had promised that complaints about security matters would be brought before the Commission for Supervision and Prevention, it was surprising that he had chosen the forum of the Assembly to cast doubts on Costa Rica's commitment to remain neutral *vis-à-vis* armed conflicts in other countries. Costa Rica had been demilitarized since 1949, with no military bases, installations or operations on its territory, even for defence purposes.

Honduras-Nicaragua dispute and armed incidents

Letters were again received from both Honduras and Nicaragua, throughout 1984, on alleged armed incidents between them. The letters were addressed to either the Secretary-General or the Security Council President and generally contained communications which had been exchanged between the respective Foreign Ministers. In February, the Security Council met at Nicaragua's request.

Communications (5 January–3 February). On 5 January,[49] Nicaragua forwarded a note of the same day protesting what were said to be violations of Nicaraguan territorial waters and airspace on 3 January by boats and aircraft coming from Honduras, continuing a series of acts of provocation and open violation of Nicaraguan sovereignty and territorial integrity. Another communication of the same date contained a 2 January note[50] from Nicaragua protesting a stated air violation of 1 January and calling on Honduras to cease supporting and tolerating mercenary forces attacking Nicaragua from Honduras.

On 6 January,[51] Nicaragua transmitted a communication of the same date protesting an alleged attack by two aircraft from Honduran territory on 5 January resulting in the death of one civilian and the wounding of four others. On 9 January,[52] Nicaragua forwarded a protest sent to Honduras on 7 January regarding what were described as boat and aircraft attacks from Honduras on 6 January.

On 11 January,[53] Nicaragua forwarded a note of the previous day, stating that on 8 January a group of Somozan mercenaries, in combination with Honduran troops, had attacked a Nicaraguan patrol in Nicaragua; participation of the Honduran army in provocative acts conformed with United States plans to cause a confrontation between the two States and thus make it possible for the United States to intervene in Central America.

On 13 January,[54] Honduras transmitted a 12 January communication, stating that on 11 January an unarmed United States army helicopter had been hit in Honduran territory by gun-fire from Nicaragua, killing a United States officer, thereby further reflecting Nicaragua's intention to undermine the Contadora Group's peace efforts.

Nicaragua, on 17 January,[55] transmitted a communication of the previous day, stating that on 12 January a Honduran army patrol had made an incursion into Nicaragua and a helicopter had violated its airspace. Another communication, of 23 January,[56] transmitted a Nicaraguan Foreign Ministry communiqué of 20 January, stating that Honduras had announced that a permanent joint Honduras–United States military base was to be built in the area of Puerto Castilla on the Atlantic coast of Honduras, at a cost of some $160 million. Nicaragua said this was in opposition to the Contadora Group's efforts, being part of aggressive United States plans.

Honduras, on 20 January,[57] transmitted notes of 16 and 19 January protesting acts of aggression said to have occurred on 7 and 8 January. The former note referred to the Nicaraguan army allegedly firing on a Honduran military post, and the latter to a mine said to have been planted in Honduras by the army and which had killed a peasant. Responding by a note of 23 January,[58] transmitted two days later, Nicaragua denied the allegations; if the incidents had occurred, they were more likely criminal acts of Honduran-based mercenary groups with the complicity of the Honduran army.

Also on 25 January,[59] Nicaragua circulated a note of 21 January protesting what was said to be the kidnapping of 30 Nicaraguan peasants on 16 January by Somozan mercenaries coming from Honduran territory and calling for the repatriation of the 29 remaining in the hands of the mercenaries.

A Nicaraguan communication of 26 January[60] transmitted a note of 24 January stating that the 1980 Nobel Peace Prize winner, Adolfo Pérez Esquivel, had charged that some 200 Nicaraguan citizens of Miskito origin had been murdered by a Honduran military patrol on 6 January as they were attempting to return to Nicaragua, and calling on Honduras to hold an urgent inquiry. Attached was a communiqué of the Nicaraguan Foreign Ministry stating that co-operation in elucidating the charge had been sought from a number of inter- and non-governmental organizations. Responding in a 25 January note forwarded two days later,[61] Honduras denied the accusation and stated that any impartial investigation would prove that it was in Nicaragua that Miskitos were being persecuted and exterminated; the Honduran Ambassador in Argentina had been asked to confer with Mr. Pérez Esquivel to ascertain if he had made such a charge.

A 25 January communiqué[62] of the Nicaraguan Foreign Ministry was forwarded on 26 January, stating that on 21 January two speedboats and an aircraft had fired on a Nicaraguan vessel and other actions had taken place in its territorial waters and airspace. Attention was drawn to the prolonged presence of United States warships off Nicaraguan shores, stated to support the assumption that those ships were being used to transport the speedboats which were constantly attacking Nicaragua. A further communication of 26 January[63] transmitted a 25 January note, protesting alleged violations of Nicaraguan airspace on 22 and 24 January and the abduction of 30 Nicaraguan farmers by Somozan mercenaries on the latter date to Honduran territory, and requesting their immediate release.

A further alleged kidnapping of six peasants, also on 24 January, by mercenaries was made by Nicaragua on 26 January and transmitted the next day.[64]

By a letter of 3 February,[65] Nicaragua circulated a note of 2 February, stating that on that day six military aircraft of the Honduran air force had attacked a military unit of the San-dinist People's Army and a civilian communications centre, killing three soldiers and wounding three others; a new dimension had been added to the existing conflict in Central America, responsibility for which rested with those financing, organizing and permitting provocative acts against Nicaragua.

SECURITY COUNCIL CONSIDERATION (February)

In a further letter of 3 February,[66] Nicaragua requested the immediate convening of the Security Council to consider the situation created by what it termed the new escalation of acts of aggression to which it had been subjected by Somozan and mercenary counter-revolutionary forces trained and financed by the United States and in which foreign armies were increasingly involved.

The Security Council met later that day, with Honduras being invited, at its request, to participate without the right to vote.

Meeting number. SC 2513.

Nicaragua stressed it was again facing dangerous events, aimed at bringing about a war of destruction in Central America; qualitatively, they were the most serious events of the past two years and could be the precursors of a war between Honduras and Nicaragua provoked by the United States to justify intervention. Nicaragua gave further details of the previous day's alleged attack, stating there had been, in 1983, more than 620 violations of Nicaraguan airspace by United States surveillance aircraft, with over 400 helicopters and aircraft flying from Honduran soil, and on one mission an American pilot had been killed. There had also been 19 air attacks in the same year. Currently, for the first time, war-planes had been used against Nicaraguan military units deep inside its territory. It was not necessary to advance proof of CIA participation but it was clear that Nicaraguan defeats of counter-revolutionary forces coming from Honduras had led to new wide-scale aggression and war exercises against Nicaragua aimed apparently at being converted into a real war. The United States and its allies had been put into a difficult position within the Contadora Group because of the constructive attitude of Nicaragua and the sincere intentions of the Group itself, Nicaragua said.

Honduras said that Nicaragua had again tried to involve Honduras in the problems it was having with its own citizens and, by creating confrontations, was seeking to divert attention from those problems. The accusation made by Nicaragua in calling for the Council meeting was unfounded, since no military aircraft had left its base; Nicaragua made charges whenever peace initiatives of the Contadora Group were progressing, and it had stated that the Nobel peace laureate had accused Honduras of being implicated in genocide, but he had denied ever making such an accusation. Referring to charges of a foreign military base in Honduras, it pointed out that on earlier occasions it had stated that what was involved was a military training centre established by Honduras, directed by its officers, and intended to train Honduran troops and also those of friendly countries. It welcomed assistance from experts not only from the United States, but also from anywhere in Central or South America with which co-operation was maintained. Honduras registered its agreements relating to armed forces with the United Nations and wished Nicaragua would do likewise and make public the agreements under which it received foreign weapons and advisers, which promoted the arms race, the destabilization of democratically elected Governments and terrorism in Central America.

The United States said the Council's dignity was abused every several months by Nicaragua's allegations of aggression by the United States and neighbouring Governments in Central America. The United States had not engaged in aggression against Nicaragua and did not plan to. However, it intended to co-operate with its friends in Central America, as elsewhere, in defence of freedom, self-determination and the institutions of democratic pluralism of which the Sandinist régime had deprived its people. It was that betrayal of the principles of its own revolution which had caused substantial numbers of Nicaraguans to take up arms against that régime.

Communications (6 February–1 November). On 6 February,[67] Nicaragua transmitted a note dated 3 February, stating that that day four aircraft flying from Honduran territory attacked a Nicaraguan army unit, killing a militiaman. On 7 February,[68] Honduras transmitted notes dated 3 and 6 February, rejecting the accusations by Nicaragua of 2 February[65] and 3 February[67] of Honduran air attacks. In a letter to the Secretary-General also of 7 February,[69] Honduras transmitted a formal declaration of 6 February concerning the same charges, stating that they were made to justify Nicaragua's arms race, its policy of intervention and hostility towards other Central American countries and the maintenance of a state of emergency enabling it to continue denying Nicaraguans a democratic system of government.

On 14 February,[70] Nicaragua transmitted a note to Honduras of 13 February stating that on 7 February some 20 Somozan mercenaries coming from Honduran territory had entered Nicaragua and threatened and interrogated local inhabitants before withdrawing; it also alleged airspace violations of 8, 9 and 12 February and territorial water violations of 12 February. Honduras, on 22 February,[71] transmitted a 20 February note rejecting the allegations as unfounded.

On 5 March,[72] Nicaragua transmitted a note of 4 March, stating that since 1 March Somozan mercenaries, with the Honduran army's collaboration, had been launching mortar attacks on Nicaraguan frontier villages from positions they occupied in Honduran territory; on 3 March, a helicopter coming from Honduran territory was said to have launched a rocket attack, while 50 Honduran troops had harassed a Nicaraguan observation post. Replying on 5 March, by a note transmitted the next day,[73] Honduras stated that it was obvious that the internal struggle in Nicaragua was becoming general and was a pretext for initiating an international confrontation involving the entire Central American region.

A Nicaraguan note of 5 March, transmitted on 6 March,[74] alleged that on that day launches and aircraft had attacked three Nicaraguan coastguard vessels in the Gulf of Fonseca, killing three crew members and wounding three more. On 7 March,[75] Nicaragua transmitted a note of 6 March to Honduras, alleging further attacks by Somozan mercenaries on 4 and 6 March, accompanied on the latter date by Honduran soldiers; the incidents had led to the wounding of a Nicaraguan soldier and the killing of a one-year-old girl. On 8 March,[76] Nicaragua transmitted a 7 March note, stating that the day before launches had attacked Nicaraguan military installations three times. Honduras rejected the allegations of 5, 6 and 7 March as being without foundation; if Nicaragua was subject to foreign aggression, Honduras was neither the source nor a participant, it said in an 8 March note, transmitted on 12 March.[77]

Nicaragua, on 13 March,[78] conveyed a note of 12 March, stating that two days earlier Honduran soldiers had attacked a Nicaraguan observation post while, in another incident, Somozan mercenaries in conjunction with the Honduran army had attacked a second post; and on 11 March, the mercenaries had conducted a further attack, also in conjunction with the Honduran army. A second Nicaraguan communication of 13 March,[79] forwarding a note of 12 March, said that on 11 March mercenaries coming from Honduras had tried to sabotage an electric power sub-station in Nicaragua, while on 12 March, others had destroyed pylons.

Honduras, on 20 March,[80] transmitted a 15 March note charging that Nicaragua had changed the location of boundary markers and proposing that a technical commission of engineers from both States visit the sector involved.

Nicaragua, on 26 March,[81] forwarded a 25 March note stating that a combined Honduran army/Somozan mercenary force had that day carried out an artillery attack on a Nicaraguan community. On 26 March,[82] Nicaragua said that, the previous day, Honduran military personnel had attacked Nicaraguan forces; such involvement by the Government of Honduras brought the risk of regional conflagration ever nearer.

Honduras, on 26 March,[83] transmitted a note of 23 March stating that on 22 March a group of 50 Nicaraguans had invaded Honduran territory seizing 539 cattle; the same group, or a similar one, had during the night of 21 March seized 250 cattle. A letter of 28 March[84] from

Honduras transmitted a communication of 27 March, stating that the Nicaraguan Minister of Defence had announced the possibility of local guerrilla groups proceeding to mine the ports of other Central American countries, from Guatemala to Panama—a public admission that subversive groups were operating with the support of the Nicaraguan Government.

On 29 March,[85] Nicaragua forwarded a note of the same date, stating that on 27 March 30 Honduran soldiers had attacked a Nicaraguan patrol, while on the same day boats and aircraft from Honduras had been involved in an attack on a Nicaraguan coastguard vessel; on 28 March a boat coming from Honduras had attacked a Panamanian vessel in Nicaraguan waters. On 2 April,[86] Nicaragua transmitted a 30 March note, stating that on 29 March Honduran army personnel had mounted an attack on Nicaraguan territory. Another communication, of 30 April, transmitted on 1 May,[87] said that, after a marked reduction in attacks and acts of provocation by Honduran army troops, there had been attacks on 23 April, an aircraft violation of Nicaraguan airspace on 29 April, and a commando group attack from Honduran territory on 30 April. On 7 May,[88] Nicaragua transmitted a note of 4 May, stating that the Honduran army had that day attacked a Nicaraguan frontier post. That attack, said Honduras in a 4 May note transmitted on 7 May,[89] had been carried out by the Nicaraguan army as part of a systematic repetition of aggressive acts coinciding with similar escalation of such acts against Costa Rica. On 8 May,[90] Nicaragua transmitted two 7 May protest notes rejecting Honduras's assertion and stating that the aggressor of 4 May was Honduras and that a further attack had been made on 6 May.

On 9 May,[91] Nicaragua transmitted an 8 May note, stating that on that day two military helicopters from Honduras had penetrated its airspace and one had been shot down, an investigation showing that it belonged to the United States armed forces; two Honduran air force identity cards were also found giving proof of Honduran direct participation in the covert war against Nicaragua, master-minded by the United States. On 9 May,[92] Honduras transmitted a note and a press communiqué of 8 May protesting against what it said was a brutal act of aggression by Nicaragua against an unarmed helicopter, carrying eight Hondurans who had perished; the helicopter was said to have deviated from its scheduled route because of bad weather and given no warning by Nicaragua before being shot down. On 10 May,[93] Honduras accused Nicaragua of making false accusations in trying to turn to its advantage the downing of the unarmed helicopter; contrary to the Nicaraguan assertion of two

helicopters, only one was involved; Nicaragua's aggressive attitude contrasted with Honduran behaviour in similar cases when it had returned unharmed personnel violating its airspace. Another communication from Honduras of 11 May[94] stated that, because of the Nicaraguan attitude towards the incident, the Nicaraguan Ambassador in Honduras had been declared *persona non grata*.

Also on 11 May,[95] Nicaragua, in a letter to the President of the Security Council, said that the expulsion of its Ambassador aggravated the tense relations between the two countries. In communiqués of 8 and 11 May annexed to the letter, Nicaragua regretted the death of the Hondurans, victims of the United States policy in the region, and appealed to Honduras to end its irresponsible policy of risking Honduran lives by increasingly involving them in the CIA's aggression against Nicaragua; it was ready to let Honduras send a mission, accompanied by Contadora Group representatives, to the site where the military helicopter was downed.

A further Nicaraguan communication of 11 May[96] concerning the incident listed air and naval attacks said to have been launched from Honduran territory between April 1983 and March 1984 near the area where the helicopter was shot down. Regarding the assertion that the helicopter, which recent investigations showed to have belonged to the Honduran air force, had deviated because of bad weather, Nicaragua stated that meteorological reports from the area showed that at the time the wind was calm, visibility unlimited and temperatures normal.

Honduras, on 21 May,[97] transmitted a 16 May note stating that it was encouraging that Nicaragua had acknowledged that the helicopter belonged to the Honduran air force; regarding the weather conditions, it said Nicaragua had ignored meteorological reports of thick cloud and fog which were normal for the time of year. Also, if visibility was unlimited, then the assertion was self-incriminating since the Sandinist army, despite this, had fired on an unarmed, clearly marked helicopter.

On 22 May,[98] Nicaragua charged that on 21 May there had been a new violation of its territorial waters by fishing boats flying the Honduran flag.

On 22 June,[99] Honduras transmitted a letter of 21 June, stating that on 19 June some 100 members of the Sandinist army had entered Honduras and another contingent on the same day had tried to attack a military post in an engagement in which three Sandinist soldiers were killed and two taken prisoner; prompted by humanitarian philosophy, Honduras was prepared to return the bodies and prisoners. On 6 July,[100] Honduras transmitted a note of 5 July stating that three

Nicaraguans apprehended by Honduras, stated by Nicaragua to be fishermen who had lost their way, were not so because they had been carrying weapons and had tried to hide in a suspicious manner. A further Honduran letter of 19 July[101] transmitted a 17 July note, stating that on 2 July a six-member Sandinist army patrol had crossed into Honduras and engaged in a firing incident with the Honduran army. On 11 October,[102] Honduras transmitted a 9 October note, stating that on 2 October a Honduran fishing vessel in Honduran waters had been fired on by a Nicaraguan patrol boat, killing a fisherman and wounding two others.

Nicaragua, on 12 October,[103] forwarded a letter stating that on 10 October approximately 25 mercenaries had entered from Honduras and, in an engagement supported by the Honduran army, two Nicaraguan militiamen had been killed and another wounded; conditions were being prepared for a major military offensive against Nicaragua based on the concentration in Honduras of mercenary forces in the service of the United States. On 1 November,[104] Nicaragua transmitted a letter of 31 October stating that that day there had been new airspace violations by unidentified aircraft coming from Honduras, actions coinciding with increased occurrence of violations, including overflights by United States aircraft dropping unidentified objects in Nicaraguan waters; these incidents were in line with CIA plans to impede the Nicaraguan electoral process.

Nicaragua-United States dispute

Relations between Nicaragua and the United States deteriorated during 1984, a situation reflected by the exchange of communications between the countries and those addressed to the United Nations. Communications to the Secretary-General and/or the Security Council President mostly transmitted texts which had been exchanged between the Nicaraguan Foreign Minister and the United States Secretary of State. The Council met in March/April, September and November to consider Nicaragua's complaints of aggression against it. A draft resolution put forward in April was not adopted because of the negative vote of a permanent Council member, the United States.

Communications (9 January–29 March). On 9 January,[105] Nicaragua forwarded a 7 January note protesting that, the previous day, two Piraña-type speedboats and an unidentified aircraft had attacked a Nicaraguan sugar refinery and neighbouring residential areas; the continued presence of United States warships in Nicaraguan waters led it to assume that the boats came from United States vessels.

On 29 February,[106] Nicaragua forwarded a note of 28 February, stating that launches supplied by the CIA to counter-revolutionary forces operating from Honduras and Costa Rica had launched attacks against Nicaragua and laid mines in its waters, resulting in the sinking of a Nicaraguan motorized vessel and damage to two others, and wounding seven people and leaving two missing.

On 7 March,[107] Nicaragua transmitted a note of 2 March complaining of further mining and stating that United States plans to impose a military blockade on Nicaragua were revealed ever more clearly.

Another note from Nicaragua of 8 March, transmitted the same day,[108] complained of additional attacks by launches, mining and acts of sabotage, stating that these incidents were part of a new strategy aimed at spreading terror in Nicaragua.

On 13 March,[109] Nicaragua transmitted a government statement of that date saying that the virtual occupation of Honduras had converted that country into a United States base ready to launch large-scale operations, with United States military personnel and equipment, against El Salvador and Nicaragua. Counter-revolutionaries had been installed in both Honduras and Costa Rica, and the United States was attempting a commercial blockade of Nicaragua.

On 15 March,[110] India forwarded a communiqué adopted by the Co-ordinating Bureau of the Movement of Non-Aligned Countries, expressing concern over the new escalation of hostile acts against Nicaragua and the reported mining of its seaports.

Nicaragua, on 21 March,[111] transmitted a Foreign Ministry communiqué of 20 March stating that a Soviet vessel carrying oil to Nicaragua had been damaged in its waters by a device placed there by mercenaries in the service of the United States, resulting in the wounding of five Soviet seamen.

On 27 March,[112] a Nicaraguan Government communiqué of the previous day was transmitted, stressing that there must be an end to the escalation of the stationing of troops in Central America by withdrawal of those sent in the past few weeks, together with espionage aircraft, aircraft-carriers and warships recently dispatched; by halting all military manoeuvres in the region; by ending attacks against Nicaragua and the mining of its harbours; and by withdrawal of a request before the United States Congress for funds to intensify terrorist activities against Nicaragua.

On 29 March,[113] Nicaragua transmitted a 28 March Foreign Ministry communiqué stating that a Liberian vessel leaving Nicaragua had struck a mine in its waters and holding the United States responsible.

SECURITY COUNCIL CONSIDERATION (March/April)

On 29 March,[114] Nicaragua requested that the Security Council meet to consider what it said was an escalation of acts of aggression against it.

The Council considered the situation at four meetings held between 30 March and 4 April.

Meeting numbers. SC 2525, 2527-2529.

At their request, Afghanistan, Algeria, Costa Rica, Cuba, Czechoslovakia, Democratic Yemen, El Salvador, Ethiopia, the German Democratic Republic, Guatemala, Guyana, Honduras, Hungary, the Lao People's Democratic Republic, the Libyan Arab Jamahiriya, Mexico, Seychelles, the Syrian Arab Republic, Viet Nam and Yugoslavia were invited to take part in the proceedings without the right to vote.

A draft resolution submitted by Nicaragua[115] to have the Council condemn and call for an immediate end to the mining of the main ports of Nicaragua, call on all States to refrain from any type of military action against any State of the region, and support the Contadora Group efforts was not adopted owing to the negative vote of a permanent Council member.

The vote was 13 to 1, with 1 abstention, as follows:

> *In favour:* China, Egypt, France, India, Malta, Netherlands, Nicaragua, Pakistan, Peru, Ukrainian SSR, USSR, Upper Volta, Zimbabwe.
> *Against:* United States.
> *Abstaining:* United Kingdom.

In statements after the vote and in explanation of vote Nicaragua and the United States explained their positions.

Nicaragua stated that it had earlier in the debate asked when the United States would hear the universal outcry and halt the undeclared war it was waging. The veto was a clear reply: it did not intend to halt its aggression or to stop mining Nicaragua's ports. For that reason Nicaragua was obliged to continue trying to acquire the appropriate technological and military means to defend itself.

The United States said that the draft resolution was seriously flawed since it expressed concern about only one kind of violence and against only one target, and expressed no concern for the many attacks on El Salvador or for the continued violation of its territorial integrity by Nicaragua's continuing arms shipments to Salvadorian guerrillas. Neither did it express concern for the repeated violations of the borders of Costa Rica or Honduras. The United States reaffirmed its commitment to peace in Central America, regional negotiations leading to settlements, demilitarization of the region, mutual respect for sovereignty and secure borders, the withdrawal of all foreign military personnel, respect for law and establishment of democratic institutions based on free elections.

The United Kingdom also felt the text lacked balance since the debate was on the problems of Central America and the positions of the United States and the other Central American countries were not to be found; nor was there a call for an immediate end to all threats, attacks and hostile acts against all States of Central America.

There was universal support for the Contadora process, while in general there was antipathy towards any attempt at an economic blockade of Nicaragua, and a large majority of the countries taking part in the debate expressed concern over the mining of Nicaraguan ports and called for an end to it. Countries advocating that course included: Afghanistan, Algeria, China, Cuba, Czechoslovakia, Democratic Yemen, Egypt, Ethiopia, France, German Democratic Republic, Guyana, India, Lao People's Democratic Republic, Libyan Arab Jamahiriya, Mexico, Netherlands, Pakistan, Peru, Seychelles, Syrian Arab Republic, Ukrainian SSR, USSR, United Kingdom, Upper Volta, Viet Nam, Yugoslavia and Zimbabwe.

France said the Central American countries must be permitted to solve their own problems and the Contadora process must aim at achieving a halt in demonstrations of strength and an end to violence and interference by countries outside the region. China urged the super-Powers to refrain from making Central America an arena for their rivalry. India said peace and progress could not be constructed by the exclusion of one State or another from the mainstream of regional development.

The Upper Volta said the real reasons for the problems arising in Central America were known to everybody, including the United States, which wanted to replace those problems with others to justify its hatred of the Sandinist revolutionary régime; the changes in Central America were not the result of an East-West ideological confrontation, as the United States claimed.

The Syrian Arab Republic accused the United States of rejecting progressive régimes, wherever they were. The Ukrainian SSR felt that because the current Government of Nicaragua was not to the liking of the United States it had decided on its overthrow. Speaking similarly, the Lao People's Democratic Republic said the United States was supporting Somozan mercenary forces which, according to CIA pronouncements, would soon amount to 18,000 armed men. Zimbabwe said that their objective was to bring down the legitimate

Government of Nicaragua. The USSR added that the United States did not attempt to conceal the fact that its principal task was to force the Nicaraguan people to turn away from their path of independent development and to restore Central America to its own total control.

Czechoslovakia said the issue was the continuing and ever-escalating acts of aggression against Nicaragua involving unlawful, hostile acts organized and financed by, or even directly carried out by, the United States in its undeclared war against an independent Central American State. Guyana said it was puzzled at the attitude of States which piously called for respect for non-intervention and peaceful settlement of disputes in other areas while brazenly violating them in Central America. Cuba said that while the United States was advocating the peaceful solution negotiated by the Contadora Group, it was preparing to invade both El Salvador and Nicaragua.

Pakistan said it firmly supported Nicaragua in its endeavours to overcome the serious problems with which it was beset, while hoping that all States in the region would help the process of peace and coexistence, permitting them to build their respective societies in accordance with their aspirations and free from outside intervention. Yugoslavia felt it was indispensable to recognize that right. Egypt added that it saw the nature of the crisis besetting Central America as but one more facet of human suffering in the third world.

The Libyan Arab Jamahiriya noted it had pointed out that it would not be the last victim in the series of American acts of aggression and the current meeting affirmed the validity of that warning. Democratic Yemen said the United States was the main source of tension, instability and the undermining of peace in the world and the Council should support Nicaragua and the other peoples of Latin America.

Algeria said the military actions against Nicaragua had assumed the characteristics of a conventional war, albeit an undeclared one, with the target nothing less than destabilization of Nicaragua and indeed the whole region.

Seychelles said it depended on the sea for its livelihood and survival and so protested wherever there was mining; the perpetrators of terrorism on the international high seas should be caught and punished.

Ethiopia said Nicaragua internally was facing the destructive activities of counter-revolutionary bandits backed by the United States; externally, in addition to many economic and financial pressures, it was also confronted with the threat of invasion by the armed forces of the United States and Honduras, the latter being one vast military base, whose political objective was the forcible overthrow of the legitimate Government of Nicaragua.

Viet Nam said a new step had been taken by the United States imperialists in their military escalation, in an attempt to wage a large-scale war of aggression against Nicaragua and to oppose the national liberation movements in El Salvador and elsewhere in Central America and the Caribbean area.

The German Democratic Republic said there was a close connection between the mining of Nicaraguan ports, the increasing attacks against Nicaragua, the use of Honduran territory and the various manoeuvres by United States armed forces in the region, at a time when millions of dollars were being spent by the United States to suppress the Central American peoples' will to freedom and to undermine legitimate Governments in that region. Afghanistan noted that the already tense situation had taken an ominous turn, with the main cause being the stepped-up United States imperialist intervention in the internal affairs of the countries of the region, including in Nicaragua.

Costa Rica believed that the Council should appeal to the countries concerned to carry out their mission in keeping with the Contadora guidelines; again appeal to the international community not to divert the nine countries involved from their chosen path; call for strict respect of the principles of international law, in particular regarding freedom of navigation; and uphold the principle that attention must be paid not only to matters relating to the security of States, but also to progress in all fields, including those dealing with political, economic and social development. Peru said the violations of Nicaragua's security and stability were a crucial link in the broader problems confronting Latin America, with the realities in the area, characterized by current circumstances and a simplistic view of the Central American crisis, obstructing dialogue and negotiations.

Mexico said what was happening in Central America reflected the major choices facing the international community: on the one hand, the absurd attempt to achieve peace by waging war and, on the other, the negotiated and rational solution of existing conflicts; the arms race on the one hand and the quest for just settlements of contemporary problems on the other. A universal consensus had been confirmed with respect to the fact that the conflicts in Central America originated in economic and social conditions and not in terms of a mechanical reflex of East-West confrontations.

The Netherlands said the crisis was closely related to the processes of change in which the countries of the region were immersed and felt that the endemic social inequalities, injustice and economic underdevelopment were at the root of the crisis, no doubt aggravated by outside interference.

Honduras believed that Nicaragua was trying to blame others for its internal conflicts, while seeking to push into the background the problems of concern to other Central American countries, such as weapons trafficking, support for all kinds of sabotage, terrorism and destabilization against other Central American Governments, the Nicaraguan arms buildup, the large numbers of Nicaraguan troops and the growing presence in Nicaragua of Eastern bloc advisers.

El Salvador pointed out that it had only emerged victorious from tragic times because of the determined democratic will of the majority of its people and the assistance offered by friendly countries, in contrast to the open foreign intervention practised by Nicaragua in Salvadorian internal affairs, embodied by the support for armed groups in El Salvador attempting to overthrow by force a legitimately constituted Government based on the people's will.

Guatemala said it had remained outside the problem of the arms race and that of exportation of armed groups and intended to continue to do so; it appealed for reconciliation among Central Americans and for them not to allow hegemonistic and extracontinental conflicts, foreign to their interest, to sweep them up.

Malta noted that in the midst of disheartening news there remained some positive elements, including the continuing peaceful overtures of Nicaragua and the belated United States recognition of the Central America crisis, of compassion for its people and of hope for its future.

Communications (30 April–4 September). On 30 April,[116] Nicaragua transmitted a government communiqué of 27 April stating that its fundamental principles and commitments were non-alignment, a mixed economy, political pluralism, and the defence of human rights and freedom of expression. It was essential to conclude treaties to guarantee the peace and security of all States in the region; delaying this until all countries could reach agreement on other regional commitments would highlight the lack of will to safeguard peace.

On 2 May,[117] Nicaragua transmitted a note of 1 May stating that launches coming from a United States ship had the previous day attacked a Nicaraguan army post. Also on 2 May,[118] Nicaragua transmitted a note of the same day stating that that day a mine had sunk a Nicaraguan fishing vessel, at a time when launches from United States ships were operating in Nicaraguan waters.

On 10 May,[119] Nicaragua transmitted excerpts from the provisional measures delivered that day by the International Court of Justice on the case Nicaragua had brought against the United States (see LEGAL QUESTIONS, Chapter I). On 15 May,[120] Nicaragua transmitted the resolution on

Nicaragua of the Third Conference of Ministers of Labour of Non-Aligned Countries and Other Developing Countries (Managua, 10-12 May), which, among other things, urged the United States to comply with the provisional measures adopted by the Court.

On 4 June,[121] Nicaragua transmitted a 2 June government communiqué stating that it had received the United States Secretary of State in a meeting with the Co-ordinator of the Governing Junta. The atmosphere had been respectful and frank with the Co-ordinator stressing that: Nicaragua was at all times ready to embark on talks to normalize relations between the two countries; verbal willingness to negotiate must be supported by practical actions, such as cessation of military manoeuvres, air and naval attacks, mining of harbours, installation of military bases and covert war; and Nicaragua stood ready at any time to conclude an agreement to guarantee peace and security in the region. Nicaragua agreed to further talks and had designated its Deputy Foreign Minister for that purpose, while stressing the need for participation in the talks of a mutually acceptable third country. The Co-ordinator also expressed his willingness to go to the United States for a meeting with its President.

On 30 August,[122] Nicaragua conveyed a note of 29 August stating that on 27 August it had shot down an American-made aircraft over its territory, killing the eight persons on board. It said the plane was one of those supplied by the CIA to mercenary bands working for the United States, and had been shot down in the area of the frontier with Honduras. Such continuing interventions by the United States belied its willingness to initiate a serious dialogue with Nicaragua.

On 4 September,[123] Nicaragua transmitted a note of 2 September stating that on 1 September it had shot down a military helicopter participating in a raid on Nicaragua which had killed four children and an adult; to date the bodies of two members of the helicopter's crew had been found.

SECURITY COUNCIL CONSIDERATION (September)

On 4 September,[124] Nicaragua requested an urgent Security Council meeting to examine the situation created by what it called the new escalation of aggression directed against it.

The Council met on 7 September.
Meeting number. SC 2557.

In the debate Nicaragua said that a few days after the United States had vetoed the text before the Council in April it had contradicted its statements by publicly acknowledging its participation in mining Nicaraguan ports. Nicaragua had then gone before the International Court of Justice, while the United States, which proclaimed itself the defender of international law, had affirmed its non-recognition of the Court's jurisdiction on the issue. Currently, there was increasing United States involvement in the no-longer-covert war against Nicaragua as evidenced by increasing air raids. In violation of United States legislation, mercenaries were being contracted, and its official policy of State terrorism was also manifested through the military presence off the coasts and on the territories of Central America, in the constant holding of joint military and naval manoeuvres and in the building of airports and other military installations in Central America. The CIA was engaging in new tactics by the presence of United States mercenaries and was trying to convert those forces into a mercenary army that could serve as a springboard during an invasion. Nicaragua invited the Council to visit it to see how well its Government was functioning and that it was not persecuting anyone; it was not and never would be a threat to the security of any Central American State, much less that of the United States.

The United States noted that this was not the first time Nicaragua had come to the Council just as the Contadora process was beginning to arrive at solutions which would cause Nicaragua to recommit itself to the democratic system it had once promised the world and its own people. Meetings that had taken place between the two States had underscored United States commitment to the Contadora negotiations as an avenue towards resolution of the Central America crisis. The baseless allegations of aggression by the United States and neighbouring Central American Governments was a tactic designed to deflect attention again from Nicaragua's reluctance to negotiate in good faith and settle its problems with its neighbours. The United States said it had not sent personnel to Nicaragua to destabilize its régime, but noted that numerous Cubans and Libyan military and security advisers were there. Together with Soviet, Palestine Liberation Organization, Basque and other foreign military personnel, they were of serious concern to the United States and Central American countries. From the nature of elections in Nicaragua, it was not surprising that many people in the world opposed them and some private American citizens had apparently become involved in that event. The guerrillas of El Salvador and the Nicaraguan Government had themselves appealed for private American aid, and some Americans also worked for the Sandinista Government. Relations had deteriorated because, instead of keeping promises about human rights and pluralistic democracy, the Sandinistas had developed increasingly close military ties to Cuba and the USSR, tightened internal repres-

sion, supported guerrilla insurgency in El Salvador and terrorism in Costa Rica and Honduras, and continued an extensive military buildup threatening regional security.

The USSR said the United States statement that it did not intend to overthrow the Nicaraguan Government was fallacious, since it openly continued to finance, arm and train mercenaries whom it had been sending to Nicaraguan territory. The issue lay elsewhere than the non-existent alleged USSR threat; the reason for United States acts of intervention against Latin American countries was its policy of not allowing the autonomous, economic, political and social development of the area and attempting to impose the kind of system it preferred. The United States had on 82 occasions used force against 11 Latin American countries.

Communications (11 September–8 November). On 11 September,[125] Nicaragua transmitted a telegram of 6 September referring to the 1 September air attack on Nicaragua (see p. 209), and stated that on 5 September the United States press had reported that the two mercenaries involved were part of a group of six sent to Honduras to carry out paramilitary activities against Nicaragua; although this violated United States criminal laws, it was not taking proceedings against those involved. A further letter, of 12 September,[126] from Nicaragua on the helicopter incident contained details of alleged United States military presence in Nicaragua, maps illustrating air operations against it and military bases in Honduras, photographs of what were said to be parts of United States–made aircraft downed in Nicaragua, including the helicopter, and newspaper articles from the United States press—documentation further confirming the double standard of the United States which, while seemingly willing to negotiate, was openly waging aggression against Nicaragua.

Refuting these allegations on 2 October,[127] the United States said they were without foundation and the United States citizens who died were not government employees, nor were they connected with its officials or activities in the region; it added that, on the date in question, several Cuban military personnel were killed in a battle with Nicaraguan freedom fighters. It was duplicitous that Nicaragua which had welcomed some 10,000 Cubans and numerous other foreign advisers and military personnel should complain about a small number of foreign individuals fighting with Nicaraguans to deliver democracy to that country.

On 18 September,[128] Nicaragua transmitted a government communiqué of the previous day stating that three frigates of the United States

Navy had repeatedly violated Nicaragua's territorial waters in acts said to be preliminary to new aggression, with likely greater involvement by the United States Army.

In the final communiqué adopted by the Meeting of Ministers for Foreign Affairs and Heads of Delegation of Non-Aligned Countries to the thirty-ninth (1984) session of the General Assembly (New York, 1-5 October), the participants noted with grave concern that the situation in the region had been further aggravated by increased recourse to imperialist policies of interference through the utilization of neighbouring territories for aggression against other States, the installation of military bases and attempts at the destabilization of the Nicaraguan Government, such as the mining of its ports and harbours in violation of international law, as well as numerous acts of aggression, pressure and economic coercion exerted against the countries of the region. The communiqué was forwarded by India on 8 October.[129]

On 15 October,[130] Nicaragua circulated the address by the Co-ordinator of the Governing Junta at the May Conference of Ministers of Labour of non-aligned and other developing countries.

On 20 October,[131] Nicaragua transmitted a document on psychological operations in guerrilla warfare said to have been prepared by the CIA for use by mercenary bands attempting to overthrow the Nicaraguan Government. The manual described how to carry out assassinations, kidnapping, assaults and other criminal activities said to contravene both international law and United States legislation. On 23 October,[132] Nicaragua transmitted a letter regarding the manual, stating that the United States President had, during a 21 October election debate, acknowledged it had been sent to the CIA chief in Nicaragua.

On 8 November,[133] Nicaragua transmitted a note of the previous day alleging further United States provocations by its frigates and violations of Nicaraguan airspace. Another note of 8 November[134] complained of an additional airspace violation said to have been committed by the United States that day, alleged to be part of a prelude to direct military intervention in Nicaragua.

SECURITY COUNCIL CONSIDERATION (November)

On 9 November,[135] Nicaragua asked the Security Council to meet to consider what it said was the serious situation created by the escalation of aggression, the repeated threats and new acts of provocation fostered by the United States.

The Council met that day.

Meeting number. SC 2562.

Nicaragua said that all the military actions, recent threatening statements by members of the United States Administration, including the President, and the daily acts of aggression which were being stepped up led it constantly to fear a military intervention. The threats against Nicaragua, including an announcement of bombing of its territory, were part of a United States policy of aggression. At the same time the United States was leaking information about ships allegedly taking USSR-made fighter planes on board and sailing for Nicaraguan ports, intensifying spy flights and preparing to put into action in Central America the airborne brigade that had invaded Grenada. Further significant measures of aggression were being prepared to discredit the successful development of the democratic process in Nicaragua, reflected by its 4 November elections which had broad and free popular participation. Nicaragua declared that no ship of any nationality was transporting fighter aircraft to Nicaraguan ports and no such aircraft had been unloaded. It denounced the United States manoeuvres and warned that Nicaraguans were prepared to respond to any call for mobilization to defend the country.

The United States felt that, since no emergency existed requiring immediate action, Nicaragua's insistence on an immediate meeting was a misuse of Council processes. The current meeting was a further occasion, resembling half a dozen others, on which the Council was convening to deal with an invented threat of invasion, alleged to emanate from the United States. Although Nicaragua's head of State had predicted an invasion by 15 October, the prediction had not come true and, with 15 November approaching, another prediction had been made, perhaps with the idea of having the issue considered at regular monthly intervals. What was true of the first alleged invasion threat was equally true of the current allegation; it was without foundation.

Communications (12-29 November). On 12 November,[136] Nicaragua transmitted notes of 10 and 11 November protesting airspace violations and naval manoeuvres and stating that such airspace violations were a daily occurrence. On 19 November,[137] Nicaragua transmitted a note of 16 November, stating that two days earlier a group of about 300 mercenaries in the service of the United States had attacked a co-operative in Nicaragua, killing 14 people, including two children; on 15 November the same bands had attacked an agricultural co-operative, killing four peasants.

Also on 19 November,[138] a further communiqué of the Co-ordinating Bureau of the non-aligned Movement, adopted that day, was transmitted by India. The Bureau reiterated that the developments, particularly intensified aerial and naval actions in Nicaraguan airspace and territorial waters, increased the dangers of regional war; it demanded the immediate cessation of all such actions.

In a note of 23 November, transmitted six days later,[139] the United States, referring to the Nicaraguan communications of 1, 7, 8, 9, 10 and 11 November, said that it was not engaging in provocative aggressive acts towards Nicaragua nor planning to invade it; Nicaragua was building up its military capability beyond any reasonable estimate of its defensive needs, thereby exacerbating tensions and helping to create a situation that had long been viewed as a serious threat by Nicaragua's neighbours.

REFERENCES

[1]A/39/71-S/16262. [2]A/39/83-S/16286. [3]A/39/95-S/16304. [4]A/39/126-S/16394. [5]A/39/110. [6]A/39/187-S/16489. [7]A/39/232. [8]A/39/226-S/16522. [9]S/16633. [10]A/39/325. [11]A/39/448-S/16723. [12]A/39/495-S/16742. [13]A/39/512. [14]S/16756. [15]A/39/555-S/16770. [16]A/39/563. [17]A/39/579. [18]A/39/588-S/16784. [19]A/39/599. [20]A/39/630. [21]A/39/629-S/16815. [22]A/39/668-S/16828. [23]A/39/637-S/16818. [24]A/39/645. [25]A/39/687. [26]A/39/135-S/16422. [27]A/39/161-S/16456. [28]A/39/539. [29]A/39/590 & Corr.1. [30]A/39/606. [31]A/39/546. [32]YUN 1983, p. 206, SC res. 530(1983), 19 May 1983. [33]*Ibid.*, p. 197, GA res. 38/10, 11 Nov. 1983. [34]A/39/562-S/16775. [35]A/39/604-S/16796. [36]A/39/L.7/Rev.1. [37]A/39/827-S/16865. [38]S/16424. [39]S/16529. [40]S/16534 & Corr.1. [41]S/16552. [42]S/16530 & Corr. 1. [43]S/16553. [44]S/16541. [45]S/16536. [46]S/16542. [47]A/39/268-S/16577. [48]A/39/545. [49]S/16250. [50]A/39/64-S/16253. [51]S/16257. [52]S/16263. [53]S/16273. [54]A/39/77-S/16279. [55]S/16280. [56]S/16284. [57]A/39/82-S/16285. [58]S/16291. [59]S/16288. [60]S/16294. [61]S/16302. [62]S/16295. [63]S/16296. [64]S/16299. [65]S/16307. [66]S/16306. [67]S/16317. [68]S/16329. [69]A/39/109. [70]S/16341. [71]S/16365. [72]S/16386. [73]S/16398. [74]S/16390. [75]S/16396. [76]S/16399. [77]S/16412. [78]S/16410. [79]S/16411. [80]S/16428. [81]S/16436. [82]S/16439. [83]S/16437. [84]S/16444. [85]S/16452. [86]S/16457. [87]S/16521. [88]S/16537. [89]S/16540. [90]S/16539. [91]S/16544. [92]S/16546 & Corr.1 (A/39/240). [93]A/39/253-S/16551. [94]A/39/256-S/16560. [95]S/16558. [96]S/16559. [97]S/16576. [98]S/16578. [99]A/39/324-S/16644. [100]S/16661. [101]S/16677. [102]S/16780. [103]S/16781. [104]A/39/628-S/16813. [105]S/16264. [106]S/16376. [107]S/16395. [108]S/16402. [109]S/16413. [110]A/39/135-S/16422. [111]S/16426. [112]A/39/155-S/16440. [113]S/16448. [114]S/16449. [115]S/16463. [116]A/39/221-S/16515. [117]S/16524. [118]S/16528. [119]S/16556. [120]A/39/260-S/16566. [121]S/16599. [122]S/16728. [123]S/16730. [124]S/16731. [125]S/16740. [126]S/16744. [127]S/16777. [128]S/16745. [129]A/39/560-S/16773. [130]A/39/581-S/16782 & Corr.1. [131]A/39/596-S/16789. [132]S/16797. [133]A/39/641-S/16823. [134]S/16824 (A/39/642). [135]S/16825. [136]A/39/648-S/16826. [137]S/16830. [138]A/39/673-S/16835. [139]A/39/766-S/16851.

Anniversary of the discovery of America

The General Assembly had decided in 1982 to consider in 1983 an item on the observance of the quincentenary of the discovery of America.[1] In 1983, it had decided to consider the item when it resumed its thirty-eighth (1983) session in 1984.[2]

On 17 September 1984, at its resumed session, the Assembly adopted decision 38/457 by which it decided to defer consideration of the item to its thirty-ninth (1984) session.

Observance of the quincentenary of the discovery of America

At its 106th plenary meeting, on 17 September 1984, the General Assembly decided to include in the draft agenda of its thirty-ninth session the item entitled "Observance of the quincentenary of the discovery of America".

General Assembly decision 38/457

Adopted without vote

Oral proposal by President; agenda item 40.

On 18 December, by decision 39/456 on the suspension of the thirty-ninth session, the Assembly decided to resume the session, at a date to be announced, to consider several agenda items, one of which was the observance of the quincentenary.

REFERENCES

[1]YUN 1982, p. 375, GA dec. 37/451, 21 Dec. 1982. [2]YUN 1983, p. 391, GA dec. 38/456, 20 Dec. 1983.

Chapter VII

Asia and the Pacific

Matters relating to Korea, the situations in Afghanistan and Kampuchea, and the Iran-Iraq war were prominent concerns in Asia brought before the United Nations in 1984.

The United Nations Command continued to monitor the 1953 Armistice Agreement between the Democratic People's Republic of Korea and the Republic of Korea. Attention focused on an October 1983 attempt on the life of the President of the Republic of Korea.

In South-East Asia, the situation in Kampuchea and border incidents—affecting that country, China, the Lao People's Democratic Republic, Thailand and Viet Nam—occupied the attention of the United Nations, with the Security Council meeting in regard to disputes along the borders both of the Lao People's Democratic Republic and Thailand, and of China and Viet Nam. The Secretary-General's Special Representative visited the area in pursuit of a peaceful solution to the problems of the region, particularly those of Kampuchea. In October, the General Assembly again called for the withdrawal of all foreign troops from Kampuchea and requested the *Ad Hoc* Committee of the International Conference on Kampuchea to continue its work (resolution 39/5).

Armed incidents affecting Afghanistan and Pakistan continued to be reported, while the Secretary-General's Personal Representative maintained his contacts with the parties leading to a new format of separate, high-level "proximity" talks regarding a political settlement. The Assembly, in November, called on all parties concerned to work for the urgent achievement of a political solution and expressed its support for the Secretary-General's efforts to that end (resolution 39/13).

The Security Council met twice in connection with the Iran-Iraq conflict, once on allegations of chemical-weapons use and the other on firings on third-party ships in the Gulf. The Secretary-General, while continuing his efforts to end the war, took a number of initiatives on particular aspects of the conflict, among them, the dispatch, out of humanitarian concern, of a mission of specialists to investigate allegations of chemical-weapons use, and the placing of United Nations teams in the area to inspect, as requested, areas of alleged shellings of civilian population centres. Concern was also raised as regards treatment of prisoners of war.

East Asia

Korean question

During 1984, the President of the Security Council received and circulated to the Council the report of the United Nations Command (UNC) concerning the maintenance of the 1953 Korean Armistice Agreement, and letters from the Democratic People's Republic of Korea and the Republic of Korea on the prevailing situation and related matters, including a bombing attack—in October 1983, at Rangoon, Burma—which had killed, among others, four cabinet ministers of the Republic of Korea.

Report of the United Nations Command. A report of UNC concerning the maintenance in 1983 of the 1953 Korean Armistice Agreement[1] was submitted by a letter of 11 June 1984 from the United States,[2] on behalf of the unified command established pursuant to a 1950 Security Council resolution.[3]

The report stated that, during the period, UNC charged the Korean People's Army/Chinese People's Volunteers with more than 4,070 Armistice Agreement violations. An appendix gave details of major incidents, including firing across the military demarcation line at a Command post in the demilitarized zone and repeated armed infiltration attempts into the Republic of Korea, and what UNC described as a terrorist bombing attack at Rangoon.

Regarding the last incident, the report stated that, on 9 October 1983, a special terrorist team from the Democratic People's Republic of Korea attempted to assassinate President Chun Du-Hwan of the Republic of Korea during his State visit to Burma by detonating an explosive device at the Martyrs' Mausoleum at Rangoon. Although the bomb blast missed its intended target, 17 citizens of the Republic of Korea, including four cabinet ministers, and four Burmese citizens were killed and scores more from both countries were injured. On 4 November, the Burmese Government announced its decision to sever diplomatic relations with the Democratic People's Republic, asserting that the latter's commandos had committed the bombing. On 22 November, the trial of two of the officers allegedly involved began at Rangoon.

Communications. In a letter of 17 September,[4] the Democratic People's Republic of Korea said the United Nations had nothing to do with the so-called United Nations forces in the Republic of Korea, where only the United States army was stationed. It stated further that annual reports of the Command, submitted by the United States to the United Nations, were propaganda documents replenished with distortions and fabrications to veil its colonial war policy; and that the Rangoon incident was a drama directed by Chun Du-Hwan to find a way out of political and economic crisis. Annexed to the letter was a December 1983 memorandum of the Foreign Ministry providing its analysis of the incident and claiming its innocence.

In pursuance of a December 1983 General Assembly resolution on protection of diplomats,[5] Burma submitted, on 10 September, a report on the findings by its Enquiry Committee on the Rangoon bomb incident,[6] which concluded that enough irrefutable evidence pointed to the culpability of three agents from the Democratic People's Republic of Korea.

By a letter of 30 October,[7] the Republic of Korea termed as groundless the Democratic People's Republic's allegation against the legality of UNC, noted the conclusions of investigation by Burma on the bombing incident, and attributed the tension on the Korean peninsula to the plans of the Democratic People's Republic to unify the country under its terms.

In October, the Meeting of Ministers for Foreign Affairs and Heads of Delegation of Non-Aligned Countries to the General Assembly's 1984 session, in its final communiqué,[8] reaffirmed support for the Korean people's desire for peaceful reunification of their homeland, the fulfilment of which, they hoped, would be enhanced by withdrawal of all foreign troops from the area.

REFERENCES

(1)YUN 1953, p. 136, GA res. 725(VIII), annex, 7 Dec. 1953. (2)S/16694. (3)YUN 1950, p. 230, SC res. 84(1950), 7 July 1950. (4)S/16743. (5)YUN 1983, p. 1117, GA res. 38/136, 19 Dec. 1983. (6)A/39/456/Add.1. (7)S/16807. (8)A/39/560-S/16773.

South-East Asia

Kampuchea situation

The situation in and around Kampuchea—particularly border incidents, allegations of chemical weapons use and Kampuchea's representation in the United Nations—continued to occupy the attention of the Organization in 1984.

The *Ad Hoc* Committee of the International Conference on Kampuchea dispatched missions to a number of countries for consultations, in its efforts to assist in seeking a settlement of the situation. In October, the General Assembly reiterated that a just and lasting solution required the withdrawal of all foreign forces; restoration and preservation of the country's independence, sovereignty and territorial integrity; the people's right to determine its destiny; and a commitment by all States to non-interference in Kampuchea's internal affairs (resolution 39/5).

Communications. A number of letters received by the Secretary-General in 1984 related to incidents on the common borders of Democratic Kampuchea, Thailand and Viet Nam.

On 13 February,[1] Thailand transmitted a list of violations of its sovereignty and territorial integrity allegedly committed by Vietnamese forces in Kampuchea between September and December 1983. They included shellings, land and sea incursions, and laying of land-mines, resulting in the death of four Thais and several injuries. Viet Nam, in a letter of 22 February,[2] rejected the Thai allegation as a deliberate act on the part of Thailand to cover up its repeated violations of the sovereignty of the People's Republic of Kampuchea and its provision of sanctuaries and aid to what Viet Nam called the genocidal Pol Pot clique and other reactionary forces. The letter alleged airspace violations and shelling in 1983 by Thailand, resulting in heavy losses of lives.

By a letter of 29 March,[3] Thailand charged that, on 25 March, Vietnamese forces had crossed from Kampuchea into Thai territory but had been pushed back by Thai artillery and an airstrike; on the same day, Viet Nam had attacked a Kampuchean civilian encampment inside Kampuchea, forcing some 10,000 Kampucheans to cross the border and seek temporary shelter inside Thailand. Officials of the International Committee of the Red Cross (ICRC) and the United Nations Border Relief Operation (UNBRO) had been dispatched to help the displaced. Thailand expressed concern over what it saw as a dangerous situation prevailing in the Thai-Kampuchean border areas, precipitated by the continuing occupation of Kampuchea by a large number of Vietnamese troops. On 1 April,[4] Viet Nam rejected the allegations and transmitted a 31 March statement by its Foreign Ministry, asserting that, over the previous five years, the Thai authorities had let the Pol Pot remnants, China's instrument, use Thai territory as their sanctuary to oppose the Kampuchean people's revival; it charged further that, in the latter half of March, many units of Thai armed forces had directly supported sabotage activities by Pol Pot remnants, including air and sea violations, and shellings.

China transmitted a 2 April Foreign Ministry statement[5] referring to the Thai protest of 29

March (see above), condemning Viet Nam for its act of aggression and supporting the Thai Government's position.

Thailand wrote on 3 April[6] alleging further military operations launched by Vietnamese troops against Kampuchean civilian encampments built by UNBRO inside Kampuchea. The additional influx of Kampucheans into Thailand as a result meant that nearly 150,000 Indo-Chinese refugees and displaced persons were currently sheltered inside Thailand, while some 230,000 Kampucheans were congregated along the border; UNBRO, whose funds were scarce and dwindling, might need additional assistance for its humanitarian relief work as a result of the current Vietnamese military operations against Kampuchean civilians.

A 16 April letter from Thailand[7] stated that Vietnamese forces had shot down an air force observation plane the previous day, while it was on a routine flight over Thai territory adjacent to the Thai-Kampuchean border, killing one crew member; a helicopter sent to search for the wreckage was also fired on and badly damaged. Viet Nam transmitted on 18 April a Foreign Ministry statement of the same date,[8] asserting that the Thai allegations were designed to cover up Thailand's repeated violations of Kampuchea's sovereignty and territory in support of the Pol Pot clique. On 14 and 15 April, the statement said, Thai reconnaissance planes and bombers had engaged in activities up to 10 kilometres into Kampuchean territory.

Another letter from Thailand of 17 April[9] mentioned that intensive Vietnamese military attacks of 14 April and an operation between 14 and 16 April had led to another influx of about 32,000 Kampucheans, and evacuation of about 45,000 Kampucheans, respectively, into Thailand; the encampments attacked were said to be under UNBRO supervision and sheltering only Kampuchean civilians.

On 23 April,[10] Indonesia transmitted a 19 April statement by the Chairman of the Standing Committee of the Association of South-East Asian Nations (ASEAN) on behalf of the ASEAN Foreign Ministers, condemning the Vietnamese forces for their military attacks in Kampuchea and Thailand. The ASEAN countries urged the international community to render assistance for the care of the displaced Kampucheans in Thailand, and called on Viet Nam to desist from further recourse to force and to adhere to United Nations resolutions, which called for withdrawal of all foreign forces from Kampuchea, a comprehensive political settlement of the Kampuchean problem and the free exercise by the Kampuchean people of their right to self-determination.

Viet Nam transmitted, on 23 April,[11] a 20 April statement by its Foreign Ministry, calling the ASEAN statement a mere repetition of the Thai and Chinese authorities' slanders, and asserting that the refugee camps along the Thai-Kampuchean border were but a screen hiding the Thai authorities' collusion with China and the United States in letting the Pol Pot gang and its accomplices use Thai territory as its commanding and training base from which to launch criminal attacks against the Kampuchean people.

By a letter of 1 May,[12] Thailand reported that, on 30 April, Vietnamese troops had shelled Thai territory about 10 kilometres from the border, killing one villager and injuring 50.

An 8 May statement of the ASEAN Foreign Ministers, transmitted by Indonesia on 10 May,[13] asserted that recent Vietnamese attacks on Kampuchean civilian encampments had driven more than 75,000 civilians into Thailand. The Foreign Ministers reaffirmed the essential elements for the survival of an independent and sovereign Kampuchea and their support for the Coalition Government of Democratic Kampuchea under the presidency of Norodom Sihanouk, and considered it desirable to convene a senior-level working group to monitor developments in the search for a comprehensive political solution.

On 14 May,[14] Viet Nam transmitted an 11 May statement made by its Foreign Ministry in response to the ASEAN statement of 8 May. Holding China and Thailand responsible for the tense situation, Viet Nam declared that its volunteers would withdraw from Kampuchea after the Pol Pot remnants and their accomplices had been eliminated and the security of the People's Republic of Kampuchea had been guaranteed. If Thailand wanted peace and stability on the border, it should consider, together with the Indo-Chinese countries, proposals for moving the refugee camps out of the areas of hostility and organizing voluntary repatriation for Kampuchean refugees.

By a letter of 9 July,[15] Thailand alleged that a Thai air force observation plane, while on a routine flight over Thai territory adjacent to the Thai-Kampuchean border, had been shot down on 7 July by Vietnamese forces and the two crew members seriously injured. Viet Nam responded on 16 July, with a 12 July statement of the Viet Nam News Agency,[16] rejecting the Thai allegation as slander covering up Thai violations and bombardment of Kampuchean territory in support of sabotage activities by the Pol Pot remnants and their accomplices.

On 6 November,[17] Thailand reported that, as a result of a 5 November Vietnamese incursion into its territory and an attack on a border patrol police base in Surin province, two Thai border patrol policemen had been killed, 25 injured and five were missing. Thai troops had been dispatched to drive out the Vietnamese forces, which continued to occupy the base the day after. A Viet Nam News Agency statement of 8 November[18] rejected the Thai allegations as a fabrication aimed at covering up Thai violations of Kampuchean territory totalling, between 25 October and 1 November alone, 377 on land, in the air and at sea.

On 23 November,[19] Thailand reported that, on 18 November, Vietnamese troops attacked a Kampuchean civilian border encampment at Nong Chan, forcing some 20,000 civilians to seek refuge at safer areas along the Thai-Kampuchean border. UNBRO, the World Food Programme, ICRC and other voluntary agencies were providing emergency relief items and medical teams. Thailand, in co-operation with UNBRO, had prepared an emergency evacuation site further inside its territory for use should Vietnamese acts of aggression force the civilians to flee their homeland.

Democratic Kampuchea, by a letter dated 26 November,[20] transmitted its Foreign Ministry statement of 21 November charging that, since 18 November, the Vietnamese aggressors had been mobilizing thousands of their troops to attack refugee camps at Nong Chan, as a result of which a large number of refugees had been killed and more than 10,000 had fled for safety. Such acts of aggression further confirmed Viet Nam's aim to annex Kampuchea, the statement concluded.

Thailand alleged, in a letter of 27 November,[21] that armed aggression by Viet Nam in the Nong Chan area in November had resulted in some of its artillery shells landing inside Thailand and causing injuries and material damage; the attacks also caused a new influx of more than 20,000 Kampucheans into Thailand. In a clash of 26 November near Ban Non Mak Mun in Thai territory, one Thai soldier was killed and eight others were injured. On 13 December,[22] Thailand reported further incidents, on 6 and 8 December, involving shelling in Trat province and an incursion into Thai territory of some 500 Vietnamese soldiers, subsequently driven out by Thai troops.

Democratic Kampuchea charged, in 1984 as in previous years, that the Vietnamese forces continued to use chemical weapons against its civilians. A letter of 25 January[23] cited a number of incidents, mostly in December 1983, of alleged poisoning of water supplies, resulting in several deaths. In a 24 January communiqué, transmitted on 27 January,[24] the Council of Ministers of the Coalition Government condemned alleged use of chemical weapons, including new mycotoxin agents. On 14 February,[25] Democratic Kampuchea transmitted information on four cases, in January, of water-supply poisoning, as well as aerial spreading of toxic chemical substances and alleged poisoning of foodstuffs and medicines, killing 30 people in one incident in January. In a 22 February statement, transmitted

on 2 March,[26] a cabinet minister of the Coalition Government charged that a Vietnamese aircraft had spread large amounts of toxic chemical products the day before in the Kampuchea-Thailand border region; that such products were also spread, in the 1983/84 dry season, by cannon- and mortar-firing and by chemical weapons experts; and that Viet Nam had caused 2.5 million deaths since its occupation of Kampuchea. The minister asserted that the Vietnamese forces had intensified chemical-weapon use to make up for the shortage of troops in Kampuchea. On 5 March,[27] and again on 5 April,[28] Democratic Kampuchea transmitted further allegations of poisoning incidents said to have occurred between January and March, causing deaths and serious illness.

The United States transmitted, on 21 February,[29] a document on the alleged use of chemical and toxic weapons in Asia; it said that, while there appeared to have been a decrease in the lethality of attacks in the Lao People's Democratic Republic and Kampuchea since it last reported in 1983, there was evidence of continuing use in those countries of an as yet unidentified, non-lethal agent or agents (see also p. 62).

In a joint communiqué of 10 July,[30] transmitted by Indonesia on 17 July to the President of the Economic and Social Council, the Foreign Ministers of ASEAN affirmed the validity of their 21 September 1983 appeal for Kampuchean independence,[31] asked the Secretary-General to continue monitoring the developments on the Thai-Kampuchean border, and again called on Viet Nam to consider a proposal for the stationing of a United Nations observer team on the Thai side of the border in conjunction with the establishment of safe areas under United Nations supervision in western Kampuchea for the displaced civilian Kampucheans encamped along the border and for those in Thailand who wished to repatriate. Noting with apprehension that there were reportedly some half a million Vietnamese settlers in Kampuchea, they reaffirmed support for the Coalition Government of Democratic Kampuchea under the presidency of Samdech Norodom Sihanouk.

Viet Nam transmitted a 5 June governmental statement on its policy regarding the use of its airspace.[32]

On 7 February,[33] the Lao People's Democratic Republic transmitted a communiqué issued at the end of a conference held at Vientiane on 28 and 29 January with the People's Republic of Kampuchea and Viet Nam. It called for a comprehensive solution based on withdrawal of all foreign armed forces from South-East Asia, an end to external intervention, and establishment in the region of a zone of peace, friendship and co-operation. Partial settlement, it continued, could be found through: total withdrawal of Vietnamese forces from Kampuchea, paired with a termination of China's hostile policy and the use of Pol Pot remnant troops and other Khmer reactionaries against the people of Kampuchea; and respect for equal security for, and the setting up of a safety zone along, both sides of the Kampuchea-Thailand border. In the mean time, a framework agreement could be reached with the ASEAN countries with a view to preventing the current situation from escalating into a major conflict and to paving the way for gradual solution of points of disagreement.

On 6 February,[34] Democratic Kampuchea submitted a 31 January statement by its Ministry of Foreign Affairs rejecting the so-called Vientiane declaration and calling for implementation of the five United Nations resolutions on the situation in Kampuchea; the Coalition Government remained ready to sign a peace and non-aggression treaty with Viet Nam once its troops were withdrawn from Kampuchea. On 17 April,[35] Democratic Kampuchea transmitted a document of 30 March prepared by the Ministry, on the situation of women and children in that country, with references to what it called mental and physical Vietnamization imposed on them.

In a 19 April document transmitted by the Lao People's Democratic Republic on 24 April,[36] the Foreign Ministry of the People's Republic of Kampuchea charged Thailand with colluding with Pol Pot and his accomplices and assisting them in their intrusion into Kampuchea. While the Thai authorities charged the Vietnamese volunteer army with attacks on refugee camps, they diverted humanitarian aid and delivered, to Pol Pot remnants using the camps as their bases, weapons and munitions from China, under the guise of goods for refugees. The People's Republic of Kampuchea urged Thailand to negotiate for a mutually agreed humanitarian solution to the refugee problem.

On 9 July,[37] Democratic Kampuchea transmitted a 6 July communiqué, issued in Beijing by its three leaders—President, Prime Minister and Vice-President in charge of Foreign Affairs—at the conclusion of their 3-6 July meeting, in which they reaffirmed the determination to achieve a political settlement based on the General Assembly resolutions. Expressing support for that communiqué, the ASEAN Foreign Ministers, in a 9 July joint statement transmitted by Malaysia,[38] again called for an early withdrawal of all Vietnamese forces from Kampuchea under international supervision. The text was submitted also to the Economic and Social Council by Indonesia.[39]

On 1 August,[40] the Lao People's Democratic Republic transmitted a document issued in April by the Ministry of Foreign Affairs of the People's Republic of Kampuchea, in which China was charged as the mastermind behind the Pol Pot régime which had committed the genocide.

Democratic Kampuchea transmitted on 23 October[41] a Foreign Ministry statement of 14 October, stating that during the last rainy season, which began in May, Viet Nam had sent some 24,000 new reinforcements as well as new war materials to Kampuchea; alleged troop withdrawals were, in fact, the discharge of tired, wounded, disabled and sick soldiers for a rest in the eastern part of Kampuchea, not even in Viet Nam.

The Meeting of Ministers for Foreign Affairs and Heads of Delegation of Non-Aligned Countries to the General Assembly at its 1984 session, in a 5 October communiqué transmitted by India,[42] reaffirmed the urgent need for a comprehensive political solution and urged all States in the region to work towards resolving their differences, establishing durable peace and stability and eliminating involvement and threats of intervention by outside Powers; it noted with approval efforts towards early establishment of a zone of peace, freedom and neutrality in the region.

ECONOMIC AND SOCIAL COUNCIL ACTION

On 24 May 1984, the Economic and Social Council, by decision 1984/148 on the right of peoples to self-determination, endorsed a February resolution of the Commission on Human Rights and expressed concern at the activities of the foreign forces in Kampuchea, particularly the continuing attacks on Kampuchean civilian encampments along the Thai-Kampuchean border.

Activities of the Committee of the Conference on Kampuchea. The 10-member *Ad Hoc* Committee of the International Conference on Kampuchea[43] met in 1984 in pursuance of an October 1983 Assembly resolution,[44] and dispatched a mission to Lagos (Nigeria), Dakar (Senegal) and Belgrade (Yugoslavia) from 17 to 24 April and another to Wellington (New Zealand), Canberra (Australia), Bangkok (Thailand) and Jakarta (Indonesia) from 2 to 12 July.

The Committee's report on its 1983/84 activities noted that the missions, in their consultations with the Governments concerned, sought the widest possible support for efforts towards a comprehensive political solution to the conflict in Kampuchea, stressing that a just and lasting settlement must be based on two principles: withdrawal of all foreign forces from Kampuchea and the right of the Kampuchean people to determine their own destiny. They also reiterated that the settlement should take account of the legitimate security concerns of the States of the region, including a commitment by all States to non-interference and non-intervention in Kampuchea's internal affairs. In the discussions with the Governments, it was noted that the recent diplomatic exchanges on the topic had not produced decisive progress towards a solution and that further efforts were required to bring about a constructive dialogue between the parties concerned.

The President of the Conference, who was briefed at Brussels, Belgium, by the July mission, subsequently visited Malaysia, Indonesia, Thailand and Singapore from 2 to 9 September. He discussed with the respective Governments the consideration of the Kampuchean question at the 1984 Assembly session and, among other things, possible actions to be undertaken within the framework of the Conference and the desirability of initiating efforts to save the temple complex of Angkor from further decay and destruction.

Concluding its report, the Committee again appealed to those Member States which had not participated in the Conference to co-operate, and to all parties to pursue dialogue and refrain from action that would further complicate the situation.

The Conference President and officers of the *Ad Hoc* Committee had an exchange of views, in New York on 28 September during the 1984 Assembly session, with the Foreign Ministers of the States members of ASEAN: Brunei Darussalam, Indonesia, Malaysia, Philippines, Singapore and Thailand.

Report of the Secretary-General. In his October 1984 report to the General Assembly,[(45)] submitted pursuant to its October 1983 resolution on Kampuchea,[(44)] the Secretary-General stated that he had maintained close contact with representatives of the States most directly concerned and with other interested parties, in the exercise of his good offices. He had held extensive discussions with the Foreign Minister of Indonesia and the Prime Minister and Foreign Minister of Thailand. His Special Representative, Rafeeuddin Ahmed, visited South-East Asia from 7 to 21 May and held consultations with the Governments of Indonesia, Malaysia, Viet Nam and Thailand; he returned to the region in July and attended the seventeenth ASEAN Ministerial Meeting at Jakarta, on the Secretary-General's behalf, and met with the Foreign Ministers and other senior officials of the ASEAN countries. The Secretary-General thereafter held further discussions with the President of Democratic Kampuchea, the Prime Minister of Malaysia, the Deputy Prime Minister and Foreign Minister of the Lao People's Democratic Republic, and the Foreign Ministers of China, Indonesia, the Philippines, Thailand and Viet Nam, as well as with other interested Governments.

The Secretary-General reported that his hopes remained unfulfilled for a more constructive dialogue emerging from contacts and diplomatic exchanges of February and March, and subsequent

armed incidents along the Thai-Kampuchean border contributed to a renewed climate of tension in the region. The consultations his Special Representative had held with the Governments in the region on resumption of the diplomatic process revealed that further efforts were necessary before a mutually acceptable agenda could be worked out, an impression confirmed by his subsequent discussions in New York.

The Secretary-General urged all parties concerned to renew their efforts towards the early initiation of the diplomatic process, while reiterating his own determination to continue exercising his good offices.

He also stated that he had continued to implement the programmes of humanitarian assistance to the Kampuchean people. Funded largely by voluntary contributions, they consisted mainly of operations within Kampuchea, at the border and within Thailand.

GENERAL ASSEMBLY ACTION

Following consideration of the situation in Kampuchea and the Secretary-General's report, the General Assembly, on 30 October 1984, adopted by recorded vote resolution 39/5.

The situation in Kampuchea

The General Assembly,

Recalling its resolutions 34/22 of 14 November 1979, 35/6 of 22 October 1980, 36/5 of 21 October 1981, 37/6 of 28 October 1982 and 38/3 of 27 October 1983,

Recalling further the Declaration on Kampuchea and resolution 1(I) adopted by the International Conference on Kampuchea,[(46)] which offer the negotiating framework for a comprehensive political settlement of the Kampuchean problem,

Taking note of the report of the Secretary-General on the implementation of General Assembly resolution 38/3,

Noting the continued effectiveness of the coalition with Samdech Norodom Sihanouk as President of Democratic Kampuchea,

Deploring that foreign armed intervention and occupation continue and that foreign forces have not been withdrawn from Kampuchea, thus causing continuing hostilities in that country and seriously threatening international peace and security,

Taking note of Economic and Social Council decision 1984/148 of 24 May 1984 on the right of peoples to self-determination and its application to peoples under colonial or alien domination or foreign occupation,

Greatly disturbed that the continued fighting and instability in Kampuchea have forced an additional number of Kampucheans to flee to the Thai-Kampuchean border in search of food and safety,

Recognizing that the assistance extended by the international community has continued to reduce the food shortages and health problems of the Kampuchean people,

Emphasizing that it is the inalienable right of the Kampuchean people who have sought refuge in neighbouring countries to return safely to their homeland,

Emphasizing further that no effective solution to the humanitarian problems can be achieved without a comprehensive political settlement of the Kampuchean conflict,

Seriously concerned about reported demographic changes being imposed in Kampuchea by foreign occupation forces,

Convinced that, to bring about durable peace in South-East Asia and reduce the threat to international peace and security, there is an urgent need for the international community to find a comprehensive political solution to the Kampuchean problem that will provide for the withdrawal of all foreign forces and ensure respect for the sovereignty, independence, territorial integrity and neutral and non-aligned status of Kampuchea, as well as the right of the Kampuchean people to self-determination free from outside interference,

Convinced further that, after the comprehensive political settlement of the Kampuchean question through peaceful means, the countries of the South-East Asian region can pursue efforts to establish a zone of peace, freedom and neutrality in South-East Asia so as to lessen international tensions and to achieve lasting peace in the region,

Reaffirming the need for all States to adhere strictly to the principles of the Charter of the United Nations, which call for respect for the national independence, sovereignty and territorial integrity of all States, non-intervention and non-interference in the internal affairs of States, non-recourse to the threat or use of force and peaceful settlement of disputes,

1. *Reaffirms* its resolutions 34/22, 35/6, 36/5, 37/6 and 38/3 and calls for their full implementation;

2. *Reiterates its conviction* that the withdrawal of all foreign forces from Kampuchea, the restoration and preservation of its independence, sovereignty and territorial integrity, the right of the Kampuchean people to determine their own destiny and the commitment by all States to non-interference and non-intervention in the internal affairs of Kampuchea are the principal components of any just and lasting resolution of the Kampuchean problem;

3. *Takes note with appreciation* of the report of the *Ad Hoc* Committee of the International Conference on Kampuchea and requests that the Committee continue its work, pending the reconvening of the Conference;

4. *Authorizes* the *Ad Hoc* Committee to convene when necessary and to carry out the tasks entrusted to it in its mandate;

5. *Reaffirms* its decision to reconvene the Conference at an appropriate time, in accordance with Conference resolution 1(I);

6. *Renews its appeal* to all States of South-East Asia and others concerned to attend future sessions of the Conference;

7. *Requests* the Conference to report to the General Assembly on its future sessions;

8. *Requests* the Secretary-General to continue to consult with and assist the Conference and the *Ad Hoc* Committee and to provide them on a regular basis with the necessary facilities to carry out their functions;

9. *Expresses its appreciation once again* to the Secretary-General for taking appropriate steps in following the situation closely and requests him to continue to do so and to exercise his good offices in order to contribute to a comprehensive political settlement;

10. *Expresses its deep appreciation once again* to donor countries, the United Nations and its agencies and other national and international humanitarian organizations that have rendered relief assistance to the Kampuchean people, and appeals to them to continue to provide emergency assistance to those Kampucheans who are still in need, especially along the Thai-Kampuchean border and in the holding centres in Thailand;

11. *Reiterates its deep appreciation* to the Secretary-General for his efforts in co-ordinating humanitarian relief assistance and in monitoring its distribution, and requests him to intensify such efforts as are necessary;

12. *Urges* the countries of South-East Asia, once a comprehensive political solution to the Kampuchean conflict is achieved, to exert renewed efforts to establish a zone of peace, freedom and neutrality in South-East Asia;

13. *Reiterates the hope* that, following a comprehensive political solution, an intergovernmental committee will be established to consider a programme of assistance to Kampuchea for the reconstruction of its economy and for the economic and social development of all States in the region;

14. *Requests* the Secretary-General to report to the General Assembly at its fortieth session on the implementation of the present resolution;

15. *Decides* to include in the provisional agenda of its fortieth session the item entitled "The situation in Kampuchea".

General Assembly resolution 39/5

30 October 1984   Meeting 43   110-22-18 (recorded vote)

55-nation draft (A/39/L.3 and Add.1); agenda item 20.

Sponsors: Antigua and Barbuda, Bangladesh, Belgium, Brunei Darussalam, Canada, Central African Republic, Chad, Chile, Colombia, Comoros, Costa Rica, Denmark, Dominica, Dominican Republic, Ecuador, Equatorial Guinea, Fiji, Gambia, Germany, Federal Republic of, Haiti, Honduras, Iceland, Indonesia, Italy, Japan, Liberia, Luxembourg, Maldives, Mauritania, Mauritius, Nepal, Netherlands, New Zealand, Niger, Nigeria, Norway, Oman, Pakistan, Papua New Guinea, Paraguay, Philippines, Saint Lucia, Saint Vincent and the Grenadines, Samoa, Senegal, Singapore, Solomon Islands, Somalia, Swaziland, Thailand, Turkey, United Kingdom, Uruguay, Zaire.

Financial implications. 5th Committee, A/39/617; S-G, A/C.5/39/28.

Meeting numbers. GA 39th session: 5th Committee 18; plenary 40-43.

Recorded vote in Assembly as follows:

In favour: Antigua and Barbuda, Argentina, Australia, Austria, Bahamas, Bahrain, Bangladesh, Barbados, Belgium, Belize, Bhutan, Bolivia, Botswana, Brazil, Brunei Darussalam, Burkina Faso, Burma, Burundi, Cameroon, Canada, Central African Republic, Chad, Chile, China, Colombia, Comoros, Costa Rica, Democratic Kampuchea, Denmark, Djibouti, Dominica, Dominican Republic, Ecuador, Egypt, El Salvador, Equatorial Guinea, Fiji, France, Gabon, Gambia, Germany, Federal Republic of, Ghana, Greece, Grenada, Guatemala, Haiti, Honduras, Iceland, Indonesia, Ireland, Israel, Italy, Ivory Coast, Jamaica, Japan, Jordan, Kenya, Kuwait, Lesotho, Liberia, Luxembourg, Malaysia, Maldives, Mali, Malta, Mauritania, Mauritius, Morocco, Nepal, Netherlands, New Zealand, Niger, Nigeria, Norway, Oman, Pakistan, Papua New Guinea, Paraguay, Peru, Philippines, Portugal, Qatar, Rwanda, Saint Lucia, Saint Vincent and the Grenadines, Samoa, Saudi Arabia, Senegal, Sierra Leone, Singapore, Solomon Islands, Somalia, Spain, Sri Lanka, Sudan, Suriname, Swaziland, Sweden, Thailand, Togo, Tunisia, Turkey, United Arab Emirates, United Kingdom, United States, Uruguay, Venezuela, Yugoslavia, Zaire, Zambia.

Against: Afghanistan, Albania, Angola, Bulgaria, Byelorussian SSR, Congo, Cuba, Czechoslovakia, Democratic Yemen, Ethiopia, German Democratic Republic, Guyana, Hungary, Lao People's Democratic Republic, Libyan Arab Jamahiriya, Mongolia, Nicaragua, Poland, Syrian Arab Republic, Ukrainian SSR, USSR, Viet Nam.

Abstaining: Algeria, Benin, Cape Verde, Finland, India, Iraq, Lebanon, Madagascar, Malawi, Mexico, Mozambique, Panama, Sao Tome and Principe, Trinidad and Tobago, Uganda, United Republic of Tanzania, Vanuatu, Zimbabwe.

In explanation of vote, Nicaragua reiterated the right of the people of Kampuchea to self-determination, rejected measures that supported the vestiges of a régime that had been abolished by the Kampuchean people, and recognized the Government of the People's Republic of Kampuchea as the sole legitimate representative of that people.

Vanuatu supported dialogue, negotiations and a comprehensive political settlement. Its support of the Secretary-General's efforts was shared by Sweden, which saw in the resolution a confirmation of principles necessary for a lasting settlement: rejection of armed intervention, respect for territorial integrity and the right to self-determination. Sweden added, however, that it did not support those elements in the text that were not, in its opinion, warranted by the facts or unlikely to facilitate a just and peaceful settlement. Ireland also supported the general thrust of the draft, adding that, as regards the fourth preambular paragraph, its position on Kampuchean representation had not changed from that of abstention on the Credentials Committee report. Ghana, Bolivia, Brazil and Burkina Faso, which also supported the thrust of the resolution, expressed reservations on that paragraph, with Burkina Faso expressing additional reservation as regards the eleventh preambular paragraph.

Participation and representation of Democratic Kampuchea in UN bodies

The question of Democratic Kampuchea's representation in United Nations bodies was again raised in 1984.

On 19 October, the Lao People's Democratic Republic conveyed a letter of 18 October[47] from Hun Sen, described as Minister for Foreign Affairs of the People's Republic of Kampuchea, stating that the Polpotists and the disguised Polpotists under the banner of Democratic Kampuchea were criminals condemned for genocide, had no right to represent the Kampuchean people and should be expelled from the United Nations; the United Nations debate on Kampuchea, in the absence of the People's Republic of Kampuchea as the only authentic and legitimate representative of the people, constituted a gross interference in the country's internal affairs.

The validity of Democratic Kampuchea's credentials to the 1984 General Assembly session was also questioned at an October meeting of the Credentials Committee.[48]

The USSR claimed that there was no such country and that only the State of the People's Republic of Kampuchea, formed on the basis of free elections, existed. Cuba also asserted that the People's Republic, as the sole representative chosen by the people, should represent Kampuchea at the United Nations. China, on the other hand, stated that the legitimacy of a State should never be challenged just because it had been subjected to

foreign aggression. Italy, Paraguay and the United States also supported the credentials of Democratic Kampuchea. The Ivory Coast said that its acceptance of credentials did not imply a position with respect to any dispute currently taking place.

Democratic Kampuchea's credentials were approved by virtue of General Assembly resolution 39/3 A, approving the Credentials Committee report.

International security in South-East Asia

A number of letters received by the United Nations in 1984 dealt with the general aspects of relations among the countries of South-East Asia (see also p. 214).

In a 2 July communiqué—transmitted on 5 July to the Secretary-General by the Lao People's Democratic Republic[49] and to the President of the Economic and Social Council by Viet Nam[50]—the Ministers for Foreign Affairs of these countries and of the People's Republic of Kampuchea, meeting at Vientiane, called for an immediate dialogue between them and ASEAN countries on problems of mutual concern, taking into account the ASEAN proposal of 21 September 1983[31] and that of the three Indo-Chinese countries put forth in a 29 January 1984 communiqué[33] (see p. 216), along with all other proposals from both sides.

Responding to the communiqué, Democratic Kampuchea, in a letter of 18 July[51] to the President of the Economic and Social Council, asserted that the Vietnamese authorities were trying to divert public opinion from the cause of the problem, which was the occupation of Kampuchea by their armed forces of 250,000 men, a contingent of 50,000 civil administrators and some 600,000 Vietnamese settlers. It also stated that Viet Nam aimed at transforming its problem with Kampuchea into a problem between the so-called Indo-Chinese countries and the ASEAN members so as to put over the plan for an "Indo-Chinese Federation", which would be nothing other than a "Greater Viet Nam".

Meeting at Jakarta, the ASEAN Foreign Ministers, in a 9 July statement,[39] reaffirmed readiness to discuss with Viet Nam a comprehensive political settlement of the Kampuchean situation. They also supported, in a 10 July communiqué,[30] the peaceful settlement of other problems in the region, including the Thai-Lao border incident (see p. 221) and Indo-Chinese refugees.

GENERAL ASSEMBLY ACTION

On an oral proposal by its President, the General Assembly adopted without vote decision 39/406.

Question of peace, stability and co-operation in South-East Asia

At its 65th plenary meeting, on 16 November 1984, the General Assembly decided to include in the provisional agenda of its fortieth session the item entitled "Question of peace, stability and co-operation in South-East Asia".

General Assembly decision 39/406

Adopted without vote

Oral proposal by President, after consultations; agenda item 37.
Meeting numbers. GA 39th session: plenary 64, 65.

China–Viet Nam dispute

Between March and June 1984, the Secretary-General received several communications from China and Viet Nam, each country charging the other with policies of annexation and aggressive acts along their common borders and elsewhere.

On 23 March, Viet Nam transmitted a 23 February communiqué[52] by its commission for investigation of what it called war crimes against it by the Chinese expansionists and hegemonists. It charged that, since March 1979, China had increased its collusion with the United States imperialists and drawn the ASEAN countries into a war of sabotage against Viet Nam, while continuing to prepare for a new war of aggression. In a series of Foreign Ministry statements—of 3,[53] 7[54] and 30 April[55] and 23 May[56]—Viet Nam alleged that China had violated its territorial integrity by resorting to artillery bombardments and intrusions into the northern provinces along the border. These allegations were repeated in a Ministry memorandum of 4 June,[57] stating that China had carried out since 2 April a campaign of large-scale shelling and armed attacks in the northern border area, as part of Beijing's scheme to conquer and annex Viet Nam.

China transmitted a Foreign Ministry statement of 26 May,[58] asserting that since early April its frontier troops had repulsed repeated attacks by intruding Vietnamese troops, destroyed some Vietnamese fortifications and positions and eliminated Vietnamese troops entrenched on China's territory.

An 8 June communiqué of Viet Nam's commission for investigation, submitted on 19 June,[59] stated that China had mobilized many divisions and army corps to reinforce the 15 divisions already stationed close to the Vietnamese border, conducted simulated attacks on Viet Nam, and launched a campaign of slander and disinformation against it.

Lao People's Democratic Republic– Thailand dispute

In 1984, the Security Council met in October to consider a border dispute between the Lao People's Democratic Republic and Thailand, and the two countries transmitted to the Secretary-General a number of communications on the topic between June and December.

Communications (June-October). The Lao People's Democratic Republic, by a letter of 14 June,[60] transmitted a statement made the previous day by its Foreign Ministry alleging that Thai troops had attacked and occupied Lao territory in May and June. Among the incidents related was a 6 June alleged Thai occupation of what it claimed were three Lao villages in Sayaboury province on the right bank of the Mekong River, followed by removal of the boundary marker the following day and a further incursion, and the hoisting of the Thai flag in the occupied villages, on 8 June. It asserted that the Thai actions were part of that country's policy of allowing its territory to be used as a staging ground for Lao reactionaries in exile, and were closely connected with Thailand's assistance to the Pol Pot clique and China's attacks along the northern border of Viet Nam.

Viet Nam, in a Foreign Ministry statement of 14 June,[61] supported the Lao People's Democratic Republic and said the Thai attacks followed the visit of the Thai army's Commander-in-Chief to China and the United States to seek military aid and came at a time when China was carrying out military escalation against Viet Nam.

In a letter of 21 June,[62] Thailand said it had been constructing roads for two years to all remote areas, particularly those villages along the border, as part of a five-year development project. A survey of the area and the Thai-Lao boundary map clearly showed the three villages to be within Thai territory, but Lao troops, in March 1984, obstructed road construction at a point about 6 kilometres inside Thai territory, claiming that the Thais had entered Lao territory. In April, Lao troops along the border were strengthened and clashes occurred in April and May; on 6 and 7 June, Thai troops were dispatched to provide security to the area, while efforts were made for a peaceful settlement. As for Viet Nam's allegation of 14 June, Thailand regarded its border problems with the Lao People's Democratic Republic as bilateral issues in which Viet Nam should not interfere.

The President of Democratic Kampuchea, in a 1 July statement transmitted the following day,[63] said that the Vientiane régime, which he called a satellite of Viet Nam, had been trying to provoke incidents on the Lao-Thai frontier, going so far as to contest the nationality of certain Thai frontier villages; he condemned, as warmongering and expansionist, the policy pursued by the Vietnamese and Lao régimes against Thailand.

The text of a press interview given on 24 July at Bangkok by the Lao Deputy Foreign Minister and head of the delegation of the National Commission for the Lao-Thai Frontier was transmitted by the Lao People's Democratic Republic on 30 July.[64] The Lao official stated that a peaceful solution called for Thai troop withdrawal from the three occupied Lao villages, repatriation of the inhabitants who had been forcibly taken to Thai territory, and the return of the situation existing before 6 June. Details were given of the Lao-Thai talks held at Bangkok on the matter, in which it was stated that the Thai position—that after its troop withdrawal, the Lao side should not send its own troops into the three villages—proved its desire for sovereignty over the villages, which had been Lao from time immemorial.

On 23 August,[65] Thailand reported that the July/August bilateral negotiations had not resulted in an agreement, and its proposal for a Thai-Lao joint team of technical personnel for an on-site survey of the boundary had been rejected. Thailand, therefore, had decided to dispatch unilaterally its technical personnel to survey and determine the boundary location, leaving open the possibility for an independent survey by impartial experts should there be any doubts as to the Thai findings.

On 27 August,[66] Thailand charged that Lao attacks on Thai positions on 18 and 26 August, resulting in the deaths and injuries of its soldiers, confirmed Lao unwillingness to settle the dispute peacefully. It urged the Lao side to refrain from further armed provocation in the area while it gathered technical data on the ground.

A memorandum and statement of 17 and 26 August, respectively, by the Lao Foreign Ministry regarding the three villages were transmitted.[67] The memorandum gave their history, details of border demarcation, allegations of premedition in the Thai occupation and collusion with China against the three Indo-Chinese countries, preparations for further hostile action, and alleged crimes against the villagers. The statement said that Thailand had unilaterally broken off the bilateral negotiations on the matter, that the central issue was not the boundary delineation according to watershed but the Thai attack on and occupation of three Lao villages, and that the Lao side had rejected the proposal for a bipartite technical survey because the existing border was clearly defined and marked and there never had been any dispute. It also alleged that Thailand had reinforced its occupation troops.

On 5 September,[68] Thailand reported that Lao soldiers had fired on two Thai posts in Uttaradit province on 1 September, killing two Thai border patrol policemen and injuring three others.

A 6 September statement by the Lao Foreign Ministry[69] placed on what it called the ultrarightist reactionaries of the Thai army the responsibility for the deaths of Thai soldiers, reaffirmed

its determination to safeguard its territorial integrity, and said it was ready to send a delegation to Bangkok again in order to negotiate on a peaceful settlement of the question.

On 18 September,[70] Thailand said that on 13 September a Thai highway official was killed and six others seriously injured in an alleged Lao ambush well inside Thai territory. A further Thai letter of 26 September[71] alleged two cases of Lao aggression on 24 September, killing a Thai soldier and a paramilitary and injuring several others.

A White Book published by the Lao Ministry of Foreign Affairs in September, entitled "The Truth about Thai-Lao Relations", was transmitted on 25 September.[72] It said Thailand was the only country in South-East Asia with expansionist and hegemonist ambitions, and presented its historical interpretation of Thai policy towards the Lao People's Democratic Republic from the thirteenth century onwards.

By a letter of 4 October,[73] Thailand drew attention to a 2 October statement by its Foreign Minister to the General Assembly, in which he asserted that the minor incidents near the Thai-Lao border, concerning only three small remote villages covering 19 square kilometres and a population of 1,100 people, had been complicated by military actions as well as by interference by a third country using the opportunity to divert world attention from its military occupation of Kampuchea. Thailand, he announced, had decided to remove its military presence from the three villages in order to defuse the situation and to bring about a peaceful solution to the problem.

SECURITY COUNCIL CONSIDERATION

On 3 October,[74] the Lao People's Democratic Republic requested a Security Council meeting to consider the situation created in the Lao-Thai border region following what it charged was an attack on and occupation of three Lao villages by Thai troops on 6 June. Asserting that the situation in the area had recently turned tense again, it rejected as a propaganda ploy the 2 October statement by the Thai Foreign Minister to the Assembly on Thai troop withdrawal.

The Council met on 9 October and, at their request, invited the Lao People's Democratic Republic and Thailand to participate in the discussion without the right to vote.

Meeting number. SC 2558.

The Lao People's Democratic Republic said the question was not a frontier dispute but a clear-cut case of premeditated aggression. The Thai stratagem was to force the Lao People's Democratic Republic to re-examine the frontier in the area of the three villages, thus creating a precedent for a wholesale revision of the common frontier; the Lao

People's Democratic Republic based its position on the principle of the inviolability of historical frontiers, as laid down in the Franco-Siamese Convention of 13 February 1904, the Franco-Siamese Treaty of 23 March 1907 and the map annexed thereto. The Thai claim of Viet Nam's intervention in the matter was only a manœuvre designed to mislead people. The Thai side must totally and unconditionally withdraw forthwith its troops and administrative personnel from the three Lao villages, send home the villagers forcibly taken to Thailand, compensate the villagers for the loss of life and property and restore the normal situation that had prevailed in the region before 6 June. The Thai statement to the General Assembly was insincere in that it did not give a precise date for the total withdrawal, renounce the maintenance of its administration or personnel, mention Lao sovereignty over the three villages, or deal with the return home of the villagers or compensation.

Thailand recapitulated its position in detail and added that, after its 2 October announcement to the Assembly on removing its military presence from the villages, the crisis had become a non-crisis because, without military protection, it was no longer possible for Thai civilians to remain in the area due to possible harassment by Lao forces. The crux of the matter was basic disagreement over the exact location of the boundary line in a small, remote, mountainous and forested area; that technical problem necessitated a joint survey to determine the watershed location. Thailand remained ready to conduct a joint technical survey with the Lao side, or to request the Secretary-General to dispatch a fact-finding mission for an on-site survey with the assistance of both Lao and Thai technical experts; if the findings were not conclusive, Thailand was prepared to resort to an impartial, independent technical expert or group of experts acceptable to both sides. The Franco-Siamese Treaty, Thailand stated, imposed undue disadvantages on Thailand for the benefit of the Lao People's Democratic Republic, then under French rule, but the Siamese Government had been in no position at that time to resist certain encroachments by the then French colonial administration.

Further communications (October-December). A statement of 14 October by the Lao Foreign Ministry[75] alleged that tension had risen in recent days regarding the three villages, that the Thai occupation troops had been reinforced rather than withdrawn, and that nearly all the villagers had been forcibly removed to Thailand. Responding to the charges, Thailand, on 17 October,[76] declared that there was no longer any Thai military or administrative presence in the three villages, that the villagers themselves had voluntarily moved and were being resettled in a safe area

nearby, and that the Lao allegations of deportation or abduction were unsubstantiated.

The Lao People's Democratic Republic, by a letter of 18 October,[77] alleged that what was actually taking place was a tactical redeployment of Thai forces, that nearly 900 Lao villagers had been deported to Thailand rather than voluntarily relocated, and that the boundary in the area followed the watershed line. By a further letter of 22 October,[78] it demanded an immediate and unconditional withdrawal of Thai forces, immediate return home of the Lao inhabitants and compensation for the loss of life and property, and resumption of negotiations which it claimed Thailand had unilaterally broken off in August. A 27 October Foreign Ministry statement, transmitted by the Lao People's Democratic Republic on 29 October,[79] reported that Thai troops had been constrained to withdraw from the three villages and Lao local authorities were once more administering them, while some of the inhabitants who had fled were gradually returning home. The situation remained tense, however, with Thai troops still occupying a position in Lao territory and assisting Lao reactionaries in exile in sabotage activities inside Lao territory; Thailand had not renounced sovereignty over the three villages or its expansionist designs on the Lao People's Democratic Republic.

Thailand, by a letter of 31 October,[80] rejected the allegation that it was still holding a position in Lao territory and called on the Lao People's Democratic Republic not to make false charges which could only exacerbate tensions.

On 6 December,[81] the Lao People's Democratic Republic said that the inhabitants of the three villages deported by Thai troops were made to perform forced labour daily and suffered from hunger and prolonged malnutrition, and women had been raped systematically. It further alleged that Thai soldiers had murdered one resident in the zone still occupied.

Thailand, on 10 December,[82] said that, since the beginning of the Thai-Lao border incidents on 15 April, the Lao side had more than 60 times violated Thailand's territorial integrity in the area, killing nine officers and one civilian and injuring 56 officers and nine civilians. The people of the three villages, it added, had told ICRC representatives that they had fled voluntarily and were determined to stay in Thailand.

By a letter of 21 December,[83] the Lao People's Democratic Republic said Thailand still occupied nine hilltops in Lao territory around the three villages and was carrying out shellings against Lao localities almost every day. It repeated charges against Thai treatment of the villagers, and added that Thailand had rejected the Lao proposal for a resumption of talks on 10 December and threatened to restrict the activities of the Lao envoy in Bangkok.

REFERENCES

(1)A/39/112-S/16343. (2)A/39/114-S/16359. (3)A/39/160-S/16453. (4)A/39/164-S/16461. (5)A/39/170-S/16467. (6)A/39/165-S/16462 & Corr.1. (7)A/39/184-S/16485. (8)A/39/190. (9)A/39/189-S/16490 & Corr.1. (10)A/39/204-S/16499. (11)A/39/205. (12)A/39/230-S/16525. (13)A/39/254-S/16555. (14)A/39/258-S/16563. (15)A/39/344-S/16666. (16)A/39/353-S/16673. (17)A/39/640-S/16822. (18)A/39/643. (19)A/39/686-S/16837. (20)A/39/694-S/16843. (21)A/39/697-S/16846. (22)A/39/824-S/16863. (23)A/39/89-S/16297. (24)A/39/92-S/16301. (25)A/39/111-S/16333. (26)A/39/121-S/16383. (27)A/39/124-S/16393. (28)A/39/172-S/16469. (29)A/39/113. (30)E/1984/139. (31)YUN 1983, p. 226. (32)A/39/309. (33)A/39/108-S/16330. (34)A/39/98-S/16326. (35)A/39/185-S/16486. (36)A/39/212-S/16505. (37)A/39/342-S/16665. (38)A/39/352-S/16672. (39)E/1984/138. (40)A/39/371 & Corr.1. (41)A/39/601-S/16795. (42)A/39/560-S/16773. (43)A/CONF.109/8. (44)YUN 1983, p. 228, GA res. 38/3, 27 Oct. 1983. (45)A/39/576. (46)YUN 1981, p. 242. (47)A/39/595. (48)A/39/574. (49)A/39/337-S/16655. (50)E/1984/130. (51)E/1984/140. (52)A/39/153. (53)A/39/169-S/16466. (54)A/39/176. (55)A/39/220. (56)A/39/274-S/16581. (57)A/39/288-S/16603. (58)A/39/279-S/16591. (59)A/39/317. (60)A/39/310-S/16626. (61)A/39/313. (62)A/39/320-S/16641. (63)A/39/334-S/16653. (64)A/39/367-S/16684. (65)A/39/426-S/16712. (66)A/39/431-S/16719. (67)A/39/451-S/16727. (68)A/39/469-S/16733. (69)A/39/475-S/16736. (70)A/39/502-S/16747. (71)A/39/524-S/16757. (72)A/39/540-S/16761. (73)A/39/550-S/16767. (74)S/16765. (75)S/16768 (A/39/586). (76)S/16787 (A/39/593). (77)S/16788. (78)S/16790. (79)S/16801 (A/39/612). (80)A/39/626-S/16811. (81)S/16852 (A/39/796). (82)A/39/809-S/16856. (83)S/16872 (A/40/59).

Western and south-western Asia

Afghanistan situation and Afghanistan-Pakistan armed incidents

The General Assembly again took up in November 1984 the situation in Afghanistan and its implications for international peace and security. By resolution 39/13, it again called for immediate foreign troop withdrawal, reaffirmed the Afghan people's right to determine their own form of government, renewed its appeal for relief assistance for the Afghan refugees, and requested the Secretary-General to continue his efforts for a political solution.

The Foreign Ministers of Afghanistan and Pakistan held discussions at Geneva in August in a new format of "proximity" talks held separately with the Secretary-General's Personal Representative, agreeing to meet again in February 1985.

Communications. In 1984, the majority of the communications addressed to the Secretary-General relating to the situation in Afghanistan concerned allegations by both Pakistan and Afghanistan of violations of airspace and territory, shellings and other attacks by one against the other.

Two of the communications dealt with an 18 December 1983 incident in the border area of Torkham inside Afghanistan,[1] in which Afghanistan had accused Pakistan of complicity. Pakistan, in a 26 December 1983 statement, transmitted on 5 January 1984,[2] rejected the charge, stating that it was the Afghan people themselves that carried on an indigenous freedom struggle throughout Afghanistan. On 19 April,[3] Afghanistan alleged that, in the course of that 1983 incident, in which a custom-house was burned, armed bandits and foreign mercenaries, assisted by Pakistan, had kidnapped and surrendered to Pakistani militia forces 37 employees of Afghan civil institutions, who were subsequently tortured in an effort to make them stay in Pakistan. Afghanistan demanded the immediate release and return of the prisoners.

By a letter of 2 February,[4] Pakistan reported that two Afghan MIG aircraft violated Pakistan's airspace near Angur Adda on 27 January, killing 42 civilians and injuring 60 others. On 26 March,[5] it reported that an Afghan MIG had crashed on its territory the day before. Afghanistan stated on 2 April[6] that the plane, on a training flight, had lost direction due to bad weather and technical problems, and crashed when its fuel was finished.

Pakistan said in a letter of 18 June[7] that two Afghan military aircraft had bombed Pakistan territory on 16 June, killing six Afghan children and injuring a woman in what it claimed was the twenty-eighth violation of Pakistan airspace from the Afghan side in 1984. Afghanistan replied on 20 June[8] that no such airspace violation had occurred, adding that, whenever the dates approached of bilateral negotiations through the Secretary-General's representative or of the General Assembly sessions, Pakistan made baseless allegations to score propagandistic gains.

Pakistan alleged further bombing attacks by Afghan military aircraft on 13 and 14 August,[9] which it said had killed 14 people and injured 10 others. Afghanistan, by a letter of 17 August,[10] rejected the allegations, adding that such claims were made to coincide with top-level officials' visits or when negotiations or the Assembly session approached; it alleged that China and the United States were behind that manœuvre, trying for their part to achieve their political objectives.

Three incidents of alleged shellings by the Afghan army across the Pakistan border at Teri Mangal on 18 and 19 August were reported by Pakistan in two letters dated 21 August: 27 Afghan refugees and nine Pakistanis were reportedly killed in two instances,[11] and two civilians were killed and four others injured in a third incident.[12] Pakistan reported that further Afghan shellings in the same area—on 21[13] and 23 August[14]—had resulted in six deaths and seven injuries.

In a 23 August letter, transmitted on 27 August,[15] Pakistan alleged that a series of violations of its territory by Afghan aircraft and artillery in August had resulted in 51 deaths. The Afghan authorities, having been frustrated in their efforts to contain the conflict raging inside that country, seemed to be seeking external diversion, Pakistan said, adding that the escalation of aggression on the eve of the Geneva talks raised doubts about Afghanistan's sincerity in searching for a just and comprehensive settlement. Pakistan hoped the Secretary-General would ask Afghanistan to desist from acts of aggression and provocation.

Afghanistan, in a note verbale to Pakistan of 22 August,[16] stated that no land or air attacks had been made against Pakistan. It asserted that Pakistan, in collusion with China and the United States, tried to block the progress of the Geneva talks and cover up the fact that its territory had been turned into a springboard of aggression and a training base for Afghan counter-revolutionary elements.

On 18 September,[17] Pakistan said another bombing of its territory by Afghan planes had taken place on 14 September. A further Afghan bombing reportedly took place on 27 September, killing 32 people in a populated commercial centre in Teri Mangal.[18] Afghanistan rejected the allegation in a note verbale to Pakistan of 1 October,[19] stating that imperialism, headed by the United States in pursuit of supremacy in the region, was behind Pakistan's anti-Afghan activities; if any explosions had occurred in the arms depots belonging to the Afghan counter-revolutionaries based in Teri Mangal, it was due to their internal conflicts and to Pakistan's policy of aiding those elements.

Afghanistan alleged on 8 October[20] that on 5 October Pakistani armed forces had fired on some Afghan helicopters inside its own territory in the Barikot area. Pakistan replied on 9 October[21] that the baseless charges were aimed at distracting international attention from the serious violations of its airspace and territory. Afghanistan[22] protested to Pakistan on 25 October that since 18 October the latter had daily conducted provocative operations inside Afghan territory, making use of mortars and other heavy weapons and killing a number of people; on 21 October, two Afghan helicopters in the Barikot area had been fired on from Pakistani territory. On 26 October,[23] Pakistan alleged that, on 21 October, a Pakistani civilian had been killed by bullets fired from the Afghanistan side and three Afghan jet aircraft violated Pakistan airspace and dropped a bomb. Afghanistan charged on 27 October[24] that heavy shelling on 24 October from Pakistan territory had resulted in several casualties. On 31 October,[25] Pakistan said four people had died in an Afghan bombing of 29 October, and denied, in a 29 October statement,[26] the Afghan allegation of a 24 October shelling. Afghanistan, on 3 November,[27] charged further firings on its

helicopters in the Barikot area from Pakistan on 29 October. On 2 November,[28] Pakistan rejected as totally false various charges made against it in October.

Afghanistan reported that further shellings had killed a child on 11 November,[29] and caused material loss in Pishangro, Barikot and Jaji districts on 16, 17 and 18 November.[30] Rejecting those charges, Pakistan, by a letter of 27 November,[31] alleged that four Afghan aircraft had carried out a bombing raid on Pakistan territory on 26 November. Earlier, Pakistan[32] had charged that a civilian had been killed in firings from the Afghan side on 14 November, a charge rejected by Afghanistan on 26 November.[33] Afghanistan[34] alleged that two Pakistani helicopters had violated its territory on 25 November and the Pakistan military forces had fired at the Barikot contingent on 26 and 27 November.

By a letter of 4 December,[35] Pakistan alleged that six Afghan jet aircraft dropped bombs and three others also violated Pakistan's airspace on 1 December. An Afghanistan information agency dispatch of 4 December[36] reported that Pakistan had shelled Afghan territory in the Barikot and Jaji regions on 1, 2 and 3 December. The Pakistani allegations of 26 November and 1 December bombings were rejected by Afghanistan on 9 December.[37]

Pakistan reported five further incidents of airspace violations by Afghanistan on 25 and 28 November and 6 December;[38] it also rejected the Afghan charges of firing and shelling incidents of 25, 26 and 27 November and of 1, 2 and 3 December. Afghanistan alleged further shellings by Pakistan on 8 and 10 December.[39] Pakistan charged further Afghan bombings of its territory on 11 December, while rejecting allegations that it had fired on Afghanistan on 8 December.[40] Afghanistan rejected the Pakistani charges of airspace violations on 11 December;[41] and, by a Foreign Ministry statement of 22 December,[42] asserted that Pakistan's firings of 18 December at the Barikot contingent had killed one person and injured eight others; it also rejected Pakistan's charges of airspace violations on 25 and 28 November and 6 December. On 27 December,[43] Pakistan denied allegations on the 18 December incident and reported that Afghanistan had again violated its airspace on 22 and 25 December, the latter involving bombings and the killing of four civilians.

Afghanistan, in a Foreign Ministry statement of 27 December,[44] claimed that Pakistan had used long-range heavy weapons in firing at Afghanistan on 19 occasions in the preceding two months alone, while charging Afghanistan with alleged air raids over Pakistan territory. Pakistan's new series of aggressions, it asserted, were related directly to the new round of Geneva negotiations; Pakistan also wanted a pretext to acquire larger quantities of the most modern offensive and destructive weapons.

A number of other 1984 communications concerned the general situation.

On 13 March,[45] Morocco transmitted documents of the Fourth Islamic Summit Conference (Casablanca, 16-19 January), including a resolution in which the Conference reaffirmed its concern over the preparation of USSR military intervention in Afghanistan, and demanded the immediate, total and unconditional withdrawal of all foreign troops from Afghanistan. It also supported the diplomatic process initiated by the Secretary-General, and thanked Pakistan for having accepted and given protection to Afghan refugees.

On 15 March,[46] Bangladesh transmitted a resolution adopted at the Fourteenth Islamic Conference of Foreign Ministers (Dhaka, 6-11 December 1983), by which the Ministers called for the immediate, total and unconditional withdrawal of all foreign troops from Afghanistan, and recommended that the Ministerial Committee— composed of the Conference Secretary-General and the Foreign Ministers of Guinea, Iran, Pakistan and Tunisia—continue exploring a political solution and co-operate with the United Nations Secretary-General in that regard.

The United States[47] transmitted a proclamation by its President, designating 21 March 1984 as Afghanistan Day, calling for the removal of the USSR troops from Afghanistan as a prerequisite for a negotiated political settlement based on the five resolutions adopted on the topic by the General Assembly. Afghanistan,[48] by a 22 March statement, called that gesture provocative and slanderous, and asserted that the United States was the organizer of the undeclared war against Afghanistan.

On 15 May,[49] France transmitted the text of a 14 May statement by the Foreign Ministers of the European Economic Community (EEC), in which they renewed their appeal to the USSR to contribute to the Secretary-General's efforts for a just and lasting settlement for all parties involved.

Afghanistan transmitted, on 10 August,[50] copies of documents said to reveal the nature of counter-revolutionary organizations established in Pakistan; the alleged communications written by such organizations to China, Egypt, France, Iran, Qatar, Saudia Arabia and the United States dealt with, among other things, military and other assistance.

The communiqué of the co-ordinating meeting of Ministers for Foreign Affairs of the Organization of the Islamic Conference (New York, 4 October), transmitted by Bangladesh on 12 October,[51] noted that the number of Afghan refugees in Pakistan exceeded 3 million, and announced that the Islamic Group would submit to the General Assembly, at its 1984 session, a draft resolution originally prepared by Pakistan (see p. 227). A similar communiqué, adopted by the Foreign Ministers at the October 1983 meeting in New York, was transmitted by the Niger on 2 May 1984.[52]

The Meeting of Ministers for Foreign Affairs and Heads of Delegation of Non-Aligned Countries to the General Assembly at its 1984 session (New York, 1-5 October),[53] in its final communiqué, reiterated a call for a political settlement on the basis of foreign troop withdrawal; full respect for the independence, sovereignty, territorial integrity and non-aligned status of Afghanistan; and strict observance of the principle of non-intervention and non-interference. It also reaffirmed the right of the Afghan refugees to return to their homes in safety and honour, and extended support to the efforts of the Secretary-General.

On 1 December,[54] Afghanistan's Bakhtar Information Agency said that, according to *The New York Times* of 28 November, the United States had decided to allocate $280 million in military aid to what Afghanistan called the Afghan counter-revolutionaries; that funding, the Agency said, was additional to the funds spent secretly by China, Israel, Saudi Arabia, the United States and others in equipping counter-revolutionary bands. The Agency further claimed that the news report also pointed to close co-operation between Pakistan and the United States in organizing, training and arming the Afghan counter-revolutionaries.

In a 21 February note verbale,[55] the United States said that chemical weapons attacks appeared to have diminished in Afghanistan during 1983; that it had not yet confirmed as valid several reports of Soviet chemical attacks in 1983; but that for 1982, on the other hand, it had strong evidence of several dozen chemical attacks in Afghanistan, resulting in over 300 chemical agent–related deaths (see also p. 62).

Report of the Secretary-General. Pursuant to a November 1983 General Assembly resolution,[56] the Secretary-General submitted to the Assembly and the Security Council in September 1984 a report on activities he had undertaken regarding the Afghanistan situation.[57]

The Secretary-General stated that he had pursued his efforts towards the achievement of a political settlement, believing the principal aim of the United Nations in that context should be to end the suffering of the Afghan people. His Personal Representative, Diego Cordovez, had returned to the area from 3 to 15 April, meeting, separately in their capitals, with the Presidents of Pakistan and Afghanistan and the Foreign Minister of Iran. At Kabul and Islamabad, a number of specific steps—both substantive and procedural—were agreed upon in order to give impetus to the diplomatic process, while Iran reiterated its support for the interests of the Afghan people.

The Secretary-General said he had visited the USSR from 11 to 13 July, at which time he exchanged views on the situation with General Secretary Konstantin Chernenko and Foreign Minister Andrei Gromyko; the USSR encouraged him to continue his efforts and reaffirmed its support for a negotiated political settlement.

A round of "proximity" talks, held separately through the intermediary of his Personal Representative, was convened at Geneva from 24 to 30 August, with the Foreign Ministers of Pakistan and Afghanistan attending; as in the past, Iran was kept informed.

The Secretary-General reported that a set of understandings worked out in April was aimed at solving, within the context of formulating the various instruments required for comprehensive settlement, some difficulties that had arisen the previous year; the procedure would allow all concerned more clearly to assess the nature, intent and interrelationships of the specific actions envisaged in the settlement. During the Geneva discussions, the interlocutors held a preliminary review of draft instruments and examined related questions, including form, legal status and formalities; they indicated their readiness for another round of talks in February 1985.

The Secretary-General, noting an increase in the number of allegations and counter-allegations between the parties about infiltration and other acts of interference, deplored those developments, particularly because they involved the loss of human lives.

GENERAL ASSEMBLY ACTION

Following consideration of the situation in Afghanistan, the General Assembly, on 15 November 1984, adopted resolution 39/13 by recorded vote.

The situation in Afghanistan and its implications for international peace and security

The General Assembly,

Having considered the item entitled "The situation in Afghanistan and its implications for international peace and security",

Recalling its resolutions ES-6/2 of 14 January 1980, 35/37 of 20 November 1980, 36/34 of 18 November 1981, 37/37 of 29 November 1982 and 38/29 of 23 November 1983,

Reaffirming the purposes and principles of the Charter of the United Nations and the obligation of all States to refrain in their international relations from the threat or use of force against the sovereignty, territorial integrity and political independence of any State,

Reaffirming further the inalienable right of all peoples to determine their own form of government and to choose their own economic, political and social system free from outside intervention, subversion, coercion or constraint of any kind whatsoever,

Gravely concerned at the continuing foreign armed intervention in Afghanistan, in contravention of the above principles, and its serious implications for international peace and security,

Noting the increasing concern of the international community over the continued and serious sufferings of the Afghan people and over the magnitude of social and economic problems posed to Pakistan and Iran by the presence on their soil of millions of Afghan refugees, and the continuing increase in their numbers,

Deeply conscious of the urgent need for a political solution of the grave situation in respect of Afghanistan,

Taking note of the report of the Secretary-General, and the status of the diplomatic process initiated by him,

Recognizing the importance of the initiatives of the Organization of the Islamic Conference and the efforts of the Movement of Non-Aligned Countries for a political solution of the situation in respect of Afghanistan,

1. *Reiterates* that the preservation of the sovereignty, territorial integrity, political independence and non-aligned character of Afghanistan is essential for a peaceful solution of the problem;

2. *Reaffirms* the right of the Afghan people to determine their own form of government and to choose their economic, political and social system free from outside intervention, subversion, coercion or constraint of any kind whatsoever;

3. *Calls* for the immediate withdrawal of the foreign troops from Afghanistan;

4. *Calls upon* all parties concerned to work for the urgent achievement of a political solution, in accordance with the provisions of the present resolution, and the creation of the necessary conditions which would enable the Afghan refugees to return voluntarily to their homes in safety and honour;

5. *Renews its appeal* to all States and national and international organizations to continue to extend humanitarian relief assistance with a view to alleviating the hardship of the Afghan refugees, in co-ordination with the United Nations High Commissioner for Refugees;

6. *Expresses its appreciation and support* for the efforts and constructive steps taken by the Secretary-General, especially the diplomatic process initiated by him, in the search for a solution to the problem;

7. *Requests* the Secretary-General to continue those efforts with a view to promoting a political solution, in accordance with the provisions of the present resolution, and the exploration of securing appropriate guarantees for the non-use of force, or threat of force, against the political independence, sovereignty, territorial integrity and security of all neighbouring States, on the basis of mutual guarantees and strict non-interference in each other's internal affairs and with full regard for the principles of the Charter of the United Nations;

8. *Requests* the Secretary-General to keep Member States and the Security Council concurrently informed of progress towards the implementation of the present resolution and to submit to Member States a report on the situation at the earliest appropriate opportunity;

9. *Decides* to include in the provisional agenda of its fortieth session the item entitled "The situation in Afghanistan and its implications for international peace and security".

General Assembly resolution 39/13

15 November 1984   Meeting 63   119-20-14 (recorded vote)

46-nation draft (A/39/L.11); agenda item 28.

Sponsors: Antigua and Barbuda, Bahrain, Bangladesh, Brunei Darussalam, Chile, Colombia, Comoros, Costa Rica, Djibouti, Dominica, Egypt, Fiji, Gambia, Guatemala, Guinea, Haiti, Honduras, Jamaica, Jordan, Kuwait, Malaysia, Maldives, Mauritania, Morocco, Nepal, Niger, Oman, Pakistan, Papua New Guinea, Paraguay, Philippines, Qatar, Saint Lucia, Saint Vincent and the Grenadines, Samoa, Saudi Arabia, Senegal, Singapore, Solomon Islands, Somalia, Sudan, Thailand, Tunisia, Turkey, United Arab Emirates, Uruguay.

Financial implications. 5th Committee, A/39/649; S-G, A/C.5/39/34.

Meeting numbers. GA 39th session: 5th Committee 25; plenary 60-63.

Recorded vote in Assembly as follows:

In favour: Albania, Antigua and Barbuda, Argentina, Australia, Austria, Bahamas, Bahrain, Bangladesh, Barbados, Belgium, Belize, Bolivia, Botswana, Brazil, Brunei Darussalam, Burma, Burundi, Cameroon, Canada, Central African Republic, Chad, Chile, China, Colombia, Comoros, Costa Rica, Democratic Kampuchea, Denmark, Djibouti, Dominica, Dominican Republic, Ecuador, Egypt, El Salvador, Equatorial Guinea, Fiji, France, Gabon, Gambia, Germany, Federal Republic of, Ghana, Greece, Grenada, Guatemala, Guinea, Guyana, Haiti, Honduras, Iceland, Indonesia, Iran, Ireland, Israel, Italy, Ivory Coast, Jamaica, Japan, Jordan, Kenya, Kuwait, Lebanon, Lesotho, Liberia, Luxembourg, Malawi, Malaysia, Maldives, Malta, Mauritania, Mauritius, Mexico, Morocco, Nepal, Netherlands, New Zealand, Niger, Nigeria, Norway, Oman, Pakistan, Panama, Papua New Guinea, Paraguay, Peru, Philippines, Portugal, Qatar, Rwanda, Saint Lucia, Saint Vincent and the Grenadines, Samoa, Saudi Arabia, Senegal, Sierra Leone, Singapore, Solomon Islands, Somalia, Spain, Sri Lanka, Sudan, Suriname, Swaziland, Sweden, Thailand, Togo, Trinidad and Tobago, Tunisia, Turkey, United Arab Emirates, United Kingdom, United Republic of Tanzania, United States, Uruguay, Vanuatu, Venezuela, Yugoslavia, Zaire, Zambia, Zimbabwe.

Against: Afghanistan, Angola, Bulgaria, Byelorussian SSR, Cuba, Czechoslovakia, Democratic Yemen, Ethiopia, German Democratic Republic, Hungary, Lao People's Democratic Republic, Libyan Arab Jamahiriya, Madagascar, Mongolia, Mozambique, Poland, Syrian Arab Republic, Ukrainian SSR, USSR, Viet Nam.

Abstaining: Algeria, Benin, Burkina Faso, Cape Verde, Congo, Cyprus, Finland, Guinea-Bissau, India, Iraq, Mali, Nicaragua, Sao Tome and Principe, Uganda.

In explanation of vote, Afghanistan, as in the past, objected to including the so-called question of Afghanistan in the Assembly's agenda, and called the draft resolution a gross violation of the Charter of the United Nations and flagrant interference in Afghanistan's internal affairs, with the sponsors advising the Afghan people, who had already chosen their path, as to the kind of social, economic and political systems it should adopt. The number of so-called refugees had been inflated for dramatic effect and for increased income, it said, adding that it had issued decrees on the general amnesty for all Afghans temporarily living abroad. It asserted that despite deliberate obstacles by Pakistan, such as preventing dissemination of those decrees and other declarations among the Afghans living in that country, many thousands of Afghans had already returned. The limited USSR contingents in Afghanistan were there at the request of the Government, solely to repel armed aggression from outside. The reason for which those contingents had been invited not only persisted but, as a result of the steady and rapid escalation of the undeclared war, lacked any realistic hope for reversal. The resolution, Afghanistan said, would in no way be binding on it, and the harmful exercise in the Assembly must be abandoned to ensure the success of direct negotiations such as it had proposed in May 1980[58] and August 1981.[59]

Cuba added that the concern expressed over Afghanistan reflected the United States desire to increase tension in the region, while distracting attention from aggressive acts of imperialism elsewhere.

Iran condemned as invalid an invitation extended, by what it called the surrogate régime in Afghanistan, to outside forces to intervene in its internal affairs, adding that those who could not rule a country without the presence of foreign troops could not have any claim to legitimacy. It asserted that problems such as the military occupation of a sovereign State, the displacement of more than 4 million people and the imposition of an unwanted Government could not be settled around negotiating tables without the presence of the true representatives of the people concerned.

Encouraged by an indication, in the Secretary-General's 1984 report, of a receptive attitude by the parties concerned for a negotiated solution, Malta said the resolution should be accepted as a spur to further efforts and an expression of the international concern. Malawi called for making the best use of the Secretary-General's good offices and promoting dialogue and diplomatic contacts. Also supporting the Secretary-General's efforts as the sole active negotiating machinery likely to lead to a political settlement, Bolivia stated that, as regards paragraph 2, it did not want to prejudge the legitimacy of the Afghan Government or question the latter's efforts to introduce social reforms and development programmes. Belgium said the international community could not remain indifferent to the sufferings of the Afghan people and it should keep up the pressure to bring about a political solution; the USSR must respond to the demand of the majority of the Member States. Mexico said a negotiated political settlement would be possible only through foreign troop withdrawal and complete cessation of all acts of foreign interference.

Other action. The Commission on Human Rights, by a resolution of 29 February 1984 on the right of peoples to self-determination as it applied to Afghanistan, called for a political settlement of the Afghanistan situation, affirmed the Afghan refugees' right to return home and appealed for humanitarian relief assistance to be extended to them, in co-operation with the United Nations High Commissioner for Refugees (see ECONOMIC AND SOCIAL QUESTIONS, Chapter XVIII, under "Self-determination of peoples").

On the Commission's recommendation, the Economic and Social Council, on 24 May, requested the Commission Chairman to appoint a special rapporteur to examine the human rights situation in Afghanistan, with a view to proposing measures for the protection of human rights of all residents of the country before, during and after the withdrawal of all foreign forces (resolution 1984/37).

REFERENCES

[1]YUN 1983, p. 233. [2]A/39/68-S/16258. [3]A/39/203-S/16496. [4]A/39/96-S/16313. [5]A/39/152-S/16435. [6]A/39/163-S/16460. [7]A/39/316-S/16635. [8]A/39/318-S/16637. [9]A/39/405-S/16701. [10]A/39/413-S/16707. [11]A/39/424-S/16710. [12]A/39/428-S/16716. [13]A/39/429-S/16717. [14]A/39/430-S/16718. [15]A/39/438-S/16720. [16]A/39/473-S/16734. [17]A/39/507-S/16748. [18]A/39/543-S/16763. [19]A/39/552-S/16769. [20]A/39/561-S/16774. [21]A/39/564-S/16778. [22]A/39/611-S/16802. [23]A/39/614-S/16804. [24]A/39/616-S/16805. [25]A/39/624-S/16809. [26]A/39/625-S/16810. [27]A/39/632-S/16816. [28]A/39/633-S/16817. [29]A/39/672-S/16834. [30]A/39/671-S/16833. [31]A/39/695-S/16844 & Corr.1. [32]A/39/679-S/16836. [33]A/39/691-S/16840. [34]A/39/721-S/16848. [35]A/39/764-S/16850. [36]A/39/811-S/16857. [37]A/39/819-S/16859. [38]A/39/823-S/16861. [39]A/39/835-S/16864. [40]A/39/854-S/16868. [41]A/39/848-S/16867. [42]A/40/60-S/16873. [43]A/40/61-S/16875. [44]A/40/62-S/16876. [45]A/39/131-S/16414 & Corr.1. [46]A/39/133-S/16417. [47]A/39/140-S/16432. [48]A/39/158-S/16445. [49]A/39/261. [50]A/39/396-S/16697. [51]A/39/585-S/16783. [52]A/39/236-S/16535. [53]A/39/560-S/16773. [54]A/39/794-S/16853. [55]A/39/113. [56]YUN 1983, p. 234, GA res. 38/29, 23 Nov. 1983. [57]A/39/513-S/16754. [58]YUN 1980, p. 303. [59]YUN 1981, p. 232.

Iran-Iraq armed conflict

In the continuing hostilities between Iran and Iraq, the Secretary-General proposed in February 1984 to send a mission to examine the damage allegedly inflicted on civilian targets, while also ascertaining the authoritative position of the parties on various issues involved in the conflict. Although both parties initially accepted the proposal, Iran cited new developments in late February and asked that political discussions be excluded from the mission's mandate. The mission did not materialize.

Moved by humanitarian concerns over the alleged use of chemical weapons in the conflict, the Secretary-General dispatched four specialists to Iran in March. Their report—and conclusion that certain such weapons had been used—was submitted both to the General Assembly and to the Security Council.

Attacks on merchant ships in the Gulf were brought to the attention of the Security Council, which, on 1 June, condemned such attacks and called on all States to respect the right of free navigation (resolution 552(1984)).

Later that month, the Secretary-General announced that Iran and Iraq had accepted his appeal to end military attacks on purely civilian population centres, and that two United Nations teams had been set up, at Baghdad and Teheran, for compliance verification.

In the General Assembly, a debate on a draft resolution proposed by Iran on preventing further use of chemical weapons was adjourned by a vote in the First Committee. The Assembly also deferred consideration of the conflict to its resumed session at a later date.

Communications (January-March). A number of communications in January and early February 1984 contained charges by both Iran and Iraq of attacks on civilian targets.

Iraq alleged such attacks by Iran between 20 December 1983 and 2 January 1984[1] and shelling of civilian targets between 4 and 22 January;[2] 30 photographs were submitted on 26 January,[3] allegedly depicting incidents of Iranian bombardment of various Iraqi civilian targets on 18 January. On 7 February,[4] Iraq submitted details of alleged Iranian attacks on civilian targets between 1 January and 6 February.

On 6 January,[5] and again on 4 February,[6] Iran invited the Secretary-General to send a fact-finding mission to both countries to update a similar mission's 1983 report[7] on the matter. In a statement transmitted on 4 February,[6] Iran asserted that the Secretary-General's 1983 report had confirmed that it had never attacked civilian targets. In a statement transmitted on 9 February,[8] Iran alleged that Iraqi attacks—involving aerial bombardments, long-range missiles and chemical weapons—on Iran's civilian and residential areas had killed some 4,600 civilians and wounded more than 22,000 in the past 40 months. Governors of three provinces in Iran, in a statement transmitted on 5 February,[9] said some 1,300 villages in those provinces had been totally destroyed by Iraq. Iran also submitted, by a note verbale of 10 January,[10] a telegram sent to the Red Crescent of Iran and the International Red Cross at Teheran by the Committee for Iraqi Refugees on alleged abuse committed by Iraq against its Kurdish population.

Iraq[11] stated on 2 February that it would strike, in self-defence against Iran's acts of aggression, selected targets in seven named towns in Iran after 6 February and called on Iranian citizens to keep away from those areas, adding on 4 February four others to be attacked after 8 February. Iran reported on those threats on 3[12] and 5 February;[13] its Foreign Minister, in a statement transmitted on 9 February,[8] said it would respond to the threats by retaliating against Iraqi industrial targets, and that the responsibility for the consequences rested with Iran and with international organizations if they failed to respond in time.

On 10 February, the Secretary-General addressed similar letters to Iran[14] and Iraq,[15] expressing concern over the grievous consequences of the conflict and a threat of escalation of the level of hostilities. In view, particularly, of the repeated allegations made by both sides of attacks on civilian targets, the Secretary-General proposed to send a mission to ascertain the facts, in order to update the previous report, and the authoritative positions of both Governments regarding other questions related to the conflict; once there was an understanding between the parties on the scope of its function, the mission could depart to the area on very short notice.

Iraq replied to the Secretary-General on 13 February,[16] reiterating support for a peaceful settlement of the conflict through implementation of Security Council resolutions, but doubting the usefulness of updating information when Iran persisted in denying—but continued almost daily— its attacks on civilian targets in Iraq and escalating the war. Iraq strongly encouraged, but could not deal with, the Secretary-General's initiative until serious assurances were given by Iran of its desire to discuss a seven-point paper covering elements of the conflict, which the Secretary-General had presented on 29 September 1983 to Iraq's Foreign Minister in the presence of Olof Palme, the Secretary-General's Special Representative on the question. Since June 1983, Iraq had proposed a special agreement, aimed at avoiding strikes against civilian targets, to be concluded with Iran under United Nations supervision; it hoped that international efforts, including those of the Secretary-General, would focus on implementing all the provisions of the October 1983 Security Council resolution.[17] Iraq also recalled its previous request that the Secretary-General dispatch a mission to investigate the treatment of prisoners of war (POWs), and added that it, as the victim of aggression, had to resort to all means to defend its security and interests.

Replying to the Secretary-General on 14 February,[18] Iran stated that the October 1983 Security Council resolution had encouraged Iraq to open new avenues of crime and to resort to chemical-weapons use; Iran accepted no imperialist-manipulated United Nations resolution and no concessionary mediations or negotiations. Iran welcomed the proposed fact-finding mission headed by a senior aide to the Secretary-General, provided the representative's mandate remained restricted to ascertaining the position of the Governments and looking into the remaining evidence of chemical weapons used by the Iraqi army.

On 16 February,[19] Iran stated that recent Iraqi attacks on innocent civilians and the callousness of the international body towards continued violation of international humanitarian law left Iran with no choice but to take appropriate action to protect its people from missile attacks and air bombardments. In view of those new developments, Iran requested that political discussion be excluded

from the mandate of the Secretary-General's mission, adding that it would welcome a fact-finding mission for the specific purpose of updating a previous report and examining the chemical-weapons use by Iraq.

On 18 February,[20] Iraq informed the Secretary-General that it welcomed the dispatch of the proposed mission for the two purposes mentioned in a 17 February letter by the Secretary-General—to ascertain the position of the respective Governments on matters relating to the conflict, and to visit areas in the two countries subjected to military attacks, with a view to updating the report of the 1983 mission.[7] Iraq agreed to the Secretary-General's suggestions regarding the mission's composition and the course of its visit to Iraq, and renewed its proposal for another mission to investigate the treatment of POWs in both Iran and Iraq.

In the mean time, both sides continued to communicate allegations of attacks on civilian targets. Iraq charged such attacks had occurred from 7 to 11 February,[21] and on 12,[22] 13,[23] 13 and 14,[24] 15[25] and 17 February.[26] Iran charged such attacks on 11, 13 and 14 February,[27] claiming that the callousness of the Security Council had forced it to take retaliatory measures in order to protect its people.

On 21 February,[28] Iraq said it had declared, on 18 February, its willingness to avoid any shelling of towns, villages or civilians, provided such commitment was subject to effective international supervision. Alleging that Iran had hit civilian targets in Iraq for five days following Iraq's 14 February declaration on a week-long non-shelling of selected targets in certain Iranian towns, Iraq requested the Secretary-General to develop mechanisms of verification and international supervision, under either the United Nations, which Iraq preferred, or any other mutually acceptable body. In another letter dated 21 February,[29] Iraq reiterated its call for such international supervision, and also pointed out that Iran had announced on 18 February that it would stop attacking civilian targets.

Iraq alleged continued shelling of civilian targets by Iran and reported such attacks on 20[30] and 21 February.[31] It further reported on 23 February[32] that, despite its 14 and 18 February announcements (see above), Iran had shelled Iraqi towns from 14 to 18 and from 19 to 23 February, with the latter coinciding with a large-scale Iranian offensive of 22/23 February; those acts proved that Iran's declarations could not be trusted and that effective international supervision was needed to prevent attacks on civilian targets. That offensive was described in a 23 February letter from Iraq,[33] which also reported that large-scale battles remained in progress on its eastern borders.

On 22 February,[34] Iran rejected the previous day's allegations of attacks on civilian targets and said Iraq had announced retaliatory attacks on Iranian cities. Iran alleged that Iraqi missile attacks on three civilian targets on 24 February[35] had killed 95 persons and injured more than 900; it also alleged that Iraq's missile attacks and aerial bombardment of 13 cities since 25 February had killed 246 and injured more than 1,500.[36] Iraq said Iran had carried out air raids on civilian areas on 24, 25 and 26 February.[37] On 5 March,[38] Iraq charged further Iranian attacks on civilian targets from 26 February through 5 March, stating also that it was Iran which blocked the Secretary-General's effort to send a mission to the two countries. On 22 February,[39] Iraq submitted information regarding what was termed Iranian aggression within the Iraqi frontier in Penjween region on 19/20 October 1983, in which 26,014 Iranians reportedly had been killed.

A number of other communications alleged the use of chemical weapons. On 29 February,[40] Iran charged that Iraq had resorted again to the use of chemical bombs; it had forwarded the information to ICRC. It also alleged that Iraq's largest chemical bombardment to date in the conflict had taken place on 28 February,[41] with symptoms clearly indicating use of mustard nitrogen gas; over 700 Iranian combatants in the Khaybar operational theatre were reportedly injured. Other chemical bombings were said to have taken place in the Hur-al-Hoveizeh area in the previous two days, with casualties reported at 400. By a letter of 5 March,[42] Iraq said its position regarding false Iranian allegations had remained unchanged since its letter of 29 November 1983 on the question,[43] and drew attention to what it said was a 27 February press release by the Permanent Mission of Iran, stating, among other things, that the new massive offensive, code-named "Khaybar", had led the Iranian troops to penetrate 40 kilometres deep inside Iraqi territory.

Iran, on 8 March,[44] said it was incumbent on the Secretary-General to inform the United Nations of the developments, since Iran had repeatedly requested an investigation of Iraq's violations of international humanitarian laws, and particularly use of internationally prohibited chemical weapons. Iran made further charges of Iraqi use of chemical weapons on 9 March in the Hur-al-Hoveizeh region.[45] On 12 March,[46] Iraq responded to an ICRC press release—on its appeals · over the wounded in the Iran-Iraq conflict—stating that it questioned the stand ICRC had taken on the issue, that those responsible in Iraq had confirmed the non-use of chemical weapons in the conflict, and that it was prepared to co-operate with any neutral authorities in investigating the allegation. Iran submitted on 13

March[47] a message from the head of its environmental protection organization, asserting that the United Nations Environment Programme, among others, should condemn Iraq's chemical-weapons use. It alleged that Iraq had used a nerve agent in three attacks against Iranian military personnel in the western Gofier region on 17 March.[48] Two victims of what was described as Iraqi chemical warfare were reported by Iran[49] to have died at Stockholm, Sweden, in early March.

Other communications during the period covered more general matters. On 29 February,[50] Iran said the United States was expanding its naval presence in the Persian Gulf and the Oman Sea, and had interfered with the movement of the Iranian air force and navy in Iranian territorial waters; charging that the activities of the United States were threatening the peace and security of the airspace and sea lanes of the region, Iran said it would exercise its rights to protect its national interests within its territorial waters. Afghanistan[51] transmitted a Foreign Ministry statement of 11 March, asserting that United States patrol operations in the Gulf had violated the norms of international law, harmed the interests of States using the air and shipping routes in that region, and served as a pretext for armed intervention in the Iran-Iraq war with a view to occupying oil resources there.

By a 9 March letter,[52] Iraq said that, in contrast to its readiness to comply with the United Nations resolutions and work towards a peaceful settlement of the conflict, Iran rejected them outright and continued the war of aggression; Iraq disapproved the United Nations silence in the face of established facts as not serving the Organization's effectiveness in advancing peace, and asked the Secretary-General to declare unequivocally his position on Iran's continued aggression and noncompliance with the United Nations resolutions, the Charter, and humanitarian laws concerning the treatment of POWs. A 24 February statement by the Iranian President, said to prove Iran's ambitions for Iraq's territory and resources, was also submitted.[53]

By a declaration of 28 February,[54] EEC appealed to Iran and Iraq to comply with Security Council resolutions and to observe international rules and conventions concerning the protection of the civilian population and the treatment of POWs; it also requested the Secretary-General to resume his mission in search of a peaceful, just and lasting solution to the conflict. On 9 March,[55] King Hassan II of Morocco, as President of the Fourth Islamic Summit Conference, appealed to the parties to the conflict to bring about an immediate end to all hostilities and resume talks in the framework of the Islamic Peace

Committee, adding that Morocco would welcome them on its soil. Morocco transmitted, on 13 March,[56] a resolution adopted at the Fourth Islamic Summit Conference (Casablanca, 16-19 January), requesting the parties to the conflict to suspend all war operations immediately and negotiate for a peaceful settlement of the dispute. Iraq transmitted, on 14 March,[57] a resolution adopted that day by the Council of the League of Arab States, at a ministerial-level emergency session at Baghdad (13 and 14 March). By that resolution—to which Democratic Yemen expressed reservations in part, and Algeria, in its entirety—the Council condemned Iran for its continued aggression against Iraq and its non-responsiveness to peace initiatives, reaffirmed solidarity with Iraq in its legitimate defence, and established a committee, consisting of the Ministers for Foreign Affairs of Democratic Yemen, Iraq, Jordan, Kuwait, Morocco and Saudi Arabia and the Secretary-General of the League of Arab States, to take actions and make international contacts aimed at ending the war and maintaining security in the region. A resolution of the Fourteenth Islamic Conference of Foreign Ministers (Dhaka, Bangladesh, 6-11 December 1983), relating to POWs in the conflict and urging co-operation with ICRC on the matter, was transmitted by Bangladesh on 15 March.[58]

Specialists' report on alleged chemical-weapons use

In March 1984, the Secretary-General submitted to the Security Council a report[59] of specialists he had appointed to investigate, out of humanitarian concern, allegations made by Iran concerning the use of chemical weapons by Iraq against Iran. The report was subsequently circulated also in the General Assembly by an April note of the Secretary-General,[60] in accordance with Iran's request of 26 April.[61]

The four specialists—from Australia, Spain, Sweden and Switzerland—made a fact-finding visit to Iran from 13 to 19 March and submitted a joint report to the Secretary-General on 21 March. In carrying out their task, they adopted several approaches, including interviews with government officials, visits to the war zone to examine evidence and to collect samples for examination in specialized laboratories located in Europe, and clinical examinations of patients allegedly exposed to a toxic-agent attack. In their report, the specialists elaborated on the munitions, as well as chemical and medical aspects of the problem. The results of the laboratory analyses and clinical examinations were reported in a number of appendices.

The specialists unanimously concluded that chemical weapons in the form of aerial bombs had been used in the areas they inspected in Iran, and that the types of chemical agents used were bis-(2-chlorethyl)-sulfide, also known as mustard gas, and ethyl N, N-dimethylphosphoroamidocyanidate, a nerve agent known as Tabun. They added that the extent to which those chemical agents had been used could not be determined within the time and resources available to them.

By a letter dated 27 March,[62] Iraq said that it had no comment on the report, that it had not used such weapons, and that the possibility could not be ruled out of Iran's fabricating circumstances aimed at diverting attention from the need to halt the war. The United Nations Secretariat, in complying for a second time with Iran's request on minor aspects of the conflict—the first being the investigation of bombing of civilian targets in 1983[7]—had disregarded Iraq's repeated request for a mission to investigate treatment of POWs in the two countries and allowed Iran to exploit the Secretary-General's role for propaganda purposes. Iraq hoped the United Nations and the Secretary-General would give priority to ending the conflict, and reiterated that it was Iran which had so far refused to co-operate in such efforts.

The Ministers for Foreign Affairs of the 10 EEC States members, in a 27 March statement,[63] expressed distress at, and condemned, the alleged use of chemical weapons in the conflict, hoped that each of the parties would agree to comply with Security Council resolutions, and expressed their readiness to support the Secretary-General in restoring peace.

SECURITY COUNCIL CONSIDERATION (March)

The Security Council met on 30 March to consider the situation between Iran and Iraq, and the President, on behalf of Council members, made the statement below:[64]

Meeting number. SC 2524.

"The members of the Security Council, having considered again the question entitled 'The situation between Iran and Iraq', and greatly concerned about the conflict which endangers international peace and security in the region, have taken note of the report of the specialists[59] appointed by the Secretary-General to investigate allegations by the Islamic Republic of Iran concerning the use of chemical weapons.

"They note with particular concern the unanimous conclusions of the specialists that chemical weapons have been used. Furthermore, they express their grave concern about all reported violations in the conflict of the rules of international law and of the principles and rules of international conduct accepted by the world community to prevent or alleviate the human suffering of warfare and affirm strongly the conclusion of the Secretary-General that these humanitarian concerns can only be fully satisfied by putting an end to the tragic conflict that continues to deplete the precious human resources of Iran and Iraq.

"The members of the Council:

"—strongly condemn the use of chemical weapons reported by the mission of specialists;

"—reaffirm the need to abide strictly by the provisions of the Geneva Protocol of 1925 for the prohibition of the use in war of asphyxiating, poisonous or other gases and of bacteriological methods of warfare;

"—call on the States concerned scrupulously to adhere to the obligations flowing from their accession to the Geneva Protocol of 1925;

"—condemn all violations of international humanitarian law and urge both parties to observe the generally recognized principles and rules of international humanitarian law which are applicable to armed conflicts and their obligations under international conventions designed to prevent or alleviate the human suffering of warfare;

"—recall relevant resolutions of the Security Council, renew urgently their calls for the strict observance of a cease-fire and for a peaceful solution of the conflict and call upon all Governments concerned to cooperate fully with the Council in its efforts to bring about conditions leading to a peaceful settlement of the conflict in conformity with the principles of justice and international law;

"—appreciate the mediation efforts of the Secretary-General and request him to continue his efforts with the parties concerned, with a view to achieving a comprehensive, just and honourable settlement acceptable to both sides; and

"—decide to keep the situation between Iran and Iraq under close review."

Communications (April/May). Communications in April/May concerned the protection of victims in international armed conflicts, allegations of possible Israeli attacks against Iraq, further charges of attacks on civilian targets and of chemical-weapons use, allegations of killing of prisoners and security in the Gulf region.

On 2 April,[65] Iran quoted article 35 of Additional Protocol I to the Geneva Conventions of 12 August 1949, relating, among other things, to the prohibition of the use of such methods or means of warfare intended or likely to cause severe damage to the natural environment. In December 1983, Iraq had challenged the existence of a convention on the safety of the environment.[66]

Iraq on 10 April[67] said there was an intensive campaign against Iraq in Western news media, similar to that preceding the 1981 Israeli aggression against Iraq's nuclear installations.[68] Asserting that Israel supplied the Iranian régime with its weapons and strove to prolong and exploit the war, it called on the Security Council to deter Israel from intensifying tension.

Iraq submitted details of alleged Iranian shelling of civilian areas inside Iraq's territory from 11 to 30 March,[69] 1 to 17 April,[70] 18 to 24 April[71] and 29 April to 15 May;[72] it reiterated its call for effective international supervision to protect the civilian areas from attack, adding that the United Nations was the only body capable of ensuring

such arrangements. Iran charged Iraqi attacks on civilian targets on 24 and 25 April,[73] 7 May[74] and 15 May.[75]

A listing, accompanied by photographs and a map, relating to the alleged Iraqi use of chemical weapons against Iran between 1980 and 5 January 1984 was submitted by Iran,[76] which renewed charges of such use on four occasions in March.[77] By a letter of 10 May,[78] Iran transmitted a 30 April letter from its Minister for Foreign Affairs, thanking the Secretary-General for having dispatched a mission to investigate chemical-weapons use and asserting that the Security Council had not taken action to stop Iraq from further use of such weapons; it demanded that specific steps be taken to stop deliveries and sale of such weapons to Iraq.

On 24 May,[79] Iraq charged that Iran had executed, on 15 March, 50 Iraqi soldiers taken prisoner; the United Nations, it added, should compel the Iranian authorities to abide by international obligations and end its crimes against Iraqi POWs.

Iran wrote on 11 May[80] that Iraq in recent months had resorted to attacking vessels belonging to other countries in order to internationalize the war, and that the United Nations should take immediate measures to contain that new development. On 25 May,[81] Iran said that, while it had allocated considerable resources and manpower to guarantee the freedom and security of navigation in the Persian Gulf and the flow of oil exports from the region, allegations of its having hit 2 or 3 vessels had brought criticism against it, when Iraq had hit 71. Some States in the area and beyond provided financial and material support and encouraged Iraq to threaten commercial shipping in the Gulf; Iran would not permit the Gulf to be closed to it and to be used by others against it. It warned the Security Council against becoming a party to the ongoing conspiracy.

Iraq replied on 27 May[82] that recent developments in the Arabian Gulf region were occasioned not by any new Iraqi movements but primarily by blatant and unjustified Iranian aggression against Kuwaiti and Saudi Arabian vessels far from the war-operations zone. While Iraq had declared a strictly delimited zone of military operations and had warned of the consequences of dispatching vessels there, Iran had decided to strike at random against vessels in neutral waters and neither approaching nor leaving Iraqi ports. Iraq struck against vessels entering or leaving Iranian ports and tightened its blockade of Iranian ports as a preventive and defensive measure, since Iran had prevented free navigation in Iraqi territorial waters and Iraqi ports.

Norway, on 22 May,[83] expressed regret that ships had been attacked in international waters outside the declared war zone, and stated that free and safe navigation should be secured in the area for international shipping. Democratic Yemen, in a 30 May statement,[84] expressed concern at the developments in the Gulf and accused the United States of using them as a pretext for adding a large number of warships and aircraft-carriers to its fleet with a view to military intervention aimed at destabilizing the countries of the Gulf region.

SECURITY COUNCIL ACTION (June)

On 21 May, Bahrain, Kuwait, Oman, Qatar, Saudi Arabia and the United Arab Emirates[85] requested that the Security Council meet urgently to consider what they called the Iranian aggressions on the freedom of navigation to and from the ports of their countries.

Accordingly, the Council convened on 25 May. Bahrain, Djibouti, Ecuador, the Federal Republic of Germany, Japan, Jordan, Kuwait, Liberia, Mauritania, Morocco, Oman, Panama, Qatar, Saudi Arabia, Senegal, Somalia, the Sudan, Tunisia, Turkey, the United Arab Emirates and Yemen were invited, at their request, to participate without the right to vote. The Secretary-General of the League of Arab States was invited to participate, at Kuwait's request,[86] under rule 39 of the Council's provisional rules of procedure.[a]

On 1 June, following consideration of the matter at five meetings, the Council adopted resolution 552(1984).

The Security Council,

Having considered the letter dated 21 May 1984 from the representatives of Bahrain, Kuwait, Oman, Qatar, Saudi Arabia and the United Arab Emirates complaining against Iranian attacks on commercial ships en route to and from the ports of Kuwait and Saudi Arabia,

Noting that Member States pledged to live together in peace with one another as good neighbours in accordance with the Charter of the United Nations,

Reaffirming the obligations of Member States with respect to the principles and purposes of the Charter,

Reaffirming also that all Member States are obliged to refrain in their international relations from the threat or use of force against the territorial integrity or political independence of any State,

Taking into consideration the importance of the Gulf region to international peace and security and its vital role to the stability of the world economy,

Deeply concerned over the recent attacks on commercial ships en route to and from the ports of Kuwait and Saudi Arabia,

Convinced that these attacks constitute a threat to the safety and stability of the area and have serious implications for international peace and security,

1. *Calls upon* all States to respect, in accordance with international law, the right of free navigation;

2. *Reaffirms* the right of free navigation in international waters and sea lanes for shipping en route to and from all ports and installations of the littoral States that are not parties to the hostilities;

3. *Calls upon* all States to respect the territorial integrity of the States that are not parties to the hostilities and to exercise the utmost restraint and to refrain from any act which may lead to a further escalation and widening of the conflict;

4. *Condemns* the recent attacks on commercial ships en route to and from the ports of Kuwait and Saudi Arabia;

5. *Demands* that such attacks should cease forthwith and that there should be no interference with ships en route to and from States that are not parties to the hostilities;

6. *Decides*, in the event of non-compliance with the present resolution, to meet again to consider effective measures that are commensurate with the gravity of the situation in order to ensure the freedom of navigation in the area;

7. *Requests* the Secretary-General to report on the progress of the implementation of the present resolution;

8. *Decides* to remain seized of the matter.

Security Council resolution 552(1984)

1 June 1984   Meeting 2546   13-0-2

6-nation draft (S/16594).
Sponsors: Bahrain, Kuwait, Oman, Qatar, Saudi Arabia, United Arab Emirates.
Meeting numbers. SC 2541-2543, 2545, 2546.

Vote in Council as follows:

In favour: China, Egypt, France, India, Malta, Netherlands, Pakistan, Peru, Ukrainian SSR, USSR, United Kingdom, United States, Upper Volta.
Against: None.
Abstaining: Nicaragua, Zimbabwe.

Explaining its vote, India said the Council should focus on defusing tensions and preventing a widening of the conflict between Iran and Iraq and the possible intervention of outside Powers. It felt that the draft, while not explicit enough, amounted to an unequivocal and categorical affirmation of the principle of freedom of navigation. The language of paragraphs 3 and 4, India added, should not be interpreted as condoning other attacks against commercial shipping in the region; on the whole, the draft could have dealt also with other aspects aimed at ending the conflict. Malta and the Upper Volta said the issue of freedom of commercial navigation could be kept separate from the main collective efforts for an early cessation of hostilities under the Council's auspices with simultaneous mediation to secure a just and honourable peace; Malta added that the restrictive formulations in paragraphs 2 through 4 could not be interpreted to derogate from the universally accepted norms of international law. The Upper Volta said its positive vote should not be interpreted as indicating a stand on the conflict. China also stated it took a strictly neutral position with regard to the conflict, and its positive vote was consistent with the principle that the right

---

[a]Rule 39 of the Council's provisional rules of procedure states: "The Security Council may invite members of the Secretariat or other persons, whom it considers competent for the purpose, to supply it with information or to give other assistance in examining matters within its competence."

to freedom of navigation on the high seas and in international sea lanes should be guaranteed, and that ships of non-belligerent parties must not come under attack. Egypt voted in favour in the hope that the resolution would contribute to ending the escalation of the conflict; it envisaged continuous efforts, both within and outside the United Nations, to create conditions conducive to a cease-fire in an impartial context. Pakistan supported as legitimate the concerns of the text's sponsors, and called also for a speedy negotiated settlement of the conflict. The Netherlands, while welcoming the text's call for respect for the territorial integrity of the littoral States not party to the conflict, felt the Council could have spoken more clearly on the need to end all hostilities in the Gulf; the right of free navigation, in paragraph 1, should not be interpreted selectively.

Zimbabwe said the Council should have appealed to both parties to end the war and to respect the right of free navigation and commerce in international waters; it abstained because it felt the text had failed to take an even-handed approach to the wider issue of the war. Nicaragua regretted that the Council had not fully reiterated the principles of free navigation and commerce and free transit and safety on the seas for all countries and in all situations; further the text should have reiterated the respect for the territorial integrity of all States, so as to prevent foreign Powers from intervening directly in Iran or Iraq.

In the Council debate, Kuwait said the question of Iran's attacks on its tankers had been taken to the Gulf Co-operation Council and to the League of Arab States, before being brought to the Security Council. Iran's aggressive behaviour, it said, was aimed, among other things, at inducing certain Powers with known objectives and interests to become parties to the dispute. The countries of the Gulf Co-operation Council, in bringing the case to the Security Council, were trying to avert complications that could lead to a direct confrontation between several Powers at the expense of the independence and the interests of the peoples in the Gulf region; unrest in the region, including a breach of the freedom of navigation, could have global implications. Similar remarks were made by Bahrain, Oman, Qatar, Saudi Arabia and the United Arab Emirates. Saudi Arabia called the attacks calculated and intentional, and rejected what it said was Iran's policy to attack a third party as a retaliation for Iraq's attacks on Iranian targets.

The United States said the acceleration of attacks against shipping in the Gulf threatened not only the safety of the non-belligerent States in the region but the world economic situation as well. The Netherlands said the matter before the Council affected the vital interests not only of the Gulf littoral States but of the whole world; in the past three years more than 60 ships—two thirds of which were commercial vessels from nations not involved in the war—had been attacked in the Gulf.

France asserted that at issue were two different matters—the Iran-Iraq conflict and unwarranted violation of the legitimate rights and interests of third States. Pakistan said, as did many other speakers, that the most recent attacks on Kuwaiti and Saudi ships represented a new dimension in the escalating conflict, threatening to disrupt the global economy and bringing about direct super-Power involvement in a conflict hitherto confined to the region. Egypt also feared that the prolongation of the conflict could destabilize the region and invite foreign intervention. The USSR said the countries in the region were threatened by the United States attempt to exploit the situation in order to impose upon them *diktat* and hegemony in the guise of military co-operation; strict observance of the principle of freedom of navigation was in the interests of all States. The United Kingdom said the attacks complained of were in clear breach of international law, and added that the Gulf should be insulated from the Iran-Iraq conflict and that the principle of freedom of navigation should be reasserted.

Of non-Council members participating in the debate, Oman saw no justification for Iran's attacks on vessels proceeding to and from the ports of States not parties to the conflict, just because Iraq had blockaded Iranian ports and attacked vessels sailing to and from them. Yemen said the Iranian aggression against the tankers should be condemned; the war had extended beyond the borders of Iran and Iraq because the Council had failed to assume its responsibilities. Bahrain and Djibouti feared Iran's acts would lead to the internationalization of the conflict. Similar views were expressed by Tunisia, which stated that the Council should work for a solution assuring dignity and honour for both belligerents. Jordan said Iran's current military actions undermined the neutrality of the Gulf and appeared aimed at stifling the Gulf States economically with the ultimate end of destabilizing them. Senegal said the Council should uphold the freedom of navigation, call for the cessation of hostilities and the continuation of mediation efforts, and request the belligerents to respect the territorial integrity of the other coastal States. Ecuador spoke in similar vein. Morocco, the Sudan and Tunisia added that the unwarranted aggression destabilized the international economy and obstructed the efforts of the developing countries to achieve progress and development. Somalia said the widening of the conflict in a region of crucial importance for world peace and economic stability carried serious consequences such as the danger of great-Power confrontation and intervention. Mauritania also felt it was imperative to discourage the repetition of hostile acts in a region of vital strategic importance. The United Arab Emirates added that the Council should, therefore, act decisively to avoid further deterioration of the situation. Jordan, as well as the Secretary-General of the League of Arab States, shared those views. Panama expressed indignation over the fact that ships flying its flag had been victims, since May 1981, of armed attacks in the Persian Gulf region, and appealed to the parties to the conflict to refrain from further such acts. Liberia expressed similar views. Japan stressed the importance of preventing the conflict from spreading to other parts of the region and beyond, and also appealed to both parties to respect the right of safe navigation in the Gulf, as did the Federal Republic of Germany and Turkey.

Communications (June-December). On 6 June,[87] Iran protested that Security Council resolution 552(1984) had given Iraq a licence for further aggression. It alleged that Iraq's 5 June bombarding of civilian targets in Baneh had, as at the latest count, killed 400 civilians and injured over 200; in view of the magnitude of the crime, 6 June was declared a national day of mourning. Iran warned that the Council, if it failed to take immediate action, must again share responsibility for the crimes Iraq perpetrated under its patronage.

Iraq submitted on 6 June[88] details of alleged Iranian attacks on civilian targets between 16 and 30 May, again urging the Secretary-General to develop international supervision to protect civilian areas from shelling. Iraq reported on 7 June[89] that, in reply to an Iranian statement of 5 June threatening an air and ground attack against 11 named Iraqi towns, it had declared its intention to reciprocate against 15 named Iranian towns. Subsequently, Iraq[90] reported Iranian attacks on the named towns and on others, as did Iran[91] in regard to Iraqi attacks.

On 9 June,[92] the Secretary-General expressed to the Presidents of Iran and Iraq profound distress over the heavy civilian casualties caused by the 5 June aerial attack on Baneh, as had been confirmed by ICRC, and the subsequent retaliatory and counter-retaliatory attacks on towns in both countries. He called on both Governments to make a solemn commitment to him to end, and in the future refrain from initiating, deliberate military attacks on purely civilian population centres. He appealed for responses by 1200 hours GMT on 11 June, with the declarations to be made effective at 0001 hours GMT on 12 June; he added that, once such declarations were received, he was prepared, if necessary, to initiate steps to introduce verification measures.

Iran and Iraq responded on 10 June. Iran[93] said it had had to retaliate only as a last resort in the last few months; ICRC had confirmed that recent Iranian retaliatory attacks began only after the 5 June attack on Baneh. Similarly, the tension in the Persian Gulf was heightened when the international forums reacted irresponsibly to repeated Iraqi aggressions on neutral vessels. To show its good faith, Iran responded positively to the Secretary-General's proposal, conditional on the total ending of Iraqi bombardment of Iranian cities. The Secretary-General's proposal would be useful only when it was adequately sanctioned by measures to identify violations through immediate dispatch of missions.

Iraq[94] said Iran had persistently denied having bombed Iraq's frontier towns and other civilian targets, even after verification by a United Nations mission. Iraq on 5 June had bombed not the civilian targets in Baneh, but a camp where a large body of Iranian forces had been concentrated in preparation for further aggression. It accepted the Secretary-General's proposal, on condition that Iran was also committed, that effective arrangements would be made for supervising the implementation of the commitments, and that other measures would also be taken, such as agreements between the parties not to place military concentrations in or near towns so as to prevent intermingling during military operations.

The Secretary-General, in similar letters of 11 June to Iran[95] and Iraq,[96] acknowledged with appreciation acceptance of his proposal, and informed them that he had instructed Diego Cordovez, Under-Secretary-General for Special Political Affairs, to contact their Permanent Representatives regarding verification measures.

On 12[97] and 15 June,[98] Iraq alleged attacks by Iran on several Iraqi civilian centres on 10 and 11 June, while Iran[99] reported similar attacks by Iraq on 11 June. On 13 June,[100] Iraq charged that Iran was continuing to shell towns, and stated that it was important to take effective measures to monitor compliance with the undertaking proposed by the Secretary-General.

The Secretary-General informed the President of the Security Council on 14 June[101] that understandings had been reached with Iran and Iraq regarding compliance verification and that he intended, as an immediate step, to set up simultaneously, as at 15 June, two teams, each consisting of three military officers drawn from the United Nations Truce Supervision Organization and one senior Secretariat official. Each inspection team would be ready to proceed to the respective country as soon as so requested by its Government and report on compliance to the Secretary-General, who, in turn, would keep the Council informed of the findings as required and in a timely manner. The Council President informed the Secretary-General the following day[102] that the Council members, with whom he had discussed the matter, agreed to the proposed measures.

On 14 June,[103] Iran said that Iraq's making its commitment contingent on residential areas not being areas of military concentration was an excuse to renew attacks on Iranian civilian centres; it was, therefore, incumbent on the United Nations to commit Iraq to unconditional implementation of the Secretary-General's humanitarian appeal. His appeal would succeed provided reports on possible violations did not meet the same destiny as the two earlier reports on investigations of attacks on civilian areas and use of chemical weapons.

Iraq[104] alleged Iranian shelling of civilian centres on 16 June in violation of the agreement, requested speedy dispatch of the verification team and warned that continued Iranian violation would force it to respond in the same way. On 19 June,[105] Iran alleged Iraqi shellings of civilian targets on 14 and 17 June. Iraq alleged on 21 June[106] that Iran had violated the agreement three times in less than 10 days, with the latest attacks on civilian targets taking place on 20 June; it also reported that a United Nations observer team was already in Iraq, but that Iran had refused to receive such a team because it intended to use the frontier for launching attacks. On 27 June,[107] Iraq submitted details of what was said to be an assemblage of numerous military units in Iranian cities, reiterating that Iran used civilian population centres for military purposes. Iran submitted, on 28 June,[108] a list of 11 incidents, between 14 and 26 June, of alleged Iraqi attacks on civilian targets.

By a note verbale of 26 June,[109] the Secretary-General informed the States parties to the Geneva Conventions of 1949 of the commitments made by Iran and Iraq to end deliberate attacks on civilian areas. At the same time, he expressed his continuing concern that serious infringements of the terms of the Conventions could bring into discredit those rules of law and universal principles relating to the treatment of POWs, and urged the States parties to give serious attention to the call by ICRC to serve as Protecting Powers. He hoped Governments would renew their determination to ensure respect for the Conventions as indispensable instruments in mitigating the effects of war.

On 29 June,[110] the Secretary-General addressed a message to the Presidents of Iran and Iraq, expressing concern over allegations that civilian population centres were being used for concentration of military forces; such actions, if true, violated the spirit of his appeal and basic standards of warfare. Deploring the use of chemical weapons, as substantiated by the specialists' mission in March (see p. 232), and expressing concern over alarming indications of the recurrent use of such weapons, the Secretary-General called on both Governments, in order to alleviate the inhumanity of warfare, to declare to him within three days that each undertook a solemn commitment not to use chemical weapons.

Iran had, on 28 June,[111] presented a table containing information on 24 chemical attacks allegedly made by Iraq between March and May. Welcoming the Secretary-General's message of 29 June (see above), Iran stated on 2 July[112] that it had never retaliated, despite Iraq's resort to chemical weapons, and that it was fully committed not to use such weapons. In addition, Iran asserted that the Iraqi claim of concentration of military forces in civilian areas was merely an excuse to bombard those areas. It transmitted, by a letter of 5 July,[113] a 3 July news dispatch originating at Teheran, alleging that in January United States military forces had delivered 2 tons of solidified gas to Iraq. By a 16 July letter,[114] the United States rejected Iran's accusations as totally false and groundless and declared that it had never supplied Iraq with chemical-warfare agents or components. On 3 August,[115] Iran asked the Secretary-General whether Iraq had responded to his month-old appeal regarding non-use of chemical weapons.

On 16 July,[116] Iran made further allegations of Iraqi attacks on cities, between 27 June and 6 July; for its part, it had adhered to the pledge of 12 June.

Other communications during the period included a charge by Iran on 7 June that Saudi Arabian fighters had shot down an Iranian air force plane over international waters and had taken the pilot to Saudi Arabia;[117] a Kuwait charge that Iranian aircraft had attacked a Kuwaiti tanker on 10 June at the entrance to the Gulf;[118] a statement on the conflict by the London Economic Summit (7-9 June), submitted by the United Kingdom;[119] and a "Baghdad Call for Peace", adopted by the International Conference on the Impact of the Gulf War on World Peace and Security (Baghdad, 8-10 July) and submitted by Iraq.[120]

On 30 August,[121] Iraq transmitted a declaration made by its Revolutionary Command Council on the release of Iranian POWs without *quid pro quo* on the occasion of Id al-Adha; they would be given the choice of returning to Iran or seeking asylum in any State consenting to receive them. Iraq added that it had invited the families of young Iranian prisoners to visit them in Iraq or any other place agreed upon, under ICRC auspices, but Iran had rejected the initiative.

In a note issued on 19 September,[122] the Secretary-General said the United Nations compliance-verification teams had been in place at Baghdad and Teheran since 20 and 26 June, respectively. On 17 September, the team at Baghdad carried out an inspection in response to the first request from Iraq to verify an attack which had allegedly taken place in the village of Abu Mughira on 12 September, approximately 20 kilometres south-east of Basra and said to be about 15 kilometres south-west of the front line. The team reported that a rocket of unknown calibre had struck in the village from a north-easterly direction four to six days prior to inspection; it concluded that the damage was caused by a lone or stray projectile and was therefore unable to say that it was a deliberately targeted attack.

Iran expressed confidence, on 18 September,[123] that the United Nations investigation team would point to Iran's full observance of the 12 June agreement; on 29 October,[124] it declared that the report of the Baghdad team had shown the baselessness of the Iraqi allegations. On 19 September,[125] it submitted a listing of what it said were more than 70 Iraqi violations of the 12 June agreement between 14 June and 8 September; details of 33 further alleged Iraqi violations between 10 September and 19 October were reported on 31 October.[126] It also submitted, on 31 December,[127] the names of 18 civilians said to have been killed in Iraqi shellings of residential areas between 27 May and 22 September, as well as details on 82 civilians injured in Abadan and Khorramshahr by Iraq's long-range artillery.

Iraq submitted, on 22 October,[128] details of 39 alleged Iranian violations between 16 June and 13 October, and charged, in a 25 October letter,[129] that Iran had opened fire on 10 October on Iraqi captives held in an Iranian camp and requested the Secretary-General to send a mission to investigate. Iran, on 7 November,[130] submitted an ICRC report which it said showed the baselessness of the Iraqi allegations. According to the report, a dispute between two Iraqi POWs triggered a camp-wide uproar, with POWs subsequently storming the camp exit; after launching tear-gas bombs and shooting in the air, the guards began firing into the crowd. On 11 October, an ICRC delegate and a medical delegate were allowed to examine three corpses and 35 wounded POWs; the corpses showed wounds on the head, caused by blows. By a letter of 7 November,[131] Iran welcomed the Secretary-General's decision to send a mission to Iran and Iraq to inquire into the concerns of both Governments regarding the situation of POWs and civilian detainees; Iran would provide full co-operation with the mission as of 15 November.

Iraq[132] submitted a 23 November statement of the ICRC President addressed to all permanent representatives at Geneva, in which he stated that, in view of the repeated and systematic violations by Iran of the third Geneva Convention relative to the Treatment of Prisoners of War, ICRC could not remain silent and jeopardize the physical and moral survival of thousands of men and future respect for humanitarian law. ICRC, which by itself had not been able in three years to obtain respect of humanitarian law in the Iraq-Iran conflict and especially to bring Iran to respect the third Geneva Convention, needed Governments' help regarding some 50,000 Iraqi POWs being held in Iran. When ICRC submitted a report on the 10 October incident to the authorities of Iraq and Iran, as was customary, Iran suspended all ICRC activities on its territory, denying for the third time in three years ICRC access to Iraqi prisoners, and undertook a slander campaign. The 10 October incident was not an isolated one, with other violent confrontations resulting in numerous deaths and injuries. ICRC's efforts to ensure protection of POWs in Iran would fail unless the Iranian authorities were brought to realize that it was the political will of the community of States to see humanitarian law observed, the statement concluded.

On 13 November,[133] Iran drew attention to a report in a Kuwaiti newspaper which was said to quote an Iraqi minister in September stating that Iraq would use chemical weapons if necessary.

Other communications relating to the conflict included: a communiqué of the co-ordinating meeting of Ministers for Foreign Affairs of the Organization of the Islamic Conference (New York, 4 October),[134] reaffirming decisions adopted on the war by previous Islamic Conferences; a communiqué of the Meeting of Ministers for Foreign Affairs and Heads of Delegation of Non-Aligned Countries to the General Assembly at its 1984 session (New York, 1-5 October),[135] reiterating the need to implement the principles of non-alignment with regard to the conflict; and a communiqué of the Supreme Council of the Co-operation Council for the Arab States of the Gulf (fifth session, Kuwait, 27-29 November),[136] noting the threat which the conflict posed to the region and calling on Iran to join in devising a solution.

Report of the Secretary-General. In a report of 31 December,[137] prepared in pursuance of Security Council resolution 552(1984), the Secretary-General submitted details of incidents regarding shipping in the Gulf since 1630 hours GMT on 1 June, as reported in response to his request by Governments and the International Maritime Organization. Of the 13 States responding, 6 (Greece, Japan, Kuwait, Switzerland, Turkey, United Kingdom) provided information on specific incidents, 2 made observations on the resolution's objectives or other aspects of the conflict, and the remaining 5 replied that they had no incidents to report. The Secretary-General also reported that he had received a telegram in October from the General Secretary of the International Transport Workers' Federation stating that, as of 10 July, 112 vessels had been hit by missiles since the start of the conflict, resulting in the death of scores of seafarers and injury to many more. In a joint telegram on 15 November, the Chairman of the International Chamber of Shipping and the President of the International Shipping Federation reported on human and material losses suffered, and appealed for international efforts to end the attacks on merchant shipping.

GENERAL ASSEMBLY ACTION

At its resumed thirty-eighth session in September 1984, the Assembly adopted decision 38/460 without vote, on an oral proposal by its President.

Consequences of the prolongation of the armed conflict between Iran and Iraq

At its 106th plenary meeting, on 17 September 1984, the General Assembly decided to include in the draft agenda of its thirty-ninth session the item entitled "Consequences of the prolongation of the armed conflict between Iran and Iraq".

General Assembly decision 38/460

Adopted without vote

Oral proposal by President; agenda item 138.

By decision 39/456 of 18 December, the Assembly decided to consider the item, among others, at its resumed thirty-ninth session at a date to be announced.

In November, Iran submitted to the Assembly's First Committee a draft resolution entitled "Preventive measures against the further use of chemical weapons",[138] by which the Assembly would have strongly condemned the use of such weapons reported by the specialists and requested the Secretary-General to continue his efforts in preventing, investigating and reporting to the Assembly on their further use.

Iraq submitted amendments to the draft which, among other things, mentioned humanitarian concerns that could be satisfied only by putting an end to the conflict between Iran and Iraq.[139] By the amendments, the Assembly would also have expressed its appreciation of the Secretary-General's efforts to mediate that conflict, welcomed that one of the parties had already expressed its willingness to settle the conflict by peaceful means, and called on the other to do likewise.

Subsequently, Iran submitted a revised text and Iraq, further amendments, both seeking to underline their divergent positions on the subject. At a still later stage, Iran withdrew the revised version and requested that action be taken on the original draft; in view of that request, Iraq stated that

it maintained the original amendments. Iraq then moved to adjourn the debate on the draft resolution and the amendments, and the First Committee approved that motion by a recorded vote of 34 to 2 (Iran, Libyan Arab Jamahiriya), with 68 abstentions.

Other action. The Fourth General Conference of the United Nations Industrial Development Organization (Vienna, Austria, 2-19 August 1984) adopted, by 44 votes to 1, with 43 abstentions, a resolution calling for a cessation of the war in the Gulf.[140]

The Commission on Human Rights, by a 12 March resolution on exploitation of child labour, called on Iran to cease using children in its armed forces, especially in time of war. In related action, both the Economic and Social Council (decision 1984/138) and the Commission on Human Rights took action on the human rights situation in Iran (see ECONOMIC AND SOCIAL QUESTIONS, Chapter XVIII).

REFERENCES

[1]A/38/771-S/16259. [2]A/38/776-S/16289. [3]A/38/779-S/16300. [4]A/38/783-S/16332. [5]S/16260. [6]S/16314. [7]YUN 1983, p. 237. [8]S/16331. [9]S/16315. [10]A/39/73. [11]A/38/784-S/16335. [12]S/16310. [13]S/16316. [14]S/16338. [15]S/16337. [16]A/38/785 (S/16342). [17]YUN 1983, p. 239, SC res. 540(1983), 31 Oct. 1983. [18]S/16340. [19]S/16352. [20]A/38/791 (S/16354). [21]A/39/788-S/16348. [22]A/38/786-S/16344. [23]A/38/787-S/16345. [24]A/38/790-S/16350. [25]A/38/789-S/16349. [26]S/16356. [27]S/16346. [28]S/16361. [29]S/16363. [30]S/16364. [31]S/16369. [32]S/16370. [33]S/16362. [34]S/16372. [35]S/16375. [36]S/16384. [37]S/16374. [38]S/16387. [39]A/38/794-S/16358. [40]S/16378. [41]S/16380. [42]S/16388. [43]YUN 1983, p. 241. [44]A/39/127 (S/16397). [45]S/16408. [46]S/16407. [47]A/39/132-S/16416. [48]S/16446. [49]S/16447. [50]S/16381. [51]A/39/134-S/16418. [52]S/16403. [53]S/16400. [54]A/39/123-S/16389. [55]A/38/796-S/16405. [56]A/39/131-S/16414 & Corr.1. [57]S/16415. [58]A/39/133-S/16417. [59]S/16433. [60]A/39/210. [61]A/39/215-S/16508. [62]S/16438. [63]A/39/161-S/16456. [64]S/16454. [65]A/38/798-S/16465. [66]YUN 1983, p. 242. [67]A/38/801-S/16476. [68]YUN 1981, p. 275. [69]A/38/802-S/16478. [70]A/38/810-S/16502. [71]A/38/811-S/16532. [72]A/38/815-S/16580. [73]S/16513. [74]S/16545. [75]S/16579. [76]A/39/182-S/16481. [77]S/16498. [78]A/39/266-S/16572. [79]S/16583. [80]S/16567. [81]S/16585. [82]S/16590. [83]S/16586. [84]S/16595. [85]S/16574. [86]S/16582. [87]S/16604. [88]A/38/817 (S/16606). [89]S/16607. [90]S/16613. [91]S/16616. [92]S/16611. [93]S/16609. [94]S/16610. [95]S/16614. [96]S/16615. [97]S/16620. [98]S/16631. [99]S/16621. [100]S/16624. [101]S/16627. [102]S/16628. [103]S/16630 & Corr.1. [104]S/16632. [105]S/16636. [106]S/16638. [107]S/16649. [108]S/16651. [109]S/16648. [110]S/16663. [111]A/39/333-S/16652. [112]S/16664. [113]S/16656. [114]S/16674. [115]A/39/374-S/16690. [116]S/16679. [117]S/16608. [118]S/16618. [119]A/38/819-S/16623. [120]A/38/832 & Corr.1. [121]A/38/833-S/16729. [122]S/16750 & Corr.1. [123]S/16753. [124]S/16806. [125]S/16751. [126]S/16808. [127]S/16878. [128]S/16793. [129]S/16799. [130]A/39/639-S/16820. [131]S/16821. [132]A/39/693-S/16842. [133]A/39/651-S/16827. [134]A/39/585-S/16783. [135]A/39/560-S/16773. [136]A/39/853. [137]S/16877 & Add.1. [138]A/C.1/39/L.46 & Rev.1. [139]A/C.1/39/L.75 & Rev.1. [140]ID/CONF.5/46 & Corr.1 (res. 13).

Chapter VIII

Mediterranean

Several political issues relating to the Mediterranean region were before the United Nations in 1984: the Cyprus question; the Libyan Arab Jamahiriya–United States dispute; and the strengthening of regional security and co-operation.

The Security Council twice extended the stationing of the United Nations Peace-keeping Force in Cyprus (UNFICYP), by resolutions 553(1984) and 559(1984). In a May decision on Cyprus (resolution 550(1984)), the Council condemned all secessionist actions, including the purported exchange of ambassadors between Turkey and the Turkish Cypriot leadership, declared them illegal and called for their immediate withdrawal, and also called for the transfer of Varosha (Famagusta) to United Nations administration. At the same time, the Council reaffirmed the good offices mandate of the Secretary-General, requested him to undertake new efforts to attain an overall solution to the Cyprus problem and called on all parties to co-operate.

In regard to his good offices mission, the Secretary-General held a number of meetings at various levels throughout the year followed by separate "proximity talks" with leaders of the two communities. In early December, he believed that a draft agreement was ready for submission to a joint high-level meeting at which an agreement could be concluded containing the necessary elements for a comprehensive solution aimed at establishing a Federal Republic of Cyprus. The Secretary-General stressed—in his annual report on the work of the Organization (p. 3)—that he remained essential to communication between the parties.

The Security Council met in March/April at the request of the Libyan Arab Jamahiriya to consider what it said was the deteriorating situation resulting from hostile American acts directed against the Jamahiriya.

Regarding the strengthening of security and co-operation in the Mediterranean region, the General Assembly, by resolution 39/153 adopted in December, reaffirmed the need for further efforts to that end while encouraging the intensification of existing forms and the promotion of new forms of co-operation, particularly those aimed at reducing tension and strengthening confidence and security in the region.

Topics related to this chapter. Africa: questions involving the Libyan Arab Jamahiriya. International Court of Justice: continental shelf delimitation (Tunisia/Libyan Arab Jamahiriya, Libyan Arab Jamahiriya/Malta).

Cyprus question

In January 1984, the Secretary-General met with Rauf R. Denktas, the leader of the Turkish Cypriot community, and President Kenan Evren of Turkey, and in February with President Spyros Kyprianou of Cyprus. In March, the Secretary-General gave Mr. Denktas a "scenario" designed to bring about a high-level meeting between the Secretary-General, President Kyprianou and Mr. Denktas.

Mr. Denktas, however, announced his intention to proceed to a "constitutional referendum" and "elections" in the north of the island in 1984, arranging also for the submission of "credentials" for the establishment of diplomatic relations with Turkey. The Secretary-General expressed regret over these developments, saying that they jeopardized his current efforts. The Security Council met in May and condemned all secessionist actions, including the purported exchange of ambassadors between Turkey and the Turkish Cypriot leadership, while requesting the Secretary-General to undertake new efforts to attain an overall solution.

In a new initiative, the Secretary-General met separately with representatives of the two sides at Vienna, Austria, in August and outlined a number of working points as a basis of high-level talks. In late August both sides responded favourably and their leaders were invited to meet with the Secretary-General separately in New York. The first round of these talks—known as "proximity talks"—was held in mid-September and addressed substantive elements with a view to elaborating the Vienna working points into a preliminary agenda and draft agreement to be submitted, as an integrated whole, to a joint high-level meeting. A second round of talks took place in mid-October.

After intensive consultations, the final round took place from late November to early December by which time the Secretary-General felt that the draft agreement was ready for submission to a joint high-level meeting that could conclude an agreement for a comprehensive solution aimed at establishing a Federal Republic of Cyprus.

In the mean time, the Security Council twice, on the recommendation of the Secretary-General, in June and December, unanimously extended the mandate of UNFICYP for a further six months, requesting the Secretary-General to continue his mission of good offices and to keep the Council informed of progress.

The Council, in its May resolution condemning secessionist actions including the purported ambassadorial exchange, had also stated that it considered any attempt to interfere with UNFICYP's status or deployment as contrary to United Nations resolutions. The Council also called for the transfer of the Varosha (Famagusta) area to United Nations administration and stated that attempts to settle any part of that area by people other than its inhabitants were inadmissible.

In December, the General Assembly decided to consider the Cyprus question in 1985.

Throughout 1984, Cyprus and Turkey addressed a number of letters to the Secretary-General. Those from Turkey transmitted letters from the Turkish Cypriot community which were signed by Rauf R. Denktas as "President of the Turkish Republic of Northern Cyprus", by Necati Munir Ertekun as "Minister for Foreign Affairs and Defence" or by Nail Atalay as "representative" of that "Republic".

Communications (January-May). Communications from the parties between January and May concerned such subjects as proposals towards a settlement, incidents along the cease-fire lines, alleged airspace violations, alleged grant of "citizenship" to mainland Turks, Turkish military exercises, the economic embargo, and purported "exchange of ambassadors" between the north and Turkey.

In a 2 February letter,[1] Cyprus stated that Turkey's letter of 22 December 1983[2] contained numerous distortions of fact and out-of-context quotations, intended to persuade the international community that the Turkish invasion of Cyprus had been a so-called peace operation, using the *coup d'état* of 15 July 1974 in Cyprus as a pretext for that invasion.

On 2 January,[3] Mr. Denktas transmitted his proposals, made to the Greek Cypriot side, on the resettlement of Varosha, the opening of Nicosia international airport, missing persons, and a general framework of relations between the two sides for progress towards a final settlement of the Cyprus problem. On 11 January,[4] Cyprus transmitted the Government's official comments of 9 January on those proposals, also calling for the withdrawal of the "declaration of independence" in the north. Also on 11 January,[5] Cyprus drew attention to President Kyprianou's statement on his submission to the Secretary-General of a framework for a settlement of the Cyprus problem.

On 16 January,[6] Mr. Atalay alleged unbecoming behaviour of Greek Cypriot soldiers on the cease-fire lines; on 3 February,[7] Cyprus said those allegations were designed to pre-empt world condemnation of Turkey for the shooting of a Cyprus National Guardsman in December 1983. On 19 April,[8] Mr. Atalay stated that a film on the incidents he had previously mentioned was available and that the UNFICYP Commander had had to intervene to end them.

On 20 January,[9] Cyprus protested and drew attention to extensive military exercises by Turkey in the north, alleging repeated violations of Cyprus airspace. Mr. Atalay on 1 February[10] stated that the exercises had taken place within the boundaries of the northern "Republic" and added that prior written notification had been made to UNFICYP.

Another exchange of letters on 17 February[11] and 9 March[12] concerned allegations by Turkey that Cyprus had mistreated nine Turks evacuated to the island from Lebanon; Cyprus replied that it gave humanitarian assistance without discrimination to all refugees, including the nine.

On 21 February,[13] Cyprus drew attention to the alleged granting of "citizenship" to 7,000 of some 50,000 settlers in the north from Turkey and their organization into a single political party. Mr. Atalay on 15 March[14] termed the allegations an audacious and contrived attempt to hatch up a case against the "Republic". Cyprus responded on 9 April[15] that Mr. Atalay had failed to reply to the particular charge. On 23 April,[16] Mr. Atalay repeated that the statements of the Greek Cypriot leadership on the subject contained the usual unfounded accusations.

On 12 March,[17] Cyprus accused the Turkish side anew of pursuing policies similar to South Africa's policy of bantustanization by its annexation, segregation and other neo-*apartheid* policies in Cyprus (see also p. 138). Refuting the accusations, Mr. Atalay, on 16 April,[18] quoted excerpts from various reports by the Secretary-General, and from British and Greek press reports speaking of the inhuman treatment inflicted on Turkish Cypriots and Turkish Cypriot refugees by Greek Cypriots from 1964 onwards.

On 5 April,[19] Cyprus protested against what it described as provocative military exercises in March by Turkish jet fighters within Cyprus airspace, while Mr. Atalay on 13 April[20] asserted that the exercises were routine, with prior notification to UNFICYP, and that the Cyprus communication was to justify its ongoing arms buildup.

On 17 April,[21] Mr. Atalay protested the Greek Cypriot economic embargo and the combined Greek and Greek Cypriot effort to strangle the Turkish Cypriot people by imposing a total ban on exports from the north to the European Economic Community (EEC). The next day,[22] he forwarded an extract from a speech attributed to the Ambassador of Greece to Cyprus which Mr. Atalay said was regarded by Turkish Cypriots as a call to continue the campaign for *enosis* (union with Greece).

On 19 April,[23] Cyprus drew attention to a 10 April decision in the north to hold a "referendum on a new constitution" in August and "general elections" in November. Cyprus said these were new illegal actions undermining the Secretary-General's efforts. On the same day,[24] Cyprus reported that, on 17 April, Turkey and the north had purportedly exchanged "ambassadors".

In view of what it said were grave developments, Cyprus, on 30 April,[25] called for an urgent meeting of the Security Council (see below). In a letter of 7 May,[26] Mr. Atalay said the exchange of "diplomatic representatives" resulting from "recognition of a new State" could not be a pretext for a Council meeting.

On 29 March,[27] France transmitted declarations adopted two days earlier by the EEC Ministers for Foreign Affairs, including one on Cyprus, reiterating support for the Council's November 1983 resolution[28] as the basis for restoring the territorial integrity and unity of the Republic of Cyprus, regretting Turkey's recognition of the "Turkish Republic of Northern Cyprus", calling for withdrawal of that recognition, and pledging support for the Secretary-General's good offices mission.

Report of the Secretary-General (May). In his report of 1 May,[29] in pursuance of Security Council resolution 544(1983)[30] on continuance of his mission of good offices, the Secretary-General summarized his activities, between November 1983 and May 1984, in particular various communications exchanged with Mr. Denktas and the visit of his Special Representative, Hugo J. Gobbi, to Cyprus in April.

The Secretary-General recalled that Mr. Denktas had, on 2 January 1984, sent a letter regarding certain goodwill measures,[3] while on 9 January President Kyprianou had presented a paper commenting on those proposals,[4] followed by an 11 January paper giving a framework for a comprehensive settlement[5] (see also above).

The Secretary-General met Mr. Denktas on 16 January at Casablanca, Morocco (where the Fourth Islamic Summit Conference was meeting), and gave him a summary of the Greek Cypriot "framework"; the following day he met with President Evren of Turkey, who urged resumption of the intercommunal talks without pre-conditions.

Immediately after these meetings, several elements of a tentative scenario which the Secretary-General was considering were further clarified with Turkish officials; these exchanges continued into March. The exchanges, the Secretary-General stated, gave him reason to feel confident that he could count on the understanding and assistance of the Turkish Government in moving forward.

Meanwhile, on 17 February, the Secretary-General met with President Kyprianou in New York, outlining in general terms his approach aimed at bringing about a high-level meeting leading to resumption of the intercommunal dialogue. President Kyprianou, the Secretary-General said, encouraged him to continue his efforts.

On 6 March, the Turkish Cypriot authorities announced their intention to adopt a flag of their own and the Secretary-General informed both Mr. Denktas and Turkey that such action was difficult to reconcile with his efforts.

The Secretary-General met Mr. Denktas in New York on 16 March and handed him a suggested scenario, aimed at opening the door to a high-level meeting and resumption of the intercommunal dialogue. To facilitate that, the parties would reach an understanding with the Secretary-General to the effect that while he was engaged in his current diplomatic effort: (*a*) there would be no further step to internationalize the Cyprus problem and initiatives under way would not be pursued; (*b*) there would be no follow-up to the 15 November 1983 declaration (of "independence") by the Turkish Cypriots and initiatives under way would not be pursued; (*c*) both sides would make reciprocal commitments to the Secretary-General not to increase qualitatively or quantitatively the military forces on the island, while agreeing to a system of UNFICYP verification inspections; (*d*) the Turkish Cypriot authorities would transfer the Varosha area (as delineated in their proposals of August 1981[31]) to the Secretary-General for placement under interim United Nations administration as part of the buffer zone controlled by UNFICYP, in a transfer phased over six to nine months; and (*e*) the parties would agree to hold a high-level meeting and to reopen the intercommunal dialogue. Regarding Varosha, the Secretary-General stated that since it would become part of the buffer zone, this implied that the process of settlement by the Greek Cypriots would be determined by the Secretary-General and that the area would not revert to the jurisdiction of the Greek Cypriots until a final settlement of the Cyprus problem was reached.

The general terms of the scenario were described to the Foreign Minister of Cyprus at a meeting in New York on 19 and 20 March.

Annexed to the report[29] were letters exchanged between the Secretary-General and Mr. Denktas.

On 30 March, Mr. Denktas gave what he described as an "interim reply" to the scenario and requested certain clarifications, to which the Secretary-General replied the next day.

On 10 April, Mr. Denktas announced that his community intended to conduct a "constitutional referendum" and "elections" in August and November, respectively. In that situation, the Secretary-General asked Mr. Gobbi to make an urgent visit to Cyprus and gave him instructions, including a letter to Mr. Denktas. In that letter, dated 14 April, the Secretary-General said he had been under the impression, after the earlier contacts, including those in Casablanca, that he could count on sympathetic consideration of the scenario by the Turkish Cypriot community. He added that the latest stated intentions of that community would tend to prejudice an essential part of the scenario but he preferred to assume that Mr. Denktas would modify those actions if agreement on the scenario were reached at that time.

On 17 April, ceremonies took place in Ankara and Nicosia, publicly described as being the submission of "credentials" for establishment of diplomatic relations, with the Turkish Cypriot leadership informing Mr. Gobbi that the ceremonies had been arranged long before. The Secretary-General stated that he deeply regretted the ceremonies and had instructed Mr. Gobbi to transmit immediately his great concern over the developments which have placed in jeopardy his current efforts.

On 18 April, Mr. Denktas replied to the 16 March scenario, saying, among other things, that if the Turkish Cypriot side was to refrain from proceeding with the implementation of the natural and legal consequences of its declaration of "independence", then it followed that the Greek Cypriot side should take corresponding action and refrain from falsely asserting that it was the Government of the whole of Cyprus and agree to refrain from all conduct appertaining to such an assumption. He said the principle of equality could be demonstrated either by the Turkish Cypriot side proceeding with the natural and legal consequences of statehood or by the Greek Cypriot side refraining from its assertion.

Regarding Varosha, Mr. Denktas stated that if the Cyprus question were raised in international forums where Turkish Cypriots were not represented or if the Greek Cypriot side did not end all restrictive measures on Turkish Cypriots in trade and other fields at the time of proposed resettlement, one year after United Nations interim administration, then Varosha would revert to Turkish Cypriot jurisdiction.

Mr. Denktas also proposed agreement in principle to reopening the Nicosia international airport for civilian traffic under an interim United Nations administration, with consultations on this matter beginning at the time of the commencement of negotiations for a comprehensive settlement.

On 18 April, Mr. Gobbi met with President Kyprianou, informing him of the situation. He left Nicosia the following day to report to the Secretary-General.

In concluding his report, the Secretary-General said that the developments spoke for themselves and that the Security Council members would wish to give careful thought to the next steps to prevent any further deterioration of the situation. He said that important requirements were maintenance of a continued process of communication and negotiation and continued deployment of UNFICYP. He was prepared to continue his mission of good offices as long as there was unambiguous support for it. The search for a peaceful settlement was vital to the interests of all the people of Cyprus, as well as to wider peace.

SECURITY COUNCIL ACTION (May)

On 30 April,[25] Cyprus requested that the Security Council meet to consider the grave situation in Cyprus caused by the actions of Turkey and take effective measures in accordance with relevant provisions of the Charter of the United Nations for the full implementation of Council resolutions regarding Cyprus.

The Council met nine times between 3 and 11 May. Non-member States invited, at their request, to participate without voting rights were: Afghanistan, Algeria, Antigua and Barbuda, Australia, Bangladesh, Bulgaria, Costa Rica, Cuba, Cyprus, Czechoslovakia, Ecuador, German Democratic Republic, Greece, Guyana, Hungary, Jamaica, Malaysia, Mongolia, Panama, Saint Lucia, Sri Lanka, Syrian Arab Republic, Turkey, Viet Nam, Yugoslavia. Mr. Denktas was invited to participate in accordance with rule 39[a] of the Council's provisional rules of procedure.

On 11 May, the Council adopted resolution 550(1984).

The Security Council,

Having considered the situation in Cyprus at the request of the Government of the Republic of Cyprus,

Having heard the statement made by the President of the Republic of Cyprus,

Taking note of the report of the Secretary-General,

Recalling its resolutions 365(1974), 367(1975), 541(1983) and 544(1983),

Deeply regretting the non-implementation of its resolutions, in particular resolution 541(1983),

Gravely concerned about the further secessionist acts in the occupied part of the Republic of Cyprus which are in violation of resolution 541(1983), namely, the purported exchange of ambassadors between Turkey and the legally invalid "Turkish Republic of Northern

[a]Rule 39 of the Council's provisional rules of procedure states: "The Security Council may invite members of the Secretariat or other persons, whom it considers competent for the purpose, to supply it with information or to give other assistance in examining matters within its competence."

Cyprus" and the contemplated holding of a "constitutional referendum" and "elections", as well as by other actions or threats of actions aimed at further consolidating the purported independent State and the division of Cyprus,

Deeply concerned about recent threats for settlement of Varosha by people other than its inhabitants,

Reaffirming its continuing support for the United Nations Peace-keeping Force in Cyprus,

1. *Reaffirms* its resolution 541(1983) and calls for its urgent and effective implementation;

2. *Condemns* all secessionist actions, including the purported exchange of ambassadors between Turkey and the Turkish Cypriot leadership, declares them illegal and invalid and calls for their immediate withdrawal;

3. *Reiterates* the call upon all States not to recognize the purported State of the "Turkish Republic of Northern Cyprus" set up by secessionist acts and calls upon them not to facilitate or in any way assist the aforesaid secessionist entity;

4. *Calls upon* all States to respect the sovereignty, independence, territorial integrity, unity and non-alignment of the Republic of Cyprus;

5. *Considers* attempts to settle any part of Varosha by people other than its inhabitants as inadmissible and calls for the transfer of that area to the administration of the United Nations;

6. *Considers* any attempts to interfere with the status or the deployment of the United Nations Peace-keeping Force in Cyprus as contrary to the resolutions of the United Nations;

7. *Requests* the Secretary-General to promote the urgent implementation of Security Council resolution 541(1983);

8. *Reaffirms* the mandate of good offices given to the Secretary-General and requests him to undertake new efforts to attain an overall solution to the Cyprus problem in conformity with the principles of the Charter of the United Nations and the provisions for such a settlement laid down in the pertinent United Nations resolutions, including resolution 541(1983) and the present resolution;

9. *Calls upon* all parties to co-operate with the Secretary-General in his mission of good offices;

10. *Decides* to remain seized of the situation with a view to taking urgent and appropriate measures, in the event of non-implementation of resolution 541(1983) and the present resolution;

11. *Requests* the Secretary-General to promote the implementation of the present resolutions and to report thereon to the Security Council as developments require.

Security Council resolution 550(1984)

11 May 1984   Meeting 2539   13-1-1

4-nation draft (S/16550).
Sponsors: India, Nicaragua, Upper Volta, Zimbabwe.
Meeting numbers. SC 2531-2539.

Vote in Council as follows:

In favour: China, Egypt, France, India, Malta, Netherlands, Nicaragua, Peru, Ukrainian SSR, USSR, United Kingdom, Upper Volta, Zimbabwe.
Against: Pakistan.
Abstaining: United States.

Pakistan, explaining its negative vote, said what was required was the giving of an open mandate to the Secretary-General to bring about conciliation of the two communities and to restart the in-

tercommunal talks, the only credible process for a just settlement. The text made no mention of such resumption and was one-sided; it hoped that despite the flawed mandate, the Secretary-General would be able to renew his contacts.

The United States said that, while condemning the so-called exchange of ambassadors between Turkey and the Turkish Cypriot leadership and other announced actions, it abstained in order to avoid any possible exacerbation of the conflict but gave the strongest support to the Secretary-General's continuing good offices mission.

Turkey rejected the text as a whole because it was based on resolution 541(1983).[28] It also objected to a number of particular provisions, its position on which had been explained during the debate (see below), such as the references to secessionist actions. Turkey also could not understand the inclusion of: the mentioning of Varosha, since the Turkish Cypriot proposals were still under discussion; and paragraph 6, as Mr. Denktas had reiterated his position *vis-à-vis* UNFICYP (see below). Turkey also objected to paragraph 3, as an expression of ostracism against the Turkish Cypriot community; paragraph 10, which had no legal basis in the Charter; and paragraph 8, linking the Secretary-General's good offices mission to resolution 541(1983), with the Council thereby setting aside high-level agreements already concluded between the two communities. Further, Turkey stressed that its forces were not occupying Cyprus but were there on the basis of the 1960 Treaty of Guarantee.

Mr. Denktas expressed similar concerns on the text but said that, despite the fact that his people did not support it, if the Secretary-General could satisfy them as to the continuing basis of his good offices in terms of paragraph 6 of Council resolution 367(1975),[32] all would be done to help him.

During the debate, President Kyprianou said Turkey's plan was and continued to be one of partitioning Cyprus. Most recently Turkey had dismissed whatever the Council had to say through an exchange of ambassadors. Unless the Council acted, there would be an end to Cyprus as an independent State and the very *raison d'être* of the United Nations would be not only undermined but ultimately destroyed. Cyprus had accepted what was unthinkable in the past, namely federation as a solution to the internal structure of the problem. None of what was currently happening would ever have happened without the occupation of 37 per cent of Cyprus by Turkish troops, and any action by the Council should be in the light of that reality. While Cyprus had nothing against the Secretary-General's good offices, if there were no abandonment of the partitionist plan, there could be no peaceful solution. The sides were working at cross purposes, with his Government working for unity of the country in conformity with United Nations resolutions, and the other side working for the destruction of the Republic of Cyprus.

Mr. Denktas said the Cyprus problem did not begin in 1974. It began before that, when the Greek Cypriot leadership set out to destroy the binational character of the State, with a view to its annexation to Greece, which was fully behind that conspiracy. Today Mr. Kyprianou was seeking a mandate to continue doing what was tried between 1963 and 1974, namely to end the bicommunal partnership. Currently an independent Republic of Cyprus (in the north) had been established as equals with the Greek Cypriots since the sovereignty of Cyprus had been given to the island's two peoples. Destruction of bicommunality by the Greek Cypriots was liberty and freedom to them, while to the Turkish Cypriots it was colonization. There had been no deliberate partitionist policy. Partition was a defence and the only reasonable alternative to *enosis*. In February 1982, the Prime Minister of Greece, Andreas Papandreou, had gone to Cyprus to state that the island was part of the national territory of Greece. The Turkish Cypriots were pushed into declaring their statehood in order to tell Mr. Papandreou and Mr. Kyprianou that in Cyprus there existed a Turkish people that would never allow such a union. The Turkish Cypriots were, however, ready to reestablish the Federal Republic, through the intercommunal talks, as a binational State. There was no crisis in Cyprus. In the south, the Greek Cypriots were prospering, and in the north, the Turkish Cypriots lived in freedom, ruling themselves. Mr. Kyprianou was not the President of Cyprus because the 1960 Constitution was in the dustbin.

Turkey said that never in the history of Cyprus had the Greek community obtained *de jure* or *de facto* the position of ruling majority *vis-à-vis* the Turkish community. There had never been a majority or a minority in Cyprus. The situation was that two national and quite separate communities continued to coexist and what was required was establishment of a political equilibrium based on the idea of equality between two nations, Turkish and Greek. Ever since the 1963 *coup d'état*, the Turkish community had continued struggling to regain its status as an equal partner in the Cypriot State, thanks to the unwavering support of Turkey. Until such restoration, the proclamation of independence of the Turkish Cypriot community was perfectly justified on moral and juridical grounds, based on the right of self-determination already exercised on an equal footing with the Greek community, the principle of self-defence and the principle according to which anyone whose rights were trampled upon may, under international law, resort to retaliation. It was not an act of secession since it aimed only at reaffirming equal status. Unless there was a final agreement on a federal solution, the decision on independence was irrevocable, as was Turkey's decision to recognize the new State. Intercommunal negotiations should resume under the auspices of the Secretary-General.

Greece, fully endorsing the views of the President of Cyprus, said that Turkey planned to achieve the partitioning of Cyprus and co-ownership of the Republic on a 50-50 basis by the two communities, one representing 80 per cent and the other 18 per cent of the population. Ankara also wanted the whole arrangement guaranteed by Turkey, thus making the Republic of Cyprus for all practical purposes a protectorate of Turkey—a first step towards total Turkish subordination. It was inconceivable that minority communities were allowed to request foreign military intervention in order to acquire disproportionate status within a State. Such acceptance would mean most United Nations members could be dismembered. The Cyprus problem stemmed directly from Turkish expansionism in the eastern Mediterranean. Whatever happened in the occupied part of Cyprus was the sole responsibility of Turkey, since it totally controlled militarily that part of the Republic. Turkey bore responsibility for the unilateral declaration of independence of the Turkish Cypriot pseudo-State. Invoking the theme of *enosis* was like calling a shadow of the past into existence to justify the crimes of the present. The question of Cyprus was one of foreign occupation of an independent Member State.

In a subsequent intervention, the representative of Cyprus said his country was participating in the Council because it represented the sole, legitimate Government, recognized by all except Turkey. The unilateral declaration of independence, condemned by the whole world, made Turkey look ridiculous, since, when Turkey invaded Cyprus in 1974, it had said it was intervening to restore independence and territorial integrity. Today there was a secessionist and illegal entity set up through uprooting the indigenous people.

Mr. Denktas in a subsequent intervention said intercommunal talks were, as named, intercommunal and the concept of a legitimate Government within or over such talks could not be supported, having regard to the facts of Cyprus. He said the hands of the Secretary-General should be untied; otherwise, the concept of the Government of Cyprus as a starting-point hindered him from doing justice to the two sides. The Greek Cypriots occupying the rest of Cyprus were usurpers and part of a 100 per cent Greek Cypriot racist régime.

Antigua and Barbuda said a principal contributor to the failure of the intercommunal talks was the continued presence of Turkish forces on

Cypriot soil. The Council should call for effective sanctions against the bogus northern "Republic" and against States seeking to give it comfort. India said the Turkish Cypriot community had taken further actions in direct contravention of resolution 541(1983)[28] and the Secretary-General's endeavours; while Mr. Denktas had said that he was not seeking partition, the course he had taken appeared to go in that direction.

Ecuador said there could be no free discussion on the destiny of a people, even when different communities were involved, as long as foreign troops were present on their territory. Egypt recalled its clear position on the declaration of the establishment of a "Republic" in the north as a grave development and took the same position regarding recent developments at variance with resolution 541(1983). Peru said neither isolated nor unrecognized unilateral acts would contribute to the common good of restoring harmony in the island. Speaking in like manner, Yugoslavia added that this was another link in the long chain of *faits accomplis*, delivering a heavy blow to efforts to resolve the problem through negotiations based on Charter principles. The Syrian Arab Republic said that negotiations on Cyprus should be based on equality, with respect for the sovereignty, territorial integrity, independence and non-aligned status of Cyprus, as well as in keeping with relevant United Nations resolutions.

Sri Lanka felt that the Council should consider the most effective ways of implementing those resolutions, preferably within a given time-frame. Nicaragua saw the problem as one of foreign military intervention and what was at stake was the Council's ability to prevent such intervention and the use of force from prevailing over the norms of international relations, contrary to international law. Panama said the *de facto* situation in Cyprus had been brought about by occupation by foreign troops and had gradually been exacerbated by a unilateral attempt to split the territory and community of Cyprus in two.

Jamaica said it was inconceivable that the international community could be expected to accept the recent measures regarding the north and urged the initiators of the proposals to withdraw them. Algeria agreed and said that the Council must give a decisive impetus to the peaceful settlement process. Similarly, Malta said that no one community could prevail over the other, nor could any one neighbour impose its will on Cyprus or any part of the island if peace was really to be secured. Zimbabwe said the grave threat to the very existence of Cyprus was the work of external forces, those forces of disintegration being the same ones that prompted the illegal 1983 declaration of the "Republic". The Upper Volta appealed to the Turkish Cypriot leaders to heed Council

resolution 541(1983) and thus enable the Secretary-General to exercise his functions. Afghanistan associated itself with the President of Cyprus in calling for appropriate measures to reverse all previous actions violating relevant United Nations resolutions. Costa Rica supported the President's proposal for complete demilitarization of the island. Guyana said Turkish Cypriots' intentions became manifest, in keeping with their partitionist policy, when they announced their intentions to hold a "referendum" and "general elections".

Viet Nam said the two communities had mingled for years without any problem before the foreign military occupation of its northern part, followed by attempts to change the demographic composition and social structure of the occupied areas; recent events were a direct consequence of plots hatched by imperialists because of the strategic significance of Cyprus. Cuba said that the rebellious attitude of the Turkish Cypriot leaders towards United Nations decisions deserved a vigorous protest and the Council should condemn their actions and discourage their continuation.

Mongolia felt that there were overt and covert attempts to turn the island into a military strategic springboard of the North Atlantic Treaty Organization (NATO), aimed at maintaining the *de facto* partition of Cyprus. The Ukrainian SSR added that the United States and its NATO allies were intent upon converting the island into a military springboard, viewing it as an important stronghold on the way to the Middle East. Czechoslovakia stressed the importance of foreign troop withdrawal from Cyprus and the liquidation of military bases; it was necessary to create as soon as possible conditions for resumption of a constructive dialogue between representatives of both communities. Hungary added that the idea of holding an international conference on Cyprus should also be borne in mind. The USSR said recent steps by the Turkish community were a flagrant violation of Council decisions, an attempt to create new *faits accomplis* and designed to split Cyprus; it attached great importance to the Secretary-General's good offices. Bulgaria opposed any efforts that might lead to secession in Cyprus, as well as its transformation into a foreign military base. The German Democratic Republic said that United Nations decisions were ignored because imperialist quarters, above all the United States, declared the whole region of the Mediterranean and the Middle East a so-called zone of vital interest and were in no way interested in settling the Cyprus question through negotiations respecting the non-alignment of the island.

Saint Lucia said at the very heart of the problem was the fundamental concern of the security of small States; the *status quo* in Cyprus was the result of a fratricidal conflict often fuelled from external sources and an example of the unwillingness or inability of the international community to act decisively to assure the security of such States.

Malaysia said the Council must assist the Secretary-General by providing the right atmosphere and proper conditions in which the intercommunal talks could go forward.

Australia saw the recent exchange of ambassadors as unhelpful. The Netherlands also rejected that exchange and hoped Mr. Denktas's words regarding a united Cyprus, within a bicommunal, bizonal and federal framework, would be translated into fact. France, too, deplored the fact that despite resolution 541(1983), Turkey had decided to establish diplomatic relations with the so-called "Republic"; it particularly favoured transferring the Famagusta area to an interim United Nations administration.

The United Kingdom felt that all parties had acted in contravention of agreements, and the long-term fundamental problem required that they co-operate with the Secretary-General in the exercise of his good offices while refraining from any action which might exacerbate the situation. China said it steadfastly supported the independence, sovereignty and territorial integrity of Cyprus, as well as its non-aligned status. It hoped the Cyprus problem would be solved through international negotiations and supported the good offices mission.

Pakistan said Cyprus was virtually divided into two separate entities; those who had allowed the distortion of the political processes in Cyprus 20 years earlier by neglecting the historical and cultural realities did not appear to have comprehended its implications or foreseen its culmination in the current impasse. The defiant course to which the Turkish Cypriot community had been obliged to resort was the product of its despair at the bleakness of efforts to ensure fulfilment of its aspirations, as guaranteed as a co-founder of the State of Cyprus under the 1960 Constitution. The one-sided nature of resolution 541(1983), from which Pakistan had dissociated itself, could not have been expected to facilitate the Secretary-General's good offices. Bangladesh spoke similarly, adding that although a sound basis existed for continuing the Secretary-General's good offices, this should not be impaired by another one-sided resolution.

Communications (May/June). Communications in May and June covered such topics as a framework for a comprehensive settlement as proposed by Cyprus and allegations of the colonization of Famagusta (Varosha).

On 9 May,[33] in a letter to the Security Council President, Vanuatu expressed its concern over the threats to the sovereignty and territorial integrity of Cyprus and similarly situated small States, urging the Council, particularly its five permanent members, to set an example by discharging their responsibilities with respect to maintaining international law and order.

The "framework for a comprehensive settlement of the Cyprus problem" was submitted to the Secretary-General by President Kyprianou during a meeting in New York on 11 January, but not made public until requested by Cyprus in a letter of 10 May.[34] It called for the withdrawal of all Turkish occupation troops together with the colonizers imported from Turkey, demilitarization of the island and creation of an international force under United Nations auspices stationed in Cyprus to secure its external defence and internal security. Effective international guarantees for the independence, territorial integrity, unity and non-alignment of the Republic of Cyprus should take the form of an international treaty from which interested Powers were to be excluded. Territorially, negotiations, notwithstanding the 18 per cent Turkish Cypriot population, would be on the basis of 23 per cent of Cyprus for the region or province to be under Turkish Cypriot administration in a federal State. If such previously heavily Greek Cypriot populated areas as Famagusta and Morphou came under Greek Cypriot administration, negotiations could be on the basis of 25 per cent of the territory to be under Turkish Cypriot administration. Constitutionally, the President would be a Greek Cypriot and the Vice-President a Turkish Cypriot, with a Federal Council of Ministers composed of 70 per cent Greek Cypriots and 30 per cent Turkish Cypriots.

On 11 May,[35] Cyprus drew attention to reports in the Turkish Cypriot press of what it said were further Turkish attempts at colonizing the town of Famagusta; Cyprus protested what it called these new aggressive actions of Turkey. On 8 June,[36] it drew urgent attention to the systematic process of colonization of Varosha which was being carried out by the Turkish occupation forces in furtherance of Ankara's objectives of partition and annexation, estimating that at least 20 houses had been settled by persons other than the rightful owners. A letter of 13 June[37] transmitted the text of an 8 June resolution unanimously adopted by the House of Representatives of the Republic of Cyprus, demanding immediate termination of the colonization of Famagusta.

Earlier, on 25 May,[38] Cyprus circulated the full text of its 30 September 1983 reply to and comments on the Secretary-General's soundings conveyed to the parties on 8 August 1983.[39]

Report of the Secretary-General (June). In his 1 June 1984 report to the Security Council on the United Nations operation in Cyprus covering 1 December 1983 to 31 May 1984,[40] the Secretary-General updated UNFICYP activities and his good offices mission.

The Secretary-General reported that, since the adoption of resolution 550(1984) on 11 May, he had held meetings with President Kyprianou on 12 May and Mr. Denktas on 14 May. Regrettably, the period under review did not record any progress but, if his mandate were continued by the Council, he would again consult the parties. It would not seem unreasonable to ask them to avoid actions that prejudiced the agreed basis for a settlement and to proceed without further delay to seek a solution on that basis, aimed at establishment of a federal State.

He recalled that, in his report of 1 May,[29] he had indicated that the continued deployment and operation of UNFICYP was more than ever indispensable in preventing any further deterioration of the situation. During the past six months, UNFICYP had continued, with the co-operation and support of both parties, to discharge its functions of supervising the cease-fire, maintaining peaceful conditions and promoting a return to normality on the island. The Force had to rely on the co-operation of those concerned, especially in maintaining the *status quo* in such sensitive places as Varosha, the status of which was directly tied to commitments of the parties under the 10-point agreement of May 1979.[41] The Secretary-General was therefore disturbed by evidence that the *status quo* was being tampered with in the north-western part of Varosha. He had conveyed his concern about this development to the party concerned.

At the Secretary-General's request, the United Nations High Commissioner for Refugees (UNHCR), as Co-ordinator of United Nations Humanitarian Assistance for Cyprus, had continued to assist the displaced and needy in the island (see ECONOMIC AND SOCIAL QUESTIONS, Chapter XXI). The report also described developments with regard to the Committee on Missing Persons in Cyprus (see ECONOMIC AND SOCIAL QUESTIONS, Chapter XVIII).

Since UNFICYP remained indispensable, the Secretary-General recommended a further extension of its mandate for six months. The Governments of Cyprus, Greece and the United Kingdom concurred with this extension, while Turkey and the Turkish Cypriot community indicated that their stand would be expounded in the Security Council.

SECURITY COUNCIL ACTION (June)

The Security Council met on 15 June to consider the Secretary-General's report and recommendation for extension of the mandate of UNFICYP. At their request, Cyprus, Greece and Turkey were invited to participate in the discussion without the right to vote; Necati Munir Ertekun was invited to participate in conformity

with rule 39[b] of the Council's provisional rules of procedure.

On that day, the Council unanimously adopted resolution 553(1984).

The Security Council,

Taking note of the report of the Secretary-General on the United Nations operation in Cyprus of 1 June 1984,

Noting the recommendation by the Secretary-General that the Security Council should extend the stationing of the United Nations Peace-keeping Force in Cyprus for a further period of six months,

Noting also that the Government of Cyprus has agreed that in view of the prevailing conditions in the island it is necessary to keep the Force in Cyprus beyond 15 June 1984,

Reaffirming the provisions of its resolution 186(1964) and other relevant resolutions,

1. *Extends once more* the stationing in Cyprus of the United Nations Peace-keeping Force established under resolution 186(1964) for a further period, ending on 15 December 1984;

2. *Requests* the Secretary-General to continue his mission of good offices, to keep the Security Council informed of the progress made and to submit a report on the implementation of the present resolution by 30 November 1984;

3. *Calls upon* all the parties concerned to continue to co-operate with the Force on the basis of the present mandate.

Security Council resolution 553(1984)

15 June 1984   Meeting 2547   Adopted unanimously

Draft prepared in consultations among Council members (S/16622).

In the debate, Cyprus stated that free unimpeded intermingling of the people had been replaced by forced segregation based on strict ethnic and racial criteria, reminiscent of *apartheid*. This policy was imposed to serve the political aims of partition and annexation of the occupied part of Cyprus to mainland Turkey. Those areas had been heavily colonized by importing thousands of aliens in furtherance of Ankara's plans to change Cyprus's demographic structure. Between 40,000 and 50,000 were already settled in the occupied areas. Further Turkish actions to colonize the Varosha area should be of special concern to the Council. Cyprus said the existence of two communities in no way pre-empted the existence of the Government of Cyprus, whose legality had been exclusively recognized by all international organizations and United Nations resolutions.

Greece said every effort was required to restore the exercise of the sovereign authority of the Government of the Republic of Cyprus over its entire territory and to safeguard its independence, unity and territorial integrity. This could be achieved through withdrawal of the Turkish forces

[b]See footnote a on p. 243.

of occupation and establishment of a democratic constitutional system providing for equal rights for all, while credibly guaranteeing the legitimate right of the Turkish Cypriot community which, with other minorities, constituted 20 per cent of the population. No just and viable solution could be reached if the demographic realities of the Republic were disregarded. Past experience demanded extreme caution. Commitments had been given to transfer Famagusta to UNFICYP while plans to start colonizing the city were already apparently final.

Mr. Ertekun said the Secretary-General's report was constructive in that it clearly stated that his current mission of good offices was entrusted to him by Security Council resolution 367(1975).[32] The Turkish Cypriot side would have agreed to extending the UNFICYP mandate provided it was done legally and constitutionally, and this required deleting the Council's reference to a Government of Cyprus. He said the "Turkish Republic of Northern Cyprus" was the sole competent authority to speak for the Turkish Cypriot partnership of the 1960 Republic of Cyprus and the northern part of the island. Nevertheless, the "Turkish Republic" was prepared to accept the presence of UNFICYP on its territory based on decisions taken solely by that Government. The "Turkish Republic" had no intention of altering the existing *status quo* of Varosha. Regarding an agreed settlement of the Cyprus question, he had that morning given the Secretary-General a comprehensive set of new proposals.

Turkey said that federation remained the ultimate goal of the "Turkish Republic of Northern Cyprus" and the Secretary-General's good offices could only be based on paragraph 6 of Council resolution 367(1975). It fully supported the new proposals Mr. Ertekun had mentioned. The current resolution, however, mentioned provisions that the "Turkish Republic" and Turkey had never accepted, prolonged a mandate rendered archaic by radical changes, and was based on supposed authorization by a so-called governmental entity having no actual or juridical existence. Turkey rejected the resolution *in toto* but it would continue to accept the presence of UNFICYP and co-operate with it.

Communications (June-August). Communications from June to August included letters from Mr. Ertekun on various activities of the Greek Cypriots and letters from Cyprus concerning actions in the north.

On 19 June,[42] Mr. Ertekun said the Greek Cypriot side had, at the Third Conference of Labour Ministers of the Non-Aligned and Other Developing Countries (Managua, Nicaragua, 10-12 May), obtained a one-sided resolution on Cyprus by removing references to resumption of the intercommunal talks; he also protested economic embargo and blockade measures against Turkish Cypriots. The text of the Conference resolution was forwarded by Cyprus on 9 July.[43]

Mr. Ertekun, on 5 July,[44] cited what he said was a Greek Cypriot press campaign undermining the Turkish Cypriot initiative concerning resumed negotiations.

In a number of letters Cyprus drew attention to what it termed secessionist acts by the Turkish Cypriot leadership, including reported plans for a free trade zone in the north (4 July),[45] creation of a central bank (5 July),[46] issuance of passports in the name of that community (31 July),[47] military exercises and parades on the anniversary of the 1974 invasion (31 July),[48] and issuance of new currency (1 August).[49]

Report of the Secretary-General (December). A December 1984 report[50] by the Secretary-General covered developments between 1 June and 12 December.

To give new impetus to his good offices mission, the Secretary-General invited both sides to designate representatives to meet him separately at Vienna on 6 and 7 August. At those meetings, he outlined a number of working points with a view to ascertaining whether they might provide a basis for convening high-level proximity talks under his auspices. On 31 August, both sides responded favourably to the proposal.

The leaders of the communities met with the Secretary-General separately in a first round of high-level proximity talks (New York, 10-20 September), whose purpose was to address a number of substantive elements, with a view to elaborating the working points proposed at Vienna into a preliminary draft agreement for submission to a joint high-level meeting. Two further rounds of proximity talks took place (New York, 15-26 October and 26 November–12 December).

At the final round, the Secretary-General presented and discussed as an integrated whole a preliminary draft for a joint high-level agreement. The package contained elements taken from different positions he thought could help in bridging the still existing gap; the Turkish Cypriot side conveyed its favourable reaction to all those elements. After further discussions with both sides, the Secretary-General sought and received from the Turkish Cypriot delegation understandings that were helpful in further narrowing the gap. By 12 December, he assessed that the documentation for a draft agreement was ready for submission to a joint high-level meeting, at which he expected that the interlocutors would conclude an agreement containing the necessary elements for a comprehensive solution of the problem, aimed at establishing a Federal Republic of Cyprus. He announced that the parties had agreed to hold such a meeting under his auspices, at a place to be decided, beginning on 17 January 1985.

The report also gave information on further work by the Committee on Missing Persons in Cyprus.

In the light of political developments and the situation on the ground, the Secretary-General recommended a further six-month extension of the UNFICYP mandate. He subsequently informed the Council that Cyprus, Greece and the United Kingdom concurred with his recommendation; Turkey and the Turkish Cypriot community would expound their positions in the Security Council.

SECURITY COUNCIL ACTION (December)

The Security Council met on 14 December to consider the Secretary-General's report and recommendation for extension of UNFICYP's mandate. At their request, Canada, Cyprus, Greece and Turkey were invited to participate in the discussion without the right to vote; Mr. Denktas was invited to participate in conformity with rule 39[c] of the Council's provisional rules of procedure.

On the same day, the Council unanimously adopted resolution 559(1984).

The Security Council,

Taking note of the report of the Secretary-General on the United Nations operation in Cyprus of 12 December 1984,

Noting the recommendation by the Secretary-General that the Security Council should extend the stationing of the United Nations Peace-keeping Force in Cyprus for a further period of six months,

Noting also that the Government of Cyprus has agreed that in view of the prevailing conditions in the island it is necessary to keep the Force in Cyprus beyond 15 December 1984,

Reaffirming the provisions of its resolution 186(1964) and other relevant resolutions,

1. *Extends once more* the stationing in Cyprus of the United Nations Peace-keeping Force established under resolution 186(1964) for a further period, ending on 15 June 1985;

2. *Requests* the Secretary-General to continue his mission of good offices, to keep the Security Council informed of the progress made and to submit a report on the implementation of the present resolution by 31 May 1985;

3. *Calls upon* all the parties concerned to continue to co-operate with the Force on the basis of the present mandate.

Security Council resolution 559(1984)

14 December 1984   Meeting 2565   Adopted unanimously

Draft prepared in consultations among Council members (S/16862).

At the outset of the debate, the President, on behalf of the Council, expressing the hope that the forthcoming high-level meeting would be useful, stated that a crossroads had been reached in the development of the Cyprus question.

During the debate, Cyprus quoted President Kyprianou to the effect that cautious optimism was justified, perhaps for the first time since 1974. In view of bitter disappointments of the recent past, Cyprus stressed that there must be no lessening of the impetus and vigilance of the international community at a time which was ripe for representations by those who could and must act in order to facilitate an agreement.

Mr. Denktas said the summit meeting was not, as suggested, between himself and the President of the Republic of Cyprus, but between the leaders of the two communities. He did not accept the current resolution because it mentioned a non-existent Government. However, UNFICYP would be accommodated on the territory of the northern "Republic" as it had been since 1983. No modification could now be made to the text of the draft agreement for the summit meeting; it did not allow for reservations of any kind.

Turkey said it was Mr. Denktas alone who had essentially contributed to the outcome of the extremely laudable efforts of the Secretary-General. Now the Turkish people of Cyprus were awaiting the unequivocal acceptance by its opposite number of the draft agreement initiated at the high-level meeting. Turkey would give it its foremost support. Regarding the resolution, Turkey's fundamental objection remained the matter of the so-called Cyprus Government. Its contacts with UNFICYP would be on the basis of decisions by the "Republic of Northern Cyprus".

Greece felt it was strange to expect President Kyprianou to come to New York in January to be presented with a document on a take-it-or-leave-it basis and then be asked to sign it; the outcome of a dialogue must always be the product of mutual agreement.

GENERAL ASSEMBLY ACTION (September)

On 17 September 1984, at the closing meeting of its resumed thirty-eighth session, the General Assembly adopted decision 38/458 without vote.

Question of Cyprus

At its 106th plenary meeting, on 17 September 1984, the General Assembly decided to include in the draft agenda of its thirty-ninth session the item entitled "Question of Cyprus".

General Assembly decision 38/458

Adopted without vote

Oral proposal by President; agenda item 41.

GENERAL ASSEMBLY ACTION (December)

On 18 December, the Assembly, by decision 39/456 on the suspension of its thirty-ninth (1984) session, deferred consideration of the Cyprus ques-

[c]See footnote a on p. 243.

tion, among other agenda items, to its resumed session, at a date to be announced (see p. 374).

Other action. The Commission on Human Rights, by a decision of 14 March, postponed the debate on human rights in Cyprus to its 1985 session (see ECONOMIC AND SOCIAL QUESTIONS, Chapter XVIII).

Peace-keeping operations

Established by the Security Council in 1964,[51] UNFICYP continued throughout 1984 to monitor, patrol and supervise the cease-fire lines of the Cyprus National Guard and of the Turkish and Turkish Cypriot forces. It also provided security for civilians in the area between the lines; used its best efforts to discharge its functions with regard to the security, welfare and well-being of Greek Cypriots living in northern Cyprus; continued regular visits to Turkish Cypriots residing in the south; and support . . . . . . relief operations.

UNFICYP kept the are . . .
lines under constant su . . .
tem of 141 observation p . . .

arranged directly or through the good offices of UNFICYP. During the 12 months ending 12 December 1984, 1,213 visits were made by Greek Cypriots to the south for family and medical reasons. During the same period, there were 67 permanent transfers of Greek Cypriots to the south and the number residing in the north fell to 788; two Turkish Cypriots transferred to the north in the same period. UNFICYP continued to verify that all transfers took place voluntarily.

Periodic visits by UNFICYP officials to Turkish Cypriots living in the south continued, and contacts were maintained with their relatives in the north. During the year, 159 reunions of separated Turkish Cypriot families were arranged under UNFICYP auspices.

UNFICYP distributed 938 tons of foodstuffs and other related items provided by the Cyprus Government and the Cyprus Red Cross to Greek Cypriots living in the north.

UNFICYP continued to provide emergency med- . . .
. . . r civilians of both communities. It . . .
. . . ish Cypriots to hospitals in the south . . .
. . . and continued to deliver medicines . . .
. . . Cypriot community on a regular

a short-term investment plan for the central area of the city, as well as a portfolio of specific investment projects based on detailed designs and feasibility studies. The World Food Programme, which provided food to schoolchildren of both communities, decided to extend the project for another three years (1985-1987).

Construction work under the second stage of the Nicosia sanitary sewerage system and domestic water supply project got under way in May. Financed by EEC and the European Investment Bank, the project involved both parts of Nicosia and laying pipes across the buffer zone. UNDP ensured proper co-ordination, with UNFICYP providing liaison and military escorts for work in the buffer zone.

The information on UNFICYP activities was provided in two reports by the Secretary-General, covering 1 December 1983 to 31 May 1984[(40)] and 1 June to 12 December 1984.[(50)] In both, he recommended extension of the Force's mandate and the Security Council twice did month period: first until 15 Decem then until 15 June 1985 (see pp. 2

Composition of UNFICYP. As

at approximately $100.5 million—excluding regular troops' pay and allowances and normal *matériel* costs—much of which was borne by the troop contributors.

As at 15 December 1984, the accumulated deficit from the operation's inception in 1964 stood at $123.1 million. Because of that deficit, payments to troop-contributing Governments (which had been absorbing costs in the order of $36.2 million every six-month period) had been made to meet claims only up to December 1977; the last such payment was made in January 1984.

CONTRIBUTIONS RECEIVED IN 1984 FOR UNFICYP
(as at 31 December 1984; in US dollars)

Country	Amount
Australia	100,800
Austria	125,000
Bahamas	2,000
Belgium	182,300
Cyprus	450,000
Denmark	120,000
	37,500
of	863,100
	739,200
	20,000
	1,000

Noting, in particular, the information contained in paragraphs 133 to 142 of that report,

Recalling its resolution 38/58 E of 13 December 1983,

Convinced that the world-wide dissemination of accurate and comprehensive information and the role of non-governmental organizations and institutions remain of vital importance in heightening awareness of and support for the inalienable rights of the Palestinian people to self-determination and to the establishment of an independent sovereign Palestinian State,

1. *Notes with appreciation* the action taken by the Department of Public Information of the Secretariat in compliance with General Assembly resolution 38/58 E;

2. *Requests* that the Department of Public Information, in full co-operation and co-ordination with the Committee on the Exercise of the Inalienable Rights of the Palestinian People, should:

(a) Continue the implementation of all parts of General Assembly resolution 38/58 E;

(b) Disseminate all information on the activities of the United Nations system relating to Palestine;

(c) Expand and update publications and audio-visual material on the facts and developments pertaining to the question of Palestine;

(d) Publish newsletters and articles in its relevant publications on Israeli violations of the human rights of the Arab inhabitants of the occupied territories;

(e) Organize fact-finding missions to the area for journalists;

(f) Organize regional and national encounters for journalists.

General Assembly resolution 39/49 C

| 11 December 1984 | Meeting 95 | 131-3-15 (recorded vote) |

17-nation draft (A/39/L.39 & Add.1); agenda item 33.

Sponsors: Afghanistan, Comoros, Cuba, Cyprus, Egypt, India, Indonesia, Lao People's Democratic Republic, Madagascar, Malaysia, Mali, Nicaragua, Pakistan, Senegal, Tunisia, Viet Nam, Yugoslavia.

Meeting numbers. GA 39th session: plenary 88-92, 94, 95.

Recorded vote in Assembly as follows:

In favour: Afghanistan, Albania, Algeria, Angola, Argentina, Austria, Bahamas, Bahrain, Bangladesh, Barbados, Belize, Benin, Bhutan, Bolivia, Botswana, Brazil, Brunei Darussalam, Bulgaria, Burkina Faso, Burma, Burundi, Byelorussian SSR, Cameroon, Cape Verde, Central African Republic, Chad, China, Colombia, Comoros, Congo, Cuba, Cyprus, Czechoslovakia, Democratic Kampuchea, Democratic Yemen, Djibouti, Dominica, Dominican Republic, Ecuador, Egypt, Equatorial Guinea, Ethiopia, Fiji, Finland, Gabon, Gambia, German Democratic Republic, Greece, Guatemala, Guinea, Guinea-Bissau, Guyana, Haiti, Honduras, Hungary, India, Indonesia, Iran, Iraq, Ivory Coast, Jamaica, Jordan, Kenya, Kuwait, Lao People's Democratic Republic, Lebanon, Lesotho, Liberia, Libyan Arab Jamahiriya, Madagascar, Malawi, Malaysia, Maldives, Mali, Malta, Mauritania, Mauritius, Mexico, Mongolia, Morocco, Mozambique, Nepal, Nicaragua, Niger, Nigeria, Oman, Pakistan, Panama, Papua New Guinea, Paraguay, Peru, Philippines, Poland, Portugal, Qatar, Romania, Rwanda, Saint Lucia, Saint Vincent and the Grenadines, Samoa, Sao Tome and Principe, Saudi Arabia, Senegal, Seychelles, Sierra Leone, Singapore, Somalia, Spain, Sri Lanka, Sudan, Suriname, Sweden, Syrian Arab Republic, Thailand, Togo, Trinidad and Tobago, Tunisia, Turkey, Uganda, Ukrainian SSR, USSR, United Arab Emirates, United Republic of Tanzania, Uruguay, Vanuatu, Venezuela, Viet Nam, Yemen, Yugoslavia, Zambia, Zimbabwe.

Against: Canada, Israel, United States.

Abstaining: Australia, Belgium, Costa Rica, Denmark, France, Germany, Federal Republic of, Iceland, Ireland, Italy, Japan, Luxembourg, Netherlands, New Zealand, Norway, United Kingdom.

In Israel's view, the text meant another wasteful drain on United Nations funds and would continue the effect of providing a sounding-board for interests and forces extraneous to the United Nations, monopolizing time and funds of DPI to the detriment of its other, legitimate responsibilities.

In the opinion of the United States, paragraph 2 *(d)* in particular provided good evidence of the caricature of fairness in the text: where was the concern for the human rights of all the region's inhabitants, it asked.

Ireland, on behalf of the EC members, said they trusted that DPI would continue to be guided in its activities by impartiality and would maintain its normal decision-making process; given the difficult financial situation, every effort should be made to avoid unnecessary burdens on the budget.

Though voting in favour, Finland said it did so with reservations.

By resolution 39/49 B, the Assembly requested the Secretary-General to ensure the continued co-operation of DPI and other Secretariat units in enabling the Division for Palestinian Rights to perform its tasks and in covering adequately the various aspects of the Palestine question.

Assistance to Palestinians

Reports of the Secretary-General. On 21 May 1984,[31] the Secretary-General reported on economic and social assistance to the Palestinians provided or planned according to information received from seven United Nations organs and 11 specialized agencies and the International Atomic Energy Agency (IAEA).

In another report, of 7 September,[32] the Secretary-General gave an overview of United Nations efforts to identify the social and economic needs of the Palestinians. As requested by the General Assembly in December 1983,[33] he had convened a meeting on economic and social assistance to the Palestinian people (Geneva, 5 and 6 July 1984), with relevant United Nations bodies and agencies participating. Represented also were PLO, Arab host countries, and intergovernmental and non-governmental organizations. In preparation for the meeting, the Director-General for Development and International Economic Co-operation had requested United Nations bodies and organizations to submit proposals for future assistance projects. The meeting called for consultations with organizations and agencies to clarify some of the proposals, including financial resources available or needed, and to identify gaps and avoid duplication. It called for a revised paper on project proposals, taking into account additional ones made at the meeting, for inter-agency review.

Concluding his report, the Secretary-General stated that, subject to discussions in the Assembly, it was intended that a review and update of the proposals discussed at the meeting be prepared for consideration and further development within the existing machinery of the inter-agency Administrative Committee on Co-ordination.

UNIDO action. Following consideration of a February 1984 report by the Executive Director of the United Nations Industrial Development Organization (UNIDO),[34] the Industrial Development Board, on 19 May,[35] requested UNIDO to intensify its efforts, in co-operation with PLO, to provide technical assistance to the Palestinians. The Board called on the Israeli occupation authorities to give UNIDO staff and experts access to the occupied territories and affirmed that the restrictive policies of those authorities inhibited the development of the Palestinian industrial sector. These calls were echoed by the UNIDO Fourth General Conference in August (resolution 14).

As reported by the Executive Director,[36] among UNIDO's activities was a survey of the manufacturing industry in the West Bank and the Gaza Strip, completed in mid-1984; it was part of a comprehensive survey by the United Nations Conference on Trade and Development of the economy of the Palestinians in the occupied territories. At the request of PLO, the final report on the UNIDO survey[37] was circulated at the Fourth General Conference of UNIDO in August 1984 (see ECONOMIC AND SOCIAL QUESTIONS, Chapter VI), and an expert group meeting on the subject was held from 10 to 13 September at Vienna.

A project on assistance to the pharmaceutical industry was approved for financing from the United Nations Industrial Development Fund and completed in 1984, while a feasibility study for a West Bank cement plant was cancelled at the request of PLO. Qualified Palestinians were invited to participate in selected UNIDO group training programmes on industrial development.

UNDP action. In early 1984, the United Nations Development Programme (UNDP) initiated a programming exercise covering an extensive array of project concepts, tentatively identifying projects for Palestinians costing at least $45 million. A total of $7.5 million from Special Programme Resources had been expended for completed projects, committed for projects under way, or allocated for approved projects which were to become operational during 1984. This full utilization of all available UNDP funding, the Administrator of UNDP stated in a March report on the programme of assistance to the Palestinians,[38] meant that the size of any future activity would depend on voluntary contributions; project identification no longer was a problem, since four years of experience in the West Bank and Gaza had enabled UNDP to identify critically important sectors and areas of concentration which called for priority action. The tentative plan for future projects represented a programme oriented more fully towards basic development activities, covering, for example: assistance to farmers, citrus producers and fishermen; development of plum and grape processing and olive and olive oil production; roads, classrooms

and water supply for rural villages; assistance in primary and secondary education and teacher training; improvement of sewage disposal; development of glass and ceramic engineering technology; agricultural and hydrological research; and strengthening health institutions.

The Administrator stated that the perceived development needs of the Palestinians were so extensive and substantial that the amount and nature of project execution should be dependent on the funding available and UNDP's delivery capabilities, rather than on arbitrarily designated spending levels. However, while a number of Governments and intergovernmental institutions had signified strong interest in supporting the programme with special contributions, only Tunisia had thus far made a definite pledge in response to appeals; he recommended that the UNDP Governing Council consider the future viability of the special programme in the light of the prevailing financial circumstances.

The Council, on 29 June,[39] expressed satisfaction with the Administrator's efforts to assist the Palestinians in the West Bank and the Gaza Strip. It noted with regret that appeals for additional special contributions of at least $8 million in the 1982-1986 programming cycle had drawn a very modest response, and reconfirmed the need for special contributions. The Council noted that, unless additional contributions were received, it would not be possible to undertake basic development projects in timely and fully effective fashion, and requested the Administrator to make proposals concerning the amount which could be utilized from Special Programme Resources to support programmes of assistance to the Palestinians.

At the 1984 United Nations Pledging Conference for Development Activities (7 and 8 November) (see ECONOMIC AND SOCIAL QUESTIONS, Chapter II), the United States announced a pledge to the programme of up to $1 million. Shortly thereafter, the Arab Gulf Programme for United Nations Development Organizations announced its intention to contribute $1 million.

UNICEF activities. The Executive Board of the United Nations Children's Fund (UNICEF), at its April/May 1984 session,[40] approved commitments totalling $1.95 million and "noted" an amount of $3.2 million, subject to the availability of specific-purpose contributions, covering the period mid-1984 to mid-1987 to support new programmes of co-operation to assist Palestinian children and mothers in Jordan, Lebanon, the Syrian Arab Republic and the occupied territories. The programmes focused on priority areas of child survival and development, pre-school, promotion of income-generating activities for women, and water supply and sanitation. Specifically, the following amounts were approved for the programme: for Jordan, a commitment of $600,000 from general resources and $450,000 from supplementary funds, subject to availability; for Lebanon, the respective amounts of $800,000 and $600,000; for the Syrian Arab Republic, $550,000 and $450,000; and for the occupied territories, $1.7 million, pledged by the Federal Republic of Germany.

Other activities. During 1984, a study on food security issues in the West Bank and the Gaza Strip was completed; the study, undertaken jointly by the Economic Commission for Western Asia and the Arab Organization for Agricultural Development, resulted in recommendations on ways to promote food production and raise nutritional standards under prevailing conditions.

Assistance to the Palestinians continued to be provided by the Food and Agriculture Organization of the United Nations (FAO) in training, including specialized training in agricultural development. FAO was the executing agency of an agricultural training centre project, with $356,000 budgeted from UNDP, to assist Palestinian families in refugee camps in the Syrian Arab Republic to improve crop and livestock production and efficiency.

ECONOMIC AND SOCIAL COUNCIL ACTION

On 25 July 1984, on the recommendation of its Third (Programme and Co-ordination) Committee, the Economic and Social Council adopted resolution 1984/56 by a roll-call vote.

Assistance to the Palestinian people

The Economic and Social Council,

Recalling General Assembly resolution 38/145 of 19 December 1983,

Recalling also Council resolution 1983/43 of 25 July 1983,

Noting the need to provide economic and social assistance to the Palestinian people,

Noting also the oral report made by the representative of the Secretary-General before the Third (Programme and Co-ordination) Committee of the Council on 9 July 1984, concerning the meeting on assistance to the Palestinian people held at Geneva on 5 and 6 July 1984 in response to General Assembly resolution 38/145,

1. *Takes note* of the report of the Secretary-General on assistance to the Palestinian people;

2. *Expresses its thanks* to the Secretary-General for convening the meeting on assistance to the Palestinian people, pursuant to General Assembly resolution 38/145;

3. *Regards* such a meeting as a valuable opportunity to assess progress in economic and social assistance to the Palestinian people and to explore ways and means of enhancing such assistance;

4. *Draws the attention* of the international community, the United Nations system and intergovernmental and non-governmental organizations to the need to ensure that their aid to the occupied Palestinian territories is disbursed only for the benefit of the Palestinian people and is not used in any manner to serve the interests of the Israeli occupation authorities;

5. *Requests* the competent programmes, organizations, agencies and organs of the United Nations system to intensify their efforts, in co-operation with the Palestine Liberation Organization, to provide economic and social assistance to the Palestinian people;

6. *Also requests* that United Nations assistance to the Palestinians in the Arab host countries should be rendered in co-operation with the Palestine Liberation Organization and with the consent of the Arab host Government concerned;

7. *Requests* the Secretary-General to report to the General Assembly at its fortieth session, through the Economic and Social Council, on the progress made in the provision of assistance to the Palestinian people.

Economic and Social Council resolution 1984/56

25 July 1984	Meeting 48	48-1 (roll-call vote)

Approved by Third Committee (E/1984/137) by vote (37-1), 13 July (meeting 6); draft by China and Mexico for Group of 77 (E/1984/C.3/L.4); agenda item 22.

Roll-call vote in Council as follows:

In favour: Algeria, Argentina, Austria, Benin, Brazil, Bulgaria, Canada, China, Colombia, Congo, Costa Rica, Djibouti, Finland, France, German Democratic Republic, Germany, Federal Republic of, Greece, Guyana, Indonesia, Japan, Lebanon, Luxembourg, Malaysia, Mexico, Netherlands, New Zealand, Pakistan, Papua New Guinea, Poland, Portugal, Qatar, Romania, Rwanda, Saint Lucia, Saudi Arabia, Sierra Leone, Somalia, Sri Lanka, Suriname, Sweden, Thailand, Tunisia, Uganda, USSR, United Kingdom, Venezuela, Yugoslavia, Zaire.

Against: United States.

Before voting on the text as a whole, the Council adopted paragraph 4 by a roll-call vote of 38 to 1, with 11 abstentions. The Committee had also voted separately on that paragraph, adopting it by 25 votes to 1, with 10 abstentions.

While reaffirming its determination to continue to assist the Palestinians, Japan said it had abstained in the vote on paragraph 4 because of an ambiguity in the final phrase.

After the vote, the United States said it was a measure of its concern for the plight of the Palestinians that it provided a major portion of the budgets for organizations such as (UNRWA) and the International Committee of the Red Cross (ICRC), which were involved in alleviating the conditions of the Palestinians. It firmly believed that such humanitarian assistance should be provided by the international community without regard to political considerations, a principle violated by the adopted text, which affirmed a role for PLO in receiving international economic and social assistance on behalf of the Palestinians. The United States did not believe that it was the Council's function to select a representative for the Palestinians or to prejudge the outcome of the eventual exercise of the Palestinians' right to select their own representatives.

Speaking for the EC members of the Council, Luxembourg pledged that they would continue to provide humanitarian assistance to the Palestinians through various channels, including food and emergency relief and the co-financing with NGOs of aid projects. Assistance would be furnished directly and through EC, as well as through the competent United Nations organizations.

Poland, for the Eastern European members of the Council, regretted that the resolution had not called for an end to the Israeli occupation of Palestinian territory and the withdrawal of all Israeli troops.

On behalf of the Arab Group of Member States, Saudi Arabia said the wording of the resolution was intended to express a humanitarian, not a political, view; in any case, PLO did not need a Council resolution to confirm that it was the genuine representative of the Palestinians. The people suffering under Israeli occupation, however, needed support and there could be no legitimate objection to paragraph 4. The Council naturally wished to declare that the Israeli occupation should be brought to an end.

In a statement after the explanations of vote, Israel said it could not receive with acclamation a resolution granting status to a terrorist organization which had inscribed on its banner the destruction of Israel; however, it was pleased to see that, unlike the corresponding 1983 resolution,[41] the 1984 text did not deplore Israel's actions, the reason for that being that Israel had done all in its power to enable authorized organizations and those with a true mandate to extend humanitarian assistance to the Palestinians. It was to be expected that some attempt would be made in the Council to malign Israel, as had been done in paragraph 4. The needs of the Palestinians would not be met by further resolutions but by concrete assistance; the reason why such assistance had not been provided on the scale required was the absence of adequate funding. Tunisia was alone among the Arab countries in making a pledge of aid to the Palestinians in response to Council and Assembly appeals.

With regard to the claim that everything possible had been done to permit assistance to the Palestinians, PLO challenged Israel to deny that fewer than 6 of the 17 projects approved by UNDP for implementation in the occupied territories had been carried out; moreover, five of the projects rejected by the Israeli authorities had been the most important: a multidisciplinary research and training centre, the planning and development of higher education, cultural heritage, a faculty of agriculture, and a housing fund. While the Council was not the appropriate place to discuss the contributions of individual countries, it was well known that many Islamic countries, the Arab Group and the Eastern European States provided assistance to the Palestinians and co-operated with PLO. More to the point was the fact that Israel had cut off access by the Arab Support Fund to the occupied territories.

GENERAL ASSEMBLY ACTION

On 18 December 1984, on the recommendation of the Second (Economic and Financial) Committee, the General Assembly adopted resolution 39/224, by recorded vote.

Assistance to the Palestinian people

The General Assembly,

Recalling its resolution 38/145 of 19 December 1983,

Recalling also Economic and Social Council resolution 1984/56 of 25 July 1984,

Recalling further the Programme of Action for the Achievement of Palestinian Rights, adopted by the International Conference on the Question of Palestine,

Noting the need to provide economic and social assistance to the Palestinian people,

1. *Takes note* of the report of the Secretary-General on assistance to the Palestinian people;

2. *Takes note also* of the report of the Secretary-General concerning the meeting on assistance to the Palestinian people which was held at Geneva on 5 and 6 July 1984 in response to General Assembly resolution 38/145;

3. *Expresses its thanks* to the Secretary-General for convening the meeting on assistance to the Palestinian people;

4. *Regards* such a meeting as a valuable opportunity to assess progress in economic and social assistance to the Palestinian people and to explore ways and means of enhancing such assistance;

5. *Draws the attention* of the international community, the United Nations system and intergovernmental and non-governmental organizations to the need to disburse their aid to the occupied Palestinian territories only for the benefit of the Palestinian people and to ensure that it is not used in any manner to serve the interests of the Israeli occupation authorities;

6. *Requests* the Secretary-General:

(a) To expedite the finalizing, through existing inter-agency mechanisms, of the co-ordinated programme of economic and social assistance to the Palestinian people requested in General Assembly resolution 38/145;

(b) To convene in 1985 a meeting of the relevant programmes, organizations, agencies, funds and organs of the United Nations system to consider the co-ordinated programme of economic and social assistance to the Palestinian people;

(c) To provide for the participation in the meeting of the Palestine Liberation Organization, the Arab host countries and relevant intergovernmental and non-governmental organizations;

7. *Requests* the relevant programmes, organizations, agencies, funds and organs of the United Nations system to intensify their efforts, in co-operation with the Palestine Liberation Organization, to provide economic and social assistance to the Palestinian people;

8. *Also requests* that United Nations assistance to the Palestinians in the Arab host countries should be rendered in co-operation with the Palestine Liberation Organization and with the consent of the Arab host Government concerned;

9. *Requests* the Secretary-General to report to the General Assembly at its fortieth session, through the Economic and Social Council, on the progress made in the implementation of the present resolution.

General Assembly resolution 39/224

18 December 1984	Meeting 104	146-2 (recorded vote)

Approved by Second Committee (A/39/789) by recorded vote (131-2), 13 November (meeting 40); 10-nation draft (A/C.2/39/L.19), orally revised; agenda item 12.

Sponsors: Algeria, Bangladesh, China, Democratic Yemen, Madagascar, Malaysia, Mali, Morocco, Tunisia, Yemen.

Meeting numbers. GA 39th session: 2nd Committee 33, 40; plenary 104.

Recorded vote in Assembly as follows:

In favour: Afghanistan, Albania, Algeria, Angola, Argentina, Australia, Austria, Bahamas, Bahrain, Bangladesh, Barbados, Belgium, Benin, Bhutan, Bolivia, Botswana, Brazil, Brunei Darussalam, Bulgaria, Burkina Faso, Burma, Burundi, Byelorussian SSR, Canada, Cape Verde, Central African Republic, Chad, Chile, China, Colombia, Congo, Costa Rica, Cuba, Cyprus, Czechoslovakia, Democratic Kampuchea, Democratic Yemen, Denmark, Djibouti, Dominican Republic, Ecuador, Egypt,

El Salvador, Equatorial Guinea, Ethiopia, Fiji, Finland, France, Gabon, Gambia, German Democratic Republic, Germany, Federal Republic of, Ghana, Greece, Guinea, Guinea-Bissau, Guyana, Haiti, Honduras, Hungary, Iceland, India, Indonesia, Iran, Iraq, Ireland, Italy, Ivory Coast, Jamaica, Japan, Jordan, Kenya, Kuwait, Lao People's Democratic Republic, Lebanon, Lesotho, Liberia, Libyan Arab Jamahiriya, Luxembourg, Madagascar, Malawi, Malaysia, Maldives, Mali, Malta, Mauritania, Mauritius, Mexico, Mongolia, Morocco, Mozambique, Nepal, Netherlands, New Zealand, Nicaragua, Niger, Nigeria, Norway, Oman, Pakistan, Panama, Papua New Guinea, Peru, Philippines, Poland, Portugal, Qatar, Romania, Rwanda, Saint Christopher and Nevis, Saint Lucia, Saint Vincent and the Grenadines, Samoa, Sao Tome and Principe, Saudi Arabia, Senegal, Sierra Leone, Singapore, Somalia, Spain, Sri Lanka, Sudan, Suriname, Swaziland, Sweden, Syrian Arab Republic, Thailand, Togo, Trinidad and Tobago, Tunisia, Turkey, Uganda, Ukrainian SSR, USSR, United Arab Emirates, United Kingdom, United Republic of Tanzania, Uruguay, Vanuatu, Venezuela, Viet Nam, Yemen, Yugoslavia, Zaire, Zambia, Zimbabwe.

Against: Israel, United States.

Introducing the draft on behalf of the sponsors, Democratic Yemen said the international community had come to recognize the need to help the Palestinians who were victims of injustices of all kinds and whose lands and natural resources were being plundered by the Israelis.

Speaking before the vote in the Committee, Israel said the text ignored, for political reasons, the fact that Israel was currently the only State engaged, directly and actively, in promoting the well-being, safety and socio-economic development of the Palestinian Arabs of Judaea, Samaria and Gaza. During the 18 years of Israeli administration, they had made spectacular progress and their situation was many times better than that of most neighbouring countries. The resolutions adopted each year on the subject presented Israel as systematically opposed to and as obstructing international aid to the Palestinians. Israel welcomed assistance through legitimate channels and would continue to co-operate with UNRWA and UNDP. The main purpose of the resolution was to emphasize the role of PLO and to attribute to it capabilities and influence it did not possess.

The United States felt that the text was contentious and not constructive; it would perpetuate unproductive, if not counter-productive, activities that would in no way resolve the serious problems in the Middle East or improve the well-being of the Palestinians. The United States continued to be actively involved in efforts to improve Palestinian life through bilateral and multilateral programmes; during the previous year, it had also inaugurated programmes to assist directly deserving Palestinian institutions in the West Bank and Gaza. Such programmes, however, were no substitute for a negotiated settlement.

Jordan expressed reservations on paragraphs 7 and 8; any assistance to Palestinian refugees in Jordan should be subject to consultations with and approval of the authorities there.

On behalf of the States members of EEC, Ireland said EEC had been increasing its assistance to improve the plight of Palestinians not only in the occupied territories but also in Lebanon and elsewhere in the region; its members continued to provide that assistance directly and through EEC and the United Nations system. Japan maintained its position concerning United Nations assistance to national liberation movements.

Gabon stressed that its vote by no means called its well-known views into question. The Libyan Arab Jamahiriya declared that its affirmative vote in no way indicated that it accepted the presence of a Zionist entity; it had reservations on any paragraph that might imply such acceptance.

Palestinian detainees

In 1984, the General Assembly and the Commission on Human Rights again took up the case of the Palestinian Ziyad Abu Eain, this time in connection with prisoners held in southern Lebanon. The Assembly and the Economic and Social Council had first considered Abu Eain's case in 1981.[42]

Action by the Commission on Human Rights. The Commission on Human Rights, in a resolution of 20 February 1984[43] on human rights violations in the occupied Arab territories, condemned Israel for its continued detention of Abu Eain and called on it to implement fully the agreement on the exchange of prisoners with PLO concluded in November 1983 with ICRC. The Commission called on Israel to release Abu Eain and others detained at Ansar (Insar) Camp, which it said must be closed under the agreement. It further called on Israel to release all Arabs detained or imprisoned as a result of their struggle for self-determination and for the liberation of their territories, and demanded that Israel cease all acts of torture and ill-treatment of Arab detainees. By another resolution, of 6 March,[44] the Commission urged Israel to release immediately all civilians arbitrarily detained since the beginning of the war in Lebanon, as well as those it rearrested and detained again at Ansar Camp, in violation of the November 1983 agreement. The Commission also urged Israel to allow ICRC to visit all detainees in all the detention centres under its control and to ensure protection for Palestinian civilians, including released detainees, in the areas under its occupation. (For further details, see ECONOMIC AND SOCIAL QUESTIONS, Chapter XVIII.)

Communication and report. On 3 October 1984,[45] Jordan transmitted a letter of the same date from PLO, containing an appeal by prisoners in the central prison of Nablus (West Bank) for support to Palestinian detainees in Israeli prisons and detention camps.

On 14 November,[46] the Secretary-General reported on the implementation of the December 1983 Assembly resolution[47] demanding the immediate release of Abu Eain as well as other prisoners who had been registered to be freed from Insar Camp and other military command posts in southern Lebanon but had not been released, and whose transfer to Algiers was to be secured in conformity with a November 1983 agreement with ICRC.[48] Referring to Israel's statement on the resolution,[49] the

Secretary-General stated that Israel had not communicated any further information in reply to his note verbale of 13 October 1984.

GENERAL ASSEMBLY ACTION

Under the agenda item on the report of the Special Committee to Investigate Israeli Practices Affecting the Human Rights of the Population of the Occupied Territories, the General Assembly, on 14 December, adopted resolution 39/95 A by recorded vote. The Assembly acted on the recommendation of the Special Political Committee.

The General Assembly,

Recalling its resolution 38/79 A of 15 December 1983,

Taking note of the report of the International Committee of the Red Cross of 13 December 1983,

Taking note of the report of the Secretary-General of 14 November 1984,

1. *Deplores* the fact that the Israeli authorities, at the last minute, took one prisoner, Ziyad Abu Eain, who had been registered before embarkation by delegates of the International Committee of the Red Cross at Tel Aviv airport;

2. *Condemns* Israel for its failure to comply with General Assembly resolution 38/79 A;

3. *Demands again* the immediate release of all prisoners, including Ziyad Abu Eain, who were duly registered to be freed from Insar Camp and other military command posts in southern Lebanon and Israel but have not, in fact, been released, and the securing of their transfer to Algiers in conformity with the agreement reached through the good offices of the International Committee of the Red Cross;

4. *Requests* the Secretary-General to report to the General Assembly as soon as possible and not later than the beginning of its fortieth session on the implementation of the present resolution.

General Assembly resolution 39/95 A

14 December 1984   Meeting 100   120-2-15 (recorded vote)

Approved by SPC (A/39/712) by recorded vote (101-2-11), 29 November (meeting 43); 25-nation draft (A/SPC/39/L.22/Rev.1); agenda item 71.

Sponsors: Afghanistan, Algeria, Bahrain, Bangladesh, Cuba, Democratic Yemen, Djibouti, India, Indonesia, Iraq, Jordan, Kuwait, Madagascar, Malaysia, Mali, Mauritania, Nicaragua, Pakistan, Qatar, Saudi Arabia, Senegal, Sudan, Syrian Arab Republic, United Arab Emirates, Yemen.

Meeting numbers. GA 39th session: SPC 31-39, 43; plenary 100.

Recorded vote in Assembly as follows:

In favour: Afghanistan, Albania, Algeria, Angola, Argentina, Austria, Bahrain, Bangladesh, Belgium, Benin, Bhutan, Bolivia, Botswana, Brazil, Brunei Darussalam, Bulgaria, Burkina Faso, Burundi, Byelorussian SSR, Cameroon, Canada, Cape Verde, Chad, China, Colombia, Congo, Costa Rica, Cuba, Cyprus, Czechoslovakia, Democratic Kampuchea, Democratic Yemen, Denmark, Djibouti, Ecuador, Egypt, El Salvador, Equatorial Guinea, Ethiopia, Fiji, Finland, France, Gabon, Gambia, German Democratic Republic, Germany, Federal Republic of, Ghana, Greece, Guinea, Guinea-Bissau, Guyana, Haiti, Hungary, India, Indonesia, Iraq, Ireland, Italy, Japan, Jordan, Kenya, Kuwait, Lao People's Democratic Republic, Lebanon, Lesotho, Libyan Arab Jamahiriya, Luxembourg, Madagascar, Malaysia, Maldives, Mali, Malta, Mauritania, Mauritius, Mexico, Mongolia, Morocco, Mozambique, Netherlands, New Zealand, Nicaragua, Niger, Nigeria, Norway, Oman, Pakistan, Papua New Guinea, Peru, Poland, Portugal, Qatar, Romania, Rwanda, Samoa, Sao Tome and Principe, Saudi Arabia, Senegal, Seychelles, Sierra Leone, Somalia, Spain, Sudan, Suriname, Sweden, Syrian Arab Republic, Togo, Tunisia, Turkey, Uganda, Ukrainian SSR, USSR, United Arab Emirates, United Kingdom, United Republic of Tanzania, Venezuela, Viet Nam, Yemen, Yugoslavia, Zambia, Zimbabwe.

Against: Israel, United States.

Abstaining: Australia, Bahamas, Barbados, Belize, Guatemala, Ivory Coast, Jamaica, Liberia, Malawi, Nepal, Panama, Paraguay, Sri Lanka, Trinidad and Tobago, Zaire.

Israel said it was highly improper for the United Nations to interfere in judicial matters which fell within the jurisdiction of a sovereign State; Abu Eain was a convicted murderer serving his prison term and Israel regretted that the activities of ICRC were being exploited for political ends.

Australia noted with concern the report of ICRC that the prisoner exchange had not been carried out fully, but voiced doubts about the practice of focusing attention in Assembly resolutions on an individual case and pointed out that there were other individuals registered to be freed who remained in detention. In Sri Lanka's view, the subject dealt with was outside the Special Committee's mandate.

Canada would have preferred more constructive language, particularly in paragraph 2, but considered it important to encourage international support for humanitarian arrangements to mitigate the suffering resulting from conflicts.

REFERENCES

[1]YUN 1983, p. 274. [2]A/39/133-S/16417. [3]A/39/378-S/16693. [4]A/39/35. [5]YUN 1976, p. 235. [6]*Ibid.*, p. 245, GA res. 31/20, 24 Nov. 1976. [7]YUN 1983, p. 276, GA res. 38/58 B, 13 Dec. 1983. [8]YUN 1967, p. 257, SC res. 242(1967), 22 Nov. 1967. [9]A/39/99-S/16327. [10]S/16450. [11]A/39/283-S/16598. [12]A/39/319-S/16640. [13]A/39/395-S/16695. [14]S/16377. [15]S/16458. [16]A/39/166. [17]A/39/177-S/16474. [18]A/39/619-S/16803. [19]A/39/201-S/16493. [20]A/39/206-S/16501. [21]A/39/257-S/16562. [22]A/39/581-S/16782 & Corr.1. [23]A/39/533. [24]YUN 1983, p. 280, 38/180 C, 19 Dec. 1983. [25]YUN 1980, p. 426, SC res. 478(1980), 20 Aug. 1980. [26]*Ibid.*, p. 425, SC res. 476(1980), 30 June 1980. [27]*Ibid.*, p. 376, GA res. 35/207, 16 Dec. 1980. [28]YUN 1981, pp. 262, 313, GA res. 36/226 A & B, 17 Dec. 1981. [29]A/39/35. [30]YUN 1983, p. 286, GA res. 38/58 E, 13 Dec. 1983. [31]A/39/265-E/1984/77 & Add.1. [32]A/39/474 & Corr.1. [33]YUN 1983, p. 284, GA res. 38/145, 19 Dec. 1983. [34]ID/B/315. [35]A/39/16 (conclusion 1984/12). [36]ID/B/332. [37]UNIDO/IO/584. [38]DP/1984/16. [39]E/1984/20 (dec. 84/13). [40]E/1984/19. [41]YUN 1983, p. 282, ESC res. 1983/43, 25 July 1983. [42]YUN 1981, p. 907. [43]E/1984/14 (res. 1984/1 A). [44]*Ibid.* (res. 1984/20). [45]A/39/548-S/16766. [46]A/39/665. [47]YUN 1983, p. 273, GA res. 38/79 A, 15 Dec. 1983. [48]*Ibid.*, p. 272. [49]*Ibid.*, p. 273.

Incidents and disputes between Arab countries and Israel

Iraq and Israel

Armed incident involving Iraqi nuclear facilities

Note and report of the Secretary-General. By a note of 6 February 1984,[1] the Secretary-General brought to the attention of the Security Council a request made by the General Assembly in November 1983[2] that the Council consider measures to deter Israel from repeating an attack such as the 1981 bombing of a nuclear research centre near Baghdad.[3] He reported on 10 August 1984[4] that by a note of 15 March he had asked Israel to inform him of the action it had decided to take with regard to the Assembly's renewed demand that it withdraw its threat to attack and destroy nuclear facilities in Iraq and other countries. Israel replied on 12 July (see immediately below).

Communications. Referring to the Secretary-General's note, Israel, by a letter of 12 July,[5] recalled a statement made on 2 May by its Prime Minister that Israel supported international arrangements which ensured the status and inviolability of nuclear facilities dedicated to peaceful purposes, and that it viewed positively the activities of organizations and agencies established by the international community for those purposes. It also drew attention to a statement of 21 May by the Director-General of the Israel Atomic Energy Commission that Israel had no policy or intention of attacking nuclear facilities dedicated to peaceful purposes, and that it supported international efforts to arrive at an early arrangement regulating nuclear facilities as well as the mission of IAEA in ensuring that nuclear energy was a safe source of peaceful development. In its letter, Israel expressed regret at the Assembly's acquiescence in being used by Iraq year after year in attempts to vilify Israel.

By a letter of 15 August,[6] Iraq said that the statements quoted by Israel made no mention of the Assembly's November 1983 resolution demanding that it withdraw its threat to attack and destroy nuclear facilities in Iraq and other countries; also, the statements were not issued by the parties who originally had made those threats and they were confined to generalities, whereas the threats were directed specifically against Iraq. The thesis of the Director-General as reported by Israel was a piece of special pleading which could not deceive the international community; moreover, the statements referred to by Israel made no mention of the international safeguards system, leaving it to the goodwill of Israel, whose aggressive designs were well known, to decide which facilities were peaceful. Iraq quoted a statement made in August 1983 by the Israeli Minister of Scientific Research, and published in a United States magazine, *Nucleonics Week*, that, as long as there was no agreement turning the Middle East into a nuclear-free zone, Israel was compelled to disrupt any Arab project when it became clear beyond doubt that the intention was to produce nuclear weapons. From the statement, Iraq concluded, it was apparent that Israel persisted in its intention to attack nuclear reactors on the basis solely of its own decision as to the nature of those reactors; it was the United Nations duty to prevent Israel from implementing its policy, which was a threat to international peace and security.

By a letter of 20 November,[7] Iraq pointed out that there was more to the Israeli Prime Minister's statement quoted in Israel's letter of 12 July. As reported on 10 May in *Nucleonics Week*, he had added that, since some régimes violated agreements and rules

of behaviour without fear of retribution, he advocated co-ordinated and unified action by democratic countries which were, in his words, capable of punishing the various international pirates. That statement, Iraq said, was not only a blatant affirmation of the aggressor's intention to repeat its acts of aggression, but also an open invitation to lawlessness.

GENERAL ASSEMBLY ACTION

On 16 November, the General Assembly adopted resolution 39/14 by recorded vote.

Armed Israeli aggression against the Iraqi nuclear installations and its grave consequences for the established international system concerning the peaceful uses of nuclear energy, the non-proliferation of nuclear weapons and international peace and security

The General Assembly,

Having considered the item entitled "Armed Israeli aggression against the Iraqi nuclear installations and its grave consequences for the established international system concerning the peaceful uses of nuclear energy, the non-proliferation of nuclear weapons and international peace and security",

Recalling the relevant resolutions of the Security Council and the General Assembly,

Taking note of the relevant resolutions of the International Atomic Energy Agency,

Viewing with deep concern Israel's refusal to comply with those resolutions, particularly Security Council resolution 487(1981) of 19 June 1981,

Noting that Israel's statements contained in its communication of 12 July 1984 continue to ignore the safeguards system of the International Atomic Energy Agency and do not specify the Iraqi nuclear installations which were the subject of the Israeli attack and subsequent threats,

Convinced that the Israeli threats to attack nuclear facilities in Iraq and in other countries will continue to endanger peace and security in the region,

1. *Reiterates its condemnation* of Israel's continuing refusal to implement Security Council resolution 487(1981), unanimously adopted by the Council on 19 June 1981;

2. *Considers* that Israel's statements contained in its communication of 12 July 1984 do not fulfil or, in the view of some, do not completely fulfil the provisions of General Assembly resolution 38/9 of 10 November 1983 which specifically demanded that Israel withdraw forthwith its threat to attack and destroy nuclear facilities in Iraq and in other countries;

3. *Further considers* that any threat to attack and destroy nuclear facilities in Iraq and in other countries constitutes a violation of the Charter of the United Nations;

4. *Demands* that Israel undertake forthwith not to carry out, in disregard of the safeguards system of the International Atomic Energy Agency, any attack on nuclear facilities in Iraq, or on similar facilities in other countries, devoted to peaceful purposes;

5. *Requests* the Security Council to consider the necessary measures to ensure Israel's compliance with Security Council resolution 487(1981) and to deter Israel from repeating its attack on nuclear facilities;

6. *Reaffirms its call* for the continuation of the consideration, at the international level, of legal measures

to prohibit armed attacks against nuclear facilities, as a contribution to promoting and ensuring the safe development of nuclear energy for peaceful purposes;

7. *Requests* the Secretary-General to report to the General Assembly at its fortieth session on the question of the implementation of Security Council resolution 487(1981) and on the consequences of Israel's non-compliance with that resolution;

8. *Decides* to include in the provisional agenda of its fortieth session the item entitled "Armed Israeli aggression against the Iraqi nuclear installations and its grave consequences for the established international system concerning the peaceful uses of nuclear energy, the non-proliferation of nuclear weapons and international peace and security".

General Assembly resolution 39/14

16 November 1984   Meeting 65   106-2-33 (recorded vote)

27-nation draft (A/39/L.13/Rev.1); agenda item 24.

Sponsors: Algeria, Bahrain, Bangladesh, Democratic Yemen, Djibouti, Indonesia, Iraq, Jordan, Kuwait, Lebanon, Libyan Arab Jamahiriya, Malaysia, Maldives, Mali, Mauritania, Morocco, Nicaragua, Oman, Pakistan, Qatar, Saudi Arabia, Somalia, Sudan, Tunisia, United Arab Emirates, Yemen, Yugoslavia.

Meeting numbers. GA 39th session: plenary 55, 56, 65.

Recorded vote in Assembly as follows:

In favour: Afghanistan, Albania, Algeria, Angola, Argentina, Austria, Bahrain, Bangladesh, Benin, Bhutan, Bolivia, Botswana, Brazil, Brunei Darussalam, Bulgaria, Burkina Faso, Burundi, Byelorussian SSR, Cameroon, Cape Verde, Central African Republic, Chad, China, Comoros, Congo, Cuba, Cyprus, Czechoslovakia, Democratic Kampuchea, Democratic Yemen, Djibouti, Egypt, Ethiopia, Gabon, German Democratic Republic, Ghana, Greece, Guinea, Guinea-Bissau, Guyana, Hungary, India, Indonesia, Iran, Iraq, Ireland, Japan, Jordan, Kenya, Kuwait, Lao People's Democratic Republic, Lebanon, Lesotho, Libyan Arab Jamahiriya, Madagascar, Malaysia, Maldives, Mali, Malta, Mauritania, Mauritius, Mexico, Mongolia, Morocco, Mozambique, Nepal, New Zealand, Nicaragua, Niger, Nigeria, Oman, Pakistan, Peru, Philippines, Poland, Portugal, Qatar, Romania, Rwanda, Sao Tome and Principe, Saudi Arabia, Senegal, Seychelles, Sierra Leone, Singapore, Somalia, Spain, Sri Lanka, Sudan, Syrian Arab Republic, Thailand, Togo, Trinidad and Tobago, Tunisia, Turkey, Uganda, Ukrainian SSR, USSR, United Arab Emirates, United Republic of Tanzania, Uruguay, Viet Nam, Yemen, Yugoslavia, Zambia, Zimbabwe.

Against: Israel, United States.

Abstaining: Australia, Barbados, Belgium, Canada, Chile, Colombia, Costa Rica, Denmark, Dominican Republic, Ecuador, Equatorial Guinea, Fiji, Finland, France, Germany, Federal Republic of, Guatemala, Haiti, Iceland, Italy, Ivory Coast, Jamaica, Liberia, Luxembourg, Malawi, Netherlands, Norway, Panama, Papua New Guinea, Paraguay, Sweden, United Kingdom, Venezuela, Zaire.

In Israel's view, the text did not seek a solution to the complex problem of protecting nuclear facilities, but rather aimed at using the issue as a pretext for an annual anti-Israel spectacle. Israel's position on the inviolability of nuclear facilities dedicated to peaceful purposes had been stated clearly four times in the previous months, while Iraq's attitude was quite different.

In the opinion of the United States, the text served no useful purpose; to bring the matter up in the Assembly year after year was unproductive. The text unfairly condemned Israel, failed to give due credit to its repeated statements that it had no policy of attacking peaceful nuclear facilities, and gave a prejudicial characterization of Israeli policy. In addition, it did not serve the interests of any IAEA member State to perpetuate a divisive political debate in that Agency on this issue.

Canada could not support the text, saying it failed to take fully into account Israel's statements in compliance with the requests of the IAEA General Conference. International public opinion on the 1981

incident had been adequately registered; unless there was something further for the Secretary-General to report upon, Canada would not support either a request for a report or a decision to include the item in the agenda.

Ecuador rejected the use and threat of force in international relations and any concept of armed reprisals, particularly against any future danger perceived on the basis of subjective unilateral analyses that could serve to justify the unacceptable sophism of preventive war; it added, however, that the United Nations had repeatedly expressed its views on the matter, which could henceforth be dealt with in the First Committee.

Sweden did not object to the continued presence on the agenda of an item devoted to the follow-up of the 1981 Security Council resolution[8] condemning Israel's attack, as long as Israel failed fully to live up to the terms of that resolution; it was to be noted, however, that in comparison with earlier statements, a clearly more forthcoming attitude by Israel had been reflected in pronouncements to the Assembly and the IAEA General Conference. Against that backdrop, it did not appear appropriate for the Assembly to pronounce itself against the Israeli attitude in terms stronger than those applied in the previous year.

Belgium considered that, in view of the declarations made and the policies followed by Israel since that attack, there was no real danger of another similar occurrence and it was, accordingly, not correct to refer to threats that would continue to endanger peace and security in the region; also, making the subject a permanent item on the agenda did not appear to further prospects for a peaceful solution to the Middle East conflict.

The Federal Republic of Germany said the text did not reflect the assessment of Israel's statements as a step in the right direction; further consideration of the item and of those statements should be undertaken within IAEA, although repeated condemnations were not conducive to promoting practical work. Also, there seemed to be no evidence that the Israeli threats referred to in the sixth preambular paragraph continued to exist.

The USSR supported the resolution aimed at preventing armed aggression against nuclear installations or threats of such aggression; it fully agreed with the concern over what it called Israel's piratical act which, it said, had serious consequences for international peace and security and the right of States to use nuclear energy for economic and social development. It declared that it was against allowing Israel to repeat such attacks in violation of United Nations resolutions and the Charter.

The Syrian Arab Republic remarked that the wording of the revised text was not in keeping with the main goal of the original draft; the sponsors had suppressed some words and paragraphs reiterating condemnation of Israel's threats to repeat its attack on nuclear facilities in Iraq and other countries, and requesting IAEA to suspend all co-operation with Israel until it complied with the 1981 Council resolution and to report thereon. The text was not commensurate with the magnitude of Israel's criminal action or with the danger that such action might be repeated.

Introducing the revised draft on behalf of the sponsors, Iraq said that Israel, in its efforts to remove all strictures on it and allow it to pursue its aggression and threats with total impunity, had called on the Assembly to defeat the draft so that it would be let off the hook it had swallowed when it committed its unprecedented act of aggression.

Complaint by Iraq

Communications. On 16 October 1984,[9] Iraq transmitted to the Secretary-General a letter of the same date from its Deputy Prime Minister and Minister for Foreign Affairs charging that, on 14 October, an Israeli patrol had intercepted and fired at an Iraqi ship, *Babel*, in Jordanian territorial waters *en route* to the Jordanian port of Aqaba.

Israel referred to those charges in a letter of 1 November,[10] saying that on 12 October the Iraqi ship *Babylon* had been sighted moving north in the Gulf of Eilat. The Israel Defence Forces had made no contact with it, and at no time had the ship been stopped, checked or fired upon.

Lebanon situation

In an October 1984 report[11] on the situation in the Middle East, the Secretary-General gave an overview of the situation in the Israel-Lebanon sector. In February, following heavy exchanges of fire in the Beirut area, the Security Council met and voted on a French draft resolution by which, had it been adopted, a United Nations force would have been constituted for the Beirut area as soon as all the elements of the four-nation multinational force (France, Italy, United Kingdom, United States) had withdrawn from Lebanese territory (see p. 284). In August and September, the Council met at Lebanon's request. By a Lebanese draft, also not adopted, the Council would have affirmed that the provisions of the 1949 Geneva Convention relative to the Protection of Civilian Persons in Time of War applied to the territories occupied by Israel in southern Lebanon, and would have demanded that Israel immediately lift all restrictions and obstacles to the restoration of normal conditions in the occupied areas (see p. 289).

In a report of 9 April[12] on UNIFIL (see p. 298), the Secretary-General stated that the Lebanese Government and the people of southern Lebanon clearly desired the restoration of Lebanese sovereignty and authority up to the internationally recognized border

at the earliest possible date. Israel, while expressing its desire to withdraw its forces from Lebanon, was concerned over the security of its northern border after the withdrawal of those forces. The security of the Palestinian refugees, especially in the camps in the Sidon area, was a matter of grave concern and responsibility.

In his 9 October report on the Force,[13] the Secretary-General noted that developments in recent weeks seemed to have brought about more positive prospects for an Israeli withdrawal and the working out of arrangements to ensure that southern Lebanon would become a zone of peace under the sovereignty and authority of the Lebanese Government. As a follow-up to the Secretary-General's own visit to the area in June, the Under-Secretary-General for Special Political Affairs visited Lebanon, the Syrian Arab Republic and Israel to discuss the situation with their authorities; there seemed to be general agreement that an expanded mandate for UNIFIL and a widening of its area of operation would be key elements in such arrangements.

Following the Secretary-General's recommendation and at Lebanon's request, the Security Council extended UNIFIL's mandate twice during the year, for six months each time (see pp. 299 and 302).

As requested by the Security Council in its October resolution extending the mandate of UNIFIL, the Secretary-General continued consultations with the Lebanese Government and other parties directly involved. On 31 October, following consultations with Lebanon and Israel, he announced the convocation of a conference of military representatives from the two countries to discuss military aspects relating to the withdrawal of Israeli forces and security arrangements in southern Lebanon. The conference, which met intermittently from 8 November, took place at UNIFIL headquarters at Naqoura.[14]

The Council also met in May to consider events at the Ein El-Helweh refugee camp near Sidon in southern Lebanon (see p. 296).

UNRWA continued to assist Palestinian refugees in Lebanon. Protection of those refugees was the subject of General Assembly resolution 39/99 I, adopted following consideration of a report by the Secretary-General (see p. 343). By resolution 39/197, the Assembly called for intensified United Nations assistance for the reconstruction and development of Lebanon (see ECONOMIC AND SOCIAL QUESTIONS, Chapter III).

Communications (January). By a letter of 4 January 1984,[15] Lebanon complained of two Israeli air raids on 3 and 4 January. On 3 January, it charged, Israeli war-planes had attacked the village of Bhamdoun, destroying houses and wounding many civilians. On 4 January, fighter-bombers had attacked a Lebanese gendarmerie barracks at Baalbek in eastern Lebanon and Immam Mousa Sadr City, causing heavy damage, killing more than 100 persons and wounding 400 others, among them 150 school-children.

In its reply of 13 January,[16] Israel expressed the hope that the Lebanese Government would soon be able to restore its sovereignty throughout Lebanon, so that it could prevent the recurrence of the uncontrolled situation which had obliged Israel to act in self-defence against terrorist bases operating with the consent and encouragement of certain United Nations Member States. Its action was directed solely against terrorist installations, training bases and launching sites, which had served as bases for some of the most heinous acts, including suicide attacks, car bombings and the shelling of civilian residential areas. Israel deeply regretted any civilian loss of life; it stressed, however, that the terrorist groups deliberately located their installations and bases in populated areas, shielding themselves behind civilians and their dwellings. Concluding, Israel reiterated its support of the full restoration of Lebanon's sovereignty, territorial integrity and independence within its internationally recognized boundaries and of the withdrawal of all foreign forces from Lebanese territory.

SECURITY COUNCIL ACTION (February)

Following a request by France on 14 February for an urgent meeting,[17] the Security Council considered the situation in Beirut at four meetings on 15, 16, 23 and 29 February. It invited Italy, Lebanon and Senegal, at their request, to participate in the discussion without the right to vote.
Meeting numbers. SC 2514-2516, 2519.

On 29 February, the Council voted on a draft resolution by France.[18] The vote was 13 to 2, as follows:

> *In favour:* China, Egypt, France, India, Malta, Netherlands, Nicaragua, Pakistan, Peru, United Kingdom, United States, Upper Volta, Zimbabwe.
> *Against:* Ukrainian SSR, USSR.

Owing to the negative vote of a permanent member, the draft was not adopted.

By the draft, which was revised twice during consultations, the Council would have again urgently appealed for an immediate cease-fire and cessation of all hostilities throughout Lebanon, to be strictly complied with; requested the Secretary-General to make without delay arrangements to enable the Observer Group Beirut to monitor compliance with the cease-fire in the Beirut area; and decided, in agreement with the Lebanese Government, to constitute immediately under the Council's authority a United Nations force composed of personnel furnished by Member States not permanent Council members and selected, if appropriate, from UNIFIL contingents. The force was to have taken up a po-

sition in the Beirut area, in co-ordination with the Lebanese authorities concerned, as soon as all elements of the multinational force had withdrawn from Lebanese territory and territorial waters. It would have had the mission of monitoring compliance with the cease-fire and helping protect civilians, including in the Palestinian refugee camps, and, without intervening in Lebanon's internal affairs for the benefit of any party, thereby assisting in re-establishing the peace necessary for restoring Lebanon's territorial integrity, unity, sovereignty and independence.

By other provisions, the Council would have requested Member States to refrain from intervening in Lebanon's internal affairs and from any action, in particular military action, that might jeopardize the re-establishment of peace and security in Lebanon, and to facilitate the task of the United Nations force. It would have invited the Secretary-General to report within 48 hours on the implementation of the resolution.

Introducing the revised text, France said the sufferings of civilians and the constant threat to peace in the region posed by the violence made it necessary for the international community to shoulder its responsibilities. The conditions that had prevailed when the multinational force was established had changed drastically and the situation in the Beirut area had further worsened; a United Nations presence should be substituted for that force. The draft took full account of the concerns expressed on all sides. France later added that, while the text was not intended to settle all the problems of peace in the region, it was a first step and a peace-making gesture intended to promote a climate of reconciliation.

The USSR considered the draft unacceptable, with, for example, ambiguous wording relating to the mandate of the United Nations force in Beirut. The text had been introduced without further consideration of the USSR's position, which favoured continuing consultations. A real settlement in Lebanon should be achieved not by separate deals and arm-twisting but on the basis of strict implementation of United Nations decisions. Among the conditions for the deployment of a United Nations force were, over and above the withdrawal of the multinational force, withdrawal of foreign warships and guarantees that there would be no resumption of artillery fire, air strikes or any other interference in Lebanon's internal affairs by the multinational force.

The Ukrainian SSR said the draft did not contain provisions which would achieve the goals the Council was pursuing, such as urgent, effective measures that would lead to peace and stability and eliminate everything hindering normalization of the situation in the country. In spite of repeated Council demands that Israel withdraw immediately, it continued to occupy one third of Lebanon's territory and was bombing other areas of the country. In May 1983,[19] Israel and the United States had imposed on Lebanon a servile agreement transforming it into an American-Israeli protectorate, which predetermined increased tension. New suffering for the Lebanese had resulted from the so-called multinational force. The Israeli occupiers and the United States fleet, participating in military actions against the patriotic forces of Lebanon, had carried out a broad campaign of threats and military provocations against the Syrian Arab Republic.

The normalization of the situation in Lebanon, the Ukrainian SSR continued, demanded a complete cessation of interference, unconditional and complete withdrawal of Israel's interventionist forces and the multinational force, the removal from Lebanon's shores of the force's warships, and an immediate end to air and artillery bombardments. Without fulfilling those conditions and protecting Lebanon's civilians, the question of United Nations assistance to Lebanon lost any real basis. The absence in the resolution of the relevant provisions and guarantees would make the mission of a United Nations force for all practical purposes unrealizable. In the light of all that, the Ukrainian SSR could not consider the draft as anything other than an attempt to justify interference in Lebanon's internal affairs in the name of the United Nations.

Addressing the vote on the text, the Netherlands regretted that the United Nations had been prevented from making even a modest contribution to the national reconciliation process in Lebanon. A United Nations force should be a peacekeeping force rather than one which would have to enforce peace, with the risks of getting itself involved in the fighting and thus intervening in Lebanon's internal affairs. A stable and effective cease-fire in the Beirut area would continue to be an essential prerequisite for such a force to carry out effectively its proposed mandate.

The United Kingdom was disappointed at the Council's inaction and could not understand that anything said during the debate justified a veto on the limited United Nations action requested by the Lebanese Government. The United Kingdom said no one had been more insistent on restricting the discussion on the draft to the smallest geographical area possible—to the city of Beirut only, not even the Beirut area—than the Council member which had explained its negative vote with statements relating to Lebanon as a whole or to parts of Lebanon other than Beirut. The United Kingdom hoped for a resumption of the dialogue on national reconciliation which, it trusted, would lead to a situation in which a new Lebanese Government, the former one having already resigned, would come into office with national ac-

claim and assert its authority through the Lebanese Army and security forces throughout the country. The United Kingdom was encouraged by the clear statements by all Governments which had forces in Lebanon that they did not intend to keep them there, despite difficulties that had to be taken into account, such as a deterioration in the internal security position in parts of the country; the United Nations, however, might be able to play a constructive part in resolving those difficulties. It was convinced that there should be an expanded United Nations role in Lebanon. The situation there was grave: the authority of the duly constituted Government was called into question, there was factional strife, and the security of ordinary people was in doubt.

In China's view, the Council should implement in earnest its resolutions on Lebanon and give consideration to other practical steps. Any Council action should be conducive to safeguarding Lebanon's territorial integrity, to eliminating foreign interference, and to promoting national reconciliation. China said its vote was based on those principles and took into consideration that the draft foresaw a clearly defined mandate—helping protect the civilians, including those in the Palestinian refugee camps, and doing so without intervening in Lebanon's internal affairs for the benefit of any party whatever. On the other hand, since the Beirut crisis was only part of the Lebanon crisis, whose root cause was Israel's invasion and occupation, the key was the withdrawal of Israeli troops. Foreign warships should not, under any pretext, carry out armed intervention in Lebanon's internal affairs.

The United States said that in voting for the draft—which was imperfect and in many ways unsatisfactory—it expressed its commitment to the view that peace in Lebanon should be brought about by the Lebanese, that all foreign forces should be withdrawn, and that the Lebanese population should be left to seek without outside interference an agreement that would respect the rights and preserve the freedom of all. Lebanon had exercised its right to self-defence and to request others to assist in reinforcing and maintaining its sovereignty; the United States had responded to that request, as had others in the multinational force. The United States vote was part of its long-standing effort to help re-establish and reinforce the peace necessary to restore Lebanon's territorial integrity and to contribute to ending the violence and protecting civilians. There had been a great deal more discussion in the Council about the internecine tribal conflicts and the presence of Israeli troops than about the more than 50,000 Syrian troops and Palestinian, Iranian and other associates in Lebanon. Much less was heard about the systematic use of violence, encouraged from outside.

Lebanon regretted that, for the second time in a few months, the Council had been unable to help in putting an end to a tragic situation. The international community, through the Council, had a great responsibility towards not only the Lebanese but the peoples of the world: to guarantee international peace and security. Lebanon appealed to the Council to reconsider the positions taken and to respond positively and quickly to any new initiative in keeping with the seriousness of the situation and by means of which the Council might be able to fulfil its tasks under the Charter.

In Malta's view, the draft attempted resolutely to address a tragic situation and would have been a step towards restoring the stability necessary to augment the prospects for a positive outcome of the national reconciliation dialogue. Malta appealed to all concerned to support the task being contemplated for United Nations personnel; that would be a move towards restoring broader peace in the Middle East after the legitimate rights of the Palestinians had finally been recognized by all.

Egypt would have preferred a clearer and stronger wording requesting unconditional and immediate Israeli withdrawal from all Lebanese territory; the situation in Lebanon, threatening the country's territorial integrity and peace in the region, was the strongest justification for a United Nations presence.

India would also have preferred a reiteration of the demand for unconditional and immediate withdrawal of Israeli forces. Further, ambiguities should be cleared up before the Council took action to deploy a United Nations force. The Upper Volta also would have liked such points as the withdrawal of all foreign troops and agreement by all parties concerned to be better spelt out. Nicaragua felt that the draft, though not perfect, could contribute to improving the situation in Lebanon.

Pakistan said the proposed Council action was not a remedy for all problems besetting Lebanon, but the presence of a United Nations force in Beirut could have become a prelude to a process which could eventually restore the country's unity and independence; only the United Nations had the capacity to meet the need for an impartial presence which could bring tranquillity to Beirut and provide a respite for Lebanese leaders to intensify their national reconciliation efforts.

Peru fully agreed with the need for effective and just United Nations action. However, the outcome of the vote was not the end of the Council's responsibilities; it should keep the matter under scrutiny and seek progress in the quest for peace in Lebanon.

The Secretary-General felt that disagreement among the Council members had prevented the United Nations from playing an expanded role in Lebanon. He appealed to the Council to continue to consider the situation there with a sense of urgency and with the intent that in the near future ways would be found for the United Nations to expand its role, not only for Lebanon's benefit, but also for the cause of international peace.

During the Council debate, France said the situation in Lebanon had become particularly serious as a result of recent events. The civilian population had been subjected to fighting and bombardment and was constantly exposed to the dangers of a resumption of violence and even military operations, further complicating the prospect for any political solution. France recalled that, in 1982, it had also suggested creating a United Nations force in Beirut,[20] but it was clear that lengthy negotiations would be required in order to reach agreement on its creation. Thus, France had responded positively to Lebanon's request for a multinational force which, for 16 months, had attempted to protect the Palestinian refugee camps of Sabra and Shatila and generally to contribute to restoring calm in Beirut and its immediate surrounds. Circumstances had changed, however, and the risks of confrontation were now such that the international community must urgently face its responsibilities. A United Nations force to replace the multinational one was necessary to ease tension; the most suitable way to provide it was to send certain detachments from UNIFIL.

Supporting France's request for a United Nations presence in and around Beirut, the United Kingdom said there was an immediate need to put an end to the fighting in Lebanon, promote national reconciliation and make possible the withdrawal of all foreign forces. The United Nations could take a number of limited steps without a new Council resolution, but they were not a substitute for more far-reaching proposals which must be considered. United Nations observers and its other representatives already in Beirut could undertake small confidence-building measures, and the Council should not stand in the way of a modest increase in the number of observers if the Secretary-General considered that helpful. Further, the United Kingdom suggested the active use by the Secretary-General of his good offices and the expansion of UNIFIL's role to facilitate Israeli withdrawal from southern Lebanon.

The United States shared France's view that the international community should assume greater responsibility for the Lebanese people and welcomed the United Kingdom's suggestions. A United Nations presence would be useful throughout Lebanon, particularly to protect Palestinian refugee camps and reinforce cease-fires. Among the available instruments in Lebanon which might be useful were: a 50-man observer group; the United Nations Truce Supervision Organization

(UNTSO), which could be doubled; and UNIFIL, which was deployed in some cases in areas where violence no longer threatened people. The United States was ready to enter into serious discussions, without pre-conditions, on the composition and deployment of United Nations forces, preferably throughout Lebanon, to achieve those goals.

What was at stake in Lebanon, said Italy, was not only such fundamental humanitarian objectives as protecting civilians and Palestinian refugees, but also the survival of a State. The political situation had deteriorated to the extent that urgent United Nations intervention was required. National reconciliation, begun in talks between Lebanon's multiple factions at Geneva in November 1983 under promising auspices, had not been continued, and the Lebanese Army seemed not to have succeeded in representing the national community. The modalities for placing a United Nations force in Beirut must be subject to the most careful evaluation, above all in connection with the replacing of the multinational force in such a way as to ensure that a dangerous vacuum was avoided; a United Nations presence must also be seen in relation to the problem of the full restoration of Lebanese sovereignty.

Lebanon approved in principle the dispatching of United Nations forces or observers to assist in restoring security and stability and enabling the legitimate authorities to exercise control over all its territory. The proposal to send international forces to the Beirut area was a positive move, which, however, remained partial and limited as long as large parts of Lebanon continued to be occupied; any international force must have the means to undertake its tasks in all of Lebanon. Setting up and dispatching United Nations forces, as well as timing their deployment and determining their tasks, must be decided in consultation with the Lebanese Government, which was ready to co-operate in drawing up and implementing any resolution that might contribute to halting the crisis.

The Netherlands called on all parties to refrain from the use of force in Lebanon and to agree to a prompt, effective cease-fire in the Beirut area, which it believed would be conducive to early renewal of the internal conciliation process in Lebanon. It urged the parties to resume that process without delay, aimed at establishing a Government which enjoyed the widest national support; such a Government would be in a better position to accomplish the complete withdrawal of all non-authorized non-Lebanese forces from Lebanese territory. The Netherlands firmly believed that all concerned should consider ways in which the United Nations could help bring about a more stable situation in the Beirut area; however, the experience of the multinational force served as an example that one should not embark too hastily on a United Nations peace-keeping mission. The most pressing problem which the Council should address was an effective cease-fire and, to that end, the Netherlands was prepared to support any constructive proposal under the following conditions: a United Nations peace-keeping force should be deployed with the permission of the host country and with the consent of all parties involved; and it should have a clearly defined mandate and the Council's full backing. As an interim measure, limited steps such as those suggested by the United Kingdom could be useful.

Senegal said it had welcomed the 1983 national reconciliation Geneva conference and the cease-fire that seemed to have been the result; however, the situation had considerably worsened following recent events. The matter had two aspects, humanitarian and political; the most urgent aspect concerned the cessation of hostilities and the protection of civilians, including Palestinian refugees. Beyond that, the Lebanese State had to be safeguarded. The Council must promote without further delay a climate of mutual confidence to enable all parties to commit themselves to the peace process and must consider the Palestine question as a whole, in particular measures for convening an International Peace Conference on the Middle East (see p. 263), which could benefit Lebanon. Senegal supported the proposal to replace the multinational force in Beirut with an international one, to avoid a dangerous vacuum. The mission and terms of a United Nations force would have to be carefully evaluated, in close consultation with all parties concerned.

The Upper Volta said the Beirut situation was but one component of the Middle East problem, the centre-piece of which remained the Palestine question. The difficulties in Lebanon stemmed also from outside interference and the will of outside Powers to control that country, it added. The presence of Israeli troops in the south and of the so-called multinational forces in Beirut and Lebanese waters was inadmissible; only their immediate withdrawal and strict respect for Lebanon's territorial integrity could create conditions favourable to a reconciliation of all its people. It was the Council's duty to hasten the restoration of peace and alleviate the suffering of the population, including the Palestinian refugees. The Upper Volta viewed favourably the proposal to send a United Nations force entrusted with maintaining peace.

India also felt that any solution to the Lebanon problem could not be divorced from the search for a comprehensive Middle East settlement, based on the exercise by the Palestinians of their national and human rights. The 1982 Israeli invasion of Lebanon[21] was part of a calculated policy to decimate the Palestinians and erode Lebanon's independence. In India's opinion, recent events demonstrated beyond any doubt that the position of the multinational force was untenable and that its continued presence could only further aggravate tension. It had become necessary for the Council to consider United Nations action to fill the vacuum that withdrawal of that force would create. The objective of a United Nations force should be clear and its mandate precisely defined before deployment. It was also essential to see some evidence of a genuine national reconciliation process so that the Lebanese people would have the opportunity to find peace and stability free from all foreign interference.

Pakistan said the deepening human tragedy in Lebanon was matched by growing political anarchy compounded by foreign intervention; the situation called for initiatives aimed at reconciliation among the Lebanese factions. The United Nations had an important role to play, supplementing efforts by responsible Governments in the region; France's initiative fit in that context. A United Nations force in the Beirut area could prove crucial in mitigating violence and ensuring a cease-fire, which would provide Lebanon with a breathing space in which national reconciliation efforts could be sustained.

Also supporting France's proposal, Egypt said the deteriorating situation in Lebanon demanded assistance in facilitating the withdrawal of the multinational force and in making possible the most rapid deployment of a United Nations force; Egypt was ready to contribute to any joint effort intended to create the atmosphere necessary to break the cycle of violence and promote a political settlement and national reconciliation and the withdrawal of all foreign forces from Lebanon.

Communications (March–August). On 2 March 1984,[22] France transmitted a declaration adopted on 28 February at a Ministerial Meeting on European Political Co-operation. The Ministers of the 10 EEC members thereby expressed concern at the recent renewal of armed confrontation in Lebanon and struggle between Lebanese political forces. They called on all the parties to reach a lasting and effective cease-fire agreement, and hoped that the international community would urgently fulfil its peace-keeping responsibilities, in particular by installing in the Beirut area, with the parties' agreement, a United Nations force which would take up position following the departure of the multinational force. The Ministers recalled that the re-establishment of Lebanese integrity and sovereignty required Lebanese reconciliation as a pre-condition and indicated their firm conviction that the process initiated during the 1983 Geneva conference should be resumed under conditions corresponding to the aspirations of all the political and religious interests.

In a declaration adopted on 27 March by the EEC Ministers for Foreign Affairs, transmitted to the Secretary-General by France on 29 March,[23] the Ministers expressed the hope that, following the current national reconciliation talks among leaders of Lebanon's major political and religious groups meeting at Lausanne, Switzerland, progress towards reconciliation in Lebanon would prove possible, and that the Lebanese Government and all political forces would continue their efforts to bring about national unity and a lasting peace by reaching a just solution to Lebanon's internal problems.

On 6 March,[24] Israel conveyed an announcement by its Prime Minister's spokesman with regard to a Lebanese Government decision unilaterally to abrogate its 17 May 1983 agreement with Israel—calling for Israeli withdrawal from Lebanon in return for political and security arrangements in southern Lebanon—which had been concluded after negotiations between the two States and with active United States participation. The main obstacle to Lebanon's independence and the main factor disturbing peace efforts in the Middle East was the Syrian Arab Republic, Israel said, which immediately after the signing of the agreement had begun to take violent action to achieve its abrogation. Israel strongly condemned the Syrian intervention and the abrogation of the agreement. In the light of the fact that Lebanon was incapable of fulfilling its international obligations or preventing southern Lebanon from being turned once again into a terrorist base, Israel itself would determine the best ways to ensure its security.

On 29 May,[25] Lebanon submitted information on Israeli practices in southern Lebanon, the western Bekaa Valley and Rashaya, alleging that ever since the area was occupied by Israel in June 1982, it had been constantly exposed to abusive and inhuman actions; not a day passed but that the occupation forces raided towns and homes, blocked roads and arrested civilians, obstructing daily life and economic activity and preventing officials and internal security forces from guaranteeing the security of the region. The international community, Lebanon added, could not allow Israel to continue to ignore international law. Annexed to the letter was a report on Israeli practices against the civilian population of southern Lebanon and the Bekaa between March and May 1984.

Israel, on 26 June,[26] rejected the Lebanese charges as unfounded, saying that Lebanon's letter must clearly be viewed as reflecting a domination of the policies of the Lebanese Government by the Syrian Arab Republic and as yet another expression of relentless efforts by Syria to exploit Lebanon for its own bellicose policies.

By a letter of 28 June,[27] Lebanon charged that Israel had committed further acts of aggression, such as air raids on the island of Aranib, 6 kilometres off Tripoli, killing 15 residents of a scout camp and wounding 30 others, and on the port of Tripoli in order to hinder rescue operations. Lebanon further charged that occupation forces had laid siege to the village of Bidyas, Tyre district, on 27 June, rounding up villagers and arresting 17, and had closed the ports of Sidon and Tyre to commercial traffic, causing substantial losses to nearly 500 fishermen.

Further charges against Israel were submitted by Lebanon on 6 July[28] alleging that Israeli warships on 29 June had seized a passenger boat bound from Cyprus to Lebanon, forcing it to Haifa where the passengers were interrogated and nine of them detained. On 3 July, after urgent representations by the Lebanese Government, in particular with ICRC, Israel had released five of those detained. In Lebanon's view, Israel's action was incompatible with international law and endangered maritime navigation to and from Lebanon.

Israel, replying on 13 July,[29] stated that it fully respected and observed the principle of freedom of navigation on the high seas. However, being exposed to an ongoing and serious terrorist threat to its maritime borders, it was fully justified in having exercised its right to self-defence in seizing the ship *Elisor Blanco*, as there had been strong indications that it carried persons closely connected with an imminent threat to Israel's security. Following a brief investigation, the ship, its crew and most of the passengers had been allowed to proceed. Two passengers strongly suspected of involvement in terrorist activity had been detained for further investigation.

On 30 July,[30] Lebanon informed the Secretary-General that Israeli forces had prevented pupils in southern Lebanon from presenting themselves for baccalaureate examinations held throughout the country; such conduct, Lebanon added, showed contempt for education and culture and violated the most elementary ethical and humanitarian principles.

Israel, on 7 August,[31] rejected Lebanon's allegations as groundless; it said it had no intention of interfering with or obstructing the matriculation examinations. The Israel Liaison Office in Dbeye had promoted co-operation between the Lebanese and Israeli authorities with a view to assisting the local population in the areas under Israeli control; by its recent unilateral decision to close that Office, Lebanon had taken on itself the responsibility for increasing the population's hardships and must be held fully accountable for the event recounted in Lebanon's letter.

SECURITY COUNCIL CONSIDERATION (August/September)

Following a Lebanese request of 24 August,[32] the Security Council met from 29 to 31 August and on 4 and 6 September to consider Israeli practices in southern Lebanon, the western Bekaa and the Rashaya region. Cuba, Democratic Yemen, Iran, Israel, Kuwait, Lebanon, Qatar, the Sudan, the Syrian Arab Republic, Turkey, the United Arab Emirates and Yemen were invited, at their request, to participate in the discussion without the right to vote. The Council also extended an invitation under rule 39 of its provisional rules of procedure[a] to the Chairman of the Committee on Palestinian rights, at his request, and, at the request of Yemen in a letter of 28 August,[33] to the Permanent Observer of the League of Arab States to the United Nations.

Meeting numbers. SC 2552-2556.

On 6 September, the Council voted on a draft resolution sponsored by Lebanon.[34] The vote was 14 to 1, as follows:

> *In favour:* Burkina Faso, China, Egypt, France, India, Malta, Netherlands, Nicaragua, Pakistan, Peru, Ukrainian SSR, USSR, United Kingdom, Zimbabwe.
> *Against:* United States.

Owing to the negative vote of a permanent member, the draft was not adopted.

By the draft, the Council would have reiterated its call for strict respect for Lebanon's sovereignty, independence, unity and territorial integrity within its internationally recognized boundaries. It would have affirmed that the Geneva Convention relative to the Protection of Civilian Persons in Time of War, of 12 August 1949 (fourth Geneva Convention), applied to the territories occupied by Israel in southern Lebanon, the western Bekaa and the Rashaya district, and that the occupying Power was duty-bound to respect and uphold the provisions of that Convention and other norms of international law. The Council would have called on Israel to respect strictly the rights of the civilians in the areas under its occupation in southern Lebanon, the western Bekaa and the Rashaya district and to comply strictly with the fourth Geneva Convention, and would have urged all parties to the Convention to ensure respect for and compliance with it in those areas. It would have demanded that Israel immediately lift all restrictions and obstacles to restoring normal conditions in the areas under its occupation that violated the Convention, particularly concerning the closing of roads and crossings, the limitation of freedom of movement of individuals and the normal flow of persons and goods between those areas and the rest of Lebanon, and the obstruction to the normal conduct of Lebanese Government institutions and personnel.

---

[a]Rule 39 of the Council's provisional rules of procedure states: "The Security Council may invite members of the Secretariat or other persons, whom it considers competent for the purpose, to supply it with information or to give other assistance in examining matters within its competence."

Referring to the vote on the text, the United States said that Israel, as the occupying Power, clearly had special rights and duties. The United States strongly supported full respect for Lebanon's sovereignty, independence, unity and territorial integrity within its internationally recognized boundaries—objectives hardly addressed in the draft resolution. An essential element in achieving those objectives was the evacuation from Lebanon of all foreign forces, also not specifically mentioned, nor was the discord in the country other than in its southern part. The draft was also silent about humanitarian concerns for the suffering elsewhere in Lebanon and there was no mention of a role in that regard for international organizations, such as ICRC. The United States said it could not be party to an unbalanced and selective resolution; it was unreasonable and unrealistic to address the question of foreign forces in southern Lebanon and humanitarian and security problems there without dealing with the same problems in all of the country.

In Israel's view, the Council's vote would not change anything in Lebanon, whose Government had sought to obtain a propaganda victory to patch up its public image. The country's main problems were not even touched upon; fires still burned in Tripoli, Beirut and its environs, car bombs were still being set off and large numbers of people were being killed as the Council concluded another series of meetings divorced from life's realities.

Lebanon regretted United States opposition to a resolution limited to humanitarian aspects. The events in some parts of Lebanon were the inescapable consequences of a 10-year crisis; it was neither correct nor fair to compare what was taking place there with what was happening in Israeli-occupied territory, or to use that as an excuse not to deal with the tragedy and its root causes. The Lebanese Government was working determinedly to spread the sovereignty of the State to all the territory of Lebanon. Adoption of the draft would have put an end to the tragedy by putting an end to arbitrary Israeli practices; it would also have supported the Lebanese Government in its efforts aimed at the ultimate liberation of the land and its unification under one legitimate authority and one national sovereignty. What must be stressed was the agreement by the Lebanese cabinet on 15 March on security arrangements with Israel, in order to ensure complete Israeli withdrawal from Lebanese territory.

The Syrian Arab Republic regretted that the Council had not been able to shoulder its responsibilities under the Charter, a stand that would lead to an escalation of terrorist activities by Israel in southern Lebanon. The United States veto amounted to permitting Israel to continue occupying southern Lebanon and engaging in practices against the Palestinians and the inhabitants there. The Syrian presence in Lebanon was based on a legitimate Lebanese request; there was a joint determination to throw out the invaders and end the Israeli occupation. The Syrian Arab Republic would continue to help Lebanon because of its traditional, historic relations with it.

The USSR pointed out that over the previous three and a half years, the United States had eight times used the veto against vital Arab interests; the latest one gave Israeli forces the go-ahead to continue outrages in a third of Lebanon's territory.

The Observer of the League of Arab States held a similar position. Moreover, whatever might have been the circumstances of the Syrian presence in Lebanon, Israel could not under any conditions equate its presence in southern Lebanon as a result of invasion with the presence of the Arab deterrent forces in the rest of the country by invitation.

Before the vote, Zimbabwe said the Council should insist on respect for Lebanon's legitimate right to territorial integrity and political sovereignty, as demanded by resolutions 508(1982)[35] and 509(1982)[36] and in accordance with the Charter. Israel had adduced its security interests as justification for its continued illegal military occupation of a third of Lebanon; the road it was following could only complicate further an already dangerous situation and risk an even bloodier conflict. It was the Council's duty to take all possible steps to avert such a prospect.

Peru would have preferred a more balanced text, including mention of other occupying forces which must also comply with the Geneva Convention. To achieve immediate restoration of Lebanon's right to independence, sovereignty, territorial integrity, unity and full exercise of its authority throughout the territory, and to produce true opportunities for the country's stabilization and pacification, it was essential that all foreign presence be removed.

The United Kingdom's vote registered the importance it attached to the scrupulous observance of the fourth Geneva Convention in occupied southern Lebanon. Israel's continued occupation was wrong and was leading to a worsening cycle of violence. The solution was clear: Israel should withdraw its forces. There was an urgent need for early talks on the subject, through intermediaries if necessary; those talks must recognize, however, that Israel had legitimate security needs, and security arrangements must ensure safety for citizens on both sides of the border. Security precautions instituted by the occupying Power must have the minimum effect on the lives of the local inhabitants and must not conflict with Israel's obligations under the Convention. The early withdrawal of all foreign forces ought to proceed hand in hand with national reconciliation. It should be the Council's objective to help promote a solution, the key to which was in constructive and actively but quietly pursued diplomacy. UNIFIL should be given a wider and more useful role in helping the Lebanese Government maintain security in southern Lebanon, particularly as Israel's withdrawal took place, in order to provide added protection for civilians.

The Netherlands agreed with the applicability to the situation in southern Lebanon of the fourth Geneva Convention and the Hague Convention of 1907; at the same time, it questioned if it was proper for the Council to single out the humanitarian situation in southern Lebanon only, without regard for other aspects of the crisis in the country which needed to be addressed as urgently. Whether the opportunity would present itself for the Council to consider making UNIFIL's mandate more effective in the context of an Israeli withdrawal would probably be known only after the formation of a new Government in Israel, where elections had been held recently. In the mean time, the Netherlands believed, the Council should avoid any actions that might be counter-productive.

Opening the debate, Lebanon said it had come before the Council on behalf of the people of Lebanon, especially those of the south, the western Bekaa and the Rashaya area where more than 800,000 inhabitants suffered from Israel's occupation and unjust arbitrary practices and lived in constant terror. Israeli weapons were always pointed at them, their normal life was interrupted, and towns and villages were stormed daily. Israeli forces laid siege to homes and institutions, detained and imprisoned an average of 368 individuals every month, closed roads and shops, imposed curfews, and destroyed crops and orchards. All those acts were prohibited by customary law and by international instruments. From time to time, Israel closed the only two harbours in the south, the ports of Sidon and Tyre. In addition, Lebanon feared a possible diversion of the water of the Litani and Wazzani rivers; the Lebanese Ministry of the Interior had information that the engineering branch of the Israeli Defence Ministry had been digging a 3-kilometre tunnel from the Lebanese-Israeli border to the township of Deir Mimas, near the Litani River, which could absorb all the river water. The occupying authorities were isolating the region from the rest of the country and subjecting it to Israeli rule despite the fourth Geneva Convention, to which both Lebanon and Israel had acceded unconditionally and which protected people and properties from the excesses of occupation.

Lebanon sought from the Council: implementation of Council resolutions calling for complete Israeli withdrawal; immediate cessation of Israeli practices against the inhabitants of the south, the western Bekaa and the Rashaya region; and respect for their legitimate right to live in peace, security and dignity. The Council should compel Israel immediately to lift its siege of the occupied territories, insist that it respect the Charter, the Universal Declaration of Human Rights, the norms of international law, the Geneva and Hague Conventions and other international instruments, and stress Lebanon's inalienable right to its waters.

For some time, Israel said, there had been a further deterioration of the situation in Lebanon arising out of ongoing internecine warfare, particularly in and around Beirut and in the north, whereas the situation in southern Lebanon, in human and political terms, was far less of a pressing problem. The Lebanese Government was totally under Syrian political and military domination; now it was turning to the Council to talk of the problems in the south, which for many years had been virtually under the rule of a terrorist organization that had reduced the life of the Lebanese to a nightmare. Shrugging off the mass killings elsewhere in the country, where foreign-backed factions were sowing disorder and destruction, the Government apparently preferred to indulge in an international diversionary exercise meant to conceal its sagging fortunes.

There could be no comparison between the frightful chaos north of the Awali River and the security situation south of it, Israel continued. The withdrawal of Israeli forces beyond the Awali in the summer of 1983 was matched by a corresponding Syrian advance into other areas of Lebanon, directly or through proxies. The area north of the Awali was racked by civil strife and bloodshed; for the umpteenth time, the cease-fire had been broken and severe fighting resumed. By contrast, to the south of the Awali, Israel had made great efforts to ease the normal life of the inhabitants in the area under its control, which until June 1982 had been a PLO state within a State. There could be no better evidence of the fact that the Lebanese civilians were aware of Israel's efforts than their massive return to the area; a recent wave of returnees had come as a result of the severe fighting to the south of Beirut in February 1984.

Israel's military presence in southern Lebanon was only provisional; that was the reason Israel left the day-to-day administration, wherever possible, to Lebanese civilian authorities, with whom it co-operated and whom it assisted. Israel's conduct in southern Lebanon met the requirements of the fourth Geneva Convention and of other rules of international law aimed at protecting the civilian population. To prevent the spreading of terror, it was necessary from time to time to detain terrorist suspects and/or proven criminals. ICRC was being kept informed of the identity of all detainees. Only sporadically and upon reliable information indicating planned terrorist activity did Israeli forces undertake searches and limited *ad hoc* security measures.

Regarding water diversion, a group of United Nations observers invited to the area by the Israel Defence Forces (IDF) saw for themselves that no work had been done in or near the springs of the Wazzani to divert it, and there was as much truth to the Lebanese calumny with regard to the Litani, Israel said.

On numerous occasions, Israel had reaffirmed that it wished to see Lebanon independent and exercising full sovereignty over all of its territory. It had no territorial ambitions in Lebanon and wanted to live in peace and maintain good-neighbourly relations with it. Israel would withdraw its forces from Lebanon as soon as adequate provisions were made for ensuring Lebanese sovereignty in the south and for the security of Israel's northern border from attack and harassment. Israel was prepared to negotiate with Lebanon to reach mutual security arrangements in the south; however, if Lebanon was either unable or unwilling to prevent its territory from being used as a base for terrorist activities against another State, it must be prepared to expect that State to take self-defence measures to protect itself and its citizens.

The USSR charged that Israel sowed undisguised terror and violence in Lebanon, seeking to perpetuate its occupation of part of yet another Arab country. For the population of southern Lebanon, Israeli occupation meant daily mass repression, shooting of unarmed inhabitants, systematic raids and arrests, overcrowded prisons and concentration camps. The occupying forces were also violating the area's economic links with the rest of the country, as well as virtually blockading the transport of local products through checkpoints and systematically destroying plantations and crops. Israel's practices demonstrated its desire to turn southern Lebanon into another field for creeping annexation, isolate it from the rest of the country and push further northwards the borders of its expansion. Such inadmissible practices must be terminated; it was the Council's duty to demand that Israel cease its policy of terror and rescind its discriminatory measures. Israel's attempts to dismember Lebanon, undermine the economic life of the occupied areas and exploit the natural resources must be rebuffed. Israel must end its illegal occupation and withdraw its troops, as called for in Council resolutions whose implementation was the key to eliminating the abnormal situation in Lebanon.

Without United States support, the entrenchment of Israeli forces in Lebanon would not have been possible. In May 1983, the United States had

assisted Israel in imposing a lopsided and insidious treaty, solidifying the gains of Israel's aggression. The fact that the American troops had been compelled to leave Lebanon and the failure of the 1983 treaty showed that attempts to impose on Lebanon systems from outside were dangerous and fruitless. The way to achieve peace in the Middle East was by a comprehensive political settlement involving collective efforts under the United Nations aegis; the best machinery for this would be an international conference. A detailed programme set forth by the USSR on 29 July 1984 (see pp. 259 and 265) provided an alternative to the continuation of Israel's policies of aggression in the guise of protecting its interests.

Similar views were expressed by the Ukrainian SSR, which said that a Middle East peace could be secured only through collective international efforts in which all parties concerned participated, as advocated by the overwhelming United Nations majority. The USSR proposal of 29 July for a comprehensive settlement was such a constructive approach. With its recent measures further exacerbating its occupation, Israel was obviously seeking to fragment Lebanon, to isolate the seized areas from the rest of the country and to entrench itself there. The continuing occupation of southern Lebanon and the gross interference by Israel and the United States in Lebanon's affairs were the fundamental causes for the crisis in and around the country. The Ukrainian SSR regarded it as the Council's duty to call for unconditional withdrawal of the armed Israeli forces from Lebanon, on the basis of resolutions 508(1982)[35] and 509(1982).[36]

China also condemned Israel's forcible occupation and its atrocities, and declared its support of the struggle of the Lebanese people and the legitimate demands of the Lebanese Government. In China's view, Israel had all along harboured ambitious designs on Lebanon; the perverse acts of its troops had reduced Lebanon to a devastated land where people lived in dire misery. It was precisely the cruel oppression by the occupying authorities that had forced the Lebanese to rise in resistance and self-defence. The Council should play an active role and implement its resolutions in earnest; in the mean time, it should consider other practical measures to preserve Lebanon's independence, sovereignty and territorial integrity and to eliminate foreign aggression and interference. The key to a solution was the withdrawal of Israeli troops.

Virtually all speakers called on Israel to respect international law, especially the fourth Geneva Convention. Among them, France stressed that Israel must respect the conventions on humanitarian law applicable to armed conflicts. The Council could not accept Israel's putting up obstacles to the accomplishment of UNIFIL's mission, it said, especially now that the Lebanese Government was making every effort to move towards national reconciliation. Lebanon must be helped to regain its independence.

In Nicaragua's opinion, Israel had taken every measure to isolate southern Lebanon, the western Bekaa and the Rashaya area. The cruel and inhuman treatment of the inhabitants of southern Lebanon was typical of Israel's conduct in all occupied Arab territories; its occupation of Lebanon was an important link in its expansionist plans, with the ultimate goal of displacing and annihilating Arabs and Palestinians. Nicaragua considered it essential that the Council use every means to make Israel implement its resolutions, seven of which in 1982 had demanded Israel's withdrawal from Lebanon. The Council must continue to demand that Israel adhere to the Charter principles, international law and the fourth Geneva Convention requiring that the occupying Power respect the basic human rights of the inhabitants of the territories it occupied. The specific problem of Lebanon could at no time be separated from the overall Middle East situation and Nicaragua considered it essential that an International Peace Conference (see p. 263) be convened as soon as possible, with the participation of the main protagonists.

Malta said the incidence of conflict elsewhere did not justify Israel's occupation of the territory of another State, even less its causing havoc and confusion through harassing Lebanese citizens. There was a growing urgency for concerted political action in the search for an enduring and equitable solution; in response to that need, the non-aligned countries of the Mediterranean were to meet in the first week of September at Valletta, in a dedicated effort at the ministerial level to chart a new course designed to reduce tension and expand co-operation. In the mean time, Malta urged Israel to turn away from its militaristic policies, respect internationally recognized principles and Council decisions, and join others in a peace process which would restore full sovereignty to the people of Lebanon within its own internationally recognized boundaries and which would also do justice to the rights of the Palestinians.

After suffering destruction and dismemberment during the civil war, Lebanon was trying to reunify itself by drawing up a national security programme, Egypt stated; yet Israel had now directed its forces to carry out completely arbitrary actions in southern Lebanon and the western Bekaa, to perpetuate a divided Lebanon. Israeli occupation practices had become more diversified and covered every segment of social, cultural, economic and human life; no city, school or village had been spared Israeli violence, which naturally brought about fierce resistance. Egypt hoped that the Council would adopt steps to make it possible to meet the Lebanese demands: to compel Israel to abide by the fourth Geneva Convention and cease all its oppressive practices in the Lebanese territory under its control; to condemn the Israeli occupation; and to implement Council resolutions demanding Israel's unconditional withdrawal.

In Burkina Faso's view, the facts reported by Lebanon were proof that Israel's true intentions were far from guaranteeing the security of its northern frontier; its practices were designed to inflame tension artificially in order to justify the perpetuation of the military occupation which it advocated as the sole means of achieving a settlement. On the basis of its conviction that no reason and no principle of international law could justify interference in the internal affairs of another country, Burkina Faso joined other non-aligned countries in demanding the withdrawal of the multinational force from Lebanon. The same conviction led it to urge Israel strictly to comply with Council resolutions and withdraw from southern Lebanon unconditionally and without delay.

Torture, harassment, detentions, raids and other inhuman practices appeared to have become the order of the day in southern Lebanon, said India; responsibility for the hardships and inhuman treatment of civilians there rested squarely with the Israeli authorities. Serious economic dislocation added to the human misery. It was appropriate that the Council should seek ways to ameliorate the situation, which could have wider repercussions for peace and stability in the region. Israel's 1982 invasion was part of its calculated policy systematically to decimate the Palestinians and completely erode Lebanon's sovereignty, India continued; its stranglehold of Lebanese territory strengthened with each day. A solution could not be divorced from the search for a comprehensive and lasting Middle East settlement, based on the exercise by the Palestinians of their national and human rights. Like most other speakers, India fully supported Lebanon's demands for immediate implementation of Council resolutions 508(1982) and 509(1982), demanding Israel's complete withdrawal and the immediate cessation of military activities in Lebanon. The time had come for the Council to act decisively to halt Israeli aggression and intransigence; India hoped that the Council would discharge its responsibility to restore the rule of law and civilized conduct in Lebanon.

The occupying forces did not shrink from any measure to intimidate the population of southern Lebanon into total submission and acquiescence in Israeli expansionist aims, Pakistan charged. The 1982 invasion was a product of the continued denial of the legitimate right of the Palestinians to an independent homeland in Palestine. The Council must not be deterred by Israel's tactics from fulfilling its responsibility of providing redress to Lebanon; it was incumbent on the Council to call on Israel to cease its inhuman practices and adhere to the norms of international law and conduct.

The Chairman of the Committee on Palestinian rights considered it the Council's duty to save Lebanon from imminent disintegration, at which Israel's practices seemed to be aimed. The framework for peace was defined by the General Assembly in a December 1983 resolution[37] which endorsed the convening of an International Peace Conference on the Middle East (see p. 263). There was an international consensus that there could be no peace there so long as the Palestine question was not settled. In the light of those considerations, the Council must discharge its mandate; it was time that the people of Lebanon, who had suffered so much, enjoyed justice, full sovereignty and integrity.

What was taking place in the occupied Lebanese territories demonstrated once again that the aim of Israel's attack on Lebanon was to create a Zionist expansionist State, the Syrian Arab Republic said. Israel's expansion northwards required expansion to the Litani River, if not beyond, plotting against Lebanon's independence and unity, and using conditions to create small states that would be satellites of Israel. Israel's practices in southern Lebanon were in line with its policy in the West Bank, the Gaza Strip and the Golan Heights, creating hardship for the inhabitants to the point where they were forced to emigrate and then preventing them from returning. All that was an attempt by Israel to lay its hand on the south, while the United States did complementary work to destroy the unity of Lebanon, trample on its sovereignty and deprive it of its national identity. Thanks to Lebanon's awareness and its heroic struggle against foreign occupation, the May 1983 agreement was aborted, leading to the withdrawal of United States Marines and aborting the international plot against Lebanon as a whole. The Syrian Arab Republic hoped that the Council would meet its responsibilities *vis-à-vis* Lebanon and its people, in particular with regard to resolution 509(1982) demanding Israel's immediate and unconditional withdrawal.

Cuba charged that the slogan "Peace for Galilee", under which the 1982 Israeli invasion had been carried out, was a futile attempt to divert attention from Israel's real objectives: to liquidate Palestinian resistance, deal blows to progressive Lebanese forces, create conditions that would allow setting up a government in Beirut subject to Tel Aviv's orders, help place United States troops in Lebanon, implement Israel's expansionist policy, lay the bases for further aggression against other Arab States, especially the Syrian Arab Republic, and consolidate Israeli presence in the other occupied territories. By intensifying its irrational policy, it seemed as though Israel was attempting to punish the Lebanese for the humiliating outcome of the multinational force and for the abrogation of the May 1983 treaty imposed with United States pressure. The international community could not go on accepting the fact that a United Nations Member continued to trample underfoot international law and Charter principles; Israel must stop its criminal actions in southern Lebanon and withdraw its invading forces.

Kuwait termed Israel's practices in southern Lebanon unspeakable crimes and obsolete colonial practices; what was happening there was proof that Israel did not intend to leave but to entrench itself and transform the country into a northern strip, adding it to the other occupied territories. If the international community did not take effective steps to restore the situation in Lebanon, it might find itself faced with another *fait accompli* imposed by Israel with full impunity.

Yemen saw Israel's actions as a link in an endless chain of unjust wars against the Arab people and attempts to annihilate the Palestinians. It called for measures to compel Israel to lift its siege of areas under its occupation and to respect Charter provisions and international law, as well as Lebanon's sovereignty over its natural resources and territory. It also called on the Council to affirm the necessity of protecting the safety and security of the Palestinians in their camps in southern Lebanon; the Palestinians must be granted their right to self-determination and statehood on their own soil.

Israel expected Lebanon to shelve the problems of Israeli occupation until annexation became a fact of life, as had been the case in the Golan Heights and Jerusalem, Democratic Yemen remarked. The misery of the Lebanese under Israeli occupation, the brutality of the invading army and Israel's designs on and plunder of Lebanon's natural resources were facts that Israel's denial could not cover up. The more barbaric the Israeli soldiers, however, the more a people dedicated to freeing its land resisted. Problems elsewhere in the country did not justify continued occupation of southern Lebanon; Israel was taking advantage of those problems, many of its own making.

In Qatar's opinion, the Israeli occupying forces had put themselves in a situation where they were subjected to natural reactions from a people whose territories had been violated and whose national sovereignty had been undermined; they had no right to invoke those reactions as a pretext to oppress civilians, deny their human rights and destroy their lives. The chain of violence would have no end unless the occupation forces withdrew. Qatar called on the Council to affirm the first part of resolution 509(1982), calling on Israel once more to withdraw all its military forces unconditionally to Lebanon's internationally recognized boundaries. The Council should affirm its resolutions 512(1982)[38] and 513(1982),[39] concerning respect for the rights of civilian populations, and put an end to the acts of violence against them. It must compel Israel to respect the Charter, the Universal Declaration of Human Rights and other relevant international instruments, and must reaffirm Lebanon's historic water rights.

According to the United Arab Emirates, it was clear that the continued Israeli occupation of southern Lebanon and the persistence of inhuman violations there were threatening international peace and security. Refusing to withdraw, Israel was consolidating its occupation. The Council had no choice but to make sure that resolutions 508(1982) and 509(1982) were implemented. If it failed to deal with the question in an integrated manner, Lebanon would time and again have to come to it to complain against Israel, and other Arab States would undoubtedly have to lodge similar complaints, all stemming from Israeli aggression and expansion and the denial of legitimate Palestinian rights.

Israel's aggression against southern Lebanon was motivated by nothing but its desire to expand, to occupy Arab territory and to plunder resources, the Sudan believed. Its practices there were an extension of its practices in the other occupied territories. The Council and the international community must protect Lebanon, and its Government must be assisted to achieve peace and unity. If the Council failed to shoulder its obligations, not only would the occupation and the suffering continue, but the aggressor would be rewarded, and the use of force encouraged and the principles that had made the Council the guardian of international peace and security undermined.

The re-establishment of Lebanese control over its territory was essential for successful national reconciliation and reconstruction, Turkey stated. A timely, judicious resolution would help Lebanon regain its sovereignty and achieve progress in that process, which was retarded by Israel's continued occupation. Israeli practices were a leading cause of tension and violence in the region and a main impediment to a Middle East settlement. In conditions acceptable to the Lebanese Government, all foreign forces in Lebanon must evacuate the country.

For 11 months prior to the June 1982 invasion of Lebanon, the Permanent Observer of the League of Arab States said, there had been no incident at the borders of southern Lebanon. Israel arrogated to itself the right to determine when and if its security was established, so the term "provisional" that Israel applied to its occupation had the seeds of permanency.

Expressing support for the struggle of the Moslem people of southern Lebanon to regain their freedom and dignity with the limited resources they had, Iran said the victims of Zionist aggression should not fall into the trap set by the American-Zionist alliance and wait passively for the Council to gain their rights for them.

Further communications (September–December). On 19 September 1984,[40] Democratic Yemen transmitted to the Secretary-General a letter of the same date from the PLO Executive Committee Chairman expressing deep concern over intelligence reports that Israel was planning to withdraw from the areas of Sidon and Tyre and to deliver those areas to its agents, the so-called armed Lebanese forces. Recalling the September 1982 massacres at the Sabra and Shatila refugee camps,[41] PLO appealed to the Secretary-General to take all measures to ensure that such genocide did not recur and to provide guarantees for the safety and security of the Palestinians in southern Lebanon.

On 14 December,[42] Lebanon protested a large-scale military action during the night of 13 December by some 4,000 Israeli forces on eight southern villages located in the zone covered by UNIFIL, resulting in four dead, dozens wounded and hundreds of civilians arrested or detained. To justify its aggression, Lebanon said, Israel claimed that some of the inhabitants of the villages had been planning to attack the Israeli forces. UNIFIL had been unable to withstand the Israeli attack because of the heavy gunfire and aerial bombing. It had been prevented by the Israeli forces from inspecting the area afterwards and from taking the dead and wounded to hospital. Lebanon reserved the right to request a special Council meeting should it deem it necessary.

Israel, on 21 December,[43] replied that Lebanon's accusations were unfounded. Acting on reliable information that terrorists were basing themselves in several villages in southern Lebanon and preparing attacks from there, IDF had carried out an operation in four villages to prevent such attacks. Israeli units had uncovered several ammunition and weapons caches and found propaganda material inciting civil disruption. Twenty suspects were arrested; in Marakah, a wanted terrorist was shot by Israeli troops. Despite precautions to avoid unnecessary casualties, a woman was fatally wounded during an unprovoked attack against Israeli forces. Expressing its commitment to preserving peace and security in southern Lebanon, Israel stressed that it would not allow terrorists to use that area as a staging ground for terrorist activities against it.

Incident at Ein El-Helweh

Communications. By a letter of 16 May 1984,[44] the Acting Chairman of the Committee on Palestinian rights drew the Secretary-General's attention to reports that Israeli troops had surrounded and entered the Ein El-Helweh Palestinian refugee camp outside Sidon in occupied southern Lebanon on 15 May in a search operation. Military action against Palestinian civilians living there resulted in 60 persons being killed or wounded and some 30 houses destroyed; in addition, 150 people were arrested. It was not yet clear, the Acting Chairman said, if the action had been a collective punitive measure; in any case, such action was prohibited by the fourth Geneva Convention.

The incident was also reported to the Security Council President in a letter of 16 May from PLO, transmitted by Egypt the following day.[45] Israel's action could only be viewed as a further link in the chain of its campaign of genocide against the Palestinians, PLO said; it called for immediate measures to put an end to that policy and to guarantee the safety and security of all Palestinians living under Israeli military occupation.

SECURITY COUNCIL CONSIDERATION

Following a request of 17 May by Kuwait as Chairman of the Arab Group,[46] the Security Council met on 21 May to consider the charge of Israeli aggression against the Ein El-Helweh refugee camp.

Meeting number. SC 2540.

The Council invited Israel, Kuwait and Lebanon, at their request, to participate in the discussion without the right to vote. It also invited the Chairman of the Committee on Palestinian rights, at his request, to participate in the debate under rule 39 of its provisional rules of procedure.[b] An invitation under that rule was also extended to the Permanent Observer of the League of Arab States, as requested by Kuwait in a letter of 21 May.[47]

At Egypt's request, in a letter of 17 May,[48] the Council decided, by 11 votes to 1 (United States), with 3 abstentions (France, Netherlands, United Kingdom), that an invitation to participate be accorded to PLO. The President stated that Egypt's proposal was not made pursuant to rule 37[c] or rule 39 of the Council's provisional rules of procedure, but, if approved, the invitation would confer on PLO the same rights as those conferred on Member States when invited to participate pursuant to rule 37.

Before the vote on that decision, the United States said the only legal basis on which the Council might grant a hearing to persons speaking on behalf of non-governmental entities was rule 39. It did not agree with the Council's recent practice which appeared selectively to try, through a departure from the rules of procedure, to enhance the prestige of those who wished to speak in the Council; that practice was without legal foundation and an abuse of the rules.

Stressing that it did not wish to convey the impression that PLO should not be heard by the Council, the Netherlands said its reservation related only to the procedure followed, which was designed to grant PLO a status similar to a Member State. It was a political gesture that did not reflect PLO's true relationship to the United Nations.

Lebanon said the events during the night of 15/16 May and on 17 May in the Ein El-Helweh camp south-east of Sidon deserved the Council's serious attention. IDF had launched a large-scale assault, attacking the camp with three contingents and then overrunning it, blowing up several houses, some with the occupants still inside. They killed or wounded many inhabitants and arrested approximately 150, who were transported to a concentration camp. Such an attack could not be justified; no attempt to distort the facts could absolve the occupying Power of its responsibility. Since its occupation of southern Lebanon, Israel had consistently launched oppressive military campaigns and carried out inhuman practices against Lebanese citizens and against Palestinians in their camps. Lebanon called on the Council to denounce, deplore and condemn those practices, which were in flagrant violation of the Charter and of human rights, to recognize the real situation in southern Lebanon, and to do its duty to preserve the safety of the population there and restore to Lebanon the usurped territory. It did not advocate the accumulation of resolutions that remained dead letters, it said, but would continue to call for implementation of earlier Council resolutions until that call was heeded. It was incumbent on the Council to put an end to the current state of affairs by prevailing on Israel to withdraw completely from southern Lebanon so that Lebanese sovereignty and authority could be regained and the south transformed into a zone of peace and security. If the Council did not take a position commensurate with the gravity of Israel's practices, it would pave the way for Israel to persist in its attempt to change the geographic and demographic character of southern Lebanon in order to further its own designs under the false pretext of protecting its own security.

[b]See footnote a on p. 289.

[c]Rule 37 of the Council's provisional rules of procedure states: "Any Member of the United Nations which is not a member of the Security Council may be invited, as the result of a decision of the Security Council, to participate, without vote, in the discussion of any question brought before the Security Council when the Security Council considers that the interests of that Member are specially affected, or when a Member brings a matter to the attention of the Council in accordance with Article 35 (1) of the Charter."

Israel said IDF had had reliable information about large quantities of arms and ammunition at the camp, and, acting on that information, it had conducted extensive search activities on the night of 15/16 May. One house was entered, in which arms and ammunition were found. The searchers encountered some resistance, as a result of which a resident of the house was injured and transferred to a local hospital; another who tried to escape was also injured. Explosives and weapons were found in a courtyard. It was feared that they were booby-trapped; the only safe course was to supervise their immediate detonation, which caused some damage to adjacent houses. IDF had already confirmed that Israel would assist the owners of the damaged houses to make the necessary repairs. During the search, a considerable number of weapons and large quantities of magazines and ammunition were uncovered. On 16 and 17 May, demonstrations and disturbances were staged by and involved only local residents; they were a direct outcome of the ongoing conflict between the rival factions of the PLO terrorists, which were all represented at the camp. During the disturbances, there were two fatalities—not 60, as PLO had claimed. Israel held that the problems of the Middle East lay elsewhere: in the Persian Gulf, the Iran-Iraq war, the invasion of Afghanistan, the periodic massacres of tens of thousands of Syrians by their own Government, and the situation in Lebanon proper where hundreds, if not thousands, of casualties had occurred in recent months, primarily in Beirut.

Kuwait said the events of 15 May were only one more link in a chain of inhuman crimes which Israel continued to commit in its desperate attempts to strengthen its grasp over the occupied territories; the latest crime again showed that Israel was convinced that the Palestinian presence constituted a danger to its territorial dreams. In dealing with that presence, Israel had resorted to defaming the Palestinians, transforming them in the eyes of the world into nothing more than a group of terrorists. Israel had the mistaken illusion that the extermination of the Palestinians and the terror through which it was trying to stifle their movement could dissuade them from carrying on their national struggle. As occupying authority, Israel was fully responsible for what was occurring in the occupied territories; it must not only put an end to the massacres, dispersal, torture and imprisonment of civilians and the destruction of their houses, but protect the population and their goods. The Arab world appealed to the Council to fulfil its responsibilities as defined in the Charter and ensure implementation of all its resolutions.

The PLO representative called the incident at Ein El-Helweh a racist and genocidal crime. He understood that, according to a report, members of the so-called Palestinian National Guard—which he said was a unit of the Israeli occupation troops—had fired at boys burning tyres on 17 May; the boys were trying to prevent the advance of Israeli troops further inside the refugee camp. The population in southern Lebanon, be they Lebanese citizens or Palestinian refugees, were only exercising a legitimate right to resist foreign occupation. PLO trusted that the Council would take proper action, as outlined by Lebanon, to ensure Israel's compliance with Council resolutions and see to it that the safety and security of the civilians in the occupied territories were guaranteed. It was the Council's duty to insist that Israel respect the Charter and international conventions; PLO called on the Council to invoke the powers vested in it and impose mandatory sanctions on a Member that violated the Charter, committed crimes and failed to respect conventions.

The Chairman of the Committee on Palestinian rights said the operation carried out at Ein El-Helweh represented a systematic denial of Palestinian rights and was a flagrant violation of human rights. Israel was trying to silence the Palestinians who were legitimately protesting the occupation of their territory and was pursuing illegal plans to annex the West Bank and Gaza. Its policies exacerbated tension in the region and endangered international peace and security. More than ever it was necessary to consider the Palestine question in its entirety at an international conference on peace in the Middle East, from which Lebanon particularly would benefit. The constant outbreaks of violence often sprang from the Palestinian cause and the failure to settle the Middle East question. Without further delay, the Council must put an end to the tragic events and seek to promote a climate of mutual confidence which would allow the renewal of dialogue between all the parties concerned.

India regarded the tragic events at the camp as clear evidence of increasing Israeli brutality and repression in the occupied territories, where similar attacks had been reported and where raids, indiscriminate killing, torture, imprisonment and harassment of Palestinians had become daily occurrences. Relentlessly pursuing its policy of intimidating the population, Israel was consolidating its stranglehold on the territories. Responsibility for the atrocities at Ein El-Helweh rested squarely with the Israeli forces. The need of the hour was to put an immediate end to bloodshed and harassment and restore peace and order; Israel should be made to discharge its obligations under the international conventions that dictated civilized behaviour by occupying Powers towards the people of occupied territories. It must withdraw all its military forces unconditionally to the internationally recognized boundaries of Lebanon. At the same time, it was imperative that the international community seek a comprehensive, just and lasting Middle East peace, to the achievement of which the Movement of Non-Aligned Countries attached paramount importance.

The Israeli occupation authorities had created and trained a so-called Palestinian National Guard which frequently fired on the unarmed population, Egypt said; the mobilization of such agents was clearly aimed at sowing discord and dissent among the Palestinians. Collective punishment and the harassment and murder of Palestinian refugees should be vigorously denounced and condemned, and effective and immediate measures adopted to protect the civilians and refugees and guarantee their safety and security; the events at Ein El-Helweh proved the urgent need for such action. The United Nations must act decisively to ensure compliance with its decisions demanding complete Israeli withdrawal.

In Pakistan's opinion, the resort to reprisals such as the intrusion into the refugee camp clearly pointed to the difficulties Israel was facing in its continuing occupation of southern Lebanon; it had been able to overrun southern Lebanon in 1982, but had not been able to crush the spirit of the inhabitants. Israel's sinister scheme to divide the population and recruit a mercenary militia also had proved futile. In choosing refugee camps as the target of retaliatory measures, Israel had demonstrated once again its animosity and ruthlessness towards the Palestinians. Israel's steps towards consolidating its control and asserting its dominance in the region appeared to follow the pattern set earlier in the West Bank, Gaza and the Golan Heights. The Council's immediate task was to secure Israel's withdrawal from Lebanon, a first step towards solution of the Middle East problem, at the heart of which was the denial of Palestinian national rights.

The Observer of the League of Arab States reiterated that the central issue of the Middle East situation and the major source of tension and potential conflict remained Israel's usurpation of Palestinian rights, its annexation of Jerusalem and the Golan Heights, its establishment and proliferation of illegal settlements, its continued occupation of southern Lebanon, and its attempts to create quislings in the occupied territories. Israel, stating that the Council was not dealing with the central and more explosive issues, had introduced tangential issues in order to reduce the importance of the events at Ein El-Helweh and to cover up its annexationist policies. The Arab Group and the Arab League had come to the United Nations because they believed that, although there had not been enough evidence to that effect, it was possible through the Council to bring about a just and peaceful settlement.

Peace-keeping operation

UNIFIL activities

During 1984, the Security Council twice extended the mandate of the United Nations Interim Force in Lebanon, in April and October—by resolutions 549(1984) and 555(1984), respectively—each time for a six-month period, as recommended by the Secretary-General. UNIFIL had been established by the Council in 1978,[49] following an Israeli invasion of Lebanon.[50] Its terms of reference were to confirm the withdrawal of Israeli forces, to restore international peace and security and to assist the Lebanese Government in ensuring the return of its effective authority in the area. A second Israeli invasion, launched in June 1982,[21] radically altered the situation in which UNIFIL had to function. Following the invasion, the Council instructed the Force, as interim tasks, to maintain its positions in its area of deployment and provide protection and humanitarian assistance to the local population.[51]

Communications. By letters of 9 April[52] and 8 October 1984,[53] Lebanon twice requested the Security Council to extend for another six months the mandate of UNIFIL, which was to expire on 19 April and 19 October. It stated that, despite the current circumstances in southern Lebanon, UNIFIL continued to be an important factor in providing stability; its presence represented the United Nations commitment to support Lebanon's independence, sovereignty and territorial integrity. In its April letter, Lebanon also expressed the belief that the time had come for the Council to reassess UNIFIL's mission in the light of current developments, so that it could perform a more dynamic role.

Report of the Secretary-General (April). In a report of 9 April,[12] the Secretary-General described the activities of UNIFIL since the previous extension of its mandate in October 1983.[54] While the situation in Lebanon had been cause for great concern during those six months, the situation in the UNIFIL area of deployment had remained relatively peaceful, he said. UNIFIL's presence was regarded as essential by the Lebanese Government and had been of benefit to the much-increased population in its area of deployment. As requested by Lebanon,[52] the Secretary-General recommended that the Council extend UNIFIL's mandate for another interim period.

None the less, the Secretary-General stated, the Force's current role did not measure up to its original mandate or to the intentions of later Council resolutions adopted in 1982,[55] under which the withdrawal of Israeli forces and the restoration of peace, normality and the authority and sovereignty of the Lebanese Government were main objectives.

In recent weeks, he added, he had been considering further means to achieve those objectives by focusing on the common interests which all concerned had in changing the situation in southern Lebanon. Positions varied less on the general objective than on the conditions in which it was to be achieved.

During the period under review, UNIFIL continued to operate check-points and conduct patrols in its area of deployment, with a view to contributing to the maintenance of order and ensuring the security of the local population. The situation in its area had remained relatively quiet, although there had been an increasing number of incidents involving the Israel Defence Forces and local militia groups armed and uniformed by them. There was a further influx of displaced persons from the north, particularly from the Beirut area, and many new houses were being built.

The presence of IDF within the UNIFIL area remained at approximately battalion strength. The Israeli forces normally limited their activities to patrolling main roads but, on occasion, for stated reasons of security, they erected road-blocks, cordoned off villages, searched houses and detained local inhabitants.

There was a growing resistance by the local population to the presence of IDF. Strikes, demonstrations and other forms of protest were held on several occasions in reaction to arrests of local inhabitants. A serious confrontation had occurred at Marakah on 24 February, in which one villager was killed, 10 wounded and 10 others arrested. Another incident, during which a villager was killed and two arrested, had taken place at Qana on 6 March, when the local population protested against earlier arrests of villagers and attempted to prevent IDF personnel from entering the village. UNIFIL also recorded some 22 incidents involving exploded or unexploded roadside bombs.

During the reporting period, IDF continued its efforts to recruit and arm selected villagers in the UNIFIL area, but a plan to establish "village committees" under Israeli guidance had met with little success. UNIFIL continued its efforts to contain the activities of the Lebanese irregulars armed and controlled by IDF. Most of the incidents involving those irregulars were related to firing at or near UNIFIL personnel and attempts at hijacking UNIFIL vehicles.

UNIFIL continued to co-operate with the Lebanese authorities as well as UNRWA, UNICEF and ICRC in assisting the local population. Approximately 9,000 Lebanese civilians were treated in UNIFIL medical centres. The medical personnel of the Force, in co-operation with UNICEF, assisted the Lebanese Government in carrying out vaccinations and water analysis. In addition, UNIFIL cleared mined land and provided equipment and engineering assistance for public works.

The Commander of the Force and his staff maintained contact with the Lebanese Government, its regional authorities and the Israeli authorities. In March and April, the Under-Secretary-General for Special Political Affairs had held discussions with high officials of the Governments in the region.

The Lebanese internal security forces continued to co-operate with UNIFIL in maintaining order; they carried out independent patrols and assisted UNIFIL in special investigations. IDF continued to deny access to Tyre, Sidon and all areas adjacent to the coastal road. UNIFIL convoys to Beirut had to be suspended, and air and sea shipments diverted to Tel Aviv and Haifa. Flight clearance was on occasion denied by Israeli military authorities on the grounds that it would interfere with activities of the Israeli air force. Negotiations had been initiated with the Lebanese authorities to secure a suitable landing site, so that air communications between UNIFIL headquarters and logistics personnel in Beirut could be re-established.

In addition to its other tasks, UNIFIL continued to search for and defuse unexploded mines, shells and bombs.

The Secretary-General suggested that the Council consider a future course of action, to include the following elements, to make UNIFIL's mandate more effective, specifically in southern Lebanon, in the context of the withdrawal of Israeli forces from the area: temporary deployment of UNIFIL, with elements of the Lebanese Army and internal security forces, in areas vacated by Israeli forces; immediate deployment of UNIFIL elements in the Sidon area on Israeli withdrawal, to assure the safety and security of the population, including Palestinian refugees in the area's camps; and working out arrangements to ensure that southern Lebanon became a zone of peace under the sovereignty and authority of the Lebanese Government.

The Secretary-General again drew attention to the financial difficulties faced by the Force; as a result of the accumulated shortfall in the UNIFIL account, the Organization was falling far behind in reimbursing troop-contributing countries. He appealed for prompt payment of assessments and for voluntary contributions.

SECURITY COUNCIL ACTION (April)

The Security Council, by resolution 549(1984) of 19 April, extended UNIFIL's mandate for six months.

The Security Council,

Recalling its resolutions 425(1978), 426(1978), 501(1982), 508(1982), 509(1982) and 520(1982), as well as all its resolutions on the situation in Lebanon,

Having studied the report of the Secretary-General on the United Nations Interim Force in Lebanon of 9 April 1984 and taking note of the observations expressed therein,

Taking note of the letter of the Permanent Representative of Lebanon to the Secretary-General of 9 April 1984,

Responding to the request of the Government of Lebanon,

1. *Decides* to extend the present mandate of the United Nations Interim Force in Lebanon for a further interim period of six months, that is, until 19 October 1984;

2. *Reiterates* its strong support for the territorial integrity, sovereignty and independence of Lebanon within its internationally recognized boundaries;

3. *Re-emphasizes* the terms of reference and general guidelines of the Force as stated in the report of the Secretary-General of 19 March 1978, approved by resolution 426(1978), and calls upon all parties concerned to co-operate fully with the Force for the full implementation of its mandate;

4. *Reiterates* that the Force should fully implement its mandate as defined in resolutions 425(1978), 426(1978) and all other relevant resolutions;

5. *Requests* the Secretary-General to continue consultations with the Government of Lebanon and other parties directly concerned on the implementation of the present resolution and to report to the Council thereon.

Security Council resolution 549(1984)

19 April 1984   Meeting 2530   13-0-2

Draft prepared in consultations among Council members (S/16491).
Vote in Council as follows:

In favour: China, Egypt, France, India, Malta, Netherlands, Nicaragua, Pakistan, Peru, United Kingdom, United States, Upper Volta, Zimbabwe.
Against: None.
Abstaining: Ukrainian SSR, USSR.

Israel and Lebanon were invited, at their request, to participate in the discussion without the right to vote.

Following adoption of the resolution, the USSR said that discussion of the abnormal situation in Lebanon had been a permanent feature of Council activities for six years. The time had come for the Council to take another serious look at the root causes of the dangerous tension—Israeli aggression against Lebanon and its continued illegal occupation of more than a third of Lebanese territory, which had turned Lebanon into a constantly smouldering source of war. In the light of Lebanon's request and the Secretary-General's recommendations, the USSR had no particular objection to extending the mandate of UNIFIL. At the same time, it assumed that during the extension period the Council would take every step necessary to end the Israeli occupation. If Israel failed to withdraw its troops from Lebanon, the Council would have to carry out the task entrusted to it by the Charter and consider the adoption of practical steps. Confirming its position of principle, the USSR said the Force should not impinge on Lebanon's sovereign rights, it should not be entrusted with functions not in accordance with its duties, it should not intervene in Lebanon's affairs, and full account should be taken of Israel's responsibility for deeds it had perpetrated. All expenses related to dealing with the consequences of

its armed aggression against Lebanon should be borne by Israel, as the aggressor; as in the past, the USSR would not participate in defraying expenses connected with UNIFIL's establishment and functioning.

The United States stressed that it was its understanding that the adopted text did not go beyond the October 1983 Council resolution on the Force's mandate,[54] but simply extended it.

Sharing the concern expressed in the Secretary-General's report, France said UNIFIL had not been able to live up completely to the hopes of the international community and the Lebanese people. It was to be hoped that the abnormal situation wherein Israeli forces continued to operate in the UNIFIL area of deployment would soon end. UNIFIL should contribute to re-establishing peace in southern Lebanon and ensure more effective security for the civilians there, under the authority of the Lebanese Government. France was prepared to consider an extension of UNIFIL's mandate and deployment area, especially if such a request were made by the Lebanese Government.

Reaffirming its view of the importance of UNIFIL's presence as an expression of the United Nations commitment to the Lebanese Government in regaining authority over the area, Egypt called for the complete withdrawal of all foreign forces, including Israel's, from Lebanese territory.

The Netherlands said its decision to retain a limited contingent in UNIFIL was based on its conviction that the Force could and should play a more meaningful role; a Council decision that would reactivate UNIFIL's role was long overdue. The Netherlands urged all parties to make use of the potential of the peace-keeping operations to restore international peace and security. It added that, although UNIFIL had been set up to facilitate the withdrawal of Israeli forces, it would be unfair and unrealistic to ignore other aspects of the crisis which also needed to be addressed urgently. In that context, the Netherlands called on all parties to agree to a cease-fire, and stressed the need for a resumption without delay of the process of conciliation and negotiation aimed at establishing a Government which enjoyed the widest possible national support and exercised its authority throughout Lebanon, whose territorial integrity and sovereignty required the withdrawal of all unauthorized foreign forces.

The United Kingdom considered it the Council's duty to help restore peace and stability and uphold Lebanon's territorial integrity. It agreed that the Council should reassess and expand UNIFIL's mission so that it could perform a more dynamic role, and it interpreted the resolution as endorsing further exploration of such possibilities by the Secretary-General.

In Lebanon's opinion also, it was time for the Council to reassess UNIFIL's mission. Lebanon strongly supported: the initiative called for by the Secretary-General to enable UNIFIL, in consultation with the Lebanese Government and the parties concerned, to achieve respect for Lebanon's territorial integrity, sovereignty and political independence within its internationally recognized boundaries, as well as Israel's withdrawal; his proposal for temporary deployment of UNIFIL in vacated areas; and UNIFIL's expanded deployment to assist in restoring Lebanese authority, as well as in working out arrangements to ensure the speedy transformation of southern Lebanon into a zone of peace under government authority. Lebanon hoped that the main arterial roads in the south would soon be brought under United Nations supervision; it called for an opening of all crossing-points leading to the south and for an end to all activities against the population. It did not recognize any military formations that had not legitimately been established, including the so-called South Lebanese Army.

Israel reaffirmed its view that, in the circumstances surrounding the situation in Lebanon since June 1982, UNIFIL had outlived its usefulness in southern Lebanon; the growing recognition of that viewpoint had also been evidenced in recent months by the position of a number of troop-contributing countries which, seeing no effective mission for UNIFIL in its area of deployment, had reduced their contingents. The security of southern Lebanon should eventually be guaranteed by Lebanese forces; UNIFIL could perform a useful role by serving as a buffer separating the Israeli and the Syrian forces and could fulfil a useful function north of the IDF deployment area, where it could serve as a genuine peace-keeping force.

Israel had general reservations on much of the Secretary-General's report. It could not regard the 1978 resolutions on the establishment of UNIFIL[56] and three 1982 resolutions calling for withdrawal of Israeli forces[55] as the basis of the Council's consideration, as the situation clearly demonstrated that it was not Israel's military presence in southern Lebanon that was at the root of the country's instability. The USSR, through its stooges, Israel said, had been instrumental in destabilizing Lebanon for a decade and more, which was a root cause of the current situation in that country. Israel regretted that the report made no mention of the Syrian presence and terrorist forces in Lebanon, of their well-documented responsibility for destabilizing the country and of their role in depriving the Lebanese Government of its authority; consequently, it could not accept the approach suggested by the Secretary-General. It was equally regrettable that the report made no mention of resolutions which referred to the withdrawal of all foreign forces from Lebanese territory, for example resolution 520(1982).[57] Israel also regarded the report as incomplete in its treatment of the numerous terrorist incidents whose perpetrators' identities were omitted.

Report of the Secretary-General (October). On 9 October 1984,[13] the Secretary-General reported on the activities of the Force since 10 April. During that period, as in the previous period, UNIFIL had continued to operate checkpoints and conduct patrols in its area of deployment. Though relatively quiet, there again had been an increasing number of incidents in the area involving IDF and local militia groups, and population continued to flow from the north.

IDF remained at battalion strength and acts of resistance against it increased. UNIFIL recorded the arrest of 423 civilians in 75 separate incidents, most of them later released. There had been a number of incidents when IDF, entering villages to search and arrest, was violently resisted by local inhabitants; IDF had reacted at times by firing, which resulted in casualties. During confrontations at Marakah, on 12 May and 27 June, a girl was shot, four other local inhabitants were injured and 119 men were arrested. Similar incidents occurred in other villages. On 11 June, Israeli personnel in civilian clothes and cars entered Burj Rahal and opened fire when the villagers demonstrated against their presence; one man was killed and another wounded.

UNIFIL also recorded some 65 incidents involving roadside bombs; some exploded, causing casualties and damage, others were demolished. During a mine-clearing operation near Ett Taibe on 20 June, five soldiers were injured.

During the reporting period, IDF attempted to recruit soldiers from the local population to build up the so-called South Lebanese Army. UNIFIL continued its efforts to contain the activities of those and other Lebanese irregulars armed and controlled by IDF; incidents involving UNIFIL and such irregulars were related to firing at or near UNIFIL positions.

UNIFIL continued to co-operate with the Lebanese authorities, UNRWA, UNICEF and ICRC in assisting the local population. UNIFIL medical personnel at Naqoura performed 315 surgical operations and treated 487 in-patients; UNIFIL helped carry out vaccinations, water analysis programmes and public works projects.

After June 1984, UNIFIL sent light convoys to Beirut. However, because of the poor quality of the road, the nature of the terrain and the unstable security situation, it was not possible to set up a normal supply and provisioning system which would permit using the Beirut International Airport and seaport.

During the period, the Commander of UNIFIL and his staff maintained contact with the Lebanese Government and regional authorities; they also maintained contact with the Israeli authorities on matters pertaining to the functioning of the Force.

In June, the Secretary-General had travelled to the Middle East for discussions with high officials of the Lebanese Government and other Governments in the region; he also visited UNIFIL headquarters and some of its contingents. The Under-Secretary-General for Special Political Affairs also had held discussions with government officials in Lebanon, the Syrian Arab Republic and Israel in September. From those contacts, the Secretary-General derived the impression that there was general agreement on the objective of Israeli withdrawal from southern Lebanon and on the necessity of working out arrangements to ensure peace and security in the region and to restore Lebanese authority and sovereignty in the wake of Israel's withdrawal. There were a number of outstanding questions on the means by which the objectives could be achieved, and various alternatives had been discussed; it was generally agreed that an expanded mandate for UNIFIL and a widening of its area of operation would be key elements in such arrangements. The Secretary-General hoped that it would be possible in the near future to move to an agreement on the necessary practical arrangements.

With regard to the future role of UNIFIL, it was not possible to make a detailed forecast of its actual task or functions in an extended role or to estimate accurately what increase in strength would be necessary. The Secretary-General believed that it would be particularly important to provide UNIFIL with a mandate which it could successfully implement, which would command the necessary support and co-operation, and which would provide the necessary reassurances to all the parties concerned.

In the light of Lebanon's request, the Secretary-General recommended that UNIFIL's mandate be extended for another interim period of six months. Repeating his suggestions made in his April report (see p. 298) on action to make UNIFIL's mandate more effective in the context of a withdrawal of the Israeli forces, he stated that developments in recent weeks seemed to have brought about more positive prospects for the realization of those suggestions. He attached great importance to taking advantage of the current, relatively favourable situation with regard to an Israeli withdrawal.

UNIFIL's existence should not be taken for granted indefinitely, the Secretary-General stated. The Council and the troop-contributing

countries had shown great patience and understanding during the previous two years when UNIFIL had been forced by circumstances to play a role not envisaged at its inception. If positive developments did not take place in a relatively short time, it would not be fair to count on the indefinite participation of the troop-contributing countries, all the more so in view of the financial liability it entailed. He reiterated his appeal for prompt payment of assessments and for voluntary contributions to reimburse troop contributors.

SECURITY COUNCIL ACTION (October)

By resolution 555(1984) of 12 October, the Security Council extended UNIFIL's mandate for another six months.

The Security Council,

Recalling its resolutions 425(1978), 426(1978), 501(1982), 508(1982), 509(1982) and 520(1982), as well as all its resolutions on the situation in Lebanon,

Having studied the report of the Secretary-General on the United Nations Interim Force in Lebanon of 9 October 1984, and taking note of the observations expressed therein,

Taking note of the letter of the Permanent Representative of Lebanon addressed to the Secretary-General of 8 October 1984,

Responding to the request of the Government of Lebanon,

1. *Decides* to extend the present mandate of the United Nations Interim Force in Lebanon for a further interim period of six months, that is, until 19 April 1985;

2. *Reiterates* its strong support for the territorial integrity, sovereignty and independence of Lebanon within its internationally recognized boundaries;

3. *Re-emphasizes* the terms of reference and general guidelines of the Force as stated in the report of the Secretary-General of 19 March 1978, approved by resolution 426(1978), and calls upon all parties concerned to co-operate fully with the Force for the full implementation of its mandate;

4. *Reiterates* that the Force should fully implement its mandate as defined in resolutions 425(1978), 426(1978) and all other relevant resolutions;

5. *Requests* the Secretary-General to continue consultations with the Government of Lebanon and other parties directly concerned on the implementation of the present resolution and to report to the Council thereon.

Security Council resolution 555(1984)

12 October 1984	Meeting 2559	13-0-2

Draft prepared in consultations among Council members (S/16779).
Vote in Council as follows:

In favour: Burkina Faso, China, Egypt, France, India, Malta, Netherlands, Nicaragua, Pakistan, Peru, United Kingdom, United States, Zimbabwe.
Against: None.
Abstaining: Ukrainian SSR, USSR.

Speaking after the vote, Lebanon, which had been invited, at its request, to participate without the right to vote, associated itself with the Secretary-General's observations and suggestions; a complete Israeli withdrawal and proper security arrangements would make it necessary to revise the functions and task of UNIFIL and the number of its troops, extend its deployment area and increase its effectiveness. UNIFIL would then be in a position to contribute, together with the Lebanese Army and the internal security forces, to the extension of the authority of the State to the internationally recognized borders, so that the south might become an area of peace and security. That new contribution of UNIFIL would be a temporary necessity during the proposed Israeli withdrawal phase, until the legitimate Lebanese forces could assume full and definitive responsibility for security.

In view of Lebanon's request, the USSR did not object to an extension of the mandate; at the same time, it emphasized its growing concern at the abnormal situation in which the Council was obliged systematically to extend the Force's mandate while conditions existed that prevented it from performing its functions. The reason for that dangerous situation was the continued illegal occupation by Israel.

The United Kingdom again advocated an expanded United Nations presence in Lebanon; it agreed with the Secretary-General's suggestion that United Nations machinery be made available to the parties to facilitate the reaching of agreements and provide facilities for the necessary discussions. It interpreted the text as endorsing further action by the Secretary-General on those lines, agreeing with him that the current opportunity must not be missed.

The Netherlands considered it obvious in the circumstances that the Council should extend UNIFIL's mandate for a limited period, pending the outcome of negotiations on arrangements to realize the overall objectives of Israeli withdrawal, peace and security in the region, and restoration of Lebanese authority and sovereignty. UNIFIL's future would be jeopardized by a failure of the parties concerned to agree on the necessary arrangements, and the Netherlands called on them to resolve their outstanding differences.

In France's view, UNIFIL was essential for the return to normal conditions in southern Lebanon and it reiterated its readiness to consider the new tasks which the Council might decide to entrust to the Force. The United States said it hoped that the resolution extending UNIFIL's mandate would contribute to peace in the area.

Composition

As of October 1984, the composition of UNIFIL was as follows:

Infantry battalions	
Fiji	629
Finland	503
France	606
Ghana	558
Ireland	637
Netherlands	160
Norway	634
Senegal	565
Headquarters camp command	
Ghana	146
Ireland	87
Logistics units	
France	767
Italy	44
Norway	205
Sweden	142
	5,683

In addition, UNIFIL was assisted by 63 military observers of UNTSO, organized as Observer Group Lebanon. Those unarmed observers were under the operational control of the UNIFIL Commander. Another observer group in Lebanon, Observer Group Beirut, composed of 50 observers headed by an officer-in-charge under the overall command of the UNTSO Chief of Staff, was established pursuant to a 1982 Security Council resolution[58] and given the task of monitoring the situation in and around Beirut.

The military observers of UNTSO continued to man the five observation posts along the Lebanese side of the Israel-Lebanon armistice demarcation line and to maintain teams at Tyre, Metulla and Château de Beaufort; in addition, they operated four mobile teams.

The Lebanese internal security forces continued to co-operate with UNIFIL in maintaining order in its area of operation. They carried out independent patrols and assisted UNIFIL in special investigations of mutual concern. The Lebanese Army unit serving with UNIFIL maintained a strength of 150 all ranks, deployed in the UNIFIL area and attached to different battalions.

Between 13 October 1983 and 9 October 1984, six members of the Force died, two of them from the accidental discharge of a weapon, the others in traffic accidents. Since UNIFIL's establishment in 1978, 102 members of the Force had died, 41 of them as a result of firing and mine explosions, 48 in accidents and 13 from natural causes. Also, some 125 were wounded in armed clashes, shellings and mine explosions.

The French battalion, which had been temporarily reduced at France's request in September 1982, was brought back to full strength with the arrival of three companies on 5 February 1984. In accordance with a decision of Senegal, repatriation of the Senegalese battalion was completed on 1 November. On 15 November,[59] the Secretary-General informed the President of the Security Council that, with the departure of the

Senegalese battalion, the number of troops had been reduced to approximately 5,200, well below its authorized strength of 7,000; subject to the usual consultations, the Secretary-General intended to accept Nepal's offer to provide a replacement battalion of about 650 men.

On 19 November,[60] the Council President informed the Secretary-General that the Council members had that day considered the matter in informal consultations and agreed with the Secretary-General's proposals.

Palestinian cultural property

In a 2 October 1984 report on the situation in the Middle East (see p. 260), the Secretary-General dealt with implementation of a December 1983 General Assembly resolution[61] condemning the plunder of the Palestinian cultural heritage and calling on Israel to make restitution of all cultural property belonging to Palestinian institutions. The Secretary-General stated that Israel, in a reply to his request for information dated 28 August 1984, had recalled its statement before the Assembly in December 1983 that it had returned the files referred to in the resolution; also, he had been informed by ICRC that, in the context of the release by Israel of Palestinian prisoners, it had received from Israeli authorities several hundred boxes, containing books and files taken from the Palestine Research Centre, which had been flown to Algiers on 23/24 November 1983 and had been handed over to PLO representatives. In addition, the Secretary-General had been kept informed of efforts by the Director-General of the United Nations Educational, Scientific and Cultural Organization (UNESCO) since 1982 to assess the extent of the destruction of Palestinian educational and cultural institutions in Lebanon and to determine the priority needs of those institutions within UNESCO's areas of responsibility. The Director-General was pursuing his contacts with the Lebanese authorities and the United Nations Co-ordinator of Assistance for the Reconstruction and Development of Lebanon in order to obtain the information required for that purpose.

Israel and the Syrian Arab Republic

In 1984, the General Assembly, as well as the Commission on Human Rights, dealt with the situation in the Syrian Golan Heights since Israel's December 1981 decision to impose its laws, jurisdiction and administration on the Israeli-occupied territory (see p. 322).

The United Nations Disengagement Observer Force, established in 1974[62] in accordance with the Agreement on Disengagement of Forces between Israel and the Syrian Arab Republic,[63] continued in 1984 to supervise the observance of the cease-fire between Israel and the Syrian Arab

Republic in the Golan Heights area and to ensure, in accordance with its mandate, that there were no military forces in the area of separation. On the Secretary-General's recommendation, the Security Council extended UNDOF's mandate twice during the year, in May and November, by resolutions 551(1984) and 557(1984) (see p. 305).

Peace-keeping operation

UNDOF activities

Reports of the Secretary-General. Prior to the expiration of the six-month mandates of UNDOF on 31 May and 30 November 1984, the Secretary-General submitted reports on the activities of the Force for the periods from 22 November 1983 to 21 May 1984[64] and 22 May to 16 November 1984.[65]

In both reports, the Secretary-General stated that UNDOF had continued to fulfil its tasks, with the co-operation of the parties and facilitated by the close contact of the Force Commander and his staff with the military liaison staffs of Israel and the Syrian Arab Republic. The cease-fire had been maintained and no complaints concerning the UNDOF area of operation had been lodged by either party.

In accordance with the terms of the Agreement on Disengagement, UNDOF continued to conduct fortnightly inspections of armament and forces in the area of limitation, carried out with the assistance of liaison officers from the parties. UNDOF had continued to receive the co-operation of both parties, although it continued to seek the lifting of restrictions on movement and inspection placed on its teams in certain areas by both sides.

Intensified patrolling on new mine-cleared paths and, from time to time, the establishment of standing patrols had helped prevent or reduce incidents involving Syrian shepherds, as had the grazing security fence in the southern part of the area of separation.

UNDOF was continuing its efforts to make the area of operation safe from mines. It also assisted ICRC with facilities for handing over mail and prisoners of war; for example, on 28 June, 297 prisoners, 16 civilians and the remains of 77 persons were exchanged between Israel and the Syrian Arab Republic.

Despite the current quiet in the sector, the Secretary-General stated, the Middle East situation as a whole continued to be potentially dangerous and was likely to remain so unless a comprehensive settlement covering all aspects of the Middle East problem could be reached. In the circumstances, he considered the continued presence of UNDOF to be essential and recommended, in each report, with the assent of the Syrian Arab

Republic and the agreement of Israel, that the Council extend its mandate for a further period of six months.

SECURITY COUNCIL ACTION

On 30 May, without debate, the Security Council unanimously adopted resolution 551(1984), thereby extending UNDOF's mandate for six months, until 30 November.

The Security Council,
Having considered the report of the Secretary-General on the United Nations Disengagement Observer Force,
Decides:

(a) To call upon the parties concerned to implement immediately Security Council resolution 338(1973);

(b) To renew the mandate of the United Nations Disengagement Observer Force for another period of six months, that is, until 30 November 1984;

(c) To request the Secretary-General to submit, at the end of this period, a report on the developments in the situation and the measures taken to implement resolution 338(1973).

Security Council resolution 551(1984)

30 May 1984   Meeting 2544   Adopted unanimously

Draft prepared in consultations among Council members (S/16592).

On 28 November, without debate, the Council unanimously adopted resolution 557(1984), extending UNDOF's mandate for a further six months, until 31 May 1985.

The Security Council,
Having considered the report of the Secretary-General on the United Nations Disengagement Observer Force,
Decides:

(a) To call upon the parties concerned to implement immediately Security Council resolution 338(1973);

(b) To renew the mandate of the United Nations Disengagement Observer Force for another period of six months, that is, until 31 May 1985;

(c) To request the Secretary-General to submit, at the end of this period, a report on the developments in the situation and the measures taken to implement resolution 338(1973).

Security Council resolution 557(1984)

28 November 1984   Meeting 2563   Adopted unanimously

Draft prepared in consultations among Council members (S/16845).

Following adoption of each resolution, the President made the following statement on behalf of the Council:[66]

"As is known, the report of the Secretary-General on the United Nations Disengagement Observer Force states, in paragraph 26: 'despite the present quiet in the Israel-Syria sector, the situation in the Middle East as a whole continues to be potentially dangerous and is likely to remain so, unless and until a comprehensive settlement covering all aspects of the Middle East problem can be reached'. That statement of the Secretary-General reflects the view of the Security Council."

Composition

As at 16 November 1984, the composition of UNDOF was as follows:

Austria	531
Canada	224
Finland	395
Poland	150
United Nations military observers (detailed from UNTSO)	6
	1,306

In addition, UNTSO observers assigned to the Israel-Syria Mixed Armistice Commission assisted UNDOF as required.

REFERENCES

[1]S/16318. [2]YUN 1983, p. 288, GA res. 38/9, 10 Nov. 1983. [3]YUN 1981, p. 275. [4]A/39/379. [5]A/39/349. [6]A/39/406-S/16702. [7]A/39/674. [8]YUN 1981, p. 282, SC res. 487(1981), 19 June 1981. [9]S/16785. [10]S/16812. [11]A/39/600-S/16792. [12]S/16472. [13]S/16776. [14]S/17093. [15]A/39/63-S/16252. [16]A/39/75-S/16276. [17]S/16339. [18]S/16351/Rev.2. [19]YUN 1983, p. 298. [20]YUN 1982, p. 440. [21]*Ibid.*, p. 428. [22]A/39/123-S/16389. [23]A/39/161-S/16456. [24]A/39/125 (S/16391). [25]A/39/282-S/16597. [26]A/39/328-S/16645. [27]A/39/330-S/16650. [28]A/39/340-S/16660. [29]A/39/350-S/16671. [30]A/39/365-S/16682. [31]A/39/377-S/16691. [32]S/16713. [33]S/16722. [34]S/16732. [35]YUN 1982, p. 450, SC res. 508(1982), 5 June 1982. [36]*Ibid.*, SC res. 509(1982), 6 June 1982. [37]YUN 1983, p. 278, GA res. 38/58 C, 13 Dec. 1983. [38]YUN 1982, p. 451, SC res. 512(1982), 19 June 1982. [39]*Ibid.*, p. 452, SC res. 513(1982), 4 July 1982. [40]A/39/509-S/16749. [41]YUN 1982, p. 481. [42]A/39/837-S/16866. [43]A/40/58-S/16871. [44]A/39/263-S/16568. [45]S/16570. [46]S/16569. [47]S/16575. [48]S/16571. [49]YUN 1978, p. 312, SC res. 425(1978), 19 Mar. 1978. [50]*Ibid.*, p. 295. [51]YUN 1982, p. 450, SC res. 511(1982), 18 June 1982. [52]S/16471. [53]S/16772. [54]YUN 1983, p. 299, SC res. 538(1983), 18 Oct. 1983. [55]YUN 1982, p. 432, SC res. 501(1982), 25 Feb. 1982; p. 450, SC res. 508(1982), 5 June 1982; *ibid.*, SC res. 509(1982), 6 June 1982. [56]YUN 1978, p. 312, SC res. 425(1978) and 426(1978), 19 Mar. 1978. [57]YUN 1982, p. 476, SC res. 520(1982), 17 Sep. 1982. [58]*Ibid.*, 1982, p. 475, SC res. 516(1982), 1 Aug. 1982. [59]S/16831. [60]S/16832. [61]YUN 1983, p. 285, GA res. 38/180 B, 19 Dec. 1983. [62]YUN 1974, p. 205, SC res. 350(1974), 31 May 1974. [63]*Ibid.*, p. 198. [64]S/16573 & Corr.1. [65]S/16829. [66]S/16593 & S/16847.

Financing of peace-keeping forces

United Nations peace-keeping operations in the Middle East comprised two peace-keeping forces—the United Nations Disengagement Observer Force and the United Nations Interim Force in Lebanon—and one observer mission, the United Nations Truce Supervision Organization.

The General Assembly, following the recommendations of the Advisory Committee on Administrative and Budgetary Questions (ACABQ) and the Fifth (Administrative and Budgetary) Committee, approved appropriations for UNDOF for operations from 1 June 1984 to 31 May 1985 totalling more than $35 million. For UNIFIL's operations from 19

April 1984 to 18 April 1985, the Assembly appropriated $141 million.

Contributions to UNDOF in 1984 totalled nearly $34 million, while assessments for the year were $35 million; contributions outstanding since UNDOF's inception in 1974 amounted to some $57 million. Of close to $140 million assessed for UNIFIL in 1984, only about $109 million was paid; contributions outstanding since the Force's inception in 1978 totalled nearly $267 million.

In view of the difficult financial situation of the two peace-keeping forces, the Assembly authorized suspension of certain provisions of the United Nations Financial Regulations to enable UNDOF and UNIFIL to retain a "surplus balance" of about $5 million and $6 million, respectively.

The last revision of standard rates of reimbursement to countries which contributed troops to the forces having taken place in 1980, the Assembly requested the Secretary-General to review existing rates with a view to ensuring an equitable reimbursement.

UNDOF financing

Report of the Secretary-General. In an October 1984 report on the financing of UNDOF,[1] the Secretary-General stated that as at 30 September, $620.5 million in contributions for UNDOF together with the second United Nations Emergency Force (UNEF II) had been received since the latter's inception in 1973 to 30 November 1984. The unpaid balance totalled $82.2 million, of which $28.8 million represented amounts apportioned among Member States which did not intend to pay, and $36 million assessed contributions due from China between 25 October 1971 and 31 December 1981 which had been transferred to a special account in accordance with a 1981 Assembly resolution.[2]

According to the Secretary-General, there was a shortfall of approximately $5.2 million in the UNDOF Special Account in respect of the periods between 25 October 1979 and 30 November 1984. The shortfall for periods before 24 October 1979, together with UNEF II until its liquidation in 1980, was estimated at $59.6 million. In the circumstances, troop contributors had not been reimbursed fully or on time; they had again conveyed to the Secretary-General their very serious concern over the situation.

For the operation of UNDOF beyond 30 November 1984, the Secretary-General estimated monthly costs of $2,976,333 gross ($2,932,917 net) from 1 December onwards, assuming an average strength of 1,320 troops. For the period 1 June to 30 November 1984, an appropriation of $17,489,496 gross ($17,280,000 net) would be required.

ACABQ recommendations. In a November 1984 report,[3] ACABQ noted that, of the outstanding contributions of $82.2 million, only $17.4 million was

estimated to be collectible. It also noted that no voluntary contributions had been received in response to an Assembly appeal of December 1983.[4]

On a related matter, ACABQ had been informed that the audited accounts for 1982-1983 indicated, for the UNEF/UNDOF Special Account, a "surplus balance" of $4,824,613 as at 31 December 1983 representing excess of income over expenditure, due to interest and miscellaneous credits accrued. According to the Secretary-General, "income" included assessed contributions, irrespective of collectibility. However, because of States withholding contributions, the surplus balance had in effect been drawn upon to the full to supplement the income from contributions for meeting expenses of the Forces. The $4,824,613 thus represented merely a theoretical surplus.

ACABQ recommended that the Secretary-General's estimate for the cost of UNDOF in 1984-1985 be approved. Requirements for the 12 months from 1 December 1984 to 30 November 1985 should not exceed $35,705,000 gross ($35,184,000 net). ACABQ further recommended that the Secretary-General be permitted the usual flexibility to transfer credits between items of expenditure, should it be necessary in the interest of good management and efficiency. The total increase in 1984-1985 was $635,000 on a net basis, or 1.8 per cent; although most of that increase was attributable to inflation, part of it related to the Secretary-General's requests for 14 additional posts, bringing the total number of staff to 154. The Committee recommended acceptance of the staffing proposals.

GENERAL ASSEMBLY ACTION

In November 1984, on the recommendation of the Fifth Committee, the General Assembly adopted two resolutions—39/28 A and B—on the financing of UNDOF.

On 30 November, the Assembly adopted resolution 39/28 A by vote.

The General Assembly,

Having considered the report of the Secretary-General on the financing of the United Nations Disengagement Observer Force, as well as the related report of the Advisory Committee on Administrative and Budgetary Questions,

Bearing in mind Security Council resolutions 350(1974) of 31 May 1974, 363(1974) of 29 November 1974, 369(1975) of 28 May 1975, 381(1975) of 30 November 1975, 390(1976) of 28 May 1976, 398(1976) of 30 November 1976, 408(1977) of 26 May 1977, 420(1977) of 30 November 1977, 429(1978) of 31 May 1978, 441(1978) of 30 November 1978, 449(1979) of 30 May 1979, 456(1979) of 30 November 1979, 470(1980) of 30 May 1980, 481(1980) of 26 November 1980, 485(1981) of 22 May 1981, 493(1981) of 23 November 1981, 506(1982) of 26 May 1982, 524(1982) of 29 November 1982, 531(1983) of 26 May 1983, 543(1983) of 29 November

1983, 551(1984) of 30 May 1984 and 557(1984) of 28 November 1984,

Recalling its resolutions 3101(XXVIII) of 11 December 1973, 3211 B (XXIX) of 29 November 1974, 3374 C (XXX) of 2 December 1975, 31/5 D of 22 December 1976, 32/4 C of 2 December 1977, 33/13 D of 8 December 1978, 34/7 C of 3 December 1979, 35/44 of 1 December 1980, 35/45 A of 1 December 1980, 36/66 A of 30 November 1981, 37/38 A of 30 November 1982 and 38/35 A of 1 December 1983,

Reaffirming its previous decisions regarding the fact that, in order to meet the expenditures caused by such operations, a different procedure is required from that applied to meet expenditures of the regular budget of the United Nations,

Taking into account the fact that the economically more developed countries are in a position to make relatively larger contributions and that the economically less developed countries have a relatively limited capacity to contribute towards peace-keeping operations involving heavy expenditures,

Bearing in mind the special responsibilities of the States permanent members of the Security Council in the financing of such operations, as indicated in General Assembly resolution 1874(S-IV) of 27 June 1963 and other resolutions of the Assembly,

I

Decides to appropriate to the Special Account referred to in section II, paragraph 1, of General Assembly resolution 3211 B (XXIX) the amount of $17,489,496 gross ($17,280,000 net) authorized and apportioned by section III of Assembly resolution 38/35 A for the operation of the United Nations Disengagement Observer Force for the period from 1 June to 30 November 1984, inclusive;

II

1. *Decides* to appropriate to the Special Account an amount of $17,852,500 for the operation of the United Nations Disengagement Observer Force for the period from 1 December 1984 to 31 May 1985, inclusive;

2. *Decides further*, as an *ad hoc* arrangement, without prejudice to the positions of principle that may be taken by Member States in any consideration by the General Assembly of arrangements for the financing of peace-keeping operations, to apportion the amount of $17,852,500 among Member States in accordance with the scheme set out in Assembly resolution 3101(XXVIII) and the provisions of section II, paragraphs 2 *(b)* and 2 *(c)*, and section V, paragraph 1, of resolution 3374 C (XXX), section V, paragraph 1, of resolution 31/5 D, section V, paragraph 1, of resolution 32/4 C, section V, paragraph 1, of resolution 33/13 D, section V, paragraph 1, of resolution 34/7 C, section V, paragraph 1, of resolution 35/45 A, section V, paragraph 1, of resolution 36/66 A and section V, paragraph 1, of resolution 37/38 A, in the proportions determined by the scale of assessments for the years 1983, 1984 and 1985;

3. *Decides* that there shall be set off against the apportionment among Member States, as provided in paragraph 2 above, their respective share in the estimated income of $10,000 other than staff assessment income approved for the period from 1 December 1984 to 31 May 1985, inclusive;

4. *Decides* that, in accordance with the provisions of its resolution 973(X) of 15 December 1955, there shall

be set off against the apportionment among Member States, as provided for in paragraph 2 above, their respective share in the Tax Equalization Fund of the estimated staff assessment income of $250,500 approved for the period from 1 December 1984 to 31 May 1985, inclusive;

III

Authorizes the Secretary-General to enter into commitments for the United Nations Disengagement Observer Force at a rate not to exceed $2,975,416 gross ($2,932,000 net) per month for the period from 1 June to 30 November 1985, inclusive, should the Security Council decide to continue the Force beyond the period of six months authorized under its resolution 557(1984), the said amount to be apportioned among Member States in accordance with the scheme set out in the present resolution;

IV

1. *Stresses* the need for voluntary contributions to the United Nations Disengagement Observer Force, both in cash and in the form of services and supplies acceptable to the Secretary-General;

2. *Requests* the Secretary-General to take all necessary action to ensure that the United Nations Disengagement Observer Force is conducted with a maximum of efficiency and economy;

V

1. *Decides* that Brunei Darussalam shall be included in the group of Member States mentioned in paragraph 2 *(c)* of General Assembly resolution 3101(XXVIII) and that its contribution to the United Nations Disengagement Observer Force shall be calculated in accordance with the provisions of the resolution adopted by the Assembly at the current session regarding the scale of assessments;

2. *Decides* that Saint Christopher and Nevis shall be included in the group of Member States mentioned in paragraph 2 *(d)* of General Assembly resolution 3101(XXVIII) and that its contribution to the United Nations Disengagement Observer Force shall be calculated in accordance with the provisions of the resolution adopted by the Assembly at the current session regarding the scale of assessments;

3. *Decides further* that, in accordance with regulation 5.2 *(c)* of the Financial Regulations of the United Nations, the contributions to the United Nations Disengagement Observer Force until 30 November 1984 of the Member States referred to in paragraphs 1 and 2 of the present section shall be treated as miscellaneous income to be set off against the appropriations apportioned in section II above.

General Assembly resolution 39/28 A

30 November 1984	Meeting 81	98-2-12

Approved by Fifth Committee (A/39/719) by vote (88-1-14), 29 November (meeting 37); 8-nation draft (A/C.5/39/L.11, part A); agenda item 119 *(a)*.

Sponsors: Austria, Canada, Denmark, Finland, Ireland, Netherlands, Norway, Sweden.

Speaking before the vote in the plenary Assembly, Albania said its objection to the financing of United Nations peace-keeping forces was based on ample evidence that those forces could not serve the defence of freedom and independence or of international peace and security; developments over the previous year had reinforced that impression.

Algeria, Iran, the Libyan Arab Jamahiriya, Maldives and the Syrian Arab Republic declared that they would not participate in the vote on either text; the financing of UNDOF was the responsibility of the aggressor. Iraq and Yemen announced that they would abstain for the same reason.

In the opinion of the USSR, the Force constituted a significant step towards the liberation of the occupied Arab territories; the increase in appropriations was excessive, however, and placed too heavy a financial burden on Member States. Moreover, the increase in posts could be avoided if UNDOF's work were better organized.

The United States supported the recommendations for the financing of UNDOF. Israel said that in the current complex situation, UNDOF was the best of the possible solutions.

Introducing both drafts in the Committee, Canada stated that peace-keeping forces played an integral role in promoting global security and respect for the Charter. The withholding of contributions placed an unfair and increasingly disproportionate burden on troop-contributing countries, particularly the developing countries; the financial burden must be shared equitably.

Also on 30 November, the Assembly adopted resolution 39/28 B by vote.

The General Assembly,

Having regard to the financial position of the Special Account for the United Nations Emergency Force and the United Nations Disengagement Observer Force, as set forth in the report of the Secretary-General, and referring to paragraph 5 of the report of the Advisory Committee on Administrative and Budgetary Questions,

Mindful of the fact that it is essential to provide the United Nations Disengagement Observer Force with the necessary financial resources to enable it to fulfil its responsibilities under the relevant resolutions of the Security Council,

Concerned that the Secretary-General is continuing to face growing difficulties in meeting the obligations of the Forces on a current basis, particularly those due to the Governments of troop-contributing States,

Recalling its resolutions 33/13 E of 14 December 1978, 34/7 D of 17 December 1979, 35/45 B of 1 December 1980, 36/66 B of 30 November 1981, 37/38 B of 30 November 1982 and 38/35 B of 1 December 1983,

Recognizing that, in consequence of the withholding of contributions by certain Member States, the surplus balances in the Special Account for the United Nations Emergency Force and the United Nations Disengagement Observer Force have, in effect, been drawn upon to the full extent to supplement the income received from contributions for meeting expenses of the Forces,

Concerned that the application of the provisions of regulations 5.2 *(b)*, 5.2 *(d)*, 4.3 and 4.4 of the Financial Regulations of the United Nations would aggravate the already difficult financial situation of the Forces,

Decides that the provisions of regulations 5.2 *(b)*, 5.2 *(d)*, 4.3 and 4.4 of the Financial Regulations of the United Nations shall be suspended in respect of the amount of $4,824,613, which otherwise would have to be surrendered pursuant to those provisions, this amount to be entered in the account referred to in the operative part of General Assembly resolution 33/13 E and held in suspense until a further decision is taken by the Assembly.

General Assembly resolution 39/28 B

30 November 1984   Meeting 81   98-11-5

Approved by Fifth Committee (A/39/719) by vote (88-11-6), 29 November (meeting 37); 8-nation draft (A/C.5/39/L.11); agenda item 119 *(a)*.
Sponsors: Austria, Canada, Denmark, Finland, Ireland, Netherlands, Norway, Sweden.

Explaining its negative vote in Committee, the USSR said the unused balance to be entered into the Special Account should be returned to Member States in accordance with the Financial Regulations.

CONTRIBUTIONS TO UNDOF

(as at 31 December 1984; in US dollars)

Country	Assessments in 1984	Paid in 1984	Total contributions outstanding*	Country	Assessments in 1984	Paid in 1984	Total contributions outstanding*
Afghanistan	349	—	3,703	Brazil	96,965	50,000	306,498
Albania	698	—	21,994	Brunei Darussalam	1,267	—	1,267
Algeria	9,068	—	60,526	Bulgaria	12,556	—	132,116
Angola	349	—	2,117	Burkina Faso	349	—	3,177
Antigua and Barbuda	349	—	1,184	Burma	698	346	698
Argentina	49,529	33,599	64,584	Burundi	349	—	10,806
Australia	547,371	513,156	305,511	Byelorussian SSR	125,512	104,435	823,337
Austria	261,483	259,200	131,883	Cameroon	698	2,497	698
Bahamas	698	1,032	352	Canada	1,073,823	1,064,448	541,599
Bahrain	698	692	352	Cape Verde	349	—	6,046
Bangladesh	1,047	1,548	528	Central African Republic	698	—	21,769
Barbados	698	346	698	Chad	349	—	10,806
Belgium	446,265	675,433	225,596	Chile	4,884	4,840	2,464
Belize	349	346	176	China	373,173	369,816	188,265
Benin	349	—	10,806	Colombia	7,674	3,802	3,872
Bhutan	349	346	176	Comoros	349	—	7,405
Bolivia	698	—	14,026	Congo	698	—	21,994
Botswana	349	802	176	Costa Rica	1,396	1,396	—

Country	Assessments in 1984	Paid in 1984	Total contributions outstanding*	Country	Assessments in 1984	Paid in 1984	Total contributions outstanding*
Cuba	6,278	—	21,200	Nepal	349	516	176
Cyprus	698	692	352	Netherlands	620,585	615,168	313,001
Czechoslovakia	264,970	260,120	979,733	New Zealand	90,648	89,856	45,720
Democratic Kampuchea	698	—	21,994	Nicaragua	698	—	2,038
Democratic Yemen	349	—	5,886	Niger	349	—	1,480
Denmark	261,483	259,200	131,883	Nigeria	13,254	5,748	20,526
Djibouti	349	—	1,861	Norway	177,808	176,256	89,680
Dominica	349	—	2,571	Oman	698	908	698
Dominican Republic	2,092	1,036	12,664	Pakistan	4,186	6,186	2,112
Ecuador	1,396	1,004	1,084	Panama	1,396	1,311	21,076
Egypt	4,884	4,840	2,464	Papua New Guinea	349	173	176
El Salvador	698	—	7,327	Paraguay	698	—	21,994
Equatorial Guinea	698	—	15,761	Peru	4,884	—	34,378
Ethiopia	349	—	1,179	Philippines	6,278	3,100	9,345
Fiji	698	692	352	Poland	251,024	703,749	126,608
Finland	167,349	165,888	84,405	Portugal	12,556	18,764	12,296
France	2,760,633	2,735,796	1,392,735	Qatar	2,092	—	9,560
Gabon	1,396	—	10,674	Romania	13,254	—	116,997
Gambia	698	1,377	—	Rwanda	349	173	349
German Democratic Republic	484,615	476,269	1,879,785	Saint Christopher and Nevis	530	—	530
Germany, Federal Republic of	2,977,419	2,951,424	1,501,707	Saint Lucia	349	1,232	606
Ghana	1,396	1,384	704	Saint Vincent and the Grenadines	349	173	
Greece	27,903	27,646	14,080	Samoa	349	—	1,831
Grenada	349	—	1,020	Sao Tome and Principe	349	—	1,936
Guatemala	1,396	—	2,767	Saudi Arabia	59,992	29,720	59,992
Guinea	349	547	315	Senegal	349	554	—
Guinea-Bissau	349	873	692	Seychelles	349	—	522
Guyana	698	1,025	698	Sierra Leone	698	179	12,956
Haiti	349	—	10,142	Singapore	6,278	6,220	3,168
Honduras	698	2,038	—	Solomon Islands	349	170	2,401
Hungary	16,043	118,978	143,303	Somalia	349	—	1,179
Iceland	10,460	10,368	5,276	South Africa	142,944	—	3,073,380
India	25,113	24,882	12,672	Spain	134,636	128,494	202,652
Indonesia	9,068	17,074	4,576	Sri Lanka	698	692	352
Iran	40,460	—	232,811	Sudan	349	170	511
Iraq	8,371	—	112,684	Suriname	349	—	1,260
Ireland	62,756	62,208	31,652	Swaziland	698	—	21,994
Israel	16,043	15,836	8,678	Sweden	460,211	680,381	232,115
Italy	1,303,928	646,272	1,303,928	Syrian Arab Republic	2,092	—	32,306
Ivory Coast	2,092	—	3,128	Thailand	5,580	5,528	2,816
Jamaica	1,396	1,321	767	Togo	698	512	2,026
Japan	3,598,006	3,536,041	3,598,006	Trinidad and Tobago	2,092	2,072	1,056
Jordan	698	661	698	Tunisia	2,092	2,054	2,092
Kenya	698	1,611	698	Turkey	22,321	20,878	15,530
Kuwait	17,439	17,278	8,800	Uganda	349	—	7,880
Lao People's Democratic Republic	349	—	2,654	Ukrainian SSR	460,211	383,778	3,061,267
Lebanon	1,396	679	21,807	USSR	4,469,595	3,677,869	27,810,231
Lesotho	349	1,644	176	United Arab Emirates	11,162	8,251	22,127
Liberia	698	—	14,848	United Kingdom	1,980,362	1,962,544	999,090
Libyan Arab Jamahiriya	18,137	—	233,061	United Republic of Tanzania	349	—	8,010
Luxembourg	20,919	20,736	10,551	United States	10,738,310	10,627,420	5,424,600
Madagascar	698	1,130	2,660	Uruguay	2,790	—	10,038
Malawi	349	517	175	Vanuatu	349	173	1,011
Malaysia	6,278	13,447	—	Venezuela	38,367	—	122,128
Maldives	349	—	997	Viet Nam	1,396	—	19,530
Mali	349	1,126	323	Yemen	349	—	10,406
Malta	698	346	698	Yugoslavia	32,088	26,507	79,008
Mauritania	698	—	12,261	Zaire	698	—	5,449
Mauritius	698	1,032	648	Zambia	698	1,044	—
Mexico	61,388	30,412	61,388	Zimbabwe	698	346	1,038
Mongolia	698	692	8,793				
Morocco	3,488	—	12,123	Total	35,008,804	33,693,091	56,976,614
Mozambique	349	—	8,951				

*Includes contributions due for UNDOF from its inception on 31 May 1974 through 31 May 1985, as at 31 December 1984, and those due for UNEF II (1973-1979); between 1974 and 1979 there was a single account for the two Forces.

SOURCE: ST/ADM/SER.B/276.

UNIFIL financing

Report of the Secretary-General. In November 1984,[5] the Secretary-General reported that, as at 30 September, contributions totalling $717.2 million had been received for the operation of UNIFIL out of $945.3 million apportioned among Member States for the periods between the inception of the Force in 1978 and 18 October 1984. The balance due of $228.1 million included $179.4 million apportioned among Members which had stated that they did not intend to pay and $19.6 million of assessments due from China between 25 October 1971 and 31 December 1981, transferred to a special account in accordance with a

1981 Assembly resolution.[2] Accordingly, only $29.1 million of the unpaid balance might be considered collectible, leaving a shortfall of $199 million.

Commitments were entered into for UNIFIL in the amount of $70,446,000 gross ($69,486,000 net) for the six months from 19 April to 18 October. The costs for the period from 19 October 1984 to 18 April 1985 were estimated at the same gross amount ($69,446,000 net), based on an average Force strength of 5,550 troops. The Secretary-General requested ACABQ's concurrence for entering into UNIFIL commitments of $23,482,000 gross ($23,148,667 net) for the period from 19 October to 18 December 1984, that amount being a one-third share of the estimate for the six months from 19 October 1984 to 18 April 1985.

Should the Security Council renew the Force's mandate beyond that date, the Assembly was requested to authorize commitments for UNIFIL for the period to 18 December 1985 at a rate not to exceed $11,741,000 gross ($11,574,333 net) per month.

The shortfall in the account because of non-payment of contributions by some Members placed an increasingly heavy burden on the troop-contributing countries, the Secretary-General said, particularly the less wealthy, and, if not remedied, could jeopardize the functioning of the operation. He appealed to all Member States to pay their assessments without delay and to make voluntary contributions.

ACABQ recommendations. In a November 1984 report,[6] ACABQ recommended that the Assembly appropriate $70,446,000 gross ($69,486,000 net) for UNIFIL for the period from 19 April to 18 October 1984; for 19 October 1984 to 18 April 1985, it recommended an appropriation of the same gross amount ($69,446,000 net). Despite differences in troop strength used as the basis for cost estimates for the preceding period, the amount requested and authorized for the period ended 18 October was the same. Noting that current estimates, on a net basis, were less than the two previous mandate-period estimates, ACABQ was informed that gains on currency exchange were expected to more than offset the effects of inflation.

Concurring with the Secretary-General's estimates, ACABQ agreed to the request to enter into commitments for the period from 19 October to 18 December 1984 in the amount requested. As for the remaining four months of the mandate period (19 December 1984–18 April 1985), ACABQ had no objection to the overall estimate; it recommended that the Assembly appropriate $46,964,000 gross ($46,297,333 net), with the Secretary-General being given the usual flexibility to revise apportionments between objects of expenditure.

ACABQ recommended approval of the amounts that the Secretary-General asked that he be authorized to commit monthly between 19 April and 18 December 1985, if the Force's mandate was renewed.

GENERAL ASSEMBLY ACTION

In December 1984, acting on the recommendation of the Fifth Committee, the General Assembly adopted two resolutions—39/71 A and B—dealing with the financing of UNIFIL.

On 13 December, the Assembly adopted resolution 39/71 A by recorded vote.

The General Assembly,

Having considered the report of the Secretary-General on the financing of the United Nations Interim Force in Lebanon and the related report of the Advisory Committee on Administrative and Budgetary Questions,

Bearing in mind Security Council resolutions 425(1978) and 426(1978) of 19 March 1978, 427(1978) of 3 May 1978, 434(1978) of 18 September 1978, 444(1979) of 19 January 1979, 450(1979) of 14 June 1979, 459(1979) of 19 December 1979, 474(1980) of 17 June 1980, 483(1980) of 17 December 1980, 488(1981) of 19 June 1981, 498(1981) of 18 December 1981, 501(1982) of 25 February 1982, 511(1982) of 18 June 1982, 519(1982) of 17 August 1982, 523(1982) of 18 October 1982, 529(1983) of 18 January 1983, 536(1983) of 18 July 1983, 538(1983) of 18 October 1983, 549(1984) of 19 April 1984 and 555(1984) of 12 October 1984,

Recalling its resolutions S-8/2 of 21 April 1978, 33/14 of 3 November 1978, 34/9 B of 17 December 1979, 35/44 of 1 December 1980, 35/115 A of 10 December 1980, 36/138 A of 16 December 1981, 36/138 C of 19 March 1982, 37/127 A of 17 December 1982 and 38/38 A of 5 December 1983,

Reaffirming its previous decisions regarding the fact that, in order to meet the expenditures caused by such operations, a different procedure from the one applied to meet expenditures of the regular budget of the United Nations is required,

Taking into account the fact that the economically more developed countries are in a position to make relatively larger contributions and that the economically less developed countries have a relatively limited capacity to contribute towards peace-keeping operations involving heavy expenditures,

Bearing in mind the special responsibilities of the States permanent members of the Security Council in the financing of peace-keeping operations decided upon in accordance with the Charter of the United Nations,

I

Decides to appropriate to the Special Account referred to in section I, paragraph 1, of General Assembly resolution S-8/2 an amount of $70,446,000 gross ($69,486,000 net), being the amount authorized with the prior concurrence of the Advisory Committee on Administrative and Budgetary Questions and apportioned under the provisions of section VI of Assembly resolution 38/38 A for the operation of the United Nations Interim Force in Lebanon from 19 April to 18 October 1984, inclusive;

II

Decides to appropriate to the Special Account an amount of $23,482,000 gross ($23,148,667 net), being the amount authorized with the prior concurrence of the Advisory Committee on Administrative and Budgetary Questions and apportioned under the provisions of section VI of General Assembly resolution 38/38 A for the operation of the United Nations Interim Force in Lebanon from 19 October to 18 December 1984, inclusive;

III

1. *Decides* to appropriate to the Special Account an amount of $46,964,000 for the operation of the United Nations Interim Force in Lebanon for the period from 19 December 1984 to 18 April 1985, inclusive;

2. *Decides further*, as an *ad hoc* arrangement, without prejudice to the positions of principle that may be taken by Member States in any consideration by the General Assembly of arrangements for the financing of peace-keeping operations, to apportion the amount of $46,964,000 among Member States in accordance with the scheme set out in Assembly resolution 33/14 and the provisions of section V, paragraph 1, of resolution 34/9 B, section VI, paragraph 1, of resolution 35/115 A, section VI, paragraph 1, of resolution 36/138 A and section IX, paragraph 1, of resolution 37/127 A, in the proportions determined by the scale of assessments for the years 1983, 1984 and 1985;

3. *Decides* that there shall be set off against the apportionment among Member States, as provided for in paragraph 2 above, their respective share in the estimated income of $13,333 other than staff assessment income approved for the period from 19 December 1984 to 18 April 1985, inclusive;

4. *Decides* that, in accordance with the provisions of its resolution 973(X) of 15 December 1955, there shall be set off against the apportionment among Member States, as provided for in paragraph 2 above, their respective share in the Tax Equalization Fund of the estimated staff assessment income of $653,334 approved for the period from 19 December 1984 to 18 April 1985, inclusive;

IV

Authorizes the Secretary-General to enter into commitments for the operation of the United Nations Interim Force in Lebanon at a rate not to exceed $11,741,000 gross ($11,574,333 net) per month for the period from 19 April to 18 December 1985, inclusive, should the Security Council decide to continue the Force beyond the period of six months authorized under its resolution 555(1984), subject to obtaining the prior concurrence of the Advisory Committee on Administrative and Budgetary Questions for the actual level of commitments to be entered into for each mandate period that may be approved subsequent to 19 April 1985, the said amount to be apportioned among Member States in accordance with the scheme set out in the present resolution;

V

1. *Renews its invitation* to Member States to make voluntary contributions to the United Nations Interim Force in Lebanon both in cash and in the form of services and supplies acceptable to the Secretary-General;

2. *Invites* Member States to make voluntary contributions in cash to the Suspense Account established in accordance with its resolution 34/9 D of 17 December 1979;

VI

Requests the Secretary-General to take all necessary action to ensure that the United Nations Interim Force in Lebanon shall be administered with a maximum of efficiency and economy;

VII

1. *Decides* that Brunei Darussalam shall be included in the group of Member States mentioned in section I, paragraph 2 *(c)*, of General Assembly resolution S-8/2 and that its contribution to the United Nations Interim Force in Lebanon shall be calculated in accordance with the provisions of the resolution adopted by the Assembly at the current session regarding the scale of assessments;

2. *Decides* that Saint Christopher and Nevis shall be included in the group of Member States mentioned in section I, paragraph 2 *(d)*, of General Assembly resolution S-8/2 and that its contribution to the United Nations Interim Force in Lebanon shall be calculated in accordance with the provisions of the resolution adopted by the Assembly at the current session regarding the scale of assessments;

3. *Decides further* that, in accordance with regulation 5.2 *(c)* of the Financial Regulations of the United Nations, the contributions to the United Nations Interim Force in Lebanon until 18 December 1984 of the Member States referred to in paragraphs 1 and 2 of the present section shall be treated as miscellaneous income to be set off against the apportionments authorized in section III above.

General Assembly resolution 39/71 A

13 December 1984   Meeting 98   121-15-3 (recorded vote)

Approved by Fifth Committee (A/39/767) by recorded vote (88-12-3), 4 December (meeting 41); 13-nation draft (A/C.5/39/L.15, part A, approved together with part B (see below)); agenda item 119 *(b)*.

Sponsors: Austria, Canada, Denmark, Finland, France, Ghana, Iceland, Ireland, Italy, Lebanon, Netherlands, Norway, Sweden.

Recorded vote in Assembly as follows:

In favour: Argentina, Australia, Austria, Bahamas, Bahrain, Bangladesh, Barbados, Belgium, Belize, Bhutan, Bolivia, Botswana, Brazil, Brunei Darussalam, Burkina Faso, Burma, Burundi, Cameroon, Canada, Cape Verde, Central African Republic, Chad, Chile, China, Congo, Costa Rica, Cyprus, Democratic Kampuchea, Denmark, Djibouti, Dominican Republic, Ecuador, Egypt, El Salvador, Equatorial Guinea, Ethiopia, Fiji, Finland, France, Gabon, Gambia, Germany, Federal Republic of, Ghana, Greece, Guatemala, Guinea, Guinea-Bissau, Guyana, Haiti, Honduras, Iceland, India, Indonesia, Ireland, Israel, Italy, Ivory Coast, Jamaica, Japan, Jordan, Kenya, Kuwait, Lebanon, Liberia, Luxembourg, Madagascar, Malawi, Malaysia, Mali, Malta, Mauritania, Mauritius, Mexico, Morocco, Nepal, Netherlands, New Zealand, Nicaragua, Niger, Nigeria, Norway, Oman, Pakistan, Panama, Papua New Guinea, Paraguay, Peru, Philippines, Portugal, Qatar, Romania, Rwanda, Saint Lucia, Saint Vincent and the Grenadines, Samoa, Saudi Arabia, Senegal, Sierra Leone, Singapore, Somalia, Spain, Sri Lanka, Sudan, Suriname, Sweden, Thailand, Togo, Trinidad and Tobago, Tunisia, Turkey, Uganda, United Arab Emirates, United Kingdom, United Republic of Tanzania, United States, Uruguay, Venezuela, Yugoslavia, Zaire, Zambia, Zimbabwe.

Against: Afghanistan, Albania, Bulgaria, Byelorussian SSR, Cuba, Czechoslovakia, German Democratic Republic, Hungary, Lao People's Democratic Republic, Mongolia, Poland, Syrian Arab Republic, Ukrainian SSR, USSR, Viet Nam.

Abstaining: Iraq, Maldives, Yemen.

Also on 13 December, by the same recorded vote, the Assembly adopted resolution 39/71 B.

The General Assembly,

Having regard to the financial position of the Special Account for the United Nations Interim Force in Lebanon, as set forth in the report of the Secretary-General, and referring to paragraph 7 of the report of the Advisory Committee on Administrative and Budgetary Questions,

Mindful of the fact that it is essential to provide the United Nations Interim Force in Lebanon with the necessary financial resources to enable it to fulfil its responsibilities under the relevant resolutions of the Security Council,

Concerned that the Secretary-General is continuing to face growing difficulties in meeting the obligations of the United Nations Interim Force in Lebanon on a current basis, particularly those due to the Governments of troop-contributing States,

Recalling its resolutions 34/9 E of 17 December 1979, 35/115 B of 10 December 1980, 36/138 B of 16 December 1981, 37/127 B of 17 December 1982 and 38/38 B of 5 December 1983,

Recognizing that, in consequence of the withholding of contributions by certain Member States, the surplus balances in the Special Account for the United Nations Interim Force in Lebanon have, in effect, been drawn upon to the full extent to supplement the income received from contributions for meeting expenses of the Force,

Concerned that the application of the provisions of regulations 5.2 *(b)*, 5.2 *(d)*, 4.3 and 4.4 of the Financial Regulations of the United Nations would aggravate the already difficult financial situation of the United Nations Interim Force in Lebanon,

Decides that the provisions of regulations 5.2 *(b)*, 5.2 *(d)*, 4.3 and 4.4 of the Financial Regulations of the United Nations shall be suspended in respect of the amount of $6,035,305, which otherwise would have to be surrendered pursuant to those provisions, this amount to be entered in the account referred to in the operative part of General Assembly resolution 34/9 E and held in suspense until a further decision is taken by the Assembly.

General Assembly resolution 39/71 B

13 December 1984   Meeting 98   121-15-3 (recorded vote)

Approved by Fifth Committee (A/39/767) by recorded vote (88-12-3), 4 December (meeting 41); 13-nation draft (A/C.5/39/L.15, part B, approved together with part A (see above)); agenda item 119 *(b)*.

Sponsors: Austria, Canada, Denmark, Finland, France, Ghana, Iceland, Ireland, Italy, Lebanon, Netherlands, Norway, Sweden.

[For recorded vote in Assembly, see above under resolution 39/71 A.]

Introducing the drafts on behalf of the sponsors, the Netherlands said that the great majority of Member States supported the concept of peace-keeping and accepted the notion that the costs of peace-keeping forces should be borne by Members according to their assessed contributions. It was most regrettable that the resulting financial obligations were not fulfilled; lack of financial resources not only threatened to undermine peace-keeping operations in general and UNIFIL's operations in particular, but also made it increasingly difficult to find States willing to take part in the operations. The situation would improve only if States withholding contributions discharged their financial responsibilities.

Holding a similar view, Ireland added that the withholding of contributions could jeopardize the efficient functioning of peace-keeping operations

and hinder efforts to ensure a wide geographical representation in the composition of the forces, with unforeseeable consequences for the United Nations ability to fulfil its role in maintaining international peace and security.

Indonesia viewed the financial situation of peace-keeping operations in the Middle East as unsatisfactory and shared the Secretary-General's concern that delayed payments to contributing countries placed an additional burden on them.

Lebanon said the United Nations presence was an essential guarantee required to safeguard Lebanon's independence, sovereignty and territorial integrity, which were indispensable pre-conditions for its progressive pacification; a withdrawal of that presence for financial reasons would have extremely serious repercussions, not only in Lebanon itself but also in the Middle East as a whole. The situation regarding the financing of UNIFIL could even jeopardize efforts being made to resolve the financial crisis of the United Nations as a whole. Maintaining UNIFIL for some time to come was indispensable; Lebanon urged Governments to adopt a more regular procedure for the payment of contributions and hoped that the Secretary-General's appeal for voluntary contributions would be favourably received.

Peace-keeping operations were by definition temporary and could be no substitute for a peaceful settlement, Israel said; yet peace-keeping forces in the Middle East were becoming a permanent feature because of the enmity towards Israel and Arab unwillingness to accept Israel's presence. If the Secretary-General was to implement the Security Council's decisions, he must be given the financial means.

The USSR said it would not share in the financing of UNIFIL; all costs incurred in eradicating the results of Israel's armed aggression should be borne by the aggressor. Similar positions were held by the German Democratic Republic, Iran, Iraq, Mongolia, the Syrian Arab Republic, Viet Nam and Yemen. Poland believed that expenditures on peace-keeping operations did not come within the scope of either Article 17 or 19 of the Charter (stipulating, respectively, that the expenses of the Organization shall be borne by the Members as apportioned by the Assembly, and that a Member in arrears for more than two years shall have no vote in the Assembly). Iran and the Libyan Arab Jamahiriya declared that, for positions of principle, they would not participate in the vote.

Albania explained that its negative vote was in conformity with its general position on the dispatching and financing of United Nations forces.

While southern Lebanon was the victim of Israeli aggression and atrocities, the United Arab Emirates said, UNIFIL's task was a humanitarian one and must be supported.

CONTRIBUTIONS TO UNIFIL
(as at 31 December 1984; in US dollars)

Country	Assessments in 1984	Paid in 1984	Total contributions outstanding*	Country	Assessments in 1984	Paid in 1984	Total contributions outstanding*
Afghanistan	1,390	—	8,760	Jamaica	5,557	5,578	3,970
Albania	2,779	—	20,235	Japan	14,335,624	10,298,018	14,335,624
Algeria	36,124	—	240,691	Jordan	2,779	3,383	1,389
Angola	1,390	—	8,882	Kenya	2,779	—	10,600
Antigua and Barbuda	1,390	—	5,322	Kuwait	69,467	34,742	34,725
Argentina	197,288	—	386,039	Lao People's Democratic Republic	1,390	—	9,748
Australia	2,180,903	2,101,210	1,170,623	Lebanon	5,557	3,157	2,400
Austria	1,041,833	1,042,290	520,688	Lesotho	1,390	7,391	695
Bahamas	2,779	5,470	1,389	Liberia	2,779	—	20,235
Bahrain	2,779	1,390	2,779	Libyan Arab Jamahiriya	72,246	—	454,612
Bangladesh	4,170	2,994	4,170	Luxembourg	83,347	83,384	41,655
Barbados	2,779	1,390	6,072	Madagascar	2,779	2,153	14,922
Belgium	1,778,063	2,196,275	888,642	Malawi	1,390	1,390	695
Belize	1,390	522	1,563	Malaysia	25,008	41,326	12,501
Benin	1,390	—	9,748	Maldives	1,390	695	3,614
Bhutan	1,390	695	695	Mali	1,390	2,722	3,816
Bolivia	2,779	—	20,235	Malta	2,779	2,780	1,389
Botswana	1,390	1,850	1,390	Mauritania	2,779	—	20,235
Brazil	386,242	100,000	1,303,191	Mauritius	2,779	3,386	3,440
Brunei Darussalam	3,671	—	3,671	Mexico	244,528	—	366,820
Bulgaria	50,018	—	328,356	Mongolia	2,779	—	20,235
Burkina Faso	1,390	—	9,748	Morocco	13,894	—	68,211
Burma	2,779	3,386	1,389	Mozambique	1,390	—	11,813
Burundi	1,390	—	9,748	Nepal	1,390	1,390	1,153
Byelorussian SSR	500,080	—	3,889,919	Netherlands	2,472,617	3,013,060	1,235,766
Cameroon	2,779	3,304	8,422	New Zealand	361,170	361,328	180,506
Canada	4,278,463	4,280,338	2,138,294	Nicaragua	2,779	—	8,864
Cape Verde	1,390	—	5,441	Niger	1,390	—	7,641
Central African Republic	2,779	3,713	16,522	Nigeria	52,795	—	90,714
Chad	1,390	—	9,748	Norway	708,447	590,632	354,068
Chile	19,450	34,741	9,723	Oman	2,779	2,780	1,389
China	1,486,714	1,487,096	743,166	Pakistan	16,673	20,967	8,834
Colombia	30,566	14,576	31,277	Panama	5,557	3,563	32,980
Comoros	1,390	—	9,748	Papua New Guinea	1,390	297	1,390
Congo	2,779	—	20,235	Paraguay	2,779	—	20,235
Costa Rica	5,557	—	31,902	Peru	19,450	—	121,719
Cuba	25,008	—	209,101	Philippines	25,008	10,714	53,514
Cyprus	2,779	3,386	1,389	Poland	1,000,160	—	11,130,204
Czechoslovakia	1,055,725	—	8,185,740	Portugal	50,018	96,338	50,018
Democratic Kampuchea	2,779	—	20,235	Qatar	8,337	17,042	7,875
Democratic Yemen	1,390	—	9,748	Romania	52,795	—	398,904
Denmark	1,041,833	1,042,290	520,688	Rwanda	1,390	695	2,369
Djibouti	1,390	—	7,212	Saint Christopher and Nevis	1,977	—	1,977
Dominica	1,390	—	10,040	Saint Lucia	1,390	—	7,614
Dominican Republic	8,337	—	51,940	Saint Vincent and the Grenadines	1,390	695	1,390
Ecuador	5,557	8,132	4,063	Samoa	1,390	—	5,853
Egypt	19,450	19,453	9,723	Sao Tome and Principe	1,390	—	8,281
El Salvador	2,779	—	19,208	Saudi Arabia	238,969	119,515	238,969
Equatorial Guinea	2,779	—	20,235	Senegal	1,390	—	7,704
Ethiopia	1,390	—	7,869	Seychelles	1,390	303	2,235
Fiji	2,779	3,386	1,389	Sierra Leone	2,779	—	20,039
Finland	666,773	667,066	333,240	Singapore	25,008	25,014	12,501
France	10,998,306	11,001,128	5,497,742	Solomon Islands	1,390	303	10,039
Gabon	5,557	—	32,899	Somalia	1,390	791	5,445
Gambia	2,779	—	20,235	South Africa	569,535	—	4,216,535
German Democratic Republic	1,930,864	—	13,933,267	Spain	536,293	825,380	567,559
Germany, Federal Republic of	11,863,008	11,868,208	5,928,904	Sri Lanka	2,779	2,780	1,389
Ghana	5,557	2,779	2,778	Sudan	1,390	303	2,792
Greece	111,148	111,176	55,560	Suriname	1,390	—	2,388
Grenada	1,390	—	4,433	Swaziland	2,779	—	20,235
Guatemala	5,557	—	9,548	Sweden	1,833,625	1,834,430	916,410
Guinea	1,390	—	4,033	Syrian Arab Republic	8,337	—	56,282
Guinea-Bissau	1,390	—	7,134	Thailand	22,230	20,981	11,112
Guyana	2,779	5,553	1,389	Togo	2,779	1,041	11,537
Haiti	1,390	—	9,748	Trinidad and Tobago	8,337	8,340	4,167
Honduras	2,779	2,510	6,158	Tunisia	8,337	4,170	10,155
Hungary	63,911	—	600,401	Turkey	88,917	84,399	74,367
Iceland	41,672	41,692	20,826	Uganda	1,390	—	8,967
India	100,033	121,874	50,004	Ukrainian SSR	1,833,625	—	14,458,268
Indonesia	36,124	22,364	36,124	USSR	17,806,784	—	133,810,561
Iran	161,165	—	1,114,503	United Arab Emirates	44,460	52,635	76,392
Iraq	33,344	—	225,115	United Kingdom	7,889,724	8,229,668	7,256,289
Ireland	250,039	273,627	—	United Republic of Tanzania	1,390	—	9,748
Israel	63,911	63,928	31,947	United States	42,819,684	42,818,576	21,410,396
Italy	5,195,275	3,596,031	4,198,020	Uruguay	11,115	—	32,738
Ivory Coast	8,337	—	32,362				

Country	Assessments in 1984	Paid in 1984	Total contributions outstanding*	Country	Assessments in 1984	Paid in 1984	Total contributions outstanding*
Vanuatu	1,390	—	5,322	Zaire	2,779	—	25,713
Venezuela	152,829	—	549,334	Zambia	2,779	2,861	1,308
Viet Nam	5,557	—	53,971	Zimbabwe	2,780	606	8,394
Yemen	1,390	—	9,748				
Yugoslavia	127,820	125,292	340,287	Total	139,515,477	108,902,817	266,529,271

*Covers the period from the inception of UNIFIL (19 March 1978) to 18 April 1985, as at 31 December 1984.
SOURCE: ST/ADM/SER.B/276.

Review of reimbursement rates to troop-contributors

GENERAL ASSEMBLY ACTION

On 13 December, on the recommendation of the Fifth Committee, the General Assembly adopted resolution 39/70 by recorded vote.

Review of the rates of reimbursement to the Governments of troop-contributing States

The General Assembly,

Recalling its decision of 29 November 1974, taken at its twenty-ninth session, by which it established, as from 25 October 1973, standard rates of reimbursement to the Governments of troop-contributing States for pay and allowances of their troops serving in the United Nations Emergency Force and the United Nations Disengagement Observer Force, and its decision 32/416 of 2 December 1977, by which it revised those rates of reimbursement as from 25 October 1977,

Recalling also its decision of 15 December 1975, taken at its thirtieth session, by which it approved the principle of reimbursing the troop-contributing States for the usage factor for personal clothing, gear and equipment, and the related report of the Secretary-General to the General Assembly at its thirty-first session establishing the rates therefor as from 25 October 1973,

Recalling further its resolution S-8/2 of 21 April 1978, by which it applied the same standard rates of reimbursement in effect for the United Nations Emergency Force and the United Nations Disengagement Observer Force to those Governments of States contributing troops to the United Nations Interim Force in Lebanon,

Recalling further its resolution 35/44 of 1 December 1980, by which these rates were once again revised as from 1 December 1980 in the case of the United Nations Disengagement Observer Force and as from 19 December 1980 in the case of the United Nations Interim Force in Lebanon,

Taking note of the concerns that escalating troop costs have adversely affected in real terms the existing standard rates of reimbursement,

Requests the Secretary-General to review, in consultation with the States contributing troops to the United Nations Disengagement Observer Force and the United Nations Interim Force in Lebanon and with other interested Member States, the existing standard rates of reimbursement, with a view to ensuring an equitable rate of reimbursement to the Governments of troop-contributing States, and to report on this matter to the General Assembly at its fortieth session.

General Assembly resolution 39/70

13 December 1984   Meeting 98   119-15-6 (recorded vote)

Approved by Fifth Committee (A/39/767) by recorded vote (89-11-5), 4 December (meeting 41); 18-nation draft (A/C.5/39/L.12), orally amended by United States; agenda item 119 *(b)*.

Sponsors: Austria, Belgium, Canada, Denmark, Fiji, Finland, France, Ghana, Greece, Iceland, Ireland, Italy, Lebanon, Nepal, Netherlands, Nigeria, Norway, Sweden.

Recorded vote in Assembly as follows:

In favour: Argentina, Australia, Austria, Bahamas, Bahrain, Bangladesh, Barbados, Belgium, Belize, Bhutan, Bolivia, Botswana, Brazil, Brunei Darussalam, Burkina Faso, Burma, Burundi, Cameroon, Canada, Cape Verde, Central African Republic, Chad, Chile, China, Congo, Costa Rica, Cyprus, Democratic Kampuchea, Denmark, Djibouti, Dominican Republic, Ecuador, Egypt, El Salvador, Equatorial Guinea, Ethiopia, Fiji, Finland, France, Gabon, Gambia, Germany, Federal Republic of, Ghana, Greece, Guatemala, Guinea, Guinea-Bissau, Guyana, Honduras, Iceland, India, Indonesia, Ireland, Israel, Italy, Ivory Coast, Jamaica, Japan, Jordan, Kenya, Kuwait, Lebanon, Lesotho, Liberia, Luxembourg, Madagascar, Malawi, Malaysia, Mali, Malta, Mauritania, Mauritius, Mexico, Morocco, Nepal, Netherlands, New Zealand, Nicaragua, Niger, Norway, Oman, Pakistan, Panama, Papua New Guinea, Paraguay, Peru, Philippines, Portugal, Qatar, Rwanda, Saint Lucia, Saint Vincent and the Grenadines, Samoa, Saudi Arabia, Senegal, Sierra Leone, Singapore, Somalia, Spain, Sri Lanka, Sudan, Suriname, Sweden, Thailand, Togo, Trinidad and Tobago, Tunisia, Turkey, Uganda, United Arab Emirates, United Kingdom, United Republic of Tanzania, United States, Uruguay, Venezuela, Yugoslavia, Zaire, Zambia, Zimbabwe.

Against: Afghanistan, Albania, Bulgaria, Byelorussian SSR, Cuba, Czechoslovakia, German Democratic Republic, Hungary, Lao People's Democratic Republic, Mongolia, Poland, Syrian Arab Republic, Ukrainian SSR, USSR, Viet Nam.

Abstaining: Benin, Democratic Yemen, Iraq, Maldives, Romania, Yemen.

Introducing the text on behalf of the sponsors, the Netherlands said that, since the last revision of the standard rates of reimbursement to troop-contributing States in 1980,[7] troop costs in the countries concerned had increased in some cases by more than 40 per cent and the existing rates should be reviewed as they might no longer be adequate.

In the view of the United States, consultations on reimbursement rates should not be limited to troop-contributing countries; since peace-keeping operations were funded from the regular budget, all Member States should be able to participate. The United States orally suggested in the Committee that the operative paragraph be amended to permit other interested Member States to participate in the consultations; this was accepted by the sponsors.

The USSR observed that reimbursements to troop contributors were the main items of expenditure for UNDOF and UNIFIL; it believed that the existing rates were already excessive. The noble cause of maintaining international peace must not give rise to inappropriate expenditures and become a source of income for some countries. The Secretary-General's 1985 report should also indicate all the criteria used to devise acceptable reimbursement rates.

Ireland said that since the latest review of reimbursement rates dated back almost five years, and in view of the significant increases in costs and inflation, a further review was needed in order to ensure that reimbursements were paid at equitable rates.

Indonesia stated that escalating costs had adversely affected the existing reimbursement and it was high time that the Assembly took steps to ensure more equitable rates.

Recalling their positions of principle on peace-keeping operations in the Middle East, Iran and the Libyan Arab Jamahiriya did not participate in the vote.

REFERENCES

(1)A/39/468. (2)YUN 1981, p. 1299, GA res. 36/116 A, 10 Dec. 1981. (3)A/39/653. (4)YUN 1983, p. 307, GA res. 38/35 A, 1 Dec. 1983. (5)A/39/650. (6)A/39/685. (7)YUN 1980, p. 369, GA res. 35/44, 1 Dec. 1980.

Territories occupied by Israel

During 1984, the situation in the territories occupied by Israel as a result of previous armed conflicts in the Middle East was again considered by the General Assembly and its Special Committee to Investigate Israeli Practices Affecting the Human Rights of the Population of the Occupied Territories (Committee on Israeli practices). The territories comprised the West Bank of the Jordan River (including East Jerusalem), the Golan Heights and the Gaza Strip.

The Assembly, in December, adopted eight resolutions (39/95 A-H) dealing with specific aspects of the report of the Committee. By resolution 39/95 A, it demanded the release of Ziyad Abu Eain and other prisoners (see p. 280). By resolution 39/95 E, it reiterated its demand that Israel rescind orders expelling and imprisoning the Mayors of Hebron and Halhul and expelling the Islamic Judge of Hebron. The Assembly also demanded that Israel comply with the 1949 Geneva Convention relative to the Protection of Civilian Persons in Time of War (fourth Geneva Convention) (39/95 B) and desist from any action which would change the status and composition of the Palestinian and other Arab territories occupied since 1967 (39/95 C). The Assembly condemned Israeli policies and practices in the Syrian Golan Heights (39/95 F) as well as those taken against Palestinian students and faculties of educational institutions (39/95 G) and in a number of other areas (39/95 D), demanding that Israel desist from those practices. The Assembly also demanded

information from Israel on the results of the investigations of assassination attempts against three Palestinian mayors in 1980 (39/95 H).

By resolution 39/146 A, it declared that peace in the Middle East must be based on a comprehensive, just and lasting solution which ensured the complete and unconditional withdrawal of Israel from the Palestinian and other occupied Arab territories, including Jerusalem; condemned Israeli occupation of those territories and its policies and practices there; and considered that Israel would be encouraged in those policies by the 1981 strategic co-operation agreements between the United States and Israel.

Concern about legislation on settlement activities in the occupied territories, under consideration by the Israeli parliament, was expressed by the Security Council in January, which urged that no measures be taken to aggravate tensions in the area.

Communications. Israeli measures in the occupied territories, including Jerusalem, continued to be at issue in a number of communications addressed during the year to the Secretary-General and to the President of the Security Council.

On 23 February[1] and 5 March,[2] Egypt transmitted letters of 22 February and 5 March, respectively, from the Permanent Observer of PLO to the United Nations detailing several hostile measures by Israelis against Palestinians, including acts of vandalism and usurping of land in a Palestinian village, a massive arrest campaign, and attacks against a refugee camp, a cemetery, and a bus carrying Palestinian workers.

On 24 February,[3] the Chairman of the Committee on Palestinian rights protested what he called discriminatory action against a representative of an Israel-based non-governmental organization who had been banned from continuing his education at the Institute of Technology at Haifa. By a letter of 8 August,[4] the Chairman reiterated the Committee's serious concern about the situation of the Palestinian Arabs in the occupied territories and drew the Secretary-General's attention to reports prepared by ILO, WHO and UNESCO on the situation of workers, on health conditions and on educational and cultural institutions in the occupied territories; the reports were annexed to the letter. By a letter of 26 November,[5] the Chairman expressed grave concern at reports of renewed acts of repression against Palestinians by Israeli forces on 21 and 22 November, including the shooting and tear-gassing of unarmed demonstrators, resulting in the deaths of two students.

In April, Israel expressed concern about a PLO exhibit at the United Nations Information Centre at Harare, Zimbabwe (see p. 365).

By a letter of 13 April,[6] Israel recounted what it called an act of PLO gangsterism, which involved the hijacking of a bus with some 30 Israeli civilians *en route* from Tel Aviv to Ashkelon; in the course of the rescue operation, eight people were wounded, one of whom subsequently died, and four of the attackers were killed. The Popular Front for the Liberation of Palestine, a PLO group headquartered at Damascus, Syrian Arab Republic, had claimed responsibility, Israel said. Referring to that communication in identical letters[7] of 1 May to the Security Council President and 23 July to the Secretary-General, the Syrian Arab Republic accused Israel of attempting to divert attention from the atrocities it had committed and continued to commit against the Arab people. Annexed to the letters were a list of what Syria called some of the most important terrorist acts committed by Zionist gangs from 1937 to the present, and an article and excerpts from four books on violence in the Middle East.

On 29 August,[8] Yemen transmitted a letter of the same date from PLO with regard to an attempted storming of the town of Um el Fahm that day by an armed group headed by a member of the Israeli Knesset (parliament); it had led to a violent confrontation with the Palestinian inhabitants, as a result of which six demonstrators were wounded.

By a letter of 8 October,[9] India transmitted the final communiqué adopted by the Meeting of Ministers for Foreign Affairs and Heads of Delegation of Non-Aligned Countries (New York, 1-5 October). The communiqué rejected the Israeli practices and policies in the occupied territories, including alteration of their geographic features and demographic composition, and declared all Israeli-established settlements there illegal.

In addition, communications were received regarding incidents in Jerusalem (see p. 272).

Action by the Commission on Human Rights. Violations of human rights in the occupied territories were the subject of four resolutions adopted by the Commission on Human Rights on 20 February 1984. By the first,[10] it condemned a number of specific practices; by the second,[11] it condemned Israel's failure to acknowledge the applicability of the fourth Geneva Convention of 1949; by the third,[12] it called on Israel to rescind decisions imposing its laws and administration on the Syrian Golan Heights; and, by the fourth,[13] it called for immediate Israeli withdrawal from the occupied Palestinian territories. By a resolution of 29 February[14] reaffirming the Palestinians' right to self-determination, the Commission condemned Israel's continued occupation of the Palestinian and other Arab territories, its aggression and practices against the Palestinians in and outside those territories, and the September 1982 massacres in the Sabra and Shatila refugee camps,[15] and rejected agreements that en-

couraged Israel to persist in its policies. (See ECONOMIC AND SOCIAL QUESTIONS, Chapter XVIII.)

Report of the Committee on Israeli practices. In its annual report, approved on 14 September 1984 and transmitted to the General Assembly by the Secretary-General,[16] the Committee on Israeli practices, established in 1968,[17] presented information on Israeli policy in the occupied territories and on various aspects of the situation there, as well as information on annexation and settlement, treatment of civilians and detainees, and judicial remedies sought by the civilian population. An annexed map showed Israeli settlements established, planned or under construction since 1967. As in previous years, the Committee worked without the co-operation of Israel.

During the reporting period (19 August 1983–31 August 1984), the Committee held three series of meetings. At the first, held at Geneva from 9 to 13 January 1984, it reviewed its mandate, examined information on the situation in the occupied territories, including communications on alleged human rights violations, and decided on the organization of its work for the year. At the second series of meetings, which took place at Geneva, Amman (Jordan) and Damascus (Syrian Arab Republic) from 25 May to 5 June, the Committee examined a number of communications pertaining to its mandate, heard testimony from persons living in the West Bank, the Gaza Strip and the Golan Heights, and discussed various aspects of its mandate with the Minister for Occupied Territories Affairs and the Minister for Foreign Affairs of Jordan, and the Director-General of the International Organizations Department in the Ministry of Foreign Affairs of the Syrian Arab Republic. The Committee convened again from 10 to 14 September to examine updated information and adopt its report.

In its conclusions, the Committee noted that Israeli statements made over the reporting period reflected an intention to annex the territories occupied in 1967 and thus were in violation of the fourth Geneva Convention. The Committee pointed out that the announced ''new policy''— aimed, avowedly, at deterring Arab retaliation against Jews and Jewish vigilante action—had led to ever harsher sentences for Palestinian civilians, an increase in violent incidents and the emergence of large-scale organized groups of Israelis striving to expand and consolidate Israeli settlement and annexation of the occupied territories.

The Committee concluded that although the so-called ''village leagues'' were no longer imposed, Israeli presence in the occupied territories had been further consolidated through the Israeli municipal authorities of the principal West Bank and Gaza Strip towns who had been nominated by the military. The Committee drew special attention to collective punishment measures by the Israeli authorities, including demolition of houses. Measures of reprisal included sealing houses, closing down shops, restricting movement and destroying of crops and water resources. With regard to deportations, the Committee noted in particular the case of Abdel Aziz Shahin who, after serving a 15-year prison sentence, had been the subject of an expulsion order.

Noting that the lawless behaviour of Israeli settlers had drawn protests in some sectors of Israeli society, the Committee cited the example of a 1982 report commissioned by the Israeli Ministry of Justice, made public in February 1984, which found that Israeli settlers acted in many respects outside the law, virtually beyond control by any authority. In 1984, a series of so-called "Jewish underground" groups were discovered; several persons were charged with offences ranging from attempted assassination to planning the bombing of public transportation, but no serious measures had yet been taken to put an end to the phenomenon. The Committee reiterated that under the fourth Geneva Convention Israel remained fully responsible for the acts of the settlers.

The Committee reported that Palestinian civilian leaders had been the subject of arbitrary orders restricting their freedom of movement. Freedom of education was also affected (see p. 333).

In the Committee's view, an on going censorship of publications and other forms of expression had the sole aim of stifling any attempt at Palestinian patriotic expression and went beyond the scope of the fourth Geneva Convention. Information received indicated that in the reporting period Israel continued annexation and settlement practices in the occupied territories with renewed vigour, planning 27 settlements for an area north of Jerusalem by the year 2010 and expropriating property. As for treatment of detainees, the Committee detected an increase in the number of allegations of ill-treatment. It reported that prison conditions had led to hunger-strikes and other protests, and noted particularly the harsh conditions in the so-called "Fara'a detention centre", opened for youthful offenders awaiting trial on minor offences. In that context, the Committee stressed that existing judicial remedies were of a temporary nature, as the courts' authority was circumscribed by the discretionary powers vested in the military occupation authorities.

The Committee concluded that the reporting period had witnessed a deterioration of the human rights situation in the territories, while at the same time hundreds of thousands were denied the right to return there and their property was taken over for the establishment of Israeli settlements. The Committee reiterated the need for the international community to prevent further deterioration and protect the basic rights of the civilians in the occupied territories.

Pursuant to a 1983 request by the General Assembly,[18] the Secretary-General, in November 1984,[19] reported on the facilities he had continued to provide to the Committee, including additional staff, circulation of its reports and coverage of its activities in press releases, publications and radio and television programmes.

GENERAL ASSEMBLY ACTION

Under the agenda item on the report of the Special Committee to Investigate Israeli Practices Affecting the Human Rights of the Population of the Occupied Territories, the General Assembly, on 14 December 1984, adopted by recorded vote resolution 39/95 D. The action was taken on the recommendation of the Special Political Committee.

The General Assembly,

Guided by the purposes and principles of the Charter of the United Nations and by the principles and provisions of the Universal Declaration of Human Rights,

Bearing in mind the provisions of the Geneva Convention relative to the Protection of Civilian Persons in Time of War, of 12 August 1949, as well as of other relevant conventions and regulations,

Recalling all its resolutions on the subject, in particular resolutions 32/91 B and C of 13 December 1977, 33/113 C of 18 December 1978, 34/90 A of 12 December 1979, 35/122 C of 11 December 1980, 36/147 C of 16 December 1981, 37/88 C of 10 December 1982 and 38/79 D of 15 December 1983, and also those adopted by the Security Council, the Commission on Human Rights, in particular its resolutions 1983/1 of 15 February 1983 and 1984/1 of 20 February 1984, and other United Nations organs concerned and by the specialized agencies,

Having considered the report of the Special Committee to Investigate Israeli Practices Affecting the Human Rights of the Population of the Occupied Territories, which contains, *inter alia*, self-incriminating public statements made by officials of Israel, the occupying Power,

Taking note of the report of the Secretary-General of 6 November 1984,

1. *Commends* the Special Committee to Investigate Israeli Practices Affecting the Human Rights of the Population of the Occupied Territories for its efforts in performing the tasks assigned to it by the General Assembly and for its thoroughness and impartiality;

2. *Deplores* the continued refusal by Israel to allow the Special Committee access to the occupied territories;

3. *Demands* that Israel allow the Special Committee access to the occupied territories;

4. *Reaffirms* the fact that occupation itself constitutes a grave violation of the human rights of the civilian population of the occupied Arab territories;

5. *Condemns* the continued and persistent violation by Israel of the Geneva Convention relative to the Pro-

tection of Civilian Persons in Time of War, of 12 August 1949, and other applicable international instruments, and condemns in particular those violations which the Convention designates as "grave breaches" thereof;

6. *Declares once more* that Israel's grave breaches of that Convention are war crimes and an affront to humanity;

7. *Strongly condemns* the following Israeli policies and practices:

(*a*) Annexation of parts of the occupied territories, including Jerusalem;

(*b*) Imposition of Israeli laws, jurisdiction and administration on the Syrian Golan Heights, which has resulted in the effective annexation of the Syrian Golan Heights;

(*c*) Illegal imposition and levy of heavy and disproportionate taxes and dues;

(*d*) Establishment of new Israeli settlements and expansion of the existing settlements on private and public Arab lands, and transfer of an alien population thereto;

(*e*) Eviction, deportation, expulsion, displacement and transfer of Arab inhabitants of the occupied territories and denial of their right to return;

(*f*) Confiscation and expropriation of private and public Arab property in the occupied territories and all other transactions for the acquisition of land involving the Israeli authorities, institutions or nationals on the one hand and the inhabitants or institutions of the occupied territories on the other;

(*g*) Excavations and transformations of the landscape and the historical, cultural and religious sites, especially at Jerusalem;

(*h*) Pillaging of archaeological and cultural property;

(*i*) Destruction and demolition of Arab houses, the most recent of which have been in the Jordan Valley;

(*j*) Collective punishment, mass arrests, administrative detention and ill-treatment of the Arab population;

(*k*) Ill-treatment and torture of persons under detention;

(*l*) Interference with religious freedoms and practices as well as family rights and customs;

(*m*) Interference with the system of education and with the social and economic development of the population in the occupied Palestinian and other Arab territories;

(*n*) Interference with the freedom of movement of individuals within the occupied Palestinian and other Arab territories;

(*o*) Illegal exploitation of the natural wealth, resources and population of the occupied territories;

8. *Strongly condemns* the arming of Israeli settlers in the occupied territories to commit acts of violence against Arab civilians and the perpetration of acts of violence by these armed settlers against individuals, causing injury and death and wide-scale damage to Arab property;

9. *Reaffirms* that all measures taken by Israel to change the physical character, demographic composition, institutional structure or legal status of the occupied territories, or any part thereof, including Jerusalem, are null and void, and that Israel's policy of settling parts of its population and new immigrants in the occupied territories constitutes a flagrant violation of the Geneva Convention and of the relevant resolutions of the United Nations;

10. *Demands* that Israel desist forthwith from the policies and practices referred to in paragraphs 7, 8 and 9 above;

11. *Calls upon* Israel, the occupying Power, to take immediate steps for the return of all displaced Arab and Palestinian inhabitants to their homes or former places of residence in the territories occupied by Israel since 1967;

12. *Urges* the international organizations and the specialized agencies, in particular the International Labour Organisation, to examine the conditions of Arab workers in the occupied Palestinian and other Arab territories, including Jerusalem;

13. *Reiterates its call* upon all States, in particular those States parties to the Geneva Convention, in accordance with article 1 of that Convention, and upon international organizations and the specialized agencies not to recognize any changes carried out by Israel in the occupied territories and to avoid actions, including those in the field of aid, which might be used by Israel in its pursuit of the policies of annexation and colonization or any of the other policies and practices referred to in the present resolution;

14. *Requests* the Special Committee, pending early termination of Israeli occupation, to continue to investigate Israeli policies and practices in the Arab territories occupied by Israel since 1967, to consult, as appropriate, with the International Committee of the Red Cross in order to ensure the safeguarding of the welfare and human rights of the population of the occupied territories and to report to the Secretary-General as soon as possible and whenever the need arises thereafter;

15. *Requests* the Special Committee to continue to investigate the treatment of civilians in detention in the Arab territories occupied by Israel since 1967;

16. *Condemns* Israel's refusal to permit persons from the occupied territories to appear as witnesses before the Special Committee and to participate in conferences and meetings held outside the occupied territories;

17. *Requests* the Secretary-General:

(*a*) To provide all necessary facilities to the Special Committee, including those required for its visits to the occupied territories, with a view to investigating the Israeli policies and practices referred to in the present resolution;

(*b*) To continue to make available additional staff as may be necessary to assist the Special Committee in the performance of its tasks;

(*c*) To ensure the widest circulation of the reports of the Special Committee and of information regarding its activities and findings by all means available through the Department of Public Information of the Secretariat and, where necessary, to reprint those reports of the Special Committee which are no longer available;

(*d*) To report to the General Assembly at its fortieth session on the tasks entrusted to him in the present paragraph;

18. *Requests* the Security Council to ensure Israel's respect for and compliance with all the provisions of the Geneva Convention relative to the Protection of Civilian Persons in Time of War, of 12 August 1949, in the Palestinian and other Arab territories occupied since 1967, including Jerusalem, and to initiate measures to halt Israeli policies and practices in those territories;

19. *Decides* to include in the provisional agenda of its fortieth session the item entitled "Report of the Special Committee to Investigate Israeli Practices Affecting the Human Rights of the Population of the Occupied Territories".

General Assembly resolution 39/95 D

14 December 1984   Meeting 100   115-2-28 (recorded vote)

Approved by SPC (A/39/712) by recorded vote (93-2-23), 29 November (meeting 43); 13-nation draft (A/SPC/39/L.25); agenda item 71.
Sponsors: Afghanistan, Bangladesh, Cuba, Egypt, India, Indonesia, Madagascar, Malaysia, Mali, Nicaragua, Pakistan, Qatar, Senegal.
Financial implications. 5th Committee, A/39/769; S-G, A/C.5/39/69, A/SPC/39/L.30.
Meeting numbers. GA 39th session: SPC 31-39, 43; 5th Committee 43; plenary 100.

Recorded vote in Assembly as follows:

In favour: Afghanistan, Albania, Algeria, Angola, Argentina, Bahrain, Bangladesh, Benin, Bhutan, Bolivia, Botswana, Brazil, Brunei Darussalam, Bulgaria, Burkina Faso, Burma, Burundi, Byelorussian SSR, Cameroon, Cape Verde, Central African Republic, Chad, China, Colombia, Congo, Costa Rica,* Cuba, Cyprus, Czechoslovakia, Democratic Kampuchea, Democratic Yemen, Djibouti, Ecuador, Egypt, El Salvador, Equatorial Guinea, Ethiopia, Fiji, Gabon, Gambia, German Democratic Republic, Ghana, Greece, Guatemala, Guinea, Guinea-Bissau, Guyana, Hungary, India, Indonesia, Iraq, Jamaica, Jordan, Kenya, Kuwait, Lao People's Democratic Republic, Lebanon, Lesotho, Libyan Arab Jamahiriya, Madagascar, Malaysia, Maldives, Mali, Malta, Mauritania, Mauritius, Mexico, Mongolia, Morocco, Mozambique, Nepal, Nicaragua, Niger, Nigeria, Oman, Pakistan, Panama, Papua New Guinea, Peru, Philippines, Poland, Portugal, Qatar, Romania, Rwanda, Samoa, Sao Tome and Principe, Saudi Arabia, Senegal, Seychelles, Sierra Leone, Singapore, Somalia, Spain, Sri Lanka, Sudan, Suriname, Syrian Arab Republic, Thailand, Togo, Trinidad and Tobago, Tunisia, Turkey, Uganda, Ukrainian SSR, USSR, United Arab Emirates, United Republic of Tanzania, Uruguay, Venezuela, Viet Nam, Yemen, Yugoslavia, Zambia, Zimbabwe.
Against: Israel, United States.
Abstaining: Australia, Austria, Bahamas, Barbados, Belgium, Belize, Canada, Denmark, Dominican Republic, Finland, France, Germany, Federal Republic of, Haiti, Iceland, Ireland, Italy, Ivory Coast, Japan, Liberia, Luxembourg, Malawi, Netherlands, New Zealand, Norway, Paraguay, Sweden, United Kingdom, Zaire.
*Later advised the Secretariat it had intended not to participate.

Paragraph 6 was approved in the Committee by a recorded vote of 84 to 18, with 17 abstentions, and in the Assembly by a recorded vote of 99 to 18, with 25 abstentions.

Sweden said that, while supporting most of the text, in particular the condemnation in paragraph 7, it was not convinced that all the formulations in that paragraph were justified. It also believed that the text went beyond the competence of the Assembly. Austria agreed with the general thrust of the text, but also considered some of the formulations to be unacceptable. Argentina felt that some of the wording was not consistent with the Special Committee's findings. The United States reiterated its position expressed in 1983;[20] the texts pertaining to this agenda item contained inflammatory rhetoric and unjustified allegations, were counter-productive, one-sided and harmed the credibility of the United Nations.

The Libyan Arab Jamahiriya said that, while it supported the resolutions, it reaffirmed its position on the substance of the Palestine question and therefore expressed reservations about anything in them that might signify that it would recognize the Zionist entity or confer legitimacy on it.

The Fifth Committee on 5 December decided, by a recorded vote of 88 to 2, with 19 abstentions, that an additional appropriation of $237,300 would be required for 1984-1985 to implement the resolution.

In resolution 39/49 C of 11 December on dissemination of information relating to Palestine, the General Assembly requested the Secretariat's Department of Public Information to publish newsletters and articles on Israeli violations of the human rights of the Arab inhabitants of the occupied territories.

Settlements policy

Throughout 1984, various communications addressed to the President of the Security Council and the Secretary-General continued to focus on Israel's policy of establishing settlements in the occupied territories. In January, the Council urged that no steps be taken to aggravate the situation. The question was also considered by the General Assembly, the Committee on Israeli practices, the Committee on Palestinian rights and the Commission on Human Settlements (see ECONOMIC AND SOCIAL QUESTIONS, Chapter XVII). The impact of Israeli settlements on the living conditions of Palestinians was examined in a report by the Secretary-General (see p. 327).

Communications (January–June). On 5 January,[21] Egypt transmitted a letter of 4 January to the Security Council President from PLO, charging that legislation seeking to extend the applicability of emergency regulations in the occupied territories, considered by the Israeli Knesset, violated international law and Security Council resolutions. Concern about the legislation was also expressed in a message from the Deputy Prime Minister and Minister for Foreign Affairs of Egypt dated 5 January, transmitted by Egypt on 6 January to the Council President[22] and the Secretary-General,[23] and in a letter of 9 January[24] from the Chairman of the Committee on Palestinian rights.

Israel stated, in identical letters of 11[25] and 13 January[26] to the Council President and the Secretary-General, that the most recent extension of the validity of emergency regulations, which were reviewed periodically, had been passed on 2 January 1984 in conformity with the recognized principle of international law that a State may apply its laws to its nationals in respect of acts committed by them beyond its territorial jurisdiction; the regulations did not affect the existing local legislation.

In a statement issued by the President of the Security Council on 26 January,[27] after consultations that day with the Council members concerning the above communications, the Council recalled its previous resolutions stressing the applicability of the fourth Geneva Convention and urged that no steps be taken which could lead to further aggravation of tension in the area.

On 29 February,[28] Jordan transmitted information from its Minister for Occupied Territories Affairs on Israeli settlement activity between November 1983 and January 1984, which included land confiscations and decisions to establish new settlements in the West Bank. Information on Israeli settlement activity during March, April and May, which involved confiscation of land, establishment of and plans to establish new settlements and consolidation of settlement activity, was provided by Jordan in letters of 1 May,[29] 25 May[30] and 22 June,[31] respectively.

On 15 March,[32] Bangladesh transmitted resolutions adopted by the Fourteenth Islamic Conference of Foreign Ministers (Dhaka, 6-11 December 1983), among them a resolution condemning Israel for its refusal to comply with the Security Council resolutions on Israeli settlements and for its plans to remove the Palestinian refugee camps in the West Bank and Gaza Strip.

By a letter of 23 February,[33] the Chairman of the Committee on Palestinian rights drew attention to what he called the intensification of Israel's activities against Palestinians, particularly with regard to the renewal of Jewish presence in Hebron and a planned new settlement between Ramallah and Nablus. The Acting Chairman of that Committee expressed concern, in a letter of 26 March,[34] over Israel's persistence in annexing the occupied territories, as exemplified by the establishment of another new settlement named Eruvin, north of Hebron, and the suggested expansion of Jerusalem's municipal limit to the north-east areas of the West Bank. On 25 June,[35] the Committee Chairman stated that Israel had reportedly approved the establishment of three new settlements—to be called Eli-Shemaa, Nirya and Yaarit—on the West Bank; the measure had been opposed by the Israeli Minister for Justice on the grounds that the land belonged to Palestinians.

Activities of the Committee on Palestinian rights. In 1984, the Committee on Palestinian rights continued to keep the situation in the occupied territories under close review. Reporting to the General Assembly on its activities during the year,[36] the Committee stated that in communications to the Secretary-General and the Security Council President it had expressed concern over Israeli policies of establishing illegal Jewish settlements in the occupied territories, the confiscation of Arab-owned land and widespread violation by Israel of the rights of the Palestinian people. The Israeli actions led the Committee to urge the Council to reactivate, as a matter of priority, its 1979 Commission set up to examine the situation relating to Israeli settlements.[37] The Committee pointed out that the Commission's latest report had not been considered by the Council since it was submitted in November 1980.[38]

Noting that Israel persisted with its settlement policy despite the illegality of such action, the censure of international opinion, United Nations de-

cisions and domestic parliamentary questioning, the Committee suggested that Israel was aiming at a projected minimum of 100,000 Israeli settlers by 1987 and 190,000 by the year 2010. The Committee also pointed out that, according to Israeli and Jordanian sources, by the end of 1983 Israel had expropriated 47.4 per cent of the West Bank territory and assumed control of between 50 and 60 per cent of the land in the occupied territories.

Fourth Geneva Convention

In 1984, the General Assembly and the Commission on Human Rights took up the question of whether the Geneva Convention relative to the Protection of Civilian Persons in Time of War, of 12 August 1949 (fourth Geneva Convention), was applicable to the Israeli-occupied territories. Both the Assembly (in resolutions 39/95 B and C) and the Commission reaffirmed the Convention's applicability, as did the Committee on Israeli practices (see p. 316).

In February 1984,[39] the Secretary-General drew the Security Council's attention to a December 1983 request of the Assembly[18] that the Council ensure Israel's respect for and compliance with the fourth Geneva Convention.

Action by the Commission on Human Rights. In one[11] of four resolutions on human rights violations in the occupied Arab territories adopted on 20 February 1984, the Commission on Human Rights reaffirmed that the fourth Geneva Convention was applicable to all those territories, including Jerusalem. Condemning Israel's failure to acknowledge its applicability and expressing deep concern over the consequences of that position, the Commission called on Israel to abide by the obligations arising from the Convention and other international instruments, and urged all States parties to that Convention to ensure respect for and compliance with it in the occupied territories.

In the other three resolutions, the Commission reaffirmed that the Convention continued to apply to Syrian territory occupied by Israel[12] and that Israel's persistent colonization of those territories constituted grave violations of the Convention,[13] and confirmed its declaration that Israel's grave breaches were war crimes and an affront to humanity.[10] (See ECONOMIC AND SOCIAL QUESTIONS, Chapter XVIII.)

GENERAL ASSEMBLY ACTION

In December 1984, the General Assembly adopted two resolutions (39/95 B and C) demanding that Israel comply with the Convention; both were discussed under the agenda item on the report of the Committee on Israeli practices. On 14 December, on the recommendation of the Special Political Committee, the Assembly adopted resolution 39/95 B by recorded vote.

The General Assembly,

Recalling its resolutions 3092 A (XXVIII) of 7 December 1973, 3240 B (XXIX) of 29 November 1974, 3525 B (XXX) of 15 December 1975, 31/106 B of 16 December 1976, 32/91 A of 13 December 1977, 33/113 A of 18 December 1978, 34/90 B of 12 December 1979, 35/122 A of 11 December 1980, 36/147 A of 16 December 1981, 37/88 A of 10 December 1982 and 38/79 B of 15 December 1983,

Recalling also Security Council resolution 465(1980) of 1 March 1980 in which, *inter alia,* the Council affirmed that the Geneva Convention relative to the Protection of Civilian Persons in Time of War, of 12 August 1949, is applicable to the Arab territories occupied by Israel since 1967, including Jerusalem,

Considering that the promotion of respect for the obligations arising from the Charter of the United Nations and other instruments and rules of international law is among the basic purposes and principles of the United Nations,

Bearing in mind the provisions of the Geneva Convention,

Noting that Israel and those Arab States whose territories have been occupied by Israel since June 1967 are parties to that Convention,

Taking into account that States parties to the Convention undertake, in accordance with article 1 thereof, not only to respect but also to ensure respect for the Convention in all circumstances,

1. *Reaffirms* that the Geneva Convention relative to the Protection of Civilian Persons in Time of War, of 12 August 1949, is applicable to the Palestinian and other Arab territories occupied by Israel since 1967, including Jerusalem;

2. *Condemns once again* the failure of Israel, the occupying Power, to acknowledge the applicability of that Convention to the territories it has occupied since 1967, including Jerusalem;

3. *Strongly demands* that Israel acknowledge and comply with the provisions of that Convention in the Palestinian and other Arab territories it has occupied since 1967, including Jerusalem;

4. *Urgently calls upon* all States parties to that Convention to exert all efforts in order to ensure respect for and compliance with its provisions in the Palestinian and other Arab territories occupied by Israel since 1967, including Jerusalem.

General Assembly resolution 39/95 B

14 December 1984   Meeting 100   140-1-3 (recorded vote)

Approved by SPC (A/39/712) by recorded vote (117-1-3), 29 November (meeting 43); 13-nation draft (A/SPC/39/L.23); agenda item 71.

Sponsors: Afghanistan, Bangladesh, Cuba, Egypt, India, Indonesia, Madagascar, Malaysia, Mali, Nicaragua, Pakistan, Qatar, Senegal.

Meeting numbers. GA 39th session: SPC 31-39, 43; plenary 100.

Recorded vote in Assembly as follows:

In favour: Afghanistan, Albania, Algeria, Angola, Argentina, Australia, Austria, Bahamas, Bahrain, Bangladesh, Barbados, Belgium, Belize, Benin, Bhutan, Bolivia, Botswana, Brazil, Brunei Darussalam, Bulgaria, Burkina Faso, Burma, Burundi, Byelorussian SSR, Cameroon, Canada, Cape Verde, Chad, Chile, China, Colombia, Congo, Costa Rica, Cuba, Cyprus, Czechoslovakia, Democratic Kampuchea, Democratic Yemen, Denmark, Djibouti, Dominican Republic, Ecuador, Egypt, El Salvador, Equatorial Guinea, Ethiopia, Fiji, Finland, France, Gabon, Gambia, German Democratic Republic, Germany, Federal Republic of, Ghana, Greece, Guatemala, Guinea, Guinea-Bissau, Guyana, Haiti, Hungary, Iceland, India, Indonesia, Iraq, Ireland, Italy, Ivory Coast, Jamaica, Japan, Jordan, Kenya, Kuwait, Lao People's Democratic Republic, Lebanon, Lesotho, Libyan Arab Jamahiriya, Luxembourg, Madagascar, Malawi, Malaysia, Maldives, Mali, Malta, Mauritius, Mexico, Mongolia, Morocco, Mozambique, Nepal, Netherlands, New Zealand, Nicaragua, Niger, Nigeria, Norway, Oman, Pakistan, Panama, Papua New Guinea, Paraguay, Peru, Philippines, Poland, Portugal, Qatar, Romania, Rwanda, Samoa, Sao Tome and Principe, Saudi Arabia, Senegal, Seychelles, Sierra Leone, Singapore, Somalia, Spain, Sri Lanka, Sudan, Suriname, Sweden, Syrian Arab Republic, Thailand, Togo, Trinidad and Tobago, Tunisia, Turkey, Uganda, Ukrainian SSR, USSR, United Arab Emirates, United Kingdom, United Republic of Tanzania, Uruguay, Venezuela, Viet Nam, Yemen, Yugoslavia, Zambia, Zimbabwe.

Against: Israel.

Abstaining: Liberia, United States, Zaire.

The Committee adopted paragraph 1 of the text by a recorded vote of 119 to 1. The Assembly did so by a recorded vote of 143 to 1.

The United States said its explanation of vote[40] on a similar resolution in 1983[41] applied equally to the current text.

Also on 14 December, on the recommendation of the Special Political Committee, the Assembly adopted resolution 39/95 C by recorded vote.

The General Assembly,

Recalling its resolutions 32/5 of 28 October 1977, 33/113 B of 18 December 1978, 34/90 C of 12 December 1979, 35/122 B of 11 December 1980, 36/147 B of 16 December 1981, 37/88 B of 10 December 1982 and 38/79 C of 15 December 1983,

Recalling also Security Council resolution 465(1980) of 1 March 1980,

Expressing grave anxiety and concern at the present serious situation in the occupied Palestinian and other Arab territories, including Jerusalem, as a result of the continued Israeli occupation and the measures and actions taken by Israel, the occupying Power, designed to change the legal status, geographical nature and demographic composition of those territories,

Confirming that the Geneva Convention relative to the Protection of Civilian Persons in Time of War, of 12 August 1949, is applicable to all Arab territories occupied since June 1967, including Jerusalem,

1. *Determines* that all such measures and actions taken by Israel in the Palestinian and other Arab territories occupied since 1967, including Jerusalem, are in violation of the relevant provisions of the Geneva Convention relative to the Protection of Civilian Persons in Time of War, of 12 August 1949, and constitute a serious obstruction to the efforts to achieve a just and lasting peace in the Middle East and therefore have no legal validity;

2. *Strongly deplores* the persistence of Israel in carrying out such measures, in particular the establishment of settlements in the Palestinian and other occupied Arab territories, including Jerusalem;

3. *Demands* that Israel comply strictly with its international obligations in accordance with the principles of international law and the provisions of the Geneva Convention;

4. *Demands once more* that Israel, the occupying Power, desist forthwith from taking any action which would result in changing the legal status, geographical nature or demographic composition of the Palestinian and other Arab territories occupied since 1967, including Jerusalem;

5. *Urgently calls upon* all States parties to the Geneva Convention to respect and to exert all efforts in order to ensure respect for and compliance with its provisions in all Arab territories occupied by Israel since 1967, including Jerusalem.

General Assembly resolution 39/95 C

14 December 1984   Meeting 100   143-1-1 (recorded vote)

Approved by SPC (A/39/712) by recorded vote (117-1-1), 29 November (meeting 43); 13-nation draft (A/SPC/39/L.24); agenda item 71.

Sponsors: Afghanistan, Bangladesh, Cuba, Egypt, India, Indonesia, Madagascar, Malaysia, Mali, Nicaragua, Pakistan, Qatar, Senegal.

Meeting numbers. GA 39th session: SPC 31-39, 43; plenary 100.

Recorded vote in Assembly as follows:

In favour: Afghanistan, Albania, Algeria, Angola, Argentina, Australia, Austria, Bahamas, Bahrain, Bangladesh, Barbados, Belgium, Belize, Benin, Bhutan, Bolivia, Botswana, Brazil, Brunei Darussalam, Bulgaria, Burkina Faso, Burma, Burundi, Byelorussian SSR, Cameroon, Canada, Central African Republic, Chad, Chile, China, Colombia, Congo, Costa Rica, Cuba, Cyprus, Czechoslovakia, Democratic Kampuchea, Democratic Yemen, Denmark, Djibouti, Dominican Republic, Ecuador, Egypt, El Salvador, Equatorial Guinea, Ethiopia, Fiji, Finland, France, Gabon, Gambia, German Democratic Republic, Germany, Federal Republic of, Ghana, Greece, Guatemala, Guinea, Guinea-Bissau, Guyana, Haiti, Hungary, Iceland, India, Indonesia, Iraq, Ireland, Italy, Ivory Coast, Jamaica, Japan, Jordan, Kenya, Kuwait, Lao People's Democratic Republic, Lebanon, Lesotho, Liberia, Libyan Arab Jamahiriya, Luxembourg, Madagascar, Malawi, Malaysia, Maldives, Mali, Malta, Mauritania, Mauritius, Mexico, Mongolia, Morocco, Mozambique, Nepal, Netherlands, New Zealand, Nicaragua, Niger, Nigeria, Norway, Oman, Pakistan, Panama, Papua New Guinea, Paraguay, Peru, Philippines, Poland, Portugal, Qatar, Romania, Rwanda, Samoa, Sao Tome and Principe, Saudi Arabia, Senegal, Seychelles, Sierra Leone, Singapore, Somalia, Spain, Sri Lanka, Sudan, Suriname, Sweden, Syrian Arab Republic, Thailand, Togo, Trinidad and Tobago, Tunisia, Turkey, Uganda, Ukrainian SSR, USSR, United Arab Emirates, United Kingdom, United Republic of Tanzania, Uruguay, Venezuela, Viet Nam, Yemen, Yugoslavia, Zaire, Zambia, Zimbabwe.

Against: Israel.

Abstaining: United States.

Israel said the texts reflected their sponsors' hostility and irresponsibility.

The question of the Convention's applicability was raised in other actions by the Assembly. By resolution 39/95 D, the Assembly condemned Israel's continued and persistent violation of the Convention, particularly the "grave breaches" declared as war crimes and an affront to humanity. Israel's systematic repression against Palestinian educational institutions in contravention of the Convention was condemned by resolution 39/95 G.

Golan Heights

In 1984, developments in the Golan Heights—a part of the Syrian Arab Republic occupied by Israel since 1967—brought action by the General Assembly (resolutions 39/95 F and 39/146 B) and the Commission on Human Rights.

Israel's refusal to abide by the relevant Assembly and Security Council resolutions was condemned by the Ministers and heads of delegation of non-aligned countries in the final communiqué adopted at their October 1984 meeting and transmitted by India on 8 October.[9]

Action by the Commission on Human Rights. On 20 February 1984,[12] the Commission on Human Rights declared once more that Israel's 14 December 1981 decision to impose its laws, jurisdiction and administration on the occupied Syrian Golan Heights[42] had no legal validity, called on Israel to rescind that decision, and emphasized the necessity of total and unconditional Israeli withdrawal. The Commission declared that Israeli practices and inhuman treatment of the

Syrian Arab population constituted a grave violation of the 1948 Universal Declaration of Human Rights,[43] the fourth Geneva Convention and United Nations resolutions. It reaffirmed that the Hague Convention of 1907 and the fourth Geneva Convention continued to apply to the occupied Syrian territory, and strongly condemned Israel for its attempts to impose Israeli citizenship and identity cards on Syrian citizens. (See ECONOMIC AND SOCIAL QUESTIONS, Chapter XVIII.)

Report of the Secretary-General. On 1 October 1984,[44] the Secretary-General reported on the implementation of a December 1983 Assembly resolution[45] which condemned Israel for refusing to rescind its 1981 decision to impose its laws, jurisdiction and administration on the Golan Heights, and called on Member States not to recognize such measures. He reported that, in reply to a note verbale of 15 March 1984, Israel had stated on 28 August that its position had been set out fully in a letter of 29 December 1981.[46] The Secretary-General also stated that, in response to notes verbales of 15 March to all other Member States, he had received information on the implementation of the resolution from Argentina, Bangladesh, Benin, Botswana, Cyprus, Czechoslovakia, Kuwait, Lesotho, Poland, Romania, Sierra Leone and Uganda, whose replies were annexed to his report. The reply of the German Democratic Republic on that subject was annexed to another October 1984 report by the Secretary-General (see p. 260).

GENERAL ASSEMBLY ACTION

In December 1984, the General Assembly adopted two resolutions dealing with the situation in the Golan Heights. On 14 December, under the agenda item on the report of the Committee on Israeli practices, the Assembly, on the recommendation of the Special Political Committee, adopted resolution 39/95 F by recorded vote.

The General Assembly,

Deeply concerned that the Arab territories occupied since 1967 have been under continued Israeli military occupation,

Recalling Security Council resolution 497(1981) of 17 December 1981 and General Assembly resolutions 36/226 B of 17 December 1981, ES-9/1 of 5 February 1982, 37/88 E of 10 December 1982 and 38/79 F of 15 December 1983,

Having considered the report of the Secretary-General of 1 October 1984,

Recalling its previous resolutions, in particular resolutions 3414(XXX) of 5 December 1975, 31/61 of 9 December 1976, 32/20 of 25 November 1977, 33/28 and 33/29 of 7 December 1978, 34/70 of 6 December 1979 and 35/122 E of 11 December 1980, in which it, *inter alia*, called upon Israel to put an end to its occupation of the Arab territories and to withdraw from all those territories,

Reaffirming once more the illegality of Israel's decision of 14 December 1981 to impose its laws, jurisdiction and administration on the Syrian Golan Heights, which has resulted in the effective annexation of that territory,

Reaffirming that the acquisition of territory by force is inadmissible under the Charter of the United Nations and that all territories thus occupied by Israel must be returned,

Recalling the Geneva Convention relative to the Protection of Civilian Persons in Time of War, of 12 August 1949,

1. *Strongly condemns* Israel, the occupying Power, for its refusal to comply with the relevant resolutions of the General Assembly and the Security Council, particularly Council resolution 497(1981), in which the Council, *inter alia*, decided that the Israeli decision to impose its laws, jurisdiction and administration on the occupied Syrian Golan Heights was null and void and without international legal effect and demanded that Israel, the occupying Power, should rescind forthwith its decision;

2. *Condemns* the persistence of Israel in changing the physical character, demographic composition, institutional structure and legal status of the occupied Syrian Arab Golan Heights;

3. *Determines* that all legislative and administrative measures and actions taken or to be taken by Israel, the occupying Power, that purport to alter the character and legal status of the Syrian Golan Heights are null and void and constitute a flagrant violation of international law and of the Geneva Convention relative to the Protection of Civilian Persons in Time of War, of 12 August 1949, and have no legal effect;

4. *Strongly condemns* Israel for its attempts and measures to impose forcibly Israeli citizenship and Israeli identity cards on the Syrian citizens in the occupied Syrian Arab Golan Heights and calls upon it to desist from its repressive measures against the population of the Syrian Arab Golan Heights;

5. *Calls once again upon* Member States not to recognize any of the legislative or administrative measures and actions referred to above;

6. *Requests* the Secretary-General to submit to the General Assembly at its fortieth session a report on the implementation of the present resolution.

General Assembly resolution 39/95 F

14 December 1984   Meeting 100   141-1-3 (recorded vote)

Approved by SPC (A/39/712) by recorded vote (116-1-3), 29 November (meeting 43); 13-nation draft (A/SPC/39/L.27); agenda item 71.

Sponsors: Afghanistan, Bangladesh, Cuba, Egypt, India, Indonesia, Madagascar, Malaysia, Mali, Nicaragua, Pakistan, Qatar, Senegal.

Meeting numbers. GA 39th session: SPC 31-39, 43; plenary 100.

Recorded vote in Assembly as follows:

In favour: Afghanistan, Albania, Algeria, Angola, Argentina, Australia, Austria, Bahamas, Bahrain, Bangladesh, Barbados, Belgium, Belize, Benin, Bhutan, Bolivia, Botswana, Brazil, Brunei Darussalam, Bulgaria, Burkina Faso, Burma, Burundi, Byelorussian SSR, Cameroon, Canada, Cape Verde, Central African Republic, Chad, Chile, China, Colombia, Congo, Costa Rica, Cuba, Cyprus, Czechoslovakia, Democratic Kampuchea, Democratic Yemen, Denmark, Djibouti, Dominican Republic, Ecuador, Egypt, El Salvador, Equatorial Guinea, Ethiopia, Fiji, Finland, France, Gabon, Gambia, German Democratic Republic, Germany, Federal Republic of, Ghana, Greece, Guatemala, Guinea, Guinea-Bissau, Guyana, Haiti, Hungary, Iceland, India, Indonesia, Iraq, Ireland, Italy, Ivory Coast, Jamaica, Japan, Jordan, Kenya, Kuwait, Lao People's Democratic Republic, Lebanon, Lesotho, Libyan Arab Jamahiriya, Luxembourg, Madagascar, Malawi, Malaysia, Maldives, Mali, Malta, Mauritania, Mauritius, Mexico, Mongolia, Morocco, Mozambique, Nepal, Netherlands, New Zealand, Nicaragua, Niger, Nigeria, Norway, Oman, Pakistan, Panama, Papua New Guinea, Peru, Philippines, Poland, Portugal, Qatar, Romania, Rwanda, Samoa, Sao Tome and Principe, Saudi Arabia, Senegal, Seychelles, Sierra Leone, Singapore, Somalia, Spain, Sri Lanka,

Sudan, Suriname, Sweden, Syrian Arab Republic, Thailand, Togo, Trinidad and Tobago, Tunisia, Turkey, Uganda, Ukrainian SSR, USSR, United Arab Emirates, United Kingdom, United Republic of Tanzania, Uruguay, Venezuela, Viet Nam, Yemen, Yugoslavia, Zambia, Zimbabwe.

Against: Israel.

Abstaining: Liberia, United States, Zaire.

The United States reiterated its position expressed in 1983[47] relating to its call on Israel to fulfil its obligations to the population in the Golan Heights, but considered that the text went beyond the Security Council's 1981 resolution[48] declaring Israel's decision null and void. Sweden pointed out that its support for the resolution did not alter its opposition[49] to a February 1982 Assembly resolution[50] mentioned in the text, on the situation in the occupied Arab territories.

On 14 December 1984, under the agenda item "The situation in the Middle East", the General Assembly adopted resolution 39/146 B by recorded vote.

The General Assembly,

Having discussed the item entitled "The situation in the Middle East",

Having considered the report of the Secretary-General of 2 October 1984,

Recalling Security Council resolution 497(1981) of 17 December 1981,

Reaffirming its resolutions 36/226 B of 17 December 1981, ES-9/1 of 5 February 1982, 37/123 A of 16 December 1982 and 38/180 A of 19 December 1983,

Recalling its resolution 3314(XXIX) of 14 December 1974, in which it defined an act of aggression, *inter alia*, as "the invasion or attack by the armed forces of a State of the territory of another State, or any military occupation, however temporary, resulting from such invasion or attack, or any annexation by the use of force of the territory of another State or part thereof" and provided that "no consideration of whatever nature, whether political, economic, military or otherwise, may serve as a justification for aggression",

Reaffirming the fundamental principle of the inadmissibility of the acquisition of territory by force,

Reaffirming once more the applicability of the Geneva Convention relative to the Protection of Civilian Persons in Time of War, of 12 August 1949, to the occupied Palestinian and other Arab territories, including Jerusalem,

Noting that Israel's record, policies and actions establish conclusively that it is not a peace-loving Member State and that it has not carried out its obligations under the Charter of the United Nations,

Noting further that Israel has refused, in violation of Article 25 of the Charter, to accept and carry out the numerous relevant decisions of the Security Council, in particular resolution 497(1981), thus failing to carry out its obligations under the Charter,

1. *Strongly condemns* Israel for its failure to comply with Security Council resolution 497(1981) and General Assembly resolutions 36/226 B, ES-9/1, 37/123 A and 38/180 A;

2. *Declares once more* that Israel's continued occupation of the Golan Heights and its decision of 14 December 1981 to impose its laws, jurisdiction and administration on the occupied Syrian Golan Heights constitute

an act of aggression under the provisions of Article 39 of the Charter of the United Nations and General Assembly resolution 3314(XXIX);

3. *Declares once more* that Israel's decision to impose its laws, jurisdiction and administration on the occupied Syrian Golan Heights is illegal and therefore null and void and has no validity whatsoever;

4. *Declares* all Israeli policies and practices of, or aimed at, annexation of the occupied Palestinian and other Arab territories, including Jerusalem, to be illegal and in violation of international law and of the relevant United Nations resolutions;

5. *Determines once more* that all actions taken by Israel to give effect to its decision relating to the occupied Syrian Golan Heights are illegal and invalid and shall not be recognized;

6. *Reaffirms its determination* that all relevant provisions of the Regulations annexed to the Hague Convention IV of 1907, and the Geneva Convention relative to the Protection of Civilian Persons in Time of War, of 12 August 1949, continue to apply to the Syrian territory occupied by Israel since 1967, and calls upon the parties thereto to respect and ensure respect of their obligations under these instruments in all circumstances;

7. *Determines once more* that the continued occupation of the Syrian Golan Heights since 1967 and their annexation by Israel on 14 December 1981, following Israel's decision to impose its laws, jurisdiction and administration on that territory, constitute a continuing threat to international peace and security;

8. *Strongly deplores* the negative vote by a permanent member of the Security Council which prevented the Council from adopting against Israel, under Chapter VII of the Charter, the "appropriate measures" referred to in resolution 497(1981) unanimously adopted by the Council;

9. *Further deplores* any political, economic, financial, military and technological support to Israel that encourages Israel to commit acts of aggression and to consolidate and perpetuate its occupation and annexation of occupied Arab territories;

10. *Firmly emphasizes once more* its demand that Israel, the occupying Power, rescind forthwith its illegal decision of 14 December 1981 to impose its laws, jurisdiction and administration on the Syrian Golan Heights, which resulted in the effective annexation of that territory;

11. *Reaffirms once more* the overriding necessity of the total and unconditional withdrawal by Israel from all the Palestinian and other Arab territories occupied since 1967, including Jerusalem, which is an essential prerequisite for the establishment of a comprehensive and just peace in the Middle East;

12. *Determines once more* that Israel's record, policies and actions confirms that it is not a peace-loving Member State, that it has persistently violated the principles contained in the Charter and that it has carried out neither its obligations under the Charter nor its commitment under General Assembly resolution 273(III) of 11 May 1949;

13. *Calls once more upon* all Member States to apply the following measures:

(a) To refrain from supplying Israel with any weapons and related equipment and to suspend any military assistance that Israel receives from them;

(b) To refrain from acquiring any weapons or military equipment from Israel;

(c) To suspend economic, financial and technological assistance to and co-operation with Israel;

(d) To sever diplomatic, trade and cultural relations with Israel;

14. *Reiterates its call* to all Member States to cease forthwith, individually and collectively, all dealings with Israel in order totally to isolate it in all fields;

15. *Urges* non-member States to act in accordance with the provisions of the present resolution;

16. *Calls upon* the specialized agencies and other international organizations to conform their relations with Israel to the terms of the present resolution;

17. *Requests* the Secretary-General to report to the General Assembly at its fortieth session on the implementation of the present resolution.

General Assembly resolution 39/146 B

14 December 1984   Meeting 101   88-22-32 (recorded vote)

32-nation draft (A/39/L.20 & Corr.1 & Add.1); agenda item 36.

Sponsors: Afghanistan, Algeria, Bahrain, Bangladesh, Byelorussian SSR, Comoros, Cuba, Democratic Yemen, Djibouti, India, Indonesia, Iraq, Jordan, Kuwait, Lao People's Democratic Republic, Lebanon, Malaysia, Maldives, Mauritania, Mongolia, Morocco, Nicaragua, Oman, Pakistan, Qatar, Saudi Arabia, Syrian Arab Republic, Tunisia, United Arab Emirates, Viet Nam, Yemen, Yugoslavia.

Meeting numbers. GA 39th session: plenary 72-77, 101.

Recorded vote in Assembly as follows:

In favour: Afghanistan, Albania, Algeria, Angola, Bahrain, Bangladesh, Benin, Bhutan, Botswana, Brunei Darussalam, Bulgaria, Burkina Faso, Burundi, Byelorussian SSR, Cameroon, Cape Verde, Central African Republic, Chad, China, Comoros, Congo, Cuba, Cyprus, Czechoslovakia, Democratic Yemen, Djibouti, Equatorial Guinea, Ethiopia, Gabon, Gambia, German Democratic Republic, Ghana, Greece, Guinea, Guinea-Bissau, Guyana, Hungary, India, Indonesia, Iran, Iraq, Jordan, Kenya, Kuwait, Lao People's Democratic Republic, Lebanon, Lesotho, Libyan Arab Jamahiriya, Madagascar, Malaysia, Maldives, Mali, Malta, Mauritania, Mexico, Mongolia, Morocco, Mozambique, Nepal, Nicaragua, Niger, Nigeria, Oman, Pakistan, Poland, Qatar, Rwanda, Sao Tome and Principe, Saudi Arabia, Senegal, Seychelles, Somalia, Sri Lanka, Sudan, Syrian Arab Republic, Togo, Tunisia, Turkey, Uganda, Ukrainian SSR, USSR, United Arab Emirates, United Republic of Tanzania, Viet Nam, Yemen, Yugoslavia, Zambia, Zimbabwe.

Against: Australia, Belgium, Canada, Denmark, Finland, France, Germany, Federal Republic of, Haiti, Iceland, Ireland, Israel, Italy, Japan, Liberia, Luxembourg, Netherlands, New Zealand, Norway, Portugal, Sweden, United Kingdom, United States.

Abstaining: Argentina, Austria, Bahamas, Barbados, Belize, Bolivia, Brazil, Burma, Colombia, Dominica, Dominican Republic, Ecuador, Egypt, Fiji, Guatemala, Honduras, Ivory Coast, Jamaica, Malawi, Panama, Papua New Guinea, Paraguay, Peru, Philippines, Saint Vincent and the Grenadines, Samoa, Singapore, Spain, Thailand, Trinidad and Tobago, Uruguay, Venezuela.

Before adopting the text, the Assembly rejected by 69 votes to 28, with 23 abstentions, a motion by the United States that this resolution, and another which became Assembly resolution 39/146 A, constituted "recommendations with respect to the maintenance of international peace and security" within the meaning of that phrase as it appears in Article 18, paragraph 2, of the Charter, and would therefore require a two-thirds majority vote for adoption (for details, see p. 261).

In Israel's view, the text was an attempt to harm and isolate it, as well as to legitimize Arab aggressions of the past and embolden such attacks in the future. Instead of condemning the Syrian Arab Republic, which had repeatedly launched attacks from the Golan Heights, the text castigated Israel; instead of calling for negotiations, it appealed to States to refrain from supplying Israel with means to defend itself.

The United States protested against the text's thrust and overall purpose, and objected to what it called the singularly offensive treatment it received in the resolution, particularly with regard to the practice of selective name-calling.

Australia found that a number of elements in the text were contrary to its policy and noted that they would only aggravate an already tense situation; specifically, a call for measures to isolate Israel discounted the need for all parties to seek negotiated solutions. Ireland, on behalf of the EC members, reiterated their call for a balanced approach, and stressed the unacceptability of formulations criticizing a permanent member of the Security Council for exercising its right under the Charter.

New Zealand was disappointed that the text did not adequately reflect the balance of principles in Council resolution 242(1967)[51] and thus could hardly contribute to a negotiated settlement.

Norway felt that some paragraphs, rather than promoting peace and understanding, were disruptive and could lead in the opposite direction. Its objections to paragraphs 12 to 16 related to their substance as well as to the fact that they could not be reconciled with the division of responsibilities between the Assembly and the Council envisaged by the Charter.

Portugal dissociated itself from any initiative that it felt could make negotiations more difficult, pointing out that the resolution's language had discriminatory or judicial implications detrimental to a dialogue towards a peaceful solution.

Austria said it was consistently opposed to the singling out for criticism of particular countries and did not believe that breaking relations with Israel could bring closer a solution of the Middle East problem. It was also against any formulation which could be interpreted as impinging on the principle of universality of United Nations membership, a view shared by Ecuador, which also said that decisions that were the prerogatives of sovereign States should not be subordinate to decisions or exhortations from third parties or international organizations.

Singapore felt that the draft was selective and unbalanced in its condemnation, and impinged on the sovereign rights of third countries having diplomatic relations with Israel.

Honduras also believed that its international, consular and diplomatic relations with other States were not given the necessary respect in the text, and that the singling out of countries with which it enjoyed such relations was unjustifiable; if this matter of principle was not taken into consideration, it could have a negative impact on the achievement of United Nations aims.

Brazil did not want to reduce the possibilities for the withdrawal of the occupation forces by the diplomatic isolation of a party to the conflict, even if its actions were incompatible with international law and United Nations resolutions.

Malawi's abstention was motivated by its conviction that there was still room for a just and amicable solution through negotiation.

The Philippines said that, to promote peace, resolutions should be balanced and should not prejudice the sovereign right of States to conduct their own international policy as they saw fit.

Bolivia said that the approach and treatment in some paragraphs precluded its support of the text, a view also held by Argentina, which believed, as did Venezuela, that certain judgements were not conducive to a solution.

Egypt remarked that it could not subscribe to certain aspects of the text, particularly parts of paragraph 13.

While endorsing the text's spirit, Spain stressed that it could not vote for it because of the legal problems and the political implications of the penultimate preambular paragraph, as well as paragraphs 8, 9 and 12 to 14. Nepal found the text's general thrust in keeping with its position; however, it reserved its position on the same operative paragraphs and on the fourth and eighth preambular paragraphs, which it said ran counter to its declared policies on the Middle East. It also believed that the initiation of measures called for in the operative paragraphs was the prerogative of the Security Council.

Greece said that, if separate votes had been taken, it would have abstained on paragraphs 8 and 13 *(c)* and *(d)*, and would have voted against paragraph 14.

Mexico said its vote demonstrated commitment to United Nations resolutions, despite its reservations on paragraphs 12 to 14. Bhutan had reservations on the use of certain phrases and determinations in the eighth preambular paragraph and paragraph 12.

Iran's reservation concerned the fact that the text made no distinction between the territories occupied before 1967 and those occupied since.

The Libyan Arab Jamahiriya reaffirmed its opposition to any reference that could be interpreted, directly or indirectly, as a recognition of what it called the Zionist entity or legitimization of a *fait accompli* imposed by force.

By resolution 39/146 A, the Assembly strongly condemned the imposition by Israel of its laws, jurisdiction and administration in the occupied Syrian Golan Heights.

West Bank officials

The issue of three West Bank officials deported by Israel in 1980[52] was again addressed by the General Assembly in 1984. The Assembly called on Israel to allow the return of the three Palestinian leaders, so that they could resume the functions for which they had been elected and appointed. The officials had been charged with inciting the local Arab population to acts of violence and subversion. The Assembly also considered again the 1980 assassination attempts against the Palestinian Mayors of Nablus, Ramallah and Al Bireh.[53]

Expulsion of Hebron and Halhul Mayors and of the Islamic Judge of Hebron

Report of the Secretary-General. In a 27 September 1984 report[54] to the General Assembly on the implementation of its December 1983 resolution[55] regarding the illegal expulsion and imprisonment of the Mayors of Hebron and Halhul and the expulsion of the Sharia (Islamic) Judge of Hebron, the Secretary-General said he had received no response from Israel in reply to a note verbale of 15 March 1984.

GENERAL ASSEMBLY ACTION

Under the agenda item on the report of the Committee on Israeli practices, the General Assembly, on 14 December 1984, acting on the recommendation of the Special Political Committee, adopted by recorded vote resolution 39/95 E.

The General Assembly,

Recalling Security Council resolutions 468(1980) of 8 May 1980, 469(1980) of 20 May 1980 and 484(1980) of 19 December 1980 and General Assembly resolutions 36/147 D of 16 December 1981, 37/88 D of 10 December 1982 and 38/79 E of 15 December 1983,

Taking note of the report of the Secretary-General of 27 September 1984,

Deeply concerned at the expulsion by the Israeli military occupation authorities of the Mayors of Hebron and Halhul and of the Sharia Judge of Hebron,

Recalling the Geneva Convention relative to the Protection of Civilian Persons in Time of War, of 12 August 1949, in particular article 1 and the first paragraph of article 49, which read as follows:

"*Article 1*

"The High Contracting Parties undertake to respect and to ensure respect for the present Convention in all circumstances."

"*Article 49*

"Individual or mass forcible transfers, as well as deportations of protected persons from occupied territory to the territory of the occupying Power or to that of any other country, occupied or not, are prohibited, regardless of their motive . . .",

Reaffirming the applicability of the Geneva Convention to the Palestinian and other Arab territories occupied by Israel since 1967, including Jerusalem,

1. *Demands once more* that the Government of Israel, the occupying Power, rescind the illegal measures taken by the Israeli military occupation authorities in expelling and imprisoning the Mayors of Hebron and Halhul and in expelling the Sharia Judge of Hebron and that it facilitate the immediate return of the expelled Palestinian leaders so that they can resume the functions for which they were elected and appointed;

2. *Requests* the Secretary-General to report to the General Assembly as soon as possible and not later than the beginning of its fortieth session on the implementation of the present resolution.

General Assembly resolution 39/95 E

14 December 1984   Meeting 100   143-1-1 (recorded vote)

Approved by SPC (A/39/712) by recorded vote (121-1-1), 29 November (meeting 43); 13-nation draft (A/SPC/39/L.26); agenda item 71.

Sponsors: Afghanistan, Bangladesh, Cuba, Egypt, India, Indonesia, Madagascar, Malaysia, Mali, Nicaragua, Pakistan, Qatar, Senegal.

Meeting numbers. GA 39th session: SPC 31-39, 43; plenary 100.

Recorded vote in Assembly as follows:

In favour: Afghanistan, Albania, Algeria, Angola, Argentina, Australia, Austria, Bahamas, Bahrain, Bangladesh, Barbados, Belgium, Belize, Benin, Bhutan, Bolivia, Botswana, Brazil, Brunei Darussalam, Bulgaria, Burkina Faso, Burma, Burundi, Byelorussian SSR, Cameroon, Canada, Cape Verde, Central African Republic, Chad, Chile, China, Congo, Costa Rica, Cuba, Cyprus, Czechoslovakia, Democratic Kampuchea, Democratic Yemen, Denmark, Djibouti, Dominican Republic, Ecuador, Egypt, El Salvador, Equatorial Guinea, Ethiopia, Fiji, Finland, France, Gabon, Gambia, German Democratic Republic, Germany, Federal Republic of, Ghana, Greece, Guatemala, Guinea, Guinea-Bissau, Guyana, Haiti, Hungary, Iceland, India, Indonesia, Iraq, Ireland, Italy, Ivory Coast, Jamaica, Japan, Jordan, Kenya, Kuwait, Lao People's Democratic Republic, Lebanon, Lesotho, Liberia, Libyan Arab Jamahiriya, Luxembourg, Madagascar, Malawi, Malaysia, Maldives, Mali, Malta, Mauritania, Mauritius, Mexico, Mongolia, Morocco, Mozambique, Nepal, Netherlands, New Zealand, Nicaragua, Niger, Nigeria, Norway, Oman, Pakistan, Panama, Papua New Guinea, Paraguay, Peru, Philippines, Poland, Portugal, Qatar, Romania, Rwanda, Samoa, Sao Tome and Principe, Saudi Arabia, Senegal, Seychelles, Sierra Leone, Singapore, Somalia, Spain, Sri Lanka, Sudan, Suriname, Sweden, Syrian Arab Republic, Thailand, Togo, Trinidad and Tobago, Tunisia, Turkey, Uganda, Ukrainian SSR, USSR, United Arab Emirates, United Kingdom, United Republic of Tanzania, Uruguay, Venezuela, Viet Nam, Yemen, Yugoslavia, Zaire, Zambia, Zimbabwe.

Against: Israel.

Abstaining: United States.

The United States reiterated its position[56] on the corresponding 1983 resolution[55] when it had acknowledged that deportation was contrary to the fourth Geneva Convention, but noted omission of factors contributing to that action.

Prosecution in assassination attempts

Report of the Secretary-General. On 9 July 1984,[57] the Secretary-General reported to the General Assembly on implementation of its December 1983 resolution[58] concerning the 1980 assassination attempts against the Mayors of Nablus, Ramallah and Al Bireh. The Secretary-General stated that, in reply to a note verbale of 15 March 1984, Israel had informed him, on 28 June, that a number of suspected perpetrators of those attacks had been apprehended by the Israeli authorities and indicted, and were currently standing trial in the Jerusalem District Court.

GENERAL ASSEMBLY ACTION

Under the agenda item on the report of the Committee on Israeli practices, the General Assembly, on 14 December 1984, acting on the recommendation of the Special Political Committee, adopted by recorded vote resolution 39/95 H.

The General Assembly,

Recalling Security Council resolution 471(1980) of 5 June 1980, in which the Council condemned the assassination attempts against the Mayors of Nablus, Ramallah and Al Bireh and called for the immediate apprehension and prosecution of the perpetrators of those crimes,

Recalling also General Assembly resolutions 36/147 G of 16 December 1981, 37/88 G of 10 December 1982 and 38/79 H of 15 December 1983,

Taking note of the report of the Secretary-General of 9 July 1984,

Recalling once again the Geneva Convention relative to the Protection of Civilian Persons in Time of War, of 12 August 1949, in particular article 27, which states, *inter alia:*

"Protected persons are entitled, in all circumstances, to respect for their persons . . . They shall at all times be humanely treated, and shall be protected especially against all acts of violence or threats thereof . . .",

Reaffirming the applicability of that Convention to the Arab territories occupied by Israel since 1967, including Jerusalem,

1. *Demands* that Israel, the occupying Power, inform the Secretary-General of the results of the investigations and prosecution relative to the assassination attempts;

2. *Requests* the Secretary-General to submit to the General Assembly at its fortieth session a report on the implementation of the present resolution.

General Assembly resolution 39/95 H

14 December 1984   Meeting 100   143-2 (recorded vote)

Approved by SPC (A/39/712) by recorded vote (121-2-1), 29 November (meeting 43); 13-nation draft (A/SPC/39/L.29); agenda item 71.

Sponsors: Afghanistan, Bangladesh, Cuba, Egypt, India, Indonesia, Madagascar, Malaysia, Mali, Nicaragua, Pakistan, Qatar, Senegal.

Meeting numbers. GA 39th session: SPC 31-39, 43; plenary 100.

Recorded vote in Assembly as follows:

In favour: Afghanistan, Albania, Algeria, Angola, Argentina, Australia, Austria, Bahamas, Bahrain, Bangladesh, Barbados, Belgium, Belize, Benin, Bhutan, Bolivia, Botswana, Brazil, Brunei Darussalam, Bulgaria, Burkina Faso, Burma, Burundi, Byelorussian SSR, Cameroon, Canada, Cape Verde, Central African Republic, Chad, Chile, China, Colombia, Congo, Costa Rica, Cuba, Cyprus, Czechoslovakia, Democratic Kampuchea, Democratic Yemen, Denmark, Djibouti, Dominican Republic, Ecuador, Egypt, El Salvador, Equatorial Guinea, Ethiopia, Fiji, Finland, France, Gabon, Gambia, German Democratic Republic, Germany, Federal Republic of, Ghana, Greece, Guatemala, Guinea, Guinea-Bissau, Guyana, Haiti, Hungary, Iceland, India, Indonesia, Iraq, Ireland, Italy, Ivory Coast, Jamaica, Japan, Jordan, Kenya, Kuwait, Lao People's Democratic Republic, Lebanon, Lesotho, Liberia, Libyan Arab Jamahiriya, Luxembourg, Madagascar, Malawi, Malaysia, Maldives, Mali, Malta, Mauritania, Mauritius, Mexico, Mongolia, Morocco, Mozambique, Nepal, Netherlands, New Zealand, Nicaragua, Niger, Nigeria, Norway, Oman, Pakistan, Panama, Papua New Guinea, Peru, Philippines, Poland, Portugal, Qatar, Romania, Rwanda, Samoa, Sao Tome and Principe, Saudi Arabia, Senegal, Seychelles, Sierra Leone, Singapore, Somalia, Spain, Sri Lanka, Sudan, Suriname, Sweden, Syrian Arab Republic, Thailand, Togo, Trinidad and Tobago, Tunisia, Turkey, Uganda, Ukrainian SSR, USSR, United Arab Emirates, United Kingdom, United Republic of Tanzania, Uruguay, Venezuela, Viet Nam, Yemen, Yugoslavia, Zaire, Zambia, Zimbabwe.

Against: Israel, United States.

The United States expressed confidence in the ability of Israel's legal system to produce a fair result and therefore considered any interference by the United Nations unjustified.

Ireland, for the EC members, stated reservations about the appropriateness of the language in paragraph 1, since the Israeli authorities had already begun proceedings against the alleged perpetrators.

Economic and social conditions

Concerned about the deteriorating economic and social conditions in the occupied territories,

the United Nations continued its efforts in 1984 to remedy the situation. A report of the Secretary-General focused on the living conditions of Palestinians in the occupied territories, a subject taken up in December by the General Assembly in resolution 39/169. Also in December, the Assembly adopted resolution 39/223 on economic development projects in those territories. Several economic and social assistance activities for Palestinians were undertaken by UNDP, UNIDO, UNICEF and other organizations (see p. 276).

Nicaragua, by a letter of 15 October,[59] transmitted to the Secretary-General, among other documents of the Third Conference of Ministers of Labour of Non-Aligned Countries and Other Developing Countries (Managua, 10-12 May), a resolution calling on ILO to increase technical assistance to the Palestinian workers in the occupied territories, and a draft resolution presented by the Group of Arab States condemning Israel for its continued occupation of Palestinian and other Arab territories, and for establishing settlements, destroying housing and expelling the members of workers' unions.

Living conditions of Palestinians

Report of the Secretary-General. In May 1984, the Secretary-General submitted a report[60] on the living conditions of Palestinians in the occupied territories, pursuant to a December 1983 request of the Assembly.[61] The report was prepared with the help of three experts, although, as in the previous year, they had not been permitted by Israel to visit the territories and thus had to rely on secondary sources of information. From 22 January to 28 February, they had held discussions in Egypt, Jordan and the Syrian Arab Republic with government and United Nations officials. Meetings were also held with PLO officials in Damascus and Amman, as well as with the former Minister of Awqaf and Holy Places, the former Mayors of Jerusalem, Halhul and Hebron, former professors from the West Bank, and Palestinians who had recently returned from the territories. Some of the material for analysis had been gathered from United Nations bodies and organizations.

In contrast to previous years, when general conditions of occupation had been analysed, the 1984 report focused on the direct impact of Israeli settlements on the living conditions of the Palestinians in the territories. It provided an overview of Israeli settlement trends and plans, and assessed the effect of the continuing Israeli settlement practices and policies on the growth of Palestinian towns and villages, on water resources and housing, on the economy of the occupied territories, on the social life and religious practices of the Palestinians, and on the judicial and local government systems.

The experts concluded that the policies designed to promote, protect and develop the settlements diminished the amount of land and water resources available to Palestinians. According to some sources, Israel controlled between 50 and 60 per cent of the land in the occupied territories, and almost all of the Jordan Valley's potentially cultivable land had been expropriated for the Israeli settlements. Although water supplies in the West Bank were substantially better than in the critically dry Gaza, Israel had imposed restrictive measures on the indigenous population, while providing preferential water supply services to Israeli settlers.

The increasing control by the occupation authorities over agricultural and industrial production, marketing and building, as well as the absence of a financial system and the continuous devaluation of the Israeli shekel, had contributed to important structural changes in the economy of the territories, diminished the potential for development and led to the West Bank's and Gaza's total dependence on the occupying Power. The report noted that Israel continued to establish settlements in a manner that impaired the expansion of Palestinian towns and villages. The already serious housing situation, exacerbated by the continuing punitive demolition and sealing of houses, was expected to worsen due to the absence of construction to replace substandard units and restrictive policies on building permits and on the transfer of funds from abroad.

The experts pointed to widely disparate conditions under which Israelis and Palestinians lived. While the settlers enjoyed subsidies, assured markets, guaranteed prices and all the benefits of full citizenship, Palestinians were impeded by various restrictions, had no access to credit, were denied national insurance and home improvement opportunities and were discouraged from investing in industry. Their social life was adversely affected by the increasing number of new Israeli settlers who often interfered with Palestinians' farming, religious and educational activities. The settlers' status as a privileged class had given rise to increased confrontation between the two groups, often leading to violence. Another factor contributing to the deteriorating situation was the existence of two different judicial and local government systems. Justice was dispensed to the Israeli settlers through Israeli courts, whereas Palestinians were subject to the jurisdiction of military courts, the judgement of which could not be appealed.

The report also noted the inadequacy of health and education facilities available to Palestinians, in contrast to quality services that Israeli settlers had access to. In addition, Palestinians were restricted in their social and cultural activities by frequent curfews, whereas the Israeli settlers were free to pursue those interests within the territories.

By a letter of 10 October 1984,[62] Israel transmitted its comments on the Secretary-General's May report, as well as on a June report[63] on permanent sovereignty over national resources in the occupied territories (see p. 334). Israel said the May report, merely summarizing the June report, did not add anything to the water resources issues.

ECONOMIC AND SOCIAL COUNCIL ACTION

In July 1984, on the recommendation of its First (Economic) Committee, the Economic and Social Council adopted decision 1984/173 without vote.

Living conditions of the Palestinian people in the occupied Palestinian territories

At its 49th plenary meeting, on 26 July 1984, the Council took note of the report of the Secretary-General on the living conditions of the Palestinian people in the occupied Palestinian territories and decided to transmit it to the General Assembly at its thirty-ninth session for consideration.

Economic and Social Council decision 1984/173

Adopted without vote

Approved by First Committee (E/1984/146) without vote, 18 July (meeting 12); oral proposal by Chairman; agenda item 15.

GENERAL ASSEMBLY ACTION

On 17 December 1984, on the recommendation of the Second Committee, the General Assembly adopted resolution 39/169 by recorded vote.

Living conditions of the Palestinian people in the occupied Palestinian territories

The General Assembly,

Recalling the Vancouver Declaration on Human Settlements, 1976, and the relevant recommendations for national action adopted by Habitat: United Nations Conference on Human Settlements,

Recalling also its resolution 38/166 of 19 December 1983,

Gravely alarmed by the continuation of the Israeli settlement policies, which have been declared null and void and a major obstacle to peace,

Recognizing the need to investigate ways and means of arresting the deterioration in the economy of the occupied Palestinian territories,

1. *Takes note with concern* of the report of the Secretary-General on the living conditions of the Palestinian people in the occupied Palestinian territories;

2. *Takes note also* of the statement made on 29 October 1984 by the Observer of the Palestine Liberation Organization;

3. *Rejects* the Israeli plans and actions intended to change the demographic composition of the occupied Palestinian territories, particularly the increase and expansion of the Israeli settlements, and other plans and actions creating conditions leading to the displacement and exodus of Palestinians from the occupied Palestinian territories;

4. *Expresses its alarm* at the deterioration, as a result of the Israeli occupation, in the living conditions of the Palestinian people in the Palestinian territories occupied since 1967;

5. *Affirms* that the Israeli occupation is contradictory to the basic requirements for the social and economic development of the Palestinian people in the occupied Palestinian territories;

6. *Requests* the Secretary-General:

(a) To organize, in 1985, a seminar on remedies for the deterioration of the economic and social conditions of the Palestinian people in the occupied Palestinian territories;

(b) To make the necessary preparations for the seminar providing for the participation of the Palestine Liberation Organization;

(c) To invite experts to present papers to the seminar;

(d) To invite also relevant intergovernmental and non-governmental organizations;

(e) To report to the General Assembly at its fortieth session, through the Economic and Social Council, on the seminar.

General Assembly resolution 39/169

17 December 1984   Meeting 103   143-2-2 (recorded vote)

Approved by Second Committee (A/39/790/Add.10) by recorded vote (129-2-2), 13 November (meeting 40); 5-nation draft (A/C.2/39/L.11), orally revised; agenda item 80 (j).

Sponsors: Madagascar, Mali, Qatar, Senegal, Tunisia.

Financial implications. 5th Committee, A/39/699; S-G, A/C.2/39/L.27, A/C.5/39/41 and Add.1.

Meeting numbers. GA 39th session: 2nd Committee 18-20, 22, 23, 26-28, 33, 37, 40; 5th Committee 36; plenary 103.

Recorded vote in Assembly as follows:

In favour: Afghanistan, Albania, Algeria, Angola, Argentina, Australia, Austria, Bahamas, Bahrain, Bangladesh, Barbados, Belgium, Benin, Bhutan, Bolivia, Botswana, Brazil, Brunei Darussalam, Bulgaria, Burkina Faso, Burma, Burundi, Byelorussian SSR, Cameroon, Canada, Cape Verde, Central African Republic, Chad, Chile, China, Colombia, Congo, Cuba, Cyprus, Czechoslovakia, Democratic Kampuchea, Democratic Yemen, Denmark, Djibouti, Dominican Republic, Ecuador, Egypt, El Salvador, Equatorial Guinea, Ethiopia, Fiji, Finland, France, Gambia, German Democratic Republic, Germany, Federal Republic of, Ghana, Greece, Guatemala, Guinea, Guinea-Bissau, Guyana, Haiti, Honduras, Hungary, Iceland, India, Indonesia, Iran, Iraq, Ireland, Italy, Jamaica, Japan, Jordan, Kenya, Kuwait, Lao People's Democratic Republic, Lebanon, Lesotho, Liberia, Libyan Arab Jamahiriya, Luxembourg, Madagascar, Malawi, Malaysia, Maldives, Mali, Malta, Mauritania, Mauritius, Mexico, Mongolia, Morocco, Mozambique, Nepal, Netherlands, New Zealand, Nicaragua, Niger, Nigeria, Norway, Oman, Pakistan, Panama, Papua New Guinea, Paraguay, Peru, Philippines, Poland, Portugal, Qatar, Romania, Rwanda, Samoa, Sao Tome and Principe, Saudi Arabia, Senegal, Sierra Leone, Singapore, Somalia, Spain, Sri Lanka, Sudan, Suriname, Swaziland, Sweden, Syrian Arab Republic, Thailand, Togo, Trinidad and Tobago, Tunisia, Turkey, Uganda, Ukrainian SSR, USSR, United Arab Emirates, United Kingdom, United Republic of Tanzania, Uruguay, Vanuatu, Venezuela, Viet Nam, Yemen, Yugoslavia, Zaire, Zambia, Zimbabwe.

Against: Israel, United States.

Abstaining: Gabon, Ivory Coast.

Israel said the text exhibited no sound reasoning or political maturity, but reflected its sponsors' hypocrisy and intent to slander Israel rather than help Palestinians. It also failed to mention several documents submitted by Israel. With regard to paragraph 3, Israel said it was not possible for a handful of Israelis to change the demography of 1.9 million Arabs. It also described as absurd the reference to the alleged deterioration of the Palestinian Arabs' living conditions and stated that the outcome of the proposed seminar would doubtless be empty rhetoric.

The United States believed that the Secretary-General's report was biased and wilfully distorted, and the resolution itself was inaccurate; the seminar would incur expenditures which could be employed instead to benefit Palestinians. While sharing the international community's concerns about the quality of Palestinian life, the United States rejected the use of condemnatory language.

The German Democratic Republic, speaking also on behalf of Bulgaria, the Byelorussian SSR, Czechoslovakia, Hungary, Mongolia, Poland, the Ukrainian SSR and the USSR, said their vote was an expression of support for a just and comprehensive Middle East solution, but regretted that the text did not call for an end to the Israeli occupation of Palestinian territory and the withdrawal of all Israeli troops.

Despite its affirmative vote, Australia said it was concerned about the financial implications of the seminar. Ireland, speaking for the EEC members, believed that considerable resources must be allocated to alleviate the problems of the region, but stressed that the seminar should be held within existing resources. Ireland and Japan observed that holding the seminar at Vienna rather than Nairobi, headquarters of the United Nations Centre for Human Settlements, contradicted the Assembly's 1976 decision[64] on holding meetings away from headquarters. Finland, on behalf of the Nordic countries, said their vote did not prejudice their position on how programme budget implications should be presented, and termed the relevant statement inadequate.

The Libyan Arab Jamahiriya pointed out that its vote should not be interpreted as a recognition of any *fait accompli* or of the entity in occupied Palestine. Iran stressed that its vote reflected its support of Palestinian rights; it was, however, opposed to the inclusion of any paragraph which accorded recognition to the régime occupying the Palestinian territories.

In Jerusalem and in the Gaza Strip, several Palestinian residential quarters had been destroyed by the occupation authorities to make way for colonial settlements, the PLO representative said, and in the West Bank Palestinian farmers had been forced to give up their land for "security" purposes so that settlements could be built. They were being established to facilitate annexation of the territories, isolate them from other Arab countries, destroy the Palestinian identity and prevent the achievement of a just peace in the region. In addition, Israel's current economic difficulties were also detrimental to the living conditions of Palestinians in the occupied territories, since those territories had been made economically dependent on the Israeli economy.

The Fifth Committee on 28 November decided, by recorded vote of 92 to 2, with 11 abstentions, that, should the Assembly adopt the text, an additional appropriation of $36,200 would be required for 1984-1985.

On 18 December 1984, on the recommendation of the Second Committee, the General Assembly adopted resolution 39/223 by recorded vote.

Economic development projects in the occupied Palestinian territories

The General Assembly,

Aware of the Israeli restrictions imposed on the foreign trade of the occupied Palestinian territories,

Aware also of the imposed domination of the Palestinian market by Israel,

Taking into account the need to give Palestinian firms and products direct access to external markets without Israeli interference,

1. *Calls* for the urgent lifting of the Israeli restrictions imposed on the economy of the occupied Palestinian territories,

2. *Recognizes* the Palestinian interest in establishing a seaport in the occupied Gaza Strip to give Palestinian firms and products direct access to external markets;

3. *Calls upon* all concerned to facilitate the establishment of a seaport in the occupied Gaza Strip;

4. *Also calls upon* all concerned to facilitate the establishment of a cement plant in the occupied West Bank and a citrus plant in the occupied Gaza Strip;

5. *Requests* the Secretary-General to report to the General Assemby at its fortieth session, through the Economic and Social Council, on the progress made in the implementation of the present resolution.

General Assembly resolution 39/223

18 December 1984   Meeting 104   138-2-7 (recorded vote)

Approved by Second Committee (A/39/789) by recorded vote (115-2-9), 13 November (meeting 40); 7-nation draft (A/C.2/39/L.18/Rev.1), orally revised; agenda item 12.
Sponsors: Algeria, Bangladesh, Madagascar, Morocco, Pakistan, Tunisia, Yemen.
Meeting numbers. GA 39th session: 2nd Committee 28-33, 40; plenary 104.

Recorded vote in Assembly as follows:

In favour: Afghanistan, Albania, Algeria, Angola, Argentina, Austria, Bahamas, Bahrain, Bangladesh, Barbados, Belgium, Benin, Bhutan, Bolivia, Botswana, Brazil, Brunei Darussalam, Bulgaria, Burkina Faso, Burma, Burundi, Byelorussian SSR, Cape Verde, Chad, Chile, China, Colombia, Congo, Costa Rica, Cuba, Cyprus, Czechoslovakia, Democratic Kampuchea, Democratic Yemen, Denmark, Djibouti, Dominican Republic, Ecuador, Egypt, El Salvador, Equatorial Guinea, Ethiopia, Fiji, France, Gabon, Gambia, German Democratic Republic, Germany, Federal Republic of, Ghana, Greece, Guatemala, Guinea, Guinea-Bissau, Guyana, Haiti, Honduras, Hungary, India, Indonesia, Iran, Iraq, Ireland, Italy, Ivory Coast, Jamaica, Japan, Jordan, Kenya, Kuwait, Lao People's Democratic Republic, Lebanon, Lesotho, Liberia, Libyan Arab Jamahiriya, Luxembourg, Madagascar, Malawi, Malaysia, Maldives, Mali, Malta, Mauritania, Mauritius, Mexico, Mongolia, Morocco, Mozambique, Nepal, Netherlands, New Zealand, Nicaragua, Niger, Nigeria, Oman, Pakistan, Panama, Papua New Guinea, Peru, Philippines, Poland, Portugal, Qatar, Romania, Rwanda, Saint Vincent and the Grenadines, Samoa, Sao Tome and Principe, Saudi Arabia, Senegal, Sierra Leone, Singapore, Somalia, Spain, Sri Lanka, Sudan, Suriname, Swaziland, Syrian Arab Republic, Thailand, Togo, Trinidad and Tobago, Tunisia, Turkey, Uganda, Ukrainian SSR, USSR, United Arab Emirates, United Kingdom, United Republic of Tanzania, Uruguay, Vanuatu, Venezuela, Viet Nam, Yemen, Yugoslavia, Zaire, Zambia, Zimbabwe.
Against: Israel, United States.
Abstaining: Australia, Canada, Finland, Iceland, Norway, Paraguay, Sweden.

Israel rejected the political connotations of the text, pointing out that products originating in

the administered territories had free access to external markets, that development projects were considered solely on the basis of their economic merits, and that the ports of Ashdod and Haifa were at the disposal of the inhabitants of Judaea, Samaria and the Gaza District.

Canada, as well as Sweden (speaking also for Finland, Iceland and Norway), agreed with the general thrust of the text, but cited as their reasons for abstaining the absence of documentation on the specific projects and lack of adequate justification for them. Australia had reservations about their cost, funding and feasibility.

Ireland, for the EC members, pointed out that their vote did not imply any commitment on their part and stressed the need for economic and technical viability of development projects. Austria withheld judgement on the economic, technical and financial aspects of specific projects for lack of adequate information. The position of Bulgaria, the Byelorussian SSR, Czechoslovakia, the German Democratic Republic, Hungary, Mongolia, Poland, the Ukrainian SSR and the USSR, as well as Iran, was the same as on other 1984 resolutions on the subject.

In December, the General Assembly also adopted, on the recommendation of the Second Committee, decision 39/442 by recorded vote.

Israeli economic practices in the occupied Palestinian and other Arab territories

At its 104th plenary meeting, on 18 December 1984, the General Assembly, on the recommendation of the Second Committee, requested the Secretary-General to submit to the Assembly at its fortieth session, through the Economic and Social Council, the comparative study on the Israeli practices in the occupied Palestinian and other Arab territories and its obligations under international law, requested in Assembly resolution 38/144 of 19 December 1983 as adopted.

General Assembly decision 39/442

145-2 (recorded vote)

Approved by Second Committee (A/39/789) by recorded vote (115-2), 13 November (meeting 40); 4-nation draft (A/C.2/39/L.17), orally revised; agenda item 12.
Sponsors: Madagascar, Pakistan, Qatar, Tunisia.
Meeting numbers. GA 39th session: 2nd Committee 33, 40; plenary 104.

Recorded vote in Assembly as follows:

In favour: Afghanistan, Albania, Algeria, Angola, Argentina, Australia, Austria, Bahamas, Bahrain, Bangladesh, Barbados, Belgium, Benin, Bhutan, Bolivia, Botswana, Brazil, Brunei Darussalam, Bulgaria, Burkina Faso, Burma, Burundi, Byelorussian SSR, Canada, Cape Verde, Central African Republic, Chad, Chile, China, Colombia, Congo, Costa Rica, Cuba, Cyprus, Czechoslovakia, Democratic Kampuchea, Democratic Yemen, Denmark, Djibouti, Dominican Republic, Ecuador, Egypt, El Salvador, Equatorial Guinea, Ethiopia, Fiji, Finland, France, Gabon, Gambia, German Democratic Republic, Germany, Federal Republic of, Ghana, Greece, Guatemala, Guinea, Guinea-Bissau, Guyana, Haiti, Honduras, Hungary, Iceland, India, Indonesia, Iran, Iraq, Ireland, Italy, Ivory Coast, Jamaica, Japan, Jordan, Kenya, Kuwait, Lao People's Democratic Republic, Lebanon, Lesotho, Liberia, Libyan Arab Jamahiriya, Luxembourg, Madagascar, Malawi, Malaysia, Maldives, Mali, Malta, Mauritania, Mexico, Mongolia, Morocco, Mozambique, Nepal, Netherlands, New Zealand, Nicaragua, Niger, Nigeria, Norway, Oman, Pakistan, Panama, Papua New Guinea, Paraguay, Peru, Philippines, Poland, Portugal, Qatar, Romania,

Rwanda, Saint Vincent and the Grenadines, Samoa, Sao Tome and Principe, Saudi Arabia, Senegal, Sierra Leone, Singapore, Somalia, Spain, Sri Lanka, Sudan, Suriname, Swaziland, Sweden, Syrian Arab Republic, Thailand, Togo, Trinidad and Tobago, Tunisia, Turkey, Uganda, Ukrainian SSR, USSR, United Arab Emirates, United Kingdom, United Republic of Tanzania, Uruguay, Vanuatu, Venezuela, Viet Nam, Yemen, Yugoslavia, Zaire, Zambia, Zimbabwe.

Against: Israel, United States.

Israel said the text had been derived from a December 1983 Assembly resolution[65] based on questionable premises which predetermined a one-sided outcome; the comparative study requested would be an elaboration of a 1983 report[66] rejected by Israel. The text disregarded the economic and social welfare of the inhabitants of the administered territories, and Israel's compliance with international law had already been repeatedly explained.

Ireland, for the EC members, said that, while the text requested a useful study, they reaffirmed their position of principle with regard to the 1983 resolution. Japan said it was sympathetic to the position of the Arab States on the problem of natural resources. Australia pointed out that its vote implied no commitment to support related future decisions.

Mediterranean–Dead Sea canal project

Israel's plan of March 1981[67] to build a 67-mile canal linking the Mediterranean Sea to the Dead Sea for electric power generation was the subject of a General Assembly resolution (39/101) and a decision of the United Nations Environment Programme (UNEP). Following up on their 1983 study[68] of the effects of the planned conduit, which was to pass through the Israeli-occupied Gaza Strip, a team of United Nations experts provided updated information on the project's impact on agricultural development, mineral production, and recreation and tourism.

On 15 March,[32] Bangladesh transmitted to the Secretary-General, among other documents of the Fourteenth Islamic Conference of Foreign Ministers (Dhaka, 6-11 December 1983), a resolution strongly condemning the canal project as detrimental to the vital interests of the Palestinian people and Jordan, and calling on States and Governments not to contribute to its execution.

UNEP Council action. Recalling that the Assembly had demanded in December of 1982[69] and 1983[70] that Israel not construct the canal and cease all actions or plans towards implementing this project, the UNEP Governing Council, on 28 May 1984,[71] deplored Israel's non-compliance with the Assembly resolutions and its refusal to receive the United Nations team of experts. The UNEP Executive Director was asked to facilitate the Secretary-General's

work in monitoring and assessing all aspects—especially ecological ones—of the adverse effects on Jordan and on the occupied Arab territories, including Jerusalem, arising from the project, as well as in the preparation of the Secretary-General's 1984 report to the Assembly.

Report of the Secretary-General. Pursuant to a December 1983 Assembly request,[70] the Secretary-General submitted in August 1984 a report[72] on Israel's decision to build a canal. Bringing up to date the available information on the project, it contained the conclusions of a team of United Nations experts who assessed the effects of a canal on agricultural development, mineral production, recreation and tourism. As Israel had considered that no useful purpose would be served by a visit of the experts to Israel and the occupied territories—their mandate being, Israel said, not to study the project but to determine its harmful effects, without addressing themselves to its merits—the team based its report on the information provided by authorities during a visit to Jordan from 30 May to 7 June 1984.

The experts reported an advanced stage of planning for the project, with $4 million (out of $24 million allocated for preparatory work from 1983 to 1985) slated to be used for drilling an exploratory tunnel from the Dead Sea shore to the site of a planned underground power plant. In their view, inundation from the proposed canal could have a significant impact on existing or future agricultural development projects, particularly in the southern and northern regions of the Dead Sea, affecting the lands being developed through the Mujib and Southern Ghors Irrigation Project. Approximately 660 hectares of irrigable land would be inundated and lost to cultivation; other areas would be adversely affected by poor drainage, increased salinity and the possible uprooting of up to 3,000 people. Annual loss of agricultural production was estimated to be from $7.9 million to $15 million, based on the 2,500 hectares of land to be affected upon the completion of the canal in 1993.

The experts stressed that the raising of the Dead Sea would have especially serious consequences for Jordan's only known mineral resources, potassium and phosphate. Inflow of large quantities of Mediterranean sea water would decrease potash production, largely dependent on the density of Dead Sea brine, and require raising of dikes and additional pumping facilities, thus reducing profitability.

A change in the level of the Dead Sea would also affect a number of recreation, tourism and health care facilities; the three main recreation and tourist centres already developed or planned would be totally or mostly inundated. Concerns were also expressed about the potential flooding of health care facilities planned to take advantage of hot springs at various locations along the eastern shore of the Dead Sea.

GENERAL ASSEMBLY ACTION

On 14 December 1984, on the recommendation of the Special Political Committee, the General Assembly adopted resolution 39/101 by recorded vote.

Israel's decision to build a canal linking the Mediterranean Sea to the Dead Sea

The General Assembly,

Recalling its resolutions 36/150 of 16 December 1981, 37/122 of 16 December 1982 and 38/85 of 15 December 1983,

Recalling the rules and principles of international law relative to the fundamental rights and duties of States,

Bearing in mind the principles of international law relative to belligerent occupation of land, including the Geneva Convention relative to the Protection of Civilian Persons in Time of War, of 12 August 1949, and reaffirming their applicability to all Arab territories occupied since 1967, including Jerusalem,

Having considered the report of the Secretary-General,

Recognizing that the proposed canal, to be constructed partly through the Gaza Strip, a Palestinian territory occupied in 1967, would violate the principles of international law and affect the interests of the Palestinian people,

Confident that the canal linking the Mediterranean Sea with the Dead Sea, if constructed by Israel, will cause direct, serious and irreparable damage to Jordan's rights and legitimate and vital interests in the economic, agricultural, demographic and ecological fields,

Deeply concerned at the digging activities in the Dead Sea area at the envisaged site of that end of the canal,

Noting with regret the non-compliance by Israel with General Assembly resolution 36/150,

1. *Deplores* Israel's non-compliance with General Assembly resolutions 37/122 and 38/85 and its refusal to receive the team of experts;

2. *Emphasizes* that the canal linking the Mediterranean Sea with the Dead Sea, if constructed, is a violation of the rules and principles of international law, especially those relating to the fundamental rights and duties of States and to belligerent occupation of land;

3. *Demands once again* that Israel not construct this canal and cease forthwith all actions taken and/or digging plans made towards the execution of this project;

4. *Calls upon* all States, specialized agencies and governmental and non-governmental organizations not to assist, directly or indirectly, in the preparation and execution of this project, and strongly urges national, international and multinational corporations to do likewise;

5. *Requests* the Secretary-General to monitor and assess, on a continuing basis and through a competent expert organ, all aspects—juridical, political, economic, ecological and demographic—of the adverse effects on Jordan and on the Arab territories occupied since 1967, including Jerusalem, arising from the implementation of the Israeli decision to construct this canal and to forward the findings of that organ on a regular basis to the General Assembly;

6. *Requests* the Secretary-General to report to the General Assembly at its fortieth session on the implementation of the present resolution;

7. *Decides* to include in the provisional agenda of its fortieth session the item entitled "Israel's decision to build a canal linking the Mediterranean Sea to the Dead Sea".

General Assembly resolution 39/101

14 December 1984   Meeting 100   143-2-1 (recorded vote)

Approved by SPC (A/39/716) by recorded vote (115-2-1), 7 December (meeting 50); 19-nation draft (A/SPC/39/L.34); agenda item 77.

Sponsors: Bahrain, Bangladesh, Democratic Yemen, Iraq, Jordan, Kuwait, Malaysia, Mauritania, Morocco, Oman, Pakistan, Qatar, Saudi Arabia, Senegal, Somalia, Sudan, Tunisia, United Arab Emirates, Yemen.

Financial implications. 5th Committee, A/39/788; S-G, A/SPC/39/L.35, A/C.5/39/81.

Meeting numbers. GA 39th session: SPC 47-50; 5th Committee 45; plenary 100.

Recorded vote in Assembly as follows:

In favour: Afghanistan, Albania, Algeria, Angola, Argentina, Australia, Austria, Bahamas, Bahrain, Bangladesh, Barbados, Belgium, Belize, Benin, Bhutan, Bolivia, Botswana, Brazil, Brunei Darussalam, Bulgaria, Burkina Faso, Burma, Burundi, Byelorussian SSR, Cameroon, Canada, Cape Verde, Central African Republic, Chad, Chile, China, Colombia, Congo, Costa Rica, Cuba, Cyprus, Czechoslovakia, Democratic Kampuchea, Democratic Yemen, Denmark, Djibouti, Dominican Republic, Ecuador, Egypt, El Salvador, Equatorial Guinea, Ethiopia, Fiji, Finland, France, Gabon, Gambia, German Democratic Republic, Germany, Federal Republic of, Ghana, Greece, Guatemala, Guinea, Guinea-Bissau, Guyana, Haiti, Honduras, Hungary, Iceland, India, Indonesia, Iraq, Ireland, Italy, Ivory Coast, Jamaica, Japan, Jordan, Kenya, Kuwait, Lao People's Democratic Republic, Lesotho, Liberia, Libyan Arab Jamahiriya, Luxembourg, Madagascar, Malawi, Malaysia, Maldives, Mali, Malta, Mauritania, Mauritius, Mexico, Mongolia, Morocco, Mozambique, Nepal, Netherlands, New Zealand, Nicaragua, Niger, Nigeria, Norway, Oman, Pakistan, Panama, Papua New Guinea, Paraguay, Peru, Philippines, Poland, Portugal, Qatar, Romania, Rwanda, Samoa, Sao Tome and Principe, Saudi Arabia, Senegal, Seychelles, Sierra Leone, Singapore, Somalia, Spain, Sri Lanka, Sudan, Suriname, Sweden, Syrian Arab Republic, Thailand, Togo, Trinidad and Tobago, Tunisia, Turkey, Uganda, Ukrainian SSR, USSR, United Arab Emirates, United Kingdom, United Republic of Tanzania, Uruguay, Venezuela, Viet Nam, Yemen, Yugoslavia, Zambia, Zimbabwe.

Against: Israel, United States.

Abstaining: Zaire.

On 11 December, the Fifth Committee Chairman proposed, on the basis of recommendations of ACABQ, that the Secretary-General be authorized to commit up to $54,000 to monitor and assess the canal project; no additional appropriations would be required under the 1984-1985 budget. The Committee approved the proposal by a recorded vote, requested by Israel, of 98 to 2, with 10 abstentions.

The United States said there was no point in passing a resolution on an abstract proposal, since according to some reports the canal was not going to be constructed.

Explaining its position in the Committee, Israel said that the experts' report was one-sided, focusing only on the purported negative effects of the canal project, while ignoring economic and ecological benefits, as well as specific problems concerning the Dead Sea and relevant studies on those problems, particularly one by the University of Jordan which warned against a further drop in the Dead Sea level and recommended a canal as a solution. In Israel's view, the project did not violate international law or the relevant Hague Regulations.

Jordan said that the project was part of Israel's effort to control all underground and surface water resources of the occupied territories in order to deprive Palestinians and force them to abandon their lands.

The Syrian Arab Republic stressed that the proposed canal violated international law, in particular of principles relating to the fundamental duties of States in respect of the occupation of territories by force.

Education

As requested by the General Assembly, the Secretary-General submitted on 18 September 1984 a report[73] on implementation of a December 1983 resolution[74] demanding that Israel rescind all measures against educational institutions in the occupied territories. Responding to a note verbale of 15 March 1984, Israel, in a reply of 28 August annexed to the report, rejected the accusations it said were levelled against it in that resolution. It pointed out that the school system in the areas in question was staffed by several thousand local Arab teachers and that since 1967 the total number of pupils in governmental, UNRWA and private schools had increased by 90.6 per cent and the number of classes by almost 90 per cent. In addition, Israel had enabled the establishment of a number of institutions of higher learning in Judaea and Samaria, including four universities. While not interfering in academic activity there, when security was endangered by hostile gatherings and exhibitions within the campus, as well as incidents such as stoning of vehicles on highways, authorities were obliged by international law to restore public order and safety; therefore it was unacceptable to interpret Israel's actions as a systematic campaign of repression against and closing of universities.

Information on measures affecting the right to freedom of education was also provided by the Committee on Israeli practices in the occupied territories in its 1984 report.[16] Those measures included a three-month closing by the West Bank military government of the Bir Zeit University's old campus in February, and its new campus for one month in April following student clashes with security forces and student demonstrations. In July, the Nablus Civil Administration ordered the closure of Al-Najah University for four months following the seizure of alleged pro-PLO propaganda at a student campus exhibition. The Committee noted that the occupation authorities had continued to subject the tenure of academic staff to the issuance of annual permits. Another serious problem was the continuing practice of mass transfers of teachers and students from one region of the occupied territories to another. The Committee emphasized that measures taken, especially in requiring signed undertakings of a political character, had introduced a political element into the academic context, leading to confrontation between the military authorities and teachers and students.

On 3 February,[75] Egypt transmitted a letter of the same date from PLO, informing the Security Council President that, on 31 January, there had been a strike by students of Bir Zeit University protesting what PLO said was an attempt by Zionist settlers to blow up the Al-Aqsa Mosque in Jerusalem, and that, on 2 February, the Israeli occupation authorities had closed down the University's old campus for three months, depriving 1,400 Palestinian students of schooling. The letter placed that move in the context of Israeli policy of direct interference in the academic affairs of educational institutions.

By a letter of 8 August,[4] the Chairman of the Committee on Palestinian rights reiterated the Committee's concern about violations of academic freedom in the occupied territories. Annexed to the letter was a report detailing UNESCO's action on behalf of educational and cultural institutions in the territories.

GENERAL ASSEMBLY ACTION

On 14 December 1984, under the agenda item on the report of the Committee on Israeli practices, the General Assembly, on the recommendation of the Special Political Committee, adopted resolution 39/95 G by recorded vote.

The General Assembly,

Bearing in mind the Geneva Convention relative to the Protection of Civilian Persons in Time of War, of 12 August 1949,

Deeply concerned at the continued harassment by Israel, the occupying Power, against educational institutions in the occupied Palestinian territories,

Recalling its resolution 38/79 G of 15 December 1983,

Taking note of the report of the Secretary-General of 18 September 1984,

1. *Reaffirms* the applicability of the Geneva Convention relative to the Protection of Civilian Persons in Time of War, of 12 August 1949, to the Palestinian and other Arab territories occupied by Israel since 1967, including Jerusalem;

2. *Condemns* Israeli policies and practices against Palestinian students and faculties in schools, universities and other educational institutions in the occupied Palestinian territories, especially the policy of opening fire on defenceless students, causing many casualties;

3. *Condemns* the systematic Israeli campaign of repression against and closing of universities and other educational and vocational institutions in the occupied Palestinian territories, restricting and impeding the academic activities of Palestinian universities by subjecting the selection of courses, textbooks and educational programmes, the admission of students and the appointment of faculty members to the control and supervision of the military occupation authorities, in clear contravention of the Geneva Convention;

4. *Demands* that Israel, the occupying Power, comply with the provisions of that Convention, rescind all

actions and measures against all educational institutions, ensure the freedom of those institutions and refrain forthwith from hindering the effective operation of the universities and other educational institutions;

5. *Requests* the Secretary-General to report to the General Assembly as soon as possible and not later than the beginning of its fortieth session on the implementation of the present resolution.

General Assembly resolution 39/95 G

14 December 1984   Meeting 100   117-2-26 (recorded vote)

Approved by SPC (A/39/712) by recorded vote (93-2-26), 29 November (meeting 43); 13-nation draft (A/SPC/39/L.28); agenda item 71.
Sponsors: Afghanistan, Bangladesh, Cuba, Egypt, India, Indonesia, Madagascar, Malaysia, Mali, Nicaragua, Pakistan, Qatar, Senegal.
Meeting numbers. GA 39th session: SPC 31-39, 43; plenary 100.

Recorded vote in Assembly as follows:

In favour: Afghanistan, Albania, Algeria, Angola, Argentina, Austria, Bahamas, Bahrain, Bangladesh, Belize, Benin, Bhutan, Bolivia, Botswana, Brazil, Brunei Darussalam, Bulgaria, Burkina Faso, Burundi, Byelorussian SSR, Cameroon, Cape Verde, Central African Republic, Chad, China, Colombia, Congo, Costa Rica, Cuba, Cyprus, Czechoslovakia, Democratic Kampuchea, Democratic Yemen, Djibouti, Dominican Republic, Ecuador, Egypt, El Salvador, Equatorial Guinea, Ethiopia, Fiji, Gabon, Gambia, German Democratic Republic, Ghana, Greece, Guinea, Guinea-Bissau, Guyana, Haiti, Hungary, India, Indonesia, Iraq, Jamaica, Jordan, Kenya, Kuwait, Lao People's Democratic Republic, Lebanon, Lesotho, Libyan Arab Jamahiriya, Madagascar, Malawi, Malaysia, Maldives, Mali, Malta, Mauritania, Mauritius, Mexico, Mongolia, Morocco, Mozambique, Nepal, Nicaragua, Niger, Nigeria, Oman, Pakistan, Papua New Guinea, Peru, Philippines, Poland, Portugal, Qatar, Romania, Samoa, Sao Tome and Principe, Saudi Arabia, Senegal, Seychelles, Sierra Leone, Singapore, Somalia, Spain, Sri Lanka, Sudan, Suriname, Sweden, Syrian Arab Republic, Thailand, Togo, Trinidad and Tobago, Tunisia, Turkey, Uganda, Ukrainian SSR, USSR, United Arab Emirates, United Republic of Tanzania, Venezuela, Viet Nam, Yemen, Yugoslavia, Zambia, Zimbabwe.

Against: Israel, United States.

Abstaining: Australia, Barbados, Belgium, Burma, Canada, Chile, Denmark, Finland, France, Germany, Federal Republic of, Guatemala, Iceland, Ireland, Italy, Ivory Coast, Japan, Liberia, Luxembourg, Netherlands, New Zealand, Norway, Panama, Paraguay, United Kingdom, Uruguay, Zaire.

The United States reiterated its position expressed in 1983[66] on the parallel 1983 resolution;[74] while certain aspects of Israeli policies were open to criticism, it found the text's condemnatory language unacceptable.

Sweden said that because of recent events it voted in favour of the text, despite the somewhat categorical wording of paragraph 2.

Permanent sovereignty over resources

Report of the Secretary-General. Pursuant to a December 1983 Assembly resolution,[65] the Secretary-General submitted in June 1984 a report[63] on permanent sovereignty over national resources in the occupied Palestinian and other Arab territories. Annexed to it was a report by a team of experts engaged to collect information on the subject. Unable to carry out on-site inquiries in Israel and the occupied territories, the team based its findings on data gathered by individual members during discussions with local officials and PLO representatives in the Syrian Arab Republic and Jordan in February/March and during visits to a number of United Nations agencies in April/May. Under the circumstances, no new data on land, economy, and social, cultural and political institutions in the territories could be obtained,

and the report was therefore limited to an examination of Israeli policies and practices relating to the exploitation of water resources. Lack of access to the relevant sites also precluded making a comparison between the practices of Israel and its obligations under international law.

The issues covered in the report included water policies and their impact; principles of water ownership; water allocation, control and administration systems; special zones or areas; protection of water rights; financial policies of water resources management; and the impact of occupation policies on water. The experts concluded that Israeli policies and practices had undergone a basic revision since 1967, with the major changes relating to water rights held by the water users, the pattern of administrative water management responsibilities and water allocation, and the fact that the system of water management operated by decision of Israeli authorities alone. Given the Israeli policies of preventing increases in the use of water in the West Bank and of supporting fully the water needs of Israeli settlements, it was difficult to see, in the experts' opinion, how the established water management system could operate without discrimination. They also believed that the extent to which the basic public water services in the occupied territories were dependent on Israeli water services would make it very difficult and costly to separate their respective water administrations.

The report also contained a list of Israeli military orders issued with regard to water resources in the territories in the period 1967-1982. In a letter of 15 May transmitting the list, Jordan stated that the orders were in contravention of the relevant principles of international law and had the aim of strangulating Arab farmers' activities in the West Bank and the other occupied Arab territories.

The negative impact of Israeli policies on the territories' resources, especially water, was underscored by the Committee on Palestinian rights, which noted in its 1984 report[36] the imposition of restrictive measures on water usage by the Palestinians, along with preferential treatment by the occupying authorities in supplying water to the Israeli settlers.

Communications. By a letter of 8 June 1984,[76] Israel transmitted a report entitled "Judaea-Samaria and the Gaza District—A sixteen-year survey", constituting a shortened version of a government report on the economic and social developments in those areas during 1967 to 1983. The content of the report was refuted by Jordan in a letter of 6 July;[77] Jordan's arguments were in turn rebutted by Israel on 20 July.[78]

By a letter dated 10 October,[62] Israel transmitted its comments on the Secretary-General's June report[63] on permanent sovereignty over national resources (see above), as well as his May report[60] on living conditions of the Palestinians in the occupied territories (see p. 327). The June report contained, in Israel's view, inaccuracies and misrepresentations. Israel's letter went on to summarize the principles guiding Israeli water resources administration in the territories and challenged statements in the report on, *inter alia*: the extension of Israeli legislation concerning water ownership, the availability of water, water transfers to Israel, integration of local water systems with Israeli systems and discrimination in water rates.

ECONOMIC AND SOCIAL COUNCIL ACTION

In July, the Economic and Social Council adopted without vote decision 1984/181.

Permanent sovereignty over national resources in the occupied Palestinian and other Arab territories

At its 49th plenary meeting, on 26 July 1984, the Council took note of the report of the Secretary-General on permanent sovereignty over national resources in the occupied Palestinian and other Arab territories, prepared in pursuance of General Assembly resolution 38/144 of 19 December 1983, and decided to transmit it to the Assembly at its thirty-ninth session for consideration.

Economic and Social Council decision 1984/181

Adopted without vote

Oral proposal by President; agenda item 8.

GENERAL ASSEMBLY ACTION

By decision 39/445, the General Assembly took note of several reports, among them the Secretary-General's June 1984 report on permanent sovereignty over national resources in the occupied territories.

REFERENCES

[1]S/16360. [2]S/16392. [3]A/39/117-S/16373. [4]A/39/403. [5]A/39/692-S/16841. [6]S/16479. [7]A/39/360 (S/16520). [8]A/39/449-S/16724. [9]A/39/560-S/16773. [10]E/1984/14 (res. 1984/1 A). [11]*Ibid.* (res. 1984/1 B). [12]*Ibid.* (res. 1984/2). [13]*Ibid.* (res. 1984/3). [14]*Ibid.* (res. 1984/11). [15]YUN 1982, p. 481. [16]A/39/591. [17]YUN 1968, p. 555, GA res. 2443(XXIII), 19 Dec. 1968. [18]YUN 1983, p. 314, GA res. 38/79 D, 15 Dec. 1983. [19]A/39/620. [20]YUN 1983, p. 315. [21]S/16249. [22]S/16255. [23]A/39/67. [24]A/39/70-S/16261. [25]S/16269. [26]A/39/74. [27]S/16293. [28]A/39/119-S/16379 & Corr.1. [29]A/39/237-S/16538. [30]A/39/278-S/16589. [31]A/39/321-S/16642. [32]A/39/133-S/16417. [33]A/39/116-S/16366. [34]A/39/157-S/16442. [35]A/39/329-S/16646. [36]A/39/35. [37]YUN 1979, p. 400, SC res. 446(1979), 22 Mar. 1979. [38]YUN 1980, p. 416. [39]S/16334. [40]YUN 1983, p. 327. [41]*Ibid.*, p. 326, GA res. 38/79 B, 15 Dec. 1983. [42]YUN 1981, p. 308. [43]YUN 1948-49, p. 535, GA res. 217 A (III), 10 Dec. 1948. [44]A/39/532 & Corr.1. [45]YUN 1983, p. 328, GA res. 38/79 F, 15 Dec. 1983. [46]YUN 1981, p. 312. [47]YUN 1983, p. 328. [48]YUN 1981, p. 312, SC res. 497(1981), 17 Dec. 1981. [49]YUN 1982, p. 507. [50]*Ibid.*, p. 515, GA res. ES-9/1, 5 Feb. 1982. [51]YUN 1967, p. 257, SC res. 242(1967), 22 Nov. 1967. [52]YUN 1980, p. 411. [53]*Ibid.*, p. 413. [54]A/39/527. [55]YUN 1983, p. 331, GA res. 38/79 E, 15 Dec. 1983. [56]*Ibid.*, p. 332. [57]A/39/339. [58]YUN 1983, p. 332, GA res. 38/79 H, 15 Dec. 1983. [59]A/39/581-S/16782 & Corr.1. [60]A/39/233-E/1984/79. [61]YUN 1983, p. 335, GA res. 38/166, 19 Dec. 1983. [62]A/C.2/39/7. [63]A/39/326-E/1984/111. [64]YUN 1976, p. 908, GA res. 31/140, 17 Dec. 1976. [65]YUN 1983, p. 340, GA res. 38/144, 19 Dec. 1983. [66]*Ibid.*, p. 339. [67]YUN 1981, p. 318. [68]YUN 1983, p. 336. [69]YUN 1982, p. 541, GA res. 37/122, 16 Dec. 1982. [70]YUN 1983, p. 337, GA res. 38/85, 15 Dec. 1983. [71]A/39/25 (dec. 12/7). [72]A/39/142. [73]A/39/501. [74]YUN 1983, p. 338, GA res. 38/79 G, 15 Dec. 1983. [75]S/16311. [76]A/39/295-E/1984/124. [77]A/39/347-E/1984/132. [78]A/39/356-E/1984/151.

Palestine refugees

UN Agency for Palestine refugees

In 1984, the United Nations Relief and Works Agency for Palestine Refugees in the Near East continued to render assistance to Palestine refugees in Jordan, Lebanon, the Syrian Arab Republic and the Israeli-occupied territories of the West Bank and the Gaza Strip. Its operations were administered from its headquarters at Vienna and Amman, Jordan, five field offices and liaison offices in New York and Cairo, Egypt. Providing both emergency relief measures and regular support operations, the Agency maintained its own schools, training establishments, clinics and health centres, and procured and distributed food rations to needy refugees.

UNRWA activities and various aspects of the Palestine refugee problem were addressed by the General Assembly, which in December adopted 11 resolutions on: assistance to Palestine refugees (39/99 A); the Working Group on the Financing of UNRWA (39/99 B); assistance to displaced persons (39/99 C); scholarships for higher education and vocational training (39/99 D); Palestine refugees in the Gaza Strip (39/99 E); ration distribution to Palestine refugees (39/99 F); refugees displaced since 1967 (39/99 G); revenues from refugee properties (39/99 H); refugee protection (39/99 I); Palestine refugees in the West Bank (39/99 J); and a proposed University of Jerusalem for Palestine refugees (39/99 K).

UNRWA activities

Emergency operations launched in the aftermath of the June 1982 Israeli invasion of Lebanon[1] continued to dominate UNRWA's relief efforts for most of 1984. Again, UNRWA was providing emergency assistance to large numbers of refugees affected by the fighting that persisted almost without interruption throughout Lebanon, as well as by the Israeli occupation of the south. Emergency food rations, distributed to all displaced refugees through the winter, were phased out in March, except for the issues to approximately 24,000 destitute. The Agency proceeded with repairing and reconstructing its installations, despite interference from continuing clashes and turmoil.

UNRWA also maintained its regular programme, with particular emphasis on education (see p. 340).

Another area receiving high priority was health services provided by the Agency under the professional guidance of WHO to 1.7 million eligible Palestine refugees, the main focus being on preventive care and environmental sanitation in the refugee camps. Out-patient services were delivered through UNRWA's 98 health units and by special arrangement at one clinic run by a voluntary agency and 22 run by Governments. The Agency also operated 27 dental clinics, three central health laboratories and 24 clinical laboratories.

Expenditure on health and relief services in 1984 totalled almost $44 million and $23 million, respectively.

Report of the Commissioner-General. Describing UNRWA's activities over the period 1 July 1983 to 30 June 1984,[(2)] the Commissioner-General noted that the ongoing intra-Palestinian and intra-factional conflict in Lebanon had forced the Agency to change planned priorities for relief and reconstruction operations. UNRWA encountered the same difficulties in carrying out its emergency operations as in the previous period (July 1982–June 1983), but the situation was exacerbated by the duration of the crisis. The Commissioner-General reported that in January 1984 in Lebanon, an Israeli air raid on Baalbek had killed 15 refugees and wounded 125, destroyed the accommodations of seven refugee families and 52 individual shelters, and damaged an additional 66 shelters as well as Agency installations in the Wavell camp. After heavy fighting broke out in the Beirut area in February, the Lebanon Field Office premises had to be closed and non-essential international staff briefly evacuated. Disturbed by the situation, the Commissioner-General alerted Lebanon and Israel and other Governments considered to be influential, and drew public attention to the alarming state of affairs. Nevertheless, towards the end of the reporting period there continued to be serious threats to the security of Palestine refugees in the south. In June and early July 1984, the Shi'ite Amal militia several times attacked Shatila and Burj el-Barajneh camps in the Beirut area. Moreover, in July and August, factional fighting in the Tripoli area disrupted UNRWA operations in northern Lebanon (see also p. 343). The report noted that the discontinuation of the emergency rations had drawn protests from the refugees and prompted their refusal, in the Tyre area, to accept for a time any Agency services.

With regard to the financial situation, the Commissioner-General expressed grave concern about 1985 and the years beyond and appealed to the international community to ensure that UNRWA was supplied with the resources it needed to carry out the will of the General Assembly.

GENERAL ASSEMBLY ACTION

On 14 December, on the recommendation of the Special Political Committee, the General Assembly adopted resolution 39/99 A by recorded vote.

Assistance to Palestine refugees

The General Assembly,

Recalling its resolution 38/83 A of 15 December 1983 and all previous resolutions on the question, including resolution 194(III) of 11 December 1948,

Taking note of the report of the Commissioner-General of the United Nations Relief and Works Agency for Palestine Refugees in the Near East, covering the period from 1 July 1983 to 30 June 1984,

1. *Notes with deep regret* that repatriation or compensation of the refugees as provided for in paragraph 11 of General Assembly resolution 194(III) has not been effected, that no substantial progress has been made in the programme endorsed by the Assembly in paragraph 2 of its resolution 513(VI) of 26 January 1952 for the reintegration of refugees either by repatriation or resettlement and that, therefore, the situation of the refugees continues to be a matter of serious concern;

2. *Expresses its thanks* to the Commissioner-General and to all the staff of the United Nations Relief and Works Agency for Palestine Refugees in the Near East, recognizing that the Agency is doing all it can within the limits of available resources, and also expresses its thanks to the specialized agencies and private organizations for their valuable work in assisting the refugees;

3. *Reiterates its request* that the headquarters of the United Nations Relief and Works Agency for Palestine Refugees in the Near East should be relocated to its former site within its area of operations as soon as practicable;

4. *Notes with regret* that the United Nations Conciliation Commission for Palestine has been unable to find a means of achieving progress in the implementation of paragraph 11 of General Assembly resolution 194(III), and requests the Commission to exert continued efforts towards the implementation of that paragraph and to report to the Assembly as appropriate, but no later than 1 September 1985;

5. *Directs attention* to the continuing seriousness of the financial position of the United Nations Relief and Works Agency for Palestine Refugees in the Near East, as outlined in the report of the Commissioner-General;

6. *Notes with profound concern* that, despite the commendable and successful efforts of the Commissioner-General to collect additional contributions, this increased level of income to the United Nations Relief and Works Agency for Palestine Refugees in the Near East is still insufficient to cover essential budget requirements in the present year and that, at currently foreseen levels of giving, deficits will recur each year;

7. *Calls upon* all Governments as a matter of urgency to make the most generous efforts possible to meet the anticipated needs of the United Nations Relief and Works Agency for Palestine Refugees in the Near East, particularly in the light of the budgetary deficit projected in the report of the Commissioner-General, and therefore urges non-contributing Governments to contribute regularly and contributing Governments to consider increasing their regular contributions.

General Assembly resolution 39/99 A

14 December 1984   Meeting 100   145-0-1 (recorded vote)

Approved by SPC (A/39/715) by recorded vote (109-0-1), 12 November (meeting 29); draft by United States (A/SPC/39/L.7); agenda item 75.

Meeting numbers. GA 39th session: SPC 11-18, 23, 29; plenary 100.

Recorded vote in Assembly as follows:

In favour: Afghanistan, Algeria, Angola, Argentina, Australia, Austria, Bahamas, Bahrain, Bangladesh, Barbados, Belgium, Belize, Benin, Bhutan, Bolivia, Botswana, Brazil, Brunei Darussalam, Bulgaria, Burkina Faso, Burma, Burundi, Byelorussian SSR, Cameroon, Canada, Cape Verde, Central African Republic, Chad, Chile, China, Colombia, Congo, Costa Rica, Cuba, Cyprus, Czechoslovakia, Democratic Kampuchea, Democratic Yemen, Denmark, Djibouti, Dominican Republic, Ecuador, Egypt, El Salvador, Equatorial Guinea, Ethiopia, Fiji, Finland, France, Gabon, Gambia, German Democratic Republic, Germany, Federal Republic of, Ghana, Greece, Guatemala, Guinea, Guinea-Bissau, Guyana, Haiti, Honduras, Hungary, Iceland, India, Indonesia, Iraq, Ireland, Italy, Ivory Coast, Jamaica, Japan, Jordan, Kenya, Kuwait, Lao People's Democratic Republic, Lebanon, Lesotho, Liberia, Libyan Arab Jamahiriya, Luxembourg, Madagascar, Malawi, Malaysia, Maldives, Mali, Malta, Mauritania, Mauritius, Mexico, Mongolia, Morocco, Mozambique, Nepal, Netherlands, New Zealand, Nicaragua, Niger, Nigeria, Norway, Oman, Pakistan, Panama, Papua New Guinea, Paraguay, Peru, Philippines, Poland, Portugal, Qatar, Romania, Rwanda, Samoa, Sao Tome and Principe, Saudi Arabia, Senegal, Seychelles, Sierra Leone, Singapore, Somalia, Spain, Sri Lanka, Sudan, Suriname, Sweden, Syrian Arab Republic, Thailand, Togo, Trinidad and Tobago, Tunisia, Turkey, Uganda, Ukrainian SSR, USSR, United Arab Emirates, United Kingdom, United Republic of Tanzania, United States, Uruguay, Venezuela, Viet Nam, Yemen, Yugoslavia, Zaire, Zambia, Zimbabwe.

Against: None.

Abstaining: Israel.

Speaking before the Assembly vote on the 11 draft resolutions on UNRWA, Israel said that they all acquiesced in the artificial perpetuation of the refugee problem and lacked balance, fairness and historical accuracy. The resolution on assistance to refugees, for example, while regretting the non-implementation of paragraph 11 of Assembly resolution 194(III) of 1948[3] on the partition of Palestine, failed to manifest regret for the Arab rejection of all offers of negotiation and attempts to implement constructive United Nations projects. Israel was repeatedly censured in the 11 texts, but there was no condemnation of the Arab States.

In the Committee, Ireland, speaking on behalf of the 10 EC members, said they fully supported the resolution and believed that all Member States should contribute to the financing of UNRWA.

UNRWA financing and administration

Financing

Total income received by UNRWA for all funds in cash and in kind in 1984 was $181.2 million. This included a one-time receipt of $8.9 million transferred to the Agency's vocational and teacher-training programme after the closure of the United Nations Emergency Operation Trust Fund. Total expenditure was $191.3 million. The General Fund received $162.1 million of unrestricted income in cash and in kind; in addition, $8.4 million in contributions for special projects was received during 1984 prior to the adoption of full fund accounting and was credited to the General Fund. Regular programme expenditures totalled $177.5 million, with an additional $3.1 million allocated to special projects. During 1984, UNRWA had 15 projects funded by special contributions.

Working Group on financing UNRWA. On 12 October 1984, the Working Group on the Financing of the United Nations Relief and Works Agency for Palestine Refugees in the Near East, established in 1970,[4] submitted a report[5] on its activities and on UNRWA's financial situation in 1984. On 3 October, the Commissioner-General had provided the Working Group with up-to-date information on the financial situation.

While pleased that no major reductions in UNRWA services were expected before the end of 1984, the Group expressed concern over the slow growth of income and the apparent trend towards lower contributions. It also noted that it would not be possible to avoid a financial crisis in 1985 if the existing trends in expenditure and income continued. Indicating that an estimated $225.3 million of net cash would be required in 1985 from voluntary contributions from Governments and intergovernmental agencies, the Group noted the difficulties in meeting that requirement as compared with 1984, when an $8.9 million one-time contribution was available and $17 million was drawn from the cash-balance reserve, which was expected to contain only $5 million at the beginning of 1985. The Group agreed that international financial support of UNRWA must be increased.

The Group noted that the willingness of some of the major contributors to convert their contributions in kind into cash had been a decisive factor in maintaining the educational programme at its current level, and expressed hope that they would continue to assist the Agency in that respect. Describing UNRWA's humanitarian services as indispensable, the Group urged non-contributing Governments to contribute, and those that had contributed before to strive for increasingly generous contributions and to pay as early as possible in the calendar year.

JIU recommendations. In September 1984,[6] the Secretary-General submitted a report on the implementation of recommendations made in several reports by the Joint Inspection Unit (JIU), among them a report of August 1983[7] on UNRWA's programme and operations, management problems and institutional questions. He reported that, out of 15 JIU recommendations, those implemented dealt with encouraging refugee self-help projects, solicitation of books for UNRWA school libraries and re-orientation of the role of UNESCO to strengthen high priority education programmes; the recommendation on United Nations liability for separation benefits was addressed to the Assembly; others had been implemented in part or were in the process of implementation (for further details, see pp. 339, 340, and 343).

***Ad Hoc* Committee for the announcement of contributions.** The *Ad Hoc* Committee of the General Assembly for the Announcement of Volun-

CONTRIBUTIONS TO UNRWA GENERAL FUND, 1984

(as at 31 December 1984; in US dollar equivalent)

Contributor	Payments in kind	Payments in cash	Total	Contributor	Payments in kind	Payments in cash	Total
Australia	—	2,201,000	2,201,000	Morocco	—	38,000	38,000
Austria	—	132,000	132,000	Netherlands	—	1,437,265	1,437,265
Bahamas	—	500	500	New Zealand	—	75,882	75,882
Bahrain	—	15,000	15,000	Norway	—	7,671,780	7,671,780
Bangladesh	—	5,000	5,000	Oman	—	25,000	25,000
Barbados	—	1,000	1,000	Pakistan	—	20,927	20,927
Belgium	—	283,172	283,172	Panama	—	500	500
Burkina Faso	—	1,445*	1,445*	Philippines	—	3,658	3,658
Burma	—	1,000	1,000	Portugal	—	15,000	15,000
Canada	—	4,272,557	4,272,557	Republic of Korea	—	5,000	5,000
Chile	—	5,000	5,000	Saudi Arabia	—	3,200,000	3,200,000
China	—	50,000	50,000	Seychelles	—	500	500
Cyprus	—	1,822	1,822	Spain	—	1,000,000	1,000,000
Denmark	—	547,886	547,886	Sri Lanka	2,000	—	2,000
European Economic Community	752,626	29,518,247	30,270,873	Sudan	—	12,047*	12,047*
Finland	—	529,770	529,770	Sweden	—	7,475,013	7,475,013
France	117,755	1,025,998	1,143,753	Switzerland	2,001,628	790,330	2,791,958
Gaza authorities	101,872	—	101,872	Syrian Arab Republic	144,137	—	144,137
Germany, Federal Republic of	—	3,453,007	3,453,007	Thailand	—	15,640	15,640
Greece	—	55,000	55,000	Trinidad and Tobago	—	4,975	4,975
Holy See	—	14,500	14,500	Turkey	—	19,123	19,123
Iceland	—	9,500	9,500	United Kingdom	—	7,255,500	7,255,500
Indonesia	—	18,000	18,000	United States	—	67,000,000	67,000,000
Iraq	—	3,500,000*	3,500,000*	Yemen	—	2,000*	2,000*
Ireland	—	295,865	295,865	Yugoslavia	35,850	—	35,850
Israel	276,051	—	276,051	Zimbabwe	—	5,134	5,134
Italy	—	1,311,475	1,311,475				
Jamaica	—	3,000	3,000	Subtotal	6,243,572	153,369,855	159,613,427
Japan	1,828,615	8,500,000	10,328,615				
Jordan	953,736	—	953,736	*United Nations and specialized agencies:*			
Kuwait	—	600,000	600,000				
Lebanon	29,302	—	29,302	United Nations	—	8,870,839	8,870,839
Libyan Arab Jamahiriya	—	926,581	926,581	UNESCO	899,939	—	899,939
Luxembourg	—	6,319	6,319	WHO	467,200	—	467,200
Malaysia	—	5,000	5,000				
Maldives	—	1,000	1,000	Subtotal	1,367,139	8,870,839	10,237,978
Malta	—	872	872				
Mauritius	—	1,250	1,250	*Non-governmental sources*	247,642	761,607	1,009,249
Mexico	—	3,000	3,000				
Monaco	—	815	815	Total	7,858,353	163,002,301	170,860,654

*Written off.

NOTE: In addition to the cash contributions, $6,142,889 was allocated from the United Nations regular budget for UNRWA international staff costs. Of this allocation, $7,889 was outstanding at year-end.

SOURCE: A/40/5/Add.3.

tary Contributions to UNRWA met at United Nations Headquarters on 19 November 1984. In his closing statement,[8] the Commissioner-General stressed that the contributions pledged, although most encouraging, would not assure the Agency sufficient income in 1985, since budget expenditures had risen to an estimated $258 million. He voiced deep concern about the financial prospects for 1985.

GENERAL ASSEMBLY ACTION

On 14 December 1984, on the recommendation of the Special Political Committee, the General Assembly adopted resolution 39/99 B without vote.

Working Group on the Financing of the United Nations Relief and Works Agency for Palestine Refugees in the Near East

The General Assembly,

Recalling its resolutions 2656(XXV) of 7 December 1970, 2728(XXV) of 15 December 1970, 2791(XXVI) of 6 December 1971, 2964(XXVII) of 13 December 1972, 3090(XXVIII) of 7 December 1973, 3330(XXIX) of 17 December 1974, 3419 D (XXX) of 8 December 1975, 31/15 C of 23 November 1976, 32/90 D of 13 December 1977, 33/112 D of 18 December 1978, 34/52 D of 23 November 1979, 35/13 D of 3 November 1980, 36/146 E of 16 December 1981, 37/120 A of 16 December 1982 and 38/83 B of 15 December 1983,

Recalling also its decision 36/462 of 16 March 1982, whereby it took note of the special report of the Working Group on the Financing of the United Nations Relief and Works Agency for Palestine Refugees in the Near East and adopted the recommendations contained therein,

Having considered the report of the Working Group on the Financing of the United Nations Relief and Works Agency for Palestine Refugees in the Near East,

Taking into account the report of the Commissioner-General of the United Nations Relief and Works Agency for Palestine Refugees in the Near East, covering the period from 1 July 1983 to 30 June 1984,

Gravely concerned at the critical financial situation of the United Nations Relief and Works Agency for Palestine

Refugees in the Near East, which has already reduced the essential minimum services being provided to the Palestine refugees and which threatens even greater reductions in the future,

Emphasizing the urgent need for extraordinary efforts in order to maintain, at least at their present minimum level, the activities of the United Nations Relief and Works Agency for Palestine Refugees in the Near East,

1. *Commends* the Working Group on the Financing of the United Nations Relief and Works Agency for Palestine Refugees in the Near East for its efforts to assist in ensuring the Agency's financial security;

2. *Takes note with approval* of the report of the Working Group;

3. *Requests* the Working Group to continue its efforts, in co-operation with the Secretary-General and the Commissioner-General of the United Nations Relief and Works Agency for Palestine Refugees in the Near East, for the financing of the Agency for a further period of one year;

4. *Requests* the Secretary-General to provide the necessary services and assistance to the Working Group for the conduct of its work.

General Assembly resolution 39/99 B

14 December 1984   Meeting 100   Adopted without vote

Approved by SPC (A/39/715) without vote, 12 November (meeting 29); 18-nation draft (A/SPC/39/L.8); agenda item 75.
Sponsors: Austria, Bangladesh, Canada, Denmark, Germany, Federal Republic of, India, Indonesia, Liberia, Malaysia, Netherlands, New Zealand, Nigeria, Pakistan, Philippines, Spain, Sri Lanka, Sweden, Yugoslavia.
Financial implications. S-G, A/SPC/39/L.19.
Meeting numbers. GA 39th session: SPC 11-18, 23, 29; plenary 100.

Accounts for 1983

For the year ended 31 December 1983, expenditure and commitments of UNRWA amounted to $210,918,091 under its General Fund.[9] The Board of Auditors noted that requests for carry-over of funds submitted to headquarters by the field offices did not provide sufficient information for a proper review by the Budget Division. Several provisions of the Manual of Supply Procedures on procurement of supplies and equipment had not been sufficiently adhered to, such as specifications of items for purchase, bidding procedures, the role of the Committee on Contracts and the timing of procurement, and the Board's 1982 recommendations on the establishment of a list of slow-moving stocks had not been implemented. The Board also commented on other budgetary and administrative matters, including several problems related to temporary assistance guidelines, travel authorizations and reimbursement claims, financial accounting of revenue-producing activities (greeting cards and calendars), assignment of internal auditors to field operations and reporting of *ex gratia* payments.

In a September report[10] on financial reports and audited financial statements and reports of the Board of Auditors, ACABQ shared the Board's concern and urged that the administration pay closer attention to all aspects of the procurement process, both to ensure full compliance with the applicable rules and to achieve optimum use of available resources.

The Assembly, by resolution 39/66, accepted the audited financial statements of UNRWA and requested remedial action as required by the Board's comments and observations.

Personnel questions

Reporting on the status of implementation of the 1983 JIU recommendations,[6] the Secretary-General noted that the recommendation on measures to be taken to improve the geographical distribution and academic qualifications and Arabic knowledge of international professional UNRWA staff had been implemented, subject to the Commissioner-General's reservation of November 1983 on academic qualification requirements.[11] The Secretary-General also reported that work was under way to define occupational groups, redefine job classifications, and develop training programmes in an effort to implement a recommendation on the area staff formulating a comprehensive career planning system. A review of UNRWA's computerized personnel record system was in progress, with a view to modernization.

Staff security

Report of the Commissioner-General. In his report for the year ended 30 June 1984,[2] the Commissioner-General stated that the number of staff members arrested and detained by the local authorities, though smaller than in the previous year, was none the less a cause for concern, with a total of 40 persons arrested without charge, though later released. As of 30 June, three staff members were in detention, two of whom had been removed from Lebanon to Israel. On 29 March, the Syrian Arab Republic, without giving any reason, had required the Director of UNRWA Affairs in that country to leave within 48 hours. The Commissioner-General had protested that action and the Secretary-General had conveyed his deep concern and hope that the matter would receive serious consideration. The Agency continued to face problems in other areas: in Jordan, staff were called upon to perform military service; in the West Bank and the Gaza Strip, Israeli-imposed restrictions on duty travel were not lifted; interrogation of staff by Israeli authorities persisted in the Gaza Strip; and in Lebanon UNRWA staff faced repeated threats to their lives.

Organizational structure

Reporting on the implementation of the 1983 JIU recommendations,[6] the Secretary-General stated that the recommendation on the reorganization of the administrative structures of UNRWA had been implemented, subject to the

Commissioner-General's reservation of November 1983 concerning integration of the Management and Budget Divisions.[12] With regard to the recommended transfer of some UNRWA headquarters functions from Vienna back to the region of operations, the Secretary-General reported that, although the situation was kept under review, no change in the location of headquarters units at Vienna had so far proved possible.

The Assembly, in resolution 39/99 A, reiterated its request that UNRWA headquarters be relocated to its former site within its area of operations as soon as practicable.

Other aspects

Assistance to displaced persons

In 1984, the General Assembly again endorsed UNRWA efforts to provide humanitarian assistance, on an emergency basis and as a temporary measure, to persons displaced as a result of the June 1967 and subsequent hostilities in the Middle East.

GENERAL ASSEMBLY ACTION

On 14 December 1984, on the recommendation of the Special Political Committee, the General Assembly adopted resolution 39/99 C without vote.

Assistance to persons displaced as a result of the June 1967 and subsequent hostilities

The General Assembly,

Recalling its resolution 38/83 C of 15 December 1983 and all previous resolutions on the question,

Taking note of the report of the Commissioner-General of the United Nations Relief and Works Agency for Palestine Refugees in the Near East, covering the period from 1 July 1983 to 30 June 1984,

Concerned about the continued human suffering resulting from the hostilities in the Middle East,

1. *Reaffirms* its resolution 38/83 C and all previous resolutions on the question;

2. *Endorses*, bearing in mind the objectives of those resolutions, the efforts of the Commissioner-General of the United Nations Relief and Works Agency for Palestine Refugees in the Near East to continue to provide humanitarian assistance as far as practicable, on an emergency basis and as a temporary measure, to other persons in the area who are at present displaced and in a serious need of continued assistance as a result of the June 1967 and subsequent hostilities;

3. *Strongly appeals* to all Governments and to organizations and individuals to contribute generously for the above purposes to the United Nations Relief and Works Agency for Palestine Refugees in the Near East and to the other intergovernmental and non-governmental organizations concerned.

General Assembly resolution 39/99 C

14 December 1984   Meeting 100   Adopted without vote

Approved by SPC (A/39/715) without vote, 12 November (meeting 29); 20-nation draft (A/SPC/39/L.9); agenda item 75.

Sponsors: Austria, Belgium, Canada, Cyprus, Denmark, Finland, Germany, Federal Republic of, Greece, Indonesia, Ireland, Italy, Japan, Malaysia, Mali, Netherlands, Norway, Pakistan, Philippines, Sri Lanka, Sweden.

Meeting numbers. GA 39th session. SPC 11-18, 23, 29; plenary 100.

Education and training services

Schools and teacher-training centres

In 1984, UNRWA spent $121 million on education and training, which accounted for 63 per cent of its total expenditure on regular programmes.[13]

The general education programme strengthened its position as the largest single Agency activity. In October 1984, a total of 345,844 pupils were enrolled in the 640 Agency elementary and preparatory schools in all the five Field Office areas, served by 10,163 teachers. An additional 100,896 refugee pupils were known to be enrolled in government and private elementary and secondary schools, and about 52,400 non-eligible children were in Agency schools. Construction of five new school buildings in 1983/84 could not solve the classroom-deficit problem, as a result of which 489 schools (75 per cent of the total) were involved in double-shifting.

In 1983/84, 3,720 training places were available to Palestine refugees in vocational and technical courses at UNRWA training centres, and 43 refugees were trained in private institutions. Having taken part in the Agency's teacher-training programme, 201 trainees graduated in October from its basic two-year, specialized two-year preparatory, and professional one-year courses and were recognized by UNRWA as professionally qualified teachers. Pre-service teacher training continued to be provided at three Agency centres, with 663 teacher trainees graduating at the end of the 1983/84 training year.

Reporting on implementation of JIU's 1983 recommendations,[6] the Secretary-General said efforts were continuing to replace unsatisfactory rented schools, financed through a special capital provision. A study of inadequate heating of classrooms was in progress.

Proposed University of Jerusalem "Al-Quds"

As requested by the General Assembly in December 1983,[14] the Secretary-General reported in September 1984 on the latest efforts to establish a university for Palestine refugees at Jerusalem.[15] He had appointed a consultant to assist him in completing a technical feasibility study requested by the Assembly in 1981,[16] a task requiring the consultant to visit all the areas and campuses concerned and to meet with the competent authorities. In an exchange of correspondence with Israel, it had been stressed that it would be difficult for the Secretary-General to take the necessary measures for establishing the university without Israel's co-operation. Israel had replied that no action could be taken on the matter, since the points it had raised in 1981 had so far not been clarified; these touched on the eligibility of students for admission, the earmarking of significant amounts of limited United Nations resources for a specific group of refugees, the compatibility of such a separate institution with policies aimed at rehabilitating refugees through their integration into the general population, and how such a university could operate in the light of the principles of the Charter and the Universal Declaration of Human Rights as well as within the framework of local legislation relating to higher education. In a subsequent letter to Israel, it had been suggested that those points might best be considered during the consultant's visit. Israel had replied that, in the absence of the clarifications it had requested, its position remained unchanged. In the absence of a positive response from Israel, the Secretary-General considered that the technical feasibility study could not be completed.

Assessing the feasibility of creating a voluntary fund for an advanced fellowship programme, endorsed by the Assembly in 1982,[17] the Secretary-General concluded that replies received in response to his inquiry to United Nations Member and non-member States, as well as to Arab regional development banks and intergovernmental organizations, did not provide a sufficient basis for creating a trust fund.

The Secretary-General also noted that the Council of the United Nations University, at its July 1984 session,[18] had reiterated its support for the establishment of a university and agreed to keep itself informed about the prospects of its offer of assistance to conduct a feasibility study of the project.

GENERAL ASSEMBLY ACTION

On 14 December 1984, on the recommendation of the Special Political Committee, the General Assembly adopted resolution 39/99 K by recorded vote.

University of Jerusalem "Al-Quds" for Palestine refugees

The General Assembly,

Recalling its resolutions 36/146 G of 16 December 1981, 37/120 C of 16 December 1982 and 38/83 K of 15 December 1983,

Having examined the report of the Secretary-General on the question of the establishment of a university at Jerusalem,

Having also examined the report of the Commissioner-General of the United Nations Relief and Works Agency for Palestine Refugees in the Near East, covering the period from 1 July 1983 to 30 June 1984,

1. *Commends* the constructive efforts made by the Secretary-General, the Commissioner-General of the United Nations Relief and Works Agency for Palestine Refugees in the Near East, the Council of the United

Nations University and the United Nations Educational, Scientific and Cultural Organization, which worked diligently towards the implementation of General Assembly resolution 38/83 D and other relevant resolutions;

2. *Further commends* the close co-operation of the competent educational authorities concerned;

3. *Emphasizes* the need for strengthening the educational system in the Arab territories occupied since 5 June 1967, including Jerusalem, and specifically the need for the establishment of the proposed university;

4. *Requests* the Secretary-General to continue to take all necessary measures for establishing the University of Jerusalem "Al-Quds", in accordance with General Assembly resolution 35/13 B of 3 November 1980, giving due consideration to the recommendations consistent with the provisions of that resolution;

5. *Calls upon* Israel, the occupying Power, to co-operate in the implementation of the present resolution and to remove the hindrances which it has put in the way of establishing the University of Jerusalem;

6. *Requests* the Secretary-General to report to the General Assembly at its fortieth session on the progress made in the implementation of the present resolution.

General Assembly resolution 39/99 K

14 December 1984   Meeting 100   144-2 (recorded vote)

Approved by SPC (A/39/715) by recorded vote (126-2), 12 November (meeting 29); 8-nation draft (A/SPC/39/L.17); agenda item 75.

Sponsors: Afghanistan, Bangladesh, Egypt, India, Jordan, Malaysia, Pakistan, Yugoslavia.

Financial implications. 5th Committee, A/39/802/Rev.1; S-G, A/C.5/39/47, A/SPC/39/L.18.

Meeting numbers. GA 39th session: SPC 11-18, 23, 29; 5th Committee 41; plenary 100.

Recorded vote in Assembly as follows:

In favour: Afghanistan, Albania, Algeria, Angola, Argentina, Australia, Austria, Bahamas, Bahrain, Bangladesh, Barbados, Belgium, Belize, Benin, Bhutan, Bolivia, Botswana, Brazil, Brunei Darussalam, Bulgaria, Burkina Faso, Burma, Burundi, Byelorussian SSR, Cameroon, Canada, Cape Verde, Central African Republic, Chad, Chile, China, Colombia, Congo, Costa Rica, Cuba, Cyprus, Czechoslovakia, Democratic Kampuchea, Democratic Yemen, Denmark, Djibouti, Dominican Republic, Ecuador, Egypt, El Salvador, Equatorial Guinea, Ethiopia, Fiji, Finland, France, Gabon, Gambia, German Democratic Republic, Germany, Federal Republic of, Ghana, Greece, Guatemala, Guinea, Guinea-Bissau, Guyana, Haiti, Honduras, Hungary, Iceland, India, Indonesia, Iraq, Ireland, Italy, Ivory Coast, Jamaica, Japan, Jordan, Kenya, Kuwait, Lao People's Democratic Republic, Lebanon, Lesotho, Liberia, Libyan Arab Jamahiriya, Luxembourg, Madagascar, Malawi, Malaysia, Maldives, Malta, Mauritania, Mauritius, Mexico, Mongolia, Morocco, Mozambique, Nepal, Netherlands, New Zealand, Nicaragua, Niger, Nigeria, Norway, Oman, Pakistan, Panama, Papua New Guinea, Paraguay, Peru, Philippines, Poland, Portugal, Qatar, Romania, Rwanda, Samoa, Sao Tome and Principe, Saudi Arabia, Senegal, Seychelles, Sierra Leone, Singapore, Somalia, Spain, Sri Lanka, Sudan, Suriname, Sweden, Syrian Arab Republic, Thailand, Togo, Trinidad and Tobago, Tunisia, Turkey, Uganda, Ukrainian SSR, USSR, United Arab Emirates, United Kingdom, United Republic of Tanzania, Uruguay, Venezuela, Viet Nam, Yemen, Yugoslavia, Zaire, Zambia, Zimbabwe.

Against: Israel, United States.

On 4 December, the Fifth Committee decided that, on the basis of ACABQ's recommendations, no additional appropriations would be required under the 1984-1985 budget to cover the remaining $22,700 estimated cost of consultant services in connection with the proposed university. The Committee approved the proposal by a recorded vote, requested by the United States, of 92 to 2, with 6 abstentions.

Israel described the call for a university as a move to institutionalize the refugee problem through the proliferation of new bodies, and characterized it as an absurdity in educational terms and as showing disregard for sound administration and restraint in the use of international funding.

Scholarships

During the academic year 1983/84, UNRWA[2] awarded 346 scholarships to Palestine refugees to study at Arab universities. The scholarships, partly funded from special contributions, were awarded for one year but were renewable subject to the end-of-year examinations.

Report of the Secretary-General. In a report submitted to the General Assembly in August 1984[19] in accordance with a December 1983 request,[20] the Secretary-General presented information on responses by Member States and United Nations agencies to the Assembly's numerous appeals for special allocations for grants and scholarships to Palestine refugees. He reported that one graduate from the Gaza Strip and one from the West Bank had begun courses in the Federal Republic of Germany, while negotiations continued on other scholarships offered by that country in 1983. The World Intellectual Property Organization had invited the UNRWA Commissioner-General to propose scholarship candidates for 1984 and had selected two of them by the date of the report. The Universal Postal Union had reiterated its willingness to continue considering applications for scholarships in the postal field. UNESCO had granted five fellowships to Palestine refugee education staff in UNRWA for special courses of training overseas, and FAO had reported on two programmes of training assistance and ILO on its preparation of projects for implementation by UNDP. UNRWA had declared its readiness to act as the recipient and trustee of special allocations and scholarships for Palestine refugees.

GENERAL ASSEMBLY ACTION

On 14 December 1984, on the recommendation of the Special Political Committee, the General Assembly adopted resolution 39/99 D by recorded vote.

Offers by Member States of grants and scholarships for higher education, including vocational training, for Palestine refugees

The General Assembly,

Recalling its resolution 212(III) of 19 November 1948 on assistance to Palestine refugees,

Recalling also its resolutions 35/13 B of 3 November 1980, 36/146 H of 16 December 1981, 37/120 D of 16 December 1982 and 38/83 D of 15 December 1983,

Cognizant of the fact that the Palestine refugees have, for the last three decades, lost their lands and means of livelihood,

Having examined the report of the Secretary-General on offers of grants and scholarships for higher education for Palestine refugees and on the scope of the implementation of resolution 38/83 D,

Having also examined the report of the Commissioner-General of the United Nations Relief and Works Agency for Palestine Refugees in the Near East, covering the period from 1 July 1983 to 30 June 1984, dealing with this subject,

1. *Urges* all States to respond to the appeal contained in General Assembly resolution 32/90 F of 13 December 1977 in a manner commensurate with the needs of Palestine refugees for higher education and vocational training;

2. *Strongly appeals* to all States, specialized agencies and non-governmental organizations to augment the special allocations for grants and scholarships to Palestine refugees in addition to their contributions to the regular budget of the United Nations Relief and Works Agency for Palestine Refugees in the Near East;

3. *Expresses its appreciation* to all Governments, specialized agencies and non-governmental organizations that responded favourably to General Assembly resolution 38/83 D;

4. *Invites* the relevant specialized agencies and other organizations of the United Nations system to continue, within their respective spheres of competence, to extend assistance for higher education to Palestine refugee students;

5. *Appeals* to all States, specialized agencies and the United Nations University to contribute generously to the Palestinian universities in the territories occupied by Israel since 1967, including, in due course, the proposed University of Jerusalem "Al-Quds" for Palestine refugees;

6. *Also appeals* to all States, specialized agencies and other international bodies to contribute towards the establishment of vocational training centres for Palestine refugees;

7. *Requests* the United Nations Relief and Works Agency for Palestine Refugees in the Near East to act as the recipient and trustee for such special allocations and scholarships and to award them to qualified Palestine refugee candidates;

8. *Requests* the Secretary-General to report to the General Assembly at its fortieth session on the implementation of the present resolution.

General Assembly resolution 39/99 D

14 December 1984   Meeting 100   145-0-1 (recorded vote)

Approved by SPC (A/39/715) by recorded vote (115-0-1), 12 November (meeting 29); 8-nation draft (A/SPC/39/L.10); agenda item 75.

Sponsors: Afghanistan, Bangladesh, Egypt, Indonesia, Jordan, Malaysia, Pakistan, Yugoslavia.

Meeting numbers. GA 39th session: SPC 11-18, 23, 29; plenary 100.

Recorded vote in Assembly as follows:

In favour: Afghanistan, Algeria, Angola, Argentina, Australia, Austria, Bahamas, Bahrain, Bangladesh, Barbados, Belgium, Belize, Benin, Bhutan, Bolivia, Botswana, Brazil, Brunei Darussalam, Bulgaria, Burkina Faso, Burma, Burundi, Byelorussian SSR, Cameroon, Canada, Cape Verde, Central African Republic, Chad, Chile, China, Colombia, Congo, Costa Rica, Cuba, Cyprus, Czechoslovakia, Democratic Kampuchea, Democratic Yemen, Denmark, Djibouti, Dominican Republic, Ecuador, Egypt, El Salvador, Equatorial Guinea, Ethiopia, Fiji, Finland, France, Gabon, Gambia, German Democratic Republic, Germany, Federal Republic of, Ghana, Greece, Guatemala, Guinea, Guinea-Bissau, Guyana, Haiti, Honduras, Hungary, Iceland, India, Indonesia, Iraq, Ireland, Italy, Ivory Coast, Jamaica, Japan, Jordan, Kenya, Kuwait, Lao People's Democratic Republic, Lebanon, Lesotho, Liberia, Libyan Arab Jamahiriya, Luxembourg, Madagascar, Malawi, Malaysia, Maldives, Mali, Malta, Mauritania, Mauritius, Mexico, Mongolia, Morocco, Mozambique, Nepal, Netherlands, New Zealand, Nicaragua, Niger, Nigeria, Norway, Oman, Pakistan, Panama, Papua New Guinea, Paraguay, Peru, Philippines, Poland, Portugal, Qatar, Romania, Rwanda, Samoa, Sao Tome and Principe, Saudi Arabia, Senegal, Seychelles, Sierra Leone, Singapore, Somalia, Spain, Sri Lanka, Sudan, Suriname, Sweden, Syrian Arab Republic, Thailand,

Togo, Trinidad and Tobago, Tunisia, Turkey, Uganda, Ukrainian SSR, USSR, United Arab Emirates, United Kingdom, United Republic of Tanzania, United States, Uruguay, Venezuela, Viet Nam, Yemen, Yugoslavia, Zaire, Zambia, Zimbabwe.
Against: None.
Abstaining: Israel.

Food aid

Reporting on the status of implementation of JIU's 1983 recommendations,[6] the Secretary-General observed that, to the extent resources permitted, UNRWA had implemented the suggested approaches to the relief programme; these had included merging special hardship assistance and basic ration distribution into one aid programme to refugees in need, and establishing a priority assistance category; the gradual introduction of food coupons was to replace distribution in kind, the annual ceiling on ration-eligible refugees should be abolished, the shelter component of the relief programme should receive more of the available resources, and health and education field officers should maintain UNRWA premises.

Report of the Commissioner-General. In his report for the year ended 30 June 1984,[2] the Commissioner-General stated that, given the efforts to implement the Assembly's March 1982 decision[21] on Agency financing and the lack of sufficient resources, UNRWA could not comply with the Assembly's December 1983 request[22] to resume the interrupted general ration distribution to Palestine refugees in all fields. The Agency nevertheless continued to provide emergency food aid to some 158,750 registered and non-registered Palestine refugees in Lebanon and until March 1984 to registered refugees from Lebanon who were displaced in the Syrian Arab Republic. In addition, some 24,000 refugees in Lebanon were treated as hardship cases, receiving food aid throughout the reporting period. Food rations continued to be distributed to hardship cases, which included widows, orphans, the aged, the physically and mentally handicapped and the chronically ill. The Commissioner-General noted that UNRWA's ability to assist the destitute largely depended on the availability of additional resources. By the end of June, the programme of assistance to hardship cases was benefiting 97,213 destitute persons Agency-wide.

GENERAL ASSEMBLY ACTION

On 14 December 1984, acting on the recommendation of the Special Political Committee, the General Assembly adopted resolution 39/99 F by recorded vote.

Resumption of the ration distribution to Palestine refugees

The General Assembly,

Recalling its resolutions 36/146 F of 16 December 1981, 37/120 F of 16 December 1982, 38/83 F of 15 December 1983 and all previous resolutions on the question, including resolution 302(IV) of 8 December 1949,

Having considered the report of the Commissioner-General of the United Nations Relief and Works Agency for Palestine Refugees in the Near East, covering the period from 1 July 1983 to 30 June 1984,

Deeply concerned at the interruption by the United Nations Relief and Works Agency for Palestine Refugees in the Near East, owing to financial difficulties, of the general ration distribution to Palestine refugees in all fields,

1. *Regrets* that resolutions 37/120 F and 38/83 F have not been implemented;

2. *Calls once again upon* all Governments, as a matter of urgency, to make the most generous efforts possible and to offer the necessary resources to meet the needs of the United Nations Relief and Works Agency for Palestine Refugees in the Near East, particularly in the light of the interruption by the Agency of the general ration distribution to Palestine refugees in all fields, and therefore urges non-contributing Governments to contribute regularly and contributing Governments to consider increasing their regular contributions;

3. *Requests* the Commissioner-General of the United Nations Relief and Works Agency for Palestine Refugees in the Near East to resume on a continuing basis the interrupted general ration distribution to Palestine refugees in all fields;

4. *Requests* the Secretary-General, in consultation with the Commissioner-General, to report to the General Assembly at its fortieth session on the implementation of the present resolution.

General Assembly resolution 39/99 F

14 December 1984   Meeting 100   122-19-4 (recorded vote)

Approved by SPC (A/39/715) by recorded vote (94-19-6), 12 November (meeting 29); 7-nation draft (A/SPC/39/L.12); agenda item 75.
Sponsors: Afghanistan, Bangladesh, Egypt, Indonesia, Malaysia, Pakistan, Yugoslavia.
Meeting numbers. GA 39th session: SPC 11-18, 23, 29; plenary 100.

Recorded vote in Assembly as follows:

In favour: Afghanistan, Algeria, Angola, Argentina, Bahamas, Bahrain, Bangladesh, Barbados, Belize, Benin, Bhutan, Bolivia, Botswana, Brazil, Brunei Darussalam, Bulgaria, Burkina Faso, Burma, Burundi, Byelorussian SSR, Cameroon, Cape Verde, Central African Republic, Chad, Chile, China, Colombia, Congo, Cuba, Cyprus, Czechoslovakia, Democratic Kampuchea, Democratic Yemen, Djibouti, Dominican Republic, Ecuador, Egypt, El Salvador, Equatorial Guinea, Ethiopia, Fiji, Gabon, Gambia, German Democratic Republic, Ghana, Greece, Guatemala, Guinea, Guinea-Bissau, Guyana, Haiti, Honduras, Hungary, India, Indonesia, Iraq, Ivory Coast, Jamaica, Jordan, Kenya, Kuwait, Lao People's Democratic Republic, Lebanon, Lesotho, Liberia, Libyan Arab Jamahiriya, Madagascar, Malawi, Malaysia, Maldives, Mali, Malta, Mauritania, Mauritius, Mexico, Mongolia, Morocco, Mozambique, Nepal, Nicaragua, Niger, Nigeria, Oman, Pakistan, Panama, Papua New Guinea, Paraguay, Peru, Philippines, Poland, Qatar, Romania, Rwanda, Samoa, Sao Tome and Principe, Saudi Arabia, Senegal, Seychelles, Sierra Leone, Singapore, Somalia, Sri Lanka, Sudan, Suriname, Syrian Arab Republic, Thailand, Togo, Trinidad and Tobago, Tunisia, Turkey, Uganda, Ukrainian SSR, USSR, United Arab Emirates, United Republic of Tanzania, Uruguay, Venezuela, Viet Nam, Yemen, Yugoslavia, Zambia, Zimbabwe.
Against: Australia, Belgium, Canada, Denmark, Finland, France, Germany, Federal Republic of, Iceland, Ireland, Israel, Italy, Japan, Luxembourg, Netherlands, New Zealand, Norway, Sweden, United Kingdom, United States.
Abstaining: Austria, Portugal, Spain, Zaire.

Sweden said that without sufficient financial resources, resuming the general ration distribution would endanger UNRWA's vital educational, health and relief activities; the categorical way in which the text was formulated did not give the Commissioner-General any leeway to exercise discretion and maintain the necessary priorities.

Refugee protection

Describing Palestine refugees in Lebanon as the victims, and in many instances specific targets, of violence, the UNRWA Commissioner-General expressed, in his report for the year ended 30 June 1984,[2] especially grave concern about their safety in the south of the country. The Lebanon Field Office having reported 25 violent deaths, 13 kidnappings and numerous other serious incidents, the Commissioner-General had repeatedly drawn attention to the lack of security for Palestinians in the south and made representations to the occupying Power, pointing out that it had the responsibility for safeguarding the welfare of the civilian population. In response to an appeal to Israel made by the Commissioner-General on 15 February to stem the ongoing campaign of harassment and violence, Israel had given assurances that the Israel Defence Forces were doing everything possible to defend refugees in the area. In May, however, further serious incidents occurred in Ein El-Helweh camp, resulting in injury to several refugees and damage to a number of shelters. The deteriorating situation in the camp was the subject of a Security Council meeting on 21 May (see p. 296), and a strong protest had been addressed to Israel by UNRWA on 6 June.[23]

Report of the Secretary-General. Protection of Palestine refugees was the subject of a 2 October 1984 report[23] prepared by the Secretary-General in response to a December 1983 General Assembly resolution[24] calling on Israel to take a number of measures to improve the security and safety of Palestine refugees in the occupied territories. The Secretary-General reported that, on 22 March 1984, he had brought the resolution to Israel's attention, requesting information on its implementation.

Israel had responded on 29 June that its March 1983 description of the situation in southern Lebanon[25] remained valid; it drew attention to the Commissioner-General's reference at a press conference on 18 March 1984 to Israeli intervention, on at least one occasion, to prevent the massacre of Palestinian Arabs in Lebanon. The Secretary-General observed that the Commissioner-General's reference had been to an approach he had made to Israeli authorities in February 1983, following which attacks on Palestine refugees in southern Lebanon had decreased. The Secretary-General also pointed out that there was a continuing concern about maintaining security after Israeli withdrawal, recalling in this connection his 9 April 1984 report[26] to the Security Council on UNIFIL, in which he had suggested the immediate deployment of UNIFIL elements in areas vacated by Israeli forces (see p. 298).

The Secretary-General also outlined UNRWA activities in the West Bank (see p. 349) and the Gaza Strip (see p. 347) and the Agency's efforts to restore services to Palestine refugees in Lebanon (see p. 335).

GENERAL ASSEMBLY ACTION

On 14 December 1984, acting on the recommendation of the Special Political Committee, the General Assembly adopted resolution 39/99 I by recorded vote.

Protection of Palestine refugees
The General Assembly,

Recalling Security Council resolutions 508(1982) of 5 June 1982, 509(1982) of 6 June 1982, 511(1982) of 18 June 1982, 512(1982) of 19 June 1982, 513(1982) of 4 July 1982, 515(1982) of 29 July 1982, 517(1982) of 4 August 1982, 518(1982) of 12 August 1982, 519(1982) of 17 August 1982, 520(1982) of 17 September 1982 and 523(1982) of 18 October 1982,

Recalling General Assembly resolutions ES-7/5 of 26 June 1982, ES-7/6 and ES-7/8 of 19 August 1982, ES-7/9 of 24 September 1982, 37/120 J of 16 December 1982 and 38/83 I of 15 December 1983,

Having considered the report of the Secretary-General of 2 October 1984,

Having also considered the report of the Commissioner-General of the United Nations Relief and Works Agency for Palestine Refugees in the Near East, covering the period from 1 July 1983 to 30 June 1984,

Referring to the humanitarian principles of the Geneva Convention relative to the Protection of Civilian Persons in Time of War, of 12 August 1949, and to the obligations arising from the Regulations annexed to the Hague Convention IV of 1907,

Deeply concerned at the lack of security for the Palestine refugees in occupied southern Lebanon resulting in scores of violent deaths, woundings, kidnappings, disappearances, evictions in the face of threats, explosions and arsons,

Deeply distressed at the sufferings of the Palestinians resulting from the Israeli invasion of Lebanon,

Reaffirming its support for Lebanese sovereignty, unity and territorial integrity, within its internationally recognized boundaries,

1. *Urges* the Secretary-General, in consultation with the United Nations Relief and Works Agency for Palestine Refugees in the Near East, to undertake effective measures to guarantee the safety and security and the legal and human rights of the Palestine refugees in all the territories under Israeli occupation in 1967 and thereafter;

2. *Holds* Israel responsible for the security of the Palestine refugees in occupied southern Lebanon, and calls upon it to fulfil its obligations as the occupying Power in this regard, in accordance with the pertinent provisions of the Geneva Convention relative to the Protection of Civilian Persons in Time of War, of 12 August 1949;

3. *Calls once again upon* Israel, the occupying Power, to release forthwith all detained Palestine refugees, including the employees of the United Nations Relief and Works Agency for Palestine Refugees in the Near East;

4. *Also calls upon* Israel to desist forthwith from preventing those Palestinians registered as refugees in Lebanon from returning to their camps in Lebanon;

5. *Further calls upon* Israel to allow the resumption of health, medical, educational and social services rendered by the United Nations Relief and Works Agency for Palestine Refugees in the Near East to the Palestinians in the refugee camps in southern Lebanon;

6. *Requests* the Commissioner-General of the United Nations Relief and Works Agency for Palestine Refugees in the Near East to co-ordinate his activities in rendering these services with the Government of Lebanon, the host country;

7. *Urges* the Commissioner-General to provide housing, in consultation with the Government of Lebanon, to the Palestine refugees whose houses were demolished or razed by the Israeli forces;

8. *Calls once again upon* Israel to compensate the United Nations Relief and Works Agency for Palestine Refugees in the Near East for the damage to its property and facilities resulting from the Israeli invasion of Lebanon, without prejudice to Israel's responsibility for all damages resulting from that invasion;

9. *Requests* the Secretary-General, in consultation with the Commissioner-General, to report to the General Assembly, before the opening of its fortieth session, on the implementation of the present resolution.

General Assembly resolution 39/99 I

14 December 1984   Meeting 100   127-2-18 (recorded vote)

Approved by SPC (A/39/715) by recorded vote (105-2-16), 12 November (meeting 29); 8-nation draft (A/SPC/39/L.15); orally revised in Assembly; agenda item 75.
Sponsors: Afghanistan, Bangladesh, Cuba, Egypt, Indonesia, Malaysia, Pakistan, Yugoslavia.
Meeting numbers. GA 39th session: SPC 11-18, 23, 29; plenary 100.

Recorded vote in Assembly as follows:

In favour: Afghanistan, Albania, Algeria, Angola, Argentina, Austria, Bahamas, Bahrain, Bangladesh, Barbados, Benin, Bhutan, Bolivia, Botswana, Brazil, Brunei Darussalam, Bulgaria, Burkina Faso, Burma, Burundi, Byelorussian SSR, Cameroon, Cape Verde, Central African Republic, Chad, Chile, China, Colombia, Congo, Costa Rica, Cuba, Cyprus, Czechoslovakia, Democratic Kampuchea, Democratic Yemen, Djibouti, Dominican Republic, Ecuador, Egypt, El Salvador, Equatorial Guinea, Ethiopia, Fiji, Finland, France, Gabon, Gambia, German Democratic Republic, Ghana, Greece, Guatemala, Guinea, Guinea-Bissau, Guyana, Haiti, Honduras, Hungary, India, Indonesia, Iraq, Jamaica, Japan, Jordan, Kenya, Kuwait, Lao People's Democratic Republic, Lebanon, Lesotho, Libyan Arab Jamahiriya, Madagascar, Malawi, Malaysia, Maldives, Mali, Malta, Mauritania, Mauritius, Mexico, Mongolia, Morocco, Mozambique, Nepal, New Zealand, Nicaragua, Niger, Nigeria, Oman, Pakistan, Papua New Guinea, Paraguay, Peru, Philippines, Poland, Qatar, Romania, Rwanda, Samoa, Sao Tome and Principe, Saudi Arabia, Senegal, Seychelles, Sierra Leone, Singapore, Somalia, Spain, Sri Lanka, Sudan, Suriname, Sweden, Syrian Arab Republic, Thailand, Togo, Trinidad and Tobago, Tunisia, Turkey, Uganda, Ukrainian SSR, USSR, United Arab Emirates, United Republic of Tanzania, Uruguay, Venezuela, Viet Nam, Yemen, Yugoslavia, Zambia, Zimbabwe.
Against: Israel, United States.
Abstaining: Australia, Belgium, Belize, Canada, Denmark, Germany, Federal Republic of, Iceland, Ireland, Italy, Ivory Coast, Liberia, Luxembourg, Netherlands, Norway, Panama, Portugal, United Kingdom, Zaire.

The Special Political Committee adopted paragraph 2 of the draft that became resolution 39/99 I by a recorded vote of 98 to 2, with 23 abstentions. In the Assembly, the sponsors orally modified the paragraph, changing the position of "the occupying Power" from holding "Israel, the occupying Power," to follow the call on Israel "to fulfil its obligations as the occupying Power".

Israel said that the incidents referred to in the sixth preambular paragraph had not occurred in southern Lebanon; it considered that the text was an instrument of political warfare, which ignored Syrian occupation and interference by the Syrian Arab Republic in the internal affairs of Lebanon as the root of the problem, and therefore should be rejected.

While stressing the need to protect effectively all Palestine refugees, the EC member States, on whose behalf Ireland spoke, had doubts about some of the wording, for example in paragraph 2. In relation to paragraph 1, they stressed the importance of Israel's fundamental responsibility as the occupying Power for the protection of the civilian population. Sweden and Finland said their vote demonstrated their deep concern for the security and rights of the Palestine refugees, but also felt that the Secretary-General should not be given responsibility for the safety of refugees, a task which, in Sweden's view, rested with the occupying Power. Uruguay held a similar view. Finland also had doubts about the effectiveness of paragraphs 1 and 8, while Sweden wished that paragraph 2 was less ambiguous about the legal obligation of the occupying Power to ensure the refugees' security.

Ecuador believed that paragraph 2 was not well balanced, and stressed that the principles of self-determination and non-interference in the internal affairs of States should be observed without any discrimination. New Zealand explained its vote as an expression of concern for the welfare of the Palestine refugees and support for UNRWA. However, it had reservations about paragraph 1, which did not take into account the Secretary-General's stated inability to protect the refugees, and felt that paragraph 5 should have called on Israel to allow the full resumption of the services mentioned.

Property rights

Report of the Secretary-General. On 6 September 1984, the Secretary-General submitted a report[27] on revenues derived from Palestine refugee properties, as the Assembly had requested in December 1983.[28] He reported that on 29 February and 22 March 1984, respectively, he had brought the Assembly's 1983 resolutions on UNRWA[29] to the attention of the Chairman of the United Nations Conciliation Commission for Palestine and to Israel's attention, requesting the latter to communicate to him information on their implementation. On 23 March and 9 July, he had also requested information from States on their implementation of the relevant provisions of those resolutions, including the call to Governments concerned, especially Israel, to assist him in implementing the resolution on revenues from Palestine refugee properties.

In a reply of 29 June, Israel had stated that its position regarding revenues from such properties had been set out fully in November 1981 before the Special Political Committee.[30] The Secretary-General said there were no replies from any other State; however, in an October 1984 addendum to his report, he informed the Assembly that he had received a reply from Cyprus dated 21 September, reiterating its support to Palestinian Arab refugees, who were entitled to property rights and to the income deriving from that property.

Report of the Conciliation Commission. In its report covering the period from 1 October 1983 to 30 September 1984,[31] the United Nations Conciliation Commission for Palestine stated that the complex situation which had limited its possibilities of action with regard to compensation for Palestine refugee properties had remained essentially unchanged. In response to a formal request from PLO for permission to obtain a copy of the microfilm on property and land in Palestine in the Commission's custody, the relevant documents had been transmitted to the Office of the Permanent Observer of PLO to the United Nations.

GENERAL ASSEMBLY ACTION

On 14 December 1984, on the recommendation of the Special Political Committee, the General Assembly adopted resolution 39/99 H by recorded vote.

Revenues derived from Palestine refugee properties

The General Assembly,

Recalling its resolutions 35/13 A to F of 3 November 1980, 36/146 C of 16 December 1981, 37/120 H of 16 December 1982, 38/83 H of 15 December 1983 and all its previous resolutions on the question, including resolution 194(III) of 11 December 1948,

Taking note of the reports of the Secretary-General of 6 September and 12 October 1984,

Taking note also of the report of the United Nations Conciliation Commission for Palestine, covering the period from 1 October 1983 to 30 September 1984,

Recalling that the Universal Declaration of Human Rights and the principles of international law uphold the principle that no one shall be arbitrarily deprived of his or her private property,

Considering that the Palestine Arab refugees are entitled to their property and to the income derived from their property, in conformity with the principles of justice and equity,

Recalling, in particular, its resolution 394(V) of 14 December 1950, in which it directed the United Nations Conciliation Commission for Palestine, in consultation with the parties concerned, to prescribe measures for the protection of the rights, property and interests of the Palestinian Arab refugees,

Taking note of the completion of the programme of identification and evaluation of Arab property, as announced by the United Nations Conciliation Commission for Palestine in its twenty-second progress report, of 11 May 1964, and of the fact that the Land Office had a schedule of Arab owners and file of documents defining the location, area and other particulars of Arab property,

1. *Requests* the Secretary-General to take all appropriate steps, in consultation with the United Nations Conciliation Commission for Palestine, for the protection and administration of Arab property, assets and property rights in Israel, and to establish a fund for the receipt of income derived therefrom, on behalf of the rightful owners;

2. *Calls upon* Israel to render all facilities and assistance to the Secretary-General in the implementation of the present resolution;

3. *Calls upon* all other Governments of Member States concerned to provide the Secretary-General with any pertinent information in their possession concerning Arab property, assets and property rights in Israel, which would assist the Secretary-General in the implementation of the present resolution;

4. *Deplores* Israel's refusal to co-operate with the Secretary-General in the implementation of the resolutions on the question;

5. *Requests* the Secretary-General to report to the General Assembly at its fortieth session on the implementation of the present resolution.

General Assembly resolution 39/99 H

14 December 1984   Meeting 100   123-2-21 (recorded vote)

Approved by SPC (A/39/715) by recorded vote (99-2-20), 12 November (meeting 29); 8-nation draft (A/SPC/39/L.14); agenda item 75.
Sponsors: Afghanistan, Bangladesh, Cuba, Egypt, India, Indonesia, Malaysia, Pakistan.
Meeting numbers. GA 39th session: SPC 11-18, 23, 29; plenary 100.

Recorded vote in Assembly as follows:

In favour: Afghanistan, Albania, Algeria, Angola, Argentina, Bahamas, Bahrain, Bangladesh, Barbados, Belize, Benin, Bhutan, Bolivia, Botswana, Brazil, Brunei Darussalam, Bulgaria, Burkina Faso, Burma, Burundi, Byelorussian SSR, Cameroon, Cape Verde, Central African Republic, Chad, Chile, China, Colombia, Congo, Costa Rica, Cuba, Cyprus, Czechoslovakia, Democratic Kampuchea, Democratic Yemen, Djibouti, Dominican Republic, Ecuador, Egypt, El Salvador, Equatorial Guinea, Ethiopia, Fiji, Gabon, Gambia, German Democratic Republic, Ghana, Greece, Guatemala, Guinea, Guinea-Bissau, Guyana, Haiti, Honduras, Hungary, India, Indonesia, Iraq, Jamaica, Jordan, Kenya, Kuwait, Lao People's Democratic Republic, Lebanon, Lesotho, Libyan Arab Jamahiriya, Madagascar, Malawi, Malaysia, Maldives, Malta, Mauritania, Mauritius, Mexico, Mongolia, Morocco, Mozambique, Nepal, Nicaragua, Niger, Nigeria, Oman, Pakistan, Panama, Papua New Guinea, Paraguay, Peru, Philippines, Poland, Portugal, Qatar, Romania, Rwanda, Samoa, Sao Tome and Principe, Saudi Arabia, Senegal, Seychelles, Sierra Leone, Singapore, Somalia, Spain, Sri Lanka, Sudan, Suriname, Syrian Arab Republic, Thailand, Togo, Trinidad and Tobago, Tunisia, Turkey, Uganda, Ukrainian SSR, USSR, United Arab Emirates, United Republic of Tanzania, Uruguay, Venezuela, Viet Nam, Yemen, Yugoslavia, Zambia, Zimbabwe.
Against: Israel, United States.
Abstaining: Australia, Austria, Belgium, Canada, Denmark, Finland, France, Germany, Federal Republic of, Iceland, Ireland, Italy, Ivory Coast, Japan, Liberia, Luxembourg, Netherlands, New Zealand, Norway, Sweden, United Kingdom, Zaire.

In Israel's opinion, the text ran counter to the basic tenets of international law, since property rights and regulations within the borders of a sovereign State were exclusively subject to domestic law and United Nations interference with that was unthinkable. Ireland (on behalf of the 10 EC members), Sweden and the United States considered that the resolution concerned an issue which should be addressed in negotiations on a peace settlement.

Proposed repatriation

Report of the Secretary-General. Pursuant to a December 1983 General Assembly request,[32] the Secretary-General submitted on 21 August 1984 a report[33] on population and refugees displaced since 1967. In response to his request of 22 March for information on Israeli steps to facilitate the return of displaced inhabitants, Israel had stated on 29 June that its position had been set out in successive annual replies, most recently on 26 August 1983.[34] It added that, since the submission of that reply and until the end of January 1984, another 2,735 persons had returned to Judaea and Samaria, bringing the total number of returnees since 1967 to 63,790.

The Secretary-General also reported that he had obtained information from the UNRWA Commissioner-General on the return of refugees registered with the Agency; those data were based on requests by returning registered refugees for transfer of their entitlements for services to the areas to which they had returned. Between 1 July 1983 and 30 June 1984, 230 refugees registered with UNRWA had returned to the West Bank and 125 to the Gaza Strip. This had brought the estimated total number of known displaced registered refugees who had returned to the occupied territories since June 1967 to 10,530.

GENERAL ASSEMBLY ACTION

On 14 December 1984, on the recommendation of the Special Political Committee, the General Assembly adopted resolution 39/99 G by recorded vote.

Population and refugees displaced since 1967
The General Assembly,

Recalling Security Council resolution 237(1967) of 14 June 1967,

Recalling also General Assembly resolutions 2252(ES-V) of 4 July 1967, 2452 A (XXIII) of 19 December 1968, 2535 B (XXIV) of 10 December 1969, 2672 D (XXV) of 8 December 1970, 2792 E (XXVI) of 6 December 1971, 2963 C and D (XXVII) of 13 December 1972, 3089 C (XXVIII) of 7 December 1973, 3331 D (XXIX) of 17 December 1974, 3419 C (XXX) of 8 December 1975, 31/15 D of 23 November 1976, 32/90 E of 13 December 1977, 33/112 F of 18 December 1978, 34/52 E of 23 November 1979, ES-7/2 of 29 July 1980, 35/13 E of 3 November 1980, 36/146 B of 16 December 1981, 37/120 G of 16 December 1982 and 38/83 G of 15 December 1983,

Having considered the report of the Commissioner-General of the United Nations Relief and Works Agency for Palestine Refugees in the Near East, covering the period from 1 July 1983 to 30 June 1984, and the report of the Secretary-General of 21 August 1984,

1. *Reaffirms* the inalienable right of all displaced inhabitants to return to their homes or former places of residence in the territories occupied by Israel since 1967 and declares once more that any attempt to restrict, or to attach conditions to, the free exercise of the right of return by any displaced person is inconsistent with that inalienable right and inadmissible;

2. *Considers* any and all agreements embodying any restriction on or condition for the return of the displaced inhabitants as null and void;

3. *Strongly deplores* the continued refusal of the Israeli authorities to take steps for the return of the displaced inhabitants;

4. *Calls once more upon* Israel:

(a) To take immediate steps for the return of all displaced inhabitants;

(b) To desist from all measures that obstruct the return of the displaced inhabitants, including measures affecting the physical and demographic structure of the occupied territories;

5. *Requests* the Secretary-General, after consulting with the Commissioner-General of the United Nations Relief and Works Agency for Palestine Refugees in the Near East, to report to the General Assembly before the opening of its fortieth session on Israel's compliance with paragraph 4 above.

General Assembly resolution 39/99 G

14 December 1984   Meeting 100   127-2-17 (recorded vote)

Approved by SPC (A/39/715) by recorded vote (100-2-18), 12 November (meeting 29); 9-nation draft (A/SPC/39/L.13); agenda item 75.

Sponsors: Afghanistan, Bangladesh, Cuba, Egypt, India, Indonesia, Malaysia, Pakistan, Yugoslavia.

Meeting numbers. GA 39th session: SPC 11-18, 23, 29; plenary 100.

Recorded vote in Assembly as follows:

In favour: Afghanistan, Albania, Algeria, Angola, Argentina, Bahamas, Bahrain, Bangladesh, Barbados, Belize, Benin, Bhutan, Bolivia, Botswana, Brazil, Brunei Darussalam, Bulgaria, Burkina Faso, Burma, Burundi, Byelorussian SSR, Cameroon, Cape Verde, Central African Republic, Chad, Chile, China, Colombia, Congo, Costa Rica, Cuba, Cyprus, Czechoslovakia, Democratic Kampuchea, Democratic Yemen, Djibouti, Dominican Republic, Ecuador, Egypt, El Salvador, Equatorial Guinea, Ethiopia, Fiji, Gabon, Gambia, German Democratic Republic, Ghana, Greece, Guatemala, Guinea, Guinea-Bissau, Guyana, Haiti, Honduras, Hungary, India, Indonesia, Iraq, Ivory Coast, Jamaica, Japan, Jordan, Kenya, Kuwait, Lao People's Democratic Republic, Lebanon, Lesotho, Liberia, Libyan Arab Jamahiriya, Madagascar, Malawi, Malaysia, Maldives, Mali, Malta, Mauritania, Mauritius, Mexico, Mongolia, Morocco, Mozambique, Nepal, Nicaragua, Niger, Oman, Pakistan, Panama, Papua New Guinea, Paraguay, Peru, Philippines, Poland, Portugal, Qatar, Romania, Rwanda, Samoa, Sao Tome and Principe, Saudi Arabia, Senegal, Seychelles, Sierra Leone, Singapore, Somalia, Spain, Sri Lanka, Sudan, Suriname, Syrian Arab Republic, Thailand, Togo, Trinidad and Tobago, Tunisia, Turkey, Uganda, Ukrainian SSR, USSR, United Arab Emirates, United Republic of Tanzania, Uruguay, Venezuela, Viet Nam, Yemen, Yugoslavia, Zaire, Zambia, Zimbabwe.

Against: Israel, United States.

Abstaining: Australia, Austria, Belgium, Canada, Denmark, Finland, France, Germany, Federal Republic of, Iceland, Ireland, Italy, Luxembourg, Netherlands, New Zealand, Norway, Sweden, United Kingdom.

Sweden said that, while it upheld the right of displaced Palestinians to return to their homes, the formulation of the text seemed to rule out negotiations on the modalities of repatriation.

In another resolution of the same date—39/99 A on assistance to Palestine refugees—the Assembly noted with regret that repatriation or compensation of the refugees had not been effected and that no substantial progress had been made in the reintegration of refugees by repatriation or resettlement. The Assembly requested the United Nations Conciliation Commission to exert continued efforts towards that goal and to report to it not later than 1 September 1985.

Palestine refugees in the Gaza Strip

Report of the Secretary-General. In September 1984,[35] the Secretary-General submitted a report on Palestine refugees in the Gaza Strip, in accordance with a December 1983 General Assembly resolution[36] asking for a report on Israeli measures concerning resettlement of the refugees and on the destruction of their shelters. He reported that, on 22 March 1984, he had requested information from Israel relevant to that resolution. On 29 June, Israel had replied that its position had been set out in successive annual replies, the latest dated 26 August 1983.[37] As to the situation since then, Israel added that it had provided housing for more than 8,000 families within the refugee voluntary rehabilitation programme, with another 1,500 families to be housed under the same programme in 1984.

The Secretary-General also stated that, according to the UNRWA Commissioner-General's reports, no demolition of refugee shelters on punitive grounds had taken place during the year under review, but that the families affected by such measures in 1983[37] had not yet been provided with alternative shelters. On the question of rehousing refugees affected by demolitions in 1971,[38] the Agency was able to review, following its discussions with Israel, the status of the 88 families categorized previously as hardship cases, 41 of whom were still in hardship or inadequately housed. Regarding demolition in 1983 of refugee shelters that Israel considered built without proper authority on State land outside camp boundaries,[37] the Commissioner-General had received information that demolition in the Rafah camp had been stopped after the death of a child in an accident, and that an injunction by the High Court of Israel early in 1984 had stopped an Israeli-ordered removal of shelters in the Jabalia camp. In July, however, 10 shelter rooms belonging to 15 refugee families were demolished. The 35 families from the Beach camp shelters demolished in 1983 had not been rehoused.

In related developments, refugee shelters in the Khan Yunis camp had been surveyed by the Israeli authorities in January; in February/March, special forms were issued by the Israeli authorities to all Jabalia camp inhabitants to be filled out with their family particulars; and Israel informed UNRWA about its plans to construct a security road along the beach at Deir El Balah, which could entail demolition of some 400 shelter rooms.

According to information available to the Commissioner-General, 748 refugee families (4,594 persons) had moved to 550 plots of land in Israeli-sponsored housing projects during the reporting period. As a pre-condition, this had required the demolition of 579 Agency-built shelter rooms, 64 rooms built with Agency assistance and 420 rooms built without such assistance. By the reporting date, Israel had allocated 3,364 plots of land in the Gaza Strip for housing. Houses built by refugees on 1,873 plots and by non-refugees on 100 plots were occupied by 2,480 refugee families and 100 non-refugee families, comprising 15,241 refugees and 666 non-refugees; 384 plots were under construction and 1,007 stood vacant. In addition, 2,940 families (17,665 persons) and 14 non-refugee families (65 persons) had moved into completed houses. Construction in three new housing projects in Beit Lahiya and Nazleh (near Jabalia camp) and Tel-el-Sultan (near Rafah camp) was still under way.

Since the re-establishment of the border between Egypt and the Gaza Strip in 1982, 791 shelter rooms affecting 266 refugee families (1,669 persons) and 86 shelter rooms affecting 28 non-refugee families (203 persons) had been demolished at the instance of Israeli authorities to make way for a security zone and border fence. Compensation had been paid to the families concerned. However, 80 families in Rafah had obtained an injunction against the demolitions from the High Court of Israel.

GENERAL ASSEMBLY ACTION

On 14 December 1984, on the recommendation of the Special Political Committee, the General Assembly adopted resolution 39/99 E by recorded vote.

Palestine refugees in the Gaza Strip

The General Assembly,

Recalling Security Council resolution 237(1967) of 14 June 1967,

Recalling also General Assembly resolutions 2792 C (XXVI) of 6 December 1971, 2963 C (XXVII) of 13 December 1972, 3089 C (XXVIII) of 7 December 1973, 3331 D (XXIX) of 17 December 1974, 3419 C (XXX) of 8 December 1975, 31/15 E of 23 November 1976, 32/90 C of 13 December 1977, 33/112 E of 18 December 1978, 34/52 F of 23 November 1979, 35/13 F of 3 November 1980, 36/146 A of 16 December 1981, 37/120 E of 16 December 1982 and 38/83 E of 15 December 1983,

Having considered the report of the Commissioner-General of the United Nations Relief and Works Agency for Palestine Refugees in the Near East, covering the period from 1 July 1983 to 30 June 1984, and the report of the Secretary-General of 4 September 1984,

Recalling the provisions of paragraph 11 of its resolution 194(III) of 11 December 1948 and considering that measures to resettle Palestine refugees in the Gaza Strip away from the homes and property from which they were displaced constitute a violation of their inalienable right of return,

Alarmed by the reports received from the Commissioner-General that the Israeli occupying authorities, in contravention of Israel's obligation under international law, persist in their policy of demolishing shelters occupied by refugee families,

1. *Reiterates its demand* that Israel desist from the removal and resettlement of Palestine refugees in the Gaza Strip and from the destruction of their shelters;

2. *Requests* the Secretary-General, after consulting with the Commissioner-General of the United Nations Relief and Works Agency for Palestine Refugees in the Near East, to report to the General Assembly, before the opening of its fortieth session, on Israel's compliance with paragraph 1 above.

General Assembly resolution 39/99 E

14 December 1984   Meeting 100   145-2 (recorded vote)

Approved by SPC (A/39/715) by recorded vote (117-2), 12 November (meeting 29); 9-nation draft (A/SPC/39/L.11); agenda item 75.

Sponsors: Afghanistan, Bangladesh, Cuba, Egypt, India, Indonesia, Malaysia, Pakistan, Yugoslavia.

Meeting numbers. GA 39th session: SPC 11-18, 23, 29; plenary 100.

Recorded vote in Assembly as follows:

In favour: Afghanistan, Albania, Algeria, Angola, Argentina, Australia, Austria, Bahamas, Bahrain, Bangladesh, Barbados, Belgium, Belize, Benin, Bhutan, Bolivia, Botswana, Brazil, Brunei Darussalam, Bulgaria, Burkina Faso, Burma, Burundi, Byelorussian SSR, Cameroon, Canada, Cape Verde, Central African Republic, Chad, Chile, China, Colombia, Congo, Costa Rica, Cuba, Cyprus, Czechoslovakia, Democratic Kampuchea, Democratic Yemen, Denmark, Djibouti, Dominican Republic, Ecuador, Egypt, El Salvador, Equatorial Guinea, Ethiopia, Fiji, Finland, France, Gabon, Gambia, German Democratic Republic, Germany, Federal Republic of, Ghana, Greece, Guatemala, Guinea, Guinea-Bissau, Guyana, Haiti, Honduras, Hungary, Iceland, India, Indonesia, Iraq, Ireland, Italy, Ivory Coast, Jamaica, Japan, Jordan, Kenya, Kuwait, Lao People's Democratic Republic, Lebanon, Lesotho, Liberia, Libyan Arab Jamahiriya, Luxembourg, Madagascar, Malawi, Malaysia,

Maldives, Mali, Malta, Mauritania, Mauritius, Mexico, Mongolia, Morocco, Mozambique, Nepal, Netherlands, New Zealand, Nicaragua, Niger, Nigeria, Norway, Oman, Pakistan, Panama, Papua New Guinea, Paraguay, Peru, Philippines, Poland, Portugal, Qatar, Romania, Rwanda, Samoa, Sao Tome and Principe, Saudi Arabia, Senegal, Seychelles, Sierra Leone, Singapore, Somalia, Spain, Sri Lanka, Sudan, Suriname, Sweden, Syrian Arab Republic, Thailand, Togo, Trinidad and Tobago, Tunisia, Turkey, Uganda, Ukrainian SSR, USSR, United Arab Emirates, United Kingdom, United Republic of Tanzania, Uruguay, Venezuela, Viet Nam, Yemen, Yugoslavia, Zaire, Zambia, Zimbabwe.
Against: Israel, United States.

The United States said it opposed unrealistic and one-sided resolutions which singled out Israel while ignoring action taken against UNRWA and the refugees by other Governments and parties in the area. In its view, the text would oppose any effort by Israel to improve the fate of certain refugees. Ireland, expressing support for the text on behalf of the 10 EC member States, said that nothing should interfere with the refugees' freedom to choose where they wished to live.

Palestine refugees in the West Bank

Report of the Commissioner-General. In his report on UNRWA activities for the year ended 30 June 1984,[(2)] the Commissioner-General stated that hardship had been caused to the refugee population in the West Bank, particularly the aged and the very young, by curfews imposed by the Israeli authorities and by the barricading of camp entrances. Entrances to the Arroub, Dheisheh and Kalandia camps were blocked with bricks and cement and some of the paths to the main streets in Jalazone and Askar camps were also blocked, leading to stone-throwing incidents. The costs of the barricades at Askar camp were imposed on the refugee families living nearby. Rooms in eight shelters in Aida and Jalazone camps and part of a shelter unit in the Balata camp were sealed as punitive measures against families for hostile acts said to have been committed by their members.

Report of the Secretary-General. On 8 August 1984, the Secretary-General submitted a report[(39)] on the resettlement of Palestine refugees in the West Bank and destruction of their camps, as requested in a December 1983 resolution,[(40)] by which the Assembly had called on Israel to abandon any such plans or actions. He reported that, in response to his request for all relevant information, Israel had stated on 29 June that its position on the matter had been set out in December 1983 before the General Assembly,[(41)] adding, however, that the proposal in question was still being looked into by the Israeli Government. The Secretary-General also pointed out that UNRWA, while not opposing measures voluntarily accepted by refugees to improve their living conditions, would strongly object to any attempt to force the refugees to comply with any particular scheme. The Agency expected to continue providing services to any

relocated refugees, since their eligibility for UNRWA services would not be affected by the mere fact of such relocation. At the time of the report, of the 349,000 registered refugees in the West Bank, 260,000 lived outside the camps.

GENERAL ASSEMBLY ACTION

On 14 December 1984, the General Assembly, acting on the recommendation of the Special Political Committee, adopted resolution 39/99 J by recorded vote.

Palestine refugees in the West Bank

The General Assembly,

Recalling Security Council resolution 237(1967) of 14 June 1967,

Recalling also General Assembly resolution 38/83 J of 15 December 1983,

Having considered the report of the Secretary-General of 8 August 1984,

Having also considered the report of the Commissioner-General of the United Nations Relief and Works Agency for Palestine Refugees in the Near East, covering the period from 1 July 1983 to 30 June 1984,

Alarmed by Israel's plans to remove and resettle the Palestine refugees of the West Bank and to destroy their camps,

Recalling the provisions of paragraph 11 of its resolution 194(III) of 11 December 1948 and considering that measures to resettle Palestine refugees in the West Bank away from the homes and property from which they were displaced constitute a violation of their inalienable right of return,

1. *Calls upon* Israel to abandon its plans and to refrain from the removal, and from any action that may lead to the removal and resettlement, of Palestine refugees in the West Bank and from the destruction of their camps;

2. *Requests* the Secretary-General, in co-operation with the Commissioner-General of the United Nations Relief and Works Agency for Palestine Refugees in the Near East, to keep the matter under close supervision and to report to the General Assembly, before the opening of its fortieth session, on any developments regarding this matter.

General Assembly resolution 39/99 J

14 December 1984   Meeting 100   145-2 (recorded vote)

Approved by SPC (A/39/715) by recorded vote (123-2), 12 November (meeting 29); 9-nation draft (A/SPC/39/L.16); agenda item 75.

Sponsors: Afghanistan, Bangladesh, Cuba, Egypt, India, Indonesia, Malaysia, Pakistan, Yugoslavia.

Meeting numbers. GA 39th session: SPC 11-18, 23, 29; plenary 100.

Recorded vote in Assembly as follows:

In favour: Afghanistan, Albania, Algeria, Angola, Argentina, Australia, Austria, Bahamas, Bahrain, Bangladesh, Barbados, Belgium, Belize, Benin, Bhutan, Bolivia, Botswana, Brazil, Brunei Darussalam, Bulgaria, Burkina Faso, Burma, Burundi, Byelorussian SSR, Cameroon, Canada, Cape Verde, Central African Republic, Chad, Chile, China, Colombia, Congo, Costa Rica, Cuba, Cyprus, Czechoslovakia, Democratic Kampuchea, Democratic Yemen, Denmark, Djibouti, Dominican Republic, Ecuador, Egypt, El Salvador, Equatorial Guinea, Ethiopia, Fiji, Finland, France, Gabon, Gambia, German Democratic Republic, Germany, Federal Republic of, Ghana, Greece, Guatemala, Guinea, Guinea-Bissau, Guyana, Haiti, Honduras, Hungary, Iceland, India, Indonesia, Iraq, Ireland, Italy, Ivory Coast, Jamaica, Japan, Jordan, Kenya, Kuwait, Lao People's Democratic Republic, Lebanon, Lesotho, Liberia, Libyan Arab Jamahiriya, Luxembourg, Madagascar, Malawi, Malaysia, Maldives, Mali, Malta,

Mauritania, Mauritius, Mexico, Mongolia, Morocco, Mozambique, Nepal, Netherlands, New Zealand, Nicaragua, Niger, Nigeria, Norway, Oman, Pakistan, Panama, Papua New Guinea, Paraguay, Peru, Philippines, Poland, Portugal, Qatar, Romania, Rwanda, Samoa, Sao Tome and Principe, Saudi Arabia, Senegal, Seychelles, Sierra Leone, Singapore, Somalia, Spain, Sri Lanka, Sudan, Suriname, Sweden, Syrian Arab Republic, Thailand, Togo, Trinidad and Tobago, Tunisia, Turkey, Uganda, Ukrainian SSR, USSR, United Arab Emirates, United Kingdom, United Republic of Tanzania, Uruguay, Venezuela, Viet Nam, Yemen, Yugoslavia, Zaire, Zambia, Zimbabwe.

Against: Israel, United States.

Israel said the resolution defied logic by calling on it to abandon plans at bettering the housing conditions of the refugees and demanding that they remain in their camps presumably for ever. Ireland, on behalf of the 10 EC member States, considered that the fifth preambular paragraph and paragraph 1 perhaps did not accurately describe the status of the "plans" to which they referred. Sweden interpreted the wording of paragraph 1 as an affirmation of Israel's responsibility to refrain from resetting Palestine refugees against their will.

REFERENCES

[1]YUN 1982, p. 428. [2]A/39/13. [3]YUN 1948-49, p. 174, GA res. 194(III), 11 Dec. 1948. [4]YUN 1970, p. 280, GA res. 2656(XXV), 7 Dec. 1970. [5]A/39/575. [6]A/39/145. [7]YUN 1983, p. 345. [8]A/AC.223/SR.1. [9]A/39/5/Add.3. [10]A/39/510. [11]YUN 1983, p. 347. [12]*Ibid.*, p. 349. [13]A/40/13 & Add.1 & Add.1/Corr.1. [14]YUN 1983, p. 350, GA res. 38/83 K, 15 Dec. 1983. [15]A/39/528. [16]YUN 1981, p. 339, GA res. 36/146 G, 16 Dec. 1981. [17]YUN 1982, p. 563, GA res. 37/120 C, 16 Dec. 1982. [18]A/40/31. [19]A/39/375. [20]YUN 1983, p. 351, GA res. 38/83 D, 15 Dec. 1983. [21]YUN 1982, p. 552, GA dec. 36/462, 16 Mar. 1982. [22]YUN 1983, p. 352, GA res. 38/83 F, 15 Dec. 1983. [23]A/39/538. [24]YUN 1983, p. 354, GA res. 38/83 I, 15 Dec. 1983. [25]*Ibid.*, p. 353. [26]S/16472. [27]A/39/464 & Add.1. [28]YUN 1983, p. 356, GA res. 38/83 H, 15 Dec. 1983. [29]*Ibid.*, pp. 342-60, GA res. 38/83 A-K, 15 Dec. 1983. [30]YUN 1981, p. 336. [31]A/39/455. [32]YUN 1983, p. 357, GA res. 38/83 G, 15 Dec. 1983. [33]A/39/411. [34]YUN 1983, p. 357. [35]A/39/457. [36]YUN 1983, p. 359, GA res. 38/83 E, 15 Dec. 1983. [37]*Ibid.*, p. 358. [38]YUN 1971, p. 198. [39]A/39/372. [40]YUN 1983, p. 360, GA res. 38/83 J, 15 Dec. 1983. [41]*Ibid.*, p. 360.

Chapter X

Other political questions

Under the broad scope of political issues falling within its competence, the General Assembly continued, in 1984, to consider questions related to information, atomic radiation and Antarctica.

After consideration by its Committee on Information of various aspects of information, the Assembly, in December, adopted resolutions on the work of the United Nations Educational, Scientific and Cultural Organization (UNESCO) (39/98 B) and on United Nations public information programmes (39/98 A).

With regard to the levels, effects and risks of atomic radiation, the Assembly commended the United Nations Scientific Committee on the Effects of Atomic Radiation for its activities and requested that it continue its work (resolution 39/94).

By resolution 39/152, the Assembly took note of a report by the Secretary-General on Antarctica.

Topics related to this chapter. Disarmament: public information. Africa: South Africa and *apartheid*—public information. Middle East: Palestine question—public information. Communications. General questions relating to colonial countries: public information. Namibia: public information. Other administrative and management questions: UN communications satellite.

Information

Fostering public understanding and support of the United Nations and promoting balanced dissemination of information in the world were the two major areas of United Nations information activities in 1984. UNESCO and the Department of Public Information of the Secretariat (DPI) carried out most of the related substantive work, with the Committee on Information continuing to coordinate activities within the United Nations system and to report to the General Assembly.

The Assembly addressed a broad spectrum of issues related to the establishment of a new world information and communication order in resolution 39/98 B, adopted on 14 December. The main thrust of resolution 39/98 A, adopted the same day, was directed towards the role of DPI in disseminating objective information about the activities of the United Nations. Both texts were based largely on the recommendations of the Commit-

tee on Information, established by the Assembly in 1978[1] to examine United Nations public information policies and activities. After a one-day organizational session on 19 March, the Committee held its sixth substantive session in New York from 18 June to 6 July and on 6 September 1984. In its report to the Assembly,[2] the Committee made 59 recommendations on promoting a new information order and enhancing United Nations public information activities—all later approved by the Assembly.

Mass communication

UNESCO activities. UNESCO concentrated its efforts in 1984 on the application of the International Programme for the Development of Communication (IPDC)—a project aimed at helping developing countries to build communication infrastructure—the establishment of a new world information and communication order (see p. 355) and a study of how modern communication technologies affected societies. The organization's activities in those areas were highlighted in a report by the UNESCO Director-General, prepared in response to a December 1983 Assembly request[3] and transmitted by the Secretary-General in September.[4]

At its fifth session (Paris, 3-9 May 1984), the IPDC Intergovernmental Council approved for funding 32 projects (14 interregional and regional and 18 national). The 14 interregional and regional projects dealt with: equipment to expand exchanges benefiting the developing countries; computerization of the International Network of Documentation Centres on Communication Research and Policies; the mass media and public health (Asia); training in book publishing (Asia-Pacific); training in radio broadcasting (South Pacific Commission); Asia-Pacific Institute for Broadcasting Development; a Latin American centre to evaluate communication technologies; manuals on transmission and production of radio programmes (Latin America); international exchange of programmes by satellite (Africa); training for radio broadcasting in Africa; a coordinated exchange system in the Andean region; a training centre for graphic and pictorial arts for multimedia projects (Latin America and the Caribbean); radio programme production (Organization of African Unity); and a regional communications institute for the Great Lakes countries. The 18 national projects approved for funding were submitted by Angola, the Central African Republic, the Gambia, Ghana, Kenya, Uganda and the United Republic of Tanzania, for Africa; Somalia and the Sudan, for the Arab States; Bangladesh, Indonesia, Kiribati, Maldives, Mongolia, Pakistan and Tuvalu, for Asia and the Pacific; and Bolivia and Guyana, for Latin America and the Caribbean.

The Council also approved by-phase funding for interregional and regional projects endorsed earlier, recommended a number of feasibility missions and approved without funding several projects submitted by international and regional organizations.

Field-based development projects, numbering over 100 in Africa, the Arab States, Asia and the Pacific, and Latin America and the Caribbean, continued to play a dominant role in UNESCO's regular and extrabudgetary communication programmes, accounting for more than $25 million in ongoing activities. Trust funds, the largest source of finance for the projects, received major contributions from the Arab Gulf Programme for United Nations Development Organizations (comprising Bahrain, Iraq, Kuwait, Oman, Qatar, Saudi Arabia and the United Arab Emirates), the Federal Republic of Germany, the Netherlands and the Scandinavian countries. Despite a decrease in United Nations Development Programme (UNDP) resources, it still played an important role, contributing to projects in Bangladesh, Uganda, the Asia-Pacific region and the Caribbean. By 27 March 1984, contributions to the special account amounted to over $5.5 million. Training activities formed an estimated 70 per cent of communication development expenditure, with an increasing emphasis on the training of trainers. There was a greater emphasis on the development of endogenous human and physical resources, modern computer-based techniques and film and sound archives. (For other 1984 UNESCO activities related to communications, see PART TWO, Chapter IV.)

Recommendations of the Committee on Information. In its 1984 report to the General Assembly,[2] the Committee on Information recommended that the United Nations system and all others concerned should be urged to support UNESCO in its information and communication activities. It suggested that that system, particularly UNESCO, should provide all possible support to the developing countries to meet their needs in information. The Committee stressed the need to promote the access of the developing countries to various kinds of communication technology. It urged the United Nations and the developed countries to assist the developing countries in strength-

ening their information and communication infrastructures, pointing to IPDC as an important step in that direction. The Committee recommended that the Secretary-General be requested to submit to its 1985 session a study on co-ordination among UNDP, UNESCO, IPDC and the International Telecommunication Union (ITU) in support of those infrastructures.

The Committee also made recommendations with regard to the proposed new world information and communication order (see p. 355) and DPI activities to ensure better information coverage of the United Nations and its work (see p. 363).

GENERAL ASSEMBLY ACTION

Acting on the recommendation of the Special Political Committee, the General Assembly on 14 December adopted resolution 39/98 B by recorded vote. The resolution was adopted under the agenda item on questions relating to information.

The General Assembly,

Recalling its resolutions 34/181 and 34/182 of 18 December 1979, 35/201 of 16 December 1980, 36/149 A of 16 December 1981, 37/94 A and B of 10 December 1982 and 38/82 A of 15 December 1983,

Recalling the relevant provisions of the Political Declaration of the Seventh Conference of Heads of State or Government of Non-Aligned Countries, held at New Delhi from 7 to 12 March 1983, in which the importance of the establishment of a new world information and communication order was stressed anew, as well as the relevant provisions of the Final Declaration of the Sixth Conference of Heads of State or Government of Non-Aligned Countries, held at Havana from 3 to 9 September 1979, and particularly the final documents of the Conference of the Ministers of Information of Non-Aligned Countries, held at Jakarta from 26 to 30 January 1984,

Recalling the relevant resolutions adopted by the Assembly of Heads of State and Government of the Organization of African Unity at its eighteenth ordinary session, held at Nairobi from 24 to 27 June 1981,

Recalling article 19 of the Universal Declaration of Human Rights, which provides that everyone has the right to freedom of opinion and expression and that this right includes freedom to hold opinions without interference and to seek, receive and impart information and ideas through any media and regardless of frontiers, and article 29, which stipulates that these rights and freedoms may in no case be exercised contrary to the purposes and principles of the United Nations,

Recalling the relevant provisions of the Final Act of the Conference on Security and Co-operation in Europe, signed at Helsinki on 1 August 1975, and those of the Concluding Document of the meeting of representatives of the participating States of the Conference on Security and Co-operation in Europe, held at Madrid from 11 November 1980 to 9 September 1983,

Recalling also resolutions 4/19 and 4/21 adopted on 27 October 1980 by the General Conference of the United Nations Educational, Scientific and Cultural Organization at its twenty-first session, as well as resolution 2/03 adopted on 3 December 1982 by the General Conference at its fourth extraordinary session,

Recalling in particular part VI of resolution 4/19 of the General Conference of the United Nations Educational, Scientific and Cultural Organization and, in this context, expressing anew the wish that that organization demonstrate its willingness to contribute to the clarification, elaboration and application of the concept of a new world information and communication order,

Recalling the Declaration on Fundamental Principles concerning the Contribution of the Mass Media to Strengthening Peace and International Understanding, to the Promotion of Human Rights and to Countering Racialism, *Apartheid* and Incitement to War, adopted on 28 November 1978 by the General Conference of the United Nations Educational, Scientific and Cultural Organization,

Recalling also the relevant provisions of the Declaration on the Preparation of Societies for Life in Peace,

Considering that international co-operation in the field of communication development should take place on the basis of equality, justice, mutual advantage and the principles of international law,

Conscious that, in order progressively to remedy existing imbalances, it is essential to strengthen and intensify the development of infrastructures, networks and resources in the communication field and thus encourage a wider and better balanced dissemination of information,

Conscious also that diverse solutions to information and communication problems are required because social, political, cultural and economic problems differ from one country to another,

Emphasizing its full support for the International Programme for the Development of Communication of the United Nations Educational, Scientific and Cultural Organization, which constitutes an essential instrument for the development of the infrastructures of communication in the developing countries and the establishment of a new world information and communication order,

Recognizing the central role of the United Nations Educational, Scientific and Cultural Organization in the field of information and communication within its mandate, as well as the progress accomplished by that organization in that field,

1. *Takes note with satisfaction* of the report of the Director-General of the United Nations Educational, Scientific and Cultural Organization on the implementation of the International Programme for the Development of Communication, on the activities relating to the establishment of a new world information and communication order, and on the social, economic and cultural impact of the new communication technologies;

2. *Appeals* to the mass media all over the world to explore all possible avenues for more equitable international co-operation in the field of information and communication and to respond in a positive way to the exceptional opportunities now available to them in the field of international relations, in order to open new vistas of progress for the world community;

3. *Underlines* the importance of efforts made to implement the principles set forth in the Declaration on Fundamental Principles concerning the Contribution of the Mass Media to Strengthening Peace and International Understanding, to the Promotion of Human Rights and to Countering Racialism, *Apartheid* and Incitement to War;

4. *Reiterates its appeal* to all Member States and all organizations of the United Nations system, international, governmental and non-governmental organizations and professional organizations in the field of communication to exert every effort to make better known through all means at their disposal the issues underlying the demand for the development of communication capacities in developing countries as a step towards the establishment of a new world information and communication order;

5. *Considers* that the International Programme for the Development of Communication of the United Nations Educational, Scientific and Cultural Organization represents a significant step towards the establishment of a new world information and communication order and welcomes the decisions adopted by the Intergovernmental Council of the Programme at its fifth session, held in Paris from 3 to 9 May 1984;

6. *Notes with satisfaction* the co-operation existing between the United Nations, the United Nations Educational, Scientific and Cultural Organization and all other organizations of the United Nations system, particularly the International Telecommunication Union, the Food and Agriculture Organization of the United Nations and the Universal Postal Union, whose projects have been approved by the Intergovernmental Council of the International Programme for the Development of Communication;

7. *Expresses its appreciation* to all Member States that have made or pledged a contribution towards the implementation of the International Programme for the Development of Communication;

8. *Reiterates its request* to Member States and organizations and bodies of the United Nations system as well as other international governmental and non-governmental organizations and concerned public and private enterprises to respond to the appeals of the Director-General of the United Nations Educational, Scientific and Cultural Organization to make an increased contribution to the International Programme for the Development of Communication by making greater financial resources available, as well as more staff, equipment, technologies and training resources;

9. *Notes with satisfaction* the progress made under the Global Satellite Project for Dissemination and Exchange of Information, executed by the United Nations Educational, Scientific and Cultural Organization in co-operation with the regional radio broadcasting unions in Africa, Asia and the Arab States and supported by the International Programme for the Development of Communication;

10. *Takes note* of the final report[4] submitted by the United Nations Educational, Scientific and Cultural Organization relating to the Symposium on the Cultural, Social and Economic Impact of New Communication Technologies, held at Rome from 12 to 16 December 1983, as well as the final report[5] of the Round Table on a New World Information and Communication Order organized jointly by the United Nations and the United Nations Educational, Scientific and Cultural Organization, held at Igls, Austria, from 14 to 19 September 1983;

11. *Notes* that very few countries have so far responded positively to resolution 4/22 concerning the

reduction of telecommunication tariffs for news exchanges, adopted on 27 October 1980 by the General Conference of the United Nations Educational, Scientific and Cultural Organization at its twenty-first session, and calls once again upon Member States to respond positively and effectively and to take the necessary steps in order to implement that resolution;

12. *Reaffirms* its strong support for the United Nations Educational, Scientific and Cultural Organization, its Constitution, the ideals reflected in it, its activities and for its efforts to further enhance its capabilities with a view to promoting the establishment of a new world information and communication order;

13. *Invites* the Director-General of the United Nations Educational, Scientific and Cultural Organization to prepare a study on the progress made by that organization in the field of research on a new world information and communication order, analyse the conclusions reached and, if necessary, broaden the basis for the study;

14. *Encourages* the United Nations Educational, Scientific and Cultural Organization to continue and intensify its studies, programmes and activities with a view to identifying new technological trends in information, communication, telematics and informatics and assess their socio-economic and cultural impact on the development of peoples, and in this context requests it to provide periodic studies relevant to these topics;

15. *Invites* the Director-General of the United Nations Educational, Scientific and Cultural Organization to continue his efforts in the information and communication field and to submit to the General Assembly, at its fortieth session, a detailed report on the implementation of the International Programme for the Development of Communication and the activities relating to the establishment of a new world information and communication order, as well as on the social, economic and cultural effects of the accelerated development of communication technologies.

General Assembly resolution 39/98 B

14 December 1984   Meeting 100   122-6-17 (recorded vote)

Approved by SPC (A/39/714) by recorded vote (98-6-17), 10 December (meeting 51); draft by Egypt, for Group of 77 (A/SPC/39/L.21/Rev.1); agenda item 74.
Meeting numbers. GA 39th session: SPC 19-21, 23, 25-30, 50, 51; plenary 100.

Recorded vote in Assembly as follows:

In favour: Afghanistan, Algeria, Angola, Argentina, Bahamas, Bahrain, Bangladesh, Barbados, Belize, Benin, Bhutan, Bolivia, Botswana, Brazil, Brunei Darussalam, Bulgaria, Burkina Faso, Burma, Burundi, Byelorussian SSR, Cameroon, Cape Verde, Central African Republic, Chad, Chile, China, Colombia, Congo, Costa Rica, Cuba, Cyprus, Czechoslovakia, Democratic Kampuchea, Democratic Yemen, Djibouti, Dominican Republic, Ecuador, Egypt, El Salvador, Equatorial Guinea, Ethiopia, Fiji, Gabon, Gambia, German Democratic Republic, Ghana, Guatemala, Guinea, Guinea-Bissau, Guyana, Haiti, Honduras, Hungary, India, Indonesia, Iraq, Ivory Coast, Jamaica, Jordan, Kenya, Kuwait, Lao People's Democratic Republic, Lebanon, Lesotho, Liberia, Libyan Arab Jamahiriya, Madagascar, Malawi, Malaysia, Maldives, Mali, Malta, Mauritania, Mauritius, Mexico, Mongolia, Morocco, Mozambique, Nepal, Nicaragua, Niger, Nigeria, Oman, Pakistan, Panama, Papua New Guinea, Paraguay, Peru, Philippines, Poland, Qatar, Romania, Rwanda, Sao Tome and Principe, Saudi Arabia, Senegal, Seychelles, Sierra Leone, Singapore, Somalia, Sri Lanka, Sudan, Suriname, Syrian Arab Republic, Thailand, Togo, Trinidad and Tobago, Tunisia, Turkey, Uganda, Ukrainian SSR, USSR, United Arab Emirates, United Republic of Tanzania, Uruguay, Venezuela, Viet Nam, Yemen, Yugoslavia, Zaire, Zambia, Zimbabwe.

Against: Germany, Federal Republic of, Israel, Japan, Netherlands, United Kingdom, United States.

Abstaining: Australia, Austria, Belgium, Canada, Denmark, Finland, France, Greece, Iceland, Ireland, Italy, Luxembourg, New Zealand, Norway, Portugal, Spain, Sweden.

Introducing the draft in the Committee, Egypt pointed out that the Group of 77, while not totally satisfied with the text, believed that it reflected the interests of many delegations; the Group, however, would not sacrifice its principles.

In explanation of vote, Australia, Austria, Canada, Finland for the Nordic countries, France, the Federal Republic of Germany, Japan, the Netherlands, Portugal, the United Kingdom and the United States objected that there was no mention in the text of the consensus reached in 1983 at UNESCO, according to which the new world information order was seen as "an evolving and continuous process". The United Kingdom added that the phrase did not imply, as some had alleged, that a great deal of time would be necessary for such evolution to take place or that practical assistance for the process was not desirable; it also pointed out that, because of its intention of giving notice to withdraw from UNESCO, it had difficulty with the paragraph reaffirming blanket support for that organization. The Federal Republic of Germany stressed that it was not within the province of the Committee on Information or the General Assembly to modify concepts developed by UNESCO and added that it did not agree with all aspects of UNESCO's work—a fact not reflected in paragraph 12. The Netherlands felt that the text ignored UNESCO's central role in information. Japan objected in particular to paragraphs 13 to 15. Italy stressed that it could not support the definition of the order as set forth in the text. The United States added that there were numerous references to regional meetings and United Nations resolutions which the United States had not attended or supported.

Israel said information should be disseminated freely and not used as a weapon in the hands of a State; it specifically objected to the third preambular paragraph because of what it called its authoritarian implications.

Turkey described its vote as a token of hope for a more constructive attitude but regretted that the text, while reflecting certain essential facts, events and concerns, had omitted others equally important. Colombia, Ecuador and Malaysia expressed regret over absence of consensus.

Albania did not participate in the vote because of several reservations, including the mention in the text of the Final Act of the 1975 Helsinki Conference on Security and Co-operation in Europe, which it saw as a super-Power farce to reinforce spheres of influence.

Proposed new world information and communication order

The leading role in the United Nations effort to promote a new world information and communication order continued to be played by UNESCO and DPI in 1984.

UNESCO activities. Further exploration of the concept of a new world information and communication order remained a thrust of UNESCO's activities in 1984. Reporting on them in September,[4] the UNESCO Director-General said that a number of studies focused on such issues as democratization of communication, plurality of information, censorship, self-censorship and other obstacles to a better balanced dissemination of information, with special emphasis on the right to communicate, access to and participation in communication, and the contribution of the media to international understanding. As a follow-up to a September 1983 joint UNESCO/United Nations round table on a new order,[5] UNESCO contributed to a number of international meetings and seminars on related subjects held in 1984 by various non-governmental organizations and professional associations.

Another key element of UNESCO's work in regard to the new world order was investigation of information flow, particularly between the industrialized and the developing worlds. A study on the international flow of television materials was concluded in 1984, spanning almost 10 years and incorporating data from about 60 countries. A major report on the global flow of information, synthesizing the results of research around the world, was also completed.

With regard to reducing telecommunication tariffs, a goal actively pursued by UNESCO, the Director-General reported that a January 1984 Conference of information ministers of non-aligned countries (Jakarta, Indonesia) had decided to reduce such tariffs by at least 50 per cent in the 11 countries hosting the distribution centres of the Non-Aligned News Agencies Pool. UNESCO was also involved in preparing a May meeting of some of those ministers at Cairo, Egypt, held in pursuance of a Conference decision. In addition, questions concerning the reduction of telecommunications tariffs were considered by a UNESCO working group and in a joint study with ITU. IPDC provided assistance to regional broadcasting unions in Africa, the Arab States and Asia and the Pacific in setting up their own satellite television news-exchange system. UNESCO also assisted in holding a seminar at New Delhi, India, to examine measures for improving the services of the Non-Aligned News Agencies Pool. The impact of postal tariffs on the circulation of books and other educational, scientific and cultural material was the subject of a UNESCO memorandum to the June/July 1984 Congress of the Universal Postal Union (UPU), which outlined possible ways of facilitating the international exchange of various categories of printed matter.

Activities of the Committee on Information. In its 1984 report to the General Assembly,[2] the Committee on Information presented a list of recommendations on promoting a new world information and communication order, which were sub-

sequently approved by the Assembly when it adopted resolution 39/98 A. The Committee again recommended that all countries, the United Nations system and others concerned should collaborate in establishing a new order based on the free circulation and wider and better balanced dissemination of information, guaranteeing the diversity of sources of information and free access to it. The Committee noted, in particular, the urgent need to change the dependence of the developing countries in information and communication.

Following the Assembly's invitation and the Committee's recommendation,[6] the Executive Director of the United Nations Centre on Transnational Corporations (UNCTC), in a memorandum of 16 May,[7] provided information on UNCTC documents pertinent to a new order. They included studies dealing with the political, legal, economic and social effects of transnational corporations, as well as the impact of their practices in transborder data flows and in specific industry sectors.

Communications. By a letter of 13 March,[8] Morocco transmitted documents of the Fourth Islamic Summit Conference (Casablanca, January), which adopted a resolution on information in which it stressed the need for continued close cooperation among States to contribute to the establishment of a new, more equitable and objective information order.

On 15 March,[9] Bangladesh transmitted the resolutions of the Fourteenth Islamic Conference of Foreign Ministers (Dhaka, December). The Conference, conscious of the need for a new order, deemed it necessary to draw up an Islamic strategy for information in keeping with that order.

India, on 20 March,[10] transmitted a declaration of the Conference of the Ministers of Information of Non-Aligned Countries (Jakarta, January) in which the Conference noted that the dominance of the transnational news agencies and corporate structures in the international mass media had given rise to imbalances in the flow of news to the disadvantage of the developing countries, making it essential to advance a new world information and communication order.

GENERAL ASSEMBLY ACTION

In resolution 39/98 B of 14 December, the Assembly reiterated its appeal to Member States and United Nations and other organizations in the communications field to make better known the issues underlying the demand for the development of communication capacities in developing countries as a step towards establishing a new world information and communication order. The Assembly reaffirmed its support for UNESCO's efforts to promote that order, considering IPDC a significant step in that direction. That support was also reaffirmed in resolution 39/98 A.

UN public information

Activities of the Committee on Information.
The Committee on Information, in its 1984 report to the General Assembly,[2] made a number of recommendations on United Nations public information activities, including specific suggestions for the work of DPI, which were later approved by the Assembly when it adopted resolution 39/98 A. In connection with the fortieth (1985) anniversary of the United Nations (see p. 382), the Committee proposed that DPI support the Preparatory Committee in publicizing the goals and accomplishments of the United Nations. It urged DPI to co-operate closely with relevant international organizations and bodies, such as UNESCO, ITU, UNDP and the Non-Aligned News Agencies Pool. The Committee again took up the question of the United Nations acquiring a communications satellite (see ADMINISTRATIVE AND BUDGETARY QUESTIONS, Chapter IV) and made specific proposals aimed at enhancing the activities of DPI radio, television and press and publications services, as well as improving the work of its information centres (for details, see below, under respective headings). It also emphasized DPI's role in the World Disarmament Campaign (see p. 86).

GENERAL ASSEMBLY ACTION

Under the agenda item on questions relating to information, the General Assembly, on 14 December, adopted resolution 39/98 A by recorded vote. The action was taken on the recommendation of the Special Political Committee.

The General Assembly,

Recalling its resolutions 3535(XXX) of 17 December 1975, 31/139 of 16 December 1976, 33/115 A to C of 18 December 1978, 34/181 and 34/182 of 18 December 1979, 35/201 of 16 December 1980, 36/149 B of 16 December 1981, 37/94 B of 10 December 1982 and 38/82 B of 15 December 1983 on questions relating to information,

Recalling article 19 of the Universal Declaration of Human Rights, which provides that everyone has the right to freedom of opinion and expression and that this right includes freedom to hold opinions without interference and to seek, receive and impart information and ideas through any media and regardless of frontiers, and article 29, which stipulates that these rights and freedoms may in no case be exercised contrary to the purposes and principles of the United Nations,

Recalling also articles 19 and 20 of the International Covenant on Civil and Political Rights,

Recalling the relevant provisions of the Political Declaration of the Seventh Conference of Heads of State or Government of Non-Aligned Countries, held at New Delhi from 7 to 12 March 1983, in which the importance of the establishment of a new world information and communication order was stressed anew, as well as the relevant provisions of the Final Declaration of the Sixth Conference of Heads of State or Government of Non-Aligned Countries, held at Havana from 3 to 9

September 1979, and particularly the final documents of the Conference of the Ministers of Information of Non-Aligned Countries, held at Jakarta from 26 to 30 January 1984,

Recalling its resolutions 3201(S-VI) and 3202(S-VI) of 1 May 1974, containing the Declaration and the Programme of Action on the Establishment of a New International Economic Order, 3281(XXIX) of 12 December 1974, containing the Charter of Economic Rights and Duties of States, and 3362(S-VII) of 16 September 1975 on development and international economic co-operation,

Recalling the Declaration on Fundamental Principles concerning the Contribution of the Mass Media to Strengthening Peace and International Understanding, to the Promotion of Human Rights and to Countering Racialism, *Apartheid* and Incitement to War, as well as the relevant resolutions on information and mass communications adopted by the General Conference of the United Nations Educational, Scientific and Cultural Organization at its nineteenth, twentieth, twenty-first and twenty-second sessions,

Recalling the relevant provisions of the Final Act of the Conference on Security and Co-operation in Europe, signed at Helsinki on 1 August 1975, and those of the Concluding Document of the meeting of representatives of the participating States of the Conference on Security and Co-operation in Europe, held at Madrid from 11 November 1980 to 9 September 1983,

Recalling also the relevant provisions of the Declaration on the Preparation of Societies for Life in Peace,

Conscious of the need for all countries, the United Nations system as a whole and all others concerned, to collaborate in the establishment of a new world information and communication order based, *inter alia*, on the free circulation and wider and better balanced dissemination of information, guaranteeing diversity of sources of information and free access to information, and, in particular, the urgent need to change the dependent status of the developing countries in the field of information and communication, as the principle of sovereign equality among nations extends also to this field, and intended also to strengthen peace and international understanding, enabling all persons to participate effectively in political, economic, social and cultural life and promoting understanding and friendship among all nations and human rights,

Reaffirming that the establishment of a new world information and communication order is linked to the new international economic order and is an integral part of the international development process,

Emphasizing the important role that public information plays in promoting understanding of and support for the establishment of the new international economic order and international co-operation for development,

Emphasizing the role that public information plays in promoting support for universal disarmament and in increasing awareness of the relationship between disarmament and development among as broad a public as possible,

Reaffirming the primary role which the General Assembly is to play in elaborating, co-ordinating and harmonizing United Nations policies and activities in the field of information, and recognizing the central and important role of the United Nations Educational, Scientific and Cultural Organization in the field of information and communication, and that the United Nations system as a whole and all others concerned, should give that organization adequate support and assistance in the field of information and communication,

Recognizing the importance of the co-ordination and co-operation between the Department of Public Information of the Secretariat, the United Nations Development Programme, the United Nations Educational, Scientific and Cultural Organization and its International Programme for the Development of Communication in the promotion of the establishment of a new world information and communication order,

Fully aware and cognizant of the important contribution which the mass media world-wide can make in enhancing and strengthening peace, deepening international understanding, promoting justice, equality, national independence, development, the exercise of human rights and the establishment of a new world information and communication order,

Noting that the celebration in 1985 of the fortieth anniversary of the creation of the United Nations will provide a unique opportunity to promote and publicize the noble goals and accomplishments of the United Nations as a major forum for pooling the efforts of States to contribute to the solution of vital world problems,

Noting that the year 1985 will also mark the twenty-fifth anniversary of the adoption of the historic Declaration on the Granting of Independence to Colonial Countries and Peoples, contained in General Assembly resolution 1514(XV) of 14 December 1960, and the important role that the United Nations plays in its implementation,

Expressing its satisfaction with the successful co-ordination and co-operation displayed by the Department of Public Information with the Non-Aligned News Agencies Pool, as well as with news agencies of other developing and developed countries, and convinced that such efforts have contributed significantly to progress towards a new world information and communication order,

Taking note of the implementation by the Department of Public Information of those parts relevant to public information of the Paris Declaration on Namibia and the Programme of Action on Namibia, adopted by the International Conference in Support of the Struggle of the Namibian People for Independence, as well as of the Bangkok Declaration and Programme of Action on Namibia, adopted by the United Nations Council for Namibia on 25 May 1984 at its extraordinary plenary meetings, held at Bangkok, in order to develop and further strengthen the dissemination of information regarding the struggle for independence of the people of Namibia, with a view to reaching the broadest possible public by means of a more systematic and better co-ordinated information campaign in accordance with General Assembly resolution 38/36 D of 1 December 1983,

Taking note also of the implementation by the Department of Public Information of those parts of the Programme of Action for the Achievement of Palestinian Rights relevant to information, in accordance with General Assembly resolution 38/58 E of 13 December 1983,

Taking note of the report of the Joint Inspection Unit on publications policy and practice in the United Nations system,

Expressing its satisfaction with the work of the Committee on Information as reflected in its report,

Taking note with satisfaction of the report of the Secretary-General on questions relating to information,

Taking note with satisfaction of the report of the Director-General of the United Nations Educational, Scientific and Cultural Organization,

1. *Approves* the report of the Committee on Information, and all the recommendations contained in paragraph 86 of that report and annexed to the present resolution, and affirms the requests and appeals reproduced therein as well as all the provisions of General Assembly resolution 38/82 B, and particularly all those unimplemented recommendations, and urges their full implementation;

2. *Reaffirms* the mandate given to the Committee on Information by the General Assembly in its resolution 34/182;

3. *Requests* the Committee on Information, keeping in mind its mandate, the essential tasks of which are to continue to examine the policies and activities of the Department of Public Information of the Secretariat and to promote the establishment of a new, more just and effective world information and communication order, to continue to seek the co-operation and active participation of all organizations of the United Nations system, particularly the United Nations Educational, Scientific and Cultural Organization and the International Telecommunication Union, while taking all possible steps to avoid any overlapping of activities on this subject;

4. *Reaffirms* its strong support for the United Nations Educational, Scientific and Cultural Organization, its Constitution and the ideals reflected therein, its activities and for its efforts to further enhance its capabilities with a view to promoting the establishment of a new world information and communication order;

5. *Reiterates its appeal* to Member States, to the information and communication media, both public and private, as well as to non-governmental organizations, to disseminate more widely objective and better balanced information about the activities of the United Nations and, *inter alia*, about the efforts of the developing countries towards their economic, social and cultural progress and about the efforts of the international community to achieve international social justice and economic development, international peace and security with the promotion of disarmament and the progressive elimination of international inequities and tensions; and the promotion of human rights and fundamental freedoms and the right of peoples to self-determination; such dissemination being aimed at achieving a more comprehensive and realistic image of the activities and potential of the United Nations system in all its purposes and endeavours;

6. *Urges* the Department of Public Information to give the widest possible dissemination of information pertaining to the observance of the twenty-fifth anniversary of the Declaration on the Granting of Independence to Colonial Countries and Peoples with a view to strengthening international commitment to the total eradication of colonialism in all its forms;

7. *Urges* the Department of Public Information to strengthen its co-operation with the Non-Aligned News Agencies Pool and in particular to ensure that its daily dispatches are received by the United Nations Office at Geneva and United Nations Headquarters in New York;

8. *Requests* the Department of Public Information to continue its follow-up programmes in further implementation of those parts relevant to public information of the Paris Declaration on Namibia and the Programme of Action on Namibia, adopted by the International Conference in Support of the Struggle of the Namibian People for Independence, as well as of the Bangkok Declaration and Programme of Action on Namibia, and to report thereon to the Committee on Information at its substantive session in 1985;

9. *Requests* the Department of Public Information to cover adequately policies and practices which violate the principles of international law relative to belligerent occupation, in particular the Geneva Convention relative to the Protection of Civilian Persons in Time of War, of 12 August 1949, wherever they occur, especially those policies and practices which frustrate the attainment and exercise of the inalienable and national legitimate rights of the Palestinian people in accordance with the relevant resolutions of the United Nations, and to report thereon to the Committee on Information at its substantive session in 1985;

10. *Reiterates* the recommendation contained in its resolution 35/201 of 16 December 1980 that additional resources for the Department of Public Information should be commensurate with the increase in the activities of the United Nations which the Department is called upon to cover for the purpose of public information, and that the Secretary-General should provide such resources to the Department to this end where needed;

11. *Reaffirms* the importance of the rapidly increasing role of United Nations public information programmes in fostering public understanding and support of United Nations activities and requests the Department of Public Information to consider the recommendations contained in the report of the Joint Inspection Unit on publications policy and practice in the United Nations system and to report to the Committee on Information at its substantive session in 1985;

12. *Decides* to increase the membership of the Committee on Information from sixty-seven to sixty-nine and appoints China and Mexico as new members;

13. *Requests* the Secretary-General to report to the Committee on Information, at its substantive session in 1985, on the implementation of all the recommendations contained in the Committee's report and annexed to the present resolution;

14. *Requests* the Secretary-General to consider the proposals of the Governments of Benin and Poland on the opening of United Nations information centres, in the light of recommendation 37 of the Committee on Information and of the criteria established in General Assembly resolution 38/82 B, and to report to the General Assembly at its fortieth session;

15. *Also requests* the Secretary-General to report to the General Assembly at its fortieth session on the implementation of the present resolution and, in particular, on the implementation of all the recommendations contained in the annex to the present resolution;

16. *Requests* the Committee on Information to report to the General Assembly at its fortieth session;

17. *Decides* to include in the provisional agenda of its fortieth session the item entitled "Questions relating to information".

ANNEX
Recommendations of the Committee on Information

1. The recommendations of the Committee on Information approved by the General Assembly in its resolution 38/82 B of 15 December 1983, as well as all provisions of the resolution, should be reiterated, taking into account the views expressed by delegations at the 98th plenary meeting of the thirty-eighth session of the Assembly on 15 December 1983. Those recommendations should be implemented in full, and the Secretary-General should be requested to report to the Committee on Information at its substantive session in 1985 on measures taken for the implementation of those recommendations and provisions pending implementation.

2. The mandate of the Committee on Information should be renewed as set forth in General Assembly resolution 34/182 of 18 December 1979 and reaffirmed in Assembly resolutions 35/201 of 16 December 1980, 36/149 of 16 December 1981, 37/94 B of 10 December 1982 and 38/82 B of 15 December 1983.

Promotion of the establishment of a new, more just and more effective world information and communication order intended to strengthen peace and international understanding and based on the free circulation and wider and better balanced dissemination of information

3. All countries, the United Nations system as a whole, and all others concerned, should collaborate in the establishment of a new world information and communication order based, *inter alia*, on the free circulation, and wider and better balanced dissemination of information, guaranteeing the diversity of sources of information and free access to information, and, in particular, the urgent need to change the dependent status of the developing countries in the field of information and communication, as the principle of sovereign equality among nations extends also to this field, and intended also to strengthen peace and international understanding, enabling all persons to participate effectively in political, economic, social and cultural life, and promoting understanding and friendship among all nations and human rights.

4. The United Nations system should reiterate its appeal to the international media and increase its efforts for action by the international community towards global development and, in particular, the efforts of the developing countries to achieve economic, social and cultural progress.

5. Under the current international climate of political conflicts and economic disorders, the Committee on Information, fully aware and cognizant of the important contribution that the mass media world-wide can make in enhancing and strengthening peace, deepening international understanding, promoting justice, equality, national independence, development, the exercise of human rights and the establishment of a new world information and communication order, recommends that the General Assembly appeal to the mass media to respond in a positive way to opportunities available to them in this field, in order to open new vistas of progress for the world community.

6. Aware of the existence of structural imbalances in the international distribution of news affecting the two-way flow of news, the Committee on Information recommends that urgent attention should be given to the elimination of existing inequalities and all other

obstacles in the free flow and wider and better balanced dissemination of information, ideas and knowledge by, *inter alia*, diversifying the sources of information as a step towards free and more balanced information and the promotion of the establishment of a new world information and communication order.

7. The Committee on Information recommends that the need be stressed to ensure and promote the access of the developing countries to communication technology including communication satellites, modern electronic information systems, informatics and other advanced information and communication facilities with a view to improving their own information and communication systems corresponding to the specific conditions prevailing in each country.

8. The Committee on Information, expressing its satisfaction with the successful co-ordination and co-operation displayed by the Department of Public Information of the Secretariat with the Non-Aligned News Agencies Pool, as well as with news agencies of other developing and developed countries, and convinced that such efforts have contributed significantly to progress towards a new world information and communication order, recommends that the Department of Public Information strengthen its co-operation with the Pool and with the agencies of developing countries as this co-operation constitutes a concrete step towards a more just and equitable flow of information thus contributing to the establishment of a new world information and communication order.

9. The Committee on Information, while recognizing the importance of the co-ordination and co-operation between the Department of Public Information, the United Nations Development Programme, the United Nations Educational, Scientific and Cultural Organization and its International Programme for the Development of Communication in the promotion of the establishment of a new world information and communication order, recommends that the Secretary-General should be requested to prepare a consolidated study, within existing resources, on the contributions, effects and levels of co-ordination between those organizations and the International Telecommunication Union in support of the development of information and communication infrastructure and systems in the developing countries for submission to the Committee on Information at its substantive session in 1985.

10. The United Nations system as a whole as well as the developed countries should be urged to co-operate in a concerted manner with the developing countries towards strengthening the information and communication infrastructures of the latter countries, in accordance with the priorities attached to such areas by the developing countries, with a view to enabling them to develop their own information and communication policies freely and independently and in the light of their history, social values and cultural traditions. In this regard, full support for the International Programme for the Development of Communication, which constitutes an important step in the development of these infrastructures, should always be emphasized.

11. The United Nations system should co-operate in a concerted manner, through its information services, in promoting, as a matter of high priority, the development activities of the United Nations and, in particular, the improvement of the conditions of the lives of the people of developing countries.

12. The United Nations system should constantly promote the creation of a climate of confidence in relations among States, as a means of easing tension and facilitating the establishment of a new world information and communication order.

13. Reaffirming the primary role which the General Assembly is to play in elaborating, co-ordinating and harmonizing United Nations policies and activities in the field of information and recognizing the central and important role of the United Nations Educational, Scientific and Cultural Organization in the field of information and communication, the Committee on Information recommends that the United Nations system as a whole and all others concerned should be urged to give that organization adequate support and assistance in the field of information and communication. The Department of Public Information in particular should co-operate more regularly with the United Nations Educational, Scientific and Cultural Organization, especially at the working level, with a view to maximizing the contributions of the Department to the efforts of that organization in promoting the establishment of a new world information and communication order and to disseminating as widely as possible information on the activities of that organization in this respect.

14. The Secretary-General should be requested to submit to the General Assembly at its thirty-ninth session information concerning the arrangements for the convening, jointly with the United Nations Educational, Scientific and Cultural Organization, of a round table in 1985 on a new world information and communication order.

15. The Department of Public Information should be urged to monitor, as appropriate, important meetings of the Movement of Non-Aligned Countries, as well as of regional intergovernmental organizations devoted to information and communication questions, within existing resources.

16. The United Nations system, particularly the United Nations Educational, Scientific and Cultural Organization, should aim at the provision of all possible support and assistance to the developing countries, within existing resources, with due regard to their interests and needs in the field of information and to actions already adopted within the United Nations system, including, in particular:

(a) Assistance to developing countries in training journalists and technical personnel and in setting up appropriate educational institutions and research facilities;

(b) The granting of favourable conditions to provide access to developing countries to such communication technology as is requisite for the establishment of a national information and communication system and correspondent with the specific situation of the country concerned;

(c) The creation of conditions that will gradually enable the developing countries to produce the communication technology suited to their national needs, as well as the necessary programme material, specifically for radio and television broadcasting, by using their own resources;

(d) Assistance in establishing telecommunication links at subregional, regional and interregional levels, especially among developing countries, free from conditions of any kind.

17. All the information activities of the Department of Public Information should be guided by, and carried out in conformity with, the principles of the Charter of the United Nations and the aspiration for a new world information and communication order, as well as conform to the consensus reached among States in resolutions 4/19, 4/21 and 4/22 adopted on 27 October 1980 by the General Conference of the United Nations Educational, Scientific and Cultural Organization at its twenty-first session.

18. The role of the Department of Public Information as the focal point for the formulation and implementation of information activities of the United Nations should be re-emphasized, and in this regard the Committee on Information recommends that the proliferation of information units in the Secretariat independent of the Department should be discouraged.

19. The Secretary-General should be requested to ensure that the activities of the Department of Public Information, as the focal point of the public information tasks of the United Nations, should be strengthened, keeping in view the principles of the Charter of the United Nations and along the lines established in the pertinent resolutions of the General Assembly and the recommendations of the Committee on Information, to ensure a more coherent coverage of and a better knowledge about the United Nations and its work, especially in its priority areas, such as those stated in section III, paragraph 1, of Assembly resolution 35/201, including international peace and security, disarmament, peace-keeping and peace-making operations, decolonization, the promotion of human rights, the struggle against *apartheid* and racial discrimination, economic, social and development issues, the integration of women in the struggle for peace and development, the establishment of the new international economic order and of a new world information and communication order, the work of the United Nations Council for Namibia and programmes on women and youth.

20. The final documents of the Conference of the Ministers of Information of the Non-Aligned Countries, held at Jakarta from 26 to 30 January 1984, should be noted.

21. The Department of Public Information should maintain editorial independence and accuracy in reporting for all material produced by the Department and should promote to the greatest possible extent an informed understanding of the work and purposes of the United Nations among the people of the world. It should take the necessary measures to ensure that its output contains objective and equitable information about issues before the Organization, reflecting divergent opinions where they occur.

22. The resolution adopted at the Conference of the Ministers of Information and Communication of the countries acting as centres of redistribution of the Non-Aligned News Agencies Pool, meeting in Cairo on 9 and 10 May 1984, on the establishment and consolidation of an information network for news and broadcasting agencies of the Movement of Non-Aligned Countries should also be noted.

23. The relevant resolution on the question relating to information of the Fourth Islamic Summit Conference, held at Casablanca from 16 to 19 January 1984, should be noted.

Continuation of examination of United Nations public information policies and activities in the light of the evolution of international relations, particularly during the past two decades, and of the imperatives of the establishment of the new international economic order and of a new world information and communication order

24. In connection with the forthcoming celebration of the fortieth anniversary of the creation of the United Nations, the Department of Public Information should be urged to give appropriate support to the Preparatory Committee for the Fortieth Anniversary of the United Nations in promoting and publicizing the noble goals and accomplishments of the United Nations as a major forum for pooling efforts of States to contribute to the solution of vital world problems.

25. The Department of Public Information should continue to ensure that the daily dispatches of the Non-Aligned News Agencies Pool that it receives are appropriately utilized in the performance of the public information tasks of the United Nations:

(a) With a view to further promotion and development of a functional and mutually beneficial cooperation between the Department and the Pool, the existing arrangements in the Department for the conduct of this co-operation should be established on a more regular basis;

(b) In view of the successful joint coverage by the Pool of important conferences and other events within the United Nations system, this practice should be continued and further strengthened;

(c) The Department should consider the possibility of utilizing the dispatches received from the Pool to establish a data base on the information and communication facilities in the non-aligned countries.

26. In connection with its annual training programme for journalists and broadcasters from developing countries, the Department of Public Information should allocate the last week of the programme for a visit by them to one of the developing countries that expresses readiness to receive them for the purpose of acquainting themselves with the ways in which information on the United Nations is received and utilized.

27. The interim report of the International Telecommunication Union on the World Communications Year should be noted and the Secretary-General should be requested to make available to the Committee on Information at its substantive session in 1985 a comprehensive report on the outcome of the activities of the International Telecommunication Union with regard to the Year.

28. The exchange of information between the Committee on Information and the Commission on Transnational Corporations in matters pertaining to the mandate of the Committee should again be encouraged.

29. The report of the Secretary-General on the acquisition by the United Nations of its own communications satellite should be noted. The Secretary-General should be requested to submit to the Committee on Information at its substantive session in 1985 a complementary report on the acquisition of a United Nations communications satellite, in compliance with recommendation 36 made by the Committee to the General Assembly at its thirty-seventh session.

30. The attention of the pertinent organs of the General Assembly and of the United Nations system

as a whole should be drawn to the findings of the International Telecommunication Union set forth in its interim report, especially as concerns the problem of the geostationary orbit reflected, *inter alia*, in paragraphs 33 and 49 of that report, taking into account the needs of the developing countries.

31. With regard to its co-operation with the Non-Aligned News Agencies Pool as well as with the regional news agencies in developing countries, the Department of Public Information should co-operate, as appropriate, with the United Nations Educational, Scientific and Cultural Organization in assisting that organization, within existing resources, in the following activities:

(a) In the preparation and implementation of a plan of integrated communication network and regional data and communication centres;

(b) In providing facilities for meetings on data and communication exchange of the public information bodies of the non-aligned countries;

(c) In the preparation for observance of 1985 as the Year of Communication for information bodies in the non-aligned countries.

32. The Department of Public Information should closely co-operate with the United Nations Educational, Scientific and Cultural Organization and the Non-Aligned News Agencies Pool to organize a workshop, within existing resources, in 1985 for familiarization of news agencies of developing countries with modern technology of relevance to news agencies, and for the standardization of teaching methods and syllabuses, and to produce training manuals in various languages for the training centres of the Pool.

33. The Secretary-General should be requested once again to maintain the functions of the Middle East/Arabic Unit as the producer of Arabic television and radio programmes, and to strengthen and expand this unit to enable it to function in an effective manner, and to report to the Committee on Information at its substantive session in 1985 on the measures taken in implementation of this recommendation.

34. In view of the importance of United Nations broadcasting for the European region, steps should be taken to maintain and enhance the functions of the European Unit in the Radio Service through redeployment of existing resources.

35. The Department of Public Information should be requested to use the official General Assembly languages adequately in its documents and audio-visual documentation in order to inform the public better about the activities of the United Nations. It should also make available to the French Language Production Section of the Press and Publications Division of the Department, within existing resources, the means that will allow it to distribute consistent press releases in sufficient quantity to satisfy the needs of numerous delegations that use French as a working language.

36. Effective steps should be taken to ensure that the United Nations information centres give adequate services in local languages. Such steps are to be taken within existing resources. The Committee on Information should be informed about the implementation of this recommendation at its substantive session in 1985.

37. The Secretary-General may be requested to consider the proposals of the Governments of Benin and Poland on the opening of United Nations information centres in their respective countries in the light of criteria established in General Assembly resolution 38/82 B, through the redeployment of resources, and to report to the General Assembly at its thirty-ninth session.

38. United Nations information centres should continue to assist press and information media in their respective countries, and, *inter alia*, promote the establishment of a new world information and communication order.

39. While the co-operation between the Department of Public Information and the United Nations Development Programme in the field should be promoted to the maximum extent, it is also important to bear in mind the intrinsic functions of United Nations information centres as distinct from those of the United Nations development activities. The information centres should redouble their efforts to publicize the activities and achievements of operational activities for development, including those of the United Nations Development Programme, taking into account the priorities determined by the General Assembly.

40. The report of the Secretary-General concerning measures to improve the effectiveness of United Nations information centres should be noted and the Secretary-General should be encouraged to implement his proposals, within the existing resources allocated to the Department of Public Information.

41. The Department of Public Information should focus on and give wider coverage to the economic, social and development activities throughout the United Nations system aimed at achieving a more comprehensive image of the activities and potential of the United Nations system, taking into account the priorities set by the General Assembly, particularly in the light of the forthcoming fortieth anniversary of the United Nations.

42. The Department of Public Information should promote an informed understanding of the work of the United Nations in the area delineated in General Assembly resolutions 34/146 of 17 December 1979, 36/109 of 10 December 1981, 37/108 of 16 December 1982 and 38/130 and 38/136 of 19 December 1983.

43. Pending the possible acquisition by the United Nations of its own short-wave radio network and taking into account the study carried out by the Department of Public Information on this subject, the Secretary-General should be requested to report on the question raised in the study, and to inform the Committee on Information on the working of such a system and to submit an evaluation report on daily short-wave radio broadcasts from Headquarters.

44. The United Nations information centres should intensify direct and systematic communication exchange with local information and educational communities in a mutually beneficial way, especially in areas of particular interest to host countries.

45. The Secretary-General should continue his efforts to develop a system for monitoring and evaluating the effectiveness of the activities of the Department of Public Information, particularly in the priority areas determined by the General Assembly.

46. The Department of Public Information should improve, within existing resources, its data-collection procedures with regard to the actual use made by redisseminators of materials distributed by the Department and its information centres and submit a report to the Committee on Information at its substantive session in 1985 on progress made in this area.

47. Future reports of the Department of Public Information to the Committee on Information and to the General Assembly, in particular on new programmes or on the expansion of existing programmes, should contain:

(a) More adequate information on the output of the Department in respect of each topic included in its work programme, which forms the basis of its programme budget;

(b) The costs of the activities undertaken in respect of each topic;

(c) More adequate information on target audiences, end-use of the Department's products, and analysis of feedback data received by the Department;

(d) The Department's evaluation of the effectiveness of its different programmes and activities;

(e) A statement detailing the priority level that the Secretary-General has attached to current or future activities of the Department in documents dealing with such activities.

48. The Secretary-General should be requested to strengthen the Planning, Programming and Evaluation Unit of the Department of Public Information through the redeployment of existing resources.

49. The steps taken by the Department of Public Information in redressing the imbalance in its staff should be noted. The Department should continue to intensify its efforts to that end and the Secretary-General should be requested to take urgent steps to increase the representation of underrepresented developing countries, and of other underrepresented groups of countries, especially at the senior levels, in conformity with the relevant provisions of the Charter of the United Nations, and to submit a report to the Committee on Information at its substantive session in 1985.

50. Member States should be called upon once again to make voluntary contributions to the United Nations Trust Fund for Economic and Social Information.

51. Quality, usefulness and coverage of the daily press releases and the weekly news summary issued by the Department of Public Information in all working languages should be further enhanced and improved in view of the important public information tasks that they can perform. Services provided at the Press Section of the Department both for the media and the delegations should be further improved. The Department should continue to co-operate closely with and provide assistance to the United Nations Correspondents Association.

52. The Department of Public Information should review, and report thereon to the Committee on Information at its substantive session in 1985, the present system of charging the Member States and the media for video tapes, audio tapes and news photographs of important United Nations events such as General Assembly and Security Council debates with a view to reducing the present prohibitive costs of those materials so as to enable the media in the Member States, particularly in the developing countries, to give wider publicity to such events.

53. The interim report of the Secretary-General entitled "The Department of Public Information as the Focal Point for the Formulation and Implementation of Information Activities of the United Nations" should be noted and the Secretary-General should be requested to submit his final report on the subject to the General Assembly at its thirty-ninth session.

54. The operations of the Non-Governmental Liaison Services (Geneva and New York) as inter-agency projects on international development issues reaching specific target audiences in the industrialized countries should be continued on a stable financial basis through the United Nations participation in those services. The Secretary-General should be requested once again to urge all the specialized agencies to make long-term contributions to the financing of those services, thereby stressing their inter-agency character.

55. The Joint United Nations Information Committee, as the essential instrument for inter-agency co-ordination and co-operation in the field of public information, should be further strengthened and given more responsibility for the public information activities of the entire United Nations system.

56. Since *Development Forum* is the only inter-agency publication of the United Nations system that concentrates on development issues, the Secretary-General should, while continuing his efforts to secure a sound and independent financial basis for the periodical, make such arrangements through the regular budget as necessary to ensure its continued publication. All the specialized agencies and other organizations of the United Nations system should be urged to contribute to the financing of this system-wide publication, thereby recognizing its inter-agency character.

57. The Secretary-General should continue to ensure that *Development Forum* retains its editorial policy of intellectual independence, thus enabling this publication to continue to serve as a world-wide forum in which diverse opinions on issues related to economic and social development can be freely expressed.

58. The Secretary-General should be encouraged to continue and intensify his efforts to explore all possibilities outside the regular budget of the United Nations of securing the adequate resources for the continuation of the *World Newspaper Supplement* project.

59. The World Disarmament Campaign should give full consideration to the role of mass media as the most effective way to promote in world public opinion a climate of understanding, confidence and co-operation conducive to peace and disarmament, the enhancement of human rights and development. Within the World Disarmament Campaign and Disarmament Week, the Department of Public Information should fulfil the role assigned to it by the General Assembly by utilizing its expertise and resources in public information to ensure its maximum effectiveness.

General Assembly resolution 39/98 A

14 December 1984   Meeting 100   132-6-7 (recorded vote)

Approved by SPC (A/39/714) by recorded vote (108-6-7), 10 December (meeting 51); draft by Egypt, for Group of 77 (A/SPC/39/L.20/Rev.1); agenda item 74.

Financial implications. 5th Committee, A/39/826; S-G, A/C.5/39/86, A/SPC/39/L.31 & Add.1.

Meeting numbers. GA 39th session: SPC 19-21, 23, 25-30, 50, 51; 5th Committee 49; plenary 100.

Recorded vote in Assembly as follows:

In favour: Afghanistan, Algeria, Angola, Argentina, Austria, Bahamas, Bahrain, Bangladesh, Barbados, Belize, Benin, Bhutan, Bolivia, Botswana, Brazil, Brunei Darussalam, Bulgaria, Burkina Faso, Burma, Burundi, Byelorussian SSR, Cameroon, Cape Verde, Central African Republic, Chad, Chile, China, Colombia, Congo, Costa Rica, Cuba, Cyprus, Czechoslovakia, Democratic Kampuchea, Democratic Yemen, Denmark, Djibouti, Dominican Republic, Ecuador, Egypt, El Salvador, Equatorial Guinea, Ethiopia, Fiji, Finland, Gabon, Gambia, German Democratic Republic, Ghana, Greece, Guatemala, Guinea, Guinea-Bissau, Guyana, Haiti, Honduras, Hungary, Iceland, India, Indonesia, Iraq, Ireland, Ivory Coast, Jamaica, Jordan, Kenya, Kuwait, Lao People's Democratic Republic, Lebanon, Lesotho, Liberia, Libyan Arab Jamahiriya, Madagascar, Malawi, Malaysia, Maldives, Mali, Malta, Mauritania, Mauritius, Mexico, Mongolia, Morocco,

Mozambique, Nepal, Nicaragua, Niger, Nigeria, Norway, Oman, Pakistan, Panama, Papua New Guinea, Paraguay, Peru, Philippines, Poland, Portugal, Qatar, Romania, Rwanda, Sao Tome and Principe, Saudi Arabia, Senegal, Seychelles, Sierra Leone, Singapore, Somalia, Spain, Sri Lanka, Sudan, Suriname, Sweden, Syrian Arab Republic, Thailand, Togo, Trinidad and Tobago, Tunisia, Turkey, Uganda, Ukrainian SSR, USSR, United Arab Emirates, United Republic of Tanzania, Uruguay, Venezuela, Viet Nam, Yemen, Yugoslavia, Zaire, Zambia, Zimbabwe.

Against: Germany, Federal Republic of, Israel, Japan, Netherlands, United Kingdom, United States.

Abstaining: Australia, Belgium, Canada, France, Italy, Luxembourg, New Zealand.

Explaining their votes, Canada, France, the Federal Republic of Germany, Japan, the Netherlands, the United Kingdom and the United States pointed out that the text failed to mention a 1983 UNESCO resolution which characterized a new world information order as an evolving and continuous process. Italy could not support the text's definition of that order. In addition, Canada, the Federal Republic of Germany, the United Kingdom and the United States found difficulty with paragraph 10 which they felt contradicted the programme budget implications; the latter three States and Japan also regretted the text's politicization. The Federal Republic of Germany felt that its disagreement with certain aspects of UNESCO's work was not adequately reflected in paragraph 1, and said paragraph 9 was unacceptable. Israel rejected that paragraph as having nothing to do with information and described the draft as parochial and unbalanced. The United Kingdom added that, because of its intention of giving notice to withdraw from UNESCO, it had difficulty with the paragraph reaffirming blanket support for that organization. The United States also felt that paragraphs dealing only with the question of Namibia and the needs of the Palestinian people, to the exclusion of other urgent international concerns, diverted attention from the text's proper subject. Australia expressed reservations about paragraphs 4 and 10.

Albania's non-participation in the vote was due to a number of reservations, including the text's mention of the Final Act of the 1975 Helsinki Conference on Security and Co-operation in Europe which it said was a farce perpetrated by the super-Powers.

Barbados, while voting in favour, expressed concern about implementation of paragraph 1, hoping that the Assembly's affirmation therein of its 1983 resolution[6] would further strengthen the work of the Caribbean Unit of the Radio Service of DPI. Benin, Colombia, Ecuador and Malaysia regretted the absence of consensus. The USSR said it would take due account of the draft's financial implications. Finland, on behalf of the Nordic countries, Portugal and Turkey expressed reservations concerning certain aspects and omissions in the text.

In many other 1984 resolutions, the Assembly called for efforts by the United Nations and others to disseminate information on specific subjects, including disarmament, *apartheid*, Israeli–South African relations, Palestine, Namibia, cultural development, racial discrimination, human rights and decolonization (for details, see relevant chapters).

DPI activities

In 1984, DPI continued to act as a focal point for formulating and implementing United Nations information activities, enhancing the work of and co-ordinating the various media at its disposal, including radio, visual and publications services, and information centres (for details, see below under respective headings). The Department also played an active role in ensuring the effectiveness of the World Disarmament Campaign and Disarmament Week (see p. 90).

With regard to administrative questions, the Secretariat reported in May[11] on the progress made over the previous four years concerning the distribution of staff by nationality in posts subject to geographical distribution in DPI. Statistics breaking down the total staff into distribution by region showed that the greatest gain in overall percentage of staff and in staff at the Senior Officer level and above had been achieved by Africa.

Re-emphasizing the role of DPI as the focal point of United Nations information activities, the Committee on Information recommended[2] that they should be carried out in conformity with the United Nations Charter, the aspiration for a new world information and communication order and the consensus of relevant resolutions adopted at the 1980 session of the UNESCO General Conference. DPI should promote an informed understanding of the United Nations as delineated in the 1979 Assembly resolution on the International Convention against the Taking of Hostages,[12] 1981[13] and 1983[14] resolutions on measures to prevent international terrorism, and 1982[15] and 1983[16] resolutions on protecting diplomatic and consular missions and representatives. The Committee stressed the need for DPI to maintain its editorial independence and objectivity.

DPI was urged to support the Preparatory Committee for the Fortieth (1985) Anniversary of the United Nations, to monitor important meetings of the non-aligned countries and regional intergovernmental organizations on information questions, to utilize the daily dispatches of the Non-Aligned News Agencies Pool, and to assist it, in co-operation with UNESCO, in preparing an integrated communication network plan, meetings on data and communication exchange and for observance of 1985 as the Year of Communication. Other suggested co-operative efforts included a 1985 workshop on modern technology and a project to standardize teaching methods and produce manuals for the Pool's training centres.

DPI was also advised to allocate a week of its annual training programme for journalists from developing countries for on-the-spot acquaintance with utilization of information on the United Nations.

The Committee called for adequate use of official Assembly languages, wider coverage of United Nations economic, social and development activities, and improvement of DPI data-collection procedures, daily press releases and weekly news summaries; it also called for DPI to fulfil its role assigned by the Assembly concerning the use of the mass media to promote the World Disarmament Campaign and Disarmament Week. With regard to DPI staff, the Secretary-General was urged to increase representation of underrepresented countries and to report to the Committee at its 1985 session. (For Committee action on other matters, see below under the relevant subject headings.)

Radio and Visual Services Division

Various aspects of the work of DPI's Radio and Visual Services Division were the subject of two 1984 reports by the Secretary-General, submitted in response to December 1983 requests by the General Assembly.[6]

In May 1984, the Secretary-General presented to the Committee on Information a report[17] on the viability of a world-wide United Nations short-wave network. The report assessed possible transmission schedules and frequencies, outlined staffing, construction, equipment and operational cost requirements, and discussed alternative approaches. In its conclusions, the report noted that, while an attempt had been made to be as comprehensive as possible, gaps in information remained, particularly with regard to the potential audience. Serious doubts were also expressed regarding the viability of a United Nations world news service. Therefore, the report could not go beyond general statements emphasizing the growing popularity of short-wave broadcasting and the expansion by established broadcasters of their activities. Although those trends pointed to a significant potential for short-wave broadcasting by the United Nations, no empirical data were available to support such a conclusion. As a way of obtaining sufficient listener response data for judging the viability of a short-wave network, the Secretary-General suggested that current United Nations short-wave broadcasts be transmitted on a daily basis throughout the year over leased transmitters. That course of action, however, was not feasible within available resources.

The Committee on Information, in its annual report to the Assembly,[2] recommended that, pending the possible acquisition by the United Nations of its own short-wave radio network, the Secretary-General should follow up on the question, inform the Committee on the working of such a system and present an evaluation report on daily short-wave radio broadcasts from Headquarters.

In a September report,[18] the Secretary-General addressed aspects of United Nations radio programming not considered by the Committee in 1984. With regard to Portuguese-language programming in the African Unit of the Radio Service, the Secretary-General reported that his 1983 proposals[19] had been fully implemented during 1984, with the recruitment of a radio producer and initiation of weekly news and feature programmes for the Portuguese-speaking regions of Africa. The Asian Unit had begun the production of a weekly programme in Bengali and a monthly programme in Indonesian, while seeking qualified candidates for two newly created writer/producer posts. Concerning co-operation with the Union of National Radio and Television Organizations of Africa and its member radio stations, DPI continued to explore ways of expanding the use of United Nations radio programmes by national broadcasting organizations in five African countries.

The Committee on Information recommended[2] that the Secretary-General strengthen and expand the Middle East/Arabic Unit as the producer of Arabic television and radio programmes and report the results to the Committee's 1985 session. DPI was also requested to report at that session on the current system of charging Member States and the media for video and audio tapes and news photographs of important United Nations events, with a view to reducing costs of those materials so as to enable the media, particularly in developing countries, to give such events wider publicity.

The Committee's recommendations were approved by the Assembly in resolution 39/98 A.

UN information centres and services

Pursuant to the Secretary-General's 1983 suggestions on United Nations information centres and relevant recommendations of the Committee on Information,[20] the Secretariat submitted to the Committee, in May 1984,[21] a note containing proposals aimed at increasing the centres' effectiveness within DPI's existing resources.

With regard to enhancing centres' discretionary authority in implementing their work programmes, the suggested measures included updating the Information Policy and Operations Manual; improving the centres' reports to Headquarters and co-ordination with substantive departments in the Secretariat; and better adaptation of information materials to regional needs. To improve the centres' flexibility in connection with special United Nations observances, it was proposed to convene a meeting of relevant departmental and unit representatives at the beginning of each year. Centre directors were also encouraged to co-operate at the local level with representatives of other United Nations agencies, while a DPI staff member was to ensure interdepartmental co-ordination at Headquarters. The problem of delays in getting information from Headquarters to centres, though not totally within DPI control, could be solved through improved co-ordination with the cable office and the pouch service and assignment of DPI staff to expedite action by substantive departments and respective divisions in DPI. The importance of closer co-operation at the interdepartmental and inter-agency levels was emphasized as a way of avoiding duplication in communication with the centres.

Regarding personnel matters, the Secretariat note pointed out that the level of centre directors was under constant review, and three P-5 and three P-4 posts were reclassified to D-1 and P-5 levels, respectively, in the proposed programme budget for 1984-1985. In an effort to improve the position of supporting staff, a national information officer category was established in 22 centres. With a view to increasing contacts between centre directors and DPI at Headquarters, senior DPI staff as well as centre directors were encouraged to visit the centres while on official business or home leave. The note stated that DPI maintained an appropriate level of mobility of the centres' Professional staff; in relation to the training of newly recruited reference and information assistants, a review of the training programmes was to be completed in 1984.

With regard to the centres' material and financial resources, the Secretariat reported, *inter alia*, that $100,000 had been provided for the installation of telex equipment at 10 additional centres; greater inter-agency sharing of office equipment in the field was encouraged; and several steps were planned to improve directors' capacity to travel, translate and produce information material and organize seminars and exhibits within available resources.

Responding to the Assembly's December 1983 recommendations,[6] the Secretary-General reported, in September,[18] that negotiations had been initiated with Indonesia on the reopening of the United Nations Information Centre at Jakarta—which had been closed since 1965[22]—and that the appointments of full-time directors for the centres at Yaoundé, Cameroon, and Bujumbura, Burundi, were under active consideration.

An activity at the United Nations Information Centre at Harare, Zimbabwe, was the subject of a 13 April letter by Israel.[23] Referring to an exhibition of the Palestine Liberation Organization held at the Centre in January, Israel protested at the staging of an exhibit on United Nations premises containing what it said was pictorial material which was offensive to Israel and those of the Jewish faith.

It noted, however, that the Centre had had no official involvement with the project.

In its recommendations to the Assembly,[2] the Committee on Information stressed the need for centres to give adequate services in local languages, to assist local information media and to intensify communication exchange with education communities, particularly in promoting a new world information and communication order and in areas of interest to host countries. It also suggested that the Secretary-General be requested to consider proposals on the opening of centres in Benin and Poland. While recognizing the distinction between development activities and the centres' intrinsic functions, the Committee urged centres to give greater publicity to United Nations activities for development. The Committee also felt that the Secretary-General should be encouraged to implement proposals made by the Secretariat on the centres' effectiveness,[21] within existing DPI resources.

The Assembly, in resolution 39/98 A, approved the Committee's recommendations and requested the Secretary-General to consider the proposals of Benin and Poland on the opening of information centres there and to report to the Assembly in 1985.

Speaking in the Special Political Committee, Benin pointed out that it had made a request, rather than a proposal, for the opening of an information centre in the country.

Programme evaluation

Following a 1983 recommendation of the Committee on Information,[24] the Secretary-General submitted, in May 1984, a report[25] on the establishment of systematic procedures for monitoring and evaluation of DPI activities. He reported progress in simplifying data-collection forms and obtaining data for the monitoring system through improved co-operation with the Radio Service and major DPI publications and better response from information centres. Better logging systems had been devised and consultations were under way to computerize the growing data base. The data gathered through the monitoring system had greatly facilitated the preparation of the Programme Performance Report for the 1982-1983 biennium to the Committee for Programme and Co-ordination (CPC).

As recommended in May 1983 by CPC,[24] DPI began examining the distribution of photo materials and radio tapes to determine and, ultimately, enhance their effectiveness. The results of the study, involving an inventory of all radio programmes and canvassing of DPI producers and radio stations utilizing United Nations tapes, were to be summarized in a final report. In an effort to ensure a better use of available resources by reviewing its current activities, DPI continued consultations with the Joint Inspection Unit (JIU).

The Committee on Information[2] stressed that the Secretary-General should continue efforts to develop a system for monitoring and evaluating DPI's effectiveness and to strengthen DPI's Planning, Programming and Evaluation Unit. DPI was requested to provide in its reports to the Committee and the Assembly more adequate information on the Department's output, as well as the costs, target audiences, effectiveness, and priorities of current and future activities.

The Committee's recommendations were approved by the Assembly in resolution 39/98 A.

Co-ordination in the UN system

JUNIC activities. Co-ordination of information activities in the United Nations system remained the responsibility of the inter-agency Joint United Nations Information Committee (JUNIC), which held its eleventh session in Paris from 3 to 6 April 1984.[26] At the session, JUNIC discussed the work of the Committee on Information in 1983 and considered subsequent developments in the Assembly on questions relating to information. It also reviewed a 1984 DPI report to the Administrative Committee on Co-ordination (ACC) on enhancement of United Nations public information activities. With regard to reportage missions, JUNIC requested its secretariat to provide information to all members on such joint projects and to establish a general roster of journalists who had taken part in media events organized by United Nations agencies. After considering a report of its task force on international expositions, JUNIC decided to inform the authorities of Expo '85 (Tsukuba, Japan) of its intention to participate in the event as a unified system, and also agreed to participate at Expo '86 (Vancouver, Canada) subject to satisfactory financial and other arrangements.

Regarding international conferences and years, JUNIC endorsed recommendations of its two task forces for International Youth Year (1985) (see ECONOMIC AND SOCIAL QUESTIONS, Chapter XX) and the 1985 World Conference to Review and Appraise the Achievements of the United Nations Decade for Women (see ECONOMIC AND SOCIAL QUESTIONS, Chapter XIX). The Committee agreed to co-operate actively with the August 1984 International Conference on Population (see ECONOMIC AND SOCIAL QUESTIONS, Chapter XIV) and the July 1984 International Conference on Assistance to Refugees in Africa (see ECONOMIC AND SOCIAL QUESTIONS, Chapter XXI), and considered reports relating to the activities of ITU, UNIDO and the World Food Council.

JUNIC renewed the call to United Nations entities to help finance *Development Forum* as the only United Nations inter-agency publication concentrating on development issues, and requested that a conceptual paper on the role, function and place of the Non-Governmental Liaison Services (NGLS) in New York and Geneva be submitted to its 1985 session. Regarding audio-visual matters, JUNIC noted that "The Message from the South" series, scheduled for completion in the third quarter of 1984, in addition to being broadcast on television, would be available to educational groups and non-governmental organizations and to all members of JUNIC through world-wide non-commercial distribution rights acquired by DPI. A series of 24 half-hour television programmes on the general theme of disarmament was planned for completion by the third quarter of 1985. JUNIC recommended the continued publishing of *Playback*, a DPI bulletin on audio-visual matters, welcomed the offer by the DPI Radio and Visual Services Division to compile a central registry of all United Nations film and videotape materials and requested another meeting of the Audio-Visual Working Group. With regard to a survey of JUNIC members' attitudes towards film and television, the Committee said the exercise had produced useful results. It also favoured co-production arrangements with outside producers, but considered undesirable a centralized JUNIC production service, consolidated JUNIC film missions and centralized placement of its visual products.

JUNIC also considered a report of its Working Group on Development Education, agreeing to have host organizations chair the Group on a rotating basis and to designate NGLS (Geneva) as its substantive secretariat. On other matters, JUNIC endorsed the introductory section of its plan of action for 1984-1985, authorizing the secretariat to finalize it on the basis of the session's results and future contributions from members. JUNIC also decided to continue to review the possibilities of assisting the *World Newspaper Supplement* project.

Following 1983 recommendations of the Committee on Information and CPC,[27] JUNIC submitted, in May 1984, for consideration by both Committees, a consolidated report[28] on its programme and activities. The report described the philosophy behind joint planning of public information activities within the United Nations system, highlighted the discussions at its April session, and outlined its plan of action for 1984-1985. Special emphasis was placed on assessing various aspects of the *Development Forum* project. With regard to a possible sales policy, JUNIC came to the following conclusions: a single-copy charge would not be financially beneficial; any charging policy would seriously reduce the effectiveness of the publication; charging for bulk supplies to certain categories of readers offered the best approach; and, on balance, the goal of reaching a reader of value to the United Nations was more important than obtaining payments.

Report of the Secretary-General. Responding to a 1983 request of the Committee on Information that he study the full implications of DPI's role as a focal point, the Secretary-General reported in May 1984[29] that the situation had remained substantially as described in his 1982 report to CPC.[30] The Secretary-General noted that, in the mean time, he was setting up a Secretariat-wide task force to propose appropriate steps and would present recommendations to the Committee on Information upon completing the review.

CPC consideration. After considering in May 1984[31] the report on JUNIC's programme and activities,[28] CPC requested that future reports should contain more information on the orientation, mandates and degree of co-ordination among United Nations organizations. In its view, the report could have reflected more completely the activities contained in the JUNIC plan of action for 1984-1985, and also could have highlighted all of the measures taken to ensure their effectiveness. CPC stressed a number of other specific points, including the relationship between disarmament and development, the campaign to improve awareness of development issues, the need for a continuing review of a *Development Forum* sales policy, and the problem of *apartheid*.

Action by the Committee on Information. The Committee on Information[2] recommended that JUNIC should be further strengthened and given more responsibility for the public information activities of the entire United Nations system. Noting that *Development Forum* was the only system-wide publication concentrating on development issues, the Committee felt that the Secretary-General should provide for its continuing publication through the regular budget and ensure its editorial policy of intellectual independence. Other United Nations entities were urged to contribute to its financing. The Committee also recommended that the Secretary-General should actively explore possibilities outside the United Nations regular budget to secure resources for the continuation of the *World Newspaper Supplement* project.

GENERAL ASSEMBLY ACTION

The General Assembly, in resolution 39/98 A, approved the Committee's recommendations, and, in resolution 39/98 B, noted with satisfaction the co-operation between the United Nations, UNESCO and all other organizations within the system, particularly ITU, FAO and UPU.

UN publications policy

With approximately 4,000 titles (including periodicals) produced each year, publications were an important programme activity of the United Nations system in 1984.

JIU report. At the request of several participating organizations, JIU prepared a report on United Nations publications policy and practice, transmitted to the General Assembly by the Secretary-General in May 1984.[32] Based largely on responses to a questionnaire sent to all JIU participating organizations, United Nations regional commissions and a number of autonomous institutions, the report outlined the main features of United Nations publishing and publications policy and practice, examined specific issues related to sales and free distribution, the role of the director of publications, management information and quantity of published material, and discussed possibilities for inter-agency co-operation. In its recommendations, JIU stressed the importance of timeliness of publications and said that departments and units seeking permission to produce publications should be required to justify a production and distribution schedule. If a time-frame could not be met, services of a commercial publisher should be sought to have the publication appear on time. JIU also emphasized that each publication from the earliest stage should be directed to a specific and identifiable readership, which should be the guideline for the whole process of writing and production.

On the question of sales and free distribution, JIU recommended that approval of any publication should be based on proper information on the prospective readership, the marketing concept and sales plans; that governing bodies should, at intervals of two to three years, test the validity of the grounds for publication; and that no publication should serve merely as proof that an activity had taken place. With regard to quality control, it emphasized the role of directors of publications, whose professional talents should be encouraged, scope of action enlarged and status recognized. Noting that some United Nations organizations lacked adequate information on important aspects of publishing, JIU specifically stressed the need for appropriate accounting systems to enable them to distinguish between the direct costs of publications and those of documents. It also called for a redistribution of publications resources to allocate more money for marketing, promotion and distribution. Governing bodies should demand stricter controls on what was published and for whom and consider budgetary arrangements to redress the imbalance between production and diffusion. With regard to inter-agency co-operation, JIU recommended that ACC invite JUNIC to advise on the public information aspects of publications and suggested that resources of DPI and its information centres could be used for promoting United Nations publications.

Commenting on the JIU report in August,[33] the Secretary-General pointed out a number of difficulties in implementing its recommendations, including: the United Nations had its own facilities for internal reproduction of publications at a reduced cost and therefore could not be compared to a small agency contracting out such services; publications in the United Nations system were accorded a relatively low priority in view of the more pressing need to produce documentation; and various categories of United Nations publications, because of their specific characteristics, did not lend themselves entirely to the approaches advocated in the report. In detailed comments on the specific recommendations of JIU, the Secretary-General demonstrated how those basic considerations affected United Nations publications policy and practice.

The usefulness of the JIU recommendations was stressed by ACC in its comments, transmitted to the Assembly by the Secretary-General in October.[34] ACC based its observations on responses to the report from various United Nations organizations.

The JIU report, together with the comments of the Secretary-General and ACC, was also considered by the Advisory Committee on Administrative and Budgetary Questions (ACABQ), which submitted its views to the Assembly in October.[35] ACABQ also stressed the generally positive reaction to JIU's recommendations, noting that a number of them were already being implemented. It suggested that the medium-term plan for 1984-1989[36] should serve as the background for their implementation and offered comments on selected issues raised by JIU.

With regard to sales and free distribution, ACABQ recommended that: the Secretary-General should periodically canvass recipients of free publications and submit the results to the relevant intergovernmental bodies; a sales staff increase should be considered through the ACC machinery; decisions on the appropriateness of recurrent publications should initially be taken by intergovernmental bodies during examination of their work programmes; marketing and sales considerations might not be the determining factor in approving a publication; governing bodies should periodically review the publications programme on the basis of readership and distribution data available; and the Secretary-General should review the pricing policy to enhance sales through a more realistic pricing formula. In relation to quality control, ACABQ concurred with the Secretary-General's suggestion to set up publications committees in main office locations and large author departments and his call for increased co-operation among bookstores of specialized agencies, regional commissions and information centres. It also agreed

with JIU that statistical and other information on the costs of publications should be made available.

GENERAL ASSEMBLY ACTION

The Assembly, in section II of resolution 39/242, concurred with ACABQ's recommendations and requested the Secretary-General to implement them.

REFERENCES
[1]YUN 1978, p. 1043, GA res. 33/115 C, 18 Dec. 1978. [2]A/39/21. [3]YUN 1983, p. 363, GA res. 38/82 A, 15 Dec. 1983. [4]A/39/497. [5]YUN 1983, p. 366. [6]*Ibid.*, GA res. 38/82 B, 15 Dec. 1983. [7]A/AC.198/81. [8]A/39/131-S/16414 & Corr.1. [9]A/39/133-S/16417. [10]A/39/139-S/16430. [11]A/AC.198/80. [12]YUN 1979, p. 1143, GA res. 34/146, 17 Dec. 1979. [13]YUN 1981, p. 1221, GA res. 36/109, 10 Dec. 1981. [14]YUN 1983, p. 1113, GA res. 38/130, 19 Dec. 1983. [15]YUN 1982, p. 1381, GA res. 37/108, 16 Dec. 1982. [16]YUN 1983, p. 1117, GA res. 38/136, 19 Dec. 1983. [17]A/AC.198/74. [18]A/39/479. [19]YUN 1983, p. 379. [20]*Ibid.*, p. 381. [21]A/AC.198/75. [22]YUN 1964, p. 190. [23]A/39/180 & Corr.1. [24]YUN 1983, p. 383. [25]A/AC.198/76. [26]ACC/1984/15. [27]YUN 1983, p. 385. [28]A/AC.198/77. [29]A/AC.198/82. [30]YUN 1982, p. 575. [31]A/39/38. [32]A/39/239. [33]A/39/239/Add.1 & Add.1/Corr.1. [34]A/39/239/Add.2. [35]A/39/602. [36]YUN 1982, p. 1433.

PUBLICATION
The New World Information and Communication Order: A Selective Bibliography (ST/LIB/SER.B/35), Sales No. E/F.84.I.15.

Radiation effects

The study of the levels, effects and risks of ionizing radiation from all sources continued in 1984 to be the main concern of the United Nations Scientific Committee on the Effects of Atomic Radiation. At its thirty-third session (Vienna, Austria, 25-29 June),[1] the Committee focused on such topics as radiation-induced cancer, developmental effects induced by irradiation *in utero*, early effects caused in man by high radiation doses, and hereditary effects of radiation in man and other mammalian species. Attention was also given to natural sources of radiation, exposures resulting from nuclear explosions and the associated production cycles, the radiological impact of the nuclear fuel cycle, and exposures due to medical uses of radiation and radioisotopes. It also held general discussions on evaluating, measuring and expressing the radiation-induced detriment to health. Stressing that the completeness of its conclusions rested on data produced by others, the Committee requested increased assistance from United Nations Member States, the specialized agencies, including WHO and IAEA, and other scientific organizations. The Committee also expressed appreciation to UNEP for its support, thereby enabling the Committee to carry out its mandate.

On 14 December 1984, the General Assembly, on the recommendation of the Special Political Committee, adopted resolution 39/94 without vote.

Effects of atomic radiation

The General Assembly,

Recalling its resolution 913(X) of 3 December 1955, by which it established the United Nations Scientific Committee on the Effects of Atomic Radiation, and its subsequent resolutions on the subject, including resolution 38/78 of 15 December 1983, by which it, *inter alia*, requested the Scientific Committee to continue its work,

Taking note with appreciation of the report of the United Nations Scientific Committee on the Effects of Atomic Radiation,

Reaffirming the desirability of the Scientific Committee continuing its work,

Concerned about the potentially harmful effects on present and future generations, resulting from the levels of radiation to which man is exposed,

Conscious of the continued need to examine and compile information about atomic and ionizing radiation and to analyse its effects on man and his environment,

Taking note of the decision of the Scientific Committee to submit shorter reports with scientific supporting documents on the specialized topics mentioned in its report as soon as the relevant studies are completed,

1. *Commends* the United Nations Scientific Committee on the Effects of Atomic Radiation for the valuable contribution it has been making in the course of the past twenty-nine years, since its inception, to wider knowledge and understanding of the levels, effects and risks of atomic radiation and for fulfilling its original mandate with scientific authority and independence of judgement;

2. *Notes with satisfaction* the continued and growing scientific co-operation between the Scientific Committee and the United Nations Environment Programme;

3. *Requests* the Scientific Committee to continue its work, including its important co-ordinating activities, to increase knowledge of the levels, effects and risks of ionizing radiation from all sources;

4. *Endorses* the Scientific Committee's intentions and plans for its future activities of scientific review and assessment on behalf of the General Assembly;

5. *Requests* the Scientific Committee to continue at its next session the review of the important problems in the field of radiation and to report thereon to the General Assembly at its fortieth session;

6. *Requests* the United Nations Environment Programme to continue providing support for the effective conduct of the Scientific Committee's work and for the dissemination of its findings to the General Assembly, the scientific community and the public;

7. *Expresses its appreciation* for the assistance rendered to the Scientific Committee by Member States, the specialized agencies, the International Atomic Energy Agency and non-governmental organizations, and invites them to increase their co-operation in this field;

8. *Invites* Member States and the organizations of the United Nations system and non-governmental organizations concerned to provide further relevant data about doses, effects and risks from various sources of radiation, which would greatly help in the preparation of the Scientific Committee's future reports to the General Assembly.

General Assembly resolution 39/94

14 December 1984   Meeting 100   Adopted without vote

Approved by SPC (A/39/609) without vote, 9 October (meeting 4); 26-nation draft (A/SPC/39/L.2); agenda item 70.

Sponsors: Argentina, Australia, Austria, Canada, Chile, Colombia, Czechoslovakia, Denmark, Ecuador, Egypt, France, Germany, Federal Republic of, Indonesia, Japan, Netherlands, New Zealand, Nigeria, Oman, Peru, Poland, Sri Lanka, Sweden, USSR, United Kingdom, United States, Uruguay.

Meeting numbers. GA 39th session: SPC 3, 4; plenary 100.

REFERENCE

[1]A/39/341.

Antarctica

Report of the Secretary-General. In October 1984, the Secretary-General submitted to the General Assembly a report[1] prepared in response to its December 1983 request[2] for a comprehensive and factual study of all aspects of Antarctica, taking fully into account the 1959 Antarctic Treaty system and other relevant factors. The study, examining physical, legal, political, economic and scientific aspects of Antarctica, was largely based on information provided by Member States, United Nations entities and other international organizations, following the Secretary-General's request for assistance. As of 29 October 1984, he had received replies from 54 States, whose views were presented in Part II of the report. The Secretary-General noted that most of those replies had been received during the final drafting of the analytical part of the report and some States had indicated that their replies were of an introductory or general nature. A number of important international organizations conducting research on the subject had requested more time to prepare substantive information. The Secretary-General suggested that such data could be used in future undertakings on Antarctica.

Communications. By a letter of 8 October,[3] India transmitted the text of the final communiqué adopted by an October 1984 Meeting of Ministers for Foreign Affairs and Heads of Delegation of Non-Aligned Countries to the 1984 session of the General Assembly, by which it welcomed the December 1983 Assembly resolution on Antarctica[2] and expressed hope that the study and the discussions at the 1984 session would contribute to widening international co-operation on that continent. By a letter of 29 November,[4] France transmitted a communiqué of that date by its Ministry of Foreign Affairs, reaffirming, on the occasion of the twenty-fifth anniversary of the Antarctica Treaty, France's intention to abide by that agreement. Communications in connection with the anniversary were also transmitted by Belgium, on 3 December,[5] and Norway, on 11 December.[6] In statements by their respective Foreign Ministries on 1 December, Belgium and Norway expressed support for the Treaty as a valuable instrument of international co-operation.

GENERAL ASSEMBLY ACTION

On 17 December 1984, the General Assembly, on the recommendation of the First Committee, adopted resolution 39/152 without vote.

Question of Antarctica

The General Assembly,

Recalling its resolution 38/77 of 15 December 1983,

Having considered the item entitled "Question of Antarctica",

Taking note of the study on the question of Antarctica,

Conscious of the increasing international awareness of and interest in Antarctica,

Bearing in mind the Antarctic Treaty and the significance of the system it has developed,

Taking into account the debate on this item at its thirty-ninth session,

Convinced of the advantages of a better knowledge of Antarctica,

Affirming the conviction that, in the interest of all mankind, Antarctica should continue forever to be used exclusively for peaceful purposes and that it should not become the scene or object of international discord,

Recalling the relevant paragraphs of the Economic Declaration adopted at the Seventh Conference of Heads of State or Government of Non-Aligned Countries, held at New Delhi from 7 to 12 March 1983,

1. *Expresses its appreciation* to the Secretary-General for the study on the question of Antarctica;

2. *Decides* to include in the provisional agenda of its fortieth session the item entitled "Question of Antarctica".

General Assembly resolution 39/152

17 December 1984   Meeting 102   Adopted without vote

Approved by First Committee (A/39/756) without vote, 30 November (meeting 55); 12-nation draft (A/C.1/39/L.83); agenda item 66.

Sponsors: Antigua and Barbuda, Bangladesh, Brunei Darussalam, Indonesia, Malaysia, Mali, Oman, Pakistan, Philippines, Singapore, Sri Lanka, Thailand.

Meeting numbers. GA 39th session; 1st Committee 50, 52-55; plenary 102.

REFERENCES

[1]A/39/583 (Part I) & Corr.1-3; A/39/583 (Part II) & Corr.1, vols. I-III. [2]YUN 1983, p. 387, GA res. 38/77, 15 Dec. 1983. [3]A/39/560-S/16773. [4]A/C.1/39/6. [5]A/39/731. [6]A/39/834.

Chapter XI

Institutional machinery

With the admission of Brunei Darussalam, United Nations membership rose to 159 in 1984.

The Security Council, in addition to its agenda, continued to examine ways of enhancing its role as an instrument for the maintenance of international peace and security, concentrating on those aspects of its work designed to promote agreement on practical measures to strengthen its effectiveness.

The General Assembly resumed and concluded its thirty-eighth session in 1984. It held the major part of its thirty-ninth session, considering 123 items of its 143-item agenda; the remainder were to be considered in 1985.

Missions of good offices and other diplomatic contacts were an important aspect of the Secretary-General's political activities during the year, with the focus on Afghanistan, Cyprus, the Falkland Islands (Malvinas), Iran-Iraq and Kampuchea. In his annual report to the Assembly on the Organization's work (p. 3), he emphasized the need to use international institutional machinery effectively.

Co-operation between the United Nations and intergovernmental organizations was the subject of five Assembly resolutions.

Preparations continued for the observance of the fortieth anniversary of the United Nations in 1985.

Topics related to this chapter. Africa: co-operation between OAU and the UN system. Regional economic and social activities: Africa—co-operation between the Southern African Development Co-ordination Conference and the United Nations. Institutional arrangements: Intergovernmental Bureau for Informatics; organizational structure—General Assembly Second Committee. Intergovernmental organizations and international law: draft standard rules of procedure for conferences. Treaties and agreements: co-operation between the United Nations and the Asian-African Legal Consultative Committee. Other administrative and management questions: calendar of meetings.

UN Members

In 1984, the membership of the United Nations rose to 159, with the admission of Brunei Darus-

salam by the General Assembly on 26 September (resolution 39/1), as recommended by the Security Council (resolution 548(1984)).

Brunei Darussalam

Brunei Darussalam, on the island of Borneo in South-East Asia and a former Territory administered by the United Kingdom, having attained independence on 1 January 1984, applied for membership by a letter of 8 February.[1]

SECURITY COUNCIL ACTION

On 24 February, the Security Council unanimously adopted resolution 548(1984).

The Security Council,

Having examined the application of Brunei Darussalam for admission to the United Nations,

Recommends to the General Assembly that Brunei Darussalam should be admitted to membership in the United Nations.

Security Council resolution 548(1984)

24 February 1984   Meeting 2518   Adopted unanimously

Draft by Committee on the Admission of New Members (S/16367).
Meeting numbers. SC: 2517, 2518.

GENERAL ASSEMBLY ACTION

On 26 September, acting on the recommendation of the Security Council, as transmitted by its President on 24 February,[2] the General Assembly adopted resolution 39/1 by acclamation.

Admission of Brunei Darussalam to membership in the United Nations

The General Assembly,

Having received the recommendation of the Security Council of 24 February 1984 that Brunei Darussalam should be admitted to membership in the United Nations,

Having considered the application for membership of Brunei Darussalam,

Decides to admit Brunei Darussalam to membership in the United Nations.

General Assembly resolution 39/1

21 September 1984   Meeting 3   Adopted by acclamation

114-nation draft (A/39/L.1/Rev.1 & Rev.1/Add.1); agenda item 19.
Sponsors: Algeria, Antigua and Barbuda, Australia, Austria, Bahamas, Bahrain, Bangladesh, Barbados, Belgium, Belize, Bhutan, Bolivia, Brazil, Burkina Faso, Burma, Burundi, Cameroon, Canada, Chad, Chile, China, Colombia, Costa Rica, Cyprus, Democratic Kampuchea, Democratic Yemen, Denmark, Djibouti, Dominica, Dominican Republic, Ecuador, Egypt, El Salvador, Equatorial Guinea, Fiji, Finland, France, Gambia, Germany, Federal Republic of, Greece, Grenada, Guatemala, Guinea, Guyana, Honduras, India, Indonesia, Iran, Iraq, Ireland, Italy, Jamaica, Japan, Jordan, Kenya, Kuwait, Lebanon, Libyan Arab Jamahiriya, Lux-

embourg, Madagascar, Malawi, Malaysia, Maldives, Mali, Malta, Mauritania, Mauritius, Morocco, Nepal, Netherlands, New Zealand, Nicaragua, Norway, Oman, Pakistan, Papua New Guinea, Paraguay, Peru, Philippines, Portugal, Qatar, Romania, Rwanda, Samoa, Sao Tome and Principe, Saudi Arabia, Senegal, Singapore, Solomon Islands, Somalia, Sri Lanka, Sudan, Suriname, Swaziland, Sweden, Syrian Arab Republic, Thailand, Togo, Trinidad and Tobago, Tunisia, Turkey, Uganda, United Arab Emirates, United Kingdom, United Republic of Tanzania, United States, Uruguay, Vanuatu, Venezuela, Yemen, Yugoslavia, Zaire, Zambia, Zimbabwe.

REFERENCES
[1]A/39/362 (S/16353). [2]A/39/363.

Security Council

The Security Council held 57 meetings in 1984 and adopted 14 resolutions.

Meeting numbers. SC: 2509-2565.

On 28 September, in accordance with a decision taken during consultations held on the same date, on the Secretary-General's 1982 report on the work of the Organization,[1] the Council President issued the following note:[2]

"1. The members of the Security Council, in the context of their constant endeavours to enhance the effectiveness of the Security Council, and against the persistent background of a precarious international situation, continued their consideration of the role of the Council in the maintenance of international peace and security.

"2. Subject to other priorities demanding immediate attention, 10 meetings in informal consultations were devoted to this subject, in an effort carefully to analyse proposals and identify views enjoying general acceptance.

"3. In order again to structure the discussion, the members retained the five main aspects agreed to last year, as detailed in paragraph 2 of document S/15971, dated 12 September 1983, and initiated a new round of discussions on the basis of the 19 points contained in that document, to which this note is an addition.

"4. In these discussions, the members of the Council welcomed the additional relevant observations contained in the Secretary-General's report to the thirty-eighth session, as well as the considered views of members newly elected to the Council in 1984. An effort was also made to take into account all known contributions so far made by Member States on the work of the Council.

"5. Discussion this year tended to concentrate more specifically, and in detail, on particular aspects of the work of the Council, designed to promote agreement on concrete and practical measures to strengthen the effectiveness of the Security Council; conscious efforts were made to advance ideas which offered the best prospects of producing agreement.

"6. A consistent theme in the presentations was the importance of a renewed dedication by Member States for strict compliance with the purposes and principles of the Charter of the United Nations, and the Charter itself, whose vitality and validity were strongly reaffirmed, as well as the consequent obligation of all members to accept and carry out the decisions of the Security Council.

"7. Due emphasis was given to the special responsibility of the Council, acting on behalf of the international community, in collective maintenance of peace and security. In this connection, members again stressed the need for prompt, relevant and current information on matters before the Council.

"8. The primary responsibility of the Council for the maintenance of international peace and security, as well as its responsibility for the prevention of international conflicts, and the Council's corresponding powers and functions under the Charter, were also emphasized. Ideas were advanced on ways and means of improving the use of procedures to enable the Security Council to contribute more effectively to the prevention of international conflicts and to the peaceful settlement of disputes.

"9. The necessity strictly to implement decisions of the Council in accordance with the Charter was also stressed, and consideration was given to ways and means to follow them up with appropriate support and action.

"10. It was again emphasized that the procedures of the Council were sufficiently flexible to adapt to conceivable requirements and that a collegial approach within the Council was desirable to facilitate considered and concerted action by the Council as the main instrument for international peace.

"11. The role of fact-finding missions undertaken by the Council was explored and modalities for their utilization suggested.

"12. The forthcoming fortieth anniversary of the founding of the United Nations was identified as an occasion to which the Security Council could make an appropriate contribution.

"13. Members of the Council value the exchange of views they have held. They are determined to continue the exercise, which they have found of intrinsic importance, stimulating valuable contact, frank dialogue and concentrated analysis."

The foregoing issues were taken up by the General Assembly in a number of resolutions relating to the Security Council's work. By resolution 39/63 K on disarmament and international security, the Assembly called on the Council to hold a series of meetings to consider the escalating arms race—particularly the nuclear arms race—with a view to initiating procedures for bringing it to a halt. By resolutions dealing with implementation of the Declaration on the Strengthening of International Security, the Assembly recommended that the Council give priority consideration to strengthening the system of collective security provided for in the Charter (resolution 39/154), and emphasized the need for the Council to consider holding periodic meetings to review outstanding problems and also to ensure effective implementation of its decisions in compliance with relevant Charter provisions (resolution 39/155). By resolution 39/156 on strengthening of international security, the Assembly reaffirmed the obligation of States to accept and carry out the Council's decisions. Expressing awareness of the Council's functions and powers, the Assembly noted the concentration of discussion on specific aspects of the work of the Council, stressed its primary responsibility in the collective maintenance of peace and security, and encouraged it to intensify efforts in the prevention of international conflict and the peaceful settlement of disputes through systematic meetings under the five main aspects mentioned in the Council President's note of September 1983.[3] The Assembly also welcomed further periodic information from the Council on the progress achieved.

The role of the Council in maintaining international peace and security was also considered in 1984 by the Special Committee on the Charter of the United Nations and on the Strengthening of the Role of the Organization.[4] Discussions focused on a working paper on prevention and removal of threats to peace and of situations leading to international friction, submitted by Belgium, the Federal Republic of Germany, Italy, Japan, New Zealand and Spain[5] (see LEGAL QUESTIONS, Chapter IV).

Agenda

Fifteen agenda items were considered by the Security Council during 1984—its thirty-ninth year. As in previous years, it adopted at each meeting the agenda for that meeting. (For list of agenda items, see APPENDIX IV.)

Eight of the items were included for the first time in the Council's agenda.[6] They concerned complaints lodged by Bahrain, Kuwait, Oman, Saudi Arabia and the United Arab Emirates against Iran (one item); by the Lao People's Democratic Republic against Thailand (one item); by the Libyan Arab Jamahiriya against the United States (one item); by Nicaragua against Honduras (one item) and against the United States (three items); and by the Sudan against the Libyan Arab Jamahiriya (one item).

In a 14 September note,[7] the Secretary-General notified the General Assembly, in accordance with Article 12, paragraph 2, of the United Nations Charter, of 13 matters relative to the maintenance of international peace and security which the Council had discussed since his previous annual notification.[8] The Secretary-General also listed 103 other matters not discussed by the Council during the period, but of which it remained seized.

GENERAL ASSEMBLY ACTION

Acting on an oral proposal by its President, the General Assembly in November adopted decision 39/405 without vote.

Notification by the Secretary-General under Article 12, paragraph 2, of the Charter of the United Nations

At its 54th plenary meeting, on 8 November 1984, the General Assembly took note of the note by the Secretary-General dated 14 September 1984.

General Assembly decision 39/405

Adopted without vote

Oral proposal by President; agenda item 7.

In other actions related to the Security Council's responsibilities for the maintenance of peace and security, the Assembly urged the Council, by resolution 39/72 A, to consider totally excluding South Africa from the United Nations family and to give special attention to action against it under Chapter VII of the Charter. By resolution 39/72 G, the Assembly further urged the Council to take steps for the strict implementation of the 1977 mandatory arms embargo[9] and to secure an end to military and nuclear co-operation with South Africa and to the import from it of military equipment supplies. With regard to Israeli practices in the occupied Arab territories, the Assembly requested the Council, in resolution 39/95 D, to ensure Israel's respect for and compliance with the 1949 Geneva Convention relative to the Protection of Civilian Persons in Time of War, and to initiate measures to halt Israeli policies and practices in those territories.

Members

In 1984, as in the previous year, the question of equitable representation on and increase in the membership of the Security Council was not considered.

GENERAL ASSEMBLY ACTION

In December, acting on an oral proposal by its President, who pointed out that there had been no request to consider the Council's membership at the current session, the General Assembly adopted decision 39/455 without vote.

Question of equitable representation on and increase in the membership of the Security Council

At its 105th plenary meeting, on 18 December 1984, the General Assembly decided to include in the provisional agenda of its fortieth session the item entitled "Question of equitable representation on and increase in the membership of the Security Council".

General Assembly decision 39/455

Adopted without vote

Oral proposal by President; agenda item 39.

Burkina Faso

On 13 August 1984,[10] the President of the Security Council confirmed that following an official notification of 6 August that the name of Upper Volta had been changed to Burkina Faso, Council members decided,[6] in informal consultations held earlier on 13 August, that the current Council President (Burkina Faso) would continue in office during August and would also hold the presidency in October.

Report for 1983/1984

The Security Council report to the General Assembly for the period 16 June 1983 to 15 June 1984 was adopted by the Council in January 1985. In preparing the report, the Council shortened it by dropping summaries of official Council documents and by indicating only the subject-matter of those related to procedural matters.

REFERENCES

[1]YUN 1982, p. 3. [2]S/16760. [3]YUN 1983, p. 389. [4]A/39/33. [5]A/AC.182/L.38. [6]S/INF/40. [7]A/39/490. [8]YUN 1983, p. 390. [9]YUN 1977, p. 161, SC res. 418(1977), 4 Nov. 1977. [10]S/16696.

PUBLICATION
Index to Proceedings of the Security Council, Thirty-ninth Year, 1984 (ST/LIB/SER.B/S.21), Sales No. E.85.I.11. *Resolutions and Decisions of the Security Council, 1984,* S/INF/40.

General Assembly

The General Assembly met in two separate sessions during 1984, to conclude its thirty-eighth regular session and to hold the major part of its thirty-ninth session.

The first part of the thirty-eighth session had been held from 20 September to 20 December 1983;[1] the session was resumed in 1984 on 26 June and on 17 September, closing that day.

The thirty-ninth regular session was opened on 18 September and continued until its suspension on 18 December. During the general debate, from 24 September to 11 October, the Assembly heard 150 statements by heads of State or Government and heads or members of delegations.

GENERAL ASSEMBLY ACTION

Following a statement by its President that, with the exception of 11 items and two sub-items, consideration of the agenda had been concluded, the General Assembly in December adopted decision 39/456 without vote.

Suspension of the thirty-ninth session

At its 105th plenary meeting, on 18 December 1984, the General Assembly decided to resume its thirty-ninth session, at a date to be announced, for the sole purpose of considering the following agenda items:

Item 11: Report of the Security Council;
Item 12: Report of the Economic and Social Council;
Item 17 (i): Confirmation of the appointment of the Secretary-General of the United Nations Conference on Trade and Development;
Item 25: The situation in Central America: threats to international peace and security and peace initiatives;
Item 38: Launching of global negotiations on international economic co-operation for development;
Item 41: Observance of the quincentenary of the discovery of America;

Item 42: Question of Cyprus;
Item 43: Implementation of the resolutions of the United Nations;
Item 44: Consequences of the prolongation of the armed conflict between Iran and Iraq;
Item 81 (j): Liquidation of the United Nations Emergency Operation Trust Fund and allocation of the remaining balance;
Item 110: Programme planning;
Item 115: Scale of assessments for the apportionment of the expenses of the United Nations;
Item 140: Celebration of the one-hundred-and-fiftieth anniversary of the emancipation of slaves in the British Empire.

General Assembly decision 39/456

Adopted without vote

Oral proposal by President; agenda item 8.

Agenda

As it had decided in December 1983,[2] the General Assembly resumed its thirty-eighth session in 1984 to consider five items and one sub-item (on elections) remaining on that session's agenda. On 26 June, it elected a member of the Economic and Social Council (see APPENDIX III); and, by decision 38/448 B, decided to maintain the item on global negotiations on international economic co-operation for development on the session's agenda. On 17 September, that item and the remaining four—on the quincentenary of the discovery of America, Cyprus, implementation of United Nations resolutions, and the Iran-Iraq conflict—were deferred for inclusion in the thirty-ninth session's draft agenda by decisions 38/448 C and 38/457 to 38/460, respectively.

The thirty-ninth session had 143 items on its agenda, of which 141 were adopted by the Assembly on 21 September and two were added to the list on 9 October.[3] Inclusion of the items in the agenda, as well as their allocation to the Assembly's Main Committees or directly to plenary meetings, was recommended by the General Committee,[4] which acted on all items without vote. On 19 September, it approved a 141-item agenda on the basis of preliminary[5] and annotated[6] lists of items, a 139-item provisional agenda,[7] a one-item supplementary list,[8] and two requests for inclusion of additional items: on the anniversary of the emancipation of slaves in the British Empire[9] and on drought-stricken countries[10] (see ECONOMIC AND SOCIAL QUESTIONS, Chapters XVIII and III, respectively). It also suggested deferring an item concerning East Timor (see TRUSTEESHIP AND DECOLONIZATION, Chapter IV) to the fortieth (1985) session. On 9 October, the Committee recommended approval of two additional items proposed during the session, on the use of outer space for peaceful purposes[11] (see p. 75) and on the inadmissibility of state terrorism[12] (see p. 121).

In September and in October, after examining the recommendations of the General Committee, the Assembly adopted decision 39/402 without vote.

Adoption of the agenda and allocation of agenda items

At its 3rd and 27th plenary meetings, on 21 September and 9 October 1984, the General Assembly, on the recommendations of the General Committee as set forth in its first, second and third reports, adopted the agenda and the allocation of agenda items for the thirty-ninth session.

At its 3rd plenary meeting, on 21 September 1984, the General Assembly, on the recommendation of the General Committee, decided to include in the provisional agenda of its fortieth session the item entitled "Question of East Timor".

General Assembly decision 39/402

Adopted without vote

Approved by General Committee (A/39/250 & Add.1,2), 19 and 21 September and 9 October; agenda item 8.
Meeting numbers. GA 39th session: General Committee 1-4; plenary 3, 27, 32.

Organization of work

In its first report of 19 September 1984,[13] the General Committee made a number of recommendations concerning the organization of the thirty-ninth session, which were based on suggestions by the Secretary-General[14] and the Committee on Conferences.[15]

The recommendations provided for a schedule of daily meetings and set the duration of the general debate and 18 December as the session's closing date. Other organizational arrangements called for limits on explanations of vote and meeting records and for agreement among regional groups on the distribution of Main Committee chairmanships for the following sessions, set 1 December as the deadline for submitting draft resolutions with financial implications as well as deadlines for submitting subsidiary organ reports requiring consideration by the Fifth (Administrative and Budgetary) Committee, and provided for a 48-hour interval between submission of and voting on proposals involving expenditure, to permit preparation of statements of administrative and financial implications. The Assembly was to urge all Member States to exercise maximum restraint in requesting circulation of material as official documents.

The General Committee also recommended authorization—subsequently granted by Assembly decision 39/403—for a number of subsidiary organs to meet during the session, and recalled a 1983 decision prohibiting smoking in small conference rooms and discouraging it in large ones.[16]

Acting on the General Committee's recommendations, the Assembly in September adopted decision 39/401 without vote.

Organization of the thirty-ninth session

At its 3rd plenary meeting, on 21 September 1984, the General Assembly, on the recommendations of the General Committee as set forth in its first report, adopted a number of provisions concerning the organization of the thirty-ninth session.

General Assembly decision 39/401

Adopted without vote

Approved by General Committee (A/39/250 & Add.2) without vote, 19 September, 21 September and 9 October (meetings 1-4); agenda item 8.
Meeting numbers. GA 39th session: General Committee 1; plenary 3.

Representatives' credentials

At its first meeting on 11 October 1984, the Credentials Committee examined a memorandum of the previous day from the Secretary-General, reporting that 127 Member States had submitted formal credentials to the General Assembly's thirty-ninth session. The Legal Counsel indicated that the Secretary-General would report later on those Members participating in the session whose formal credentials had not been received. The Committee also heard several statements in connection with the credentials of Afghanistan, Chile and Democratic Kampuchea.

China and the United States, while not objecting to the credentials of Afghanistan, pointed out that their position should not be interpreted as acquiescence in the situation resulting from foreign aggression against that country; the USSR considered those pronouncements a distortion of facts and an interference in the internal affairs of a Member State. The USSR also reaffirmed its non-recognition of the credentials of Chile and reiterated its opposition to those of Democratic Kampuchea, an opposition shared by Cuba. On the other hand, China, Italy, Paraguay and the United States supported the validity of the credentials of Democratic Kampuchea, while the Ivory Coast noted that its acceptance of all the credentials under consideration in no way implied that it had taken a position on any ongoing international dispute. Paraguay and the United States also held that there was no basis for questioning Chile's credentials.

Acting on an oral proposal by its Chairman, the Committee adopted without vote a resolution by which it accepted the credentials received, taking into account the various reservations expressed. It also recommended for adoption a draft resolution by which the Assembly would approve the Committee's first report.[17]

On 13 December, the Committee examined a memorandum of the previous day by the

Secretary-General indicating that, since the Committee's October meeting, additional formal credentials had been submitted by 29 Member States and that the appointment of the representatives of Angola and Vanuatu had been communicated to him.

Several statements were made concerning the credentials of Grenada. Expressing reservations on them, Cuba said that the current régime had been elected without the free expression of the people and therefore represented only the interests of the occupying forces. Supporting that view, the USSR stressed that acceptance of a puppet régime's credentials would be inconsistent with the United Nations Charter and the Assembly's November 1983 resolution on Grenada[18] and would harm the Organization's image. Noting that those comments raised matters that were not before the Committee, the United States said there was no basis for objecting to Grenada's credentials since they were in order.

The Committee, acting without vote, adopted a resolution orally proposed by its Chairman by which it accepted the credentials received and took into account the reservations expressed. It also submitted a draft resolution to the Assembly recommending approval of its second report.[19]

GENERAL ASSEMBLY ACTION

Acting on the recommendations of the Credentials Committee, the General Assembly adopted two resolutions on representatives' credentials.

On 17 October, it adopted resolution 39/3 A without vote.

The General Assembly
Approves the first report of the Credentials Committee.

General Assembly resolution 39/3 A

17 October 1984   Meeting 32   Adopted without vote

Approved by Credentials Committee (A/39/574) without vote, 11 October (meeting 1); draft orally proposed by Chairman; agenda item 3.

Before adopting the resolution, the Assembly decided, by a recorded vote of 80 to 41, with 22 abstentions, not to act on an amendment by Iran to reject the credentials of Israel. The Assembly acted on a motion by Denmark also on behalf of Finland, Iceland, Norway and Sweden. Reservations about Israel's credentials had been entered by 52 States (see p. 268).

On 17 December, the Assembly adopted resolution 38/3 B without vote.

The General Assembly
Approves the second report of the Credentials Committee.

General Assembly resolution 39/3 B

17 December 1984   Meeting 102   Adopted without vote

Approved by Credentials Committee (A/39/574/Add.1) without vote, 13 December (meeting 2); draft orally proposed by Chairman; agenda item 3.

Representation of Kampuchea in United Nations bodies was also the subject of several 1984 communications (see p. 220).

Rationalization of UN procedures

Pursuant to a December 1983 request by the General Assembly,[20] the Special Committee on the Charter of the United Nations and on the Strengthening of the Role of the Organization, at its April 1984 session,[21] (see LEGAL QUESTIONS, Chapter IV) resumed its consideration of States' proposals on rationalizing the existing procedures of the United Nations.

An open-ended Working Group of the Committee held eight meetings between 2 and 26 April, at which it resumed consideration of the proposals contained in a draft list prepared by the Philippines and Romania,[22] which included working papers submitted by a number of other States.

Based on the Group's work, the Special Committee adopted agreed conclusions, which were forwarded to the Assembly and annexed to its resolution below.

GENERAL ASSEMBLY ACTION

On 13 December, acting on the recommendation of the Sixth (Legal) Committee, the General Assembly adopted resolution 39/88 B without vote.

The General Assembly,
Recalling its resolution 2837(XXVI) of 17 December 1971 on the rationalization of the procedures and organization of the General Assembly,

Having considered the conclusions of the Special Committee on the Charter of the United Nations and on the Strengthening of the Role of the Organization contained in paragraph 151 of its report on the work of the session it held in 1984,

Conscious of the need to discharge in the most efficient manner the functions incumbent upon it under the Charter of the United Nations,

1. *Approves* the conclusions of the Special Committee on the Charter of the United Nations and on the Strengthening of the Role of the Organization as set forth in the annex to the present resolution;

2. *Decides* that the conclusions referred to in paragraph 1 above shall be reproduced as an annex to the rules of procedure of the General Assembly.

ANNEX
Conclusions of the Special Committee on the Charter of the United Nations and on the Strengthening of the Role of the Organization concerning the rationalization of the procedures of the General Assembly
1. The agenda of the sessions of the General Assembly should be simplified as much as possible by grouping or merging related items, after consultation and with the agreement of the delegations concerned.*
2. Specific items should be referred, where relevant, to other United Nations organs or to specialized agencies. The right of States to request that specific items be discussed in the General Assembly should remain unimpaired.

3. The recommendation in paragraph 28 of annex V to the rules of procedure of the General Assembly, according to which the Assembly should ensure, as far as possible, that the same questions, or the same aspects of a question, are not considered by more than one Main Committee, should be more fully implemented, except when it would be helpful for the Sixth Committee to be consulted on the legal aspects of questions under consideration by other Main Committees.

4. The General Committee should play more fully its role under rule 42 of the rules of procedure and paragraphs 1 and 2 of General Assembly decision 34/401, reviewing periodically the work of the Assembly and making the necessary recommendations.

5. The Chairmen of the Main Committees should take the initiative, in the light of past experience, to propose the grouping of similar or related items and the holding of a single general debate on them.

6. The Chairmen of the Main Committees should propose to the Committee the closing of the list of speakers on each item at a suitably early stage.

7. Agreed programmes of work should be respected. To this end, meetings should start at the scheduled time and the time allotted for meetings should be fully utilized.

8. The officers of each Main Committee should review periodically the progress of work. In case of need, they should propose appropriate measures to ensure that the work remains on schedule.

9. Negotiation procedures should be carefully selected to suit the particular subject-matter.

10. The Secretariat should facilitate informal consultations by providing adequate conference services.†

11. The mandate of subsidiary organs should be carefully defined in order to avoid overlapping and duplication of work. The General Assembly should also review periodically the usefulness of its subsidiary organs.

12. Resolutions should be as clear and succinct as possible.

---

*The view was expressed that the agreement of the delegations concerned was not an essential condition.

†The view was expressed that this recommendation was not intended to have any financial implications whatsoever and was approved subject to that condition.

General Assembly resolution 39/88 B

13 December 1984   Meeting 99   Adopted without vote

Approved by Sixth Committee (A/39/781) without vote, 6 December (meeting 64); 35-nation draft (A/C.6/39/L.18 & Corr.1); agenda item 133.
Sponsors: Argentina, Australia, Belgium, Bolivia, Brazil, Brunei Darussalam, Chile, Congo, Cyprus, Egypt, Germany, Federal Republic of, Indonesia, Italy, Ivory Coast, Japan, Kenya, Malaysia, Mexico, New Zealand, Nigeria, Papua New Guinea, Paraguay, Philippines, Romania, Rwanda, Samoa, Sao Tome and Principe, Senegal, Singapore, Spain, Thailand, Venezuela, Yugoslavia, Zaire, Zambia.
Meeting numbers. GA 39th session: 6th Committee 23-31, 64; plenary 99.

REFERENCES
[1]YUN 1983, p. 391. [2]*Ibid.*, GA dec. 38/456, 20 Dec. 1983. [3]A/39/251 & Add.1. [4]A/39/250 & Add.1,2. [5]A/39/50. [6]A/39/100 & Add.1. [7]A/39/150. [8]A/39/200. [9]A/39/241. [10]A/39/242 & Add.1. [11]A/39/243. [12]A/39/244. [13]A/39/250. [14]A/BUR/39/1. [15]A/39/482 & Add.1. [16]YUN 1983, p. 392. [17]A/39/574. [18]YUN 1983, p. 214, GA res. 38/7, 2 Nov. 1983. [19]A/39/574/Add.1. [20]YUN 1983, p. 1122, GA res. 38/141, 19 Dec. 1983. [21]A/39/33. [22]YUN 1983, p. 1121.

PUBLICATIONS
Index to Proceedings of the General Assembly, Thirty-ninth session—1984/1985: Part I—Subject Index; Part II—Index to Speeches (ST/LIB/SER.B/A.38 (Parts I & II)), Sales No. E.85.I.22 (Parts I & II). *Resolutions and Decisions adopted by the General Assembly during its Thirty-ninth Session, 18 September–18 December 1984 and 9-12 April 1985,* A/39/51 & Add.1.

Secretary-General

In his September 1984 annual report to the General Assembly on the work of the Organization (p. 3), the Secretary-General, voicing concern over the increasing questioning of the rules, instruments and modalities of multilateral co-operation, emphasized the need for the effective and correct use of international institutional machinery.

In December, the Assembly took note of the report by decision 39/413.

Good offices

During 1984, the Secretary-General pursued a number of missions of good offices entrusted to him by either the Security Council or the General Assembly. He also continued or initiated other diplomatic efforts aimed at promoting peaceful settlements of disputes. These contacts concerned Afghanistan, Cyprus, the Falkland Islands (Malvinas), Iran-Iraq and Kampuchea.

The Secretary-General's efforts towards a political settlement of the Afghanistan situation continued through a diplomatic process (see p. 227). His mission in Cyprus was aimed at promoting a just and lasting settlement of the conflict between the Greek Cypriot and Turkish Cypriot communities (see p. 240). He pursued his exchanges with Argentina and the United Kingdom to try to assist them to resume negotiations to find a peaceful solution to their sovereignty dispute over the Falkland Islands (Malvinas) (see TRUSTEESHIP AND DECOLONIZATION, Chapter IV). His mediation efforts in the Iran-Iraq conflict also continued, and in June both sides agreed to his appeal not to attack civilian population centres (see p. 229). The Kampuchea situation remained a priority matter for the Secretary-General, who maintained close contacts with representatives of the States most directly concerned and other interested parties within the framework of his good offices (see p. 218).

Co-operation with other intergovernmental organizations

Co-operation between the United Nations and other intergovernmental organizations was the subject in 1984 of five General Assembly resolutions and an Economic and Social Council decision. Those organizations were: the League of Arab States, and the Organization of the Islamic Conference (see below); the Organization of African Unity (see p. 191); the Intergovernmental Bureau for Informatics, and the Southern African Development Co-ordination Conference (see ECONOMIC AND SOCIAL QUESTIONS, Chapters XXIV and VII, respectively); and the Asian-African Legal Consultative Committee (see LEGAL QUESTIONS, Chapter VII).

League of Arab States

As requested by the General Assembly in October 1983,[1] the Secretary-General submitted on 4 September 1984 a progress report[2] on developing co-operation between the United Nations and the League of Arab States. The report gave account of high-level consultations between the two organizations, described action taken on recommendations made at their 1983 meeting held at Tunis, Tunisia,[3] and provided information on preparations for a meeting on food and agriculture to be held in late September 1984 (see below) and a proposed meeting on social development.

Concerning implementation of the Tunis recommendations, the Secretary-General noted that, since most of the specific proposals were of a bilateral nature, follow-up action would be taken by the relevant organizations without reference to the League's General Secretariat or to the United Nations. At the multilateral level, where 37 proposals had to be dealt with, joint sectoral inter-agency working groups were to be set up after United Nations bodies and the League had completed identifying areas of direct interest to them. The Secretary-General also summarized reports received from United Nations bodies describing their action on the recommendations. The replies pertained to six main areas of co-operation: political matters; economic, financial and technical co-operation for development; food and agriculture; social development, labour, human resources and cultural affairs; refugees, disaster prevention and emergency relief, and human rights; and information and communication. While covering both bilateral and multilateral proposals, some replies contained information on action already taken; others reviewed areas of co-operation or made suggestions for further joint activities.

In an October addendum to his report,[4] the Secretary-General informed the Assembly about a joint United Nations/League of Arab States meeting on food and agriculture in the Arab region, held at Rome, Italy, on 27 and 28 September. Upon reviewing the current situation, the League's General Secretariat and the United Nations, as well as a number of specialized agencies on each side which took part in the meeting, called for a substantial increase in capital investment and for agricultural development strategies aimed at increasing productivity. The meeting examined ways of enhancing co-operation by formal agreements and mechanisms and agreed to strengthen collaboration by joint regional studies in food security, agricultural development planning, agricultural integration and integrated rural development; co-sponsorship of regional seminars and other technical meetings; technical co-operation; joint efforts to increase investment flows; co-operation between the Food and Agriculture Organization of the United Nations (FAO) and affiliated regional programmes and Arab organizations and centres; and promotion of information exchange.

During the year, the Secretary-General of the League and its Permanent Observer to the United Nations made statements at four Security Council meetings, to which they had been invited in accordance with rule 39[a] of the Council's provisional rules of procedure. Those meetings dealt with the dispute between Iran and Iraq, and the situation in Lebanon and the Middle East.

GENERAL ASSEMBLY ACTION

On 8 November, the General Assembly adopted resolution 39/9 by recorded vote.

Co-operation between the United Nations and the League of Arab States

The General Assembly,

Recalling its previous resolutions on the promotion of co-operation between the United Nations and the League of Arab States, in particular resolutions 36/24 of 9 November 1981, 37/17 of 16 November 1982 and 38/6 of 28 October 1983,

Having considered the report of the Secretary-General on co-operation between the United Nations and the League of Arab States,

Having heard the statement of the Permanent Observer of the League of Arab States on co-operation between the United Nations and the League of Arab States and having noted the emphasis placed therein on follow-up projects, actions and procedures on the recommendations adopted at the meeting between representatives of the General Secretariat of the League of Arab States and its specialized organizations and the secretariats of the United Nations and other organizations of the United Nations system, held at Tunis from 28 June to 1 July 1983, as well as on various sectoral activities related to development priorities in the Arab region,

Recalling the relevant Articles of the Charter of the United Nations which encourage activities through regional arrangements for the promotion of the purposes and principles of the United Nations,

---

[a]Rule 39 of the Council's provisional rules of procedure states: "The Security Council may invite members of the Secretariat or other persons, whom it considers competent for the purpose, to supply it with information or to give it other assistance in examining matters within its competence."

Noting with appreciation the desire of the League of Arab States to consolidate and develop the existing ties with the United Nations in all areas relating to the maintenance of international peace and security, and to co-operate in every possible way with the United Nations in the implementation of United Nations resolutions relating to the question of Palestine and the situation in the Middle East,

Aware of the vital importance for the countries members of the League of Arab States of achieving a just, comprehensive and durable solution to the Middle East conflict and the question of Palestine, the core of the conflict,

Realizing that the strengthening of international peace and security is directly related, *inter alia*, to disarmament, decolonization, self-determination and the eradication of all forms of racism and racial discrimination,

Convinced that the strengthening and furtherance of co-operation between the United Nations and the organizations of the United Nations system and the League of Arab States contribute to the work of the United Nations system and to the promotion of the purposes and principles of the United Nations,

Noting that the Tunis meeting defined the framework of co-operation between the United Nations and the League of Arab States in certain priority sectors, without determining specific projects that could lend themselves to joint implementation,

Recognizing the need for closer co-operation between the United Nations system and the League of Arab States and its specialized organizations in realizing the goals and objectives set forth in the Strategy for Joint Arab Economic Development adopted by the Eleventh Arab Summit Conference, held at Amman from 25 to 27 November 1980,

1. *Takes note with satisfaction* of the report of the Secretary-General;

2. *Expresses its appreciation* to the Secretary-General for his efforts towards the implementation of the recommendations of the meeting between representatives of the General Secretariat of the League of Arab States and its specialized organizations and the secretariats of the United Nations and other organizations of the United Nations system, as well as to the specialized agencies and other organizations of the United Nations system for their substantial contributions to that meeting;

3. *Expresses its satisfaction* at the results achieved at the meeting on food and agriculture in the Arab region, held in Rome on 27 and 28 September 1984, within the framework of the Food and Agriculture Organization of the United Nations;

4. *Requests* the Secretary-General to strengthen co-operation with the General Secretariat of the League of Arab States for the purpose of implementing United Nations resolutions relating to the question of Palestine and the situation in the Middle East in order to achieve a just, comprehensive and durable solution to the Middle East conflict and the question of Palestine, the core of the conflict;

5. *Requests* the Secretariat of the United Nations and the General Secretariat of the League of Arab States, within their respective fields of competence, to intensify their co-operation towards the realization of the purposes and principles of the Charter of the United Nations, the strengthening of international peace and security, disarmament, decolonization, self-deter-mination and the eradication of all forms of racism and racial discrimination;

6. *Requests* the Secretary-General to strengthen co-operation and co-ordination between the United Nations and the organizations of the United Nations system and the League of Arab States in order to enhance their capacity to serve the mutual interests of the two organizations in the political, economic, social and cultural fields;

7. *Takes note* of the proposals and recommendations contained in the report of the Secretary-General and requests him to take the necessary steps to ensure their implementation, including the following measures:

 (a) Setting up of joint sectoral inter-agency working groups for follow-up of multilateral projects;

 (b) Promotion of contacts and consultations regarding projects of a multilateral nature between the counterpart agencies, programmes and bodies concerned;

 (c) Follow-up of the implementation of the approved proposals mentioned in paragraph 8 of the report of the Secretary-General;

8. *Calls upon* the competent bodies of the United Nations, the specialized agencies and other organizations of the United Nations system:

 (a) To give urgent consideration to the various recommendations contained in the report of the Secretary-General and to inform him not later than 15 May 1985, of the action taken on them;

 (b) To promote contacts and consultations regarding projects of a bilateral nature between the counterpart agencies, programmes and bodies concerned;

9. *Reaffirms* its recommendation contained in resolution 38/6 that another sectoral meeting on social development be organized in April 1985, under the aegis of the General Secretariat of the League of Arab States, in a country member of that organization, to give careful consideration to projects prepared for joint implementation, in conformity with the priorities set forth in paragraphs 61 and 62 of the report of the Secretary-General, including joint sectoral meetings;

10. *Requests* the Secretary-General to co-operate closely with the Secretary-General of the League of Arab States concerning arrangements for the organization of the above-mentioned meeting and to provide all necessary assistance and facilities to ensure its success;

11. *Also requests* the Secretary-General, in close co-operation with the Secretary-General of the League of Arab States, to convene *ad hoc* meetings between representatives of the Secretariat of the United Nations and of the General Secretariat of the League of Arab States for consultations on follow-up policies, projects, actions and procedures;

12. *Further requests* the Secretary-General to submit to the General Assembly, at its fortieth session, a progress report on the implementation of the present resolution;

13. *Decides* to include in the provisional agenda of its fortieth session the item entitled "Co-operation between the United Nations and the League of Arab States".

General Assembly resolution 39/9

8 November 1984   Meeting 54   134-2-2 (recorded vote)

Draft by Jordan (A/39/L.10/Rev.1); agenda item 23.
Financial implications. 5th Committee, A/39/638; S-G, A/C.5/39/32.
Meeting numbers. GA 39th session: 5th Committee 22; plenary 54.

Recorded vote in Assembly as follows:

In favour: Albania, Algeria, Argentina, Australia, Austria, Bahamas, Bahrain, Bangladesh, Belgium, Benin, Bolivia, Brazil, Brunei Darussalam, Bulgaria, Burkina Faso, Burma, Burundi, Byelorussian SSR, Cameroon, Canada, Cape Verde, Central African Republic, Chad, Chile, China, Colombia, Costa Rica, Cuba, Cyprus, Czechoslovakia, Democratic Kampuchea, Democratic Yemen, Denmark, Ecuador, Egypt, El Salvador, Equatorial Guinea, Fiji, Finland, France, Gabon, German Democratic Republic, Germany, Federal Republic of, Ghana, Greece, Grenada, Guatemala, Guinea, Guinea-Bissau, Guyana, Haiti, Honduras, Hungary, Iceland, India, Indonesia, Iran, Iraq, Ireland, Italy, Ivory Coast, Jamaica, Japan, Jordan, Kenya, Kuwait, Lao People's Democratic Republic, Lebanon, Lesotho, Liberia, Libyan Arab Jamahiriya, Luxembourg, Madagascar, Malawi, Malaysia, Maldives, Mali, Malta, Mauritania, Mauritius, Mexico, Mongolia, Morocco, Mozambique, Nepal, Netherlands, New Zealand, Nicaragua, Niger, Nigeria, Norway, Oman, Pakistan, Panama, Papua New Guinea, Paraguay, Peru, Philippines, Poland, Portugal, Qatar, Romania, Rwanda, Sao Tome and Principe, Saudi Arabia, Senegal, Seychelles, Sierra Leone, Singapore, Somalia, Spain, Sri Lanka, Sudan, Suriname, Swaziland, Sweden, Syrian Arab Republic, Thailand, Togo, Trinidad and Tobago, Tunisia, Turkey, Uganda, Ukrainian SSR, USSR, United Arab Emirates, United Kingdom, United Republic of Tanzania, Uruguay, Venezuela, Viet Nam, Yemen, Yugoslavia, Zambia.

Against: Israel, United States.

Abstaining: Ethiopia, Zaire.[a]

[a]Later advised the Secretariat that it had intended to vote in favour.

Before adopting the text as a whole, the Assembly voted separately, at the request of the United States, on paragraph 4, retaining it by a recorded vote of 108 to 2, with 24 abstentions.

Israel said that it was voting against that paragraph and the text as a whole in view of the League's policies and activities, which contradicted the United Nations Charter and encouraged a radical approach to the Arab-Israeli conflict, as well as intransigence and terrorism against Israel.

Stressing that the paragraph referred to many resolutions repudiating fundamental United States policies for peace in the Middle East, thus compelling it to vote also against the text as a whole, the United States said it could not support resolutions requesting the Secretary-General to take actions it opposed, and had reservations about additional costs for conference servicing. Ireland, on behalf of the 10 members of the European Community, said they considered it best if resolutions of the kind just adopted, which depended on the unanimous support of the international community, addressed the question of co-operation without introducing divisive elements, and also without placing further burdens on the United Nations budget—a position shared by Japan. As to paragraph 4, the Ten drew particular attention to the fact that they had not supported all the resolutions mentioned and to the need to avoid prejudicing the Secretary-General's role.

Denmark, speaking also for five Nordic countries, said that they had abstained in the vote on paragraph 4 and voted in favour of the resolution on the understanding that the elements with political implications were not relevant and could not prejudice their positions on the substantive matter.

Ethiopia expressed its strong reservation on the text by its abstention, stating that its acceptance might be misconstrued as endorsement of the League's decisions, which Ethiopia had consistently rejected.

Organization of the Islamic Conference

In 1984, co-operation continued between the United Nations system and the Organization of the Islamic Conference on a broad range of political, economic, social and cultural matters, which were highlighted by the Secretary-General in a September report[5] on implementing the General Assembly's October 1983 resolution on such co-operation.[6] The report noted that, within the framework of consultations between the two organizations, the Secretary-General addressed the Fourth Islamic Summit Conference (Casablanca, Morocco, 16-19 January), at which he also exchanged views with several heads of State or Government. The Conference adopted a series of resolutions on political, economic, social and information matters. The resolutions, reports and a final communiqué were transmitted to the Secretary-General by Morocco on 13 March.[7] Throughout the year, the two organizations continued to exchange views and information on such topics as international peace and security, decolonization and *apartheid*, outer space, and disarmament.

Pursuant to a decision of the Task Force on Science and Technology for Development of the Administrative Committee on Co-ordination, the Executive Director of the Centre for Science and Technology for Development held consultations with the Islamic Foundation for Science and Technology for Development (Jeddah, Saudi Arabia, 14 May). They agreed to confine co-operation initially to such questions as the impact of national budgets on scientific and technological capabilities. The consultations were a follow-up to the July 1983 joint meeting of the secretariats of the Islamic Conference and the United Nations system,[8] which designated lead agencies for five priority areas of co-operation. The need for a priority programme to complete various studies was emphasized by a joint working group on agricultural co-operation, which met at the headquarters of FAO (Rome, April), the lead agency for agricultural matters. The report also highlighted activities of United Nations bodies to promote economic, social and cultural co-operation with the Conference, as well as proposals for strengthening such co-operation.

At their annual co-ordinating meeting (New York, 4 October),[9] the Foreign Ministers of the Conference reviewed questions on the agenda of the Assembly's 1984 session of interest to Conference members. They adopted a communiqué, which Bangladesh transmitted to the Secretary-General on 12 October.[10] The communiqué adopted at a similar meeting in October 1983 had been transmitted earlier by Niger, on 2 May.[11] A message from the Secretary-General was delivered to the Fifteenth Islamic Conference of Ministers for Foreign Affairs (Sana'a, Yemen Arab Republic, 18-22 December). In its resolution on co-operation between the two organizations, the Conference called on its member States to give priority to the celebration in 1985 of the fortieth anniversary of the United Nations (see below) and the twenty-fifth anniversary of the Declaration on the Granting of Independence to Colonial Countries and Peoples (see TRUSTEESHIP AND DECOLONIZATION, Chapter I). It also called for support of programmes drawn up by the 1984 Assembly session and for co-operation with the United Nations Conference on Disarmament. A package of documents adopted by the Fourteenth (1983) Islamic Conference of Foreign Ministers had been transmitted to the Secretary-General by Bangladesh on 15 March.[12]

Regarding co-operation in the peaceful uses of outer space, training courses on remote sensing applications in forestry and agriculture, co-sponsored, respectively, by the USSR and FAO in co-operation with Italy (see p. 100), were attended by participants from Conference member States.

Various United Nations entities explored further avenues of co-operation on economic, social and cultural matters. The United Nations Educational, Scientific and Cultural Organization discussed principal areas of co-operation in promoting literacy with the Deputy Director-General for Education of the Islamic Education, Scientific and Cultural Organization (Paris, October). The United Nations Industrial Development Organization helped organize the Second Organization of the Islamic Conference Ministerial Consultation on Industrial Co-operation (Istanbul, Turkey, November 1984). The United Nations Conference on Trade and Development assisted the Permanent Committee of the Islamic Conference on Economic and Commercial Co-operation in preparing its first meeting (Istanbul, 12-16 November), and, jointly with the Islamic Centre for Development of Trade, held a seminar on the generalized system of trade preferences (Casablanca, Morocco, 26-29 November).

GENERAL ASSEMBLY ACTION

On 8 November 1984, the General Assembly adopted resolution 39/7 without vote.

Co-operation between the United Nations and the Organization of the Islamic Conference

The General Assembly,

Having considered the report of the Secretary-General on co-operation between the United Nations and the Organization of the Islamic Conference,

Taking into account the desire of both organizations to co-operate more closely in their common search for solutions to global problems, such as questions relating to international peace and security, disarmament, self-

determination, decolonization, fundamental human rights and the establishment of a new international economic order,

Noting the strengthening of co-operation between the specialized agencies and other organizations of the United Nations system and the Organization of the Islamic Conference,

Noting also the progress achieved in the implementation of the decisions of the first annual meeting, held at Geneva on 15 July 1983, between representatives of the secretariat of the Organization of the Islamic Conference and the secretariats of the United Nations and other organizations of the United Nations system, particularly the multisectoral contacts between the focal points of the two organizations,

Taking note of the encouraging results obtained and the urgent need to assure the co-ordination and follow-up of the decisions adopted during the meeting,

Convinced of the need to strengthen further the co-operation between the organizations of the United Nations system and the Organization of the Islamic Conference,

Recalling its resolutions 35/36 of 14 November 1980, 36/23 of 9 November 1981, 37/4 of 22 October 1982 and 38/4 of 28 October 1983,

1. *Takes note with satisfaction* of the report of the Secretary-General;

2. *Requests* the United Nations and the Organization of the Islamic Conference to continue co-operation in their common search for solutions to global problems, such as questions relating to international peace and security, disarmament, self-determination, decolonization, fundamental human rights and the establishment of a new international economic order;

3. *Encourages* the specialized agencies and other organizations of the United Nations system to continue to expand their co-operation with the Organization of the Islamic Conference, particularly by negotiating co-operation agreements, and invites them to multiply the contacts and meetings of focal points for co-operation in priority areas of interest to the United Nations and the Organization of the Islamic Conference;

4. *Requests* the Secretary-General to continue to take steps to strengthen the co-ordination of the activities of the United Nations system in this field with a view to intensifying co-operation between the United Nations and the Organization of the Islamic Conference;

5. *Requests* the Secretary-General to strengthen co-operation and co-ordination between the United Nations and other organizations of the United Nations system and the Organization of the Islamic Conference to serve the mutual interests of the two organizations in the political, economic, social and cultural fields;

6. *Also requests* the Secretary-General to strengthen the mechanism for co-ordination between the two organizations, taking into account the results of the meeting at Geneva, namely, contacts pursued with focal points in the five priority fields, evaluation of their activities and preparation of the second annual meeting as provided for in General Assembly resolution 37/4;

7. *Further requests* the Secretary-General to report to the General Assembly at its fortieth session on the state of co-operation between the United Nations and the Organization of the Islamic Conference;

8. *Decides* to include in the provisional agenda of its fortieth session the item entitled "Co-operation between

the United Nations and the Organization of the Islamic Conference''.

General Assembly resolution 39/7

8 November 1984   Meeting 54   Adopted without vote

Draft by Bangladesh (A/39/L.5); agenda item 21.

Other intergovernmental organizations

At the request of the host Governments of several intergovernmental conferences, the main documents of those meetings were transmitted to the Secretary-General during 1984 for circulation as documents of the General Assembly, the Security Council or both, as follows:

—Final documents of the Conference of the Ministers of Information of Non-Aligned Countries (Jakarta, Indonesia, 26-30 January 1984);[13] report of the Rapporteur and other documents of the Third Conference of Ministers of Labour of Non-Aligned Countries and Other Developing Countries (Managua, Nicaragua, 10-12 May);[14] final communiqué adopted by the Meeting of Ministers for Foreign Affairs and Heads of Delegation of the Non-Aligned Countries to the thirty-ninth session of the General Assembly (New York, 1-5 October).[15]

—Declarations adopted on 27 March by the Ministers for Foreign Affairs of the 10 States members of the European Economic Community.[16]

—Declaration on Democratic Values by the Tenth Economic Summit (London, 7-9 June).[17]

—Part of a joint communiqué issued on 10 July by the Ministerial Meeting of the Association of South-East Asian Nations.[18]

—Resolutions adopted by the Seventy-second Inter-Parliamentary Conference (Geneva, 29 September).[19]

—Final communiqué adopted by the Fifth Session of the Supreme Council of the Co-operation Council for the Arab States of the Gulf (Kuwait, 27-29 November).[20]

REFERENCES

[1]YUN 1983, p. 394, GA res. 38/6, 28 Oct. 1983. [2]A/39/418. [3]YUN 1983, p. 394. [4]A/39/418/Add.1. [5]A/39/481 & Corr.1. [6]YUN 1983, p. 397, GA res. 38/4, 28 Oct. 1983. [7]A/39/131-S/16414 & Corr.1. [8]YUN 1983, p. 396. [9]A/40/657. [10]A/39/585-S/16783. [11]A/39/236-S/16535. [12]A/39/133-S/16417. [13]A/39/159-S/16430. [14]A/39/581-S/16782. [15]A/39/560-S/16773. [16]A/39/161-S/16456. [17]A/39/307. [18]E/1984/139. [19]A/39/590 & Corr.1. [20]A/39/853 & Corr.1.

Other institutional questions

Fortieth anniversary of the United Nations (1985)

Pursuant to a December 1983 decision of the General Assembly,[1] the Preparatory Committee for the Fortieth Anniversary of the United Nations began its work in 1984, holding five meetings in May, June, September and December. After extensive deliberations, the 98-member Committee (as at 14 December 1984) made recommendations on the observance of the fortieth anniversary, which formed the basis of a resolution and a decision adopted by the Assembly (see below). The Committee's report[2] described action initiated or envisaged by the United Nations system in connection with the anniversary. This included an Economic and Social Council decision to assess in 1985 the role of the United Nations in promoting international economic and social co-operation (see also below); and a resolution endorsing the 1984 conclusions and recommendations of the Committee for Programme and Co-ordination,[3] among them that an overview study of the objectives and plans of United Nations entities in the social, economic and humanitarian fields should be published by the Secretariat in connection with the anniversary (see ECONOMIC AND SOCIAL QUESTIONS, Chapter XXIV).

Intergovernmental organizations also addressed the question of the anniversary observance at their 1984 forums. In October, the Meeting of Foreign Ministers and Heads of Delegation of the Non-Aligned Countries to the thirty-ninth session of the General Assembly called on all members to play an active role in the preparation for and the conduct of commemorative activities and stressed the significance of the participation of their heads of State or Government at the 1985 Assembly session.[4] In September, a resolution on the anniversary was adopted by the Seventy-second Inter-Parliamentary Conference at Geneva, requesting a study of ways whereby the Inter-Parliamentary Union could be associated with the commemoration and make a contribution to it.[5]

ECONOMIC AND SOCIAL COUNCIL ACTION

On 27 July 1984, acting on an oral proposal by its President, the Economic and Social Council adopted resolution 1984/82 without vote.

Fortieth anniversary of the United Nations in 1985

The Economic and Social Council,

Recalling General Assembly decision 38/455 of 20 December 1983 on the commemoration of the fortieth anniversary of the United Nations in 1985,

Considering that the economic and social sectors of the United Nations system should contribute effectively to the observance of the anniversary,

1.   *Decides* that, at the second regular session of 1985 of the Economic and Social Council, in the context of the general debate, special attention should be devoted to an assessment of the role of the United Nations in promoting international economic and social co-operation and to the consideration of ways of strengthening the role of the Organization and of further enhancing its effectiveness in this regard, and calls upon

the Secretary-General to ensure that appropriate preparations are made for these discussions;

2. *Recommends* that the regional commissions and other subsidiary bodies of the Council and the specialized agencies and other organizations of the United Nations system should take full cognizance of the fortieth anniversary of the United Nations and participate actively in its observance;

3. *Invites* the competent intergovernmental organizations and non-governmental organizations in consultative status with the Council to develop appropriate activities in support of the anniversary.

Economic and Social Council resolution 1984/82

27 July 1984   Meeting 50   Adopted without vote

Oral proposal by President; agenda item 2.

GENERAL ASSEMBLY ACTION

In December, the General Assembly took two actions relating to the preparations for the anniversary.

On 17 December, acting on the recommendation of the Preparatory Committee for the Fortieth Anniversary of the United Nations, the Assembly adopted resolution 39/161 A without vote.

The General Assembly,

Recalling its decision 38/455 of 20 December 1983, by which it established the Preparatory Committee for the Fortieth Anniversary of the United Nations and entrusted it with the task of considering and recommending to the General Assembly at its thirty-ninth session proposals for suitable activities in connection with the observance in 1985 of the fortieth anniversary of the United Nations,

Having considered the report of the Preparatory Committee,

1. *Decides* that the theme of the fortieth anniversary of the United Nations shall be "United Nations for a better world" and expresses the hope and desire that the year 1985 will mark the beginning of an era of durable and global peace and justice, social and economic development and progress and independence of all peoples;

2. *Takes note* of the programmes and activities, including those recommended by the Preparatory Committee for the Fortieth Anniversary of the United Nations, to be undertaken by the United Nations and its related organizations, as well as the programmes and activities suggested for the consideration of Governments of Member States and non-governmental organizations;

3. *Decides* that the Preparatory Committee, established at its thirty-eighth session, shall continue to function in that capacity, under the chairmanship of the President of the thirty-ninth session of the General Assembly, until the observance of the anniversary, with the purpose of drawing up and co-ordinating plans and organizing suitable activities for the anniversary to be undertaken by the United Nations, in the light of the present resolution and the report of the Preparatory Committee;

4. *Decides* that a commemorative session of the General Assembly shall be held for a short period, cul-

minating on 24 October 1985 and coinciding with the proclamation of the International Year of Peace;

5. *Requests* the Preparatory Committee to draw up a suitable text for a final document or documents to be considered for signature and/or adoption during the commemorative session;

6. *Expresses the hope* that Heads of State or Government will find it possible to participate in the commemorative session in order to enhance its significance;

7. *Decides* that the year 1985 shall be observed as Year of the United Nations;

8. *Requests* the Secretary-General to provide the necessary facilities for implementing the provisions of the present resolution and the recommendations contained in the report of the Preparatory Committee.

General Assembly resolution 39/161 A

17 December 1984   Meeting 103   Adopted without vote

Draft by Preparatory Committee for the Fortieth Anniversary of the United Nations (A/39/49); agenda item 40.

In December, acting on an oral proposal by its President, the Assembly adopted decision 39/425 without vote.

Observance of the fortieth anniversary of the United Nations

At its 103rd plenary meeting, on 17 December 1984, the General Assembly, on the recommendation of the Preparatory Committee for the Fortieth Anniversary of the United Nations:

(a) Invited the Governments of Member States:

(i) To organize appropriate observance of the fortieth anniversary of the United Nations in their respective countries, involving the widest possible participation;

(ii) To consider the establishment of national committees with the purpose of evaluating and publicizing the contribution of the United Nations system over the past four decades, its continuing relevance in the current international situation and ways and means by which the United Nations could be strengthened and made more effective;

(iii) To implement General Assembly resolution 1511(XV) of 12 December 1960, entitled "Teaching of the purposes and principles, the structure and activities of the United Nations and its related agencies";

(b) Invited the specialized agencies and other organizations of the United Nations system as well as other international organizations associated with the United Nations to participate actively in the observance of the fortieth anniversary of the United Nations and to formulate such plans and programmes as were appropriate for the occasion;

(c) Urged the Department of Public Information of the Secretariat and the specialized agencies and other international organizations to give the widest possible dissemination to information pertaining to the United Nations;

(d) Appealed to the international mass media, both public and private, as well as non-governmental organizations and educational institutions to contribute more effectively to dissemination of information on United Nations activities.

General Assembly decision 39/425

Adopted without vote

Oral proposal by President; agenda item 40.

By resolution 39/161 B of the same date, the Assembly decided that the events commemorating the fortieth anniversary should reflect the observance of the twenty-fifth anniversary, also in 1985, of the Declaration on the Granting of Independence to Colonial Countries and Peoples. In resolution 39/98 A, it urged the Department of Public Information of the Secretariat to support the Preparatory Committee in connection with the upcoming celebration.

Composition of UN organs

In 1984, as in previous years since 1979, consideration of the question of the composition of the relevant organs of the United Nations was deferred.

GENERAL ASSEMBLY ACTION

Acting on the recommendation of the Special Political Committee, the General Assembly in December adopted decision 39/422 without vote.

Question of the composition of the relevant organs of the United Nations

At its 100th plenary meeting, on 14 December 1984, the General Assembly, on the recommendation of the Special Political Committee, decided to include in the provisional agenda of its fortieth session the item entitled "Question of the composition of the relevant organs of the United Nations".

General Assembly decision 39/422

Adopted without vote

Approved by SPC (A/39/670) without vote, 12 November (meeting 28); oral proposal by Chairman; agenda item 79.
Meeting numbers. GA 39th session: SPC 28; plenary 100.

REFERENCES

[1]YUN 1983, p. 398, GA dec. 38/455, 20 Dec. 1983. [2]A/39/49. [3]A/39/38. [4]A/39/560-S/16773. [5]A/39/590 & Corr.1.

PUBLICATION

Basic Facts about the United Nations (DPI/822), Sales No. E.84.I.12.

Economic and social questions

Chapter I

Development policy and international economic co-operation

The weak and uneven character of the world economic recovery and the poor prospects of the developing countries, particularly the least developed among them, were reviewed by numerous United Nations bodies throughout 1984. The need for urgent action regarding both the critical state of sub-Saharan Africa and the serious external debt situation of developing countries was stressed in several economic reports and during discussions on the world economic situation.

In his annual report on the work of the Organization (p. 3), the Secretary-General noted that criticism of United Nations economic institutions was easy since they often fell short of their high aims. However, only intensified multilateral co-operation could solve global economic problems in an increasingly economically interdependent world.

The Committee established to carry out the first review and appraisal of the implementation of the International Development Strategy for the Third United Nations Development Decade considered progress made towards achieving the Strategy's goals and the strengthening of its implementation. Despite the Committee's work and contributions from many United Nations sources, the exercise was not completed.

In December, the General Assembly commemorated the tenth anniversary of the adoption of the Charter of Economic Rights and Duties of States and decided on a thorough review of its implementation in 1985.

Reiterating concern first expressed in 1983 about the impact of political tensions on international economic co-operation, the Assembly requested the Secretary-General to continue consultations on the scope of possible confidence-building measures in international economic relations. The Assembly deplored the continued application of coercive economic measures against developing countries.

Discussions continued on the launching of global negotiations on international economic co-operation for development, originally scheduled to start in 1980; in December, in suspending its 1984 session, the Assembly decided to keep the item open and to reconvene to consider any agreements that might emerge from informal consultations. Discussions also continued on various aspects of the proposed new international economic order, including its legal aspects.

Economic co-operation among developing countries (ECDC) continued to be discussed within the United Nations Conference on Trade and Development (UNCTAD), while the Fourth General Conference of the United Nations Industrial Development Organization (UNIDO) decided to accord high priority in UNIDO's activities to industrial co-operation among those countries. The mandates of, and problems addressed by, the United Nations system in economic and technical co-operation among developing countries were discussed by the Committee for Programme and Co-ordination (CPC) and the Economic and Social Council. The Assembly urged the United Nations system to intensify support for ECDC. Support by the system for economic and technical co-operation among developing countries was also discussed by the Organization's co-ordination bodies, while the Council considered promotion of such co-operation at the interregional level.

The *World Economic Survey 1984*, which gave an account of trends and policies in the world economy, was the background document for the annual discussion in the Council on international economic and social policy. UNCTAD published the fourth annual report on trade and development issues, the *Trade and Development Report, 1984*, which, in addition to analysing the world economic situation, focused on the international trade and payments system. A further assessment of the economic situation was carried out by the Committee for Development Planning (CDP), which identified priority areas for urgent international attention.

Broad areas of economic and social development were considered in several United Nations forums during the year. The improvement of various aspects of development planning, education, administration and information continued to be studied. The Seventh Meeting of Experts on the United Nations Programme in Public Administration and Finance took place and the programme of technical co-operation for public administration continued.

The work of the United Nations system in rural development was reviewed, with particular emphasis on alleviating the poverty of the poorest and drought-stricken countries.

Action on behalf of countries particularly affected by the world economic situation was again urged by the Assembly, which again called for immediate measures in favour of the developing countries. Preparations intensified throughout the system for the 1985 mid-term global review of the Substantial New Programme of Action for the 1980s (SNPA) for the Least Developed Countries (LDCs); to carry out the review, the Assembly decided to convene a high-level meeting of the UNCTAD Intergovernmental Group on the Least Developed Countries. That review was discussed by UNCTAD's Trade and Development Board and the UNCTAD secretariat published *The Least Developed Countries 1984 Report*, the first such annual report. Country review meetings continued to be organized for individual LDCs by the United Nations Development Programme (UNDP), which also administered the special fund for them. UNIDO's Fourth General Conference recommended that industrialization be taken fully into account in the mid-term review and requested UNIDO to strengthen its industrial development assistance to LDCs. In July, the Economic and Social Council requested CDP to consider adding Kiribati and Tuvalu to the list of the 36 LDCs and in December a request for consideration of Vanuatu was made by the General Assembly.

The particular problems of land-locked and island developing countries were kept under consideration by the UNCTAD Trade and Development Board and by the Assembly which renewed calls for action on their behalf. The Assembly also renewed its appeal for contributions to the United Nations Special Fund for Land-locked Developing Countries.

Topics related to this chapter. Disarmament: disarmament and development. Economic assistance, disasters and emergency relief: Africa—critical economic situation. Operational activities for development. International trade and finance. Regional economic and social activities: economic and social trends—Africa, Asia and the Pacific, Europe, Latin America, Western Asia; development policy and regional economic co-operation—Africa, Asia and the Pacific, Europe, Latin America, Western Asia. Social and cultural development: social aspects of development planning; popular participation in development; family in development; social aspects of rural development. Human rights: right to development; proposed new international economic order and human rights. Women: women in development. Statistics: economic statistics.

International economic relations

Development and economic co-operation

During 1984, aspects of development and economic co-operation were debated in several United Nations bodies, including the General Assembly and the Economic and Social Council. In resolution 39/226, the Assembly requested the Secretary-General to continue consulting Governments and United Nations organizations on confidence-building measures in international economic relations. In resolution 39/210, it deplored the continued, and in some cases increased, application of economic measures against developing countries as a means of coercion. ECDC was widely discussed, with the Assembly urging increased assistance in this area (39/216).

Substantive discussions took place on the first review and appraisal of the implementation of the International Development Strategy for the Third United Nations Development Decade, both within the Committee established for that purpose and in various other United Nations bodies which contributed to its work. By resolution 39/162, the Assembly expressed disappointment that the Committee had been unable to complete its mandate successfully and requested the Secretary-General to suggest arrangements for a resumed session of the Committee in 1985. The Assembly also decided, in resolution 39/163, to review the implementation of the 1974 Charter of Economic Rights and Duties of States during 1985.

Proposals for global economic negotiations and a new international economic order continued to be considered in various United Nations forums throughout the year, with no agreement being reached.

Concern was expressed by most United Nations bodies over the economic situation in Africa, particularly in the sub-Sahara: such concerns included the fall in incomes, decreasing employment prospects and the debt-servicing problems of those countries.

CDP activities. At its May 1984 session,[1] CDP noted that while economic optimism had returned in some industrialized countries, many developing countries were struggling to contain social disintegration and potential political turmoil as living conditions deteriorated. It drew attention to three areas to which the international community should devote urgent attention: reform of the international monetary and financial system; the international debt situation (see also Chapter IV of this section); and development assistance on concessional terms to LDCs (see below under "Least developed countries"). The serious position of sub-Saharan Africa, where incomes in most countries had fallen steadily for a decade and in some had dropped below the levels of the mid-1960s, was also singled out by CDP as requiring special and immediate attention.

Measures proposed by CDP to assist the developing countries and safeguard the world economy included: substantial increases in the resources available to the International Monetary Fund (IMF) and in the annual lending programme of the World Bank; debt relief through capping interest payments, adding unpaid interest to principal or extending maturities; a new round of North-South trade negotiations to subject quotas and other non-tariff barriers to more effective international discipline; a substantial new allocation of IMF special drawing rights (SDRs) to restore the reserves of developing countries; the achievement of the targeted level of $12 billion for the seventh three-year replenishment of the International Development Association (IDA); and more abundant and flexible multilateral and official development assistance to sub-Saharan Africa.

Two CDP working groups met during the year: one on interdependence and multilateralism (Geneva, 12-14 October) and the other on domestic economic policies and surveillance (Geneva, 16 and 17 November).

ACC activities. At its first regular session of 1984 (London, 16-18 April), the Administrative Committee on Co-ordination (ACC) discussed a paper prepared by the International Labour Organisation (ILO) on employment and development: problems and perspectives. The paper, annexed to the ACC annual report to the Economic and Social Council,[2] was designed to raise issues for discussion rather than present a comprehensive analysis or suggest solutions. Trends and prospects for world economic recovery and industrial development in the developing countries were described and it was noted that an adjustment process had to take place under three major constraints: inflation; the balance-of-payments disequilibrium; and mounting unemployment and underemployment. The paper suggested several guidelines to make adjustment measures more tolerable: slashing of unproductive spending, including armaments, and conspicuous luxury consumption; protection of the poorest and preservation of their productive capacity; concentration of resources on more economically productive and socially useful programmes and development of

human skills; building up of physical infrastructure to absorb manpower while creating productive permanent assets; increasing labour mobility in occupational and geographic terms; and avoidance of protectionism, aiming instead at self-reliant development.

ACC members commented on various aspects of the paper from the perspective of their respective organizations. Some points made included: the need to create jobs and employment in all countries; the need for short-term adjustment programmes in developing countries to be supplemented by longer-term structural adjustment, for which large-scale development assistance was critical; the need for integrated rural development programmes to increase agricultural production and non-agricultural employment opportunities in rural areas where the majority of the population of developing countries lived; the need for development of the industrial sector in developing countries and for manpower training; and the need for basic adjustment in the agricultural policies of some developed countries with regard to subsidized production and trade.

ACC noted that United Nations organizations had made substantial contributions to the employment and development issue which was extremely complicated and not amenable to easy solution; there was, however, a need for greater sharing of views and experiences both bilaterally between organizations and system-wide. ACC adopted a decision[3] by which it decided that its Task Force on Long-Term Development Objectives should carry out a follow-up study on employment and development and that the ILO background paper, as revised to reflect the ACC discussion, be brought to the attention of CDP.

The Task Force devoted its thirteenth session (Geneva, 28-30 November)[4] to the question of employment and development: medium- and long-term perspectives and problems. It noted a deterioration in the employment situation in many developing countries. In Latin America, reported unemployment had increased significantly since 1980 and informal sector activities had grown, reversing a long-term trend towards more regular full-time employment, at least in urban areas. The urban unemployment situation had also deteriorated in Africa where, for some countries, estimates suggested that it could be as high as 25 per cent of the labour force. Even in Asia, urban unemployment had increased in some countries. Youth unemployment was a particularly disturbing feature of the situation.

The prospects for obtaining employment in the developing world were alarming, the Task Force noted. Projections indicated that between 1980 and the turn of the century, the working-age population (between 15 and 64 years of age) would increase by 85 per cent in Africa, 66 per cent in Latin America, 64 per cent in South Asia and 44 per cent in East Asia. The 15- to 19-year-old age group—of special importance, since it constituted the new entrants to the working-age population—would increase by more than 60 per cent in the developing world as a whole. The Task Force noted some calculations which determined that a 7 per cent per annum rate of economic growth would be required to provide employment to the fast-growing labour force.

Changes in the external environment which the Task Force considered could contribute to increasing production and employment in developing countries included: more rapid economic growth in the industrialized countries which could generate policies more favourable to co-operation with the developing world; the adoption of appropriate employment policies in the developed countries to ease adjustment to the evolving international division of labour; reduction of protectionism and establishment of a more stable organization of trade relations; maintenance of financial flows to developing countries; and increased emphasis on technical assistance, especially human resource development.

The Task Force suggested possible internal policies for the developing countries to maximize chances for rapid economic growth and for greater absorption of the expanding labour force, including: employment promotion measures at all levels from central government to local communities, involving participation by workers' and employers' organizations, co-operatives and farmers' associations; employment concerns to be built into development plans; development of broad-based education and training systems for a flexible labour force; production of goods for domestic consumption to be carried out in small and medium-sized enterprises; and the establishment of price and income (especially wages) policies.

World Economic Survey 1984. During its annual discussion of international economic and social policy, which took place in July (see below), the Economic and Social Council had before it the *World Economic Survey 1984,*[5] prepared by the United Nations Department of International Economic and Social Affairs (DIESA) and based on information available as at 31 March 1984.

Following its analysis of recent trends and prospects in the world economy (see below), the *Survey* concluded that there were a number of directions that current policy should take to improve the international economic environment and set the stage for sustained, non-inflationary growth: easing of import constraints and increased export capacities in developing countries and a progressive adjustment of productive structures in developed countries would improve growth

prospects; lower interest rates would stimulate investment in developed and developing countries and ease the debt-service burden of many of the latter; relaxation of cautious fiscal policies in Japan and Western Europe could result in higher growth rates; redesigning the national and group-wide economic policies of the European centrally planned economies would achieve and sustain a higher pace of growth; halting and reversing protectionist measures would restore dynamism to international trade; an immediate issue of SDRs could alleviate the liquidity problems of many developing countries; revival of trade among developing countries would foster diversification and economic growth; increased food aid and improved food distribution would alleviate the critical situation in sub-Saharan Africa; greater flows of bilateral and multilateral official development assistance would facilitate structural adjustment and reactivate development in low-income countries; resumption of international lending to highly indebted countries would avoid further retrenchment as would conversion of medium- to long-term debt instruments; increased availability of long-term capital would help revive investment in developing countries; and programmes to correct balance-of-payments disequilibria of developing countries should combine demand-management policies and supply-side measures.

In the general discussion of international economic and social policy in the Economic and Social Council,[6] opinions differed on whether to characterize the world recovery as soundly based or as weak and fragile, but there was consensus on the need to avoid complacency since many developing countries, particularly in Africa and those caught in debt-servicing difficulties, continued to face critical situations. It was widely recognized that the social dimension should be more explicitly taken into account in programming adjustment.

Of particular concern was the question of how to improve upon the outlook for the remainder of the decade. Attention focused on more efficient use of resources, increasing employment, accelerating structural adjustment and fostering the development of human resources. Possibilities for reform and adaptation of international monetary, financial and trade relations were discussed, as were developments in sectoral and regional areas of co-operation and in the broad framework of international economic co-operation.

Report of the Secretary-General. In his September 1984 report to the General Assembly on the work of the Organization (p. 3), the Secretary-General stated that global economic relations had changed significantly since the post-war years when most international economic institutions began their work. Developing countries looked on these institutions as insufficiently responsive to their needs, a perception strengthened by recent serious economic difficulties. United Nations economic institutions often fell short of their aims; nevertheless, multilateral co-operation had achieved much and, despite the difficulties involved, it would be short-sighted to turn away from the concept and the institutions which embodied it.

In the domain of global issues, many United Nations contributions were in less tangible forms, such as raising global consciousness on key issues and shaping international debates on major problems. It was in no small measure due to the discussions on the International Development Strategy for the Third United Nations Development Decade[7] that the world community was giving priority to the cause of development.

Regarding politicization of economic issues in the United Nations, the Secretary-General pointed out that this reflected the frustrations which developing countries felt in their long attempt to reshape their economic destiny.

A new consensus on economic issues in the light of world economic and political realities had not yet emerged, said the Secretary-General, but its absence need not prevent progress in critical areas. In a world of growing economic interdependence, impoverished people faced perpetually with overwhelming economic and social crises constituted not only a challenge to international conscience but a threat to international stability.

Communications. Several communications dealing with general aspects of international economic relations were received by the Secretary-General in 1984.

On 9 February,[8] Ecuador transmitted the text of the Quito Declaration and Plan of Action, a Latin American and Caribbean response to the economic crisis affecting the region, agreed to at the Latin American Economic Conference (Quito, Ecuador, 9-13 January). The Declaration expressed anxiety over conditions prevailing in the world economy which seriously affected the region's development and stability (see Chapter VIII of this section).

In a communiqué transmitted by Morocco on 13 March,[9] the Fourth Islamic Summit Conference (Casablanca, Morocco, 16-19 January) indicated policies to be adopted by member Governments to strengthen economic co-operation among them and to consolidate the Islamic World Development Programme.

On 15 March,[10] Bangladesh transmitted the resolutions and final declaration adopted by the Fourteenth Islamic Conference of Foreign Ministers (Dhaka, Bangladesh, 6-11 December 1983); a resolution on the world economy and the Islamic countries urged international co-operation to accelerate the development of the developing countries.

In a declaration of 19 May transmitted by Argentina, Brazil, Colombia and Mexico on 21 May,[11] their Presidents proposed that measures be adopted to transform international financial and trade policy (see also Chapter IV of this section).

On 12 June,[12] the United Kingdom transmitted the London Economic Declaration issued at the tenth Economic Summit (London, 7-9 June), attended by the heads of State or Government of seven major industrialized countries (Canada, France, Federal Republic of Germany, Italy, Japan, United Kingdom, United States) and the President of the Commission of the European Communities. The Declaration outlined economic and financial policies which would spread the benefits of economic recovery within the industrialized countries and also to the developing countries. A letter to the participants in the London Summit from the President of Panama, transmitted by Panama on 11 June,[13] drew attention to the serious economic situation in Latin America and that of the developing countries in general and requested the participants to initiate a North-South dialogue to spur on global economic negotiations (see below). On 12 June,[14] Argentina, Brazil, Colombia, Ecuador, Mexico, Peru and Venezuela transmitted a letter from their Presidents to the Summit participants calling for the situation of the Latin American economies, particularly the issues of trade, financing and external debt, to be considered at the Summit and drawing attention to the Quito Declaration and Plan of Action.[8]

On 18 June,[15] Yugoslavia transmitted the text of the final statement adopted at the second session of the Interaction Council (Brioni, Yugoslavia, 24-26 May). The Council, comprising 26 former heads of State or Government, suggested policies to deal with the debt crisis, promote development, improve trade relations, co-ordinate policy and institutions, and reform international monetary arrangements.

The USSR, on 22 June,[16] transmitted a statement on further development and intensification of economic, scientific and technical co-operation among the member countries of the Council for Mutual Economic Assistance (CMEA) which met in a high-level Economic Conference at Moscow (12-14 June). Also transmitted was the declaration of the CMEA members on maintenance of peace and international economic co-operation.

On 26 June,[17] Argentina, Bolivia, Brazil, Chile, Colombia, the Dominican Republic, Ecuador, Mexico, Peru, Uruguay and Venezuela transmitted the text of the Cartagena Consensus on the economic, social and financial situation of Latin America, signed by their Ministers for Foreign Affairs and of Finance at Cartagena, Colombia, on 22 June (see also Chapter IV of this section). On

3 October,[18] the same countries forwarded the text of the Mar del Plata Communiqué, signed at Mar del Plata, Argentina, on 14 September, which supplemented and developed the Cartagena Consensus.

A Declaration adopted at the eighth annual meeting of the Ministers for Foreign Affairs of the Group of 77 developing countries, held in New York (26-28 September) on the Group's twentieth anniversary, was transmitted by Mexico on 28 September.[19] The Declaration covered economic issues of multilateral co-operation for development as well as other issues of concern to the General Assembly.

A statement annexed to a letter of 4 October[20] from the German Democratic Republic described aid provided by that State to developing countries and national liberation movements in 1983. Information on Czechoslovakia's economic assistance to developing countries was transmitted on 6 December.[21]

In the final communiqué adopted by the Meeting of Ministers for Foreign Affairs and Heads of Delegation of Non-Aligned Countries (New York, 1-5 October), transmitted by India on 8 October,[22] the participants expressed grave concern at the persistent world economic crisis and its impact on the developing countries.

The communiqué of the thirty-ninth session of CMEA[23] (Havana, Cuba, 29-31 October) was transmitted by Cuba on 5 November. The participants reaffirmed their determination to carry out the programme of action developed by the Economic Conference for improving international economic relations (see above).

On 15 November,[24] France transmitted the Lisbon Declaration on North-South: Europe's role, adopted by a Conference on the subject organized by the Parliamentary Assembly of the Council of Europe (Lisbon, Portugal, 9-11 April).

On 29 November,[25] Romania forwarded an extract from a report on recent and future activities of the Romanian Communist Party in economic and social development, as well as the direction of Romania's foreign policy.

GENERAL ASSEMBLY ACTION

The General Assembly's Second (Economic and Financial) Committee devoted a major part of its 1984 session to development and international economic co-operation, making recommendations on a large number of specific topics (see APPENDIX IV, agenda item 80). A list of pertinent documents was included in part I of the Committee's report on this item.[26] The Assembly took note of part I in December when it adopted decision 39/426 as orally proposed by the President.

Development and international economic co-operation

At its 103rd plenary meeting, on 17 December 1984, the General Assembly took note of part I of the report of the Second Committee.

General Assembly decision 39/426

Adopted without vote

Oral proposal by President; agenda item 80.
Meeting numbers. GA 39th session: 2nd Committee 16-23, 26-28, 31, 33, 35-37, 39-47, 50, 53-55; plenary 103.

In resolution 39/218 of 18 December, the Assembly requested the Secretary-General to ascertain the views of Member States on expanding international co-operation in money, finance, debt and resource flows, including development assistance and trade, with special attention to the interests of developing countries and the effects of the economic crisis on their development, and to report to the Assembly in 1985.

Proposed global economic negotiations

Discussion on launching a round of global negotiations on international economic co-operation for development, originally scheduled to begin in 1980,[27] continued throughout 1984.

On 11 June,[13] Panama transmitted a letter from its President, who was also President of the thirty-eighth session of the General Assembly, to the London Economic Summit of the seven major industrialized countries. He recalled that the General Assembly's 1979 decision to launch global negotiations[27] was a response to the concern of the international community, and particularly of the developing countries, regarding lack of tangible progress towards establishing a new international economic order. He drew attention to the economic crisis which had serious repercussions on the great majority of developing countries and requested the Summit participants to consider initiating a new high-level North-South dialogue in order to spur on the global negotiations.

Communications forwarded by Bangladesh,[10] India,[22] Mexico[19] and the USSR[16] also called for early launching of the negotiations.

GENERAL ASSEMBLY ACTION

On 26 June, at the resumed thirty-eighth session of the General Assembly, the Assembly President gave an account of consultations which had been taking place since the beginning of the year and noted the successful conclusion in February of the exploratory process, begun during the Assembly's 1983 session. The Assembly, therefore, adopted decision 38/448 B without vote, on the President's oral proposal.

At its 105th plenary meeting, on 26 June 1984, the General Assembly decided that the item be maintained on the agenda of its thirty-eighth session and that contacts among delegations on this question be continued with a view to the convening of another round of informal meetings in the early part of September to consider appropriate action by the Assembly before the closure of the session.

Adopted without vote

Oral proposal by President; agenda item 38.

At the closing meeting of the resumed thirty-eighth session on 17 September, after the President again reported on the informal consultations and pointed out that it had not been possible to make further substantive progress, the Assembly adopted decision 38/448 C without vote.

At its 106th plenary meeting, on 17 September 1984, the General Assembly decided to include in the draft agenda of its thirty-ninth session the item entitled "Launching of global negotiations on international economic co-operation for development".

Adopted without vote

Oral proposal by President; agenda item 38.

When the Assembly again took up the matter, in December, the President reported that informal consultations had continued during the thirty-ninth session. He reminded Member States of the continuing validity of the concept of global negotiations, and appealed to them to renew their commitment to co-operate so as to launch the negotiations at the earliest practicable date.

On 18 December, the Assembly adopted decision 39/454 A without vote, as orally proposed by the President.

At its 105th plenary meeting, on 18 December 1984, the General Assembly decided to keep the item open in order to allow for the continuation of informal consultations after the suspension of the session and to reconvene on short notice to consider any decisions or agreements that might emerge from the negotiations.

Adopted without vote

Oral proposal by President; agenda item 38.

Also on 18 December, the Assembly decided by decision 39/456 to resume its thirty-ninth session, at a date to be announced, to consider several agenda items, one of which was on the launching of global negotiations.

International Development Strategy for the Third UN Development Decade

The year 1984 saw the beginning of the review and appraisal of the implementation of the International Development Strategy for the Third United Nations Development Decade (the 1980s), as provided for in the Strategy adopted by the Assembly in 1980[7] and reaffirmed in 1982.[28] Guidelines for conducting the system-wide review and appraisal procedure were contained in a December 1983 Assembly resolution.[29]

UNCTAD action. In accordance with a 1983 UNCTAD Trade and Development Board decision,[30] a high-level intergovernmental group of officials met (Geneva, 30 January–10 February) to consider the review and appraisal of the Strategy's implementation. The group had before it two related 1983 reports by the UNCTAD secretariat.[31] The group decided to annex to its report to the Board[32] documents presented by the Group of 77, Group D (centrally planned economies) and Mongolia, and Group B (developed market economies), and texts resulting from informal discussions.

In introducing the report to the thirteenth special session of the Trade and Development Board (Geneva, 2-6 April), the Vice-Chairman of the high-level group pointed out that, while the texts resulting from informal discussions reflected a large measure of agreement, square brackets in the text indicated some phrases on which agreement had not been reached or which represented the individual positions of different groups. The group had agreed that negotiations would continue in order to improve on broad areas of consensus and had discussed the introduction to the text but not completed its consideration. The question of review and appraisal *per se* was not discussed and was to be taken up by the Board. However, the views of regional groups were reflected in the documents annexed to the high-level group's report.

On 6 April, the Board decided[33] to transmit the text of the introduction, together with the texts resulting from the informal discussions of the high-level group and the report on its thirteenth special session, to the Committee on the Review and Appraisal of the Implementation of the International Development Strategy for the Third United Nations Development Decade (see below). The Board noted that progress had been made during its twenty-eighth (March/April 1984) regular session on a programme of work on protectionism and structural adjustment and on a set of conclusions on the debt and development problems of developing countries (see Chapter IV of this section), matters which were of direct relevance to the Strategy's review and appraisal.

The text, which was annexed to the Board's decision, represented UNCTAD's contribution to the review and appraisal process. The introduction comprised a number of basic ideas regarding the context, scope and intent of the review and appraisal; as in the case of the composite text, it contained some paragraphs in square brackets on which regional groups had not been able to reach agreement. The composite text dealt with areas falling within UNCTAD's competence: commodities, international trade, financial and monetary issues for development, least developed countries, technology, shipping, land-locked developing countries, island developing countries, trade relations among countries having different economic and social systems, and ECDC.

UNIDO action. In a 19 May conclusion[34] on follow-up to the Third (1980) General Conference of UNIDO and the eleventh special session of the General Assembly,[35] held in 1980 to assess progress made by the United Nations system towards establishing a new international economic order, the UNIDO Industrial Development Board agreed that the conclusions of the review and appraisal of the Strategy's implementation could be taken into account for accelerating the industrialization process in developing countries.

ACC action. ACC, in its overview report for 1983/84,[2] stated that it attached the greatest importance to the review and appraisal of the Strategy's implementation and noted that United Nations organizations were contributing to the process. The results of sectoral reviews conducted in the governing and legislative organs of a number of organizations were being submitted to the Committee on the Review and Appraisal of the Strategy (see below), as was the report of the ACC Task Force on Long-Term Development Objectives on the subject.[30]

ACC also carried out a system-wide review of the implementation of the Strategy concerning the environment which was included in its annual report to the Governing Council of the United Nations Environment Programme (UNEP) (see below).

UNEP action. At its twelfth session (Nairobi, Kenya, 16-29 May), the UNEP Governing Council had before it the annual report of ACC to the Council, with an addendum reviewing the Strategy's implementation as far as environment was concerned.[36] The review outlined progress made and ways of accelerating it. Progress in dealing with environment in the United Nations on a system-wide basis was assessed, as were overall indicators of progress. The review discussed environmental aspects of some development sectors such as food and agriculture, health, energy, industry, human settlements, and trade. Desertification control activities were also assessed.

The report concluded that progress made to give effect to environment-related directives had not been adequate to achieve environmental goals, although consciousness of environmental changes and appreciation of their bearing on social and economic well-being had grown in the developing countries. However, unless the environmental issue was integrated into decision-making on development, the Strategy's goal of sustainable development would remain elusive.

In a 28 May decision on co-ordination,[37] the UNEP Council took note of the ACC report, reiterated the importance of environmental considera-

tions for the successful implementation of the Strategy and invited the Committee on the Review and Appraisal to stress those considerations.

Committee on the Strategy. The Committee on the Review and Appraisal of the Implementation of the International Development Strategy for the Third United Nations Development Decade, established with universal membership by the General Assembly in 1982,[28] held its 1984 substantive session in New York from 7 to 25 May and from 10 to 18 September,[38] an organizational session having been held in December 1983.[39] In accordance with an Assembly resolution of the same month,[29] the Committee held informal consultations on 20 January to review the preparation of documentation and held substantive informal consultations from 23 April to 4 May. Informal consultations were also held at Geneva in July during the second regular session of the Economic and Social Council (see below). On 10 September, the Committee established an informal drafting group which considered an informal negotiating text prepared by the Chairman; the group was not able to complete its discussions on that text.

In its 1982 resolution,[28] the Assembly had requested the Secretary-General to submit to it, through the Committee and the Economic and Social Council, a comprehensive report and other documentation on the subject, a request reiterated in 1983.[29]

The Secretary-General submitted such a report in March 1984[40] assessing progress made in the first years of the Decade towards the Strategy's goals and objectives and in implementing the policy measures recommended for realizing them. The report indicated reasons for shortfalls in performances, discussed changes in economic circumstances since the Strategy's adoption, and considered prospects for and measures needed over the balance of the Decade. It drew extensively on recent work by the specialized agencies and other United Nations organizations on trends and policies and on review and appraisal of the Strategy itself. Particular use was made of papers submitted to and discussions within inter-agency meetings convened under the auspices of ACC.[30]

The report's introduction noted that the adoption of the Strategy in 1980, at a time when the economic situation was deteriorating, had reaffirmed the need for collective action to create an international environment more supportive of national development efforts. Few foresaw, however, that the recession would be so prolonged, would compel so many countries to retrench so deeply and would bring the system of international economic relations into such severe straits.

The actual economic performance of developing countries since 1980 was in stark contrast to the growth path traced in the Strategy: as a group, per capita output declined in each of the Decade's first three years; adverse trends in international trade and finance brought their external accounts under pressure and depressed domestic production and investment; export earnings, particularly from primary commodities, fell and the net inflow of financial resources contracted; and external payments difficulties were exacerbated by the debt-service burden which had been transformed by rising interest rates, shortened repayment periods and additional borrowing.

Looking at the balance of the Decade, the report discussed the likely evolution of the world economy and suggested some main issues confronting the international community in reaccelerating development. In the short term, the report noted two striking characteristics of the current evolution of the world economy: while recovery was taking place in the developed market economies, it did not follow that developing countries would be drawn into a similar upswing in activity; and economic events and policies within each group of countries were a major influence on performance of the others but not necessarily mutually reinforcing, and many of them were contradictory.

Addressing future prospects, the report projected an aggregate growth in the developing world between 1986 and 1990 in the range of 3.5 to 4.5 per cent per annum, yielding very modest increases in per capita output over the Decade as a whole, with the least developed and other low-income countries recording the slowest rates of economic expansion. The rate of growth of gross domestic project (GDP) in the developed market economies could be in the range of no more than 2.5 to 3 per cent per annum for the same period, due mainly to loss of dynamism of capital formation.

The third section of the report assessed trends and policies in individual sectors of both national economies and the international economy. It reviewed progress in implementing policy measures recommended in the Strategy and considered needed changes for the future in: international trade; industrialization; food and agriculture; financial resources for development; international monetary issues; technical co-operation; science and technology for development; energy; transport; economic and technical co-operation among developing countries; least developed, developing island and land-locked developing countries; environment; human settlements; disaster relief; and social development.

In comparing actual performance of developing countries with targets set in the Strategy for some of these areas, the report noted that for international trade, volumes of exports and imports of goods and services were to expand at annual rates of 7.5 and 8 per cent respectively, whereas in 1983 they had fallen to -0.5 and -7 per cent. Manufacturing production had grown by less than 2 per cent per annum during 1981-1982 against the target of 9 per cent. The growth target for agricultural production in developing countries was set at 4 per cent per annum, which was exceeded in 1981. However, there was a sharp slow-down in 1982 with particularly pronounced shortfalls in Africa. The target for gross domestic saving was to reach 24 per cent of GDP by 1990, with those countries having a ratio of less than 15 per cent to make efforts to raise it to 20 per cent as early as possible; estimates indicated that the saving rate had declined steadily from almost 25 per cent in 1980 and by 1983 might have been close to 20 per cent.

The Strategy set a target for official development assistance (ODA) by all developed countries to reach and possibly surpass 0.7 per cent of their gross national product (GNP) by 1985 and in any case not later than in the second half of the Decade, with a target of 1 per cent to be reached as soon as possible thereafter. The report stated that ODA from all sources declined in both 1981 and 1982. For the developed market economies, the share of ODA in GNP in 1982 was 0.38 per cent, little different from that recorded in 1980. Although members of the Organization of Petroleum Exporting Countries (OPEC) had a combined ODA/GNP ratio of about 1.2 per cent for 1982, assistance had declined since 1980 due to their worsening balance-of-payments position. Among centrally planned economies, the USSR reported an increase in net economic assistance to developing countries from 0.9 per cent of GNP in 1976 to 1.3 per cent in 1980 and 1981, Bulgaria reported 0.79 per cent of net national product over the period 1976 to 1981, Czechoslovakia reported 0.74 per cent of national income in 1982, and the German Democratic Republic reported 0.78 per cent of such income in 1981 and 0.79 per cent in 1982.

The report was complemented by a separate report on social aspects of development, requested by the Economic and Social Council in 1983 (see Chapter XIII of this section).

Among other documents submitted to the Committee's May session were a formal proposal by Mexico on behalf of the Group of 77 setting out policy measures for further implementation of the Strategy, and informal proposals by China, the European Economic Community (EEC), Japan, the Nordic countries and the United States, all of which were annexed to the Committee's report.[38]

Also brought to the attention of the Committee, the General Assembly and the Economic and Social Council was a letter of 26 April,[41] by which the Ukrainian SSR, also on behalf of Bulgaria, the Byelorussian SSR, Czechoslovakia, the German Democratic Republic, Hungary, Mongolia, Poland and the USSR, transmitted a joint statement on the review and appraisal of the Strategy's implementation. By a letter of 23 May,[42] the USSR transmitted a communication to the three bodies on its contribution to the Strategy's implementation.

CPC/ACC Joint Meetings. The implementation of the Strategy, with special emphasis on Africa, was discussed at Joint Meetings of CPC and ACC (Geneva, 2 and 3 July).[43] They concluded that overall progress in the Strategy's implementation had been disappointingly slow and limited. This was widely perceived as a symptom of the overall crisis of the international economy and of multilateral co-operation. Within the context of the Strategy, the crucial nature of the problems facing African countries was recognized. The Secretary-General's initiative in consulting his colleagues in the United Nations system with regard to the unprecedented economic and social crisis in Africa was welcomed and the importance of a coherent and co-ordinated approach to that question stressed. It was also recognized that attention should be paid to both the immediate needs and the medium- and longer-term developmental requirements in addressing the problems of Africa. The importance of taking into account the social dimension of development was emphasized and it was suggested that the 1985 Meetings could discuss the follow-up of the Strategy's implementation in the light of the outcome of the review and appraisal.

ECONOMIC AND SOCIAL COUNCIL ACTION

The Committee on the Review and Appraisal held informal consultations during the July session of the Economic and Social Council and, on 20 July, the Committee Chairman informed the Council that although the Committee had reached wide agreement, there were several key issues (mobilization of financial resources for development, international monetary and financial questions, and industrialization) on which there had not been a sufficient meeting of minds. Therefore, he was to prepare a negotiating text for the Committee's September meetings (see above).

On the proposal of its President, the Council adopted decision 1984/159 without vote.

Review and appraisal of the implementation of the International Development Strategy for the Third United Nations Development Decade

At its 46th plenary meeting, on 20 July 1984, the Council:

(*a*) Took note of the oral report made by the Chairman of the Committee on the Review and Appraisal of the Implementation of the International Development Strategy for the Third United Nations Development

Decade on the work of the Committee and decided to endorse the arrangements outlined therein for the completion of the work of the Committee;

(*b*) Decided that the final report of the Committee should be submitted directly to the General Assembly at its thirty-ninth session;

(*c*) Decided to invite all Governments to make every effort to ensure the successful conclusion of the work of the Committee.

Economic and Social Council decision 1984/159

Adopted without vote

Oral proposal by President; agenda item 5.

On the same date, on the proposal of the President, the Council adopted decision 1984/160 without vote.

Reports of the Secretary-General relating to the review and appraisal of the implementation of the International Development Strategy for the Third United Nations Development Decade

At its 46th plenary meeting, on 20 July 1984, the Council took note of the reports of the Secretary-General on the review and appraisal of the implementation of the International Development Strategy for the Third United Nations Development Decade, prepared in pursuance of General Assembly resolutions 37/202 of 20 December 1982 and 38/152 of 19 December 1983, and on the social aspects of development, prepared in pursuance of Economic and Social Council decision 1983/123 of 26 May 1983, and decided to transmit those reports to the General Assembly at its thirty-ninth session for consideration.

Economic and Social Council decision 1984/160

Adopted without vote

Oral proposal by President; agenda item 5.

In a 26 July resolution (1984/61 B), the Council took note of the report of the Chairmen of CPC and ACC on their Joint Meetings devoted to the implementation of the Strategy.

GENERAL ASSEMBLY ACTION

On 17 December, on the recommendation of the Second Committee, the Assembly adopted resolution 39/162 without vote.

Review and appraisal of the implementation of the International Development Strategy for the Third United Nations Development Decade

The General Assembly,

Recalling its resolutions 3201(S-VI) and 3202(S-VI) of 1 May 1974, containing the Declaration and the Programme of Action on the Establishment of a New International Economic Order, 3281(XXIX) of 12 December 1974, containing the Charter of Economic Rights and Duties of States, and 3362(S-VII) of 16 September 1975 on development and international economic co-operation,

Recalling also its resolution 35/56 of 5 December 1980, the annex to which contains the International Development Strategy for the Third United Nations Development Decade,

Bearing in mind its resolution 37/202 of 20 December 1982, in which it established a committee of universal membership to undertake the first review and appraisal exercise called for in paragraphs 169 to 180 of the International Development Strategy,

Recalling its resolution 38/152 of 19 December 1983, in which it reaffirmed that the process of review and appraisal of the implementation of the Strategy should consist of systematic scrutiny, within the context of an overall review of the international economic situation, of the progress made towards achieving the goals and objectives of the Strategy, and should ensure its effective implementation and strengthen it as an instrument of policy,

Taking note of the report on the work of the Committee on the Review and Appraisal of the Implementation of the International Development Strategy for the Third United Nations Development Decade, as well as of the report of the Secretary-General,

Deeply concerned that the first review and appraisal of the implementation of the International Development Strategy has not been successfully carried out,

1. *Expresses grave disappointment* that the Committee on the Review and Appraisal of the Implementation of the International Development Strategy for the Third United Nations Development Decade was unable to carry out successfully its mandate, in accordance with resolutions 37/202 and 38/152;

2. *Reaffirms* for the Third United Nations Development Decade the validity of the goals and objectives of the International Development Strategy and the need to achieve them;

3. *Reaffirms also* the urgent need to carry out the adjustment, intensification or reformulation of the policy measures set out in the Strategy, as may be necessary in the light of evolving needs and developments, in order for the instrument to contribute effectively to the development of developing countries, with a view to the establishment of the new international economic order;

4. *Requests* the Secretary-General to undertake consultations and to submit his suggestions to the Economic and Social Council, at its organizational session for 1985, on the timing, duration and necessary documentation for the resumed session of the Committee on the Review and Appraisal of the International Development Strategy for the Third United Nations Development Decade.

General Assembly resolution 39/162

17 December 1984   Meeting 103   Adopted without vote

Approved by Second Committee (A/39/790/Add.1) without vote, 11 December (meeting 59); draft by Vice-Chairman (A/C.2/39/L.136), based on informal consultations on draft by Egypt, for Group of 77 (A/C.2/39/L.122); agenda item 80 *(a)*.
Meeting numbers. GA 39th session: 2nd Committee 56, 59; plenary 103.

The draft approved by the Second Committee differed from that put forward by the Group of 77 in that, in addition to drafting changes, the Group's text referred to a mid-term review and appraisal rather than the first. In paragraph 1, the Assembly would have deeply regretted that the Committee had been unable to carry out its mandate, and, in paragraph 3, would have reaffirmed further the urgent need to carry out the necessary adjustments, intensification or reformulation of the Strategy's policy measures.

Also on 17 December, by decision 39/427, the Assembly took note of the Secretary-General's report on social aspects of development. In resolution 39/222 of 18 December, on the United Nations Children's Fund, the Assembly reaffirmed the Strategy's goals with reference to children, in particular the goals of ensuring children's immunization against major diseases by 1990 and of reducing the infant mortality rate to fewer than 50 per 1,000 live births by the year 2000.

Proposed new international economic order

During 1984, aspects of a new international economic order, called for by the General Assembly in 1974,[44] continued to be discussed in several United Nations bodies.

In March, the Commission on Human Rights recommended that the Economic and Social Council should arrange for a study on the new order and the promotion of human rights, completed in 1983,[45] to be published and given wide distribution in all United Nations official languages. By decision 1984/133 of 24 May, the Council agreed to the Commission's recommendation (see Chapter XVIII of this section).

In October, the United Nations Institute for Training and Research submitted to the General Assembly the third and final phase of an analytical study on the progressive development of the principles and norms of international law relating to the new international economic order, plus a summary and outline of the study to facilitate debate. On 13 December, in resolution 39/75, the Assembly urged Member States to submit their comments on the study, including proposals for further action (see LEGAL QUESTIONS, Chapter VI).

At its June/July session, the United Nations Commission on International Trade Law (UNCITRAL) had before it a report of its Working Group on the New International Economic Order concerning a draft legal guide on drawing up contracts for construction of industrial works. The Commission agreed that, in order to expedite the Group's work on the legal guide, it should hold two sessions prior to UNCITRAL's 1985 session. In September,[46] the UNCTAD Trade and Development Board took note of UNCITRAL's report. On 13 December, in resolution 39/82, the Assembly called on UNCITRAL to continue to take account of its 1974 and 1975 resolutions concerning the new international economic order and commended UNCITRAL for progress made towards preparing the legal guide (see LEGAL QUESTIONS, Chapter VI).

In other related action, the Assembly, by resolution 39/8 of 8 November, reaffirmed the determination of the United Nations to work closely with the Organization of African Unity towards the establishment of the new order. In resolution 39/162 of 17 December (see above), the Assembly reaffirmed the need to adjust, intensify or reformulate the International Development Strategy's policy measures in order for it to contribute effectively to the development of developing countries, with a view to establishing the new order.

Confidence-building measures

In response to a 1983 General Assembly request,[47] the Secretary-General in June 1984 submitted to the Assembly through the Economic and Social Council a report on confidence-building in international economic relations.[48] As requested by the Assembly, he had asked all States and United Nations bodies concerned for their views on confidence-building measures to promote and accelerate international economic co-operation.

The report comprised excerpts from replies received from 21 Member States which, in general, addressed three clusters of largely mutually supportive measures: reaffirmation of the basic principles and instruments of international economic co-operation; co-operative efforts to promote recovery, accelerate development and achieve progress in negotiations, including those dealing with reduction of military expenditures; and new measures to promote or reinforce confidence in co-operation, including methods for exchanging information and an international mechanism with consultative or conciliatory functions. The replies received from United Nations bodies were summarized.

In concluding remarks, the report stated that the measures proposed by those replying covered a wide range of issues and the general tone was that the United Nations had a major role to play in strengthening confidence in economic relations. However, the number of responses did not provide a sufficient basis for the Secretary-General to recommend a specific course of action. He had on several occasions drawn Member States' attention to the need for urgent action to improve the state of the global economy and especially to accelerate the development of developing countries. It was clear that the problems faced in improving international economic relations could not be separated from the parallel deterioration of the political climate in the international community and action on several fronts appeared to be required.

A working paper on confidence-building, transmitted to the Council[49] and the Assembly[50] by Poland, suggested that, in addition to disarmament, the United Nations might focus on confidence-building in finance, trade, science and technology, food and general guidelines of behaviour.

ECONOMIC AND SOCIAL COUNCIL ACTION

In July, on the proposal of its President, the Economic and Social Council adopted without vote decision 1984/186.

Report of the Secretary-General on confidence-building in international economic relations

At its 50th plenary meeting, on 27 July 1984, the Council took note of the report of the Secretary-General on confidence-building in international economic relations, prepared in response to General Assembly resolution 38/196 of 20 December 1983.

Economic and Social Council decision 1984/186

Adopted without vote

Oral proposal by President; agenda item 3.
Meeting numbers. ESC 47, 49, 50.

A draft resolution on the same topic, sponsored by Benin, the Libyan Arab Jamahiriya, Poland and the Syrian Arab Republic,[51] was withdrawn after informal consultations. By this text, the Council would have invited States and United Nations bodies to continue exchanging views in order to identify measures to reinforce confidence in economic relations, requested CDP to consider such measures, requested the Secretary-General to prepare a study on the scope of possible confidence-building measures and the role of the United Nations in the exercise, and recommended that the Assembly consider the issue as one of the vital notions in commemorating the United Nations fortieth anniversary in 1985.

GENERAL ASSEMBLY ACTION

On 18 December, on the recommendation of the Second Committee, the General Assembly adopted by recorded vote resolution 39/226.

Confidence-building in international economic relations

The General Assembly,

Taking note of the report of the Secretary-General prepared in response to its resolution 38/196 of 20 December 1983 on confidence-building in international economic relations,

Recalling that the spirit of mutual confidence made possible the founding of the United Nations nearly forty years ago,

Convinced that the state of, and trends prevailing in, the world economy, as well as the deteriorating international climate, call for new efforts aimed at enhancing confidence in international economic relations,

Convinced also that there can be no sustained global development unless there is an improvement in the economic situation of the developing countries, which depends, *inter alia*, on structural adjustments in the international financial and trading system and on the reinforcement of confidence among all States in their economic relations,

Reiterating its concern over the impact of political tensions on international economic co-operation and over the increasing departure from the multilateral platform of economic exchanges and negotiations on key development issues,

1. *Invites* all States and the United Nations bodies and organizations concerned to continue the exchange of views on confidence-building in international economic relations and on ways and means of enhancing such confidence;

2. *Requests* the Secretary-General to continue his consultations with Governments and the United Nations bodies and organizations concerned on the scope of possible confidence-building measures in international economic relations and on the role of the United Nations in that endeavour, and to present his analysis and conclusions thereon to the General Assembly at its forty-first session, through the Economic and Social Council.

General Assembly resolution 39/226

18 December 1984   Meeting 104   111-17-12 (recorded vote)

Approved by Second Committee (A/39/789) by recorded vote (93-18-10), 30 November (meeting 54); draft by Poland (A/C.2/39/L.30), orally corrected; agenda item 12. *Meeting numbers.* GA 39th session: 2nd Committee 41, 54; plenary 104.

Recorded vote in Assembly as follows:

In favour: Afghanistan, Algeria, Angola, Argentina, Bahamas, Bahrain, Bangladesh, Barbados, Benin, Bhutan, Bolivia, Botswana, Brunei Darussalam, Bulgaria, Burkina Faso, Burma, Burundi, Byelorussian SSR, Cape Verde, China, Colombia, Congo, Costa Rica, Cuba, Cyprus, Czechoslovakia, Democratic Kampuchea, Democratic Yemen, Dominican Republic, Ecuador, Egypt, El Salvador, Equatorial Guinea, Ethiopia, Fiji, Gambia, German Democratic Republic, Ghana, Greece, Guatemala, Guinea, Guinea-Bissau, Guyana, Haiti, Honduras, Hungary, Indonesia, Iran, Iraq, Jamaica, Kenya, Kuwait, Lao People's Democratic Republic, Lesotho, Liberia, Libyan Arab Jamahiriya, Madagascar, Malawi, Malaysia, Maldives, Mali, Malta, Mauritania, Mauritius, Mexico, Mongolia, Mozambique, Nepal, Nicaragua, Niger, Nigeria, Oman, Pakistan, Panama, Papua New Guinea, Paraguay, Peru, Philippines, Poland, Qatar, Romania, Rwanda, Saint Christopher and Nevis, Saint Lucia, Saint Vincent and the Grenadines, Samoa, Sao Tome and Principe, Saudi Arabia, Sierra Leone, Somalia, Sri Lanka, Suriname, Swaziland, Syrian Arab Republic, Thailand, Togo, Trinidad and Tobago, Tunisia, Uganda, Ukrainian SSR, USSR, United Arab Emirates, United Republic of Tanzania, Uruguay, Vanuatu, Viet Nam, Yemen, Yugoslavia, Zaire, Zambia, Zimbabwe.

Against: Australia, Belgium, Canada, France, Germany, Federal Republic of, Iceland, Ireland, Israel, Italy, Japan, Luxembourg, Netherlands, New Zealand, Norway, Portugal, United Kingdom, United States.

Abstaining: Austria, Chad, Chile, Denmark,[a] Finland, Gabon, Ivory Coast, Morocco, Senegal, Spain, Sweden, Turkey.

[a]Later advised the Secretariat it had intended to vote in favour.

The recorded vote in the Second Committee was requested by the United States. Explaining their votes, Egypt, India and Pakistan regretted that a draft on confidence-building had been put to a vote, while the Sudan gave that reason for its non-participation. The German Democratic Republic, speaking on behalf of the socialist States of Eastern Europe and Mongolia, said it was deplorable that some delegations had been unable to support the draft since it set forth a minimum of the mutual understanding and practical measures required to establish confidence in international economic relations. Saint Lucia, referring to paragraph 2, stated that the methodology to be used in no way bound its future position.

Coercive economic measures against developing countries

Pursuant to a December 1983 General Assembly request,[52] the Secretary-General in September 1984 submitted a report on the adoption and

effects of economic measures taken by developed countries as a means of political and economic coercion against developing countries.[53] The report was based on information provided by 24 States members of UNCTAD in response to a request for such information from the UNCTAD Secretary-General. The texts of the replies received were annexed to the report.

Summarizing the replies, the report stated that they reflected the view that the 1983 resolution[52] remained largely unimplemented and in that connection some Governments made suggestions for its full implementation, which could be studied during any further work. The majority felt that the United Nations should continue to play the major role in studying and compiling information provided by Governments and also had to keep its leading position in elaborating measures to eliminate any political and economic coercion from international economic relations in order to restore a climate of peaceful co-operation among States, as well as to accelerate development in the developing countries.

GENERAL ASSEMBLY ACTION

On 18 December, on the recommendation of the Second Committee, the General Assembly adopted by recorded vote resolution 39/210.

Economic measures as a means of political and economic coercion against developing countries

The General Assembly,

Recalling the relevant principles set forth in the Charter of the United Nations,

Recalling also its resolutions 2625(XXV) of 24 October 1970, containing the Declaration on Principles of International Law concerning Friendly Relations and Co-operation among States in accordance with the Charter of the United Nations, 3201(S-VI) and 3202(S-VI) of 1 May 1974, containing the Declaration and the Programme of Action on the Establishment of a New International Economic Order, and 3281(XXIX) of 12 December 1974, containing the Charter of Economic Rights and Duties of States,

Reaffirming article 32 of the Charter of Economic Rights and Duties of States, which declares that no State may use or encourage the use of economic, political or any other type of measures to coerce another State in order to obtain from it the subordination of the exercise of its sovereign rights,

Bearing in mind the general principles governing international trade and trade policies for development contained in its resolution 1995(XIX) of 30 December 1964, resolution 152(VI) of 2 July 1983 of the United Nations Conference on Trade and Development entitled "Rejection of coercive economic measures", and the principles and rules of the General Agreement on Tariffs and Trade and paragraph 7 (iii) of the Ministerial Declaration adopted on 29 November 1982 by the Contracting Parties of the General Agreement on Tariffs and Trade at their thirty-eighth session,

Reaffirming its resolution 38/197 of 20 December 1983,

Taking note of the report of the Secretary-General on the adoption and effects of economic measures taken by developed countries as a means of political and economic coercion against developing countries,

Gravely concerned that the use of coercive measures adversely affects the economies and development efforts of developing countries and that, in some cases, those measures have worsened, creating a negative impact on international economic co-operation,

1. *Deplores* the fact that some developed countries continue to apply and, in some cases, have increased the scope of economic measures that have the purpose of exerting coercion on the sovereign decisions of developing countries subject to those measures;

2. *Reaffirms* that developed countries should refrain from threatening or applying trade restrictions, blockades, embargoes and other economic sanctions, incompatible with the provisions of the Charter of the United Nations and in violation of undertakings contracted multilaterally or bilaterally, against developing countries as a form of political and economic coercion which affects their economic, political and social development;

3. *Requests* the Secretary-General to prepare a comprehensive report on the economic measures mentioned in paragraph 2 above, taken by developed countries for coercive purposes, including their impact on international economic relations, with a view to assisting in concrete international actions against those measures, and to submit that report to the General Assembly at its fortieth session;

4. *Also requests* the Secretary-General, in preparing the comprehensive report, to request further comments from Governments and to use inputs from competent organizations of the United Nations system, particularly the United Nations Conference on Trade and Development and the regional commissions;

5. *Appeals* to Governments to provide the necessary information to the Secretary-General, as requested in paragraph 4 above.

General Assembly resolution 39/210

18 December 1984   Meeting 104   116-19-6 (recorded vote)

Approved by Second Committee (A/39/790/Add.3) by recorded vote (102-19-6), 6 December (meeting 56); draft by Egypt, for Group of 77 (A/C.2/39/L.75); agenda item 80 *(c)*.

Meeting numbers. GA 39th session: 2nd Committee 53, 56; plenary 104.

Recorded vote in Assembly as follows:

In favour: Afghanistan, Albania, Algeria, Angola, Argentina, Bahamas, Bahrain, Bangladesh, Barbados, Benin, Bhutan, Bolivia, Botswana, Brazil, Brunei Darussalam, Bulgaria, Burkina Faso, Burma, Burundi, Byelorussian SSR, Cape Verde, Chad, Chile, China, Colombia, Congo, Costa Rica, Cuba, Cyprus, Czechoslovakia, Democratic Kampuchea, Democratic Yemen, Djibouti, Dominican Republic, Ecuador, Egypt, El Salvador, Equatorial Guinea, Ethiopia, Fiji, Gabon, Gambia, German Democratic Republic, Ghana, Guatemala, Guinea, Guinea-Bissau, Guyana, Haiti, Honduras, Hungary, India, Indonesia, Iran, Jordan, Kenya, Kuwait, Lao People's Democratic Republic, Lebanon, Liberia, Libyan Arab Jamahiriya, Malawi, Malaysia, Maldives, Mali, Malta, Mauritania, Mauritius, Mexico, Mongolia, Morocco, Mozambique, Nepal, Nicaragua, Niger, Nigeria, Oman, Pakistan, Panama, Papua New Guinea, Paraguay, Peru, Philippines, Poland, Qatar, Romania, Rwanda, Saint Vincent and the Grenadines, Samoa, Sao Tome and Principe, Saudi Arabia, Senegal, Sierra Leone, Singapore, Somalia, Sri Lanka, Sudan, Suriname, Swaziland, Syrian Arab Republic, Thailand, Togo, Trinidad and Tobago, Tunisia, Uganda, Ukrainian SSR, USSR, United Arab Emirates, United Republic of Tanzania, Uruguay, Venezuela, Viet Nam, Yemen, Yugoslavia, Zaire, Zambia.

Against: Australia, Belgium, Canada, Denmark, France, Germany, Federal Republic of, Iceland, Ireland, Israel, Italy, Japan, Luxembourg, Netherlands, New Zealand, Norway, Portugal, Turkey, United Kingdom, United States.

Abstaining: Austria, Finland, Greece, Ivory Coast, Spain, Sweden.

Almost all those who spoke in explanation of vote in the Second Committee said that they held the same position they had voiced at the adoption of the 1983 resolution on the subject.[54] Austria and Sweden said they had rejected coercive economic measures when not taken in the framework of à Security Council decision; the current text did not meet the criterion of universality. Similarly, Israel said the draft was restrictive. Ireland (on behalf of the EEC members) agreed, adding that, in general, they subscribed to the 1970 Declaration on Principles of International Law concerning Friendly Relations and Co-operation among States in accordance with the Charter of the United Nations,[55] under which no State might use or encourage coercive measures. Portugal believed the text was unilateral and of a political nature. Turkey felt the question was not within UNCTAD's competence.

Economic rights and duties of States

Pursuant to a 1982 General Assembly request,[56] by which it decided to conduct in 1984 a review of the implementation of its 1974 Charter of Economic Rights and Duties of States,[57] the Secretary-General submitted a report on the subject in July, with a later addendum,[58] to the Assembly through the Economic and Social Council. In accordance with that request, the Secretary-General had invited Governments, intergovernmental organizations and United Nations bodies to communicate to him information on their application of the Charter's provisions. The report contained synoptic tables and summaries reflecting information provided by 25 Governments, one intergovernmental organization and nine United Nations bodies.

ECONOMIC AND SOCIAL COUNCIL ACTION

On 26 July, the Economic and Social Council adopted by a roll-call vote resolution 1984/64.

Charter of Economic Rights and Duties of States

The Economic and Social Council,

Recalling the Declaration and the Programme of Action on the Establishment of a New International Economic Order, contained in General Assembly resolutions 3201(S-VI) and 3202(S-VI) of 1 May 1974, the Charter of Economic Rights and Duties of States, contained in Assembly resolution 3281(XXIX) of 12 December 1974, and Assembly resolution 3362(S-VII) of 16 September 1975 on development and international economic co-operation, which laid down the foundations of the new international economic order,

Bearing in mind the adoption by the General Assembly, on 12 December 1974, of the Charter of Economic Rights and Duties of States,

Recalling General Assembly resolution 37/204 of 20 December 1982, in which the Assembly decided to carry out, at its thirty-ninth session, a comprehensive review of the implementation of the Charter, as provided for in article 34 thereof,

1. *Recommends* the General Assembly, at its thirty-ninth session, to commemorate the tenth anniversary of the adoption of the Charter of Economic Rights and Duties of States in a suitable and appropriate manner at a plenary meeting on 12 December 1984;

2. *Invites* Governments and intergovernmental organizations which have not yet done so to submit to the Secretary-General their comments on the implementation of the Charter, in accordance with General Assembly resolution 37/204.

Economic and Social Council resolution 1984/64

26 July 1984   Meeting 49   39-1-8 (roll-call vote)

Draft by Mexico, for Group of 77 (E/1984/L.38); agenda item 3.
Meeting numbers. ESC 47, 49.

Roll-call vote in Council as follows:

In favour: Algeria, Argentina, Austria, Benin, Bulgaria, China, Colombia, Congo, Costa Rica, Djibouti, Ecuador, Finland, German Democratic Republic, Greece, Guyana, Indonesia, Lebanon, Malaysia, Mexico, New Zealand, Pakistan, Papua New Guinea, Poland, Portugal, Qatar, Romania, Rwanda, Saint Lucia, Saudi Arabia, Sri Lanka, Sweden, Suriname, Thailand, Tunisia, Uganda, USSR, Venezuela, Yugoslavia, Zaire.
Against: United States.
Abstaining: Canada, France, Germany, Federal Republic of, Japan, Luxembourg, Netherlands, Somalia,[a] United Kingdom.

[a]Later stated it had intended to vote in favour.

Speaking in explanation of vote, Poland said that, in the opinion of the socialist countries of Eastern Europe, the Secretary-General's report was not an adequate or appropriate response to the Assembly's 1982 resolution; the Secretariat should ensure that a full review of activities in implementation of the Charter could be submitted to the Assembly later in 1984.

The United Kingdom said that a commemoration of the Charter's adoption, as proposed in the draft, would be a waste of time and money.

By decision 1984/187 of 27 July on reports considered in connection with its general discussion of international economic and social policy (see below, under "Economic surveys and trends"), the Council took note of the Secretary-General's report.

GENERAL ASSEMBLY ACTION

In accordance with the Council's recommendation, a General Assembly plenary meeting was held on 12 December to commemorate the tenth anniversary of the adoption of the Charter of Economic Rights and Duties of States.

On 17 December, on the recommendation of the Second Committee, the Assembly adopted by recorded vote resolution 39/163.

Charter of Economic Rights and Duties of States
The General Assembly,
Recalling its resolutions 3201(S-VI) and 3202(S-VI) of 1 May 1974, containing the Declaration and the Programme of Action on the Establishment of a New International Economic Order, 3281(XXIX) of 12 December 1974, containing the Charter of Economic Rights and Duties of States, and 3362(S-VII) of 16 September 1975 on development and international economic co-operation, which laid down the foundations of the new international economic order,

Bearing in mind article 34 of the Charter of Economic Rights and Duties of States and General Assembly resolution 3486(XXX) of 12 December 1975, relating to the review of the implementation of the Charter,

Recalling its resolution 37/204 of 20 December 1982, in which it decided to conduct at its thirty-ninth session, on the occasion of the tenth anniversary of the adoption of the Charter of Economic Rights and Duties of States, a comprehensive review of its implementation, as provided for in article 34 thereof,

Having examined the report of the Secretary-General on the implementation of the Charter of Economic Rights and Duties of States, submitted in accordance with General Assembly resolution 37/204,

Deeply concerned at the gravity of the world economic situation and its impact on the developing countries,

1. *Decides* to undertake a thorough and systematic review of the implementation of the Charter of Economic Rights and Duties of States, taking into account the evolution of all the economic, social, legal and other factors related to the principles upon which the Charter is based and to its purpose, in order to identify the most appropriate actions for the implementation of the Charter that would lead to lasting solutions to the grave economic problems of developing countries within the framework of the United Nations;

2. *Decides also* to establish an *Ad Hoc* Committee of the Whole to Review the Implementation of the Charter of Economic Rights and Duties of States, to be convened for three weeks in 1985, to carry out the review mentioned in paragraph 1 above, and requests the Committee to report thereon to the General Assembly at its fortieth session;

3. *Requests* the Secretary-General to prepare a report on the implementation of the Charter of Economic Rights and Duties of States, to be submitted to the *Ad Hoc* Committee in 1985.

General Assembly resolution 39/163

17 December 1984   Meeting 103   125-10-12 (recorded vote)

Approved by Second Committee (A/39/790/Add.2) by recorded vote (101-11-12), 6 December (meeting 56); draft by Egypt, for Group of 77 (A/C.2/39/L.98); agenda item 80 *(b)*.
Financial implications. 5th Committee, A/39/815; S-G, A/C.2/39/L.113, A/C.5/39/85.
Meeting numbers. GA 39th session: 2nd Committee 55, 56; 5th Committee 45, plenary 103.

Recorded vote in Assembly as follows:

In favour: Afghanistan, Algeria, Angola, Argentina, Bahamas, Bahrain, Bangladesh, Barbados, Benin, Bhutan, Bolivia, Botswana, Brazil, Brunei Darussalam, Bulgaria, Burkina Faso, Burma, Burundi, Byelorussian SSR, Cameroon, Cape Verde, Central African Republic, Chad, Chile, China, Colombia, Costa Rica, Cuba, Cyprus, Czechoslovakia, Democratic Kampuchea, Democratic Yemen, Djibouti, Dominican Republic, Ecuador, Egypt, El Salvador, Equatorial Guinea, Ethiopia, Fiji, Gabon, Gambia, German Democratic Republic, Ghana, Greece, Guatemala, Guinea, Guinea-Bissau, Guyana, Haiti, Honduras, Hungary, India, Indonesia, Iran, Iraq, Ivory Coast, Jamaica, Jordan, Kenya, Kuwait, Lao People's Democratic Republic, Lebanon, Lesotho, Liberia, Libyan Arab Jamahiriya, Madagascar, Malawi, Malaysia, Maldives, Mali, Malta, Mauritania, Mauritius, Mexico, Mongolia, Morocco, Mozambique, Nepal, Nicaragua, Niger, Nigeria, Oman, Pakistan, Panama, Papua New Guinea, Paraguay, Peru, Philippines, Poland, Qatar, Romania, Rwanda, Saint Lucia, Samoa, Sao Tome and Principe, Saudi Arabia, Senegal, Sierra Leone, Singapore, Somalia, Sri Lanka, Sudan, Suriname, Swaziland, Syrian Arab Republic, Thailand, Togo, Trinidad and Tobago, Tunisia, Turkey, Uganda, Ukrainian SSR, USSR, United Arab Emirates, United Republic of Tanzania, Uruguay, Vanuatu, Venezuela, Viet Nam, Yemen, Yugoslavia, Zaire, Zambia, Zimbabwe.
Against: Belgium, Canada, Denmark, France, Germany, Federal Republic of, Italy, Japan, Luxembourg, United Kingdom, United States.
Abstaining: Australia, Austria, Finland, Iceland, Ireland, Israel, Netherlands, New Zealand, Norway, Portugal, Spain, Sweden.

Speaking in explanation of vote in the Second Committee, Portugal said it had always supported the Charter but did not agree with the review procedure provided for in the draft. The Netherlands said its position with respect to the Charter had not changed—some provisions were important but others gave rise to serious reservations; a review process was desirable, but the solution in the draft resolution was not the best one, particularly because of its financial implications; a meeting during the spring 1985 session of the Economic and Social Council would have been preferable. Sweden said it had supported the 1974 adoption of the Charter, despite some reservations; it had doubts about the usefulness of the procedure envisaged for improving the North-South dialogue. Speaking similarly, Finland added that the text would not promote rationalization of economic activities nor enhance the Organization's credibility. Australia said that it continued to support the Charter but did not find the proposed review mechanism justified. The resolution's sponsors had also failed to indicate why a three-week meeting should be organized or what its objectives, agenda and procedures would be. Austria was not convinced of a need to set up a Charter Committee which, it felt, might duplicate the Sixth (Legal) Committee's work on the new international economic order.

Economic co-operation among developing countries

During 1984, the United Nations continued to promote ECDC, mainly through UNCTAD. Technical co-operation among developing countries (TCDC) received the support of UNDP (see next chapter).

UNCTAD activities. At its March/April 1984 session,[59] the UNCTAD Trade and Development Board endorsed a 1983 report by its Committee on Economic Co-operation among Developing Countries.[60]

As recommended by the Committee in 1983, a 1984 meeting was held by the secretariats of economic co-operation and integration groupings of developing countries and multilateral development finance institutions to examine the problems of promoting and financing integration projects (Geneva, 4-8 June).[61] The meeting agreed to a series of recommendations for follow-up concerning pre-investment funds for and promotion of integration projects, financing of such projects and guarantee requirements.

UNIDO action. On 19 August, the Fourth General Conference of UNIDO (see Chapter VI of this section) adopted a resolution on strengthening ECDC[62] by which it recommended that the developing countries co-operate in sharing information and facilitating the flow of human, scientific, technological, energy and financial resources, as well as in increasing direct investment among themselves and collaboration, and in increasing South-South trade and other exchanges. The Conference invited the developed countries to support ECDC through increased voluntary contributions to UNDP and the United Nations Industrial Development Fund. It decided to give high priority to industrial co-operation among developing countries in UNIDO's activities, and requested that body to provide more active support for the implementation of such co-operation within the overall context of ECDC and TCDC and to assist subregional, regional and interregional co-operation efforts of developing countries in various areas of industrial development. UNIDO was also requested to strengthen its information, project development, industrial investment promotion and technical assistance activities in ECDC. The Conference also recommended that UNIDO co-ordinate more closely with various international organizations in ECDC to avoid duplication of effort and to ensure optimum use of resources.

Co-ordination in the UN system

ACC activities. In accordance with a July 1983 Economic and Social Council resolution on Joint Meetings of CPC and ACC on ECDC and TCDC,[63] ACC considered its informal draft report on support by the United Nations system for such co-operation at its first regular session of 1984 (London, 16-18 April).[2] The draft outlined measures to be undertaken to respond to the concern of Governments as expressed in the 1983 Council resolution.

At its April session, ACC adopted a decision[64] by which it approved the draft report, the final version of which was to be submitted to CPC after the 1984 CPC/ACC Joint Meetings (see below).

CPC activities. In response to a 1983 Economic and Social Council resolution,[63] a report by the Secretary-General analysing the mandates of, and problems addressed by, the United Nations system in ECDC and TCDC[65] was submitted to the General Assembly through CPC. The report was to be the basis for preparation of a cross-organizational programme analysis of ECDC and TCDC to be carried out by CPC in 1985. The Assembly, in December 1983,[66] had endorsed the Council resolution and requested it, as well as CPC, to consider the initial report.

The report first traced the origins of the concept of ECDC and TCDC and went on to describe the legislative mandates of the United Nations system directly referring to co-operation among developing countries going back to 1964, when the first United Nations Conference on Trade and Development was convened. The report stated that such mandates ranged from comprehensive policy statements to specific actions to be taken in narrowly defined fields. For the United Nations, a total of 405 global and regional mandates for action were identified. In addition, 40 resolutions adopted by the governing bodies of the specialized agencies related directly to ECDC and TCDC.

The report described major areas of activity of the United Nations system in ECDC and TCDC which included trade, monetary and financial co-operation, industrial development, transport and communications, science and technology, food and agriculture, natural resources and energy, development planning and administration, health, social development and other areas.

In its conclusions and recommendations, the report stated that operationally usable criteria had to be found for determining which United Nations system activities should be deemed to support ECDC and TCDC and thus be included in the cross-organizational programme analysis. A further task would be to see whether an analysis of activities in ECDC and TCDC could help to clarify the distinction beween the two. In order to structure the disparate elements of the system's activities into a comprehensive whole for analysis, the report proposed that the content of each activity be classified using several different categories. The key elements of the proposed classification structure were the main and subsidiary areas of activity covered and the nature of United Nations system support for ECDC and TCDC. It was also proposed that information collected on each activity include estimated biennial cost for 1982-1983 and for 1984-1985, its source of funding and the nature of co-operation in its planning and execution with other organizations, both within and outside the system.

At its twenty-fourth session (New York, 23 April–1 June),[67] CPC endorsed the methodology proposed in the Secretary-General's report for the preparation of the cross-organizational programme analysis, especially the elements relating to collection of information on financial data, funding sources and co-operation with other organizations. It considered, however, that some aspects of the criteria proposed needed further refinement.

CPC felt that the report on the programme analysis should critically assess the United Nations system's role and the relationship between its activities and mandates, in order to permit CPC to make recommendations for improving the United Nations work in ECDC and TCDC.

Regarding the distinction between ECDC and TCDC, the programme analysis should consider whether problems existed in defining the relative competence of UNDP and UNCTAD or in co-ordinating their activities. It was also recommended that the relevant activities of the World

Bank, IMF and the International Fund for Agricultural Development (IFAD) be included in the analysis.

The Committee decided that the 1984 CPC/ACC Joint Meetings should consider an ACC report on a follow-up to the 1983 joint discussions.[68].

CPC/ACC Joint Meetings. A report on support by United Nations organizations for ECDC and TCDC[69] was submitted by ACC to its July 1984 Joint Meetings with CPC. Prepared as a follow-up to the 1983 discussions, the report examined policy issues related to United Nations support, described measures taken or proposed to enhance the effectiveness of United Nations activities in support of co-operation, and suggested areas in which such activities could be reoriented or strengthened.

Possible areas for enhanced United Nations support included: improved access to the flow of information from the system; support of South-South information activities; support of negotiations; new initiatives in operational activities; reorientation of research; and long-term programming.

It was generally agreed by the Joint Meetings[43] that the ACC report reflected a positive reaction by the system to the previous year's discussions, although more needed to be done. It was suggested that a new inter-agency mechanism might be required to promote better co-ordination of activities in the field and to serve as a link with the Group of 77 developing countries.

With respect to the cross-organizational programme analysis to be presented to CPC in 1985, it was pointed out that the interrelationship between ECDC and implementation of United Nations decisions on restructuring of international economic relations and on the establishment of a new international economic order should be taken into account.

ECONOMIC AND SOCIAL COUNCIL ACTION

In a 26 July resolution (1984/61 A, section VI) on the report of CPC, the Economic and Social Council requested the Secretary-General to ensure that future cross-organizational programme analyses, particularly that of ECDC and TCDC, would provide a critical analysis of gaps in coverage of the activities mandated and of priorities, as well as of overlaps and co-ordination, taking into consideration problems in defining the relative competences of UNDP and UNCTAD or in co-ordinating their activities. The Secretary-General was also requested to refine further the criteria proposed in his report[65] for identifying activities to be included in the cross-organizational programme analysis of ECDC and TCDC. The Council recommended that the analysis should contain a critical analytical assessment of the role of the United

Nations system and the relationship between its activities and mandates, including difficulties encountered.

In a decision of 26 July (1984/176) on reports considered by the Council in connection with the question of international co-operation and co-ordination within the United Nations system, the Council took note of the Secretary-General's report[65] and transmitted it to the General Assembly.

GENERAL ASSEMBLY ACTION

On 18 December, the General Assembly took action with regard to ECDC and TCDC.

On the recommendation of the Second Committee, it adopted resolution 39/216 without vote.

Activities of the United Nations system in support of economic co-operation among developing countries

The General Assembly,

Recognizing that economic co-operation among developing countries is an integral part of the efforts to establish the new international economic order, without being a substitute for or an alternative to co-operation between developed and developing countries, and that the Caracas Programme of Action adopted by the High-level Conference on Economic Co-operation among Developing Countries, held at Caracas from 13 to 19 May 1981, provides their basic framework for specific activities and arrangements in the field of economic co-operation among developing countries,

Mindful of the various resolutions adopted within the United Nations system in support of economic co-operation among developing countries and calling for appropriate action on them,

Looking forward to the cross-organizational programme analysis on economic co-operation among developing countries, to be considered by the Committee for Programme and Co-ordination at its twenty-fifth session, and to the cross-organizational programme review of the activities of the United Nations system on the same subject, to be held at the second regular session of the Economic and Social Council in 1985,

1. *Urges* the organs and organizations of the United Nations system to provide and to intensify support and assistance, in accordance with their mandates, to economic co-operation among developing countries, giving due regard to the Caracas Programme of Action;

2. *Urges* the Secretary-General, giving due consideration to the conclusions emerging from the ongoing cross-organizational programme analysis, to pay careful attention to economic co-operation among developing countries in preparing his programme budget proposals for the biennium 1986-1987 and to include in his future performance reports on the programme budget specific information on the implementation of activities for economic co-operation among developing countries;

3. *Requests* the Secretary-General, in consultation with the executive heads of the bodies and organizations of the United Nations system and of the specialized agencies, to keep the activities of the United Nations system in support of economic co-operation among developing countries under periodic review in the existing inter-agency machinery;

4. *Recommends* that the documentation being prepared for the cross-organizational programme review of medium-term plans in economic and technical co-operation among developing countries and for the cross-organizational programme analysis should be combined into one report so as to ensure an integrated approach to this area;

5. *Requests* the executive secretaries of the regional commissions to continue to intensify activities to support economic co-operation among developing countries at the subregional, regional and interregional levels and to include an assessment of progress made in their reports to the Economic and Social Council;

6. *Requests* the Secretary-General of the United Nations Conference on Trade and Development, in view of its key role in the area of economic co-operation among developing countries, to continue to intensify activities in this area, in accordance with its mandate;

7. *Requests* the Secretary-General to report to the General Assembly at its fortieth session on the implementation of the present resolution.

General Assembly resolution 39/216

18 December 1984   Meeting 104   Adopted without vote

Approved by Second Committee (A/39/790/Add.7) without vote, 14 December (meeting 60); draft by Vice-Chairman (A/C.2/39/L.137) — based on informal consultations on draft by Egypt, for Group of 77 (A/C.2/39/L.48) — orally revised and further orally amended by Egypt, for Group of 77; agenda item 80 *(g)*.

Meeting numbers. GA 39th session: 2nd Committee 44, 60; plenary 104.

The Vice-Chairman's draft was orally amended by Egypt on behalf of the Group of 77, to delete, in paragraph 7, after "*Requests* the Secretary-General", the phrase "giving due regard to the support of the United Nations system for the implementation, by the developing countries, of the Caracas Programme of Action".

The text approved by the Second Committee differed in a number of respects from the original draft by the Group of 77. That text did not include the third preambular paragraph or paragraphs 4 and 6. By the second preambular paragraph, the Assembly would have called for full implementation of, rather than appropriate action on, United Nations resolutions on ECDC.

By paragraph 1, the Assembly would have urged increased support and assistance to ECDC, in particular implementation of the 1981 Caracas Programme of Action.[70] Paragraph 2 would not have included the phrase "giving due consideration to the conclusions emerging from the ongoing cross-organizational programme analysis" and the Assembly would have urged increased rather than careful attention to ECDC.

The Group's text had included a request by the Assembly for the United Nations system to intensify efforts in support of ECDC by increasing utilization of technical and other capabilities of developing countries. In reporting on the resolution's implementation, the Secretary-General would have been requested to take account of the Caracas Programme of Action and the 1979 Arusha Programme for Collective Self-Reliance and Framework for Negotiations.[71]

As recommended by the Second Committee, the Assembly adopted decision 39/435 without vote.

Report of the Secretary-General on analysis of the mandates of, and problems addressed by, the United Nations system in economic and technical co-operation among developing countries

At its 104th plenary meeting, on 18 December 1984, the General Assembly, on the recommendation of the Second Committee, took note of the report of the Secretary-General on analysis of the mandates of, and problems addressed by, the United Nations system in economic and technical co-operation among developing countries.

General Assembly decision 39/435

Adopted without vote

Approved by Second Committee (A/39/790/Add.7) without vote, 14 December (meeting 60); oral proposal by Chairman; agenda item 80 (g).

Co-operation among regional commissions

Following up a July 1983 Economic and Social Council resolution on promoting interregional economic and technical co-operation among developing countries,[72] the Secretary-General submitted to the Council in June 1984 a report on progress made in implementing that resolution.[73] The report stated that the executive secretaries of the regional commissions had consulted with concerned United Nations organizations and agencies on operational aspects for joint promotion and an initial review of the views of those bodies showed that there was a positive attitude towards the need for and the potential benefits from increased co-ordination. There was also a considerable degree of consensus on the need to translate ECDC and TCDC into concrete action.

Parallel to the consultation process, the regional commissions had taken action to continue promoting interregional ECDC and TCDC. It had been agreed that the Economic Commission for Europe (ECE) would disseminate to the other regions technical information and expertise available within ECE in a number of sectors relevant to economic and social development, such as energy and transport. Some regional commissions were moving towards the operative stage, and the Economic Commission for Africa and the Economic Commission for Latin America had prepared a joint promotional project in mining and had exchanged draft proposals for a project on trade promotion between a selected group of countries from the two regions. Consultations had been held between the Economic and Social Commission for Asia and the Pacific and the Economic Commission for Western Asia on a transport and communications decade for Asia and the Pacific (1985-1994) (see Chapter VIII of this section).

In its conclusions and recommendations, the report stated that it was of primary importance that the first periodic consultation between the regional commissions and United Nations organizations active at the regional and interregional levels be convened at an early date, possibly during the second 1984 session of ACC to be held on 22 and 23 October. Agenda items could be: the examination of answers received from United Nations organizations and agencies on operational modalities for setting up and executing joint projects to promote and support interregional ECDC and TCDC; the identification of project ideas in selected priority areas; possible co-ordinated actions in international financial co-operation; and activities that had been carried out or were being planned in specific aspects of interregional co-operation.

ECONOMIC AND SOCIAL COUNCIL ACTION

On 27 July, on the proposal of its President, the Economic and Social Council adopted without vote decision 1984/185.

Promotion of interregional economic and technical co-operation among developing countries

At its 50th plenary meeting, on 27 July 1984, the Council:

(a) Took note of the conclusions and recommendations contained in the report of the Secretary-General on the progress made in the implementation of Council resolution 1983/66 of 29 July 1983 on the promotion of interregional economic and technical co-operation among developing countries;

(b) Decided to request the Secretary-General to continue to implement resolution 1983/66 and to report thereon to the Council at its second regular session of 1985.

Economic and Social Council decision 1984/185

Adopted without vote

Oral proposal by President; agenda item 9.

On 18 July, a draft resolution on promotion of interregional economic and technical co-operation among developing countries[74] was introduced in the Council's First (Economic) Committee by Mexico on behalf of the Group of 77 developing countries. By this text, which was subsequently withdrawn, the Council would have: called on Member States to support the regional commissions in promoting such co-operation; endorsed the conclusions and recommendations in the Secretary-General's report;[73] and decided that the first periodic consultation between the regional commissions and the United Nations organizations concerned should be convened during the October session of ACC. The Secretary-General would have been requested: to continue to ensure co-ordination and co-operation in preparing and implementing programmes and activities of the regional commissions; to assess the capacities and potentials of the specialized agencies and other

United Nations bodies to increase support for ECDC and TCDC, to suggest ways of strengthening activities in that area, and to report to the General Assembly in 1985 through the Council; and to take into account the need to intensify activities in ECDC and TCDC in preparing the 1986-1987 programme budget. The Council would also have recommended that the United Nations system maintain close contact with developing countries so as to improve the system's effectiveness and its responsiveness to their needs. It would have recommended that the Assembly continue to provide resources to the regional commissions to meet their responsibility with regard to ECDC and TCDC, and request the Secretary-General to inform the Assembly, through the Council, of progress in promoting subregional, regional and interregional co-operation.

REFERENCES

[1]E/1984/17.   [2]E/1984/66.   [3]ACC/1984/DEC/1-12 (dec. 1984/4). [4]ACC/1985/11. [5]*World Economic Survey 1984: Current Trends and Policies in the World Economy* (E/1984/62), Sales No. E.84.II.C.1. [6]A/39/3. [7]YUN 1980, p. 503, GA res. 35/56, annex, 5 Dec. 1980. [8]A/39/118-E/1984/45. [9]A/39/131-S/16414 & Corr.1. [10]A/39/133-S/16417. [11]A/39/269-E/1984/102. [12]A/39/304. [13]A/39/302. [14]A/39/303-E/1984/125. [15]A/39/314. [16]A/39/323. [17]A/39/331-E/1984/126. [18]A/39/554. [19]A/39/536. [20]A/C.2/39/4. [21]A/C.2/39/14. [22]A/39/560-S/16773. [23]A/C.2/39/10. [24]A/C.2/39/12. [25]A/39/720. [26]A/39/790. [27]YUN 1979, p. 468, GA res. 34/138, 14 Dec. 1979. [28]YUN 1982, p. 608, GA res. 37/202, 20 Dec. 1982. [29]YUN 1983, p. 407, GA res. 38/152, 19 Dec. 1983. [30]*Ibid.*, p. 406. [31]*Ibid.* [32]TD/B/984 & Add.1. [33]A/39/15, vol. I (dec. 283(S-XIII)). [34]A/39/16 (1984/2). [35]YUN 1980, p. 486. [36]UNEP/GC.12/8/Add.1 & Add.1/Corr.1. [37]A/39/25 (dec. 12/2). [38]A/39/48 & Corr.1,2. [39]YUN 1983, p. 409. [40]A/39/115-E/1984/49 & Corr.1. [41]A/39/228-E/1984/94. [42]A/39/273-E/1984/103. [43]E/1984/119. [44]YUN 1974, p. 324, GA res. 3201(S-VI), 1 May 1974. [45]YUN 1983, p. 854. [46]A/39/15, vol. II. [47]YUN 1983, p. 412, GA res. 38/196, 20 Dec. 1983. [48]A/39/312-E/1984/106 & Corr.1 & Add.1,2. [49]E/1984/127. [50]A/C.2/39/2. [51]E/1984/L.37. [52]YUN 1983, p. 412, GA res. 38/197, 20 Dec. 1983. [53]A/39/415. [54]YUN 1983, p. 413. [55]YUN 1970, p. 789, GA res. 2625(XXV), annex, 24 Oct. 1970. [56]YUN 1982, p. 598, GA res. 37/204, 20 Dec. 1982. [57]YUN 1974, p. 403, GA res. 3281(XXIX), 12 Dec. 1974. [58]A/39/332-E/1984/105 & Add.1. [59]A/39/15, vol. I. [60]YUN 1983, p. 414. [61]TD/B/C.7/67. [62]ID/CONF.5/46 & Corr.1 (res. 7). [63]YUN 1983, p. 416, ESC res. 1983/50, 28 July 1983. [64]ACC/1984/DEC/1-12 (dec. 1984/1). [65]A/39/154-E/1984/46 & Corr.1. [66]YUN 1983, p. 987, GA res. 38/227 B, 20 Dec. 1983. [67]A/39/38. [68]YUN 1983, p. 416. [69]E/1984/104. [70]YUN 1981, p. 383. [71]YUN 1979, p. 487. [72]YUN 1983, p. 418, ESC res. 1983/66, 29 July 1983. [73]E/1984/113. [74]E/1984/C.1/L.11.

Economic and social trends and policy

Economic reports prepared by the United Nations Secretariat in 1984 stressed the weak and uneven character of the world economic recovery which had begun in 1983. Two major reports, which were submitted as background documents for the annual discussion of international economic and social policy in the Economic and Social Council and the Trade and Development Board, expressed particular concern over the subdued rates of growth of international trade and the severe difficulties being faced by many countries in meeting their debt-servicing obligations (see Chapter IV of this section).

Economic surveys and trends

The *World Economic Survey 1984*,[1] prepared by DIESA and issued in mid-1984, reported that, after the most protracted global recession since the 1930s, the prospects for sustained and broad-based growth were still not satisfactory.

The *Survey*, which was based on information available as at 31 March, stated that, while a reversal of recessionary trends began in 1983, recovery had not become general. North America and some developing countries of South and East Asia were experiencing quite a rapid advance in income, and output and economic growth in the centrally planned economies had accelerated. However, most developing countries were beset by problems which hindered their prospects, and recovery in Western Europe had been weak. Preliminary estimates indicated that world output had expanded at a rate of about 2 per cent in 1983, and could accelerate to between 3.5 and 4 per cent in 1984 and 1985. Those rates, while markedly higher than those attained in the first three years of the decade, were modest for a period of economic recovery.

In the developing countries, the *Survey* noted that, although per capita GDP, on average, declined for the third consecutive year, a weak recovery was gradually emerging. Revised estimates indicated that average growth rates of GDP fell from 0.5 per cent in 1982 to a preliminary estimate of virtual stagnation in 1983. However, it was projected that the annual growth rate of GDP was likely to increase to 3.5 per cent in developing countries as a whole in 1984-1985. There was also significant diversity of economic performance among regions. While most countries in South and East Asia were likely to achieve economic growth rates considerably higher than population growth, for a large number of developing countries in other regions per capita GDP would remain stagnant.

During 1983, the world economy was not conducive to reactivating growth in the developing countries for the following reasons: weak demand in industrial countries for developing countries' exports; a substantial fall in oil prices and a modest upswing in other commodity prices; and, among markets for exports of manufactures from developing countries, only North America exhibited strong expansion. The precarious liquidity positions and serious balance-of-payments problems of most developing countries were a constraint on economic growth throughout the early 1980s. However, from mid-1982, external debt and the associated debt-service burden considerably worsened the external payments situation, especially in Latin America.

Among the developed market economies, a normal cyclical upswing in the United States and continued growth in Japan were accompanied by a recovery in Western Europe which was limited to some countries and was cyclically weak. While an expansionary fiscal policy aided recovery in the United States, some Western European countries pursued relatively restrictive fiscal policies to reduce structural budget deficits and the size of the government sector. Lack of demand had restrained expansion of output in Western Europe; intra-European trade had been adversely affected by weak aggregate demand, and exports to developing countries had contracted in absolute terms. In those countries generally, a significant decline in inflation and a slow-down in wage increases had improved business confidence, and rates of investment were picking up. However, the average unemployment rate remained unusually high at about 9 per cent, although its increase rate had slowed significantly. Because of the strength of the recovery in the United States, the unemployment rate there decreased sharply. The average growth rate of GDP for the developed market economies for 1983 was estimated at 2 per cent, compared with a revised estimate for 1982 of -0.2 per cent, and a rate of 4 per cent was forecast by the *Survey* for 1984.

The pace of economic activity in the centrally planned economies rose from a revised estimate of 3.7 per cent in 1982 to an estimated 4.3 per cent in 1983. Nevertheless, that average masked a number of important differences in the performance of various countries: the Asian planned economies continued their strong performance, with aggregate output growing by about 6 per cent, with somewhat higher growth in China; the USSR attained several key plan targets with overall output growth at about 3.5 per cent, and industry and agriculture reaching 4 and 5 per cent growth, respectively; and the 3.4 per cent growth of Eastern Europe was in sharp contrast to the sluggish performance of the preceding four years. While the economic performance of the Eastern European centrally planned economies improved over 1982, it remained well below post-war trends. The continuation of austerity measures adopted in the early 1980s in several Eastern European countries made the short-term outlook for growth not too bright and it would be extremely difficult to achieve a number of key output growth targets of current (1981-1985) medium-term plans.

The *Survey* stated that prospects for a more sustained revival of investment and growth in the developed market economies were threatened by their policy stances which could either persist in leaning towards deflationary restraint or provoke a reversion to deflationary measures. Deflationary policies remained inescapable for much of the developing world as a consequence of the debt burden, high interest rates and the weak recovery in world trade. More important for the medium term was the fact that the functioning of the international trading and financial system had been seriously impaired by events of recent years. Restoration and improvement of that system were essential for the reactivation of development.

International trade and payments issues were also addressed in the *Survey* (see Chaper IV of this section) and an annex on selected sectoral trends dealt with the food crisis in Africa in the context of global production and trade, and the situation in world energy markets.

A *Supplement* to the *Survey*[(2)] contained articles on exchange rate volatility in an interdependent world economy, some changes in trade among developing countries between 1965 and 1980, and wage behaviour in the developed economies.

In its account of recent and prospective trends in the world economy, the *Trade and Development Report, 1984*[(3)] focused on their quantitative impact on trade and development.

The *Report*, based on information and data available in June 1984, indicated that the impact of the continuing economic decline experienced by most developing countries was increasingly being felt in the social as well as in the economic sphere. Unemployment, underemployment and poverty were on the rise, social infrastructures and public services were under severe pressure, and there was growing evidence of difficulty in insulating health and education from the effects of the crisis. Physical investment was also severely constrained in many countries, reflecting both a drying-up of private investment in the face of economic recession and the atrophy of public investment following pressures to reduce public expenditure. All these factors placed development in jeopardy.

Although causes for this set-back varied from country to country, severe strains in external payments were a common factor. The debt crises in Africa, Latin America and some Asian countries were characterized by a cut-back in new private financial flows, which was particularly severe in Latin America. The modest growth of world trade and hesitant rise of commodity prices failed to produce a decided recovery in export earnings. Also, adverse weather conditions affected agricultural output in a number of countries, particularly in Africa, thereby reducing exports and increasing the need for essential imports. Oil-exporting developing countries suffered a severe drop in export earnings, as energy conservation and the development of productive capacity outside the major developing oil exporters compounded the impact of the recession. For a number of developing countries in South and East Asia, growth was on the whole satisfactory: in East Asia, the major exporters of manufactures enjoyed a significant increase in export demand from the United States; in South Asia, the large size of some countries, their lesser degree of openness, the relatively low level of indebtedness and large dependence on concessional financial flows provided the region with some insulation from external shocks.

For the developed market-economy countries, increases in output during the latter half of 1983 and the opening months of 1984 indicated that, as a group, they were emerging from the recession. Moreover, the pace of inflation in most countries slowed appreciably and the expansion was proceeding without signs of re-emerging inflationary pressures. The experience of individual developed market-economy countries varied considerably, with the most remarkable turn-around being that of the United States, in which GDP rose by 3.4 per cent in 1983 after a decline of 1.9 per cent in 1982. However, the impact of increased United States imports on developing countries was marginal as it accounted for only about one fifth of their total exports. Thus, despite an increase of some $3.2 billion in exports to the United States, developing countries' total exports fell by some $35 billion in 1983 from the 1982 level. Recovery of the developing countries would be hampered by indebtedness and protectionism. The recent increase in interest rates was a strongly negative factor for most debtor developing countries, as imports would be constrained by the amount of debt service to be paid. Since developing countries accounted for about a quarter of total exports of developed market economies, this would influence world demand so as to reduce transmission of economic recovery among developed market-economy countries themselves.

There was evidence, said the *Report*, that a turn-around in economic activity had taken place during 1981-1982 in the socialist countries of Eastern Europe other than the USSR, while in the latter country growth continued moderately. For those countries as a whole, the salient feature of external trade in 1983 was the smaller increase in the value of exports from 6.9 per cent in 1982 to 4.9 per cent in 1983, and the faster rise in imports from 0.9 per cent to 3.4 per cent. The faster import growth was a result of a reactivation of trade among the countries of the region, including the

socialist countries of Asia; imports from developed market-economy countries and from developing countries continued to decline. Although positive balances on current account in 1982 and 1983 significantly improved the international financial position of the socialist countries of Eastern Europe, balance-of-payments constraints continued to play a key role in the external sector plans of most of them in 1984 and were likely to remain a major concern for 1985. In China, progress towards attaining the targets set by that country's 1981-1985 plan continued, with further strong economic growth predicted for 1984.

ECONOMIC AND SOCIAL COUNCIL ACTION

By decision 1984/187, adopted without vote on the proposal of its President, the Economic and Social Council took note of the *World Economic Survey* and other reports submitted in connection with its general discussion of international economic and social policy, including the Secretary-General's report on the implementation of the Charter of Economic Rights and Duties of States (see above, under "Economic rights and duties of States") and those prepared on current economic conditions in Africa, Asia and the Pacific, Europe, Latin America and Western Asia (see Chapter VIII of this section).

Reports considered by the Economic and Social Council in connection with its general discussion of international economic and social policy, including regional and sectoral developments

At its 50th plenary meeting, on 27 July 1984, the Council took note of the following documents:

(a) Report of the Secretary-General on the implementation of the Charter of Economic Rights and Duties of States;

(b) *World Economic Survey 1984: Current Trends and Policies in the World Economy;*

(c) Summary of the economic and social survey of Asia and the Pacific, 1983;

(d) Summary of the economic survey of Latin America, 1983;

(e) Summary of the survey of economic and social conditions in Africa, 1982-1983;

(f) Summary of the survey of economic and social developments in the region of the Economic Commission for Western Asia, 1983;

(g) Report on recent economic developments in the region of the Economic Commission for Europe.

Economic and Social Council decision 1984/187

Adopted without vote

Oral proposal by President; agenda item 3.
Meeting numbers. ESC 24-33, 42-45, 50.

Resources, environment, people and development

During 1984, the ACC Consultative Committee on Substantive Questions (Programme Matters) (CCSQ(PROG)) continued to deal with inter-agency co-ordination of the programme of work on inter-relationships between resources, environment, people and development, and to screen projects proposed for financing under the general trust fund for the programme, established in June 1981.[4]

At its first regular session (Geneva, 26-30 March),[5] CCSQ(PROG) was briefed by the Food and Agriculture Organization of the United Nations (FAO) and the United Nations Educational, Scientific and Cultural Organization (UNESCO) on a project on carrying capacity in Kenya, and by UNEP on a project on deforestation in the Himalayan foothills. A paper on tropical forestry ecology systems in West and Central Africa, based on requests for assistance submitted to the United Nations Financing System for Science and Technology for Development, was circulated to the Committee, which agreed that the United Nations would consult on it with the organizations concerned. It was also agreed that an attempt would be made to develop future project proposals for consideration by CCSQ(PROG).

At its second regular session (New York, 4-9 October),[6] CCSQ(PROG) was again briefed on the two projects and heard a report on the status of the trust fund. Of a total of some $300,000, $185,000 had been expended on the project in Kenya and $100,000 earmarked for that in the Himalayas.

It was agreed that further projects needed to be developed and it was noted that the Designated Officials for Environmental Matters had suggested proceeding with an interrelationships study in the Sudano-Sahelian region. CCSQ(PROG) decided to address that question in 1985 based on an updated note covering proposals for further action in the area.

In a 28 May decision on population and the environment, the Governing Council of UNEP requested the UNEP Executive Director to accord priority to the work towards harmonious interaction between population, resources, development and the environment (see Chapter XVI of this section).

REFERENCES

(1)World Economic Survey 1984: Current Trends and Policies in the World Economy (E/1984/62), Sales No. E.84.II.C.1. (2)Supplement to World Economic Survey 1984 (ST/ESA/158), Sales No. E.84.II.C.2. (3)Trade and Development Report, 1984 (UNCTAD/TDR/4/Rev.1), Sales No. E.84.II.D.23. (4)YUN 1981, p. 391. (5)ACC/1984/5. (6)ACC/1984/19.

Development planning, education, administration and information

During 1984, various aspects of development planning, education, administration and information were considered by United Nations bodies, including CDP which studied development issues against the background of the uneven world economic recov-ery. The Seventh Meeting of Experts on the United Nations Programme in Public Administration and Finance met to review the needs of developing countries in that area and to review the United Nations work programme. The Joint United Nations Information Committee (JUNIC) continued to co-ordinate preparation of United Nations educational materials.

Development planning

CDP activities. The Committee for Development Planning held its twentieth session in New York from 17 to 21 May 1984.[1] The dates of the session, originally planned for April, were changed by the Economic and Social Council in May (see below).

Composed of 24 experts appointed by the Council, CDP examined the state of the world economy, considered the outlook under existing policies and discussed needed changes in national and international policies (see above, under "Development and economic co-operation"). The debt crisis and development finance were considered (see Chapter IV of this section) as were the particular problems of the least developed and other low-income countries (see below, under "Least developed countries"). CDP had before it the 1983 reports by its working groups on development priorities and policies for the remainder of the 1980s,[2] and on the international monetary and financial system.[3]

In a statement at the conclusion of the session, which was incorporated in its report[1] to the Economic and Social Council, CDP drew the attention of the international community to three areas requiring urgent responses: reform of the international monetary and financial system, international debt, and the situation of the poorest countries. It believed that, without action in at least those key areas, the crisis would deepen and bring incalculable suffering in human and national terms.

Regarding arrangements for its future work, CDP proposed meeting twice a year for a total of six days instead of having one session of 10 days. The twenty-first session would be scheduled in the last quarter of 1984 and the first quarter of 1985. Following approval of this proposal by the Council (see below), CDP met at Geneva from 19 to 21 November for the first part of its twenty-first session.[4] The session was preceded by working group meetings at Geneva on interdependence and multilateralism (12-14 October) and on domestic economic policies and surveillance (16 and 17 November).

ECONOMIC AND SOCIAL COUNCIL ACTION

In May, following consideration of a note by the Secretariat,[5] which stated that newly appointed members of CDP were unable to attend the CDP session on its originally scheduled dates, the Council adopted decision 1984/110 without vote, as orally proposed by its President.

Change of date of the twentieth session of the Committee for Development Planning

At its 6th plenary meeting, on 2 May 1984, the Council, having considered a note by the Secretariat, decided that the twentieth session of the Committee for Development Planning would be held at United Nations Headquarters from 17 to 21 May 1984 instead of from 4 to 13 April 1984.

Economic and Social Council decision 1984/110

Adopted without vote

Oral proposal by President; agenda item 1.

On 5 July, the Chairman of CDP introduced the Committee's report[1] to the Council, which on 27 July adopted resolution 1984/83 by roll-call vote.

Report of the Committee for Development Planning on its twentieth session

The Economic and Social Council,

Having considered the report of the Committee for Development Planning on its twentieth session and taking note of the statement made by the Committee at the conclusion of its work,

Taking note also of the statement made before the Council on 5 July 1984 by the Chairman of the Committee for Development Planning,

1. *Decides* to advance the session of the Committee for Development Planning scheduled for April 1985 to the last quarter of 1984, as proposed, and to hold that session at Geneva, and to consider the proposed schedule of meetings of the Committee at the organizational session for 1985 of the Council;

2. *Expresses its appreciation* of the programme of work of the Committee for Development Planning and invites the Committee to continue to present action-oriented recommendations.

Economic and Social Council resolution 1984/83

27 July 1984	Meeting 50	32-1-11 (roll-call vote)

5-nation draft (E/1983/L.42), orally revised; further orally revised and sponsored by Mexico, for Group of 77, and orally amended by Greece; agenda item 3.
Sponsors: Argentina, India, Malaysia, Saint Lucia, Yugoslavia.
Meeting numbers. ESC 24, 49, 50.

Roll-call vote in Council as follows:

In favour: Algeria, Argentina, Austria, Brazil, Canada, China, Colombia, Costa Rica, Ecuador, Finland, Greece, Guyana, Indonesia, Lebanon, Malaysia, Mexico, New Zealand, Pakistan, Qatar, Romania, Saint Lucia, Saudi Arabia, Somalia, Sri Lanka, Suriname, Sweden, Thailand, Tunisia, Uganda, Venezuela, Yugoslavia, Zaire.

Against: United States.

Abstaining: Bulgaria, France, German Democratic Republic, Germany, Federal Republic of, Japan, Luxembourg, Netherlands, Poland, Portugal, USSR, United Kingdom.

Before adoption of the text as a whole, Greece proposed that paragraph 1 of the original draft— by which the Council would have decided that CDP meetings be held at Geneva and in New York, in accordance with the schedule of meetings proposed by CDP—be amended to the subsequently adopted text except that the proposed schedule was to be considered at the General Assembly's 1984 session. After informal consultations, Greece orally reworded its amendment as adopted. The United States proposed an amended text by which the Council, in a single operative paragraph, would simply have considered, at its organizational session for 1985, the proposed schedule of meetings of CDP. That amendment was rejected by a roll-call vote of 24 to 10, with 7 abstentions. The Council then adopted paragraph 1, as proposed by Greece, by a roll-call vote of 31 to 2, with 11 abstentions.

Speaking in explanation of vote, the United States, stating that the resolution was designed to spend more money on the Council itself, hoped the Council would take its responsibility for ensuring fiscal integrity more seriously and see that most of the money distributed by multilateral organizations went where it was supposed to go.

Japan said it had voted against paragraph 1 and abstained on the resolution as a whole as it believed that the proposal, which affected the Council's 1985 work programme, should be decided at its 1985 organizational session. The USSR said it believed in ensuring maximum economy in the United Nations budget and the proposed change would have financial implications; CDP should hold only one session and that in New York. The United Kingdom agreed and said it would watch carefully for financial implications when the matter was addressed again.

Finland said it could find no substantive argument in favour of the steps suggested in paragraph 1 and was concerned that important resolutions were introduced at the end of the Council's session. Greece said it fully supported the work of CDP which knew best how to carry out its work and should determine its own work programme. At the end of two years, CDP and the Council could assess the new pattern of sessions and decide whether to continue it. Mexico said Council members should study the results produced by CDP, especially at its May 1984 session.

Development administration

In 1984, the United Nations Department of Technical Co-operation for Development carried out an $11.7-million programme of assistance to Governments in public administration and finance. The programme encompassed a wide range of activities in institution-building by reforming existing administrative structures and creating new ones, training and personnel management, and improvements in planning and implementing strategies for greater efficiency and effectiveness in managing the public sector. The main source of funds was UNDP, which provided $9.9 million.[6]

During the year, over 134 technical co-operation projects were executed in 63 developing countries, primarily in the areas of administrative reform, training and personnel administration, financial and public enterprise management, resource mobilization and management information systems.[7]

The Seventh Meeting of Experts on the United Nations Programme in Public Administration and Finance was held at Geneva from 17 to 26 October[8] to review public administration and finance in developing countries in the 1980s, analyse the needs of developing countries, particularly the least developed, especially in training and institution-building, review the United Nations work programme, recommend action at national and international levels, and increase the effectiveness of United Nations technical co-operation activities in this area. The Meeting, originally planned for May 1984, was rescheduled by a February decision of the Economic and Social Council (see below).

The Meeting agreed that developing countries should give precedence to improving the performance and productivity of existing institutions, personnel, policies and mechanisms over creating new institutions and further expanding the system. Identified as priorities were personnel policies, resource mobilization and management, decentralization and citizens' rights. The Meeting paid special attention to the crisis in sub-Saharan Africa and in that regard identified the following priority areas for which the international community should find ways to promote and undertake joint programmes: personnel management systems and management development institutions; financial management and fiscal administration; supplies, procurement and maintenance management; transport management; and modern management information systems.

Regarding the 1984-1985 United Nations programme in public administration and finance, the Meeting urged the Secretary-General to pursue vigorously his consultations with Governments on establishing an international centre for public accounting and auditing, as requested by the Economic and Social Council in 1982.[9] Among measures to improve the impact of the programme were: strengthening of information and dissemination activities; promoting exchange of comparative experience among countries; strengthening evaluation of activities; and ensuring that recommendations for administrative change in developing countries were realistic in the light of local conditions and needs. The Meeting took note of informal inter-agency consultations on public administration and finance (15 and 16 October), recognized the need for better co-ordination of activities and suggested that existing mechanisms for that purpose should be fully utilized. It was recommended that the next Meeting be held in 1987.

ECONOMIC AND SOCIAL COUNCIL ACTION

Having considered a note by the Secretary-General,[10] who proposed that the Seventh Meeting be rescheduled so that it could consider the outcome of several meetings on public administration and finance to be held in the first half of 1984, the Council, in February, adopted decision 1984/103 without vote.

Seventh Meeting of Experts on the United Nations Programme in Public Administration and Finance

At its 2nd plenary meeting, on 10 February 1984, the Council, having considered the note by the Secretary-General, decided that the Seventh Meeting of Experts on the United Nations Programme in Public Administration and Finance would be held at Geneva from 17 to 26 October 1984 instead of at United Nations Headquarters from 16 to 25 May 1984.

Economic and Social Council decision 1984/103
Adopted without vote

Draft by President, for Bureau (E/1984/L.14 & Corr.1); agenda item 2.

Development education and information

Development education

At its April 1984 session,[11] JUNIC (see POLITICAL AND SECURITY QUESTIONS, Chapter X) reviewed the work of its Working Group on Development Education, designated the chairmanship of that body to host organizations on a rotating basis and appointed the Group's substantive secretariat. During consideration of the work of its *Ad Hoc* Working Group on Development Support Communication, JUNIC was briefed on the status of UNESCO's International Programme for Development of Communication. Its co-ordinators were negotiating $10 million of assistance and several countries had conveyed offers of training; 55 projects were receiving assistance from the Programme.

Information Systems Unit

In response to a 1983 request by CPC,[12] the Secretary-General submitted a report[13] on the location of the Information Systems Unit (ISU) within the Secretariat to CPC's April-June 1984 session. CPC had proposed that the possible integration of ISU, currently in DIESA, within the Dag Hammarskjöld Library be examined by the Secretary-General. A 1983 report by the Advisory Committee for the Co-ordination of Information Systems[12] had dealt with the institutional arrangements for ISU and recommended establishing it as a distinct unit within the Library. The Secretary-General stated that he was reviewing the institutional and financial arrangements for ISU to continue working at its current high level of effectiveness and intended to formulate relevant proposals under the proposed programme budget for 1986-1987.

In April,[14] CPC recommended that a final solution to ISU's institutional and financial base be provided by the Secretary-General in the 1986-

1987 budget, and that it should continue its useful work as a distinct administrative unit.

REFERENCES

(1)E/1984/17. (2)YUN 1983, p. 407. (3)*Ibid.*, p. 560. (4)E/1985/29. (5)E/1984/L.18. (6)DP/1985/43/Add.3. (7)DP/1985/43/Add.1. (8)E/1985/39/Add.1. (9)YUN 1982, p. 745, ESC res. 1982/43, 27 July 1982. (10)E/1984/L.13. (11)ACC/1984/15. (12)YUN 1983, p. 427. (13)E/AC.51/1984/9. (14)A/39/38.

PUBLICATION

Crisis or Reform: Breaking the Barriers to Development. Views and recommendations of the Committee for Development Planning (ST/ESA/153), Sales No. E.84.II.C.4.

Agrarian reform and rural development

During 1984, rural development activities being carried out throughout the United Nations system were reviewed by ACC, CPC and the Economic and Social Council. FAO, in a four-year review of agrarian reform and rural development, concluded that, without more equitable distribution of assets and income, economic growth alone would not alleviate the high level of rural poverty. In August, the Fourth General Conference of UNIDO recommended industrial policies to achieve rural development and self-sufficiency in food in developing countries.

Rural development

In accordance with a 1981 CPC request,[1] ACC in 1984 prepared a report on review and appraisal of the work of its Task Force on Rural Development since 1981,[2] which was considered by the Task Force itself, ACC, CCSQ(PROG) and CPC before being forwarded to the Economic and Social Council. The report noted that the momentum of reorientation of United Nations rural development activities towards alleviating the poverty of the world's poorest groups had been basically maintained from 1981 to 1983. The Task Force had contributed to that momentum by: receiving regular reports from its members on their rural development activities; promoting internal staff workshops, seminars and training sessions; and publishing (since 1983) a newsletter on the rural development activities and experiences of United Nations organizations.

Regarding joint action at the country and regional levels, the report stated that, since 1981, policy review missions organized by FAO as a follow-up to the 1979 World Conference on Agrarian Reform and Rural Development (WCARRD)[3] had built up joint inter-agency participation and, by the end of 1983, 13 such missions had taken place. International assistance in key components of national rural development planning provided as follow-up to review missions totalled $50 million by the end of 1983. Regional action was promoted by the Task Force through annual or biennial inter-agency consultations in Africa, Asia and the Pacific, Latin America and the Near East and it had also been involved with newly established intergovernmental regional rural development centres. A Task Force panel on people's participation had met three times in 1981-1983 and published studies of obstacles and approaches to people's participation as reference documents. It also prepared draft general guidelines on the monitoring and evaluation of people's participation in rural development and gave special attention to guidelines for promoting women's participation. The panel, at an inter-agency workshop in Bangladesh, promoted the exchange of experiences among developing countries, especially regarding group-based savings and credit schemes in Asian countries. Similar activities were planned in other regions. A panel on monitoring and evaluation had also met three times and produced a set of guiding principles for monitoring and evaluating rural development projects and programmes.

Regarding the main areas of the Task Force's future programme of work, it was proposed that they continue to be: monitoring reorientation of rural development activities of the United Nations system to benefit the rural poor; joint action at country and regional levels; promoting people's participation; and monitoring and evaluation. A new aspect was also proposed, namely the administrative and institutional infrastructure for rural development, the initial step of which would be to analyse difficulties experienced in establishing and operating national co-ordinating mechanisms and to identify additional assistance required from Task Force members.

Task Force members agreed to exchange information on the main components of future rural development programmes to identify areas for collaboration.

ACC action. The Task Force on Rural Development (Rome, Italy, 22-24 February)[4] reviewed work accomplished since its 1983 meeting[5] in its three priority areas: joint action at country and regional levels; people's participation in rural development; and monitoring and evaluation. It also discussed and approved the report on review and appraisal of its work since 1981[2] (see above) and discussed an FAO report on review and analysis of agrarian reform and rural development (see below). A 1984-1986 work programme, which included provision for country-level inter-agency missions and regional inter-agency meetings and round tables, was adopted.

The Task Force's report was considered in March by CCSQ(PROG),[6] which noted the Task Force's work since 1981 and agreed that it was working in the right direction towards the important objectives of its priority areas. It was noted, however, that much remained to be done and that the challenges were complex. The Committee stressed that, in preparing for and follow-up of country missions, there was need for fuller involvement of all agencies concerned and for wider multidisciplinary involvement of the country concerned.

A review of the work of the Task Force was included in the ACC annual overview report for 1983/84,[7] and, at its April session, ACC adopted a decision[8] by which it approved the report on review and appraisal of the work of the Task Force since 1981 for submission to the Economic and Social Council through CPC.

CPC action. In May 1984,[9] CPC took note of the ACC report on review and appraisal of the work of its Task Force since 1981,[2] approved the Task Force's future work programme and recommended that it be implemented flexibly and pragmatically, while taking into account the objectives of WCARRD.

By decision 1984/166 (see below), the Economic and Social Council took note of the ACC report, approved the Task Force's future work programme and endorsed the CPC recommendation that it should be implemented taking into account the objectives of WCARRD.

UNIDO action. On 19 August, the Fourth General Conference of UNIDO (see Chapter VI of this section) adopted a resolution on industrial policies and measures to achieve rural development and self-sufficiency in food supplies of developing countries.[10] It recommended that developing countries develop small enterprises in rural areas to attract private investment and entrepreneurship, as well as develop State and co-operative enterprises. All countries, especially the developed ones, were invited to provide technical and financial assistance to developing countries, particularly the drought-stricken, to implement rural industrialization programmes.

The Conference recommended that UNIDO, in co-operation with other organizations: assist in intensifying rural development in developing countries, especially the African and least developed; assist in implementing industrial components for rural development programmes; continue work on rural industrialization; study the possibility of projects in consultancy service centres and rural industrial workshops; strengthen activities in fertilizer and pesticide production, agricultural machinery and equipment, storage facilities and the rural artisan sector; and pay greater attention to small enterprises and to the informal sector in rural areas.

Agrarian reform

Pursuant to a 1981 Economic and Social Council decision,[11] the Secretary-General, in May 1984, transmitted to the Council a report, prepared by FAO in collaboration with other United Nations bodies, reviewing and analysing agrarian reform and rural development.[12] By its 1981 decision, the Council had agreed to FAO's suggestion that such reports be submitted every four years, beginning in 1984.

The report discussed rural population and economic growth trends, incidence of poverty, food supply and rural poverty, land availability, agricultural prices and terms of trade, export orientation, and public expenditure and inflow of external resources. It also reviewed and analysed government policies for agrarian reform and rural development in the major areas of the WCARRD Programme of Action: access to land, people's participation, integration of women in development, access to inputs and services, agricultural extension and training, and rural non-farm employment. Noting that special strategies, policies and programmes were needed to meet the basic needs of the poor, one section of the report was devoted to such needs (food, health services, education, housing) in the context of rural development.

In its conclusions, the report noted that a relatively high level of rural poverty existed across developing countries at all income levels, and across all regions, indicating that economic growth alone, without measures for more equitable distribution of assets and income, was not enough to alleviate rural poverty. The results of monitoring by countries under the WCARRD Programme of Action had shown weaknesses in data and monitoring capabilities in developing countries and showed the need to collect data separately for rural areas and for women and other disadvantaged groups, since policy and action implications could be quite different for them as opposed to urban areas and other groups.

ECONOMIC AND SOCIAL COUNCIL ACTION

In July, the Economic and Social Council, acting on the recommendation of its First Committee, adopted decision 1984/166 without vote.

Review and analysis of agrarian reform and rural development

At its 48th plenary meeting, on 25 July 1984, the Council:

(a) Commended the Food and Agriculture Organization of the United Nations for its comprehensive and systematic review of the progress achieved in agrarian reform and rural development in the context of the implementation of the Programme of Action as adopted by the World Conference on Agrarian Reform and Rural Development and looked forward to a similar review in four years' time;

(b) Took note of the report of the Administrative Committee on Co-ordination concerning progress achieved by its Task Force on Rural Development;

(c) Approved the proposed future programme of work of the Task Force and endorsed the recommendation of the Committee for Programme and Co-ordination that the programme of work should be implemented taking into account the objectives of the World Conference on Agrarian Reform and Rural Development.

Economic and Social Council decision 1984/166

Adopted without vote

Approved by First Committee (E/1984/144) without vote, 20 July (meeting 14); draft by Netherlands (E/1984/C.1/L.14); agenda item 12.

REFERENCES

[1]YUN 1981, p. 401. [2]E/1984/50. [3]YUN 1979, p. 500. [4]ACC/1984/11. [5]YUN 1983, p. 428. [6]ACC/1984/5. [7]E/1984/66. [8]ACC/1984/DEC/1-12 (dec. 1984/5). [9]A/39/38. [10]ID/CONF.5/46 & Corr.1 (res. 5). [11]YUN 1981, p. 400, ESC dec. 1981/185, 23 July 1981. [12]E/1984/72.

Special economic areas

In 1984, the General Assembly, by resolution 39/175, again called for immediate measures in favour of developing countries and for action to deal with the specific problems of particular groups of developing countries. In resolution 39/174, the Assembly decided to convene in 1985 a high-level meeting of the UNCTAD Intergovernmental Group on the Least Developed Countries to carry out the mid-term global review of the implementation of the Substantial New Programme of Action for the 1980s for the Least Developed Countries. In resolution 39/221, the Assembly renewed its appeal for resources for the United Nations Special Fund for Land-locked Developing Countries and, in resolution 39/209, urged increased assistance to them. A call for intensified efforts to implement action in favour of island developing countries was made by the Assembly in resolution 39/212.

Developing countries

In 1984, the General Assembly again took up the question of immediate measures in favour of the developing countries, having, by a December 1983 resolution,[1] urged Governments to negotiate towards adopting concrete measures in specific areas. In response to that same resolution, the Secretary-General, in August 1984, submitted a report[2] on its implementation, stating that some measures had been taken in the five areas singled out for urgent action—food and agriculture, money and finance, trade and raw materials, energy resources, and LDCs—but they had been few in number and inadequate to cope with the seriousness of the situation.

GENERAL ASSEMBLY ACTION

On 17 December, on the recommendation of the Second Committee, the Assembly adopted without vote resolution 39/175.

Immediate measures in favour of the developing countries

The General Assembly,

Recalling its resolutions 3201(S-VI) and 3202(S-VI) of 1 May 1974, containing the Declaration and the Programme of Action on the Establishment of a New International Economic Order, 3281(XXIX) of 12 December 1974, containing the Charter of Economic Rights and Duties of States, and 3362(S-VII) of 16 September 1975 on development and international economic co-operation,

Reaffirming its resolution 38/200 of 20 December 1983,

Gravely concerned that the immediate measures referred to in resolution 38/200 are far from being implemented fully and that the critical problems facing developing countries in areas identified in that resolution still exist and in many cases have worsened further, particularly in Africa,

1. *Calls upon* all Governments, in particular those of developed countries, to adopt and intensify measures aimed at the full implementation of General Assembly resolution 38/200 and to fulfil, as a matter of urgency, the existing international commitments in the areas identified in that resolution;

2. *Requests* the relevant organs, organizations and bodies of the United Nations system to intensify their efforts to develop specific proposals and expedite actions for the implementation of resolution 38/200;

3. *Requests* the Secretary-General, in co-operation with the heads of organs, organizations and bodies of the United Nations system, to follow up on the actions taken by the agencies and to submit a report on the progress made in the implementation of the present resolution to the General Assembly at its fortieth session.

General Assembly resolution 39/175

17 December 1984   Meeting 103   Adopted without vote

Approved by Second Committee (A/39/790/Add.15) without vote, 30 November (meeting 55); draft by Vice-Chairman (A/C.2/39/L.53), based on informal consultations on draft by Egypt, for Group of 77 (A/C.2/39/L.9); agenda item 80 *(o)*. *Meeting numbers.* GA 39th session: 2nd Committee 28, 55; plenary 103.

In the original draft by the Group of 77, the Assembly, in the third preambular paragraph, would have expressed grave concern that the measures in its 1983 resolution[1] had not been implemented and that, as a result, the critical problems had worsened further, omitting the phrase "still exist and in many cases". By paragraph 1, the Assembly would have called only on Governments of developed countries and paragraph 2 would have referred to programmes rather than proposals.

Least developed countries

The special problems of the 36 officially designated LDCs were considered in several United Nations forums during 1983, including the UNCTAD Trade and Development Board, the

Governing Council of UNDP, the Fourth General Conference of UNIDO, ACC and the General Assembly. The Economic and Social Council requested CDP to consider including Kiribati and Tuvalu in the list of LDCs while the Assembly asked that similar consideration be given to Vanuatu. In a statement at the conclusion of its May 1984 session,[3] CDP cited the plight of the poorest countries as one of three areas to be urgently addressed by the international community. It said LDCs and other low-income countries were feeling the full brunt of the world economic downturn, often compounded by natural disaster. The lack of response to those countries' hardships had been distressing, as overall volumes of ODA had virtually stagnated while needs had increased and alternative sources diminished. With regard to the low-income countries of sub-Saharan Africa, CDP stressed the extreme urgency of their recovery and development needs for the balance of the 1980s.

Programme of Action for the 1980s

During 1984, the United Nations system continued to monitor the implementation of the Substantial New Programme of Action (SNPA) for the 1980s for the Least Developed Countries, adopted in 1981 by the United Nations Conference on the Least Developed Countries[4] and endorsed later that year by the General Assembly.[5]

In response to a December 1983 General Assembly resolution,[6] the Secretary-General submitted in October 1984 a report[7] on the implementation of that resolution, by which the Assembly had, *inter alia*, urged all countries and international institutions to implement their commitments under SNPA and again invited United Nations bodies to take measures for effective implementation and follow-up. The report, prepared by the UNCTAD secretariat, gave a brief account of the recent economic performance of the 36 LDCs,[8] noting that as a group they had recorded a growth rate of only 2 per cent in 1982. Since population was growing by as much as 2.6 per cent per year, per capita GDP declined in 1982 to a level of $210, less than a quarter of the level for developing countries as a group. Estimates of 1983 GDP growth indicated that it had regained its former low rate of 3 per cent, while for 1984 and 1985 UNCTAD forecast a slight improvement, to almost 4 per cent.

With regard to national action to implement SNPA, the report noted that, because of the increasingly harsh external environment, a number of Governments of LDCs had had to resort to shorter-term emergency measures, instead of pursuing longer-term development goals. Since the 1981 Conference, 24 countries had elaborated strategies, plans and programmes and discussed them with their development partners in order to obtain the support required.

The report noted that, although SNPA embodied aid targets for donor countries to provide 0.15 per cent of their GNP to LDCs, or to double their ODA to them by 1985 or as soon as possible thereafter, the transfer of external resources to LDCs had been disappointing. In 1981, ODA flows from all major groups had decreased and in 1982 the most noticeable improvement was among OPEC bilateral donors, with a real increase of almost 50 per cent over 1981. ODA from Development Assistance Committee (DAC) members of the Organisation for Economic Co-operation and Development remained at 0.08 per cent of GNP in 1981 and 1982, compared with 0.09 per cent in 1980. Among individual DAC members, Denmark, the Netherlands, Norway and Sweden had exceeded the 0.15 per cent target before adoption of SNPA and had continued to do so. Belgium exceeded it for the first time in 1981 and attained the target again in 1982. In 1982, 12 of the 17 DAC member countries had not met either SNPA target.

The report also contained information on action taken by organizations of the United Nations system and on inter-agency consultations held in April 1984 (see below under relevant headings).

The report concluded that progress in implementing SNPA had been slow and that the economic situation of LDCs had deteriorated. Conditions in Africa had reached crisis proportions, which had further affected the 26 LDCs on that continent. Of the 34 drought-affected and food-aid-dependent countries, 20 were among the least developed. All donors, the report stated, should consider responding positively to requests from LDCs to alleviate their debt-service burden in respect of ODA loans. It was also essential to consider additional measures to alleviate their debt-service obligations to both public and private lenders.

Of the greatest importance was that all donor countries and institutions fulfil by 1985 the ODA targets called for in SNPA. It was also essential that the international community respond expeditiously to the urgent needs and requirements of LDCs, as called for in SNPA and in UNCTAD resolution 142(VI).[9]

The serious resource situation of most United Nations organizations which accorded high priority to LDCs had adversely affected the ability of a number of them to provide adequate assistance. There was urgent need for donor countries to provide substantially greater resources through IDA, UNDP and its Special Measures Fund for LDCs, the United Nations Capital Development Fund and IFAD.

As to the role of country review meetings in implementing SNPA, the report said that they provided the necessary forum for fruitful dialogue between LDCs and their development partners on plans, programmes and support, and enabled better programming by Governments of LDCs of resources likely to be obtained from external sources. Therefore, LDCs that had not yet held their first review meeting should consider doing so as soon as possible and preferably before the mid-term review of SNPA's implementation, scheduled for 1985.

UNCTAD action. In accordance with UNCTAD resolution 142(VI)[9] and the 1983 General Assembly resolution on LDCs,[6] the UNCTAD Trade and Development Board at its March/April 1984 session discussed the convening of a Third Meeting of Multilateral and Bilateral Financial and Technical Assistance Institutions with Representatives of LDCs, as part of the preparation for the 1985 mid-term global review of the implementation of SNPA. Following a debate in a sessional committee, the Board on 6 April decided[10] to convene such a meeting to consider: areas for possible improvement of aid practices and management with respect to LDCs, particularly improved co-ordination of assistance programmes, measures already being taken by LDCs with the support of the international community and possible additional ones for accelerating progress of LDCs and implementing SNPA, and ways of better adapting implementation of assistance programmes to their specific needs, taking into account the 1982 agreed conclusions of the Second Meeting;[11] and organizational issues related to the mid-term review.

Also on 6 April, the Board adopted a decision on debt and development problems of poorer developing countries, in particular the least developed (see Chapter IV of this section).

In 1984, as a contribution to the global monitoring of SNPA implementation, the UNCTAD secretariat launched a series of annual reports on LDCs, each of which would contain a global review of recent socio-economic developments in LDCs and highlight recent developments in each of them. A theme of particular importance to SNPA's implementation would also be studied in each issue and that chosen for the first issue, *The Least Developed Countries 1984 Report,*[12] was the role of exports in their economic development. An annex to the report contained basic data on LDCs in tabular form.

ACC action. In accordance with a December 1983 General Assembly resolution[6] and a 1981 ACC decision,[13] a third inter-agency consultation on SNPA follow-up was held at Geneva on 9 and 10 April 1984.[14] The consultation reviewed experience gained from country review meetings and heard reports on action taken by individual United Nations organizations on their activities and work programmes relevant to LDCs. It discussed arrangements for the 1985 mid-term review to be carried out by a high-level meeting of the UNCTAD Intergovernmental Group on the Least Developed Countries. It noted that two more inter-agency consultations might be held before the mid-term review, with the main objective of the first being to consider preparations for the review.

In its annual overview report,[15] ACC said it continued to attach priority to co-ordination of operational activities dealing with assistance to LDCs. The consultation process between them and their donor partners and ways of financing projects identified during that process were being strengthened, and inter-agency consultations were being held regularly.

UNDP action. Together with the World Bank, UNDP continued to serve as lead agency in organizing country review meetings, whose aim was to enable individual LDCs to consult with their aid partners on the recipient country's economic situation, on progress in SNPA implementation, on aid conditions and on needs for additional assistance. During 1984,[16] such round-table review meetings were held with UNDP assistance for Burundi, the Comoros, the Gambia, Guinea-Bissau, Lesotho and Malawi. Other countries elected to have the World Bank assist them with review meetings.

Funding for the round-table process and for other activities benefiting LDCs was provided by the UNDP Special Measures Fund for LDCs. Contributions to the Fund in 1984 totalled $13.6 million and nine countries pledged $5.3 million for 1985. Expenditures on round-table conferences from the Fund were limited to $100,000 for each LDC. Resources from a trust fund established in 1983[17] for a special contribution from the Netherlands for LDCs were used to prepare four round-table conferences. The trust fund was also used to finance follow-up activities to conferences held in recent years.

(For 1984 payments and 1985 pledges to the Special Measures Fund, see next chapter: table "Contributions to UNDP, 1984 and 1985".)

During 1984, UNDP continued to give highest priority to assisting the poorest countries (for UNDP indicative planning figures and project expenditures, see next chapter). In addition, by the end of the year the United Nations Capital Development Fund (UNCDF) had approved capital assistance to LDCs in the amount of $38.3 million for projects to meet the basic needs and develop the productive capacity of the poorest segments of the population.[18]

On 29 June,[19] the UNDP Governing Council requested the UNDP Administrator to submit in 1985 an evaluation report on UNDP's role in implementing SNPA, focusing particularly on experiences gained through round-table conferences, with particular emphasis on: the dialogue between

LDCs and the donor community; co-ordination and utilization of aid available to LDCs; management of aid by Governments of LDCs and social and economic policy measures undertaken by them; impact on the level and flow of aid in line with commitments undertaken in SNPA; and appropriate modalities for follow-up to the round-table conferences. The Council reiterated its appeal for increased aid to LDCs through voluntary contributions to UNCDF and the Special Measures Fund, and through other channels. The Administrator was requested to continue assistance to LDCs in the follow-up to round-table conferences, and the appointment of a co-ordinator of assistance to LDCs was welcomed.

UNIDO action. By a 19 August resolution on the implementation of SNPA,[20] the Fourth General Conference of UNIDO (see Chapter VI of this section) recommended that industrialization be taken fully into account during the 1985 mid-term review, and that co-operation between LDCs and other developing countries be promoted in order to accelerate industrial development in the former. All countries and international organizations were invited to continue assistance to LDCs in promoting domestic processing of raw materials, developing human resources, utilizing their industrial capacities and preparing surveys of resources. UNIDO was requested to strengthen its industrial development assistance to LDCs, and, within the framework of SNPA, to co-operate more closely with UNDP, the World Bank and other organizations in organizing round-table conferences, and to improve the efficiency of its solidarity meetings for LDCs and consider their expansion.

GENERAL ASSEMBLY ACTION

On the recommendation of the Second Committee, the General Assembly, on 17 December 1984, adopted resolution 39/174 without vote.

Implementation of the Substantial New Programme of Action for the 1980s for the Least Developed Countries

The General Assembly,

Recalling its resolutions 3201(S-VI) and 3202(S-VI) of 1 May 1974, containing the Declaration and the Programme of Action on the Establishment of a New International Economic Order, 3281(XXIX) of 12 December 1974, containing the Charter of Economic Rights and Duties of States, and 3362(S-VII) of 16 September 1975 on development and international economic co-operation,

Reaffirming the provisions of the International Development Strategy for the Third United Nations Development Decade relating to the least developed countries,

Reaffirming the Substantial New Programme of Action for the 1980s for the Least Developed Countries, adopted unanimously by the United Nations Conference on the Least Developed Countries and endorsed by the General Assembly in its resolution 36/194 of 17 December 1981,

Expressing serious concern at the continued deterioration of the economic and social situation of the least developed countries in spite of their national efforts at development, as well as efforts made by the international community, including donor countries, even three years after the adoption of the Substantial New Programme of Action, and stressing the immediate need for greatly expanded support measures, including a major increase in the transfer of additional resources for the realization of the objectives of the Programme,

Deeply concerned at the very slow pace at which the Substantial New Programme of Action is being implemented,

Recalling resolution 142(VI) of 2 July 1983 of the United Nations Conference on Trade and Development on progress in the implementation of the Substantial New Programme of Action for the 1980s for the Least Developed Countries,

Recalling also its resolution 38/195 of 20 December 1983,

Taking note of the report of the Secretary-General on the implementation of the Substantial New Programme of Action for the 1980s for the Least Developed Countries,

Recognizing that the mid-term global review of the implementation of the Substantial New Programme of Action will provide an opportunity for the international community to consider ways and means of enhancing the implementation of the Programme during the rest of the 1980s and adjusting it, as appropriate, in the second half of the decade of the 1980s,

1. *Emphasizes* that, in view of their deteriorating socio-economic situation, the least developed countries need the urgent and special attention of the international community and its large-scale support on a continuous basis to enable them to progress towards self-reliant development, consistent with the plans and programmes of each least developed country;

2. *Reaffirms* the commitment of the international community to the Substantial New Programme of Action for the 1980s for the Least Developed Countries and urges all countries, international institutions and others concerned to implement fully and effectively their commitments under the Programme;

3. *Decides* to convene the high-level Meeting of the Intergovernmental Group on the Least Developed Countries of the United Nations Conference on Trade and Development from 30 September to 11 October 1985 to carry out, *inter alia*, the mid-term global review of the implementation of the Substantial New Programme of Action and readjust, as appropriate, the Programme for the second half of the Decade of the 1980s in order to ensure its full implementation, pursuant to paragraph 9 of General Assembly resolution 36/194 and paragraph 119 of the Substantial New Programme of Action;

4. *Urges* all countries as well as multilateral and bilateral financial and technical assistance institutions to take the necessary steps to ensure appropriate preparations for an in-depth review at the high-level meeting;

5. *Stresses* the importance of the timely preparation of all necessary documentation, as requested in the Programme, including specific recommendations for the full and expeditious implementation of the Substantial New Programme of Action by the United Nations Confer-

ence on Trade and Development and other competent organizations;

6. *Welcomes* decision 284(XXVIII) of 6 April 1984 of the Trade and Development Board, in which the Board decided to convene from 1 to 10 May 1985, as part of the preparatory process for the mid-term global review of the progress made towards the implementation of the Substantial New Programme of Action, a meeting of governmental experts of donor countries and multilateral and bilateral financial and technical assistance institutions with representatives of the least developed countries to consider the following:

(a) Areas for possible improvement of aid practices and management with respect to the least developed countries, taking into account the experience to be drawn from the national review meetings, and in particular:

(i) Measures to improve the co-ordination of assistance programmes;

(ii) Measures that the least developed countries are already taking with the support of the international community, as well as possible additional measures that could be undertaken for accelerated progress of the least developed countries and full and expeditious implementation of the Substantial New Programme of Action, taking into account the economic situation of the least developed countries;

(iii) Ways of better adapting the implementation of development assistance programmes to the specific needs of the least developed countries, taking into account the agreed conclusions of the Second Meeting of Multilateral and Bilateral Financial and Technical Assistance Institutions with Representatives of the Least Developed Countries, held at Geneva from 11 to 20 October 1982;

(b) Organizational issues related to the 1985 mid-term global review of the implementation of the Substantial New Programme of Action, including the state of preparation of documentation for that review, especially documents concerning the economic situation of the least developed countries;

7. *Takes note* of decision 289(XXVIII) of 6 April 1984 of the Trade and Development Board, in which the Board decided that the results of the comprehensive review, to be carried out at its thirtieth session in March 1985, of the implementation of section A of its resolution 165(S-IX) of 11 March 1978, called for in paragraph 1 of United Nations Conference on Trade and Development resolution 161(VI) of 2 July 1983, and of the implementation of resolution 165(S-IX) as stated in the Substantial New Programme of Action and in Conference resolution 142(VI), are to be taken into account during the preparatory process for the mid-term global review;

8. *Emphasizes* the need for the conclusion of the first round of remaining country review meetings for the least developed countries as soon as possible and, at the latest, before the mid-term global review;

9. *Requests* all relevant organs, organizations and bodies of the United Nations system to submit reports containing a review of the implementation of the Substantial New Programme of Action within their fields of competence and proposals for further action as input into the preparation for the mid-term global review;

10. *Requests* the Director-General for Development and International Economic Co-operation, in conformity with paragraph 123 of the Substantial New Programme of Action, to continue, in close collaboration with the Secretary-General of the United Nations Conference on Trade and Development, the executive secretaries of the regional commissions and the lead agencies for the aid consultative groups, to ensure at the secretariat level the full mobilization and co-ordination of the United Nations system for the purpose of implementation and follow-up of the Substantial New Programme of Action, taking into account, in particular, the mid-term global review;

11. *Requests* the Secretary-General to obtain extrabudgetary resources to ensure effective participation of the representatives of the least developed countries, through provision of necessary resources to finance travel expenses of at least two representatives from each least developed country to attend the high-level Meeting on the mid-term global review of the implementation of the Substantial New Programme of Action and one representative from each least developed country to attend the meeting referred to in paragraph 6 above;

12. *Further requests* the Secretary-General to submit to the General Assembly at its fortieth session a report on the high-level Meeting on the mid-term global review and on the implementation of the present resolution.

General Assembly resolution 39/174

17 December 1984   Meeting 103   Adopted without vote

Approved by Second Committee (A/39/790/Add.14) without vote, 6 December (meeting 56); draft by Vice-Chairman (A/C.2/39/L.110), based on informal consultations on draft by Egypt, for Group of 77 (A/C.2/39/L.83); agenda item 80 (n).
Meeting numbers. GA 39th session: 2nd Committee 53, 56; plenary 103.

In addition to drafting changes, the Group of 77 draft differed from the adopted text in that, by paragraph 11, the Assembly would simply have requested the Secretary-General to ensure participation of LDC representatives in the meetings referred to in the text.

The Declaration on the Critical Economic Situation in Africa, adopted by the Assembly on 3 December (resolution 39/29), stated that full and speedy implementation of SNPA, particularly with regard to the ODA level, would greatly augment resource flows to many African countries. In a resolution of 17 December (39/166), the Assembly stressed that advances in food and agricultural research and technology needed to be sustained and made more widespread, and in that context the needs of African countries and LDCs should be given special attention. The need to increase food and agricultural production and to raise nutritional standards in the developing countries, particularly in Africa and LDCs, was also emphasized.

Identification of LDCs

During 1984, CDP was requested to consider the eligibility of three countries for inclusion in the list of LDCs. The consideration of Kiribati and Tuvalu was requested by the Economic and Social Council in resolution 1984/58 (see below), while the consideration of Vanuatu was requested by the General Assembly in resolution 39/198 (see Chapter III of this section).

ECONOMIC AND SOCIAL COUNCIL ACTION

On 26 July, the Council, on the recommendation of its Third (Programme and Co-ordination) Committee, adopted resolution 1984/58 without vote.

Inclusion of Kiribati and Tuvalu in the list of the least developed countries

The Economic and Social Council,

Recalling General Assembly resolution 3421(XXX) of 8 December 1975 on the implementation of the Declaration on the Granting of Independence to Colonial Countries and Peoples, in which the Assembly urged the specialized agencies and other organizations within the United Nations system to extend assistance to the newly independent and emerging States,

Recalling also General Assembly resolutions 31/156 of 21 December 1976, 32/185 of 19 December 1977, 34/205 of 19 December 1979, 35/61 of 5 December 1980 and 37/206 of 20 December 1982, in which the Assembly urged all Governments, in particular those of the developed countries, to lend their support, in the context of their assistance programmes, for the implementation of the specific action envisaged in favour of island developing countries, and in which it also called upon all organizations of the United Nations system to implement, within their respective spheres of competence, appropriate specific action in favour of island developing countries,

Recalling further resolutions 98(IV) of 31 May 1976, 111(V) of 3 June 1979 and 138(VI) of 2 July 1983 of the United Nations Conference on Trade and Development, concerning specific action related to the particular needs and problems of island developing countries,

Recognizing the special problems faced by island developing countries, because of their smallness, remoteness, constraints in transport and communications, distance from market centres, limited internal markets, lack of natural resources, dependence on a few commodities, natural disasters, shortage of administrative personnel and heavy financial burdens,

Taking into account the fact that Kiribati and Tuvalu are island developing countries and are small and archipelagic, which makes the provision of services difficult and causes disproportionately high costs because of inter-island distances and the distribution of the population in small isolated pockets,

Concerned at the cumulative effect of the severe constraints on the economic development of Kiribati and Tuvalu, particularly those resulting from their geographical isolation,

Concerned also at the continued structural imbalances in the economies of the two countries, particularly their unavoidable dependence on imports,

1. *Calls the attention* of the international community to the special problems confronting Kiribati and Tuvalu as island developing countries with small populations;

2. *Appeals* to Member States, regional and interregional organizations and other intergovernmental organizations to provide financial, material and technical assistance to Kiribati and Tuvalu to enable them to establish the social and economic infrastructure that is essential for the well-being of their people;

3. *Invites* the Economic and Social Commission for Asia and the Pacific, the United Nations Conference on Trade and Development, the United Nations Industrial Development Organization, the United Nations Children's Fund, the United Nations Development Programme, the World Food Programme, the International Labour Organisation, the Food and Agriculture Organization of the United Nations, the United Nations Educational, Scientific and Cultural Organization, the International Civil Aviation Organization, the World Health Organization, the World Bank, the International Telecommunication Union, the World Meteorological Organization, the International Maritime Organization, the International Monetary Fund and the International Fund for Agricultural Development to bring to the attention of their governing bodies, for their consideration, the special needs of Kiribati and Tuvalu;

4. *Requests* the Secretary-General to mobilize the financial, technical and economic assistance of the international community, in particular the developed countries and the appropriate organizations of the United Nations system, with a view to meeting the short-term and long-term development needs of Kiribati and Tuvalu;

5. *Requests* the appropriate organizations and programmes of the United Nations system to maintain and increase their current and future programmes of assistance to Kiribati and Tuvalu, to co-operate closely with the Secretary-General in organizing an effective international programme of assistance, and to report periodically to him on the steps they have taken and the resources they have made available to help those countries;

6. *Requests* the Committee for Development Planning, at its twenty-first session, as a matter of priority, to give due consideration to the question of the inclusion of Kiribati and Tuvalu in the list of the least developed countries and to submit its conclusions to the Economic and Social Council at its second regular session of 1985;

7. *Also requests* the Secretary-General to prepare as soon as possible a mission which will assess the needs of, and prepare a programme of assistance for, Kiribati and Tuvalu and, if possible, to apprise the General Assembly at its thirty-ninth session of the findings of the mission;

8. *Further requests* the Secretary-General to report to the Economic and Social Council at its second regular session of 1985 on the priority needs of Kiribati and Tuvalu and the assistance required from the international community.

Economic and Social Council resolution 1984/58

26 July 1984   Meeting 49   Adopted without vote

Approved by Third Committee (E/1984/148) without vote, 20 July (meeting 14); 17-nation draft (E/1984/C.3/L.5); agenda item 18.

Sponsors: Australia, Bangladesh, China, Costa Rica, Guyana, Indonesia, Japan, Malaysia, New Zealand, Pakistan, Papua New Guinea, Saint Lucia, Sierra Leone, Thailand, Tunisia, United Kingdom, United States.

Land-locked developing countries

During 1984, the special needs and problems of land-locked developing countries were considered by UNCTAD and the General Assembly. Matters relating to the United Nations Special Fund for Land-locked Developing Countries were taken up by the UNDP Governing Council and the Assembly.

UNCTAD action. In accordance with UNCTAD resolution 137(VI),[21] the UNCTAD Secretary-General appointed an *Ad Hoc* Group of Experts to Study Ways and Means of Improving Transit-transport Infrastructures and Services for Land-locked Developing Countries, which met at Geneva from 4 to 8 June 1984.[22]

In the area of transit facilities and co-operation, the Group recommended: that land-locked developing countries and transit countries establish joint obligations and responsibilities for financing, operating or managing transit facilities and organizations related to transit transport, and that they arrange for the land-locked developing countries to participate in major decisions affecting their transportation activities; that land-locked developing countries be permitted to establish, with transit countries' support, free-port areas at ocean ports and trans-shipment points; that third-party involvement in establishing transit facilities and procedures be accepted and that this involvement be addressed by donor agencies when providing concessionary or aid financing of transit facilities; that donor agencies provide for transit-transport projects within subregional or transit corridor development plans, and evaluate transit-transportation proposals from the perspective of an overall development strategy for land-locked developing countries, particularly in view of the importance of alternative transport routes to the long-run political survival of those nations; that organizations and countries involved in transit matters develop corridor transit plans establishing agreed project priorities, including trade-facilitation measures and other non-physical matters; and that provision be made for aid-supported investment in small projects aimed at improving the security of goods in transit and the efficiency of transit traffic.

Regarding technical and procedural matters involving transit, the Group recommended: that national trade facilitation programmes be introduced in all transit countries, that the creation of regional trade facilitation commissions be encouraged and that international agreements related to transit trade and inter-country transport be implemented by transit and land-locked countries; that donor agencies encourage adoption of international conventions when providing aid support for transit facilities; that the UNCTAD secretariat prepare a report on simplifying trade documentation and transit procedures and alleviating non-physical transit barriers; and that land-locked countries be encouraged to create agencies to monitor transit-

transport problems, and that the UNCTAD secretariat advise and consult with those agencies.

With respect to general development of land-locked developing countries, the Group recommended: that donor countries, United Nations organizations and regional economic groupings encourage development programmes focusing on internal economic development; that special attention be paid to air-freight alternatives and telecommunication facilities both internally and internationally; that UNCTAD, UNDP and the regional commissions undertake studies on expanding the external trade sector of land-locked developing countries; and that regional and subregional economic groupings of developing countries also intensify their efforts in that regard.

As to action by international agencies the Group recommended: that an approach be formulated to remedy problems of manpower deficiencies in all areas of transit-transport, including trade facilitation; that UNCTAD accumulate and disseminate information on transit-transport matters; that UNCTAD, in co-operation with the regional commissions and specialized agencies, continue to study the relationship between the evolving trade structure of land-locked developing countries and existing transport facilities; and that technical assistance to land-locked and transit developing countries be expanded.

Also in accordance with UNCTAD resolution 137(VI),[21] the UNCTAD secretariat submitted to the September session of the Trade and Development Board a July progress report with a later addendum on implementing specific action for the land-locked developing countries.[23] The report was based on information supplied by Governments and organizations and on UNCTAD's own work on land-locked developing countries.

There was evidence, concluded the report, that the international community had maintained the momentum to help land-locked developing countries, but at an inadequate level. The main observation was that several major donors did not have particular development assistance policies in favour of those countries but recognized that they faced particular problems resulting from their geographical disadvantages. There was also a growing awareness that acute transport problems in such countries hampered efforts to accelerate development in other sectors of the economy. Major donors had given particular attention to developing and improving transport and communications infrastructures in southern Africa within the framework of the Southern African Development Co-ordination Conference, of which six land-locked countries were members. There was an urgent need for greater political support for international conventions related to transit trade and transport; problems of implementation could be tackled subsequent to signing or ratification. Unless reservations, particularly by the transit countries, were reversed, valuable international instruments would be of little practical effect.

On 21 September, the Trade and Development Board adopted a decision[24] on transit-transport infrastructures and services for land-locked developing countries. It invited member States to provide to the UNCTAD Secretary-General their comments on the report of the *Ad Hoc* Group of Experts,[22] and requested him to report on those comments to the Board in 1985. The decision consisted of the final three paragraphs of a draft resolution submitted by the Group of 77. The Board agreed that the remainder of that draft should be considered in 1985.

Also on 21 September, the Board decided to transmit the UNCTAD secretariat progress report[23] to the General Assembly, together with comments made thereon during the Board's session.

GENERAL ASSEMBLY ACTION

For its consideration of the question, the Assembly had before it a September note with a later addendum by the Secretary-General,[25] transmitting the UNCTAD secretariat progress report,[23] and a note by the Secretariat[26] containing a draft resolution referred for consideration by a 1983 Assembly decision.[27]

In December, the Assembly, on the recommendation of the Second Committee, took two actions on the needs of land-locked developing countries.

On 18 December, it adopted without vote resolution 39/209.

Specific action related to the particular needs and problems of land-locked developing countries

The General Assembly,

Reiterating the specific actions related to the particular needs of the land-locked developing countries stated in resolutions 63(III) of 19 May 1972, 98(IV) of 31 May 1976, 123(V) of 3 June 1979 and 137(VI) of 2 July 1983 of the United Nations Conference on Trade and Development,

Recalling the provisions of its resolutions 31/157 of 21 December 1976, 32/191 of 19 December 1977, 33/150 of 20 December 1978, 34/198 of 19 December 1979, 35/58 of 5 December 1980 and 36/175 of 17 December 1981 and other resolutions of the United Nations relating to the particular needs and problems of land-locked developing countries,

Bearing in mind various other resolutions adopted by the General Assembly, its related organs and the specialized agencies, emphasizing special and urgent measures in favour of land-locked developing countries,

Recalling the relevant provisions of the International Development Strategy for the Third United Nations Development Decade,

Recalling the United Nations Convention on the Law of the Sea, adopted on 10 December 1982,

Recognizing that the lack of territorial access to the sea, aggravated by remoteness and isolation from world markets, and the prohibitive transit, transport and transshipment costs impose serious constraints on the socioeconomic development of land-locked developing countries,

Noting with concern that the measures taken so far in favour of land-locked developing countries and the assistance given fall far short of their needs,

1. *Reaffirms* the right of access of land-locked countries to and from the sea and freedom of transit through the territory of transit States by all means of transport, in accordance with article 125 of the United Nations Convention on the Law of the Sea;

2. *Appeals* to all States, international organizations and financial institutions to implement, as a matter of urgency and priority, the specific actions related to the particular needs and problems of land-locked developing countries envisaged in resolutions 63(III), 98(IV), 123(V) and 137(VI) of the United Nations Conference on Trade and Development, in the International Development Strategy for the Third United Nations Development Decade, in the Substantial New Programme of Action for the 1980s for the Least Developed Countries and in other relevant resolutions of the United Nations;

3. *Urges* all concerned countries as well as international organizations to provide land-locked developing countries with the appropriate financial and technical assistance in the form of grants or concessional loans for the construction and improvement of their transport and transit infrastructures and facilities;

4. *Urges also* the international community and multilateral and bilateral financial institutions to intensify efforts in raising the net flow of resources to all land-locked developing countries to help offset the adverse effects of their disadvantageous geographical situation on their economic development efforts, in keeping with the overall development needs of each land-locked developing country;

5. *Invites* transit countries and the land-locked developing countries to co-operate effectively in harmonizing transport planning and promoting other joint ventures in the field of transport at the regional, subregional and bilateral levels;

6. *Further invites* the international community to give financial, technical and other support to interested transit and land-locked developing countries in the construction of alternative routes to the sea;

7. *Commends* the United Nations Development Programme, the United Nations Conference on Trade and Development and other United Nations agencies for their work and the assistance they have provided to the land-locked developing countries and invites them to continue to take appropriate and effective measures to respond to the specific needs of those countries;

8. *Recommends* continued and intensified activities relating to the conducting of necessary studies and the implementation of special actions and specific measures for the land-locked developing countries, including those in the area of economic co-operation among developing countries, as well as those that have been envisaged in the programme of work of the United Nations Conference on Trade and Development, the regional commissions and other programmes and activities at the regional and subregional levels;

9. *Takes note* of the report of the *Ad Hoc* Group of Experts to Study Ways and Means of Improving Transit-

transport Infrastructures and Services for Land-locked Developing Countries;

10. *Requests* Member States to transmit to the Secretary-General of the United Nations Conference on Trade and Development their views and comments on the report of the *Ad Hoc* Group of Experts;

11. *Requests* the Secretary-General of the United Nations Conference on Trade and Development to submit to the General Assembly at its fortieth session a report on the geographical disadvantages of land-locked developing countries and their consequences for the development of those countries.

General Assembly resolution 39/209

18 December 1984   Meeting 104   Adopted without vote

Approved by Second Committee (A/39/790Add.3) without vote, 10 December (meeting 58); draft by Secretariat (A/C.2/39/L.3), amended by Nepal (A/C.2/39/L.134), orally revised; agenda item 80 *(c)*.

The Nepalese amendments made drafting changes and added the references to the 1982 United Nations Convention on the Law of the Sea[28] and to UNC-TAD resolution 137(VI).[21] The amendments also replaced two paragraphs, by which the Assembly would have recommended that UNCTAD VI (1983) take action on the question and requested the United Nations Secretary-General to report to the Assembly in 1983, by paragraphs 9 to 11 of the adopted text. Paragraph 1, as amended, was approved by a recorded vote, requested by Ireland, of 86 to none, with 29 abstentions; the other amendments were approved without vote.

In explanation of its abstention on paragraph 1, Senegal said it had reservations on its content. Liberia was convinced that right of access was a bilateral issue. Ghana, although abstaining, said it would continue to co-operate closely with its land-locked neighbours. Ireland, on behalf of the EEC members, said that matters of a State's sovereignty should be decided only by consensus. The Congo said it had abstained because of institutional arrangements between it and neighbouring land-locked countries, although its position did not detract from its willingness to co-operate with the countries concerned. Mauritania said its non-participation in the vote did not affect its readiness to co-operate with neighbouring land-locked countries.

Ecuador's vote in favour of paragraph 1 did not imply acceptance of the Convention on the Law of the Sea and was based on the understanding that the laws and rights of transit States would be respected. Finland's support for the paragraph did not imply acceptance of interference in the decision-making processes of multilateral financial institutions regarding allocation of their resources, to which paragraph 4 might be interpreted as referring. Brazil and India said their bilateral agreements with neighbouring countries using their territory for transit purposes would not be affected by the resolution's adoption. Algeria said that application of paragraph 1 remained subject to the principles which had been made explicit at the 1980 Assembly discussions on the subject.[29]

Turkey's joining in the consensus on the resolution as a whole did not imply that it accepted the Convention on the Law of the Sea. Liberia had not opposed the resolution because it understood the serious problems of land-locked developing countries. The United States said it did not find the category of land-locked countries meaningful and was opposed to special categories of developing countries other than the least developed. Djibouti had reservations regarding the operative part of the resolution. Peru said it had joined the consensus on the understanding that the rights of transit States and existing agreements would be respected. Canada supported the development of land-locked developing countries but did not consider them a separate category in its development assistance programme.

Also on 18 December, the Assembly adopted without vote decision 39/434, dealing with land-locked developing countries and the Agreement Establishing the Common Fund for Commodities (see Chapter IV of this section).

Specific action related to the particular needs and problems of the land-locked developing countries; status of the Agreement Establishing the Common Fund for Commodities

At its 104th plenary meeting, on 18 December 1984, the General Assembly, on the recommendation of the Second Committee, took note of the following documents:

(*a*) Note by the Secretary-General transmitting a progress report by the secretariat of the United Nations Conference on Trade and Development on progress in the implementation of specific action related to the particular needs and problems of the land-locked developing countries;

(*b*) Report of the Secretary-General on the status of the Agreement Establishing the Common Fund for Commodities.

General Assembly decision 39/434

Adopted without vote

Approved by Second Committee (A/39/790Add.3) without vote, 14 December (meeting 60); oral proposal by Chairman; agenda item 80 *(c)*.

UN Special Fund for Land-locked Developing Countries

The annual report of the UNDP Administrator for 1984[30] stated that contributions to the United Nations Special Fund for Land-locked Developing Countries and resultant interest earnings had declined steadily in recent years. It was estimated that only $37,692 would be available in 1985, which meant that during the 1985-1986 biennium the Fund would approach a point when its income would fall below its administrative costs. In 1984, $116,738 was received from 10 States and 13 States pledged $37,692 for 1985 (see table below). Most of these States were themselves land-locked. During the year, expenditures from the Fund for projects in the Central African Republic, Malawi and Swaziland totalled some $111,000.[31]

GENERAL ASSEMBLY ACTION

On 18 December, on the recommendation of the Second Committee, the Assembly adopted resolution 39/221 by recorded vote.

United Nations Special Fund for Land-locked Developing Countries

The General Assembly,

Recalling its resolution 31/177 of 21 December 1976, by which it approved the statute of the United Nations Special Fund for Land-locked Developing Countries, and its subsequent resolutions on the Fund, including resolution 38/174 of 19 December 1983,

Taking note of resolution 137(VI) of 2 July 1983 of the United Nations Conference on Trade and Development and decision 83/28 of 24 June 1983 of the Governing Council of the United Nations Development Programme,

Recalling the relevant provisions of the International Development Strategy for the Third United Nations Development Decade,

Also recalling the relevant paragraphs of the Substantial New Programme of Action for the 1980s for the Least Developed Countries,

Convinced that access to world markets at the least possible cost is an integral part of the meaningful economic development of land-locked developing countries,

Expressing deep concern at the very low level of contributions that have been consistently pledged to the Fund since its establishment,

Noting that the demands for assistance from the Fund are additional to, and generally different from, the types of activities financed from other sources in the United Nations system,

1. *Expresses concern* at the lack of implementation of its resolutions on the United Nations Special Fund for Land-locked Developing Countries;

2. *Renews its appeal* for adequate resources to be provided to the Fund;

3. *Urges* the international community to give full consideration to the special constraints facing the land-locked developing countries in their economic and social development;

4. *Requests* the Administrator of the United Nations Development Programme, in consultation with the Secretary-General of the United Nations Conference on Trade and Development and the executive heads of the organs, organizations and bodies of the United Nations system, to continue to pursue action in favour of the land-locked developing countries within the framework of the interim arrangements, bearing in mind that each country concerned should receive appropriate technical and financial assistance.

General Assembly resolution 39/221

18 December 1984   Meeting 104   124-0-22 (recorded vote)

Approved by Second Committee (A/39/791) by recorded vote (101-0-22), 10 December (meeting 58); draft by Egypt, for Group of 77 (A/C.2/39/L.97); agenda item 81 *(f)*.

Meeting numbers. GA 39th session: 2nd Committee 48-53, 55, 58; plenary 104.

Recorded vote in Assembly as follows:

In favour: Afghanistan, Algeria, Angola, Argentina, Bahamas, Bahrain, Bangladesh, Barbados, Benin, Bhutan, Bolivia, Botswana, Brazil, Brunei Darussalam,

Bulgaria, Burkina Faso, Burma, Burundi, Byelorussian SSR, Cape Verde, Chad, Chile, China, Colombia, Congo, Costa Rica, Cuba, Cyprus, Czechoslovakia, Democratic Kampuchea, Democratic Yemen, Djibouti, Dominican Republic, Ecuador, Egypt, El Salvador, Equatorial Guinea, Ethiopia, Fiji, Gabon, Gambia, German Democratic Republic, Ghana, Guatemala, Guinea, Guinea-Bissau, Guyana, Haiti, Honduras, Hungary, India, Indonesia, Iran, Iraq, Israel, Ivory Coast, Jamaica, Jordan, Kenya, Kuwait, Lao People's Democratic Republic, Lebanon, Lesotho, Liberia, Libyan Arab Jamahiriya, Madagascar, Malawi, Malaysia, Maldives, Mali, Malta, Mauritania, Mauritius, Mexico, Mongolia, Morocco, Mozambique, Nepal, Nicaragua, Niger, Nigeria, Oman, Pakistan, Panama, Papua New Guinea, Paraguay, Peru, Philippines, Poland, Qatar, Romania, Rwanda, Saint Lucia, Saint Vincent and the Grenadines, Samoa, Sao Tome and Principe, Saudi Arabia, Senegal, Sierra Leone, Singapore, Somalia, Sri Lanka, Sudan, Suriname, Swaziland, Syrian Arab Republic, Thailand, Togo, Trinidad and Tobago, Tunisia, Turkey, Uganda, Ukrainian SSR, USSR, United Arab Emirates, United Republic of Tanzania, Uruguay, Venezuela, Viet Nam, Yemen, Yugoslavia, Zaire, Zambia, Zimbabwe.

Against: None.

Abstaining: Australia, Austria, Belgium, Canada, Denmark, Finland, France, Germany, Federal Republic of, Greece, Iceland, Ireland, Italy, Japan, Luxembourg, Netherlands, New Zealand, Norway, Portugal, Spain, Sweden, United Kingdom, United States.

Explaining its vote, the United States said it felt that the category of land-locked developing countries was not a meaningful one and it opposed the establishment of special categories of developing countries other than the least developed. Ireland, on behalf of the EEC members, said that action in favour of the land-locked developing countries had to be related to their individual situation and level of development and be aimed at offsetting their geographical handicaps. EEC would channel aid to such countries through existing bilateral and multilateral institutions. The USSR said it understood the special needs of the land-locked developing countries and considered them in its trade relations, assisting them with special transport problems.

CONTRIBUTIONS TO THE UN SPECIAL FUND FOR LAND-LOCKED DEVELOPING COUNTRIES, 1984 AND 1985

(as at 31 December 1984; in US dollar equivalent)

Country	1984 payment	1985 pledge
Afghanistan	—	5,000
Bhutan	—	1,580
Bolivia	—	500
Brazil	10,000	—
Lao People's Democratic Republic	1,000	1,000
Lesotho	6,000	847
Malawi	1,468	1,315
Nepal	2,000	2,000
Philippines	1,484	500
Senegal	—	1,000
Thailand	1,000	1,000
Tunisia	432	445
Zambia	88,137	18,367
Zimbabwe	5,217	4,138
Total	116,738	37,692

SOURCE: A/40/5/Add.1.

Appointment of an Executive Director

In 1984, the General Assembly again considered the question of appointing an Executive Director of the Special Fund. The Secretary-General submitted a note[32] in which he recalled the circumstances surrounding the establishment of the Fund and the interim arrangements for its management by the UNDP Administrator, gave details of the amount pledged for its 1985 operations (see above) and stated that he was not submitting an appointment for the post of Executive Director.

GENERAL ASSEMBLY ACTION

On 10 December, on the oral proposal of its President, the General Assembly adopted decision 39/316 without vote.

Confirmation of the appointment of the Executive Director of the United Nations Special Fund for Land-locked Developing Countries

At its 93rd plenary meeting, on 10 December 1984, the General Assembly took note of the information contained in the note by the Secretary-General.

General Assembly decision 39/316

Adopted without vote

Oral proposal by President; agenda item 17 *(k)*.

Election of a Board of Governors

GENERAL ASSEMBLY ACTION

On an oral proposal of its President, the General Assembly adopted decision 39/313 without vote.

Election of the members of the Board of Governors of the United Nations Special Fund for Land-locked Developing Countries

At its 93rd plenary meeting, on 10 December 1984, the General Assembly decided to defer until its fortieth session the election of the members of the Board of Governors of the United Nations Special Fund for Land-locked Developing Countries, since no candidate had been put forward by the regional groups.

General Assembly decision 39/313

Adopted without vote

Oral proposal by President; agenda item 16 *(e)*.

Island developing countries

UNCTAD action. In accordance with UNCTAD resolution 138(VI) on UNCTAD activities concerning island developing countries (IDCs),[33] the UNCTAD secretariat submitted a report[34] on the implementation of that resolution to the September 1984 session of the Trade and Development Board. The report also responded to a 1982 General Assembly resolution[35] by which the Secretary-General had been requested to report on measures taken by the international community to respond to the specific needs of those countries. The UNCTAD report described their particular problems and went on to review the implementation of action related to those problems; the latter part of the report was based on information supplied by Governments and international organizations in response to a request from the UNCTAD Secretary-General.

The report concluded that a number of the IDCs' constraints were due to smallness rather than insularity *per se*. Other characteristics were linked to insularity and remoteness but it appeared that, even in those cases, small islands faced more acute problems than large ones, combining smallness with insularity. Scepticism had been expressed by some States and institutions as to whether IDCs indeed had special needs and problems; this was possibly because problems of large developing islands were not unlike those of large developing mainland countries. The report suggested that consideration be given to defining the concept of small IDCs more precisely and to limiting specific action to them.

Many problems of IDCs, said the report, could be handled by the United Nations regional commissions and the regional development banks, with the commissions promoting co-operation among IDCs. In the Pacific and Caribbean subregions, there were fairly well-structured mechanisms for inter-island co-operation receiving considerable outside support which, the report recommended, should be continued.

At the interregional or global level, the future role of the UNCTAD secretariat should involve: defining the specific problems of IDCs, or small developing countries, and making operational recommendations based on those findings; providing for exchange of information and experience; and continuing or developing specific support measures to implement development strategies of IDCs.

Most areas of interest to IDCs were covered by UNCTAD and General Assembly resolutions and were not dealt with in the report. Examples of common subject-areas that merited continued attention were: national strategies and planning problems of small IDCs; transport and communications; natural disaster planning and prevention; environment; development of marine resources; market access and earnings stabilization; the role of invisibles and emigrants' remittances in foreign exchange earnings; and establishing an information exchange system for IDCs.

On 21 September, the Trade and Development Board decided to transmit the report to the General Assembly, together with comments made thereon during the Board's session.

GENERAL ASSEMBLY ACTION

By a 28 September note,[36] the Secretary-General transmitted to the General Assembly the UNCTAD secretariat report on island developing countries.

On 18 December, the Assembly adopted without vote resolution 39/212, on the recommendation of the Second Committee.

Specific measures in favour of island developing countries

The General Assembly,

Recalling the Declaration and the Programme of Action on the Establishment of a New International Economic Order, contained in its resolutions 3201(S-VI) and 3202(S-VI) of 1 May 1974, the Charter of Economic Rights and Duties of States, contained in its resolution

3281(XXIX) of 12 December 1974, its resolution 3362(S-VII) of 16 September 1975 on development and international economic co-operation and the International Development Strategy for the Third United Nations Development Decade, contained in the annex to its resolution 35/56 of 5 December 1980,

Recalling also its resolutions 31/156 of 21 December 1976, 32/185 of 19 December 1977, 34/205 of 19 December 1979, 35/61 of 5 December 1980 and 37/206 of 20 December 1982, relating to the special needs and problems of island developing countries,

Reiterating the call for specific action in favour of island developing countries contained in resolutions 98(IV) of 31 May 1976, 111(V) of 3 June 1979 and 138(VI) of 2 July 1983 of the United Nations Conference on Trade and Development,

Recognizing the difficult problems faced by island developing countries, in particular those which suffer handicaps due especially to their smallness, remoteness, vulnerability to natural disasters, constraints in transport, great distances from market centres, a highly limited internal market, lack of natural resources, heavy dependence on a few commodities, shortage of administrative personnel and heavy financial burdens,

Mindful of the fact that timely additional efforts are needed to implement the specific measures required to assist island developing countries in offsetting the major handicaps which retard their development process,

1. *Reaffirms* its resolution 37/206 and other relevant resolutions of the United Nations and of the United Nations Conference on Trade and Development, and calls for their immediate and effective implementation;

2. *Takes note* of the note by the Secretary-General on measures taken by the international community and recommendations for future action in favour of island developing countries;

3. *Expresses its appreciation* to all States and organizations which have facilitated the implementation of resolutions in favour of island developing countries;

4. *Notes with concern* that the specific measures envisaged in the relevant resolutions of the United Nations and the United Nations Conference on Trade and Development, including Conference resolution 138(VI), have not yet been fully implemented and calls upon States and international organizations to respond positively in this regard;

5. *Requests* the Secretary-General of the United Nations Conference on Trade and Development, in co-operation with Governments and regional and other competent institutions, to continue the programme of in-depth studies of the common problems of island economies and of the constraints inhibiting their economic growth and development carried out by the secretariat of the United Nations Conference on Trade and Development, with a view to proposing concrete specific actions, taking into account, *inter alia*, the geographical factors, traditional island life and institutions, the physical environment, development priorities and the problems of island developing countries in the international economy;

6. *Also requests* the Secretary-General of the United Nations Conference on Trade and Development to seek the views of the representatives of island developing countries and other interested countries on the implementation of the specific measures in favour of island developing countries, taking into account studies undertaken thus far and the studies envisaged in paragraph 5 above;

7. *Calls upon* all States and international organizations and financial institutions to intensify efforts to implement specific actions in favour of island developing countries in accordance with the relevant resolutions of the United Nations and of the United Nations Conference on Trade and Development;

8. *Requests* the competent organs and organizations of the United Nations system, in particular the regional commissions, to take adequate measures to respond positively to the particular needs of island developing countries;

9. *Requests* the United Nations Conference on Trade and Development to pursue further its role, not only as a focal point for specific action at the global level in favour of island developing countries but also, where necessary, as a catalyst in this regard, *inter alia*, by organizing and facilitating cross-regional interchange of information and experience in full co-operation with regional and subregional organizations;

10. *Requests* the competent organizations of the United Nations system, in particular the United Nations Conference on Trade and Development, the United Nations Development Programme, the United Nations Industrial Development Organization and the United Nations Capital Development Fund, to take adequate measures in order to respond positively to the particular needs of island developing countries;

11. *Requests* the Secretary-General, in co-operation with the organs, organizations and bodies of the United Nations system, to explore the possibility of organizing a follow-up meeting to the interregional workshop held in Saint Vincent and the Grenadines in November 1983, with the participation of representatives of island developing countries and other interested countries;

12. *Also requests* the Secretary-General to report to the General Assembly at its forty-first session on the measures taken by the international community to respond to the specific needs of island developing countries, as called for in this and other relevant resolutions of the United Nations, in order to permit the Assembly to undertake at that session a comprehensive review of the problems and needs of the island developing countries.

General Assembly resolution 39/212

18 December 1984   Meeting 104   Adopted without vote

Approved by Second Committee (A/39/790/Add.3) without vote, 6 December (meeting 56); draft by Vice-Chairman (A/C.2/39/L.114), based on informal consultations on draft by Egypt, for Group of 77 (A/C.2/39/L.82); agenda item 80 (c).

Meeting numbers. GA 39th session: 2nd Committee 53, 56; plenary 104.

The draft approved by the Second Committee differed in a number of ways from that put forward by the Group of 77. By the Group's text, the Assembly, in the third preambular paragraph, would have reiterated the programme of specific action envisaged in various UNCTAD resolutions. In the fifth preambular paragraph, it would have referred to urgent and additional efforts. In paragraph 4, the Assembly would have noted with concern that some States and international organizations had not responded positively to the action programme in favour of IDCs. Paragraphs 5 and

6 of the final text replaced a paragraph in the original draft, by which the Assembly would have requested the Secretary-General to seek the views of IDCs and other interested countries in order to review the implementation of the programme of specific action in favour of IDCs and to propose further action. In paragraph 9 of the final text, the phrases "where necessary" and "in full co-operation with regional and subregional organizations" were added. Paragraph 10 of the final text replaced one by which the Assembly would have invited UNDP to support UNCTAD, the regional commissions and other competent United Nations organizations in implementing relevant resolutions. By paragraph 11 of the Group's draft, the Assembly would have simply requested a follow-up meeting to the 1983 workshop, and in paragraph 12 would have requested the Secretary-General to recommend further action to permit the Assembly to undertake its review.

UN Special Fund

GENERAL ASSEMBLY ACTION

There being no proposal pertaining to the United Nations Special Fund,[37] the General Assembly adopted decision 39/430 without vote.

United Nations Special Fund

At its 103rd plenary meeting, on 17 December 1984, the General Assembly took note of part XIII of the report of the Second Committee.

General Assembly decision 39/430

Adopted without vote

Oral proposal by President; agenda item 80 *(I)*.

REFERENCES

[1]YUN 1983, p. 429, GA res. 38/200, 20 Dec. 1983. [2]A/39/398. [3]E/1984/17. [4]YUN 1981, p. 406. [5]*Ibid.*, p. 410, GA res. 36/194, 17 Dec. 1981. [6]YUN 1983, p. 433, GA res. 38/195, 20 Dec. 1983. [7]A/39/578. [8]YUN 1982, p. 616. [9]YUN 1983, p. 432. [10]A/39/15, vol. I (dec. 284(XXVIII)). [11]YUN 1982, p. 613. [12]*The Least Developed Countries 1984 Report* and *Annex: Basic Data* (TD/B/1027 & Add.1), Sales No. E.84.II.D.25, vols. I and II. [13]YUN 1981, p. 408. [14]ACC/1984/12. [15]E/1984/66. [16]DP/1985/11/Add.1. [17]YUN 1983, p. 431. [18]DP/1985/11 & Corr.1. [19]E/1984/20 (dec. 84/10). [20]ID/CONF.5/46 & Corr.1 (res. 6). [21]YUN 1983, p. 435. [22]TD/B/1002. [23]TD/B/1007 & Corr.1,2 & Add.1. [24]A/39/15, vol. II (dec. 298(XXIX)). [25]A/39/462 & Add.1. [26]A/C.2/39/L.3. [27]YUN 1983, p. 436, GA dec. 38/437, 19 Dec. 1983. [28]YUN 1982, p. 181. [29]YUN 1980, p. 549. [30]DP/1985/5/Add.1. [31]DP/1985/5/Add.6. [32]A/39/798. [33]YUN 1983, p. 438. [34]TD/B/1006. [35]YUN 1982, p. 620, GA res. 37/206, 20 Dec. 1982. [36]A/39/463. [37]A/39/790/Add.12.

Chapter II

Operational activities for development

In 1984, total official development assistance transferred through all the organizations of the United Nations system to developing countries amounted to $6.6 billion dollars. Total contributions for the system's development activities amounted to $5.7 billion, a decline compared with $6 billion in 1983. A number of countries increased the national currency value of their contributions, but, as several reports on operational activities indicated, part of the increase was lost due to the strength of the United States dollar.

In his annual report on the work of the Organization (p. 3), the Secretary-General said that the United Nations Development Programme (UNDP) with the specialized agencies, had come to represent a vital source of economic and technical assistance for developing countries. High priority was being given to the low-income countries and, in a period of restricted resources, efforts were continuing to ensure more effective operational co-operation within the system.

The three major issues which illustrated the new technical co-operation requirements claiming the attention of UNDP in 1984 were the debt problems of developing countries, their needs in shaping and implementing macroeconomic policies, and the crisis in Africa. Programme adjustments were initiated by UNDP to respond to the emergency in Africa, which was widely perceived to be a development issue. Field expenditures in the region, by and through UNDP, amounted to more than $300 million over the year.

The work of UNDP in technical co-operation among developing countries during the year included a major interregional project through which 133 activities were financed at a cost of $1.28 million.

The General Assembly, by resolution 39/220 of 18 December 1984, recognized the contributions of Governments to UNDP and called on the UNDP Governing Council, while considering the level of resources of the fourth programming cycle (1987-1991), to take into account the increased needs of the developing countries in technical co-operation and the need for real growth in resources.

The United Nations Department of Technical Co-operation for Development (DTCD) delivered a technical co-operation programme of almost $111 million in 1984 which was almost comparable to that of 1983 despite a drop in the level of budgets.

In 1984, the United Nations Volunteers programme (UNV) attached the highest priority to assisting the most severely affected African countries to utilize emergency relief assistance more effectively. Twenty-seven countries were selected to receive such assistance, requests for which were predominantly in the areas of aid co-ordination, food distribution, and vehicle, water pump and borehole maintenance.

The United Nations Capital Development Fund approved $36.8 million for 17 new projects. In programming its assistance, the Fund gave priority to drought-affected areas of Africa and to projects related to food production and distribution, primary health care and water-related projects.

Topics related to this chapter. Africa: South Africa and *apartheid*—aid programmes and inter-agency co-operation. Middle East: aid programmes for Palestinians. Development policy and international economic co-operation: economic co-operation among developing countries. Economic assistance, disasters and emergency relief. International trade and finance: UNCTAD technical co-operation. Development finance. Regional economic and social activities—technical co-operation. Food: food aid. Health and human resources: human resources. Refugees: refugee assistance. Institutional arrangements: organizational structure. Namibia: international assistance.

General aspects

In his annual report on United Nations technical co-operation activities for 1984,[1] the Secretary-General gave information on the activities of the United Nations Department of Technical Co-operation for Development (DTCD) and of other entities of the system responsible for technical co-operation. The steep decline in DTCD's field programme in 1982 and 1983 levelled off in 1984 when a programme of nearly $111 million was delivered. This was achieved as a result of DTCD's improved rate of delivery;

although the Department's financial situation still gave rise to concern. Of the Department's total expenditures, $76.7 million was for UNDP-financed projects, $11.4 for UNFPA, $7 million under the United Nations Regular Programme of Technical Co-operation and $11.9 million under trust funds. Compared with 1983, the budget fell by $4.7 million, but expenditures remained practically the same. By geographic area, budgets for 1984 grew by 2 per cent in Africa, but decreased in all other regions. The distribution of expenditure, however, was little changed from 1983, with Africa remaining the most important programme accounting for nearly $43 million, or 38 per cent of the total, followed by Asia with over $29 million or 26 per cent. By sector, natural resources and energy continued to account for the largest share of the programme, representing $50 million in expenditures, or 45 per cent. Development planning was the second most important activity, although its share of delivery dropped from 22 per cent in 1983 to 19 per cent, and from $25 to $21 million in monetary terms.

In his annual report on operational activities of the United Nations system,[2] the Director-General for Development and International Economic Co-operation (DIEC) stated that some $6,604 million in official development assistance (ODA) was transferred through all the organizations of the United Nations system to developing countries in 1984, amounting to about 15 per cent of net ODA received by those countries. Disbursements of both the International Development Association (IDA) and the International Fund for Agricultural Development (IFAD) on a net transfer basis increased during the year to reach $2,515 million. Grant financed expenditures on field programmes amounted to $2,297 million, the fourth successive year for which there had been no increase in nominal dollar terms. Developing countries thus experienced a real decline in United Nations system assistance.

Other features of 1984 programme expenditures highlighted in the report included: the stagnation in expenditures reflected the contribution situation, although a stronger United States dollar which had a depressive effect on contributions had a beneficial effect on programme expenditures; the decline in expenditures financed by UNDP and from the regular budget of agencies were offset by increased expenditures by the World Food Programme (WFP) and by organizations from extrabudgetary resources; the agriculture, forestry and fisheries, health and natural resources sectors absorbed about 50 per cent of total technical co-operation expenditures, little change from 1983; expenditures in sub-Saharan Africa continued to grow: the allocation of ex-

penditures continued to shift towards least developed countries (LDCs) and other low-income groups; and total UNDP activities financed 45 per cent of total system-wide technical co-operation of $1,374 million (excluding the World Bank), as in 1983. Expenditures of the organizations participating in the Joint Consultative Group on Policy (UNDP, UNFPA, UNICEF and WFP) totalled $1,657 million, or about three quarters of system-wide expenditures.

Introducing to the General Assembly's Second Committee, his annual report for 1984,[3] which covered mainly 1983 activities,[4] the DIEC Director-General said developments over the preceding year had shown that the system had been adapting its programmes to meet the new requirements of the developing countries. Nevertheless, there was a need to modify some existing programmes and to consider social issues more explicitly in formulating adjustment and economic recovery programmes. Resource constraints had adversely affected the system's capacity to assist developing countries. However, in both 1983 and 1984, a number of countries, particularly developing ones, had increased their contributions in national currencies. A number of Member States had announced larger national currency contributions at the November 1984 United Nations Pledging Conference for Development Activities (see below), but the overall situation gave no grounds for complacency.

A November 1984 report of the Secretary-General[5] on implementing a 1977 resolution on restructuring the economic and social sectors of the United Nations system[6] contained a section on operational activities. It was noted that a practice had been established of triennial policy reviews of operational activities by the Assembly and the Economic and Social Council, and annual reviews by the Assembly itself, based on reports submitted by the Director-General. Provisions of the 1977 resolution relating to the establishment of a single pledging conference, the designation of a single official at the country level, and the carrying out of comprehensive policy reviews, had been carried out, while those relating to the use of the UNDP country programming process as a frame of reference for operational activities had proceeded more slowly. No specific action had been taken by intergovernmental bodies to integrate existing United Nations programmes and funds for development financed from extrabudgetary resources; nor had a uniform pattern emerged with regard to resource mobilization.

ACC activities. The Administrative Committee on Co-ordination (ACC), through its Consultative Committee on Substantive Questions (Operational Activities) (CCSQ(OPS)), also discussed operational activities.[7] The Committee met twice in 1984, in March and December. At its March session,[8] it discussed links between technical co-operation and investment and agreed on an agenda for an *ad hoc* meeting on investment promotion, and on items to be considered at a seminar, to be followed by an informal inter-agency consultation, on enhancing the role of United Nations agencies in implementing technical assistance financed by multi-lateral development banks, both to be held later in the year.

Also considered were: simplification and harmonization of aid modalities; strengthening of technical backstopping of operational activities; feasibility of in-depth reviews of selected multisectoral projects; and follow-up to a 1983 Assembly resolution on a comprehensive policy review of operational activities for development.[9]

At its December 1984 session,[10] CCSQ(OPS) discussed the conclusions and recommendations of the seminar and the *ad hoc* meeting (Washington, D.C. 14-15 May; Vienna, Austria, 11-12 October). It also continued its consideration of simplification and harmonization of aid modalities, based on a report on evaluation and project reporting prepared by UNDP and the World Health Organization (WHO). Other subjects discussed included: policy issues associated with tied aid procurement; influencing the direction and flow of bilateral aid by the United Nations system; administrative costs of fellowships; and the Committee's own 1985-1986 work programme.

ECONOMIC AND SOCIAL COUNCIL ACTION

In July, on the recommendation of its Third (Programme and Co-ordination) Committee, the Economic and Social Council adopted without vote decision 1984/171.

Reports considered by the Economic and Social Council in connection with the question of operational activities for development

At its 48th plenary meeting, on 25 July 1984, the Council took note of the following reports:

(a) Report of the Executive Board of the United Nations Children's Fund;

(b) Extract from the report of the Governing Council of the United Nations Development Programme on its organizational meeting for 1984 and its thirty-first session;

(c) Report of the Secretary-General on the establishment of a technical unit for technical co-operation among developing countries in ground-water resources development within the Centre for Waters at Zagreb, Yugoslavia;

(d) Report of the Secretary-General on United Nations technical co-operation activities.

Economic and Social Council decision 1984/171

Adopted without vote

Approved by Third Committee (E/1984/149) without vote, 19 July (meeting 13); oral proposal by Chairman and in light of paragraph 5 *(e)* of Council decision 1984/101; agenda item 19.

GENERAL ASSEMBLY ACTION

In resolution 39/220, the General Assembly reaffirmed the central responsibility of developing countries in co-ordinating external assistance, including determining local co-ordination arrangements. The Secretary-General was requested to ensure that the United Nations system was responsive to developing countries[2] requests for assistance in strengthening their co-ordination capabilities. The DIEC Director-General was requested to provide data on issues identified in the 1983 Assembly resolution on the policy review of operational activities for development[9] and to report in 1985 on progress achieved. He was also requested to include in that report information on: steps being considered to improve the effectiveness of round-table meetings in the light of the experience gained in the 1985 mid-term review of the implementation of the Substantial New Programme of Action for the 1980s for the Least Developed Countries (1981), (see p. 413) in close collaboration with the UNDP Administrator; the situation in the United Nations system regarding tied contributions and the outcome of discussions on the issue by ACC; data on procurement undertaken by United Nations organizations engaged in operational activities; data on and analysis of the relationship between programme delivery and administrative and support costs of those organizations; and information on action to help strengthen developing countries' co-ordination capabilities.

Financing of operational activities

In a report on United Nations system regular and extrabudgetary technical co-operation expenditures financed from sources other than UNDP,[11] the UNDP Administrator indicated that, in 1984, 27 organizations and five regional commissions (excluding Governments, non-governmental organizations (NGOs) and the development banks) reported expenditures of almost $841 million financed from services other than UNDP central funds. Although total expenditure was the same as that for 1983, regular technical co-operation expenditures went down by some 14 per cent and UNFPA-financed expenditures fell from $123 million in 1983 to $120 million in 1984. However, expenditures funded by sources other than UNDP, UNFPA and UNDP-administered funds rose to $420 million in 1984 from $397 million in 1983. Those financed by UNDP-administered funds rose sharply to $81 million as opposed to $64 million in 1983.

The DIEC Director-General stated that indications suggested that there had been a halt in the erosion of contributions during 1984.

1984 EXPENDITURES BY THE UN SYSTEM ON OPERATIONAL ACTIVITIES FOR DEVELOPMENT AND NON-DEVELOPMENT ASSISTANCE, BY RECIPIENT COUNTRY AND REGION
(in thousands of US dollars)

RECIPIENT	Development assistance*	Other assistance†	RECIPIENT	Development assistance*	Other assistance†	RECIPIENT	Development assistance*	Other assistance†
Developing Member States			Hungary	110,929	—	Sri Lanka	108,104	—
Afghanistan	8,098	20	India	976,918	—	Sudan	106,646	49,163
Albania	3,371	—	Indonesia	574,851	4,476	Suriname	527	—
Algeria	9,698	3,588	Iran	(73,923)	7,804	Swaziland	1,449	1,567
Angola	18,452	6,712	Iraq	(8,821)	—	Syrian Arab Republic	26,870	—
Antigua and Barbuda	408	—	Ivory Coast	125,513	—	Thailand	143,120	32,497
Argentina	(21,019)	4,512	Jamaica	3,974	—	Togo	30,082	0
Bahamas	183	—	Jordan	20,621	—	Trinidad and Tobago	(6,379)	—
Bahrain	891	—	Kenya	121,344	3,793	Tunisia	27,664	—
Bangladesh	357,398	—	Kuwait	171	—	Turkey	303,572	1,266
Barbados	4,900	—	Lao People's Democratic Republic	15,527	936	Uganda	87,831	5,996
Belize	1,934	—	Lebanon	20,744	1,248	United Arab Emirates	(134)	—
Benin	26,647	539	Lesotho	19,124	863	United Republic of Tanzania	77,583	5,838
Bhutan	12,212	—	Liberia	17,124	—	Uruguay	33,962	—
Bolivia	(7,287)	20	Libyan Arab Jamahiriya	1,006	—	Vanuatu	930	—
Botswana	23,955	1,420	Madagascar	34,592	106	Venezuela	(23,502)	—
Brazil	652,521	—	Malawi	79,427	—	Viet Nam	25,438	3,992
Bulgaria	1,483	—	Malaysia	(14,341)	7,874	Yemen	44,203	—
Burkina Faso	36,594	20	Maldives	2,492	—	Yugoslavia	136,634	1,868
Burma	91,731	10	Mali	51,910	166	Zaire	44,157	9,928
Burundi	40,902	1,229	Malta	196	—	Zambia	21,539	3,709
Cameroon	29,021	1,070	Mauritania	16,826	42	Zimbabwe	58,795	3,335
Cape Verde	11,682	20	Mauritius	22,727	—			
Central African Republic	20,364	—	Mexico	215,557	10,182	Subtotal	7,044,436	386,616
Chad	27,223	49	Mongolia	1,808	—			
Chile	11,716	—	Morocco	159,171	—	**Developing non-member States/Territories**		
China	305,351	4,295	Mozambique	39,471	429			
Colombia	199,750	226	Nepal	58,322	25	Bermuda	32	—
Comoros	8,113	—	Nicaragua	21,784	1,875	Democratic People's Republic of Korea	3,458	—
Congo	10,209	—	Niger	36,524	54	Hong Kong	171	4,984
Costa Rica	6,882	8,269	Nigeria	169,622	1,227	Namibia	3,761	—
Cuba	5,446	—	Oman	19,308	—	Republic of Korea	149,028	—
Cyprus	1,399	7,644	Pakistan	209,908	87,145	Tonga	857	—
Czechoslovakia	394	—	Panama	19,159	—	Other countries	(26,744)	33,635
Democratic Kampuchea	6,116	—	Papua New Guinea	21,238	—			
Democratic Yemen	40,068	—	Paraguay	36,980	13	Subtotal	130,563	38,619
Djibouti	4,533	3,869	Peru	71,895	850			
Dominica	2,898	—	Philippines	55,972	9,343	Total	7,174,999	425,235
Dominican Republic	7,916	—	Poland	1,543	—			
Ecuador	31,959	218	Portugal	19,535	595	**Developed countries**	(79,749)	8,350
Egypt	221,153	2,583	Qatar	11	—			
El Salvador	9,304	—	Romania	(118,312)	—	TOTAL (all countries)	7,095,250	433,585
Equatorial Guinea	5,953	—	Rwanda	34,876	4,439			
Ethiopia	89,310	16,808	Saint Lucia	815	—	**Intercountry**		
Fiji	(2,877)	9	Saint Vincent and the Grenadines	674	—	Regional Africa	77,112	224
Gabon	(2,080)	—	Samoa	1,815	—	Regional Americas	26,075	812
Gambia	16,421	—	Sao Tome and Principe	2,417	—	Regional Arab States	40,258	802
Ghana	58,927	30	Saudi Arabia	2,084	—	Regional Asia	66,982	—
Greece	11,086	1,341	Senegal	37,419	1,484	Regional Europe	13,555	—
Grenada	687	—	Seychelles	847	—	Interregional	153,569	—
Guatemala	(11,641)	—	Sierra Leone	10,599	—	Global	76,340	29,240
Guinea	32,802	148	Singapore	(15,191)	—			
Guinea-Bissau	11,015	—	Solomon Islands	2,026	—	Total	453,891	31,078
Guyana	1,105	—	Somalia	72,236	44,105			
Haiti	40,855	—	Spain	(31,505)	1,229	**Not elsewhere classified**	5,213	162,820
Honduras	41,674	12,505						
						GRAND TOTAL	7,554,354	627,483

*Represents the sum of operational activities financed under regular United Nations and agency budgets ($220.1 million), the UNDP main programme ($454.5 million), UNDP-administered funds ($81 million), UNFPA ($119.9 million), UNICEF ($244.4 million), other extrabudgetary funds ($317.4 million) and WFP ($678.9 million), plus net transfers from the World Bank ($2,797.1 million), IDA ($2,326.7 million) and IFC ($126.6 million) and net IFAD disbursements ($187.7 million).

†Represents expenditure financed by UNHCR ($458.5 million), UNRWA ($161.7 million) and UNDRO ($7.1 million).

NOTE: Figures in parentheses are negative.

SOURCE: A/40/698.

1984 CONTRIBUTIONS TO THE UN SYSTEM FOR OPERATIONAL ACTIVITIES FOR DEVELOPMENT
(in thousands of US dollars)

CONTRIBUTOR	Amount	CONTRIBUTOR	Amount	CONTRIBUTOR	Amount
Member States		Guinea	91	Saudi Arabia	102,850
		Guinea-Bissau	31	Senegal	1,832
Afghanistan	91	Guyana	332	Seychelles	22
Albania	29	Haiti	1,874	Sierra Leone	151
Algeria	3,023	Honduras	1,672	Singapore	351
Angola	31	Hungary	18,784	Solomon Islands	35
Antigua and Barbuda	4	Iceland	372	Somalia	570
Argentina	12,730	India	16,470	South Africa	4,150
Australia	69,186	Indonesia	9,466	Spain	47,271
Austria	30,951	Iran	1,337	Sri Lanka	3,631
Bahamas	150	Iraq	2,418	Sudan	602
Bahrain	1,007	Ireland	5,454	Suriname	46
Bangladesh	5,112	Israel	708	Swaziland	1,890
Barbados	66	Italy	136,140	Sweden	194,987
Belgium	50,989	Ivory Coast	362	Syrian Arab Republic	398
Belize	4	Jamaica	2,297	Thailand	1,874
Benin	87	Japan	1,264,008	Togo	267
Bhutan	23	Jordan	1,028	Trinidad and Tobago	2,218
Bolivia	457	Kenya	764	Tunisia	1,129
Botswana	796	Kuwait	1,958	Turkey	2,310
Brazil	23,306	Lao People's Democratic Republic	73	Uganda	1,677
Bulgaria	1,283	Lebanon	6,615	Ukrainian SSR	3,158
Burkina Faso	96	Lesotho	70	USSR	24,913
Burma	3,022	Liberia	163	United Arab Emirates	1,442
Burundi	59	Libyan Arab Jamahiriya	8,505	United Kingdom	251,077
Byelorussian SSR	943	Luxembourg	1,449	United Republic of Tanzania	44
Cameroon	1,867	Madagascar	43	United States	1,674,144
Canada	263,212	Malawi	134	Uruguay	1,806
Cape Verde	21	Malaysia	1,375	Vanuatu	51
Central African Republic	32	Maldives	26	Venezuela	5,774
Chad	22	Mali	351	Viet Nam	77
Chile	2,827	Malta	101	Yemen	2,298
China	7,525	Mauritania	27	Yugoslavia	3,157
Colombia	3,255	Mauritius	1,988	Zaire	13,839
Comoros	21	Mexico	33,319	Zambia	627
Congo	3,017	Mongolia	202	Zimbabwe	7,350
Costa Rica	1,411	Morocco	955	*Not elsewhere classified*	7,188
Cuba	1,723	Mozambique	3,566		
Cyprus	328	Nepal	743	Total	5,476,164
Czechoslovakia	2,612	Netherlands	132,977		
Democratic Kampuchea	23	New Zealand	6,229	*Non-member States/Territories*	
Democratic Yemen	550	Nicaragua	433		
Denmark	143,695	Niger	167	Bermuda	3
Djibouti	50	Nigeria	19,786	Democratic People's Republic of	
Dominica	42	Norway	173,805	Korea	375
Dominican Republic	887	Oman	1,127	Republic of Korea	2,164
Ecuador	1,518	Pakistan	4,437	Switzerland	52,051
Egypt	3,529	Panama	3,318	Tonga	24
El Salvador	267	Papua New Guinea	210	Other	2,366
Equatorial Guinea	28	Paraguay	323		
Ethiopia	1,966	Peru	1,300	Total	56,983
Fiji	436	Philippines	1,728		
Finland	53,788	Poland	2,463	TOTAL (all countries)	5,533,147
France	179,691	Portugal	1,711	*Inter/non-governmental*	
Gabon	2,541	Qatar	6,518	Arab Gulf Programme for	
Gambia	888	Romania	1,002	UN Development Organizations	10,875
German Democratic Republic	3,726	Rwanda	273	European Communities	84,725
Germany, Federal Republic of	339,714	Saint Lucia	20	Other intergovernmental	65,557
Ghana	192	Saint Vincent and the Grenadines	23	Non-governmental	45,327
Greece	2,239	Samoa	25		
Grenada	52	Sao Tome and Principe	26	Total	206,484
Guatemala	646			GRAND TOTAL	5,739,631

*Includes contributions from Governments and other sources to UNHCR, UNRWA, UNDRO, UNEP and Trust Fund for Special Economic Assistance Programmes.
NOTE: Totals may differ from sum of figures because of rounding.
SOURCE: A/40/698.

GENERAL ASSEMBLY ACTION

On 18 December 1984, on the recommendation of the Second (Economic and Financial) Committee, the General Assembly adopted resolution 39/220 without vote.

Financing of operational activities for development

The General Assembly,

Recalling its resolutions 3201(S-VI) and 3202(S-VI) of 1 May 1974, containing the Declaration and the Programme of Action on the Establishment of a New International Economic Order, 3281(XXIX) of 12 December 1974, containing the Charter of Economic Rights and Duties of States, and 35/56 of 5 December 1980, the annex to which contains the International Development Strategy for the Third United Nations Development Decade,

Recalling further its resolutions 2688(XXV) of 11 December 1970 on the capacity of the United Nations development system and 3405(XXX) of 28 November 1975 on new dimensions in technical co-operation,

Reiterating its resolutions 32/197 of 20 December 1977, 33/201 of 29 January 1979 and 35/81 of 5 December 1980 on a comprehensive policy review of operational activities for development, 36/199 of 17 December 1981 and 37/226 of 20 December 1982 on operational activities for development of the United Nations system,

Reaffirming the exclusive responsibility of the Government of the recipient country in formulating its national development plan, priorities and objectives, as set out in the consensus contained in the annex to General Assembly resolution 2688(XXV), and emphasizing that the integration of the operational activities of the United Nations system with national programmes would enhance the impact and relevance of those activities,

Stressing the urgent need to strengthen multilateral co-operation for development, including increased voluntary contributions to operational activities for development of the United Nations system,

Having considered the report of the Director-General for Development and International Economic Co-operation on operational activities for development of the United Nations system,

1. *Reaffirms* its resolutions 38/171 and 38/172 of 19 December 1983;

2. *Notes* the positive signs at the 1984 United Nations Pledging Conference for Development Activities, which nevertheless follow a stagnation in resources for operational activities for development in 1983 compared to 1982, bearing in mind that the continuing needs of developing countries require greater efforts to strengthen that positive trend to lead to a process of growth in resources by increasing significantly the level of contributions on a more equitable basis;

3. *Stresses* the need for the successful completion of the first replenishment of the International Fund for Agricultural Development, and urges all countries concerned, bearing in mind the particular contribution of the developed countries, to reach agreement on a priority basis for the second replenishment, in order to enable the Fund to continue its effective contribution at an adequate level;

4. *Urges* developed countries to provide supplementary financing for the seventh replenishment of the International Development Association in order to cover the shortfall and enable the Association to increase its assistance to developing countries, particularly in the development of food and agriculture;

5. *Reaffirms* the unique and central role of the United Nations Development Programme in the field of technical co-operation for development;

6. *Recognizes* the contribution of Governments to the United Nations Development Programme, particularly those which have increased their contributions by 14 per cent, bearing in mind decision 80/30 of 26 June 1980 of the Governing Council of the Programme, reaffirms the imperativeness of providing the Programme with adequate resources, and calls upon the Governing Council, while considering the level of resources of the fourth programming cycle, to take fully into account, in accordance with the principles of the consensus of 1970, the increased needs of the developing countries in the

area of technical co-operation and the need for achieving real growth in resources;

7. *Reaffirms also* the central responsibility of Governments of developing countries in the process of co-ordination of external assistance, including the determination of local co-ordination arrangements;

8. *Requests* the Secretary-General to ensure that the United Nations system is responsive to assisting developing countries, at their request, in strengthening their capabilities in exercising co-ordination;

9. *Requests* the Director-General for Development and International Economic Co-operation, in his annual report for 1985, to continue to provide data on the various issues identified in General Assembly resolution 38/171, particularly in its paragraphs 15 and 24, and to report to the Assembly, at its fortieth session, on the progress achieved with regard to paragraphs 19, 23 and 27 of that resolution, and also requests the Director-General to include in his report information on the following:

(a) Steps being considered to improve the process and effectiveness of round-table meetings in the light of the experience gained in the mid-term global review of the implementation of the Substantial New Programme of Action for the 1980s for the Least Developed Countries, in close collaboration with the Administrator of the United Nations Development Programme;

(b) The prevailing situation in various organizations and programmes of the United Nations system with regard to tied contributions in the light of paragraph 8 of resolution 38/171 and the outcome of discussions on this issue by the Administrative Committee on Co-ordination;

(c) Data on procurement undertaken by organizations of the United Nations system engaged in operational activities;

(d) Further data on and analysis of the relationship between programme delivery and administrative and support costs of those organizations;

(e) Information on specific action taken in response to paragraph 8 of the present resolution.

General Assembly resolution 39/220

18 December 1984   Meeting 104   Adopted without vote

Approved by Second Committee (A/39/791) without vote, 14 December (meeting 61); draft by Vice-Chairman (A/C.2/39/L.138/Rev.1), based on informal consultations on draft by Egypt, for Group of 77 (A/C.2/39/L.96); agenda item 81 *(a)*.
Meeting numbers. GA 39th session: 2nd Committee 48-53, 55, 56, 58, 61; plenary 104.

Apart from drafting changes, the adopted text differed substantially from that submitted by the Group of 77. The second, third and fourth preambular paragraphs were added. In the provision that became the fifth preambular paragraph, the Assembly would have referred to a significant increase in ODA rather than increased voluntary contributions to the United Nations. Paragraph 2 of the final text comprised three paragraphs of the earlier draft by which the Assembly would have: stressed the importance of operational activities for the development process of developing countries, and emphasized that their deteriorating economic situation and the critical economic situation in Africa required an urgent increase in financial resources to strengthen multilateral co-operation; expressed deep concern at the decrease in resources for operational activities in 1983 compared with 1982, especially when the latter was considered a crisis year by the Assembly; and also expressed deep concern that, despite positive signs at the 1984 Pledging Conference for Development Activities, overall resource levels remained far below requirements. Omitted from the final text was a paragraph by which the Assembly would have strongly reiterated the need for an assured, substantial increase in resources, to enable the system to increase operational programmes, and called on Member States, particularly developed countries whose overall performance was not commensurate with their capacities, to increase their contributions to attain and, where possible, surpass planned funding levels of UNDP and its administered funds. Also deleted was a call to United Nations financial institutions to use DTCD's experience and operational capabilities fully, while paragraph 5 was added.

Other changes included the following: by the provision that became paragraph 3, the Assembly would have urged developed countries to fulfil their pledges under the IFAD first replenishment and to announce contributions for the second on a priority basis; by what became paragraph 4, it would have urged developed countries to agree on supplementary funding of IDA of not less than $3 billion; and by a provision corresponding to paragraph 6, it would have reaffirmed the 14 per cent annual growth rate for UNDP resources, and called on the UNDP Governing Council, in considering the fourth programming cycle, to take account of developing countries' increased technical co-operation needs and international targets warranting a steady increase of ODA over the decade.

Paragraphs 8 and 9 comprised four earlier provisions, by which, in addition to the requests contained in the final text, the Assembly would have requested the DIEC Director-General to provide in 1985 information on action taken to assist developing countries in strengthening co-ordination. Sub-paragraphs 9 (c), (d) and (e) were also added to the Group of 77's draft.

Expenditures

Total ODA transferred through all United Nations organizations to developing countries amounted to $6,604 million in 1984, or about 15 per cent of net ODA received. Excluding the concessional funds provided by IDA and IFAD, the share of developing countries net-ODA receipts channelled through the system was a little over 6 per cent, the level attained in earlier years. Disbursements of both IDA and IFAD on a net transfer basis increased to $2,515 million, a significant increase over 1983, largely due to rapid growth in

UN SYSTEM TECHNICAL CO-OPERATION EXPENDITURES IN 1984, BY EXECUTING BODY
(in thousands of US dollars)

Executing body	UNDP	Other sources	Total
UNIDO	56,234	29,812	86,046
UNCTAD	7,161	2,115	9,276
UN Centre on Transnational Corpo-rations	—	484	484
ECA	5,891	8,328	14,219
ECE	650	306	956
ECLA	1,340	5,312	6,652
ECWA	632	2,174	2,806
ESCAP	5,452	9,185	14,637
UNHCR	—		0
UNCHS	10,495	4,885	15,380
Other UN	76,230	34,388	110,618
Subtotal UN	164,085	96,989	261,074
IAEA	2,249	28,947	31,196
ILO	37,242	45,268	82,510
FAO	109,270	164,576	273,846
UNESCO	36,367	63,721	100,088
WHO	13,187	260,910*	274,097
World Bank and IDA	33,705	2,837†	36,542
ICAO	23,527	20,925	44,452
UPU	1,596	970	2,566
ITU	18,454	4,919	23,373
WMO	11,825	10,230	22,055
IMO	6,536	3,459	9,995
WIPO	1,191	2,190	3,381
ITC	5,707	8,425	14,132
UNDP	39,000	38,212	77,212
UNFPA	—	22,879	22,879
UNICEF	—	6,520	6,520
Subtotal other UN system	339,856	684,988	1,024,844
World Tourism Organization	543	—	543
Asian Development Bank	4,677	—	4,677
Arab Fund for Economic and Social Development	62	—	62
Governments	18,272‡	49,833	68,105
Non-governmental organizations	—	9,224	9,224
Subtotal non-UN system	23,554	59,057	82,611
Total	527,495	841,034	1,368,529

*Including support costs.
†Excluding $845 million financed by World Bank loans and IDA credits.
‡Excluding government cash counterpart expenditures of $5,095,000.
NOTE: Figures for UNDP are provisional data covering IPFs, Special Programme Resources, Special Measures Fund for Least Developed Countries, Special Industrial Services, cost-sharing and trust funds established by the Administrator, where applicable; UNDP-administered funds outside the Programme's central resources are included in the "other sources" column.
SOURCE: DP/1985/65.

IDA disbursements. IFAD disbursements continued to quicken in the light of the large pipeline of commitments.

Grant financed expenditures on field programmes totalled $2,297 million, the fourth successive year for which there had been no increase in nominal dollar terms. Such stagnation reflected the overall contributions situation although the stronger United States dollar which had a depressive effect on contributions had a beneficial effect on expenditures. Expenditures in sub-Saharan Africa continued to grow, from $472 million in 1979 (30 per cent of total country and regional programmes) to $766 million in 1984 (41 per cent), a reflection of the importance attached by the international community to the region's severe economic problems. Allocation of expenditures continued to shift towards least developed countries (LDCs) and other low-income groups with LDCs receiving 41 per cent of the system's country and regional activities, compared with 33 per cent in 1979.

Expenditures on refugee, humanitarian, and disaster relief activities, amounted to $628 million in 1984, a slight increase over previous years' figures but still below the level attained in the earlier part of the decade. Those expenditures were likely to increase, particularly in view of the United Nations response to the crisis in Africa.

Total UNDP project expenditures decreased from $560 million in 1983 to $527 (not including $5.1 million in government cash counterpart expenditures) in 1984. Non-UNDP-financed technical co-operation expenditures, however, remained at the 1983 level amounting to $841 million. Nevertheless, the majority of executing bodies continued to have the larger part of their technical co-operation expenditures financed by UNDP, exceptions being IAEA, ILO, FAO, UNESCO, WHO, WIPO, ITC, ESCAP and the Centre on Transnational Corporations (see table above).

Contributions

Total contributions from Governments and other official and non-official sources to development activities of the United Nations system, amounted to $5.7 billion in 1984 (see table above) compared with $6 billion the previous year. Covered in the totals were all United Nations funds and programmes, the operational activities of the specialized agencies and WFP.

Aggregate contributions to United Nations funds and programmes amounted to $1,352 million, a slight increase over 1983. Contributions to UNDP-administered trust funds and to other United Nations funds and programmes amounted to $182 million. Contributions to the main programme resources of UNDP stagnated at less than $700 million for the fifth consecutive year. Despite a number of countries increasing their 1984 pledges to UNDP, the effect was lost as a result of the appreciation of the United States dollar against most other currencies.

Extrabudgetary contributions for the technical co-operation activities of the specialized agencies and IAEA increased in 1984 to $376 million, the same level attained in 1982, largely the result of an increase in contributions from developing countries. Cost-sharing and self-supporting contributions amounted to $205 million in 1984, an increase over 1982 and 1983.

Contributions to IDA and IFAD declined from the 1982 and 1983 levels, totalling $2,776 million in 1984; however, year-to-year changes reflected the bunching of IDA payments.

Contributions for humanitarian, refugee, disaster relief and special economic assistance programmes—not included in the above data—

amounted to $556 million in 1984, an increase over 1983 but below the earlier years of the decade. In 1985, contributions were expected to show a more rapid increase, in view of the response to the critical situation in Africa.

Regarding the resource outlook for 1985 to 1988, UNDP, UNFPA, UNICEF and WFP estimated that contributions to the four organizations would amount to $1,900 million in 1985 compared with about $1,750 million received in 1984. For 1986-1988, those organizations were planning for total contributions of $6,300 million compared with the $5,437 million collected and estimated for 1985 for the immediate preceding three years.

In response to a 1983 General Assembly request,[9] the DIEC Director-General, in his report to the 1984 Assembly,[3] included an examination of the extent and implications of the trend towards tying contributions for operational activities to the procurement of goods and services in the donor country. The report stated that the UNDP Governing Council, at its 1984 session, had discussed the issue in the context of earlier Council decisions to authorize the UNDP Administrator to accept trust funds conditioned on procurement from a donor country for three funds (see below under "Technical co-operation through UNDP"). Based on the Administrator's conclusion that acceptance of such trust funds had enabled those funds to provide significant additional assistance, the Council, while emphasizing the importance of preserving the principles of multilateralism, expressed concern for the needs of LDCs, particularly those afflicted by drought and desertification, which urgently needed additional resources, and decided to extend the period granted to the Administrator to accept trust funds conditioned on procurement in a donor country for the funds in question through April 1986.

The Director-General also reported that the Chairman of ACC CCSQ(OPS) was exploring with interested organizations issues associated with tied procurement. The purpose of the consultations was to ascertain whether organizations felt that tied procurement contributions were increasing, to consider the experience of organizations with such contributions and to assess the implications for multilateral development co-operation. Consideration would also be given to the need for action, including improving the transparency of information on tied procurement.

UN Pledging Conference for Development Activities. The 1984 United Nations Pledging Conference for Development Activities was held at United Nations Headquarters on 7 and 8 November to receive government pledges for 1985 to United Nations funds and programmes concerned with development and related assistance.

Contributions to the funds and programme participating in the Pledging Conference totalled $1,020

CONTRIBUTIONS TO FUNDS AND PROGRAMMES INCLUDED IN THE
UN PLEDGING CONFERENCE FOR DEVELOPMENT ACTIVITIES, 1984 AND 1985
(1984, as at 31 December 1984; 1985, as at 30 June 1985;
in thousands of US dollars)

	1984 PAYMENT		1985 PLEDGE	
FUND OR PROGRAMME	Amount	Number of donor countries	Amount	Number of donor countries
UN Development Programme	651,136	136	629,405	128
Special Measures Fund for the Least Developed Countries	13,598	9	9,352	9
Energy Account	73	2	73	2
UN Children's Fund	181,716	134	179,708	102
UN Fund for Population Activities	122,449	81	141,795	87
UN Capital Development Fund	21,160	37	20,303	41
UN Industrial Development Fund	11,076	85	12,817	87
UN Fund for Drug Abuse Control	6,492	36	14,954	42
UN Habitat and Human Settlements Foundation	1,333*	36	1,931	39
Voluntary Fund for the UN Decade for Women	3,097	39	2,373	42
UN Revolving Fund for Natural Resources Exploration	191	5	2,354	6
UN Trust Fund for African Development Activities	2,006	NA	114	7
UN Institute for Training and Research	1,953	48	1,492	44
Special Voluntary Fund for the UN Volunteers	725	18	808	20
Trust Fund for the UN Centre on Transnational Corporations	894	NA	225	4
UN Trust Fund for Social Defence	722	13	436	9
UN Trust Fund for Sudano-Sahelian Activities	571	7	5,332	14
UN Financing System for Science and Technology for Development	350	23	207	21
UN Trust Fund for the International Research and Training Institute for the Advancement of Women	484	16	449	19
UN Special Fund for Land-locked Developing Countries	117	10	34	13
UN Trust Fund for the Transport and Communications Decade in Africa	32	NA	18	5
UN Environment Programme	NA	NA	28	65
International Year of Shelter for the Homeless	NA	NA	315	7
Total	1,020,175		1.024,523	

*Amount pledged for 1984, as at 30 June 1985.
NA = Not available.
SOURCES: For 1984, A/40/5/Add.1,2,4,7-9 and unpublished documents; for 1985, A/CONF.126/2.

million in 1984. Pledges for 1985, as at 30 June 1985, amounted to $1,025 million, more than half of which was for UNDP.

GENERAL ASSEMBLY ACTION

In resolution 39/220, the General Assembly noted the positive signs at the 1984 Pledging Conference, which followed a stagnation in resources for operational activities in 1983, bearing in mind that the needs of developing countries required greater efforts to strengthen that positive trend in order to lead to a process of growth in resources by increasing contributions on a more equitable basis.

Inter-agency co-operation

ACC action

The Administrative Committee on Co-ordination (ACC), in its overview report for 1983/84,[7] stated that it was heartened by the somewhat higher pledges made at the 1983 Pledging Conference[12] but continued to view with concern the lack of certainty and inadequate level of resources being made available to assist developing countries.

During discussion of a 1983 General Assembly resolution on operational activites[9] ACC's CCSQ

(OPS), at its March 1984 session,[10] addressed the need for more concerted United Nations country-level action, the role of resident co-ordinators, the need to strengthen the evaluation capacity of developing countries and the issue of tied procurement. Special attention was given to efforts being made within the system to simplify and harmonize aid modalities. ACC felt that further harmonization of procedures should aim to make it easier for donor and recipient Governments to collaborate through the multilateral system. Since the bulk of aid inputs handled by United Nations organizations originated from a relatively limited number of central funds, it was important to bring those organizations together to simplify and harmonize their procedures.

Evaluation

In September 1984, the Secretary-General submitted to the General Assembly a report on implementing recommendations by the Joint Inspection Unit (JIU),[13] including 1983 recommendations on United Nations system co-operation in developing evaluation by Governments.[14] The report stated that in October 1983, a Bureau for Programme Policy and Evaluation had been created in the UNDP Central Evaluation Office to assist the regional bureaux in UNDP and executing agencies in assisting developing countries to enhance their evaluation capacity. The new proposed guidelines on monitoring, evaluating and reporting on UNDP projects and programmes stressed the role of national and regional resources in UNDP's evaluation work and specifically required that evaluation be undertaken as a tripartite exercise with full participation of Government(s) concerned. Specific technical co-operation projects to strengthen government evaluation capacity were under discussion with Nepal and Yemen. UNDP also issued a directory of evaluation offices and institutions in developing countries to aid exchanges of ideas and experience among them. With regard to training, UNDP participated in two seminars for development planners in Africa (Botswana, April 1984).

Guidelines on evaluation were re-drafted and it was hoped to develop a common evaluation system covering all United Nations operational and trust-fund activities, which would simplify the task of recipient Governments.

In February, the UNDP Administrator submitted to the UNDP Governing Council a progress report on an interorganizational evaluation study of women's participation in development (see Chapter XIX of this section). (For other UNDP programme evaluation activities, see below.)

REFERENCES

[1]DP/1985/43 & Add. 1-3. [2]A/40/698 & Corr. 1. [3]A/39/417. [4]YUN 1983, p.440. [5]A/39/476. [6]YUN 1977, p. 438, GA res. 32/197, 20 Dec. 1977. [7]E/1984/66. [8]ACC/1984/4. [9]YUN 1983, p.442, GA res. 38/171, 19 Dec. 1983. [10]ACC/1984/24. [11]DP/1985/65. [12]YUN 1983, p. 451. [13]A/39/145. [14]YUN 1983, p. 453.

Technical co-operation through UNDP

In his annual report for 1984,[1] the UNDP Administrator stated that the year had witnessed a progressive clarification of issues in the development dialogue as donors, recipients and development institutions focused on the orientation and enhancement of development assistance efforts. Three major issues, which illustrated the new technical co-operation requirements claiming UNDP's attention, had preoccupied the development community: the debt problems of developing countries; the needs of developing countries, particularly the least developed, in shaping and implementing macro-economic policies; and the crisis of drought and famine in Africa.

As an example of debt-related issues to which UNDP had already started to respond, the Administrator cited a project initiated in Costa Rica

in 1982 through which UNDP provided consultancy services on a broad range of financial issues arising from the country's debt crisis. He also mentioned UNDP support for the African Centre for Monetary Studies (Dakar, Senegal), which provided advice on monetary and banking matters to Governments of the region; assistance to the Office of Debt Management in Zaire, executed by the World Bank, which helped to marshal data on the country's debt sources in an integrated information system; and support services in Panama, linked to a World Bank adjustment loan.

Sub-Saharan Africa's worsening condition greatly occupied international policy attention in 1984, placing urgent demands on UNDP's resources and underscoring the need for renewed programming efforts throughout the United Nations system. UNDP offices in the region assisted immediate relief efforts, often acting as centres for logistical support and co-ordination as well as for important country information. Recognizing the close link between emergency assistance and medium- and longer-term development programmes, UNDP reorganized its field offices in affected countries to ensure that emergency work did not pre-empt continued development activities. Steps towards longer-term solutions were being taken through UNDP's existing and planned programmes for Africa. Core indicative planning figure (IPF) inputs to sub-Saharan Africa for 1982-1986 would total nearly $1 billion, of which $200 million was budgeted in 1984. UNDP had drawn up a threefold plan of action to be carried out in co-operation with its agency partners: the focusing of resources on projects in agricultural development, food production, processing and storage, forestry development, meteorology and drought management, and development planning and public administration; the redirection of inputs towards production-oriented activities involving grass-roots communities and aimed at stimulating their income-generating potential; and the reinforcement of macro-economic policy formulating capabilities, and strengthening of government planning mechanism.

A significant phenomenon in 1984, stated the Administrator, was the deepening resolve of major donors to support aid co-ordination mechanisms which led to improved strategies for national self-reliance. The 115 UNDP field offices' interaction with host Governments and activities such as emergency aid co-ordination, the provision of management and administrative services, trust fund management, and the preparation of cross-sectoral feasibility studies offered a useful basis for an expanded UNDP co-ordinating role. An evaluation of the round-table process had shown where there was scope for improvement in the format, venue and work methods of such consultations.

With regard to UNDP's efforts to improve the quality of technical assistance, the Administrator stated that updated financial management guidelines for field personnel were helping to expedite key decision-making, accounting and reporting functions, as were recently-introduced control systems for budget management and data processing. Measures were also continuing to rationalize the diverse efforts of funds administered by UNDP, to collaborate with agency partners in joint programming exercises and to harmonize UNDP's numerous special mandates with its central programmes. In addition, the recently-established Central Evaluation Office (CEO) was fulfilling its promise as an in-house analytical tool. As an example of enhanced technical assistance performance, the Administrator cited the transfer in December 1983 of funds from the United Nations Emergency Operation Trust Fund to a UNDP trust fund for developing countries affected by drought and related catastrophes.[2] In little more than a year, 98 per cent of a total of $33.9 million had been committed to over 95 projects in affected countries, with about $26 million going to sub-Saharan Africa. The single most powerful means to improve effectiveness, said the Administrator, remained the country programme which was the result of collaborative effort between the Government, UNDP and the United Nations agencies and organizations.

Highlights of UNDP action following the June 1984 Governing Council session were: efforts at closer collaboration with organizations of the United Nations system and other institutions in assisting African countries affected by the economic and social crisis constituted a major thrust in UNDP programming in 1984, and UNDP channelled exceptional funding of $1.5 million, authorized by the Council from Special Programme Resources, to provide increased numbers of United Nations volunteers for emergency programmes in the region; field office capacities in Africa were surveyed to determine measures needed to ensure adequate country-level support; and consultations were held on preparations for the fourth programming cycle (1987-1991).

At the United Nations Pledging Conference for Development Activities in November (see p. 432), nine of UNDP's 16 major donors maintained the real value of their contributions in national currencies and six of the nine substantially exceeded that minimum level. A total of 31 countries (27 of them developing countries) met or exceeded the 14 per cent growth rate set for the third programming cycle (1982-1986) in terms of their national currencies. Canada, Denmark, Italy and Sweden pledged a further $13.1 million in supplementary contributions for 1984. Nevertheless, the strength and volatility of the United States dollar main-

tained an adverse influence on the Programme's resource outlook. In current dollar terms, the value of pledges to UNDP remained static from 1981 onward at around $675 million.

Despite central resource constraints, a substantial increase in supplementary contributions enabled UNDP to maintain its services to developing countries. Sources of those funds included cost-sharing, trust funds, government cash counterpart contributions and contributions to the Special Measures Fund for LDCs. In 1984, those resources amounted to $148.4 million or 18 per cent of the Programme's resources, compared with $85.1 million or 11 per cent in 1981.

Reflecting the growth in supplementary resources, five new trust funds were established in 1984; income received for these funds amounted to the equivalent of $6.8 million. In addition, 14 sub-trust funds were established on behalf of the United Nations Sudano-Sahelian Office (UNSO), five on behalf of the United Nations Financing System for Science and Technology for Development (UNFSSTD) and one on behalf of the United Nations Capital Development Fund (UNCDF). Total 1984 income for those sub-trust funds amounted to the equivalent of $13.1 million. Voluntary pledges for the numerous special-purpose funds administered by UNDP declined slightly in 1984 to $38.6 million against $45.5 million for 1983. However, cost-sharing and sub-trust fund income received by those special funds increased from $17.7 million in 1983 to $25.8 in 1984.

Total contributions to central resources, special purpose funds and sub-trust fund and cost-sharing arrangements amounted to $834.5 million in 1984, a decline in United States dollar terms of almost 10 per cent compared with 1983. In that context, resource mobilization efforts by UNDP field offices and complementary financing attracted by UNDP-assisted projects took on renewed significance. Figures reported by 46 UNDP field offices indicated that an additional $145 million in third-party co-financing and parallel financing was directly generated by UNDP-assisted activities in 1984.

Total expenditures under UNDP in 1984 amounted to $717.7 million, of which $532.6 million (including $5.1 million in government cash counterpart expenditures) was for field programme activities, while the balance was for agency support costs, administrative and programme support, sectoral support and other field-level costs. In addition, 86 field offices reported assistance in implementing more than 1,600 non-UNDP-financed projects with total expenditures of approximately $243.2 million.

While the value of new projects approved in 1984 declined again from the previous year, their number increased from 945 to 1,074. New approvals by sector followed the pattern of the preceding year with one exception. In 1983, the three leading sectors, in order of their numerical share of new approvals, were: industry; agriculture, forestry and fisheries; and development policy and planning; in 1984, the order changed with development policy and planning taking second place to industry.

The Secretary-General's December 1984 decision to establish the United Nations Office for Emergency Operations in Africa (OEOA), under the Administrator's direction, underlined the major adjustment required of the Programme in 1984. Field expenditures in Africa by and through UNDP amounted to over $300 million, with UNDP core resources accounting for $255 million of that total (see p. 468).

Programmable resources for the Asia and Pacific region for 1982-1986 totalled $1,100 million, of which $875 million had been committed for financing 1,587 country and intercountry projects by the end of 1984. During the year, 28 of the region's 34 operational programmes were reviewed as part of the preparation for the fourth programming cycle, to assess their continuing validity and impact. The majority of those reviews demonstrated that, while the orientation and content of country programmes were still largely valid, progress in implementation was not as rapid as expected. The reviews also revealed trends reflecting some of the new technical co-operation modalities endorsed by the Governing Council in June, including: greater reliance on government execution; increasing use of national experts; and more effective aid co-ordination. At a major meeting organized by UNDP at Bangkok (Thailand) in May, government aid co-ordinators were consulted on how to improve the substance, co-ordination and operation of the intercountry programme. The meeting also provided a forum for clarifying technical co-operation procedures with senior government officials and afforded the seven LDCs in the region an opportunity to evaluate the results of the UNDP-assisted round-table process and discuss further improvements in such consultations. Statistical data on the regional programme revealed two trends: an increase in resources directed to the industrial sector and a decrease in funds spent on equipment. Expenditure patterns also confirmed the increasing importance of the human factor in development.

Through region-wide consultations in Latin America and the Caribbean, carried out by UNDP during 1984, three characteristics were noted as being of special concern: evident stagnation in many national economies; deteriorating social conditions; and acute vulnerability to external factors. Following UNDP consultations with Governments of the region, the Economic Commission for Latin America and the Caribbean (ECLAC), United Nations agencies and numerous regional and intergovernmental bodies, a meeting of the regional bureau attended by representatives of all parties to those consultations was held at Santo Domingo (Dominican Republic) in November. Areas envisaged for future multilateral technical assistance included: public policy formulation, implementation and management; alleviation of urban and rural poverty; and the transfer of high technology. Technical co-operation among developing countries (TCDC) continued to play an important part in the region with several new initiatives during the year. Brazil signed an agreement with UNDP under which it would make available 200 persons/months of consultancies, host 30 study tours, organize six international seminars and receive 12 in-service trainees in the field of energy. Those inputs were to be applied towards any United Nations-assisted technical co-operation projects in any developing country. Argentina signed agreements with Costa Rica, Nicaragua and Peru for the export of goods and services.

Between 1983 and 1984, 14 of the 20 country programmes in the Arab States were reviewed in the context of changing national policies in both oil-exporting and non-oil-exporting countries. In 1984, 22 in-depth project evaluations were also conducted. Adjustments in several country programmes reflected a shift from policies of economic expansion to those emphasizing consolidation and the optimal use of existing capacities. Declining oil revenues led a number of countries to cut back some important cost-sharing arrangements with UNDP resulting in revised priorities. In several countries, human resources development activities and management training were stepped up. Maintenance of existing investments and development of post-investment strategies were among new emphases while aid co-ordination received renewed attention, notably in the region's five LDCs, three of which—Djibouti, Somalia and the Sudan—were also affected by drought, necessitating special emergency relief and co-ordination measures and redirection of their country programmes.

Other UNDP activities in which there had been notable developments during 1984 were: TCDC; project evaluation; inter-agency relations; transfer of knowledge through expatriate nationals; the Projects Annotated Listing (PAL, i.e. project profiles aimed at bringing additional resource requirements to the attention of potential donors); staff development and training; and emergency activities in addition to those in Africa.

UNDP also administered the following Special Funds in 1984: UNCDF; the United Nations Volunteers Programme (UNV); the United Nations Revolving Fund for Natural Resources Exploration; the UNDP Energy Account; UNSO; UNFSSTD; the Voluntary Fund for the United Nations Decade for Women (VFDW); the Programme of Assistance to the Palestinian People; the Trust Fund for Assistance to Colonial Countries and Peoples; and the United Nations Special Fund for Land-locked Developing Countries.

In his 1983 annual report,[2] submitted to the June 1984 session of the UNDP Governing Council, the Administrator reported on measures taken to establish a more solid resource foundation for the Programme, on new activities for resource mobilization at the country level, and on steps taken to expand UNDP's service to the development community, while exploring new measures to meet the changing technical co-operation needs of the 1980s.

The Administrator submitted a separate note on measures to promote better understanding of UNDP's role and activities and of its resource needs (see below, under "UNDP financing").

UNDP Council action. The UNDP Governing Council held an organizational meeting in New York on 22 and 23 February, and its thirty-first session at Geneva from 4 to 30 June 1984.[3] The Council resolved itself into a Committee of the Whole,[4] which held meetings between 4 and 8 June to discuss country and intercountry programmes and projects and evaluation and made a number of recommendations taken into consideration by the Council in its decisions.

Financial, budgetary and administrative matters were considered by the Council's Budgetary and Finance Committee[5] between 4 and 29 June.

In February, the Council adopted two decisions, on its 1984 programme and organization of work[6] and on the joint United Nations/UNDP/United Nations Industrial Development Organization (UNIDO) evaluation concerning manufactures (see p. 570).

The 46 decisions adopted by the Council in June dealt with assistance to the national liberation movements recognized by the Organization of African Unity (OAU) (see p. 168); assistance to the Palestinian people (see p. 276); implementation of the Substantial New Programme of Action (SNPA) for the 1980s for LDCs (see p. 414); implementation in the Sudano-Sahelian region of the Plan of Action to Combat Desertification (see Chapter XVI of this section) and of a medium-term and long-term recovery and rehabilitation programme (see p. 509); alternative ways of financing the United Nations Sudano-Sahelian Office–UNDP/UNEP joint venture beyond 1984-1985; action taken following the liquidation of the United Nations Emergency Operation Trust Fund (see p. 522), and on the use of United Nations volunteers to assist the most severely affected African countries in implementing emergency assistance programmes (see p. 458); the United Nations Revolving Fund for Natural Resources Exploration (see Chapter IX of this section); programmes in energy development (see Chapter X of this section); the United Nations Fund for

Population Activities (see Chapter XIV of this section); the role of qualified national personnel in the social and economic development of developing countries (see Chapter XV of this section); assistance to Namibia (see TRUSTEESHIP AND DECOLONIZATION, Chapter III); and other matters affecting UNDP's work (for details see below). Two decisions dealt with the agenda, and organization of work of the Council's 1984 session,[6] and by others the Council decided on the agenda and arrangements[7] for its meetings in 1985. By another decision,[8] the Council took note of various reports submitted to its 1984 session.

Having considered the Administrator's 1983 annual report,[2] the Council on 29 June[9] welcomed the steps he had taken to improve the UNDP's effectiveness, particularly the enhanced services extended by its field offices at the country level and the increased emphasis on evaluation, and noted with appreciation his vigorous implementation of a 1983 Council decision on measures to mobilize increased resources on a more predictable, continuous and assured basis.[10] The Council encouraged him to mobilize additional resources at the country level, requested him to survey Council members to ascertain the usefulness of documents issued for the 1984 session, the results of the survey to be discussed in 1985, and encouraged him to continue his efforts to ensure the timely preparation and distribution of documents for the Council's consideration.

GENERAL ASSEMBLY ACTION

In December, the General Assembly adopted decision 39/439 without vote.

Operational activities for development

At its 104th plenary meeting, on 18 December 1984, the General Assembly, on the recommendation of the Second Committee, took note of the following documents:

(a) Note by the Secretary-General transmitting the report of the Joint Inspection Unit entitled "Office for Projects Execution of the United Nations Development Programme" and comments of the Secretary-General thereon;

(b) Note by the Secretary-General on the role of qualified national personnel in the social and economic development of developing countries;

(c) Report of the Governing Council of the United Nations Development Programme on its organizational meeting for 1984 and its thirty-first session.

General Assembly decision 39/439

Adopted without vote

Approved by Second Committee (A/39/791) without vote, 14 December (meeting 61); oral proposal by Chairman; agenda item 81 *(b)*.

Policy review

As background for the Governing Council's 1984 policy review of United Nations technical co-operation activities, the Administrator submitted in April a report on measures to be taken to meet the changing technical co-operation requirements of the developing countries.[11]

The report analysed achievements in technical co-operation over the preceding 35 years, contrasted them with a range of unsolved problems and examined the basic philosophy of technical co-operation in terms of the objective of self-reliance. The report then outlined some changing requirements in technical co-operation that were likely to gain prominence in future, and drew attention to the continuing needs of the poorer countries. It also discussed some essential functions of UNDP as measures of response to the changing requirements which had implications for the processes of programming, co-ordination, evaluation, resources mobilization and project planning and execution.

On 29 June,[12] the Governing Council noted the Administrator's findings and stressed the importance of maintaining a balanced approach in meeting technical co-operation needs and the necessity of enhanced effectiveness in programming and implementation. The Council affirmed the need to maintain UNDP's capacity to respond flexibly to changing needs in widely varying local conditions and to pursue "continuous programming" within the framework of country programmes as an effective response to a country's changing technical co-operation needs. The United Nations system was urged to co-operate with UNDP in using the country programming process as a frame of reference for technical co-operation. The Council considered that assessing and planning overall technical co-operation needs could provide a framework for co-ordinating technical assistance from external sources and that the process could be useful in that respect, and requested the Administrator to assist Governments in formulating country programmes. Governments were encouraged, when preparing programmes, to take account of the global themes and priorities expressed in intergovernmental resolutions as they related to their national plans and to consider bringing smaller projects into "umbrella projects" to reduce administrative workload and to gain in programming impact.

Executing agencies were invited to continue improving procedures to ensure that their technical knowledge was accessible to Governments, irrespective of project execution. The World Bank and regional development banks were urged to continue collaborating with UNDP.

The Council reaffirmed the importance of pre-investment and investment as an integral part of the UNDP technical co-operation programme and welcomed the field office network's expanded role in management and support services and in resource mobilization.

In high technology and other areas where changing economic and social cirumstances made new demands, the Council endorsed the Administrator's view that the more advanced developing countries continued to require multilateral technical co-operation from UNDP and urged UNDP to ensure that the emerging needs of low-income developing countries also received adequate attention. It also urged UNDP to continue responding to the technical assistance needs of LDCs, particularly towards implementing the SNPA for the 1980s for the LDCs (see p. 413), expressed appreciation to the Administrator for assisting them in preparing round-table meetings and urged him to pay special attention to their follow-up.

The Council welcomed his emphasis on grass-roots approaches for development and his strengthening of UNDP assistance to Governments through collaboration with the private sector. It stressed the importance of covering both the short- and long-term needs of developing countries for skilled manpower and requested the Administrator to address those needs, including a proposal for a human resources facility, and to report thereon to the Council in 1985. The Administrator was also invited to consider how Governments could be assisted in strengthening their central planning and co-ordination capabilities. The Council recognized that UNDP could provide recipient Governments with complementary means to achieve more effective country-level co-ordination of external assistance and reaffirmed that the UNDP country programming process should be used as a frame of reference for co-ordinating United Nations operational activies at the country level, under the responsibility of the resident co-ordinator, in order to facilitate the host country's task in co-ordinating external assistance, achieving improved coherence of action, reducing administrative overhead costs and avoiding duplication.

The Council appealed to participating United Nations organizations to join with UNDP in the efforts of the host Government for more effective development country-level co-operation and requested the Administrator to strengthen the co-ordination capability of UNDP field offices and to report to the Council thereon in 1985.

UNDP operational activities

Country and intercountry programmes

In a report[13] to the UNDP 1984 Governing Council, the UNDP Administrator examined trends and problems evident in the seven country programmes (Afghanistan, Benin, Bolivia, El Salvador, Lebanon, Singapore and Swaziland) being submitted to the Council for approval. The report dealt with the timing of the programmes and related aspects, the nature of the preparatory work, financial aspects, major development objectives and orientation, allocation of resources, pre-investment and investment support activities and global priorities.

In a section of his annual report for 1984[1] on project results of the global/interregional programme and special funds, the Administrator stated that expanded demand from the programme in 1984 was met through concentrated efforts in areas of acknowledged developmental significance. Agriculture, water supply and sanitation, special public works, housing and health and energy assessment and management continued to receive sustained attention. Basic research, technology development and transfer, and management support constituted major programme thrusts while human resources development activities were intensified.

In another section, dealing with programme implementation, he described representative project achievements reported by field offices during the year.

Following a discussion of selected country and intercountry programmes, global and interregional projects, the Committee of the Whole made several recommendations on which the Council acted in June (see below). However, the Committee did not reach a consensus on a recommendation regarding the programme for Afghanistan.

UNDP Council action. In June,[14] the Governing Council took note of the Administrator's reports on: trends and problems in the country programmes proposed for approval; and on the implementation of selected country programmes in Africa,[15] the Arab States,[16] Asia and the Pacific,[17] Europe,[18] and Latin America and the Caribbean.[19] The Council approved country programmes for: Benin and Swaziland (Africa); Lebanon (Arab States); Singapore (Asia and the Pacific); and Bolivia and El Salvador (Latin America). It also decided to extend the country programme for Guatemala through 1984 and that for Suriname through 1984 and 1985. The Council authorized the Administrator to appraise and approve requests for assistance for projects falling within each country programme, in accordance with a 1981 decision that expenditures be kept in conformity with the relevant indicative planning figures, increased with government cost-sharing contributions.

The Council also approved follow-up assistance for the following global projects: international rice testing and improvement programme (phase II); international maize testing programme and training activities; maximizing crop production through biological nitrogen fixation; and survey and identification of world marine fish resources.

Indicative planning figures

In a report to the 1984 Governing Council on the mid-term review of the third programming cycle (1982-1986),[20] the Administrator also discussed specific issues such as indicative planning figures (IPFs). Unless substantial resources were made available, he stated, he was not in a position to make any recommendations with regard to adjustments of the illustrative IPFs. The amount of $99.5 million, set aside in 1980 as unallocated reserve for future participants and for revisions of IPFs, would have been available only if voluntary contributions had reached the target level. Given the current shortfall in resources, no such funds were available as all actual and projected resources had been allocated to maintain the current programming levels of approved IPFs. In those circumstances, neither a general review of the illustrative IPFs nor a specific review of those countries whose economic situation had deteriorated substantially appeared to be useful.

Based on these and other observations in the Administrator's report, the Governing Council on 29 June 1984[21] decided that no general revision of IPFs could be made in the prevailing resource situation, but that such a revision might be considered to the extent that improvement in the UNDP resource position would permit in the future, and to the extent that it would not result in reducing other programmes. The Council noted the Administrator's implementation of its 1983 decision[22] in respect of programme levels of countries with small IPFs, and further noted his actions to increase resource flows to, and improve the co-ordination of, activities for LDCs.

The Council decided that, for the purpose of determining the carry-forward to the fourth programming cycle (1987-1991), the norm against which positive or negative carry-forwards would be calculated would be derived using 55 per cent of the illustrative IPF, except for the smaller IPFs covered by the 1983 decision.

The Council approved the following conditions for borrowing from fourth-cycle IPFs: borrowing would be authorized to the extent that it did not threaten the financial integrity of the Programme and that total expenditures were kept within available resources, only for countries in a region up to a maximum of expected under-expenditures in the 1982-1986 cycle in respect of other countries in the region, only for countries where the fourth-cycle IPF was expected to be larger than the 1982-1986 illustrative IPF, and only up to a maximum of 15 per cent of the 1982-1986 illustrative IPF for each country qualifying for borrowing; borrowing for intercountry programmes would be allowed up to the estimated extent of underspending in other intercountry programmes, not to exceed 15 per cent of each 1982-1986 illustrative IPF; for the purpose of borrowing from the fourth cycle, the global and interregional programmes could be counted together; the borrowed amount would constitute a first charge against the corresponding fourth-cycle IPF; and the Administrator would report to the Council on his use of selective borrowing from the fourth cycle.

The Council approved a pro-rated illustrative IPF for St. Helena of $330,000 for 1984-1986. It took note of: the continued lack of data to calculate illustrative IPFs for Democratic Kampuchea and Lebanon, for which provisional illustrative IPFs of $25.5 million and $10 million, respectively, would remain in effect until sufficient data were available; the fact that, while revised data were available for Hungary, its illustrative IPF remained unchanged at $3.5 million; and the independence of Brunei Darussalam and the consequent revision of its illustrative IPF to $730,000.

Pre-investment activities

In accordance with a 1982 decision,[23] the Administrator submitted to the June 1984 Governing Council a report[24] on progress achieved in strengthening UNDP's pre-investment role. The Administrator reported on the co-operative arrangement with FAO whereby the expertise of the FAO Investment Centre was used to enhance the investment potential of UNDP-assisted projects and to promote them with sources of finance. Similar co-operative arrangements with other executing agencies were being undertaken or were under consideration. The report covered the first year of operation of the investment feasibility study facility, under which special programme resources were used to finance on a reimbursable basis feasibility studies for investment projects. Measures for strengthening UNDP's pre-investment role which had continued to prove effective, as the Administrator stated in his report on 1984 activities,[1] included: co-operative arrangements with agencies; training courses in investment development for UNDP staff; strengthened relations with sources of finance through special interest arrangements; and the use of a facility for financing investment feasibility studies on a reimbursable basis.

Investment development training for UNDP staff continued to be provided through the World Bank Economic Development Institute. In addition, in conjunction with the Asian Development Bank, UNDP launched a new training course in investment project preparation and management for its staff and host government staff in the Asia and Pacific region. Under umbrella projects in Burma, China and Sri Lanka, supported by UNDP and executed by the World Bank, several smaller projects were packaged and approved at the same time to reserve funds for important activities while preserving the flexibility to substitute individual pre-investment studies within each package.

On 29 June,[25] the Governing Council noted progress made in financing feasibility studies from the special account of $1 million established in 1982,[23] from Special Programme Resources and endorsed the efforts of the Administrator and the agencies to increase pre-investment activities. The Council took note of the relationship established between UNDP and development finance sources

to promote complementarity of programming and follow-up investment to Programme-assisted pre-investment activities, and requested the Administrator to continue such relationships and consider broadening their scope to include other sources of finance. The Council noted the progress made under pre-investment training programmes and requested the Administrator to continue such training.

Investment follow-up

In his report on 1984 activities,[1] the Administrator noted that investment commitments related to UNDP-assisted projects totalled $10.2 billion compared with $9.6 billion in 1983. Investment commitments reported as follow-up to UNDP-supported projects rose steeply to $9.3 billion in 1984 as against $6.4 billion in 1983. Transport and communications continued to attract the largest amount of reported follow-up commitments ($3.07 billion), followed by natural resources ($2.3 billion), agriculture, forestry and fisheries ($1.54 billion), human settlements ($810 million), industry ($580 million), and education ($290 million). Developing countries provided the most substantial source of financing, accounting for $4.06 billion. The World Bank group contributed $1.92 billion, bilateral agencies $1.82 billion while the private sector in both developed and developing countries provided $640 million.

Results of UNDP's co-operative arrangements with agencies included: $422.1 million in follow-up investments for 16 projects prepared with FAO assistance; and $36.8 million for two projects prepared with ILO assistance.

UNDP programme planning and execution

Programme evaluation

The Administrator reported[1] that in 1984 UNDP moved further ahead in strengthening its procedures relating to project evaluation. The UNDP Central Evaluation Office (CEO) established in October 1983 completed and circulated to field offices draft revised procedures to be used for evaluation activities on a trial basis. In 1984, 239 evaluations were carried out. CEO, in consultation with Governments and United Nations agencies, prepared a schedule of thematic evaluations to be carried out in 1985 and 1986 covering projects related to aquaculture, the generalized system of preferences, small businesses and agrometeorology. Other activities pursued by CEO in 1984 included helping Governments to stress their own evaluation capacity, and extending evaluation practices and policies developed in the context of IPF-financed projects to those supported by the various special funds administered by UNDP.

In response to a 1983 Governing Council decision,[26] the Administrator in a report[27] to the Council's June 1984 session, described measures taken to improve evaluation policies and procedures. Approaches to strengthening the evaluation capacity of Governments were discussed and the results of a preliminary analysis of a sample of project evaluations were described. Summaries of thematic evaluations studies on national agricultural research and training of industrial manpower were annexed to the report. Separate reports were submitted to the Council on the joint United Nations/UNDP/UNIDO evaluation of UNDP-financed technical co-operation activities of UNIDO on manufactures (see p. 564), and on an interorganizational evaluation of women's participation in development (see Chapter XIX of this section).

On 29 June,[28] the Council, having considered a 1983 JIU report on the evaluation system of UNDP[29] and the Secretary-General's comments thereon,[30] accepted the JIU recommendations, noting that a central evaluation unit had been set up.

Preparations for 1987-1991 programming cycle

In May 1984, the Administrator transmitted to the Governing Council a report on preparations for the fourth programming cycle (1987-1991).[31] The report raised issues on which the views of the Council would be needed to enable him to make proposals on the scope and magnitude of fourth-cycle programmes to the Council's June 1985 session. Those issues included: shortening or extending the cycle; the target magnitude of resources and principles to govern their indicative distribution and setting of IPFs; programming of assistance; methods of delivery of technical co-operation; and administrative costs and efficency of operation.

On 29 June 1984,[32] the Governing Council, having considered the report, took note of the proposed timetable for Council action in preparing the fourth cycle, and decided to consider the subject at a special meeting in early 1985 with a view to finalizing a decision at its 1985 session. The Administrator was requested to submit alternative scenarios for the fourth cycle and to arrange informal consultations during the latter half of 1984 among all participating Governments on the size of resources to be taken into account for the next cycle, and to submit to the 1985 Council an elaboration of suggestions contained in his report regarding an increase in the Programme's Operational Reserve and an enlargement of its scope to overcome its current limitations as a liquidity reserve.

In his report for 1984,[1] the Administrator stated that UNDP had organized informal consultations with all participating Governments. In an effort to establish clear parameters for identifying resource prospects, UNDP had described specific alternative scenarios based on different possible assumptions.

Through the consultations, some 13 options were reviewed leading to the clarification of four alternatives which could obtain in the next cycle, providing a basis for discussions at a special meeting to be held in 1985.

Projects execution

In his annual report,[1] the Administrator stated that total project expenditures by the Office for Projects Execution (OPE) in 1984 amounted to $65.9 million, a slight increase over 1983. The total share of OPE in UNDP core expenditures fell to $35.7 million compared with $37.8 million in 1983. However, expenditures on behalf of other funding sources increased to $30.3 million from $27.3 million.

Non-IPF projects executed by OPE included: construction of rural feeder roads in West Africa on behalf of UNSO; technical support and equipment procurement for UNCDF; and loan administration on behalf of IFAD. OPE services were also sought in connection with the Ethiopian Rehabilitation Programme and the Development Training and Communications Programme at Bangkok (Thailand), which was incorporated as a new OPE service unit in 1984. OPE also executed two major projects to combat opium production in Pakistan and Thailand on behalf of the United Nations Fund for Drug Abuse and Control.

The majority of OPE project activites were concerned with limited services and with cases where recipient Governments were principally responsible for managing technical inputs. Projects tended to be specific in character, with clearly defined, often short-term objectives, such as resource surveys, installation of computer systems and feasibility studies. OPE had developed mechanisms for locating and mobilizing expertise from the public and private sector. Consulting groups and subcontracted services of private firms, public institutions, State corporations and non-governmental organizations played an important role in enabling OPE to meet the technical requirements of projects entrusted to it.

JIU report. In February, the Secretary-General submitted to the General Assembly a JIU report on OPE.[33] The Inspectors noted that, since direct execution of technical co-operation projects by UNDP began in 1973, OPE's operations had given rise to controversy between UNDP and the major technical United Nations agencies which considered that OPE's activities had outgrown their original purpose and encroached upon the agencies' sectors of technical competence.

After studying the various facets of UNDP execution and noting the main views expressed for and against it, the Inspectors concluded that the growth of OPE as an executing agency had had an adverse effect on UNDP's relationship with the agencies and that UNDP should bring the performance of the executing agencies to a more acceptable level where necessary. The Inspectors recommended: (1) that the UNDP Governing Council provide new terms of reference for UNDP direct execution, limiting it to projects requiring general management and direction and to those of a non-technical nature, reducing OPE staff and other resources correspondingly over a three-year transitional period; and (2) that ACC, assisted by the Inter-Agency Task Force at UNDP Headquarters, examine OPE procedures with a view to recommending for use by all organizations those that had proven their worth in technical co-operation delivery.

Commenting in April[34] on the JIU report, the Secretary-General addressed three issues: the purpose of technical co-operation; accountability of the UNDP Administrator; and OPE operations in relation to other organizations' activities. Regarding the first issue, he noted that responsiveness to developing countries' requirements should be the overriding consideration for determining the most suitable executing arrangements for UNDP-assisted projects, and that the main consideration in project execution should be provision by the United Nations to developing countries of sound and flexible mechanisms to ensure the quality and timeliness of project inputs and outputs.

Regarding the Administrator's accountability, the Secretary-General stated that it was the Administrator's responsibility to determine, after consulting agencies and governments, appropriate arrangements for executing UNDP-assisted projects. The Administrator had maintained the practice of giving first consideration to the United Nations and specialized agencies in selecting executing agents for UNDP asistance.

The Secretary-General said that a comparative analysis of efficiency in project execution by OPE and by other executing agencies and an assessment of cost-effectiveness of sub-contracting, not contained in the JIU report, would be required for a full discussion of OPE's activities.

In his comments on specific recommendations, the Secretary-General agreed that the UNDP Governing Council should be invited to provide a consolidated framework for OPE's future role but could not accept limiting OPE's operations and reducing its staff and other resources. He welcomed the JIU recommendation that ACC, assisted by the Inter-Agency Task Force, examine OPE procedures. The Secretary-General added that the UNDP guidelines for direct execution, which provided for consultation with agencies on the designation of UNDP as its own executing agent, needed to be rigorously observed and the consultations carried out prior to final decision-making by UNDP.

In his comments on the JIU report to the 1984 Governing Council,[35] the Administrator dealt in a general way with the main issues and in more detail with specific points raised by JIU. Regard-

ing JIU's first recommendation, the Administrator felt that arguments adduced by JIU in its favour were based on premises which would undermine his responsibility to the Council for the Programme's good management and, if applied in a general way, would undermine the rationale for UNDP's existence. He welcomed the recommendation that ACC examine OPE working practices that had proven their worth with a view to proposing their use by other agencies.

The Administrator also submitted to the Council comments on the JIU report by United Nations organizations other than UNDP.[36] All organizations which had commented, with two exceptions, generally supported the first recommendation with varying degrees of emphasis. Almost all supported the second recommendation.

UNDP Council action. On 29 June,[28] the Governing Council—recalling a 1970 General Assembly resolution[37] concerning the Administrator's responsibility, in consultation with Governments, to select the agency by which Programme assistance would be implemented, and further recalling his full responsibility for all aspects of the Programme's implementation—did not accept JIU recommendation 1 but accepted recommendation 2. The Council welcomed the Administrator's statement of his adherence to the principle of partnership as set out in the 1970 consensus[38] regarding the designation of executing agencies, bearing in mind his obligation to provide the best possible services to developing countries. It reaffirmed that OPE was established with the Council's full approval in recognition of the Administrator's need for an instrument to provide direct project services to Governments, and approved the continued use of OPE as an agent for implementing projects where the Administrator decided in consultation with the Government and executing agencies concerned that the services required were such that delivery through OPE would best serve the interests of the country concerned. He was requested to pursue vigorously the goal of self-reliance, as expressed in a 1975 Council decision on new dimensions for technical co-operation, endorsed by the Assembly in the same year,[39] by promoting the modality of government execution and the innovative use of OPE as a co-operating organization.

By decision 39/439, the Assembly took note of the Secretary-General's note transmitting the JIU report and his comments.[34]

UNDP financing

Financial situation

In his annual report on the UNDP financial situation in 1984,[40] the Administrator stated that

(continued on p. 445)

CONTRIBUTIONS TO UNDP, 1984 AND 1985
(as at 31 December 1984; in US dollar equivalent)

| | 1984 PAYMENT | | | | | | 1985 PLEDGE | | |
| | UNDP Account | Fund for LDCs | Government cost-sharing | Government cash counterpart | Assessed programme costs | Total | UNDP Account* | Fund for LDCs | Total |
CONTRIBUTOR									
Afghanistan	33,000	—	—	—	—	33,000	33,000	—	33,000
Albania	5,714	—	—	—	—	5,714	6,571	—	6,571
Algeria	834,000	—	1,383,287	130,461	—	2,347,748	834,000	—	834,000
Argentina	300,000	—	705,441	—	—	1,005,441	—	—	—
Australia	13,445,378	—	642,683	—	—	14,088,061	—	—	—
Austria	6,737,080	—	—	—	—	6,737,080	7,169,721	—	7,169,721
Bahamas	50,290	—	73,188	—	—	123,478	14,945	—	14,945
Bahrain	56,000	—	979,337	—	—	1,035,337	56,000	—	56,000
Bangladesh	193,900	—	—	—	—	193,900	228,000	—	228,000
Barbados	29,390	—	—	—	—	29,390	33,506	—	33,506
Belgium	10,256,410	—	321,324	—	—	10,577,734	9,756,098	—	9,756,098
Bermuda	3,403	—	—	—	—	3,403	—	—	—
Bhutan	—	—	—	—	—	—	5,700	1,580	7,280
Bolivia	—	—	415,093	—	—	415,093	60,000	—	60,000
Botswana	14,060	—	737,000	—	—	751,060	20,608	—	20,608
Brazil	1,391,638	—	4,096,516	155,862	—	5,644,016	—	—	—
British Virgin Islands	7,500	—	—	—	—	7,500	—	—	—
Bulgaria	670,050	—	—	—	—	670,050	771,573	—	771,573
Burkina Faso	—	—	—	—	—	—	2,128	—	2,128
Burma	885,406	—	—	—	—	885,406	104,651	—	104,651
Burundi	33,344	—	—	—	—	33,344	—	—	—
Byelorussian SSR	173,077	—	—	—	—	173,077	158,265	—	158,265
Cameroon	570,796	—	674,443	364,426	—	1,609,665	180,851	—	180,851
Canada	49,952,912	—	961,706	—	—	50,914,618	—	—	—
Cayman Islands	18,808	—	14,327	—	—	33,135	5,700	—	5,700
Chile	820,000	—	181,903	43,805	—	1,045,708	820,000	—	820,000
China	1,750,000	—	1,740,000	20,000	—	3,510,000	1,880,000	—	1,880,000
Colombia	101,365	—	1,275,222	340,166	—	1,716,753	988,100	—	988,100
Comoros	—	—	—	—	—	—	1,000	—	1,000
Congo	—	—	2,904,546	—	—	2,904,546	12,766	—	12,766
Cook Islands	36,459	—	101,989	—	—	138,448	5,000	—	5,000
Costa Rica	235,527	—	863,618	216,991	—	1,316,136	210,000	—	210,000
Cuba	784,000	—	—	—	—	784,000	860,989	—	860,989
Cyprus	174,000	—	39,483	—	—	213,483	199,000	—	199,000
Czechoslovakia	573,224	—	2,762	—	—	575,986	—	—	—
Democratic People's Republic of Korea	242,915	—	—	—	—	242,915	242,915	—	242,915
Democratic Yemen	10,600	—	456,395	—	—	466,995	12,100	—	12,100
Denmark	40,436,576	—	—	—	—	40,436,576	—	—	—
Djibouti	—	—	27,500	—	—	27,500	1,000	—	1,000
Dominica	18,188	—	—	—	—	18,188	—	—	—
Dominican Republic	149,695	—	661,326	—	—	811,021	—	—	—
Ecuador	1,011,219	—	618,777	(305)	—	1,629,691	494,000	—	494,000
Egypt	691,979	21,166	449,674	1,167,213	—	2,330,032	691,979	21,166	713,145
El Salvador	244,000	—	(100)	—	—	243,900	210,032	—	210,032
Equatorial Guinea	6,854	—	—	—	—	6,854	—	—	—
Ethiopia	144,928	—	48,000	—	—	192,928	—	—	—
Fiji	50,000	—	—	—	—	50,000	40,000	—	40,000
Finland	8,504,773	701,754	93,200	—	—	9,299,727	8,976,378	787,402	9,763,780
France	27,479,173	1,851,852	100,592	—	—	29,431,617	26,276,596	744,681	27,021,277
Gabon	—	—	2,460,213	—	—	2,460,213	—	—	—
Gambia	4,882	—	—	—	—	4,882	5,000	—	5,000
German Democratic Republic	384,586	—	—	—	—	384,586	327,869	—	327,869
Germany, Federal Republic of	41,323,808	—	284,617	—	—	41,608,425	38,360,656	—	38,360,656
Ghana	—	—	105,968	—	—	105,968	—	—	—
Greece	882,022	—	103,942	—	—	985,964	1,037,400	—	1,037,400
Grenada	31,353	—	—	—	—	31,353	8,827	—	8,827
Guatemala	189,000	—	312,229	50,000	—	551,229	189,000	—	189,000
Guinea	12,346	—	55,727	—	—	68,073	1,000	—	1,000
Guyana	277,334	—	—	—	—	277,334	141,177	—	141,177
Haiti	32,500	—	171,012	—	—	203,512	2,000	—	2,000
Holy See	4,000	—	—	—	—	4,000	2,000	—	2,000
Honduras	43,500	—	1,499,186	63,481	—	1,606,167	62,500	—	62,500
Hong Kong	23,219	—	—	—	—	23,219	—	—	—
Hungary	695,147	—	5,723	—	—	700,870	658,162	—	658,162
Iceland	105,360	—	(878)	—	—	104,482	87,005	—	87,005
India	7,042,254	—	25,000	72,939	—	7,140,193	7,172,996	—	7,172,996
Indonesia	2,802,430	—	5,461,199	10,000	—	8,273,629	2,796,000	—	2,796,000
Iran	—	—	398,206	—	—	398,206	50,000	—	50,000
Iraq	—	—	245,272	—	—	245,272	—	—	—
Ireland	1,058,340	—	—	—	—	1,058,340	1,090,724	—	1,090,724
Israel	133,272	—	—	—	—	133,272	70,000	—	70,000
Italy	26,256,983	—	194,449	—	—	26,451,432	31,578,947	—	31,578,947
Ivory Coast	42,553	—	38,208	—	—	80,761	—	—	—

CONTRIBUTOR	1984 PAYMENT						1985 PLEDGE		
	UNDP Account	Fund for LDCs	Government cost-sharing	Government cash counterpart	Assessed programme costs	Total	UNDP Account*	Fund for LDCs	Total
Jamaica	—	—	268,604	600,402	—	869,006	51,250	—	51,250
Japan	38,400,000	—	200,000	—	—	38,600,000	—	—	—
Jordan	539,650	—	(49,698)	—	—	489,952	—	—	—
Kenya	222,433	—	286,144	142,857	—	651,434	79,576	—	79,576
Kiribati	—	—	—	—	—	—	—	—	—
Kuwait	570,000	—	487,914	—	—	1,057,914	—	—	—
Lao People's Democratic Republic	39,200	—	—	—	—	39,200	19,600	—	19,600
Lebanon	—	—	379,500	—	—	379,500	—	—	—
Lesotho	—	—	—	—	—	—	25,706	—	25,706
Liberia	—	—	140,000	—	—	140,000	—	—	—
Libyan Arab Jamahiriya	—	—	1,323,792	—	—	1,323,792	—	—	—
Luxembourg	70,472	—	—	—	—	70,472	60,732	—	60,732
Madagascar	—	—	—	—	—	—	158,751	—	158,751
Malawi	29,008	1,424	62,283	—	—	92,715	25,503	1,252	26,755
Malaysia	385,000	—	501,026	20,000	—	906,026	385,000	—	385,000
Maldives	1,800	—	—	—	—	1,800	1,800	—	1,800
Mali	—	—	—	—	—	—	1,000	—	1,000
Malta	73,093	—	—	—	—	73,093	—	—	—
Mauritius	55,922	—	—	—	—	55,922	—	—	—
Mekong Committee	—	—	—	21,274	—	21,274	—	—	—
Mexico	992,471	—	623,936	—	—	1,616,407	—	—	—
Monaco	3,333	—	—	—	—	3,333	3,404	—	3,404
Mongolia	172,880	—	—	—	—	172,880	157,961	—	157,961
Montserrat	32,222	—	—	—	—	32,222	—	—	—
Morocco	192,001	—	110,118	122,850	—	424,969	177,728	—	177,728
Mozambique	61,176	—	—	—	—	61,176	—	—	—
Nepal	69,200	—	617,733	—	—	686,933	57,500	—	57,500
Netherlands	46,477,878	—	2,874,413	—	—	49,352,291	41,739,130	—	41,739,130
Netherlands Antilles	—	—	492,751	—	—	492,751	—	—	—
New Zealand	1,282,895	—	—	—	—	1,282,895	1,282,895	—	1,282,895
Nicaragua	7,418	—	388,383	—	—	395,801	—	—	—
Nigeria	651,400	—	4,729,636	—	—	5,381,036	—	—	—
Niue	5,000	—	—	—	—	5,000	5,000	—	5,000
Norway	45,625,902	2,838,710	754,717	—	—	49,219,329	45,197,740	—	45,197,740
Oman	75,000	—	929,992	—	—	1,004,992	75,000	—	75,000
Pakistan	1,815,454	—	—	1,569,917	—	3,385,371	1,718,963	—	1,718,963
Panama	389,000	—	772,513	—	—	1,161,513	389,000	—	389,000
Papua New Guinea	36,283	—	77,800	19,223	—	133,306	26,882	—	26,882
Paraguay	58,527	—	249,896	(8,136)	—	300,287	30,000	—	30,000
Peru	214,824	—	806,861	—	—	1,021,685	429,647	—	429,647
Philippines	631,399	—	—	—	—	631,399	385,965	—	385,965
Poland	568,907	—	5,723	—	—	574,630	496,230	—	496,230
Portugal	114,583	—	1,049,849	(9,400)	—	1,155,032	120,482	—	120,482
Qatar	—	—	1,206,904	—	—	1,206,904	200,000	—	200,000
Republic of Korea	893,000	—	30,500	27,619	—	951,119	893,000	—	893,000
Romania	550,491	—	—	—	—	550,491	—	—	—
Rwanda	15,000	—	213,600	—	—	228,600	—	—	—
Saint Christopher and Nevis	18,255	—	—	—	—	18,255	—	—	—
Saint Vincent and the Grenadines	16,765	—	—	—	—	16,765	—	—	—
Samoa	6,329	—	—	—	—	6,239	—	—	—
Sao Tome and Principe	938	469	—	703	—	2,110	1,244	444	1,688
Saudi Arabia	3,500,000	—	14,225,815	2,254,449	—	19,980,264	3,500,000	—	3,500,000
Senegal	144,544	—	—	—	—	144,544	100,000	—	100,000
Seychelles	1,000	—	—	—	—	1,000	1,000	—	1,000
Sierra Leone	76,000	1,000	—	—	—	77,000	76,000	1,000	77,000
Singapore	100,000	—	41,600	—	—	141,600	—	—	—
Solomon Islands	8,500	—	—	—	—	8,500	4,500	—	4,500
Somalia	—	—	—	507,069	—	507,069	—	—	—
Spain	2,568,472	—	91,670	—	71,528	2,731,670	2,726,344	—	2,726,344
Sri Lanka	875,183	—	139,152	—	—	1,014,335	857,736	—	857,736
Sudan	78,125	—	382,436	—	—	460,561	200,000	—	200,000
Suriname	—	—	—	—	—	—	40,000	—	40,000
Swaziland	9,036	—	223,159	—	—	232,195	16,950	—	16,950
Sweden	44,955,071	5,972,757	335,755	—	—	51,263,583	—	1,339,286	1,339,286
Switzerland	16,968,610	2,208,333	618,886	—	—	19,795,829	—	2,400,000	2,400,000
Syrian Arab Republic	283,526	—	—	—	—	283,526	—	—	—
Thailand	1,001,030	—	94,279	50,112	—	1,145,421	1,001,030	—	1,001,030
Togo	233,334	—	—	—	—	233,334	—	—	—
Tokelau	2,500	—	70,000	—	—	72,500	2,850	—	2,850
Tonga	—	—	—	—	—	—	10,000	—	10,000
Trinidad and Tobago	—	—	2,110,750	—	—	2,110,750	—	—	—
Trust Territory of the Pacific Islands	—	—	78,039	—	—	78,039	—	—	—
Tunisia	254,730	—	284,539	130,920	—	670,189	254,635	—	254,635
Turkey	318,867	—	760,968	16,753	—	1,096,588	1,100,000	—	1,100,000
Turks and Caicos Islands	6,032	—	—	—	—	6,032	—	—	—
Uganda	—	—	1,646,400	—	—	1,646,400	15,929	—	15,929
Ukrainian SSR	432,692	—	—	—	—	432,692	395,662	—	395,662
USSR	1,923,077	—	—	—	—	1,923,077	1,758,499	—	1,758,499

	1984 PAYMENT						1985 PLEDGE		
CONTRIBUTOR	UNDP Account	Fund for LDCs	Government cost-sharing	Government cash counterpart	Assessed programme costs	Total	UNDP Account*	Fund for LDCs	Total
United Arab Emirates	7,549	—	828,028	—	—	835,577	—	—	—
United Kingdom	26,805,394	—	139,750	—	—	26,945,144	24,213,075	—	24,213,075
United Republic of Tanzania	56,754	—	(80,653)	—	—	(23,899)	—	—	—
United States	155,000,000	—	(40,000)	—	—	154,960,000	165,000,000	—	165,000,000
Uruguay	200,000	—	278,664	7,406	—	486,070	—	—	—
Vanuatu	—	—	34,020	—	—	34,020	2,000	—	2,000
Venezuela	2,200,000	—	1,697,004	227,363	—	4,124,367	1,100,000	—	1,100,000
Viet Nam	10,004	—	—	12,500	—	22,504	13,000	—	13,000
Yemen	16,212	—	1,266,552	—	—	1,282,764	13,110	—	13,110
Yugoslavia	973,866	—	1,930	—	—	975,796	949,711	—	949,711
Zambia	209,794	—	58,544	—	—	268,338	142,857	—	142,857
Zimbabwe	78,261	—	172,414	74,130	—	324,805	68,966	—	68,966
Arab Fund for Economic and Social Development	—	—	33,168	—	—		—	—	—
Arab Gulf Programme for UN Development Organizations	—	—	2,115,820	—	—	150,000	—	—	—
Caribbean Development Bank	—	—	120,000	—	—	34,000	—	—	—
Central African Development Bank	—	—	—	—	—	2,794	—	—	—
Inter-American Development Bank	—	—	400,000	—	—	200,000	—	—	—
IFAD	—	—	207,500	—	—	150,000	—	—	—
IMF	—	—	125,000	—	—	135,400	—	—	—
ITU	—	—	7,000	—	—	20,033	—	—	—
Latin American Association for Integration	—	—	62,690	—	—	73,500	—	—	—
Latin American Centre for Development Administration	—	—	9,852	—	—	57,403	—	—	—
OPEC Special Fund	—	—	1,944,100	—	—	4,846,520	—	—	—
United Nations	—	—	30,000	—	—	258,500	—	—	—
United Nations Centre for Human Settlements	—	—	125,000	—	—	(6,481)	—	—	—
UNDRO	—	—	200,000	—	—	—	—	—	—
UNICEF	—	—	—	—	—	50,000	—	—	—
UNHCR	—	—	145,410	—	—	—	—	—	—
United Nations Trust Fund for Sudano-Sahelian Activities	—	—	276,243	—	—	—	—	—	—
UNESCO	—	—	—	—	—	10,303	—	—	—
World Bank	—	—	255,000	—	—	66,250	—	—	—
Miscellaneous	—	—	991,402	110,000	—	113,118	—	—	—
Total	651,135,792	13,597,465	83,972,081	8,533,050	71,528	757,309,916	442,764,978	5,296,811	448,061,789

*Includes only those pledges made in 1984.
SOURCE: A/40/5/Add.1.

total income amounted to $789.7 million ($85.7 million lower than forecast), while total expenditure was $717.7 million. As a result of surplus main programme income over expenditure, the UNDP revenue reserve increased from $57.9 million at the end of 1983 to $116.5 million at 31 December 1984. Income from voluntary contributions amounted to $651.1 million, which was lower than the forecast by $53.1 million, mainly because further strengthening of the United States dollar reduced the value of pledges and because a number of pledges were not paid before the end of the year, including an amount of $20 million from one donor.

Field programme expenditure in 1984 was $532.6 million, of which $436.6 million represented expenditure against IPFs, $73.5 million against cost-sharing and $22.5 million against supplementary programmes. The total expenditure represented a reduction of $27.5 million from 1983 or approximately 4.6 per cent. Although it had been intended during 1984 to reverse the trend towards a lower level of programming, IPF expenditures for 1984

amounted to only $436.6 million, a reduction of 6.4 per cent compared with 1983. Again, this was mainly due to the strength of the United States dollar *vis-à-vis* other currencies. However, caution on the part of UNDP resident representatives, executing agencies and recipient Governments in developing and approving projects in the face of continuing uncertainty over the availability of resources and unfavourable conditions in a number of countries resulting from natural disasters, civil disorders and other security related problems were additional factors. While recognizing the influence of those factors on programme delivery, the Administrator was concerned about reduction in programme expenditures, as well as about the ability of UNDP and the agencies to forecast expenditures accurately and plan utilization of resources. He had therefore initiated a joint study on improving programme delivery in 1985 and future years. Such measures would relate to improved project budgeting and monitoring to ensure that the strength of the United States dollar and decreasing inflationary rates in many countries were reflected in UNDP project budgets. In co-operation with Governments concerned, steps would also be taken to achieve a greater rate of project approvals and implementation.

In his report for 1984,[1] the Administrator again referred to the trend towards lower programming levels arising from resource uncertainties which was reflected in declining overall expenditures. Field programme delivery, however, was not affected to the same extent. The static pattern of contributions, evident since 1982, prevailed again in 1984, despite efforts by major donors to increase pledges in national currency terms. Referring to the strength of the United States dollar, the Administrator stated that lower total recorded expenditure disguised the significant delivery purchased in certain components, as well as increased expenditure in particular areas such as training fellowships and equipment purchases. While central resources had been constrained in dollar terms for three years, in part through currency fluctuations beyond governmental control, increased supplementary contributions enabled UNDP to maintain its services to developing countries.

In aggregate, total contributions to central resources, special purpose funds under UNDP administration and all sub-trust fund and cost-sharing arrangements amounted to $834.5 million in 1984, a decline in United States dollar terms of almost 10 per cent compared with the 1983 total of $927 million. An additional amount of over $145 million in third-party co-financing and parallel financing was directly generated in the course of the year.

In his annual report to the 1984 UNDP Governing Council,[2] the Administrator noted that country-level resource mobilization had come to play an increasingly important role in UNDP financing.

The Council, on 29 June,[32] requested the Administrator to arrange informal consultations during the latter half of 1984 among all participating Governments to discuss the size of resources for the fourth programming cycle (1987-1991).

Mid-term review of 1982-1986 programming cycle

In response to a 1980 UNDP Governing Council decision, which called for a mid-term review of the 1982-1986 programming cycle, the Administrator submitted to the June 1984 Council session a report[20] containing a review of voluntary contributions to UNDP from 1982 to 1984 and of his actions to control the Programme's financial integrity in the light of stagnating contributions. The report also discussed the resource outlook for 1984-1986 and gave updated information on the movement of countries to net contributor status. An addendum to the report dealt with the resource needs of the global programme.

The Administrator expressed confidence that growth in contributions would resume as economic recovery among donor countries progressed and exchange rates stabilized. Even so, significant increases would be needed to maintain the momentum of the 1982-1986 programming cycle. He recommended that no upward adjustments be made of any illustrative IPFs since they would have to be accompanied by corresponding downward adjustments in others. He proposed a flat across-the-board reduction in all illustrative IPFs to 55 per cent of their original levels, with the exception of countries with small IPFs covered by a 1983 Council decision on the subject.[22] The Administrator asked the Council to note his intention to authorize selective, limited borrowing from the 1987-1991 cycle and the proposed guidelines for such borrowing.

On 29 June,[21] the Governing Council noted both the Administrator's review of contributions—particularly that, over the preceding four years, they had increased by an average of 7.2 per cent annually in pledged currencies but declined by an average of 1.2 per cent annually expressed in United States dollars—and his projection of resumed growth in contributions for 1985 and 1986, although at a level below that envisaged for the cycle. The Council urged all countries in a position to do so to increase their contributions to achieve adequate real growth of the Programme's resources during the remaining years of the 1982-1986 cycle, and took note of the Administrator's actions to safeguard UNDP's financial and substantive integrity. The Council also took note of the information on movements towards net contributor status and urged countries which had not made progress towards the targets outlined in a 1980 Council decision[41] to increase their efforts to do so.

Review of financial situation in 1983

In a report[42] to the 1984 UNDP Governing Council, the Administrator provided a comprehensive financial review of UNDP-financed activities during 1983 and of the financial position at the end of that year. The report included estimates of resources and expenditures for 1984 and 1985, and provided information on cost-sharing activities; utilization of accumulated non-convertible currencies; collection of outstanding accounts receivable; placement of UNDP funds; the Operational Reserve; the status of Special Programme Resources and of the Special Measures Fund for LDCs and of the Reserve for Construction Loans to Governments. The Administrator also brought to the Council's attention a request from the International Telecommunication Union (ITU) for additional support cost reimbursement (see below).

Based on a recommendation contained in the Administrator's report, the Governing Council on 29 June adopted a decision[43] by which it took note of his steps to ensure that the level of programme delivery was consistent with resource availability and encouraged him to continue to make available for projects and programmes in developing countries the maximum possible level of resources in conformity with the financial liability of UNDP. The Council expressed satisfaction at the prompt payment of pledges by many donors and urged all Governments to continue making such payments as early in the year as possible. Governments were also urged to increase contributions to UNDP on a more predictable, continuous and assured basis. The Council requested the Administrator to investigate possible alternatives to utilize accumulated non-convertible roubles and to report thereon in 1985. The decision also dealt with support to executing agencies, including ITU (see below).

Promoting the resource needs and role of UNDP

In response to recommendations by the UNDP Inter-sessional Committee of the Whole and a 1983 Governing Council decision,[10] the Administrator submitted to the 1984 Council a note on measures taken to promote better understanding of the role and activities of UNDP and its resource needs.[44] He reported significant progress in implementing such measures despite severe limitations of authorized information resources; the UNDP Division of Information continued to operate under severe staff and other resource constraints. The chief feature of progress had been the bringing of information about UNDP closer to country levels with improved data on the impact of the Programme in the development efforts of developing countries. This had involved the combined efforts of the UNDP secretariat and other elements of the United Nations system, Governments, and non-governmental organizations.

On 29 June,[45] the Governing Council requested the Administrator to submit in 1985 specific proposals, together with budgetary implications, for strengthening the Division of Information and its activities.

Expenditures

In his annual report for 1984,[1] the Administrator stated that total expenditures for the year under UNDP amounted to $717.7 million, of which $532.6 million were for field programme activities, $70.1 million for agency support costs, $114.7 million for UNDP administrative and programme support costs and $3.3 million for sectoral support and other field-level costs. A credit of $3 million against miscellaneous expenditures in previous years was also received in 1984.

Of field programme expenditures, $436.6 million was expended under IPF resources, $73.5 million under cost-sharing arrangements, $5.3 million

under Special Programme Resources, $1.8 million under Special Industrial Services, $10.3 million under the Special Measures Fund for the LDCs and $5.1 million in government cash-counterpart funds. All these components declined below 1983 levels, apart from cost-sharing which advanced by $4.8 million over the preceding year and Special Programme Resources which increased by $1.3 million. In 1984, 86 field offices reported assistance in implementing more than 1,600 non-UNDP-financed projects with total expenditures of approximately $243.2 million. Of that amount, UNDP field offices provided major services and support for 1,062 projects with expenditures amounting to $225.4 million and a further 531 projects were assisted to a lesser degree.

Actual expenditures on the various components of Programme delivery financed from UNDP central resources in 1984 were: $279.6 million for project international personnel; $94.9 million for equipment; $68.8 million for subcontracts; $63.3 million for fellowships; and $21.2 million for miscellaneous expenditures. In addition, government cash counterpart expenditures were $5.1 million.

UNDP EXPENDITURES, 1984
(in US dollars)

UNDP account:	
Programme expenditure:	
Project costs:	
Indicative planning figures	436,648,869
From government cost-sharing contributions	73,468,976
Special Measures Fund for the Least Developed	
Countries	10,281,806
From government cash counterpart contributions	5,095,019
Special Programme Resources	5,313,508
Special Industrial Services	1,782,230
Subtotal project costs	532,590,408
Other programme expenditure:	
Reimbursement of programme support costs to	
participating and executing agencies	70,126,728
UNDP sectoral support	3,288,016
Expert hiatus financing and extended sick leave	949,508
Adjustments to 1982 programme expenditure and	
programme support costs (net)	(3,912,849)
Subtotal other programme expenditure	70,451,403
UNDP biennial budget expenditure	107,803,154
UNDP extrabudgetary expenditure	6,794,308
Adjustments for institutional support of	
UNDP/UNEP joint venture	56,518
Total UNDP account	114,653,980
Trust funds:	
UN Capital Development Fund*	32,402,250
UN Financing System for Science and Technology	
for Development†	7,790,579
UN Trust Fund for Sudano-Sahelian Activities	10,206,304
UN Revolving Fund for Natural Resources	
Exploration	4,879,206
UNDP Energy Account	3,562,256
UN Volunteers	1,863,737
UNDP Trust Fund for the Nationhood Programme	
of the Fund for Namibia‡	1,593,267
UNDP Trust Fund for projects financed by the	
Voluntary Fund for the UN Decade for Women§	3,254,015
UN Trust Fund for Operational Programme	
in Lesotho	516,777
Trust Fund for Technical Assistance to	
World Bank Projects in Jamaica, Panama and Zambia	3,878,146

Trust funds: (cont.)

Trust Fund for the Training in the USSR of Specialists from Developing Countries	1,643,652
Initial Initiative against Avoidable Disablement (IMPACT)	151,029
UNDP Trust Fund for Action on Development Issues	686,791
UN Trust Fund for Provision of Operational Personnel in Swaziland	49,882
UN Special Fund for Land-locked Developing Countries	198,347
Trust Fund for Assistance to Colonial Countries and Peoples	601,587
UNDP Development Study Programme	38,116
Fund of the United Nations for the Development of West Irian	43,694
Trust Fund Programme for the Republic of Zaire	11,330
Trust Fund for Special Netherlands Contributions for the Least Developed Countries	373,503
UNEP Trust Fund for Developing Countries Afflicted by Famine and Malnutriton	8,160,238
UNDP Trust Fund for Economic and Technical Co-operation Among Developing Countries	37,719
Trust Fund for the Norwegian Contribution to the Angolan Petroleum Training in Sumbe	1,895,601
Total trust funds	83,838,026
Junior Professional Officers' Programme	7,357,100
GRAND TOTAL	205,849,106

*Includes four sub-trust funds established by the Administrator: Trust Fund for Rehabilitation of Rural Water Reservoirs ($631,486), Trust Fund for the Community Water Supply and Sanitation Project in Nepal ($439,473), Trust Fund for Rice Irrigation in Tombouctou Province, Mali ($153,662) and Trust Fund for Construction and Maintenance of Priority Feeder Roads ($34,118).

†Includes eight sub-trust funds established by the Administrator: Special Purpose Contribution Agreements with Federal Republic of Germany ($575,917), Trust Fund for the Establishment of the Beijing Institute for Computer Software ($231,193), Technological Information Pilot System ($197,403), Regional Nondestructive Testing Network for Latin America and the Caribbean—Phase II ($180,688), Strengthening the National Capacity for Mineral Prospection ($107,904), Application of Technologies Appropriate for Rural Areas—Phase II ($53,753), Trust Fund for Project Formulation and Design ($23,681) and Goodwill Mission (-$3,848).

‡Includes a transfer to the United Nations of $371,917 in interest earned by the Fund.

§Includes additional contributions of $236,186 to UNDP in support of such projects and a transfer to the United Nations of $540,282 in interest earned by the Fund.

SOURCE: A/40/5/Add.1.

Budget for 1984-1985

On 29 June,[46] the Governing Council approved revised appropriations of $332,615,200 gross for 1984-1985 covering the administrative costs of the main Programme and of seven other activities managed by UNDP: UNV, UNCDF, UNRFNRE, the Information Referral System for TCDC (see below), the Consultative Group on International Agricultural Research, UNSO, and the UNSO UNDP/UNEP joint venture (see Chapter XVI of this section). The Council resolved that income estimates of $70,296,900 be used to offset the gross appropriations, resulting in net appropriations of $262,318,300.

The Council approved a contingency provision not to exceed 3 per cent of approved gross appropriations, with the authority for its use, which would be subject to the prior concurrence of ACABQ, to be limited to unforeseen requirements due to currency movements, inflation or General Assembly decisions affecting administrative costs in the biennial budget, and requested the Adminis-

trator to report on the use of that authority to the 1985 Governing Council. The Council took note of a carry-forward of $700,000 of 1982-1983 support cost earnings of the Office for Projects Execution for use in 1984-1985.

The figures approved by the Council were based on May 1984 recommendations of the Advisory Committee on Administrative and Budgetary Questions (ACABQ).[47] In April,[48] the Administrator had proposed net appropriations of $262,318,300, or $17,212,800 less than the Council had approved in 1983.[49] The decrease resulted primarily from currency movements during 1983, revised inflation figures and other factors and was partially offset by increases for staff benefits, Governing Council documentation and lower income estimates. ACABQ had no objection to the estimates and recommended their approval.

Sectoral support

On June 1984,[50] the Governing Council approved $912,000 to 11 executing agencies for sectoral support activities in 1986—principally interregional advisers and short-term missions of experts—designed to complement similar activities by the agencies from their own resources. The Council approved in addition $2,031,000 for the largest programme of that type, the Senior Industrial Development Field Advisers (SIDFAs), managed by UNIDO (see p. 573).

These allocations were recommended by the Administrator in a February 1984 report,[51] In his report, the Administrator also proposed that sectoral support to a number of the smaller executing agencies be extended to the end of 1986.

The Council also requested the Administrator to report to it in 1985 on sectoral support development, taking into account the link between sectoral support and sectoral analysis, and to consult with executive heads of agencies to ensure that sectoral advisers were associated with the preparation of round-table meetings for LDCs.

Agency supports costs

As requested by the Governing Council in 1983,[49] the Administrator submitted his first ex post facto report on agency support costs to the June 1984 Council session.[52] The report covered expenditures relating to salaries, official travel and general operating expenses and other administrative costs incurred during 1982-1983 by agencies executing UNDP projects. On 29 June 1984, the Council requested the Administrator to continue submitting such reports biennially.[53]

In another report, reviewing UNDPs financial situation in 1983 (see above), the Administrator brought to the Council's attention a request from ITU for additional support cost reimbursement in connection with ITU's implementation of UNDP-financed projects. The Council, also on 29 June,[43] decided that support to executing agencies, including ITU, should made in accordance with 1980[54] and 1981[55] Council decisions.

Contributions

At the 1984 United Nations Pledging Conference for Development Activities (see p. 432), nine of UNDP's 16 major donors maintained the real value of their contributions in national currencies in accordance with Governing Council appeals. Six of the nine substantially exceeded that minimum level. A total of 31 countries (27 of them developing countries) met or exceeded the 14 per cent growth rate set for the 1982-1986 programming cycle in terms of their national currencies. Canada, Denmark, Italy and Sweden pledged a further $13.1 million in supplementary contributions for 1984. However, due to the strength and volatility of the United States dollar, the value of pledges in dollar terms had remained static since 1981 at around $675 million.

While central resources had been constrained, a substantial increase in supplementary contributions had enabled UNDP to maintain its services to developing countries. Sources included cost-sharing, trust funds, government cash counterpart contributions and contributions to the Special Measures Fund for LDCs. In 1984, those resources amounted to $148.4 million or 18 per cent of UNDP's resources compared with $85.1 million or 11 per cent in 1981.

Reflecting the growth in supplementary resources, five new trust funds were established during 1984, income for which amounted to the equivalent of $6.8 million. In addition, 14 sub-trust funds were established, for which income received during the year totalled the equivalent of $13.1 million (see below).

Pledges for the numerous special-purpose funds administered by UNDP declined from $45.5 million for 1983 to $38.6 million for 1984. However, cost-sharing and sub-trust fund income received by those funds increased from $17.7 million in 1983 to $25.8 million in 1984.

In the aggregate, contributions to UNDP amounted to $834.5 million, a decline in United States dollar terms of almost 10 per cent compared with the 1983 total of $927 million. Figures reported by 46 UNDP field offices in 1984 indicated an additional amount of over $145 million in third-party co-financing and parallel financing which was directly generated by UNDP-assisted activities during the year. That amount combined with the total contributions to UNDP and its special funds, brought some $980 million in development funding to the overall operations of UNDP in 1984.[2]

Government contributions to local office costs

In accordance with a 1982 Governing Council decision,[56] the Administrator submitted to the Council's June 1984 session a progress report on host government contributions to local office costs.[57] He stated that UNDP had negotiated with host Governments to agree on the level of their contributions to field offices from 1 January 1984. Regarding the authority to waive in part contributions, the following formula had been applied, based on 1978 per capita gross national product: over $3,000—no waiver; from $1,501 to $3,000—25 per cent waiver; from $500 to $1,500—50 per cent waiver; and less than $500—75 per cent waiver.

Noting that a significant number of negotiations were still in progress, the Administrator stated that results of those already concluded were: of 113 host Governments, 35 were either contributing towards local office costs in excess of the minimum required or had pledged to meet the 1984 target; 24 had agreed to provide some increase or maintain their level of contributions; 8 had requested special consideration due to conditions prevailing in their countries; and 46 were expected to provide official confirmation of anticipated contributions. The Administrator considered that additional negotiations would be helpful but recommended that effective 1 January 1985, an accounting linkage be established between Governments' contributions to local office costs and their contributions to UNDP general resources, and proposed a draft decision along those lines for adoption by the Council. In an addendum to his report, the Administrator informed the Council that during further discussions with several Governments, it had been suggested that shortfalls in contributions to local office costs should be met first by contributions to voluntary programme costs which were initially intended to meet the cost of support services in host countries to the UNDP-financed programme.

On 29 June 1984,[58] the Council called on Governments to increase their contributions at least to the level of their commitments. The Administrator was requested: to pursue negotiations with Governments and conclude them by the end of 1984; to ensure that resident representatives held consultations with host Governments before submitting their biennial budget requests; and to provide the Council with information on the net flow of contributions to and payments from UNDP in respect of each participating Government. The Administrator was authorized to establish from 1 January 1985 an accounting linkage of voluntary contributions, contributions to voluntary programme costs and contributions to local office costs, in such a manner that contributions were first accounted for against local office costs and to report in 1985 on progress achieved.

Recommendations of the Joint Inspection Unit (JIU) related to field offices were dealt with in another Council decision (see below).

Extrabudgetary resources

In an April 1984 report to the Governing Council,[59] the Administrator reviewed the definition, origin and use of extrabudgetary resources. The report described the rationale of the concept of such resources, identified the four basic categories of support service to which they related and gave their historical development; its annex accounted in detail for the uses for which extrabudgetary resources were required.

Extrabudgetary resources shared three commom elements; they were under the authority of the Administrator; UNDP provided them with central administrative services; and the Administrator was accountable to the Governing Council for their operations. With respect to UNDP core activities, extrabudgetary resources related to four basic categories of support service: Support services provided by UNDP core activities to UNDP non-core activities, other organizations and trust funds administered by UNDP; administrative support of activities by the Reserve for Construction Loans to Governments; programme support concerning energy; programme and administrative support related to field office activities.

On 29 June,[60] the Council requested the Administrator to submit to it in 1985 a comprehensive report on the structure, financing and interrelation of all funds administered by him.

Support costs

Reimbursement for field office services

The Administrator submitted to the June 1984 Governing Council a report[61] describing difficulties experienced by UNDP in implementing a 1982 Council decision[62] on reimbursement of services provided by UNDP field offices to executing agencies. He stated that in the majority of cases, UNDP and the agencies concerned had been able to implement the decision in a spirit of constructive dialogue and co-operation, and UNDP had been able to provide the required services within the approved resources. However, he had to seek the Council's guidance regarding a situation in one country where he had been seeking the resources necessary to finance services rendered to agencies to support their funds-in-trust activities. He suggested two options for the Council's consideration: that the agencies involved be requested to reimburse UNDP for services rendered in the country concerned; or that the Council authorize 13 new posts for the respective field office and appropriate $600,000 for 1984-1985.

On 29 June 1984,[63] the Council decided that UNDP should be reimbursed for services provided to trust-fund activities of other United Nations bodies, unless the trust-fund donor or the host Government directly reimbursed the Programme.

Trust funds

In 1984, the Administrator established 25 trust funds, 14 on behalf of UNSO, 5 each on behalf of UNDP and the United Nations Financing System for Science and Technology for Development (UNFSSTD), and 1 on behalf of the United Nations Capital Development Fund (UNCDF). In addition, further contributions were received to a USSR/UNDP Trust Fund established in 1982, to continue the funding of the training of specialists from developing countries in the USSR. Overall income for 1984 from these resources amounted to $19.9 million.[64]

On 29 June 1984,[65] the Governing Council requested that he provide each year detailed information on trust funds established by him, as well as on individual projects financed from them.

Trust funds conditioned on procurement from donor countries

As requested by the Governing Council in 1983,[66] the Administrator submitted to the Council's June 1984 session a comprehensive report[67] on trust funds conditioned on procurement from a donor country in respect of UNSO, UNCDF and UNFSSTD. The Administrator concluded that the authority to accept such trust funds granted under a 1982 Council decision[68] and extended in 1983,[66] had not distorted the basic principles of multilateralism of UNDP, but had enabled the three funds to provide additional assistance of significant importance. He proposed that the mandate to accept trust funds conditioned on procurement from a donor country be extended until 30 April 1986.

On 29 June 1984,[69] the Council decided: with regard to UNFSSTD to extend its 1983 decision until 30 April 1986; and to extend the experimental period with regard to UNCDF and UNSO to the same date by which time it would take a final decision on trust funds conditioned on procurement from a donor country.

With regard to UNCDF and UNSO, the Administrator could accept such trust funds provided that: the donor country had not decreased its contributions in national currency to UNDP general resources; that it was a contributor in the same year to the general resources of the United Nations Capital Development and UNSO, respectively; and that the contribution did not exceed 10 per cent in the case of UNCDF and 15 per cent in the case of UNSO, of the donor's contributions to the general resources of the Programme and the Fund or Office. All Governments were urged to increase their contributions to the Fund's or Office's general resources so that their activities could expand without recourse to contributions conditioned on procurement from a donor country.

The Council requested the Administrator to make a full report, with recommendations, to its 1986 session, including an evaluation of the sectoral and geographical distribution of the use of such funds and on procurement procedures utilized and the effects obtained.

Allocations from UN Emergency Operations Trust Fund

In accordance with a 1983 resolution by which the General Assembly liquidated the United Nations Emergency Operation Trust Fund,[70] the Secretary-General submitted a June 1984 progress report[71] on the implementation of that resolution. Of the $48,516,744 available when the Trust Fund was formally liquidated on 31 December 1983, $33,961,722 was transferred to a UNDP Special Account entitled Trust Fund for Countries Afflicted by Famine and Malnutrition, $5,822,008 was transferred to a UNDP Special Account entitled Trust Fund for Economic and Technical Co-operation between Developing Countries, and the balance was transferred to the United Nations Relief and Works Agency for Palestine Refugees in the Near East (see p. 337).

At meetings held between the Director-General for Development and International Economic Co-operation for Development and the Administrator on allocation and utilization of the funds channelled through UNDP, it was agreed that projects to be approved out of the Trust Fund for Countries Afflicted by Famine and Malnutrition would be primarily in the food and agricultural sectors and approximately 80 per cent of the funds should be earmarked for Africa. As of 30 April 1984, UNDP had approved out of that Trust Fund 76 projects in 43 countries, totalling $20,287,400. As at 31 March, there were no projects approved from the other trust fund.

In a report to the June Governing Council,[72] the Administrator presented updated information on those trust funds. Under the fund for countries afflicted by famine and malnutrition, as of 31 May, 81 projects in 48 countries had been approved or accepted, entailing total budgets in the amount of $24,955,400. With regard to the fund for economic and technical co-operation among developing countries, consultations with developing countries were still continuing. It had been agreed that developing countries would initiate project proposals to be reviewed by the Administrator and, where appropriate, endorsed for implementation.

The Council, on 29 June,[73] expressed satisfaction at the speedy action taken by the Administrator in approving assistance to projects in countries afflicted by famine and malnutrition, took note of the arrangements for initiating project proposals concerning activities in economic and technical co-operation among developing countries, and requested him to report further in 1985.

Accounts and auditing

Accounts for 1983

The financial statements of UNDP for the year ended 31 December 1983, together with the report of the Board of Auditors, were submitted to the General Assembly in June 1984.[74] The statements also covered the trust funds for which the Administrator had been assigned responsibility.

In its report, the Board observed that owing to a slight increase in pledges collected and a sharp decrease in main programme expenditures, UNDP's financial situation as at 31 December 1983 appeared less critical than anticipated. Unpaid pledges amounted to $13.2 million at the end of 1983, which compared favourably with $39.6 million in 1982. Factors contributing to the decline of programme expenditures were the continued strengthening of the United States dollar, the progressively declining limitations on IPF expenditures, and cautious planning by many Governments and resident representatives resulting in major reductions in project approvals. Additional savings were realized from the cancelling of some obligations by executing agencies which had originally been established in 1982 and were subsequently found to be unnecessary. The Board recommended that the Administration continue to monitor closely the smooth transition to the lower level of programming decided on in 1982.

With regard to general programme matters, the Board recommended: more explicit guidelines for examining and assessing project financial statements to avoid unanticipated overruns and setting limits to extensions of experts' assignments; continuous updating of computerized information on long duration projects, reviews of which were seriously impeded by incompleteness of such information; special projects' implementation reviews by all regional bureaux; improvement of terminal assessment reports; and examination of the effectiveness of agency performance reviews.

In its review of projects, the Board mainly examined regional projects executed by UNDP/OPE and recommended that: measures be taken to streamline further communication, approval and monitoring procedures on budgetary and administrative matters related to those projects; any increase, redeployment or rephasing of project budget components be reflected in substantive revisions; executing agencies provide explanations for budgetary changes and transfers; and that the usefulness of guidelines for preparing round-table projects be considered. Regarding the employment of experts and consultants, the Board recommended that procedures and internal controls on their recruitment be improved and that the authority of the Contracts Committee should be respected. It also recommended that informal procedures to evaluate experts be streamlined and adhered to. Further comments related to functioning of the UNDP liaison office at Addis Ababa, Ethiopia, emergency payroll advances, travel and communications costs, and cases of fraud or presumptive fraud.

In response to the Board's observations and recommendations, the Administrator noted that although the reduced levels of expenditures in 1982 and 1983 made possible gradual increases in programme delivery during the final year of the third programming cycle (1982-1986), the build-up of programme budgets would continue to be carefully monitored to ensure that programme delivery was consistent with resource availability.

The Administrator also stated that action had been taken on several of the Board's other recommendations.

Commenting on the Board's findings, ACABQ, in a September 1984 report,[75] stated that, with regard to travel costs, a UNDP decision to apply the most economical full economy fare (business class) when a flight exceeded six hours was less economical than the standard applied in the United Nations. With regard to the employment of experts and consultants, ACABQ was of the view that the practice of signing contracts with consultants after their services had commenced should be discontinued, unless there was an overriding reason to the contrary.

Audit reports for 1982

The Governing Council, on 29 June 1984,[76] took note of the Administrator's note transmitting the audit reports of the participating and executing agencies for 1982 relating to funds allocated to them by UNDP,[77] as well as of his comments on the observations made by the external auditors and a description of action taken in response to the Council's June 1983 decision on audit reports.[66] The Council emphasized again the importance it attached to receiving long-form narrative audit reports covering areas identified in earlier Council decisions, including the audit of the effectiveness of financial management. The Administrator was requested to bring the Council's decision and the views of the Budgetary and Finance Committee on the matter to the attention of the Panel of External Auditors and of the executing agencies. He was further requested to convey the Council's views to the executive heads of the executing agencies for them to advise their legislative bodies for further action. The Council agreed with the proposal by the external auditors of the Asian Development Bank to carry out additional audit procedures and authorized the Administrator to reimburse the Bank for additional audit costs. The Administrator was requested to make available at future Council sessions copies of the latest annual audited financial statements of UNDP, the report of the United Nations Board of Auditors thereon and the Administrator's financial

report for that year as well as copies of the General Assembly decision on the audit report, and to report orally to the Council on those matters.

Financial regulations

The Governing Council on 29 June 1984,[78] decided that, notwithstanding the absence of a consensus in respect of some of the financial regulations proposed in 1983 (dealing with the currencies of contributions),[79] all other regulations approved by the Council in 1981[80] were fully in effect and that with respect to those on which consensus had not been reached, existing regulations would apply until a decision was reached in 1985. The Council further decided that the Budgetary and Finance Committee would consider at its 1985 meetings the parts of the regulations and other questions on which consensus had not been achieved in 1984.

Annexes and amendments to financial regulations

In response to a 1981 Governing Council decision,[80] the Administrator proposed in a March 1984 note[81] two annexes to the UNDP Financial Regulations to meet the specific requirements of UNCDF and the United Nations Revolving Fund for Natural Resources Exploration (UNRFNRE). In a May report,[82] ACABQ stated that it had no objection to the proposals regarding UNCDF and UNRFNRE apart from the deletion of a proposed regulation on reimbursement of co-operating agencies which was unnecessary in view of an existing regulation.

ACABQ suggested improvements in the presentation of both annexes and recommended acceptance of the Administrator's other proposals contained in his note, concerning a text change in the financial regulations concerning UNFPA (see Chapter XIV of this section); an amendment regarding the annual submission of UNDP accounts to the United Nations Board of Auditors, and a proposal to amend the Information annex to the UNDP Financial Regulations which contained additional terms of reference governing the audit of the accounts by the United Nations Board of Auditors.

On 29 June,[83] the Governing Council approved the additions and amendments and requested the Administrator to revise the UNDP Financial Regulations accordingly.

Guidelines for procurement

In response to a 1983 Governing Council request,[84] the Administrator in a March 1984 note,[85] summarized action taken by UNDP in cooperation with executing agencies to harmonize procurement procedures. In April, the Inter-Agency Procurement Working Group (IAPWG) considered responses received from 28 agencies to a comprehensive questionnaire on agency procurement practices. The Working Group agreed that unification of procurement procedures was necessary in order to facilitate increased transparency of the procurement process of the United Nations system, although some differences in individual agency rules and practices would continue to exist. IAPWG established a sub-group to prepare specific recommendations on unified procurement procedures based on replies to the questionnaire. The sub-group, which met in June, discussed inequality of access to procurement opportunities which adversely affected the underutilized major donor and developing countries.[86]

On 29 June,[87] the Council requested the Administrator to continue his efforts to harmonize procurement procedures to make available in 1985 the analysed results of the IAPWG study on agency practices and report on developments.

UNDP administration and staff

Field offices

Following consideration of a 1983 JIU report on UNDP field offices[79] and the Secretary-General's comments thereon,[84] the Governing Council, on 29 June 1984,[88] accepted the JIU recommendation on strengthening field offices, but took note of the Secretary-General's comment that a policy recommendation on general contributions to their costs should await a full examination of all field offices of all organizations of the system and that the resident co-ordinator's role should be taken into account. The Council also took note of the Administrator's intention to review the staffing and other needs of field offices, particularly in the least developed countries in Africa. It urged recipient Governments to make available on secondment to UNDP field offices in their countries qualified persons to serve as programme officers. The Council accepted several JIU recommendations on policy implementation, substantive programme functions and personnel questions but did not accept a recommendation regarding utilization of competitive examinations organized by the United Nations in the light of reservations expressed by the Administrator.

The Governing Council decision was summarized by the Secretary-General in a September report[89] to the General Assembly on implementation of JIU recommendations (see ADMINISTRATIVE AND BUDGETARY QUESTIONS, Chapter II).

REFERENCES

[1]DP/1985/5 & Add.1-6. [2]DP/1984/5 & Add.1-6. [3]E/1984/20. [4]DP/1984/L.7 & Add.1. [5]DP/1984/75 & Corr.1. [6]E/1984/20 (dec. 84/1 & dec. 84/3). [7]*Ibid.* (dec. 84/44 & 84/45). [8]*Ibid.* (dec. 84/46). [9]*Ibid.* (dec. 84/5). [10]YUN 1983, p. 462. [11]DP/1984/4. [12]E/1984/20 (dec. 84/4). [13]DP/1984/21. [14]E/1984/20 (dec. 84/17). [15]DP/1984/22. [16]DP/1984/23 & Corr.1. [17]DP/1984/24. [18]DP/1984/26. [19]DP/1984/25 & Corr.1.
[20]DP/1984/20 & Add.1. [21]E/1984/20 (dec.84/16). [22]YUN 1983, p. 457. [23]YUN 1982, p. 642. [24]DP/1984/11. [25]E/1984/20 (dec. 84/8). [26]YUN 1983, p. 461. [27]DP/1984/18. [28]E/1984/20 (dec. 84/6). [29]YUN 1983, p. 460. [30]DP/1984/9. [31]DP/1984/27. [32]E/1984/20 (dec. 84/20). [33]A/39/80. [34]A/39/80/Add.1. [35]DP/1984/8. [36]DP/1984/74. [37]YUN 1970, p. 350, GA res. 2688(XXV), annex, 11 Dec. 1970. [38]*Ibid.*, p. 345. [39]YUN 1975, p. 414, GA res. 3405(XXX), 28 Nov. 1975. [40]DP/1985/54 & Add.1. [41]YUN 1980, p. 582. [42]DP/1984/53. [43]E/1984/20 (dec. 84/31). [44]DP/1984/10. [45]E/1984/20 (dec. 84/7). [46]E/1984/20 (dec. 84/32). [47]DP/1984/56. [48]DP/1984/54. [49]YUN 1983, p. 468. [50]E/1984/20 (dec. 84/41). [51]DP/1984/64. [52]DP/1984/62. [53]E/1984/20 (dec. 84/39). [54]YUN 1980, p. 592. [55]YUN 1981, p. 449. [56]YUN 1982, p. 654. [57]DP/1984/12 & Corr.1,2, & Add.1. [58]E/1984/20 (dec. 84/9). [59]DP/1984/55 & Corr.1. [60]DP/1984/20 (dec. 84/33). [61]DP/1984/73. [62]YUN 1982, p. 650. [63]E/1984/20 (dec.84/42). [64]DP/1985/59 & Corr.1. [65]E/1984/20 (dec. 84/34). [66]YUN 1983, p. 471. [67]DP/1984/58 & Add.1. [68]YUN 1982, p. 655. [69]E/1984/20 (dec. 84/35). [70]YUN 1983, p. 537, GA res. 38/201, 20 Dec. 1983. [71]A/39/284. [72]DP/1984/71 & Add.1. [73]E/1984/20 (dec. 84/14). [74]A/39/5/Add.1. [75]A/39/510. [76]E/1984/20 (dec. 84/40). [77]DP/1984/63 & Add.1 & Add.1/Corr.1. [78]E/1984/20 (dec. 84/36). [79]YUN 1983, p. 473. [80]YUN 1981, p. 451. [81]DP/1984/61 & Add.1,2. [82]DP/1984/56. [83]E/1984/20 (dec. 84/38). [84]YUN 1983, p. 474. [85]DP/1984/59. [86]DP/1985/61. [87]E/1984/20 (dec. 84/37). [88]E/1984/6 (dec. 84/6). [89]A/39/145 & Corr.1.

Other technical co-operation

UN programmes

In 1984, the United Nations, mainly through its Department of Technical Co-operation for Development (DTCD), continued to provide technical assistance to developing countries in the economic and social sectors by supplying experts and advisory services, awarding fellowships and organizing workshops and study tours. The activities covered a broad range of subjects, including development planning and administration, rural and social development, international trade, industrial development, transnational corporations, mineral resources, energy, ocean economics, environment, science and technology, population, women, human rights and statistics.

In 1984, the United Nations delivered a technical co-operation programme of $254 million compared with $255 million in 1983, a 0.4 per cent decrease in project expenditures. The programme executed by DTCD amounted to $110.8 million compared with $112 million in 1983.

Technical co-operation activities were also carried out under the United Nations regular programme for technical co-operation. Funds from that programme, totalling some $15 million, financed activities by a number of United Nations entities, including DTCD, the Centre for Human Rights, the Centre for Social Development and Humanitarian Affairs, the United Nations Centre for Human

Settlements (Habitat), the United Nations Conference on Trade and Development (UNCTAD), the regional commissions and the United Nations Industrial Development Organization.

In a report to the UNDP Governing Council on technical co-operation activities carried out by the United Nations in 1984,[1] the Secretary-General identified major concerns of developing countries, including structural adjustment programmes and institution-building for recovery and development, and discussed the response and modalities required to provide assistance commensurate with the enormity of the problems faced by those countries.

DTCD made particular efforts during 1984 to expand its collaboration with its traditional funding partners and sought out new arrangements with organizations within the system as well as with Governments and other financial institutions. In August, for example, the joint DTCD/UNDP Task Force started to explore ways to promote closer collaboration between DTCD and UNDP's OPE in the use of their respective capabilities. A closer working relationship had evolved with the World Bank with frequent staff consultations taking place at all levels between the Bank and DTCD in a number of sectors including development planning, development administration, and mineral resources development. Similar linkages had been strengthened with the regional development banks. In view of the scarcity of funds available to developing countries under their IPF, a number of Governments had decided to provide resources to finance DTCD-executed projects in their countries. DTCD had also been involved in preparing technical specifications for procuring equipment which bilateral programmes made directly available to developing countries.

The report also singled out specific areas of concern to DTCD, among them: the application of new technologies; support to UNDP round-tables; LDCs; participation of women in development; and pre-investment and investment follow-up.

Measures to be taken to meet the changing technical co-operation requirements of the developing countries were analysed by the UNDP Administrator in an April 1984 report to the UNDP Governing Council (see p. 438).

In an April report[2] to the Governing Council, the Secretary-General provided an overview of the work during 1983 of all United Nations organizations with responsibility for technical co-operation and detailed information on the activities of DTCD. The Governing Council, on 29 June,[3] and the Economic and Social Council, in decision 1984/171, took note of that report.

GENERAL ASSEMBLY ACTION

Following consideration of the Secretary-General's report on 1983 activities,[2] the General Assembly

in December adopted decision 39/441 without vote, as recommended by the Second Committee.

Report of the Secretary-General on United Nations technical co-operation activities

At its 104th plenary meeting, on 18 December 1984, the General Assembly, on the recommendation of the Second Committee, took note of the report of the Secretary-General on United Nations technical co-operation activities.

General Assembly decision 39/441

Adopted without vote

Approved by Second Committee (A/39/791) without vote, 14 December (meeting 61); oral proposal by Chairman; agenda item 81 *(i)*.

Meeting numbers. GA 39th session: 2nd Committee 49, 51, 52, 61; plenary 104.

DTCD activities

In a report to the UNDP Governing Council,[1] the Secretary-General described activities undertaken by DTCD during 1984 in its main substantive areas of development issues and policies, natural resources and energy, development administration and finance, statistics, rural development, ocean economics and technology and humanitarian affairs. The report also described the Department's work with regard to evaluation, technical assistance recruitment and project personnel administration and its work in conjunction with the World Food Programme (WFP) and the Voluntary Fund for the United Nations Decade for Women.

The Department's programme of technical co-operation projects at the end of 1984, amounted to $140 million in approved budgets, with expenditures totalling $110.8 million. Of those expenditures, $76.7 million was for UNDP–financed projects, $11.4 million for UNFPA, $7 million under the United Nations Regular Programme of Technical Co-operation and $11.9 million under trust funds. Budgets fell by $4.7 million compared with 1983, but the level of expenditures remained practically the same. Budgets grew by 2 per cent in Africa but decreased in all other regions. Expenditure, on the other hand, was little changed from 1983 with Africa remaining the most important programme, accounting for nearly $43 million, or 38 per cent of the total, followed by Asia with over $29 million or 26 per cent.

By sector, natural resources and energy continued to account for the largest share of the programme, representing $50 million in expenditures, or 45 per cent, an increase of $1.4 million in monetary terms. Development planning was the second most important activity although its share of delivery dropped from 22 per cent in 1983 to 19 per cent, and from $25 million to $21 million in monetary terms. Population and statistics remained essentially steady at $16 million and $12 million respectively, and public administration accounted for approximately 11 per cent of the programme, with expenditures of $11.7 million, up from $10.9 million in 1983. Social development projects increased from $3.1 million in 1983 to $3.8 million in 1984.

During the year, DTCD executed 210 field projects in 84 countries in economic and social development, including rural development. In addition, 165 weeks of project-related and direct advisory missions were undertaken by Headquarters staff. Important activities in integrated rural development included: multidisciplinary grass-roots development in the Central African Republic and Liberia; a community development project for the Bedouin population in Democratic Yemen; and assistance to a centre for applied research and training in community development in Saudi Arabia. DTCD continued to emphasize assistance to LDCs, including preparation for, participation in and follow-up activities to international donors' round-tables (see p. 414).

Activities in natural resources and energy included: 55 minerals projects covering mineral exploration, institution-building and strengthening, mine development and rehabilitation, training, planning, mining legislation and contract negotiation, equipment supply, and application of computer techniques; 88 energy projects in the three main areas of conventional energy, electric power and new and renewable resources; 90 water resources projects, half of which were directed towards alleviating arid conditions in Africa; and 20 cartography projects covering institution-building, transfer of technical expertise to national cartographic and hydrographic institutions, training and equipment. Public works activities focused on executing projects financed by UNDP and other sources.

In public administration and finance, DTCD backstopped over 134 projects in 63 developing countries, mostly in administrative reform, training and personnel administration, financial and public enterprise management, resource mobilization and management information systems. In the area of statistics, technical co-operation was provided in 151 country projects in such activities as statistical organization, national accounts, demographic and social statistics, industrial trade statistics and data processing. The Department executed 100 UNFPA-supported demographic projects in 1984, of which approximately 33 per cent were in demographic training, 47 per cent in analysis of census and survey data, and 20 per cent in population policy and development.

In social development and humanitarian affairs, activities relating to youth received priority attention with the approach of International Youth Year (1985). With regard to crime prevention and criminal justice, advisory services were provided to 13 countries in areas such as juvenile offenders, corrections, the judiciary, economic crimes, crime prevention, computerization of the judicial system, penitentiary systems and police departments.

Support services provided by DTCD included the selection and appointment of experts and consultants to advise Governments on various aspects of social and economic development. In 1984, 1,020 experts and consultants were appointed compared with 818 in 1983. A total of 3,820 fellowships were implemented of which 2,000 were in developing countries to further TCDC. The 1984 edition of the *Directory of Training Courses and Programmes for Europe and Neighbouring Areas* included information on more than 500 courses in all fields of DTCD competence.

Because of the critical situation in Africa and other parts of the developing world both WFP and DTCD gave priority attention to the low-income, food-deficit and most seriously affected countries. A high-level meeting was held between the two organizations to strengthen collaboration between them and to establish a framework for DTCD's involvement in implementing WFP's new project cycle.

The Department also continued to execute projects, funded by the Voluntary Fund for the United Nations Decade for Women, to help to involve rural and poor urban women to achieve development goals. During 1984, DTCD expended $164,997 provided by the Fund.

UNDP Council action. The Governing Council, on 29 June 1984,[3] noted that DTCD had streamlined its organizational structure and reduced its administrative costs, and endorsed the Department's efforts to promote a more integrated approach to programme and project management and to improve its procedures with a view to achieving greater effectiveness in delivering its services to developing countries. The Council noted with concern the decline in resources necessary to maintain vital programmes and projects, reiterated its request for action to strengthen the Department's role as the main operational arm of the United Nations for technical co-operation activities, in pursuance of a 1977 Assembly resolution,[4] and invited financial and funding institutions to take account of the Department's special competence, experience and operational capability when designating an executing agency or advising Governments on sources of assistance for implementation of projects.

The Council reaffirmed its support of DTCD's work programme under the regular programme of technical co-operation and endorsed the more flexible use of the regular programme as seed money for innovative activities, including pilot projects, as well as for the Department's programme of interregional advisory services for the least developed, island developing, land-locked developing and other particularly disadvantaged countries. The Council endorsed the DTCD's efforts in support of the Secretary-General's initiative for Africa (see p. 465) and recommended that consideration be given to establishing within the Department a flexible procedure to cover the initial cost of project formulation and recruitment of experts, including the review of any financial implications.

JIU recommendations. At its 1984 session,[5] the Committee for Programme and Co-ordination (CPC) considered a 1983 JIU report on DTCD[6] and the Secretary-General's comments thereon.[7] CPC recognized that DTCD's activities were of great importance to developing countries and warranted full support. Since there were competing claims for an organizational structure that emphasized substance over geography, the Department needed constantly to review its structure in order to function as effectively as possible. The Committee supported most of the JIU recommendations but recognized that lack of extrabudgetary resources would hamper DTCD's efforts to implement them fully. It acknowledged that the JIU recommendations on structure and operation were not yet fully implemented and requested that their implementation be reported on.

CPC recommended that: the Department be given a clear mandate involving clustering within it all technical co-operation functions in the Secretariat and co-ordination of guidelines and methods relating to those functions, including UNDP's OPE; in recognition of the need to strengthen co-ordination of DTCD's field activities, the machinery proposed by JIU could be resorted to; the Department's existing capabilities should be used to the full; and evaluation should be given continuous attention.

In a September 1984 report on implementation of JIU recommendations,[8] the Secretary-General stated that information relevant to the JIU report on DTCD would be included in his 1984 report to the Assembly on restructuring the economic and social sectors of the United Nations system (see Chapter XXIV of this section). In that report,[9] the Secretary-General stated that the 1983 reorganization of DTCD into four Divisions (Policy, Programming and Development Planning; Natural Resources and Energy; Development Administration; and Programme Support), in line with JIU recommendations, was to promote a more integrated approach to programme management and to place the major emphasis and locus of responsibility on the substantive aspects of technical co-operation.

In the context of implementation of the 1977 Assembly resolution on restructuring the economic and social sectors of the United Nations,[4] and subsequent reports of the Secretary-General and JIU, the following issues needed further consideration: identification of further modalities for collaboration between DTCD and United Nations entities that had been designated executing agencies, especially the regional commissions and the avoidance of further proliferation of executing agencies; more effective harmonization of technical co-operation in statistics, with DTCD exercising more fully integrated management responsibility for operational activities in development planning, public administration and demography, falling within its purview; and greater use of the Department's technical and executing capabilities within existing funding mechanisms.

In follow-up to the Secretary-General's comments on the JIU report on UNDP's OPE (see p. 442), UNDP and DTCD established a task force to review ways of promoting closer collaboration which would match OPE's approach to project execution with DTCD's technical knowledge and services.

In decision 1984/178, the Economic and Social Council took note of the 1983 JIU report and of the Secretary-General's comments.

The General Assembly, in resolution 39/242, took note of the Secretary-General's report on implementing the JIU recommendations and renewed its invitation to United Nations organs to bear in mind the importance of specific, clear decisions on those recommendations.

United Nations Volunteers

In 1984, the guiding principle of the United Nations Volunteers (UNV) programme continued to be its marked recipient orientation, the objective of which was the harnessing of volunteers' dedication and technical competence for the fulfilment of the interests of the developing countries as defined by them. Another important characteristic was the programme's universality in terms both of the availability to all participating countries of a cost-effective alternative form of technical assistance and of the origin of the volunteers. At the end of the year, 942 volunteers from 78 countries were involved in field projects in 64 developing countries. In addition, 145 volunteers were en route to assignments and 519 were under recruitment, bringing established posts to 1,606, the highest since UNV's founding; 420 volunteers concluded assignments and 490 new volunteers were placed.

In his report on UNV activities in 1984,[10] the UNDP Administrator said the programme had demonstrated that, in addition to its regular functions, it could be particularly effective in dealing with both operational assistance and emergency operations and could also be instrumental in promoting participatory development activities. Over 45 per cent of volunteers in the field as of December 1984 were directly attached to government departments, mainly in operational assistance capacities in LDCs and UNV attached high priority to a project to provide emergency assistance to drought-affected countries in Sub-Saharan Africa (see below).

The second annual UNV Consultative Meeting was held in April 1984 at Geneva with representatives of Governments and co-sponsoring organizations from donor and developing countries to discuss ways of improving the selection, recruitment, utilization and backstopping of volunteers. Efforts were to continue to raise the level of participation of industrialized country nationals in the programme, which was below the optimum.

In the Asia and Pacific region, Bhutan hosted the largest programme with volunteers functioning within a multisectoral project covering key sectors of the economy. In the Trust Territory of the Pacific Islands, 31 UNV posts were established in skills ranging from small-scale industry development to medical services. In Western Samoa, a rural medical service was being developed and modernized through a number of medical officers to be recruited from Asian countries, in keeping with the policy of favouring a TCDC approach where possible. In the Cook Islands, a multisectoral project provided for 15 volunteers.

The Africa region, which absorbed close to 50 per cent of the volunteers, was to receive an even larger contingent as the emergency assistance project became fully operational (see below). Madagascar, Nigeria and Zaire requested volunteers for the first time and Angola received the first three of eight volunteers financed under its IPF. Botswana would soon host one of the largest contingents of UNVs on the continent and steady expansion was projected for Lesotho. Projects were also being developed or under way in Burundi, the Central African Republic, Gabon, Guinea, Guinea-Bissau, Mali, Rwanda, Togo and the United Republic of Tanzania.

Eleven countries in Latin America and the Caribbean had UNVs assigned to their programmes with the largest presence in Jamaica where an additional 20 volunteers in the health field were to complement the 17 already in place. In Honduras, four volunteers were assigned near border areas for work related to asylum and resettlement. In Haiti, the second phase of an ILO project for artisanal development and employment promotion was being prepared involving a team of seven volunteers.

Requests for posts from Arab States registered a 46 per cent increase over 1983. Qatar, Turkey and the United Arab Emirates participated in the programme for the first time, with the establishment of posts in education, meteorology and vocational rehabilitation of the disabled. Programmes were also under way in Democratic Yemen, Somalia, and Yemen.

During 1984, 40 UNV posts were fully funded by the following donor Governments: Belgium, the Federal Republic of Germany, Finland, Norway, Sweden, Switzerland and the United States.

The main thrust of the UNV youth and domestic development services (DDS) programme continued to be the regional IPF-funded

activities in Asia and the Pacific. That regional project was extended to 1986, bringing the total allocation to $2 million with a total of 260 UNV/DDS volunteers assigned by the end of 1984. Geographically, the programme expanded to include an additional six countries—Bhutan, Fiji, India, Solomon Islands, Tonga and Vanuatu—bringing the number of participating countries to 16 together with Papua New Guinea, which endorsed the project in 1984. The UNV participatory development programme for Africa became fully operational with the fielding of the project manager and opening of the project office in Zambia in December 1984. The assignment of UNV specialists and the first group of DDS volunteers in Mali, Rwanda and Zambia was scheduled for early 1985.

Preparatory work of UNV at the local level in relation to International Youth Year (1985) also continued (see Chapter XX of this section).

Expenditures from the UNV Special Voluntary Fund during 1984 totalled some $2.03 million, approximately 94 per cent of which was utilized to meet the external costs of volunteers from developing countries for whom no other financing was available. Contributions received during 1984 totalled $724,807.

The UNDP Administrator submitted his annual report on UNV activities in 1983[11] to the June 1984 session of the UNDP Governing Council.

CONTRIBUTIONS TO THE SPECIAL VOLUNTARY FUND
FOR THE UN VOLUNTEERS, 1984 AND 1985
(as at 31 December 1984; in US dollar equivalent)

Country	1984 payment	1985 pledge
Austria	10,000	10,000
Bangladesh	1,098	1,210
Belgium	162,602	162,602
Bhutan	—	900
Botswana	376	338
Brazil	10,000	—
Cameroon	—	42,553
China	20,000	20,000
Denmark	48,158	—
Germany, Federal Republic of	—	74,098
India	5,000	5,000
Italy	105,263	131,579
Lesotho	2,000	1,412
Netherlands	76,982	—
Norway	129,032	112,994
Philippines	1,000	500
Republic of Korea	10,000	10,000
Sri Lanka	3,000	3,000
Sudan	—	1,000
Switzerland	131,462	200,000
Syrian Arab Republic	5,064	—
Thailand	—	1,500
Tunisia	3,770	3,795
Total	724,807	782,481

SOURCE: A/40/5/Add.1.

UNV PROJECT EXPENDITURES, 1984
(as at 31 December 1984; in thousands of US dollars)

Country/Territory	Amount	Country/Territory	Amount	Country/Territory	Amount
Afghanistan	13	Honduras	10	Somalia	93
Angola	7	Indonesia	7	Sri Lanka	459
Bahrain	9	Ivory Coast	6	Sudan	21
Bangladesh	20	Jamaica	56	Swaziland	20
Benin	39	Kenya	45	Syrian Arab Republic	16
Bhutan	61	Lao People's Democratic Republic	16	Thailand	11
Botswana	27	Lesotho	61	Togo	3
Burkina Faso	8	Liberia	29	Tonga	10
Burundi	11	Malawi	5	Trinidad and Tobago	6
Cameroon	3	Malaysia	3	Trust Territory of the Pacific Islands	26
Cape Verde	5	Maldives	6	Tuvalu	1
Central African Republic	41	Mali	6	Uganda	24
Chad	10	Mauritania	24	United Republic of Tanzania	89
China	6	Mozambique	7	Vanuatu	9
Comoros	25	Namibia	9	Yemen	82
Congo	9	Nepal	4	Zaire	2
Cook Islands	49	Niger	23	Zimbabwe	19
Democratic Yemen	12	Niue	9		
Djibouti	10	Pakistan	2	Total	1,955
Dominica	6	Papua New Guinea	18		
Equatorial Guinea	29	Paraguay	1	*INTERCOUNTRY*	
Ethiopia	11	Philippines	6	*Global*	57
Fiji	3	Rwanda	25	*Regional*	
Gabon	35	Samoa	50	Asia and the Pacific	(1)
Gambia	22	Sao Tome and Principe	13	Latin America and the Caribbean	14
Ghana	28	Senegal	2		
Guatemala	3	Seychelles	2	Total	70
Guinea	1	Sierra Leone	11	GRAND TOTAL	2,025
Guinea-Bissau	78	Singapore	12		
Guyana	9	Solomon Islands	6		

SOURCE: DP/1985/5/Add.6.

Use of UNV for African emergency programme

The Administrator submitted to the June 1984 session of the UNDP Governing Council of the same month a note,[12] on using United Nations volunteers to assist the most severely affected African countries in implementing the emergency assistance programmes. He stated that the UNV programme could secure at short notice the large numbers of experienced logistic and technical personnel necessary to ensure that emergency assistance had the maximum impact on the intended beneficiaries.

The Administrator estimated that some 200 volunteers would be required at the regional level and recommended to the Council that it approve an allocation from Special Programme Resources of $1.5 million to provide the services of approximately 100 volunteers to the most severely affected African countries with a minimum lead time. A regional project south of the Sahara would be designed for the smooth functioning of the scheme. Such an arrangement would also enable individual donor countries to participate by providing complementary contributions under the cost-sharing modality. The Administrator appealed to donor countries to consider such contributions favourably.

On 29 June,[13] the Governing Council approved, on the understanding that it would not be a precedent, the allocation of $1.5 million for the regional project and took note of the Administrator's assur-

ance that fully structured assignments would be worked out with recipient Governments prior to sending the volunteers.

Technical co-operation among developing countries

In 1984, UNDP, with other United Nations organizations, continued to carry out its special responsibility for technical co-operation among developing countries (TCDC)—a major effort by developing countries to promote their collective self-reliance. Those activities paralleled action in favour of economic co-operation among developing countries (ECDC), taken by UNCTAD and others. Support by the United Nations system for ECDC and TCDC and the preparation of a cross-organizational programme analysis of ECDC and TCDC were discussed by several United Nations bodies during the year (see p. 400).

In his annual report for 1984,[14] the Administrator stated that action programmes recommended by the High-level Committee on the Review of Technical Co-operation among Developing Countries in 1983,[15] and financed under Special Programme Resources, had gathered momentum. Through a major interregional project, 133 TCDC activities costing some $1.28 million were financed from those resources: 57 in Latin America and the Caribbean; 34 in Africa; 15 in the Arab States; 11 in Asia and the Pacific; and 5 in Europe. Sectors covered by the project included agriculture, forestries and fisheries, general development issues, policy and planning, natural resources, transport and communications, and industry.

Progress continued in the expansion and use of the TCDC multi-sectoral Information Referral System (INRES), which launched its computerized inquiry service in the latter half of 1984. Its data bank contained information on some 2,300 institutions in 97 developing countries and comprised 50,000 line items with details on the facilities and capabilities of those institutions in such areas as education and training, research and technology development, expert services, and project-related experiences with multilateral and bilateral programmes. In its first few months INRES processed 170 queries from 45 developing countries.

In 1984, UNDP examined the use being made by recipient countries of their IPF allocations in support of TCDC. Despite the scaling down of IPFs in the 1982-1986 period, 17 developing countries were using those resources specifically for TCDC measures, an indication of the priority attached to those activities.

A significant trend was the growing preference of Governments for single "umbrella" projects covering all TCDC donor and/or recipient activities in their respective countries, underscoring their determination to make the most coherent use of scarce funds.

In May 1984,[16] the Secretary-General reported on the possibility of establishing a technical unit for TCDC in ground-water resources development within the Centre for Waters (Zagreb, Yugoslavia) (see Chapter IX of this section).

Allocation from Special Programme Resources

In a May 1984 report to the Governing Council,[17] the Administrator presented an accounting of the use of an allocation of $600,000 from Special Programme Resources, approved by the Council in 1983,[18] for specific promotional activities for TCDC during 1984-1985. The Administrator established an interregional project with an initial budget allocation of $400,000 for which the UNDP Office for Projects Execution was designated executing agency. The objectives of the project were: to provide intercountry level support by training and exchange of expertise and to promote the exchange of technical resources, skills and capacities; and to provide direct support to developing countries with a view to strengthening their TCDC capacities and potential.

As at 15 March 1984, 66 requests costing an estimated $778,400 had been received from 59 countries. The project's budget was therefore increased to $800,000 by adding the balance of the funds approved by the Council plus another $200,000 from savings from previous allocations. Since 15 March, other requests had been received on which action had been postponed because of paucity of funds.

The report gave a breakdown of the distribution of funds by region and component and noted that each request also involved major cost-sharing between donor and recipient countries. The experience gained suggested that the project was successfully strengthening TCDC at the regional, interregional and global levels. The Administrator recommended that the Council approve an additional $800,000 from Special Programme Resources for 1984-1986 to ensure continuation of promotional activities for TCDC.

On 29 June,[19] the Council approved that recommendation, requesting him to submit a detailed report in 1985 on the use of the funds.

Use of country IPFs for TCDC

Pursuant to a 1983 decision of the High-level Committee for the Review of TCDC,[15] the Administrator submitted to the Governing Council a February report on the possibility of introducing greater flexibility in the use of country IPFs for TCDC activities.[20] The report was to be considered at the Council's organizational meeting for 1985. The Governing Council had asked the Administrator to study the consequences of the following proposals made by the Committee: allowing country IPFs to cover fully the local currrency expenditure on TCDC projects financed from IPF resources; permitting the reimbursement in convertible currency of the local currency expenditure on TCDC projects covered by country IPFs; and ensuring procurement, in TCDC projects, of equipment, service, experts, etc., from developing countries.

Following a brief review of the rationale underlying established policies governing the use of country IPFs for TCDC activities, the report discussed the consequences of each of the three proposals and advanced recommendations for further streamlining some of the relevant procedures.

The Administrator concluded that: to allow the use of country IPFs to fully finance TCDC projects would be inconsistent with the principle that TCDC activities should be primarily financed by developing countries themselves and that UNDP's role was only supportive and catalytic; reimbursement of local currency expenditures from the IPF should continue to be made in that currency when UNDP had accumulated holdings of it and, when holdings were insufficient, UNDP should continue to puchase the needed currency, resulting in convertible currency accruing to the country's banking system; and for procurement of equipment and supplies for TCDC projects, bids from developing countries should be given a 15 per cent cost preferential treatment over other bids but other regulations pertaining to the bidding procedures should be maintained.

Activities and staffing of Special Unit for TCDC

In accordance with a 1983 Governing Council decision,[18] the Administrator submitted to that body a report on the activities and staffing of the UNDP Special Unit for TCDC.[21] The report reviewed the background and mandate of the Unit and then described its functions as: programming of TCDC action-oriented promotional activities funded through the Special Programme Resources; developing new ideas, for promoting TCDC; reporting to and servicing the High-level Committee; programme support; maintaining liaison with TCDC focal points of Governments and assisting developing countries to strengthen their TCDC co-ordination mechanisms; collecting and disseminating information on potential sources for financing; organizing training programmes for government officials and United Nations personnel; expanding and maintaining the UNDP Information Referral System (INRES) and establishing links with national and regional information systems; and supporting public information programmes on TCDC.

With regard to staffing, the Administrator noted that, since 1982, the Unit had consisted of five Professional-level posts and six General Service posts and if all the functions proposed for the Unit by the Committee were to be meaningfully developed and implemented at the levels expected, additional staff would be required. However, those needs had to be weighed against other needs in the organization. If he was to contain the size of the administrative budget, the Administrator could not propose an increase in the Unit's staff, although he was fully cognizant of the importance of TCDC. Continued efforts would be made to further enhance TCDC within available budgetary resources.

On 29 June 1984,[22] the Governing Council, noting UNDP's financial constraints and the Administrator's conclusion that additional staff could not be recommended, requested him to keep the issue under review, particularly in preparing the 1986-1987 budget.

Information Referral System for TCDC

In response to a 1983 Governing Council decision,[23] the Administrator submitted a March 1984 progress report to the Council on the TCDC Information Referral System (INRES).[24] The report stated that INRES had reached the operational stage and arrangements had been made for technical support to be provided by the UNDP Division of Management Information Services. However, the Special Unit for TCDC (see above) continued to operate the information service including dispatch and receipt of questionnaires, data validation, coding and entry, operation of the enquiry service, monitor-

ing of the use and general promotion of INRES among potential users.

As requested by the High-level Committee on TCDC in 1983,[23] the report also reviewed the activities of INRES in relation to the other multisectoral information systems in UNDP and the regional commissions. The Administrator stated that there was an overlap between INRES and the regional commissions in the collection, storage and dissemination of information on institutions and that he would consult further with them on modalities for ensuring better policy and operational co-ordination. He had also instructed the UNDP Central Evaluation Office to include in its work plan an evaluation of the global and regional information systems supported by UNDP. Better co-ordination of United Nations information systems would be further facilitated by the Advisory Committee for the Co-ordination of Information Systems established in 1983.[25]

The Administrator proposed to keep the situation under review and would report to both the High-level Committee on TCDC and the Governing Council in 1985.

Skilled workers

In his annual report to the Governing Council on 1984 UNDP activities,[14] the Administrator stated that the programme for the Transfer of Knowledge through Expatriate Nationals (TOKTEN) continued to attract increasing support from Governments which had found skilled expatriates from its growing roster to be invaluable short-term consultants. By the end of 1984, the TOKTEN scheme had delivered more than 1,000 consultancies in 15 participating countries, contributing to resolving some of the problems created by the brain drain from developing countries.

On 6 April,[26] the UNCTAD Trade and Development Board took note of consultations held between the UNCTAD Secretary-General and Governments, as requested by the High-level Committee on the Review of TCDC in 1983.[23] The Board urged Governments to respond positively to the invitation addressed to the Board in 1983 by the High-level Committee, including the convening of a group of governmental experts on co-operative exchange of skills among developing countries, and to take a decision thereon at its September 1984 session.

On 21 September,[27] the Board requested the UNCTAD Secretary-General to convene in 1985 a meeting of governmental experts to examine the modalities for co-operation analysed in a 1983 study on institutional and policy issues relating to the co-operative exchange of skills,[23] recommend ways of systematically promoting such an exchange among developing countries, and submit its findings to the Board for transmittal to the High-level Committee in 1985. The UNCTAD Secretary-General was further requested to attempt to obtain financial resources outside the UNCTAD regular budget in order to facilitate participation of experts from LDCs in the meeting.

REFERENCES
[1]DP/1985/43 & Add.1-3. [2]DP/1984/42 & Add.1-3. [3]E/1984/20 (dec. 84/22). [4]YUN 1977, p. 439, GA res. 32/197, annex, 20 Dec. 1977. [5]A/39/38. [6]YUN 1983, p. 478. [7]*Ibid.*, p. 479. [8]A/39/145. [9]A/39/476. [10]DP/1985/44 & Add.1. [11]YUN 1983, p. 481. [12]DP/1984/22/Add.1. [13]E/1984/20 (dec. 84/19). [14]DP/1985/5 & Add.1-6. [15]YUN 1983, p. 485. [16]E/1984/101. [17]DP/1984/46/Add.1. [18]YUN 1983, p. 486. [19]E/1984/20 (dec. 84/25). [20]DP/1984/47. [21]DP/1984/46. [22]E/1984/20 (dec. 84/24). [23]YUN 1983, p. 487. [24]DP/1984/48. [25]YUN 1983, p. 1208. [26]A/39/15, vol.I (dec. 290(XXVIII)). [27]A/39/15, vol. II (res. 300(XXIX)).

UN Capital Development Fund

In his annual report on the United Nations Capital Development Fund (UNCDF) for 1984,[1] the Administrator described the Fund's programme activities, gave the conclusions of evaluation studies of a number of projects, and provided information on the Fund's financial status.

Programme operations. In 1984, UNCDF approved $36.8 million for 27 new projects plus $2.1 million for increases in existing project budgets, bringing outstanding commitments at year-end to $144 million. Of the total amount approved, $20.6 million was funded directly from UNCDF general resources while the balance was funded through cost-sharing and trust fund arrangements.

In programming its assistance during the year, UNCDF gave priority to drought-affected areas in Africa and to projects that would increase food production and facilitate its distribution, and improve primary health care services and community water-supply systems. Of the new projects and grant increases approved, 19 were for 12 LDCs in Africa.

UNCDF began 1984 with 194 ongoing projects with $143.7 million in outstanding commitments. The projects were located in 41 countries and were designed to be implemented primarily by government agencies. Some required specialized assistance which was provided by eight co-operating agencies of the United Nations system. Project expenditure amounted to some $30 million compared with $24.8 million for 1983. An additional $1 million was disbursed against trust fund and cost-sharing arrangements.

As authorized by the UNDP Governing Council in 1983,[2] UNCDF continued to accept trust funds conditioned on procurement in the donor country and in 1984 negotiated one new tied

trust fund of $12.96 million from Italy for a project in Ethiopia.

In 1984, UNCDF and the Arab Gulf Programme for United Nations Development Organizations concluded cost-sharing agreements, with the latter contributing $0.5 million for two projects, bringing its total cost-sharing contributions to $2.6 million for six projects.

UNCDF also obtained funding towards 13 of its new projects from two UNDP-administered trust funds. Twelve projects were to be funded in part by the UNDP Trust Fund for Developing Countries Afflicted by Drought, Famine and Malnutrition, which, as decided by the General Assembly in 1983,[3] financed urgently needed projects, primarily in the food and agricultural sectors in countries afflicted by famine and malnutrition resulting from severe or prolonged drought. UNCDF received $4.8 million in contributions from that trust fund, of which $4 million was allocated to nine projects in Africa. It also obtained $2.5 million from a special Netherlands trust fund for LDCs to fund a project in Haiti (see also p. 414).

During the year, six programming missions were fielded by the Fund to identify new projects and, as a follow-up to those and earlier project identifications, 26 formulations missions were dispatched to 14 countries, resulting in the approval of 15 projects.

UNCDF also participated in four round-table donor meetings for LDCs organized by Burundi, Comoros, Lesotho and Malawi, with UNDP assistance.

Programme resources. Voluntary contributions received by UNCDF in 1984 amounted to $21.2 million (down from $24.2 in 1983). In addition, UNCDF received $0.6 million in trust fund contributions and cost-sharing arrangements while additional joint financing modalities for $18.5 million were also concluded during the year. As at 31 December, pledges for 1985 amounted to $14.3 million (see table).

Of the 10 major donors contributing to UNCDF, eight made their contributions in national currencies which were converted to the United States dollar equivalent. The strength of the dollar had the effect of substantially reducing the dollar equivalent of both pledges and amounts paid in despite increased levels of national currency pledges from several countries.

At the beginning of the year, outstanding commitments funded from general resources totalled $143.7 million and the Fund approved $20.6 million in new project commitments. Project expenditures of $30 million and project savings and cancelled obligations of $13.8 million reduced the year-end commitments to $120.3 million. The difference between outstanding project commitments and available resources, exclusive of the

UNCDF PROJECT EXPENDITURES, 1984
(as at 31 December 1984; in thousands of US dollars)

Country	Amount*	Country	Amount*	Country	Amount*
Angola	598	Gambia	310	Senegal	1,010
Bangladesh	2,351	Guinea	1,042	Somalia	914
Benin	1,171	Guinea-Bissau	189	Sudan	95
Bhutan	1,065	Haiti	850	Togo	370
Bolivia	218	Lao People's Democratic Republic	297	Tonga	130
Botswana	349	Lesotho	238	Uganda	785
Burkina Faso	1,800	Malawi	800	United Republic of Tanzania	3,168
Burundi	615	Maldives	97	Viet Nam	46
Cape Verde	332	Mali	1,471	Yemen	708
Central African Republic	1,310	Mauritania	499		
Chad	526	Nepal	1,689	Subtotal	30,862
Comoros	757	Nicaragua	396		
Democratic Yemen	489	Niger	996	Regional Africa	31
Djibouti	56	Rwanda	983		
Equatorial Guinea	702	Samoa	1	Total	30,893
Ethiopia	1,353	Sao Tome and Principe	86		

*Figures are estimates not necessarily corresponding to audited figures given in text.
SOURCE: DP/1985/5/Add.6.

CONTRIBUTIONS TO UNCDF, 1984 AND 1985
(as at 31 December 1984; in US dollar equivalent)

Country	1984 payment	1985 pledge	Country	1984 payment	1985 pledge
Afghanistan	2,000	2,000	Malawi	6,107	5,369
Algeria	37,000	37,000	Maldives	600	600
Austria	13,953	14,085	Mali	—	500
Bangladesh	3,633	4,275	Mauritius	1,044	—
Belgium	—	487,805	Nepal	1,250	1,250
Bhutan	—	1,810	Netherlands	3,693,331	3,362,319
Botswana	3,759	6,757	Norway	3,367,974	3,050,847
Burkina Faso	—	1,064	Sao Tome and Principe	1,876	444
Cameroon	1,762	—	Senegal	—	10,410
China	144,928	110,701	Sierra Leone	1,000	1,000
Cuba	23,068	22,222	Sweden	3,822,565	—
Cyprus	1,000	1,000	Switzerland	1,764,583	1,694,000
Democratic Yemen	1,760	1,940	Tunisia	3,654	2,843
Denmark	1,994,048	—	Turkey	136,356	153,153
Finland	958,333	1,039,370	United Republic of Tanzania	1,135	—
France	—	106,383	United States	2,100,000	2,000,000
Greece	10,000	10,000	Viet Nam	834	1,000
Guatemala	1,000	—	Yugoslavia	88,800	85,492
Iraq	71,612	—	Zambia	49,402	15,306
Italy	1,842,105	2,105,263	Zimbabwe	5,217	4,138
Japan	1,000,000	—			
Lao People's Democratic Republic	1,500	1,500	Total	21,160,189	14,343,258
Lesotho	3,000	1,412			

SOURCE: A/40/5/Add.1.

operational reserve, of $41.3 million was expected to be covered by resources pledged for 1985 and by part of the anticipated contributions for 1986. The Fund's total available resources at year-end amounted to $103.1 million, including the operational reserve of $24.1 million.

Expenditures in 1984 were $31.1 million—$28.8 million in project costs and $2.3 million for administrative and programme support costs.

REFERENCES

[1]DP/1985/45. [2]YUN 1983, p. 488. [3]Ibid., p. 537, GA res. 38/201, 20 Dec. 1983.

Chapter III

Economic assistance, disasters and emergency relief

Through a number of organizations, the United Nations continued in 1984 to provide special assistance to countries with serious economic difficulties. Those problems were frequently aggravated by natural or other disasters. Of particular concern was the critical economic situation in Africa which was compounded by a prolonged drought in certain regions. Both the Economic and Social Council and the General Assembly added an item to their agenda for the first time on that situation. In a December resolution (39/29), the Assembly adopted the Declaration on the Critical Economic Situation in Africa, expressing concern at the crisis which over the previous few years had assumed alarming proportions, seriously jeopardizing not only the development process, but also the very survival of millions of people. By the Declaration, the Assembly outlined the problems and proposed remedial measures.

In order to view firsthand the effects of widespread drought, food shortages, livestock epidemics and dwindling resources, the Secretary-General travelled to eight countries in West Africa from 17 January to 4 February. On his return, he remarked that the dimensions of the human tragedy became all the more poignant during his trip, and he called on the international community to respond urgently and adequately, as lives were threatened and the economic survival of many African countries was at stake. In addition to problems of food, health, water supply, refugees, transportation and communication, the international community needed to deal with the causes of the crisis, he said. In December, the Secretary-General established the United Nations Office for Emergency Operations in Africa; the Administrator of the United Nations Development Programme (UNDP) was appointed to direct the new Office. The most urgent problem was famine, which was complicated by problems of transport, storage and distribution of food.

With regard to countries suffering grave economic difficulties, the Economic and Social Council in July called for assistance to Guinea (resolution 1984/59), and in December the Assembly adopted a series of resolutions calling for economic assistance to Benin (39/185), Cape Verde (39/189), the Central African Republic (39/180), Chad (39/195), the Comoros (39/193), Democratic Yemen (39/184), Djibouti (39/200), Equatorial Guinea (39/181), the Gambia (39/203), Guinea (39/202), Guinea-Bissau (39/186), Haiti (39/196), Lesotho (39/183), Liberia (39/182), Mozambique (39/199), Nicaragua (39/204), Sao Tome

and Principe (39/187), Sierra Leone (39/192), Uganda (39/188) and Vanuatu (39/198).

The United Nations system continued to respond to emergency situations arising from natural disasters, mainly through action co-ordinated by the Office of the United Nations Disaster Relief Coordinator (UNDRO). The Assembly (in resolutions 39/190, 39/191, 39/194, 39/201, 39/205 and 39/206) and the Council (in resolutions 1984/3, 1984/5, 1984/6 and 1984/7 and decision 1984/106) dealt with assistance needs resulting from the continuing drought in certain areas in Africa, particularly the Sudano-Sahelian region and East Africa; cyclones and floods in Madagascar; a cyclone in Swaziland; and an earthquake in Yemen. Both the Assembly and the Council, in resolutions 39/207 and 1984/60 respectively, called for strengthening the United Nations capacity to respond to disasters.

In addition to special economic assistance and disaster relief, emergency humanitarian assistance was provided to Lebanon. Lebanon had been unable to carry out its reconstruction programme due to renewed fighting and disorder and the military situation in the south. The Assembly, in resolution 39/197, called for assistance for the reconstruction and development of Lebanon, as did the Council in decision 1984/174.

Topics related to this chapter. Development policy and international economic co-operation: special economic areas—developing countries. Regional economic and social activities: Africa—economic and social trends; Asia and the Pacific—typhoons. Food: food aid. Environment: desertification. Children—emergency relief. Refugees: assistance to refugees.

Economic assistance

In response to requests by the General Assembly, the United Nations in 1984 continued to provide special assistance to a number of developing countries faced with particularly severe economic problems. A wide range of adverse economic conditions, often accompanied by damaging climatic events, had jeopardized the development of those countries.

The Secretary-General, by various 1982 and 1983 resolutions, had been requested to report to the Assembly in 1984 on the economic situation and on the progress made in organizing and implementing special programmes of economic assistance for a number of developing countries. Each of the countries concerned was asked whether it would prefer the report to be based on the findings of a visiting review mission or whether it would wish to provide the information to be used in a brief, interim report to the Assembly. Eleven of the countries concerned chose the latter form; accordingly, the Secretary-General, in September and October,[1] submitted summary reports for 11 countries for which special programmes of economic assistance were being implemented, based on information supplied by them. The summaries—for Bolivia, Ecuador and Peru; Chad; the Comoros; Djibouti; Equatorial Guinea; the Gambia; Sierra Leone; Tonga; and Uganda—addressed the main developments in the respective economies and the status of the special programme of economic assistance.

The Secretary-General also submitted individual reports on assistance rendered to Benin,[2] Cape Verde,[3] the Central African Republic,[4] Democratic Yemen,[5] Guinea,[6] Lesotho,[7] Mozambique,[8] Nicaragua,[9] Sao Tome and Principe[10] and Vanuatu.[11] In a further report to the Assembly,[12] he described assistance provided by the United Nations system to 20 countries: Benin, Bolivia, Cape Verde, Central African Republic, Chad, Comoros, Djibouti, Ecuador, Equatorial Guinea, Gambia, Ghana, Guinea-Bissau, Lesotho, Mozambique, Peru, Sao Tome and Principe, Sierra Leone, Tonga, Uganda, Vanuatu. The summaries of aid to those countries were based on information provided by specialized agencies and other United Nations bodies, programmes and organizations that had rendered technical and other forms of assistance within their various fields of competence: FAO, UNESCO, WHO, the World Bank and IDA, IMF, ICAO, UPU, ITU, WMO, IMO, WIPO, IFAD, UNDP, UNCTAD, UNICEF, UNIDO, UNCDF, UNCHS, WFP, WFC, UNFPA, UNDRO, DTCD and UNHCR. (See below for details on individual countries.)

The Assembly took note of the Secretary-General's report on system-wide assistance when it adopted decision 39/431 on 17 December.

Speaking to the Assembly's Second (Economic and Financial) Committee on 2 November, the Under-Secretary-General for Special Political Questions and Co-ordinator for Special Economic Assistance Programmes, Abdulrahim Abby Farah, reported that nine additional countries (Bolivia, Ecuador, Guinea, Kiribati, Madagascar, Peru, Swaziland, Tuvalu and Vanuatu) had been added during the year to those for which special programmes of economic assistance had been established, bringing the total to 25. Reports on 20

of them were before the Committee; another, on Guinea, was under preparation. Of the 18 African States included, 14 had been classified by the United Nations as least developed countries (LDCs). The effects of the prolonged drought had compounded their situation.

Many of the countries concerned had heavy debt-servicing burdens which obliged them to request rescheduling of their external debts. Noting that a number of the countries had taken austerity measures, the Co-ordinator called on the international community to support those efforts by increasing the flow of financial and other assistance. A number of the countries had mobilized additional external resources by organizing donor conferences and round-tables which deserved the support of the international community. On behalf of the Secretary-General, he appealed to bilateral and multilateral donors to respond generously.

In an October report to the Assembly,[13] the Secretary-General described the implementation of the Substantial New Programme of Action for the 1980s for the Least Developed Countries (SNPA), adopted by the 1981 United Nations Conference on the Least Developed Countries[14] and endorsed that year by the Assembly.[15] SNPA was aimed at helping LDCs achieve a self-sustained economy and enabling them to attain internationally accepted minimum standards of nutrition, health, housing and education. The report, prepared by the secretariat of UNCTAD, gave a brief account of the recent economic performance of LDCs (see p. 413).

GENERAL ASSEMBLY ACTION

The General Assembly, acting on the recommendation of the Second Committee, adopted without vote decision 39/431.

Special programmes of economic assistance

At its 103rd plenary meeting, on 17 December 1984, the General Assembly, on the recommendation of the Second Committee:

(a) Took note of the summary reports of the Secretary-General on Bolivia, Ecuador and Peru, and on Tonga;

(b) Took note of the oral report made on 5 November 1984 by the United Nations Disaster Relief Co-ordinator on the steps taken to implement General Assembly resolution 38/217 of 20 December 1983, entitled "Special assistance to alleviate the economic and social problems faced in regions of Honduras and Nicaragua as a result of the May 1982 floods and other subsequent natural disasters";

(c) Took note of the report of the Secretary-General on assistance provided by the United Nations system.

General Assembly decision 39/431

Adopted without vote

Approved by Second Committee (A/39/793) without vote, 30 November (meeting 54); oral proposal by Chairman; agenda item 83 (b).
Meeting numbers. GA 39th session: 2nd Committee 32, 34, 54; plenary 103.

Africa

Critical economic situation

According to several 1984 United Nations reports, the economic and social situation in Africa continued to deteriorate. The crisis reflected the cumulative impact of a variety of internal and external factors, such as natural disasters, inadequate resources, slow economic growth, structural weaknesses, global economic recession, strife and adverse climatic conditions.

For the first time, in 1984 the Economic and Social Council and the General Assembly included in their agenda an item on the critical economic situation in Africa.

In an April report to the Council,[16] the Secretary-General described the nature and magnitude of the critical social and economic situation in Africa, identified the most pressing needs, and called for concerted and co-ordinated action from the international community. As a result of economic stagnation or decline combined with rapid population growth, average per capita income in many African countries was, in real terms, less than it had been 15 years earlier. Despite some gains in the quality of life in Africa over the previous two decades, social conditions were far from acceptable and were threatened with deterioration. In recent years, the number of people living at subsistence level had increased sharply and vulnerable groups (women, children, the disabled, rural communities) were especially endangered. The situation was manifested in lack of basic health care and safe drinking-water, high infant mortality rates, high unemployment and inadequate housing.

To some extent, the economic difficulties stemmed from the limited production base of African countries, usually restricted to a few primary commodities and mineral products, requiring reliance on industrialized countries, and from a lack of transport and communications infrastructure. Food production had failed to keep pace with population growth. The industrial sector remained small in most countries and heavily dependent on imported inputs and spare parts.

The impact of the recent global economic recession and of inflation on the already vulnerable economies of Africa had been devastating. It had led to a sharp drop in commodity prices, which in 1982, in real terms, had been at their lowest level in 40 years. Between 1981 and 1983 alone, the total value of African developing countries' exports fell by more than 15 per cent. As a result of declining commodity prices, the terms of trade of those countries declined by approximately 50 per cent between 1977 and 1981. To curb growing trade deficits, many countries had to reduce overall imports while accommodating a growing need for food imports. Many had no alternative but to request the rescheduling of their external debt, which provided only temporary relief. Faced with financial imbalances, a number of countries had undertaken adjustment programmes in association with IMF and/or the World Bank, usually calling for reduced government expenditures, such as the reduction of subsidies for basic consumer goods and for strategic production inputs such as fertilizer, as well as major currency devaluations. While the purpose of the programmes was to restore financial equilibrium, the immediate impact was often a further worsening of living conditions. The Secretary-General said that increased official development assistance (ODA) was vital during the adjustment period until better financial balance was restored.

The most pressing need was for food. Almost half of Africa's population was threatened by severe hunger and malnutrition and in some cases by starvation. There was little prospect that those needs could be met from domestic production in the near future due to the continuation of drought. FAO estimated that Africa would require 3.3 million tons of food aid during the 1983/84 season. In addition to food, assistance was needed to ensure its distribution and to rehabilitate agricultural production. Programmes to develop water supplies and basic health services were urgently needed. The development of human resources was a key priority.

Economic assistance was needed for balance-of-payments support to meet urgent import requirements and to achieve fuller utilization of existing industrial and agricultural capacity. In the Secretary-General's view, international action was required to help stabilize prices of African export commodities and reduce barriers to markets for African goods. In recent years, aid flows and private flows of equity capital to Africa had been declining. While bilateral aid would remain the major component in ODA, multilateral aid was also essential.

Within the United Nations, an effort was being made to achieve a better co-ordinated approach, beginning with asking the United Nations resident co-ordinators in African countries to consult with each Government, as well as with the local representatives of bilateral and multilateral agencies and non-governmental organizations (NGOs), to identify specific country needs. Specific needs had also been identified by numerous United Nations organizations, many of which were active in 1984 in dealing with the African crisis.

In a July addendum[17] to the April report, the Secretary-General updated selected issues of the emergency situation in the most affected food-deficient countries. The report was prepared by his Special Representative for the African crisis on the basis of information from Governments supplied to the resident co-ordinators and to United Nations organizations and bodies participating in the activities of the Special Representative's office at Nairobi, Kenya. In addition to presenting the emergency needs of African countries and assessing domestic and international responses, the report dealt with strengthening the preparedness of the affected countries for future emergency situations. As at mid-1984, there remained a food-aid gap for 1983/84 in the range of 500,000 tons, and pledges were urgently needed to fill it. The estimated emergency requirements, amounting to about $225 million, related mainly to water, transport and distribution, health, nutrition, energy and the provision of emergency agricultural input for the next planting season.

Food production in 1983/84 in the 24 most affected countries, as identified by FAO, had declined by 10 per cent from the poor crop yields of 1982/83, and by 14 per cent from that of the last normal year, 1981. The shortfall in production had been severe in both West Africa, particularly in the Sahelian countries, and southern Africa, which had suffered from drought in 1982 and 1983. In East Africa, the drought had been very severe in some areas, and there had been widespread starvation. As at the end of May 1984, FAO and WFP estimated that 3 million tons of food aid had to be provided in 1983/84.

Other critical problems were: water shortages; lack of transportation for food, water and medicines to the affected populations; population displacement within and outside national boundaries; lack of adequate basic health services; livestock diseases; and insufficient energy supply.

Reviewing the preparedness of countries for coping with emergency situations, the Special Representative found that, in slightly more than half of the countries surveyed, a national emergency or reconstruction plan did not exist. One third had national plans to cope with the emergency/drought situation, but in only a few cases did such plans contain financial and sectoral details. In 13 of the 18 countries in which a national relief co-ordinating mechanism existed, the internal co-ordinating capacity could be rated from adequate to strong.

A global drought/food early warning system (EWS) had been set up by FAO, but it needed improvement, as did national and area EWS capabilities. Timely and reliable data and trained manpower were also needed. A major bottle-neck occurred in the scheduling of food-aid deliveries to the distribution sites. United Nations resident co-ordinators—who were the UNDP resident representatives in all African countries—acted as focal points for the United Nations system at the country level for matters concerning economic crises and the drought-induced emergency; in general they had many responsibilities and were understaffed.

While the international community had concentrated on the provision of food, it was also essential to provide the means to resume normal agricultural production, i.e. crop seeds and fertilizers, agricultural materials, equipment and spare parts, technical assistance and agricultural rehabilitation. Aid in the form of seeds, fertilizers, pesticides, insecticides, animal vaccines, animal feed, vehicles, and agricultural tools and equipment was provided through FAO and UNDP. FAO had drawn up plans for expanding food and seed reserves—an important element in preparing for emergency situations—while WHO had established health emergency stocks at six African locations.

The Special Representative had convened a special meeting of African intergovernmental organizations and financial institutions at Geneva on 20 July to explore their capacities in the solution of short-, medium- and long-term problems and how those capacities could be synchronized with donors' efforts.

In an October report to the Assembly,[18] also prepared by the Special Representative, the Secretary-General provided supplementary information, reviewing the emergency situations as at 31 August 1984 in 36 African countries, of which 27 were identified by an FAO/WFP special task force monitoring food-aid requirements, pledges and deliveries as countries facing abnormal food shortages, and nine were identified by the Conference of Ministers of the Economic Commission for Africa (ECA) (tenth meeting, Addis Ababa, Ethiopia, 24-28 May 1984) as also being drought-affected. The critical areas were actual or impending shortages of food and water; serious losses of livestock; massive imports of food, placing severe strain on already weak transport, storage and distribution systems; increased malnutrition and health risks; and further displacement of drought-affected populations. Projections of food harvests and supply were constantly changing and were merely indicative of the magnitude of needs. The report also discussed briefly the longer-term aspects of structural adjustment, with particular emphasis on actions required from African Governments and from donors, multilateral aid institutions and NGOs.

The crisis was affecting the economies of the entire continent. Gross output of developing Africa declined by 0.1 per cent in 1983 and a marginal growth of 1.8 per cent was projected for 1984. As a result, per capita income had consistently declined since 1980 at an average annual rate of 4.1 per cent. While there were structural defects in the economies of many African countries, their current position was largely the result of an unfavourable international economic environment. The economies were also affected by the degradation and loss of agricultural soils, the destruction of vegetal cover, the desertification of pasture lands and the depletion of ground water. By September 1984, food-aid pledges from donors had reached 2.6 million metric tons (with an estimated value of over $500 million), comprising 88 per cent of requirements, for 24 countries identified as having high cereal-import requirements for 1983/84.

The Secretary-General concluded that the situation remained precarious and that greater efforts would be required in 1984/85 since drought was again affecting a number of countries. Moreover, several were unlikely to meet import targets through commercial purchases because of foreign exchange constraints; continuous assessment was recommended. Transport, storage and distribution of relief supplies continued to be a main bottle-neck, and donor support was essential in this sector. Addressing the longer-term structural requirements, the Secretary-General said that the primary responsibility rested with the African Governments themselves in such areas as formulation of national rehabilitation and development programmes, improved management of the economy, and development of entrepreneurship in all economic sectors. Such efforts should be complemented with international support in the interrelated areas of primary commodity export, external debt and financial flows. Compensatory mechanisms should be made as flexible as possible and bilateral creditors should make efforts to alleviate the debt burden through new rescheduling schemes and the waiving of debt-service payments over an agreed period of time.

The Secretary-General, in a note of 1 November,[19] stressed that, even though the dimensions of the drought and the imminence of mass starvation had abated somewhat over the previous year, a large number of Africans were still struggling to survive and many of the countries were still in a critical situation. A week earlier he had issued an urgent appeal for immediate assistance to Ethiopia, where almost a million people were facing the prospect of death from starvation. The situation was also ominous in Angola, Chad, Mali and the Niger.

The Secretary-General urged that the international community increase net financial flows to Africa, particularly concessional flows through bilateral channels and multilateral organizations such as the World Bank and the other United Nations funding institutions. In regard to the African countries' external debt, country-specific solutions were required, but as for public debt, the measures provided for in a 1978 UNCTAD resolution[20] on debt and development problems of developing countries should be implemented for the least developed and other poor countries of Africa. In order to improve those countries' commodity export earnings, the Secretary-General said steps must be taken to enable the Common Fund for Commodities, a mechanism intended to stabilize the commodities market by helping to finance buffer stocks of specific commodities and commodity development activities, to become operative as soon as possible (see Chapter IV of this section).

Progress was also needed in negotiating individual commodity agreements and in improving compensatory financing arrangements. Increasing agricultural production for domestic consumption and export was also a priority area.

United Nations action had included efforts to assist countries through specific programmes and the mobilization of concessional resources. The Secretary-General called for greater administrative flexibility as well as adequate financing, through the reallocation of existing resources, co-financing arrangements or from additional resources. Action was needed in three broad areas: first, strengthening support for national programmes for developing human resources, particularly in management and administration, including technical assistance in resources management and training programmes on skills needed in rural areas; second, protection of underprivileged groups, the most vulnerable of whom were women and children, including increasing child survival programmes and programmes to provide drinking-water and health education and medicine; and third, maintenance and repair of production, transport and communications infrastructures.

In a report issued in June with a later addendum,[21] the Secretary-General described special measures taken by the United Nations system, in accordance with a 1980 Assembly resolution,[22] for the social and economic development of Africa in the 1980s (see Chapter VIII of this section). The report focused on measures for implementing the Lagos Plan of Action for the Implementation of the Monrovia Strategy for the Economic Development of Africa,[23] adopted by the Organization of African Unity (OAU) at Lagos, Nigeria, in 1980 as the major framework for the continent's development plans.

The Administrative Committee on Co-ordination (ACC) reviewed the critical economic situation in Africa at its April[24] and October 1984[25] sessions. In April, it adopted a decision[26] endorsing three areas for immediate and high priority action by the United Nations system, as identified by its Sub-Committee on Nutrition at its tenth session (Rome, Italy, 5-9 March). Two of these concerned Africa: initiative Africa for the strengthening of institutions, specifically the FAO/WHO/OAU Regional Food and Nutrition Commission for Africa; and a co-ordinated country-level approach in food and nutrition—based on a Sub-Committee analysis of problems and opportunities of a selected African country. The third pertained to the control of vitamin A and iodine deficiency.

At the end of 1984, the Secretary-General took measures to strengthen the system's response to the emergency situation and provide a broad framework for international action, emphasizing the linkage between emergency relief, rehabilitation and long-term development.

In June,[27] the Secretary-General transmitted to the Council the Special Memorandum on Africa's Economic and Social Crisis, adopted by the ECA Conference of Ministers in May (see Chapter VIII of this section). The ministers responsible for economic development and planning addressed the current crisis and its causes, the emergency needs of the 24 most affected countries, the short- and medium-term measures needed to combat the crisis in those and 10 other drought-prone countries, and the long-term structural adjustment measures for the whole continent in accordance with the Lagos Plan of Action. In an addendum, the Secretary-General transmitted the Addis Ababa Declaration on Africa's External Indebtedness, adopted by the African Ministers of Finance at a regional meeting on the topic (Addis Ababa, 18-20 June).

The twentieth ordinary session of the Assembly of Heads of State and Government of OAU (Addis Ababa, 12-15 November) adopted two declarations and a series of resolutions which were transmitted by Djibouti to the Secretary-General on 10 January 1985.[28] One of the declarations, on the critical economic situation in Africa, called for measures to be taken at the national, regional and international levels to alleviate emergency relief and rehabilitation problems and meet longer-term development requirements. It urged all donor countries to respond positively to the proposals put forward by the recent World Bank report entitled *Towards Sustained Development of Sub-Saharan Africa: A Joint Programme of Action*, which called for additional bilateral and multilateral disbursements of about $2 billion yearly for the region, and suggested that the Bank consider establishing special facilities for the realization of those objectives. By a resolution on the economic problems of Africa, the OAU Assembly endorsed the recommendations made by the ECA Conference of Ministers in its Special Memorandum, and requested its Secretary-General to submit the declaration and the Memorandum to the 1984 session of the General Assembly.

UNDP activities. The Administrator of UNDP, in his annual report for 1984,[29] described the programme adjustments made by UNDP during the year due to the crisis in Africa. Drought had advanced over large areas of sub-Saharan Africa that year, further harming fragile economies already sapped by the effects of collapses in commodity prices, static ODA in real terms, unprecedentedly heavy debt-service burdens and volatile currency exchange rates. In December 1984, the Secretary-General established the United Nations Office for Emergency Operations in Africa (OEOA) with the UNDP Administrator serving as its head. That decision underlined the major adjustment required of UNDP. The emergency in Africa was widely perceived to be foremost a development issue. As the central funding and co-ordinating body for United Nations tech-

nical co-operation, UNDP was called upon to respond to requests for medium- and long-term rehabilitation as the necessary corollary of emergency relief actions.

UNDP field offices, in partnership with United Nations agencies, notably UNDRO, FAO, UNHCR, UNICEF and WFP, acted jointly as on-the-spot centres for information and emergency aid co-ordination. Following an appraisal of UNDP staff capacities, a redeployment exercise was carried out aimed at strengthening field offices in the most seriously affected countries, and further staffing needs were identified. In addition, UNDP reviewed its assistance to over 20 countries, and programmes and projects were adjusted to complement new relief and rehabilitation efforts. The adjustments were similar to the recommendations adopted by the ECA Conference of Ministers in May and endorsed by the OAU Assembly. UNDP identified its priority areas as: food production; water supply sources and systems; communications infrastructures to alleviate difficulties affecting the transportation, storage and distribution of food and medical supplies; and co-ordination of rehabilitation programmes with the resettlement of displaced populations. Within available resources, UNDP also gave priority to health services in affected countries, livestock management projects, renewable energy development and drought management and control. It also helped national authorities to define policy to ensure the efficient use of available development funds.

Field expenditures in Africa by and through UNDP amounted to over $300 million over the year. UNDP core resources accounted for $255 million of the total. Resource mobilization efforts were increased by promoting third-party cost-sharing projects which became a significant source of additional financing in the region.

The Administrator established in November the UNDP Trust Fund to Combat Poverty and Hunger in Africa. The Fund was to be used for projects in the priority areas of food self-sufficiency, water, energy for household use, primary health care, rural roads and anti-desertification and reforestation. Its resources could also be used for emergency assistance to African countries when exceptional circumstances warranted such action.

By a decision of 29 June on the economic and social crisis in Africa,[30] the UNDP Governing Council reaffirmed the importance of the central co-ordinating role of UNDP in assisting African Governments to meet their urgent needs as well as their medium- and long-term technical co-operation requirements for development. The Administrator was invited to continue his efforts to collaborate with organizations of the United Nations development system in such areas as assistance flows, resource mobilization and development of priority activities to help meet immediate and long-term development needs in Africa. The Council expressed appreciation for UNDP assistance in organizing round-table conferences of donors, requested the Administrator to support future conferences, and urged donor countries to support African countries' efforts, through United Nations funds and programmes, to plan and implement development projects. The Council supported the Administrator's initiative to channel an increased number of United Nations volunteers and technical personnel to the most severely affected African countries, and endorsed his intention to review the capacity of African field offices to undertake the additional work-load. It noted his speedy action to implement the General Assembly's 1983 request[31] to liquidate the United Nations Emergency Operation Trust Fund and allocate the remaining balance to existing funds, including 70 per cent to UNDP-administered funds to finance urgently needed projects, primarily for food in African countries afflicted by drought (see p. 451).

By another decision of the same date,[32] the Governing Council approved an allocation of $1.5 million for a regional project in sub-Saharan Africa to counter the effects of the prolonged drought there by providing United Nations volunteers (see p. 458).

The UNDP Administrator, in an April report to the Governing Council,[33] described special programmes of assistance for specific countries. The report was made in response to a number of 1983 General Assembly resolutions calling for expanded aid to several countries (Benin, Bolivia, Cape Verde, Central African Republic, Ecuador, Gambia, Guinea-Bissau, Lesotho, Peru, Sierra Leone, Uganda, Vanuatu) and inviting UNDP and other United Nations organizations to consider their special needs.

Communications. Japan, in a letter of 5 September 1984,[34] referring to the Secretary-General's appeal of 16 February for assistance to countries affected by the crisis besetting Africa, described its response, including food assistance to Ethiopia, Ghana, Mozambique, Senegal and Somalia, aid for refugees in Burundi, Ethiopia, Somalia, the Sudan, Uganda, Zaire and Zimbabwe and WFP-channelled food aid for refugees in Chad, Somalia and the Sudan. On 29 November,[35] Japan transmitted an appeal to the international community for assistance to Africa issued by its Foreign Minister after a trip that month to observe the effects of the drought. The Minister announced Japanese supplemental food and agricultural aid of $50 million, in addition to the food-related assistance of more than $115 million it had already approved for 1984.

On 6 December,[36] the United Republic of Tanzania transmitted a letter of 28 November to the Secretary-General from its President in his capacity

as Chairman of OAU. The Chairman endorsed the Secretary-General's call, made when he attended the twentieth OAU summit session in November 1984, for an international conference under United Nations auspices to consider action on the famine and hunger which afflicted most of Africa. He drew attention to the summit's decision to establish an African Fund for Emergency Assistance for Drought and Famine Problems and to its endorsement of the World Bank's proposal for a special fund for sub-Saharan Africa to contribute to Africa's medium- and longer-term recovery and development needs.

On 14 December,[37] the United States transmitted a communiqué from the Development Assistance Committee of the Organisation for Economic Co-operation and Development (OECD), which met in Paris on 3 and 4 December to discuss means of strengthening ODA and international co-operation to meet the acute problems of developing countries, in particular to respond more effectively to the economic and social crisis in sub-Saharan Africa. The Committee members said they were committed to working with the Secretary-General to organize effective international emergency action and were providing food and other assistance either directly or through international institutions and NGOs. They welcomed the efforts by the World Bank to strengthen aid co-ordination and to promote local arrangements for co-ordination, and UNDP's related efforts to strengthen the co-ordination capability of round-tables for LDCs.

ECONOMIC AND SOCIAL COUNCIL ACTION

In July, the Economic and Social Council adopted decision 1984/188 without vote.

Critical economic situation in Africa

At its 50th plenary meeting, on 27 July 1984, the Council decided:

(a) To request the General Assembly to include in the provisional agenda of its thirty-ninth session an item entitled "Critical economic situation in Africa" so as to bring to a successful conclusion the initiatives taken by the Council at its second regular session of 1984;

(b) To transmit to the General Assembly at its thirty-ninth session the documents relating to that question which were before the Council at its second regular session of 1984, together with the relevant summary records.

Economic and Social Council decision 1984/188

Adopted without vote

Oral proposal by Vice-President; agenda item 4.
Meeting numbers. ESC 34-41, 50.

Algeria, a Council Vice-President, expressed regret that an informal Council working group on Africa, which had met under his chairmanship, had been unable to produce a declaration on guidelines for concerted action for Africa acceptable to all interested parties. In lieu of a declaration, the group had proposed the draft decision. Algeria said that the failure might be attributed to differences of approach between developed and African countries on action to be taken on such matters as commodity price stability and compensatory financing, and to differences with regard to objectives. Some developed countries thought primarily in terms of emergency humanitarian aid, whereas African countries considered that the main objective should be to bring about the conditions necessary for recovery and the renewal of development.

Consideration by the Committee for Development Planning. The Committee for Development Planning (CDP), at the first part of its twenty-first session (Geneva, 19-21 November 1984), made recommendations on the critical economic situation in Africa.[38] In a statement issued on 21 November, it said that in 1984-1985, over 5 million tons of grain would be required to avert severe malnutrition and starvation in 27 countries. Tens of thousands were dying in the most severely affected countries, especially in Chad, Ethiopia and Mozambique. CDP observed, however, that emergency food aid could have little impact on the deeper sources of the current crisis: rapid population growth, civil strife, external destabilization, the state of the world economy and natural disasters.

The circumstances could be overcome, according to CDP, and one of the means involved relatively small external support—less than one tenth of 1 per cent of the gross national product (GNP) of the OECD countries. The World Bank, ECA, the African Development Bank and the overwhelming majority of African Governments agreed that sustained development could begin over the next three to five years through domestic policy reform and improved external support. Increased support for agriculture, through restructured institutions and incentives, was the crux of the required domestic policy change.

CDP recommended that the international community agree no later than at its resumed session, to be held in April 1985, on a joint financing plan for Africa along the lines recommended by the World Bank, requiring total new commitments of at least $6 billion per year over the next three years. That much was needed merely to maintain net flows at the levels of recent years. Of that amount, at least $2 billion should be channelled into a special financing facility to be administered by the World Bank and IDA for use in low-income countries in Africa. The Committee recommended that both bilateral aid and African Governments' economic policies be monitored. It also called for IMF, the World Bank and other sources of finance to review African access to international liquidity and bridging finance.

GENERAL ASSEMBLY ACTION

On 3 December, the Assembly adopted without vote resolution 39/29, thereby adopting the Declaration on the Critical Economic Situation in Africa.

**Declaration on the Critical Economic
Situation in Africa**

The General Assembly,

Alarmed by the critical economic situation currently prevailing in Africa,

Commending the efforts of the Secretary-General in sensitizing the international community to the plight of Africa,

Noting the increased concern of the international community for the worsening plight of African countries affected by the crisis,

Having considered the critical economic situation in Africa, the note by the Secretary-General and his report on the subject,

Taking note of the Declaration on the Critical Economic Situation in Africa and the resolutions adopted by the Assembly of Heads of State and Government of the Organization of African Unity at its twentieth ordinary session, held at Addis Ababa from 12 to 15 November 1984,

Taking note also of the statement of the Committee for Development Planning, at the conclusion of its twenty-first session, held at Geneva from 19 to 21 November 1984, on the critical economic situation in Africa,

Convinced of the need for concerted action by the international community to assist the efforts of the African Governments by providing immediate emergency relief, and medium-term and long-term development aid,

1. *Adopts* the Declaration on the Critical Economic Situation in Africa set forth in the annex to the present resolution;

2. *Requests* the Secretary-General to take all appropriate measures for the full and speedy implementation of the objectives contained in the Declaration;

3. *Also requests* the Secretary-General to bring the Declaration to the attention of all States, and intergovernmental and non-governmental organizations;

4. *Further requests* the Secretary-General to continue to monitor the situation, to assess the needs and the responses thereto, and to report thereon to the General Assembly at its fortieth session through the Economic and Social Council.

ANNEX
**Declaration on the Critical Economic
Situation in Africa**

1. We the States Members of the United Nations express our deep concern at the profound economic and social crisis that Africa is experiencing. Over the last few years the situation has assumed alarming proportions, seriously jeopardizing not only the development process but, more ominously, the very survival of millions of people.

2. We are alarmed by the spectre of widespread famine hanging over many African countries. Over one hundred and fifty million people are facing hunger and malnutrition. Prolonged unprecedented drought, accelerating desertification and other natural disasters have compounded an already serious situation, dislocating normal life all over the continent. Alarming shortages in food and water supplies and the depletion of livestock have led to the displacement of millions of people within and across borders.

3. All these factors are further straining fragile economies crippled by deep-rooted structural deficiencies, that is to say, weak physical and social infrastructures, lack of trained human resources and dependence on the export of a few primary commodities.

4. Africa, despite its enormous potential, remains the least developed of all continents, lagging far behind

by every economic indicator. Economic performance of many African countries is characterized by declining per capita incomes and stagnant or negative rates of growth. Furthermore, food production has not kept pace with population growth. According to all projections, prospects for recovery, growth and development remain very dim unless the efforts currently under way in African countries are fully supported by the international community.

5. Furthermore, the international economic environment continues to affect developing countries adversely and, particularly, it had a devastating impact on the already fragile African economies. This is manifested in deteriorating terms of trade, sharp declines in export earnings, the heavy burden of external debt and stagnating resource flows to African countries.

6. We are aware that African countries recognize they have the primary responsibility for their development and for addressing the present crisis. They have therefore undertaken and continue to undertake painful adjustment measures at very high social and political costs. While recognizing the determined efforts of African countries and the support provided by the international community, much more needs to be done as the situation remains very grave.

7. We recognize that, in dealing with the present crisis, African regional and subregional efforts towards economic co-operation and integration as well as enhanced economic and technical co-operation among developing countries play an important role in the achievement of national and collective self-reliance and sustained development in Africa.

8. We are aware that the maintenance of peace and security and the strengthening of international co-operation are important for meeting the challenge of development.

9. We fully recognize that emergency relief aid on a massive scale is urgently needed in the following areas: additional food aid and other emergency supplies, together with the technical and financial assistance necessary for their transportation, storage and distribution to the affected populations; improvement of water supplies; improvement of health and nutrition, particularly for vulnerable groups, including refugees and displaced persons; safeguarding national nuclei of herds of livestock; establishment of income-generating projects and promotion of new and renewable energy projects, particularly in rural areas. In addition to the assistance already provided by the international community, further urgent assistance from bilateral and multilateral donors and non-governmental organizations is required to meet the above and other identified emergency needs in a comprehensive manner, as well as to strengthen the emergency prevention and preparedness capacities of African countries.

10. Of particular importance is the need to undertake urgent action to speed up and support the recovery and rehabilitation process in African countries, especially of the agricultural and industrial sectors as well as for physical and social infrastructures. Assistance for increasing the import capacity for vital imports, through adequate balance-of-payments support and other relevant measures, would help to establish a sound basis for the resumption and acceleration of sustained economic and social development in Africa.

11. We agree that in confronting the challenge of development, national policies and measures, such as those outlined in the Lagos Plan of Action for the Implementation of the Monrovia Strategy for the Economic Development of Africa adopted by the Assembly of Heads of State and Government of the Organization of African Unity and the Special Memorandum on Africa's Economic and Social Crisis adopted by the Conference of Ministers of the Economic Commission for Africa, provide a framework for national and subregional action and international support.

12. We recognize that, in view of the high priority attached by African countries to food and agriculture, the first urgent task is the early attainment of national and collective self-reliance in food production. In this connection, as highlighted in the Harare Declaration on the food crisis in Africa adopted on 25 July 1984 by the thirteenth FAO Regional Conference for Africa, national food strategies and integrated rural development plans play an important role, especially in the achievement of food security. Moreover, we recognize the important role of women in rural development, particularly in food production, a role for which greater support is needed. Also important are the provision of appropriate incentives, credit, improvement of storage and transport, reduction of food losses, in particular post-harvest losses, achievement of a better balance between agricultural export commodities and food production, diversification of agricultural production and utilization of irrigation potential, particularly in the drought-prone areas.

13. Urgent action is needed at the international level to support national and regional efforts to implement the Regional Plan of Action to Combat the Effects of Drought in Africa and the Plan of Action to Combat Desertification.

14. Increased resources for rapid implementation of the Industrial Development Decade for Africa and the Transport and Communications Decade in Africa are required. Furthermore, efforts at national, subregional and regional levels to develop the necessary and much needed skilled manpower, and to build technological capacities, require increased international support.

15. We fully acknowledge that, in the light of the worsening economic situation in Africa, the interrelationship between the debt problem, concessional flows and export earnings and their direct impact on recovery, growth and development assume even greater significance. It is vital, therefore, to take urgent and mutually reinforcing measures in those areas, taking into account the Special Memorandum on Africa's Economic and Social Crisis, the Addis Ababa Declaration on Africa's External Indebtedness adopted by the African Ministers of Finance and the World Bank Special Programme for Sub-Saharan Africa, in order to complement and support domestic adjustment efforts in African countries.

16. Africa is experiencing a very serious debt problem, repayment and servicing of which is taking a very high percentage of already reduced export earnings. The problem is further exacerbated by factors such as deteriorating terms of trade, decline in concessional flows in real terms and increased use of short-term commercial credit. Without an increase in net capital inflows and urgent debt relief measures, prospects for recovery and development in Africa will be undermined.

17. Bilateral and multilateral creditors should take concerted measures to ease the debt burden of African countries. For official and officially guaranteed debt, total or partial conversion of official development assistance debts into grants, longer maturities and grace periods, lower or concessional interest rates and extended multi-

year rescheduling are among the measures to be dealt with urgently within the framework of close consultation with each of the debtor countries concerned, as well as any other measures to be agreed upon. It is essential to ensure the full and urgent implementation of Trade and Development Board resolution 165(S-IX) of 11 March 1978. Multilateral financial institutions should expedite resource disbursement. Reduction in international interest rates would further alleviate the debt burden. Moreover, the full co-operation of commercial banks is indispensable. The capacity of African countries to manage their debt should be improved through the provision of technical assistance, particularly by international agencies.

18.   We recognize that African countries, in view of their heavy dependence on concessional financial flows and their limited access to alternative sources of external finance, require a substantial and sustained increase in the volume of these flows through bilateral donors and multilateral channels for development finance and technical co-operation. The international community, in particular the developed countries and the multilateral financial institutions, should endeavour to provide the additional financial resources to maintain and increase a net transfer of resources to African countries. The World Bank is strongly urged to explore with donors possible approaches, including a special facility, in mobilizing the resources required to implement the Bank's Special Programme for Sub-Saharan Africa.

19.   The full and speedy implementation of the Substantial New Programme of Action for the 1980s for the Least Developed Countries, particularly with regard to the official development assistance level, would greatly augment resource flows to many African countries. Supplementary funding for the International Development Association and the early completion of the replenishment of the International Fund for Agricultural Development would ensure at least the maintenance of the real value of resources channelled to Africa.

20.   The heavy dependence of African countries on the export of a few primary commodities renders them particularly vulnerable to the sharp price fluctuations that result in drastic shortfalls in export earnings. Urgent action is therefore needed to stabilize commodity prices on long-term trends and to improve and increase the use of compensatory financing arrangements for export earnings shortfalls, such as the Compensatory Financing Facility of the International Monetary Fund. Improved market access for African primary and processed products, efforts of African countries to diversify production, and the early and effective operation of the Common Fund for Commodities require intensified international action.

21.   The modalities and quality of official development assistance flows in terms of a greater grant element, untied resources and simplified procedures for aid delivery should be improved through, *inter alia*, speedier disbursements and greater reliance on more flexible forms of assistance, such as non-project programme and sector aid, including local and recurrent costs.

22.   We acknowledge that there is room for further improvement in the co-ordination of assistance and the efficient and effective use of resources. Co-ordination of multilateral as well as bilateral assistance is primarily the responsibility of recipient Governments and, in this connection, effective national co-ordinating mechanisms can play an important role. The United Nations system should extend technical assistance in this field to Govern-

ments, upon request, and should pursue its own efforts to enhance co-ordination at the programme and operational levels, in conformity with relevant General Assembly resolutions.

23.   We are convinced that in addressing the critical needs of African countries there are many areas where the United Nations could play an important role both in mobilizing the necessary resources and in carrying out specific activities. In this respect, existing resources allocated for programmes in Africa should, in consultation with African Governments, be refocused to address identified priority areas. There is need for further improvement in the efficiency and programme delivery of United Nations activities in Africa. Furthermore, additional voluntary contributions should be mobilized to ensure the implementation of projects and programmes in priority areas.

24.   We urge all organs, organizations and bodies of the United Nations system to give greater attention to Africa and to continue to mobilize resources for assisting African countries in dealing with the current crisis and its longer-term ramifications.

25.   We further urge bilateral and multilateral donors, as well as non-governmental organizations, to take all necessary measures to support the efforts of the African countries aimed at alleviating the critical economic situation in Africa.

26.   We request the Secretary-General to continue his commendable efforts in alerting and sensitizing the international community to the plight of African countries, in mobilizing additional assistance to Africa, as well as in co-ordinating the activities of the United Nations system in Africa and in monitoring the situation, and to present periodic reports thereon.

27.   We are convinced that unless urgent action is taken the rapidly deteriorating situation in Africa may well lead to disaster. We are therefore fully committed to supporting the efforts of African countries to meet the dual challenge of survival and development by taking concerted and urgent measures commensurate with the needs outlined in the present Declaration.

General Assembly resolution 39/29

3 December 1984   Meeting 83   Adopted without vote

Draft by Cameroon (A/39/L.22), orally amended by co-ordinator following consultations; agenda item 139.
Meeting numbers. GA 39th session: plenary 47-52, 83.

Japan, the co-ordinator of informal consultations on this agenda item, orally informed the Assembly of amendments agreed to in paragraph 17 following consultations: the measures listed to ease the debt burden of African countries became measures "to be dealt with urgently" rather than measures "which deserved urgent action", and the word "Furthermore" was removed from the beginning of the following sentence.

In a separate action, the Assembly, in resolution 39/239 A on the financial emergency of the United Nations, called for a special postage stamp issue to sensitize the international community to the social and economic crisis in Africa, half the revenues from which were to be earmarked to implement objectives of the Declaration on the Critical Economic Situation in Africa.

By resolution 39/8 on co-operation between the United Nations and OAU, the Assembly commended the Secretary-General for his updated report on the critical economic situation in Africa.[18] It expressed appreciation for his initiative in alerting the international community to the situation and for organizing special programmes of economic assistance for African States, and welcomed his steps to facilitate international co-operation to assist Africa. Appreciation was also expressed to the World Bank, UNDP and other international financial institutions for their response to the critical situation as well as their assistance in organizing round-table and donor conferences in favour of African LDCs and those requiring special economic assistance programmes. The Assembly called on Member States and organizations to participate in measures to deal with the economic crisis in Africa, and on the international community to provide long-term assistance to the affected African States, particularly those suffering from natural disasters; appreciation was expressed to UNDRO, WFP, FAO, WHO and UNICEF for their assistance in this regard. Member States and United Nations organizations were called on to increase assistance to the African States affected by serious economic problems, in particular problems of displaced persons, and the organizations' attention was drawn to the need to publicize the social and economic development of Africa, in particular the critical economic situation.

Resolution 39/165 dealt with a related problem—the critical food and agriculture situation in Africa.

Benin

As requested by the General Assembly in 1983,[39] the Secretary-General reported on special economic and disaster relief assistance to Benin, which was classified by the United Nations as an LDC. The September 1984 report[2] was based on the findings of a review mission sent to Benin from 18 to 22 June.

Benin had appealed to the international community on 26 January for assistance in dealing with urgent economic and social problems resulting from drought and abnormal rainfall which had caused food shortages, estimated by the Government to be 50,000 to 70,000 metric tons of cereals, rural water shortages and electrical power outages. UNDP and UNDRO had responded promptly. An *ad hoc* United Nations emergency committee was established, consisting of all relevant United Nations representatives and experts in the country. In co-operation with the Government, UNDRO formulated a plan of action, focusing on improving wells, water distribution, providing and transporting food, a vaccination campaign and livestock protection; its estimated cost was $1.7 million and, by April, the

necessary funds had been provided, mainly by bilateral donors. The drought appeared to have ended in 1984, although water shortages continued in many parts of the country and total rainfall was still below normal. Long-term solutions to water availability and storage problems were needed, and a significant food gap remained.

Following the donors' round-table in March 1983,[40] Benin had revised many of the projects initially presented as its national development and investment programme for 1983-1987 and revised cost estimates.

GENERAL ASSEMBLY ACTION

On 17 December, the General Assembly, acting on the recommendation of the Second Committee, adopted resolution 39/185 without vote.

Special economic assistance to Benin

The General Assembly,

Recalling its resolutions 35/88 of 5 December 1980, 36/208 of 17 December 1981, 37/151 of 17 December 1982 and 38/210 of 20 December 1983, in which it appealed to the international community to provide effective and continuous financial, material and technical assistance to Benin so as to help that country overcome its financial and economic difficulties,

Recalling also Security Council resolution 419(1977) of 24 November 1977, in which the Council appealed to all States and all appropriate international organizations, including the United Nations and its specialized agencies, to assist Benin,

Having heard the statement made by the representative of Benin on 5 November 1984, in which he described the serious economic and financial situation of his country and the action taken by his Government to tackle these difficulties,

Having considered the report of the Secretary-General on assistance to Benin,

Noting from the report that, in spite of various unfavourable factors, Benin continues to achieve some positive results in its development efforts thanks to the action taken by the Government and the assistance provided by the international community,

Deeply concerned, nevertheless, by the fact that Benin continues to experience serious economic and financial difficulties, characterized by a marked balance-of-payments disequilibrium, heavy burdens of its external debt and a lack of resources to implement its planned economic and social development programme,

Noting also that the persisting unfavourable climatic conditions in the coastal and northern regions of Benin have led to losses in agricultural and livestock production,

Noting that a round-table conference of partners in the economic and social development of Benin was held at Cotonou in March 1983 and that the Government took steps to organize the follow-up of its results,

Taking into consideration the objectives of Benin's national development plan for 1983-1987,

Having noted the efforts made by the Government of Benin to mobilize international support for the country's development plan by organizing the round-table conference held at Cotonou in March 1983 with the assistance of the United Nations Development Programme,

Considering that Benin is one of the least developed countries,

1. *Expresses its appreciation* to the Secretary-General for the steps he has taken to organize and mobilize support for the international programme of economic assistance to Benin;

2. *Takes note* of the report of the review mission sent to Benin in June 1984;

3. *Notes with satisfaction* the interest and support which the participants in the round-table conference have shown for Benin's development plan;

4. *Expresses its appreciation* for the assistance already provided or pledged to Benin by Member States, United Nations bodies and regional, interregional and intergovernmental organizations;

5. *Appeals* to Member States, international financial institutions, the specialized agencies and other United Nations bodies to respond generously and urgently to the needs of Benin as set forth in that country's development plan for 1983-1987;

6. *Requests* the appropriate programmes and organizations of the United Nations system—in particular the United Nations Development Programme, the Food and Agriculture Organization of the United Nations, the International Fund for Agricultural Development and the United Nations Children's Fund—to maintain and expand their programmes of assistance to Benin, to co-operate closely with the Secretary-General in organizing an effective international programme of assistance and to report periodically to him on the measures they have taken and the resources they have made available to help that country;

7. *Invites* the United Nations Development Programme, the United Nations Children's Fund, the World Food Programme, the World Health Organization, the Food and Agriculture Organization of the United Nations, the World Bank and the International Fund for Agricultural Development to bring to the attention of their governing bodies, for their consideration, the special needs of Benin and to report the decisions of those bodies to the Secretary-General by 15 July 1985;

8. *Requests* the Secretary-General:

(a) To continue his efforts to mobilize the necessary resources for implementing the projects of the special programme of economic assistance to Benin;

(b) To render appropriate assistance to the Government of Benin for mobilizing the resources necessary for implementing its national development plan;

(c) To keep the situation in Benin under constant review and, in consultation with the Government of Benin, to report to the General Assembly as soon as necessary.

General Assembly resolution 39/185

17 December 1984   Meeting 103   Adopted without vote

Approved by Second Committee (A/39/793) without vote, 30 November (meeting 54); 29-nation draft (A/C.2/39/L.43); agenda item 83 *(b)*.

Sponsors: Algeria, Angola, Bangladesh, Benin, Bhutan, Botswana, Burkina Faso, Central African Republic, China, Congo, Cyprus, Democratic Yemen, Djibouti, Egypt, Ethiopia, France, Gambia, Ghana, Guinea-Bissau, Lebanon, Liberia, Madagascar, Malawi, Niger, Pakistan, Togo, Tunisia, Vanuatu, Viet Nam.

Meeting numbers. GA 39th session: 2nd Committee 32-37, 44, 54; plenary 103.

Cape Verde

Special economic assistance to Cape Verde was the subject of an August 1984 report[3] by the Secretary-General, as requested by the General As-

sembly in 1983.[41] A United Nations mission which visited that country from 9 to 16 June 1984 noted that the Government was operating with a deficit forecast for 1984 of approximately $6.3 million and there was a continuing trade deficit. In 1984, the total external debt stood at $119.5 million, representing 150 per cent of the gross domestic product (GDP). Debt service for the year was estimated at $4.5 million.

The food situation was seriously affected by erratic rainfall—drought followed by torrential rains in September—and, taking into account existing stocks, estimated domestic production, commercial imports and food aid pledged, there remained an estimated food deficit of 36,871 tonnes for 1984. Under WFP, over 43,000 persons were receiving food aid. The Government had concluded long-term food aid agreements with France, Switzerland, the United States and the European Economic Community (EEC) and was seeking similar arrangements with other donors. The Government strengthened mechanisms for food aid distribution to vulnerable groups by mobilizing army and civil administration resources, but external assistance was needed to implement its water supply, job creation and livestock preservation programmes.

UNCTAD, in a January 1985 report on its assistance to Cape Verde, Uganda and Vanuatu,[42] said it had undertaken activities relating to trade and regional economic integration in Cape Verde, financed by UNDP. As an LDC, Cape Verde was eligible to benefit from measures provided for in SNPA, adopted in 1981,[14] and, as an island developing country, it was entitled to other benefits from UNCTAD. In a resolution of 6 April,[43] the Trade and Development Board requested that the UNCTAD Secretary-General, in co-operation with UNDP, identify Cape Verde's assistance needs within UNCTAD's competence and make efforts to meet those needs. Among the projects identified by the Secretary-General's mission to Cape Verde, there were two (institutional reinforcement of commerce, and a stabilization fund for food security) which were eligible for UNCTAD support.

UNDP continued implementing the Cape Verde country programme for 1983-1986, expending $1.2 million on priority projects in 1984, according to a March 1985 report of the Administrator.[44] Two projects approved for urgent implementation were a desalination plant, and procurement of spare parts for rural development activities for controlling desertification.

GENERAL ASSEMBLY ACTION

On 17 December, the Assembly, acting on the recommendation of the Second Committee, adopted resolution 39/189 without vote.

Assistance to Cape Verde

The General Assembly,

Recalling its resolutions on assistance to Cape Verde, in particular its resolution 38/219 of 20 December 1983, in which the international community was requested to provide an appropriate level of resources for the implementation of the programme of assistance to Cape Verde as envisaged in the reports of the Secretary-General,

Recalling resolutions 142(VI) and 138(VI) of 2 July 1983 of the United Nations Conference on Trade and Development on the progress in the implementation of the Substantial New Programme of Action for the 1980s for the Least Developed Countries, and on activities in the field of island developing countries,

Noting that Cape Verde is one of the least developed countries and a small archipelagic State, with a fragile and open economy, aggravated by endemic and severe drought,

Reiterating that increased substantial, continuous and predictable assistance from the international community is needed for the effective completion of the First National Development Plan (1982-1985),

Gravely concerned at the critical food situation in Cape Verde resulting from the failure of seasonal rains, the continuing recurrence of drought and the spreading desertification,

Recognizing the strenuous efforts deployed by the Government and people of Cape Verde in the process of the economic and social development of their country despite existing constraints,

1. *Takes note* of the report of the Secretary-General, to which is annexed the report of the review mission sent to Cape Verde in response to General Assembly resolution 38/219;

2. *Expresses its appreciation* to the Secretary-General for the efforts deployed in mobilizing resources for the implementation of the programme of assistance to Cape Verde;

3. *Expresses its gratitude* to States and to international, regional and interregional organizations and other intergovernmental organizations for their contribution to the programme of assistance to Cape Verde;

4. *Reaffirms* the need for all Governments and international organizations to implement their commitments undertaken within the framework of the Substantial New Programme of Action for the 1980s for the Least Developed Countries, particularly those undertaken at the round-table conference of Cape Verde's partners in development, held at Praia from 21 to 23 June 1982;

5. *Urges* Governments and international, regional and interregional organizations and other intergovernmental organizations to extend and intensify substantially their assistance for the early implementation of the programme of assistance to Cape Verde;

6. *Invites* the international community, in particular donor countries, to take appropriate and urgent measures to support the effective completion of the First National Development Plan (1982-1985) of Cape Verde;

7. *Requests* the organs, organizations and bodies of the United Nations system to continue and increase their assistance to Cape Verde, to co-operate with the Secretary-General in his efforts to mobilize resources for the implementation of the programme of assistance and to report periodically to him on the measures they have taken and the resources they have made available to help that country;

8. *Calls upon* the international community to continue to contribute generously to all appeals for food and fodder assistance made by the Government of Cape Verde, or on its behalf by the specialized agencies and other competent organizations of the United Nations system, to help it cope with the critical situation in the country;

9. *Once again draws the attention* of the international community to the special account established at United Nations Headquarters by the Secretary-General, in accordance with General Assembly resolution 32/99, for the purpose of facilitating the channelling of contributions to Cape Verde;

10. *Invites* the United Nations Development Programme, the United Nations Conference on Trade and Development, the United Nations Children's Fund, the World Food Programme, the World Health Organization, the United Nations Industrial Development Organization, the Food and Agriculture Organization of the United Nations, the World Bank and the International Fund for Agricultural Development to continue to consider, through their governing bodies, the special needs of Cape Verde and to report the decisions of those bodies to the Secretary-General by 15 July 1985;

11. *Requests* the Secretary-General:

(a) To continue his efforts to mobilize the necessary resources for implementing the programme of development assistance to Cape Verde;

(b) To keep the situation in Cape Verde under constant review, to apprise the Economic and Social Council, at its second regular session of 1985, of the progress made in the implementation of the present resolution and to report thereon to the General Assembly at its fortieth session;

(c) To arrange for a review of the economic situation in Cape Verde and, in consultation with the Government of Cape Verde, to make a substantive report on the implementation of the special programme of economic assistance for Cape Verde to be considered by the General Assembly at its forty-first session.

General Assembly resolution 39/189

17 December 1984   Meeting 103   Adopted without vote

Approved by Second Committee (A/39/793) without vote, 30 November (meeting 54); 48-nation draft (A/C.2/39/L.49); agenda item 83 *(b)*.

Sponsors: Afghanistan, Algeria, Angola, Argentina, Austria, Bangladesh, Brazil, Burkina Faso, Cameroon, Canada, Cape Verde, Central African Republic, Chad, China, Congo, Cuba, Dominican Republic, Egypt, France, Ghana, Guinea, Guinea-Bissau, Iceland, India, Italy, Japan, Libyan Arab Jamahiriya, Madagascar, Mali, Mauritania, Mozambique, Nicaragua, Niger, Pakistan, Panama, Portugal, Sao Tome and Principe, Senegal, Spain, Sudan, Sweden, Trinidad and Tobago, United Republic of Tanzania, United States, Vanuatu, Yugoslavia, Zambia, Zimbabwe.

Meeting numbers. GA 39th session: 2nd Committee 32-37, 45, 54; plenary 103.

Central African Republic

The Secretary-General, in response to a 1983 request of the General Assembly,[45] arranged for a review mission to visit the Central African Republic from 9 to 16 June 1984 in order to report on the economic situation there and on implementing the special programme of economic assistance. According to the mission's report, annexed to the Secretary-General's August report,[4] the Central African Republic, a land-locked LDC, continued to suffer the effects of a November 1982–May 1983 drought, including bush fires, pests, loss of crops, electricity shortages, disease and interruption of transport. Accordingly, it had been included on the FAO/WFP list of countries in need of exceptional international assistance. The general slow-down in economic activity resulted in loss of revenues and worsening balance-of-payments deficits. Efforts were under way to implement a 1983-1985 national action plan, designed to improve agriculture, forestry, livestock, fisheries and rural infrastructure, in particular transport, sanitation, water supply, social services, education and health. The 1983/84 production of staple crops declined significantly, and the projected earnings for 1984 decreased by 40 per cent.

The country's GDP, of which agriculture accounted for one third, increased in 1984 by 9.2 per cent over 1983, and the economy grew at an estimated 6 per cent. At the end of 1984, external debt was $262 million, representing 44 per cent of GNP and 166.7 per cent of exports of goods and services. External debt-service payments represented 4.7 per cent of GDP. By June 1984, of the 17 projects in the special programme of economic assistance awaiting funding in 1982, six had been fully funded, five partially funded, two had good funding prospects, two had not received any financing, and two had been withdrawn by the Government.

GENERAL ASSEMBLY ACTION

Acting on the recommendation of the Second Committee, the Assembly adopted on 17 December resolution 39/180 without vote.

Assistance for the reconstruction, rehabilitation and development of the Central African Republic

The General Assembly,

Recalling its resolution 35/87 of 5 December 1980, in which it affirmed the urgent need for international action to assist the Government of the Central African Republic in its efforts for reconstruction, rehabilitation and development of the country and invited the international community to provide sufficient resources to carry out the programme of assistance to the Central African Republic,

Recalling also its resolutions 36/206 of 17 December 1981, 37/145 of 17 December 1982 and 38/211 of 20 December 1983, in which it noted with concern that the assistance provided had not been adequate to meet the urgent needs of the country,

Recalling further its resolution 38/195 of 20 December 1983 on the implementation of the Substantial New Programme of Action for the 1980s for the Least Developed Countries,

Considering that the Central African Republic is landlocked and is classified as one of the least developed countries,

Taking note of the statement made by the Minister for Foreign Affairs and International Co-operation of the Central African Republic on 11 October 1984, in which he described the economic problems of concern to the Central African Republic and stated that, because of the lack of financial means, external aid continued to be essential to the country,

Also taking note of the statement made by the representative of the Central African Republic on 6 November 1984, according to which, despite an incipient economic recovery, his country continued to be faced by enormous difficulties in implementing its socio-economic development programmes,

Particularly concerned that the Government of the Central African Republic is unable to provide the population with adequate health, educational and other essential social and public services because of an acute shortage of financial and material resources,

Taking account of the losses suffered by the Central African economy following the great drought of 1982-1983,

Noting with satisfaction the considerable efforts exerted by the Government and people of the Central African Republic for national reconstruction, rehabilitation and development, despite the limitations confronting them,

Also noting the intention of the Central African Government to organize, with the assistance of the United Nations Development Programme, a round-table conference of donors in 1985,

Taking note of the report of the Secretary-General, submitted pursuant to General Assembly resolution 38/211, to which was annexed the report of the review mission sent to the Central African Republic in June 1984,

Also taking note of table 7 of the annex to the report of the Secretary-General according to which substantial additional assistance for the special programme of economic assistance is needed to finance projects which have only been implemented in part and others for which finance has not yet been obtained, including new high-priority projects specified therein,

1. *Expresses its appreciation* to the Secretary-General for the efforts he has made to mobilize resources for carrying out the programme of assistance to the Central African Republic;

2. *Reiterates its appreciation* to States, international, regional and interregional organizations and other intergovernmental organizations for their contribution to the programme of assistance to the Central African Republic;

3. *Notes with concern,* however, that the assistance provided under this heading continues to fall far short of the country's urgent needs;

4. *Urgently draws the attention* of the international community to table 7 of the annex to the Secretary-General's report, which indicates the projects still in need of financing;

5. *Reiterates its appeal* to all States to contribute generously, through bilateral or multilateral channels, to the reconstruction, rehabilitation and development of the Central African Republic;

6. *Urges* all States, organizations and financial institutions to participate in the round-table conference of donors scheduled for 1985 and to contribute to the financing of the projects to be submitted;

7. *Requests* the appropriate programmes and organizations of the United Nations system—in particular the United Nations Development Programme, the World Bank, the International Monetary Fund, the Food and Agriculture Organization of the United Nations, the International Fund for Agricultural Development, the World Food Programme, the World Health Organization, the United Nations Children's Fund, the United Nations Fund for Population Activities and the United Nations Industrial Development Organization—to maintain their programmes of assistance to the Central African Republic, to co-operate closely with the Secretary-General in his efforts to organize an effective international programme of assistance and to report periodically to him on the steps they have taken and the resources they have made available to help that country;

8. *Invites* regional and interregional organizations and other intergovernmental and non-governmental organizations to give urgent consideration to the establishment of a programme of assistance to the Central African Republic or, where one is already in existence, to the expansion and considerable strengthening of that programme with a view to its implementation as soon as possible;

9. *Urges* all States and relevant United Nations bodies—in particular the United Nations Development Programme, the World Food Programme, the United Nations Children's Fund, the World Health Organization, the United Nations Fund for Population Activities and the United Nations Industrial Development Organization—to provide all possible assistance to help the Government of the Central African Republic to cope with the critical humanitarian needs of the population and to provide, as appropriate, food, medicines and essential equipment for schools and hospitals, as well as to meet the emergency needs of the population in the drought-stricken areas of the country;

10. *Invites* the United Nations Development Programme, the United Nations Children's Fund, the World Food Programme, the World Health Organization, the United Nations Industrial Development Organization, the Food and Agriculture Organization of the United Nations, the World Bank and the International Fund for Agricultural Development to bring to the attention of their governing bodies, for their consideration, the special needs of the Central African Republic and to report the decisions of those bodies to the Secretary-General by 15 July 1985;

11. *Again draws the attention* of the international community to the special account opened by the Secretary-General at United Nations Headquarters, in accordance with General Assembly resolution 35/87, for the purpose of facilitating the channelling of contributions to the Central African Republic;

12. *Requests* the Secretary-General:

(*a*) To continue his efforts to organize a special emergency assistance programme with regard to food and health, especially medicaments, vaccines, hospital equipment, generating sets for field hospitals, water pumps and food products in order to help the vulnerable populations;

(*b*) To continue also his efforts to mobilize necessary resources for an effective programme of financial, technical and material assistance to the Central African Republic;

(*c*) To ensure that the necessary financial and budgetary arrangements are made to continue the organization of the international programme of assistance to the Central African Republic and the mobilization of that assistance;

(*d*) To keep the situation in the Central African Republic under constant review, to maintain close contact with Member States, specialized agencies, regional and other intergovernmental organizations and the international financial institutions concerned and to apprise the Economic and Social Council, at its second regular session of 1985, of the status of the special programme of economic assistance for the Central African Republic;

(*e*) To report on the progress made in the economic situation of the Central African Republic and in organizing and implementing the special programme of eco-nomic assistance for that country in time for the matter to be considered by the General Assembly at its fortieth session.

General Assembly resolution 39/180

17 December 1984   Meeting 103   Adopted without vote

Approved by Second Committee (A/39/793) without vote, 30 November (meeting 54); 39-nation draft (A/C.2/39/L.38), orally revised following informal consultations; agenda item 83 (*b*).

Sponsors: Benin, Cameroon, Cape Verde, Central African Republic, Chad, China, Comoros, Congo, Cyprus, Democratic Kampuchea, Djibouti, Egypt, Equatorial Guinea, Ethiopia, France, Gabon, Ghana, Guinea, Guinea-Bissau, Haiti, Japan, Lesotho, Liberia, Madagascar, Mali, Mauritania, Niger, Nigeria, Pakistan, Rwanda, Sao Tome and Principe, Sierra Leone, Swaziland, Thailand, Togo, Uganda, Yugoslavia, Zaire, Zambia.

Meeting numbers. GA 39th session: 2nd Committee 32-37, 45, 54; plenary 31, 103.

When the draft text was introduced in the Second Committee, Kuwait proposed an amendment[46] to paragraph 8 to delete mention of IFAD and specific non–United Nations regional, interregional and other intergovernmental and non-governmental organizations in its invitation to such bodies to consider establishing a programme of assistance to the Central African Republic. The Secretary later informed the Committee that, during informal consultations, it had been agreed that the text should be revised by inserting UNFPA in paragraph 7 and by replacing paragraph 8 with the text subsequently adopted. Kuwait then withdrew its amendment.

Chad

Chad, an LDC, had experienced civil unrest since 1965, which continued to affect the economic situation, the Secretary-General reported to the General Assembly in September 1984.[1] The very slight increase in GDP between 1980 and 1984 in nominal terms indicated that no real economic growth had taken place. As a result largely of an increased cotton harvest, which accounted for two thirds of export revenue, and a reduced import bill, Chad's trade balance moved from a deficit in 1983 to a small surplus in 1984. Food production generally fell in 1983/84, due in large part to the shortage of rain, but also to the displacement of people fleeing from combat zones. The food deficit for the 1983/84 season was estimated at 138,000 tonnes. In response to Chad's request to the international community for 57,000 tonnes of emergency assistance, 67,430 tonnes were pledged and, as at 31 May 1984, 16,208 tonnes had been received. The transport capacity for food was considered adequate, although there were operating problems for ferries on the Chari River and storage capacity needed to be expanded. Additional health supplies were also needed.

An emergency assistance programme for Chad consisting of 122 projects costing $341 million was drawn up. Of the total, 32 projects received funding, amounting to $107 million, 59 were considered as in the pipeline or as the subject of further negotiations with interested donors, and 31 were without response.

On 17 December, the Assembly, on the recommendation of the Second Committee, adopted resolution 39/195 without vote.

Special economic assistance to Chad

The General Assembly,

Recalling its resolution 38/214 of 20 December 1983 and its previous resolutions on assistance in the reconstruction, rehabilitation and development of Chad, emergency humanitarian assistance to Chad and special economic assistance to that country,

Having considered the reports of the Secretary-General on special economic assistance to Chad, relating, *inter alia*, to the economic and financial situation of Chad, the status of assistance provided for the rehabilitation and reconstruction of the country and the progress made in organizing and executing the programme of assistance for that country,

Gravely concerned by the unprecedented drought which is wreaking havoc in Chad at the present time, compounding the already precarious food and health situation and thus compromising all the country's efforts at reconstruction,

Considering that the drought has occasioned a massive displacement of population,

Taking note of the appeal of the Secretary-General dated 1 November 1984 and the numerous appeals launched by the Government of Chad and governmental and non-governmental organizations regarding the gravity of the food and health situation in Chad,

Considering that Chad is one of the least developed countries and therefore entitled to the benefits provided for in the various relevant resolutions of the General Assembly,

Recognizing the need for emergency humanitarian assistance to Chad,

Also recognizing the need for assistance in the reconstruction and development of Chad,

Taking note of the intention of the Government of Chad to organize in 1985, with the assistance of the United Nations Development Programme, a conference of donors and contributors of funds, as agreed at the International Conference on Assistance to Chad, held in November 1982,

1. *Expresses its gratitude* to the States and governmental and non-governmental organizations which responded and are continuing to respond generously to the appeals of the Government of Chad and of the Secretary-General by furnishing assistance to Chad;

2. *Further expresses its appreciation* to the Secretary-General for his efforts to make the international community aware of the difficulties of Chad and to mobilize assistance for that country;

3. *Appeals* to the international community to provide the necessary emergency humanitarian assistance to the people of Chad who have suffered from the war and the drought;

4. *Renews the request* made to States, appropriate organizations and programmes of the United Nations system and international economic and financial institutions to contribute to the rehabilitation and reconstruction of Chad;

5. *Again requests* the Administrator of the United Nations Development Programme to give all the necessary assistance to Chad for the preparation and organization of the conference of donors and contributors of funds, in accordance with General Assembly resolution 38/214;

6. *Invites* States and governmental and non-governmental organizations to take part in the conference of donors and contributors of funds and to accord particular attention to the projects to be presented there with a view to financing them;

7. *Requests* the Secretary-General:

(a) To continue his efforts to organize the special programme of economic assistance for Chad;

(b) To monitor, in close collaboration with the humanitarian agencies concerned, the humanitarian needs, particularly in the areas of food and health, of the people displaced by the war and the drought;

(c) To mobilize special humanitarian assistance for persons who have suffered as a result of the war and the drought and for the resettlement of displaced persons;

(d) To keep the situation in Chad under review and to report thereon to the General Assembly at its fortieth session.

General Assembly resolution 39/195

17 December 1984   Meeting 103   Adopted without vote

Approved by Second Committee (A/39/793) without vote, 30 November (meeting 54); 38-nation draft (A/C.2/39/L.60); agenda item 83 *(b)*.

Sponsors: Bangladesh, Burkina Faso, Burma, Burundi, Cameroon, Cape Verde, Central African Republic, Chad, Chile, China, Comoros, Democratic Kampuchea, Djibouti, Dominican Republic, Egypt, Equatorial Guinea, Ethiopia, France, Gabon, Gambia, Ghana, Guinea, Guinea-Bissau, Haiti, Italy, Japan, Liberia, Madagascar, Mali, Mozambique, Niger, Pakistan, Sierra Leone, Swaziland, Togo, United States, Vanuatu, Zaire.

Meeting numbers. GA 39th session: 2nd Committee 32-37, 45, 54; plenary 103.

Comoros

The Comoros, an archipelago country poor in natural resources, was unable to produce adequate food for its population of about 400,000 and relied on imports of upwards of 20,000 tonnes of rice annually, according to a September 1984 report of the Secretary-General.[1] Rapid population growth (3.5 per cent per annum) and long periods of drought exacerbated the situation. Lack of trained human resources in all sectors of the economy and inadequate health conditions and care were also factors. The primary sector—agriculture, animal husbandry, fisheries and forestry—employed more than 80 per cent of the active population and accounted for almost all export earnings. Those earnings depended heavily on a few cash crops subject to strong price fluctuations over which the country had no control.

The Government presented an investment programme for a 1983-1986 development plan to a donors' round table—the first international solidarity conference for the development of the Comoros—held at Moroni from 2 to 4 July 1984. The programme of 19 priority projects, estimated to cost $89.7 million, stressed food self-sufficiency, improvement of inter-island communications, energy, water supply, health programmes and training.

GENERAL ASSEMBLY ACTION

On 17 December, the Assembly, on the recommendation of the Second Committee, adopted resolution 39/193 without vote.

Assistance to the Comoros

The General Assembly,

Recalling its resolution 38/209 of 20 December 1983 and its previous resolutions on assistance to the Comoros, in which it appealed to the international community to provide effective and continuous financial, material and technical assistance to the Comoros in order to help that country overcome its financial and economic difficulties,

Taking note of the special problems confronting the Comoros as an island developing country and as one of the least developed countries,

Noting that the Government of the Comoros has given priority to the questions of infrastructure, transport and telecommunications,

Noting also the economic difficulties arising from the country's scarcity of natural resources, compounded by the recent drought and cyclones,

Noting further the grave budgetary and balance-of-payments problems facing the Comoros,

Bearing in mind the holding at Moroni, from 2 to 4 July 1984, of the first international solidarity conference for the development of the Comoros,

Having examined the summary report of the Secretary-General,

1. *Expresses its appreciation* to the Secretary-General for the steps he has taken to mobilize assistance for the Comoros;

2. *Notes with satisfaction* the response by various Member States, organizations of the United Nations system and other organizations to its appeals and those of the Secretary-General for assistance to the Comoros;

3. *Notes with concern,* however, that the assistance thus far provided continues to fall short of the country's urgent requirements and that assistance is still urgently required in order to implement the projects described in the report of the Secretary-General;

4. *Appeals* to those States and organizations which participated in the first international solidarity conference for the development of the Comoros, to put into effect as soon as possible their declaration of intent;

5. *Renews its appeal* to Member States, the appropriate organs, programmes and organizations of the United Nations system, regional and international organizations and other intergovernmental bodies and non-governmental organizations, as well as international financial institutions, to provide the Comoros with assistance to enable it to cope with its difficult economic situation and pursue its development goals;

6. *Requests* the appropriate programmes and organizations of the United Nations system to increase their current programmes of assistance to the Comoros, to co-operate closely with the Secretary-General in organizing an effective international programme of assistance and to report periodically to him on the steps they have taken and the resources they have made available to help that country;

7. *Requests* the Secretary-General:

(a) To continue his efforts to mobilize the necessary resources for an effective programme of financial,

technical and material assistance to the Comoros;

(b) To keep the situation in the Comoros under constant review, to maintain close contact with Member States, the specialized agencies, the regional and other intergovernmental organizations and international financial institutions concerned, and to apprise the Economic and Social Council, at its second regular session of 1985, of the status of the special programme of economic assistance for the Comoros;

(c) To report on the evolution of the economic situation of the Comoros and the progress made in organizing and implementing the special programme of economic assistance for that country in time for the matter to be considered by the General Assembly at its fortieth session.

General Assembly resolution 39/193

17 December 1984   Meeting 103   Adopted without vote

Approved by Second Committee (A/39/793) without vote, 30 November (meeting 54); 38-nation draft (A/C.2/39/L.57); agenda item 83 (b).

Sponsors: Angola, Bahamas, Bangladesh, Burkina Faso, Central African Republic, Chad, China, Colombia, Comoros, Congo, Cyprus, Democratic Kampuchea, Djibouti, Egypt, Ethiopia, France, Gabon, Ghana, Guinea, Guinea-Bissau, Indonesia, Ivory Coast, Japan, Liberia, Madagascar, Malawi, Morocco, Niger, Oman, Pakistan, Sao Tome and Principe, Senegal, Singapore, Somalia, Sudan, Thailand, United Republic of Tanzania, United States.

Meeting numbers. GA 39th session: 2nd Committee 32-37, 45, 54; plenary 103.

Djibouti

Djibouti, an LDC not endowed with many natural resources, continued in 1984 to suffer from a prolonged drought; in order to assess the situation, the Secretary-General sent a mission there as requested by the Economic and Social Council in resolution 1984/6 (see p. 513). As it almost totally lacked an agricultural sector, Djibouti needed to import practically all its foodstuffs, according to a September report of the Secretary-General.[1] Other factors contributing to its fragile economic situation were a high population growth rate (3 per cent) and a continuing influx of refugees (approximately 15,000, or nearly 5 per cent of the Djibouti population), most of whom were drought victims from Ethiopia and Somalia. Nevertheless, by the end of 1984, the slowing down of the Djibouti economy appeared to have ceased.

The Government estimated the GDP growth rate for 1984 at 0.6 per cent. While the per capita GDP was estimated at $450 for the year, the expatriate community accounted for a sizeable share of GDP and, given the population growth, real per capita income declined. Djibouti's balance of payments continued to decline in 1984. Almost all exports and imports reflected activities of non-residents, since most products merely passed through Djibouti, thus making minimal contribution to the economy. Less than 50 per cent of the recorded imports were for the consumption of Djiboutians; most were sent to a French military base. The decline in export earnings was also due to budgetary constraints exercised by France with regard to its activities in Djibouti and to the appreciation of the Djibouti franc in relation to the French franc.

A special investment programme of 117 projects amounting to $570 million was drawn up at a round-table of development partners held in Djibouti in November 1983.[47] As of mid-1984, 93 had been funded; the remainder had either been partially funded or were under negotiation with potential donors.

GENERAL ASSEMBLY ACTION

On the recommendation of the Second Committee, the Assembly on 17 December adopted resolution 39/200 without vote.

Assistance to Djibouti

The General Assembly,

Recalling its resolution 38/213 of 20 December 1983 and its previous resolutions on assistance to Djibouti, in which it drew the attention of the international community to the critical economic situation confronting Djibouti and to the country's urgent need for assistance,

Deeply concerned at the adverse effects of the prolonged drought on the economic and social development of Djibouti,

Recalling also its resolution 37/176 of 17 December 1982, in which it called upon the international community to continue to support the efforts made by the Government of Djibouti to cope with the needs of the refugee population,

Bearing in mind its resolution 37/133 of 17 December 1982, in which it decided to include Djibouti in the list of the least developed countries,

Having examined the summary report of the Secretary-General,

Noting the critical economic situation of Djibouti and the list of urgent and priority projects formulated by the Government that require international assistance,

1. *Expresses its appreciation* to the Secretary-General for the steps he has taken to organize an international programme of economic assistance for Djibouti;

2. *Notes with appreciation* the assistance already provided or pledged to Djibouti by Member States, organizations of the United Nations system and other organizations;

3. *Draws the attention* of the international community to the difficult economic situation confronting Djibouti and to the severe structural constraints to its development;

4. *Renews its appeal* to Member States, the appropriate organs, organizations and programmes of the United Nations system, regional and international organizations and other intergovernmental bodies and non-governmental organizations, as well as international financial institutions, to provide assistance bilaterally and multilaterally, as appropriate, to Djibouti in order to enable it to cope with its difficult economic situation and to implement its development strategies, including the programme of assistance that was presented at the round-table of development partners convened by the Government of Djibouti in November 1983;

5. *Appeals* to the international community to provide financial, material and technical assistance, as a matter of urgency, to alleviate the sufferings of the population affected by drought and for the implementation of the drought-related projects and programmes;

6. *Requests* the appropriate specialized agencies and other organizations of the United Nations system to maintain and increase their current and future programmes of assistance to Djibouti, to co-operate closely with the Secretary-General in organizing an effective international programme

of assistance and to report periodically to him on the steps they have taken and the resources they have made available to help that country;

7. *Requests* the Secretary-General:

(*a*) To continue his efforts to mobilize the necessary resources for an effective programme of financial, technical and material assistance to Djibouti;

(*b*) To keep the situation in Djibouti under constant review, to maintain close contact with Member States, the specialized agencies, regional and other intergovernmental organizations and the international financial institutions concerned, and to apprise the Economic and Social Council, at its second regular session of 1985, of the current status of the special programme of economic assistance for Djibouti;

(*c*) To report on the progress made in the economic situation of Djibouti and in organizing and implementing the special programme of economic assistance for that country in time for the matter to be considered by the General Assembly at its fortieth session.

General Assembly resolution 39/200

17 December 1984   Meeting 103   Adopted without vote

Approved by Second Committee (A/39/793) without vote, 30 November (meeting 54); 31-nation draft (A/C.2/39/L.65); agenda item 83 *(b)*.

Sponsors: Algeria, Bahrain, Bangladesh, Benin, Central African Republic, Chad, Comoros, Democratic Yemen, Djibouti, Ethiopia, Ghana, Guinea-Bissau, Japan, Jordan, Kuwait, Lebanon, Liberia, Libyan Arab Jamahiriya, Madagascar, Mali, Mauritania, Oman, Pakistan, Qatar, Saudi Arabia, Senegal, Sierra Leone, Somalia, Tunisia, Uganda, Yemen.

Meeting numbers. GA 39th session: 2nd Committee 32-37, 47, 54; plenary 103.

In a related text, the Assembly, in resolution 39/205, urged the establishment of an assistance programme for six drought-stricken countries of East Africa, including Djibouti.

Equatorial Guinea

Equatorial Guinea, an LDC with a climate and soil suited to food production, had communications and transportation problems due to its geographical situation and a literacy rate believed to be about 30 per cent, according to the Secretary-General's September 1984 report.[1]

Outstanding external public debt was estimated at $90 million, some 50 per cent more than estimated GDP. Total debt was about six times the value of exports. Main export crops were cocoa, timber and coffee.

The majority of projects in the country's 1982-1984 programme presented to a donors' conference in 1982[48] had been funded, although some sectors, particularly water and sanitation, had received practically no funding.

GENERAL ASSEMBLY ACTION

On 17 December, the Assembly, on the recommendation of the Second Committee, adopted resolution 39/181 without vote.

Assistance for the reconstruction, rehabilitation and development of Equatorial Guinea

The General Assembly,

Recalling its resolutions 35/105 of 5 December 1980,

36/204 of 17 December 1981 and 37/133 of 17 December 1982,

Recalling also its resolution 38/224 of 20 December 1983, in which it appealed to all Member States to respond generously, through bilateral or multilateral channels, to the reconstruction and development needs of Equatorial Guinea as presented at the International Conference of Donors for the Economic Reactivation and Development of Equatorial Guinea, and called upon regional and interregional organizations and other intergovernmental and non-governmental organizations, as well as international financial and development institutions, to give urgent consideration to the establishment of a programme of assistance to Equatorial Guinea or, where one was already in existence, to its expansion in accordance with the programme established by the International Conference of Donors,

Recalling further that Equatorial Guinea is one of the least developed countries,

Having considered the summary report of the Secretary-General, submitted pursuant to General Assembly resolution 38/224,

Noting with concern that Equatorial Guinea continues to be beset by serious economic and financial difficulties, and continues to suffer from a food situation made precarious by the absence of large-scale food-crop production projects,

Recognizing once again the essential role of both short-term and long-term international assistance in support of the efforts of the Government of Equatorial Guinea in the difficult task of reconstruction, rehabilitation and development of the country,

Bearing in mind the statement made by the Minister of State in charge of External Affairs and Co-operation of Equatorial Guinea, on 11 October 1984, on the progress achieved in the sphere of regional co-operation,

Recognizing the efforts made by the Government and people of Equatorial Guinea towards the internal economic recovery and the social development of the country,

1. *Reaffirms* its resolution 38/224 and other relevant resolutions and calls for their implementation;

2. *Takes note* of the summary report of the Secretary-General;

3. *Expresses its thanks* to the Secretary-General for his efforts to organize and mobilize the necessary resources for an effective programme of assistance to Equatorial Guinea;

4. *Reiterates its appeal* to all Member States to continue to respond generously, through bilateral or multilateral channels, so as to meet, in full, the needs indicated in the 1982-1984 three-year programme presented in 1982 at the International Conference of Donors for the Economic Reactivation and Development of Equatorial Guinea;

5. *Notes* the entry of Equatorial Guinea into the Central African Customs and Economic Union and the Bank of Central African States;

6. *Expresses its thanks* to States and international, regional and interregional organizations and other intergovernmental organizations for their assistance to Equatorial Guinea;

7. *Earnestly calls upon* all Member States and international and regional organizations and other intergovernmental organizations, as well as international financial and development institutions and appropriate programmes of the United Nations system, especially the United Nations Development Programme and the United Nations Institute for Training and Research, to establish, maintain and expand their programmes of assistance to Equatorial Guinea, particularly in the areas of public administration and public finance in which a general transformation is required as a result of Equatorial Guinea's entry into the Central African Customs and Economic Union and the Bank of Central African States;

8. *Requests* the Secretary-General:

(a) To intensify his efforts to mobilize the necessary resources for an effective programme of financial, technical and material assistance to Equatorial Guinea;

(b) To keep the situation in Equatorial Guinea under review, to maintain close contact with Member States, the specialized agencies, regional and other intergovernmental organizations and competent international financial institutions and to apprise the Economic and Social Council, at its second regular session of 1985, of the status of assistance to Equatorial Guinea;

(c) To submit to the General Assembly at its fortieth session a report on the economic situation of Equatorial Guinea and the progress made in implementing the present resolution;

9. *Also requests* the Secretary-General to include in his report, in close collaboration with the Administrator of the United Nations Development Programme, information on the response of the international community to the 1982-1984 three-year programme presented at the International Conference of Donors for the Economic Reactivation and Development of Equatorial Guinea.

General Assembly resolution 39/181

17 December 1984   Meeting 103   Adopted without vote

Approved by Second Committee (A/39/793) without vote, 30 November (meeting 54); 35-nation draft (A/C.2/39/L.39), orally revised following informal consultations; agenda item 83 *(b)*.

Sponsors: Afghanistan, Argentina, Bahamas, Barbados, Burundi, Cameroon, Central African Republic, Chad, Congo, Democratic Kampuchea, Dominican Republic, Egypt, El Salvador, Equatorial Guinea, Ethiopia, France, Gabon, Ghana, Guinea, Guinea-Bissau, Indonesia, Kenya, Liberia, Madagascar, Morocco, Nigeria, Pakistan, Panama, Somalia, Spain, Sudan, Tunisia, United Republic of Tanzania, Uruguay.

Meeting numbers. GA 39th session: 2nd Committee 32-37, 44, 54; plenary 31, 103.

After the draft resolution was presented, the Secretary informed the Second Committee that, during informal consultations, it had been agreed that paragraph 8 *(c)*—originally asking the Secretary-General to include in his 1985 report, in particular, the international community's response to the three-year programme presented at the 1982 donors' conference—would be divided into two paragraphs, 8 *(c)* and 9.

Gambia

The Gambia, an LDC, had an annual population growth rate of 3.5 per cent. Per capita GDP for 1983/84 was estimated at $280, a decline of 13 per cent from 1982/83. About 80 per cent of the population depended on agriculture for its livelihood. The 1983/84 fiscal year was the poorest agricultural season since 1978/79, although the impact of the drought varied greatly from crop to crop. Ground-nuts, the principal source of income (normally 85 to 90 per cent of export earnings), were subject to fluctuations in production and prices due to weather and world demand. The UNDP Administrator observed in a 1985 report[44] that the situation was exacerbated by an increase in imports which affected the country's balance of payments, and by reduced government revenue. Financing required to cover the deficit amounted to 15 per cent of GDP in 1983/84. Local food production normally covered about 70 per cent of the country's requirements; some 35,000 tonnes of cereals, mainly rice, were imported annually.

In 1983/84, drought was even more severe than in previous years, with rainfall at 50 per cent of the normal level, resulting in a loss of about half of the Gambia's cereal production. Following the Government's appeal in August 1983 for food assistance,[49] food pledges were made; however, as at May 1984, a deficit of 10,657 tonnes of cereals remained to be met.

In his September report on special programmes of economic assistance,[1] the Secretary-General mentioned that six projects worth $18.5 million, which had been recommended for aid in 1982,[50] had received no external funding.

A round-table donors' conference, held at Banjul in November 1984 with UNDP assistance, endorsed recommendations for follow-up activities and co-ordination. The donors expressed interest in specific projects, and/or made commitments to give support.

GENERAL ASSEMBLY ACTION

On the recommendation of the Second Committee, the Assembly, on 17 December, adopted resolution 39/203 without vote.

Assistance to the Gambia

The General Assembly,

Recalling its resolution 38/212 of 20 December 1983, in which it, *inter alia,* noted that the Gambia is a least developed country with acute economic and social problems arising from its weak economic infrastructure and that it also suffers from many of the serious problems common to countries of the Sahelian region, notably drought and desertification,

Having considered the summary report of the Secretary-General, in which the recent economic situation in the Gambia is described,

Concerned that the Gambia continues to encounter serious balance-of-payments and budgetary problems and noting that the lack of domestic resources is the most important constraint on development, since the Government lacks the funds to meet the counterpart costs of donor-assisted projects,

Noting that external assistance is still required to enable the Government of the Gambia to implement the six projects recommended by the Secretary-General in his report,

Aware that a round-table conference of donors was held in the Gambia in November 1984, with the assistance of the United Nations Development Programme, to discuss the country's development needs and to consider ways and means of helping the Government in its efforts to meet those needs,

1. *Takes note* of the summary report of the Secretary-General;

2. *Expresses its appreciation* to the Secretary-General for the steps he has taken to mobilize assistance for the Gambia;

3. *Expresses its appreciation also* to those States and organizations that have provided assistance to the Gambia;

4. *Draws the attention* of the international community to the need for assistance for the projects and programmes identified by the Secretary-General in his report;

5. *Renews its urgent appeal* to Member States, specialized agencies and other organizations of the United Nations system, regional and interregional organizations and other intergovernmental and non-governmental organizations, as well as international development and financial institutions, to give generous assistance to the Gambia, through bilateral or multilateral channels, and to provide financial, technical and material assistance for the implementation of the projects and programmes recommended by the Secretary-General in his report;

6. *Urges* donors, as appropriate, to provide financial assistance to the Gambia to help meet the local counterpart costs of externally assisted projects, bearing in mind that the Gambia is classified as a least developed drought-stricken country;

7. *Urges* Member States, organizations and programmes of the United Nations system, regional and interregional bodies, financial and development institutions, as well as intergovernmental and non-governmental organizations, to respond generously to the needs of the Gambia at the round-table conference of donors held in November 1984;

8. *Requests* the appropriate organizations and programmes of the United Nations system—in particular the United Nations Development Programme, the United Nations Children's Fund, the United Nations Fund for Population Activities, the World Food Programme, the World Health Organization, the United Nations Industrial Development Organization, the Food and Agriculture Organization of the United Nations and the International Fund for Agricultural Development—to increase their current and future programmes of assistance to the Gambia, to co-operate closely with the Secretary-General in organizing an effective international programme of assistance and to report periodically to him on the steps they have taken and the resources they have made available to assist that country;

9. *Invites* the United Nations Development Programme, the United Nations Children's Fund, the World Food Programme, the World Health Organization, the United Nations Industrial Development Organization, the Food and Agriculture Organization of the United Nations, the World Bank and the International Fund for Agricultural Development to bring to the attention of their governing bodies, for their consideration, the special needs of the Gambia and to report the decisions of those bodies to the Secretary-General by the end of June 1985;

10. *Requests* the Secretary-General:

(a) To continue his efforts to mobilize the necessary resources for an effective programme of financial, technical and material assistance to the Gambia;

(b) To keep the situation in the Gambia under constant review, to maintain close contact with Member States, the specialized agencies, regional and other intergovernmental organizations and the international financial institutions concerned, and to apprise the Economic and Social Council, at its second regular session of 1985, of the status of the special programme of economic assistance for the Gambia;

(c) To report on the progress made in the economic situation of the Gambia and in organizing and implementing the special programme of economic assistance for that country in time for the matter to be considered by the General Assembly at its fortieth session.

General Assembly resolution 39/203

17 December 1984   Meeting 103   Adopted without vote

Approved by Second Committee (A/39/793) without vote, 30 November (meeting 54); 20-nation draft (A/C.2/39/L.71), orally revised following informal consultations; agenda item 83 *(b)*.

Sponsors: Algeria, Bangladesh, Ethiopia, Gambia, Ghana, Guinea, Guinea-Bissau, Lesotho, Liberia, Madagascar, Mali, Niger, Nigeria, Pakistan, Saint Lucia, Senegal, Sierra Leone, Somalia, United Arab Emirates, United States.

Meeting numbers. GA 39th session: 2nd Committee 32-37, 47, 54; plenary 103.

Before approval of the resolution in the Second Committee, the Secretary informed the members that, during informal consultations, it had been agreed to add UNFPA in paragraph 8 and to invite organizations mentioned in paragraph 9 to report by the end of June 1985, rather than by 1985.

Ghana

In 1984, Ghana experienced its first solid economic gains since 1978. Normal weather ended three consecutive years of drought, and food production increased. Food prices declined and the high inflation rate of 1983 (over 174 per cent at one time) decreased to 23 per cent by August 1984. Hydroelectric power was restored, resulting in increased industrial production. After three years of decline, trade volume increased in 1984, even though it was still only slightly more than 50 per cent of that of 1980. Imports increased, but were insufficient to meet the need for raw materials, spare parts and equipment required for Ghana's economic recovery programme.

The Secretary-General reported[12] that special economic assistance provided to Ghana by the United Nations system was for mining, population statistics and development planning by DTCD; technologies for rural women by ILO; logistics arrangements at ports, distribution networks and storage facilities by UNDRO and ILO; agricultural development by IFAD; industrial planning and programming in the brick and tile industries by UNDP and UNIDO; water supply, planning and formal education by UNICEF; emergency food aid and development projects by WFP; forest energy resources and natural resources development, agricultural planification, forestry, crops, agricultural statistics and rural development by FAO; maritime training by IMO; postal services fellowships by UPU; civil aviation training and equipment by ICAO; financial data compilation and processing by IMF; and loans for oil refinery and export rehabilitation and oil palm projects by the World Bank.

UNDP helped co-ordinate aid with regard to Ghana's 1984-1986 emergency economic recovery programme, which focused on rebuilding infrastructure and mobilizing traditional exports: cocoa, timber and gold. Following a mid-term review in November 1984, it was agreed that the programme needed some reorientation, with the major focus of UNDP assistance shifting to rural development and planning. A consultative group meeting of the World Bank was held in Paris in December to mobilize resources for Ghana, and donors expressed support for its economic recovery programme, launched in April 1983.[51]

Guinea

Guinea, an LDC, grew at a relatively low rate of 2.3 per cent per annum since 1980, reflecting a deterioration in the health situation. As a direct consequence, there had been an increase in the infant mortality rate to almost 200 per 1,000 in 1983, the highest in the world. Per capita GDP was estimated at $270. The rural sector accounted for 37.9 per cent of GDP, but the agricultural output had not ensured food self-sufficiency. Apart from mining, Guinea's development had been based solely on the public sector. Public enterprises were producing at less than 15 per cent of capacity and registered heavy losses.

The Secretary-General, in a November 1984 report on assistance to Guinea,[6] said that Guinea, on 8 June, had requested emergency aid from the international community. In July, the Economic and Social Council had asked him, in consultation with Guinea, to organize an assistance mission.

ECONOMIC AND SOCIAL COUNCIL ACTION

On 26 July, the Economic and Social Council adopted resolution 1984/59 without vote. It acted on the recommendation of its Third (Programme and Co-ordination) Committee.

Critical situation in Guinea

The Economic and Social Council,

Noting the statement made on 18 July 1984 before the Third (Programme and Co-ordination) Committee of the Council by the Minister for Planning and Statistics of Guinea concerning the difficult situation of his country, characterized by a subsistence economy, a lack of infrastructure, a low per capita income, a chronic deficit in the State budget and a very heavy foreign debt,

Noting also the reference by the Minister to the letter dated 8 June 1984 from the Head of State of Guinea to the Secretary-General, describing the social and economic situation of his country and requesting emergency aid from the international community and the United Nations in the economic, social and humanitarian fields,

Confirming the urgent need for international action to assist the Government of Guinea in its national reconstruction and rehabilitation efforts, taking account of the fact that Guinea is classified as one of the least developed countries,

1. *Appeals urgently* to all Member States and to intergovernmental and non-governmental organizations and international financial institutions to contribute generously to the reconstruction and rehabilitation of Guinea;

2. *Requests* the organizations and bodies of the United Nations system to expand their programmes of assistance to Guinea and to co-operate closely with the Secretary-General in organizing an effective international programme of assistance;

3. *Requests* the Secretary-General, in consultation with the Government of Guinea, to organize a programme of social, economic and humanitarian assistance to support the actions of the Government with a view to discharging the urgent tasks of national reconstruction and rehabilitation;

4. *Invites* the Secretary-General, after consultation with the Government of Guinea, to report to the General Assembly, at its thirty-ninth session, the requisite information concerning the action to be taken or the proposals to be made with a view to providing the necessary aid to the Government of Guinea.

Economic and Social Council resolution 1984/59

26 July 1984	Meeting 49	Adopted without vote

Approved by Third Committee (E/1984/148) without vote, 23 July (meeting 15); 5-nation draft (E/1984/C.3/L.8), orally corrected; agenda item 18.
Sponsors: Bangladesh, France, Pakistan, Senegal for African Group, United States.

Secretary-General's report. Pursuant to the Council's 26 July resolution, the Secretary-General sent a mission to Guinea from 19 to 24 August and submitted its report to the Assembly in November.[6] The mission, led by the Assistant Administrator of UNDP and Regional Director, Regional Bureau for Africa, surveyed the economic situation, described the country's economic policies and development strategies, and made recommendations for follow-up action. It concluded that Guinea, despite its diverse natural resources, had been suffering for many years from a decline in agricultural production, especially food; deterioration of social services, especially education and health care; losses in government revenues and foreign exchange; inefficient operation of many State enterprises; and inefficient administration. Causes included an unofficial market which provided 80 per cent of consumer goods, the world economic recession, the fall in prices of raw materials, an overly centralized government apparatus, drought, and the mass influx of Guinean refugees who were returning after liberalization measures were instituted in April 1984 by the new Government. In order to rehabilitate

the economy, and with the help of the World Bank and IMF, the Government had introduced economic, monetary and social reforms.

The per capita GDP of Guinea was $270, one of the lowest in the world. Since 1980, the annual growth rate of per capita GDP had been declining, decreasing by 20 per cent in 1983.

The mission recommended a two-pronged approach by the international community to help Guinea: a 12-month emergency humanitarian assistance programme to provide food, veterinary products, pharmaceuticals, school supplies and laboratory equipment; and a 1985-1987 interim programme of economic rehabilitation to restore productive capacity, provide essential services, promote the private sector and improve government performance. The mission proposed that once the Government's request had been reviewed by the specialized agencies, the Secretary-General should appeal for donations to cover the emergency programme. The Government would also require technical assistance in economic and administrative planning. In addition, the mission recommended that a second mission, in which UNDP, DTCD and the World Bank were represented, visit Guinea to help it programme the external assistance requirements and prepare an interim programme of key technical assistance needs. A joint UNDP/World Bank mission to Guinea in October defined more precisely the Government's needs in technical assistance, equipment and logistic support for preparing the interim programme.

GENERAL ASSEMBLY ACTION

Addressing the General Assembly on 4 October, Guinea said the end of a 26-year régime on 3 April 1984 had left Guinea facing a disastrous economic situation, with the public treasury depleted and a people discouraged by the prospect of a future lacking food, hospitals, medicines, schools, decent housing, transport and good roads, a people whose needs were immense. He pointed out that, in the framework of open and mutually beneficial co-operation, a new investment code, which provided sufficient incentive, had recently been prepared and published.

The Assembly, acting without vote on the recommendation of the Second Committee, adopted resolution 39/202 on 17 December.

Economic and financial assistance to Guinea
The General Assembly,

Having considered the report of the Secretary-General on assistance to Guinea,

Recalling Economic and Social Council resolution 1984/59 of 26 July 1984, in which the Council confirmed the urgent need for international action to assist the Government of Guinea in its efforts to bring about national reconstruction, rehabilitation and development,

Noting the statement made by the Minister for Foreign Affairs of Guinea on 4 October 1984, in which he described his country's serious socio-economic and financial problems,

Noting with concern the grave balance-of-payments problems facing Guinea,

Deeply concerned by the weakness and underdevelopment of Guinea's economic and social infrastructure, which constitutes a major obstacle to the country's economic development and to raising the living standard of its population,

Taking note, in this context, of the results of the United Nations Conference on the Least Developed Countries, in particular the Substantial New Programme of Action for the 1980s for the Least Developed Countries,

Recalling that Guinea is one of the least developed countries,

1. *Takes note* of the report of the Secretary-General;

2. *Expresses its gratitude* for the support which Member States, specialized agencies and other United Nations bodies and regional organizations have provided to assist the people of Guinea in their reconstruction and rehabilitation efforts;

3. *Appeals urgently* to all Member States, specialized agencies and other United Nations bodies, as well as to international economic and financial institutions and other aid donors, to contribute generously, through bilateral or multilateral channels, to the reconstruction, rehabilitation and development of Guinea;

4. *Requests* the Secretary-General to continue his efforts and to mobilize financial, technical and economic assistance from the international community for Guinea, so as to enable it to meet its short-term and long-term needs within the framework of its development programme;

5. *Invites* the United Nations Development Programme, the World Health Organization, the Food and Agriculture Organization of the United Nations, the United Nations Educational, Scientific and Cultural Organization, the World Bank, the International Fund for Agricultural Development, the United Nations Children's Fund and the World Food Programme to bring to the attention of their governing bodies, for priority consideration, the special needs of Guinea, and to keep the Secretary-General informed of decisions taken in that regard;

6. *Requests* the Secretary-General to apprise the Economic and Social Council, at its second regular session of 1985, and the General Assembly, at its fortieth session, of the results achieved in the implementation of the present resolution.

General Assembly resolution 39/202

17 December 1984   Meeting 103   Adopted without vote

Approved by Second Committee (A/39/793) without vote, 30 November (meeting 54); 50-nation draft (A/C.2/39/L.69), orally revised, following informal consultations; agenda item 83 (b).

Sponsors: Afghanistan, Algeria, Argentina, Bangladesh, Benin, Burkina Faso, Cameroon, Cape Verde, Central African Republic, Chad, China, Comoros, Congo, Democratic Kampuchea, Egypt, Equatorial Guinea, Ethiopia, France, Gabon, Gambia, Ghana, Guatemala, Guinea, Guinea-Bissau, Haiti, India, Japan, Lesotho, Liberia, Madagascar, Mali, Mauritania, Morocco, Nepal, Nicaragua, Niger, Nigeria, Pakistan, Romania, Sao Tome and Principe, Senegal, Sierra Leone, Spain, Sudan, Togo, Tunisia, Uganda, United Republic of Tanzania, Yugoslavia, Zaire.

Meeting numbers. GA 39th session: 2nd Committee 32-37, 47, 54; plenary 21, 103.

Following informal consultations, the Secretary informed the Second Committee that it had been agreed to revise paragraph 6 by specifying the Coun-

cil's second 1985 session. On 28 December, the Secretary-General appealed to Member States to contribute to an emergency humanitarian assistance programme for Guinea.

Guinea-Bissau

In May 1984, the first round-table donors' conference for assistance to Guinea-Bissau was organized at Lisbon, Portugal, for which UNDP, UNCTAD and DTCD helped in the preparations. Some $2.1 million of UNDP indicative planning figure resources were expended on projects for the country, a drought-stricken LDC. Other United Nations assistance was provided in several areas, including: dam building, electricity, public finance, development planning and training for civil servants by DTCD; water supply by UNICEF and UNCHS; medical and paramedical personnel training, family health, sex education, and maternal and child health statistics by UNFPA; food development projects and emergency operations by WFP; agricultural planning, seed improvement, fisheries, livestock, food security, and development of natural resources by FAO; funding for transportation by the World Bank and IDA; studies on manufacturing by UNIDO; training in civil aviation, airport improvement and supply of equipment by ICAO; vocational training by ILO; rice development by IFAD; banking expertise by IMF; and navigation and ship maintenance by IMO.

GENERAL ASSEMBLY ACTION

On 17 December, the Assembly, on the recommendation of the Second Committee, adopted resolution 39/186 without vote.

Special economic assistance to Guinea-Bissau

The General Assembly,

Recalling its resolution 35/95 of 5 December 1980, in which it renewed its appeal to the international community to continue to provide effective financial, material and technical assistance to Guinea-Bissau to help it overcome its financial and economic difficulties and to permit the implementation of the projects and programmes recommended by the Secretary-General in his report submitted pursuant to General Assembly resolution 34/121 of 14 December 1979,

Recalling also its resolution 36/217 of 17 December 1981,

Recalling further its resolution 3339(XXIX) of 17 December 1974, in which it invited Member States to provide economic assistance to the then newly independent State of Guinea-Bissau, and its resolutions 32/100 of 13 December 1977 and 33/124 of 19 December 1978, in which it, *inter alia*, expressed deep concern at the gravity of the economic situation in Guinea-Bissau and appealed to the international community to provide financial and economic assistance to that country,

Recalling that Guinea-Bissau is one of the least developed countries,

Noting with concern that Guinea-Bissau continues to experience serious economic and financial difficulties,

Noting also with concern that the gross national product of Guinea-Bissau has decreased in real terms, that the balance-of-payments deficit continues to rise, that the external debt is imposing a heavy burden on the country's fragile economy and that the budget deficit has also grown substantially,

Noting that Guinea-Bissau is one of the drought-stricken countries,

Noting also that Guinea-Bissau continues to have problems in supplying staple foodstuffs to satisfy the needs of its population,

Noting with satisfaction the main features of the first four-year development plan (1983-1986) of Guinea-Bissau and the implementation of the 1983-1984 stabilization programme,

Also noting with satisfaction the results of the round-table conference of donors for Guinea-Bissau, held at Lisbon in May 1984,

1. *Expresses its appreciation* to the Secretary-General for the steps he has taken to mobilize assistance for Guinea-Bissau;

2. *Draws the attention* of the international community to the assistance required for implementing the projects and programmes submitted at the round-table conference;

3. *Expresses its gratitude* to the Member States and international organizations concerned for the food aid generously provided to Guinea-Bissau;

4. *Expresses its gratitude* to the States and organizations that have responded to the appeal of Guinea-Bissau and to the appeals of the Secretary-General by providing assistance to Guinea-Bissau;

5. *Renews its urgent appeal* to Member States, regional and interregional organizations and other intergovernmental organizations to continue to provide financial, material and technical assistance to Guinea-Bissau to help it overcome its economic and financial difficulties and to permit the implementation of the projects and programmes specified in its first four-year development plan;

6. *Urges* Member States, United Nations bodies, regional and interregional bodies, financing and development institutions and governmental and non-governmental organizations to respond very generously and urgently to the needs of Guinea-Bissau in accordance with the dialogue held between Guinea-Bissau and its partners at the round-table conference of donors;

7. *Appeals* to the international community to contribute to the special account opened by the Secretary-General at United Nations Headquarters, in accordance with General Assembly resolution 32/100, in order to facilitate the payment of contributions for Guinea-Bissau;

8. *Invites* the United Nations Development Programme, the United Nations Children's Fund, the World Food Programme, the World Health Organization, the Food and Agriculture Organization of the United Nations, the World Bank and the International Fund for Agricultural Development to bring to the attention of their governing bodies, for their consideration, the special and pressing needs of Guinea-Bissau and to report the decisions of those bodies to the Secretary-General before 15 July 1985;

9. *Requests* the specialized agencies and other appropriate United Nations bodies to report periodically to the Secretary-General on the steps they have taken and the resources they have made available to assist Guinea-Bissau;

10. *Requests* the Secretary-General:

(a) To continue his efforts to mobilize the necessary resources for an effective programme of financial, technical and material assistance to Guinea-Bissau;

(b) To keep the situation in Guinea-Bissau under constant review, to maintain close contact with Member States, specialized agencies, regional and other intergovernmental organizations and the international financial institutions concerned, and to apprise the Economic and Social Council, at its second regular session of 1985, of the status of the special programme of economic assistance for Guinea-Bissau;

11. *Also requests* the Secretary-General to carry out, in close collaboration with the Administrator of the United Nations Development Programme, an evaluation of the results of the round-table conference of donors and of the progress made in organizing and implementing the special programme of economic assistance for Guinea-Bissau, in time for the status of this programme to be considered by the General Assembly at its fortieth session.

General Assembly resolution 39/186

17 December 1984   Meeting 103   Adopted without vote

Approved by Second Committee (A/39/793) without vote, 30 November (meeting 54); 47-nation draft (A/C.2/39/L.44), orally revised following informal consultations; agenda item 83 *(b)*.

Sponsors: Algeria, Angola, Bahamas, Bangladesh, Benin, Brazil, Burkina Faso, Cameroon, Cape Verde, Chad, Comoros, Congo, Cuba, Djibouti, Equatorial Guinea, Ethiopia, France, Gabon, Ghana, Guinea, Guinea-Bissau, Haiti, India, Italy, Japan, Liberia, Libyan Arab Jamahiriya, Madagascar, Mali, Mauritania, Mongolia, Mozambique, Nicaragua, Niger, Nigeria, Pakistan, Portugal, Rwanda, Sao Tome and Principe, Senegal, Sudan, Thailand, Togo, Vanuatu, Yugoslavia, Zaire, Zambia.

Meeting numbers. GA 39th session: 2nd Committee 32-37, 45, 54; plenary 103.

The draft was orally revised in informal consultations in the Second Committee. The Secretary said it had been agreed that a provision originally designated as paragraph 10 *(c)* would be reformulated as paragraph 11. The original text had not mentioned the collaboration of the UNDP Administrator.

Lesotho

The Secretary-General arranged for a mission to Lesotho from 14 to 20 May 1984, led by the Joint Co-ordinator for Special Economic Assistance Programmes, in response to the Assembly's 1983 request[52] that he consult the Government on the question of migrant workers returning from South Africa, continue to mobilize resources for assistance, and report on the economic situation of Lesotho and on the special programme of economic assistance. The mission's report was submitted by the Secretary-General to the Assembly in September 1984.[7]

The mission noted that, with a per capita income of less than $300 per year, Lesotho was regarded by the United Nations as an LDC. Lesotho's size, geographical position and limited natural resources resulted in heavy dependence on South Africa, a country with whose social and political policies it was in basic disagreement. Lesotho bought capital and consumer goods, including much of its grain supply, from South Africa. Income earned by migrant miners and other workers in South Africa was equal to or greater than the income generated within the country. The two major goals of Lesotho's development policy were to reduce its dependence on South Africa and to improve the well-being of its people. The 1980-1985 development programme focused on promoting high-value crops, improving livestock, expanding irrigation, broadening the export base, import substitution, and diversifying markets, credit facilities and marketing channels. The most serious constraints on development remained Lesotho's geopolitical situation and the need for financial assistance, in particular grants and concessional aid.

Lesotho's balance of payments was characterized by large trade deficits financed mainly by remittances from migrant workers and transfers. It was estimated that exports covered less than 15 per cent of import costs. Agriculture remained the most important sector, accounting for about 70 per cent of total domestic employment and providing subsistence for about 50 per cent of the rural population. However, only 13 per cent of the land was suitable for farming. Prolonged drought had a serious impact on agriculture and, on 4 April, the Prime Minister had declared a state of national food emergency for the second year in succession. Under normal circumstances, Lesotho needed to import approximately 150,000 tonnes of grain, but requirements for 1984 were estimated to be double that amount.

Industrial development remained at a small scale, and manufacturing, including handicrafts, contributed only 4 to 5 per cent of GDP. The major factors inhibiting manufacturing included the small domestic market, competition from South Africa, and the shortage of skilled manpower.

The mission reported on progress in implementing the 10 specific projects identified by the Secretary-General's mission in 1983[53] in response to a 1982 request by the Security Council.[54]

Lesotho, with UNDP support, convened a donors' round-table conference at Maseru from 14 to 17 May, at which it presented 38 projects valued at $67 million, as well as the proposed highlands water project (see p. 184), which in 1980 had been estimated to cost $1.4 billion. The projects fell under the sectoral headings of administration; rural development and co-operatives; agriculture; industry, trade and tourism; water, mineral resources and power; roads, transportation and communication; education; health; and urban development.

GENERAL ASSEMBLY ACTION

On 17 December, the General Assembly, on the recommendation of the Second Committee, adopted resolution 39/183 without vote.

Assistance to Lesotho

The General Assembly,

Recalling Security Council resolution 402(1976) of 22 December 1976, in which the Council, *inter alia,* expressed concern at the serious situation created by South Africa's closure of certain border posts between South Africa and Lesotho aimed at coercing Lesotho into according recognition to the bantustan of the Transkei,

Recalling also Security Council resolution 535(1983) of 29 June 1983, in which the Council endorsed the report of the mission dispatched to Lesotho in response to resolution 527(1982) of 15 December 1982,

Commending the decision of the Government of Lesotho not to recognize the Transkei, in compliance with United Nations decisions, particularly General Assembly resolution 31/6 A of 26 October 1976,

Also commending the Government of Lesotho for its steadfast opposition to *apartheid* and its generosity to the South African refugees,

Fully aware that the decision of the Government of Lesotho not to recognize the Transkei and its acceptance of refugees from South Africa have imposed special economic burdens upon its people,

Strongly endorsing the appeals for assistance to Lesotho made in Security Council resolutions 402(1976) of 22 December 1976, 407(1977) of 25 May 1977 and 535(1983) of 29 June 1983, in General Assembly resolutions 32/98 of 13 December 1977, 33/128 of 19 December 1978, 34/130 of 14 December 1979, 35/96 of 5 December 1980, 36/219 of 17 December 1981, 37/160 of 17 December 1982 and 38/215 of 20 December 1983,

Having examined the report of the Secretary-General, submitted in response to General Assembly resolution 38/215, which contains a review of the economic situation and of the progress made in the implementation of the special programme of economic assistance for Lesotho,

Noting the priority which the Government of Lesotho accords to raising levels of food production through increased productivity, thus lessening the country's dependency on South Africa for food imports,

Aware that the high prices paid by Lesotho for its imports of petroleum products as a result of the oil embargo on South Africa have become a serious impediment to the development of the country,

Recognizing, in connection with such embargoes, the obligation of the international community to help countries such as Lesotho that act in support of the Charter of the United Nations and in compliance with General Assembly resolutions,

Recalling its resolutions 32/160 of 19 December 1977 and 33/197 of 29 January 1979 concerning the Transport and Communications Decade in Africa and, in this regard, noting Lesotho's geopolitical situation, which necessitates the urgent development of air and telecommunication links with neighbouring countries of Africa and the rest of the world,

Taking account of Lesotho's need for a national network of roads, both for its planned social and economic development and to lessen its dependence on the South African network, to reach various regions of the country affected by the imposition of travel restrictions by South Africa,

Taking note of Lesotho's special problems associated with the employment of large numbers of its able-bodied men in South Africa,

Taking note also of the priority which the Government of Lesotho has accorded to the problem of absorbing into the economy the young generation, as well as migrant workers returning from South Africa,

Welcoming the action taken by the Government of Lesotho to make more effective use of women in the development process by promoting their participation in the economic, social and cultural life of the country,

Taking account also of Lesotho's position as a least developed, most seriously affected and land-locked country,

Recalling its resolution 32/98, in which it, *inter alia,* recognized that the continuing influx of refugees from South Africa imposed an additional burden on Lesotho,

1. *Expresses its concern* at the difficulties that confront the Government of Lesotho as a result of its decision not to recognize the so-called independent Transkei, and of its rejection of *apartheid* and acceptance of refugees from *apartheid* oppression;

2. *Endorses fully* the assessment of the situation contained in the report of the mission to Lesotho annexed to the report of the Secretary-General;

3. *Takes note* of the requirements of Lesotho, as described in the report of the mission to Lesotho, including initial projects presented by the Government of Lesotho to the round-table conference of donors held in Lesotho from 14 to 17 May 1984;

4. *Expresses its appreciation* to the Secretary-General for the measures he has taken to organize an international programme of economic assistance for Lesotho;

5. *Notes with appreciation* the response made thus far by the international community to the special programme of economic assistance for Lesotho, which has enabled it to proceed with the implementation of parts of the recommended programme;

6. *Reiterates its appeal* to Member States, regional and interregional organizations and other intergovernmental bodies to provide financial, material and technical assistance to Lesotho for the implementation of the projects identified in the report of the mission to Lesotho;

7. *Calls upon* Member States and the appropriate agencies, organizations and financial institutions to provide assistance to Lesotho so as to enable it to achieve a greater degree of self-sufficiency in food production;

8. *Also calls upon* Member States to give all possible assistance to Lesotho to ensure an adequate and regular supply of oil to meet its national requirements;

9. *Further calls upon* Member States to assist Lesotho in developing its internal road and air systems and its air communication with the rest of the world;

10. *Commends* the efforts of the Government of Lesotho to integrate women more fully into development efforts and requests the Secretary-General to consult with the Government on the type and amount of assistance it will require to achieve this objective;

11. *Draws the attention* of the international community to the round-table conference of donors held in Lesotho from 14 to 17 May 1984 and urges Member States and the appropriate agencies and organizations to provide assistance to Lesotho in accordance with the outcome of that meeting;

12. *Also draws the attention* of the international community to the special account which was established at United Nations Headquarters by the Secretary-General, in accordance with Security Council resolution 407(1977), for the purpose of facilitating the channelling of contributions to Lesotho;

13. *Invites* the United Nations Development Programme, the United Nations Children's Fund, the World Health Organization, the United Nations Industrial Development Organization, the Food and Agriculture Organization of the United Nations and the International Fund for Agricultural Development to bring further to the attention of their governing bodies the special needs of Lesotho and to report to the Secretary-General by 15 July 1985 on the steps they have taken;

14. *Requests* the appropriate specialized agencies and other organizations of the United Nations system to co-operate closely with the Secretary-General in organizing an effective international programme of assistance to Lesotho and to report periodically to him on the steps they have taken and the resources they have made available to assist that country;

15. *Requests* the Secretary-General:

(a) To continue his efforts to mobilize the necessary resources for an effective programme of financial, technical and material assistance to Lesotho;

(b) To consult with the Government of Lesotho on the question of migrant workers returning from South Africa and to report on the type of assistance which the Government requires in order to establish labour-intensive projects to deal with their absorption into the economy;

(c) To keep the situation in Lesotho under constant review, to maintain close contact with Member States, the specialized agencies, regional and other intergovernmental organizations and international financial institutions concerned and to apprise the Economic and Social Council, at its second regular session of 1985, of the current status of the special programme of economic assistance for Lesotho;

(d) To report on the progress made in the economic situation of Lesotho and in organizing and implementing the special programme of economic assistance for that country in time for the matter to be considered by the General Assembly at its fortieth session.

General Assembly resolution 39/183

17 December 1984   Meeting 103   Adopted without vote

Approved by Second Committee (A/39/793) without vote, 30 November (meeting 54); 16-nation draft (A/C.2/39/L.41), orally corrected following informal consultations; agenda item 83 *(b).*

Sponsors: Afghanistan, Algeria, Bangladesh, Botswana, Cameroon, Central African Republic, Gambia, Ghana, Lesotho, Liberia, Madagascar, Malawi, Nigeria, Pakistan, Swaziland, Zambia.

Meeting numbers. GA 39th session: 2nd Committee 32-37, 45, 54; plenary 103.

Liberia

In 1984, Liberia continued to face serious economic and financial problems. The situation was the result of such external factors as the global economic recession which yielded reduced earnings from Liberia's primary commodity exports, the strength of the United States dollar (the legal tender in Liberia) and high overseas interest rates. Domestic problems included a large external debt, a prolonged outflow of capital and an increase in recurrent public expenditure. With an estimated population growth of 3.3 per cent, real per capita income in Liberia deteriorated between 1980 and 1984 by 25 per cent. The balance of payments continued to show a deficit in 1983/84 estimated at $87 million, or 8 per cent of GDP, due mainly to the decline in export earnings and the increasing interest payments on public debt ($52 million in 1983/84) and private transfers abroad ($36 million).

The United Nations provided assistance within the framework of the special programme of economic assistance and followed up on implementation of projects identified by a donors' round-table conference in October 1983.[55]

GENERAL ASSEMBLY ACTION

On the recommendation of the Second Committee, the General Assembly adopted resolution 39/182 on 17 December without vote.

Special economic assistance to Liberia

The General Assembly,

Recalling its resolutions 36/207 of 17 December 1981 and 37/149 of 17 December 1982, in which it appealed to all Member States, the specialized agencies and other organizations of the United Nations system and international development and financial institutions to provide all possible assistance for the reconstruction, rehabilitation and development of Liberia,

Recalling also the summary report of the Secretary-General,

Noting from the report that, despite a variety of adverse factors, Liberia continues to make some progress in its development efforts as a result of the measures adopted by the Government,

Having noted the efforts of the Government of Liberia to mobilize international support for the country's development plan through the organization of a round-table conference of donors, held at Berne in October 1983 with the assistance of the United Nations Development Programme,

Deeply concerned that Liberia continues to experience serious economic and financial difficulties, characterized by a severe balance-of-payments problem, heavy burden of external debt and shortfall in export earnings, which have contributed to the lack of resources to implement its planned economic and social development programmes,

1. *Expresses its appreciation* to the Secretary-General for the measures he has taken to organize and mobilize support for the international economic assistance programme for Liberia;

2. *Notes with satisfaction* the interest in the development plan of Liberia expressed by participants in the round-table conference of donors;

3. *Appeals* to all States, international financial institutions and organizations of the United Nations system to respond generously and urgently to the needs of Liberia as set forth in that country's development plan, taking into account its current critical economic situation;

4. *Takes note* of the measures being taken by the Government of Liberia to strengthen the economy of the country through institutional and economic policy reforms;

5. *Reiterates once again its appeal* to all States, international financial institutions and organizations of the United Nations system to provide substantial and appropriate assistance, through bilateral and multilateral channels, preferably in the form of grants-in-aid or loans granted on concessionary terms, in order to enable Liberia to carry out fully the recommended economic assistance programme;

6. *Requests* the Secretary-General:

(a) To continue his efforts to mobilize the necessary resources for an effective programme of financial, technical and material assistance to Liberia;

(b) To keep the situation regarding assistance to Liberia under constant review, to maintain close contact with

Member States, specialized agencies, regional and other intergovernmental organizations and the international financial institutions concerned and to apprise the Economic and Social Council, at its second regular session of 1985, of the status of the special programme of economic assistance for Liberia;

(c) To arrange for a review of the economic situation in Liberia and the status of the special programme of economic assistance and to report thereon to the General Assembly at its fortieth session.

General Assembly resolution 39/182

17 December 1984   Meeting 103   Adopted without vote

Approved by Second Committee (A/39/793) without vote, 30 November (meeting 54); 33-nation draft (A/C.2/39/L.40); agenda item 83 *(b)*.

Sponsors: Afghanistan, Bangladesh, Barbados, Benin, Central African Republic, China, Comoros, Djibouti, Dominican Republic, Egypt, Equatorial Guinea, Ethiopia, France, Gambia, Ghana, Guinea-Bissau, India, Indonesia, Japan, Kenya, Lebanon, Lesotho, Liberia, Madagascar, Malawi, Nepal, Nigeria, Pakistan, Senegal, Sierra Leone, Sudan, Tunisia, United States.

Meeting numbers. GA 39th session: 2nd Committee 32-37, 44, 54; plenary 103.

Mozambique

The Secretary-General, in response to a 1983 General Assembly request[56] that he consult with Mozambique on its special assistance needs, arranged for a mission to go there from 5 to 12 May 1984, led by the Under-Secretary-General for Special Political Questions. The mission's report, issued in August,[8] described the economic and financial situation of the country and made recommendations for priority development projects. Noting that Mozambique's situation was extremely serious and that it urgently needed food, petroleum and agricultural inputs, the Secretary-General, in transmitting the mission's report to the Assembly, stated his intention to consult with the Government with a view to formulating a new special programme of economic assistance based on current conditions and on the new development principles which the Government was in the process of defining. Meanwhile, during this interim period the country urgently needed assistance. There was a critical problem of starvation and malnutrition, and vital inputs were required to permit the economy to function. Some initial priority programmes were needed to establish a basis for future development.

The economic situation had deteriorated mainly as a result of natural disasters and destabilization. With a per capita income of about $125 in 1983, Mozambique was an LDC, and a further decline was foreseen for 1984. Government revenues decreased by 5 per cent in 1984 while expenditures increased by 10 per cent. The infant mortality rate in 1983 was estimated at 240 per 1,000, the literacy rate at 10 per cent and life expectancy was 46 years. Health and education services were unavailable to a large part of the population. During the first half of 1984, starvation and malnutrition were prevalent in many areas where relief supplies could not be transported.

The majority of the population was engaged in subsistence agriculture, with over 80 per cent residing in rural and often remote areas. Agriculture was oriented towards export crops such as cotton, sugar, tea and cashews. The country had promising agricultural, fishery and forestry potential, though most of those resources had not been developed. Energy resources included hydroelectricity and coal, which were normally exported, but due to instability which prevented transport to ports, coal had not been exported for a year.

By the end of 1984, the outstanding external debt totalled $2.4 billion. Mozambique had often had a trade deficit, with the value of exports covering only about one third of the cost of imports. That had been partly compensated by remittances from migrant miners working in South Africa, but a decrease in their employment from about 120,000 in 1978 to 40,000 in recent years had aggravated the balance-of-payments situation. A second major source of foreign exchange, the international transit of goods through Mozambique's ports and railways, had suffered drastic reductions due to instability in the region. Cargo tonnage declined from 17.5 million tonnes in 1978 to 3.3 million in 1983. The country faced a serious foreign exchange shortage that had restricted its ability to import the raw materials and other inputs necessary. The drop in export revenues had prohibited Mozambique from meeting its debt-service obligations, expected to exceed export earnings by far. Mozambique had requested debt rescheduling, but until such an agreement was reached, external borrowing to withstand its economic crisis would generally be unavailable.

Further complicating the economic situation, externally supported armed elements had disrupted transportation and energy lines and forced substantial expenditures for defence. Mozambique also suffered from a prolonged drought in the south and central regions, and a cyclone in January 1984 hit the one region in the central-southern part of the country that had not been devastated by the drought. Cyclone damage was estimated at $75 million, with heavy losses in the communications and transportation and water supply systems, and to agriculture and livestock.

Although the agricultural sector accounted for approximately 41 per cent of the gross social product and 85 per cent of employment, Mozambique was never self-sufficient in food.

The Government informed the mission of its immediate needs, emphasizing petroleum products, and basic inputs and consumer goods for the agricultural sector. Minimum requirements for 1984 were an estimated 600,000 tonnes of crude oil and 190,000 tonnes of other fuel; as at May 1984, arrangements had been made for 260,000 tonnes of crude oil. In addition, some 700,000 tonnes of food imports were required.

The mission made recommendations for 11 specific projects as the most urgent, with values of $26.7 million for agriculture (food security reserves, seeds, water supply and irrigation), $4 million for transportation (repairs to the railway line to Swaziland), $3.8 million for industrial development (raw materials essential for domestic industries), $1.3 million for health (medical supplies and equipment), $5 million for water supply (borehole drilling), and education, for which an estimate was not available.

GENERAL ASSEMBLY ACTION

On 17 December, the General Assembly, on the recommendation of the Second Committee, adopted resolution 39/199 without vote.

Assistance to Mozambique

The General Assembly,

Recalling Security Council resolution 386(1976) of 17 March 1976, in which the Council appealed to all States to provide, and requested the Secretary-General, in collaboration with the appropriate organizations of the United Nations system, to organize, with immediate effect, financial, technical and material assistance to enable Mozambique to carry out its economic development programme,

Recalling further its resolution 38/208 of 20 December 1983 and its earlier resolutions, in which it urged the international community to respond effectively and generously with assistance to Mozambique,

Having considered the report of the Secretary-General submitted in response to its resolution 38/208, to which is annexed the report of the mission to Mozambique,

Deeply concerned at the loss of life and the destruction of essential infrastructures such as roads, railways, bridges, petroleum facilities, electricity supply, schools and hospitals, as identified in the reports of the Secretary-General,

Noting with deep concern that Mozambique has continued to suffer from a prolonged drought causing heavy losses in food production and livestock and resulting in dislocation of its people,

Also noting with deep concern the extensive damage caused by the cyclone "Demoina" at the end of January 1984,

Noting that Mozambique faces an emergency food situation of an exceptional scale and needs imports of 700,000 tonnes of cereals in 1984/1985 to meet its food requirements,

Recognizing that substantial international assistance is required for the implementation of a number of reconstruction and development projects,

1. *Strongly endorses* the appeals made by the Security Council and the Secretary-General for international assistance to Mozambique;

2. *Expresses its appreciation* to the Secretary-General for the measures he has taken to organize an international economic assistance programme for Mozambique;

3. *Also expresses its appreciation* for the assistance provided to Mozambique by various States and regional and international organizations and humanitarian institutions;

4. *Regrets*, however, that the total assistance provided to date falls far short of Mozambique's pressing needs;

5. *Appeals* to the international community to provide adequate food aid to Mozambique to prevent further starvation and malnutrition;

6. *Draws the attention* of the international community to the two areas for immediate action—the supply of crude oil and petroleum products and the supply of basic inputs and consumer goods for the agricultural sector—that are critical for the functioning of the economy;

7. *Also draws the attention* of the international community to the additional financial, economic and material assistance identified in the annex to the report of the Secretary-General as urgently required by Mozambique;

8. *Calls upon* Member States, regional and interregional organizations and other governmental, intergovernmental and non-governmental organizations to provide financial, material and technical assistance to Mozambique, wherever possible in the form of grants, and urges them to give special consideration to the early inclusion of Mozambique in their programmes of development assistance, if it is not already included;

9. *Urges* Member States and organizations that are already implementing or negotiating assistance programmes for Mozambique to strengthen them, wherever possible;

10. *Also appeals* to the international community to contribute to the special account for Mozambique established by the Secretary-General for the purpose of facilitating the channelling of contributions to Mozambique;

11. *Requests* the appropriate organizations and programmes of the United Nations system—in particular the United Nations Development Programme, the Food and Agriculture Organization of the United Nations, the International Fund for Agricultural Development, the World Food Programme, the World Health Organization, the United Nations Children's Fund and the United Nations Fund for Population Activities—to maintain and increase their current and future programmes of assistance to Mozambique, to co-operate closely with the Secretary-General in organizing an effective international programme of assistance and to report periodically to him on the steps they have taken and the resources they have made available to help that country;

12. *Requests* the Secretary-General:

(a) To continue his efforts to mobilize the necessary resources for an effective programme of financial, technical and material assistance to Mozambique;

(b) To keep the situation in Mozambique under constant review, to maintain close contact with Member States, the specialized agencies, regional and other intergovernmental organizations, international financial institutions and other bodies concerned, and to apprise the Economic and Social Council, at its second regular session of 1985, of the current status of the special programme of economic assistance for Mozambique;

(c) To prepare, on the basis of sustained consultations with the Government of Mozambique, a report on the development of the economic situation and the implementation of the special programme of economic assistance for that country in time for the matter to be considered by the General Assembly at its fortieth session.

General Assembly resolution 39/199

17 December 1984   Meeting 103   Adopted without vote

Approved by Second Committee (A/39/793) without vote, 30 November (meeting 54); 32-nation draft (A/C.2/39/L.64), orally revised following informal consultations; agenda item 83 *(b)*.

Sponsors: Afghanistan, Algeria, Angola, Bangladesh, Botswana, Brazil, Burkina Faso, Cape Verde, Congo, Cuba, Democratic Yemen, Ethiopia, France, German Democratic Republic, Ghana, Guinea-Bissau, Italy, Lesotho, Madagascar, Malawi, Mongolia, Mozambique, Nicaragua, Nigeria, Pakistan, Portugal, Sao Tome and Principe, Swaziland, Sweden, United Republic of Tanzania, Zambia, Zimbabwe.

Meeting numbers. GA 39th session: 2nd Committee 32-37, 47, 54; plenary 103.

After informal consultations, the Secretary of the Second Committee announced that it had been agreed to include UNFPA in paragraph 11.

Sao Tome and Principe

In response to the General Assembly's 1982 request[57] that he report on the economic situation and the special programme of economic assistance for Sao Tome and Principe, the Secretary-General arranged for a mission to go there from 5 to 9 June 1984 and issued its report in September.[10] The Government had informed the mission that the major constraints to economic development were geographic isolation, dependence on a single export crop (cocoa provided almost 80 per cent of export earnings), and lack of trained manpower and of suitable machinery for efficient government administration. The Government had attempted to reduce the dependence on cocoa for foreign exchange, particularly as the amount produced and the price on the world market had declined. The drought that affected some parts of the country in 1982 and 1983, combined with erratic rainfall in other areas, had had a negative effect on the already fragile situation. The limited production of staple foods declined, and cocoa production was reduced by almost two thirds.

Sao Tome and Principe, an archipelagic LDC, had an annual population growth rate of 2.8 to 3 per cent.

Economic growth had fluctuated radically over the previous few years, the mission reported, with GDP dropping 1.9 per cent in 1983. In real terms, GDP had declined steadily since 1980 and in 1984 was less than 70 per cent of the 1980 level. Per capita GDP had declined to $330 in 1984 from $486 in 1980. The balance of payments was characterized by a persistent trade deficit. There was a significant improvement in the trade balance in 1983 and 1984, but it was achieved through drastic measures to reduce imports, which had serious implications for the economy, given the country's reliance on imports not only for food but also for inputs, particularly oil, necessary to development. The country relied on short-term loans to finance the deficit, resulting in heavy debt-service obligations.

The agricultural sector dominated the economy, accounting for 41 per cent of GDP. Government efforts to rehabilitate agricultural production had been hampered by the 1982-1983 drought. Export crops took up about 90 per cent of the cultivable land; efforts were being made to expand livestock production and fishing. Lack of energy sources and transportation remained serious problems limiting international trade.

Of the 18 projects for special economic assistance identified by a 1982 mission,[58] at a value of $50 million, eight had received total or partial financing, and negotiations were in progress with regard to two major projects—establishment of vegetable-oil plants and construction of a hydroelectric plant. No financing had been obtained for the remaining eight projects. The Government had proposed to the 1984 mission 15 others in such areas as agricultural inputs and equipment, increasing production of staple food crops, studies on orchards and flowers, use of forest resources, a building-construction organization, increasing electricity, road maintenance, public transportation, medical supplies and housing. The total cost was estimated at $43 million.

GENERAL ASSEMBLY ACTION

On the recommendation of the Second Committee, the Assembly, on 17 December, adopted resolution 39/187 without vote.

Assistance to Sao Tome and Principe
The General Assembly,

Recalling its resolutions 32/96 of 13 December 1977, 33/125 of 19 December 1978, 34/131 of 14 December 1979, 35/93 of 5 December 1980, 36/209 of 17 December 1981 and 37/146 of 17 December 1982, in which it reiterated its appeal to the international community to provide financial, material and technical assistance to Sao Tome and Principe to enable it to establish the necessary social and economic infrastructure for development,

Aware that the economic and social development of Sao Tome and Principe has been seriously hindered by fragile infrastructure, inadequate health, educational and housing facilities and by insufficient external assistance, and that urgent improvement in these sectors is a prerequisite for the country's future progress,

Aware also that, at independence, the country inherited a plantation economy that made it dependent on imports to meet its national food requirements,

Noting with appreciation the concerted efforts undertaken by the Government of Sao Tome and Principe to increase national food production and to decrease dependence on food imports,

Concerned that the severe drought in 1982-1983 followed by abnormally heavy rains and floods in 1984 have seriously affected agricultural production, increased the national food deficit and reduced the ability of the country to pay for food imports,

Taking into account the decision of the Government of Sao Tome and Principe to convene, with the assistance of the United Nations Development Programme, a round-table conference of donors in September-October 1985 at Sao Tome, preparatory to the launching of a national development plan for 1986-1990,

Having examined the report of the Secretary-General, to which is annexed the report of the review mission sent to Sao Tome and Principe,

1. *Expresses its appreciation* to the Secretary-General for the steps he has taken to mobilize assistance to Sao Tome and Principe;

2. *Endorses fully* the assessment and recommendations contained in the annex to the report of the Secretary-General;

3. *Expresses its appreciation* to the Member States, international organizations, and other intergovernmental

and non-governmental organizations which have provided assistance to Sao Tome and Principe;

4. *Renews its appeal* to Member States, the appropriate organs, organizations and programmes of the United Nations system, regional and interregional organizations and other intergovernmental bodies and non-governmental organizations, as well as international financial institutions, to provide financial, technical and material assistance to Sao Tome and Principe through bilateral and multilateral channels, as appropriate, to enable it to strengthen its social and economic infrastructure and to implement the special programme of economic assistance;

5. *Urges* Member States, organizations and programmes of the United Nations system, regional and interregional bodies, financial and development institutions and intergovernmental and non-governmental organizations to participate in the round-table conference of donors to be held in 1985 and to provide all possible assistance for the implementation of the national development plan of Sao Tome and Principe;

6. *Calls upon* the international community to continue its food assistance programmes for Sao Tome and Principe in order to help it cope with the critical food situation in the country and to provide all possible assistance to enable the country to produce more food and reduce its dependence on food imports;

7. *Requests* the Secretary-General:

(a) To keep the situation in Sao Tome and Principe under constant review and to apprise the Economic and Social Council, at its second regular session of 1985, of the current status of the special programme of economic assistance for Sao Tome and Principe;

(b) To report on the progress made in the economic situation of Sao Tome and Principe and in organizing and implementing the special programme of economic assistance for that country in time for the matter to be considered by the General Assembly at its fortieth session.

General Assembly resolution 39/187

17 December 1984   Meeting 103   Adopted without vote

Approved by Second Committee (A/39/793) without vote, 30 November (meeting 54); 32-nation draft (A/C.2/39/L.45); agenda item 83 (b).

Sponsors: Afghanistan, Algeria, Angola, Argentina, Bangladesh, Barbados, Belize, Brazil, Burkina Faso, Cape Verde, China, Congo, Cuba, France, Gabon, Ghana, Guinea, Guinea-Bissau, Italy, Japan, Libyan Arab Jamahiriya, Madagascar, Mozambique, Nicaragua, Nigeria, Pakistan, Panama, Portugal, Sierra Leone, Tunisia, United States, Vanuatu.

Meeting numbers. GA 39th session: 2nd Committee 32-37, 45, 54; plenary 103.

Sierra Leone

Sierra Leone, favourably endowed with agricultural, mineral and water resources, had the potential to achieve self-sustaining growth, but it had experienced serious economic difficulties, due partly to the slow-down in global economic activity and partly to structural imbalances in its economy, according to a September 1984 report by the Secretary-General.[1] The economy was being undermined by severe scarcities of imported raw materials and spare parts for industry, fewer trade and commercial credits, large arrears in commercial payments and strains on government finances. Commercial activity and employment had fallen. The Government had adopted a strategy which emphasized expanding domestic productive activities, but Sierra

Leone, an LDC, required substantial external assistance to ameliorate its financial situation, permit project implementation and enable it to realize its economic potential. An understanding had been reached with IMF on a policy to restore long-term growth and stability by restrictive fiscal and monetary policies aimed at improving the balance of payments.

Agriculture, which contributed 30 per cent or more of GDP, was the principal source of livelihood for about 70 per cent of the population and the largest sector in the economy. Mining, trade, transport, communications and public services were the other sectors contributing 10 per cent or more; manufacturing and handicrafts together contributed less than 5 per cent. GDP was estimated to have increased by barely 1 per cent per annum in real terms from 1978/79 to 1983/84, while the population was increasing at more than 2 per cent per year; this represented a deterioration of the trend of the 1970s when GDP growth kept pace with population increases. The overall deficit in 1983/84 was 8 per cent of GDP as compared to 11 to 13 per cent during the years 1978/79 to 1982/83.

Of the 71 priority projects identified in 1983 for an assistance programme costing $275 million, 27 projects, costing $124 million, were considered especially urgent.[59] As at mid-1984, less than 3 per cent of the resources required to implement the priority projects had been mobilized, excluding $12 million allocated by the World Bank for renovating power systems, to be applied when co-financing could be arranged.

GENERAL ASSEMBLY ACTION

On 17 December, the General Assembly, acting on the recommendation of the Second Committee, adopted resolution 39/192 without vote.

Assistance to Sierra Leone

The General Assembly,

Recalling its resolutions 37/158 of 17 December 1982 and 38/205 of 20 December 1983, in which it appealed to all States, the specialized agencies and international development and financial institutions to provide all possible assistance for the development of Sierra Leone,

Further recalling its resolution 37/133 of 17 December 1982, in which it decided to include Sierra Leone in the list of the least developed countries,

Having considered the summary report of the Secretary-General,

Noting with concern that the economy of Sierra Leone is being undermined by severe scarcities of imported raw materials and spare parts for industry, a drying-up of trade and commercial credits, large commercial payment arrears and unmitigated strains on government finances,

Concerned that unusually low rainfall in 1984 has seriously affected the food production of the country and considerably worsened its balance-of-payments position,

Noting that the Government of Sierra Leone, in co-operation with the United Nations Development Pro-

gramme, has initiated preparatory activities for a round-table of partners in development of Sierra Leone, to be organized with the assistance of the Programme early in 1985,

Reiterating the need for effective mobilization of international assistance, in order to implement fully the programme of development outlined in the report of the multiagency mission,

1. *Expresses its appreciation* to the Secretary-General for the steps he has taken to mobilize assistance for Sierra Leone;

2. *Urgently reiterates its appeal* to the international community, including the specialized agencies and other organizations and bodies of the United Nations system, to contribute generously, through bilateral or multilateral channels, to the economic and social development of Sierra Leone;

3. *Urges* all States and relevant United Nations bodies—in particular the United Nations Development Programme, the World Food Programme, the United Nations Industrial Development Organization, the United Nations Children's Fund, the World Health Organization, the United Nations Educational, Scientific and Cultural Organization and the United Nations Fund for Population Activities—to provide all possible assistance to help the Government of Sierra Leone meet the critical humanitarian needs of the population and to provide, as appropriate, food, medicines and essential equipment for hospitals and schools;

4. *Invites* the United Nations Development Programme, the United Nations Children's Fund, the World Food Programme, the World Health Organization, the United Nations Industrial Development Organization, the Food and Agriculture Organization of the United Nations, the World Bank and the International Fund for Agricultural Development to bring to the attention of their governing bodies, for their consideration, the special needs of Sierra Leone and to report the decisions of those bodies to the Secretary-General by 15 July 1985;

5. *Appeals* to all States and international organizations to participate at a high level in the round-table of partners in development of Sierra Leone to be held early in 1985, and to contribute generously to the programme of action that will be presented by the Government of Sierra Leone;

6. *Requests* the Secretary-General:

(a) To continue his efforts to mobilize the necessary resources for an effective programme of financial, technical and material assistance to Sierra Leone;

(b) To apprise the Economic and Social Council, at its second regular session of 1985, of the assistance granted to Sierra Leone;

(c) To keep the situation regarding assistance to Sierra Leone under review and to report to the General Assembly at its fortieth session on the implementation of the present resolution.

General Assembly resolution 39/192

17 December 1984   Meeting 103   Adopted without vote

Approved by Second Committee (A/39/793) without vote, 30 November (meeting 54); 19-nation draft (A/C.2/39/L.56); agenda item 83 *(b)*.

Sponsors: Afghanistan, Angola, Bangladesh, Burkina Faso, Chad, Ethiopia, Ghana, Guinea, Japan, Lesotho, Liberia, Madagascar, Malawi, Nepal, Pakistan, Sao Tome and Principe, Sierra Leone, Singapore, Uganda.

Meeting numbers. GA 39th session: 2nd Committee 32-37, 45, 54; plenary 103.

Uganda

Uganda, a land-locked country, was classified by the United Nations as an LDC. Its serious socio-economic situation, according to a September 1984 summary report by the Secretary-General,[1] had been caused or aggravated by the economic and social policies in effect from 1972 to 1980, the liberation war of 1979, and drought and famine in 1979 and 1981, compounded by the widespread drought of 1983 and 1984 that affected southern Uganda and neighbouring countries. A recovery programme for 1982-1984, drawn up by the Government, was revised in November 1983 to cover the period 1983-1985, and, in January 1984, it was endorsed by a Consultative Group on Uganda at a meeting in Paris organized by the World Bank. The revised programme, while continuing to emphasize short-term revival of the production sector, reallocated resources from mining, energy and transport to industry and infrastructure, partly to reflect donors' preferences. During 1984, problems of internal security and inadequate skilled human resources and infrastructure continued to be major constraints in programme implementation.

Uganda's economy was reversed in 1981 from a declining trend towards positive growth. Since then, GDP had risen every year, and in 1983 real GDP rose by 7.3 per cent. New government policies put into effect in 1981 provided incentives to farmers that elicited a substantial increase in production, nearly doubling coffee, cotton, tea and tobacco crop yields by 1983/84. Uganda's trade deficit declined from $122.5 million in 1982 to an estimated $51.6 million in 1983 and was expected to be reduced to $25.5 million in 1984. The estimated costs of imports for 1984 was less than one half that for 1982. However, the Government's budget remained in deficit despite the rise in revenue. With the mediation of the World Bank, Uganda, Kenya and the United Republic of Tanzania had signed in December 1983 the Arusha Accord which addressed the division of the assets and liabilities of the former East African Community. The Accord provided for reimbursements to Uganda of $145 million by Kenya and $46 million by the United Republic of Tanzania and provided guidelines for future co-operation.

UNCTAD reported[42] that it had helped formulate import and export, exchange rate and pricing policies, improve managerial capabilities, and develop transit transport services. In a resolution of 6 April,[43] the UNCTAD Trade and Development Board took note of UNCTAD's assistance, with UNDP support, to Uganda and requested the UNCTAD Secretary-General to contribute to the implementation of the revised recovery programme and to report to the Board in 1985.

The UNDP Administrator reported[44] that an overall review was carried out by the UNDP field office with the Government between February and June 1984, which resulted in the termination of selected projects as well as the revision of others. The new programme consisted of some 30 projects in agriculture, transport, communications, industry, public administration, planning, banking and finance.

GENERAL ASSEMBLY ACTION

On 17 December, the General Assembly adopted resolution 39/188 without vote, acting on the recommendation of the Second Committee.

Assistance to Uganda

The General Assembly,

Recalling its resolutions 35/103 of 5 December 1980, 36/218 of 17 December 1981, 37/162 of 17 December 1982 and 38/207 of 20 December 1983 on assistance to Uganda,

Bearing in mind the enormous economic and social setbacks suffered by Uganda and the resultant precipitous decline in the well-being of its people,

Taking into account the revised recovery programme (1983-1985) presented by the Government of Uganda to the meeting of the Consultative Group on Uganda, held in Paris in January 1984 under the auspices of the World Bank,

Recognizing that Uganda is not only land-locked but also one of the least developed and most seriously affected countries,

Noting the appeals of the Secretary-General for assistance to Uganda,

Taking note of the summary report of the Secretary-General, in which it is stated that substantial additional assistance is required to finance the remaining projects in the revised recovery programme which have not yet attracted the support of the international community,

Reaffirming the urgent need for further international action to assist the Government of Uganda in its continuing efforts for national reconstruction, rehabilitation and development,

Encouraged that the economic policies of the Government of Uganda and the support assistance provided by the donor countries and international organizations have produced positive signs of economic recovery,

1. *Expresses its appreciation* to the Secretary-General for the steps he has taken to mobilize assistance for Uganda;

2. *Further expresses its appreciation* to those States and organizations that have provided assistance to that country;

3. *Reiterates its endorsement* of the assessment and recommendations contained in the annex to the report of the Secretary-General submitted to the General Assembly at its thirty-seventh session;

4. *Invites* the international community, in particular the United Nations system and donor countries and organizations, to make available more resources to implement the country's revised recovery programme (1983-1985) and meet the remaining needs described in the Secretary-General's summary report;

5. *Urgently renews its appeal* to all Member States, specialized agencies and other organizations of the United Nations system and international economic and financial institutions to contribute generously, through bilateral and multilateral channels, to the reconstruction, rehabilitation and development needs of Uganda and to its emergency requirements;

6. *Requests* the appropriate organizations and programmes of the United Nations system to maintain and increase their current and future programmes of assistance to Uganda and to report periodically to the Secretary-General on the steps they have taken and the resources they have made available to help that country;

7. *Invites* the United Nations Conference on Trade and Development, the United Nations Industrial Development Organization, the United Nations Children's Fund, the United Nations Development Programme, the World Food Programme, the International Fund for Agricultural Development, the International Labour Organisation, the Food and Agriculture Organization of the United Nations, the United Nations Educational, Scientific and Cultural Organization, the World Health Organization and the World Bank to bring to the attention of their governing bodies, for their consideration, the special needs of Uganda and to report the decisions of those bodies to the Secretary-General by 15 July 1985;

8. *Requests* the United Nations High Commissioner for Refugees to continue his humanitarian assistance programmes in Uganda;

9. *Requests* the Secretary-General:

(a) To continue his efforts to mobilize the necessary resources for an effective programme of financial, technical and material assistance to Uganda;

(b) To keep the situation in Uganda under constant review, to maintain close contact with Member States, the specialized agencies, regional and other intergovernmental organizations and the international financial institutions concerned, and to apprise the Economic and Social Council, at its second regular session of 1985, of the current status of the special programme of economic assistance for Uganda;

(c) To report on the progress made in the economic situation in Uganda and in organizing international assistance for that country in time for the matter to be considered by the General Assembly at its fortieth session.

General Assembly resolution 39/188

17 December 1984   Meeting 103   Adopted without vote

Approved by Second Committee (A/39/793) without vote, 30 November (meeting 54); 16-nation draft (A/C.2/39/L.46); agenda item 83 (b).

Sponsors: Afghanistan, Bangladesh, Botswana, Burundi, Central African Republic, Democratic Yemen, Djibouti, Ghana, Guinea, Kenya, Madagascar, Pakistan, Tunisia, Uganda, United Republic of Tanzania, Zambia.

Meeting numbers. GA 39th session: 2nd Committee 32-37, 44, 54; plenary 103.

The Assembly, in resolution 39/205, called for assistance programmes for the drought-stricken areas of six East African countries, including Uganda.

Other regions

Democratic Yemen

The Secretary-General, as requested by the General Assembly in 1983,[60] reported in October 1984[5] on international assistance to Democratic Yemen, which had suffered heavy damage, estimated at $950 million, as a result of nation-wide flooding in March 1982.[61] Aid for relief operations to the LDC was provided by UNDRO (beds, blankets), UNICEF (tents, blankets), UNDP (mattresses, blankets, stoves), WFP (flour, fat, dates) and WHO

(medicines). Long-term rehabilitation assistance was provided by UNDP (technical assistance for flood control and roads), UNCDF (crops), WFP (rehabilitation of flood damaged areas), FAO (irrigation and flood control), UNESCO (rehabilitation works) and IDA (roads and erosion control). Fifteen countries gave assistance on a bilateral basis; 17 Red Cross/Red Crescent national or regional organizations and three other organizations provided relief aid and long-term rehabilitation assistance.

GENERAL ASSEMBLY ACTION

The General Assembly, on the recommendation of the Second Committee, adopted resolution 39/184 without vote on 17 December.

Assistance to Democratic Yemen

The General Assembly,

Recalling its resolution 38/206 of 20 December 1983 and Economic and Social Council resolutions 1982/6 of 28 April 1982 and 1982/59 of 30 July 1982 concerning the extensive devastation caused by the heavy floods in Democratic Yemen,

Recalling also resolution 107(IX) of 11 May 1982 of the Economic Commission for Western Asia, in which the Commission called for the urgent establishment of a programme for the rehabilitation and reconstruction of the flood-stricken areas of Democratic Yemen,

Having considered the report prepared by the Office of the United Nations Disaster Relief Co-ordinator on the extent and nature of the damage caused by the floods,

Taking note of the report of the Secretary-General on assistance to Democratic Yemen,

Recognizing that Democratic Yemen, as one of the least developed countries, is unable to bear the mounting burden of rehabilitation and reconstruction of the affected areas,

Recognizing also the efforts made by Democratic Yemen to alleviate the suffering of the victims of the floods,

1. *Expresses its appreciation* to the Secretary-General for the steps he has taken regarding assistance to Democratic Yemen;

2. *Expresses its gratitude* to those States and international, regional and intergovernmental organizations that have provided assistance to Democratic Yemen;

3. *Requests* the Secretary-General to continue to mobilize the necessary resources for an effective, comprehensive programme of financial, technical and material assistance to Democratic Yemen in order to help mitigate the damage inflicted on it and implement its rehabilitation and reconstruction plans;

4. *Appeals* to Member States to contribute generously through bilateral or multilateral channels to the reconstruction and development process in Democratic Yemen;

5. *Requests* the appropriate organizations and programmes of the United Nations system—in particular the United Nations Development Programme, the World Bank, the World Food Programme, the Food and Agriculture Organization of the United Nations, the International Fund for Agricultural Development, the World Health Organization, the United Nations Fund for Population Activities, the United Nations Children's Fund and the United Nations Industrial Development Organization—to maintain and expand their programmes of assistance to Democratic Yemen and to co-operate closely

with the Secretary-General in organizing an effective programme of assistance to that country;

6.   *Calls upon* regional and interregional organizations and other intergovernmental and non-governmental organizations to continue their assistance to the development requirements of Democratic Yemen;

7.   *Requests* the Secretary-General to keep the situation in Democratic Yemen under review and to report to the General Assembly at its fortieth session on the progress made in the implementation of the present resolution.

General Assembly resolution 39/184

17 December 1984   Meeting 103   Adopted without vote

Approved by Second Committee (A/39/793) without vote, 30 November (meeting 54); 31-nation draft (A/C.2/39/L.42); agenda item 83 *(b)*.

Sponsors: Afghanistan, Algeria, Argentina, Bahrain, Bangladesh, Benin, Cuba, Cyprus, Czechoslovakia, Democratic Yemen, Djibouti, Ethiopia, France, India, Jordan, Kuwait, Lebanon, Libyan Arab Jamahiriya, Madagascar, Mongolia, Mozambique, Oman, Pakistan, Qatar, Saudi Arabia, Sudan, Tunisia, United Arab Emirates, Viet Nam, Yemen, Yugoslavia.

Meeting numbers. GA 39th session: 2nd Committee 32-37, 44, 54; plenary 103.

Haiti

Haiti was the only country in the western hemisphere in 1984 to be classified as an LDC by the United Nations. Per capita GDP in 1983 was estimated at $320. Malnutrition was widespread, especially in the rural areas, and infant mortality was high—120 per 1,000 births—largely the result of malnutrition. Life expectancy was 53 years. Estimates indicated that in 1984 real GDP increased by 3 per cent after remaining stagnant for the previous two years. The balance of payments was characterized by a persistent surplus of imports over exports. External debt grew to $493.9 million in 1984 from $449.9 million in 1983. Since most external borrowing was on concessional terms, the debt-service ratio remained low, approximately 5.5 per cent of the value of exports of goods and services in 1984, but that figure did not include short-term borrowing or the use of IMF resources.

Despite its economic situation, Haiti had considerable potential. It could be self-sufficient in food and enjoyed an advantage in some export crops (bananas, coffee, rice, sugar). Proximity to North American markets and the possibilities for increasing tourism were other advantages.

GENERAL ASSEMBLY ACTION

On the recommendation of the Second Committee, the General Assembly on 17 December adopted resolution 39/196 without vote.

Economic assistance to Haiti

The General Assembly,

Recalling its resolution 36/194 of 17 December 1981, in which it endorsed the Substantial New Programme of Action for the 1980s for the Least Developed Countries,

Recalling that Haiti is one of the least developed countries and is therefore entitled to the assistance provided for in the relevant General Assembly resolutions for the more intensive development of those countries,

Noting with concern that Haiti continues to face serious economic and financial difficulties owing to the severe constraints on the economy consequent upon the decline in gross national product in real terms, the balance-of-payments deficit, the external debt and the budgetary deficit,

Deeply concerned at the complete collapse of the tourist industry and the termination of bauxite mining consequent upon the exhaustion of reserves, two of the country's principal sources of foreign exchange,

Gravely concerned at the impoverishment of the rural population resulting from the total elimination of the pig population as a result of swine fever,

Bearing in mind the damage caused by cyclone "Allen" in 1981 to a substantial area of Haiti's coffee plantations,

Taking into account that the Government of Haiti, in view of the serious economic situation, has implemented, with the assistance of the International Monetary Fund and the World Bank, an intensive economic and financial stabilization programme,

1.   *Expresses its gratitude* to Member States and to international, regional and interregional organizations for their assistance to Haiti;

2.   *Renews its urgent appeal* to all Governments and international organizations which, at the United Nations Conference on the Least Developed Countries, assumed commitments under the Substantial New Programme of Action for the 1980s for the Least Developed Countries to honour their pledges generously;

3.   *Urges* Governments of Member States and international, regional, interregional and intergovernmental organizations to increase and intensify their assistance to Haiti substantially to help it cope with its economic and financial difficulties and implement successfully its development plan for the biennium 1985-1986;

4.   *Invites* all organizations and programmes of the United Nations system, particularly the United Nations Development Programme, the United Nations Children's Fund, the United Nations Fund for Population Activities, the World Food Programme, the World Health Organization, the Food and Agriculture Organization of the United Nations, the World Bank, the International Fund for Agricultural Development and the United Nations Industrial Development Organization, as well as the Department of Technical Co-operation for Development of the Secretariat, to take account of Haiti's specific needs and to apprise the Secretary-General of their decisions;

5.   *Requests* the Secretary-General:

(a)   To send a mission to Haiti to assess the priority needs of the country, to prepare a programme for assisting the country in coping with the present economic crisis and to pursue its efforts to obtain supplementary international assistance;

(b)   To apprise the Economic and Social Council of the mission at its second regular session of 1985 and to report to the General Assembly at its fortieth session on the implementation of the present resolution.

General Assembly resolution 39/196

17 December 1984   Meeting 103   Adopted without vote

Approved by Second Committee (A/39/793) without vote, 30 November (meeting 54); 35-nation draft (A/C.2/39/L.61), orally revised following informal consultations; agenda item 83 *(b)*.

Sponsors: Algeria, Antigua and Barbuda, Argentina, Bahamas, Bangladesh, Belize, Botswana, Canada, Cape Verde, Central African Republic, Chad, Chile, Comoros,

Dominican Republic, Ecuador, Egypt, Equatorial Guinea, Ethiopia, Gabon, Guinea, Guinea-Bissau, Guyana, Haiti, Ivory Coast, Liberia, Madagascar, Nepal, Pakistan, Panama, Senegal, Sierra Leone, Somalia, Suriname, Trinidad and Tobago, Vanuatu.
Meeting numbers. GA 39th session: 2nd Committee 32-37, 45, 54; plenary 103.

Following informal consultations, the Secretary informed the Second Committee that it had been agreed to add UNFPA to the bodies mentioned in paragraph 4.

Nicaragua

In August 1984,[9] the Secretary-General, in response to a 1983 request by the General Assembly,[62] reported on assistance to Nicaragua, based on information from Member States and United Nations bodies and organizations. In 1983, Nicaragua had been pledged $65.6 million from multilateral agencies and $350 million from bilateral sources. For the first quarter of 1984, bilateral sources pledged $58.9 million in aid. Czechoslovakia, Ecuador, the German Democratic Republic, Norway and Sweden had submitted information on their assistance to Nicaragua. United Nations assistance during the period 19 July 1979 to 1 April 1984 amounted to $258.5 million, of which $149.6 million was in financial assistance and $108.9 million in technical assistance.

GENERAL ASSEMBLY ACTION

On 17 December, the General Assembly adopted resolution 39/204 without vote. It acted on the recommendation of the Second Committee.

Assistance to Nicaragua

The General Assembly,

Recalling its resolutions 34/8 of 25 October 1979, 35/84 of 5 December 1980, 36/213 of 17 December 1981, 37/157 of 17 December 1982 and 38/223 of 20 December 1983 concerning assistance for the reconstruction of Nicaragua,

Recalling also Economic and Social Council decision 1982/168 of 29 July 1982,

Taking note of the report of the Secretary-General on assistance to Nicaragua,

Noting with satisfaction the support that Member States, the specialized agencies and other organizations of the United Nations system have given to the efforts of the Government of Nicaragua for the reconstruction of the country,

Bearing in mind that, in the past few years, the Nicaraguan economy has been negatively affected by various events, among them natural disasters such as the floods and drought of 1982,

Considering that, despite the efforts of the Government and people of Nicaragua, the economic situation has not returned to normal and continues to worsen,

Deeply concerned that Nicaragua is experiencing serious economic difficulties directly affecting its development efforts,

1. *Expresses its appreciation* to the Secretary-General for his efforts regarding assistance to Nicaragua;

2. *Expresses its appreciation also* to the States and organizations that have provided assistance to Nicaragua;

3. *Urges* all Governments to continue contributing to the reconstruction and development of Nicaragua;

4. *Requests* the organizations of the United Nations system to continue and to increase their assistance in this endeavour;

5. *Recommends* that Nicaragua should continue to receive treatment appropriate to the special needs of the country until the economic situation returns to normal;

6. *Requests* the Secretary-General to report to the General Assembly at its fortieth session on the progress made in the implementation of the present resolution.

General Assembly resolution 39/204

17 December 1984   Meeting 103   Adopted without vote

Approved by Second Committee (A/39/793) without vote, 30 November (meeting 54); 74-nation draft (A/C.2/39/L.72); agenda item 83 *(b)*.

Sponsors: Afghanistan, Algeria, Angola, Argentina, Austria, Bangladesh, Barbados, Belize, Benin, Bolivia, Brazil, Bulgaria, Burkina Faso, Burundi, Canada, Cape Verde, China, Colombia, Congo, Costa Rica, Cuba, Cyprus, Czechoslovakia, Democratic Yemen, Denmark, Dominican Republic, Ecuador, Egypt, Equatorial Guinea, Ethiopia, France, German Democratic Republic, Ghana, Greece, Guatemala, Guinea, Guinea-Bissau, Guyana, India, Lao People's Democratic Republic, Lebanon, Lesotho, Libyan Arab Jamahiriya, Madagascar, Mauritania, Mexico, Mongolia, Mozambique, Nepal, Nicaragua, Niger, Nigeria, Norway, Pakistan, Panama, Peru, Romania, Saint Lucia, Sao Tome and Principe, Seychelles, Spain, Suriname, Sweden, Syrian Arab Republic, Trinidad and Tobago, Uganda, United Republic of Tanzania, Uruguay, Vanuatu, Venezuela, Viet Nam, Yugoslavia, Zambia, Zimbabwe.

Meeting numbers. GA 39th session: 2nd Committee 32-37, 48, 54; plenary 103.

In decision 39/431, the Assembly took note of an oral report made in the Second Committee on 5 November by the United Nations Disaster Relief Co-ordinator on implementation of a 1983 Assembly resolution[63] on special assistance to Nicaragua following floods in May 1982 and subsequent natural disasters[64] (see p. 504).

Tonga

In October 1984, the Secretary-General issued a summary report on the special programme of economic assistance to Tonga,[65] as requested by the General Assembly in 1982.[66] The report was based on information provided by Tonga from the mid-term review of its fourth development plan, 1980-1985. A major constraint in Tonga's planning was the lack of comprehensive, accurate and timely data.

The effects of a 1982 cyclone and subsequent drought which lasted most of 1983 continued to affect the economy in 1984; a large proportion of available aid resources had to be diverted from development priorities to rehabilitation and reconstruction. To overcome the economic slow-down that occurred after those natural disasters, the Government had proposed measures to stimulate economic activity, such as: liberalizing wage, price and export controls; promoting the leasing of agricultural land; amending tax laws to increase disposable income; revising import duties to encourage tourism; providing incentives for new industries; raising local revenues for development purposes; and tightening government expenditures.

In the period 1980/81 to 1982/83, total GDP increased by 6.9 per cent in real terms, and the net per capita increase in GDP in that period was 5.2 per cent. The trade figures showed a widening gap: between 1978 and 1982, imports doubled, while export revenues had been decreasing since 1980. Tonga had presented to a 1982 inter-agency mission 48 projects for which assistance was needed at a cost of $58.1 million,[67] oriented to short- and medium-term development needs. The 1984 report described the status of those projects as at 30 September 1984.

GENERAL ASSEMBLY ACTION

By decision 39/431, the General Assembly on 17 December took note of two summary reports of the Secretary-General, including the one on Tonga.

Vanuatu

An inter-agency mission led by the Under-Secretary-General for Special Political Questions and Co-ordinator for Special Economic Assistance Programmes visited Vanuatu from 18 to 24 June 1984 to consult with the Government and to report on the country's urgent development needs. Its report, issued in August 1984[11]—in response to the General Assembly's 1983 request[68] that the Secretary-General mobilize assistance for Vanuatu—provided information on the economic, financial and social conditions, described requirements for Vanuatu's development and proposed projects for international assistance, giving estimated costs.

Vanuatu, an archipelago with a relatively high population growth rate of 3 per cent, had significant fishery resources but only a small fishing industry. About 41 per cent of the land was considered arable and 17 per cent was under cultivation. Explorations were under way to determine possible mineral deposits. Under its first national development plan for 1982-1986, Vanuatu had set out development objectives with emphasis on transport and communications, utilization of the country's agricultural and human resources, encouragement of national entrepreneurism, preservation of its cultural and environmental heritage, and the long-term goal of national reliance.

The mission stated that the economy, having gradually recovered from a set-back following pre-independence disturbances, had expanded steadily since 1981. GDP growth in real terms was estimated to have accelerated from about 2 per cent that year to about 4 per cent in 1983, and there were indications of good economic performance in 1984. Real incomes for 1984 were estimated to have grown by 4 to 5 per cent over 1983. Construction, tourism and investment had increased since independence in 1980. Agriculture accounted for about one fifth of GDP, despite the fact that 85 per cent of the workforce was engaged in agriculture, and for over 80 per cent of the country's total exports. Vanuatu's export base was dominated by copra, which brought in over 70 per cent of export earnings. In 1984, copra exports increased nearly 20 per cent, doubling copra export earnings. The Government introduced in 1982 a copra price stabilization scheme, and stabili-

zation schemes for cocoa and other primary commodities were under consideration.

Vanuatu's trade deficit was $2.2 million in 1983; earnings from tourism more than made up for the outflow of money. With international assistance, Vanuatu had attained a favourable balance of payments. Import duties were the largest revenue source.

Four road projects had been identified for priority implementation, subject to availability of funding. Inter-island shipping services, air transport facilities and telecommunications also needed improvement. The country was dependent on imported petroleum for commercial energy requirements, although three quarters of its energy consumption was in the form of local biomass. Only 8 per cent of the population had electricity, almost entirely restricted to two urban centres. Other areas of concern were education, health, water supply and sewerage, and natural disaster preparedness.

The mission reviewed the development projects proposed by the Government for financing by the international community in the agriculture, transport, telecommunications, energy, social services, local government and natural disaster preparedness sectors, and recommended them for favourable action. It divided the 35 proposed projects, worth some $74.6 million, into an order of priorities.

In a resolution of 6 April,[43] the Trade and Development Board of UNCTAD requested the UNCTAD Secretary-General, in co-operation with UNDP, to identify, respond to and report on Vanuatu's assistance needs within UNCTAD's competence. UNCTAD had participated in the June mission to Vanuatu, with special reference to transport problems. According to an UNCTAD secretariat report,[42] by the end of 1984 no requests for assistance for projects within UNCTAD's competence had been received.

The UNDP Administrator reported[44] that, during 1984, the UNDP field office at Suva, Fiji, which covered Vanuatu, sent three missions there to monitor and review ongoing UNDP country and regional projects and to co-ordinate third-party cost-sharing and other multi- and bilateral arrangements with donors. Assistance to Vanuatu in 1984 was facilitated by the move of the United Nations Development Advisory Team from Fiji to Vanuatu, where it was combined with the Pacific Office of the Economic and Social Commission for Asia and the Pacific (ESCAP) to form the new ESCAP Pacific Operations Centre at Vila, the capital of Vanuatu.

GENERAL ASSEMBLY ACTION

On 17 December, the General Assembly, acting on the recommendation of the Second Committee, adopted resolution 39/198 without vote.

Economic assistance to Vanuatu

The General Assembly,

Recalling its resolution 38/218 of 20 December 1983, in which it requested the Secretary-General to mobilize the financial, technical and economic assistance of the international community, in particular the developed countries and the appropriate organizations of the United Nations system, with a view to meeting the development needs of Vanuatu,

Recalling also its resolutions 31/156 of 21 December 1976, 32/185 of 19 December 1977, 34/205 of 19 December 1979, 35/61 of 5 December 1980 and 37/206 of 20 December 1982, in which it urged all Governments, in particular those of the developed countries, to lend their support, in the context of their assistance programmes, for the implementation of the specific action envisaged in favour of island developing countries, and in which it also called upon all organizations of the United Nations system to implement, within their respective spheres of competence, appropriate specific actions in favour of island developing countries,

Noting the difficult problems faced by island developing countries, owing mainly to their smallness, remoteness, constraints in transport, great distances from market centres, highly limited internal markets, lack of natural resources, heavy dependence on a few commodities, shortage of administrative personnel and heavy financial burdens,

Taking into account the fact that Vanuatu is an island developing country, that it is a geographically remote archipelago with a small population, that it has demographic disadvantages, that its dependence on imports is overwhelming and that it has a scarcity of adequate transportation and communications links, all of which pose special development problems, making the provision of services difficult and entailing very high overhead costs,

1. *Calls the attention* of the international community to the report of the Secretary-General on assistance to Vanuatu;

2. *Endorses* the assessment and recommendations contained in the annex to the report of the Secretary-General;

3. *Expresses its appreciation* to the Secretary-General for the steps he has taken to mobilize assistance for Vanuatu;

4. *Also expresses its appreciation* to those States and organizations which have provided assistance to that country;

5. *Further calls the attention* of the international community to the special problems confronting Vanuatu as an island developing country with a small but rapidly growing and unevenly distributed population, a severe shortage of development capital and declining budgetary support from present donors;

6. *Requests* the appropriate organizations and programmes of the United Nations system to maintain and expand their current and future programmes of assistance to Vanuatu, to co-operate closely with the Secretary-General in organizing an effective international programme of assistance and to report periodically to him on the steps they have taken and the resources they have made available to help that country;

7. *Invites* the Economic and Social Commission for Asia and the Pacific, the United Nations Conference on Trade and Development, the United Nations Industrial Development Organization, the United Nations Children's Fund, the United Nations Fund for Population Activities, the United Nations Development Programme, the World Food Programme, the International Labour Organisation, the Food and Agriculture Organization of the United Nations, the United Nations Educational, Scientific and Cultural Organization, the International Civil Aviation Organization, the World Health Organization, the World Bank, the International Telecommunication Union, the World Meteorological Organization, the International Maritime Organization and the International Fund for Agricultural Development to bring to the attention of their governing bodies, for their consideration, the special needs of Vanuatu and to report the decisions of those bodies to the Secretary-General by 15 July 1985;

8. *Requests* the Committee for Development Planning at its twenty-first session, as a matter of priority, to give due consideration to the question of the inclusion of Vanuatu in the list of the least developed countries and to submit its conclusions to the Economic and Social Council at its second regular session of 1985;

9. *Calls upon* Member States, pending consideration by the Committee for Development Planning at its twenty-first session of the report submitted to it and in view of the critical economic situation of Vanuatu, to accord Vanuatu special measures and, as a matter of priority, to give special consideration to the early inclusion of Vanuatu in their programmes of development assistance;

10. *Requests* the Secretary-General:

(*a*)   To continue his efforts to mobilize the necessary resources for an effective programme of financial, technical and material assistance to Vanuatu;

(*b*)   To keep the situation in Vanuatu under constant review, to maintain close contact with Member States, the specialized agencies, regional and other intergovernmental organizations and the international financial institutions concerned, and to apprise the Economic and Social Council, at its second regular session of 1985, of the current status of the special programme of economic assistance for Vanuatu;

(*c*)   To report on the progress made in the economic situation in Vanuatu and in organizing international assistance for that country in time for the matter to be considered by the General Assembly at its fortieth session.

General Assembly resolution 39/198

17 December 1984   Meeting 103   Adopted without vote

Approved by Second Committee (A/39/793) without vote, 30 November (meeting 54); 60-nation draft (A/C.2/39/L.63), orally revised following informal consultations; agenda item 83 *(b)*.

Sponsors: Afghanistan, Algeria, Angola, Australia, Bahamas, Bangladesh, Belize, Benin, Bolivia, Botswana, Burundi, Cameroon, Cape Verde, Chad, China, Cyprus, Democratic Yemen, Dominican Republic, Ecuador, Egypt, Ethiopia, Fiji, Guinea-Bissau, Guyana, Haiti, India, Japan, Libyan Arab Jamahiriya, Madagascar, Maldives, Mozambique, New Zealand, Nicaragua, Niger, Nigeria, Pakistan, Panama, Papua New Guinea, Portugal, Romania, Rwanda, Samoa, Sao Tome and Principe, Senegal, Sierra Leone, Solomon Islands, Swaziland, Syrian Arab Republic, Trinidad and Tobago, Uganda, United Kingdom, United Republic of Tanzania, United States, Uruguay, Vanuatu, Venezuela, Viet Nam, Yemen, Yugoslavia, Zambia.

Meeting numbers. GA 39th session: 2nd Committee 32-37, 45, 54; plenary 103.

The draft was revised in informal consultations, where it was agreed to add UNFPA to the list of organizations in paragraph 7.

REFERENCES

[1]A/39/392 & Add.1. [2]A/39/383. [3]A/39/389. [4]A/39/384. [5]A/39/381. [6]A/39/572. [7]A/39/385. [8]A/39/382. [9]A/39/391. [10]A/39/394. [11]A/39/388. [12]A/39/393 & Add.1. [13]A/39/578. [14]YUN 1981, p. 406. [15]*Ibid.*, p. 410, GA res. 36/194, 17 Dec. 1981. [16]E/1984/68. [17]E/1984/68/Add.1. [18]A/39/594. [19]A/39/627. [20]YUN 1978, p. 429. [21]A/39/289-E/1984/107 & Add.1. [22]YUN 1980, p. 557, GA res. 35/64, 5 Dec. 1980.

[23]*Ibid.,* p. 548. [24]E/1984/66. [25]E/1985/57. [26]ACC/1984/DEC/1-12 (dec. 1984/2). [27]E/1984/110 & Add.1. [28]A/40/87. [29]DP/1985/5/Add.1. [30]E/1984/20 (dec. 84/18). [31]YUN 1983, p. 537, GA res. 38/201, 20 Dec. 1983. [32]E/1984/20 (dec. 84/19). [33]DP/1984/17. [34]A/39/477. [35]A/39/724 & Corr.1. [36]A/39/797-S/16854. [37]A/39/833. [38]E/1985/29. [39]YUN 1983, p. 492, GA res. 38/210, 20 Dec. 1983. [40]*Ibid.,* p. 492. [41]*Ibid.,* p. 494, GA res. 38/219, 20 Dec. 1983. [42]TD/B/1038. [43]A/39/15, vol. I (res. 292(XXVIII)). [44]DP/1985/19. [45]YUN 1983, p. 496, GA res. 38/211, 20 Dec. 1983. [46]A/C.2/39/L.74. [47]YUN 1983, p. 500. [48]YUN 1982, p. 685. [49]YUN 1983, p. 502. [50]YUN 1982, p. 686. [51]YUN 1983, p. 504. [52]*Ibid.,* p. 508, GA res. 38/215, 20 Dec. 1983. [53]*Ibid.,* p. 507. [54]YUN 1982, p. 317, SC res. 527(1982), 15 Dec. 1982. [55]YUN 1983, p. 510. [56]*Ibid.,* p. 511, GA res. 38/208, 20 Dec. 1983. [57]YUN 1982, p. 693, GA res. 37/146, 17 Dec. 1982. [58]*Ibid.,* p. 693. [59]YUN 1983, p. 512. [60]*Ibid.,* p. 515, GA res. 38/206, 20 Dec. 1983. [61]YUN 1982, p. 698. [62]YUN 1983, p. 515, GA res. 38/223, 20 Dec. 1983. [63]*Ibid.,* p. 532, GA res. 38/217, 20 Dec. 1983. [64]*Ibid.,* p. 532. [65]A/39/392/Add.1. [66]YUN 1982, p. 700, GA res. 37/164, 17 Dec. 1982. [67]*Ibid.,* p. 699. [68]YUN 1983, p. 516, GA res. 38/218, 20 Dec. 1983.

Disasters

During 1984, UNDRO continued its work in co-ordinating the relief activities of the United Nations system in response to natural disasters such as drought, floods, storms and earthquakes. Besides responding to disasters, UNDRO continued its work in promoting preparedness for such events.

Both the General Assembly and the Economic and Social Council called for assistance to deal with special needs resulting from the continuing drought in certain areas in Africa, particularly the Sudano-Sahelian region (Assembly resolution 39/206) and East Africa (Council resolutions 1984/5, 1984/6 and 1984/7, and Assembly resolutions 39/201 and 39/205); cyclones and floods in Madagascar (Council resolution 1984/3 and Assembly resolution 39/191); a cyclone in Swaziland (Council decision 1984/106 and Assembly resolution 39/194); and an earthquake in Yemen (Assembly resolution 39/190). In addition, the Assembly and the Council (resolutions 39/207 and 1984/60 respectively) recommended measures for strengthening the United Nations capacity to respond to disasters, stressed the importance of UNDRO activities and appealed to the international community to contribute to the UNDRO Trust Fund.

Office of the United Nations Disaster Relief Co-ordinator

UNDRO activities

In 1984, UNDRO continued to provide assistance at the request of Governments to reduce the economic and social impact of disasters on developing countries. Its activities were dominated by the emergency situation in Africa (see p. 465), involving some 18 countries and an estimated 30 million people out of a total population of 161 million. That situation was caused by a combination of drought and, in some cases, civil strife, coupled with administrative and logistical difficulties and underdevelopment problems. UNDRO continued its functions of assessing relief needs, monitoring and co-ordinating donor response, and providing information on requirements in individual countries and the evolution of the emergency situation there. In addition to on-site assessment of damage and needs once a disaster struck and provision of emergency relief, UNDRO activities included the interrelated areas of disaster preparedness and prevention (see p. 520) and dissemination of information throughout the world. UNDRO's activities between 1 April 1983 and 31 March 1985 were described in reports of the Secretary-General to the Economic and Social Council and/or the General Assembly issued in June 1984[1] and May 1985.[2] The first of two addenda to the 1984 report dealt with strengthening the United Nations capacity to respond to natural disasters and other disaster situations; the second contained the text of a proposed draft convention on expediting the delivery of emergency assistance (see p. 504).

Maintaining close working relationships with Governments—both donors to relief efforts and those suffering disasters—was an important element of UNDRO's work. High-level missions visited a number of countries in both categories. In August and November, after consultations with the Economic Commission for Latin America and the Caribbean (ECLAC), a mission visited the headquarters of the Latin American Economic System (know by its Spanish acronym, SELA) at Caracas, Venezuela, to develop co-operation between the two organizations. (SELA translated and relayed UNDRO situation reports on disasters in the region to member States.) Questionnaires developed for joint preparedness and prevention activities aimed at assessing the current state of disaster management capability in Latin American countries. In that connection, UNDRO undertook assessment missions to Colombia, Ecuador, Panama, Paraguay and Peru, while SELA sent a consultant to Argentina, Bolivia, Brazil, Chile and Uruguay for that purpose. UNDRO continued consultations with intergovernmental and non-governmental humanitarian organizations to share information. To that end, the second international meeting of mobile disaster units (groups organized for relief activities at disaster sites outside their own countries) (Geneva, 22-24 May) made recommendations on logistics and stockpiles of relief goods covering pre-disaster planning, assessment and intervention.

Activities in public information were expanded, with the crisis in Africa adding urgency to the need to acquire and disseminate up-to-date information on disaster prevention technology, pre-disaster planning, public education, assessment of relief needs and other aspects of disaster management. The bimonthly *UNDRO News* contained the latest technical information on disasters and on UNDRO emergency-related activities, including a table on the latest situation in the African countries affected by drought and other disasters. New publications included the latest volume of the UNDRO/UNEP *Compendium on Disaster Prevention and Mitigation—Preparedness Aspects*; the final report on the meeting on mobile disaster units, and the proceedings of the 1983 Balkan Regional Seminar on Earthquake Preparedness.[3] A brochure was published describing the functions, purposes and uses of the Trust Fund of UNDRO. UNDRO also co-operated in making two documentary films, one on relief activities following a typhoon in the Philippines and disaster prevention and preparedness work in the Caribbean, and the other on the causes and effects of the drought in Africa. The press was informed of UNDRO activities through periodic press releases, briefings on emergency operations and topical articles.

New components were introduced into the computerized Disaster Information System and UNDRO's telecommunications system. Implementation of the computerized Disaster Information Data Base system continued. A new component, the Bibliographic Data Base, was completed. The UNDRO Data Bank, a collection of disaster-related material, was expanded, with particular attention to training, education and audio-visual material, as well as to the map library. UNDRO also provided systems and services for use by other organizations, including UNHCR and UNICEF, which were provided direct access to the Disaster Information Data Base, and UNHCR was given the use of the UNDRO computerized telex transmission system. Portable mini-computers, capable of computer-to-computer interchange of information with UNDRO headquarters at Geneva, were introduced in disaster-stricken countries to record contributions and assist in managing the logistics of receipt and distribution of relief goods.

During 1984, the United Nations concluded an agreement with the International Telecommunications Satellite Corporation (INTELSAT), permitting the free use of INTELSAT satellites for peace-keeping and disaster relief operations. Field tests were carried out using portable satellite transmitters for emergency communications from the field to UNDRO headquarters.

In addition to examining a number of disaster situations concerning which the General Assembly and the Economic and Social Council took action to provide relief assistance (see below, under "Disaster relief"), UNDRO took note of numerous other disasters, such as those listed below, often launching international appeals at the request of the Govern-

ments concerned, providing technical assistance, issuing situation reports or providing cash grants.

—*Afghanistan.* An earthquake struck a region bordering Pakistan on 31 December 1983, destroying 1,316 houses and forcing 6,580 persons to evacuate their homes. UNDRO issued an international appeal on 30 January 1984 and provided a cash grant of $20,000 for construction material.

—*Benin.* After deficient rainfall throughout 1983 which led to crop failures and a significant lowering of water-tables, UNDRO sent an inter-agency mission to Benin from 11 to 25 February 1984. At the request of the Government, the mission formulated a six-month, $1-million relief programme to provide drinking-water, emergency food aid and medical supplies. A multisectoral drought-relief programme planned by UNDRO was completed on 30 September, which involved drilling of boreholes and repair of wells, provision of food aid and agricultural and medical supplies, and reconstruction of villages.

—*Botswana.* Rainfall continued to be insufficient in 1984, resulting in lack of drinking-water and malnutrition. At the request of the Government, UNDRO appealed for international assistance.

—*Burma.* A serious fire on 24 March at Mandalay destroyed 2,700 houses and rendered 23,250 persons homeless. Loss of property was estimated at $33 million. An appeal was launched on 13 April for assistance to the homeless. UNDRO provided an emergency grant for fire equipment. Contributions as at 8 November amounted to $377,236.

—*Chad.* In November, the Government appealed for relief assistance to the drought-affected population. UNDRO sent a representative there to help assess relief needs.

—*Colombia.* Flooding and landslides in October affected 194,000 persons. The Government appealed for international assistance on 13 November. UNDRO released an emergency grant and sent a representative to assist in assessing damage and relief needs.

—*Mali.* Following a poor 1982/83 growing season, Mali appealed for international assistance and UNDRO sent an evaluation mission there in May 1984 to establish a list of emergency relief needs. A cholera outbreak in July 1984 lasted through the rainy season. A UNDRO/WFP/FAO mission in October/November evaluated stock-breeding, agricultural production and emergency relief and determined a need for 202,000 metric tons of food.

—*Mauritania.* In response to a 14 December 1983 request from the Government, UNDRO organized an inter-agency mission from 14 to 21 February 1984 to review the implementation of the emergency action plan for combating the effects of the drought and to strengthen the relief effort. The mission called for additional food aid, trucks and contributions towards transport costs, assistance in nutritional monitoring and strengthening of medical facilities, as well as short-term measures in agriculture, cattle raising, hydrology and utilization of labour.

—*Mozambique.* In addition to suffering a prolonged drought, Mozambique was hit by a cyclone in late January, which caused 109 deaths and affected 300,000 persons. Agricultural land, irrigation systems and water supply for Maputo were severely damaged. UNDRO led a multi-agency mission to assess the emergency needs and identify relief distribution problems. Following an international appeal, UNDRO reported over $87 million in contributions as at 24 February.

—*Niger*. UNDRO launched an international appeal for assistance, as requested by the Niger on 19 December as a result of the drought. UNDRO was also asked to provide logistics support and to obtain the necessary funding.

—*Philippines*. Three strong typhoons hit the Philippines between August and November, causing flooding which destroyed crops and livestock and damaged roads, bridges and buildings. More than 3.2 million people were affected and damage was estimated at $337 million. UNDRO provided an emergency grant to cover immediate relief needs. Air transport was arranged for much of the relief distribution.

—*Viet Nam*. A typhoon struck coastal provinces in November, followed by heavy rains which extended to other parts of the country. About 650,000 people were seriously affected and considerable damage was caused to crops and housing. Responding to an appeal for emergency assistance, the international donor community provided cash to purchase medicines and food, and contributions in kind.

ECONOMIC AND SOCIAL COUNCIL ACTION

On 26 July, the Economic and Social Council adopted resolution 1984/60 without vote. The draft was recommended by the Third Committee.

Office of the United Nations Disaster Relief Co-ordinator

The Economic and Social Council,

Recalling General Assembly resolutions 2816(XXVI) of 14 December 1971, by which the Assembly established the Office of the United Nations Disaster Relief Co-ordinator, 36/225 of 17 December 1981, by which it reaffirmed the mandate and strengthened the capacity of the Office, and 38/202 of 20 December 1983, in which it, *inter alia*, noted with interest the steps taken to strengthen the capacity of the Office, and of the United Nations system as a whole, to respond to disasters, and called for a further report on the matter to be submitted to the Assembly at its thirty-ninth session, through the Economic and Social Council at its second regular session of 1984,

Noting with appreciation the effective responses of the Office of the United Nations Disaster Relief Co-ordinator, and of the international community, to recent major and continuing disaster situations,

Recognizing that shortage of resources continues to hamper the full achievement of the aim of rapid and effective response to the needs of countries affected by disasters and that, if this shortage is to be overcome, further efforts will be required by the international community to provide both funds and assistance in kind,

Considering that all possible new and innovative approaches should be examined with a view to improving further the rapid delivery of emergency relief,

Noting the wealth of expertise and training facilities that exists and that could be drawn upon by disaster-prone developing countries,

Recalling the importance attached in the Substantial New Programme of Action for the 1980s for the Least Developed Countries to the reduction of losses caused by disasters of all kinds and the creation of infrastructures which would be beneficial in this regard,

Convinced of the absolute necessity of maintaining a sound financial basis, in accordance with repeated requests by the General Assembly, to ensure the continuation of the work of the Office of the United Nations Disaster Relief Co-ordinator at its present level as a minimum,

Appreciating the contributions made by donors in supporting international relief operations, including those made to the Trust Fund of the Office of the United Nations Disaster Relief Co-ordinator,

1. *Takes note with profound satisfaction* of the report of the Secretary-General on the activities of the Office of the United Nations Disaster Relief Co-ordinator and of the statement made by the Co-ordinator before the Third (Programme and Co-ordination) Committee of the Council on 17 July 1984, as well as of the report of the Secretary-General on strengthening the capacity of the United Nations system to respond to natural disasters and other disaster situations, called for in paragraph 12 of General Assembly resolution 38/202;

2. *Recognizes* that information is one of the essential elements for the fulfilment of the mandate of the Office of the United Nations Disaster Relief Co-ordinator as the focal point of the United Nations system for disaster relief co-ordination, and emphasizes the importance of improving the flow and quality of information during disaster relief operations so that a more complete picture of relief channels and activities, assistance received and unmet requirements may be available to all concerned;

3. *Stresses*, in this regard, the primary importance of inter-agency assessment missions organized by the Office of the United Nations Disaster Relief Co-ordinator with the participation of the appropriate organizations of the United Nations system and other relief bodies in order to ensure the effective co-ordination of disaster relief activities, assistance and requirements;

4. *Recognizes* the value of united appeals, launched after the joint development with the agencies concerned of concerted relief programmes based upon the findings of inter-agency assessment missions, to be sent at the invitation of the Government concerned, as a most effective tool for co-ordination, and urges Governments to continue to respond to such appeals accordingly;

5. *Requests* the Secretary-General to adapt procedures for the procurement of supplies by the Office of the United Nations Disaster Relief Co-ordinator in order to permit a timely response to the special and immediate requirements of countries exposed to disasters or facing an emergency situation;

6. *Calls upon* those contributing assistance in kind to provide, when appropriate, special grants to cover the costs of transport and distribution of the assistance to and within the affected country;

7. *Requests* the Office of the United Nations Disaster Relief Co-ordinator to study, in co-operation with the parties concerned, the most appropriate steps to ensure the ready availability of relief supplies and transport equipment;

8. *Urges* Governments to increase their efforts to reduce delays in the provision of food assistance in response to natural disasters and other disaster situations;

9. *Recommends* that, as the United Nations Disaster Relief Co-ordinator phases out his emergency co-ordination responsibility in a given country, he should contribute to ensuring the necessary transition to the re-

habilitation and reconstruction phase by passing on relevant data to competent organs and agencies of the United Nations system;

10. *Calls upon* Governments and international relief organizations to put at the disposal of the United Nations Disaster Relief Co-ordinator the names and specializations of qualified disaster personnel available, in case of need, for inter-agency assessment missions, the execution of relief programmes or other disaster mitigation activities, and to inform him of existing disaster management training capabilities and opportunities for such training which could be offered to officials from developing countries;

11. *Encourages* the Co-ordinator to review, if necessary with the assistance of specialists made available by appropriate international bodies, the internal evaluation system of the Office;

12. *Recognizes* the importance of disaster prevention and preparedness at the regional and national levels in mitigating the effects of disasters, appreciates the work which the Office of the United Nations Disaster Relief Co-ordinator has performed in this area as far as the resources available in its Trust Fund have allowed, and encourages Governments to continue to draw upon the services available from the Office and other organizations concerned and to provide the necessary resources for this aspect of technical co-operation;

13. *Emphasizes* the essential need for the work of the Office of the United Nations Disaster Relief Co-ordinator to be placed and kept on a sound financial basis, and appeals to the international community to make contributions to the Trust Fund for General Disaster Relief or to the Trust Fund of the Office of the United Nations Disaster Relief Co-ordinator for the purposes set out in the report of the Secretary-General on the activities of the Office.

Economic and Social Council resolution 1984/60

26 July 1984   Meeting 49   Adopted without vote

Approved by Third Committee (E/1984/148) without vote, 23 July (meeting 15); 11-nation draft (E/1984/C.3/L.9), orally revised; agenda item 18.

Sponsors: Argentina, Austria, Bangladesh, Canada, Kuwait, Lebanon, Pakistan, Portugal, Saint Lucia, Senegal for African Group, Turkey.

Following the sponsors' oral proposal to add the last preambular paragraph, Canada withdrew an oral amendment it had made to add a final operative paragraph to the same effect. Japan also orally proposed, but later withdrew, an amendment to add a preambular paragraph recognizing that primary responsibility for administration of relief operations and disaster preparedness lay with the affected countries and that the major part of the material assistance and human effort in disaster relief came from those countries' Governments.

GENERAL ASSEMBLY ACTION

Addressing the Second Committee on 5 November 1984, the United Nations Disaster Relief Co-ordinator stressed the considerable needs of the countries affected by the drought in Africa. A common feature of the relief programmes recently prepared for those countries had been the emphasis

on the need for support for the transport and distribution of relief supplies.

With regard to disaster preparedness and prevention, increasing use was being made of modern techniques in monitoring situations which might develop into emergencies. UNDRO had significantly strengthened its information service, an essential instrument for liaison and co-operation with other organizations.

The Assembly adopted resolution 39/207, on the recommendation of the Second Committee, without vote on 17 December.

Office of the United Nations Disaster Relief Co-ordinator

The General Assembly,

Recalling its resolutions 2816(XXVI) of 14 December 1971, by which the Office of the United Nations Disaster Relief Co-ordinator was established, 36/225 of 17 December 1981, by which it reaffirmed the mandate of the Office and strengthened its capacity, and 38/202 of 20 December 1983, in which it, *inter alia*, noted with interest the steps taken to strengthen the capacity of the Office, and of the United Nations system as a whole, to respond to disasters, and called for a further report on the matter to be submitted to the Assembly at its thirty-ninth session, through the Economic and Social Council at its second regular session of 1984,

Recalling also Economic and Social Council resolution 1984/60 of 26 July 1984,

Noting with appreciation the effective response of the Office of the Co-ordinator and of the international community to recent major and continuing disaster situations,

Recognizing that shortage of resources continues to hamper the full achievement of the aim of rapid and effective response to the needs of countries affected by disasters and that, if this shortage is to be overcome, further efforts will be required by the international community to provide both funds and assistance in kind,

Considering that all possible new and innovative approaches should be examined with a view to improving further the rapid delivery of emergency relief,

Noting the wealth of expertise and training facilities that exists and that could be drawn upon by disaster-prone developing countries,

Recalling the importance attached in the Substantial New Programme of Action for the 1980s for the Least Developed Countries to the reduction of losses caused by disasters of all kinds and the creation of infrastructures which would be beneficial in this regard,

Convinced of the absolute necessity of maintaining a sound financial basis, in accordance with repeated requests by the General Assembly, to ensure the continuation of the work of the Office of the Co-ordinator at its present level as a minimum,

Appreciating the contributions made by donors in supporting international relief operations, including those made to the Trust Fund of the Office of the United Nations Disaster Relief Co-ordinator,

1. *Takes note with satisfaction* of the report of the Secretary-General on the work of the Office of the United Nations Disaster Relief Co-ordinator, as well as his report on strengthening the capacity of the United Nations system to respond to natural disasters and other

disaster situations, called for in paragraph 12 of General Assembly resolution 38/202, and of the statement made by the Co-ordinator on 5 November 1984;

2. *Recognizes* that information is one of the essential elements for the fulfilment of the mandate of the Office of the Co-ordinator as the focal point of the United Nations system for disaster relief co-ordination, and emphasizes the importance of improving the flow and quality of information during disaster relief operations so that a more complete picture of relief channels and activities, assistance received and unmet requirements may be available to all concerned;

3. *Stresses*, in this regard, the primary importance of inter-agency assessment missions organized by the Office of the Co-ordinator with the participation of the appropriate organizations of the United Nations system and other relief bodies in order to ensure the effective co-ordination of disaster relief activities, assistance and requirements;

4. *Recognizes* the value of united appeals, launched after the joint development with the agencies concerned of concerted relief programmes based upon the findings of inter-agency assessment missions, to be sent at the invitation of the Government concerned, as a most effective tool for co-ordination and urges Governments to continue to respond to such appeals accordingly;

5. *Requests* the Secretary-General to modify existing United Nations procurement procedures, as necessary, to permit, on the part of the Office of the Co-ordinator, a timely and more effective response to the special and immediate requirements of countries exposed to disasters or facing an emergency situation;

6. *Calls upon* those contributing assistance in kind to provide, when appropriate, special grants to cover the costs of transport and distribution of the assistance to and within the affected country;

7. *Requests* the Office of the Co-ordinator to study, in co-operation with the parties concerned, the most appropriate steps to ensure the ready availability of relief supplies and transport equipment;

8. *Urges* Governments to increase their efforts to reduce delays in the provision of food assistance in response to natural disasters and other disaster situations;

9. *Recommends* that as the Co-ordinator phases out his emergency co-ordination responsibility in a given country, he should contribute to ensuring the necessary transition to the rehabilitation and reconstruction phase by passing on relevant data to competent organs and agencies of the United Nations system;

10. *Calls upon* Governments and international relief organizations to put at the disposal of the Co-ordinator the names and specializations of qualified disaster personnel available, in case of need, for inter-agency assessment missions, the execution of relief programmes or other disaster mitigation activities, and to inform him of existing disaster management training capabilities and opportunities for such training which could be offered to officials from developing countries;

11. *Requests* the Co-ordinator to review and improve, if necessary with the assistance of specialists made available by appropriate international bodies, the internal evaluation system of the Office of the Co-ordinator in order to ensure that experience obtained from disaster relief operations is fully taken into account in the future work of the Office;

12. *Recognizes* the importance of disaster prevention and preparedness at the regional and national levels in mitigating the effects of disasters, appreciates the work which the Office of the Co-ordinator has performed in this area as far as the resources available in the Trust Fund of the Office have allowed, and encourages Governments to continue to draw upon the services available from the Office and other organizations concerned and to provide the necessary resources for this aspect of technical co-operation;

13. *Requests* the Office of the Co-ordinator to increase its fund-raising efforts through the means available to it;

14. *Emphasizes* the essential need for the work of the Office of the Co-ordinator to be placed and kept on a sound financial basis and requests the Secretary-General to assign a higher priority to this;

15. *Reiterates* in particular its appeals to the international community in resolutions 35/107 of 5 December 1980, 36/225 of 17 December 1981, 37/144 of 17 December 1982 and 38/202 of 20 December 1983 for urgent increased contributions to the Trust Fund established pursuant to its resolution 3243(XXIX) of 29 November 1974 for the purposes set out in the reports of the Secretary-General concerning the activities of the Office of the Co-ordinator.

General Assembly resolution 39/207

17 December 1984 　　　　Meeting 103 　　　　Adopted without vote

Approved by Second Committee (A/39/793Add.1) without vote, 6 December (meeting 56); draft by Vice-Chairman (A/C.2/39/L.103), based on informal consultations on 28-nation draft (A/C.2/39/L.70); agenda item 83 *(a)*.

Meeting numbers. GA 39th session: 2nd Committee 32-37, 47, 56; plenary 103.

In his oral report to the Second Committee on 5 November, the Co-ordinator reported on steps taken to implement a 1983 Assembly resolution[4] on special assistance to alleviate the economic and social problems faced in regions of Honduras and Nicaragua as a result of the May 1982 floods and other subsequent natural disasters. Nicaragua had requested technical assistance for earthquake and volcanic prediction; UNDRO, through the UNDP representatives, had offered technical assistance services of experts in pre-disaster planning. Honduras had also defined the specific areas where assistance was needed, and a technical mission was currently being organized.

The Assembly, by decision 39/431, took note of the oral report.

Draft convention on expediting aid delivery

In an addendum[5] to his June 1984 report on UNDRO activities,[1] the Secretary-General submitted UNDRO's proposed draft convention on expediting the delivery of emergency assistance following disasters. The text dealt with measures to facilitate the receipt of aid, such as transit rights, visas and the necessary privileges, immunities and security for relief units, to facilitate export and import of relief goods, to ensure access to telecommunications for relief purposes, to provide transportation of relief consignments, and to assign liability in connection with assistance provided by States and organizations to affected States. Comments of the

United Nations Legal Counsel and of the International Red Cross had been taken into consideration and some modifications made. The text was submitted so that the Economic and Social Council could decide on a further review by a group of governmental experts.

ECONOMIC AND SOCIAL COUNCIL ACTION

In July, the Council adopted decision 1984/175, without vote, on the recommendation of its Third Committee.

Reports of the Secretary-General relating to special economic, humanitarian and disaster relief assistance

At its 49th plenary meeting, on 26 July 1984, the Council:

(a) Took note of the reports of the Secretary-General on a proposed draft convention on expediting the delivery of emergency relief and on the implementation of the medium-term and long-term recovery and rehabilitation programme in the Sudano-Sahelian region and decided to transmit those reports to the General Assembly;

(b) Took note of the summary report of the Secretary-General on the special economic assistance programme for Swaziland.

Economic and Social Council decision 1984/175

Adopted without vote

Approved by Third Committee (E/1984/148) without vote, 23 July (meeting 15); oral proposal by Chairman; agenda item 18.

UNDRO financing

The activities of UNDRO were financed mainly from the United Nations regular budget and voluntary contributions to the UNDRO Trust Fund. In addition, the Trust Fund for General Disaster Relief was used as a reserve and a revolving fund to guarantee and, if necessary, advance sums pledged by donors for particular relief operations, bridging the gap between the date of the pledge and actual receipt of the donation. For the 1984-1985 biennium, the General Assembly had appropriated $5,236,400 in December 1983,[6] which was revised to $4,794,000 in December 1984 by resolution 39/237 A. In 1984, contributions from Governments to the UNDRO Trust Fund totalled $7,783,779. Expenses for the Office amounted to $2,496,757, most of which was spent on salaries and common staff costs.

Expenditures under the Trust Funds during 1984 were $7,073,936, including $5,022,385 to 33 individual countries and the Caribbean. The UNDRO Trust Fund had sub-accounts for strengthening UNDRO, for emergency relief assistance (unearmarked, to supplement regular budget grants, and earmarked, for particular countries) and for technical assistance in disaster prevention and predisaster planning. Contributions from 19 Governments and EEC paid to the Funds in 1984 totalled $7,783,779 (see tables below).

In his June report on UNDRO,[1] the Secretary-General emphasized that, to maintain the current level of activity, there was need for resources and the reversal of the unsatisfactory trend in voluntary contributions, which paid for one third of UNDRO's work, over the previous two years. In 1984, steps had to be taken to restrict the length of staff contracts to the funds known to be available and UNDRO had been compelled to draw upon the very limited reserves brought forward from previous years in order to continue its work. However, the Co-ordinator reported orally on 5 November to the Assembly's Second Committee that there had been a reversal of the downward trend in voluntary contributions to the Trust Fund.

CONTRIBUTIONS TO THE TRUST FUNDS FOR
DISASTER RELIEF ASSISTANCE, 1984
(as at 31 December 1984; in US dollar equivalent)

PURPOSE/CONTRIBUTOR	AMOUNT PAID
Disaster relief in Angola	
European Economic Community	394,761
Netherlands	103,188
Norway	127,000
Subtotal	624,949
Disaster relief in Burma	
Philippines	250
United States	10,000
Subtotal	10,250
Disaster relief in Chad	
Denmark	30,000
Disaster relief in Ethiopia	
Canada	587,164
European Economic Community	1,962,039
Italy	262,095
Norway	8,392
United States	300,000
Subtotal	3,119,690
Disaster relief in Guinea	
European Economic Community	80,458
Switzerland	30,734
United States	10,000
Subtotal	121,192
Disaster relief in Madagascar	
Australia	22,560
Canada	38,402
United States	76,500
Subtotal	137,462
Disaster relief in Mali	
Denmark	20,000
Italy	1,048,381
Netherlands	20,000
Switzerland	24,000
United Kingdom	55,000
Subtotal	1,167,381
Disaster relief in Mauritania	
Denmark	20,408
Norway	18,286
Switzerland	15,000
Subtotal	53,694

PURPOSE/CONTRIBUTOR	AMOUNT PAID
Disaster relief in Mozambique	
Australia	23,612
Ireland	16,763
Italy	612,639
Subtotal	653,014
Disaster relief in Nicaragua	
Italy	117,347
Disaster relief in the Niger	
Denmark	20,000
Disaster relief in Rwanda	
Germany, Federal Republic of	47,510
United Kingdom	47,720
Subtotal	95,230
Disaster relief in Sri Lanka	
Cyprus	300
Disaster relief in Swaziland	
Australia	47,225
Canada	40,254
Subtotal	87,479
Strengthening of UNDRO	
Australia	110,556
Bahamas	1,500
Barbados	1,000
Canada	190,804
Greece	10,000
Italy	265,521
Japan	50,000
New Zealand	6,457
Norway	50,000
Switzerland	60,000
Tunisia	5,101
United Kingdom	6
Subtotal	750,945
UNDRO Pan Caribbean Projects	
Canada	456,078
European Economic Community	13,268
United States	275,500
Subtotal	744,846
Disaster prevention and pre-disaster planning	
Norway	50,000
Total	7,783,779

SOURCE: Accounts for the 12-month period ended 31 December 1984 of the 1984-1985 biennium—schedules of individual trust funds.

EXPENDITURES UNDER THE TRUST FUNDS FOR
DISASTER RELIEF ASSISTANCE, 1984
(as at 31 December 1984; in US dollars)

ACCOUNT/PURPOSE	AMOUNT
Disaster relief assistance	
Afghanistan	20,000
Angola	2,147
Argentina	20,000
Benin	539,361
Bolivia	20,400
Botswana	10,200
Burkina Faso	20,000
Burma	10,489
Cape Verde	19,880
Caribbean	801,706
Chad	48,962
Colombia	225,745
Ecuador	217,583
Ethiopia	2,368,448
Fiji	9,425
Ghana	30,318
Guinea	147,743
Honduras	2,885

ACCOUNT/PURPOSE	AMOUNT
Disaster relief assistance (cont.)	
Indonesia	122
Lebanon	15,596
Madagascar	105,721
Mali	165,936
Mauritania	42,309
Mozambique	428,536
Nepal	25,000
Niger	54,293
Paraguay	13,011
Peru	95,762
Philippines	32,467
Portugal	25,000
Somalia	24,648
Swaziland	104,850
Turkey	355,003
Viet Nam	18,839
Subtotal	5,022,385
General disaster relief operations	80,725
Strengthening of UNDRO	698,112
UNDRO/UNEP projects	16,720
Disaster prevention and pre-disaster planning	255,994
Total	7,073,936

SOURCE: Accounts for the 12-month period ended 31 December 1984 of the 1984-1985 biennium—schedules of individual trust funds.

In resolution 1984/60, the Economic and Social Council emphasized the need for UNDRO's work to be on a sound financial basis and appealed to the international community to contribute to the Trust Funds set up to support that work.

The General Assembly, in resolution 39/207, requested UNDRO to increase its fund-raising efforts and also emphasized the need for UNDRO's work to be on a sound financial basis; the Secretary-General was asked to assign a higher priority to that goal. The Assembly reiterated its appeals to the international community for urgent increased contributions to the UNDRO Trust Fund.

Co-ordination in the UN system

The Secretary-General, in an addendum[7] to his June report on UNDRO,[1] made proposals for strengthening the capacity of the United Nations system to respond to natural and other disaster situations, as requested by the General Assembly in 1983.[8] The report was a follow-up to recommendations in a 1983 report on the same subject.[9]

The Secretary-General recommended that, once a feasibility study had been done, UNDRO should conduct, on an experimental basis, its headquarters' consultations with agencies through a teleconferencing system.

The Secretary-General proposed that Member States recognize the value of united appeals—launched for an affected country, particularly in the case of major compound disasters, after the joint development of relief programmes with the agencies concerned—as a most effective tool for co-ordination and that they continue to respond to those appeals. UNDRO, in co-operation with the agencies concerned, monitored and reported on contributions and needs as they became known or changed.

Addressing the difficulties in delivering relief supplies, he recommended that, in special cases, contributions in kind be accompanied by a provision for cash grants to cover the transport of relief goods to reach those in need, with donors acting in consultation with UNDRO. A study should be undertaken to determine with potential donors ways to ensure the availability of relief supplies and to mobilize transport equipment promptly in disaster cases, and to explore ways of concluding agreements with major manufacturers and suppliers so as to ensure their immediate availability. As a start, the Co-ordinator would contact emergency units in donor countries to study the feasibility of such a proposal. Member States were urged to reduce the delays in providing emergency food aid through WFP. This could be done, the Secretary-General said, by making physically available at the beginning of each fiscal year at least part of the pledged contributions to the International Emergency Food Reserve.

Another recommendation called for Governments and international relief organizations to transmit to UNDRO the names and specializations of qualified disaster experts who could be sent on assessment missions. States were also urged to inform UNDRO of existing disaster-management training capabilities in disaster-prone countries, with an indication of possible funding and scholarships.

Drawing attention to the uses for unearmarked emergency relief funds available through the Trust Fund for General Disaster Relief, the Secretary-General proposed that an appeal be made to all States to help in increasing the Fund's financial resources from its current level of approximately $800,000. States were also urged to contribute to the technical co-operation sub-account of the UNDRO Trust Fund, used for preparedness and prevention in disaster-prone countries by early warnings and information. He suggested that UNDRO's systematic internal evaluation be reviewed, if necessary with the assistance of specialists.

The Secretary-General, in following up 1982 and 1983 resolutions by which the General Assembly had called for special assistance to 20 countries, requested United Nations bodies and the specialized agencies to submit information on such assistance. The information—on aid, provided by UNDRO, DTCD, WFC, WFP, UNICEF, UNHCR, UNCTAD, UNFPA, UNDP, UNIDO, UNCHS, UNCDF, ILO FAO, UNESCO, WHO, the World Bank and IDA, IMF, ICAO, UPU, ITU, WMO, IMO, WIPO and IFAD—was communicated to the Assembly in a report on special assistance provided by the United Nations system[10] (see p. 464).

UNDRO continued to serve as the focal point for co-ordinating United Nations assistance in cases of disaster. The June report on UNDRO activities from 1 April 1983 to 31 March 1984[1] said that a total of 442 alerts were recorded by its global monitoring system and had been brought to the attention of the international community when warranted; in 43 cases, such alerts had involved UNDRO assistance, following a request from the stricken country, as against 35 such cases the preceding 12 months. During the reporting year, 23 relief assessment missions were undertaken either by UNDRO or jointly with other agencies, sometimes covering more than one country. Co-ordination of the activities was improved through meetings at headquarters, field missions and meetings in the affected countries. Meetings at the country level were usually organized under the chairmanship of the UNDP resident representative/resident co-ordinator. Contacts were maintained with international airlines to secure free transportation for both freight and passenger travel. In addition to working with United Nations bodies, UNDRO co-ordinated relief from other intergovernmental and non-governmental organizations, in particular EEC, the League of Arab States and OAU. A growing number of NGOs were associated with relief programmes and some were sub-contracted to execute UNDRO-financed relief operations, for example, the Red Cross of the Federal Republic of Germany, the Middle East Council of Churches, OXFAM and World Vision International.

Disaster relief

Drought-stricken areas of Africa

According to the Secretary-General's report on UNDRO activities from 1 April 1984 to 31 March 1985,[2] perhaps the chief factor that distinguished that period from earlier years was the emergency situation in Africa, which was caused by drought and resulted in famine. Failure, either partial or complete, of seasonal rainfall resulted in crop losses. The land had lost much of its fertility through years of over-grazing, and insufficient capital was available for fertilizers, reforestation and soil conservation projects. Consequent problems included malnutrition, disease, loss of human lives, sharp depletion of animal stocks, increased poverty—particularly among disadvantaged groups—desiccation of water resources, and increased migration especially to urban areas.

The Scientific Round-Table on the Climatic Situation and Drought in Africa (Addis Ababa, 20-23 February 1984) was organized by ECA in co-sponsorship with five other United Nations bodies—UNEP, UNSO, FAO, UNESCO and WMO—and OAU. The ECA Executive Secretary's report on its outcome was transmitted to the Economic and Social Council in June.[11] The meeting was attended by experts on climate, land, water and soil resources, ecology and the environment from 26 ECA member countries, observers from 11 other countries, and representatives from three intergovernmental and non-governmental organizations as well as 11 United Nations organs and specialized agencies. The meeting reviewed the situation, assessed the impact of drought on the socio-economic systems, as well as human responses to drought, and adopted a Regional Plan of Action, detailing measures for the short, medium and long terms at the national, regional and international levels to combat the impact of drought in Africa, which had begun in 1968 and had not yet ended, despite a brief lull during which near normal rainfalls had been experienced in the Sahel region in 1974 and 1975. The severity of the food shortages could be seen from the fact that the 1983 cereal production in 24 drought-affected countries registered a shortfall of 3.3 million tons as compared to 1981.

The meeting suggested that an inter-agency regional working group on drought in Africa, with a secretariat at ECA, be established to monitor the Plan of Action and to strengthen inter-agency collaboration. African countries were urged to encourage inter-State exchange of information on the impact of the drought, to consider establishing subregional drought control organizations similar to the Permanent Inter-State Committee on Drought Control in the Sahel (CILSS), and to encourage training and research activities. Members of the international community were called on to increase assistance to affected countries, and the United Nations and other organizations should help train manpower in areas related to drought, strengthen institutional capabilities of meteorological and hydrological services, ensure that data necessary for detecting and for warning of drought were available, and establish subregional climatic data banks. Drought-stricken and disaster-prone countries should adopt long-term measures for 1990 and beyond with a view to devising strategies to make national economies more versatile and less vulnerable to climatic variability and minimize the impact of drought.

The Plan of Action was approved by the ECA Conference of Ministers on 26 May 1984 (see Chapter VIII of this section). The Conference urged ECA members to implement the Plan and called on the international community and United Nations organizations to assist the drought-stricken African countries to combat the impact of drought, rehabilitate their economies and implement the Plan.

Drought and desertification issues were also considered by the Ministerial Conference for a joint policy to combat desertification in the member States of CILSS and the Economic Community of West African States (ECOWAS), as well as the Maghreb countries, Egypt and the Sudan (Dakar, Senegal, 18-27 July 1984). The final resolution of the Conference, transmitted to the Secretary-General by Senegal on 26 September,[12] contained recommen-

dations for States on combating desertification at the national, regional and international levels, involving political commitment, strategies and planning, and operational and financial co-operation. In addition to Egypt and the Sudan, the participating countries were Cape Verde, Chad, the Gambia, Mali, Mauritania, the Niger, Senegal and the Upper Volta (CILSS); Benin, Ghana, Guinea, Guinea-Bissau, the Ivory Coast, Liberia, Nigeria, Sierra Leone and Togo (ECOWAS); Algeria, Morocco and Tunisia (the Maghreb countries).

The Assembly, in resolution 39/208, welcomed the results of the Conference. It recommended that the international community, above all the developed countries, should continue to provide short-, medium- and long-term assistance to the countries stricken by desertification and drought in order to support the rehabilitation process—in particular through reafforestation—and the renewal of agricultural production in the affected countries, particularly in Africa.

UNDRO, as a member of the Secretary-General's Advisory Group and Task Force for Africa, had been associated from the outset with this initiative. In his June report on UNDRO activities,[1] the Secretary-General observed that the Group had held an information meeting for representatives of the donor community on 2 February to inform them of the critical situation in Africa and actions envisaged by UNDRO to step up relief assistance. As at 31 March, the total donations for the six countries involved (Benin, Chad, Ethiopia, Mauritania, Mozambique, Somalia), not counting contributions of food and in kind, amounted to $124 million, including $4 million through UNDRO. In another June report,[13] the Secretary-General described and provided data on the food and agriculture situation in Africa (see Chapter VIII of this section).

The food and agriculture situation was also of concern to UNDP. The Administrator issued in May a report[14] on activities of the United Nations Sudano-Sahelian Office (UNSO) (see below) and assistance to other drought-stricken countries in Africa during 1983, covering the eight CILSS members and other African countries particularly affected by drought. He emphasized that the problems related to the drought, which was becoming increasingly structural and endemic, could be solved in a lasting manner only through an increased global effort, based on ongoing discussions between the countries concerned and the international community as a whole. Medium- and long-range plans for integrated economic and social development were needed, encompassing water control, food production and human and livestock health, with a view to food self-sufficiency, rehabilitation and protection of the environment. The resources devoted thus far to development assistance for the African countries fell far short of the needs.

In a 29 June decision,[15] the UNDP Governing Council expressed satisfaction at the action taken by the Administrator, in pursuance of a 1983 General Assembly resolution on the liquidation of the United Nations Emergency Operation Trust Fund and allocation of the balance,[16] in approving assistance to urgently needed projects, primarily in the food and agricultural sectors in countries afflicted by famine and malnutrition, with special emphasis on drought-stricken African countries.

By resolution 39/165, the General Assembly took action on the critical problems of food and agriculture in Africa, calling on the international community to support African countries in their efforts to increase food production.

The UNEP Governing Council, after reviewing the implementation of the 1977 Plan of Action to Combat Desertification,[17] adopted on 28 May a decision[18] noting that desertification had continued to spread in developing countries, particularly in Africa, and proposing measures to ameliorate the problem. It endorsed the UNEP Executive Director's view that implementation should focus on the most affected countries, with priority to areas offering the best chances for rehabilitation. The Council decided that a further overall assessment of progress in implementation of the Plan of Action should be carried out in 1992.

In resolution 39/208, the Assembly took note of the UNEP Governing Council's decision and called for its implementation. By resolution 39/168 A, the Assembly endorsed UNEP's decision on a 1992 assessment of progress.

Sudano-Sahelian region

UNSO, under the authority and supervision of UNDP, continued in 1984 to carry out its mandate in support of drought-related medium- and long-term recovery and rehabilitation programmes in the eight countries of the Sudano-Sahelian region which were members of CILSS, assisting those countries in dealing with the impact of drought, which began in 1968 and created a severe emergency in 1984. The activities carried out in 1983 with UNSO financing were described by the Secretary-General in an April 1984 report, with a later addendum,[19] and updated through 1984 in a 1985 report.[20] In addition, UNSO, which co-operated closely with CILSS, continued its programme to combat desertification (see Chapter XVI of this section).

In 1984, project commitments to the United Nations Trust Fund for Sudano-Sahelian Activities (see p. 512) in the form of cost-sharing and specific trust funds for drought-related recovery and rehabilitation projects of the CILSS Governments amounted to over $7.5 million. In addition, UNSO mobilized almost $6 million for desertification-control projects in the CILSS countries, making a total of about $13.5 million.

A number of regional projects were continued in 1984. Among them was the construction and maintenance of a region-wide system of all-weather secondary roads in the Sahel, with the aim of guaranteeing the transport of emergency food to remote areas. The secondary road programme, executed by UNDP, was an important element of the overall development process in the Sahel. As at the end of 1984, almost 2,040 of the 3,000 kilometres of roads for which there was financing were completed. The plan for the entire system was to construct 5,000 kilometres, carried out for the most part by national public works departments. Under the project for the ecological rehabilitation of the Fouta-Djallon massif in Guinea, the watershed area for the main rivers of West Africa, a plan was drawn up for socioeconomic and hydrological studies to be carried out in 1985 by consultants. As part of an ongoing programme for developing and producing fuel-efficient cooking stoves to reduce demand for ligneous materials for domestic energy, national stoves projects were begun in Burkina Faso and the Gambia. The Institute of the Sahel, a specialized agency of CILSS, continued to benefit from UNSO assistance in carrying out some of its activities, including training in management and conservation of pasture lands.

According to the UNDP Administrator,[21] UNSO had since its inception, together with UNDP and UNEP, supported wide-ranging desertification control programmes such as those currently under way in 21 affected countries in East and West Africa (two more than in 1983), including the Sudano-Sahelian countries, through measures such as stabilizing and fixing sand dunes.

The Administrator also reported in April 1984[22] on ways of financing, beyond the 1984-1985 biennium, the UNDP/UNEP joint venture which assisted in carrying out UNSO's desertification control mandate. UNSO's administrative and programme expenditures were financed entirely from extrabudgetary sources, and the contributions of UNDP and UNEP to the joint venture constituted only a part of UNSO's operating costs. Those contributions were used mainly as "seed" money for project identification, formulation and development, and resource mobilization. The Administrator concluded that most of the financial sources within UNDP, UNEP and the United Nations did not present means of financing the venture beyond 1985. He believed that the current ways of financing it should be maintained—by the UNDP administrative budget, the African and the Arab States' regional indicative planning figures, and the UNEP Fund for the Environment.

In addition to desertification-control projects, UNSO-supported national projects included: livestock management in Burkina Faso; rehabilitation of an airport, exploration and utilization of water resources, soil and water conservation, and a desalination and power plant in Cape Verde; a campaign against rinderpest, re-establishment of a tree nursery, and training in agriculture and livestock projects in Chad; well maintenance, ground-water and natural resource management, and bush-fire control in the Gambia; a tree plantation, agro-sylvo-pastoral development of the Niger River flood plain, and installation of hand pumps on existing boreholes in Mali; agricultural statistics, training in forestry, development of deep-bore wells, and dam construction in Mauritania; establishment of green belts around towns, manufacture of agricultural tools and equipment, gum arabic production, and plan-ning for dam construction in the Niger; and reafforestation studies, and development of energy sources and energy conservation in Senegal. Road-construction projects continued in all those coun-tries except Chad.

UNSO, besides co-operating closely with a num-ber of United Nations bodies, also worked with the West African Economic Community on the joint programming and financing of activities. A joint programme for food storage, harvesting cereal and transport was under way.

In 1983,[23] the General Assembly had invited the Governing Council of UNEP to examine the pos-sibility of including Ghana and Togo in the list of countries which received assistance through UNSO in implementing in the Sudano-Sahelian region the 1977 Plan of Action to Combat Desertification.[17] The UNEP Council on 28 May 1984,[18] supported by the UNDP Governing Council on 29 June,[24] decided that those countries would be included.

The UNDP Council, in a 29 June decision[25] on implementation of the recovery and rehabilitation programme in the Sudano-Sahelian region, took note of the Secretary-General's report on the sub-ject,[19] and commended the Administrator for his priority attention to the needs of the region's drought-affected countries and for the results achieved by UNSO. It appealed for increased support for UNSO and requested UNSO to continue to co-operate with CILSS.

The Economic and Social Council, by decision 1984/175, also took note of the Secretary-General's report and transmitted it to the General Assembly.

UNCTAD also contributed to the implementation of the region's recovery and rehabilitation pro-gramme, as its secretariat reported in June.[26] As part of its mandate to assist LDCs and land-locked and island developing countries, UNCTAD provided assistance to Burkina Faso, Cape Verde, the Cen-tral African Republic, Chad, the Gambia, Mali, the Niger and Senegal. Such support was provided for projects in the areas of trade analysis, advisory services for trade policy, price controls and tariffs, trade statistics, transit transport for land-locked coun-tries, road construction, training activities related

to preferences and the transfer of technology, trade facilitation, shipping and debt management. On 21 September,[27] the Trade and Development Board transmitted the secretariat's note to the General Assembly, invited the Assembly to con-sider intensifying United Nations activities on behalf of the region, through UNSO, and to entrust UNC-TAD to carry out a study, in co-operation with UNSO and other bodies concerned, on the impact of the drought on the foreign trade of the CILSS member States as well as on the role of foreign trade for the development of those countries. The UNCTAD Secretary-General was invited to intensify the tech-nical assistance activities for the countries in the programme.

In September,[28] the Secretary-General reported to the Assembly on non-implementation of recom-mendations made by the Joint Inspection Unit, in-cluding those in a 1983 report on UNSO activities.[29] The recommendation that had not been im-plemented was the proposal that UNSO should en-courage the formulation of a global strategy for com-bating African drought and desertification by co-ordinating the activities of an inter-agency group which would draw up a document for considera-tion by a regional seminar that it would organize, bringing together national technical services, regional organizations, relevant United Nations bodies and donors. While UNSO had not established the pro-posed group, it had helped organize national and regional seminars and workshops on desertification, assisted CILSS in preparing an inventory of priority needs, and contributed to the funding of and par-ticipated in the July 1984 Ministerial Conference convened by Senegal (see p. 508).

GENERAL ASSEMBLY ACTION

On 17 December, the General Assembly adopted without vote resolution 39/206, as recommended by the Second Committee.

Implementation of the medium-term and long-term recovery and rehabilitation programme in the Sudano-Sahelian region

The General Assembly,

Recalling its resolutions 3054(XXVIII) of 17 October 1973, 3253(XXIX) of 4 December 1974, 3512(XXX) of 15 December 1975, 31/180 of 21 December 1976, 32/159 of 19 December 1977, 33/133 of 19 December 1978, 34/16 of 9 November 1979, 35/86 of 5 December 1980, 36/203 of 17 December 1981, 37/165 of 17 December 1982 and 38/225 of 20 December 1983,

Taking note of decision 84/28 of 29 June 1984 of the Governing Council of the United Nations Development Programme concerning the implementation of the medium-term and long-term recovery and rehabilitation programme in the Sudano-Sahelian region,

Deeply concerned by the tragic consequences of a disas-trous and persistent drought involving a substantial decrease in food and agricultural production in the Sudano-Sahelian countries,

Noting with satisfaction the efforts made by the United Nations Sudano-Sahelian Office in helping to combat the effects of drought and to implement the medium-term and long-term recovery and rehabilitation programme adopted by the States members of the Permanent Inter-State Committee on Drought Control in the Sahel, as well as in mobilizing the necessary resources for financing priority projects,

Also noting with satisfaction the collaboration between the Permanent Inter-State Committee on Drought Control in the Sahel and the Club du Sahel and urging that this collaboration be continued and strengthened,

Welcoming the inclusion in the agenda of its thirty-ninth session of the items entitled "Countries stricken by desertification and drought" and "Critical economic situation in Africa",

Bearing in mind the statements made by many delegations during the current session of the General Assembly in which they emphasized the continuing and increasing seriousness of the drought and desertification in the Sudano-Sahelian countries and in other regions of Africa and their devastating impact on the economic and social situation,

Considering that, owing to the nature and magnitude of the needs of the States members of the Permanent Inter-State Committee on Drought Control in the Sahel, the solidarity action taken by the international community to support the recovery and economic development efforts of those countries should be continued and intensified,

Having considered the report of the Secretary-General on the implementation of the medium-term and long-term recovery and rehabilitation programme in the Sudano-Sahelian region,

1. *Takes note* of the report of the Secretary-General;

2. *Expresses its gratitude* to the Governments, United Nations bodies, intergovernmental and non-governmental organizations and individuals that have contributed to the implementation of the medium-term and long-term recovery and rehabilitation programme in the Sudano-Sahelian region;

3. *Requests* all Governments to increase the resources of the United Nations Sudano-Sahelian Office by making voluntary contributions on the occasion of the United Nations Pledging Conference for Development Activities, as well as through other, in particular bilateral, channels so as to enable it to respond more fully to the priority requirements of the Governments of States members of the Permanent Inter-State Committee on Drought Control in the Sahel;

4. *Requests* the international community to support the implementation of the Second-Generation Programme of the States members of the Inter-State Committee on Drought Control in the Sahel, *inter alia*, by providing more assistance in all its forms for carrying out the following activities:

(*a*) Development projects already formulated and approved by the Governments;

(*b*) Regional projects to combat desertification;

(*c*) Surveys needed for establishing development potentials at national and regional levels;

(*d*) Strengthening and/or establishing national and subregional research and training institutes designed to find solutions to the problems confronting the Sahelian countries;

(*e*) Strengthening of national and subregional capacity for planning, management and evaluation of integrated development activities;

5. *Requests* all Governments and all organs, organizations and programmes of the United Nations system to give special attention to the increasingly critical food situation in the countries of the Sahel;

6. *Welcomes* the results achieved by the Administrator of the United Nations Development Programme, through the United Nations Sudano-Sahelian Office, in assisting the States members of the Permanent Inter-State Committee on Drought Control in the Sahel to implement their medium-term and long-term recovery and rehabilitation programme;

7. *Reaffirms* the role of the United Nations Sudano-Sahelian Office in co-ordinating United Nations efforts to help the countries of the Sahel to implement their recovery and rehabilitation programme;

8. *Invites* the United Nations Sudano-Sahelian Office to continue to strengthen its co-operation with the States members of the Permanent Inter-State Committee on Drought Control in the Sahel and with the Committee itself, with a view to expediting implementation of the medium-term and long-term recovery and rehabilitation programme in the Sudano-Sahelian region, and in particular to help those countries to formulate and implement national medium-term and long-term plans to combat desertification and drought, with a view to achieving food self-sufficiency;

9. *Requests* the Secretary-General to continue to report to the General Assembly, through the Governing Council of the United Nations Development Programme and the Economic and Social Council, on the implementation of the medium-term and long-term recovery and rehabilitation programme in the Sudano-Sahelian region.

General Assembly resolution 39/206

17 December 1984   Meeting 103   Adopted without vote

Approved by Second Committee (A/39/793) without vote, 30 November (meeting 54); 19-nation draft (A/C.2/39/L.47), orally revised following informal consultations; agenda item 83 *(c)*.

Sponsors: Algeria, Benin, Burkina Faso, Cape Verde, Chad, Comoros, Egypt, Gabon, Gambia, Ghana, Guinea, Guinea-Bissau, Liberia, Mali, Mauritania, Niger, Pakistan, Senegal, Togo.

Meeting numbers. GA 39th session: 2nd Committee 32-37, 45, 54; plenary 103.

Following informal consultations, the Secretary of the Second Committee announced that it had been agreed to add the fifth preambular paragraph. It was also agreed to add the phrase at the end of paragraph 8 inviting help in particular for formulating and implementing national plans with a view to CILSS members' achieving food self-sufficiency.

In resolution 39/208, the Assembly requested the UNDP Administrator to have UNSO establish biennial programmes for the implementation of the Plan of Action to Combat Desertification, with the requirement that those programmes be submitted for approval by the Administrator and the UNEP Executive Director, and emphasized the need for increased financial support by the international community for UNSO and UNEP activities.

In resolution 39/168 A, the Assembly took measures to improve implementation of the Plan of Action and called for increased support for UNSO.

UN Trust Fund for Sudano-Sahelian Activities

Expenditures from the United Nations Trust Fund for Sudano-Sahelian Activities totalled $14,147,000 in 1984. Seven Governments paid a total of $571,011 to the Fund during the year (see tables below).

PROGRAMME EXPENDITURES UNDER THE UN TRUST FUND
FOR SUDANO-SAHELIAN ACTIVITIES, 1984
(as at 31 December 1984; in thousands of US dollars)

Country/Region	Amount
Benin	87
Burkina Faso	633
Cape Verde	1,871
Chad	67
Djibouti	117
Ethiopia	454
Gambia	1,079
Guinea	28
Guinea-Bissau	6
Mali	195
Mauritania	1,411
Niger	3,497
Senegal	3,423
Somalia	251
Sudan	299
Subtotal	13,418
Regional Africa	729
Total	14,147

SOURCE: DP/1985/5/Add.6.

CONTRIBUTIONS TO THE UN TRUST FUND FOR
SUDANO-SAHELIAN ACTIVITIES, 1984 AND 1985
(as at 31 December 1984; in US dollar equivalent)

Country	1984 payment	1984 pledge for 1985
Algeria	20,000	20,000
Cameroon	8,929	18,085
Chile	—	5,000
Denmark	208,333	—
Finland	—	94,488
Greece	—	20,000
Italy	315,789	526,316
Mali	—	500
Philippines	5,000	500
Portugal	10,000	10,000
Senegal	—	10,000
Sudan	—	3,000
Sweden	—	2,285,714
Yugoslavia	2,960	3,886
Total	571,011	2,997,489

SOURCE: A/40/5/Add.1 & Add.1/Corr.1.

East Africa

In October 1984, the Secretary-General issued a note[30] on assistance to drought-stricken areas in East Africa—Djibouti, Ethiopia, Kenya, Somalia, the Sudan and Uganda—as requested by the General Assembly in December 1983.[31] During 1983 and 1984, most parts of the East African countries again experienced severe drought. While arrangements had not been finalized between the Governments concerned for an intergovernmental body to combat the effects of drought, as proposed by the Assembly, the Secretary-General had taken measures to increase the effectiveness of existing channels in dealing with the situation. To facilitate contacts with

Governments and to resolve urgent problems expeditiously, he appointed Adebayo Adedeji, Executive Secretary of ECA, as his Special Representative on the African crisis. In addition, a temporary office was set up in Nairobi to provide the Special Representative with the necessary support.

Plans for establishing the intergovernmental body were discussed at a meeting of the Foreign Ministers of the six countries in New York on 4 October 1984. Sudan informed the Secretary-General on 8 October[32] of the results of that meeting; the Ministers had affirmed their decision to meet on 15 January 1985 in Djibouti to finalize the necessary arrangements.

Djibouti, Ethiopia and Somalia, in notes verbales to the President of the Economic and Social Council, requested him to include in the agenda of the first regular 1984 session of the Council an item on emergency assistance to victims of the drought in their countries.

On 24 April,[33] Ethiopia said that its emergency situation had affected the entire country. Hundreds of thousands of people had been forced to flee to relief camps and cities in search of food; 5.2 million people were in a virtually helpless situation. The available food supply was barely sufficient for two months, even at a rate significantly below the starvation ration (400 grams). Starvation currently afflicted about 20 per cent of the Ethiopian population.

Djibouti informed the President on 10 May[34] of its emergency situation that had arisen because of the two-year drought, affecting 80,000 people. The situation had led to food shortages, endemic diseases and increased malnutrition, particularly among children. The nomadic people had lost 70 per cent of their livestock, which constituted their means of living. Despite the Government's emergency measures, Djibouti lacked adequate food, medical and logistic resources to meet the growing needs.

On 11 May,[35] Somalia said that, as a result of adverse climatic conditions, it was experiencing serious deficiencies in food needed to sustain the massive refugee population which Somalia had taken in. In addition to the drought, other factors over which Somalia had no control had aggravated the situation. For the previous two years, Somalis in certain parts of the country had received much less food than the agreed minimum.

On 14 February, after a Government-requested mission had visited Somalia from 6 to 13 February, UNDRO launched an appeal requesting relief assistance for the affected areas in north-west Somalia until the rainy season of April 1984. Similarly, UNDRO launched an appeal on 3 April to deal with the drought emergency in Ethiopia, immediately after the Government alerted the international donor community to the rapidly deteriorating situation. UNDRO representatives, permanently in the country since August 1983, continued to assess needs and transmit data to possible donors. In November, the Secretary-General appointed Kurt Jansson as Assistant Secretary-General for Emergency Operations in Ethiopia. UNDRO implemented and/or financed a number of relief programmes with cash contributions totalling $3.5 million for internal transport and distribution of relief supplies, bagging of food for air-dropping, and procurement of fuel, spare parts and equipment, seeds and blankets. The drought situation in the Sudan, aggravated by a renewed influx of people, was taken under review by UNDRO in October.

ECONOMIC AND SOCIAL COUNCIL ACTION

The Economic and Social Council on 17 May 1984 adopted without vote resolutions 1984/5, 1984/6 and 1984/7 on emergency assistance to Ethiopia, Djibouti and Somalia, respectively.

Emergency assistance to the drought victims in Ethiopia

The Economic and Social Council,

Having heard the statement made by the Commissioner for Relief and Rehabilitation of Ethiopia concerning the critical food situation in the drought-affected regions of Ethiopia,

Deeply disturbed at the gravity of the food situation and the prospect of mass starvation as a result of the drought that has affected the entire country recently,

Aware that a lasting solution to the problem of drought and environmental degradation can best be reached through regional and subregional co-operation as envisaged for the East African subregion in General Assembly resolution 35/90 of 5 December 1980 and Economic and Social Council resolution 1983/46 of 28 July 1983,

Recognizing, however, that, as a result of the unprecedented drought affecting the entire country, an emergency situation has arisen which requires prompt attention,

Noting with appreciation the continued efforts made by the Office of the United Nations Disaster Relief Coordinator, the United Nations Development Programme, the United Nations Children's Fund, the Food and Agriculture Organization of the United Nations, the World Food Programme and other organs and organizations of the United Nations system, as well as the invaluable support of non-governmental organizations,

Noting further that, despite the generous assistance offered to the Government of Ethiopia by Member States, organs and organizations of the United Nations system and voluntary agencies, enormous difficulties of relief and rehabilitation still persist,

1. *Takes note* of the statement made by the Commissioner for Relief and Rehabilitation of Ethiopia on the extremely critical food situation in the drought-affected regions of Ethiopia;

2. *Expresses its concern* at the difficulties that confront the Government of Ethiopia as a result of the unprecedented drought;

3. *Notes with appreciation* the response made thus far by the international community, organs and organizations of the United Nations system and voluntary agencies to assist the victims of the drought in Ethiopia;

4. *Appeals* to Governments of Member States, organs and organizations of the United Nations system, governmental and non-governmental organizations and all voluntary agencies to intensify and increase urgently their assistance to the Government of Ethiopia for emergency relief and rehabilitation for the victims of the drought, as well as for the recovery of the drought-affected areas of Ethiopia;

5. *Decides* to keep the matter under review.

Economic and Social Council resolution 1984/5

17 May 1984	Meeting 15	Adopted without vote

19-nation draft (E/1984/L.24); agenda item 1.

Sponsors: Algeria, Cuba, Cyprus, Djibouti, Egypt, Ethiopia, Gambia, India, Lesotho, Liberia, Madagascar, Pakistan, Rwanda, Sierra Leone, Tunisia, Uganda, Viet Nam, Yugoslavia, Zimbabwe.

Meeting numbers. ESC 5, 11, 15.

Emergency assistance to the drought victims in Djibouti

The Economic and Social Council,

Having heard the statement made by the representative of Djibouti on the distressing situation of the victims of the prolonged drought in that country,

Deeply concerned at the distressing emergency situation of the victims of the drought in Djibouti,

Aware of the adverse effects of the prolonged drought on the economic and social development of Djibouti,

Aware also of the regional character of the drought currently prevailing in the countries of East Africa,

Appreciating the unremitting efforts being made by the Government of Djibouti to meet the growing needs of the victims of the drought, in spite of the slenderness of its economic resources,

Recalling the resolutions adopted by the General Assembly and the Economic and Social Council on assistance in cases of natural disaster, in particular Assembly resolutions 2816(XXVI) of 14 December 1971 and 2959(XXVII) of 12 December 1972,

1. *Takes note* of the statement made by the representative of Djibouti on the critical situation of the victims of the drought in that country;

2. *Appreciates* the assistance provided to date by Member States, United Nations organizations and intergovernmental and non-governmental organizations to the relief programme for the victims of drought in Djibouti;

3. *Appeals* to Member States, international, governmental and non-governmental organizations and the specialized agencies to contribute generously to help the populations affected by drought in Djibouti by providing, as a matter of urgency, financial, material and technical assistance;

4. *Requests* the Secretary-General to send to Djibouti, as a matter of urgency, after consultation with the Government of Djibouti, an inter-agency mission with the task, in particular, of making a study of the situation in the drought-stricken areas of the country and evaluating the short-term, medium-term and long-term needs of the Government in the face of that situation, and to report to the General Assembly at its thirty-ninth session, through the Economic and Social Council at its second regular session of 1984, on the results of that mission and on the progress achieved in the implementation of the present resolution.

Economic and Social Council resolution 1984/6

17 May 1984   Meeting 15   Adopted without vote

41-nation draft (E/1984/L.25); agenda item 1.
Sponsors: Algeria, Austria, Bangladesh, Benin, Botswana, China, Cuba, Cyprus, Djibouti, Egypt, Ethiopia, France, Gambia, Greece, India, Italy, Japan, Kenya, Lebanon, Liberia, Madagascar, Malawi, Mali, Mexico, Morocco, Pakistan, Qatar, Rwanda, Saint Lucia, Saudi Arabia, Sierra Leone, Somalia, Sri Lanka, Swaziland, Syrian Arab Republic, Thailand, Tunisia, Uganda, Yugoslavia, Zaire, Zambia.
Meeting numbers. ESC 11, 15.

Emergency assistance to the drought victims in Somalia

The Economic and Social Council,

Having heard the statement made by the representative of Somalia on the critical need for emergency assistance to the drought victims in Somalia,

Recognizing the alarming situation which is developing in Somalia as a result of successive failures of seasonal rains in several regions of the country,

Cognizant of the emergency situation which, as a consequence, has overtaken the entire country, posing the severe threat of mass starvation to both people and livestock,

Appreciating the ongoing response of the Office of the United Nations Disaster Relief Co-ordinator, the United Nations Development Programme, the United Nations Children's Fund, the Food and Agriculture Organization of the United Nations, the World Food Programme and international voluntary agencies, and the vital bilateral contributions of friendly States,

Concerned, nevertheless, that despite those responses the serious food crisis in Somalia continues to escalate,

1. *Takes note* of the statement made by the representative of Somalia;

2. *Notes with appreciation* the response of the Government and people of Somalia and the favourable reaction to date of the international community, the United Nations and voluntary agencies to the crisis caused by the drought;

3. *Appeals* to the Governments of Member States, United Nations organizations and voluntary agencies urgently to increase their assistance to the Government of Somalia so that all victims of the drought currently afflicting Somalia may receive the necessary aid, with a minimum of delay;

4. *Decides* to keep the situation in Somalia under review.

Economic and Social Council resolution 1984/7

17 May 1984   Meeting 15   Adopted without vote

28-nation draft (E/1984/L.26); agenda item 1.
Sponsors: Algeria, Bangladesh, China, Cyprus, Djibouti, Egypt, Gambia, Greece, India, Italy, Japan, Lebanon, Madagascar, Morocco, Pakistan, Qatar, Saint Lucia, Saudi Arabia, Sierra Leone, Singapore, Somalia, Suriname, Swaziland, Thailand, Tunisia, Yugoslavia, Zaire, Zambia.
Meeting numbers. ESC 14, 15.

GENERAL ASSEMBLY ACTION

On 17 December, the General Assembly adopted resolution 39/205, on assistance to the drought-stricken areas of six East African countries, and resolution 39/201, on assistance to the drought-stricken areas of Ethiopia. Both texts were recommended by the Second Committee and adopted by the Assembly without vote.

Assistance to the drought-stricken areas of Djibouti, Ethiopia, Kenya, Somalia, the Sudan and Uganda

The General Assembly,

Recalling its resolutions 35/90 and 35/91 of 5 December 1980, 36/221 of 17 December 1981, 37/147 of 17 December 1982 and 38/216 of 20 December 1983 and Economic and Social Council resolution 1983/46 of 28 July 1983 on assistance to the drought-stricken areas of Djibouti, Ethiopia, Kenya, Somalia, the Sudan and Uganda,

Having considered the note by the Secretary-General on assistance to the drought-stricken areas of those countries,

Alarmed by the catastrophic effects of the prolonged and persistent drought that poses an imminent threat to human survival and the development prospects of the affected countries of the region,

Deeply disturbed by the grave food situation and the spectre of widespread famine in the drought-stricken areas of the region,

Taking into account the regional nature of the drought and the practical and regional arrangements for co-operation that already exist among the affected countries,

Bearing in mind the urgent need for the international community to render assistance to Member States in the event of natural disasters,

1. *Reaffirms* its resolutions 35/90, 35/91, 36/221, 37/147 and 38/216 on assistance to the drought-stricken areas of Djibouti, Ethiopia, Kenya, Somalia, the Sudan and Uganda;

2. *Takes note* of the note of the Secretary-General on assistance to the drought-stricken areas of those countries;

3. *Notes with satisfaction* the decision taken by the Governments of Djibouti, Ethiopia, Kenya, Somalia, the Sudan and Uganda to establish an intergovernmental body to combat the effects of drought and other natural disasters, as recommended by the General Assembly in resolution 35/90 and to meet in Djibouti on 15 January 1985 to finalize the necessary arrangements for the establishment of that body;

4. *Notes with appreciation* the assistance thus far rendered by the international community and the measures taken by the Secretary-General, in co-operation with the specialized agencies and other organizations of the United Nations system, to ensure the speediest and most effective relief aid for the victims of drought and other natural disasters in Djibouti, Ethiopia, Kenya, Somalia, the Sudan and Uganda;

5. *Urges* all States, organizations of the United Nations system, governmental and non-governmental organizations and international financial institutions concerned, to give urgent consideration to the establishment of a programme of assistance for the six countries in the East African subregion, supporting their efforts:

(a) To meet the grave and urgent needs of the people of those countries;

(b) To combat the effects of drought and other natural calamities and to deal with the problem of medium-term and long-term recovery and rehabilitation in a concerted manner;

6. *Invites* the Secretary-General, in close co-operation with the Administrator of the United Nations Development Programme, and within existing resources, to extend to Djibouti, Ethiopia, Kenya, Somalia, the Sudan

and Uganda the technical assistance needed to finalize the necessary arrangements for the establishment of the proposed intergovernmental body;

7. *Requests* the Secretary-General, in close co-operation with the Administrator of the United Nations Development Programme and the appropriate specialized agencies and other organizations of the United Nations system, to continue to extend all necessary assistance to those countries in their efforts to combat the effects of drought on the basis of the recommendations of various multi-agency missions;

8. *Also requests* the Secretary-General, in close co-operation with the Administrator of the United Nations Development Programme and the appropriate specialized agencies and other organizations of the United Nations system, to assist the Governments of the region, at their request, in establishing or improving national machinery to combat the effects of drought and other natural disasters, to apprise the Economic and Social Council, at its second regular session of 1985, of the progress made in the implementation of the present resolution and to report thereon to the General Assembly at its fortieth session.

General Assembly resolution 39/205

17 December 1984   Meeting 103   Adopted without vote

Approved by Second Committee (A/39/793) without vote, 30 November (meeting 54); 11-nation draft (A/C.2/39/L.73), orally revised, following informal consultations; agenda item 83 *(b)*.
Sponsors: Afghanistan, Bangladesh, Djibouti, Ethiopia, Gambia, Ghana, Kenya, Pakistan, Somalia, Sudan, Uganda.
Meeting numbers. GA 39th session: 2nd Committee 32-37, 47, 54; plenary 103.

The last preambular paragraph was orally revised, as agreed following informal consultations, so as to refer to the urgent, rather than imperative, need for assistance.

Assistance to the drought-stricken areas of Ethiopia

The General Assembly,

Recalling Economic and Social Council resolution 1984/5 of 17 May 1984 on emergency assistance to the drought victims in Ethiopia,

Noting with appreciation the appeals made by the President of the General Assembly and the Secretary-General for emergency assistance to Ethiopia,

Having heard the statement made by the Commissioner for Relief and Rehabilitation of Ethiopia on 2 November 1984 concerning the critical food situation and the sad state of affairs that prevails in the disaster-stricken areas of Ethiopia,

Alarmed by the catastrophic effects of the serious and persistent drought that poses imminent danger to the survival of millions of drought victims,

Deeply disturbed by the grave food situation and the widespread and deadly famine that prevails in the disaster-stricken areas,

Convinced that long-term solutions are imperative in order to avoid the recurrence of a tragic human drama such as the one which is currently unfolding in the disaster-stricken areas,

1. *Commends* the generous response of the international community to the tragic situation in Ethiopia;

2. *Expresses its deep gratitude* to all States, governmental and non-governmental organizations and individuals that have provided emergency humanitarian assistance to Ethiopia;

3. *Urges* all Member States, organs and organizations of the United Nations system, specialized agencies and non-governmental organizations to assist the Government of Ethiopia in its efforts to provide for the emergency needs of the drought victims and to deal with the problem of medium-term and long-term recovery and rehabilitation;

4. *Requests* the Secretary-General to continue his efforts:

(a) To mobilize resources for relief and rehabilitation, including assistance for the victims of drought who wish to resettle in areas less prone to drought;

(b) To apprise the Economic and Social Council, at its first regular session of 1985, of the situation of the drought victims and the response of the international community to their plight.

General Assembly resolution 39/201

17 December 1984   Meeting 103   Adopted without vote

Approved by Second Committee (A/39/793) without vote, 30 November (meeting 54); 93-nation draft (A/C.2/39/L.68/Rev.1); agenda item 83 *(b)*.
Sponsors: Afghanistan, Algeria, Angola, Argentina, Australia, Austria, Bahamas, Bangladesh, Belgium, Benin, Botswana, Brazil, Bulgaria, Burkina Faso, Burundi, Cameroon, Canada, Cape Verde, Central African Republic, Chad, Chile, China, Colombia, Comoros, Congo, Costa Rica, Cuba, Cyprus, Czechoslovakia, Democratic Yemen, Denmark, Djibouti, Dominican Republic, Ecuador, Egypt, Equatorial Guinea, Ethiopia, France, Gambia, German Democratic Republic, Ghana, Guinea, Guinea-Bissau, Haiti, Hungary, India, Ireland, Italy, Ivory Coast, Jamaica, Japan, Kenya, Lao People's Democratic Republic, Lebanon, Lesotho, Liberia, Madagascar, Malawi, Mali, Mauritania, Mexico, Mongolia, Morocco, Mozambique, Nepal, Nicaragua, Nigeria, Norway, Pakistan, Peru, Romania, Rwanda, Sao Tome and Principe, Senegal, Sierra Leone, Sri Lanka, Sudan, Suriname, Swaziland, Sweden, Trinidad and Tobago, Tunisia, Uganda, United Republic of Tanzania, Uruguay, Vanuatu, Venezuela, Viet Nam, Yemen, Yugoslavia, Zaire, Zambia, Zimbabwe.
Meeting numbers. GA 39th session: 2nd Committee 32-37, 50, 54, 55; plenary 103.

Floods and storms

Floods in Bolivia, Ecuador and Peru

In February 1984,[36] UNDRO reported on emergency assistance provided to Bolivia, Ecuador and Peru, which had been struck by heavy flooding in late 1982 and 1983 as a result of a widespread climatic change associated with disturbances in the ocean current known as "El Niño".[37] According to UNDRO, as at 31 January 1984, the international community had contributed more than $87 million following the Secretary-General's appeal on 10 August 1983 for assistance to those countries.

In his September 1984 report[38] on special economic and disaster relief assistance to 10 countries (see p. 464), the Secretary-General described the nature and extent of damage resulting from the flooding in the three countries, as reported by a 1983 inter-agency mission sent there,[39] and on drought in the Bolivian-Peruvian plateau. Losses to Bolivia were estimated at $836.5 million. The mission, in consultation with the Government, identified projects amounting to $129.4 million for which external funding was sought. As of June 1984, approximately $50 million and some equipment had been provided, while a number of projects were under discussion with bilateral donors. Damages to Ecuador were estimated at $640.6 million. Of the $97 million sought for recommended projects, $33.35 million was received as of 1 July. Peru suffered $2,001.8 million in damage. Projects identified by the mission for international funding amounted to $180.8 million, of which $68.6 million was donated.

The Secretary-General, in his annual report on UNDRO issued in June,[1] stated that the international response to UNDRO's appeal for aid for Bolivia had resulted in assistance valued at $2 million. He noted in his September report on assistance provided by the United Nations system[10] that UNDRO had dispatched a field delegate to Bolivia from October 1983 to April 1984 to assist the resident co-ordinator and the national body responsible for the distribution of emergency relief.

By decision 39/431, the General Assembly took note of the summary reports of the Secretary-General on Bolivia, Ecuador and Peru.[38]

Cyclones and floods in Madagascar

Madagascar, by a letter of 20 April to the Secretary-General,[40] requested that the Economic and Social Council include in the agenda of its first regular 1984 session an item on measures to be taken following the cyclones and floods in Madagascar (1983-1984). It explained that between December 1983 and April 1984, Madagascar had been hit by four cyclones. The most destructive one, in April, killed at least 68 people. In the stricken areas, there was an urgent need for food, medical care, shelter and clothing. Damage was estimated to exceed $600 million. Reconstruction was needed for port and airport facilities, roads, bridges and dikes. Damage to merchant and fishing vessels, plants, irrigation channels, crops and livestock was extensive.

ECONOMIC AND SOCIAL COUNCIL ACTION

On 11 May, the Economic and Social Council adopted resolution 1984/3 by consensus.

Measures to be taken following the cyclones and floods in Madagascar

The Economic and Social Council,

Having heard the statements made by the observer for Madagascar and the representative of the Office of the United Nations Disaster Relief Co-ordinator concerning the four tropical cyclones and the floods which severely affected all parts of Madagascar in December 1983 and January and April 1984,

Recognizing that these climatic phenomena have resulted in loss of life and the destruction of several towns and have inflicted serious damage on the economic and social infrastructures and on the agricultural, stock-farming and agro-industrial sectors,

Taking into account the fact that those sectors are of fundamental importance to the economy of the country,

Recalling the resolutions of the General Assembly and the Economic and Social Council on assistance in cases of natural disaster, in which appeals have been made to the international community to give special attention to these phenomena,

Taking into account the fact that the provision of assistance to countries stricken by natural disasters is an expression of the international solidarity proclaimed in the Charter of the United Nations,

Noting the efforts made by the Government of Madagascar to relieve the suffering of the victims of the cyclones and floods,

Noting with satisfaction the emergency assistance provided by a number of States, international and regional organizations, specialized agencies and voluntary agencies,

1.   *Expresses its profound sympathy* with the people and Government of Madagascar for the loss of life and the serious damage which the recent cyclones and floods have inflicted on the economy of the country;

2.   *Urges* all States to participate or to continue to participate in relief operations and in the implementation of programmes for the rehabilitation and reconstruction of the areas affected by the cyclones and floods;

3.   *Requests* international and regional organizations, specialized agencies and voluntary agencies, particularly those most directly concerned, to lend their support, within the framework of their respective programmes, to the efforts of the Secretary-General and the United Nations Disaster Relief Co-ordinator to mobilize relief and assistance, and also to consider urgently the requests for assistance made by the Government of Madagascar during the phase of rehabilitation and reconstruction;

4.   *Expresses the hope* that the United Nations Development Programme, the World Bank and all other international and regional financial institutions concerned will give sympathetic and urgent consideration to requests for assistance which the Government of Madagascar may submit under its rehabilitation, reconstruction and development programmes and with a view to improving the existing disaster warning and protection systems;

5.   *Requests* the Secretary-General:

(a)   To send an inter-agency mission to Madagascar with a view to evaluating the damage, the priority needs of the country following the cyclones and floods and the medium-term and long-term impact of those disasters on the national economy, and to compiling the data relevant to the promotion of concerted international assistance;

(b)   To transmit the report of the mission to the international community;

(c)   To take the necessary action to help the Government prepare a reconstruction and recovery programme for the regions and sectors affected;

6.   *Further requests* the Secretary-General to apprise the Economic and Social Council at its second regular session of 1984 and to report to the General Assembly at its thirty-ninth session on the implementation of the present resolution.

Economic and Social Council resolution 1984/3

11 May 1984   Meeting 11   Adopted by consensus

30-nation draft (E/1984/L.21), orally revised; agenda item 1.

Sponsors: Algeria, Argentina, Bangladesh, Benin, Botswana, Colombia, Congo, Cuba, Cyprus, Djibouti, Ecuador, Ethiopia, France, Liberia, Malawi, Mali, Mexico, Nigeria, Pakistan, Romania, Rwanda, Saint Lucia, Sierra Leone, Somalia, Suriname, Swaziland, Tunisia, Uganda, Viet Nam, Zaire.

Meeting numbers. ESC 5, 11.

Report of the inter-agency mission. As requested by the Council in resolution 1984/3, the Secretary-General sent an inter-agency mission to Madagascar from 24 May to 5 June. Its report was transmitted to the General Assembly in August.[41] An oral report had been made to the Council at its second regular session of 1984.

The report surveyed the general economic situation of the country, which suffered problems of many other developing countries—the effects of the international economic recession, whether in terms of decreased demand for exports, fluctuations in the prices of raw materials, deteriorating terms of trade, exchange rate fluctuations or increases in interest rates. Agriculture constituted the backbone of the economy, contributing close to 40 per cent of GNP and over 80 per cent of export earnings. In recent years, agricultural production had been stagnant, due in large part to the inadequate transportation system. The Government drew up measures in 1983 for short-term economic recovery, as well as a long-term development strategy, complementing the main targets of its second national development plan, 1982-1987, aimed at achieving self-sufficiency in foodstuffs and energy, increasing exports, promoting industrial development, and improving training and health. The Government's plans included such steps as ensuring adequate price incentives in the agricultural sector, improving irrigation and transport systems, diversifying crops, supporting private enterprises, facilitating the growth of the private sector and reducing public expenditures.

Damage caused by the cyclones of late 1983 and early 1984 was estimated at $36.12 million to agriculture and at $4.9 million to related infrastructure (agro-industrial plants, access roads, irrigation systems). Reconstruction costs for the transport sector were estimated at $13.69 million, and for the industrial sector, $11.79 million. Housing and other buildings, and power plants and lines were also damaged. UNDRO played the leading role in coordinating the responses to Madagascar's appeal.

The mission outlined a special economic assistance programme to assist Madagascar. Although the main goal of the programme was reconstruction and rehabilitation, the projects were consistent with the objectives and strategy of its current national development plan. Thirty-nine projects were proposed in agriculture, transportation (including roads, ports and airports), industry, public buildings, energy and disaster preparedness, at a total cost of $39,181,000.

GENERAL ASSEMBLY ACTION

On 17 December, the General Assembly, acting on the recommendation of the Second Committee, adopted resolution 39/191 without vote.

Assistance to Madagascar

The General Assembly,

Recalling Economic and Social Council resolution 1984/3 of 11 May 1984 on measures to be taken following the cyclones and floods in Madagascar in December 1983 and January and April 1984,

Recognizing that these climatic phenomena have resulted in loss of life and the destruction of several towns and have inflicted serious damage on the economic and social infrastructures and on the agricultural, stock-farming, transport and industrial sectors,

Concerned by the fact that the damage caused by these natural disasters is hampering the development efforts of Madagascar,

Taking note of the report of the Secretary-General on assistance to Madagascar, prepared pursuant to Economic and Social Council resolution 1984/3,

Having considered the special economic assistance programme prepared by the inter-agency mission which visited Madagascar from 24 May to 5 June 1984,

Noting the efforts of the people and Government of Madagascar to deal with the emergency situation and to initiate a reconstruction and rehabilitation programme,

Noting also the emergency assistance provided by several States, international and regional organizations, specialized agencies and voluntary agencies,

Affirming the need for prompt and concerted international action to assist the people and Government of Madagascar in carrying out the reconstruction and rehabilitation of the stricken regions and sectors,

1. *Expresses its gratitude* to the States, programmes and organizations of the United Nations system and intergovernmental, non-governmental and voluntary organizations which provided assistance to Madagascar during the emergency;

2. *Urges* all States to participate generously through bilateral or multilateral channels in projects and programmes for the reconstruction and rehabilitation of Madagascar;

3. *Requests* the international and regional organizations, the specialized agencies and voluntary agencies to continue and increase their assistance in response to the reconstruction, rehabilitation and development needs of Madagascar;

4. *Requests* the programmes and organizations of the United Nations system, in particular the United Nations Development Programme, the World Bank, the Food and Agriculture Organization of the United Nations, the International Fund for Agricultural Development and the United Nations Industrial Development Organization, and all other international and regional financial institutions concerned, to give sympathetic and urgent consideration to requests for assistance submitted by the Government of Madagascar under its reconstruction, rehabilitation and development programmes;

5. *Requests* the Secretary-General:

(a) To take the necessary steps, in collaboration with the programmes and organizations of the United Nations system, to mobilize the resources needed for implementing the reconstruction, rehabilitation and development programmes of Madagascar;

(b) To keep the question of assistance for the reconstruction and rehabilitation of Madagascar under constant review;

6. *Further requests* the Secretary-General to apprise the Economic and Social Council, at its second regular session of 1985, of the progress made in the implementation of the present resolution and to report thereon to the General Assembly at its fortieth session.

17 December 1984   Meeting 103   Adopted without vote

Approved by Second Committee (A/39/793) without vote, 30 November (meeting 54); 65-nation draft (A/C.2/39/L.52); agenda item 83 *(b)*.

Sponsors: Afghanistan, Algeria, Angola, Argentina, Bangladesh, Benin, Botswana, Burkina Faso, Burundi, Cameroon, Cape Verde, Central African Republic, Chad, China, Comoros, Congo, Cuba, Cyprus, Democratic Yemen, Djibouti, Dominican Republic, Ecuador, Egypt, Equatorial Guinea, Ethiopia, France, Ghana, Guinea, Guinea-Bissau, Haiti, India, Japan, Lebanon, Lesotho, Liberia, Libyan Arab Jamahiriya, Malawi, Mali, Mauritania, Mauritius, Mozambique, Nepal, Nicaragua, Niger, Nigeria, Pakistan, Philippines, Romania, Rwanda, Sao Tome and Principe, Seychelles, Sierra Leone, Somalia, Sudan, Suriname, Swaziland, Tunisia, Uganda, United Republic of Tanzania, Vanuatu, Viet Nam, Yugoslavia, Zaire, Zambia, Zimbabwe.

Meeting numbers. GA 39th session: 2nd Committee 32-37, 45, 54; plenary 103.

Cyclone in Swaziland

In a letter of 9 February to the President of the Economic and Social Council,[42] Swaziland said it had been hit by a cyclone between 28 and 30 January, which caused about 100 deaths and severe damage to property. The cyclone "Domoina" and subsequent floods damaged approximately 80 per cent of the roads and railways. The exact extent of the disaster was still unknown, since several areas were inaccessible. As a land-locked country whose economy was almost totally export-oriented, the lines of communication to seaports were essential, and for that reason Swaziland appealed for economic and technical assistance. It hoped that the Council would recommend a special economic assistance programme and that the Secretary-General would send an inter-agency mission to Swaziland to help it assess priority needs and the medium- and long-term implications of the floods on the economy.

The Secretary-General reported in June[1] that, at the request of the Government, UNDRO launched an appeal on 2 February and allocated a cash grant of $20,000 for air drops of relief supplies. Total contributions reported in cash and in kind as at 29 February amounted to $862,320.

ECONOMIC AND SOCIAL COUNCIL ACTION

The Economic and Social Council adopted decision 1984/106 without vote.

Special economic assistance programme for Swaziland

At its 2nd plenary meeting, on 10 February 1984, the Council, having considered the letter dated 9 February 1984 from the Permanent Representative of Swaziland to the United Nations addressed to the President of the Council, decided to request the Secretary-General to send, as soon as possible and within existing resources, an inter-agency mission to Swaziland to assess that country's priority needs in the light of the cyclone of January 1984 and its medium-term and long-term implications for the economy, and to consider the matter at its first regular session of 1984, under the item entitled "Adoption of the agenda and other organizational matters", should the report of the mission be available at that time.

Adopted without vote

Oral proposal by President; agenda item 2.

Report of the inter-agency mission. As the Council had requested, the Secretary-General arranged for an inter-agency mission, led by the Under-Secretary-General for Special Political Questions, to visit Swaziland from 30 April to 5 May. As the mission's report was not available in time for consideration at the Council's first regular 1984 session, as envisaged in decision 1984/106, the Council, on an oral proposal of its President, decided on 1 May, without adopting a formal decision, to consider the report at its July 1984 session. A preliminary summary report, outlining specific requirements as a basis for immediate action, was submitted by the Secretary-General to the Council on 13 July;[43] the Council took note of it on 26 July, when it adopted decision 1984/175. The complete report, describing the economic situation, damage, emergency response, and outstanding requirements for assistance, was submitted in August to the Council[44] and in October to the General Assembly.[45]

The mission noted that Swaziland had a per capita income of approximately $880 at the 1982 exchange rate. Agriculture played a vital role in the economy, generating approximately 25 per cent of GDP, 71 per cent of export earnings and employment for 75 per cent of the labour force (6 per cent worked in the mines of South Africa). Recession in the economy of its main trading partner, South Africa, during the previous two years had had an adverse effect on the Swazi economy: real GDP declined in 1982 and 1983.

The total cyclone damage was estimated at $65.4 million, most of which was the result of flooding. The total losses to the economy represented an amount equivalent to 45 per cent of the Government's total annual expenditures, or 12 per cent of its GDP. Confirmed deaths numbered 53, but the actual total was probably higher. Immediately following the cyclone, the Government appealed for assistance directly to donors and through the Secretary-General. Relief co-ordination meetings of United Nations organizations, donors and NGOs were organized by the resident co-ordinator. From the launching of UNDRO's emergency appeal on 2 February to the end of the initial emergency period at mid-year, more than $2.5 million of assistance had been made available. There remained a need for international assistance, in particular concessional assistance, if Swaziland was to succeed in its reconstruction and rehabilitation and achieve economic development.

The mission presented an outline of a special economic assistance programme at a total cost of $44 million. Twenty-three projects were proposed for bridge and road repair, agriculture, power, water supply and public facilities. The proposals did not include approximately $8.4 million for rehabilitation of the railways, since repairs had to be undertaken immediately and were financed by the Government.

GENERAL ASSEMBLY ACTION

On 17 December, the General Assembly, on the recommendation of the Second Committee, adopted resolution 39/194 without vote.

Special economic assistance for Swaziland
The General Assembly,
Recalling Economic and Social Council decision 1984/106 of 10 February 1984, in which the Council requested the Secretary-General to send an inter-agency mission to Swaziland to assess that country's priority needs in the light of the cyclone of January 1984 and its medium-term and long-term implications for the economy,
Having heard the statement made by the Minister for Foreign Affairs of Swaziland on 11 October 1984, in which he expressed appreciation for the assistance rendered by Governments, the United Nations system and other organizations during the difficult period following the cyclone,
Having considered the report of the Secretary-General, to which was annexed the report of the inter-agency mission which visited Swaziland from 30 April to 5 May 1984,
Noting from the report the serious damage to the economic infrastructure of Swaziland and the efforts made by the Government and people of Swaziland to cope with the problems of reconstruction,
Taking note of the recommended programme of assistance for Swaziland drawn up by the inter-agency mission, in consultation with the Government, concerning priority projects designed to permit the resumption of normal economic activity,
1. *Draws attention* to the urgent need for international action to assist the Government and people of Swaziland in their efforts for reconstruction and rehabilitation;
2. *Expresses its appreciation* to the Secretary-General for his prompt action and for the report of the inter-agency mission on the economic situation of Swaziland and the additional assistance required by that country to cope with the problems of reconstruction and rehabilitation;
3. *Expresses its gratitude* to all States and organizations that have provided emergency assistance to Swaziland;
4. *Endorses* the assessment and recommendations of the inter-agency mission contained in the annex to the report of the Secretary-General;
5. *Requests* the appropriate organizations and programmes of the United Nations system, in particular the United Nations Development Programme, the World Bank, the Food and Agriculture Organization of the United Nations, the International Fund for Agricultural Development, the World Food Programme, the World Health Organization, the United Nations Children's Fund and the United Nations Industrial Development Organization, to maintain and expand their programmes of assistance to Swaziland, to co-operate closely with the Secretary-General in his efforts to organize an effective international programme of assistance and to report to him by mid-1985 on the steps they have taken and the resources they have made available to help that country;
6. *Calls upon* regional and interregional organizations and other intergovernmental bodies and non-governmental

organizations as well as international financial institutions to give urgent consideration to the establishment of a programme of assistance for Swaziland or, where one is already in existence, to the expansion of that programme;
7. *Requests* the Secretary-General:
(*a*) To continue his efforts to mobilize the necessary resources for an effective programme of international assistance for Swaziland;
(*b*) To keep the situation regarding assistance to Swaziland under constant review, to maintain close contact with Member States, the specialized agencies, regional and other intergovernmental organizations and the international financial institutions concerned and to apprise the Economic and Social Council, at its second regular session of 1985, of the current status of the special economic assistance programme for Swaziland;
(*c*) To report on the progress made in the economic situation of Swaziland and in organizing and implementing the programme of assistance for that country in time for the matter to be considered by the General Assembly at its fortieth session.

General Assembly resolution 39/194

17 December 1984　　Meeting 103　　Adopted without vote

Approved by Second Committee (A/39/793) without vote, 30 November (meeting 54); 19-nation draft (A/C.2/39/L.59); agenda item 83 (*b*).
Sponsors: Afghanistan, Bangladesh, Botswana, Cameroon, Central African Republic, Chad, Ethiopia, Gambia, Ghana, Lesotho, Madagascar, Malawi, Mozambique, Nepal, Pakistan, Suriname, Swaziland, Zambia, Zimbabwe.
Meeting numbers. GA 39th session: 2nd Committee 32-37, 45, 54; plenary 30, 103.

Earthquake in Yemen

As requested by the General Assembly in 1983,[46] the Secretary-General, in October 1984,[47] reported on assistance for the reconstruction programme of Yemen needed after an earthquake in December 1982.[48] Approximately 1,500 people had been killed, over 265,000 were affected, 42,000 residential buildings were damaged, and loss was estimated at $2 billion. Immediately following the earthquake, the resident co-ordinator acted as co-ordinator for relief assistance. An *ad hoc* committee of Yemen-based government officials and representatives of United Nations bodies and bilateral and non-governmental organizations was established; the office of the UNDP Resident Representative in Sana'a acted as its secretariat. The committee helped with the acquisition and supply of relief items. An international joint mission of representatives of the Economic Commission for Western Asia, the World Bank, the Arab Fund for Economic and Social Development, the Kuwait Fund for Arab Economic Development and the Organization of Arab Petroleum Exporting Countries visited Yemen and drew up reconstruction programmes, which included construction of earthquake-resistant dwellings in safe sites.

The Government had undertaken a three-phase reconstruction programme, at a total cost of $620 million: relief, reconstruction and assistance to rural development. The relief phase was completed in 1983. Reconstruction would involve the repair of

17,000 houses and construction of 25,000. Assistance for rural development in the earthquake-affected areas was to be organized once the reconstruction was completed.

GENERAL ASSEMBLY ACTION

On 17 December, the General Assembly adopted without vote resolution 39/190, on the recommendation of the Second Committee.

Assistance to Yemen

The General Assembly,

Recalling its resolutions 37/166 of 17 December 1982 and 38/204 of 20 December 1983 and resolution 150(VI) of 2 July 1983 of the United Nations Conference on Trade and Development,

Fully aware of the grave devastation and substantial loss of life and property caused by the earthquake that struck large areas of Yemen on 12 December 1982,

Concerned about the damage caused to infrastructure, which has a far-reaching effect on the implementation of the national development plan in that country,

Taking note of the report of the Secretary-General, which outlines the reconstruction programme of the Government of Yemen, the cost of which is estimated at $620 million,

Taking into account that the various phases of reconstruction have placed a strain on the Government of Yemen, largely exhausted the resources available and hindered development plans,

Recognizing that Yemen, as one of the least developed countries, is unable to bear the mounting burden of the relief efforts and the reconstruction of the affected areas,

1. *Appeals* to all countries, especially the developed countries, to continue to contribute generously to the relief efforts and the reconstruction of the affected areas through financial contributions and the provision of the construction materials and equipment necessary to restore infrastructure and basic services in the affected areas;

2. *Requests* the appropriate organizations and programmes of the United Nations system to maintain and expand their programmes of assistance to Yemen;

3. *Expresses its gratitude* to the States, the international and regional organizations and the non-governmental organizations that have participated in the ongoing efforts undertaken for the reconstruction of the affected areas in Yemen;

4. *Requests* the Secretary-General to apprise the Economic and Social Council, at its second regular session of 1985, and the General Assembly, at its fortieth session, of the progress made in the implementation of the present resolution.

General Assembly resolution 39/190

17 December 1984   Meeting 103   Adopted without vote

Approved by Second Committee (A/39/793) without vote, 30 November (meeting 54); 24-nation draft (A/C.2/39/L.51); agenda item 83 *(b)*.

Sponsors: Afghanistan, Algeria, Bahrain, Bangladesh, Cyprus, Democratic Yemen, Djibouti, Egypt, Ethiopia, Jordan, Kuwait, Lebanon, Libyan Arab Jamahiriya, Madagascar, Mauritania, Oman, Pakistan, Qatar, Saudi Arabia, Somalia, Sudan, Tunisia, United Arab Emirates, Yemen.

Meeting numbers. GA 39th session: 2nd Committee 32-37, 45, 54; plenary 103.

Disaster preparedness and prevention

In addition to responding to immediate disaster relief needs, UNDRO in 1984 continued its activities in pre-disaster planning.[1] UNDRO's concept of disaster preparedness was the integration of human and material resources into a national system of readiness in order to minimize the loss of lives and damage when a disaster struck. Its technical assistance programmes were aimed at establishing national structures capable of immediate action. It also sought to improve communication channels between central and local preparedness units, as well as damage-reporting systems to determine relief assistance. Early-warning systems and public education to cope with natural and other hazards were other components of disaster preparedness. During the year, the number of requests for UNDRO assistance in disaster preparedness planning had increased, whereas contributions to the sub-account for technical assistance of the UNDRO Trust Fund had decreased. It had become necessary for UNDRO to identify donors prepared to finance individual projects before it could respond to such requests.

An example of projects in this area was the Co-ordination and Information Centre for Emergencies, at N'djamena, Chad, set up by UNDRO with assistance from the Swiss Disaster Relief Unit. The Centre, which became operational in 1983, gathered information on the arrival and movement of relief goods, published a monthly statement of stocks and distribution, and processed and disseminated information on disaster needs. After an inter-agency mission was sent to Vanuatu in June, UNDRO agreed to that Government's request to provide the services of an expert in disaster management.[2] Preparedness projects were also planned or under way in Indonesia, Madagascar, Nicaragua, the Sudan and the United Republic of Tanzania.

At the international level, the Typhoon Committee, an intergovernmental organization established in 1968 to reduce the effects of typhoons through improved forecasting, completed its four-year Typhoon Operational Experiment with a final evaluation meeting at Tokyo in March. UNDRO and the League of Red Cross Societies, joint co-ordinators for the Warning Dissemination and Information Exchange component, presented to the meeting an evaluation report with follow-up proposals. The WMO/ESCAP Panel on Tropical Cyclones helped organize a Regional Seminar on Disaster Preparedness (Male, Maldives, 28 February–3 March), at which disaster managers from Bangladesh, India, Maldives, Nepal, Pakistan, Sri Lanka and Thailand adopted recommendations on actions to be taken by national, regional and international bodies.

As requested by the Tropical Cyclone Committee for the South-West Indian Ocean, a regional body of eight countries created by WMO to enhance national capabilities and regional co-operation in forecasting and warning of tropical cyclones, UNDRO, jointly with the League of Red Cross Societies, organized a training seminar in disaster prevention and preparedness for disaster management personnel from the member countries (Mauritius, 21-25 May). Another regional project was UNDRO's financing of the participation of relief officials from five countries—Bangladesh, Burma, Pakistan, Sri Lanka and Thailand—in a training programme in India in disaster management. A Regional Meeting on Disaster Prevention and Preparedness in Africa (Addis Ababa, 24 and 25 February) was organized jointly with ECA and OAU. Representatives from 21 African countries, United Nations agencies and NGOs assessed the situation with regard to natural disasters other than drought and considered measures to mitigate their harmful impact. The meeting adopted a strategy and recommendations put forward in an UNDRO/ECA paper on the subject. A project in the Balkan region was completed in April 1984 followed by the establishment of a permanent International Governmental Committee for Earthquake Risk Reduction.

UNDRO provided expert services for two workshops in Titograd, Yugoslavia, on vulnerability and seismic-risk analysis, and continued technical advisory services to Yugoslavia throughout the year; a study was made on earthquake vulnerability. Assistance was provided to Egypt for flood-risk analysis and flood-prevention techniques, and to Mozambique for strengthening national disaster prevention and counter-disaster operations. A disaster plan for a province in Papua New Guinea, drawn up in 1983, was applied in early 1984 when typical precursors to volcanic eruptions occurred.

In July 1984 an earthquake engineer and seismologist visited Cyprus to advise both the Greek and Turkish communities on earthquake risk reduction methods for the Nicosia Master Plan, a UNCHS project.

Preparedness for industrial accidents was another area of UNDRO activity, including participation with the International Atomic Energy Agency in such projects as the preparation of a "Handbook for assessing off-site consequences of accidents in nuclear power plants" and the compilation of "Guidelines for mutual emergency assistance arrangements in connection with a nuclear accident or radiation emergency"; as well as a joint UNIDO/UNDRO/WHO/UNEP project for the institution and co-ordination of national contingency plans for emergencies associated with industrial installations in the West and Central African region. A regional workshop related to the latter project was held at Dakar in February, at which 15 Governments were represented. The final report contained recommendations for action.

The Pan-Caribbean Disaster Preparedness and Prevention Project, a multi-agency project begun in 1981 and covering 28 Caribbean countries and territories, involved UNDRO's technical supervision of prevention and preparedness activities, including the provision of two full-time experts and an emergency telecommunications programme. Activities in 1984 included regional seminars or workshops in Antigua, Barbados, Cuba, Puerto Rico, and Saint Christopher and Nevis, on such subjects as search and rescue, oil spill, hurricane preparedness, emergency shelter and other aspects of disaster management. An air crash simulation exercise was held in Antigua. Technical assistance missions developed national disaster plans and training programmes in the British Virgin Islands, Dominica, Grenada, Guyana, Jamaica, Montserrat, Saint Christopher and Nevis, and Saint Vincent and the Grenadines.

Prevention activities included studies on vulnerability of buildings and infrastructure to hurricanes in Dominica and Saint Lucia, and workshops and manuals to illustrate techniques to minimize hurricane and earthquake damage. Emergency communications equipment between national emergency offices was in operation and a procedures manual was prepared. The Pan-Caribbean project stimulated the creation of national emergency offices and, by the end of 1984, 23 of the 28 member countries had programmes in disaster preparedness and prevention.

In April, UNDRO, ECLAC and the Pan American Health Organization/WHO sponsored a seminar at Mexico City to develop a methodology to assess relief needs following sudden natural disasters. As a follow-up, in August 1984 an UNDRO representative visited ECLAC headquarters to discuss plans for future action in pre-disaster planning in Latin America.

Reporting on some of its emergency operations in 1984,[49] UNICEF said it had circulated the second draft of its emergency manual to most field offices in Africa and a number of selected offices in other regions. The manual provided guidelines on policies, procedures and possible programme interventions in emergency situations. It was also sent for comment to emergency units of United Nations organizations and others with particular expertise in emergency aid. The Eastern and Southern Africa Regional Office in Nairobi organized a workshop in June to train staff in responding to emergency situations.

The Economic and Social Council, in resolution 1984/60, and the General Assembly, in resolution 39/207, expressed recognition of the importance of disaster prevention and preparedness at the regional and national levels in mitigating the effects of disasters, and appreciation of UNDRO's work in that area as far as resources allowed. It encouraged Governments to continue to draw upon the services available from UNDRO and other organizations and to provide the necessary resources for that aspect of technical co-operation.

REFERENCES

[1]A/39/267-E/1984/96 & Corr.1 & Add.1,2. [2]E/1985/75. [3]YUN 1983, p. 534. [4]*Ibid.*, p. 532, GA res. 38/217, 20 Dec. 1983. [5]A/39/267/Add.2-E/1984/96/Add.2. [6]YUN 1983, p. 1150, GA res. 38/236 A, 20 Dec. 1983. [7]A/39/267/Add.1-E/1984/96/Add.1. [8]YUN 1983, p. 522, GA res. 38/202, 20 Dec. 1983. [9]*Ibid.*, p. 521. [10]A/39/393 & Add.1. [11]E/1984/109. [12]A/39/530. [13]A/39/270. [14]DP/1984/52 & Add.1. [15]E/1984/20 (dec. 84/14). [16]YUN 1983, p. 537, GA res. 38/201, 20 Dec. 1983. [17]YUN 1977, p. 509. [18]A/39/25 (dec. 12/10). [19]A/39/211-E/1984/58 & Add.1. [20]E/1985/65. [21]DP/1985/5/Add.2 (part II). [22]DP/1984/51 & Corr.1,2. [23]YUN 1983, p. 777, GA res. 38/164, 19 Dec. 1983. [24]E/1984/20 (dec. 84/27). [25]*Ibid.* (dec. 84/28). [26]TD/B/1004. [27]A/39/15, vol. II (res. 295(XXIX)). [28]A/39/145. [29]YUN 1983, p. 526. [30]A/39/386. [31]YUN 1983, p. 529, GA res. 38/216, 20 Dec. 1983. [32]A/C.2/39/5. [33]E/1984/64. [34]E/1984/90. [35]E/1984/95. [36]UNDRO/84/8. [37]YUN 1983, p. 529. [38]A/39/392. [39]YUN 1983, p. 530. [40]E/1984/67. [41]A/39/404. [42]E/1984/31. [43]E/1984/135. [44]E/1984/135/Add.1. [45]A/39/598. [46]YUN 1983, p. 533, GA res. 38/204, 20 Dec. 1983. [47]A/39/380. [48]YUN 1983, p. 533. [49]E/ICEF/1985/11.

Emergency relief and assistance

Lebanon

As a result of the renewed fighting and disorder in late 1983 and early 1984 in Lebanon (see p. 283), the country's economy declined and its reconstruction programme was set back. The United Nations Co-ordinator of Assistance for the Reconstruction and Development of Lebanon, reporting orally to the Economic and Social Council on 17 July, noted that despite many difficulties work on reconstruction projects had continued wherever conditions allowed.

The Secretary-General, in a September 1984 report[1] to the General Assembly, requested in December 1983,[2] described the general situation in Lebanon and summarized developments there since his 1983 report[3] on assistance for Lebanon's reconstruction and development. He said tension remained at a high level and heavy fighting had taken place in late 1983 between Palestinian and other groups in the Bekaa Valley and around Tripoli. In December 1983, a truce was arranged and a large contingent of Palestine Liberation Organization fighters left Tripoli in ships flying the United Nations flag. While sporadic fighting was going on in the Shouf mountains in February 1984, hostilities broke out in West Beirut, again splitting the city along the so-called "Green Line". A new Government was formed in May and Parliament gave it special powers to legislate by decree. Under those powers, the Government adopted a security plan by which it reopened the Beirut port, airport and traffic passageways between the eastern and western parts of the city.

The worsening security problem eroded the ability of the Lebanese economy to function. The reces-sion had deepened throughout 1983 and continued during the first half of 1984. An estimated 30 per cent of the active labour force was unemployed. Economic disruptions were aggravated by restrictions imposed by Israeli forces on movements of goods and people to and from southern Lebanon. Government expenditures increased due to the security situation, contributing to a deficit in the balance of payments of around $900 million. The economy still had characteristics that would enable it to recover, but some of this potential, both human and financial, was being drained away by migration. According to the Secretary-General, the consolidation of security on a stable basis would be the most important single factor in facilitating economic recovery.

The situation in the south (including western Bekaa) posed especially difficult problems for reconstruction. Two thirds of the industrial plants there were closed and agricultural production was 40 per cent below normal. Schools, medical facilities and essential services were not functioning properly. The war damage of 1982 remained largely unrepaired, and the latest Shouf and Beirut outbreaks brought an influx of displaced persons (approximately 20,000 families), straining local resources. Continued Israeli occupation of the region isolated it from the rest of the country and disrupted normal life and economic activity. The Government accorded high priority to basic relief needs and rehabilitation projects in housing, education, road reconstruction, drinking-water and waste management, electricity and health.

The United Nations continued to have a substantial and active presence in Lebanon. Many specialized agencies and other United Nations organizations maintained regional offices in Beirut, namely UNICEF, UNHCR, ILO, FAO, UNESCO, WHO, UNDP, WFP and UNRWA. The United Nations Interim Force in Lebanon had been stationed in southern Lebanon since 1978 and, in addition to peace-keeping operations, it conducted humanitarian activities (see p. 298). Closure of the airport and insecurity had obliged ILO and UNICEF to move their regional offices temporarily out of Lebanon to Geneva and Amman, respectively, and UNDP was obliged to reduce its operations in Lebanon. The principal focus of United Nations activities was emergency relief assistance to victims of the fighting.

Under a 1980 arrangement between the Government and UNICEF, a rehabilitation programme comprising education, health, water and self-help projects continued. In addition to the initial reconstruction of the south project ($26.5 million), UNICEF funded and organized a $44-million programme aimed at repairing the damage caused during the 1982 Israeli invasion. On behalf of the Government and with Arab aid funds, UNICEF was executing a $100-million programme of rebuilding hospitals, schools and water-supply systems. Reporting on its emergency operations in 1984 (excluding Africa),[4] UNICEF said that, following civil violence in February which disrupted the water supply in the southern suburbs of Beirut and in the Shouf mountains, it helped supply power generators and repair damaged pipes, rehabilitated damaged wells and sanitation facilities and trucked water to 37 centres for displaced families.

The second country programme for Lebanon[5] was submitted in March to the UNDP Governing Council for consideration and approval. It was based on a request by Lebanon for UNDP assistance for 1984-1986 and drawn up in collaboration with the UNDP resident representative. The Government's primary concern was the reconstruction of basic facilities as elaborated in its reconstruction project. That project, which called for expenditures in the order of $15 billion over 10 years, provided the overall framework for public sector actions and policies, beginning with the rehabilitation of physical and social infrastructures. The World Bank, at the Government's request, finalized in early 1983 a reconstruction assessment report which foresaw an initial investment of $230 million for education, housing, urban development, water supply, telecommunications, port facilities and highway maintenance.

Other assistance by the United Nations was provided by DTCD, UNCTAD, UNIDO, UNFPA, the Division of Narcotic Drugs, WFP, UNHCR, IAEA, FAO, UNESCO, WHO and ITU.

Speaking to the General Assembly's Second Committee on 6 November, the Co-ordinator of Assistance for the Reconstruction and Development of Lebanon said that Lebanon's reconstruction programme had been interrupted by renewed fighting in the mountains in September 1983 and in the Beirut suburbs in February 1984, affecting some 500,000 persons on each occasion; nevertheless, Lebanon had been able to implement about 27 per cent of the programme. At the request of Lebanon, the Secretary-General had issued appeals both times for international emergency relief. It was estimated on each occasion that $10 million was needed. Tens of thousands would remain in need of assistance for some time to come. The Lebanese Government was currently working on a new programme for 1985 and onwards which would have to take into account the damage caused by fighting and disorder over the previous 12 to 15 months.

The Fourth General Conference of UNIDO (see Chapter VI of this section, under "Programme and finances of UNIDO"), in a resolution of 19 August,[6] requested UNIDO to provide Lebanon with immediate, medium- and long-term assistance so as to enable it to reconstruct its industrial sector. It called on member States to assist UNIDO in its reindustrialization efforts for Lebanon.

ECONOMIC AND SOCIAL COUNCIL ACTION

The Economic and Social Council, on the recommendation of the Third Committee, adopted decision 1984/174 without vote.

Assistance for the reconstruction and development of Lebanon

At its 49th plenary meeting, on 26 July 1984, the Council:

(a) Took note with appreciation of the oral report made on 17 July 1984 by the United Nations Co-ordinator of Assistance for the Reconstruction and Development of Lebanon pursuant to General Assembly resolution 38/220 of 20 December 1983 and of the statement made on 18 July 1984 by the Permanent Representative of Lebanon to the United Nations Office at Geneva before the Third (Programme and Co-ordination) Committee of the Council;

(b) Expressed its appreciation for the relentless efforts undertaken by the Government of Lebanon in the implementation of the initial phase of reconstruction of the country, despite adverse circumstances;

(c) Appealed to all Member States and organs, organizations and bodies of the United Nations system to continue and intensify their efforts to mobilize all possible assistance for the reconstruction and development of Lebanon, in accordance with the relevant resolutions and decisions of the General Assembly and the Economic and Social Council.

Economic and Social Council decision 1984/174
Adopted without vote

Approved by Third Committee (E/1984/148) without vote, 23 July (meeting 15); 5-nation draft (E/1984/C.3/L.7); agenda item 18.
Sponsors: Bangladesh, Pakistan, Tunisia, United States, Venezuela.

GENERAL ASSEMBLY ACTION

On the recommendation of the Second Committee, the General Assembly, on 17 December, adopted resolution 39/197 without vote.

Assistance for the reconstruction and development of Lebanon

The General Assembly,

Recalling its resolutions 33/146 of 20 December 1978, 34/135 of 14 December 1979, 35/85 of 5 December 1980, 36/205 of 17 December 1981, 37/163 of 17 December 1982 and 38/220 of 20 December 1983 on assistance for the reconstruction and development of Lebanon,

Recalling also Economic and Social Council resolution 1980/15 of 29 April 1980 and decisions 1983/112 of 17 May 1983 and 1984/174 of 26 July 1984,

Noting with deep concern the continuing heavy loss of life and the additional destruction of property, which have caused further extensive damage to the economic and social structures of Lebanon,

Also noting with concern the serious economic situation in Lebanon,

Welcoming the determined efforts of the Government of Lebanon in undertaking its reconstruction and rehabilitation programme,

Reaffirming the urgent need for further international action to assist the Government of Lebanon in its continuing efforts for reconstruction and development,

Taking note of the report of the Secretary-General and of the statement made on 6 November 1984 by the United Nations Co-ordinator of Assistance for the Reconstruction and Development of Lebanon,

1.   *Expresses its appreciation* to the Secretary-General for his report and for the steps he has taken to mobilize assistance to Lebanon;

2.   *Commends* the United Nations Co-ordinator of Assistance for the Reconstruction and Development of Lebanon and his staff for their valuable and unstinting efforts in the discharge of their duties;

3.   *Expresses its appreciation* for the relentless efforts undertaken by the Government of Lebanon in the implementation of the initial phase of reconstruction of the country, despite adverse circumstances, and for the steps it has taken to remedy the economic situation;

4.   *Requests* the Secretary-General to continue and intensify his efforts to mobilize all possible assistance within the United Nations system to help the Government of Lebanon in its reconstruction and development efforts;

5.   *Requests* the organs, organizations and bodies of the United Nations system to intensify their programmes of assistance and to expand them in response to the needs of Lebanon;

6.   *Also requests* the Secretary-General to report to the Economic and Social Council at its second regular session of 1985 and to the General Assembly at its fortieth session on the progress achieved in the implementation of the present resolution.

General Assembly resolution 39/197

17 December 1984   Meeting 103   Adopted without vote

Approved by Second Committee (A/39/793) without vote, 30 November (meeting 54); 43-nation draft (A/C.2/39/L.62); agenda item 83 *(b)*.

Sponsors: Australia, Austria, Bahrain, Bangladesh, Belgium, Burkina Faso, Canada, Colombia, Cyprus, Democratic Yemen, Djibouti, Dominican Republic, Ecuador, Egypt, Ethiopia, France, Gambia, Italy, Japan, Jordan, Kuwait, Lebanon, Liberia, Libyan Arab Jamahiriya, Madagascar, Mauritania, Morocco, Nicaragua, Oman, Pakistan, Panama, Qatar, Saudi Arabia, Senegal, Spain, Sudan, Tunisia, United Arab Emirates, United Kingdom, United States, Uruguay, Yemen, Yugoslavia.

Meeting numbers. GA 39th session: 2nd Committee 32-37, 45, 54; plenary 103.

REFERENCES

[1]A/39/390. [2]YUN 1983, p. 536, GA res. 38/220, 20 Dec. 1983. [3]*Ibid.*, p. 535. [4]E/ICEF/1985/11. [5]DP/CP/LEB/2. [6]ID/CONF.5/46 & Corr.1 (res. 12).

Chapter IV

International trade and finance

In 1984, the year in which the United Nations Conference on Trade and Development (UNCTAD) commemorated its twentieth anniversary, debate in the UNCTAD Trade and Development Board centred on the debt problems of developing countries and the need to deal simultaneously with the interdependent problems of trade, development finance and the international monetary system. At its two 1984 regular sessions, the Board also considered matters arising from recommendations of the sixth session of the Conference (UNCTAD VI) held in 1983; a special session (the Board's thirteenth) was devoted to the review and appraisal of the implementation of the International Development Strategy for the Third United Nations Development Decade.

In his annual report on the work of the Organization (p. 3), the Secretary-General stated that there was a high degree of frustration in United Nations activities at the global level in trade, money and finance, where the Organization's achievements could not be measured simply in terms of the number of treaties and agreements negotiated and signed. Many of the Organization's contributions were in much less tangible forms, such as shaping the framework of international debates on major problems. For example, he had consistently stressed the importance of finding solutions to the acute debt problems, solutions going beyond the short term and taking into account the need to ensure growth in the export earnings of developing countries.

In a December resolution (39/214), the General Assembly addressed several specific areas of UNCTAD's work programme and called on countries to strengthen international economic co-operation by revitalizing the development process and dealing with structural problems in the global economy.

Following its third annual review of protectionism and structural adjustment, the Trade and Development Board adopted a programme with respect to its continuing work on the issue, full implementation of which was called for by the Assembly in December.

The International Trade Centre continued to assist developing countries in promoting their exports and facilitating movement of goods in international commerce and took steps to strengthen its export market development activities in commodities, in line with an UNCTAD VI recommendation.

Although additional States adhered during 1984 to the 1980 Agreement Establishing the Common Fund for Commodities, by year's end it had not entered into force. With regard to individual commodities, the International Sugar Conference culminated in July with the adoption of the International Sugar Agreement, 1984. Progress was made at two sessions of the United Nations Cocoa Conference towards completing negotiations on a successor agreement to the 1980 International Cocoa Agreement and it was decided to reconvene the Conference. Although neither the International Tropical Timber Agreement, 1983, nor the International Agreement on Jute and Jute Products, 1982, received sufficient ratifications to enter into force, the latter Agreement entered into force provisionally by a decision of the Governments which had signed or ratified it, or had given notice that they would apply it provisionally. Meetings were held during the year to review the market situation of iron ore and tungsten.

A set of draft guidelines on consumer protection was discussed by the Economic and Social Council and forwarded to the General Assembly (resolution 1984/63), which in December decided to consider adopting them in 1985 (decision 39/444).

Concerning international financial relations, the debt problems of developing countries were considered to require urgent international action, as was the need for reform of the international monetary and financial system. Those issues were taken up in United Nations bodies and the Organization's major economic reports, which all stressed the close link between international monetary and financial matters and international trade issues. In December, the Assembly requested the Secretary-General to ascertain the views of Governments and United Nations bodies on expanding international co-operation in money, finance, debt and resource flows, including development assistance and trade (resolution 39/218). In April, the Trade and Development Board adopted agreed conclusions on the debt problems of developing countries. In December, the Assembly called on the international community to address those problems taking into account the Board's action.

In the area of trade-related finance, an expert group on the compensatory financing of export earnings shortfalls held three sessions in 1984 and made recommendations regarding a proposed complementary facility to finance commodity-related shortfalls.

Topics related to this chapter. Development policy and international economic co-operation. Economic assistance, disasters and emergency relief: Africa—critical economic situation. Transport. Industrial development. Regional economic and social activities: international trade and finance—Africa, Asia and the Pacific, Europe, Latin America, Western Asia. Science and technology: technology transfer. International economic law: international trade law.

UNCTAD VI follow-up

During 1984, the UNCTAD Trade and Development Board discussed matters arising from the decisions of the sixth (1983) session of the Conference (UNCTAD VI).[1] As mandated by the Conference, the Board, at its twenty-eighth session (Geneva, 26 March–6 April),[2] adopted a resolution on the work programme on protectionism and structural adjustment and decisions on the debt-servicing and debt and development problems of poorer developing countries (see under relevant subject headings below). At its twenty-ninth session (Geneva, 10-27 September),[3] the Board adopted a resolution on the UNCTAD technical co-operation programme on the generalized system of preferences, and decisions on trade relations among countries having different economic and social systems and on the International Trade Centre (see under relevant subject headings below). Action was also taken on organizational matters at both Board sessions (see below, under "Organizational questions").

Other matters dealt with by the Board in accordance with UNCTAD VI action included: implementation of the medium- and long-term recovery and rehabilitation programme in the Sudano-Sahelian region (see p. 509); technical co-operation among developing countries—co-operative exchange of skills among developing countries (see p. 480); assistance to the peoples of Namibia (see TRUSTEESHIP AND DECOLONIZATION, Chapter III) and those of South Africa (see p. 168); land-locked developing countries (see p. 417); and island developing countries (see p. 422).

GENERAL ASSEMBLY ACTION

After considering the Trade and Development Board's 1984 work, the General Assembly adopted a resolution on the Board's activities, taking a number of decisions in specific areas (see under related subject headings in this chapter). On 18 December, on the recommendation of the Second (Economic and Financial) Committee, the Assembly adopted resolution 39/214 without vote.

Report of the Trade and Development Board
The General Assembly,

Recalling its resolutions 3201(S-VI) and 3202(S-VI) of 1 May 1974, containing the Declaration and the Programme of Action on the Establishment of a New International Economic Order, 3281(XXIX) of 12 December 1974, containing the Charter of Economic Rights and Duties of States, and 3362(S-VII) of 16 September 1975 on development and international economic co-operation,

Recalling further its resolution 38/155 of 19 December 1983,

Recognizing the need for reversing the negative trends in international co-operation for development and, in particular, their detrimental effects on developing countries,

Recognizing also the importance of achieving a sustained world economic recovery, in particular the reactivation of the economies of developing countries, and ensuring rapid expansion of international trade that is supportive of economic growth and development, in particular that of developing countries,

1. *Takes note* of the report of the Trade and Development Board on its twenty-eighth, thirteenth special and twenty-ninth sessions;

2. *Notes* that the *Trade and Development Report, 1984* was of great interest to Governments in the valuable debate on the interdependence of problems of trade, development, finance and the international monetary system, which took place at the twenty-ninth session of the Trade and Development Board;

3. *Calls* for early and full implementation of the work programme on protectionism and structural adjustment adopted by the Trade and Development Board at its twenty-eighth session;

4. *Calls upon* the international community to continue to address, in an adequate and appropriate manner, the debt problems of developing countries, taking into account the agreed conclusions of the Trade and Development Board at its twenty-eighth session on the review of the implementation of the agreed features contained in (Board) resolution 222(XXI) of 27 September 1980 and in pursuance of resolution 161(VI) of 2 July 1983 of the United Nations Conference on Trade and Development;

5. *Takes note* of Trade and Development Board decision 297(XXIX) of 21 September 1984, concerning further work in the field of trade relations among countries having different economic and social systems and all trade flows resulting therefrom;

6. *Welcomes* Trade and Development Board decision 301(XXIX) of 21 September 1984, in which the Interim Committee was requested to report to the Board at its thirtieth session with a view to the taking of a decision to hold a ministerial session in the autumn of 1985 and, to this end, invites all Governments to exert efforts to ensure the successful outcome of the consultations;

7. *Expresses its concern* at the current state of commodity markets, and urges all Governments to expedite the implementation of the Integrated Programme for Commodities through, *inter alia*, positive and constructive decisions at the sessions of the Committee on Commodities in 1985 and at the fourteenth special session of the Trade and Development Board;

8. *Reaffirms* the importance of the Common Fund for Commodities, and urges all States that have not yet done so to sign and ratify the Agreement establishing the Fund without any further delay so that the Common Fund would become operational;

9. *Calls upon* all countries to exert every effort to strengthen international economic co-operation by adopting and implementing the measures necessary for revitalization of the development process of the developing countries and for dealing with structural problems in the global economy, and reiterates the continuing important role of the United Nations Conference on Trade and Development in this regard;

10. *Requests* the Trade and Development Board and the subsidiary organs of the United Nations Conference on Trade and Development to take the appropriate necessary action on the resolutions and decisions adopted by the Conference at its sixth session.

General Assembly resolution 39/214

18 December 1984   Meeting 104   Adopted without vote

Approved by Second Committee (A/39/790/Add.3) without vote, 14 December (meeting 61); draft by Vice-Chairman (A/C.2/39/L.141), based on informal consultations on draft by Egypt, for Group of 77 (A/C.2/39/L.109); agenda item 80 *(c)*.
Meeting numbers. GA 39th session: 2nd Committee 53, 56, 58, 60, 61; plenary 104.

In addition to drafting and other changes, the adopted text differed in a number of major respects from that put forward by the Group of 77 and subsequently withdrawn. The Group's draft included five additional operative paragraphs by which the Assembly would have: urged developed countries to eliminate restrictive measures incompatible with their international commitments and draw up a programme to eliminate protectionist measures which adversely affected the trade of developing countries; reaffirmed the need for stability in the generalized system of preferences, and called on preference-giving countries to ensure continuity, improvement and broadening of their schemes and avoid the introduction into the system of discriminatory measures; affirmed the importance for the development of developing countries of their attaining self-reliance in services and called on UNCTAD to assist them; emphasized the need to accelerate the flow of financial resources to developing countries; and emphasized that the developed countries should facilitate structural adjustment, taking into account an equitable international division of labour.

REFERENCES
[1]YUN 1983, p. 539. [2]A/39/15, vol. I. [3]*Ibid.*, vol. II.

PUBLICATION
The History of UNCTAD, 1964-1984 (UNCTAD/PSG/286), Sales No. E.85.II.D.6.

International trade

During 1984, international trade issues were considered by various United Nations bodies, with the close link between trade issues and international monetary and financial matters being stressed by both the Trade and Development Board and the Committee for Development Planning (CDP). An UNCTAD secretariat report prepared for the Board's annual review of protectionism and structural adjustment noted continued protectionist pressures and stated that some actions by developed countries were in breach of a commitment undertaken at UNCTAD VI to halt protectionism. In April, the Board adopted a work programme on protectionism and structural adjustment, implementation of which was called for by the Assembly in December.

UNCTAD continued its work on trade preferences, which included a new UNCTAD technical assistance project on the generalized system of preferences following the conclusion of a joint UNCTAD/United Nations Development Programme (UNDP) project. Meetings also continued on establishing a global system of trade preferences among developing countries.

A 19-member group of experts met to consider ways to expand trade and economic relations between countries having different economic and social systems and suggested ways in which the Trade and Development Board could act more effectively to facilitate such trade.

The International Trade Centre, operated jointly by UNCTAD and the General Agreement on Tariffs and Trade (GATT), continued to serve as the focal point for United Nations assistance to developing countries in formulating and implementing trade promotion programmes, and steps were taken to strengthen its support of the UNCTAD Integrated Programme for Commodities. The UNCTAD Intergovernmental Group of Experts on Restrictive Business Practices held its third session in 1984.

Widely fluctuating commodity prices continued to cause concern during the year and several meetings on individual commodities were held within UNCTAD. By 31 December, the Agreement establishing the Common Fund for Commodities had still not been ratified by a sufficient number of countries for it to enter into force.

A set of draft guidelines on consumer protection was considered by the Economic and Social Council and by the General Assembly, which decided to consider adopting them at a resumed session in 1985.

Trade policy

For the developing countries, the modest growth of world trade and hesitant rise of commodity prices during 1983 failed to produce a decided recovery of export earnings, said the UNCTAD *Trade and Development Report, 1984.*[1] In addition, adverse weather conditions affected agricultural output in a number of countries, particularly in Africa, thereby reducing exports and increasing the need for essential imports. The developed market-economy countries, on the other hand, were emerging from the most protracted recession of the post-war period, with Canada and the United States experiencing the most remarkable turnaround.

In 1983, the terms of trade of developing countries as a whole fell slightly due to contradictory movements in terms of trade of oil- and of non-oil-exporting developing countries. Growth of import volume for developing countries as a whole was about 1.1 per cent. The increase was largely accounted for by major exporters of manufactures, with an increase of 5.1 per cent, and was confined essentially to the Asian countries. The least developed countries (LDCs), a large number of which were in sub-Saharan Africa, were forced to cut imports by about 3 per cent for the second consecutive year. Developing countries' export volumes increased by 1.1 per cent in 1983, but remained far below 1980 levels. Exports from major oil exporters continued to decrease, but much more slowly than in the two previous years. Export growth in net oil-importing countries fell to 2.8 per cent in 1983, from 4 per cent in 1982; were it not for the major exporters of manufactures, whose export volumes rose by 10.1 per cent, there would have been an absolute decline. In China, after three years of import restraints, import volumes increased by 29.4 per cent in 1983; export volumes increased by 10.5 per cent. In spite of the slower growth of exports relative to imports, the trade balance on a customs basis registered a surplus of $800 million.

Among the developed market-economy countries in 1983, there was considerable diversity of economic experience resulting from differences in fiscal stance. There was a large deterioration in the current account of the United States, which was largely offset by a widening Japanese surplus and reductions in the deficits of France, Italy and the smaller developed market-economy countries. Thus, while lower exports had a negative influence on overall domestic activity, the deterioration in the trade account of the United States imparted, albeit unevenly, an impetus to activity elsewhere, most markedly in Japan, Canada and some smaller European economies. Signs of improvement in the export sector became evident in other Western European countries by mid-1983.

Although the terms of trade of the socialist countries of Eastern Europe deteriorated slightly in 1983, the trade surplus increased. The salient feature of their external trade was the smaller increase in the value of exports from 6.9 per cent

in 1982 to 4.9 per cent in 1983, and the faster rise in imports from 0.9 per cent to 3.4 per cent. However, the faster import growth resulted from reactivation of trade among the countries of the region (including the socialist countries of Asia). Imports from developed market-economy and developing countries continued to decline, by 4 per cent and 0.9 per cent respectively.

In order to explore the changing role of the international trade and payments system, the *Report* devoted a section to following the main lines of evolution which the international monetary, financial and trading systems had undergone in the post-war period. A further section discussed possible reform of the trade and payments system. The *Report* noted that both the trade and payments system and national economies had been left in a weakened condition by the recent crisis and their capacity to bear additional strain was therefore limited. Prudent policy planning called for urgent examination of how the trade and payments system could be restructured to promote better economic performance of national economies. A viable system needed to reaffirm the emphasis on employment and growth that underlay the design of the post-war systems and also to establish mechanisms to ensure adequate growth opportunities for all the system's members. Under the existing arrangements, decisions on the international monetary and financial system, although having a deep impact on both developed and developing countries, were circumscribed by narrow monetary and financial considerations. Also, developing countries were not represented in international monetary negotiations.

An alternative approach, suggested the *Report*, would be to reform the system on the basis of the interdependence of trade and payments and the mutual dependence of employment and development. The *Report* listed several fundamental questions which needed to be addressed by Governments, but stated that the most urgent issue was that of debt (see below, under "Debt problems of developing countries").

The international trade and payments situation was also discussed in a chapter of the *World Economic Survey 1984.*[2] Developments since early 1983, said the *Survey*, had illustrated the crucial interaction between the evolution of international economic and financial variables and the strength and spread of world economic recovery. Although the economic upswing in some developed market economies had given some impetus to world trade, external financial constraints had caused a broad decline in the imports of developing countries, and that had dampened the growth of exports and output in developed and developing countries alike. Unless their export earnings grew sufficiently, developing countries would not contribute significantly to the expansion of world trade, since their imports were constrained by a scarcity of foreign exchange. Their exports would be further affected if recent protectionist threats were acted upon.

Those subdued prospects for export earnings were of particular concern to countries in debt-servicing difficulties, said the *Survey*. The drying up of capital inflows from international capital markets, large amortization payments coming due and high interest rates forced many developing countries into unprecedented reductions in imports in 1983. In spite of severe adjustment, several countries were unable to service their external debt normally. Inadequate international liquidity was an even more widespread problem among developing countries than external debt. Also cited as important problems clouding the international trade and payments picture were rising protectionist pressures and actions and exchange rate fluctuations.

At its May 1984 session,[3] CDP expressed concern about the separation of the issues of trade on the one hand and international monetary and financial matters on the other. It was necessary, CDP stated, to harmonize the sprawling process of re-examining the international economic system, bearing in mind the interrelated areas of money, finance and trade. Most pressing was the need to begin an effective dialogue and prepare the way for negotiation and action.

CDP also called for efforts to reverse the inroads made by protectionism on international markets and drew particular attention to the proliferation of non-tariff barriers.

International trading system

Having considered the matter informally at its March/April session, the Trade and Development Board in September discussed the organization of a review and in-depth study of the international trading system in line with UNCTAD resolution 159(VI).[4] The Board had before it a report[5] prepared by the UNCTAD secretariat which pointed out that the Conference's resolution had evolved from a 1979 Conference decision (132(V))[6] which had requested the Board to undertake a global evaluation of the Tokyo Round of multilateral trade negotiations (MTNs) conducted by GATT (see also PART TWO, Chapter XVII). At a 1981 Board session,[7] Gabon had submitted a draft resolution on behalf of the Group of 77, calling for an annual review by the Board of developments in the international trading system, covering, in particular, the rules and principles governing its functioning. There was no agreement on that draft which was subsequently remitted to each of the Board's 1982, 1983 and 1984 sessions; finally, it was withdrawn by the sponsors in September 1984.

The UNCTAD report identified the following features of what it described as the post-MTN system: the fact that tariffs were no longer relied upon as the principal means of protection; the introduction of flexible or contingent measures of protection, such as subsidies or dumping; the trend towards "managed" trade occurring outside the framework of GATT; and the fact that the unconditional most-favoured-nation treatment principle had ceased to be the guiding principle of international trade relations.

With regard to the review called for in Conference resolution 159(VI), the report said that the formulation of recommendations would require an international consensus: first, as to what was wrong with the current system and, second, as to the fundamental concepts upon which a strengthened and improved system should be based.

On 21 September, the Board took note of the positions of the various groups and decided to annex to its report draft conclusions on the international trading system submitted by Argentina on behalf of the Group of 77.

By the draft conclusions, the Board would have noted that recent developments had further accentuated the need for action to improve and strengthen the international trading system. While recognizing that the review and in-depth study was a continuing activity, the Board would have agreed that the process be accelerated and intensified to permit it at its thirty-first session (September 1985) to make recommendations and proposals. The UNCTAD Secretary-General would have been invited to prepare studies on: the state of implementation of commitments in favour of developing countries; developments in international trade in textiles and clothing; the adverse impact of tariff and non-tariff measures on trade in commodities; and the special problems of LDCs. The Board would also have invited Governments to contribute to accelerating the fulfilment of the mandate in Conference resolution 159(VI).

Protectionism and structural adjustment

Trade and Development Board activities. The Trade and Development Board at its March/April session undertook its annual review of protectionism and structural adjustment in conjunction with monitoring the implementation of part I of UNCTAD resolution 159(VI) dealing with ways to combat protectionism and facilitate structural adjustment.[8] In accordance with Conference decision 160(VI) and a follow-up 1983 Board decision,[9] the question of establishing a work programme on protectionism and structural adjustment was also discussed.

The sessional committee established to deal with the issue had before it an UNCTAD secretariat report on protectionism and structural adjustment in the world economy, Part I[10] of which analysed major policy issues and requirements and, in addenda, summarized information received from 36 UNCTAD States members and the European Economic Community (EEC) on changes in tariffs, quantitative restrictions and measures of equivalent effect, anti-dumping and countervailing duties, and differential and more favourable treatment for developing countries. The report stated that 1983 had witnessed continued protectionist pressures and that a number of actions by developed countries—most of which involved manufactured and semi-manufactured products—were in breach of the commitment undertaken in Conference resolution 159(VI) to halt protectionism.

In developing countries, balance-of-payments difficulties were the main cause of import restrictions and balance-of-payments considerations also justified import barriers in a few developed countries. However, the majority of actions taken were to protect domestic, import-competing industries. Textiles, steel, footwear and ceramic products, together with various electronic goods, remained major targets for protective actions, and controls were further tightened in those sectors. Exporters affected continued to be low-cost producers of textiles and the fast-growing exporters of manufactures in all groups of countries.

The report underlined a number of developments in 1983, the most disturbing of which was the number of actions taken after UNCTAD VI when the developed countries had committed themselves to halting protectionism. On the positive side, it was noted that some concrete actions had been taken to liberalize trade.

The report drew the attention of the Board to two matters in particular: the increasingly ominous implications of international debt problems for both creditor and debtor countries and the contribution that appropriate trade policy initiatives could make in alleviating those problems; and the future work of the UNCTAD secretariat on trade, protectionism and structural adjustment.

Part II of the report[11] discussed developments during the first three years of the 1980s in world production and trade in agriculture, manufactures and services.

Other UNCTAD secretariat reports prepared for the Board's review of protectionism and structural adjustment dealt with an improved and more efficient safeguard system[12] and anti-dumping and countervailing duty practices.[13]

On 6 April, following its discussion of the item, the Board adopted a resolution on its work programme on protectionism and structural adjustment,[14] by which it decided that, in the context of its annual review of the topics, the Board should: monitor implementation of Conference resolution 159(VI) and, where necessary, make recommen-

dations on general problems of protectionism and continue the work on non-tariff barriers in pursuance of that resolution and of Conference resolution 131(V);[15] and exchange information, discuss members' experience and review progress regarding structural adjustment, and review and monitor developments in trade. The Board also decided that, in carrying out the reviews, attention should be given to: all sectors, including agriculture, manufactures and services, and all countries; all factors relevant to the issues, including the links between international trade and balance-of-payments problems and the link between the evolution of work trade and the structure of industries; fostering greater transparency concerning policies and practices in this area; policies to facilitate structural adjustment; strengthening participation of developing countries in agro-industrial production and trade; industrial collaboration arrangements; identifying trends important to the structural adjustment process and to production; with regard to the work on non-tariff barriers, the questions relating to definitions and to dissemination of the results of the inventory; and the special problems and needs of LDCs. The Board instructed the sessional committee to consider other measures to assist developing countries to promote and diversify their exports.

States members of UNCTAD were invited to: provide information on actions relevant to agreements and commitments in Conference resolution 159(VI), to assist the Board in monitoring its implementation; continue to provide information on their experience with regard to structural adjustment; and continue to supply information for UNCTAD secretariat studies. The Board decided to follow closely progress in GATT on a more efficient safeguard system and invited the UNCTAD Secretary-General and the GATT Director-General to hold consultations.

GENERAL ASSEMBLY ACTION

In resolution 39/214 on the Trade and Development Board's report (see above), the Assembly called for early and full implementation of the work programme on protectionism and structural adjustment adopted by the Board in April.

When it was considering the Board's report, the Second Committee also had before it a draft resolution contained in a note by the Secretariat.[16] The draft, originally submitted in 1980 on behalf of the Group of 77[17] and revised by the sponsors in 1981,[18] was considered in 1982[19] and in 1983 when it was referred to the Assembly's 1984 session.[20]

By the draft the Assembly would have urged the developed countries to limit protectionist policies and facilitate measures to increase the share of developing countries in international trade. A table containing suggestions by some developed countries for changes in the draft was annexed to it.

In December, the Assembly, on the recommendation of the Second Committee, adopted decision 39/432 without vote.

Protectionism and structural adjustment

At its 104th plenary meeting, on 18 December 1984, the General Assembly, on the recommendation of the Second Committee, decided to refer to its fortieth session for consideration the draft resolution entitled "Protectionism and structural adjustment".

General Assembly decision 39/432

Adopted without vote

Approved by Second Committee (A/39/790/Add.3) without vote, 6 December (meeting 56); oral proposal by Vice-Chairman; agenda item 80 *(c)*.

Services

In accordance with part IV of Conference resolution 159(VI),[9] the Trade and Development Board at its September 1984 session considered the subject of trade in services. The Board had before it an UNCTAD secretariat study on services and the development process and a summary of that report.[21] The report noted that recent technological developments had given rise to new services and to new interlinkages among services and between goods and services, and that services in a development context had not so far been addressed. The report concentrated on two main issues: the role of services in the growth and development of the domestic economy, with special emphasis on the developing countries, particularly the least developed; and services in the international context which might be relevant to the development process. The report also examined the rationale behind regulations on services at the national and international levels and summarized the current international debate on services in governmental and non-governmental circles.

Among other documents before the Board for its discussion of this issue were: an UNCTAD secretariat report[22] containing replies from international organizations on relevant activities, including technical assistance; background reports on technology[23] and insurance;[24] and a contribution by the United Nations Centre on Transnational Corporations on transborder data flows in the context of services and the development process.[25]

On 21 September, the Board took note of the positions of the various groups and decided to annex to its report a draft decision on services submitted on behalf of the Group of 77. By this draft, the Board would have recognized that an improved knowledge of services in the development process was fundamental and that future UNCTAD work

in the sector should safeguard and promote a self-reliant and accelerated process of development by: considering the definitional aspects of services; strengthening and refining the data base at the national, regional and international levels; carrying out further in-depth studies of the role of services in development; and providing technical assistance to member States. The UNCTAD Secretary-General would have been requested to invite UNDP and other sources to provide financial assistance for technical assistance on services.

Trade preferences

During 1984, the joint UNCTAD/UNDP technical assistance project on the generalized system of preferences came to an end and a new UNCTAD technical assistance project was launched. Discussions continued on a proposed global system of trade preferences among developing countries.

Generalized system of preferences

The Trade and Development Board's Special Committee on Preferences held its twelfth session at Geneva from 24 April to 4 May 1984[26] and had before it the UNCTAD secretariat's eighth general report on implementing the generalized system of preferences (GSP).[27] The report described changes and improvements in the system since the previous review in 1982.[28]

The report noted that total most-favoured-nation dutiable imports by preference-giving countries of the Organisation for Economic Co-operation and Development (OECD) amounted to $132.1 billion in 1982, of which $62.2 billion (or 47 per cent) were covered by GSP. Imports which actually received preferential treatment amounted to $27.8 billion. The addition of preferential imports into Hungary for 1980 and the USSR for 1981 would bring total preferential imports under GSP to $31.1 billion.

With regard to special tariff treatment by preference-giving countries to LDCs, the report noted that total imports of 10 OECD preference-giving countries from LDC beneficiaries amounted to an annual figure of $1,270 million in 1981-1982. However, only one third of that fell within the purview of GSP. Imports which actually received preferential treatment were valued at $115.5 million. The addition of imports from LDCs into Hungary for 1980 and the USSR for 1981 would bring total preferential imports from such countries under GSP to $291.6 million. The report observed that only a fraction of exports from LDCs were eligible under GSP, either because of narrow product coverage of agricultural products under the schemes or because officials of those countries did not have the skills and experience to deal with the complexities of the schemes and their rules of origin.

Following the general review of GSP, the Special Committee on 4 May decided to annex to its report a draft resolution submitted at its 1982 session on behalf of the Group of 77.[29]

At its April/May 1984 session, the Special Committee also considered a report[30] on technical co-operation activities in connection with GSP during 1982 and 1983.[31] The report noted that the UNCTAD/UNDP project of assistance to developing countries for the fuller utilization of GSP had expired on 31 December 1983, following a UNDP decision not to continue its funding. It would, however, continue with minimum activities until 30 June 1984, pending the launching of a new two-year technical assistance programme under a trust fund or GSP account which was to begin on 1 July (see below). The new programme would be in line with Conference resolution 159(VI).[31]

In other action, the Special Committee held consultations on harmonizing and improving the rules of origin, used to ensure that preferential tariff treatment under GSP was given only to goods originating in preference-receiving countries, and decided to recommend that the Working Group on Rules of Origin be reconvened in 1985.

Technical co-operation

During 1984, technical assistance to developing countries on utilizing GSP continued with limited funding from UNDP until 30 June, during which time the UNCTAD secretariat attempted to mobilize support for future GSP technical assistance activities. In addition to cash contributions to a newly established trust fund, assistance was provided by several States in the form of experts, seminar financing, hosting of seminar/workshop activities and certificates of origin. On 1 September, a new scaled-down UNCTAD GSP project was initiated for a period of one year.

Regional or national seminars under the aegis of the UNCTAD/UNDP project and the new UNCTAD project were held in Honduras, the Ivory Coast, Nepal, Pakistan, Sri Lanka and Thailand. These seminars trained some 414 developing-country government officials who administered GSP and representatives of the private sector from 29 countries.

Trade and Development Board action. On 21 September, the Trade and Development Board took note of the report of the Special Committee on Preferences,[26] and adopted a resolution[32] in which it reiterated its invitations to UNDP to renew its financial support for the UNCTAD technical co-operation programme on GSP and invited member States to provide extrabudgetary contributions to the UNCTAD trust fund.

Global system of trade preferences among developing countries

In accordance with a 1983 Trade and Development Board resolution,[33] a meeting enabling the developing countries participating in the negotiations on a global system of trade preferences among developing countries to continue the necessary work towards the establishment of the system was held at Geneva from 14 to 25 May 1984.[34] Following an informal exchange of views on five working papers prepared by a technical group within the Group of 77, it was decided to hold a further meeting in 1984. The second meeting was held at Geneva from 8 to 19 October and a report[35] to the 1985 session of the Committee on Economic Co-operation among Developing Countries, comprising an account of its proceedings, was adopted.

Trade among countries having different economic and social systems

In accordance with a 1983 Trade and Development Board decision,[36] an *ad hoc* group of experts was convened at Geneva from 28 May to 1 June 1984 to consider ways of expanding trade and economic relations between countries having different economic and social systems. The group's mandate included studying the outstanding issues referred to in Conference decision 145(VI).[33]

The group had before it: a study by the UNCTAD secretariat on ways of expanding such trade and economic relations,[37] and a study on new forms of trade and economic co-operation between developing countries and the USSR,[38] prepared by an UNCTAD consultant.

In its report,[39] the 19-member group stated that, while trade and economic co-operation among countries having different economic and social systems had expanded, it was not commensurate with the economic potential of the different groups of countries. UNCTAD, said the group, should study the various problems and constraints in trade and economic co-operation between the different groups and ensure implementation of its decisions aimed at expanding trade flows. A principal target would be to ensure observance of generally accepted norms of international trade as embodied in international agreements, including the United Nations Charter and GATT. Given UNCTAD's experience in assisting States to develop trade and economic relations among countries with different economic and social systems, the group considered that UNCTAD's work needed to be reinforced by concrete activities, including studies of a practical nature, giving due regard to the developments of the previous two decades in the world economy and in international economic relations.

The group also recommended: strengthening co-operation between UNCTAD and the United Nations regional commissions; additional efforts by partners in East-West trade to restore confidence in their relations; further expansion of trade and economic relations between socialist and developing countries; attention to the special problems of LDCs; improved information on foreign trade policies of trading partners and identification of unexploited trade opportunities; and intensification of UNCTAD's technical assistance activities.

The group suggested several actions by which the Trade and Development Board could act more effectively to facilitate trade and economic relations among the different groups of countries: continue efforts to finalize the informal text annexed to Conference decision 145(VI)[33] and to resolve outstanding issues in that text; continue studying ways of expanding and diversifying trade and economic co-operation among those countries; consider convening meetings of groups of experts to discuss those or similar issues; request member countries to provide more information on trade flows, commodity composition and various instruments of expansion of trade and co-operation; organize meetings among developing countries to share experience of trade promotion with socialist countries; and consider measures for better use of consultative machinery within UNCTAD.

Trade and Development Board action. In addition to the report of the *ad hoc* group of experts,[39] the Trade and Development Board, at its September session, had before it an UNCTAD secretariat report[40] which analysed developments in trade between the socialist countries of Eastern Europe and other groups of countries. The report's annex contained statistics in tabular form. A further UNCTAD secretariat report[41] on recent developments in East-West co-operation in third countries and in tripartite co-operation evaluated the impact and benefits of that kind of co-operation for developing countries.

On 21 September,[42] the Board decided to remit to its thirty-first (1985) session the informal text annexed to Conference decision 145(VI).[33] The Board requested the UNCTAD Secretary-General to prepare studies contributing to the promotion of economic co-operation between countries having different economic and social systems, paying particular attention to trade interests of developing countries, including case-studies on the co-operation of LDCs with the socialist countries of Eastern Europe and on the establishment of joint ventures and mixed companies with the participation of the enterprises of those socialist countries, in order to explore forms of and experiences in economic co-operation with the participation of countries having different systems.

The UNCTAD Secretary-General was also requested to prepare an evaluation report on the UNCTAD consultative machinery and to submit it, together with proposals for improving the machinery, to the Board's thirty-first session. He was further requested to ensure adequate support for UNCTAD technical assistance projects and programmes in the area of trade of developing

countries, particularly the least developed, with the socialist countries of Eastern Europe, with a view to strengthening developing countries' participation in trade and economic negotiations. UNDP was invited to contribute to their financing and voluntary contributions were also invited.

In resolution 39/214 of 18 December, the General Assembly took note of the Board's decision.

Technical co-operation

During 1984, under a special arrangement set up in 1983[36] under the USSR/UNDP Trust Fund for Training in the USSR of Specialists from Developing Countries, a regional seminar was organized in Moscow and Tashkent (USSR) and Sofia (Bulgaria) in co-operation with the Economic and Social Commission for Asia and the Pacific. The seminar, the aim of which was to explore the potential for expanding trade between the countries of the Asia and Pacific region and the socialist countries of Eastern Europe, was attended by officials from foreign trade ministries and the private business sector. A subregional seminar for senior officials from eastern and southern Africa was held at Nairobi (Kenya), Moscow and Berlin, in co-operation with the Economic Commission for Africa. The Nairobi segment was organized with the Eastern and Southern Africa Trade Promotion and Training Centre. Foreign trade policies and practices of the socialist countries of Eastern Europe were studied as were possibilities for expanding trade and economic co-operation between the two groups of countries. An expert group meeting was held in Moscow to evaluate the results of a 1983 regional seminar for Arab countries; five experts from Arab countries and six from socialist countries participated.

A UNDP-funded regional project on economic relations between Latin American countries and countries members of the Council for Mutual Economic Assistance was completed in 1984. A seminar was held at Buenos Aires (Argentina) to review the project and to explore the possibilities of strengthening economic relations between the two groups of countries.

Trade promotion and facilitation

During 1984, United Nations bodies continued to assist developing countries to promote their exports and to facilitate the movement of goods in international commerce by harmonizing procedures, standardizing documents and developing new data processing and communication methods for exports, imports and transit. The main originator of technical co-operation projects in this area was the International Trade Centre (ITC). An UNCTAD Intergovernmental Group of Experts met to consider ways of eliminating restrictive business practices as barriers to trade flows.

International Trade Centre

During 1984, the International Trade Centre, under the joint sponsorship of UNCTAD and GATT, continued its technical co-operation activities, serving as the focal point for United Nations assistance to developing countries in formulating and implementing trade promotion programmes.[43]

ITC reported that expenditure on project implementation in 1984 remained at approximately the same level as in 1983. However, since expenditure was recorded in United States dollars, which appreciated considerably during the year, ITC activities in fact expanded. The value of UNDP-financed activities executed by ITC continued to rise, reflecting the importance attached by developing countries to improving their trade performance. The percentage share of UNDP financing in the total value of ITC activities increased, as it had in 1983.

In Africa, national projects increased from 19 to 20 in 1984 and regional projects from 9 to 13; 12 of these projects were in African LDCs. In Asia and the Pacific, country projects increased to 32 from 28, while regional projects remained at 7. In Latin America, there were 21 country projects, compared with 16 in 1983, and 10 regional projects compared with 12 the previous year. In Europe, the Mediterranean and the Middle East, ITC activities were again affected by limited financial resources and delays in approving new project proposals.

ITC activities regarding institutional infrastructure for trade promotion at the national level in 1984 included a comparative study of export promotion systems in selected Latin American and Caribbean countries. In addition to the study itself, guidelines were prepared on export development programmes, medium-term export strategies and the formulation of work programmes for export promotion organizations, and case-studies were prepared on export promotion systems used in the selected countries. This material was distributed to all Spanish-speaking Latin American countries.

In accordance with Conference resolution 158(VI),[44] in 1984 ITC strengthened export market development activities in the area of commodities and in support of UNCTAD's Integrated Programme for Commodities (IPC). Comprehensive, long-term research, development and training programmes, including technical co-operation project proposals, were prepared for cocoa, coconut products, coffee, jute, meat, rubber, tropical timber and vegetable oils. Through its trade information supply services, ITC's Import-Export Contact Programme dealt with some 1,400 requests in 1984, an 8 per cent increase over 1983. ITC continued to collect and disseminate company profiles on exporters in developing countries and importers in developed and developing countries. By the end of the year, profiles in the computerized data base reached 21,000, an increase of more than 60 per cent over 1983. Fifty issues of "Trade Contacts"—studies containing both contact data on exporters/importers and selection data, such as type of activity, year of establishment, number of employees and description of products handled— were published in 1984, compared with only 13 in 1983. The UNDP-financed Market News Service consolidated its world-wide operations during 1984, with some 93 receiving centres in exporting developing countries participating. It provided numerous consulting services, mainly in Africa, to assist exporting developing countries in interpreting, analysing and locally disseminating information.

In the area of specialized national trade promotion services, a training course for packaging designers from Cuba was held at Havana, a seminar on food packaging was arranged at Karachi, Pakistan, and an export packaging symposium was held at Cairo, Egypt. Shorter presentations on packaging were given in various countries. Substantive support was also provided to a UNDP-financed export packaging development project for the 12 member countries of the Asian Packaging Federation.

With regard to multinational trade promotion, ITC continued market promotion projects for jute and jute products in Western Europe and the United States. The projects, started by ITC in 1981, were extended to cover 1984 with multilateral and UNDP support. ITC continued to provide support to IPC and FAO in identifying and formulating market promotion programmes for hard fibres.

ITC's special programme of technical co-operation with LDCs focused on assisting those countries to widen their limited export product base through better use of domestic resources. Trade promotion activities oriented to rural development included technical assistance to Bangladesh, Malawi, Senegal, Swaziland and a number of Sahelian countries.

Total ITC expenditure in 1984 was $25.4 million. Of this amount, technical co-operation activities accounted for $15 million, compared with $14.9 million in 1983. Trust fund contributions furnished $8.4 million of the 1984 amount for technical co-operation; the remainder was provided by UNDP. The Centre's 1984 regular budget of $8 million, covering operations at its Geneva headquarters, was contributed in equal parts by the United Nations and GATT. As at 31 December,

ITC had a headquarters-based staff of 75 Professionals and 129 in the General Service category. It had 65 experts assigned to projects during the year.

JAG action. The Joint Advisory Group (JAG) on ITC, at its seventeenth session (Geneva, 9-16 April),[45] urged the Centre to continue efforts to increase trust fund contributions and diversify its sources of financing to ensure an expanded technical co-operation programme. Among other recommendations were: that continued attention be given to identifying products with export potential and to developing products for export; that market development publications be issued in English, French and Spanish, preferably simultaneously; that ITC implement project proposals on marketing and distribution of commodities, in accordance with Conference resolution 158(VI);[44] and that it take measures to expand direct training opportunities for developing countries. Recommended areas of emphasis for ITC activities were: promotion of trade among developing countries; integration of market and product development; and increased participation in training programmes in the socialist countries of Eastern Europe.

The Group endorsed the future orientation of ITC's global technical co-operation activities in Africa, south of the Sahara, and recommended that priority be given to its implementation.

Trade and Development Board action. On 13 September, the Trade and Development Board took note of the JAG report. By a decision of 21 September[46] on voluntary contributions to ITC, the Board welcomed the response by Governments of some donor countries to the appeal for increased resources in Conference resolution 158(VI),[44] and invited Governments to announce voluntary contributions to ITC for its activities in 1985 and 1986.

Accounts for 1982-1983

Reporting in 1984 on its audit of ITC for the biennium 1982-1983,[47] the Board of Auditors found that salaries of some staff members in 1982 had been charged to the regular budget instead of to the Programme Support Costs Fund, that the terms of reference of the Centre's Contracts Review Committee were not clearly defined, and that procurement and travel procedures were not being fully complied with.

Commenting on the Board's report, the Advisory Committee on Administrative and Budgetary Questions (ACABQ)[48] noted that a consultant had been retained to review distribution of posts between the regular budget and the support costs budget and establish a rationale for such distribution. ACABQ recommended that the study's results be reflected in the proposed 1986-1987 pro-

gramme budget. With regard to procurement practices, ACABQ urged the ITC administration to pay closer attention to all aspects of the procurement process to ensure compliance with the rules and achieve optimum use of resources.

On 13 December, by resolution 39/66, the General Assembly accepted the financial reports and accounts reviewed by the Board of Auditors of various United Nations programmes, including that of ITC, concurred with the ACABQ comments and requested the ITC Executive Director to take remedial action as required by the Board.

Trade facilitation

During 1984, the UNCTAD Special Programme on Trade Facilitation (FALPRO) continued to provide the focal point in an international network of national trade facilitation bodies and interested international organizations. Technical co-operation activities during the year included two interregional projects: a trade facilitation field programme financed by UNDP and advisory and training services in trade facilitation financed by the Swedish International Development Authority. Advisory missions were carried out in Bolivia, Colombia, Djibouti, Haiti, Paraguay and the United Republic of Tanzania. A trade facilitation symposium, attended by officials and private sector representatives from all six members of the Association of South-East Asian Nations, was organized in December at Kuala Lumpur, Malaysia.

Various manuals, directories and code systems in trade facilitation, established jointly by UNCTAD and the Economic Commission for Europe (ECE), were maintained and updated during the year. Four issues of *Trade Facilitation News* were published by ECE and FALPRO in 1984.

Restrictive business practices

The UNCTAD Intergovernmental Group of Experts on Restrictive Business Practices, established as a forum for consultation on matters related to the Set of Multilaterally Agreed Equitable Principles and Rules for the Control of Restrictive Business Practices, adopted in 1980,[49] held its third session at Geneva from 7 to 16 November 1984.[50]

The Group had before it revised versions of a study on collusive tendering[51] and of elements for provisions of a model law on restrictive business practices,[52] prepared by the UNCTAD secretariat. The original versions of these documents had been considered at the Group's 1983 session.[53] Other documentation prepared by the UNCTAD secretariat for the Group's discussions included a study on tied purchasing,[54] a note on restrictive business practices in the services sector by consulting firms and other enterprises in relation to the design and manufacture of plant and equipment,[55] a note giving views by States and suggestions concerning the improvement and further development of the Principles and Rules,[56] a review of the implementation of technical assistance, advisory and training programmes on restrictive business practices,[57] and a note giving replies by States and regional groupings on steps taken to meet their commitments to the Principles and Rules.[58]

On 16 November, the Group adopted a resolution[59] by which it expressed concern about the resort to restrictive business practices, underlined the importance of adequate implementation of the Principles and Rules and called on States to implement them. The Group regretted that no action had been taken to implement the technical assistance, advisory and training programmes on restrictive business practices as agreed in the Principles and Rules and invited States to consider taking the issue up at the ongoing General Assembly session. International organizations and financing programmes, particularly UNDP, were urged to provide resources to finance those programmes, and all countries, particularly developed ones, were invited to make voluntary financial and other contributions. The Group requested the UNCTAD secretariat to proceed as early as possible with preparing a handbook on restrictive business practices legislation and requested the UNCTAD Secretary-General to arrange for publication of the revised study on collusive tendering,[51] together with the comments made during the session by regional group spokesmen. The Group noted that no information was supplied by States for the study on the use of restrictive business practices in the services sector,[55] reiterated its request to States to provide information on the issue, and requested the UNCTAD secretariat to develop the study in the light of new information provided. The secretariat was also requested to develop further the study on tied purchasing[54] in the light both of additional information to be supplied by Governments and of comments expressed at the session. The Group noted the revised draft of the model law or laws on restrictive business practices[52] and the comments made thereon during the session, and requested the secretariat to continue work on the model law taking into account the comments made and the importance which the Group attached to the handbook's preparation. The UNCTAD Secretary-General was requested to prepare documents for the 1985 United Nations Conference on Restrictive Business Practices and to present outlines of possible future studies.

Also on 16 November, the Group decided to annex to its report a draft resolution submitted on behalf of the Group of 77. By this draft, the Group of Experts would have agreed to make the following proposals to the 1985 Conference: to consider

that the Principles and Rules be made legally binding; to recommend to the Assembly the creation of a special committee to monitor their application and implementation and devise ways to facilitate multilateral co-operation to exchange information and experience in controlling restrictive business practices; to recommend to the Assembly the convening of a conference in 1990 to review all aspects of the revised Principles and Rules; and to request the Assembly to allocate resources to carry out technical assistance activities, as decided on in the Principles and Rules.

Commodities

During 1984, several meetings were held within UNCTAD to discuss individual commodities. By resolutions 155(VI) and 156(VI),[60] UNCTAD VI had requested the convening of a special session of the Committee on Commodities to examine the role of international commodity agreements negotiated within UNCTAD and to elaborate frameworks for international co-operation in processing, marketing and distribution of commodities of export interest to developing countries, a report on which was to be submitted to the Trade and Development Board not later than 31 December 1984. In adopting a 21 September decision on the calendar of meetings,[61] the Board postponed the dates of the second special session of the Committee and the fourth session of the Permanent Sub-Committee on Commodities from their original dates of October and September 1984, respectively, to January 1985.

In a chapter on international trade and payments, the *World Economic Survey 1984*[2] noted that during 1983 prices for internationally traded non-fuel primary commodities had begun to recover from the sharp slide of the preceding two years. Little progress had been made to improve international institutions to stabilize prices of primary commodities, the *Survey* noted. In particular, the Common Fund for Commodities had not been ratified by a sufficient number of countries (see below). It was unlikely that commodity prices would experience a generalized decline in the next two years but, if international price stabilizing mechanisms were not improved during that period, commodity prices and the export earnings of developing countries could continue to exhibit wide fluctuations.

The *Trade and Development Report, 1984*[1] noted that prices of non-oil commodities exported by developing countries were likely to maintain an upward trend in 1984 and 1985. With the deceleration of growth foreseen in the United States for 1984-1985 and a moderate pace of recovery in the rest of the industrial world, the non-oil commodity price index was expected to rise less in those two years than in 1983. For the first and second quarters of 1984, the UNCTAD price indices of non-oil primary commodities exported by developing countries were 14.7 and 7.3 per cent higher, respectively, than during the corresponding quarters of 1983. Those increases, reflecting strengthening of tropical beverages and vegetable oil prices, and continuing depressed levels of mineral and metal prices, seemed to indicate a deceleration in the overall rise of prices.

Common Fund for Commodities

Preparations continued in 1984 on arrangements for the Common Fund for Commodities, a mechanism intended to stabilize the commodities market by helping to finance buffer stocks of specific commodities as well as commodity development activities such as research and marketing. Although additional States adhered to the 1980 Agreement Establishing the Common Fund for Commodities,[62] by the end of the year it had not been ratified, accepted or approved by the required minimum of 90 States necessary for its entry into force.

Signatures and ratifications

As at 31 December 1984, the 1980 Agreement Establishing the Common Fund for Commodities had been signed by 112 States and EEC, and 82 States had formally adhered by ratifying, accepting or approving it.[63] Of these, 2 States signed the Agreement and 14 adhered during 1984.

The States which adhered in 1984 were: Afghanistan, Bhutan, Brazil, Cape Verde, Chad, Comoros, Greece, Italy, Nepal, Nicaragua, Samoa, Somalia, Spain, Togo. Those which signed were: Djibouti, Saint Lucia.

Report of the Secretary-General. For the General Assembly's review of the implementation of its December 1983 resolution on signature and ratification of the Agreement Establishing the Common Fund,[64] the Secretary-General submitted in October 1984 a report[65] on the status of that Agreement. The report recalled that the Agreement was to enter into force after: (i) it had been ratified, accepted or approved by a minimum of 90 States, accounting for at least two thirds of the Fund's directly contributed capital of $470 million; and (ii) at least 50 per cent of the $280 million target for pledges of voluntary contributions to the Second Account had been met. While the latter requirement had been met by 31 March 1982, the initial deadline for entry into force, the former requirement had not. In June 1982,[66] the deadline had been extended until 30 September 1983. As of 11 October 1984, the Agreement had been signed by 114 States and ratified, accepted or approved by 81 States, accounting for 47.3 per cent of the Fund's capital. Therefore, conditions

for entry into force had not been fulfilled and it was not possible for the Fund to begin operations by 1 January 1984, as called for in UNCTAD resolution 153(VI).[67]

The report noted that, since the States that had adhered to the Agreement were empowered to decide on a new period for fulfilment of requirements for its entry into force, the UNCTAD Secretary-General would be consulting the States concerned.

GENERAL ASSEMBLY ACTION

Following discussions in the Second Committee, the Assembly, on that Committee's recommendation, adopted decision 39/434 by which it took note of the Secretary-General's report.[65]

In resolution 39/214 on the report of the Trade and Development Board, the Assembly reaffirmed the importance of the Common Fund for Commodities and urged all States to sign and ratify the Agreement establishing the Fund without delay so that the Fund would become operational.

In its Declaration on the Critical Economic Situation in Africa, annexed to resolution 39/29, the Assembly noted that the heavy dependence of African countries on the export of a few primary commodities rendered them vulnerable to sharp price fluctuations resulting in drastic shortfalls in export earnings. In that regard, early and effective operation of the Common Fund required intensified international action.

Individual commodities

During 1984, the UNCTAD secretariat issued the revised versions of commodity-by-commodity processing and marketing studies, as originally called for by UNCTAD resolution 124(V).[68] The published versions included written comments on the studies by Governments and other bodies, together with comments made in the Permanent Sub-Committee on Commodities at its 1982[69] and 1983[70] sessions. Studies were issued for the following commodities: bauxite/alumina/aluminium;[71] cocoa;[72] coffee;[73] copper;[74] hard fibres (sisal and henequen);[75] jute and jute products;[76] manganese;[77] phosphates;[78] sugar;[79] and tea.[80] UNCTAD secretariat reports were also prepared on the marketing, distribution and transportation of iron ore,[81] on the processing of tin,[82] and on the marketing and distribution of tin.[83]

The studies and reports examined obstacles to increased participation by developing countries in processing, marketing and distributing the particular commodities, starting from the premise that appropriate international action in that area concerned policies to ensure that the international economic environment supported efforts to promote development. Among issues identified as seeming amenable to intergovernmental negotiation were:

control of restrictive business practices; transfer of technology and dissemination of information on techniques and suppliers; market transparency in terms of market functioning, outlets and other commercial information; investment financing; technical assistance for processing and marketing in developing countries; and reduction of tariff and non-tariff barriers facing exports of developing countries.

Agricultural commodities

Cocoa. In 1984, a United Nations Cocoa Conference was held in two parts at Geneva (7-25 May and 8 October–2 November) under the auspices of UNCTAD to negotiate a successor agreement to the 1980 International Cocoa Agreement.[84] In a note dealing with some policy issues,[85] the UNCTAD secretariat stated that the effectiveness of the 1980 Agreement had been seriously weakened by the International Cocoa Council's incapacity to deal with surplus production during the Agreement's first two years, and by inadequate finance for buffer stocking. Non-membership of the leading exporter (Ivory Coast) and the leading importer (United States) constituted an additional handicap. Among the principal issues expected to arise in relation to the economic provisions of a new agreement were: the price objective; economic mechanisms; size, financing and operating arrangements of the buffer stock; and export quotas. Also before the Conference was a paper by the secretariat of the International Cocoa Organization which was adopted by the International Cocoa Council as a working document for the Conference.

At the conclusion of the first part of the Conference (May), a resolution[86] was adopted, by which the Conference, noting significant progress made in preparing a successor agreement, requested the UNCTAD Secretary-General to reconvene the Conference for three weeks in October, with a possible extension until 2 November, and requested the Conference President to undertake consultations to facilitate its work.

The second part of the Conference (October/November) adopted a resolution[87] by which, noting further progress in preparing a successor agreement, it reaffirmed the readiness of producing and consuming countries to complete the negotiations on a new agreement. The UNCTAD Secretary-General was requested to maintain contacts with producing and consuming countries to assist the Conference in achieving a successful conclusion, and to reconvene the Conference for a period of three weeks, as soon as possible after mid-February 1985.

Hides and skins. In the light of UNCTAD resolution 155(VI),[60] in which the Committee on Commodities was requested to provide a forum for interested Governments to consider project proposals or other arrangements on hides and skins within the context of the Integrated Programme for Commodities, the UNCTAD secretariat in October 1984 prepared for the Committee's 1985 session a report[88] on hides and skins in raw and processed forms: features of the market and elements of a programme of developmental measures.

The report described changes in the volume, structure and pattern of international trade in hides, skins and leather over the previous two decades and compared the sector in developed and developing countries, illustrating the disparity in efficiency in the two groups of countries. Problems of the hides and skins sector in developing countries were discussed and elements of a development programme for the sector outlined. Priority areas to be covered in such a programme were: research, development and training to increase the availability and improve the quality of hides, skins and leather; improving statistical information; and improving marketing, particularly through better market intelligence and strengthening promotion activities for exports from developing countries. In implementing such a programme, the objective would be to extend and complement multilateral and bilateral technical assistance already being provided and to avoid duplication. The programme would need to differentiate between short-term projects and activities in the longer term.

The report noted that the Committee on Commodities might wish to recommend convening an *ad hoc* intergovernmental meeting on hides and skins to consider whether a development programme, eligible for financing from the Second Account of the Common Fund, should be instituted and what elements it should contain. Such a specialized meeting would need to make recommendations on: preparation of research and development projects; the extent to which those projects could form part of a special section of the programme on meat; and institutional arrangements for co-ordinating implementation of a programme on hides and skins.

Jute. The International Agreement on Jute and Jute Products, 1982,[89] which was negotiated and concluded in the framework of the Integrated Programme for Commodities, entered into force provisionally on 9 January 1984. Although requirements for entry into force of the Agreement on the part of exporting countries were fulfilled in 1983,[90] on the importers' side fewer than the required number of 20 countries—representing 65 per cent of net world imports—had definitively signed, ratified, accepted, approved or acceded to it.

Under the terms of the Agreement, the United Nations Secretary-General convened a meeting of

Governments which had signed or ratified it, or had notified the depositary that they would apply it provisionally. The meeting (Dhaka, Bangladesh, 9 January) decided[91] to put the Agreement as a whole into effect immediately on a provisional basis, and further decided that it would enter into force definitively when its requirements had been met, without necessitating a further meeting of Governments concerned. The meeting was followed immediately by the first session of the International Jute Council, the main organ of the International Jute Organization which was established by the Agreement.

By 31 December 1984,[63] 14 importing countries had definitively signed, ratified, accepted, approved or acceded to the Agreement, while a further 8 importing countries, plus EEC, had provisionally applied it.

Sugar. At its third session (Geneva, 12 June–5 July 1984), the United Nations Sugar Conference, 1983, which had met twice that year,[90] established the text of the International Sugar Agreement, 1984.[92] On 5 July, the Conference adopted a resolution[93] by which it requested the United Nations Secretary-General to arrange for the Agreement to be open for signature at United Nations Headquarters, and invited States and intergovernmental organizations to become parties to it.

Like the International Sugar Agreement, 1973,[94] the 1984 Agreement was administrative in nature without economic provisions because of unresolved issues in connection with a regulatory mechanism to keep world sugar prices within an agreed zone. The Agreement's objectives were to further international co-operation in sugar matters and to provide a framework for the possible renegotiation of a new international sugar agreement with economic provisions.

The target date for entry into force was 1 January 1985, immediately upon expiration of the 1977 International Sugar Agreement.[95] The Agreement was opened for signature from 1 September to 31 December 1984 and was to enter into force when ratified, accepted, approved or acceded to by Governments holding 50 per cent of the votes of exporting countries and by those holding 50 per cent of the votes of importing countries. Should requirements for entry into force not be met by 1 January 1985, the Agreement was to enter into force provisionally if notifications of provisional application were deposited by Governments satisfying the above percentage requirements. Once in force, either definitively or provisionally, it would remain in force until 31 December 1986, unless terminated or extended by the International Sugar Council of the International Sugar Organization.

Tropical timber. Following the adoption of the International Tropical Timber Agreement in 1983,[90] and in accordance with a resolution adopted by the 1983 United Nations Conference on Tropical Timber,[96] the UNCTAD Secretary-General convened a meeting of the Preparatory Committee for the International Tropical Timber Council at Geneva from 2 to 6 July 1984.[97] The Preparatory Committee considered preparations for the establishment of the Council and of the International Tropical Timber Organization, envisaged under the 1983 Agreement. No consensus was reached on the location of a headquarters site for the organization and no recommendation was made regarding its Executive Director as no candidates had been put forward.

The Committee endorsed a request of the 1983 Conference for the UNCTAD Secretary-General to convene the first session of the Council as soon as possible after the entry into force of the Agreement. In view of the number and importance of issues on which the Council would have to decide, the Committee recommended that the first session should be for two weeks.

On 6 July, the Preparatory Committee adopted a resolution by which it welcomed action taken by 17 Governments regarding signature and/or ratification of the 1983 Agreement and strongly urged Governments which had not done so to sign and ratify it to enable it to enter into force on 1 October 1984. Earlier, in May, the Governing Council of the United Nations Environment Programme had also urged Governments to sign and ratify it (see Chapter XVI of this section).

The Agreement was opened for signature from 2 January and was to enter into force on 1 October or any date thereafter, if 12 Governments of producing countries holding at least 55 per cent of the total votes and 16 Governments of consuming countries holding at least 70 per cent of the total votes had signed the Agreement definitively or had ratified, accepted, approved or acceded to it. As at 31 December, eight States (Denmark, Japan, Indonesia, Ireland, Malaysia, Norway, Sweden, United Kingdom) had ratified or accepted the Agreement.[63] Therefore, there was insufficient adherence for the Agreement to enter into force.

Minerals and metals

Iron ore. The Third Preparatory Meeting on Iron Ore was held at Geneva from 9 to 13 April 1984[98] to review the iron ore market situation and short-term outlook, consider international measures and recommend follow-up action.

Because of the time lapse since the second preparatory meeting in 1978,[99] the UNCTAD secretariat prepared a note[100] summarizing that meeting's conclusions regarding both the establishment of an annual statistical programme on iron ore and the preparation of an outline of a study of problems of the iron ore industry and the steps taken in pursuance of them. Other material prepared by the UNCTAD secretariat included a description of developments in the world iron ore market and the short-term outlook[101] and updated statistical information.[102]

In its adopted conclusions, the Meeting: requested the UNCTAD secretariat to prepare a report indicating possible gaps in iron ore statistics and to suggest improvements in their quality and coverage; invited Governments to make proposals regarding studies to be undertaken on technological and economic factors relating to the iron ore sector; requested the UNCTAD secretariat to prepare a report on alternative forms of co-operation and dialogue between exporting and importing countries; and requested the UNCTAD Secretary-General to convene a fourth preparatory meeting not later than the end of 1985.

Tungsten. At its sixteenth session (Geneva, 10-14 December 1984),[103] the UNCTAD Committee on Tungsten established a sessional working group on the tungsten market situation. As requested by the Committee in 1983,[96] the UNCTAD secretariat prepared a note on the establishment of such a group,[104] which examined procedural and substantive aspects and contained draft terms of reference and operating procedures, which were amended and adopted by the Committee.

Also pursuant to a 1983 request,[96] the Committee had before it an UNCTAD secretariat note[105] which reviewed developments in tungsten price indicators, structural and technological change within the industry and the demand for tungsten in key sectors. The note also reported on ways to further the Committee's work.

In order to facilitate the Committee's examination of the current tungsten market situation and outlook, the UNCTAD secretariat provided a note[106] covering developments in 1983 and part of 1984. In response to suggestions made in 1983[96] on improving the quality and timeliness of the quarterly bulletin *Tungsten Statistics*, the secretariat also prepared a note on that subject[107] for the Committee's consideration.

Manufactures

In response to a 1980 request of the Committee on Manufactures,[108] the UNCTAD secretariat issued in 1984 a report on international trade in textiles, with special reference to the problems faced by developing countries.[109] After examining the pattern of world trade in textiles and clothing during the 1970s and restrictions on such trade, the report suggested elements to be taken into account in arresting the trend towards greater protection and discrimination and towards erosion of multilateral disciplines in the sector. It was essential for the future of the international trading system, concluded the report, that bilateralism and unilateralism be replaced by a multilateral approach based on equity and the common good.

Also at the Committee's request, the UNCTAD secretariat issued in 1984 a report on international trade in the fertilizer sector.[110] The report analysed problems related to the access to developed-country markets for exports of fertilizer products from developing countries, concentrating on tariff and non-tariff barriers to trade and on preferential treatment.

Consumer protection

During 1984, a set of draft guidelines on consumer protection, which had been considered by the Economic and Social Council and the General Assembly in 1983,[111] was taken up again by those bodies. In accordance with a December 1983 Assembly resolution,[112] the Council, in decision 1984/101 of 10 February (see Chapter XXIV of this section), decided that an informal sessional working group of the whole should review the draft guidelines during the Council's May session and report thereon to its July session, with a view to the Assembly's adopting them in 1984.

Reporting to the July session,[113] a Council Vice-President stated that the working group, which had met from 7 to 10 May, had completed the first reading of the draft guidelines and agreed that delegations' comments made during the discussions should be made available to the Council in July. Also before the Council was an April note with a later addendum by the Secretary-General,[114] containing a synopsis of comments from 20 Governments, which were in addition to those submitted to the Assembly in 1983.[115]

ECONOMIC AND SOCIAL COUNCIL ACTION

On 26 July, the Economic and Social Council adopted without vote resolution 1984/63, as recommended by its Third (Programme and Co-ordination) Committee.

Consumer protection
The Economic and Social Council,

Recalling its resolution 1981/62 of 23 July 1981, in which it requested the Secretary-General to continue consultations on consumer protection with the aim of pursuing, *inter alia,* the elaboration of a set of general guidelines for consumer protection, taking particularly into account the needs of the developing countries,

Recalling further its decision 1983/174 of 28 July 1983 and General Assembly resolution 38/147 of 19 December 1983,

Taking note of the discussions held during its first and second regular sessions of 1984,

Decides to transmit to the General Assembly for consideration with a view to their adoption, at its thirty-ninth session as agreed in resolution 38/147, the draft guidelines on consumer protection contained in the report of the Secretary-General on that question submitted to the Council in 1983, as well as the comments of States thereon.

Economic and Social Council resolution 1984/63

26 July 1984   Meeting 49   Adopted without vote

Approved by Third Committee (E/1984/150) without vote, 23 July (meeting 15); draft by Vice-President (E/1984/C.3/L.11); agenda item 20.

In September,[116] the Secretary-General transmitted the government comments to the Assembly.

GENERAL ASSEMBLY ACTION

In December, on the recommendation of the Second Committee, the General Assembly adopted without vote decision 39/444.

Consumer protection

At its 104th plenary meeting, on 18 December 1984, the General Assembly, on the recommendation of the Second Committee:

(a) Took note of the consensus reached, on an *ad referendum* basis, on the guidelines for consumer protection annexed to the draft resolution contained in document A/C.2/39/L.139;

(b) Decided to consider the draft resolution for adoption at a resumed session in 1985.

General Assembly decision 39/444

Adopted without vote

Approved by Second Committee (A/39/789/Add.2) without vote, 14 December (meeting 60); draft by Vice-Chairman (A/C.2/39/L.139), based on informal consultations on draft by Bangladesh, Colombia, Egypt, Guinea, India, Nepal, Nicaragua, Nigeria, Pakistan, Peru, Singapore, Sri Lanka, Sudan, Trinidad and Tobago, Venezuela, Zimbabwe (A/C.2/39/L.37/Rev.1); agenda item 12.
Meeting numbers. GA 39th session: 2nd Committee 41, 60; plenary 104.

By the 16-nation draft, which was withdrawn by the sponsors, the Assembly would have adopted the guidelines and requested the Secretary-General to disseminate them as widely as possible and advise and assist Governments in their implementation.

REFERENCES

[1]*Trade and Development Report, 1984* (UNCTAD/TDR/4/Rev.1), Sales No. E.84.II.D.23. [2]*World Economic Survey 1984: Current Trends and Policies in the World Economy* (E/1984/62), Sales No. E.84.II.C.1. [3]E/1984/17. [4]YUN 1983, p. 543. [5]TD/B/1005. [6]YUN 1979, p. 561. [7]YUN 1981, p. 539. [8]YUN 1983, p. 544. [9]*Ibid.*, p. 545. [10]TD/B/981 (Part I) & Corr.1,2 & Add.1,2. [11]*Ibid.* (Part II) & Corr.1. [12]TD/B/978 & Corr.1. [13]TD/B/979 & Corr.1. [14]A/39/15, vol. I (res. 286(XXVIII)). [15]YUN 1979, p. 560. [16]A/C.2/39/L.4. [17]YUN 1980, p. 627. [18]YUN 1981, p. 542. [19]YUN 1982, p. 727. [20]YUN 1983, p. 546, GA dec. 38/438, 19 Dec. 1983. [21]TD/B/1008 & Corr.1 & Summary. [22]TD/B/1009. [23]TD/B/1012. [24]TD/B/1014. [25]TD/B/1016. [26]TD/B/998. [27]TD/B/C.5/90 & Corr.1. [28]YUN 1982, p. 728. [29]*Ibid.*, p. 729. [30]TD/B/C.5/88. [31]YUN 1983, p. 547. [32]A/39/15, vol. II (res. 296(XXIX)). [33]YUN 1983, p. 548. [34]TD/B/C.7/66. [35]TD/B/C.7/69. [36]YUN 1983, p. 549. [37]TD/B/AC.38/2. [38]TD/B/AC.38/2/Add.1 & Add.1/Corr.1. [39]TD/B/1001. [40]TD/B/1003 & Add.1. [41]TD/B/1000. [42]A/39/15, vol. II (dec. 297(XXIX)). [43]ITC/AG(XVIII)/95 & Add.1. [44]YUN 1983, p. 550. [45]ITC/AG(XVII)/93 & Corr.1. [46]A/39/15, vol. II (dec. 299(XXIX)). [47]A/39/5 (vol. II). [48]A/39/510. [49]YUN 1980, p. 626. [50]TD/B/1030. [51]TD/B/RBP/12/Rev.1. [52]TD/B/RBP/15/Rev.1 & Corr.1,2. [53]YUN 1983, p. 551. [54]TD/B/RBP/18. [55]TD/B/RBP/19. [56]TD/B/RBP/20 & Add.1. [57]TD/B/RBP/21 & Add.1,2.
[58]TD/B/RBP/22 & Add.1-4. [59]TD/B/1030 (res. 3(III)). [60]YUN 1983, p. 553. [61]A/39/15, vol. II (dec. 303(XXIX)). [62]YUN 1980, p. 621. [63]*Multilateral Treaties Deposited with the Secretary-General: Status as at 31 December 1984* (ST/LEG/SER.E/3), Sales No. E.85.V.4. [64]YUN 1983, p. 555, GA res. 38/156, 19 Dec. 1983. [65]A/39/192. [66]YUN 1982, p. 734. [67]YUN 1983, p. 554. [68]YUN 1979, p. 561. [69]YUN 1982, p. 733. [70]YUN 1983, p. 552. [71]*Studies in the Processing, Marketing and Distribution of Commodities. The Processing and Marketing of Bauxite/Alumina/Aluminium: Areas for International Co-operation* (TD/B/C.1/PSC/19/Rev.1), Sales No. E.84.II.D.15. [72]*Ibid. The Processing before Export of Cocoa: Areas for International Co-operation* (TD/B/C.1/PSC/18/Rev.1), Sales No. E.84.II.D.16. [73]*Ibid. The Processing and Marketing of Coffee: Areas for International Co-operation* (TD/B/C.1/PSC/31/Rev.1), Sales No. E.84.II.D.11. [74]*Ibid. The Processing and Marketing of Copper: Areas for International Co-operation* (TD/B/C.1/PSC/30/Rev.1), Sales No. E.84.II.D.24. [75]*Ibid. The Marketing of Hard Fibres (Sisal and Henequen): Areas for International Co-operation* (TD/B/C.1/PSC/21/Rev.1), Sales No. E.84.II.D.21. [76]*Ibid. The Marketing of Jute and Jute Products: Areas for International Co-operation* (TD/B/C.1/PSC/32/Rev.1), Sales No. E.84.II.D.9. [77]*Ibid. The Processing and Marketing of Manganese: Areas for International Co-operation* (TD/B/C.1/PSC/20/Rev.1), Sales No. E.84.II.D.18. [78]*Ibid. The Processing and Marketing of Phosphates: Areas for International Co-operation* (TD/B/C.1/PSC/22/Rev.1), Sales No. E.84.II.D.13. [79]*Ibid. The Processing and Marketing of Sugar: Areas for International Co-operation* (TD/B/C.1/PSC/29/Rev.1), Sales No. E.84.II.D.14. [80]*Ibid. The Marketing and Processing of Tea: Areas for International Co-operation* (TD/B/C.1/PSC/28/Rev.1), Sales No. E.84.II.D.10. [81]TD/B/C.1/PSC/41 & Corr.1. [82]TD/B/C.1/PSC/39. [83]TD/B/C.1/PSC/38 & Corr.1. [84]YUN 1980, p. 622. [85]TD/COCOA.7/3. [86]TD/COCOA.7/7. [87]TD/COCOA.7/9. [88]TD/B/C.1/255. [89]YUN 1982, p. 737. [90]YUN 1983, p. 556. [91]TD/JUTE/12. [92]*International Sugar Agreement, 1984* (TD/SUGAR.10/11/Rev.1), Sales No. E.85.II.D.9. [93]TD/SUGAR.10/10. [94]YUN 1973, p. 348. [95]YUN 1977, p. 477. [96]YUN 1983, p. 557. [97]ITTC(I)/5. [98]TD/B/IPC/IRON ORE/17. [99]YUN 1978, p. 493. [100]TD/B/IPC/IRON ORE/14. [101]TD/B/IPC/IRON ORE/16. [102]TD/B/IPC/IRON ORE/15. [103]TD/B/C.1/268. [104]TD/B/C.1/TUNGSTEN/52. [105]TD/B/C.1/TUNGSTEN/54. [106]TD/B/C.1/TUNGSTEN/53. [107]TD/B/C.1/TUNGSTEN/51. [108]YUN 1980, p. 625. [109]*International Trade in Textiles, with Special Reference to the Problems Faced by Developing Countries* (TD/B/C.2/215/Rev.1), Sales No. E.84.II.D.7. [110]*International Trade in the Fertilizer Sector: Implications for Developing Countries* (TD/B/C.2/213/Rev.1), Sales No. E.84.II.D.17. [111]YUN 1983, p. 558. [112]*Ibid.*, p. 559, GA res. 38/147, 19 Dec. 1983. [113]E/1984/121. [114]E/1984/51 & Add.1. [115]YUN 1983, p. 559. [116]A/C.2/39/L.2.

OTHER PUBLICATIONS

Production and Trade in Services: Policies and Their Underlying Factors Bearing upon International Service Transactions (TD/B/941/Rev.1), Sales No. E.84.II.D.2. *Development and Recovery: The Realities of the New Interdependence* (TD/271/Rev.1), Sales No. E.84.II.D.4. *Handbook of International Trade and Development Statistics, 1984 Supplement* (TD/STAT/12), Sales No. E/F.84.II.D.12. *UNCTAD Commodity Yearbook, 1984* (TD/B/C.1/STAT/1), Sales No. E.84.II.D.22. *UNCTAD Statistical Pocket Book* (TAD/INF/PUB.84/4), Sales No. E.84.II.D.20.

Finance

The debt difficulties of developing countries received particular attention during 1984 in the various United Nations bodies which considered international financial and monetary issues. At its March/April session, the Trade and Development Board reviewed the implementation of agreed features to deal with the debt problems of developing countries, and considered the debt issue again at its September session.

The interdependence of problems of trade, development finance and the international monetary system was another major item on the Board's agenda at both its 1984 sessions, while in December the General Assembly requested the Secretary-General to carry out consultations and prepare a report for 1985 on international co-operation in money, finance, debt and resource flows, including development assistance and trade.

In May, the Economic and Social Council approved the future work programme of the *Ad Hoc* Group of Experts on International Co-operation in Tax Matters.

Financial policy

The Committee for Development Planning (CDP), meeting in May,[1] called attention to the urgent need for international action regarding reform of the international monetary and financial system, noting that there was disorder verging on chaos in several areas critical to the economic life of all nations: in currency and capital markets, in international debt and international trade, in the funding of international institutions, and in international financial flows. In particular, the debt situation, which threatened the world economy at a level of gravity not experienced since the 1930s, demanded immediate attention.

CDP drew attention to the close link between trade issues and international monetary and financial matters and noted that there was a need to consider those interrelated areas simultaneously. The need to reform the trade and payments system on the basis of the interdependence of the problems in those areas was also stressed in both the *Trade and Development Report, 1984*[2] and the *World Economic Survey 1984*[3] (see p. 528).

GENERAL ASSEMBLY ACTION

On 18 December, on the recommendation of the Second Committee, the Assembly adopted by recorded vote resolution 39/218.

Development and international economic co-operation

The General Assembly,

Emphasizing the vital importance of issues related to money, finance, debt, resource flows and trade for development, prosperity and good relations among peoples and the urgency of measures to promote wider co-operation among nations on these issues,

Emphasizing also the need for consistency between the international trade, monetary and financing systems and policies,

1. *Requests* the Secretary-General to consult Governments of States Members of the United Nations and members of the specialized agencies and to ascertain their specific views on expanding international co-operation in the fields of money, finance, debt and resource flows, including

development assistance and trade, with special attention to the interests of the developing countries, taking into account the effects of the economic crisis on their economic and social development;

2. *Also requests* the Secretary-General to seek the views of the relevant organs, organizations and bodies of the United Nations system, in particular the United Nations Conference on Trade and Development, the International Monetary Fund and the World Bank, as well as the General Agreement on Tariffs and Trade, on enhancing their effectiveness to support in every respect the actions taken by States to strengthen international co-operation in these areas;

3. *Further requests* the Secretary-General to prepare a report based on the outcome of the consultations in relation to the issues referred to in paragraphs 1 and 2 above to be circulated to Governments not later than the first quarter of 1985 and to be updated subsequently, as appropriate, for submission to the General Assembly at its fortieth session.

General Assembly resolution 39/218

18 December 1984   Meeting 104   123-14-8 (recorded vote)

Approved by Second Committee (A/39/790/Add.17) by recorded vote (102-14-7), 14 December (meeting 60); draft by Egypt, for Group of 77 (A/C.2/39/L.128); agenda item 80.

Meeting numbers. GA 39th session: 2nd Committee 56, 57, 60; plenary 104.

Recorded vote in Assembly as follows:

In favour: Afghanistan, Algeria, Angola, Argentina, Bahamas, Bahrain, Bangladesh, Barbados, Benin, Bhutan, Bolivia, Botswana, Brazil, Brunei Darussalam, Bulgaria, Burkina Faso, Burma, Burundi, Byelorussian SSR, Cape Verde, Chad, Chile, China, Colombia, Congo, Costa Rica, Cuba, Cyprus, Czechoslovakia, Democratic Kampuchea, Democratic Yemen, Djibouti, Dominican Republic, Ecuador, Egypt, El Salvador, Equatorial Guinea, Ethiopia, Fiji, Gabon, Gambia, German Democratic Republic, Ghana, Greece, Guatemala, Guinea, Guinea-Bissau, Guyana, Haiti, Honduras, Hungary, India, Indonesia, Iran, Iraq, Ivory Coast, Jamaica, Jordan, Kenya, Kuwait, Lao People's Democratic Republic, Lebanon, Lesotho, Liberia, Libyan Arab Jamahiriya, Madagascar, Malawi, Malaysia, Maldives, Mali, Malta, Mauritania, Mauritius, Mexico, Mongolia, Morocco, Mozambique, Nepal, Nicaragua, Niger, Nigeria, Oman, Pakistan, Panama, Papua New Guinea, Paraguay, Peru, Philippines, Poland, Qatar, Romania, Rwanda, Saint Lucia, Saint Vincent and the Grenadines, Samoa, Sao Tome and Principe, Saudi Arabia, Senegal, Sierra Leone, Singapore, Somalia, Sri Lanka, Sudan, Suriname, Swaziland, Syrian Arab Republic, Thailand, Togo, Trinidad and Tobago, Tunisia, Turkey, Uganda, Ukrainian SSR, USSR, United Arab Emirates, United Republic of Tanzania, Uruguay, Venezuela, Viet Nam, Yemen, Yugoslavia, Zaire, Zambia.

Against: Australia, Belgium, Canada, Denmark, France, Germany, Federal Republic of, Ireland, Israel, Italy, Japan, Luxembourg, Netherlands, United Kingdom, United States.

Abstaining: Austria, Finland, Iceland, New Zealand, Norway, Portugal, Spain, Sweden.

A draft resolution submitted by Mexico[4] on the same subject was withdrawn. By that text, the Assembly would have requested the Secretary-General: to consult Governments on ways to expand international co-operation in money, finance, debt and trade, with special attention to the developing countries; to seek the opinion of the United Nations system on those subjects; and to report to the Assembly not later than at its 1985 session. He would also have been requested to prepare a report, in consultation with relevant bodies of the system, on the economic problems of developing countries, to be submitted to Governments by March 1985, and to undertake a study of proposals and reports on international monetary, financial, debt and trade problems for the 1985 Assembly. The Assembly would have decided to include an item on money, finance, debt and trade for development in its 1985 agenda.

In the Second Committee, before the vote on the Group of 77's draft, the United States proposed a draft decision by which the Assembly would have referred the Group's draft to its 1985 session. The Committee rejected the draft decision by a recorded vote of 97 to 22, with 1 abstention. Explaining its position before the vote, the USSR said that the request made to the Secretary-General in paragraph 3 of the draft resolution precluded the adoption of the measure proposed by the United States.

Explaining their votes on the approved text in the Committee, Austria, Canada, France, the Federal Republic of Germany, Japan, the United Kingdom and the United States stated that more appropriate forums existed to discuss questions of money, finance and trade, and drew particular attention to the special sessions of the International Monetary Fund (IMF) Interim Committee and the World Bank/IMF Development Committee which were scheduled for April 1985 to consider those issues.

Finland said that a report on money, finance, debt, resource flows and trade for development should be prepared particularly carefully, a requirement not taken into account in paragraph 3 of the resolution.

Debt problems of developing countries

The international debt situation was one of three issues identified by CDP[1] as requiring the urgent attention of the international community, and recent debt crises were too numerous to be dismissed as isolated incidents. In 1983, some $70 billion of debt service was rescheduled, 10 times as much as in 1981 and 1982 combined. Of the 22 largest developing-country debtors, 10 were Latin American, 7 African and 5 Asian.

An important part of the solution to the problem, stated CDP, lay in a new and significant increase in IMF quotas to restore the Fund's resources in relation to world trade to the level of the 1960s. There was also need for a substantial increase in the World Bank's annual lending programme and hence in its net transfer.

The *Trade and Development Board Report, 1984*[2] stated that many proposals had been put forward regarding the way in which debt problems of developing countries might be alleviated. However, one of the more important issues was how resolving current debt difficulties could be made compatible with high and rising financial flows to debtor countries in future years. The debt problem was also closely related to the monetary policies of developed market-economy countries, the growth of activity in those economies and the access of developing countries to foreign markets. Thus the debt question could only be resolved in the context of reform of the international trade and payments system, while the system itself would inevitably be affected, and its long-term evolution influenced, by decisions regarding debt.

Trade and Development Board action. By a 6 April decision,[5] the Trade and Development Board adopted agreed conclusions on the review of the implementation of the agreed features to deal with the debt problems of developing countries contained in a 1980 Board resolution[6] and in pursuance of UNCTAD resolution 161(VI) on external debt.[7]

The agreed conclusions, annexed to the decision, stated that the review had taken place at the Board's March/April 1984 session when broader aspects of the indebtedness of developing countries were also discussed, recognizing the importance of the following: analysing those countries' difficulties in order to find solutions to them; expanding the exports of indebted countries; and enhancing international co-operation in support of policies of debtor countries which aimed to maintain or restore their creditworthiness. In order to improve implementation of the agreed features, particular attention was to be given by Governments to the following agreed points: debt rescheduling operations should be undertaken within the context of a thorough analysis; international action on debt difficulties of developing countries should be conducted flexibly to improve efficiency and timeliness; special attention should be given to rescheduling the debts of the poorer developing countries, particularly the least developed; bilateral negotiations following multilateral agreement reached in official creditor groups should be accelerated; and Governments should maintain efforts to improve implementation of the agreed features and to solve the debt problems of developing countries. The conclusions also stated that the World Bank's important role in helping developing countries formulate medium-term investment programmes and in supporting such programmes financially should be underlined and that the Board should review implementation of the guidelines, taking into account the above conclusions, in 1987.

In undertaking its review, the Board had before it an UNCTAD secretariat report[8] on the review of the implementation of the Board's 1980 resolution[6] and a note[9] giving conclusions drawn by the secretariat following consultations in pursuance of Conference resolution 161(VI).[7]

With regard to the debt and development problems of poorer developing countries, particularly the least developed, on 6 April the Board decided[10] to carry out in 1985 a review of the implementation of a 1978 Board resolution on the subject,[11] with the results of that review being taken into account during preparations for the 1985 midterm review of the implementation of the Substantial New Programme of Action for the 1980s for the Least Developed Countries (see p. 413).

Communications. Several communications dealing with the debt problems of developing countries were received by the Secretary-General in 1984. On

21 May,[12] Argentina, Brazil, Colombia and Mexico transmitted a 19 May declaration by their Presidents, proposing the adoption of measures to transform international financial and trade policy, the effect of which would include relieving the burden of indebtedness, and stressing that it was particularly necessary to establish adequate amortization and grace periods and to reduce interest rates, margins, commissions and other financial charges. A letter of 12 June[13] from Argentina, Brazil, Colombia, Ecuador, Mexico, Peru and Venezuela transmitted the text of a communication from their Presidents to the London Economic Summit of major industrialized countries (see p. 389). The Presidents urged that the situation and prospects of the economies of Latin America, particularly issues of trade, financing and external debt, be considered at the London talks; they stressed that the need for concerted action was particularly obvious in the case of indebtedness and that constructive dialogue between creditor and debtor countries to identify measures to relieve the external debt burden was necessary.

On 18 June,[14] Yugoslavia transmitted the text of the final statement adopted by the second session of the Interaction Council at Brioni (see also p. 389) which contained a section on the debt crisis and debt management. Measures suggested by the Council to contain annual debt repayments where they became excessive were: restriction of annual debt-service payments to an agreed maximum; consolidation of short-term debts to medium-term fixed interest bonds; multiyear rescheduling instead of shortest-term practice; capitalization of interest; and special measures as required for developing countries on a case-by-case basis.

On 26 June,[15] Argentina, Bolivia, Brazil, Chile, Colombia, the Dominican Republic, Ecuador, Mexico, Peru, Uruguay and Venezuela transmitted the text of the Cartagena Consensus on the economic and financial situation of Latin America, signed by the Ministers for Foreign Affairs and of Finance of those countries at Cartagena, Colombia, on 22 June. The Ministers stressed that the Latin American economic crisis was largely due to external factors, particularly the repeated increases in interest rates, which had brought about the region's grave external-debt situation. They proposed a series of measures to alleviate the debt problem, including a drastic reduction of nominal and real interest rates on international markets.

On 3 October,[16] the same countries forwarded the text of the Mar del Plata Communiqué, signed by their Foreign and Finance Ministers at Mar del Plata, Argentina, on 14 September, which supplemented the Cartagena Consensus. The Ministers noted with concern the loss of a sense of urgency in industrialized countries with respect to solving the external-debt crisis and that in recent debt-restructuring negotiations some principles stated

in the Consensus regarding terms, costs and conditions had been adopted. However, it was important to seek lasting solutions to all external-debt problems so that Governments of creditor countries, multilateral financial agencies and the banking community would make contributions comparable to efforts exerted by debtor countries in their adjustment process. They felt it was essential to invite Governments of industrialized countries to participate in a direct political dialogue, to be held preferably in the first half of 1985.

GENERAL ASSEMBLY ACTION

In resolution 39/214, the General Assembly called on the international community to continue to address the debt problems of developing countries, taking into account the agreed conclusions adopted by the Trade and Development Board on 6 April.

In its Declaration on the Critical Economic Situation in Africa, annexed to resolution 39/29, the Assembly stated that Africa was experiencing a serious debt problem, repayment and servicing of which was taking a high percentage of already reduced export earnings. The Assembly indicated measures to be taken by bilateral and multilateral creditors to ease the debt burden of African countries.

Development finance

The *World Economic Survey 1984*[3] noted that official development assistance (ODA) had been behaving erratically during the early 1980s. In real terms, ODA receipts of developing countries were practically unchanged in 1981 and dropped sharply in 1982. There were no indications that those flows had increased in 1983. Regarding multilateral development co-operation, trends were disquieting; following a decade of rapid expansion averaging 22.5 per cent per annum, net multilateral disbursements in the 1980s were going through a phase of slow growth and, in some cases, absolute stagnation. Major donors had agreed that the delayed seventh replenishment of the International Development Association (IDA) should be at a level of $9 billion for three years, in contrast to the initially agreed $12 billion under the sixth replenishment. The tentative agreement on the second replenishment of the International Fund for Agricultural Development (IFAD) reached in March 1984 indicated that contributions for 1985-1987 would not exceed those originally pledged for 1981-1983. As at the end of March 1984, pledges to the World Food Programme for 1985-1986 were less than 50 per cent of its target of $1.35 billion.

Certain efforts had been made, especially in 1983, to increase some categories of official resource transfers. The World Bank and regional development banks increased their share of total project financing and accelerated disbursement of funds. The Bank also sought to expand its structural adjustment lending and programme lending in support of sectoral adjustment. On the other hand, those departures from past practice had to be financed from regular resources, implying the need to restrict other lending programmes or acquire new capital resources.

In the report on its May 1984 session,[1] CDP pointed out that development assistance on concessional terms to the least developed and other low-income countries from all groups of donors had virtually stagnated, while needs had increased and alternative sources diminished. The situation of IDA was particularly alarming. The under-funding of IDA and other multilateral institutions for development finance and technical co-operation was reflected in an overall reduction in the multilateral share of total ODA flows. Analyses of the effectiveness of bilateral and multilateral ODA provided no justification for a trend towards bilateralization. Multilateral assistance, not least from the multilateral development banks, had a particularly impressive record in the poorer countries in such key areas as agriculture.

A comparison of ODA flows for 1980 to 1982 with targets set in the International Development Strategy for the Third United Nations Development Decade (the 1980s)[17] was contained in a report of the Secretary-General on the Strategy's review and appraisal[18] (see p. 392).

GENERAL ASSEMBLY ACTION

In December, a draft decision[19] was submitted to the General Assembly's Second Committee by Egypt on behalf of the Group of 77 developing countries. By the draft, the Assembly would have requested the Secretary-General urgently to consult with Governments on an international conference on money and finance for development and to report to the Assembly not later than at its fortieth (1985) session.

On 18 December, on the Committee's recommendation, the Assembly adopted decision 39/438 without vote.

International conference on money and finance for development

At its 104th plenary meeting, on 18 December 1984, the General Assembly, on the recommendation of the Second Committee, decided to refer to its fortieth session for consideration the draft decision entitled "International conference on money and finance for development".

General Assembly decision 39/438

Adopted without vote

Approved by Second Committee (A/39/790/Add.17) without vote, 14 December (meeting 60); oral proposal by Vice-Chairman; agenda item 80.
Meeting numbers. GA 39th session: 2nd Committee 57, 60; plenary 104.

In its Declaration on the Critical Economic Situation in Africa, annexed to resolution 39/29, the Assembly recognized that African countries required a substantial increase in concessional financial flows through bilateral donors and multilateral channels for development finance and technical co-operation. The World Bank was urged to explore possible approaches, including a special facility, in mobilizing the resources required to implement its Special Programme for Sub-Saharan Africa. Implementation of the Substantial New Programme of Action for the 1980s for the Least Developed Countries (see p. 413), particularly with regard to ODA, would greatly augment resource flows to many African countries, and supplementary funding of IDA and the early completion of the replenishment of IFAD would ensure maintenance of the real value of resources channelled to Africa. The modalities and quality of ODA flows in terms of a greater grant element, untied resources and simplified procedures for aid delivery should be improved through speedier disbursements and greater reliance on more flexible assistance, such as non-project programme and sector aid.

Trade-related finance

Export earnings

Pursuant to UNCTAD resolution 157(VI),[20] the UNCTAD Secretary-General convened in 1984 an expert group on the compensatory financing of export earnings shortfalls. The group met at Geneva in three sessions (9-13 April, 30 July–3 August, 1 and 2 November)[21] and considered: the nature, causes and effects of export earnings instability; export earnings stabilization options; existing programmes and their limitations in dealing with commodity sector stabilization; and the need for and nature of a complementary facility for compensatory financing shortfalls.

The group stated that existing international programmes did not adequately address the causes of commodity supply instability and agreed that the reduction of such instability was desirable for the developing countries, given the importance of commodity earnings to their economies, the instability in those earnings and the deleterious impact of such instability on the economic welfare of those countries. The group also agreed that measures addressing the causes of supply instability had advantages over measures that dealt with its effects and that, while efforts by individual developing countries to deal with instability were necessary, they were likely to be of limited success without international support. A new programme should have an explicit policy objective, identified resources and built-in evaluation procedures and should be consistent with international commodity objectives and arrangements.

In considering whether a complementary compensatory financing facility could address effectively

the causes of supply instability, the group emphasized two points: that its definition of compensatory finance which included supply adjustment measures was different from that used in the IMF
compensatory financing facility; and that the group's
focus on a facility to deal with supply instability
did not mean that there could not be other useful
measures to address that problem.

The group considered the following to be essential
characteristics of a prototype commodity-specific
facility: the principal objective would be to reduce
supply instability in specific commodity sectors consonant with national and international policies and
arrangements; membership would be open to all
States; all primary commodities would be eligible,
except for fuels, gold, diamonds and precious stones;
governmental contributions along the lines of the
Common Fund for Commodities would be appropriate, with voluntary contributions to cover conces-
sionality; the facility would operate on self-financing
and commercial principles; access would be limited
to developing countries suffering a shortfall in earnings
from a specific commodity accounting for a certain share of the country's export earnings; loans
would be provided after an agreement was signed
between the facility and the applicant on a programme
to address the causes of the instability; and repayment would occur over a fixed maximum period.

The group thought that such a facility should
not be established as an independent institution.
A suitable location would be as a third account with
the Common Fund for Commodities when it became operational. Should the Fund not become operational within a reasonable period, a separate window
within the World Bank would be a possible arrangement.

Taxation

Following the completion in December 1983, by
the *Ad Hoc* Group of Experts on International Co-
operation in Tax Matters, of a set of guidelines on
international co-operation to combat international
tax evasion and avoidance,[22] the Secretary-General
submitted to the Economic and Social Council's
May 1984 session a report on the work of the *Ad
Hoc* Group.[23] The report stated that, having completed the guidelines, the Group proposed, within
its terms of reference as defined in a 1982 Council
resolution,[24] to: continue examining the United
Nations Model Double Taxation Convention between Developed and Developing Countries, adopted
by a predecessor group in 1979, and consider the
experiences of countries in bilateral applications
of that Model Convention; and study the possibilities
of reducing potential conflicts among tax laws of
various countries and of enhancing the efficiency
of tax administrations and formulate suggestions
regarding policy and methodology.

The Secretary-General endorsed the wish of the
Group that the Council should appeal to Member
States to provide information about their experiences
in applying the Model Convention by replying to
a Secretariat questionnaire, and in replying that
they be urged to indicate which issues they would
like to be studied, with a view to reducing possible incompatibilities among tax systems. He hoped
that, in accordance with the Group's wish, voluntary contributions would be forthcoming to finance
regional seminars on the Model Convention, to be
organized by the regional commissions in co-operation
with the Secretariat.

General and specific comments on the guidelines
were submitted to the Council's May session by the
International Chamber of Commerce,[25] a non-
governmental organization.

ECONOMIC AND SOCIAL COUNCIL ACTION

On 16 May, the Economic and Social Council
adopted without vote decision 1984/114, on an oral
proposal of its President.

International co-operation in tax matters

At its 14th plenary meeting, on 16 May 1984, the Council
took note of the report of the Secretary-General on the
work of the *Ad Hoc* Group of Experts on International
Co-operation in Tax Matters and approved the recommendations contained therein.

Economic and Social Council decision 1984/114

Adopted without vote

Oral proposal by President; agenda item 9.

REFERENCES

[1]E/1984/17. [2]*Trade and Development Report, 1984* (UNC-
TAD/TDR/4/Rev.1), Sales No. E.84.II.D.23. [3]*World Economic
Survey 1984: Current Trends and Policies in the World Economy* (E/1984/62),
Sales No. E.84.II.C.1. [4]A/C.2/39/L.116. [5]A/39/15, vol. I
(dec. 288(XXVIII)). [6]YUN 1980, p. 616. [7]YUN 1983, p. 563.
[8]TD/B/980. [9]TD/B/990. [10]A/39/15, vol. I (dec. 289(XXVIII)).
[11]YUN 1978, p. 429. [12]A/39/269-E/1984/102. [13]A/39/303-
E/1984/125. [14]A/39/314. [15]A/39/331-E/1984/126. [16]A/39/554.
[17]YUN 1980, p. 503, GA res. 35/56, annex, 5 Dec. 1980.
[18]A/39/115-E/1984/49 & Corr.1. [19]A/C.2/39/L.115. [20]YUN
1983, p. 566. [21]*Compensatory Financing of Export Earnings Shortfalls*
(TD/B/1029/Rev.1), Sales No. E.85.II.D.3. [22]YUN 1983, p. 567.
[23]E/1984/37. [24]YUN 1982, p. 746, ESC res. 1982/45, 27 July
1982. [25]E/1984/NGO/4.

OTHER PUBLICATIONS
*Journal of Development Planning, No. 14. World Recovery and Mone-
tary Reform* (ST/ESA/135), Sales No. E.84.II.A.6. *Accrual Accounting
in Developing Countries* (ST/ESA/SER.E/37), Sales No. E.84.II.H.2.

Programme and finances of UNCTAD

The February/March 1984 session of the UNC-
TAD Working Party on the Medium-term Plan and
the Programme Budget considered the UNCTAD sections of the United Nations medium-term plan for
1984-1989, revisions to which were required due

to the adoption by UNCTAD VI (1983) of resolutions affecting UNCTAD's work programme. The revisions were approved by the Economic and Social Council.

UNCTAD's technical assistance programme was also reviewed by the Working Party in 1984.

UNCTAD programme

The Trade and Development Board—the executive body of UNCTAD—held three sessions in 1984, all at Geneva. Its twenty-eighth session was held from 26 March to 6 April; its thirteenth special session from 2 to 6 April, in conjunction with the Board's twenty-eighth session, in order to consider UNCTAD's contribution to the review and appraisal by the General Assembly of the implementation of the International Development Strategy for the Third United Nations Development Decade (see p. 391); and its twenty-ninth session from 10 to 27 September.

The Board adopted eight resolutions and 23 decisions during 1984. The four resolutions adopted in April dealt with the UNCTAD work programme on protectionism and structural adjustment (see p. 529), assistance to Cape Verde, Uganda and Vanuatu (see pp. 474, 494, 498), timely issuance of UNCTAD documentation and the scheduling of the Board's second regular session (see below). The four resolutions adopted in September dealt with implementation of the recovery and rehabilitation programme in the Sudano-Sahelian region (see p. 509), financial support for the UNCTAD technical co-operation programme on the generalized system of preferences (see p. 531), technical co-operation among developing countries: co-operative exchange of skills among developing countries (see p. 460), and assistance to the peoples of Namibia (see TRUSTEESHIP AND DECOLONIZATION, Chapter III) and South Africa (see p. 168).

The Board's report for 1984[1] was considered by the General Assembly, which took note of it in resolution 39/214 and which on 17 and 18 December adopted seven other resolutions on various aspects of the UNCTAD programme. In these resolutions, the Assembly dealt with: the implementation of the Substantial New Programme of Action for the 1980s for the Least Developed Countries[2] (resolution 39/174); specific action related to the needs and problems of land-locked developing countries (39/209); development aspects of the reverse transfer of technology (39/211); specific measures in favour of island developing countries (39/212); the United Nations Conference on Conditions for Registration of Ships (39/213 A and B); and activities of the United Nations system in support of economic co-operation among developing countries (39/216).

Programme policy decisions

The eighth session of the Trade and Development Board's Working Party on the Medium-term Plan and the Programme Budget (Geneva, 27 February–9 March and 19 March 1984)[3] was devoted mainly to updating the UNCTAD sections of the United Nations medium-term plan for 1984-1989[4] and reviewing UNCTAD technical assistance activities. Programme evaluation was also discussed.

On 19 March, the Working Party adopted agreed conclusions in which it: considered that the UNCTAD chapters of the revised medium-term plan should reflect the mandates contained in the decisions of the General Assembly and of intergovernmental bodies and conferences of UNCTAD, particularly UNCTAD VI; recommended to the Trade and Development Board that it request the UNCTAD Secretary-General to submit to the Working Party at its tenth (October 1985) session a report on implementing the medium-term plan and the programme budget for 1984-1985, containing resources committed, studies undertaken and accomplishments of the objectives of the secretariat for each subprogramme, and that it further request him to submit to the Working Party's ninth (April 1985) session a document on options for the 1986-1987 programme budget relating to redistribution of resources and to priorities; requested the UNCTAD Secretary-General, for the Working Party's 1986 review of UNCTAD technical assistance activities for 1984, to submit an updated and expanded report; and invited him to elaborate further his proposals for an effective programme evaluation system within UNCTAD for presentation to the Working Party's ninth session.

Also annexed to the Working Party's report were position papers on the updating of the medium-term plan submitted by the Group of 77 developing countries and by Group D (centrally planned economies), comments on a report by the UNCTAD Secretary-General on the updating of the plan[5] submitted by Group B (developed market economies) and by China, and a note by the UNCTAD secretariat on requests for documentation made in the Working Party's agreed conclusions.

On 6 April, the Trade and Development Board decided to transmit the Working Party's report, together with comments made at the Board's session, to the appropriate United Nations bodies.

Other related action. At its twenty-fourth session (New York, 23 April–1 June 1984),[6] the Committee for Programme and Co-ordination (CPC) recommended that the Assembly should adopt, with a number of modifications, proposed revisions to the 1984-1989 medium-term plan[7] dealing with international trade and development finance. References to UNCTAD VI and Trade and Development Board resolutions were included in the revisions.

In resolution 1984/61 A of 26 July, the Economic and Social Council endorsed the CPC conclusions and recommendations on the proposed revisions to the medium-term plan to incorporate the programme implications of resolutions and decisions adopted by intergovernmental organs or international conferences.

By resolution 39/238 of 18 December, the Assembly adopted the revisions as modified by CPC and approved by the Council.

Technical co-operation

Total project expenditure incurred by UNCTAD in 1984 for technical co-operation activities amounted to some $9.3 million. Allocations from UNDP totalling $7.2 million were the main source of funds.

The main sectors in which UNCTAD provided assistance were: maritime and multimodal transport; economic co-operation among developing countries; assistance to least developed, land-locked and island developing countries; money, finance and development; manufactures and semi-manufactures; trade in commodities; transfer of technology; insurance and reinsurance; trade among countries having different economic and social systems; and trade facilitation.

In addition to these activities, ITC continued to provide technical assistance for trade promotion (see p. 533).

The fourth annual report[8] on UNCTAD technical co-operation activities, prepared by the UNCTAD secretariat for the tenth (1985) session of the Working Party on the Medium-term Plan and the Programme Budget, reviewed UNCTAD's activities and their financing in detail and included a comprehensive chapter on evaluation of technical co-operation activities. The report noted two general trends in 1984: an increase in requests for assistance from developing countries for debt registration and monitoring; and an increased number of multidisciplinary projects, showing an integrated approach by Governments to national economic development.

Organizational questions

Conferences and meetings

Calendar of UNCTAD meetings

By a 6 April decision,[9] the Trade and Development Board approved a calendar of meetings for the remainder of 1984 and a tentative schedule for 1985. On 21 September,[10] following a further review, the Board approved the 1984 and 1985 calendars and the tentative schedules for 1986 and 1987.

Pursuant to 1983 discussions on holding a ministerial session during 1985,[11] the Board decided on 6 April[12] to establish an *ad hoc* consultative committee to consider the subject. In the light of the 19-member committee's report, the Board, at its September 1984 session, was to decide on the exact dates and the agenda for the ministerial session and the establishment of a preparatory committee.

The *Ad Hoc* Consultative Committee met in September.[13] It agreed that a two- to three-day ministerial meeting should be held as part of a regular Board session, preferably in autumn 1985, and that the two-item agenda would be a guideline for ministers, who would be free to discuss issues of particular concern to them. The items, which could be considered together, were: the world economic situation in the context of the interrelationship of issues and interdependence of national economies, with particular reference to development problems; and substantive issues in the areas of competence of UNCTAD.

On 21 September,[14] the Board noted the agreed conclusions of the *Ad Hoc* Consultative Committee and decided to establish an interim committee under the chairmanship of the Board's President and to entrust it with the mandate to seek agreement on issues where full consensus had not emerged. The Board further decided that the interim committee would comprise 19 members and would report to the Board in 1985 with a view to its deciding to hold the session in the autumn of that year and to initiating the preparatory process, and that the UNCTAD Secretary-General would be associated with all stages of that process.

GENERAL ASSEMBLY ACTION

In resolution 39/214, the General Assembly welcomed the Trade and Development Board's decision and invited all Governments to exert efforts to ensure the successful outcome of the consultations.

Scheduling of Trade and Development Board meetings

On 6 April,[15] the Trade and Development Board, following consideration of a July 1983 Economic and Social Council decision[16] in which the Board was invited to consider rescheduling its meetings, and a similar request contained in a December 1983 General Assembly decision,[17] regretted that it was unable to respond positively to the Council's invitation. The Board reaffirmed that its second regular session would continue to be held in the autumn of each year, but in sufficient time for its report to be available to the Assembly in all its working languages in accordance with the Assembly's request. The matter of scheduling the Board's sessions would be reviewed subsequently in the light of the results of rationalization exercises under way in those parts of the United Nations system concerned with economic and development matters, particularly the Economic and Social Council.

ECONOMIC AND SOCIAL COUNCIL ACTION

Following consideration of a 17 April letter[18] from the President of the Trade and Development Board informing the Economic and Social Council President of the Board's decision, the Council in July adopted decision 1984/161 without vote.

Scheduling of the sessions of the Trade and Development Board

At its 48th plenary meeting, on 25 July 1984, the Council decided to authorize the President of the Economic and Social Council to continue his consultations with the President of the Trade and Development Board on the question of the scheduling of the sessions of the Board and to report thereon to the Council at its organizational session for 1985.

Economic and Social Council decision 1984/161

Adopted without vote

Oral proposal by President; agenda item 23.

Appointment of UNCTAD Secretary-General

In an 18 December 1984 note[19] to the General Assembly, the Secretary-General stated that, despite consultations with the regional groups, he was not in a position to present a name for the post of Secretary-General of UNCTAD to succeed the incumbent whose term would end on 31 December. He would continue his consultations in the hope that he could present a name in early 1985. In the interim, he would appoint a senior Deputy Secretary-General of UNCTAD to act as officer-in-charge.

GENERAL ASSEMBLY ACTION

In December, the General Assembly adopted decision 39/324 without vote.

Confirmation of the appointment of the Secretary-General of the United Nations Conference on Trade and Development

At its 105th plenary meeting, on 18 December 1984, the General Assembly took note of the information contained in the note by the Secretary-General.

General Assembly decision 39/324

Adopted without vote

Oral proposal by President; agenda item 17 *(i)*.

Documentation

The timely issuance of UNCTAD documentation in all official languages was taken up by the Trade and Development Board in March/April 1984. It considered a report[20] by its *Ad Hoc* Working Group on Documentation, established by the Board in 1983.[21]

On 4 April, the Board adopted a resolution[22] based on a draft suggested by the Working Group. By the resolution, the Board decided, with respect to Board members: that requests for documentation should be kept to a minimum; that States members should, when directing that documents be prepared, request the UNCTAD Secretary-

General to give them a time-frame in the light of the existing document work-load; that the Board should review the implementation of its 1982 decision[23] on the length of its annual report to the General Assembly, and also review the length of reports of its own subsidiary bodies; and that the Board should establish a 32-page limit for reports of its expert groups. With respect to the UNCTAD secretariat, the Board requested the UNCTAD Secretary-General: to issue, in advance of his consultations on the calendar of meetings, a status report on preparation of documents for meetings during the following six months, in order for the secretariat to co-ordinate with the United Nations Office at Geneva so that decisions regarding rescheduling of meetings could be taken in due time; and to improve arrangements within the secretariat for co-ordinating and organizing document preparation to ensure timely submission to that Office. With respect to that Office, the Board decided that UNCTAD documents should be distributed simultaneously in the official languages of UNCTAD.

The Board recognized the importance of official language versions of in-session documents being available expeditiously and requested the UNCTAD Secretary-General to consider the issue in informal consultations and to report to the Board at its September 1984 session.

In a decision of 21 September[24] on control and limitation of documentation, the Board: decided to continue preparing an annual report to the Assembly and a fuller account of its proceedings; adopted revised guidelines, annexed to the decision, for preparing such reports, to take effect from its first session of 1985; requested the Rapporteurs of the Board and of its sessional bodies to produce succinct reports; urged representatives to be brief in their statement summaries; decided to dispense with summary records for its plenary meetings; and instructed its main Committees and other subsidiary bodies to ensure that their reports were concise and did not exceed 32 pages.

REFERENCES

[1]A/39/15, vols. I & II. [2]YUN 1981, p. 406. [3]TD/B/995. [4]YUN 1982, p. 1433. [5]TD/B/WP/33 & Corr.1-4. [6]A/39/38. [7]A/39/6 & Corr.1. [8]TD/B/WP/41 & Add.1. [9]A/39/15, vol. I (dec. 294(XXVIII)). [10]*Ibid.*, vol. II (dec. 303(XXIX)). [11]YUN 1983, p. 569. [12]A/39/15, vol. I (dec. 287(XXVIII)). [13]TD/B/1017. [14]A/39/15, vol. II (dec. 301(XXIX)). [15]*Ibid.*, vol. I (res. 291(XXVIII)). [16]YUN 1983, p. 1003, ESC dec. 1983/184, 29 July 1983. [17]*Ibid.*, p. 1008, GA dec. 38/429, 19 Dec. 1983. [18]E/1984/76. [19]A/39/852. [20]TD/B/988. [21]YUN 1983, p. 569. [22]A/39/15, vol. I (res. 282(XXVIII)). [23]YUN 1982, p. 726. [24]A/39/15, vol. II (dec. 302(XXIX)).

Chapter V

Transport and communications

The United Nations Conference on Trade and Development (UNCTAD) and its subsidiary bodies, particularly the Committee on Shipping (eleventh session, Geneva, 19-30 November) of the UNCTAD Trade and Development Board, continued in 1984 to deal with problems of transport.

The United Nations Conference on Conditions for Registration of Ships (Geneva, 16 July-3 August) made progress in, but did not complete, preparing an international agreement, and the General Assembly, in December, agreed that the Conference meet in resumed session in 1985 (resolution 39/213 A).

In July, the Economic and Social Council called for the promotion of a system of customs transit for goods applicable world-wide (resolution 1984/79).

The outcome of World Communications Year (1983) was considered by the Committee on Information at its June/July session.

Topics related to this chapter. Development policy and economic co-operation: land-locked countries. Regional economic and social activities: Africa—Transport and Communications Decade in Africa; Asia—Transport and Communications Decade in Asia and the Pacific; Europe—Europe-Africa link through the Strait of Gibraltar.

Transport

Maritime transport

The UNCTAD secretariat, in its annual *Review of Maritime Transport, 1984*[1] prepared in accordance with the work programme of the Committee on Shipping,[2] stated that in 1984, for the first time in five years, the total volume of international seaborne trade increased and reached 3.3 billion tons—a 6.7 per cent rise over 1983. At the same time, the size of the world fleet declined from 686 million deadweight tons (dwt) in mid-1983 to 674.5 million dwt by mid-1984, with the fleets of developed market-economy countries undergoing the largest decrease. The low participation of developing countries in the world merchant fleet (15.9 per cent of dwt) continued to be disproportionate to their share of international seaborne trade (37 per cent); developed market-economy countries owned

75 per cent of world tonnage while generating 56 per cent of world trade.

Among other developments: the surplus of tonnage and laid-up dwt decreased from the previous year; except for liner freight and dry cargo tramp trip charter indices, freight rate indices experienced a minimal change over the 12-month period; and the proportion of freight charges to 1983 cost, insurance, freight (c.i.f.) import values for developing countries continued to be twice as high as that of developed market-economy countries (10.8 per cent and 5.4 per cent, respectively). Two liner companies introduced round-the-world container services during the last quarter of 1984.

Data on the true management and beneficial ownership of open-registry fleets between 1 July 1983 and 1 July 1984, also prepared for the Committee on Shipping by the UNCTAD secretariat[3] and covering 98.6 per cent of the dwt registered under five open-registry flags (Cyprus, the Bahamas, Bermuda, Liberia and Panama), pointed out that the total dwt registered under such arrangements increased from 202 million to 202.5 million, while the number of ships increased from 6,403 to 6,615. Tanker tonnage under flags of convenience continued to decline, from 100.9 million to 97 million dwt, while that of dry bulk and combined carriers increased from 67.6 million to 68.6 million dwt. Other ships showed a significant increase in dwt from 33.5 million to 37 million.

As in past years, three countries and one territory (Greece, Japan, the United States, Hong Kong) were true managers of 66.4 per cent and beneficial owners of 72.3 per cent of the world dwt of the open-registry fleet.

In another report,[4] prepared in response to a 1983 UNCTAD request[5] and submitted to the Committee on Shipping, the secretariat presented a draft programme of action for co-operation among developing countries in shipping, ports and multimodal transport. The report observed that the resources and capacity—in matters of finance, manpower and market access—were not equally distributed among developing countries, and that those countries, by pooling resources and entering into joint ventures and other co-operative arrangements among themselves, would be able to increase their ownership in the world tonnage and their participation in the carriage of their seaborne trade. Noting the role of shipping in the socio-economic development of developing countries, the draft programme identified, as major areas of possible co-operation, the protection of shippers' interests, provision of shipping services, development of trans-shipment ports, harmonization of port statistics and port tariffs, joint dredging and marine salvage operations, technical expertise exchange, training, harmonization of regulatory policies and administrative procedures, multilateral action relating to infrastructure, and establishment of multimodal transport operators (MTOs) and of regional organizations of MTOs.

Annexed to the report were the relevant recommendations, adopted at a meeting of Experts on Services Related to Trade, of the Group of 77 developing countries (Guatemala City, Guatemala, 23-27 January 1984), held in accordance with the 1981 Caracas Programme of Action.[6]

A *Directory of Services for Technical Assistance in Shipping, Ports and Multimodal Transport to Developing Countries*, issued in November by the UNCTAD secretariat,[7] listed bilateral and multilateral sources of such assistance.

Shipping

Committee on Shipping consideration. At the 1984 session of the Committee on Shipping, the UNCTAD Secretary-General observed that the problems in the world shipping industry— persistent overtonnaging, structural imbalances and increased protectionism—remained serious and formed part of the overall problems facing the world economy, and that there was a need to analyse the issues affecting international co-operation in shipping.

The Deputy Director of the secretariat's Shipping Division stated that, in view of the heavy workload against the increasing budgetary constraints, agreement had been reached with the International Maritime Organization secretariat on the division of work on maritime liens and mortgages and with the United Nations Commission on International Trade Law secretariat in regard to the work on rights and duties of terminal operators.

The Committee on Shipping, by a 30 November resolution[8] on co-operation among developing countries in shipping, ports and multimodal transport, decided to consider further the draft programme of action proposed by the UNCTAD secretariat (see above) and invited the UNCTAD Secretary-General to convene in 1986 an *ad hoc* intergovernmental group of senior officials to develop relevant proposals. It also requested the secretariat to compile an inventory of existing co-operation agreements; urged developing countries to create and strengthen regional institutional mechanisms of shippers, shipowners, port and maritime authorities for co-operation and harmonization of policies and practices; and invited UNCTAD members and international institutions to provide technical assistance and financial support for implementing co-operation programmes and projects among developing countries.

Report by the UNCTAD secretariat. The UNCTAD secretariat, in a November report to the Trade and Development Board on shipping in the context of services and the development process,[9] reviewed UNCTAD's evolving role in shipping services, discussed the role of shipping in the economy, the problems pertaining to shipping services and policy measures to alleviate them, as well as future challenges and strategies. It stated that transport and communication were a vital prerequisite for any form of economic and political integration of States, and that development in shipping contributed decisively to integrating developing countries into the world economy. It listed instability, restrictive practices, structural overtonnaging in the shipping industry and barriers to the entry of developing countries to shipping as some of the immediate problems facing Governments and the industry. According to the report, self-regulation through market forces had not proved effective because of the existing market structures and the traditional concentration of ownership of shipping; structurally built-in inertia had inhibited normal transfer of operations to shipowners from developing countries and that, coupled with the flags of convenience phenomenon, was aggravating an overtonnaging situation and structural disequilibria. It also pointed out that the universal problems facing the shipping industry had to be addressed so that developing countries could have a fair opportunity to develop their fleets.

UN conference on registration of ships

The United Nations Conference on Conditions for Registration of Ships met at Geneva from 16 July to 3 August 1984[10] in pursuance of a 1982 General Assembly resolution,[11] to consider an international agreement concerning the conditions under which vessels should be accepted on national shipping registers.

A draft composite text of such an agreement— containing alternative phrasings on key issues such as manning of ships, the role of flag countries in managing shipowning companies and vessels, and equity participation in capital—had been prepared in 1983 by an Intergovernmental Preparatory Group for the Conference. The text was annexed, along with other proposals, to the report of the Preparatory Committee.[12]

Ninety-two States were represented at the Conference, and two other States participated as observers. In addition, a number of specialized agencies and intergovernmental and non-governmental organizations were present.

Summing up the work of the Conference, its President, Lamine Fadika, Minister of Marine Affairs of the Ivory Coast, said the Conference did not complete its work as an agreement was yet to be reached on the scope of application of the future international instrument. However, consensus had emerged that the future agreement should, among other things, define certain major elements linking the vessel and the flag State, confirm that the flag State must have an adequate maritime administration and ensure under its laws and regulations access to information on those owning ships which fly its flag, and possibly contain provisions to safeguard the interests of labour-supplying countries. A composite text of the proposed agreement was annexed to the report of the Conference.[10]

The Conference, by a resolution of 3 August on its future work, agreed to hold a resumed session at Geneva from 28 January to 15 February 1985 and recommended that its President continue consultations with Governments. In December, the President submitted a report on inter-sessional consultations he had held, and proposals derived from them, for consideration by the Conference.[13] The UNCTAD secretariat estimated the cost of the resumed session at $412,000.

In an October note to the General Assembly,[14] the United Nations Secretary-General transmitted the resolution adopted by the Conference and estimated the costs of a resumed session at $448,600.

GENERAL ASSEMBLY ACTION

On 18 December 1984, under the agenda item on trade and development, the General Assembly, on the recommendation of the Second (Economic and Financial) Committee, adopted without vote resolution 39/213 A.

The General Assembly,

Recalling its resolution 37/209 of 20 December 1982, by which it decided to convene the United Nations Conference on Conditions for Registration of Ships,

Taking note of the note by the Secretary-General on the United Nations Conference on Conditions for Registration of Ships,

Noting that the Conference adopted on 3 August 1984 a resolution, by which it took note of the significant progress achieved towards the preparation and adoption of an international agreement on conditions for registration of ships and recognized that there is a need for a resumed session of three weeks' duration in order to complete its work,

1. *Endorses* the resolution adopted on 3 August 1984 by the United Nations Conference on Conditions for Registration of Ships, and decides to convene a resumed session of the Conference to be held at Geneva from 28 January to 15 February 1985;

2. *Requests* the Secretary-General of the United Nations Conference on Trade and Development to make all the necessary arrangements for holding the resumed session of the United Nations Conference on Conditions for Registration of Ships.

General Assembly resolution 39/213 A

18 December 1984   Meeting 104   Adopted without vote

Approved by Second Committee (A/39/790/ Add.3) without vote, 6 December (meeting 56); draft by Egypt, for Group of 77 (A/C.2/39/L.84); agenda item 80 *(c)*.
Financial implications. S-G, A/C.2/39/L.100, A/C.5/39/65.
Meeting numbers. GA 39th session: 2nd Committee 53, 56; plenary 104.

In explanation of position on the programme budget implications of the text, the United States expressed hope that the Secretary-General, when later submitting a consolidated statement of Conference-servicing requirements, would take into account the necessary appropriations for those requirements, calculated on a full-cost basis.

Convention on code of conduct for liner conferences

The Convention on a Code of Conduct for Liner Conferences,[15] which entered into force in 1983,[12] had 59 States parties as at 31 December 1984.[16]

In a September note,[17] prepared for the Committee on Shipping, the UNCTAD secretariat reported on the status of the Convention as at 31 August 1984 and noted that eight countries, which had signed the Convention in 1974 and 1975, had not yet deposited with the Secretary-General an instrument of ratification, acceptance or approval. The secretariat, which was preparing a comprehensive report on national measures taken by the contracting States to implement the Code, reported that a number of them had expressed their concern about the tardiness in follow-up by many of the countries which had declared their intention to implement it.

Another secretariat report, also submitted to the Committee in May, dealt with the formulae and methods used for calculating and applying liner conferences surcharges.[18] The report highlighted problem areas, suggested elements which could be used to establish policy guidelines, and proposed, among other things, that shippers' organizations should co-operate at subregional and regional levels in order to strengthen their consultations with conferences and shipowners on surcharges and freight rates.

On 30 November,[19] the Committee on Shipping invited States members of UNCTAD which had not yet become contracting parties to the Convention to consider ratifying or acceding to it; called upon States members of UNCTAD which were contracting parties to the Convention to enter into multilateral or bilateral consultations to implement it; and requested the UNCTAD secretariat to report to the Committee in 1986 on the implementation of the Convention.

Bulk cargoes

In a September 1984 report on the participation by developing countries in the maritime transportation of dry bulk cargoes,[20] the UNCTAD secretariat observed that there were indications that access to cargoes was the most important factor affecting their participation in dry bulk shipping.

The report pointed out that the dry bulk carrier fleet of developing countries increased from 3.8 million to 33.1 million dwt between 1970 and 1983, while their percentage participation in the world dry bulk fleet increased from 5.3 to 15.4 per cent. Although their participation had improved, it was still limited to a small number of countries, and the lack of participation by developing countries in Africa was particularly noticeable since many in that region had substantial dry bulk cargo export and/or import flows. A comprehensive report on that matter would be submitted to the Committee at its 1986 session.

In March, a Group of Experts on International Sea Transport of Liquid Hydrocarbons in Bulk (second session, Geneva, 30 January–3 February)[21] also submitted to the Committee a report based on information supplied by 312 companies in the hydrocarbon trade in 37 countries (of which 200 companies were importers, exporters or traders, and the others providers of shipping services) which had responded to the Group's questionnaire.

The Group unanimously agreed on recommendations for consideration by the Committee, covering: maritime legislation, administration and training; dissemination of information; clauses for sales/purchase contracts; terms of shipment; shipbroking centres; regional co-operation; ship financing; restrictive port regulations; joint ventures; and international consultations on the supply/demand situation in the tanker market.

The Committee on Shipping, on 30 November,[22] asked that States members of UNCTAD urge commercial parties involved in the sea transport of liquid hydrocarbons in bulk to implement the Group's recommendations on dissemination of information, clauses for sales/purchase contracts and terms of shipment. In addition, the Committee requested developing States members to encourage their shipping companies to develop joint ventures, and it requested the UNCTAD secretariat to report on: trends in the supply-and-demand imbalance in world shipping; progress by developing countries in the carriage of crude oil and petroleum products; ways and means of establishing on a regional basis ship-broking centres in developing countries; and recent developments in the global pattern of container shipping services. It further called on the secretariat to bring the Group of Experts' recommendation on restrictive port regulations to the attention of the International

Maritime Organization (IMO); to take into account the Group's recommendations on maritime legislation, administration and training and joint ventures when updating its report on ship and port financing for developing countries; and to provide technical assistance to developing countries seeking to enact codes of maritime legislation and to set up ship registers and maritime administrations.

International shipping legislation

In 1984, the Working Group on International Shipping Legislation (tenth session, Geneva, 24 September–5 October)[23] continued its consideration of marine insurance and adopted a set of standard clauses as a non-mandatory international model for hull and cargo policies. A new item on maritime liens and mortgages was taken up by its Subgroup which urged a study of economic aspects of the question.

An *Ad Hoc* Intergovernmental Group to Consider Means of Combating All Aspects of Maritime Fraud, Including Piracy, met at Geneva from 6 to 17 February 1984 (see below, under "Maritime fraud").

The UNCTAD secretariat submitted, in October, a report to the Committee on Shipping on the treatment of merchant vessels in ports at the regional level[24]—a topic which was last considered in depth in 1977. Of the 36 States members of UNCTAD supplying information upon request, 14 reported that such regional arrangements were in force in their national ports and two others said that the measures were in force in foreign ports. The replies indicated that the only existing arrangements were those covered by a Paris memorandum of understanding on port State control, signed in 1982 with a view to ensuring harmonized and effective implementation of relevant conventions by the maritime authorities of 14 Western European countries.

On 30 November,[25] the Committee called on States members of UNCTAD to inform the IMO and UNCTAD secretariats of actual commercial and economic consequences they had noted for their merchant ships due to port State control at the regional level; recognized the competence of UNCTAD in the area of maritime liens and mortgages; and asked the Rapporteur of the Working Group on International Shipping Legislation to submit to the Trade and Development Board in 1985 his final report on standard marine hull and cargo insurance clauses.

Ports

In October 1984, the UNCTAD secretariat submitted a progress report[26] in which it examined the principles that should underlie the measurement of port congestion and determination of such surcharges. It noted that while neither shippers nor ship operators were motivated to seek rationalization of surcharge procedures because basic freight rates were already conditioned by fluctuating market pressures, the trading community as a whole, and thus world-wide economic development, would benefit from fair surcharges and elimination of congestion. A set of principles for the levy of surcharges was suggested with comments on each principle.

Among other documents issued by the secretariat in October were: a pilot study on container terminals data,[27] as part of a possible port data bank; measures for improving port performance;[28] and outlines of the studies[29] on port financing, bulk terminals and trans-shipment.

At its 1984 session, the Committee on Shipping, by decision 54(XI) of 30 November on development and improvement of ports, requested the secretariat to complete studies on port financing, bulk terminals and trans-shipment ports and to prepare a report describing ongoing port-related training activities; invited the UNCTAD Secretary-General to convene, not later than 1986, an *ad hoc* intergovernmental group of port experts to review the practical problems relevant to the development, improvement and operation of ports; and recommended the continuation and possible expansion of the UNCTAD interregional advisory service on ports.

Technical assistance and training

During 1984, the UNCTAD secretariat executed 44 technical assistance projects, financed mainly by the United Nations Development Programme (UNDP), as compared with 36 in 1983.[30] Those projects included advisory or sectoral support services, training, technical studies, publications, and the SHIPASSIST Directory of technical assistance available to developing countries. Eleven projects were initiated and 10 were completed. The total project budget was $2.2 million.

Seminars held during the year dealt with: port operations (Leningrad, USSR), container terminal management (Antwerp, Belgium), port statistics (Marseilles, France) and port finances (Le Havre, France). With funds contributed by the Swedish International Development Authority, training materials on port performance improvement were prepared for use by ports and port training institutes in developing countries. Seminars designed to train instructors to teach management of general cargo operations were given at Mombasa, Kenya, and Sharjah, United Arab Emirates. Under the TRAINMAR interregional training programme,[31] courses were prepared on: multimodal transport, general cargo operations and port administration, port financial management, management of container terminal operations, and cargo storage and warehousing.

By a September note,[32] the UNCTAD secretariat reported on the effect of the UNDP financial crisis on UNCTAD technical assistance and training activities in shipping, ports and multimodal transport. It pointed out that fund-raising efforts had failed in setting up an advisory service and, therefore, the future financing of the central support element of TRAINMAR was at stake.

The Committee on Shipping, on 30 November,[33] requested the UNCTAD Secretary-General to allocate, as a priority, the funds to carry out existing technical assistance programmes, and asked UNDP to continue financing such assistance and training projects. It also invited the UNCTAD Secretary-General to communicate to UNDP the Committee's concern over the future financing of TRAINMAR.

Maritime fraud

An *Ad Hoc* Intergovernmental Group to Consider Means of Combating All Aspects of Maritime Fraud, Including Piracy, held its first session in 1984 (Geneva, 6-17 February) and submitted a report[34] in April to the UNCTAD Trade and Development Board. It was noted at the session that an alarming increase in the number of reported cases of maritime fraud and related acts had been estimated by the shipping community to have involved $1 billion a year.

By a 17 February resolution, annexed to its report, the Group recommended that the Trade and Development Board invite States to consider adoption of suggestions by UNCTAD and others involving improved transportation, handling, storage and document procedures. It requested the Board to: recommend that States deal with acts of piracy, reconvene the *Ad Hoc* Intergovernmental Group in 1985 to finalize its work, instruct the UNCTAD secretariat to study such matters as international co-operation and the feasibility of a banking super-service scheme, and invite international and commercial organizations to study measures for combating maritime fraud and piracy.

Transport of dangerous goods

The problem of the transport of dangerous goods continued to be dealt with in 1984 by the Committee of Experts on the Transport of Dangerous Goods (thirteenth session, Geneva, 3-12 December)[35] which considered the following: amendments to, and new texts for, the United Nations Recommendations on the Transport of Dangerous Goods; activities of international organizations concerned with regulations or recommendations on the topic; and recommendations made by its Group of Rapporteurs. The Committee also considered a draft manual of tests and criteria for the classification of explosive substances and articles which had been completed by its Group of Experts on Explosives (twenty-fourth session, Geneva, 6-10 August).[36]

Multimodal and container transport

In September 1984, the UNCTAD secretariat submitted to the Committee on Shipping a report on national policy measures concerning multimodal transport operations and containerization,[37] based on information submitted by 49 mostly developing countries responding to the secretariat questionnaire. The report found that many developing countries needed assistance in preparing guidelines governing the qualifications and practices of MTOs and national regulations on multimodal transport. It urged those countries which had not yet done so to consider becoming contracting parties to the United Nations Convention on International Multimodal Transport of Goods,[38] and suggested that the Committee might consider establishing a group of governmental experts to recommend a set of related principles.

Another secretariat report to the Committee concerned adaptation to multimodal transport and containerization in developing countries.[39] In addition, it submitted notes on the use of computer software programmes in shipping companies and MTOs;[40] elaboration of a standard form and model provisions for multimodal transport documents;[41] and review of developments in the standardization of containers and related activities.[42]

A Group of Experts on Model Rules for Multimodal Container Tariffs held two sessions at Geneva (16-20 January, 7-11 May 1984) and recommended principles for developing rules for possible use by commercial parties in establishing the terms and conditions of carriage.[43] Its report with recommended principles was subsequently transmitted to the Committee on Shipping by the UNCTAD Secretary-General. The secretariat provided, in an April report,[44] examples of how the principles agreed upon by the Group at its January session appeared against the background of an existing tariff.

On 30 November,[45] the Committee on Shipping requested the UNCTAD Secretary-General to convene a meeting of experts in 1986 to propose model rules for multimodal container tariffs consistent with the principles recommended by the Group (see above). It also requested the secretariat to: submit to the Committee at its 1986 session a final draft of a standard form and model provisions for multimodal transport documents and to prepare a report containing guidelines concerning the establishment of MTOs in developing countries; prepare a study on the economic and commercial implications of the United Nations Convention on the Carriage of Goods by Sea, 1978 (Hamburg Rules),[46] and

the Convention on International Multimodal Transport of Goods;[38] and examine technological developments in data processing, with a view to suggesting how developing countries might introduce data processing to enhance the competitive position of their multimodal transport services.

Customs transit for goods

ECONOMIC AND SOCIAL COUNCIL ACTION

A system of customs transit for goods applicable world-wide under cover of *transport international routier* (TIR) carnets, which concerns the transport of merchandise by road vehicles between customs ports without inspection by customs agents, was considered by the Economic and Social Council.

On 27 July 1984, the Council, on the recommendation of its First (Economic) Committee, adopted without vote resolution 1984/79.

**Promotion of a system of customs transit
for goods applicable world-wide**

The Economic and Social Council,

Taking into account the need to facilitate the international exchange of goods,

Aware of the role played by transport in the international exchange of goods,

Taking into account also the economic requirements for the facilitation of transport and, to that end, the need for a system of customs transit applicable world-wide,

Convinced that it is possible to make significant progress in this direction by the adoption of a system of customs transit to be used in all regions of the world,

Noting from the experience gained in the application of the Customs Convention on the International Transport of Goods under Cover of TIR Carnets, concluded under the auspices of the United Nations at Geneva on 14 November 1975, that the TIR system can meet the criteria of world-wide application and the requirements connected with the technical possibilities of implementation,

Convinced also that the world-wide application of the TIR system could contribute to the facilitation not only of customs transit as such, but also of transport as a whole, by reducing transport costs and bringing a number of additional technical and economic advantages in the international exchange of goods,

1. *Recommends* that Governments which have not yet done so should consider the possibility of accepting the Customs Convention on the International Transport of Goods under Cover of TIR Carnets of 14 November 1975[47] and should consequently introduce the TIR system in their national legislation and regulations;

2. *Recommends also* that the international, intergovernmental and non-governmental organizations directly or indirectly concerned, particularly the regional commissions of the United Nations, should be encouraged to undertake the promotion of the TIR system and should endeavour to include this matter, wherever possible, in their own work programmes;

3. *Invites* the Secretary-General to reallocate available resources in order to make possible appropriate action with a view to promoting the world-wide application of

the Customs Convention on the International Transport of Goods under Cover of TIR Carnets of 14 November 1975.

Economic and Social Council resolution 1984/79

27 July 1984   Meeting 50   Adopted without vote

Approved by First Committee (E/1984/142/Add.1) without vote, 24 July (meeting 17); 4-nation draft (E/1984/C.1/L.8); agenda item 9.
Sponsors: Austria, Bulgaria, Morocco, Yugoslavia.

REFERENCES

(1)*Review of Maritime Transport, 1984* (TD/B/C.4/289), Sales No. E.85.II.D.18. (2)TD/B/1034. (3)TD/B/C.4/290. (4)TD/B/C.4/273. (5)YUN 1983, p. 571. (6)YUN 1981, p. 383. (7)UNCTAD/SHIP/196/Rev.1. (8)TD/B/1034 (res.53(XI)). (9)TD/B/1013. (10)TD/RS/CONF/10 & Add.1 & Corr.1 & Add.2. (11)YUN 1982, p. 748, GA res. 37/209, 20 Dec. 1982. (12)YUN 1983, p. 572. (13)TD/RS/CONF/12. (14)A/39/558. (15)YUN 1974, p. 460. (16)*Multilateral Treaties Deposited with the Secretary-General: Status as at 31 December 1984* (ST/LEG/SER.E/3), Sales No. E.85.V.4. (17)TD/B/C.4/281. (18)TD/B/C.4/265. (19)TD/B/1034 (dec. 50(XI)). (20)TD/B/C.4/271. (21)TD/B/C.4/263. (22)TD/B/1034 (res. 51(XI)). (23)TD/B/C.4/283. (24)TD/B/C.4/275. (25)TD/B/1034 (dec. 52(XI)). (26)TD/B/C.4/279. (27)TD/B/C.4/272. (28)TD/B/C.4/277. (29)TD/B/C.4/280. (30)UNCTAD/ST/SHIP/10. (31)TD/B/C.4/282. (32)TD/B/C.4/276. (33)TD/B/1034 (dec. 56(XI)). (34)TD/B/985. (35)ST/SG/AC.10/10 & Add.1-7. (36)ST/SG/AC.10/C.1/12. (37)TD/B/C.4/278 & Corr.1. (38)YUN 1980, p. 1020. (39)TD/B/C.4/274. (40)TD/B/C.4/268. (41)TD/B/C.4/269. (42)TD/B/C.4/270 & Corr.1. (43)TD/B/C.4/267. (44)TD/B/C.4/AC.5/6. (45)TD/B/1034 (res. 55(XI)). (46)YUN 1978, p. 955. (47)YUN 1975, p. 523.

Communications

World Communications Year

In May 1984, the Secretary-General submitted to the Committee on Information (18 June–6 July) a note[1] stating that, pending collection of information from all pertinent sources, he was forwarding to the Committee, in an annex to the note, an interim report prepared by the International Telecommunication Union (ITU) on activities carried out during World Communications Year (WCY) (1983).[2] In 1983,[3] the General Assembly had requested the Secretary-General to provide the Committee in 1984 with a report on the outcome of such ITU activities.

ITU, the lead agency for WCY, reported that 78 countries had set up national committees to promote appreciation of communications for development and to establish priorities on investment needs. A number of seminars and meetings were held at regional and national levels, and several broadcasting organizations promoted the objectives of the Year. The WCY secretariat provided basic documentation for the national committees and made available audio-visual materials.

The Committee on Information, at its 1984 session,[4] requested the Secretary-General to make available to its 1985 session a comprehensive report on ITU activities in relation to the Year.

In resolution 39/98 A of 14 December 1984, the General Assembly approved the recommendations of the Committee including that on ITU.

REFERENCES

(1)A/AC.198/79. (2)YUN 1983, p. 576. (3)*Ibid.*, p. 366, GA res. 38/82 B, 15 Dec. 1983. (4)A/39/21.

Chapter VI

Industrial development

Difficult conditions of world trade were exerting unfavourable effects on the industrialization of developing countries, concluded the Fourth General Conference of the United Nations Industrial Development Organization (UNIDO) in 1984. The Conference recognized that protectionism in many countries was harmful to trade and industrial development, and agreed that it should be resisted and reversed. Furthermore, the Conference found that the broad objectives contained in the 1975 Lima Declaration and Plan of Action on Industrial Development and Co-operation[1] and the 1980 New Delhi Declaration and Plan of Action on Industrialization of Developing Countries and International Co-operation for their Industrial Development[2] were far from attainment. UNIDO's goal was to assist developing countries to increase their share of world industrial production to 25 per cent in 2000; since 1975, their share had risen from 10 to 11.9 per cent.

In December 1984, the General Assembly expressed concern that the Conference had not yielded results commensurate with the problems (resolution 39/232), took note of the Conference's report (decision 39/448), and urged developed countries to pursue policies that would facilitate world industrial restructuring (resolution 39/235). It referred a draft resolution on mobilizing financial resources for industrial development to its 1985 session (decision 39/447).

The Assembly also requested that the Secretary-General continue his efforts to convert UNIDO into a United Nations specialized agency (resolution 39/231), and confirmed the appointment of the UNIDO Executive Director for an additional two years (decision 39/315).

The Executive Director stated that UNIDO's annual expenditures of between $120 million and $130 million were glaringly inadequate. Funds had to be spread thin because all countries had an equal right to request assistance from UNIDO; thus, it was currently active in 136 countries, carrying out 1,503 projects of varying complexity.

The Industrial Development Board, the principal UNIDO body, held its eighteenth session (Vienna, Austria, 2-19 May) and expressed concern at the lack of progress during the preceding four years in increasing the developing countries' share of world industrial production. The Board adopted 16 conclusions on various programme, industrial and organizational matters. They included

technical assistance to Namibians (see TRUSTEE-SHIP AND DECOLONIZATION, Chapter III) and Palestinians (see p. 276), and integration of women in development (see Chapter XIX of this section). In addition, it adopted a resolution on the Industrial Development Decade for Africa (IDDA) (see Chapter VIII of this section). The Board's Permanent Committee held its twenty-first session (Vienna, 19-23 November).

By decision 1984/167, the Economic and Social Council in July transmitted the report of the UNIDO Board on its session as well as a report on IDDA to the General Assembly.

As a result of the admission of Brunei Darussalam to the United Nations, the Assembly added it to the list of States eligible for UNIDO Board membership (resolution 39/234).

Topics related to this chapter. Regional economic and social activities: implementation of the programme for the Industrial Development Decade for Africa. Energy: industrial uses. Science and technology: technology transfer. Environment: environment and industry. Women: women in development.

Programme and finances of UNIDO

Programme policy

During 1984, UNIDO maintained its role as the central co-ordinating organ of the United Nations system for promoting and accelerating the industrial development of developing countries. It contributed to co-operation between industrialized and developing countries, provided a forum for negotiations, encouraged investment and facilitated the transfer of technology. On the basis of studies and surveys, UNIDO helped to formulate industrial development plans in the public, co-operative and private sectors. It organized technical assistance, including training programmes and advisory services, and published industrial statistics. It carried out its activities during the year taking into account the International Development Strategy for the Third United Nations Development Decade (the 1980s)[3] and related Assembly decisions and recommendations.

At the eighteenth (May 1984) session of the Industrial Development Board, the UNIDO Executive Director submitted a report[4] on progress in 1983/84 in follow-up action to the 1980 decisions of the Third General Conference and of the eleventh special session of the General Assembly on development and international economic co-operation. Because follow-up action in a number of priority areas was the subject of separate reports, the Executive Director's report contained mainly references to documents covering industrial technology, energy-related technology, development of human resources, industrial production, special measures for the least developed countries, the System of Consultations, industrial restructuring, social aspects of industrialization, industrial financing, the Industrial Development Decade for Africa, and monitoring.

The Board, on 19 May,[5] expressed concern at the lack of progress over the preceding four years in increasing the share of the developing countries in world industrial production. It recognized the importance, particularly in the current international economic situation, of financial flows to industrial development in developing countries, and requested the Executive Director to continue improving UNIDO's capacity to assist developing countries in designing industrial projects. It was unable to agree on his proposals for setting up an international bank for industrial development, and asked him to submit a report on the question in 1985.

Fourth General Conference of UNIDO

The Fourth General Conference of UNIDO was held at Vienna from 2 to 19 August 1984.[6] Representatives of 139 countries and 34 United Nations bodies, Secretariat units and specialized and other agencies attended, as well as observers from 29 intergovernmental and 33 international non-governmental organizations and four liberation movements—the African National Congress of South Africa, the Palestine Liberation Organization, the Pan-Africanist Congress of Azania and the South West Africa People's Organization. Namibia, represented by the United Nations Council for Namibia, also took part as a full member. (For participants and officers, see APPENDIX III.)

The Conference reviewed the progress and considered the prospects of industrial development *vis-à-vis* the Lima and New Delhi Declarations, examined national and international action in nine areas of industrial development for the period 1985-2000 identified as critical, looked at activities for the Industrial Development Decade for Africa (the 1980s), proclaimed in 1980,[7] and discussed UNIDO's co-ordinating role in the United Nations system. It adopted 12 resolutions by consensus; the preamble to the report, with conclusions and recommendations, and three resolutions were adopted by vote. The Conference referred

two draft resolutions to the General Assembly (see below, under "Redeployment of industrial production to developing countries" and "Industrial financing").

Preparations for the Conference

Among the 1984 regional preparatory meetings for the Conference, at which positions were discussed and formulated on the main issues of the Conference, were: the Economic and Social Commission for Asia and the Pacific (ESCAP) Preparatory Meeting of Ministers of Industry (Bangkok, Thailand, 15 and 16 March); the Seventh Conference of African Ministers of Industry, organized jointly by the Economic Commission for Africa (ECA), the Organization of African Unity (OAU) and UNIDO (Addis Ababa, Ethiopia, 26-28 March); a Latin American intergovernmental technical meeting (Santiago, Chile, 7-10 May); a high-level Latin American co-ordination meeting organized by the Latin American Economic System (Havana, Cuba, 22-25 May); the Sixth Conference on Industrial Development for Arab States, organized by the Arab Industrial Development Organization (AIDO) in co-operation with UNIDO (Damascus, Syrian Arab Republic, May); and an AIDO-organized meeting of Under-Secretaries of Ministries of Industry of Arab States (Tunis, Tunisia, 4-6 July).

In addition, the open-ended working group of the Industrial Development Board, established in 1982[8] to meet periodically and with the UNIDO secretariat to exchange information and views on Conference preparations, met on 19 January, and the Group of 77 developing countries held an interregional preparatory meeting at Vienna on 31 July and 1 August. A non-governmental organizations (NGOs) forum was held at Vienna on 6 and 7 February to elicit involvement of NGOs in the Conference. A regional workshop for African countries on the integration of women in the industrial planning and development process (Harare, Zimbabwe, 9-17 April) was the first of three such workshops to bring Conference issues to the participants and their views to the Conference; the others were for Caribbean countries (Georgetown, Guyana, 6-12 May) and Asian countries (Bangkok, 5-12 July) (see Chapter VIII of this section).

At its May 1984 session, the Industrial Development Board, which functioned as the Preparatory Committee for the Conference, reviewed Conference preparations. On 19 May,[9] it took note of the preparatory arrangements and appealed to member States and international organizations for voluntary contributions to make possible the participation in the Conference of the least developed countries. Noting progress in informal consultations, held on 29 February, 28 March and 18 and 25 April under the chairmanship of the Board

President, on Conference-related issues to identify areas of potential agreement on or convergence around agenda items, the Board endorsed the President's report on the consultations, to which were annexed the areas of agreement, and reconfirmed his mandate to continue consultations on procedural and substantive issues. It asked him to submit to the Conference President recommendations on outstanding procedural and organizational issues and to inform him of the outcome of consultations on substantive issues.

Work of the Conference

The Conference, following the proposal of the Industrial Development Board as Preparatory Committee, assigned various agenda items to two main committees for consideration and for preparation of draft resolutions and other decisions to be adopted by the Conference. In addition, a Drafting Committee prepared the preamble, containing the conclusions and recommendations of the Conference. The plenary Conference held a general debate jointly with its consideration of the Lima and New Delhi Declarations and Plans of Action: retrospective and perspective.

Committee I. Committee I held 15 meetings at which it considered action concerning four of the nine critical areas of industrial development for 1985-2000: the mobilization of financial resources for industrial development; world industrial restructuring and redeployment; implementation of the Substantial New Programme of Action (SNPA) for the 1980s for the Least Developed Countries (LDCs), adopted in 1981 by the United Nations Conference on LDCs;[10] and strengthening economic co-operation among developing countries. In addition, the Committee reviewed progress and proposals on how to achieve the objectives of IDDA.

On the question of *mobilizing financial resources*, it was agreed that access to resources was essential for existing industries, new industries and structural adjustment in developing countries. The current economic situation made it more difficult for developing countries to secure financing.

Many delegations spoke of the obstacles to industrialization arising from high debt-servicing requirements; some supported a proposal that a debt-servicing ratio of 25 per cent of total export earnings be viewed as an upper limit for developing countries. Many delegations called for increased official development assistance (ODA), with priority given to LDCs; others pointed out the complementarity of external and domestic financing, many considering that a major objective should be to increase domestic resources, particularly long-term capital, through savings incentives and appropriate taxation policies. However, many stated that domestic financing systems alone

could not generate sufficient resources. Industrialized countries were urged to provide more financing on better terms and in more appropriate forms; UNIDO was urged to continue examining mechanisms for increasing the transfer of external resources to industry in a stable manner. Many supported the establishment of a bank for industrial development, but others opposed the proposal.

Industrial restructuring and redeployment were said to be issues of greater concern than ever owing to the unfavourable economic situation. Several delegations emphasized the importance of government intervention, the State's regulatory role, the benefits of State enterprises, and the advantages of long- and medium-term planning. Others stressed that the restructuring process resulted primarily from market forces and private enterprise, and Governments' role should be limited to facilitating adjustment to that process. Many referred to the negative impact of protectionism, transnational corporations and the debt burden on the restructuring process in the developing countries. Others drew attention to the need to learn from the successful domestic policies followed by certain newly industrializing countries.

General concern was expressed at the deteriorating situation confronting *the least developed countries* when measured against the economic growth and industrial output targets set in SNPA. Many delegations emphasized the impact of rapid population growth, natural disasters, adverse terms of trade, low rates of investment, poor agricultural performance and the failure of the manufacturing sector to contribute significantly to the economy. Several delegations mentioned the expenditure for arms of resources that could otherwise be used for industrial development. A group of countries called for extensive international supportive measures, including a doubling of ODA by 1985, the conversion of outstanding ODA loans into grants, the facilitation of technology transfer, simplification of preferential schemes, and co-operation between developing countries.

It was agreed that *economic and technical co-operation for industrialization* should be strengthened among developing countries; many delegations recognized that, while financial and technical support from developed countries and international organizations remained necessary, such co-operation was primarily the responsibility of developing countries themselves. South-South co-operation, many delegations emphasized, was not a substitute for North-South co-operation; the two were complementary. A number of delegations requested UNIDO to accord high priority to industrial co-operation and to play a promotional and catalytic role in that regard. Many attached particular importance to solidarity meetings, joint programmes in specific sectors, the development of standards institutes, expansion of information exchange systems, and strengthening of centres for research and training.

A review of the progress of the *Industrial Development Decade for Africa* highlighted concern about the crisis facing many African countries, whose economic difficulties were compounded by drought and desertification (see Chapter XVI of this section). The economic difficulties, in the view of many delegations, were due to the region's dependence on the export of a few primary commodities. World market prices for those commodities had declined, while prices for imported manufactures continued to rise; the lack of trained manpower, low productivity, underutilization of installed capacity and inadequate integration of industry with other sectors, primarily agriculture, were cited as other causes. Implementation of OAU's 1980 Lagos Plan of Action for the Implementation of the Monrovia Strategy for the Economic Development of Africa[11] was supported by many as a means of providing a lasting solution.

Committee II. Committee II held 16 meetings at which it considered international action and national policies relating to five of the nine critical areas of industrial development for the period 1985-2000: accelerated development of human resources for industrial development; strengthening of scientific and technological capacities for industrial development; energy and industrialization; policies for domestic industrial processing of raw materials; and policies for rural development and self-sufficiency in food supplies. The Committee also discussed UNIDO's co-ordinating role within the United Nations system in industrial development. An informal drafting group formulated resolutions on the various topics.

The *role of human resources* in the development process was considered central by all delegations. Many spoke of the numerous difficulties in developing those resources, of the current imbalance between supply and demand of skills in developing countries, and of the "brain drain" phenomenon. It was a key responsibility of each State, according to some, to adapt training policies to its own level of industrialization, specific conditions and development policy; human resources development should be carried out as a part of broad social and economic changes. Staff retraining, the integration of women and youth in the development process, the training of trainers and the development of local entrepreneurship were recognized by some as priorities. Many called for UNIDO to expand its activities in human resources development; several supported a proposal by the International Labour Organisation (ILO) for the convening of a world conference on training.

The *importance of science and technology* for accelerating industrialization was emphasized by a number of delegations. While many described the useful role that private foreign investment could play in the transfer of technology to developing countries, others stressed that the public sector could strengthen those countries' technological development, in accordance with their national interests. The transfer of technology should not be used, several delegations asserted, to exert economic and political pressure or hinder international co-operation. One group of countries pointed out that the growing technology gap between developed and developing countries was bound to aggravate the imbalance in international economic relations. Many delegations referred to the implications of technological advances, such as micro-electronics, genetic engineering, biotechnology and new materials, and stressed the need for developing countries to be able to work in those areas. The value of technological information exchange systems and the need for co-ordination among United Nations bodies undertaking similar work were commented upon.

It was generally recognized that *energy* was a high priority in the industrialization of developing countries. Most delegations welcomed the attention given by UNIDO to energy-related activities; many underscored the importance of integrating energy plans into overall industrial, social, environmental and economic policies. The benefits of energy conservation programmes as a low-cost option producing immediate results were widely recognized. Proposals for North-South co-operation included technology transfer for the manufacture of energy equipment and for energy conservation, energy development, technical assistance and training; suggestions for South-South co-operation included the setting up of regional centres to design energy plans and conduct research on energy conservation and development of new and renewable sources of energy, the exchange of experience on technology, and joint manufacturing and marketing ventures.

There was a consensus that *domestic industrial processing of raw materials* would enable developing countries to improve their balance of payments, make better use of their natural resources, provide new job opportunities and contribute to overall economic development of certain areas or countries. The colonialist attitude of some countries was referred to by some delegations as the cause of the current situation, and the need for sovereignty over natural resources was pointed out. Some delegations emphasized the importance of small-scale and co-operative industries in processing domestic raw materials. Several stressed the need to process raw materials locally to facilitate the vertical integration of industries, while many said that, although they supported domestic processing in principle, it might not always be justified; only a detailed study could determine its viability.

It was generally agreed that industrial development was crucial for *rural development and self-sufficiency in food supplies*. Many delegations stressed the need for an integrated systems approach to tackle simultaneously problems at the multisectoral level. The social aspects of rural development and the importance of social overhead investments which, in the long run, produced economic returns were emphasized. The Committee recognized that industrialization in rural development involved both forward and backward linkages with agriculture. The interdependent nature of industrial and agricultural development was emphasized by many delegations, a number of which urged the creation of agro-industrial complexes, village industrial clusters and settlements. Great importance was attached by the Committee to the attainment of food self-sufficiency by developing countries. A group of countries emphasized the need for regional food security plans.

Committee II reaffirmed the central *co-ordinating role of UNIDO in the United Nations system* for activities related to industrialization, a role which many delegations felt should be strengthened. It was agreed that duplication and overlap of activities with other agencies should be avoided as much as possible. Many delegations called on member States to provide United Nations organizations with the legislative authority, through decisions of their governing bodies, to help avoid duplication of mandates and activities.

Preamble and resolutions

The preamble to the report of the Fourth General Conference contained its conclusions and recommendations. The Conference adopted the preamble on 19 August by 79 votes to 1, with 12 abstentions, as submitted by the Drafting Committee.

Reaffirming the importance of industrialization as a major factor in the development of the developing countries and in the promotion of a dynamic world economy, the Conference found that the objectives contained in the Lima and New Delhi Declarations and Plans were far from attainment. It reaffirmed the international community's commitment to SNPA and IDDA.

Since the Second General Conference in Lima in 1975,[(1)] the developing countries' share in world manufacturing value added had risen from 10 to 11.9 per cent. The period since the Third General Conference in New Delhi in 1980[(2)] had been characterized by widespread economic stagnation and crisis, which had had a particularly severe impact on developing countries. A recovery had begun in some industrialized nations, but developing countries continued to face critical situations that were adversely affecting their industrial development prospects, and industrial growth had been unevenly spread.

Rapid developments in technology, an important element in industrialization strategies, had not been fully available to developing countries; the Conference recognized the importance of facilitating the transfer of technology.

A constrictive international economic environment (recession, slack demand for exports, protectionist pressures) and difficult conditions of trade on the world market were exerting unfavourable effects on the industrialization of developing countries. Protectionism in many countries was hindering the attainment of a more just and effective international division of labour. The Conference recognized that protectionism was harmful to trade and industrial development and agreed that it should be reversed. Developed countries agreed to work towards reducing and eliminating quantitative restrictions and similar measures.

The development of developing countries, particularly in industrialization, depended on external financing; however, the current world economic situation had seen net financial outflows from a number of developing countries to developed countries. It was also necessary to reverse that situation.

Further efforts were needed to improve the functioning of the international monetary and financial systems. Donor countries should increase, if possible, their ODA, especially for LDCs and sub-Saharan countries, which were those most affected by the current economic situation.

The increasing debt-servicing burden, aggravated by high interest rates, was one of the major constraints to development. The Conference invited the international community and financial institutions to give due attention to the need for increased flows of concessional as well as non-concessional industrial finances to developing countries.

The Conference agreed on special and immediate action by the international community, and particularly the developed countries and UNIDO, to support efforts by the least developed and African countries, and to implement SNPA and IDDA more rapidly; it asked UNIDO to increase its aid to the drought-stricken areas.

Developing countries' strategies should aim at structural changes to enlarge the economic and social roles of industry and guarantee people's participation, should take cognizance of past experiences, should take into account the options and priorities they themselves had defined, should include sound domestic economic policies, and should encourage the mobilization and optimal use of human and material resources, promote internal structural change, adopt positive adjustment policies, strengthen links with other sectors of the economy, particularly agriculture, and broaden links between the public and private sectors and between small, medium-scale and large-scale industries.

The international economic system should be reformed to provide a more equitable framework for developing countries to pursue their industrialization policies, in accordance with their socio-economic structure and development level and recognizing their sovereign right to choose their policies free from external coercion. There was also a need to enhance co-operation between developing countries, and UNIDO should strengthen its role in promoting and facilitating such co-operation.

The Conference reaffirmed UNIDO's mandate to provide sustained co-operation to developing countries in their industrialization efforts. It requested UNIDO to complement the activities of regional organizations and promote joint action to maximize the effectiveness of available funds. It recognized the important function of other United Nations agencies—the United Nations Development Programme and the World Bank—and regional development banks in regard to the financing of technical assistance and project preparation and implementation. It affirmed the importance of UNIDO's technical assistance activities and called for increased contributions to the Industrial Development Fund to the agreed desirable level of $50 million per annum. It also welcomed the outcome of consultations on the conversion of UNIDO into a specialized agency.

The 15 resolutions adopted by the Conference concerned the following: accelerated development of human resources for industrial development; strengthening of scientific and technological capacities for industrial development in developing countries; energy and industrialization, with special emphasis on development of energy resources and manufacture of equipment (see Chapter X of this section); domestic industrial processing of raw materials in developing countries; rural development and self-sufficiency in food supplies (see Chapter XI of this section); implementation of SNPA (see p. 415); strengthening economic co-operation among developing countries (see p. 400); IDDA (see Chapter VIII of this section); integration of women in industrial development (see Chapter XIX of this section); the Industrial Development Fund; UNIDO's co-ordinating role in the United Nations system on industrial development; immediate assistance to Lebanon for the reconstruction of its industrial sector (see p. 522); cessation of the war in the Gulf (see p. 239); technical assistance to the Palestinian people (see p. 276); and technical assistance to the southern

African national liberation movements recognized by OAU (see p. 168).

Two draft resolutions, on the mobilization of financial resources for industrial development and world industrial restructuring and redeployment, were forwarded to the General Assembly for consideration.

GENERAL ASSEMBLY ACTION

On 18 December 1984, on the recommendation of the Second (Economic and Financial) Committee, the General Assembly adopted by recorded vote resolution 39/232.

Industrial development co-operation

The General Assembly,

Recalling its resolutions 3201(S-VI) and 3202(S-VI) of 1 May 1974, containing the Declaration and the Programme of Action on the Establishment of a New International Economic Order, 3281(XXIX) of 12 December 1974, containing the Charter of Economic Rights and Duties of States, 3362(S-VII) of 16 September 1975 on development and international economic co-operation and 35/56 of 5 December 1980, the annex to which contains the International Development Strategy for the Third United Nations Development Decade, in which, *inter alia*, the importance of industrialization in the development of developing countries is stressed,

Recalling also the Lima Declaration and Plan of Action on Industrial Development and Co-operation, in which were laid down the main measures and principles for industrial development and co-operation within the framework of the establishment of the new international economic order, and the New Delhi Declaration and Plan of Action on Industrialization of Developing Countries and International Co-operation for their Industrial Development, in which a strategy was spelt out for the further industrialization of developing countries,

Reaffirming its resolution 38/192 of 20 December 1983, as well as all other relevant resolutions in the field of industrial development co-operation,

Concerned about the continuing negative impact of the world economic crisis on the economic development and industrialization of the developing countries,

Urging developed countries to take fully into account the broad international implications of their policy decisions, including their impact on developing countries and industrial development,

Also urging developed countries to promote conditions conducive to the sustained world economic recovery so necessary for revitalizing the industrialization of developing countries by, *inter alia*, substantially increasing their financial and technical assistance,

Stressing the importance of economic co-operation among developing countries as an integral part of a global development effort and of an interdependent world economy and urging the enhancement of such co-operation in the field of industrialization,

Reaffirming the role of the United Nations Industrial Development Organization as the central co-ordinating organ in the United Nations system having a primary responsibility for promoting the transfer of industrial technology to developing countries and for the promotion and acceleration of their industrial development,

Expressing its concern that contributions to the United Nations Industrial Development Fund have remained far below the agreed desirable level of $50 million and that the level of the Fund has gradually declined in real terms since its establishment,

Reaffirming the importance and effectiveness of the Senior Industrial Development Field Advisers Programme in implementing the wide range of programmes and services rendered by the United Nations Industrial Development Organization,

Expressing its concern that the availability of funds from the United Nations Development Programme, which is the main source of funding for the technical assistance activities of the United Nations Industrial Development Organization, has been reduced substantially in the past few years,

Recognizing that the efforts of developing countries to develop their industrial technological capabilities should be supported by the international community and the importance of facilitating the transfer of technology to developing countries,

Having considered the report of the Fourth General Conference of the United Nations Industrial Development Organization, held at Vienna from 2 to 19 August 1984, and the report of the Industrial Development Board on its eighteenth session,

I
Report of the Fourth General Conference of the
United Nations Industrial Development Organization

1.   *Takes note* of the report of the Fourth General Conference of the United Nations Industrial Development Organization;

2.   *Notes with concern* that the Conference was unable to yield results commensurate with the dimensions of the problems confronting the developing countries concerning their industrialization and confronting the world economy as a whole;

3.   *Endorses* the resolutions adopted by the Conference and calls for their immediate and effective implementation;

4.   *Notes with regret* that the Conference could not adopt two draft resolutions concerning world industrial restructuring and redeployment and the mobilization of financial resources for industrial development;

5.   *Welcomes* the decision of the Conference to accord high priority to industrial co-operation among developing countries in the activities and programmes of the United Nations Industrial Development Organization;

6.   *Welcomes also* the decision of the Conference to give priority to strengthening the technological capabilities of developing countries, which are an important element in the industrialization process;

7.   *Decides* that adequate resources should be provided in the budget of the United Nations Industrial Development Organization to implement fully all its mandates, particularly those in support of the activities established in priority areas, and authorizes the Secretary-General to take appropriate action to this end;

8.   *Welcomes* the announcements to allocate new and additional voluntary contributions to the United Nations Industrial Development Fund, including contributions through trust funds, and calls upon all countries, in particular the developed countries, to contribute or to increase their contributions to the United Nations Industrial Development Fund so as to reach, at the earliest

date possible, the agreed desirable funding level of $50 million a year;

9.   *Requests* the United Nations Industrial Development Organization to take appropriate action to implement the resolutions and recommendations of the Conference;

10.   *Calls upon* all organs, organizations and bodies of the United Nations system to respond positively to the relevant resolutions and recommendations addressed to them by the Conference;

II
Report of the Industrial Development Board
on its eighteenth session

1.   *Takes note* of the report of the Industrial Development Board on its eighteenth session;

2.   *Decides* that in 1985 the regular budget of the United Nations will provide for maintaining the total number of existing posts in the Senior Industrial Development Field Advisers Programme, taking into account the allocation in the budget of the United Nations Development Programme, as well as voluntary funding through the United Nations Industrial Development Organization, and requests the Secretary-General to take appropriate action to this end;

3.   *Appeals* to developed countries to provide maximum voluntary contributions for the Senior Industrial Development Field Advisers Programme;

4.   *Reaffirms* its support for strengthening the system of consultations, in the light of experience gained, with the objective of increasing the industrial capacities of developing countries.

General Assembly resolution 39/232

18 December 1984   Meeting 104   118-2-27 (recorded vote)

Approved by Second Committee (A/39/790/Add.4) by recorded vote (92-2-28), 10 December (meeting 58); draft by Egypt, for Group of 77 (A/C.2/39/L.34); agenda item 80 *(d)*.

Financial implications. 5th Committee, A/39/830; S-G, A/C.2/39/L.93, A/C.5/39/91.

Meeting numbers. GA 39th session: 2nd Committee 39, 58; 5th Committee 52, 53; plenary 104.

Recorded vote in Assembly as follows:

In favour: Afghanistan, Algeria, Angola, Argentina, Austria, Bahamas, Bahrain, Bangladesh, Barbados, Benin, Bhutan, Bolivia, Botswana, Brazil, Brunei Darussalam, Burkina Faso, Burma, Burundi, Canada, Cape Verde, Chad, Chile, China, Colombia, Congo, Costa Rica, Cuba, Cyprus, Democratic Kampuchea, Democratic Yemen, Djibouti, Dominican Republic, Ecuador, Egypt, El Salvador, Equatorial Guinea, Ethiopia, Fiji, Gabon, Gambia, Ghana, Greece, Guatemala, Guinea, Guinea-Bissau, Guyana, Haiti, Honduras, India, Indonesia, Iran, Iraq, Ivory Coast,[a] Jordan, Kenya, Kuwait, Lao People's Democratic Republic, Lebanon, Lesotho, Liberia, Libyan Arab Jamahiriya, Madagascar, Malawi, Malaysia, Maldives, Mali, Malta, Mauritania, Mauritius, Mexico, Morocco, Mozambique, Nepal, Nicaragua, Niger, Nigeria, Oman, Pakistan, Panama, Papua New Guinea, Paraguay, Peru, Philippines, Qatar, Romania, Rwanda, Saint Christopher and Nevis, Saint Lucia, Saint Vincent and the Grenadines, Samoa, Sao Tome and Principe, Saudi Arabia, Senegal, Sierra Leone, Singapore, Somalia, Sri Lanka, Sudan, Suriname, Swaziland, Syrian Arab Republic, Thailand, Togo, Trinidad and Tobago, Tunisia, Turkey, Uganda, United Arab Emirates, United Republic of Tanzania, Uruguay, Vanuatu, Venezuela, Viet Nam, Yemen, Yugoslavia, Zaire, Zambia, Zimbabwe.

Against: Israel, United States.

Abstaining: Australia, Belgium, Bulgaria, Byelorussian SSR, Czechoslovakia, Denmark, Finland, France, German Democratic Republic, Germany, Federal Republic of, Hungary, Iceland, Ireland, Italy, Japan, Luxembourg, Mongolia, Netherlands, New Zealand, Norway, Poland, Portugal, Spain, Sweden, Ukrainian SSR, USSR, United Kingdom.

[a]Later advised the Secretariat it had intended to abstain.

Separate recorded votes were taken in both the Second Committee and the Assembly on section II, paragraph 2, before approval of the text as a whole. The Committee adopted the paragraph by

91 votes to 14, with 17 abstentions, and the Assembly by 117 votes to 16, with 15 abstentions.

The Fifth (Administrative and Budgetary) Committee on 15 December, by a recorded vote of 71 to 17, with 11 abstentions, decided to inform the Assembly that an additional $1,135,000 appropriation would be required in 1985 to finance nine Senior Industrial Development Field Adviser (SIDFA) posts.

Explaining its negative vote in the Second Committee, the United States said the draft resolution was faulty because it spoke of the continuing negative impact of the world economic crisis instead of noting the positive trends in the world economy. It did not mention the domestic policy decisions that were needed for industrial development in the third world, focusing only on the developed countries' policies, it gave too negative a view of the results of the Fourth General Conference, and it allocated more than $1 million to the SIDFA Programme (see below, under "Industrial development activities"). Israel said it supported UNIDO aims but had voted against the text because section I, paragraph 3, endorsed some resolutions which it had opposed.

Japan, noting that it had abstained on the draft as a whole, explained that it voted against section II, paragraph 2, because the decision taken in 1983[12] authorizing an allocation from the United Nations regular budget for the SIDFA Programme had been in response to exceptional circumstances which no longer prevailed.

The United Kingdom also objected to financing the SIDFA Programme from the regular budget and felt that the text did not reflect a balanced assessment of the results of the Fourth General Conference.

The Ukrainian SSR, on behalf also of Bulgaria, the Byelorussian SSR, Czechoslovakia, the German Democratic Republic, Hungary, Mongolia, Poland and the USSR, said they fully supported the position of principle regarding the need to hold down budgetary growth, and had therefore been forced to vote against section II, paragraph 2, and abstain in the vote as a whole, although that did not reflect any change in their support for the national economic development plans of the developing countries.

Denmark had serious concern regarding the principles involved in, and the significant financial implications of, the text. The vote had disregarded the Committee's efforts to adopt resolutions having financial implications by consensus. The Federal Republic of Germany also said it could not go along with the financial implications.

On the same date, on the recommendation of the Second Committee, the Assembly adopted without vote decision 39/448.

Report of the Fourth General Conference of the United Nations Industrial Development Organization

At its 104th plenary meeting, on 18 December 1984, the General Assembly, on the recommendation of the Second Committee, took note of the report of the Fourth General Conference of the United Nations Industrial Development Organization.

General Assembly decision 39/448

Adopted without vote

Approved by Second Committee (A/39/790/Add.4) without vote, 14 December (meeting 60); oral proposal by Chairman; agenda item 80 (d).

Work programme for 1984-1985

The Committee for Programme and Co-ordination (CPC) at its 1984 session (New York, 23 April–1 June)[13] reviewed the implementation of its recommendations[14] on UNIDO's 1984-1985 work programme that the Economic and Social Council had endorsed in 1983,[15] mainly those concerning proposed changes in the System of Consultations (see below, under "Industrial co-operation"). It also heard a statement by the secretariat on issues related to avoiding duplication and organizing UNIDO's work programme more rationally.

Proposed work programme for 1986-1987

The UNIDO Executive Director submitted a proposed work programme for the biennium 1986-1987[16] to the November 1984 session of the Industrial Development Board's Permanent Committee. The programme of activities focused on policy co-ordination, industrial studies and research, and industrial operations, and reflected resolutions adopted at the Fourth General Conference of UNIDO. Following consideration of the proposed programme, the Permanent Committee[17] requested the Executive Director to reflect the views expressed during the session in a revised programme and to convey it to the Secretary-General.

Evaluation

A UNIDO secretariat report[18] to the Permanent Committee described the changes made in UNIDO's self-evaluation system for field projects resulting from an assessment of the system's first year of operation which began in May 1982. It also introduced a new system for evaluating group training projects. The report was updated to mid-December 1984 in the UNIDO Executive Director's annual report for 1984.[19]

From May to December 1982, 52 project evaluation reports (PERs) were prepared; in 1983, the total was 88, and in 1984, 104. In addition, 15 terminal PERs were prepared in 1982, 19 in 1983 and 18 in 1984. A gradual increase in compliance indicated that the system was becoming well established, accompanied not only by a significant improvement in the quality of information received from the field but also by an improvement in the speed and quality of headquarters feedback.

On 19 May 1984,[20] the Industrial Development Board decided that the item "Evaluation", covering all aspects, was to be included in the provisional agenda of the 1984 session of the Permanent Committee and would be discussed only once every year.

On 23 November,[17] the Permanent Committee noted with appreciation the application of the system, encouraged the secretariat to continue to improve it, including field staff training programmes and in-depth evaluation, and re-emphasized the important role of participating States in the evaluation process.

A report[21] by the Secretary-General evaluating UNIDO's technical co-operation activities in manufactures was submitted to CPC's 1984 session; a secretariat note[22] on the matter was presented to the Permanent Committee (see below, under "Industrial development activities").

Institutional machinery

Proposed organizational change

As at 31 December 1984, 138 States had signed the Constitution adopted by a United Nations conference in 1979[23] to establish UNIDO as a specialized agency; 118 had ratified, accepted or approved it.

The States that had adhered to the Constitution (the five in italics acted during 1984) were:

Afghanistan, Algeria, Argentina, Australia, Austria, Bangladesh, Barbados, Belgium, Benin, Bhutan, Bolivia, Brazil, Burkina Faso, Burundi, Cameroon, Canada, *Cape Verde*, Central African Republic, Chile, China, Colombia, Congo, Cuba, Cyprus, Democratic People's Republic of Korea, Democratic Yemen, Denmark, Dominica, Dominican Republic, Ecuador, Egypt, *Equatorial Guinea*, Ethiopia, Fiji, Finland, France, Gabon, Germany, Federal Republic of, Ghana, Greece, Guatemala, Guinea, Guinea-Bissau, *Guyana*, Haiti, Honduras, Hungary, India, Indonesia, Iraq, *Ireland*, Israel, Ivory Coast, Jamaica, Japan, Jordan, Kenya, Kuwait, Lao People's Democratic Republic, Lebanon, Lesotho, Libyan Arab Jamahiriya, Luxembourg, Madagascar, Malawi, Malaysia, Mali, Malta, Mauritania, Mauritius, Mexico, Mozambique, Nepal, Netherlands, Nicaragua, Niger, Nigeria, Norway, Oman, Pakistan, Panama, Paraguay, Peru, Philippines, *Portugal*, Republic of Korea, Romania, Rwanda, Saint Lucia, Senegal, Seychelles, Sierra Leone, Somalia, Spain, Sri Lanka, Sudan, Suriname, Swaziland, Sweden, Switzerland, Syrian Arab Republic, Thailand, Togo, Trinidad and Tobago, Tunisia, Turkey, Uganda, United Arab Emirates, United Kingdom, United Republic of Tanzania, United States, Uruguay, Venezuela, Viet Nam, Yemen, Yugoslavia, Zaire, Zambia.

Twenty States had signed but not formally adhered to the Constitution as at 31 December (the one in italics acted during 1984):

Angola, Antigua and Barbuda, Bulgaria, Byelorussian SSR, Chad, Comoros, *Costa Rica*, Czechoslovakia, Djibouti, El Salvador, German Democratic Republic, Iran, Italy, Liberia, Mongolia, Morocco, Poland, Sao Tome and Principe, Ukrainian SSR, USSR.

In accordance with its article 25, the Constitution was to enter into force when at least 80 States that had deposited instruments of ratification, acceptance or approval notified the depositary (the Secretary-General) that they had agreed, after consultations among themselves, that the Constitution would enter into force. The Secretary-General said in a report to the General Assembly in August 1984[24] that consultations requested by the Assembly in December 1983[25] took place in April and May 1984 at Vienna. He said there was a consensus on the desirability of establishing the new agency on a universal basis and that an equitable geographical representation should be maintained at all secretariat levels; in addition, the agency's competent organs were expected, after it came into being, to review the totality of its operations.

GENERAL ASSEMBLY ACTION

On 18 December 1984, on the recommendation of the Second Committee, the General Assembly adopted without vote resolution 39/231.

Conversion of the United Nations Industrial Development Organization into a specialized agency

The General Assembly,

Recalling its resolutions 37/213 of 20 December 1982 and 38/193 of 20 December 1983,

Bearing in mind that the Constitution of the United Nations Industrial Development Organization has been ratified, accepted or approved by more than the minimum number of States whose agreement is required for its entry in force,

1. *Takes note with interest* of the consensus reached at the consultations on the conversion of the United Nations Industrial Development Organization into a specialized agency that were held at Vienna prior to and in April and May 1984;

2. *Endorses* the contents of the report of the Secretary-General on the conversion of the United Nations Industrial Development Organization into a specialized agency and calls upon all countries to abide by the outcome of the consultations as set out in that report;

3. *Expresses its confidence* that the new organization will honour the contents of the report of the Secretary-General;

4. *Calls upon* those States that have not yet done so to ratify the Constitution of the United Nations Industrial Development Organization without further delay;

5. *Decides* that adequate resources should be provided in the regular budget of the United Nations Industrial Development Organization for the biennium 1984-1985 to ensure the provision of the necessary funds,

in accordance with paragraph 7 of General Assembly resolution 34/96 of 13 December 1979, for the first General Conference of the United Nations Industrial Development Organization, to be held in two parts for a total duration of no more than thirteen days, and other costs associated with the conversion of the organization into a specialized agency;

6. *Decides further* that, in anticipation of the speedy conversion of the United Nations Industrial Development Organization into a specialized agency, the Secretary-General should adjust the calendar of conferences and meetings of the United Nations for the biennium 1984-1985 so that only one session of the Industrial Development Board will be held in 1985;

7. *Requests* the Secretary-General to continue his efforts, in accordance with General Assembly resolution 38/193, for the immediate conversion of the United Nations Industrial Development Organization into a specialized agency.

General Assembly resolution 39/231

18 December 1984   Meeting 104   Adopted without vote

Approved by Second Committee (A/39/790Add.4) without vote, 10 December (meeting 58); draft by Vice-Chairman (A/C.2/39/L.121), based on informal consultations on draft by Egypt, for Group of 77 (A/C.2/39/L.32); agenda item 80 *(d)*.
Financial implications. 5th Committee, A/39/830; S-G, A/C.2/39/L.78, A/C.2/39/L.123, A/C.5/39/92.
Meeting numbers. GA 39th session: 2nd Committee 39, 58; 5th Committee 49; plenary 104.

The Secretary-General estimated that an additional $1,034,100 would be required to service the first General Conference after UNIDO's conversion into a specialized agency, $924,500 for temporary assistance for meetings and $109,600 for various administrative support costs. The Advisory Committee on Administrative and Budgetary Questions (ACABQ), reporting orally to the Fifth Committee on 13 December, recommended reducing temporary assistance costs to $900,000 and administrative costs to $26,000, for a total of $926,000. On 13 December, the Fifth Committee decided without vote to inform the Assembly that that amount would be required under the 1984-1985 budget.

On 18 December, the Assembly adopted resolution 39/237 A on the United Nations budget, section 17 of which was increased to accommodate the above appropriation.

Appointment of the Executive Director

In a note of 7 December 1984,[26] the Secretary-General proposed to reappoint Abd-El Rahman Khane as UNIDO Executive Director for a further two-year period ending on 31 December 1986, or until the date on which the Director-General of the new UNIDO assumed office, whichever came first.

GENERAL ASSEMBLY ACTION

On 10 December, the General Assembly adopted without vote decision 39/315.

Confirmation of the appointment of the Executive Director of the United Nations Industrial Development Organization

At its 93rd plenary meeting, on 10 December 1984, the General Assembly confirmed the appointment by the Secretary-General of Mr. Abd-El Rahman Khane as Executive Director of the United Nations Industrial Development Organization for a further period of two years ending on 31 December 1986, or until the date on which the Director-General of the United Nations Industrial Development Organization assumed office, whichever was earlier.

General Assembly decision 39/315

Adopted without vote

Oral proposal by President; agenda item 17 *(h)*.

Report of the Industrial Development Board

ECONOMIC AND SOCIAL COUNCIL ACTION

In July 1984, on the recommendation of its First (Economic) Committee, the Economic and Social Council adopted without vote decision 1984/167.

Industrial development co-operation

At its 48th plenary meeting, on 25 July 1984, the Council:

(a) Took note of the report of the Industrial Development Board on the work of its eighteenth session and decided to transmit it, together with the recommendations of the Board, to the General Assembly at its thirty-ninth session for consideration;

(b) Took note also of the note by the Secretary-General transmitting the third progress report of the Executive Director of the United Nations Industrial Development Organization and the Executive Secretary of the Economic Commission for Africa on the Industrial Development Decade for Africa and decided to transmit it to the General Assembly at its thirty-ninth session for consideration.

Economic and Social Council decision 1984/167

Adopted without vote

Approved by First Committee (E/1984/133) without vote, 10 July (meeting 5); oral proposal by Chairman; agenda item 13.

GENERAL ASSEMBLY ACTION

On 18 December, the General Assembly adopted resolution 39/232, in section II of which it took note of the Board's report.

Eligibility for membership in the Industrial Development Board

As a result of the admission to the United Nations of Brunei Darussalam in September 1984 (see p. 371), the General Assembly decided to include that country in the list of States eligible for membership in the Industrial Development Board.

GENERAL ASSEMBLY ACTION

On 18 December, on the recommendation of the Second Committee, the General Assembly adopted without vote resolution 39/234.

Revision of the lists of States eligible for membership in the Industrial Development Board

The General Assembly,

Recalling section II, paragraph 4, of its resolution 2152(XXI) of 17 November 1966 on the United Nations Industrial Development Organization,

Decides to include Brunei Darussalam in list A of the annex to resolution 2152(XXI).

General Assembly resolution 39/234

18 December 1984   Meeting 104   Adopted without vote

Approved by Second Committee (A/39/790/Add.4) without vote, 10 December (meeting 58); draft by Vice-Chairman (A/C.2/39/L.130), based on informal consultations; agenda item 80 *(d)*.

Co-ordination in the UN system

During 1984, UNIDO continued its efforts to enhance the cost-effectiveness of its co-ordination activities in the use of the United Nations system's resources for industrial development co-operation. Co-ordination activities were carried out at the policy-making, intersecretariat and country levels. UNIDO accepted 164 invitations to participate in meetings of policy-making bodies, or technical meetings, organized by other United Nations organizations; it declined 257 others because of budgetary constraints. It also took part in eight intersecretariat co-ordinating bodies and joint technical working group meetings.

On the country level, co-ordination was pursued through the offices of United Nations resident co-ordinators, UNDP resident representatives and SIDFAs.

On 19 August 1984,[27] the Fourth General Conference of UNIDO adopted a resolution on UNIDO's co-ordinating role. It recommended that UNIDO strengthen its co-ordination with work-related United Nations, governmental, inter-governmental and non-governmental organizations; strengthen promotion and facilitation of industrial co-operation between developing countries in the context of economic and technical co-operation among those countries; analyse its co-ordination activities, including objectives, costs, benefits and problems; make optimal use of existing co-ordination mechanisms; and strengthen field co-ordination in co-operation with UNDP. It also welcomed the efforts of the General Assembly to achieve more effective system-wide co-ordination through harmonization of inter-agency programmes.

An October report[28] of the secretariat to the November session of the Permanent Committee of the Industrial Development Board described industrial development co-ordination activities of UNIDO between November 1983 and October 1984. It covered co-ordination objectives, costs, benefits and problems, and noted UNIDO activities in the field of economic co-operation among developing countries. The report pointed out three basic co-ordination problems: parallel mandates of various United Nations organizations; the inadequacy of resources for carrying out through UNIDO both an industrial development technical co-operation programme and co-ordination activities; and institutional weaknesses in co-ordination machinery.

On 23 November,[17] the Permanent Committee requested the secretariat to strengthen its co-ordination role in respect of economic co-operation among developing countries in accordance with the Fourth General Conference's resolution. The Committee called on the secretariat to continue efforts to harmonize the planning, programming, budgeting and evaluation of UNIDO co-ordination activities, with a view to drawing up a co-ordination programme, and requested it to provide at its 1985 session a cost breakdown of those activities.

CPC, at its April-June 1984 session, recommended that a report on questions raised in a 1983 Economic and Social Council resolution,[15] notably the problem of co-ordination and rationalization of UNIDO's activities, be submitted to it in 1985.

Documents control

The secretariat, in a September 1984 covering note[29] to the Permanent Committee, recalled that the General Assembly on numerous occasions had appealed to United Nations bodies to consider ways to reduce documentation; to facilitate discussion, it transmitted a note[30] by the Secretary-General containing the Assembly's decisions and recommendations on control and limitation of documentation.

On 23 November,[17] the Permanent Committee suggested that the Executive Director's annual report should serve as a reference document to avoid unnecessary reproduction, and asked him to report to its 1986 session on action taken to limit documentation.

Financial questions

UN Industrial Development Fund

In 1984, the secretariat continued to programme United Nations Industrial Development Fund (UNIDF) resources according to nine priority areas endorsed by the Industrial Development Board, which included energy-related and other industrial technology, industrial production, human resources development, special measures for LDCs, the System of Consultations, restructuring world industrial production, industrial financing, IDDA and monitoring.

Total pledges for UNIDF reached $15.7 million, an increase of about 13 per cent over 1983 pledges.

The increase related entirely to special-purpose contributions; general-purpose convertible contributions decreased by approximately 10 per cent.

Projects amounting to $11.16 million were approved, as follows: Africa, including African Arab States, $2.23 million (20 per cent); Americas, $710,000 (6.4 per cent); Arab States, excluding African Arab States, $50,000 (0.4 per cent); Asia and the Pacific, $1.49 million (13.4 per cent); Europe, $280,000 (2.5 per cent); and global and interregional, $6.4 million (57.3 per cent). A number of innovative projects were conducted. For example, in Pakistan, assistance was given in developing through genetic manipulation and genetic engineering a new species of yeast which was particularly efficient in breaking down cellulosic material, of importance in connection with the utilization of biomass.

A Symposium on Lactic Acid Fermentation in Food Industry (Mexico City, 27-29 November) considered state-of-the-art application of genetic engineering and biotechnology to fermented foods.

An Interregional Seminar on Energy Saving in the Cement Industry (Paris, 11-29 June) aimed at providing information to developing countries on energy management and conservation in that industry.

On 19 May,[31] the Industrial Development Board approved the UNIDO Executive Director's programme for UNIDF for 1985 and plan for 1985-1986,[32] and agreed to continue to delegate authority to him to approve projects for UNIDF financing in 1985 and 1986. It expressed concern about UNDP's continuing financial difficulties, which had affected UNIDO as an executing agency. Noting that contributions to the Fund had increased in 1984, but that its value had declined since its establishment, the Board urged countries to raise their contributions, with maximum flexibility, so that the Fund might achieve the desirable annual funding level of $50 million. It urged the secretariat to continue activities in the nine priority areas, particularly in projects concerning LDCs, to minimize delays in implementation and to try for greater balance between allocated and actual share of Fund-financed priority-area activities. It asked the Executive Director for annual progress reports as well as terminal reports on projects, within six months of completion, to donor and recipient States.

On 19 August,[33] the Fourth General Conference pointed out that Fund contributions remained far below the desirable target and called particularly on the developed countries to increase their contributions.

The General Assembly on 18 December, in resolution 39/232, also called for increased contributions to the Fund.

CONTRIBUTIONS TO THE UN INDUSTRIAL DEVELOPMENT FUND, 1984 AND 1985

(as at 31 December 1984; in US dollar equivalent)

Country	1984 payment	1985 pledge	Country	1984 payment	1985 pledge
Afghanistan	1,500	1,500	France	1,005,917	904,255
Algeria	—	40,000	German Democratic Republic	474,748	105,960
Australia	138,657	168,067	Germany, Federal Republic of	2,214,093	2,317,881
Austria	552,387	651,163	Greece	7,200	36,000
Bahrain	5,000	5,000	Guatemala	—	5,000
Bangladesh	6,025	2,420	Guyana	5,167	706
Barbados	2,000	2,000	Honduras	2,000	1,000
Belgium	360,244	393,443	Hungary	66,445	62,779
Benin	3,714	—	India	200,000	1,000,000
Bhutan	—	1,320	Indonesia	50,000	50,000
Bolivia	—	1,000	Italy	—	2,105,263
Botswana	4,717	—	Ivory Coast	126,551	
Bulgaria	—	101,523	Jamaica	4,000	4,000
Burkina Faso	2,273	—	Japan	1,229,801	—
Burma	1,000	1,000	Kenya	29,203	15,252
Burundi	846	—	Kuwait	75,000	—
Central African Republic	713	—	Lao People's Democratic Republic	1,500	1,500
Chile	10,000	10,000	Lebanon	5,579	—
China	373,973	365,830	Lesotho	2,000	—
Colombia	5,711	5,700	Luxembourg	5,472	4,754
Congo	9,579	11,000	Madagascar	2,359	1,629
Costa Rica	8,924	12,250	Malawi	2,290	2,349
Cuba	24,306	23,333	Malaysia	39,550	20,000
Cyprus	885	1,210	Mauritania	4,302	—
Czechoslovakia	153,374	167,504	Mauritius	676	—
Democratic Yemen	—	4,000	Mexico	15,000	—
Dominica	1,840	—	Mongolia	2,155	2,082
Ecuador	4,700	6,500	Nepal	700	—
Egypt	278,620	72,492	Netherlands	—	441,176
Ethiopia	1,122	1,111	Nigeria	150,000	50,000
Fiji	1,070	1,000	Oman	12,000	12,000
Finland	429,558	—	Pakistan	70,175	73,684

Country	1984 payment	1985 pledge		Country	1984 payment	1985 pledge
Panama	2,000	2,000		Tunisia	22,120	19,953
Paraguay	—	6,000		Turkey	174,814	223,529
Peru	15,000	20,000		Uganda	2,000	—
Philippines	8,901	1,000		USSR	591,017	586,854
Poland	184,332	226,291		United Kingdom	485,363	152,047
Portugal	15,000	15,000		United Republic of Tanzania	1,135	—
Qatar	—	30,000		Uruguay	830	—
Republic of Korea	30,000	30,000		Venezuela	—	7,376
Rwanda	4,000	—		Viet Nam	—	1,000
Saudi Arabia	1,000,000	1,000,000		Yemen	32,000	—
Senegal	—	3,000		Yugoslavia	133,333	194,596
Sierra Leone	—	2,000		Zaire	1,029	—
Sri Lanka	6,057	3,000		Zambia	1,770	9,804
Sudan	15,235	15,000		Zimbabwe	11,538	8,966
Suriname	—	2,000				
Swaziland	1,639	—		Subtotal	11,041,853	12,883,390
Switzerland	65,390	1,056,338				
Syrian Arab Republic	5,372	—		*Non-governmental organizations*	34,028	—
Thailand	23,084	—				
Togo	2,273	—		Total	11,075,881	12,883,390
Trinidad and Tobago	20,000	—				

SOURCE: A/40/5/Add.9.

Budgetary resources

The General Assembly decided on 18 December, in resolution 39/232, that adequate resources should be provided in the UNIDO budget to implement all its mandates, particularly priority-area activities, and authorized the Secretary-General to take action towards that end.

Also on 18 December, the Assembly adopted resolution 39/237 A, increasing the UNIDO budget by $2,173,800 for the biennium 1984-1985, from $72,149,500 to $74,323,300.

REFERENCES

[1]YUN 1975, p. 473. [2]YUN 1980, p. 647. [3]*Ibid.*, p. 503, GA res. 35/56, annex, 5 Dec. 1980. [4]ID/B/322. [5]A/39/16 (conclusion 1984/2). [6]ID/CONF.5/46 & Corr.1. [7]YUN 1980, p. 662, GA res. 35/66 B, 5 Dec. 1980. [8]YUN 1982, p. 758, GA res. 37/212, 20 Dec. 1982. [9]A/39/16 (conclusion 1984/7). [10]YUN 1981, p. 406. [11]YUN 1980, p. 548. [12]YUN 1983, p. 580, GA res. 38/192, 20 Dec. 1983. [13]A/39/38. [14]YUN 1983, p. 592. [15]*Ibid.*, p. 986, ESC res. 1983/49, 28 July 1983. [16]ID/B/C.3/133. [17]ID/B/327. [18]ID/B/C.3/129. [19]ID/B/340. [20]A/39/16 (conclusion 1984/14). [21]E/AC.51/1984/7 & Corr.1. [22]ID/B/C.3/130. [23]YUN 1979, p. 618. [24]A/39/376. [25]YUN 1983, p. 584, GA res. 38/193, 20 Dec. 1983. [26]A/39/800. [27]ID/CONF.5/46 & Corr.1 (res. 11). [28]ID/B/C.3/132. [29]ID/B/C.3/128. [30]A/INF/39/1. [31]A/39/16 (conclusion 1984/8). [32]ID/B/325. [33]ID/CONF.5/46 & Corr.1 (res. 10).

Industrial development activities

Technical co-operation

The UNIDO technical co-operation programme amounted to $87.2 million in 1984, compared to $78 million in 1983, according to a report of the Secretary-General[1] to the UNDP Governing Council; 1,503 projects were conducted in 136 countries. Activities were funded from UNDP main programmes (64.9 per cent) and UNDP-administered trust funds (4.2 per cent), from UNIDF and other trust funds (25.9 per cent) and from the regular programme (4.2 per cent).

Approved were 633 new projects totalling $73.5 million, compared to 509 valued at $70.5 million in 1983. The total value of new project approvals for LDCs exceeded $20 million, compared to $11.1 million the previous year.

The main areas of implementation, according to the Executive Director,[2] were the chemical, engineering and agricultural industries. The main thrust of the programme continued to be on industrial planning and programming (including the preparation of feasibility studies), industrial manpower development, industrial infrastructure, agro-based industries, and promotion of small- and medium-scale industries as well as rural industries based on local resource use.

Asia and the Pacific accounted for 35.8 per cent of project delivery; Africa, including African Arab States, 34.5 per cent; Arab States, excluding African Arab States, 4.7 per cent; the Americas, 10.3 per cent; Europe, 4.2 per cent; and global and interregional projects, 10.5 per cent. Of 1,132 newly appointed experts, 258 or 22.8 per cent came from developing countries.

Chemical industries accounted for $22.1 million of technical co-operation activities; engineering industries, $13.9 million; institutional infrastructure, $10.4 million; agro-industries, $9.7 million; metallurgical industries, $6.3 million; industrial planning, $5.8 million; training, $5.7 million; feasibility studies, $4.3 million; and factory establishment, $2.9 million. About $6.1 million was allotted to related activities.

By project component, personnel accounted for $42.5 million (48.7 per cent); sub-contracts, $12.2 million (14 per cent); fellowships and training, $11.7

million (13.4 per cent); equipment, $18.6 million (21.4 per cent); and miscellaneous, $2.2 million (2.5 per cent).

In Africa, UNIDO paid increasing attention to the need of countries to reorient their industrial policies and maximize use of domestic resources; emphasis was also placed on the production of key mass-consumption goods, including pharmaceuticals, low-cost building materials and agricultural implements, processing of agricultural products, promotion of small-scale industries, use of renewable energy resources, and manpower training. In the Americas, the development of capital goods industries continued to be emphasized in a number of countries; others aimed at satisfying basic food and health care needs, optimal use of local natural resources and aid to agro-based industries. Projects in the Arab States centred on provision of industrial advisory services, improvement of the capacity utilization of industries, processing of locally available raw materials and strengthening of industrial infrastructure. In Asia and the Pacific, assistance focused on the support of strategies adopted by Governments to strengthen their economies, with continued emphasis on metallurgical, engineering and textile industries. European requests for assistance were connected mainly with the strengthening of research institutions, acquisition of sophisticated technologies and training of national staff abroad.

Under the regular programme, UNIDO's activities amounted to $3.7 million. The regular programme was used essentially for the training of personnel from developing countries, particularly LDCs, in various industries. Group training was provided in the iron and steel industry and industrial information in the USSR, in the textile industry in Belgium, in management of industrial public enterprises in Madagascar, in energy efficiency for LDCs in the Philippines, in industrial utilization of medicinal herbs in Romania and in the expansion of small industrial enterprises in the United Republic of Tanzania. UNIDO received in 1984 an additional $1 million allocation from the regular budget for IDDA and for assistance to African countries and intergovernmental organizations in the formulation and implementation of programmes for the Decade.

A revision[3] of the tentative allocations of the reduced appropriation for the UNIDO regular programme of technical co-operation (allocations based on a requested $6,823,500 were revised downward to $6,610,600) for 1984-1985 was submitted by the Executive Director to the Industrial Development Board's 1984 session. On 19 May,[4] noting with concern that the real value of the resources for the UNIDO regular programme had been declining steadily since 1980 and stressing again the programme's importance, the Board

recommended to the General Assembly that its real value be maintained and approved the revised tentative allocations.

Evaluation study

The Secretary-General submitted to the 1984 session of CPC a comprehensive evaluation[5] of the UNDP-financed technical co-operation activities of UNIDO in the field of manufactures. Requested by CPC in 1980, the evaluation was based on a full staff evaluation report of 1 February 1983 prepared by three independent evaluation co-ordinators representing the United Nations Department of International Economic and Social Affairs, UNDP and UNIDO. The Secretary-General's study reviewed the recommendations contained in the staff report in terms of their acceptability to the bodies concerned and the extent to which they were being implemented.

Fifty-nine individual proposals were put forward under seven broad recommendations: redefining the roles, responsibilities, accountability and authority of the parties of the tripartite system (Governments, UNDP and the executing agency—in this case UNIDO); expansion of the country programme concept to include problem-solving at the sectoral and subsectoral levels; measures to improve essential elements in the project cycle (problem identification, formulation and approval, implementation, completion and follow-up); improvements in recruitment, staff training and staff redeployment; measures to improve UNIDO's functioning and effectiveness; redefining UNDP staff responsibilities, and changes in project design concepts and evaluation methodology; and follow-up action.

Neither of the intergovernmental bodies concerned—UNDP's Governing Council and UNIDO's Permanent Committee—was able to arrive at a consensus on any recommendation, but expressed their views on each proposal, for or against or with reservations. The Secretary-General recommended the continued assessment of the recommendations already being implemented, proposed follow-up action on recommendations considered feasible, and suggested approaches to recommendations which required further consideration or which appeared to be currently impracticable.

CPC's discussion, at its April-June session, focused on general comments on the evaluation and the methodology employed.[6] It was generally agreed that it would not deal with the substance of specific recommendations, but would concern itself with the modalities proposed by the Secretary-General for follow-up and monitoring of UNDP's and UNIDO's responses. It felt that in some cases technical clarifications were needed regarding the classification of certain of those responses. It asked that care be taken to ensure that resources devoted to evaluation did not adversely affect programme delivery.

A report[7] by the UNDP Administrator on which of the recommendations UNDP might accept was submitted to the 1984 organizational meeting of the UNDP Governing Council; on 23 February,[8] the Council noted that many of the recommendations had already been implemented, transmitted the report to CPC, and requested the Administrator to report on further action taken or on his recommendations for action. The Administrator reported[9] to the Council's June session on 28 recommendations directed to UNDP, including proposed follow-up actions; among the actions envisaged were studies to correct problem analysis and baseline data to clarify project design standards, and the modification of project formulation guidelines and of training for programming. On 18 June,[10] the Council endorsed the Administrator's proposed course of action.

A note by the secretariat,[11] reviewing the developments that followed discussions of the staff evaluation report by the UNIDO Permanent Committee at its 1983 session,[12] was submitted to the Committee at its November 1984 session. It included comments and observations on the Economic and Social Council's 26 July resolution (see immediately below) inviting the Industrial Development Board to take action on the recommendations in the staff report, and gave information on planned and carried-out activities by the secretariat regarding those recommendations. On 23 November,[13] the Committee requested the secretariat to report to it on future developments in order to assist the Board to keep implementation of the recommendations under review.

ECONOMIC AND SOCIAL COUNCIL ACTION

On 26 July, in considering the CPC report on its 1984 session, the Economic and Social Council adopted resolution 1984/61 A on programme planning and co-ordination, section V of which dealt with the evaluation of the UNDP-financed technical co-operation activities of UNIDO in the field of manufactures.

The Council invited the governing bodies of UNIDO and UNDP: to ensure that the recommendations reported as implemented under existing procedures and policies prior to the staff report would continue to be implemented systematically and followed up; to adopt and implement the recommendations reported as feasible but for which resources were not sufficient; and to give careful consideration to recommendations reported as requiring the attention of governing bodies and member States, to those reported by secretariats as being doubtful or unacceptable, and to others inviting the keeping under review of the recommendations on redefin-

UNIDO TECHNICAL CO-OPERATION AND SUPPORT EXPENDITURES BY PROGRAMME COMPONENT, 1984

(as at 31 December 1984; in thousands of US dollars)

Programme component	Technical co-operation	Support
Policy-making organs	—	1,963
Executive direction and management*	22	1,606
Policy co-ordination		
Economic co-operation among developing countries	266	450
Field reports monitoring	283	728
Inter-agency programme co-ordination	—	484
Least developed countries	136	558
Negotiations	246	2,030
New York Liaison Office	—	401
Non-governmental organizations	31	370
Programme development and evaluation	—	1,786
Programme formulation and direction	—	1,193
Subtotal	952	8,000
Industrial operations		
Agro-industries	9,675	1,027
Chemical industries	22,083	1,565
Engineering industries	13,913	912
Factory establishment and management	2,914	703
Feasibility studies	4,274	632
Industrial planning	5,794	707
Institutional infrastructure	10,407	1,065
Investment co-operative programme	3,178	1,327
Metallurgical industries	6,307	702
Programme formulation and direction	490	1,060
Project personnel recruitment†	—	1,457
Purchase and contract	—	1,155
Training	5,705	1,077
Subtotal	84,740	13,389
Industrial studies		
Development and transfer of technology	275	1,064
Global and conceptual studies	20	1,114
Industrial and Technological Information Bank	—	289
Industrial information	(1)	525
Programme formulation and direction	95	1,081
Regional and country studies	842	1,626
Sectoral studies	47	1,260
Technological advisory services	16	219
Subtotal	1,294	7,178
Conference services, public information and external relations	207	—
Conference service	—	6,153
Governments and intergovernmental organizations relations	—	354
IDB secretariat	—	266
Programme formulation and direction	—	242
Public information	—	666
Subtotal	207	7,681
Administrative and common services		
Financial service	—	2,241
General services	—	1,568
Legal service	—	185
Personnel service	—	2,067
Programme direction‡	—	1,855
Subtotal	—	7,916
Unspecified	(24)	—
Total	87,191	47,733

NOTE: Numbers in parentheses represent negative quantity.

*Including UNIDO representation at Geneva.

†Including Technical Assistance Recruitment Service at Geneva and in New York.

‡Including electronic data processing.

SOURCE: ID/B/340.

ing the roles within the tripartite system and calling attention to recommendations to which there was no response. Secretariats were to report further on the last-mentioned recommendations as well as on those reported as requiring their further attention, and Member States were invited to give careful consideration to those reported as being implemented and as requiring their attention.

Training of personnel

Expenditures for fellowships and training components in technical co-operation projects implemented by UNIDO in 1984 amounted to $11.7 million, compared to $11.4 million in 1983. Of that total, $6.3 million was spent for fellowships and study tours and $5.4 million for group training activities and meetings. A total of 196 projects were completed or being implemented.

The number of individual training programmes (fellowships) initiated in 1984 was 4.8 per cent higher than in 1983 (1,278 compared to 1,220), while the number of placement arrangements by host countries was higher by 11.1 per cent (2,166 compared to 1,949). Of those placements, 448 or 20.7 per cent were arranged in developing countries; 167 (13.1 per cent) of the trainees came from LDCs and 141 (11 per cent) were female.

Under a programme to build up institutions in developing countries to serve as training centres, training in production management techniques was transferred during 1984 from the University of Louvain in Belgium to the University of Douala in Cameroon; training activities related to institution building, the training of trainers, industry/university linkage and repair and maintenance. Cameroon agreed to share its training capacities with other French-speaking African countries as well as Lebanon to stimulate those countries to set up their own training programmes.

Special emphasis was given to the training of trainers in in-plant programmes on grain milling and storage in the USSR and on maintenance and repair of diesel engines in Czechoslovakia.

In Gabon, a multisectoral Institute of Applied Technology, Planning and Project Evaluation was established to train government officials and personnel of the Central African Customs and Economic Union. In the Ivory Coast, the Government contributed 70 per cent of the cost of strengthening the Centre ivoirien de gestion des entreprises, which offered courses and consultancy services in industrial management. In Nigeria, the Centre for Industrial Research and Development was assisted in organizing courses on the development of small-scale industry.

The Governing Council of the Association of African Development Finance Institutions approved, at Tunis in May, a five-year training programme for such institutions, aimed at fostering co-operation among them on institution building and the training of trainers from the national to the interregional level.

Industrial training activities involved the design of large-scale projects for which countries had been able to secure loans from the World Bank, including a rehabilitation programme for the sugar industry in the Sudan and extension of an industrial training and development centre in Turkey. UNIDO also co-operated with Turkey in assessing training and manpower needs with the objective of establishing a technological and manpower development centre for the iron and steel industry. In co-operation with the International Centre for Public Enterprises in Developing Countries, a group training programme was organized at Ljubljana, Yugoslavia, for manpower planning managers. A mission to selected Latin American countries identified training needs in repair and maintenance.

Within the framework of IDDA, a regional project of assistance to African countries and institutions in the development of manpower training was implemented. Egypt and Nigeria were selected on a pilot basis to host training programmes in 1985 for some 25 African managers in the foundry, sheet-metalworking and leather industries. A special training programme was developed for managers of management training institutions in African LDCs.

To enhance the role of women in the industrialization process, a workshop for the training of women industrial managers was organized (Vienna, 3-7 December) by UNIDO and the International Research and Training Institute for the Advancement of Women. The establishment of a training centre for women entrepreneurs at Indorra, India, was being considered by India and UNDP.

On 19 August,[14] the Fourth General Conference of UNIDO invited developing countries to make their education systems more responsive to changing industrial manpower needs and to consider establishing high-level co-ordinating bodies for human resources development programmes. They were invited to give special attention to the training of trainers and of women, youth and the disabled. It recommended that measures be taken against the brain drain and to promote the repatriation of skilled workers and professionals. It also recommended that UNIDO, with ILO, UNESCO and other United Nations agencies, help developing countries determine requirements and work out plans of action; organize training programmes for contract negotiators, energy management and the training of trainers; publish manuals, guidelines and check-lists on industrial plant maintenance; seek more expert assistance from developing countries; establish information channels between developing countries; continue efforts towards setting up international training in technology; and accord priority to African countries. It urged that developed countries increase their contributions to UNIDF for human resource development programmes for industrialization, particularly regional and subregional training centres. In addition, co-operation with development finance institutions should be strengthened, industrial projects should, where appropriate, include training as part of their costs, bilateral assistance should increasingly incorporate training programmes, assistance for travel of trainees should be provided, and contracts for the transfer of technology should include provisions for the necessary training.

Strengthening the SIDFA Programme

In 1984, the General Assembly, the Permanent Committee of the UNIDO Industrial Development Board and the UNDP Governing Council devoted considerable attention to the Senior Industrial Development Field Advisers (SIDFA) Programme and its financing. SIDFAs assisted in programming and implementing technical co-operation projects.

A February 1984 report by the UNDP Administrator[15] concluded that, while SIDFAs served a vital function and enjoyed broad support in developing countries, the Programme's financial foundation remained shaky; the Administrator proposed that UNDP continue to provide financial support to the SIDFA Programme to the end of 1986. On 29 June,[16] the Governing Council approved an allocation of $2,031,000, subject to resource availability, for SIDFAs in 1986, together with any savings from previous years. It also authorized the Administrator to finance the maximum number of advisers possible; urged continued consultations with UNIDO and recipient countries on cost-sharing; urged continued close collaboration of SIDFAs with other United Nations agency field representatives; reaffirmed that priority be given in the provision of SIDFA services to those countries which had shared in their cost; appealed for voluntary contributions to increase SIDFAs; and asked the Administrator to report in 1985 on the current and future development of sectoral support, and to ensure that sectoral advisers were associated with the preparation of round-table meetings for LDCs.

On 19 May,[17] the Industrial Development Board decided that the SIDFA Programme would be discussed by the Permanent Committee at its November session. A September report[18] by the Executive Director on the UNIDO network of SIDFAs included a statistical breakdown of SIDFAs contracted by region since 1967, and information on the Programme's financial situation and perspectives for 1985 and 1986. The Permanent Committee noted on 23 November[13] that the available resources might decline, invited the UNDP Council to explore ways of locating additional resources, renewed an appeal to all member States, particularly developed countries, to make contributions, and requested the Executive Director to seek additional resources. The Committee stressed that the Programme should be maintained in 1985 at 30 posts and recommended that the General Assembly consider the question. The Executive Director was to report on progress to the Board in 1985.

In December, the Assembly, in section II of resolution 39/232, appealed to developed countries to provide maximum contributions for the SIDFA Programme, and decided that in 1985 provision would be made in the regular budget for maintaining the existing number of SIDFA posts. Paragraph 2 of section II, deciding on the 1985 budget provision, was adopted by recorded vote in the Second Committee and the Assembly (for votes and explanations of vote see above, under "Programme and finances of UNIDO"). Subsequently, the Assembly granted UNIDO an additional $1,135,000 from the regular budget for 1985 to finance nine SIDFA posts.

Contributions to SIDFA had been received in the past from Austria, Finland and Japan. Italy announced a contribution in 1984, the details of which were to be negotiated. Some developing countries had also contributed to UNDP for the local cost of SIDFA offices; others were indirectly contributing to the SIDFA Programme by sharing the cost of UNDP offices.

At the end of 1984, 29 SIDFAs and one project manager acting as a SIDFA were in place. A second regional SIDFA meeting for Latin America and the Caribbean (Mexico City, 10-15 December) analysed UNIDO activities in the region and identified ways SIDFAs might strengthen them.

Despite budgetary constraints, the Junior Professional Officer (JPO) programme, which supported UNIDO technical co-operation projects, was expanded in 1984; 22 new JPOs were recruited, and the number of JPOs was increased to 65, from 55 in 1983. A training course in project design, formulation and evaluation, attended by 13 JPOs and representatives of several donor countries, was held in November. At the end of the year, the programme was receiving support from Belgium, Denmark, Finland, the Federal Republic of Germany, Italy, Japan, the Netherlands, Norway, Sweden and Switzerland.

Special Industrial Services

The Special Industrial Services (SIS) programme enabled UNIDO to meet urgent requests for assistance from developing countries by providing them with high-level advisory missions.

During 1984, 86 new projects were approved and 25 projects were extended at a cost of $2.7 million. Assistance was provided mainly to the metallurgical and chemical industries, agro-industries, engineering industries and factory establishment and management.

In Ethiopia, SIS drew up a rehabilitation and development plan for a fibreboard plant. In the Cook Islands, it studied the possibilities of creating a cottage industry for salt production. In Mongolia, it repaired and calibrated tensile testing machinery at a leather research centre at Ulan Bator. In Bolivia, technical problems at a glass factory were diagnosed and a plan for improvements formulated. In the Dominican Republic, recommendations were made in connection with the introduction of new technology at a sugar plant. In Sierra Leone, the operations of a garment manufacturing plant were brought up to date.

Industrial co-operation

System of Consultations

The Industrial Development Board began an appraisal of the System of Consultations, a mechanism for identifying possible areas for technical co-operation, at its May 1984 session and decided to continue the appraisal in 1985. The secretariat undertook to examine the implementation of recommendations made by the consultation meetings, to discover areas of strength and weakness, and to consider possible corrective measures. Problems in co-ordination had come to light and possibilities had been identified for greater interaction between member States and the secretariat.

Three sectoral consultations were held in 1984: on the fertilizer industry (the fourth on this topic), on the leather and leather products industry (third) and on the food-processing industry with special emphasis on vegetable oils and fats (second), bringing to 24 the number of consultation meetings since 1977.

On 19 May 1984,[19] the Board took note of the UNIDO Executive Director's report on the 1983 consultations.[20] Responding to a July 1983 request by the Economic and Social Council,[21] the Board decided that work on wood and the wood products industry and on industrial financing should continue and that the question of including pesticides within the System of Consultations was to be taken up in 1985. The Board endorsed a proposed co-sponsorship with the United Nations Centre for Human Settlements of the first consultation on the building materials industry. To obtain a better appraisal of the System, it requested the UNIDO Executive Director to provide, each biennium, detailed information on expenditure for its activities, and invited member States to transmit to him their views on possible improve-

ments; the Board President was asked to organize informal open-ended meetings with member States to exchange views on the States' suggestions. To ensure greater participation by LDCs in consultation meetings, the General Assembly should determine the sources from which to pay the costs for 50 representatives from those countries in 1984-1985.

On 23 May,[22] CPC took note of the Board's decision when it considered the UNIDO work programme for 1984-1985. Following a statement by the secretariat on implementation of its 1983 suggestions[20] on revising or merging various programme elements of the System of Consultations, endorsed by the Economic and Social Council,[21] CPC said it regretted it had not been provided with the requested report on that programme. CPC agreed that the financial aspects should be considered by ACABQ, and recommended that UNIDO continue to see to the improvement of the System, taking into account the views of the developing countries concerned.

On 18 December, in adopting resolution 39/235 on world industrial restructuring and redeployment, the General Assembly recommended that the System of Consultations should cover industrial sectors of particular interest to developing countries, hold more regional consultation meetings, in particular in relation to IDDA, seek to identify specific areas and forms of co-operation, and explore ways to promote industrial co-operation at subregional, regional and international levels.

Co-operation among developing countries

UNIDO activities to promote economic and technical co-operation among developing countries during 1984 again focused on: organizing solidarity ministerial meetings in LDCs and round-table ministerial meetings, to bring together developing countries for the promotion of industrial development; following up decisions made at such meetings; developing joint programmes for specific industrial subsectors; implementing recommendations reached through the System of Consultations (see above); and developing a work programme based on the recommendations adopted by the 1981 High Level Conference on Economic Co-operation among Developing Countries.[23] Particular emphasis was placed on activities in support of IDDA.

Solidarity meetings were organized in Yemen (25-30 March) and Rwanda (5-8 June) in 1984. Offers of assistance to Yemen included grants from Oman and Algeria for specific projects; training from India; expert services in cotton ginning and shelling from China; and a feasibility study of the tannery industry from Yugoslavia. Offers of assistance to Rwanda were received for pre-investment and feasibility studies, training and provision of equipment, such as an offer by China to carry out a study on the production of cement bags and an offer by Yugoslavia to assist in the establishment of industrial estates.

In co-operation with ESCAP, a seminar for promoting co-operation in manufacturing and popularization of agricultural machinery, tools and equipment was held in China from 8 to 25 May. A joint UNIDO/Yugoslavia programme at the fifty-first International Agricultural Fair (Novi Sad, 14-17 May) promoted co-operation in the development of agro-industries with emphasis on food processing. Regional workshops on the integration of women in the industrial planning and development process (Harare, 9-17 April; Georgetown, 6-12 May; Bangkok, 5-12 July) considered joint activities, an improved information flow, and possible joint information networks. Orientation visits and exchanges of experience continued to form part of the co-operation programme of UNIDO.

A new approach to co-operation between two or more countries in programmes financed under trust-fund arrangements was studied. An agreement was concluded between China and the Libyan Arab Jamahiriya in December, under which Chinese manufacturing enterprises would provide directly, or through UNIDO, plant operational personnel in the iron and steel and petrochemical industries.

On 19 August,[24] the Fourth General Conference of UNIDO adopted a resolution recommending that the developing countries co-operate in sharing information and facilitating the flow of human, scientific, energy and financial resources as well as increasing direct investment among themselves and increasing South-South trade. It invited the developed countries to support economic co-operation among developing countries through increased contributions to UNDP and UNIDF. It requested UNIDO to accord high priority to and support more actively industrial co-operation among developing countries and assist their efforts undertaken for such purposes as planning industrial development and carrying out studies on industrial technology, co-ordinating industrialization policies and carrying out consultations, exchanging information, studying and adopting industrial agreements, establishing joint ventures, promoting investments, increasing capital investment flow and establishing regional consultancy networks. It also requested UNIDO to improve its programme of solidarity ministerial meetings for LDCs, strengthen its technological information exchange mechanisms and project development services, and arrange joint industrial investment promotion ventures. (See also p. 400.)

International trade aspects

Work on trade and trade-related aspects of industrial collaboration was conducted during 1984 as a complement to activities carried out in implementing the recommendations of sectoral consultations. Activities relating to contractual arrangements between enterprises included the preparation of check-lists, guidelines and model forms of agreements for the fertilizer, petrochemical, pharmaceutical, agricultural machinery, leather and leather products and food-processing industries as well as training. An exchange of information took place with other international institutions whose work touched on similarly relevant areas.

A report[25] on industrial collaboration at the enterprise level reviewed its main characteristics and the factors conducive to its further development.

On 19 May,[19] following its consideration of the System of Consultations (see above), the Industrial Development Board reconfirmed a 1982 Board decision[26] to examine further joint UNCTAD/UNIDO work on trade and trade-related aspects of industrial collaboration arrangements, and asked the Executive Director to report to it in 1985.

Industrial co-operation contracts

UNCITRAL activities. The Working Group on the New International Economic Order of the United Nations Commission on International Trade Law (UNCITRAL), at its fifth session (New York, 23 January–3 February 1984),[27] considered draft chapters of the legal guide on drawing up international contracts for the supply and construction of industrial works. The chapters dealt with variation clauses, assignment, suspension of construction, termination, inspection and tests, failure to perform and damages. The guide's format also was discussed. There was general agreement that work on the guide should proceed as quickly as possible and that whenever feasible the Working Group should hold two sessions every year.

At its sixth session (Vienna, 10-20 September),[28] the Working Group took up additional chapters of the guide. These covered the scope and quality of works, completion, acceptance and take-over, allocation of risk of loss or damage, liquidated damages and penalty clauses, insurance, sub-contracting, and security for performance. The UNCITRAL Secretary stated that the secretariat would submit to the Group's seventh session in 1985 a revised draft outline of the guide's structure that would reflect the Group's deliberations and contain some rearrangement and amalgamation of certain chapters.

At its June/July session,[29] UNCITRAL expressed satisfaction with the work on the guide thus far, and agreed that two sessions of the Working Group should be held before the Commission's 1985 session. (See also LEGAL QUESTIONS, Chapter VI.)

Industrial development of LDCs

UNIDO continued its efforts in 1984 to assist LDCs, with the main thrust of technical co-operation programmes focusing on industrial planning and programming (including the preparation of pre-feasibility and feasibility studies), industrial manpower development, industrial infrastructure, agro-based industries, and promotion of small- and medium-scale as well as rural industries based on the utilization of local resources.

Despite financial constraints, new project approvals increased significantly in 1984 compared to 1983, although some of the UNDP-financed projects had been developed in 1983 or earlier but constraints had deferred their approval.

UNIDO continued to try to mobilize additional resources through contacts with such agencies as the United Nations Capital Development Fund (UNCDF), the World Bank and regional financial institutions. Co-operation with UNCDF led to the development of additional projects to be carried out by UNIDO and funded jointly by UNDCF and UNDP, two of which were approved in 1984. A number of projects developed in co-operation with the World Bank were being implemented.

Financial support was provided to enable the representatives of LDCs to participate at consultation meetings on fertilizers, leather and leather products and food processing (see above). UNIDO fielded seven programme review and six project formulation missions in a number of LDCs.

As part of UNIDO's advisory services, an investment promotion meeting was held at Kathmandu, Nepal (4-7 June); a portfolio of projects was distributed to financial institutions and private investors attending the meeting. Within its energy programme, UNIDO provided technical assistance to the Niger in developing improved cooking stoves, and conducted studies on the establishment of a mini-hydroelectric plant and a unit for the promotion of solar equipment in Mali. Preparatory work also was initiated to develop mini-hydroelectric plants for rural areas in selected LDCs in Africa. In manpower development, UNIDO accorded high priority to group training programmes and seminars designed for LDCs, covering small-scale foundry operations, energy conservation, medicinal plants, project preparation and evaluation, and management of small-scale industries. Projects in water management, agricultural implement production and energy

were begun in the Sudano-Sahelian zone and two projects in building materials were initiated in Chad. UNIDO completed three studies on resource-based industries, bringing the total to 11, and also completed two country industrial development reviews.

On 19 May,[30] the Industrial Development Board expressed concern about the continued limitation of resources for the UNIDO programme of technical co-operation for LDCs, and reiterated its call on the industrialized countries in particular to increase their contributions to UNIDF, with flexibility of use, and to raise special-purpose contributions for the Fund component on special measures for industrial development of the least developed, land-locked and island developing countries. It requested the secretariat to contribute to and participate in the mid-term global review of the implementation of the Substantial New Programme of Action for the 1980s for LDCs,[31] scheduled for 1985.

Serious concern was expressed at the Fourth General Conference of UNIDO about the continuing deterioration of the economic and social situation of LDCs, the low level of industrialization and the slow growth in manufacturing value added in those countries.

On 19 August,[32] the Conference reaffirmed the commitment of the international community to SNPA, called on countries to facilitate the transfer of technology and provide assistance to LDCs, and recommended the promotion of co-operation between LDCs and other developing countries. It requested UNIDO to strengthen further its programme for LDCs and its capacity to assist them in formulating industrial policies, to assist in the establishment of pilot plants and other instruments to promote technology suited to their needs and in studying LDC potential in raw materials processing, to co-operate more closely with UNDP and other organizations in organizing round-table conferences of consultative groups, and to improve the efficiency of and expand its solidarity meetings for LDCs. (See also p. 415.)

Redeployment of industrial production to developing countries

In a February 1984 report[33] to the Industrial Development Board, the Executive Director gave a global overview of the findings of UNIDO studies in 1983 on industrial redeployment and restructuring. He stated that the pace and scope of structural adjustment were being constrained by worldwide low economic growth, structural rigidities and social considerations in developed countries and inefficiencies in resource allocations and other constraints in developing countries. Development in third world countries was being hampered by prevailing uncertainties, trade and industrial policies, and the large gaps between existing and optimum industrial structures and between available and required resources. Both export-oriented industrial development and endeavours to upgrade production structures were being restrained by falling export earnings in developing countries and protectionism in developed countries.

He concluded that it would seem crucial to support national restructuring efforts, to formulate international and regional approaches, to identify new modes of co-operation reflecting the need for technological upgrading and rehabilitation of industry in developing countries and the need for market access in developed countries, and to establish schemes for South-South co-operation.

On 19 May,[34] the Board reaffirmed the continuing need for UNIDO to study the process of restructuring world industrial production, urged member States to facilitate restructuring through international co-operation, and requested the Executive Director to report in 1985 on how UNIDO could strengthen its role.

In a letter of 17 September,[35] the President of the Fourth General Conference of UNIDO transmitted to the Secretary-General for consideration by the General Assembly a draft resolution on world industrial restructuring and redeployment which had been considered by the Conference; in spite of several efforts, Conference Committee I had been unable to produce a text acceptable for adoption by the Conference.

GENERAL ASSEMBLY ACTION

The Second Committee was informed on 14 December that a consensus had been reached, following informal consultations, on the text of the draft resolution on world industrial restructuring which had been referred to the Assembly by the Fourth General Conference.

On 18 December, on the recommendation of the Second Committee, the Assembly adopted the consensus text without vote as resolution 39/235.

World industrial restructuring and redeployment
The General Assembly,

Recalling the Lima Declaration and Plan of Action on Industrial Development and Co-operation, in which were laid down the main measures and principles for industrial development and co-operation within the framework of the establishment of the new international economic order, and the New Delhi Declaration and Plan of Action on Industrialization of Developing Countries and International Co-operation for their Industrial Development, in which a strategy was spelt out for the further industrialization of developing countries,

Recalling that the Lima Declaration and Plan of Action on Industrial Development and Co-operation elaborated a framework for global industrial restructuring and redeployment and established a target for the developing countries' share of world industrial production,

Reaffirming that the attainment of the targets contained in the International Development Strategy for the Third United Nations Development Decade, aimed at, *inter alia*, raising the share of the developing countries in world industrial production in accordance with the Lima Declaration and Plan of Action, calls for far-reaching changes in the structure of world production,

Further reaffirming that policies that maintain internationally less competitive industries through subsidies and other protective measures should be avoided, thus facilitating redeployment of such industries from developed to developing countries,

Bearing in mind that new technological advances and the current global economic situation require innovative approaches to world industrial restructuring,

Stressing the importance of redeployment of industry from industrialized to developing countries on the principle of dynamic comparative advantage, in conjunction with structural adjustment, and reaffirming that restructuring and redeployment should be carried out in accordance with the national policies and priorities of Member States, in particular of the developing countries,

Affirming that industrial restructuring as a long-term process should encompass not only the establishment of manufacturing capacities in the developing countries but also the capacity to manage, expand, adapt and direct industrial development as part of their national development process,

Recalling resolution 159(VI) of 2 July 1983 of the United Nations Conference on Trade and Development, in which it stressed the importance of access to international markets for products of developing countries,

Bearing in mind the importance of economic and social effects of restructuring and redeployment,

Recalling that the System of Consultations, as an important and established activity of the United Nations Industrial Development Organization, is, *inter alia*, a valuable framework for identifying problems associated with the industrialization of developing countries, for considering ways and means at the national, regional and international levels to accelerate their industrialization and for fostering closer industrial co-operation among member countries, in accordance with the Lima Declaration and Plan of Action, as well as other relevant conclusions, decisions and resolutions agreed upon in the past by the United Nations,

Convinced that industrial financing is a key factor in this context in each case,

Stressing that the appraisal of the System of Consultations initiated by the Industrial Development Board at its eighteenth session should result in the improving of the System and in making it more result-oriented in order to achieve its fundamental objectives as laid down in the Lima Declaration and Plan of Action, and in the principles, objectives and characteristics of the System of Consultations,

Affirming that the System of Consultations should provide avenues for the exchange of information and views and therefrom, *inter alia*, to the identification of specific areas and forms of co-operation, and would also permit negotiations among interested parties, at their request, at the same time as or after the Consultations,

Recognizing the increasing interdependence of all countries of the world as a base of international economic co-operation,

1. *Invites* developing countries to co-ordinate their efforts and policies in order to facilitate world industrial restructuring and redeployment;

2. *Calls upon* developing countries to promote their own regional multinational enterprises for the implementation of industrial projects of common interest;

3. *Urges* developed countries to pursue appropriate positive adjustment policies and measures that facilitate world industrial restructuring with minimal disruptions, which policies should seek to avoid negative effects on the industrial development of developing countries;

4. *Invites* the developed countries to fulfil their commitments to halt protectionism by fully implementing and strictly adhering to the stand-still provisions they have accepted, in particular concerning imports from developing countries, and to work systematically towards reducing and eliminating quantitative restrictions and measures having similar effect and to support efforts by developing countries to attain full utilization of industrial capacity, with importance being attached by interested countries to the promotion of foreign and domestic investment through an adequate and mutually beneficial framework for investment;

5. *Requests* the United Nations Industrial Development Organization:

(a) To strengthen its activities in the fields of technical assistance, feasibility studies, advisory services, analysis of opportunities, assistance in the formulation of national development programmes and investment promotion in sectors in which industrial restructuring is taking place, in order to facilitate industrial restructuring and redeployment;

(b) To improve its ability to respond adequately and promptly to requests from Member States for information relating to industrial restructuring and related policies and, for this purpose, to maintain close collaboration with the relevant United Nations bodies and organizations working in this field, as well as with relevant economic research institutes;

(c) To continue, in accordance with its mandate, to work in close co-operation and collaboration with the United Nations Conference on Trade and Development and relevant international organizations in industrial restructuring and redeployment;

(d) To continue to prepare case studies on social and economic implications of industrial restructuring and redeployment in developing countries;

6. *Recommends* that the System of Consultations should:

(a) Cover industrial sectors of particular interest to developing countries;

(b) Hold more regional consultation meetings, in particular in relation to the Industrial Development Decade for Africa, within the agreed framework for the System;

(c) Seek to identify specific areas and forms of co-operation;

(d) Explore means and practical measures for the promotion of industrial co-operation at subregional, regional and international levels;

7. *Recommends* strengthening the Investment Promotion Services of the United Nations Industrial Development Organization by continuing, where appropriate, to build a network of national promotion centres in developed and developing countries; that these services should actively mobilize outside resources for identified investment projects, especially those related to the implementation of the Industrial Development Decade for Africa, maintain close co-ordination with developing countries' industrial development programmes and promote projects falling within the national objectives and priorities of developing countries.

General Assembly resolution 39/235

18 December 1984   Meeting 104   Adopted without vote

Approved by Second Committee (A/39/790/Add.4) without vote, 14 December (meeting 60); draft by Vice-Chairman (A/C.2/39/L.140), based on informal consultations on draft referred by Fourth General Conference of UNIDO (ID/CONF.5/C.1/L.13); agenda item 80 (d).

The Ukrainian SSR, on behalf of the Eastern European States, pointed out that, although they had not opposed the adoption of the draft, those States believed that proposals to intensify investment activities should be considered solely in the context of assistance to developing countries; the vain attempts by certain Western countries during the informal consultations on the draft to convince other delegations of the "great importance" of foreign investments were inadmissible. Neither the System of Consultations nor any other UNIDO activity should be used as a means for private foreign capital to penetrate developing countries' economies.

On 18 December, on the recommendation of the Second Committee, the Assembly adopted without vote decision 39/446.

World industrial restructuring and redeployment

At its 104th plenary meeting, on 18 December 1984, the General Assembly, on the recommendation of the Second Committee, requested the Secretary-General to issue the text of resolution 39/235 as an addendum to the report of the Fourth General Conference of the United Nations Industrial Development Organization.

General Assembly decision 39/446

Adopted without vote

Approved by Second Committee (A/39/790/Add.4) without vote, 14 December (meeting 60); oral proposal by Vice-Chairman; agenda item 80 (d).

Industrial financing

On 19 May,[19] the Industrial Development Board decided, with respect to the work programme of the System of Consultations (see above), that work on industrial financing should be pursued with regard to each sector on which consultations had been scheduled.

The President of the Fourth General Conference of UNIDO in September forwarded to the Secretary-General[35] a draft resolution on mobilization of financial resources for industrial development on which no consensus agreement had been reached, with a request that the General Assembly consider it at its 1984 session. By the draft, the Conference, in agreed provisions, would have: recommended that consideration be given to providing adequate financial support for the developing countries to meet their industrialization needs and that developed countries promote increased investment in the developing countries; invited member States to consider promoting agreements on co-production, joint ventures, export-oriented manufacturing and the incorporation of technology through licensing and engineering contracts; and urged developed countries to implement their commitments on aid volume as set out in the International Development Strategy for the Third United Nations Development Decade[36] and SNPA.[31] It would have urged the international community to intensify financial and technical co-operation with African countries and regional and subregional industrial development organizations. It also would have requested UNIDO: to co-operate increasingly with regional organizations and international financial institutions, particularly the World Bank; to prepare projects for consideration by multilateral development institutions; to continue its studies of the industrial investment requirements of selected developing countries and assist them, especially LDCs, to design industrial projects that would attract domestic and foreign resources; and to study mechanisms used by developed and developing countries for mobilizing savings and utilizing financial resources effectively.

GENERAL ASSEMBLY ACTION

On 18 December, on the recommendation of the Second Committee, the General Assembly adopted without vote decision 39/447.

Mobilization of financial resources for industrial development

At its 104th plenary meeting, on 18 December 1984, the General Assembly, on the recommendation of the Second Committee, decided to refer to its fortieth session for consideration the draft resolution entitled "Mobilization of financial resources for industrial development", annexed to the letter dated 17 September 1984 from the President of the Fourth General Conference of the United Nations Industrial Development Organization to the Secretary-General.

General Assembly decision 39/447

Adopted without vote

Approved by Second Committee (A/39/790/Add.4) without vote, 14 December (meeting 60); oral proposal by Vice-Chairman; agenda item 80 *(d)*.

Proposed international bank for industrial development

At its May 1984 session, the Industrial Development Board again considered a 1981 proposal[37] by the UNIDO Executive Director for the establishment of an international bank for industrial development. The Board was unable to come to an agreement, and requested[38] the Executive Direc-

tor to submit a report on the question in 1985 in the light of deliberations at the Fourth General Conference.

Investment promotion

The network of UNIDO Investment Promotion Services, almost exclusively supported by host country contributions, made it possible for developing countries to have direct access to technological, managerial and financial sources in industrialized countries. Currently, UNIDO had Services in Cologne, New York, Paris, Tokyo, Vienna, Warsaw and Zurich. The Brussels Service was phased out at the end of October. Negotiations were under way for a Service to be opened in Milan, Italy, in 1985, as well as in Seoul, Republic of Korea, and discussions were under way with Brazil, India, Mexico and countries of the Gulf region. The Tokyo Service was again extended, to 30 June 1986.

During the year, the Services launched 47 industrial projects in 26 developing countries with a known total investment value of about $165 million. Sixteen country presentation meetings were organized for Cameroon, the Caribbean countries, Chile, China, Nepal, Senegal, Sri Lanka, the South Pacific countries and Uruguay; representatives of developing countries met with industrialists, financiers and members of professional and government institutions and informed them about their countries' material and human resources, investment laws and potential investment sectors and projects.

Five national and regional investment promotion meetings (investors' forums) were held for Nepal (Kathmandu, 4-7 June), Colombia (Bogotá, 2-5 July), Caribbean countries (Bridgetown, Barbados, 22-25 October), the South Pacific (Suva, Fiji, 26-30 November) and west Africa (Dakar, Senegal, 3-6 December). At the Kathmandu meeting, 51 industrial investment projects were discussed, resulting in the signing of 16 letters of intent. The investors' forum at Bogotá considered 97 projects. The Caribbean meeting discussed 177 proposals and concluded with the signing of at least 15 letters of intent, while the South Pacific meeting took up 109 proposals and some 30 letters of intent were signed. At the west Africa forum, 155 projects were presented and promoted.

In adopting resolution 39/235 on 18 December, concerning world industrial restructuring and redeployment, the Assembly recommended that UNIDO's Investment Promotion Services continue building a network of national promotion centres in developed and developing countries, and that they actively mobilize outside resources for identified investment projects, maintain close coordination with developing countries' industrial development programmes and promote projects within national objectives and priorities.

Industrial processing of raw materials

On 19 August,[39] the Fourth General Conference of UNIDO recommended that developing countries adopt policies for the domestic processing of raw materials in order to achieve their optimal utilization, and that UNIDO promote such processing, especially in LDCs and African countries, prepare specific case-studies on the subject, identify training opportunities, examine approaches, existing standards and new product standards, and intensify its technical co-operation programmes. It invited countries to facilitate finance flow and the development of technology, capital and human resources for domestic industrial processing, and invited developed countries to halt protectionism by adhering to accepted standstill provisions.

Rural areas

To cope with problems such as rural unemployment and economic stagnation, UNIDO rural industrialization activities concentrated in 1984 on creating development poles around which industries could be interlinked. Projects were developed to offer special facilities, including training and production centres, pilot and demonstration plants and mobile facilities for on-the-spot technical assistance. Mobile facilities were put into operation in Zaire and Zambia, providing repair and maintenance service for industrial machinery in isolated areas.

The Fourth General Conference of UNIDO stressed the importance of rural development, of which rural industrialization was the prime catalyst. There was a trend in developing countries towards more intensive valorization of locally available raw materials in rural areas to reduce imports.

On 19 August,[40] the Conference called for co-operation in agro-industrial development. It recommended the establishment of national industrial development centres, programmes to develop small rural enterprises to attract private investment as well as State and co-operative enterprises, and programmes to minimize the effects of natural calamities. It recommended that UNIDO: assist in developing policies for integrated rural development and in implementing industrial components for rural development programmes; continue its studies relating to rural industrialization; examine the possibility of projects relating to consultancy service centres and rural industrial workshops; strengthen its activities in fertilizer and pesticide production, agricultural machinery, storage facilities and the rural artisan sector; and pay greater attention to the small enterprises of different social and organizational structures. It invited all countries to provide technical, financial and other assistance to developing countries and invited the developed countries to fulfil commitments to halt protectionism concerning imports from developing countries.

Industrial management

During 1984, industrial management assistance continued for the improvement of production capacity in sectors ranging from shipbuilding to fruit processing and textile production. Solutions included the introduction of micro-computers with appropriate software. UNIDO expenditures for factory establishment and management amounted to $2.9 million, with some 90 per cent supplied by UNDP; 50 projects were implemented.

Overall trends continued to indicate the need of developing countries for self-reliance in management, business development, production and plant organization. In view of limited funds for large-scale factory construction projects, a different approach to technical co-operation was being adopted, whereby seminars would tackle specific management problems, particularly in Africa.

Management problems, involving organization, production processes, equipment and plant maintenance, materials handling, inventory control, financial management, marketing and distribution, had proved most intractable in Africa. They had been aggravated by the adverse world economic situation, the shortage of foreign exchange for spare parts and raw materials, and environmental difficulties such as drought.

In Somalia and Malawi, assistance continued on improving the performance of industrial enterprises. Sectoral approaches to management problems showed positive results in the Sudan. A project to improve the financial management of enterprises in Zaire continued, with the Government requesting 14 additional experts and UNDP increasing its funding. In Mauritania, assistance provided by UNIDF enabled the setting up of a programme for industrial promotion, which included entrepreneurship development and management assistance to enterprises.

Two projects in energy management were initiated in Sri Lanka: the first provided energy measuring equipment for principal industrial subsectors as well as training programmes and consultancy services; the second concerned the establishment of an industrial energy management unit. In the Philippines, energy audits identified potential savings of $5 million in 30 facilities through more efficient use of fuel. Energy management proposals were prepared for the African region in connection with IDDA and energy-related activities were also being pursued in Thailand, Turkey and Viet Nam.

Efforts were also made to assist developing countries in the use of computers and in designing software. A computer-based management information system was designed for a Barbados development corporation. A workshop on dynamic simulation and operational gaming as teaching and research tools was held at Balaton Fured, Hungary, from 2 to 7 September. Other computer-related projects were designed for Cuba, Democratic Yemen, Fiji, Mexico, the Philippines, Somalia, the Sudan and Zaire.

A substantial number of countries, particularly in Africa, expressed interest in obtaining UNIDO assistance in the rehabilitation of industries. In Senegal, changes undertaken in management/marketing and the technical organization of shipyards at Dakar resulted in increased productivity as well as better use of machinery and infrastructure. A project in Somalia brought about improvements in the only textile factory in the country, where UNIDO was currently arranging training programmes for technical and management staff. In Sierra Leone, a fruit-processing factory producing jams and jellies received rehabilitation assistance.

A number of requests for industrial consultancy were met, as efforts to develop local consultancy capacities continued. In Egypt, short-term consultancy services were provided in numerous fields, while experts strengthened functions at the Ministry of Industry, eliminated obstacles at plant level, developed products for export, and advised on marketing. Experts provided by Spain through UNIDO developed local consultancy services in Uruguay. In the Syrian Arab Republic, in co-operation with the University of Aleppo, assistance was provided in developing a consultancy programme for the establishment and management of factories.

Industrial planning

Expenditures on industrial planning in 1984 totalled $5.8 million, with 80 per cent coming from UNDP. Of that amount, Africa accounted for 41 per cent; the Americas, 17 per cent; Arab States, 4 per cent; Asia and the Pacific, 36 per cent; and Europe and interregional/global, 1 per cent each. A total of 67 projects were implemented or being implemented.

Planning activities included: an assessment of industrial development at sectoral and subsectoral levels; the identification of subsectors with development potential and comparative advantage; formulation of medium- and long-range master plans; preparation of subsectoral plans, particularly for the capital goods industry; restructuring; formulation of policies and policy measures; strengthening of technical and institutional capabilities; and promotion of multinational and regional co-operation.

The number of requests for UNIDO assistance in preparing medium-term industrial master plans with long-term perspectives increased during 1984. A study was completed of 14 industrial subsectors under the industrial master plan project in Malaysia. Similar assistance was provided by UNIDO in the Ivory Coast and Mali, and a plan for the manufacturing sector was prepared for Kenya. In Cameroon, the second phase of preparing a master plan began, under which sectoral studies were to cover the key subsectors of iron and steel, aluminium, petrochemicals and wood and agro-industries; market analysis and projections for selected industrial products would be made to the year 2000.

Many developing countries sought UNIDO assistance in reorienting their industrial structures. In Thailand, UNIDO helped to examine the structure and performance of the automotive, mechanical, iron and steel, petrochemicals and textile subsectors; a number of seminars were organized on industrial restructuring. Similar assistance was provided in Guinea and the Ivory Coast.

Consultancy services to Qatar focused on the diversification of its oil-based economic structure. Pakistan was assisted in establishing a computerized data bank for formulating and monitoring industrial plans and policies.

In Latin America, emphasis continued to be placed on programmed development of capital goods industries. A large-scale development programme in Mexico focused on the reorientation of its capital goods programme in the light of the financial crisis; an analysis was made of steel fabrication plants, with recommendations for production streamlining, technological improvements and financial requirements. A project in Venezuela concentrated on strategies for the development of the capital goods sector, production in the petroleum and electric sectors, a programme for manufacturers of equipment for the foundry, forging and steel industries, and development of a technological information centre.

Industrial planning in many developing countries suffered from insufficient co-ordination between the ministry of industry and other ministries and institutions. In 1984, UNIDO assisted several countries, among them Mali and Guinea, with those matters.

Within the framework of IDDA, assistance was given to African countries in putting together integrated subregional industrial promotion programmes and to regional organizations in identifying projects for key industrial subsectors and strengthening subregional co-operation. The West African Economic Community was assisted in sectoral studies in the glass container, fertilizer and iron and steel industries, with a view to creating viable subregional industrial units; market studies were conducted and projections prepared for periods of 10 to 15 years.

An expert group meeting on industrial planning (Kiev, Ukrainian SSR, 21-25 May) was held for senior planners and economists from countries around the world. Another (Vienna, 10-13 September) followed up on a survey by UNIDO consultants of the manufacturing industry in the West Bank and Gaza Strip; ways of improving current economic conditions in the occupied territories were considered.

Industrial studies

Through its industrial studies and research programme, whose activities were closely interrelated at the global, regional, country and sectoral levels, UNIDO aimed at a balance between examining in detail the whole range of problems related to accelerating industrialization and providing conceptual, empirical and statistical background for use by decision makers and in technical co-operation programmes.

During 1984, UNIDO studied the impact of world economic developments on industrialization in developing countries. A preliminary assessment of the impact of the protectionist policies of the European Economic Community was made, and an empirical study of the foreign exchange benefits and costs of exporting manufactures was initiated. Up-to-date estimates and short-term forecasts of the growth of economic and industrial output were prepared on a country, regional and global basis. Other studies included assessments of the effect on developing countries of recent changes in the automotive industry; the implications for developing countries of structural changes taking place in member countries of the Council for Mutual Economic Assistance; and industrial policies in developing countries brought about by the uncertain external environment. Global models continued to be applied in analysing the international industrial restructuring process; a new simulation model—Trade Impact Analysis Model—was developed to measure the interrelated impact of various export growth scenarios on income, production and imports in 12 regions of the world. An analysis was made of the role of the energy sector in alternative industrialization scenarios for the year 2000. Three surveys on conceptual topics were published, on the use of capital in developing countries, industrial and manufacturing activities in the informal sector, and the Lima target and South-South co-operation.

Studies at the regional and subregional levels focused on potentialities for industrial co-operation, underscoring factors of particular significance to country groupings such as linkages between large- and small-scale industries. A series

of country industrial development reviews covered Algeria, Argentina, Bangladesh, India, Indonesia, Kenya, Malaysia, Paraguay, Peru, the Philippines, Sri Lanka, the Sudan, Thailand, the United Republic of Tanzania and Uruguay; each provided an overview of the industrial sector, including industrial training and financial requirements.

A three-stage approach continued to characterize sectoral studies—analytical appraisal of current and future trends, elaboration of alternative strategies, and practical application of research findings. Work was started on a regional survey of the fisheries industry, the effects of ocean shipping costs on the location of wood-processing facilities, the production of pesticides, a study of the lime industry, and the emerging role of new developing-country producers in the petrochemical industry. Work continued on updating the 1990 regional and global scenarios for the iron and steel industry, on preparing guidelines for capital cost control in fertilizer plants and on monitoring the current restructuring of the agricultural machinery industry in industrialized countries. A study of the building materials industry and a techno-economic appraisal of the manufacture of chloroquine phosphate and its chemical intermediates were completed.

Statistical research included efforts to standardize the valuation concepts used by different countries in reporting their industrial statistics and to enhance the scope of the UNIDO industrial data base with particular attention to small-scale establishments.

Industrial technology

The work of the technology programme in 1984 continued to be directed towards two interrelated goals: to encourage appropriate policy responses by developing countries to the changing technological scene as well as strengthening their technological capabilities; and to help developing countries in the selection, acquisition and development of technology.

For example, UNIDO initiated studies on microelectronics in developing countries to identify their needs and the most suitable forms of technical co-operation. Efforts to promote a regional microelectronics network in Latin America continued. Emphasis was given in 1984 to the concept of software as an industry. State-of-the-art reports in microelectronics were prepared for Bangladesh, India, Pakistan, the Republic of Korea and Venezuela. Studies were completed on optical fibre technology and its implications for developing countries and on the telecommunications industry in Brazil. Other areas receiving attention were genetic engineering and biotechnology and new materials (ceramics, non-metallic, mineral-based) as well as technological co-operation in small-scale industries.

In a March report[41] to the Industrial Development Board, the UNIDO Executive Director analysed the activities undertaken by the secretariat during 1983 in the field of development and transfer of technology (including the role of the Industrial and Technological Information Bank (INTIB) (see below)) against the general background of industrial technology for the 1980s, highlighting considerations relating to integration of technological advances with ongoing industrial and technology development efforts of developing countries.

On 19 May,[42] the Board took note of the Executive Director's report; reiterated the high priority it attached to the transfer of technology to developing countries, stressing UNIDO's role in this area; and requested early action on previous decisions calling for strengthening institutional arrangements for the programme within the UNIDO secretariat. It requested the Executive Director to submit in 1985 a report on UNIDO's work in the development and transfer of technology, including INTIB.

On 19 August,[43] the Fourth General Conference of UNIDO adopted a resolution on the strengthening of scientific and technological capacities for industrial development in developing countries. It recommended that those countries: allocate more funds to developing such capacities; establish the means to forecast, monitor and assess technological trends and their implications; and consider formulating national technology policies. It recommended promotion of the exchange of scientists, education and training programmes, links between universities and intergovernmental agreements on co-operation, and studies on more efficient linkages and co-operation between centres for selected technologies.

It recommended that UNIDO: assist in promoting national research and development capacities in developing countries, in establishing national development policies and in building up technological capabilities; promote technological co-operation between small- and medium-sized enterprises of developing and developed countries; identify energy-related technologies and equipment; help developing countries, particularly through INTIB, to process technological information; provide special assistance to African countries for development of technological capacities; promote an international referral system to identify scientists and technologists; pursue new technological co-operation initiatives; use the capabilities of developing countries more; continue aid for sectoral technological centres and information systems; help improve capabilities for identifying and preparing projects in new technological opportunities; adopt an integrated approach linking technology with other relevant factors; and co-operate with other organizations in developing, promoting and transferring technology. It urged that technology be transferred to developing countries on just and equitable terms, encouraged fair, just and equitable contracts and called for increased ODA earmarked for industrial technical assistance.

(For further information on technology transfer, see Chapter XII of this section.)

Industrial and Technological Information Bank

During 1984, the Industrial and Technological Information Bank strengthened contacts with sources of information and users and continued to process and disseminate industrial and technological information. INTIB linkages with a number of industrial and technological information data bases in developed countries were improved. Malaysia was assisted in the establishment and improvement of industrial information organizations.

About 1,300 inquiries were received by INTIB's Industrial Inquiry Service from industrial enterprises, information centres, United Nations organizations, research institutions, engineering and consulting firms, government officials, universities, professional organizations and development banks. They dealt with chemicals and pharmaceuticals, agro-industries, food processing, capital goods, fabricated metal products, non-metallic minerals, basic metal industries, textiles and leather goods, pulp and paper, and wood and wood processing.

Work continued on a consolidated edition of the *Industrial Development Abstracts* data base, which contained 14,000 entries. Work also proceeded on the revision and expansion of sources of industrial information within the On-Line-Information Key data base. A directory of institutions engaged in solar research was issued. The *UNIDO Newsletter* continued to be published monthly in five languages (Chinese, English, French, Russian, Spanish).

On 19 May,[41] the Industrial Development Board stressed the usefulness of INTIB to developing countries, in particular its regional linkages and its programmes assisting small- and medium-scale industries, and the importance of co-operation among relevant United Nations bodies in that field.

REFERENCES

[1]DP/1985/43/Add.2. [2]ID/B/340. [3]ID/B/323. [4]A/39/16 (conclusion 1984/6). [5]E/AC.51/1984/7 & Corr.1 & Add.1. [6]A/39/38. [7]DP/1984/1. [8]E/1984/20 (dec. 84/2). [9]DP/1984/68. [10]E/1984/20 (dec. 84/15). [11]ID/B/C.3/130. [12]YUN 1983, p. 589. [13]ID/B/327. [14]ID/CONF.5/46 & Corr.1 (res. 1). [15]DP/1984/64. [16]E/1984/20 (dec. 84/41). [17]A/39/16 (conclusion 1984/15). [18]ID/B/C.3/131. [19]A/39/16 (conclusion 1984/4). [20]YUN 1983, p. 592. [21]*Ibid.*, p. 986, ESC res. 1983/49, 28 July 1983. [22]A/39/38. [23]YUN 1981, p. 383. [24]ID/CONF.5/46 & Corr.1 (res. 7). [25]UNIDO/PC.101. [26]YUN 1982, p. 768. [27]A/CN.9/247.

(28)A/CN.9/259. (29)A/39/17. (30)A/39/16 (conclusion 1984/9).
(31)YUN 1981, p. 406. (32)ID/CONF.5/46 & Corr.1 (res. 6).
(33)ID/B/316. (34)A/39/16 (conclusion 1984/3). (35)A/C.2/39/8.
(36)YUN 1980, p. 503, GA res. 35/56, annex, 5 Dec. 1980.
(37)YUN 1981, p. 591. (38)A/39/16 (conclusion 1984/2).
(39)ID/CONF.5/46 & Corr.1 (res. 4). (40)*Ibid.* (res. 5).
(41)ID/B/318. (42)A/39/16 (conclusion 1984/5).
(43)ID/CONF.5/46 & Corr.1 (res. 2).

Development of specific industries

During 1984, many of UNIDO's technical co-operation activities related to specific industrial sectors or industries. The major sectors were agro-industries, and chemical, engineering, and metallurgical and mineral industries.

Agro-industries

Technical co-operation activities under the heading agro-industries amounted to $9.7 million in 1984, with some 70 per cent financed from UNDP resources. Of the total, Africa accounted for 17 per cent; the Americas, 19; the Arab States (excluding those in Africa), 3; Asia and the Pacific, 52; Europe, 2; and interregional/global, 7. A total of 158 projects were implemented or being implemented, 13 of them greater than $1 million in value, 53 greater than $150,000 and 92 below $150,000.

Projects covered the following light industries: wood products and processing, including timber engineering; textile production and garment making; food-processing and agro-industrial complexes; leather and leather products; and rubber products and packaging.

Clothing and textile industry

The majority of projects in the textile and garment-making sector were large-scale projects. In 1984, 10 such projects, all financed by UNDP, were under implementation in Bangladesh, Egypt, India, Sri Lanka, the United Republic of Tanzania and Viet Nam. Nine concerned the establishment or strengthening of institutions to serve the industry, following a trend towards indirect assistance; all other projects related to direct assistance. In Bangladesh, for example, a project to provide central testing laboratories for jute goods neared completion, while in Sri Lanka a textile training and service centre was established and in Viet Nam aid was given to textile factories in the south to improve maintenance and production management.

A diagnostic study on the restructuring needs of the Argentine textile industry was completed. A seminar organized by UNIDO and the International Institute for Cotton at Manchester, United Kingdom, in April demonstrated the application of computer programs in establishing knitting parameters; to share the new technique, regional workshops were conducted at Coimbatore, India, and Mexico City, funded by the United Kingdom. In Sierra Leone, UNIDO provided expertise in technical and managerial activities, including staff training, enabling a garment manufacturing company to operate as an independent and viable enterprise.

Fisheries industry

Case-studies were undertaken in Chile and Peru so as to understand better the problems faced by developing countries in the fisheries sector. A group of experts, meeting at Vienna in February, identified priority areas for international co-operation, including harvesting techniques and equipment manufacture, shipbuilding, technology, training, market research, research in packaging, freezing, processing, storage and transport. Co-ordination was maintained with the Food and Agriculture Organization of the United Nations (FAO), with the participation of UNIDO in meetings in preparation for the 1984 FAO World Conference on Fisheries Management and Development (see PART TWO, Chapter III).

Food industry

In view of the food crisis in Africa, UNIDO gave priority during 1984 to activities in the food-processing industries that would encourage self-sufficiency. Assistance in rehabilitation, modernization and expansion was provided to plants in Angola, Guinea, Mozambique, Rwanda and Sierra Leone. Attention was given to the utilization of agro-based raw materials such as meat, sugar, bakery products, passion-fruit and cassava.

A research project on the use of the fruit of *Balanites aegyptiaca* was completed in the Sahelian region for commercial production of edible oil and animal feed. A study was completed on establishing a plant in a west African country to produce cereal products with composite flour from local and other cereals by extrusion.

Technical assistance continued in Argentina, El Salvador and Ecuador to food-processing research, development and quality control. The grape-processing industry of Bolivia was the recipient of assistance. A project was initiated in Peru, in co-operation with the United Nations Fund for Drug Abuse Control, to eradicate drug crops and develop the food industry.

The Second Consultation on the Food-Processing Industry with Special Emphasis on Vegetable Oils and Fats was held at Copenhagen, Denmark, from 15 to 19 October,[1] attended by 143 participants from 58 countries and observers from 10 international organizations. Preparations in 1984 included an expert group meeting

(Vienna, 6-8 February) on downstream processing; it completed issue, background and study papers, and considered constraints to the diversification of processing activities in developing countries. Although the emphasis of the Consultation was on vegetable oils and fats, the interlinkages of that sector with animal feed, meat processing and dairy products also received consideration. Within that framework, the Consultation discussed an integrated approach to food processing and the role of co-operatives and small- and medium-scale enterprises.

On an integrated approach to food processing, the Consultation agreed that such an approach could often be the most appropriate strategy for development of the food-processing industry in developing countries; that both Governments and industries should interact to utilize installed capacity fully, embracing inputs of raw materials, technology, upgrading, marketing and planning; and that regional consultations should be organized. It recommended that UNIDO undertake a technical assistance project, upon request, in a developing country to illustrate the application of the integrated approach to the oil-seed-protein subsystem, including meat and dairy industries; consider organizing regional consultations in the sector to examine regional collaboration arrangements for the manufacture of components and spare parts and instruments; arrange for periodic review by independent advisers of developments in the vegetable oils and fats processing industry; promote the increasing production of edible oils and fats in developing countries; and strengthen training activities for personnel in processing, maintenance of equipment, quality control, management and marketing.

On the role of co-operatives and small- and medium-scale enterprises, the Consultation concluded that in co-operation arrangements a clear distinction must be made between aid and commercial relations and that the nature of the latter must reflect the level of industrialization in the partner country. It further concluded that increased involvement of co-operatives as well as small- and medium-scale enterprises in international co-operation for the food-processing industry would be highly beneficial to production, processing and marketing operations; that Governments should create favourable conditions for co-operatives; that international, governmental and non-governmental organizations had an important task in supporting an increase in the involvement of co-operatives; and that UNIDO's role was of special importance. The Consultation recommended that UNIDO prepare case-studies on specific projects and measures to stimulate co-operation, promote an increased flow of information, and contribute to improved co-ordination of activities.

Leather industry

Technical assistance activities in the leather and leather products sector were directed in 1984 towards an integrated programme approach to maximize the industry's potential in developing countries, as recommended by the Third Consultation on the Leather and Leather Products Industry (Innsbruck, Austria, 16-19 April).[2] The Consultation was attended by 108 participants from 46 countries and 11 observers from nine international organizations.

In order to maximize the industry's potential, the Consultation concluded that an integrated programme approach at the national level could provide a relevant framework for international co-operation; it recommended that UNIDO examine practical ways of establishing regional training centres, and that particular attention should be given to working conditions, safety and health. It also recommended that UNIDO assess and evaluate the potential of the industry in individual developing countries; advise on practical ways of securing the necessary sectoral programme financing; and assist in the provision of technical services, management and marketing know-how.

On the issue of measures to facilitate the production and acquisition of tanning chemicals and footwear auxiliaries in developing countries, the Consultation concluded that procurement of tanning chemicals was a significant constraint in many developing countries, and recognized that the manufacture of those chemicals required substantial economies of scale to be viable. It recommended that UNIDO undertake technical and economic studies of the raw-material base and other necessary facilities existing in developing countries that could lead to the production of tanning chemicals.

In Africa, UNIDO activities aimed at increasing the utilization of domestic resources. Under a World Bank–financed project, UNIDO provided aid to the United Republic of Tanzania in setting up an infrastructure for its leather, footwear and leather products sector. Another project expedited the start-up of a tannery in Burundi. One phase of a multi-stage project in leather products development was completed in Ethiopia. Assistance was also given to Kenya, Lesotho, Madagascar and the Sudan.

In China, the Philippines and Sri Lanka, large-scale projects of assistance to leather centres reached their final stages, while new projects were started in Burma and Mongolia to solve technological problems.

Packaging industry

Under a project to establish a national food-packaging centre at Campinas, Brazil, fellowships and study tours were arranged and experts' services and equipment delivered. Projects in Jamaica and Turkey involved strengthening research and development centres. Specialists in the economics, industrial production and standardization of paper, board, plastics, metals and glass packaging were analysing the packaging industry in Mexico. A project in Mali introduced a less expensive packaging system for locally produced fruit juices. A regional packaging centre became operational in Morocco. Other projects were implemented in Cuba, Guinea-Bissau and the Republic of Korea.

Wood-using industry

Small wood and wood product industry projects in 1984 were designed to provide highly specific technical assistance, funded mainly through the SIS programme or UNIDF. Further assistance was given to African countries within the framework of the ECA/FAO/UNIDO Forest Industries Advisory Group for Africa.

A furniture factory in Guinea received production assistance; a match factory in the Congo was being rehabilitated. Other projects included assistance to the production of wood-based panels and school furniture in Rwanda and the manufacture of bentwood chairs in the Sudan. In Asia and the Pacific, demonstrations were offered of the structural use of coconut wood and rubber wood; model houses were built in the Philippines using coconut wood. New projects were undertaken in Nicaragua and Peru utilizing the UNIDO low-cost modular prefabricated wooden bridge system, and a survey of the furniture industry was initiated in Guyana. Training courses, workshops or seminars were held in Costa Rica, Honduras, Italy, Mauritius and New Zealand.

On 19 May,[3] the Industrial Development Board took note of the recommendations of the First Consultation on the Wood and Wood Products Industry, held in 1983,[4] and decided that work on the industry should continue.

Chemical industries

In 1984, technical co-operation expenditures for chemical industries amounted to $22.1 million, with some 45 per cent financed from UNDP resources. Of that amount, Africa accounted for 47 per cent; the Americas, 5; Arab States (excluding those in Africa), 3; Asia and the Pacific, 30; Europe, 6; and interregional/global, 9. A total of 311 projects were implemented or under implementation, 33 of them greater than $1 million in value, 99 less than that but greater than $150,000, and 179 less than $150,000.

Activities concentrated on five broad subsectors: basic chemicals, environment and pulp and paper; building materials and construction industries; fertilizers, pesticides and organic chemicals indus-

tries; petrochemical industries; and pharmaceutical industries. UNIDO experts were assigned to paper mills in Bolivia, the Democratic People's Republic of Korea, Turkey and Viet Nam. To make optimum use of existing plant capacities for the pulp and paper industry in developing countries, assistance was provided to the industries which produced essential basic chemicals: salt, caustic soda and chlorine. Salt production projects were assisted in Benin and the Niger. Since 60 per cent of pulp and paper production in developing countries was based on non-wood fibres, UNIDO continued to aid non-wood fibre-pulping and paper-making research. Projects for utilizing bamboo were under way in Burma and China. In addition, activities to control industrial pollution were expanded. Several projects were implemented on air pollution monitoring and control, marine pollution control, waste treatment and utilization, development of non-waste technologies for chemical processes, advisory services for environmental protection, training in industrial pollution control, and recycling and conservation of environmental resources (see Chapter XVI of this section).

Building materials industry

Activities related to the building materials and construction industries focused on fuller use of local, non-metallic raw materials, developing innovative methods of construction and introducing new materials. Large-scale projects were implemented on constructing low-cost housing, earthquake-resistant technologies and base isolation techniques. UNIDO projects included work on rubber-steel mounts for base isolation of buildings in earthquake-prone areas, a technique which was applied in the construction of the City Hall of San Bernardino, California, United States. In Africa, a mobile mechanized brickmaking plant was introduced, to be based in the United Republic of Tanzania. UNIDO advised a brickmaking company in the Niger on utilizing an old production line for the manufacture of unfired bricks with or without lime stabilization. Brick-plant production was also assisted in Cameroon and the Gambia. A project continued in Ethiopia to rehabilitate the marble and stone industries and develop low-cost building materials based on volcanic tuff. A ceramic research and development laboratory was opened in Sri Lanka. A manual was published on the manufacture of rice husk ash cement to promote it as a high-quality building material. The cement industry was also aided in Botswana, China, Egypt and the Libyan Arab Jamahiriya. A global preparatory meeting was held (Vienna, 24-28 September) for the first consultation on the building materials industry, to be convened in 1985.

Fertilizer industry

Much of UNIDO's work in the chemical sector dealt with projects for the fertilizer and pesticides industries.

A survey of ways to promote co-operation in the production of phosphate fertilizer was begun in member countries of the Common African and Mauritian Organization. The survey included an evaluation of the technical, natural and economic conditions of each country producing fertilizer.

Two projects were completed in India on the use of low-grade raw materials for fertilizer production, involving the production of sulphur and sulphuric acid from low-grade pyrites and the processing of low-grade phosphate rock into fertilizers.

The Fourth Consultation on the Fertilizer Industry (New Delhi, India, 23-27 January)[5] was attended by 134 participants from 52 countries and 21 observers from 13 international organizations. It recommended that two model forms of contract presented by the secretariat for the construction of a fertilizer plant—the semi-turnkey and the licensing and engineering services agreement—should be finalized by two international expert groups. (The groups agreed on the final drafts of the model contracts at meetings in July at Vienna.) The Consultation also formulated specific recommendations aimed at enhancing co-operation among developing countries, for example through training programmes and the study of joint-venture arrangements. It requested UNIDO to prepare a pre-contracting manual for the fertilizer industry as well as guidelines for project management and capital cost control; to continue promoting co-operation on mini fertilizer plants between potential contractors and engineering companies and buyers from developing countries; and to undertake work in co-operation with other organizations on new technologies and environmental pollution. It referred the issue of pesticides to the Industrial Development Board.

On 19 May,[3] the Board took note of the conclusions and recommendations of the Fourth Consultation.

Petrochemical industry

In the petrochemical subsector, UNIDO activities were concentrated during 1984 on the development of polymer industries—plastics, rubbers, synthetic fibres—in developing countries as well as on the manufacture of basic petrochemicals essential to processing industries.

The Indian Petrochemical Corporation was provided with simulator training facilities and software for various technological processes. Petrochemical research and development programmes were started in the Democratic People's Republic of Korea and Yugoslavia. A regional project to establish a petroleum training centre in Angola was approved and a mission undertaken to countries of the region

to select trainees. Workshops were organized on petroleum processing, production planning, energy management and maintenance, and plant inspection.

In Saudi Arabia, a symposium on the petrochemical industry was held in three cities—Riyadh, Dammam and Jeddah—to encourage entrepreneurs to set up downstream processing industries for plastics, rubbers and synthetic fibres. Recommendations for North-South co-operation were formulated by the first Expert Group Meeting on International Co-operation on Petrochemicals, while a meeting of the Advisory Panel on Petrochemicals helped to prepare a programme for South-South co-operation; both meetings were held at Vienna in September.

The secretariat established a data base for 25 petrochemicals to determine world supply and demand.

Pesticides industry

Pesticide research and development were given particular emphasis in developing countries during 1984. The first phase of a UNDP/UNIDF project to modernize the toxicological department of a research institute in China was completed, and a similar project in the Republic of Korea was begun. Assistance in the development of pesticides continued to be given to a laboratory and institute in India and Hungary.

A regional network in the Philippines for the production, marketing and control of pesticides in Asia and the Pacific organized expert group meetings on quality control of pesticides (Dhaka, Bangladesh, 13-17 May) and on trade and tariff considerations (Colombo, Sri Lanka, 13-17 August). The network also encouraged an exchange of expertise and arranged study tours.

Pharmaceutical industry

Among the UNIDO activities in 1984 to increase pharmaceutical production in developing countries were the use of indigenous medicinal plants and petrochemical by-products, the adaptation of technology for local production, the promotion of biologicals to enhance preventive measures, and the strengthening of national research and development capabilities.

The utilization of medicinal and aromatic plants received particular attention in projects in Afghanistan, Burkina Faso, Cameroon, Mali, Nepal, Rwanda, Thailand, Turkey and the United Republic of Tanzania. Exploratory projects were initiated in Burundi, Guatemala and Madagascar. Plants for the bulk production of essential synthetic drugs were nearing completion in Cuba and under construction in Brazil and Iran. Expansion of facilities for manufacturing the anti-malarial drug chloroquine diphosphate in India was completed. In Guinea, a project for the formulation and packaging of pharmaceuticals was also completed, and, in Zambia, a project for local production of oral rehydration salts was begun.

An advisory panel on preventive medicine, composed of representatives from industry, government and United Nations bodies such as WHO and UNICEF, was set up to guide a new UNIDO programme on the industrial production of biologicals. The panel met twice: at Vienna on 27 and 28 February, and at Bogotá on 22 and 23 November. A directory to sources of supply for 26 essential bulk drugs, their chemical intermediates and some raw materials was revised during 1984 for distribution in 1985. Programmes for vaccine production were prepared with assistance from Hungary and the Netherlands.

On 19 May,[3] the Industrial Development Board took note of the conclusions and recommendations of the Second Consultation on the Pharmaceutical Industry, held in 1983.[6]

Engineering industries

In 1984, technical co-operation expenditures under the heading engineering industries amounted to $13.9 million, about 90 per cent of which was financed by UNDP. Africa accounted for 19 per cent; the Americas, 9; Arab States (excluding those in Africa), 5; Asia and the Pacific, 60; Europe, 6; and inter-regional/global, 1. A total of 170 projects were completed or being implemented, of which 27 were greater than $1 million in value, 66 greater than $150,000, and 77 less than $150,000.

Activities aimed at the creation of new or improvement of existing production capacities and diversification of products. The main subsectors receiving assistance were: agricultural machinery and implements; electronic and electrical machinery and products; computer and computer-related equipment; metal-working and machine tools; land-based or water-borne transport equipment; and energy-related equipment. The first three categories accounted for the majority of requests.

Genetic engineering

A reconvened Plenipotentiary Meeting on the Establishment of the International Centre for Genetic Engineering and Biotechnology (Vienna, 3 and 4 April 1984), which had first met in 1983,[6] decided to locate the Centre in two components at Trieste and New Delhi. The Italian component would be concerned with energy, industrial microbiology and protein engineering; the Indian component would work on agriculture, human and animal health and productivity. Activities were expected to begin in 1985.

The Preparatory Committee on the establishment of the Centre held three sessions in 1984, all at Vienna (24-27 January, 2 and 3 April and 17-19 September). At its September session, a panel of scientific advisers was constituted to advise on

preparations. Financing for the preparatory activities had been pledged by Italy under a technical co-operation trust-fund agreement.

Also, by the end of 1984, 36 countries had signed the statutes establishing the Centre. The statutes would enter into force when at least 24 States, including the host States, had deposited instruments of ratification and had ascertained that sufficient financial resources were ensured.

Programmes in genetic engineering and biotechnology included symposia on biotechnology (New Delhi, 19-25 February) and on lactic acid fermentation (Mexico City, 27-29 November), and joint research and pilot studies by universities and institutes on the cloning of cellulosic genes (Brazil/Federal Republic of Germany) and on high-cellulose-producing yeast species (Ireland/Pakistan). A Latin American biotechnology network was initiated through joint UNIDO/UNDP/UNESCO efforts, and a project was approved to establish a regional research and development centre in Mexico.

Agricultural machinery

Following up a recommendation of the Second Consultation on the Agricultural Machinery Industry held in 1983,[6] an expert group meeting was convened (Guangzhou, China, 15-18 November 1984) to promote the manufacture of agricultural machinery and rural and food-related equipment at multi-purpose plants in developing countries. Work was begun by the secretariat to investigate factors relevant to the elaboration of a framework for industrial co-operation in this sector.

Assistance in the manufacture of agricultural tools and machinery was provided to Burkina Faso, Lesotho, Somalia, Togo and Uganda. A regional programme for 12 Latin American and Caribbean countries on the repair, maintenance and reconditioning of sugar industry equipment was undertaken. A joint UNIDO/FAO mission was fielded in January to finalize a 10-year mechanization plan for Cameroon.

On 19 May,[3] the Industrial Development Board took note of the conclusions and recommendations of the Second Consultation on the Agricultural Machinery Industry.

Metallurgical and mineral industries

In 1984, technical co-operation expenditures under the heading metallurgical industries amounted to $6.3 million, with about 85 per cent financed by UNDP. Of that amount, Africa accounted for 32 per cent; the Americas, 12; Arab States (excluding those in Africa), 4; Asia and the Pacific, 42; and Europe, 10. A total of 136 projects were completed or under way, 13 of them greater than $1 million in value, 46 less than that but greater than $150,000, and 77 less than $150,000.

Activities accelerated in extractive and physical metallurgy, covering light and heavy non-ferrous metals (aluminium, titanium, copper, lead, zinc), the iron and steel industry, ferrous and non-ferrous foundries and other metal transformation and forming processes (rolling, forging, heat treatment, extruding, welding), and about 15 projects dealt with establishing or strengthening centres for metallurgical research. About 25 projects involved the planning, establishment, expansion and operation of metallurgical plants. Other assistance was provided to the establishment of pilot plants, particularly for foundry industry development.

Emphasis was given to projects assisting developing countries in the evaluation, concentration and beneficiation of ores and minerals, and promoting the integrated development of the mineral dressing and processing sector. Projects were under way in China, Cuba, Greece, India, Iran, Mauritania, Mongolia, Sri Lanka and Viet Nam.

The transfer of technology was promoted through a number of projects, including the production of silicon for the electrical and semi-conductor industry in Pakistan, the electro-refining of copper in Peru, the manufacture of magnetic materials for use in electronic engineering in Viet Nam, the elaboration of a new process (combismelt) for the processing of iron ore to steel in Mexico, and the utilization of low-grade ores and low calorific coals in Hungary.

In Paraguay, processes were introduced on a pilot scale for the production of metallurgical charcoal for use in blast furnaces. A project in Chile dealt with the handling and recovery of ore residues from effluents and slurries of mining and metallurgical operations.

UNIDO continued to provide advisory services to Egypt in computerized maintenance and completed the installation of a computer system for process control. A regional demonstration workshop on maintenance in the metallurgical and foundry industries for African countries was held at Cairo (17 November–7 December). A technical consultancy and training centre opened in Czechoslovakia, providing services to local industry as well as developing countries; also established in Czechoslovakia was a computerized management information system for small piece and batch manufacturing.

In co-operation with the African Regional Centre for Engineering Design and Manufacturing, a study tour and workshop in core metallurgical and engineering industries was conducted in Hungary (8-25 October) for 20 participants from 10 African countries, including six LDCs.

Aluminium industry

In Yugoslavia, work progressed in 1984 on the establishment of an aluminium institute at Titograd. Equipment was supplied and a research programme was elaborated.

A demonstration unit for an alumina calciner designed to reduce fuel-oil consumption was being established at Korba, India. Under another project, sub-contracting was arranged for a conceptual design study on the production of super-pure aluminium at the same company and UNIDO was also requested to assist in a study of the production of special aluminas and the optimization of rolling mill operations. De-ironed refractory-grade bauxite production was the subject of a project in Greece.

A training course in alumina production and aluminium electrolysis was organized in China, within the framework of the Joint UNIDO/Hungary Aluminium Industry Programme; seven Hungarian experts lectured to 32 Chinese nationals. Hungarian experts prepared and UNIDO published in 1984 a design study for aluminium extrusion and anodizing plants.

Foundries

Projects related to the development of the foundry and metal transformation sector were being implemented in 1984 in Afghanistan, Angola, Democratic Yemen, Ethiopia, Malta, Morocco, Mozambique, Nepal, Nicaragua, the Niger, the Republic of Korea, Somalia, the United Republic of Tanzania and Viet Nam.

In Angola, a master plan was elaborated for the modernization and development of the foundry industry sector; 15 Angolans were sent for a year's training in Brazil. Assistance was also provided to Morocco through the establishment of a foundry laboratory designed to act as a quality testing centre. A pilot and demonstration foundry was opened in Kathmandu in March; it produced spare parts worth about $2 million for a wide range of industries. Study tours to the foundry were organized for specialists from Afghanistan and Ethiopia. Two seminars to improve the quality of castings were organized at the foundry in March and July for technicians from various enterprises in Nepal.

UNIDO participated in the International Foundry Fair (Düsseldorf, Federal Republic of Germany, June), during which it responded to some 600 requests for information, held 60 consultations, and organized a foundry seminar and a study tour to foundry and metallurgical plants in the vicinity.

Iron and steel industry

The crisis in the iron and steel industry and its implications for developing countries were analysed during 1984. The connection between the iron and steel and capital goods sectors, as well as the possibilities of financing infrastructure and training in iron and steel projects, were also examined. At the same time, work began on a methodology for training and on defining the degrees of technological complexity and the skills required to master it.

An international iron and steel seminar (Karachi, Pakistan, 19-29 May) discussed an integrated approach to the iron and steel, capital goods, construction and other sectors, considered mini steel plants as a route for developing countries, and identified new perspectives for the financing of projects. A study was begun on integrated planning for the iron and steel industry and other industrial sectors.

Technical assistance continued to be given to foundry and steel-rolling operations in Mozambique, including on-the-job training in Bulgaria. In Angola, a centre to collect and process scrap for the country's only steel plant was being built. Maintenance assistance was provided to Zimbabwe, which in turn lent assistance to steel industries in Ethiopia, Mozambique and Uganda. The possibility of establishing a steel industry in the United Republic of Tanzania was studied; tests of Tanzanian chromium, titanium and vanadium were carried out. A concurrent top and bottom blown converter for steelmaking was installed at the Research and Development Centre of the Steel Authority of India. An interregional workshop on welding technology was held in co-operation with the National Welding Research Institute of India (Tiruchirapalli, 30 January–4 February). Advice was provided to Bolivia, Gabon and Guinea on the exploitation of their iron ores, natural gas and other raw materials.

Non-ferrous metals

In preparation for a forthcoming first consultation on the non-ferrous metals industry, activities in this sector focused on an analysis of information and trends in each component of the industry (aluminium, zinc, copper, nickel, lead, tin).

Other activities during 1984 included an analysis of energy requirements and their impact on the increase in industrial processing of non-ferrous metals in developing countries; a joint United Nations Centre on Transnational Corporations/UNIDO programme to analyse the strategies of Governments and transnational corporations in the industry; and the completion of the first part of a three-part study of its development and restructuring.

Preparatory work was started on a typology of countries as well as a set of scenarios and medium- and long-term forecasting to determine broad strategies for processing non-ferrous metals in developing countries.

UNIDO provided assistance to Chile in assessing a research and development programme on an innovative bacterial leaching process for treating copper ores. Expert services were provided in Peru on advanced technologies for copper production and advice was given on establishing a pilot operation for electro-refining of copper.

Other industrial categories

Export-oriented industries

In co-operation with members of the Association of South-East Asian Nations—traditionally commodity exporters—UNIDO launched in 1984 a group training programme on export industry development to upgrade the skills of government and industry policy-makers in applying modern management techniques to the production of high-quality products for the international market.

A project in Sri Lanka involved building the investment promotion capabilities of the Greater Colombo Economic Commission; it was expected that, through better feasibility studies, improved administrative services and the use of wide international contacts, including UNIDO's Investment Promotion Services, the flow of capital to Sri Lanka would increase. A project in Burma aimed at preparing feasibility studies on the establishment of industrial plants outside a metropolis, which would alleviate rural unemployment. ESCAP and UNIDO implemented a project in Fiji to review industrial development strategy for an isolated island nation.

Small-scale industry

Technical assistance in the development of small- and medium-scale industries covered a broad spectrum of activities in 1984, ranging from institution-building to direct assistance to enterprises. There was a noticeable trend towards the upgrading of raw materials available in rural areas. Efforts focused on the creation of development poles in rural areas around which industries could be interlinked. Mobile facilities were put into operation which provided repair and maintenance services for industrial machinery in isolated areas.

Assistance continued to the Société nationale d'études et promotion industrielles in Senegal, the Office de promotion de l'entreprise nigérienne in the Niger, the Small Industry Development Organization in Zambia, the Ethiopian Handicraft and Small Industries Development Agency, and the Kenya Industrial Estate. Small-scale industrial development was promoted in provincial, semi-urban and rural areas of Burundi, the Comoros, Madagascar and Rwanda.

REFERENCES

(1)ID/329. (2)ID/318. (3)A/39/16 (conclusion 1984/4). (4)YUN 1983, p. 600. (5)ID/314. (6)YUN 1983, p. 602.

PUBLICATIONS

Industry and Development, No. 10 (ID/SER.M/10 & Add.1), Sales No. E.84.II.B.1 & addendum; No. 11 (ID/SER.M/11 & Add.1), Sales No. E.84.II.B.2 & addendum. *Rice Bran: An Under-Utilized Raw Material* (ID/320), Sales No. E.84.II.B.3.

Chapter VII

Transnational corporations

The impact of the activities of transnational corporations (TNCs) on the changing world economy continued to be a major concern of the international community in 1984. The positive contribution of TNCs to development, especially to that of low-income and least developed countries, was overshadowed by the consequences of the world economic recession.

The draft code of conduct on TNCs continued to be discussed at a special session of the Commission on Transnational Corporations, reconvened in January and June 1984. As certain outstanding issues—which included a definition of TNCs and the scope of the code's application, international obligations *vis-à-vis* national legislation, settlement of disputes, and non-collaboration with racist minority régimes in southern Africa—could not be resolved during discussions, the negotiations on the draft code reached an impasse. The General Assembly, in December (decision 39/443), requested the Chairman of the Commission to initiate consultations aimed at overcoming that impasse and decided to reconvene the special session in 1985.

International standards of accounting and reporting—a question related to the world-wide growth of TNCs—were examined by an intergovernmental group. In addition to assisting in the work on the draft code and preparing studies for the intergovernmental group, the United Nations Centre on TNCs continued to develop a comprehensive information system, carried out research, and conducted and supervised technical co-operation activities. An important element in the Centre's work continued to be research on TNC activities in South Africa and Namibia. The Centre also participated in the work of an *Ad Hoc* Committee on preparations for public hearings on those activities (see p. 149). These aspects of the Centre's work and other matters related to TNC activities were considered by the Commission on TNCs at its tenth regular session (New York, 17-27 April).

Topics related to this chapter. Africa: transnational corporations. Development policy and international economic co-operation: International Development Strategy for the Third United Nations Development Decade. International trade: trade policy. Human rights: human rights violations—Africa.

Draft code of conduct

Special session of the Commission (January). Pursuant to a December 1983 General Assembly decision,[1] a special session of the Commission on TNCs, open to the participation of all States, was reconvened (New York, 9-13 January 1984) to continue—at six formal and a number of informal meetings—discussion of a draft code of conduct on TNCs.[2] Not being able to solve the key outstanding issues, the Commission recommended that the Economic and Social Council again reconvene the special session to complete work on the code.

At its tenth session in April,[3] the Commission urged that every effort be made to conclude negotiations on the code.

ECONOMIC AND SOCIAL COUNCIL ACTION

In February, the Economic and Social Council adopted decision 1984/109 without vote.

Reconvened special session of the Commission on Transnational Corporations

At its 3rd plenary meeting, on 21 February 1984, the Council, having assessed the work undertaken by the Commission on Transnational Corporations at its reconvened special session on the draft code of conduct on transnational corporations and of the divergencies still to be overcome in that regard, decided:

(*a*) To reconvene further the special session of the Commission on Transnational Corporations from 11 to 29 June 1984, with a view to completing the work on the formulation of the draft code of conduct on transnational corporations for submission to the General Assembly at its thirty-ninth session through the Economic and Social Council at its second regular session of 1984;

(*b*) That the question of the participation of expert advisers in the reconvened special session should be considered by the Commission on Transnational Corporations at its tenth session, taking into account the proposal made by the delegation of Mexico, on behalf of the States Members which are members of the Group of 77, during the organizational session for 1984 of the Council; and that the recommendations of the Commission would be considered, for appropriate action, by the Council at its first regular session of 1984.

Economic and Social Council decision 1984/109

Adopted without vote

Draft by President, for Bureau (E/1984/L.15), orally revised following informal consultations; agenda item 4.

Financial implications. S-G, E/1984/9/Add.1.
Meeting numbers. ESC 2, 3.

During informal consultations in the Council on the draft submitted by the President, two proposals were made concerning the question of the participation of expert advisers in the reconvened special session; the first would have the Council refer consideration of the matter back to the Commission, while the second would have the Council recommend that the Commission consider the question at its regular session in April, taking into account the proposals by the Group of 77. Following further consultations, an agreement was reached to add the second paragraph to the draft decision.

In a February statement on the financial implications of reconvening the Commission's special session, the Secretary-General estimated conference servicing requirements at $309,400, on the assumption that the session would last for three weeks, be serviced in six languages and require two meetings a day and 160 pages of documentation. It was possible, however, that four meetings per day might be required; should the Council approve that arrangement, additional costs would total $207,600. Should the Council decide that expert advisers should participate, $94,800 would be needed for travel and per diem expenses for 16 advisers.

In May, the Council adopted decision 1984/120 without vote.

Question of the participation of expert advisers in the reconvened special session of the Commission on Transnational Corporations

At its 11th plenary meeting, on 11 May 1984, the Council, having considered the note by the Secretary-General,[4] decided to invite expert advisers to participate in the work of the reconvened special session of the Commission on Transnational Corporations, to be held from 11 to 29 June 1984, during the last three days of the second week of the session, within existing resources.

Economic and Social Council decision 1984/120

Adopted without vote

Draft by Commission on TNCs (E/1984/18); agenda item 1.

In an April note to the Council,[4] the Secretary-General stated that, should the Council decide to approve the Commission's recommendation with regard to the participation of 16 expert advisers in its reconvened special session, programme budget implications would arise in respect of the travel and per diem expenses. Additional resources ($34,000) would be required only for travel costs; per diem costs ($12,400) would be absorbed within existing resources of the 1984-1985 programme budget.

Speaking before the Council, the Director of the Centre on TNCs said the Secretariat had given further consideration to the financial implications set forth in the Secretary-General's note and expected to be able to absorb all the costs indicated within existing resources.

Reconvened special session (June). In accordance with Council decision 1984/109, the Commission reconvened its special session (New York, 11-29 June),[5] focusing again on the draft code's key outstanding issues. In both formal and informal meetings, it considered definitions and scope of application; respect for national sovereignty and observance of domestic laws, regulations and administrative practices; treatment of TNCs by the countries in which they operated; nationalization and settlement of disputes; conflicts of jurisdiction; non-interference in internal affairs; the free transfer by TNCs of payments relating to their investments; and non-collaboration by TNCs with racist minority régimes in southern Africa.

Most delegations stated that they could accept as a compromise the 1983 proposals by the Chairman and the Rapporteur on the outstanding issues,[6] provided that all other delegations would accept them; however, they would also consider other proposals. Such proposals made by delegations at the reconvened special session were presented in an October report of the Centre on TNCs.[7]

Expert advisers from 15 countries—Argentina, Brazil, Canada, China, France, Federal Republic of Germany, Italy, Netherlands, Philippines, USSR, United Kingdom, United States, United Republic of Tanzania, Upper Volta, Uruguay—took part in the discussions.

At the end of the session, the Commission discussed future work on the draft code and stressed the importance of completing and adopting it.

ECONOMIC AND SOCIAL COUNCIL ACTION

In July, on the recommendation of its First (Economic) Committee, the Economic and Social Council adopted decision 1984/163 without vote.

Report of the Commission on Transnational Corporations on its reconvened special session

At its 48th plenary meeting, on 25 July 1984, the Council took note of the report of the Commission on Transnational Corporations on its reconvened special session, held from 11 to 29 June 1984, and decided to transmit it to the General Assembly at its thirty-ninth session for consideration.

Economic and Social Council decision 1984/163

Adopted without vote

Approved by First Committee (E/1984/141) without vote, 17 July (meeting 10); oral proposal by Chairman; agenda item 10.

GENERAL ASSEMBLY ACTION

In December, on the recommendation of the Second (Economic and Financial) Committee, the General Assembly adopted decision 39/443 without vote.

Reconvened special session of the Commission on Transnational Corporations

At its 104th plenary meeting, on 18 December 1984, the General Assembly, on the recommendation of the Second Committee:

(a) Took note of the report of the Commission on Transnational Corporations on its reconvened special session, held from 11 to 29 June 1984;

(b) Decided to request the Chairman, together with the other officers of the Commission on Transnational Corporations at its recovened special session, and with the assistance of the United Nations Centre on Transnational Corporations, to initiate consultations aimed at overcoming the current impasse regarding the negotiations on the draft code of conduct on transnational corporations, bearing in mind, *inter alia*, the proposals of the Chairman and the Rapporteur and the progress achieved thus far during the special session;

(c) Decided to request the United Nations Centre on Transnational Corporations to prepare a study on the outstanding issues in the draft code of conduct, including, *inter alia*, the questions of international law and international obligations *vis-à-vis* national legislation, to be circulated to Governments prior to the reconvened special session;

(d) Decided to reconvene the special session of the Commission on Transnational Corporations for one week in June 1985 for the Commission to examine the study requested in subparagraph (c) above and, in the light of that examination and the results of the consultations mentioned in subparagraph (b) above, to prepare a report, including suggestions regarding the most appropriate steps to be taken to complete the code of conduct, to be submitted, for consideration, to the Economic and Social Council at its second regular session of 1985 and to the General Assembly at its fortieth session.

General Assembly decision 39/443

Adopted without vote

Approved by Second Committee (A/39/789/Add.1) without vote, 10 December (meeting 58); draft by Vice-Chairman (A/C.2/39/L.132), based on informal consultations on draft by Egypt, for Group of 77 (A/C.2/39/L.107); agenda item 12. *Financial implications.* 5th Committee, A/39/831; S-G, A/C.2/39/L.117, A/C.5/39/90. *Meeting numbers.* GA 39th session: 2nd Committee 28-32, 56, 58; 5th Committee 49; plenary 104.

The United Kingdom hoped the date for the reconvened special session would be chosen with the aim of minimizing conference servicing costs. The United States explained that its support of the text was predicated both on substantive grounds and on the expectation that the Secretary-General would absorb those costs. The Ukrainian SSR, speaking also on behalf of Bulgaria, the Byelorussian SSR, Czechoslovakia, the German Democratic Republic, Hungary, Mongolia, Poland and the USSR, stated that negotiations on the draft code, already in progress for eight years, had reached an impasse because of the negative position of certain Western countries which were blocking the "package proposal" of the special session's Chairman, which the socialist countries continued to view as a sensible compromise.

Introducing the original draft, Egypt expressed the concern of the Group of 77 that the code was not finished or adopted.

The adopted text differed from the original draft in that it requested the Commission Chairman to initiate consultations with the additional assistance of the Centre.

Definition of TNC

The question of the definition of TNCs had been considered by the Commission since its first session in 1975. Background information on the question was provided in a February 1984 report by the Centre's secretariat.[8] The question had generally been deferred pending the outcome of negotiations on a draft code of conduct (see above), in which definition was a major issue.

An important point of disagreement about the definition of TNCs related to the nature of the ownership of the enterprise; opinions differed as to whether the code was applicable to State-owned or public enterprises as well as those of private or mixed ownership. Also, a major point of divergence was whether the definition should underline the comprehensive character of its ambit by including the words "whether of public, private or mixed ownership" or whether a definition which made no explicit reference to the nature of ownership would be sufficient.

At its reconvened special session in January,[2] the Commission did not examine specific proposals; however, the Chairman mentioned a number of possible solutions to the question of definitions and scope of application.

During its regular session in April,[3] the Commission again took up the question. Some delegations emphasized the importance for the definition of TNCs to be all-inclusive, covering all types of enterprises operating in two or more countries, including those State-owned. Others stated that an emphasis on State-owned enterprises was a diversion and that they were quite different from TNCs.

At its reconvened special session in June,[5] the Commission examined a variety of texts put forward by delegations, but reached no agreement.

Bilateral, regional and international arrangements relating to TNCs

In 1984, the Centre on TNCs intensified its work on the collection and analysis of international, regional and bilateral arrangements relating to TNCs, taking steps to develop methods for storing, updating and retrieving relevant material, so as to respond better to the growing number of requests for information in that area. Bilateral investment treaties remained the most frequently concluded among the international instruments. The Centre initiated a number of studies on the subject.

In accordance with a June 1983 Commission decision to include in its agenda a sub-item on those arrangements, approved by the Economic and Social Council in July of that year,[9] the Centre on TNCs submitted a report as a basis for discussion of the matter at the Commission's April 1984 session.[10] The report reviewed the principal intergovernmental arrangements and discussed bilateral arrangements dealing with investment protection and promotion as well as taxation. It examined regional arrangements, including instruments adopted by regional economic integration groupings, and international arrangements dealing with specific economic, social and political issues, in addition to the draft code on TNCs. The report concluded that all instruments relating to TNCs adopted so far were limited in terms of substantive or geographic coverage; none addressed the full range of international concerns that had to be dealt with. They were no substitute for a comprehensive, effective and universally applicable code of conduct.

The Commission took note of the report and requested the Centre to update it for the Commission's 1986 session.[3]

REFERENCES

[1]YUN 1983, p. 606, GA dec. 38/428, 19 Dec. 1983. [2]E/1984/9. [3]E/1984/18. [4]E/1984/L.19. [5]E/1984/9/Add.2. [6]YUN 1983, p. 605. [7]E/C.10/1985/5. [8]E/C.10/1984/17. [9]YUN 1983, p. 610, ESC dec. 1983/182, 29 July 1983. [10]E/C.10/1984/8.

Standards of accounting and reporting

The Intergovernmental Working Group of Experts on International Standards of Accounting and Reporting, established by the Economic and Social Council in 1982,[1] held its second session in New York from 12 to 23 March 1984.[2] Before it were three studies prepared by the Centre on TNCs on the following topics: the work of standard-setting bodies in home and host countries;[3] TNC accounting and reporting policies;[4] and issues identified during the development of an information system on TNC activities (see below).[5] In addition, a working paper was submitted by Egypt for the members of the Group of 77 which were Working Group members, on harmonization of corporate accounting and reporting.

The Executive Director of the Centre on TNCs pointed out that divergent accounting and reporting practices continued to cause concern about the comparability of information in financial statements in different countries. The Chairman observed that many issues reflected different schools of thought about corporate accounting and reporting, issues related to the world-wide growth of TNCs, the diversity of their operations, their impact on the countries in which they operated, and their role in the utilization of capital, technology and human resources. The Group recognized that there was concern in three main areas— information disclosure, divergent accounting practices, and accounting education, training and research—and agreed on the need for harmonizing accounting and reporting practices.

The Group considered issues of accounting and reporting arising from the comprehensive information system developed and maintained by the Centre on TNCs (see below), and outstanding issues identified by the *Ad Hoc* Intergovernmental Working Group of Experts on International Standards of Accounting and Reporting in 1982.[6] Those outstanding issues included: movements in certain assets, among them land and buildings, equipment, long-term investments, patents and trade marks, and long-term deferred charges; government subsidies to business enterprises; and value added as a result of operations of business enterprises. The Group agreed that there was a need for disclosure of information in those areas. In dealing with transfer pricing, another outstanding issue, the Group agreed that policies followed in determining the prices for transactions among associated and similar enterprises should be disclosed, as should the volume of such transactions.

All delegations that spoke at the April session of the Commission on TNCs on the question of international standards of accounting and reporting agreed that the Group had made progress in fulfilling its mandate. One delegation, also speaking on behalf of several others, stressed that the Group's purpose was not to set accounting standards. Some delegations considered that the Group's list of accounting and reporting issues, annexed to its report, was too ambitious.

On 24 April, the Commission took note of the Group's report and approved the provisional agenda and documentation for its 1985 session.[7]

REFERENCES

[1]YUN 1982, p. 788, ESC res. 1982/67, 27 Oct. 1982. [2]E/C.10/1984/9. [3]E/C.10/AC.3/1984/2 & Corr.1 & Add.1. [4]E/C.10/AC.3/1984/3. [5]E/C.10/AC.3/1984/4. [6]YUN 1982, p. 787. [7]E/1984/18 (dec. I).

Centre on TNCs

During 1984, the United Nations Centre on TNCs, the principal Secretariat unit for TNC-related matters, assisted in formulating a code of conduct, prepared studies for the Intergovernmental Working Group of Experts on International

Standards of Accounting and Reporting, and continued to survey international, regional and bilateral arrangements on TNCs (see p. 593). It undertook economic and legal research, and research on the political, social and cultural effects of TNCs. It expanded its information system on TNC activities and trends and provided advisory and information services to Governments (see below). It co-operated in updating a consolidated list of products whose consumption and/or sale had been banned, withdrawn, severely restricted or, in the case of pharmaceuticals, not approved by Governments (see Chapter XVI of this section).

Research on TNC activities in South Africa and Namibia continued to be an important element of the Centre's work. As requested by the Economic and Social Council in July (resolution 1984/53), the Centre assisted in the work of the *Ad Hoc* Committee on the preparations for the public hearings on TNC activities at its two series of meetings in 1984 (July and September) (see p. 149). For those meetings, the Centre prepared a list of studies and reports issued by the United Nations on TNCs in South Africa and Namibia. For the 1984 session of the Commission on TNCs, the Centre prepared a report dealing with measures adopted by home countries with respect to TNCs operating there in violation of United Nations resolutions and decisions.

The Commission considered the activities of the Centre at its April session, taking note of the Secretary-General's report on its activities since mid-1983,[1] and requesting the Centre to report in 1986 on its utilization of resources during 1984-1985.[2]

Information system

In 1984, the Centre on TNCs continued to develop its comprehensive information system.[3] The system focused on six areas in which information was collected, processed and analysed: trends in TNC activities; studies on TNC activities in specific sectors; individual corporations; policies, laws and regulations relating to TNCs; contracts and agreements between TNCs and government agencies and local enterprises; and information sources.

To discern trends in TNC activities, the system collected macro-economic data, including information on flows and stocks of foreign investment, investment income payments from developing countries, and payments to TNCs for technology and services. During 1984, all statistics were updated and refinements were made both in the data collected and in the processing of data. The categories in which data were collected and analysed and the coding systems for those categories were made to conform to evolving United Nations classification standards.

Studies were made on TNCs in specific industry sectors such as construction and engineering; computers and data processing; computer services; banking; biotechnology; synthetic fibres, textiles and clothing; pharmaceuticals; armaments; non-fuel minerals; trade in data and data services; telecommunications; plastics; agricultural trade; pesticides; primary commodities; and semiconductors.

The fifth report on national legislation and regulations relating to TNCs was completed. The Centre also collected a significant number of bilateral and multilateral investment treaties and related agreements. Its collection of contracts and agreements between TNCs and host government organizations was greatly enlarged by the acquisition of 350 petroleum contracts covering the regions of Asia and Australasia, South America and southern and central Africa.

On 24 April 1984,[2] the Commission on TNCs took note of the February progress report on the Centre's information system[4] and requested another report in 1985. The Commission approved the recommendations of the Centre for the modification of its corporate information system. The modifications dealt mainly with increased selectivity in collecting corporate information, increased co-ordination between the analysis of corporate information and the Centre's advisory services and sectoral studies, and the redesign of corporate profiles to make them more uniform and more useful to Governments. The Centre expanded its collection of information on the largest industrial companies from 382 to 700 such companies; the data items collected included total and foreign components of sales, net assets, earnings, research and development expenditure, capital expenditure, and wages and salaries.

The Centre responded to 498 requests for information from Governments and intergovernmental organizations, about half of the requests coming from developing countries. A total of 521 requests were received from non-governmental organizations, including trade unions, business organizations, academic institutions, public interest organizations and the media.

In response to the concern expressed by several delegations at the Commission's April session that the Centre's work might not be reaching the government organizations that most needed them, a note verbale was sent to United Nations missions requesting the names of government and other organizations that should receive Centre publications. Approximately 30 Governments responded, nearly doubling the Centre's mailing list to some 650 organizations, most of them in developing countries.

The Intergovernmental Working Group of Experts on International Standards of Accounting and Reporting, in March 1984 (see above), considered issues of accounting and reporting arising from the Centre's information system. The Group noted that, in collecting data on TNC activities from various sources, the Centre had identified two key issues—the availability and the comparability of data—which concerned the disclosure of financial and non-financial information items, segmentation of aggregate figures, units of measurement, methods of accounting and formats of presentation. The Group agreed that the Centre, in developing its information system, should take into account the agreed lists of minimum items for general purpose reporting, identified by the *Ad Hoc* Intergovernmental Working Group in 1982.[(5)]

The Centre also co-operated in preparing the first revised issue of a list of chemical products deemed toxic or hazardous. In resolution 39/229, the Assembly urged the Centre to continue co-operating fully in updating the list. It further urged countries to avail themselves of the Centre's information facilities.

Joint units with regional commissions

Joint units established between the Centre on TNCs and the United Nations regional commissions in developing areas continued to operate in 1984 in Africa, Asia and the Pacific, Europe, Latin America and Western Asia. Designed for the region's specific needs and to complement the work of the Centre, each unit engaged in research on the economic, social and institutional issues of TNCs, information dissemination, and training and advisory services.

Two Secretariat reports described the work of the units during the year; one covering May 1983 to March 1984,[(6)] submitted to the Commission on TNCs at its April 1984 session, and the other covering April 1984 to March 1985,[(7)] prepared for its 1985 session.

In 1984, the joint unit of the Centre and the Economic Commission for Africa (ECA) concentrated on research. A study on the role of transnational banks and financial institutions in Africa's development process was completed, as were two case-studies on Liberia and Nigeria. Studies were also finalized on TNCs in the non-food agricultural industry and in agricultural food processing. Another study dealt with the structures, policies and operations of TNCs in the mining industry in Africa. The role of TNCs in the African mining industry was also the subject of a regional workshop (Manzini, Swaziland) for English-speaking African countries. A report was prepared on Morocco's experience in relation to the establishment of African multinational enterprises. Collection and dissemination of information was intensified and requests for information on TNCs were sent to all ECA member States.

The activities of the unit established between the Centre and the Economic Commission for Europe (ECE) were mainly focused on in-house research. A comprehensive survey on the extent, dimensions and structure of foreign direct investments in developed countries was completed, while work began on a project on TNCs in the economic integration of the economies of the countries of the ECE region. The unit also aided the Centre in its technical assistance and advisory projects related to specific industries.

In Latin America, case-studies of Bolivia and Peru with respect to transnational banks and external financing were completed as part of an ongoing research project, as was a report on the role of TNCs in the foreign commercial flows of the region. Two studies in the area of commodities were finished, dealing with a global approach for strengthening the bargaining power of countries and with the role of the public sector and TNCs in the development of the mining sector in Latin America. A survey was made of 30 major TNCs in Colombia, and case-studies of Argentina and Colombia were started as part of an ongoing series of reports on the importance of TNCs in various countries. The joint unit also provided advisory services to several countries and co-operated in training activities of the Latin American Institute for Economic and Social Planning of the Economic Commission for Latin America and the Caribbean.

Among the activities of the joint unit with the Economic Commission for Western Asia were preparations for a report on the status of the draft code of conduct on TNCs, with special reference to Arab countries. Negotiations were started with the Arab Industrial Development Organization for a joint study on the role of TNCs in the transfer of technology in the region.

The joint unit with the Economic and Social Commission for Asia and the Pacific (ESCAP) completed a project on transnational trading corporations in selected countries (Republic of Korea, Sri Lanka, Thailand) and a survey of TNCs based in developing countries of the region. A revised version of a study on the taxation of mining projects in the region was issued, as was a study on costs and conditions of technology transfer. A preliminary overview of TNC involvement and foreign investment in Nepal was also completed. The unit provided administrative and technical support to several national and regional workshops organized by the Centre and continued to establish focal points in several ESCAP member countries so as to respond efficiently to their information needs on TNC-related matters.

Research

Centre research activities fell into five broad categories: studies related to a code of conduct and other international arrangements and agreements relating to TNCs, including international standards of accounting and reporting (see p. 594); analyses of general trends in TNC operations; examination of measures strengthening the negotiating capacity of Governments in their relations with TNCs; analysis of the political, social and cultural impact of TNCs on host developing countries; and studies of TNCs in specific areas and selected sectors.[8]

An important element in the Centre's work continued to be research on TNC activities in South Africa and Namibia (see p. 146). The role of TNCs was examined in relation to various other selected areas, including international trade and banking, industry, employment and technology transfer.

The Centre continued to follow closely developments relating to environmental aspects of TNC activities. It was involved in a research programme, carried out jointly with the United Nations Environment Programme, intended to increase the understanding of the role of TNCs in relation to sustained development, national environment policies, location of pollution-intensive industries, environmental management practices and international environmental co-operation.

The Centre published a study on TNCs in the pharmaceutical industry of developing countries and completed drafts of studies on TNCs in the international semiconductor, construction and engineering, and man-made fibre, textile and clothing industries.

Recommendations for the Centre's research and advisory programmes were made by the Secretary-General in a report to the Commission's April 1984 session,[9] based on suggestions made at an August/September 1983 interregional seminar on TNCs in primary commodity exports. Most of the proposals fell within the Centre's existing mandate, the Secretary-General noted, and could be initiated within the programme elements and resources allocated for 1984-1985. He suggested that further research could be undertaken on TNCs in agricultural trade and in non-fuel minerals, and on TNCs and taxation, in co-ordination with the United Nations Conference on Trade and Development, the Food and Agriculture Organization of the United Nations, and the Division of Natural Resources and Energy of the United Nations Department of Technical Co-operation for Development.

During the discussion at the Commission's April session,[2] some delegations stressed the need to avoid duplication of the work of other organizations both inside and outside the United Nations system. Others felt that insufficient attention had been devoted to the negative implications of TNC activities. Several delegations suggested that the Centre should continue its research on the role of TNCs in the least developed countries; others

stressed the importance of further research on conflicting jurisdictions on TNCs in a manner that would mitigate such conflicts. Among other research topics suggested were: technology transfer and reverse transfer of technology; export processing zones; finance and international indebtedness; trade and the balance of payments; interference in the internal affairs of States; political and social impact of TNCs; capital flows and outflows; and armaments and the transfer of military technology. One delegation indicated opposition to research on the last subject, noting the predominant role of Governments in that area and the difficulty in obtaining information.

The Commission requested the Centre, in implementing its research programme, to take into account the delegations' views.

TNCs and development

A major focus of the Centre's research activities was the role of TNCs in world development. Submitted to the Commission at its April 1984 session were: a report on TNCs in world development,[10] updating a survey completed in 1983;[11] and a report on their role in the implementation of the International Development Strategy for the Third United Nations Development Decade.[12]

The first report contained a review of developments in three areas in which international co-operation, including the involvement of TNCs, could be beneficial: finance and trade, where major adjustments were needed to compensate for the decline in lending to developing countries by transnational banks; the role of TNCs in employment; and their role in low-income countries. The report concluded that new and more imaginative forms of co-operation between essential public flows of capital and certain types of foreign private flows were needed.

The second report concluded that the contribution of TNCs to achieving the Strategy's objectives was overshadowed by the consequences of the world economic recession. Foreign direct investment, international lending, the growth of manufactured exports from developing countries and industrialization for the domestic market were adversely affected by the impact of that recession on international trade and payments, trade policies and policies for domestic stabilization. Especially for the majority of the low-income countries and the least developed areas, TNCs might not be able to make a substantial contribution to achieving the objectives of the Strategy that related to resource flows, redeployment and industrialization. The liberalization of restrictions on foreign direct investment had also been a feature of structural adjustment programmes undertaken as a condition for restoring access to international credits, a trend that could reduce developing countries' ability to regulate the activities of TNCs; there remained a need for national and international action to strengthen the negotiating position of developing countries.

In that connection, the report stressed the need for early adoption of a code of conduct (see p. 592) as an instrument for orienting the international environment towards encouraging a positive contribution of TNCs to achieving the objectives of the Strategy. Consideration could also be given to careful scrutiny of foreign investment policies to ensure that a liberalization of restrictions did not erode the real gains made by developing countries in channelling TNC activities towards their national development objectives; further refinement of the policies of host countries towards TNCs and co-operation among developing countries could improve their bargaining power, help reduce the negative effects of TNCs and promote a positive contribution on their part towards achieving the Strategy's objectives.

The Commission on TNCs, at its April 1984 session,[2] decided to transmit the second report in 1985 to the Committee on the Review and Appraisal of the Implementation of the International Development Strategy for the Third United Nations Development Decade. It requested the Centre to prepare for 1988 a fourth survey on TNCs in development. The Commission postponed consideration of a five-nation (Canada, Federal Republic of Germany, Italy, Japan, Sweden) draft resolution, requesting the Centre to prepare a study on the activities of State-owned enterprises, in particular in developing countries.

Transborder data flows

In view of the growing importance of transborder data flows for all countries, especially developing ones, it was stressed at the Commission's April 1984 session that further work on the subject was required.[2] Corporate transborder data flows, in particular, were becoming increasingly important for the conduct of international business.

National and international policies in that area still being rudimentary or non-existent, a Centre report to the Commission[13] proposed that the Centre focus on research on the subject, preparing country case-studies and selected industry studies, and highlighting the impact of new information technologies on the structure and decision-making of TNCs and the role of TNCs in international data and data-services trade.

During the Commission's discussion of the report, it was suggested that a forum be created, in the form of an *ad hoc* working group of experts, in which the implications and impact of transborder data flows on the development process of developing countries could be discussed. Some

delegations felt, however, that such a group was not currently needed and that the Centre should proceed along the path taken so far, which included informal seminars. A draft decision submitted by Mexico, for the members of the Group of 77 which were Commission members, on the establishment of such a working group was withdrawn by the sponsors.

The Commission reaffirmed the importance it attached to the Centre's work on the subject and took note of the Centre's intention to concentrate in the following year on one project area. It requested the Centre's Executive Director to include in the 1985 report on the role of TNCs in transborder data flows suggestions for the future course of action of the Commission on the question, taking into account also consultations with international bodies and other organizations.

Information on studies dealing with the impact of TNCs on transborder data flows and documents on other aspects of TNCs in the context of a new world information and communication order (see p. 354) was submitted in a May 1984 note by the Centre on TNCs to the Committee on Information.

Technical co-operation

The programme of technical co-operation in advisory, information and training services of the Centre on TNCs continued in 1984 to respond to a wide variety of requests from developing countries in numerous sectors and areas.[14] During the year, the Centre completed or initiated 90 advisory and information projects in 33 countries and organized 13 training workshops for some 500 participants. Of those projects, 50 were carried out in low-income countries in response to a growing interest in institution-building. Forty-six were undertaken in 17 African countries or areas, 37 in 11 Asian and Pacific countries or areas, 5 in 3 Latin American countries, and one each in a Western Asian and a European country.

Governments were provided with assistance in formulating new or revising existing policies, institutional arrangements, laws, regulations and model contracts on TNC participation in the economy generally, relating to foreign investment and technology policies and legislation, or in specific sectors, such as petroleum, mining, forestry, pharmaceuticals and electronics. Forty-six projects of that type were conducted, several resulting in legislation approved by Cabinet or enacted by Parliament.

Other services related to the negotiation of specific contractual arrangements and a whole range of issues involving TNCs, with regard to wholly-owned direct investment, joint venture, technology, management, turnkey, financing and other contracts in the context of specific domestic projects. Forty-four projects of that kind were conducted in 1984, approximately one half in the natural resource sectors (petroleum, mining, agriculture, forestry and fisheries) and the remaining half in manufacturing and service industries (fertilizer, pesticide, soda ash, cement, airline, hotel, international loan).

The Centre, partly through its comprehensive information system (see p. 595), delivered basically two types of information: on the organizational structure, experience and financial position of specific TNCs; and on policies, laws and contractual arrangements with TNCs in developing countries.

Training services provided by the Centre comprised workshops, study tours and support to institutions of higher learning and of management and public administration in developing countries. Of the 13 training workshops conducted in 1984, 3 were general, dealing with cross-sectoral issues between TNCs and host Governments, and 10 were specialized programmes on petroleum, mining, loan negotiations, acquisition of technology and, for the first time, international accounting and reporting and international leasing. Nine of the workshops were given in Asia, two in Africa and one each in Western Asia and Latin America.

Study tours were organized for senior officials of the Government of Pakistan to visit foreign investment and technology screening bodies in Malaysia, the Republic of Korea and the Philippines, and for senior officials from Ghana to study, in New York and Washington, D.C., tax and accounting issues related to TNC transactions.

The Centre completed preparation of detailed curricula, related bibliographies and case material for graduate courses on TNCs and economic development, business policy and law, and a non-degree course for practitioners. The curricula were reviewed by scholars in the participating countries (Bangladesh, India, Indonesia, Malaysia, Philippines, Singapore, Sri Lanka, Thailand) and subsequently finalized by the Centre and distributed to participating institutions.

Other training services initiated in 1984 included a programme of assistance to national and regional institutes of management and public administration in Africa; the programme called for assistance in developing institutes' course curricula, the training of lecturers, preparation of teaching manuals and organization of workshops on TNC-related matters.

Among other technical co-operation activities was continued support to intergovernmental organizations that dealt with TNC-related matters. Assistance was provided to a subregional organization in Africa in drafting a charter on multinational industrial enterprises and in analysing fiscal incentives and investment régimes in member countries. The Centre also initiated a project with the secretariat of the Andean Pact to assist member States in adopting uniform requirements for the registration of foreign investment.

In carrying out its technical co-operation programmes, the Centre co-operated with a variety of organizations within and outside the United Nations system.

The Commission on TNCs, in April,[2] reaffirmed the importance it attached to the Centre's technical co-operation programme.

Financing

The Centre implemented technical co-operation activities substantially through the use of extrabudgetary resources, comprised primarily of voluntary contributions by Governments to the Trust Fund for the Centre and resources made available by the United Nations Development Programme (UNDP) for project execution. Total income in 1984 was $2,608,331. That amount included contributions of $764,206 by eight Governments (Finland, $26,474; Netherlands, $125,944; Norway, $190,223; Republic of Korea, $8,558; Sweden, $175,131; Switzerland, $233,645; Zaire, $500; Zambia, $3,731), interest and miscellaneous income of and $193,590 and $1,061,635 from UNDP. Expenditures during the year came to $1,601,635, of which the UNDP share was 66.3 per cent, up from 60.4 per cent in 1983.[15]

REFERENCES

[1]E/C.10/1984/4 & Corr.1. [2]E/1984/18. [3]E/C.10/1985/11. [4]E/C.10/1984/15. [5]YUN 1982, p. 787. [6]E/C.10/1984/5. [7]E/C.10/1985/4. [8]E/C.10/1985/10. [9]E/C.10/1984/13. [10]E/C.10/1984/2. [11]YUN 1983, p. 609. [12]E/C.10/1984/3. [13]E/C.10/1984/14. [14]E/C.10/1985/14. [15]YUN 1983, p. 610.

PUBLICATION

The CTC Reporter, No. 17, Sales No. E.84.II.A.3.

Commission on TNCs

Agenda for the 1985 regular session

ECONOMIC AND SOCIAL COUNCIL ACTION

In July 1984, acting on the recommendation of its First Committee, the Economic and Social Council adopted decision 1984/162 without vote.

Provisional agenda and documentation for the eleventh session of the Commission on Transnational Corporations

At its 48th plenary meeting, on 25 July 1984, the Council approved the provisional agenda and documentation for the eleventh session of the Commission on Transnational Corporations, set out below.

**Provisional agenda and documentation for
the eleventh session of the
Commission on Transnational Corporations**

1. Election of officers.
2. Adoption of the agenda and organization of work.
3. Recent developments related to transnational corporations and international economic relations.
   Documentation
   > Report of the Secretariat on recent developments related to transnational corporations and international economic relations
   > Report of the Secretariat on transnational corporations in international trade and foreign direct investment by transnational corporations, including capital inflows and outflows
4. Activities of the United Nations Centre on Transnational Corporations.
   Documentation
   > Report of the Secretary-General on the activities of the United Nations Centre on Transnational Corporations and on the activities of the joint units with the regional commissions
5. Work related to the formulation of a code of conduct and other international arrangements and agreements:
   (a) Code of conduct;
   Documentation
   > Report of the Secretariat on the code of conduct on transnational corporations
   (b) Other international arrangements and agreements.
   Documentation
   > Report of the Secretariat on developments under other international arrangements and agreements on matters related to transnational corporations
6. Transnational corporations in South Africa and Namibia:
   (a) Activities of transnational corporations in South Africa and Namibia and collaboration of such corporations with the racist minority régime in that area;
   Documentation
   > Report of the Secretariat
   (b) Organization of public hearings on the activities of transnational corporations in South Africa and Namibia;
   Documentation
   > Report of the *Ad Hoc* Committee on the Preparations for the Public Hearings on the Activities of Transnational Corporations in South Africa and Namibia
   (c) Responsibilities of home countries with respect to the transnational corporations operating in South Africa and Namibia in violation of the relevant resolutions and decisions of the United Nations.
   Documentation
   > Report of the Secretariat

7. Ongoing and future research.
   Documentation
   > Report of the Secretariat
8. Comprehensive information system.
   Documentation
   > Report of the Secretariat on the comprehensive information system on transnational corporations
9. International standards of accounting and reporting.
   Documentation
   > Report of the Intergovernmental Working Group of Experts on International Standards of Accounting and Reporting on its third session
10. The role of transnational corporations in transborder data flows.
    Documentation
    > Report of the Secretariat
11. Technical co-operation:
    (a) Review of the programme of technical co-operation;
    Documentation
    > Report of the Secretariat on the programme of technical co-operation
    (b) Measures to strengthen the negotiating capacity of developing countries in their dealings with transnational corporations
    Documentation
    > Report of the Secretariat
12. Work related to the definition of transnational corporations.
    Documentation
    > Report of the Secretariat on the question of the definition of transnational corporations
13. Issues arising from decisions of the General Assembly and the Economic and Social Council.
    Documentation
    > Note by the Secretariat
14. Provisional agenda for the twelfth session of the Commission.
15. Adoption of the report of the Commission.

Economic and Social Council decision 1984/162

Adopted without vote

Approved by First Committee (E/1984/141) without vote, 17 July (meeting 10); draft by Commission on TNCs (E/1984/18); agenda item 10.

Cycle of meetings

Following a request by the Economic and Social Council (in decision 1984/104) that its subsidiary bodies currently meeting annually consider adopting, on an experimental basis, a biennial cycle of meetings, the Commission decided at its April 1984 session to revert to that question in 1985.[1]

REFERENCE

[1]E/1984/18 (dec. II).

Chapter VIII

Regional economic and social activities

In 1984, the five regional commissions held their regular intergovernmental sessions: the Economic Commission for Latin America (changing its nomenclature to the Economic Commission for Latin America and the Caribbean (ECLAC)), at Lima, Peru (29 March–6 April); the Economic Commission for Europe (ECE) at Geneva (3-14 April); the Economic and Social Commission for Asia and the Pacific (ESCAP) in Tokyo (17-27 April); the Economic Commission for Western Asia (ECWA) at Baghdad, Iraq (22-26 April); and the Economic Commission for Africa (ECA) and its Conference of Ministers at Addis Ababa, Ethiopia (24-28 May).

Among issues of concern to the regional commissions considered by the General Assembly in 1984 were: the Transport and Communications Decade in Africa (resolution 39/230), the Industrial Development Decade for Africa (39/233), the Transport and Communications Decade for Asia and the Pacific (39/227) and co-operation between the United Nations and the Southern African Development Coordination Conference (39/215). The Assembly endorsed, in principle, the proposed construction projects at both ECA and ESCAP headquarters (sections III and XI of resolution 39/236) to expand their conference facilities. It authorized the Secretary-General to take measures to enable ECWA to meet its personnel requirements (resolution 39/243).

The Economic and Social Council, in July, took action on: the Transport and Communications Decade in Africa (resolution 1984/68), development of a remote-sensing programme in Africa (1984/69), the Industrial Development Decade for Africa (1984/70), water resources development in Africa (1984/73), the Europe-Africa permanent link through the Strait of Gibraltar (1984/75), ECA's women's programme (1984/77) and the Transport and Communications Decade for Asia and the Pacific (1984/78). Other Council actions dealt with strengthening the ECA role as an executing agency (1984/74), matters arising from ECA Executive Secretary's 1982-1983 report (1984/76), policy-making structure (1984/80) and staff and administrative questions of ECWA (1984/81), and the terms of reference of ECLAC and ESCAP (1984/67 and 1984/66).

Summaries of the annual survey of current economic conditions in each region, prepared by commission secretariats, were taken note of by the Council in July during its discussion of the world economic situation (see p. 406).

Topics related to this chapter. Middle East: assistance to Palestinians. Development policy and international economic co-operation: economic and social trends and policy. Operational activities for development. Economic assistance, disasters and emergency relief. Food. Environment.

Regional co-operation

The Secretary-General reported to the Economic and Social Council, in a June 1984 report on regional co-operation,[1] on the work of the regional commissions and on issues calling for Council action or attention. As part of their ongoing contacts, the executive secretaries of the five regional commissions met at Geneva on 9 July, under the chairmanship of the Director-General for Development and International Economic Co-operation, and reviewed a wide range of issues, including the economic situation and the promotion of interregional economic and technical co-operation among developing countries (see p. 403).[2]

ECONOMIC AND SOCIAL COUNCIL ACTION

The Economic and Social Council, on the recommendation of its First (Economic) Committee, adopted decision 1984/184 without vote. The documents taken note of in the decision are discussed later in this chapter.

Reports considered by the Economic and Social Council in connection with the question of regional co-operation

At its 50th plenary meeting, on 27 July 1984, the Council took note of the following documents:

(*a*) Report of the Joint Inspection Unit entitled "Contribution of the United Nations system to the conservation and management of Latin American cultural and natural heritage" and the comments of the Secretary-General thereon;

(*b*) Note by the Secretary-General transmitting the progress report of the Executive Secretary of the Economic Commission for Africa on the implementation of the programme for the Transport and Communications Decade in Africa;

(*c*) Report of the Secretary-General on special measures for the social and economic development of Africa in the 1980s;

(*d*) Progress report of the Joint Inspection Unit on the implementation of recommendations on regional programmes in the conservation and management of African wildlife and the comments of the Secretary-General thereon;

(e) Note by the Secretary-General transmitting the report of the Executive Secretary of the Economic Commission for Africa on the outcome of the round-table meeting on the climatic situation and drought in Africa;

(f) Report of the Secretary-General on regional co-operation;

(g) Report of the Secretary-General on progress made in the implementation of Economic and Social Council resolution 1983/66 on interregional co-operation among developing countries;

(h) Note by the Secretary-General transmitting the interim report of the Executive Secretaries of the Economic Commission for Africa and the Economic Commission for Europe on a Europe-Africa permanent link through the Strait of Gibraltar;

(i) Note by the Secretary-General transmitting the report of the Executive Secretary of the Economic Commission for Africa on particular problems facing Zaire with regard to transport, transit and access to foreign markets.

Economic and Social Council decision 1984/184

Adopted without vote

Approved by First Committee (E/1984/142/Add.1) without vote, 24 July (meeting 17); oral proposal by Chairman; agenda item 9.

Strengthening of regional commissions

The Secretary-General reported in April 1984[3] that efforts to achieve decentralization and restructuring, in accordance with a 1982 General Assembly resolution on the topic,[4] should not lead to fragmentation of Secretariat activities, but promote mutually reinforcing activities and contribute to the cohesiveness of the work of the United Nations. The consultations held on the question had confirmed a definite need to encourage genuine co-operation and closer and continuing interaction between units of regional commissions and Headquarters on programme matters and to pursue decentralization with flexibility, taking into account the requirements of each commission. The Secretary-General believed that the overwhelming proportion of the work involved would be undertaken at the regional level, while Headquarters would retain responsibility for global synthesis and analysis and for presenting outputs to central legislative bodies. A number of joint activities, with Headquarters having the main responsibility but with greater involvement by the commissions, were suggested in programmes relating to population, social development, science and technology, and development issues and policies and public administration.

In a November report,[5] the Secretary-General noted that advances had been made with regard to delegation of authority and decentralization. In the administrative area, clear-cut policies had gradually emerged, leading to a considerable delegation of personnel and financial authority to the regional commissions; in relation to substantive programmes, it had generally proved more difficult to develop

and apply uniform approaches and criteria. Arrangements were being made to promote a more systematic involvement of the executive secretaries at all stages of programme planning and budgeting, and a new practice had been initiated involving the holding of intersecretariat meetings following sessions of the General Assembly and the Economic and Social Council to determine the most effective distribution of responsibilities for implementing their resolutions. Collaboration continued to be strengthened between the regional commissions on the one hand and the United Nations Development Programme (UNDP) and the Department of Technical Co-operation for Development (DTCD) on the other. The promotion of subregional and regional co-operation, the main *raison d'etre* of the commissions, was acquiring important new dimensions with the increasing emphasis being placed by developing countries on the concept of self-reliance and economic and technical co-operation among them.

On interregional co-operation among developing countries, the Secretary-General, in a June report[6] on progress made in implementing a 1983 Council resolution,[7] emphasized the need for an intersecretariat meeting to examine operational modalities for setting up and executing joint projects for promoting such co-operation, the application of an operational framework to priority areas for joint action, possible co-ordinated activities in the high-priority sphere of international financial co-operation, and activities in certain specific aspects of interregional economic and technical co-operation among developing countries (see p. 403).

The Committee for Programme and Co-ordination (CPC),[8] having studied the Secretary-General's April report, concluded that several fundamental questions of decentralization—such as measures to avoid compartmentalization or duplication of activities—had yet to be analysed before it could take decisions. It recommended that the Secretary-General should further clarify and identify the specific activities for decentralization and present concrete proposals in order to ensure the most economical and effective use of resources.

The Assembly took note of the Secretary-General's April report in decision 39/437.

REFERENCES

[1]E/1984/112 & Corr.1-3. [2]E/1985/106. [3]A/39/97-E/1984/59. [4]YUN 1982, p. 828, GA res. 37/214, 20 Dec. 1982. [5]A/39/476. [6]E/1984/113. [7]YUN 1983, p. 418, ESC res. 1983/66, 29 July 1983. [8]A/39/38.

Africa

In 1984, Africa faced the most critical economic conditions which, for some countries on the continent experiencing famine and malnutrition, came down to the question of sheer survival. Some 36 countries were affected by drought and were dependent on food aid. In addition, several disasters disrupted transport and communications with wide-ranging long-term effects (see p. 465).

Meeting from 24 to 26 May at its headquarters at Addis Ababa, the Economic Commission for Africa (nineteenth session) and its Conference of Ministers (tenth meeting)[1]—the highest policy body of ECA—focused on the critical economic situation, external indebtedness, food and agriculture, effects of the climatic situation and drought, and development issues. The Conference of Ministers adopted 43 substantive resolutions covering all aspects of socio-economic development, including a Regional Plan of Action to Combat the Impact of Drought in Africa, and a Kilimanjaro Programme of Action on Population and Self-Reliant Development. In addition, it adopted a final communiqué and a Special Memorandum on Africa's Economic and Social Crisis, to which was annexed a Declaration on Africa's External Indebtedness, adopted in June by the African Ministers of Finance.

The Commission's activities focused on achieving the goals and objectives of the Lagos Plan of Action for the Implementation of the Monrovia Strategy for the Economic Development of Africa, adopted by the Organization of African Unity (OAU)[2] and taken note of by the General Assembly in 1980.[3]

Economic and social trends

The overall economic situation in Africa in 1982-1983 was one of stagnation of output, according to a summary of the ECA survey of economic and social conditions in Africa.[4] After declining by 2.7 per cent in 1981, the regional product remained practically constant in 1983, and only a handful of countries had grown at rates exceeding the population growth or comparable to the average of the 1970s. There was a steep decline in per capita income to a level estimated at 10 per cent lower than in 1980. The major factors behind the recession affecting Africa were decline in demand for its exports, resulting from the recession of the industrialized economies, and the drought. The exports of oil-producing Nigeria and the Libyan Arab Jamahiriya, for instance, fell by 55 and 48 per cent, respectively, between 1980 and 1983, while other primary commodity prices fell sometimes to record lows. Lower export revenues led to acute shortages of imported raw materials and inputs for industry, leading to production slow-downs and even close-ups; capacity utilization fell to 20 per cent in some cases.

Continuing drought in the west and southern subregions depressed agricultural production (see p. 509), with diverse consequences on the external balance as well as the industrial sector which was highly dependent on agriculture for supplies.

Other factors leading to the poor economic performance pertained to the policies followed by Governments, tending in many instances to create an unfavourable framework for production activities.

The survey foresaw a recovery in 1984, although prospects beyond 1984 were not favourable.

The summary was noted by the Economic and Social Council in decision 1984/187.

The survey for 1983-1984[5] indicated that Africa's economic performance continued to be affected by, among other factors, the catastrophic drought, which covered a vast area from the Sahel to eastern and southern Africa, with a population of nearly 182 million in a total of 27 countries. A substantial tightening of budget policies was noted in the region in 1983-1984, the terms of trade improved slightly in 1984 and the total external debt of developing Africa at the end of 1984 was estimated at some $158 billion (see p. 606).

Critical economic situation

Special Memorandum

In May 1984, the ECA Conference of Ministers adopted a Special Memorandum on Africa's Economic and Social Crisis,[6] consisting of a preamble and five parts dealing with the nature and causes of the crisis, the emergency needs of the 24 most affected countries, short- and medium-term measures, long-term structural adjustment measures for the continent, and conclusions.

In the preamble, grave concern was expressed over the alarming and significant deterioration in the economic and social conditions of the African countries, the effects of the drought affecting 34 member States, and the devastating impact of the global economic recession on Africa, with the collapse in commodity prices, unexpectedly high interest rates, sharp exchange-rate fluctuations, increased protectionism, balance-of-payments difficulties, mounting external debt and decline in real terms of official development assistance (ODA). (See also p. 468.)

In analysing the current crisis and its causes, the Special Memorandum noted that the crisis stemmed mainly from the interaction of widespread, severe and persistent drought and the rapidly deteriorating international economic environment; solution was beyond the ability of African countries, for many of which the issue was that of sheer survival. In particular, the prolonged drought had led to severe food scarcity and had triggered off famine, malnutrition and related diseases, loss of human lives, depletion of livestock, water shortages and severe dislocation of normal life and the fragile African economies. The food situation had deteriorated so drastically that in the 34 drought-stricken countries, the imports of cereals had increased from some 4 million metric tons in 1970 to over 23 million tons in 1982.

The emergency situation had also aggravated the movement of persons in search of food and water.

In addition to emergency requirements such as food aid, the African Ministers appealed to the International Monetary Fund (IMF) and the World Bank to liberalize the conditionalities of their loans and aid, and to all creditors to grant a moratorium to loan servicing and repayments to the 24 countries so as to enable them to cope with the emergency situation. Immediate balance-of-payments support and direct credit to enable reactivation of under-utilized industrial capacities was requested.

In the Memorandum's conclusions, the ECA members expressed the belief that Africa should not continue to be the weakest link in the network of world economic interdependence, and that it was in the interest of world peace and stability for the international community to co-operate fully with African Governments in averting the impending economic and social disaster and in putting Africa on the path of growth and development.

In a special appeal to the London Summit, in June, of seven major industrialized countries, the ECA Conference of Ministers called on the participants to mobilize massive resources to assist African countries.

A Declaration on Africa's External Indebtedness, adopted by the African Ministers of Finance at a regional ministerial meeting in June (see p. 606), was subsequently annexed to the Special Memorandum in accordance with a decision of the ECA Conference of Ministers.

Activities in 1984

Development policy and regional economic co-operation

Implementation of the 1980 Lagos Plan of Action

In a report submitted to the General Assembly and the Economic and Social Council in June, with a July addendum,[7] the Secretary-General discussed, in response to a December 1983 Assembly request,[8] the activities of the United Nations system in relation to the social and economic development of Africa, and progress made in implementing the 1980 Lagos Plan of Action,[2] covering areas such as human resources development, investment studies and activities, technology development and transfer, and technical assistance and co-operation projects.

The report pointed out that, while the ODA component in bilateral assistance continued to decline in real terms, more aid was anticipated in response to the Secretary-General's appeal for assistance to deal with the current critical economic situation and as a result of the Economic and Social Coun-

cil's special consideration of the matter at its second regular session of 1984. The Secretary-General said he would continue to allocate the necessary resources to ECA, taking into account its role as the main economic and social development centre within the United Nations system for the African region. The report was taken note of by the Council in decision 1984/184 and by the General Assembly in decision 39/445.

In May, the ECA Conference of Ministers took note of the 1982-1983 report of the Executive Secretary, expressed concern that ECA did not have the necessary resources for evaluating its programmes and projects, and appealed to the international community to contribute to the United Nations Trust Fund for African Development. Further, it urged UNDP, and requested the Secretary-General, to increase allocations to ECA. By another action, the Ministers requested the ECA and OAU secretariats to intensify their technical and logistic support to the African countries prior to and during international negotiations on development issues.

The Commission's Multinational Programming and Operational Centres (MULPOCs) continued to promote and sustain economic co-operation and integration activities in the region.

ECONOMIC AND SOCIAL COUNCIL ACTION

On 27 July 1984, the Economic and Social Council, on the recommendations of its First Committee, adopted resolution 1984/76 without vote.

Matters arising from the biennial report of the Executive Secretary of the Economic Commission for Africa for 1982-1983

The Economic and Social Council,

Recalling resolution 403(XVI), adopted on 10 April 1981 by the Conference of Ministers of the Economic Commission for Africa, on the biennial report of the Executive Secretary of the Commission for 1979-1980,

Recalling also section IV of the annex to General Assembly resolution 32/197 of 20 December 1977 on the restructuring of the economic and social sectors of the United Nations system, in which, *inter alia*, it is stipulated that the regional commissions should be enabled fully to play their role under the authority of the General Assembly and the Economic and Social Council as the main general economic and social development centres within the United Nations system for their respective regions,

Recalling further General Assembly resolution 38/199 of 20 Decmeber 1983 on special measures for the social and economic development of Africa in the 1980s, in which, *inter alia*, the Assembly urged donor countries to provide substantial and sustained levels of resources for promoting the accelerated development of African countries and the effective implementation of the Lagos Plan of Action for the Implementation of the Monrovia Strategy for the Economic Development of Africa and the Final Act of Lagos and to contribute generously to the United Nations Trust Fund for African Development,

Convinced that a strengthened secretariat of the Economic Commission for Africa is an imperative necessity for the States members of the Commission, both individually and collectively, particularly in view of the current economic and social crisis facing Africa,

1. *Appeals* to the international community, particularly the developed countries of Western and Eastern Europe, North America, Japan and the members of the Organization of the Petroleum Exporting Countries, other developing countries in a position to do so, and international and regional financial institutions to contribute generously at the Fifth Biennial Pledging Conference for the United Nations Trust Fund for African Development;

2. *Requests* the Secretary-General to provide additional resources to the Economic Commission for Africa as the centre for general social and economic development within the United Nations system for the African region so as to enable it, in general, to assist member States more effectively and, in particular, to develop the required capacity and capability in the field of evaluation of programmes and projects.

Economic and Social Council resolution 1984/76

27 July 1984   Meeting 50   Adopted without vote

Approved by First Committee (E/1984/142) without vote, 23 July (meeting 16); draft by ECA (E/1984/21); agenda item 9.

Development planning

The Joint Conference of African Planners, Statisticians and Demographers (third session, Addis Ababa, 5-14 March) prepared five draft resolutions for consideration by the ECA Conference of Ministers, on short-term forecasting in the African region, perspective studies in Africa, demographic training institutes, infrastructure posts for the ECA secretariat in the population field, and the Pan-African Documentation and Information System (PADIS).

In May, the Conference of Ministers called on African countries to undertake and strengthen short-term outlook activities, and to undertake perspective studies on their respective economies. It also decided to establish a regional technical committee, which would set a policy for PADIS and oversee project execution.

Implementation of the International Development Strategy

The ECA Conference of Ministers, in May, expressed concern over the lack of progress in implementing, in Africa, the International Development Strategy for the Third United Nations Development Decade (the 1980s).[9] It urged African Governments to renew their efforts to remove obstacles to the Strategy's implementation, invited them to bring such impediments to the attention of the Economic and Social Council, and requested the Executive Secretary to prepare a progress report.

Least developed countries

The Conference of Ministers of African Least Developed Countries (LDCs) held its fourth meeting at Addis Ababa from 22 to 25 May 1984.

The ECA Conference of Ministers, also in May, urged African LDCs to prepare themselves for the 1985 mid-term global review, by an intergovernmental expert group of the United Nations Conference on Trade and Development (UNCTAD), of the Substantial New Programme of Action (SNPA) for the 1980s for LDCs.[10] It also urged donor countries and multilateral financial institutions to provide financial assistance to the African LDCs on favourable terms and conditions, and to alleviate their debt burden through retroactive adjustment measures or complete cancellation of debts. (See also p. 412.)

International trade and finance

The Ministerial Follow-up Committee on Trade and Finance for African Development (third meeting, Addis Ababa, 9-14 May) considered trade issues of concern to Africa, including the implication of UNCTAD VI on the region's development; it also called on the secretariat to seek dialogue with the socialist countries of Eastern Europe on trade and economic relations and co-operation.

The ECA Conference of Ministers, in May, asked the 26 African LDCs to bring up to date their institutional pricing structures and to make appropriate price-fixing arrangements for agricultural producers, and invited IMF and the World Bank to make compensatory arrangements regarding pricing policies. In another action, the Ministers accepted Togo's offer to host the Fourth All-Africa Trade Fair at Lomé in 1985 and created an organizing committee of 15 countries for the Fair.

Secretariat activities placed special emphasis on identifying domestic trade distribution channels, bearing in mind the region's food crisis; high priority was given to the preparatory work for setting up an African Monetary Fund.

Intraregional trade

The Federation of African Chambers of Commerce was established in September 1984 with 24 national chambers of commerce, industry, mines and agriculture signing its constitution: the ECA secretariat was designated to serve as the Federation's interim secretariat until January 1986.

Preferential Trade Area for Eastern and Southern African States

GENERAL ASSEMBLY ACTION

In November 1984, Zimbabwe, on behalf also of 11 other African States, submitted a draft resolution[11] to the General Assembly's Second (Economic and Financial) Committee, which would have had the Assembly request donor Governments to provide financial and technical assistance to the Preferential Trade Area for Eastern and Southern African States—established by a treaty signed at Lusaka, Zambia, in 1981[12]—to accelerate its development into an economic community by 1992.

In December, the Assembly adopted decision 39/433 without vote.

Preferential Trade Area for Eastern and Southern African States

At its 104th plenary meeting, on 18 December 1984, the General Assembly, on the recommendation of the Second Committee, decided to refer to its fortieth session for consideration the draft resolution entitled "Preferential Trade Area for Eastern and Southern African States".

General Assembly decision 39/433

Adopted without vote

Approved by Second Committee (A/39/790/Add.3) without vote, 6 December (meeting 56); oral proposal by Vice-Chairman; agenda item 80 *(c)*.
Meeting numbers. GA 39th session: 2nd Committee 53, 56; plenary 104.

Other action. The ECA Conference of Ministers appealed to member States which had not done so to sign and ratify the 1981 treaty, urged those which had not done so to ratify the treaty establishing the Economic Community of Central African States, called for measures to strengthen MULPOCs and appealed for assistance for projects whose final objective was establishment of an African economic community by the year 2000.

External debt

The African Ministers of Finance—at a regional ministerial meeting, held at Addis Ababa from 18 to 20 June 1984—adopted a Declaration on Africa's External Indebtedness.[13] In addition to a preamble, the Declaration contained sections dealing with the causes of the external indebtedness; measures for implementation at national, subregional, regional, interregional and international levels; and conclusions.

The Declaration noted that Africa's external debt was $150 billion, out of the total third-world indebtedness of $785 billion in 1983, with rates of overall debt and debt servicing as compared to exports, respectively, at 223.5 per cent and 25.1 per cent, far ahead of Asia (81.4 per cent and 10.8 per cent) and closer to Latin America (288.5 per cent and 44 per cent); the available margin for internal adjustments was much smaller in Africa because of the large number of countries classified as LDCs facing the vagaries of the weather and food problems.

Among measures called for at the international level were possible cancellation of external debts of developing African countries; improved debt rescheduling; a moratorium, for at least 3 to 5 years, on debt servicing of both public and private lenders; containing debt services at a reasonable percentage

of export earnings and gross national product; and introduction of fairer and more far-reaching multilateral arrangements for reorganizing debt-servicing obligations. IMF was called on to adopt more concrete measures for balance-of-payments support at an increased level.

Further, the Declaration saw a need for increased ODA in view of the substantial reduction in private resource flows to Africa, and for consideration by the industrialized countries of reducing international interest rates, setting a ceiling on interest rates, and writing off accumulated arrears in interest payments or converting them into grants. It recommended the convening of international conferences—one to deal with the external indebtedness of African countries, and another on money and finance for development.

The Declaration was annexed to the Special Memorandum on Africa's Economic and Social Crisis (see p. 603), as previously agreed to by the ECA Conference of Ministers.

Africa's external debt problem was also dealt with by the General Assembly in resolution 39/29, on the Declaration on the Critical Economic Situation in Africa.

Transport and communications

Transport and Communications Decade in Africa (1978-1988)

The second phase (1984-1988) of the Transport and Communications Decade for Africa (1978-1988)[14] was launched by the Conference of African Ministers of Transport, Communications and Planning (fourth session, Conakry, Guinea, 7-11 February 1984), which also reviewed the implementation of the first phase (1980-1983) and approved the programme for the second phase.

The Secretary-General submitted to the Assembly, in May,[15] a listing and financial analysis of the work programme developed for 1984-1985, and reported that no response had been made to his March appeal for voluntary contributions towards the unappropriated resources required. The Committee for Programme and Co-ordination,[16] on 8 May, took note of the report and requested the Secretary-General to submit to the Assembly at its 1984 session an updated report indicating all activities foreseen and the status of resources available for their implementation.

In his annual progress report on the implementation of the programme for the Decade, submitted in June to the Assembly and the Council,[17] the ECA Executive Secretary discussed the preparation and presentation of the second-phase programme, consisting of 1,053 projects costing $18.36 billion. Of those, 581 projects were for transport ($14.43 billion) and 472 for communications

($3.93 billion). Some 37 per cent of the funds required for the former, and 46 per cent for the latter, had been or were about to be secured. The Secretary-General also reported in June to the Assembly and the Council[18] that the second-phase programme reflected ECA efforts to prepare a rational programme based on the evaluation of the first-phase activities. Emphasis was placed on certain categories of projects that were both critical and would have the greatest impact on the physical integration of the continent, namely, maintenance and rehabilitation, human resources development, transit corridors and inter-country and subregional projects.

Evaluation of the first phase showed that, during implementation, the initial programme had increased from 771 to 1,091 projects and costs had risen from an estimated $9 billion to $15.4 billion; of the $7.1 billion secured for the first phase, some $5.2 billion, or 75 per cent, was provided by the African countries themselves. It was considered that a firm base had been established during the first phase for the eventual solution of Africa's major transport and communications problems.

The ECA Conference of Ministers, in May, endorsed the programme for the second phase and called on donor countries and international financial institutions to provide African countries with technical and financial resources on liberal terms for implementing the new phase, giving particular attention to projects of land-locked countries. The Secretary-General and the UNDP Administrator were also asked to secure and provide funds.

ECONOMIC AND SOCIAL COUNCIL ACTION

On 27 July 1984, the Economic and Social Council, on the recommendation of its First Committee, took note of the ECA Executive Secretary's progress report (decision 1984/184) and adopted resolution 1984/68 without vote.

Transport and Communications Decade in Africa

The Economic and Social Council,

Recalling resolution 291(XIII), adopted on 26 February 1977 by the Conference of Ministers of the Economic Commission for Africa, Council resolution 2097(LXIII) of 29 July 1977 and General Assembly resolution 32/160 of 19 December 1977, by which the Assembly proclaimed a Transport and Communications Decade in Africa during the years 1978-1988,

Recalling also resolutions 435(XVII) and 464(XVIII), adopted on 30 April 1982 and 2 May 1983 by the Conference of Ministers of the Economic Commission for Africa,

Referring to Council resolution 1982/54 of 29 July 1982 and General Assembly resolutions 37/140 of 17 December 1982 and 38/150 of 19 December 1983,

Considering that the programme for the Decade requires regular adjustment throughout the Decade,

Noting with satisfaction the efforts made by the Executive Secretary of the Economic Commission for Africa

in the preparation of the plan of action for the second phase (1984-1988) of the Decade and the approval of that plan of action by the Conference of African Ministers of Transport, Communications and Planning at its fourth meeting, held at Conakry from 7 to 11 February 1984,

Noting with satisfaction also that the Secretary-General has provided funds for the preparation and organization of the four consultative technical meetings to be held during the second phase of the Decade,

Aware of the report of the Executive Secretary on the implementation of the plan of action for the first phase (1980-1983) of the Decade and the approved plan of action for the second phase (1984-1988),

Considering that the Conference of Ministers of the Economic Commission for Africa has endorsed the plan of action for the second phase of the Decade with regard to the transport and communications routes accorded priority in the Lagos Plan of Action for the Implementation of the Monrovia Strategy for the Economic Development of Africa and the Final Act of Lagos,

1. *Expresses its appreciation* to the Secretary-General for the financial support he has provided for the organization of the consultative technical meetings and the preparations for the second phase of the Transport and Communications Decade in Africa;

2. *Requests* the Secretary-General to make every effort to secure and provide to the Economic Commission for Africa the additional resources needed for the implementation of the activities requested by the General Assembly in paragraph 9 of its resolution 38/150;

3. *Further requests* the Secretary-General to make available to the Economic Commission for Africa, within existing resources, sufficient financial resources to enable it to ensure the preparation of relevant financing documents and the prompt follow-up of the interest expressed by donors and financial institutions during consultative technical meetings in financing projects for the Decade.

Economic and Social Council resolution 1984/68

25 July 1984   Meeting 50   Adopted without vote

Approved by First Committee (E/1984/142) without vote, 23 July (meeting 16); draft by ECA (E/1984/21), orally amended during informal consultations; agenda item 9.

GENERAL ASSEMBLY ACTION

On 18 December 1984, the General Assembly, on the recommendation of the Second (Economic and Financial) Committee, took note of the two reports of the Secretary-General relating to the Decade (decision 39/445) and adopted resolution 39/230 by recorded vote.

Transport and Communications Decade in Africa

The General Assembly,

Recalling its resolution 38/150 of 19 December 1983 on the Transport and Communications Decade in Africa, by which it approved the organization of technical consultative meetings and studies on the harmonization and co-ordination of the various modes of transport and communications,

Recalling also Economic and Social Council resolution 1984/68 of 27 July 1984,

Considering the priority attached to transport and communications in the Lagos Plan of Action for the Implementation of the Monrovia Strategy for the Economic Development of Africa and the Final Act of Lagos, and the endorsement of the programme for the second phase (1984-1988) of the Transport and Communications Decade in Africa by the Conference of Ministers of the Economic Commission for Africa in its resolution 487(XIX) of 26 May 1984,

Noting the approval of the programme for the second phase of the Decade by the Conference of African Ministers of Transport, Communications and Planning at its fourth session, held at Conakry from 7 to 11 February 1984, and the efforts made by the Executive Secretary of the Economic Commission for Africa in the preparation of the plan,

Bearing in mind that the programme for the Decade requires regular adjustment throughout the Decade,

Taking note of the note by the Secretary-General transmitting the progress report of the Executive Secretary of the Economic Commission for Africa on the implementation of the programme for the first phase (1980-1983) of the Decade and the approved programme for the second phase (1984-1988),

1. *Reaffirms* its resolution 38/150 on the Transport and Communications Decade in Africa and calls for its immediate and effective implementation;

2. *Endorses* the programme for the second phase of the Transport and Communications Decade in Africa approved by the Conference of Ministers of the Economic Commission for Africa in its resolution 487(XIX);

3. *Notes* the financial support provided by the Secretary-General and the Administrator of the United Nations Development Programme to the Economic Commission for Africa for the preparation of the programme for the second phase of the Decade and for the continued operations of the Decade Co-ordination Unit;

4. *Invites* all Governments, particularly those of the developed countries, and international financial institutions to increase substantially their financial support for the programme for the second phase of the Decade and to accord particular attention to the financing and implementation of transport and communications projects of the land-locked countries, to participate fully and positively in the scheduled technical consultative meetings and to provide financial and technical resources on liberal terms to African countries for the implementation of the programme for the second phase of the Decade;

5. *Appeals* to the international community and international financial institutions to provide the Economic Commission for Africa with experts for short terms who would carry out specialized activities in the programme for the Decade, including the preparation of project documents;

6. *Appeals also* to the United Nations Development Programme to continue to provide the Economic Commission for Africa with funds during the next programming cycle;

7. *Requests* the Secretary-General to provide the Economic Commission for Africa with adequate financial resources from the regular budget of the United Nations to enable it:

(a) To fully implement the activities previously mandated in paragraph 9 of General Assembly resolution 38/150;

(b) To ensure the preparation of relevant financial and technical documents of selected projects for the programme for the second phase of the Decade;

(c) To ensure prompt follow-up on interest expressed by Governments and international financial institutions, during technical consultative meetings, in financing Decade projects;

8. *Further* requests the Secretary-General to ensure the implementation of the present resolution and to submit to the General Assembly at its fortieth session a report on the progress achieved in the implementation of the Decade programme.

General Assembly resolution 39/230

18 December 1984   Meeting 104   130-1-18 (recorded vote)

Approved by Second Committee (A/39/789/Add.1) by recorded vote (105-1-20), 10 December (meeting 58); draft by Egypt, for Group of 77 (A/C.2/39/L.33); agenda item 12.

Financial implications. 5th Committee, A/39/831; S-G, A/C.2/39/L.79, A/C.5/39/93.

Meeting numbers. GA 39th session, 2nd Committee 39, 58; 5th Committee 53; plenary 104.

Recorded vote in Assembly as follows:

In favour: Afghanistan, Algeria, Angola, Argentina, Australia, Austria, Bahamas, Bahrain, Bangladesh, Barbados, Benin, Bhutan, Bolivia, Botswana, Brazil, Brunei Darussalam, Burkina Faso, Burma, Burundi, Cape Verde, Central African Republic, Chad, Chile, China, Colombia, Congo, Costa Rica, Cuba, Cyprus, Democratic Kampuchea, Democratic Yemen, Denmark, Djibouti, Dominican Republic, Ecuador, Egypt, El Salvador, Equatorial Guinea, Ethiopia, Fiji, Finland, France, Gabon, Gambia, Ghana, Greece, Guatemala, Guinea, Guinea-Bissau, Guyana, Haiti, Honduras, Iceland, India, Indonesia, Iran, Iraq, Israel, Ivory Coast, Jamaica, Jordan, Kenya, Kuwait, Lao People's Democratic Republic, Lebanon, Lesotho, Liberia, Libyan Arab Jamahiriya, Madagascar, Malawi, Malaysia, Maldives, Mali, Malta, Mauritania, Mauritius, Mexico, Morocco, Mozambique, Nepal, New Zealand, Nicaragua, Niger, Nigeria, Norway, Oman, Pakistan, Panama, Papua New Guinea, Paraguay, Peru, Philippines, Portugal, Qatar, Romania, Rwanda, Saint Christopher and Nevis, Saint Lucia, Saint Vincent and the Grenadines, Samoa, Sao Tome and Principe, Saudi Arabia, Senegal, Sierra Leone, Singapore, Somalia, Spain, Sri Lanka, Sudan, Suriname, Swaziland, Sweden, Syrian Arab Republic, Thailand, Togo, Trinidad and Tobago, Tunisia, Turkey, Uganda, United Arab Emirates, United Republic of Tanzania, Uruguay, Vanuatu, Venezuela, Viet Nam, Yemen, Yugoslavia, Zaire, Zambia, Zimbabwe.

Against: United States.

Abstaining: Belgium, Bulgaria, Byelorussian SSR, Canada, Czechoslovakia, German Democratic Republic, Germany, Federal Republic of, Hungary, Ireland, Italy, Japan, Luxembourg, Mongolia, Netherlands, Poland, Ukrainian SSR, USSR, United Kingdom.

On 15 December, the Fifth (Administrative and Budgetary) Committee, by a recorded vote of 73 to 17, with 9 abstentions, decided to inform the Assembly that the resolution's adoption would entail an additional appropriation of $1,439,600 in the 1984-1985 budget.

Paragraphs 4 and 7 were approved in the Second Committee by recorded votes of 102 to 1, with 22 abstentions, and 94 to 14, with 17 abstentions, respectively. In explanation of vote on the text as a whole, the Federal Republic of Germany, the Ukrainian SSR (also on behalf of Bulgaria, the Byelorussian SSR, Czechoslovakia, the German Democratic Republic, Hungary, Mongolia, Poland and the USSR) and the United States objected to the financial implications. Denmark further objected to a departure from the Committee's efforts to adopt by consensus those resolutions having financial implications. Similarly, Japan and the United Kingdom felt that paragraph 7 (a) contravened the arrangements set forth in the December 1983 Assembly resolution on the topic[19] whereby financing was assured for the 1984-1985 biennium.

Air transport

A Conference on Freedoms of the Air (Mbabane, Swaziland, 19-23 November 1984)—organized, in response to a December 1983 Assembly request,[19] by ECA in collaboration with OAU, the African Civil Aviation Commission and the African Airlines Association—adopted the Mbabane Declaration, thereby creating a technical committee to, among other things, take inventory of existing or potential main routes necessary for the economic development and physical integration of Africa, and to promote multinational airlines or joint operations at subregional levels.

Satellite communications and remote sensing

An extraordinary meeting of experts of transport, communications and planning (Addis Ababa, March) reviewed the activities of the Inter-Agency Co-ordinating Committee in conducting a feasibility study on an African satellite communications system.

Conscious of the benefits to be derived from the applications of remote sensing to communications and natural resources development and to the solution of many of the phenomena affecting Africa's social and economic development, the Conference of Ministers requested the Economic and Social Council and the Secretary-General to provide ECA with adequate resources on a regular basis for development of the African remote-sensing programme.

ECONOMIC AND SOCIAL COUNCIL ACTION

On 27 July 1984, the Economic and Social Council, on the recommendations of its First Committee, adopted resolution 1984/69 without vote.

Development of the African remote-sensing programme

The Economic and Social Council,

Noting with appreciation the steps taken by the Executive Secretary of the Economic Commission for Africa, as highlighted in his biennial report for 1982-1983, towards the implementation of resolution 280(XII), adopted on 28 February 1975 by the Conference of Ministers of the Economic Commission for Africa, concerning the introduction of remote-sensing technology into Africa, and resolution 313(XIII), adopted on 1 March 1977 by the Conference of Ministers, concerning the establishment of a remote-sensing programme in Africa,

Recalling that the achievements reported by the Executive Secretary have been accomplished principally through the utilization of extrabudgetary resources which have continued to be inadequate for the development of the programme,

Mindful of General Assembly resolution 37/90 of 10 December 1982 on the Second United Nations Conference on the Exploration and Peaceful Uses of Outer Space,

Requests the Executive Secretary of the Economic Commission for Africa to review the current programme of the Commission, with a view to reallocating funds for the implementation and development of the African remote-sensing programme.

Economic and Social Council resolution 1984/69

27 July 1984   Meeting 50   Adopted without vote

Approved by First Committee (E/1984/142) without vote, 23 July (meeting 16); draft by ECA (E/1984/21), orally amended during informal consultations; agenda item 9.

Strait of Gibraltar

The Executive Secretaries of ECA and ECE, in an interim report submitted to the Economic and Social Council through the Secretary-General in June,[20] stated that all transport work in the Mediterranean region should take into account the possibility that a permanent link would be built between Africa and Europe through the Strait of Gibraltar by the end of the century. They expressed the hope that material resources would be allocated to the project, which they believed was essential for communications between the two continents.

In May, the ECA Conference of Ministers adopted a resolution similar to that subsequently adopted by the Council (see below).

ECONOMIC AND SOCIAL COUNCIL ACTION

On 27 July, the Economic and Social Council, on the recommendation of its First Committee, adopted resolution 1984/75 without vote.

Europe-Africa permanent link through the Strait of Gibraltar

The Economic and Social Council,

Recalling its resolutions 1982/57 of 30 July 1982 and 1983/62 of 29 July 1983 on the proposed Europe-Africa permanent link through the Strait of Gibraltar,

Recalling also the conclusions contained in the interim report prepared by the Economic Commission for Africa and the Economic Commission for Europe,

Bearing in mind the need to take into account the principles of good-neighbourliness and co-operation among all parties interested in and concerned with the pursuit of this project,

1. *Invites* the Governments of Morocco and Spain to continue to provide information to, and to consult and co-operate with, Governments, international organizations, research institutions and universities in the Mediterranean area and elsewhere, the Economic Commission for Africa and the Economic Commission for Europe and to make concerted efforts in the pursuit of the development of the project for the Europe-Africa permanent link through the Strait of Gibraltar;

2. *Also invites* Governments, international organizations, research institutions and universities in the Mediterranean area and elsewhere to continue to co-operate with the Governments of Morocco and Spain and with the Economic Commission for Africa and the Economic Commission for Europe and to make concerted efforts in the pursuit of this project;

3. *Requests* the Secretary-General to provide the Economic Commission for Africa and the Economic Commission for Europe, within available resources, with the additional resources necessary for the implementation of the recommendations on the proposed permanent link through the Strait of Gibraltar;

4. *Requests* the Executive Secretaries of the Economic Commission for Africa and the Economic Commission for Europe to submit an interim report on the progress made with regard to the studies on this project, through the Economic Commission for Africa and the Economic Commission for Europe, to the Economic and Social Council at its second regular session of 1985.

Economic and Social Council resolution 1984/75

27 July 1984   Meeting 50   Adopted without vote

Approved by First Committee (E/1984/142) without vote, 23 July (meeting 16); draft by Vice-Chairman (E/1984/C.1/L.21), based on informal consultations on draft by ECA (E/1984/21) and orally amended during those consultations; agenda item 9.

Transport and trade of Zaire

In 1984, the Secretary-General submitted to the Council a June note,[21] later taken note of in Council decision 1984/184, transmitting the report of the ECA Executive Secretary on the results of the first round-table meeting organized in 1983[22] to assist the semi-land-locked country of Zaire with its international trade and transit problems. It was reported that—due to project cancellation or suspension, or cost adjustment since the 1983 meeting—the number of projects had been reduced from 59 to 56, while the total cost of the programme had increased from $2,239 million to $2,526 million.

Tourism

A Regional Conference on Tourism, organized in collaboration with the World Tourism Organization (Niamey, Niger, 2-6 October), decided to establish a Conference of African Ministers of Tourism to be convened every two years; it also asked for studies on the possibility of establishing an *ad hoc* machinery for co-ordinating the activities of regional and subregional tourism development institutions.

Industrial development

Implementation of the programme for the Industrial Development Decade for Africa (1980-1990)

Efforts continued to focus in 1984 on implementing the programme for the Industrial Development Decade for Africa (IDDA) (1980-1990).[23]

The OAU Council of Ministers, at its February-March 1984 session, urged the international community to give increased assistance to African countries in their effort to implement industrial programmes and projects within the IDDA framework.

The Seventh Conference of African Ministers of Industry (Addis Ababa, March) reviewed the progress made, endorsed the programme of activities for 1985-1990, and formulated and approved a common African position for the Fourth General Conference of the United Nations Industrial Development Organization (UNIDO). It noted that, out of 36 countries classified by the United Nations as least developed, 26 were in Africa, and 21 of the 34 countries classified by the World Bank as "low-income" developing countries were located in the region; in 1980, the industrial sector in Africa accounted for 9.8 per cent of the region's GDP and for only 0.9 per cent of world manufacturing output. It stressed the need for international support, adding that preliminary estimates for some of the core projects in the DDA programme stood at $140 billion.

The ECA Conference of Ministers, in May, reiterated the need to accord priority to developing strategic core industries, providing sectoral linkages and essential inputs for the production and processing of natural resources, especially food and agricultural products. It also noted that the African Industrial Development Fund, which the Conference of African Ministers of Industry in 1979 had requested ECA and the African Development Bank to establish,[24] had become operational with 15 member States—three more than the minimum number required—having signed or ratified the Fund's constitution. It agreed that the African Development Bank should manage the Fund under the policy direction of the Ministers of Industry.

UNIDO action. On 19 May, the Industrial Development Board (IDB) of UNIDO[25] requested the UNIDO Executive Director, in co-operation with OAU and ECA, to assist African countries and intergovernmental organizations in implementing the programmes endorsed by the Seventh Conference of African Ministers of Industry. It welcomed the 1983 Assembly decision[26] to increase allocations to IDDA by $1 million (see p. 611) and noted with interest the appeal expressed by the Seventh Conference that the Assembly allocation be increased to an annual minimum level of $5 million and be put on a permanent basis.

A third progress report on IDDA, prepared in response to a 1983 Assembly request[26] by the UNIDO Executive Director, in co-operation with the ECA Executive Secretary, and considered by IDB, was later submitted by the Secretary-General[27] to the Assembly through the Economic and Social Council. The report described co-operation between, and activities by the secretariats of, ECA, OAU and UNIDO in implementing the IDDA programme.

On 19 August,[28] the Fourth General Conference of UNIDO invited the Assembly to consider the appeal for a permanent allocation of an annual minimum of $5 million to IDDA. It also recommended that UNIDO assist African countries and organizations in a wide range of industrial development endeavours, including developing industries based on locally available natural resources, especially those promoting self-sufficiency in food supplies and creating employment in rural areas.

ECONOMIC AND SOCIAL COUNCIL ACTION

On 27 July 1984, the Economic and Social Council, on the recommendation of its First Committee, adopted resolution 1984/70 without vote.

Implementation of the programme for the Industrial Development Decade for Africa

The Economic and Social Council,

Recalling General Assembly resolution 35/66 B of 5 December 1980, by which the Assembly proclaimed the 1980s as the Industrial Development Decade for Africa, section II of Assembly resolution 36/182 of 17 December 1981, section II of Assembly resolution 37/212 of 20 December 1982 and section II of Assembly resolution 38/192 of 20 December 1983, concerning the Industrial Development Decade for Africa,

Recalling also resolutions 442(XVII), adopted on 30 April 1982 by the Conference of Ministers of the Economic Commission for Africa, concerning the formulation and implementation of a programme for the Industrial Development Decade for Africa, and 466(XVIII), adopted on 2 May 1983 by the Conference of Ministers, concerning the implementation of the programme for the Industrial Development Decade for Africa,

Welcoming resolution CM/Res.941(XL), adopted by the Council of Ministers of the Organization of African Unity at its fortieth ordinary session, held at Addis Ababa from 27 February to 5 March 1984,

Reiterating the need to accord priority to the development of strategic core industries that provide intrasectoral and intersectoral linkages and essential input for the production and processing of natural resources, especially food and agricultural products,

Convinced of the need to undertake concerted action for the mobilization of financial resources, including technical assistance from the secretariats of the Economic Commission for Africa, the United Nations Industrial Development Organization and the Organization of African Unity and from other African and international organizations and bilateral and multilateral donor agencies, for the implementation of the programme for the Decade,

1. *Expresses its appreciation* to the General Assembly for its decision, in section II of resolution 38/192, to increase the allocation to the United Nations Industrial Development Organization from the regular budget of the United Nations by $1 million in 1984 for assistance to African countries and to intergovernmental organizations in the implementation of the programme for the Industrial Development Decade for Africa, notes with interest the appeal made by the Seventh Conference of African Ministers of Industry, held at Addis Ababa from 26 to 28 May 1984, that the allocations made by the General Assembly for the Decade should reach an annual level of at least $5 million and be placed on a permanent basis, and calls upon the General Assembly to give it due attention; to this end, a similar arrangement should be considered for the Economic Commission for Africa to enable it and its Multinational Programming and Operational Centres to assist member States at the subregional level in their consultations, negotiations and investment promotion for multi-country projects;

2. *Welcomes with appreciation* the generous financial contributions made by a number of countries to the Economic Commission for Africa, the United Nations Industrial Development Organization and some African regional centres for the implementation of activities related to the Decade;

3. *Reiterates* the repeated appeals made to the international community, particularly the United Nations Development Programme, the World Bank, the African Development Bank, the Fund for International Development of the Organization of Petroleum Exporting Countries, the Arab Bank for Economic Development in Africa and other international organizations, multilateral and bilateral agencies and financial institutions to increase and intensify their technical and financial assistance, on preferential conditions, to African countries and to intergovernmental organizations in the formulation and implementation of the programme for the Decade.

Economic and Social Council resolution 1984/70

27 July 1984   Meeting 50   Adopted without vote

Approved by First Committee (E/1984/142) without vote, 23 July (meeting 16); draft by ECA (E/1984/21), orally amended during informal consultations; agenda item 9.

In related action, the Council, by decision 1984/167, took note of, and transmitted to the General Assembly, the IDB report and the Secretary-General's note transmitting the third progress report on IDDA.

Financing. In response to a December 1983 Assembly decision[26] to increase the allocation to UNIDO by $1 million in 1984 for assistance in IDDA programme implementation, the Secretariat reported to CPC in April 1984[29] that reviews and consultations had been initiated on various possibilities for savings from the 1984-1985 programme budget or redeployment aimed at meeting the allocation target, but that little could be said before a review was made of submissions from units within the Secretariat for the first programme budget performance report in September. CPC recommended in May,[16] that the Secretary-General speed up efforts to present a comprehensive report on his proposal to achieve the necessary reimbursement of funds.

The Secretary-General reported to the Fifth Committee in November[30] that savings of $127,100 had been identified from the 1984-1985 programme budget and that, during the current biennium, a balance of $872,900—required to reimburse fully the $1 million drawn from savings in the 1982-1983 programme budget—was expected from further savings and redeployments. The Advisory Committee on Administrative and Budgetary Questions (ACABQ) endorsed the approach taken by the Secretary-General; since the budget was approved on a two-year basis, savings could not be reported unless it was certain that an activity would not be implemented in either year. In November, the Fifth Committee[31] took note of the Secretary-General's report and approved certain transfer of funds and reduction of income estimates.

GENERAL ASSEMBLY ACTION

On 18 December 1984, the General Assembly, on the recommendation of the Second Committee, adopted resolution 39/233 by recorded vote.

Industrial Development Decade for Africa

The General Assembly,

Recalling its resolutions 3201(S-VI) and 3202(S-VI) of 1 May 1974, containing the Declaration and the Programme of Action on the Establishment of a New International Economic Order, 3281(XXIX) of 12 December 1974, containing the Charter of Economic Rights and Duties of States, 3362(S-VII) of 16 September 1975 on development and international economic co-operation and 35/56 of 5 December 1980, the annex to which contains the International Development Strategy for the Third United Nations Development Decade, in which, *inter alia*, the importance of industrialization in the development of developing countries is stressed,

Recalling its resolutions 38/192 and 38/199 of 20 December 1983 and Economic and Social Council resolution 1983/70 of 29 July 1983 emphasizing the Industrial Development Decade for Africa as one of the most important industrial development programmes of the United Nations Industrial Development Organization,

Considering that the provision of adequate levels of resources by donor countries will contribute immensely to promoting the accelerated industrial development of African countries and the effective implementation of the Lagos Plan of Action for the Implementation of the Monrovia Strategy for the Economic Development of Africa,

Recalling Economic and Social Council resolution 1984/70 of 27 July 1984, in which the Council noted the appeal to the General Assembly to increase substantially the allocation to the United Nations Industrial Development Organization from the regular budget of the United Nations for assistance to African countries and to intergovernmental organizations in the implementation of the programme for the Industrial Development Decade for Africa to an annual minimum level of $5 million and to place that allocation on a permanent basis,

Reaffirming resolution 8 adopted on 19 August 1984 by the Fourth General Conference of the United Nations Industrial Development Organization, concerning the Industrial Development Decade for Africa,

Reaffirming also Industrial Development Board resolution 57(XVIII) of 19 May 1984, in which the Board, *inter alia*, reaffirmed its request to the United Nations Development Programme to allocate adequate financial resources to the programme for the Decade, taking into account the high priority attached to it by the General Assembly, the Industrial Development Board and the African countries,

Taking note of resolution CM/Res.941(XL) adopted by the Council of Ministers of the Organization of African Unity at its fortieth ordinary session, concerning the implementation of the programme for the Industrial Development Decade for Africa,

Mindful of the need for African countries to undertake the priority activities designated for the preparatory phase of the programme for the Decade,

Mindful also of the high level of investment expenditure required for promoting the objectives of the Decade,

1. *Reaffirms* its resolutions 38/192 and 38/199 and calls for their immediate and effective implementation;

2. *Takes note with satisfaction* of the third progress report on the Industrial Development Decade for Africa, prepared jointly by the Executive Director of the United Nations Industrial Development Organization and the Executive Secretary of the Economic Commission for Africa;

3. *Welcomes* the efforts that the United Nations Industrial Development Organization continually deploys in order to assist African countries and intergovernmental organizations in defining national and subregional programmes for the Industrial Development Decade for Africa and in order to maintain permanent and harmonious co-ordination with the secretariat of the Organization of African Unity, the Economic Commission for Africa and the other international organizations concerned;

4. *Endorses* resolution 8 of the Fourth General Conference of the United Nations Industrial Development Organization and requests the General Conference, in co-ordination with other bodies and organizations of the United Nations system, as well as with technical and financial institutions in both Africa and the donor countries, to take appropriate measures for the implementation of that resolution, in particular paragraph 9 thereof;

5. *Endorses also* Industrial Development Board resolution 57(XVIII) in which, *inter alia*, the Board requested the Executive Director of the United Nations Industrial Development Organization to provide, to the extent possible, in co-operation with the Secretary-General of the Organization of African Unity and the Executive Secretary of the Economic Commission for Africa, assistance to African countries and intergovernmental organizations concerned in the implementation of the initial integrated industrial promotion programmes at the subregional level, including the convening of follow-up subregional meetings to review the progress made in their implementation;

6. *Endorses further* the appeal made by the Seventh Conference of African Ministers of Industry, held at Addis Ababa from 26 to 28 March 1984, for the allocation of at least $5 million, on a permanent annual basis, from the regular budget of the United Nations in order to enable the United Nations Industrial Development Organization to assist the African countries and the intergovernmental organizations concerned in the implementation of the programme for the Industrial Development Decade for Africa;

7. *Reiterates its appeal* to all countries, particularly the developed countries, and to multilateral financial institutions to increase their contributions to the United Nations Industrial Development Fund, taking into account the financial requirements of projects directed towards the implementation of the programme for the Industrial Development Decade for Africa;

8. *Urges* the international community, in particular the developed countries and international financial institutions, to intensify and increase their technical and financial assistance to African countries for the implementation of programmes and the execution of projects at the national, subregional and regional levels, in the context of the Industrial Development Decade for Africa;

9. *Requests* the Executive Director of the United Nations Industrial Development Organization, in cooperation with the Economic Commission for Africa, to submit to the General Assembly at its fortieth session, through the Industrial Development Board and the Economic and Social Council at its second regular session of 1985, a report on the progress made in the implementation of the programme for the Industrial Development Decade for Africa.

General Assembly resolution 39/233

18 December 1984   Meeting 104   120-1-28 (recorded vote)

Approved by Second Committee (A/39/790/Add.4) by recorded vote (93-1-28), 10 December (meeting 58); draft by Egypt, for Group of 77 (A/C.2/39/L.35); agenda item 80 *(d)*.

Financial implications: 5th Committee, A/39/830; S-G, A/C.2/39/L.94, A/C.5/39/94.

Meeting numbers. GA 39th session: 2nd Committee 39, 58; 5th Committee 53; plenary 104.

Recorded vote in Assembly as follows:

In favour: Afghanistan, Algeria, Angola, Argentina, Austria, Bahamas, Bahrain, Bangladesh, Barbados, Benin, Bhutan, Bolivia, Botswana, Brazil, Brunei Darussalam, Burkina Faso, Burma, Burundi, Cape Verde, Central African Republic, Chad, Chile, China, Colombia, Congo, Costa Rica, Cuba, Cyprus, Democratic Kampuchea, Democratic Yemen, Djibouti, Dominican Republic, Ecuador, Egypt, El Salvador, Equatorial Guinea, Ethiopia, Fiji, Gabon, Gambia, Ghana, Greece, Guatemala, Guinea, Guinea-Bissau, Guyana, Haiti, Honduras, India, Indonesia, Iran, Iraq, Israel, Ivory Coast, Jamaica, Jordan, Kenya, Kuwait, Lao People's Democratic Republic, Lebanon, Lesotho, Liberia, Libyan Arab Jamahiriya, Madagascar, Malawi, Malaysia, Maldives, Mali, Malta, Mauritania, Mauritius, Mexico, Morocco, Mozambique, Nepal, Nicaragua, Niger, Nigeria, Oman, Pakistan, Panama, Papua New Guinea, Paraguay, Peru, Philippines, Qatar, Romania, Rwanda, Saint Christopher and Nevis, Saint Lucia, Saint Vincent and the Grenadines, Samoa, Sao Tome and Principe, Saudi Arabia, Senegal, Sierra Leone, Singapore, Somalia, Sri Lanka, Sudan, Suriname, Swaziland, Syrian Arab Republic, Thailand, Togo, Trinidad and Tobago, Tunisia, Turkey, Uganda, United Arab Emirates, United Republic of Tanzania, Uruguay, Vanuatu, Venezuela, Viet Nam, Yemen, Yugoslavia, Zaire, Zambia, Zimbabwe.

Against: United States.

Abstaining: Australia, Belgium, Bulgaria, Byelorussian SSR, Canada, Czechoslovakia, Denmark, Finland, France, German Democratic Republic, Germany, Federal Republic of, Hungary, Iceland, Ireland, Italy, Japan, Luxembourg, Mongolia, Netherlands, New Zealand, Norway, Poland, Portugal, Spain, Sweden, Ukrainian SSR, USSR, United Kingdom.

In the Second Committee, paragraphs 5 and 6 were approved by recorded votes of 90 to 10, with 21 abstentions, and 91 to 22, with 8 abstentions, respectively.

All those speaking in explanation of vote objected to the draft's financial implications. The United States felt it was inappropriate to spend large sums of money for the purpose indicated in the text at a time when millions of people were starving. The Ukrainian SSR (also on behalf of Bulgaria, the Byelorussian SSR, Czechoslovakia, the German Democratic Republic, Hungary, Mongolia, Poland, and the USSR) spoke of the need to check budgetary growth. The United Kingdom opposed the financing of operational activites from the regular budget, and the idea of a permanent annual allocation. Sweden felt the draft went much further than the resolution adopted by consensus by UNIDO. For Denmark, the action on the draft disregarded the Committee's efforts to adopt, by consensus, resolutions having financial implications. The Federal Republic of Germany stated that its support for the text's objectives notwithstanding, it could not go along with the financial implications.

On 15 December, by a recorded vote of 71 to 18, with 10 abstentions, the Fifth Committee decided to inform the Assembly that the resolution's adoption would entail an additional appropriation of $5 million in the 1984-1985 budget.

In related action, the Assembly, in resolution 39/29 on the Declaration on the Critical Economic Situation in Africa, noted the need for increased resources and international support for rapid implementation of IDDA.

Natural resources and energy

In 1984, ECA activities in mineral resources focused on strengthening the Eastern and Southern African Mineral Resources Development Centre (Dodoma, United Republic of Tanzania), by providing technical and administrative assistance. An extraordinary Governing Council meeting took place in December to enable the Central African Mineral Resources Development Centre (Brazzaville, Congo) to become operational.

In the energy field, work continued on an inventory of potential resources, coal, oil and gas production and oil refinaries, and thermal and hydropower stations and transmission lines. Preparations were made for an African Regional Centre for Solar Energy.

The ECA Conference of Ministers, in May, endorsed the undertaking of a comprehensive study on the pipeline distribution, and a comparison of various modes of transport, of African natural gas for marketing within Africa and possible transport to Europe.

National capabilities for marine resources management were studied at an African intergovernmental meeting on aspects of applications of the provisions of the United Nations Convention on the Law of the Sea (Addis Ababa, September).

Water

ECONOMIC AND SOCIAL COUNCIL ACTION

On 27 July, the Economic and Social Council, on the recommendation of its First Committee, adopted without vote resolution 1984/73 on water resources development and follow-up to the 1977 Mar del Plata Action Plan.[32]

Water resources development and follow-up to the Mar del Plata Action Plan

The Economic and Social Council,

Recalling General Assembly resolution 32/158 of 19 December 1977, by which the Assembly adopted the report of the United Nations Water Conference and approved the Mar del Plata Action Plan,

Guided by resolution VIII of the United Nations Water Conference, in which the regional commissions were called upon to play a central role in the promotion of intergovernmental co-operation as a follow-up to the Mar del Plata Action Plan on integrated water resources development and management,

Recalling also Council resolutions 2043(LXI) of 5 August 1976, in which it requested the Secretary-General to make adequate provisions so as to enable the regional commissions to carry out their activities effectively, and 1979/67 of 3 August 1979, in which it recommended that the secretariats of the regional commissions should be provided with sufficient manpower and financial resources to enable them to discharge the expanded responsibilities assigned to them by the United Nations Water Conference in relation to the execution of the Mar del Plata Action Plan,

Recalling further the recommendation on institutional strengthening at the regional level contained in paragraph 82 (iii) of the Lagos Plan of Action for the Implementation of the Monrovia Strategy for the Economic Development of Africa,

Requests the Secretary-General to continue to strengthen the secretariat of the Economic Commission for Africa in the area of water resources so that water experts can be deployed to the Multinational Programming and Operational Centres to assist member States in the planning and execution of their water development activities and in the follow-up to the recommendations contained in the Mar del Plata Action plan.

Economic and Social Council resolution 1984/73

27 July 1985   Meeting 50   Adopted without vote

Approved by First Committee (E/1984/142) without vote, 23 July (meeting 16); draft by ECA (E/1984/21), orally amended during informal consultations; agenda item 9.

Food and agriculture

In 1984, hunger, famine and malnutrition threatened Africa with greater force than ever before, the Secretary-General informed the General Assembly in a June report,[33] prepared in response to a December 1983 Assembly request.[34] He reported that, by the end of 1983, the number of African countries threatened by food shortages had risen from 22 to 24, that the line of vegetation on the southern fringes of the Sahara desert had moved 200 kilometres southwards from 1982 to 1983, and that a large majority of the countries were failing to meet increased food demand from domestic production. (See also Chapter XI of this section.) In the mean time, the sub-Saharan population—which had grown by 87 per cent since 1960 to 393 million—continued to increase by some 3 per cent annually, the fastest growth rate in the world. The climatic conditions continued to worsen in southern and eastern Africa. It was observed that one of the prime objectives of the Lagos Plan of Action[2]—the acceleration of food programmes and actions for greater collective food self-sufficiency by the turn of the century—could not be achieved if current trends continued. The report examined recent trends, some possible causes, outlook for the future, and issues consituting a basis for possible action; it called for greater policy adjustments, the setting of priorities and stepped-up investments for reversing the unfavourable trends.

A Conference for Africa, held by the Food and Agriculture Organization of the United Nations (FAO) at Harare, Zimbabwe, in July, adopted the Harare Declaration and a resolution appealing for additional international food aid to Africa (see PART II, Chapter III).

The Sub-Committee on Nutrition of the Administrative Committee on Co-ordination (ACC) (tenth session, Rome, Italy, 5-9 March),[35] decided that information on nutrition assistance contained in United Nations development assistance reports should be collated and that three institutions in Africa south of the Sahara should be identified, strengthened and expanded to provide regional competence in food and nutrition training, research and advisory services. Its suggestion for investigating the possibility of strengthening the Joint FAO/WHO/OAU Regional Food and Nutrition Commission for Africa was reiterated by ACC in its annual overview report for 1983/84.[36]

The World Food Council (tenth session, Addis Ababa, 11-15 June)[37] noted the gravity of the food crisis facing Africa, expecially the sub-Saharan region, and the estimates by FAO that almost half the African countries, with some 150 million people, were facing food shortages. It called on donors to step up emergency and relief supplies to the highly affected African countries, while underlining the importance of greater integration of short-term relief with medium-term rehabilitation measures and the longer-term social and economic objectives of the Lagos Plan of Action. The Council believed that resources should be concentrated during the next decade on such areas as human resources development, restructuring of grain markets and improving pricing policies, greater integration of consumption and nutritional factors in production programmes, and expanding irrigation schemes. International support should be given to regional or subregional efforts in water management, agricultural research, trade organization, management of agricultural commodity markets and the fight against desertification.

The United Nations/FAO Committee on Food Aid Policies and Programmes (eighteenth session, Rome, 29 October–8 November) urged donor countries to provide more emergency assistance in terms of food and logistical support for those African nations facing imminent threats of starvation and malnutrition. It also urged affected countries to mobilize local resources for transportation and distribution of available food, and resident representatives of international organizations to co-ordinate in assisting recipient nations to ensure the effective and efficient delivery of emergency food aid.

The ECA Conference of Ministers, in May, having examined a report prepared by the Executive Secretary, in collaboration with FAO, on a study to ascertain the causes of the apparent discrepancy between the increasing resource allocation to food and agriculture and the declining performance of that sector, called on African States to undertake such studies at the national level and report to the Conference in 1985.

GENERAL ASSEMBLY ACTION

On 17 December 1984, the General Assembly, on the recommendation of the Second Committee, adopted resolution 39/165 without vote.

Critical situation of food and agriculture in Africa

The General Assembly,

Recalling its resolutions 3201(S-VI) and 3202(S-VI) of 1 May 1974, containing the Declaration and the Programme of Action on the Establishment of a New International Economic Order, 3281(XXIX) of 12 December 1974, containing the Charter of Economic Rights and Duties of States, and 3362(S-VII) of 16 September 1975 on development and international economic cooperation,

Gravely concerned at the dramatic deterioration in food and agricultural production in Africa, as a result of which there has been an alarming increase in the number of people exposed to hunger, malnutrition and even starvation,

Recognizing the special emphasis placed upon food and agriculture and the undertaking and resolve of Africa to devote its scarce resources on a priority basis to the rehabilitation of food and agricultural production as reflected in and in accordance with the Lagos Plan of Action for the Implementation of the Monrovia Strategy for the Economic Development of Africa,

Taking note of the report of the Secretary-General on the critical situation of food and agriculture in Africa,

Noting the exacerbation of Africa's food and agricultural crisis by the adverse impact of prolonged drought and accelerating desertification and, moreover, that the African countries have been hit by adverse external forces, including falling trade earnings resulting from the global economic recession, the worsening terms of trade and the debt crisis,

Convinced that the food and agricultural crisis in Africa has a long genesis and has been rendered more acute by natural factors, such as poor rainfall, widespread bush fires, unusually severe crop infestation, and epidemics of plant and animal diseases,

Welcoming the adoption, on 25 July 1984, by the Thirteenth FAO Regional Conference for Africa, of the Harare Declaration on the food crisis in Africa, prepared by the African Ministers for Agriculture and Rural Development,

1. *Reaffirms* its resolution 38/159 of 19 December 1983, as well as all other relevant resolutions on the critical situation of food and agriculture in Africa, and calls for their immediate and effective implementation;

2. *Welcomes* the conclusions and recommendations of the World Food Council at its tenth ministerial session, held at Addis Ababa from 11 to 15 June 1984, in particular those relating to the African region;

3. *Notes with appreciation* the encouraging response by the international community to the various appeals made for the alleviation of the present critical food supply situation in Africa;

4. *Welcomes* the unanimous adoption by the Committee on Food Aid Policies and Programmes on 8 November 1984 of a resolution on the food crisis in Africa, and calls for its full and prompt implementation;

5. *Urges* the international community, in view of the continued critical food supply situation in a large number of African countries, to sustain and increase its efforts to provide the additional food aid required on an emergency basis, as well as technical and other forms of assistance needed in that connection;

6. *Urges* the international community also to respond generously to the urgent need for agricultural inputs for the rehabilitation of agriculture and animal husbandry;

7. *Calls upon* the international community to continue to support efforts undertaken by African countries at the national, subregional and regional levels to increase food production through, *inter alia*, the provision, on a priority and long-term basis, of additional financial and technical assistance to Africa by organizations of the United Nations system, such as the International Fund for Agricultural Development, the United Nations Development Programme and other organizations involved in the financing of agricultural development, and through an increase in lending by the World Bank to the agricultural sector in Africa;

8. *Takes note* of the efforts already undertaken by African countries in the field of food and the formulation of agricultural policies, and encourages them to pursue and strengthen these efforts, especially in the definition and implementation of national food strategies, plans and programmes;

9. *Requests* the Secretary-General to submit to the General Assembly at its fortieth session, through the Economic and Social Council at its second regular session of 1985, a progress report on the implementation of the present resolution, with particular emphasis on the role and activities of the United Nations system in assisting the African countries towards the solution of their food and agricultural problems.

General Assembly resolution 39/165

17 December 1984   Meeting 103   Adopted without vote

Approved by Second Committee (A/39/790/Add.6) without vote, 30 November (meeting 54); draft by Vice-Chairman (A/C.2/39/L.54), based on informal consultations on draft by Egypt, for Group of 77 (A/C.2/39/L.13); agenda item 80 *(f)*.
Meeting numbers. GA 39th session: 2nd Committee 31, 54; plenary 103.

In a related action, the Assembly—by a 27-paragraph Declaration on the Critical Economic Situation in Africa, annexed to resolution 39/29—expressed deep concern over Africa's economic and social crisis, which, it said, had assumed alarming proportions seriously jeopardizing the very survival of millions of people. It recognized the urgent need for massive international emergency relief aid in: additional food and other emergency supplies, together with the technical and financial assistance necessary for their transportation, storage and distribution; improvement in water supplies; improvement of health and nutrition, including the needs of refugees and displaced persons; safeguarding national nuclei of livestock herds; establishment of income-generating projects; and promotion of new and renewable energy projects, particularly in rural areas. Urgent international action was required to support national and regional efforts to implement the Plan of Action to Combat Desertification. The Assembly also recognized the need for, among other things, an early attainment of national and collective self-reliance in food production, the provision of appropriate incentives, improvement of storage and transport, reduction of food losses, achievement of a better balance between agricultural export commodities and food production, diversification of agricultural production and utilization of irrigation potential, particularly in drought-prone areas.

In resolution 39/166, the Assembly called on the international community for greater flow of resources in support of programmes and policies for increasing food and agricultural production and raising nutritional standards in the developing countries, particularly in Africa.

Science and technology in Africa

In May, the ECA Conference of Ministers approved recommendations of the Intergovernmental Committee of Experts for Science and Technology Development, which had met in 1983,[38] and thanked India and the Federal Republic of Germany for financial support in promoting rural technologies and mobilizing adaptive technology potential in African economies.

Social development

In May, the ECA Conference of Ministers expressed concern about the increasing criminality of different forms and dimensions in many African countries, endorsed the report of the 1983 African Regional Preparatory Meeting for the Seventh (1985) United Nations Congress on the Prevention of Crime and the Treatment of Offenders,[39] and urged member States to consider crime prevention and criminal justice in the context of overall development. The United Nations system was invited to assist African States in achieving a concerted socio-economic development within the context of the Lagos Plan of Action in order to improve living conditions, thereby reducing crime tendencies resulting from poverty, unemployment and overcrowded slums.

On the question of youth and the 1985 International Youth Year (IYY), the Conference of Ministers endorsed the conclusions and recommendations of an ECA report on the situation of African youth in the 1980s and the report of the 1983 regional meeting on IYY, including a regional plan of action on youth (see Chapter XX of this section).

In resolution 1984/71, the Economic and Social Council requested the Secretary-General to continue strengthening the ECA secretariat in order to enable it to fulfil its extended mandate in the field of youth, including implementation of the regional plan of action.

Population

The Second African Population Conference, meeting at Arusha, United Republic of Tanzania, from 9 to 13 January, adopted a Kilimanjaro Programme of Action for African Population and Self-Reliant Development.

The Programme of Action,[40] comprised of principles and objectives and 93 recommendations, noted that the current African population of about 439 million was likely to double by 2010, that half the population was under 20 years old and that the current high levels of fertility and mortality caused concern about the region's ability to maintain even living standards already attained since independence.

Among objectives, the Programme listed the formulation and implementation of comprehensive population policies which provided lasting solutions to the major problems of high mortality and fertility, uneven population distribution, growing unemployment, stagnation of living standards and unequal income distribution. The recommendations dealt with population and development strategy and policy; fertility and family planning; morbidity and mortality; urbanization and migration; the changing role of women in the development process; children and youth; population data collection, analysis, training and research; population information; community involvement and the role of private and non-governmental organizations; and actions by the international community. It asserted that population should be seen as a central component in formulating and implementing policies and programmes for accelerated socio-economic development.

In May, the ECA Conference of Ministers approved the Kilimanjaro Programme of Action and urged the United Nations Fund for Population Activities (UNFPA) to reactivate certain posts for ECA in the population field. It also urged African Governments to support, administratively and financially, the Regional Institute for Population Studies in Ghana and the Institut de formation et de recherche démographiques in Cameroon.

The UNDP Governing Council, in June, supported continued assistance to regional and interregional demographic training and research centres, taking into account the particular needs of the centres located in Africa south of the Sahara (see p. 722).

ECA activities in 1984 included assistance to member States in preparation for the International Conference on Population in Mexico (see p. 714).

Human resources development

In May, the ECA Conference of Ministers called on United Nations agencies and other organizations carrying out activities in the field of human resources development to give preference to using and strengthening existing African institutions in order to assist the continent in achieving self-sufficiency in human resources supply.

Environment

The ECA Conference of Ministers, discussing the critical economic and social conditions in Africa which were being aggravated by drought and other natural calamities, noted that 34 African countries, including 16 LDCs, were affected by drought and desertification (see also p. 756). It adopted a Regional Plan of Action to Combat the Impact of Drought in Africa, which had been approved by the Scientific Round-Table on the Climatic Situation and Drought in Africa (Addis Ababa, 20-23 February) with a view to equipping the African countries with the means better to monitor and predict the drought and deal with its adverse impacts (see p. 507).

The Conference of Ministers also called on ECA and the World Meteorological Organization to explore the feasibility of establishing an advanced centre for meteorology in Africa to assist in applying meteorological services for development and for combating drought.

On environment and development, it called for the promotion of technical co-operation, information exchange, technology and expertise for combating desertification in Africa; invited African Governments to increase awareness of environmental issues and concerns, particularly in the rural population; and recommended that Governments take immediately all precautionary measures for environmental protection in industrial development by adapting into national industrial development programmes the guidelines developed on the topic by the United Nations Environment Programme (UNEP), and develop national environmental institutions. Further, the Conference urged the Economic and Social Council and the General Assembly to consider including the United Republic of Tanzania in the terms of reference of the United Nations Sudano-Sahelian Office (UNSO) so that it could receive assistance in combating desertification, and expanding UNSO's scope so as to assist members of the Southern African Development Co-ordination Conference (see p. 620) in implementing programmes to combat desertification and drought.

The report of the Joint Intergovernmental Regional Committee on Human Settlements and Environment (second meeting, Addis Ababa, January) (see also p. 618) was considered by the Conference of Ministers.

Related action. The UNEP Governing Council, at its May 1984 session,[41] requested its Executive Director, within available resources, to strengthen the Regional Office for Africa and to study the establishment of subregional offices in the future.

African wildlife

A training seminar on implementation of the Convention on International Trade in Endangered Species of Wild Fauna and Flora (CITES) for African parties was held in Belgium in June, organized by the CITES secretariat and financed by UNEP, the Commission of the European Communities and European CITES parties.

JIU report. A progress report on the implementation of recommendations in regional programmes in the conservation and management of African wildlife,[42] prepared by the Joint Inspection Unit (JIU) in 1983[43] and taken note of by the Economic and Social Council in decision 1984/184 of 27 July 1984, found that the implementation of the 1979 JIU recommendations on the topic[44] had been piecemeal, without a lead organization in the United Nations system charged with co-ordination or co-operation in that regard.

JIU asserted that the success of an integrated regional conservation programme depended on full co-operation not only among ECA member States but also among United Nations organizations concerned, in particular members of the Ecosystem Conservation Group (FAO, UNEP, UNESCO and the International Union for Conservation of Nature and Natural Resources) in close co-operation with ECA. JIU recommended specific support measures by ECA, FAO, UNDP, UNEP and UNESCO for the Ecole de faune (Garoua, Cameroon) and the College of African Wildlife Management (Mweka, United Republic of Tanzania)—which JIU had identified in 1979 as highly successful regional training entities—and assistance to other institutes in developing regional training programmes. It added that ECA should inform relevant organizations of member States' request for co-operation in formulating and implementing an integrated regional living resources conservation strategy and programme, while ECA, FAO and OAU should consult with member States with a view to establishing a single, formal technical forum to bring together agencies in member States responsible for wildlife resources administration and management. Encouragement should be given to more member States to ratify or accede to the OAU African Convention on the Conservation of Nature and Natural Resources and related treaties and agreements.

The Secretary-General, in his February 1984 comments[45] on the JIU report, noted actions being taken in relation to the JIU recommendations, and said consultations with the Governments concerned indicated that the most suitable arrangement for the Garoua and Mweka institutions was for them to continue operating under their respective Government's execution while housing regional programmes. In a September report to the Assembly on implementation of JIU recommendations,[46] the Secretary-General discussed the funding arrangements for the two institutions and stated that the establishment of a task force had been suggested for implementing the JIU recommendations, examining alternative options and formulating strategies for collaboration among United Nations agencies.

Human settlements

In 1984, the Joint Intergovernmental Regional Committee on Human Settlements and Environment, in addition to recommending measures against desertification in Africa (see p. 617), adopted resolutions on establishing a regional programme for protection and restoration of the environment and human settlements in the case of natural disasters and earthquakes in Africa, a plan of action regarding the 1987 International Year of Shelter for the Homeless, promotion of local building materials and ECA human settlements activities in 1984-1985.

The Commission on Human Settlements,[47] by resolution of 9 May, requested the Executive Director of the United Nations Centre for Human Settlements to continue providing assistance to the Company for Habitat and Housing in Africa (Shelter-Afrique), based at Nairobi, Kenya (see also p. 780).

Women in development in Africa

The Joint ECA/OAU Regional Intergovernmental Preparatory Meeting for the 1985 World Conference on the United Nations Decade for Women/Third Regional Conference on the Integration of Women in Development (Arusha, 8-12 October) adopted strategies for the advancement of women in Africa beyond the end of the Decade (1976-1985). The Conference was followed, on 13 October, by a donors' round-table on assistance to women in Africa, which took note of a new strategy drafted by an expert group.

In May, the ECA Conference of Ministers called for the full and equitable participation of African women in the development process and for measures to ensure recruitment or promotion of African women to senior-level and decision-making positions in ECA and elsewhere in the United Nations system.

ECONOMIC AND SOCIAL COUNCIL ACTION

On 27 July 1984, the Economic and Social Council, on the recommendation of its First Committee, adopted resolution 1984/77 without vote.

Mobilization of human and financial resources for the women's programme of the Economic Commission for Africa beyond the United Nations Decade for Women: Equality, Development and Peace

The Economic and Social Council,

Aware that the goals and objectives of the United Nations Decade for Women: Equality, Development and Peace have not yet been fully achieved, especially in Africa,

Recalling General Assembly resolution 33/143 of 20 December 1978, in section III of which the Assembly requested the Secretary-General to take the necessary measures to increase the number of women in posts in the United Nations Secretariat subject to geographical distribution to 25 per cent of the total over a four-year period,

Recalling General Assembly resolution 37/235 B of 21 December 1982, in which the Assembly requested the Secretary-General to intensify his efforts to implement fully section III of Assembly resolution 33/143 and section V of Assembly resolution 35/210 of 17 December 1980,

Recalling also resolution 21 adopted by the World Conference of the United Nations Decade for Women: Equality, Development and Peace, in which the Secretary-General was requested, as an interim measure, to explore the possibility of redeploying vacant posts within the regional commissions to the women's programmes, and General Assembly resolution 35/136 of 11 December 1980,

Recalling further General Assembly resolution 38/106 of 16 December 1983, in which the Assembly urged the Secretary-General, in consultation with the executive secretaries of the regional commissions, _inter alia,_ to take urgently appropriate measures to ensure that all temporary and permanent senior women's programme officers posts in the regional commissions should be continued within the regular budgetary resources available to them,

1. _Urges_ the Secretary-General and the Executive Secretary of the Economic Commission for Africa to do all in their power to provide a core group of posts from regular budgetary resources, through the redeployment of vacant posts and in the context of the proposals for the programme budget for the biennium 1986-1987, to the African Training and Research Centre for Women and to the women's programmes of the Multinational Programming and Operational Centres in order to ensure their long-term viability beyond the United Nations Decade for Women;

2. _Expresses its appreciation_ to the United Nations Development Programme, the Voluntary Fund for the United Nations Decade for Women and the international community for the financial and technical assistance provided for the women's programme of the Economic Commission for Africa.

Economic and Social Council resolution 1984/77

27 July 1984   Meeting 50   Adopted without vote

Approved by First Committee (E/1984/142) without vote, 23 July (meeting 16); draft by ECA (E/1984/21); agenda item 9.

The General Assembly, by resolution 39/127, expressed concern over a lack of progress in regularizing senior women's programme officers posts at the regional commissions, and requested the Secretary-General to take corrective measures.

Statistics

In 1984, the ECA Conference of Ministers, acting on the recommendations of the Joint Conference of African Planners, Statisticians and Demographers (see also p. 605), called on all African countries to undertake and strengthen short-term forecasting activities and appealed to member States to undertake perspective studies on their respective economies. The secretariat activities focused on the African Household Survey Capability Programme, the statistical training programme and the regional advisory service in demographic statistics. Work on statistical data-base development was also carried out.

Programme, organizational and administrative questions concerning ECA

ECA as executing agency

Using funds from United Nations, multilateral and bilateral sources, ECA continued in 1984 to engage in diverse technical co-operation activities. In addition to United Nations regular programme funds, resources were provided by UNDP, UNFPA, the Voluntary Fund for the United Nations Decade for Women, UNEP and the United Nations Trust Fund for African Development.

In May, the ECA Conference of Ministers, supporting the strengthening of ECA as an executing agency, requested the Secretary-General to relax certain administrative constraints by realigning the rules of recruitment and procurement with those of other United Nations executing agencies to enable ECA to execute projects promptly.

ECONOMIC AND SOCIAL COUNCIL ACTION

On 27 July 1984, the Economic and Social Council, on the recommendation of its First Committee, adopted resolution 1984/74 without vote.

Strengthening of the role of the Economic Commission for Africa as an executing agency

The Economic and Social Council,

Recalling General Assembly resolution 33/202 of 29 January 1979 on the restructuring of the economic and social sectors of the United Nations system, in which, *inter alia,* the Assembly decided that the regional commissions should have the status of executing agencies, in their own right, in respect of the categories of project described in and in conformity with paragraph 23 of the annex to its resolution 32/197 of 20 December 1977,

Recalling also the agreement signed on 1 March 1977 between the United Nations Development Programme and the Economic Commission for Africa, designating the Commission as a participating and executing agency

for the inter-country projects of the United Nations Development Programme,

Noting with satisfaction the progress that has been achieved within a short space of time by the Commission acting as an executing agency for the inter-country projects of the United Nations Development Programme and other such projects, with the result that it is currently one of the largest executing agencies for the inter-country projects in Africa financed by the Programme,

Noting with concern the administrative difficulties being experienced by the Commission in the implementation of those projects, owing to the lack of differentiation between the rules and procedures that apply to its role as an executing agency and those that govern its regular budgetary activities, both in the recruitment of project personnel residing outside Africa and those above level L-5 and in the procurement of project equipment and supplies costing more than $20,000,

Noting with regret that the rate of implementation by the Commission of the inter-country projects of the United Nations Development Programme and other such projects has decreased substantially, owing to the above-mentioned constraints, which create unnecessary delays,

Bearing in mind the current critical economic situation in Africa and the expectation of member States that the secretariat of the Commission should play an increasing role in assisting them in the expeditious execution of operational projects funded from the resources of the United Nations system,

Requests the Secretary-General to consider the possibility of streamlining and, if necessary, relaxing the above-mentioned administrative constraints by aligning the rules and procedures of the Commission governing recruitment and procurement with those of other United Nations executing agencies so that the Commission will be able to execute projects promptly, thereby placing it on the same basis as the other executing agencies of the United Nations system.

Economic and Social Council resolution 1984/74

27 July 1984   Meeting 50   Adopted without vote

Approved by First Committee (E/1984/142) without vote, 23 July (meeting 16); draft by ECA (E/1984/21), orally amended during informal consultations; agenda item 9.

Expansion of Addis Ababa conference facilities

In a follow-up to developments in 1983[48] on a proposal for new conference facilities at ECA headquarters at Addis Ababa, including the General Assembly decision[49] to defer consideration until 1984, the Secretary-General, in September,[50] reported that the Government of Ethiopia had officially confirmed its offer of a parcel of land immediately adjacent to ECA's existing site free of charge to the United Nations. It had also confirmed that materials and furniture and equipment required for constructing the conference facilities would be exempt from duty or sales taxes.

The Secretary-General reiterated his proposal for the construction of one large, two medium and four small conference rooms, and recommended that the Assembly accept Ethiopia's offer of land of approximately 42,400 square metres. He also recommended that the Assembly approve, in principle, the project at a total estimated cost of $89,360,000; an appropriation of $3,120,000 for 1984-1985 in order to formulate detailed designs; and $111,400 for the same period for a proposed planning unit.

ACABQ, also in September,[51] recommended approval, in principle, of the project at an estimated cost of $73,501,000. Its other recommendations were the same as those of the Secretary-General.

GENERAL ASSEMBLY ACTION

On 18 December 1984, the General Assembly, on the recommendation of the Fifth Committee, adopted section III of resolution 39/236 by recorded vote.

Conference facilities of the Economic Commission for Africa at Addis Ababa

[*The General Assembly . . .*]

Having considered the reports of the Secretary-General on the adequacy of the conference facilities of the Economic Commission for Africa at Addis Ababa, and the related report of the Advisory Committee on Administrative and Budgetary Questions,

1. *Concurs* with the comments and observations of the Advisory Committee as contained in its report;

2. *Accepts with appreciation* the generous offer by the Government of Ethiopia of approximately 42,400 square metres of land immediately adjacent to the existing site of the Economic Commission for Africa, taking due account of the assurance by that Government that all goods will be exempt from duty and sales taxes;

3. *Approves*, in principle, the project at an estimated cost of $73,501,000, excluding the cost of the Planning Unit at the Economic Commission for Africa;

4. *Decides* that the appropriation of $3,120,000 approved for the biennium 1984-1985 in order to formulate detailed designs should be placed in a construction account and any unexpended balance carried forward until the completion of the project;

5. *Requests* the Secretary-General to submit annual progress reports thereon to the General Assembly;

. . .

General Assembly resolution 39/236, section III

18 December 1984   Meeting 105   122-5-16 (recorded vote)

Approved by Fifth Committee (A/39/839) by recorded vote (83-3-13), 16 October (meeting 12); oral proposal by Chairman; agenda item 109.

Recorded vote in Assembly as follows:

In favour: Afghanistan, Algeria, Angola, Antigua and Barbuda, Argentina, Austria, Bahamas, Bahrain, Bangladesh, Barbados, Benin, Bhutan, Bolivia, Botswana, Brazil, Brunei Darussalam, Bulgaria, Burkina Faso, Burma, Burundi, Byelorussian SSR, Cameroon, Cape Verde, Central African Republic, Chad, China, Colombia, Congo, Costa Rica, Cuba, Cyprus, Czechoslovakia, Democratic Kampuchea, Democratic Yemen, Djibouti, Dominican Republic, Ecuador, Egypt, Ethiopia, Fiji, Gabon, Gambia, German Democratic Republic, Ghana, Greece, Guatemala, Guinea, Guinea-Bissau, Guyana, Honduras, Hungary, India, Indonesia, Iraq, Italy, Ivory Coast, Jamaica, Jordan, Kenya, Kuwait, Lao People's Democratic Republic, Lebanon, Lesotho, Liberia, Libyan Arab Jamahiriya, Madagascar, Malawi, Malaysia, Maldives, Mali, Malta, Mauritania, Mauritius, Mexico, Mongolia, Morocco, Mozambique, Nepal, Nicaragua, Niger, Nigeria, Oman, Pakistan, Panama, Papua New Guinea, Paraguay, Peru, Philippines, Poland, Qatar, Romania, Rwanda, Samoa, Sao Tome and Principe, Saudi Arabia, Senegal, Sierra Leone, Singapore, Somalia, Sri Lanka, Sudan, Suriname, Swaziland, Syrian Arab Republic, Thailand, Togo, Trinidad and Tobago, Tunisia, Turkey, Uganda, Ukrainian SSR, USSR, United Arab Emirates, United Republic of Tanzania, Vanuatu, Venezuela, Viet Nam, Yemen, Yugoslavia, Zaire, Zambia, Zimbabwe.

Against: Belgium, Luxembourg, Netherlands, United Kingdom, United States.

Abstaining: Australia, Canada, Denmark, El Salvador, Finland, France, Germany, Federal Republic of, Iceland, Ireland, Israel, Japan, New Zealand, Norway, Portugal, Spain, Sweden.

Before acting on the draft, the Committee rejected—by 73 votes to 21, with 2 abstentions—a motion by the United States, seconded by the United Kingdom, to adjourn the debate on the topic, while consideration was given to other proposals of possible greater utility. Egypt, on behalf of the Group of 77, and Ethiopia spoke against the motion.

The United States requested the recorded vote on the draft.

In explanation of vote, Belgium and Norway expressed reservations about the intended use of the ECA facilities for holding a major United Nations conference and the consequences of establishing such a precedent.

Ethiopia spoke of the need for a new ECA complex, and added that ACABQ had taken account of the need for economy and was advocating a lesser facility. Egypt and Cameroon stressed the need for better facilities at ECA, and, along with Cuba, expressed readiness to accept the ACABQ proposal despite their preference for the Secretary-General's original recommendations. Cameroon and Cuba rejected attempts to link the question with other agenda items, with Cuba dismissing what it saw as the implied criticism that the project represented an undesirable transfer of resources. Brazil felt ACABQ had conducted a careful examination of the project. While supporting the draft, Italy stressed the need for effective monitoring of project execution to ensure careful spending of resources.

Regional institutions

In 1984, the ECA Conference of Ministers considered a report submitted by an *ad hoc* committee it had created in 1983 to evaluate and harmonize the activities of the African multinational institutions sponsored by ECA and OAU, and extended the committee's mandate by a year so that it could complete its work.

Commission sessions

The ECA Conference of Ministers decided to continue meeting annually subject to a review in 1988.

1985 session

ECONOMIC AND SOCIAL ACTION

In July, the Economic and Social Council adopted decision 1984/183 by roll-call vote.

Venue of the twentieth session of the Economic Commission for Africa

At its 50th plenary meeting, on 27 July 1984, the Council decided to accept the invitation of the Government of

Guinea to hold the twentieth session of the Economic Commission for Africa and eleventh meeting of the Conference of Ministers of the Commission at Conakry, in April 1985.

Economic and Social Council decision 1984/183

32-9-7 (roll call vote)

Approved by First Committee (E/1984/142) by roll-call vote (26-9-7), 23 July (meeting 16); oral proposal by Chairman; agenda item 9.

Roll-call vote in Council as follows:

In favour: Algeria, Argentina, Austria, Benin, Brazil, China, Colombia, Costa Rica, Djibouti, Ecuador, Guyana, Indonesia, Japan, Lebanon, Malaysia, Mexico, Pakistan, Qatar, Romania, Rwanda, Saint Lucia, Saudi Arabia, Somalia, Sri Lanka, Suriname, Swaziland, Thailand, Tunisia, Uganda, Venezuela, Yugoslavia, Zaire.

Against: Canada, France, Germany, Federal Republic of, Luxembourg, Netherlands, New Zealand, Portugal, United Kingdom, United States.

Abstaining: Bulgaria, Finland, German Democratic Republic, Greece, Poland, Sweden, USSR.

Delegations expressing opposition or reservations on the text said the funds could be better spent for Africa's development.

Co-operation between the United Nations and the Southern African Development Co-ordination Conference

In an August 1984 report to the General Assembly,[52] submitted in pursuance of its December 1983 request,[53] the Secretary-General described the co-operation between the United Nations and the Southern African Development Co-ordination Conference (SADCC)—a subregional organization, established in 1980 to forge links between member States (Angola, Botswana, Lesotho, Malawi, Mozambique, Swaziland, United Republic of Tanzania, Zambia, Zimbabwe)—for promoting and harmonizing mutual contacts. He reported that the fifth SADCC conference (Lusaka, 2 and 3 February) focused on agriculture, in the context of additional burdens created by the drought conditions.

The fifth SADCC summit (Gaborone, Botswana, 6 July) appealed to donor Governments and agencies not to use their aid programmes in attempts to divide SADCC member States.

GENERAL ASSEMBLY ACTION

On 18 December 1984, the General Assembly, on the recommendation of the Second Committee, adopted resolution 39/215 without vote.

Co-operation between the United Nations and the Southern African Development Co-ordination Conference

The General Assembly,

Recalling its resolutions 37/248 of 21 December 1982 and 38/160 of 19 December 1983, by which it, *inter alia,* requested the Secretary-General to promote co-operation between the organs, organizations and bodies of the United Nations system and the Southern African Development Co-ordination Conference and urged intensification of contacts in order to accelerate the achievement of the objectives envisaged in resolution 37/248,

Having considered the report of the Secretary-General on co-operation between the United Nations and the Southern African Development Co-ordination Conference,

Noting that progress is being made by organs, organizations and bodies of the United Nations system in formulating co-operation programmes with the Conference,

1. *Takes note* of the report of the Secretary-General concerning the progress made in the implementation of General Assembly resolution 37/248;

2. *Commends* the organs, organizations and bodies of the United Nations system that have already established concrete contacts with the Southern African Development Co-ordination Conference;

3. *Requests* the Secretary-General, in consultation with the Executive Secretary of the Conference, to continue contacts aimed at promoting and harmonizing co-operation between the Conference and the United Nations;

4. *Also requests* the Secretary-General to submit to the General Assembly at its fortieth session a report on the implementation of the present resolution.

General Assembly resolution 39/215

18 December 1984   Meeting 104   Adopted without vote

Approved by Second Committee (A/39/790/Add.7) without vote, 13 November (meeting 40); draft by Vice-Chairman (A/C.2/39/L.29), based on informal consultations on draft by SADCC members (A/C.2/39/L.15); agenda item 80 *(g).*

Meeting numbers. GA 39th session: 2nd Committee 35, 40; plenary 104.

REFERENCES

[1]E/1984/21. [2]YUN 1980, p. 548. [3]*Ibid.,* p. 557, GA res. 35/64, 5 Dec. 1980. [4]E/1984/75. [5]E/1985/81. [6]E/1984/110. [7]A/39/289-E/1984/107 & Add.1. [8]YUN 1983, p. 618, GA res. 38/199, 20 Dec. 1983. [9]YUN 1980, p. 503, GA res. 35/56, annex, 5 Dec. 1980. [10]YUN 1981, p. 406. [11]A/C.2/39/L.80. [12]YUN 1981, p. 612. [13]E/1984/110/Add.1. [14]YUN 1977, p. 603, GA res. 32/160, 19 Dec. 1977. [15]A/39/223. [16]A/39/38. [17]A/39/271-E/1984/98. [18]A/39/272-E/1984/99. [19]YUN 1983, p. 629, GA res. 38/150, 19 Dec. 1983. [20]E/1984/114. [21]E/1984/115. [22]YUN 1983, p. 630. [23]YUN 1980, p. 662, GA res. 35/66 B, 5 Dec. 1980. [24]YUN 1979, p. 728. [25]A/39/16 (res. 57(XVIII)). [26]YUN 1983, p. 581, GA res. 38/192, sect. II, 20 Dec. 1983. [27]A/39/301-E/1984/108. [28]ID/CONF.5/46 & Corr.1 (res. 8). [29]E/AC.51/1984/11 & Corr.1. [30]A/C.5/39/42. [31]A/39/839. [32]YUN 1977, p. 555. [33]A/39/270-E/1984/97. [34]YUN 1983, p. 621, GA res. 38/159, 19 Dec. 1983. [35]ACC/1984/13. [36]E/1984/66. [37]A/39/19. [38]YUN 1983, p. 627. [39]*Ibid.,* p. 632. [40]E/ECA/CM.10/14. [41]A/39/25 (dec. 12/17 B). [42]E/1984/3. [43]YUN 1983, p. 625. [44]YUN 1979, p. 1224. [45]E/1984/3/Add.1. [46]A/39/145 & Corr.1. [47]A/39/8 (res. 7/6). [48]YUN 1983, p. 634. [49]*Ibid.,* GA res. 38/234, sect. XXIII, 20 Dec. 1983. [50]A/C.5/39/8. [51]A/39/7/Add.2. [52]A/39/408. [53]YUN 1983, p. 633, GA res. 38/160, 19 Dec. 1983.

PUBLICATIONS

Survey of Economic and Social Conditions in Africa, 1983-1984, Sales No. E.87.II.K.2; *1984-1985,* Sales No. E.87.II.K.3.

Asia and the Pacific

The Economic and Social Commission for Asia and the Pacific (ESCAP), at its fortieth session (Tokyo, 17-27 April, 1984),[1] focussed on technology for development, reviewed the implementation of the International Development Strategy for the Third United Nations Development Decade (the 1980s)[2] as well as the Substantive New Programme of Action (SNPA) for the 1980s for the Least Developed Countries

(LDCs),[3] and considered the transport and communications needs of the region.

The Commission—headquartered at Bangkok, Thailand—called for a further review of the functioning of its legislative committees, recommended including in the 1984-1989 medium-term plan a new programme on marine affairs, and reviewed the functioning of the regional institutions and the special projects.

Vanuatu, which had been an associate member of the Commission since joining the United Nations membership in 1981, became a full ESCAP member in February 1984, and the Economic and Social Council, accordingly, revised the Commission's terms of reference (resolution 1984/66).

In December, the General Assembly, on the recommendation of the Council (resolution 1984/78), proclaimed a Transport and Communications Decade for Asia and the Pacific (1985-1994) to improve the infrastructure and services of developing member countries of the region (resolution 39/227). The Assembly also approved a three-year construction project to expand ESCAP conference facilities at a total estimated cost of $44 million (resolution 39/236).

Economic and social trends

The *Economic and Social Survey of Asia and the Pacific, 1983*,[4] the summary of which was noted by the Economic and Social Council in resolution 1984/187 of 27 July, found that, although the developing countries of the ESCAP region showed greater resilience than those of other regions, there was a definite and significant downward trend in growth rates in almost all the developing economies in the region prior to 1984. However, the survey for 1984[5] showed that the seven LDCs in the region—Afghanistan, Bangladesh, Bhutan, Lao People's Democratic Republic, Maldives, Nepal and Samoa—did not share either the general resilience displayed by others during the 1980-1983 recession or the improvement in growth rates achieved in 1983-1984, with a dire scarcity of resources and vulnerability to weather fluctuations seriously hampering their efforts to achieve better economic growth and development.

Activities in 1984

Development policy and planning

In reviewing the implementation of the International Development Strategy for the Third United Nations Development Decade,[2] the Commission identified four areas for immediate policy implementation: monetary and financial issues; trade and raw materials, including trade liberalization and price stabilization; energy; and food and agriculture. The Commission felt that emphasis should be placed on collective co-operation for self-reliance.

With regard to implementation of the SNPA for the 1980s for LDCs,[3] the Commission urged immediate action to improve the basic standards of living in those countries and to transform their economies towards self-sustained development.

The Committee on Development Planning (fifth session, Bangkok, 17-20 December) noted the negligible progress made in implementing the Strategy and SNPA, and the need to provide LDCs with financial resources at concessional terms, technical assistance, and the transfer of technology; liberalization of commercial policies in developed countries would also contribute to development.

The Asian and Pacific Development Centre continued training and research activities.

Mekong River basin development

The Interim Committee for Co-ordination of Investigations of the Lower Mekong Basin held two sessions in 1984 in Thailand (nineteenth, Chiang Mai, 16-21 January; twentieth, Bangkok, 30 July-3 August)[6] and endorsed projects for the revision of the Indicative Basin Plan (1970-2000). It also held a special session at Bangkok (30 April-2 May) and approved, effective as of 1985, the recommendations made by UNDP on restructuring the Committee's secretariat to render it more operational and cost-effective.

Technical co-operation and assistance

Under the United Nations regular programme for technical co-operation,[7] ESCAP conducted 28 missions during 1984 to meet requests from 41 Governments—mostly of LDCs and island developing countries—for technical and advisory services.

The United Nations Development Advisory Team for the South Pacific at Suva, Fiji, and the ESCAP Pacific Liaison Office at Nauru were merged on 1 July into the ESCAP Pacific Operating Centre (EPOC), based at Port Vila, Vanuatu.

The Commission,[1] in April, welcomed the establishment of EPOC, and requested the Executive Secretary to assist Kiribati and Tuvalu in preparing materials that would enable them to be included in the United Nations list of LDCs.

International trade

The Commission,[1] which continued to attach importance to trade in raw materials and commodities, welcomed the establishment of the International Jute Organization at Dhaka, Bangladesh, in January 1984 (see p. 538); noted the progress made by the members of the Regional Consultative Group on Silk in implementing specific co-operative activities; and welcomed the holding of an Asian Silk Fair at Hong Kong in August. It urged more member countries to join the Asian Clearing Union, the Asian Reinsurance Corporation and the Bangkok Agreement for the further promotion of intraregional trade. There was agreement in the Commission that a meeting of ministers of trade should be held.

The Committee on Trade (twenty-fifth session, Bangkok, 6-12 November) noted with concern that the majority of developing countries in the region, which were mainly exporters of primary products, had not as yet benefited significantly from renewed world trade growth as prices of such products remained depressed; it urged, among other things, that current tendencies towards intensification of trade restrictions be arrested and that efforts be made to promote foreign trade expansion particularly through diversification of external markets and exploration of new export possibilities.

Transport and communications

In 1984, the General Assembly, on the recommendation of the Economic and Social Council, proclaimed a Transport and Communications Decade for Asia and the Pacific (1985-1994), with a view to raising the relevant infrastructural facilities of developing countries of ESCAP to a level commensurate with their development objectives and priorities (resolution 39/227).

Transport and communications decade (1985-1994)

In April, the Commission[1] proclaimed the Transport and Communications Decade for Asia and the Pacific, 1985-1994, endorsing the recommendation of its *ad hoc* intergovernmental group, which, at one session each in 1983[8] and 1984 (Bangkok, January), had formulated objectives, an action programme and organizational arrangements for the decade.

The Decade was aimed at improving the transport and communications infrastructural facilities of developing member countries, with special attention to the needs of the least developed, landlocked and island developing countries of the region; promoting a more effective and efficient integrated network; and encouraging effective co-ordination and co-operation. In proclaiming the Decade, the Commission noted that the deleterious effects of inadequate attention paid to the transport and communication sectors in the region had been compounded by several oil price crises, worsening terms of trade and economic recession; scarce resources had been diverted from infrastructure maintenance and improvement to the more immediately evident need to cover day-to-day operating costs.

ECONOMIC AND SOCIAL COUNCIL ACTION

In a June report informing the Economic and Social Council of the ESCAP proclamation of the Decade,[9] known as the Tokyo Proclamation, the Secretary-General noted that the intergovernmental group had estimated the first quinquennium of the regional action programme to cost some US$20 million, and had proposed setting up an inter-agency co-ordinating committee for the Decade. The

Secretary-General also reported that, in pursuance of a 1983 Council resolution,[10] the ESCAP secretariat had consulted with ECWA on Decade activities applicable to the latter region.

On 27 July, the Economic and Social Council, on the recommendation of its First Committee, adopted resolution 1984/78 without vote.

Transport and Communications Decade for Asia and the Pacific, 1985-1994

The Economic and Social Council,

Noting resolution 236(XL) of 27 April 1984 of the Economic and Social Commission for Asia and the Pacific, concerning a transport and communications decade for Asia and the Pacific during the period 1985-1994,

Bearing in mind the imperative need to mobilize funds for the decade through reprogramming or extrabudgetary contributions,

Recalling paragraph 30 of the International Development Strategy for the Third United Nations Development Decade, annexed to General Assembly resolution 35/56 of 5 December 1980,

Recalling also the section of the Substantial New Programme of Action for the 1980s for the Least Developed Countries relevant to the improvement of transport and communications infrastructure,

Recalling further Council resolution 1983/69 of 29 July 1983 concerning a transport and communications decade in Asia and the Pacific during the period 1985-1994,

Convinced of the critical role of all modes and means of transport and communications as enabling elements in economic development and the importance, therefore, of the improvement and growth of transport and communications infrastructure and services in a manner commensurate with the anticipated growth of all sectors of the economy generating the demand for transport and communications,

Recognizing the need for an integrated approach to the planning of transport and communications development and taking into account the positive contribution which the proclamation of a transport and communications decade for Asia and the Pacific during the period 1985-1994 would make towards the mobilization of support for such an approach,

Taking note of the report of the Secretary-General on the implementation of Economic and Social Council resolution 1983/69 concerning the proclamation of a transport and communications decade in Asia and the Pacific,

1. *Endorses* resolution 236(XL) of the Economic and Social Commission for Asia and the Pacific, with a view to:

(a) Raising the transport and communications infrastructural facilities of developing member countries to a level commensurate with their development objectives and priorities, giving particular attention to the special needs of the least developed, land-locked and island developing countries of the region;

(b) Identifying systematically and in a comprehensive manner the problems of transport and communications in the region and working out feasible solutions;

(c) Promoting a more effective and efficient transport and communications network comprising all modes and means in an integrated way, in particular for development of intraregional and interregional transport and communications linkages, as well as in the fields of maintenance and co-ordination of networks, tariff setting and physical planning;

(d) Encouraging effective co-ordination and co-operation in the field of transport and communications in the region;

2. *Recommends* the General Assembly to proclaim a Transport and Communications Decade for Asia and the Pacific during the period 1985-1994, in accordance with resolution 236(XL) of the Economic and Social Commission for Asia and the Pacific;

3. *Urges* all relevant international organizations, particularly the United Nations Development Programme, to contribute effectively to the implementation of the regional action programme for the Decade;

4. *Requests* the Secretary-General to extend, within existing resources, all necessary facilities and support to the Executive Secretaries of the Economic and Social Commission for Asia and the Pacific and the Economic Commission for Western Asia in their elaboration of a practical and integrated regional action programme for the Decade and to mobilize the necessary international support for the successful implementation of the programmes for the Decade;

5. *Calls upon* the Secretary-General to promote intergovernmental and inter-agency co-ordination at the regional and subregional levels;

6. *Invites* all Governments, in particular those of the developed countries and others in a position to do so, to contribute and participate effectively in the implementation of the regional action programme for achieving the objectives of the Decade;

7. *Requests* the Secretary-General to submit a report on the implementation of the present resolution to the Economic and Social Council at its second regular session of 1986, and every two years thereafter until the end of the Decade.

Economic and Social Council resolution 1984/78

27 July 1984   Meeting 50   Adopted without vote

Approved by First Committee (E/1984/142) without vote, 23 July (meeting 16); draft by Vice-Chairman (E/1984/C.1/L.20), based on informal consultations on 8-nation draft (E/1984/C.1/L.6); agenda item 9.
Sponsors: Australia, Bangladesh, China, Indonesia, Japan, Malaysia, Sri Lanka, Thailand.

GENERAL ASSEMBLY ACTION

On 18 December 1984, the General Assembly, on the recommendation of the Second Committee, adopted resolution 39/227 without vote.

Transport and Communications Decade for Asia and the Pacific

The General Assembly,

Recalling the relevant paragraphs of the International Development Strategy for the Third United Nations Development Decade, annexed to General Assembly resolution 35/56 of 5 December 1980,

Recalling also Economic and Social Council resolutions 1983/69 of 29 July 1983 and 1984/78 of 27 July 1984,

Taking note of resolution 236(XL) of 27 April 1984 of the Economic and Social Commission for Asia and the Pacific, concerning a transport and communications decade for Asia and the Pacific during the period 1985-1994,

Recalling the section of the Substantial New Programme of Action for the 1980s for the Least Developed Countries relevant to the improvement of transport and communications infrastructure,

Convinced of the critical role of transport and communications in economic development and the importance, therefore, of the improvement and growth of transport and communications infrastructure and services in a manner commensurate with the anticipated growth of all sectors of the economy generating the demand for transport and communications,

1. *Endorses* the recommendation made in paragraph 2 of Economic and Social Council resolution 1984/78 and proclaims a Transport and Communications Decade for Asia and the Pacific during the period 1985-1994, with a view to:

(a) Raising the transport and communications infrastructural facilities of States members of the Economic and Social Commission for Asia and the Pacific which are developing countries to a level commensurate with their development objectives and priorities, giving particular attention to the special needs of the least developed, land-locked and island developing countries of the region;

(b) Identifying systematically and in a comprehensive manner the problems of transport and communications in the region and working out feasible solutions;

(c) Promoting a more effective and efficient transport and communications network comprising all modes and means in an integrated way, in particular for development of intraregional and interregional transport and communications linkages, as well as in the fields of maintenance and co-ordination of networks, tariff setting and physical planning;

(d) Encouraging effective co-ordination and co-operation in the field of transport and communications in the region;

2. *Requests* the Secretary-General to extend all necessary facilities and support to the Executive Secretaries of the Economic and Social Commission for Asia and the Pacific and the Economic Commission for Western Asia in their development of the regional action programme for the Decade in a practical and integrated manner and to mobilize the necessary international support for the successful implementation of the programmes for the Decade, bearing in mind the contents of the seventh preambular paragraph of resolution 236(XL) of the Economic and Social Commission for Asia and the Pacific;

3. *Urges* all relevant international organizations, particularly the United Nations Development Programme, to contribute to and provide assistance for the effective implementation of the regional action programme for the Decade;

4. *Invites* all Governments, in particular those of the developed countries, to contribute to and participate effectively in the implementation of the regional action programme for achieving the objectives of the Decade;

5. *Requests* the Secretary-General to submit a report on the implementation of the present resolution to the Economic and Social Council at its second regular session of 1986, and every two years thereafter until the end of the Decade.

General Assembly resolution 39/227

18 December 1984   Meeting 104   Adopted without vote

Approved by Second Committee (A/39/789) without vote, 6 December (meeting 56); draft by Vice-Chairman (A/C.2/39/L.112), based on informal consultations on draft by Egypt, for Group of 77 (A/C.2/39/L.31); agenda item 12.
Meeting numbers. GA 39th session: 2nd Committee 28-32, 39, 56; plenary 104.

Explaining its position, the United States said that, given the absence of indication as to the availability of sufficient extrabudgetary funds for the proposed activities, it questioned whether participation in the Decade was the most prudent way for ESCAP to use its scarce resources.

Regional remote sensing programme

A regional remote sensing programme, funded by UNDP, continued to promote information exchange and co-operation among the developing ESCAP countries in upgrading national facilities for the surveying, mapping and monitoring of natural resources. The Commission, which executed the programme, called for UNDP funding of the programme beyond 1986.

Industrial development

At its April 1984 session,[1] ESCAP endorsed the report of its Preparatory Meeting (Bangkok, 15 and 16 March) of Ministers of Industry for the Fourth General Conference of UNIDO (UNIDO IV, Vienna, Austria, 2-18 August) as the regional position for submission to the Conference.[11] (See also Chapter VI of this section.) In so doing, the Commission noted the heterogeneity of the ESCAP region, and stressed the need for a gradual increase in the developing countries' share in world industrial production as part of the process of global industrial restructuring. It agreed to establish a technical advisory group to assist in implementing projects at the national level, and urged that a follow-up to the industrial survey be carried out by ESCAP, the Asian Development Bank and the South Pacific Bureau for Economic Co-operation, with a view to further promoting industrial initiatives in the Pacific islands region.

The Committee on Industry, Technology and Human Settlements and the Environment (eighth session, Bangkok, 11-17 September)[12] suggested, among other things, that developing Asian and Pacific countries should pursue joint ventures and tripartite forms of industrial co-operation.

Transnational corporations

The ESCAP/United Nations Centre on Transnational Corporations (UNCTC) Joint Unit on Transnational Corporations organized in 1984 a Ministerial Round Table on Transnational Corporations and the Developing Pacific Island Countries (Samoa, 27 February–2 March). It also provided administrative and technical support to advisory missions and workshops, and continued to process information on transnational corporations in the region.

Natural resources and energy

The Committee on Natural Resources (eleventh session, Bangkok, 16-22 October) made a series of recommendations[13] on exploitation and management of natural resources and energy in the ESCAP region.

The Committee felt that ESCAP and other international agencies should help initiate regional collaboration on specific projects and management problems as well as promote and strengthen efforts towards integrated energy planning. It noted the importance of alternative sources of energy and the potential for regional co-operation in exploring and harnessing energy technology; stressed the need to improve rural energy supplies; and reiterated that ESCAP should review and assess technological capabilities of the region and suggest action plans. The Committee also endorsed, in general, the recommendations on energy-sector strategies under the ESCAP Plan of Action on Technology for Development (see below, under "science and technology"), and the priorities and recommendations of the Meeting of Focal Points on New and Renewable Sources of Energy (Bangkok, June) and the High-level Regional Consultative Meeting for the Mobilization of Financial Resources for New and Renewable Sources of Energy (Bangkok, September).

Activities remaining from the first phase (1982-1983) of the regional energy development programme were completed. In July, UNDP approved the project document for the second phase (1984-1986).

The Committee for Co-ordination of Joint Prospecting for Mineral Resources in South Pacific Offshore Areas (CCOP/SOPAC), at an extraordinary meeting held in the Cook Islands in May 1984, approved a Memorandum of Understanding, which conferred on CCOP/SOPAC the status of a regional intergovernmental organization. The Committee for Co-ordination of Joint Prospecting for Mineral Resources in Asian Offshore Areas and the Regional Mineral Resources Centre continued to implement their work programmes.

Food and agriculture

In 1984, several meeting were held on drought-related food shortages, pesticide use and marketing, agro-climatic assessment techniques, farm broadcasting and rural savings mobilization and agriculture banking systems.

The ESCAP Committee on Industry, Technology and Human Settlements and the Environment[12] recommended that the middle- and low-income countries of the region should not overlook the importance of agricultural development and its contribution to increasing employment and income.

The Regional Network for Agricultural Machinery—an inter-country project aimed at increasing agricultural output and land productivity in the participating countries (India, Indonesia, Iran, Pakistan, Philippines, Republic of Korea, Sri Lanka, Thailand)—continued to operate with additional funding from Australia, Japan and UNDP.

The Governing Board of the Regional Co-ordination Centre for Research and Development of Coarse Grains, Pulses, Roots and Tuber Crops in the Humid Tropics of Asia and the Pacific (second session, Bogor, Indonesia, 6-8 March) suggested that the Centre focus on agro-economic and socio-economic aspects of developing such crops.

Science and technology

In April 1984, the Commission[1] adopted the ESCAP Plan of Action on Technology for Development as a guideline for further activating technology-related activities in order to accelerate socio-economic development in the region. Prepared by the High-level Expert Group Meeting on Technology for Development, and endorsed by the Intergovernmental Meeting on Technology for Development (Bangkok, February), the Plan[14] stated that most developing countries in the ESCAP region lacked integration of technological considerations in the overall national development planning process; it analysed common issues and policies, considered national action plans and discussed the role of, and the need to strengthen, ESCAP's technology units.

The Committee on Industry, Technology, Human Settlements and the Environment[12] called for assigning priority to projects on technology transfer among small- and medium-scale industries, technological needs and capabilities of LDCs, and technological information sharing. Further, it endorsed the draft statute of the Regional Centre for Technology Transfer (RCTT), and called on the Centre to organize a special training programme on technological forecasting and monitoring.

Social and cultural development

At its 1984 session,[1] ESCAP urged Governments to give special attention to the social impact of policies relating to integrated rural development programmes.

Cultural and natural heritage. In a 1983 report, transmitted by the Secretary-General to the Economic and Social Council in April 1984,[15] JIU discussed the United Nations contribution to conservation and management of cultural and natural heritage in Asia and the Pacific.

The Inspectors found that demographic and other problems deriving partly from national modernization imperatives hindered heritage conservation and management in the region, which had more than half of the world's population and the highest population density. That, coupled with large-scale development schemes, urbanization and industrialization processes exerted increasing pressure on the carrying capacity of land and heritage resources, often leading to deforestation, desertification and the near extinction of some wildlife species. Natural disasters and poverty also posed intractable environmental problems and escalated the costs of heritage

conservation and management. While impressed by what had been done, the Inspectors thought it desirable for Governments of the region to formulate comprehensive and coherent long-term conservation strategies involving the full participation of all segments of the population.

The Inspectors recommended that ESCAP, UNEP, FAO and UNESCO encourage and support Governments of the region to formulate long-term national strategies as recommended by the 1980 World Conservation Strategy.[16] It was also recommended that FAO, UNDP and UNESCO direct their efforts towards helping train technical and management personnel with a view to ensuring national self-reliance in regard to wildlife and national parks; develop and enforce administrative and legislative aspects for cultural heritage protection and management; and ensure completion of operations and achievement of project objectives within planned time-frames and resources. Further, the Inspectors suggested that FAO, UNDP and UNEP explore with Governments of the region possibilities of assisting the wildlife training facilities in Dhera Dun, India, and Ciawi, Indonesia, to develop and operate regional and subregional training programmes, and establishing two new subregional centres in other suitable locations. It was recommended that UNESCO encourage establishment of a network of co-operation linking restoration and conservation laboratories in the region.

The Secretary-General[17] supported the JIU recommendations.

Population

The ESCAP Population Division and its information services continued to receive institutional support from UNFPA.[7] ESCAP also received funds for regional advisory services on population census and surveys and data preparation and processing, technical assistance and training in demography and population statistics, fellowships for demographers for training at the International Institute for Population Studies in India, and for various demographic studies.

Environment

At its April 1984 session,[1] ESCAP adopted a resolution on prevention of oil pollution of the marine environment, expressing grave concern over the fact that severe oil pollution had occurred in the region, and calling on Governments to refrain from action which might cause such pollution.

The ESCAP Committee on Industry, Technology, Human Settlements and Environment[12] welcomed the initiative taken by the member countries of South Asia in formulating a regional seas programme for that sub-region under the auspices of the South Asia Co-operative Environment Programme and UNDP, and in designating 1988 as the Year of Trees for South

Asia in response to a UNEP Governing Council decision. Work continued on a draft declaration and action plan for consideration at a ministerial-level conference on environment in Asia, scheduled for 1985.

The UNEP Governing Council in a 28 May resolution on regional activities in Asia and the Pacific, requested its Executive Director to accord continued higher priority to, and seek support and funds for, the region's environmental programmes, including the regional seas programme and the preparatory activities for a new South Asian seas action plan (see p. 745).

Typhoons

In 1984, ESCAP organized a number of roving missions on improving typhoon damage information compilation or disaster prevention systems. It organized, in co-operation with the World Meteorological Organization (WMO), a seminar on the application of remote sensing techniques to flood hazard assessment and to flood loss prevention and management (Bangkok, November) for the members of its Typhoon Committee and the WMO/ESCAP Panel on Tropical Cyclones.

The Typhoon Committee (seventeenth session, Manila, Philippines, 4-10 December) recognized the need for institutional support to put into more stable status its planning and co-ordinating role.

Human settlements

The Committee on Industry, Technology, Human Settlements and Environment[12] agreed that development of small and intermediate towns and rural hinterlands would provide an alternative to unbalanced human settlement patterns, that optimum land use be seriously pursued and that sanitation and water supply was a basic factor in improving the habitat of the poor.

The Executive Director of UNCHS reported to the Commission on Human Settlements in February 1984[18] that a small working group had met at Manila, Philippines, in January, and discussed a proposal for a financial and advisory institution for human settlements in Asia and the Pacific. The group had recommended, among other things, that the Habitat Executive Director initiate high-level consultations with selected countries of the region and the Asian Development Bank to explore the role the Bank might play, and that a regional forum be selected to discuss the proposal and make arrangements for establishing the institution.

Statistics

The Working Group of Statistical Experts (fourth session, Bangkok, July) considered the multidisciplinary approach adopted by the secretariat in advisory services, emerging issues relating to na-

tional capability-building in statistics and the allocation of national resources for statistical services. The Statistical Institute for Asia and the Pacific continued to offer training courses in general statistics and automatic data processing.

Programme, organizational and administrative questions concerning ESCAP

Amendment of terms of reference

On 27 April,[1] ESCAP noted the decision by Vanuatu[19]—an associate member since the country's admission to the United Nations membership in 1981—to become a full member of the Commission as at 17 February 1984, and adopted a draft resolution for action by the Economic and Social Council to amend paragraphs 3 and 4 of the Commission's terms of reference containing, respectively, the listing of full and associate members.

ECONOMIC AND SOCIAL COUNCIL ACTION

On 27 July, on the recommendation of its First Committee, the Economic and Social Council adopted resolution 1984/66 without vote.

> **Amendment of the terms of reference of the Economic and Social Commission for Asia and the Pacific: membership of Vanuatu**
>
> *The Economic and Social Council,*
>
> *Noting* that Vanuatu has become a member of the Economic and Social Commission for Asia and the Pacific in accordance with paragraph 3 of the terms of reference of the Commission,
>
> *Decides* to amend paragraphs 3 and 4 of the terms of reference of the Economic and Social Commission for Asia and the Pacific accordingly.

Economic and Social Council resolution 1984/66

27 July 1984   Meeting 50   Adopted without vote

Approved by First Committee (E/1984/142) without vote, 23 July (meeting 16); agenda item 9.

Conference facilities

The Secretary-General, who had informed the General Assembly in 1983[20] of the need to expand conference facilities at ESCAP headquarters at Bangkok, Thailand, reported to the Assembly in October 1984[21] that, with the assistance of a secretariat advisory group, a design, which provided a total built-up area of 47,244 square metres, was selected through international bidding and competition. The construction project, if begun in January 1985 and completed early in 1988, was estimated to cost $44,177,700. The Secretary-General suggested that the Assembly approve the project at that total estimated cost, including an appropriation of $5,126,305 for 1984-1985.

The Secretary-General also proposed establishing a team in the Secretariat's Office of General Services in New York to direct and control all overseas con-

struction projects. As a counterpart to the Headquarters team, in the case of the ESCAP project, he
proposed setting up a small planning unit in the
Commission's Division of Administration, for which
the Secretary-General asked the Assembly to provide necessary appropriations.

ACABQ recommended in November[22] that the
Assembly approve the construction project and provide the appropriations requested.

In a letter dated 28 November,[23] Thailand assured the Secretary-General that the terms and conditions concerning the lease agreement on the additional land it had offered for the construction
project would not be less favourable than those applicable to the current lease and that the necessary
imported construction materials and equipment
would be tax-exempted.

GENERAL ASSEMBLY ACTION

On 18 December, the General Assembly, on the
recommendation of the Fifth Committee, adopted
resolution 39/236, section XI, by recorded vote.

Expansion of the conference facilities of the Economic and Social Commission for Asia and the Pacific at Bangkok

[The General Assembly . . .]

Having considered the report of the Secretary-General
on the expansion of the conference facilities of the Economic and Social Commission for Asia and the Pacific
at Bangkok and the related report of the Advisory Committee on Administrative and Budgetary Questions,

Taking note of the assurances given by the Government
of Thailand, as contained in the letter dated 27 November 1984 addressed to the Secretary-General,

1. *Approves,* in principle, the construction project for
expansion of the conference facilities of the Economic
and Social Commission for Asia and the Pacific at a total
estimated cost of $44,177,700, excluding the cost of the
Planning Unit at the Commission;

2. *Decides* that the appropriation of $5,126,300 ap-
proved for the biennium 1984-1985 for the construction
project should be placed in a construction account and
any unexpended balance carried forward until the completion of the project;

3. *Requests* the Secretary-General to submit annual
progress reports to the General Assembly on the progress
of the construction project;

. . .

General Assembly resolution 39/236, section XI

18 December 1984   Meeting 105   126-10-10 (recorded vote)

Approved by Fifth Committee (A/39/839) by recorded vote (104-11-8), 30 Novem-
ber (meeting 39); oral proposal by Chairman; agenda item 109.
Financial implications. ACABQ, A/39/7/Add.7; S-G, A/C.5/39/24.
Meeting numbers. GA 39th session: 5th Committee 39, 40, 55; plenary 105.

Recorded vote in Assembly as follows:

In favour: Afghanistan, Algeria, Angola, Antigua and Barbuda, Argentina, Australia,
Austria, Bahamas, Bahrain, Bangladesh, Benin, Bhutan, Bolivia, Botswana, Brazil,
Brunei Darusalam, Burkina Faso, Burma, Burundi, Cameroon, Cape Verde, Central
African Republic, Chad, Chile, China, Colombia, Congo, Costa Rica, Cuba, Cyprus,
Democratic Kampuchea, Democratic Yemen, Denmark, Djibouti, Dominican Repub-
lic, Ecuador, Egypt, El Salvador, Equatorial Guinea, Ethiopia, Fiji, Finland, Gabon,
Gambia, Ghana, Greece, Guatemala, Guinea, Guinea-Bissau, Guyana, Haiti, Hon-
duras, Iceland, India, Indonesia, Iran, Iraq, Ireland, Ivory Coast, Jamaica, Japan,

Jordan, Kenya, Kuwait, Lao People's Democratic Republic, Lebanon, Lesotho,
Liberia, Libyan Arab Jamahiriya, Madagascar, Malawi, Malaysia, Maldives, Mali,
Malta, Mauritania, Mauritius, Mexico, Morocco, Mozambique, Nepal, New Zealand,
Nicaragua, Niger, Nigeria, Norway, Oman, Pakistan, Panama, Papua New Guinea,
Paraguay, Peru, Philippines, Qatar, Romania, Rwanda, Saint Lucia, Samoa, Sao
Tome and Principe, Saudi Arabia, Senegal, Sierra Leone, Singapore, Somalia,
Sri Lanka, Sudan, Suriname, Swaziland, Sweden, Syrian Arab Republic, Thailand,
Togo, Trinidad and Tobago, Tunisia, Turkey, Uganda, United Arab Emirates, United
Republic of Tanzania, Vanuatu, Venezuela, Viet Nam, Yemen, Yugoslavia, Zaire,
Zambia, Zimbabwe.

Against: Bulgaria, Byelorussian SSR, Czechoslovakia, German Democratic Republic, Hungary, Poland, Ukrainian SSR, USSR, United Kingdom, United States.

Abstaining: Belgium, Canada, France, Germany, Federal Republic of, Israel,
Italy, Luxembourg, Netherlands, Portugal, Spain.

In the Fifth Committee, a recorded vote was taken
on the draft, at the request of the United States.

In explanation of vote, the United Kingdom said
the provision of expensive new conference facilities was not a priority at a time of widespread economic difficulty and United Nations budgetary restraint. Sharing that view, the United States said
it regarded the proposed project a burden. The
USSR said the proposed expansion was unnecessary because meeting requirements could be satisfied
by existing facilities and by the construction of a
number of small conference rooms.

Canada and the Federal Republic of Germany
said they would have preferred a more modest project
than the one proposed. Sweden, while voting in
favour, shared the misgivings as regards priority
under the current critical economic situation. Ireland
supported the proposal on the understanding that
the project would cover the needs of ESCAP alone
and would not result in the establishment of another
international conference centre.

While agreeing that the economic situation was
not favourable, Japan considered the project reasonable in view of ESCAP's long-term needs; it added
that, in order to ensure proper execution of the
project, there be close co-operation between Headquarters and ESCAP, and that the Secretary-General
include detailed financial information in his progress
reports. Brazil, Egypt and Pakistan felt the project
should be started immediately.

REFERENCES

[1]E/1984/24. [2]YUN 1980, p. 503, GA res. 35/56, annex, 5
Dec. 1980. [3]YUN 1981, p. 406. [4]*Economic and Social Survey
of Asia and the Pacific 1983* (ST/ESCAP/263), Sales No. E.84.II.F.1
(summary, E/1984/69). [5]E/1985/66. [6]MKG/110.
[7]DP/1985/43/Add.2. [8]YUN 1983, p. 639. [9]E/1984/116.
[10]YUN 1983, p. 639, ESC res. 1983/69, 29 July 1983.
[11]E/ESCAP/352. [12]E/ESCAP/409. [13]E/ESCAP/403 & Corr.1.
[14]E/ESCAP/398. [15]E/1984/52. [16]YUN 1980, p. 717.
[17]E/1984/52/Add.1. [18]HS/C/7/2/Add.2. [19]E/ESCAP/361.
[20]YUN 1983, p. 641. [21]A/C.5/39/24. [22]A/39/7/Add.7.
[23]A/C.5/39/62.

PUBLICATIONS

*The Integration of Tax Planning into Development Planning in the ESCAP
Region* (ST/ESCAP/231), Sales No. E.84.II.F.3. *Fuels for the Transport
Sector: Compressed Natural Gas (CNG)* (ST/ESCAP/260), Sales No.
E.84.II.F.5. *Proceedings of the Meeting on Water Resources Develop-
ment in the South Pacific* (ST/ESCAP/SER.F/57), Sales No. E.84.II.F.7.
Quarterly Bulletin of Statistics for Asia and the Pacific, vol. XIV: No. 1
(March 1984) (ST/ESCAP/287), Sales No. EF.84.II.F.11; No. 2

(June 1984) (ST/ESCAP/304), Sales No. E.84.II.21; No. 3 (September 1984) (ST/ESCAP/341), Sales No. E.85.II.F.12; No. 4 (December 1984) (ST/ESCAP/360), Sales No. E.85.II.F.15. *Proceedings of the Seminars on Flood Vulnerability Analysis and on the Principles of Floodplain Management for Flood Loss Prevention* (ST/ESCAP/SER.F/58), Sales No. E.84.II.F.12. *Proceedings of the Ninth Session of the Committee on Natural Resources* (ST/ESCAP/265), Sales No. E.84.II.F.13. *Updated Guidebook on Biogas Development* (ST/ESCAP/275), Sales No. E.84.II.F.14. *Small Industry Bulletin for Asia and the Pacific, No. 19* (ST/ESCAP/SER.M/37), Sales No. E.84.II.F.17. *Energy in the ESCAP Region: Policies, Issues and the Potential for Regional Co-operation* (ST/ESCAP/306), Sales No. E.84.II.F.22. *Economic and Social Survey of Asia and the Pacific, 1984* (ST/ESCAP/313), Sales No. E.85.II.F.1. *Economic Bulletin for Asia and the Pacific,* vol. XXXV: No. 1 (ST/ESCAP/335), Sales No. E.85.II.F.16; No. 2 (ST/ESCAP/344), Sales No. E.85.II.F.18. *Statistical Yearbook for Asia and the Pacific, 1984* (ST/ESCAP/340), Sales No. E/F.85.II.F.21. *Foreign Trade Statistics of Asia and the Pacific, 1981-1984* (ST/ESCAP/441), vol. XVII, Series B, Sales No. E.86.II.F.18.

Europe

The Economic Commission for Europe (ECE) at its thirty-ninth session (Geneva, 3-14 April 1984)[1] reviewed the economic situation in the region, discussed the activities of its subsidiary bodies[2] and approved plans for its future work.

In a resolution of 14 April on its work and future activities, ECE called on its members to continue taking full advantage of its potential as an instrument for dialogue and for strengthening economic relations and multilateral co-operation in the region. It noted the importance, to that end, of full respect for the principles guiding relations among States as set out in the Final Act of the 1975 Helsinki (Finland) Conference on Security and Co-operation in Europe (CSCE) and those contained in the Concluding Document of the Madrid Meeting of Representatives of the Participating States of CSCE. ECE also requested its subsidiary bodies to take into account in their activities its possible contribution to the United Nations programmes designed to assist developing countries and the necessity of effective co-operation with other international organizations.

Among several decisions taken in April, the Commission adopted a Declaration of Policy on the Rational Use of Water and a set of 18 principles governing its use, took note of the decision by the Senior Economic Advisers to ECE Governments to prepare an overall economic perspective to the year 2000, and invited member Governments to submit proposals to improve the efficiency of the work of its Sessional Committee.

Economic trends

In 1984, the economies of the ECE region— Europe and North America—continued their recovery from the longest post-war recession, with real output growth exceeding 4 per cent, the highest rate since 1978.[3]

In the market economies, the western European recovery was influenced by the strength of United States import demand, and of the dollar, as well as the high United States interest rates. Average GDP growth in western Europe in 1984 was about 2.5 per cent, as against the United States rate of around 7 per cent. The volume of western European exports of goods and services rose some 6 per cent compared with about 2 per cent in 1983. Imports accelerated sharply, but the net balance on goods and services nevertheless contributed about 14 per cent of the increase in GDP in the four large economies and some 20 to 25 per cent in the smaller ones; however, in the United States much of the increase in domestic expenditure had gone into imports, and the current account deficit, which had risen from under 1 per cent of GNP at the beginning of 1983 to over 3 per cent in the last quarter of 1984, had become an increasing drag on the growth of domestic output. The recovery of the preceding two years had not been accompanied by an upsurge in inflation rates; moderate wage increases and rising productivity not only had helped to reduce such pressures but had also contributed to the significant rise in profits in 1984, supporting the recovery of business investment. Recovery had a marked effect on employment and unemployment only in the United States, where the former increased by about 4.5 per cent in 1984 and the latter fell from 8 to 7 per cent of the labour force in the course of the year. In western Europe, unemployment generally remained a rising trend, at a little over 9.5 per cent (19 million people) of the total labour force.

In southern Europe, the export-led recovery of output growth, of nearly 3 per cent, had not prevented a further increase in unemployment or stopped the persistent and dramatic fall in fixed investment. The still high levels of inflation in the subregion had required caution towards any stimulus of domestic demand.

In the centrally planned economies, aggregate net material product (NMP) increased by some 3.5 per cent in eastern Europe and the USSR in 1984, thus continuing the upturn in economic growth which had started in 1983. In eastern Europe, the growth of NMP accelerated to about 5 per cent in 1984, while the rate of growth weakened in the USSR due to stagnation of agricultural output. In eastern Europe, in contrast, agricultural output rose by about 7 per cent. It was estimated that labour productivity continued to grow at rates close to those of NMP, while capital productivity probably continued to decline in most countries, although at a more moderate pace. There was a further strengthening of the eastern European countries' financial position in 1984, as reflected in larger current-account surpluses, a rising accumulation of assets, declining net debt (from $70 billion at the end of the 1983 to some $62 billion at the end of 1984) and increasing access to a wider vaiety of credit instruments, including commercial credits from international banks.

The volume of world trade increased at a rapid pace—some 8 per cent—in 1984, with the import boom in the United States accounting for about half of the rise, and a considerable impetus also coming from the nearly 6 per cent growth in imports into the European ECE countries. United States exports grew nearly as fast as those from Europe, though at less than one third of the rate of import growth. While the United States deficit continued to widen mainly from the upsurge in imports, both market and centrally planned economies in Europe showed some improvement in current accounts, due largely to favourable export developments. Because of the large share of intra-regional flows in European trade, a 39 per cent rise in western European exports and a 50 per cent rise in eastern European exports, both to the United States, accounted for a small portion of their overall export growth in 1984.

In 1984, east-west trade continued to expand. Western trade with eastern Europe showed a pronounced pickup, with a further widening of deficit in the former, while Western trade with the USSR slowed substantially. The volume of trade rose between the eastern European countries and the USSR, probably reflecting fuel and raw material deliveries to the former for the upswing of production growth there.

By decision 1984/187, the Economic and Social Council took note of a document[4] prepared by ECE on recent economic developments in the region.

Activities in 1984

Regional economic co-operation

The Senior Economic Advisers to ECE Governments (twentieth session, 20-24 February), continuing to explore wider co-operation, especially between countries having different economic and social systems, agreed to prepare an overall economic perspective (OEP) to the year 2000. In April, ECE expressed the hope for a timely preparation of OEP, including main economic variables.

Ad hoc working groups, convened for OEP preparation, discussed science and technology, human resources and synthesis work, agreed on a scenario, and identified other topics for analysis. Work was initiated on international trade and co-operation, employment and labour productivity, development of production capacities and investment, patterns of consumption and possible constraints of future economic growth.

Co-operation among Mediterranean countries

In pursuance of an April ECE request, its Executive Secretary participated in a seminar on economic, scientific and cultural co-operation in the Mediterranean (Venice, Italy, 16-26 October) in the light of the CSCE Final Act and co-operated with ECA and ECWA in convening a meeting on transport development in the Mediterranean region (Thessaloniki, Greece, 2-4 October). At the Thessaloniki meeting, there was general agreement that transport study centres be established at Barcelona, Spain, for the western Mediterranean, and Volos, Greece, for the eastern Mediterranean, as well as a training centre in Turkey.

International trade

The Committee on the Development of Trade (thirty-third session, 3-7 December) decided to continue work on an inventory of obstacles to trade, and agreed to convene expert meetings in 1985: one on prospects for east-west trade in the 1980s, and another on industrial co-operation. The Working Party on Facilitation of International Trade Procedures (March, September) concentrated on efforts towards harmonization in automatic trade-data interchange, while the Group of Experts on International Contract Practices in Industry (July, December) continued preparing a guide on drawing up contracts for services relating to maintenance, repair and operation of industrial and other works.

Transport and communications

The Inland Transport Committee (forty-fifth session, 30 January–3 February) completed work on methodological aspects of an intermodal evaluation of policy measures affecting international transport; a set of operational guidelines had been formulated to facilitate integrated development of the different transport modes.

The Working Party on Road Transport (June, November) adopted a consolidated resolution on the facilitation of road transport and new technical regulations for motor vehicle equipment and parts. The Group of Experts on Combined Transport (June) studied commercial attitudes of users and providers of piggyback services, the economic viability of piggyback transport and delays in international combined transport. Other subsidiary bodies meeting during the year finalized a draft text of an international instrument relating to the development of a European railway network; made further progress in preparing an updated version of the European Code for Inland Waterways; settled administrative, technical and legal questions related to the practical application of the 1975 Customs Convention on the International Transport of Goods under Cover of TIR Carnets; and promoted accession to the International Convention on the Harmonization of Frontier Controls of Goods. The Group of Experts on Transport Statistics (April/May) decided to meet annually, instead of every 18 months.

Countries participating in the Trans-European North-South Motorway (TEM) agreed to continue the project after 1986 so that TEM would become a permanent ECE activity; with the end of phase II, most of the physical and operational standards had been finalized and a set of recommended practices for border crossing operations had been adopted. By the end of 1984, 2,200 kilometres of motorway were in operation and 3,700 kilometres were in various stages of design or construction.

Standardization of summer time

The Commission recommended in April[1] that all Governments pursue their efforts to standardize over a medium-term period the application of summer time in Europe.

Industry

The Chemical Industry Committee (seventeenth session, 26-28 September) assessed market trends and selected techno-economic issues affecting the industry. It decided to continue work on the recycling of waste rubber and initiated an analysis of new developments in the field of additives for polymers, particularly thermoplastics. Internationally comparable statistics were being developed on aromatic hydrocarbons, olefins and polyamides.

The Steel Committee (fifty-second session, 24-26 October) examined factors influencing the structure of steel production costs and improvement of steel consumption forecasting, and decided to revive the Working Party on Steel Statistics. A study on the evaluation of the specific consumption of steel was published.

The Working Party on Engineering Industries and Automation (fourth session, 7-9 March) continued studies of techno-economic aspects of introducing new manufacturing concepts and methods. Three studies were finalized—on the use of industrial robots, energy-effective engineering equipment, and equipment for better waste-water management—and outlines for two new studies were agreed, on a review of recent trends in electrical and electronic engineering and use of digital image processing in biomedical engineering. Work was begun on a study of telematics equipment and application of information technology.

The Commission,[1] in April, decided to consider in 1985 the request made by the Working Party to be upgraded to a principal subsidiary body with the title of a committee.

Water

In April 1984, the Commission[1] adopted a Declaration of Policy on the Rational Use of Water—consisting of 18 principles—in recognition of the need for co-ordinated efforts to formulate and apply strategies of water-demand management to cope with limited water supply. It decided that national water policies and planning should pay specific attention to protecting ground water from the possibility of pollution and over-use.

The principles emphasized the need for a unified national strategy for water withdrawal, distribution, treatment, use and discharge; integrated water use, attaching priority to drinking-water requirements and environmental protection; water-demand management and preventive measures so as to avoid water shortages and pollution; non-structural measures aimed at increasing operation efficiency of existing water schemes; co-ordinated utilization of both surface and ground-water, with priority to public drinking-water supply in ground-water use; and measures to combat harmful effects of water, such as flooding and soil erosion.

In a related action, the Commission recognized the significance of developing and strengthening co-operation among the ECE countries in water-pollution control matters, including transboundary water pollution.

In further implementation of the ECE Declaration, the Committee on Water Problems (sixteenth session, 19-23 November) decided to elaborate a set of guidelines on ground-water management, in view of the importance of the problems associated with the over-exploitation of aquifers and the hazards resulting from long-term effects of ground-water pollution. A seminar on co-operation in the field of transboundary waters (Düsseldorf, Federal Republic of Germany, October) drew up a set of recommendations to Governments and prepared draft principles on international co-operation in the harmonious development, use and conservation of water resources shared by two or more countries.

Energy resources

The Steering Committee of the inter-country project on international co-operative research in low-calorie fuel technology held its first session in March and, in accordance with decisions taken, an *ad hoc* meeting was convened in December of Governments interested in participating in the project (Bulgaria, Greece, Hungary, Poland, Romania, Spain, Turkey, USSR, Yugoslavia).

No consensus was reached in 1984 on the convening of the Senior Advisers to ECE Governments on Energy prior to the 1985 session of the Commission. In the mean time, work on general energy problems concentrated on research on energy balances, energy conservation, and new and renewable sources of energy. Long-term series of energy production, exports, imports and consumption by sector on a comparable basis had been established as a result of the preparation by the ECE secretariat of an updated version of abridged energy balances, 1965-1982. The secretariat also prepared studies on waste energy recovery and the efficient use of energy in industry in the ECE region.

The Coal Committee (eightieth session, 1-4 October) considered the current situation and prospects of coal demand, supply and use, with special focus on world coal trade and updated world and ECE-region coal prospects to the year 2000.

The Committee on Electric Power (forty-second session, 16-20 January) discussed problems of planning and operating large power systems, electric power stations and the relationship between electricity and the environment.

The Committee on Gas (thirtieth session, 23-26 January) examined the current situation in the ECE region, natural gas markets, availabilities, and import possibilities, and the future role of gas in the energy requirements of the region.

Agriculture and timber

The Committee on Agricultural Problems (thirty-fifth session, 12-16 March) concentrated on programmes to assist Governments in the gradual reorientation of the agricultural sector in the light of difficult production and market conditions created, in part, by the general economic situation, population trends, balances of trade and payments and foreign indebtedness. Among the activities undertaken in that regard, the Working Party on Standardization of Perishable Produce (November), after 35 years of work on quality standards, began revising the overall framework of its work, with a possibility of finishing the task in 1985.

The Timber Committee (forty-second session, 8-12 October) focused its efforts on preparing a new study of long-term timber trends and prospects in Europe, including development of more sophisticated demand projection models for wood, a review of the outlook for non-wood goods and services of the forest, and an attempt to assess the impact of forest damage on forest productivity and future supply.

The Joint FAO/ECE/ILO Committee on Forest Working Techniques and Training of Forest Workers held its fifteenth session in Turkey in May, together with a seminar and study tour on the rehabilitation of low-productivity forests.

Science and technology

The Senior Advisers to ECE Governments on Science and Technology (twelfth session, 17-21 September) reviewed changes which had occurred in national science and technology policies over the previous four years and analysed those policies aimed

at increasing the effectiveness of research and development activities. The Senior Advisers decided to extend the coverage of the *Manual of Licensing Procedures in Member Countries of the United Nations Economic Commission for Europe* by inviting six industrialized countries from outside the region (Australia, Brazil, India, Japan, Mexico, New Zealand) to contribute national chapters.

Environment

The Senior Advisers to ECE Governments on Environmental Problems (twelfth session, 7-10 February) completed a plan for the elaboration of a strategy for environmental protection and rational use of natural resources in member countries up to the year 2000 and beyond. An *ad hoc* meeting, subsequently held in November, developed the basic elements and structure of a long-term regional strategy as well as a tentative schedule and method of work.

The Commission, in April,[1] adopted decisions on air pollution, a conference on the causes and prevention of damage to forests and water through air pollution in Europe (see below), monitoring and evaluation of transboundary water pollution, and co-operation in the field of protection and improvement of the environment. The Commission, among other things, invited the Senior Advisers to pursue efforts at drawing up a compendium on non-waste technology, to intensify activities regarding air pollution matters not covered by the Convention on Long-range Transboundary Air Pollution, and to elaborate proposals for protecting flora and fauna and their habitats in the ECE region.

A multilateral conference on the causes and prevention of damage to forests and water by air pollution in Europe (Munich, Federal Republic of Germany, June) strengthened and enhanced the work carried out under the Convention on Long-range Transboundary Air Pollution. The Executive Body for the Convention (second session, September) adopted, and 16 contracting parties subsequently signed, a protocol on long-term financing of the Co-operative Programme for Monitoring and Evaluation of the Long-range Transmission of Air Pollutants in Europe, setting forth mandatory annual contributions and a scale for sharing the costs among the contributors. The Executive Body also recognized the need for reducing by 1995 the total annual national emissions of nitrogen oxides from stationary and mobile sources or their transboundary fluxes, as well as for internationally harmonized assessment methods and systems for monitoring forest damage in relation to air pollution.

An *ad hoc* meeting in November recommended ways for the Senior Advisers to contribute to the comprehensive protection of flora, fauna and their habitats, including the elaboration of an all-European declaration.

Human settlements

The Committee on Housing, Building and Planning (forty-fifth session, 10–14 September) discussed long-term perspectives for human settlements development in the region. The fifth Conference on Urban and Regional Research (Lisbon, Portugal, May) evaluated research on long-term perspectives as related to management structures, and a seminar on the city and its transportation (Moscow, USSR, October), organized jointly with the Inland Transport Committee, considered problems and policies related to the integration of transportation infrastructure into the urban structure.

Statistics

The Conference of European Statisticians (thirty-second session, 18-22 June) concentrated on revising and harmonizing economic classifications and on developing the United Nations System of National Accounts and its linking with the System of Balances of the National Economy of the Council for Mutual Economic Assistance. Continuing attention was paid to the European Comparison Programme of the International Comparison Project. The first phase of the inter-country project on use of computers for statistical purposes was completed at the end of 1984, with a number of software products arising from the project ready for use.

Standardization

The Government Officials Responsible for Standardization Policies (eighth meeting, 20-24 February) continued to promote mutual recognition of certification systems and tests, and adopted, among other things, a revised ECE Standardization List. The Commission, in April,[1] agreed to consider in 1985 the convening of a ninth meeting of the group.

The Group of Experts on Standardization Policies decided to compile a directory of international, regional and national certification systems, arrangements and other agreements.

REFERENCES

(1)E/1984/23. (2)E/ECE/1086. (3)E/1985/101. (4)E/1984/82.

PUBLICATIONS

Study of Regulations, Codes and Standards Related to Energy Use in Buildings (ECE/HBP/41), Sales No. E.84.II.E.7. *Agricultural Trade in Europe,* No. 21, 1983 (ECE/AGRI/77), Sales No. E.84.II.E.9. *The Evolution of the Specific Consumption of Steel* (ECE/STEEL/45), Sales No. E.84.II.E.17. *Strategies, Technologies and Economics of Waste Water Management in ECE Countries* (ECE/WATER/36), Sales No. E.84.II.E.18. *ECE Compendium of Model Provisions for Building Regulations* (ECE/HBP/55), Sales No. E.84.II.E.19. *Waste Energy Recovery in the Industry in the ECE Region* (ECE/ENERGY/9), Sales No. E.84.II.E.21. *Engineering Equipment and Automation Means for Waste Water Management in ECE Countries,* Parts I & II (ECE/ENG.AUT/18, vols. I & II), Sales No. E.84.II.E.13 & 23. *Policies for Integrated Water Management* (E/ECE/1084, ECE/WATER/38), Sales No. E/F/R.84.II.E.24. *Measures for Improving Engineering Equipment with a View to More Effective Energy Use* (ECE/ENG.AUT/16), Sales No. E.84.II.E.25. *Forecasting and Programming of Housing* (ECE/HBP/51),

Sales No. E.84.II.E.26. *The Steel Market, 1984* (ECE/STEEL/49), Sales No. E.85.II.E.28. *Statistics of Air Quality: Some Methods,* No. 36, Sales No. E.84.II.E.29. *Regulations and Legislation on Food Additives and Chemicals for Food Packaging* (ECE/CHEM/54), Sales No. E.84.II.E.30. *Economic Survey of Europe, 1984/85,* Sales No. E.85.II.E.1. *Annual Bulletin of Housing and Building Statistics for Europe, 1984,* vol. XXVIII, Sales No. E/F/R.85.II.E.3. *Annual Bulletin of Electric Energy Statistics for Europe, 1984,* vol. XXX, Sales No. E/F/R.85.II.E.4. *Annual Bulletin of Steel Statistics for Europe, 1984,* vol. XII, Sales No. E/F/R.85.II.E.5. *Annual Bulletin of Gas Statistics for Europe, 1984,* vol. XXX, Sales No. E/F/R.85.II.E.6. *Annual Bulletin of Transport Statistics for Europe, 1984,* vol. XXXVI, Sales No. E/F/R.85.II.E.7. *Annual Bulletin of Coal Statistics for Europe, 1984,* vol. XIX, Sales No. E/F/R.85.II.E.8. *Statistics of World Trade in Steel, 1984,* Sales No. E/F/R.85.II.E.10. *Statistics of Road Traffic Accidents in Europe, 1984,* vol. XXXI, Sales No. E/F/R.85.II.E.12. *Agricultural Review for Europe,* No. 27, *1983 and 1984:* vols. I-VI (ECE/AGRI/83, vols. I-VI), Sales No. E.85.II.E.21-26. *Annual Bulletin of Trade in Chemical Products, 1984,* vol. XI, Sales No. E/F/R.85.II.E.42. *Annual Review of Engineering Industries and Automation, 1983-84,* vols. I & II (ECE/ENG.AUT/19), Sales No. E.85.II.E.43. *Annual Bulletin of General Energy Statistics for Europe, 1984,* vol. XVII, Sales No. E/F/R.86.II.E.8. *Bulletin of Statistics on World Trade in Engineering Products, 1984,* Sales No. E/F/R.86.II.E.10. *Annual Review of the Chemical Industry, 1984* (ECE/CHEM/59), Sales No. E.86.II.E.12. *Prices of Agricultural Products and Selected Inputs in Europe and North America,* No. 34, *1983-84* (ECE/AGRI/82), Sales No. E.85.II.E.13; No. 35, *1984-85* (ECE/AGRI/88), Sales No. E.86.II.E.13. *Quarterly Bulletin of Steel Statistics for Europe, 1984,* vol. XXXV, No. 3. *Forest Products Market Trends in 1983 and Prospects for 1984,* vol. XXXVI, Supplement 3.

Latin America and the Caribbean

The economic crisis and the future prospects of Latin America and the Caribbean, the internal adjustment policies and the renegotiation of external debt were among the topics discussed by the Economic Commission for Latin America,[1] as it held its twentieth session at Lima, Peru, from 29 March to 6 April 1984. Regarding internal adjustment policies and renegotiation of the external debt, the Commission stressed that responsibility must be shared by both the debtor and the developed countries, international private banks and multilateral financial agencies.

After considering the Commission's recommendations, the Economic and Social Council, in July, approved the Commission's name change to Economic Commission for Latin America and the Caribbean (ECLAC) and the decision to admit Portugal as a full member and the British Virgin Islands and the United States Virgin Islands as associate members (resolution 1984/67).

The Commission—headquartered at Santiago, Chile—also reviewed the work and recommendations of its subsidiary bodies and approved the programme of work for 1986-1987. Four sessional committees of the Commission examined the topics of water, human settlements, co-operation among developing countries and regions, and population, the latter in preparation for the 1984 International Conference on Population, held in Mexico in August.

With the Council's approval, the Commission's Committee of the Whole held a one-day special meeting at United Nations Headquarters on 28 June (p. 638).

Among other developments in the region was the holding in January, at Quito, Ecuador, of the Latin American Economic Conference, in response to an initiative by the President of that country; and a June meeting, at Cartagena, Colombia, of Ministers of Foreign Affairs and of Finance of 11 countries of the region.

Economic trends

The economic evolution of Latin America in 1983 was characterized by the falling GDP, worsening employment situation and accelerating rate of inflation, according to the *Economic Survey of Latin America, 1983*. The Economic and Social Council took note of a summary of the survey[2] in its decision 1984/187 of 27 July 1984.

There was further exacerbation of the crisis which, by 1982, had already reached dimensions not witnessed since the economic depression of the 1930s. Many economies of the region made adjustment efforts in order to reduce the profound disequilibria that had developed in the external sector over previous years. For the second consecutive year, an extraordinary contraction was observed of net capital inflows, accompanied by the transfer of resources abroad by Latin American countries.

In 1984,[3] a weak and inadequate recovery of economic activity was seen, along with a sharp increase in the rate of inflation for the fourth consecutive year and an improvement in the external sector situation. It was estimated that Latin America's total GDP increased by 3.3 per cent, after having fallen by a little over 3 per cent in 1983. The interruption of the downward trend that economic activity had been showing since 1981 was widespread, since GDP increased in 14 of the 19 countries for which comparable data were available. However, inasmuch as the economic recovery was very slight in most countries, and also as a result of population growth, the per capita product rose in 1984 by only 0.9 per cent in the region as a whole and once again diminished in 10 of the 19 countries. Thus, Latin America's per capita product was almost 9 per cent lower in 1984 than in 1980 and was similar to that already obtained by the region in 1977. The inadequacy of the recovery was also evidenced by the fact that urban unemployment rates continued to rise or remained unusually high in most of the countries.

As a result of the adjustment effort and of more favourable world trade trends in 1984, Latin America succeeded in further reducing its balance-of-payments deficit on current account, to barely $2.1 billion, or 95 per cent less than that recorded on average during 1981-1982.

After plummeting from a record peak of $37.7 billion in 1981 to barely $4.4 billion in 1983, the net amount of loans and investments obtained by Latin America rose to $12.4 billion in 1984. Thanks to that increase and also to the reduced deficit on current account, the balance of payments closed in 1984 with a surplus of more than $10 billion. Although that positive balance—the first since 1980—permitted a partial recovery in the level of international reserves, the net inflow of capital continued to fall far short of the amount of net remittances of interest and profits. In 1984, therefore, Latin America was obliged for the third consecutive year to make a substantial transfer of resources abroad, of approximately $25 billion—a sum which, although lower than the $30 billion recorded in 1983, implied a reduction in the region's capacity to import equivalent to about 22 per cent of the value of exports of goods and services.

In 1984, as the growth rate of Latin America's total external debt was slower than that of exports, the debt-export coefficient decreased for the first time in four years, although at a level still very high in internationally comparable terms and far exceeding those recorded in Latin America up to 1982.

Activities in 1984

Development policy and regional economic co-operation

At its 1984 session,[1] the Commission adopted a number of resolutions concerning economic co-operation and development. It decided that its Committee of the Whole should examine in 1985 those aspects of long-term economic and social development policies which could help the countries of the region meet the challenges arising from the changing international economy. By a second resolution, the Commission reaffirmed that the serious economic problems of the region, aggravated by processes of adjustment and renegotiation of external debt, had been caused by factors beyond their control; and that it was the economic policies of some developed countries which had led to a constant deterioration of the terms of trade, a decline in trade, an excessive increase in interest rates and an abrupt reversal of capital flows, as a result of which the countries of the region had become net exporters of capital. Calling the situation untenable, unfair and irrational, the Commission stressed that responsibility for the external debt problems must be shared by both the region's debtor countries and by the developed countries of and outside the region, the international private banks and the multilateral financial agencies. The ECLAC secretariat was called on to undertake studies to identify trends, limitations and alternatives for the region regarding domestic adjustment processes and external indebtedness.

In a third resolution, the Commission approved

a secretariat report[4] on the review and appraisal of the regional implementation of the International Development Strategy for the Third United Nations Development Decade (1980s),[5] containing an appraisal of the current economic and social situation in the region and of the implementation of the Regional Programme of Action for Latin America in the 1980s,[6] as well as policies and measures for action which took into account, among other things, the agreements reached at the Latin American Economic Conference at Quito, Ecuador, in January 1984 (see below). The report viewed it as essential to change the framework in which the external negotiations of the region were being held, with the region mobilizing its bargaining power in order to guarantee import levels compatible with its socio-economic objectives. The Commission requested its Executive Secretary to transmit the report to the Economic and Social Council and to the General Assembly's Committee on the Review and Appraisal of the Implementation of the International Development Strategy for the Third United Nations Development Decade.

In December, the Technical Sub-Committee of the Latin American Institute for Economic and Social Planning (ILPES) met in preparation for the fifth (1985) conference of ministers and heads of planning of Latin America and the Caribbean and the 1985 meeting of the ILPES Technical Committee.

Latin American Economic Conference. In 1984, high-level representatives of 26 Latin American and Caribbean countries—including 5 heads of government—attended the Latin American Economic Conference (Quito, Ecuador, 9-13 January), held in close co-operation with the Latin American Economic System and in response to the 1983 Santo Domingo Pledge[7] resulting from the initiatives of the President of Ecuador. The Conference adopted the Quito Declaration and Plan of Action,[8] containing various measures for reactivating the economy and dealing with the external debt.

The Declaration stated that the countries of the region faced the most serious and intense economic and social crisis of the century, manifesting itself in an unprecedented level of unemployment and reduction of personal incomes and living standards, with grave consequences for the political and social stability of its peoples. It recognized the need for concerted regional and international action, including efforts at achieving and maintaining regional food security; and called for an attitude of shared responsibility by the Governments of creditor countries, the international financing organizations and the international private banks in solving the external debt problem. It also stressed an urgent need to reform the international monetary and financial system, expressed alarm over the increase in protectionist measures of industrialized countries, called for dynamic price stabilization for export commodities for the region, and asked support for the Latin American Energy Organization.

The Plan of Action for intraregional co-operation covered measures dealing with financing, trade, regional food security, energy co-operation, and services.

In a letter dated 12 June,[9] the Presidents of Argentina, Brazil, Colombia, Ecuador, Mexico, Peru and Venezuela informed the Secretary-General of the communiqué they had sent to the heads of State or Government participating in the London Summit meeting, asking them to consider the situation and prospects of Latin America's economies, particularly as regards issues of trade, financing and the external debt.

Caribbean area

In 1984, the Caribbean Development and Co-operation Committee (eighth session, Port-au-Prince, Haiti, 6-12 June) admitted the United States Virgin Islands and the British Virgin Islands as associate members; in other action, it noted the completion of a Caribbean Draft Maritime Search and Rescue Plan, the first of its kind produced in the developing world.

In April,[1] ECLAC requested the Commission's Executive Secretary to accelerate efforts to seek and to channel funding and resources to the ECLAC subregional Headquarters for the Caribbean.

International trade and finance

In an April 1984 resolution on actions affecting the freedom of trade and economic development of Central America, the Commission[1] noted the need to banish from the subregion all foreign intervention striking against its peace and economic development (see also POLITICAL AND SECURITY QUESTIONS, Chapter VI), and urged backing for the work of the Action Committee in Support of the Economic and Social Development of Central America.

A study on international economic relations and regional co-operation in Latin America was presented to the eighth session of the Committee of High-level Government Experts (Montevideo, Uruguay, 19-23 January) and, in expanded and revised form, to the 1984 session of the Commission.

As in past years, the Commission's bimonthly bulletin on *Facilitation of commerce and transport—Latin America and the Caribbean* reported on the latest worldwide advances in reducing or eliminating non-tariff barriers to international trade.

The Second Ibero-American Conference on Economic Co-operation was held at Lima, Peru, 30 March–3 April. In July, a seminar met at Buenos Aires, Argentina, on economic relations between Latin American countries and member countries of the Council for Mutual Economic Assistance.

External debt

Meeting on 21 and 22 June at Cartagena, Colombia, Ministers of Foreign Affairs and of Finance of Argentina, Bolivia, Brazil, Chile, Colombia, Dominican Republic, Ecuador, Mexico, Peru, Uruguay and Venezuela signed on 22 June the Cartagena Consensus statement on the international economic situation, with particular reference to external debt.[10]

In a series of proposals contained in the statement, they called for a drastic and immediate reduction by Governments of the industrialized countries of nominal and real interest rates on international markets; the use by international banks, during renegotiation of debt agreement and negotiation of new loans, of reference interest rates not exceeding the true cost of raising funds in the market-place; and the elimination of commissions and cancellation, during renegotiation periods, of interest payments on arrears. Other proposals called for reactivating flows of finance to debtor countries and revising the procedures of IMF, the World Bank Group and the Inter-American Development Bank. It was also proposed that debtor countries should be accorded longer repayment periods and new credit lines on preferential terms and in amounts enabling them to avert suspension of imports; and that immediate attention should be paid to developing countries' demands with respect to stabilizing commodity prices, and to eliminating the industrialized countries' tariff and non-tariff barriers restricting access to their markets.

The Ministers agreed on regional consultation and follow-up machinery, to facilitate exchange of information and experience, promote contacts outside the region with other developing countries, and promote dialogue with Governments of the creditor countries and possibly with multilateral financial institutions and the international banking system.

A North-South round-table meeting at ECLAC headquarters, 27-29 February, discussed the adjustment process, the renegotiation of external debt and the terms established by IMF for the creditor countries.

Technical co-operation

In co-operation with ILPES and the Latin American Demographic Centre, ECLAC continued to provide advisory services and regional training courses in socio-economic planning and policy. Interregional technical or economic co-operation among developing countries continued to be promoted and the Commission prepared with ECA a joint project document for promoting such co-operation in developing the mineral resources of both regions; the project was submitted to UNDP for funding.

At its 1984 session,[1] ECLAC requested identification of methods and procedures for co-operation among the countries of the region which made fullest possible use of financial resources in national currencies and promotion of joint interregional technical and economic co-operation activities with other regional commissions.

Technical co-operation in Central America and the Caribbean

The first of a two-part report of JIU on United Nations technical co-operation in Central America and the Caribbean—volume I on Central America[11] and volume II on the Caribbean (issued in 1985)[12]—was transmitted to the Economic and Social Council in November 1984 by the Secretary-General.

The report on Central America—covering Belize, Costa Rica, El Salvador, Guatemala, Honduras, Nicaragua and Panama—examined the extent to which such co-operation had helped mitigate the social and economic problems, enhance self-reliance at the national level, and develop their co-operation potential in the subregion. Focusing attention on the development of national and regional institutional frameworks for policy formulation, planning and programme management, and on population—as elements critical to the socio-economic development and political stability of the region—the Inspectors drew conclusions based on projects supported with resources from UNDP and UNFPA.

The Inspectors recommended, among other things, that a balance be struck between programmes for social development and those for economic development, that every opportunity be exploited for joint programmes so as to enhance mutual co-operation and a harmonious development process in the region, and that efforts be made to speed up the pool of trained human resources.

In commenting on the JIU recommendations, the Secretary-General[13] said the aim of a more balanced distribution between social and economic development projects should be viewed as a recognition that Governments were ultimately responsible for deciding which projects required external assistance. He observed that the effectiveness and impact of United Nations and other technical co-operation in the subregion depended on a climate of political stability, accompanied by programmes aimed at enhancing the countries' capabilities for self-reliance and addressing the most basic needs of their population.

Transport

The Commission continued in 1984 to provide technical assistance and convene meetings to assist its member countries to improve land, river, maritime and multimodal transport. Its Transport and Communications Division considered, at the request of the Latin American Integration Association (ALADI), a study on a system of information on international transport.

Industrial development

A diagnosis of events in the industrial sector in the region and long-term policies in industrialization was considered by the Latin American Technical Meeting on Industrialization (Santiago, Chile, May), whose conclusions were used in establishing the position of the countries of the region at the Fourth General Conference of UNIDO (UNIDO IV) (see p. 758).

The Regional Programme on Industrial Reorganization was initiated toward the end of 1984 in conjunction with UNIDO. Its aim was to provide Governments of the region with analytical information relating to trends in industrial and technical reorganization within the industrialized countries, to assess the repercussions of such changes on the region's industrialization process and to assist countries in formulating appropriate strategies and policies. The first meeting of the working party on industrial reorganization in the region was held at Santiago in November.

Natural resources and energy

In 1984, articles of association of the Latin American Mining Agency were approved at a meeting at Lima, Peru, 3-4 April, with delegates from 13 countries in the region participating.

In the field of water resources, the Commission decided in 1984 to pursue, at the request of Governments, efforts supporting the national and regional implementation of the Mar del Plata Plan of Action, adopted at the 1977 United Nations Water Conference,[14] and urged Governments to co-operate in preparing a progress report on the Plan's implementation. It was recommended that the ECLAC secretariat also continue its support for activities in connection with the International Drinking Water Supply and Sanitation Decade (1981-1990).[15]

A meeting on global energy issues and their relation to Latin American energy policies and options (Santiago, 1-3 March) made a number of proposals, including the creation of a Latin American prospecting fund for petroleum as a way of mobilizing international sources of high-risk capital.

In the field of new and renewable sources of energy (NRSE), a number of technical missions and meetings were organized on the economics of solar energy, development of NRSE projects in Latin America and the Caribbean, and developing a plan of action on rural energy in the region, with special reference to NRSE.[16]

Food and agriculture

Work continued in 1984 on research projects on rural poverty in Latin America, agricultural policies and rural development, and structure and operation of national food systems.

The subject of rural poverty was tackled with technical and financial help from FAO, including the preparation of country case studies and documents of regional scope. A round-table on rural poverty in Latin America and the Caribbean (Santiago, May) enabled government and private-sector experts from 17 countries of the region, working together with experts from 9 international institutions, to evaluate the Commission's activities in the field. Other 1984 meetings dealt with rural development, farm finance techniques, and farming systems.

Science and technology

In 1984, the Committee of High-level Government Experts (ninth session, Montevideo, Uruguay, 23-24 January), at a session devoted to science and technology for development, reviewed regional developments relating to the implementation of the Vienna Programme of Action on Science and Technology for Development (VPA) and its Operational Plan—adopted at the 1979 United Nations Conference on Science and Technology for Development, at Vienna, Austria.[17]

The Committee adopted a series of proposals for future action dealing, among other things, with promotion of mechanisms for co-operation among the countries of the region; modification of conditions contributing to the exodus of qualified personnel; regulation of importation of technology built into capital goods and reorienting the demand for such goods to suppliers in the region; monitoring practices of transnational corporations that worked against national policies; protection and promotion of national capabilities in engineering, consultant services and technological management; stressing the importance of standardization, measurement and quality control; allocation to science and technology of resources equivalent to twice the present percentage of GDP; and strengthening training in priority areas.

The Commission continued to study the possible impact of the incorporation of new techniques—such as biotechnology, including genetic engineering, robotization and microelectronics—on the economic and social development of the countries of the region. The Second Meeting of High-Level Government Experts on Science and Technology (Caracas, Venezuela, May) expressed support for a co-operative programme of action in microelectronics, including recommendations for the establishment of a regional microelectronics network.

Social and cultural development

The Commission, at its 1984 session,[1] urged Governments to encourage the full integration of women into the economic and social development processes of their countries, to adopt short- and medium-term policies to that end, and to prepare a comprehensive diagnosis of the situation of women.

Governments were also urged to adopt policies aimed at slowing down the migration to the cities of women and their families, to improve the working conditions of women in rural areas and to extend or increase effectively the coverage of social security schemes.

In July, the Economic and Social Council requested the Secretary-General to assist in holding a regional meeting in 1985 to review the implementation of the Regional Plan of Action for Latin America and the Caribbean for the International Youth Year (see below, resolution 1984/67, sect. II).

Conservation of cultural property

In September 1984,[18] the Secretary-General submitted to the General Assembly information on the implementation of the 1982 JIU recommendations on the United Nations contribution to the conservation and management of Latin American cultural and natural heritage.[19] The Secretary-General, in commenting on the JIU report in 1983,[20] had generally concurred with the Inspectors' observations, including the view that the United Nations system needed to be fully attuned to the exigencies of a conservation-oriented approach to development in the region. In his 1984 report, the Secretary-General noted that the creation of a single regional intergovernmental forum on heritage conservation, if the region so decided, might be explored most appropriately in the framework of the established international or regional organizations.

Population

The Latin American Demographic Centre (CELADE), whose work programme had been approved by ECLAC member countries, continued to focus on demographic statistics and projections of population trends, population and development, and education and training.

The Commission, at its 1984 session,[1] recognized the collaboration given by UNFPA, a major funding agency for CELADE, in supporting the efforts of the countries of the region in the population field, and urged increased contributions to UNFPA to enable it to respond more adequately to the region's growing assistance needs.

Environment

The Commission continued studies and research aimed at promoting horizontal co-operation, advisory services and training. Work continued on efforts to incorporate the environmental dimension in development planning processes. In August, a new project on tourism and the environment in the Caribbean was begun.

At its May 1984 session,[21] the UNEP Governing Council urged the Governments of the region to continue strengthening co-operation and promot-

ing exchange of experience. Among the meetings held in 1984 was one of high-level experts designated by Governments to review regional environmental programmes (Peru, April) (see also Chapter XVI of this section).

Statistics

In 1984, the Commission continued to maintain, up-date and improve statistics contained in the External Trade Data Bank for Latin America and the Caribbean (BADECEL), broadening work in the areas of national accounts, external trade and external indebtedness, income distribution, consumption, prices, production and population, as well as social development.

Recognizing the importance of access to reliable and timely statistics in achieving the economic integration of the region, the Commission, in 1984,[1] noted with satisfaction the progress made in launching and operating BADECEL, urged regional integration bodies to continue collaborating with the ECLAC secretariat in creating a regional system of foreign trade statistics, and urged Governments to give priority to improving and processing their foreign trade statistics.

Programme, organizational and administrative questions

Special meeting

ECONOMIC AND SOCIAL COUNCIL ACTION

The Economic and Social Council, on 21 May 1984, adopted decision 1984/116 without vote, on an oral proposal by its President.

Special meeting of the Committee of the Whole of the Economic Commission for Latin America

At its 16th plenary meeting, on 21 May 1984, the Council, in pursuance of the request made by the Economic Commission for Latin America at its twentieth session, decided to approve the convening of a one-day special meeting of the Committee of the Whole of the Commission at United Nations Headquarters on 28 June 1984, in order to approve the conclusions and recommendations submitted to it by the Caribbean Development and Co-operation Committee.

Economic and Social Council decision 1984/116

Adopted without vote

Oral proposal by President, on request by Economic Commission for Latin America; agenda item 1.

At the one-day special meeting at United Nations Headquarters on 28 June, the ECLAC Committee of the Whole[22] approved the conclusions and recommendations submitted to it by the Caribbean Development and Co-operation Committee and, in a resolution on response to the emergency economic situation in El Salvador, recommended that the country, though not officially listed by the General

Assembly among LDCs, be accorded a similar treatment until normalcy returned.

Composition, terms of reference and work programme

In April, ECLAC approved its draft programme of work for 1986-1987.

ECONOMIC AND SOCIAL COUNCIL ACTION

On 27 July, the Council, on the recommendation of its First Committee, adopted resolution 1984/67 without vote.

Composition, terms of reference and programme of work of the Economic Commission for Latin America

The Economic and Social Council,

Noting with satisfaction the results of the twentieth session of the Economic Commission for Latin America, held at Lima from 29 March to 6 April 1984,

Having considered the decisions and recommendations adopted by the Commission at that session,

I

Composition and terms of reference of the Commission

1. *Decides* to change the name of the Economic Commission for Latin America to "Economic Commission for Latin America and the Caribbean", as recommended by the Commission in its resolution 455(XX) of 6 April 1984;

2. *Endorses* Commission resolution 452(XX) of 6 April 1984, by which the Commission welcomed the request of the Government of Portugal and decided to admit that country as a full member of the Commission;

3. *Approves* the recommendation of the Commission that the French and Spanish versions of its terms of reference and rules of procedure should be amended by replacing the words "la région des Antilles" by "la région des Caraïbes" and the words "la región de las Antillas" by "la región del Caribe";

4. *Decides,* therefore, to amend the terms of reference and rules of procedure of the Commission in order to incorporate the decisions contained in paragraphs 1 to 3 of the present resolution;

5. *Takes note with satisfaction* of Commission resolutions 453(XX) and 454(XX) of 6 April 1984, in which the Commission decided to admit the British Virgin Islands and the United States Virgin Islands as associate members of the Commission;

II

Programme of work and calendar of conferences of the Commission

6. *Takes note* of resolution 465(XX) of 6 April 1984 of the Economic Commission for Latin America on its programme of work and calendar of conferences, in particular the recommendations contained therein on the holding by the Commission of regional preparatory meetings for United Nations world conferences, and requests the Secretary-General to make every effort to reallocate existing resources for the holding in 1985 of a regional meeting to review the implementation of the Regional Plan of Action for Latin America and the Caribbean for the International Youth Year.

Economic and Social Council resolution 1984/67

27 July 1984   Meeting 50   Adopted without vote

Approved by First Committee (E/1984/142) without vote, 23 July (meeting 16); orally amended by Secretary, following informal consultations; agenda item 9.
Financial implication. S-G, E/1984/C.1/L.19.

REFERENCES

[1]E/1984/22. [2]E/1984/71. [3]E/1985/98. [4]E/CEPAL/G.1307. [5]YUN 1980, p. 503, GA res. 35/56, annex, 5 Dec. 1980. [6]YUN 1981, p. 661. [7]YUN 1983, p. 647. [8]A/39/118-E/1984/45. [9]A/39/303-E/1984/125. [10]A/39/331-E/1984/126. [11]E/1985/3. [12]E/1985/3/Add.2 & 3. [13]E/1985/3/Add.1. [14]YUN 1977, p. 555. [15]YUN 1980, p. 712, GA res. 35/18, 10 Nov. 1980. [16]E/1986/34. [17]YUN 1979, p. 635. [18]A/39/145 & Corr.1. [19]YUN 1982, p. 871. [20]A/38/170. [21]A/39/25. [22]LC/G.1327 (PLEN.17/L.5/Rev.1.

PUBLICATIONS

CEPAL Review, No. 22 (April 1984) (E/CEPAL/G.1296), Sales No. E.84.II.G.3; No. 23, Sales No. E.84.II.G.4. *Statistical Yearbook for Latin America and the Caribbean, 1983* (E/CEPAL/G.1313), Sales No. E/S.84.II.G.2; *1984* (LC/G.1337), Sales No. E/S.85.II.G.1. *Economic Survey of Latin America and the Caribbean, 1984*, volumes I & II (LC/G.1398 & Add.1), Sales No. E.86.II.G.2.

Western Asia

The Economic Commission for Western Asia (ECWA) held its eleventh session at its headquarters at Baghdad, Iraq, from 22 to 26 April 1984.[1] Major issues discussed included regional co-operation and integration, food security and agricultural development and development of human resources. In reviewing the implementation of the International Development Strategy for the Third United Nations Development Decade (the 1980s)[2] (see also p. 391) discussions focused on how negatively the deteriorating world economic conditions, the declining prices in the oil market and the continuation of the Iran-Iraq war had affected the capacity of the region to extend assistance to third world countries.

The Commission adopted nine resolutions, two of which were for consideration by the Economic and Social Council. In July, the Council approved the two texts, thereby designating ECWA's Standing Committee for the Programme as the Technical Committee (resolution 1984/80), and recommending to the General Assembly a proposal for recruiting staff for the ECWA secretariat from among the Commission's members, including the Palestine Liberation Organization (PLO). The Assembly subsequently adopted the proposal in December (resolution 39/243).

Other ECWA resolutions concerned a 1983 study of the economic and social conditions and potential of the Palestinian Arab people,[3] participation in the Fourth General Conference of UNIDO (UNIDO IV, August 1984) (see p. 558), a regional conference on population and the Amman Declaration on Population in the Arab World, strengthening of national capabilities in household surveys, increasing the participation of Arab women in development, developing the ECWA information system, and social and economic studies on the Palestinian people in the occupied territories.

Economic and social trends

The summary of the survey of economic and social development in the ECWA region,[4] taken note of by the Economic and Social Council in its resolution 1984/187 of 27 July, found that the region, comprising some of the most open economies among the developing countries, was vulnerable to external factors which adversely affected the efforts at achieving many of the targets of the current International Development Strategy.[2] While the Strategy called for an average annual GDP growth rate of 7 per cent for developing countries, the region averaged a negative growth rate of 6.4 per cent (at constant 1980 prices) during 1980-1983.

The ECWA region, facing lower oil prices and sharply reduced exports, experienced the disturbing effects of declining revenues and the consequent curtailment in expenditures; the region's oil revenues, which provided the major source of funds for development, had fallen in 1983 to only 49 per cent of those received in 1980. The deterioration in the balance of payments and sharp decline in oil revenues had also affected the non-oil and least developed economies in the region, which largely depended on economic assistance from the oil-exporting countries to finance their development endeavours. Nevertheless, the performance of the oil-exporting countries of the region remained above the Strategy's target in terms of concessional aid, and was better than the actual performance of the developed countries in connection with official development assistance. However, if oil revenues did not pick up and development expenditures continued to be constrained, many countries would be seriously affected in terms of foreign exchange earnings, return migration and settlement, and consequent aggravation of domestic employment situation.

Activities in 1984

Development policy and regional economic co-operation

A follow-up report was completed in 1984, on the regional implementation of the Substantial New Programme of Action for the 1980s for the Least Developed Countries[5] (see also p. 413); the report was submitted to the Commission's 1985 session. Advisory services and assistance to Yemen concentrated on budgetary, monetary and foreign exchange issues, as well as on establishing a department for investment encouragement at the Ministry of Economy and Industry. Democratic Yemen was given

assistance in applying modern techniques in project planning and monitoring.

At its 1984 session,[1] the Commission, during an examination of current issues in regional co-operation and integration, noted that the Council for Arab Economic Unity had expanded the membership of the Arab Common Market, and the accession to membership of the least developed Arab countries had been facilitated by means of a compensation fund.[6] It was stressed that co-operation and co-ordination among Arab and international organizations and institutions and among Arab businessmen and investors through their chambers of commerce or federations could greatly contribute to the strengthening of joint Arab economic action.

International trade and finance

A number of reports on international trade and development finance were completed in 1984, including a review and analysis of developments in the external trade and payment situation of ECWA member countries, and the role of joint ventures in regional co-operation and integration.

Development assistance

Technical co-operation

The Commission, under the support programme of UNDP,[7] continued to provide short-term regional advisory services to ECWA member countries in such areas as development planning, industrial project identification, formulation and appraisal, financial management, human resources development, household surveys and demography, national accounts and economic statistics, transport and communication, new and renewable sources of energy and industrial and mechanical engineering.

Activities undertaken in co-operation with the Voluntary Fund for the United Nations Decade for Women included case studies of women's position in national plans, a project in institutional development for rural women and training activities for income-generation (see also Chapter XIX of this section).

Transport and communications

In 1984, the data and information necessary for preparing a study on a transport development strategy for the region were collected and analysed, in addition to a comparative analysis of national transport plans in ECWA member countries. In co-operation with UNCTAD, the Commission explored the feasibility of an intraregional maritime information system and subregional centres for the TRAINMAR project.

Studies were completed or published on development of national merchant marines and promotion of multinational shipping enterprises, development of inland waterways and coastal shipping, improvements of road maintenance, and on transport harmonization and standardization of documents. A report on legal aspects of the simplification of border crossing facilities in countries of Western Asia was circulated.

Industrial development

A techno-economic study on the integrated development of manufacturing facilities for automotive activities was completed, and a project was initiated for a feasibility study on development of diesel engines and components at the Arab regional level. A work plan was formulated regarding preparation of master plans for developing technological capabilities in oil refining, petrochemicals and fertilizers; capital goods and heavy engineering; and iron and steel. Preparations continued for a solidarity meeting for Democratic Yemen, to be held in 1985 in the context of industrial programming for LDCs.

The Commission, at its April 1984 session,[1] requested the Executive Secretary to continue providing member countries with information and studies on the topics for discussion at UNIDO IV, and to maintain co-ordination with the Arab Industrial Development Organization in that respect.

Transnational corporations

Work continued on a report on the status of formulating the draft code of conduct relating to transnational corporations (TNCs) (see also p. 591), with special reference to the participation of Arab countries. Studies were initiated on the impact of TNC operations on development in Western Asia, and on TNC operations in the industrial sector in Bahrain. An interim report on the scope of TNC operations in Western Asia was completed and incorporated in a mid-term review of the International Development Strategy.

Preparations were made for a joint project with the Arab Industrial Development Organization on the role of TNCs in the transfer of technology in Arab countries.

Natural resources, environment and energy

A study was completed on co-operation and co-ordination of activities in the field of water and sea resources in the region. Work continued on identifying the activities of ECWA member States and international agencies in water resources development during 1980-1985.

A report on industrial pollution control in the ECWA region was completed with recommendations for pollution abatement and integration of environmental dimensions in industrial development programmes.

Work continued towards establishing a regional network on new and renewable sources of energy (NRSE), aimed at mobilizing and strengthening existing capabilities in the region and at fostering regional co-operation.

Food and agriculture

In the context of encouraging development in environmentally less favourable areas of the region, three studies were completed on integrated development of mountain farming areas. A report was submitted to the Commission on the progress and impact of national and intercountry action programmes to combat desertification.

As a joint undertaking with the Arab Organization of Agricultural Development, food security issues in the West Bank and Gaza were studied.

Science and technology

Agreements were reached with institutions in Jordan, Kuwait and Saudi Arabia on promoting subregional and regional co-operation for strengthening national scientific and technological capabilities. A review was made of progress in the ECWA region since the 1979 Vienna Conference on Science and Technology for Development.[8]

Social development

In 1984, an Expert Group Meeting on a strategy for the advancement of Arab women in the ECWA region to the year 2000 (Baghdad, 29-31 October) and a regional preparatory meeting (Baghdad, 3-6 December) for the 1985 World Conference to Review and Appraise the Achievements of the United Nations Decade for Women considered two documents prepared in relation to the Conference: the assessment of the conditions of Arab women in Western Asia during the Decade for Women (1976-1985) and a regional strategy to the year 2000. The first document gave special reference to the issues of women and peace in the region, especially those concerning Palestinian women and the Iran-Iraq war. The second document formulated priority areas, such as policies and programmes for political participation and improvements in legal status, employment and production, and education and training.

The Commission, at its April 1984 session,[1] had urged the Executive Secretary to establish contacts with the League of Arab States and other Arab regional organizations in connection with the holding of a regional preparatory meeting for the 1985 Conference, and requested a report on a possible regional project (see also Chapter XIX of this section).

The secretariat continued to provide technical assistance to regional projects financed by the Voluntary Fund for the United Nations Decade for Women, dealing with subjects such as the role of rural women in economic development and education and training for income generation.

A report was completed on the situation and needs of youth, with emphasis on education and employment.

Population

A regional population conference for the Arab world—meeting at Amman, Jordan, from 25 to 29 March, in preparation for the International Conference on Population (Mexico, August 1984) (see Chapter XIV of this section)—adopted the Amman Declaration on Population in the Arab World,[9] containing recommendations on development strategies and population policies; components of population policy; data, research, exchange of information and training; and intraregional and international co-operation. Noting that the Arab population, of some 180 million in 1984, was expected to rise to over 250 million by the end of the century, the development strategies and population policies recommended included planning designed to meet basic needs in employment, education, health, food, housing, clothing and social security by the year 2000, and pursuit, in each sector, of a demographic course of action conducive to achieving the objectives of an integrated population policy and providing an appropriate minimum level of family income. Among other specific recommendations was a call to halt support and assistance to Israel, whose policy, the Declaration asserted, affected the demographic character of the occupied Arab territories.

The Amman Declaration was subsequently endorsed by ECWA at its April 1984 session.[1]

Other developments in 1984 included the meeting of an Arab parliamentary conference on development and population (Tunisia, May).

Human settlements

Preparation of country profiles—intended as a basis for formulating human settlement policies and strategies—commenced in Egypt, Iraq and Kuwait, while one on Yemen was published and those on Democratic Yemen and Jordan were finalized.

Work continued in preparing a study on the status of the building material industry and the requirements and potentials for its development, and in assessing alternative energy-saving building materials and low-cost housing designs and projects.

Statistics

The seventh issue of *Statistical Abstract of the Region of the Economic Commission for Western Asia*, covering 1973-1982, was published with main statistical data on population, social statistics, national accounts, agriculture, forestry and fishing, industry, energy, foreign trade, finance and transport, communications and tourism. Among other publications were a 1984 issue of *National Accounts Studies* and that of *External Trade Bulletin of the ECWA Countries*.

The Commission, in April 1984,[1] urged financial and technical assistance to enable its member countries to carry out their national household survey programmes.

Programme, organizational and administrative questions

Information system

At its 1984 session,[1] ECWA asked its Executive Secretary to elaborate a comprehensive programme of work to develop the secretariat's information infrastructure, and to co-operate with Arab, regional and international organizations in co-ordinating the programme.

Organizational structure

ECONOMIC AND SOCIAL COUNCIL ACTION

On 27 July 1984, the Economic and Social Council, on the recommendation of its First Committee, adopted resolution 1984/80 without vote.

ECWA, at its April 1984 session,[1] had recommended that its Standing Committee for the Programme of ECWA be designated as the Technical Committee, with related changes in its agenda and rules of procedure.

General policy-making structure of the Economic Commission for Western Asia

The Economic and Social Council,

Recalling its resolution 1982/64 of 30 July 1982, by which it established, within the Economic Commission for Western Asia, a Standing Committee for the Programme, composed of all members of the Commission, as the main subsidiary organ of the Commission to assist it in the execution of its responsibilities for programme planning and review,

Desirous of ensuring representation at the ministerial level at the annual sessions of the Commission,

1. *Takes note* of the decision of the Economic Commission for Western Asia that rule 1 (a) of the Commission's provisional rules of procedure should be amended to read: "Normally annually, beginning on the Saturday of the third week of April";

2. *Decides* to designate the Standing Committee for the Programme of the Economic Commission for Western Asia as the Technical Committee and to add to its terms of reference, set out in paragraph 5 of Commission resolution 114(IX) of 12 May 1982, the consideration of the items of the provisional agenda for the annual session of the Commission, in preparation for the Commission's meeting at the ministerial level;

3. *Decides also* that the Technical Committee should meet for a four-day period immediately prior to a two-day meeting of the Economic Commission for Western Asia at the ministerial level.

Economic and Social Council resolution 1984/80

27 July 1984   Meeting 50   Adopted without vote

Approved by First Committee (E/1984/142/Add.1) without vote, 24 July (meeting 17); 3-nation draft (E/1984/C.1/L.16); agenda item 9.
Sponsors: Iraq, Lebanon, Qatar.

Staffing

ECONOMIC AND SOCIAL COUNCIL ACTION

On 27 July, the Economic and Social Council, on the recommendation of its First Committee, adopted resolution 1984/81 by roll-call vote. In April, ECWA[(1)] had adopted a resolution with essentially the same wording.

Staff and administrative questions of the Economic Commission for Western Asia

The Economic and Social Council,

Deeply concerned about the high vacancy rate which has prevailed in the Economic Commission for Western Asia for a number of years,

Convinced that the high vacancy rate has had a serious impact on the work programme of the Commission,

Recognizing that repeated efforts have been made by the secretariat of the Commission to find qualified staff from unrepresented or underrepresented States in the region covered by the Commission but that difficulties still persist in the recruitment of such staff,

Recognizing also the importance of knowledge of the Arabic language by the staff of the Commission for the effective performance of their work,

1. *Urges* unrepresented and under-represented States to endeavour to encourage competent personnel to work in the secretariat of the Economic Commission for Western Asia as staff members on a regular or fixed-term basis;

2. *Proposes* to the General Assembly that it should authorize the Secretary-General to take all necessary measures to enable the Economic Commission for Western Asia to recruit staff from any State member of the Commission to meet the Commission's personnel requirements;

3. *Also proposes* to the General Assembly that all members of the Economic Commission for Western Asia should be treated in a manner consistent with their full membership in the Commission with regard to employment in the secretariat of the Commission.

Economic and Social Council resolution 1984/81

27 July 1984   Meeting 50   47-1 (roll-call vote)

Approved by First Committee (E/1984/142/Add.1) by roll-call vote (40-1-2), 24 July (meeting 17); 6-nation draft (E/1984/C.1/L.17), orally amended by Chairman, by Ireland (for European Community), after informal consultations, and by Secretary, after informal consultations; agenda item 9.

Sponsors: Democratic Yemen, Iraq, Libyan Arab Jamahiriya, Qatar, Saudi Arabia, Tunisia.

Roll-call vote in Council as follows:

In favour: Algeria, Argentina, Austria, Benin, Brazil, Bulgaria, Canada, China, Colombia, Costa Rica, Djibouti, Ecuador, Finland, France, German Democratic Republic, Germany, Federal Republic of, Greece, Guyana, Indonesia, Japan, Lebanon, Luxembourg, Malaysia, Mexico, Netherlands, New Zealand, Pakistan, Poland, Portugal, Qatar, Romania, Rwanda, Saint Lucia, Saudi Arabia, Somalia, Sri Lanka, Suriname, Swaziland, Sweden, Thailand, Tunisia, Uganda, USSR, United Kingdom, Venezuela, Yugoslavia, Zaire.

Against: United States.

Abstaining: None.

GENERAL ASSEMBLY ACTION

The text of Council resolution 1984/81 was transmitted to the General Assembly in December by the Secretary-General.[(10)]

The Assembly, on the recommendation of the Fifth Committee, adopted resolution 39/243 on 18 December by recorded vote.

Staff and administrative questions of the Economic Commission for Western Asia

The General Assembly,

Recalling Economic and Social Council resolution 1984/81 of 27 July 1984,

Deeply concerned about the high vacancy rate and difficulties in recruitment which have prevailed for a number of years in the regional commissions, particularly in the Economic Commission for Western Asia,

Convinced that the high vacancy rate has had a serious impact on the work programme of the Economic Commission for Western Asia,

Recognizing that repeated efforts have been made by the secretariat of the Economic Commission for Western Asia to find qualified staff from unrepresented or underrepresented States in the region covered by the Commission, but that the difficulties still persist in the recruitment of such staff,

Recognizing also the importance of knowledge of the Arabic language by the staff of the Economic Commission for Western Asia for the effective performance of their work,

1. *Urges* unrepresented and underrepresented States to endeavour to encourage competent personnel to work in the secretariat of the Economic Commission for Western Asia as staff members on a regular or fixed-term basis;

2. *Authorizes* the Secretary-General to take all necessary measures to enable the Economic Commission for Western Asia to recruit staff from any State member of the Commission to meet its personnel requirements;

3. *Decides* that all members of the Economic Commission for Western Asia should be treated in a manner consistent with their full membership in the Commission in regard to employment in the secretariat of the Commission.

General Assembly resolution 39/243

18 December 1984   Meeting 105   123-2-20 (recorded vote)

Approved by Fifth Committee (A/39/845) by recorded vote (72-2-17), 15 December (meeting 53); 8-nation draft (A/C.5/39/L.17), orally amended by Indonesia; agenda item 116.

Sponsors: Bahrain, Democratic Yemen, Egypt, Iraq, Qatar, Saudi Arabia, United Arab Emirates, Yemen.

Meeting numbers. GA 39th session: 5th Committee 49, 53; plenary 105.

Recorded vote in Assembly as follows:

In favour: Afghanistan, Algeria, Angola, Antigua and Barbuda, Argentina, Austria, Bahrain, Bangladesh, Benin, Bhutan, Bolivia, Botswana, Brazil, Brunei Darussalam, Bulgaria, Burkina Faso, Burma, Burundi, Byelorussian SSR, Cameroon, Cape Verde, Central African Republic, Chad, China, Colombia, Congo, Costa Rica, Cuba, Cyprus, Czechoslovakia, Democratic Kampuchea, Democratic Yemen, Djibouti, Ecuador, Egypt, El Salvador, Equatorial Guinea, Ethiopia, Fiji, Finland, Gabon, Gambia, German Democratic Republic, Ghana, Greece, Guatemala, Guinea, Guinea-Bissau, Guyana, Haiti, Honduras, Hungary, India, Indonesia, Iraq, Ireland, Ivory Coast, Jordan, Kenya, Kuwait, Lao People's Democratic Republic, Lebanon, Lesotho, Liberia, Libyan Arab Jamahiriya, Madagascar, Malawi, Malaysia, Maldives, Mali, Malta, Mauritania, Mauritius, Mexico, Mongolia, Morocco, Mozambique, Nepal, Nicaragua, Niger, Nigeria, Oman, Pakistan, Panama, Papua New Guinea, Paraguay, Peru, Philippines, Poland, Qatar, Romania, Rwanda, Samoa, Sao Tome and Principe, Saudi Arabia, Senegal, Sierra Leone, Singapore, Somalia, Spain, Sri Lanka, Sudan, Suriname, Swaziland, Sweden, Syrian Arab Republic, Thailand, Togo, Tunisia, Turkey, Uganda, Ukrainian SSR, USSR, United Arab Emirates, United Republic of Tanzania, Uruguay, Vanuatu, Venezuela, Yemen, Yugoslavia, Zaire, Zambia, Zimbabwe.

Against: Israel, United States.

Abstaining: Australia, Bahamas, Barbados, Belgium, Canada, Denmark, France, Germany, Federal Republic of, Iceland, Italy, Jamaica, Japan, Luxembourg, Netherlands, New Zealand, Norway, Portugal, Saint Christopher and Nevis, Saint Lucia, United Kingdom.

The Assistant Secretary-General for Personnel Services told the Fifth Committee, before the vote, that the draft's second preambular paragraph seemed not to reflect reality, as a recent cable from ECWA indicated the current number of vacant posts as 10; the situation in the other regional commissions likewise did not seem to be a matter of concern to their respective executive secretaries. Egypt, however, reiterated that a high vacancy rate had long been a problem in ECWA.

Israel said the exclusion of Israel and the inclusion of a non-State in ECWA were in violation of the United Nations Charter; it protested the recruitment of members of PLO for service in the Commission's secretariat.

The United States asserted that the expedient proposed in the draft would create a bad precedent as it would allow ECWA to violate the principle of equal employment opportunities for nationals of all Member States and even to offer employment to members which were neither Governments nor States nor Members of the United Nations but organizations which paid no

assessment and therefore had no claim to be represented in the secretariat. Moreover, the statistics cited by the Assistant Secretary-General seemed to indicate that the critical situation no longer existed.

Speaking also on behalf of the States members of the European Economic Community, Ireland said it understood that the draft was of a temporary nature intended to resolve problems in ECWA and that it should not constitute a precedent for any other regional commission or United Nations body, particularly in respect of States which were already overrepresented.

REFERENCES

[1]E/1984/25. [2]YUN 1980, p. 503, GA res. 35/56, annex, 5 Dec. 1980. [3]YUN 1983, p. 653. [4]E/1984/78 & Corr.1. [5]YUN 1981, p. 406. [6]E/1984/112. [7]DP/1985/43/Add.2. [8]YUN 1979, p. 635. [9]E/ECWA/POP/CONF.5/15. [10]A/C.5/39/87.

Chapter IX

Natural resources and cartography

During 1984, the United Nations Revolving Fund for Natural Resources Exploration (UNRFNRE) continued to assist developing countries. Programme expenditures in 1984 were estimated at $3.7 million, a decline of some $1 million from the previous year. Concern over the Fund's diminishing financial capacity was expressed by the administering body, the Governing Council of the United Nations Development Programme (UNDP).

A Global Plan of Action for the Conservation, Management and Utilization of Marine Mammals, prepared by the United Nations Environment Programme (UNEP) in co-operation with the Food and Agriculture Organization of the United Nations (FAO), was endorsed by the UNEP Governing Council.

The Economic and Social Council decided that the Third United Nations Regional Cartographic Conference for the Americas should be held in 1985 instead of 1984 (decision 1984/105) and that the Conference should meet in New York rather than at Buenos Aires, Argentina (decision 1984/117).

In decision 1984/112, the Council took note of an offer by Turkey to host the Eleventh United Nations Regional Cartographic Conference for Asia and the Pacific in 1987.

Topics related to this chapter. Law of the sea: sea-bed mining. Middle East: permanent sovereignty over natural resources in the occupied territories. Regional economic and social activities. Energy. Namibia: natural resources.

General aspects of natural resources

Exploration

UN Revolving Fund for Natural Resources Exploration

Activities

UNRFNRE continued to provide developing countries with comprehensive assistance, including project design, execution and follow-up, as well as high-risk financing, expertise, advanced technology and help in obtaining investment. The Fund's 1984 activities, administered by UNDP, were described in a March 1985 report[1] by the UNDP Administrator.

Inadequate financial support remained the major constraint to assisting more developing countries in natural resources exploration and development (see below).

In the mining sector, severely depressed metal prices caused a general lack of investment. Lack of investment in the San Bartolomé silver deposit in Ecuador illustrated the situation, but was also indicative of the long lead time experienced in mining projects and the long-term nature of the Fund's operations.

Work was completed during 1984 on projects in Burkina Faso and Suriname. A project in Mali neared termination, and a new project was begun in Peru. At the end of the year, only three projects—in Haiti, Peru and Sierra Leone—were fully operational.

Detailed geological mapping, two geophysical campaigns, trenching and sampling were carried out in Haiti, concentrating on two areas: at La Mine, polymetallic sulphide mineralization (zinc, copper, gold and barite) was discovered within a three-kilometre zone of acid volcanics; in the structurally complex Faille area, widespread gold showings were found.

In Peru, investigation of gold contained within high-altitude glacial moraine deposits at San Antonio de Poto dominated activities. Most heavy equipment had been received, drill access and drilling pads were prepared, a processing plant was constructed at Ananea, and project headquarters and a final processing laboratory had been installed at Arequipa. Meanwhile, initial exploration for zinc and other base metals was completed over the Orquideas prospect near San Ramon.

In Sierra Leone, field work was initiated, target areas with gold mineralization were identified, and detailed investigations were being conducted in two areas: the southern portion of the Sula Mountains-Kangari Hills for bedrock gold and the Pampana River flood plain, which drains part of the bedrock area, for placer gold. The Administrator recommended that the UNDP Governing Council take note of his approval of the minimum work for gold exploration in the Sula Mountains-Kangari Hills at a cost of $0.97 million and approve the project involving a maximum expenditure of $2.72 million. On 29 June,[2] the Council approved the project, subject to availability of funds.

Other project development work was continued by the Fund. Areas in southern Rwanda with good indications of gold mineralization were appraised positively, and a phosphate exploration project in Chile was endorsed by UNRFNRE's Joint Operations Group (JOG). Missions to Brazil and Ghana had positive results. Work proceeded well in Guatemala, where a positive project recommendation was expected in 1985.

A gold deposit was identified in Suriname and determined to be of sufficient grade and tonnage to support a small mining operation.

Further testing was undertaken to provide Governments and potential investors with more detailed analyses of the Fund's discoveries in Benin and the Congo. In Benin, laboratory evaluation of a kaolin deposit resulted in a decision to proceed to applied industrial testing of a large bulk sample. The deposit could be of value in the manufacture of cement, tiles, paint and paper. Similarly, following successful completion of a second phase of explorations for offshore phosphates near Pointe Noire in the Congo, bulk sample tests were being financed by UNRFNRE. Some 25 million tons of mixed shell/phosphorite for use as quality fertilizers for the sugar-cane industry were believed to be recoverable using simple, cost-effective offshore mining methods.

In Kenya, an additional $350,000 was allocated for detailed geophysical work, geological studies and additional drilling for a copper-silver mineralization project.

After field work in Mali demonstrated no economic potential at the In Darset gold prospect and the Adrar Tadhak alkaline complex, the project was closed down. Tin and tungsten possibilities in the Tessalit/Kidal area produced no signs of mineralization, while drilling of the Immanal carbonatites and Tessalit sulphides uncovered sub-economic mineralization. In Burkina Faso, nickel-laterite and gold were discovered, but the mineralization was insufficient.

Although a negative assessment was made in Burundi, the Fund continued to study follow-up possibilities uncovered by UNDP and the United Nations Department of Technical Co-operation for Development (DTCD) in Cibitoke Province.

Advanced geothermal energy projects were pursued in several countries. A project in Mexico at Las Planillas, near Guadalajara, was endorsed by JOG, following two Fund missions; if successful, the project was expected to lead to the development of a large block of power to assist industry in the area. In Saint Lucia, pre-feasibility studies resulted in a positive appraisal of the Qualibou Caldera prospect near Soufrière for a Fund project, estimated at $5 million, to meet all Saint Lucia's electrical requirements and thereby replace imported diesel oil as the main power source. Discussions took place with

the Government and the United States Agency for International Development for possible co-financing. An appraisal mission visited the Seferihisar prospect near Izmir, Turkey, in October 1984. A DTCD consultant appraised two prospects in Bolivia, for one of which a project was set up at Laguna Colorada by UNDP using Italian bilateral funding.

Contributions and expenditures

In 1984, programme expenditures were estimated at $3.7 million, a decline of about $1 million from 1983. Contributions in 1984 totalled $190,462; thus contributions fell far short of the level needed for new projects. Some 40 proposals for exploration projects were under consideration.

CONTRIBUTIONS TO UNRFNRE, 1984 AND 1985
(as at 31 December 1984; in US dollar equivalent)

Country	1984 payment	1985 pledge
Bangladesh	1,064	1,210
Belgium	171,253	—
Chile	5,000	5,000
Indonesia	10,000	10,000
Norway	—	338,983
Sierra Leone	—	1,000
Zambia	3,145	—
Total	190,462	356,193

SOURCE: A/40/5/Add.1.

UNRFNRE PROJECT EXPENDITURES, 1984
(as at 31 December 1984; in thousands of US dollars)

Country	Amount
Argentina	(24)
Benin	33
Bolivia	15
Botswana	11
Brazil	2
Burkina Faso	161
Burma	(1)
Burundi	13
Chile	22
China	(5)
Colombia	2
Cyprus	4
Dominica	(1)
Ecuador	(5)
Ghana	8
Guatemala	26
Guyana	17
Haiti	421
Honduras	19
Iraq	2
Ivory Coast	17
Kenya	(19)
Liberia	42
Mali	790
Mexico	63
Panama	12
Peru	1,670
Philippines	37
Rwanda	31
Saint Lucia	30
Sierra Leone	488
Sudan	25
Turkey	43
Vanuatu	2
Zambia	4
Zimbabwe	4
Other	(320)
Total	3,639

SOURCE: DP/1985/5/Add.6.

The Fund's cumulative expenditure on completed projects, including its current programme commitments and an actuarial estimate for subsequent work, was $32.8 million as at 31 December 1984.

Although it was uncertain how quickly negotiations on various projects would proceed with Governments, it was clear that funding capacity was rapidly being exhausted. If projects endorsed by JOG, in addition to others in an advanced stage of development, were approved by the UNDP Governing Council, estimated funding for other new programming would be reduced to $1.5 million.

On 29 June,[2] the Governing Council expressed concern about the deteriorating capacity of the Fund to meet the demands of developing countries, appealed for significant voluntary contributions, and requested the UNDP Administrator to pursue co-financing as a means of increasing resources.

REFERENCES

[1]DP/1985/46 & Add.1. [2]E/1984/20 (dec. 84/23).

Mineral resources

Technical co-operation

During 1984, DTCD, in addition to UNRFNRE, carried out activities related to mineral exploration, institution building and strengthening, rehabilitation of mines, mine development, formal and on-the-job training, mineral sector planning, mining legislation and contract negotiation, supply of equipment, and application of computer techniques in mineral exploration and development.

A total of 55 projects were operational in 1984 funded from the United Nations regular programme of technical co-operation, UNDP and trust funds, with total expenditures of almost $14 million; about 10 projects were in the final stages of becoming operational. The projects were described in an addendum to a report by the Secretary-General on United Nations technical co-operation activities.[1]

An increase was reported in the number of projects to strengthen national institutions—geological surveys, bureaux of mines, ministry departments, State mining companies—and training, in several cases in conjunction with other activities, such as exploration for non-metallic and metallic minerals. The projects included operational assistance to the Ghana State Gold Mining Corporation, together with rehabilitation of its mines; a training programme for geologists and mining engineers from Namibia; mineral exploration, evaluation and development planning in the United Republic of Tanzania; supervision of the evaluation of gold mineralization in Suriname; and three projects in co-operation with the Indian Bureau of Mines.

The United Nations and Colombia completed an economic and technical evaluation of a major mineral deposit, containing molybdenum and copper. Since the deposit was located in mountainous terrain, near the southern village of Mocoa, supplies and personnel had to be flown in by helicopter. Project activities included not only diamond core drilling, metallurgical testing, preliminary investigation of infrastructure requirements and cash flow estimates but the training of Colombian nationals in mining, engineering, geology, and computer applications in mineral exploration. It was concluded that the molybdenum-copper reserves were comparable to those in deposits in production around the world but, as prices for the two metals were at historically low levels, development of a mine was currently unlikely.

Exploration for metals and minerals continued in many countries. In Burundi, a search went on for precious and other minerals and metals; training in the application of computer techniques to mineral exploration and development also was being given. In Jamaica, non-metallic minerals were investigated. In Paraguay, geological, hydrogeological and metallogenic maps were prepared. In Saint Vincent and the Grenadines, a volcano monitoring system was installed and local personnel were trained in its operation.

Several projects continued to explore for precious metals, especially gold, which were among the relatively few mineral commodities suffering less severely from low prices and slow rates of growth in consumption. In addition, the United Nations co-operated in the rehabilitation of existing gold mines.

Advisory services were made available to developing countries under the United Nations regular programme of technical co-operation. About 20 missions were undertaken in regard to mining legislation, contract negotiations and mineral sector planning. Other advisory missions were concerned with electronic data processing in mineral exploration and development, mining engineering, geochemistry and geophysics.

In November, a Group of Experts on Electronic Data Processing in Mineral Exploration and Development held a meeting and an interregional seminar in Brazil; more than 80 persons from developing countries attended.

REFERENCE

[1]DP/1985/43/Add.1.

PUBLICATION

Price-forecasting Techniques and Their Application to Minerals and Metals in the Global Economy (ST/ESA/140), Sales No. E.84.II.C.3.

Water and marine resources

Water resources development

During 1984, some 90 water resources projects were carried out by DTCD in 50 countries at a cost of more than $18 million.[1] More than 60 technical and interregional advisory missions were undertaken. Some 20 projects were started at a cost of $8.3 million; half of them were to alleviate arid conditions in Africa, four in direct response to drought. In Burkina Faso, the United Nations Emergency Operation Trust Fund (UNEOTF) provided $80,000 to deepen wells which had dried. In the Central African Republic, UNDP gave $250,000 to construct 22 new wells and deepen 23 existing ones. In the Comoros, UNEOTF contributed $300,000 to strengthen drilling operations on Grand Comoros Island. In Somalia, new pumping equipment was installed at 15 deep wells, 35 others were repaired, and 50 well operators were given maintenance training.

In Mauritania, UNDP contributed $1 million to repair and maintain wells. In the Niger, UNDP and the United Nations Children's Fund contributed $1.5 million and $1.7 million, respectively, to the second phase of a project to develop ground water in rural areas. In Chad, a preparatory rural water-supply project was completed, prior to a full-scale project.

Elsewhere, a project was under way to assist the assessment of ground-water resources in a major grain-producing plains area of northern China through consultant services, scientific equipment and training programmes. Assistance was provided to Viet Nam in the exploration for ground-water resources; hydrogeological maps were prepared and exploration teams organized. Argentina received assistance in ground-water exploration, flood forecasting, river basin planning, laboratory research and information systems. In the Turks and Caicos Islands, water legislation was drafted.

Pursuant to a 1983 Economic and Social Council resolution,[2] the Secretary-General submitted a report in May 1984 concerning the establishment of a technical unit for technical co-operation among developing countries in ground-water resources development within the Centre for Waters at Zagreb, Yugoslavia.[3] He had held consultations with UNDP and Yugoslavia on the possibilities of establishing such a unit, whose objectives would be to encourage technical co-operation and to strengthen technical capabilities. The unit's activities would include organization of round-table discussions, establishment of an information network and data bank, a newsletter, a roster of experts, and the provision of consultancy services.

To carry out the unit's activities, it was estimated that $200,000 for non-local costs would be required during its first two years of operation, as follows: training and meetings of representatives of developing countries, $100,000; *ad hoc* consultants, $40,000; information and documentation, $40,000; and travel, office and miscellaneous expenses, $20,000. In support of the unit, Yugoslavia would provide a director and a hydrogeologist and would be responsible for the costs of secretarial and administrative services and local facilities.

Limited funds might be forthcoming from multilateral sources to support fellows from least developed countries, the Secretary-General said. He added that, in view of the modest level of funding required, interested Member States and multilateral funding agencies should be encouraged to assist in setting up the unit.

On 25 July, the Economic and Social Council took note of the Secretary-General's report on the unit when it adopted decision 1984/171.

The Intersecretariat Group for Water Resources of the Administrative Committee on Co-ordination (ACC) held its fifth session at Vienna, Austria, from 29 October to 2 November 1984.[4] It considered such matters as implementation of the Mar del Plata Action Plan for the development of water resources, adopted by the United Nations Water Conference in 1977;[5] the International Drinking Water Supply and Sanitation Decade (1981-1990), proclaimed by the General Assembly in 1980;[6] and integrated approaches to education and training in water resources, in accordance with a 1981 Economic and Social Council resolution.[7] The Group reviewed draft reports by the Secretary-General and the Economic Commission for Africa (ECA) on implementation of the Mar del Plata Action Plan. It also dealt with co-ordination among organizations of the United Nations system in implementing their programmes under the Action Plan and, in that connection, emphasized the need for full utilization of the substantive and operational capabilities of the different organizations in allocating responsibility for projects.[8]

Other Group activities included[9] the preparation of a briefing note on the involvement of organizations in water resources development; the completion of a *Consolidated Catalogue of Publications on Water Resources in Print from 1971 to 1981;*[10] and the compilation of information on bilateral and international assistance programmes, with a view to increasing the flow of financial resources.

UNEP activities. As a consequence of socio-economic development, and especially water resources development in the river basins of the world, freshwater ecosystems were becoming more and more complex in their structural, spatial and temporal dimensions, the Executive Director of UNEP said in his annual report for 1984.[11]

Perceptions of the functions of freshwater bodies (rivers, lakes, aquifers) also changed during development, he pointed out. Fresh water was not only a renewable natural resource for which no substitute existed, but formed a very important part of ecosystems and landscapes. Contrary to the prevailing practice, which focused almost exclusively on the function of fresh water as a natural resource, all the related functions should be considered simultaneously. That meant environmental effects could not be viewed only in the context of specific water projects, but also on a basin-wide scale, which was particularly important in regard to international water systems.

Against this background, UNEP concentrated in 1984 on the environmental aspects of water resources management; support for the International Drinking Water Supply and Sanitation Decade; freshwater ecosystems; and preparation of a comprehensive water programme.

Emphasis was given to Africa, in the light of the serious drought it was experiencing. Ground-water management and erosion control in Africa were considered by an International Symposium on Challenges in African Hydrology and Water Resources, organized by the International Association of Hydrological Sciences (IAHS) and Zimbabwe at Harare in July 1984. The participation of 12 African experts was financed by UNEP; the proceedings of the Symposium, containing several African case-studies, were published by IAHS in co-operation with UNEP, the United Nations Educational, Scientific and Cultural Organization and the World Meteorological Organization.

In keeping with a 1983 UNEP Governing Council decision concerning the UNEP water programme,[12] UNEP began in 1984 a programme on the environmental management of the common river system of the Zambezi whose aim was to prepare a plan for sound management of the Zambezi by the basin countries and to co-ordinate the efforts of interested United Nations organizations. It was hoped that eventually an international treaty would be concluded.

As part of an effort to rehabilitate agricultural systems and control schistosomiasis, diarrhoeal diseases and malaria in a group of 31 villages in the large Gezira-Managil Scheme in central Sudan, a strategy for health and water supply improvements was developed under a joint UNEP/World Health Organization (WHO) project on integrated irrigation.

Providing support to the International Drinking Water Supply and Sanitation Decade was a major activity. UNEP took part in the twelfth meeting of the Steering Committee for Co-operative Action at Vienna in October. Two new projects were begun during the year in co-operation with WHO, one to test methods and guidelines for the control of drinking-water quality in rural areas and the other to evaluate the health hazards of and provide guidelines for waste water reuse. UNEP participated in an international seminar on waste water reuse organized by WHO at Al Manamah, Bahrain, in September. The seminar concluded that waste water reuse was not only a desirable but an absolutely necessary method of meeting water demands in arid regions, especially in Arab countries, and that the permissible limits of waste water reuse in relation to health risks should be determined.

Among the training courses given in 1984 were three organized by the International Training Centre for Water Resources Management and supported by UNEP. A four-week course on rural community water supply for 17 participants from English-speaking African countries was held at Arusha, United Republic of Tanzania, in September-October. Two four-week courses on sanitation in urban areas were given, one for French-speaking and the other for English-speaking African countries, with 18 and 16 participants, respectively; the planning, operation and maintenance of water supply and sanitation schemes were discussed.

Several other meetings were held. An Inter-Parliamentary Conference on Environment, organized by UNEP (Nairobi, Kenya, 26 November–1 December), recommended that parliamentarians urge their Governments to use international rivers rationally and to maintain the quality of their waters. The importance of sound environment management principles for lake ecosystems was stressed at a conference at Otsu, Japan, in August; the conference adopted a number of recommendations concerning official activity in drainage basins, environmental impact assessment, international co-operation among countries sharing drainage basins, public awareness, popular organization, education and training and the international exchange of information. The second meeting of the UNEP Advisory Group on Water Resources was held at Geneva in June; the Group reviewed UNEP water activities, discussed a draft programme on environmentally sound management of inland waterways, and made recommendations for future UNEP water activities.

The UNEP Governing Council, on 28 May 1984,[13] noted the establishment of the Advisory Group in 1983[14] and the convening of a working group on large-scale water projects.

On 27 July 1984, the Economic and Social Council adopted resolution 1984/73, concerning the strengthening of the secretariat of the ECA in the area of water resources (see Chapter VIII of this section).

Marine resources

CPC consideration. In its annual overview report for 1983/84,[9] ACC noted that the Committee for Programme and Co-ordination (CPC) had recommended in May 1983,[15] that United Nations organizations co-operate closely in the follow-up to the United Nations Convention on the Law of the Sea,[16] using existing ACC mechanisms, and that the follow-up had been influenced by several developments at the intergovernmental level (see p. 108).

The ACC report also dealt with assistance to developing countries in marine science, technology and ocean service infrastructures.

CPC considered at its twenty-fourth session (New York, 23 April–1 June 1984)[17] the follow-up to a cross-organizational programme analysis of United Nations activities in marine affairs, which it had taken up in 1983. It had before it a note by the Secretary-General transmitting a report by the Secretaries-General of the International Maritime Organization (IMO) and the United Nations Conference on Trade and Development (UNCTAD).[18] The report was submitted in response to a CPC request that IMO and UNCTAD increase their co-operation in maritime transport and report to CPC. Considering the report as preliminary, CPC requested them to take into account the need to eliminate duplication and overlap in their activities and to clarify further a proposed arrangement to meet the needs of developing countries for maritime transport. CPC also requested additional information on the proposed involvement of the regional commissions.

Marine mammals: Global Plan of Action

In response to a 1981 decision of the UNEP Governing Council,[19] a draft Global Plan of Action for the Conservation, Management and Utilization of Marine Mammals and a financial plan for its implementation were submitted to the May 1984 session of the Council by the UNEP Executive Director.[20] The Plan was prepared by UNEP in co-operation with FAO. Early in 1984, the Executive Director reported,[11] representatives of UNEP, FAO, the International Union for Conservation of Nature and Natural Resources, the Scientific Committee on Antarctic Research of the International Council of Scientific Unions, and the International Whaling Commission met at Rome, Italy, revised the draft Plan and agreed on a final draft.

Under the Plan, marine mammals were taken to include those mammals which spent all or a large proportion of their time in the sea and obtained their food predominantly from it; a few species whose ancestors were marine but which had moved into fresh waters also were included. They belonged to four groups: cetaceans, pinnipeds, sirenians and others. Their populations had been severely depleted by human activities, mainly by hunting but also by fishing, destruction of their habitats and disturbance of breeding colonies; pollution had seriously affected some species. The most seriously depleted large whales were the right

and bowhead whales and to a lesser extent the blue and humpback whales. The fin and sei whales, although less depleted, were well below their most productive levels in most areas.

There was greater uncertainty about the status of a number of small cetaceans, but those probably in the most dire circumstances were some of the freshwater forms whose habitats had been gravely impoverished by the construction of dams and water pollution. Many of the pinnipeds which had been seriously reduced by hunting had made good recoveries; those in the most danger currently were several species of monk seals, whose habitat requirements made them particularly susceptible to coastal modification and disturbance, and some fur seals and sea-lions. The sirenians, which lived in coastal and fresh waters in tropical areas, had been severely reduced throughout much of their range.

The Plan put forward a series of recommendations dealing with the identification of conservation and management objectives and actions to meet current critical situations, to increase current knowledge so as to provide a basis for further stages of the Plan, and to improve the overall machinery of conservation.

Nine projects in support of the Plan were listed at a total cost of $11,841,500 for 1984-1985. The projects were: review of harvesting operations on marine mammals which were not under international control, $40,000; determination of safe catch limits and scientific sampling in protected areas, $100,000; assistance to developing countries in the protection of threatened marine mammal populations and training of additional scientists, $1,150,000; international co-ordination and support for the Plan, $340,000; information systems and research to support conservation—large cetaceans, $3,083,500, small cetaceans, $2,687,000, and pinnipeds, sirenians and some otters, $4,246,000; legal aspects of conservation, $95,000; and increasing public awareness, $100,000.

On 28 May 1984,[13] the UNEP Governing Council endorsed the Plan as a timely and valuable framework for policy formulation by the international community. It noted the efforts of the Executive Director to prepare a financial plan and appealed to Governments and international organizations to make firm commitments. It requested the Executive Director to promote a broad-based response to the Plan, to circulate to potential donors fact sheets on the nine projects, and to investigate the possibility of adopting a regional approach to the funding of projects with a strong regional component.

REFERENCES

[1]DP/1985/43/Add.1. [2]YUN 1983, p. 667, ESC res. 1983/57, 28 July 1983. [3]E/1984/101. [4]ACC/1985/PG/1. [5]YUN 1977,

p. 555. [6]YUN 1980, p. 712, GA res. 35/18, 10 Nov. 1980. [7]YUN 1981, p. 681, ESC res. 1981/80, 24 July 1981. [8]E/1985/57. [9]E/1984/66. [10]*Consolidated Catalogue of Publications on Water Resources in Print from 1971 to 1981* (ST/ESA/137), Sales No. E/F/S.84.II.A.15. [11]UNEP/GC.13/2. [12]YUN 1983, p. 667. [13]A/39/25 (dec. 12/12). [14]YUN 1983, p. 667. [15]*Ibid.*, p. 669. [16]YUN 1982, p. 181. [17]A/39/38. [18]E/AC.51/1984/4. [19]YUN 1981, p. 834. [20]UNEP/GC.12/15.

OTHER PUBLICATIONS

Treaties concerning the Utilization of International Watercourses for Other Purposes than Navigation: Africa (ST/ESA/141), Sales No. E/F.84.II.A.7. *The Use of Non-Conventional Water Resources in Developing Countries*, Natural Resources/Water Series No. 14 (ST/ESA/149), Sales No. E.84.II.A.14.

Cartography

Projects, missions and fellowships

In 1984, cartography continued to receive a high priority from DTCD in many developing countries and 20 projects were carried out.[1]

Technical co-operation projects, including geodetic surveying, mapping, hydrography, photogrammetry and map production, were active in Bhutan, Burundi, the Cayman Islands, Ethiopia, Fiji, Jamaica, the Lao People's Democratic Republic, Madagascar, Nepal, the Philippines, Saudi Arabia, Trinidad and Tobago, and Viet Nam.

Advisory and preparatory assistance missions to identify future projects or extend activities were made to Honduras, Iraq, Madasgascar, Nepal, Qatar, Trinidad and Tobago, the United Arab Emirates and Viet Nam.

A total of 22 fellowships and 12 grants for study tours were awarded for studies in surveying, cartography, photogrammetry and hydrography to candidates from Bhutan, Burundi, the Cayman Islands, Ethiopia, Nepal, Trinidad and Tobago, and Viet Nam.

Conferences

The Secretary-General, in response to a 1981 Economic and Social Council request,[2] submitted a report to the Council on the desirability and feasibility of holding United Nations interregional cartographic conferences.[3] He had consulted widely on the question and at the Fifth United Nations Regional Cartographic Conference for Africa (Cairo, Egypt, 28 February–7 March 1983) and the Tenth United Nations Regional Cartographic Conference for Asia and the Pacific[4] had obtained the views of delegations. He concluded that regional conferences provided a unique forum for the senior administrative, technical and management personnel of the various Governments to discuss mutual problems, exchange of information, transfer of technology and exchange

programmes. They were the only conferences at which the subject-matter covered the full range of surveying and mapping according to the United Nations definition of cartography; discussion was at the executive and management level, in line with social and economic aims rather than the scientific and scholarly aims of most international professional associations; and technical subjects were weighed by participants in terms of policy, programme and production implications.

The regional conferences should continue to be held, the Secretary-General said, but at four-year intervals (instead of the current three-year intervals), and their length should be shortened to 10 working days. The question of holding interregional conferences could be deferred in view of the 1983 Economic and Social Council decision[5] endorsing the convening of the Eleventh United Nations Regional Cartographic Conference for Asia and the Pacific in 1987 (see below). Moreover, the question should be further considered to avoid duplication by international organizations and to give particular attention to the needs of small countries. The provisional agenda for the 1987 meeting and other recommendations for future regional cartographic conferences were provided in an annex to the report.

ECONOMIC AND SOCIAL COUNCIL ACTION

On 4 May 1984, the Economic and Social Council adopted without vote decision 1984/111.

Report of the Secretary-General on United Nations interregional cartographic conferences

At its 7th plenary meeting, on 4 May 1984, the Council took note of the report of the Secretary-General on United Nations interregional cartographic conferences, prepared in pursuance of its resolution 1981/6 of 4 May 1981.

Economic and Social Council decision 1984/111

Adopted without vote

Oral proposal by President; agenda item 8.
Meeting numbers. ESC 6, 7.

Eleventh UN Cartographic Conference for Asia and the Pacific

In a 4 April 1984 note verbale addressed to the Secretary-General,[6] Turkey stated that it was prepared to host the Eleventh United Nations Regional Cartographic Conference for Asia and the Pacific, scheduled for the first half of 1987.[5]

ECONOMIC AND SOCIAL COUNCIL ACTION

On 4 May, the Economic and Social Council adopted without vote decision 1984/112.

Eleventh United Nations Regional Cartographic Conference for Asia and the Pacific

At its 7th plenary meeting, on 4 May 1984, the Council took note of the offer made by the Government of

Turkey to act as host to the Eleventh United Nations Regional Cartographic Conference for Asia and the Pacific to be held in 1987, and decided to revert to the matter at its first regular session of 1985.

Economic and Social Council decision 1984/112

Adopted without vote

Oral proposal by President; agenda item 8.
Meeting numbers. ESC 6, 7.

Third UN Cartographic Conference for the Americas

In a letter of 8 February 1984[7] to the President of the Economic and Social Council, Argentina requested that the Third United Nations Regional Cartographic Conference for the Americas, which was to have been held from 3 to 14 September 1984 at Buenos Aires, be deferred until the first quarter of 1985, owing to the change-over that had taken place in the national, provincial and municipal authorities of Argentina on 10 December 1983 and the need to make adequate preparations for the Conference.

ECONOMIC AND SOCIAL COUNCIL ACTION

On 10 February 1984, the Economic and Social Council adopted with vote decision 1984/105.

Third United Nations Regional Cartographic Conference for the Americas

At its 2nd plenary meeting, on 10 February 1984, the Council, having considered the letter dated 8 February 1984 from the Permanent Representative of Argentina to the United Nations addressed to the President of the Council, decided that the Third United Nations Regional Cartographic Conference for the Americas should be held at Buenos Aires during the first quarter of 1985 instead of from 3 to 14 September 1984.

Economic and Social Council decision 1984/105

Adopted without vote

Oral proposal by President, on request by Argentina (E/1984/27); agenda item 2.

On 21 May, the Council, having heard its President state that Argentina had informed the Secretary-General that it was not in a position to host the Conference, adopted without vote decision 1984/117.

Third United Nations Regional Cartographic Conference for the Americas

At its 16th plenary meeting, on 21 May 1984, the Council decided that the Third United Nations Regional Cartographic Conference for the Americas would be held at United Nations Headquarters from 19 February to 1 March 1985 instead of at Buenos Aires during the first quarter of 1985 as decided by the Council in its decision 1984/105 of 10 February 1984.

Economic and Social Council decision 1984/117

Adopted without vote

Oral proposal by President; agenda item 1.

REFERENCES

[1]DP/1985/43/Add.1. [2]YUN 1981, p. 688, ESC res. 1981/6, 4 May 1981. [3]E/1984/36. [4]YUN 1983, p. 671. [5]*Ibid.*, ESC dec. 1983/121, 26 May 1983. [6]E/1984/63. [7]E/1984/27.

Chapter X

Energy resources

In 1984, United Nations entities continued their work in trying to diminish world-wide dependence on depletable sources of energy, focusing special attention on the energy needs of developing countries. In an effort to accelerate progress in the development of their energy resources, the General Assembly, in resolution 39/176, urged improved international co-operation and consideration of new avenues for financing. The United Nations Development Programme (UNDP) remained a major force in mobilizing funds in support of developing countries' energy efforts through collaboration with the World Bank, the international donor community and various co-financing arrangements. As an instrument for channelling additional voluntary resources into high priority projects, the UNDP Energy Account had, at the end of 1984, $18 million allocated to projects. Transfer of technology and expertise to developing countries was a key element in energy-related activities of the United Nations Conference on Trade and Development (UNCTAD) and the Secretariat's Department of Technical Co-operation for Development (DTCD), while the United Nations Industrial Development Organization (UNIDO) focused on assisting developing countries in integrating national industrial and energy policies and improving industrial energy efficiency.

The 1981 Nairobi Programme of Action for the Development and Utilization of New and Renewable Sources of Energy provided the basis for another sphere of United Nations efforts concerning such sources in 1984. Practical problems concerning its implementation were examined at the second session of the Committee on the Development and Utilization of New and Renewable Sources of Energy, which made recommendations to that end. In resolution 39/173, the Assembly called for early action on them, expressing concern over the slow pace of the Programme's implementation.

With regard to nuclear energy, most United Nations work continued to be carried out by the International Atomic Energy Agency (IAEA). After considering IAEA's annual report for 1983, the Assembly urged, in resolution 39/12, international co-operation in promoting the use of nuclear energy for peaceful purposes, strengthening technical assistance to developing countries, and promoting nuclear safety. By resolution 39/74, the Assembly decided that the United Nations Conference for the Promotion of International Co-operation in the Peaceful Uses of Nuclear Energy would be held at Geneva in November 1986.

Topics related to this chapter. Disarmament: nuclear weapons. Peaceful uses of outer space. Regional economic and social activities: energy resources—Africa; Asia and the Pacific; Europe; Latin America. Statistics: energy statistics.

General aspects

Energy resources development

Report of the Secretary-General. In August 1984, the Secretary-General presented to the General Assembly an expanded analysis of the development of energy resources in developing countries,[1] as requested by the Assembly in December 1983.[2] Designed to complete his June 1983 analysis,[3] the report focused on the process of real capital formation in the energy industries of the developing world, particularly what were termed domestic energy enterprises, that is, organizations such as national oil companies, private coal producers and public utilities with headquarters in developing countries, which had a considerable effect on energy resources development.

In assessing energy investment requirements of developing countries for the period 1982-2000, the report identified the major participants in energy resources development in each of the main energy sectors and estimated their future capital expenditures and investment needs. It concluded that in aggregate, the domestic energy enterprises of developing countries must invest up to $1,489 billion over the 19-year period, with 62 per cent of the projected investment going for hydrocarbon exploration and development.

The report also examined the supply of capital to the energy industries of developing countries. After reviewing three major financing sources of energy enterprises in the developing world—funds generated internally from operations, new loans, and new infusions of equity capital—it assessed prospects for energy capital supplies from conventional sources. The report concluded that with the exception oil-exporting and potential coal-exporting countries, the capacity of domestic energy enterprises in the developing countries to finance their own investment programmes from their own operations was very limited, implying an increasing recourse to governmental funds in competition with other development aims. Estimating the cumulative flow of funds to domestic energy enterprises, the report assumed some shift in the relative importance of individual sources of funds by the year 2000 and predicted that cash from operations and new equity would rise to represent 55 and 14 per cent of cumulative financing, respectively, and drop to 31 per cent with regard to new debt.

The report examined the balance between the demand for and supply of energy capital to developing countries and considered policy measures which might be appropriate under the circumstances. It was estimated that about $311 billion or 60 per cent of the overall gap between investment requirements and funds likely to be forthcoming was centred on the hydrocarbons sector. In primary electricity, where investment requirements and funds available came closest in relative terms, the gap was $124 billion or 40 per cent, while in oil and gas, coal and new and renewable sources of energy requirements exceeded funds by 50 per cent or more. The report suggested that, due to their considerable financing gaps in hydrocarbons, coal, primary electricity and new and renewable sources of energy, over the rest of the century energy-deficient countries would suffer one half of the overall energy investment requirements deficit among the developing countries as a whole. It was noted, however, that the expected $520 billion total deficit of domestic energy enterprises in the developing countries reflected only investment and its financing and thus significantly underestimated the overall imbalance between future uses and sources of funds in upstream energy in those countries.

To help redress that imbalance, the report proposed a number of policy measures at national and international levels. Promotion of energy conservation and direct foreign investments as well as a greater use of small-scale energy resources were described as effective ways of reducing the investment burden of the developing countries without sacrificing rapid economic growth. Those policies were to be complemented by various efforts to maximize the capital available to domestic energy enterprises, mainly through an increase of domestic energy prices to reflect opportunity costs of the energy provided.

The need for joint international action to augment purely national policies in reducing the deficit between energy investment demand and supply was also emphasized. Bilateral economic and technical co-operation among developing countries as well as through various regional programmes yielded promising results in exploring petroleum resources and developing hydro-electric potential of major river systems. The energy situation could also be improved through political and diplomatic means. External support, however, reflected a slow-down in world economic growth, especially with regard to bilateral assistance. Under these circumstances the international community needed, the report maintained, to consider additional institutional arrangements to supplement the flow of external capital to developing countries. Reviewing such proposals as the creation of an energy affiliate of the World Bank or exploration insurance and energy development funds, the report stressed that the main difficulty lay in achieving a political consensus on the need for further institutional innovation at the international level.

UNDP activities. Throughout 1984, UNDP worked closely together with the World Bank to provide developing countries, donors and investors with assessments of pressing energy issues and options for dealing with them. These activities were carried out within the framework of the joint UNDP/World Bank Energy Sector Assessments Programme, with the Energy Management Assistance Programme (ESMAP) serving as the primary vehicle for ensuring appropriate action on the Assessments Programme recommendations.[4] Most ESMAP operations were related to pre-feasibility or pre-investment studies, particularly with regard to energy needs of African countries. The projects concentrated on rehabilitation of power generation and transmission systems, conservation of energy and its efficient use in industry and transport, creation of peri-urban fuelwood plantations and assistance in developing improved woodstoves. At the end of 1984, there were 86 completed or ongoing pre-investment projects in 35 countries, with a potential for co-financing and pre-investment activities in another six, in association with eight donors.

In addition to the core resources available from UNDP, the international donor community and the World Bank, ESMAP received funds for pre-feasibility studies through collaboration with a number of individual donors under various co-financing arrangements, among them third-party cost-sharing arrangements with the UNDP inter-regional programme, a trust fund facility and various country programmes.

Another instrument for channelling additional voluntary resources by interested donors into high priority energy projects in developing countries, was the UNDP Energy Account. In his 1984 report on UNDP's main programme record,[5] the Administrator stated that as at 31 December, $18 million of the Account's $21.12 million total resources had been allocated to projects. $9.3 million of the allocated funds went to cover ESMAP and Energy Sector Assessment Programme activities. Among Energy Account–sponsored programmes, training continued to receive heightened emphasis. A seminar on energy assessment and planning for senior developing country officials was organized together with the Office of the Director-General for Development and International Economic Co-operation, while a Sub-Saharan Energy Seminar was a joint effort with the Economic Development Institute of the World Bank. Several major efforts were also launched in the area of new and renewable sources of energy (see p. 661).

UNDP ENERGY ACCOUNT PROJECT EXPENDITURES, 1984

(in thousands of US dollars)

Country/Region	Amount
Barbados	69
Colombia	501
Djibouti	104
Fiji	11
Honduras	40
Jamaica	(7)
Namibia	221
Viet Nam	3
Subtotal	942
Africa	39
Latin America and the Caribbean	7
Global and Interregional	2,667
Subtotal	2,713
Total	3,655

SOURCE: DP/1985/5/Add.6.

CONTRIBUTIONS TO UNDP ENERGY ACCOUNT, 1984 AND 1985

(as at 31 December 1984; in US dollar equivalent)

Source	1984 payment	1985 pledge*
Colombia	300,000	125,300
Denmark	100,000	181,818
Iceland	40,000	40,000
Jamaica	33,947	—
Netherlands	556,518	242,029
New Zealand	32,895	—
Norway	338,983	150,000
OPEC Fund	225,275	5,774,725
Sweden	—	240,000
Switzerland	813,008	800,000
United Nations	176,989	—
World Bank	767,500	—
Other income†	1,047,695	—
Total	4,432,810	7,553,872

*Approximate amounts to be converted at prevailing exchange rate when received.

†Income from the Information Centre for Heavy Crude and Tar Sands, miscellaneous income and interest.

SOURCE: DP/1985/52/Add.1.

In May,[6] the Committee on new and renewable sources of energy (see below, under "Non-conventional energy sources") recommended that the UNDP Governing Council should review the current interim arrangements for the Energy Account with a view to strengthening its activities.

In connection with that review, the UNDP Administrator proposed in a May report[7] to the UNDP Governing Council that he be authorized to transform the Energy Account into a stable funding arrangement and strengthen its activities concerning new and renewable sources of energy. He also proposed to increase participation of United Nations development system organizations in implementing programmes and projects and to expand the funding base by appealing for increased contributions to the Account.

Having considered the Administrator's report and the Committee's recommendations, the UNDP Governing Council, by a decision of 29 June,[8] authorized him to continue with the Energy Account, as established by the Council in 1980,[9] as long as it received adequate donor support, and called on Governments in a position to do so to increase their contributions. In addition, the Administrator was requested to harmonize Account-financed activities with regular Programme projects and to report more comprehensively to the Council's 1985 session on the results.

UNU activities. Energy-related activities of the United Nations University (UNU) were aimed at developing the concept and methodology of integrated energy systems and providing needed information for and training to third world planners and technicians.[10] Working within the framework of that programme area, the Integrated Rural Energy Systems Association expanded the number of its projects to 12 and held its first official meeting at Cairo, Egypt, in March 1984. A project group of four institutions in Argentina, Brazil, France and India which dealt with energy planning and management was expanded to include the University of Chile and received support from the International Development Research Centre of Canada. Following a 1983 agreement on joint energy research with the Centre,[11] the UNU Energy Research Group held its second meeting at Singapore in April 1984 and decided that the members should referee the 120 commissioned research papers and generate a synthesis document to reflect the Group's position.

The year 1984 also saw an expansion of the Abstracts of Selected Solar Energy Technology (ASSET) network to more than 1,100 members from 115 developing countries. Nine issues of *Asset* were published, while an agreement with Spain on a Spanish translation provided for a greater input from Spanish-language nations into the *Asset* data base. A project on biogas technology involved the use of videotape for disseminating information on biogas utilization among rural communities in Guyana.

As of December 1984, 18 fellows and 4 special fellows had completed training while 5 others were in training.[12]

GENERAL ASSEMBLY ACTION

On 17 December 1984, on the recommendation of the Second (Economic and Financial) Committee, the Assembly adopted resolution 39/176 without vote.

Development of the energy resources of developing countries

The General Assembly,

Recalling the Declaration and the Programme of Action on the Establishment of a New International Economic Order, contained in its resolutions 3201(S-VI) and 3202(S-VI) of 1 May 1974, the Charter of Economic Rights and Duties of States, contained in its resolution 3281(XXIX) of 12 December 1974, its resolution 3362(S-VII) of 16 September 1975 on development and international economic co-operation, and the International Development Strategy for the Third United Nations Development Decade contained in the annex to its resolution 35/56 of 5 December 1980,

Recalling its resolutions 37/251 of 21 December 1982 and 38/151 of 19 December 1983,

Considering that the principal impediments to the realization of the indigenous energy potential of the developing countries are, in addition to inadequate exploration, the scarcity of financial resources, insufficient exploration data, inadequate access to technology and a shortage of skills,

Reaffirming the principle of the full and permanent sovereignty of each State over its natural resources,

Reaffirming also that effective and urgent measures need to be taken by the international community to assist and support the efforts of the developing countries, in particular the energy-deficient among them, for developing their energy resources, in order to meet their needs through co-operation, assistance and investment in the field of conventional and of new and renewable sources of energy, consistent with their national plans and priorities, as called for in the International Development Strategy,

1. *Reaffirms* its resolution 38/151 and calls for the immediate and effective implementation of all its provisions;

2. *Requests* the Secretary-General to improve further and update the contents of his report on the development of the energy resources of the developing countries and, in so doing, to consider all sources of energy, including new and renewable sources of energy, in a balanced and integrated manner and to submit a consolidated and comprehensive report to the General Assembly at its fortieth session;

3. *Urges,* in this connection, early consideration of possible avenues that would increase energy financing, including, *inter alia,* the mechanisms being examined by the World Bank, such as an energy affiliate, and calls upon Member States to take appropriate measures to this end in the relevant forums;

4. *Requests* the Secretary-General, in consultation with the organs and organizations of the United Nations system, to promote international co-operation for the development of internal technological and other capabilities in developing countries in order to achieve the development of their energy resources;

5. *Requests* the Secretary-General to prepare and submit to the General Assembly at its fortieth session a report on the implementation of the present resolution and to include in that report the results of symposia and similar undertakings in support of efforts by developing countries for the exploration and development of their energy resources.

General Assembly resolution 39/176

17 December 1984   Meeting 103   Adopted without vote

Approved by Second Committee (A/39/790/Add.16) without vote, 6 December (meeting 56); draft by Vice-Chairman (A/C.2/39/L.89), based on informal consultations on draft by Egypt, for Group of 77 (A/C.2/39/L.14); agenda item 80 *(p)*.

Financial implications. S-G, A/C.2/39/L.50, A/C.2/39/L.102, A/C.5/39/77.

Meeting numbers. GA 39th session: 2nd Committee 31, 55, 56; 5th Committee 45; plenary 103.

In addition to drafting changes, the adopted text differed from that of the Group of 77, which was withdrawn. Added in the preamble was the Assembly's reaffirmation of the principle of each State's sovereignty over its natural resources. Paragraph 5 was also expanded to have the Secretary-General include in his report the results of undertakings in support of efforts by developing countries to explore their energy resources.

Technology transfer

UNCTAD activities. Following a December 1983 General Assembly request[2] and recommendations by the 1982 Meeting of Governmental Experts on the Transfer, Application and Development of Technology in the Energy Sector,[13] UNCTAD continued in 1984 to analyse issues related to strengthening the technological capacity of developing countries' energy resources. As part of that effort the UNCTAD secretariat presented six reports to the October session of the UNCTAD Committee on Transfer of Technology.

An August progress report on UNCTAD activities in that sphere over the previous year[14] reviewed the current application of energy policy in developing countries, assessed the results of country studies in such areas as transfer of petroleum exploration technology, power plant procurement and development of renewable energy technology, and indicated possible directions for UNCTAD's future work. The report found that an increasing number of developing countries were beginning to establish a comprehensive policy for their energy sector, while the studies on selected individual technology issues confirmed the importance of strengthening the domestic technological capability for the sector's development. The following areas were outlined for in-depth expert examination under UNCTAD auspices: enhancement of institutional mechanisms for exchange of experiences among developing countries; assessment of potential benefits for individual participants of a forum of public power plant utilities; co-operation between developed and developing countries in research and development and transfer of energy technology; and ways of building a skilled manpower base in developing countries.

Factual information, which served as the basis for the above conclusions, was supplied by several national-level case-studies undertaken by UNCTAD with financial support by Sweden. A report on Peru, for example, focused on developing the technological capability of the petroleum industry.[15] It concluded that in order to satisfy its growing petroleum requirements, the country must adapt its petroleum contracts without reducing the necessary technological development effort. Noting the importance of Peruvian experience for other developing countries, the report stressed the significance of conserving skilled human resources by ensuring proper higher education, technical training and remuneration. It also suggested that the contribution of national industry could be extended by developing preferential regional markets and that the investments which Peru planned for petroleum exploration over the coming 15 years would act as an incentive for the development of service industries.

A comparative analysis of oil exploration in Cameroon, Guinea-Bissau and the Ivory Coast[16] highlighted the methods used by those West African countries to strengthen their technological capacity in oil exploration and production and difficulties they had encountered. It emphasized the strategic role of contacts among the three and other developing countries with wider experience, especially in formulating a legal and fiscal framework, in drawing up a strategy for negotiating contracts, and for training personnel.

Another UNCTAD report studied power alcohol technology in Kenya and Zimbabwe.[17] Assessing its attractiveness for developing countries, the report concluded that power alcohol might reduce their strategic dependence on imported fossil fuels and have a positive effect on the balance of payments, as well as on increased rural development, employment opportunities and indigenous technical capacity. It also listed factors influencing the effectiveness of power alcohol application and recommended strategies to enhance its viability.

A report dealing with the experience of the power plant sector in the Republic of Korea[18] analysed the effect of government procurement policy on the technological development of the domestic energy industry and appraised implications of the Korean experience for other developing countries. Technology issues of small-scale hydropower projects in Nepal were the subject of another report,[19] which recommended specific means for strengthening overall development in that sphere. The report concluded that even a least developed country could acquire and develop small-scale hydropower technology and thus contribute to solving some of its energy problems.

DTCD activities. Introduction of new and high technology to developing countries was a key element of Department of Technical Co-operation for Development (DTCD) energy-related technical co-operation projects in 1984.[20] The Department provided advanced equipment and expertise for a geophysical survey using reflection seismic techniques in China and supplied the most modern three dimensional seismic technology to India. It contributed to establishing a computer-based system for coal-operation management in Romania and assisted Yugoslavia in exploiting oil shale. DTCD was also developing microcomputer-based software for energy planning to be provided on request to the developing countries with which it had technical co-operation projects. Interregional advisory missions in petroleum legislation, formulation of legal codes for exploration and production of oil, and model agreements applicable to the petroleum industry were provided to 12 developing countries; six countries were assisted in coal resource development and one in energy planning.

Of 31 electricity supply development projects under way in 1984, many concentrated on computerization of utility management, the application of new technologies in thermal power plant fuel cycles and use of computerized training simulators. They included establishment of a centre in China to train thermal power plant operators and a training simulator in India to study management of high voltage interconnections between different areas and power systems. Introduction of computerized techniques for electricity supply planning and management was involved in projects carried out in Egypt and the United Arab Emirates. DTCD also assisted developing countries in assessing technical problems arising with the greater use of solid fuels and in establishing research and test facilities. As part of the latter effort, two projects to create national centres for testing power plant facilities were launched in Bhutan and Iran. DTCD's conventional energy effort included 15 projects in planning and economics, and 24 in petroleum and coal.

UNIDO action. Issues related to the transfer of technology in the energy industry of developing countries were also considered by the Fourth General Conference of UNIDO in August. The Conference, which considered the transfer of technology in conjunction with other aspects of energy and industrialization (see below), urged the further promotion of the transfer of energy-related industrial technologies to developing countries on equitable terms.[21] It also recommended that UNIDO and other relevant United Nations entities should support local manufacture of energy equipment in developing countries and facilitate the transfer of the necessary technology, particularly through the activities of the UNIDO Industrial and Technological Information Bank (see Chapter VI of this section).

Energy resources in industry

The principal objectives of developing countries in the field of energy and industrialization were identified in August at the Fourth General Conference of UNIDO (see p. 558), which had a separate agenda item devoted to energy. The objective included development of integrated national industrial and energy policies, strengthening of the energy resource base, enhancement of capital goods manufacture, maintenance of energy-related capital equipment, and improvement of industrial energy efficiency. Describing the organization's 1984 activities in pursuance of those goals, the UNIDO Executive Director reported completion of approximately 90 projects with an estimated expenditure of $8.4 million, representing about 9 per cent of the total amount spent on technical assistance.[22]

During the year, UNIDO expanded its activities to foster improved industrial energy efficiency, holding interregional seminars, workshops and training programmes on energy conservation techniques and energy savings in the cement, glass, and sugar beet industries and in petroleum refineries. Sri Lanka was assisted in launching an industrial energy conservation programme and establishing an energy management unit. An energy conservation project was initiated in the energy-intensive sectors of European developing countries. In Colombia, a project was started to provide assistance in manufacturing energy-related capital goods. Special attention was also devoted to new and renewable sources of energy (see below).

After considering various questions related to energy and industrialization, particularly with regard to development and application of energy resources and manufacture of equipment, the Fourth General Conference, on 19 August,[21] invited developing countries to promote co-operation among themselves at different levels and to develop capital goods manufacture and services. It also invited all countries, especially developed ones, to provide adequate resources to developing countries to help them utilize their indigenous energy resources. The Conference recommended that UNIDO, together with other United Nations entities, assist developing countries in such areas as: integration of development, industrial and energy policies; formulation of industrial energy projects; implementation of a technical assistance programme in regard to hydroelectric power plants; rational use of energy in industry; harmonization of electric power supplies and interconnections in the various subregions; and industrial application and development of appropriate energy options in the industrial sector.

REFERENCES

[1]A/39/420 & Corr.1. [2]YUN 1983, p. 676, GA res. 38/151, 19 Dec. 1983. [3]*Ibid.*, p. 674. [4]DP/1985/5/Add.2 (Part II). [5]DP/1985/5/Add.1. [6]A/39/44. [7]DP/1984/37 & Corr.1. [8]E/1984/20 (dec. 84/30). [9]YUN 1980, p. 586. [10]A/39/31. [11]YUN 1983, p. 675. [12]E/1985/55. [13]YUN 1982, p. 891. [14]TD/B/C.6/115. [15]TD/B/C.6/103 & Corr.1. [16]TD/B/C.6/117 & Corr.1. [17]TD/B/C.6/104. [18]TD/B/C.6/105. [19]TD/B/C.6/116. [20]DP/1985/43/Add.1. [21]ID/CONF.5/46 & Corr.1 (res. 3). [22]ID/B/340.

PUBLICATIONS

Energy Statistics Yearbook, 1984 (ST/ESA/STAT/SER.J/28), Sales No. E.86.XVII.2. *Energy Balances and Electricity Profiles, 1984* (ST/ESA/STAT/SER.W/3), Sales No. E.86.XVII.14. *Energy Resources Development Problems in the ESCAP Region* (ST/ESCAP/306), Sales No. E.84.II.F.22. *Waste Energy Recovery in the Industry in the ECE Region* (ECE/ENERGY/9), Sales No. E.84.II.E.21. *Measures for Improving Engineering Equipment with a View to More Effective Energy Use* (ECE/ENG.AUT/16), Sales No. E.84.II.E.25.

Non-conventional energy sources

Implementation of the 1981 Nairobi Programme of Action

Throughout 1984, various United Nations bodies continued their efforts to implement the Nairobi Programme of Action for the Development and Utilization of New and Renewable Sources of Energy, endorsed by the General Assembly in 1981.[1]

As requested by the Assembly in December 1983,[2] the Secretary-General submitted a report[3] to the April/May 1984 session of the Committee on the Development and Utilization of New and Renewable Sources of Energy (see below) describing the contribution of consultative meetings to the mobilization of additional resources and the finalization of projects aimed at implementing the Nairobi Programme of Action. The Secretary-General reported that the United Nations system had undertaken extensive preparatory work at the national, regional and global levels. A number of national round-table conferences and consultative group meetings, organized with the assistance of UNDP and the World Bank, considered energy projects related to new and renewable sources of energy and had resulted in pledges of support.

Proposals on further ways of mobilizing financial resources for new and renewable sources of energy were presented by the Secretary-General in a March report to the Committee,[4] as also requested by the Assembly.[2] Focusing mainly on financial resources for technical co-operation, the report stressed the crucial role of supporting actions and pre-investment activities for the development of new and renewable resources, generally financed as regular programmes or through the resources of UNDP and its associated funds. The way to increase those financial flows, in the Secretary-General's view, was through strengthening the UNDP Energy Account as an active mechanism with a potential for expanding its activities. A review of the interim arrangements could result in turning that account into an energy fund with the responsibility for promoting the mobilization of additional voluntary resources. Such a strengthening and expansion, the Secretary-General noted, could benefit a wider variety of new and renewable sources, improve geographical coverage and diversify the types of projects undertaken in the executing agencies.

Annexed to the report was a list of projects approved for financing from the Energy Account, and updates of the Secretary-General's 1982 reports[5] on the role of United Nations entities and the regional, subregional and other financial institutions in new and renewable sources of energy. In 1982-1983, the World Bank was reported to have lent $1.56 billion for those activities, planning another $1.54 billion for the period ending 1984-1985, the bulk of which would go to hydropower development. The World Bank's volume of lending, although the largest for any single agency, was still relatively small and was unlikely to exceed an annual average of $4 billion over the 1983-1987 period due to resource constraints. Also included were summaries of ongoing projects financed by UNDP and its associated funds.

In relation to regional banks and other official financial institutions, the report noted an increase in their assistance programmes to developing countries, which totalled $1.6 billion in annual financial commitments and was estimated to surpass $2 billion in 1985. While funding for hydropower projects represented more than two thirds of the total financing, there was a perceptible move by some institutions to other new and renewable energy sources which accounted for about 8 per cent of the total energy-related activities financed by regional institutions.

As requested by the Assembly in December 1982,[6] the Secretary-General also submitted to the Committee an analysis[7] of information on resource commitments and flows and activities undertaken in implementation of the Nairobi Programme of Action. From 1980 to 1984 the United Nations system committed resources for 750 activities and projects amounting to $2,782 million, the dominant part of which (93.2 per cent) was related to financial co-operation projects. There was a substantial increase in resource commit-

ments for activities under the regular programme for the 1982-1983 biennium; however, resource constraints made it difficult to maintain the momentum in the 1984-1985 biennium. Fluctuations in resource commitments for UNDP-funded technical co-operation projects brought the 1982 high of $48 million down to $14 million in 1983 and the decrease was expected to continue in 1984-1985. Commitments for financial co-operation projects funded from World Bank resources also registered considerable fluctuations but showed no commensurate increase.

As regards the regional distribution of resource commitments for both technical and financial co-operation projects, Asia and the Pacific and Latin America and the Caribbean accounted for 47.4 and 35.1 per cent respectively, and developing areas in Europe and Africa for 9.5 and 7.9 per cent respectively of the total, while Western Asia received under 0.1 per cent. The regional distribution for technical co-operation projects showed a slightly different pattern, with Asia and the Pacific accounting for more than half of the total and Africa for one third. The balance was committed for Latin America and the Caribbean and for Europe; a minor share went to Western Asia.

Broken down by source of energy, commitments allocated for large-scale hydropower development totalled 74.4 per cent, fuelwood received 12.7 per cent and geothermal development 5.0 per cent of the total. Most of the remaining commitments were allocated for planning, energy conservation, biomass and multi-source projects. Large-scale hydropower development was the focus of reported bilateral and intergovernmental commitments as well as mobilized domestic resources for the implementation of World Bank–funded projects. Reported resource commitments for the development and utilization of new and renewable sources of energy amounted to an annual average of approximately $2,231 million during 1982 and 1983. The Secretary-General concluded that even if the reported commitments reached about half the actual total commitments for supporting actions and pre-investment in developing countries, it would still be well below the estimated requirement of some $1,000 million.

ACC action. Established by the Administrative Committee on Co-ordination (ACC) in 1983 to increase the United Nations responsiveness to the Nairobi Programme of Action and to improve co-ordination within the system,[8] the Inter-Agency Group on New and Renewable Sources of Energy held its third session in New York on 18 and 19 April and 2 and 4 May 1984.[9] The Group assessed progress in implementing the Nairobi Programme, discussed joint planning activities and considered contributions by United Nations bodies to the second session of the Committee on new and renewable sources of energy which was taking place at the same time (see below).

In its report, the Group noted that more complete information should be provided to the focal point in the Department of International Economic and Social Affairs (DIESA) on the synopsis of projects and their expected output, as well as the need for an improvement of the verification process. Regarding the consultative meetings, it examined the status and time schedules of their preparation and, while noting appreciable progress at all levels, called for the speediest convening of the regional and global meetings.

The Group also considered avenues for carrying out its co-ordinating responsibilities and agreed on ways to avoid overlapping with the DIESA focal point of information. It was decided that the Inter-Agency Group, as an ACC task force, should be ready to assist the Secretary-General in assessing progress in the implementation of relevant projects as well as in updating existing and preparing new proposals. After considering the joint planning of energy activities financed through regular budgets, the Group identified UNESCO and DTCD as the lead agencies in the two areas of: energy information systems; and research and training for energy assessment, planning and utilization, respectively. The Group agreed that if it were entrusted with joint planning, it would be able to undertake that responsibility in co-operation with the identified lead agencies.

In October,[10] the ACC Consultative Committee on Substantive Questions (Programme Matters) expressed satisfaction with the Group's work, agreeing that it could serve as a forum for prior consultations on proposed programme budgets for the 1986-1987 biennium in all areas covered by its mandate.

Activities of the Committee on new and renewable sources of energy. The Committee on the Development and Utilization of New and Renewable Sources of Energy, established by the General Assembly in December 1982[6] to promote implementation of the Nairobi Programme of Action, held its second session in New York from 23 April to 4 May 1984. In its report,[11] the Committee reiterated the need for early implementation of the Programme of Action and characterized the development of new and renewable sources of energy as a long-term endeavour, implying wide multilateral action. It reaffirmed the importance of the Programme's areas for priority action, recognizing at the same time their need to reflect the specific circumstances of each country or region. While the primary responsibility for promoting the development of new and renewable energy sources rested with individual countries, implementing the Programme of Action required

continuous commitment of the world community and a balance between national efforts and international support. The Committee stressed that countries with economic and managerial potential had a particular responsibility to support efforts for an effective energy transition.

Having examined the Secretary-General's reports (see above), the Committee characterized them as useful but limited in scope and lacking balanced information on financing and on operational experience of ongoing or completed projects. The Committee was concerned about the delay in preparing consultative meetings, particularly at the regional level, and about the generally slow pace of Programme implementation, especially in such priority areas as mobilizing financial resources. The Committee also welcomed the establishment and operation of the focal point for information, reaffirmed the validity of the mandates already given to United Nations entities and reiterated that action-oriented plans and programmes should be part of integrated efforts at the national, subregional, regional and global levels.

Emphasizing the medium- and long-term goals in the implementation of the Programme of Action, the Committee agreed on a number of recommendations and policy guidelines. It requested the UNDP Governing Council to review the current interim arrangements for the Energy Account (see above) and called for improved co-operation among United Nations bodies involved in the development of new and renewable energy sources. In accordance with the main thrusts of the proposed guidelines, the Secretary-General was requested to submit to the Committee in 1985 the following: an analytical report on monitoring the implementation of the Programme, with a special emphasis on co-ordination activities, the performance of the Inter-Agency Group, utilization of experts and consultants from developing countries, and the results of *ad hoc* technical panels and expert meetings; a progress report on consultative meetings and the performance of the consultative mechanism in general, including an update of his report on further ways of mobilizing financial resources, as well as information on the UNDP Governing Council's review of the Energy Account current interim arrangements; and a progress report on implementing projects and programmes as outlined at the Committee's April 1983 session,[8] including an update of existing and formulation of new proposals.

The Committee called on the international community to take urgent action to make available additional financial resources for the needs of developing countries. Reiterating its call for the convening of consultative meetings, the Committee encouraged developing countries to launch them at the national level. It stressed that at regional and subregional levels responsibility rested with the regional commissions and, globally, with the Director General for Development and International Economic Co-operation. It urged Governments and United Nations entities to provide all relevant data to the focal point for information of the Secretariat Unit on New and Renewable Sources of Energy and requested the Secretary-General to prepare a brief guide for improving its co-operation with national focal points. The Committee also invited the international community to use existing institutional arrangements in the Secretariat more efficiently, called on United Nations entities to support economic and technical co-operation among developing countries, and drew particular attention to the needs of the least developed countries. In addition, it recommended that the United Nations system consider improving the statistical coverage of new and renewable sources of energy.

UNDP activities. Some project results concerning new and renewable sources were described by the Administrator in his 1984 annual report.[12] The UNDP Energy Office, charged with supervising the optimal use of Energy Account resources, assisted the United Nations Institute for Training and Research (UNITAR) in holding the Third International Conference on Heavy Crude and Tar Sands as well as a conference on the development of shallow oil and gas resources. Together with the World Bank and the European Economic Community it participated in supporting the improvement of biomass gasifiers through demonstration activities in numerous developing countries. Stepping up its support for country-level operations, the Office contributed $1 million to geothermal resource identification in Djibouti, which catalysed a total financial package from multiple sources valued at $16.6 million. In Morocco, a feasibility study on utilizing and transporting natural gas from the Essaouira field for industrial applications had elicited donor interest, while in the Dominican Republic joint preparations with the Government and the OPEC Fund for rehabilitating a mini-hydro station were finalized. A mini-hydro proposal for Fiji was also being developed.

UNIDO action. Projects related to new and renewable sources of energy constituted a sizeable part of UNIDO activities throughout 1984, with a special emphasis placed on small hydropower, biomass and solar energy. In his 1984 annual report,[13] the UNIDO Executive Director noted that a six-volume manual on the design of Pelton, cross-flow and axial turbines, regulators and control systems, prepared in co-operation with the Latin American Energy Organization (OLADE), was particularly useful to developing countries wishing to manufacture equipment for small

hydropower stations. Another project involved assessing techno-economic possibilities for establishing a small hydroelectric plant in Mali. With regard to biomass, new initiatives included: an interregional project for the use of fermentation enthanol as fuel and chemical feedstock; a bio-fuels demonstration programme in Ethiopia; improvements in industrial charcoal production in Somalia; a pilot plant for the production of alcohol from cellulosic raw material in the Philippines; assistance in the manufacture of efficient wood-burning stoves in Samoa; the industrial use of cane-sugar by-products in Colombia; and—in co-operation with the French Government—a consultative meeting on energy production from agro-industrial by-products and wastes. Solar energy efforts ranged from construction of a prototype solar timber drying kiln in Guyana and assistance in establishing a salt industry in the Solomon Islands, to a fact-finding mission in Maldives for the manufacture and application of solar collectors and a research and development programme on renewable energy in Madagascar.

Working to implement the Nairobi Programme of Action, UNIDO prepared, in co-operation with the Special Co-ordinator for New and Renewable Sources of Energy, specific proposals for a global consultative meeting to be held in 1985. It also submitted proposals for the regional consultative meeting in Asia and the Pacific (see Chapter VIII of this section) and participated in the work of the Inter-Agency Group on new and renewable sources (see above).

In August, the Fourth General Conference of UNIDO recommended[14] that the organization should assist developing countries in obtaining energy from new and renewable sources and promote co-operation between institutions engaged in their research and development.

DTCD activities. During 1984, DTCD aimed many of its technical co-operation activities towards the development of new and renewable sources of energy to assist developing countries in reducing their dependence on energy imports.[15] Over the year geothermal energy projects were carried out in China, Djibouti, Ethiopia, India, Kenya, the Philippines, Romania, Thailand and Yugoslavia. Projects in wind, solar, and bio-energy, as well as energy conservation and rural energy supplies, were implemented in Argentina, Cape Verde, China, Egypt, India, Maldives, Mauritius, Mongolia, Pakistan, Romania, Seychelles and Yugoslavia. As part of a programme for developing small hydropower resources, 33 of a targeted 48 developing countries were surveyed by the end of the year with funding from Japan, Norway and Sweden. The Department also provided advisory services to Argentina, Haiti, Indonesia, Iran, Maldives, Mauritius, Mexico, Mongolia, Nigeria, Romania, Saint Lucia, Thailand and Yugoslavia. Cost analysis reports, prepared by DTCD for photovoltaic systems in developing countries and solar, wind and diesel-pumping at village sites in Nigeria, Somalia and Zimbabwe, were circulated to UNDP offices.

ECONOMIC AND SOCIAL COUNCIL ACTION

In July, acting on the recommendation of its First (Economic) Committee, the Economic and Social Council adopted without vote decision 1984/170.

Development and utilization of new and renewable sources of energy

At its 48th plenary meeting, on 25 July 1984, the Council took note of the report of the Committee on the Development and Utilization of New and Renewable Sources of Energy on its second session, and of the recommendations contained therein and decided to transmit the report to the General Assembly at its thirty-ninth session for consideration.

Economic and Social Council decision 1984/170

Adopted without vote

Approved by First Committee (E/1984/134) without vote, 9 July (meeting 3); oral proposal by Chairman; agenda item 17.

GENERAL ASSEMBLY ACTION

On the recommendation of the Second Committee, the General Assembly, on 17 December 1984, adopted without vote resolution 39/173.

Implementation of the Nairobi Programme of Action for the Development and Utilization of New and Renewable Sources of Energy

The General Assembly,

Recalling the Declaration and the Programme of Action on the Establishment of a New International Economic Order, contained in its resolutions 3201(S-VI) and 3202(S-VI) of 1 May 1974, the Charter of Economic Rights and Duties of States, contained in its resolution 3281(XXIX) of 12 December 1974, its resolution 3362(S-VII) of 16 September 1975 on development and international economic co-operation, and the International Development Strategy for the Third United Nations Development Decade, contained in the annex to its resolution 35/56 of 5 December 1980,

Reaffirming the importance of the Nairobi Programme of Action for the Development and Utilization of New and Renewable Sources of Energy as the basic framework of reference for action by the international community in this field,

Emphasizing the need for development of new and renewable sources of energy in order to improve the welfare of the people,

Bearing in mind the need for financial and technical support by the international community and the vital role to be played in this respect by the United Nations system and emphasizing in this context that special attention should be paid to the development of new and renewable sources of energy of developing countries in accordance with their national plans and priorities,

Recalling its resolutions 36/193 of 17 December 1981,

37/250 of 21 December 1982 and 38/169 of 19 December 1983 on the immediate implementation of the Nairobi Programme of Action,

Having considered the report of the Committee on the Development and Utilization of New and Renewable Sources of Energy on its second session,

1. *Takes note* of the report of the Committee on the Development and Utilization of New and Renewable Sources of Energy on its second session;

2. *Notes with concern* that the implementation of the Nairobi Programme of Action for the Development and Utilization of New and Renewable Sources of Energy had been slow and falls far short of the urgent needs of developing countries, and, in this regard, stresses the need for continuous commitment and action by the international community at the national, regional and global levels, in particular with respect to the mobilization of financial resources, to which the General Assembly has attached high priority;

3. *Calls* for the early and effective implementation of the Nairobi Programme of Action and of the conclusions and recommendations adopted to this end by the Committee at its second session;

4. *Expresses its concern* at the results of the few regional consultative meetings thus far convened and reiterates that thorough preparation, as well as financial and technical support, is necessary for ensuring the convening and success of such meetings at the national, regional and global levels;

5. *Requests* the Secretary-General to report to the General Assembly at its fortieth session on the implementation of the present resolution.

General Assembly resolution 39/173

17 December 1984   Meeting 103   Adopted without vote

Approved by Second Committee (A/39/790/Add.13) without vote, 30 November (meeting 55); draft by Vice-Chairman (A/C.2/39/L.88), based on informal consultations on draft by Egypt, for Group of 77 (A/C.2/39/L.8); agenda item 80 *(m)*. *Meeting numbers.* GA 39th session: 2nd Committee 28, 55; plenary 103.

The adopted text contained, apart from drafting changes, several additions when compared with that put forward on behalf of the Group of 77 and subsequently withdrawn by its sponsors: two new preambular paragraphs on the need for development of new and renewable energy sources and the need for financial and technical support by the international community; while in paragraph 2, the need for continuous commitment by the international community was stressed.

REFERENCES

(1)YUN 1981, p. 691, GA res. 36/193, 17 Dec. 1981. (2)YUN 1983, p. 682, GA res. 38/169, 19 December 1983. (3)A/AC.218/6. (4)A/AC.218/7 & Corr.1. (5)YUN 1982, pp. 900-901. (6)YUN 1982, p. 896, GA res. 37/250, 21 Dec. 1982. (7)A/AC.218/5. (8)YUN 1983, p. 681. (9)ACC/1984/PG/5. (10)ACC/1984/19/Corr.1. (11)A/39/44. (12)DP/1985/5/Add.2 (Part II). (13)ID/B/340. (14)ID/CONF.5/46 (res. 3). (15)DP/1985/43/Add.1.

PUBLICATION

Updated Guidebook on Biogas Development (ST/ESCAP/275), Sales No. E.84.II.F.14.

Nuclear energy

United Nations technical work regarding nuclear energy continued to be dealt with mainly by the International Atomic Energy Agency (IAEA) in 1984. (For information on IAEA activities during the year, see PART II, Chapter I.)

IAEA report

The IAEA report for 1983 and a later addendum were transmitted to the 1984 General Assembly session by the Secretary-General in September.[1]

Updating the report in a statement before the Assembly on 12 November, the IAEA Director General reiterated that despite the persistent shrinking of energy demand in industrialized countries due to the economic recession, the past year had witnessed a continued rise in electricity demands and a steady growth world-wide in the production of nuclear power. As the nuclear industry strove to become more efficient and economical, there were increased efforts to develop nuclear reactors for heat production or co-generation of heat and electricity and growing interest among manufacturers in small and medium-sized plants, especially useful for developing countries. The development of new generations of power reactors, such as breeders, and research on nuclear fusion were described by the Director General as areas of great potential importance, with IAEA providing an international forum for exchange of experience and joint projects.

With regard to safety, he said that the Agency's review covering 1983 detected no health or environment-endangering radiation accidents at any of the more than 300 nuclear power plants in operation. IAEA also examined on request the operational safety of plants in several countries and launched, jointly with the Nuclear Energy Agency of the Organisation for Economic Co-operation and Development (OECD), an international system designed to monitor all accidents and incidents with safety implications. Continuing to serve as a centre for reaching an international consensus on nuclear waste management standards, the Agency undertook a review of the dumping of low-level radioactive wastes into the deep ocean.

Although the majority of developing countries would not be introducing nuclear power in the foreseeable future, the Director General pointed to the IAEA role in assisting them in energy planning and infrastructure development, as well as in applying nuclear techniques for food production and health improvement. The use of radioisotopes and nuclear techniques in food and agriculture, particularly in developing countries, was given special prominence in 1984 as IAEA and FAO marked the twentieth anniversary of joint work to promote those applications. IAEA technical co-operation programmes in nuclear techniques had been steadily expanding, with the total volume of activities oriented towards developing countries reaching in excess of $60 million in 1984.

With regard to the transfer of nuclear technologies and hardware producing or making use of fissionable material, the Director General described it as a complex problem requiring a mutually acceptable accommodation of the interests of the suppliers and importing States, since the former were concerned about the potential misuse of nuclear fuel for military purposes and the latter depended on a reliable supply of fuel and technology. While seeking to reconcile these interests in its Committee on Assurances of Supply, the Agency was also acquiring extensive experience of systematic on-site verification which might be of use in connection with future arms control agreements. The Director General also reported progress in IAEA verification of peaceful nuclear activities in the nuclear-weapon States, including a negotiated agreement with the USSR following its voluntary offer to accept IAEA's safeguards on some of its peaceful nuclear facilities.

Expressing regret over lack of progress in nuclear disarmament, he hoped to see further efforts in applying nuclear technology for peaceful purposes and cited substantial gains in the international transfer of technology, despite a decrease in funds available for technical assistance and co-operation with developing countries.

With regard to the consequences of Israel's 1981 attack on an Iraqi nuclear research reactor[2] (see p. 280) and South Africa's nuclear potential (see p. 39), the Director General said that IAEA had again urged both countries to accept comprehensive safeguards. He noted, however, that while the safeguards aspects of the two issues fell within IAEA statutory obligations, a perennial consideration of the broader political ramifications placed a strain on the Agency.

GENERAL ASSEMBLY ACTION

On 13 November 1984, the General Assembly adopted resolution 39/12 without vote.

Report of the International Atomic Energy Agency

The General Assembly,

Having received the report of the International Atomic Energy Agency to the General Assembly for the year 1983,

Taking note of the statement of the Director General of the International Atomic Energy Agency of 12 November 1984, which provides additional information on the main development of the Agency's activities during 1984,

Recognizing the importance of the work of and the relevance for the International Atomic Energy Agency to promote further the application of nuclear energy for peaceful purposes, as envisaged in its statute, and to improve further its technical assistance and promotional programmes for the benefit of developing countries,

Conscious of the importance of the work of the International Atomic Energy Agency in the implementation of the safeguards provisions of the Treaty on the Non-Proliferation of Nuclear Weapons and other international treaties, conventions and agreements designed to achieve similar objectives, as well as ensuring, as far as it is able, that the assistance provided by the Agency or at its request or under its supervision or control is not used in such a way as to further any military purpose, as stated in article II of its statute,

Recognizing the importance of the work of the International Atomic Energy Agency on nuclear safety, which increases public confidence in nuclear power,

Recalling that 1984 marked the twentieth anniversary of the establishment by the Food and Agriculture Organization of the United Nations and the International Atomic Energy Agency of the joint Division of Isotope and Radiation Applications of Atomic Energy for Food and Agricultural Development as well as of the establishment of the International Centre for Theoretical Physics of Trieste, and expressing its satisfaction at the valuable work carried out with the use of nuclear techniques to increase food production and at the development of physical and mathematical sciences in developing countries,

Bearing in mind resolutions GC(XXVIII)/RES/423, GC(XXVIII)/RES/424, GC(XXVIII)/RES/425 and GC(XXVIII)/RES/439, as adopted on 28 September 1984 by the General Conference of the International Atomic Energy Agency at its twenty-eighth regular session,

1. *Takes note* of the report of the International Atomic Energy Agency;

2. *Affirms* its confidence in the role of the International Atomic Energy Agency in the application of nuclear energy for peaceful purposes;

3. *Urges* all States to strive for effective and harmonious international co-operation in carrying out the work of the International Atomic Energy Agency, pursuant to its statute, in promoting the use of nuclear energy and the application of nuclear science and technology for peaceful purposes; in strengthening technical assistance and co-operation for developing countries; in ensuring the effectiveness and efficiency of the Agency's safeguards system; and in promoting nuclear safety;

4. *Requests* the Secretary-General to transmit to the Director General of the International Atomic Energy Agency the records of the thirty-ninth session of the General Assembly relating to the Agency's activities.

General Assembly resolution 39/12

13 November 1984   Meeting 59   Adopted without vote

3-nation draft (A/39/L.15), orally revised; agenda item 14.
Sponsors: Australia, Egypt, German Democratic Republic.
Meeting numbers. GA 39th session: plenary 58, 59.

The related topics of nuclear disarmament and nuclear power sources in outer space were the subject of several other resolutions adopted by the Assembly in 1984 (see POLITICAL AND SECURITY QUESTIONS, Chapters I and II).

Preparations for the Conference on nuclear energy

Preparatory Committee activities. The Preparatory Committee for the United Nations Conference for the Promotion of International Co-operation in the Peaceful Uses of Nuclear Energy, established by the General Assembly in 1980,[3] held its fifth session at Geneva from 25 June to 6 July 1984 during which it held 19 formal and a number of informal meetings, and reported the results to the Assembly.[4]

After several years of unsuccessful attempts to resolve basic matters pertaining to the Conference, the Committee agreed on a provisional agenda and approved draft provisional rules of procedure. While not entirely satisfactory to all delegations, the agenda represented a compromise, specifically in relation to an item dealing with the principles of international co-operation in the peaceful uses of nuclear energy, drafted with an understanding that relevant decisions in the Conference should be adopted by consensus. The draft provisional rules of procedure were approved on the understanding that questions relating to elections of officers and records of meetings would be considered at the Committee's October 1985 session. Following a proposal that summary records should not be provided for the Conference, the Committee agreed to consider that issue in 1985 and requested the Secretary-General to provide a statement of administrative and financial implications of the proposal.

The Committee also considered a report by the Secretary-General on the preparations for the Conference and documentation[5] which reviewed contributions to the preparations by Member States, IAEA, the specialized agencies and other United Nations organizations. Noting lack of concrete information in material received from contributors, the Secretary-General reported that a broad list of relevant issues had been sent to all Governments on 19 March 1984 and that a comprehensive evaluation of the forthcoming data would be prepared upon receipt of responses. Concerning the input of international institutions, the OECD Nuclear Energy Agency offered to prepare a paper on a suitable topic. Interest in the Conference was expressed, among others, by the International Centre for Theoretical Physics, the International Institute for Applied Systems Analysis, and the World Energy Conference. Regional preparations involved two interrelated sets of activities: studies on regional experiences, problems and priorities in the peaceful uses of nuclear energy and follow-up regional meetings by expert groups. The Secretary-General also briefly reviewed the status of preparations with regard to invitations, documents on decisions and conclusions, and public information activities highlighting the Conference's goals and purposes.

The Committee emphasized the importance of adequate preparations and asked the Secretary-General to continue his efforts as outlined in the report, keeping in mind the Committee's suggestions. It also agreed to begin formal inter-sessional intergovernmental work with its 1985 session and recommended that the Assembly request the Committee's Chairman and the Conference Secretary-General to continue individual and group consultations to expedite preparations. The Committee decided that contributions from specialized agencies and other United Nations bodies should conform to Assembly directives on the control of documentation and be specifically related to the Conference. It was agreed that the Committee should receive input materials before their distribution for the Conference. The Committee recommended that the Assembly should provide resources for a meeting of a 15-member advisory group of internationally eminent experts drawn on equitable geographical distribution, to be held some six months prior to the Conference. Another recommendation concerned potential participants.

The Committee further decided that if no invitations were forthcoming from Member States, the Conference should be held at Geneva for three weeks during September-November 1986.

GENERAL ASSEMBLY ACTION

On 13 November 1984, the General Assembly adopted resolution 39/74 without vote.

United Nations Conference for the Promotion of International Co-operation in the Peaceful Uses of Nuclear Energy

The General Assembly,

Reaffirming the principles and provisions of its resolution 32/50 of 8 December 1977,

Recalling its subsequent resolutions 33/4 of 2 November 1978, 34/63 of 29 November 1979, 35/112 of 5 December 1980, 36/78 of 9 December 1981, 37/167 of 17 December 1982 and 38/60 of 14 December 1983,

Noting that the pending issues related to the United Nations Conference for the Promotion of International Co-operation in the Peaceful Uses of Nuclear Energy were successfully resolved at the fifth session of the Preparatory Committee for the Conference as reflected in its report to the General Assembly,

Noting that the Preparatory Committee once again emphasized the importance of adequate preparations for the Conference and agreed on the importance of inter-sessional intergovernmental consultations and contacts,

Noting also that the Preparatory Committee agreed to begin formal/official inter-sessional intergovernmental work with its sixth session,

Noting further the decision of the Preparatory Committee relating to the convening of a meeting of a group of internationally eminent experts to provide advice on major issues of concern to the Conference,

1. *Approves* the recommendations and decisions contained in the report of the Preparatory Committee for the United Nations Conference for the Promotion of International Co-operation in the Peaceful Uses of Nuclear Energy on its fifth session;

2. *Expresses its appreciation* for the efforts of the Chairman of the Preparatory Committee and the Secretary-General of the Conference in pursuance of paragraph 2 of General Assembly resolution 38/60;

3. *Requests* the Chairman of the Preparatory Committee and the Secretary-General of the Conference, on the basis of the practice successfully used before the fifth session of the Committee, to continue informal individual and group consultations, as necessary, in order to assist the Committee in expediting the necessary procedural and substantive preparations for the Conference;

4. *Notes with appreciation* the progress made in the preparations for the Conference and requests the Secretary-General of the Conference to continue with the preparations as outlined in the report of the Secretary-General to the Preparatory Committee at its fifth session;

5. *Decides* that the Preparatory Committee shall hold its sixth session at Vienna from 21 October to 1 November 1985 to consider, *inter alia*, the mechanism for formal/official inter-sessional intergovernmental work and the commencement of preparation of the concluding document or documents of the Conference, as well as the mandate and composition of the group of internationally eminent experts;

6. *Decides* that the United Nations Conference for the Promotion of International Co-operation in the Peaceful Uses of Nuclear Energy shall be held at Geneva from 10 to 28 November 1986;

7. *Invites* the International Atomic Energy Agency, the specialized agencies and other relevant organizations of the United Nations system to ensure that their contributions to the input documents for the Conference, including reports of the regional expert group meetings, should be concise and comprehensive and specifically related to the purpose, aims and objectives of the Conference, including in particular suggestions regarding practical and effective ways and means for the promotion of international co-operation in the peaceful uses of nuclear energy, so as to achieve meaningful results from the Conference in accordance with the objectives of General Assembly resolution 32/50;

8. *Invites* all States to co-operate actively in the preparation of the Conference and to make available, as soon as possible, the information requested in paragraph 9 of General Assembly resolution 36/78 and in the broad questionnaire circulated by the Secretary-General of the Conference in March 1984;

9. *Decides* to include in the provisional agenda of its fortieth session the item entitled "United Nations Conference for the Promotion of International Co-operation in the Peaceful Uses of Nuclear Energy".

General Assembly resolution 39/74

13 December 1984   Meeting 99   Adopted without vote

3-nation draft (A/39/L.26); agenda item 35.
Sponsors: Egypt, Germany, Federal Republic of, Poland.
Financial implications. 5th Committee, A/39/822; S-G, A/C.5/39/84 & Add.1.

REFERENCES

(1)A/39/458/Add.1. (2)YUN 1981, p. 275. (3)YUN 1980, p. 164, GA res. 35/112, 5 Dec. 1980. (4)A/39/47. (5)A/CONF.108/PC/11 & Add.1.

Chapter XI

Food

Faced with a persisting dichotomy, when hundreds of millions of people in the world went hungry and malnourished just as ample food was available at a global level, various United Nations entities stepped up their efforts in 1984 to tackle the gamut of food problems through emergency operations, development aid and policy planning assistance.

In a year that marked the tenth anniversary of the World Food Conference, the World Food Council (WFC) reviewed progress in the implementation of the Conference objectives and identified major tasks to be addressed by the international community and individual countries to ensure food security and eradicate hunger and malnutrition. WFC's recommendations were endorsed by the Economic and Social Council (resolution 1984/54) and welcomed by the General Assembly (resolution 39/166), which called on Governments and international organizations to give particular attention to the measures proposed by WFC. The role of fisheries in ensuring national self-reliance in food production was high on the agenda of the World Conference on Fisheries Management and Development, which mapped out a strategy and associated programmes of action, endorsed subsequently by the Assembly (resolution 39/225).

For the World Food Programme (WFP), 1984 brought record levels of activity in providing food aid to developing countries. As compared with the previous year, WFP food commitments increased by 48 per cent to reach 2.1 million metric tons. By 31 December 1984, a total of $999.8 million had been pledged to the regular WFP budget for 1985-1986. That represented 74 per cent of the $1.35 billion WFP target for the period, the need for achieving which was stressed by the Assembly in resolution 39/166. The governing body of WFP, the 30-member Committee on Food Aid Policies and Programmes, held its seventeenth and eighteenth sessions, approving projects at a total cost of more than $770 million.

Topics related to this chapter. Law of the sea. Economic assistance, disasters and emergency relief. Regional economic and social activities: Africa—food and agriculture. Natural resources and cartography: marine resources. Health and human resources: nutrition. Human rights: right to food. Women: women in rural areas. Children: nutrition.

Food problems

Following a 1982 decision of WFC,[1] an independent seven-member panel of experts sponsored by Australia, Canada and the Netherlands prepared a report[2] on the world food and hunger problem over the 1974-1984 period for submission to the tenth ministerial session of WFC (see below). Assessing progress in meeting food objectives since the 1974 World Food Conference[3] and the priority tasks which remained to be achieved, the report examined in particular the impact of the current food balance on low-income, food-deficit countries. It noted that many of the dire forecasts in 1974 had not been borne out. Aggregate food and agricultural production was at record levels and the threat of global food scarcity seemed remote, although the possibility of major production shortfalls was still evident and chronic malnutrition proved to be a much more intractable problem than previously thought.

The report specifically focused on the key paradox of the current food situation—alongside a growing output, an estimated 400 million to 600 million people, especially in the low-income countries of Asia, Africa and Latin America, went without adequate food. It sought to make a distinction between the world hunger problem and the world food problem, noting that while increased food production was important to deal with hunger, ultimate success was impossible until the undernourished had access to meaningful employment and income-generating opportunities, which could come about mainly through greater output and productivity of the food and agriculture sectors. Therefore, in the panel's view, the problem of hunger had to be tackled at the national level where most of the economic and financial decisions influencing the overall food situation were made.

The report identified the global food problem as the inability to reconcile the increasing commercialization of domestic and international agricultural trade with divergent national agricultural policies and expanding food surpluses. To deal with it, the panel called on the industrially advanced countries to begin shaping their national agricultural policies by understanding their implications for international prices and the low-income countries, the nexus where the global food and hunger problems came together.

Another assessment effort, initiated by WFC in response to a 1982 decision,[1] was a progress report by the Executive Director covering the past decade, with focus on the role of multilateral agencies in eradicating hunger.[4] Describing multilateral resources as a salient factor in implementing the 1974 World Food Conference resolutions, the report concluded that they had been applied in conformity with the Conference's objectives and the evolving needs of the developing countries. The main emphasis was placed on low-income countries, the small farmer and rural poor, with considerable resources assigned to technical assistance for strengthening individual and institutional capacity and to application of improved technologies. At the same time, however, the report noted faltering support in the 1980s for the work of the multilateral agencies, demonstrated by dwindling resources available multilaterally for food and agriculture. In the Executive Director's view, sustained progress in attaining the Conference's goals could be achieved only if multilateral institutions were to play a central role in concerting national and international efforts. Despite certain co-ordination problems (see below), the report affirmed the importance of continued support for multilateral agencies, emphasizing that strategic decisions to that end by the world community were unavoidable.

Specific problems related to co-ordination among multilateral agencies were reviewed by the Executive Director in another report[5] prepared for the tenth ministerial session of WFC. The review was limited to examining two related areas of inter-agency co-ordination: the delineation of institutional policies and resource allocation, and the co-ordination of project and programme implementation. The report concluded that co-operation among the multilateral agencies was more pervasive than had been generally recognized. However, to overcome jurisdictional disputes and further improve co-ordination, Governments and agencies should work together towards eradicating hunger and malnutrition. The importance of an expanded policy framework raised what the Executive Director saw as the central co-ordination issue: how to assure convergence of action at the country level in order to implement a coherent set of policies and programmes that promoted food and nutrition objectives.

The most difficult problems were found in the least developed countries, especially in Africa. Inability of their Governments to keep up with management and co-ordination requirements, while receiving aid from a multiplicity of agencies, highlighted the importance of a more unified multi-agency approach under United Nations

auspices and underscored a key role for United Nations resident co-ordinators, who continued to be responsible for co-ordinating United Nations operational activities for development in individual countries (see Chapter II of this section).

A mutual political and diplomatic accord among aid agencies and host Governments on the direction of development efforts, rather than creation of additional co-ordination mechanisms, was seen by the Executive Director as a prerequisite for raising the effectiveness of co-ordination in solving the food problem. In Africa, the food sector could be a unifying theme for all development activities, with a comprehensive "Accord on food" serving to galvanize the necessary political and financial support, providing a focal point for a broader consensus on meeting immediate needs and achieving national food self-determination, and becoming the driving force for sustained development. A better integration of aid in support of national food strategies could improve operational co-ordination of external assistance.

As requested by the Economic and Social Council in July 1983,[6] a global assessment of resource flows through the United Nations system to the food and agriculture sector[7] was prepared for consideration by WFC at its tenth session. Focusing on development assistance as well as expenditures for policy, research and related activities, the study covered the 1974-1982 period and was based on roughly 14,000 data entries collected from 22 organizations. It found a 13.7 per cent annual increase, in real terms, of resource flows to the food and agriculture sector through the United Nations system, with the World Bank supplying more than half of all external resources. Other major sources included WFP, trust funds, the United Nations Development Programme and, towards the latter part of the period, the International Fund for Agricultural Development (IFAD). Among United Nations agencies responsible for programme execution in developing countries, the Food and Agriculture Organization of the United Nations (FAO) remained the major one. Among regions, Asia and the Pacific received 18.5 per cent annual increases in disbursements, expanding its share of all external flows from 29.4 to 43 per cent. By comparison, flows to Africa and to the least developed countries rose annually at 12.1 per cent.

The study found the most rapid growth to be in the subsectors of agricultural credit, forestry and rural development—each in excess of 21 per cent annually. Resource flows to land and water had an annual incease of 16.7 per cent to comprise more than 25 per cent of total resource flows by 1982, whereas flows to nutrition, livestock, crops and agricultural support services declined as a percentage of total flows. The report noted that since 1974 the international community had accelerated its resource commitments and disbursements in response to the consensus achieved at the World Food Conference. None the less, the magnitude of resource flows, bilateral as well as multilateral, had remained short of widely acknowledged resource needs. In addition, the rate of growth of commitments for food and agriculture was declining, with a consequential effect on disbursements in the near future.

WFC activities. Marking the tenth anniversary of the World Food Conference, WFC met for its tenth ministerial session at Addis Ababa, Ethiopia, from 11 to 15 June 1984.[8] The 36-member Council—the world's highest-level body dealing with food problems—reviewed the progress made during the past decade, noting that the global food situation had become more complex and was characterized by large imbalances and the increasing risks of food insecurity in many low-income developing countries despite an improved supply of food world-wide. While conceding that the Conference's goal of eliminating hunger and malnutrition within a decade had proved unattainable, WFC reaffirmed the feasibility of reaching that objective in the foreseeable future and stressed the need for much greater emphasis on food and development problems. It described sub-Saharan Africa as the centre of the food problem, and noted that Asia, although progressing towards self-reliance, still had most of the world's chronically undernourished, while Latin America's advances in the commercial food and agricultural sector had been made largely at the expense of the subsistence farm sector. Citing the persisting instability of agricultural markets, WFC recommended that all countries avoid self-centred policies and promote real dialogue for improving international commodity and financial markets.

To meet the World Food Conference objectives, WFC concluded that the following major tasks had to be addressed: increased food production and improved access to food supplies by the developing countries; an accelerated reduction of chronic hunger and malnutrition; resolution of the African food and development crisis; further negotiation of measures to aid developing countries in the event of global food shortages; reduction of trade protectionism and international market instability; resolution of the serious financial problems of developing countries; and sustained development assistance, with a strengthened role for multilateral agencies and improved international assistance coordination. The Council also reaffirmed that peace and disarmament were prerequisites to enhanced food security and that food was a universal human right.

Special emphasis was placed on national food policies and agro-food systems. WFC stressed the urgent need for more autonomous economic growth strategies and national food strategies, which encouraged improved co-ordination of food and agricultural policies with technical operations and investments. It recognized that an integrated food strategy approach would be of even greater importance in the future, when feeding large urban populations and providing employment for the vastly increased rural and urban populations would become the two priority objectives at the national level. With regard to the problems of chronic hunger and malnutrition, WFC resolved that it must put greater emphasis on removing political, economic and social barriers to more equitable access to food by all people. It also called for increased support for small-holders, underlining the importance of beneficial pricing policies, and of co-operatives and agricultural institutions blending modern management practices with traditional cultural patterns.

Concerning the situation in Africa, WFC noted that the region faced a food crisis of the gravest proportions and called on donors and multilateral agencies to step up emergency supplies to the highly affected countries. It also stressed the need for additional financial resources for logistic support, called for greater integration of short-term relief with medium-term rehabilitation measures and longer-term social and economic objectives, identified the major priority areas for concentrating internal and external resources during the next decade, and stressed the need for regional and subregional co-operation. WFC requested further steps to promote co-operation between Africa and other regions and supported efforts of the Secretary-General to increase international awareness of the economic and social crisis in Africa and to promote additional international support.

The Council attached great importance to the fact that, since 1974, multilateral agencies had implemented many of the specific proposals called for by the World Food Conference to deal with emergencies and food security. The means for meeting emergency situations had been much improved, it said. Among them, the Global Information and Early Warning System of FAO could identify production shortfalls and potential food crises, and the International Emergency Food Reserve, administered by WFP, proved to be effective in mobilizing emergency assistance. There had been a better conceptualization of the elements that comprised food security and their application: FAO now related many of its ongoing programme activities to an integrated food-security concept and was attracting extrabudgetary resources to help make national food systems operational; WFC had placed world food security within the context of national food strategies, as well as of international policies; food aid, as carried out by WFP, now operated as a development resource and as a transfer of income, usually to the most needy people in the poorest countries; and the cereal facility of the International Monetary Fund (IMF), though used only on limited occasions since its establishment in mid-1981, provided balance-of-payments relief to food-deficit countries experiencing temporary increases in the cost of their cereal imports.

With regard to the role of multilateral agencies, WFC noted that, although a larger proportion of total food aid was moving through their channels, needs were larger than a decade ago and food aid levels were way below the growing cereal-import requirements of many low-income developing countries. The Council also stressed the role of multilateral agencies in rendering technical and financial support, particularly in promoting measures to increase income and employment, as well as other poverty-related measures for reaching chronically hungry groups. Expressing deep concern that the world-wide recession had set back prospects of increased food security for developing countries, WFC agreed on the value of more open trade and reaffirmed its position against the use of food as an instrument of political pressure. Another matter of concern was an apparent erosion of the 1974 international understanding for increased financial assistance in support of the food and agricultural sectors of developing countries, although the impetus of the World Food Conference had resulted in a doubling of external resources, in real terms, during the 1970s. Referring to the global assessment of resource flows,[7] the Council emphasized the need to reverse the tide of declining aid; it supported the Executive Director's recommendation that donor countries devote more of their aid flows (at least $5 billion over five years, starting in 1986) to promoting the implementation of food strategies of low-income developing countries.

Improvements in international co-operation and changes in national decision-making structures were seen by WFC as an integral part of the commitment to eliminate hunger and malnutrition. It stressed that the real problem of co-ordination lay not only in the food agencies themselves, but also in the different objectives and policy orientations of non-food agencies, particularly financial institutions. Additionally, there was a need for greater participation of non-governmental organizations in a better co-ordinated international co-operative effort.

In conclusion, WFC affirmed that hunger was largely a man-made phenomenon resulting from human error and neglect; asserted that its most important task was to maintain confidence that hunger could be eradicated in our time and that, to achieve that goal, it was WFC's responsibility to monitor and advocate innovative approaches; expressed commitment to act as a catalyst for concerted action; commended to the Economic and Social Council that a special session of the General Assembly on Africa be convened; and invited the international community to renew its commitment to eradicate hunger and malnutrition by no later than the end of the century.

The WFC conclusions and recommendations were reiterated by its Executive Director in his statement before the General Assembly's Second (Economic and Financial) Committee on 17 October 1984.

ECONOMIC AND SOCIAL COUNCIL ACTION

On 25 July, on the recommendation of its First (Economic) Committee, the Economic and Social Council adopted resolution 1984/54 without vote.

Tenth anniversary of the World Food Conference

The Economic and Social Council,

Recalling the Universal Declaration on the Eradication of Hunger and Malnutrition as adopted by the World Food Conference and the Programme of Action as adopted by the World Conference on Agrarian Reform and Rural Development,

Recalling also Economic and Social Council resolution 1983/71 of 29 July 1983 and General Assembly resolution 38/158 of 19 December 1983,

Noting with appreciation the documentation prepared for the tenth session of the World Food Council, in particular the report prepared in co-operation with the Department of International Economic and Social Affairs of the United Nations Secretariat on the global assessment of resource flows through the United Nations system to the food and agriculture sector, requested by the Economic and Social Council in paragraph 10 of its resolution 1983/77 of 29 July 1983,

1. *Welcomes* the report of the World Food Council on the work of its tenth session, held at Addis Ababa from 11 to 15 June 1984, endorses the conclusions and recommendations of the Council, as adopted, and recommends them to the General Assembly at its thirty-ninth session for consideration;

2. *Recommends* that the General Assembly, at its thirty-ninth session, should appropriately mark the tenth anniversary of the World Food Conference, held at Rome from 5 to 16 November 1974, taking into account the ten-year assessment of the world food economy carried out by the World Food Council.

Economic and Social Council resolution 1984/54

25 July 1984   Meeting 48   Adopted without vote

Approved by First Committee (E/1984/143) without vote, 20 July (meeting 15); 21-nation draft (E/1984/C.1/L.18), orally revised; agenda item 11.

Sponsors: Australia, Bangladesh, Canada, Egypt, Ethiopia, France, Germany, Federal Republic of, Ghana, Italy, Kenya, Malaysia, Mexico, Netherlands, Nigeria, Pakistan, Papua New Guinea, Thailand, Tunisia, United Republic of Tanzania, United States, Venezuela.

GENERAL ASSEMBLY ACTION

On 17 December, on the recommendation of the Second Committee, the General Assembly adopted resolution 39/166 without vote.

Food and agricultural problems

The General Assembly,

Recalling the Declaration and the Programme of Action on the Establishment of a New International Economic Order, contained in its resolutions 3201(S-VI) and 3202(S-VI) of 1 May 1974, the Charter of Economic Rights and Duties of States, contained in its resolution 3281(XXIX) of 12 December 1974, its resolution 3362(S-VII) of 16 September 1975 on development and international economic co-operation, and the International Development Strategy for the Third United Nations Development Decade, contained in the annex to its resolution 35/56 of 5 December 1980,

Stressing the imperative need to keep food and agricultural issues at the centre of global attention,

Having considered the grave situation of food and agriculture in many developing countries, especially the critical and deteriorating situation in Africa, further exacerbated by prolonged drought and accelerating desertification, and the persistent problem of food shortages in food-deficit developing countries, particularly the least developed countries,

Recognizing that, although the overall aggregate world food supply situation has steadily improved over the past decade, the numbers of hungry and malnourished are increasing and the risks of food insecurity are now greater for many developing countries, and that the situation thus demands additional efforts,

Reaffirming that food and agricultural problems in developing countries should be considered in a comprehensive manner in their different dimensions, as well as in their immediate short-term and long-term perspectives,

Reaffirming the Universal Declaration on the Eradication of Hunger and Malnutrition, adopted ten years ago by the World Food Conference, and the Programme of Action adopted by the World Conference on Agrarian Reform and Rural Development,

1. *Reaffirms* its resolutions 38/158 of 19 December 1983 on food problems and 38/159 of 19 December 1983 on the critical situation of food and agriculture in Africa, as well as all other relevant resolutions concerning food and agriculture, and calls for their immediate and effective implementation;

2. *Welcomes* the conclusions and recommendations of the World Food Council at its tenth ministerial session, held at Addis Ababa from 11 to 15 June 1984;

3. *Welcomes* the ninth annual report of the Committee on Food Aid Policies and Programmes;

4. *Urges* the international community, on the occasion of the tenth anniversary of the World Food Conference, to rededicate itself to the objective of that Conference and intensify concerted efforts for the fulfilment of its commitment to eliminate hunger and malnutrition as soon as possible, and definitely by the end of the present century, and in this regard, calls upon Governments and international organizations to give particular attention to the measures agreed to by the World Food Council at its tenth ministerial session as the major tasks for achieving the objectives of that Conference;

5. *Reaffirms* that the maintenance of peace and security and the strengthening of international co-operation in food and agriculture are important for improved economic conditions and enhanced food security;

6. *Reaffirms* that the right to food is a universal human right which should be guaranteed to all people, and, in that context, believes in the general principle that food should not be used as an instrument of political pressure;

7. *Reaffirms* that urgent action should be taken to increase food production, which is one of the most important elements in meeting the food needs of the developing countries, and that, in this regard, sustained efforts at the national, regional and international levels should be pursued and that the national food strategies, plans and programmes of developing countries should play a central role in the process of establishing priorities, in co-ordinating national and international funding and in the application of technology, in order to promote food production and increase the national self-reliance of the developing countries;

8. *Calls upon* the international community to support the efforts of the developing countries facing constraints in the development of their food and agricultural production to enable them to achieve self-reliance;

9. *Stresses* that measures taken by developed countries to reduce future food and agricultural production should not adversely affect the food problems faced by developing countries;

10. *Calls upon* the international community to accord greater support towards realization of the enlarged and integrated concept of world food security, focusing on the adequacy of food supplies and production, stability of food supplies and markets, and security of access to supplies, as defined by the Committee on World Food Security of the Food and Agriculture Organization of the United Nations at its eighth session;

11. *Stresses* that significant advances in food and agricultural research and technology and their application in developing countries need to be sustained, improved and made more widespread to encompass all of those countries; in this context, the needs of the African countries and the least developed countries should be given special attention;

12. *Emphasizes* the need to reverse any declining trends in aid commitments to food and agriculture and calls upon the international community, particularly the developed countries, to increase the flow of resources to adequate levels, through all channels, in support of programmes and policies for increasing food and agricultural production and raising nutritional standards in the developing countries, particularly in Africa and the least developed countries, keeping in view the proposal made by the Executive Director of the World Food Council at its tenth session for increases of at least $5 billion in external resources over five years, starting in 1986, in roughly equal proportions for both capital and programme assistance, to be channelled through existing agencies and programmes;

13. *Stresses* the need for the successful completion of the first replenishment of the International Fund for Agricultural Development, and urges all countries concerned, bearing in mind the particular contribution of the developed countries, to reach agreement on a priority basis for the second replenishment, in order to enable the Fund to continue its effective contribution at an adequate level;

14. *Further urges* developed countries to provide supplementary financing for the seventh replenishment of the International Development Association in order to

cover the shortfall and enable the Association to increase its assistance to developing countries, particularly in the development of food and agriculture;

15. *Further stresses* the need to ensure achievement of the agreed target for regular resources of the World Food Programme of $1.35 billion for the biennium 1985-1986;

16. *Emphasizes* the need for effective implementation of the 1980 Food Aid Convention, which has been extended until 30 June 1986;

17. *Expresses deep concern* that the food-financing facility of the International Monetary Fund has been used only on limited occasions since its establishment and, in this regard, looks forward to the upcoming review of the facility by the Fund;

18. *Considers* that improvement of the conditions of farmer groups particularly affected by the small size of holdings or other constraints is critical;

19. *Emphasizes* the role of women as part of the rural family, calls for more policy attention to the role of women in relation to food systems, and stresses the need to involve women in the formulation, implementation and follow-up of national food strategies, plans and projects;

20. *Urges* the international community to respond immediately, adequately and in a concerted manner to the initiative of the Secretary-General and the appeal of the Director-General of the Food and Agriculture Organization of the United Nations in favour of the African countries threatened by severe food shortages by continuing and increasing emergency food and technical assistance to those countries, as well as by augmenting all forms of assistance towards rehabilitation of their food and agricultural sectors;

21. *Notes* that the proliferation of import restrictions and increasing export subsidization are seen to have contributed to international market instability and to growing resource allocation distortions in developed and developing countries, that all countries should demonstrate the requisite political will by refraining from creating tariff obstacles to agricultural imports, especially those from developing countries, and that exporting countries should endeavour to limit export subsidies and analogous practices which might hinder trade, especially that of developing countries;

22. *Stresses, inter alia,* that in order to attain an overall solution of food and agricultural problems, efforts should be made to resolve the serious financial problems in general, and liquidity problems in particular, confronting the developing countries, which are caused to a large degree by the impact of the increases in interest rates;

23. *Reaffirms* the commitment to sustained and increased development assistance in the food sector, with a strengthened role for multilateral co-operation and improved international assistance co-ordination;

24. *Stresses* the need for strengthening subregional, regional and interregional co-operation for the promotion of food security and the development of agriculture in developing countries and, in this context, calls upon the relevant entities of the United Nations system to accord priority support to economic and technical co-operation among developing countries in food and agriculture;

25. *Welcomes* the comprehensive and systematic review of the progress in agrarian reform and rural development carried out by the Food and Agriculture Organization of the United Nations in the context of the implementation of the Programme of Action as adopted by the World Conference on Agrarian Reform and Rural Development and looks forward to a similar review in four years.

General Assembly resolution 39/166

17 December 1984   Meeting 103   Adopted without vote

Approved by Second Committee (A/39/790/Add.6) without vote, 6 December (meeting 56); draft by Vice-Chairman (A/C.2/39/L.118), based on informal consultations on draft by Egypt, for Group of 77 (A/C.2/39/L.10); agenda item 80 (f).
Meeting numbers. GA 39th session: 2nd Committee 28, 31, 54, 56; plenary 103.

Apart from drafting changes, the adopted text differed from the original draft submitted by the Group of 77 in a number of ways. The fourth preambular paragraph and operative paragraphs 5, 9 and 23 were added, while a provision dealing with the FAO World Conference on Fisheries Management and Development (see below) was deleted. Paragraphs 4 and 10 were expanded to draw attention, respectively, to the measures agreed at WFC's June session, and the adequacy, stability and security of food supplies, production and markets. A number of paragraphs were reworded considerably, changing emphasis. Thus, instead of urging developed countries to fulfil their pledges under the first replenishment of IFAD and announce their contributions for the second, as proposed in the draft, the adopted text, in paragraph 13, stressed the need for successful completion of the first replenishment and urged all countries concerned, bearing in mind the particular contribution of the developed ones, to agree on the second replenishment. Paragraph 17 expressed concern over the limited use of IMF's financing facility, whereas the draft only requested a review to liberalize its use. While focusing on the same general subject, paragraph 21 did not express, as did the original, the urgent need for developed countries to refrain from imposing various import barriers and using export subsidies.

The USSR did not press to a vote an oral amendment to paragraph 5 by which the Assembly would have reaffirmed that, apart from peace and security, disarmament was also important for improved economic conditions and enhanced food security.

Food problems, particularly with regard to Africa, figured prominently in two other 1984 Assembly resolutions. In its Declaration on the Critical Economic Situation in Africa, adopted by resolution 39/29 (see Chapter III of this section), the Assembly recognized early attainment of national and collective self-reliance in food production by African countries as the first urgent task, noting that national food strategies and integrated rural development plans played an important role, especially in achieving food security. It also recognized the important role of women in food production and stressed the necessity for providing incentives and credit, improving storage and transport, reducing food losses, balancing out agricultural export commodities and food production, diversifying agricultural production and utilizing irrigation potential. In resolution 39/165 on the critical situation of food and agriculture in Africa (see Chapter VIII of this section), the Assembly welcomed WFC's conclusions and recommendations, particularly those relating to the African region. It noted with appreciation the encouraging response by the international community to appeals for alleviating the critical food supply situation there, and called for continued international support of African efforts to increase food production and for additional financial and technical assistance. African countries were encouraged to strengthen their efforts, especially in defining and implementing national food strategies.

Fisheries management and development

Utilization of world fishery resources with a view to enhancing food security of developing countries and their national self-reliance in food production became an important area of activity for various United Nations entities in 1984, culminating in the World Conference on Fisheries Management and Development (see below). Problems related to the application of remote sensing for assessing and harvesting aquatic food supplies were addressed at the ninth annual joint United Nations/FAO international training course, held for 20 participants from 19 developing countries at Rome, Italy, in September.[9]

World Conference on Fisheries

The role of fisheries in solving food problems was high on the agenda of the FAO World Conference on Fisheries Management and Development, which met at Rome from 27 June to 6 July (see PART II, Chapter III). The Conference endorsed a Strategy for Fisheries Management and Development, whose text formed a part of the Conference's report, transmitted to the General Assembly in October,[10] as requested by the Economic and Social Council (see below). The Strategy covered such key areas as the contribution of fisheries to national economic, social and nutritional goals; improvement of national self-reliance in fisheries; rational management and optimum use of fish resources; the special role and needs of small-scale fisheries; international trade in fish and fish products; investment in fisheries; and economic and technical co-operation and international collaboration in fisheries. The Conference also approved five programmes of action, which covered the following interlinked elements: planning, management and development of fisheries; small-scale fisheries development; aquacul-

ture development; international trade in fish and fish products; and the role of fisheries in alleviating undernutrition.

On 17 July, the Secretary-General of the Conference highlighted its results in a statement before the First Committee of the Economic and Social Council.

ECONOMIC AND SOCIAL COUNCIL ACTION

In July, the Council, on the recommendation of its First Committee, adopted decision 1984/164 without vote.

World Conference on Fisheries Management and Development

At its 48th plenary meeting, on 25 July 1984, the Council:

(a) Noted with satisfaction the statement made on 17 July 1984 before the First (Economic) Committee by the Secretary-General of the World Conference on Fisheries Management and Development, convened by the Food and Agriculture Organization of the United Nations at Rome from 27 June to 6 July 1984;

(b) Decided to invite the Director-General of the Food and Agriculture Organization of the United Nations to submit the report of the World Conference on Fisheries Management and Development to the General Assembly at its thirty-ninth session for consideration.

Economic and Social Council decision 1984/164

Adopted without vote

Approved by First Committee (E/1984/143) without vote, 20 July (meeting 15); 5-nation draft (E/1984/C.1/L.13); agenda item 11.
Sponsors: Australia, Canada, Mexico, Netherlands, Pakistan.

GENERAL ASSEMBLY ACTION

On 18 December, on the recommendation of the Second Committee, the General Assembly adopted resolution 39/225 without vote.

World Conference on Fisheries Management and Development

The General Assembly,

Recognizing that the recent developments in the law of the sea have created new opportunities and responsibilities for States and that national and international objectives and policies for fisheries management and development are being re-examined and adjusted,

Recognizing also the relevant provisions of the United Nations Convention on the Law of the Sea,

Bearing in mind the importance of the need to promote improvements in the production and distribution of all food and agricultural products, including those from fisheries, and to raise levels of nutrition and standards of living,

Noting with appreciation the convening of the Food and Agriculture Organization of the United Nations World Conference on Fisheries Management and Development at Rome from 27 June to 6 July 1984, with a view to promoting the optimum utilization of world fishery resources from the economic, social and nutritional points of view, increasing the contribution of fisheries to national self-reliance in food production and towards food security, enhancing the capacity of developing countries in the management and development of fisheries and fostering international co-operation in fisheries between developed and developing countries and among developing countries themselves,

1. *Endorses* the Strategy for Fisheries Management and Development and the associated programmes of action adopted by the World Conference on Fisheries Management and Development;

2. *Invites* States and international organizations concerned to take into account the principles and guidelines contained in the Strategy when planning the management and development of fisheries;

3. *Urges* all bilateral and multilateral donor agencies and financing institutions to provide the support required for the effective implementation of the programmes of action;

4. *Invites* the Food and Agriculture Organization of the United Nations, in collaboration with the organs, organizations and bodies concerned within the United Nations system, to continue to play its important role in assisting States in their efforts towards the improved management and development of fishery resources.

General Assembly resolution 39/225

18 December 1984   Meeting 104   Adopted without vote

Approved by Second Committee (A/39/789) without vote, 30 November (meeting 54); draft by Vice-Chairman (A/C.2/39/L.86), based on informal consultations on draft by Bangladesh, Canada, China, France, Guinea, Jamaica, Mexico, Netherlands, Nicaragua, Pakistan and Philippines (A/C.2/39/L.28); agenda item 12. *Meeting numbers.* GA 39th session: 2nd Committee 41, 54; plenary 104.

In addition to drafting changes, the adopted text differed from the original in its inclusion of the second preambular paragraph.

REFERENCES

[1]YUN 1982, p. 912. [2]WFC/1984/6. [3]YUN 1974, p. 488. [4]WFC/1984/2. [5]WFC/1984/3. [6]YUN 1983, p. 703, ESC res. 1983/77, 29 July 1983. [7]WFC/1984/9. [8]A/39/19. [9]A/AC.105/347. [10]A/C.2/39/6.

PUBLICATION

Rice Bran: An Under-utilized Raw Material (ID/320 & abstract), Sales No. E.84.II.B.3.

Food aid

World Food Programme

For a second consecutive year, 1984 marked record levels of activity for WFP,[1] a joint undertaking of the United Nations and FAO charged with providing food aid to developing countries to support development projects and meet emergency needs. Commitments for both development projects and emergency operations rose substantially as compared with 1983, as did the total amount of food shipped.

Responding to the critical need for food aid in sub-Saharan Africa, WFP increased its emergency assistance, allocating over two thirds of its emergency operations to that region and establishing an Africa Task Force Secretariat as a focal point for all its activities related to the crisis. WFP also worked to strengthen co-ordination between donors and recipient countries, and took steps to lessen, with financial help from the World Bank, the logistical problems impeding the flow of emergency food aid to and within developing countries.

It reviewed various issues related to the function and cost of food aid as a development resource, arranged to strengthen its project cycle and continued work on design and implementation of built-in monitoring and evaluation systems to improve project management and performance assessment.

Highlighting WFP's 1984 activities in his address to the General Assembly's Second Committee, the WFP Executive Director stressed that food aid constituted some 10 per cent of total global development assistance. In order for it to be effective for development, food aid must be co-ordinated with technical and financial assistance, which prompted WFP's efforts to improve co-operation with the World Bank and seek closer ties with the African Development Bank and IFAD. The Executive Director saw WFP's role in helping co-ordinate all food aid as its greatest contribution in major emergencies, but emphasized that this was a highly specialized and complex task requiring further strengthening of WFP capabilities.

Food aid policies and programmes

CFA activities. At its seventeenth session, held at Rome from 28 May to 9 June 1984,[2] the Committee on Food Aid Policies and Programmes (CFA), the WFP governing body, conducted its ninth annual review of food aid policies and programmes, focusing mainly on the use of food aid in sub-Saharan Africa in support of an employment-led, equitable growth strategy for rural areas. The Committee generally agreed that the problem of hunger must be tackled at the national level, where decisions should be made on a whole range of agricultural, economic, financial and social matters, and unanimously upheld the view that food aid should be integrated into the national development plans of recipient countries, to provide an incentive for increased production and to support humanitarian objectives. It urged all donors to stimulate food production in, and trade among, developing countries in order to make food aid more effective. The Committee noted that despite significant advances in implementing the recommendations of the 1974 World Food Conference, the minimum annual food aid target of 10 million tons of grain had yet to be attained and forward planning of food aid on a multi-annual basis had been undertaken only on a limited scale. Total food aid had not increased and the ability of low-income countries to purchase their food imports on commercial terms had declined.

The Committee approved 34 projects, among them 17 project expansions, at a total cost of $557.5 million and 13 budget increases for approved projects; the combined value of projects and budget increases amounted to over $600 million or an equivalent of 1.2 million metric tons of food.

The Committee held its eighteenth session at Rome from 29 October to 8 November 1984.[3] It considered a report of the United Nations Joint Inspection Unit (JIU) on WFP personnel problems and an interim report by WFP and FAO reviewing the basis of costing of services provided by FAO. As a result of the JIU report, the Secretary-General and the FAO Director-General decided to establish a task force to review problems between WFP and FAO. The Committee urged the task force to address all matters regarding the interpretation of rights and responsibilities. It agreed that the basic relationship with the United Nations and FAO should be preserved and improved, and that there was no question of WFP becoming a separate agency.

Continuing its review of selected national experiences, the Committee supported efforts to use food aid as a broad-based development resource to augment Lesotho's drive to increase production, employment and incomes in rural areas. In view of the serious food crisis in many African countries, the Committee allocated an additional $10 million to the 1984 emergency budget from WFP's regular resources. It also adopted a resolution calling on donors to provide more emergency assistance to the African nations facing starvation and malnutrition, and urging the affected countries to make the utmost effort in distributing food with the co-ordinating assistance of in-country representatives of international organizations.

The Committee approved 22 projects at a total cost of $216.1 million and 16 budget increases for approved projects. The combined value amounted to approximately $240 million, equivalent to about 520,000 tons of food. In addition, 11 projects had been approved by the Executive Director from 1 January to 30 June, at a total cost to WFP of $16.7 million.

ECONOMIC AND SOCIAL COUNCIL ACTION

In July 1984, on the recommendation of its First Committee, the Economic and Social Council adopted decision 1984/165 without vote.

Ninth annual report of the Committee on Food Aid Policies and Programmes

At its 48th plenary meeting, on 25 July 1984, the Council welcomed the ninth annual report of the Committee on Food Aid Policies and Programmes.[4]

Economic and Social Council decision 1984/165

Adopted without vote

Approved by First Committee (E/1984/143) without vote, 20 July (meeting 15); oral proposal by Chairman; agenda item 11.

GENERAL ASSEMBLY ACTION

The ninth annual report of CFA was also welcomed by the General Assembly, in resolution 39/166. In resolution 39/165, the Assembly welcomed the unanimous adoption by CFA on 8 November of a resolution on the food crisis in Africa, and called for its full and prompt implementation (see Chapter VIII of this section).

Development assistance

In 1984, the level of WFP commitments for development projects rose by 33 per cent over the previous year, from $696 million to a record $925 million, while the amount of food shipped grew by 48 per cent, from 1.4 million tons to an unprecedented 2.1 million tons.[1] The programme increase was also reflected in the number of projects approved, which rose from 67 (valued at $577 million) in 1983 to 82 (valued at $808 million) in 1984—a 22 per cent increase. Of the 57 developing countries which received WFP development commitments in 1984, 38 belonged to the low-income or least developed categories. Commitments to low-income, food-deficit countries amounted to $706 million, with an increasing share going to the least developed countries—$348 million, up from $250 million in 1983.

With a prevailing emphasis throughout the year on assistance to sub-Saharan Africa, WFP commitments to that region increased from $168 million to $325 million. In Latin America and the Caribbean, both the volume of assistance and number of projects increased, while commitments in Asia and the Pacific reached an all-time record of $339 million, despite a 5 per cent drop in relative terms from the 42 per cent share in 1983.

Emergency operations

In 1984, WFP committed $233.1 million to provide 740,100 tons of food to 63 emergency operations in 38 countries, as well as $595,700 as a cash subsidy for three operations approved in 1983. This was an almost 12 per cent increase over 1983 in dollar terms and a 13 per cent rise in food volume. Of the 17.6 million people receiving WFP emergency food aid in 1984, the principal beneficiaries (57 per cent) were victims of drought. Of WFP's emergency assistance, 54 per cent (in dollar terms) went for 43 operations in sub-Saharan Africa, 35 per cent for 8 operations in Asia, 9 per cent for 8 operations in Latin America and 2 per cent for 4 operations in North Africa and the Near East.

As in previous years, WFP was involved throughout 1984 in a number of large-scale emergency operations. It continued co-ordinating the procurement and delivery of food aid to Kampuchea and to relief operations along the Thai/Kampuchean border. By the end of 1984, the total cumulative cost of this aid stood at about $367 million, with 237,000 tons of food provided from the International Emergency Food Reserve (IEFR) and 580,000 tons bilaterally. The necessary funds had been mobilized through pledging conferences held in New York in 1984, with pledges of $35 million, and other special appeals. WFP committed 222,500 tons of food for the 2 million Afghan refugees in Pakistan, bringing its total commitment to them since 1979 to over 1 million tons, mainly drawn from IEFR. In sub-Saharan Africa, WFP emergency assistance was implemented in all of the 10 countries identified as most seriously affected by drought and other calamities, as well as nine other affected countries with total commitments amounting to more than 350,000 tons. Additional quantities were committed for countries struck by poor harvests in 1984. WFP's contribution towards the cost of internal transport, storage and handling of its emergency food supplies in seven African countries amounted to $2.8 million; and eight logistical missions were dispatched to assist in identifying measures to improve and accelerate the delivery of food aid. On behalf of bilateral donors, WFP also purchased, shipped or monitored more than 350,000 tons of food to 24 African countries. Eight emergency operations were approved for six Latin American countries, mainly for refugees and displaced persons—victims of the persistent civil strife in the region.

Two evaluations of selected WFP emergency operations were carried out during the year. The evaluations drew attention to the remaining problems of refugee enumeration and food aid planning and scheduling; as a longer-term strategy, the phasing out of free food distribution in favour of food and cash for work was suggested.

WFP resources

Pledges and contributions

By the end of 1984, announced contributions to WFP from 21 donors amounted to 655,449 tons of food at a value of $173 million. Of the total 1984 contributions, 87 per cent were channelled multilaterally through WFP. During the year, the Programme received $150.1 million in cash, of which $104 million came from regular contributions; the balance came from IEFR ($20.1 million), Food Aid Convention (FAC) contributions ($3.1 million), government contributions towards local operating costs ($1 million) and other miscellaneous income. By the end of the year, almost the entire quantity of commodities at the disposal of WFP, including both regular pledges and FAC contributions of all donors, had been called forward and, for the most part, shipped. FAC grains contributed outside the regular programme or IEFR amounted to 38,000 tons, valued at approximately $8.5 million. For the third time since the inception of IEFR, its target of 500,000 tons of cereals was reached in 1984.

By 31 December 1984, pledges by 69 countries totalled $999.8 million or 74 per cent of the $1.35 billion regular pledges target for 1985-1986. Approximately 49 per cent of that goal was reached at the WFP Pledging Conference held in New York on 6 March 1984,[5] when 52 countries pledged $658.3 million worth of contributions.

GENERAL ASSEMBLY ACTION

In resolution 39/166, the General Assembly stressed the need to ensure achievement of the agreed target for WFP regular resources of $1.35 billion for 1985-1986 (see above, under "Food problems").

REFERENCES

[1]E/1985/110.   [2]WFP/CFA:17/21.   [3]WFP/CFA:18/19.
[4]E/1984/117. [5]A/CONF.124/SR.1,2.

FOOD AID FOR DEVELOPMENT

(Projects approved in 1984 by CFA)

Country	Field of activity	Amount (in US dollars)	Country	Field of activity	Amount (in US dollars)
Angola	Assistance to Namibian refugees (SWAPO settlement)	8,094,600	Cape Verde	Assistance to vulnerable groups	7,576,000
	Assistance to peasant associations in Malange province	15,995,000	Chad	Vulnerable group rehabilitation programme	21,009,300
Bangladesh	National relief works programme for land and water development	35,502,300	China	Command area development, Xicha irrigation project, Gansu province	8,630,000
	Feeding and rehabilitation of vulnerable groups	59,329,800		Improvement of camellia tea-oil plantations, Hunan province	14,153,000
Bhutan	Cereal price stabilization scheme	3,077,000		Irrigation in Gansu province	14,251,000
	Construction and improvement of roads and bridges	4,036,500		The Nanwuniu scheme of the Donglei irrigation project, Shanxi province	16,082,000
Botswana	Assistance to primary schoolchildren and vulnerable groups	14,054,000		Rural road construction for developing mountainous areas, Shanxi province	7,390,800
Brazil	Feeding of pre-school and primary schoolchildren in depressed areas	38,881,000		Development of aquaculture in low-lying saline-alkaline areas, Hangzhou Bay, Zhejiang province	9,420,000

Country	Field of activity	Amount (in US dollars)
China *(cont.)*	Development of fish and forage production in low-lying, saline-alkaline areas, Tianjin municipality	11,310,000
	Improvement through irrigation of low-yielding lands, Haidong prefecture, Qinghai province	18,745,000
	Command area development, Songtao reservoir, Hainan island	14,884,000
Comoros	Multi-purpose rural development	11,517,700
Cuba	Dairy development, Jimaguayu basin	35,065,000
Cyprus	Assistance to schools and institutions	3,718,400
Democratic Yemen	Development of the fishery sector	14,357,000
	Agricultural development schemes	7,861,600
El Salvador	Rural housing and community infrastructure in agrarian reform areas	3,922,000
Ghana	Forest plantations	9,250,000
	Assistance to oil-palm plantations and rubber estates	10,029,250
	Assistance to railways and ports rehabilitation project	11,372,000
	Rehabilitation of export sector	41,500,000
Guatemala	Community development	10,486,000
Guinea	Multi-purpose rural development	3,473,000
Guinea-Bissau	Multi-purpose rural development	8,383,000
Honduras	Forestry development	4,594,000
	Construction of basic infrastructure and promotion of productive activities in rural and suburban areas	6,603,000
India	Watershed development and afforestation, Uttar Pradesh	31,417,000
Jamaica	Primary school feeding	6,151,600
Jordan	Assistance to primary schools	6,808,000
Lesotho	Primary school feeding	24,373,000
Madagascar	Dairy development	15,389,000
Nepal	Feeding of mothers, infants and children	19,909,000
	Construction and improvement of hill tracks	4,220,000
Nicaragua	Assistance to rural development schemes	8,229,500
Niger	Multi-purpose project in the fields of training, forestry and inland fisheries, rural infrastructure, food security at village level	12,507,000
Pakistan	Supplementary feeding of pre-school children, pregnant women and nursing mothers	32,959,000
	Rural development works, North-West Frontier province	5,122,200
Senegal	Integrated rural development, Fodor and Matam region	2,834,400
	Irrigation development, Senegal River valley	5,302,000
	Conservation and development of natural vegetation	14,952,000
Somalia	Institutional feeding	10,693,000
	Rangeland development and reforestation	6,679,000
Sudan	Assistance to the settlement of Ethiopian and Ugandan refugees	16,238,000
Swaziland	Institutional feeding in the health sector	4,487,000
	Assistance to the education sector	4,251,000
Syrian Arab Republic	Feeding of women trainees, vulnerable groups and primary schoolchildren	30,140,000
United Republic of Tanzania	Dairy development, Zanzibar	1,951,000
Zambia	Infant feeding and prevention of malnutrition	4,257,000
Total		773,422,950

SOURCE: WFP/CFA:17/21, WFP/CFA:18/19.

EMERGENCY ALLOCATIONS APPROVED IN 1984

Country	Nature of emergency	Amount (in US dollars) IEFR	WFP
Angola	Displaced Persons	2,054,700	—
Bangladesh	Flood	6,184,500	5,035,500
	Flood	4,599,000	—
Botswana	Drought	537,000	—
Burkina Faso	Drought	3,296,600	345,200
Burundi	Drought	607,700	243,600
Cameroon	Drought	—	1,288,000
Chad	Drought	1,985,400	3,292,600
	Drought	4,453,000	3,350,000
Colombia	Floods	—	690,000
Djibouti	Drought	1,403,000	312,000
El Salvador	Displaced persons	5,341,100	—
	Displaced persons	4,898,000	—
Ethiopia	Drought	7,345,100	1,690,800
	Refugees	1,518,200	669,300
	Drought	7,119,000	144,000
	Refugees	987,400	—
	Drought	—	420,900
Gambia	Drought	1,634,400	93,600
	Drought	660,000	26,000
Ghana	Drought	4,714,200	—
Guinea	Drought	—	64,800
Honduras	Refugees	1,151,000	471,100
	Refugees	—	1,314,000
Indonesia	Refugees	501,200	164,000
Jordan	Droughts	1,566,900	235,800
Kenya	Drought	2,681,300	947,000
	Drought	4,822,000	1,613,700
Lao People's Democratic Republic	Drought	1,044,000	—
Lebanon	Civil disturbance	567,700	746,700
Lesotho	Drought	1,264,300	—
Mali	Drought	—	110,000
Mauritania	Drought	23,400	—
Mexico	Refugees	1,122,400	846,000
Morocco	Drought	1,940,000	—
Mozambique	Drought	204,500	658,800
	Drought	—	670,200
	Drought	1,980,000	—
Nicaragua	Displaced persons	2,298,000	1,385,100
Niger	Drought	—	1,254,600
	Drought	2,384,000	756,000
Pakistan	Refugees	31,109,000	9,776,000
	Refugees	18,544,200	500
	Refugees	3,840,000	910,000
Peru	Drought	791,300	461,500
Philippines	Typhoon	855,000	195,000
Rwanda	Refugees/returnees	875,800	120,800
	Drought	3,505,000	786,500
Senegal	Drought	2,520,000	—
Somalia	Refugees	4,046,800	—
	Refugees	6,305,700	1,298,300
	Drought	2,791,300	1,242,100
	Refugees	—	3,759,800
Sudan	Refugees	6,491,100	966,900
	Refugees	943,000	260,000
	Drought	1,190,000	—
	Drought	1,531,400	—
	Refugees	2,093,600	228,000
	Drought	3,562,000	1,680,000

Country	Nature of emergency	Amount (in US dollars) IEFR	WFP	Country	Nature of emergency	Amount (in US dollars) IEFR	WFP
Syrian Arab Republic	Refugees	115,100	73,200	Zambia	Drought	1,298,200	1,405,000
Uganda	Displaced persons	591,000	539,900	Zimbabwe	Displaced persons	491,900	354,900
	Drought	—	905,000		Drought	1,483,200	324,000
United Republic of Tanzania	Drought	1,541,500	137,500	Total		179,405,100	54,264,200

SOURCE: WFP/CFA:19/10.

CONTRIBUTIONS UNDER THE INTERNATIONAL EMERGENCY FOOD RESERVE
(as at 31 December 1984)

Contributor	Contribution	Quantity (in metric tons)	Estimated value (including costs for transportation) (in US dollars)	Contributor	Contribution	Quantity (in metric tons)	Estimated value (including costs for transportation) (in US dollars)
Multilateral					Vegetable oil	1,250	1,693,198
Australia	Rice	6,855	1,168,660		SKr 14,675,000	9,468	1,836,792
	Grain	25,000	5,160,000		SKr 15,000,000	1,351	1,808,593
Austria	Grain	5,000	1,800,000		$US 25,000	—	25,000
Belgium	Grain	7,000	1,941,500	Switzerland	Grain	26,469	3,127,870
Canada	$Can 7,000,000	13,700	5,785,124		Sorghum	374	101,000
	$Can 15,000,000	33,759	12,004,900		Dried whole milk	146	408,700
	$Can 3,732,000	6,300	2,848,900	Thailand	Rice	200	50,000
Denmark	DKr 25,000,000	11,722	2,847,091	United Kingdom	Grain	5,000	1,020,000
EEC	Grain	45,000	7,831,850	United States	Various commodities	232,215	70,535,040
	Vegtable oil	1,000	1,153,230				
	Sugar	302	169,714	Subtotal		573,304	155,378,605
Finland	Fmk 11,700,000	1,050	1,993,270				
France	Grain	20,000	4,425,800	*Bilateral*			
Germany, Federal Republic of	Grain	51,000	8,156,000				
				Australia	Grain	18,145	4,735,845
Iceland	$US 8,700	31	8,700	Belgium	Grain	3,000	783,000
Japan	$US 2,000,000	8,500	2,000,000	France	Grain	10,000	2,610,000
Netherlands	Grain	8,250	1,991,430	Italy	$US 5,000,000	20,300	5,000,000
	$US 25,000	—	25,000		Rice	29,000	2,610,000
New Zealand	$NZ 350,000	705	188,523	United States	Various commodities	1,700	1,614,000
Norway	Grain	10,000	2,610,000				
	NKr 7,000,000	1,157	998,203	Subtotal		82,145	17,352,845
	$US 40,000	—	40,000				
Sri Lanka	Rice	500	160,000	Total		655,449	172,731,450
Sweden	Grain	40,000	9,464,517				

SOURCE: WFP/CFA:19/4/Add.1.

CONTRIBUTIONS UNDER THE FOOD AID CONVENTION MADE AVAILABLE TO WFP
(as at 31 December 1984; in US dollars)

CONTRIBUTOR	CROP YEAR 1984/85 Commodity (metric tons)	Value	CASH	CROP YEAR 1985/86 Commodity (metric tons)	Value	CASH
Food Aid Convention net						
Ireland	4,024	663,960	241,440	4,024	643,840	241,440
Norway	30,000	4,950,000	1,800,000	—	—	—
Subtotal	34,024	5,613,960	2,041,440	4,024	643,840	241,440
Convention through regular programme						
Australia	200,000	28,275,000	10,000,000	200,000	28,275,000	10,000,000
Belgium	13,000	2,145,000	780,000	—	—	—
EEC	70,000	11,550,000	4,200,000	70,000	11,200,000	4,200,000
Finland	20,000	3,300,000	1,200,000	20,000	3,200,000	1,200,000
Germany, Federal Republic of	15,000	2,475,000	900,000	15,000	2,400,000	900,000
Netherlands	16,750	3,188,000	1,005,000	16,750	3,188,000	1,005,000
Sweden	40,000	7,131,000	2,400,000	40,000	7,131,000	2,400,000
United Kingdom	50,000	8,250,000	3,000,000	50,000	8,000,000	3,000,000
Subtotal	424,750	66,314,000	23,485,000	411,750	63,394,000	22,705,000

CONTRIBUTOR	CROP YEAR 1984/85			CROP YEAR 1985/86		
	Commodity (metric tons)	Value	CASH	Commodity (metric tons)	Value	CASH
Convention through IEFR*						
Australia	31,855	5,022,000	1,307,000	—	—	—
Belgium	5,000	825,000	485,000	—	—	—
EEC	40,000	6,600,000	3,880,000	40,000	6,400,000	3,880,000
Germany, Federal Republic of	20,000	3,300,000	1,417,000	20,000	3,200,000	1,940,000
Netherlands	8,250	1,361,000	800,000	8,250	1,320,000	800,000
Switzerland	10,000	1,650,000	970,000	10,000	1,600,000	970,000
United Kingdom	5,000	825,000	485,000	5,000	800,000	485,000
Subtotal	120,105	19,583,000	9,344,000	83,250	13,320,000	8,075,000
Total	578,879	91,510,960	34,870,440	499,024	77,357,840	31,021,440

*Under IEFR, donor countries cover all transportation costs.

SOURCE: WFP/CFA:19/4/Add.1.

CONTRIBUTIONS TO THE WORLD FOOD PROGRAMME, 1984

(as at 31 December 1984; in US dollar equivalent)

Contributor	Commodities	Cash and services	Total	Contributor	Commodities	Cash and services	Total
Algeria	—	132,250	132,250	Kuwait	—	500,000	500,000
Angola	—	10,201	10,201	Lao People's Democratic Republic	—	1,000	1,000
Argentina	1,396,704	—	1,396,704	Lebanon	—	21,791	21,791
Australia	16,280,679	6,463,372	22,744,051	Luxembourg	—	11,887	11,887
Austria	2,319,145	300,000	2,619,145	Malaysia	—	4,274	4,274
Belgium	505,934	610,872	1,116,806	Morocco	—	18,321	18,321
Benin	—	5,083	5,083	Mozambique	—	2,108	2,108
Bolivia	—	10,000	10,000	Netherlands	13,798,079	6,679,452	20,477,531
Brazil	—	150,000	150,000	New Zealand	356,505	175,439	531,944
Burundi	—	1,269	1,269	Norway	11,228,407	5,180,607	16,409,014
Canada	89,579,954	15,444,246	105,024,200	Pakistan	348,142	—	348,142
Chile	—	25,000	25,000	Panama	—	1,000	1,000
China	—	300,000	300,000	Portugal	—	45,000	45,000
Colombia	—	3,000	3,000	Republic of Korea	—	50,000	50,000
Cuba	492,986	—	492,986	Saudi Arabia	14,038,936	6,875,000	20,913,936
Cyprus	—	1,755	1,755	Somalia	—	641	641
Denmark	9,957,424	4,944,924	14,902,348	Spain	—	200,000	200,000
Ecuador	—	4,753	4,753	Sri Lanka	56,883	—	56,883
Egypt	161,024	—	161,024	Suriname	—	7,500	7,500
EEC	50,340,885	9,485,250	59,826,135	Sweden	6,087,275	2,988,506	9,075,781
Finland	5,282,123	1,877,966	7,160,089	Switzerland	1,258,324	1,087,963	2,346,287
France	2,499,850	2,080,455	4,580,305	Thailand	35,000	—	35,000
Germany, Federal Republic of	8,018,223	6,180,808	14,199,031	Togo	—	3,317	3,317
Greece	147,255	—	147,255	Tunisia	—	36,400	36,400
Honduras	—	10,000	10,000	Turkey	(42,711)	—	(42,711)
Hungary	100,972	—	100,972	United Kingdom	9,801,678	4,654,240	14,455,918
Iceland	—	20,000	20,000	United Republic of Tanzania	—	15,201	15,201
India	673,447	—	673,447	United States	92,188,930	22,128,051	114,316,981
Ireland	833,164	383,963	1,217,127	Uruguay	—	1,902	1,902
Israel	—	2,500	2,500	Venezuela	—	46,512	46,512
Italy	58,547	2,105,263	2,163,810	Yemen	—	3,000	3,000
Japan	4,675,333	2,337,667	7,013,000	Yugoslavia	540,000	—	540,000
Jordan	—	37,500	37,500	Total	343,019,097	103,668,049	446,687,146
Kenya	—	840	840				

SOURCE: WFP/CFA:20/15.

Chapter XII

Science and technology

Responding to demands for a restructuring of international scientific and technological relations, the United Nations continued in 1984 its efforts to strengthen the related capacities of developing countries by mobilizing financial resources, upgrading institutional arrangements and balancing the international flows of technology within the framework provided by the 1979 Vienna Programme of Action. A major effort to review progress in implementing the Vienna Programme's operational plan and map out further measures needed to accelerate the process was undertaken in analytical reports by the Secretary-General and the Director-General for Development and International Economic Co-operation (DIEC). Several *ad hoc* panels and workshops met in 1984 to provide expert advice on such specific problems as long-term perspectives on science and technology, scientific and technological indicators for development, and integration of emerging and traditional technologies.

A central role in financing various activities was played by the United Nations Financing System for Science and Technology for Development (UNFSSTD). Although uncertainty about its long-term financial prospects had hindered the mobilization of resources through regular pledging procedures, UNFSSTD initiated a number of new projects and programming activities with funds provided directly from Governments and from such non-core mechanisms as cost-sharing and trust funds, which yielded $4.7 million in 1984. Long-term financial and institutional arrangements of UNFSSTD were considered by the General Assembly, which decided in December to establish an informal open-ended intergovernmental working group for a speedy conclusion of the arrangements, while urging all countries to contribute to the System's operation under existing procedures (decision 39/428).

The Intergovernmental Committee on Science and Technology for Development, the main directing and policy-making body, held its sixth session in May/June 1984, focusing special attention on implementation of the Vienna Programme, on strengthening the role of the Committee and on improving the effectiveness of its work methods. The Assembly, in December, supported those initiatives, in particular the Committee's decision to select in advance the themes for its sessions (resolution 39/164). The Committee also considered activities of its Advisory Committee on Science and Technology for Development, which met for its fourth session in February, and of the United Nations Centre for Science and Technology for Development. Charged with the task of providing substantive assistance to the Intergovernmental Committee and co-ordinating United Nations activities at the Secretariat level, the Centre proceeded with efforts to initiate the Advance Technology Alert System, continued its feasibility study of indicators for measuring the impact of science and technology on national development and prepared the first biennial review of United Nations implementation of the Vienna Programme. In the area of inter-agency co-operation, it provided assistance to the Task Force on Science and Technology for Development, which held its fifth session in January, adopting recommendations on a variety of issues, including United Nations joint activities, criteria for building endogenous capacities of developing countries, and further actions by United Nations entities to strengthen their role in science and technology.

The problem of balancing flows of technology between industrialized and developing countries remained high on the agenda of United Nations bodies in 1984, particularly the United Nations Conference on Trade and Development (UNCTAD). UNCTAD's Committee on Transfer of Technology, at its first special session in February, took up the question of a strategy for the technological transformation of developing countries; at its fifth regular session in December, it considered a broad spectrum of economic, commercial, developmental, legal and organizational issues related to the international transfer of technology. The question of the reverse transfer of technology, or brain drain, was again a concern of the General Assembly which requested, in resolution 39/211, the organizing of further meetings of governmental experts and of the Inter-Agency Group on Reverse Transfer of Technology.

Topics related to this chapter. Disarmament: peaceful uses of science and technology. Operational activities for development: technical co-operation among developing countries. Industrial development: industrial technology. Regional economic and social activities: science and technology in Africa; Asia and the Pacific—science and technology; Europe—science and technology. Human rights: human rights and science and technology. Women: science and technology and women.

Implementation of the Vienna Programme of Action

General aspects

Efforts to implement the 1979 Vienna Programme of Action on Science and Technology for Development[1] and improve the effectiveness of its 1981 operational plan[2] constituted a significant part of United Nations activities in science and technology throughout 1984. As requested by the Intergovernmental Committee on Science and Technology for Development in June 1983,[3] the Secretary-General submitted to the Committee's May/June 1984 session an analytical report[4] reviewing the progress made by the United Nations system in implementing the operational plan over the 1982-1983 budgetary cycle. The report appraised the principal activities of United Nations bodies under each of the plan's eight programme areas and assessed their overall impact, focusing primarily on the programmes which had received major resources. Aimed mainly at providing information and advisory services to science and technology institutions and personnel in developing countries, those activities proved to have direct impact in areas such as development of institutional and human infrastructure and resulted in valuable exchanges of views and knowledge in other fields. The report concluded that, despite positive developments, there continued to be substantial scope and potential for further improvement, in both the formulation and implementation of United Nations programmes.

Further measures to accelerate implementation of the Vienna Programme of Action were considered by the Secretary-General in another report to the Intergovernmental Committee.[5] Progress could be achieved, in his view, by improving co-ordination of the medium-term plans and programme budgets of the United Nations system, promoting action at the national level, and enhancing the role of funding institutions and inter-governmental and non-governmental organizations (NGOs). With regard to evaluation and follow-up measures, the report pointed to the need to streamline the Committee's review process, establish country review mechanisms and develop indicators on science and technology for development. The question of upgrading United Nations joint activities was tackled by the DIEC Director-General in a March report[6] which reviewed financing and consultation processes and mapped out venues for additional joint ventures (see below, under "Institutional arrangements").

Implementation of the Vienna Programme of Action was high on the agenda of the fifth session (Rome, Italy, 17-19 January) of the Task Force on Science and Technology for Development of the Administrative Committee on Co-ordination (ACC). Among key issues under consideration were the status of joint activities, criteria for building endogenous capacities in developing countries and further actions by United Nations entities to strengthen their role in science and technology. In a report on the session,[7] the Task Force noted that there had been serious efforts in formulating joint activities, but underscored the need for extrabudgetary resources and suggested methods of improving contacts with funding institutions and donor countries. The Task Force stressed that it was up to the countries and financing bodies to determine priorities and advised against a search for additional joint projects. With regard to building endogenous capacities in the developing countries, three ways of action were proposed: providing information to the Intergovernmental Committee on assessment studies by other United Nations organizations; contracting national institutions to study criteria for endogenous capacities; and launching joint inter-agency missions under the Task Force's authority to assist selected countries in capacity-building. In relation to further action to strengthen the role of the United Nations system in science and technology, the Task Force agreed that it would not currently be opportune to identify new areas for joint planning and that efforts should be made to implement fully existing activities.

Various other issues related to implementation of the Vienna Programme, including science and technology indicators, the Advance Technology Alert System and a global network of scientific and technological information, were considered by the Advisory Committee on Science and Technology for Development in February (see below).

Intergovernmental Committee action. The Intergovernmental Committee, on 8 June,[8] noted the Secretary-General's biennial review of United Nations activities[4] and the DIEC Director-General's report on United Nations joint activities in implementation of the Vienna Programme.[6] The Committee emphasized the need for greater co-ordination of United Nations science and technology programmes. It invited the Economic and Social Council to request United Nations entities to consider ways of enhancing co-ordination and give special consideration to the Vienna Programme, its operational plan and the Intergovernmental Committee's resolutions. In another resolution of the same date,[9] the Committee recommended that the Vienna Programme be popularized in a small booklet and that the Advisory Committee review to what extent the scientific progress since 1979 had influenced its implementation.

In July 1984, on the recommendation of its First (Economic) Committee, the Economic and Social Council adopted decision 1984/168 without vote.

Implementation of the Vienna Programme of Action on Science and Technology for Development

At its 48th plenary meeting, on 25 July 1984, the Council requested the organs and organizations of the United Nations system to consider ways and means of enhancing the co-ordination of their medium-term plans and programme budgets in the field of science and technology for development and to give special consideration to the guidelines of the Vienna Programme of Action on Science and Technology for Development and its operational plan and to the resolutions of the Intergovernmental Committee on Science and Technology for Development.

Economic and Social Council decision 1984/168

Adopted without vote

Approved by First Committee (E/1984/147) without vote, 20 July (meeting 14); oral proposal by Chairman; agenda item 16.

In resolution 39/164 of 17 December, the General Assembly took note of Council decision 1984/168.

NGO participation

In accordance with a June 1983 recommendation of the Intergovernmental Committee,[10] the Centre for Science and Technology for Development convened at Amsterdam, Netherlands, from 24 to 26 January 1984, the first meeting of the NGO Steering Committee, established in 1983. The meeting recommended a series of specific tasks for NGOs regarding implementation of the Vienna Programme.

Advisory Committee consideration. Reviewing the results of an April 1983 panel of experts on the role of regional associations[11] and endorsing its recommendations, the Advisory Committee, at its February 1984 session,[12] emphasized that NGOs could provide essential inputs to the development process. The Committee felt that NGOs could be particularly effective in defining research and development priorities, objectives and programmes, as well as in assisting countries that did not possess a critical mass of scientists and technologists and in developing working relationships with regional intergovernmental and international organizations. The Committee urged the popularization of science and technology, with due attention to aspirations of women and youth. Noting that one of the most serious obstacles to popularization efforts in developing countries was the lack of good science communicators, it recommended that NGOs enhance their role in that area.

Intergovernmental Committee action. In a resolution of 8 June,[13] the Intergovernmental Committee encouraged the Centre for science and technology to involve NGOs more in its activities. By a decision of the same date,[14] it took note of the oral report of the Chairman of the Steering Committee of the Centre's NGO Advisory Group on its January meeting at Amsterdam (see above) and encouraged NGOs to continue to co-operate with the Intergovernmental Committee in implementing the Vienna Programme.

Scientific and technological policies

Long-term perspectives

The adverse impact of the world economic recession on implementation of the Vienna Programme continued to be a cause of particular concern in 1984. Following up on its February 1983 proposal,[15] the Advisory Committee considered in February 1984[12] the scope of the topic for an *ad hoc* panel of specialists on long-term global perspectives of science and technology for development, to be held later in the year. The Committee outlined the main issues to be covered by the panel; it stressed that the interaction among the various changes and trends should also be examined in relation to such key issues as endogenous development, industrialization, productivity and international competitiveness.

After a preliminary informal meeting of a small group of experts at Laxenburg, Austria, from 1 to 3 August, the panel met at Mbabane, Swaziland, from 21 to 26 November.[16] It examined the economic and social turbulence and rapid advances in science and technology since 1979 which it said had created a critical situation for the developing countries. The slow-down in economic growth was leading to sharp decreases and fluctuations in the demand for scientific and technological activities and services. In short, the closer links between scientific capabilities, developments in technology and economic growth, the increasing cost of scientific research, the accelerating obsolescence of research capabilities, the emergence of new transdisciplinary fields and the growing complexity of the institutional setting for research were making it more difficult for most developing countries to take advantage of scientific and technological advances.

The panel identified four key dimensions involved in the design of new strategies for science and technology for development: the need to take into account the specific situation of a developing country and its international context; the importance of combining different types of technology, from traditional to advanced, in productive and service activities, the so-called "management of technological pluralism"; the need to enhance the innovative capabilities of society at all levels, from industrial firms to communities; and the necessity of combining defensive measures with the exploitation of opportunities in international markets and with the building of long-term capabilities.

The panel also emphasized a need to devise new sets of policy instruments and to promote international co-operation.

Science and technology indicators for development

Responding to the growing need for measuring ever more complicated scientific activities and their impact on development, the Advisory Committee, at its February 1984 session, decided to convene a panel of experts to give impetus to the construction of appropriate indicators.

The *ad hoc* panel of specialists on the measurement of the impact of science and technology on development objectives met at Graz, Austria, from 2 to 7 May. Reporting on the results of the meeting,[17] the panel described science and technology indicators as tools to be discussed in the context of improving policy management and assessment, and stressed the importance of developing skills to create adequate indicators and the need to demonstrate their utility and limitations to senior decision-makers. It suggested launching a number of pioneer projects to test new and old indicators in specific situations in developing countries and holding training courses on development and utilization of indicators. It stressed that the goal was not to create fixed indicators for universal application, but to evolve methodologies for devising indicators best suited to specific situations.

Advance Technology Alert System

As requested by the Intergovernmental Committee in June 1983,[11] a progress report on the launching of an Advance Technology Alert System (ATAS) was submitted to the Committee in March 1984.[18] Three major components had been proposed for ATAS: a semi-annual bulletin designed to inform policy-makers in developing countries about new and emerging technologies and their implications for the development process; advisory services to Governments and national and regional organizations on the implications of new technologies; and establishment of a network of research institutes, individuals, regional and international organizations and the scientific community to better the link between institutes for science and technology forecasting and assessment in developing countries with those in developed countries.

In an effort to promote the ATAS network, the Centre for Science and Technology for Development contacted over 100 potential contributors in order to prepare a review of some leading technology forecasting and assessment institutes

around the world for inclusion in the first issue of the *ATAS Bulletin*. Assessing the progress in launching ATAS, the Advisory Committee, in February,[12] recommended that the *Bulletin* be geared to a diversified audience and urged the Centre to draw directly on the expertise of its members. In addition, it made a number of editorial suggestions.

The Intergovernmental Committee, in a resolution of 8 June,[13] noted the launching of ATAS and expressed its appreciation for the prepublication version of the first issue of the *Bulletin*. The Committee requested that the publication continue to present information on new and emerging technologies and assess their impact on developing countries, taking into consideration relevant recommendations of the Advisory Committee. The first issue of the *ATAS Bulletin* was published in November, with 3,500 copies distributed to governmental and non-governmental organizations, as well as to scientists and technologists in both developed and developing countries.[19]

With regard to assistance to Member States, another ATAS objective, the Centre assisted the Organization of African Unity and the Economic Commission for Africa in the convening of an African expert group meeting to assess the implications of new technologies for implementation of the 1980 Lagos Plan of Action for the Implementation of the Monrovia Strategy for the Economic Development of Africa[20] (see Chapter I of this section). The meeting (Mbabane, Swaziland, 22-26 October) was attended by more than 60 experts and representatives of Governments and organizations; it recognized the need for specific measures to examine on a continuous basis the implications of new technologies to the development of the region. The Centre also undertook a preliminary study of the implications of new technologies to the Caribbean regional development efforts, responding to a request by the Caribbean Council for Science and Technology.

Scientific research and development

Emerging and traditional technologies

As proposed by the Advisory Committee in February 1983,[11] an international workshop on pioneer projects on the integration of emerging and traditional technologies was held in April 1984 in Tokyo by the Centre for science and technology jointly with the Japanese Association for Promotion of International Co-operation. Also following an Advisory Committee request, the International Labour Organisation published a compilation of case-studies on the blending of new and traditional technologies, showing how microelectronics, biotechnologies, satellite technology and photovoltaic power could be blended with traditional economic activities in various sectors.

On 8 June, the Intergovernmental Committee expressed its appreciation for the workshop and the compilation of case-studies.[9]

Research-production link

In considering, at its February 1984 session,[12] questions related to the linkages between research and development activities and the production system, the Advisory Committee had before it the results of an October 1983 panel of specialists at Lima, Peru.[21] The Committee emphasized that new conceptual approaches would be needed to stimulate research and development that met the needs of developing countries for advances in agricultural and industrial production. The aim of those efforts was to increase productivity by enhancing the effectiveness of technological choices and practices on the working environment. The Committee felt that improving the linkages between research and development and production would make it easier to integrate emerging and traditional technologies in agriculture, industry and services.

The Committee recommended that research and development institutions provide technical services on a continuously updated basis and correlated with production and service needs, including such services as the development of demonstration plants; assistance to end-users in implementation; trouble-shooting; industrial surveys; industrial staff training; process improvement; technical extension and liaison activities; and information collection and dissemination.

The Committee felt that research and development and production activities should be viewed in their relation to national development goals. It urged Governments to use a variety of policy and planning instruments to promote linkages and stressed that development banks could play an important role; it recommended that Governments direct their national development financial institutions to provide loans for the promotion and commercialization of research and development results. The Committee proposed that an independent expert team review the impact of loans by multilateral and bilateral funding agencies on the research and development sectors.

The Advisory Committee's views were noted with appreciation by the Intergovernmental Committee on 8 June.[9]

Scientific and technological information

The Vienna Programme placed considerable emphasis on the development of national systems of scientific and technological information and the linking of such systems with regional and international information networks. As requested by the Intergovernmental Committee in June 1983,[11] the Centre for science and technology submitted in March 1984 a progress report on the preparation of a study on the long-term plan of action for the establishment of a global scientific and technological information network.[22] The report stated that 16 Member States had expressed interest in all or some of the joint activities related to the global network. The report also noted the Centre's co-operation with the ACC Task Force and described its contacts with intergovernmental organizations within and outside the United Nations system, several of which declared their willingness to co-operate.

Following up on another June 1983 request of the Intergovernmental Committee,[11] the Secretary-General submitted also in March 1984 a note describing progress in establishing a data base on approved United Nations programmes and projects in the area of science and technology for development, geared towards endogenous capacity-building of developing countries.[23] The Secretary-General outlined criteria derived from the Vienna Programme for determining whether a particular activity could contribute towards endogenous capacity-building. He proposed input data elements and a possible output design. The data base was to be established in two phases, the first to cover all the regular United Nations work programmes and projects funded by the United Nations Development Programme (UNDP), and the second phase to cover the remaining agencies' activities financed through trust funds and other extrabudgetary resources.

Questions related to the establishment of a global scientific and technological information network were taken up by the Advisory Committee at its February session.[12] The Committee suggested a review of established and planned multi-country information systems both within and outside the United Nations system and an assessment of the needs of users in developing countries, including cost consideration. It also distinguished between two different uses of the term "network", one referring to physical communications facilities and the other describing an informal system of institutions responding to users' needs; the Committee stressed that an initial study should focus on the latter type. It believed that the development of networks of co-operating institutions could lead to immediate benefits to the users in developing countries.

The Intergovernmental Committee, in a resolution of 8 June,[9] noted the Advisory Committee's comments and suggested that in 1985 a panel of specialists be convened on the subject, taking into account the need to use existing information systems. It also took note of the Advisory Committee's views on the report of the panel on the role of regional organizations in popularizing science and technology[11] and recommended that panel and workshop reports be extensively disseminated.

UNCTAD activities. Pursuant to a 1982 request of the Committee on Transfer of Technology,[24] the UNCTAD secretariat submitted to the Committee's December 1984 session a report on the access of developing countries to technological information.[25] Examining the range of technologies available to developing countries and the role of small and medium-sized enterprises as technology sources (see below, under "Technology transfer"), the report also reviewed the main channels through which developing countries could gain access to information, including on-line data bases, information systems of government-sponsored organizations or non-profit groups, national and regional data bases in developing countries, and United Nations information systems. A number of measures to improve access to information were suggested, such as an increase in the use of small and medium-sized enterprises as suppliers of technology, greater utilization of government-sponsored information systems and improvement of the technological information base of developing countries.

With regard to possible future action, the report proposed that UNCTAD should develop better links with on-line data bases, establish a suitable referral base for expeditious provision of information to requesting countries, and set up a basic register of small and medium-sized technology suppliers in developed and developing countries. Further, UNCTAD could play an important role in improving developing countries' access to information technologies from non-enterprise, governmental sources, and, in the longer run, increase its assistance to help those countries build up their national technology information systems and develop their interlinkages with regional systems. The report also suggested that UNCTAD organize a meeting of specialists to work out methods for improving developing countries' access to information on technologies available from small and medium-sized enterprises and non-enterprise sources.

By a resolution of 20 December 1984,[26] the Committee on Transfer of Technology recognized that small and medium-sized enterprises were an important source of technological know-how and innovation, in many cases well adapted to the needs of developing countries. It requested the UNCTAD Secretary-General to complete case-studies and to submit them to it in 1986.

Other activities. Among related activities, a technology information pilot system entered in 1984 its preparatory phase, jointly sponsored by UNFSSTD and Italy (see below). The main objective of the project was to establish a mechanism for information exchange on selected energy and industrial technologies, mainly among developing countries. Initially, it linked 10 developing countries through national bureaux established for that purpose; if proven viable, it was supposed to lead to the design of a wider, subscription-based, multisectoral information network.

GENERAL ASSEMBLY ACTION

In resolution 39/164 of 17 December, the General Assembly noted that information systems for science and technology for development had been selected as the theme for consideration at the seventh (1985) session of the Intergovernmental Committee.

REFERENCES

(1)YUN 1979, p. 636. (2)YUN 1981, p. 734. (3)YUN 1983, p. 706. (4)A/CN.11/45. (5)A/CN.11/43 & Corr.1. (6)A/CN.11/44. (7)ACC/1984/3. (8)A/39/37 (res. 1(VI)). (9)*Ibid.* (res. 2(VI)). (10)YUN 1983, p. 713. (11)*Ibid.*, p. 707. (12)A/CN.11/47 & Corr.1,2. (13)A/39/37 (res. 4(VI)). (14)*Ibid.* (dec. 1(VI)). (15)YUN 1983, p. 714. (16)A/CN.11/AC.1/V/3 & Corr.1. (17)A/CN.11/AC.1/V/2. (18)A/CN.11/51. (19)A/CN.11/58. (20)YUN 1980, p. 548. (21)YUN 1983, p. 708. (22)A/CN.11/49. (23)A/CN.11/50 & Corr.1. (24)YUN 1982, p. 948. (25)TD/B/C.6/124. (26)TD/B/1035 (res. 28(V)).

Financing

UN Financing System

Operative since January 1982,[1] the United Nations Financing System for Science and Technology for Development continued throughout 1984 to help developing countries enhance their scientific and technological capacities as envisaged by the 1979 Vienna Programme of Action. A report on UNFSSTD's operations in 1984,[2] prepared by the Administrator of UNDP, in consultation with the DIEC Director-General, noted that uncertainty regarding long-term financial and institutional arrangements had hindered the mobilization of resources through normal pledging procedures, although a number of new projects and programming activities were initiated with funds provided directly by Governments and from other sources. Major emphasis was placed on project development activities, as UNFSSTD prepared itself for a potential decrease of traditional grant resources.

Operational activities

In the absence of a substantial inflow of new core resources through the traditional pledging conference, UNFSSTD succeeded in attracting over $20 billion for project funding through such non-core mechanisms as cost-sharing and trust funds. In addition, co-operative arrangements were set up with Governments and NGOs whereby non-financial resources were allocated to scientific and technological capacity-building in developing countries. By the end of 1984, despite a slow-down, the total number of official project requests from developing countries was more than 1,000. Intensified co-operation with UNDP and its field network allowed UNFSSTD in 1984 to bring to bear a broad range of technical expertise to its own project operations.

Following the primary component of its mandate to strengthen endogenous scientific and technological capacities, approximately 18 per cent of UNFSSTD expenditures was directly applied to training. Since 1982, nearly 1,800 fellows had been trained under UNFSSTD-financed projects, with 86 per cent of training fellowships in the developing countries themselves. A major emphasis was on project evaluation, with seven evaluations completed by the end of the year.

Among the main operational projects assisted by UNFSSTD in 1984, projects in Botswana, Burundi, Lesotho and Zimbabwe focused on the integration of science and technology policies and planning with overall economic and social development. In Fiji, the emphasis was on strengthening policy-making capabilities and employment opportunities. Other policy-making and planning efforts included a project in the Dominican Republic and the creation of a new Institute of Fundamental Studies in Sri Lanka. Working to strengthen scientific and technological infrastructure, UNFSSTD assisted in: establishing a Central Metallurgical Centre in Nigeria, a geo-technical section at the State Commissariat for National Resources in Guinea-Bissau and a Centre for Earth Sciences and Geological Cartography in Tunisia; improving the information and documentation capability of the Institute for Agriculture Research in Senegal; raising efficiency of the Centre for Oceanographic Research in Madagascar; and launching a two-phased undertaking to establish an Institute of Oceanography in Yemen. In the area of technology acquisition and transfer, UNFSSTD assisted projects in Burundi, Cape Verde, the Gambia, Indonesia, Maldives, Mauritius, Nepal and Seychelles. Assistance in developing technical manpower in Africa included projects in Ethiopia and Kenya and a joint venture with the Economic Commission for Western Asia. In Latin America and the Caribbean, training projects were completed in such fields as artisanal coastal fishery (Haiti); chemistry of natural products (Paraguay); mathematics, physics, chemistry, biology and engineering (Peru); and certification of non-destructive testing operators (regional).

Strengthening information networks was the subject of projects in Kenya and Senegal, while at the interregional level UNFSSTD assisted the members of the League of Arab States in establishing a computer-based information system and undertook a mid-term evaluation of the Andean Technological Information System. Various aspects of linking research and development activities to the productive sphere were tackled by projects in Bangladesh (herbal and plant-based drugs); Cape Verde, the Gambia, Lesotho, Mauritius and Seychelles (renewable energy technologies); Jordan (low-cost housing techniques); Malawi (tea research); Papua New Guinea (sago-starch village factories); and the Republic of Korea (petrochemical waste recycling). Four pilot projects in Latin America neared completion: Brazil and Honduras (carbon fibre production and replacement of fuel oil by charcoal); Jamaica (bauxite processing); and Uruguay (inactivation of the foot-and-mouth disease virus).

Owing to the fact that UNFSSTD core resources had not been substantially replenished, trust fund operations, originally conceived as one of several funding modes, became an important funding source. In 1984, five trust fund projects valued at $6.1 million were approved. They included a technological information pilot system for 10 countries in all regions ($1,472,600) (see above, under "Implementation of the Vienna Programme of Action"); development of national scientific and technological capacity in natural resources remote sensing in Ethiopia ($118,650); application of technologies for rural areas in Indonesia ($2,190,000); strengthening of national capacity for mineral prospecting in Costa Rica ($658,000); and a regional non-destructive testing network in 13 countries in Latin America and the Caribbean ($1,711,450). Commitments were received for nine more, with an input of $12.5 million, which were expected to become operational in 1985.

Project development

In an effort to lay the groundwork for further operational activities, UNFSSTD pursued in 1984 a variety of measures to obtain alternative sources of project funding. In June, it entered the Project Annotated List, co-ordinated by UNDP and designed to match unmet assistance requirements of developing countries with the special resources available in developed countries and from multilateral financing institutions. It also launched a number of special initiatives to strengthen co-operation among developing countries. In November, it sponsored jointly with the African Regional Centre for Technology a meeting at Rome of high-level scientists and technologists from over 20 African and other developing countries, to discuss selected co-operative projects in food and energy.

In October/November, it co-sponsored with the Permanent Inter-State Committee on Drought Control in the Sahel an international seminar on research and dissemination strategies for the Sahelian region.

In addition to its monitoring and support of projects under implementation and the processing of new commitments, UNFSSTD worked out plans to hold several technical meetings during 1985-1986, at Addis Ababa (Ethiopia), Seychelles, São Paulo (Brazil) and Beijing (China), to promote more effective utilization of project inputs among developing countries and explore possibilities for follow-up action. UNFSSTD also continued its cooperative arrangements with non-governmental and private organizations in order to focus the widest possible range of expertise and resources on the scientific and technological components of programmes within its purview.

Financial situation

By a resolution of 8 June 1984,[3] the Intergovernmental Committee expressed concern that it had not been possible to convene a pledging conference for UNFSSTD as decided by the General Assembly in December 1983.[4] Taking into account the fact that the available financial resources would not permit the System to continue beyond the end of 1984, the Committee invited the Secretary-General to convene such a conference as early as possible during the 1984 Assembly session and requested him to report to the Assembly after consulting with Governments and arranging a preparatory meeting to enable them to indicate their contributions.

The Secretary-General, in a note of 12 June[5] on programme, financial and administrative implications of the Committee resolution, estimated conference-servicing requirements on a full-cost basis at $32,500, while the estimated cost of a two-day preparatory meeting was $109,000. He also informed the Committee that the convening of a preparatory meeting would be a departure from the calendar of conferences and as such would be subject to the approval of the Committee on Conferences.

In another resolution of 8 June,[6] the Committee decided to consider mobilization of resources for science and technology for development as a possible theme for its 1986 session.

As requested by the Intergovernmental Committee, a preparatory meeting was convened on 30 and 31 October. Earlier, on 31 July, the Secretary-General had sent an appeal to Governments, calling for a successful conclusion of negotiations on UNFSSTD. The meeting had also been preceded by consultations with individual countries and major groups of countries, undertaken by the DIEC Director-General and the UNDP Administrator on behalf of the Secretary-General. Reporting to the General Assembly's Second (Economic and Financial) Committee on the results of those consultations, the Director-General noted that the significance of science and technology for development had received full recognition and that interested Governments had stated their wish to continue mobilizing resources for the System.

At the meeting, 16 Governments and the interested member States of the European Economic Community (EEC) stated their readiness to contribute a total of about $10 million for the first year of the long-term Financing System (1985), with three of them indicating financial contributions for the succeeding two years. Twelve Governments withheld their intended contributions until a later time, several others noted they were not in the position to state their intentions at the meeting and still others expressed interest in providing substantial amounts of non-core resources. Since the amount of available resources was substantially below the envisaged target, an important requirement for launching the System on a long-term basis had not been met. The meeting reviewed the implications of the shortfall and suggested that an informal open-ended intergovernmental working group be constituted to continue negotiations on long-term arrangements and prepare recommendations for the Intergovernmental Committee's 1985 session.

Both the DIEC Director-General and the UNDP Administrator reiterated the Secretary-General's appeal for contributions to UNFSSTD at the annual United Nations Pledging Conference for Development Activities on 7 and 8 November 1984 (see Chapter II of this section).

GENERAL ASSEMBLY ACTION

In December 1984, on the recommendation of the Second Committee, the General Assembly adopted decision 39/428 without vote.

Long-term financial and institutional arrangements for the United Nations Financing System for Science and Technology for Development

At its 103rd plenary meeting, on 17 December 1984, the General Assembly, on the recommendation of the Second Committee, recalling the Vienna Programme of Action on Science and Technology for Development, containing, *inter alia*, the features of the long-term financial and institutional arrangements for the United Nations Financing System for Science and Technology for Development:

(a) Decided to establish an Informal Open-ended Intergovernmental Working Group on the Long-term Financial and Institutional Arrangements for the United Nations Financing System for Science and Technology for Development, which should meet to permit a broad exchange of views on ways and means to facilitate the bringing into effect of the arrangements;

(b) Recommended that the Working Group should begin its deliberations as soon as possible and meet as necessary, so as to complete its work before the seventh session of the Intergovernmental Committee on Science and Technology for Development to be held from 28 May to 7 June 1985;

(c) Decided to continue the existing operating procedures of the Financing System and urged all countries to contribute to its operation.

General Assembly decision 39/428

Adopted without vote

Approved by Second Committee (A/39/790/Add.5) without vote, 10 December (meeting 58); draft by Vice-Chairman (A/C.2/39/L.131), based on informal consultations on draft by Egypt, for Group of 77 (A/C.2/39/L.108); agenda item 80 *(e)*. *Financial implications.* 5th Committee, A/39/829; S-G, A/C.2/39/L.120, A/C.5/39/95. *Meeting numbers.* GA 39th session: 2nd Committee 56, 58; 5th Committee 49; plenary 103.

Contributions and expenditures

Continuing uncertainty over long-term measures to maintain the operational momentum of UNFSSTD affected its resource prospects in 1984, when voluntary pledges amounted to under $250,000. Cost-sharing and trust funds established by the UNDP Administrator yielded $4.7 million, providing funds for several new projects and activities.

EXPENDITURES OF THE UN FINANCING SYSTEM FOR SCIENCE AND TECHNOLOGY FOR DEVELOPMENT BY COUNTRY OR AREA, 1984

(as at 31 December 1984; in thousands of US dollars)

Country/area	Amount
Bangladesh	58
Bolivia	21
Brazil	151
Burundi	129
China	352
Costa Rica	164
Cuba	1
Djibouti	7
Fiji	9
Gambia	64
Guinea	608
Guinea-Bissau	2
Haiti	70
Honduras	121
India	511
Indonesia	41
Ivory Coast	16
Jamaica	30
Jordan	322
Kenya	105
Lesotho	300
Madagascar	895
Malawi	174
Maldives	105
Mexico	3
Mongolia	75
Mozambique	35
Nepal	113
Nigeria	377
Pakistan	37
Paraguay	300
Peru	60
Philippines	21
Senegal	21
Seychelles	88
Sierra Leone	57
Somalia	128
Sri Lanka	127
Sudan	82
Swaziland	590
Thailand	436

Country/area	Amount
United Republic of Tanzania	16
Uruguay	30
Subtotal	6,852
Regional Africa	357
Regional Arab States	669
Regional Asia and the Pacific	106
Regional Latin America and the Caribbean	677
Global and interregional	379
Subtotal	2,188
Total	9,040

SOURCE: DP/1985/5/Add.6.

CONTRIBUTIONS TO THE UN FINANCING SYSTEM FOR SCIENCE AND TECHNOLOGY FOR DEVELOPMENT, 1984 AND 1985

(as at 31 December 1984; in US dollar equivalent)

Country	1984 payment	1985 pledge
Bangladesh	2,280	2,600
Belgium	48,780	—
Bhutan	—	1,580
Congo	2,353	—
Cyprus	503	500
Democratic Yemen	—	2,000
Egypt	25,000	—
Fiji	1,000	909
Guyana	2,133	941
Honduras	2,000	2,000
Indonesia	12,000	12,000
Jamaica	2,492	—
Jordan	39,975	—
Kenya	—	61,008
Madagascar	—	3,236
Malawi	—	1,678
Mongolia	293	264
Pakistan	63,314	61,392
Panama	2,000	2,000
Philippines	10,000	1,000
Republic of Korea	30,000	30,000
Senegal	—	2,000
Seychelles	1,000	409
Sierra Leone	1,000	1,000
Sri Lanka	15,000	—
Thailand	25,000	—
Yugoslavia	20,000	—
Zambia	37,943	30,612
Zimbabwe	6,261	4,828
Total	350,327	221,957

SOURCE: A/40/5/Add.1.

REFERENCES

[1]YUN 1982, p. 937. [2]A/CN.11/60. [3]A/39/37 (res. 3(VI)). [4]YUN 1983, p. 711, GA res. 38/157, 19 Dec. 1983. [5]A/CN.11/L.84. [6]A/39/37 (res. 6(VI)).

Institutional arrangements

National focal points

Further efforts were made in 1984 to encourage the establishment of national focal points—originally set up for the 1979 United Nations Conference on Science and Technology for Development—and to integrate them into the national system for science and technology, as called for by the operational plan for the implementation of the Vienna Programme of Action.

As requested by the Intergovernmental Committee in 1982,[1] the Secretary-General, on 1 March 1984,[2] presented a list of national focal points, updated as of 1 February 1984, and including information provided by Member States since March 1983, when the initial registry had been compiled.[3] The registry listed the 158 Member States of the United Nations and five non-member States maintaining permanent observer missions at United Nations Headquarters. In 17 cases, the designation of the national focal point had been made on a temporary basis, and in two cases the Centre for science and technology was awaiting the requisite information. In the mean time, the registry listed the respective Permanent Mission to the United Nations in New York or, in its absence, the Ministry of Foreign Affairs.

Intergovernmental Committee

Review of work methods

As decided by the Intergovernmental Committee in June 1983,[4] the DIEC Director-General submitted to the Committee's May/June 1984 session a report on strengthening its role and effectiveness.[5] After reviewing the Committee's functions and activities, the Director-General made several proposals, largely based on formal and informal consultations with a wide range of interested parties. With regard to inter-agency co-operation, he recommended more specific requests for such co-operation in the Committee's decisions and resolutions, improved interaction between the Committee and other intergovernmental bodies, increased efforts to mobilize financial resources for joint activities, and greater involvement of the ACC Task Force in deliberations of the Committee. In his view, the Committee should also explore avenues of enhancing interaction with the regional commissions and NGOs in the implementation of the Vienna Programme and should better utilize the capabilities of the Advisory Committee through more direct requests for its technical advisory support and participation of the Advisory Committee Chairman in the relevant discussions.

Concerning organizational matters, the Director-General discussed the respective advantages and modalities of biennial or annual cycles of the Committee's meetings, noting that it might be advisable to keep to annual sessions for the time being and consider the matter at a later stage. The introduction of a biennial cycle of meetings had been suggested by the General Assembly in December 1983.[6] In order to improve the efficiency of its work, he proposed that the Committee reduce the number of reports and reviews, plan ahead the work of each session, and hold a short organizational Bureau meeting six weeks before the regular session. In relation to the methods of

work, the Director-General proposed specific, in-depth, selective examination of substantive issues, with more extensive preparatory work to collect, process and analyse information on science and technology policies. By focusing on those matters, the Committee could provide opportunities for an exchange of views and experiences among Governments and for initiating or strengthening multilateral and bilateral co-operation. For the Committee to include in-depth consideration of such substantive issues in its deliberations, he proposed that it select a special theme or themes for its annual session, for the preparation and implementation of which he outlined a certain mechanism.

The financial and administrative implications of the Director-General's proposals were assessed by the Secretary-General in a note of 5 June,[7] in which he concluded that, should the Committee decide to recommend adoption of the proposals, the estimated financial requirements for participation of the Advisory Committee Chairman would be $5,600 for each session of the Intergovernmental Committee, and the convening of an intergovernmental *ad hoc* expert group or meeting to prepare work on the annual theme(s) would require an estimated $87,000. Conference-servicing requirements for 1984-1985 were estimated at $1,108,800 for annual sessions and $554,400 for a biennial session.

The Intergovernmental Committee, in a resolution of 8 June 1984,[8] decided to place on the agenda of each of its sessions one or two specific themes to be determined two years in advance. To this end, it invited: the Centre for science and technology to concentrate on inter-agency co-ordination and analytical preparation for the discussions; ACC to give special attention to the examination of national, regional or global needs in the areas corresponding to the selected themes; the Advisory Committee to give attention to an in-depth investigation of the selected themes; and the international community to assist the in-depth investigation of those themes. The Committee identified as possible themes for its 1986 session the mobilization of resources for science and technology for development, and technology applied to agricultural development. It invited Governments to send their comments on those themes to the Secretary-General before 1 October 1984 and requested the Committee Chairman to decide on the theme or themes and to inform the General Assembly at its 1984 session.

Other provisions included a request to the Centre to prepare a report on United Nations activities in science and technology for development; a second report on the biennial review of the implementation of the Vienna Programme; and a report on the issues left unresolved by the 1979 United Nations Conference on Science and Technology for Development.[9]

Certain aspects of the Intergovernmental Committee's organization and methods of work were also discussed by the ACC Task Force at its January session (see below).

Report of the Committee

The report of the Intergovernmental Committee on its sixth (1984) session (New York, 29 May–8 June)[10] was submitted to the Economic and Social Council at its July session.

ECONOMIC AND SOCIAL COUNCIL ACTION

In July, on the recommendation of its First Committee, the Council adopted decision 1984/169 without vote.

Report of the Intergovernmental Committee on Science and Technology for Development

At its 48th plenary meeting, on 25 July 1984, the Council took note of the report of the Intergovernmental Committee on Science and Technology for Development on its sixth session and decided to transmit it to the General Assembly at its thirty-ninth session for consideration.

Economic and Social Council decision 1984/169

Adopted without vote

Approved by First Committee (E/1984/147) without vote, 20 July (meeting 14); oral proposal by Chairman; agenda item 16.

GENERAL ASSEMBLY ACTION

By a telegram of 9 November,[11] the Chairman of the Intergovernmental Committee for 1984 informed the President of the General Assembly about the Committee's review of its methods of work. In response to the Committee's invitation, comments on the two proposed themes for the Committee's 1986 session had been received as at 1 November 1984 from 31 Governments, the majority of them endorsing the selection of both. On the basis of those replies, mobilization of resources and technology applied to agricultural development would be the themes for in-depth analysis at the 1986 Committee session.

On 17 December 1984, on the recommendation of the Second Committee, the Assembly adopted resolution 39/164 without vote.

Report of the Intergovernmental Committee on Science and Technology for Development

The General Assembly,

Recalling the Vienna Programme of Action on Science and Technology for Development and General Assembly resolution 34/218 of 19 December 1979,

Noting the forthcoming mid-decade review of the implementation of the Vienna Programme of Action to be considered by the Intergovernmental Committee at its seventh session in the context of the review and appraisal of the International Development Strategy for the Third United Nations Development Decade,

1. *Takes note* of the report of the Intergovernmental Committee on Science and Technology for Development

on its sixth session and of Economic and Social Council decisions 1984/168 and 1984/169 of 25 July 1984;

2. *Supports* the initiatives of the Intergovernmental Committee with a view to strengthening its role and effectiveness and, in particular, its decision to adopt a selective approach that will enable it, at each of its sessions, to conduct deliberations of greater depth by selecting in advance themes for consideration;

3. *Notes*, in this context, that information systems for science and technology for development have been selected as the theme for consideration at the seventh session of the Intergovernmental Committee in 1985 and that the two themes selected for the eighth session are mobilization of resources for science and technology for development for developing countries and technology applied to agricultural development and related development areas.

General Assembly resolution 39/164

17 December 1984   Meeting 103   Adopted without vote

Approved by Second Committee (A/39/790/Add.5) without vote, 10 December (meeting 58); draft by Vice-Chairman (A/C.2/39/L.126), resulting from informal consultations; agenda item 80 *(e)*.

Meeting numbers. GA 39th session: 2nd Committee 57, 58; plenary 103.

The draft resolution was originally sponsored by the German Democratic Republic. Following informal consultations, however, the Chairman informed the Second Committee that the text should be considered as a Vice-Chairman's text.

Advisory Committee

The Advisory Committee on Science and Technology for Development held its fourth session in New York from 14 to 21 February 1984;[12] it reviewed follow-up measures to two 1982 panels and considered the reports of three 1983 panels on: the role of regional organizations in strengthening research and development (see above, under "NGO participation"); linkages between research and development and the production system (see above, under "Research-production link"); and science and technology and women.[13] Discussing further steps to implement the Vienna Programme of Action, the Committee dealt with perspectives of science and technology for development, the launching of ATAS and creation of a global network of scientific and technological information (see above, under "Implementation of the Vienna Programme of Action"). The Advisory Committee recommended that one of its panels in 1985 should focus on the mobilization of resources and decided to postpone a final decision on the topic of a second 1985 panel until its February 1985 session.

By a resolution of 8 June 1984,[14] the Intergovernmental Committee took note of the Advisory Committee's report and expressed appreciation to Peru, Tunisia, the United States, Japan and Austria for their co-operation in holding the panels and workshops in 1983 and 1984. It recommended that the panel and workshop reports be disseminated extensively, the Vienna Programme be publicized in a small booklet, and the Advisory Committee continue emphasizing the practical problems confronting the developing countries and assess the influence of scientific progress on the implementation of the Programme. It requested the Advisory Committee to discuss in 1985 the possibility of involving members personally in implementing the Vienna Programme, noted that mobilization of resources for scientific and technological development was the subject for one of the 1985 panels and suggested that the topic for the other should be the global network of scientific and technological information.

Certain aspects of the Advisory Committee's work were also covered in other Committee resolutions of the same date (see above, under "Review of work methods", and immediately below).

Centre for science and technology

The United Nations Centre for Science and Technology for Development continued, throughout 1984, to assist the DIEC Director-General in implementing the 1979 Vienna Programme of Action, particularly in providing substantive support to the Intergovernmental Committee and its subsidiary bodies, and in promoting and co-ordinating United Nations scientific and technological activities at the Secretariat level.

In the area of policy analysis and research, the Centre continued to collect additional data to review the progress achieved in implementing the operational plan for implementing the Programme of Action. It proceeded with efforts to initiate ATAS and studied the feasibility of developing suitable indicators for measuring the impact of science and technology on national development (see above, under "Implementation of the Vienna Programme of Action"). The Centre expanded its substantive secretariat services to the Advisory Committee, organizing the *ad hoc* panels of specialists (see above, under "Long-term perspectives" and "Science and technology indicators for development"). Continuing to maintain co-operation and consultation with relevant United Nations organizations, it prepared the first biennial review of United Nations activities to implement the Vienna Programme (see above, under "Implementation of the Vienna Programme of Action"). The Centre also provided support to the ACC Task Force (see below), participated in discussions in science and technology committees of the five regional commissions, and co-ordinated the preparation of the main United Nations programme on science and technology of the medium-term plan for 1984-1989. A major part of its activities concerned financing for science and technology, including efforts to mobilize resources and to appraise projects in co-operation with

UNFSSTD. The Centre maintained regular interaction with national focal points, Governments and NGOs in support of activities related to the Vienna Programme. It continued to publish its newsletter *UPDATE*, which covered progress in implementing the Programme. In an effort to strengthen co-operation among developing and developed countries, the Centre co-sponsored an international workshop in April in Tokyo (see above, under "Implementation of the Vienna Programme of Action").

The Intergovernmental Committee, on 8 June,[15] took note of the Secretary-General's report on the Centre's activities for the period March 1983–February 1984.[16] It noted the support provided by the Centre to the ACC Task Force and its various working groups, and encouraged the Centre to involve NGOs more closely in its activities. The Centre was requested to focus its attention on the themes selected by the Intergovernmental Committee for its future sessions, as well as on programmes emerging from the work of the Advisory Committee panels and on analytical preparation of documents aimed at promoting international co-operation. Reviewing its own work methods, the Intergovernmental Committee, in another resolution of the same date,[8] addressed several other aspects of the Centre's activities (see above).

Co-ordination in the system

The Task Force on Science and Technology for Development, established by ACC as a mechanism of inter-agency co-operation in implementing tasks assigned to the Intergovernmental Committee, held its fifth session at Rome from 17 to 19 January 1984.[17] Discussing the implementation of the Vienna Programme in the light of the June 1983 decisions of the Intergovernmental Committee,[18] the Task Force made recommendations on joint activities and their follow-up; criteria for building endogenous capacities in developing countries; assessment of current means of United Nations support to developing countries' science and technology programmes; and further actions to be taken by United Nations entities to enhance their role in science and technology (see above, under "Implementation of the Vienna Programme of Action").

To allow United Nations organizations to become more involved in the *ad hoc* panels of the Advisory Committee, the Task Force agreed that close interaction be continued or established between its members and the panels, extending to identification and organization of future panels. With regard to the Intergovernmental Committee's effectiveness, the Task Force noted the need for a more coherent agenda, greater attention to substantive policy issues, and shortened and better-focused subjects.

Recalling an agreement reached in 1983, designating the Task Force as the lead agency for examining and following up proposals of the Organization of the Islamic Conference and United Nations bodies in science and technology, the Task Force stressed that the Centre should be kept fully informed about direct contacts of individual bodies with the Conference and that the co-operation of the Islamic Fund for Science and Technology for Development be sought to finance joint activities.

Progress in establishing a data base on the activities of United Nations organizations in science and technology was described by the Secretary-General in a March 1984 note[19] (see above, under "Implementation of the Vienna Programme of Action").

By a resolution of 8 June,[20] the Intergovernmental Committee emphasized the need for greater co-ordination and harmonization of United Nations science and technology programmes. It took note of United Nations organizations' efforts to evolve joint activities, called for further efforts in that regard, and invited the Economic and Social Council to request United Nations entities to consider ways of enhancing co-ordination. By other resolutions of the same date, the Committee noted the support provided by the Centre to the ACC Task Force[15] and invited ACC, through its Task Force, to give special attention to the examination of national, regional and global needs in areas corresponding to the themes selected by the Committee and to inter-agency co-ordination on the same themes.[8]

REFERENCES

[1]YUN 1982, p. 936. [2]A/CN.11/INF/6. [3]YUN 1983, p. 712. [4]*Ibid.*, p. 713. [5]A/CN.11/53 & Corr.1. [6]YUN 1983, p. 1008, GA dec. 38/429, 19 Dec. 1983. [7]A/CN.11/L.77. [8]A/39/37 (res. 6(VI)). [9]YUN 1979, p. 640. [10]A/39/37. [11]A/C.2/39/11. [12]A/CN.11/47 & Corr.1,2. [13]YUN 1983, p. 922. [14]A/39/37 (res. 2(VI)). [15]*Ibid.* (res. 4(VI)). [16]A/CN.11/49. [17]ACC/1984/3. [18]YUN 1983, p. 716. [19]A/CN.11/50 & Corr.1. [20]A/39/37 (res. 1(VI)).

Technology transfer

The problem of technological choice, acquisition and transfer—a critical aspect in achieving greater technological self-reliance in developing countries—was high on the agenda of several United Nations organizations throughout 1984, particularly UNCTAD and the United Nations Industrial Development Organization (UNIDO). The trends of United Nations activities in this sphere—corresponding to programme area III of

the Vienna Programme's operational plan—were appraised in the Secretary-General's biennial review of United Nations activities in science and technology for development,[1] which noted that programmes had generally taken the form of studies dealing with alternative technological choice or increasing national capability for exercising suitable choice and acquisition, including laws and regulations and institutional arrangements regarding foreign technology and indigenous technological development. The report stressed that United Nations activities had had a considerable impact on policies and measures related to technological choice and acquisition, prompting greater consideration of technological alternatives and improving awareness of the legal and regulatory measures suitable in different country situations. The Secretary-General concluded that there was a need for a continuing assessment of the latest trends in technology policies, co-ordination of institutional arrangements relating to technology acquisition, and integration of technology choice and acquisition measures into broader programmes of scientific and technological development. Greater emphasis was also necessary in the case of the least developed countries, as well as with regard to programmes for rural areas and communities in developing countries.

UNCTAD's Advisory Service on Transfer of Technology continued to provide technical and operational assistance. Questions of technology development and transfer in industry were covered in a report by UNIDO's Executive Director and in a conclusion of the Industrial Development Board (see Chapter VI of this section).

UNCTAD activities. The Committee on Transfer of Technology held its first special session at Geneva from 13 to 22 February 1984[2] to consider a 1982 report by the UNCTAD secretariat on a strategy for the technological transformation of developing countries,[3] transmitted to the Committee on a request by the Conference in July 1983.[4] After discussing the subject, the Committee adopted on 22 February a resolution on further elaboration and implementation of the strategy,[5] by which the Committee decided to continue work on the subject with a view to completing it at its fifth session (see below) and invited the UNCTAD Secretary-General and the Committee Chairman to prepare the appropriate documentation. The Committee also decided to annex to its report two draft resolutions, by the Group of 77 developing countries and by Group B (developed market economies), and two documents outlining the strategy by the Group of 77 and by Group D (centrally planned economies).

The Committee held its fifth session at Geneva from 3 to 20 December.[6] On 20 December, it adopted a resolution[7] setting out a number of measures to accelerate the technological transformation of developing countries and topics related to technology transfer, including an international code of conduct (see below); national laws and regulations on technology transfer, acquisition and development (see below); implementation of UNCTAD resolutions 87(IV),[8] 112(V)[9] and 143(VI),[4] on strengthening the technological capacity of developing countries; economic, commercial and developmental aspects of new and emerging technologies; the commercialization of the results of United Nations–funded research and development; promotion and encouragement of technological innovation; the role of small and medium-sized enterprises in international technology transfer; economic, commercial and developmental aspects of the industrial property system (see below); and follow-up to the 1979 Conference on Science and Technology for Development.

Also on 20 December, the Committee decided to resume work at its 1986 session on the strategy for the technological transformation of developing countries, with a view to finalizing it;[10] to annex to its report three draft texts on the strategy submitted by the Group of 77, Group B and Group D;[11] and to transmit to the Trade and Development Board in 1985 two texts, submitted by the Group of 77 and Group B, on technical and operational assistance provided by the Advisory Service on Transfer of Technology.[12]

The Committee also considered a number of reports by the UNCTAD secretariat related to technology transfer and technological transformation.

Draft code of conduct

In March 1984,[13] the Secretary-General reported to the Intergovernmental Committee on the state of negotiations on issues left unresolved by the 1979 United Nations Conference on Science and Technology for Development.[14] He stated that the Committee on Transfer of Technology had made further progress in drafting an international code of conduct on the transfer of technology. Progress had also been made with regard to a draft code of conduct on transnational corporations, which contained a provision on transfer of technology.

Taking note of the report, the Intergovernmental Committee, on 8 June 1984,[15] regretted that work on both draft codes had not been completed and urged that they be finalized as early as possible. The Committee wished to be kept informed of relevant developments and decided to take up the unresolved issues at its next session.

In a resolution of 20 December,[7] the Committee on Transfer of Technology recognized that an international code of conduct would help promote the international transfer of technology under terms advantageous to all parties. It welcomed the decision to convene in 1985 the sixth session of the United Nations Conference on an International Code of Conduct on the Transfer of Technology (initially convened in 1978 under UNCTAD auspices[16]), urging full participation by all Governments in order to complete the negotiations on the code. It invited the UNCTAD Secretary-General to make all necessary arrangements, including informal consultations with regional groups and Governments, as mandated by the General Assembly in December 1983.[17]

Other aspects of technology transfer

Industrial property

In a resolution of 20 December 1984,[7] the Committee on Transfer of Technology invited the UNCTAD secretariat to continue its work on the industrial property system, and invited the UNCTAD Secretary-General, in consultation with regional groups, to convene a meeting of the Group of Governmental Experts on the Economic, Commercial and Developmental Aspects of Industrial Property in the Transfer of Technology to Developing Countries.

In a progress report submitted to the Committee,[18] the UNCTAD secretariat stated that it had not proved practicable to convene the Group of Experts before the Committee's December 1984 session; however, the Group would meet in time to report in 1986. The report suggested that the Group might want to give particular consideration to: effects of new patent policies in developing countries; trade marks and generic names of pharmaceuticals and consumer protection; and industrial property protection of new and emerging technologies. Annexed to the report was a summary of comments by 19 States and three intergovernmental organizations on a study on trade marks and generic names of pharmaceuticals and consumer protection, submitted to a 1982 meeting of the Group of Experts.[19]

Laws and regulations

As requested by the Committee on the Transfer of Technology in 1982,[20] the UNCTAD secretariat submitted to the Committee's December 1984 session three reports dealing with laws and regulations on the transfer and acquisition of technology. The first summarized the views of 12 Governments and two United Nations bodies on matters related to common approaches to such laws and regulations.[21] For further possible action by the Committee in that regard, the report suggested that it request the UNCTAD secretariat to expand its report and to convene groups of experts to consider ways of harmonizing laws and regulations. The second report analysed the experience of two countries—Nigeria and Portugal—in implementing laws on technology transfer, offering some preliminary conclusions.[22] Another report[23] contained the first periodic review of policies, laws and regulations conducive to technology development, transfer and acquisition, covering national, bilateral and multilateral developments during 1979-1983.

The Committee, in a resolution of 20 December 1984,[7] recognized the importance of a legal and institutional framework for technology transfer, acquisition and development for increasing the technological capacity of developing countries and the contribution of technology to overall social and economic development. The Committee invited Governments to continue to inform the UNCTAD Secretary-General of new laws and regulations and modifications of existing ones. It requested him to continue studies on the topic, taking into account government views on the documentation prepared so far. The Committee recommended that appropriate action be taken at its 1986 session.

Commercialization of results of UN-funded research

In August 1984, the UNCTAD secretariat reported to the Committee on Transfer of Technology on research and development activities applicable to the production process.[24] Those activities, comprising design/engineering of new products and processes as well as updating or upgrading of existing technologies, and carried out by public as well as private, national or international entities, were an important tool for the technological transformation and economic growth in particular of the developing countries, the report stated. The report, submitted in accordance with UNCTAD resolution 143(VI),[4] summarized information from several United Nations bodies on resources for, results of, and policies and practices relating to research and development.

In a resolution of 20 December,[7] the Committee on Transfer of Technology took note of the preliminary work undertaken by UNCTAD as the lead agency in issues relating to the commercialization of results of United Nations–funded research and development. It requested the UNCTAD Secretary-General to continue work on the matter by preparing a study covering issues such as technologies and inventions emanating from such research; benefits from the commercialization of its results; and assertion of United Nations property rights. The Committee invited him to examine those issues in the context of inter-agency meetings and to report in 1986.

Promotion of technological innovation

As requested by the Committee on Transfer of Technology in 1982,[20] the UNCTAD secretariat prepared a preliminary review of policies and instruments used by developed countries to promote and encourage technological innovation, especially in industry. The report,[25] meant to assist developing countries in formulating policies, was submitted to the Committee in December 1984.

In a resolution of 20 December,[7] the Committee requested the UNCTAD secretariat to continue its studies in the field and to submit them to the Committee in 1986. The studies were to consider the influence of factors, such as risk-taking, incentives and linkages between research and production, on the creation of an innovative environment.

REFERENCES

[1]A/CN.11/45. [2]TD/B/986. [3]*A Strategy for the Technological Transformation of Developing Countries* (TD/277/Rev.1), Sales No. E.84.II.D.19. [4]YUN 1983, p. 717. [5]TD/B/986 (res. 26(S-I)). [6]TD/B/1035. [7]*Ibid.* (res. 28(V)). [8]YUN 1976, p. 397. [9]YUN 1979, p. 595. [10]TD/B/1035 (dec. 27(V)). [11]*Ibid.* (dec. 29(V)). [12]*Ibid.* (dec. 30(V)). [13]A/CN.11/14/Add.3. [14]YUN 1979, p. 640. [15]A/39/37 (res. 5(VI)). [16]YUN 1978, p. 503. [17]YUN 1983, p. 718, GA res. 38/153, 19 Dec. 1983. [18]TD/B/C.6/110 & Add.1. [19]YUN 1982, p. 951. [20]*Ibid.*, p. 953. [21]TD/B/C.6/107. [22]TD/B/C.6/112. [23]TD/B/C.6/111 & Corr.1,2. [24]TD/B/C.6/121. [25]TD/B/C.6/123.

PUBLICATION

Technology and Development Perspectives of the Pharmaceutical Sector in Ethiopia (UNCTAD/TT/58), Sales No. E.84.II.D.6.

Brain drain

The negative economic, political and social effects of the reverse transfer of technology, also described as the brain drain of skilled personnel from developing to developed countries, was a major area of concern for UNCTAD and the General Assembly throughout 1984.

UNCTAD activities. In accordance with a December 1983 Assembly resolution,[1] the Second Meeting of Governmental Experts on the Reverse Transfer of Technology was held at Geneva from 27 August to 5 September 1984. The Meeting examined studies by the UNCTAD secretariat on: an integrated approach to international skill exchange, including proposals for policy and action on reverse transfer of technology; measures to mitigate the brain drain's adverse impact on developing countries; major components for an internationally agreed set of principles, definitions and standards on reverse transfer of technology; and improvement of the collection and dissemination of information on the brain drain.

The Meeting adopted several conclusions and recommendations, which were annexed to its report to the Trade and Development Board.[2] It emphasized the importance of efficient skill utilization for developing countries and adequate protection of the interests of all countries affected by brain drain, calling for a comprehensive and integrated approach to obviate its adverse effects. The Meeting recommended that all the developed countries should support measures encouraging greater use of skilled personnel within the developing countries. Developed countries which received skilled migrants should consider arrangements to allow the developing countries to share in the benefits and should assist in building up a better data base on skilled migration, while developing countries should monitor skilled outflows and take remedial measures. Regarding international action, the Meeting suggested that the UNCTAD Secretary-General convene a third and fourth meeting of governmental experts—the third meeting, scheduled for 1985, focusing on formulation of an integrated programme of action on reverse transfer of technology—and requested him to invite several other United Nations bodies to provide information on their activities in the field. It also invited the Secretaries-General of the United Nations and UNCTAD to consult with Governments and regional groups to obtain their full participation at the meetings, and recommended that the UNCTAD secretariat continue studying the problem.

The Trade and Development Board took note on 21 September of the Meeting's conclusions and recommendations and decided on 27 September to transmit them, together with the statements by delegations, to the Assembly.[3]

Development aspects of the reverse transfer of technology and the question of co-operative exchange of skills were the subject of another UNCTAD secretariat report to the Committee on Transfer of Technology.[4]

Inter-agency group meetings. As requested by the Assembly in December 1983,[1] two meetings of a newly established Inter-Agency Group on Reverse Transfer of Technology were held on 22 March and on 12 and 13 July 1984 under the chairmanship of UNCTAD. The report of the Group, annexed to a note of 6 September by the Secretary-General,[5] stressed that the main thrust of the discussions was on co-ordination of measures and, in particular, enhancement of United Nations effectiveness in responding to the needs of the countries concerned. Noting that all outflows of skilled manpower constituted not only a movement of people, but also a transfer of productive resources, the Group stressed that losses incurred by developing countries should be properly accounted for, and called for concerted United Nations efforts and concrete international measures to help solve the problem of the reverse transfer of technology. The Group held it necessary to elaborate internationally agreed norms and standards, formulate methodologies for measuring flows of human resources, move from recommendations to sub-

stantive conclusions, and enhance an orderly South-South migration of skilled manpower or co-operative exchange of skills. The Group pointed to the necessity of meeting on a regular basis and considered it useful to associate intergovernmental organizations outside the United Nations, as well as NGOs, with the work carried out by the United Nations in the area.

GENERAL ASSEMBLY ACTION

On 18 December, the General Assembly, on the recommendation of the Second Committee, adopted resolution 39/211 by recorded vote.

Development aspects of the reverse transfer of technology

The General Assembly,

Recalling its resolutions 3201(S-VI) and 3202(S-VI) of 1 May 1974, containing the Declaration and the Programme of Action on the Establishment of a New International Economic Order, 3281(XXIX) of 12 December 1974, containing the Charter of Economic Rights and Duties of States, 3362(S-VII) of 16 September 1975 on development and international economic co-operation, 35/56 of 5 December 1980, the annex to which contains the International Development Strategy for the Third United Nations Development Decade, and all relevant resolutions concerning the reverse transfer of technology,

Convinced that the search for durable solutions to the problem of the reverse transfer of technology requires the full participation of all parties concerned,

1. *Takes note* of the report of the Inter-Agency Group on Reverse Transfer of Technology, covering meetings held at Geneva on 22 March and 12 and 13 July 1984;

2. *Takes note also* of the outcome of the Second Meeting of Governmental Experts on the Reverse Transfer of Technology, held at Geneva from 27 August to 5 September 1984;

3. *Requests* the Secretary-General of the United Nations Conference on Trade and Development to convene the requisite meetings of governmental experts on the reverse transfer of technology, as provided for in General Assembly resolution 38/154;

4. *Invites* the Secretary-General to undertake intensive consultations with all Governments with a view to obtaining their full participation in the meetings of governmental experts on the reverse transfer of technology;

5. *Requests* the Trade and Development Board to include, in its report to the General Assembly at its fortieth session, a section on the outcome of the Third Meeting of Governmental Experts on the Reverse Transfer of Technology;

6. *Requests* the Secretary-General to convene further meetings of the Inter-Agency Group on Reverse Transfer of Technology and to report on the results of those meetings to the General Assembly at its fortieth session.

General Assembly resolution 39/211

18 December 1984   Meeting 104   119-21-1 (recorded vote)

Approved by Second Committee (A/39/790/Add.3) by recorded vote (105-21), 14 December (meeting 60); draft by Egypt, for Group of 77 (A/C.2/39/L.76); agenda item 80 *(c)*.

Meeting numbers. GA 39th session: 2nd Committee, 53, 58, 60; plenary 104.

Recorded vote in Assembly as follows:

In favour: Afghanistan, Algeria, Angola, Argentina, Bahamas, Bahrain, Bangladesh, Barbados, Benin, Bhutan, Bolivia, Botswana, Brazil, Brunei Darussalam, Bulgaria, Burkina Faso, Burma, Burundi, Byelorussian SSR, Cape Verde, Chad, Chile, China, Colombia, Congo, Costa Rica, Cuba, Cyprus, Czechoslovakia, Democratic Kampuchea, Democratic Yemen, Djibouti, Dominican Republic, Ecuador, Egypt, El Salvador, Equatorial Guinea, Ethiopia, Fiji, Gabon, Gambia, German Democratic Republic, Ghana, Guatemala, Guinea, Guinea-Bissau, Guyana, Haiti, Honduras, Hungary, India, Indonesia, Iran, Iraq, Ivory Coast, Jamaica, Jordan, Kenya, Kuwait, Lao People's Democratic Republic, Lebanon, Liberia, Libyan Arab Jamahiriya, Malawi, Malaysia, Maldives, Mali, Malta, Mauritania, Mauritius, Mexico, Mongolia, Morocco, Mozambique, Nepal, Nicaragua, Niger, Nigeria, Oman, Pakistan, Panama, Papua New Guinea, Paraguay, Peru, Philippines, Poland, Qatar, Romania, Rwanda, Saint Vincent and the Grenadines, Samoa, Sao Tome and Principe, Saudi Arabia, Senegal, Sierra Leone, Singapore, Somalia, Sri Lanka, Sudan, Suriname, Swaziland, Syrian Arab Republic, Thailand, Togo, Trinidad and Tobago, Tunisia, Turkey, Uganda, Ukrainian SSR, USSR, United Arab Emirates, United Republic of Tanzania, Uruguay, Venezuela, Viet Nam, Yemen, Yugoslavia, Zaire, Zambia.

Against: Australia, Austria, Belgium, Canada, Denmark, Finland, France, Germany, Federal Republic of, Greece, Iceland, Ireland, Italy, Japan, Luxembourg, Netherlands, New Zealand, Norway, Portugal, Spain, Sweden, United States.

Abstaining: United Kingdom.[a]

[a]Later advised the Secretariat it had intended to vote against.

Speaking in the Second Committee for the EEC members, Ireland said the approach taken to the important question of the reverse transfer of technology was not right; it was necessary first to determine whether human resource flows and their consequences could be measured, a task not suited to the mandate of the Meeting of Governmental Experts. In the view of the United States, no progress was possible in the work of the United Nations in the current context; the problem of the outflow of trained personnel was a domestic one and its solution lay in creating incentives in the developing countries. Canada supported international efforts to formulate policies, but stressed that no account had been taken of the fact that the problem of human resource flows was of a universal nature with implications in the North-South and East-West contexts; it termed unfeasible UNCTAD's suggestion that a value be set on emigrating human capital and that receiving countries should pay compensation, and pointed out that there was no framework allowing participation by all the groups concerned. Finland regretted that operative paragraph 3 linked the text to the December 1983 Assembly resolution on reverse technology transfer,[1] against which it had voted. The German Democratic Republic, on behalf of the Eastern European countries, explained that the outflow of professional personnel from the developing to some Western countries was a form of neocolonialism and linked to the required democratic restructuring of international economic relations. States benefiting from the outflow of trained personnel should compensate the States affected; however, the measures provided for in the adopted resolution must be financed without any increase in the regular United Nations budget.

Introducing the draft on behalf of the Group of 77, Egypt said it was essentially procedural and sought to ensure continuation of relevant United Nations activities; the positive outcome of the Meeting of Governmental Experts should facilitate adoption of the text.

REFERENCES

[1]YUN 1983, p. 719, GA res. 38/154, 19 Dec. 1983. [2]TD/B/1018. [3]A/39/15, vol. II. [4]TD/B/C.6/129. [5]A/39/397.

Chapter XIII

Social and cultural development

Available evidence on the social aspects of development suggested a mixed picture, with large groups in Asia improving their standards of living, poverty increasing dramatically in Africa, and both the poor and middle-income social groups in Latin America experiencing a deterioration in their living conditions.

Reviewing activities of the Joint Committee for the Promotion of Aid to Co-operatives (COPAC), a liaison body of the United Nations, the Food and Agriculture Organization of the United Nations, the International Labour Organisation and four international non-governmental organizations, the Secretary-General recommended that the United Nations remain a member of COPAC and continue to contribute to it in 1985. The Advisory Committee on Administrative and Budgetary Questions and the General Assembly concurred with the Secretary-General's recommendation.

The United Nations Research Institute for Social Development continued in 1984 its research programme covering such issues as food systems and society, popular participation, improvement of development data and refugee settlements.

Preparations continued to be made during 1984 for the Seventh (1985) United Nations Congress on the Prevention of Crime and the Treatment of Offenders. Interregional preparatory meetings were held on four of the five substantive items to be taken up by the Congress and the Committee on Crime Prevention and Control, acting as the preparatory body, met for its eighth session at Vienna, Austria, in March. Both the Economic and Social Council and the General Assembly took action on the preparations. The Council accepted an invitation from Italy to hold the Congress at Milan (decision 1984/154) and decided that it would be held from 26 August to 6 September 1985 with the general theme of "Crime prevention for freedom, justice, peace and development" (resolution 1984/45). The Assembly called for broad participation and welcomed the Council's recommendations to the Congress, particularly one on finalizing guidelines on crime prevention and criminal justice in the context of development (resolution 39/112).

A draft declaration on the rights of victims of crimes or other illegal acts involving the abuse of power was discussed and finalized at an interregional preparatory meeting for the 1985 Congress. Draft minimum rules for the administration

of juvenile justice were also recommended to the Congress for consideration. At another preparatory meeting, draft guidelines on the independence of the judiciary were revised, finalized and recommended to the Congress as a matter of highest priority.

Following the Committee's recommendations, the Council adopted several resolutions on other topics related to criminal justice: crime prevention and criminal justice in the context of development (1984/48); fair treatment of women by the criminal justice system (1984/49); alternatives to imprisonment (1984/46); and technical co-operation in crime prevention and criminal justice (1984/51). The Council also approved safeguards guaranteeing protection of the rights of those facing the death penalty (resolution 1984/50) and approved revised procedures for the effective implementation of the 1955 Standard Minimum Rules for the Treatment of Prisoners (1984/47).

The Director-General of the United Nations Educational, Scientific and Cultural Organization proposed the proclamation of a World Decade for Cultural Development beginning in 1986.

Topics related to this chapter. Development policy. Health: disabled persons. Human rights: arbitary and summary executions; rights of detained persons; popular participation. Women: violence against women.

Social development and welfare

Social aspects of development

The Secretary-General, in response to a May 1983 Economic and Social Council decision,[1] submitted in April 1984 a report on the social aspects of development[2] reviewing progress achieved since 1981 in realizing the social goals set forth in the International Development Strategy for the Third United Nations Development Decade (see Chapter I of this section). Those goals included the elimination of poverty, the eradication of hunger and malnutrition, full and productive employment, longer life expectancy, and health, education, literacy and shelter for all. The Strategy also called for the participation by the entire population in development, including equal status for women and the integration into society of vulnerable groups, especially children, youth and disabled persons.

The time-frame set in the Strategy for achieving those objectives extended generally to the year 2000, the Secretary-General said. Only a broad assessment could be made of the extent to which social conditions had changed up to now. In some parts of the developing world, notably in Asia, large groups had improved their standards of living. Elsewhere, particularly in Africa, poverty had increased dramatically; in many countries of Latin America, both the poor and the middle-income groups had experienced a deterioration in their living conditions.

As the labour force continued to expand rapidly and recession or reduced economic growth prevailed, the goal of full employment appeared to be more and more out of reach, added the Secretary-General. Thus, the first prerequisite for the participation of people in the development process could not be met. On the other hand, there were signs of a greater involvement of women and of specific groups in social change. Many demands were voiced, sometimes by the poorest people themselves, for changes in social structures and social mores.

The Strategy outlined policy measures, both national and international, for achieving development goals. One condition was creation by the international community of an environment supportive of national and collective efforts. Such an environment was lacking in the first years of the Decade. Not only was the world economy unstable and in recession, but international cooperation was strained, political tensions had become more pronounced and conflicts persisted or erupted in various parts of the world. More efforts and resources were devoted to military purposes, and the conviction that development was a common cause appeared to falter.

GENERAL ASSEMBLY ACTION

In December 1984, the General Assembly, on the recommendation of the Second (Economic and Financial) Committee, adopted decision 39/427 without vote.

Report of the Secretary-General on social aspects of development

At its 103rd plenary meeting, on 17 December 1984, the General Assembly, on the recommendation of the Second Committee, took note of the report of the Secretary-General on social aspects of development.

General Assembly decision 39/427

Adopted without vote

Approved by Second Committee (A/39/790/ Add.1) without vote, 11 December (meeting 59); oral proposal by Chairman; agenda item 80 *(a)*.
Meeting numbers. GA 39th session: 2nd Committee 59; plenary 103.

Popular participation

Following adoption of a resolution on 6 March 1984 by the Commission on Human Rights,[3] the Economic and Social Council adopted on 24 May decision 1984/131 on popular participation as an important factor in development and in the realization of human rights (see Chapter XVIII of this section).

Co-operatives

In April, the Secretariat submitted a note to the Economic and Social Council on the financial arrangements between the United Nations and COPAC.[4] It stated that, in considering the proposed 1984-1985 programme budget, the Advisory Committee on Administrative and Budgetary Questions (ACABQ) had recommended in 1983 that the financial arrangements between the United Nations and COPAC be reviewed by the Secretary-General. During consideration of the matter in November 1983 in the General Assembly's Fifth (Administrative and Bugetary) Committee, Sweden had proposed that the resources related to COPAC be approved only for 1984, pending the outcome of a review of the financial arrangements by ACABQ; the Fifth Committee had endorsed that proposal on the understanding that the review by the Secretary-General would be submitted to the Assembly in 1984, through the Council.

Established in 1970, COPAC was a liaison body composed of the United Nations, the Food and Agriculture Organization of the United Nations (FAO), the International Labour Organisation (ILO) and four international non-governmental organizations. The United Nations share of COPAC's expenditures was $24,400 in 1984.

The Secretary-General submitted his review also in April.[5] Examining the arrangements against the background of an analysis of COPAC's activities and its contribution to United Nations development efforts, he said he believed that the United Nations should not terminate its financial support to COPAC; such a move could be interpreted as diminished commitment to the cooperative movement and could trigger similar action by other COPAC members. He recommended that the United Nations remain a member of COPAC and that provision be made for a financial contribution to it for 1985; the current level of the United Nations contribution, which was about 15 per cent of COPAC's regular budget, was reasonable and could be maintained, subject to a periodic review.

In an October 1984 report,[6] ACABQ concurred with the Secretary-General's recommendation regarding membership of COPAC and had no objection to the proposed financial arrangements, subject to the observation that, when the United Nations was a party to inter-agency arrangements involving financial commitments, the Secretary-General should make specific reference to those arrangements in future budget submissions.

ECONOMIC AND SOCIAL COUNCIL ACTION

In May 1984, the Economic and Social Council, on the recommendation of its Second (Social) Committee, adopted decision 1984/155 without vote.

Financial arrangements between the United Nations and the Committee for the Promotion of Aid to Co-operatives

At its 21st plenary meeting, on 25 May 1984, the Council:

(a) Took note of the note by the Secretariat on financial arrangements between the United Nations and the Committee for the Promotion of Aid to Co-operatives and of the conclusions on the convergence of the specific objectives of the Committee and the activities of the United Nations contained in the report of the Secretary-General on the question;

(b) Took note of the recommendation of the Secretary-General that the United Nations should remain a member of the Committee.

Economic and Social Council decision 1984/155

Adopted without vote

Approved by Second Committee (E/1984/92) without vote, 23 May (meeting 20); oral proposal by Chairman; agenda item 11.

GENERAL ASSEMBLY ACTION

On 18 December, the General Assembly, on the recommendation of the Fifth Committee, adopted section IV of resolution 39/236 without vote.

Financial arrangements between the United Nations and the Committee for the Promotion of Aid to Co-operatives

[*The General Assembly . . .*]

Having considered the report of the Secretary-General on the financial arrangements between the United Nations and the Committee for the Promotion of Aid to Co-operatives and the related report of the Advisory Committee on Administrative and Budgetary Questions,

Concurs with the observations and recommendations of the Advisory Committee as contained in its report;
. . .

General Assembly resolution 39/236, section IV

18 December 1984   Meeting 105   Adopted without vote

Approved by Fifth Committee (A/39/839) without objection, 22 October (meeting 15); oral proposal by Chairman; agenda item 109.
Meeting numbers. GA 39th session: 5th Committee 15; plenary 105.

Institutional machinery

UN Research Institute for Social Development

In 1984, the United Nations Research Institute for Social Development (UNRISD) continued its research programme[7] which covered issues such

as food systems and society, popular participation, improvement of development data, and refugee settlements.

A study on the impact of social change on women in Burkina Faso, the Ivory Coast and Senegal was completed in 1984. The research was viewed as a first stage of work under way in West Africa on food systems and society; findings showed that, with the expansion of cash crops for export and the modernization of agriculture, some groups had prospered, while others were worse off. At the same time, studies on urban food security problems were conducted in Ouagadougou, Burkina Faso; Abidjan, Ivory Coast; and Dakar, Senegal.

Discussions with the United Nations Children's Fund (UNICEF), which had a large programme on child nutrition in China, led to an agreement under which UNRISD would make available to UNICEF research funds earmarked for China by the United Nations Development Programme (UNDP).

Research continued to identify the determinants of food insecurity in eastern India, a food-deficit region. The work was being conducted in collaboration with the Centre for Regional Ecological and Science Studies in Development Alternatives. In 1984, approximately 2,400 householders in 10 village clusters were surveyed, and seasonal patterns of income, expenditure, food availability and consumption, and morbidity were recorded.

In 1984, UNRISD's income was over $1.6 million, including contributions of $935,822 from nine Governments, and its expenditures amounted to nearly $1.4 million.

REFERENCES

[1]YUN 1983, p. 726, ESC dec. 1983/123, 26 May 1983. [2]A/39/171-E/1984/54. [3]E/1984/14 (res. 1984/15). [4]E/1984/65. [5]A/C.5/38/3. [6]A/39/7/Add.3. [7]E/CN.5/1985/10.

PUBLICATION

The Family Model for Providing Comprehensive Services for Family and Child Welfare (ST/ESA/138), Sales No. E.84.IV.2.

Crime

UN congresses on crime

Preparations for Seventh Congress (1985)

Preparations continued in 1984 for the Seventh (1985) United Nations Congress on the Prevention of Crime and the Treatment of Offenders, with the Committee on Crime Prevention and Control (Committee on crime) functioning as the preparatory committee.[1] Regional and interregional preparatory meetings as well as interagency consultations were held, experts assisted in preparing documentation for the Congress, and a public information programme was carried out.

Interregional meetings were also held on substantive items of the provisional agenda of the Congress, namely: topic 2, criminal justice processes and perspectives in a changing world (Budapest, Hungary, 4-8 June);[2] topic 3, victims of crime (Ottawa, Canada, 9-13 July);[3] topic 4, youth, crime and justice (Beijing, China, 14-18 May);[4] and topic 5, formulation and application of United Nations standards and norms in criminal justice (Varenna, Italy, 24-28 September).[5] Among other recommendations, the meeting in China approved standard minimum rules for the administration of juvenile justice, while the Canada meeting drafted a declaration on the rights of victims. At Varenna, draft guidelines on the independence of the judiciary were revised, finalized and recommended to the Congress for adoption as a matter of highest priority; the meeting also assessed the impact achieved as well as the difficulties encountered in applying the Standard Minimum Rules for the Treatment of Prisoners. The purpose of those and other interregional meetings was to provide a theoretical and technical framework for defining, at the 1985 Congress, new guiding principles for crime prevention and criminal justice in the context of overall development planning.

The Committee on crime also considered the preparations for the Congress.[6] The preparatory activities were outlined by the Executive Secretary of the Congress who described the co-operation provided by the regional commissions and intergovernmental and non-governmental organizations, as well as the assistance given by the United Nations regional crime institutes.

ECONOMIC AND SOCIAL COUNCIL ACTION

On 25 May, the Economic and Social Council, on the recommendation of its Second Committee, adopted resolution 1984/45 by vote.

Continuation of preparations for the Seventh United Nations Congress on the Prevention of Crime and the Treatment of Offenders

The Economic and Social Council,

Recalling General Assembly resolutions 415(V) of 1 December 1950, 32/60 of 8 December 1977 and 36/21 of 9 November 1981,

Recalling also Council resolutions 1982/29 and 1982/30 of 4 May 1982,

Having considered the report of the Secretary-General and the note by the Secretariat relating to preparations for the Seventh United Nations Congress on the Prevention of Crime and the Treatment of Offenders,

Conscious of the need to increase the publicity relating to the Seventh Congress, and the impact of its results,

Aware of the important work to be accomplished by the interregional preparatory meetings,

1. *Takes note* of the reports of the regional preparatory meetings with their respective recommendations on the substantive items of the provisional agenda for the Seventh United Nations Congress on the Prevention of Crime and the Treatment of Offenders;

2. *Takes note also* of the discussion guide for the regional and interregional preparatory meetings for the Seventh Congress;

3. *Recommends* the Seventh Congress to consider in depth the resolutions adopted at the regional preparatory meetings;

4. *Recommends also* the Seventh Congress to finalize, under item 3 of its provisional agenda, the guiding principles for crime prevention and criminal justice in the context of development and a new international economic order as reviewed by the Committee on Crime Prevention and Control on the basis of the observations made at the regional preparatory meetings, and to make every effort to secure their adoption for the strengthening of international co-operation in this field;

5. *Decides* that the Seventh Congress should be held from 26 August to 6 September 1985, with two days of pre-Congress consultations;

6. *Decides also* that items 1, 2, 3 and 8 of the provisional agenda should be considered in plenary meeting, and that items 4 and 7 should be allocated to Committee I and items 5 and 6 to Committee II;

7. *Decides further* that the general theme for the Seventh Congress should be "Crime prevention for freedom, justice, peace and development";

8. *Approves* the documentation for the Seventh Congress as outlined by the Secretary-General;

9. *Invites* Governments to finalize national preparations related to the Seventh Congress, including the submission of national papers, and to consider the inclusion of national correspondents in their delegations to the Congress;

10. *Invites* representatives of the Committee on Crime Prevention and Control attending the interregional preparatory meetings for the Seventh Congress to ensure that reports of the meetings, with related recommendations, are in conformity with the policy guidelines given by the Committee;

11. *Requests* the Secretary-General to appoint a Secretary-General for the Seventh Congress, in accordance with the standard practice for major United Nations conferences;

12. *Also requests* the Secretary-General to invite 25 expert consultants to participate in the Seventh Congress, at the expense of the United Nations, as was done on the occasion of the Sixth Congress, so as to ensure that adequate expertise is provided to the Congress by each region for each substantive item of the provisional agenda;

13. *Further requests* the Secretary-General, in the organization of the Seventh Congress, to include the following activities:

(*a*) Lectures to be given by outstanding experts and scholars selected on the basis of equitable geographical distribution;

(*b*) Research workshop on youth crime and juvenile justice, to be organized with the joint co-operation of the United Nations Social Defence Research Institute, the United Nations regional institutes for the prevention of crime and the treatment of offenders and competent national and international research institutes;

(c) Ancillary meetings of non-governmental organizations in consultative status with the Economic and Social Council concerning items of the provisional agenda, in accordance with existing legislative regulations;

(d) Meetings for professional and geographical interest groups;

(e) General meeting of national correspondents;

14. *Urges* the Secretary-General to strengthen the information programme related to the Seventh Congress.

Economic and Social Council resolution 1984/45

25 May 1984	Meeting 21	41-1-5

Approved by Second Committee (E/1984/92) by recorded vote (39-1-4), 21 May (meeting 19); draft by Committee on crime (E/1984/16); agenda item 11.
Financial implications. ACABQ, A/39/7/Add.6; S-G, A/C.5/39/25, E/1984/16/ Add.1.

Mexico said that it supported the text but that it would make known its final position once it had fully studied the text. China, Pakistan, Romania and Saudi Arabia pointed out that they could not take part in consideration of the draft resolutions based on the report of the Committee on crime since the report had been distributed too late to be studied.

The United States, which requested the vote, voted against the text due to its financial implications. Canada supported the text because of its strong interest in the 1985 Congress, but said that it should be implemented within the resources allocated. Although voting in favour, the United Kingdom mentioned it would take up in the Fifth Committee the financial implications which seemed excessive.

In November, ACABQ said additional costs should be absorbed from within existing resources.

In resolution 1984/51, the Council took note of the recommendations contained in the resolutions adopted at the regional preparatory meetings for the 1985 Congress.

GENERAL ASSEMBLY ACTION

On 14 December, on the recommendation of the Third (Social, Humanitarian and Cultural) Committee, the General Assembly adopted resolution 39/112 without vote.

Seventh United Nations Congress on the Prevention of Crime and the Treatment of Offenders

The General Assembly,

Bearing in mind the responsibility assumed by the United Nations in the field of the prevention of crime and criminal justice under General Assembly resolution 415(V) of 1 December 1950, in particular by convening the quinquennial congresses on the prevention of crime and the treatment of offenders,

Recalling its resolution 36/21 of 9 November 1981, in which it requested the Secretary-General to take the necessary measures for the fullest implementation of the Caracas Declaration and for the appropriate preparation of the Seventh United Nations Congress on the Prevention of Crime and the Treatment of Offenders,

Recalling also Economic and Social Council resolutions 1982/29 of 4 May 1982, in which the Council approved the provisional agenda for the Seventh Congress, and 1984/45 of 25 May 1984 on the continuation of preparations for the Congress, as well as Council resolution 1984/51 of 25 May 1984 on technical co-operation in crime prevention and criminal justice,

Taking note of Economic and Social Council decision 1984/154 of 25 May 1984, in which it accepted the invitation of the Government of Italy to hold the Seventh Congress at Milan from 26 August to 6 September 1985,

Acknowledging that criminality, particularly violent and organized crime, constitutes a serious threat to the development and security of nations,

Recognizing that constraints of an economic and technical nature impede many countries in their fight against crime,

Reiterating the necessity for the international community to make concerted and systematic efforts to strengthen technical and scientific co-operation in crime prevention and criminal justice and to formulate fair, humane and effective policies directed towards crime control in the context of different political and cultural systems, economic and social development and social values and changes,

Convinced of the important role played by the previous congresses in promoting understanding, awareness and co-operation and in achieving further progress in this field,

Stressing the need to improve further regional, interregional and international co-operation and co-ordination in order to intensify the struggle against crime,

1. *Expresses its appreciation* to the Government of Italy for its offer to act as host to the Seventh United Nations Congress on the Prevention of Crime and the Treatment of Offenders;

2. *Reaffirms its hope* that the Seventh Congress will make an important and useful contribution to the solution of problems related to crime prevention and criminal justice;

3. *Welcomes* Economic and Social Council resolutions 1982/29 and 1984/45 and, in particular, the recommendation that the Seventh Congress finalize new guiding principles on crime prevention and criminal justice in the context of development;

4. *Welcomes also* the recommendations made by the Economic and Social Council in its resolution 1984/51 on improved modalities of technical co-operation in crime prevention and criminal justice;

5. *Takes note* of the preparatory work carried out by the Committee on Crime Prevention and Control, as the preparatory body for the Seventh Congress, at its eighth session and by the regional and interregional preparatory meetings convened in co-operation with the regional commissions, interregional and regional crime prevention institutes and interested Governments;

6. *Calls upon* Governments, United Nations bodies, the specialized agencies and other intergovernmental organizations, as well as interested non-governmental organizations in consultative status with the Economic and Social Council, to participate in the Seventh Congress and to intensify and expand their technical and scientific preparations for it;

7. *Invites* the Economic and Social Council at its first regular session of 1985 to approve the provisional rules of procedure of the Seventh Congress;

8. *Requests* the Seventh Congress, under item 3 of its provisional agenda, to give urgent attention to the

strengthening of technical co-operation in crime prevention and criminal justice, in pursuance of the recommendations of the regional preparatory meetings and the Committee on Crime Prevention and Control;

9. *Invites* the Seventh Congress to pay particular attention to the question of illicit drug trafficking;

10. *Appeals* to Member States to consider contributing to the United Nations Trust Fund for Social Defence, in order to enable the Fund to undertake activities of assistance to countries requesting it, and to allocate an appropriate portion of their resources to programmes for the reduction of crime and the improvement of criminal justice;

11. *Requests* the Secretary-General to ensure that the substantive and organizational work of the Seventh Congress is fully adequate for its successful outcome;

12. *Also requests* the Secretary-General to submit to the General Assembly at its fortieth session, in accordance with past practice, a report on the implementation of the recommendations of the Sixth Congress, to be prepared for the Seventh Congress in pursuance of paragraph 4 of Economic and Social Council resolution 1982/29;

13. *Further requests* the Secretary-General to submit to the General Assembly at its fortieth session his views and recommendations on the implementation of the conclusions of the Seventh Congress;

14. *Decides* to include in the provisional agenda of its fortieth session an item entitled "Crime prevention and criminal justice: report of the Seventh United Nations Congress on the Prevention of Crime and the Treatment of Offenders".

General Assembly resolution 39/112

14 December 1984   Meeting 101   Adopted without vote

Approved by Third Committee (A/39/700) without vote, 6 December (meeting 64); 31-nation draft (A/C.3/39/L.74); agenda item 12.

Sponsors: Bangladesh, Belgium, Bolivia, Canada, China, Colombia, Costa Rica, Denmark, Finland, France, Greece, Hungary, Indonesia, Italy, Ivory Coast, Japan, Morocco, Norway, Portugal, Samoa, Sierra Leone, Spain, Sudan, Sweden, Thailand, Togo, United States, Uruguay, Venezuela, Zaire, Zambia.

Meeting numbers. GA 39th session: 3rd Committee 61, 64; plenary 101.

Venue of Congress

On 29 March 1984, Italy informed the Committee on crime that it wished to act as host to the 1985 Congress and, the following day, the Committee took note of the offer with appreciation.[7]

On 27 April 1984, by a note verbale to the Secretary-General,[8] Italy proposed that the Congress be held in Milan.

ECONOMIC AND SOCIAL COUNCIL ACTION

In May, on the recommendation of its Second Committee, the Economic and Social Council adopted decision 1984/154 without vote.

Seventh United Nations Congress on the Prevention of Crime and the Treatment of Offenders

At its 21st plenary meeting, on 25 May 1984, the Council took note with appreciation of the invitation of the Government of Italy to hold the Seventh United Nations Congress on the Prevention of Crime and the Treatment of Offenders at Milan and decided to accept that invitation.

Economic and Social Council decision 1984/154

Adopted without vote

Approved by Second Committee (E/1984/92) without vote, 23 May (meeting 20); 3-nation draft (E/1984/C.2/L.9); agenda item 11.

Sponsors: Costa Rica, Japan, Sri Lanka.

Before the vote, the Secretary of the Council said that it was the Secretary-General's understanding that Italy would defray any additional costs of holding the Congress within its territory.

GENERAL ASSEMBLY ACTION

In resolution 39/112, the General Assembly expressed its appreciation to Italy for its offer to host the Congress.

Provisional rules of procedure

ECONOMIC AND SOCIAL COUNCIL ACTION

In May 1984, on the recommendation of its Second Committee, the Economic and Social Council adopted decision 1984/152 without vote.

Provisional rules of procedure for United Nations congresses on the prevention of crime and the treatment of offenders

At its 21st plenary meeting, on 25 May 1984, the Council decided to defer until its first regular session of 1985 the consideration of draft resolution I, entitled "Provisional rules of procedure for United Nations congresses on the prevention of crime and the treatment of offenders", contained in the report of the Committee on Crime Prevention and Control on its eighth session.

Economic and Social Council decision 1984/152

Adopted without vote

Approved by Second Committee (E/1984/92) without vote, 23 May (meeting 20); oral proposal by Chairman; agenda item 11.

If adopted, the rules would supersede those approved by the Council in 1979.[9]

Committee on crime

The Committee on crime held its eighth session at Vienna, Austria, from 21 to 30 March 1984. In its report to the Council,[10] it recommended draft resolutions on: provisional rules of procedure for United Nations crime congresses; preparations for the 1985 Congress; alternatives to imprisonment; procedures for implementing the Standard Minimum Rules for the Treatment of Prisoners; crime prevention and criminal justice in the context of development; fair treatment of women by the criminal justice system; safeguards guaranteeing protection of the rights of those facing the death penalty; and technical co-operation in crime prevention and criminal justice.

The Committee recommended that the Council transmit to the 1985 Congress draft resolutions on guiding principles for crime prevention and criminal justice in the context of development and a new international economic order,[11] and on a model agreement on the transfer of foreign prisoners.[12] It further recommended that the Council: endorse draft guidelines on the independence of the judiciary; invite the interregional preparatory meeting on United Nations standards and norms in criminal justice to finalize those draft guidelines in co-operation with all parties concerned; and request the Secretary-General to submit the finalized text to the 1985 Congress for adoption.[13] By a fourth decision,[14] the Committee recommended to the Council to forward draft rules on standard minimum rules for the administration of juvenile justice, proposed in a report of the Secretary-General, to the Congress through the interregional meeting on youth, crime and justice. Following consideration of another report of the Secretary-General on the Code of Conduct for Law Enforcement Officials, the Committee, noting that more information would be required to assess the Code's implementation, recommended that the Council request the Secretary-General to invite Member States to provide the necessary information, so that a comprehensive report could be submitted to the 1985 Congress.[15] A resolution on victims of crimes and of abuses of power, adopted by the Committee on 29 March 1984,[16] was also brought to the Council's attention, as were two decisions by which the Committee took note of two reports of the Secretary-General: on procedures for the effective implementation of the Standard Minimum Rules for the Treatment of Prisoners,[17] and on United Nations activities in crime prevention and criminal justice.[18]

ECONOMIC AND SOCIAL COUNCIL ACTION

In May 1984, on the recommendation of its Second Committee, the Economic and Social Council adopted decision 1984/153 without vote.

Report of the Committee on Crime Prevention and Control on its eighth session and provisional agenda and documentation for the ninth session of the Committee

At its 21st plenary meeting, on 25 May 1984, the Council:

(a) Took note of the report of the Committee on Crime Prevention and Control on its eighth session;

(b) Approved the recommendations made by the Committee in its decisions 8/1, 8/2, 8/3, as amended, 8/4 and 8/5;

(c) Approved the provisional agenda and documentation for the ninth session of the Committee set out below.

Provisional agenda and documentation for the ninth session of the Committee on Crime Prevention and Control

1. Election of officers.
2. Adoption of the agenda.
3. Review of the rules of procedure for United Nations congresses on the prevention of crime and the treatment of offenders (rule 62 of the provisional rules

of procedure for United Nations congresses on the prevention of crime and the treatment of offenders).
   Documentation
   Note by the Secretary-General
4. Progress report on United Nations activities in crime prevention and control.
   Documentation
   Report of the Secretary-General on United Nations activities in crime prevention and control
5. Preparations for the Eighth United Nations Congress on the Prevention of Crime and the Treatment of Offenders.
   Documentation
   Report of the Secretary-General on the implementation of the conclusions and recommendations of the Seventh United Nations Congress on the Prevention of Crime and the Treatment of Offenders
   Note by the Secretary-General on the preparations for the Eighth United Nations Congress on the Prevention of Crime and the Treatment of Offenders
6. Crime prevention and criminal justice in the context of development (Economic and Social Council resolution 1979/19).
   Documentation
   Report of the Secretary-General on crime prevention and criminal justice in relation to socio-economic change and development
7. Consideration of the provisional agenda for the tenth session of the Committee.
8. Adoption of the report of the Committee.

Economic and Social Council decision 1984/153

Adopted without vote

Approved by Second Committee (E/1984/92) without vote, 23 May (meeting 20); draft by Committee on crime (E/1984/16), orally amended by Second Committee Chairman; agenda item 11.

Subparagraph *(b)* was inserted on the oral proposal by the Second Committee Chairman.

Questions related to criminal justice

Crime prevention and development

In January 1984, the Secretary-General submitted to the Committee on crime two reports on crime prevention and criminal justice in the context of development. In the first, on the relationship between crime and specific socio-economic issues,[19] prepared pursuant to a 1980 General Assembly resolution,[20] he considered demographic, economic, social and cultural factors that accompanied high and low crime rates, and found that some very tentative conclusions seemed justifiable. Phenomena such as misery or extreme poverty, despair and hopelessness, lack of opportunities, glaring social injustices, exploitation, maltreatment and humiliation of minorities and different kinds of discrimination and segregation appeared to contribute to social disorganization and thus to the probability of criminal behaviour. The family seemed to play a crucial role in generating law-abiding behaviour. In some circumstances, socio-economic development, rapid social change, demographic growth, urbanization, rural-urban migration, etc. might have a harmful influence on individuals, especially young people, and social structure and might lead to crime. However, socio-economic change was not necessarily criminogenic; only when carried out in an unplanned and socially disorganizing fashion did it become a source of anti-social behaviour.

It appeared particularly important to protect young people from the dysfunctional effects of social change. Policies aimed at providing them with educational and employment opportunities, as well as full participation in the development and political processes of their countries, could reduce youth crime rates, the Secretary-General continued. The mass media could be used more extensively in crime prevention, for example, by promoting social values. A dynamic perspective of interrelated activities and functions in legislation, law enforcement, the judicial process and the treatment of offenders might prove useful in ensuring coherence between national planning and crime prevention and criminal justice planning. There seemed to be an acute need for studies assessing current and future socio-economic issues of development and crime trends.

A second report, on crime trends and crime prevention strategies,[21] submitted in response to a May 1983 Economic and Social Council decision,[22] concerned the second United Nations survey of crime trends, operations of criminal justice systems and crime prevention strategies, based on a questionnaire sent to Member States of which 52 replied. The results of the questionnaire were analysed at a 1983 meeting.[23]

The preliminary results of the survey reinforced the concerns of the 1980 United Nations Congress on the Prevention of Crime and the Treatment of Offenders which had noted a world-wide need to develop reliable statistical information about crime.[24] The results indicated that adequate comparable data were not available to provide the basis for a comprehensive analysis of crime trends. Therefore, preparation of a manual on the collection and analysis of crime data would be a major step towards improving the availability of comparable statistics for national and international use, the Secretary-General concluded.

On 30 March 1984, the Committee adopted a decision on guiding principles for crime prevention and criminal justice in the context of development and a new international economic order.[11] The principles covered crime prevention and a new economic order, national development and the prevention of crime, the responsiveness of the

criminal justice system to development and human rights, and international co-operation in crime prevention and criminal justice. The Committee recommended that the Economic and Social Council transmit the principles to the 1985 Congress.

ECONOMIC AND SOCIAL COUNCIL ACTION

On 25 May 1984, on the recommendation of its Second Committee, the Economic and Social Council adopted resolution 1984/48 without vote.

Crime prevention and criminal justice in the context of development

The Economic and Social Council,

Having considered the report of the Committee on Crime Prevention and Control in respect of crime trends, operations of criminal justice systems and crime prevention strategies in the context of social and economic change, and with respect to the different facets of development,

Emphasizing the progress made towards the provision of assistance to Member States in improving national crime-related statistics, the establishment of a United Nations crime-related data base, and the long-term nature of such programmes of work,

1. *Takes note, with appreciation,* of the reports of the Secretary-General on the relationship between crime and specific socio-economic issues and on crime trends and crime prevention strategies;

2. *Recommends* the Seventh United Nations Congress on the Prevention of Crime and the Treatment of Offenders to give detailed consideration both to the further development of such studies, including specific questions such as the relationship between criminality and particular socio-economic factors, for example, the transmission of social values and changes in family functions, and to concrete problems of crime and criminal justice data, in the light of the Second United Nations Survey of Crime Trends, Operations of Criminal Justice Systems and Crime Prevention Strategies, and the proposed manual on the collection and analysis of crime statistics;

3. *Requests* the Secretary-General to submit a report on crime prevention and criminal justice in relation to socio-economic change and development to the Committee on Crime Prevention and Control at its ninth session;

4. *Also requests* the Secretary-General to maintain and develop the United Nations crime-related data base by continuing to conduct quinquennial surveys of crime trends, operations of criminal justice systems and crime prevention strategies, and to report periodically to the Committee on Crime Prevention and Control on the progress made;

5. *Further requests* the Secretary-General to develop concrete projects of technical co-operation for assistance in the collection and analysis of criminal justice data to Member States requesting such assistance.

Economic and Social Council resolution 1984/48

25 May 1984   Meeting 21   Adopted without vote

Approved by Second Committee (E/1984/92) without vote, 23 May (meeting 20); draft by Committee on crime (E/1984/16); agenda item 11.

In resolution 1984/51, the Council called on States, in considering crime prevention and criminal justice in the context of development, to encourage the exchange of data, information and experiences, and other regional activities. It requested United Nations bodies to strengthen support for technical co-operation in crime prevention between developed and developing countries, and also among developing countries.

Prevention of abuses of power

The Secretary-General submitted to the Committee on crime in March 1984 three reports on: criminal abuses of power—their patterns, trends and impact; prevention and control; and guidelines for measures on behalf of victims.

The first report examined criminal acts involving abuses of power, as well as a typology of offenders and victims.[25] More knowledge was required about illegal acts involving abuses of power, the kinds of victimization they caused and the types of victims and victimizers if adequate policies for their prevention and control were to be instituted nationally and complementary international and regional action was to be taken for abuses that cut across national frontiers, the Secretary-General said, and in-depth investigations, including case-studies, should help to further explore the socio-economic and political context in which abuses of power occurred. The development of forecasting techniques and more effective evaluation methods could also assist in tracing trends of offences linked to abuses of power.

A second report on legislative provisions against abuses of power and measures used for their prevention and control,[26] submitted in response to a May 1983 Economic and Social Council decision,[22] was based on information supplied by 31 Member States. The vast majority of the replies described existing legislation to prevent or control illicit abuses of economic, public or political power. Some material was provided on proposed or envisaged draft legislation, and on the assessment of the effectiveness of existing provisions and practices. Generally, it was agreed that international co-operation to avoid and remedy abuses of economic and public or political power was necessary.

Guidelines for measures on behalf of victims of crime and abuses of power were considered in a third report,[27] following a recommendation of the 1980 Congress.[24] Among the issues to be covered by those guidelines were their purposes and principles, a definition of "victim", harms for which redress or sanction should be provided, procedures to determine violations and identify victims, indemnification and other forms of redress, services and support for victims, parties responsible for redress and/or subject to sanctions, and preventive and corrective strategies.

For problems such as those of victims of crime and abuses of power, the most wide-ranging, comprehensive and concerted strategies were called for, involving national, regional and international action and starting with action to meet the most urgent needs as well as providing medium- and long-term perspectives, the Secretary-General concluded. The formulation of guidelines was a prerequisite. A draft declaration on the rights of victims of crimes or other illegal acts involving the abuse of power was presented for discussion in an annex to the report. The draft declaration was considered at an interregional meeting held in July at Ottawa, Canada.

On 29 March, the Committee adopted a resolution on victims of crimes and abuses of power,[16] by which it took note of the Secretary-General's reports; welcomed efforts made as a valuable basis for future work; recommended that the interregional preparatory meeting for the 1985 Congress seek a comprehensive agreement on a draft declaration; and further recommended that continued priority be given to the question of victimization and the means of its containment and redress.

Treatment of prisoners

Minimum rules for treatment of prisoners

The Secretary-General, responding to a recommendation of the 1980 Congress,[24] submitted to the Committee on crime in January 1984 a report[28] on procedures for implementing the 1955 United Nations Standard Minimum Rules for the Treatment of Prisoners, endorsed by the Economic and Social Council in 1957.[29] He pointed out that those Rules were never intended to describe in detail a model penal system, but attempted to set out principles and practice for the social rehabilitation of prisoners, having in mind the great variety of legal, social, economic and geographical conditions. A revised text of the procedures on the basis of discussions at the 1980 Congress and comments from Member States was appended to the report. On 30 March 1984,[17] the Committee took note of the report.

An interregional preparatory meeting (Varenna, Italy) for the 1985 Congress assessed the impact achieved as well as the difficulties encountered in applying the Standard Minimum Rules.

ECONOMIC AND SOCIAL COUNCIL ACTION

On 25 May 1984, on the recommendation of its Second Committee, the Economic and Social Council adopted resolution 1984/47 without vote.

Procedures for the effective implementation of the Standard Minimum Rules for the Treatment of Prisoners

The Economic and Social Council,

Considering the importance of the recommendations contained in the Standard Minimum Rules for the Treatment of Prisoners adopted by the First United Nations Congress on the Prevention of Crime and the Treatment of Offenders, and approved by the Council in its resolution 663 C (XXIV) of 31 July 1957,

Noting with satisfaction the impact of the Rules on national laws and practices,

Concerned, however, that there still exist obstacles of various kinds to the full implementation of the Rules, as evidenced in the periodic United Nations reports on their implementation,

Recalling the recommendations of the Fifth United Nations Congress on the Prevention of Crime and the Treatment of Offenders, and Council resolution 1993(LX) of 12 May 1976, in which the Committee on Crime Prevention and Control was requested at its fourth session to study the range of application of the Rules and to formulate a set of implementing procedures for the Rules,

Taking note with appreciation of the work accomplished in pursuance of that mandate by the Committee on Crime Prevention and Control at its fourth session in 1976 and at its eighth session in pursuance of the recommendations of the Sixth United Nations Congress on the Prevention of Crime and the Treatment of Offenders, which invited the Committee to finalize the procedures in the light of its report,

1. *Approves* the procedures for the effective implementation of the Standard Minimum Rules for the Treatment of Prisoners, as set out in the annex to the present resolution;

2. *Invites* Member States to take the procedures annexed hereto into consideration in the process of implementing the Rules and in their periodic reports to the United Nations;

3. *Requests* the Secretary-General to bring the present resolution to the attention of the Governments of the Member States, and to assist them at their request in implementing the Rules in accordance with the procedures annexed hereto.

ANNEX
Procedures for the effective implementation of the Standard Minimum Rules for the Treatment of Prisoners

Procedure 1

All States whose standards for the protection of all persons subjected to any form of detention or imprisonment fall short of the Standard Minimum Rules for the Treatment of Prisoners shall adopt the Rules.

Commentary

The General Assembly, in its resolution 2858(XXVI) of 20 December 1971, invited the attention of Member States to the Standard Minimum Rules and recommended that they should be effectively implemented in the administration of penal and correctional institutions and that favourable consideration should be given to their incorporation in national legislation. Some States may have standards that are more advanced than the Rules, and the adoption of the Rules is therefore not requested on the part of such States. Where States feel that the Rules need to be harmonized with their legal system and adapted to their culture, the emphasis is placed on the substance rather than the letter of the Rules.

Procedure 2

Subject, as necessary, to their adaptation to the existing laws and culture but without deviation from the spirit and purpose of the Rules, the Standard Minimum Rules shall be embodied in national legislation and other regulations.

Commentary

This procedure emphasizes that it is necessary to embody the Rules within national legislation and regulations, thus covering also some aspects of procedure 1.

Procedure 3

The Standard Minimum Rules shall be made available to all persons concerned, particularly to law enforcement officials and correctional personnel, for purposes of enabling their application and execution in the criminal justice system.

Commentary

This procedure stresses that the Rules, as well as national statutes and regulations implementing the Rules, should be made available to all persons concerned with their implementation, in particular law enforcement officials and correctional personnel. The effective implementation of the Rules might also involve the organization of training courses by the central administration in charge of correctional matters. The dissemination of procedures is discussed in procedures 7 to 9.

Procedure 4

The Standard Minimum Rules, as embodied in national legislation and other regulations, shall also be made available and understandable to all prisoners and all persons under detention, on their admission and during their confinement.

Commentary

To achieve the goal of the Standard Minimum Rules, it is necessary to make the Rules, as well as the implementing national statutes and regulations, available to prisoners and all persons under detention (rule 95), in order to further the awareness that the Rules represent the minimum conditions that are accepted as suitable by the United Nations. Thus, this procedure supplements the provisions contained in procedure 3.

A similar requirement, that the Rules be made available to the persons for whose protection they have been elaborated, has been already established in the four Geneva Conventions of 12 August 1949, of which articles 47 of the first Convention, 48 of the second, 127 of the third and 144 of the fourth state in common:

"The High Contracting Parties undertake, in time of peace as in time of war, to disseminate the text of the present Convention as widely as possible in their respective countries, and, in particular, to include the study thereof in their programmes of military and, if possible, civil instruction, so that the principles thereof may become known to the entire population, in particular to the armed fighting forces, the medical personnel and the chaplains."

Procedure 5

States shall inform the Secretary-General of the United Nations every five years of the extent of the implementation and the progress made with regard to the application of the Standard Minimum Rules, and of the factors and difficulties, if any, affecting their implementation, by responding to the Secretary-General's questionnaire. This questionnaire should, following a specified schedule, be selective and limited to specific questions in order to secure an in-depth review and study of the problems selected. Taking into account the reports of Governments as well as other relevant information available within the United Nations system, the Secretary-General shall prepare independent periodic reports on progress made with respect to the implementation of the Standard Minimum Rules. In the preparation of those reports the Secretary-General may also enlist the co-operation of specialized agencies and of the relevant intergovernmental organizations and non-governmental organizations in consultative status with the Economic and Social Council. The Secretary-General shall submit the above-mentioned reports to the Committee on Crime Prevention and Control for consideration and further action, as appropriate.

Commentary

It will be recalled that the Economic and Social Council, in its resolution 663 C (XXIV) of 31 July 1957, recommended that the Secretary-General be informed every five years of the progress made with regard to the application of the Standard Minimum Rules and authorized the Secretary-General to make arrangements for the publication, as appropriate, of such information and to ask for supplementary information if necessary. Seeking the co-operation of specialized agencies and relevant intergovernmental and non-governmental organizations is a well-established United Nations practice. In the preparation of his independent report, on progress made with respect to the implementation of the Standard Minimum Rules, the Secretary-General will take into account, *inter alia,* information available in the human rights organs of the United Nations, including the Commission on Human Rights, the Sub-Commission on Prevention of Discrimination and Protection of Minorities, the Human Rights Committee functioning under the International Covenant on Civil and Political Rights, and the Committee on the Elimination of Racial Discrimination. The implementation work under the future convention against torture could also be taken into account, as well as any information which might be gathered under the body of principles for the protection of prisoners and detainees currently under preparation in the General Assembly.

Procedure 6

As part of the information mentioned in procedure 5 above, States should provide the Secretary-General with:

(a) Copies or abstracts of all laws, regulations and administrative measures concerning the application of the Standard Minimum Rules to persons under detention and to places and programmes of detention;

(b) Any data and descriptive material on treatment programmes, personnel and the number of persons under any form of detention, and statistics, if available;

(c) Any other relevant information on the implementation of the Rules, as well as information on the possible difficulties in their application.

Commentary

This requirement derives from both resolution 663 C (XXIV) of the Economic and Social Council and the recommendations of the United Nations congresses on the prevention of crime and the treatment of offenders. Although the items of information suggested here are not specifically provided for, it seems feasible to collect such information in order to assist Member States in overcoming difficulties through an exchange of experience. Furthermore, the request for such information is analogous to the existing periodic reporting system on human rights originally established by the Economic and Social Council in its resolution 624 B (XXII) of 1 August 1956.

Procedure 7

The Secretary-General shall disseminate the Standard Minimum Rules and the present implementing procedures, in as many languages as possible, and make them available to all States and intergovernmental and non-governmental organizations concerned, in order to ensure the widest circulation of the Rules and the present implementing procedures.

Commentary

The need for the widest possible dissemination of the Standard Minimum Rules is self-evident. Close co-operation with all appropriate intergovernmental and non-governmental organizations is important to secure more effective dissemination and implementation of the Rules. Therefore, the Secretariat should maintain close contacts with such organizations and should make relevant information and data available to them. It should also encourage those organizations to disseminate information about the Standard Minimum Rules and the implementing procedures.

Procedure 8

The Secretary-General shall disseminate his reports on the implementation of the Rules, including analytical summaries of the periodic surveys, reports of the Committee on Crime Prevention and Control, reports prepared for the United Nations congresses on the prevention of crime and the treatment of offenders as well as the reports of the congresses, scientific publications and other relevant documentation as from time to time may be deemed necessary to further the implementation of the Standard Minimum Rules.

Commentary

This procedure reflects the present practice of disseminating such reports as part of the documentation for the United Nations bodies concerned, as United Nations publications or as articles in the *Yearbook on Human Rights* and the *International Review of Criminal Policy,* the *Crime Prevention and Criminal Justice Newsletter* and any other relevant publications.

Procedure 9

The Secretary-General shall ensure the widest possible reference to and use of the text of the Standard Minimum Rules by the United Nations in all its relevant programmes, including technical co-operation activities.

Commentary

It should be ensured that all relevant United Nations bodies include or make reference to the Rules and the implementing procedures, thus contributing to wider dissemination and increasing the awareness of specialized agencies, governmental, intergovernmental and non-governmental bodies and the general public of the Rules and of the commitment of the Economic and Social Council and the General Assembly to their implementation.

The extent to which the Rules have any practical effect on correctional administrations depends to a great extent on the measures through which they permeate local legislative and administrative practices. They should be known and understood by a wide range of professionals and non-professionals throughout the world. Therefore there is a great need for more publicity in any form, which could also be attained by frequent references to the Rules, accompanied by public information campaigns.

Procedure 10

As part of its technical co-operation and development programmes the United Nations shall:

(a) Aid Governments, at their request, in setting up and strengthening comprehensive and humane correctional systems;

(b) Make available to Governments requesting them the services of experts and regional and interregional advisers on crime prevention and criminal justice;

(c) Promote national and regional seminars and other meetings at the professional and non-professional levels to further the dissemination of the Standard Minimum Rules and the present implementing procedures;

(d) Strengthen substantive support to regional research and training institutes in crime prevention and criminal justice that are associated with the United Nations.

The United Nations regional research and training institutes in crime prevention and criminal justice, in co-operation with national institutions, shall develop curricula and training materials, based on the Standard Minimum Rules and the present implementing procedures, suitable for use in criminal justice educational programmes at all levels, as well as in specialized courses on human rights and other related subjects.

Commentary

The purpose of this procedure is to ensure that the United Nations technical assistance programmes and the training activities of the United Nations regional institutes are used as indirect instruments for the application of the Standard Minimum Rules and the present implementing procedures. Apart from regular training courses for correctional personnel, training manuals and the like, particularly at the policy and decision-making level, provision should be made for expert advice on the questions submitted by Member States, including an expert referral system to interested States. This expert referral system seems particularly necessary in order to implement the Rules according to their spirit and with a view to the socio-economic structure of the countries requesting such assistance.

Procedure 11

The United Nations Committee on Crime Prevention and Control shall:

(a) Keep under review, from time to time, the Standard Minimum Rules, with a view to the elaboration of new rules, standards and procedures applicable to the treatment of persons deprived of liberty;

(b) Follow up the present implementing procedures, including periodic reporting under procedure 5 above.

Commentary

As most of the information collected in the course of periodic inquiries as well as during technical assistance missions would be brought to the attention of the Committee on Crime Prevention and Control, ensuring the effectiveness of the Rules in improving correctional practices rests with the Committee, whose recommendations would determine the future course in the application of the Rules, together with the implementing procedures. The Committee should therefore clearly define existing shortcomings in or the reasons for the lack of implementation of the Rules, *inter alia,* through contacts with the judiciary and ministries of justice of the countries concerned, with the view to suggesting appropriate remedies.

Procedure 12

The Committee on Crime Prevention and Control shall assist the General Assembly, the Economic and Social Council and any other United Nations human rights bodies, as appropriate, with recommendations relating to reports of *ad hoc* inquiry commissions, with respect to matters pertaining to the application and implementation of the Standard Minimum Rules.

Commentary

As the Committee on Crime Prevention and Control is the relevant body to review the implementation of the Standard Minimum Rules, it should also assist the above-mentioned bodies.

Procedure 13

Nothing in the present implementing procedures should be construed as precluding resort to any other means or remedies available under international law or set forth by other United Nations bodies and agencies for the redress of violations of human rights, including the procedure on consistent patterns of gross violations of human rights under Economic and Social Council resolution 1503(XLVIII) of 27 May 1970, the communication procedure under the Optional Protocol to the International Covenant on Civil and Political Rights and the communication procedure under the International Convention on the Elimination of All Forms of Racial Discrimination.

Commentary

Since the Standard Minimum Rules are only partly concerned with specific human rights issues, the present procedures should not exclude any avenue for redress of any violation of such rights, in accordance with existing international or regional standards and norms.

Economic and Social Council resolution 1984/47

25 May 1984   Meeting 21   Adopted without vote

Approved by Second Committee (E/1984/92) without vote, 23 May (meeting 20); draft by Committee on crime (E/1984/16); agenda item 11.

GENERAL ASSEMBLY ACTION

On 14 December 1984, on the recommendation of the Third Committee, the General Assembly adopted resolution 39/118 without vote.

Human rights in the administration of justice

The General Assembly,

Mindful of articles 3, 5, 9, 10 and 11 of the Universal Declaration of Human Rights, as well as the relevant provisions of the International Covenant on Civil and Political Rights, in particular article 6, which explicitly states that no one shall be arbitrarily deprived of his life,

Recalling its resolutions 2858(XXVI) of 20 December 1971 and 3144(XXVIII) of 14 December 1973 on human rights in the administration of justice,

Recalling also Economic and Social Council resolutions 1984/47 and 1984/50 of 25 May 1984, in which, *inter alia*, the Council approved the procedures for the effective implementation of the Standard Minimum Rules for the Treatment of Prisoners and the safeguards guaranteeing protection of the rights of those facing the death penalty,

Acknowledging the important work accomplished by the Committee on Crime Prevention and Control at its eighth session,

Aware that the Seventh United Nations Congress on the Prevention of Crime and the Treatment of Offenders, to be held from 26 August to 6 September 1985, will consider the issues related to the formulation and application of United Nations standards and norms in the administration of justice under item 7 of its provisional agenda, in accordance with Economic and Social Council resolution 1982/29 of 4 May 1982,

Convinced of the need for further co-ordinated and concerted action in promoting respect for the principles embodied in the aforementioned articles of the Universal Declaration of Human Rights,

1. *Reaffirms* the existing prohibition under international law of every form of cruel, inhuman or degrading treatment or punishment, and strongly condemns the practice of arbitrary and summary executions;

2. *Endorses* the recommendations contained in Economic and Social Council resolutions 1984/47 and 1984/50 on procedures for the effective implementation of the Standard Minimum Rules for the Treatment of Prisoners and on safeguards guaranteeing protection of the rights of those facing the death penalty, respectively, as well as the provisions of their annexes;

3. *Calls upon* Member States to spare no effort in providing for adequate mechanisms, procedures and resources so as to ensure the implementation of these recommendations, both in law and in practice;

4. *Requests* the Seventh United Nations Congress on the Prevention of Crime and the Treatment of Offenders, under item 7 of its provisional agenda, to give urgent attention to the matter of devising ways and means to ensure more effective application of existing standards and to report thereon to the General Assembly at its fortieth session;

5. *Requests* the Secretary-General to discharge fully his tasks in connection with the implementation of the Standard Minimum Rules for the Treatment of Prisoners, particularly with regard to procedures 7, 8, 9 and 10 contained in the annex to Economic and Social Council resolution 1984/47, and to employ his best endeavours in cases where the safeguards guaranteeing the protection of the rights of those facing the death penalty are violated;

6. *Requests* the Economic and Social Council, through the Committee on Crime Prevention and Control, to keep these matters under constant review;

7. *Invites* the specialized agencies and other organizations of the United Nations system, as well as intergovernmental and non-governmental organizations concerned, to continue to co-operate with the Secretary-General in these endeavours by providing assistance, as may be appropriate, and by submitting proposals for relevant action to the Seventh Congress;

8. *Decides* to consider at its fortieth session the question of human rights in the administration of justice.

General Assembly resolution 39/118

14 December 1984   Meeting 101   Adopted without vote

Approved by Third Committee (A/39/700) without vote, 7 December (meeting 66); 14-nation draft (A/C.3/39/L.82), orally revised; agenda item 12.

Sponsors: Austria, Belgium, Bolivia, Colombia, Costa Rica, Germany, Federal Republic of, Japan, Netherlands, New Zealand, Norway, Samoa, Sweden, Uruguay, Zambia.

Meeting numbers. GA 39th session: 3rd Committee 61, 66; plenary 101.

Minimum rules for administration of juvenile justice

Following a recommendation of the 1980 Congress on crime prevention,[24] the Secretary-General submitted to the Committee on crime in January 1984 a report on standard minimum rules for the administration of juvenile justice.[30] The draft rules, he said, were based on current legislation, procedures, practices and experiences of many countries in all regions and were the result of studies, research and meetings in which the impact of various institutions and forms had been taken into account. The proposed rules were included in the report with commentary.

On 30 March,[14] the Committee recommended that the Economic and Social Council forward the draft rules, after necessary modifications, to the 1985 Congress, through the interregional preparatory meeting on youth, crime and justice. The meeting, held in May at Beijing, China, approved the rules and recommended them to the Congress for consideration.

Treatment of women by criminal justice system

In January 1984, the Secretary-General submitted a report to the Committee on crime on the fair treatment of women by the criminal justice system,[31] in response to a recommendation of the 1980 Congress.[24] The report gave an overview of preliminary findings of a global survey to which 48 countries had responded. It dealt with female administrators in the criminal justice system, female criminality and delinquency, differential treatment of female offenders, and female victimization.

The Secretary-General concluded that an initial step forward had been taken in collecting internationally comparable data. While in some parts of the world, female criminality did not seem to be a particular problem, in others it assumed serious proportions or characteristics. Such criminality required criminal justice systems to respond in an equitable and humane way, with consideration of the special needs and problems of females while in custody. Many respondents had emphasized that greater attention should be paid to the victimization of females, through sex offences, violence, abuse, abduction, slave-like practices and forced labour, and that greater regional and international co-operation was needed. The role of the United Nations was stressed, especially in disseminating the results of research and in providing technical advisory services and policy guidelines.

ECONOMIC AND SOCIAL COUNCIL ACTION

On 25 May 1984, on the recommendation of its Second Committee, the Economic and Social Council adopted resolution 1984/49 without vote.

Fair treatment of women by the criminal justice system

The Economic and Social Council,

Having considered the report of the Secretary-General on the fair treatment of women by the criminal justice system,

Taking into account resolution 9 of the Sixth United Nations Congress on the Prevention of Crime and the Treatment of Offenders, on the specific needs of women prisoners,

1. *Takes note* of the report of the Secretary-General on the fair treatment of women by the criminal justice system;

2. *Reaffirms* resolution 9 of the Sixth United Nations Congress on the Prevention of Crime and the Treatment of Offenders, in particular paragraph 4 thereof, in which the Congress requested that, at future Congresses and their preparatory meetings, as well as in the work of the Committee on Crime Prevention and Control, time should be allotted for the study of women as offenders and victims;

3. *Decides* that the question of the fair treatment of women by the criminal justice system and the question of the situation of women as victims of crime should be included in the provisional agenda for the Seventh United Nations Congress on the Prevention of Crime and the Treatment of Offenders under the items entitled "Criminal justice processes and perspectives in a changing world" and "Victims of crime", respectively;

4. *Requests* the Secretary-General to submit reports on the two above-mentioned questions to the Seventh Congress.

Economic and Social Council resolution 1984/49

25 May 1984   Meeting 21   Adopted without vote

Approved by Second Committee (E/1984/92) without vote, 23 May (meeting 20); draft by Committee on crime (E/1984/16); agenda item 11.

On 24 May, the Council adopted resolution 1984/19 on physical violence against detained women that was specific to their sex.

Safeguards protecting those facing death penalty

Pursuant to a May 1983 Economic and Social Council resolution,[32] the Secretary-General submitted to the Committee on crime in January 1984 a note on arbitrary and summary executions.[33] Following a summary of the relevant activities of the Commission on Human Rights and its Sub-Commission on Prevention of Discrimination and Protection of Minorities (see Chapter XVIII of this section), he considered draft guidelines to guarantee a fair trial for those sentenced to death; international standards reaffirming the right to life; and relevant human rights provisions. The Secretary-General concluded that the prevalence of summary and arbitrary executions was such that the Committee might wish to take up in depth all related issues as a high priority matter, endorse the draft guidelines, and consider the social, economic and political conditions in which executions took place. In addition, he said, ways should be found to increase the awareness of those in power, of law enforcement officials and of the public of the incompatibility of the executions with a humane and fair system of justice.

On 30 March, the Committee on crime adopted a resolution on safeguards guaranteeing protection of the rights of those facing the death penalty, which it recommended for adoption by the Economic and Social Council.

ECONOMIC AND SOCIAL COUNCIL ACTION

On 25 May, on the recommendation of its Second Committee, the Economic and Social Council adopted resolution 1984/50 without vote.

Safeguards guaranteeing protection of the rights of those facing the death penalty

The Economic and Social Council,

Having regard to the provisions bearing on capital punishment in the International Covenant on Civil and Political Rights, in particular article 2, paragraph 1, and articles 6, 14 and 15 thereof,

Recalling General Assembly resolution 38/96 of 16 December 1983, in which, *inter alia,* the Assembly expressed its deep alarm at the occurrence on a large scale of summary or arbitrary executions,

Recalling also General Assembly resolution 36/22 of 9 November 1981, in which the Committee on Crime Prevention and Control was requested to examine the problem with a view to making recommendations,

Recalling further Council resolution 1983/24 of 26 May 1983, in which it decided that the Committee on Crime Prevention and Control should further study the question of death penalties that did not meet the acknowledged minimum legal guarantees and safeguards, as contained in the International Covenant on Civil and Political Rights and other international instruments, and welcomed the intention of the Committee that the issue should be discussed at the Seventh United Nations Congress on the Prevention of Crime and the Treatment of Offenders,

Acknowledging the work done by the Commission on Human Rights and the Sub-Commission on Prevention of Discrimination and Protection of Minorities in the areas of summary or arbitrary executions, including the reports of the Special Rapporteur,

Considering the relevant views and comments of the Human Rights Committee established under the International Covenant on Civil and Political Rights,

Expressing its concern at the tragic incidence of arbitrary or summary executions in the world,

Having considered the note by the Secretary-General on arbitrary and summary executions,

Guided by the desire to continue to contribute to the strengthening of the international instruments relating to the prevention of arbitrary or summary executions,

1. *Takes note* of the note by the Secretary-General on arbitrary and summary executions;

2. *Again strongly condemns and deplores* the brutal practice of arbitrary or summary executions in various parts of the world;

3. *Approves* the safeguards guaranteeing protection of the rights of those facing the death penalty, recommended by the Committee on Crime Prevention and Control and annexed to the present resolution, on the understanding that they shall not be invoked to delay or to prevent the abolition of capital punishment;

4. *Invites* the Seventh United Nations Congress on the Prevention of Crime and the Treatment of Offenders to consider the safeguards with a view to establishing an implementation mechanism, within the framework of the item of its provisional agenda entitled "Formulation and application of United Nations standards and norms in criminal justice".

ANNEX
Safeguards guaranteeing protection of the rights of those facing the death penalty

1. In countries which have not abolished the death penalty, capital punishment may be imposed only for the most serious crimes, it being understood that their scope should not go beyond intentional crimes with lethal or other extremely grave consequences.

2. Capital punishment may be imposed only for a crime for which the death penalty is prescribed by law at the time of its commission, it being understood that if, subsequent to the commission of the crime, provision is made by law for the imposition of a lighter penalty, the offender shall benefit thereby.

3. Persons below 18 years of age at the time of the commission of the crime shall not be sentenced to death, nor shall the death sentence be carried out on pregnant women, or on new mothers, or on persons who have become insane.

4. Capital punishment may be imposed only when the guilt of the person charged is based upon clear and convincing evidence leaving no room for an alternative explanation of the facts.

5. Capital punishment may only be carried out pursuant to a final judgement rendered by a competent court after legal process which gives all possible safeguards to ensure a fair trial, at least equal to those contained in article 14 of the International Covenant on Civil and Political Rights, including the right of anyone suspected of or charged with a crime for which capital punishment may be imposed to adequate legal assistance at all stages of the proceedings.

6. Anyone sentenced to death shall have the right to appeal to a court of higher jurisdiction, and steps should be taken to ensure that such appeals shall become mandatory.

7. Anyone sentenced to death shall have the right to seek pardon, or commutation of sentence; pardon or commutation of sentence may be granted in all cases of capital punishment.

8. Capital punishment shall not be carried out pending any appeal or other recourse procedure or other proceeding relating to pardon or commutation of the sentence.

9. Where capital punishment occurs, it shall be carried out so as to inflict the minimum possible suffering.

Economic and Social Council resolution 1984/50

25 May 1984   Meeting 21   Adopted without vote

Approved by Second Committee (E/1984/92) without vote, 23 May (meeting 20); draft by Committee on crime (E/1984/16); amended by Austria, Costa Rica, Italy, Netherlands, Sweden, Uruguay (E/1984/C.2/L.8), orally revised; agenda item 11.

In the Second Committee, two 6-nation amendments were approved. In paragraph 3, the phrase "not be invoked to delay or to prevent the abolition of capital punishment" replaced "not be interpreted as affecting the consideration of the question of the abolition or retention of capital punishment"; the amendment was adopted by 29 votes to 1, with 17 abstentions. Also approved was the insertion of "In countries which have not abolished the death penalty," at the beginning of paragraph 1 of the annex. Following consultations, a further amendment by the same six nations to the annex, to add, at the end of paragraph 8, the phrase "and in any case not until a minimum period of three months has elapsed after judgement has become final", was withdrawn by the sponsors.

Before adopting the text as a whole, the Council, by 23 votes to 6, with 16 abstentions, rejected an oral amendment by the United States calling for reinstatement of the original wording of paragraph 3. The United States felt that the text approving the safeguards should be kept separate from the debate on the retention or abolition of capital punishment and that neutral language with regard to its abolition or retention would better promote its underlying goal.

GENERAL ASSEMBLY ACTION

In resolution 39/118, the General Assembly endorsed the Economic and Social Council recommendations on safeguards guaranteeing protection of the rights of those facing the death penalty and requested the Council to keep the matter under review. The Assembly called on States to ensure implementation of those recommendations, and requested the Secretary-General to employ his best endeavours in cases where the safeguards were violated.

The Assembly also dealt with summary or arbitrary executions in resolution 39/110, and adopted resolution 39/137 on the elaboration of a second optional protocol to the International Covenant on Civil and Political Rights aiming at the abolition of the death penalty (see Chapter XVIII of this section).

Implementation of the 1979 Code of Conduct for Law Enforcement Officials

A report on the United Nations Code of Conduct for Law Enforcement Officials, adopted in 1979,[34] was submitted by the Secretary-General to the Committee on crime in January 1984[35] in response to a 1982 Committee recommendation. The Secretary-General noted that, as of 30 September 1983, 29 countries had replied to a request for information on implementation of the Code, and that nearly all had indicated that they had legal provisions reflecting its principles or going beyond it. Most said that they supported the Code and that law enforcement officials were required to observe its statutes.

On 30 March 1984,[15] the Committee noted that more information would be needed to determine the degree of implementation of the Code, and recommended that the Economic and Social Council request the Secretary-General to invite Member States to provide such information, so that he could submit a comprehensive report to the 1985 Congress.

An interregional preparatory meeting for the Congress, held at Varenna, Italy, in September 1984, unanimously adopted recommendations for more effective implementation of the Code of Conduct.

Alternatives to imprisonment

On a recommendation of the 1980 Congress on crime prevention,[24] the Secretary-General submitted to the Committee on crime in January 1984 a report on alternatives to imprisonment and measures for the social resettlement of prisoners.[36] He stated that, as at 15 September 1983, replies to a request for information had been received from 52 countries and the Holy See. Those replies showed that efforts in most countries were being directed towards a reduction in prison sentences, with priority given to re-socialization through community-based measures. The application of those alternatives did not lead to any substantial increase in crime, especially when they were properly planned and implemented, and received the full support of the community and public at large.

The Secretary-General stressed that the public must be informed and made aware of the importance of the new trends in crime prevention and treatment of offenders, whose final goals—reduction of criminality and recidivism—should be seen in the context of the whole socio-economic situation of each country as well as in a broader international perspective. For that reason, and to achieve positive results in crime prevention, increasing international co-operation and exchange of views seemed all the more necessary.

ECONOMIC AND SOCIAL COUNCIL ACTION

On 25 May, the Economic and Social Council, on the recommendation of its Second Committee, adopted resolution 1984/46 without vote.

Alternatives to imprisonment

The Economic and Social Council,

Recalling resolutions 8 and 10 of the Sixth United Nations Congress on the Prevention of Crime and the Treatment of Offenders,

Acknowledging the importance of further developing alternatives to the sanction of imprisonment,

Considering the noticeable progress made in various countries in intensifying contacts between sentenced persons and the community at large,

Aware that further progress is needed in order to reduce the social and psychological costs related to imprisonment,

1. *Takes note with appreciation* of the report of the Secretary-General on alternatives to imprisonment and measures for the social resettlement of offenders;

2. *Encourages* Member States to increase their efforts in order to further expand the use of such measures;

3. *Calls the attention* of Member States to the recommendation of the Sixth United Nations Congress on the Prevention of Crime and the Treatment of Offenders that the principles on linking the rehabilitation of offenders to related social services should be taken into account when formulating strategies for deinstitutionalization within the overall framework of crime prevention;

4. *Welcomes* the recommendation of the Committee on Crime Prevention and Control that these matters should be considered by the Seventh United Nations Congress on the Prevention of Crime and the Treatment of Offenders, under the item of the provisional agenda entitled "Formulation and application of United Nations standards and norms in criminal justice";

5. *Requests* the Secretary-General to update the report on alternatives to imprisonment, on the basis of information to be provided by Member States and other sources, including relevant non-governmental organizations and professional organizations, for submission to the Seventh Congress.

Economic and Social Council resolution 1984/46

25 May 1984   Meeting 21   Adopted without vote

Approved by Second Committee (E/1984/92) without vote, 23 May (meeting 20); draft by Committee on crime (E/1984/16); agenda item 11.

UN activities in crime prevention

A progress report on United Nations activities in crime prevention and criminal justice covering the period from May 1980 to August 1983 was submitted by the Secretary-General to the Committee on crime in January 1984.[37] On 30 March,[18] the Committee took note of the report.

Technical co-operation in crime prevention

The Economic and Social Council in May 1984 adopted a resolution on technical co-operation in crime prevention and criminal justice. By that resolution, it took note of recommendations made in 1983 at four regional preparatory meetings for the 1985 Congress.[38] The Council noted also that the African Regional Preparatory Meeting had viewed with great concern the delay in the establishment of an African regional institute on crime prevention, which it had requested in 1979.[39]

ECONOMIC AND SOCIAL COUNCIL ACTION

On 25 May 1984, the Economic and Social Council, on the recommendation of its Second Committee, adopted resolution 1984/51 without vote.

Technical co-operation in crime prevention and criminal justice

The Economic and Social Council,

Recalling General Assembly resolution 36/21 of 9 November 1981, in which the Assembly urged the Department of Technical Co-operation for Development of the United Nations Secretariat and the United Nations Development Programme to increase their level of support to programmes of technical assistance in the field of crime prevention and criminal justice, and to encourage technical co-operation among developing countries,

Recalling also General Assembly resolution 35/171 of 15 December 1980, in which the Assembly endorsed the Caracas Declaration annexed thereto, wherein it was stressed that appropriate measures should be taken to strengthen, as necessary, the activities of the competent United Nations organs concerned with crime prevention and the treatment of offenders, especially activities at the regional and subregional levels,

Recalling further Economic and Social Council resolution 1979/20 of 9 May 1979, in which the Council took note, *inter alia,* of the growing number of countries that expressed a need for interregional and technical advisory services capable of assisting Governments in planning and implementing their crime prevention policies, and Council resolution 1979/21 of 9 May 1979,

Convinced of the crucial importance of international co-operation in crime prevention and criminal justice, both among developing countries and between developed and developing countries,

Conscious of the financial and other difficulties encountered by many countries in their efforts to introduce efficient and humane crime prevention policies,

Recognizing the vital role performed by the United Nations regional training and research institutes in effectively supporting various forms and modalities of technical co-operation despite serious financial and budgetary constraints,

Recognizing also the important role of the United Nations Social Defence Research Institute in United Nations efforts to strengthen research in an interregional context,

Aware that the existing interregional and regional institutes are heavily dependent for financial support on the host countries,

Noting that the post of Interregional Adviser in the area of crime prevention and criminal justice was re-established in 1981,

Aware that, since the appointment of an Interregional Adviser in July 1982, Governments of developing countries have requested his advisory services on fifty-six occasions,

1. *Takes note* of the recommendations concerning regional and international co-operation in crime prevention and criminal justice contained in the resolutions adopted by the Asia and Pacific, Latin American, African and Western Asia Regional Preparatory Meetings for the Seventh United Nations Congress on the Prevention of Crime and the Treatment of Offenders;

2. *Notes also* that the African Regional Preparatory Meeting, in its resolution on subregional, regional and interregional co-operation in crime prevention and criminal justice, viewed with great concern the delay in the establishment of an African regional institute on the prevention of crime and the treatment of offenders;

3. *Emphasizes* the usefulness of regional co-operation as fostered by the United Nations Latin American Institute for the Prevention of Crime and the Treatment of Offenders, the United Nations Asia and Far East Institute for the Prevention of Crime and the Treatment of Offenders and the Helsinki Institute for Crime Prevention and Control, affiliated with the United Nations;

4. *Urges* the Secretary-General and all the organizations and agencies involved in the establishment of the institute for the African region to take steps to ensure its prompt creation, if possible before the Seventh United Nations Congress on the Prevention of Crime and the Treatment of Offenders, and also appeals to Governments in that region to co-operate fully and act expeditiously in this respect;

5. *Recommends* the regional commissions and the regional institutes to increase their co-operation in undertaking joint activities;

6. *Requests* the organs, organizations and bodies of the United Nations to strengthen appropriate arrangements for the support of technical co-operation in crime prevention and criminal justice between developed and developing countries and also among developing countries, in the spirit of the Buenos Aires Plan of Action for Promoting and Implementing Technical Co-operation among Developing Countries and General Assembly resolutions 35/171 and 36/21 and Economic and Social Council resolutions 1979/20 and 1979/21;

7. *Urges* the Secretary-General to ensure increased support for the critically needed interregional advisory services in the field of crime prevention and criminal justice, and to provide additional interregional and regional advisers as quickly as budgetary resources will permit, especially to serve the needs of those regions without regional institutes;

8. *Also urges* the Secretary-General to find appropriate means to strengthen the financial capacity of the existing interregional and regional institutes;

9. *Calls upon* Member States in each region, in considering crime prevention and criminal justice in the context of development, to encourage the exchange of data, information and experiences, to engage in joint activities for training and research, to assist in demonstration projects of a bilateral and multilateral nature, to enter into agreements on the provision of human, financial and material resources in support of regional and subregional seminars involving the various modalities of technical co-operation, and to encourage the involvement in such efforts of scientific and professional non-governmental organizations active in the field of crime prevention and criminal justice.

Economic and Social Council resolution 1984/51

25 May 1984   Meeting 21   Adopted without vote

Approved by Second Committee (E/1984/92) without vote, 23 May (meeting 20); draft by Committee on crime (E/1984/16); agenda item 11.

UN Trust Fund for Social Defence

In 1984, the United Nations Trust Fund for Social Defence supplied $624,164 to the United Nations Social Defence Research Institute in Rome, Italy. The Trust Fund was established pursuant to a 1965 resolution of the Economic and

Social Council to strengthen United Nations work in social defence.[40]

Contributions to the Trust Fund in 1984 totalled $721,592, from the following 13 countries: Canada ($9,231), Cyprus ($246), Denmark ($8,602), France ($38,456), Greece ($7,475), Israel ($2,000), Italy ($340,880), Japan ($58,978), Saudi Arabia ($220,000), Sweden ($23,349), Switzerland ($9,375), Thailand ($1,000) and Yugoslavia ($2,000). Pledges for future years amounted to $375,726 from five countries.

The General Assembly, in resolution 38/112, appealed to States to consider contributing to the Fund, to enable it to respond to countries' requests for assistance.

REFERENCES

[1]E/AC.57/1984/7 & Add.1 & Add.1/Corr.1. [2]A/CONF.121/IPM/2. [3]A/CONF.121/IPM/4 & Add.1 & Corr.1. [4]A/CONF.121/IPM/1. [5]A/CONF.121/IPM/3. [6]E/1984/16 & Add.1 & Add.1/Corr.1. [7]E/1984/16 (dec. 8/8). [8]E/1984/74. [9]YUN 1979, p. 774, ESC dec. 1979/25, 9 May 1979. [10]E/1984/16. [11]*Ibid.* (dec. 8/1). [12]*Ibid.* (dec. 8/2). [13]*Ibid.* (dec. 8/3). [14]*Ibid.* (dec. 8/4). [15]*Ibid.* (dec. 8/5). [16]*Ibid.* (res. 8/1). [17]*Ibid.* (dec. 8/6). [18]*Ibid.* (dec. 8/7). [19]E/AC.57/1984/5. [20]YUN 1980, p. 787, GA res. 35/171, 15 Dec. 1980. [21]E/AC.57/1984/11 & Corr.1. [22]YUN 1983, p. 739, ESC dec. 1983/125, 26 May 1983. [23]YUN 1983, p. 738. [24]YUN 1980, p. 779. [25]E/AC.57/1984/13. [26]E/AC.57/1984/12. [27]E/AC.57/1984/14. [28]E/AC.57/1984/10. [29]YUN 1957, p. 254, ESC res. 663 C I (XXIV), 31 July 1957. [30]E/AC.57/1984/2. [31]E/AC.57/1984/15. [32]YUN 1983, p. 845, ESC res. 1983/24, 26 May 1983. [33]E/AC.57/1984/16. [34]YUN 1979, p. 779, GA res. 34/169, annex, 17 Dec. 1979. [35]E/AC.57/1984/4. [36]E/AC.57/1984/9. [37]E/AC.57/1984/17. [38]YUN 1983, p. 738. [39]YUN 1979, p. 781, ESC res. 1979/20, 9 May 1979. [40]YUN 1965, p. 409, ESC res. 1086 B (XXXIX), 30 July 1965.

Cultural development

Proposed World Decade for Cultural Development

By a letter of 6 February 1984,[1] the Director-General of the United Nations Educational, Scientific and Cultural Organization (UNESCO) transmitted to the Secretary-General a proposal on the proclamation of a World Decade for Cultural Development. The Director-General suggested that the Decade be proclaimed in 1986, following approval by the General Assembly. Annexes to the letter contained a 1983 UNESCO General Conference resolution on the Decade and the Director-General's comments on the objectives of the Decade, with some proposals for action.

The Economic and Social Council took note of the letter in decision 1984/176.

REFERENCE

[1]E/1984/53.

Chapter XIV

Population

The major United Nations event in the area of population in 1984 was the International Conference on Population which culminated in the adoption of the Mexico City Declaration on Population and Development and 88 recommendations for the further implementation of the 1974 World Population Plan of Action. The Conference reaffirmed the validity of that Plan, which was aimed at improving standards of living and quality of life for all peoples in promotion of their common destiny in peace and security. In December, the General Assembly endorsed the report of the Conference and welcomed the Mexico City Declaration (resolution 39/228).

During the year, the United Nations system continued to support the population programmes of Member States through the United Nations Fund for Population Activities which spent 72.5 per cent of country programme resources on 53 priority countries, exceeding the goal of two thirds set by the Governing Council of the United Nations Development Programme. In June, the Governing Council supported continued assistance to seven regional and interregional demographic training and research centres and approved assistance to large-scale programmes or projects for seven developing countries.

In addition to January and March meetings as the Preparatory Committee for the Population Conference, the Population Commission met in January to assess the progress of the Secretariat's work in population and to formulate its future work programme. In May, acting on the Commission's recommendation, the Economic and Social Council adopted the work programme (resolution 1984/4) and emphasized the importance of maintaining the effectiveness of the global and regional population programmes and of strengthening co-ordination among the departments and organizations of the United Nations system in planning and executing population programmes.

Topics related to this chapter. Regional economic and social activities—population: Africa; Asia and the Pacific; Latin America and the Caribbean; Western Asia. Statistics: population and housing censuses.

The 1984 Conference on Population

The International Conference on Population was held at Mexico City from 6 to 14 August 1984 to appraise the implementation of the World Population Plan of Action,[1] adopted in 1974 at Bucharest, Romania, by the World Population Conference. The 1984 Conference was preceded on 5 August by consultations on procedural and organizational matters, while activities in preparation for the Conference were organized during early 1984 throughout the United Nations system (see below).

The Conference was attended by 146 Member States, as well as by representatives of the Secretariat, regional commissions and other United Nations organizations and five specialized agencies. Also represented were 13 intergovernmental organizations, 154 non-governmental organizations (NGOs) and three national liberation movements: the African National Congress of South Africa, the Palestine Liberation Organization and the Pan-Africanist Congress of Azania. The United Nations Council for Namibia represented Namibia.

At its first meeting on 6 August, the Conference elected as its President Manuel Bartlett Diaz (Mexico); it also elected a Rapporteur-General and 28 Vice-Presidents. (For Conference participants and officers, see APPENDIX III.)

The Conference's inaugural ceremony heard a message from the United Nations Secretary-General, who addressed the Conference on 13 August. Statements were also made by the Secretary-General of the Conference and by Miguel de la Madrid Hurtado, President of Mexico, who reviewed the global situation and described measures adopted in Mexico to carry out the population policy elaborated in the preceding decade.

Speaking to the Conference, the United Nations Secretary-General said that the population problem was not merely a matter of statistics but concerned human beings whose well-being had to be based not only on adequate living conditions but also on respect for their human rights, including the right to decide the size of their families. He hoped that the Conference's results would guide and inspire efforts to deal with the challenge of an expanding population at the global level.

On 14 August,[2] the Conference adopted the Mexico City Declaration on Population and Development in which it reaffirmed the full validity of the principles and objectives of the 1974 Plan of Action and adopted by consensus[a] a set of recommendations for its further implementation. Those recommendations comprised a preamble, a short section on peace, security and population, 76 recommendations for action by Governments, and 12 recommendations for implementation.

In its Declaration, the Conference stated that, although the world had undergone far-reaching changes since 1974, population growth, high mortality and morbidity, and migration problems continued to be causes of great concern requiring immediate action. The Conference confirmed that the principal aim of social, economic and human development, of which population goals and policies were integral parts, was to improve people's living standards and quality of life. The Declaration constituted a solemn undertaking by the nations and international organizations gathered in Mexico City, to respect national sovereignty, combat all forms of racial discrimination, including *apartheid*, and promote social and economic development, human rights and individual freedom.

Regarding the global population growth rate, the Declaration noted that it had declined from 2.03 to 1.67 per cent per year in the previous decade, but would decline more slowly in the next. Moreover, the annual increase in numbers was expected to continue and could reach 90 million by the year 2000. Ninety per cent of the increase would occur in developing countries and 6.1 billion people were expected to inhabit the Earth. Demographic differences between developed and developing countries remained striking with an average life expectancy of 73 years in developed countries and only 57 years in developing countries. In addition, families in the latter tended to be much larger. This caused concern since social and population pressures could contribute to continuing the wide disparity in welfare and the quality of life between developing and developed countries.

Although progress had been made since 1974, millions still lacked access to safe, effective family planning methods. Major efforts were needed to ensure that all could exercise their basic human right to decide freely the number and spacing of their children and to have the information and means to do so.

Also emphasized in the Declaration were: the importance of recognizing the link between population and development; the positive influence of improving the status of women on family life and size; the need to increase funding to develop new contraceptive methods; the need for special attention to be given to maternal and child health services; and rapid urbanization and migratory movements.

The preamble to the recommendations for the further implementation of the Plan of Action stated that the Plan had served as a guide to action and that its principles and objectives remained valid.

Major challenges and problems of primary concern to the international community included: reducing poverty, expanding employment and encouraging economic growth; promoting the status of women; reducing population growth rates; changes in population structures; infant and maternal mortality; unmet family planning needs; internal and international migration and high urbanization rates; and the increasing number of persons lacking sufficient food, pure water, shelter, health care, education and other facilities.

The 88 recommendations for action to implement further the 1974 World Population Plan of Action dealt with socio-economic development, the environment and population (see p. 769); the role and the status of women; the development of population policies; population goals and policies; morbidity and mortality; reproduction and the family; population distribution and internal migration; international migration; population structure; promotion of knowledge and policy; the role of national Governments and international co-operation in implementing the Plan; and the monitoring, review and appraisal of the Plan's implementation.

The Conference stressed the need to take account of the interrelationships between population, resources, environment and development and recommended that Governments take population trends into account when formulating development plans and implement policies to redress imbalances in population growth and resources and environmental requirements.

In connection with the role and status of women, Governments were urged to integrate women into all phases of development and take measures with regard to their legal rights and status, education, training, employment and access to health care, while continuing to support their role as mothers. The age of entry into marriage should be raised to encourage delay in child-bearing, and Governments should promote men's active involvement in all areas of family responsibility, and ratify the 1979 Convention on the Elimination of All Forms of Discrimination against Women.[3]

Governments were urged to adopt mutually reinforcing population and social and economic policies and to provide resources and adopt innovative measures to implement population policy.

In recommendations on population goals and policies, the Conference invited countries which considered that their population growth rates hindered the attainment of national goals to consider relevant demographic policies which respected human rights, including the right of each individual and

---

[a]Reservations were entered on a number of the recommendations: recommendation 3 (Ukrainian Soviet Socialist Republic, USSR, the United States); recommendation 18(e) (Sweden); recommendation 36 (United States); recommendation 88 (India, Mexico).

couple to determine the size of its own family. All Governments were urged to reduce morbidity and mortality levels and improve health among all population groups. Countries with higher mortality levels should aim for a life expectancy of at least 60 years and an infant mortality rate of fewer than 50 per 1,000 live births by the year 2000; those with intermediate mortality levels should aim for a life expectancy of at least 70 years and an infant mortality rate of fewer than 35 per 1,000 by that year. It was strongly urged that governmental action in mortality and health involve all sectors of national and community development.

Governments were urged to identify the underlying causes of infant and child morbidity and mortality and to attack those conditions. To reduce maternal morbidity and mortality by at least 50 per cent by the year 2000, Governments should provide prenatal and perinatal care, emphasize the nutritional needs of pregnant women and nursing mothers, help women avoid abortion, support family planning, and encourage community education to change attitudes which countenanced pregnancy and child-bearing at young ages. Action was urged to expand the use of techniques which could achieve a virtual revolution in child survival, including breast-feeding. In countries with many illiterate women, a supplementary effort should be made to extend mass education.

With regard to adult morbidity and mortality, Governments were urged to implement disease control programmes, provide potable water and sanitation facilities and implement other elements of primary health care. Provision of health care information and the taking of measures to eliminate occupational health hazards were urged.

In the area of reproduction and the family, the Conference recommended to Governments that they provide information and the means to assist people to achieve their desired number of children and that resources be allocated for family planning services, including the family-life and sex education of adolescents. The right to decide the number and spacing of children should be assured and legislation and policies in that regard should be neither coercive nor discriminatory. Policies should be sensitive to the need for financial and other support to families and development policies known to reduce fertility levels, such as improved health, education, integration of women and social equity, should be adopted.

With regard to internal migration, the Conference recommended that population distribution policies be consistent with international human rights instruments and that socio-economic policies to minimize adverse spatial consequences should be implemented through incentives. It also recommended other policies to assist internal migrants which should be integrated into the overall develop-ment planning process, including establishing labour exchanges to provide information on employment in receiving areas, directing rural development programmes towards increasing rural production and efficiency and adopting policies to assist women migrants and women, children and the elderly left behind in rural areas.

The Conference recommended that international migration policies should respect basic human rights and fundamental freedoms and that Governments of receiving countries should take into account the well-being of migrants and the demographic implications of migration. Governments of countries of origin concerned with the outflow of skilled workers and professionals should seek to retain them and encourage their return. It was also recommended that high priority be placed on rehabilitating expelled and homeless people displaced by natural and man-made catastrophes.

Recommendations on documented migrant workers urged the adoption of measures to promote normalization of their family life and the undertaking of information activities to increase migrants' awareness of their legal position and rights. Dissemination of information to promote public understanding of migrant workers was also urged. Recommendations were also made regarding the protection of the basic human rights of undocumented migrants.

The Conference recommended that States accede to international instruments on refugees while Governments and international agencies were urged to find durable solutions to problems related to refugees and their movements.

With regard to the question of population structure, the Conference called for Governments to give due attention to the needs of children and youth. It also called for further efforts in connection with the aging (see Chapter XX of this section).

The Conference's recommendations on the promotion of knowledge and policy urged Governments to develop capabilities in the collection and analysis of population statistics and to tabulate and publish such data while safeguarding individual privacy. Governments were also urged to increase resources for research in human reproduction and fertility regulation, and give priority to social research into the determinants and consequences of fertility.

Governments were urged to develop population programmes and increase their support to existing ones dealing with management, training, information, education and communications. They were invited to develop a trained corps to formulate and implement integrated population and development policies, plans and programmes at all levels.

The Conference's recommendations for implementation of the Plan of Action by national Governments dealt with management of population programmes, and utilization of technical co-operation among developing countries. With regard to international co-operation in the Plan's implementation, the Conference recommended the provision of substantial international support by developed countries, other donor countries and intergovernmental organizations and NGOs. Areas identified as requiring particular emphasis by the international community included: research and action programmes; integration of population planning in the development process; improving the status of women; biomedical and social science research; collection and analysis of data; identification of successful programmes and dissemination of information on them; implementation of monitoring and evaluation systems; promotion of exchanges between countries with common experiences; and education and training. The Conference also urged Governments to increase assistance for population activities, urged further strengthening of UNFPA and invited national NGOs and other groups and individuals to assist in developing and implementing population policies and programmes.

Finally, the Conference stated that the monitoring of population trends and policies would continue to be undertaken by the Secretary-General and the next review and appraisal of progress made towards achieving the goals and recommendations of the Plan of Action would be in 1989.

Among documents before the Conference was a report of the Secretary-General[4] on the review and appraisal of the 1974 World Population Plan of Action. The report, revised in the light of the discussions of the Preparatory Committee for the Conference (see below), was organized in six chapters: socio-economic development and population; development of population policies; population trends, prospects, goals and policies; promotion of knowledge; role of national Governments and the international community; and monitoring, review and appraisal of the 1974 Plan.

A note by the Secretariat[5] transmitted those draft recommendations on which the Preparatory Committee had been able to reach agreement (see below) and a further report of the Secretary-General[6] transmitted the recommendations of the United Nations regional commissions for the further regional implementation of the 1974 Plan of Action.

GENERAL ASSEMBLY ACTION

On 18 December 1984, on the recommendation of the Second (Economic and Financial) Committee, the General Assembly adopted resolution 39/228 without vote.

International Conference on Population
The General Assembly,

Recalling Economic and Social Council resolution 1981/87 of 25 November 1981 on the convening of an international conference on population in 1984,

Recalling also Economic and Social Council resolutions 1982/7 of 30 April 1982, 1982/42 of 27 July 1982 and 1983/6 of 26 May 1983,

Recalling further General Assembly resolution 38/148 of 19 December 1983,

1. *Endorses* the report of the International Conference on Population, containing the recommendations for the further implementation of the World Population Plan of Action;

2. *Welcomes and strongly supports* the Mexico City Declaration on Population and Development, adopted by the Conference on 14 August 1984;

3. *Expresses its appreciation* to the Government and people of Mexico for their generous hospitality, co-operation and support;

4. *Commends* the Secretary-General of the United Nations and the Secretary-General of the Conference for the successful organization of the Conference;

5. *Affirms* that the principal aim of social, economic and human development, of which population goals and policies are integral parts, is to improve the standards of living and quality of life of the people;

6. *Also affirms* that population growth, high mortality and morbidity and migration problems continue to be causes of great concern requiring immediate action;

7. *Emphasizes* the need, in implementing the recommendations of the Conference, to respect national sovereignty, to combat all forms of racial discrimination, including *apartheid*, and to promote social and economic development, human rights and individual freedom;

8. *Reaffirms* the importance attached by the Conference to the formulation and implementation of concrete policies which will enhance the status and role of women in the area of population policies and programmes, and the need to pay attention to specific problems of population structures;

9. *Invites* Governments to consider the recommendations for action at the national level and to implement appropriate population policies and programmes, in the context of their national plans, needs and requirements;

10. *Emphasizes* that international co-operation in the field of population is essential for the implementation of recommendations adopted at the Conference and, in that context, calls upon the international community to provide adequate and substantial international support and assistance for population activities, particularly through the United Nations Fund for Population Activities, in order to ensure more effective delivery of population assistance in the light of growing needs and the increasing efforts being made by developing countries;

11. *Invites* the Population Commission, at its twenty-third session, to review, within its area of competence, the recommendations of the Conference and their implications for the activities of the United Nations system, and to transmit its views to the Economic and Social Council at its first regular session of 1985;

12. *Requests* the Economic and Social Council to examine, at its first regular session of 1985, the recommendations of the Conference for the further implementation of the World Population Plan of Action, in order to provide overall policy guidelines within the United Nations system on population questions, and to undertake or to continue, on an appropriate basis, the review, monitoring and appraisal of the Plan of Action, in accordance with the Plan and relevant recommendations of the Conference;

13. *Requests* the Secretary-General to take, without delay, appropriate steps regarding the relevant recommendations, in particular recommendation 83, for further implementation of the World Population Plan of Action concerning the role of international co-operation, taking note also of the suggestions offered by various delegations and benefiting, in the process, from the deliberations of the Economic and Social Council, and to report to the General Assembly, through the Economic and Social Council, on their implementation as soon as possible but not later than 1986.

General Assembly resolution 39/228

18 December 1984   Meeting 104   Adopted without vote

Approved by Second Committee (A/39/789) without vote, 6 December (meeting 56); draft by Vice-Chairman (A/C.2/39/L.106), based on informal consultations on 20-nation draft (A/C.2/39/L.36); agenda item 12.

Meeting numbers. GA 39th session: 2nd Committee 39, 56; plenary 104.

The 20-nation draft (mainly developing countries and 4 Western countries), which was withdrawn, did not include "and strongly supports" in paragraph 2, the references to racial discrimination, including *apartheid*, and social and economic development in paragraph 7, or the final phrase in paragraph 8 on the need to attend to problems of population structures. Paragraph 10 of the earlier draft had referred to the increasing commitment of developing countries rather than the increasing efforts being made by them. By paragraph 12, the Economic and Social Council would have been requested to keep under review, on a regular basis, the monitoring and appraisal of the World Population Plan of Action.

Following approval of the draft in the Second Committee, two States explained their positions. Israel had not asked for a separate vote on paragraphs 1 and 7 in a spirit of co-operation, although it maintained its reservations regarding Conference recommendation 36—concerning population distribution being consistent with the 1949 Geneva Convention relative to the Protection of Civilian Persons in Time of War—which it felt had been introduced for political reasons. The United States said that it endorsed recommendations for the further implementation of the 1974 Plan of Action subject to its reservations expressed at the Conference regarding its positions on recommendation 3 on commodity agreements or future lending resources for international financial institutions; and recommendation 36 which it felt was politically divisive and extraneous.

Preparations for the Conference

To prepare for the Conference, the Population Commission, acting as the Preparatory Committee for the International Conference on Population, met in New York from 23 to 27 January and in a resumed session authorized by the Economic and Social Council (see below) from 12 to 17 March; membership of the Committee was open to all States.

Its report[7] contained recommendations for the further implementation of the 1974 World Population Plan of Action. It also made recommendations to the Council regarding the Conference's provisional agenda, rules of procedure and other organizational matters.

Within the United Nations system, the Administrative Committee on Co-ordination (ACC) Task Force on the Conference met in New York on 30 and 31 January[8] and discussed the Committee's January meeting, arrangements for the Committee's report to be discussed by the regional commissions, arrangements for drafting proposals for further implementation of the 1974 Plan of Action at the regional level, and contributions for the report on the review and appraisal of that Plan. Task Force members were invited to submit to the Conference secretariat their written suggestions to improve a 1983 report of the Secretary-General[9] on the further implementation of the 1974 Plan.

At its April 1984 session,[10] the ACC Joint United Nations Information Committee (JUNIC) heard oral reports on information activities being conducted by agencies in preparation for the Conference. JUNIC agreed to extend full co-operation in implementing the information programme for the Conference (see p. 366).

In other action leading up to the Conference, the Governing Council of the United Nations Environment Programme (UNEP) urged UNEP to participate fully (see also p. 769). At the regional level, two intergovernmental meetings were held in 1984: the Second African Population Conference (Arusha, United Republic of Tanzania, 9-13 January) convened by the Economic Commission for Africa (see p. 616); and the Third Regional Population Conference in the Arab World (Amman, Jordan, 25-29 March) convened by the Economic Commission for Western Asia and the League of Arab States (see p. 642). Other regional meetings had been held in 1982[11] and 1983.[12]

A commemorative stamp on the Conference was issued in February (see ADMINISTRATIVE AND BUDGETARY QUESTIONS, Chapter IV).

ECONOMIC AND SOCIAL COUNCIL ACTION

In February, the Economic and Social Council, having considered a letter from the Chairman of the Conference Preparatory Committee,[13] adopted decision 1984/102 without vote.

Preparatory Committee for the International Conference on Population, 1984

At its 2nd plenary meeting, on 10 February 1984, the Council, having considered the letter from the Chairman of the Preparatory Committee for the International Conference on Population, 1984 to the President of the Council, decided to authorize the Preparatory Committee to hold a resumed session at United Nations Headquarters from 12 to 16 March 1984, and to report to the Council at its first regular session of 1984.

Economic and Social Council decision 1984/102
Adopted without vote

Draft by President, for Bureau (E/1984/L.14 and Corr.1); agenda item 2.

In May, following its consideration of the Preparatory Committee's report,[7] the Council adopted without vote decision 1984/118 by which it amended a recommendation on the organization of the Conference and one of the provisional rules of procedure.

Report of the Preparatory Committee for the International Conference on Population, 1984

At its 17th plenary meeting, on 22 May 1984, the Council:

(a) Decided to revise paragraph (e) of recommendation 5 of the Preparatory Committee for the International Conference on Population, 1984, to read as follows:

"(e) In view of the constraints of time, it is desirable that statements in the general debate on item 4 be limited to seven minutes for the representatives of each State and three minutes for other participants";

(b) Recommended the following text as rule 6 of the provisional rules of procedure for the International Conference on Population, 1984:

"The Conference shall elect the following officers: a President, two Vice-Presidents for co-ordination, twenty-six other Vice-Presidents, a Rapporteur-General and a Presiding Officer for the Main Committee established in accordance with rule 45";

(c) Took note of the report of the Preparatory Committee for the International Conference on Population, 1984 and of the recommendations contained therein, as revised, and decided to transmit them to the Conference.

Economic and Social Council decision 1984/118
Adopted without vote

Oral proposal by President; draft recommended by Preparatory Committee (E/1984/28 & Add.1), amended by USSR (E/1984/L.27), orally amended by Mexico, based on informal consultations; agenda item 6.
Meeting numbers. ESC 12-14, 17.

The paragraph concerning the Preparatory Committee's recommendation 5, amended by the USSR, had not included the words "it is desirable that". Rule 6, orally amended by Mexico, and on which the Preparatory Committee had not reached agreement, had stated that there should be only 24 other Vice-Presidents.

REFERENCES

(1)YUN 1974, p. 552. (2)*Report of the International Conference on Population, 1984, Mexico City, 6-14 August 1984* (E/CONF.76/19 & Corr.1), Sales No. E.84.XIII.8. (3)YUN 1979, p. 895, GA res. 34/180, annex, 18 Dec. 1979. (4)E/CONF.76/4 & Corr.1. (5)E/CONF.76/5. (6)E/CONF.76/6 & Corr.1. (7)E/1984/28 & Add.1. (8)ACC/1984/PG/3. (9)YUN 1983, p. 752. (10)ACC/1984/15. (11)YUN 1982, p. 847. (12)YUN 1983, p. 749. (13)E/1984/26.

OTHER PUBLICATIONS

Review and Appraisal of the World Population Plan of Action, 1984 Report (ST/ESA/SER.A/99), Sales No. E.86.XIII.2. *World Population Prospects, Estimates and Projections as Assessed in 1984* (ST/ESA/SER.A/98 & Corr.1), Sales No. E.86.XIII.3.

UN Fund for Population Activities

Activities

In 1984, the United Nations Fund for Population Activities (UNFPA) concentrated its efforts on the International Conference on Population and also continued its work on involving women in population and development issues and on the priority programme areas outlined by the Governing Council of the United Nations Development Programme (UNDP) in 1981[1]: family planning, including training of personnel and research into contraceptive methods; population education and information dissemination; basic data collection; population dynamics on the effects of population trends; and population policy formulation, implementation and evaluation. Details of these activities and special programmes were described by the UNFPA Executive Director in his annual report for 1984.[2]

Total UNFPA income in 1984 was $138.4 million compared with $134.7 million in 1983. Project allocations, which totalled $139 million, are broken down in the tables below by major function and executing agency, and geographically. Expenditures were $137.9 million ($122.6 million in 1983), including $82.5 million for country programmes, $33 million for intercountry programmes, $4.7 million for the budgets of the UNFPA Deputy Representatives and Senior Advisers on Population, $5.9 million for overhead costs, and $11.8 million for the administrative budgets.

At year's end, UNFPA was assisting 2,180 projects—1,682 country, 220 regional, 116 interregional and 162 global. New projects approved in 1984 numbered 453, amounting to $29.8 million, compared with 271 in 1983, amounting to $15.2 million. In 1984, 187 projects were completed, bringing the cumulative total to 2,193.

UNFPA assistance for family planning programmes came to $68 million, or 50.8 per cent of total allocations, and focused on projects to enhance delivery of family planning services and information, education and motivational programmes in support of such services. Particular assistance was given to strengthening distribution channels for services and supplies, such as health and community networks and private and public sector sources, and to projects directed towards hard-to-reach groups, such as rural populations, marginal groups in urban areas and adolescents. The Fund continued assistance in areas closely connected with the improvement of services: personnel training and logistic support including transport, medical equipment and contraceptive supplies. In its support for family planning research, it again contributed $2 million in 1984 to the WHO Special Programme of Research, Development and Research Training in Human Reproduction. With respect to trends in family planning programmes supported by the Fund, the integration of family planning into maternal/child health-care and general health services was becoming the rule, with delivery systems becoming more community-oriented and the use of traditional midwives and village health volunteers more widespread.

Guidelines governing UNFPA assistance for family planning activities were revised to indicate that, since abortion was not a method of contraception, UNFPA did not extend assistance, and was particularly careful to assure that none of its assistance was used, for that purpose. The guidelines reiterated that every nation had the sovereign right to determine its population policies and programmes and all couples and individuals had the basic right to decide freely and responsibly the number and spacing of their children.

Support for population education and communication activities totalled $20 million, or 14.9 per cent of all allocations. An increased interest by many Governments in initiating these activities continued in 1984 and was partly met by combining bilateral funding with UNFPA support. Population education projects were conducted in school systems in Africa, Asia, Latin America and the Middle East, and also in some non-school settings where family-life education programmes were introduced. Communication strategies for creating demand for family planning services involved both channelling information to target audiences and obtaining feedback from them to best meet their needs.

Some $13.9 million, or 10.5 per cent of all allocations, was devoted to research on population dynamics. This included analysis of demographic and socio-economic data and their interrelationships and research into the social and economic consequences of population trends. Support for formulation and evaluation of population policies totalled $8.2 million or 6.2 per cent of total allocations. A major area of UNFPA support in this category continued to be for projects to promote awareness and understanding of interrelationships between population factors and development planning. UNFPA assistance to policy implementation in 1984

totalled $1.1 million or 0.8 per cent of total allocations.

Assistance for basic data collection was $11.7 million, or 8.8 per cent of all allocations. Although this was a smaller share than allocated for 1983 (10.7 per cent), the amount rose slightly from $10.8 million due to support for second-time population censuses. As in the past, censuses took the largest share of data collection resources followed by civil registration and vital statistics systems, and demographic surveys and related statistical activities.

UNFPA assistance to special programmes relating to women, population and development and to the issue of aging totalled $2.0 million, or 1.5 per cent of total allocations.

Of programmes and projects funded by UNFPA and executed by various United Nations bodies and NGOs, a major portion was executed by the United Nations Department of Technical Co-operation for Development (see p. 728).

UNFPA ALLOCATIONS BY MAJOR FUNCTION, 1984

	Amount (in millions of US dollars)	Percentage of total programme
Family planning	67.9	50.8
Communication and education	19.9	14.9
Population dynamics analysis	13.9	10.5
Basic data collection	11.7	8.8
Multisector activities	8.7	6.5
Formulation and evaluation of population policies	8.2	6.2
Special programmes	2.0	1.5
Implementation of policies	1.1	0.8
Total*	133.7	100.0

*Excludes allocations of $5.5 million for Deputy Representatives and Senior Advisers on Population, overhead for government-executed projects and infrastructure; differs from the sum of the figures due to rounding.
SOURCE: DP/1985/28 (Part I).

UNFPA ALLOCATIONS BY EXECUTING AGENCY, 1984

	Amount (in millions of US dollars)	Percentage of total programme
Governments (directly executed)	41.1	30.8
UNFPA	23.8	17.8
WHO	20.6	15.4
United Nations	14.8	11.1
Non-governmental organizations	9.8	7.4
Regional commissions	6.9	5.2
ILO	6.4	4.8
UNESCO	6.2	4.7
UNICEF	1.9	1.5
FAO	1.7	1.3
Total*	133.7	100.0

*Differs from the sum of the figures due to rounding.
SOURCE: DP/1985/28 (Part I).

UNFPA PROJECT ALLOCATIONS, 1984
(in US dollars)

COUNTRY, TERRITORY AND REGIONAL PROJECTS	ALLOCATION	COUNTRY, TERRITORY AND REGIONAL PROJECTS	ALLOCATION	COUNTRY, TERRITORY AND REGIONAL PROJECTS	ALLOCATION
Africa south of the Sahara		*Asia and the Pacific* (cont.)		*Latin America and the Caribbean* (cont.)	
Angola*	197,101	Iran	35,225	Saint Christopher and Nevis	26,260
Benin*	409,238	Kiribati	99,092	Saint Lucia	108,860
Botswana	533,892	Lao People's Democratic		Saint Vincent and the Grenadines	64,276
Burkina Faso*	973,436	Republic*	393,514	Suriname	10,137
Burundi*	611,089	Malaysia	1,024,972	Trinidad and Tobago	12,600
Cameroon	520,871	Maldives*	170,861	Turks and Caicos Islands	9,800
Cape Verde	71,376	Mongolia	453,418	Uruguay	216,000
Central African Republic'	271,459	Nepal*	2,290,254	Venezuela	19,018
Chad*	15,180	Pakistan*	2,694,850	Regional	3,155,300
Comoros*	179,824	Papua New Guinea	98,730		
Congo	652,587	Philippines	1,398,966	Subtotal	17,381,604
Equatorial Guinea*	127,279	Republic of Korea	489,464		
Ethiopia*	2,034,730	Samoa*	205,832	*Middle East and the Mediterranean*	
Gambia*	169,943	Singapore	17,427		
Ghana*	518,024	Solomon Islands*	54,092	Algeria	22,506
Guinea*	500,883	Sri Lanka*	1,919,467	Bahrain	178,164
Guinea-Bissau	77,795	Thailand	1,875,774	Democratic Yemen*	874,289
Ivory Coast	225,123	Tonga	88,049	Djibouti	142,354
Kenya*	496,796	Trust Territory of the Pacific		Egypt*	1,686,364
Lesotho*	225,934	Islands	272,183	Iraq	22,413
Liberia*	693,716	Tuvalu	39,230	Jordan	607,556
Madagascar*	617,961	Vanuatu	83,007	Libyan Arab Jamahiriya	4,300
Malawi*	635,664	Viet Nam*	1,582,910	Morocco	1,160,773
Mali*	630,408	Regional	5,440,702	Somalia*	830,505
Mauritania*	904,516			Sudan*	1,320,608
Mauritius	258,286	Subtotal	63,338,363	Syrian Arab Republic	881,342
Mozambique*	1,078,036			Tunisia	735,193
Niger*	404,839	*Latin America and the Caribbean*		Turkey	338,547
Nigeria	1,199,526			Yemen*	781,017
Rwanda*	550,190	Anguilla	2,603	Regional	1,809,445
Sao Tome and Principe*	204,735	Antigua and Barbuda	18,413		
Senegal*	1,091,090	Bahamas	2,300	Subtotal	11,395,376
Seychelles	71,431	Barbados	83,343		
Sierra Leone*	523,458	Belize	124,463	*Europe*	
Swaziland	426,830	Bermuda	1,940		
Togo	301,929	Bolivia	601,501	Albania	196,800
Uganda*	222,356	Brazil	371,042	Bulgaria	151,632
United Republic of Tanzania*	1,057,449	British Virgin Islands	15,820	Czechoslovakia	1,856
Zaire*	522,471	Chile	10,474	Greece	63,095
Zambia*	713,265	Colombia	588,295	Hungary	109,087
Zimbabwe*	774,930	Costa Rica	566,199	Poland	1,596
Regional	5,174,628	Cuba	1,041,850	Portugal	126,482
		Dominica*	94,135	Romania	72,157
Subtotal	26,870,274	Dominican Republic	788,730	Yugoslavia	142,908
		Ecuador	520,706	Regional	532,705
Asia and the Pacific		El Salvador	739,498		
		Grenada	6,600	Subtotal	1,398,318
Afghanistan*	546,518	Guatemala	800,048		
Bangladesh*	4,343,709	Guyana	46,063	*INTERREGIONAL AND GLOBAL PROJECTS*	
Bhutan*	269,412	Haiti*	992,875		
Burma*	196,991	Honduras	652,852	Interregional	14,168,689
China*	6,428,678	Jamaica	375,279	Global	4,623,191
Cook Islands	58,217	Mexico	2,712,758		
Democratic People's Republic		Montserrat	11,700	Subtotal	18,791,880
of Korea	53,000	Nicaragua	610,767		
Fiji	973,685	Panama	319,021	Total	139,175,815
Hong Kong	46,526	Paraguay	564,846		
India*	27,093,043	Peru	1,095,232		
Indonesia*	2,600,565				

*Classified as a priority country for UNFPA assistance.
SOURCE: DP/1985/30 Parts I and II.

Country and intercountry programmes

In 1984, UNFPA continued to focus on the needs of the 53 countries given priority status in 1982,[3] of which 30 were in Africa, 16 in Asia and the Pacific, 2 in Latin America and the Caribbean, and 5 in the Middle East and the Mediterranean. Of the year's total amount of resources for country programmes and projects, $71.6 million or 72.5 per cent was allocated to those 53 countries.

Intercountry activities accounted for $35 million in allocations in 1984, comprising $16.1 million for regional projects, $14.2 for interregional projects and $4.6 million for global projects.

On 29 June 1984,[4] the UNDP Governing Council noted the increase in UNFPA assistance for the 53 priority countries, and reiterated the goal of devoting up to two thirds of country programme assistance to those countries. It requested the UNFPA Executive Director to strengthen his efforts to reduce the proportion of assistance from the Fund allocated to intercountry activities and to report to the Council's 1986 session, clarifying the definition of intercountry activities and reviewing the possibility of revising the definition and the 25 per cent target set for intercountry programme activities. The Council also approved Fund assistance to large-scale country programmes for the Central African Republic, China, Dominican Republic, Peru, Togo, Viet Nam and Zambia.

Further to a 1983 request,[5] the UNFPA Executive Director submitted to the Governing Council a 28 March report[6] on the programmes of the regional and interregional demographic training and research centres for which UNFPA assistance had been approved for the four-year cycle, 1984-1987. The seven centres, in Cameroon, Chile, Egypt, Ghana, India, Romania and the USSR, were to receive assistance up to a maximum of $3.5 million per year. UNFPA support was based on the concept of the attainment of self-reliance and gradual phasing out of international assistance. The centres, therefore, were required to adopt training strategies that were cost-effective, predominantly self-supporting and responsive to the needs of the countries and of the region. The UNFPA Executive Director reported that the centres were complying with the principles, which the Council had endorsed, to provide direction to the training programmes, and stated that he would report further in 1986.

In June 1984,[4] the Council supported continued assistance to the centres, taking into account the particular needs of those in Africa south of the Sahara, and requested the Executive Director to report to the Council's 1986 session on the extent to which all the centres had incorporated the agreed principles on funding and programming, including steps to achieve self-reliance. African Governments were urged to increase and provide prompt contributions to the institutes south of the Sahara.

Family planning research

In response to a 1983 decision of the UNDP Governing Council,[5] which stated that the level of UNFPA contributions to the WHO Special Programme of Research, Development and Research Training in Human Reproduction would be reviewed annually by the Council, the UNFPA Executive Director submitted a March 1984 report on the UNFPA strategy for support of contraceptive research.[7] The report outlined principles for assistance and gave details of organizations en-

gaged in contraceptive research and development: two to which UNFPA provided assistance (the WHO Special Programme and the Program for the Introduction and Adaptation of Contraceptive Technology, an NGO with headquarters in Seattle, United States); and several others, both NGOs and national institutions in developing countries considered to be appropriate entities to receive UNFPA funds for contraceptive research projects.

As its immediate strategy for funding such research, the report proposed that UNFPA consult with developing countries and NGOs active in the field to ascertain their needs, that it continue to make available country programme funds for developing countries to carry out their own biomedical contraceptive research, and that in addition to providing an annual $2 million contribution to the WHO Special Programme, UNFPA should, within funding limitations and availability, increase its assistance during 1985-1987.

On 29 June,[4] the UNDP Governing Council approved the general principles outlined in the report,[7] decided that the Fund's contribution to the WHO Special Programme should be fixed at $2 million for 1985, approved the Executive Director's strategy for immediate funding, and requested him to report briefly to the Council in 1985 on the results of the recommendations of the Special Programme's Policy and Co-ordination Committee, and recommend UNFPA funding for 1986-1989.

Work programmes

The UNFPA work plan for 1985-1988 was prepared by its Executive Director,[8] based on expected income for 1984 of $142 million and projected income of $152 million for 1985, $165 million for 1986, $179 million for 1987 and $194.5 million for 1988. After deductions for operational costs and additions to the operational reserve, programmable resources were expected to total $547.2 million for the four years of the work plan: $121.5 million for 1985; $131.2 million for 1986; $142.0 million for 1987; and $152.5 million for 1988. Intercountry activities would account for 25 per cent of total programmable resources, and priority countries two thirds of new programmable resources for country projects. Other criteria for allocations, including the possibility of increased shares for family planning and population communication, would also be taken into account.

On 29 June 1984,[4] the UNDP Governing Council approved the 1985-1988 work plan on the understanding that the Executive Director would limit approval of projects to available resources, and gave approval authority for 100 per cent of the 1985 figures and smaller proportions (75, 50 and 25 per cent respectively) of total anticipated spending for the three following years. The net additional amounts approved were $48.4 million for 1985, $44.9 million for 1986, $41.5 million for 1987 and $38 million for 1988.

The Council also expressed appreciation for the Executive Director's report on the status of financial implementation of Council-approved UNFPA programmes and projects[9] and requested future similar reports to be annexed to the work plan.

Programme planning and evaluation

During 1984, eight independent, in-depth evaluations were undertaken of UNFPA-assisted programmes and projects in China, Democratic Yemen, the English-speaking Caribbean, Indonesia, Kenya/Sierra Leone, Malawi/Zambia, Mexico and Rwanda, the results of which were presented to the UNDP Governing Council in the report of the UNFPA Executive Director for 1984.[2]

He also submitted to the Council a March 1984 report[10] on UNFPA evaluation activities, describing in-depth evaluations conducted during 1982-1983, with emphasis on their results, discussing the utilization of such results and presenting UNFPA's plans for future evaluation activities. There was a need, said the report, to assess how evaluations were actually used for the projects evaluated, for similar projects elsewhere and for policy-making; this would require an analysis of the results by substantive sectors. Although progress had been made in developing built-in evaluation and making independent, in-depth evaluations more useful, additional improvements were needed, including training of personnel in formulating and implementing evaluation plans, and efforts were being made within the Fund to deal with those issues.

On 29 June,[4] the Governing Council endorsed that approach to future evaluation activities and noted that a report would be made to the Council at its 1986 session on the comparative results of past evaluations.

In a 12 April report[11] to the Governing Council, the Executive Director traced the evolution of UNFPA's programming system, described the programme development process, outlined the steps required to formulate, appraise, and approve projects, decribed the monitoring and evaluation system and summarized trends and improvements in the programming and monitoring process of UNFPA.

A 24 April report of the Executive Director on programme planning[12] described the UNFPA planning process, including resource distribution constraints and efforts being made towards full resource utilization.

On 29 June,[4] the Council expressed appreciation for the reports and requested him to further improve programme planning and procedures.

Financial and administrative questions

Budget for 1984-1985

On 1 January 1984, UNFPA's balance was $19,168,557. During the year the Fund received income of $138,568,989 and had expenditures of $137,127,662—an excess of income over expenditure of $1,331,327. The Fund's balance as at 31 December was $17,499,884; unspent allocations amounted to $19,292,199.

In June 1984,[4] the UNDP Governing Council gave to the UNFPA Executive Director an approval authority for 1984 of $142 million (see above, under "Work programmes"). At year end, project allocations amounted to $139,184,707, including $16,852,461 in unspent allocations from 1983. Net appropriations for the 1984-1985 biennial budget totalled $24,577,523, as approved by the Council in 1983.[13]

Contributions

During 1984, 81 countries and territories paid a total of $122.5 million in voluntary contributions to UNFPA (see table below), compared with $130.3 million from 84 countries and territories in 1983.[14] This figure, together with additions and adjustments to pledges for prior years, exchange-rate and currency revaluation adjustments, interest, donations and other miscellaneous income, made up a total 1984 income of $138.6 million. Pledges for 1985 from 76 countries and territories totalled $109.8 million as at 31 December 1984 (see table below), compared with $69 million from 75 countries and territories at the end of the previous year.[14]

On 29 June 1984,[4] the UNDP Governing Council urged all countries that were able to do so to increase their contributions and urged that payments be made as early as possible.

CONTRIBUTIONS TO UNFPA, 1984 AND 1985

(as at 31 December 1984 in US dollar equivalent)

Country or territory	1984 payment	1985 pledge	Country or territory	1984 payment	1985 pledge
Afghanistan	—	2,000	Barbados	6,000	3,000
Albania	1,143	1,429	Belgium	314,726	325,203
Australia	1,060,650	969,828	Bhutan	—	1,990
Austria	36,200	93,000	Bolivia	—	5,000
Bangladesh	14,500	15,950	Botswana	—	946

Country or territory	1984 payment	1985 pledge	Country or territory	1984 payment	1985 pledge
Bulgaria	30,457	30,457	Netherlands	9,494,102	10,434,783
Burkina Faso	–	2,128	New Zealand	232,470	–
Burma	6,143	5,814	Norway	10,903,819	10,734,463
Cameroon	2,379	–	Oman	20,000	10,000
Canada	8,769,145	–	Pakistan	321,712	325,000
Chile	5,000	5,000	Panama	1,250	1,500
China	400,000	450,000	Papua New Guinea	–	1,075
Colombia	40,000	40,000	Paraguay	–	15,000
Cyprus	750	750	Philippines	125,376	–
Democratic Yemen	–	2,200	Poland	9,276	16,393
Denmark	4,528,690	4,545,455	Portugal	35,966	20,000
Ecuador	2,000	22,000	Qatar	–	30,000
Egypt	228,921	228,921	Republic of Korea	82,000	41,000
Fiji	2,000	2,000	Romania	4,208	–
Finland	1,523,571	1,692,913	Rwanda	1,000	–
France	273,292	234,043	Saint Christopher and Nevis	999	–
Germany, Federal Republic of	12,468,390	12,131,148	Sao Tome and Principe	469	667
Greece	5,000	5,000	Saudi Arabia	30,000	30,000
Guyana	267	941	Senegal	17,747	5,000
Haiti	1,400	–	Seychelles	–	100
Honduras	10,000	10,000	Sierra Leone	1,000	1,000
Hungary	11,074	12,151	Spain	88,000	90,878
Iceland	–	2,600	Sri Lanka	7,500	10,000
India	300,469	337,553	Sudan	25,391	25,000
Indonesia	150,000	150,000	Suriname	5,000	–
Italy	1,742,105	1,842,105	Sweden	5,733,847	12,114,286
Jamaica	317	2,500	Switzerland	1,666,667	2,000,000
Japan	19,550,000	–	Syrian Arab Republic	5,500	–
Jordan	42,354	–	Thailand	48,400	48,400
Kenya	3,237	149	Trust Territory of the Pacific	1,000	–
Kuwait	25,000	25,000	Tunisia	29,400	17,948
Lao People's Democratic Republic	1,000	500	Turkey	5,000	10,000
Lesotho	1,500	–	Uganda	–	2,124
Luxembourg	10,759	4,309	United Kingdom	3,879,885	4,539,952
Madagascar	1,463	5,000	United States	38,000,000	46,000,000
Malawi	990	870	Uruguay	17,900	–
Maldives	871	871	Viet Nam	834	1,000
Mali	872	500	Yemen	–	2,850
Malta	436	–	Yugoslavia	6,684	2,876
Mauritius	2,776	–	Zambia	35,176	2,041
Mexico	5,414	–	Zimbabwe	25,668	2,069
Mongolia	499	449	Total	122,448,756	109,750,828
Nepal	3,750	3,750			

SOURCE: A/40/5/Add.7.

Accounts for 1983

In 1984, following an audit of the UNFPA financial statements for the year ended 31 December 1983, the Board of Auditors made a series of observations and recommendations.[15]

With regard to project delivery, the Board found that in many projects, expenditures had exceeded allotments or were incurred without them, while in some projects allotments remained unutilized; it recommended strengthened control of project allotments and expenditures and strict adherence to new instructions for approval of project budgets. The Board's examination of consultant services revealed insufficient adherence to instructions on the use of former staff members as consultants and procedures for follow-up and evaluation of consultant services; it recommended compliance with the relevant instructions. Noting that UNFPA travel procedures were not fully cost-effective, the Board recommended that they be closely examined. The Board's examination of communications costs disclosed weaknesses in internal controls with regard to long distance and personal telephone calls; it advised

that the control system be strengthened. The Board also noted with concern that the unexpended balance of trust funds increased in 1983 to $4,676,450; it was of the opinion that firm measures were required to initiate an adequate use of available funds.

In response, the UNFPA Executive Director indicated that attempts would be made to comply with the Board's recommendations. UNFPA travel procedures and arrangements would be examined in consultation with UNDP, which established such procedures.

By resolution 39/66 of 13 December 1984, the General Assembly accepted the UNFPA financial reports when it accepted various other 1983 financial reports and audited statements and the Auditors' opinions, concurred with ACABQ's observations on UNDP travel costs—including those of UNFPA (see p. 452), and requested the executive heads to take such remedial action as might be required.

Audited accounts, 1982

On 29 June 1984,[4] the Governing Council noted that the audited accounts of the participating and executing agencies of UNFPA for 1982[16] and prior years had not been accompanied by narrative audit reports. The Council emphasized the importance attached to such reports and requested the UNFPA Executive Director to bring the Council's decision and the views of the Budgetary and Finance Committee to the attention of the Panel of External Auditors and the administrations of the participating and executing agencies, and to report to the Council on their reaction. The Executive Director was further requested to provide an annual oral report to the Budgetary and Finance Committee regarding the annual audit submitted to the General Assembly and the Fund's response to such audit.

Financial regulations

In view of the UNDP Administrator's proposed amendments to UNDP financial regulations (see p. 452), the UNFPA Administrator proposed similar amendments to the UNFPA Financial Regulations,[17] as they were based on those of UNDP. Acceptance of the proposed changes was recommended by ACABQ.[18]

On 29 June,[4] the UNDP Governing Council approved the proposed amendment to the Fund's Financial Regulations relating to the submission of annual accounts to the United Nations Board of Auditors. It noted amendments to the annex to the Financial Regulations of the United Nations, made by the General Assembly in 1983,[19] and noted that they would be reflected in the information annex to the Fund's Financial Regulations.

Staffing

In response to a June 1983 request,[20] the Executive Director submitted to the UNDP Governing Council a report[21] on including UNFPA's Deputy Representatives and Senior Advisors on Population (DRSAPs) in the regular staffing table. The report reviewed the background to the practice of funding DRSAPs and auxiliary support staff in the field from projects funds and described the changed situation which was largely the result of the continued growth of the UNFPA programme. It was noted that, under current employment conditions, DRSAPs could only be offered successive two-year contracts with no opportunities for advancement except within the UNFPA field service. The resulting lack of opportunity for movement from field to headquarters and vice versa had created a sense of separation for field staff and impeded adequate career development.

It was recommended that the Council approve the incorporation into the regular staffing table of those DRSAP posts which qualified based on selected criteria, which would include programme needs, size and complexity of the programme, relative permanency, continuity, and degree of commitment to population programmes. Should the Council approve the transfer of DRSAP posts to the regular staffing table, the Executive Director would propose consideration of the related question of auxiliary support personnel in the field.

With regard to financial implications, the Executive Director stated that his proposals related exclusively to the transfer of posts and that, while the administrative and programme support budget would appear larger, no additional expenditure would be involved.

ACABQ was unable to recommend Council acceptance of the proposal.[18] While aware of the importance of career development and equitable treatment of staff, ACABQ pointed out that those issues had to be viewed in the context of the Fund's overall needs and financial position; it was concerned that the potential gain in flexibility in administering the staffing table could be at the expense of the necessary flexibility to respond to changes in UNFPA's situation, such as a decline in income.

Should the Council approve the proposal, however, ACABQ recommended that, in the implementation plan to be submitted by the Executive Director in 1984, careful attention should be paid to the criteria to be applied in determining which DRSAP posts should be included in the regular staffing table. Those criteria should relate to the nature of the functions performed and should also be applicable to auxiliary support staff in the field.

On 29 June 1984,[4] the Council requested the UNFPA Executive Director, in preparing the Fund's budget for 1986-1987, to include all international and local staff at headquarters and in field offices, without prejudice to the Council's final decision on the appropriate format which would be taken in 1985. When considering the 1986-1987 budget, the Council would also consider if and to what extent field posts should be established on a permanent or temporary basis and the criteria which should be applied in determining posts to be included in the regular staffing table, taking into account the ACABQ recommendation. The Council noted the Executive Director's intention to prepare a detailed implementation plan and revised staffing table to be included in his document on the Fund's basic manpower requirements to be considered by the Council in 1985.

REFERENCES
[1]YUN 1981, p. 781. [2]DP/1985/28 (Parts I, II). [3]YUN 1982, p. 970. [4]E/1984/20 (dec. 84/21). [5]YUN 1983, p. 746. [6]DP/1984/41. [7]DP/1984/36. [8]DP/1984/31. [9]DP/1984/32. [10]DP/1984/33. [11]DP/1984/35 & Corr.1. [12]DP/1984/34. [13]YUN 1983, p. 747. [14]YUN 1983, p. 748. [15]A/39/5/Add.7. [16]DP/1984/39. [17]DP/1984/77. [18]DP/1984/40. [19]YUN 1983, p. 1162, GA dec. 39/408, 25 Nov. 1983. [20]YUN 1983, p. 749. [21]DP/1984/38 & Corr.1.

Other population activities

Population Commission

The Population Commission held its twenty-second session in New York from 18 to 20 January 1984[1] when it discussed action by the United Nations to implement the recommendations of the 1974 World Population Conference,[2] including monitoring trends and policies, and reviewed progress and outlined the future population work of the United Nations (see under subject headings below).

The Commission recommended to the Economic and Social Council the adoption of a draft resolution on the work programme concerning population and a draft decision on the provisional agenda and documentation for the twenty-third (1985) session of the Commission.

ECONOMIC AND SOCIAL COUNCIL ACTION

On 16 May, the Economic and Social Council adopted without vote resolution 1984/4.

Work programme in the field of population
The Economic and Social Council,

Recalling General Assembly resolution 3344(XXIX) of 17 December 1974, in which the Assembly affirmed that the World Population Plan of Action was an instrument of the international community for the promotion of economic development, quality of life, human rights and fundamental freedoms within the broader context of the internationally adopted strategies for national and international progress,

Recalling also Council resolution 1981/28 of 6 May 1981 on the strengthening of actions concerned with the fulfilment of the World Population Plan of Action,

Reaffirming the role of the Population Commission in advising the Council on population questions, and noting with satisfaction the holding of the twenty-third session of the Population Commission in February and March 1985,

Taking note of the report of the Population Commission on its twenty-second session and the discussion contained therein on the progress of work and the work programme in the field of population,

Bearing in mind recommendations that may emanate from the International Conference on Population, 1984, for the further implementation of the World Population Plan of Action,

1. *Takes note with satisfaction* of the progress of work towards the implementation of the work programme for the biennium 1984-1985 and the medium-term plan for the period 1984-1989;

2. *Requests* the Secretary-General:

(a) To continue vigorously the work on the monitoring of world population trends and policies and the work necessary for the review and appraisal of the World Population Plan of Action;

(b) To continue the work on world population trends and structure, paying attention to studies of fertility, mortality, internal and international migration, and particularly:

(i) To pursue vigorously the expansion of the data base for the measurement of the levels, trends, characteristics and demographic consequences of international migration;

(ii) To continue the work on patterns and factors of urbanization in relation to development, with special attention to internal migration;

(iii) To continue the work on the measurement and analysis of trends in mortality levels and differentials, the factors which affect them and their consequences; although special emphasis should be given to situations in developing countries, research related to developed countries should receive due recognition;

(iv) To complete a global assessment of nuptiality patterns and trends, making full use of the 1980 round of censuses;

(v) To undertake in the medium term a major global assessment of age patterns of fertility, including a special study of adolescent fertility;

(c) To continue the work on world demographic estimates and projections;

(d) To continue work on the interrelations of population and development, paying due attention both to the implications of population trends for development and to the impact of social and economic change on demographic trends, with a view to promoting the integration of demographic factors in national and international development strategies and plans, and to expedite the preparation of manuals for the use of national planners on methods of incorporating demographic factors in development planning;

(e) To continue the work undertaken by the United Nations Working Group on Comparative Analysis of World Fertility Survey Data, using all available data from the World Fertility Survey;

(f) To continue the work on the population policy data bank in order to broaden the scope and analytic capacity of research on population policy formulation, implementation and evaluation;

(g) To pursue research on the formulation, implementation and evaluation of all aspects of population policies, including mortality, fertility and the family, population distribution and international migration;

(h) To continue work on the interrelationships between population, resources, environment and development;

(i) To pursue and intensify the efforts of the international Population Information Network (POPIN) towards identifying and establishing better ways to improve the flow of population information;

(j) To continue the United Nations programme of technical co-operation in the field of population for countries requesting such assistance, in close co-ordination with funding agencies, in particular the United Nations Fund for Population Activities, taking full account of experience gained through technical co-operation projects on population, and making necessary programme modifications in the light of the recommendations of the International Conference on Population, 1984;

(k) To pursue the United Nations programme of training in population, giving appropriate support to the United Nations–sponsored regional and interregional demographic training and research centres, and assisting the further development of national training insti-

tutions, in order to provide interdisciplinary training in population, emphasizing specific policy-oriented training in and studies of population and development, and also to consider restoring the block grants for allocation for training fellowships;

To assist Governments, at their request, to exploit the full potential of population censuses and survey data by developing national capacities for demographic analysis and studies, including the further development and utilization of emerging computer software for demographic evaluation and analysis and preparation of total and sectoral population projections as inputs to national development planning;

To further assist Governments, at their request, in establishing or strengthening national institutions, such as population units and population committees, whose purpose is to co-ordinate all population activities, particularly those relating to development planning, to integrate population factors in national development and to assist Governments in the formulation, implementation, follow-up and evaluation of population policies and programmes;

To effect the more timely publication of all population studies and projections and to promote a wide dissemination of those publications in order to provide Governments with information relevant for the formulation of policies;

3. *Requests* the Secretary-General, in carrying out the programme set out in paragraph 2 above, to seek any further needed resources only from extrabudgetary contributions;

4. *Emphasizes* the importance of maintaining the effectiveness and efficiency of the global and regional population programmes and of continuing to strengthen co-ordination and collaboration among the Department of International Economic and Social Affairs, the Department of Technical Co-operation for Development, the regional commissions, the United Nations Fund for Population Activities and organizations of the United Nations system in the planning and execution of their population programmes, as well as the need for organizations of the United Nations system to strengthen collaboration and co-ordination with national research organizations.

Economic and Social Council resolution 1984/4

16 May 1984   Meeting 14   Adopted without vote

Draft recommended by Population Commission (E/1984/12); agenda item 6.

On the same date, the Council adopted decision 1984/115, also without vote.

Provisional agenda and documentation for the twenty-third session of the Population Commission

At its 14th plenary meeting, on 16 May 1984, the Council approved the provisional agenda and documentation for the twenty-third session of the Population Commission set out below.

Provisional agenda and documentation for the twenty-third session of the Population Commission

1. Election of officers.
2. Adoption of the agenda and other organizational matters.

3. International Conference on Population, 1984: follow-up action to be taken by the United Nations:
   (a) Consideration of the recommendations of the Conference;
   (b) Implications of the recommendations of the Conference on the work programme on population.
   Documentation
   Review of the implications of the recommendations of the Conference on the work programme on population: report of the Secretary-General
4. Action by the United Nations to implement the recommendations of the International Population Conference, 1984: monitoring of population trends and policies.
   Documentation
   Addendum to the concise report on monitoring of population trends and policies: report of the Secretary-General (E/CN.9/1984/2 and Corr.1)
5. Programme of work in the field of population for the biennium 1986-1987, and implementation of the programme budget for 1984-1985.
   Documentation
   Note by the Secretary-General on the proposed programme in the field of population for the biennium 1986-1987
   Report of the Secretary-General on progress of work in the field of population for 1984-1985
6. Provisional agenda for the twenty-fourth session of the Commission.
7. Adoption of the report of the Commission on its twenty-third session.

Economic and Social Council decision 1984/115

Adopted without vote

Draft recommended by Population Commission (E/1984/12); agenda item 6.

Progress of work, 1981-1983

For its review of the United Nations Secretariat's work in population from 1981 to 1983, the Population Commission had before it reports of the Secretary-General on progress achieved by the Department of International Economic and Social Affairs (DIESA) and by the Department of Technical Co-operation for Development (DTCD).[3]

The Secretary-General described DIESA's activities in world demographic analysis, demographic projections, population policy, population and development, monitoring of population trends and policies, factors affecting patterns of reproduction and dissemination of population information. It was noted that the latter part of the programme period had been affected by the additional responsibilities of providing substantive support to the International Conference on Population, 1984 (see above).

In his report on the activities of DTCD, the Secretary-General stated that the Department had continued to expand its programme of technical co-operation in population to countries requesting assistance. This was done mainly with the financial support of UNFPA and UNDP. DTCD had continued to give high priority to support for activities related to training national personnel in population, with the aim of strengthening national capabilities of self-sufficiency in that area. Support was also provided by DTCD for evaluation and analysis of basic population and demographic data and for population policy planning and development planning. In order to assist developing countries to evaluate and analyse demographic data and population projections to provide timely input into the development planning process, DTCD had also been involved in developing and increasing the availability of computer software programs for demographic analysis. The Department had also continued to work on a series of publications which provided Governments with information on new methodologies and innovative technical approaches in the design and delivery of technical co-operation services in population. Other activities included a significant contribution by DTCD to the International Conference and the preparations leading up to it.

1984 activities

In a report on the Secretariat's 1984 activities,[4] the Secretary-General stated that DIESA's major focus of activity during the year was the Population Conference (see above), it being responsible for the substantive preparations and providing most of the substantive services. DIESA also continued to work on implementing the regular work programme on substantive, technical and information dissemination activities, which included preparation of an addendum to a report on monitoring of population trends and policies (see below), and continued work on an investigation of socio-economic correlates of child mortality, based on case studies in 15 developing countries, and on a comprehensive analysis of sex differentials in mortality in both developing and developed countries.

Reports were under preparation or issued on various subjects, including: determinants of mortality change and differentials in developing countries; consequences of mortality trends and differentials; data bases for mortality measurement; socio-economic development and fertility decline; population distribution and migration; updating of global demographic estimates and projects; population policies of five of the world's 20 largest cities; and the institutional framework for the formulation of population policies and goals.

Population Policy Compendium reports for 10 countries were issued during the year, bringing to 56 the number of countries for which reports had been issued.

A major activity within the framework of the Population Information Network (POPIN) was the organization of a reference centre at the International Conference on Population consisting of a working library and computerized population information data bases. A report on developments related to population information since the 1974 World Population Conference was featured in a special issue of the *POPIN Bulletin*.

From July 1983 to June 1984 DTCD continued to provide technical co-operation concerning population to countries requesting assistance, mainly with financial support from UNFPA and UNDP. This required substantive, technical and managerial support and monitoring by Headquarters staff of approximately 100 projects in 65 countries dealing with demography training through country projects and through interregional centres and programmes, evaluation and analysis of basic population data, population policy planning and development planning, evaluation of technical co-operation activities in population and through activities related to the 1984 Population Conference.

DTCD's work in demography training included technical support for the Cairo Demographic Centre, which undertook a major curriculum revision by introducing population and development planning and population dynamics as core courses, technical support for the United Nations–Romania Demographic Centre, whose operations closed in June 1984, and for the United Nations/USSR Interregional Demographic Training and Research Programme in Population and Development Planning. A total of 67 new awards were provided for population study at institutions other than United Nations-sponsored training centres, with an increase in the number of awards to students from African countries but fewer to Asian students.

Regarding data analysis, DTCD provided major assistance in the evaluation of demographic and socio-economic data from censuses and surveys while DIESA took major responsibility for assisting in the collection of population data. DTCD also evaluated computer software for use by developing countries in population data analysis and helped establish national population units for the formulation of population objectives.

The Department continued to evaluate the technical co-operation aspects of teaching in population and development, preparing proposals for a curriculum for publication, and examined the impact of the population training fellowhips provided by the United Nations. It also participated in the Population Conference.

Population trends and policies

In accordance with a recommendation of the 1974 World Population Plan of Action,[2] the Secretary-General submitted to the Population Commission his biennial report monitoring population trends and policies;[5] subsequently, the Commission requested him to prepare an addendum to that report.[6]

The report said that the world population stood at 4.5 billion in 1980 and was projected to reach 6.1 billion in the year 2000. The rate of growth had declined from a peak of 2.1 per cent at the end of the 1960s to 1.7 per cent at the beginning of the 1980s. Two components of natural increase, mortality and natality, had changed markedly over the preceding 10 years. The expectation of life at birth increased by almost four years to 58.9 at the beginning of the 1980s although life expectancy in the developed regions was 16 years higher than in developing ones. The decline in fertility which began in the early 1960s had spread to many developing countries where the total fertility rate diminished by almost 26 per cent since the early 1970s to a little more than four births per woman in the early 1980s. Excluding China, however, where the decrease was reported to be 54 per cent, the decline in developing countries between 1970 and 1980 was no more than 15 per cent.

The report also gave trends in world and regional population growth, mortality, fertility, contraception, urbanization, international migration, age structure and interrelationships between population, resources, the environment and development and described Government perceptions and policies relating to population growth, mortality and morbidity, fertility, internal migration, and international migration. An annex showed changes in selected demographic indicators by level of development and region from 1970 to 2025 as assessed in 1982.

The addendum[6] updated demographic trends showing that analysis of the data from 35 recent censuses indicated that the gradual slow-down of global population growth was still holding— estimated at 1.65 per cent per year compared to 2.0 per cent during the 1960s.

A section of the report[5] was devoted to an appraisal of demographic perceptions and policies of Members of the United Nations system (168 countries as at 1 July 1983) based mainly on data from a fifth inquiry among Governments, to which 109 countries had responded by 15 September 1983. The report on that inquiry among Governments,[7] which was carried out as a contribution towards the continous monitoring of population trends and policies as called for in the 1974 Plan of Action[2] and as requested by the Economic and Social Council in 1981,[8] was also before the Commission.

In March 1984, the Secretary-General submitted to the General Assembly, through the Economic and Social Council, a summary and conclusions[9] of the biennial report on the world population situation in 1984.[5]

ECONOMIC AND SOCIAL COUNCIL ACTION

Acting on a proposal by its President, the Economic and Social Council adopted decision 1984/119 without vote.

Report of the Secretary-General on the world population situation in 1984

At its 17th plenary meeting, on 22 May 1984, the Council took note of the report of the Secretary-General on the world population situation in 1984, and decided to transmit it to the General Assembly at its thirty-ninth session.

Economic and Social Council decision 1984/119

Adopted without vote

Oral proposal by President; agenda item 6.

GENERAL ASSEMBLY ACTION

By decision 39/445, the General Assembly, on the recommendation of the Second Committee, took note of the Secretary-General's report.[9]

UN Population Award

On 3 October 1984, the Secretary-General transmitted to the General Assembly a report by the UNFPA Executive Director describing activities related to the United Nations Population Award for 1984.[10]

The Committee for the Award had received 35 nominations, which was fewer than in 1983 because it had decided to limit each nominator to one nomination, instead of allowing multiple ones. It held four meetings in January and February 1984 and selected two laureates: Dr. Carmen A. Miro, a demographer from Panama who had helped to create and develop a variety of Latin American population institutions; and Dr. Sheldon J. Segal of the United States, a leader in contraceptive development and family planning promotion. The 1984 Award was presented to the laureates by the Secretary-General at a ceremony held at Mexico City on 13 August, in conjunction with the Population Conference.

The balance of the trust fund for the award stood at $412,266 at the beginning of 1984.

GENERAL ASSEMBLY ACTION

On the recommendation of the Second Committee, the General Assembly adopted decision 39/440.

Report of the Executive Director of the United Nations Fund for Population Activities on the United Nations Population Award and Trust Fund

At its 104th plenary meeting, on 18 December 1984, the General Assembly, on the recommendation of the

Second Committee, took note of the note by the Secretary-General transmitting the report of the Executive Director of the United Nations Fund for Population Activities on the United Nations Population Award and Trust Fund.

General Assembly decision 39/440

Adopted without vote

Approved by Second Committee (A/39/791, draft decision II) without vote, 14 December (meeting 61); oral proposal by Chairman; agenda item 81(d).
Meeting numbers. GA 39th session: 2nd Committee 48-53, 55, 56, 58, 61; plenary 104.

REFERENCES

[1]E/1984/12. [2]YUN 1974, p. 552. [3]E/CN.9/1984/4 & Add.1. [4]E/CN.9/1985/3 & Add.1. [5]E/CN.9/1984/2 & Corr.1. [6]E/CN.9/1984/2/Add.1. [7]E/CN.9/1984/3 & Corr. 1,2. [8]YUN 1981, p. 786, ESC res. 1981/29, 6 May 1981. [9]A/39/128-E/1984/35. [10]A/39/537.

PUBLICATIONS

Population Bulletin of the United Nations: No. 16, *1984* (ST/ESA/SER.N/16), Sales No. E.84.XIII.6; No. 17, *1985* (ST/ESA/SER.N/17), Sales No. E.84.XIII.13. *Studies to Enhance the Evaluation of Family Planning Programmes* (ST/ESA/SER.A.87), Sales No. E.84.XIII.9. *Population and Vital Statistics Report, 1984 Special Supplement* (ST/ESA/STAT/SER.A/149), Sales No. E.84.XIII.2. *Demographic Yearbook 1984* (ST/ESA/STAT/SER.R/14), Sales No. E/F.85.XIII.1.

Chapter XV

Health and human resources

Health conditions in 1984 continued to be very poor in large parts of the developing world. Malnutrition and improper sanitation and water supply accounted for high incidences of diseases and mortality rates, and much remained to be done to improve primary health care and availability of medication.

At least 350 million of some 500 million disabled persons throughout the world were reportedly living in areas where disability services were inadequate or unavailable. In November, the General Assembly called upon Member States and other donors to contribute to the United Nations trust fund for the disabled persons, and requested the Secretary-General to convene in 1987 a meeting of experts to evaluate the progress of the United Nations Decade for Disabled Persons (1983-1992) (resolution 39/26).

In December, the Assembly stressed the importance of training qualified national personnel for the social and economic development of developing countries (resolution 39/219). It welcomed the continuing emphasis of the United Nations Institute for Training and Research (UNITAR) on economic and social training and research (39/178), and requested the preparation of a comprehensive study on UNITAR activities, funding and future role (39/177).

The Assembly noted the advance made by the United Nations University in its activities and emphasized the University's continuing need to strengthen the capacity of existing scholarly and scientific institutions in developing countries (39/179).

Topics related to this chapter. Operational activities for development: skilled workers. Food: food problems; food aid. Science and technology: brain drain. Environment: protection against harmful products. Human rights: human rights of disabled persons. Children: UNICEF programmes by sector.

Health

General aspects

In an April 1984 report on the social aspects of development (see Chapter XIII of this section),[1] submitted in response to a 1983 Economic and Social Council request,[2] the Secretary-General stated that, despite improvement in the past decades, health conditions remained very poor in large parts of the developing world, with high disparities in health conditions among social groups even increasing in those countries affected by economic recession. In the mean time, international efforts, such as immunization campaigns or safe water supply, continued with the support of the United Nations Children's Fund (UNICEF) and the World Health Organization (WHO).

Current projections on mortality rates indicated that the target of a minimum life expectancy of 60 years by the year 2000 would not be achieved in 54 developing countries—a majority of them African. Infant mortality was expected to remain above 50 per 1,000 in 71 developing countries. The high mortality rates were associated with a high incidence of diseases endemic in areas affected by malnutrition and improper sanitation and water supply.

Six major communicable diseases—diphtheria, whooping cough, tetanus, poliomyelitis, measles and tuberculosis—caused the deaths of some 5 million children annually in the developing world (1 million in Africa), and crippled, blinded or caused mental damage to perhaps 5 million more. An expanded programme of immunization against the six major communicable diseases, launched by WHO in 1974 to reach all children by 1990, needed acceleration to achieve its goal.

In view of an alarming increase over the past decade in the incidence of malaria, trypanosomiasis and schistosomiasis, WHO had launched a Special Programme for Research and Training in Tropical Diseases; research by the world scientific community and the pharmaceutical industry had been insufficient, and current control methods frequently were inadequate or too costly and cumbersome for widespread use.

In developing countries, diarrhoeal diseases—transmitted by faecal contamination of soil, food and water—were among the leading causes of death among children. Further mobilization of domestic and international resources was needed to provide an ample supply of potable water and adequate sanitation in order to control such diseases.

Severe mental illness was considered to affect some 40 million people in the world; at least twice that many were seriously disabled by drug dependence, alcohol-related problems, mental retardation and organic disorders of the nervous system.

While Governments of most developing countries had reviewed their development strategies to provide greater support for primary health care programmes, total public capital and operating expenditures per capita for health in such countries ranged around 2 or 3 per cent of their gross national product. A substantial proportion of those extremely limited resources was spent for curative rather than preventive health efforts, in fixed investments (hospitals, dispensaries), in maintaining routine services and paying salaries. The recent slow-down of overall external economic assistance had further impaired the capacity of many developing countries to implement their health programmes.

Efforts continued to be made for improving the availability and utilization of drugs, maximizing the use of limited manpower and financial resources, and promoting the production and distribution of effective drugs of acceptable quality at the least possible cost.

While a broad base of inexpensively trained, less skilled personnel at the community level was lacking, there had been excessive investment in training programmes for medical students and doctors who required sophisticated facilities and equipment. WHO, which estimated that there were 1,000 medical personnel per 100,000 inhabitants in the developed countries and 200 per 100,000 in developing countries, currently recommended a review of the functions of different types of health personnel in order to improve the accessibility of health services for the less privileged social groups.

Global strategy

By a June 1984 note[3] to the Economic and Social Council, the Secretary-General reported that the thirty-seventh World Health Assembly (Geneva, 7-17 May 1984) considered the report of the WHO Executive Board on progress made in implementing the Global Strategy for Health for All by the Year 2000,[4] and had adopted three resolutions relating to the Strategy—health for all, technical co-operation among developing countries in support of that goal and monitoring progress.

In decision 1984/176, the Economic and Social Council took note of the Secretary-General's note.

Disabled persons

Of an estimated 500 million physically, mentally or sensorially disabled persons in the world, at least 350 million were living in areas where services were insufficient or unavailable, in particular in the rural parts of developing countries and among

the poorest social groups, the Secretary-General mentioned in his April 1984 report on social aspects of development.[1] An average of 20 to 25 per cent of the population of developing countries was estimated to be affected by disability (see Chapter XIII of this section).

While the situation of disabled persons in developing countries remained difficult and precarious, conditions for progress had improved with the visibility of the problem, the social awareness that disability did not necessarily mean marginalization, and the attitudes of the disabled themselves in promoting their rights. The 1981 International Year of Disabled Persons (IYDP)[5] had helped establish national committees, and many Governments had drawn up national plans or taken measures to facilitate the participation of disabled persons in life and society in accordance with the 1982 World Programme of Action concerning Disabled Persons.[6] Further, there was a growing tendency to replace institutionalized treatment with programmes that helped families and communities to care for the disabled in their normal social environment.

Implementation of the Programme of Action

UN activities

The second inter-agency meeting on the United Nations Decade of Disabled Persons (1983-1992) (Vienna, Austria, 3 and 4 September 1984)[7]— convened following a 1983 proposal[8] of the Consultative Committee on Substantive Questions (Programme Matters) of the Administrative Committee on Co-ordination (ACC)—recommended the adoption of a framework, proposed by the United Nations Centre for Social Development and Humanitarian Affairs, for monitoring the implementation of the 1982 World Programme of Action concerning Disabled Persons.[6] The framework dealt with: community-based rehabilitation, equalization of opportunities, government responsibility, socio-economic factors relating to disability, and international co-operation. The inter-agency meeting further agreed that interorganizational task forces should be established on public education, disability concepts, human resources development, technical aids and regional rehabilitation programmes, and that the Council of World Organizations Interested in the Handicapped as well as Disabled Peoples' International should be invited to participate in them.

Among other recommendations of the meeting were the strengthening of the United Nations Trust Fund, making the inter-agency meetings on disability as permanent arrangements, and holding a further session at Vienna in 1985 before that year's first regular session of the Economic and Social Council.

In response to a 1982 General Assembly request,[9] the Secretary-General submitted a report to the Assembly in October 1984[10] on the implementation by the United Nations system of the World Programme of Action. He noted, among other things, that the Centre for Social Development and Humanitarian Affairs, which the Programme had designated as the focal point for coordinating and monitoring its implementation, was assisting requesting Governments in designing national disability policies and programmes and data-collection operations. The Centre also conducted studies on legislation aimed at equalizing opportunities for disabled persons, and on the causes and consequences of disability. Regional economic commissions as well as specialized agencies conducted programmes within their areas of competence to promote disability prevention and rehabilitation of the disabled.

In resolution 1984/26, the Economic and Social Council encouraged the Secretary-General to obtain the views of United Nations bodies and other organizations on ways to prevent human rights violations which might cause disabilities (see Chapter XVIII of this section).

GENERAL ASSEMBLY ACTION

On 23 November 1984, the General Assembly, on the recommendation of the Third (Social, Humanitarian and Cultural) Committee, adopted resolution 39/26 without vote.

United Nations Decade of Disabled Persons
The General Assembly,
Recalling its resolutions 37/52 of 3 December 1982, by which it adopted the World Programme of Action concerning Disabled Persons, and 37/53 of 3 December 1982 by which, *inter alia*, it proclaimed the period 1983-1992 United Nations Decade of Disabled Persons as a long-term plan of action,
Recalling its resolution 38/28 of 22 November 1983, in which it recognized the desirability of the continuation of the United Nations Trust Fund for the International Year of Disabled Persons throughout the Decade,
Noting Economic and Social Council resolution 1983/19 of 26 May 1983, in which the Secretary-General was requested to monitor and support the implementation of the World Programme of Action concerning Disabled Persons by enlisting extrabudgetary resources,
Noting with satisfaction Commission on Human Rights resolution 1984/31 of 12 March 1984 and the draft resolution of the Sub-Commission on Prevention of Discrimination and Protection of Minorities, concerning violations of human rights and fundamental freedoms and disability, and the appointment of a special rapporteur to study this issue in collaboration with the Centre for Social Development and Humanitarian Affairs of the Secretariat,
Noting with great appreciation the generous voluntary contributions and pledges made by Governments and other donors to the Trust Fund, as well as other voluntary contributions to support activities concerning disabled persons,

Noting also with appreciation the results achieved so far through funding from the Trust Fund during the International Year of Disabled Persons and its follow-up activities, as well as through other voluntary contributions,
Desirous of ensuring effective implementation of the World Programme of Action, and aware that, if this is to be achieved, Member States, organs, organizations and bodies of the United Nations system, non-governmental organizations and organizations of disabled persons must be encouraged to continue the activities already undertaken and to initiate new programmes and activities,
Stressing that the primary responsibility for the realization of the objectives of the World Programme of Action rests with individual countries and that international action should be directed towards assisting and supporting national efforts in this regard,
Noting the emergence of organizations of disabled persons in all parts of the world and their importance to the implementation of the World Programme of Action,
Convinced that high priority must continue to be assigned to the planning, management and financing of the activities and programmes relating to the United Nations Decade of Disabled Persons,
Convinced that the Decade will give a meaningful and forceful impetus to the implementation of the World Programme of Action and to a broader understanding of its importance,
Concerned that developing countries are experiencing increasing difficulties in mobilizing adequate resources for meeting pressing needs in the field of disability prevention, rehabilitation and equalization of opportunities for the millions of persons with disabilities, particularly in the face of pressing demands from other high-priority sectors concerned with basic needs,
Recalling that in paragraph 157 of the World Programme of Action concerning Disabled Persons it is stated that the Trust Fund should be used to meet requests for assistance from developing countries and organizations of disabled persons and to further the implementation of the World Programme of Action and, in paragraph 158, it is indicated that there is a need to increase the flow of resources to developing countries to implement the objectives of the World Programme of Action, and that, therefore, the Secretary-General should explore new ways and means of raising funds and take the necessary follow-up measures for mobilizing resources, and that voluntary contributions from Governments and from private sources should be encouraged,
Stressing the importance of an effective system for collection and dissemination of technical information on disability,
Stressing further the importance of public information and education activities in the field of prevention, rehabilitation and equalization of opportunities,
Having considered the report of the Secretary-General on the implementation of the World Programme of Action concerning Disabled Persons,
1. *Expresses its appreciation* to all Member States which elaborated national policies and programmes for the implementation of the World Programme of Action concerning Disabled Persons and for the United Nations Decade of Disabled Persons, and urges those which have not yet formulated such programmes to do so;

2.   *Notes with appreciation* the activities relating to the implementation of the World Programme of Action undertaken by the United Nations system and by relevant non-governmental organizations;

3.   *Urges* Member States to make every effort to attain the objectives of the World Programme of Action in co-operation with non-governmental organizations concerned and to involve disabled persons in planning and decision-making related to the implementation of the Programme;

4.   *Invites* Member States as a matter of priority to reinforce or establish national committees or similar bodies for the Decade at the highest level with participation of organizations of disabled persons to plan, co-ordinate and encourage the execution of activities in support of the objectives of the Decade at the national and local levels;

5.   *Requests* the Secretary-General to elaborate the guidelines for priority actions during the Decade based on his report to the current session and on the replies received from Member States and organizations including those of disabled persons;

6.   *Reiterates its request* that the Secretary-General strengthen the Centre for Social Development and Humanitarian Affairs of the Secretariat through a reallocation of existing resources to enable the Centre to continue to serve as the focal point in the field of disability, particularly for purposes of paragraph 5 above;

7.   *Requests* the Secretary-General and relevant organizations of the United Nations system to develop specific programmes to publicize the Decade and the goals of the World Programme of Action, and invites Member States and non-governmental organizations to assist in this undertaking;

8.   *Invites* Member States, organizations of the United Nations system, as well as non-governmental organizations to make available resources in the form of funds and personnel for the purpose of planning, managing and financing the Decade at the national, regional and interregional levels;

9.   *Urges* all organizations of the United Nations system to take into consideration the interests of disabled persons as well as the effective implementation of the World Programme of Action in the pursuance of their overall objectives in their respective areas of competence;

10.   *Decides* that, pending completion of the elaboration and the adoption of the guidelines referred to in paragraph 5 above, the United Nations Trust Fund for the International Year of Disabled Persons should continue to support activities in accordance with paragraph 157 of the World Programme of Action and paragraph 4 of General Assembly resolution 38/28;

11.   *Calls upon* Member States and other donors to continue to contribute generously to the Trust Fund;

12.   *Requests* the Secretary-General to promote the recruitment of more disabled persons within the United Nations system;

13.   *Again requests* the Secretary-General to convene in 1987 a meeting of experts, consisting largely of disabled persons, to evaluate progress at the mid-point of the Decade and to prepare a report that would enable him to help the General Assembly at its forty-second session to evaluate the implementation of the World Programme of Action, as provided for in paragraph 3 of resolution 37/52;

14.   *Requests* the Secretary-General to report on the implementation of the present resolution, including detailed information on the activities relating to the Trust Fund, to the General Assembly at its fortieth session and decides to include in the provisional agenda of that session an item entitled "Implementation of the World Programme of Action concerning Disabled Persons and the United Nations Decade of Disabled Persons".

General Assembly resolution 39/26

23 November 1984   Meeting 71   Adopted without vote

Approved by Third Committee (A/39/661) without vote, 13 November (meeting 37); 37-nation draft (A/C.3/39/L.14); agenda item 91.

Sponsors: Austria, Bangladesh, Belgium, Burkina Faso, Canada, Central African Republic, Chile, China, Costa Rica, Democratic Kampuchea, Dominican Republic, Guinea, Guinea-Bissau, Kenya, Mali, Mauritania, Morocco, Nepal, Nigeria, Oman, Pakistan, Panama, Papua New Guinea, Paraguay, Peru, Philippines, Romania, Saudi Arabia, Senegal, Somalia, Sudan, Trinidad and Tobago, United States, Uruguay, Venezuela, Yugoslavia, Zaire.

Financial implications. 5th Committee, A/39/684; S-G, A/C.3/39/L.22 & Add.1, A/C.5/39/40.

Meeting numbers. GA 39th session: 3rd Committee 16-23, 27, 37; 5th Committee 32; plenary 71.

Employment of disabled persons by the UN

In 1984, the Secretary-General recommended that United Nations organizations encourage the employment of disabled persons system-wide and make their facilities totally barrier-free.[10] He also recommended that the ACC policy statement on the employment of disabled persons[11] be applied to all United Nations organizations as a guideline for recruitment and provision of services to the disabled.

The General Assembly, in resolution 39/26, requested the Secretary-General to promote the recruitment of more disabled persons within the United Nations system.

National action

Several Member States reported the adoption of national disability plans, and measures taken covered legislation, education, employment, rehabilitation, prevention, bilateral technical co-operation, housing and accessibility, recreation, and data collection aimed at the equalization of opportunities.[9] Following the proclamation of the 1981 IYDP, approximately 45 countries had collected benchmark data on the disabled; some 15 others planned similar action.

Most of the national committees set up during IYDP were reported to be still functioning. Governments had been encouraged to proclaim national days for the disabled, and Finland, Haiti and Japan stated that such days had been observed.

In response to a May 1983 Economic and Social Council request,[12] the Secretary-General submitted, in November 1984, a progress report[13] on national experiences in implementing the World Programme of Action concerning Disabled Persons, and on developing criteria for monitoring the Programme. He reported that inter-agency consultations (see above) had been held, and would continue, to develop the monitoring procedures.

The General Assembly, in resolution 39/26, urged Member States to reinforce or establish national committees for the United Nations Decade of Disabled Persons and requested the Secretary-General to elaborate the guidelines for priority actions during the Decade.

NGO activities

Several international non-governmental organizations (NGOs) of and for disabled persons reported on their activities.[10] Among them, Disabled Peoples' International—founded in 1981 with partial support from the United Nations Trust Fund for IYDP—provided expertise, resources and training to assist disabled persons in acquiring self-help skills. It also sponsored leadership training seminars at Dakar, Senegal; at Bangkok, Thailand; and in Barbados. The World Federation for Mental Health and the International League of Societies for Persons with Mental Handicaps expressed interest in implementing the goals of the World Programme of Action.

By resolution 39/26, the General Assembly noted with appreciation the activities undertaken by NGOs, and urged Member States to co-operate with them in attaining the World Programme's objectives.

Trust Fund for the Year

UN Trust Fund

In 1984, the United Nations Trust Fund for IYDP had a total income of $260,021 and expenditures of $321,584. Contributions to the Trust Fund were made by Austria ($7,203), France ($20,497), Greece ($5,000), Saudi Arabia ($45,200) and Senegal ($1,699).

Since its inception, the Trust Fund had provided financial support in areas such as advisory and consultative services, cultural activities and community programmes, and support services, including training courses, seminars and workshops.

The Secretary-General recommended in 1984[10] that the Trust Fund be renamed United Nations Fund for Disability, which would more accurately reflect the need to utilize its resources for activities under the World Programme of Action, particularly during the Decade, as recommended by the General Assembly in 1983.[14] The Trust Fund would be classified as a general-purpose trust fund in accordance with United Nations rules and procedures.

The second inter-agency meeting on the United Nations Decade of Disabled Persons[7] also took note of the suggestions made by the Centre for Social Development and Humanitarian Affairs for a new name, new terms of reference and new institutional arrangements for the Trust Fund.

The General Assembly, in resolution 39/26, decided that, pending adoption of new guidelines, the Trust Fund should continue to support activities as previously agreed; it called on Member States and other donors to contribute generously to the Fund.

Trust Fund for Norway's contribution to the International Year

In 1984, the income of the Trust Fund for Norway's Contribution to the International Year of Disabled Persons totalled $97,822; expenditures totalled $98,103.

Nutrition

In its annual overview report for 1983/84, issued in May 1984,[15] ACC discussed the work of its Sub-Committee on Nutrition in carrying out the inter-agency work (see Chapter XXIV of this section).

Three priority areas for co-ordinated action—Africa's food and nutrition problems, a co-ordinated country-level approach to nutrition activities, and control of vitamin A and iodine deficiencies—were identified by the Sub-Committee and endorsed by the Consultative Committee on Substantive Questions (Programme Matters) and ACC at its first regular session of 1984. The Sub-Committee's ongoing efforts included supporting the inclusion of nutritional considerations in the projects of regional development banks and international agricultural research centres; identifying research priorities; determining the most effective use of food aid for the greatest nutritional impact; linking at the country level of inputs from individual United Nations agencies; and examining primary health care systems as a vehicle for improving nutrition.

The Sub-Committee, at its tenth session (Rome, Italy, 5-9 March),[16] discussed its work programme and decided, among other things, that its Advisory Group on Nutrition would continue to support long-term research on nutrition activities within primary health care programmes; clarify problems associated with energy in nutrition; and assist in designing the country-level examination of problems, opportunities and co-ordinating mechanisms in nutrition.

The United Nations University[17] (see below) reported that it had conducted activities relating to: the food-energy nexus, focusing on the linkages between food and energy and their implications for policy options and integrated development planning, and food, nutrition, biotechnology and poverty, dealing with the social and economic effects of inadequate nutrition and the practical effects of existing health-care and agricultural policies on nutrition.

REFERENCES

[1]A/39/171-E/1984/54. [2]YUN 1983, p. 726, ESC dec. 1983/123, 26 May 1983. [3]E/1984/122. [4]YUN 1982, p. 1538. [5]YUN

1981, p. 795. [6]YUN 1982, p. 980. [7]ACC/1984/PG/7. [8]YUN 1983, p. 760. [9]YUN 1982, p. 983, GA res. 37/53, 3 Dec. 1982. [10]A/39/191 & Corr.1. [11]ACC/1983/9. [12]YUN 1983, p. 758, ESC res. 1983/19, 26 May 1983. [13]E/1985/4. [14]YUN 1983, p. 758, GA res. 38/28, 22 Nov. 1983. [15]E/1984/66. [16]ACC/1984/13. [17]A/39/31.

Human resources

Human resources development

The General Assembly, in a 1982 resolution on the role of qualified national personnel in the social and economic development of developing countries,[1] requested the Secretary-General to prepare and distribute periodic and analytical surveys of national reports on experiences in human resources development and international co-operation in training, and to consult with Member States and the United Nations system on possible elements of general guidelines on principles, objectives and structures of education and training of such personnel.

In 1984, the Governing Council of the United Nations Development Programme (UNDP), at its thirty-first session,[2] considered a May report by the UNDP Administrator,[3] in which he stated that UNDP would require additional resources of some $100,000 to comply with the request made by the Secretary-General under the 1982 Assembly resolution to collect information and consult on guidelines.

By a June note,[4] the Secretary-General drew the attention of the Assembly and the Economic and Social Council to the report of the UNDP Administrator.

On 29 June, the UNDP Governing Council requested the UNDP Administrator to inform the Secretary-General that UNDP could not implement the 1982 Assembly request from its available resources.[5]

Recommendations on co-operation regarding vocational training and human resources development were made by the Third Conference of Ministers of Labour of Non-Aligned Countries and Other Developing Countries (Managua, Nicaragua, 10-12 May 1984).[6]

GENERAL ASSEMBLY ACTION

On 18 December 1984, the General Assembly, on the recommendation of the Second (Economic and Financial) Committee, adopted resolution 39/219 without vote.

Role of qualified national personnel in the social and economic development of developing countries

The General Assembly,

Referring to its resolutions 33/135 of 19 December 1978, 35/80 of 5 December 1980 and 37/228 of 20 December 1982 on the role of qualified national personnel in the social and economic development of developing countries,

Referring also to its resolutions 3201(S-VI) and 3202(S-VI) of 1 May 1974, containing the Declaration and the Programme of Action on the Establishment of a New International Economic Order, and 3281(XXIX) of 12 December 1974, containing the Charter of Economic Rights and Duties of States,

Desiring to promote full implementation of the provisions of the International Development Strategy for the Third United Nations Development Decade concerning the important role of qualified national personnel in the achievement of the development goals of the developing countries,

Noting with regret that the report on the implementation of resolution 37/228, including possible elements of general guidelines on principles, objectives and structures of education and training of personnel of developing countries, has not yet been prepared,

1. *Reaffirms* the importance of implementing the provisions of its resolution 37/228;

2. *Requests* the Secretary-General, in the implementation of that resolution, to consult as soon as possible with the Governments of Member States on their experience in establishing and developing their systems of training qualified national personnel, particularly on the principles, objectives and structures of those systems;

3. *Also requests* the Secretary-General to compile and summarize the information provided by the Governments and to submit it to the General Assembly at its fortieth session.

General Assembly resolution 39/219

18 December 1984　　　　Meeting 104　　　Adopted without vote

Approved by Second Committee (A/39/791) without vote, 10 December (meeting 58); draft by Vice-Chairman (A/C.2/39/L.124), based on informal consultations on 18-nation draft (A/C.2/39/L.85/Rev.1); agenda item 81.
Meeting numbers. GA 39th session: 2nd Committee 53, 58; plenary 104.

UN Institute for Training and Research

Activities of UNITAR

The activities of the United Nations Institute for Training and Research (UNITAR), an autonomous organization within the United Nations system, were described by its Executive Director in reports to the General Assembly for the periods 1 July 1983 to 30 June 1984[7] and 1 July 1984 to 30 June 1986.[8]

In 1984, the UNITAR Board of Trustees (twenty-second session, New York, 19-23 March) approved the UNITAR draft work programme for 1984-1985, discussed long-term financing arrangements (see below) and adopted the budget for 1984.

Stressing that the UNITAR programme should deal with the issues of most concern to Member States, the Board suggested that: research projects could deal with the effectiveness of the United Nations in maintaining peace and security, and the information revolution and its impact on third world countries; training projects might include advising the organizations of the United Nations system on the quality of their training programmes, and studying the establishment by UNITAR of a development-oriented staff training institution for national and international organizations involved in development co-operation with third world countries; and a UNITAR documentation centre on world issues could be created.

The UNITAR Executive Director, in a November statement before the Assembly's Second Committee, said there was a general lack of awareness of the unique role of UNITAR in enhancing the effectiveness of the United Nations through training and research.

Among the training courses conducted by UNITAR in 1984 were seminars for new members of permanent missions (New York, 24-27 January; Geneva, 12-16 November); a course on the drafting of treaties, resolutions and other international instruments (New York, 9-13 and 18 April); a seminar on trade and economic relations between countries having different economic and social systems (Geneva, 3 and 4 September); and a workshop on international negotiation (New York, 11-14 September). Training for other government officials included: a United Nations/UNITAR fellowship programme in international law (The Hague, Netherlands, 2 July–10 August) and a regional training and refresher course in international law for Africa (Yaoundé, Cameroon, 12-24 November).

In response to *ad hoc* requests, UNITAR provided: a training course on international co-operation and multilateral diplomacy for junior diplomats from French-speaking African countries (Paris/Geneva/Brussels/Berlin/Bonn, 16 April–15 June); training for conference officers from Kuwait (Geneva, 8-25 May); basic diplomatic training for government officials from Gabon (Libreville, 1 July–27 September) and from Namibia (Geneva/New York, 3 August–2 November); and briefing seminars on multilateral diplomacy through the United Nations for junior diplomats from Saudi Arabia (New York, 17-20 September).

With financial support from the Italian Government, UNITAR established in 1984 an International Centre for Small Energy Resources at Rome to conduct research on renewable as well as non-renewable energy resources.

Other research activities included: an evaluation of United Nations efforts to alleviate absolute poverty; a seminar on strategies for the future of Asia (Bangkok, Thailand, January); a workshop on population movements within the English-speaking Caribbean (Saint Vincent, February); a first international conference on the development of shallow oil and gas resources (Oklahoma, United States, 25 July–3 August); and a symposium on the urban population explosion (Geneva, November).

Among the publications issued by UNITAR during the year were *African and Arab Co-operation for Development, Co-operation in the 1980s: Principles and Prospects, The Prevention of Nuclear War: A United States Approach, World Leadership and International Development*, and *Worlds Apart: Technology and North-South Relations in the Global Economy.*

An analytical study, *The Principle of Participatory Equality of Developing Countries in International Economic Relations*, was also published. The Secretary-General submitted a report to the Assembly containing a summary and outline of the study.[9]

GENERAL ASSEMBLY ACTION

On 17 December 1984, the General Assembly, on the recommendation of the Second Committee, adopted resolution 39/178 without vote.

United Nations Institute for Training and Research
The General Assembly,
Recalling its resolution 38/177 of 19 December 1983 on the United Nations Institute for Training and Research,
Having considered the report of the Executive Director of the United Nations Institute for Training and Research, covering the period from 1 July 1983 to 30 June 1984, and his introductory statement of 9 November 1984,
Recalling the important role assigned to the Institute for the purpose of enhancing the effectiveness of the United Nations in achieving its major objectives, in particular the maintenance of peace and security and the promotion of economic and social development,
Recalling also the need for the Institute to continue to evolve clear, long-term priorities in the training and research programmes of the Institute that would emphasize its role in the promotion and strengthening of the development process,
Noting with satisfaction the emphasis being placed by the Institute on the revitalization of its programme, the dissemination of the results of its research and the improvement of its management, and on the mobilization of adequate resources to enable it to perform its functions satisfactorily,
Sharing the concern of the Executive Director that only a small number of States are contributing to the General Fund of the United Nations Institute for Training and Research, as well as his concern over the inadequacy of the resources available to the Institute for its work,
1. *Takes note with appreciation* of the report of the Executive Director of the United Nations Institute for Training and Research and of the measures taken in 1984 to improve the management and the budgeting process of the Institute;
2. *Also takes note* of the priorities and work programme for the biennium 1984-1985 approved by the Board of Trustees of the United Nations Institute for Training and Research;
3. *Welcomes* the continuing emphasis of the United Nations Institute for Training and Research on economic and social training and research and the inclusion of specific projects on the problems that exist in the areas identified by the General Assembly at its sixth and seventh special sessions, in the relevant decisions adopted

at its twenty-ninth and subsequent sessions, and in the International Development Strategy for the Third United Nations Development Decade, taking into consideration the statements on the programme of work of the Institute made at the current session;

4. *Takes note* of the clarification provided by the Executive Director on the mandate and the future role of the United Nations Institute for Training and Research as they relate to the mandates and roles of other institutions active in the Institute's field of competence, and notes with satisfaction the efforts being made to strengthen co-operation with those institutions;

5. *Calls upon* all States that have not yet contributed to the United Nations Institute for Training and Research to do so, and urges once again all donor countries, especially those that are not contributing at a level commensurate with their capacity, to increase their voluntary contributions in order to meet the urgent financial needs of the Institute during the biennium 1984-1985;

6. *Again requests* all States to continue to announce their contributions to the United Nations Institute for Training and Research early and, if possible, not later than the annual United Nations Pledging Conference for Development Activities, and to speed up the payment of their voluntary contributions to the Institute.

General Assembly resolution 39/178

17 December 1984   Meeting 103   Adopted without vote

Approved by Second Committee (A/39/792) without vote, 10 December (meeting 58); draft by Vice-Chairman (A/C.2/39/L.133), based on informal consultations on 23-nation draft (A/C.2/39/L.67); agenda item 82 *(a)*.

Meeting numbers. GA 39th session: 2nd Committee 38-39, 41, 47, 58; 5th Committee 49; plenary 103.

Finances of UNITAR

Income and expenditures in 1984

As at 31 December 1984,[10] UNITAR's General Fund income totalled $2,412,845 and expenditures $2,345,140. The income of the Special Purpose Grants Fund was $1,773,226, and expenditures $1,795,574.

In December, the General Assembly called on States that had not yet contributed to UNITAR to do so and urged donor countries to increase their contributions to meet the urgent financial needs during 1984-1985 (resolution 39/178).

Accounts for 1983

As at 31 December 1983,[11] the General Fund income was $2,051,137 and expenditures $3,016,108, a deficit of $964,971. The income of the Special Purpose Grants Fund totalled $920,147 and expenditures $2,071,486, a deficit of $1,151,339.

In December 1983, the General Assembly approved, exceptionally, an advance of $886,000 to cover the deficit in the Institute's 1983 budget.[12] The Board of Auditors—which, in 1984, examined UNITAR's financial report for

1983—noted the need for effective budgetary control, and recommended compliance with the financial rules for incurring expenditures, as well as more appropriate reviews of the status of allotments reports. It added that the Administration had agreed to take the necessary measures.

The Advisory Committee on Administrative and Budgetary Questions (ACABQ)[13] had no comments on the Board of Auditors' report on UNITAR's financial statement.

By resolution 39/66, the Assembly accepted the UNITAR financial report and audited financial statement for the period ended 31 December 1983.

CONTRIBUTIONS TO THE UNITAR GENERAL FUND, 1984
(as at 31 December 1984; in US dollar equivalent)

Country	Amount
Afghanistan	1,000
Algeria	14,485
Austria	26,500
Bahamas	1,000
Barbados	250
Belgium	138,327
Botswana	500
Canada	69,219
Chile	8,000
China	20,000
Democratic Yemen	1,265
Denmark	42,290
Egypt	5,000
Finland	35,168
France	54,581
Germany, Federal Republic of	174,520
Greece	5,000
India	45,000
Indonesia	8,000
Ireland	12,518
Israel	6,000
Italy	86,592
Jamaica	2,000
Japan	100,000
Kuwait	20,000
Libyan Arab Jamahiriya	80,000
Luxembourg	1,733
Malawi	1,123
Malta	600
Netherlands	45,225
New Zealand	4,650
Nigeria	12,469
Norway	126,815
Oman	10,000
Pakistan	10,000
Philippines	10,000
Saudi Arabia	72,834
Spain	20,000
Sweden	90,165
Switzerland	67,754
Trinidad and Tobago	8,292
Tunisia	3,037
USSR	40,000
United Republic of Tanzania	8,336
United States	422,000
Venezuela	29,947
Yugoslavia	5,000
Zambia	5,970
Total	1,953,165

SOURCE: A/40/5/ Add.4.

Long-term financing

UNITAR Board of Trustees consideration. In an effort to avoid budget deficits, the UNITAR Executive Director submitted to the UNITAR Board of Trustees[7] a balanced budget for 1984, eliminating from the work programme financed by the General Fund most of the research activities and restricting other expenses. The Executive Director stressed the importance of an urgent decision by the Assembly that would place the Institute's long-term financing on a more predictable, assured and continuous basis, as called for in 1982.[13]

The Board of Trustees reaffirmed in 1984 that the minimum budgetary level required for a training and research programme for 1984-1985 was $3 million per year, and concluded that the existing pattern of annual contributions gave no promise of meeting minimal needs. It therefore approved three methods proposed by the Executive Director for long-term financing: setting up of a reserve fund of $15 million through grants and soft loans, adoption of a replenishment system under which a target amount would be subscribed to by a large group of contributors, and establishment of an endowment fund of at least $50 million. The Board indicated its preference for an endowment fund, and recommended that the Secretary-General take up personally with Governments his conviction as to the essential role of UNITAR and the necessity of ensuring its long-term financing.

Report of the Secretary-General. In an October 1984 report on long-term financing arrangements for UNITAR,[14] submitted to the General Assembly in response to its 1982 request,[15] the Secretary-General stated that UNITAR's training and research activities helped improve the functioning of multilateral institutions and diplomacy, and that he remained convinced of the validity of the reasons which had led to the establishment of UNITAR in 1965.[16] He reported that the consultations he had held with Governments on the funding proposal by the UNITAR Board of Trustees indicated that they were not in a position to implement any of the three proposals. It was up to the Assembly, therefore, to decide on measures that would ensure the long-term financial viability of UNITAR; in the absence of agreement on such measures, it would be necessary to close down the Institute.

GENERAL ASSEMBLY ACTION

On 17 December, the General Assembly, on the recommendation of the Second Committee, adopted resolution 39/177 by recorded vote.

Long-term financing and the future role of the United Nations Institute for Training and Research

The General Assembly,

Recalling its resolutions 37/142 of 17 December 1982 and 38/177 of 19 December 1983, in which it called upon the Secretary-General to submit a report on long-term financing arrangements for the United Nations Institute for Training and Research which would place its financing on a more predictable, assured and continuous basis,

Having considered the report of the Secretary-General and the statements made by the Executive Director of the United Nations Institute for Training and Research on 9 and 14 November 1984 on the financial difficulties of the Institute,

Taking note of the priorities and work programme for the biennium 1984-1985 approved by the Board of Trustees of the United Nations Institute for Training and Research,

Noting with concern that the 1984 United Nations Pledging Conference for Development Activities, held on 7 and 8 November 1984, was unable to provide the General Fund of the United Nations Institute for Training and Research during 1985 with the level of resources considered by the Board of Trustees of the Institute as the minimum required to maintain the Institute as a viable entity,

Acknowledging with regret that the system of voluntary contributions, instituted to provide resources for the operation of the Institute, has thus far failed fully to guarantee the minimum level of resources needed by the Institute for its General Fund,

Noting with regret that the three options for long-term financing arrangements for the Institute recommended by the Board of Trustees, namely, the setting up of a reserve fund, the adoption of a replenishment system and the establishment of an endowment fund, have not been found acceptable by the major contributors,

1. *Expresses its appreciation* to the Secretary-General for his report;

2. *Endorses* the view of the Secretary-General about the continuing importance of the role of the United Nations Institute for Training and Research;

3. *Requests* the Secretary-General to prepare a comprehensive study on the United Nations Institute for Training and Research, its activities in training and research, its funding and its future role, keeping in mind related activities within the United Nations system and the relevant provisions of the Statute of the Institute, in order to determine the most effective manner of discharging those functions;

4. *Further requests* the Secretary-General to submit his report, together with the comments of the Board of Trustees of the United Nations Institute for Training and Research thereon, to the General Assembly at its fortieth session;

5. *Decides* to grant the United Nations Institute for Training and Research up to $1.5 million, on an exceptional basis, to supplement the funds raised through voluntary contributions for the General Fund of the Institute, in order to enable the Institute to carry out a minimum training and research programme in 1985 at a level to be decided by the Board of Trustees of the Institute at its forthcoming special session, but not exceeding $3 million;

6. *Requests* that the Board of Trustees of the United Nations Institute for Training and Research and, if it agrees, the Advisory Committee on Administrative and Budgetary Questions, examine urgently the programme and budget proposals of the Institute for 1985, with a view to obtaining savings in its budget;

7. *Decides* to take a decision at its fortieth session on the basis of the report of the Secretary-General on the future, programmes and funding arrangements of the United Nations Institute for Training and Research.

General Assembly resolution 39/177

17 December 1984   Meeting 103   127-10-11 (recorded vote)

Approved by Second Committee (A/39/792) by recorded vote (101-10-12), 10 December (meeting 58); 4-nation draft (A/C.2/39/L.66/Rev.1); agenda item 82 (a).
Sponsors: Bangladesh, Canada, Guinea-Bissau, Pakistan.
Financial implications. 5th Committee, A/39/828; S-G, A/C.2/39/L.105, A/C.5/39/96.
Meeting numbers. GA 39th session: 2nd Committee 38-41, 45, 47, 58; 5th Committee 49; plenary 103.

Recorded vote in Assembly as follows:

In favour: Afghanistan, Algeria, Angola, Argentina, Bahamas, Bahrain, Bangladesh, Barbados, Benin, Bhutan, Bolivia, Botswana, Brunei Darussalam, Burkina Faso, Burma, Burundi, Cameroon, Canada, Cape Verde, Central African Republic, Chad, Chile, China, Congo, Costa Rica, Cuba, Cyprus, Democratic Kampuchea, Democratic Yemen, Denmark, Djibouti, Dominican Republic, Ecuador, Egypt, El Salvador, Equatorial Guinea, Ethiopia, Fiji, Finland, Gabon, Gambia, Ghana, Greece, Guatemala, Guinea, Guinea-Bissau, Guyana, Haiti, Honduras, Iceland, India, Indonesia, Iran, Iraq, Ireland, Israel, Italy, Ivory Coast, Jamaica, Jordan, Kenya, Kuwait, Lao People's Democratic Republic, Lebanon, Lesotho, Liberia, Libyan Arab Jamahiriya, Madagascar, Malawi, Malaysia, Maldives, Mali, Malta, Mauritania, Mauritius, Mexico, Morocco, Mozambique, Nepal, Netherlands, New Zealand, Nicaragua, Niger, Nigeria, Norway, Oman, Pakistan, Panama, Papua New Guinea, Paraguay, Peru, Philippines, Portugal, Qatar, Rwanda, Saint Lucia, Samoa, Sao Tome and Principe, Saudi Arabia, Senegal, Sierra Leone, Singapore, Somalia, Spain, Sri Lanka, Sudan, Suriname, Swaziland, Sweden, Syrian Arab Republic, Thailand, Togo, Trinidad and Tobago, Tunisia, Turkey, Uganda, United Arab Emirates, United Republic of Tanzania, Uruguay, Vanuatu, Venezuela, Viet Nam, Yemen, Yugoslavia, Zaire, Zambia, Zimbabwe.

Against: Bulgaria, Byelorussian SSR, Czechoslovakia, German Democratic Republic, Hungary, Mongolia, Poland, Ukrainian SSR, USSR, United States.

Abstaining: Australia, Austria, Belgium, Brazil, Colombia, France, Germany, Federal Republic of, Japan, Luxembourg, Romania, United Kingdom.

As regards budgetary implications of the text, ACABQ noted that preparation of the envisaged study would require four work-months of a high-level consultant at a cost of $30,000 in fees and travel but, since that requirement would be covered under the provisions for consultants in the programme budget, no additional funds would be required.

Before taking action on the text as a whole, the Assembly adopted paragraph 5 by a separate recorded vote of 103 to 15, with 25 abstentions; subsequently, the Lao People's Democratic Republic said it had intended to abstain. The Second Committee had approved the paragraph by a recorded vote of 83 to 15, with 23 abstentions.

In explanation of vote on the paragraph, Belgium, recalling that the Assembly had envisioned UNITAR to be financed by voluntary contributions, cautioned that adopting the text might lead to new mandatory contributions and reduce voluntary contributions. The United States declared that if the Assembly approved the text, it might reduce its voluntary contribution up to the amount of its share of the regular-budget cost of the proposed grant—a statement which it repeated in the Fifth Committee. Cameroon held that UNITAR was being punished for a crime it had not committed; if the statute under which UNITAR was to be financed by voluntary contributions had been complied with, there would have been no request for funds from the regular budget.

On the resolution as a whole, the Ukrainian SSR, speaking on behalf also of Bulgaria, the Byelorussian SSR, Czechoslovakia, the German Democratic Republic, Hungary, Mongolia, Poland and the USSR, expressed opposition to financial subsidies from the regular budget and any other proposals to change the voluntary financing of the Institute. Similarly, Australia, Japan and the United Kingdom voted against paragraph 5 and abstained on the draft as a whole because they believed that voluntarily funded institutions should not receive supplementary funding from the regular budget. Agreeing that UNITAR should continue to be financed voluntarily, France abstained in both votes.

While abstaining on paragraph 5, Argentina, Denmark, Italy and the Netherlands voted for the text because of their support for and interest in UNITAR. Norway also supported the resolution with the understanding that the Assembly would consider in 1985 all aspects of UNITAR's activities and its future.

In the Fifth Committee, the USSR, the United Kingdom and the United States reiterated their opposition concerning UNITAR's funding and felt that UNITAR's work programme should be kept within its resources.

The Fifth Committee adopted—by a recorded vote of 60 to 15, with 17 abstentions—a proposal by its Chairman informing the Assembly that, should it adopt the revised draft, an additional appropriation of $1.5 million would be required under the programme budget for 1984-1985. Sweden, while supporting that proposal, expressed concern over the fact that the Institute would receive a grant for the third time in four years.

UN University

Activities of the University

In 1984, the United Nations University (UNU), an autonomous academic institution within the United Nations framework, made progress in setting up its research and training centres, signing a formal Agreement with Finland on the World Institute for Development Economics Research (WIDER), and initialling a draft Memorandum of Understanding with the Ivory Coast on the Institute for Natural Resources in Africa.[17] A proposal to establish in Japan an institute of advanced studies was endorsed by the UNU Council.

Thirty-five projects and some 50 subprojects were in operation during the year under the five themes of UNU's medium-term perspective (1982-1987),[18] which dealt with: peace, security, conflict resolution and global transformation; the global economy; hunger, poverty, resources and the environment; human and social development and the coexistence of peoples, cultures and social systems; and science and technology and their social and ethical implications.

The University continued to expand its involvement in activities of international concern. It sponsored a symposium on conditions essential for maintaining outer space for peaceful purposes (The Hague, Netherlands, March) and a symposium on the science and praxis of complexity (Montpellier, France, May). Among the meetings it co-sponsored were: the North-South Roundtable of the Society for International Development (Santiago, Chile, February); the fourth annual lecture in a Global Lecture Series on peace and development (Tokyo, March); and a workshop on the integration of emerging and traditional technologies, organized by the Japanese Association for Promotion of International Co-operation (Tokyo, April). It participated, among others, in a joint meeting—at Rome, Italy, in January—of the Independent Commission on International Development Issues (Brandt Commission) and the Independent Commission on Disarmament and Security Issues (Palme Commission).

The core group of the Special Committee on Africa project held its first planning meeting at Nairobi, Kenya, in August; implementation of the project would begin with a series of three symposia, starting in 1985.

The University's new planning process was broadened in April, to include programme directors, project co-ordinators, University consultants and a former and a present Fellow; the responsibility for training was assigned to the Global Learning Division. In January 1984, the University welcomed its first Visiting Scholar, Kenneth Boulding.

Progress was made in preparatory work for the University's permanent headquarters, with the allocation of a budgetary provision for 1984-1985 for planning activities, including an overall study of architectural needs and the collection of information for basic design.

Institutions associated with UNU numbered 37. The University had over 100 research and training units carrying out its work in more than 60 countries. The number of University Fellows in training was about 70; as at November 1984, about 450 Fellows had completed training.

By a decision adopted on 18 October 1984, the Executive Board of the United Nations Educational, Scientific and Cultural Organization, among other things, urged UNU to secure greater diversity in the choice of co-operating institutions and countries.

Among the University's publications in 1984 were *Development as Social Transformation: Reflections on the Global Problématique; Energy and Agriculture: Their Interacting Futures; Food as a Human Right; In Search of Peace in the Nuclear Age; Maintaining Outer Space for Peaceful Purposes; Social, Economic and Institutional Aspects of Agro-Forestry; The Transformation of the World Economy and Society (vol. 2); Transforming the World Economy: Nine Critical Essays on the New International Economic Order;* and *Visions of Desirable Societies.*

GENERAL ASSEMBLY ACTION

On 17 December 1984, the General Assembly, on the recommendation of the Second Committee, adopted resolution 39/179 without vote.

United Nations University

The General Assembly,

Recalling its resolutions 2951(XXVII) of 11 December 1972, 3081(XXVIII) of 6 December 1973, 3313(XXIX) of 14 December 1974, 3439(XXX) of 9 December 1975, 31/117 and 31/118 of 16 December 1976, 32/54 of 8 December 1977, 33/108 of 18 December 1978, 34/112 of 14 December 1979, 35/54 of 5 December 1980, 36/45 of 19 November 1981, 37/143 of 17 December 1982 and 38/178 of 19 December 1983,

Having considered the report of the Council of the United Nations University on the work of the University,

Noting with appreciation the continuing interest of the Government of Japan in, and its support for, the University in regard to the construction of a permanent headquarters building,

Noting decision 5.2.1 adopted on 18 October 1984 by the Executive Board of the United Nations Educational, Scientific and Cultural Organization at its one hundred and twentieth session,

1. *Notes with satisfaction,* as the United Nations University reaches the middle of its medium-term perspective (1982-1987), the progress achieved by the University in realizing the main objectives set forth in the perspective, namely, developing and implementing the University programme focused on five themes relevant to the pressing global problems of human survival, development and welfare that are also the concerns of the United Nations and the specialized agencies, and embarking on a new phase of institutional development, with emphasis on establishing the University's own research and training centres as called for in its Charter;

2. *Welcomes* the reports of external evaluation teams indicating the positive results of the United Nations University's research, institutional relations and post-graduate training, particularly the advanced training of University Fellows who have returned to their home institutions, in collaboration with the University's associated and co-operating institutions in both developing and industrialized countries;

3. *Welcomes also* the progress made in setting up the World Institute for Development Economics Research, the United Nations University's first research and training institution, at Helsinki, and expresses its appreciation for the leading role and invaluable support of the Government of Finland in establishing the Institute by providing financial and other forms of support;

4. *Notes with satisfaction* the advance made towards establishing the proposed Institute for Natural Resources in Africa and an international programme in biotechnology in Venezuela;

5. *Emphasizes* the continuing need of the United Nations University to strengthen the capacity of existing scholarly and scientific institutions in developing countries;

6. *Notes* the need to further continue, expand and intensify co-operative activities of the United Nations University with the United Nations, its bodies and the specialized agencies, on the one hand, and with the international academic and scientific community, on the other, which enhance the responsiveness of the University to global issues and problems and bring its work into closer relation with the concerns of the United Nations system and the world academic community in regard to global issues and problems;

7. *Recognizes* that the United Nations University needs to intensify its fund-raising efforts to build up its Endowment Fund and Operating Fund and to ensure the development of its activities in a well-co-ordinated manner in accordance with its Charter;

8. *Earnestly appeals* to all Member States to take cognizance of the progress made by the United Nations University and the relevance of its work to the concerns of the United Nations and to contribute urgently and generously to its Endowment Fund and, additionally or alternatively, to make operating contributions to the University to enable it to fulfil its mandate effectively, in accordance with its Charter and with the relevant resolutions of the General Assembly.

General Assembly resolution 39/179

17 December 1984   Meeting 103   Adopted without vote

Approved by Second Committee (A/39/792) without vote, 30 November (meeting 55); draft by Vice-Chairman (A/C.2/39/L.87), based on informal consultations on 20-nation draft (A/C.2/39/L.58); agenda item 82 *(b)*.
Meeting numbers. GA 39th session: 2nd Committee 38-39, 45, 55; plenary 103.

Activities of the Council

The UNU Council met twice during 1984, holding its twenty-third session[17] at Oxford, United Kingdom, from 1 to 6 July, and its twenty-fourth session[18] in Tokyo from 10 to 14 December.

In July, the Council, among other things, reviewed the programmes of the University for the first half of the medium-term perspective, and approved a proposal to establish a programme of research and training in biotechnology at Caracas, Venezuela, and a research and training centre in Japan. It designated the following as associated institutions of UNU: Institute of Nutrition and Food Science of the University of Dhaka (Bangladesh); University of Guelph (Canada); Universidad de los Andes (Colombia); Addis Ababa University (Ethiopia); Institute for World Economics of the Hungarian Academy of Sciences (Hungary); and Korea Advanced Institute of Science and Technology (Republic of Korea).

In December, the Council adopted the supplemental programme and budget for 1984-1985, and took note of progress reports on the permanent headquarters of the University and the report of the University for Peace. The Council's fourth colloquium on distance learning systems was held during the session to allow Council members to be involved in greater depth in the University's work.

Finances of the University

As at December 1984, the total pledges to the UNU Endowment and Operating Funds were $176 million, of which $137 million had been received. Expenditures amounted to $10.4 million for the 12-month period ending 31 October 1984. Planned expenditures for 1985 were set at $18.4 million.

CONTRIBUTIONS TO UNU, 1984 AND 1985
(as at 31 December 1984; in US dollar equivalent)

COUNTRY	1984 payment	1985 pledge
Endowment Fund		
Austria	15,270	—
Germany, Federal Republic of	368,700	—
Ghana	250,000	—
Japan	2,000,000	—
Nigeria	10,940	—
Trinidad and Tobago	20,730	—
Venezuela	1,996,512	—
Zambia	8,400	—
Subtotal	4,670,552	—
General Operating Fund		
Austria	59,398	—
France	167,190	—
Greece	40,000	—
Norway	126,815	—
Sri Lanka	5,000	16,666
Tunisia	4,962	—
Subtotal	403,365	16,666
WIDER Trust Fund—Endowment Fund		
Finland	6,000,000	19,000,000
Subtotal	6,000,000	19,000,000
WIDER Trust Fund—Operating Fund		
Finland	416,667	2,033,898
Subtotal	416,667	2,033,898
Total	11,490,584	21,050,564

SOURCE: UNU.

Recognizing that UNU needed to intensify its fund-raising efforts to build up its Endowment and Operating Funds, the General Assembly, in resolution 39/179, appealed to Member States to contribute to them.

Accounts for 1982-1983

The Advisory Committee on Administrative and Budgetary Questions[13] had no comments on the Board of Auditors' report on the financial statements of UNU for 1982-1983.

In resolution 39/66, the General Assembly accepted the financial statements and the Board's report.

REFERENCES
[1]YUN 1982, p. 986, GA res. 37/228, 20 Dec. 1982. [2]E/1984/20. [3]DP/1984/65. [4]A/39/308-E/1984/118. [5]E/1984/20 (dec. 84/43). [6]A/39/581-S/16782. [7]A/39/14. [8]A/41/14. [9]A/39/504/Add.1. [10]A/40/5/Add.4. [11]A/39/5/Add.4. [12]YUN 1983, p. 763, GA res. 38/177, 19 Dec. 1983. [13]A/39/510. [14]A/39/148. [15]YUN 1982, p. 988, GA res. 37/142, 17 Dec. 1982. [16]YUN 1965, p. 517. [17]A/39/31. [18]E/1985/55.

Chapter XVI

Environment

The United Nations Environment Programme (UNEP) was able to make scant headway against the rising tide of environmental destruction in 1984, according to the UNEP Executive Director. It undertook a global campaign to engender a better understanding of the central role of environmental issues in the broader economic and social context.

The Governing Council of UNEP held its twelfth session in 1984. After reviewing implementation of the Plan of Action to Combat Desertification from 1978 to 1984, the Council noted with great concern that desertification was continuing to spread, particularly in Africa; it proposed further measures to ameliorate the problem. By resolution 39/208, the General Assembly called on the international community, particularly the developed countries, to assist countries stricken by desertification and drought. The Economic and Social Council (resolution 1984/65) and the Assembly (resolution 39/168 A) urged increased assistance to those countries. The Assembly also emphasized the need to redouble efforts to combat the problem in the Sudano-Sahelian region (resolution 39/168 B). To develop a joint policy for combating desertification, the 21 countries affected held a regional Ministerial Conference in Senegal in July.

The Economic and Social Council, by resolution 1984/72, urged the Assembly to expand the scope of work of the United Nations Sudano-Sahelian Office (UNSO) to assist additional States to tackle desertification.

The Global Environmental Monitoring System of Earthwatch, the assessment arm of UNEP, continued to monitor renewable resources, climate, health, pollutants and oceans. A Convention for the Protection of the Ozone Layer was drafted. The International Register of Potentially Toxic Chemicals continued to expand its global information network. Draft guidelines were being developed for the management of hazardous wastes. Other UNEP activities included world climate impact studies, management of tropical forests and world soil resources, wildlife conservation, protection of the marine environment, and linkages between environment and development, industry, population and human settlements.

By resolution 39/229, the Assembly decided that a list of products whose consumption and/or sale had been banned, withdrawn, severely restricted or not approved by Governments should be issued annually. By resolution 39/167, it regretted that no concrete measures had been taken to solve the problem of material remnants of war and requested the Secretary-General to assist countries affected in their efforts to detect and clear them.

Forty-eight new projects were approved by the Environment Fund in 1984; 53 projects were concluded. The Fund disbursed $17 million for programme activities; government contributions totalled $29.5 million.

Topics related to this chapter. Africa: co-operation with the Organization of African Unity. Asia: Iran-Iraq armed conflict. Middle East: Mediterranean–Dead Sea canal project. Economic assistance, disasters and emergency relief: drought-stricken areas of Africa. Regional economic and social activities: environment. Natural resources: water resources. Energy resources: nuclear energy. Health. Human settlements.

Programme and finances of UNEP

The twelfth session of the Governing Council of UNEP was held at UNEP headquarters, Nairobi, Kenya, from 16 to 29 May 1984. The Council adopted 26 decisions on environmental and administrative matters.

Programme policy

On 28 May,[1] the UNEP Council took note of the reports of the UNEP Executive Director on emerging environmental issues[2] and on environmental events in 1983[3] and requested him to update annually the list of emerging issues; it found that air pollution in cities of developing countries and biotechnology should be taken into account when preparing UNEP's biennial programme budgets.

The Council decided that a comprehensive report on the state of the environment should be prepared every 10 years, the next such report to be submitted in 1992. It further decided that population and the environment and environmental aspects of emerging agricultural technology should be examined in the Executive Director's 1985 report.[4] The Council also took note of his intention to produce a final version of the state-of-the-environment report for 1984.[5]

ECONOMIC AND SOCIAL COUNCIL ACTION

In July, the Economic and Social Council, on the recommendation of its First (Economic) Committee, adopted decision 1984/179 without vote.

Report of the Governing Council of the United Nations Environment Programme on the work of its twelfth session

At its 49th plenary meeting, on 26 July 1984, the Council took note of the report of the Governing Council of the United Nations Environment Programme on the work of its twelfth session and decided to transmit it to the General Assembly at its thirty-ninth session for consideration.

Economic and Social Council decision 1984/179

Adopted without vote

Approved by First Committee (E/1984/145) without vote, 20 July (meeting 14); oral proposal by Chairman; agenda item 14.

Two draft resolutions concerning international co-operation on the environment were introduced in the First Committee and later withdrawn. By the first,[6] introduced by Norway on behalf of 18 nations, the Council would have welcomed the establishment of a Special Commission on the Environmental Perspective to the Year 2000 and Beyond (see below), and would have noted with concern the meagre pledges made to the UNEP Fund. By the other draft,[7] submitted by a Vice-Chairman on the basis of informal consultations on the first, the Council would have recalled in the preamble that in a 1983 Assembly resolution[8] it had been stated that the continuing increase in the production, stockpiling and risk of use of weapons of mass destruction not only posed a major threat to the environment and even to life on earth, but also competed for limited resources that could be better used.

GENERAL ASSEMBLY ACTION

In December, the General Assembly, on the recommendation of the Second (Economic and Financial) Committee, adopted decision 39/429 without vote.

Environment

At its 103rd plenary meeting, on 17 December 1984, the General Assembly, on the recommendation of the Second Committee:

(a) Took note of the report of the Governing Council of the United Nations Environment Programme on the work of its twelfth session;

(b) Took note of the note by the Secretary-General transmitting the report of the Executive Director of the United Nations Environment Programme on international conventions and protocols in the field of the environment.[9]

General Assembly decision 39/429

Adopted without vote

Approved by Second Committee (A/39/790/Add.9) without vote, 14 December (meeting 60); oral proposal by Chairman; agenda item 80 (i).

Meeting numbers. GA 39th session: 2nd Committee 37, 50, 54, 58, 60; plenary 103.

In the Committee, Norway submitted and subsequently withdrew a draft resolution on international co-operation in the field of the environment on behalf of 20 nations.[10] It would have had the Assembly welcome the establishment of the Special Commission on the Environmental Perspective; note with concern the status of government pledges to the UNEP Fund; and endorse a series of Governing Council decisions.

The USSR proposed inserting a preambular paragraph referring to the threat posed by weapons of mass destruction to the environment and life on earth.[11] Pakistan orally proposed revising the amendment to state that the continuing arms accumulation in many regions and the risk of their use was a major danger for the environment and competed for limited resources. Iraq proposed revising Pakistan's text to refer to the stockpiling of weapons of mass destruction (see below, under "Arms race and the environment").

State of the environment

In response to a May 1983 UNEP Council decision,[12] the Executive Director submitted a report on the state of the environment in 1984.[13] The topic selected for consideration was environment in the dialogue between and among developed and developing countries. Among other things, the report discussed interdependence between economic and environmental issues, and environmental standards in relation to international investment and trade.

The report concluded that a broad understanding of the economic and social context, one in which the environment was seen to play an all-pervading role, was required. Environmental and resource management issues transcended international boundaries; solutions to those problems required extensive international co-operation and mutual assistance. The dialogue between developed and developing countries was crucial in that respect. Since many environmental problems tended to be technical and politically neutral, environmental agreements could have a unifying impact and help create a favourable climate for attacking more controversial problems.

Three addenda to the report concerned emerging environmental issues,[2] preparation and presentation of environmental data[14] and environmental events in 1983.[3]

By a decision of 28 May 1984,[5] the UNEP Council noted with appreciation the Executive Director's intention to produce a final version of the report, taking into account government views. It encouraged him to continue suggesting specific action, encouraged governmental bodies to continue their efforts for sustained global progress with special focus on developing countries' needs, and agreed to continued support by UNEP for the dialogue between developed and developing countries (see also below, under "Environmental aspects of political, economic and other issues"). As requested by the Council, the final report was to be transmitted to the General Assembly, its Committee on the Review and Appraisal of the Implementation of the International Development Strategy for the Third United Nations Development Decade and other United Nations bodies.

In July, UNEP organized a workshop in London to discuss the publication of environmental indicators, requested in a UNEP Council decision of 28 May.[15] The workshop was attended by representatives of the International Institute for Environment and Development, the Monitoring and Assessment Research Centre of the University of London, and the World Resources Institute, which were to co-operate with UNEP in compiling the data. Publication was planned for 1986.

Environmental Perspective

In 1984, the UNEP Council again took up the question of preparing an Environmental Perspective to the Year 2000 and Beyond, to be submitted in 1987. In March 1984, the Executive Director reported on the state of the preparations.[16] Pursuant to a December 1983 General Assembly resolution,[17] an Intergovernmental Inter-sessional Preparatory Committee was being set up to assist the Council in preparing the Perspective; a 22-member Special Commission, also known as the World Commission on Environment and Development, would develop proposals. An interim special account for voluntary contributions, from which disbursements were to be made for the Special Commission, was established in February 1984.

On 29 May,[18] the UNEP Council decided on the 30 members of the Committee. The Commission held at Geneva an organizational meeting in May and an inaugural meeting in October (see APPENDIX III).

Regional activities

Regional activities in Africa, Asia and the Pacific, and Latin America and the Caribbean were dealt with in UNEP Council decisions of 28 May.[19] The Council welcomed the outcome of a meeting of the African subregional environment groups (Lusaka, Zamba, 10-13 April), in particular its draft programme of action on the African environment, and requested the Executive Director to continue assisting in convening an African ministerial conference to approve a regional plan of action, to strengthen the Regional Office for Africa and to study the establishment of subregional offices, considering the offer of Morocco to host the subregional office for North Africa.

The Council also requested him to continue to accord high priority to the programmes of the Asia and Pacific region and to intensify his efforts to seek funds for them, while urging that he use his discretionary authority to increase funds for the high-priority regional seas programme.

The Council thanked Peru for convening the third (1984) Regional Intergovernmental Meeting on the Environment in Latin America and the Caribbean, and the Executive Director for the Meeting of High-level Experts Designated by Governments to Review Regional Environmental Programmes in Latin America and the Caribbean (Lima, Peru, 8-12 April). It requested him to provide financial support for strengthening regional activities, to set in motion as soon as possible regional programmes of common interest, and to incorporate those in the 1986-1987 budget. It called his attention to the request by the Meeting of High-level Experts that he compile information on innovative means of financing, while Governments and international organizations were urged to intensify their support to the following programmes co-ordinated by UNEP: the Action Plan for the Caribbean Environment; the Environmental Training Network for Latin America and the Caribbean (see p. 771); and the Action Plan for the Protection of the Marine Environment and Coastal Areas of the South-East Pacific.

The Council, in another decision of 28 May,[20] urged States to support fully regional conventions and protocols for the protection and development of the marine environment and coastal areas (see "Regional seas programme" below).

Towards regional and technical co-operation, the Executive Director pointed out in his annual report,[21] UNEP continued to provide support to: staff of UNEP regional offices, including regional advisers; individual experts from developing countries wishing to participate in environment-related meetings, symposia, workshops and seminars; the environment co-ordinating units in the United Nations regional commissions; and a limited number of small technical co-operation projects. The importance of regional co-operation was also stressed in the area of education and training. A regional approach was also taken in combating desertification (see p. 756).

Co-ordination

United Nations co-ordination

In a report to the UNEP Governing Council at its 1984 session on co-ordination of environment activities,[22] the Administrative Committee on Co-ordination (ACC) continued to keep under review preparation of the Environmental Perspective to the Year 2000 and Beyond, reiterating that member organizations were ready to participate in the process. It decided to contribute to the ongoing review of the environment component of the International Development Strategy for the Third United Nations Development Decade (see p. 391), and noted that a clearing-house facility established by UNEP to act as intermediary between donors and recipients in helping developing countries deal with environmental problems was becoming operational (see below).

Reviewing preparations to assess the progress in implementing the 1977 Plan of Action to Combat Desertification, ACC noted with concern that, although there was growing consciousness of the need to combat the problem, particularly in the Sudano-Sahelian region, insufficient financing was seriously limiting United Nations efforts to implement the Plan (see p. 756).

In an addendum to the report, ACC reviewed, within the context of the International Development Strategy, the evolution of United Nations system-wide co-ordination on the environment (see p. 392).

On 28 May 1984,[23] the UNEP Council expressed appreciation for the report and noted the progress made by UNEP in its co-ordinating role.

On 23 October,[24] ACC approved its report to the 1985 UNEP Council session.

During 1984, 87 UNEP Fund projects were being implemented in co-operation with other United Nations agencies and organizations, including FAO (22 projects), UNESCO (17), WHO (13), WMO (8) and UNSO (6).

Co-operation with UNCHS

Noting the report of the Executive Director[25] on the sixth joint meeting of UNEP and the United Nations Centre for Human Settlements (UNCHS) in December 1983,[26] the UNEP Council, on 28 May 1984,[23] requested him to increase co-operation between both entities and reaffirmed that such meetings were no longer necessary.

In its report on co-ordination of environment activities (see above), ACC pointed out that UNEP and UNCHS had prepared guidelines for developing human settlements along environmentally sound lines. It was envisaged that technical and other assistance to developing countries in applying the guidelines would be increased. However, ACC noted that very little progress had been made in improving the environmental aspects of human settlements in those countries (see p. 768).

UNEP clearing-house mechanism

On 28 May 1984,[27] the UNEP Council decided to extend for three years the clearing-house mechanism for the mobilization of resources over and above regular contributions to meet serious environmental problems in developing countries. The clearing-house concept, which had emerged in 1982,[28] incorporated programming and technical assistance elements, with UNEP acting as a catalyst and co-ordinator, rather than as a financing agency. Also on 28 May, the Council requested the Executive Director to establish a Clearing-house Unit with no more than five Professional staff plus support services; to seek funding for long-term programmes; to initiate programmes for integrating environmental considerations into development planning processes; to consider other means of promoting the clearing-house concept; and to ensure that clearing-house projects were formulated in co-ordination with other United Nations organizations, bilateral donors and non-governmental organizations. The Council called on Governments for support in cash or in kind.

In extending the clearing-house experiment, the Council followed a suggestion by the Executive Director in a March progress report.[29] Describing different types of projects, the report concluded that the mechanism was not only successful in promoting environmental improvement but was also an innovative financial mechanism.

Several projects presented for financing in 1984 focused on specific environmental problems, improving national environmental legislation, training central government administrators, and organizing nation-wide discussions of environmental priorities. Early in 1984, long-term strategies for tackling serious environmental problems were completed in Botswana, Indonesia, Jordan and Peru. During the year, funds were committed or pledged to the clearing-house by Argentina, the Federal Republic of Germany, the Netherlands, Norway, Sweden and the Arab Gulf Programme for United Nations Development Organizations. Discussions continued with Argentina, which established a five-year line of credit for use by other developing countries in dealing with environmental problems. Malaysia offered facilities and staff for training technicians of other countries in environmental controls in the palm-oil and rubber industries.

Co-ordination with intergovernmental organizations

The number of intergovernmental organizations participating in environmental activities continued to grow in 1984. Several worked closely with UNEP in such areas as regional seas, desertification, toxic and contaminated matter, and environmental education and training.

In Europe, the Council for Mutual Economic Assistance (CMEA) joined with the UNEP International Register of Potentially Toxic Chemicals and the ILO/WHO/UNEP International Programme on Chemical Safety in a training seminar (Moscow, 19-30 November) on the optimal use of health risk evaluations. UNEP took part in the twentieth session of the CMEA Board for Environmental Protection (Poznan, Poland, 25-28 April) and in the environmental activities of the Council of Europe and the Organisation for Economic Co-operation and Development (OECD), including the OECD International Conference on Environment and Economics (Paris, 18-21 June).

Outside the industrialized world, UNEP continued to act as a focal point for intergovernmental co-operation. It provided a secretariat for the third Regional Intergovernmental Meeting on the Environment in Latin America and the Caribbean (Lima, April). In Asia and the Pacific, it collaborated with the Association of South-East Asian Nations (ASEAN), giving technical assistance in nature conservation, environmental impact assessment, and education and training. UNEP regional seas specialists continued to assist the ASEAN countries with projects on oil pollution, chemical dispersants and ambient oceanographic and meteorological phenomena. In the South Pacific, UNEP worked with the South Pacific Commission, the South Pacific Bureau for Economic Co-operation and individual Governments in developing the South Pacific Regional Environment Programme and a regional seas plan of action. Moreover, it was involved in the South Asia Co-operative Environment Programme as well as the launching of the South Asian Seas programme.

In the Middle East, UNEP continued to collaborate with the League of Arab States, particularly the Conference on Environmental Pollution and Its Problems in Arab Countries (Amman, Jordan, July); the Conference proposed that a meeting of Arab ministers on the environment be organized in 1985. Long-standing ties with the Arab League Educational, Cultural and Scientific Organization (ALECSO) were formalized by UNEP in a memorandum of understanding in January; UNEP was also working with ALECSO in regional seas activities for the Red Sea and the Gulf of Aden, environment projects in the Mediterranean, and green belt projects in North Africa and the Syrian desert.

In Africa, UNEP co-operated with the Organization of African Unity and various subregional governmental organizations.

Relations with NGOs

On 28 May,[23] the UNEP Council welcomed UNEP's increasing co-operation with non-governmental organizations (NGOs) and endorsed the efforts of the Executive Director to extend that co-operation.

UNEP continued in 1984 to provide financial assistance to the Nairobi-based Environment Liaison Centre (ELC), which maintained a network of more than 6,000 NGOs dealing with environment issues. A substantial part of that assistance was used for ELC's programme of collecting and disseminating information.

Preparatory work for a Global Meeting on Environment and Development for NGOs was supported financially by UNEP through ELC; the preparatory committee met at Nairobi (27-30 September).

UNEP gave priority to NGO activities in a number of ways. Several NGOs participated in about 20 projects on nature conservation and terrestrial ecosystems, information and publicity campaigns, and meteorological and oceanographic research. UNEP continued to support the World Resources Institute, particularly its data collection programmes, and maintained close co-operation with the Global Tomorrow Coalition, which brought together a large number of community groups and NGOs in the United States.

With financial support from UNEP and under the auspices of the Inter-Parliamentary Union, 98 delegates from 44 parliaments met at UNEP headquarters to exchange views on environmental management and legislation.

A World Industry Conference on Environmental Management (Versailles, France, 14-16 November) was jointly sponsored by UNEP, major industries and the International Chamber of Commerce (see below, under "Environmental activities").

UNEP Fund

During 1984, the Environment Fund disbursed $22,254,930 for programme activities—excluding $588,348 for activities under the programme reserve—in the following areas: environmental awareness, $3,709,109; Earthwatch, $3,088,379; oceans, $2,761,444; environment and development, $2,589,976; terrestrial ecosystems, $2,582,074; health and human settlements, $2,509,876; desertification, $2,314,359; regional and technical co-operation, $2,107,614; water, $477,098; and arms race and the environment, $115,000.

Forty-eight new projects were approved in 1984, compared with 44 in 1983; 53 projects were closed. At the end of 1984, 294 projects were still open. Geographical distribution of Fund commitments was as follows: global, $14,013,559 (61 per cent); regional, $6,596,354 (29 per cent); and inter-regional, $2,233,365 (10 per cent).

On 28 May,[30] the UNEP Council authorized the Executive Director to draw up a programme of Fund activities resulting in project expenditures of about $50 million in 1986-1987, and requested him to present the programme at the Council's 1985 session in such a way as to facilitate the consideration of programme priorities. Also on 28 May,[31] the Council approved his recommendation to set the financial reserve of the Fund at $6.86 million in 1984 and $7.35 million in 1985, and requested him to report in 1985 on the usefulness of an increased reserve in reducing undercommitment of funds. The Council confirmed the appropriation of $26,020,000 for programme and programme support costs for 1984-1985, and requested the Executive Director to continue to attempt to limit those costs to within 33 per cent of estimated contributions in 1984.

Contributions

On 28 May,[30] the UNEP Council requested the Executive Director to seek increased contributions to the Fund so that projects costing about $50 million in 1986-1987 could be implemented.

Accounts for 1982-1983

As at 31 December 1983, total income of the UNEP Fund for 1982-1983 amounted to $62,939,418, while expenditures totalled $65,886,931, leaving an excess of expenditure over income of $2,947,513.

Commenting on the audited accounts,[32] the Board of Auditors noted that some pledges for 1980-1981 remained unpaid and that in certain cases expenditure was incurred either in excess of or without allotments. There was a need to strengthen the periodic review and follow-up procedure for settling overdue accounts. Further, in one project substantial expenditure had been unnecessarily incurred owing to inadequacy in the project design; also, reporting on various projects was not timely, and inventory control and monitoring of project activities inadequate. In contravention of existing rules, internationally recruited General Service staff members were being paid 70 per cent of their salary in convertible currency.

The Advisory Committee on Administrative and Budgetary Questions (ACABQ), in a September 1984 report,[33] noted that the maximum proportion authorized by United Nations Headquarters for payment in convertible currency to such staff was 25 or 50 per cent, depending on dependency status. ACABQ had been informed that, so far as was known at Headquarters, the situation was restricted to some 30 UNEP staff; consul-

CONTRIBUTIONS TO THE UNEP FUND, 1984

(as at 31 December 1984)

Country	Amount (in US dollars)	Country	Amount (in US dollars)	Country	Amount (in US dollars)
Algeria	11,000	Greece	7,000	Philippines	2,349
Argentina	70,000	Hungary	21,041	Poland	24,590
Australia	386,775	Iceland	4,500	Portugal	3,000
Austria	300,000	India	100,000	Qatar	10,000
Bahamas	500	Indonesia	12,000	Saudi Arabia	500,000
Bangladesh	5,167	Ireland	19,234	Seychelles	100
Barbados	1,000	Italy	249,420	Singapore	1,000
Belgium	171,375	Ivory Coast	4,211	Somalia	203
Benin	1,713	Japan	4,000,000	Spain	258,876
Botswana	902	Jordan	5,000	Sri Lanka	3,000
Brazil	20,000	Kenya	45,000	Swaziland	1,074
Bulgaria	10,152	Kuwait	200,000	Sweden	2,079,168
Byelorussian SSR	16,666	Lao People's		Switzerland	491,135
Canada	903,000	Democratic Republic	6,000	Syrian Arab Republic	12,721
Chile	5,000	Lesotho	388	Thailand	10,000
China	96,552	Luxembourg	5,218	Trinidad and Tobago	5,000
Colombia	35,000	Malawi	1,291	Tunisia	15,180
Congo	7,370	Malaysia	15,000	Turkey	6,000
Costa Rica	103	Malta	1,526	Ukrainian SSR	41,026
Cyprus	2,000	Mexico	29,494	USSR	3,361,540
Czechoslovakia	24,773	Mongolia	880	United Kingdom	915,000
Democratic Yemen	1,840	Morocco	10,277	United States	9,924,938
Denmark	322,047	Nepal	1,000	Venezuela	100,000
Egypt	24,340	Netherlands	502,076	Yugoslavia	8,640
Finland	600,000	New Zealand	63,066	Zambia	7,353
France	758,586	Nigeria	20,289	Zimbabwe	5,134
German Democratic		Norway	772,211		
Republic	133,787	Oman	10,000	Total	29,407,309
Germany, Federal		Pakistan	4,984		
Republic of	1,596,028	Panama	3,500		

SOURCE: UNEP/GC.14/2.

tations were being carried out between Headquarters and UNEP.

In resolution 39/66, accepting the 1983 financial reports of various United Nations funds and programmes, including the Environment Fund, the General Assembly concurred with ACABQ's observations and requested remedial action.

Other administrative questions

UNEP public information

Significant progress in reforming the UNEP information programme was achieved during 1984, the Executive Director reported.[21] Among the priorities was the development of a production schedule for the newsletter *UNEP News*, which was to be published every two months in English, French and Spanish beginning in January 1985, in accordance with a UNEP Council decision on the reform of the UNEP Information Service (see below). UNEP issued 20 publications during 1984.

Bilateral publications and information support programmes continued with China and the USSR. A publications support programme was initiated with France for the translation, editing, publishing and distribution of selected UNEP publications in French.

An audio-visual catalogue of all films, videotapes and slide shows available on loan from UNEP was produced. A colour transparency library of 10,000 photographs was catalogued. Arabic versions of the films *The State of the Planet* and *Water: A Vital Resource* were distributed.

The Desertification Information Campaign was a major UNEP activity. A total of 6,000 media packs, with a selection of articles on the implementation of the Plan of Action to Combat Desertification (see p. 759), were distributed world-wide. A film on desertification, *Seeds of Despair*, made in Ethiopia, elicited widespread interest in Europe and contributed to a large-scale fund-raising effort in the United Kingdom for famine relief. In Japan, it helped to raise $5.2 million. The Campaign stimulated the creation of a Television Trust for the Environment, aimed at promoting public understanding of environmental issues, which was sponsored by UNEP and Central Independent Television of the United Kingdom. Representatives of the international media visited a drought-affected area in northern Kenya where desertification control methods were demonstrated (Marsabit, 16-18 March). To promote environmental awareness, UNEP worked with a number of press and media agencies.

Following recommendations of the first meeting of the Advisory Committee of the International Referral System for sources of environmental information (INFOTERRA) (Athens, Greece, October 1983), four special sectoral sources were established in 1984 on environmental legislation, water supply, sanitation and renewable energy, toxic chemicals, and the impact of industry on the environment.

An on-line INFOTERRA information search service was set up; a *Thesaurus of Environmental Terms* and a supplement to the *International Directory of Sources* on some 1,000 environmental topics were published.

During the year, INFOTERRA conducted six national seminars, three training courses, and a workshop on the role of environmental information in decision-making.

Reform of the Information Service

By a decision of 28 May,[34] the UNEP Council agreed with the Executive Director[35] that reform of the Information Service should be gradual. The priorities were: identification of information needs, in particular those of the developing countries; streamlining the publications programme; identification of non-traditional forms of information; intensification of UNEP use of United Nations information centres and services; co-operation with NGOs; and establishment of environmental information training fellowships. The Council considered that a regular flagship publication was currently not essential and therefore agreed to replace *UNITERRA* and *Report to Governments* with a newsletter; it also decided to discontinue at the end of 1984 support for *Mazingira*, a journal published every two months which provided news and comments on environment and development issues, and to apply the resources to regional information activities and non-traditional forms of information. The Council further decided that concise information on newly approved projects, evaluation of closed ones and in-depth evaluation of selected projects should be distributed to Governments twice a year.

UN accommodation at Nairobi

The UNEP Council, on 28 May,[36] welcomed the announcement by the President of Kenya, on 21 May, granting an additional 40 acres of land for United Nations accommodation at Nairobi, and recommended that the General Assembly accept the donation. It also welcomed Kenya's announcement that access roads would be improved, and commended the Executive Director for the completion of the accommodation on schedule and within the approved cost estimates.

(For further details on accommodation at Nairobi, see ADMINISTRATIVE AND BUDGETARY QUESTIONS, Chapter IV).

Smoking in meeting rooms

The UNEP Council decided on 28 May 1984 that a no-smoking rule would be observed in all its meeting rooms beginning with the 1985 session, and encouraged all meetings on environmental issues to observe the same restriction.[37]

REFERENCES

[1]A/39/25   (dec. 12/3 B).   [2]UNEP/GC.12/11/Add.1. [3]UNEP/GC.12/11/Add.3.   [4]A/39/25   (dec. 12/3 C). [5]*Ibid.* (dec. 12/3 A). [6]E/1984/C.1/L.4. [7]E/1984/C.1/L.10. [8]YUN 1983, p. 769, GA res. 38/165, 19 Dec. 1983. [9]A/39/432. [10]A/C.2/39/L.24/Rev.1. [11]A/C.2/39/L.55. [12]YUN 1983, p. 771. [13]UNEP/GC.12/11 & Corr.1,2. [14]UNEP/GC.12/11/Add.2.   [15]A/39/25   (dec. 12/11). [16]UNEP/GC.12/3/Add.1. [17]YUN 1983, p. 771, GA res. 38/161, 19 Dec. 1983. [18]A/39/25 (dec. 12/1). [19]*Ibid.* (dec. 12/17 A-D). [20]*Ibid.* (dec. 12/12). [21]UNEP/GC.13/2 & Corr.1. [22]UNEP/GC.12/8 & Corr.1. [23]A/39/25 (dec. 12/2). [24]ACC/1984/DEC/14-22 (dec. 1984/22). [25]UNEP/GC.12/10. [26]YUN 1983, p. 774. [27]A/39/25 (dec. 12/4). [28]YUN 1982, p. 999. [29]UNEP/GC.12/4. [30]A/39/25 (dec. 12/18). [31]*Ibid.* (dec. 12/19). [32]A/39/5/Add.6. [33]A/39/510. [34]A/39/25 (dec. 12/15). [35]UNEP/GC.12/6 & Add.1. [36]*Ibid.* (dec. 12/9). [37]*Ibid.* (dec. 12/8).

Environmental activities

Environmental monitoring

Environmental assessment and monitoring continued to be one of the key tasks of UNEP in 1984. Its environment assessment programme, Earthwatch, was designed as a global system of national facilities and services to study the interaction between man and the environment, provide early warning of potential environmental hazards and determine the state of selected natural resources. The corner-stone of Earthwatch was the Global Environmental Monitoring System (GEMS), a collective international effort to acquire the data needed for rational management of the environment. The activities of GEMS, operational since 1975, were divided in 1984 into five major programmes: renewable resource monitoring, climate-related monitoring, health-related monitoring, long-range transport of pollutants monitoring, and ocean monitoring.

Among GEMS projects in 1984 was a pilot project conducted jointly with UNESCO and WMO on integrated monitoring in temperate forest biosphere reserves, focusing on the behaviour of pollutants in the various ecosystem "media": soil, air, water, plants and animals. The project involved data collection in the Torres del Paine Biosphere Reserve in Chile and the Olympic National Park in the United States as well as exchanges of information and specialists between the two countries.

Data on sulphates in precipitation were examined. A project was begun with the Economic Commission for Europe (ECE) to assess the effects of acidifying deposition on forest resources in the ECE countries, and to recommend a unified methodology of assessing damage to forests from air pollution. Other ongoing activities included glacier observation and assessment of radioactivity in the South Pacific.

On 28 May,[1] the UNEP Governing Council invited the Executive Director to begin publication in 1985 of as many as possible of the environmental indicators listed in his report on the preparation and presentation of environmental data,[2] continuing with routine updates and presenting the indicators so as to highlight trends in the global environment. He was also invited to start compiling a list of selected environmental data sources; to continue the publication of assessments of important environmental problems; and to utilize the annual environmental indicators publications in preparing comprehensive reports on the state of the environment. The Council also dealt with other aspects of environmental monitoring, such as protection against harmful products (see below).

Also on 28 May,[3] the Council addressed nine issues concerning environmental management: marine mammals, the World Soils Policy, tropical forest and woodlands, water, genetic resources, wildlife conservation and management, industry and environment, marine pollution and regional seas (see below).

Protection against harmful products

UNEP activities. Following a 1982 UNEP Council decision,[4] an *Ad Hoc* Working Group of Experts for the Exchange of Information on Potentially Harmful Chemicals (in Particular Pesticides) in International Trade was established and held its first session (Noordwijkerhout, Netherlands, 26-30 March 1984).[5] As global guidelines for such an information exchange, the Group recommended a provisional notification scheme for banned and severely restricted chemicals, which was adopted by the Council on 28 May.[6] It called on Governments and the Executive Director to bring the scheme into effect as soon as possible, and requested him to report in 1986 on Governments' experience in implementing it.

Among reports considered by the Working Group was one on the state of information on potentially harmful chemicals in international trade, which described the work of UNEP's International Register of Potentially Toxic Chemicals and its attempts to facilitate access to information on chemicals and promote international procedures for collection, validation, processing and exchange of data necessary for hazard assessment and control of chemicals in commerce.[7]

Another report summarized national legislation and regulatory programmes, as well as activities and programmes of international organizations and bodies, related to the exchange of information on potentially harmful chemicals.[8]

The use of pesticides in agriculture had been growing in both developed and developing countries, the Executive Director pointed out in his annual report.[9] That growth had led to an increase in the health problems of rural communities, particularly in countries with agriculture-based economies. The principal cause was misuse or abuse of pesticides by farm workers who were often unaware of their health hazards or the safety procedures to be observed during application. Many of those toxic chemicals, though freely sold in developing countries, were banned or tightly controlled in their countries of origin.

The situation had been aggravated by the development of resistant strains of pests and vectors, demanding increases in dosage as well as the introduction of new, usually more toxic, chemicals. As a result, NGOs, headed by the Pesticide Action Network, had demanded that industry make more information available to the public.

The FAO/UNEP Panel of Experts on Integrated Pest Control held its twelfth session (Rome, Italy, 22 and 23 October) and published guidelines on integrated control of cotton pests and on the economic aspects of integrated pest control research. The FAO Committee of Experts on Pest Control (third session, Rome, 24-26 October) guided activities under the Co-operative Action Programme on Plant Health (including UNEP-supported programmes on integrated pest control).

FAO, IAEA, the United Nations Centre on Transnational Corporations, UNEP, UNIDO and WHO held a thematic programming meeting on pesticides (Rome, 10 and 11 April), identifying activities for 1986-1987.

The UNEP Council, on 28 May 1984,[1] noted the report of the Executive Director on the list of environmentally dangerous chemical substances and processes of global significance.[10] It requested him to obtain comments on the report from Governments, international organizations, industry and NGOs and to submit an updated version in 1987, evaluating the extent to which developing and developed countries participated in the production, distribution and release of environmentally dangerous chemical substances.

Reports of the Secretary-General. In accordance with a December 1983 General Assembly request,[11] the Secretary-General submitted in June 1984, to both the Economic and Social Council and the Assembly, a report on the exchange of information on banned hazardous chemicals and unsafe pharmaceutical products.[12] The report reviewed activities of United Nations bodies and other organizations, which could be grouped in three principal categories: the establishment of mechanisms for information exchange; the development of guiding instruments; and the preparation of technical information. Among recent developments of special interest were: the provisional notification scheme for banned and severely restricted chemicals (see above); draft guiding principles being developed in OECD on the exchange of information related to export of banned or severely restricted chemicals; the work of the Council of Europe with regard to the sale of European pharmaceutical products in developing countries; and the preparation by the Organization of American States of a list of substances prohibited or significantly restricted in the United States.

There was an increasing awareness by both importing and exporting countries of the need for information exchange on internal control measures taken by exporting countries, the report concluded. The principle of notifying importing countries of measures designed to ban or severely restrict specific products had gained wide acceptance, but further negotiations were needed. The provisional notification scheme was an important step towards harmonizing the different positions, while improved use of the WHO Certification Scheme on the Quality of Pharmaceutical Products Moving in International Commerce adopted in 1975 would enhance the quality and safety of imported pharmaceuticals. A code of conduct on the distribution and use of pesticides, drafted by FAO, was submitted to Governments for review.

Progress appeared to have been made with regard to the legislative and administrative capability of developing countries to control the manufacture, import, sale and use of chemical and pharmaceutical products. In addition to technical co-operation assistance by various organizations, developing countries could benefit from exchange of information on administrative and legislative models followed by other countries; in that context, the activities of FAO and WHO should be noted.

Also requested by the Assembly in December 1983[11] was a report on a consolidated list of products whose consumption and/or sale had been banned, withdrawn, severely restricted or, in the case of pharmaceuticals, not approved by Governments. In the report, submitted in September 1984, the Secretary-General described the role and content of the list and steps taken in its preparation.[13]

The first issue of the list had been transmitted to Governments on 31 December 1983. A revised first issue contained information on regulatory decisions by 60 Governments relating to nearly 500 pharmaceutical products, agricultural and industrial chemicals, and consumer products. Also included was information provided by NGOs.

However, the report stated, the list still needed to be expanded, both in terms of the numbers of countries included and products reported. Further information was needed from Governments on legislative measures and the regulatory context in which, and the health or environmental reasons for which, those measures were taken, as well as on the nature of limitations imposed on the manufacture, import, sale and use of products.

ECONOMIC AND SOCIAL COUNCIL ACTION

In decision 1984/176 of 26 July, the Economic and Social Council took note of the Secretary-General's report on the exchange of information on banned hazardous chemicals and transmitted it to the Assembly.

GENERAL ASSEMBLY ACTION

On 18 December, on the recommendation of the Second Committee, the General Assembly adopted resolution 39/229 by recorded vote.

Protection against products harmful to health and the environment

The General Assembly,

Reaffirming its resolutions 37/137 of 17 December 1982 and 38/149 of 19 December 1983,

Taking note with satisfaction of the report of the Secretary-General on products harmful to health and the environment,

Bearing in mind the report of the Secretary-General on the exchange of information on banned hazardous chemicals and unsafe pharmaceutical products, and welcoming the effort being made in various international forums with regard to the exchange of information on such products,

1. *Expresses its appreciation* to the Secretary-General and commends him for the distribution of the first issue of the consolidated list of products whose consumption and/or sale have been banned, withdrawn, severely restricted or, in the case of pharmaceuticals, not approved by Governments;

2. *Reiterates its appreciation* for the co-operation extended by Governments in the preparation of the consolidated list, and urges all Governments that have not yet done so to provide the necessary information for inclusion in the updated versions of the list;

3. *Notes with satisfaction* the co-operation provided by the appropriate organs, organizations and bodies of the United Nations system and other intergovernmental organizations in the issuance of the list and urges them, particularly the Food and Agriculture Organization of the United Nations, the World Health Organization, the International Labour Organisation, the United Nations Environment Programme, the General Agreement on Tariffs and Trade and the United Nations Centre on Transnational Corporations, to continue to co-operate fully in the preparation of the updated versions of the list;

4. *Expresses its appreciation* for the co-operation provided by non-governmental organizations in this regard, and urges them to continue to extend co-operation to the Secretary-General in the preparation of the consolidated list, particularly in the identification of potential sources of information among national Governments and in obtaining governmental information on relevant regulatory actions;

5. *Decides* that:

(a) An updated consolidated list should be issued annually and that the data should be made available to Governments and other users in such a form as to permit direct computer access to it;

(b) In order to keep costs to a minimum, the consolidated list should be published and made available in all the official languages of the United Nations in sets of alternating languages each year, with no more than three languages per year and with the same frequency for each language;

(c) The format of the consolidated list should be kept under continuing review with a view to its improvement, in accordance with General Assembly resolution 37/137, in co-operation with the relevant organs, organizations and bodies of the United Nations system, taking into account the complementary nature of the list, the experiences obtained and the views expressed by Governments on this matter, and that the next review should be submitted by the Secretary-General to the General Assembly at its forty-first session;

(d) The review of the consolidated list should cover particularly the advantages and disadvantages of introducing to the list such information as the legal, public health and commercial context of the regulatory actions, as well as complementary information on safe uses of the products;

6. *Urges* importing countries, bearing in mind the extensive legal, public health and safety information already provided to the United Nations Centre on Transnational Corporations, the United Nations Environment Programme, the International Labour Organisation, the Food and Agriculture Organization of the United Nations, the World Health Organization and the General Agreement on Tariffs and Trade, to avail themselves of the information provision facilities of those organizations, which include, in some cases, direct computer access;

7. *Requests* the Secretary-General, with the assistance of the appropriate specialized agencies, to submit to the General Assembly at its forty-first session a report on a review of the various information exchange schemes now in operation within the United Nations system;

8. *Requests* the Secretary-General and the competent organs, organizations and bodies of the United Nations system to continue to provide the necessary technical assistance to the developing countries, at their request, for the establishment or strengthening of national systems for managing hazardous chemicals and pharmaceutical products, as well as for an adequate monitoring of the importation, manufacture and use of those products;

9. *Also requests* the Secretary-General, through the Economic and Social Council, to inform the General Assembly at its forty-first session and every three years thereafter about the implementation of resolutions 37/137 and 38/149 and of the present resolution;

10. *Further requests* the Secretary-General to take the necessary measures for the implementation of the present resolution.

General Assembly resolution 39/229

18 December 1984   Meeting 104   147-1 (recorded vote)

Approved by Second Committee (A/39/789/Add.1) by recorded vote (127-1), 10 December (meeting 58); draft by Sweden (A/C.2/39/L.135), orally revising draft by Vice-Chairman (A/C.2/39/L.125), based on informal consultations on draft by Algeria, Argentina, Bangladesh, Colombia, Dominican Republic, Ecuador, Egypt, Honduras, India, Mexico, Nicaragua, Nigeria, Oman, Pakistan, Peru, Qatar, Rwanda, Saudi Arabia, Senegal, Sudan, Trinidad and Tobago, Uruguay, Venezuela, Viet Nam (A/C.2/39/L.25); agenda item 12.

Financial implications. 5th Committee, A/39/831; S-G, A/C.2/39/L.127, A/C.5/39/89.

Meeting numbers. GA 39th session: 2nd Committee 38, 58; 5th Committee 49; plenary 104.

Recorded vote in Assembly as follows:

In favour: Afghanistan, Albania, Algeria, Angola, Argentina, Australia, Austria, Bahamas, Bahrain, Bangladesh, Barbados, Belgium, Benin, Bhutan, Bolivia, Botswana, Brazil, Brunei Darussalam, Bulgaria, Burkina Faso, Burma, Burundi, Byelorussian SSR, Canada, Cape Verde, Central African Republic, Chad, Chile, China, Colombia, Congo, Costa Rica, Cuba, Cyprus, Czechoslovakia, Democratic Kampuchea, Democratic Yemen, Denmark, Djibouti, Dominican Republic, Ecuador, Egypt, El Salvador, Equatorial Guinea, Ethiopia, Fiji, Finland, France, Gabon, German Democratic Republic, Germany, Federal Republic of, Ghana, Greece, Guatemala, Guinea, Guinea-Bissau, Guyana, Haiti, Honduras, Hungary, Iceland, Indonesia, Iran, Iraq, Ireland, Israel, Italy, Ivory Coast, Jamaica, Japan, Jordan, Kenya, Kuwait, Lao People's Democratic Republic, Lebanon, Lesotho, Liberia, Libyan Arab Jamahiriya, Luxembourg, Madagascar, Malawi, Malaysia, Maldives, Mali, Malta, Mauritania, Mauritius, Mexico, Mongolia, Morocco, Mozambique, Nepal, Netherlands, New Zealand, Nicaragua, Niger, Nigeria, Norway, Oman, Pakistan, Panama, Papua New Guinea, Paraguay, Peru, Philippines, Poland, Portugal, Qatar, Romania, Rwanda, Saint Christopher and Nevis, Saint Lucia, Saint Vincent and the Grenadines, Samoa, Sao Tome and Principe, Saudi Arabia, Senegal, Sierra Leone, Singapore, Somalia, Spain, Sri Lanka, Sudan, Suriname, Swaziland, Sweden, Syrian Arab Republic, Thailand, Togo, Trinidad and Tobago, Tunisia, Turkey, Uganda, Ukrainian SSR, USSR, United Arab Emirates, United Kingdom, United Republic of Tanzania, Uruguay, Vanuatu, Venezuela, Viet Nam, Yemen, Yugoslavia, Zaire, Zambia, Zimbabwe.

Against: United States.

The text was based on a draft submitted by a Committee Vice-Chairman following informal consultations on a text introduced by Venezuela on behalf of 24 nations. The Vice-Chairman's draft was withdrawn, but reintroduced by Sweden with several oral revisions. Those revisions included the addition, at the end of paragraph 4, of the words "particularly in the identification of potential sources of information among national Governments and in obtaining governmental information on relevant regulatory actions". From paragraph 5 (d), the words "and also give due consideration to the possible advantages and disadvantages of streamlining its content, so that users, when alerted to the potential hazards of a product, may be directed to sources of more complete information" were deleted. Paragraph 7 was replaced; by the Vice-Chairman's draft, the Assembly would have invited the specialized agencies to provide an evaluation of the information collection and dissemination procedures in operation, bearing in mind the need to increase their efforts to make available to Governments information on national regulatory action taken with regard to products within their respective spheres of responsibility, and would have requested a report in 1986 on the results of that evaluation.

Deleted from the Vice-Chairman's draft were five preambular paragraphs, referring to the need for access to information on products in international trade that had been banned or severely restricted; recognizing that several specialized agencies had programmes on the collection, evaluation and dissemination of information related to the hazards associated with products in international trade, and noting UNEP's provisional notification

scheme for exchange of information on potentially harmful chemicals, in particular pesticides; noting that the May 1984 World Health Assembly had called for an expert meeting in 1985 on the rational use of drugs; noting that FAO was preparing a code of conduct on the distribution and use of pesticides; and seeking to gain full participation by Governments in response to a 1982 Assembly resolution on protection against harmful products[14] and to resolve outstanding issues.

Apart from those and other drafting changes, the adopted text differed from the original 24-nation draft in that it did not contain a paragraph requesting the Secretary-General to strengthen arrangements to provide for legal analysis, risk assessment, commercial marketing analysis, and liaison with Governments and organizations, and for the improvement in quality and quantity of international product safety information. Also, instead of a review of the consolidated list, as called for in paragraph 5 (d) of the adopted text, the original draft would have had the Assembly consider that the list be developed further, with particular emphasis on the legal, public health and commercial context of regulatory actions and with information on safe uses of products. In addition, the final version did not include preambular provisions by which the Assembly would have reiterated that products banned from domestic consumption and sale should be sold abroad only on request from an importing country, and that countries which had severely restricted or not approved domestic consumption and sale of specific products should make available full information on them, including clear labelling in a language acceptable to the importing country.

On 13 December, the Fifth (Administrative and Budgetary) Committee decided by a recorded vote of 91 to 4, with 2 abstentions, to inform the Assembly that, should it adopt the draft resolution, additional appropriations of $89,700 would be required under the 1984-1985 budget. In making that decision, the Committee followed the Secretary-General's estimates, as orally endorsed by ACABQ.

Before the vote in the Fifth Committee, the United States reiterated its objection to the request for additional funding. For the States members of the European Economic Community (EEC), Ireland stated that the financial implications had been incorrectly presented in the original statement to the Second Committee; it hoped that that would not be a precedent. Venezuela said the Secretariat had recognized that it had begun to implement the 1982 resolution on the subject[14] with insufficient resources. The USSR remarked that, as far as the draft's budgetary aspects were concerned, the Secretary-General's statement gave the impression that activities would be starting from scratch while, in fact, they were already in progress and could be pursued with existing resources and staff.

In the Second Committee, the United States agreed that Member States should have a reference source for identifying regulatory actions by other States, but warned that sketchy information, as contained in the current consolidated list, was inappropriate and dangerous. Inquiries should be directed to the sources of complete information both in the notifying countries and in the competent specialized agencies. The United States also objected to the financial implications of the text which, it said, endorsed an ongoing project already provided for in the 1984-1985 budget; a draft resolution should have financial implications only when it provided for substantial new activities.

Canada felt that the consolidated list should be continued, but considered it important to avoid duplication and unnecessary expansion. Ireland, on behalf of the EEC members, asserted that they had always been in favour of a consolidated list; at the same time, many issues relating to the list—including that of information duplication—remained to be resolved. Venezuela stated that the sponsors of the original 24-nation draft would have preferred an expansion of the consolidated list with respect to the legal, public health and commercial context of regulatory actions concerning the products on the list; nevertheless, they believed that the adopted text was a very important step forward.

The Ukrainian SSR, also on behalf of Bulgaria, the Byelorussian SSR, Czechoslovakia, the German Democratic Republic, Hungary, Mongolia, Poland and the USSR, declared that they attached great importance to providing developing countries with information on unsafe chemicals or harmful pharmaceutical products, banned in the West but marketed abroad by transnational corporations. Necessary resources for implementing the text should be found through savings and redeployment of existing resources, with no increase in the regular budget.

International Register of Potentially Toxic Chemicals

The International Register of Potentially Toxic Chemicals (IRPTC), established in 1976, continued in 1984 to expand the global information network on chemicals and their effects on health and the environment. New contacts were made with organizations, national institutions and industry.

During the year, IRPTC prepared an update of its loose-leaf manual on toxic chemicals, and continued to develop its computerized profiles of chemicals of international significance; 450 of those profiles were currently stored in its data bank.

The IRPTC Query-Response Service received more than 200 inquiries on chemicals, mostly

agrochemicals, 36 per cent from developing countries. The Legal File, published in 1983 and containing data on regulatory measures and recommendations for hazard control on 400 chemicals covering 12 countries and six international organizations, was expanded to include all the chemicals for which regulatory information was available. Waste management data were collected for 500 chemicals on the IRPTC Working List of Selected Chemical Substances.

Two issues of the *IRPTC Bulletin* were published in English, French, Russian and Spanish and distributed to about 9,000 recipients; the *Bulletin* contained information on the activities of IRPTC and other organizations in relation to chemicals, the results of risk assessments of chemicals, and chemicals that were causing concern or were the subject of controls or bans. An IRPTC/INFOTERRA directory of information sources on chemical safety was published; it provided descriptions of more than 400 institutions, bibliographies on chemical safety and hazard control, lists of IRPTC national correspondents and INFOTERRA focal points. With ILO, IRPTC updated the ILO publication *Occupational Exposure Limits for Airborne Toxic Substances*, which contained data on more than 1,100 substances from 19 countries and one international organization. In co-operation with the USSR, IRPTC continued publishing the series *Scientific Reviews of Soviet Literature on Toxicity and Hazards of Chemicals*, which comprised 79 publications; an English version of a reference book, *Problems of Industrial Toxicology*, and a collection of lectures delivered during a 1983 training course in preventive toxicology were published in 1984 under this co-operative arrangement.

A training seminar was conducted by CMEA, the International Programme on Chemical Safety and IRPTC on the optimal use of international health risk evaluations (Moscow, 19-30 November). A three-week training course (Geneva, October/November) aimed at assisting developing countries to establish national information systems on chemicals.

In response to a 28 May UNEP Council decision,[1] IRPTC prepared a final report on the list of environmentally dangerous chemical substances and processes and submitted it to Governments and organizations. IRPTC also assisted in implementing the provisional notification scheme for chemicals (see above). By the end of the year, 40 Governments had designated national authorities for participation in implementing the scheme.

IRPTC also assisted in preparing the consolidated list of products whose consumption and/or sale had been banned, withdrawn, severely restricted or, in the case of pharmaceuticals, not approved by Governments (see above). Jointly with the Directorate-General for Employment, Social

Affairs and Education and the Environmental Chemicals Data and Information Network of the Commission of the European Communities, it undertook a study of substances to which workers were exposed at the workplace and which were easily absorbed through the skin.

Draft guidelines for management of hazardous wastes

In accordance with a 1982 UNEP Governing Council decision,[4] an *Ad Hoc* Working Group of Experts on the Environmentally Sound Management of Hazardous Wastes met (first session, Munich, Federal Republic of Germany, 28 February–5 March 1984;[15] second session, Geneva, 3-7 December[16]) to develop guidelines for transfrontier movements, storage and disposal of hazardous wastes.

On 28 May,[6] the UNEP Council expressed satisfaction at the results of the session; requested the Executive Director to continue the work initiated by the Group and to continue collaborating with other United Nations bodies in elaborating the guidelines; and called on Governments to participate actively.

The draft guidelines[17] were to be further reviewed by the Group in 1985.

Health and environment

In 1984, UNEP promoted increased awareness of environmental health problems through publications, training and demonstration programmes.

The International Programme on Chemical Safety (IPCS), sponsored jointly by ILO, UNEP and WHO, provided evaluations of chemicals and their effects on human health and the environment. Fourteen reports in the series "Environmental Health Criteria" were published in 1984, bringing the total to 42. A food inspection manual was produced with FAO. A network of IPCS national focal points was being established to facilitate the dissemination of information.

At the fourth meeting of the IPCS Programme Advisory Committee (Nairobi, 1-5 October), a new memorandum of understanding between the three participating agencies was formulated, broadening IPCS activities to include the effect of chemicals on species other than man and on natural and man-made resources. The fourth meeting of the FAO/UNEP/WHO Panel of Experts on Environmental Management for Vector Control was held (Geneva, 1-5 October).

Further to a programme developed in 1983 by UNEP in co-operation with the Egyptian Academy for Scientific Research and Technology on the control of water-borne diseases in rural areas, a meeting of national institutions from Brazil, Egypt, Ethiopia, the Federal Republic of Germany, Kenya, the Sudan, the United Kingdom and the United States was held (Cairo, Egypt, 12-15 March 1984).

A training course on food contamination control, with emphasis on mycotoxins, was held for 16 participants from developing countries (Moscow and Tbilisi, USSR, 2 April–2 June).

In September, the Secretary-General submitted to the General Assembly a report on products harmful to health and the environment,[13] which described the role and content of a consolidated list of products whose consumption and/or sale had been banned, withdrawn, severely restricted or, in the case of pharmaceuticals, not approved by Governments. In June,[12] he reported on the exchange of information on banned hazardous chemicals and unsafe pharmaceutical products (see above).

Atmosphere

Protection of the ozone layer

Preparations for a global convention for the protection of the ozone layer neared completion in 1984. The *Ad Hoc* Working Group of Legal and Technical Experts for the Elaboration of a Global Framework Convention for the Protection of the Ozone Layer (Vienna, Austria, 16-20 January;[18] Geneva, 22-26 October[19]) continued elaborating a draft convention and a draft protocol on chlorofluorocarbons. A further meeting was to be held in January 1985.

UNEP supported the work on the draft convention with up-to-date assessments of ozone layer modification and its impacts. An assessment of ozone layer depletion, prepared by the UNEP Coordinating Committee on the Ozone Layer in April 1983,[20] was published in January 1984. Because, in the mean time, advances in understanding atmospheric chemistry had taken place, a new assessment was undertaken by the Committee at its seventh session (Geneva, 15-19 October).

The UNEP Council, on 28 May,[6] requested the Executive Director to convene in the first quarter of 1985 a diplomatic conference to finalize and adopt a global convention and consider a report concerning further work on a protocol. It called on Governments and organizations to participate and appealed to Governments to provide financial resources and facilities. It asked the Coordinating Committee to continue to provide evaluations and to examine, if possible within two years, the likely effects of the substances listed in an annex to the draft convention.

Climate impact studies

The World Climate Impact Studies Programme (WCIP) of UNEP concentrated in 1984 on three areas: improving methodologies to be applied in the studies; reducing the vulnerability of food systems to climate; and assessing the carbon dioxide/climate issue.

WCIP's Scientific Advisory Committee, which held its third meeting at Stockholm, Sweden, noted that reliable methodologies were the linchpins of successful climate impact study. A major volume on climate impact assessment, concerning the interaction of climate and society—a joint project of the Scientific Committee on Problems of the Environment and UNEP—was in the final stages of preparation.

Another project, developed jointly by the International Institute for Applied Systems Analysis and UNEP, was concerned primarily with food production in different types of climate-sensitive regions.

The implementation plan for an international satellite land surface climatology project was completed. Project activities in 1984 included a series of workshops to develop a field experiment to validate ways of using satellite data for determining climate-related variables at the Earth's surface and a workshop on vegetation indices (Graz, Austria, 27 June), in conjunction with the Committee on Space Research Symposium on Space Observations for Climate Studies.

A number of WCIP projects were concerned primarily with agriculture. Under a study on the reduction of the vulnerability of food systems to climate in eastern India, jointly sponsored by the United Nations Research Institute for Social Development and UNEP, data on rainfall, temperature, floods, agricultural practices and food production were analysed. A new project, started in late 1984 by UNEP and the UNESCO/WMO/FAO Inter-Agency Group on Agricultural Biometeorology, sought to evaluate the impact of climate on socio-economic systems in the tropics of South America.

An inter-agency planning committee was established for a second assessment of the role of carbon dioxide in climate variations. At a Scientific Round Table on the Climatic Situation and Drought in Africa (Addis Ababa, Ethiopia, 20-23 February), organized by UNEP, the Economic Commission for Africa (ECA) and other organizations, a Regional Plan of Action to Combat the Adverse Impacts of Drought in Africa was drafted, which was adopted by the ECA Conference of Ministers in May (see p. 508).

A second edition of the UNEP inventory of climate impact studies was circulated to the scientific community for updating before distribution to Governments.

In resolution 39/148 F on the climatic effects of nuclear war: nuclear winter, the General Assembly requested the Secretary-General to compile and distribute as a United Nations document excerpts of all national and international scientific studies on the climatic effects of nuclear war published up to 31 July 1985.

Ecosystems

Terrestrial ecosystems

Desertification control

The 17-year-old Sudano-Sahelian drought intensified severely in 1984, causing famine in Chad, Ethiopia, Mali, Mauritania, the Niger and the Sudan and severe food shortages in the other countries of the region.[21]

In a February report to the UNEP Governing Council assessing progress in implementing the 1977 Plan of Action to Combat Desertification (see below), the Executive Director confirmed the scale and urgency of the problem of desertification which continued to spread and intensify. The Council on 28 May also noted with great concern that desertification had continued to spread, particularly in Africa.[22]

Desertification control was part of the programme of the United Nations Sudano-Sahelian Office (UNSO), jointly sponsored by the United Nations Development Programme (UNDP) and UNEP (see p. 509). With the inclusion of Ghana and Togo among those receiving assistance, UNSO's desertification mandate covered 21 countries. Parallel to emergency relief operations, UNSO helped carry out rehabilitation and medium- to long-term programmes aimed at mitigating the effects of drought and preventing future similar disasters; project commitments totalling $17.8 million were made in the form of cost-sharing and project-specific funds through the Trust Fund for Sudano-Sahelian Activities. A mission was sent to Ghana in November to formulate a project for the development of agro-forestry. UNSO also took part in a UNDP mission to Ethiopia in December to design a programme for coping with future droughts; the programme was being financed with a contribution of $25 million to $27 million from Italy.

The UNDP Governing Council, in a 29 June decision[23] on implementation in the Sudano-Sahelian region of the 1977 Plan of Action, urged all countries of the affected areas to intensify their co-ordination efforts in combating desertification.

On 24 August 1984,[24] Senegal transmitted to the Secretary-General a request from a Ministerial Conference on desertification (Dakar, Senegal, 18-27 July) that an item on countries stricken by desertification and drought be included in the agenda of the 1984 General Assembly session. By a memorandum transmitted on 20 September,[25] Senegal explained the history and causes of desertification and its effects. On 26 September,[26] it transmitted the final resolution adopted by the 21 nations attending the Conference (Algeria, Benin, Cape Verde, Chad, Gambia, Ghana, Guinea, Guinea-Bissau, Ivory Coast, Liberia, Mali, Mauritania, Morocco, Niger, Nigeria, Senegal, Sierra Leone, Sudan, Togo, Tunisia, Upper Volta) on a joint policy to combat desertification.

Other action. Three resolutions on desertification control were adopted by ECA on 26 May (see p. 617). By the first,[27] ECA recommended that African Governments promote technical co-operation, information exchange, and expertise for combating desertification. By the second,[28] it adopted a Regional Plan of Action to combat drought (see above) and urged increased funds and assistance to the affected countries. By the third,[29] it urged member States to support the development of national meteorological services in order to help mitigate the effects of drought and other weather-related disasters in Africa.

The Trade and Development Board of the United Nations Conference on Trade and Development (UNCTAD), on 21 September,[30] requested the UNCTAD Secretary-General to carry out a study, in collaboration with UNSO, on the impact of drought on the foreign trade of the affected countries (see p. 510).

ECONOMIC AND SOCIAL COUNCIL ACTION

On 27 July, on the recommendation of its First Committee, the Economic and Social Council adopted resolution 1984/72 without vote.

Environment and development in Africa

The Economic and Social Council,

Recalling General Assembly resolution 35/56 of 5 December 1980, containing the International Development Strategy for the Third United Nations Development Decade, which, *inter alia*, calls for methods to be devised to assist interested developing countries in dealing more adequately with the environmental aspects of development activities, for the international community to increase substantially its financial and technical support to drought-stricken countries suffering from desertification, for consideration to be given by all countries to the environmental aspects of industrialization in the formulation and implementation of their industrial policies and plans and for the improvement of the quality of life and the environment through, *inter alia*, the strengthening, in the context of human settlements planning, of measures to improve housing conditions,

Taking note of decisions 10/4 and 10/6 of 31 May 1982 of the Governing Council of the United Nations Environment Programme, in which the Governing Council called for assistance to be provided to developing countries in addressing serious environmental problems related to poverty and underdevelopment,

Recalling also resolution 446(XVII), adopted on 30 April 1982 by the Conference of Ministers of the Economic Commission for Africa, on the need to intensify regional co-operation for combating desertification in Africa, resolution 473(XVIII), adopted on 2 May 1983 by the Conference of Ministers, in which the Confer-

ence called for the organization of a scientific round-table on the climatic situation and drought in Africa, and resolution 474(XVIII), adopted on 2 May 1983 by the Conference of Ministers, in which the Conference called for the strengthening of African capabilities in environmental matters, especially the environmental co-ordination capabilities of the Commission, and for the encouragement of the development of environmental education and training programmes in member States,

Urges the General Assembly to consider seriously:

(a) The inclusion of reference to the United Republic of Tanzania in the terms of reference of the United Nations Sudano-Sahelian Office in order to enable that country to receive assistance in the implementation of programmes for combating desertification;

(b) The expansion of the scope of the work of the United Nations Sudano-Sahelian Office so as to enable it to assist the States members of the Southern African Development Co-ordination Conference in implementing the recommendations of the United Nations Environment Programme on combating desertification and drought, in the same way as the Office is currently assisting the States members of the Permanent Inter-State Committee on Drought Control in the Sahel.

Economic and Social Council resolution 1984/72

27 July 1984   Meeting 50   Adopted without vote

Approved by First Committee (E/1984/142) without vote, 23 July (meeting 16); draft by ECA (E/1984/112 & Corr.1-3); agenda item 9.

GENERAL ASSEMBLY ACTION

On 17 December, on the recommendation of the Second Committee, the General Assembly adopted resolution 39/208 without vote.

Countries stricken by desertification and drought

The General Assembly,

Deeply concerned about the tragic consequences of the acceleration of desertification, combined with a persistent drought—the most serious recorded this century—which have been reflected in a substantial drop in agricultural production in many developing countries and which, in particular, have contributed to the worsening of Africa's current economic crisis,

Noting with great anxiety that desertification continues to spread and intensify in developing countries, particularly in Africa,

Deeply alarmed by recent trends indicating that far-reaching climatic changes have taken place in Africa and are making the current situation extremely critical, as demonstrated, in particular, by the disturbing outlook noted by the Scientific Round Table on the Climatic Situation and Drought in Africa held at Addis Ababa from 20 to 23 February 1984,

Recalling its resolutions 32/172 of 19 December 1977, 35/73 of 5 December 1980, 38/163 and 38/164 of 19 December 1983 and 38/225 of 20 December 1983,

Aware that desertification and drought problems are increasingly assuming a structural and endemic character and that real and permanent solutions must be found in increased global efforts based on concerted action by the stricken countries and the international community,

Bearing in mind that the majority of the countries affected by desertification and drought are low-income countries and, for the most part, belong to the group of the least developed countries, particularly those in Africa,

Noting the efforts made by the affected countries themselves and by the international community, including the organizations of the United Nations system, to combat desertification and drought, particularly in Africa,

Bearing in mind the results of the Ministerial Conference for a joint policy to combat desertification in the countries of the Permanent Inter-State Committee on Drought Control in the Sahel and the Economic Community of West African States, in the Maghreb countries and in Egypt and the Sudan, held at Dakar from 18 to 27 July 1984,

Aware that the prime responsibility in the struggle against desertification and the effects of the drought rests with the countries concerned and that such action is an essential component of their development,

Considering the interdependence between developed countries and those affected by desertification and drought, and the negative impact of those phenomena on the economies of the countries concerned,

Noting the positive action taken by the United Nations Sudano-Sahelian Office as part of a joint effort by the United Nations Development Programme and the United Nations Environment Programme to help twenty-one African countries, on behalf of the United Nations Environment Programme, in implementing the Plan of Action to Combat Desertification,

Welcoming the praiseworthy efforts of the Permanent Inter-State Committee on Drought Control in the Sahel in fighting the drought in the Sahel region and its fruitful co-operation with Governments and with organizations and agencies of the United Nations system,

Taking note of the decision made by six East African countries—Djibouti, Ethiopia, Kenya, Somalia, the Sudan and Uganda—to set up an intergovernmental body in order to combat the effects of the drought in those countries,

Recognizing that, given the scope and intensity of desertification, the attainment of the objectives of programmes to fight it requires financial and human resources beyond the means of the affected countries,

1. *Welcomes* the results of the Ministerial Conference for a joint policy to combat desertification in the countries of the Permanent Inter-State Committee on Drought Control in the Sahel and the Economic Community of West African States, in the Maghreb countries and in Egypt and the Sudan, convened at Dakar on the initiative of the President of Senegal, and notes with satisfaction the final resolution adopted by the Conference;

2. *Recommends* that high priority should be given in the development plans and programmes of the affected countries themselves to the problem of desertification and to problems resulting from drought;

3. *Recognizes* that particular attention should be given to countries stricken by desertification and drought and that special efforts should be made by the international community, particularly the developed countries, in support of action taken individually or collectively by the affected countries;

4. *Recommends* that the international community, above all the developed countries, should continue to provide coherent short-term, medium-term and long-term assistance to the countries stricken by desertification and drought in order to support effectively the re-

habilitation process—in particular through intensive reafforestation—and the renewal of growth of agricultural production in the affected countries, particularly in Africa;

5. *Recommends* that, within the framework of bilateral and multilateral aid programmes, the fight against desertification and drought should be granted priority in view of the extent of those problems;

6. *Takes note* of decision 12/10 of 28 May 1984 on desertification, adopted by the Governing Council of the United Nations Environment Programme, calls for its full and speedy implementation, requests the Administrator of the United Nations Development Programme to have the United Nations Sudano-Sahelian Office establish specific biennial programmes for the ongoing implementation of the Plan of Action to Combat Desertification, with the requirement that these programmes be submitted for the consideration and joint approval of the Administrator of the United Nations Development Programme and the Executive Director of the United Nations Environment Programme, and, lastly, emphasizes the urgent need for increased financial support by the international community for the activities of the Office and of the United Nations Environment Programme;

7. *Emphasizes* the fundamental importance of all forms of South-South co-operation in executing programmes to combat desertification and drought;

8. *Appeals* to all members of the international community, organs and agencies of the United Nations system, regional and subregional financial institutions, as well as non-governmental organizations, to continue to provide full support, in all forms—including financial, technical, or any other form of assistance—to the development efforts of countries stricken by desertification and drought;

9. *Welcomes* the decision of the Trade and Development Board to request the Secretary-General of the United Nations Conference on Trade and Development to prepare a study on the impact of desertification and drought on the external trade of the countries affected;

10. *Requests* the appropriate organs and agencies of the United Nations to provide the Secretary-General with all relevant studies carried out in their respective spheres of competence, in particular with respect to food and agricultural production, development of water resources, industrialization and raw materials, for transmission to the stricken countries;

11. *Requests* the Secretary-General to ensure that in the activities of the organs and agencies of the United Nations, emphasis should also be placed on scientific knowledge of the causes and effects of the phenomena of desertification and drought and on the use of the most appropriate technology to overcome them;

12. *Also requests* the Secretary-General to place greater emphasis on the situation and prospects of the countries stricken by desertification and drought in the *World Economic Survey;*

13. *Further requests* the Secretary-General to take all necessary steps to ensure the implementation of the different activities mentioned above and to report to the General Assembly, at its fortieth session, through the Economic and Social Council, on the evolution of the situation in these countries, and to formulate proposals for specific, co-ordinated action.

General Assembly resolution 39/208
17 December 1984   Meeting 103   Adopted without vote

Approved by Second Committee (A/39/652) without vote, 2 November (meeting 33); draft by Vice-Chairman (A/C.2/39/L.26), based on informal consultations on 84-nation draft (A/C.2/39/L.16 and Corr.1); agenda item 141.
Meeting numbers. GA 39th session: 2nd Committee 24, 25, 27, 31, 33; plenary 103.

The adopted text differed from the original draft in that paragraph 6 was redrafted to specify the responsibilities of the competent United Nations bodies.

As urged by the Economic and Social Council in resolution 1984/72 (see above), the Assembly in resolution 39/168 A requested the UNEP Council to examine in 1985 possible inclusion of the United Republic of Tanzania in the terms of reference of UNSO.

Plan of Action to Combat Desertification

A first general assessment of the 1977 Plan of Action to Combat Desertification[31] was carried out by UNEP in 1984.[32] The Plan presented a detailed set of recommendations for sustaining co-operative efforts to reinforce and integrate national, regional and global actions against desertification, both inside and outside the United Nations system. The period 1978-1984 was chosen for implementation of the immediate action required, with a general assessment of progress at the end of those first seven years.

UNEP Council action. Two reports on implementation of the Plan of Action, and specifically on its implementation in the Sudano-Sahelian region, were submitted by the UNEP Executive Director. The reports were transmitted to the General Assembly in September 1984.[33]

On 28 May,[22] the UNEP Council reconfirmed the validity of the Plan. It endorsed the Executive Director's view that implementation had to be more focused on the most affected countries and on action to arrest desertification, and authorized him to assist Governments in applying land-use policies. It urged Governments and international bodies to examine ongoing and planned projects to ensure maximum effectiveness in combating desertification, revising policies which impeded local control and establishing national monitoring mechanisms.

The Council reaffirmed UNEP's central role in co-ordinating and assessing implementation of the Plan. It invited the General Assembly to expand the role of the Consultative Group for Desertification Control and Governments to become more involved in the Group's work. It requested the Executive Director to examine the functions of the Inter-Agency Working Group on Desertification and to recommend in 1985 changes to ensure full co-operation between United Nations agencies. The Council decided that a further overall assessment of progress in implementing the Plan should

be carried out in 1992. In the mean time, the Executive Director would report to the Council annually.

Following an invitation by the Assembly in December 1983,[34] the Council decided to include Ghana and Togo among those eligible to receive assistance through UNSO in implementing the Plan, bringing the number of countries covered by UNSO's desertification mandate to 21.

UNDP action. In April 1984, the UNDP Administrator submitted to the UNDP Council his annual report on UNSO assistance to the countries in the Sudano-Sahelian region in implementing the Plan of Action.[35] As called for in the Plan, UNSO also helped prepare an assessment of desertification in the region, scheduled for review by the UNEP Council together with a global assessment. The assessment showed that the most successful areas in which the Plan had been carried out had been in sensitizing Governments and population to the importance of anti-desertification measures and national planning, as well as institutional machinery, projects with a specific focus such as sand-dune fixation, and projects which allowed for involvement of the people affected.

The UNDP Governing Council, on 29 June,[23] endorsed the UNEP Council decision to include Ghana and Togo among those eligible for UNSO assistance and commended the UNDP Administrator on the progress achieved in assisting the countries of the region in implementing the Plan. Governments, United Nations bodies and organizations were urged to intensify their assistance, and the Administrator was requested to continue to report annually on implementation of the Plan.

ECONOMIC AND SOCIAL COUNCIL ACTION

On 26 July, on the recommendation of its First Committee, the Economic and Social Council adopted resolution 1984/65 without vote.

Implementation of the Plan of Action to Combat Desertification

The Economic and Social Council,

Recalling General Assembly resolution 32/172 of 19 December 1977, by which the Assembly approved the Plan of Action to Combat Desertification,

Recalling also paragraph 8 of General Assembly resolution 38/165 of 19 December 1983, by which the Assembly welcomed the decision of the Governing Council of the United Nations Environment Programme to devote two days, during its twelfth session, to a detailed assessment of the implementation of the Plan of Action to Combat Desertification,

Having considered the reports of the Governing Council of the United Nations Environment Programme on the general assessment of progress in the implementation of the Plan of Action to Combat Desertification, 1978-1984, on the implementation of the Plan of Action to Combat Desertification, submitted in response to General Assembly resolution 32/172 and subsequent resolutions, in particular resolution 37/218 of 20 December 1982, and on the implementation in the Sudano-Sahelian region of the Plan of Action to Combat Desertification, submitted in response to paragraph 7 of General Assembly resolution 38/164 of 19 December 1983,

I
Implementation of the Plan of Action to Combat Desertification

1. *Takes note with appreciation* of the report of the Governing Council of the United Nations Environment Programme on the general assessment of progress in the implementation of the Plan of Action to Combat Desertification, 1978-1984, submitted pursuant to paragraph 9 of the Plan of Action approved by the General Assembly in resolution 32/172, and transmits it to the Assembly for consideration;

2. *Takes note with appreciation also* of the report of the Governing Council on the implementation of the Plan of Action to Combat Desertification, submitted pursuant to General Assembly resolution 37/218, and transmits it to the Assembly for consideration;

3. *Takes note* of Governing Council decision 12/10 of 28 May 1984;

4. *Expresses its deep concern* that, during the seven years since the United Nations Conference on Desertification in 1977, desertification has continued to spread and intensify in developing countries, particularly in Africa;

5. *Welcomes* the reconfirmation by the Governing Council of the validity of the Plan of Action to Combat Desertification, the reaffirmation of the central role of the United Nations Environment Programme in catalysing, co-ordinating and assessing the implementation of the Plan of Action at the international level, and the approval by the Governing Council of concrete, time-bound activities to combat desertification over the next fifteen years;

6. *Concurs* with the invitation of the Governing Council to the General Assembly to expand the role of the Consultative Group for Desertification Control, which is financed from voluntary contributions, and invites all Governments, particularly those of donor members, to become more involved in the work of the Consultative Group;

7. *Urges* Governments of countries prone to or suffering from desertification to give priority to the establishment of national programmes to combat desertification and to consider setting up appropriate national machinery or assigning responsibility to existing national machinery, where appropriate, to that end;

8. *Urges* all Governments to increase their assistance, through appropriate channels, to countries suffering from desertification, including the financing of regional and subregional programmes;

9. *Welcomes* the decision of the Governing Council that a further overall assessment of progress in the implementation of the Plan of Action to Combat Desertification should be carried out in 1992;

II
Implementation in the Sudano-Sahelian region of the Plan of Action to Combat Desertification

10. *Takes note with appreciation* of the report of the Governing Council of the United Nations Environment Programme on the implementation in the Sudano-Sahelian region of the Plan of Action to Combat Deser-

tification, submitted pursuant to General Assembly resolutions 33/88 of 15 December 1978, 34/187 of 18 December 1979 and 38/164 of 19 December 1983, transmits it to the Assembly for consideration, and notes the decision of the Governing Council to include Ghana and Togo among the countries eligible to receive assistance through the United Nations Sudano-Sahelian Office;

11. *Expresses its satisfaction* at the positive assessment by the Governing Council of the activities carried out by the United Nations Sudano-Sahelian Office, as a joint venture of the United Nations Environment Programme and the United Nations Development Programme, to assist the countries of the Sudano-Sahelian region, on behalf of the United Nations Environment Programme, in implementing the Plan of Action to Combat Desertification;

12. *Welcomes* the decisions of the Governing Councils of the United Nations Environment Programme and the United Nations Development Programme on the continuation of the joint venture of the two Programmes, aimed at ensuring the timely and effective provision of assistance to the group of designated countries by the United Nations Sudano-Sahelian Office, on behalf of the United Nations Environment Programme, in combating desertification in the Sudano-Sahelian region;

13. *Expresses its appreciation* to Governments, organizations of the United Nations system, and intergovernmental and non-governmental organizations that have contributed to the implementation in the Sudano-Sahelian region of the Plan of Action to Combat Desertification;

14. *Urges* all Governments, organizations of the United Nations system and other intergovernmental and non-governmental organizations to strengthen their financial and technical support to the countries of the Sudano-Sahelian region to assist them in the implementation of the Plan of Action to Combat Desertification.

Economic and Social Council resolution 1984/65

26 July 1984   Meeting 49   Adopted without vote

Approved by First Committee (E/1984/145) without vote, 17 July (meeting 10); draft by Vice-Chairman (E/1984/C.1/L.7), based on informal consultations on draft by Algeria, Bahrain, Botswana, Canada, Congo, France, Gabon, Germany, Federal Republic of, Ghana, Japan, Kenya, Malaysia, Nigeria, Norway, Senegal, Sudan, Tunisia, Uganda, United Republic of Tanzania, Yugoslavia (E/1984/C.1/L.3); agenda item 14.

The original draft did not note in paragraph 6 that the Consultative Group for Desertification Control was financed by voluntary contributions; and in paragraph 7 it did not mention existing national machinery. In paragraph 14 of the original, the Council would have called for support bilaterally, or through UNSO or any other intermediary.

GENERAL ASSEMBLY ACTION

On 17 December, on the recommendation of the Second Committee, the General Assembly adopted resolution 39/168 A without vote.

Implementation of the Plan of Action to Combat Desertification

The General Assembly,

Recalling its resolution 32/172 of 19 December 1977, by which it approved the Plan of Action to Combat Desertification,

Recalling also paragraph 8 of its resolution 38/165 of 19 December 1983, by which it welcomed section VIII of decision 11/1 of the Governing Council of the United Nations Environment Programme, in which the Council decided to devote two days, during its twelfth session, to a detailed assessment of the implementation of the Plan of Action to Combat Desertification,

Taking note of Economic and Social Council resolution 1984/65 of 26 July 1984 on the Implementation of the Plan of Action to Combat Desertification,

Having considered the views of the Governing Council of the United Nations Environment Programme on the general assessment of progress in the implementation of the Plan of Action to Combat Desertification during the period 1978-1984,

Having also considered Economic and Social Council resolution 1984/72 of 27 July 1984 on environment and development in Africa,

Bearing in mind the current serious problem of prolonged drought and desertification that has contributed to the widespread economic catastrophe in a large number of African countries south of the Sahara,

1. *Takes note with appreciation* of the views of the Governing Council of the United Nations Environment Programme on the general assessment of progress in the implementation of the Plan of Action to Combat Desertification during the period 1978-1984;

2. *Also takes note with appreciation* of the report of the Governing Council on the implementation of the Plan of Action to Combat Desertification;

3. *Takes note with interest* of Governing Council decision 12/10 of 28 May 1984 on desertification;

4. *Notes with great concern* that, during the seven years since the United Nations Conference on Desertification in 1977, desertification has continued to spread and intensify in developing countries, particularly in Africa;

5. *Welcomes* the reconfirmation by the Governing Council of the United Nations Environment Programme of the validity of the Plan of Action to Combat Desertification, the reaffirmation of the central role of the Programme in catalysing, co-ordinating and assessing the implementation of the Plan of Action at the international level, and the approval by the Governing Council of concrete, time-bound activities to combat desertification over the next fifteen years;

6. *Decides* to expand the role of the Consultative Group for Desertification Control, which is financed from voluntary contributions, to include explicitly responsibility for advising the Executive Director on:

(*a*) The progress and effectiveness of activities implemented under the Plan of Action, identifying constraints and possible solutions to problems, taking account of relevant evaluations and case-studies;

(*b*) Programme priorities of the United Nations Environment Programme related to problems of desertification;

(*c*) Measures required to improve implementation of the Plan of Action on a regional and world-wide basis;

7. *Calls upon* the Consultative Group for Desertification Control to intensify further its efforts to assist the Executive Director of the United Nations Environment Programme in the mobilization of resources for the implementation of the Plan of Action;

8. *Urges* Governments of countries prone to or suffering from desertification to give priority to the establishment of national programmes to combat desertification

and to consider setting up appropriate national machinery or assigning responsibility to existing national machinery, where appropriate, to that end;

9. *Requests* the Governing Council of the United Nations Environment Programme to examine, at its thirteenth session, the possibility of:

(*a*) The inclusion of reference to the United Republic of Tanzania in the terms of reference of the United Nations Sudano-Sahelian Office in order to enable that country to receive assistance in the implementation of programmes for combating desertification;

(*b*) The expansion of the scope of the work of the United Nations Sudano-Sahelian Office so as to enable it to assist the States members of the Southern African Development Co-ordination Conference in implementing the recommendations of the United Nations Environment Programme on combating desertification and drought, in the same way as the Office is currently assisting the States members of the Permanent Inter-State Committee on Drought Control in the Sahel;

10. *Urges* all Governments to increase their assistance, *inter alia*, by financing regional and subregional programmes, through appropriate channels, including the Special Account created under General Assembly resolution 32/172 of 19 December 1977, to countries suffering from desertification;

11. *Endorses* the decision of the Governing Council in paragraph 28 of its decision 12/10 that a further overall assessment of progress in the implementation of the Plan of Action to Combat Desertification should be carried out in 1992.

General Assembly resolution 39/168 A

17 December 1984   Meeting 103   Adopted without vote

Approved by Second Committee (A/39/790/Add.9) without vote (parts A and B together), 30 November (meeting 54); draft by Vice-Chairman (A/C.2/39/L.92, part A), based on informal consultations on draft by Algeria, Egypt, Ethiopia, Kenya, Liberia, Mozambique, Sudan, Togo, Uganda, United Republic of Tanzania, Yemen, Zambia (A/C.2/39/L.20); agenda item 80 *(i)*.

Meeting numbers. GA 39th session: 2nd Committee 37, 50, 54; plenary 103.

By the original draft, the Assembly, in paragraph 3, would have endorsed the UNEP Council decision on desertification. In paragraph 8, it also would have urged Governments to accord priority to combating desertification in their development plans and in their requests for development assistance. In the original, subparagraph 9 *(b)* was not included.

Also on 17 December, the Assembly adopted resolution 39/168 B without vote.

Implementation in the Sudano-Sahelian region of the Plan of Action to Combat Desertification

The General Assembly,

Recalling its resolutions 36/190 of 17 December 1981, 37/216 of 20 December 1982 and 38/164 of 19 December 1983,

Taking note of decision 12/10 of 28 May 1984 of the Governing Council of the United Nations Environment Programme on desertification,

Taking note of Economic and Social Council resolutions 1984/65 of 26 July 1984 on the implementation in the Sudano-Sahelian region of the Plan of Action to Combat Desertification and 1984/72 of 27 July 1984 on the environment and development in Africa,

Taking note also of the inclusion of Ghana and Togo in the list of countries to be covered by the United Nations Sudano-Sahelian Office under the Plan of Action to Combat Desertification,

Having considered the report of the Governing Council of the United Nations Environment Programme on the implementation in the Sudano-Sahelian region of the Plan of Action to Combat Desertification,

Bearing in mind the special review undertaken by the Governing Council of the progress made in implementing the Plan of Action, based, *inter alia*, on the general assessment by the Executive Director of progress in the implementation of the Plan of Action during the period 1978-1984, and on the document on the assessment of desertification in the Sudano-Sahelian region,

Aware that the prime responsibility in the struggle against desertification and the effects of drought rests upon the countries concerned, and noting the efforts of those countries to combat desertification and drought,

1. *Takes note* of the report of the Governing Council of the United Nations Environment Programme on the implementation in the Sudano-Sahelian region of the Plan of Action to Combat Desertification;

2. *Notes with concern:*

(a) That the persistent drought in the Sahel has intensified and spread into other parts of Africa, assuming the catastrophic proportions of a generalized drought;

(b) That the inadequacy of financial resources continues to place a serious constraint on the fight against desertification;

(c) That struggle against desertification requires financial and human resources beyond the means of the affected countries;

3. *Expresses its appreciation* of the progress made towards overcoming these obstacles by the United Nations Sudano-Sahelian Office, on behalf of the United Nations Environment Programme, as part of a joint action by the United Nations Environment Programme and the United Nations Development Programme to assist the Governments of the region in combating desertification;

4. *Expresses its appreciation also* for the efficient and co-ordinated manner in which the Executive Director of the United Nations Environment Programme and the Administrator of the United Nations Development Programme have continued to develop this joint action through the United Nations Sudano-Sahelian Office;

5. *Requests* the Governing Council of the United Nations Environment Programme and the Governing Council of the United Nations Development Programme to continue to provide and increase their support to the United Nations Sudano-Sahelian Office in order to enable it to respond fully to the urgent needs of the countries of the Sudano-Sahelian region;

6. *Expresses its gratitude* to the Governments, United Nations bodies, intergovernmental organizations and other organizations which have contributed to the implementation in the Sudano-Sahelian region of the Plan of Action to Combat Desertification;

7. *Emphasizes* the need to redouble the efforts in order to implement in the Sudano-Sahelian region the Plan of Action to Combat Desertification and urges all Governments to respond favourably to the requests submitted by the Governments of the countries of the Sudano-Sahelian region for assistance in combating desertification;

8. *Requests* the Governing Council of the United Nations Environment Programme to make the neces-

sary arrangements at each session for submitting a report to the General Assembly, through the Economic and Social Council, on the implementation in the Sudano-Sahelian region of the Plan of Action to Combat Desertification.

General Assembly resolution 39/168 B

17 December 1984   Meeting 103   Adopted without vote

Approved by Second Committee (A/39/790/Add.9) without vote (parts A and B together), 30 November (meeting 54); draft by Vice-Chairman (A/C.2/39/L.92, part B), based on informal consultations on draft by Burkina Faso, Cape Verde, Chad, Egypt, Gambia, Ghana, Guinea, Guinea-Bissau, Liberia, Mali, Niger, Senegal, Togo (A/C.2/39/L.23, orally revised); agenda item 80 *(i)*.

Meeting numbers. GA 39th session: 2nd Committee 37, 50, 54; plenary 103.

The original draft did not contain the last preambular paragraph or subparagraph 2 *(c)*.

In the Declaration on the Critical Economic Situation in Africa, adopted by Assembly resolution 39/29, the United Nations Member States declared that urgent international action was needed to support regional and national efforts to implement the Plan of Action.

Financing of UNSO-UNDP/UNEP joint venture

Approved budgets for the UNSO-UNDP/UNEP joint venture for 1984-1985 amounted to $1,973,200 for institutional support and $2,000,000 for programme support. The UNDP Governing Council approved on 29 June 1984 revised appropriations of $2,190,100 gross ($986,600 net) for institutional support of the joint venture during the biennium.[36]

Ways of financing the joint venture beyond that time were examined in an April 1984 report of the UNDP Administrator.[37] He concluded that the current methods of financing the joint venture—involving the use of UNDP's administrative budget for institutional support and the Africa and Arab States' regional indicative planning figures (IPFs) for programme support, and the use of UNEP's Environment Fund for support to both budget components—remained the most practical for the time being.

By another decision of 29 June,[38] the UNDP Council noted with satisfaction the provisions made to ensure that the costs of UNDP's participation in the joint venture for 1984-1985 were fully secured despite the tight resource situation of the regional IPF. The Council endorsed the Administrator's recommendation that, pending availability of alternative funding sources, the joint venture should continue to be funded from regional IPFs and the UNDP administrative budget, and requested him to ensure that under the venture additional resources were made available to the countries of the Sudano-Sahelian region in their efforts to combat desertification.

Management of tropical forests

World-wide concern about the rapid destruction of tropical forest ecosystems continued to increase in 1984. Consequently, UNEP gave high priority to assisting in environmentally sound management policies for tropical forest areas.

As a part of joint UNEP/UNESCO activities, pilot research and training projects were established in various tropical countries. A project in the Ivory Coast resulted in a comprehensive report on management of a humid tropical forest environment, which was expected to be useful in promoting conservation of the remaining West African forests.

A model for planning total resource utilization in tropical ecosystems was prepared for UNEP by Dartmouth College (Hanover, New Hampshire, United States). With UNEP support, the Kenya Wildlife Fund Trustees completed an ecological survey of the easternmost remnant of the African equatorial forests, and management guidelines for the area were formulated. UNEP also sponsored attendance by participants from Brazil, Malaysia and Senegal at an International Union of Forestry Research Organizations Symposium on Human Impacts on Forests (Strasbourg, France, September). FAO for its part published an updated report on national and international activities and co-operation in tropical forestry.

The UNEP Council, on 28 May,[3] welcomed the adoption of the International Tropical Timber Agreement in 1983[39] and urged Governments to sign and ratify it to enable it to enter into force on the appointed date of 1 October 1984. The Council authorized the Executive Director to co-operate with the International Tropical Timber Organization. Despite the Council's call, the number of signatures and ratifications remained insufficient for the Agreement to enter into force (see p. 539).

Soil management

Implementation of the World Soils Policy

Excessive loss of topsoil from croplands in the four major food-producing countries (China, India, USSR, United States) was roughly estimated at 13.2 billion tons per year. If the rates of soil erosion for the rest of the world were similar, the world was losing an estimated 25.4 billion tons of soil per year from croplands in excess of new soil formation, the UNEP Executive Director concluded in his annual report.[9] To meet these problems, the UNEP secretariat prepared a Plan of Action for the Implementation of the 1982 World Soils Policy.[40] The Plan was structured into five major programmes: to enhance international awareness of the importance of land degradation and conservation issues; to assist countries in formulating national soils policies; to provide assistance to countries through missions, field projects, training courses, seminars and technical

publications; to develop the technical and scientific knowledge necessary to promote rational use of the world's soils; and to collect, compile and disseminate data on the world's soil resources, their use and management.

The UNEP Council endorsed the Plan on 28 May.[3] It noted the efforts of the Executive Director to prepare a financial plan for its implementation; requested him to promote a broad response to the Plan of Action, to circulate fact sheets on projects to potential donors and to investigate the possibility of a regional approach to funding; and appealed to Governments and international organizations to make commitments.

Also on 28 May,[41] the Council decided that, in the Plan of Action, highest priority should be given to training national technical cadres for executing national plans on soils policy and that training and research programmes should be carried out in existing institutions. The Council called on the Executive Director to assess the feasibility of convening a world conference to achieve co-operation in implementing the World Soils Policy.

Other activities

A meeting on integrated land-soil management in mountain ecosystems was held in March 1984 at Sofia, Bulgaria, and a course to train specialists from developing countries in the subject was also given at Sofia from 22 September to 14 October. A workshop on the impact of agricultural management on the environment at the regional level was held in Georgia, USSR, in October. A joint UNEP/Zambia project on watershed management, with special reference to soil and water conservation, started in October.

In co-operation with FAO, UNEP published a Spanish version of the *Guidelines for the Control of Soil Degradation*. As a result of a project on the impact of agricultural management on the environment, jointly undertaken by UNEP and the USSR Commission for UNEP, the first of four volumes on *The Natural Dimensions of Agriculture* was prepared.

Wildlife conservation

Illegal trade, indiscriminate hunting, destruction of habitats, expansion of agriculture, continued overgrazing by domestic livestock and the presence of toxic chemicals in the environment continued to endanger the survival of many wild animal and plant species.

Exercising its co-ordinating role in the implementation of the 1980 World Conservation Strategy,[42] UNEP continued to provide secretariat services to the Ecosystem Conservation Group (ECG), consisting of FAO, UNESCO, UNEP and the International Union for Conservation of Nature and Natural Resources (IUCN). Expert missions were sent to a number of countries to help prepare national conservation strategies. A project on wildlands, protected areas and wildlife management in Latin America and the Caribbean was identified as a pilot activity of ECG.

UNEP also continued its support to the IUCN Species Survival Commission and its more than 60 specialist groups and to the Commission on National Parks and Protected Areas, in their roles as major sources of data for the UNEP-supported IUCN Conservation Monitoring Centre.

According to the Centre, there were nearly 3,000 protected areas in the world, which covered some 400 million hectares but fell far short of truly protecting biological diversity. A project was started in September 1984 to ensure that guidance was available to Governments on existing protected areas and their management in the Afro-tropical, Indo-Malayan and Oceanian/Antarctic realms. With UNEP support, action plans were prepared for groups of species, including Asian elephants and rhinoceroses, cats and polar bears.

A draft Action Plan for Biosphere Reserves was adopted by the International Co-ordinating Council of the UNESCO Man and the Biosphere (MAB) programme in December. The Council then requested the MAB secretariat to submit the Plan to the governing bodies of FAO, IUCN and UNEP for implementation during 1985-1989.

In co-operation with FAO, IUCN and UNESCO, UNEP continued to assist Governments in implementing international and regional measures for conservation of wild animals and plants and their habitats. Two regional training seminars on the implementation of the Convention on International Trade in Endangered Species of Wild Fauna and Flora (CITES) were organized in 1984 (Brussels, Belgium, June; Kuala Lumpur, Malaysia, October). The Standing Committee of the Conference of the Parties to CITES met from 2 to 6 July at Gland, Switzerland. Its Technical Committee met in July at Brussels to deal with several problems, particularly the ivory trade; a meeting of the regional co-ordinators of the Technical Committee was held in conjunction with the Kuala Lumpur seminar.

The UNEP Council, in a 28 May decision on environmental management,[3] took note of the report of the Joint Inspection Unit on the contribution of the United Nations system to the conservation of the Latin American cultural and natural heritage and its progress report on regional programmes in the conservation of African wildlife, as well as the comments of the Executive Director on the two reports (see p. 617).

In another decision of the same date,[6] the Council welcomed the intention of the Federal Republic of Germany to host the first meeting of the Conference of the Parties to the Convention on the Conservation of Migratory Species of Wild Animals in 1985 (see p. 770).

Genetic resources

The International Board for Plant Genetic Resources (IBPGR), supported by UNEP, continued in 1984 to co-ordinate the exploration, collection and conservation of crop plant genetic resources. Research centres in almost 100 countries were supporting that programme. The material collected was deposited in various gene banks, including those forming part of the network housing the World Base Collection; that network consisted of 38 centres in 29 countries, storing material from 30 crops or groups of crops that produced seeds. During the year, IBPGR began to designate centres to hold clonally propagated crops.

A network of centres to collect the seeds of multi-purpose arboreal species from arid and semi-arid zones was started by FAO, IBPGR and UNEP. Eight countries were co-operating in the network during 1984: Chile, Democratic Yemen, India, Mexico, Pakistan, Peru, Senegal and the Sudan. With UNEP support, FAO identified three countries—Cameroon, Malaysia and Peru—for pilot projects developing and testing methodologies for *in situ* conservation of forest genetic resources within existing protected areas.

Similarly, UNEP continued to support the conservation of animal genetic resources. In a joint FAO/UNEP project, the University of Khartoum (Sudan) was planning the creation of a nucleus herd of the Kenana cattle breed. The French Government's Laboratoire de Contrôle des Reproducteurs began collecting semen from the Gobra breed in Senegal for shipment to the first FAO/UNEP gene bank.

UNEP also continued its support to regional Microbiological Resource Centres in Brazil, Egypt, Guatemala, Kenya, Senegal and Thailand. The Centres organized training activities, provided research fellowships and grants, and produced several state-of-the-art reports. UNEP identified pilot projects to be carried out by the Centres for environmental application of microbial resources for soil fertility, pest and vector control, degradation of persistent environmental pollutants and organic residue utilization.

Significant developments took place in the application of biological nitrogen fixation for enhancing soil fertility and increasing legume production in small farms while moving away from the use of costly and potentially polluting nitrogenous fertilizers. Activities included the establishment of pilot plants for *Rhizobium* inoculant production; trials on legume inoculation; testing of peat resources as inoculant carriers; training of local biological nitrogen fixation professionals and technicians; and information dissemination.

The FAO/UNEP Advisory Panel on Biological Nitrogen Fixation held its first meeting at Nairobi in conjunction with the first conference of the African Association of Biological Nitrogen Fixation (23-27 July), which was co-sponsored by FAO, UNDP, UNEP and Nairobi University.

The World Data Centre for Micro-organisms at Brisbane, Australia—established to promote access to information about culture collections and to produce specialized inventories of microbial genetic resources of environmental and economic value—continued to receive support from UNEP. The first meeting of the Working Group on the International Microbial Strain Data Network (Bangkok, Thailand, 23-25 November) was organized by UNEP in conjunction with the Fifth Congress of Culture Collections.

On 28 May,[3] the UNEP Council welcomed the adoption by FAO in 1983 of the International Undertaking on Plant Genetic Resources,[43] urged Governments to support it and authorized the Executive Director to co-operate with the FAO Commission on Plant Genetic Resources in its implementation.

Freshwater ecosystems

The environmental aspects of water resources management and freshwater ecosystems were important areas of UNEP activities in 1984 (see p. 648).

Marine ecosystems

Protection of the marine environment

During 1984, UNEP continued to assess marine pollution problems; much of that work was carried out through the regional seas programme (see below).

The Joint Group of Experts on the Scientific Aspects of Marine Pollution was the main interagency mechanism to review problems of marine pollution. Through it, hazard evaluations for cadmium, lead and tin were completed, and work was in progress on the evaluation of arsenic, carcinogens, major nutrients, mercury and organosilicons. The air/sea transport of pollutants in the Mediterranean region was reviewed; analyses of marine pollution implications of ocean energy development and of the effects of thermal discharges on the marine environment were completed; and an oceanographic model for the dispersion of waste disposal into the sea was prepared. A major review of the global flux of pollutants from land-based sources and of the feasibility of integrated global ocean monitoring was initiated. Guidelines for the environmental impact assessment of land-based sources of pollution were applied in two case-studies, in Chile and Thailand.

The *Ad Hoc* Working Group of Experts on the Protection of the Marine Environment against Pollution from Land-based Sources held its second session at Geneva in November to develop global guidelines to control marine pollution from sources such as rivers and coastal outfalls.[44] The UNEP Council, on 28 May 1984,[6] expressed satisfaction at the results of the Working Group's first session in November/December 1983[45] and welcomed Canada's offer to host a future session.

Work was undertaken with several agencies on the formulation and testing of reference methods for marine pollution studies. The work was conducted under the technical co-ordination of the IAEA International Laboratory of Marine Radioactivity, which served as the global quality control (intercalibration) centre for most of the pollutants monitored through UNEP-sponsored activities. Approximately 20 reference methods had been issued, and their application provided the basis for the global comparability of data collected through the regional seas programme.

UNEP reached an agreement with the Intergovernmental Oceanographic Commission (IOC) of UNESCO, providing that IOC would co-sponsor the Group of Experts on Methods, Standards and Intercalibration. The aim of the agreement was to ensure the widest possible involvement of experts in the formulation, testing and application of reference methods.

A number of global, regional and specialized directories and bibliographies were published in co-operation with the FAO Aquatic Sciences and Fisheries Abstracts system.

The UNEP Council, on 28 May,[3] welcomed the increased co-operation between UNEP and IOC. It noted the progress made with regard to a review of environmental implications of the disposal of radioactive wastes at sea, as requested in 1983,[45] and urged the Executive Director to continue to co-operate with IAEA and other organizations in studying the impact of the disposal of radioactive wastes on the sea-bed as well as sea-bed mining.

Living marine resources

In 1984, UNEP efforts in regard to living marine resources focused on a Global Plan of Action for the Conservation, Management and Utilization of Marine Mammals prepared in co-operation with FAO (see p. 650).

Regional seas programme

Since May 1984, UNEP's Regional Seas Programme Activity Centre had been pursuing activities in 10 regions involving more than 120 coastal States, more than 30 global and regional organizations and a network of approximately 250 national institutions. By the end of 1984, action plans had been adopted in eight regions and regional conventions signed in six. Preparations for the adoption of one more action plan and two more conventions advanced significantly. UNEP continued to provide overall co-ordination for the regional seas programme and served as the secretariat for four action plans and three conventions.

Activities under the regional seas programme included:

Mediterranean. Assessments were published of microbial pollution of beaches and shellfish-growing areas and of pollution by mercury; control measures were imposed. The regional monitoring programme was strengthened through national monitoring agreements signed with six countries. The Mediterranean Trust Fund supported 116 projects.

Kuwait Action Plan region. UNEP continued to assist the Regional Organization for the Protection of the Marine Environment to co-ordinate the implementation of four major projects in co-operation with IAEA, IOC, IUCN and UNESCO, and to prepare for negotiations on a protocol on the prevention of pollution from land-based sources. The Marine Emergency Mutual Aid Centre in Bahrain held several technical meetings to formulate surveillance programmes to determine the extent of pollution.

Caribbean. The first ratification of the Convention for the Protection and Development of the Marine Environment of the Wider Caribbean Region and its Protocol concerning Co-operation in Combating Oil Spills, signed in 1983,[46] was received in 1984. A total of 10 projects were negotiated with 11 organizations or Governments for implementation in 1984 and 1985; they dealt with marine pollution monitoring and control, oil spill preparedness planning, environmental education and public awareness, tourism development and environmental management, environmental impact assessment of industrial projects, environmental training, protected natural areas and endangered wildlife species.

West and Central Africa. The Convention for Co-operation in the Protection and Development of the Marine and Coastal Environment of the West and Central African Region and the Protocol concerning Co-operation in Combating Pollution in Cases of Emergency entered into force on 5 August 1984. Implementation of priority projects dealing with contingency planning for pollution emergencies, marine pollution research and coastal erosion control continued with the co-operation of FAO, IAEA, IMO, IOC, UNESCO and WHO.

East Africa. A second meeting of experts was convened (Nairobi, October) to complete negotiations on a regional convention for the protection, management and development of the marine and coastal environment, a protocol concerning protected areas and wild fauna and flora, and a protocol on co-operation in combating marine pollution in cases of emergency. The experts reached consensus on nearly all of the provisions of those instruments and recommended that a conference of plenipotentiaries be convened in 1985 for adoption of the final texts.

Red Sea and Gulf of Aden. The Regional Convention for the Conservation of the Red Sea and Gulf of Aden

Environment and the Protocol concerning Regional Co-operation in Combating Pollution by Oil and Other Harmful Substances in Cases of Emergency, adopted in 1982,[47] were ratified by the Sudan. UNEP continued its support to marine pollution research and monitoring activities through ALECSO.

South Pacific. Negotiations continued on a draft convention for the protection and development of the natural resources and environment of the region and on two protocols. A large number of projects on research, monitoring, environmental education, training and information were begun through two networks of national and regional institutions. Workshops were convened on trace metal analysis, coastal mapping, water resources of small islands, and marine pollution prevention, response and control, the last in co-operation with IMO and the United States Coast Guard.

South-east Pacific. A programme for research on and monitoring of marine pollution from domestic, agricultural, mining and industrial sources, involving 15 institutions from all five participating States, became operational. Global guidelines for environmental impact assessment were applied to a case-study in Chile in co-operation with the Economic Commission for Latin America and the Caribbean (ECLAC).

East Asian seas. The Action Plan was built around five major projects co-ordinated by the national institutions of the participating States: assessment of levels of pollutants and their effects on the marine and coastal environment; study of coral resources and their protection from pollution; research on the toxicity of oil and oil dispersants; development of regional data exchange systems; and study of maritime meteorological phenomena influencing the environment of the region. The projects were financed by the East Asian Seas Trust Fund, with matching funds from the Environment Fund.

South Asian seas. A meeting of national focal points on the development of an action plan was convened by UNEP, in co-operation with the South Asia Co-operative Environment Programme, in March 1984. The meeting considered the geographical scope of the plan and its main objectives, identified priority areas, discussed financial arrangements, and agreed on the preparation of studies and reviews.

UNEP Council action. On 28 May,[3] the UNEP Council noted the progress made in implementing the regional seas programme. It urged States to support the adoption and ratification of regional conventions and protocols and invited them to pay their contributions to the trust funds for the regional action plans.

Environmental aspects of political, economic and other issues

Arms race and the environment

Following a 1981 UNEP Council request,[48] regular analysis of the impact of the arms race on nature was included in the 1984-1989 system-wide medium-term environment programme.

Work on an annotated bibliography on military activities and the human environment continued in 1984, as a joint project begun in 1983 of UNEP and the Stockholm International Peace Research Institute. Under the same project, two books were published in 1984: *Environmental Warfare: A Technical, Legal and Political Appraisal*, and *Herbicides in War: The Long-term Ecological and Human Consequences*. A book on mitigating the environmental effects of explosive remnants of war was completed.

A UNEP study on collateral damage likely from chemical warfare was expected to be completed in 1985. Another study examined the impact of the massive use of lethal anti-personnel nerve agents on crops, livestock, forest, grassland, wildlife, aquatic biota and soil biota.

Among other developments, Iran, by a letter of 13 March to the Secretary-General,[49] charged that Iraq's recent use of chemical weapons in its attacks on Iran (see p. 229) not only endangered human life and natural resources but polluted the environment; Iran's Environmental Protection Organization expected all international organizations, particularly UNEP, to condemn such inhuman action.

Material remnants of war

Pursuant to a December 1983 General Assembly request,[50] the Secretary-General submitted in October 1984 a report on the problem of remnants of war.[51] He stated that the Executive Director had sought the views of all States on the recommendations of a July 1983 high-level group of experts dealing with legal, informational, technical, institutional and other aspects of the problem.[52] By 28 August 1984, only 10 States had replied: Angola, Belgium, Burkina Faso, Liberia, Mexico, Netherlands, New Zealand, Senegal, Sweden, Uganda.

Of those, three said they had no comments. Two States reiterated their position that the question should be resolved bilaterally, that the subject had already been introduced into international law (Protocol II to the Convention on Prohibitions or Restrictions on the Use of Certain Conventional Weapons Which May Be Deemed to Be Excessively Injurious or to Have Indiscriminate Effects, adopted in 1980[53]) and that discussions on responsibility and compensation should be avoided. As for a United Nations conference or a meeting of government-nominated experts, two States considered that a meeting would be convenient while two others opposed the proposal. Two countries considered it convenient to consult the International Court of Justice, while one indicated its opposition to that procedure. Two States felt that the United Nations system had a role with regard to technical assistance. One State suggested

that a tax on the military budgets of the superPowers be considered.

The Secretary-General concluded that the limited responses had made it difficult to comply with the Assembly's request that he intensify his efforts to urge the States concerned to conduct bilateral consultations leading to agreements.

GENERAL ASSEMBLY ACTION

On 17 December 1984, on the recommendation of the Second Committee, the General Assembly adopted resolution 39/167 by recorded vote.

Remnants of war

The General Assembly,

Recalling its resolutions 3435(XXX) of 9 December 1975, 35/71 of 5 December 1980, 36/188 of 17 December 1981, 37/215 of 20 December 1982 and 38/162 of 19 December 1983 concerning the problem of remnants of war,

Recalling also decisions 80(IV) of 9 April 1976, 101(V) of 25 May 1977, 9/5 of 25 May 1981 and 10/8 of 28 May 1982 of the Governing Council of the United Nations Environment Programme,

Recalling further resolution 32 adopted by the Fifth Conference of Heads of State or Government of Non-Aligned Countries, held at Colombo from 16 to 19 August 1976, and resolution 26/11-P adopted by the Eleventh Islamic Conference of Foreign Ministers, held at Islamabad from 17 to 22 May 1980,

Convinced that the responsibility for the removal of the remnants of war should be borne by the countries that planted them,

Recognizing that the presence of the material remnants of war, including mines, in the territories of developing countries seriously impedes their development efforts and causes loss of life and property,

1. *Takes note* of the report of the Secretary-General on the problem of remnants of war;

2. *Regrets* that no concrete measures have been taken to solve the problem of remnants of war despite the various resolutions and decisions adopted thereon by the General Assembly and the Governing Council of the United Nations Environment Programme;

3. *Reiterates its support* of the just demands of the developing countries affected by the implantation of mines and the presence of other remnants of war in their territories for compensation and for complete removal of those obstacles by the States that implanted them;

4. *Requests* the Secretary-General, in co-operation with the United Nations Environment Programme and other organizations of the United Nations system, within their mandates, to collect all information on expertise and available equipment, so as to evaluate, on request, the actual needs of the developing countries affected and to assist those countries in their efforts to detect and clear material remnants of war;

5. *Calls upon* all States to co-operate with the appropriate organizations of the United Nations system in carrying out the task assigned to them in paragraph 4 above;

6. *Also calls upon* those developed countries directly responsible for the presence of remnants of war to intensify bilateral consultations with the aim of conclud-

ing, without undue delay, agreements for the solution of those problems;

7. *Requests* all States to inform the Secretary-General of actions they have taken in the implementation of the present resolution;

8. *Requests* the Secretary-General to submit to the General Assembly at its fortieth session a detailed and comprehensive report on the implementation of the present resolution.

General Assembly resolution 39/167

17 December 1984　　　Meeting 103　　　121-0-24 (recorded vote)

Approved by Second Committee (A/39/790/Add.9) by recorded vote (105-0-23), 30 November (meeting 54); 43-nation draft (A/C.2/39/L.12/Rev.1); agenda item 80 *(i)*.

Sponsors: Afghanistan, Algeria, Bahrain, Bangladesh, Benin, Burkina Faso, Cape Verde, Comoros, Cuba, Democratic Yemen, Djibouti, Egypt, Ghana, Guinea, Guinea-Bissau, Iran, Kuwait, Lao People's Democratic Republic, Libyan Arab Jamahiriya, Madagascar, Maldives, Mali, Malta, Mauritania, Mexico, Mongolia, Morocco, Nicaragua, Nigeria, Oman, Pakistan, Qatar, Sao Tome and Principe, Saudi Arabia, Sierra Leone, Suriname, Syrian Arab Republic, Tunisia, United Arab Emirates, Viet Nam, Yemen, Zambia, Zimbabwe.

Meeting numbers. GA 39th session: 2nd Committee 37, 50, 54; plenary 103.

Recorded vote in Assembly as follows:

In favour: Afghanistan, Albania, Algeria, Angola, Argentina; Bahamas, Bahrain, Bangladesh, Barbados, Benin, Bhutan, Bolivia, Botswana, Brazil, Brunei Darussalam, Bulgaria, Burkina Faso, Burma, Burundi, Byelorussian SSR, Cameroon, Cape Verde, Central African Republic, Chad, Chile, China, Colombia, Costa Rica, Cuba, Cyprus, Czechoslovakia, Democratic Kampuchea, Democratic Yemen, Djibouti, Dominican Republic, Ecuador, Egypt, El Salvador, Ethiopia, Fiji, Gabon, German Democratic Republic, Ghana, Guatemala, Guinea, Guinea-Bissau, Guyana, Haiti, Honduras, Hungary, India, Indonesia, Iran, Iraq, Ivory Coast, Jamaica, Jordan, Kenya, Kuwait, Lao People's Democratic Republic, Lesotho, Liberia, Libyan Arab Jamahiriya, Madagascar, Malawi, Malaysia, Maldives, Mali, Malta, Mauritania, Mauritius, Mexico, Mongolia, Morocco, Mozambique, Nepal, Nicaragua, Niger, Nigeria, Oman, Pakistan, Panama, Papua New Guinea, Paraguay, Peru, Philippines, Poland, Qatar, Romania, Rwanda, Saint Lucia, Samoa, Sao Tome and Principe, Saudi Arabia, Sierra Leone, Somalia, Sri Lanka, Sudan, Suriname, Swaziland, Syrian Arab Republic, Thailand, Togo, Trinidad and Tobago, Tunisia, Turkey, Uganda, Ukrainian SSR, USSR, United Arab Emirates, United Republic of Tanzania, Uruguay, Vanuatu, Venezuela, Viet Nam, Yemen, Yugoslavia, Zaire, Zambia, Zimbabwe.

Against: None.

Abstaining: Australia, Austria, Belgium, Canada, Denmark, Finland, France, Gambia, Germany, Federal Republic of, Greece, Iceland, Ireland, Italy, Japan, Luxembourg, Netherlands, New Zealand, Norway, Portugal, Senegal, Spain, Sweden, United Kingdom, United States.

Speaking also on behalf of Italy and the United Kingdom, the Federal Republic of Germany said the text raised issues that fell within bilateral relations; reference to the just demands of the developing countries for compensation was not acceptable as it prejudged the outcome of bilateral relations; also, the concept of responsibility of certain States did not have any foundation under international law. In Sweden's view, the possibility of practical results would be furthered if the question of international responsibility and compensation were left aside; instead of giving the Secretary-General tasks which could not be carried out, it would be more constructive to try to co-operate along lines envisaged in article 9 of Protocol II to the 1980 Convention on prohibiting the use of excessively injurious weapons. India pointed out that the text applied only to actions resulting from colonial and imperialist wars.

Introducing the draft, Malta said that unexploded war devices continued threatening life and property in many developing countries and jeopardizing their economic development; it was time for the countries which had been involved in the Second World War to join in clearing the war debris, for they alone had the necessary technology. Egypt, on behalf of the Group of 77 developing countries, said the remnants constituted further aggression against the people of the countries where they had been planted.

Environmental aspects of *apartheid*

In response to a May 1983 UNEP Council decision,[54] the Executive Director submitted in January 1984 a report on the environmental impacts of *apartheid*, with specific reference to industry in urban townships and rural bantustans.[55] In particular, the report reviewed the impact of industrial relocation in black areas on the environment, and discussed the environmental problems related to black urban townships. According to available information, compliance with environmental standards required was often lax, but no hard evidence could be obtained on the extent of environmental damage caused by industry. However, considering that most of the industries in the so-called homelands were related to manufacturing, a wide spectrum of environmental pollution could be expected unless preventive measures were taken. The environment in which the black population of the urban townships lived reflected South Africa's racial laws; although the Government had drawn up plans for urban renewal and the provision of housing, the translation of those plans into action could not be taken for granted.

Taking note of the report, the UNEP Council, on 28 May,[56] noted with concern that serious environmental deterioration was continuing with the establishment of polluting industries. The Council reaffirmed its solidarity with the victims of *apartheid* and its condemnation of that system. It requested the Executive Director to continue monitoring the environmental impacts of *apartheid*, including the adverse conditions under which black people worked, especially in mines, and to respond, in conjunction with other United Nations agencies, to appeals from national liberation movements for assistance to the victims.

Mediterranean—Dead Sea canal project

On 28 May 1984,[57] the UNEP Council adopted a decision on Israel's decision to build a canal linking the Mediterranean Sea to the Dead Sea (see POLITICAL AND SECURITY QUESTIONS, Chapter IX).

Environment and development

Guidance on the integration of environmental considerations into development decision-making was provided by UNEP throughout 1984. Among its activities was an analysis of Japanese experience in integrating physical and socio-economic planning with environmental considerations.

A survey of the methods utilized in centrally planned economies to analyse natural resources in relation to development goals was undertaken by UNEP, the CMEA International Institute of Economic Problems and the USSR Commission for UNEP.

Action aimed at demonstrating the feasibility of integrating nature conservation into major development projects was begun by UNEP and the IUCN Conservation for Development Centre. The Centre, with UNEP support, prepared a review of environmental impact assessment procedures used in developing countries. The review served as a background paper at an international seminar on the topic (Feldafing, Federal Republic of Germany, 9-12 April). A survey of the environmental aspects of the activities of transnational corporations was prepared by UNEP with the United Nations Centre on Transnational Corporations.

The fifth meeting of the Committee of International Development Institutions on the Environment (Luxembourg, 13-15 June) reviewed progress made in implementing the Declaration of Environmental Policies and Procedures Relating to Economic Development; three workshops on the environmental dimension in development planning were held by UNEP in co-operation with ECLAC in May (Argentina, Chile, Colombia); a training course on the evaluation of development projects from the standpoint of environmental economics was co-sponsored by UNEP and the East-West Environment and Policy Institute of the University of Hawaii (Honolulu, United States, 4-15 June).

Regional meetings of employers' organizations on environment and development in Asia and the Pacific (Bangkok, 12-16 March) and in Africa (Nairobi, 15-19 October) were convened by ILO and UNEP; an expert group meeting on environmental accounting and its use in development policy and planning was held by UNEP and the World Bank (Washington, D.C., 5-9 November).

On 28 May,[58] the UNEP Council took note of the review of the implementation of the environmental aspects of the International Development Strategy for the Third United Nations Development Decade (the 1980s) in a report prepared under the aegis of the Administrative Committee on Co-ordination (see p. 392). The Council reiterated the importance it attached to environmental considerations for the success of the Strategy and authorized the Executive Director to transmit the report with the Council's comments to the Committee on review and appraisal of the Strategy.

The Council, in another decision of the same date,[59] encouraged governmental bodies engaged in environmental activities to continue their efforts for sustained global progress with special focus on the needs of developing countries, thus contributing to a continuing dialogue between and among developed and developing countries. It agreed to continued support by UNEP of that dialogue, with a view to facilitating agreements and elaborating actions for environmental undertakings.

The World Commission on Environment and Development, established to help prepare the Environmental Perspective to the Year 2000 and Beyond (see p. 744), held an organizational meeting in May and an inaugural meeting in October (see APPENDIX III).

Environment and industry

As called for by the Executive Director in 1983,[60] a World Industry Conference on Environmental Management (Versailles, 14-16 November) was sponsored jointly by world industry and UNEP, in co-operation with the International Chamber of Commerce (ICC); more than 500 representatives from over 70 countries took part. Emerging from the Conference was that: environmental management should be an integral part of economic development; economic growth could be made compatible with environmental protection; cost-benefit analysis was an essential element of environmental decision-making and should be improved in an attempt to quantify the value of critical elements in our cultural heritage; the direct cost of environmental protection as well as the cost to society of environmental damage must be considered; and a preventive approach was preferable to correcting environmental problems after they had occurred.

In addition, the Conference agreed on 15 major recommendations. Of particular interest to UNEP was that ICC should convene a small group of chief executive officers representative of both geographical areas and industrial sectors to serve as advisers for industry, and case-studies on companies' experience in environmental management were to be prepared under the auspices of UNEP and industrial associations.

Following the Conference, UNEP co-ordinated work on a strategy for industrial and intersectoral environmental planning.

Population and environment

Environment received significant attention at the International Conference on Population (Mexico City, August 1984) (see p. 714). The Conference declared that priority should be given to the protection of the physical environment and the prevention of its further deterioration.

On 28 May,[61] the UNEP Council requested the Executive Director to give priority to the work towards harmonious interaction between population, resources, development and the environment, and to treat the issue of population and the environment in the state-of-the-environment report for 1985 in the light of the Conference's results.

Human settlements and environment

Faced with increasing environmental pressures on urban regions, UNEP continued to collaborate with other United Nations agencies, notably UNCHS (see p. 744), in combating deteriorating environmental standards. As part of its efforts for the International Year of Shelter for the Homeless (1987) (see p. 776), UNEP approved a pilot project on environmentally sound planning of human settlements in Democratic Yemen.

A joint UNEP/UNCHS project assisting the United Republic of Tanzania in planning its new capital of Dodoma was completed. Technical missions were undertaken by UNEP and UNCHS to upgrade slum and squatter settlements in Rio de Janeiro, Brazil.

An international conference on the ecological approach to urban planning was held by UNEP and UNESCO (Suzdal, USSR, 23-30 September).

A third volume of guidelines for environmental planning and management of human settlements was prepared; the guidelines were being tested in field projects before their scheduled publication in 1985.

Environmental law

Three working groups of experts had been established for the priority topics under the 1981 Montevideo Programme for the Development and Periodic Review of Environmental Law.[62] The groups dealt with: protection of the marine environment; management of hazardous wastes; and information on potentially harmful chemicals (see above).

The Working Group of Experts on Environmental Law met (Washington, D.C., 26-29 June 1984) to develop principles and goals for environmental impact assessment.

On 28 May,[6] the UNEP Council welcomed the financial support by the United States for the Working Group session and called on Governments to participate in the Group. The Council also expressed satisfaction at the results of the first sessions of the three working groups and requested the Executive Director to continue co-operation with other United Nations bodies in preparing international guidelines.

The legal status of non-obligatory guidelines and principles was one of the issues considered at an expert workshop on the future of international environmental law, convened in November by the United Nations University and the Hague Academy of International Law with UNEP participation.

International instruments

Pursuant to a 1975 General Assembly resolution,[63] the Secretary-General transmitted in September 1984 a report of the Executive Director on international conventions and protocols in the field of the environment.[64] The report contained information on nine recent conventions and protocols and changes in the status of existing conventions. It recorded the conventions and protocols for which corrections had been introduced and other conventions pertaining to the environment.

The Register of international treaties and other agreements in the field of the environment was revised to reflect membership status as of 15 August; the revised Register listed 118 multilateral instruments relating to the environment.

By a 28 May decision,[6] the UNEP Council authorized the Executive Director to transmit his report and the Register to the Assembly, and requested him to continue collecting and disseminating information on international and national environmental law. In accordance with the same decision, the secretariat of the Convention on the Conservation of Migratory Species of Wild Animals was established at Bonn in October under UNEP administration with support from the Federal Republic of Germany. The Council authorized the Executive Director to call the first meeting of the Conference of the Parties to the Convention for 1985.

Preparations for a global convention for the protection of the ozone layer neared completion, and global guidelines for transfrontier movements, storage and disposal of hazardous wastes were being developed (see above).

Following a request by the States parties to the 1973 Convention on International Trade in Endangered Species of Wild Fauna and Flora, the secretariat of the Convention (located at Lausanne, Switzerland) was administered from November 1984 by the UNEP Executive Director and fully financed from the trust fund established for that purpose.

In decision 39/429, the General Assembly took note of the Secretary-General's note transmitting the Executive Director's report on conventions and protocols.

Environmental education and training

Many UNEP projects contained an education and training component. The UNEP/UNESCO International Programme in Environmental Education in its ninth year in 1984 promoted general environmental education through teacher training, studies, publications, dissemination of technical materials, workshops, and technical assistance to Governments. A review of the Programme found that priority should be placed on the implementation of activities rather than on further elaboration of a theoretical basis for them; that instructional and reference materials had to be adapted and augmented for local use; and that more attention should be devoted to incorporating environmental education into technical and vocational school curricula.

In addition to specialized environmental training, there was general training of groups whose decisions and activities had direct impact on the environment. During 1984, 200 officials and professionals received such general training in environmental management from UNEP. The seventh and eighth international graduate courses on resource management and environmental impact assessment in developing countries, organized by UNEP, UNESCO and the German Democratic Republic at the Technical University of Dresden, ended in July and began in October, respectively.

Under a joint ILO/UNEP project started in 1980, ILO continued to test training modules at five ILO-sponsored training institutions in Asia and the Pacific.

Co-operation between UNEP and the International Centre for Training in Environmental Sciences, which began in 1975, ended with the dissolution of the Centre in 1984. Subsequently, UNEP focused its support on training activities in the Network of Environmental Training Institutions in Latin America and the Caribbean. The Network concentrated on assisting Governments in preparing a regional environmental training programme.

Recommendations for a programme of action for environmental education and training in Africa, made at an April 1983 meeting of experts,[65] were submitted to the UNEP Council by the Executive Director in January 1984.[66] The recommendations dealt with assessing national needs, developing national plans, establishing national co-ordination machinery and steering committees, and promoting regional co-operation among national institutions.

The Council, on 28 May,[67] endorsed the recommendations. It requested the Executive Director to formulate a regional programme in co-operation with Governments and UNESCO, and to report in 1985 on progress achieved. The Council recommended that the countries of Latin America and the Caribbean agree soon on a general programme for the regional Environmental Training Network and that the environmental training activities of various agencies be co-ordinated. It requested the Executive Director to explore the possibilities of co-operation among the regions that were undertaking an effort similar to the Network and urged him to continue budgetary support to the Network. The Council recommended that the countries of the region study a co-ordination project with the aim of attaining the signature of an instrument that would guarantee financing for the Network up to 1987.

REFERENCES

[1]A/39/25 (dec. 12/11). [2]UNEP/GC.12/11/Add.2. [3]A/39/25 (dec. 12/12). [4]YUN 1982, p. 1010. [5]UNEP/WG.96/5. [6]A/39/25 (dec. 12/14). [7]UNEP/WG.96/2. [8]UNEP/WG.96/3. [9]UNEP/GC.13/2 & Corr.1. [10]UNEP/GC.12/16. [11]YUN 1983, p. 779, GA res. 38/149, 19 Dec. 1983. [12]A/39/290-E/1984/120. [13]A/39/452. [14]YUN 1982, p. 1011, GA res. 37/137, 17 Dec. 1982. [15]UNEP/WG.95/5. [16]UNEP/WG.111/3. [17]UNEP/WG.95/4. [18]UNEP/WG.94/10. [19]UNEP/WG.110/4. [20]YUN 1983, p. 781. [21]DP/1985/50. [22]A/39/25 (dec. 12/10). [23]E/1984/20 (dec. 84/27). [24]A/39/242. [25]A/39/242/Add.1. [26]A/39/530. [27]E/1984/21 (res. 496(XIX)). [28]Ibid. (res. 499(XIX)). [29]Ibid. (res. 528(XIX)). [30]A/39/15, vol. II (res. 295(XXIX)). [31]YUN 1977, p. 509. [32]UNEP/GC.12/9 & Corr.1. [33]A/39/433. [34]YUN 1983, p. 777, GA res. 38/164, 19 Dec. 1983. [35]DP/1984/50. [36]E/1984/20 (dec. 84/32). [37]DP/1984/51 & Corr.1,2. [38]E/1984/20 (dec. 84/29). [39]YUN 1983, p. 556. [40]YUN 1982, p. 1021. [41]A/39/25 (dec. 12/13). [42]YUN 1980, p. 717. [43]YUN 1983, p. 1230. [44]UNEP/WG.109/4. [45]YUN 1983, p. 783. [46]Ibid., p. 784. [47]YUN 1982, p. 1022. [48]YUN 1981, p. 835. [49]A/39/132-S/16416. [50]YUN 1983, p. 786, GA res. 38/162, 19 Dec. 1983. [51]A/39/580. [52]YUN 1983, p. 786. [53]YUN 1980, p. 77. [54]YUN 1983, p. 787. [55]UNEP/GC.12/5. [56]A/39/25 (dec. 12/6). [57]Ibid. (dec. 12/7). [58]Ibid. (dec. 12/2). [59]Ibid. (dec. 12/3). [60]YUN 1983, p. 788. [61]A/39/25 (dec. 12/5). [62]YUN 1981, p. 839. [63]YUN 1975, p. 443, GA res. 3436(XXX), 9 Dec. 1975. [64]A/39/432. [65]YUN 1983, p. 789. [66]UNEP/GC.12/13. [67]A/39/25 (dec. 12/16).

Chapter XVII

Human settlements

Progress in implementing the work programme of
the United Nations Centre for Human Settlements
(UNCHS), also known as Habitat, continued to be
made during 1984, with the completion of 16 technical co-operation projects and the beginning of
41 new ones.

The seventh session of the Commission on
Human Settlements was held at Libreville, Gabon,
from 30 April to 11 May 1984. Among the items
on its agenda were the 1987 International Year of
Shelter for the Homeless (IYSH), human settlements activities of the United Nations system, and
systematic approaches to training and information
for human settlements. The Commission adopted
15 resolutions and one decision; two of the resolutions, concerning IYSH and the living conditions
of the Palestinian people in the Israeli-occupied
territories (see POLITICAL AND SECURITY QUES-
TIONS, Chapter IX), required General Assembly
action.

The Secretary-General presented a cross-
organizational programme analysis of United
Nations human settlements activities to the Committee for Programme and Co-ordination (CPC),
which made several recommendations to improve
their system-wide co-ordination.

The Economic and Social Council, by resolution 1984/57 A, encouraged the Commission to
continue helping developing countries to develop
human settlements and urged it to support technical co-operation among those countries.

The Council, by resolution 1984/57 B, requested United Nations agencies and organizations to review their programmes with a view to
incorporating in their activities the objectives of
IYSH.

By resolution 39/170 A, the Assembly took note
of the Commission's report on its 1984 session and
made a renewed appeal to Governments to contribute to the United Nations Habitat and Human
Settlements Foundation. By resolution 39/170 B,
the Assembly welcomed the Secretary-General's
intention to review the arrangements regarding
UNCHS participation in the work of the Administrative Committee on Co-ordination (ACC). By
resolution 39/171, the Assembly urged Governments to intensify their activities for IYSH and to
assess prospects and resources regarding shelter
and settlements, leading to the formulation of national shelter strategies applicable until the year
2000.

Topics related to this chapter. Middle East:
territories occupied by Israel—living conditions of
Palestinians; settlements policy. Regional economic
and social activities.

Programme and finances of UNCHS

Programme policy

The report of the Commission on Human Settlements on its 1984 session[1] was considered by
both the Economic and Social Council and the
General Assembly.

The Council in July, by resolution 1984/57 A,
encouraged the Commission to continue to contribute to the efforts of developing countries in developing human settlements, and urged it to provide adequate support for technical co-operation
among developing countries in formulating and
implementing their human settlements programmes. Further, the Council expressed support
for the efforts of the Commission and UNCHS to
achieve greater co-ordination of human settlements activities in the United Nations system.

The Assembly, by resolution 39/170 A of 17 December, expressed appreciation to those who had
made voluntary contributions to the United
Nations Habitat and Human Settlements Foundation in support of the work of UNCHS, and
renewed its appeal to Governments, especially
those of developed countries, to begin making
regular contributions.

ECONOMIC AND SOCIAL COUNCIL ACTION

On 26 July, the Economic and Social Council,
on the recommendation of its First (Economic)
Committee, adopted without vote resolution
1984/57 A.

Report of the Commission on Human Settlements
The Economic and Social Council,
Recalling General Assembly resolutions 3201(S-VI) and
3202(S-VI) of 1 May 1974, containing the Declaration
and the Programme of Action on the Establishment of
a New International Economic Order, 3281(XXIX) of
12 December 1974, containing the Charter of Economic
Rights and Duties of States, and 3362(S-VII) of 16 September 1975 on development and international economic
co-operation,

Recalling also General Assembly resolutions 32/162 of 19 December 1977 on institutional arrangements for international co-operation in the field of human settlements and 34/116 of 14 December 1979 on the strengthening of human settlements activities,

Reaffirming its belief that access to decent shelter is a basic human need and entitlement,

Reaffirming also its conviction that human settlements activities can play a major role in national economic and social development, particularly in the developing countries,

Recognizing the need for greater co-ordination and co-operation in the field of human settlements, as noted in the report of the Committee for Programme and Co-ordination on the work of its twenty-fourth session,

Taking note of Commission on Human Settlements resolution 7/4 of 10 May 1984, concerning the participation of youth in the solution of housing problems under conditions of lasting peace and security,

Having considered the report of the Commission on Human Settlements on the work of its seventh session,

1. *Takes note* of the report of the Commission on Human Settlements on the work of its seventh session and the resolutions and decision contained therein;

2. *Takes note in particular* of Commission on Human Settlements resolution 7/5 of 9 May 1984 on the question of a biennial cycle of sessions for the Commission, and again requests the Commission, pursuant to General Assembly decision 38/429 of 19 December 1983 and Economic and Social Council decision 1984/104 of 10 February 1984, to consider adopting a biennial cycle of sessions;

3. *Encourages* the Commission on Human Settlements to continue to contribute to the efforts of the developing countries in the development of human settlements;

4. *Recommends* to the General Assembly, for consideration and action at its thirty-ninth session, the resolutions adopted by the Commission at its seventh session which require action by the Assembly;

5. *Urges* the Commission on Human Settlements to continue to take account of and to provide adequate support for technical co-operation among developing countries in the formulation and implementation of its programmes on human settlements;

6. *Supports* the efforts of the Commission on Human Settlements and the United Nations Centre for Human Settlements (Habitat) to achieve greater harmonization and co-ordination of human settlements activities in the United Nations system, as envisaged by the General Assembly in resolutions 32/162 of 19 December 1977, 35/77 C of 5 December 1980 and 37/223 C of 20 December 1982, and the recommendations related to the cross-organizational programme analysis of the activities of the United Nations system in human settlements made by the Committee for Programme and Co-ordination at its twenty-fourth session.

Economic and Social Council resolution 1984/57 A

26 July 1984   Meeting 49   Adopted without vote

Approved by First Committee (E/1984/146) without vote (parts A and B together), 18 July (meeting 12); draft by Vice-Chairman (E/1984/C.1/L.12, part A), based on informal consultations on draft by Canada, Kenya, Netherlands, Sri Lanka and Uganda (E/1984/C.1/L.5, part A); agenda item 15.

The original 5-nation draft did not contain reference to the resolutions and decision in the Commission's report, as did paragraph 1 of the adopted text. Paragraph 3 was redrafted; by the original version, the Council would have commended the Commission on the significant contribution it continued to make to the efforts of developing countries in human settlements development. In paragraph 6, the Council would have endorsed the efforts of the Commission and UNCHS to achieve greater co-ordination of United Nations human settlements activities; the original version also did not include reference to the recommendations of CPC related to the cross-organizational programme analysis of those activities (see Chapter XXIV of this section).

GENERAL ASSEMBLY ACTION

On 17 December 1984, on the recommendation of the Second (Economic and Financial) Committee, the General Assembly adopted without vote resolution 39/170 A.

Report of the Commission on Human Settlements

The General Assembly,

Recalling its resolutions 3201(S-VI) and 3202(S-VI) of 1 May 1974, containing the Declaration and the Programme of Action on the Establishment of a New International Economic Order, 3281(XXIX) of 12 December 1974, containing the Charter of Economic Rights and Duties of States, and 3362(S-VII) of 16 September 1975 on development and international economic co-operation,

Recalling also its resolutions 32/162 of 19 December 1977 on institutional arrangements for international co-operation in the field of human settlements and 34/116 of 14 December 1979 on the strengthening of human settlements activities,

Seriously concerned at the continued low level of voluntary contributions being made available to the United Nations Centre for Human Settlements (Habitat) in support of the human settlements activities of the United Nations,

Taking note of Economic and Social Council resolution 1984/57 A of 26 July 1984 on international co-operation in the field of human settlements,

Having considered the report of the Commission on Human Settlements on the work of its seventh session,

1. *Takes note* of the report of the Commission on Human Settlements on the work of its seventh session and the resolutions contained therein;

2. *Expresses its appreciation* to those Governments and others which have made voluntary contributions to the United Nations Habitat and Human Settlements Foundation in support of the work of the United Nations Centre for Human Settlements (Habitat) and commends in particular those which have done so on a regular basis;

3. *Renews its appeal* to all Governments, particularly those of the developed countries, to begin making regular voluntary contributions to the United Nations Habitat and Human Settlements Foundation of the Centre, if they have not already done so, and, if they have, to consider increasing the amount of their contributions.

General Assembly resolution 39/170 A

17 December 1984   Meeting 103   Adopted without vote

Approved by Second Committee (A/39/790/ Add.10) without vote (parts A and B together), 30 November (meeting 55); draft by Vice-Chairman (A/C.2/39/L.90, part A), based on informal consultations on draft by Canada, Colombia, Ethiopia, Gabon, India, Jamaica, Kenya, Liberia, Netherlands, Philippines, Sri Lanka, Uganda and Zambia (A/C.2/39/L.21, part A); agenda item 80 *(j)*.

Meeting numbers. GA 39th session: 2nd Committee 33, 37, 40, 55; plenary 103.

The original 13-nation draft did not contain reference to the resolutions contained in the report of the Commission. In paragraph 3 of the original version, the Assembly would have made a strong appeal to Member States, particularly the developed countries, and others in a position to do so, to begin making contributions.

Administrative and budgetary questions

Extrabudgetary resources

The Commission on Human Settlements, by a decision of 10 May 1984,[2] took note of a February report[3] of the UNCHS Executive Director on financial matters, specifically the use of extrabudgetary resources of UNCHS during 1982-1983.[4]

UN Habitat and Human Settlements Foundation

Accounts for 1982-1983

The 1982-1983 accounts of the United Nations Habitat and Human Settlements Foundation,[5] together with observations of the Board of Auditors,[6] were submitted to the General Assembly at its regular 1984 session. The Advisory Committee on Administrative and Budgetary Questions, in a September report,[7] stated that it had no comments on the accounts.

By resolution 39/66 on the accounts of various United Nations programmes and funds, the General Assembly accepted the Foundation's accounts for 1982-1983.

Contributions

In 1984, a total of $1.3 million in contributions for the Foundation was received from 36 countries, while pledges for future years amounted to $2.1 million.

CONTRIBUTIONS TO THE UN HABITAT
AND HUMAN SETTLEMENTS FOUNDATION
(as at 31 December 1984; in US dollar equivalent)

Country	1984 payment	Pledges for future years
Algeria	8,500	—
Bangladesh	5,000	—
Barbados	1,000	—
Belgium	—	163,934
Belize	—	2,000
Botswana	1,727	3,521
Cameroon	1,190	31,915

Country	1984 payment	Pledges for future years
Canada	134,109	—
Chile	5,000	5,000
Colombia	4,000	12,000
Congo	—	2,128
Cyprus	370	500
Denmark	340,150	325,000
Egypt	30,246	15,213
Finland	86,583	125,984
France	77,019	69,149
Gabon	31,000	—
Ghana	2,500	—
Hungary	—	40,000
India	49,000	100,000
Indonesia	—	10,000
Jamaica	10,000	10,000
Japan	—	500,000
Kenya	27,874	45,000
Kuwait	15,000	15,000
Lesotho	3,000	6,000
Malawi	—	872
Malaysia	10,000	—
Netherlands	—	159,152
Nigeria	46,980	—
Norway	68,288	112,994
Pakistan	—	5,000
Papua New Guinea	5,294	4,839
Philippines	150,000	2,000
Qatar	—	30,000
Republic of Korea	40,000	20,000
Somalia	641	874
Sri Lanka	4,000	—
Sudan	10,000	—
Swaziland	4,113	3,339
Sweden	—	208,860
Tunisia	21,004	18,979
Turkey	33,832	50,000
Uganda	3,437	2,146
Venezuela	69,878	25,815
Yemen	500	—
Zaire	31,968	—
Zimbabwe	—	4,348
Total	1,333,203	2,131,562

SOURCE: HS/C/8/INF.4.

REFERENCES

[1]A/39/8. [2]*Ibid.* (dec. 7/16). [3]HS/C/7/8. [4]YUN 1983, p. 791. [5]A/39/5/Add.8 & Corr.1. [6]YUN 1983, p. 792. [7]A/39/510.

Human settlements activities

Activities of UNCHS

The 1984 activities of UNCHS[1] were structured on the basis of eight subprogrammes, as approved by the Commission in 1981:[2] settlements policies and strategies; settlements planning; shelter and community services; development of the indigenous construction sector; low-cost infrastructure for human settlements; land; mobilization of finance for human settlements development; and human settlements institutions and management.

The year started with 120 technical co-operation projects; of those, 16 were completed, while 41 new projects were started during 1984. Consequently, at the end of the year, 145 projects were ongoing, a 20.8 per cent increase over 1983.

Work under the settlements policies and strategies subprogramme included the preparation of a theme paper on planning and management of settlements, with emphasis on small and intermediate towns and local growth points, for the Commission's 1985 session. A report was also prepared for the International Conference on Population, held in August at Mexico City (see Chapter XIV of this section), giving particular attention to national population redistribution policies. Another report, concerning human settlements policies and institutions: issues, options, trends and guidelines, contained case-studies on national policies in Brazil, Costa Rica, Hungary, Kenya, Mexico, the Philippines and Sri Lanka. Work continued throughout the year on the quinquennial *Global Report on Human Settlements*. Fifteen technical co-operation projects were in progress, of which two were completed, while two new projects were started.

Under the settlements planning subprogramme, two reports were completed for publication in 1985. They were on road networks and electricity reticulation networks, two volumes of the series providing guidelines for the planning of rural settlements and infrastructure. An interim report was prepared on the use of urban data management systems supported by microcomputers in developing countries, following a survey conducted through *Habitat News*. Integration of environmental policies into settlements planning was a continuing activity, and reports produced in co-operation with the United Nations Environment Programme (UNEP) were reviewed. At the end of the year, 33 technical co-operation projects were in progress, of which 10 were new projects in 1984. Three projects were completed during the year.

Strategies and options available to Governments for the rehabilitation of inner-city slums were identified by UNCHS research under the shelter and community services subprogramme. The research was based on an appraisal of rehabilitation programmes in Lagos, Nigeria; Cairo, Egypt; Bangkok, Thailand; and Bombay, India. A project on training for community participation in low-income settlements improvement was approved by the Danish International Development Agency; agreements were reached with Sri Lanka and Zambia on training courses, and training materials were developed for road planning in squatter areas, community participation in sites-and-services projects and sanitation programmes, cost recovery and affordability, and project support communication. Research outlines were drawn up on the co-operative promotion of shelter programmes and the role of community services

in the development of low-income communities. Thirty-two technical co-operation projects were in progress at the end of 1984, of which seven were started during the year; six projects were completed in 1984.

Under the subprogramme on the development of the indigenous construction sector, a report on small-scale building materials production in the context of the informal economy was published. In co-operation with the Economic Commission for Africa, work continued on reformulating building codes in African countries. Four case-studies on the use of indigenous building materials and technologies in Colombia, Ecuador, Honduras and Zambia were completed. A workshop and international colloquium on earth construction technologies appropriate to developing countries was held at Brussels, Belgium (10-12 December 1984). Seven technical co-operation projects continued throughout the year.

Under the low-cost infrastructure for human settlements subprogramme, discussions were held with the Economic and Social Commission for Asia and the Pacific (ESCAP) on future co-operation related to new and renewable energy sources, and it was agreed to produce jointly a video film on solar energy utilization in developing countries. Two reports—on energy requirements and utilization in rural and urban low-income settlements and on the use of solar energy and natural cooling in the design of buildings in developing countries—were published. A series of technical memoranda on low-cost transport for developing countries was initiated in co-operation with the International Labour Organisation; the first memorandum, on animal-drawn carts, was prepared, as was a study on human settlements and transportation policies in the context of energy and national development goals. A review of technologies for the provision of basic infrastructure in low-income settlements was published. A demonstration project on low-cost sanitation technologies in rural settlements was begun, in co-operation with Jordan and the United Nations Children's Fund. Ten technical co-operation projects were in progress at the beginning of 1984; two were completed, and five were added, leaving 13 ongoing at the end of the year.

Research was carried out under the land subprogramme aimed at bringing about an effective public/private partnership in land development. At the end of 1984, three technical co-operation projects were ongoing, two of which started during the year. Among them, a research project, based on regional reports from Africa, Asia and Latin America, identified land-use planning and management problems with respect to data collection and administration.

Under the subprogramme on the mobilization of finance for human settlements development, research sought to identify effective structures and procedures for financing shelter, infrastructure and services in developing countries. Comparative analysis of case-studies was aimed at identifying innovative finance mechanisms. Technical reports on the promotion of non-conventional approaches to housing finance for low-income groups and community-based finance institutions were published. Research continued on a housing software package which could be tailored to the type of housing loan and the needs and repayment capacities of individual borrowers. Seven technical co-operation projects were in progress at the end of the year, two of which were added in 1984.

Work continued on the first of two case-studies on urban management in large and middle-sized cities under the human settlements institutions and management subprogramme. However, the main thrust of activity under that subprogramme was on training and improving the urban and rural habitat. A number of regional workshops, seminars and courses were held, among them: a workshop on housing in development, co-sponsored by UNCHS and the Catholic University of Leuven (Belgium) (Nairobi, Kenya, 16-27 January), with a follow-up course at Leuven (27 August–26 October); a course on planning, financing and managing city growth, co-sponsored by UNCHS and the Economic Development Institute of the World Bank (Bangkok, 29 June–11 August), including a high-level seminar on the same subject (5-10 August); and a seminar/workshop on the management of human settlements in hot and dry climates, sponsored by UNCHS in co-operation with the United Nations Educational, Scientific and Cultural Organization and the Arab League Educational, Cultural and Scientific Organization (Khartoum, Sudan, 19-29 February). A trilingual thesaurus (English, French, Spanish) on human settlements was prepared with the Swedish Institute of Building Documentation. Three technical co-operation projects were completed during 1984, while 13 new projects were started, making 35 ongoing projects at the end of the year.

Member States expressed interest in innovative data management techniques for human settlements planning. A training package on data management, based on UNCHS workshops, was issued.

Short-term advisory services and preparatory assistance to field projects, with emphasis on supporting human settlements activities in the least developed, land-locked and island developing countries, were provided by UNCHS. In 1984, 42 short-term missions were fielded.

Co-operation with intergovernmental and non-governmental organizations

A report highlighting the co-operation between UNCHS, intergovernmental organizations outside the United Nations system, financial institutions (intergovernmental as well as private, foundations, etc.) and international and national non-governmental organizations (NGOs) was submitted by the Executive Director to the Commission in March 1984.[3]

UNCHS maintained regular contact with many organizations and took part in their meetings.

Other co-operative activities related to information and training. A number of films were produced with, among others, the National Film Board of Canada and the Asian Institute of Technology (Bangkok); most of the films were designed for training in upgrading slums and squatter settlements. UNCHS provided assistance to regional information systems, including the Latin American Information Network on Human Settlements (Bogotá, Colombia) and the Human Settlements Information Network/Africa (Nairobi). A basic list of documents for human settlements libraries in developing countries was being prepared with the Swedish Institute of Building Documentation. The International Development Research Centre (Ottawa, Canada) made a major contribution to human settlements information exchange by providing 10 sets of microfiche of some 2,000 previously unpublished technical reports.

Several universities and training institutes collaborated with UNCHS on courses, seminars, workshops and surveys. For example, the Housing Research and Development Unit of the University of Nairobi made available resource people and undertook field research in connection with UNCHS training courses. Similar collaboration existed with universities in other regions. Resource people from various universities served as consultants and experts to the UNCHS Training Unit (see below).

International Year of Shelter for the Homeless (1987)

A report on the International Year of Shelter for the Homeless (1987) was submitted by the UNCHS Executive Director to the Commission in February 1984.[4] The report pointed out that guidelines on the selection of IYSH projects had been distributed, also in February, to Governments, the United Nations and other international and non-governmental organizations. Also distributed was an IYSH brochure in several languages.

Pointing out that the Commission and the General Assembly had previously agreed that IYSH would not be an end in itself, the Executive Director said that 1987 was intended to be a transitional period between the demonstration and testing of practical action (1984-1986) and the application of new or revised national strategies, policies and programmes (1988-2000). Four major reporting goals needed to be achieved by the end of 1986 for the Year to be a significant transition period, he added. The reports would cover the results of IYSH projects around the world; shelter and settlement conditions and priorities in various countries; IYSH policy and technical options; and shelter in relation to national economic and social development.

The ACC Consultative Committee on Substantive Questions (Programme Matters) considered IYSH at an October 1984 meeting. It was agreed that all United Nations agencies, including the regional commissions, would provide UNCHS with a copy of their current and 1986-1987 work programmes, annotated to indicate those elements that might be relevant to IYSH. It was also agreed that each agency would designate at least one project as an IYSH project.

Meetings were held with United Nations Development Programme (UNDP) resident coordinators who were active in promoting IYSH. In September 1984, the Economic Commission for Latin America and the Caribbean and the United Nations University sponsored a Latin American mayors' conference that focused on low-cost shelter and infrastructure issues. The UNCHS Executive Director spoke on urban explosion and IYSH at a World Social Prospects Association meeting, sponsored by the United Nations Institute for Training and Research at Geneva in November.

On 10 May, the Commission on Human Settlements adopted two resolutions on IYSH. One recommended a draft resolution for adoption by the General Assembly.[5] The Assembly would appeal to Governments that had not made a voluntary contribution to IYSH to do so and to international financial institutions and intergovernmental and non-governmental organizations to provide support. The Commission's resolution included an annex on national action required, including the selection of projects, the distribution of guidelines, the establishment of procedures for reporting on the progress of projects, and the formulation of national shelter strategies to the year 2000. By the second resolution,[6] the Commission invited the developed countries, in co-operation with developing countries and international financial agencies, to consider increasing until 1987 the percentage of financing for shelter and allied services for the most disadvantaged.

ECONOMIC AND SOCIAL COUNCIL ACTION

On 26 July, the Economic and Social Council, on the recommendation of its First Committee, adopted resolution 1984/57 B without vote.

International Year of Shelter for the Homeless
The Economic and Social Council,
Recalling its resolution 1981/69 B of 24 July 1981, in which it noted the recommendation of the Commission on Human Settlements and recommended to the General Assembly that it should proclaim the year 1987 International Year of Shelter for the Homeless,
Recalling also General Assembly resolution 37/221 of 20 December 1982, in which the Assembly proclaimed

the year 1987 International Year of Shelter for the Homeless,
Noting with great appreciation the strong support which the proclamation of an International Year of Shelter for the Homeless has received from Governments and from intergovernmental and non-governmental organizations throughout the world, as evidenced by the fact that more than one hundred countries have already designated national focal points for the Year,
Convinced that, in the implementation of strategies, programmes and projects for the International Year of Shelter for the Homeless, all possible means of co-operation—bilateral, multilateral and multi-bilateral—between and among international agencies and governmental and non-governmental organizations should be utilized to the full,
Having considered the conclusions and recommendations of the Commission on Human Settlements contained in its resolution 7/1 of 10 May 1984,
1. *Welcomes* the conclusions and recommendations of the Commission on Human Settlements contained in its resolution 7/1;
2. *Recommends* the General Assembly to adopt, at its thirty-ninth session, the draft resolution recommended for adoption by the Assembly in Commission on Human Settlements resolution 7/1;
3. *Expresses its appreciation* to those Governments and other institutions that have made pledges of voluntary contributions to the International Year of Shelter for the Homeless, noting that more than 80 per cent of the amount of such pledges to date has come from developing countries;
4. *Again urges* those Governments that have not yet done so to announce their voluntary contributions as soon as possible and appeals to those that have already made pledges to consider increasing, if possible, the amount of such pledges;
5. *Requests* United Nations agencies and organizations, including the regional commissions, bilateral and multilateral financing institutions and other intergovernmental and non-governmental organizations concerned to review their policies and programmes with a view to incorporating in their activities the objectives of the International Year of Shelter for the Homeless.

Economic and Social Council resolution 1984/57 B

26 July 1984   Meeting 49   Adopted without vote

Approved by First Committee (E/1984/146) without vote (parts A and B together), 18 July (meeting 12); draft by Vice-Chairman (E/1984/C.1/L.12, part B), based on informal consultations on draft by Canada, Kenya, Netherlands, Sri Lanka and Uganda (E/1984/C.1/L.5, part B); agenda item 15.

By the original 5-nation draft, the Council would have endorsed, rather than welcomed, the 10 May Commission resolution on IYSH,[5] and would have strongly urged, rather than again urged, Governments to announce their contributions.

GENERAL ASSEMBLY ACTION

On 17 December 1984, on the recommendation of the Second Committee, the General Assembly adopted resolution 39/171 without vote.

International Year of Shelter for the Homeless

The General Assembly,

Recalling its resolutions 37/221 of 20 December 1982 and 38/168 of 19 December 1983 on the International Year of Shelter for the Homeless, as well as Economic and Social Council resolution 1980/67 of 25 July 1980,

Noting with appreciation that over one hundred countries have established national focal points for the International Year of Shelter for the Homeless and that national programmes and projects for the Year are already under way in many countries,

Noting also that most of the voluntary contributions pledged to date have been pledged by developing countries and that further voluntary contributions are needed in order to carry out effectively the overall plans endorsed by the General Assembly for the activities before and during the International Year of Shelter for the Homeless,

Bearing in mind the need for Governments to integrate the objectives of the International Year of Shelter for the Homeless into their current and future national development plans,

Having considered the conclusions and recommendations of the Commission on Human Settlements contained in its resolution 7/1 of 10 May 1984, and Economic and Social Council resolution 1984/57 B of 26 July 1984 on the International Year of Shelter for the Homeless,

1. *Urges* all Governments to intensify their activities related to the International Year of Shelter for the Homeless and in particular to undertake or designate as soon as possible suitable human settlements projects that can serve as demonstration projects in accordance with the guidelines established under the programme for the International Year of Shelter for the Homeless;

2. *Further urges* all Governments to initiate a comprehensive assessment of prospects, priorities and resources regarding shelter and settlements, leading to the formulation of national shelter strategies applicable until the year 2000;

3. *Expresses its appreciation* to those Governments that have already made voluntary contributions and pledges to the International Year of Shelter for the Homeless;

4. *Appeals* to all Governments that have not yet announced voluntary contributions to do so, and to international financial institutions, intergovernmental and non-governmental organizations to provide adequate financial and other support for the programme for the International Year of Shelter for the Homeless;

5. *Invites* the specialized agencies and other organizations of the United Nations system, including the regional commissions, to review their policies and programmes with a view to incorporating and promoting therein activities which serve the objectives of the International Year of Shelter for the Homeless;

6. *Requests* the Secretary-General to submit to the General Assembly at its fortieth session a report on progress achieved in the implementation of the approved programme of measures and activities to be undertaken before and during the International Year of Shelter for the Homeless;

7. *Decides* to include in the provisional agenda of its fortieth session the item entitled "International Year of Shelter for the Homeless".

General Assembly resolution 39/171

17 December 1984   Meeting 103   Adopted without vote

Approved by Second Committee (A/39/790/Add.10) without vote, 30 November (meeting 55); draft by Vice-Chairman (A/C.2/39/L.91), based on informal consultations on draft by Canada, Colombia, Ecuador, India, Jamaica, Kenya, Liberia, Netherlands, Philippines, Romania, Sri Lanka, Uganda and Zambia (A/C.2/39/L.22); agenda item 80 *(j)*.

Meeting numbers. GA 39th session: 2nd Committee 33, 37, 40, 55; plenary 103.

The original 13-nation draft did not contain the provision that became paragraph 2 of the adopted text and, in the first preambular paragraph, did not refer to the 1980 Economic and Social Council resolution putting forward guidelines for international years.[7] By the original, the Assembly would have appealed for voluntary contributions from all Governments, especially those of developed countries and others in a position to do so, instead of merely appealing to all Governments that had not announced contributions. Also, instead of inviting United Nations agencies and organizations to review their policies and programmes, the Assembly would have requested them to do so.

National action for human settlements

In accordance with a 1979 General Assembly request,[8] the UNCHS Executive Director submitted in January 1984 to the Commission a progress report[9] on the implementation of the recommendations for national action adopted in 1976 by Habitat: United Nations Conference on Human Settlements.[10] Nineteen countries—Costa Rica, Egypt, Finland, France, Gabon, Greece, Hungary, Israel, Kenya, the Netherlands, New Zealand, Norway, Peru, the Philippines, Solomon Islands, Sweden, Thailand, Turkey and the United Arab Emirates—had responded to a UNCHS request for information. The Executive Director stated that the information collected might have been more valid had the response rate been higher. He suggested that information provided in the future be based on a regular assessment by Governments of their human settlements strategies, policies and programmes. A synthesis of those national reports would undoubtedly be more productive than questionnaire responses.

By a resolution of 10 May,[11] the Commission invited all Member States to submit at its 1986 session a report on the implementation over the past decade, 1976-1985, of the Habitat recommendations.

Human settlements information

In response to a 1982 Commission resolution,[12] the UNCHS Executive Director submitted in January 1984 a report on a systematic and comprehensive approach to information for human settlements.[13] Four main areas of concern were identified—statistical data; scientific and technological knowledge; "popular", or indigenous, knowledge; and communication techniques. A number of measures at the national and international levels which might be undertaken to integrate information activities into a coherent system were recommended. Among them were making Governments aware of the need for more effective utilization of information; providing technical support for the establishment of information systems; developing compatible standards and common methods of information processing; encouraging municipal governments to concentrate on basic data collection, such as cadastral surveys; increasing dissemination of research and technical project results through publications and bibliographical data bases; and training staff for documentation and information services. A list of basic human settlements data requirements and a summary of UNCHS information activities were annexed to the report.

The Commission, by a resolution of 10 May,[14] endorsed the report. It urged Governments to formulate human settlements information and communication policies and requested the Executive Director to assist them in that regard. By another resolution of the same date,[15] it invited UNCHS, in co-operation with UNDP and the United Nations Industrial Development Organization, to disseminate information on construction technologies among developing countries.

Human settlements training

The UNCHS Executive Director, responding to a 1982 Commission resolution,[12] submitted in January 1984 a report on human settlements training.[16] Reviewing training in human settlements for developing countries, the report stated that the overriding training issue was the need to evolve new forms of regional and subregional collaboration, and that current systems of national action and international support were failing to establish training institutions on a realistic scale. Collaborative approaches were required to produce locally based training materials, to train local trainers, and to maintain a flow of information to Governments, national training institutions, aid agencies, NGOs and community groups.

The report discussed multilateral and bilateral approaches to training, the dominant role of university training in developed countries, and the deficiencies of current training efforts, and made recommendations to developed and developing countries and to UNCHS, among them: Developing countries should encourage their training institutions to focus on practical problem-solving and to be interdisciplinary and innovative; accept primary responsibility for financing their own internal training programmes; and create a cadre of skilled trainers. Training as a development process required the active participation of bilateral and multilateral agencies in the developed countries. Bilateral agencies should ensure that there was a strong training component in every development project they supported; funding agencies should explore local and regional training capabilities before sending trainees to developed countries. UNCHS should sponsor collaboration with other United Nations organizations, funding agencies and international NGOs, in order to improve training activities. It should take a leading role in designing methods for analysing training needs and capabilities.

By a resolution of 10 May,[17] the Commission outlined a systematic approach to training for human settlements. It endorsed the report of the Executive Director and took note of the recommendations made in *Sharing Responsibilities and Roles for Training in Planning and Development*, a report prepared by a seminar of experts, organized by the Centre for Human Settlements, University of British Columbia (Vancouver, Canada). It urged Governments to expand their training programmes and requested the Executive Director to take specific steps to enhance manpower development. Among the steps recommended were the devising of criteria for assessing manpower and training needs, the preparation of manpower development strategies and the identification of training institutions that could facilitate collective self-reliance in manpower development.

Assistance to developing countries

A report on financial and other assistance to developing countries for human settlements was submitted by the UNCHS Executive Director to the Commission in February 1984,[18] pursuant to a 1979 General Assembly resolution.[19] The report focused on the distribution of aid for human settlements among developing countries according to regional distribution, distribution by level of income, and distribution among the 36 least developed and the other developing countries. It identified bilateral and multilateral donors and the recipients of such aid, as well as emerging trends and issues, and discussed the results of a questionnaire sent to Member States; it found that while responses were few, they expressed some useful viewpoints. For example, the United States Agency for International Development cited several problems associated with human settlements assistance, including absorptive capacity which limited where funds could be used, project delays, lack of co-ordination and subsidized interest rates. In conclusion, the report pointed out the low, and even declining, priority that the human settlements sector commanded in donor aid. It suggested that the question of targets in assistance levels be considered, a question never addressed in the human settlements field.

Rather than directing attention exclusively to increasing the flow of assistance to human settlements, it was important to find ways to make more effective the existing flow, the report concluded. Consideration should be given to broadening the channels through which assistance was provided; in that context, community organizations and church groups had a valuable role to play. A co-ordinating UNCHS information centre that could identify the various needs of developing countries for assistance in human settlements was needed. On a national level, focal points for human settlements could be established within national aid agencies, also to facilitate an exchange of views and experiences.

By a resolution of 10 May,[20] the Commission requested the Executive Director to improve information on financial and other assistance; it called on major donor and lending agencies to give him full support and on Governments to submit their views on the policies followed for such assistance. By another resolution of the same date,[6] the Commission invited developed countries, within a new approach to the financing of housing in the framework of IYSH (see above), to consider providing for or increasing financing for shelter and services for the most disadvantaged.

Proposed financial and advisory institution for Asia and the Pacific

In response to a May 1983 resolution of the Commission on Human Settlements,[21] a further step was taken in relation to the establishment of an Asian human settlements bank. The UNCHS Executive Director reported to the Commission in February 1984 that he had called a meeting of a small working group of governmental experts and others.[22] The group, composed of experts from India, the Philippines and ESCAP, an observer from the Asian Development Bank, an expert consultant and a UNCHS officer, met at Manila, Philippines, from 25 to 28 January 1984. The group recommended that the Executive Director initiate high-level consultations with countries of the region and the Asian Development Bank to explore the role the Bank might play in creating the proposed institution. It also recommended that a regional forum discuss the proposal and appoint a committee of prospective member countries which, in co-operation with UNCHS and other concerned parties, would finalize its charter.

Human settlements in territories occupied by Israel

At its 1984 session, the Commission on Human Settlements adopted two resolutions relating to Israel's policy of establishing settlements in the territories occupied by it as a result of previous armed conflict in the Middle East (see p. 316). By the first resolution, adopted on 9 May,[23] the Commission condemned Israel's settlement policies in the occupied Palestinian territories and rejected its actions to change their demographic composition. It reaffirmed the need for a comprehensive report on the impact of the Israeli settlements on the security and social, economic and cultural life of the Palestinians, and requested that a UNCHS senior representative accompany United Nations experts to the territories in order to prepare the report for the Commission's 1985 session. It also requested that the General Assembly take appropriate measures if Israel refused to co-operate in implementing the 1983 Assembly[24] and Commission resolutions.[21]

By the second resolution, of 10 May 1984,[25] the Commission recommended that the UNCHS Executive Director consider the possibility, in connection with IYSH, of carrying out a housing programme for the Palestinians in the occupied territories. It requested him to submit a study on the subject in 1985.

Assistance to Africa

In 1984, UNCHS co-operated with various institutions in Africa, including the Organization of African Unity (OAU) and Shelter-Afrique (see below). It also maintained regular contact with the Africa Union of Architects (AUA), a member of the International Union of Architects.

A financial contribution was made by UNCHS to a Seminar on Education of Architects, Planners and Designers of the Human Habitat (Yamoussukro, Ivory Coast, January). AUA provided UNCHS, at its request, with a list of members who could assist in the training of skilled personnel for the construction industry in Africa. Representatives of UNCHS attended the first triennial World Congress of AUA (Yaoundé, Cameroon, May).

Assistance to victims of apartheid

By a resolution of 9 May 1984,[26] the Commission on Human Settlements strongly condemned South Africa's *apartheid* régime for its inhuman repression and its illegal occupation of Namibia, as well as its acts of aggression against the front-line and other neighbouring States. It commended the UNCHS Executive Director for his efforts to aid the victims of *apartheid*, in implementation of its May 1983 resolution,[27] and further commended OAU member States and others for their support of efforts against *apartheid*. The Executive Director was requested to continue to provide additional assistance to those countries in which human settlements had been disrupted or overburdened by the South African régime, and to report in 1985 on progress made.

Co-operation with Shelter-Afrique

Having noted the various organizational steps taken to enable Shelter-Afrique (a specialized housing finance institution) to commence operations at its headquarters at Nairobi, the Commission on Human Settlements, by a resolution of 9 May 1984,[28] requested the UNCHS Executive Director to continue to provide assistance to Shelter-Afrique and to report in 1985 on the specific nature of that assistance and on the progress made in finalizing the draft memorandum of understanding, identifying specific areas and the forms of co-operation. The draft memorandum had been prepared by UNCHS.

Participation of youth in the solution of human settlements problems

By a resolution of 10 May 1984,[29] the Commission on Human Settlements acknowledged that the solution of housing problems was a long-term process, requiring the participation of all population groups, and that the participation of youth in the solution of those problems was feasible only under conditions of lasting peace and security. The Commission urged Governments to curb the arms race and focus their efforts on ensuring that the social and economic needs of youth for shelter, education and related infrastructure were met. It invited all countries to prepare information on their national experience with the participation of youth in solving housing problems, and requested the UNCHS Executive Director to report on that experience in 1986.

REFERENCES

[1]HS/C/8/2. [2]YUN 1981, p. 846. [3]HS/C/7/INF.3. [4]HS/C/7/5. [5]A/39/8 (res. 7/1). [6]*Ibid.* (res. 7/10). [7]YUN 1980, p. 1029, ESC res. 1980/67, 25 July 1980. [8]YUN 1979, p. 709, GA res. 34/116, 14 Dec. 1979. [9]HS/C/7/7 & Add.1. [10]YUN 1976, p. 444. [11]A/39/8 (res. 7/11). [12]YUN 1982, p. 1038. [13]HS/C/7/4. [14]A/39/8 (res. 7/9). [15]*Ibid.* (res. 7/15). [16]HS/C/7/3. [17]A/39/8 (res. 7/14). [18]HS/C/7/6. [19]YUN 1979, p. 708, GA res. 34/114, 14 Dec. 1979. [20]A/39/8 (res. 7/12). [21]YUN 1983, p. 798. [22]HS/C/7/2/Add.2. [23]A/39/8 (res. 7/2). [24]YUN 1983, p. 335, GA res. 38/166, 19 Dec. 1983. [25]A/39/8 (res. 7/8). [26]*Ibid.* (res. 7/3). [27]YUN 1983, p. 799. [28]A/39/8 (res. 7/6). [29]*Ibid.* (res. 7/4).

Organizational questions

Co-ordination in the UN system

Report of the Secretary-General. Pursuant to a December 1983 General Assembly resolution,[1] the Secretary-General submitted to the Assembly in October 1984 a report[2] on his efforts to arrange UNCHS participation in all aspects of the work of ACC in order to strengthen the co-ordination of human settlements programmes within the United Nations system. He said that UNCHS had been kept informed on matters under consideration in ACC and its subsidiary bodies, and had been invited to participate in those meetings in which it had a direct interest. He would review those arrangements in

the near future, bearing in mind the UNCHS mandate and relevant Assembly resolutions. In that context, he noted the relevant comments of CPC at its 1984 session and Economic and Social Council resolution 1984/57 A concerning the need for greater co-ordination on human settlements (see below).

GENERAL ASSEMBLY ACTION

The General Assembly, on the recommendation of the Second Committee, adopted resolution 39/170 B without vote on 17 December 1984.

Co-ordination of human settlements programmes within the United Nations system

The General Assembly,

Reaffirming its resolution 35/77 C of 5 December 1980, in which it invited the Secretary-General to arrange, in consultation with the members of the Administrative Committee on Co-ordination, for the United Nations Centre for Human Settlements (Habitat) to participate in all aspects of the work of that Committee and its subsidiary machinery,

Recalling its resolution 37/223 C of 20 December 1982, in which it requested the Secretary-General to accelerate his efforts in arranging for such participation and to report thereon to the General Assembly at its thirty-eighth session,

Recalling also its resolution 38/167 B of 19 December 1983 in which it took note of the report of the Secretary-General summarizing decision 1983/18 of 27 October 1983 of the Administrative Committee on Co-ordination, which decision it noted did not completely meet the requirement of its earlier resolutions 35/77 C and 37/223 C, and requested the Secretary-General to report to the General Assembly at its thirty-ninth session on the implementation of its resolutions on the question,

Noting the views of the Economic and Social Council, contained in its resolution 1984/57 A of 26 July 1984, particularly paragraph 6 thereof,

Having considered the report of the Secretary-General concerning the co-ordination of human settlements programmes within the United Nations system, prepared in response to General Assembly resolution 38/167 B,

1. *Takes note* of the report of the Secretary-General;

2. *Takes note,* in particular, of resolution 7/5 of 9 May 1984 of the Commission on Human Settlements, on the question of a biennial cycle of sessions for the Commission, and again requests the Commission, pursuant to General Assembly decision 38/429 of 19 December 1983 and Economic and Social Council decision 1984/104 of 10 February 1984, to consider adopting a biennial cycle of sessions;

3. *Welcomes,* in particular, the intention of the Secretary-General to review in the near future the existing arrangements regarding the participation of the United Nations Centre for Human Settlements (Habitat) in the work of the Administrative Committee on Co-ordination in the light of the Centre's mandate and responsibilities and the relevant General Assembly resolutions;

4. *Requests* the Secretary-General to report to the General Assembly at its fortieth session on the implementation of its resolutions on this question, taking into account the pertinent comments of the Committee for Programme and Co-ordination at its twenty-fourth session.

General Assembly resolution 39/170 B

17 December 1984   Meeting 103   Adopted without vote

Approved by Second Committee (A/39/790/ Add.10) without vote (parts A and B together), 30 November (meeting 55); draft by Vice-Chairman (A/C.2/39/L.90, part B), based on informal consultations on draft by Canada, Colombia, Ethiopia, Gabon, India, Jamaica, Kenya, Liberia, Netherlands, Philippines, Sri Lanka, Uganda and Zambia (A/C.2/39/L.21, part B); agenda item 80 *(j)*.

Meeting numbers. GA 39th session: 2nd Committee 33, 37, 40, 55; plenary 103.

The adopted text did not contain a provision included in the original 13-nation draft. By that provision, the Assembly would have restated its conviction that full participation by UNCHS in all aspects of the work of ACC and its subsidiary machinery was necessary for the effective co-ordination of United Nations human settlements programmes. By the original draft, the Assembly also would have taken note of, rather than welcomed, the Secretary-General's intention to review arrangements of such participation.

Cross-organizational programme analysis

In response to a 1982 CPC decision,[3] the Secretary-General presented in April 1984 a cross-organizational programme analysis (COPA) of the human settlements activities of the United Nations system.[4] Two innovations were particularly important for that analysis: an initial review by the Commission on Human Settlements, at its 1983 session,[5] of the structure of activities in relation to national needs and the use of information on activities over three bienniums.

A number of conclusions could be drawn which suggested a need for remedial action, the analysis stated. The first was that a practical working definition of what constituted a human settlements activity did not exist; without such a definition, effective programming and co-ordination were extremely difficult.

None the less, it seemed that the United Nations human settlements activities responded to Governments' needs, but there were problems concerning priorities and emphasis. Total resources seemed to have increased since the 1976 Habitat Conference,[6] a growth accounted for almost entirely by the World Health Organization. Although UNCHS had also had some real growth, there had been no real growth in human settlements activities as a whole and their share of total programme resources had declined. Moreover, while inter-governmental bodies had emphasized a number of areas—shelter, public participation, regional planning and finance—there were few discrete programme activities in those areas, and there had been no real change in emphasis among programmes since the 1976 Conference, despite modifications in emphasis by the General Assembly in the International Development Strategy for the Third United Nations Development Decade and by the Commission on Human Settlements.

The analysis showed that the degree of co-operation among the organizations concerned with human settlements was not so high as in other activities which had been the subject of COPAs. The Commission had yet to play a decisive role in co-ordinating system-wide activities.

A number of possible recommendations flowed from the conclusions. First, there should be a thorough review of programme priorities. In addition, CPC might wish to recommend: that an urgent effort be made to elaborate a practical working definition of human settlements activities and to establish sub-categories for them; that a more deliberate effort be made to improve the flow of information about human settlements, with all organizations of the system adjusting their information systems under the guidance of the Advisory Committee for the Co-ordination of Information Systems; and that the Commission co-ordinate activities better, with UNCHS supporting the Commission's work more actively.

Over the longer term, a few areas should emerge with particularly high priority in which many organizations would be involved, the analysis stated. For those areas, CPC might wish to recommend that joint thematic reviews be carried out by specialist staff, patterned along the model of thematic programming used in the preparation of the system-wide medium-term environment programme.

Commenting on the analysis in May 1984,[7] CPC noted that human settlements conditions remained for developing countries, especially the least developed, a matter of grave concern. Certain groups were identified as requiring special attention, for example the elderly, the disabled, youth and women. CPC pointed out that although the Commission on Human Settlements had been consulted on the preliminary analysis, it had not been able to review the final version and therefore its substantive comments had not been available to CPC. CPC also noted that, while most relevant activities had been included, those of the Office of the United Nations High Commissioner for Refugees had not and full information on the rural settlements activities of the World Bank also had been omitted. It observed that the imperatives agreed upon by the 1976 Conference did not seem to have led to fundamental changes in the *de facto* orientation of United Nations human settlements activities.

CPC made several general recommendations. It affirmed its earlier recommendations that COPAs, together with CPC's conclusions and recommendations, be reviewed and followed up by the competent intergovernmental bodies, and in the case of the human settlements COPA, CPC recommended that it be placed before the Commission on Human Settlements in 1985 and that CPC deal with the question again in 1986. It further recommended that the analysis be the subject of a joint CPC/ACC meeting, should subsequent developments make that desirable. Specifically, CPC stated that a more precise definition of human settlements activities was necessary. It recommended that intergovernmental bodies, in particular the Commission on Human Settlements, review the question of programme priorities; that co-ordination be reinforced at both the inter-agency and intergovernmental levels; and that new efforts be undertaken to identify ways to optimize human settlements resources.

CPC further recommended that the Commission carry out its co-ordination function more vigorously and that UNCHS assist the Commission; for that purpose, the Centre should help organize a systematic exchange of information, promote programme cohesion through prior consultations on programme budgets, and determine possible revisions to the medium-term plan.

It also recommended that the tools for co-ordination of operational activities—the resident United Nations co-ordinators and assistance to Governments in country programming—be focused more effectively on human settlements, stressing in particular information exchange among concerned organizations.

In section VI of resolution 1984/61 A, the Economic and Social Council invited the Commission on Human Settlements to give due consideration to the analysis and the CPC recommendations and, with UNCHS, to exercise vigorously its co-ordination role.

In resolution 1984/57 A on the Commission's report (see above), the Council expressed support for the efforts of the Commission and UNCHS to achieve greater harmonization of United Nations human settlements activities and for CPC's recommendations.

The General Assembly, in resolution 39/238, approved the CPC recommendations (see Chapter XXIV of this section).

Joint meetings with UNEP

Noting the May 1983 decision of the UNEP Governing Council expressing the view that annual joint meetings with UNCHS would no longer be necessary after 1984 because of the expected proximity of the headquarters of both organizations at Nairobi,[8] the Commission on Human Settlements, by a resolution of 10 May 1984,[9] recognized that changes in the practice of holding those annual joint meetings had institutional implications. It requested the UNCHS Executive Director to assess the implications of the discontinuation and decided to take up the question in 1985.

Commission on Human Settlements

Biennial cycle of sessions

Following a decision (1984/104) by the Economic and Social Council to request its subsidiary bodies that currently met on an annual basis to consider on an experimental basis a biennial cycle of meetings (see Chapter XXIV of this section), the UNCHS secretariat expressed its views with regard to that request in a March note to the Commission on Human Settlements.[10] Should the Commission decide to adopt a biennial cycle of sessions, the note stated, the timing of the change-over was crucial. If the Commission were to go on a biennial cycle as of the conclusion of its 1985 session, for example, it would not meet again until 1987, the International Year of Shelter for the Homeless. As a matter of practical necessity and legislative injunction, it would appear that such a change-over should not take place before IYSH. Since there were numerous other implications, the note suggested that the Commission might wish to take up the issue again in 1985.

On 9 May 1984,[11] the Commission decided to consider the matter at its 1985 session on the basis of a report to be prepared by the UNCHS Executive Director.

Both the Council (resolution 1984/57 A) and the General Assembly (resolution 39/170 B) took note of the Commission's resolution and again requested it to consider adopting a biennial cycle of sessions.

1986 Commission session

Two possible themes—public participation, and building materials and technology—that might be discussed by the Commission in 1986 were put forward in February 1984.[12]

The Commission, by a resolution of 10 May,[13] decided that the theme at its 1986 session should be community participation in human settlement work, and invited the UNCHS Executive Director to submit an outline for the theme paper in 1985.

REFERENCES

[1]YUN 1983, p. 799, GA res. 38/167 B, 19 Dec. 1983. [2]A/39/547. [3]YUN 1982, p. 1240. [4]E/AC.51/1984/5 & Corr.1. [5]YUN 1983, p. 800. [6]YUN 1976, p. 441. [7]A/39/38. [8]YUN 1983, p. 774. [9]A/39/8 (res. 7/13). [10]HS/C/7/9. [11]A/39/8 (res. 7/5). [12]HS/C/7/10/Add.1. [13]A/39/8 (res. 7/7).

Chapter XVIII

Human rights

In 1984, the United Nations continued its efforts to foster human rights and fundamental freedoms world-wide and to curtail their violation. Through its Commission on Human Rights and Sub-Commission on Prevention of Discrimination and Protection of Minorities, it responded to the challenges posed by discrimination in all its aspects and violations of the entire range of civil and political, as well as economic, social and cultural, rights. Engaging a large part of its attention were denial of the right to self-determination of peoples and gross human rights violations in various countries, primarily the system of *apartheid*, and violations of the human rights of the individual. The Secretary-General added his concern for individuals whose rights might have been violated and stated his commitment to seek to facilitate the release of those who might have been imprisoned for political reasons (p. 8).

In addition to its endeavours to define the rights to development, to food, and to education and employment, the United Nations broadened its activities in the area of scientific and technological progress in relation to human rights.

During the year, the Convention against Torture and Other Cruel, Inhuman or Degrading Treatment or Punishment was adopted, marking an achievement in United Nations efforts towards eventual respect for all human rights through international human rights instruments. Adherence to these instruments continued to be encouraged, and elaboration of other international standards moved forward on behalf of the child, those detained due to mental ill-health, indigenous populations, migrant workers, minorities and non-citizens, on the rights to development and to promote human rights, and in respect of computerized files.

Actions on these and other human rights taken by the Commission, at its fortieth session held at Geneva from 6 February to 16 March 1984,[1] were embodied in 64 resolutions and 17 decisions; those taken by the Sub-Commission, at its thirty-seventh session, held also at Geneva, from 6 to 31 August,[2] in 37 resolutions and six decisions. Action taken on their recommendations by the Economic and Social Council was embodied in 22 resolutions and 25 decisions; those taken by the General Assembly, in 31 resolutions and two decisions.

Topics related to this chapter. International peace and security. Africa: South Africa and *apartheid*. Americas: Central America situation. Asia and the Pacific: Kampuchea situation; Afghanistan situation; Iran-Iraq armed conflict. Mediterranean: Cyprus question. Middle East: Middle East situation; territories occupied by Israel; Palestinian prisoners. Social and cultural development. Health and human resources. Women. Namibia. Other colonial Territories.

Discrimination

Racial discrimination

Second Decade to Combat Racism and Racial Discrimination (1983-1993)

Implementation of the Programme for the Decade

In 1984, in keeping with a 1983 General Assembly resolution,[3] the Programme for the first Decade for Action to Combat Racism and Racial Discrimination (1973-1983)[4] continued to be applied and implemented, pending adoption of a plan of activities for 1985-1989 requested of the Secretary-General by the same resolution.

As called for in the Programme, the Secretary-General submitted to the Economic and Social Council in April 1984 two reports on activities relating to the Decade. His annual report on this topic, with later addenda,[5] summarized actions, suggestions and trends emerging from deliberations of United Nations bodies, specialized agencies and other international and regional organizations, and transmitted information on activities by non-governmental organizations (NGOs). The second report, also with later addenda,[6] summarized replies received from Governments on legislative, administrative and other measures they had taken to implement the Programme.

Action by the Commission on Human Rights. On 28 February 1984,[7] the Commission on Human Rights took note of the 1983 Declaration and Programme of Action for the Second Decade to Combat Racism and Racial Discrimination.[8] Stressing the need for vigorous action to implement United Nations resolutions on *apartheid*, racism and racial discrimination, the Commission endorsed the September 1983 decision of its Sub-Commission[9] to include in a study to be carried out by Asbjorn Eide (Norway) recommendations on ways of ensuring such implementation.

ECONOMIC AND SOCIAL COUNCIL ACTION

Having considered the Secretary-General's reports on implementation of the Programme for the first Decade, the Economic and Social Council, in May 1984, adopted decision 1984/151 without vote.

Reports of the Secretary-General relating to the Second Decade to Combat Racism and Racial Discrimination

At its 20th plenary meeting, on 24 May 1984, the Council took note of the reports of the Secretary-General submitted in accordance with paragraphs 18 *(e)* and *(f)* of the Programme for the Decade for Action to Combat Racism and Racial Discrimination and paragraph 7 of General Assembly resolution 38/14 of 22 November 1983 on the Second Decade to Combat Racism and Racial Discrimination.

Economic and Social Council decision 1984/151

Adopted without vote

Oral proposal by President; agenda item 3.

Plan of activities for 1985-1989

In line with the goals of the Programme of Action for the Second Decade, the Secretary-General submitted to the General Assembly, through the Economic and Social Council, a draft plan for 1985-1989, as well as a statement of programme budget implications for the activities recommended for 1985.[10]

The draft plan suggested specific activities, such as the preparation of model legislation; training courses for legislative draftsmen; a review of national legislation in conjunction with the Council's review of the Programme of Action for the Decade; and periodic examination of the functioning of the 1973 International Convention on the Suppression and Punishment of the Crime of *Apartheid*[11] and of the 1965 International Convention on the Elimination of All Forms of Racial Discrimination.[12] Priority could be assigned to completing the ongoing elaboration of a draft convention on the rights of migrant workers and their families, a draft declaration on the rights of minorities and draft standards on the human rights of indigenous populations (see below).

Teaching materials to promote educational activities against racism and racial discrimination, with particular emphasis at the primary and secondary levels of education, could be prepared by the United Nations Educational, Scientific and Cultural Organization (UNESCO), and an information programme developed and carried out by the United Nations Department of Public Information. International and regional seminars could be organized on topics such as human rights of persons belonging to ethnic groups in countries of immigration, and equality of treatment for persons belonging to ethnic and racial minorities and disadvantaged groups.

Also suggested were an updating of a 1976 revised special study on racial discrimination in all spheres,[13] studies on racial discrimination and world peace and racial discrimination in immigration laws and practices, as well as publication of a manual of existing models of national institutions promoting tolerance and harmony and combating racism and racial discrimination.

The following activities were recommended for 1985: convening of an international seminar on community relations commissions and their functions, preparation and publication of a global compilation of national legislation against racial discrimination, a study on the role of private group action to combat racism and racial discrimination, and publication and dissemination of pamphlets on problems of racial discrimination.

ECONOMIC AND SOCIAL COUNCIL ACTION

On 24 May 1984, the Economic and Social Council adopted resolution 1984/43 by recorded vote.

Second Decade to Combat Racism and Racial Discrimination

The Economic and Social Council,

Welcoming the proclamation by the General Assembly in its resolution 38/14 of 22 November 1983 of the Second Decade to Combat Racism and Racial Discrimination,

Bearing in mind the Programme of Action for the Second Decade approved by the General Assembly in its resolution 38/14,

Mindful of the responsibilities conferred upon it by the General Assembly of co-ordinating the implementation of the Programme of Action and of evaluating the activities to be undertaken during the Second Decade,

Recalling the guidance provided to the Secretary-General by the General Assembly in its resolution 38/14 for the preparation of the plan of activities for the period 1985-1989 for implementing the Programme of Action and achieving the objectives of the Second Decade,

Having considered the plan of activities for the period 1985-1989 proposed by the Secretary-General,

1. *Welcomes* the adoption by the General Assembly of the Programme of Action for the Second Decade to Combat Racism and Racial Discrimination;

2. *Takes note* of the plan of activities for the period 1985-1989 proposed by the Secretary-General;

3. *Requests* the Secretary-General to submit to the General Assembly at its thirty-ninth session a revised plan of activities for the period 1985-1989, taking into account the priorities reflected in the Programme of Action for the Second Decade and the relevant resolutions and recommendations, including the Programme for the Decade for Action to Combat Racism and Racial Discrimination and the programme of activities to be undertaken during the second half of that Decade, as contained in General Assembly resolutions 3057(XXVIII) of 2 November 1973, particularly paragraphs 18 *(b)* and *(e)* thereof, and 34/24 of 15 November 1979;

4. *Invites* all Governments, United Nations bodies, the specialized agencies and other intergovernmental or-

ganizations, as well as interested non-governmental organizations in consultative status with the Economic and Social Council, to participate in the implementation of the plan of activities for the Second Decade by intensifying and expanding their efforts to ensure the rapid elimination of *apartheid* and all forms of racism and racial discrimination;

5. *Decides* to consider on an annual basis an item entitled "Implementation of the Programme of Action for the Second Decade to Combat Racism and Racial Discrimination".

Economic and Social Council resolution 1984/43

24 May 1984   Meeting 20   43-5-2 (recorded vote)

19-nation draft (E/1984/L.29); agenda item 2.
Sponsors: Algeria, Benin, Botswana, Congo, Djibouti, Egypt, Gambia, Liberia, Mali, Morocco, Nigeria, Rwanda, Sierra Leone, Somalia, Swaziland, Tunisia, Uganda, Zaire, Zambia.
Meeting numbers. ESC 17, 20.

Recorded vote in Council as follows:

In favour: Algeria, Argentina, Austria, Benin, Botswana, Brazil, Bulgaria, China, Colombia, Congo, Costa Rica, Djibouti, Ecuador, Finland, German Democratic Republic, Greece, Indonesia, Japan, Lebanon, Malaysia, Mali, Mexico, Pakistan, Papua New Guinea, Poland, Portugal, Qatar, Romania, Rwanda, Saudi Arabia, Sierra Leone, Somalia, Sri Lanka, Suriname, Swaziland, Sweden, Thailand, Tunisia, Uganda, USSR, Venezuela, Yugoslavia, Zaire.
Against: Canada, Germany, Federal Republic of, Luxembourg, Netherlands, United Kingdom.
Abstaining: France, New Zealand.

Before adoption of the draft resolution as a whole, a vote was taken on the second part of paragraph 3 at Finland's suggestion. The wording was retained by a recorded vote of 34 to 7, with 7 abstentions.

Among the States explaining their negative votes on the paragraph, Canada and the Federal Republic of Germany said it reintroduced elements that had broken the unity of the campaign against racism and racial discrimination during the first Decade, in particular the 1979 Assembly resolution on racial discrimination.[14] France pointed out that the 1979 resolution included passages it could not accept. Luxembourg also objected to the reference to that resolution. Canada, along with New Zealand, recalled that it had voted against that resolution because of its political aspects which were alien to the campaign. In the opinion of the Netherlands, paragraph 3 changed the mandate given to the Secretary-General by the Assembly in November 1983,[3] a change that Canada, the Federal Republic of Germany, Luxembourg and the United Kingdom claimed the Council did not have the right to make. France considered such a change irregular. Adoption of the text, the Netherlands added, might jeopardize its co-operation with respect to the Second Decade.

Of those abstaining on paragraph 3, Japan regretted the reference to the 1979 Assembly resolution and said that, in requesting the Secretary-General to submit a revised plan, the Council exceeded the powers conferred on it. Greece noted that the paragraph mentioned resolutions it did not support; similarly, Costa Rica said the para-

graph referred to resolutions defining racism in a manner it rejected. Portugal felt it would have been preferable to defer consideration of substantive questions to the Assembly's 1984 session and to avoid reopening questions which made it impossible to maintain a consensus.

Finland gave as reason for its abstention on the paragraph that it contained elements which jeopardized the consensus without which it would be difficult to obtain the goals of the Decade. Austria said it might destroy consensus and did not contribute to the joint effort to eliminate racism. Sweden hoped that the African Group of Member States at the United Nations would try to restore the consensus reached at the previous Assembly session.

Argentina stressed that its positive vote on the text did not mean that it agreed with United Nations resolutions which were not consistent with its foreign policy. Though voting in favour of retaining the second part of paragraph 3, Mexico reiterated its reservations with regard to the programme of activities for the second half of the first Decade adopted in 1979.[15]

The USSR said it did not see what there was to arouse such strong objections among certain Western countries; the text did not directly condemn Israel's racist and genocidal policies nor did it advocate specific measures against the South African *apartheid* régime, and it did not even mention the deterioration of the situation concerning racial discrimination in the world. The resolutions referred to in paragraph 3 had been adopted by an absolute majority and the Council therefore must refer to them and observe their provisions; moreover, the draft plan of activities did not follow the Programme of Action adopted by the Assembly, hence the need to request the Secretary-General to submit a revised plan.

Algeria stated that, for a large number of countries, reaching a consensus meant negotiating a position of principle on zionism or *apartheid* rather than agreeing on the specific means—such as boycotting the racist South African régime—in achieving a common objective.

The United States did not participate in the vote, saying it had decided to discontinue its participation in the activities of the Decade after adoption of the 1975 Assembly resolution calling zionism a form of racism;[16] since that travesty of the notion of racism had been retained in the Programme of Action for the Second Decade, the United States had no choice but to abstain from all participation in the proposed activities.

The Observer for Israel noted that paragraph 3 of the adopted text referred to the 1979 Assembly resolution adopting the programme of activities for the second half of the first Decade;[14] Israel had rejected paragraphs 8 and 23 of that programme. In calling on United Nations organizations to continue investigating Israeli policies and practices based on various forms of racial discrimination, paragraph 8 made the implication, without any attempt to establish the facts, that such policies existed in Israel.

The Observer for Saudi Arabia expressed surprise that some countries were protesting against the reference to an Assembly resolution defining zionism as a form of racial discrimination but not at the Israeli practices—genocide, torture and resettlement of the population—in the occupied territories.

CERD activities. In March and August 1984, the Committee on the Elimination of Racial Discrimination (CERD) (see below) considered the draft plan of activities for 1985-1989, among other documents, and examined ways to contribute to the realization of the objectives of the Second Decade. It concluded that the two studies on articles 4 (on promotion of ideas against racial discrimination) and 7 (calling for measures to combat prejudices leading to racial discrimination) of the 1965 International Convention on the Elimination of All Forms of Racial Discrimination,[12] which it had contributed to the Second World Conference to Combat Racism and Racial Discrimination in August 1983,[17] would constitute useful tools for carrying out the activities for the Decade. Accordingly, CERD requested the General Assembly on 21 August 1984[18] to authorize publication of the studies so as to give them the widest possible dissemination.

Sub-Commission action. Noting the plan of activities proposed for 1985-1989, the Sub-Commission on 28 August 1984[19] recommended implementation of the proposed activities in education, information dissemination, research and advisory services. It emphasized that, in preparing teaching materials and aids, special attention should be paid to removing derogatory references to race and xenophobia from all educational literature. Drawing attention to the continued existence of organizations founded on racism and preaching violence, the Sub-Commission expressed the wish that legal measures be taken against them.

GENERAL ASSEMBLY ACTION

As requested by the Council, the Secretary-General submitted in September 1984 for the General Assembly's consideration a report containing additions to the plan for 1985-1989.[20] These included specific action to combat *apartheid*, international and regional activities, and measures for programme co-ordination and reporting.

On 23 November 1984, acting on the recommendation of the Third (Social, Humanitarian and Cultural) Committee, the Assembly adopted resolution 39/16 without vote.

Second Decade to Combat Racism and Racial Discrimination

The General Assembly,

Reaffirming its objective contained in the Charter of the United Nations to achieve international co-operation in solving international problems of an economic, social, cultural or humanitarian character, and in promoting and encouraging respect for human rights and fundamental freedoms for all without distinction as to race, sex, language or religion,

Reaffirming its firm determination and its commitment to eradicate totally and unconditionally racism in all its forms, racial discrimination and *apartheid,*

Recalling the Universal Declaration of Human Rights, the International Convention on the Elimination of All Forms of Racial Discrimination, the International Convention on the Suppression and Punishment of the Crime of *Apartheid* and the Convention against Discrimination in Education adopted by the United Nations Educational, Scientific and Cultural Organization on 14 December 1960,

Recalling also its resolution 3057(XXVIII) of 2 November 1973, on the first Decade for Action to Combat Racism and Racial Discrimination, and its resolution 38/14 of 22 November 1983, on the Second Decade to Combat Racism and Racial Discrimination,

Recalling further the two World Conferences to Combat Racism and Racial Discrimination, held at Geneva in 1978 and 1983, respectively,

Taking note once again of the *Report of the Second World Conference to Combat Racism and Racial Discrimination,*

Convinced that the Second World Conference represented a positive contribution by the international community towards attaining the objectives of the Decade, through its adoption of a Declaration and an operational Programme of Action for the Second Decade to Combat Racial Discrimination,

Noting with concern that, despite the efforts of the international community, the first Decade for Action to Combat Racism and Racial Discrimination did not attain its principal objectives and that millions of human beings continue to this day to be the victims of varied forms of racism, racial discrimination and *apartheid,*

Emphasizing the necessity of attaining the objectives of the Second Decade to Combat Racism and Racial Discrimination,

Convinced of the need to take more effective and sustained international measures for the elimination of all forms of racism and racial discrimination and the total eradication of *apartheid* in South Africa,

1. *Resolves once again* that all forms of racism and racial discrimination, particularly in their institutionalized form, such as *apartheid*, or resulting from official doctrines of racial superiority or exclusivity, are among the most serious violations of human rights in the contemporary world and must be combated by all available means;

2. *Appeals* to the international community, in general, and the United Nations, in particular, to continue to give the highest priority to programmes for combating racism, racial discrimination and *apartheid*, and to intensify its own efforts, during the Second Decade to Combat Racism and Racial Discrimination, to provide assistance and relief to the victims of racism and all forms of racial discrimination and *apartheid*, especially in South Africa and Namibia and in occupied territories and territories under alien domination;

3. *Appeals* to all Governments and to international and non-governmental organizations to increase and intensify their activities to combat racism, racial discrimination and *apartheid* and to provide relief and assistance to the victims of these evils;

4. *Appeals* to all Governments to review their laws and enact appropriate legislation with a view to ensuring that any victim of racism or racial discrimination has adequate protection, avenues of recourse and assistance;

5. *Invites* the concerned organs of the United Nations, in particular the Committee on the Elimination of Racial Discrimination, the Commission on Human Rights and its Sub-Commission on Prevention of Discrimination and Protection of Minorities, as well as the relevant specialized agencies, to continue exercising vigilance in identifying actual or emergent situations of racism or racial discrimination, to draw attention to them where discovered and to suggest appropriate remedial measures;

6. *Invites* the Secretary-General to proceed immediately with the implementation of the activities outlined in his report on the plan of activities for the period 1985-1989;

7. *Requests* the Secretary-General to give the highest priority to actions to combat *apartheid* in the implementation of the plan of activities;

8. *Further requests* the Secretary-General, in implementing the plan of activities, to take fully into account the following elements:

(a) Universal recognition and implementation of the International Convention on the Elimination of All Forms of Racial Discrimination and other related international instruments;

(b) Assistance from the United Nations and the specialized agencies to States in their efforts to embark on concrete programmes to eradicate racial discrimination;

(c) Study of the effects of racial discrimination in the field of education, training and employment as it affects the children of minorities, in particular, those of migrant workers;

9. *Calls upon* the Secretary-General to maintain close contacts with the Special Committee against *Apartheid*, the United Nations Council for Namibia and other relevant United Nations committees and international and regional organizations, as well as non-governmental organizations, as to their respective roles in implementing the plan of activities;

10. *Requests* Governments to forward a report every two years on the action taken under the Programme of Action for the Second Decade to Combat Racism and Racial Discrimination, on the basis of a questionnaire circulated by the Secretary-General, which reports shall be transmitted to the Economic and Social Council for its consideration;

11. *Requests* the Economic and Social Council, during the period of the Decade, to submit an annual report to the General Assembly, containing, *inter alia:*

(a) An enumeration of the activities undertaken or contemplated to achieve the objectives of the Second Decade, including the activities of Governments, United Nations bodies, the specialized agencies and other international and regional organizations, as well as non-governmental organizations;

(b) A review and appraisal of those activities;

(c) Its suggestions and recommendations;

12. *Invites* the Secretary-General to report to the General Assembly at its fortieth session on the implementation of the present resolution;

13. *Decides* to keep the item entitled "Implementation of the Programme of Action for the Second Decade to Combat Racism and Racial Discrimination" on its agenda throughout the Second Decade and to consider it as a matter of the highest priority at its fortieth session.

General Assembly resolution 39/16

23 November 1984   Meeting 71   Adopted without vote

Approved by Third Committee (A/39/656) by consensus, 8 November (meeting 34); draft by Ethiopia, for African Group (A/C.3/39/L.17); agenda item 86.
Financial implications. 5th Committee, A/39/683; S-G, A/C.3/39/L.23, A/C.5/39/38.
Meeting numbers. GA 39th session: 3rd Committee 4-15, 30, 34; 5th Committee 32; plenary 71.

Following the request of CERD (see above), the Assembly, in resolution 39/21, requested the Secretary-General to explore the possibilities of issuing the two CERD studies on articles 4 and 7 of the International Convention on the Elimination of All Forms of Racial Discrimination.

Other measures to combat racism and racial discrimination

On 12 March 1984,[21] the Commission on Human Rights appealed to States to encourage educational institutions to incorporate in their curricula the concept of the oneness of the human race and interdependence of all peoples, who shared the same basic needs and aspirations. It invited UNESCO and all other organizations concerned to continue to use every means at their disposal to emphasize the importance of education in combating all forms of prejudice.

Earlier, on 28 February,[22] the Commission recommended for adoption a draft text which served as the basis for the Economic and Social Council resolution below.

ECONOMIC AND SOCIAL COUNCIL ACTION

On 24 May, the Economic and Social Council, acting on the recommendation of its Second (Social) Committee, adopted resolution 1984/24 without vote.

Measures to combat racism and racial discrimination

The Economic and Social Council,

Mindful of resolution 1983/10 of 5 September 1983 of the Sub-Commission on Prevention of Discrimination and Protection of Minorities and Commission on Human Rights resolution 1984/9 of 28 February 1984 on measures to combat racism and racial discrimination,

1. *Authorizes* the Sub-Commission on Prevention of Discrimination and Protection of Minorities to entrust Mr. Asbjorn Eide with carrying out a study on the achievements made and obstacles encountered during the Decade for Action to Combat Racism and Racial Discrimination, with special emphasis on the progress made in this field, if any, between the first[23] and sec-

ond[17] world conferences to combat racism and racial discrimination, taking into account also any resolutions the General Assembly might adopt on the report of the Second World Conference to Combat Racism and Racial Discrimination and the first stage of the implementation of the Programme of Action for the Second Decade;

2. *Recommends* that the study should propose new or additional measures in this field which can be taken up for examination by the Sub-Commission;

3. *Requests* the Secretary-General to give all necessary assistance to Mr. Asbjorn Eide in his work;

4. *Requests* that the study be presented to the Sub-Commission at its thirty-eighth session.

Economic and Social Council resolution 1984/24

24 May 1984   Meeting 20   Adopted without vote

Approved by Second Committee (E/1984/91) without vote, 17 May (meeting 15); draft by Commission on Human Rights (E/1984/14); agenda item 10.

The United States said it did not join in the consensus because it believed that the text was intrinsically linked to the first Decade for Action to Combat Racism and Racial Discrimination, in which it had ceased to participate since the Assembly's 1975 resolution equating zionism with racism.[16] The United States affirmed its full commitment to the elimination of racial discrimination but deeply regretted that United Nations activities in that field had been over-politicized.

Convention on the Elimination of Racial Discrimination

Accessions and ratifications

As at 31 December 1984, there were 124 parties to the International Convention on the Elimination of All Forms of Racial Discrimination, adopted by the General Assembly in 1965[12] and in force since 1969.[24] In 1984, two States—Maldives and Suriname—became parties; Peru made the declaration under article 14 of the Convention recognizing the competence of CERD to receive and consider communications from individuals or groups of individuals claiming to be victims of violations of any of the rights under the Convention.

In the Secretary-General's annual report to the Assembly on the status of the Convention,[25] the same number of States were listed as having signed, ratified and acceded to the Convention as at 1 September 1984.

GENERAL ASSEMBLY ACTION

On 23 November, acting on the recommendation of the Third Committee, the General Assembly adopted resolution 39/20 without vote.

Status of the International Convention on the Elimination of All Forms of Racial Discrimination

The General Assembly,

Recalling its resolutions 3057(XXVIII) of 2 November 1973, 3135(XXVIII) of 14 December 1973, 3225(XXIX) of 6 November 1974, 3381(XXX) of 10 November 1975, 31/79 of 13 December 1976, 32/11 of 7 November 1977, 33/101 of 16 December 1978, 34/26 of 15 November 1979, 35/38 of 25 November 1980, 36/11 of 28 October 1981, 37/45 of 3 December 1982 and 38/18 of 22 November 1983,

Expressing its satisfaction at the entry into force, on 3 December 1982, of the competence of the Committee on the Elimination of Racial Discrimination to accept and to examine communications from persons or groups of persons under article 14 of the International Convention on the Elimination of All Forms of Racial Discrimination,

1. *Takes note* of the report of the Secretary-General on the status of the International Convention on the Elimination of All Forms of Racial Discrimination;

2. *Expresses its satisfaction* at the increase in the number of States that have ratified the Convention or acceded thereto;

3. *Reaffirms once again its conviction* that ratification of or accession to the Convention on a universal basis and implementation of its provisions are necessary for the realization of the objectives of the Second Decade to Combat Racism and Racial Discrimination;

4. *Requests* those States that have not yet become parties to the Convention to ratify it or accede thereto;

5. *Calls upon* States parties to the Convention to consider the possibility of making the declaration provided for in article 14 of the Convention;

6. *Requests* the Secretary-General to continue to submit to the General Assembly annual reports concerning the status of the Convention, in accordance with Assembly resolution 2106 A (XX) of 21 December 1965.

General Assembly resolution 39/20

23 November 1984   Meeting 71   Adopted without vote

Approved by Third Committee (A/39/658) without vote, 8 November (meeting 34); 29-nation draft (A/C.3/39/L.8), amended by 12 nations (A/C.3/39/L.10); agenda item 88 *(c)*.

Sponsors of draft: Algeria, Argentina, Australia, Bahamas, Bangladesh, Barbados, Belgium, Bulgaria, Burkina Faso, Colombia, Cuba, Cyprus, Denmark, Egypt, Germany, Federal Republic of, Guinea-Bissau, Hungary, India, Morocco, New Zealand, Pakistan, Portugal, Rwanda, Spain, Suriname, Syrian Arab Republic, Trinidad and Tobago, Venezuela, Yugoslavia.

Sponsors of amendments: Colombia, Costa Rica, Ecuador, France, Iceland, Italy, Netherlands, Norway, Senegal, Somalia, Sweden, Uruguay.

Meeting numbers. GA 39th session: 3rd Committee 4-15, 27, 34; plenary 71.

Before approving the draft resolution as a whole, the Third Committee adopted, by 83 votes to none, with 40 abstentions, amendments sponsored by 12 nations. The amendments added the second preambular paragraph and paragraph 5.

Implementation of the Convention

Communication. By a letter of 16 January 1984,[26] Israel drew attention to what it called an ominous upsurge of anti-Semitism at the United Nations in recent years (for further details, see p. 259).

CERD activities. The Committee on the Elimination of Racial Discrimination, set up under article 8 of the Convention, held two sessions in 1984: the twenty-ninth, from 5 to 23 March, in New York; and the thirtieth, from 6 to 24 August, at Geneva.

Over two thirds of the sessions' meetings were devoted to an examination of reports and additional information submitted by 41 States and by Namibia through the United Nations Council for Namibia under article 9 of the Convention, on measures to give effect to the Convention's provisions. The CERD annual report to the General Assembly[27] summarized members' views on each country report and statements made by the States parties concerned, and reported on action taken to ensure submission of reports.

As authorized by article 15 of the Convention, also examined were copies of petitions, reports and other information relating to Trust and Non-Self-Governing Territories transmitted by the Trusteeship Council (see TRUSTEESHIP AND DECOLONIZATION, Chapter II) and by the Special Committee on the Situation with regard to the Implementation of the Declaration on the Granting of Independence to Colonial Countries and Peoples. The reports related to African Territories, including Namibia; Pacific and Indian Ocean Territories; and Atlantic Ocean and Caribbean Territories, including Gibraltar. CERD observed that the continued existence of colonial régimes in the Territories was hampering full implementation of the Convention; and that the reports on the Pacific and Indian Ocean Territories, and on Anguilla and Bermuda, did not contain relevant information to enable it to fulfil its functions under article 15 in respect of those Territories.

As to the reporting obligations of States parties under article 9 of the Convention, which it had been invited to consider by a November 1983 Assembly resolution,[28] CERD on 22 March 1984[29] underlined the importance of strict compliance with reporting—one of the main mechanisms through which the Committee could promote elimination of racial discrimination. CERD was of the opinion that amending the Convention, either to extend the two-year period for submitting reports or to require a four-year substantive report and a two-year interim one, would weaken the obligations assumed by States parties under the Convention and have a negative impact on the struggle against racism and racial discrimination. CERD stated its readiness to assist States with reporting difficulties by providing training and advisory services. With the increase in the number of States parties, it would amend its rules of procedure to respond adequately to a corresponding increase in the number of reports.

Following examination of the initial report on Namibia, CERD on 20 August[30] expressed concern at the inability of the Council for Namibia to apply the provisions of the Convention in the Territory owing to South Africa's policy of *apartheid*. It strongly condemned that policy and decided to keep the situation in Namibia under constant review.

Also in August, CERD began to consider, in conformity with article 14 of the Convention, communications from individuals or groups of individuals claiming violation of their rights under the Convention by a State party recognizing CERD competence to receive and consider such communications. Eleven of the 124 States parties—Costa Rica, Ecuador, France, Iceland, Italy, the Netherlands, Norway, Peru, Senegal, Sweden and Uruguay—had declared such recognition. By the end of the August session, work under the article had not reached the reporting stage.

GENERAL ASSEMBLY ACTION

On 23 November, the General Assembly, acting on the recommendation of the Third Committee, adopted resolution 39/21 by recorded vote.

Report of the Committee on the Elimination of Racial Discrimination

The General Assembly,

Recalling its resolutions 38/21 of 22 November 1983 on the report of the Committee on the Elimination of Racial Discrimination and 39/20 of 23 November 1984 on the status of the International Convention on the Elimination of All Forms of Racial Discrimination, as well as its other relevant resolutions on the implementation of the Programme of Action for the Second Decade to Combat Racism and Racial Discrimination,

Having considered the report of the Committee on the Elimination of Racial Discrimination on the work of its twenty-ninth and thirtieth sessions, submitted under article 9, paragraph 2, of the International Convention on the Elimination of All Forms of Racial Discrimination,

Emphasizing that it is important for the success of the struggle against all instances of racial discrimination, including vestiges and manifestations of racist ideologies wherever they exist, that all Member States be guided in their internal and foreign policies by the basic provisions of the Convention,

Bearing in mind the fact that the Convention is being implemented in different economic, social and cultural conditions prevailing in individual States parties,

Mindful of the obligation of all States parties to comply fully with the provisions of the Convention,

Aware of the importance of the contribution of the Committee on the Elimination of Racial Discrimination to the implementation of the Programme of Action for the Second Decade to Combat Racism and Racial Discrimination,

Taking note of the decisions adopted and the recommendations made by the Committee at its twenty-ninth and thirtieth sessions,

1. *Takes note with appreciation* of the report of the Committee on the Elimination of Racial Discrimination on the work of its twenty-ninth and thirtieth sessions;

2. *Strongly condemns* the policy of *apartheid* in South Africa and Namibia as a crime against humanity and urges all Member States to adopt effective political, economic and other measures in conformity with the relevant resolutions of the General Assembly, the Security Council and other United Nations bodies, in order to support the legitimate struggle of the oppressed people

of South Africa and Namibia for their national liberation and human dignity, and to secure the elimination
of the racist *apartheid* system;

3. *Takes note with appreciation* of the report submitted
to the Committee by the United Nations Council for
Namibia as the legal Administering Authority for Namibia until independence and encourages the Council
in its determined endeavours towards the elimination
of *apartheid* from the Territory and the attainment of independence of the people of Namibia;

4. *Commends* the Committee for its continuous endeavours towards the elimination of *apartheid* in South
Africa and Namibia and of all forms of discrimination
based on race, colour, descent or national or ethnic origin, wherever it exists;

5. *Takes note with appreciation* of the Committee's decision to participate actively in the implementation of
the Programme of Action for the Second Decade to
Combat Racism and Racial Discrimination;

6. *Requests* the Secretary-General to explore the possibilities of issuing as United Nations publications the
two studies prepared by the Committee on articles 4 and
7 of the International Convention on the Elimination
of All Forms of Racial Discrimination;

7. *Welcomes* the efforts of the Committee aimed at
the elimination of all forms of discrimination against
national or ethnic minorities, persons belonging to such
minorities and indigenous populations, wherever such
discrimination exists, and the attainment of the full enjoyment of their human rights through the implementation of the principles and provisions of the Convention;

8. *Welcomes further* the efforts of the Committee aimed
at the elimination of all forms of discrimination against
migrant workers and their families, the promotion of
their rights on a non-discriminatory basis and the
achievement of their full equality, including the freedom
to maintain their cultural characteristics;

9. *Calls upon* all Member States to adopt effective
legislative, socio-economic and other necessary measures in order to ensure the prevention or elimination
of discrimination based on race, colour, descent or national or ethnic origin;

10. *Further calls upon* States parties to the Convention
to protect fully, by the adoption of the relevant legislative and other measures, in conformity with the Convention, the rights of national or ethnic minorities and
persons belonging to such minorities, as well as the rights
of indigenous populations;

11. *Commends* States parties to the Convention on
measures taken to ensure, within their jurisdiction, the
availability of appropriate recourse procedures for the
victims of racial discrimination;

12. *Reiterates its invitation* to the States parties to the
Convention to provide the Committee, in accordance
with its general guidelines, with information on the implementation of the provisions of the Convention, including information on the demographic composition
of their population and on their relations with the racist régime of South Africa;

13. *Calls upon* the United Nations bodies concerned
to ensure that the Committee is supplied with all relevant information on all the Territories to which General
Assembly resolution 1514(XV) of 14 December 1960 applies and urges again the administering Powers to co-
operate with these bodies by providing all the necessary
information in order to enable the Committee to dis-

charge fully its responsibilities under article 15 of the
Convention;

14. *Appeals* to the States parties to take fully into consideration their obligation under the Convention to submit their reports in due time;

15. *Takes note* of the decision of the Committee to hold
its session in one of the African countries at the appropriate time and requests the Secretary-General to explore
the possibilities and financial implications of holding that
session within the context of the Second Decade to Combat Racism and Racial Discrimination and to inform
the General Assembly and the Committee on his
findings;

16. *Requests* the Secretary-General to take the necessary steps to ensure wider publicity of the work of the
Committee, which would facilitate its task to implement
effectively its functions under the Convention.

General Assembly resolution 39/21

23 November 1984   Meeting 71   145-1 (recorded vote)

Approved by Third Committee (A/39/658) by recorded vote (137-1), 9 November
(meeting 35); 16-nation draft (A/C.3/39/L.9), orally revised; agenda item 88 *(a)*.
Sponsors: Angola, Argentina, Bangladesh, Bolivia, Cape Verde, China, Cuba, Jor-
dan, Madagascar, Morocco, Nigeria, Pakistan, Yemen, Yugoslavia, Zambia,
Zimbabwe.
Meeting numbers. GA 39th session: 3rd Committee 4-15, 27, 34, 35; plenary 71.

Recorded vote in Assembly as follows:

In favour: Afghanistan, Albania, Algeria, Angola, Antigua and Barbuda, Ar-
gentina, Australia, Austria, Bahamas, Bahrain, Bangladesh, Barbados, Belgium,
Benin, Bhutan, Bolivia, Botswana, Brazil, Brunei Darussalam, Bulgaria, Burkina
Faso, Burma, Burundi, Byelorussian SSR, Cameroon, Canada, Cape Verde, Cen-
tral African Republic, Chad, Chile, China, Colombia, Comoros, Congo, Costa
Rica, Cuba, Cyprus, Czechoslovakia, Democratic Kampuchea, Democratic
Yemen, Denmark, Djibouti, Dominican Republic, Ecuador, Egypt, Equatorial
Guinea, Ethiopia, Fiji, Finland, France, Gabon, Gambia, German Democratic
Republic, Germany, Federal Republic of, Ghana, Greece, Grenada, Guinea,
Guinea-Bissau, Guyana, Haiti, Honduras, Hungary, Iceland, India, Indonesia, Iran,
Iraq, Ireland, Italy, Ivory Coast, Jamaica, Japan, Jordan, Kenya, Kuwait, Lao Peo-
ple's Democratic Republic, Lebanon, Lesotho, Liberia, Libyan Arab Jamahiriya,
Luxembourg, Madagascar, Malawi, Malaysia, Maldives, Mali, Malta, Maurita-
nia, Mexico, Mongolia, Morocco, Mozambique, Nepal, Netherlands, New
Zealand, Nicaragua, Niger, Nigeria, Norway, Oman, Pakistan, Panama, Papua
New Guinea, Peru, Philippines, Poland, Portugal, Qatar, Romania, Rwanda, Saint
Lucia, Samoa, Sao Tome and Principe, Saudi Arabia, Senegal, Sierra Leone,
Singapore, Somalia, Spain, Sri Lanka, Sudan, Suriname, Swaziland, Sweden,
Syrian Arab Republic, Thailand, Togo, Trinidad and Tobago, Tunisia, Turkey,
Uganda, Ukrainian SSR, USSR, United Arab Emirates, United Kingdom, United
Republic of Tanzania, Uruguay, Venezuela, Viet Nam, Yemen, Yugoslavia, Zaire,
Zambia, Zimbabwe.
Against: United States.

Before adopting the text as a whole, the Assembly voted separately on paragraphs 2, 3 and 12
(specifically the phrase "including information on
the demographic composition of their population
and on their relations with the racist régime of
South Africa"). The paragraphs were retained by
recorded votes of, respectively: 123 to 1, with 20
abstentions; 139 to none, with 6 abstentions; and
120 to none, with 22 abstentions.

The same paragraphs had also been voted on
in the Third Committee and were retained by
recorded votes of, respectively: 115 to 1, with 20
abstentions; 130 to none, with 6 abstentions; and
116 to none, with 20 abstentions.

Explaining its vote against paragraph 2 and the
text as a whole, the United States said it regretted
that the sponsors had withdrawn their revisions
to paragraphs 2 and 4 (to replace "a crime against

humanity" by "the most abhorrent form of racial discrimination" in the first paragraph and, in the second, to delete "in South Africa and Namibia" after the words "the elimination of *apartheid*"). The legal definition of *apartheid* as a crime against humanity, to which the sponsors had reverted, was a definition adopted by the Assembly in the context of the 1973 Convention against *apartheid*[11] and had no place in a draft resolution dealing with the CERD report.

Australia, which abstained on paragraph 2, likewise voiced regret that the revision to that paragraph had been withdrawn, saying it would have been more judicious to draw attention to the definition elsewhere.

The Niger, which voted for the paragraph and the text as a whole, emphasized that *apartheid* was clearly a crime against humanity.

Ecuador regarded certain paragraphs as tendentious, biased and improperly worded. Ireland, speaking for the member States of the European Economic Community (EEC), stated reservations to paragraphs 2 and 12; in their view, it was not for the Third Committee to direct the work of CERD, which was an independent body established by an international convention and must not be induced to exceed its mandate by adopting positions or undertaking work not directly linked to the struggle to eliminate racial discrimination. Canada regretted that the attempts to achieve a compromise on paragraph 2 had failed; it also had strong reservations on paragraphs 3 and 12. Reservations to paragraphs 2 and 12 were expressed by Finland on behalf of the Nordic countries; in their view, neither the Assembly nor CERD could impose on Member States or States parties obligations clearly beyond the Convention's mandate. Austria held that paragraphs 2 and 12 went further than allowed for by the Convention and CERD's mandate. In Japan's opinion, paragraph 2 had no legal value.

Though voting in favour of paragraph 12, Algeria had reservations about the call on States parties to include information on the demographic composition of their population which, it felt, did not serve any practical purpose; such a request was not contained in the Convention and was merely a recommendation made by CERD in 1973. The Byelorussian SSR supported restoration of the original text; the vote had shown, it added, who were the real partisans of the right to self-determination and the struggle against *apartheid* and who were those content with verbal assurances. Expressing firm support for paragraphs 2 and 4 in their unrevised form, Mauritania regretted that certain countries which preached the defence of human rights had voted against the text. Chile reaffirmed its firm opposition to all forms of racial discrimination, in particular to South

Africa's *apartheid* policy. The whole text was endorsed by Honduras.

Measures against nazism and fascism

Action by the Commission on Human Rights. On 12 March 1984,[31] the Commission on Human Rights again condemned all totalitarian or other ideologies and practices, including Nazi, Fascist and neo-Fascist, based on racial exclusiveness or intolerance, hatred, terror, or systematic denial of human rights and fundamental freedoms. It urged States to draw attention to threats to democratic institutions by such ideologies and practices and called for intensified measures against them. The Commission called on States to commemorate the fortieth anniversary of the conclusion of the Second World War, and recommended that, for the occasion, the Economic and Social Council should request the General Assembly to hold a special commemorative meeting in 1985, at which it would also discuss measures to counter the spread of totalitarian ideologies and practices.

Report of the Secretary-General and communications. Responding to an Assembly request of December 1983,[32] the Secretary-General in April 1984 submitted a report, with later addenda,[33] summarizing comments from 20 States, a specialized agency and 18 NGOs on ongoing and future measures to eradicate nazism, fascism and related ideologies and practices.

Additional comments were transmitted by the USSR on 4 December.[34] In this connection, Israel, on 13 December,[35] rejected what it called vilifications included in those comments, namely, that it had adopted the ideas of national and racial superiority that had been the foundations of Hitlerism. Israel said it could only assume that USSR efforts to malign zionism, the national liberation movement of the Jewish people, were aimed at seeking justification for the brutal and racist oppression of Jews in the USSR.

ECONOMIC AND SOCIAL COUNCIL ACTION

Following consideration of the Secretary-General's report, the Economic and Social Council, acting on the recommendation of its Second Committee, in May adopted decision 1984/149 without vote.

Report of the Secretary-General on measures to be taken against Nazi, Fascist and neo-Fascist activities and all other forms of totalitarian ideologies and practices based on racial intolerance, hatred and terror

At its 20th plenary meeting, on 24 May 1984, the Council took note of the report of the Secretary-General on measures to be taken against Nazi, Fascist and neo-Fascist activities and all other forms of totalitarian ideologies and practices based on racial intolerance, hatred and terror and decided to transmit it to the General Assembly at its thirty-ninth session.

Economic and Social Council decision 1984/149
Adopted without vote

Approved by Second Committee (E/1984/91) without vote, 17 May (meeting 16); oral proposal by Chairman; agenda item 10.

GENERAL ASSEMBLY ACTION

On 14 December 1984, acting on the recommendation of the Third Committee, the General Assembly adopted resolution 39/114 without vote.

Measures to be taken against Nazi, Fascist and neo-Fascist activities and all other forms of totalitarian ideologies and practices based on racial intolerance, hatred and terror

The General Assembly,

Recalling that the United Nations emerged from the struggle against nazism, fascism, aggression and foreign occupation, and that the peoples expressed their resolve in the Charter of the United Nations to save future generations from the scourge of war,

Bearing in mind the suffering, destruction and death of millions of victims of aggression, foreign occupation, nazism and fascism,

Recalling also the close relationship between all totalitarian ideologies and practices based on racial or ethnic exclusiveness or intolerance, hatred and terror and the systematic denial of human rights and fundamental freedoms,

Considering that the fortieth anniversary of the victory over nazism and fascism in the Second World War will occur in 1985 and should serve to mobilize efforts of the world community in its struggle against Nazi, Fascist and neo-Fascist and all other totalitarian ideologies and practices based on racial intolerance, hatred and terror,

Reaffirming the purposes and principles laid down in the Charter, which are aimed at maintaining international peace and security, developing friendly relations among nations based on respect for the principle of equal rights and the self-determination of peoples, and achieving international co-operation in promoting and encouraging respect for human rights and fundamental freedoms for all,

Firmly convinced that the best bulwark against nazism and racial discrimination is the establishment and maintenance of democratic institutions, that the existence of genuine political, social and economic democracy is an effective vaccine and an equally effective antidote against the formation or development of Nazi movements and that a political system which is based on freedom and effective participation by the people in the conduct of public affairs, and under which economic and social conditions are such as to ensure a decent standard of living for the population, makes it impossible for fascism, nazism or other ideologies based on terror to succeed,

Emphasizing that all totalitarian or other ideologies and practices, including Nazi, Fascist and neo-Fascist, based on racial or ethnic exclusiveness or intolerance, hatred, terror or systematic denial of human rights and fundamental freedoms, or which have such consequences, may jeopardize world peace and constitute obstacles to friendly relations between States and to the realization of human rights and fundamental freedoms,

Acknowledging with satisfaction the fact that many States have established systems based on the inherent dignity and the equal and inalienable rights of all human beings, which are the basis of a democratic society and the best bulwark against totalitarian ideologies and practices,

Noting that, nevertheless, in the contemporary world there continue to exist various forms of totalitarian ideologies and practices which entail contempt for the individual or a denial of the intrinsic dignity and equality of all human beings, of equality of opportunity in civil, political, economic, social and cultural spheres, and of social justice,

Reaffirming that the prosecution and punishment of war crimes and crimes against peace and humanity, as laid down in General Assembly resolutions 3(I) of 13 February 1946 and 95(I) of 11 December 1946, constitute a universal commitment for all States,

Mindful of the principles of international co-operation in the detection, arrest, extradition and punishment of persons guilty of war crimes and crimes against humanity, set forth in General Assembly resolution 3074(XXVIII) of 3 December 1973,

Recalling also its resolutions 2331(XXII) of 18 December 1967, 2438(XXIII) of 19 December 1968, 2545(XXIV) of 11 December 1969, 2713(XXV) of 15 December 1970, 2839(XXVI) of 18 December 1971, 34/24 of 15 November 1979, 35/200 of 15 December 1980, 36/162 of 16 December 1981, 37/179 of 17 December 1982 and 38/99 of 16 December 1983,

Recalling further the Declaration on Social Progress and Development, the United Nations Declaration on the Elimination of All Forms of Racial Discrimination, the Declaration on the Granting of Independence to Colonial Countries and Peoples and the Declaration on the Elimination of All Forms of Intolerance and of Discrimination Based on Religion or Belief,

Underlining the importance of the Universal Declaration of Human Rights, the International Covenants on Human Rights, the International Convention on the Elimination of All Forms of Racial Discrimination, the Convention on the Prevention and Punishment of the Crime of Genocide, the Convention on the Non-Applicability of Statutory Limitations to War Crimes and Crimes against Humanity, the International Convention on the Suppression and Punishment of the Crime of *Apartheid* and other relevant international instruments,

Reaffirming that totalitarian or other ideologies and practices, including Nazi, Fascist and neo-Fascist, based on racial or ethnic or other exclusiveness or intolerance, hatred, terror or systematic denial of human rights and fundamental freedoms, or which have such consequences, are incompatible with the purposes and principles of the Charter of the United Nations and the above-mentioned international instruments,

Conscious of the need to counter the spread of totalitarian ideologies and practices based on the systematic denial of human rights and fundamental freedoms, racial intolerance, hatred and terror,

Acknowledging the fact that a number of States have set up legal regulations which are suited to prevent the activities of Nazi, Fascist and neo-Fascist groups and organizations,

Noting again with deep concern that the proponents of Fascist ideologies have, in a number of countries, intensified their activities and are increasingly co-ordinating them on an international scale,

Expressing its concern that Fascist and Nazi and other totalitarian ideologies and practices are inherited, *inter alia*, by repressive racist régimes practising gross and flagrant violations of human rights and systematic denial of human rights and fundamental freedoms,

1. *Again condemns and expresses its determination* to resist all totalitarian or other ideologies and practices, including Nazi, Fascist and neo-Fascist, based on racial or ethnic exclusiveness or intolerance, hatred and terror, which deprive people of basic human rights and fundamental freedoms and of equality of opportunity;

2. *Urges* all States to draw attention to the threat to democratic institutions by the above-mentioned ideologies and practices and to consider taking measures, in accordance with their national constitutional systems and with the provisions of the Universal Declaration of Human Rights and the International Covenants on Human Rights, to prohibit or otherwise deter activities by groups or organizations or whoever is practising those ideologies;

3. *Invites* Member States to adopt, in accordance with their national constitutional systems and with the provisions of the Universal Declaration of Human Rights and the International Covenants on Human Rights, as a matter of high priority, measures declaring punishable by law any dissemination of ideas based on racial superiority or hatred and of war propaganda, including Nazi, Fascist and neo-Fascist ideologies;

4. *Calls upon* States to assist each other in detecting, arresting and bringing to trial persons suspected of having committed war crimes and crimes against humanity and, if they are found guilty, in punishing them;

5. *Appeals* to all States that have not yet done so to ratify or to accede or to give serious consideration to acceding to the International Covenants on Human Rights, the Convention on the Prevention and Punishment of the Crime of Genocide, the International Convention on the Elimination of All Forms of Racial Discrimination, the Convention on the Non-Applicability of Statutory Limitations to War Crimes and Crimes against Humanity and the International Convention on the Suppression and Punishment of the Crime of *Apartheid;*

6. *Calls upon* the appropriate specialized agencies, as well as intergovernmental and international non-governmental organizations, to initiate or intensify measures against the ideologies and practices described in paragraph 1 above;

7. *Invites* all States, on the occasion of the fortieth anniversary of the conclusion of the Second World War, to renew their efforts to counter the spread of ideologies and practices described in paragraph 1 above and to initiate measures in accordance with the Charter of the United Nations to maintain international peace and security;

8. *Gives expression* to the respect felt by today's generations for the victims of and the struggle of peoples against nazism and fascism in the Second World War and for establishing the United Nations in order to save mankind from the scourge of war and to reaffirm faith in fundamental human rights and in the dignity and worth of the human person;

9. *Declares* that 8 and 9 May 1985 will be the days of the fortieth anniversary of victory over nazism and

fascism in the Second World War and of that struggle against them;

10. *Requests* the Secretary-General to ensure that the Department of Public Information of the Secretariat pays due attention to the dissemination of information on this anniversary and the founding of the United Nations, exposing the ideologies and practices described in paragraph 1 above;

11. *Reiterates its request* to the Commission on Human Rights to consider this subject at its forty-first session;

12. *Calls once again upon* all States to provide the Secretary-General with their comments on this question;

13. *Requests* the Secretary-General to submit a report, through the Economic and Social Council, to the General Assembly at its fortieth session in the light of the discussion that will take place in the Commission on Human Rights and on the basis of comments provided by States and international organizations.

General Assembly resolution 39/114

14 December 1984   Meeting 101   Adopted without vote

Approved by Third Committee (A/39/700) without vote, 6 December (meeting 64); 14-nation draft (A/C.3/39/L.76); agenda item 12.
Sponsors: Afghanistan, Angola, Bulgaria, Byelorussian SSR, Cuba, Czechoslovakia, German Democratic Republic, Hungary, Lao People's Democratic Republic, Mongolia, Nicaragua, Poland, Ukrainian SSR, Viet Nam.
Meeting numbers. GA 39th session: 3rd Committee 54-56, 58, 59, 61, 64; plenary 101.

Other aspects of discrimination

Implementation of the 1981 Declaration against religious intolerance

ECONOMIC AND SOCIAL COUNCIL ACTION

Acting without vote on the recommendation of its Second Committee, the Economic and Social Council, on 24 May 1984, adopted resolution 1984/39. The text was based on a draft recommended by the Commission on Human Rights on 15 March.[36]

Implementation of the Declaration on the Elimination of All Forms of Intolerance and of Discrimination Based on Religion or Belief

The Economic and Social Council,

Conscious of the need to promote universal respect for, and observance of, human rights and fundamental freedoms for all without distinction as to race, sex, language or religion,

Recalling General Assembly resolution 36/55 of 25 November 1981, in which the Assembly proclaimed the Declaration on the Elimination of All Forms of Intolerance and of Discrimination Based on Religion or Belief,[37]

Bearing in mind Commission on Human Rights resolution 1983/40 of 9 March 1983,

Welcoming the appointment by the Sub-Commission on Prevention of Discrimination and Protection of Minorities of a Special Rapporteur to undertake the comprehensive and thorough study requested in that resolution,

Noting Sub-Commission resolution 1983/31 of 6 September 1983,

Aware that intolerance and discrimination on the grounds of religion or belief continue to occur in many parts of the world,

1. *Authorizes* the Sub-Commission on Prevention of Discrimination and Protection of Minorities to entrust the Special Rapporteur, Mrs. Odio Benito, with the preparation of a study, in accordance with the terms of Sub-Commission resolution 1983/31,[38] on the current dimensions of the problems of intolerance and of discrimination on grounds of religion or belief;

2. *Requests* the Secretary-General to give the Special Rapporteur all the assistance she may require in her work;

3. *Requests* the Special Rapporteur to submit her study to the Sub-Commission at its thirty-seventh session;

4. *Requests* the Commission on Human Rights to consider this matter further at its forty-first session under the item entitled "Implementation of the Declaration on the Elimination of All Forms of Intolerance and of Discrimination Based on Religion or Belief".

Economic and Social Council resolution 1984/39

24 May 1984   Meeting 20   Adopted without vote

Approved by Second Committee (E/1984/91) without vote, 17 May (meeting 16); draft by Commission on Human Rights (E/1984/14); agenda item 10.

Sub-Commission action. Complying with the Economic and Social Council's request that the study on discrimination based on religion or belief be submitted to the Sub-Commission at its August 1984 session, Special Rapporteur Elizabeth Odio Benito (Costa Rica), appointed to undertake the study, prepared a preliminary report[39] in view of the shortness of time. The report contained a proposed outline for the study and annexed a questionnaire for information gathering.

Having discussed the preliminary report, the Sub-Commission on 30 August[40] requested the Special Rapporteur to submit a progress report in 1985 and a final one in 1986, and asked the Secretary-General to provide all possible assistance to her.

Activities of the Secretary-General. A Seminar on the Encouragement of Understanding, Tolerance and Respect in Matters relating to Freedom of Religion or Belief took place at Geneva from 3 to 14 December 1984. It was organized by the Secretary-General in accordance with a Commission on Human Rights request that had been endorsed by the Economic and Social Council in May 1983.[41] The results were not available for consideration by the 1984 General Assembly session.

GENERAL ASSEMBLY ACTION

On 14 December 1984, acting without vote on the recommendation of the Third Committee, the General Assembly adopted resolution 39/131.

Elimination of all forms of religious intolerance

The General Assembly,

Conscious of the need to promote universal respect for, and observance of, human rights and fundamental freedoms for all without distinction as to race, sex, language or religion,

Reaffirming its resolution 36/55 of 25 November 1981, in which it proclaimed the Declaration on the Elimination of All Forms of Intolerance and of Discrimination Based on Religion or Belief,

Recalling its resolutions 37/187 of 18 December 1982 and 38/110 of 16 December 1983, in which it requested the Commission on Human Rights to consider what measures might be necessary to implement the Declaration,

Welcoming Economic and Social Council resolution 1984/39 of 24 May 1984, in which the Council authorized the Sub-Commission on Prevention of Discrimination and Protection of Minorities to entrust its Special Rapporteur with the preparation of a study, in accordance with the terms of Sub-Commission resolution 1983/31 of 6 September 1983, on the current dimensions of the problems of intolerance and of discrimination based on religion or belief,

Taking note of the proposed outline for the study presented by the Special Rapporteur to the Sub-Commission at its thirty-seventh session,

Welcoming the fact that the Secretary-General organized at Geneva, from 3 to 14 December 1984, within the framework of the advisory services programme, the Seminar on the Encouragement of Understanding, Tolerance and Respect in Matters relating to Freedom of Religion or Belief,

Recognizing that it is desirable to enhance the promotional and public information activities of the United Nations in matters relating to freedom of religion or belief and that both Governments and non-governmental organizations have an important role to play in this domain,

Aware that intolerance and discrimination based on religion or belief continue to exist in many parts of the world,

Believing that further efforts are, therefore, required to promote and protect the right to freedom of thought, conscience, religion or belief,

1. *Reaffirms* that everyone has the right to freedom of thought, conscience, religion or belief;

2. *Urges* all States to give continuing attention to the need for adequate legislation to prohibit discrimination based on religion or belief in the recognition, exercise and enjoyment of human rights and fundamental freedoms;

3. *Also urges* all States to take all appropriate measures to combat intolerance and to encourage understanding, tolerance and respect in matters relating to freedom of religion or belief;

4. *Requests* the Commission on Human Rights to continue its consideration of measures to implement the Declaration on the Elimination of All Forms of Intolerance and of Discrimination Based on Religion or Belief and to report, through the Economic and Social Council, to the General Assembly at its fortieth session;

5. *Requests* the Secretary-General to submit, to this end, the report of the Seminar on the Encouragement of Understanding, Tolerance and Respect in Matters relating to Freedom of Religion or Belief to the Commission on Human Rights at its forty-first session and to the General Assembly at its fortieth session;

6. *Invites* the Secretary-General to continue to give high priority to the dissemination of the text of the Declaration on the Elimination of All Forms of Intolerance and of Discrimination Based on Religion or Be-

lief, in all official languages of the United Nations, and to take all appropriate measures to make the text available for use both by United Nations information centres and by other interested bodies;

7. *Requests* the Secretary-General in this context to invite interested non-governmental organizations to consider what further role they could envisage playing regarding the dissemination of the Declaration in national and local languages;

8. *Decides* to include in the provisional agenda of its fortieth session the item entitled "Elimination of all forms of religious intolerance" and to consider the report of the Commission on Human Rights in the context of that item.

General Assembly resolution 39/131

14 December 1984   Meeting 101   Adopted without vote

Approved by Third Committee (A/39/704) without vote, 3 December (meeting 57); 24-nation draft (A/C.3/39/L.51); agenda item 95.
Sponsors: Australia, Austria, Belgium, Canada, Costa Rica, Dominican Republic, Fiji, Finland, France, Germany, Federal Republic of, Ireland, Italy, Ivory Coast, Japan, Morocco, Netherlands, New Zealand, Norway, Rwanda, Samoa, Suriname, Sweden, Uganda, United States.
Meeting numbers. GA 39th session: 3rd Committee 44-52, 56, 57; plenary 101.

Indigenous populations

Action by the Commission on Human Rights. Having received information on the 1983 activities of the Sub-Commission's Working Group on Indigenous Populations,[42] the Commission on Human Rights on 12 March 1984[43] welcomed the Group's efforts with respect to the review of developments in the promotion and protection of the human rights of indigenous populations and to the evolution of international standards. It took note of the Group's discussion of a possible voluntary fund to facilitate participation by representatives of indigenous populations in the work of the Group and commended its efforts to establish a long-term programme of work. The Commission looked forward to receiving material for the formulation of draft international standards.

Working Group activities. In its review of developments in the promotion of the human rights of indigenous populations at its third session (Geneva, 30 July–2 August and 6 August 1984), the Working Group on Indigenous Populations focused on the right to land and to natural resources. With respect to international standards, the kind of instrument to be elaborated and the complex issue of a definition of indigenous populations were discussed. Consideration continued of the various proposals for the establishment and administration of a voluntary fund to encourage indigenous participation in the Group's work. An action plan for 1985 was adopted. These activities were described in the Group's report[44] to the Sub-Commission at its August 1984 session.

Study on discrimination against indigenous populations. The final report on a study of the problem of discrimination against indigenous populations[45] was presented to the Sub-Commission at its 1984 session. This final or third part of the study, completed by Special Rapporteur José R. Martínez Cobo (Ecuador) in 1983,[42] outlined his findings and a series of recommendations for action by the United Nations, the specialized agencies (specifically the International Labour Organisation (ILO), UNESCO, the World Health Organization and the Food and Agriculture Organization of the United Nations (FAO)), intergovernmental organizations (the Organization of American States and the Inter-American Commission on Human Rights) and NGOs. Special areas for action included health, housing, education, language, culture, employment, land, political and religious rights, and equality in the administration of justice. Also outlined were concepts and criteria for the definition of indigenous populations, as well as principles that could form the basis for a declaration on the rights of indigenous populations.

Sub-Commission action. On 30 August 1984, the Sub-Commission recomended a two-part draft resolution for adoption by the Commission on Human Rights.[46] By part A, the Commission would recommend that the Economic and Social Council authorize the Secretary-General to arrange for the publication and widest possible distribution of a condensed version of the study. By part B, the Commission would recommend adoption of a resolution by which the Council would establish a United Nations Voluntary Fund for Indigenous Populations, with specifications as to its uses and administration.

On the same date,[47] the Sub-Commission authorized the Chairman of the Working Group on Indigenous Populations, Erica-Irene A. Daes (Greece), to attend the Conference of Indigenous Peoples, to be held in Panama from 23 to 30 September. The costs involved were to be borne by the United Nations Centre for Human Rights.

GENERAL ASSEMBLY ACTION

In resolution 39/21, the General Assembly welcomed CERD efforts aimed at eliminating all forms of discrimination against indigenous populations, among others. It called on States parties to the 1965 Convention against racial discrimination[12] to adopt legislative and other measures, in conformity with the Convention, in order to protect fully the rights of such populations.

Migrant workers

Draft convention

In March 1984, the Commission on Human Rights considered the progress made by the Working Group on the Drafting of an International Convention on the Protection of the Rights of All Migrant Workers and Their Families, as described in the Group's reports on its May/June inter-sessional meeting and September/October session in 1983.[48] On 15 March 1984,[49] as in the previous year, the Commission invited Member States to continue to co-operate with the Group and reiterated its hope for an early completion of the convention's elaboration.

ECONOMIC AND SOCIAL COUNCIL ACTION

Acting without vote on the recommendation of its Second Committee, the Economic and Social Council adopted resolution 1984/41 on 24 May 1984.

Measures to improve the situation and ensure the human rights and dignity of all migrant workers and their families

The Economic and Social Council,

Mindful of the need for international co-operation in solving international problems of an economic, social, intellectual or humanitarian nature and in developing and encouraging respect for human rights and fundamental freedoms for all, without distinction as to race, sex, language or religion,

Recalling in that regard the provisions of the Universal Declaration of Human Rights, of the International Convention on the Elimination of All Forms of Racial Discrimination and of the International Covenants on Human Rights,

Mindful of the contribution made by migrant workers to the economic growth and the social and cultural development of the host countries,

Noting, in particular, that the problems of migrant workers, which are becoming more serious in some regions for political and economic reasons and for social and cultural reasons, constitute a matter of grave concern and continue to be of the greatest importance to certain countries,

Mindful of the important contribution made by the International Labour Organisation in the protection of the rights of all migrant workers,

Appreciating also the efforts of the United Nations Educational, Scientific and Cultural Organization in matters relating to migrant workers,

Deeply concerned at the fact that, despite the general effort made by Member States, regional intergovernmental organizations and various United Nations bodies, migrant workers are still unable fully to exercise their rights in the social field and in the labour field, as defined in the Universal Declaration of Human Rights,

Emphasizing, therefore, the efforts that must still be made effectively to protect the rights of all migrant workers and their living conditions,

Recalling its resolutions 1981/21 of 6 May 1981 and 1983/40 of 27 May 1983, and Commission on Human Rights resolution 1984/61 of 15 March 1984,

Recalling also its resolutions 1980/16 of 30 April 1980 and 1981/35 of 8 May 1981,

1. *Welcomes* the progress made by the Working Group on the Drafting of an International Convention on the Protection of the Rights of All Migrant Workers and Their Families, established in pursuance of General Assembly resolution 34/172 of 17 December 1979;

2. *Expresses again its conviction* that the drafting of that convention will further facilitate the exchanges of views needed for protecting the human rights and improving the situation of migrant workers and their families;

3. *Expresses the hope* that substantial progress will be made by the Working Group during the two meetings to be held in 1984 in accordance with General Assembly resolution 38/86 of 16 December 1983, with a view to completing the drafting of the convention during the thirty-ninth session of the Assembly;

4. *Decides* to consider at its first regular session of 1985 the question of measures to improve the situation and ensure the human rights and dignity of all migrant workers and to monitor the status of work done with a view to protecting the rights of all migrant workers and their families.

Economic and Social Council resolution 1984/41

24 May 1984   Meeting 20   Adopted without vote

Approved by Second Committee (E/1984/91) without vote, 17 May (meeting 16); 17-nation draft (E/1984/C.2/L.5); agenda item 10.

Sponsors: Algeria, Argentina, Bangladesh, Colombia, Costa Rica, Ecuador, Egypt, Finland, France, Greece, Italy, Mexico, Morocco, Pakistan, Portugal, Sweden, Yugoslavia.

Following adoption of the text, the Federal Republic of Germany said that, despite its reservations on the content and scope of the draft convention as envisaged, it had joined in the consensus on the resolution and would continue to participate in the Group's work.

Working Group activities. The open-ended Working Group on the Drafting of an International Convention on the Protection of the Rights of All Migrant Workers and Their Families, established by the General Assembly in 1979,[50] convened in New York in 1984 for its fourth intersessional meeting, between 29 May and 8 June,[51] and for its fifth session, from 25 September to 5 October.[52]

At the end of those meetings, the Group had concluded the first reading of the draft convention's provisions defining the term "migrant worker" and the categories of workers included and excluded under that term, the articles relating to the rights of documented and undocumented migrant workers and of project-tied migrant workers, and the articles on declarations of exclusions upon signature or ratification. Provisional agreement on those articles concluded the first reading of parts I on scope and definitions, II and III on fundamental and other rights of migrant workers, and VII and VIII on general and final provisions. The first reading was also concluded of parts IV on provisions applicable to particular categories of migrant workers and VI on the convention's application.

Thus completed, the stage had been set for a second reading of the consolidated text, which included the preamble and other parts previously agreed upon provisionally.[53]

GENERAL ASSEMBLY ACTION

Having examined the reports of the Working Group, the General Assembly, acting without vote on the recommendation of the Third Committee, adopted resolution 39/102 on 14 December 1984.

Measures to improve the situation and ensure the human rights and dignity of all migrant workers

The General Assembly,

Reaffirming once more the permanent validity of the principles and standards embodied in the basic instruments regarding the international protection of human rights, in particular in the Universal Declaration of Human Rights, the International Covenants on Human Rights, the International Convention on the Elimination of All Forms of Racial Discrimination and the Convention on the Elimination of All Forms of Discrimination against Women,

Bearing in mind the principles and standards established within the framework of the International Labour Organisation and the United Nations Educational, Scientific and Cultural Organization, and the importance of the task carried out in connection with migrant workers and their families in other specialized agencies and in various organs of the United Nations,

Reiterating that, in spite of the existence of an already established body of principles and standards, there is a need to make further efforts to improve the situation and ensure the human rights and dignity of all migrant workers and their families,

Recalling its resolution 34/172 of 17 December 1979, by which it decided to establish a working group open to all Member States to elaborate an international convention on the protection of the rights of all migrant workers and their families,

Recalling also its resolutions 35/198 of 15 December 1980, 36/160 of 16 December 1981, 37/170 of 17 December 1982 and 38/86 of 16 December 1983, by which it renewed the mandate of the Working Group on the Drafting of an International Convention on the Protection of the Rights of All Migrant Workers and Their Families and requested it to continue its work,

Having examined the progress made by the Working Group during its fourth inter-sessional meeting, held from 29 May to 8 June 1984, as well as the report of the Working Group during the current session of the General Assembly, during which the Working Group concluded the first reading of the draft convention,

1. *Takes note with satisfaction* of the reports of the Working Group on the Drafting of an International Convention on the Protection of the Rights of All Migrant Workers and Their Families and commends it for concluding, in its first reading, the drafting of the preamble and articles, which will serve as the basis for the second reading of the draft convention;

2. *Decides* that, in order to enable it to complete its task as soon as possible, the Working Group shall again hold an inter-sessional meeting of two weeks' duration in New York, immediately after the first regular session of 1985 of the Economic and Social Council;

3. *Invites* the Secretary-General to transmit to Governments the reports of the Working Group so as to enable the members of the Group to undertake the second reading of the preamble and the articles during the inter-sessional meeting to be held in the spring of 1985, as well as to transmit the results obtained at that meeting to the General Assembly for consideration during its fortieth session;

4. *Also invites* the Secretary-General to transmit the above-mentioned documents to the competent organs of the United Nations and to international organizations concerned, for their information, so as to enable them to continue their co-operation with the Working Group;

5. *Decides* that the Working Group shall meet during the fortieth session of the General Assembly, preferably at the beginning of the session, to continue the second reading of the draft international convention on the protection of the rights of all migrant workers and their families.

General Assembly resolution 39/102

14 December 1984   Meeting 101   Adopted without vote

Approved by Third Committee (A/39/700) without vote, 30 November (meeting 55); 25-nation draft (A/C.3/39/L.56); agenda item 12.
Sponsors: Algeria, Argentina, Cameroon, Colombia, Ecuador, Egypt, Finland, France, Greece, India, Italy, Jordan, Mexico, Morocco, Nicaragua, Norway, Pakistan, Philippines, Portugal, Rwanda, Spain, Sweden, Tunisia, Turkey, Yugoslavia.
Financial implications. 5th Committee, A/39/805/Rev.1; S-G, A/C.3/39/L.60, A/C.5/39/71.
Meeting numbers. GA 39th session: 3rd Committee 54, 55; 5th Committee 44, 45; plenary 101.

In resolution 39/21 on elimination of racial discrimination, the Assembly welcomed CERD efforts to eliminate discrimination against migrant workers and their families, to promote their rights and to achieve full equality, including freedom to maintain their cultural characteristics.

Exploitation of labour

Acting on the recommendation of its Second Committee, the Economic and Social Council adopted resolution 1984/30 without vote on 24 May 1984. The text had been submitted by the Sub-Commission in August 1983[54] and recommended for Council action by the Commission on Human Rights, by 42 votes to 1, on 12 March 1984.[55]

Report on the exploitation of labour through illicit and clandestine trafficking

The Economic and Social Council

1. *Decides:*

(a) That the report prepared by the Special Rapporteur, Mrs. H. E. Warzazi, on the exploitation of labour through illicit and clandestine trafficking[56] should be printed and given the widest possible distribution;

(b) To transmit the report for comments and observations to Governments and relevant United Nations bodies and specialized agencies, other intergovernmental organizations and non-governmental organizations;

2. *Requests* the Secretary-General to report to the Sub-Commission on Prevention of Discrimination and Protection of Minorities at its thirty-seventh session on those comments and observations, as well as on other significant developments regarding the human rights of migrant workers.

Economic and Social Council resolution 1984/30

24 May 1984   Meeting 20   Adopted without vote

Approved by Second Committee (E/1984/91) without vote, 17 May (meeting 15); draft by Commission on Human Rights (E/1984/14); agenda item 10.

Protection of minorities

At its February/March 1984 session, the Commission on Human Rights continued to consider, through an informal working group open to its membership, a draft declaration on the rights of persons belonging to national, ethnic, religious and linguistic minorities. A revised, consolidated draft text, prepared in 1980 and submitted to the Commission in 1981,[57] had formed the basis of discussions of each working group set up annually since then. The work accomplished by the 1984 working group, at meetings held between 27 February and 9 March at Geneva, consisted of preliminary agreement on the draft declaration's title and preamble, and a continuation of the first reading of article 1.

Taking note of the group's report,[58] the Commission on 15 March[59] decided to set up another working group in 1985 to continue elaboration of the draft declaration and requested its Sub-Commission to define the term "minority", taking account of related studies and government views.

A definition was accordingly proposed at the August 1984 session of the Sub-Commission. Following a brief discussion, the Sub-Commission, on 27 August,[60] postponed further consideration of the question to its 1985 session.

GENERAL ASSEMBLY ACTION

In resolution 39/21 on elimination of racial discrimination, the General Assembly welcomed CERD efforts to eliminate all forms of discrimination against national or ethnic minorities, among others. It called on States parties to the 1965 Convention against racial discrimination[12] to adopt legislative and other measures, in conformity with the Convention, so as to protect fully the rights of such minorities.

Draft declaration on the human rights of non-citizens

A Working Group, set up by the General Assembly in December 1983[61] and open to all United Nations Members, met in New York between 3 October and 20 November 1984 to continue drafting a declaration on the human rights of individuals not citizens of the country in which they lived. At those meetings, the Group adopted the following provisions in second reading: article 4 (paragraph 1 *(d)* on the right to marry and found a family, and paragraph 2 on additional fundamental rights); article 7 prohibiting expulsion of legal aliens and defining exceptions to it; article 8 defining economic and social rights; article 9 prohibiting arbitrary deprivation of lawfully acquired assets; and article 10 on freedom of communication. The agreed provisions were annexed to the Group's report.[62]

GENERAL ASSEMBLY ACTION

Acting without vote on the recommendation of the Third Committee, the General Assembly adopted resolution 39/103 on 14 December 1984.

Question of the international legal protection of the human rights of individuals who are not citizens of the country in which they live
The General Assembly,

Bearing in mind Economic and Social Council resolutions 1790(LIV) of 18 May 1973 and 1871(LVI) of 17 May 1974 concerning the question of the international legal protection of the human rights of individuals who are not citizens of the country in which they live,

Recalling Commission on Human Rights resolutions 8(XXIX) of 21 March 1973, 11(XXX) of 6 March 1974, 16(XXXV) of 14 March 1979 and 19(XXXVI) of 29 February 1980 on the same subject,

Recalling also resolution 9(XXXI) of 13 September 1978 of the Sub-Commission on Prevention of Discrimination and Protection of Minorities,

Recalling that the Economic and Social Council, by its resolution 1980/29 of 2 May 1980, decided to transmit to the General Assembly at its thirty-fifth session the text of the draft declaration on the human rights of individuals who are not citizens of the country in which they live, prepared by the Special Rapporteur of the Sub-Commission on Prevention of Discrimination and Protection of Minorities and amended by the Sub-Commission, together with the comments on the text received from Member States in response to Council decision 1979/36 of 10 May 1979, and recommended that the Assembly should consider the adoption of a declaration on the subject,

Recalling also its resolutions 35/199 of 15 December 1980, 36/165 of 16 December 1981, 37/169 of 17 December 1982 and 38/87 of 16 December 1983, by which it decided to establish an open-ended working group for the purpose of concluding the elaboration of the draft declaration on the human rights of individuals who are not citizens of the country in which they live,

Having considered the comments submitted by Governments, specialized agencies, regional and intergovernmental organizations and the competent organs of the United Nations pursuant to General Assembly resolution 37/169 on the reports of the open-ended working groups established at the thirty-fifth, thirty-sixth, thirty-seventh and thirty-eighth sessions of the Assembly,

Having considered the report of the Working Group established for the purpose of concluding the elaboration of the draft declaration on the human rights of individuals who are not citizens of the country in which they live,

1. *Takes note* of the report of the Working Group and of the fact that, although the Working Group has done useful work, it has not had sufficient time to conclude its task;

2. *Decides* to establish, at its fortieth session, an open-ended working group for the purpose of concluding the elaboration of the draft declaration on the human rights of individuals who are not citizens of the country in which they live;

3. *Requests* the Secretary-General to invite Governments to submit further comments and views on the draft declaration as a whole, taking into consideration

the progress made by the Working Group and the present state of the draft, in time for their inclusion in a report of the Secretary-General to be submitted to the General Assembly at its fortieth session;

4. *Expresses the hope* that a draft declaration on the human rights of individuals who are not citizens of the country in which they live will be adopted by the General Assembly at its fortieth session.

General Assembly resolution 39/103

14 December 1984   Meeting 101   Adopted without vote

Approved by Third Committee (A/39/700) without vote, 30 November (meeting 55); 6-nation draft (A/C.3/39/L.58); agenda item 12.

Sponsors: Costa Rica, Dominican Republic, Greece, Italy, Mexico, Morocco.

Financial implications. 5th Committee, A/39/805/Rev.1; S-G, A/C.3/39/L.61, A/C.5/39/72.

Meeting numbers. GA 39th session: 3rd Committee 54, 55; 5th Committee 44, 45; plenary 101.

Discrimination in criminal justice

Acting on the recommendation of its Second Committee, the Economic and Social Council in May adopted decision 1984/141 without vote. The text had been submitted by the Sub-Commission in August 1983[63] and recommended for Council action by the Commission on Human Rights on 12 March 1984.[64]

Measures to combat racism and racial discrimination

At its 20th plenary meeting, on 24 May 1984, the Council, noting Commission on Human Rights decision 1984/107 of 12 March 1984, decided that the report prepared by Mr. Abu Sayeed Chowdhury, Special Rapporteur of the Sub-Commission on Prevention of Discrimination and Protection of Minorities, entitled "Study on discriminatory treatment of members of racial, ethnic, religious or linguistic groups at the various levels in the administration of criminal justice, such as police, military, administrative and judicial investigations, arrest, detention, trial and execution of sentences, including the ideologies or beliefs which contribute or lead to racism in the administration of criminal justice",[65] in accordance with section A of Sub-Commission resolution 4(XXXIII) of 5 September 1980, should be printed and given the widest possible distribution, including distribution in Arabic.

Economic and Social Council decision 1984/141

Adopted without vote

Approved by Second Committee (E/1984/91) without vote, 17 May (meeting 16); draft by Commission on Human Rights (E/1984/14); agenda item 10.

REFERENCES

[1]E/1984/14 & Corr.1. [2]E/CN.4/1985/3. [3]YUN 1983, p. 806, GA res. 38/14, 22 Nov. 1983. [4]YUN 1973, p. 524, GA res. 3057(XXVIII), annex, 2 Nov. 1973. [5]E/1984/56 & Add.1,2. [6]E/1984/34 & Add.1-3. [7]E/1984/14 (res. 1984/8). [8]YUN 1983, p. 807, GA res. 38/14, 22 Nov. 1983. [9]*Ibid.*, p. 814. [10]A/39/167-E/1984/33 & Add.1. [11]YUN 1973, p. 103, GA res. 3068(XXVIII), annex, 30 Nov. 1973. [12]YUN 1965, p. 440, GA res. 2106 A (XX), annex, 21 Dec. 1965. [13]YUN 1976, p. 580. [14]YUN 1979, p. 805, GA res. 34/24, 15 Nov. 1979. [15]*Ibid.*, p. 806, GA res. 34/24, annex, 15 Nov. 1979. [16]YUN 1975, p. 599, GA res. 3379(XXX), 10 Nov. 1975. [17]YUN 1983, p. 802. [18]A/39/18 (dec. 2(XXX)). [19]E/CN.4/1985/3 (res. 1984/5). [20]A/39/167/Add.2-E/1984/33/Add.2. [21]E/1984/14 (res. 1984/36). [22]*Ibid.* (res. 1984/9). [23]YUN 1978, p. 662. [24]YUN 1969, p. 488. [25]A/39/459. [26]A/39/79 & Corr.1. [27]A/39/18. [28]YUN 1983, p. 817, GA res. 38/20, 22 Nov. 1983. [29]A/39/18 (dec. 1(XXIX)). [30]*Ibid.* (dec. 1(XXX)). [31]E/1984/14 (res. 1984/42). [32]YUN 1983, p. 818, GA res. 38/99, 16 Dec. 1983. [33]A/39/168-E/1984/39 & Add.1,2. [34]A/C.3/39/11. [35]A/39/836. [36]E/1984/14 (res. 1984/57). [37]YUN 1981, p. 881, GA res. 36/55, 25 Nov. 1981. [38]YUN 1983, p. 820. [39]E/CN.4/Sub.2/1984/28. [40]E/CN.4/1985/3 (res. 1984/31). [41]YUN 1983, p. 820, ESC dec. 1983/150, 27 May 1983. [42]*Ibid.*, p. 821. [43]E/1984/14 (res. 1984/32). [44]E/CN.4/Sub.2/1984/20. [45]E/CN.4/Sub.2/1983/21/Add.8. [46]E/CN.4/1985/3 (res. 1984/35). [47]*Ibid.* (dec. 1984/102). [48]YUN 1983, p. 823. [49]E/1984/14 (res. 1984/61). [50]YUN 1979, p. 875, GA res. 34/172, 17 Dec. 1979. [51]A/C.3/39/1. [52]A/C.3/39/4 & Corr.1. [53]A/C.3/39/WG.1/WP.1. [54]YUN 1983, p. 824. [55]E/1984/14 (res. 1984/38). [56]YUN 1976, p. 607. [57]YUN 1981, p. 883. [58]E/CN.4/1984/74. [59]E/1984/14 (res. 1984/62). [60]E/CN.4/1985/3 (dec. 1984/101). [61]YUN 1983, p. 825, GA res. 38/87, 16 Dec. 1983. [62]A/C.3/39/9 & Corr.1. [63]YUN 1983, p. 826. [64]E/1984/14 (dec. 1984/107). [65]YUN 1982, p. 1068.

PUBLICATION

The United Nations and Human Rights (DPI/808), Sales No. E.84.I.6.

Civil and political rights

Covenant on Civil and Political Rights and Optional Protocol

Accessions and ratifications

As at 31 December 1984, the International Covenant on Civil and Political Rights and the Optional Protocol thereto, adopted by the General Assembly in 1966[1] and in force since 1976,[2] had been ratified or acceded to by 80 and 34 States, respectively. Cameroon, Togo and Zambia became parties to the Covenant in 1984. Cameroon, France and Zambia acceded to the Protocol. Two States—Ecuador and Peru—made the declaration under article 41 of the Covenant recognizing the competence of the Human Rights Committee to receive and consider communications to the effect that a State party claimed that another was not fulfilling its obligations under the Covenant.

In his report on international covenants on human rights to the Assembly,[3] the Secretary-General provided information on the status of the Covenant and the Protocol as at 1 September 1984.

Implementation of the Covenant and the Optional Protocol

Action by the Commission on Human Rights. On 6 March,[4] the Commission on Human Rights expressed appreciation that the Human Rights Committee continued to strive for uniform standards in implementing the Covenant and the Optional Protocol and invited States to become parties to them and to consider making the declaration under article 41. In emphasizing the importance of the strictest compliance with those instruments, the Commission stressed the obligation of a State party availing itself (in time of public emergency) of the right of derogation from the Covenant's provisions in accordance with article 4, paragraph 1, immediately to inform the other States parties, through the Secretary-General, of the provisions from which it had derogated and its reasons for doing so.

The Commission welcomed the measures taken by the Secretary-General to publish the Committee's documentation in annual bound volumes and requested him to make available the resources necessary to produce the remaining volumes. The Commission encouraged Governments to give the Covenant and the Protocol the widest possible publicity. It took note of a December 1983 General Assembly request[5] that the Secretary-General continue to ensure the ability of the United Nations Centre for Human Rights to assist the Committee in its functions under the Covenant.

Human Rights Committee activities. The Human Rights Committee, established under article 28 of the Covenant, held three sessions in 1984: the twenty-first in New York, from 26 March to 13 April; the twenty-second and twenty-third at Geneva, from 9 to 27 July, and from 22 October to 9 November.

The Committee considered reports and additional information submitted by 12 States (Byelorussian SSR, Canada, Chile, Democratic People's Republic of Korea, Egypt, Gambia, German Democratic Republic, India, Panama, Trinidad and Tobago, USSR, Venezuela) under article 40 of the Covenant. The Committee also concluded consideration of and adopted views on five communications from individuals claiming that their rights under the Covenant had been violated and that they had exhausted all available domestic remedies. The cases concerned Uruguay (4) and Zaire (1). The Committee decided that six other such communications—from five individuals and from a group of associations for the rights of the disabled and handicapped—were inadmissible.

As authorized by the Assembly in December 1983,[6] Arabic language services were provided as from the Committee's twenty-first session. On 27 July 1984, the Committee unanimously adopted its eighth annual report[7] to the Assembly.

ECONOMIC AND SOCIAL COUNCIL ACTION

In decision 1984/101 of 10 February on its basic work programme for 1984, the Economic and Social Council requested the Secretary-General to transmit the annual report of the Human Rights Committee, among others, directly to the Assembly for consideration, on the understanding that the Council would again consider the reschedul-

ing of the Committee's meetings. The Council had invited the Committee to consider that possibility in 1983 so that, starting in 1984, it could submit its report to the Assembly through the Council at the latter's first regular session, during the second quarter of the year.

Drawing attention to that decision on 4 May 1984, the President informed the Council that the Committee wished to maintain its current schedule of meetings, contending that transmitting its report to the Assembly through the Council at the end of its yearly session in July, as currently practised, enabled the Assembly to consider the most up-to-date information on the Committee's work and other important human rights developments. The President had also been informed of the extreme difficulties a rescheduling of meetings would pose to Committee members, who served in their personal capacity as experts and as such had other commitments. In the circumstances, the Committee would find ways of accommodating the Council's requests for information. It could transmit its general comments based on reports received from States parties, as provided for by article 40, paragraph 4, of the Covenant.

Finland was of the view that article 45 of the Covenant—stipulating that the Committee report annually on its activities to the Assembly through the Council—did not limit the Council's role to a strictly procedural forwarding of the Committee's report to the Assembly; however, it recognized that there were substantive arguments against giving the report the same degree of consideration in the Council as in the Assembly's Third Committee. Consequently, Finland recommended that serious thought be given to defining an appropriate division of functions between the Council and the Assembly in this regard.

Austria said it was not aware that the Committee had ever transmitted general comments to the Council. Interpreting the term "specialized agencies" to include the Human Rights Committee, Austria pointed out that Article 64 of the Charter of the United Nations, entitling the Council to obtain regular reports from specialized agencies, also applied to the issue before the Council. Meticulous application of that Article and of article 40, paragraph 4, of the Covenant, could strengthen the role of the Council and contribute to its revitalization.

Following those statements, the Council adopted resolution 1984/2 without vote on 8 May 1984.

Scheduling of the sessions of the Human Rights Committee established under the International Covenant on Civil and Political Rights

The Economic and Social Council,

Recalling paragraph 5 (g) of its decision 1984/101 of 10 February 1984,

Having heard the statement made by the President of the Economic and Social Council on 4 May 1984 regarding the outcome of his consultations with the Chairman of the Human Rights Committee on the question of the scheduling of the sessions of that Committee, and the views expressed by delegations on the matter,

Decides to request the President of the Economic and Social Council to continue further his consultations with the Chairman of the Human Rights Committee and to report thereon to the Council at its organizational session for 1985.

Economic and Social Council resolution 1984/2

8 May 1984   Meeting 9   Adopted without vote

Oral proposal by President; agenda item 5.
Meeting numbers. ESC 7, 9.

GENERAL ASSEMBLY ACTION

In resolution 39/136, the General Assembly took note of the Human Rights Committee report and expressed satisfaction with the serious and constructive manner in which the Committee was continuing to perform its functions. The Assembly urged States to become parties to the Covenant and to consider acceding to the Optional Protocol. It invited States parties to make the declaration under article 41 of the Covenant and emphasized the importance of strictest compliance with their obligations under the Covenant and Optional Protocol. It urged those parties requested by the Committee to provide additional information to do so. It also urged the Secretary-General to take determined steps within existing resources to give publicity to the Committee's work and to continue to expedite publication of its official public records in bound volumes, starting with its first session. The Assembly further requested him to keep the Committee informed of the relevant activities of the Assembly, the Council and selected United Nations organs.

States of siege or emergency

On 6 March 1984,[8] the Commission on Human Rights stated that it looked forward to the first annual report on compliance with national and international rules governing the legality of the declaration of a state of siege or emergency, including a list of countries in which such a state had been declared or terminated. It decided to examine the report in 1985 as a matter of priority, to determine what further action should be taken on the question. The report was to be submitted by the Sub-Commission in connection with its September 1983 decision[9] to include in its agenda an item on implementation of the right of derogation provided for under article 4 of the Covenant.

Preparation of the report and list was among the topics discussed by the 1984 Working Group on Detention (see below, under "Rights of detained persons") in August. Agreeing that preparation of the list was premature, the Group suggested that the Sub-Commission invite one of its members to conduct a technical study on a method of work for drafting such a report and list.

Accordingly, the Sub-Commission on 30 August[10] requested from one of its members a paper on how best to accomplish the yearly preparation of such a report. It recommended to the Commission a draft resolution for adoption by the Economic and Social Council, which would authorize the Sub-Commission to appoint a special rapporteur to prepare the annual report. The rapporteur, who would be asked to submit the first report to the Sub-Commission in 1986, would be provided with the necessary assistance by the Secretary-General.

Also in March 1984, the Commission called on Chile to put an end to the régime of exception and to the practice of declaring states of emergency (see below, under "Human rights violations"); it invited Paraguay to do the same (see below).

Paraguay

Seriously concerned at the permanent application of the state of siege in Paraguay since 1954, the Commission on Human Rights, by a roll-call vote of 36 to 1, with 5 abstentions, taken on 13 March 1984,[11] invited the Government to consider ending the state of siege in order to encourage the promotion of and respect for human rights in the country.

By 19 votes to none, on 28 August,[12] the Sub-Commission, taking note of the statements of Paraguay before the Commission about an eventual project for the abrogation of the state of siege, requested the Commission to recommend to the Government to persevere in its aim to co-operate with the Commission towards that end and to consider enacting a measure of amnesty to allow popular participation in the country's public affairs. The Sub-Commission asked the Secretary-General to transmit information to it in 1985 on developments on the question of ending the state of siege.

Self-determination of peoples

In six resolutions adopted at its February/March 1984 session, the Commission on Human Rights dealt with the right of peoples to self-determination (see below). It reaffirmed that right for Palestinians,[13] South Africans as a whole and Namibians,[14] Kampucheans,[15] the people of Western Sahara,[16] Afghans,[17] and the people of Grenada.[18]

The Commission's actions and debate, and actions taken by the Economic and Social Council in 1984, were summarized by the Secretary-General in a report to the General Assembly on the universal realization of the right to self-determination.[19] Also summarized were responses to two November 1983 Assembly resolutions on the topic[20] from 16 Governments, three United Nations organs, six specialized agencies and four NGOs. An additional response, from the USSR, was transmitted on 10 November 1984.[21]

In 1984, as in the previous year, the Assembly adopted two resolutions on the right to self-determination (see below)—a right it repeatedly reaffirmed for individual Non-Self-Governing Territories (see TRUSTEESHIP AND DECOLONIZATION, Chapter IV). The Assembly also urged States to respect that right, as well as peoples' right freely to choose their socio-political system and to pursue their political, economic, social and cultural development, in its resolution 39/159 on the inadmissibility of State terrorism in relation to the sovereignty and political independence of States.

GENERAL ASSEMBLY ACTION

Acting on the recommendation of the Third Committee, the General Assembly adopted two resolutions on 23 November 1984 concerning the right of peoples to self-determination. The first, resolution 39/17, was adopted by recorded vote.

Importance of the universal realization of the right of peoples to self-determination and of the speedy granting of independence to colonial countries and peoples for the effective guarantee and observance of human rights

The General Assembly,

Reaffirming its faith in the importance of the implementation of the Declaration on the Granting of Independence to Colonial Countries and Peoples contained in its resolution 1514(XV) of 14 December 1960,

Reaffirming the importance of the universal realization of the right of peoples to self-determination, national sovereignty and territorial integrity and of the speedy granting of independence to colonial countries and peoples as imperatives for the full enjoyment of all human rights,

Reaffirming the obligation of all Member States to comply with the principles of the Charter of the United Nations and the resolutions of the United Nations regarding the exercise of the right to self-determination by peoples under colonial and foreign domination,

Recalling its resolutions 2649(XXV) of 30 November 1970, 2955(XXVII) of 12 December 1972, 3070(XXVIII) of 30 November 1973, 3246(XXIX) of 29 November 1974, 3382(XXX) of 10 November 1975, 33/24 of 29 November 1978, 34/44 of 23 November 1979, 35/35 of 14 November 1980, 36/9 of 28 October 1981, 37/43 of 3 December 1982 and 38/17 of 22 November 1983, and Security Council resolutions 418(1977) of 4 November 1977 and 421(1977) of 9 December 1977,

Recalling also its resolutions 1514(XV) of 14 December 1960, 2465(XXIII) of 20 December 1968, 2708(XXV) of 14 December 1970, 33/44 of 13 December 1978, 35/119 of 11 December 1980, 36/68 of 1 December 1981, 37/35 of 23 November 1982 and 38/54 of 7 December 1983, concerning the implementation of the

Declaration on the Granting of Independence to Colonial Countries and Peoples,

Recalling further its resolutions 3103(XXVIII) of 12 December 1973, 3314(XXIX) of 14 December 1974 and 38/137 of 19 December 1983, as well as Security Council resolutions 405(1977) of 14 April 1977, 419(1977) of 24 November 1977, 496(1981) of 15 December 1981 and 507(1982) of 28 May 1982, in which the United Nations condemned the recruiting and the use of mercenaries, in particular against developing countries and national liberation movements,

Recalling further its resolutions on the question of Namibia, in particular resolution ES-8/2 of 14 September 1981, and Security Council resolutions 532(1983) of 31 May 1983 and 539(1983) of 28 October 1983,

Recalling the Paris Declaration on Namibia and the Programme of Action on Namibia, adopted by the International Conference in Support of the Struggle of the Namibian People for Independence,

Bearing in mind the outcome of the International Conference on the Alliance between South Africa and Israel, held at Vienna from 11 to 13 July 1983,

Welcoming the holding at Tunis from 7 to 9 August 1984 of the Conference of Arab Solidarity with the Struggle for Liberation in Southern Africa,

Recalling resolutions CM/Res.934(XL) on Namibia, CM/Res.935(XL) on South Africa and CM/Res.936(XL) on the situation in southern Africa adopted by the Council of Ministers of the Organization of African Unity at its fortieth ordinary session, held at Addis Ababa from 27 February to 5 March 1984,

Reaffirming that the system of *apartheid* imposed on the South African people constitutes a violation of the fundamental rights of that people, a crime against humanity and a constant threat to international peace and security,

Gravely concerned at the continuation of the illegal occupation of Namibia by South Africa and the continued violations of the human rights of the people in the Territory and of the other peoples still under colonial domination and alien subjugation,

Expressing its profound indignation and its preoccupation at the brutal repression which followed the imposition of the so-called "new constitution" by the *apartheid* régime of South Africa in defiance of world public opinion,

Reaffirming its resolution 39/2 of 28 September 1984 and recalling Security Council resolution 554(1984) of 17 August 1984, which rejected the so-called "new constitution" as null and void,

Deeply concerned at the continued terrorist acts of aggression committed by the Pretoria régime against independent African States in the region,

Deeply indignant at the continued occupation of part of the territory of Angola by the troops of the racist régime of South Africa,

Recalling Security Council resolutions 527(1982) of 15 December 1982 and 535(1983) of 29 June 1983 on Lesotho,

Reaffirming the national unity and territorial integrity of the Comoros,

Recalling the Political Declaration adopted by the First Conference of Heads of State and Government of the Organization of African Unity and the League of Arab States, held at Cairo from 7 to 9 March 1977,

Recalling further its relevant resolutions on the question of Palestine, in particular resolutions 3236(XXIX)

and 3237(XXIX) of 22 November 1974, 36/120 of 10 December 1981, ES-7/6 of 19 August 1982, 37/86 of 10 December 1982 and 38/58 of 13 December 1983,

Recalling the Geneva Declaration on Palestine and the Programme of Action for the Achievement of Palestinian Rights, adopted by the International Conference on the Question of Palestine,

Considering that the denial of the inalienable rights of the Palestinian people to self-determination, sovereignty, independence and return to Palestine and the repeated acts of aggression by Israel against the people of the region constitute a serious threat to international peace and security,

Deeply shocked and alarmed at the deplorable consequences of the Israeli invasion of Lebanon and recalling all the relevant resolutions of the Security Council, in particular resolutions 508(1982) of 5 June 1982, 509(1982) of 6 June 1982, 520(1982) of 17 September 1982 and 521(1982) of 19 September 1982,

1. *Calls upon* all States to implement fully and faithfully all the resolutions of the United Nations regarding the exercise of the right to self-determination and independence by peoples under colonial and foreign domination;

2. *Reaffirms* the legitimacy of the struggle of peoples for their independence, territorial integrity, national unity and liberation from colonial domination, *apartheid* and foreign occupation by all available means, including armed struggle;

3. *Reaffirms* the inalienable right of the Namibian people, the Palestinian people and all peoples under foreign and colonial domination to self-determination, national independence, territorial integrity, national unity and sovereignty without foreign interference;

4. *Strongly condemns* those Governments that do not recognize the right to self-determination and independence of all peoples still under colonial domination and alien subjugation, notably the peoples of Africa and the Palestinian people;

5. *Calls* for the full and immediate implementation of the declarations and programmes of action on Namibia and on Palestine adopted by the international conferences on those questions;

6. *Reaffirms* its vigorous condemnation of the continued illegal occupation of Namibia by South Africa;

7. *Condemns* the policy of "bantustanization" and reiterates its support for the oppressed people of South Africa in its just and legitimate struggle against the racist minority régime of Pretoria;

8. *Reaffirms* its rejection of the so-called "new constitution" as null and void and reiterates that peace in South Africa can only be guaranteed by the establishment of majority rule through the full and free exercise of adult suffrage by all the people in a united and undivided South Africa;

9. *Strongly condemns* the wanton killing of peaceful and defenceless demonstrators and workers on strike, as well as the arbitrary arrests of the leaders and activists of the United Democratic Front and other mass organizations;

10. *Condemns* South Africa for its increasing oppression of the Namibian people, for the massive militarization of Namibia and for its armed attacks launched against the States in the region in order to destabilize them politically and to sabotage and destroy their economies;

11. *Strongly condemns* the establishment and use of armed terrorist groups by South Africa with a view to pitting them against the national liberation movements and destabilizing the legitimate Governments of southern Africa;

12. *Strongly condemns* the continued occupation of parts of southern Angola and demands the immediate and unconditional withdrawal of the South African troops from Angolan territory;

13. *Strongly reaffirms* its solidarity with the independent African countries and national liberation movements that are victims of murderous acts of aggression and destabilization by the racist régime of Pretoria, and calls upon the international community to render increased assistance and support to these countries in order to enable them to strengthen their defence capacity, defend their sovereignty and territorial integrity and peacefully rebuild and develop;

14. *Reaffirms* that the practice of using mercenaries against sovereign States and national liberation movements constitutes a criminal act and calls upon the Governments of all countries to enact legislation declaring the recruitment, financing and training of mercenaries in their territories and the transit of mercenaries through their territories to be punishable offences, and prohibiting their nationals from serving as mercenaries, and to report on such legislation to the Secretary-General;

15. *Strongly condemns* the continued violations of the human rights of the peoples still under colonial domination and alien subjugation, the continuation of the illegal occupation of Namibia, South Africa's attempts to dismember its territory, the perpetuation of the racist minority régime in southern Africa and the denial to the Palestinian people of their inalienable national rights;

16. *Further strongly condemns* the racist régime of Pretoria for its acts of destabilization, armed aggression and economic blockade against Lesotho and strongly urges the international community to extend maximum assistance to Lesotho to enable it to fulfil its international humanitarian obligations towards refugees and to use its influence on the racist régime to desist from its terrorist acts against Lesotho;

17. *Denounces* the collusion between Israel and South Africa and expresses support for the Declaration of the International Conference on the Alliance between South Africa and Israel;

18. *Strongly condemns* the policy of those Western States, Israel and other States whose political, economic, military, nuclear, strategic, cultural and sports relations with the racist minority régime in South Africa encourage that régime to persist in its suppression of the aspirations of peoples to self-determination and independence;

19. *Again demands* the immediate application of the mandatory arms embargo against South Africa, imposed under Security Council resolution 418(1977), by all countries and more particularly by those countries that maintain military and nuclear co-operation with the racist Pretoria régime and continue to supply it with related *matériel;*

20. *Calls* for the full implementation of the provisions of the Paris Declaration on Sanctions against South Africa and the Special Declaration on Namibia adopted by the International Conference on Sanctions against

South Africa, held under the auspices of the United Nations and the Organization of African Unity;

21. *Demands once again* the immediate implementation of its resolution ES-8/2 on Namibia;

22. *Urges* all States, specialized agencies, competent organizations of the United Nations system and other international organizations to extend their support to the Namibian people through its sole and legitimate representative, the South West Africa People's Organization, in its struggle to gain its right to self-determination and independence in accordance with the Charter of the United Nations;

23. *Reaffirms* the resolutions on the question of Western Sahara adopted by the Assembly of Heads of State and Government of the Organization of African Unity at its eighteenth and nineteenth ordinary sessions, held at Nairobi from 24 to 27 June 1981 and at Addis Ababa from 6 to 12 June 1983, and calls for their immediate implementation;

24. *Notes* the contacts between the Government of the Comoros and the Government of France in the search for a just solution to the problem of the integration of the Comorian island of Mayotte in the Comoros, in accordance with the resolutions of the Organization of African Unity and the United Nations on this question;

25. *Calls* for a substantial increase in all forms of assistance given by all States, United Nations organs, specialized agencies and non-governmental organizations to the victims of racism, racial discrimination and *apartheid* through their national liberation movements recognized by the Organization of African Unity;

26. *Demands* the immediate release of women and children detained in Namibia and South Africa;

27. *Strongly condemns* the constant and deliberate violations of the fundamental rights of the Palestinian people, as well as the expansionist activities of Israel in the Middle East, which constitute an obstacle to the achievement of the self-determination and independence by the Palestinian people and a threat to peace and stability in the region;

28. *Further strongly condemns* the massacre of Palestinians and other civilians at Beirut and the Israeli aggression against Lebanon, which endangers stability, peace and security in the region;

29. *Demands* the immediate and unconditional release of all persons detained or imprisoned as a result of their struggle for self-determination and independence, full respect for their fundamental individual rights and compliance with article 5 of the Universal Declaration of Human Rights, under which no one shall be subjected to torture or to cruel, inhuman or degrading treatment;

30. *Urges* all States, specialized agencies, competent organizations of the United Nations system and other international organizations to extend their support to the Palestinian people through its sole and legitimate representative, the Palestine Liberation Organization, in its struggle to regain its right to self-determination and independence in accordance with the Charter;

31. *Expresses its appreciation* for the material and other forms of assistance that peoples under colonial rule continue to receive from Governments, organizations of the United Nations system and intergovernmental organizations and calls for a substantial increase in this assistance;

32. *Urges* all States, specialized agencies and other competent organizations of the United Nations system to do their utmost to ensure the full implementation of the Declaration on the Granting of Independence to Colonial Countries and Peoples and to intensify their efforts to support peoples under colonial, foreign and racist domination in their just struggle for self-determination and independence;

33. *Requests* the Secretary-General to give maximum publicity to the Declaration on the Granting of Independence to Colonial Countries and Peoples and to give the widest possible publicity to the struggle of oppressed peoples for the achievement of their self-determination and national independence and to report periodically to the General Assembly on his activities;

34. *Decides* to consider this item again at its fortieth session on the basis of the reports that Governments, organizations of the United Nations system and intergovernmental and non-governmental organizations have been requested to submit concerning the strengthening of assistance to colonial territories and peoples.

General Assembly resolution 39/17

23 November 1984   Meeting 71   121-17-7 (recorded vote)

Approved by Third Committee (A/39/657) by recorded vote (105-17-9), 8 November (meeting 34); draft by Ethiopia, for African Group (A/C.3/39/L.3); agenda item 87.

Meeting numbers. GA 39th session: 3rd Committee 4-15, 27, 30, 34, 35; plenary 71.

Recorded vote in Assembly as follows:

In favour: Afghanistan, Albania, Algeria, Angola, Antigua and Barbuda, Argentina, Bahamas, Bahrain, Bangladesh, Barbados, Benin, Bhutan, Bolivia, Botswana, Brazil, Brunei Darussalam, Bulgaria, Burkina Faso, Burma, Burundi, Byelorussian SSR, Cameroon, Cape Verde, Central African Republic, Chad, Chile, China, Colombia, Comoros, Congo, Cuba, Cyprus, Czechoslovakia, Democratic Kampuchea, Democratic Yemen, Djibouti, Dominican Republic, Ecuador, Egypt, Equatorial Guinea, Ethiopia, Fiji, Gabon, Gambia, German Democratic Republic, Ghana, Grenada, Guinea, Guinea-Bissau, Guyana, Haiti, Honduras, Hungary, India, Indonesia, Iran, Iraq, Ivory Coast, Jamaica, Jordan, Kenya, Kuwait, Lao People's Democratic Republic, Lebanon, Lesotho, Liberia, Libyan Arab Jamahiriya, Madagascar, Malaysia, Maldives, Mali, Malta, Mauritania, Mexico, Mongolia, Morocco, Mozambique, Nepal, Nicaragua, Niger, Nigeria, Oman, Pakistan, Panama, Papua New Guinea, Peru, Philippines, Poland, Qatar, Romania, Rwanda, Saint Lucia, Samoa, Sao Tome and Principe, Saudi Arabia, Senegal, Sierra Leone, Singapore, Somalia, Sri Lanka, Sudan, Suriname, Swaziland, Syrian Arab Republic, Thailand, Togo, Trinidad and Tobago, Tunisia, Turkey, Uganda, Ukrainian SSR, USSR, United Arab Emirates, United Republic of Tanzania, Uruguay, Venezuela, Viet Nam, Yemen, Yugoslavia, Zambia, Zimbabwe.

Against: Australia, Belgium, Canada, Denmark, Finland, France, Germany, Federal Republic of, Iceland, Israel, Italy, Luxembourg, Netherlands, New Zealand, Norway, Sweden, United Kingdom, United States.

Abstaining: Austria, Greece, Ireland, Japan, Malawi, Portugal, Spain.

Speaking on behalf of the 10 European Community members, Ireland said they found the text—submitted without the usual wide consultations among all the groups—negative, unbalanced and unacceptable in several respects. These concerned southern Africa and the Middle East, the encouragement of armed action to solve international problems, wording to the effect that maintaining relations with a State was equivalent to approval or encouragement of its policies, and the references to violations of peoples' right to self-determination in certain situations but not to flagrant violations of it in Afghanistan and Kampuchea. In Canada's opinion, the text contained excessive and polemical language and presented a biased view of various international situations.

Portugal said certain provisions gave rise to reservations; in addition to the eighth, ninth and twenty-third preambular paragraphs and paragraphs 18 and 27, it could not agree with the endorsement of armed struggle in paragraph 2. It maintained its previously expressed reservations on the declarations and action programmes mentioned in paragraph 5. Its reservations on paragraphs 17 and 20 stemmed from references to conferences it had not attended. Finally, while it had affirmed its support for Namibia on numerous occasions, it did not believe that isolating South Africa was the best way to promote a solution to the Namibia problem.

Austria said it had to abstain because paragraph 2 legitimized "all means" of struggle for independence. Greece could not support the wording of paragraph 19, and Spain could not endorse either paragraph.

Burma recalled that it had consistently supported the right of peoples to self-determination and the speedy granting of independence to colonial countries and peoples; however, it voiced reservations on what it regarded as the excessive language of some provisions. Ecuador shared Portugal's reservations on references to conferences it had not attended and on the implementation called for in paragraph 5, which it felt was exclusively for a State to decide in the exercise of its sovereignty. Honduras remarked that the text, while not sufficiently emphasizing peaceful settlement of disputes, contained objectives compatible with those of Honduran foreign policy: the struggle against colonialism, *apartheid* and racism; non-use of force; and support for self-determination of peoples. In the Committee, where Honduras abstained, it noted that the text was too selective. Malta affirmed its support for resolutions expressing dissatisfaction with the *apartheid* policies of South Africa, but stated that such support did not imply full agreement with the provisions or language of the text under consideration.

Among others voicing some reservations were the Byelorussian SSR and the Dominican Republic. Argentina took issue with the wording of some paragraphs. With regard to paragraph 2, Peru stressed that only peaceful means of struggle in accordance with the United Nations Charter were legitimate. Uruguay regarded armed struggle as contrary to the Charter principles and purposes; it also objected to paragraph 18, terming it biased. Turkey regretted that Western countries were expressly condemned in paragraph 18. Chile also particularly objected to the inclusion of armed struggle as a means of struggling for independence, saying that on the other hand the text failed to mention well-known situations such as those in Afghanistan and Kampuchea. Brazil and Mexico had reservations especially on paragraph 17; con-

cerning paragraph 5, Brazil pointed to its comments on certain parts of the documents mentioned.

For the USSR, the legitimacy of the struggle of peoples for independence, reaffirmed in paragraph 2, was beyond all doubt. Colombia supported the text because it believed that dialogue was a better means of resolving problems than physical or verbal violence.

The second resolution, 39/18, was adopted by the Assembly without vote.

Universal realization of the right of peoples to self-determination

The General Assembly,

Reaffirming the importance, for the effective guarantee and observance of human rights, of the universal realization of the right of peoples to self-determination enshrined in the Charter of the United Nations and embodied in the International Covenants on Human Rights, as well as in the Declaration on the Granting of Independence to Colonial Countries and Peoples contained in General Assembly resolution 1514(XV) of 14 December 1960,

Welcoming the progressive exercise of the right to self-determination by peoples under colonial, foreign or alien occupation and their emergence into sovereign statehood and independence,

Deeply concerned at the continuation of acts or threats of foreign military intervention and occupation that are threatening to suppress, or have already suppressed, the right to self-determination of an increasing number of sovereign peoples and nations,

Expressing grave concern that, as a consequence of the persistence of such actions, millions of people have been and are being uprooted from their homes as refugees and displaced persons, and emphasizing the urgent need for concerted international action to alleviate their conditions,

Recalling the relevant resolutions regarding the violation of the right of peoples to self-determination and other human rights as a result of foreign military intervention, aggression and occupation, adopted by the Commission on Human Rights at its thirty-sixth, thirty-seventh, thirty-eighth, thirty-ninth and fortieth sessions,

Reiterating its resolutions 35/35 B of 14 November 1980, 36/10 of 28 October 1981, 37/42 of 3 December 1982 and 38/16 of 22 November 1983,

Taking note of the report of the Secretary-General,

1. *Reaffirms* that the universal realization of the right of all peoples, including those under colonial, foreign and alien domination, to self-determination is a fundamental condition for the effective guarantee and observance of human rights and for the preservation and promotion of such rights;

2. *Declares its firm opposition* to acts of foreign military intervention, aggression and occupation, since these have resulted in the suppression of the right of peoples to self-determination and other human rights in certain parts of the world;

3. *Calls upon* those States responsible to cease immediately their military intervention and occupation of foreign countries and territories and all acts of repression, discrimination, exploitation and maltreatment,

particularly the brutal and inhuman methods reportedly employed for the execution of these acts against the peoples concerned;

4. *Deplores* the plight of the millions of refugees and displaced persons who have been uprooted by the aforementioned acts and reaffirms their right to return to their homes voluntarily in safety and honour;

5. *Requests* the Commission on Human Rights to continue to give special attention to the violation of human rights, especially the right to self-determination, resulting from foreign military intervention, aggression or occupation;

6. *Requests* the Secretary-General to report on this issue to the General Assembly at its fortieth session under the item entitled "Importance of the universal realization of the right of peoples to self-determination and of the speedy granting of independence to colonial countries and peoples for the effective guarantee and observance of human rights".

General Assembly resolution 39/18

23 November 1984   Meeting 71   Adopted without vote

Approved by Third Committee (A/39/657) without vote, 8 November (meeting 34); 21-nation draft (A/C.3/39/L.4); agenda item 87.

Sponsors: Brunei Darussalam, Chile, Comoros, Costa Rica, Djibouti, Ecuador, Jordan, Kuwait, Malaysia, Morocco, Oman, Pakistan, Papua New Guinea, Philippines, Qatar, Saudi Arabia, Singapore, Somalia, Sudan, Suriname, Thailand.

Meeting numbers. GA 39th session: 3rd Committee 4-15, 27, 30, 34; plenary 71.

Afghanistan

Action by the Commission on Human Rights. On 29 February 1984,[17] the Commission on Human Rights, by a roll-call vote of 31 to 8, with 4 abstentions, reaffirmed its profound concern that the people of Afghanistan continued to be denied their right to self-determination, to determine their own form of government, and to choose their economic, political and social system free from outside intervention, subversion, coercion or constraint. It called for a political settlement based on immediate foreign troop withdrawal from Afghanistan; full respect for that country's independence, sovereignty, territorial integrity and non-aligned status; and strict observance of the principle of non-interference. It urged a settlement that would also enable the Afghan refugees to return to their homes. The Commission requested the Secretary-General to continue to promote a political solution, urged all concerned to continue to co-operate with him, and appealed for humanitarian relief assistance to alleviate, in coordination with the United Nations High Commissioner for Refugees (UNHCR), the hardship of Afghan refugees.

Concerned over the continued presence of foreign forces and reports of extensive human rights violations in Afghanistan, the Commission also recommended on 15 March,[22] by a roll-call vote of 27 to 8, with 6 abstentions, a text which served as the basis for the Economic and Social Council resolution below.

ECONOMIC AND SOCIAL COUNCIL ACTION

Acting on the recommendation of its Second Committee on 24 May 1984, the Economic and Social Council adopted resolution 1984/37 by recorded vote.

Situation of human rights in Afghanistan

The Economic and Social Council,

Mindful of resolution 1983/20 of 5 September 1983 of the Sub-Commission on Prevention of Discrimination and Protection of Minorities and Commission on Human Rights resolution 1984/55 of 15 March 1984,

1. *Requests* the Chairman of the Commission on Human Rights to appoint an individual of recognized international standing as Special Rapporteur with the mandate to examine the human rights situation in Afghanistan, with a view to formulating proposals which could contribute to ensuring full protection of the human rights of all residents of the country, before, during and after the withdrawal of all foreign forces;

2. *Authorizes* the Special Rapporteur to seek relevant information from specialized agencies, intergovernmental organizations and non-governmental organizations;

3. *Requests* the Special Rapporteur to submit a comprehensive report to the Commission at its forty-first session.

Economic and Social Council resolution 1984/37

24 May 1984   Meeting 20   35-4-12 (recorded vote)

Approved by Second Committee (E/1984/91) by vote (33-4-11), 17 May (meeting 16); draft by Commission on Human Rights (E/1984/14); agenda item 10.

Recorded vote in Council as follows:

In favour: Argentina, Austria, Botswana, Canada, China, Colombia, Costa Rica, Djibouti, France, Germany, Federal Republic of, Greece, Japan, Lebanon, Liberia, Luxembourg, Malaysia, Mexico, Netherlands, New Zealand, Pakistan, Papua New Guinea, Portugal, Qatar, Rwanda, Saint Lucia, Saudi Arabia, Sierra Leone, Somalia, Suriname, Swaziland, Sweden, Thailand, United Kingdom, United States, Venezuela.

Against: Bulgaria, German Democratic Republic, Poland, USSR.

Abstaining: Algeria, Benin, Brazil, Congo, Ecuador, Finland, Mali, Sri Lanka, Tunisia, Uganda, Yugoslavia, Zaire.

Before the Committee approved the draft resolution, it rejected, by a roll-call vote of 34 to 6, with 8 abstentions, a proposal by the German Democratic Republic that no decision should be taken on the draft.

In the Council, Afghanistan reiterated its objections to the text's adoption and said it did not consider itself bound by it. Commission and Council consideration of the so-called human rights situation in Afghanistan, it stressed, was a violation of the Charter and interference in Afghanistan's internal affairs. To consider that artificial issue in open meetings while it was under discussion in private by the Sub-Commission ran counter to the procedures set forth by the Council in 1970.[23] The sponsors of the text were politically motivated, Afghanistan asserted, since they chose to ignore the efforts of its Government to ensure full protection of human rights. Moreover, submitting the draft just when the indirect negotiations between Afghanistan and Pakistan had entered a delicate stage could torpedo those negotiations. Afghanistan also objected to what it called defamatory tactics through the irresponsible appointment of special rapporteurs.

The USSR—speaking also for Bulgaria, the German Democratic Republic and Poland—said there was no reason for the resolution because it dealt with a non-existent problem. The USSR joined Afghanistan in labelling the text a gross interference in the affairs of a sovereign State, adding that it was not conducive to a settlement of the situation in the region.

Brazil had reservations on the appointment of a special rapporteur and expressed its desire to avoid any intervention which might hinder the Secretary-General's recent steps with regard to Afghanistan.

Tunisia called for urgent action by the international community to alleviate the suffering of the Afghans by seeking a political settlement which would ensure increased assistance to refugees, allow them to return to their country and guarantee respect for international law, which prohibited the use of force or threat of force and outside interference. The situation in Afghanistan merited particular attention if the Council wished to help the Afghans to recover their sovereignty and independence and to exercise their right to self-determination.

Sub-Commission action. By 13 votes to 4, with 2 abstentions, on 28 August 1984,[24] the Sub-Commission, gravely concerned by the continued, systematic bombardment of the civilian population in Afghanistan, requested the Commission urgently to call on the authorities in Afghanistan to end the bombardment and to ask its Special Rapporteur on Afghanistan to investigate the consequent human and material losses.

Central America

In 1984, the Commission on Human Rights followed up on a Sub-Commission resolution of August 1983,[25] calling for support of the Contadora Group's efforts towards peace in Central America so that Nicaragua's right to self-determination might be assured. On 12 March 1984,[26] the Commission expressed firmest support for the Group's efforts and noted other regional efforts to establish or improve democratic, representative and pluralistic systems. It reaffirmed the right of the region's countries to live in peace and to decide their own future, free from outside interference, and repudiated the acts of aggression against their sovereignty, independence and territorial integrity, which were causing loss of life and irreparable damage to their economies.

(For details on the situation in Central America and Nicaragua, see p. 195.)

East Timor

In a July 1984 report,[27] the Secretary-General summarized the consultations he had held with In-

donesia and Portugal since he assumed office at the beginning of 1982, for the purpose of improving the humanitarian situation in East Timor and promoting efforts towards a comprehensive settlement of the problem there. He also outlined the results of those consultations up to the time of reporting (see TRUSTEESHIP AND DECOLONIZATION, Chapter IV, under "East Timor question").

On 29 August 1984,[28] the Sub-Commission, by 8 votes to 1, with 11 abstentions, welcomed the report and requested the Secretary-General to continue his efforts to encourage all parties concerned, including the administering Power, to co-operate towards achieving a durable solution, taking the interests of the people of East Timor into full consideration. The Sub-Commission also requested the Indonesian authorities to facilitate without restrictions the activities of humanitarian organizations in East Timor, and recommended that the Commission study the evolution of the situation of human rights and fundamental freedoms there.

Grenada

Recalling that the General Assembly had considered the question of Grenada at its 1983 session and reaffirmed the sovereign and inalienable right of that country to determine its own political, economic and social system,[29] the Commission on Human Rights on 12 March 1984[18] called on all States to show the strictest respect for Grenada's sovereignty, independence and territorial integrity and reaffirmed their obligation not to interfere or intervene in its internal affairs. The Commission reaffirmed the right of Grenadians to exercise fully their human rights and fundamental freedoms, decide their own future and hold free elections to choose their Government democratically without external interference or pressure.

Kampuchea

On 29 February 1984, the Commission on Human Rights, by a roll-call vote of 27 to 10, with 4 abstentions,[15] reiterated its condemnation of persistent human rights violations in Kampuchea. It reaffirmed that the continued occupation of Kampuchea by foreign forces deprived Kampucheans from exercising their right to self-determination, which currently constituted the primary violation of human rights in that country. The Commission emphasized that withdrawal of those foreign forces, restoration of Kampuchea's independence, sovereignty and territorial integrity, recognition of the Kampucheans' right to self-determination and a commitment by all States to non-interference were essential components for a solution to the Kampuchea problem. It reiterated its call for a cessation of hostilities and for an immediate withdrawal of foreign forces, to enable Kampucheans to exercise their human rights free from foreign interference and to determine their future through free and fair elections under United Nations supervision; to enable the United Nations to offer its services in the field of human rights; and to make possible efforts towards a political solution according to the 1981 Declaration on Kampuchea[30] and relevant United Nations resolutions, and also the return of all Kampuchean refugees.

The Commission requested the *Ad Hoc* Committee of the International Conference on Kampuchea to continue its work pending a reconvening of the Conference and the Secretary-General to monitor the situation in Kampuchea and intensify his efforts towards a political settlement and restoration of human rights; and recommended that the Economic and Social Council continue to implement recommendations for the achievement by the Kampucheans of the full enjoyment of human rights and freedoms, in particular the right to self-determination.

Report of the Secretary-General. In keeping with a May 1983 decision of the Economic and Social Council,[31] the Secretary-General submitted a list and description of the responses received, as at 1 May 1984,[32] to his request for information on developments in Kampuchea, including violations of humanitarian principles perpetrated against Kampuchean refugees by occupation troops along the Kampuchea-Thailand border. The responses were from 12 Governments (two stating they had no infomation), four United Nations bodies (three had no information), three specialized agencies (two had no information), and two intergovernmental and two non-governmental organizations.

ECONOMIC AND SOCIAL COUNCIL ACTION

Acting on the recommendation of its Second Committee, the Economic and Social Council adopted decision 1984/148 by recorded vote.

Right of peoples to self-determination and its application to peoples under colonial or alien domination or foreign occupation

At its 20th plenary meeting, on 24 May 1984, the Council fully endorsed Commission on Human Rights resolution 1984/12 of 29 February 1984, by which the Commission, *inter alia*, reaffirmed that the continuing occupation of Kampuchea by foreign forces deprived the people of Kampuchea of the exercise of their right to self-determination and constituted the primary violation of human rights in Kampuchea at present. The Council reaffirmed its decisions 1981/154 of 8 May 1981, 1982/143 of 7 May 1982 and 1983/155 of 27 May 1983 and reiterated its call for the withdrawal of all foreign forces from Kampuchea in order to allow the people of Kampuchea to exercise their fundamental freedoms and human rights, including the right to self-determination as contained in the Declaration on Kampuchea adopted by the International Conference on Kampuchea on 17 July 1981 and in General Assembly resolutions 34/22

of 14 November 1979, 35/6 of 22 October 1980, 36/5 of 21 October 1981, 37/6 of 28 October 1982 and 38/3 of 27 October 1983.

The Council expressed its grave concern at the activities of the foreign forces in Kampuchea, particularly the continuing attacks on Kampuchean civilian encampments along the Thai-Kampuchean border, resulting in serious loss of life and property of Kampucheans and forcing even larger numbers of Kampuchean civilians to flee into Thailand.

The Council took note with appreciation of the note by the Secretary- General, prepared pursuant to its decision 1983/155, requested him to report to the Council any further violations of humanitarian principles perpetrated against Kampuchean civilian refugees by the foreign occupying troops along the border, and also requested him to continue to monitor closely the developments in Kampuchea and to intensify efforts, including the use of his good offices, to bring about a comprehensive political settlement of the Kampuchean problem and the restoration of fundamental human rights in Kampuchea.

The Council noted with appreciation the ongoing efforts of the *Ad Hoc* Committee of the International Conference on Kampuchea and requested that the Committee continue its work, pending the reconvening of the Conference.

Economic and Social Council decision 1984/148

40-6-6 (recorded vote)

Approved by Second Committee (E/1984/91) by recorded vote (39-5-5), 17 May (meeting 16); 29-nation draft (E/1984/C.2/L.2); agenda item 10.

Sponsors: Bangladesh, Belgium, Canada, Costa Rica, Fiji, Gambia, Germany, Federal Republic of, Italy, Japan, Liberia, Luxembourg, Malaysia, Nepal, Netherlands, New Zealand, Pakistan, Papua New Guinea, Philippines, Saint Lucia, Samoa, Singapore, Solomon Islands, Somalia, Sudan, Swaziland, Thailand, United Kingdom, Uruguay, Zaire.

Financial implications. S-G, E/1984/C.2/L.7.

Recorded vote in Council as follows:

In favour: Argentina, Austria, Botswana, Brazil, Canada, China, Colombia, Costa Rica, Djibouti, Ecuador, France, Germany, Federal Republic of, Greece, Indonesia, Japan, Liberia, Luxembourg, Malaysia, Netherlands, New Zealand, Pakistan, Papua New Guinea, Portugal, Qatar, Rwanda, Saint Lucia, Saudi Arabia, Sierra Leone, Somalia, Sri Lanka, Suriname, Swaziland, Sweden, Thailand, Tunisia, United Kingdom, United States, Venezuela, Yugoslavia, Zaire.

Against: Benin, Bulgaria, Congo, German Democratic Republic, Poland, USSR.

Abstaining: Algeria, Finland, Lebanon, Mali, Mexico, Uganda.

Viet Nam stated that information relating to alleged violations of human rights in Kampuchea was at variance with reality and ambiguous with regard to attacks on so-called civilian encampments, since the refugees were being used as a buffer and the encampments as bases by Khmer reactionaries. The text represented interference in the internal affairs of an independent and sovereign State, and was an attempt to restore the régime that had brought calamity to the Kampuchean people and thereby impede Kampuchea's recovery.

The Lao People's Democratic Republic urged the international community to do its utmost to contribute to that recovery and encourage the parties—which the text would not—to restore peace, stability and co-operation in South-East Asia.

The Congo called the draft one-sided, for it failed to take a stand with respect to the Pol Pot régime and was clearly directed against Viet Nam, whose role in liberating Kampuchea from that régime it ignored; a presentation of the situation outside of its historical perspective distorted the problem, even before an attempt could be made to resolve it. The USSR, speaking also on behalf of Bulgaria, the German Democratic Republic and Poland, shared the view—as did Benin—that the text was an interference in Kampuchea's internal affairs and violated the right of Kampucheans to self-determination. They opposed efforts being made to use the United Nations to help criminals and hoped that the political manœuvres within the Council would soon end and common sense prevail.

Democratic Kampuchea said the adoption of the text proved that Viet Nam's lies and slanders had failed to cause anyone to forget that the solution of the problem of Kampuchea lay in stopping Viet Nam's war of aggression and USSR-supported expansionist policy which violated the Charter. The Kampucheans and their coalition Government were determined to pursue their struggle until all Vietnamese forces were withdrawn in accordance with the relevant United Nations resolutions.

Sweden pointed out that it did not subscribe to all provisions of the 1984 Commission on Human Rights resolution (see above) endorsed by the Council.

(For details on the Kampuchea situation, see p. 214.)

Palestinians

The Commission on Human Rights, by a resolution adopted on 29 February 1984 by a roll-call vote of 28 to 7, with 8 abstentions,[13] condemned the continued occupation of Palestinian and other Arab territories by Israel and demanded its immediate, unconditional and total withdrawal. The Commission reaffirmed the right of the Palestinian people to self-determination without external interference and to an independent and sovereign State of Palestine, and called for the return of Palestinians to their homes and property in exercise of that right. It recognized the right of Palestinians to regain their rights by all means in accordance with the Charter and reaffirmed that their future could be decided only with their participation in all efforts through their representative, the Palestine Liberation Organization (PLO).

The Commission rejected all partial agreements and separate treaties in so far as they violated the rights of Palestinians and contradicted the principles of just and comprehensive Middle East solutions, as well as the "autonomy" plan proposed in the 1978 "Camp David accords", declaring

those accords to be without validity. States, United Nations bodies and other international organizations were urged to extend support to Palestinians, through PLO, in the struggle to restore their rights.

The Commission adopted several other resolutions dealing with human rights violations in the occupied Arab territories (see below, under "Human rights violations").

South Africa and Namibia

By a resolution of 29 February 1984, adopted by a roll-call vote of 31 to 5, with 7 abstentions,[14] the Commission on Human Rights called on States to take steps to enable the dependent people of South Africa and Namibia to exercise fully and without further delay their right to self-determination. It reaffirmed the right of Namibians to freedom and national independence in a united Namibia, as well as the legitimacy of their struggle and that of the oppressed people of South Africa by all means, including armed struggle. It urged States to provide them with moral and material assistance and called for immediate implementation of the 1983 Paris Declaration and Programme of Action on Namibia.[33] It demanded not only full respect for the human rights of all people detained or imprisoned by South Africa because of their struggle for independence, but also their immediate release.

The Commission condemned South Africa's illegal occupation of Namibia, including attempts to dismember its territory. It condemned the so-called constitutional reforms and the policy of "bantustanization" as contrary to the principle of self-determination and inconsistent with genuine independence and national unity. It reaffirmed that continued colonialism in all forms—including racism, racial discrimination, *apartheid*, exploitation of economic and human resources by foreign and other interests, and colonial wars to suppress national liberation movements—was incompatible with the United Nations Charter, the 1948 Universal Declaration of Human Rights[34] and the 1960 Declaration on the Granting of Independence to Colonial Countries and Peoples.[35]

The Commission also condemned South Africa's acts of aggression and destabilization against independent African States, in particular Angola, Botswana, Lesotho, Mozambique and Zimbabwe, and demanded an immediate end to such acts and the withdrawal of South Africa's forces from Angola.

Reaffirming once again that the use of mercenaries against national liberation movements and sovereign States was a criminal act and that the mercenaries themselves were criminals, the Commission called on Governments: to enact legislation declaring the recruitment, financing and training of mercenaries, as well as transit of mercenaries through their territories, to be punishable offences and to prohibit their nationals from serving as mercenaries; and to report on such legislation to the Secretary-General.

Pursuant to a similar provision of a February 1983 Commission resolution on self-determination as it applied to South Africa and Namibia,[36] 13 Governments provided the information requested, which the Secretary-General summarized in a report[37] submitted to the Commission at its 1984 session.

(For details on legislation against mercenaries, see LEGAL QUESTIONS, Chapter II, under "Draft convention against mercenaries".)

In two related resolutions adopted on 28 February, the Commission reaffirmed[38] the inalienable right of the oppressed people of South Africa and Namibia to self-determination and independence, and declared[39] that that right could be legally exercised by the Namibian people only in accordance with conditions determined by the Security Council in 1978.[40]

Western Sahara

On 29 February 1984,[16] the Commission on Human Rights, having considered the question of Western Sahara, took note of a resolution on the topic, adopted unanimously by the Assembly of Heads of State and Government of the Organization of African Unity (OAU) in June 1983 and quoted in full in a December 1983 General Assembly resolution.[41] OAU had urged the parties to the conflict to negotiate for a cease-fire so as to create the condition necessary for a peaceful and fair referendum for self-determination of Western Sahara under OAU and United Nations auspices. The Commission decided to follow the development of the situation in Western Sahara and to consider the question in 1985 as a matter of priority. (See also TRUSTEESHIP AND DECOLONIZATION, Chapter IV.)

Rights of detained persons

In 1984, an open-ended working group of the General Assembly's Sixth (Legal) Committee continued work on a draft Body of Principles for the Protection of All Persons under Any Form of Detention or Imprisonment. In December, the Assembly decided to establish a similar working group in 1985 to expedite finalization of the draft.

The human rights of persons subjected to any form of detention or imprisonment were the subject of a report by the Secretary-General to the Sub-Commission. The Sub-Commission's sessional Working Group on Detention, meeting in August, considered a draft declaration against the unacknowledged detention of persons and the

question of compliance with rules governing the declaration of a state of siege or emergency (see below).

In March, the Commission on Human Rights adopted a resolution dealing with persons detained by Israel and another with persons detained solely for exercising the right to freedom of expression as laid down by the International Covenant on Civil and Political Rights (see below, under "Human rights violations").

In two related actions, the Economic and Social Council called for appropriate measures to eradicate physical violence against detained women that was specific to their sex (see p. 905) and approved a set of procedures for the effective implementation of the 1955 Standard Minimum Rules for the Treatment of Prisoners (see p. 701).

Treatment of prisoners and detainees

Report of the Secretary-General. In accordance with the Sub-Commission's annual review of developments in the administration of justice and human rights of detainees, the Secretary-General in May 1984 submitted a report, with later addenda,[42] summarizing reliably attested information on the subject from 26 Governments, four specialized agencies and a regional intergovernmental organization.

Activities of the Working Group on Detention. A five-member sessional Working Group on Detention, set up by the Sub-Commission on 7 August 1984, met between 13 and 21 August, with John Roche (United States) as Chairman/Rapporteur.[43]

The Group considered the first draft of a declaration aimed at eliminating unacknowledged detention and related practices (see below). It discussed ways of preparing the yearly report on compliance with rules guaranteeing the legality of a state of emergency and list of countries instituting or terminating such a state (see above). In addition, the Group began to conduct annual hearings and to receive information on torture (see below).

The Group postponed to 1985 examination of the proposals which the Sub-Commission had referred to it in September 1983,[44] on the period of detention after arrest, the right to a fair trial, abolition of capital punishment particularly in politically related cases, and the suspension of penal law permitting retroactive changes in jurisdiction or procedure in a state of emergency.

Draft principles for protection of detainees

In 1984, a Working Group open to all members of the General Assembly's Sixth Committee continued work on a draft Body of Principles for the

Protection of All Persons under Any Form of Detention or Imprisonment. The draft originated from a text adopted by the Sub-Commission in 1978,[45] which had since undergone revisions by a succession of working groups: of the Third Committee in 1980;[46] and of the Sixth Committee in 1981,[47] 1982[48] and 1983.[49]

Established pursuant to an Assembly decision of December 1983,[50] the 1984 Working Group met in New York between 26 September and 26 November, with Tullio Treves (Italy) as Chairman/Rapporteur. It resumed work on the draft at principle 19 and left off at principle 22, paragraph 1. These covered specific rights of persons detained or imprisoned, including, during their interrogation, prohibitions against self-incrimination or testimony against others, threats or violent methods of interrogation, and medical or scientific experimentation; and the right to recording and certification of their interrogation in all of its aspects and of access to such record, to free medical examination upon detention and thereafter as necessary, and to a second medical opinion. The approved provisional texts were annexed to the Group's report.[51]

GENERAL ASSEMBLY ACTION

Acting without vote on the recommendation of the Sixth Committee, the General Assembly in December adopted decision 39/418.

Draft Body of Principles for the Protection of All Persons under Any Form of Detention or Imprisonment

At its 99th plenary meeting, on 13 December 1984, the General Assembly, on the recommendation of the Sixth Committee:

(a) Took note with appreciation of the report of the Working Group on the Draft Body of Principles for the Protection of All Persons under Any Form of Detention or Imprisonment, established in accordance with General Assembly decision 37/427 of 16 December 1982 to elaborate a final version of the draft Body of Principles, a task which it had not been able to conclude;

(b) Decided that an open-ended working group of the Sixth Committee would be established at its fortieth session with a view to expediting the finalization of the draft Body of Principles for the Protection of All Persons under Any Form of Detention or Imprisonment;

(c) Decided to request the Secretary-General to circulate to Member States the report of the open-ended Working Group established at the thirty-ninth session;

(d) Decided to include in the provisional agenda of its fortieth session the item entitled "Draft Body of Principles for the Protection of All Persons under Any Form of Detention or Imprisonment".

General Assembly decision 39/418

Adopted without vote

Approved by Sixth Committee (A/39/784) without vote, 4 December (meeting 62); draft by Sweden (A/C.6/39/L.15); agenda item 136.
Meeting numbers. GA 39th session: 6th Committee 3, 61, 62; plenary 99.

Torture and cruel treatment

In 1984, a working group of the Commission on Human Rights completed elaboration of a draft convention against torture and other cruel, inhuman or degrading treatment or punishment. Work on the draft had begun in 1978 and had been carried out yearly since by a Commission working group set up by authority of the Economic and Social Council before each Commission session. The final text, submitted to the Commission by the 1984 working group, was transmitted to the General Assembly through the Council.

Contributions to the United Nations Voluntary Fund for Victims of Torture were once again called for by the Commission in March and by the Assembly in December.

The 1984 sessional Working Group on Detention (see above) began to conduct annual hearings and to receive information on torture and other cruel treatment, as called for by the Sub-Commission in 1982[52] and authorized by the Commission in 1983.[53] Information was provided by six NGOs, among them Amnesty International, which drew attention to a 12-point programme for the prevention of torture, which it launched with the publication of its report entitled "Torture in the 1980s".

Convention against torture

Working group activities. As authorized by the Economic and Social Council in May 1983,[54] the Commission on Human Rights set up an open-ended working group before its February/March 1984 session to complete work on a draft convention against torture and other cruel, inhuman or degrading treatment or punishment. Elaboration of the convention, requested of the Commission by the General Assembly in 1977[55] and in progress since 1978,[56] had been pursued by a succession of similar working groups authorized yearly by the Council. The 1984 working group, meeting at Geneva between 30 January and 16 February, with Jan Herman Burgers (Netherlands) as Chairman/Rapporteur, considered the unresolved portions of the 1983 text.

The title and the preamble were left unchanged. Article 3, paragraph 2, was adopted following deletion of "a State policy of *apartheid*, racial discrimination or genocide, colonialism or neo-colonialism, the suppression of national liberation movements or the occupation of foreign territory" and insertion of "flagrant or mass". Articles 5, 6 and 7 remained unaltered and were adopted without prejudice to the reservations expressed. In article 16, a reference to article 14 was deleted.

As to the provisions on implementation, article 17 was amended to increase the number of experts to 10 and the term of office to four years. A new paragraph on meeting expenses was added to article 18. Since no agreement was reached on the proposal to replace "comments or suggestions" by "general comments" in article 19, or on the question of giving the proposed inquiry system an optional character in article 20, both articles could not be adopted. Articles 21 to 24 remained unchanged and were adopted.

As to the final clauses, articles 25 to 27 and 31 were adopted without change. Article 28 was amended by the insertion of "within four months from the date of such communication" in the third sentence. A new article on dispute settlement was added and numbered 29; former articles 29 to 31 were thus renumbered 30 to 32. A new paragraph was added to article 30 and the references in article 31 were changed due to the renumbering.

The draft convention as provisionally adopted was annexed to the group's report.[57]

Action by Commission on Human Rights. On 6 March 1984,[58] the Commission on Human Rights, having examined the working group's report, decided to transmit it to the General Assembly, through the Economic and Social Council, together with the summary records of the Commission's debate on the item. The Commission recommended that the Assembly consider the draft convention with a view to its early adoption. It requested the Secretary-General to bring the documents mentioned to the attention of Governments and to obtain their comments, preferably before 1 September, for submission to the 1984 Assembly session.

ECONOMIC AND SOCIAL COUNCIL ACTION

Acting without vote on the recommendation of its Second Committee, the Economic and Social Council in May adopted decision 1984/134.

Draft convention against torture and other cruel, inhuman or degrading treatment or punishment

At its 20th plenary meeting, on 24 May 1984, the Council, noting Commission on Human Rights resolution 1984/21 of 6 March 1984, decided to transmit to the General Assembly the report of the working group established by the Commission to draw up a draft convention against torture and other cruel, inhuman or degrading treatment or punishment, as well as the summary records of the Commission's debate on the question during its fortieth session. The Council further noted the Commission's request to the Secretary-General to submit the comments received from Governments on the draft convention, in conformity with Commission resolution 1984/21, to the General Assembly at its thirty-ninth session, and the Commission's recommendation that the Assembly should consider, pursuant to its resolution 38/119 of 16 December 1983, the draft convention contained in the annex to the working group's report as a matter of priority, with a view to the early adoption of a convention against torture and other cruel, inhuman or degrading treatment or punishment.

Economic and Social Council decision 1984/134
Adopted without vote

Approved by Second Committee (E/1984/91) without vote, 17 May (meeting 16); draft by Commission on Human Rights (E/1984/14); agenda item 10.

GENERAL ASSEMBLY ACTION

Responding to the Commission's request of 6 March (see above), the Secretary-General submitted to the Assembly in October a report with later addenda,[59] summarizing the comments communicated by 31 Governments on the draft convention.

Acting on the recommendation of the Third Committee, the Assembly adopted resolution 39/46 without vote on 10 December 1984.

Convention against Torture and Other Cruel, Inhuman or Degrading Treatment or Punishment

The General Assembly,

Recalling the Declaration on the Protection of All Persons from Being Subjected to Torture and Other Cruel, Inhuman or Degrading Treatment or Punishment, adopted by the General Assembly in its resolution 3452(XXX) of 9 December 1975,

Recalling also its resolution 32/62 of 8 December 1977, in which it requested the Commission on Human Rights to draw up a draft convention against torture and other cruel, inhuman or degrading treatment or punishment, in the light of the principles embodied in the Declaration,

Recalling further that, in its resolution 38/119 of 16 December 1983, it requested the Commission on Human Rights to complete, at its fortieth session, as a matter of highest priority, the drafting of such a convention, with a view to submitting a draft, including provisions for the effective implementation of the future convention, to the General Assembly at its thirty-ninth session,

Taking note with satisfaction of Commission on Human Rights resolution 1984/21 of 6 March 1984, by which the Commission decided to transmit the text of a draft convention against torture and other cruel, inhuman or degrading treatment or punishment, contained in the annex to the report of the Working Group, to the General Assembly for its consideration,

Desirous of achieving a more effective implementation of the existing prohibition under international and national law of the practice of torture and other cruel, inhuman or degrading treatment or punishment,

1. *Expresses its appreciation* for the work achieved by the Commission on Human Rights in preparing the text of a draft convention against torture and other cruel, inhuman or degrading treatment or punishment;

2. *Adopts* and opens for signature, ratification and accession the Convention against Torture and Other Cruel, Inhuman or Degrading Treatment or Punishment contained in the annex to the present resolution;

3. *Calls upon* all Governments to consider signing and ratifying the Convention as a matter of priority.

ANNEX
Convention against Torture and Other Cruel, Inhuman or Degrading Treatment or Punishment

The States Parties to this Convention,

Considering that, in accordance with the principles proclaimed in the Charter of the United Nations, recognition of the equal and inalienable rights of all members of the human family is the foundation of freedom, justice and peace in the world,

Recognizing that those rights derive from the inherent dignity of the human person,

Considering the obligation of States under the Charter, in particular Article 55, to promote universal respect for, and observance of, human rights and fundamental freedoms,

Having regard to article 5 of the Universal Declaration of Human Rights and article 7 of the International Covenant on Civil and Political Rights, both of which provide that no one shall be subjected to torture or to cruel, inhuman or degrading treatment or punishment,

Having regard also to the Declaration on the Protection of All Persons from Being Subjected to Torture and Other Cruel, Inhuman or Degrading Treatment or Punishment, adopted by the General Assembly on 9 December 1975,

Desiring to make more effective the struggle against torture and other cruel, inhuman or degrading treatment or punishment throughout the world,

Have agreed as follows:

Part I
Article 1

1. For the purposes of this Convention, the term "torture" means any act by which severe pain or suffering, whether physical or mental, is intentionally inflicted on a person for such purposes as obtaining from him or a third person information or a confession, punishing him for an act he or a third person has committed or is suspected of having committed, or intimidating or coercing him or a third person, or for any reason based on discrimination of any kind, when such pain or suffering is inflicted by or at the instigation of or with the consent or acquiescence of a public official or other person acting in an official capacity. It does not include pain or suffering arising only from, inherent in or incidental to lawful sanctions.

2. This article is without prejudice to any international instrument or national legislation which does or may contain provisions of wider application.

Article 2

1. Each State Party shall take effective legislative, administrative, judicial or other measures to prevent acts of torture in any territory under its jurisdiction.

2. No exceptional circumstances whatsoever, whether a state of war or a threat of war, internal political instability or any other public emergency, may be invoked as a justification of torture.

3. An order from a superior officer or a public authority may not be invoked as a justification of torture.

Article 3

1. No State Party shall expel, return ("*refouler*") or extradite a person to another State where there are substantial grounds for believing that he would be in danger of being subjected to torture.

2. For the purpose of determining whether there are such grounds, the competent authorities shall take into account all relevant considerations including, where applicable, the existence in the State concerned of a consistent pattern of gross, flagrant or mass violations of human rights.

Article 4

1. Each State Party shall ensure that all acts of torture are offences under its criminal law. The same shall apply to an attempt to commit torture and to an act

by any person which constitutes complicity or participation in torture.

2. Each State Party shall make these offences punishable by appropriate penalties which take into account their grave nature.

Article 5

1. Each State Party shall take such measures as may be necessary to establish its jurisdiction over the offences referred to in article 4 in the following cases:

(*a*) When the offences are committed in any territory under its jurisdiction or on board a ship or aircraft registered in that State;

(*b*) When the alleged offender is a national of that State;

(*c*) When the victim is a national of that State if that State considers it appropriate.

2. Each State Party shall likewise take such measures as may be necessary to establish its jurisdiction over such offences in cases where the alleged offender is present in any territory under its jurisdiction and it does not extradite him pursuant to article 8 to any of the States mentioned in paragraph 1 of this article.

3. This Convention does not exclude any criminal jurisdiction exercised in accordance with internal law.

Article 6

1. Upon being satisfied, after an examination of information available to it, that the circumstances so warrant, any State Party in whose territory a person alleged to have committed any offence referred to in article 4 is present shall take him into custody or take other legal measures to ensure his presence. The custody and other legal measures shall be as provided in the law of that State but may be continued only for such time as is necessary to enable any criminal or extradition proceedings to be instituted.

2. Such State shall immediately make a preliminary inquiry into the facts.

3. Any person in custody pursuant to paragraph 1 of this article shall be assisted in communicating immediately with the nearest appropriate representative of the State of which he is a national, or, if he is a stateless person, with the representative of the State where he usually resides.

4. When a State, pursuant to this article, has taken a person into custody, it shall immediately notify the States referred to in article 5, paragraph 1, of the fact that such person is in custody and of the circumstances which warrant his detention. The State which makes the preliminary inquiry contemplated in paragraph 2 of this article shall promptly report its findings to the said States and shall indicate whether it intends to exercise jurisdiction.

Article 7

1. The State Party in the territory under whose jurisdiction a person alleged to have committed any offence referred to in article 4 is found shall in the cases contemplated in article 5, if it does not extradite him, submit the case to its competent authorities for the purpose of prosecution.

2. These authorities shall take their decision in the same manner as in the case of any ordinary offence of a serious nature under the law of that State. In the cases referred to in article 5, paragraph 2, the standards of evidence required for prosecution and conviction shall

in no way be less stringent than those which apply in the cases referred to in article 5, paragraph 1.

3. Any person regarding whom proceedings are brought in connection with any of the offences referred to in article 4 shall be guaranteed fair treatment at all stages of the proceedings.

Article 8

1. The offences referred to in article 4 shall be deemed to be included as extraditable offences in any extradition treaty existing between States Parties. States Parties undertake to include such offences as extraditable offences in every extradition treaty to be concluded between them.

2. If a State Party which makes extradition conditional on the existence of a treaty receives a request for extradition from another State Party with which it has no extradition treaty, it may consider this Convention as the legal basis for extradition in respect of such offences. Extradition shall be subject to the other conditions provided by the law of the requested State.

3. States Parties which do not make extradition conditional on the existence of a treaty shall recognize such offences as extraditable offences between themselves subject to the conditions provided by the law of the requested State.

4. Such offences shall be treated, for the purpose of extradition between States Parties, as if they had been committed not only in the place in which they occurred but also in the territories of the States required to establish their jurisdiction in accordance with article 5, paragraph 1.

Article 9

1. States Parties shall afford one another the greatest measure of assistance in connection with criminal proceedings brought in respect of any of the offences referred to in article 4, including the supply of all evidence at their disposal necessary for the proceedings.

2. States Parties shall carry out their obligations under paragraph 1 of this article in conformity with any treaties on mutual judicial assistance that may exist between them.

Article 10

1. Each State Party shall ensure that education and information regarding the prohibition against torture are fully included in the training of law enforcement personnel, civil or military, medical personnel, public officials and other persons who may be involved in the custody, interrogation or treatment of any individual subjected to any form of arrest, detention or imprisonment.

2. Each State Party shall include this prohibition in the rules or instructions issued in regard to the duties and functions of any such persons.

Article 11

Each State Party shall keep under systematic review interrogation rules, instructions, methods and practices as well as arrangements for the custody and treatment of persons subjected to any form of arrest, detention or imprisonment in any territory under its jurisdiction, with a view to preventing any cases of torture.

Article 12

Each State Party shall ensure that its competent authorities proceed to a prompt and impartial investigation, wherever there is reasonable ground to believe that an act of torture has been committed in any territory under its jurisdiction.

Article 13

Each State Party shall ensure that any individual who alleges he has been subjected to torture in any territory under its jurisdiction has the right to complain to, and to have his case promptly and impartially examined by, its competent authorities. Steps shall be taken to ensure that the complainant and witnesses are protected against all ill-treatment or intimidation as a consequence of his complaint or any evidence given.

Article 14

1. Each State Party shall ensure in its legal system that the victim of an act of torture obtains redress and has an enforceable right to fair and adequate compensation, including the means for as full rehabilitation as possible. In the event of the death of the victim as a result of an act of torture, his dependants shall be entitled to compensation.

2. Nothing in this article shall affect any right of the victim or other persons to compensation which may exist under national law.

Article 15

Each State Party shall ensure that any statement which is established to have been made as a result of torture shall not be invoked as evidence in any proceedings, except against a person accused of torture as evidence that the statement was made.

Article 16

1. Each State Party shall undertake to prevent in any territory under its jurisdiction other acts of cruel, inhuman or degrading treatment or punishment which do not amount to torture as defined in article 1, when such acts are committed by or at the instigation of or with the consent or acquiescence of a public official or other person acting in an official capacity. In particular, the obligations contained in articles 10, 11, 12 and 13 shall apply with the substitution for references to torture of references to other forms of cruel, inhuman or degrading treatment or punishment.

2. The provisions of this Convention are without prejudice to the provisions of any other international instrument or national law which prohibits cruel, inhuman or degrading treatment or punishment or which relates to extradition or expulsion.

Part II

Article 17

1. There shall be established a Committee against Torture (hereinafter referred to as the Committee) which shall carry out the functions hereinafter provided. The Committee shall consist of ten experts of high moral standing and recognized competence in the field of human rights, who shall serve in their personal capacity. The experts shall be elected by the States Parties, consideration being given to equitable geographical distribution and to the usefulness of the participation of some persons having legal experience.

2. The members of the Committee shall be elected by secret ballot from a list of persons nominated by States Parties. Each State Party may nominate one person from among its own nationals. States Parties shall bear in mind the usefulness of nominating persons who

are also members of the Human Rights Committee established under the International Covenant on Civil and Political Rights and who are willing to serve on the Committee against Torture.

3. Elections of the members of the Committee shall be held at biennial meetings of States Parties convened by the Secretary-General of the United Nations. At those meetings, for which two thirds of the States Parties shall constitute a quorum, the persons elected to the Committee shall be those who obtain the largest number of votes and an absolute majority of the votes of the representatives of States Parties present and voting.

4. The initial election shall be held no later than six months after the date of the entry into force of this Convention. At least four months before the date of each election, the Secretary-General of the United Nations shall address a letter to the States Parties inviting them to submit their nominations within three months. The Secretary-General shall prepare a list in alphabetical order of all persons thus nominated, indicating the States Parties which have nominated them, and shall submit it to the States Parties.

5. The members of the Committee shall be elected for a term of four years. They shall be eligible for re-election if renominated. However, the term of five of the members elected at the first election shall expire at the end of two years; immediately after the first election the names of these five members shall be chosen by lot by the chairman of the meeting referred to in paragraph 3 of this article.

6. If a member of the Committee dies or resigns or for any other cause can no longer perform his Committee duties, the State Party which nominated him shall appoint another expert from among its nationals to serve for the remainder of his term, subject to the approval of the majority of the States Parties. The approval shall be considered given unless half or more of the States Parties respond negatively within six weeks after having been informed by the Secretary-General of the United Nations of the proposed appointment.

7. States Parties shall be responsible for the expenses of the members of the Committee while they are in performance of Committee duties.

Article 18

1. The Committee shall elect its officers for a term of two years. They may be re-elected.

2. The Committee shall establish its own rules of procedure, but these rules shall provide, *inter alia*, that:

(a) Six members shall constitute a quorum;

(b) Decisions of the Committee shall be made by a majority vote of the members present.

3. The Secretary-General of the United Nations shall provide the necessary staff and facilities for the effective performance of the functions of the Committee under this Convention.

4. The Secretary-General of the United Nations shall convene the initial meeting of the Committee. After its initial meeting, the Committee shall meet at such times as shall be provided in its rules of procedure.

5. The States Parties shall be responsible for expenses incurred in connection with the holding of meetings of the States Parties and of the Committee, including reimbursement to the United Nations for any expenses, such as the cost of staff and facilities, incurred by the United Nations pursuant to paragraph 3 of this article.

Article 19

1. The States Parties shall submit to the Committee, through the Secretary-General of the United Nations, reports on the measures they have taken to give effect to their undertakings under this Convention, within one year after the entry into force of the Convention for the State Party concerned. Thereafter the States Parties shall submit supplementary reports every four years on any new measures taken and such other reports as the Committee may request.

2. The Secretary-General of the United Nations shall transmit the reports to all States Parties.

3. Each report shall be considered by the Committee which may make such general comments on the report as it may consider appropriate and shall forward these to the State Party concerned. That State Party may respond with any observations it chooses to the Committee.

4. The Committee may, at its discretion, decide to include any comments made by it in accordance with paragraph 3 of this article, together with the observations thereon received from the State Party concerned, in its annual report made in accordance with article 24. If so requested by the State Party concerned, the Committee may also include a copy of the report submitted under paragraph 1 of this article.

Article 20

1. If the Committee receives reliable information which appears to it to contain well-founded indications that torture is being systematically practised in the territory of a State Party, the Committee shall invite that State Party to co-operate in the examination of the information and to this end to submit observations with regard to the information concerned.

2. Taking into account any observations which may have been submitted by the State Party concerned, as well as any other relevant information available to it, the Committee may, if it decides that this is warranted, designate one or more of its members to make a confidential inquiry and to report to the Committee urgently.

3. If an inquiry is made in accordance with paragraph 2 of this article, the Committee shall seek the co-operation of the State Party concerned. In agreement with that State Party, such an inquiry may include a visit to its territory.

4. After examining the findings of its member or members submitted in accordance with paragraph 2 of this article, the Committee shall transmit these findings to the State Party concerned together with any comments or suggestions which seem appropriate in view of the situation.

5. All the proceedings of the Committee referred to in paragraphs 1 to 4 of this article shall be confidential, and at all stages of the proceedings the co-operation of the State Party shall be sought. After such proceedings have been completed with regard to an inquiry made in accordance with paragraph 2, the Committee may, after consultations with the State Party concerned, decide to include a summary account of the results of the proceedings in its annual report made in accordance with article 24.

Article 21

1. A State Party to this Convention may at any time declare under this article that it recognizes the competence of the Committee to receive and consider communications to the effect that a State Party claims that

another State Party is not fulfilling its obligations under this Convention. Such communications may be received and considered according to the procedures laid down in this article only if submitted by a State Party which has made a declaration recognizing in regard to itself the competence of the Committee. No communication shall be dealt with by the Committee under this article if it concerns a State Party which has not made such a declaration. Communications received under this article shall be dealt with in accordance with the following procedure:

(a) If a State Party considers that another State Party is not giving effect to the provisions of this Convention, it may, by written communication, bring the matter to the attention of that State Party. Within three months after the receipt of the communication the receiving State shall afford the State which sent the communication an explanation or any other statement in writing clarifying the matter, which should include, to the extent possible and pertinent, reference to domestic procedures and remedies taken, pending or available in the matter;

(b) If the matter is not adjusted to the satisfaction of both States Parties concerned within six months after the receipt by the receiving State of the initial communication, either State shall have the right to refer the matter to the Committee, by notice given to the Committee and to the other State;

(c) The Committee shall deal with a matter referred to it under this article only after it has ascertained that all domestic remedies have been invoked and exhausted in the matter, in conformity with the generally recognized principles of international law. This shall not be the rule where the application of the remedies is unreasonably prolonged or is unlikely to bring effective relief to the person who is the victim of the violation of this Convention;

(d) The Committee shall hold closed meetings when examining communications under this article;

(e) Subject to the provisions of subparagraph (c), the Committee shall make available its good offices to the States Parties concerned with a view to a friendly solution of the matter on the basis of respect for the obligations provided for in this Convention. For this purpose, the Committee may, when appropriate, set up an *ad hoc* conciliation commission;

(f) In any matter referred to it under this article, the Committee may call upon the States Parties concerned, referred to in subparagraph (b), to supply any relevant information;

(g) The States Parties concerned, referred to in subparagraph (b), shall have the right to be represented when the matter is being considered by the Committee and to make submissions orally and/or in writing;

(h) The Committee shall, within twelve months after the date of receipt of notice under subparagraph (b), submit a report:

(i) If a solution within the terms of subparagraph (e) is reached, the Committee shall confine its report to a brief statement of the facts and of the solution reached;

(ii) If a solution within the terms of subparagraph (e) is not reached, the Committee shall confine its report to a brief statement of the facts; the written submissions and record of the oral submissions made by the States Parties concerned shall be attached to the report.

In every matter, the report shall be communicated to the States Parties concerned.

2. The provisions of this article shall come into force when five States Parties to this Convention have made declarations under paragraph 1 of this article. Such declarations shall be deposited by the States Parties with the Secretary-General of the United Nations, who shall transmit copies thereof to the other States Parties. A declaration may be withdrawn at any time by notification to the Secretary-General. Such a withdrawal shall not prejudice the consideration of any matter which is the subject of a communication already transmitted under this article; no further communication by any State Party shall be received under this article after the notification of withdrawal of the declaration has been received by the Secretary-General, unless the State Party concerned has made a new declaration.

Article 22

1. A State Party to this Convention may at any time declare under this article that it recognizes the competence of the Committee to receive and consider communications from or on behalf of individuals subject to its jurisdiction who claim to be victims of a violation by a State Party of the provisions of the Convention. No communication shall be received by the Committee if it concerns a State Party which has not made such a declaration.

2. The Committee shall consider inadmissible any communication under this article which is anonymous or which it considers to be an abuse of the right of submission of such communications or to be incompatible with the provisions of this Convention.

3. Subject to the provisions of paragraph 2, the Committee shall bring any communications submitted to it under this article to the attention of the State Party to this Convention which has made a declaration under paragraph 1 and is alleged to be violating any provisions of the Convention. Within six months, the receiving State shall submit to the Committee written explanations or statements clarifying the matter and the remedy, if any, that may have been taken by that State.

4. The Committee shall consider communications received under this article in the light of all information made available to it by or on behalf of the individual and by the State Party concerned.

5. The Committee shall not consider any communications from an individual under this article unless it has ascertained that:

(a) The same matter has not been, and is not being, examined under another procedure of international investigation or settlement;

(b) The individual has exhausted all available domestic remedies; this shall not be the rule where the application of the remedies is unreasonably prolonged or is unlikely to bring effective relief to the person who is the victim of the violation of this Convention.

6. The Committee shall hold closed meetings when examining communications under this article.

7. The Committee shall forward its views to the State Party concerned and to the individual.

8. The provisions of this article shall come into force when five States Parties to this Convention have made declarations under paragraph 1 of this article. Such declarations shall be deposited by the States Parties with the Secretary-General of the United Nations, who shall

transmit copies thereof to the other States Parties. A declaration may be withdrawn at any time by notification to the Secretary-General. Such a withdrawal shall not prejudice the consideration of any matter which is the subject of a communication already transmitted under this article; no further communication by or on behalf of an individual shall be received under this article after the notification of withdrawal of the declaration has been received by the Secretary-General, unless the State Party has made a new declaration.

Article 23

The members of the Committee and of the *ad hoc* conciliation commissions which may be appointed under article 21, paragraph 1 *(e)*, shall be entitled to the facilities, privileges and immunities of experts on mission for the United Nations as laid down in the relevant sections of the Convention on the Privileges and Immunities of the United Nations.

Article 24

The Committee shall submit an annual report on its activities under this Convention to the States Parties and to the General Assembly of the United Nations.

Part III
Article 25

1. This Convention is open for signature by all States.

2. This Convention is subject to ratification. Instruments of ratification shall be deposited with the Secretary-General of the United Nations.

Article 26

This Convention is open to accession by all States. Accession shall be effected by the deposit of an instrument of accession with the Secretary-General of the United Nations.

Article 27

1. This Convention shall enter into force on the thirtieth day after the date of the deposit with the Secretary-General of the United Nations of the twentieth instrument of ratification or accession.

2. For each State ratifying this Convention or acceding to it after the deposit of the twentieth instrument of ratification or accession, the Convention shall enter into force on the thirtieth day after the date of the deposit of its own instrument of ratification or accession.

Article 28

1. Each State may, at the time of signature or ratification of this Convention or accession thereto, declare that it does not recognize the competence of the Committee provided for in article 20.

2. Any State Party having made a reservation in accordance with paragraph 1 of this article may, at any time, withdraw this reservation by notification to the Secretary-General of the United Nations.

Article 29

1. Any State Party to this Convention may propose an amendment and file it with the Secretary-General of the United Nations. The Secretary-General shall thereupon communicate the proposed amendment to the States Parties with a request that they notify him whether they favour a conference of States Parties for the purpose of considering and voting upon the proposal. In the event that within four months from the date of such communication at least one third of the States Parties favours such a conference, the Secretary-General shall convene the conference under the auspices of the United Nations. Any amendment adopted by a majority of the States Parties present and voting at the conference shall be submitted by the Secretary-General to all the States Parties for acceptance.

2. An amendment adopted in accordance with paragraph 1 of this article shall enter into force when two thirds of the States Parties to this Convention have notified the Secretary-General of the United Nations that they have accepted it in accordance with their respective constitutional processes.

3. When amendments enter into force, they shall be binding on those States Parties which have accepted them, other States Parties still being bound by the provisions of this Convention and any earlier amendments which they have accepted.

Article 30

1. Any dispute between two or more States Parties concerning the interpretation or application of this Convention which cannot be settled through negotiation shall, at the request of one of them, be submitted to arbitration. If within six months from the date of the request for arbitration the Parties are unable to agree on the organization of the arbitration, any one of those Parties may refer the dispute to the International Court of Justice by request in conformity with the Statute of the Court.

2. Each State may, at the time of signature or ratification of this Convention or accession thereto, declare that it does not consider itself bound by paragraph 1 of this article. The other States Parties shall not be bound by paragraph 1 of this article with respect to any State Party having made such a reservation.

3. Any State Party having made a reservation in accordance with paragraph 2 of this article may at any time withdraw this reservation by notification to the Secretary-General of the United Nations.

Article 31

1. A State Party may denounce this Convention by written notification to the Secretary-General of the United Nations. Denunciation becomes effective one year after the date of receipt of the notification by the Secretary-General.

2. Such a denunciation shall not have the effect of releasing the State Party from its obligations under this Convention in regard to any act or omission which occurs prior to the date at which the denunciation becomes effective, nor shall denunciation prejudice in any way the continued consideration of any matter which is already under consideration by the Committee prior to the date at which the denunciation becomes effective.

3. Following the date at which the denunciation of a State Party becomes effective, the Committee shall not commence consideration of any new matter regarding that State.

Article 32

The Secretary-General of the United Nations shall inform all States Members of the United Nations and all States which have signed this Convention or acceded to it of the following:

(a) Signatures, ratifications and accessions under articles 25 and 26;

(b) The date of entry into force of this Convention under article 27 and the date of the entry into force of any amendments under article 29;

(c) Denunciations under article 31.

Article 33

1. This Convention, of which the Arabic, Chinese, English, French, Russian and Spanish texts are equally authentic, shall be deposited with the Secretary-General of the United Nations.

2. The Secretary-General of the United Nations shall transmit certified copies of this Convention to all States.

General Assembly resolution 39/46

10 December 1984   Meeting 93   Adopted without vote

Approved by Third Committee (A/39/708 and Corr.2) without vote, 5 December (meeting 60); 25-nation draft (A/C.3/39/L.40), orally revised; amended by Byelorussian SSR (A/C.3/39/L.66) and further amended by 10 nations (A/C.3/39/L.49); agenda item 99.

Sponsors of draft: Argentina, Australia, Austria, Belgium, Bolivia, Colombia, Costa Rica, Denmark, Dominican Republic, Finland, France, Gambia, Greece, Iceland, Italy, Netherlands, New Zealand, Norway, Panama, Portugal, Samoa, Singapore, Spain, Sweden, United Kingdom.

Sponsors of amendment: Afghanistan, Bulgaria, Czechoslovakia, German Democratic Republic, Hungary, Mongolia, Poland, Ukrainian SSR, USSR, Viet Nam.

Financial implications. S-G, A/C.3/39/L.62.

Meeting numbers. GA 39th session: 3rd Committee 44-52, 56, 57, 60; plenary 93.

During its consideration by the Third Committee, the draft convention underwent several modifications. In addition to oral revisions made to paragraphs 1 and 5 of article 20, the sponsors agreed to the 10-nation amendments, according to which, in paragraph 3 of article 19, the word "general" was inserted before "comments" and the phrase "or suggestions on the report" was deleted; also deleted were, in paragraph 4, the words "or suggestions". A new article 28 proposed by the Byelorussian SSR was accepted and the subsequent articles renumbered accordingly.

Also in Committee, Iran introduced, but did not press to a vote, a draft resolution[60] which would have had the Assembly condemn all acts of torture as contrary to human dignity and request States to prohibit trade in instruments of torture and to ban their development and production.

Fund for victims of torture

On 6 March 1984,[61] the Commission on Human Rights again called on Governments, organizations and individuals to contribute to the United Nations Voluntary Fund for Victims of Torture, established in 1981.[62] The Commission asked the Secretary-General to transmit its appeal to Governments for further contributions and to assist the Board of Trustees in efforts to give publicity to the Fund's humanitarian work. It also asked him to keep the Commission informed of the Fund's operations.

The Secretary-General stated in his annual report on the status of the Fund as at 31 October 1984[63] that the Board, which met in a third session at Geneva from 27 to 29 August, had recommended to him approval of grants for 18 projects, including follow-up grants for ongoing projects, totalling $518,700. The projects were to assist rehabilitation centres for torture victims at Copenhagen (Denmark) and Toronto (Canada), to finance training courses or seminars on treatment and rehabilitation, and to support other projects such as those providing medical and psychological aid to victims.

In 1984, the Fund recorded a total income of $646,793 and a total expenditure of $80,031.

GENERAL ASSEMBLY ACTION

Acting without vote on the recommendation of the Third Committee, the General Assembly adopted resolution 39/113 on 14 December 1984.

United Nations Voluntary Fund for Victims of Torture

The General Assembly,

Recalling article 5 of the Universal Declaration of Human Rights, which states that no one shall be subjected to torture or to cruel, inhuman or degrading treatment or punishment,

Recalling also the Declaration on the Protection of All Persons from Being Subjected to Torture and Other Cruel, Inhuman or Degrading Treatment or Punishment,

Recalling further its resolution 36/151 of 16 December 1981, in which it noted with deep concern that acts of torture took place in various countries, recognized the need to provide assistance to the victims of torture in a purely humanitarian spirit and established the United Nations Voluntary Fund for Victims of Torture,

Convinced that the struggle to eliminate torture includes the provision of assistance in a humanitarian spirit to the victims and their family members,

Taking note of the report of the Secretary-General on the United Nations Voluntary Fund for Victims of Torture,

1. *Expresses its gratitude and appreciation* to those Governments, organizations and individuals that have already contributed to the United Nations Voluntary Fund for Victims of Torture;

2. *Calls upon* all Governments, organizations and individuals in a position to do so to respond favourably to requests for initial as well as further contributions to the Fund;

3. *Expresses its appreciation* to the Board of Trustees of the Fund for the work it has carried out;

4. *Expresses its appreciation* to the Secretary-General for the support given to the Board of Trustees;

5. *Requests* the Secretary-General to make use of all existing possibilities to assist the Board of Trustees of the Fund, *inter alia* through the preparation, production and dissemination of information materials, in its efforts to make the Fund and its humanitarian work better known and in its appeal for contributions.

General Assembly resolution 39/113

14 December 1984   Meeting 101   Adopted without vote

Approved by Third Committee (A/39/700) without vote, 6 December (meeting 64); 16-nation draft (A/C.3/39/L.75); agenda item 12.

Sponsors: Australia, Bolivia, Costa Rica, Cyprus, Denmark, Finland, France, Germany, Federal Republic of, Greece, Iceland, Kenya, Mexico, Netherlands, Norway, Sweden, United States.

Meeting numbers. GA 39th session: 3rd Committee 61, 64; plenary 101.

Penalty of amputation

Noting the existence of legislation or practices in various countries providing for the penalty of amputation, the Sub-Commission, by a vote of 10 to 5, with 9 abstentions, taken on 29 August 1984,[64] recommended to the Commission on Human Rights that it urge Governments having such legislation or practices to take measures to provide for other punishment consonant with article 5 (providing that no one should be subjected to torture or to cruel, inhuman or degrading treatment or punishment) of the Universal Declaration of Human Rights.[34]

Principles of Medical Ethics

Pursuant to a General Assembly request of December 1983,[65] the Secretary-General submitted in September 1984 a report, with later addenda,[66] summarizing information communicated to him on steps taken to disseminate and implement the 1982 Principles of Medical Ethics[67] relevant to the role of health personnel in the protection of prisoners and detainees against torture and other cruel treatment. Information was received from 12 Governments, two specialized agencies, an intergovernmental organization outside the United Nations, and seven NGOs.

Detention on grounds of mental illness

In 1984, work remained to be completed on a draft body of principles, guidelines and guarantees for the protection of persons detained on grounds of mental ill-health or suffering from mental disorder. The draft text had been annexed to a final report on the subject, submitted to the Sub-Commission in 1983.[68]

Acting on the Sub-Commission's draft proposals of September 1983 calling for the report's publication and priority consideration of the draft body of principles,[69] the Commission on Human Rights, on 13 March 1984, decided to recommend the following for Economic and Social Council action: a draft decision, which it recommended by 36 votes to none, with 6 abstentions,[70] and a draft resolution,[71] both of which served as the bases for the Council actions below.

ECONOMIC AND SOCIAL COUNCIL ACTION

Acting without vote on the recommendation of the Second Committee, the Economic and Social Council in May adopted decision 1984/142.

Principles, guidelines and guarantees for the protection of persons detained on grounds of mental ill-health or suffering from mental disorder

At its 20th plenary meeting, on 24 May 1984, the Council, noting Commission on Human Rights decision 1984/108 of 13 March 1984, decided that the report entitled "Principles, guidelines and guarantees for the protection of persons detained on grounds of mental ill-

health or suffering from mental disorder" should be published, without annex III, and given the widest possible distribution in all the official languages of the United Nations.

Economic and Social Council decision 1984/142

Adopted without vote

Approved by Second Committee (E/1984/91) without vote, 17 May (meeting 16); draft by Commission on Human Rights (E/1984/14); agenda item 10.

Also on the recommendation of the Second Committee, the Council adopted resolution 1984/33 without vote on 24 May.

Principles, guidelines and guarantees for the protection of persons detained on grounds of mental ill-health or suffering from mental disorder

The Economic and Social Council,

Mindful of resolution 1983/39 of 7 September 1983 of the Sub-Commission on Prevention of Discrimination and Protection of Minorities and Commission on Human Rights resolution 1984/47 of 13 March 1984,

1. *Expresses its deep appreciation* to the Special Rapporteur, Mrs. Erica-Irene A. Daes, for her work in preparing her report on principles, guidelines and guarantees for the protection of persons detained on grounds of mental ill-health or suffering from mental disorder;

2. *Requests* the Sub-Commission on Prevention of Discrimination and Protection of Minorities to establish a sessional working group and to allocate to it appropriate time and facilities for a further examination, as a matter of high priority, of the draft body of principles, guidelines and guarantees annexed to the report of the Special Rapporteur and to submit the draft body of principles, guidelines and guarantees to the Commission on Human Rights at its forty-second session.

Economic and Social Council resolution 1984/33

24 May 1984   Meeting 20   Adopted without vote

Approved by Second Committee (E/1984/91) without vote, 17 May (meeting 15); draft by Commission on Human Rights (E/1984/14); agenda item 10.

Working group activities. In accordance with the Council's request, the Sub-Commission set up a sessional working group in August 1984 to examine further the draft body of principles, guidelines and guarantees. With Erica-Irene A. Daes (Greece) as Chairman/Rapporteur, the group convened in five meetings between 9 and 23 August, during which it heard brief comments by five NGOs and completed a first reading of articles 25 to 40 and 45 to 47. The first reading of articles 1 to 7 had been completed in 1982 and of articles 8 to 24 in 1983.

As to articles 41 to 44, concerning minors and juvenile patients, it was agreed to postpone their consideration to the group's next session, owing to a lack of a comprehensive study on the terms and because the question of the aged, who were not necessarily affected by mental disorder, might be discussed under that part of the draft.

The full revised text of the draft body of principles was annexed to the group's report.[72]

Acting on the recommendation of the Third Committee on 14 December 1984, the General Assembly adopted resolution 39/132 without vote.

Implications of scientific and technological developments for human rights

The General Assembly,

Recalling its resolution 33/53 of 14 December 1978, in which it requested the Commission on Human Rights to urge the Sub-Commission on Prevention of Discrimination and Protection of Minorities to undertake, as a matter of priority, a study of the question of the protection of those detained on the grounds of mental ill-health, with a view to formulating guidelines,

Recalling also its resolution 38/111 of 16 December 1983, in which it urged the Commission on Human Rights and the Sub-Commission to expedite their consideration of this question, so that the Commission could submit its views and recommendations, including a draft body of guidelines, principles and guarantees, to the General Assembly at its fortieth session, through the Economic and Social Council,

Recalling further Economic and Social Council resolution 1984/33 and decision 1984/142 of 24 May 1984,

Noting that the Commission on Human Rights will not be in a position to submit its views and recommendations to the General Assembly at its fortieth session through the Economic and Social Council because the Sub-Commission has still not concluded its consideration of the draft body of guidelines, principles and guarantees,

Noting with satisfaction the progress made by the Sub-Commission on this question,

Reaffirming its conviction that detention of persons in mental institutions on account of their political views or on other non-medical grounds is a violation of their human rights,

Again urges the Commission on Human Rights and, through it, the Sub-Commission on Prevention of Discrimination and Protection of Minorities to expedite their consideration of the draft body of guidelines, principles and guarantees, so that the Commission can submit its views and recommendations, including a draft body of guidelines, principles and guarantees, to the General Assembly at its forty-first session, through the Economic and Social Council.

General Assembly resolution 39/132

14 December 1984   Meeting 101   Adopted without vote

Approved by Third Committee (A/39/705) without vote, 3 December (meeting 57); 21-nation draft (A/C.3/39/L.46); agenda item 96.

Sponsors: Bolivia, Botswana, Colombia, Costa Rica, Cyprus, Fiji, Gambia, Italy, Ivory Coast, Jamaica, Mexico, Morocco, Netherlands, Norway, Philippines, Sierra Leone, Singapore, Sweden, Togo, Trinidad and Tobago, United Kingdom.

Meeting numbers. GA 39th session: 3rd Committee 44-52, 56, 57; plenary 101.

Draft declaration against unacknowledged detention

Consideration by Working Group on Detention. As requested by the Sub-Commission in September 1983,[73] the 1984 sessional Working Group on Detention (see above) began work in August on the first draft of a declaration aimed at eliminating unacknowledged detention and related practices. The declaration was to apply to detention not only by Governments, but also by so-called private armies, death squads or groups that appeared to be tolerated by authorities.

The initial text, submitted by the Group's Chairman/Rapporteur, consisted of a preamble, article I (prohibition of unacknowledged detention), article II (right of notification), article III (duty of record-keeping), article IV (non-secret places of detention), article V (remedies), article VI (definitions) and article VII (non-restriction of rights).

Sub-Commission action. On 29 August 1984,[74] the Sub-Commission thanked the Working Group for the work it had accomplished on the draft declaration and requested it to submit, for possible review in 1985, a revised text in the light of the comments expressed at the Group's August 1984 meetings. The Sub-Commission asked the Secretary-General to provide it and the Group with any available documentation for this purpose.

Capital punishment

On 14 February 1984,[75] the Commission on Human Rights decided to transmit a telegram to the President of Malawi to the effect that the Commission had learned that the Malawi National Traditional Court of Appeal had turned down the appeal of Orton Chirwa and his wife against the death sentence passed on them for treason.[76] Based on a purely humanitarian concern deriving from its recognition of the singular importance of the right to life, the Commission appealed most respectfully and strongly that clemency be granted to them.

Proposed second optional protocol to the Covenant on Civil and Political Rights

The idea of a second optional protocol to the International Covenant on Civil and Political Rights, aimed at the abolition of the death penalty, originated in the General Assembly in 1980.[77] Government views on it were reported to the Assembly in 1981[78] and again in 1982,[79] when the Assembly requested the Commission on Human Rights to undertake the task of elaborating the protocol.[80]

Accordingly, the Commission on 6 March 1984[81] transmitted to its Sub-Commission the draft of a second optional protocol, together with the pertinent documents, and invited it to consider, at its 1984 session, elaborating the protocol and setting up a sessional working group for the purpose. The Commission asked the Secretary-General to inform the Assembly of these actions.

Taking note of the documents transmitted to it, the Sub-Commission on 28 August[82] recommended to the Commission a draft resolution by which the Economic and Social Council would authorize the Sub-Commission to entrust Marc Bossuyt (Belgium) with the preparation of an analysis concerning the proposal, taking into account the views expressed for and against it, and to present recommendations for Sub-Commission consideration in 1986. The Council would request the Secretary-General to provide the assistance necessary to complete that task.

GENERAL ASSEMBLY ACTION

On 14 December 1984, acting on the recommendation of the Third Committee, the General Assembly adopted resolution 39/137 by recorded vote.

Elaboration of a second optional protocol to the International Covenant on Civil and Political Rights, aiming at the abolition of the death penalty

The General Assembly,

Recalling its decision 35/437 of 15 December 1980 and its resolution 36/59 of 25 November 1981 concerning the idea of elaborating a draft of a second optional protocol to the International Covenant on Civil and Political Rights, aiming at the abolition of the death penalty,

Recalling also its resolution 37/192 of 18 December 1982, in which it requested the Commission on Human Rights to consider the idea of elaborating a draft of a second optional protocol to the International Covenant on Civil and Political Rights, aiming at the abolition of the death penalty,

Taking note of Commission on Human Rights resolution 1984/19 of 6 March 1984 and the action taken by the Sub-Commission on Prevention of Discrimination and Protection of Minorities to implement that resolution,

Taking note also of the report of the Secretary-General,

1. *Requests* the Commission on Human Rights and the Sub-Commission on Prevention of Discrimination and Protection of Minorities to consider further the idea of elaborating a draft of a second optional protocol to the International Covenant on Civil and Political Rights, aiming at the abolition of the death penalty;

2. *Invites* Member States which are in a position to do so, specialized agencies and international organizations to assist the Commission and the Sub-Commission in the consideration of this question;

3. *Requests* the Secretary-General to inform the General Assembly at its forty-second session of the consideration given to this question by the Commission and the Sub-Commission;

4. *Decides* to continue its consideration of this question at its forty-second session, in the light of the action taken by the Commission and the Sub-Commission, under the item entitled "International Covenants on Human Rights".

General Assembly resolution 39/137

14 December 1984   Meeting 101   64-19-55 (recorded vote)

Approved by Third Committee (A/39/707) by recorded vote (57-18-50), 5 December (meeting 60); 26-nation draft (A/C.3/39/L.48/Rev.1), orally revised; agenda item 98 *(c)*.

Sponsors: Argentina, Austria, Belgium, Cape Verde, Colombia, Costa Rica, Cyprus, Denmark, Dominican Republic, Ecuador, Finland, Germany, Federal Republic of, Greece, Honduras, Iceland, Italy, Luxembourg, Netherlands, Nicaragua, Norway, Panama, Portugal, Solomon Islands, Spain, Sweden, Uruguay.

Meeting numbers. GA 39th session: 3rd Committee 44-52, 56, 57, 60; plenary 101.

Recorded vote in Assembly as follows:

In favour: Argentina, Australia, Austria, Belgium, Bolivia, Brazil, Burundi, Canada, Cape Verde, Central African Republic, Chile, Colombia, Costa Rica, Cyprus, Denmark, Dominican Republic, Ecuador, El Salvador, Fiji, Finland, France, Germany, Federal Republic of, Ghana, Greece, Guatemala, Guinea, Guyana, Haiti, Honduras, Iceland, Ireland, Israel, Italy, Ivory Coast, Jamaica, Japan, Kenya, Liberia, Luxembourg, Mali, Malta, Mauritania, Mexico, Netherlands, New Zealand, Nicaragua, Norway, Panama, Papua New Guinea, Peru, Portugal, Rwanda, Samoa, Sao Tome and Principe, Seychelles, Spain, Sweden, Togo, Trinidad and Tobago, Turkey, United Kingdom, United States, Uruguay, Venezuela.

Against: Bahrain, Bangladesh, Iran, Iraq, Jordan, Kuwait, Libyan Arab Jamahiriya, Maldives, Oman, Pakistan, Qatar, Saudi Arabia, Senegal, Singapore, Somalia, Sudan, Syrian Arab Republic, United Arab Emirates, Yemen.

Abstaining: Afghanistan, Algeria, Angola, Bahamas, Barbados, Belize, Benin, Bhutan, Botswana, Brunei Darussalam, Bulgaria, Burkina Faso, Burma, Byelorussian SSR, Cameroon, China, Congo, Cuba, Czechoslovakia, Democratic Kampuchea, Egypt, Equatorial Guinea, Ethiopia, Gabon, Gambia, German Democratic Republic, Hungary, India, Lao People's Democratic Republic, Lebanon, Lesotho, Madagascar, Malawi, Malaysia, Mauritius, Mongolia, Nepal, Niger, Nigeria, Paraguay, Poland, Saint Vincent and the Grenadines, Sri Lanka, Swaziland, Thailand, Tunisia, Uganda, Ukrainian SSR, USSR, United Republic of Tanzania, Viet Nam, Yugoslavia, Zaire, Zambia, Zimbabwe.

In the Committee, Saudi Arabia explained that it had called for a vote because abolition of the death penalty was incompatible with the Islamic principle that premeditated murder must be punished by the death penalty. The United Arab Emirates said that, since the text was procedural, it would have preferred its adoption without vote. Along with Yemen, it also said that the text was contrary to Islamic principles. Kuwait stated that it could not support any formulation that might be interpreted as consent to abolish capital punishment. Morocco did not participate in the vote but said it would be the first to vote against the abolition of capital punishment.

Referring to its position on the death penalty as the reason for its abstention, the Byelorussian SSR said that paragraph 2 should have been formulated differently because only Commission and Sub-Commission members could assist in the consideration of the elaboration of a second optional protocol.

A number of States—Burundi, Canada, Japan, Mali, Rwanda, the United Kingdom and the United States among them—said they had no problem supporting a text that was procedural; they variously explained, however, that their vote was not to be interpreted as in any way affecting their countries' position on the death penalty.

Introducing the revised draft on behalf of the sponsors, the Federal Republic of Germany said they felt that the purely procedural text did not run counter to the interests of any State; however, the question would require further thorough examination by the Commission and the Sub-Commission before the Assembly could take a decision on the substance of the proposal to abolish the death penalty.

Other action. In resolution 1984/50, the Economic and Social Council approved the safeguards guaranteeing protection of the rights of those facing the death penalty, recommended by the Committee on Crime Prevention and Control (see Chapter XIII of this section), on the understanding that they should not be invoked to delay or prevent the abolition of capital punishment.

Extra-legal executions

In conformity with an Economic and Social Council request of May 1983,[83] Special Rapporteur S. Amos Wako (Kenya) submitted to the Commission on Human Rights in February 1984 a second report[84] on summary or arbitrary executions. The report took account of observations made on the topic at the Commission's 1983 session and of new information received since then from 34 Governments, two United Nations bodies, six specialized agencies, a regional intergovernmental organization and 12 NGOs. This included information on national legislation of various countries analysed within the context of the relevant international instruments.

The report concluded that developments since the first report[85] continued to bear out the fact that summary or arbitrary executions remained widespread and that respect for the right to life was far from being a universal reality. In 1983, persons alleged to have been summarily or arbitrarily executed numbered in the thousands, even excluding those who had died from counter-insurgency or anti-guerrilla measures and thus not classified as having been executed under the terms of international conventions. National legislation in some cases was in conflict with those conventions in that it permitted situations where executions could take place; in others, they had taken place despite meticulously stipulated safeguards for the right to life. Situations under which executions occurred involved multiple factors, among them political upheavals, internal armed conflicts, suppression of opposition groups or individuals, abuse of power by the law enforcement sector, and campaigns against crime.

In addition to reiterating the recommendations of the first report—among them the setting up by the Commission of a mechanism to monitor practices or situations of summary or arbitrary executions and to keep them under continuous review—the second report suggested that, in an all-out international effort to bring such executions to a halt, the United Nations Department of Public Information could convene a high-level meeting of regional editors aimed at strengthening the role of the press and mass media; and the Committee on Crime Prevention and Control could examine ways of effectively controlling law enforcement and security authorities to prevent excesses, with perhaps the co-operation of the International Criminal Police Organization (INTERPOL). Periodic reporting by Governments on their efforts to give effective protection to the right to life could be given consideration.

ECONOMIC AND SOCIAL COUNCIL ACTION

Acting without vote on the recommendation of its Second Committee, the Economic and Social Council on 24 May 1984 adopted resolution 1984/35. It was based on a text submitted for Council action by the Commission on Human Rights on 14 March,[86] following its examination of the Special Rapporteur's report.

Summary or arbitrary executions

The Economic and Social Council,

Recalling the Universal Declaration of Human Rights, which guarantees the right to life, liberty and security of person,

Having regard to the provisions of the International Covenant on Civil and Political Rights, which states that every human being has the inherent right to life, that this right shall be protected by law and that no one shall be arbitrarily deprived of his life,

Recalling General Assembly resolution 34/175 of 17 December 1979, in which the Assembly reaffirmed that mass and flagrant violations of human rights were of special concern to the United Nations and urged the Commission on Human Rights to take timely and effective action in existing and future cases of mass and flagrant violations of human rights,

Mindful of General Assembly resolutions 36/22 of 9 November 1981, 37/182 of 17 December 1982 and 38/96 of 16 December 1983,

Taking note of resolution 1982/13 of 7 September 1982 of the Sub-Commission on Prevention of Discrimination and Protection of Minorities, in which the Sub-Commission recommended that effective measures should be adopted to prevent the occurrence of summary and arbitrary executions,

Taking note also of the work done by the Committee on Crime Prevention and Control in the area of summary and arbitrary executions, including the elaboration of minimum legal guarantees and safeguards to prevent recourse to such extra-legal executions, to be considered by the Seventh United Nations Congress on the Prevention of Crime and the Treatment of Offenders in 1985,

Deeply alarmed about the occurrence on a large scale of summary or arbitrary executions, including extra-legal executions,

1. *Strongly deplores,* once again, the large number of summary or arbitrary executions, including extra-legal executions, which continue to take place in various parts of the world;

2. *Appeals urgently* to Governments, United Nations bodies, the specialized agencies, regional intergovernmental organizations and non-governmental organizations to take effective action to combat and eliminate summary or arbitrary executions, including extra-legal executions;

3. *Takes note with appreciation* of the report of the Special Rapporteur, Mr. S. Amos Wako;

4. *Decides* to continue the mandate of the Special Rapporteur for another year, in order to enable him to submit further conclusions and recommendations to the Commission on Human Rights;

5. *Requests* the Special Rapporteur in carrying out his mandate to continue to examine situations of sum-

mary or arbitrary executions and to pay special attention to cases in which a summary or arbitrary execution is imminent or threatened;

6. *Requests* the Special Rapporteur in carrying out his mandate to respond effectively to information that comes before him;

7. *Considers* that the Special Rapporteur in carrying out his mandate should continue to seek and receive information from Governments, United Nations bodies, specialized agencies, regional intergovernmental organizations and non-governmental organizations in consultative status with the Economic and Social Council;

8. *Requests* the Secretary-General to continue to provide all necessary assistance to the Special Rapporteur so that he may carry out his mandate effectively;

9. *Urges* all Governments and all others concerned to co-operate with and assist the Special Rapporteur;

10. *Requests* the Commission on Human Rights to consider the question of summary or arbitrary executions as a matter of high priority at its forty-first session, under the item entitled "Question of the violation of human rights and fundamental freedoms in any part of the world, with particular reference to colonial and other dependent countries and territories".

Economic and Social Council resolution 1984/35

24 May 1984 Meeting 20 Adopted without vote

Approved by Second Committee (E/1984/91) without vote, 17 May (meeting 16); draft by Commission on Human Rights (E/1984/14); agenda item 10.

In resolution 1984/50 on the rights of those facing the death penalty, the Council again strongly condemned and deplored the brutal practice of arbitrary or summary executions.

GENERAL ASSEMBLY ACTION

On 14 December 1984, acting without vote on the recommendation of the Third Committee, the General Assembly adopted resolution 39/110.

Summary or arbitrary executions

The General Assembly,

Recalling the provisions of the Universal Declaration of Human Rights, which states that every human being has the right to life, liberty and security of person and that everyone is entitled in full equality to a fair and public hearing by an independent and impartial tribunal,

Having regard to the provisions of the International Covenant on Civil and Political Rights, which states that every human being has the inherent right to life, that this right shall be protected by law and that no one shall be arbitrarily deprived of his life,

Recalling also its resolution 34/175 of 17 December 1979, in which it reaffirmed that mass and flagrant violations of human rights are of special concern to the United Nations and urged the Commission on Human Rights to take timely and effective action in existing and future cases of mass and flagrant violations of human rights,

Recalling further its resolution 36/22 of 9 November 1981, in which it condemned the practice of summary or arbitrary executions, and its resolutions 37/182 of 17 December 1982 and 38/96 of 16 December 1983,

Deeply alarmed at the occurrence on a large scale of summary or arbitrary executions, including extra-legal executions,

Recalling resolution 1982/13 of 7 September 1982 of the Sub-Commission on Prevention of Discrimination and Protection of Minorities, in which the Sub-Commission recommended that effective measures should be adopted to prevent the occurrence of summary or arbitrary executions,

Taking note of the work done by the Committee on Crime Prevention and Control in the area of summary or arbitrary executions, including the elaboration of minimum legal guarantees and safeguards to prevent recourse to such extra-legal executions, to be considered by the Seventh United Nations Congress on the Prevention of Crime and the Treatment of Offenders, to be held from 26 August to 6 September 1985,

Convinced of the need for appropriate action to combat and eventually eliminate the practice of summary or arbitrary executions, which represents a flagrant violation of the most fundamental human right, the right to life,

1. *Strongly deplores* the large number of summary or arbitrary executions, including extra-legal executions, which continue to take place in various parts of the world;

2. *Welcomes* Economic and Social Council resolutions 1982/35 of 7 May 1982, in which the Council decided to appoint for one year a special rapporteur to examine the questions related to summary or arbitrary executions, and 1983/36 of 26 May 1983, in which it decided to continue the mandate of the Special Rapporteur for another year;

3. *Also welcomes* Economic and Social Council resolution 1984/35 of 24 May 1984, in which the Council decided to continue the mandate of the Special Rapporteur, Mr. S. A. Wako, for a further year and requested the Commission on Human Rights to consider the question of summary or arbitrary executions as a matter of high priority at its forty-first session;

4. *Appeals* to all Governments to co-operate with and assist the Special Rapporteur of the Commission on Human Rights in the preparation of his report;

5. *Requests* the Special Rapporteur, in carrying out his mandate, to respond effectively to information that comes before him, in particular when a summary or arbitrary execution is imminent or threatened;

6. *Considers* that the Special Rapporteur, in carrying out his mandate, should continue to seek and receive information from Governments, United Nations bodies, specialized agencies, regional intergovernmental organizations and non-governmental organizations in consultative status with the Economic and Social Council;

7. *Requests* the Secretary-General to provide all necessary assistance to the Special Rapporteur so that he may effectively carry out his mandate;

8. *Again requests* the Secretary-General to continue to use his best endeavours in cases where the minimum standard of legal safeguards provided for in articles 6, 14 and 15 of the International Covenant on Civil and Political Rights appear not to be respected;

9. *Requests* the Commission on Human Rights at its forty-first session, on the basis of the report of the Special Rapporteur to be prepared in conformity with Economic and Social Council resolutions 1982/35, 1983/36 and 1984/35, to make recommendations concerning ap-

propriate action to combat and eventually eliminate the practice of summary or arbitrary executions.

General Assembly resolution 39/110

14 December 1984   Meeting 101   Adopted without vote

Approved by Third Committee (A/39/700) without vote, 6 December (meeting 64); 24-nation draft (A/C.3/39/L.72); agenda item 12.
Sponsors: Argentina, Austria, Belgium, Canada, Costa Rica, Cyprus, Denmark, Dominican Republic, Ecuador, Finland, France, Gambia, Greece, Iceland, Ivory Coast, Japan, Kenya, Morocco, Netherlands, Nicaragua, Norway, Portugal, Sweden, Zambia.
Meeting numbers. GA 39th session: 3rd Committee 61, 64; plenary 101.

In resolution 39/118, on human rights in the administration of justice, the Assembly reaffirmed the prohibition under international law of every form of cruel, inhuman or degrading treatment or punishment, and strongly condemned the practice of arbitrary and summary executions.

Amnesty

In 1984, a preliminary report on a study of amnesty laws and their role in safeguarding and promoting human rights, prepared by Special Rapporteur Louis Joinet (France),[87] was before the Sub-Commission, in keeping with its request of September 1983.[49] The study was intended to draw, from a comparative examination of State laws and practices, a set of common rules to serve as a framework for instituting amnesty, assessing the impact of amnesty laws, drafting legislation and promoting amnesties generally. Examined were texts of amnesty laws obtained from 76 States, and information from a United Nations information centre, four specialized agencies, a regional intergovernmental organization and five NGOs.

The report defined the scope of the study as being limited to amnesty in the following sense: whether or not a person amnestied had been tried or convicted, or served a sentence, his or her conduct was deemed not to have constituted an offence and the penalty never to have been enforced. The report concluded that amnesty dealt only with the effects of national dissension especially upon the institution of a state of emergency. The same held true when violations of the most rudimentary cultural, social or economic rights were at the root of civil dissension. Therefore, an amnesty process could be effective only if coupled with measures to eradicate the causes of dissension, including political (such as the repeal of emergency laws and the holding of genuine elections, as stipulated by article 21 of the 1948 Universal Declaration of Human Rights[34]), social and economic measures. The programmes for social and economic rehabilitation provided for by the 1982 amnesty decree of Colombia were cited as examples.

On 28 August 1984,[88] the Sub-Commission expressed appreciation to the Special Rapporteur for his preliminary report and requested him to continue work on the study for submission in 1985.

It asked the Secretary-General to remind States, specialized agencies, regional intergovernmental and non-governmental organizations to transmit to the Special Rapporteur, if they had not already done so, their observations and documents on amnesty laws.

Taking into consideration the emphasis which the report placed on the positive nature of the amnesty process under way in Colombia, the Sub-Commission, on 29 August,[89] further requested the Special Rapporteur to include in his final report the evolution of that process and its effects on the safeguarding and promotion of human rights and fundamental freedoms.

In related actions, the Sub-Commission requested the Commission on Human Rights to recommend to Paraguay that it end its state of siege (in force since 1954) and consider enacting an amnesty measure (see above, under "States of siege or emergency"); and urged Uruguay to speed up the process of setting free persons detained and/or sentenced for alleged offences against State security and internal order (see below, under "Human rights violations").

Human rights in states of siege or emergency were also dealt with in connection with the rights of detained persons (see above).

Persons detained by Israel

Reaffirming that fundamental human rights established by international instruments were fully applicable in armed conflict, the Commission on Human Rights, by a roll-call vote of 41 to 1, with 1 abstention, taken on 6 March 1984,[90] urged Israel to recognize, in accordance with the 1949 Geneva Convention relative to the Treatment of Prisoners of War, the status of prisoner of war for all combatants captured during the war in Lebanon and to treat them accordingly.

The Commission also urged Israel to release immediately all civilians arbitrarily detained since the beginning of that war, as well as those subsequently rearrested and detained again in Insar (Ansar) Camp in southern Lebanon in violation of a November 1983 agreement on prisoner exchange (see p. 279); to co-operate with the International Committee of the Red Cross (ICRC) and allow it to visit all detainees in detention centres under its control; and to ensure protection for Palestinian civilians, including released detainees, in the areas under its occupation, in conformity with the 1949 Geneva Convention relative to the Protection of Civilian Persons in Time of War and The Hague Convention of 1907. It called on all parties to the conflict to furnish ICRC with information concerning persons who were missing or who disappeared following the Israeli invasion of Lebanon.

By a 20 February resolution[91] on human rights violations in the occupied Arab territories (see below, under "Human rights violations"), the Commission called on Israel to release all Arabs detained or imprisoned as a result of their struggle for self-determination and demanded that Israel cease all acts of torture and ill-treatment of Arab detainees. It further called on Israel to release the Palestinian Ziyad Abu Eain and others from Insar Camp, which must be closed under the November 1983 agreement.

Disappearance of persons

Communication. On 17 January 1984,[92] the United States transmitted to the Secretary-General a statement issued the same day by the United States Department of State. According to the statement, the date marked the thirty-ninth anniversary of the disappearance of Raoul Wallenberg, a Swedish diplomat who had been escorted away by USSR authorities from Budapest, Hungary, never to return. The statement continued that, while the USSR had stated in 1957, in reply to repeated inquiries, that Mr. Wallenberg had perished in prison 10 years before, questions as to his whereabouts continued to persist; it therefore called on the USSR to provide a full account of his fate.

Action by the Commission on Human Rights. On 6 March 1984,[93] the Commission on Human Rights, taking note of the 1983 report of the Working Group on Enforced or Involuntary Disappearances,[94] extended the Group's mandate for one year and requested that it submit in 1985 a report on its work, together with recommendations, including those for the effective fulfilment of its mandate. The Group was requested to discharge that mandate with discretion so as to protect persons providing information or to limit dissemination of information from Governments. The Commission renewed its request that the Secretary-General appeal for government cooperation and continue to provide the Group with assistance.

Noting that Viscount Colville of Culross (United Kingdom) was resigning from the chairmanship of the Group, which he had held since the Group's inception in 1980, the Commission, also on 6 March,[95] expressed appreciation to him for the skill and dedication with which he had carried out his tasks.

Working Group activities. The five-member Working Group on Enforced or Involuntary Disappearances, established in 1980,[96] held three sessions in 1984: the thirteenth from 4 to 8 June in New York; the fourteenth from 3 to 11 October at San José, Costa Rica; and the fifteenth from 5 to 14 December at Geneva.[97]

At those sessions, the Group continued to address communications on enforced or involuntary disappearances, some 2,900 of which were received in 1984. It transmitted reports on some 2,000 newly reported cases of missing persons to the Governments concerned, with a request for information on the fate of those alleged to have disappeared. It retransmitted summaries of all cases unclarified since the Group's inception, with a request that the information be either confirmed or disproved. Reports not transmitted were being held for further information from the reports' sources or were found not to fall within the Group's mandate (assassinations, torture, arbitrary detentions, harassment).

The Group held 12 meetings with government representatives—from Argentina, Bolivia, Colombia, Haiti, Honduras, Nicaragua, Peru and the Philippines; 5 with members of parliaments; and 26 with representatives of organizations, associations or witnesses directly concerned with reports of disappearances. The Group also discussed with Argentina, Bolivia, El Salvador, Guatemala, Peru and the Philippines its wish to visit those countries to enable it to fulfil its mandate more effectively.

The Group concluded that a major breakthrough in efforts to eradicate enforced disappearances could not be claimed. Its findings indicated no reversal of the trend where the practice had been rampant, and an alarming increase where it had been considered incipient. The Group recommended to the Commission that it appeal to the Governments concerned to set up national organs to investigate reports of missing persons and to respond to the Group's requests for information on steps they had taken to implement the 1978 General Assembly resolution on disappeared persons.[98] It also recommended that the Commission elaborate an international instrument against enforced or involuntary disappearances and renew the Group's mandate for a further two years.

ECONOMIC AND SOCIAL COUNCIL ACTION

Acting without vote on the recommendation of its Second Committee, the Economic and Social Council in May adopted decision 1984/135.

Question of enforced or involuntary disappearances

At its 20th plenary meeting, on 24 May 1984, the Council, noting Commission on Human Rights resolution 1984/23 of 6 March 1984, approved the Commission's decision to extend for one year the mandate of the Working Group on Enforced or Involuntary Disappearances, as laid down in Commission resolution 20(XXXVI) of 29 February 1980. The Council endorsed the Commission's request to the Secretary-General to continue to provide the Working Group with all necessary assistance, in particular the staff and resources it may require to perform its functions in an effective and expeditious manner and, if necessary, to make the appropriate arrangements to ensure the continuity of the Secretariat's work.

Economic and Social Council decision 1984/135

Adopted without vote

Approved by Second Committee (E/1984/91) without vote, 17 May (meeting 16); draft by Commission on Human Rights (E/1984/14); agenda item 10.

GENERAL ASSEMBLY ACTION

Acting without vote on the recommendation of the Third Committee, the General Assembly on 14 December 1984 adopted resolution 39/111.

Question of enforced or involuntary disappearances

The General Assembly,

Recalling its resolution 33/173 of 20 December 1978, entitled "Disappeared persons", and its resolution 38/94 of 16 December 1983 on the question of enforced or involuntary disappearances,

Deeply concerned about the persistence, in certain cases, of the practice of enforced or involuntary disappearances,

Expressing its profound emotion at the anguish and sorrow of the families concerned, who should know the fate of their relatives,

Convinced of the importance of implementing the provisions of General Assembly resolution 33/173 and of the other United Nations resolutions on the question of enforced and involuntary disappearances, with a view to finding solutions for cases of disappearances and helping to eliminate such practices,

Bearing in mind Commission on Human Rights resolution 1984/23 of 6 March 1984, in which the Commission decided to extend for one year the term of the mandate of the Working Group on Enforced or Involuntary Disappearances, and Economic and Social Council decision 1984/135 of 24 May 1984, in which the Council approved the Commission's decision,

1. *Expresses its appreciation* to the Working Group on Enforced or Involuntary Disappearances for the humanitarian work it has done and to those Governments that have co-operated with it;

2. *Welcomes* the decision of the Commission on Human Rights to extend for one year the term of the mandate of the Working Group, as laid down in Commission resolution 1984/23;

3. *Also welcomes* the provisions made by the Commission on Human Rights in its resolution 1984/23 to enable the Working Group to fulfil its mandate with even greater efficiency;

4. *Appeals* to all Governments to provide the Working Group and the Commission on Human Rights with the full co-operation warranted by their strictly humanitarian objectives and their working methods based on discretion;

5. *Calls upon* the Commission on Human Rights to continue to study this question as a matter of priority and to take any step it may deem necessary to the pursuit of the task of the Working Group when it considers the report to be submitted by the Group at its forty-first session;

6. *Renews its request* to the Secretary-General to continue to provide the Working Group with all necessary assistance.

General Assembly resolution 39/111

14 December 1984   Meeting 101   Adopted without vote

Approved by Third Committee (A/39/700) without vote, 6 December (meeting 64); 15-nation draft (A/C.3/39/L.73); agenda item 12.

Sponsors: Argentina, Canada, Colombia, Costa Rica, France, Gambia, Germany, Federal Republic of, Greece, Italy, Netherlands, Nicaragua, Senegal, Spain, Sweden, United Kingdom.

Meeting numbers. GA 39th session: 3rd Committee 54-56, 58, 59, 61, 64; plenary 101.

Other aspects of civil and political rights

Slavery

Action by the Commission on Human Rights. By a roll-call vote of 35 to none, with 8 abstentions, the Commission on Human Rights on 12 March 1984[99] recognized *apartheid* as a slavery-like practice, endorsed the call for mandatory economic sanctions against South Africa and appealed for Security Council support for proposals to that effect. The Commission appealed to States to sign or ratify the relevant conventions—the 1926 Slavery Convention, the 1949 Convention for the Suppression of the Traffic in Persons and of the Exploitation of the Prostitution of Others,[100] and the 1956 Supplementary Convention on the Abolition of Slavery, the Slave Trade, and Institutions and Practices Similar to Slavery[101]—or, if unable to do so, to explain why in writing.

The Secretary-General was requested to call on the States parties to those conventions to report regularly on the situation in their countries, and to call on other States, United Nations agencies, intergovernmental and non-governmental organizations and INTERPOL to supply relevant information to the Working Group on Slavery; to transmit for comment to the Governments concerned the statements containing allegations of slavery-like practices given to the Group in 1981[102] by the Anti-Slavery Society for the Protection of Human Rights, the Minority Rights Group and the International Abolitionist Federation; and to submit to the Sub-Commission in August 1984 a report on how the work of the United Nations Development Programme (UNDP) in certain countries could be adapted to contribute to the struggle against slavery.

The Commission asked the competent United Nations bodies to offer States co-ordinated legal, technical, administrative, educational, financial and other practical assistance to eliminate conditions conducive to slavery and slavery-like situations. ILO, FAO and UNESCO were invited to participate actively in the Group's work and to include in their technical assistance programmes activities designed to eliminate slavery-type problems. The Sub-Commission was invited to involve the persons whose names appeared in the list of slavery experts more closely in the Group's work.

On 13 March,[103] the Commission recommended a draft resolution on the question of slavery and the slave trade, which served as the basis for the Economic and Social Council action below.

On 24 May 1984, acting without vote on the recommendation of its Second Committee, the Economic and Social Council adopted resolution 1984/34.

Question of slavery and the slave trade in all their practices and manifestations

The Economic and Social Council

1. *Requests* the Secretary-General to entrust a working group composed of experts designated by the Sub-Commission on Prevention of Discrimination and Protection of Minorities, the United Nations Children's Fund, the United Nations Educational, Scientific and Cultural Organization and the World Health Organization with the task of conducting a comprehensive study on the phenomenon of traditional practices affecting the health of women and children;

2. *Requests* the Secretary-General to provide the working group with all the assistance it may need to carry out the study;

3. *Requests* all interested non-governmental organizations to co-operate in the study;

4. *Requests* the working group to submit its report to the Commission on Human Rights at its forty-second session.

Economic and Social Council resolution 1984/34

24 May 1984　　　　　Meeting 20　　　　　Adopted without vote

Approved by Second Committee (E/1984/91) without vote, 17 May (meeting 16); draft by Commission on Human Rights (E/1984/14); agenda item 10.

Mission to Mauritania. In keeping with arrangements made in 1983,[104] the Sub-Commission dispatched a mission to Mauritania, consisting of an expert, Marc Bossuyt (Belgium), accompanied by three officials of the United Nations Centre for Human Rights. The visit extended from 14 to 24 January 1984. The mission, essentially one of information and consultation carried out at the invitation of Mauritania, was to acquaint itself with the situation in the country following its abolition of slavery, as proclaimed on 5 July 1980 and confirmed by an ordinance of 9 November 1981, and to determine what international aid was needed to enable Mauritania to surmount the consequences of slavery.

Based on his findings, the expert addressed a series of recommendations to Mauritania. They included ratification of or accession to the international human rights instruments; promulgation of a three-year limit for the submission of compensation claims by former slave owners; establishment of a body to co-ordinate activities against slavery and its consequences; and involvement of former slaves in those activities and, through the civil status legislation in preparation, raising their consciousness to their legal personality as free men. A circular should be issued drawing to the attention of administrative authorities their obligation to report any breach of the abolition law. A media campaign should be undertaken, in all languages and with the aid of religious authorities, to familiarize the public with the importance of the abolition and with the criminal penalties applicable to those guilty of victimizing former slaves. Schools and small-scale enterprises in handicrafts and livestock farming for former slaves were also recommended.

The recommendations addressed to the Sub-Commission formed the basis for the Sub-Commission action (see below) on the mission's report.[105]

Activities of the Working Group on Slavery. The Sub-Commission's Working Group on Slavery held its tenth session at Geneva from 30 July to 3 August 1984.[106] As in 1983, it reviewed developments in slavery and the slave trade in all their practices, including violence and coercion against women; female circumcision; servitude of domestic servants; the sale of children and exploitation of child labour; debt bondage; traffic in persons and the exploitation of the prostitution of others; and the slavery-like practices of *apartheid* and colonialism. Questions relating to the situation in Mauritania and other Sahelian countries were also discussed.

During the review, statements were made by a number of NGOs, among them the Anti-Slavery Society for the Protection of Human Rights, the International Abolitionist Federation, the International Association of Democratic Lawyers, the International Movement for Fraternal Union among Races and Peoples, and the Minority Rights Group, as well as by INTERPOL.

The Working Group put forward a series of recommendations, on which the Sub-Commission based a draft resolution on slavery for action by the Commission (see below).

Sub-Commission action. In addition to the reports of the mission to Mauritania and the Working Group on Slavery, the Sub-Commission had before it, in response to a Commission request (see above), a report by the Secretary-General[107] stating that there were no UNDP projects designed specifically to combat slavery practices, nor was UNDP in a position to create such projects, since development objectives for which UNDP resources were used were decided upon by the recipient Governments. However, UNDP would be pleased to support requests for assistance in that area within the overall UNDP-financed country or intercountry programmes.

On 30 August 1984,[108] the Sub-Commission, having considered the mission report, expressed appreciation to Mauritania for the facilities it had placed at the mission's disposal and to the expert for a valuable report, which he was asked to present to the Commission in 1985. The Sub-Commission recommended a draft resolution to the Commission, by which the Commission would transmit the report: to Mauritania, inviting it to inform the Sub-Commission of any action it felt able to take thereon; and to UNDP and its donor States, other relevant United Nations bodies and specialized agencies, and regional and subregional organizations, inviting them to provide assistance to Mauritania for the purpose of eradicating the consequences of slavery. The Commission would ask the expert to prepare a follow-up report based on replies received and to submit to the Sub-Commission an interim report in 1985 and a final one in 1986. It would ask the Secretary-General to provide the expert with assistance for the follow-up report.

Taking note of the Working Group's report, the Sub-Commission, also on 30 August,[109] considered it useful for the Group to review at each session the developments in situations it had previously considered. It recommended wider use of mass media to inform peoples of the extent of the problems and develop their awareness of their rights and responsibilities in the struggle against slavery and slavery-like practices, and recommended expert seminars for the exchange of experiences.

The Sub-Commission further recommended to the Commission a draft resolution by which the Commission would invite States to sign or ratify the 1949 Convention on prostitution, and invite the Secretary-General to pursue the matter. The Commission would request him to invite States parties to that Convention and to the 1926 and 1956 slavery conventions to report regularly on their compliance with those instruments. It would invite States, the United Nations system, intergovernmental and non-governmental organizations and INTERPOL to continue to supply relevant information to the Group. The Commission would request the Secretary-General to transmit to Governments and United Nations bodies and agencies concerned the statements on specific allegations of slavery-like practices, submitted by NGOs to the Working Group in 1984. It would also request the Sub-Commission to undertake two studies, on alleged slavery-like practices against women and children, indicating ways to rehabilitate the victims, and on debt bondage.

By other provisions of the draft, the Commission would recommend: intensified struggle at the national level against procuring, and adoption of international measures to dismantle prostitution networks and to assist and repatriate their victims; adoption by States of social and legal measures to ensure the effective reintegration of victims of prostitution into society; wide use of the mass media to publicize the evils of slavery and slavery-like practices; and use by Governments of assistance under the programme of advisory services in human rights and other programmes for

eliminating slavery, slavery-like practices and their sequels. Finally, the Commission would request UNICEF, ILO, FAO and UNESCO to give particular attention, in their technical assistance programmes, to situations where poverty led to or perpetuated slavery and slavery-like practices.

Pursuant to Economic and Social Council resolution 1984/34, the Sub-Commission on 31 August[110] designated Halima Embarek Warzazi (Morocco) and Murlidhar C. Bhandare (India) as experts to serve on a Working Group on Traditional Practices Affecting the Health of Women and Children.

Anniversary of the emancipation of slaves in the British Empire

An item entitled "Celebration of the one-hundred-and-fiftieth anniversary of the emancipation of slaves in the British Empire" was included in the 1984 agenda of the General Assembly and allocated to the plenary Assembly, on the recommendation of the General Committee. The item's inclusion was requested by Antigua and Barbuda in a letter of 24 August.[111]

In a memorandum annexed to the letter, it was proposed that the year beginning 1 August 1984 mark the anniversary, explaining that the Abolition of Slavery Act of 1 August 1834, which emancipated slaves in the British Empire, was an important advance in mankind's effort to achieve racial equality and social justice in the context of basic human rights.

A draft resolution, sponsored by Antigua and Barbuda, Barbados, Mauritius, Saint Vincent and the Grenadines, and Trinidad and Tobago, by which the Assembly would decide to commemorate the anniversary, was circulated on 21 November.[112]

In decision 39/456, on the suspension of its 1984 session, the Assembly decided to retain the item on the agenda and to include it among the items to be considered when the session resumed in 1985.

Meeting numbers. GA 39th session: General Committee 1, 2; plenary 70, 105.

Conscientious objectors

On 24 May 1984, acting on the recommendation of its Second Committee, the Economic and Social Council adopted without vote resolution 1984/27. It was based on a draft recommended by the Commission on Human Rights on 12 March,[113] following presentation to it of the 1983 report on the question of conscientious objection to military service.[114]

Conscientious objection to military service

The Economic and Social Council

1. *Decides:*

(a) That the report prepared by Mr. Eide and Mr. Mubanga-Chipoya on conscientious objection to military service should be printed and given the widest possible distribution;

(b) To transmit the report for comments and observations to Governments and relevant United Nations bodies and specialized agencies, other intergovernmental organizations and non-governmental organizations;

2. *Requests* the Secretary-General to report to the Commission on Human Rights at its forty-first session on those comments and observations and on other significant developments regarding the human rights of conscientious objectors;

3. *Requests* the Commission on Human Rights to study the report on conscientious objection to military service, including the recommendations contained therein, as well as the report of the Secretary-General containing the comments and observations, under the item entitled "The role of youth in the promotion and protection of human rights, including the question of conscientious objection to military service".

Economic and Social Council resolution 1984/27

24 May 1984   Meeting 20   Adopted without vote

Approved by Second Committee (E/1984/91) without vote, 17 May (meeting 15); draft by Commission on Human Rights (E/1984/14); agenda item 10.

Report of the Secretary-General. Pursuant to the Economic and Social Council's request (see above), the Secretary-General prepared a report[(115)] for the Commission that contained replies to his note verbale of 20 August, circulating the Special Rapporteurs' report on conscientious objection to military service with a request for comments. By the end of 1984, substantive replies had been received from five Governments, two United Nations bodies and nine NGOs.

Freedom of movement

On 24 May 1984, the Economic and Social Council, acting on the recommendation of its Second Committee, adopted without vote resolution 1984/29. It was based on a text recommended by the Commission on Human Rights on 12 March, by a vote of 34 to none, with 8 abstentions.[(116)]

Study of discrimination in respect of the right of everyone to leave any country, including his own, and to return to his country

The Economic and Social Council,

Recalling the *Study of Discrimination in Respect of the Right of Everyone to Leave Any Country, Including His Own, and to Return to His Country,* submitted to the Sub-Commission on Prevention of Discrimination and Protection of Minorities at its fifteenth session, in 1963, by the Special Rapporteur, Mr. José D. Inglés, and the draft principles respecting this right adopted by the Sub-Commission at the same session,

Also recalling Sub-Commission resolution 7(XXXIV) of 9 September 1981, by which the Sub-Commission requested the Secretary-General to submit to it at its thirty-fifth session a concise note informing it of the consideration given by the Commission on Human Rights and the Economic and Social Council to the report on the aforementioned study,

Noting the report of the Secretary-General submitted pursuant to that resolution,

Noting also Sub-Commission resolutions 1982/23 of 8 September 1982 and 1983/5 of 31 August 1983 and Commission on Human Rights resolution 1984/37 of 12 March 1984,

1. *Endorses* the appointment by the Sub-Commission on Prevention of Discrimination and Protection of Minorities of Mr. Mubanga-Chipoya to prepare an analysis of current trends and developments in respect of the right of everyone to leave any country, including his own, and to return to his country, and to have the possibility of entering other countries, without discrimination or hindrance, especially of the right to employment, taking into account the need to avoid the phenomenon of the brain drain from developing countries and the question of recompensing those countries for the loss incurred, and to study in particular the extent of restrictions permissible under article 12, paragraph 3, of the International Covenant on Civil and Political Rights;

2. *Requests* the Special Rapporteur to submit to the Sub-Commission at its thirty-seventh session for its consideration recommendations for promoting and encouraging respect for and observance of that right;

3. *Requests* the Secretary-General to give Mr. Mubanga-Chipoya all the assistance he may require in his work.

Economic and Social Council resolution 1984/29

24 May 1984   Meeting 20   Adopted without vote

Approved by Second Committee (E/1984/91) by vote (43-0-7), 17 May (meeting 15); draft by Commission on Human Rights (E/1984/14); agenda item 10.

Canada, which in the Committee had requested a vote on the text, agreed to the appointment of a special rapporteur to prepare a study of discriminatory practices affecting the right of everyone to leave any country, including one's own; it had, however, reservations on the rest of the paragraph which it termed vague and unrealistic, especially in view of the regulations enforced by most countries with regard to visas and work permits. The USSR did not object to adoption of the text without vote but said it would abstain in a vote; the subject of the proposed study was already covered by article 12 of the 1966 Covenant.

France and the Federal Republic of Germany voiced reservations particularly on the reference in paragraph 1 to the question of recompensing the developing countries for the loss incurred as a result of the brain drain; that question and the reference to the right to employment were outside the scope of the proposed study, the Federal Republic of Germany felt.

Sub-Commission action. A preliminary report on freedom of movement[(117)] by Special Rapporteur Chama L. C. Mubanga-Chipoya (Zambia) was before the Sub-Commission at its August 1984 session. The report contained a questionnaire to be used for collecting information for the analysis requested by the Council.

On 29 August,[(118)] the Sub-Commission expressed appreciation to the Special Rapporteur for his report and excellent introductory statement. It requested him to continue his work so as to present a progress report in 1985 and a final one, to include recommendations, in 1986. It also requested the Secretary-General to provide the assistance necessary to complete that task.

Freedom of speech

In 1984, the right to freedom of expression, as reaffirmed by article 19 of the 1966 International Covenant on Civil and Political Rights,[(1)] was considered by the Commission on Human Rights in view of its concern over the extensive detention in many parts of the world of persons solely for exercising that right. In that connection, it took note of a September 1983 Sub-Commission resolution that included an appeal for the release of all persons detained for their views who had neither used nor advocated violence and thus had not threatened peace and security.[(119)]

The Commission repeated that appeal to all States on 12 March 1984,[(120)] and called on them to allow full realization of that right. In an effort to promote respect for that right, it decided to review the matter in 1985.

Use of force by law enforcement officials

In response to a September 1983 Sub-Commission request,[(49)] the Secretary-General submitted an analysis of State policies and practices regarding restraints on the use of force by law enforcement officials and military personnel.[(121)] The analysis was based on information received, as at 8 June 1984, from 11 Governments, four specialized agencies, a regional intergovernmental organization, and two NGOs. The question of restraint was examined with respect to the use of firearms, arrest, detention and imprisonment, public gatherings, and states of siege or emergency. Three main directions in State policies and practices emerged from the findings: establishment of a legal framework for enforcement officials, including regulations for firearms use and guarantees against arbitrary arrest and detention; supervision of application of legislation through remedies to victims of abuse and imposition of sanctions (civil, penal and disciplinary) on persons responsible for such abuse; and education of law enforcement officials.

On 29 August,[(122)] the Sub-Commission asked the Secretary-General to issue a reminder to all concerned to communicate, if they so wished, the information he had previously requested regarding restraints on the use of force against detainees. It also asked that, on the basis of such information, he prepare a further analysis of State policies and practices. The Sub-Commission requested the 1984 Working Group on Detention to review the further analysis, together with the one already submitted, and to present in 1985 conclusions and recommendations based on that review.

Independence of the judicial system

A final report on the question of the independence and impartiality of the judiciary, jurors and assessors and the independence of lawyers from Special Rapporteur L. M. Singhvi (India)[(114)] remained pending in 1984. Hence, the Sub-Commission on 29 August[(123)] requested that the report be submitted in 1985 when it would give it priority consideration with a view to elaborating a draft body of principles on the subject.

REFERENCES

[(1)]YUN 1966, p. 423, GA res. 2200 A (XXI), annex, 16 Dec. 1966. [(2)]YUN 1976, p. 609. [(3)]A/39/461. [(4)]E/1984/14 (res. 1984/18). [(5)]YUN 1983, p. 863, GA res. 38/116, 16 Dec. 1983. [(6)]*Ibid.*, p. 827, GA res. 38/115, 16 Dec. 1983. [(7)]A/39/40 & Corr.1,2. [(8)]E/1984/14 (dec. 1984/104). [(9)]YUN 1983, p. 827. [(10)]E/CN.4/1985/3 (res. 1984/27). [(11)]E/1984/14 (res. 1984/46). [(12)]E/CN.4/1985/3 (res. 1984/9). [(13)]E/1984/14 (res. 1984/11). [(14)]*Ibid.* (res. 1984/14). [(15)]*Ibid.* (res. 1984/12). [(16)]*Ibid.* (res. 1984/13). [(17)]*Ibid.* (res. 1984/10). [(18)]*Ibid.* (res. 1984/25). [(19)]A/39/505 & Add.1. [(20)]YUN 1983, pp. 828 & 829, GA res. 38/16 & 38/17, 22 Nov. 1983. [(21)]A/C.3/39/3. [(22)]E/1984/14 (res. 1984/55). [(23)]YUN 1970, p. 530, ESC res. 1503(XLVIII), 27 May 1970. [(24)]E/CN.4/1985/3 (res. 1984/6). [(25)]YUN 1983, p. 835. [(26)]E/1984/14 (res. 1984/34). [(27)]A/39/361. [(28)]E/CN.4/1985/3 (res. 1984/24). [(29)]YUN 1983, p. 214, GA res. 38/7, 2 Nov. 1983. [(30)]YUN 1981, p. 242. [(31)]YUN 1983, p. 834, ESC dec. 1983/155, 27 May 1983. [(32)]E/1984/88. [(33)]YUN 1983, p. 1045. [(34)]YUN 1948-49, p. 535, GA res. 217 A (III), 10 Dec. 1948. [(35)]YUN 1960, p. 49, GA res. 1514(XV), 14 Dec. 1960. [(36)]YUN 1983, p. 836. [(37)]E/CN.4/1984/16. [(38)]E/1984/14 (res. 1984/6). [(39)]*Ibid.* (res. 1984/4). [(40)]YUN 1978, pp. 915-16, SC res. 435(1978), 29 Sep. 1978, & 439(1978), 13 Nov. 1978. [(41)]YUN 1983, p. 1087, GA res. 38/40, 7 Dec. 1983. [(42)]E/CN.4/Sub.2/1984/12 & Add.1-4. [(43)]E/CN.4/Sub.2/1984/16. [(44)]YUN 1983, p. 837. [(45)]YUN 1978, p. 698. [(46)]YUN 1980, p. 842. [(47)]YUN 1981, p. 900. [(48)]YUN 1982, p. 1079. [(49)]YUN 1983, p. 838. [(50)]*Ibid.*, GA dec. 38/426, 19 Dec. 1983. [(51)]A/C.6/39/L.10. [(52)]YUN 1982, p. 1082. [(53)]YUN 1983, p. 839. [(54)]*Ibid.*, ESC res. 1983/38, 27 May 1983. [(55)]YUN 1977, p. 718, GA res. 32/62, 8 Dec. 1977. [(56)]YUN 1978, p. 699. [(57)]E/CN.4/1984/72. [(58)]E/1984/14 (res. 1984/21). [(59)]A/39/499 & Add.1,2. [(60)]A/C.3/39/L.68/Rev.1. [(61)]E/1984/14 (res. 1984/22). [(62)]YUN 1981, p. 906, GA res. 36/151, 16 Dec. 1981. [(63)]A/39/662. [(64)]E/CN.4/1985/3 (res. 1984/22). [(65)]YUN 1983, p. 841, GA res. 38/118, 16 Dec. 1983. [(66)]A/39/480 & Add.1,2. [(67)]YUN 1982, p. 1081, GA res. 37/194, annex, 18 Dec. 1982. [(68)]YUN 1983, p. 841. [(69)]*Ibid.*, p. 842. [(70)]E/1984/14 (dec. 1984/108). [(71)]*Ibid.* (res. 1984/47). [(72)]E/CN.4/Sub.2/1984/19. [(73)]YUN 1983, p. 847. [(74)]E/CN.4/1985/3 (res. 1984/13). [(75)]E/1984/14 (dec. 1984/102). [(76)]YUN 1982, p. 1077. [(77)]YUN 1980, p. 789, GA dec. 35/437, 15 Dec. 1980. [(78)]YUN 1981, p. 899. [(79)]YUN 1982, p. 1078. [(80)]*Ibid.*, GA res. 37/192, 18 Dec. 1982. [(81)]E/1984/14 (res. 1984/19). [(82)]E/CN.4/1985/3 (res. 1984/7). [(83)]YUN 1983, p. 845, ESC res. 1983/36, 27 May 1983. [(84)]E/CN.4/1984/29. [(85)]YUN 1983, p. 843. [(86)]E/1984/14 (res. 1984/50). [(87)]E/CN.4/Sub.2/1984/15. [(88)]E/CN.4/1985/3 (res. 1984/8). [(89)]*Ibid.* (res. 1984/16). [(90)]E/1984/14 (res. 1984/20). [(91)]*Ibid.* (res. 1984/1 A). [(92)]A/39/81. [(93)]E/1984/14 (res. 1984/23). [(94)]YUN 1983, p. 846. [(95)]E/1984/14 (dec. 1984/105). [(96)]YUN 1980, p. 843. [(97)]E/CN.4/1985/15 & Add.1. [(98)]YUN 1978, p. 737, GA res. 33/173, 20 Dec. 1978. [(99)]E/1984/14 (res. 1984/40). [(100)]YUN 1948-49, p. 613, GA res. 317(IV), annex, 2

Dec. 1949. [101]YUN 1956, p. 228. [102]YUN 1981, p. 913.
[103]E/1984/14 (res. 1984/48). [104]YUN 1983, p. 848.
[105]E/CN.4/Sub.2/1984/23. [106]E/CN.4/Sub.2/1984/25.
[107]E/CN.4/Sub.2/1984/24. [108]E/CN.4/1985/3 (res. 1984/28).
[109]*Ibid.* (res. 1984/33). [110]E/CN.4/1985/3 (dec. 1984/104).
[111]A/39/241. [112]A/39/L.16. [113]E/1984/14 (res. 1984/33).
[114]YUN 1983, p. 850. [115]E/CN.4/1985/25 & Add.1.
[116]E/1984/14 (res. 1984/37). [117]E/CN.4/Sub.2/1984/10.
[118]E/CN.4/1985/3 (res. 1984/21). [119]YUN 1983, p. 905.
[120]E/1984/14 (res. 1984/26). [121]E/CN.4/Sub.2/1984/14.
[122]E/CN.4/1985/3 (res. 1984/10). [123]*Ibid.* (res. 1984/11).

Economic, social and cultural rights

Covenant on Economic, Social and Cultural Rights

Accessions and ratifications

As at 31 December 1984, the International Covenant on Economic, Social and Cultural Rights, adopted by the General Assembly in 1966[1] and in force since 1976,[2] had been ratified or acceded to by 83 States. Cameroon, Togo and Zambia became parties to it during 1984.

The Secretary-General reported on the status of ratifications of or accessions to the Covenant—as at 1 March, in a note to the Economic and Social Council;[3] and as at 1 September, in a report to the General Assembly.[4]

Implementation of the Covenant

The Sessional Working Group of Governmental Experts on the Implementation of the Covenant met for its sixth session in New York from 16 April to 4 May 1984.[5] Composed of States parties to the Covenant (see APPENDIX III), the Group was set up by the Economic and Social Council in 1978[6] and restructured in 1982.[7] The Group examined 25 reports received in 1984 from 24 States parties on their implementation of specific provisions of the Covenant. On each report, the Group heard statements by, and put questions to, the respective State representative. Under a programme established by the Council in 1976,[8] reports required under the Covenant were to be submitted in three biennial cycles or stages, each stage covering a related group of articles of the Covenant.

For the first stage (due 1 September 1977), the Group examined reports from Japan, Peru, Rwanda and Venezuela,[9] concerning rights covered by articles 6 to 9 (the right to work and to favourable conditions of work, the rights of trade unionists, the right to social security). At their request, consideration of the reports from Mexico and Iraq were deferred.[10] Second-stage reports (due 1 September 1983) examined came from the Byelorussian SSR, Chile, Cyprus, Denmark, Ecuador, Finland, Hungary, Mongolia, Norway, the Philippines, Spain, Sweden, the Ukrainian SSR, the USSR and Yugoslavia.[11] Those from Bulgaria and Romania[12] were received later in the year and were thus marked for consideration in 1985. Consideration of the report of the German Democratic Republic[13] was deferred at its request. Expressing deep concern over the human rights situation in Chile, Group members asked that State party to provide information reflecting the actual situation on implementation of articles 6 to 9.

The Group examined initial reports (due 1 September 1979) on rights covered by articles 10 to 12 (protection of the family, mothers and children, an adequate living standard, and physical and mental health) from Canada, India, Italy and the Netherlands.[14] Consideration of the report from Portugal[15] was deferred at its request.

Also examined were initial reports (due 1 September 1981) on implementation of articles 13 to 15 (education, including compulsory education, and participation in cultural life) from Finland and Guyana.[16] Consideration of reports from Iraq and Portugal[17] was deferred.

In addition, the Group considered two notes by the Secretary-General: one on the status of submission of reports as at 1 March 1984 (see above);[3] and another transmitting an extract from an ILO report on implementation of articles 6 to 12.[18]

The Group's recommendations to the Council included reminding States parties to submit reports under article 16 of the Covenant and urging them to cover the entire cycle of initial reports before submitting second periodic reports; drawing their attention to their reporting obligations no later than January of the year in which the reports fell due; and reminding them to implement fully their obligations in all the territories under their jurisdiction. Reports scheduled for consideration should be presented at least six weeks before the Group's session. For its examination of second periodic reports, the Group asked that it be provided also with the initial reports and related summary records. Reports should be balanced and, to render them more comprehensible, should include the necessary demographic and macroeconomic data, as well as a description of legislative and administrative acts. Descriptions of implementation should not be confined to references to annexes or to reports submitted to other United Nations bodies or specialized agencies.

The Group recommended press coverage of its proceedings, wide participation in them by the States parties, United Nations Members and specialized agencies, and attendance by NGOs and the public at large. It further recommended full composition of the Group and session attendance by all of its members, the better to accomplish its task and enhance the importance of its work.

ECONOMIC AND SOCIAL COUNCIL ACTION

The Economic and Social Council acted on the recommendations of the Group of Experts by adopting resolution 1984/9 on 24 May 1984 without vote.

Implementation of the International Covenant on Economic, Social and Cultural Rights

The Economic and Social Council,

Bearing in mind its important responsibilities under articles 16 and 17 of the International Covenant on Economic, Social and Cultural Rights,

Recalling its resolutions 1988(LX) of 11 May 1976, 1979/43 of 11 May 1979, 1983/41 of 27 May 1983 and its decision 1981/158 of 8 May 1981,

Recalling also General Assembly resolutions 37/191 of 18 December 1982 and 38/116 of 16 December 1983,

Having considered the report of the Sessional Working Group of Governmental Experts on the Implementation of the International Covenant on Economic, Social and Cultural Rights,

Mindful of the relevant resolutions and decisions adopted by the General Assembly and the Economic and Social Council on the control and limitation of documentation,

Recalling its resolution 1982/33 of 6 May 1983, by which it decided to review the composition, organization and administrative arrangements of the Sessional Working Group of Governmental Experts on the Implementation of the International Covenant on Economic, Social and Cultural Rights at its first regular session of 1985, taking into account the principle of equitable geographical distribution and the increase in the number of States parties to the Covenant,

Recalling also that the meetings of the Sessional Working Group of Governmental Experts on the Implementation of the International Covenant on Economic, Social and Cultural Rights are public, that States parties to the Covenant, States Members of the United Nations and representatives of the specialized agencies concerned may participate in its proceedings in accordance with Council decision 1978/10 of 3 May 1978, and that interested non-governmental organizations in consultative status with the Council and the public at large may attend those meetings,

Noting the concern expressed by the Sessional Working Group of Governmental Experts on the Implementation of the International Covenant on Economic, Social and Cultural Rights about the lack of publicity given to its work at the present session of the Council,

1. *Takes note* of the report of the Sessional Working Group of Governmental Experts on the Implementation of the International Covenant on Economic, Social and Cultural Rights;

2. *Invites* again all States that have not yet done so to become parties to the International Covenant on Economic, Social and Cultural Rights;

3. *Calls upon* States parties to the Covenant to submit reports required under article 16 thereof, in accordance with the programme established by Council resolution 1988(LX), and urges States parties to complete the entire cycle of initial reports before submitting second periodic reports;

4. *Invites* States parties to the Covenant to comply with the guidelines established by the Secretary-General concerning the form and content of reports and to take note of the relevant recommendations of the Sessional Working Group of Governmental Experts on the Implementation of the International Covenant on Economic, Social and Cultural Rights in preparing and submitting their reports;

5. *Requests* the specialized agencies, on the basis of experience gained in other bodies and of reports so far submitted and considered by the Sessional Working Group of Governmental Experts on the Implementation of the International Covenant on Economic, Social and Cultural Rights to report on the progress made in achieving the observance of the provisions of the Covenant falling within the scope of their activities, in accordance with article 18 of the Covenant and paragraph 6 of Council resolution 1988(LX);

6. *Requests* the Secretary-General to take all appropriate measures to ensure that the United Nations press service issues press releases on the proceedings of the next session of the Sessional Working Group of Governmental Experts on the Implementation of the International Covenant on Economic, Social and Cultural Rights;

7. *Requests* the Sessional Working Group of Governmental Experts on the Implementation of the International Covenant on Economic, Social and Cultural Rights to continue to consider including in its report to the Council brief summaries of the consideration of each country report;

8. *Requests* the Secretary-General to bring the relevant suggestions and recommendations listed in section IV of the report of the Sessional Working Group of Governmental Experts on the Implementation of the International Covenant on Economic, Social and Cultural Rights to the attention of States parties to the Covenant so that States parties may take them into account in preparing and submitting their reports under the Covenant;

9. *Also requests* the Secretary-General to submit to the Economic and Social Council at its first regular session of 1985 a report on the composition, organization and administrative arrangements of the Sessional Working Group of Governmental Experts on the Implementation of the International Covenant on Economic, Social and Cultural Rights and other bodies established in accordance with existing international instruments in the field of human rights in order to facilitate the review which the Council will undertake in accordance with its resolution 1982/33;

10. *Decides* that the review shall be conducted at an early date during its first regular session of 1985 to allow enough time for a full discussion of this important matter, taking into account any recommendations which the Sessional Working Group of Governmental Experts on the Implementation of the International Covenant on Economic, Social and Cultural Rights may agree upon at its next session.

Economic and Social Council resolution 1984/9

24 May 1984   Meeting 19   Adopted without vote

8-nation draft (E/1984/L.30/Rev.1); agenda item 3.
Sponsors: Austria, Denmark, Finland, France, Germany, Federal Republic of, Japan, Netherlands, Sweden.
Meeting numbers. ESC 16, 17, 19.

*Organizational questions
concerning the Working Group*

The Sessional Working Group recommended two draft decisions to the Economic and Social Council: one on its work programme and another on the composition of its bureau for 1985.

Acting on the first of these, the Council adopted decision 1984/121 without vote.

Provisional agenda for 1985 of the Sessional Working Group of Governmental Experts on the Implementation of the International Covenant on Economic, Social and Cultural Rights

At its 19th plenary meeting, on 24 May 1984, the Council approved the provisional agenda for 1985 of the Sessional Working Group of Governmental Experts on the Implementation of the International Covenant on Economic, Social and Cultural Rights set out below.

Provisional agenda for 1985 of the Sessional Working Group of Governmental Experts on the Implementation of the International Covenant on Economic, Social and Cultural Rights

1. Consideration of reports submitted in accordance with Council resolution 1988(LX) by States parties to the Covenant concerning rights covered by articles 10 to 12.
   Documentation
   Portugal (E/1980/6/Add.35 and Corr.1)
   Any other reports received by the Secretary-General
2. Consideration of reports submitted in accordance with Council resolution 1988(LX) by States parties to the Covenant concerning rights covered by articles 13 to 15.
   Documentation
   Iraq (E/1982/3/Add.26)
   Portugal (E/1982/3/Add.27)
3. Consideration of reports submitted in accordance with Council resolution 1983(LX) by States parties to the Covenant concerning rights covered by articles 6 to 9.
   Documentation
   Initial reports
      Mexico (E/1984/6/Add.2)
      Iraq (E/1984/6/Add.3)
   Second periodic reports
      German Democratic Republic (E/1984/7/Add.3)
      Romania (E/1984/7/Add.17)
      Bulgaria (E/1984/7/Add.18)
4. Formulation of suggestions and recommendations of a general nature based on the consideration of reports submitted by States parties to the Covenant and by the specialized agencies, in order to assist the Council to fulfil, in particular, its responsibilities under articles 21 and 22 of the Covenant.
5. Consideration of the report of the Sessional Working Group of Governmental Experts on the Implementation of the International Covenant on Economic, Social and Cultural Rights.

Economic and Social Council decision 1984/121

Adopted without vote

Draft by Group of Experts on International Covenant on Economic, Social and Cultural Rights (E/1984/83); agenda item 3.
Meeting numbers. ESC 16, 17, 19.

Acting on the Group's second recommendation, the Council adopted decision 1984/122, also without vote.

Bureau for 1985 of the Sessional Working Group of Governmental Experts on the Implementation of the International Covenant on Economic, Social and Cultural Rights

At its 19th plenary meeting, on 24 May 1984, the Council decided that the Bureau for 1985 of the Sessional Working Group of Governmental Experts on the Implementation of the International Covenant on Economic, Social and Cultural Rights should be constituted as follows:
   Chairman: Eastern European States;
   Vice-Chairmen: Asian States; Latin American States; Western European and other States;
   Rapporteur: African States.

Economic and Social Council decision 1984/122

Adopted without vote

Draft by Group of Experts on International Covenant on Economic, Social and Cultural Rights (E/1984/83); agenda item 3.
Meeting numbers. ESC 16, 17, 19.

Other action. The Commission on Human Rights, on 6 March, also dealt with the question of the realization of economic, social and cultural rights contained in the Covenant, particularly the right to development (see immediately below).

Right to development

Action by the Commission on Human Rights. By a roll-call vote of 39 to none, with 4 abstentions, taken on 6 March 1984,[19] the Commission on Human Rights expressed concern at the current situation adversely affecting the establishment of a new international economic order and the full achievement of the right to development. It reaffirmed the inalienable right of all nations to pursue freely their economic and social development and to exercise complete sovereignty over their natural resources subject to the principles referred to in article 1, paragraph 2, of the Covenant; and that foreign occupation, colonialism, *apartheid*, racism and racial discrimination, and the denial of the right to self-determination and of universally recognized human rights were serious impediments to economic and social progress.

Noting the progress made by the Working Group of Governmental Experts on the Right to Development in the elaboration of a draft declaration on the subject, as reflected in its 1983 report,[20] the Commission decided to reconvene the Group, with a request that it hold two sessions at Geneva and submit its proposals in 1985. At that time, the need to continue the Group's activities would be reviewed.

ECONOMIC AND SOCIAL COUNCIL ACTION

Acting on the recommendation of its Second Committee, the Economic and Social Council in May adopted decision 1984/132 by recorded vote.

Question of the realization in all countries of the economic, social and cultural rights contained in the Universal Declaration of Human Rights and in the International Covenant on Economic, Social and Cultural Rights, and study of special problems which the developing countries face in their efforts to achieve these human rights

At its 20th plenary meeting, on 24 May 1984, the Council, noting Commission on Human Rights resolution 1984/16 of 6 March 1984, endorsed the Commission's decision to reconvene the Working Group of Governmental Experts on the Right to Development with the same mandate as before in order to allow it to elaborate, on the basis of its report, and all the documents already submitted or to be submitted, a draft declaration on the right to development. The Council also endorsed the Commission's request to the Working Group to hold two sessions of two weeks each at Geneva.

Economic and Social Council decision 1984/132

52-0-1 (recorded vote)

Approved by Second Committee (E/1984/91) by vote (48-0-2), 17 May (meeting 16); draft by Commission on Human Rights (E/1984/14); agenda item 10.

Recorded vote in Council as follows:

In favour: Algeria, Argentina, Austria, Benin, Botswana, Brazil, Bulgaria, Canada, China, Colombia, Congo, Costa Rica, Djibouti, Finland, France, German Democratic Republic, Germany, Federal Republic of, Greece, Indonesia, Japan, Lebanon, Liberia, Luxembourg, Malaysia, Mali, Mexico, Netherlands, New Zealand, Pakistan, Papua New Guinea, Poland, Portugal, Qatar, Romania, Rwanda, Saint Lucia, Saudi Arabia, Sierra Leone, Somalia, Sri Lanka, Suriname, Swaziland, Sweden, Thailand, Tunisia, Uganda, USSR, United Kingdom, Venezuela, Yugoslavia, Zaire.
Against: None.
Abstaining: United States.

Working Group activities. Responding to the Commission's request of 6 March, as endorsed by the Council (see above), the 15-member Working Group of Governmental Experts on the Right to Development met at Geneva in two sessions in 1984: the eighth from 24 September to 5 October; and the ninth from 3 to 14 December.

At those sessions, the Group considered in detail paragraphs 6, 9, 12, 15 and 16 of the preamble to the draft declaration on the basis of a technical consolidated text and of various drafts and proposals brought forward from 1983.[20] It also considered articles 1 to 4 of the operative section. Paragraph 16 of the preamble was discussed jointly with article 1 concerning the definition of the right to development, the central feature of the declaration. An extensive exchange of views was held on articles 2 to 4 concerning the responsibility for development in its individual and collective dimensions, and the elements involved in the effective realization of the right to development. No general agreement emerged from the proposals put forward.

In its report to the Commission,[21] the Group annexed a draft declaration by the non-aligned countries and another by two experts (France and the Netherlands); the 1983 technical consolidated text; USSR proposals for article 1 and other unnumbered articles; three sets of proposals submitted at the seventh (1983) session and at the 1984 sessions; and the texts of the preamble on which general agree-

ment in principle had been reached at the seventh and ninth sessions.

GENERAL ASSEMBLY ACTION

In resolution 39/145, the General Assembly reaffirmed that the right to development was an inalienable human right and that, for its full realization, international peace and security were essential. The Assembly requested the Commission on Human Rights to take measures to promote that right and welcomed the Commission's decision that the Working Group of Governmental Experts on the Right to Development should continue elaborating a draft declaration. It requested the Secretary-General to transmit to it in 1985 a report on the Group's progress.

The new international economic order and human rights

Action by the Commission on Human Rights. Following its consideration of the study on the new international economic order and the promotion of human rights, completed by Special Rapporteur Raúl Ferrero (Peru) in 1983,[20] the Commission on Human Rights adopted a draft decision on 6 March 1984 by a roll-call vote of 39 to 1, with 3 abstentions,[22] which served as the basis for the Economic and Social Council decision below.

ECONOMIC AND SOCIAL COUNCIL ACTION

Acting on the recommendation of its Second Committee, the Economic and Social Council in May adopted decision 1984/133 by recorded vote.

The new international economic order and the promotion of human rights

At its 20th plenary meeting, on 24 May 1984, the Council noted Commission on Human Rights resolution 1984/17 of 6 March 1984 and decided that the study on the new international economic order and the promotion of human rights should be published and given the widest possible distribution in all the official languages of the United Nations.

Economic and Social Council decision 1984/133

49-1-3 (recorded vote)

Approved by Second Committee (E/1984/91) by vote (47-1-3), 17 May (meeting 16); draft by Commission on Human Rights (E/1984/14); agenda item 10.

Recorded vote in Council as follows:

In favour: Algeria, Argentina, Austria, Benin, Botswana, Brazil, Bulgaria, Canada, China, Colombia, Congo, Costa Rica, Djibouti, Ecuador, Finland, France, German Democratic Republic, Greece, Indonesia, Lebanon, Liberia, Luxembourg, Malaysia, Mali, Mexico, Netherlands, New Zealand, Pakistan, Papua New Guinea, Poland, Portugal, Qatar, Romania, Rwanda, Saint Lucia, Saudi Arabia, Sierra Leone, Somalia, Sri Lanka, Suriname, Swaziland, Sweden, Thailand, Tunisia, Uganda, USSR, Venezuela, Yugoslavia, Zaire.
Against: United States.
Abstaining: Germany, Federal Republic of, Japan, United Kingdom.

Popular participation and human rights

In 1984, the Commission on Human Rights had before it a preliminary report by the Secretary-General[23] on an analytical study he was undertaking on the right to popular participation in its various forms as an important factor in the full realization of all human rights. Submitted in accordance with a May 1983 Economic and Social Council resolution,[24] the report summarized views and comments on popular participation, in theory and in practice, in relation to respect for human rights and as a human right in itself. Included were the views expressed on the topic in the General Assembly in 1982 and in the Commission in 1983; comments received, as at 17 January 1984, from five Governments; and an overview of related activities carried out by five United Nations organs, three specialized agencies and two intergovernmental regional organizations. The summary took account of the conclusions of the 1982 International Seminar on Popular Participation.[25]

Based on the foregoing information, the report described a three-part provisional outline of the final study, indicating the main issues to be addressed. Part I would define the multi-dimensional nature of the concept of popular participation and survey its major forms and place in development. Part II would focus on popular participation and its links with the rights to self-determination, development, the enjoyment of human rights by minority groups (women, indigenous and rural populations) and other human rights in various areas (information, association, employment and management, education, cultural life, etc.). Part III would examine whether popular participation might be considered a specific human right, and what its content and place in the existing system of human rights might be.

Action by the Commission on Human Rights. By a roll-call vote of 41 to 1, taken on 6 March 1984,[26] the Commission on Human Rights, taking note of the preliminary report of the Secretary-General, requested him to take account of the views expressed in the debate on popular participation at the current session and invited all concerned to transmit their comments to him as called for by the Economic and Social Council in 1983.[24]

ECONOMIC AND SOCIAL COUNCIL ACTION

Acting on the recommendation of its Second Committee, the Economic and Social Council in May 1984 adopted decision 1984/131 by recorded vote.

Popular participation in its various forms as an important factor in development and in the full realization of all human rights

At its 20th plenary meeting, on 24 May 1984, the Council, noting Commission on Human Rights resolution 1984/15 of 6 March 1984, endorsed the Commission's request to the Secretary-General, in preparing the final study on the right to popular participation in its various forms as an important factor in development and in the full realization of all human rights, to take into account the views expressed at the fortieth session of the Commission. The Council further endorsed the Commission's invitation

to those Governments, United Nations organs and specialized agencies that have not yet done so to transmit their comments and views to the Secretary-General, as called for in Council resolution 1983/31 of 27 May 1983.

Economic and Social Council decision 1984/131

51-1 (recorded vote)

Approved by Second Committee (E/1984/91) by vote (47-1), 17 May (meeting 16); draft by Commission on Human Rights (E/1984/14); agenda item 10.

Recorded vote in Council as follows:

In favour: Algeria, Argentina, Austria, Benin, Botswana, Brazil, Bulgaria, Canada, China, Colombia, Congo, Costa Rica, Djibouti, Ecuador, Finland, France, German Democratic Republic, Germany, Federal Republic of, Greece, Indonesia, Japan, Lebanon, Liberia, Luxembourg, Malaysia, Mali, Mexico, Netherlands, New Zealand, Papua New Guinea, Poland, Portugal, Qatar, Romania, Rwanda, Saint Lucia, Saudi Arabia, Sierra Leone, Somalia, Sri Lanka, Suriname, Swaziland, Sweden, Thailand, Tunisia, Uganda, USSR, United Kingdom, Venezuela, Yugoslavia, Zaire.

Against: United States.

The United States, explaining its vote, observed that the financial implications involved raised serious questions of procedure and substance. Under the 1983 Council resolution,[24] the Secretariat had had a clear mandate to prepare not only the preliminary study but also the complete analytical study on popular participation. Thus the credits which had been approved had been intended to finance those two studies, not simply the preparation—by a consultant recruited at the P-4 level for six months at a cost of $33,200—of a preliminary report that, with the exception of 26 paragraphs, had been prepared by other United Nations organs. The United States was therefore dismayed at the Secretariat's statement that it would again be necessary to engage a consultant under similar terms to complete the study, at an estimated cost of $34,300.

Right to education and employment

In resolution 39/23, on measures for securing the enjoyment by youth of human rights, particularly the right to education and work, the General Assembly called on all States, governmental and non-governmental organizations and interested United Nations bodies and specialized agencies to pay continuous attention to implementation of measures aimed at promoting human rights and their enjoyment by youth, particularly the right to education, vocational training and work, with a view to resolving the problem of youth unemployment. The Assembly made a similar request to the Secretary-General in connection with his survey of the implementation of the Specific Programme of Measures and Activities for the International Youth Year (1985) (see p. 929). It invited national committees or organs co-ordinating activities for the Year to give priority to implementation and enjoyment by youth of human rights, particularly the right to education and work.

In resolution 39/145, the Assembly reaffirmed that, in order to facilitate full enjoyment of all rights and personal dignity, it was necessary to promote the rights to education and work, among others, through national measures, including those providing for workers' participation in management, and through international ones, including the establishment of a new international economic order.

Right to food

Pursuant to a May 1983 decision of the Economic and Social Council,[27] Special Rapporteur Asbjørn Eide (Norway) submitted to the Sub-Commission in 1984 a progress report on a study on the right to adequate food as a human right.[28] The report consisted of a draft of the first five chapters of the final report and a summary of replies received in response to a request for comments or information relevant to the preparation of the study.

Chapter I examined the nature of economic, social and cultural rights—the broad international legal framework within which the right to adequate food as a human right had been proclaimed—and addressed certain objections to the juristic quality of those rights. Chapter II surveyed the existing formulations of the right to food in international law. Chapter III covered food problems and the concept of food entitlement (defined as the command a person or family could legitimately establish over food). Chapters IV and V dealt, respectively, with food systems within their broader social context at all levels and with international efforts to co-ordinate and facilitate realization of the right to food. The remaining chapters, VI to VIII, were to deal with the normative content of the right to food including the corresponding obligations, international supervision of implementation of those obligations, and conclusions and recommendations.

Sub-Commission action. Having examined the progress report, the Sub-Commission, on 29 August 1984,[29] requested the Special Rapporteur to submit a final report in 1985. It also requested the Secretary-General to provide all the assistance required to carry out that task.

GENERAL ASSEMBLY ACTION

In resolution 39/166, the General Assembly reaffirmed that the right to food was a universal human right which should be guaranteed to all people, and, in that context, believed in the general principle that food should not be used as an instrument of political pressure.

REFERENCES

[1]YUN 1966, p. 419, GA res. 2200 A (XXI), annex, 16 Dec. 1966. [2]YUN 1976, p. 609. [3]E/1984/47. [4]A/39/461. [5]E/1984/83. [6]YUN 1978, p. 727, ESC dec. 1978/10, 3 May 1978. [7]YUN 1982, p. 1090, ESC res. 1982/33, 6 May 1982. [8]YUN 1976, p. 615, ESC res. 1988(LX), 11 May 1976. [9]E/1984/6/Add.1 & Add.1/Corr.1 & Add.4-6 & Add.6/Corr.1. [10]E/1984/6/Add.2,3. [11]E/1984/7/Add.1,2,4-16. [12]E/1984/7/Add.17,18. [13]E/1984/7/Add.3. [14]E/1980/6/Add.31-34 & Add.34/Corr.1 & Add.36. [15]E/1980/6/Add.35. [16]E/1982/3/Add.5,28,29. [17]E/1982/3/Add.26,27. [18]E/1984/55. [19]E/1984/14 (res. 1984/16). [20]YUN 1983, p. 854. [21]E/CN.4/1985/11. [22]E/1984/14 (res. 1984/17). [23]E/CN.4/1984/12 & Add.1. [24]YUN 1983, p. 730, ESC res. 1983/31, 27 May 1983. [25]YUN 1982, p. 961. [26]E/1984/14 (res. 1984/15). [27]YUN 1983, p. 857, ESC dec. 1983/140, 27 May 1983. [28]E/CN.4/Sub.2/1984/22 & Add.1,2. [29]E/CN.4/1985/3 (res. 1984/15).

Advancement of human rights

In 1984, an open-ended working group of the Commission on Human Rights continued an overall analysis of alternative ways and means within the United Nations system for improving the effective enjoyment of human rights and fundamental freedoms, as well as of other issues arising from the Commission's discussion of the further promotion and encouragement of human rights, including its programme and methods of work. The group, similar to the one established in 1983,[1] met at Geneva on 1, 7 and 12 March 1984.[2] In reviewing the work undertaken since 1978,[3] the group identified those areas on which deliberations had led to action, those concerning which it had acted merely in a "think-tank" capacity, and those considered but on which no agreement had been reached.

Actions taken included the expansion of the Commission from 32 to 43 members, extension of its sessions to six weeks with an additional week for its working groups, revision of its terms of reference to provide for Commission assistance to the Economic and Social Council in improving co-ordination of human rights activities, redesignation of the Division of Human Rights to the Centre for Human Rights, reclassification of the post of Director of the Centre to the level of Assistant Secretary-General, facilitating the Commission's conduct of its proceedings by setting a time-limit for statements, and streamlining its agenda.

Issues on which the group had played a "think-tank" role were the strengthening of the advisory services programme, public information initiatives, the Secretary-General's good-offices role, national institutions as well as regional arrangements for the promotion of human rights, and the role of the Sub-Commission in relation to the Commission.

Agreement remained to be reached on the following: inter-sessional role (organizational, substantive, emergency) of the Bureau of the Commission, rescheduling of the Commission's annual session, revision of its terms of reference for greater flexibility, a long-term work programme, creation of the post of United Nations High Commissioner for Human Rights, and a revision of the procedure for considering communications alleging denial or violation of human rights (see below, under "Human rights violations"). Some of the problems raised by these issues were also indicated. While some delegations felt that these issues could be the basis for future work, others felt that their continued discussion by the group would not be productive owing to the impasse it had reached on them.

On 15 March,[4] noting with appreciation the review by the working group, the Commission decided to consider—in the light of discussions to take place at the 1984 General Assembly session—setting up an open-ended working group in 1985 to continue the overall analysis.

GENERAL ASSEMBLY ACTION

On 14 December 1984, acting on the recommendation of the Third Committee, the General Assembly adopted resolution 39/145 by recorded vote.

Alternative approaches and ways and means within the United Nations system for improving the effective enjoyment of human rights and fundamental freedoms

The General Assembly,

Recalling that in the Charter of the United Nations the peoples of the United Nations declared their determination to reaffirm faith in fundamental human rights, in the dignity and worth of the human person and in the equal rights of men and women and of nations large and small and to employ international machinery for the promotion of the economic and social advancement of all peoples,

Recalling also the purposes and principles of the Charter to achieve international co-operation in solving international problems of an economic, social, cultural or humanitarian character, and in promoting and encouraging respect for human rights and for fundamental freedoms for all without distinction as to race, sex, language or religion,

Emphasizing the significance and validity of the Universal Declaration of Human Rights and of the International Covenants on Human Rights in promoting respect for and observance of human rights and fundamental freedoms,

Recalling its resolution 32/130 of 16 December 1977, in which it decided that the approach to the future work within the United Nations system with respect to human rights questions should take into account the concepts set forth in that resolution,

Recalling also its resolutions 34/46 of 23 November 1979, 35/174 of 15 December 1980, 36/133 of 14 December 1981 and 38/124 of 16 December 1983,

Recognizing that the human being is the main subject of development and that everyone has the right to participate in, as well as to benefit from, the development process,

Reiterating once again that the establishment of the new international economic order is an essential element for the effective promotion and the full enjoyment of human rights and fundamental freedoms for all,

Reiterating also its profound conviction that all human rights and fundamental freedoms are indivisible and interdependent and that equal attention and urgent consideration should be given to the implementation, promotion and protection of both civil and political and economic, social and cultural rights,

Reaffirming the importance of furthering the activities of the existing organs of the United Nations in the field of human rights in conformity with the principles of the Charter,

Underlining the need for the creation of conditions at the national and international levels for the promotion and full protection of the human rights of individuals and peoples,

Emphasizing that Governments have the duty to ensure respect for all human rights and fundamental freedoms,

Taking note of the work done by the Working Group of Governmental Experts on the Right to Development, as reflected in its reports to the Commission on Human Rights,

Underlining that the right to development is an inalienable human right,

Recognizing that international peace and security are essential elements for the full realization of human rights, including the right to development,

Considering that the resources which would be released by disarmament could contribute significantly to the development of all States, in particular the developing countries,

Recognizing that co-operation among all nations on the basis of respect for the independence, sovereignty and territorial integrity of each State, including the right of each people to choose freely its own socio-economic and political system, and to exercise full sovereignty over its wealth and natural resources, subject to the principles referred to in article 1, paragraph 2, and article 25 of the International Covenant on Economic, Social and Cultural Rights, is essential for the promotion of peace and development,

Convinced that the primary aim of such international co-operation must be the achievement by each human being of a life of freedom and dignity and freedom from want,

Acknowledging the progress so far achieved by the international community in the promotion and protection of human rights and fundamental freedoms,

Concerned, however, at the occurrence of violations of human rights in the world,

Reaffirming that nothing in the Universal Declaration of Human Rights or in the International Covenants on Human Rights may be interpreted as implying for any State, group or person the right to engage in any activity or perform any act aimed at the destruction of any of the rights and freedoms set forth therein,

Affirming that the ultimate aim of development is the constant improvement of the well-being of the entire population, on the basis of its full participation in the process of development and a fair distribution of the benefits therefrom,

1.   *Reiterates its request* that the Commission on Human Rights continue its current work on the overall analysis with a view to further promoting and improving human rights and fundamental freedoms, including the question of the Commission's programme and working methods, and on the overall analysis of the alternative approaches and ways and means for improving the effective enjoyment of human rights and fundamental freedoms, in accordance with the provisions and concepts of General Assembly resolution 32/130 and other relevant texts;

2.   *Affirms* that a primary aim of international co-operation in the field of human rights is a life of freedom, dignity and peace for all peoples and for each human being, that all human rights and fundamental freedoms

are indivisible and interrelated and that the promotion and protection of one category of rights should never exempt or excuse States from the promotion and protection of the others;

3. *Affirms its profound conviction* that equal attention and urgent consideration should be given to the implementation, protection and promotion of both civil and political and economic, social and cultural rights;

4. *Reaffirms* that it is of paramount importance for the promotion of human rights and fundamental freedoms that Member States should undertake specific obligations through accession to, or ratification of, international instruments in this field and, consequently, that the standard-setting work within the United Nations system in the field of human rights and the universal acceptance and implementation of the relevant international instruments should be encouraged;

5. *Reiterates once again* that the international community should accord, or continue to accord, priority to the search for solutions to mass and flagrant violations of human rights of peoples and individuals affected by situations such as those mentioned in paragraph 1 *(e)* of General Assembly resolution 32/130, paying due attention also to other situations of violations of human rights;

6. *Reaffirms* its responsibility for achieving international co-operation in promoting and encouraging respect for human rights and fundamental freedoms for all and expresses its concern at serious violations of human rights, in particular mass and flagrant violations of these rights, wherever they occur;

7. *Expresses concern* at the present situation with regard to the achievement of the objectives and goals for establishing the new international economic order and its adverse effects on the full realization of human rights, in particular the right to development;

8. *Reaffirms* that the right to development is an inalienable human right;

9. *Reaffirms also* that international peace and security are essential elements in achieving the full realization of the right to development;

10. *Recognizes* that all human rights and fundamental freedoms are indivisible and interdependent;

11. *Considers* it necessary that all Member States promote international co-operation on the basis of respect for the independence, sovereignty and territorial integrity of each State, including the right of each people to choose freely its own socio-economic and political system, and to exercise full sovereignty over its wealth and natural resources, subject to the principles referred to in article 1, paragraph 2, and article 25 of the International Covenant on Economic, Social and Cultural Rights, with a view to resolving international problems of an economic, social and humanitarian character;

12. *Expresses concern* at the disparity existing between the established norms and principles and the actual situation of all human rights and fundamental freedoms in the world;

13. *Urges* all States to co-operate with the Commission on Human Rights in the promotion and protection of human rights and fundamental freedoms;

14. *Reiterates* the need to create, at the national and international levels, conditions for the full promotion and protection of the human rights of individuals and peoples;

15. *Reaffirms once again* that, in order to facilitate the full enjoyment of all rights and complete personal dignity, it is necessary to promote the rights to education, work, health and proper nourishment through the adoption of measures at the national level, including those that provide for workers' participation in management, as well as the adoption of measures at the international level, including the establishment of the new international economic order;

16. *Requests* the Commission on Human Rights to take the necessary measures to promote the right to development, taking into account the results achieved by the Working Group of Governmental Experts on the Right to Development, which is engaged in the study of the scope and content of the right to development, and welcomes the decision of the Commission in its resolution 1984/16 of 6 March 1984 that the Working Group should continue its work with the aim of submitting as soon as possible a draft declaration on the right to development;

17. *Requests* the Secretary-General to transmit to the General Assembly at its fortieth session a report containing information on the progress made by the Working Group of Governmental Experts on the Right to Development of the Commission on Human Rights in the drafting of a declaration on the right to development;

18. *Decides* to include in the provisional agenda of its fortieth session the item entitled "Alternative approaches and ways and means within the United Nations system for improving the effective enjoyment of human rights and fundamental freedoms".

General Assembly resolution 39/145

14 December 1984   Meeting 101   131-2-12 (recorded vote)

Approved by Third Committee (A/39/711) by recorded vote (118-1-13), 30 November (meeting 55); 31-nation draft (A/C.3/39/L.36), orally revised; agenda item 102 *(a)*.

Sponsors: Algeria, Angola, Argentina, Bangladesh, Benin, Bolivia, Burkina Faso, Cape Verde, Colombia, Congo, Cuba, Democratic Yemen, Ethiopia, Guinea-Bissau, Guyana, India, Libyan Arab Jamahiriya, Madagascar, Mali, Mexico, Mozambique, Nicaragua, Nigeria, Pakistan, Panama, Romania, Sao Tome and Principe, Syrian Arab Republic, Uganda, Viet Nam, Yugoslavia.

Meeting numbers. GA 39th session: 3rd Committee 33, 34, 36, 47, 53, 55; plenary 101.

Recorded vote in Assembly as follows:

In favour: Afghanistan, Algeria, Angola, Argentina, Australia, Bahamas, Bahrain, Bangladesh, Barbados, Belgium, Belize, Benin, Bhutan, Bolivia, Botswana, Brazil, Brunei Darussalam, Bulgaria, Burkina Faso, Burma, Burundi, Byelorussian SSR, Cameroon, Cape Verde, Central African Republic, Chad, Chile, China, Colombia, Congo, Costa Rica, Cuba, Cyprus, Czechoslovakia, Democratic Kampuchea, Democratic Yemen, Djibouti, Dominican Republic, Ecuador, Egypt, El Salvador, Equatorial Guinea, Ethiopia, Fiji, France, Gabon, Gambia, German Democratic Republic, Ghana, Greece, Guatemala, Guinea, Guyana, Honduras, Hungary, India, Indonesia, Iraq, Italy, Ivory Coast, Jamaica, Jordan, Kenya, Kuwait, Lao People's Democratic Republic, Lebanon, Lesotho, Liberia, Libyan Arab Jamahiriya, Luxembourg, Madagascar, Malawi, Malaysia, Maldives, Mali, Malta, Mauritania, Mauritius, Mexico, Mongolia, Morocco, Mozambique, Nepal, Netherlands, New Zealand, Nicaragua, Niger, Nigeria, Oman, Pakistan, Panama, Papua New Guinea, Paraguay, Peru, Philippines, Poland, Portugal, Qatar, Romania, Rwanda, Saint Vincent and the Grenadines, Samoa, Sao Tome and Principe, Saudi Arabia, Senegal, Seychelles, Singapore, Somalia, Spain, Sri Lanka, Sudan, Suriname, Swaziland, Syrian Arab Republic, Thailand, Togo, Trinidad and Tobago, Tunisia, Uganda, Ukrainian SSR, USSR, United Arab Emirates, United Republic of Tanzania, Uruguay, Venezuela, Viet Nam, Yemen, Yugoslavia, Zaire, Zambia, Zimbabwe.

Against: Israel, United States.

Abstaining: Austria, Canada, Denmark, Finland, Germany, Federal Republic of, Iceland, Ireland, Japan, Norway, Sweden, Turkey, United Kingdom.

During consideration of the draft text in the Third Committee, Italy proposed two amendments which it later withdrew:[5] one was to paragraph 6, which would have substituted the text after the word "all" by "and that massive and flagrant violations and all other violations of human rights, wherever they occur, are of concern to the United Nations"; the other was to paragraph 12 (originally paragraph 13), which would have substituted the text after the word "principles" by "and the massive and flagrant and all other violations of human rights which continue to take place in many parts of the world". The Ukrainian SSR also proposed and later withdrew an amendment[6] introducing a new paragraph by which the Assembly would have reaffirmed the duty of a State to refrain from exploiting and distorting human rights issues as a means of interfering in the internal affairs of other States or creating distrust and disorder among them. Following consultations on those proposals, the draft was orally revised by the sponsors.

It was contended by the majority of States explaining their votes in the Committee that, in the absence of a universally acceptable definition of the right to development and pending the outcome of the deliberations of the Working Group charged with drafting a declaration (see above), the formulation in paragraph 8 was either unacceptable or premature. Those States included Austria, Belgium, Canada, the Federal Republic of Germany, Italy, Japan, the Netherlands, Sweden (for the Nordic countries) and the United States. The Federal Republic of Germany observed that the text, instead of reflecting the various proposals for strengthening or developing United Nations structures for a more effective protection of human rights and fundamental freedoms, referred to a number of unclear concepts for the realization of human rights; such issues as international peace and security, disarmament and development should be dealt with in more competent forums.

The United States could not accept formulations such as those in paragraphs 7 and 16, which might imply that establishment of the so-called new international economic order (NIEO) was a prerequisite to the realization of human rights and fundamental freedoms. Similar views were voiced by the Federal Republic of Germany, Sweden and the Netherlands, which also said it was by no means clear what the content of NIEO would be.

Turkey and Ireland were of the opinion that the text did not reflect the basic concept that human rights were inherent in human nature and existed independently of all other factors. Nor did it reflect the necessary balance between civil and political rights, and economic, social and cultural rights, Turkey added. The Federal Republic of Germany and Sweden made a similar observation. Sweden further explained that the Nordic countries fully supported the approach taken by the Assembly in 1977[7] to the effect that all human rights and fundamental freedoms were indivisible and interdependent and that equal attention should be given to implementing and promoting them; Sweden thus found regrettable the tendency to stress States' rights rather than the individual's, and economic and social rights rather than civil and political.

The various international human rights instruments drawn up by the United Nations had made any human rights violations a legitimate concern of the United Nations, the Federal Republic of Germany asserted; it could therefore not support formulations restricting United Nations competence in respect of such violations. Ireland said such concern was not expressed with sufficient clarity by the text. There could be no doubt, the Netherlands observed, that protection of human rights implied active United Nations involvement—an involvement that should not be restricted to mass and flagrant human rights violations.

Through the 1948 Universal Declaration of Human Rights,[8] the United Nations and its Members had committed themselves to ensuring respect for the human rights of each member of the human community, Belgium said; it thus felt that violations of the individual's rights were as grave as violations of any other rights embodied in the Covenants. Australia said it failed to understand the trepidation with which some approached the idea that all human rights violations were of concern to the United Nations; it could, therefore, only with difficulty accept the qualified reference to violations in the terms in which it appeared in paragraph 6. France regretted that the text still contained unacceptable elements and it hoped that it would be possible to produce a really balanced text on the subject in 1985.

In the view of the USSR, the text neither placed undue emphasis on social and economic rights, as opposed to the civil and political, nor did it place States' rights in opposition to the individual's. To speak of the human rights of the individual was unrealistic, the USSR felt, unless the rights of the whole people were safeguarded. The text avoided the pitfall of making human rights violations the exclusive concern of the United Nations, which would absolve States of all responsibility with respect to human rights. The USSR also remarked that the importance of the right to development could not be appreciated by countries whose position in the world was founded on colonial exploitation, and that countries emerging from colonial status could not hope to implement the 1966 International Covenants (see below), unless their enjoyment of that right was ensured.

National institutions for human rights protection

As requested by the General Assembly in December 1983,[9] the Secretary-General submitted a report[10] summarizing replies to his request for additional information on the various types of national and local institutions for the protection and promotion of human rights. As at 1 November 1984, replies were received from 12 Governments. The

Secretary-General stated that the new information tended to reinforce the basic approach of his 1983 report.[11]

GENERAL ASSEMBLY ACTION

On 14 December 1984, acting on the recommendation of the Third Committee, the General Assembly adopted resolution 39/144 without vote.

National institutions for the protection and promotion of human rights

The General Assembly,

Recalling its resolutions 32/123 of 16 December 1977, 33/46 of 14 December 1978, 34/49 of 23 November 1979, 36/134 of 14 December 1981 and 38/123 of 16 December 1983,

Mindful of the guidelines on the structure and functioning of national and local institutions for the promotion and protection of human rights, endorsed by the General Assembly in its resolution 33/46,

Mindful also of the need to create conditions, at the national, regional and international levels, for the protection and promotion of human rights,

Emphasizing the importance of the Universal Declaration of Human Rights, the International Covenants on Human Rights and other international human rights instruments for promoting respect for and observance of human rights and fundamental freedoms,

Conscious of the significant role which institutions at the national level can play in protecting and promoting human rights and fundamental freedoms and in developing and enhancing public awareness and observance of those rights and freedoms,

1. *Takes note with appreciation* of the report of the Secretary-General;

2. *Emphasizes* the importance of the integrity and independence of national institutions for the protection and promotion of human rights, in accordance with national legislation;

3. *Draws attention* to the constructive role that national non-governmental organizations can play in the work of such national institutions;

4. *Encourages* all Member States to take appropriate steps for the establishment or, where they already exist, the strengthening of national institutions for the protection and promotion of human rights;

5. *Invites* all Member States to take appropriate steps to disseminate the texts of human rights instruments, including international covenants and conventions, in their respective national or local languages, in order to give the widest possible publicity to these instruments;

6. *Recommends* that all Member States should consider including in their educational curricula material relevant to a comprehensive understanding of human rights issues;

7. *Also recommends* that all Member States should take appropriate steps to encourage the exchange of experience in the establishment of national institutions;

8. *Requests* the Secretary-General, in carrying out public information activities in the field of human rights, to give due attention to the role of national institutions and non-governmental organizations concerned with the protection and promotion of human rights;

9. *Requests* the Secretary-General to provide all necessary assistance to Member States, upon their request, in the implementation of paragraph 5 above, according high priority to the needs of developing countries;

10. *Requests* the Secretary-General to continue and, as appropriate, increase assistance in the field of human rights to Governments, at their request, within the framework of the programme of advisory services in the field of human rights;

11. *Also requests* the Secretary-General, in the light of his reports and of further information received, to prepare and submit to the General Assembly, through the Commission on Human Rights and the Economic and Social Council, a consolidated report, for eventual publication as a United Nations handbook on national institutions for the use of Governments, including information on the various types and models of national and local institutions for the protection and promotion of human rights, taking into account differing social and legal systems;

12. *Further requests* the Secretary-General to report to the General Assembly at its fortieth session on the implementation of the present resolution.

General Assembly resolution 39/144

14 December 1984   Meeting 101   Adopted without vote

Approved by Third Committee (A/39/711) without vote, 28 November (meeting 53); 8-nation draft (A/C.3/39/L.39); agenda item 102 *(b)*.
Sponsors: Australia, India, Iraq, Morocco, New Zealand, Nigeria, Peru, Sri Lanka.
Meeting numbers. GA 39th session: 3rd Committee 33, 34, 36, 47, 53; plenary 101.

UN machinery

Commission on Human Rights

Organization of work for the 1984 session

On 7 February 1984,[12] the Commission on Human Rights set up informal open-ended working groups to consider the following agenda items: torture and other cruel, inhuman or degrading treatment or punishment (see above, under "Civil and political rights"); further promotion and encouragement of human rights and fundamental freedoms, including the question of the programme and methods of work of the Commission (see above); the question of a convention on the rights of the child (see below, under "Other human rights questions"); and the rights of persons belonging to national, ethnic, religious and linguistic minorities (see above, under "Discrimination"). In keeping with its March 1983 decision arising from the recommendations of a 10-member working group on the rationalization of its 1984 agenda,[13] the Commission decided that the item on human rights and scientific and technological developments, to be considered every two years beginning in 1984, would be dealt with by the working group on the advancement of human rights.

The Commission invited special rapporteurs, experts, special representatives and other officials to participate in meetings on certain topics with which they were specifically concerned, including the Sub-Commission Chairman during consideration of the 1983 Sub-Commission report. A similar invitation was extended on 16 March 1984 in connection with the 1984 report.[14]

Also on 16 March,[15] the Commission—taking account of its heavy work schedule and that of its sessional working groups, and of the need to consider adequately all the items on its agenda—adopted a decision which served as a basis for the Economic and Social Council decision below.

ECONOMIC AND SOCIAL COUNCIL ACTION

Acting without vote on the recommendation of its Second Committee, the Economic and Social Council in May adopted decision 1984/144.

Organization of the work of the Commission on Human Rights

At its 20th plenary meeting, on 24 May 1984, the Council, noting Commission on Human Rights decision 1984/113 of 16 March 1984, decided to authorize, if possible within the existing financial resources, twenty fully-serviced additional meetings, including summary records, for the Commission's forty-first session. The Council took note of the Commission's decision to request its Chairman at the forty-first session to make every effort to organize the work of the session within the normal allotted time, the additional meetings authorized by the Council to be utilized only if such meetings prove to be absolutely necessary.

Economic and Social Council decision 1984/144

Adopted without vote

Approved by Second Committee (E/1984/91) without vote, 17 May (meeting 16); draft by Commission on Human Rights (E/1984/14); agenda item 10.

Report of the Commission

On 20 February,[16] the Commission decided not to include in its report summaries of substantive debate and to ensure that the report contained accurate and precise references to the summary records.

On 16 March, the Commission adopted the draft report on the work of its fortieth (February/March 1984) session, as amended in the course of its consideration.

ECONOMIC AND SOCIAL COUNCIL ACTION

Acting on the recommendation of its Second Committee, the Economic and Social Council in May adopted decision 1984/147 without vote.

Report of the Commission on Human Rights

At its 20th plenary meeting, on 24 May 1984, the Council took note of the report of the Commission on Human Rights on its fortieth session.

Economic and Social Council decision 1984/147

Adopted without vote

Approved by Second Committee (E/1984/91) without vote, 17 May (meeting 16); draft by Commission on Human Rights (E/1984/14); agenda item 10.

Sub-Commission on Prevention of Discrimination and Protection of Minorities

Work organization and programme

As recommended by the Sub-Commission in September 1983,[17] the Commission on Human Rights, by a vote of 34 to 1, with 4 abstentions, taken on

15 March 1984,[18] took note of a Sub-Commission decision to establish in 1984 a working group to study in depth the Sub-Commission's working methods and programme of work, including its relationship with the Commission and the United Nations Secretariat. The Commission invited an exchange of views between a spokesman of the group and the Commission in 1985, which would be reported on to the Sub-Commission later that year for its consideration.

ECONOMIC AND SOCIAL COUNCIL ACTION

Acting without vote on the recommendation of its Second Committee, the Economic and Social Council in May 1984 adopted decision 1984/139.

Review of the work of the Sub-Commission on Prevention of Discrimination and Protection of Minorities

At its 20th plenary meeting, on 24 May 1984, the Council, noting Commission on Human Rights resolution 1984/60 of 15 March 1984, noted the decision of the Sub-Commission on Prevention of Discrimination and Protection of Minorities to establish at its thirty-seventh session a working group to study in depth the working methods and the programme of work of the Sub-Commission, including its relationship with the Commission and the Secretariat, and endorsed the Commission's invitation for an exchange of views between a spokesman for that working group and the Commission or a working group of the Commission during the forty-first session of the Commission.

Economic and Social Council decision 1984/139

Adopted without vote

Approved by Second Committee (E/1984/91) by vote (49-1), 17 May (meeting 16); draft by Commission on Human Rights (E/1984/14); agenda item 10.

Working Group activities. The five-member Working Group on the Review of the Work of the Sub-Commission met at Geneva during the August 1984 session of the Sub-Commission, with Ahmed Mohamed Khalifa (Egypt) as Chairman/Rapporteur. The Group considered a wide range of complex issues relating to the name and terms of reference of the Sub-Commission, its role and functions, its relationship with the Commission on Human Rights, the programming of its studies and other tasks, and the rationalization of its procedures and methods. Among the Group's conclusions and recommendations were a series of core items for the Sub-Commission's agenda and a five-year plan of studies, for 1985-1989, constituting annexes I and II, respectively, of the Group's report.[19] The Group also recommended a procedure for the preparation of the Sub-Commission's studies, additional meetings for its session, a strengthening of the Centre for Human Rights, and an extension of the Group's mandate—all of which were embodied in the Sub-Commission's resolution below.

The regular items recommended for inclusion in the Sub-Commission's agenda for 1985-1989 were:

a review of further developments in areas with which the Sub-Commission had been concerned; racial discrimination, including updating annual studies on its adverse consequences; communications concerning human rights violations (see below); administration of justice and human rights of detained persons, including an annual review of developments in those rights; discrimination against indigenous populations; slavery and slavery-like practices; encouragement of universal acceptance of human rights instruments; future work and draft provisional agenda; and the possibility of examining certain items once every two years.

Sub-Commission action. Having considered the Working Group's report, the Sub-Commission, by 10 votes to 3, with 6 abstentions, on 31 August,[20] expressed appreciation to the Group and its Chairman/Rapporteur and endorsed their recommendations, including the long-term plan of studies and the core items to be kept on the Sub-Commission's agenda for 1985-1989. It asked the Secretary-General to inform the Commission on Human Rights of the Group's activities and decided that the Group should continue its deliberations during the Sub-Commission's 1985 session.

Besides deciding to begin its future meetings on time, the Sub-Commission recommended that the Commission consider: renaming the Sub-Commission as the Sub-Commission of Experts of the Commission on Human Rights; electing the members for a four-year term, with half of them elected every two years; authorizing 10 additional meetings per session to allow the Sub-Commission properly to execute its increasing workload and the sessional working groups to meet concurrently; and strengthening the Centre for Human Rights to enable it to provide further services to the Sub-Commission and implement its five-year plan of work. The Sub-Commission also recommended that studies undertaken under its auspices be prepared within a three-year cycle, the first year to be devoted to a concise report outlining the proposed approach, the second to a concise progress report that would also raise special questions, and the third to the final report. It was to be understood that a study, once authorized by the Council, would proceed through each of these stages without further approval by the Council, Commission or Sub-Commission.

Report of the Sub-Commission for 1984

ECONOMIC AND SOCIAL COUNCIL ACTION

Acting without vote on the recommendation of its Second Committee, the Economic and Social Council in May adopted decision 1984/146.

Report of the Sub-Commission on Prevention of Discrimination and Protection of Minorities on its thirty-sixth session

At its 20th plenary meeting, on 24 May 1984, the Council, noting Commission on Human Rights decision 1984/115

of 16 March 1984, endorsed the Commission's invitation to the Sub-Commission on Prevention of Discrimination and Protection of Minorities to be present, through its Chairman or another member it may designate, at the consideration of its report during the forty-first session of the Commission.

Economic and Social Council decision 1984/146

Adopted without vote

Approved by Second Committee (E/1984/91) without vote, 17 May (meeting 16); draft by Commission on Human Rights (E/1984/14); agenda item 10.

Calendar of meetings for 1985

On 31 August 1984,[21] the Sub-Commission adopted a schedule of meetings in 1985 for its working groups on communications, on slavery and on indigenous populations, as well as the dates for its own session. It determined the composition of those groups on the same date.[22]

Proposed UN High Commissioner for Human Rights

The question of the establishment of a post of United Nations High Commissioner for Human Rights, first proposed in 1965 by Costa Rica,[23] was again considered by the Commission on Human Rights in 1984. Two proposals on the subject were before it. One, sponsored by Colombia, Costa Rica and Peru, recommended establishment of the post and set forth its functions and responsibilities and administrative arrangements.[24] Amendments to the text were proposed by Cuba[25] and by the German Democratic Republic.[26] The other proposal, sponsored by Brazil, recommended establishment in 1985 of an open-ended working group of the Commission to continue to consider the question.[27]

Following a motion by Yugoslavia, the Commission on 15 March 1984[28] adjourned the debate on the draft resolutions until its 1985 session.

International human rights instruments

On 7 August 1984, the Sub-Commission, acting in pursuance of a 1979 resolution,[29] established a five-member sessional Working Group on the encouragement of universal acceptance of human rights instruments—such as the 1966 International Covenants on Economic, Social and Cultural Rights and on Civil and Political Rights and the latter's Optional Protocol,[30] the 1965 International Convention on the Elimination of All Forms of Racial Discrimination,[31] the 1948 Convention on the Prevention and Punishment of the Crime of Genocide,[32] the 1973 International Convention on the Suppression and Punishment of the Crime of *Apartheid*,[33] the 1926 Slavery Convention and the 1953 Protocol amending it,[34] the 1956 Supplementary Convention on the Abolition of Slavery, the Slave Trade, and Institutions and Practices Similar to Slavery,[35] the 1949 Convention for the Suppression of the Traffic in Persons and of the Exploitation of the Prostitution of Others,[36] and the 1979 Convention on the Elimination of All Forms of Discrimination against Women.[37]

Meeting at Geneva on 15, 22, 23 and 27 August 1984,[38] the Group conducted a country-by-country examination of information received from Belgium, Bolivia, Cyprus, the Federal Republic of Germany and the Netherlands; and additional information from Belgium, El Salvador and Guatemala, as summarized in two notes by the Secretary-General, both of 28 June.[39] In the course of its discussions, the Group heard statements by the observer from Senegal, and by representatives of ILO and seven NGOs.

Based on its findings, the Group made recommendations that served as the basis for the Sub-Commission action below.

Sub-Commission action. Taking note of the Working Group's report, the Sub-Commission, by 18 votes to 1, with 1 abstention, on 30 August 1984,[40] requested the Secretary-General to renew his invitation to Governments to adhere to international human rights instruments, to invite Guatemala to clarify the nature of the legal problems it had encountered with respect to the 1949 Convention on prostitution and supply information on steps taken to overcome them, to examine the idea of offering technical assistance in the drafting of legislation to enable States to ratify or accede to human rights instruments, to hold informal discussions on ratification prospects during such occasions as the General Assembly sessions, to examine the idea of designating regional advisers on international human rights standards who would also advise on acceptance and implementation of such instruments, and to prepare a table containing a country-by-country record of developments in connection with the ratification of, or accession to, the instruments.

The Sub-Commission decided to include the two Protocols additional to the 1949 Geneva Conventions in the list of human rights instruments whose universal acceptance was to be encouraged. It suspended the work of the Working Group and requested the Sub-Commission Chairman to appoint one of its members to report to it in 1985 on information received under the present resolution.

International covenants on human rights

In January 1984, the Secretary-General reported[41] to the Commission on Human Rights on the status of the 1966 International Covenants on Human Rights[30] and gave a synopsis of United Nations action taken in that context. Annexed to the report were lists of States which had signed, ratified or acceded to the Covenants, as well as to the Optional Protocol to the International Covenant on Civil and Political Rights.

Acting without vote on the recommendation of the Third Committee, the General Assembly adopted resolution 39/136 on 14 December 1984.

International Covenants on Human Rights

The General Assembly,

Recalling its resolutions 33/51 of 14 December 1978, 34/45 of 23 November 1979, 35/132 of 11 December 1980, 36/58 of 25 November 1981, 37/191 of 18 December 1982 and 38/116 and 38/117 of 16 December 1983,

Taking note of the report of the Secretary-General on the status of the International Covenant on Economic, Social and Cultural Rights, the International Covenant on Civil and Political Rights, and the Optional Protocol to the International Covenant on Civil and Political Rights,

Noting with appreciation that, following its appeal, more Member States have acceded to the International Covenants on Human Rights,

Recognizing the important role of the Human Rights Committee in the implementation of the International Covenant on Civil and Political Rights and the Optional Protocol thereto,

Taking into account the useful work of the Sessional Working Group of Governmental Experts on the Implementation of the International Covenant on Economic, Social and Cultural Rights,

Bearing in mind the important responsibilities of the Economic and Social Council in relation to the International Covenants on Human Rights,

1. *Takes note with appreciation* of the report of the Human Rights Committee on its twentieth, twenty-first and twenty-second sessions, and expresses its satisfaction with the serious and constructive manner in which the Committee is continuing to perform its functions;

2. *Expresses its appreciation* to those States parties to the International Covenant on Civil and Political Rights that have submitted their reports to the Human Rights Committee under article 40 of the Covenant and urges States parties that have not yet done so to submit their reports as speedily as possible;

3. *Urges* those States parties to the International Covenant on Civil and Political Rights that have been requested by the Human Rights Committee to provide additional information to comply with that request;

4. *Commends* those States parties to the International Covenant on Economic, Social and Cultural Rights that have submitted their reports under article 16 of the Covenant and urges States that have not yet done so to submit their reports as soon as possible;

5. *Notes with satisfaction* that the majority of States parties to the International Covenant on Civil and Political Rights, and an increasing number of States parties to the International Covenant on Economic, Social and Cultural Rights, have been represented by experts for the presentation of their reports, thereby assisting the Human Rights Committee and the Economic and Social Council in their work, and hopes that all States parties to both Covenants will arrange such representation in future;

6. *Again urges* all States that have not yet done so to become parties to the International Covenant on Economic, Social and Cultural Rights and the International Covenant on Civil and Political Rights, as well as to con-

sider acceding to the Optional Protocol to the International Covenant on Civil and Political Rights;

7. *Invites* the States parties to the International Covenant on Civil and Political Rights to consider making the declaration provided for in article 41 of the Covenant;

8. *Emphasizes* the importance of the strictest compliance by States parties with their obligations under the International Covenant on Economic, Social and Cultural Rights and the International Covenant on Civil and Political Rights and, where applicable, the Optional Protocol to the International Covenant on Civil and Political Rights;

9. *Requests* the Secretary-General to keep the Human Rights Committee informed of the relevant activities of the General Assembly, the Economic and Social Council, the Commission on Human Rights, the Sub-Commission on Prevention of Discrimination and Protection of Minorities, the Committee on the Elimination of Racial Discrimination and the Committee on the Elimination of Discrimination against Women and also to transmit the annual reports of the Human Rights Committee to those bodies;

10. *Looks forward* to the report of the Secretary-General, to be submitted to the Economic and Social Council at its first regular session of 1985, on the composition, organization and administrative arrangements of the Sessional Working Group of Governmental Experts on the Implementation of the International Covenant on Economic, Social and Cultural Rights and other bodies established in accordance with existing international instruments in the field of human rights in order to facilitate the review which the Council will undertake in accordance with its resolution 1982/33 of 6 May 1982;

11. *Welcomes* the decision by the Economic and Social Council in its resolution 1984/9 of 24 May 1984 to conduct the review at an early stage of its first regular session of 1985 to allow enough time for a full discussion of this important matter;

12. *Requests* the Secretary-General to submit to the General Assembly at its fortieth session a report on the status of the International Covenant on Economic, Social and Cultural Rights, the International Covenant on Civil and Political Rights and the Optional Protocol to the International Covenant on Civil and Political Rights;

13. *Again urges* the Secretary-General, taking into account the suggestions of the Human Rights Committee, to take determined steps within existing resources to give more publicity to the work of the Committee and, similarly, to the work of the Economic and Social Council and its Sessional Working Group and to improve administrative and related arrangements to enable them to carry out their respective functions effectively under the International Covenants on Human Rights;

14. *Urges* the Secretary-General to continue to expedite the publication of the official public records of the Human Rights Committee in bound volumes, as indicated in General Assembly resolution 37/191, starting with its first session;

15. *Requests* the Secretary-General to ensure that the Centre for Human Rights of the Secretariat effectively assists the Human Rights Committee and the Economic and Social Council in the implementation of their respective functions under the International Covenants on Human Rights.

General Assembly resolution 39/136

14 December 1984   Meeting 101   Adopted without vote

Approved by Third Committee (A/39/707) without vote, 3 December (meeting 57); 17-nation draft (A/C.3/39/L.69), orally revised; agenda item 98.

Sponsors: Australia, Bulgaria, Canada, Costa Rica, Cyprus, Denmark, Ecuador, Finland, Iceland, Italy, Netherlands, Nicaragua, Norway, Peru, Spain, Sweden, United Kingdom.
Meeting numbers. GA 39th session: 3rd Committee 44-52, 56, 57; plenary 101.

Reporting obligations of States parties

In September 1984, the Secretary-General transmitted to the Assembly a report of a meeting of the Chairmen of the Commission on Human Rights, the Human Rights Committee, the Sessional Working Group of Governmental Experts on the Implementation of the International Covenant on Economic, Social and Cultural Rights and the Committee on the Elimination of Racial Discrimination,[42] convened pursuant to a December 1983 Assembly request.[43] The meeting, which took place at Geneva on 16 and 17 August 1984, considered the 1983 report of the Secretary-General[44] on the reporting obligations of States parties to the 1965 Convention against racial discrimination[31] and the 1966 International Covenants.[30]

The Chairmen identified as the most serious problems in the functioning of the reporting procedures the failure of some States parties to submit reports at all, delays in submitting them, the varying quality of those submitted, the burden placed on States parties by several coexisting reporting systems, the lack of qualified staff to prepare reports, and the need to enhance implementation of the provisions of international conventions.

Reviewing suggestions put forward to resolve those problems, the Chairmen focused on such measures as the exchange of information among the various organs entrusted with considering reports, to enhance which they suggested consolidating in one reference document guidelines and rules of procedure and consolidating in another their observations and decisions, a table showing reports submitted and outstanding, and consolidated tables on the status of ratification of the instruments. Reporting guidelines, apart from being co-ordinated, should include a standard format for obtaining the profile (geographical and demographic characteristics, basic economic and social conditions, constitutional structure, basic legislation dealing with the rights under the 1966 Covenants) of a reporting State party. A programme of advisory services should be developed, to include regional courses, seminars and fellowships for the development of reporting skills, and regional experts who could be dispatched on short advisory missions as required.

The Chairmen were of the unanimous view that their meeting had proved valuable and felt that such a meeting should be held regularly, possibly annually or biennially and perhaps to include the Chairman of the Committee on the Elimination of Discrimination against Women. They also suggested that the Secretary-General could raise the question of ratifications when he met heads of State, Foreign Ministers or other high-level officials during Assembly sessions.

Acting without vote on the recommendation of the Third Committee, the General Assembly adopted resolution 39/138 on 14 December 1984.

Reporting obligations of States parties to United Nations conventions on human rights

The General Assembly,

Recalling its resolutions 37/44 of 3 December 1982 and 38/117 of 16 December 1983,

Considering that the General Assembly, as the principal organ of the United Nations entitled to adopt conventions on human rights, is in the position to take an overview of their implementation as an integrated system of substantive provisions and reporting obligations of States parties to the various conventions,

Conscious that the fulfilment of reporting obligations constitutes an essential element of co-operation by States parties in contributing to the assessment of their compliance with their obligations,

Bearing in mind the report of the Secretary-General on the reporting obligations of States parties under various United Nations conventions on human rights,

Having considered the report of the meeting of the Chairmen of the Commission on Human Rights, the Human Rights Committee, the Sessional Working Group of Governmental Experts on the Implementation of the International Covenant on Economic, Social and Cultural Rights and the Committee on the Elimination of Racial Discrimination held at Geneva on 16 and 17 August 1984,

Concerned about the problems experienced by the above-mentioned bodies in the functioning of the reporting procedures, including the burden which several coexisting reporting systems place upon States parties to the conventions on human rights,

Convinced, therefore, of the need to improve the existing reporting systems in order to resolve the problems experienced both by the bodies entrusted with the consideration of the periodic reports of the States parties and by the States parties to the conventions on human rights,

1. *Reiterates* the importance it attaches to the obligations established under international conventions, including their respective reporting systems;

2. *Takes note with interest* of the report of the meeting of the Chairmen of the Commission on Human Rights, the Human Rights Committee, the Sessional Working Group of Governmental Experts on the Implementation of the International Covenant on Economic, Social and Cultural Rights and the Committee on the Elimination of Racial Discrimination, which contains suggestions made by the Chairmen with regard to exchange of information among their respective bodies, co-ordination of guidelines for the submission of the reports of States parties, advisory services and assistance for States parties to the various conventions on human rights, and other matters;

3. *Expresses the view* that the presence at the above-mentioned meeting of the Chairmen of all bodies concerned with reporting obligations of States parties to United Nations conventions on human rights would have further contributed to the review of problems experienced in the functioning of reporting procedures;

4. *Acknowledges* that common problems have arisen in the functioning of the reporting procedures, thus indicating the necessity of considering them within the overall framework of reporting obligations of States parties under the various conventions on human rights;

5. *Decides* to keep under consideration the problems that have arisen from the coexistence of several different reporting systems, in particular the proliferation of reporting obligations under the various instruments, as well as the serious delays which have occurred in the submission of reports;

6. *Requests* the Secretary-General, to that effect, to submit to the General Assembly at its fortieth session a report containing:

(a) Updated information on the general situation of the submission of reports of States parties to all conventions which are already in force, thus enabling the General Assembly to take an overview of the fulfilment of all reporting obligations and to consider how to achieve an improvement, particularly in the interest of States parties with limited technical and administrative resources;

(b) A consolidated text of the guidelines of the various bodies entrusted with the consideration of the reports of States parties on the implementation of all United Nations conventions on human rights;

7. *Requests* the Commission on Human Rights to consider, in the context of its standing item concerning advisory services in the field of human rights, the suggestions made by the Chairmen;

8. *Decides* to consider the question of reporting obligations of States parties to United Nations conventions on human rights in the light of the report of the Secretary-General to be submitted in accordance with paragraph 6 above and to consider also the eventual convening of another meeting of the Chairmen of the bodies entrusted with the consideration of the reports of States parties;

9. *Invites* the bodies concerned to give particular attention to the present resolution when they next meet;

10. *Decides* to consider the question at its fortieth session, in the light of the report of the Secretary-General to be submitted in accordance with paragraph 6 above.

General Assembly resolution 39/138

14 December 1984   Meeting 101   Adopted without vote

Approved by Third Committee (A/39/707) without vote, 5 December (meeting 60); 7-nation draft (A/C.3/39/L.70), orally revised; agenda item 98.

Sponsors: Belgium, Canada, Finland, Germany, Federal Republic of, Italy, Jamaica, Japan.

Meeting numbers. GA 39th session: 3rd Committee 44-52, 56, 57, 60; plenary 101.

Other measures to advance human rights

Advisory services

In 1984, under the United Nations programme of advisory services in human rights, experts provided advisory services to Bolivia and Uganda (see below).

The Secretary-General reported[45] that, out of 73 governmental nominations received during the year, recommendations were made to award 30 individual human rights fellowships from 27 countries. He also reported that no training course was organized under the programme.

On 13 March 1984,[46] the Commission on Human Rights, having considered the Secretary-General's report on the 1983 activities under the programme,[47] expressed appreciation for his efforts to provide advisory assistance to Governments requesting it, asked him to continue to do so and further asked that, in his next report, he outline suggestions for a long-term programme of advisory services.

Bolivia

In keeping with a March 1983 request of the Commission on Human Rights to provide advisory services and other forms of human rights assistance as might be requested by the constitutional Government of Bolivia, as endorsed by the Economic and Social Council in May of that year,[48] the Secretary-General had invited Héctor Gros Espiell (Uruguay), the Special Envoy who had conducted a study of the human rights situation in Bolivia, to ascertain the assistance to be offered and that country's views on the matter. The Special Envoy did so by visiting Bolivia from 8 to 13 December 1983.

In his report to the Commission, transmitted by a January 1984 Secretariat note,[49] the Special Envoy recommended that the Secretary-General offer, through the United Nations Centre for Human Rights, assistance in the preparation of a programme of teaching human rights at the primary, secondary and higher levels of education. A seminar on the propagation and analysis of human rights in Bolivia was to form the starting point for the general reorganization of education in the country, for which the co-operation of UNESCO and of non-governmental academic or scientific institutions was to be sought. Other areas recommended for advisory and other assistance related to the country's economic and social conditions adversely affecting the effective enjoyment of human rights. Such areas included planning prison reform, presenting Bolivia's case for assistance to the international community in the best possible way, and assessing the extent of extreme poverty in the country and its implications for economic planning and social policies.

The report noted that efforts to obtain international assistance had been set in motion by two round-table meetings sponsored by Bolivia and the Secretary-General, one held at La Paz from 20 to 22 April 1983 and another on 2 April 1984.

On 13 March,[50] the Commission commended the Secretary-General for his initiative in studying an adequate way of providing United Nations assistance to Bolivia, expressed gratitude to the Special Envoy for effectively fulfilling his mandate and endorsed his recommendations for strengthening implementation of human rights and fundamental freedoms in that country. The Commission recommended a draft text which served as the basis for the Economic and Social Council resolution below.

ECONOMIC AND SOCIAL COUNCIL ACTION

On 24 May 1984, the Economic and Social Council, acting without vote on the recommendation of its Second Committee, adopted resolution 1984/32.

Advisory services in the field of human rights: assistance to the Government of Bolivia

The Economic and Social Council,

Bearing in mind Commission on Human Rights resolution 1984/43 of 13 March 1984,

Conscious of the role that the United Nations can play in promoting, protecting and strengthening human rights and fundamental freedoms throughout the world,

Bearing in mind the request by the Government of Bolivia for assistance in strengthening human rights and fundamental freedoms in that country,

1. *Requests* the Secretary-General, under the programme of advisory services in the field of human rights and in consultation with the Government of Bolivia, to examine ways and means and possible resources for rapid implementation of the projects suggested by the Special Envoy of the Commission on Human Rights in his report on assistance to Bolivia, considered by the Commission on Human Rights at its fortieth session;

2. *Invites* all Member States, United Nations organizations and humanitarian and non-governmental organizations to provide support and assistance to the Government of Bolivia in its efforts to strengthen the enjoyment of human rights and fundamental freedoms in that country;

3. *Specially invites* the International Labour Organisation, the Food and Agriculture Organization of the United Nations, the United Nations Educational, Scientific and Cultural Organization and the World Health Organization to provide the Government of Bolivia with the assistance required, in keeping with the means available to them and their spheres of competence;

4. *Requests* the Commission on Human Rights to consider this question at its forty-first session, in the light of the Secretary-General's report on the implementation of the present resolution.

Economic and Social Council resolution 1984/32

24 May 1984   Meeting 20   Adopted without vote

Approved by Second Committee (E/1984/91) without vote, 17 May (meeting 15); draft by Commission on Human Rights (E/1984/14); agenda item 10.

Equatorial Guinea

In 1984, the United Nations reiterated its offer to assist Equatorial Guinea to restore human rights in the country, in accordance with a plan of action prepared by the Secretary-General in 1981 based on the recommendations of a United Nations expert.[51] As requested by the Economic and Social Council in May 1983,[52] the Secretary-General reported[53] to the February/March 1984 session of the Commission on Human Rights that he had received no response to his request for information from Equatorial Guinea on measures it envisaged and assistance it required from the United Nations for further implementation of the plan of action. In the circumstances, no further action had been taken.

Taking note of the Secretary-General's report on 14 March,[54] the Commission recommended a draft text which served as the basis for the Council resolution below.

ECONOMIC AND SOCIAL COUNCIL ACTION

A letter of 15 April 1984 from Equatorial Guinea[55] was among the documents considered by the Economic and Social Council in the context of the situation of human rights in that country. The letter requested the circulation of a note verbale of 28 February from the Minister of State for Foreign Affairs and Co-operation, expressing gratitude for United Nations efforts on behalf of Equatorial Guinea and outlining the steps taken to restore human rights and fundamental freedoms, in particular the right of the population to participate in the management of the country's public affairs. These included approval of basic decree-laws for the country's judicial system and administration at the village, town and national levels, and elections and appointments to the corresponding administrative bodies. The Minister urged the international community to provide increased assistance, especially through the United Nations, to hasten the country's economic recovery and to support training programmes in education, health, public administration, international relations and communications.

On 24 May, acting on the recommendation of its Second Committee, the Economic and Social Council adopted without vote resolution 1984/36.

Situation of human rights in Equatorial Guinea

The Economic and Social Council,

Recalling its resolutions 1982/36 of 7 May 1982 and 1983/35 of 27 May 1983,

Bearing in mind Commission on Human Rights resolution 1984/51 of 14 March 1984,

Considering that there has been no major change in the situation of human rights in Equatorial Guinea since the events of 3 August 1979,

Noting that it has not been possible to implement all the recommendations contained in its resolution 1983/35,

1. *Urges* the Government of Equatorial Guinea to co-operate with the Secretary-General in order to ensure the full enjoyment of human rights and fundamental freedoms in that country;

2. *Requests* the Secretary-General to appoint an expert to visit Equatorial Guinea in order to study, in conjunction with the Government of that country, the best way of implementing the plan of action proposed by the United Nations;

3. *Requests* the Commission on Human Rights to keep this matter under consideration at its forty-first session.

Economic and Social Council resolution 1984/36

24 May 1984   Meeting 20   Adopted without vote

Approved by Second Committee (E/1984/91) without vote, 17 May (meeting 16); draft by Commission on Human Rights (E/1984/14); agenda item 10.

Other action. In accordance with the Council's May request (see above), the Secretary-General designated Fernando Volio Jiménez (Costa Rica), who went on a mission to Equatorial Guinea between 13 and 20 November, where he held consultations with government officials. His report was to be submitted to the Commission on Human Rights in 1985.

Uganda

Pursuant to a March 1983 request of the Commission on Human Rights,[56] the Secretary-General reported[57] to it in 1984 on his continuing negotiations with Uganda to ascertain the most appropriate methods of providing it with human rights assistance. He stated that he had advised Uganda of the positive response of UNDP and UNESCO to that country's interest in obtaining assistance to restore the law library for its High Court and Ministry of Justice, to secure the services of an expert to revise the country's laws and to train prison officers.

The Secretary-General also transmitted information received, as of 31 December 1983, in reply to his notes verbales inviting support for Uganda's efforts to continue guaranteeing the enjoyment of human rights and fundamental freedoms. The information came from eight Governments, five United Nations bodies, three specialized agencies and five NGOs.

On 13 March 1984,[58] the Commission, having considered the report of the Secretary-General, requested him to remain in contact with Uganda and, while providing it with all possible assistance within the framework of the advisory services programme, to identify and bring to its attention external sources from which it could draw assistance. The Commission invited States, United Nations bodies and agencies, as well as humanitarian and non-governmental organizations, to lend their support to Uganda, and commended those which had provided such support.

Technical assistance to strengthen legal institutions

On 29 August 1984,[59] the Sub-Commission, convinced that the strengthening of legal institutions was a prerequisite for promoting human rights, asked the Secretary-General to invite Governments receiving UNDP aid to indicate their needs with respect to: establishment or strengthening of law faculties, development of adequate law libraries, training of judges, drafting of legal texts in conformity with provisions of international instruments on human rights, publication of official law journals, and collection and classification of legal material, including legislation and digests of court decisions.

The information requested was to be followed up by UNDP resident representatives, each with the Government of his duty station. The Secretary-General was to request Governments, United Nations specialized agencies and regional organizations dispensing official development assistance to indicate the extent to which they were providing or were willing to provide assistance in the areas mentioned. He was also to submit to the Sub-Commission in 1985 a report based on the information received, with a copy to the Special Rapporteur on the independence of judges, lawyers, jurors and assessors (see above, under "Civil and political rights").

Responsibility to promote and protect human rights

Draft declaration

On 16 March 1984,[60] the Commission on Human Rights, recalling its decision of March 1983[56] to undertake work in 1985 on a draft declaration on the right and responsibility of individuals, groups and organs of society to promote and protect universally recognized human rights and fundamental freedoms, decided to establish an open-ended working group to draft such a declaration. The group would be allocated appropriate time to meet during the Commission's 1985 session.

Draft body of principles and guidelines

ECONOMIC AND SOCIAL COUNCIL ACTION

On 24 May 1984, following approval of a Commission on Human Rights recommendation of 15 March[61] by the Second Committee of the Economic and Social Council, the Council adopted without vote resolution 1984/38.

Draft body of principles and guidelines on the right and responsibility of individuals, groups and organs of society to promote and protect human rights and fundamental freedoms

The Economic and Social Council,

Recalling Commission on Human Rights resolution 1983/31 of 8 March 1983 and resolution 1982/24 of 8 September 1982 of the Sub-Commission on Prevention of Discrimination and Protection of Minorities, by which the Sub-Commission, *inter alia,* requested Mrs. Erica-Irene A. Daes to prepare draft principles on the right and responsibility of individuals, groups and organs of society to promote and protect universally recognized human rights and fundamental freedoms,

Mindful of Sub-Commission resolution 1983/40 of 7 September 1983 and Commission on Human Rights resolution 1984/56 of 15 March 1984,

Expressing its deep appreciation to the Special Rapporteur, Mrs. Erica-Irene A. Daes, for the work she has thus far accomplished in connection with the important elaboration of a study on draft principles on the right and responsibility of individuals, groups and organs of society to promote and protect universally recognized human rights and fundamental freedoms,

1. *Requests* the Special Rapporteur to continue her work on the above-mentioned study with a view to submitting, if possible, her final report to the Sub-Commission on Prevention of Discrimination and Protection of Minorities at its thirty-seventh session;

2. *Requests* the Secretary-General to transmit the relevant questionnaire, which will be prepared by the Special Rapporteur on the basis of the above-mentioned resolutions, and the comments made by the members of the Sub-Commission to Governments, specialized agencies, regional organizations, intergovernmental organizations and non-governmental organizations for their comments and replies;

3. *Further requests* the Secretary-General to give the Special Rapporteur all the assistance she may require in her work.

Economic and Social Council resolution 1984/38

| 24 May 1984 | Meeting 20 | Adopted without vote |

Approved by Second Committee (E/1984/91) without vote, 17 May (meeting 16); draft by Commission on Human Rights (E/1984/14); agenda item 10.

Sub-Commission action. In response to the Council's request (see above) for a final report on the study to the Sub-Commission, possibly in 1984, Special Rapporteur Erica-Irene A. Daes (Greece) submitted a preliminary report,[62] indicating that, as of 12 July, replies to the questionnaire on the study had been received from seven Governments, nine specialized agencies, three intergovernmental regional organizations and 20 NGOs. In view of the lack of a sufficient number of substantive replies from Governments, the Special Rapporteur considered it appropriate to postpone further elaboration of the study and body of principles until 1985; to finalize them, she indicated that she would also draw material from relevant studies, reports and resolutions of the United Nations system and consult other sources, including publications of recognized scholars and scientists.

On 28 August,[63] the Sub-Commission, expressing appreciation to the Special Rapporteur for the work she had so far accomplished, requested her to continue elaborating the study and draft body of principles. The Secretary-General was asked, in addition to giving her all the assistance required to carry out her work, to transmit a reminder to Governments and all others concerned to provide her with their views on the matter.

Regional arrangements

As requested by the General Assembly in December 1983,[64] the Secretary-General reported in October 1984[65] on replies to his invitation for comments concerning information exchanges between the United Nations and the regional organizations for the promotion and protection of human rights and on ways and means of furthering such exchanges. The report reproduced the replies received as at 13 September from three specialized agencies, two regional commissions and two regional intergovernmental organizations.

GENERAL ASSEMBLY ACTION

Acting without vote on the recommendation of the Third Committee, the General Assembly adopted resolution 39/115 on 14 December 1984.

Regional arrangements for the protection of human rights

The General Assembly,

Recalling its resolutions 32/127 of 16 December 1977, 33/167 of 20 December 1978, 34/171 of 17 December 1979, 35/197 of 15 December 1980, 36/154 of 16 December 1981,

37/171 and 37/172 of 17 December 1982 and 38/97 of 16 December 1983 concerning regional arrangements for the promotion and protection of human rights,

Having considered the report of the Secretary-General on regional arrangements for the promotion and protection of human rights,

Reaffirming that regional arrangements for the promotion and protection of human rights may make a major contribution to the effective enjoyment of human rights and fundamental freedoms and that the exchange of information and experience in this field among the regions, within the United Nations system, may be improved,

1. *Takes note* of the report of the Secretary-General;

2. *Expresses its thanks* to the specialized agencies, the regional commissions and the intergovernmental regional organizations which contributed to the preparation of that report;

3. *Requests* the Secretary-General to consider the possibility of encouraging contacts between representatives of regional bodies and United Nations bodies entrusted with the promotion of human rights with a view to exchanging information and experience in this field;

4. *Requests* the Commission on Human Rights, when considering the item on its agenda entitled "Advisory services in the field of human rights", to pay special attention to the most appropriate ways of assisting, at their request, the countries of the different regions under the programme of advisory services and to make, where necessary, the relevant recommendations;

5. *Invites* the Secretary-General to submit to the General Assembly at its forty-first session a report on the state of regional arrangements for the promotion and protection of human rights and to include therein the results of action taken in pursuance of the present resolution;

6. *Decides* to consider this question further at its forty-first session.

General Assembly resolution 39/115

14 December 1984   Meeting 101   Adopted without vote

Approved by Third Committee (A/39/700) without vote, 6 December (meeting 64); 11-nation draft (A/C.3/39/L.78); agenda item 12.
Sponsors: Australia, Austria, Belgium, Colombia, Costa Rica, Cyprus, Italy, Netherlands, Senegal, Togo, Uruguay.
Meeting numbers. GA 39th session: 3rd Committee 54-56, 58, 59, 61, 64; plenary 101.

Asia and the Pacific

In April 1984, the Secretary-General submitted to the General Assembly through the Economic and Social Council a report, with a later addendum,[66] containing comments received from six Governments—all members of the Economic and Social Commission for Asia and the Pacific—on the 1982 Seminar on National, Local and Regional Arrangements for the Promotion and Protection of Human Rights in the Asian Region.[67] The report was submitted pursuant to a 1982 General Assembly request.[68]

ECONOMIC AND SOCIAL COUNCIL ACTION

On the recommendation of its Second Committee, the Economic and Social Council adopted without vote resolution 1984/40 on 24 May 1984.

Regional arrangements for the promotion and protection of human rights

The Economic and Social Council,

Recalling General Assembly resolutions 34/171 of 17 December 1979, 35/197 of 15 December 1980 and 36/154 of 16 December 1981 on regional arrangements for the promotion and protection of human rights,

Recalling also General Assembly resolution 37/171 of 17 December 1982, by which the Assembly requested the Secretary-General to transmit the report of the Seminar on National, Local and Regional Arrangements for the Protection of Human Rights in the Asian Region, held at Colombo from 21 June to 2 July 1982, to States members of the Economic and Social Commission for Asia and the Pacific and to invite their comments thereon,

1. *Takes note* of the report of the Secretary-General on regional arrangements for the promotion and protection of human rights and the comments of States members of the Economic and Social Commission for Asia and the Pacific annexed thereto;

2. *Requests* States members of the Economic and Social Commission for Asia and the Pacific region that have not yet done so to communicate their comments on the report of the Seminar on National, Local and Regional Arrangements for the Protection of Human Rights in the Asian Region to the Secretary-General in time for submission to the General Assembly at its thirty-ninth session;

3. *Requests* the Secretary-General to transmit his report, together with further comments on the Seminar received from States members of the Economic and Social Commission for Asia and the Pacific, to the General Assembly at its thirty-ninth session.

Economic and Social Council resolution 1984/40

24 May 1984   Meeting 20   Adopted without vote

Approved by Second Committee (E/1984/91) without vote, 17 May (meeting 16); 10-nation draft (E/1984/C.2/L.4); agenda item 10.
Sponsors: Australia, Bangladesh, Bhutan, Costa Rica, India, Nepal, New Zealand, Pakistan, Papua New Guinea, Sri Lanka.

GENERAL ASSEMBLY ACTION

On 14 December 1984, acting without vote on the recommendation of the Third Committee, the General Assembly adopted resolution 39/116.

Regional arrangements for the promotion and protection of human rights in the Asian region

The General Assembly,

Recalling its resolutions 34/171 of 17 December 1979, 35/197 of 15 December 1980, 36/154 of 16 December 1981 and 37/171 of 17 December 1982,

Having considered the report of the Seminar on National, Local and Regional Arrangements for the Promotion and Protection of Human Rights in the Asian Region, held at Colombo from 21 June to 2 July 1982,

1. *Takes note* of the report of the Secretary-General on regional arrangements for the promotion and protection of human rights;

2. *Takes note with appreciation* of the comments received from Member States in the Asian and Pacific region on the report of the Seminar on National, Local and Regional Arrangements for the Promotion and Protection of Human Rights in the Asian Region;

3. *Invites* States members of the Economic and Social Commission for Asia and the Pacific that have not

yet done so to communicate their comments on the report of the Seminar to the Secretary-General as early as possible so that further consultations may be held;

4. *Requests* the Secretary-General to report to the General Assembly at its forty-first session, through the Economic and Social Council, on the responses received;

5. *Decides* to consider this question further at its forty-first session.

General Assembly resolution 39/116

14 December 1984   Meeting 101   Adopted without vote

Approved by Third Committee (A/39/700) without vote, 6 December (meeting 64); 12-nation draft (A/C.3/39/L.81); agenda item 12.

Sponsors: Australia, Bangladesh, Bhutan, Cyprus, Fiji, India, Nepal, New Zealand, Pakistan, Papua New Guinea, Samoa, Sri Lanka.

Meeting numbers. GA 39th session: 3rd Committee 54-56, 58, 59, 61, 64; plenary 101.

Public information activities

In a January 1984 report to the Commission on Human Rights,[69] the Secretary-General stated that public information activities in human rights, carried out by the United Nations system world-wide, included press, radio, television and photographic coverage of interviews, meetings and debates on human rights issues in various forums. Human rights topics were given extensive coverage in the Organization's major publications, and texts of international human rights instruments were disseminated in languages other than the official United Nations languages. Seminars, briefings and round-table conferences were held, and promotional brochures, pamphlets and posters distributed. The Secretary-General also outlined a series of future activities.

On 15 March,[70] the Commission took note of the Secretary-General's report and proposals. It invited comments on those proposals and requested Governments to facilitate publicity of United Nations human rights activities. It requested the Secretary-General to take measures to enhance and further develop the promotional and public information activities of the Centre for Human Rights, and to continue to keep the Commission informed of United Nations promotional activities, including the programme for disseminating international human rights instruments.

On 9 August, the Sub-Commission set in motion a study on the implications for human rights of recent advances in computer and micro-computer technology, with particular attention to the potential use of such technology for disseminating international human rights instruments and other information (see below, under "Other human rights questions").

In resolution 39/98 B, the General Assembly underlined the importance of efforts made to implement the principles set forth in the 1978 UNESCO Declaration on Fundamental Principles concerning the Contribution of the Mass Media to Strengthening Peace and International Understanding, to the Promotion of Human Rights and to Countering Racialism, *Apartheid* and Incitement to War.

REFERENCES

[1]YUN 1983, p. 865. [2]E/CN.4/1984/73. [3]YUN 1978, p. 711. [4]E/1984/14 (res. 1984/59). [5]A/C.3/39/L.53. [6]A/C.3/39/L.59. [7]YUN 1977, p. 734, GA res. 32/130, 16 Dec. 1977. [8]YUN 1948-49, p. 535, GA res. 217 A (III), 10 Dec. 1948. [9]YUN 1983, p. 862, GA res. 38/123, 16 Dec. 1983. [10]A/39/556 & Add.1. [11]YUN 1983, p. 861. [12]E/1984/14 (dec. 1984/101). [13]YUN 1983, p. 866. [14]E/1984/14 (dec. 1984/115). [15]Ibid. (dec. 1984/113). [16]Ibid. (dec. 1984/103). [17]YUN 1983, p. 867. [18]E/1984/14 & Corr.1 (res. 1984/60). [19]E/CN.4/Sub.2/1984/3. [20]E/CN.4/1985/3 (res. 1984/37). [21]Ibid. (dec. 1984/103). [22]Ibid. (dec. 1984/105). [23]YUN 1965, p. 494. [24]E/CN.4/1984/L.23. [25]E/CN.4/1984/L.102. [26]E/CN.4/1984/L.90. [27]E/CN.4/-L.89. [28]E/1984/14 (dec. 1984/112). [29]YUN 1979, p. 854. [30]YUN 1966, p. 419, GA res. 2200 A (XXI), annex, 16 Dec. 1966. [31]YUN 1965, p. 440, GA res. 2106 A (XX), annex, 21 Dec. 1965. [32]YUN 1948-49, p. 959, GA res. 260 A (III), annex, 9 Dec. 1948. [33]YUN 1973, p. 103, GA res. 3068(XXVIII), annex, 30 Nov. 1973. [34]YUN 1953, p. 411, GA res. 794(VIII), 23 Oct. 1953. [35]YUN 1956, p. 228. [36]YUN 1948-49, p. 613, GA res. 317(IV), annex, 2 Dec. 1949. [37]YUN 1979, p. 895, GA res. 34/180, annex, 18 Dec. 1979. [38]E/CN.4/Sub.2/1984/26. [39]E/CN.4/Sub.2/1984/27 & 39. [40]E/CN.4/1985/3 (res. 1984/36). [41]E/CN.4/1984/39. [42]A/39/484. [43]YUN 1983, p. 864, GA res. 38/117, 16 Dec. 1983. [44]Ibid., p. 817. [45]E/CN.4/1985/36. [46]E/1984/14 (res. 1984/44). [47]YUN 1983, p. 868. [48]Ibid., ESC dec. 1983/146, 27 May 1983. [49]E/CN.4/1984/46. [50]E/1984/14 (res. 1984/43). [51]YUN 1981, p. 938. [52]YUN 1983, p. 868, ESC res. 1983/35, 27 May 1983. [53]E/CN.4/1984/27. [54]E/1984/14 (res. 1984/51). [55]E/1984/C.2/1. [56]YUN 1983, p. 869. [57]E/CN.4/1984/45. [58]E/1984/14 (res. 1984/45). [59]E/CN.4/1985/3 (res. 1984/19). [60]E/1984/14 (dec. 1984/116). [61]Ibid. (res. 1984/56). [62]E/CN.4/Sub.2/1984/30. [63]E/CN.4/1985/3 (res. 1984/3). [64]YUN 1983, p. 870, GA res. 38/97, 16 Dec. 1983. [65]A/39/570. [66]A/39/174-E/1984/38 & Add.1. [67]YUN 1982, p. 1106. [68]Ibid., p. 1107, GA res. 37/171, 17 Dec. 1982. [69]E/CN.4/1984/23. [70]E/1984/14 (res. 1984/58).

Human rights violations

Situations involving alleged violations of human rights on a large scale in several countries were again examined in 1984 by the General Assembly, the Economic and Social Council and the Commission on Human Rights, as well as by special bodies and officials appointed to examine some of those situations.

In addition, situations of alleged human rights violations involving the self-determination of peoples (see above, under "Civil and political rights") were discussed with regard to Afghanistan, Grenada, Kampuchea, South Africa and Namibia, Western Sahara and the Palestinian people. The Commission also dealt with the human rights situation in Bolivia, Equatorial Guinea and Uganda, to which the United Nations provided advisory services (see above, under "Advancement of human rights").

Under a procedure established in 1970 by the Council to deal with communications alleging denial or violation of human rights,[1] the Commission held closed meetings in 1984 to study confidential documents, observations thereon submitted by Governments concerned and a confidential report by a working group set up in 1983[2] to examine the material. As announced by its Chairman on 6 March 1984, the Commission had taken confidential action with regard to Albania, Argentina, Benin, Haiti, Indonesia (East Timor), Malaysia, Pakistan, Paraguay, the Philippines, Turkey and Uruguay. By a decision adopted at a closed meeting on 6 March, and agreed to be made public the same day,[3] the Commission set up a similar working group for 1985, subject to Council approval.

ECONOMIC AND SOCIAL COUNCIL ACTION

Acting without vote on the recommendation of its Second Committee, the Economic and Social Council in May 1984 adopted decision 1984/145.

General decision concerning the establishment of a working group of the Commission on Human Rights to examine situations referred to the Commission under Economic and Social Council resolution 1503(XLVIII) and those situations of which the Commission is seized

At its 20th plenary meeting, on 24 May 1984, the Council approved the decision of the Commission on Human Rights, in its decision 1984/114 of 6 March 1984, to set up a working group composed of five of its members to meet for one week prior to the forty-first session to examine such particular situations as might be referred to the Commission by the Sub-Commission on Prevention of Discrimination and Protection of Minorities at its thirty-seventh session under Council resolution 1503(XLVIII) and those situations of which the Commission is seized.

Economic and Social Council decision 1984/145

Adopted without vote

Approved by Second Committee (E/1984/91) without vote, 17 May (meeting 16); draft by Commission on Human Rights (E/1984/14); agenda item 10.

GENERAL ASSEMBLY ACTION

In resolution 39/145 on alternative approaches for improving the enjoyment of human rights, the General Assembly reiterated once again that the international community should continue to accord priority to the search for solutions to mass and flagrant violations of human rights of peoples and individuals, paying due attention also to other situations of human rights violations. It reaffirmed its responsibility for achieving international co-operation in promoting and encouraging respect for human rights and fundamental freedoms for all and expressed its concern at serious and in particular mass and flagrant violations, wherever they occurred.

Africa

South Africa and Namibia

Working Group report. The six-member *Ad Hoc* Working Group of Experts on Southern Africa, established in 1967 by the Commission on Human Rights,[4] met at Geneva from 3 to 13 January 1984 when it adopted a progress report on developments concerning policies and practices violating human

rights in South Africa and Namibia.[5] The report was based on an analysis of published information, including relevant international instruments and United Nations resolutions, and of oral testimony and written communications provided by individuals and organizations during the Group's mission of inquiry to London from 23 to 27 May 1983.

The report noted that, in keeping with a February 1983 Commission request,[6] the United Nations Centre for Human Rights had addressed a letter to South Africa asking that the Group be allowed to conduct on-the-spot investigations of the living conditions and of the treatment of prisoners in South Africa and Namibia. South Africa had replied on 9 January 1984 that it was unable to extend such co-operation, in the light of what it called the Group's bias and of investigations frequently conducted by its own judicial and medical authorities and by ICRC.

The Group reported on a wide range of human rights violations resulting from *apartheid* and racial discrimination, including South Africa's "homelands" policy and forced removals of population; legislation providing for capital punishment, the killing of civilians by police "acting in the execution of their duties" and arbitrary searches, indefinite detention without trial and appeal, torture of detainees and political prisoners, and bannings; denial of the right to work and freedom of association; and infringements of trade union rights, the farm labour system and forced child labour. Legislation limiting the right to education and freedom of expression was described, as was opposition to such limitations by black students and white universities and by journalists. Instances of violations of the territorial integrity of States bordering South Africa by the South African armed forces were also reported.

The Group updated the list of persons deemed responsible for the crime of *apartheid* or for a serious human rights violation. It also summarized the substantive comments of States on the Group's 1981 study and draft statute of an international penal tribunal for the suppression and punishment of the crime of *apartheid*,[7] to be established under an additional protocol to the 1973 Convention against *apartheid* (see below).

The Group's conclusions and recommendations were to be submitted in a final report in 1985. That report would also contain an examination of the question of the criminal effects of *apartheid* amounting to a policy bordering on genocide.

Action by the Commission on Human Rights. By a vote of 42 to none, with 1 abstention, taken on 28 February 1984,[8] the Commission expressed appreciation for the progress report of the Working Group. It also expressed abhorrence of the system of *apartheid* and indignation at the scale and variety of human rights violations in South Africa, in particular the increased number of sentences and executions, the torture of political activists during interrogation, the ill-treatment of captured freedom fighters and other detainees, the deaths of detainees under suspicious circumstances, forced population removals and the increase in prosecutions under the Bantu "homelands" policy laws. The Commission called for the release of all political prisoners and again requested South Africa to allow an on-the-spot investigation by the Group of the living conditions and treatment of prisoners in the country.

The Commission condemned South Africa for its military attacks on neighbouring States, demanding their immediate cessation, and reaffirmed the unacceptability of any constitutional arrangement serving to perpetuate *apartheid*. In addition to requesting the Secretary-General to renew his invitation for States' comments on the Group's interim study on a proposed international penal tribunal for the punishment of the crime of *apartheid*, the Commission asked the Group to continue its study and bring to the Commission's attention in 1985 human rights violations in South Africa and Namibia. It decided to transmit the Group's findings on the violation of trade union rights to the Economic and Social Council for action.

Deeply disturbed by the gross violations of human rights in Namibia as reported by the Group, the Commission, by a vote of 39 to none, with 4 abstentions, taken also on 28 February,[9] reaffirmed the inalienable right of the Namibian people to self-determination and independence and to the rights enshrined in the 1948 Universal Declaration of Human Rights and other relevant international instruments. It condemned South Africa for its increasing oppression of the Namibians, including torture and ill-treatment of detainees and captured freedom fighters, and the massive militarization of the Territory. The Commission requested the Group to continue inquiries concerning any person who might have committed the crime of *apartheid* or a serious violation of human rights in Namibia, and renewed its request to South Africa to allow an on-the-spot investigation of prison conditions and treatment of prisoners in Namibia.

ECONOMIC AND SOCIAL COUNCIL ACTION

Acting on the recommendation of its Second Committee, the Economic and Social Council adopted decision 1984/129 by recorded vote.

Violations of human rights in southern Africa: report of the *Ad Hoc* Working Group of Experts
At its 20th plenary meeting, on 24 May 1984, the Council, noting Commission on Human Rights resolution 1984/5 of 28 February 1984, took note of the findings on the violation of trade union rights in South Africa contained in the progress report of the *Ad Hoc* Working Group of Experts on southern Africa, and endorsed the Commission's request to the *Ad Hoc* Working Group of Experts to continue its study and to bring to the attention of the Commission at its forty-first ses-

sion violations of human rights in South Africa and Namibia.

Economic and Social Council decision 1984/129
52-0-1 (recorded vote)

Approved by Second Committee (E/1984/91) by vote (49-0-1), 17 May (meeting 16); draft by Commission on Human Rights (E/1984/14); agenda item 10.

Recorded vote in Council as follows:

In favour: Algeria, Argentina, Austria, Benin, Botswana, Brazil, Bulgaria, Canada, China, Colombia, Congo, Costa Rica, Djibouti, Ecuador, Finland, France, German Democratic Republic, Germany, Federal Republic of, Greece, Indonesia, Japan, Lebanon, Liberia, Luxembourg, Malaysia, Mali, Mexico, Netherlands, New Zealand, Pakistan, Papua New Guinea, Poland, Portugal, Qatar, Romania, Rwanda, Saint Lucia, Saudi Arabia, Sierra Leone, Somalia, Sri Lanka, Suriname, Swaziland, Sweden, Thailand, Tunisia, Uganda, USSR, United Kingdom, Venezuela, Yugoslavia, Zaire.
Against: None.
Abstaining: United States.

The United States explained that it fully shared the concerns that inspired the decision and that it abstained solely on the basis of financial considerations.

Sub-Commission action. On 30 August 1984,[10] the Sub-Commission, by 16 votes to none, with 2 abstentions, reaffirmed that *apartheid* was an international crime and repudiated all efforts towards its perpetuation by the illegitimate South African régime, including the so-called new constitution and elections held in August. The Sub-Commission condemned the mass arrests of political activists, workers and students before and after those elections. It demanded the cessation of the campaign of mass terror in South Africa and Namibia against those trying to exercise their civil and political rights. It further demanded the release of all political prisoners, including all persons subjected to banning, house arrest and banishment, and of those recently arrested for their opposition to the so-called elections. The Sub-Commission requested the Secretary-General to give this resolution the widest possible dissemination.

GENERAL ASSEMBLY ACTION

In resolution 39/21 on the CERD report, the General Assembly strongly condemned the policy of *apartheid* in South Africa and Namibia as a crime against humanity and urged all Member States to adopt effective political, economic and other measures in conformity with United Nations resolutions in order *inter alia* to secure the elimination of the racist *apartheid* system.

Other action. On 20 August 1984, CERD (see above, under "Discrimination") strongly condemned the policy of *apartheid*, racial discrimination and the continuous violations of human rights and fundamental freedoms inflicted by the South African Government on the people of Namibia.

1973 Convention against apartheid

As at 31 December 1984, there were 79 parties to the 1973 International Convention on the Suppression and Punishment of the Crime of *Apartheid*.[11] In 1984, Maldives and Togo acceded to the Convention.

In his annual report to the General Assembly on the status of the Convention,[12] the Secretary-General annexed a list of States that had signed, ratified or acceded to it as at 1 September.

Activities of the Group of Three. The Group of Three—established under article IX of the Convention to consider reports by States parties on measures taken to implement the Convention's provisions, and in 1984 composed of Bulgaria, Mexico and the Syrian Arab Republic—held its seventh session at Geneva from 30 January to 3 February 1984.[13]

At that session, the Group examined initial reports from El Salvador, the Philippines and Rwanda; second reports from Cape Verde, Egypt, Mongolia and Tunisia; third reports from the Byelorussian SSR and Qatar; and a fourth report from Hungary. The examination took place in the presence of representatives of the reporting States, except Cape Verde, Qatar and Tunisia. Submitted in 1984 but scheduled for consideration the following year were reports from Algeria, the Byelorussian SSR, Cuba, Madagascar, the USSR and Yugoslavia.

Also examined was the question of whether actions of transnational corporations (TNCs) operating in South Africa came under the definition of the crime of *apartheid* and whether legal action could be taken under the Convention. It was the Group's opinion that international criminal responsibility could apply, as provided for under article III of the Convention. It felt, however, that further examination was needed, in connection with which States' views on the matter would be highly useful.

The Group expressed appreciation to the representatives of the reporting States for their participation in its work, a practice which it considered constructive and should be continued. It called on States parties to submit their periodic reports, to adhere to the reporting guidelines and to provide more information under article IV on measures to suppress *apartheid* and on the prosecution of persons responsible for acts of *apartheid* as defined in article II, including difficulties encountered in taking such measures, and on implementation of article XI on the extradition of such persons in accordance with legislation and treaties in force, as well as on measures taken in teaching and education for the fuller implementation of the Convention.

The Group recommended to the Commission on Human Rights that States be urged to ratify or accede to the Convention, and that the United Nations and other international organizations be asked to intensify dissemination of information on problems of racial discrimination in general and *apartheid* in particular. It further recommended that the States parties be invited to express their views on the extent to which TNCs were responsible for the continued existence of the system of *apartheid* in South Africa and be asked to strengthen their co-operation in implementing United Nations resolutions on *apartheid*. It drew their attention to the desirability of disseminating more information about the Convention and the Group's work.

Action by the Commission on Human Rights. By a vote of 32 to 1, with 10 abstentions, taken on 28 February 1984,[14] the Commission took note of the Group of Three's report and its recommendations, including those pertaining to the reporting obligations of States parties to the Convention against *apartheid*. The Commission drew attention to the Group's opinion on the applicability of article III of the Convention to TNC actions in South Africa and asked the Group to continue examining the question. It reiterated its request to the Secretary-General to invite States parties' views on the 1981 interim study of international machinery for punishment of the crime of *apartheid*[7] by the *Ad Hoc* Working Group of Experts on Southern Africa (see above). The Commission requested the Secretary-General to provide the Group, which would meet for not more than five days prior to the 1985 Commission session, with all the necessary assistance.

GENERAL ASSEMBLY ACTION

On 23 November 1984, acting on the recommendation of the Third Committee, the General Assembly adopted resolution 39/19 by recorded vote.

Status of the International Convention on the Suppression and Punishment of the Crime of *Apartheid*

The General Assembly,

Recalling its resolution 3068(XXVIII) of 30 November 1973, by which it adopted and opened for signature and ratification the International Convention on the Suppression and Punishment of the Crime of *Apartheid*, and its subsequent resolutions on the status of the Convention,

Reaffirming its conviction that *apartheid* constitutes a total negation of the purposes and principles of the Charter of the United Nations, a gross violation of human rights and a crime against humanity, seriously threatening international peace and security,

Convinced that the implementation of the objectives of the Second Decade to Combat Racism and Racial Discrimination proclaimed by its resolution 38/14 of 22 November 1983 and of the Programme of Action adopted by the Second World Conference to Combat Racism and Racial Discrimination will contribute to the final eradication of *apartheid* and all other forms of racism and racial discrimination,

Strongly condemning South Africa's continued policy of *apartheid* and its continued illegal occupation of Namibia, as well as its repeated acts of aggression against sovereign African States, which constitute a manifest breach of international peace and security,

Condemning the continued collaboration of certain States and transnational corporations with the racist régime of South Africa in the political, economic, military and other fields as an encouragement to the intensification of its odious policy of *apartheid*,

Underlining that the strengthening of the existing mandatory arms embargo and the application of comprehensive mandatory economic sanctions under Chapter VII of the Charter are vital in order to compel the racist régime of South Africa to abandon its policy of *apartheid*,

Firmly convinced that the legitimate struggle of the oppressed peoples in southern Africa against *apartheid*, racism and colonialism and for the effective implementation of their inalienable right to self-determination and independence demands more than ever all necessary support by the international community and, in particular, further action by the Security Council,

Underlining that ratification of and accession to the Convention on a universal basis and the implementation of its provisions without any delay are necessary for its effectiveness and would be a useful contribution towards achieving the complete elimination of *apartheid*,

1. *Takes note* of the report of the Secretary-General on the status of the International Convention on the Suppression and Punishment of the Crime of *Apartheid;*

2. *Commends* those States parties to the Convention that have submitted their reports under article VII thereof;

3. *Appeals once again* to those States that have not yet done so to ratify or to accede to the Convention without further delay, in particular those States which have jurisdiction over transnational corporations operating in South Africa and Namibia;

4. *Expresses its appreciation* of the constructive role played by the Group of Three of the Commission on Human Rights, established in accordance with article IX of the Convention, in analysing the periodic reports of States and in publicizing the experience gained in the international struggle against the crime of *apartheid;*

5. *Calls upon* all States parties to the Convention to adopt legislative, judicial and administrative measures to prosecute, bring to trial and punish, in accordance with their jurisdiction, persons responsible for, or accused of, the acts enumerated in article II of the Convention;

6. *Further calls upon* States parties to the Convention to submit their opinions on the extent and the nature of the responsibility of transnational corporations for the continued existence of the system of *apartheid* in South Africa and on the application of article III of the Convention to the activities of those corporations;

7. *Requests* the Commission on Human Rights to intensify, in co-operation with the Special Committee against *Apartheid*, its efforts to compile periodically the progressive list of individuals, organizations, institutions and representatives of States deemed responsible for crimes enumerated in article II of the Convention, as well as those against whom or which legal proceedings have been undertaken;

8. *Requests* the Secretary-General to distribute the above-mentioned list among all States parties to the Convention and all Member States and to bring such facts to the attention of the public by all means of mass communication;

9. *Appeals* to all States, United Nations organs, specialized agencies and international and national non-governmental organizations to step up their activities in enhancing public awareness by denouncing the crimes committed by the racist régime of South Africa;

10. *Requests* the Secretary-General to intensify his efforts, through appropriate channels, to disseminate information on the Convention and its implementation with a view to promoting further ratification of or accession to the Convention;

11. *Requests* the Secretary-General to include in his next annual report under General Assembly resolution 3380(XXX) of 10 November 1975 a special section concerning the implementation of the Convention.

General Assembly resolution 39/19

23 November 1984   Meeting 71   121-1-23 (recorded vote)

Approved by Third Committee (A/39/658) by recorded vote (110-1-23), 8 November (meeting 34); 21-nation draft (A/C.3/39/L.5); agenda item 88 *(c)*.

Sponsors: Afghanistan, Algeria, Angola, Bulgaria, Congo, Cuba, Czechoslovakia, Ethiopia, German Democratic Republic, Guinea, Guinea-Bissau, Hungary, Iran, Lao People's Democratic Republic, Madagascar, Mongolia, Nigeria, Rwanda, Ukrainian SSR, Viet Nam, Zambia.

Meeting numbers. GA 39th session: 3rd Committee 4-15, 27, 34, 35; plenary 71.

Recorded vote in Assembly as follows:

In favour: Afghanistan, Albania, Algeria, Angola, Antigua and Barbuda, Argentina, Bahamas, Bahrain, Bangladesh, Barbados, Benin, Bhutan, Bolivia, Botswana, Brazil, Brunei Darussalam, Bulgaria, Burkina Faso, Burma, Burundi, Byelorussian SSR, Cameroon, Cape Verde, Central African Republic, Chad, Chile, China, Colombia, Comoros, Congo, Costa Rica, Cuba, Cyprus, Czechoslovakia, Democratic Kampuchea, Democratic Yemen, Djibouti, Dominican Republic, Ecuador, Egypt, Equatorial Guinea, Ethiopia, Fiji, Gabon, Gambia, German Democratic Republic, Ghana, Grenada, Guinea, Guinea-Bissau, Guyana, Haiti, Honduras, Hungary, India, Indonesia, Iran, Iraq, Ivory Coast, Jamaica, Jordan, Kenya, Kuwait, Lao People's Democratic Republic, Lebanon, Lesotho, Liberia, Libyan Arab Jamahiriya, Madagascar, Malaysia, Maldives, Mali, Malta, Mauritania, Mexico, Mongolia, Morocco, Mozambique, Nepal, Nicaragua, Niger, Nigeria, Oman, Pakistan, Panama, Papua New Guinea, Peru, Philippines, Poland, Qatar, Romania, Rwanda, Saint Lucia, Samoa, Sao Tome and Principe, Saudi Arabia, Senegal, Sierra Leone, Singapore, Somalia, Sri Lanka, Sudan, Suriname, Syrian Arab Republic, Thailand, Togo, Trinidad and Tobago, Tunisia, Turkey, Uganda, Ukrainian SSR, USSR, United Arab Emirates, United Republic of Tanzania, Uruguay, Venezuela, Viet Nam, Yemen, Yugoslavia, Zaire, Zambia.

Against: United States.

Abstaining: Australia, Austria, Belgium, Canada, Denmark, Finland, France, Germany, Federal Republic of, Greece, Iceland, Ireland, Italy, Japan, Luxembourg, Malawi, Netherlands, New Zealand, Norway, Portugal, Spain, Swaziland, Sweden, United Kingdom.

Austria said it could not endorse measures prejudicial to the rights of the individual. Canada recalled that it had neither signed nor ratified the Convention. Ireland, speaking on behalf of the EEC members, referred to reservations they had expressed on the Convention, which they considered defective on a number of legal grounds; those reservations, however, related not to the Convention's objectives but only to the methods envisaged for achieving them. Ireland added that any step taken in pursuance of the Convention applied only to the States parties. Japan considered certain Convention provisions to be too ambiguous. Portugal explained that, while it supported the resolution's aim, its abstention stemmed from its inability to become party to the Convention because some of its provisions were at variance with Portugal's Constitution.

Uruguay said it supported the elimination of racial discrimination, but it had serious legal difficulties in ratifying the Convention. It also had reservations concerning: the jurisdiction of States parties in respect of acts committed outside their territories by persons not their nationals; the vagueness of the definition of the crime of *apartheid;* and the granting of powers, for the purpose of applying the Convention, to a United Nations body such as the Commission on Human Rights, many of whose mem-

bers had not acceded to the Convention. Chile's
and Turkey's vote was to demonstrate their opposition to *apartheid;* however, Turkey said it was unable to support the text without reservation because
the Convention presented substantial legal difficulties.

Democratic Kampuchea said the text perfectly
expressed its views, paragraph 4 in particular.

Introducing the draft resolution, the German Democratic Republic said a country's position on the Convention was a decisive indicator of its stand in the
struggle for the elimination of *apartheid.* The strengthening of the Convention was an important step in
increasing the effectiveness of measures designed
to eliminate the illegal *apartheid* régime, which could
survive only with the continued collaboration of
certain States and TNCs; that collaboration was
treated by the text as the key issue in the fight against
apartheid.

Foreign support of South Africa

Action by the Commission on Human Rights.
Having noted a July 1983 report of Special Rapporteur Ahmed Mohamed Khalifa (Egypt),[15] containing an updated list of banks, TNCs and other
organizations assisting South Africa, the Commission
on 28 February 1984, by a roll-call vote of 31 to 7,
with 5 abstentions,[16] welcomed the August 1983
decision of its Sub-Commission[15] to mandate the
Special Rapporteur to continue to update the list,
subject to annual review, for submission to the Commission through its Sub-Commission. It again called
on Governments to take legislative, administrative
or other measures so as to put a stop to the activities of their nationals and bodies corporate under
their jurisdiction operating enterprises in South Africa
and Namibia, and to end all technological assistance
or collaboration in the manufacture of arms and
military supplies, in particular in the nuclear field.
It asked the specialized agencies, particularly the
International Monetary Fund and the World Bank,
to refrain from granting any type of loans to the
South African régime.

The Commission called on the States parties to
the Convention against *apartheid* to express their views
on TNC responsibility for the continued existence
of the system of *apartheid* in South Africa.

In other actions, the Commission, also on 28 February, requested the Group of Three (see above) to
continue its examination of whether TNC actions
in South Africa came under the definition of the
crime of *apartheid* and whether legal action could
be taken under the Convention. On 29 February,
in reaffirming the right of the peoples of South Africa
and Namibia to self-determination (see above, under
"Civil and political rights"), the Commission condemned: all collaboration with South Africa, particularly nuclear, military and economic, and
demanded the cessation of such collaboration; the
policies of Western and other countries whose re-

lations with South Africa encouraged its régime to
persist in suppressing peoples' aspirations to self-
determination and independence; and the continuing
activities of foreign economic and other interests
impeding implementation of the 1960 Declaration
on the Granting of Independence to Colonial Countries
and Peoples[17] with respect to colonial Territories,
particularly Namibia.

ECONOMIC AND SOCIAL COUNCIL ACTION

On the recommendation of its Second Committee,
the Economic and Social Council adopted decision
1984/130 by recorded vote.

> **Adverse consequences for the enjoyment
> of human rights of political, military, economic
> and other forms of assistance given to colonial
> and racist régimes in southern Africa**
> At its 20th plenary meeting, on 24 May 1984, the Council,
> noting Commission on Human Rights resolution 1984/6
> of 28 February 1984, endorsed the Commission's deci-
> sion to welcome the decision of the Sub-Commission on
> Prevention of Discrimination and Protection of Minorities
> to mandate the Special Rapporteur, Mr. Ahmed Khalifa,
> to continue to update the list of banks, transnational cor-
> porations and other organizations assisting the colonial
> and racist régime in South Africa, subject to annual review,
> and to submit the revised report to the Commission, through
> the Sub-Commission.

Economic and Social Council decision 1984/130

39-7-7 (recorded vote)

Approved by Second Committee (E/1984/91) by vote (36-6-7), 17 May (meeting 16);
draft by Commission on Human Rights (E/1984/14); agenda item 10.

Recorded vote in Council as follows:

In favour: Algeria, Argentina, Benin, Botswana, Brazil, Bulgaria, China, Colombia,
Congo, Costa Rica, Djibouti, Ecuador, German Democratic Republic, Indonesia,
Lebanon, Liberia, Malaysia, Mali, Mexico, Pakistan, Papua New Guinea, Poland,
Qatar, Romania, Rwanda, Saint Lucia, Saudi Arabia, Sierra Leone, Somalia, Sri
Lanka, Suriname, Swaziland, Thailand, Tunisia, Uganda, USSR, Venezuela, Yugoslavia,
Zaire.

Against: Canada, France, Germany, Federal Republic of, Luxembourg, Netherlands,
United Kingdom, United States.

Abstaining: Austria, Finland, Greece, Japan, New Zealand, Portugal, Sweden.

Report of the Special Rapporteur. In fulfilment
of his mandate, the Special Rapporteur presented
to the Sub-Commission a revised report[18] containing a comprehensive, updated list of banks, TNCs
and other organizations assisting the South African régime. The report was based on material received
before 30 June.

Sub-Commission action. By a vote of 19 to none,
with 1 abstention, taken on 28 August,[19] the Sub-
Commission, having noted the revised report, invited the Special Rapporteur to continue updating the list, using all available material and in co-
operation with the United Nations Centre on TNCs
and the Centre against *Apartheid.* It welcomed the
Commission's call on Governments to put an end
to the activities of enterprises owned and operated
by their nationals or by bodies corporate under their
jurisdiction in South Africa and Namibia.

The Sub-Commission recommended a draft resolution, by which the Commission would call on Governments to give the updated report the widest publicity; invite the Secretary-General to do likewise and to issue the report as a United Nations publication; and request him to give all the assistance required by the Special Rapporteur, including adequate travel funds, with a view to establishing direct contacts with the Centres mentioned, to expand annotation of selected cases and to continue the computerization of future lists.

Communication. On 4 October 1984,[20] Argentina transmitted a 21 September note to the United Nations Centre for Human Rights in connection with the inclusion of Compañía Aerolíneas Argentinas in the Special Rapporteur's 1984 updated list. The note pointed out that the company had stopped operating air services between Argentina and South Africa at the beginning of 1981 and that such information had been brought to the Sub-Commission's attention in 1983. The note therefore requested deletion of the company's name from the list.

GENERAL ASSEMBLY ACTION

Acting on the recommendation of the Third Committee, the Assembly adopted resolution 39/15 by recorded vote on 23 November 1984.

Adverse consequences for the enjoyment of human rights of political, military, economic and other forms of assistance given to the racist and colonialist régime of South Africa

The General Assembly,

Recalling its resolutions 3382(XXX) and 3383(XXX) of 10 November 1975, 33/23 of 29 November 1978, 35/32 of 14 November 1980 and 37/39 of 3 December 1982,

Recalling also its resolutions 3201(S-VI) and 3202(S-VI) of 1 May 1974, containing the Declaration and the Programme of Action on the Establishment of a New International Economic Order, and 3281(XXIX) of 12 December 1974, containing the Charter of Economic Rights and Duties of States,

Mindful of its resolution 3171(XXVIII) of 17 December 1973 relating to permanent sovereignty over natural resources of both developing countries and territories under colonial and foreign domination or subjected to the *apartheid* régime,

Recalling its resolutions on military collaboration with South Africa, as well as Security Council resolutions 418(1977) of 4 November 1977 and 421(1977) of 9 December 1977,

Taking into account, in particular, the relevant decisions adopted by the Assembly of Heads of State and Government of the Organization of African Unity at its nineteenth ordinary session, held at Addis Ababa from 6 to 12 June 1983, and by the Council of Ministers of that organization at its fortieth ordinary session, held at Addis Ababa from 27 February to 5 March 1984,

Taking note of the updated report prepared by the Special Rapporteur of the Sub-Commission on Prevention of Discrimination and Protection of Minorities on the adverse consequences for the enjoyment of human rights of political, military, economic and other forms of assistance given to the racist and colonial régime in southern Africa,

Reaffirming that any collaboration with the racist régime of South Africa constitutes a hostile act against the oppressed peoples of southern Africa in their struggle for freedom and independence and a contemptuous defiance of the United Nations and of the international community,

Considering that such collaboration enables South Africa to acquire the means necessary to carry out acts of aggression and blackmail against independent African States,

Deeply concerned that the major Western and other trading partners of South Africa continue to collaborate with that racist régime and that their collaboration constitutes the main obstacle to the liquidation of that racist régime and the elimination of the inhuman and criminal system of *apartheid,*

Alarmed at the continued collaboration of certain Western States and Israel with the racist régime of South Africa in the nuclear field,

Regretting that the Security Council has not been in a position to take binding decisions to prevent any collaboration in the nuclear field with South Africa,

Affirming that the highest priority must be accorded to international action to secure the full implementation of the resolutions of the United Nations for the eradication of *apartheid* and the liberation of the peoples of southern Africa,

Conscious of the continuing need to mobilize world public opinion against the political, military, economic and other forms of assistance given to the racist and colonialist régime of South Africa,

1. *Reaffirms* the inalienable right of the oppressed peoples of southern Africa to self-determination, independence and the enjoyment of the natural resources of their territories;

2. *Again reaffirms* the right of those same peoples to dispose of those resources for their greater well-being and to obtain just reparation for the exploitation, depletion, loss or depreciation of those natural resources, including reparation for the exploitation and abuse of their human resources;

3. *Vigorously condemns* the collaboration of certain Western States, Israel and other States, as well as the transnational corporations and other organizations which maintain or continue to increase their collaboration with the racist régime of South Africa, especially in the political, economic, military and nuclear fields, thus encouraging that régime to persist in its inhuman and criminal policy of brutal oppression of the peoples of southern Africa and denial of their human rights;

4. *Reaffirms once again* that States and organizations which give assistance to the racist régime of South Africa become accomplices in the inhuman practices of racial discrimination, colonialism and *apartheid* perpetrated by that régime, as well as in the acts of aggression against the liberation movements and neighbouring States;

5. *Requests* the Security Council urgently to consider complete and mandatory sanctions under Chapter VII of the Charter of the United Nations against the racist régime of South Africa, in particular:

(a) The prohibition of all technological assistance or collaboration in the manufacture of arms and military supplies in South Africa;

(b) The cessation of all collaboration with South Africa in the nuclear field;

(c) The prohibition of all loans to, and all investments in, South Africa and the cessation of any trade with South Africa;

(d) An embargo on the supply of petroleum, petroleum products and other strategic goods to South Africa;

6. *Appeals* to all States, specialized agencies and non-governmental organizations to extend all possible co-operation to the liberation movements of southern Africa recognized by the United Nations and the Organization of African Unity;

7. *Expresses its appreciation* to the Special Rapporteur of the Sub-Commission on Prevention of Discrimination and Protection of Minorities for his updated report;

8. *Reaffirms* that the updating of the report on the adverse consequences for the enjoyment of human rights of political, military, economic and other forms of assistance given to the colonial and racist régime in southern Africa is of the greatest importance to the cause of fighting *apartheid* and other violations of human rights in South Africa and Namibia;

9. *Invites* the Special Rapporteur:

(a) To continue to update, subject to annual review, the list of banks, transnational corporations and other organizations assisting the racist and colonialist régime of South Africa, giving such details regarding enterprises listed as the Rapporteur may consider necessary and appropriate, including explanations of responses, if any, and to submit the updated report to the General Assembly at its forty-first session;

(b) To use all available material from other United Nations organs, Member States, national liberation movements recognized by the Organization of African Unity, specialized agencies and other intergovernmental and non-governmental organizations, as well as other relevant sources, in order to indicate the volume, nature and adverse human consequences of the assistance given to the racist régime of South Africa;

(c) To initiate direct contacts with the United Nations Centre on Transnational Corporations and the Centre against *Apartheid* of the Secretariat, with a view to consolidating mutual co-operation in updating his report;

10. *Requests* the Secretary-General to give the Special Rapporteur all the assistance, including adequate travel funds, that he may require in the exercise of his mandate, with a view in particular to establishing direct contacts with the United Nations Centre on Transnational Corporations and the Centre against *Apartheid*, to expanding his work on the annotation of certain selected cases as reflected in the list contained in his report and to continuing the computerization of future updated lists;

11. *Calls upon* the Governments of the countries where the banks, transnational corporations and other organizations named and listed in the updated report are based to take effective action to put a stop to their trading, manufacturing and investing activities in the territory of South Africa as well as in the Territory of Namibia illegally occupied by the racist Pretoria régime;

12. *Urgently requests* all specialized agencies, particularly the International Monetary Fund and the World Bank, to refrain from granting loans or financial assistance of any type to the racist régime of South Africa;

13. *Requests* the Secretary-General to transmit the updated report to the Special Committee against *Apartheid*, the United Nations Council for Namibia, other bodies concerned within the United Nations system and regional international organizations;

14. *Invites* the Secretary-General to give the updated report the widest dissemination, to issue it as a United Nations publication and to make it available to learned societies, research centres, universities, political and humanitarian organizations and other interested groups;

15. *Calls upon* all States, specialized agencies and regional, intergovernmental and other organizations concerned to give wide publicity to the updated report;

16. *Invites* the Commission on Human Rights to give high priority at its forty-first session to the consideration of the updated report;

17. *Decides* to consider at its forty-first session, as a matter of high priority, the item entitled "Adverse consequences for the enjoyment of human rights of political, military, economic and other forms of assistance given to the racist and colonialist régime of South Africa", in the light of any recommendations which the Sub-Commission on Prevention of Discrimination and Protection of Minorities, the Commission on Human Rights, the Economic and Social Council and the Special Committee against *Apartheid* may wish to submit to it.

General Assembly resolution 39/15

23 November 1984   Meeting 71   120-10-14 (recorded vote)

Approved by Third Committee (A/39/654) by recorded vote (104-9-17), 8 November (meeting 34); draft by Ethiopia, for African Group (A/C.3/39/L.7); agenda item 84.
Financial implications. 5th Committee, A/39/681; S-G, A/C.3/39/L.16, A/C.5/39/37.
Meeting numbers. GA 39th session: 3rd Committee 4-15, 27, 34, 35; 5th Committee 32; plenary 71.

Recorded vote in Assembly as follows:

In favour: Afghanistan, Albania, Algeria, Angola, Antigua and Barbuda, Argentina, Bahamas, Bahrain, Bangladesh, Barbados, Benin, Bhutan, Bolivia, Botswana, Brazil, Brunei Darussalam, Bulgaria, Burkina Faso, Burma, Burundi, Byelorussian SSR, Cameroon, Cape Verde, Central African Republic, Chile, China, Colombia, Comoros, Congo, Costa Rica, Cuba, Cyprus, Czechoslovakia, Democratic Kampuchea, Democratic Yemen, Djibouti, Dominican Republic, Ecuador, Egypt, Ethiopia, Fiji, Gabon, Gambia, German Democratic Republic, Ghana, Grenada, Guinea, Guyana, Haiti, Honduras, Hungary, India, Indonesia, Iran, Iraq, Ivory Coast, Jamaica, Jordan, Kenya, Kuwait, Lao People's Democratic Republic, Lebanon, Lesotho, Liberia, Libyan Arab Jamahiriya, Madagascar, Malaysia, Maldives, Mali, Malta, Mauritania, Mexico, Mongolia, Morocco, Mozambique, Nepal, Nicaragua, Niger, Nigeria, Oman, Pakistan, Panama, Papua New Guinea, Peru, Philippines, Poland, Qatar, Romania, Rwanda, Saint Lucia, Samoa, Sao Tome and Principe, Saudi Arabia, Senegal, Sierra Leone, Singapore, Somalia, Sri Lanka, Sudan, Suriname, Swaziland, Syrian Arab Republic, Thailand, Togo, Trinidad and Tobago, Tunisia, Turkey, Uganda, Ukrainian SSR, USSR, United Arab Emirates, United Republic of Tanzania, Uruguay, Venezuela, Viet Nam, Yemen, Yugoslavia, Zaire, Zambia, Zimbabwe.

Against: Belgium, Canada, France, Germany, Federal Republic of, Israel, Italy, Luxembourg, Netherlands, United Kingdom, United States.

Abstaining: Australia, Austria, Denmark, Finland, Greece, Iceland, Ireland, Japan, Malawi, New Zealand, Norway, Portugal, Spain, Sweden.

Canada said the Special Rapporteur's report covered only Western organizations, was often inaccurate or out of date and strayed too far from the topic with which it was supposed to deal. Israel declared it inadmissible for the Special Rapporteur to give vent to his personal feelings concerning Jews and to cite their sacred texts without understanding them; it therefore considered it equally inadmissible to authorize the continuation and financing of his work.

Australia regarded some paragraphs of the resolution as not conducive to more effective international co-operation in the struggle against *apartheid*. Portugal mentioned reservations on the Special Rapporteur's report and on paragraphs 3 to 5, 10 and 14. Though categorically rejecting racism, racial discrimination and *apartheid*, Spain did not see trade with South Africa as an obstacle to the liquidation of *apartheid;* with respect to paragraph 3, it felt that totally isolating a country was not the best way of inducing it to respect human rights, and the accuracy of the statement in paragraph 4 had never been demonstrated, it said. Speaking for the EEC members, Ireland said the text contained elements they found difficult to accept; the Special Rapporteur's report was not a useful basis for debating the issue at hand and the guidance outlined for him in paragraph 9 did not correspond to the title of the agenda item under consideration.

Japan, in addition to sharing doubts about the report's usefulness and the methods used in its preparation, expressed reservations on paragraphs 10 and 14. Honduras referred to the resolution's negative elements, such as its selectiveness in the choice of examples.

On behalf of the Nordic countries, Sweden said they agreed with the main thrust of the resolution but felt that it departed from its objectives in several respects. They could not accept those paragraphs containing unjustified accusations against selected countries, nor could they support recommendations that did not respect the division of competence among the different United Nations organs, as provided for in the Charter. They also noted with great regret the continued tendency to employ controversial formulations.

Voicing reservations on some paragraphs regarded as not likely to facilitate achievement of the resolution's objective were Burma and Chile. Reservations were also expressed by the Dominican Republic. Uruguay considered paragraph 3 to be biased and it interpreted paragraph 5 as by no means affecting the exclusive competence of the Security Council with respect to the application of measures under Chapter VII of the Charter. Concerning paragraph 12, it stressed that any politicization of economic agencies must be avoided. Brazil, citing paragraphs 7 and 11, said the Special Rapporteur's report, which should be improved in general, contained inaccuracies in respect of Brazil. If the information on assistance to South Africa were updated, the report would be more useful, the Bahamas felt. Singapore believed it would have been better to refrain from selectively condemning the countries named in paragraph 3—a sentiment shared by Turkey.

For the Byelorussian SSR, the text clearly indicated that any co-operation with South Africa was tantamount to being an accomplice in that country's racial discrimination policy. Similarly, the USSR said that States which gave assistance to the racist South African régime became its accomplices.

Trade union rights

In 1984, the Economic and Social Council had before it three letters relating to allegations of infringements of trade union rights in South Africa, brought to the Council's attention in 1983.[15] Those allegations—made by the International Confederation of Free Trade Unions (ICFTU) of the arrest of six South African women trade unionists, and by the World Federation of Trade Unions (WFTU) of the dismissal of 2,000 workers at the Kloof mines following a strike for improved living conditions for black miners—were to be transmitted to the Fact-Finding and Conciliation Commission on Freedom of Association of ILO, as decided by the Council in May 1983.[21]

Later that year, ICFTU and WFTU, by letters of 19 July and 5 August, respectively, expressed their reservations as to the usefulness of pursuing the matter, with ICFTU withdrawing its complaint. In the light of those reservations, the ILO Director-General, on 24 October, suggested to the Secretary-General that the matter as it had developed should again be referred to the Council. Accordingly, the Secretary-General transmitted these three letters to the Council by a note of 23 February 1984.[22]

Also before the Council were the findings of the *Ad Hoc* Working Group of Experts on Southern Africa on violations of trade union rights in South Africa (see above), transmitted by a Secretariat note of 4 May.[23]

ECONOMIC AND SOCIAL COUNCIL ACTION

In May, the Economic and Social Council, acting on the recommendation of its Second Committee, adopted a decision and resolution on the topic. Decision 1984/150 was adopted without vote.

Note by the Secretary-General on allegations regarding infringements of trade union rights

At its 20th plenary meeting, on 24 May 1984, the Council, having considered the note by the Secretary-General on allegations regarding infringements of trade union rights, decided that the matter referred to the Fact-Finding and Conciliation Commission on Freedom of Association of the International Labour Organisation through the Governing Body of the International Labour Office by its decision 1983/156 of 27 May 1983 should not be pursued.

Economic and Social Council decision 1984/150

Adopted without vote

Approved by Second Committee (E/1984/91) without vote, 17 May (meeting 16); oral proposal by Chairman; agenda item 10.

Resolution 1984/42 was adopted on 24 May, also without vote.

Report of the *Ad Hoc* Working Group of Experts of the Commission on Human Rights on allegations of infringements of trade union rights in the Republic of South Africa

The Economic and Social Council,

Recalling its resolution 1982/40 of 7 May 1982,

Having examined the extract from the progress report of the *Ad Hoc* Working Group of Experts on southern Africa,

Noting with grave concern that police and State interference in industrial disputes and repression against independent black trade union movements have persisted,

1. *Takes note* of the extract from the progress report of the *Ad Hoc* Working Group of Experts on southern Africa;

2. *Demands* the cessation of persecution of trade unionists by the Government of South Africa;

3. *Calls once again* for the immediate recognition of the unimpeded exercise of freedom of association and trade union rights by the entire population of South Africa, without discrimination of any kind;

4. *Demands* the immediate release of all imprisoned trade unionists and the lifting of the orders banning trade unionists and trade union organizations;

5. *Requests* the *Ad Hoc* Working Group of Experts to continue to study the situation and to report thereon to the Commission on Human Rights and the Council;

6. *Also requests* the *Ad Hoc* Working Group of Experts, in the discharge of its mandate, to consult with the International Labour Organisation and the Special Committee against *Apartheid*, as well as with international and African trade union confederations;

7. *Decides* to consider at its first regular session of 1985 the question of allegations of infringements of trade union rights in South Africa as a sub-item under the item entitled "Human rights questions".

Economic and Social Council resolution 1984/42

24 May 1984   Meeting 20   Adopted without vote

Approved by Second Committee (E/1984/91) without vote, 17 May (meeting 16); 7-nation draft (E/1984/C.2/L.6); agenda item 10.
Sponsors: Cuba, Djibouti, Egypt, Gambia, Somalia, Uganda, Zambia.

Asia and the Pacific

Iran

Reports by the Secretary-General. In 1984, the human rights situation in Iran was again the subject of two reports from the Secretary-General, dated 22[24] and 29 February,[25] submitted in response to a Commission on Human Rights request of March 1983.[26] The earlier report, reproducing the communications of August 1983 with Iran[26] concerning continuance of the Secretary-General's direct contacts with that country to discuss alleged human rights violations there through a representative, indicated that although efforts had been made to follow up on those communications, Iran's position remained unchanged. That position was one of scepticism about the constructive consequences of any sincere fact-finding mission.

The later report presented information, without comment as to its veracity, on alleged violations, specifically of those rights enshrined in the 1966 International Covenant on Civil and Political Rights:[27] the rights to life, to physical integrity and freedom from torture, to fair trial, and to freedom of conscience and opinion. The information was based on communications received by the United Nations from a wide variety of sources, inside and outside Iran. In conclusion, the report observed that, in the four years since the Sub-Commission was first seized of the situation of the Baha'i religious community in Iran,[28] there had been no clear evidence of improvement, Iran's being a party to the Covenant notwithstanding. Continuing allegations of human rights violations and the position taken by Iran pointed to the need for an appropriate means of fact-finding and for full co-operation between that country and the Commission.

Action by the Commission on Human Rights. On 14 March 1984, by a roll-call vote of 21 to 6, with 15 abstentions,[29] the Commission expressed deep concern at the continuing serious violations of human rights in Iran as reflected in the Secretary-General's report,[25] particularly at the evidence of summary and arbitrary executions, torture, detention without trial, religious intolerance and persecution, in particular of the Baha'is, and the lack of an independent judiciary and other recognized safeguards for a fair trial. It again urged Iran, as a State party to the Covenant on Civil and Political Rights, to respect and ensure to all individuals under its jurisdiction the rights recognized in that Covenant. The Commission requested its Chairman to appoint a special representative to establish contacts with Iran and to make a thorough study of the human rights situation there. It also requested Iran to extend its co-operation to the special representative, and the Secretary-General to give him the necessary assistance.

Also in March, the Commission called on Iran to cease using children in its armed forces (see below, under "Other human rights questions").

ECONOMIC AND SOCIAL COUNCIL ACTION

On the recommendation of its Second Committee, the Economic and Social Council in May adopted decision 1984/138 by recorded vote.

Situation of human rights in the Islamic Republic of Iran

At its 20th plenary meeting, on 24 May 1984, the Council, noting Commission on Human Rights resolution 1984/54 of 14 March 1984, endorsed the Commission's decision to request its Chairman to appoint, after consultation within the Bureau, a special representative of the Commission, whose mandate will be to establish contacts with the Government of the Islamic Republic of Iran and to make a thorough study of the human rights situation in that country based on such information as he may deem relevant, including comments and materials provided by the Government, containing conclusions and appropriate suggestions, to be submitted to the Commission at its forty-first session. The Council further endorsed the Commission's request to the Secretary-General to give all necessary assistance to the special representative of the Commission.

Economic and Social Council decision 1984/138

29-2-14 (recorded vote)

Approved by Second Committee (E/1984/91) by vote (28-2-13), 17 May (meeting 16); draft by Commission on Human Rights (E/1984/14); agenda item 10.
NGO statement: E/1984/NGO/5.

Recorded vote in Council as follows:

In favour: Argentina, Austria, Botswana, Bulgaria, Canada, Colombia, Costa Rica, Finland, France, Germany, Federal Republic of, Greece, Luxembourg, Mexico, Netherlands, New Zealand, Papua New Guinea, Poland, Portugal, Rwanda, Saint Lucia, Suriname, Swaziland, Sweden, Uganda, USSR, United Kingdom, United States, Venezuela, Zaire.
Against: Algeria, Pakistan.

Abstaining: Benin, Brazil, China, Congo, Ecuador, German Democratic Republic, Japan, Liberia, Malaysia, Sierra Leone, Sri Lanka, Thailand, Tunisia, Yugoslavia.

Sub-Commission action. On 29 August 1984, by 14 votes to 1, with 6 abstentions,[30] the Sub-Commission expressed alarm at reports of continuing gross violations of human rights in Iran, in particular of political, ethnic and national groups including the Kurds and the Baha'i religious community. It welcomed the Commission's decision to appoint a special representative to study the human rights situation in that country and requested the Secretary-General to bring to the attention of the Commission and its special representative information on grave violations received by the Sub-Commission and action taken.

Sri Lanka

On 30 January 1984, Sri Lanka provided information on the communal disturbances in the country[31] that had given rise to a September 1983 Sub-Commission decision requesting such information.[26] Describing the situation as an aberration within a tradition of intercommunal and interreligious harmony among various groups (mainly Sinhalese and Sri Lankan and Indian Tamils), Sri Lanka pointed to what it called a small dissatisfied group of Tamils as the source of the disturbances. The group—claiming active discrimination of the Tamil community with respect to economic opportunities, employment, education, land settlement, religious freedom and language—was agitating for a separate State to be called Eelam. To that end, it had set in motion a campaign in the country and abroad to justify terrorist activities in the north and to seek international support for its separatist movement.

To refute the group's claim, Sri Lanka cited constitutional legislation designed to protect civil and political rights, to provide legal relief in the event of their infringement, and to provide for both Sinhala and Tamil as national languages and for education in either of those languages. Examples of the practical application of such legislation for the benefit of all, even non-nationals, were also cited. Sri Lanka said that, in the face of a persistent campaign of terrorism, however, it was constrained to enact the Prevention of Terrorism Act to preserve the country's unity and territorial integrity. A political process was under way to deal with the issues that had led to the events of July 1983, including a conference of all political parties in January 1984. A dialogue with those parties and other groups was being maintained.

Action by the Commission on Human Rights. On 14 March 1984,[32] the Commission on Human Rights, taking note of the information voluntarily submitted by Sri Lanka, appealed to the parties to continue taking measures to maintain peace and restore harmony among the people of the country. It welcomed all measures for rehabilitation and reconciliation, including the all-party conference, expressed hope for the parties' success in achieving a lasting solution, and decided that further consideration of the matter was not necessary.

Sub-Commission action. By 11 votes to 3, with 6 abstentions, taken on 30 August,[33] the Sub-Commission, concerned about the recurrence of violence in Sri Lanka which had resulted in heavy loss of life and property, and recognizing that ultimate responsibility for the protection of all sections of the community lay with the Government, expressed hope that that Government would submit information to the Commission in 1985 on the progress of its investigation of the incidents and on the recent efforts to promote communal harmony.

Europe and the Mediterranean area

Cyprus

On 14 March 1984,[34] the Commission on Human Rights postponed debate on the question of human rights in Cyprus to its 1985 session, on the understanding that action required by previous Commission resolutions on the subject remained operative, including the request to the Secretary-General to report on their implementation.

Poland

In March 1984, Patricio Ruedas, United Nations Under-Secretary-General for Administration and Management, designated by the Secretary-General during the latter part of 1983 to update and complete on his behalf a study of the human rights situation in Poland, submitted a report[35] to the Commission on Human Rights in accordance with its resolution of March 1983.[36] The report was based on events in 1983 and on information gathered by Mr. Ruedas during two visits to Poland: once in 1983 and again in 1984, from 18 to 21 February. Mr. Ruedas interviewed representatives of the Government, Parliament, the Patriotic Movement for National Rebirth, the Roman Catholic Church, trade unions constituted under a law of 8 October 1982,[37] and individuals interned under martial law and later released.

The report reproduced a letter of 20 September 1983 from Hugo J. Gobbi, previously designated to follow the human rights situation in the country, requesting Poland for information relating to that situation, as well as a detailed questionnaire enclosed for the purpose. No reply was ever received, although the Secretary-General was later advised unofficially that Poland considered the questionnaire as not lending itself to a reply. Mr. Gobbi shortly thereafter asked to be relieved of his responsibilities following his acceptance of a government post in Argentina. The Secretary-General was thus unable to give effect to the Commission resolution on the subject.[36]

The report noted a number of legislative developments brought about by the lifting of martial law on 22 July 1983. Chief among these were the enactment of an amnesty law in respect of a number of offences committed before that date; amendments to the Constitution; special temporary regulations designed to stabilize the economy; amendments to the penal laws; and a new press law. Specific human rights violations dealt with included allegations of deaths resulting from police reaction to demonstrations, severe conditions of detention for a number of prisoners and detainees, and arrests. Inquiry was also made into the question of freedom of association and trade union rights.

In his conclusions, Mr. Ruedas stated that the resources and stamina of the people and Government of Poland were being taxed to the utmost by the difficult economic and social situation prevailing in the country since 1981. Under martial law, numerous arrests had been made and deaths had resulted from clashes between demonstrators and police: at least two in 1981, one in 1982 and two in 1983. That the figures were in dispute was not so important as that the deaths had occurred, for one single death was one too much. The lifting of martial law, the enactment and implementation of clemency measures and the amnesty law all had created conditions favourable to a reconciliation between the different sectors of the society. Of significance was the reduced number of detainees: 281 as at 18 February 1984, compared with some 1,500 at 4 January 1983.

Nevertheless, the recent legislation, though temporary, gave rise to certain questions. Thus, for example, an amendment to the penal code seemed to perpetuate a similar provision of the defunct martial law. Also, the special regulations to overcome the socio-economic crisis conferred extensive powers on the authorities in several domains, including education. However, Mr. Ruedas noted that, as to the possible exercise of those powers, he was impressed by the spirit of moderation shown by the government officials he had met, an impression that had led the Secretary-General to state that what he had heard in Poland was very encouraging on all fronts. It also seemed clear that Poland had fulfilled its stated intention to terminate the restrictive measures on the exercise of human rights in one very important aspect—the review of prison sentences—through the clemency measures and amnesty law that it had enacted and was implementing.

Action by the Commission on Human Rights. In March, a draft resolution sponsored by France, the Federal Republic of Germany, Italy and the Netherlands[38] was before the Commission on Human Rights for consideration. By the draft, the Commission would once again call for measures to enable the people of Poland to exercise fully their human rights and fundamental freedoms. On 14 March,[39] the Commission decided, by a roll-call vote of 17

to 14, with 12 abstentions, to postpone action on the draft to its 1985 session.

Latin America and the Caribbean

Chile

Report of the Special Rapporteur. In February 1984, Special Rapporteur Rajsoomer Lallah (Mauritius) reported to the Commission on Human Rights on developments in the human rights situation in Chile during the last four months of 1983.[40] Prepared in accordance with a Commission request of March of that year,[41] the report supplemented his interim report to the General Assembly in October.[42] The Special Rapporteur noted that Chile's lack of co-operation had made his task more difficult, especially since it had not provided the Secretary-General with subsequent information or comment.

The report stated that the rules of the 1980 Constitution had yet to be amended to allow exercise of the right to participate in the country's political life. To vindicate that right, "days of national protest" and other popular demonstrations had continued, leaving a trail of victims, injured, tortured and arrested. Under the continuing "state of danger due to threats of internal peace", extended for a further six months on 7 September 1983, the right of assembly remained subject to restrictions, as did freedom of information in respect of new publications other than those emanating from universities. Procedural guarantees continued to be seriously curtailed by the substantial extension of the jurisdiction of military courts, and limitations to the remedy of *amparo* applicable to persons subjected to executive action remained in force. As to violations of the right to life, the Government appeared to have no intention of shedding light on deaths resulting from demonstrations and had not allowed a commission of inquiry to be set up.

Torture continued to be a habitual practice. Judicial protection of the right to physical and moral integrity remained inadequate; however, an *ad hoc* military prosecutor was appointed on 21 October 1983 to investigate a number of allegations of torture, and, for the first time, a civil judge visited a secret place of detention where 11 students had reportedly been tortured. Arbitrary detentions and arrests substantially increased, numbering 4,306 in 1983, compared with 976 in 1982 and 871 in 1981. However, most of the arrests were reportedly made to discourage protest. While the Executive continued to hold power to prohibit entry into and to expel from the national territory, the Government, on 28 October 1983, published a consolidated list of 3,421 persons authorized to return to Chile. Restrictions to freedom of movement had been extended to apply to trade union leaders and shanty-town dwellers. Freedom of opinion in political matters remained subject to the "political recess" provided for in the Constitution's transitional provisions.

The Special Rapporteur concluded that prospects for the protection of human rights and freedoms continued to be bleak—a situation provoking widespread protest, in turn giving rise to systematic government countermeasures with increased adverse consequences for human rights. It was his considered view that the basic problem lay in the continued denial of the right to participate in the country's political life. To enforce this denial, a system of legislative, executive and administrative measures was being used, together with a restriction of all the other rights and freedoms that would give effect to that central right. This tightening of measures to nullify the positive consequences of the lifting of one of two states of emergency and the untimely breakdown of the political talks had brought into question the Government's avowed commitment to re-establish a democratic order in the near future.

The Special Rapporteur recommended that Chile be urged to co-operate with him and the Commission, immediately end the current state of emergency, completely restore the jurisdiction and independence of the judiciary, and take measures to ensure respect for the rights to life, liberty and security and for the freedom of thought, opinion and expression. Other recommendations called for a thorough investigation of disappearances; prevention of arrests and detentions by elements outside the police force; the banning of torture, secret detention sites and internal banishment; restoration of the right to work and to appropriate conditions of work; education for all and restoration of the autonomy of universities; and implementation of the rights of the indigenous population.

Action by the Commission on Human Rights. By a letter of 16 February 1984,[43] the Special Rapporteur advised the Commission of his inability to participate in the consideration of his report. Annexed to the letter was a summary of the 1983 human rights situation in Chile to assist in those deliberations.

On 15 March,[44] the Commission, by a roll-call vote of 31 to 5, with 6 abstentions, commended the Special Rapporteur for his report. It expressed distress at the persistence and increase of serious and systematic human rights violations in Chile, in particular the violent suppression of popular protests. It also expressed alarm that the repressive activities of the police and security agencies had gone unpunished. It reiterated its dismay at the disruption of the traditional democratic legal order and its institutions through the maintenance of emergency legislation, the institutionalization of states of emergency, the extension of military jurisdiction, and a Constitution that not only failed to guarantee but also suppressed human rights and fundamental freedoms.

The Commission called on the Chilean authorities to restore and respect human rights in accordance with the obligations they had assumed under various international instruments; to clarify the fate of persons arrested for political reasons and who later disappeared, and to bring to trial those responsible for such disappearance; and to respect the right of Chilean nationals to live in, freely enter and leave the country without restrictions. The Commission renewed its appeal for the restoration of the full exercise of trade union rights, in particular the right to collective bargaining and to strike. It again urged restoration of economic, social and cultural rights, in particular those intended to preserve the cultural identity and improve the social status of indigenous populations.

The Commission exhorted the Chilean authorities to co-operate with the Special Rapporteur and to submit their comments on his report to the Commission. It extended the Special Rapporteur's mandate for another year, with a request that he report to the General Assembly in 1984 and to the Commission in 1985.

ECONOMIC AND SOCIAL COUNCIL ACTION

Acting on the recommendation of its Second Committee, the Economic and Social Council in May 1984 adopted decision 1984/140 by recorded vote.

Question of human rights in Chile

At its 20th plenary meeting, on 24 May 1984, the Council, noting Commission on Human Rights resolution 1984/63 of 15 March 1984, endorsed the Commission's decision to extend the mandate of the Special Rapporteur on the situation of human rights in Chile for another year and to request him to report on the situation of human rights in that country to the General Assembly at its thirty-ninth session and to the Commission at its forty-first session. The Council requested the Secretary-General to make appropriate arrangements to ensure that the necessary financial resources and sufficient staff are provided to implement the resolution of the Commission.

Economic and Social Council decision 1984/140

35-3-12 (recorded vote)

Approved by Second Committee (E/1984/91) by recorded vote (33-3-10), 17 May (meeting 16); draft by Commission on Human Rights (E/1984/14); agenda item 10.

Recorded vote in Council as follows:

In favour: Algeria, Argentina, Austria, Benin, Botswana, Bulgaria, Canada, Congo, Costa Rica, Finland, France, German Democratic Republic, Germany, Federal Republic of, Greece, Luxembourg, Mali, Mexico, Netherlands, New Zealand, Papua New Guinea, Poland, Portugal, Romania, Rwanda, Sierra Leone, Sri Lanka, Suriname, Swaziland, Sweden, Tunisia, Uganda, USSR, United Kingdom, Venezuela, Yugoslavia.
Against: Brazil, Pakistan, United States.
Abstaining: China, Colombia, Ecuador, Japan, Lebanon, Liberia, Malaysia, Qatar, Saint Lucia, Saudi Arabia, Thailand, Zaire.

Sub-Commission action. On 30 August,[45] the Sub-Commission called on the Chilean authorities to end all repression and torture, to identify and punish those responsible for such acts and for disappearances, and to respect civil and political rights, as well as economic, social and cultural rights including those of indigenous peoples. It recommended that the Commission on Human Rights address an appeal to the same authorities to respect and promote human rights in conformity with international instruments to which Chile was a party and to co-operate with the Special Rapporteur.

Further report. As requested by the Commission in March (see above), the Special Rapporteur prepared a report on developments in the human rights situation in Chile during the first half of 1984 (January to June), taking into account subsequent data wherever possible, which the Secretary-General transmitted to the General Assembly in November.[46] The report indicated that Chile, replying to the Special Rapporteur's request for co-operation, had reiterated its decision not to collaborate based on a position of principle that it had stated on many occasions. In the circumstances, he resorted to the method of work used for previous reports: consulting official publications in Chile, including administrative and legislative provisions, 1984 court decisions of major significance, material supplied by national and international governmental and non-governmental organizations, and information supplied by individuals; sifting the data, rejecting those deemed subjective; and assessing the situation in terms of the international human rights instruments ratified by Chile and other applicable norms.

The report noted that, during the period under review, violations increased, notably of the rights to life, to physical and psychological integrity, and to liberty and security. New legislation was enacted extending application of the death penalty. Some 93 persons were reportedly injured by security agencies and another 90 subjected to acts of torture. Some 1,655 arrests were recorded, of whom 168 were put on trial and the rest released. In Santiago alone, 165 acts of persecution and intimidation occurred. Judicial supervision over arbitrary and illegal arrests was ineffective, as were proceedings for the compensation for such arrests.

Further restrictions on the freedom of expression and information were introduced by legislation. The exercise of the right of public assembly, subject to prior authorization, was continually obstructed by repeated refusals to grant authorization; those authorized were subjected to disruption. The right of association remained prohibited by "political recess" instituted by a transitional provision of the Constitution banning all political party activities until 1989 or pending promulgation of a constitutional organic law. Thus, current associations with some humanitarian, political or trade-union objectives existed outside the law.

The right to enter and leave the country remained seriously restricted due largely to the Government's interpretation of the term "national security". Recent court decisions (30 January, 9 July) confirmed that the courts were powerless to consider substantive issues raised by expulsion or prohibition of entry.

While some 5,000 persons had been allowed to return to the country (between 1983 and May 1984), the national airlines received (10 September) a list of 4,860 persons to whom tickets should not be sold without police clearance. Restrictions of movement within the country were imposed on 29 persons, a decline from 45 in 1983; also, exceptionally, a remedy of *amparo* was granted to two university students (10 May) who had been under an internal banishment order.

From his detailed examination of the status of those and other human rights, the Special Rapporteur concluded that the situation had continued to deteriorate in 1984. The central issue continued to be maintenance of the current system of government in the face of widespread popular aspirations for the protection of those rights and freedoms and for the restoration of democratic order.

The Special Rapporteur made a series of recommendations, most of which were embodied in the Assembly's resolution below.

GENERAL ASSEMBLY ACTION

Acting on the recommendation of the Third Committee, the General Assembly adopted resolution 39/121 by recorded vote on 14 December 1984.

Situation of human rights and fundamental freedoms in Chile

The General Assembly,

Aware of its responsibility to promote and encourage respect for human rights and fundamental freedoms for all and determined to remain vigilant with regard to violations of human rights wherever they occur,

Stressing the obligation of Governments to promote and protect human rights and to carry out the responsibilities they have undertaken by virtue of various international instruments,

Recalling its resolutions 3219(XXIX) of 6 November 1974, 3448(XXX) of 9 December 1975, 31/124 of 16 December 1976, 32/118 of 16 December 1977, 33/175 of 20 December 1978, 34/179 of 17 December 1979, 35/188 of 15 December 1980, 36/157 of 16 December 1981, 37/183 of 17 December 1982 and 38/102 of 16 December 1983, relating to the situation of human rights in Chile, as well as its resolution 33/173 of 20 December 1978 on disappeared persons,

Recalling also the resolutions of the Commission on Human Rights on the situation of human rights in Chile, in particular resolution 1984/63 of 15 March 1984, in which the Commission decided, *inter alia*, to extend for a year the mandate of the Special Rapporteur on the situation of human rights in Chile,

Deploring once again the fact that the repeated appeals of the General Assembly, the Commission on Human Rights and other international organs to re-establish human rights and fundamental freedoms have been ignored by the Chilean authorities, which continue to refuse to co-operate with the Commission on Human Rights and its Special Rapporteur,

Once again expressing its grave concern at the persistence of the serious situation of human rights in Chile, which, as established by the Special Rapporteur, has continued to deteriorate, and at the fact that the Chilean authorities have not been responsive to the concerns of the international community, as expressed in resolutions of the General Assembly and of the Commission on Human Rights,

Observing that, according to the conclusions of the Special Rapporteur, the right to enter and leave one's country freely is seriously restricted for Chilean nationals and that this situation has been aggravated by the issuance of a list of the names of thousands of Chileans who are not allowed to enter their country without conditions,

Taking note with utmost concern of the re-establishment of the state of siege on 6 November 1984, which has aggravated the situation of human rights and fundamental freedoms in Chile, particularly by the increase in the number of arbitrary mass arrests, of persons sent into internal exile and the practice of torture and other forms of inhuman and degrading treatment, as well as the additional restrictions on the freedom of expression and information, assembly and association,

1. *Commends* the Special Rapporteur on the situation of human rights in Chile for his report, prepared in accordance with Commission on Human Rights resolution 1984/63;

2. *Expresses its indignation* at the persistence of and increase in serious and systematic violations of human rights in Chile, as described in the report of the Special Rapporteur, and, in particular, at the violent repression of popular protest in the face of the refusal to restore the democratic order and human rights and fundamental freedoms on the part of the authorities, which have in fact committed further serious and flagrant violations of human rights, with mass arrests and numerous deaths;

3. *Reiterates once again its dismay* at the disruption in Chile of the traditional democratic legal order and its institutions, particularly through the maintenance of exceptional legislation, the institutionalization of states of emergency, the extension of military jurisdiction and the existence of a Constitution which does not reflect the will of the people freely expressed and the provisions of which not only fail to guarantee human rights and fundamental freedoms but suppress, suspend or restrict the enjoyment and exercise thereof;

4. *Expresses its alarm* at the fact that the repressive activities of the police and security agencies and, in particular, the National Information Agency continue to go unpunished, as pointed out in the report of the Special Rapporteur;

5. *Once again views with concern* the ineffectiveness of the remedies of *habeas corpus* or *amparo* and of protection, owing to the fact that the judiciary does not exercise fully its powers of investigation, monitoring and supervision in this respect and performs its functions under severe restrictions;

6. *Once again requests* the Chilean authorities to restore and respect human rights in accordance with the obligations they have assumed under various international instruments and, in particular, to put an end to the régime of exception and the practice of declaring states of emergency, under which serious and continuing violations of human rights are committed, with a view to restoring the principle of legality, democratic institutions and the effective enjoyment and exercise of civil and political rights and fundamental freedoms;

7. *Urges* the Chilean authorities to terminate the state of siege decreed on 6 November 1984 and the consequences of that state of siege;

8. *Once more urges* the Chilean authorities to investigate and clarify the fate of persons who have disappeared, including those arrested for political reasons, and to inform their families of the results of such investigation and to bring to trial and punish those responsible for their disappearance;

9. *Once again emphasizes* to the Chilean authorities the need to put an end to intimidation and persecution, as well as arbitrary or illegal arrests and imprisonment in secret places, and to respect the right of persons to life and physical integrity by halting the practice of torture and other forms of cruel, inhuman or degrading treatment which, in some cases, have resulted in unexplained deaths;

10. *Again requests* the Chilean authorities to respect, in accordance with article 12 of the International Covenant on Civil and Political Rights, the right of Chilean nationals to live in and freely enter and leave their country, without restrictions or conditions of any kind, in particular to annul the list of names of Chileans whose right to enter the country has been restricted and recent measures affecting other individuals, and to cease the practice of "relegation" (assignment of forced residence) and forced exile;

11. *Renews its appeal* to the Chilean authorities to re-establish the full enjoyment and exercise of trade union rights, in particular the right to organize trade unions, the right to collective bargaining and the right to strike, and to put an end to the system of repressing the activities of trade union leaders and their organizations;

12. *Once more urges* the Chilean authorities to respect and, where necessary, restore economic, social and cultural rights and, in particular, the rights intended to preserve the cultural identity and improve the social situation of indigenous populations, recognizing especially their right to their land;

13. *Concludes*, on the basis of the report of the Special Rapporteur, that it is necessary to keep under consideration the situation of human rights in Chile;

14. *Again requests* the Chilean authorities to co-operate with the Special Rapporteur and to submit their comments on his report to the Commission on Human Rights at its forty-first session;

15. *Invites* the Commission on Human Rights to study in depth at its forty-first session the report of the Special Rapporteur and to take the most appropriate steps for the effective restoration of human rights and fundamental freedoms in Chile, including the extension of the mandate of the Special Rapporteur for one more year, and requests the Commission to report, through the Economic and Social Council, to the General Assembly at its fortieth session.

General Assembly resolution 39/121

14 December 1984   Meeting 101   90-13-40 (recorded vote)

Approved by Third Committee (A/39/700) by recorded vote (83-15-32), 7 December (meeting 66); 15-nation draft (A/C.3/39/L.79); agenda item 12.

Sponsors: Algeria, Australia, Cuba, Denmark, France, Greece, Italy, Luxembourg, Mexico, Netherlands, Norway, Portugal, Spain, Sweden, Yugoslavia.

Meeting numbers. GA 39th session: 3rd Committee 54-56, 58, 59, 61-66; plenary 101.

Recorded vote in Assembly as follows:

In favour: Afghanistan, Algeria, Angola, Argentina, Australia, Austria, Bahrain, Barbados, Belgium, Benin, Botswana, Bulgaria, Burkina Faso, Burundi, Byelorussian SSR, Canada, Cape Verde, Congo, Costa Rica, Cuba, Cyprus, Czechoslovakia, Democratic Yemen, Denmark, Dominican Republic, Equatorial Guinea, Ethiopia, Finland, France, Gambia, German Democratic Republic, Germany, Federal Republic of, Ghana, Greece, Guinea, Guyana, Hungary, Iceland, India, Iran, Ireland, Italy, Jamaica, Kenya, Kuwait, Lao People's Democratic Republic, Lesotho, Libyan Arab Jamahiriya, Luxembourg, Madagascar, Maldives, Mali, Malta, Mauritania,

Mauritius, Mexico, Mongolia, Mozambique, Netherlands, New Zealand, Nicaragua, Norway, Poland, Portugal, Qatar, Romania, Rwanda, Samoa, Sao Tome and Principe, Senegal, Seychelles, Sierra Leone, Spain, Sri Lanka, Swaziland, Sweden, Togo, Tunisia, Uganda, Ukrainian SSR, USSR, United Arab Emirates, United Kingdom, United Republic of Tanzania, Vanuatu, Venezuela, Viet Nam, Yugoslavia, Zambia, Zimbabwe.

Against: Bangladesh, Brazil, Chile, El Salvador, Guatemala, Haiti, Indonesia, Lebanon, Morocco, Pakistan, Paraguay, United States, Uruguay.

Abstaining: Bahamas, Belize, Bhutan, Brunei Darussalam, Burma, Cameroon, Central African Republic, Chad, China, Democratic Kampuchea, Ecuador, Egypt, Fiji, Gabon, Honduras, Ivory Coast, Japan, Jordan, Liberia, Malawi, Malaysia, Nepal, Niger, Nigeria, Oman, Panama, Papua New Guinea, Peru, Philippines, Saint Vincent and the Grenadines, Saudi Arabia, Singapore, Somalia, Sudan, Suriname, Thailand, Trinidad and Tobago, Turkey, Yemen, Zaire.

Chile accused the Organization of politicizing the cause of human rights and rejected the charges against it as invalid. It called the text selective and irresponsible, and said it failed to recognize the institutional effort and democratic goal of Chile's policies.

Likewise criticizing the text as selective were Colombia, Ecuador, Guatemala, Paraguay, Peru and Uruguay, all of which referred to a discriminatory attitude towards certain Latin American countries, including Chile. The Federal Republic of Germany echoed their sentiment that human rights violations were just as serious, if not more so, in other parts of the world and that such selectivity could only undermine United Nations credibility in its efforts to promote human rights. Indonesia declared itself fully committed to promoting human rights but not at the expense of the sovereign independence of the State; the principle of a State's national authority, as enshrined in the Charter, must not be called into question.

The United States said it felt obliged to express its concern over the set-back in the re-establishment of democracy in Chile. It deplored the restrictions to and violations of fundamental freedoms, the brutal repression and the imposition of the state of emergency. It had made its views known to the Chilean Government and had urged it to take immediate steps to rectify the situation, beginning by revoking the state of emergency. As to the text, the United States would again reproach the United Nations for its double standards, claiming that the text—a mixture of truths, falsehoods and statements that the United Nations was clearly not competent to make—would require Chile to respect criteria not universally applied.

The Philippines believed that unless adequate safeguards were instituted to preserve the principle of non-intervention in domestic affairs, appointing a special rapporteur to look into the human rights situation in any Member State might infringe that principle.

Bolivia asked that its non-participation in the vote for political reasons be duly recorded.

The United Kingdom expressed deep concern over the serious and deteriorating human rights situation in Chile, which it felt was satisfactorily reflected in the draft resolution. Canada, Finland and the Federal Republic of Germany had a similar view. Nevertheless, the United Kingdom felt that the text could have been improved by a reference to the increase in terrorist violence and by some positive language calling on both sides to resume dialogue. Also, paragraph 15 unduly prejudiced the decision to extend the Special Rapporteur's mandate, which was for the Commission on Human Rights alone to make. Canada would have preferred a more balanced text attributing the increased violence not only to the Government but also to the opposition forces. The Federal Republic of Germany considered it unfortunate that the text did not refer to the complicated aspect of the situation, namely, that the legitimate democratic opposition found it difficult to define its position amid increasing violence and terrorism, which repression only served to intensify. Only by involving as many Chileans as possible in the country's redemocratization could the Government isolate the terrorist forces.

Uganda considered the text an important effort towards improving the human rights situation in Chile.

El Salvador

Report of the Special Representative. In January 1984, Special Representative José Antonio Pastor Ridruejo, in fulfilment of his mandate as extended by the Commission on Human Rights in March 1983,[47] submitted a final report on the human rights situation in El Salvador,[48] updating a November 1983 interim report to the General Assembly.[47]

The Special Representative's findings and recommendations were essentially the same as those outlined in his 1983 interim report. In reiterating his recommendations, he called for termination of the activities of "death squads" and implementation of agrarian reform.

Action by the Commission on Human Rights. By a roll-call vote of 24 to 5, with 13 abstentions, taken on 14 March 1984,[49] the Commission on Human Rights commended the Special Representative for his report and expressed deep concern over the persistence of the gravest human rights violations in El Salvador. It regretted that its appeals and those of the General Assembly and the international community had gone unheeded and that the creation of a national human rights commission and promulgation of an amnesty law[47] had not altered the situation as a whole. The Commission recommended the adoption of measures to put an immediate end to attacks on human life and requested the Government to punish those responsible for the serious violations of the right to life perpetrated by the so-called death squads, among others. It expressed concern at the consequences of the attacks on the economic infrastructure, largely attributable to the opposition forces.

Deploring the interruption in the dialogue between the Government and the other political forces, the Commission urged the parties to create conditions necessary for the search for a negotiated solution. It appealed for government action to ensure respect for human rights and fundamental freedoms by all its agencies, including the security forces and other armed organizations under its authority. It urged adoption of measures to enable the judiciary to uphold the rule of law and to prosecute and punish those responsible for grave human rights violations. It recommended that the reforms necessary to solve the economic and social problems that were at the root of the conflict be implemented so as to allow the effective exercise of human rights.

The Commission again urged States not to intervene and to suspend all manner of military assistance. It appealed to the conflicting parties not to interfere with the activities of humanitarian organizations working among the civilian population, the wounded and the imprisoned.

The Commission decided to extend the mandate of the Special Representative for another year, with a request that he present a report on further developments to the Assembly in 1984 and to the Commission in 1985. It requested the Government and all other parties to extend to him their full co-operation. It also requested the Secretary-General to give him all the necessary assistance.

ECONOMIC AND SOCIAL COUNCIL ACTION

Acting on the recommendation of its Second Committee, the Economic and Social Council in May 1984 adopted decision 1984/136 by recorded vote.

Situation of human rights in El Salvador

At its 20th plenary meeting, on 24 May 1984, the Council, noting Commission on Human Rights resolution 1984/52 of 14 March 1984, endorsed the Commission's decision to extend the mandate of the Special Representative on the situation of human rights in El Salvador for another year and to request him to submit his report on further developments in the situation of human rights in that country to the General Assembly at its thirty-ninth session and to the Commission at its forty-first session. The Council further endorsed the Commission's request to the Secretary-General to give all necessary assistance to the Special Representative of the Commission.

Economic and Social Council decision 1984/136

33-3-14 (recorded vote)

Approved by Second Committee (E/1984/91) by recorded vote (33-3-12), 17 May (meeting 16); draft by Commission on Human Rights (E/1984/14); agenda item 10.

Recorded vote in Council as follows:

In favour: Algeria, Argentina, Austria, Benin, Botswana, Bulgaria, Canada, Congo, Finland, France, German Democratic Republic, Germany, Federal Republic of, Greece, Japan, Luxembourg, Mali, Mexico, Netherlands, New Zealand, Papua New Guinea, Poland, Portugal, Qatar,ª Sierra Leone, Suriname, Swaziland, Sweden, Tunisia, Uganda, USSR, United Kingdom, Venezuela, Yugoslavia.

Against: Brazil, Saint Lucia, United States.

Abstaining: China, Colombia, Costa Rica, Ecuador, Lebanon, Liberia, Malaysia, Pakistan, Romania, Rwanda, Saudi Arabia, Sri Lanka, Thailand, Zaire.

ªLater advised that it had abstained, not voted in favour as incorrectly indicated.

The United States expressed disappointment that the Special Representative, whose mandate had just been extended, had not been able to observe at first hand the presidential elections held in El Salvador in March.

Sub-Commission action. On 30 August 1984,[50] the Sub-Commission, by 14 votes to 1, with 7 abstentions, recommended that, despite the change of government in El Salvador (see below), the Commission on Human Rights should continue to examine the human rights situation there and compliance with the 1949 Geneva Conventions. It requested the Special Representative to pay special attention to persistent reports of the systematic bombing of the civilian population by government forces and suggested that the Commission reiterate its appeal to the conflicting parties to resume talks without delay. It urged States not to intervene and to suspend military assistance so that peace might be restored and a negotiating mechanism established for a comprehensive political solution. It requested the Secretary-General to report in 1985 on the Representative's work and on the deliberations of the Commission and the General Assembly.

Further report. In November 1984, the Special Representative reported further on developments in the human rights situation in El Salvador. Prepared pursuant to the Commission's March request (see above) and transmitted to the Assembly by the Secretary-General, this interim report[51] contained 1984 information, gathered during the Special Representative's visit to El Salvador from 16 to 24 September and from interviews conducted thereafter at Geneva, San José (Costa Rica), Washington, D.C., and New York with individuals and representatives of various organizations.

A notable development was the presidential election on 25 March, with over 300 outside observers present. Since none of the candidates had obtained more than 50 per cent of the votes, a second round of voting was held on 6 May, resulting in the assumption of José Napoleon Duarte (Christian Democratic Party) to the presidency on 1 June. With a new Government set up, President Duarte met with leaders of the opposition (Frente Farabundo Martí para la Liberación Nacional–Frente Democrático Revolucionario) on 15 October, at which he presented a proposal to end the violence in the country. The proposal would guarantee unconditional amnesty to all connected with the situation of political violence; freedom of movement to the rebels and their families who would be reintegrated in society; political participation for all sectors and groups; official documents for those wanting to leave the country and arrangements for their arrival in the country of emigration; safeguards for displaced persons returning to El Salvador, with a guarantee of the right to freedom of expression and to engage in political activity, including the right to register their political party and candidates; and special programmes for the wounded and disabled.

Other information included the status of economic, social and cultural rights and, in this connection, implementation of the country's agrarian reform programme; the status of civil and political rights with respect to political murders, abductions and disappearances, political prisoners, the status of the criminal justice system, and human rights violations attributed to the guerrilla forces; the situation of refugees and displaced persons; and human rights in armed conflicts.

The Special Representative stated that the new Government was actively pursuing a policy of improving the human rights situation in the country. For example, it had disbanded the intelligence section of the Treasury Police, dismissed up to 45 local commanders, restricted the activities of "death squads" and created a separate secretariat for public security in the Ministry of Defence, as well as a special commission to investigate political crimes having international relevance. An investigation, ordered by the Minister for Defence, of the alleged participation of an army unit in a massacre of 68 peasants in July was under way.

The Special Representative found that the situation with regard to economic, social and cultural rights had worsened, owing largely to the serious economic difficulties facing El Salvador that were exacerbated by the generalized violence in the country. Serious violations of civil and political rights attributable to the State apparatus and armed paramilitary organizations continued, although political murders of non-combatants had declined. The judicial system remained inadequate and its proceedings exceedingly slow: while a guilty verdict was handed down in the trial for the 1980 murder of four United States missionaries and another trial was concluded, most human rights violations had yet to be investigated. Civilian deaths continued to be reported in the wake of bombings and attacks by the armed forces and of guerrilla activities. However, the considerable gap previously reported between government intentions to improve the human rights situation and improvements achieved had narrowed during the year.

In addition, according to information received from UNHCR, of the Salvadorian refugees living abroad (244,000 as at 31 July 1983), only some 34,300 were receiving assistance; some 1,200 had returned to the country. Displaced persons, estimated at 500,000, lived in camps under harsh conditions.

The Special Representative urged immediate termination of attacks on non-combatants and establishment of civil peace as a prerequisite for the respect of human rights. He recommended repeal of all legislative and other measures incompatible with international human rights instruments; strengthening of government control over the armed forces, security bodies, and all armed individuals and organizations, including the so-called death squads; adoption of measures to prevent, investigate and punish human rights violations, and to include the dismissal of civilian officials, armed forces personnel and security

agents guilty of such violations; intensification of mass campaigns to promote respect for human rights; and implementation of administrative and social reforms, especially agrarian reform as a foundation for the exercise of economic, social and cultural rights.

GENERAL ASSEMBLY ACTION

Acting on the recommendation of the Third Committee, the General Assembly adopted resolution 39/119 by recorded vote on 14 December 1984.

Situation of human rights and fundamental freedoms in El Salvador

The General Assembly,

Guided by the principles of the Charter of the United Nations, the Universal Declaration of Human Rights, the International Covenant on Civil and Political Rights and by the humanitarian rules set out in the Geneva Conventions of 12 August 1949 and Additional Protocols I and II thereto,

Aware that the Governments of all Member States have an obligation to promote and protect human rights and fundamental freedoms and to carry out the responsibilities they have undertaken under various international human rights instruments,

Recalling that, in its resolutions 35/192 of 15 December 1980, 36/155 of 16 December 1981, 37/185 of 17 December 1982 and 38/101 of 16 December 1983, it expressed deep concern at the situation of human rights in El Salvador,

Bearing in mind Commission on Human Rights resolutions 32(XXXVII) of 11 March 1981, in which the Commission decided to appoint a Special Representative on the situation of human rights in El Salvador, 1982/28 of 11 March 1982, 1983/29 of 8 March 1983 and 1984/52 of 14 March 1984, whereby the Commission extended the mandate of the Special Representative for another year and requested him to report, *inter alia*, to the General Assembly,

Noting that the Special Representative of the Commission on Human Rights points out in his report that, owing to the adoption of a new government policy, the number of human rights violations has markedly decreased, which is a welcome development, but that nevertheless a situation of war and generalized violence continues to exist in El Salvador, that there are still serious violations of human rights, that the number of attacks on life and the economic structure remains a cause for concern and that the capacity of the judicial system to investigate and punish human rights violations committed in the country continues to be patently unsatisfactory,

Considering that there is an armed conflict not of an international character in El Salvador in which the Government of that country and the opposition forces are obligated to apply the minimum standards of protection of human rights and of humane treatment set out in article 3 common to the Geneva Conventions of 12 August 1949, as well as Additional Protocol II thereto,

Aware that a delicate process aiming at a political solution has been initiated in El Salvador, which could be hindered if arms or military contributions of any other kind, making it possible to prolong or intensify the war, are provided from outside,

Taking into account that on 8 October 1984 the President of El Salvador stated before the General Assembly that the main task of the mandate he was given by the elections of 6 May 1984 is to achieve social harmony and internal peace in El Salvador, and that the Special Representative notes with satisfaction the obvious desire of the new Government to establish a democracy governed by the rule of law and guaranteeing full respect for human rights,

Recognizing that dialogue is the only way, in a spirit of generosity and openness, to achieve a negotiated comprehensive political solution that will promote genuine national reconciliation, put an end to the suffering of the Salvadorian people and stem the growing tide of refugees and internally displaced persons,

1. *Commends* the Special Representative of the Commission on Human Rights for his report on the situation of human rights in El Salvador;

2. *Expresses its deep concern* at the fact that, as indicated in the report of the Special Representative, although the number of human rights violations has decreased, they are still serious and numerous, resulting in suffering for the Salvadorian people;

3. *Recalls* that the right to life and liberty is paramount and therefore notes with satisfaction the measures which, according to the report of the Special Representative, the Government of El Salvador has adopted to put an end to these serious violations of human rights;

4. *Deeply regrets* that the persistence of hostilities by the armed forces of the Government has resulted in many civilian victims and material damage, and also regrets that the hostilities of the guerrilla forces have on occasion caused civilian victims and material damage to the economic infrastructure of El Salvador;

5. *Reaffirms once again* the right of the Salvadorian people freely to determine their political, economic and social future without interference from outside, through a genuine democratic process, in an atmosphere free from intimidation and terror;

6. *Requests* all States to refrain from intervening in the internal situation in El Salvador and, instead of supplying arms or helping in any way to prolong and intensify the war, to encourage the continuation of the dialogue until a just and lasting peace is achieved;

7. *Welcomes with satisfaction* the fact that, in accordance with the appeal made by the President of El Salvador before the General Assembly and the Assembly's own repeated appeals, talks were resumed between the Government of El Salvador and the Frente Farabundo Martí para la Liberación Nacional-Frente Democrático Revolucionario, which confirmed its willingness in that respect;

8. *Recognizes* that this dialogue is an important step in the process of pacification and democratization of the country and therefore calls upon the Government of El Salvador and the Frente Farabundo Martí para la Liberación Nacional-Frente Democrático Revolucionario to intensify their talks until they achieve a negotiated comprehensive political solution which will put an end to the armed conflict and establish a lasting peace based on the full exercise both of civil and political rights and of economic, social and cultural rights by all Salvadorians;

9. *Welcomes* the fact that the Government of El Salvador and the insurgent forces have agreed through indirect talks to exchange prisoners of war and allow the International Committee of the Red Cross to evacuate wounded combatants of the opposition in exchange for the release of government officials captured in combat, appeals to all States to do what they can to support operations of that kind, and urges the Government of El Salvador and the insurgent forces to continue those practices, which humanize the conflict, and to agree as early as possible to respect the medical personnel and all military hospitals, as required by the Geneva Conventions;

10. *Again reiterates its appeal* to the Government of El Salvador and to the opposition forces to co-operate fully and not to interfere with the activities of humanitarian organizations dedicated to alleviating the suffering of the civilian population, wherever these organizations operate in the country;

11. *Recommends* the continuation and broadening of the reforms necessary in El Salvador, including effective application of agrarian reform, for the solution of the economic and social problems which are the basic cause of the internal conflict in that country;

12. *Deeply deplores* the fact that the capacity of the judicial system in El Salvador to investigate, prosecute and punish violations of human rights continues to be patently unsatisfactory and therefore urges the competent authorities to continue and strengthen the process of reform of the Salvadorian penal judicial system, in order to punish speedily and effectively those responsible for the serious human rights violations which have been committed and are still being committed in that country;

13. *Calls upon* the competent authorities in El Salvador to introduce changes in the laws and other measures that are incompatible with the provisions contained in the international instruments binding on the Government of El Salvador in respect of human rights;

14. *Renews its appeal* to the Government of El Salvador, as well as to other parties concerned, to continue to co-operate with the Special Representative of the Commission on Human Rights;

15. *Decides* to keep under consideration, during its fortieth session, the situation of human rights and fundamental freedoms in El Salvador, in order to examine this situation anew in the light of additional elements provided by the Commission on Human Rights and the Economic and Social Council.

General Assembly resolution 39/119

14 December 1984   Meeting 101   93-11-40 (recorded vote)

Approved by Third Committee (A/39/700) by recorded vote (83-13-35), 7 December (meeting 66); 9-nation draft (A/C.3/39/L.43/Rev.2), orally revised following consultations; agenda item 12.

Sponsors: Algeria, Denmark, France, Greece, Mexico, Netherlands, Norway, Spain, Sweden.

Meeting numbers. GA 39th session: 3rd Committee 54-56, 58, 59, 61-66; plenary 24, 101.

Recorded vote in Assembly as follows:

In favour: Afghanistan, Albania, Algeria, Angola, Argentina, Australia, Austria, Bahrain, Barbados, Belgium, Benin, Botswana, Bulgaria, Burkina Faso, Burundi, Byelorussian SSR, Canada, Cape Verde, Colombia, Congo, Costa Rica, Cuba, Cyprus, Czechoslovakia, Democratic Yemen, Denmark, Dominican Republic, Egypt, Ethiopia, Finland, France, Gambia, German Democratic Republic, Ghana, Greece, Guinea, Guyana, Hungary, Iceland, India, Iran, Iraq, Ireland, Italy, Jamaica, Kenya, Kuwait, Lao People's Democratic Republic, Lesotho, Libyan Arab Jamahiriya, Luxembourg, Madagascar, Mali, Malta, Mauritania, Mauritius, Mexico, Mongolia, Mozambique, Netherlands, New Zealand, Nicaragua, Nigeria, Norway, Panama, Peru,[a] Poland, Portugal, Qatar, Rwanda, Saint Vincent and the Grenadines, Samoa, Sao Tome and Principe, Saudi Arabia, Senegal, Seychelles, Sierra Leone, Spain, Swaziland, Sweden, Syrian Arab Republic, Togo, Tunisia, Uganda, Ukrainian SSR, USSR, United Arab Emirates, United Republic of Tanzania, Vanuatu, Venezuela, Viet Nam, Yugoslavia, Zambia.

Against: Bangladesh, Chile, El Salvador, Guatemala, Haiti, Honduras, Indonesia, Morocco, Paraguay, United States, Uruguay.

Before approval of the revised draft resolution by the Committee, amendments sponsored by Costa Rica and Venezuela[52] had been introduced, by which they would have replaced: the words "provision of weapons and military assistance" by "foreign military intrusion" in the seventh preambular paragraph; the first full clause in paragraph 6 with "Requests all States to refrain from any military intrusion in El Salvador"; and the last phrase in paragraph 7 with the words "which expressed their willingness in that respect". The amendments were withdrawn following consultations that resulted in the oral revision of those paragraphs.

El Salvador felt that the text, despite its improvement by the oral revisions, remained tendentious: it engaged in subjective political considerations in violation of the principle of non-interference and played down the armed interventions of the left carried out under the protection of totalitarian régimes. El Salvador voiced disapproval of the way in which the text had been negotiated, for the reason that it had not been a party to those negotiations and the conclusions reached were inconsistent with those of the Special Representative. It also observed that Mexico, supposedly engaged in a good offices mission as a member of the Contadora Group, had assumed the indefensible position of making accusations against the Salvadorian Government, and that Cuba, as one of the main instigators of the disturbances in El Salvador, bore heavy responsibility for the bloodshed there.

Morocco regretted that the Salvadorian Government had not been consulted in the negotiations on the text, whereas the political opposition had been; hence, the oral amendments notwithstanding, Morocco could not accept the resulting compromise formula. Senegal likewise voiced regret at the lack of consultation. The United States felt that the text did not give enough recognition to the work accomplished by the new President or to the progress made in the country's democratization since he took office. Moreover, it tried to dictate internal policy to the Government, which was not within the competence of the United Nations to do. Indonesia said that human rights must not be promoted at the expense of a State's sovereignty and independence.

Chile, Guatemala, Honduras, Paraguay and Uruguay rejected what they called the selectivity of the text: singling out certain countries for human rights violations while maintaining silence with respect to others for the same violations. Guatemala said such a double standard weakened the credibility of human rights institutions and respect for the Charter,

while Honduras pointed to such omissions as the failure to recognize the Government's efforts to improve the situation. Uruguay referred to elements that were extraneous to human rights and constituted interference in the internal affairs of El Salvador.

Sharing the views of the latter three countries were Ecuador and Peru; Peru saw the text as a result of systematic discrimination against Latin America, and Ecuador emphasized respect for the universal defence of human rights and stressed that it should be essentially Latin Americans who should busy themselves to solve the problems of the region.

Expressing support for the Latin American countries in their fight for effective enjoyment of their independence and for the efforts of the Contadora Group in that regard, China called for cessation of all foreign interference in those countries' affairs.

The Philippines was concerned that, unless adequate safeguards were instituted to preserve the principle of non-intervention in the domestic affairs of States, as stipulated by the Charter, to appoint a special representative to look into the human rights situation in any Member State might be an infringement of that principle. In the view of the Federal Republic of Germany, the text did not adequately reflect the Salvadorian Government's positive intentions, the recent free elections that had led to the installation of a legitimate and democratic Government, and the initiation of a dialogue among all of the country's political forces.

The United Kingdom, recognizing the difficulties in producing a text to reflect satisfactorily both the progress made in El Salvador and the seriousness of the continuing problems, said that, in its revised form, the text was considerably more balanced than the resolutions previously adopted on the subject. Nevertheless, the United Kingdom found unacceptable the implicit injunction against military assistance to a Government that had an inherent right to self-defence. It considered regrettable that paragraph 8 took insufficient account of the democratic processes already under way, as well as the lack of appreciation for the extensive co-operation provided by the Government to the Special Representative.

Referring to political reasons, Bolivia did not participate in the vote and requested that its position be duly recorded.

Mozambique would have liked the text to be more precise in certain points. Albania said its vote reflected support for the just struggle of peoples, its reservations on certain paragraphs notwithstanding. Argentina stressed that human rights constituted a legitimate interest of the United Nations, and the Assembly should concern itself with violations of those rights wherever they occurred. It wanted to point out, however, that 1984 had seen positive progress in the situation in El Salvador, as demonstrated by the elections and the dialogue initiated by its President with the opposition forces. Australia said the sponsors of the draft and especially the Contadora Group should be thanked for sparing no effort to produce a text that might contribute to solving the conflict in El Salvador.

Belgium took exception to the approach to certain aspects as defined in the text, saying such definition lay within the exclusive purview not of the Assembly but of the country concerned. Canada challenged the use of the expression "a negotiated comprehensive political solution" in paragraph 8, saying that wording gave the impression that the Government and the opposition forces, the latter not having participated in the electoral process, enjoyed the same constitutional legitimacy. Those opposition forces, Canada also felt, should not be specifically named as they were in paragraphs 7 and 8.

In Venezuela's opinion, the text acknowledged the legitimacy of established authority but made clear that, to be a true political system fully respecting human rights, that authority must negotiate with those who had taken up arms. It was a matter not of deciding in advance who would hold power, but of ensuring the emergence of a true democracy from a dialogue between the Government and the opposition. While recognizing that arms shipments constituted a severe threat to peace in the region, the text did not seek to dictate El Salvador's foreign policy. Finland said its vote was to encourage a country where the situation was improving to promote dialogue among all the parties.

Colombia said the sponsors understood that the Latin American countries could contribute to the search for solutions and, recognizing the role of the Salvadorian President in taking certain initiatives, had agreed substantially to change the content and language of the text. Its vote was in recognition of this political integrity, Colombia stressed. Uganda considered the draft an important effort towards achieving improvements in the human rights situation in El Salvador.

Upon Committee approval of the revised text, a draft resolution on the same topic, sponsored by Costa Rica, Singapore and Venezuela[53]—to which amendments were submitted by Cuba[54] and by Nicaragua[55]—was withdrawn.

By that draft, the Assembly would have expressed concern that a critical situation still existed in El Salvador which impeded the enjoyment of human rights, and at the effect which the hostilities and systematic attacks on the economic infrastructure had on economic, social and cultural rights. It would have deplored that the capacity of the judicial system to investigate human rights violations showed no perceptible improvement, and would again have urged the authorities to speed up the reform of the penal system to punish those responsible for such violations. It would have called on the armed forces and the guerrilla forces to protect the health personnel, medical units and hospitals, and would have called on the Government to continue its support for the activities of the Committee of the Red Cross and other humanitarian organizations. It would have reiterated its appeal to all Salvadorian parties to the conflict to co-operate with those organizations, and would have welcomed the Salvadorian President's appeal for dialogue and the favourable response by the opposition forces. The Assembly further would have called on government and opposition forces to ensure that the national reconciliation process advanced so that conditions for a lasting peace could be established, characterized by respect for economic, social and cultural, and civil and political rights. It would have renewed its request to the Government and the parties concerned to continue to extend their co-operation to the Special Representative.

Guatemala

Report of the Special Rapporteur. In February 1984, Special Rapporteur Viscount Colville of Culross (United Kingdom) submitted to the Commission on Human Rights a report on the human rights situation in Guatemala,[56] pursuant to a Commission request of March 1983.[57] This final report contained information gathered during the Special Rapporteur's visit to Guatemala from 24 to 29 November 1983, updating his interim report to the General Assembly earlier that month.[58]

Besides providing information on the international human rights instruments to which Guatemala was or was not a party and a historical perspective from which to evaluate the situation in the country, the Special Rapporteur gave an account of his investigations, including his observations with respect to: reforms introduced, such as democratic elections with a timetable for the return to democracy beginning with constitutional elections in March 1984 or earlier, the abolition of the Council of State, and social and economic reforms; unresolved indications of abuses, among them disappearances, killings and kidnappings, compulsory service in civil patrols, infringement of religious freedom and army harassment, abduction and killing of priests and catechists ostensibly for subversive activities; and general concerns about alleged human rights violations and the problems of verifying them, the so-called protected or model villages, freedom of speech, trade unions and freedom of association, and refugees in Mexico.

The Special Rapporteur stated that economic injustice and social and racial inequalities underlay the trouble in Guatemala. Thus, unless the economic, social and cultural problems were significantly ameliorated, much of the population had little opportunity for participating in many civil and political rights. The right to life could be infringed as much by poverty and lack of medical care as by slaughter. The revolutionary movements had declared themselves anxious to effect necessary reforms, and the initiatives taken by the Government since early 1982 demonstrated that it was seeking the same goals.

The Special Rapporteur made a series of recommendations including: Commission support of government plans for rural development, to be accompanied by the granting of communal rights to land, infrastructural support in the form of access roads and water supply, advisory and educational services, and health care; electoral reform; assistance to refugees at home and abroad; a continuation of amnesties; establishment of an official system of inquiry for alleged abuses and human rights violations; a Supreme Court review of cases of persons convicted by special tribunals; and a guarantee of the freedom of speech, of the press and of association. The Special Rapporteur vigorously stressed the clearing up of disappearances, killings and kidnappings.

Action by the Commission on Human Rights. On 14 March 1984,[59] the Commission on Human Rights, by a roll-call vote of 28 to 3, with 11 abstentions, thanked the Special Rapporteur for his report and took note of his recommendations. It expressed profound concern at the continuing massive human rights violations in Guatemala, particularly the violence against non-combatants, widespread repression, massive displacement of rural and indigenous peoples, and disappearances and killings, recently reported to have increased. It urged the Government: to ensure full respect of human rights and fundamental freedoms by its authorities and agencies, including security forces; to enable persons convicted under the system of special tribunals to be retried and, if necessary, to enact new legislation for that purpose; and to establish conditions necessary for the judiciary to uphold the rule of law.

The Commission called on the Government to establish an impartial and authoritative body to investigate alleged violations, and to refrain from forcefully displacing rural and indigenous populations and from the practice of coercive participation in civilian patrols. It reiterated its appeal for the application of relevant norms of international humanitarian law for the protection of civilians in armed conflicts. It asked the Government to investigate and clarify the fate of disappeared persons and reiterated its appeal that international humanitarian organizations be allowed to assist in the investigations on behalf of relatives and to assist the civilian population in areas of conflict. Noting that constitutional elections had taken place in January 1984, the Commission urged Guatemala to adhere faithfully to the timetable for the return to democracy, which specified July 1984 for the election of a Constituent Assembly and July 1985 as the latest date for instituting a new constitutional Government, and to guarantee the free participation of all political forces.

The Commission called on Governments to refrain from giving military assistance to Guatemala as long as serious human rights violations there continued

to be reported. It extended the mandate of the Special Rapporteur for another year, with a request that he submit an interim report to the General Assembly in 1984 on subsequent developments, especially with regard to his recommendations, and a final report to the Commission in 1985. It invited the Government and all parties to extend to him their full cooperation and requested the Secretary-General to provide him with the necessary assistance.

ECONOMIC AND SOCIAL COUNCIL ACTION

Acting on the recommendation of its Second Committee, the Economic and Social Council in May adopted decision 1984/137 by vote.

Situation of human rights in Guatemala

At its 20th plenary meeting, on 24 May 1984, the Council, noting Commission on Human Rights resolution 1984/53 of 14 March 1984, endorsed the Commission's decision to extend the mandate of the Special Rapporteur on the situation of human rights in Guatemala for another year and to request him to report on the subsequent development of the situation of human rights in that country, taking into account developments in regard to the recommendations in his reports as well as information from other reliable sources, and to submit an interim report to the General Assembly at its thirty-ninth session and a final report to the Commission at its forty-first session. The Council further endorsed the Commission's request to the Secretary-General to give all necessary assistance to the Special Rapporteur.

Economic and Social Council decision 1984/137

34-1-15

Approved by Second Committee (E/1984/91) by vote (30-1-13), 17 May (meeting 16); draft by Commission on Human Rights (E/1984/14); agenda item 10.

Sub-Commission action. Taking note of the elections for the Constituent Assembly held in Guatemala on 1 July 1984 and of the electoral schedule for the coming year, the Sub-Commission on 29 August[60] expressed deep concern over the increasing and systematic human rights violations in the country, in particular acts of violence against the civilian non-combatant population, including torture, forced disappearances and massive extra-judicial executions, as well as displacements of rural and indigenous populations, their confinement in militarized hamlets and incorporation into civilian patrols organized and controlled by the army. The Sub-Commission exhorted the Government to: ensure that all authorities and dependencies, including security forces, observed total respect for human rights and fundamental freedoms; clarify the destiny of all disappeared persons; forbid clandestine prisons; sanction the authors of acts of torture; ensure enforcement of the right of *habeas corpus;* and free and provide care to imprisoned persons.

The Sub-Commission called on all parties to ensure observance of humanitarian law applicable in armed conflicts such as were occurring in Guatemala, in particular the 1949 Geneva Conventions and the Protocols additional thereto. It urged the Government to abide by the electoral schedule and to improve guarantees of participation by all political forces in the presidential elections to be held in July 1985. It also urged Governments to abstain from giving military assistance to Guatemala as long as serious human rights violations continued. It invited the Special Rapporteur to take account of the situation of the indigenous population and of all reports submitted to the Sub-Commission, which would be forwarded to him.

Further report. In keeping with the Commission's March request (see above), the Special Rapporteur prepared an interim report on developments in the human rights situation in Guatemala, which the Secretary-General transmitted to the Assembly in November.[61] The report was confined to events in 1984 and included information gathered during the Special Rapporteur's visit to Guatemala from 12 to 18 August, with one morning spent in Honduras, and to Mexico and Belize until 24 August. The report noted that the Guatemalan Government had provided every facility and posed no obstacles to his travel and interviews. Belize, Honduras and Mexico likewise had co-operated in enabling him to visit refugees.

The report noted that the first phase of the electoral process took place on 1 July 1984 as scheduled. Parties of the centre and right participated and the Supreme Electoral Tribunal carried out its duties with skill and impartiality. Despite several incidents designed to disrupt the process and invalidate the results, a Constituent Assembly was installed on 1 August. There continued to be apparent numerous examples of violations of human rights of individuals, notably murders, disappearances and woundings; information was not available as to how many of these had been cleared up, but very many had not. The allegations indicated four groups as being responsible: security forces, guerrillas, common criminals and private organizations consisting of off-duty police and military and/or right-wing political groups. A Commission for Peace, set up earlier in the year to resolve allegations, had so far failed to function. Those convicted by special tribunals had been pardoned and freed.

Freedom of speech and publication did not seem to suffer from any appreciable infringement. Trade union activities appeared extremely limited and their existence precarious. Many refugees remained in Mexico; the smaller numbers in Belize and Honduras showed little inclination to return. Refugees who had returned from abroad and internal refugees who had come out of hiding were being resettled. Amnesties were continuing.

The Special Rapporteur recommended every support for the process towards a return to a democratically elected Government, with the terms of the new Con-

stitution to be drawn up to guarantee the range of human rights contained in the 1966 International Covenants, to ensure that positions of power and responsibility at every level of central and local government were filled by civilians, and to establish independence for the judiciary. The Government should urgently seek to prevent disappearances and bring perpetrators to justice, making an inquiry into the 458 persons arrested under the system of special tribunals and another into the 117 persons who might have been detained improperly by police as test cases. There should be an improvement in the climate of violence if a wider range of political parties was to be persuaded to participate in the next elections.

Other recommendations called for continuance of distribution of land titles and technical assistance for rural development, improvement of living conditions of migrant workers, encouragement of trade union activities, strengthening of the Commission for Peace or its replacement with another system, and providing refugees, especially those in Mexico, with information to enable them to make decisions regarding their return to Guatemala.

Communication. On 16 August 1984,[62] Guatemala transmitted the text of Decree-Law No. 74-84 of 18 July, whereby complete pardon was granted to those sentenced without possibility of appeal under the abolished system of special tribunals; trials initiated under that system and later transferred to the courts were dismissed and the accused persons released.

GENERAL ASSEMBLY ACTION

Acting on the recommendation of the Third Committee, the General Assembly adopted resolution 39/120 by recorded vote on 14 December 1984.

Situation of human rights and fundamental freedoms in Guatemala

The General Assembly,

Reiterating that the Governments of all Member States have an obligation to promote and protect human rights and fundamental freedoms,

Recalling its resolutions 37/184 of 17 December 1982 and 38/100 of 16 December 1983,

Taking note of Commission on Human Rights resolution 1984/53 of 14 March 1984, in which the Commission expressed its profound concern at the continuing massive violations of human rights in Guatemala,

Mindful of resolution 1984/23 of 29 August 1984 of the Sub-Commission on Prevention of Discrimination and Protection of Minorities, in which the Sub-Commission recognized, *inter alia*, that in Guatemala there existed an armed conflict of a non-international character, which stemmed from economic, social and political factors of a structural nature,

Noting the elections to the Constituent Assembly held in July 1984, which fulfilled the first stage of the electoral process for the institution of a new constitutional Government according to the timetable proposed by the Government of Guatemala, and affirming the importance of creating conditions in which the electoral process can be pursued in a climate free from intimidation and terror,

Alarmed at the continuation of politically motivated violence in the form of killings and kidnappings,

Alarmed also at the large number of persons who have continued to disappear and the unclear fate of those reported to have been tried by the special tribunals, now abolished,

Welcoming the co-operation of the Government of Guatemala with the Special Rapporteur of the Commission on Human Rights in the fulfilment of his mandate and noting with satisfaction that a list of cases dealt with by the special tribunals has now been handed over to the Special Rapporteur,

1. *Takes note* of the interim report by the Special Rapporteur on the situation of human rights in Guatemala, prepared in accordance with Commission on Human Rights resolution 1984/53;

2. *Reiterates its deep concern* at the continuing grave and widespread violations of human rights in Guatemala, particularly the violence against non-combatants, the disappearances and killings and the widespread repression, including the practice of torture, the displacement of rural and indigenous people, their confinement in development centres and their forced participation in civilian patrols, organized and controlled by the armed forces;

3. *Once again urges* the Government of Guatemala to take effective measures to ensure that all its authorities and agencies, including its security forces, fully respect human rights and fundamental freedoms;

4. *Renews its call upon* the Government of Guatemala to refrain from the forceful displacement of people belonging to rural and indigenous populations and from the practice of coercing them into participation in civilian patrols, leading to human rights violations;

5. *Welcomes* the fact that many of the persons who were tried by the special tribunals have now been released and invites the Government of Guatemala to publish the list of cases dealt with by the special tribunals;

6. *Requests* the Government of Guatemala to investigate and clarify the fate of all persons who have been subjected to involuntary or forced disappearances and are still unaccounted for and to put an end to arbitrary detention and imprisonment in secret places;

7. *Urges* the Government of Guatemala to establish the necessary conditions to ensure the independence of the judicial system and to enable the judiciary to uphold the rule of law, including the right of *habeas corpus*, and to prosecute and punish speedily and effectively those found responsible for violations of human rights, including members of the military and security forces;

8. *Calls upon* the Government of Guatemala to allow an independent and impartial body to function in the country to monitor and investigate alleged human rights violations;

9. *Reiterates its appeal* to all parties concerned in Guatemala to ensure the application of the relevant norms of international humanitarian law applicable in armed conflicts of a non-international character to protect the civilian population and to seek an end to all acts of violence;

10. *Appeals* to the Government of Guatemala to allow international humanitarian organizations to render their assistance in investigating the fate of persons who have disappeared, with a view to informing their relatives of their whereabouts, to visit detainees or prisoners and to bring assistance to the civilian population in areas of conflict;

11. *Calls upon* Governments to refrain from supplying arms and other military assistance to Guatemala as long as serious human rights violations in that country continue;

12. *Urges* the Government of Guatemala to ensure a climate free from intimidation and terror which would allow the free participation of all in the political process;

13. *Invites* the Government of Guatemala and other parties concerned to continue co-operating with the Special Rapporteur of the Commission on Human Rights;

14. *Requests* the Commission on Human Rights to study carefully the report of its Special Rapporteur, as well as other information pertaining to the human rights situation in Guatemala, and to consider further steps for securing effective respect for human rights and fundamental freedoms for all in that country;

15. *Decides* to continue its examination of the situation of human rights and fundamental freedoms in Guatemala at its fortieth session.

General Assembly resolution 39/120

14 December 1984   Meeting 101   85-11-47 (recorded vote)

Approved by Third Committee (A/39/700) by recorded vote (79-13-39), 7 December (meeting 66); 10-nation draft (A/C.3/39/L.77); agenda item 12.

Sponsors: Austria, Canada, Denmark, France, Greece, Ireland, Netherlands, Norway, Spain, Sweden.

Meeting numbers. GA 39th session: 3rd Committee 54-56, 58, 59, 61-66; plenary 101.

Recorded vote in Assembly as follows:

In favour: Afghanistan, Algeria, Angola, Argentina, Australia, Austria, Bahrain, Barbados, Belgium, Benin, Botswana, Bulgaria, Burkina Faso, Burundi, Byelorussian SSR, Canada, Cape Verde, Congo, Cuba, Cyprus, Czechoslovakia, Democratic Yemen, Denmark, Ethiopia, Finland, France, Gambia, German Democratic Republic, Germany, Federal Republic of, Ghana, Greece, Guyana, Hungary, Iceland, India, Iran, Iraq, Ireland, Italy, Jamaica, Kenya, Kuwait, Lao People's Democratic Republic, Lesotho, Libyan Arab Jamahiriya, Luxembourg, Madagascar, Mali, Malta, Mauritania, Mauritius, Mexico, Mongolia, Mozambique, Netherlands, New Zealand, Nicaragua, Norway, Poland, Portugal, Qatar, Rwanda, Samoa, Sao Tome and Principe, Saudi Arabia, Senegal, Seychelles, Sierra Leone, Spain, Swaziland, Sweden, Syrian Arab Republic, Togo, Tunisia, Uganda, Ukrainian SSR, USSR, United Arab Emirates, United Kingdom, United Republic of Tanzania, Vanuatu, Viet Nam, Yugoslavia, Zambia, Zimbabwe.

Against: Bangladesh, Chile, El Salvador, Guatemala, Haiti, Indonesia, Morocco, Pakistan, Paraguay, United States, Uruguay.

Abstaining: Bahamas, Belize, Bhutan, Brazil, Brunei Darussalam, Burma, Central African Republic, Chad, China, Colombia, Costa Rica, Democratic Kampuchea, Dominican Republic, Ecuador, Egypt, Equatorial Guinea, Fiji, Gabon, Guinea, Honduras, Ivory Coast, Japan, Jordan, Liberia, Malawi, Malaysia, Maldives, Nepal, Niger, Nigeria, Oman, Panama, Papua New Guinea, Peru, Philippines, Romania, Singapore, Somalia, Sri Lanka, Sudan, Suriname, Thailand, Trinidad and Tobago, Turkey, Venezuela, Yemen, Zaire.

Guatemala expressed strong opposition to the text, saying it was partial, unbalanced and discriminatory and reflected the political prejudices of its sponsors. It cited references in the fourth and fifth preambular paragraphs as partial and rejected what it called the insinuation deriving from the word "unclear" in the seventh. It pointed to paragraph 2 as full of false accusations, particularly of "grave and widespread violations of human rights" and "widespread repression", and as unwarranted its references to "combatants" and "non-combatants", there being no civil war in the country but only secret terrorist groups. Guatemala objected to what it said was the intolerable presumption of the injunction in paragraph 11, underscoring its right to defend itself and to acquire the means to guarantee its security and independence and to maintain law and order. It urged that the draft not be approved for it contributed neither to peace in Guatemala nor to stability in Central America.

Uruguay and Peru echoed Guatemala's criticism of the text as discriminatory, and Paraguay as flawed by partiality and prejudice. Chile, Colombia and Ecuador referred to the selectivity of the text.

The United States said the conclusions reached in the annual report of its Department of State on the human rights situation in Guatemala were similar to those of the Special Rapporteur, namely, that problems continued but that there had been definite improvements, such as the July elections for the Constituent Assembly. Far from reflecting that progress, the draft made unfounded allegations; whence the negative vote of the United States, despite its strong wish to encourage the promotion of human rights in that country.

Morocco's position was that human rights could be defended only in an atmosphere devoid of emotionalism, political manœuvring, geopolitics, and hegemonistic and ideological ambitions. For that reason it had never approached the subject on any but a humanitarian basis. Therefore, when a draft resolution raised doubt as to its true objective, Morocco would vote accordingly.

Indonesia declared itself committed to promoting human rights, but not at the expense of the most fundamental right: the sovereign independence of the State. It observed that, when an uprising threatened the State's integrity, external interference could only exacerbate the situation. The principle of the national authority of a State, enshrined in the Charter, should not be called into question, as it was by the draft. The concern of the Philippines was safeguarding the principle of non-intervention; it felt that mandating a special rapporteur to look into the human rights situation of a Member State might infringe that principle.

Bolivia said that, for political reasons, it was not participating in the vote and wanted this position recorded.

According to the Federal Republic of Germany, the Special Rapporteur's report gave clear evidence that, despite some encouraging developments in Guatemala, the human rights situation there continued to be quite serious; the text, however, reflected the Special Rapporteur's conclusions only partially and gave the impression that the Government alone was responsible for the violence in the country and not also the guerrilla forces. Such imprecision, exhibited also by paragraph 11, could have been avoided by a reference to both government and opposition forces. Also, the text should have been more prudent in its references to rural development centres and forced participation in civilian patrols.

In Finland's view, the Government of Guatemala, where the situation was improving, should be encouraged to promote dialogue among all interested parties.

Uganda said that, since 1979, it had consistently voted for similar resolutions on the human rights situation not only in Guatemala but also in Chile and El Salvador. It felt a need to point this out because it had inadvertently abstained on the resolutions on all three countries in the Committee.

Haiti

By a decision adopted at a closed meeting on 1 March 1984 and made public[63] in accordance with a procedure established in 1970 by the Economic and Social Council for dealing with communications alleging denial or violations of human rights,[1] the Commission on Human Rights took note of a report of the Secretary-General submitted pursuant to its confidential decision relating to Haiti, adopted at a closed meeting on 28 February 1983. The Commission recommended a draft text that served as the basis for the Council decision below.

ECONOMIC AND SOCIAL COUNCIL ACTION

Acting on the recommendation of its Second Committee, the Economic and Social Council in May 1984 adopted decision 1984/143 by recorded vote.

Study of situations which appear to reveal a consistent pattern of gross violations of human rights as provided in Commission on Human Rights resolution 8(XXIII) and Economic and Social Council resolutions 1235(XLII) and 1503(XLVIII)

At its 20th plenary meeting, on 24 May 1984, the Council, noting Commission on Human Rights decision 1984/109 of 1 March 1984, decided to request the Secretary-General to continue his consultations with the Government of Haiti, as envisaged in his report to the Commission, with a view to further exploring ways and means of providing the Government of Haiti with assistance to facilitate the realization of full enjoyment of human rights for the people of Haiti, and to report to the Commission at its forty-first session on the implementation of the present decision.

Economic and Social Council decision 1984/143

45-2-3 (recorded vote)

Approved by Second Committee (E/1984/91) by vote (42-1-4), 17 May (meeting 16); draft by Commission on Human Rights (E/1984/14); agenda item 10.

Recorded vote in Council as follows:

In favour: Algeria, Argentina, Austria, Benin, Botswana, Bulgaria, Canada, China, Colombia, Congo, Costa Rica, Ecuador, Finland, France, German Democratic Republic, Germany, Federal Republic of, Greece, Japan, Lebanon, Liberia, Luxembourg, Mali, Mexico, Netherlands, New Zealand, Papua New Guinea, Poland, Portugal, Qatar, Romania, Rwanda, Saudi Arabia, Sierra Leone, Somalia, Sri Lanka, Suriname, Swaziland, Sweden, Thailand, Tunisia, Uganda, USSR, United Kingdom, Venezuela, Yugoslavia.

Against: Saint Lucia, United States.

Abstaining: Brazil, Malaysia, Zaire.

Brazil voiced strong reservations with respect to the decision's title.

Uruguay

By 17 votes to none, with 5 abstentions, on 30 August 1984,[64] the Sub-Commission—noting that Uruguay had taken measures to restore the democratic system and that national elections were scheduled for 25 November, but concerned nevertheless that measures remained in the way of the full exercise of political rights—expressed confidence that Uruguay would continue to make efforts to achieve full restoration of democratic institutions and to adopt measures to restore full exercise of human rights and fundamental freedoms. Welcoming the process begun for the liberation of persons detained or sentenced for alleged offences against the security of the State and internal order, the Sub-Commission urged the Government to speed up that process and to lift restrictions on the political rights of citizens and political parties so that free and democratic elections might be held.

Concerned that Wilson Ferreira Aldunate, a presidential candidate of one of the country's most important political forces, continued to be deprived of his liberty, thereby preventing a considerable sector from exercising its political rights, and that charges against him were basically related to his human rights activities, the Sub-Commission likewise urged the Government to set him free and remove any restrictions on political rights affecting him. It recommended that the Commission urge the Secretary-General to use his good offices to verify the information that the charges against Mr. Ferreira Aldunate included his "having made requests before specialized agencies of the United Nations", and to inform the Commission Chairman of the results of this endeavour.

Middle East

Territories occupied by Israel

In 1984, the question of human rights violations in the territories occupied by Israel as a result of the 1967 hostilities in the Middle East was again considered by the Commission on Human Rights. This was in addition to the consideration of political and other aspects by the General Assembly, its Special Committee to Investigate Israeli Practices Affecting the Human Rights of the Population of the Occupied Territories and other bodies (see p. 315).

Action by the Commission on Human Rights. Following consideration of a report by the Secretary-General[65] on measures taken to give the widest possible publicity to Commission on Human Rights resolutions of February 1983[66] on the question of human rights violations in the occupied Arab territories, including Palestine, the Commission on 20 February 1984 adopted four resolutions relating to those territories: two on the same subject, one on Israeli occupation of the Syrian Golan Heights, and another on Israeli withdrawal from those territories.

By the first of these resolutions,[67] the Commission, by 29 votes to 1, with 11 abstentions, reaffirmed that occupation itself was a fundamental violation of the human rights of the civilian population of the Palestinian and other occupied Arab territories. It denounced Israel's continued refusal to allow the Special Committee on Israeli practices access to the occupied territories and reiterated the Com-

mittee's alarm that Israel's policy in them was based on the so-called Homeland doctrine envisaging a monoreligious (Jewish) State including the occupied territories, a policy that not only denied the right to self-determination of the population but also constituted the source of systematic human rights violations. It confirmed its declaration that Israel's continuous grave breaches of the 1949 Geneva Convention relative to the Protection of Civilian Persons in Time of War (fourth Geneva Convention) and of the Additional Protocols were war crimes and an affront to humanity.

The Commission firmly rejected Israel's decision to annex Jerusalem and to change the physical character, demographic composition, institutional structure or status of the territories and considered these measures and their consequences null and void. It strongly condemned Israel's attempts to subject the West Bank and the Gaza Strip to Israeli laws.

The Commission also condemned Israeli measures to promote and expand settler colonies in the territories, as well as the following practices: annexation of parts of the territories, including Jerusalem; establishment of new Israeli settlements on Arab lands; arming of settlers to commit acts of violence against Arab civilians; evacuation, expulsion and displacement of the territories' Arab inhabitants and denial of their right to return; confiscation and expropriation of Arab property; destruction and demolition of Arab houses; mass arrests, collective punishments, detention and ill-treatment of the Arab population; pillaging of archaeological and cultural property; interference with religious freedoms and family customs; systematic repression against cultural and educational institutions; illegal exploitation of the territories' natural resources; and dismantling of municipal services by dismissing elected mayors and municipal councils and forbidding Arab aid funds.

The Commission called on Israel to take immediate steps for the return of displaced Arabs to their homes and property; to implement Security Council resolutions on the return of the expelled Mayors of Hebron and Halhul; to release all Arabs detained for their struggle for self-determination; to cease all acts of torture of Arab prisoners; and to release the Palestinian Ziyad Abu Eain and others detained in Insar Camp, which must be closed in accordance with a 1983 agreement on prisoner exchange (see p. 279).

The Commission reiterated its call to all States, international organizations and specialized agencies not to recognize any changes carried out by Israel in the territories, including Jerusalem, and to avoid taking action or extending aid which Israel might use to pursue its annexation and colonization policies. It urged Israel to refrain from policies and practices violating human rights and to report to it, through the Secretary-General, in 1985. It requested the Assembly to recommend to the Security Council, through the Economic and Social Council, to take the measures referred to in Chapter VII of the Charter against Israel for its persistent human rights violations. It asked the Secretary-General to give this resolution the widest possible publicity.

By the second resolution,[68] adopted by 32 votes to 1, with 8 abstentions, the Commission reaffirmed that the fourth Geneva Convention was applicable to all the Arab territories occupied by Israel since 1967, including Jerusalem, and condemned Israel's failure to acknowledge such applicability. It called on Israel to abide by the obligations under the Charter, the Convention and other instruments of international law and again urged all States parties to the Convention to ensure Israel's compliance.

By the third resolution,[69] adopted by a roll-call vote of 30 to 1, with 11 abstentions, the Commission condemned Israel for failure to comply with Security Council and Assembly resolutions demanding rescission of its 1981 decision to apply Israeli law to the occupied Golan Heights.[70] The Commission again declared that decision null and void, and Israeli practices and inhuman treatment of the Syrian Arab population a grave violation of the 1948 Universal Declaration of Human Rights,[71] the fourth Geneva Convention and relevant United Nations resolutions, as well as a threat to international peace and security. It condemned Israel for attempting to impose Israeli citizenship and identity cards on Syrian citizens in the occupied Golan Heights. It deplored the negative vote and pro-Israeli position of a permanent Security Council member which prevented the Council from adopting measures under Chapter VII of the Charter against Israel. The Commission emphasized the necessity of total and unconditional withdrawal from all Palestinian and Syrian territories as an essential prerequisite for a comprehensive and just peace in the Middle East.

By the fourth resolution,[72] adopted by 30 votes to 1, with 11 abstentions, the Commission, repeating its condemnation of continued Israeli occupation of the Palestinian territories, including Jerusalem, and persistence in colonizing them, called for immediate Israeli withdrawal from those territories so as to restore to the Palestinian people their inalienable national rights.

Also in February 1984, the Commission, in its resolution reaffirming the right of the Palestinian people to self-determination (see above, under "Civil and political rights") and to a fully independent and sovereign State of Palestine, condemned Israel for its aggression and practices against Palestinians in and outside the occupied territories and for its responsibility for the 1982 large-scale massacre in the Sabra and Shatila refugee camps, which it determined constituted an act of genocide.[73]

In addition, the Commission in March 1984 urged Israel to recognize the status of prisoner of war for all combatants captured during the war in Lebanon (see above, under "Rights of detained persons").

Mass exoduses

Following its consideration of a 1983 report by the Secretary-General on human rights and mass exoduses,[74] the Commission on Human Rights, on 14 March 1984,[75] welcomed his intention to utilize to the utmost the relevant United Nations machinery for the prompt analysis of information on situations that might cause mass exoduses. It noted that he had on many occasions designated special representatives on humanitarian issues on an *ad hoc* basis and noted his readiness to expand that practice.

The Commission invited Governments to intensify their co-operation and assistance in world-wide efforts to address the problem of mass exoduses in all its aspects. It appealed to them to make their views known on the subject and thus contribute to the discussion of how the international community could remove the root causes of mass exoduses and solve the problems resulting from them.

GENERAL ASSEMBLY ACTION

Acting without vote on the recommendation of the Third Committee, the General Assembly adopted resolution 39/117 on 14 December 1984.

Human rights and mass exoduses

The General Assembly,

Mindful of its general humanitarian mandate under the Charter of the United Nations to promote and encourage respect for human rights and fundamental freedoms,

Deeply disturbed by the continuing scale and magnitude of exoduses of refugees and displacements of population in many regions of the world and by the human suffering of millions of refugees and displaced persons,

Conscious of the fact that human rights violations are among the multiple and complex factors causing mass exoduses of refugees, as indicated in the study of the Special Rapporteur of the Commission on Human Rights on this subject,

Considering the efforts which have been made to address this subject within the United Nations, in particular by the Commission on Human Rights,

Deeply preoccupied by the increasingly heavy burden being imposed upon the international community as a whole, particularly upon developing countries with limited resources of their own, by these sudden mass exoduses and displacements of population,

Stressing the need for international co-operation aimed at the prevention of new massive flows of refugees along with the provision of adequate solutions to actual refugee situations,

Taking note again of the report of the Secretary-General on human rights and mass exoduses,

Recalling its resolutions 35/196 of 15 December 1980, 37/186 of 17 December 1982 and 38/103 of 16 December 1983 and Commission on Human Rights resolutions 30(XXXVI) of 11 March 1980, 29(XXXVII) of 11 March 1981, 1982/32 of 11 March 1982 and 1983/35 of 8 March 1983,

1. _Welcomes_ the steps taken so far by the United Nations to examine the problem of massive outflows of refugees and displaced persons in all its aspects, including its root causes;

2. _Invites_ Governments to intensify their co-operation and assistance in world-wide efforts to address the serious problem of mass exoduses of refugees and displaced persons;

3. _Welcomes_ the special interest which the Secretary-General has taken in this question and reiterates its request to him to follow closely developments in the field of human rights and mass exoduses;

4. _Encourages_ the Secretary-General in his efforts to enable the United Nations to anticipate and react more adequately and speedily to cases requiring humanitarian assistance, as mentioned in his report on the work of the Organization;

5. _Invites_ the Commission on Human Rights to keep the question of human rights and mass exoduses under review with the objective of making appropriate recommendations concerning further measures to be taken in this field;

6. _Decides_ to review the question of human rights and mass exoduses at its fortieth session.

General Assembly resolution 39/117

14 December 1984　　　Meeting 101　　　Adopted without vote

Approved by Third Committee (A/39/700) without vote, 7 December (meeting 66); 10-nation draft (A/C.3/39/L.80), orally revised; agenda item 12.
Sponsors: Australia, Bangladesh, Canada, Colombia, Costa Rica, Germany, Federal Republic of, Japan, Pakistan, Somalia, Sudan.
Meeting numbers. GA 39th session: 3rd Committee 54-56, 58, 59, 61-66; plenary 101.

Genocide

Report of the Special Rapporteur. In July 1984, Special Rapporteur Benjamin Charles George Whitaker (United Kingdom) submitted a preliminary report[76] on the revision and updating of a 1978 study on the prevention and punishment of the crime of genocide.[77] The report was prepared in accordance with the mandate entrusted to him by the Sub-Commission in August 1983.[78]

The report reproduced a questionnaire which the Special Rapporteur prepared and sent to Governments, specialized agencies and other United Nations bodies, regional organizations and NGOs in January 1984 for the purpose of obtaining information for the revision. As at 16 July 1984, replies had been received from 16 States, 4 specialized agencies and 12 NGOs. The Special Rapporteur proposed that he present the revised study in draft form to the Sub-Commission in 1985 and to the Commission on Human Rights in 1986, to enable him to take into consideration additional replies that might still be forthcoming. In the mean time, he invited the Sub-Commission members to provide him with their views on the issues set forth in the questionnaire, or on any other matter dealt with in the study.

Sub-Commission action. Having discussed the preliminary report of the Special Rapporteur, the Sub-Commission on 28 August 1984[79] requested him to continue his work and to submit a final report

in 1985. It requested the Secretary-General to provide him with all possible assistance to facilitate his work.

REFERENCES

[1]YUN 1970, p. 530, ESC res. 1503(XLVIII), 27 May 1970. [2]YUN 1983, p. 872. [3]E/1984/14 (dec. 1984/114). [4]YUN 1967, p. 509. [5]E/CN.4/1984/8. [6]YUN 1983, p. 874. [7]YUN 1981, p. 947. [8]E/1984/14 (res. 1984/5). [9]_Ibid._ (res. 1984/4). [10]E/CN.4/1985/3 (res. 1984/34). [11]YUN 1973, p. 103, GA res. 3068(XXVIII), annex, 30 Nov. 1973. [12]A/39/460. [13]E/CN.4/1984/48. [14]E/1984/14 (res. 1984/7). [15]YUN 1983, p. 878. [16]E/1984/14 (res. 1984/6). [17]YUN 1960, p. 49, GA res. 1514(XV), 14 Dec. 1960. [18]_Adverse Consequences for the Enjoyment of Human Rights of Political, Military, Economic and Other Forms of Assistance Given to the Racist and Colonialist Régime of South Africa_ (E/CN.4/Sub.2/1984/8/Rev.1), Sales No. E.85.XIV.4. [19]E/CN.4/1985/3 (res. 1984/4). [20]A/C.3/39/2. [21]YUN 1983, p. 879, ESC dec. 1983/156, 27 May 1983. [22]E/1984/32. [23]E/1984/85. [24]E/CN.4/1984/32. [25]E/CN.4/1984/28. [26]YUN 1983, p. 880. [27]YUN 1966, p. 423, GA res. 2200 A (XXI), annex, 16 Dec. 1966. [28]YUN 1980, p. 829. [29]E/CN.4/1984 (res. 1984/54). [30]E/CN.4/1985/3 (res. 1984/14). [31]E/CN.4/1984/10. [32]E/1984/14 (dec. 1984/111). [33]E/CN.4/1985/3 (res. 1984/32). [34]E/1984/14 (dec. 1984/117). [35]E/CN.4/1984/26. [36]YUN 1983, p. 882. [37]_Ibid._, p. 881. [38]E/CN.4/1984/L.66/Rev.1. [39]E/1984/14 (dec. 1984/110). [40]E/CN.4/1984/7. [41]YUN 1983, p. 883. [42]_Ibid._, p. 884. [43]E/CN.4/1984/20. [44]E/1984/14 (res. 1984/63). [45]E/CN.4/1985/3 (res. 1984/29). [46]A/39/631. [47]YUN 1983, p. 888. [48]E/CN.4/1984/25 & Corr.1. [49]E/1984/14 (res. 1984/52). [50]E/CN.4/1985/3 (res. 1984/26). [51]A/39/636. [52]A/C.3/39/L.83. [53]A/C.3/39/L.71. [54]A/C.3/39/L.85. [55]A/C.3/39/L.84. [56]E/CN.4/1984/30. [57]YUN 1983, p. 892. [58]_Ibid._, p. 893. [59]E/1984/14 (res. 1984/53). [60]E/CN.4/1985/3 (res. 1984/23). [61]A/39/635. [62]A/39/414. [63]E/1984/14 (dec. 1984/109). [64]E/CN.4/1985/3 (res. 1984/25). [65]E/CN.4/1984/51. [66]YUN 1983, p. 896. [67]E/1984/14 (res. 1984/1 A). [68]_Ibid._ (res. 1984/1 B). [69]_Ibid._ (res. 1984/2). [70]YUN 1981, p. 309. [71]YUN 1948-49, p. 535, GA res. 217 A (III), 10 Dec. 1948. [72]E/1984/14 (res. 1984/3). [73]YUN 1982, p. 481. [74]YUN 1983, p. 898. [75]E/1984/14 (res. 1984/49). [76]E/CN.4/Sub.2/1984/40. [77]YUN 1978, p. 723. [78]YUN 1983, p. 899. [79]E/CN.4/1985/3 (res. 1984/1).

Other human rights questions

Additional Protocols I and II to the 1949 Geneva Conventions

A list of parties as at 24 August 1984 to the two 1977 Protocols Additional to the Geneva Conventions of 12 August 1949 for the protection of war victims[1] was submitted by the Secretary-General in a report to the General Assembly.[2]

As at 31 December 1984, 47 States and the United Nations Council for Namibia had ratified or acceded to Protocol I (on protection of victims of international armed conflicts), as follows (those in italics acted in 1984):

Angola, Austria, Bahamas, Bangladesh, _Belize_, Bolivia, Botswana, _Cameroon_, _Central African Republic_, China, Congo, Costa Rica, Cuba, Cyprus, Denmark, Ecuador, El Salvador, Finland, Gabon, Ghana, _Guinea_, Jordan, Lao People's Democratic Republic, Libyan Arab Jamahiriya,

Mauritania, Mauritius, Mexico, Mozambique, Niger, Norway, *Oman*, Republic of Korea, *Rwanda*, Saint Lucia, Saint Vincent and the Grenadines, *Samoa*, *Seychelles*, Sweden, Switzerland, Syrian Arab Republic, *Togo*, Tunisia, United Arab Emirates, United Republic of Tanzania, Viet Nam, Yugoslavia, Zaire, United Nations Council for Namibia.

All of these parties had also adhered to Protocol II (on protection of victims of non-international conflicts), except Angola, Cuba, Cyprus, Mexico, Mozambique, the Syrian Arab Republic, Viet Nam and Zaire. France (acting in 1984) adhered only to Protocol II.

GENERAL ASSEMBLY ACTION

Acting without vote on the recommendation of the Sixth Committee, the General Assembly adopted resolution 39/77 on 13 December.

Status of the Protocols Additional to the Geneva Conventions of 1949 and relating to the protection of victims of armed conflicts

The General Assembly,

Recalling its resolutions 32/44 of 8 December 1977, 34/51 of 23 November 1979 and 37/116 of 16 December 1982,

Having considered the report of the Secretary-General on the status of the Protocols Additional to the Geneva Conventions of 1949 and relating to the protection of victims of armed conflicts,

Convinced of the continuing value of established humanitarian rules relating to armed conflicts and the need to respect and ensure respect for these rules in all circumstances within the scope of the relevant international instruments pending the earliest possible termination of such conflicts,

Mindful of the need for continued improvement of the implementation, and for further expansion, of the body of humanitarian rules relating to armed conflicts,

Particularly mindful of the importance of the protection of the civilian population, especially women and children, against the effects of hostilities,

Noting the virtually universal acceptance of the four Geneva Conventions of 12 August 1949 concerning the protection of victims of armed conflicts, and their binding character for all parties,

Aware, however, of the fact that so far only a limited number of States have signed, ratified or acceded to the two Protocols Additional to the Geneva Conventions,

Noting at the same time with appreciation the continuing efforts of the International Committee of the Red Cross to promote and to disseminate knowledge of the two additional Protocols,

1. *Reiterates its call*, contained in resolutions 34/51 and 37/116, to all States to consider at the earliest possible date the matter of ratifying or acceding to the two Protocols Additional to the Geneva Conventions of 1949 and relating to the protection of victims of armed conflicts;

2. *Calls upon* all States becoming parties to Protocol I to consider the matter of making the declaration provided for under article 90 of that Protocol;

3. *Requests* the Secretary-General to submit to the General Assembly at its forty-first session a report on the status of the Protocols based on information received from Member States;

4. *Decides* to include in the provisional agenda of its forty-first session the item entitled "Status of the Protocols Additional to the Geneva Conventions of 1949 and relating to the protection of victims of armed conflicts: report of the Secretary-General".

General Assembly resolution 39/77

13 December 1984   Meeting 99   Adopted without vote

Approved by Sixth Committee (A/39/772) without vote, 5 December (meeting 63); 14-nation draft (A/C.6/39/L.6/Rev.1); agenda item 122.
Sponsors: Austria, Bangladesh, Costa Rica, Denmark, Egypt, Finland, Ghana, Libyan Arab Jamahiriya, Netherlands, Norway, Suriname, Sweden, Tunisia, Yugoslavia.
Meeting numbers. GA 39th session: 6th Committee 7, 8, 63; plenary 99.

Israel stated that, while the draft resolution was by and large unobjectionable, it would have abstained had there been a vote. Despite its active role in the negotiations for the Protocols, the political terminology and transient considerations included in Protocol I prevented it from taking part in the consensus on the Protocol as a whole. The relative ease with which any group claiming to meet the political criteria of article 1, paragraph 4, could consider itself entitled to status under the Protocol served only to encourage and license terrorist activities just when the international community was trying to stamp out terrorism. Characterizing article 44 as diluting the requirements for prisoner-of-war status and for differentiating between combatants and civilians, Israel said this could increase invocation of the Protocol as a shelter for terrorist activity and the danger to the life and safety of innocent civilians.

The United States said it had taken part in the adoption of the text without prejudice to its position on the substance of the Protocols, which were under consideration by its Government.

Rights of the child

Draft convention

Working Group activities. As authorized by the Economic and Social Council in May 1983,[3] an open-ended Working Group, with Adam Lopatka (Poland) as Chairman/Rapporteur, met between 30 January and 3 February and on 2 March 1984 to continue work on a draft convention on the rights of the child.

The Group adopted articles 7 *bis*, 8 *bis*, 9 and 13. These concerned, respectively: the right of the child to freedom of thought, conscience and religion; protective measures against all forms of physical or mental injury or abuse, neglect or negligent treatment, maltreatment or exploitation including sexual abuse; access to information and material of social and cultural benefit, and protection from potentially injurious information; and the right to benefit from social security. The text of these articles, together with those previously adopted, were annexed to the Group's report.[4] Also annexed were proposed draft articles and amendments which the Group could not consider for lack of time.

Action by the Commission on Human Rights.
On 8 March,[5] the Commission on Human Rights
decided to continue its work on the elaboration of
the draft convention in 1985 as a matter of highest
priority. It requested the Economic and Social Council
to authorize a meeting of an open-ended working
group for one week prior to the 1985 Commission
session to speed up completion of the work. It recommended a draft text to that effect which served as
the basis for the Council resolution below.

ECONOMIC AND SOCIAL COUNCIL ACTION

Acting without vote on the recommendation of
its Second Committee, the Economic and Social
Council adopted resolution 1984/25 on 24 May 1984.

Question of a convention on the rights of the child

The Economic and Social Council,

Recalling General Assembly resolution 38/114 of 16 December 1983, by which the General Assembly requested
the Commission on Human Rights to give the highest
priority at its fortieth session to the question of completing
the draft convention on the rights of the child, and Economic and Social Council resolution 1983/39 of 27 May
1983, by which the Council authorized a meeting of an
open-ended working group for a period of one week prior
to the fortieth session of the Commission to facilitate and
speed up the completion of the work on a draft convention on the rights of the child,

Considering that it was not found possible to complete
the work on the draft convention during the fortieth session
of the Commission,

Taking note of Commission on Human Rights resolution 1984/24 of 8 March 1984,

1. *Authorizes* a meeting of an open-ended working group
for a period of one week prior to the forty-first session
of the Commission on Human Rights to facilitate and
speed up the completion of the work on a draft convention on the rights of the child;

2. *Requests* the Secretary-General to transmit documents relating to the draft convention on the rights of
the child to the Commission on Human Rights at its forty-first
session and to extend all facilities to the open-ended working
group during the meeting to be held prior to the forty-
first session of the Commission.

Economic and Social Council resolution 1984/25

24 May 1984   Meeting 20   Adopted without vote

Approved by Second Committee (E/1984/91) without vote, 17 May (meeting 15);
draft by Commission on Human Rights (E/1984/14); agenda item 10.

GENERAL ASSEMBLY ACTION

Acting on the recommendation of the Third Committee, the General Assembly adopted resolution
39/135 without vote on 14 December 1984.

Question of a convention on the rights of the child

The General Assembly,

Recalling its resolutions 33/166 of 20 December 1978,
34/4 of 18 October 1979, 35/131 of 11 December 1980,
36/57 of 25 November 1981, 37/190 of 18 December 1982
and 38/114 of 16 December 1983,

Recalling also Commission on Human Rights resolutions 20(XXXIV) of 8 March 1978, 19(XXXV) of 14
March 1979, 36(XXXVI) of 12 March 1980, 26(XXXVII)
of 10 March 1981, 1982/39 of 11 March 1982, 1983/52
of 10 March 1983 and 1984/24 of 8 March 1984, as well
as Economic and Social Council resolutions 1978/18 of
5 May 1978, 1978/40 of 1 August 1978, 1982/37 of 7 May
1982, 1983/39 of 27 May 1983 and 1984/25 of 24 May
1984 and Council decisions 1980/138 of 2 May 1980 and
1981/144 of 8 May 1981,

Reaffirming that children's rights are basic human rights
and call for continuous improvement of the situation of
children all over the world, as well as their development
and education in conditions of peace and security,

Recalling that the year 1984 marks the twenty-fifth anniversary of the adoption of the Declaration of the Rights
of the Child which was proclaimed to the end that the
child might have a happy childhood and enjoy for his
own good and for the good of society the rights and freedoms set forth therein and be, in all circumstances, among
the first to receive protection and relief,

Aware of the fact that, twenty-five years after the adoption
of the Declaration of the Rights of the Child, the situation of children in many parts of the world still continues
to be far from satisfactory,

Stressing again the need to keep up the momentum of
positive action for the sake of children, generated by the
International Year of the Child,

Mindful of the important role of the United Nations
Children's Fund and the United Nations in promoting
the well-being of children and their development,

Convinced of the significance of an international convention on the rights of the child as a standard-setting
accomplishment of the United Nations, in the fields of
social development and human rights, for protecting children's rights and ensuring their well-being,

Noting with satisfaction the widespread interest in the
elaboration of an international convention on the rights
of the child displayed by a great number of Member States,
representing all geographical regions and socio-political
systems, as well as by international organizations,

Noting with appreciation that further progress was made
in the elaboration of a draft convention on the rights of
the child during the fortieth session of the Commission
on Human Rights,

1. *Stresses* the significance of the twenty-fifth anniversary
of the Declaration of the Rights of the Child which has
directly stimulated the idea of elaborating an international convention on the rights of the child;

2. *Welcomes* Economic and Social Council resolution
1984/25, in which the Council authorized a meeting of
an open-ended working group of the Commission on
Human Rights for a period of one week prior to the forty-
first session of the Commission to facilitate and speed
up the completion of the work on a draft convention on
the rights of the child;

3. *Requests* the Commission on Human Rights to give
the highest priority to this question and to make every
effort at its forty-first session to complete the draft convention and to submit it, through the Economic and Social
Council, to the General Assembly at its fortieth session;

4. *Invites* all Member States to offer their effective
contribution to the completion of the draft convention
on the rights of the child at the forty-first session of the
Commission on Human Rights;

5.   *Requests* the Secretary-General to provide all necessary assistance to the working group to ensure its smooth and efficient work in the fulfilment of this important task;

6.   *Decides* to include in the provisional agenda of its fortieth session the item entitled "Question of a convention on the rights of the child".

General Assembly resolution 39/135

14 December 1984   Meeting 101   Adopted without vote

Approved by Third Committee (A/39/706) without vote, 3 December (meeting 57); 86-nation draft (A/C.3/39/L.57); agenda item 97.

Sponsors: Afghanistan, Algeria, Angola, Argentina, Australia, Austria, Bahamas, Bangladesh, Benin, Bhutan, Bolivia, Bulgaria, Burkina Faso, Byelorussian SSR, Cameroon, Canada, China, Colombia, Congo, Costa Rica, Cuba, Cyprus, Czechoslovakia, Democratic Yemen, Denmark, Egypt, Equatorial Guinea, Fiji, Finland, Gambia, German Democratic Republic, Ghana, Greece, Guinea-Bissau, Guyana, Hungary, Iceland, India, Indonesia, Iran, Iraq, Italy, Ivory Coast, Jamaica, Jordan, Kenya, Lao People's Democratic Republic, Lesotho, Liberia, Madagascar, Mali, Mauritania, Mexico, Mongolia, Morocco, Mozambique, New Zealand, Nicaragua, Nigeria, Norway, Pakistan, Panama, Philippines, Poland, Rwanda, Senegal, Sierra Leone, Spain, Sri Lanka, Suriname, Swaziland, Sweden, Syrian Arab Republic, Togo, Uganda, Ukrainian SSR, USSR, United Republic of Tanzania, Uruguay, Venezuela, Viet Nam, Yemen, Yugoslavia, Zaire, Zambia, Zimbabwe.

Meeting numbers. GA 39th session: 3rd Committee 44-52, 56, 57; plenary 101.

Child labour

On 12 March 1984, the Commission on Human Rights adopted two resolutions on child labour. By the first,[6] the Commission, noting the recommendation made by Special Rapporteur Abdelwahab Bouhdiba (Tunisia) that a seminar be held on the subject,[7] recommended a draft resolution which served as the basis for the Economic and Social Council action below.

By the second resolution,[8] the Commission called on Iran immediately to cease the use of children in the armed forces, especially in time of war. It invited the appropriate international organizations to offer all possible aid for the welfare of children currently held prisoners of war in Iraq, especially as regards their education and physical and mental health, or to assist those children desiring to settle in another Islamic country until their return to Iran became feasible.

ECONOMIC AND SOCIAL COUNCIL ACTION

Acting on the recommendation of its Second Committee, the Economic and Social Council adopted resolution 1984/28 without vote on 24 May 1984.

Exploitation of child labour

The Economic and Social Council

Requests the Secretary-General to organize, in close cooperation with the International Labour Office, a seminar on ways and means of achieving the elimination of the exploitation of child labour in all parts of the world, within the framework of the programme of advisory services in the field of human rights.

Economic and Social Council resolution 1984/28

24 May 1984   Meeting 20   Adopted without vote

Approved by Second Committee (E/1984/91) without vote, 17 May (meeting 15); draft by Commission on Human Rights (E/1984/14); agenda item 10.

Youth and human rights

In 1984, the youth-related issue of conscientious objection to military service was considered by the Commission on Human Rights and the Economic and Social Council (see above, under "Civil and political rights").

The General Assembly, in resolution 39/23, requested that the Secretary-General, in his report surveying implementation of the Specific Programme of Measures and Activities to be undertaken prior to and during the International Youth Year (1985) (see p. 929), pay adequate attention to the enjoyment by youth of human rights, particularly the right to education and to work.

Human rights of disabled persons

ECONOMIC AND SOCIAL COUNCIL ACTION

On 24 May 1984, the Economic and Social Council, acting on the recommendation of its Second Committee, adopted resolution 1984/26 without vote. It was based on a text submitted by the Commission on Human Rights on 12 March.[9]

Human rights violations and disabled persons

The Economic and Social Council,

Recalling its resolution 1983/19 of 26 May 1983,

Having regard to the Declaration on the Rights of Mentally Retarded Persons, the Declaration on the Rights of Disabled Persons and the Declaration on the Rights of Deaf-Blind Persons,

Welcoming the decision of the General Assembly, in its resolution 37/53 of 3 December 1982, to proclaim the period 1983-1992 United Nations Decade of Disabled Persons,

Deeply concerned that serious violations of human rights remain a significant cause of temporary and permanent disability,

1.   *Encourages* the efforts of the Secretary-General to obtain the views of United Nations bodies, specialized agencies, regional intergovernmental organizations, the International Committee of the Red Cross and other concerned non-governmental organizations on ways and means of preventing serious violations of human rights which may cause disabilities;

2.   *Requests* Governments to pay particular attention to ways and means of strengthening procedures whereby disabled persons may seek redress for human rights violations in accordance with resolution 1982/1 of 7 September 1982 of the Sub-Commission on Prevention of Discrimination and Protection of Minorities;

3.   *Invites* Governments, in consultation with organizations of and for disabled persons, to inform the Secretary-General of their views and policies on these issues so that he can transmit them to the Sub-Commission, in accordance with its resolution 1982/1, for consideration at its thirty-seventh session;

4.   *Requests* the Sub-Commission to appoint a special rapporteur to undertake a thorough study, in consultation with the Centre for Social Development and Humanitarian Affairs of the United Nations Secretariat, of the causal connection between serious violations of human rights and fundamental freedoms and disability and of the progress made to alleviate problems, and to submit its views and recommendations, through the Commission on Human Rights and the Commission on Social Development, to the Economic and Social Council at its first regular session of 1986;

5. *Decides* exceptionally to include in the agenda of its first regular session of 1986 a special item on disabled persons to coincide with the approach, in 1987, of the mid-point of the United Nations Decade of Disabled Persons, in order to allow for a full debate of the Special Rapporteur's report and the views and recommendations of the Sub-Commission, the Commission on Human Rights and the Commission on Social Development on these and related issues.

Economic and Social Council resolution 1984/26

24 May 1984   Meeting 20   Adopted without vote

Approved by Second Committee (E/1984/91) without vote, 17 May (meeting 15); draft by Commission on Human Rights (E/1984/14); agenda item 10.
NGO statement: E/1984/NGO/3.

Report of the Secretary-General. As requested by the Sub-Commission in 1982,[10] the Secretary-General submitted a report containing communications received in reply to his invitation for views on ways of promoting the human rights of disabled persons and for information on how the protection of such rights had been affected by reduced spending for social programmes. As at 4 July 1984, replies had been received from 11 States, 3 regional commissions, 2 United Nations bodies, 5 specialized agencies and 3 NGOs.[11]

Sub-Commission action. On 29 August 1984,[12] the Sub-Commission appointed Leandro Despouy (Argentina) as Special Rapporteur to undertake a study of human rights and disability, as requested by the Economic and Social Council in May (see above). The study was to include consideration of: human rights and humanitarian law violations resulting in disability or having an impact on disabled persons; *apartheid* in relation to disability; all forms of discrimination against the disabled; institutionalization and institutional abuse; and economic, social and cultural rights in relation to disability. It was also to include a preliminary outline of the topic of scientific experimentation in relation to disability.

The Sub-Commission requested the Special Rapporteur to take account of any relevant information received from Governments, specialized agencies, regional international organizations and NGOs, and to present the study to the Sub-Commission in 1985 for submission to the Commission in 1986. The Secretary-General was asked to provide all the assistance necessary to complete this task.

Human rights of the individual and international law

Work continued in 1984 on a study of the status of the individual and international law, mandated by the Commission on Human Rights in 1981 and authorized by the Economic and Social Council the same year.[13]

On 12 March 1984,[14] the Commission recommended for adoption a draft resolution that served as the basis for the Council action below.

ECONOMIC AND SOCIAL COUNCIL ACTION

On 24 May 1984, the Economic and Social Council, acting on the recommendation of its Second Committee, adopted resolution 1984/31 without vote.

The status of the individual and contemporary international law

The Economic and Social Council,

Mindful of resolution 1983/17 of 5 September 1983 of the Sub-Commission on Prevention of Discrimination and Protection of Minorities and Commission on Human Rights resolution 1984/41 of 12 March 1984,

Recognizing the importance and usefulness of the study on the status of the individual and contemporary international law, in particular in the field of the protection of the human rights of the individual at regional and international levels,

Expressing its deep appreciation to the Special Rapporteur, Mrs. Erica-Irene A. Daes, for her preliminary report and the excellent work she has so far accomplished in connection with the important study in progress on the status of the individual and contemporary international law,

1. *Requests* the Special Rapporteur to continue her work on the above-mentioned study with a view to submitting her final report to the Sub-Commission on Prevention of Discrimination and Protection of Minorities at its thirty-seventh session;

2. *Requests* the Secretary-General to transmit, as soon as possible, a reminder, with the relevant questionnaire, to Governments, specialized agencies, regional and other intergovernmental organizations and non-governmental organizations which have not yet replied to that questionnaire to submit, if they so wish, their comments, views and information to the Special Rapporteur;

3. *Further requests* the Secretary-General to give the Special Rapporteur all the assistance she may require in her work.

Economic and Social Council resolution 1984/31

24 May 1984   Meeting 20   Adopted without vote

Approved by Second Committee (E/1984/91) without vote, 17 May (meeting 15); draft by Commission on Human Rights (E/1984/14); agenda item 10.

Report of the Special Rapporteur. In a progress report[15] to the Sub-Commission, Special Rapporteur Erica-Irene A. Daes (Greece) stated that, in reply to the questionnaires circulated for the purpose of obtaining information for the proposed study, substantive comments had been received from 33 States, 5 specialized agencies, 2 regional organizations, 3 intergovernmental organizations, 24 NGOs and 2 liberation movements as at 10 February 1984.

The report set forth the basic purpose of the study and provided a provisional outline of its contents. It also reproduced the questionnaire addressed to Governments and that addressed to others.

Sub-Commission action. On 28 August 1984,[16] the Sub-Commission expressed appreciation to the Special Rapporteur for her progress report and requested her to continue work on the study and submit a final report in 1985. It asked the Secretary-General to give all the assistance needed for that task.

Human rights and science and technology

In 1984, human rights and scientific and technological progress was the subject of four resolutions of the Commission on Human Rights, all adopted on 12 March. Two related to the use of such progress, as embodied in a 1975 declaration and for peace; a third, dealing with the topic in general, also touched on the question of computerized personal files (see below). By the fourth resolution,[17] the Commission, taking into account the recommendations of a group of eminent experts that had convened in 1975 to discuss the balance to be established between scientific and technological progress and the intellectual, spiritual, cultural and moral advancement of humanity, decided to consider in 1986 the implications of the topics indicated in the recommendations. The Commission requested the Secretary-General to invite the views of United Nations Members, organs and specialized agencies in this regard.

In addition to the question of computerized personal files, two other aspects were dealt with by the Sub-Commission: unlawful human experimentation and computer technology for dissemination of international human rights instruments. In adopting a resolution on each of these aspects on 29 August, the Sub-Commission was mindful of a Commission request of 12 March asking it to consider areas for study in connection with human rights and scientific and technological developments (see below).

By the first resolution,[18] the Sub-Commission submitted a draft resolution to the Commission for submission to the Economic and Social Council, by which the Council would authorize the Sub-Commission to entrust Driss Dahak (Morocco) with preparing a study on the current dimensions and problems arising from unlawful human experimentation, for submission in preliminary form in 1985.

In a related action,[12] authorizing a study on human rights and disability, the Sub-Commission asked that the study include, among other material, a preliminary outline of the topic of scientific experimentation and disability (see above).

By the second resolution,[19] the Sub-Commission also submitted a draft resolution by which the Commission in turn would recommend for Council action a draft authorizing the Sub-Commission to appoint a special rapporteur to undertake a study on the implications for human rights of recent advances in computer and micro-computer technology. The study would pay particular attention to the potential uses of such technology for the increased dissemination of international human rights instruments and of other human rights information.

Report of the Secretary-General. Pursuant to a March 1983 request of the Commission on Human Rights,[20] the Secretary-General submitted to it in 1984 a report, with later addenda,[21] summarizing replies to his note verbale addressed in 1983 to all States and relevant international organizations and NGOs, inviting their views on the most effective ways of using the results of scientific and technological developments for the promotion and realization of human rights and fundamental freedoms.

As at 30 November 1983, eight States, three United Nations bodies, five specialized agencies and five NGOs had replied. Two other States replied in January 1984. Additional replies were subsequently received.

Action by the Commission on Human Rights. On 12 March 1984,[22] the Commission took note of the report of the Secretary-General and invited Member States and international organizations that had not done so to submit to him their views on the most effective ways of using scientific and technological developments to promote human rights. It requested from the Secretary-General an updated report in 1986 taking account of those views. It requested the Sub-Commission to consider areas for possible study on the subject, taking account also of those views and of existing studies.

Implementation of the 1975 Declaration on the use of scientific and technological progress

By 33 votes to none, with 10 abstentions, on 12 March 1984,[23] the Commission stressed the importance of States' implementation of the 1975 Declaration on the Use of Scientific and Technological Progress in the Interests of Peace and for the Benefit of Mankind,[24] in order to promote human rights and fundamental freedoms under conditions of scientific and technological progress. It called on States to use the achievements of such progress for peaceful economic, social and cultural development and to improve the well-being of peoples. It once again requested the Sub-Commission to undertake, as a matter of priority, a study on the use of those achievements to ensure the right to work and development.

Report of the Secretary-General. Pursuant to a December 1983 General Assembly request[25] for information on measures taken to implement the 1975 Declaration, the Secretary-General submitted a report, with a later addendum,[26] containing substantive replies received, as at 10 August 1984, from two Governments, a regional commission and five specialized agencies. A third Government replied in September.

Acting on the recommendation of the Third Committee, the General Assembly adopted resolution 39/133 on 14 December 1984, by recorded vote.

Human rights and scientific and technological developments

The General Assembly,

Noting that scientific and technological progress is one of the important factors in the development of human society,

Noting once again the great importance of the Declaration on the Use of Scientific and Technological Progress in the Interests of Peace and for the Benefit of Mankind, adopted by the General Assembly in its resolution 3384(XXX) of 10 November 1975,

Considering that implementation of the said Declaration will contribute to the strengthening of international peace and the security of peoples and to their economic and social development, as well as to international cooperation in the field of human rights,

Seriously concerned that the results of scientific and technological progress could be used for the arms race to the detriment of international peace and security and social progress, human rights and fundamental freedoms and the dignity of the human person,

Recognizing that the establishment of the new international economic order calls in particular for an important contribution to be made by science and technology to economic and social progress,

Bearing in mind that the exchange and transfer of scientific and technological knowledge is one of the important ways to accelerate the social and economic development of the developing countries,

Taking note with satisfaction of the report of the Secretary-General on human rights and scientific and technological developments,

1. *Stresses* the importance of the implementation by all States of the provisions and principles contained in the Declaration on the Use of Scientific and Technological Progress in the Interests of Peace and for the Benefit of Mankind in order to promote human rights and fundamental freedoms;

2. *Calls upon* all States to make every effort to use the achievements of science and technology in order to promote peaceful social, economic and cultural development and progress;

3. *Requests* the specialized agencies and other organizations of the United Nations system to take into account in their programmes and activities the provisions of the Declaration;

4. *Invites* those Member States, specialized agencies and other organizations of the United Nations system that have not yet done so to submit their information pursuant to General Assembly resolution 35/130 A of 11 December 1980;

5. *Requests* the Commission on Human Rights to give special attention, in its consideration of the item entitled "Human rights and scientific and technological developments", to the question of the implementation of the provisions of the Declaration, taking into consideration the information submitted by Member States, specialized agencies and other organizations of the United Nations system in accordance with General Assembly resolution 35/130 A;

6. *Decides* to include in the provisional agenda of its fortieth session the item entitled "Human rights and scientific and technological developments".

General Assembly resolution 39/133

14 December 1984   Meeting 101   127-0-21 (recorded vote)

Approved by Third Committee (A/39/705) by recorded vote (100-0-20), 3 December (meeting 57); 32-nation draft (A/C.3/39/L.65); agenda item 96.

Sponsors: Afghanistan, Algeria, Angola, Argentina, Bangladesh, Benin, Bolivia, Bulgaria, Byelorussian SSR, Cuba, Cyprus, Czechoslovakia, Democratic Yemen, German Democratic Republic, Guinea-Bissau, Hungary, Ivory Coast, Lao People's Democratic Republic, Madagascar, Mali, Mauritania, Mongolia, Morocco, Mozambique, Nicaragua, Poland, Romania, Sierra Leone, Syrian Arab Republic, Viet Nam, Zambia, Zimbabwe.

Meeting numbers. GA 39th session: 3rd Committee 44-52, 56, 57; plenary 101.

Recorded vote in Assembly as follows:

In favour: Afghanistan, Algeria, Angola, Argentina, Bahamas, Bahrain, Bangladesh, Barbados, Belize, Benin, Bhutan, Bolivia, Botswana, Brazil, Brunei Darussalam, Bulgaria, Burkina Faso, Burma, Burundi, Byelorussian SSR, Cameroon, Cape Verde, Central African Republic, Chad, Chile, China, Colombia, Congo, Costa Rica, Cuba, Cyprus, Czechoslovakia, Democratic Kampuchea, Democratic Yemen, Djibouti, Dominican Republic, Ecuador, Egypt, El Salvador, Equatorial Guinea, Ethiopia, Fiji, Gabon, Gambia, German Democratic Republic, Ghana, Greece, Guatemala, Guinea, Guyana, Haiti, Honduras, Hungary, India, Indonesia, Iran, Iraq, Ivory Coast, Jamaica, Japan, Jordan, Kenya, Kuwait, Lao People's Democratic Republic, Lebanon, Lesotho, Liberia, Libyan Arab Jamahiriya, Madagascar, Malawi, Malaysia, Maldives, Mali, Malta, Mauritania, Mauritius, Mexico, Mongolia, Morocco, Mozambique, Nepal, Nicaragua, Niger, Nigeria, Oman, Pakistan, Panama, Papua New Guinea, Paraguay, Peru, Philippines, Poland, Qatar, Romania, Rwanda, Saint Vincent and the Grenadines, Samoa, Sao Tome and Principe, Saudi Arabia, Senegal, Seychelles, Sierra Leone, Singapore, Somalia, Sri Lanka, Sudan, Suriname, Swaziland, Syrian Arab Republic, Thailand, Togo, Trinidad and Tobago, Tunisia, Turkey, Uganda, Ukrainian SSR, USSR, United Arab Emirates, United Republic of Tanzania, Uruguay, Venezuela, Viet Nam, Yemen, Yugoslavia, Zaire, Zambia, Zimbabwe.

Against: None.

Abstaining: Australia, Austria, Belgium, Canada, Denmark, Finland, France, Germany, Federal Republic of, Iceland, Ireland, Israel, Italy, Luxembourg, Netherlands, New Zealand, Norway, Portugal, Spain, Sweden, United Kingdom, United States.

Human rights and peace

On 12 March 1984,[27] the Commission on Human Rights, by a roll-call vote of 28 to 8, with 7 abstentions, reaffirmed the inherent right to life of all individuals, the safeguarding of which was an essential condition for the enjoyment of the entire range of economic, social and cultural, as well as civil and political, rights. It again stressed the need for the international community to make every effort to remove the growing threat of war, particularly nuclear war, to halt the arms race, to achieve general disarmament under effective international control and to prevent violations of the Charter principles, thus contributing to assuring the right to life. It also stressed the importance of such practical disarmament measures as releasing substantial resources that should be used for social and economic development.

The Commission appealed to States and all others concerned to take measures to ensure that the results of scientific and technological progress were used exclusively in the interests of international peace, for the benefit of mankind and for promoting universal respect for human rights and fundamental freedoms. It called on all States to take measures to prohibit any propaganda for war, in particular that intended to legitimize the first use of nuclear weapons and in general to justify the admissibility of unleashing nuclear war.

Report of the Secretary-General. In a July 1984 report to the Sub-Commission,[28] the Secretary-General analysed the effects of gross violations of human rights on international peace and security. Prepared pursuant to a September 1983 Sub-Commission request,[29] the analysis was based on views and comments on the subject, transmitted to the Secretary-General in response to his request. As at 1 June, substantive information had been received from eight Governments, three specialized agencies, two regional organizations and nine NGOs.

The Secretary-General stated that the comments stressed the close interrelationship and interdependence of human rights and international peace and security. They noted in this regard the fundamental significance of the United Nations Charter, of specific provisions of many relevant United Nations instruments, declarations and resolutions, and of some non–United Nations instruments—all of them recognizing the manifold character of this relationship.

Certain human rights or groups of rights were identified, in respect of which the correlation between gross disregard for them and threats to peace and security were considered particularly close. Among these were the right to life, identified as a most fundamental right, and the act of preparing for war, in particular the arms race, as directly threatening that right. Similarly identified was the right to self-determination in all its dimensions, the violation of which seriously threatened international peace and security. Colonialist and neo-colonialist oppression, foreign occupation, racial discrimination, racism and *apartheid*, and persecution of minorities were cited as the main causes of a large number of ongoing armed struggles and escalation of conflict, as were denial of State sovereignty over its natural resources and denial to the masses of the most basic economic and social rights. Thus the World Council of Churches saw economic injustice, oppression and exploitation as the root causes of war.

As to civil and political rights, gross violations of the freedoms of opinion, expression and association, and information were regarded as detrimental to confidence-building and as sources of international tension. The need was recognized, however, for limitations to those freedoms if exercised for war propaganda and to promote hatred. Denial of the right to leave one's country was denounced as endangering friendly relations between States, and arbitrary arrests and detentions, and resulting mass exoduses, as compounding international tension.

Several methods were suggested for dealing with such gross violations bearing directly on international peace and security, notably: a preventive strategy calling for a network of research centres to conduct case-studies of successful solutions to human rights problems; a massive human rights education programme using such case-studies and enlisting mass media co-operation; promotion of popular participation in development, especially through trade union rights; and constant monitoring of the effects of gross violations by including the subject as a regular item in the Sub-Commission's agenda.

Sub-Commission action. On 30 August 1984,[30] the Sub-Commission expressed appreciation to the Secretary-General for his comprehensive report. It stressed the threat that the arms race, particularly the nuclear-arms race, posed for social and economic progress and the universal realization of all human rights. It requested the Secretary-General to prepare a guide to conventions and United Nations resolutions and reports relating to the adverse consequences of the arms race for the realization of human rights, to be submitted to it in 1985. The Sub-Commission also requested him to transmit a reminder to Governments and NGOs which had not done so to submit their views on the effects of gross human rights violations on international peace and security.

GENERAL ASSEMBLY ACTION

Acting on the recommendation of the Third Committee, the General Assembly adopted resolution 39/134 on 14 December 1984 by recorded vote.

Human rights and use of scientific and technological developments

The General Assembly,

Reaffirming the determination of the peoples of the United Nations to save succeeding generations from the scourge of war, to reaffirm faith in the dignity and worth of the human person, to maintain international peace and security and to develop friendly relations among peoples and international co-operation in promoting and encouraging universal respect for human rights and fundamental freedoms,

Recalling the relevant provisions of the Universal Declaration of Human Rights, the International Covenant on Economic, Social and Cultural Rights and the International Covenant on Civil and Political Rights,

Recalling also the Charter of Economic Rights and Duties of States and the Declaration and the Programme of Action on the Establishment of a New International Economic Order,

Recalling further the Declaration on the Strengthening of International Security, the Declaration on the Use of Scientific and Technological Progress in the Interests of Peace and for the Benefit of Mankind, the Declaration on the Preparation of Societies for Life in Peace, and the Declaration on the Prevention of Nuclear Catastrophe, as well as General Assembly resolutions 36/92 I of 9 December 1981, on the non-use of nuclear weapons and prevention of nuclear war, and 37/100 C of 13 December 1982 and 38/73 G of 15 December 1983, on a convention on the prohibition of the use of nuclear weapons,

Bearing in mind that, in its resolution 38/75 of 15 December 1983, the General Assembly resolutely, unconditionally and for all time condemned nuclear war as being contrary to human conscience and reason, as the most monstrous crime against peoples and as a violation of the foremost human right—the right to life,

Recalling its appeal for the conclusion of an international convention on the prohibition of the use of nuclear weapons with the participation of all the nuclear-weapon States,

Taking note with appreciation of Commission on Human Rights resolutions 1982/7 of 19 February 1982, 1983/43 of 9 March 1983 and 1984/28 of 12 March 1984,

Reaffirming the inherent right to life,

Profoundly concerned that international peace and security continue to be threatened by the arms race in all its aspects, particularly the nuclear-arms race, as well as by violations of the principles of the Charter of the United Nations regarding the sovereignty and territorial integrity of States and the self-determination of peoples,

Aware that all the horrors of past wars and all other calamities that have befallen people would pale in comparison with what is inherent in the use of nuclear weapons capable of destroying civilization on Earth,

Noting the pressing need for urgent measures towards general and complete disarmament, particularly nuclear disarmament, for the sake of life on Earth,

Bearing in mind that, in accordance with the International Covenant on Civil and Political Rights, any propaganda for war shall be prohibited by law,

Recalling the historic responsibility of the Governments of all countries of the world to remove the threat of war from the lives of people, to preserve civilization and to ensure that everyone enjoys his inherent right to life,

Convinced that for no people in the world today is there a more important question than that of the preservation of peace and of ensuring the cardinal right of every human being, namely, the right to life,

1. *Reaffirms* that all peoples and all individuals have an inherent right to life and that the safeguarding of this cardinal right is an essential condition for the enjoyment of the entire range of economic, social and cultural, as well as civil and political, rights;

2. *Stresses once again* the urgent need for the international community to make every effort to strengthen peace, remove the growing threat of war, particularly nuclear war, halt the arms race and achieve general and complete disarmament under effective international control and prevent violations of the principles of the Charter of the United Nations regarding the sovereignty and territorial integrity of States and self-determination of peoples, thus contributing to ensuring the right to life;

3. *Stresses further* the foremost importance of the implementation of practical measures of disarmament for releasing substantial additional resources, which should be utilized for social and economic development, particularly for the benefit of the developing countries;

4. *Calls upon* all States, appropriate organs of the United Nations, specialized agencies and intergovernmental and non-governmental organizations concerned to take the necessary measures to ensure that the results of scientific and technological progress are used exclusively in the interests of international peace, for the benefit of mankind and for promoting and encouraging universal respect for human rights and fundamental freedoms;

5. *Again calls upon* all States that have not yet done so to take effective measures with a view to prohibiting any propaganda for war, in particular the formulation, propounding and dissemination of propaganda for doctrines and concepts aimed at unleashing nuclear war;

6. *Looks forward* to further efforts by the Commission on Human Rights with a view to ensuring the inherent right of all peoples and all individuals to life;

7. *Decides* to consider this question at its fortieth session under the item entitled "Human rights and scientific and technological developments".

General Assembly resolution 39/134

14 December 1984   Meeting 101   124-6-17 (recorded vote)

Approved by Third Committee (A/39/705) by recorded vote (97-6-17), 5 December (meeting 60); 25-nation draft (A/C.3/39/L.55); agenda item 96.

Sponsors: Afghanistan, Angola, Benin, Bulgaria, Byelorussian SSR, Cuba, Czechoslovakia, Democratic Yemen, German Democratic Republic, Guinea-Bissau, Hungary, India, Lao People's Democratic Republic, Libyan Arab Jamahiriya, Madagascar, Mauritania, Mongolia, Mozambique, Nicaragua, Nigeria, Poland, Syrian Arab Republic, Ukrainian SSR, USSR, Viet Nam.

Meeting numbers. GA 39th session: 3rd Committee 44-52, 56, 57, 60; plenary 101.

Recorded vote in Assembly as follows:

In favour: Afghanistan, Algeria, Angola, Argentina, Bahamas, Bahrain, Bangladesh, Barbados, Belize, Benin, Bhutan, Bolivia, Botswana, Brazil, Brunei Darussalam, Bulgaria, Burkina Faso, Burma, Burundi, Byelorussian SSR, Cameroon, Cape Verde, Central African Republic, Chad, Chile, China, Colombia, Congo, Costa Rica, Cuba, Cyprus, Czechoslovakia, Democratic Kampuchea, Democratic Yemen, Djibouti, Dominican Republic, Ecuador, Egypt, El Salvador, Equatorial Guinea, Ethiopia, Fiji, Gabon, Gambia, German Democratic Republic, Ghana, Greece, Guatemala, Guinea, Guyana, Haiti, Honduras, Hungary, India, Indonesia, Iran, Iraq, Ivory Coast, Jamaica, Jordan, Kenya, Kuwait, Lao People's Democratic Republic, Lebanon, Lesotho, Liberia, Libyan Arab Jamahiriya, Madagascar, Malawi, Malaysia, Maldives, Mali, Malta, Mauritania, Mauritius, Mexico, Mongolia, Morocco, Mozambique, Nepal, Nicaragua, Niger, Nigeria, Oman, Pakistan, Panama, Papua New Guinea, Peru, Philippines, Poland, Qatar, Romania, Rwanda, Saint Vincent and the Grenadines, Samoa, Sao Tome and Principe, Saudi Arabia, Senegal, Seychelles, Sierra Leone, Singapore, Somalia, Sri Lanka, Sudan, Suriname, Swaziland, Syrian Arab Republic, Thailand, Togo, Trinidad and Tobago, Tunisia, Uganda, Ukrainian SSR, USSR, United Arab Emirates, United Republic of Tanzania, Uruguay, Venezuela, Viet Nam, Yemen, Yugoslavia, Zaire, Zambia, Zimbabwe.

Against: Canada, France, Germany, Federal Republic of, Italy, United Kingdom, United States.

Abstaining: Australia, Austria, Belgium, Denmark, Finland, Iceland, Ireland, Israel, Japan, Luxembourg, Netherlands, New Zealand, Norway, Portugal, Spain, Sweden, Turkey.

France, the Federal Republic of Germany, Italy and the United States said the text dealt with issues outside the Committee's competence, issues which the United States called highly contentious. A similar opinion was expressed by the United Kingdom, which said the text was more contentious than the resolutions of previous years. Likewise, the resolution adopted by the Commission on Human Rights in March had been considerably more contentious and had led to a narrowly defeated motion by a number of Western and developing countries to take no action on it because it was irrelevant to the Commission's work. Canada's vote stemmed from the references to previous resolutions it had rejected in the belief that, by doing so, it would advance the cause of peace.

Japan and the Netherlands felt that the focus of the text was not relevant to the agenda item. Belgium did not consider itself competent to take a decision on the material contained in the text. In the view of Finland, which spoke for the five

Nordic countries, the Committee was not the competent forum to discuss elimination of the arms race. They also had reservations on the fourth and fifth preambular paragraphs and on paragraph 5, based on their expressed reservation to article 20 (on the prohibition by law of war propaganda and advocacy of national, racial or religious hatred) of the 1966 International Covenant on Civil and Political Rights.[31] Rwanda and Tunisia expressed reservations on certain formulations, primarily paragraph 5.

Introducing the draft, the USSR said it was based on the Charter and other basic documents and sought to preserve peace, the fundamental pre-condition for ensuring the right to life. Scientific and technological progress had great potential for solving the problems of hunger and illiteracy and ensuring social and economic progress, and United Nations bodies could contribute to that cause.

In China's view, nuclear disarmament was an important aspect of United Nations work and a common aspiration. It stressed, however, that it had abstained on the December 1983 resolution mentioned in the preamble by which the Assembly had condemned nuclear war[32] and that China's position in that regard had not changed.

In related actions, the Assembly, in resolution 39/11, approved a Declaration on the Right of Peoples to Peace. In resolution 39/155, on implementation of the 1970 Declaration on the Strengthening of International Security (see p. 114), the Assembly considered that respect for and promotion of human rights in their civil, political, economic, social and cultural aspects, on the one hand, and the strengthening of international peace and security, on the other, reinforced each other.

Computerized personal files

In its resolution of 12 March 1984 dealing with human rights and scientific and technological developments generally,[22] the Commission on Human Rights welcomed the 1983 final report on guidelines relating to computerized personal files,[20] presented to it by Special Rapporteur Louis Joinet (France).

On 29 August 1984,[33] the Sub-Commission, having endorsed in September 1983[20] the conclusions of the study, asked the Secretary-General to transmit to Member States and relevant international organizations the provisional draft guidelines with a request for their views thereon. Taking those views into account, the Special Rapporteur was to submit draft final guidelines to the Sub-Commission in 1985.

REFERENCES

[1]YUN 1977, p. 706. [2]A/39/465. [3]YUN 1983, p. 901, ESC res. 1983/39, 27 May 1983. [4]E/CN.4/1984/71. [5]E/1984/14 (res. 1984/24). [6]*Ibid.* (res. 1984/35). [7]YUN 1982, p. 1136. [8]E/1984/14 (res. 1984/39). [9]*Ibid.* (res. 1984/31). [10]YUN 1982, p. 1138. [11]E/CN.4/Sub.2/1984/9 & Add.1. [12]E/CN.4/1985/3 (res. 1984/20). [13]YUN 1981, p. 976, ESC dec. 1981/142, 8 May 1981. [14]E/1984/14 (res. 1984/41). [15]E/CN.4/Sub.2/1984/29. [16]E/CN.4/1985/3 (res. 1984/2). [17]E/1984/14 (res. 1984/30). [18]E/CN.4/1985/3 (res. 1984/17). [19]*Ibid.* (res. 1984/18). [20]YUN 1983, p. 904. [21]E/CN.4/1984/33 & Add.1,2. [22]E/1984/14 (res. 1984/27). [23]*Ibid.* (res. 1984/29). [24]YUN 1975, p. 631, GA res. 3384(XXX), 10 Nov. 1975. [25]YUN 1983, p. 904, GA res. 38/112, 16 Dec. 1983. [26]A/39/422 & Add.1. [27]E/1984/14 (res. 1984/28). [28]E/CN.4/Sub.2/1984/11. [29]YUN 1983, p. 905. [30]E/CN.4/1985/3 (res. 1984/30). [31]YUN 1966, p. 423, GA res. 2200 A (XXI), annex, 16 Dec. 1966. [32]YUN 1983, p. 28, GA res. 38/75, 15 Dec. 1983. [33]E/CN.4/1985/3 (res. 1984/12).

Chapter XIX

Women

Improvements in the status of women and reduction of discrimination had affected only a small minority and the condition of the majority of women in the developing world had changed at most marginally, the Secretary-General stated in an April 1984 report on social aspects of development.[1] The achievements of the United Nations Decade for Women (1976-1985) in helping women advance in the economic, social and political spheres were to be appraised by the 1985 World Conference to review the Decade.

In 1984, Governments and the United Nations system worked for the implementation of the Programme of Action for the Second Half of the United Nations Decade for Women and continued with preparations for the 1985 Conference. The Commission on the Status of Women, meeting for its second session as the preparatory body for the Conference (Vienna, Austria, 27 February–7 March), made recommendations on the preparations which were endorsed by the Economic and Social Council in May (decision 1984/125) and the General Assembly in December (resolution 39/129). Also in May, the Council considered that the objectives of the Decade had not been achieved and that activities towards equal treatment for women and their full integration in development should continue beyond 1985 (resolution 1984/16).

The Voluntary Fund for the United Nations Decade for Women continued its work to augment the flow of resources to rural and poor urban women. By the end of the year, the Fund had approved over 400 projects valued at more than $24 million. In December, the Assembly decided on future arrangements for the Fund, establishing it under the name of United Nations Development Fund for Women as a separate entity in autonomous association with the United Nations Development Programme (UNDP) (resolution 39/125).

The Commission on the Status of Women, at its thirtieth session (Vienna, 15-25 February), recommended to the Economic and Social Council 11 draft resolutions for adoption. These resolutions dealt with a number of issues relating to the status of women, women in the United Nations system and items related to the Commission's work. In closed session, the Commission considered confidential and non-confidential communications on the status of women. The Commission also reviewed the status of the 1979 Convention on the Elimination of All Forms of Discrimination against Women, to which 64 States had become parties at the end of 1984. Questions related to the Commission's work at its next (1986) session were dealt with by the Council in a resolution (1984/20) and a decision (1984/123) adopted in May.

The Committee on the Elimination of Discrimination against Women, at its third session (New York, 26 March–6 April), considered initial reports of six States parties on their implementation of the Convention. The Economic and Social Council, in May (resolution 1984/8), and the Assembly, in December (resolution 39/130), emphasized the importance of strictest compliance with the Convention and requested the parties to it to make all possible efforts to submit their implementation reports. The Council, also in May (resolution 1984/10), urged States to ratify or accede to the Convention in the light of the 1985 Conference.

In October, the Secretary-General reported on the world survey on the role of women in development. The Assembly, in December, recommended that the survey in its final form be considered in 1985 together with comments on it and related decisions by the World Conference (resolution 39/172). By resolution 39/124, it pledged to encourage the full participation of women in economic, social, cultural, civil and political affairs, and invited Governments to ensure implementation of the 1982 Declaration on the Participation of Women in Promoting International Peace and Co-operation.

The International Research and Training Institute for the Advancement of Women (INSTRAW) continued work on studies relating to issues affecting women. Its Board of Trustees, at its fourth session (Santo Domingo, Dominican Republic, 23-28 January), approved a budget of $2.5 million for 1984-1985 and approved a draft statute for the Institute which was later endorsed by the Economic and Social Council (decision 1984/124). The Assembly, in December, took note of INSTRAW's activities as a valuable contribution to an increased role of women in development (resolution 39/122).

The Assembly, also in December, adopted resolutions on the role of women in society—as mothers and as participants in economic development and in public life (39/123); on the integration of women in all aspects of development (39/128); and on the improvement of the situation of women in rural areas (39/126).

Acting on recommendations of the Commission on the Status of Women, the Economic and Social Council adopted, in May, resolutions on women under *apartheid* (1984/17), Palestinian women (1984/18), violence in the family (1984/14) and violence against detained women (1984/19). It also made recommendations for the promotion of opportunities for young women (resolution 1984/15) and requested the Secretary-General to prepare a report on the status and situation of elderly women (resolution 1984/13).

Topics related to this chapter. Middle East: territories occupied by Israel—Palestinian women. Operational activities for development: inter-agency co-operation. Industrial development: Fourth General Conference of UNIDO. Regional economic and social activities: Africa—women in development in Africa. Food: food problems. Social and cultural development: treatment of women by criminal justice system. United Nations officials: status of women in Secretariat.

REFERENCE

(1)A/39/171-E/1984/54.

Advancement of women

Decade for Women (1976-1985)

Implementation of the Programme for 1981-1985

In 1984, the United Nations continued to work with Governments and intergovernmental bodies to implement the Programme of Action for the Second Half of the United Nations Decade for Women—adopted in 1980 by the World Conference of the United Nations Decade for Women: Equality, Development and Peace, and endorsed by the General Assembly later that year.[1] In December 1984, the Secretary-General reported to the Commission on the Status of Women acting as the preparatory body for the 1985 World Conference to Review and Appraise the Achievements of the United Nations Decade for Women on forward-looking strategies of implementation and on concrete measures to overcome obstacles to the achievement of the goals of the Decade.[2]

The report focused on the overall objectives of the Decade—equality, development and peace—discussing obstacles, strategies and measures for their implementation, and considered issues of special concern, such as the situation of poor women in rural and urban areas, women in areas of armed conflict, those who were elderly, young, abused, destitute or victims of prostitution, women who were deprived of their traditional means of livelihood or were the sole supporters of families, physically and mentally disabled women, and detained women. It also considered the problems of women living under *apartheid*, Palestinian women and those who were refugees or displaced, migrants, or in minority or indigenous groups.

The report also dealt with obstacles to and strategies for international and regional co-operation and measures for implementing those strategies, such as monitoring, technical co-operation, training and advisory services, institutional co-ordination, research and policy analysis, participation in decision-making, and information dissemination.

On 16 October,[3] the Sudan transmitted to the Secretary-General a resolution adopted by the Seventy-second Inter-Parliamentary Conference at Geneva on 29 September, on the need for parliamentary and other actions to formulate initiatives to achieve equal rights and responsibilities for men and women.

ECONOMIC AND SOCIAL COUNCIL ACTION

On 24 May, on the recommendation of its Second (Social) Committee, the Economic and Social Council adopted resolution 1984/16 without vote.

Implementation of the objectives of the United Nations Decade for Women: Equality, Development and Peace

The Economic and Social Council,

Considering General Assembly resolutions 3520(XXX) of 15 December 1975 and 35/136 of 11 December 1980,

Reaffirming the objectives of the United Nations Decade for Women: Equality, Development and Peace,

Emphasizing the importance of undertaking, at the conclusion of the Decade, a critical review and appraisal of progress at the international, regional and national levels in the achievement of the goals of the Decade—equality, development and peace—and of the obstacles encountered in the implementation of the World Plan of Action for the Implementation of the Objectives of the International Women's Year and the Programme of Action for the Second Half of the United Nations Decade for Women, and also in developing a forward-looking perspective on the status of women,

Looking ahead to the World Conference to Review and Appraise the Achievements of the United Nations Decade for Women: Equality, Development and Peace, to be held in 1985, at which the achievements of the Decade and the need to continue such achievements beyond the end of the Decade will be reviewed and appraised,

Conscious that further efforts are necessary to eliminate all forms of discrimination against women in every area of human activity,

Stressing that the objectives, strategies and measures to improve the socio-economic conditions of women should be an integral part of national development plans, as well as of international and development strategies, including the efforts for the establishment of the new international economic order,

Reaffirming the existence of the undeniable link between peace and development and the imperative need to halt the arms race, thereby releasing valuable additional resources that could be used for the development of the developing countries and could contribute to the well-being and prosperity of all,

Noting that, until genuine disarmament is achieved, women and men throughout the world must maintain their vigilance and do their utmost to achieve peace,

Taking into account the fact that millions of women are still experiencing untold sufferings and violations of human dignity resulting from different forms and manifestations of colonialism, foreign domination, *apartheid* and racial discrimination,

1. *Reaffirms* the urgent need to fulfil the goals of the United Nations Decade for Women: Equality, Development and Peace and the socio-economic development objectives established by the international community, *inter alia*, the elimination of hunger and malnutrition, the achievement of full employment by the year 2000, health for all by the year 2000, appropriate population policies, the reduction of the infant mortality rate, the availability of safe water and adequate sanitary facilities by 1990, the attainment of a life expectancy of 60 years as a minimum by the year 2000, universal primary school enrolment by the year 2000, and the full participation of women as both agents and beneficiaries in all sectors and at all levels of the development process;

2. *Emphasizes* that foreign occupation, colonialism, *apartheid*, racism and racial discrimination, and the denial of the right of peoples to self-determination and of all universally recognized human rights, are serious impediments to peace and development;

3. *Recommends* that States, especially militarily significant States, in preparing their national programmes for social and economic development, should consider taking measures to convert some resources spent for military purposes to the promotion of social progress;

4. *Considers* that the objectives of the Decade—equality, development and peace—as reflected in the World Plan of Action for the Implementation of the Objectives of the International Women's Year and in the Programme of Action for the Second Half of the United Nations Decade for Women have not yet been achieved;

5. *Considers* that the activities of the world community and of the United Nations should continue beyond the end of the United Nations Decade for Women and should be directed towards equal treatment for women and their full integration in development under conditions of peace.

Economic and Social Council resolution 1984/16

24 May 1984   Meeting 19   Adopted without vote

Approved by Second Committee (E/1984/93) without vote, 10 May (meeting 9); draft by Commission on women (E/1984/15), amended by Algeria, Mexico and Yugoslavia (E/1984/C.2/L.1); agenda item 12.

The sixth preambular paragraph was inserted by the three-nation amendment.

GENERAL ASSEMBLY ACTION

In resolution 39/123, the General Assembly recommended that the 1985 World Conference take into account all aspects of the role of women in society in reviewing and appraising the achievements of the Decade and in formulating future policies.

In resolution 39/127, the Assembly stressed that the appointment of senior women's programme officers at the regional commissions represented a valuable contribution to the implementation of the goals of the Decade. It requested the Secretary-General to allocate sufficient resources in order to regularize all temporary and permanent senior women's programme officer posts at the commissions before the end of the Decade (see ADMINISTRATIVE AND BUDGETARY QUESTIONS, Chapter III).

Preparations for the 1985 Conference

The Commission on the Status of Women met at Vienna from 27 February to 7 March 1984 for its second session as the preparatory body for the 1985 World Conference. In its report on the session,[4] it recommended that the Conference be held for 10 working days from 15 to 26 July 1985, plus two days of pre-Conference consultations.

Other draft decisions calling for action by the Economic and Social Council concerned preparatory work on basic Conference documentation, including that on women and children in the occupied Arab territories and other occupied territories, rural women, women under *apartheid*, refugee and displaced women, technology, illiteracy and the family; outstanding organizational aspects; and the Conference's provisional agenda. Decisions brought to the Council's attention were: that adoption of the Conference rules of procedure would be postponed until 1985 and that the Commission endorsed the practice of electing the head of the delegation of the host country as Conference President.

The Commission considered a number of notes and reports by the Secretary-General on different aspects of Conference preparations, among them a report on statistics on the situation of women and the status of a compilation of selected statistics and indicators for the Conference.[5] The report was part of a programme begun in 1983 to improve statistics on women.[6]

Recommendations on different aspects were made by an inter-agency meeting on preparations for the Conference (Vienna, 8 and 9 March 1984).[7] The meeting recommended to the Consultative Committee on Substantive Questions (Programme Matters) (CCSQ(PROG)) of the Administrative Committee on Co-ordination that the final draft of the world survey of the role of women in development (see below, under "Women in society") be sent to lead agencies and organizations for comments. It also made recommendations concerning the format and deadline for contributions of agencies and organizations to the review and appraisal of the progress achieved and obstacles encountered at the national and international levels in attaining the goals and objectives of the Decade. It agreed that United Nations agencies and organizations would submit suggestions for strategies and concrete measures to overcome those obstacles, and that consultations of those bodies with the Conference secretariat would be ongoing. It further recommended that CCSQ(PROG) approve the convening of an inter-agency meeting immediately after the third session of the preparatory body to discuss, among other things, inter-agency mechanisms for Conference follow-up.

During the year, seven countries contributed $318,212 to the Trust Fund for the Preparatory Activities of the 1985 World Conference to Review and Appraise the Achievements of the United Nations Decade for Women.

At an April meeting (see p. 366) of the Joint United Nations Information Committee in Paris, its Task Force on the 1985 World Conference heard reports of several organizations in order to identify a number of joint activities.[8] The United Nations Children's Fund (UNICEF) drew attention to its Women and Development Kits, the World Bank stated that it was involved in issues on women and development, the United Nations Non-Governmental Liaison Service reported on its efforts to involve non-governmental organizations (NGOs) in the Conference, and the United Nations Educational, Scientific and Cultural Organization reported on its programme on the status of women, which included support for NGO activities for the Conference and an evaluation of its work since 1975 to promote women's education and training.

ECONOMIC AND SOCIAL COUNCIL ACTION

In May 1984, on the recommendation of its Second Committee, the Economic and Social Council adopted without vote decision 1984/125.

Report of the Commission on the Status of Women acting as the Preparatory Body for the World Conference to Review and Appraise the Achievements of the United Nations Decade for Women: Equality, Development and Peace on its second session

At its 19th plenary meeting, on 24 May 1984, the Council:

(a) Took note of the report of the Commission on the Status of Women acting as the Preparatory Body for the World Conference to Review and Appraise the Achievements of the United Nations Decade for Women on its second session;

(b) Approved the recommendations contained in that report and decided to transmit it to the General Assembly at its thirty-ninth session.

Economic and Social Council decision 1984/125

Adopted without vote

Approved by Second Committee (E/1984/93) without vote, 17 May (meeting 15); oral proposal by Chairman; agenda item 12.

Financial implications. S-G, A/CONF.116/PC/19/Add.1 & Add.1/Corr.1.

GENERAL ASSEMBLY ACTION

On 14 December 1984, on the recommendation of the Third (Social, Humanitarian and Cultural) Committee, the Assembly adopted resolution 39/129 without vote.

Preparations for the World Conference to Review and Appraise the Achievements of the United Nations Decade for Women: Equality, Development and Peace

The General Assembly,

Recalling its resolution 3520(XXX) of 15 December 1975, in which it endorsed, *inter alia,* the action proposals contained in the World Plan of Action for the Implementation of the Objectives of the International Women's Year,

Recalling also its resolution 3490(XXX) of 12 December 1975, in which it expressed its conviction that a comprehensive and thorough review and appraisal of progress made in meeting the goals of the World Plan of Action was of crucial importance for the success of the Plan and recognized that the results of the implementation of the Plan would contribute to the consideration of the review and appraisal of the International Development Strategy for the Second United Nations Development Decade and would consequently promote the role of women in the development process,

Recalling further that the International Development Strategy for the Third United Nations Development Decade stressed that the important set of measures to improve the status of women contained in the World Plan of Action adopted at Mexico City in 1975, and the important agreed measures relating to the International Development Strategy in the Programme of Action for the Second Half of the United Nations Decade for Women, should be implemented,

Recalling its resolution 35/136 of 11 December 1980, in which it decided to convene in 1985, at the conclusion of the United Nations Decade for Women: Equality, Development and Peace, a World Conference to Review and Appraise the Achievements of the United Nations Decade for Women,

Reaffirming the objectives of the United Nations Decade for Women: Equality, Development and Peace, with the subtheme "Employment, Health and Education",

Recalling also its resolution 37/60 of 3 December 1982, in which it welcomed the decision of the Economic and Social Council that the Commission on the Status of Women should act as the preparatory body for the Conference,

Recalling further its resolution 38/108 of 16 December 1983,

Having considered the report of the Commission on the Status of Women acting as the preparatory body for the World Conference to Review and Appraise the Achievements of the United Nations Decade for Women: Equality, Development and Peace on its second session,

Taking into consideration Economic and Social Council decision 1984/125 of 24 May 1984,

Bearing in mind the request of the Economic and Social Council in its resolution 1983/28 of 26 May 1983 that the Secretary-General should invite interested non-governmental organizations in consultative status with the Council to submit information to the preparatory body for the Conference, including their views on the progress made and the obstacles still to be overcome towards the attainment of the goals of the Decade, as

well as their views on priorities and strategies looking
to the year 2000,

Stressing the importance of the World Conference to
Review and Appraise the Achievements of the United
Nations Decade for Women,

Bearing in mind the important role of the Commission on the Status of Women acting as the preparatory
body for the Conference, as well as the need for ensuring the high quality of the documents to be submitted
to the Conference,

1. *Reiterates its appreciation* to the Government of
Kenya for its offer to act as host to the World Conference to Review and Appraise the Achievements of the
United Nations Decade for Women: Equality, Development and Peace at Nairobi from 15 to 26 July
1985;

2. *Urges all* Member States to make all efforts to
ensure the success of the Conference;

3. *Takes note* of the report of the Commission on
the Status of Women acting as the preparatory body
for the Conference on its second session and endorses
the recommendations contained therein, as approved
by the Economic and Social Council at its first regular
session of 1984;

4. *Requests* the Secretary-General to submit to the
preparatory body for the Conference at its third session all the recommendations contained in the reports
of each of the regional preparatory meetings;

5. *Also requests* the Secretary-General to submit to
the preparatory body for the Conference at its third
session a report containing information from interested non-governmental organizations in consultative status with the Economic and Social Council, in
accordance with Council resolution 1983/28;

6. *Requests* that the preparatory body for the Conference ensure the high quality of the documents to be
submitted to the Conference, which should be distributed at least six weeks before the opening of the
Conference;

7. *Decides* to include in the provisional agenda of
its fortieth session the item entitled "United Nations
Decade for Women: Equality, Development and
Peace".

General Assembly resolution 39/129

14 December 1984   Meeting 101   Adopted without vote

Approved by Third Committee (A/39/702) without vote, 28 November (meeting
53); draft by Egypt, for Group of 77 (A/C.3/39/L.21); agenda item 93 *(b)*.

Financial implications. ACABQ, A/39/7/ Add.11; 5th Committee, A/39/812; S-G,
A/C.3/39/L.44, A/C.5/39/64.

Meeting numbers. GA 39th session: 3rd Committee 23-33, 42, 47, 50, 53; 5th
Committee 45; plenary 101.

The Fifth (Administrative and Budgetary)
Committee on 11 December decided that, should
the Assembly adopt the draft that was to become
resolution 39/129, additional appropriations of
$222,200 would be required for 1984-1985. That
amount, recommended by the Advisory Committee on Administrative and Budgetary Questions (ACABQ), was $51,600 less than the
$273,800 estimated by the Secretary-General for
non-conference-servicing requirements, additional to $1,958,200 for conference-servicing
costs.

Voluntary Fund

Status of the Fund

In 1984, the Voluntary Fund for the United
Nations Decade for Women continued to provide
financial and technical assistance to promote
economic growth, employment and social equity,
with special attention to rural and poor urban
women. Contributions to the Fund by Governments totalled $3.1 million, while expenditures
were almost $3.8 million. By the end of the year,
the Fund had approved over 400 projects valued
at more than $24 million. The largest number of
projects were for employment, followed by
human resources development, planning, energy
and information activities.

In 1984, the Fund's African Investment Plan
moved into its operational phase, focusing on
credit support for projects in such sectors as
agriculture and energy. Its Food Cycle Technologies Project, carried out with the Food and
Agriculture Organization of the United Nations,
the International Labour Organisation, UNDP
and UNICEF, identified prototype food technologies of demonstrated value to women and
promoted their wider use.[9]

The Fund's activities from October 1983 to
September 1984, its financial situation and
resources, and a summary of the Consultative
Committee's recommendations at its fifteenth
and sixteenth sessions were detailed in an October report of the Secretary-General to the
General Assembly.[10]

Following a December 1983 Assembly request,[11] the Secretary-General also included in
his report extracts from the forward-looking assessment undertaken on the Fund's activities. In
conclusion, he stated that the assessment showed
that the objectives of Fund-supported projects
were consonant with regional and national
strategies for promoting development in different
areas, helping combat poverty, illiteracy and
unemployment and promoting agricultural
production, self-reliance, employment, health,
nutrition, education, training and institution-
building.

To further its role as technical co-operation
mechanism for women and development, two
major implications for the Fund emerged from
the assessment: on the one hand, it needed to
concentrate on projects whose potential multiplier effects were greatest and thus might have
the greatest impact on national development; on
the other, closer co-operation with other United
Nations and bilateral and multilateral organizations was desirable. In addition, the mobilization
of resources implied for the Fund a higher level
of visibility among the donor communities.

As at 31 December 1984, Government contributions and pledges to the Fund were as follows:

CONTRIBUTIONS AND PLEDGES TO THE VOLUNTARY FUND
FOR THE UNITED NATIONS DECADE FOR WOMEN
(as at 31 December 1984; in US dollar equivalent)

Country	1984 payment	Pledge for future years
Afghanistan	500	—
Algeria	10,000	10,000
Australia	102,487	92,437
Austria	21,000	21,000
Bangladesh	2,000	—
Belgium	—	65,574
Botswana	3,565	3,521
Cameroon	2,568	—
Canada	14,968	16,260
Chile	5,000	—
China	20,000	30,000
Colombia	—	2,000
Cyprus	—	300
Democratic Yemen	3,055	1,760
Denmark	126,618	100,000
Egypt	—	2,000
Finland	121,126	157,480
France	39,025	26,596
Germany, Federal Republic of	19,151	33,113
Greece	3,500	3,500
Guinea	—	1,000
Guyana	1,000	1,000
Honduras	1,000	1,000
Iceland	6,000	6,000
India	40,000	20,000
Indonesia	3,000	3,000
Ireland	—	20,387
Italy	554,809	184,211
Jamaica	257	235
Lao People's Democratic Republic	—	1,500
Madagascar	1,798	—
Mauritius	500	—
Mexico	2,043	—
New Zealand	7,970	—
Norway	1,347,716	790,960
Oman	10,000	10,000
Pakistan	9,294	8,772
Philippines	—	1,000
Qatar	—	5,000
Republic of Korea	2,000	2,000
Sao Tome and Principe	—	444
Senegal	887	1,500
Seychelles	—	272
Spain	—	17,647
Sri Lanka	2,000	—
Sweden	96,177	—
Thailand	3,000	—
Turkey	4,991	5,000
Uganda	—	2,146
United States	500,000	500,000
Yugoslavia	4,000	4,000
Zambia	—	2,451
Zimbabwe	4,348	—
Total	3,097,353	2,155,066

SOURCE: Interim United Nations financial statements for the 12-month period of the biennium 1984-1985 ended 31 December 1984: schedules of individual trust funds.

Recognizing that requests for funding far exceeded resources, the Consultative Committee identified two priority areas for the future: making technical assistance available to Governments to increase the involvement of women in mainstream development activities, and working with local and national women's groups to support programmes on women in development. Members of the Committee stressed the importance of preserving the Fund's unique identity and capac-ity to innovate while making even greater use of the existing development assistance agencies.

Future arrangements

In October 1984, the Secretary-General submitted two reports related to future arrangements for the Fund. By the first,[12] he presented the views of 24 Member States indicating wide agreement that the Fund should continue its activities as an autonomous unit within UNDP in order to be closely involved in its operational work.

In the second report,[13] the Secretary-General examined options for the administrative location of the Fund: under the auspices of the Centre for Social Development and Humanitarian Affairs, Department of International Economic and Social Affairs, at Vienna; under the Department of Technical Co-operation for Development in New York; or as a special fund in association with UNDP.

With regard to the last option, the Secretary-General stated that it would imply recognition of the key role already played by UNDP in the administration of more than 90 per cent of the Fund's resources; that it would provide a basis for further developing the Fund's role in promoting wider recognition of women's contribution to development, by giving it better access to follow-up and multiplier financing by other United Nations funds, and to UNDP's technical capacities, activities and other resources, including country programming and donor round-tables; that it would further the Fund's image as an integral part of United Nations development assistance; and that it would help maintain low overhead costs.

GENERAL ASSEMBLY ACTION

On 14 December 1984, on the recommendation of the Third Committee, the Assembly adopted resolution 39/125 without vote.

Arrangements for the future management of the Voluntary Fund for the United Nations Decade for Women

The General Assembly,

Recalling its resolution 31/133 of 16 December 1976, containing the criteria and arrangements for the management of the Voluntary Fund for the United Nations Decade for Women,

Recalling also its resolution 36/129 of 14 December 1981, in which it decided that the Fund should continue its activities beyond the United Nations Decade for Women: Equality, Development and Peace,

Stressing the urgency of determining at its current session the most effective arrangements for continuing the activities of the Fund beyond the Decade in view of the need for ensuring the long-term stability of the Fund,

Recalling further its resolution 38/106 of 16 December 1983, in which, *inter alia*, it decided that, when considering the reports of the Secretary-General on the future of the Fund, all possible options would be reviewed in depth,

Reaffirming that the Fund has a unique contribution to make to the achievement of the goals of the Third United Nations Development Decade, and even beyond it,

Recognizing the important actual and potential contribution by women to development, as evidenced in the forward-looking assessment of the activities assisted by the Fund and the crucial role of the Fund as a specialized resource base for development co-operation, and the need for continued assistance to activities directly benefiting women,

Considering, accordingly, that it is of paramount importance to establish a future organizational framework that will secure the ability of the Fund to act as a catalytic agent on the main United Nations development co-operation system,

Considering also the innovative and experimental activities of the Fund directed to strengthening both governmental and non-governmental institutional capacities to ensure access for women to development co-operation resources and their full participation at all levels in the development process,

Stressing that general questions of development and access of women to development resources have, as a common objective, to create conditions which will improve the quality of life for all,

Welcoming the completion of the forward-looking assessment of the activities assisted by the Fund and the findings and conclusions with regard to women and development and their implications for technical co-operation agencies and organizations,

Conscious of the highly specialized professional competence of the Fund in the area of development activities for women and the need for strengthening that competence,

Aware of the broad range of linkages of the Fund with national Governments, national women's groups, non-governmental organizations and women's research institutes, besides its close co-operation with United Nations development agencies, including the regional commissions,

Taking into consideration the moderate size of the Fund and its continued need to draw on the operational capacity of other agencies and, in this regard, expressing its appreciation to the United Nations Development Programme for its continuing technical and resource assistance to the Fund,

Expressing appreciation to the Department of International Economic and Social Affairs of the Secretariat and its Centre for Social Development and Humanitarian Affairs for their contribution to the work of the Fund during its initial operational years,

Taking note of the reports of the Consultative Committee on the Voluntary Fund for the United Nations Decade for Women on its fifteenth and sixteenth sessions, referred to in the report of the Secretary-General prepared in accordance with General Assembly resolution 38/106,

Taking note also of the reports of the Secretary-General on the Fund,

1. *Decides* that the activities of the Voluntary Fund for the United Nations Decade for Women shall be continued through establishment of a separate and identifiable entity in autonomous association with the United Nations Development Programme, which will play an innovative and catalytic role in relation to the United Nations overall system of development co-operation;

2. *Endorses* the modalities for the arrangements between the Fund and the United Nations Development Programme for the future management of the Fund, as contained in the annex to the present resolution, and decides that these arrangements shall enter into force at the latest on 1 January 1986;

3. *Reaffirms* the criteria laid down in its resolution 31/133 on the use of the resources of the Fund and the guidelines established on the advice of the Consultative Committee on the Voluntary Fund for the United Nations Decade for Women, emphasizing the use of these resources for technical co-operation benefiting women;

4. *Requests* the Consultative Committee at its seventeenth session, to be held from 25 to 29 March 1985, to propose an appropriate future title for the Fund;

5. *Stresses* the need for close and continuous working relationships between the Fund and the bodies, organs and organizations of the United Nations system concerned with women's issues and development co-operation, in particular with the Department of International Economic and Social Affairs of the Secretariat and its Centre for Social Development and Humanitarian Affairs;

6. *Expresses its appreciation* for the contributions to the Fund made by Governments and non-governmental organizations, which have a vital role to play in maintaining and increasing the financial viability of the Fund and the effectiveness of its work;

7. *Notes with concern* that contributions to the Fund have not been sufficient to enable it to respond to all the deserving requests for technical assistance that it has received;

8. *Urges*, accordingly, Governments to continue and, where possible, to increase their contributions to the Fund, and calls upon those Governments that have not yet done so to consider contributing to the Fund;

9. *Requests* the Secretary-General, after consultation with the Consultative Committee at its seventeenth session, to report to the General Assembly at its fortieth session on the arrangements he has made with the Administrator of the United Nations Development Programme for the future of the Fund;

10. *Requests* that the Consultative Committee monitor the process of implementing the arrangements for the management of the Fund contained in the annex to the present resolution and that the Committee's views on this matter be reflected fully in the annual report on the Fund to the General Assembly, particularly in its initial years.

ANNEX
Arrangements for the management of the United Nations Development Fund for Women

1. The United Nations Development Fund for Women (UNIFEM), hereinafter referred to as "the Fund", is hereby established as a separate and identifiable entity in autonomous association with the United Nations Development Programme. The Administrator of the United Nations Development Programme, hereinafter referred to as "the Administrator", shall be accountable for all aspects of the management and operations of the Fund. There shall be a Consultative Committee to advise the Administrator on all policy matters relating to the activities of the Fund in accordance with paragraph 13 below. The following arrangements for the management of the Fund shall apply:

I. Transfer of existing resources, solicitation
and acknowledgement of pledges and
collection of contributions

2. The Voluntary Fund for the United Nations Decade for Women and its subsidiary Supplementary Trust Fund, which was established by a memorandum of understanding between the Secretary-General of the United Nations and the Administrator on 25 June 1980, are hereby liquidated and their assets transferred to the Fund.

3. Governments, intergovernmental and non-governmental organizations and other donors may contribute to the Fund.

4. The Fund shall be included among the programmes for which funds are pledged at the annual United Nations Pledging Conference for Development Activities. The Administrator shall assist with the mobilization of financial resources for the Fund. The contributions to the Fund and the bank accounts into which they are deposited shall be in accordance with the applicable Financial Regulations and Rules of the United Nations Development Programme.

II. Operations and control

5. All operations of the Voluntary Fund for the United Nations Decade for Women are hereby transferred to the Fund.

6. The Administrator, in consultation with the Consultative Committee on the Voluntary Fund for the United Nations Decade for Women, shall appoint a Director of the Fund, hereinafter referred to as "the Director", bearing in mind the relevant qualifications and experience with technical co-operation, including those benefiting women. The Administrator shall appoint the staff of the Fund in consultation with the Director, pursuant to the Staff Regulations of the United Nations and the relevant provisions of the Charter of the United Nations.

7. The Administrator shall delegate the management of the Fund and its administration, including responsibility for the mobilization of resources, to the Director, who shall have the authority to conduct all matters related to its mandate and who shall be accountable directly to the Administrator.

8. The operations of the Fund shall be conducted taking into account the innovative and catalytic nature of its development co-operation activities for women and its existing criteria and operational procedures. The present procedures of the Fund, including those governing the identification, formulation, approval, appraisal, execution and evaluation of projects established in accordance with the requirements set out in the criteria adopted by the General Assembly in its resolution 31/133 and on the advice of the Consultative Committee, shall remain in force. Subject to the arrangements for the management of the Fund, the regulations, rules and directives of the United Nations Development Programme shall be applied to the operations of the Fund.

9. The resources of the Fund shall be used mainly within two priority areas: first, to serve as a catalyst, with the goal of ensuring the appropriate involvement of women in mainstream development activities, as often as possible at the pre-investment stages; secondly, to support innovative and experimental activities benefiting women in line with national and regional priorities. Fund resources should be a supplement to and not a substitute for the mandated responsibilities of other United Nations development co-operation organizations and agencies, including the United Nations Development Programme.

10. All the administrative and programme support costs of the Fund shall be met from its own resources.

11. The regional bureaux, other organizational units and field offices of the United Nations Development Programme shall continue to assist the operations of the Fund, *inter alia*, by joint programming missions to ensure the involvement of women in technical co-operation activities financed by the United Nations Development Programme and by supporting the project cycle activities of projects financed by the Fund. For its part, the Fund shall participate in existing machineries for co-ordination of technical co-operation at headquarters and field levels.

12. The proposed biennial budget for the administrative costs of the Fund shall be reviewed initially by the Consultative Committee prior to its submission by the Administrator for approval by the Governing Council of the United Nations Development Programme.

III. The Consultative Committee and the relationship of the Fund to other organizations

13. The President of the General Assembly shall designate, with due regard for the financing of the Fund from voluntary contributions and to equitable geographical distribution, five Member States to serve on the Consultative Committee for a period of three years. Each State member of the Consultative Committee shall designate a person with relevant expertise and experience in development co-operation activities, including those benefiting women, to serve on the Committee. The Committee shall advise the Administrator on all matters of policy affecting the activities of the Fund, including the application of the criteria set forth by the General Assembly in respect of the use of the Fund.

14. The Fund shall establish and maintain close and continuous working relationships with other United Nations organs, in particular the Department of International Economic and Social Affairs of the Secretariat and its Centre for Social Development and Humanitarian Affairs, the regional commissions, the United Nations Children's Fund, the United Nations Fund for Population Activities and the International Research and Training Institute for the Advancement of Women, as well as through the Administrative Committee on Co-ordination with the specialized agencies and other United Nations entities concerned, in particular the International Fund for Agricultural Development. Co-operation shall also be established for the sharing of information with the Commission on the Status of Women and other relevant global and regional intergovernmental bodies concerned with development and with women. As appropriate, the activities of the Fund may be drawn to the attention of the Committee on the Elimination of Discrimination against Women.

IV. Reporting and auditing

15. The Director shall prepare substantive and financial progress reports on the use of the Fund for the Administrator to submit to the Consultative Committee.

16. Taking into account the advice of the Consultative Committee, the Administrator shall submit to the Governing Council of the United Nations Development Programme an annual report on the operations,

management and budget of the Fund. He shall submit a similar report to the General Assembly, to be referred to the Second Committee for consideration of its technical co-operation aspects and also to the Third Committee.

17. The Commission on the Status of Women shall also be provided with the annual reports referred to in paragraph 16 above.

18. The Administrator shall be responsible for reporting all the financial transactions of the Fund and shall issue annual financial statements in accordance with the Financial Regulations and Rules of the United Nations Development Programme.

19. The Fund shall be subject to the internal and external auditing procedures provided for under the financial regulations, rules and directives of the United Nations Development Programme.

General Assembly resolution 39/125

14 December 1984   Meeting 101   Adopted without vote

Approved by Third Committee (A/39/702) without vote, 26 November (meeting 50); 26-nation draft (A/C.3/39/L.24/Rev.1); agenda item 93 (c).
Sponsors: Australia, Bolivia, Canada, Central African Republic, Colombia, Costa Rica, German Democratic Republic, Guyana, India, Ivory Coast, Jamaica, Japan, Kenya, Liberia, Mali, Morocco, Netherlands, New Zealand, Norway, Sri Lanka, Sudan, Swaziland, Sweden, Togo, Trinidad and Tobago, United Kingdom.
Meeting numbers. GA 39th session: 3rd Committee 23-33, 42, 47, 50; plenary 101.

Commission on the Status of Women

The Commission on the Status of Women held its thirtieth session at Vienna from 15 to 25 February 1984. In its report,[14] the Commission recommended 11 draft resolutions for adoption by the Economic and Social Council. These dealt with the 1979 Convention on the Elimination of All Forms of Discrimination against Women (see below), equal opportunity for women employed in the United Nations system and concerns of women within the United Nations (see ADMINISTRATIVE AND BUDGETARY QUESTIONS, Chapter III), implementation of the objectives of the United Nations Decade for Women (see above), future work of the Commission (see below) and a number of issues relating to the status of women (see below). Also for action by the Council, the Commission recommended a draft decision on the provisional agenda and documentation for its 1986 session.

In accordance with a May 1983 Council resolution,[15] the Commission appointed at its February 1984 session a five-member Working Group on Communications on the Status of Women. The Group studied a list of 121 communications and the replies of some Governments, many of them concerning the separation of families and of persons wishing to marry. The Group considered those as not within its mandate but within that of the Commission on Human Rights, since they related equally to men and women. It identified only one trend which it wished to draw to the Commission's attention: the widespread physical violence against women in official custody. After having heard the Working Group's report in closed session on 23 February, the Commission decided to adopt it and incorporate it into its own report.

ECONOMIC AND SOCIAL COUNCIL ACTION

In May, on the recommendation of its Second Committee, the Economic and Social Council adopted decision 1984/126 without vote.

Report of the Commission on the Status of Women

At its 19th plenary meeting, on 24 May 1984, the Council took note of the report of the Commission on the Status of Women on its thirtieth session.

Economic and Social Council decision 1984/126

Adopted without vote

Approved by Second Committee (E/1984/93) without vote, 17 May (meeting 15); oral proposal by Chairman; agenda item 12.

Future work of the Commission

ECONOMIC AND SOCIAL COUNCIL ACTION

On 24 May 1984, on the recommendation of its Second Committee, the Council adopted resolution 1984/20 without vote.

Future work of the Commission on the Status of Women

The Economic and Social Council,

Reaffirming the mandate of the Commission on the Status of Women established by the Economic and Social Council in resolution 11(II) of 21 June 1946,

Considering that the objectives of the United Nations Decade for Women: Equality, Development and Peace continue to be valid, are closely interrelated and constitute a significant basis for the work of the Commission on the Status of Women,

Considering that, as the end of the Decade approaches, it is urgently necessary to reinforce the future work of the Commission on the Status of Women so that it may discharge its important role in promoting the implementation of the strategies for the year 2000 that will emanate from the World Conference to Review and Appraise the Achievements of the United Nations Decade for Women: Equality, Development and Peace, to be held in 1985,

Emphasizing the importance of the role of women in development as both agents and beneficiaries,

Taking into account resolution 40 of the World Conference of the United Nations Decade for Women: Equality, Development and Peace, General Assembly resolutions 2263(XXII) of 7 November 1967, 2626(XXV) of 24 October 1970 and 35/56 of 5 December 1980, Economic and Social Council resolution 1980/38 of 2 May 1980 and any other relevant resolutions,

Welcoming the decision of the General Assembly to declare 1986 the International Year of Peace as a contribution to the improvement of the international climate, which will alleviate existing tensions and the grave threats to the maintenance of peace which jeopardize the possibility of improving the status of women,

1. *Recommends* that the Commission on the Status of Women at its thirty-first session, as a contribution to the International Year of Peace, should consider recommendations for concrete proposals to ensure the full participation of women in the establishment of conditions conducive to the maintenance of peace and to the elimination of inequality and poverty;

2. *Also recommends* that the Commission on the Status of Women at its thirty-first session should propose concrete measures to overcome the general and specific trends that impede the advancement of women, in particular by proposing the establishment, by other organs of the United Nations, of training programmes and socially and economically profitable projects that give women a part in the development process on a footing of equality.

Economic and Social Council resolution 1984/20

24 May 1984   Meeting 19   Adopted without vote

Approved by Second Committee (E/1984/93) without vote, 10 May (meeting 9); draft by Commission on women (E/1984/15); agenda item 12.

Agenda and documentation for 1986 session

ECONOMIC AND SOCIAL COUNCIL ACTION

In May 1984, on the recommendation of its Second Committee, the Council adopted decision 1984/123 without vote.

Provisional agenda and documentation for the thirty-first session of the Commission on the Status of Women

At its 19th plenary meeting, on 24 May 1984, the Council approved the provisional agenda and documentation for the thirty-first session of the Commission on the Status of Women set out below.

Provisional agenda and documentation for the thirty-first session of the Commission on the Status of Women

1. Election of officers.
2. Adoption of the agenda and other organizational matters.
3. Results of the World Conference to Review and Appraise the Achievements of the United Nations Decade for Women: Equality, Development and Peace.
   Documentation
   Report of the World Conference to Review and Appraise the Achievements of the United Nations Decade for Women: Equality, Development and Peace
   Note by the Secretary-General on the reporting system for periodic review and appraisal of progress in the advancement of women at national, regional and international levels
   Report of the Secretary-General on measures for the integration of the needs and concerns of women in planning and programme activities of the United Nations system
4. Elimination of discrimination against women in accordance with the aims of the Convention on the Elimination of All Forms of Discrimination against Women.
   Documentation
   Report of the Secretary-General on the status of the Convention on the Elimination of All Forms of Discrimination against Women
   Reports of the Committee on the Elimination of Discrimination against Women (for information)
   Reports of the Joint Inspection Unit on the status of women in the Professional category and above and other relevant reports (for information)

Report of the Secretary-General on information on family violence provided by Member States, organizations of the United Nations system and non-governmental organizations
5. Participation of women in promoting international peace and co-operation.
   Documentation
   Report of the Secretary-General on measures of assistance for women inside South Africa and Namibia and for women from South Africa and Namibia who have become refugees as a result of the practice of *apartheid*
   Progress report of the Secretary-General on the preparation of a comprehensive report on the situation of women living within and outside the occupied Arab territories
6. Role of women in development.
   Documentation
   Report of the Secretary-General on the status and situation of elderly women
7. Communications concerning the status of women.
   Documentation
   Note by the Secretary-General transmitting a non-confidential list of communications concerning the status of women
   Note by the Secretary-General transmitting a confidential list of communications concerning the status of women
   Report of the Secretary-General on information provided by Member States on physical violence against detained women that is specific to their sex
8. Programme of future work, including the provisional agenda for the thirty-second session.
9. Adoption of the report of the Commission on its thirty-first session.

Economic and Social Council decision 1984/123

Adopted without vote

Approved by Second Committee (E/1984/93) without vote, 10 May (meeting 9); draft by Commission on women (E/1984/15); agenda item 12.

1979 Convention on discrimination against women

As at 31 December 1984, there were 64 States parties to the Convention on the Elimination of All Forms of Discrimination against Women, adopted in 1979.[16] The Committee on the Elimination of Discrimination against Women (CEDAW), established in 1982 under the Convention,[17] held its third session in New York from 26 March to 6 April 1984 to consider reports of States parties submitted under article 18. The Economic and Social Council, in May, adopted two resolutions relating to the Convention's implementation and the Committee's work. The Assembly dealt with the subject in December.

Implementation of the Convention

Communication. On 16 October 1984, the Sudan transmitted to the Secretary-General a resolution adopted by the Seventy-second Inter-

Parliamentary Conference at Geneva on 29 September, urging all Governments which had not done so to become parties to the Convention.[3]

CEDAW action. At its third session,[18] CEDAW considered initial reports of six States parties on measures they had adopted to give effect to the Convention, out of 21 reports received since the Convention entered into force in 1981.[19]

Among other matters, the Committee decided that reservations and objections by States parties should be annexed to future country reports. It agreed to discuss in future how to interpret article 21 of the Convention, under which the Committee could make suggestions and general recommendations to the General Assembly, based on the examination of country reports. With regard to its contribution to the 1985 World Conference to review the Decade for Women (see above, requested by the Commission on the Status of Women as the preparatory body, the Committee agreed to recommend to the Economic and Social Council that the United Nations Secretariat prepare a report on achievements and obstacles experienced by States parties in implementing the Convention, to be discussed in draft form at the Committee's 1985 session.

The Committee adopted the report on its second session,[20] held in August 1983,[21] on 28 March 1984 and the report on its third session on 6 April.

ECONOMIC AND SOCIAL COUNCIL ACTION

On 22 May, the Economic and Social Council adopted resolution 1984/8 by vote.

Convention on the Elimination of All Forms of Discrimination against Women

The Economic and Social Council,

Recalling General Assembly resolution 34/180 of 18 December 1979, by which the Assembly adopted the Convention on the Elimination of All Forms of Discrimination against Women annexed thereto,

Recalling also General Assembly resolutions 35/140 of 11 December 1980, 36/131 of 14 December 1981, 37/64 of 3 December 1982 and 38/109 of 16 December 1983,

Taking into account Council resolutions 1983/1 of 17 May 1983 and 1984/10 of 24 May 1984,

Noting that the Committee on the Elimination of Discrimination against Women, in its rules of procedure, provided that it would have summary records and would include Arabic among its official languages,

Recognizing the importance of the summary records of bodies established to monitor the implementation of international human rights instruments,

Having considered the reports of the Committee on the Elimination of Discrimination against Women on its second and third sessions,

Welcoming the decision of the Committee to contribute to the World Conference to Review and Appraise the Achievements of the United Nations Decade for Women: Equality, Development and Peace, to be held in 1985,

1. *Takes note* of the reports of the Committee on the Elimination of Discrimination against Women on its second and third sessions;

2. *Emphasizes* the importance of the strictest compliance by States parties with their obligations under the Convention on the Elimination of All Forms of Discrimination against Women;

3. *Requests* States parties to make all possible efforts to submit their initial implementation reports in accordance with article 18 of the Convention and requests the Committee in organizing its work to ensure that the reports of States parties are adequately reviewed within the quadrennial cycle envisaged;

4. *Notes* the decision of the Committee, as contained in paragraphs 366 and 367 of the report on its third session, to consider at its fourth session the achievements and obstacles experienced by States parties in the implementation of the Convention as a contribution to the World Conference to Review and Appraise the Achievements of the United Nations Decade for Women: Equality, Development and Peace;

5. *Requests* the Secretary-General to prepare a compendium of information based upon the national reports on the achievements of and obstacles experienced by States parties in the implementation of the Convention, in conformity with article 17, paragraph 9, of the Convention, to assist the Committee in the preparation of a report on those issues as a contribution to the Conference;

6. *Takes note* of the discussion in the Committee concerning the inclusion in the agenda of a future session of an item on ways and means of implementing article 21 of the Convention, which provides that the Committee may make suggestions and general recommendations based on the examination of reports;

7. *Recommends* the General Assembly to take the necessary steps to ensure the provision and distribution in all official languages of summary records of meetings of the Committee;

8. *Invites* the Committee, once it is provided with summary records on a regular basis, to review the format and content of its report, bearing in mind the provisions of paragraphs 13, 14 and 15 of General Assembly resolution 37/14 C of 16 November 1982;

9. *Requests* the Secretary-General to transmit the reports of the Committee on the Elimination of Discrimination against Women to the General Assembly at its thirty-ninth session, as well as to the Commission on the Status of Women, for information.

Economic and Social Council resolution 1984/8

22 May 1984   Meeting 17   48-1

11-nation draft (E/1984/L.22/Rev.1); agenda item 4.
Sponsors: Austria, Bulgaria, Canada, Colombia, Greece, Mongolia, Portugal, Rwanda, Saint Lucia, Sri Lanka, Sweden.
Financial implications. S-G, E/1984/L.28.
Meeting numbers. ESC 7, 8, 16, 17.

Following introduction of the 11-nation draft resolution, a draft decision submitted by Bulgaria, Cuba and the German Democratic Republic was withdrawn.[22] By that draft, the Council would have taken note of the Committee's reports and welcomed its decision to request the Secretary-General to submit for discussion at the Committee's 1985 session a draft report on the progress achieved and the obstacles to implementing the Convention.

On 24 May, the Council, on the recommendation of its Second Committee, adopted resolution 1984/10 without vote.

Convention on the Elimination of All Forms of Discrimination against Women

The Economic and Social Council,

Bearing in mind that one of the purposes of the United Nations, set forth in Articles 1 and 55 of the Charter, is to promote universal respect for human rights and fundamental freedoms without distinction of any kind, including any distinction as to sex,

Affirming that women and men should participate equally in social, economic and political development, should contribute equally to such development and should share equally in improved conditions of life,

Recalling General Assembly resolution 34/180 of 18 December 1979, by which the Assembly adopted the Convention on the Elimination of All Forms of Discrimination against Women annexed thereto,

Recalling also General Assembly resolutions 35/140 of 11 December 1980, 36/131 of 14 December 1981, 37/64 of 3 December 1982, 38/18 of 22 November 1983 and 38/109 of 16 December 1983, and Council resolution 1983/1 of 17 May 1983,

Having taken note of the report of the Committee on the Elimination of Discrimination against Women on its first session,

1. *Notes with appreciation* the increasing number of Member States that have ratified or acceded to the Convention on the Elimination of All Forms of Discrimination against Women;

2. *Expresses its grave concern* about continuing discrimination against women and infringement of their rights in a number of States;

3. *Urges* all States that have not yet ratified or acceded to the Convention to do so as soon as possible, taking into account the World Conference to Review and Appraise the Achievements of the United Nations Decade for Women: Equality, Development and Peace, to be held in 1985;

4. *Welcomes* the fact that the Committee on the Elimination of Discrimination against Women began its work successfully and, in particular, adopted at its second session general guidelines regarding the form and content of reports received from States parties under article 18 of the Convention;

5. *Decides* to include in the agenda of the thirty-first session of the Commission on the Status of Women the question of the Convention on the Elimination of All Forms of Discrimination against Women.

Economic and Social Council resolution 1984/10

24 May 1984   Meeting 19   Adopted without vote

Approved by Second Committee (E/1984/93) without vote, 10 May (meeting 9); draft by Commission on women (E/1984/15); agenda item 12.

GENERAL ASSEMBLY ACTION

On 14 December 1984, on the recommendation of the Third Committee, the General Assembly adopted by recorded vote resolution 39/130.

Convention on the Elimination of All Forms of Discrimination against Women

The General Assembly,

Bearing in mind that one of the purposes of the United Nations, as stated in Articles 1 and 55 of the Charter, is to promote universal respect for human rights and fundamental freedoms for all without distinction of any kind, including distinction as to sex,

Affirming that women and men should participate equally in social, economic and political development, should contribute equally to such development and should share equally in improved conditions of life,

Recalling its resolution 34/180 of 18 December 1979, by which it adopted the Convention on the Elimination of All Forms of Discrimination against Women,

Recalling also its resolutions 35/140 of 11 December 1980, 36/131 of 14 December 1981, 37/64 of 3 December 1982 and 38/109 of 16 December 1983,

Taking note of the report of the Secretary-General on the status of the Convention,

Having considered the reports of the Committee on the Elimination of Discrimination against Women on its second and third sessions,

Noting that the Committee, in its rules of procedure, decided that it would have summary records and would include Arabic among its official languages and that the Economic and Social Council, in its resolution 1984/8 of 22 May 1984, recommended that the General Assembly should take the necessary steps to ensure the provision and distribution in all official languages of such records,

Recognizing the importance of the summary records of bodies established to monitor the implementation of international human rights instruments,

Noting that the Committee decided to consider the achievements and obstacles experienced by States parties in the implementation of the Convention as a contribution to the World Conference to Review and Appraise the Achievements of the United Nations Decade for Women: Equality, Development and Peace, to be held at Nairobi from 15 to 26 July 1985, and that the Economic and Social Council, in its resolution 1984/8, requested the Secretary-General to assist the Committee therein,

1. *Notes with appreciation* the increasing number of Member States that have ratified or acceded to the Convention on the Elimination of All Forms of Discrimination against Women;

2. *Invites* States that have not yet done so to become parties to the Convention by ratifying or acceding to it;

3. *Requests* the Secretary-General to submit annually to the General Assembly a report on the status of the Convention;

4. *Takes note with appreciation* of the reports of the Committee on the Elimination of Discrimination against Women on its second and third sessions and commends the Committee for its work;

5. *Emphasizes* the importance of the strictest compliance by States parties with their obligations under the Convention;

6. *Requests* States parties to make all possible efforts to submit their initial implementation reports in accordance with article 18 of the Convention, bearing in mind the Committee's general guidelines regarding the form and contents of such reports;

7. *Requests* the Committee, in organizing its work, to ensure that the reports of States parties are adequately

reviewed within the quadrennial cycle envisaged in the Convention;

8. *Takes note* of the discussion in the Committee concerning the inclusion in the agenda of a future session of an item on the discussion of article 21 of the Convention, specifically the provision that the Committee may make suggestions and general recommendations based on the examination of reports;

9. *Authorizes* the provision and distribution in all official languages of the United Nations of summary records of the meetings of the Committee and requests the Secretary-General to take appropriate measures to that end;

10. *Invites* the Committee to consider, in the light of this authorization of the provision and distribution of summary records of its meetings on a regular basis, the format and content of its future reports, bearing in mind the relevant provisions of General Assembly resolution 37/14 C of 16 November 1982.

General Assembly resolution 39/130

14 December 1984   Meeting 101   142-1-1 (recorded vote)

Approved by Third Committee (A/39/703) by recorded vote (124-1-4), 26 November (meeting 50); 37-nation draft (A/C.3/39/L.18); agenda item 94.

Sponsors: Australia, Austria, Bulgaria, Canada, Central African Republic, China, Costa Rica, Cuba, Denmark, Ecuador, Egypt, Ethiopia, France, German Democratic Republic, Greece, Hungary, Iceland, Indonesia, Jamaica, Liberia, Mexico, Mongolia, Netherlands, Nigeria, Norway, Panama, Philippines, Poland, Portugal, Rwanda, Spain, Sri Lanka, Swaziland, Sweden, Uruguay, Viet Nam, Yugoslavia.

Financial implications. 5th Committee, A/39/803; S-G, A/C.3/39/L.26, A/C.5/39/55.

Meeting numbers. GA 39th session: 3rd Committee 23-33, 42, 50; 5th Committee 41; plenary 101.

Recorded vote in Assembly as follows:

In favour: Afghanistan, Algeria, Angola, Argentina, Australia, Austria, Bahamas, Bahrain, Bangladesh, Barbados, Belgium, Belize, Benin, Bhutan, Bolivia, Botswana, Brazil, Brunei Darussalam, Bulgaria, Burkina Faso, Burma, Burundi, Byelorussian SSR, Cameroon, Canada, Cape Verde, Central African Republic, Chad, Chile, China, Colombia, Congo, Costa Rica, Cuba, Cyprus, Czechoslovakia, Democratic Kampuchea, Democratic Yemen, Denmark, Djibouti, Dominican Republic, Ecuador, Egypt, El Salvador, Equatorial Guinea, Ethiopia, Fiji, Finland, France, Gabon, Gambia, German Democratic Republic, Germany, Federal Republic of, Ghana, Greece, Guatemala, Guinea, Guyana, Haiti, Honduras, Hungary, Iceland, India, Indonesia, Iran, Iraq, Ireland, Israel, Italy, Ivory Coast, Jamaica, Japan, Jordan, Kenya, Kuwait, Lao People's Democratic Republic, Lebanon, Lesotho, Liberia, Libyan Arab Jamahiriya, Luxembourg, Madagascar, Malawi, Malaysia, Maldives, Mali, Malta, Mauritania, Mauritius, Mexico, Mongolia, Mozambique, Nepal, Netherlands, New Zealand, Nicaragua, Niger, Nigeria, Norway, Panama, Papua New Guinea, Paraguay, Peru, Philippines, Poland, Portugal, Qatar, Romania, Rwanda, Saint Vincent and the Grenadines, Samoa, Sao Tome and Principe, Saudi Arabia, Senegal, Seychelles, Sierra Leone, Singapore, Somalia, Spain, Sri Lanka, Sudan, Suriname, Swaziland, Sweden, Thailand, Togo, Trinidad and Tobago, Tunisia, Turkey, Uganda, Ukrainian SSR, USSR, United Arab Emirates, United Kingdom, United Republic of Tanzania, Uruguay, Venezuela, Viet Nam, Yemen, Yugoslavia, Zaire, Zambia.

Against: United States.

Abstaining: Morocco.

In the Third Committee, the United States explained that it had requested a recorded vote because of the financial implications of having summary records for CEDAW; it was vital to control the volume of documentation. The USSR also objected to the financial implications of providing summary records which, it felt, would not promote the efficacy of the work of CEDAW. Japan hoped that maximum efforts would be made to reduce expenditures, and Brazil reserved its position on paragraph 9 which it thought should be taken up by the Fifth Committee. Norway urged for support of its position that CEDAW be accorded the

same facilities as other bodies which monitored the implementation of human rights instruments. The United Kingdom stressed that, if CEDAW was provided with summary records, it should not include summaries of its debates in its report. Stating that certain provisions of the Convention conflicted with its national legislation, Morocco declared it would abstain for reasons which had nothing to do with financial implications.

Introducing the text on behalf of 37 nations, Sweden said CEDAW had so far been provided with summary records only on a provisional basis; the provision of summary records would place it on an equal footing with such bodies as the Human Rights Committee and the Committee on the Elimination of Racial Discrimination.

Ratifications, accessions and signatures

During 1984, 11 States (Bangladesh, Brazil, Democratic Yemen, Equatorial Guinea, Indonesia, Jamaica, Kenya, Liberia, Mauritius, Republic of Korea, Spain) ratified or acceded to the Convention, bringing to 64 the total number of States parties.[23] In a report to the General Assembly, the Secretary-General listed the States which had signed, ratified or acceded to the Convention as at 17 July 1984.[24] Annexed to the report were reservations made since 28 July 1983 by five States.

Research and Training
Institute for the Advancement of Women

In a March 1984 report to the Economic and Social Council[25] and an October note to the General Assembly's Third Committee,[26] the Board of Trustees of the International Research and Training Institute for the Advancement of Women (INSTRAW) and the Secretary-General, respectively, provided information on INSTRAW activities. The Institute continued work on a series of studies on transfer and development of technology and on the choice of technology as it affected women, and it started similar work on trade, finance and monetary issues as they affected women. Other work focused on women and the self-reliance of developing countries, the role of women in food production, and the relationship of energy policies to women. In its subprogramme on the role of women in the International Drinking Water Supply and Sanitation Decade (1981-1990) (see Chapter IX of this section), the Institute convened an interregional seminar (Cairo, Egypt, 12-16 March)[27] and issued a pamphlet on women and water supply and sanitation.

A consultative meeting (Santo Domingo, 17-22 September) reviewed nine studies on the role of women in international economic relations, and a workshop (Vienna, 3-7 December) convened jointly with the United Nations Industrial Development Organization (UNIDO) prepared modules for training women for managerial and entrepreneurial activities in industry. During the year, the Institute published a booklet on its training programme policy designed to overcome high costs and inadequate techniques of training.

The Board of Trustees of INSTRAW held its fourth session at the Institute's headquarters at Santo Domingo (23-28 January), reviewing the progress of work, the programme budget for 1984-1985 and the draft statute of the Institute.[25] The Board requested that the results of its 1982-1983 activities be published; that the Institute acquire basic equipment needed for its permanent headquarters; that particular attention be given to the role of women in international economic relations; and that the results of its activities concerning statistics on the situation of women, as well as the recommendations on the incorporation of women into development planning, be brought to the attention of relevant organizations. It also expressed satisfaction that the Steering Committee for Cooperative Action to support the International Drinking Water Supply and Sanitation Decade had adopted its strategy for enhancing women's participation in these activities and would hold its next meeting at INSTRAW headquarters. It agreed that major efforts were needed in fund-raising.

The Board approved the proposed programme budget for 1984-1985, with the exception of an element on training modules, and approved the activities and posts proposed on the basis of allocations of $2.5 million for the two years. It recommended that funds be maintained for training programmes and fellowships; stressed the value of decentralized programme implementation in cooperation with the specialized agencies and other United Nations organizations; and expressed the wish to consider a long-term plan outlining the priorities for the Institute's programme activities, indicating that each programme should have an evaluation component. The Board also adopted a draft statute for the Institute, which was later approved by the Economic and Social Council (see below).

The Board decided in principle to accept the invitation of Cuba to hold its fifth session at Havana, subject to the signing of an agreement between Cuba and the United Nations and on the understanding that all additional costs would be borne by Cuba.

GENERAL ASSEMBLY ACTION

On 14 December, on the recommendation of the Third Committee, the Assembly adopted without vote resolution 39/122.

International Research and Training Institute for the Advancement of Women

The General Assembly,

Recalling its resolutions 37/56 of 3 December 1982 and 38/104 of 16 December 1983 on the International Research and Training Institute for the Advancement of Women,

Taking note of the note by the Secretary-General on recent developments regarding the activities and statute of the Institute,

Recalling Economic and Social Council decision 1984/124 of 24 May 1984 on the statute of the Institute,

Bearing in mind that the entire operation of the Institute depends solely on voluntary contributions,

1. *Welcomes* the statute of the International Research and Training Institute for the Advancement of Women as approved by the Economic and Social Council in its decision 1984/124;

2. *Takes note with satisfaction* of the programme of activities of the Institute, which constitutes a valuable contribution to an increased role of women in the development process at all levels and is carried out in co-operation with the organizations of the United Nations system;

3. *Stresses* the relevance of programmes related to women and international economic relations;

4. *Requests* the Institute, in preparing its future activities, to take into consideration the trends in research and training relevant to women and development;

5. *Invites* Governments and intergovernmental organizations to contribute to the United Nations Trust Fund for the International Research and Training Institute for the Advancement of Women, in view of the increasing importance of research and training for the advancement of women;

6. *Requests* the Secretary-General to continue to provide support to the Institute, particularly in its fund-raising activities, by encouraging voluntary contributions to the Institute;

7. *Also requests* the Secretary-General to submit to the General Assembly at its fortieth session a report on the activities of the Institute;

8. *Decides* to include in the provisional agenda of its fortieth session a separate item entitled "International Research and Training Institute for the Advancement of Women".

General Assembly resolution 39/122

14 December 1984   Meeting 101   Adopted without vote

Approved by Third Committee (A/39/701) without vote, 26 November (meeting 50); 44-nation draft (A/C.3/39/L.25), orally revised; agenda item 92.

Sponsors: Algeria, Angola, Argentina, Austria, Bahamas, Bangladesh, Barbados, Bolivia, Cameroon, Central African Republic, Chile, Colombia, Congo, Costa Rica, Cuba, Cyprus, Denmark, Dominican Republic, Ecuador, Egypt, Fiji, France, Greece, Guatemala, Guinea-Bissau, Indonesia, Jamaica, Japan, Mali, Mexico, Morocco, Nicaragua, Nigeria, Norway, Peru, Philippines, Spain, Sri Lanka, Sudan, Trinidad and Tobago, Uruguay, Venezuela, Yugoslavia, Zaire.

Meeting numbers. GA 39th session: 3rd Committee 23-33, 42, 47, 50; plenary 101.

INSTRAW statute

Further to a December 1983 General Assembly resolution,[28] the Secretary-General prepared a draft statute of the Institute which the Board of Trustees examined in January 1984. Following an article-by-article review with the assistance of the United Nations Office of Legal Affairs, the Board made a number of changes in the draft regarding the principal functions and mode of operation of the Institute, the election of officers and provisions for its co-operation with other organizations and institutions.

The Board adopted the draft statute, as amended, and submitted it to the Economic and Social Council for approval. The statute was annexed to the Board's report on its 1984 session.[25]

ECONOMIC AND SOCIAL COUNCIL ACTION

In May, following the recommendation of its Second Committee, the Economic and Social Council adopted decision 1984/124 without vote.

Statute of the International Research and Training Institute for the Advancement of Women

At its 19th plenary meeting, on 24 May 1984, the Council, having considered the report of the Board of Trustees of the International Research and Training Institute for the Advancement of Women on its fourth session, approved the Statute of the International Research and Training Institute for the Advancement of Women contained therein and decided to transmit it to the General Assembly for its endorsement.

Economic and Social Council decision 1984/124

Adopted without vote

Approved by Second Committee (E/1984/93) without vote, 10 May (meeting 9); draft by INSTRAW Board of Trustees (E/1984/41), orally amended by Argentina; agenda item 12.

In the Committee debate, Argentina orally amended the draft decision to add specific reference to the Board's report.

GENERAL ASSEMBLY ACTION

In resolution 39/122, the Assembly welcomed the statute of INSTRAW as approved by the Council.

The statute was transmitted to the Assembly by a 26 September 1984 note of the Secretary-General.[29] ACABQ, in a report of 17 October,[30] after clarifying the wording of several provisions, recommended that the Assembly endorse the statute. In addition, it proposed that the Secretary-General review the text to ensure that maximum clarity was obtained when similar provisions were used in future statutes of other United Nations organs.

The Assembly in 1984 did not act on a draft resolution recommended to it by the Fifth Committee,[31] by which the Assembly would have endorsed the statute and concurred with the observations of ACABQ regarding its administrative and financial aspects. The Fifth Committee approved the draft, orally proposed by its Chairman, without objection on 24 October. (The matter was subsequently taken up by the Assembly in 1985.)

Meeting number. GA 39th session: 5th Committee 16.

INSTRAW finances

The INSTRAW Board of Trustees, in January 1984, approved in principle the proposed programme budget for 1984-1985, authorizing allocations up to $2.5 million. By a note of 19 Oc-

tober,[26] the Secretary-General reported to the Assembly's Third Committee that resources available to INSTRAW as of 30 June 1984 were $2.53 million and that 46 States had thus far contributed to its Trust Fund.

Contributions by Governments to the United Nations Trust Fund for INSTRAW in 1984 totalled $483,492, compared to $473,442 in 1983;[32] pledges for 1985 amounted to $459,289 (see table below).

In resolution 39/122, the General Assembly invited Governments and intergovernmental organizations to contribute to the Trust Fund.

CONTRIBUTIONS TO INSTRAW, 1984 AND 1985
(as at 31 December 1984; in US dollar equivalent)

Country	1984 payment	1985 pledge
Afghanistan	500	—
Austria	7,000	7,000
Brazil	3,000	—
Chile	(5,000)*	—
China	5,000	10,000
Congo	—	6,383
Cuba	1,153	—
Cyprus	—	500
Denmark	50,000	50,000
Egypt	500	1,000
France	81,988	53,192
Greece	2,500	2,500
Indonesia	5,000	—
Jamaica	257	235
Madagascar	—	393
Mexico	5,758	—
Norway	317,062	282,486
Pakistan	4,610	4,351
Philippines	—	1,000
Spain	—	27,176
Sudan	—	1,000
Thailand	—	3,000
Turkey	—	5,000
Yugoslavia	4,164	1,622
Zambia	—	2,451
Total	**483,492**	**459,289**

*Adjustment of prior pledge.

SOURCE: Interim United Nations financial statements for the 12-month period of the biennium 1984-1985 ended 31 December 1984: schedules of individual trust funds.

REFERENCES

[1]YUN 1980, p. 905, GA res. 35/136, 11 Dec. 1980. [2]A/CONF.116/PC/21. [3]A/39/590 & Corr.1. [4]A/CONF.116/PC/19 & Corr.1. [5]A/CONF.116/PC/16. [6]YUN 1983, p. 915. [7]ACC/1984/PG/4. [8]ACC/1984/15. [9]DP/1985/5/Add.2 (Part II). [10]A/39/569. [11]YUN 1983, p. 912, GA res. 38/106, 16 Dec. 1983. [12]A/39/146 & Corr.1 & Add.1. [13]A/39/571. [14]E/1984/15. [15]YUN 1983, p. 923, ESC res. 1983/27, 26 May 1983. [16]YUN 1979, p. 895, GA res. 34/180, annex, 18 Dec. 1979. [17]YUN 1982, p. 1149. [18]A/39/45, vol. II. [19]YUN 1981, p. 994. [20]A/39/45, vol. I. [21]YUN 1983, p. 913. [22]E/1984/L.23. [23]*Multilateral Treaties Deposited with the Secretary-General: Status as at 31 December 1984* (ST/LEG/SER.E/3), Sales No. E.85.V.4. [24]A/39/486. [25]E/1984/41. [26]A/C.3/39/6. [27]*Proceedings of the Interregional Seminar on Women and the International Drinking Water Supply and Sanitation Decade (Cairo, Egypt, 12-16 March 1984)*, Sales No. E.87.III.C.2. [28]YUN 1983, p. 916, GA res. 38/104, 16 Dec. 1983. [29]A/39/511. [30]A/39/568. [31]A/39/613. [32]YUN 1983, p. 917.

Status of women

During the year, the United Nations addressed several issues relating to the status of women, including the specific situations of women under *apartheid*, Palestinian women, young women, elderly women, and the problems of violence that were specific to women in the family and within the criminal justice system (for details, see below).

The Economic and Social Council adopted two resolutions on women in the United Nations system (see ADMINISTRATIVE AND BUDGETARY QUESTIONS, Chapter III). It requested the Secretary-General to promote the recruitment and hiring of women in Secretariat Professional posts at middle and high levels (1984/11) and to examine ways to integrate the needs and concerns of women into all planning and programme activities (1984/12).

The 1984 International Conference on Population also made a number of recommendations on the status of women (see Chapter XIV of this section). On 17 April,[1] Democratic Kampuchea transmitted a document on the situation of women and children in Democratic Kampuchea (see p. 217).

Women under *apartheid*

In January 1984,[2] the Secretary-General reported to the Commission on the Status of Women on the situation of women and children living under *apartheid*, in accordance with a 1982 Economic and Social Council decision.[3]

The report noted that political and legal restrictions and migrant labour policies meant that families very rarely lived together, since men worked as migrant labourers, leaving their families behind in impoverished bantustans, or women worked in white areas where other family members were not permitted to stay.

Apart from domestic service, where 38 per cent of all employed African women worked, employment opportunities for women were generally restricted to the two sectors with the lowest pay and the greatest exploitation—agriculture and border industries—where they were not protected by any legislation on working hours or wages. Although most African women were excluded from industrial employment, it was reported that those who did work in factories had the same conditions as men, but only half the wage. Urban domestic workers worked from 10 to 11 hours a day, and as farm labourers black women often worked 12 to 14 hours daily with no paid leave or overtime and the risk of losing their house if they lost their job.

In rural areas, only a few women had access to land and few were able to produce enough food for themselves and their children; they suffered from epidemics due to their living conditions and lack of medical services. Educational policies, which did not provide compulsory education for black children but turned hundreds away from school for lack of places, led to low attendance rates especially among girls and restricted black children to inferior education. The report also gave an overview of activities to promote awareness of the plight of women and children under *apartheid*, and of assistance to women and children in southern Africa.

In 1984, the Special Committee against *Apartheid* continued to pay special attention to the plight of women and children in South Africa (see p. 175).

ECONOMIC AND SOCIAL COUNCIL ACTION

On 24 May 1984, on the recommendation of its Second Committee, the Economic and Social Council adopted without vote resolution 1984/17.

Women under *apartheid*
The Economic and Social Council,
Taking note of the report of the Secretary-General on the situation of women and children living under racist minority régimes and in the occupied Arab territories and other occupied territories,

Bearing in mind the conclusions of the International Conference on Women and *Apartheid*, held at Brussels from 17 to 19 May 1982, and of the Declaration adopted by the Conference,

Noting the wide observance of 9 August annually as the International Day of Solidarity with the Struggle of Women in South Africa and Namibia, in accordance with General Assembly resolution 36/172 K of 17 December 1981,

1. *Expresses its appreciation* to the Special Committee against *Apartheid* and its Task Force on Women and Children for giving special attention to the plight of women and children under *apartheid*, in accordance with General Assembly resolution 36/172 K;

2. *Expresses its appreciation* to the International Committee of Solidarity with the Struggle of Women in South Africa and Namibia for undertaking activities in support of women and children living under *apartheid*, and urges the Committee to exert greater efforts in support of women and children living under *apartheid;*

3. *Urges* all Governments, United Nations bodies, international, regional, intergovernmental and non-governmental organizations, women's and anti-*apartheid* groups and other concerned groups to give the highest priority to measures of assistance to women in South Africa and Namibia until the end of the United Nations Decade for Women: Equality, Development and Peace and beyond;

4. *Invites* the Special Committee against *Apartheid* and its Task Force on Women and Children to continue their activities in promoting the widest possible dissemination of information concerning women and children living under *apartheid;*

5. *Appeals* to all Governments, United Nations bodies, international, regional, intergovernmental and non-governmental organizations, women's and anti-*apartheid* groups and other concerned groups to support the various projects of the national liberation movements and front-line States designed to assist refugee women and children from South Africa and Namibia;

6. *Requests* the Secretary-General to submit to the Commission on the Status of Women at its thirty-first session a preliminary report on measures of assistance provided to women inside South Africa and Namibia and to women from South Africa and Namibia who have become refugees as the result of the practice of *apartheid;*

7. *Calls upon* all women's organizations to support the women of Namibia in their efforts to attain independence, in accordance with Security Council resolution 435(1978) of 29 September 1978.

Economic and Social Council resolution 1984/17

24 May 1984   Meeting 19   Adopted without vote

Approved by Second Committee (E/1984/93) without vote, 10 May (meeting 9); draft by Commission on women (E/1984/15); agenda item 12.

Palestinian women

Further to a 1982 decision of the Economic and Social Council,[3] the Secretary-General reported in January 1984 to the Commission on the Status of Women on the situation of Palestinian women and children living in the occupied Arab territories,[2] where practices by the occupying authorities (see p. 315 and p. 810) seriously affected the economic status of women, their social position and psychological well-being, employment and working conditions. Since there were fewer Arab farms and villages for self-employment, more women and children worked in seasonal agriculture and in Israeli enterprises set up in the occupied territories where wages were up to 50 per cent less than for equivalent work in Israel. To work in Israel, Palestinian women and children were engaged on short-term work permits without job security or employment benefits. Palestinian women were thus drawn away from their traditional position in society without obtaining permanent jobs or prospects for advancement. This had adverse effects on family and community life, on the education of children and the preservation of traditions.

ECONOMIC AND SOCIAL COUNCIL ACTION

On 24 May 1984, on the recommendation of its Second Committee, the Economic and Social Council adopted without vote resolution 1984/18.

Situation of Palestinian women within and outside the occupied Arab territories

The Economic and Social Council,

Deeply concerned about the prevailing living conditions of Palestinian women within and outside the occupied Arab territories,

Recognizing that the mass uprooting of Palestinian women from their homeland seriously affects their participation and integration in the development process,

Noting that no comprehensive study relating to the status of Palestinian women within and outside the occupied Arab territories has been conducted in the United Nations system since the World Conference of the United Nations Decade for Women: Equality, Develop-

ment and Peace, held at Copenhagen from 14 to 30 July 1980,

Recalling the relevant resolutions of the General Assembly, the Economic and Social Council and other appropriate United Nations organizations,

Taking note of chapter II of the report of the Secretary-General on the situation of Palestinian women and children in the occupied Arab territories, submitted to the Commission on the Status of Women at its thirtieth session,

1. *Requests* the Secretary-General to submit an updated version of that report to the Commission on the Status of Women at its thirty-first session;

2. *Also requests* the Secretary-General to prepare a comprehensive report on the situation of Palestinian women living within and outside the occupied Arab territories and to submit it to the Commission on the Status of Women at its thirty-second session;

3. *Further requests* the Secretary-General to submit an interim report on the preparation of that study to the Commission on the Status of Women at its thirty-first session;

4. *Invites* all Governments, intergovernmental and non-governmental organizations and United Nations bodies to extend all necessary assistance to the Secretary-General in this regard.

Economic and Social Council resolution 1984/18

24 May 1984   Meeting 19   Adopted without vote

Approved by Second Committee (E/1984/93) without vote, 10 May (meeting 9); draft by Commission on women (E/1984/15); agenda item 12.

Young women

ECONOMIC AND SOCIAL COUNCIL ACTION

On 24 May, on the recommendation of its Second Committee, the Council adopted without vote resolution 1984/15.

Promotion of opportunities for young women

The Economic and Social Council,

Recognizing that 1985 is the culminating year of the United Nations Decade for Women: Equality, Development and Peace,

Recognizing also that 1985 has been designated International Youth Year: Participation, Development, Peace,

Recognizing further that 1985 presents an opportunity to focus on the roles of young women and their participation in all activities, such as festivals, meetings, and other international youth forums to mark the International Youth Year: Participation, Development, Peace,

Bearing in mind that young women were singled out for priority attention by the World Conference of the United Nations Decade for Women: Equality, Development and Peace, particularly in its resolution 27,

Affirming that youth is the period of growth, development and apprenticeship for the adult roles of work, citizenship and parenthood, from which all of society will benefit,

Affirming also that youth should be a period of discovery and joy in living,

Considering that young women who become mothers too early are not only deprived of their youth but are not prepared for the responsibilities of parenthood and are subject to a higher health risk,

Recognizing that, while girls and young women are found in societies at all levels of development, the world is in a period of technological revolution affecting all and women must therefore be equal partners with men in shaping and benefiting from that revolution,

Stressing that those young women who lack sufficient nutrition, education, appropriate training and health are ill-prepared for their adult roles in this changing world and are thus vulnerable to economic, social and sexual exploitation,

1. *Recommends* that Member States should take appropriate steps to ensure that girls and young women are motivated to choose, and sufficiently trained to be chosen for, work at all levels and all the functions of a developing economy and society;

2. *Recommends also* that Member States should assist families to give equal support, guidance and encouragement to young women and men;

3. *Recommends further* that Member States should direct special assistance to girls and young women who are socially and economically disadvantaged;

4. *Recommends* that specialized agencies should undertake projects to promote global, regional and local action to accelerate the improvement in the education and training, employment and health status of girls and young women in accordance with their needs and with global, regional and local conditions;

5. *Recommends also* that specialized agencies, Member States and non-governmental organizations should undertake projects to develop cultural and sports activities aimed at promoting better international understanding and the equal right of young women and young men to fitness;

6. *Recommends* that special attention should be paid, in multilateral and bilateral co-operation programmes and projects, to the training and development of young women as managers of projects and as participants in articulating the development needs of youth;

7. *Recommends* that the Advisory Committee for the International Youth Year and the Secretary-General should, in all their reports, take special account of the needs of young women in rural and urban areas and of the problems they face.

Economic and Social Council resolution 1984/15

24 May 1984   Meeting 19   Adopted without vote

Approved by Second Committee (E/1984/93) without vote, 10 May (meeting 9); draft by Commission on women (E/1984/15); agenda item 12.

Elderly women

ECONOMIC AND SOCIAL COUNCIL ACTION

On 24 May, on the recommendation of its Second Committee, the Council adopted resolution 1984/13 without vote.

Question of elderly women

The Economic and Social Council,

Recalling the important conclusions and recommendations of the International Plan of Action on Aging adopted by the World Assembly on Aging, in particular paragraphs 11, 20 *(b)* and *(c)*, 25 *(m)*, 31 *(g)*, 45, 66 (recommendations 25 and 26), 67 (recommendations 27, 28 and 29), 72 (recommendation 36 *(c)*) and 89, concerning elderly women,

Reaffirming General Assembly resolution 38/27 of 22 November 1983, in which the Assembly recognized that women had a longer life expectancy than men and that they would increasingly constitute a majority of the elderly population of the world,

Reaffirming resolution 4 of the World Conference of the United Nations Decade for Women: Equality, Development and Peace, in which the Conference emphasized that the increase in the life expectancy of women had not been dealt with comprehensively,

Appreciating that at the World Assembly on Aging special attention was given to the problems faced by some elderly women, namely, income security, education, employment, housing, health and community support services and absence of social contacts,

Believing that more data on the situation of the aging should be collected, specifically to determine the needs of elderly women and to formulate appropriate solutions,

Recalling the request made by the World Conference of the United Nations Decade for Women: Equality, Development and Peace in its resolution 4 that such data should be submitted to Member States participating in the Conference and to the Commission on the Status of Women,

1. *Requests* the Secretary-General to prepare, within existing budgetary resources and in accordance with the established priorities of the work of the Commission on the Status of Women, an information report on the status and situation of elderly women in their societies, their social, health and economic needs, and their entitlements as compared to those of men, comparing single, divorced and married women and widows on the basis of reports, discussions and recommendations, in particular those of the World Assembly on Aging;

2. *Further requests* the Secretary-General to submit that report to the Commission on the Status of Women at its thirty-first session with a view to recommending necessary action relating to the plight of elderly women throughout the world;

3. *Decides* to include the question of elderly women under the appropriate item of the agenda of the thirty-first session of the Commission on the Status of Women.

Economic and Social Council resolution 1984/13

24 May 1984   Meeting 19   Adopted without vote

Approved by Second Committee (E/1984/93) without vote, 10 May (meeting 9); draft by Commission on women (E/1984/15); agenda item 12.

Violence against women

Based on recommendations of the Commission on the Status of Women at its February 1984 session, the Economic and Social Council, in May, adopted two resolutions on the subject of violence against women. By the first, on violence in the family, it urged Member States to effect a systematic information exchange, to draw attention to the negative consequences of such violence and to formulate national solutions, and requested the Secretary-General to convene a seminar on the topic. By the second resolution, the Council called for measures to eradicate violence against detained women.

Violence in the family

ECONOMIC AND SOCIAL COUNCIL ACTION

On 24 May, on the recommendation of its Second Committee, the Council adopted resolution 1984/14 without vote.

Violence in the family

The Economic and Social Council,

Bearing in mind the goals of the United Nations Decade for Women: Equality, Development and Peace, and the subtheme "Employment, Health and Education",

Recalling resolution 5 of the World Conference of the United Nations Decade for Women: Equality, Development and Peace on battered women and violence in the family,

Recalling also Council resolution 1982/22 of 4 May 1982 on abuses against women and children,

Recognizing that violence within the family has serious negative consequences for all the individuals concerned and follows patterns of abuse that are frequently cyclical, presenting serious problems for society as a whole,

Further recognizing that violence within the family is found among various population groups,

Concerned that information on the nature of this problem and its causes is often concealed and thus is not widely available and that efforts to prevent violence in the family, to provide assistance to the victims and to prevent recurrences need greater public awareness and publicity,

Aware that many Governments and non-governmental organizations have conducted research into this issue and initiated programmes both to support victims and to treat abusers,

Recognizing that the problem of family violence is a long-standing and complex issue and needs serious and thoughtful attention,

Convinced that a more thorough exchange of information and experiences on this subject between States Members of the United Nations, organizations of the United Nations and non-governmental organizations could draw increasing attention to the problem and contribute to the development of international solutions,

1. *Calls upon* the Secretary-General to invite Member States, organizations of the United Nations and non-governmental organizations to provide the United Nations Secretariat with information on family violence and descriptions of successful programmes on the subject, or to supplement information already provided;

2. *Urges* Member States to take appropriate steps to effect a systematic exchange of information on this subject, to draw attention to the negative consequences of family violence for the men, women and children involved and for society as a whole, and to formulate solutions at the national level;

3. *Requests* the Secretary-General to convene a seminar of experts on family violence, with emphasis on its effects on women, within the resources for the biennium 1986-1987, taking into account what may emanate on this subject from the Seventh United Nations Congress on the Prevention of Crime and the Treatment of Offenders, to be held in 1985, with a view to making recommendations to combat this abuse;

4. *Decides* to include the subject of family violence under the appropriate item of the agenda of the thirty-first session of the Commission on the Status of Women on the basis of information to be supplied in response to paragraph 1 of the present resolution.

Economic and Social Council resolution 1984/14

24 May 1984　　　　Meeting 19　　　　Adopted without vote

Approved by Second Committee (E/1984/93) without vote, 10 May (meeting 9); draft by Commission on women (E/1984/15); agenda item 12.

Violence against detained women

In January 1984,[4] the Secretary-General reported to the Committee on Crime Prevention and Control on the fair treatment of women by the criminal justice system, providing an overview of preliminary findings of a global survey. On 25 May, the Economic and Social Council adopted resolution 1984/49 on the topic (see p. 708).

ECONOMIC AND SOCIAL COUNCIL ACTION

On 24 May, on the recommendation of its Second Committee, the Council adopted without vote resolution 1984/19.

Physical violence against detained women that is specific to their sex

The Economic and Social Council,

Noting with grave concern that the Commission on the Status of Women, in the report on its thirtieth session under the question of communications concerning the status of women, drew attention to a pattern of physical violence against women while detained—cases of rape and other sexual abuse, including violence against pregnant women,

Considering that women are especially vulnerable to sexual violence,

Considering also that pregnant women require special protection and care by society,

Recalling its resolutions 76(V) of 5 August 1947 and 304 I (XI) of 14 and 17 July 1950,

Recalling also its resolutions 1980/39 of 2 May 1980 and 1983/27 of 26 May 1983, by which it reaffirmed the mandate of the Commission on the Status of Women to consider communications relating to the status of women, including the replies of Governments thereon, if any, and to draw to the attention of the Council emerging trends and patterns so that it may decide what action to take,

1. *Calls upon* the Member States concerned to take appropriate measures urgently to eradicate such violations;

2. *Invites* all Member States to submit their views on physical violence against detained women that is specific to their sex to the Secretary-General to enable him to report to the Commission on the Status of Women at its thirty-first session under the appropriate item of the agenda;

3. *Decides* to authorize the Secretary-General to provide, from within existing budgetary resources, the services and facilities necessary for the implementation of the present resolution.

Economic and Social Council resolution 1984/19
24 May 1984   Meeting 19   Adopted without vote

Approved by Second Committee (E/1984/93) without vote, 10 May (meeting 9); draft by Commission on women (E/1984/15); agenda item 12.

REFERENCES
(1)A/39/185-S/16486. (2)E/CN.6/1984/10. (3)YUN 1982, p. 1162, ESC dec. 1982/123, 4 May 1982. (4)E/AC.57/1984/15.

Women in society

Considering the role of women in society—as mothers and as participants in economic development and public life—the United Nations addressed the question of the integration of women in development, including in rural areas, the role of women in science and technology, and the question of increasing the participation of women in promoting peace and co-operation.

GENERAL ASSEMBLY ACTION

On 14 December 1984, on the recommendation of the Third Committee, the General Assembly adopted without vote resolution 39/123.

The role of women in society

The General Assembly,

Reaffirming the objectives of the United Nations Decade for Women: Equality, Development and Peace, as well as the importance of the Declaration of Mexico on the Equality of Women and their Contribution to Development and Peace, 1975, the World Plan of Action for the Implementation of the Objectives of the International Women's Year and the Programme of Action for the Second Half of the United Nations Decade for Women,

Noting that just and lasting peace and social progress as well as the establishment of a new international economic order require the active participation of women in promoting international peace and co-operation and in the process of development,

Bearing in mind that economic inequality, colonialism, racism, racial discrimination, *apartheid*, acts of aggression and interference in the internal affairs of others and violations of human rights and fundamental freedoms constitute an impediment to the achievement of real and genuine equality and to the integration of women in society,

Convinced of the necessity to secure for all women full realization of the rights embodied in the Convention on the Elimination of All Forms of Discrimination against Women, in the International Covenants on Human Rights and in other relevant instruments in this field,

Recognizing that the achievement of equal and full participation of women in all spheres of activity constitutes an inseparable part of the political, economic, social and cultural development of all countries,

Aware that efforts to promote the status of women in all its aspects and their complete integration in society go beyond the problem of legal equality and that deeper structural transformations of society and changes in present-day economic relations, as well as elimination of traditional prejudices through education and dissemination of information, are required so as to create conditions for women to develop fully their intellectual and physical capacities and to participate actively in the decision-making process in political, economic, social and cultural development,

Mindful of the necessity to enlarge the possibilities for both men and women to combine parental duties and household work with paid employment and social activities,

Aware that child-bearing should not be the cause of inequality and discrimination against women, and that child-rearing demands shared responsibilities among women, men and society as a whole,

Deeply appreciating the increasing participation of women in political, economic, social and cultural life and their contribution thereto,

1. *Appeals* to all Governments, international organizations and non-governmental organizations to recognize in their activities the importance of all interrelated aspects of the role of women in society—as mothers, as participants in economic development and as participants in public life—without underestimating any one of them;

2. *Encourages* such social and economic development that would secure the participation of women in all spheres of work, equal pay for work of equal value and equal opportunities for education and professional and vocational training, taking into consideration the necessity of combining all aspects of the role of women in society;

3. *Appeals* to Governments, international organizations and non-governmental organizations to promote the creation of conditions that would enable women to participate as equal partners with men in public and political life, in the decision-making process at all levels and in the management of different spheres of life in society;

4. *Appeals* to Governments to recognize the special status and social importance of motherhood and to take, in the context of their special abilities and conditions, all necessary measures to promote the protection of motherhood, including maternity leave with pay, and to provide security for their jobs as long as necessary, so as to allow women, if they so wish, to fulfil their role as mothers without prejudice to their professional and public activities;

5. *Also appeals* to Governments to promote the establishment of appropriate facilities for child-care and education of children as a means of combining motherhood with economic, political, social, cultural and other activities of women and thus to provide assistance to women in integrating fully into their societies;

6. *Recommends* to the World Conference to Review and Appraise the Achievements of the United Nations Decade for Women: Equality, Development and Peace, to be held at Nairobi from 15 to 26 July 1985, that it take duly into account, in reviewing and appraising the achievements of the Decade and in formulating future policies in this field, all aspects of the role of women in society.

General Assembly resolution 39/123
14 December 1984   Meeting 101   Adopted without vote

Approved by Third Committee (A/39/702) without vote, 26 November (meeting 50); 13-nation draft (A/C.3/39/L.19/Rev.1); agenda item 93.
Sponsors: Argentina, Bangladesh, Bulgaria, Burkina Faso, Cuba, German Democratic Republic, Greece, Guinea-Bissau, Mongolia, Nigeria, Venezuela, Viet Nam, Zambia.
Meeting numbers. GA 39th session: 3rd Committee 23-33, 42, 47, 50; plenary 101.

Women in development

The need for full participation of women in development in developing countries, including in rural areas, was further recognized during the year by the Economic and Social Council and the General Assembly. Programmes to increase participation constituted a major focus of the Voluntary Fund for the United Nations Decade for Women and INSTRAW (see above), with UNDP and UNIDO also giving attention to the subject.

The Secretary-General, in an October 1984 report[1] on the Voluntary Fund, affirmed that women did participate in the development process but under unequal conditions, due to lower levels of education and training than men in the same socio-economic group and to a major responsibility for the unremunerated work needed for family survival.

INSTRAW Board action. The Board of Trustees of INSTRAW, at its January 1984 session,[2] requested the INSTRAW Director to bring the recommendations of the December 1983 Seminar on the Incorporation of Women into Development Planning[3] to the attention of the relevant bodies and institutions and to disseminate widely its proceedings. The Board agreed that the results of the Seminar should be used as a basis for the development of training material on the subject.

UNDP action. During the year, projects carried out with UNDP assistance[4] relating to women in development included: a community-based production project in Honduras which assisted 350 women in three economically depressed areas to start non-traditional self-sustaining enterprises such as poultry and fishpond farming, sugar milling and leather processing; cottage industries in Indonesia creating new job opportunities for rural women (over 575 participants and a further 1,374 village workers on a part-time basis), using local raw materials for making woven silk, batiks, ready-made clothing, embroidered and bamboo-plaited products, roof tiles and palm sugar; a project in northern Swaziland that trained 1,173 women to produce school uniforms and shoes, as well as teaching them leather crafts, small-unit welding and cement block-making; a pilot wool processing and training centre in Kashmir; rural sanitation training for some 1,000 participants, mostly women, in Sierra Leone; a project in Yemen to demonstrate to predominantly female farm workers new practices for diversified cultivation; training for leaders of women's cooperatives in Mexico; self-help housing construction schemes in Zimbabwe; and a new research and development centre in China for improved vegetable production, with 32 women scientists among its research staff of 61.

In February, the UNDP Administrator submitted a progress report on an interorganizational evaluation study of women's participation in development.[5] Initiated in response to a 1982 UNDP Governing Council decision,[6] the study was being undertaken by 14 United Nations organizations that were significantly concerned with women's role in development, to evaluate their effectiveness and provide a basis for recommending improved strategies to ensure that technical co-operation activities enhanced women's participation in development and the benefits they derived therefrom. The study was to be presented to the 1985 World Conference to Review and Appraise the Achievements of the United Nations Decade for Women.

On 18 June 1984,[7] the UNDP Governing Council took note of the Administrator's report.

UNIDO action. On 19 August 1984, the Fourth General Conference of UNIDO[8] called on States to promote the increased participation of women in industrial development and stressed the role UNIDO had to play in that regard. It welcomed the action of the secretariat to co-ordinate its own activities on the subject and to organize regional workshops on the integration of women in industrial planning and development, and urged the UNIDO Executive Director to take account of the integration of women in the design of technical co-operation and study activities.

On 19 May,[9] the Industrial Development Board reaffirmed the importance of involving women in the industrial sector at the national planning and management level, of training them for work in that sector and of recruiting more women to Professional posts in the UNIDO secretariat.

In his 1984 annual report,[10] the Executive Director listed three regional workshops on the integration of women in the industrial planning and development process: in Africa (Harare, Zimbabwe, 9-17 April), in the Caribbean (Georgetown, Guyana, 6-12 May) and in Asia (Bangkok, Thailand, 5-12 July).

ECONOMIC AND SOCIAL COUNCIL ACTION

In decision 1984/101 on its basic work programme, the Economic and Social Council decided to review the question of women and development during its first regular session of 1985.

GENERAL ASSEMBLY ACTION

On 14 December 1984, on the recommendation of the Third Committee, the General Assembly adopted without vote resolution 39/128.

Integration of women in all aspects of development

The General Assembly,

Recalling its resolution 37/57 of 3 December 1982, as well as Economic and Social Council resolution 1984/12 of 24 May 1984,

Recalling paragraphs 190 to 196 of the World Plan of Action for the Implementation of the Objectives of the

International Women's Year, in which the relevant agencies of the United Nations and intergovernmental, interregional and regional bodies were called upon to scrutinize all existing plans and projects with a view to extending their sphere of activities to include women and to develop new and innovative projects to include women,

Bearing in mind that development is one of the themes of the United Nations Decade for Women: Equality, Development and Peace,

Recalling paragraph 51 of the International Development Strategy for the Third United Nations Development Decade, which stated that appropriate measures should be taken for profound social and economic changes and for the elimination of the structural imbalances which compound and perpetuate women's disadvantages,

Looking ahead to the World Conference to Review and Appraise the Achievements of the United Nations Decade for Women: Equality, Development and Peace, to be held at Nairobi from 15 to 26 July 1985, and foreseeing the need to continue such achievements beyond the end of the Decade,

Convinced of the importance of integrating women fully into development in its political, economic, social, cultural and other dimensions, both as agents and as beneficiaries,

Reaffirming the central policy and advisory role of the Commission on the Status of Women within the United Nations in considering matters relating to women, including the achievement of the objectives of the Decade,

Recognizing the efforts made by the specialized agencies to integrate women into their ongoing programmes, especially into the establishment of cross-sectoral mechanisms,

Welcoming Economic and Social Council decision 1984/101 of 10 February 1984, in paragraph 7 of which the Council decided to select the question of women in development for review on a cross-organizational basis at its first regular session of 1985,

Aware that greater co-ordination and knowledge of activities in this area within the specialized agencies and the regional commissions and by Member States and non-governmental organizations would facilitate an exchange of experience and concepts and be beneficial to all,

Reaffirming that within the United Nations system the Centre for Social Development and Humanitarian Affairs of the Department of International Economic and Social Affairs of the Secretariat remains the focal point for co-ordination, consultation, promotion and advice on questions concerning women,

Deeply concerned that international efforts on behalf of women should keep pace with the increasing efforts towards establishing effective national machineries and mobilizing resources to ensure the integration of women into all stages of planning, monitoring and development activities,

Noting that the progress report of the Secretary-General requested by the General Assembly in its resolution 37/57 was submitted to the Commission on the Status of Women at its thirtieth session,

1. *Urges* the specialized agencies, regional commissions and other organs, bodies and organizations of the United Nations system which have not yet done so to develop and implement comprehensive policies regarding the concerns of women, both as agents and as beneficiaries, in technical co-operation and development activities and to establish effective review measures to ensure that women are an integral part of these policies and activities;

2. *Requests* the specialized agencies, regional commissions and other organs, bodies and organizations of the United Nations system to ensure continued co-operation and co-ordination with the Commission on the Status of Women beyond the World Conference to Review and Appraise the Achievements of the United Nations Decade for Women, in order fully to achieve the goals of the United Nations Decade for Women: Equality, Development and Peace;

3. *Endorses* the request of the Economic and Social Council in its resolution 1984/12 that the Secretary-General should report to the Commission on the Status of Women at each session on all significant developments pertaining to the advancement of women within the United Nations system that have occurred since the preceding session;

4. *Invites* the Commission on the Status of Women to give greater attention at its future sessions to the reports of the Secretary-General pertaining to the integration of women in development, by continuing to include in its agenda a specific item for that purpose, and to submit its comments on his reports to the Economic and Social Council and, as appropriate, through the Council to the General Assembly;

5. *Reaffirms* its resolution 36/127 of 14 December 1981, which provides for the consideration of issues relating to the integration of women in development in all the relevant organs of the General Assembly.

General Assembly resolution 39/128

14 December 1984   Meeting 101   Adopted without vote

Approved by Third Committee (A/39/702) without vote, 26 November (meeting 50); 38-nation draft (A/C.3/39/L.29); agenda item 93.

Sponsors: Australia, Bahamas, Bangladesh, Belgium, Bolivia, Cameroon, Canada, Central African Republic, Colombia, Costa Rica, Denmark, Ecuador, France, Gambia, Germany, Federal Republic of, Guinea, Indonesia, Ireland, Ivory Coast, Jordan, Kenya, Lesotho, Mali, Nepal, New Zealand, Norway, Philippines, Portugal, Samoa, Singapore, Spain, Sri Lanka, Suriname, Sweden, Trinidad and Tobago, United States, Venezuela, Viet Nam.

Meeting numbers. GA 39th session: 3rd Committee 23-33, 42, 47, 50; plenary 101.

In its Declaration on the Critical Economic Situation in Africa, adopted by resolution 39/29 (see Chapter III of this section), the Assembly recognized the important role of women in rural development, particularly in food production.

In resolution 39/166 on food and agricultural problems (see Chapter XI of this section), the Assembly called for more policy attention to the role of women in relation to food systems and stressed the need to involve women in formulating and implementing national food strategies and projects.

World survey

In October 1984,[11] the Secretary-General reported on the world survey on the role of women in development, providing a summary of preliminary conclusions on the role of women in industry, agriculture, science and technology, and money and finance.

The March 1984 inter-agency meeting on the preparations for the World Conference to Review and

Appraise the Achievements of the United Nations Decade for Women (see above, under "Decade for Women") agreed that the final draft of the world survey would be sent by the Conference secretariat to lead agencies and organizations for comments.[12]

GENERAL ASSEMBLY ACTION

On 17 December, on the recommendation of the Second (Economic and Financial) Committee, the General Assembly adopted without vote resolution 39/172.

World survey on the role of women in development

The General Assembly,

Recalling its resolution 35/78 of 5 December 1980 on the effective mobilization and integration of women in development, in which it, *inter alia*, called for the preparation of a comprehensive and detailed outline for an interdisciplinary and multisectoral world survey on the role of women in overall development,

Recalling also its resolution 36/74 of 4 December 1981, in which it requested the Secretary-General to prepare the survey in close collaboration with the appropriate United Nations organs, organizations and bodies, as well as the relevant national institutions, and to submit the survey in its final form to the General Assembly at its thirty-ninth session,

Bearing in mind the report of the Secretary-General on the progress made in the preparation of the survey submitted to the General Assembly at its thirty-seventh session,

Noting that the survey in its final form will be one of the basic documents at the World Conference to Review and Appraise the Achievements of the United Nations Decade for Women: Equality, Development and Peace, to be held at Nairobi from 15 to 26 July 1985,

Taking note of the report of the Secretary-General concerning the preliminary results of the survey, including the emerging awareness of the important actual and potential contribution of women to economic development around the world,

Recognizing that further efforts will be required to collect adequate data on the participation of women in economic sectors and that further research is needed to determine the steps to be taken to ensure the effective mobilization and integration of women in development, especially in relation to the formulation and implementation of economic policies and to economic production and the use of resources,

Recommends that the survey in its final form should be considered by the General Assembly at its fortieth session under the item entitled "Effective mobilization and integration of women in development", together with any comments on the survey and related decisions taken at the World Conference to Review and Appraise the Achievements of the United Nations Decade for Women: Equality, Development and Peace.

General Assembly resolution 39/172

17 December 1984   Meeting 103   Adopted without vote

Approved by Second Committee (A/39/790/ Add.11) without vote, 6 December (meeting 56); draft by Vice-Chairman (A/C.2/39/L.104), based on informal consultations on 20-nation draft (A/C.2/39/L.77); agenda item 80 (k).
Meeting numbers. GA 39th session: 2nd Committee 53, 56; plenary 103.

The adopted text was based on a 20-nation draft introduced by Norway; it incorporated several drafting changes agreed on during informal consultations in the Committee.

Women in rural areas

Further to a 1982 General Assembly request,[13] an Interregional Seminar on National Experience Relating to the Improvement of the Situation of Women in Rural Areas was held (Vienna, 17-28 September 1984), giving special emphasis to the problems of developing countries.[14] The Seminar was attended by representatives of the United Nations system and specialized agencies, by observers from Member States and intergovernmental and non-governmental organizations, and by 15 experts from all regions. It formulated recommendations on ways to improve the productivity and standard of living of rural women by increasing access to land, water, credit, technology and training, and outlined global policies that would support those recommendations.

GENERAL ASSEMBLY ACTION

On 14 December, on the recommendation of the Third Committee, the General Assembly adopted without vote resolution 39/126.

Improvement of the situation of women in rural areas

The General Assembly,

Bearing in mind the objectives of the United Nations Decade for Women: Equality, Development and Peace,

Recalling its resolution 35/136 of 11 December 1980, in which it endorsed the Programme of Action for the Second Half of the United Nations Decade for Women,

Recalling also its resolution 37/59 of 3 December 1982 on the improvement of the situation of women in rural areas,

Reaffirming the importance attached in the Programme of Action for the Second Half of the United Nations Decade for Women and in the Convention on the Elimination of All Forms of Discrimination against Women, as well as in the International Development Strategy for the Third United Nations Development Decade, to the need to improve the status of women and ensure their full participation in the development process as agents and beneficiaries of development,

1. *Notes with appreciation* the organization of the Interregional Seminar on National Experience Relating to the Improvement of the Situation of Women in Rural Areas, held at Vienna from 17 to 28 September 1984;

2. *Requests* the Secretary-General to compile the observations and comments made on the report of the above-mentioned Seminar at the World Conference to Review and Appraise the Achievements of the United Nations Decade for Women: Equality, Development and Peace, to be held at Nairobi from 15 to 26 July 1985;

3. *Also requests* the Secretary-General to submit to the General Assembly at its fortieth session the report of the Seminar, together with the observations and comments compiled in accordance with paragraph 2 above.

General Assembly resolution 39/126

14 December 1984   Meeting 101   Adopted without vote

Approved by Third Committee (A/39/702) without vote, 26 November (meeting 50); 17-nation draft (A/C.3/39/L.27); agenda item 93.
Sponsors: Bangladesh, Benin, Burkina Faso, Cameroon, Cuba, German Democratic Republic, Guinea, Ivory Coast, Mongolia, Morocco, Nicaragua, Nigeria, Philippines, Rwanda, Sierra Leone, Suriname, Viet Nam.
Meeting numbers. GA 39th session: 3rd Committee 23-33, 42, 47, 50; plenary 101.

Participation of women in promoting peace and co-operation

The General Assembly, in December 1984, invited Governments and requested the Secretary-General to promote the 1982 Declaration on the Participation of Women in Promoting International Peace and Co-operation.[15]

GENERAL ASSEMBLY ACTION

On 14 December, on the recommendation of the Third Committee, the Assembly adopted without vote resolution 39/124.

Participation of women in promoting international peace and co-operation

The General Assembly,

Reaffirming its resolution 37/63 of 3 December 1982, by which it proclaimed the Declaration on the Participation of Women in Promoting International Peace and Co-operation,

Recalling its resolution 38/105 of 16 December 1983, in which it requested the Commission on the Status of Women to consider what measures might be necessary in order to implement the Declaration,

Believing that further efforts are required to eliminate discrimination against women in all its forms and in every field of human endeavour,

Wishing to encourage the active participation of women in promoting international peace and security and co-operation,

Taking note of Economic and Social Council resolution 1984/16 of 24 May 1984, in which the Council took into account the fact that millions of women were still experiencing untold sufferings and violations of human dignity resulting from different forms and manifestations of colonialism, foreign domination, *apartheid* and racial discrimination,

Conscious of the need to implement the provisions of the Declaration,

1. *Pledges its determination* to encourage the full participation of women in the economic, social, cultural, civil and political affairs of society and in the endeavour to promote international peace and co-operation;

2. *Invites* all Governments to take the necessary measures to ensure wide publicity for the Declaration on the Participation of Women in Promoting International Peace and Co-operation and the implementation thereof;

3. *Requests* the Secretary-General to continue to take adequate steps to ensure that publicity is given to the Declaration;

4. *Invites* the United Nations Educational, Scientific and Cultural Organization, the International Labour Organisation, the World Health Organization and other appropriate bodies within the United Nations system to consider adequate measures to implement the Declaration;

5. *Requests* the Commission on the Status of Women, as the preparatory body for the World Conference to Review and Appraise the Achievements of the United Nations Decade for Women: Equality, Development and Peace, to consider measures which may be necessary to implement the Declaration in the context of forward-looking strategies for the advancement of women for the period up to the year 2000;

6. *Decides* to consider the further implementation of the Declaration at its fortieth session, in the light of the report of the World Conference to be held at Nairobi from 15 to 26 July 1985, under the item entitled "United Nations Decade for Women: Equality, Development and Peace".

General Assembly resolution 39/124

14 December 1984   Meeting 101   Adopted without vote

Approved by Third Committee (A/39/702) without vote, 26 November (meeting 50); 21-nation draft (A/C.3/39/L.20); agenda item 93.
Sponsors: Afghanistan, Angola, Congo, Cuba, Czechoslovakia, Democratic Yemen, Ethiopia, German Democratic Republic, Guinea-Bissau, Hungary, Iraq, Lao People's Democratic Republic, Madagascar, Mali, Mongolia, Mozambique, Nicaragua, Nigeria, Poland, Ukrainian SSR, Viet Nam.

Women and science and technology

The Advisory Committee on Science and Technology for Development, in February 1984 (see Chapter XII of this section), dealt with the issue of science and technology and women.[16] The Committee expressed concern that women were underrepresented in that field and were seldom in decision-making positions. It felt that research and development that served women's needs must be given higher priority. It recommended that Governments appoint women to national, regional and international bodies dealing with science and technology for development, and stressed the importance of science and technology education and training for women and the need for them to be better informed. Among other recommendations were that women scientists and engineers be given equal access to training and technological installations, and that potential users of technology participate in all stages of design and adaptation of alternative technologies. Also, the Intergovernmental Committee on Science and Technology for Development was urged to appoint more women to the Advisory Committee.

REFERENCES

[1]A/39/569. [2]E/1984/41. [3]YUN 1983, p. 915. [4]DP/1985/5/Add.2 (Part I). [5]DP/1984/19. [6]YUN 1982, . p. 1156. [7]E/1984/20 (dec. 84/15). [8]ID/CONF.5/46 (res. 9). [9]A/39/16 (conclusion 1984/13). [10]ID/B/340. [11]A/39/566. [12]ACC/1984/PG/4. [13]YUN 1982, p. 1155, GA res. 37/59, 3 Dec. 1982. [14]A/40/239. [15]YUN 1982, p. 1160, GA res. 37/63, annex, 3 Dec. 1982. [16]A/CN.11/47 & Corr.1.

PUBLICATION

Compiling Social Indicators on the Situation of Women (ST/ESA/STAT/SER.F/32), Sales No. E.84.XVII.2.

Chapter XX

Children, youth and aging persons

In 1984, the United Nations Children's Fund (UNICEF) continued its programmes for children in 117 countries—in Africa, Asia, Latin America and the Mediterranean area—reaching a total population under 16 years of age of approximately 1.3 billion. Support was provided for water supply and sanitation, primary health care, education, food and nutrition, social services and emergency relief. UNICEF promoted effective, inexpensive methods to improve children's health and reduce child mortality and morbidity. The General Assembly once more reaffirmed the goal of children's immunization against major diseases by 1990 and again called for comments from States on a draft declaration relating to children's protection and welfare, especially foster placement and adoption.

Due to the burgeoning emergency situation in many African countries, which was claiming the lives of 12,000 children each day, UNICEF strengthened its efforts in the region through redeployment of resources. An international appeal was launched for 13 of the most seriously affected countries.

Activities concerning youth—persons 15 to 24 years old—focused during the year on preparations for International Youth Year (1985) (IYY). The Assembly decided to strengthen the secretariat of the Economic Commission for Africa to enable it to fulfil its youth mandate, and to continue promoting activities relating to intergenerational matters.

Follow-up actions to implement the 1982 Vienna International Plan of Action on Aging (people aged 60 and over) continued in 1984. The Assembly called on Governments to take into account the changing age structure of the population in their economic and social development plans and to contribute to the United Nations Trust Fund for Aging. It further requested the Secretary-General to promote joint activities regarding aging and youth, especially during IYY.

Topics related to this chapter. Health and human resources. Human rights: rights of the child; youth and human rights; human rights of aging persons. Women: women and children under *apartheid*.

Children

In 1984, assistance for children in Africa, Asia, Latin America and the Mediterranean area, provided by UNICEF with the assistance of other United Nations bodies, covered areas such as water supply and sanitation, primary health care, education, food and nutrition, social services and emergency relief. UNICEF continued to support a variety of low-cost programmes aimed at improving children's health and reducing child mortality and morbidity.

The General Assembly, in resolution 39/222, reaffirmed the goals of the International Development Strategy for the Third United Nations Development Decade (the 1980s),[1] particularly those of ensuring children's immunization against major diseases by 1990 and of reducing the infant mortality rate to less than 50 per 1,000 live births in all countries by the year 2000. In resolution 39/89, the Assembly again requested the Secretary-General to report on States' comments on a draft Declaration on Social and Legal Principles relating to the Protection and Welfare of Children, with Special Reference to Foster Placement and Adoption Nationally and Internationally.

In August 1984, the International Conference on Population made recommendations aimed at reducing infant, child and maternal morbidity and mortality (see p. 714).

UN Children's Fund

In 1984, UNICEF provided assistance for children in 117 countries, with a total population under 16 years of age of approximately 1.3 billion. Total programme expenditure amounted to $345 million, an average expenditure per child of 26 cents (16 cents from general UNICEF resources and 10 cents from supplementary funds) for countries where UNICEF was co-operating in long-term programmes. Support was given to: basic maternal and child health services and nutrition in 109 countries; water supply, sanitation and social welfare services in 97; non-formal education in 96; formal education in 93; and emergency relief in 24. Of the total programme expenditure, 28 per cent was spent for water supply and sanitation, 26 per cent for basic child health, 13 per cent for planning and project support, 12 per cent for education, 8 per cent for nutrition, 7 per cent for emergency relief and 6 per cent for social services.

The UNICEF Executive Board held its regular 1984 session at Rome, Italy, from 24 April to 4 May 1984.[2] It also met in New York on 8 and 14 June to elect officers for the period 1 August 1984 to 31

July 1985. The Programme Committee met from 27 April to 2 May, and the Committee on Administration and Finance met on 2 and 3 May. In April, a session of UNICEF National Committees and the Executive Committee of the Society of the Union of the Red Cross and the Red Crescent of a number of Eastern European socialist countries met at Prague, Czechoslovakia, and adopted an appeal to UNICEF National Committees of all countries to improve the international climate, halt the arms race, strengthen peace and international security and establish equal international co-operation and mutual understanding among nations for the welfare of current and future generations.[3]

In his report covering 1984 activities,[4] the UNICEF Executive Director noted the continuing difficulties caused by the world economic situation, the organization's response to the emergency situation in many African countries and measures taken to strengthen UNICEF.

He pointed out that the economic recession of recent years had provoked major set-backs in child welfare. The combined effect of declining expenditure in the social sector and shortages of foreign exchange hampered health, potable water, sanitation, housing and other assistance, and the shortage of foreign exchange reduced the availability of imported goods. Food emergencies were declared in 22 African countries, and an increase in child and maternal malnutrition was registered in 1983 and 1984 in countries as diverse as Bolivia, Botswana, Brazil, Costa Rica, the Ivory Coast, Malawi, Peru and the Philippines.

In implementing priority child survival and development activities, progress was made during the year in immunization and oral rehydration therapy (ORT)—a method of preventing dehydration caused by diarrhoea, a major cause of child mortality; UNICEF supplied vaccines worth some $9 million, compared with $6 million in 1983, and assisted 80 countries with their immunization programmes. The Executive Director felt that the United Nations goal of universal access for children by 1990 to immunization against the six major communicable childhood diseases (diphtheria, pertussis, tetanus, measles, poliomyelitis and tuberculosis) could be achieved globally if Governments would mobilize intensive but relatively low-cost national programmes. In its efforts to promote ORT against diarrhoeal diseases and associated malnutrition, UNICEF provided over 65 million packets of "complete formula" oral rehydration salts (ORS) and assisted 20 countries in manufacturing ORS themselves. World-wide, such local production accounted for some 100 million packets annually, giving a global supply of nearly 200 million packets from all sources, compared with 1 million in 1975 when UNICEF first started to produce ORS and 20 million in 1980. UNICEF also

called for breast-feeding and proper weaning practices to prevent malnutrition, and growth monitoring to detect malnutrition early in its development.

The crisis facing African children and their families continued to preoccupy UNICEF. Actions undertaken by it to increase financial commitments and resource allocations to affected countries included: releasing $2.8 million from the Emergency Reserve Fund; earmarking $7.2 million from the Infant Mortality Reduction Reserve for child survival and development activities; fundraising for existing emergency rehabilitation and other projects; and identifying financial needs, which resulted in an appeal launched by the Executive Director in July 1984 to raise some $50 million for additional short-term projects for child survival and development activities in 13 seriously affected countries. That amount was increased to $67 million during the special meeting on Africa on 31 October (see p. 915). Measures were also taken during the year to strengthen UNICEF's capacity in Africa through redeployment of resources from headquarters and field offices in Asia.

Programme policy decisions

At its 1984 session,[2] the UNICEF Executive Board reviewed the organization's performance in 1983. With global economic depression continuing to threaten millions of children's lives, the Board's main concern was to translate the growing political support for the UNICEF child survival and development strategy into expanded country programmes, particularly in Africa.

The Board endorsed the child survival and development strategy goals, as well as programmes aimed at accelerating child survival and development activities. It reviewed UNICEF's existing emergency operations in Africa and recommended the strengthening of inter-agency co-operation in that area. The Executive Director was instructed to prepare a programme outlining short- and long-term measures for dealing with emergencies; to pursue other activities, mainly staff-related, designed to strengthen UNICEF; and, when preparing the 1986-1987 budget estimates, to take into account the need for improving UNICEF's capacity in Africa.

The Board also approved general resource commitments of some $105 million and "noted" projects of $59.5 million for financing through specific-purpose contributions. It agreed that UNICEF should co-operate with Governments and other organizations and agencies in researching, evaluating and publicizing ways to incorporate psycho-social factors in child development efforts.

In decision 1984/171 of 25 July, the Economic and Social Council took note of the report of the UNICEF Executive Board.[2]

On 18 December, the General Assembly, on the recommendation of the Second (Economic and Financial) Committee, adopted resolution 39/222 without vote.

United Nations Children's Fund

The General Assembly,

Recalling its resolution 38/175 of 19 December 1983,

Taking note of Economic and Social Council decision 1984/171 of 25 July 1984,

Having considered the report of the Executive Board of the United Nations Children's Fund on its session held at Rome from 24 April to 4 May 1984, and having noted in particular in this context the Board's discussions on achieving the child survival and child development revolution and on the present emergency situation in Africa,

Reaffirming the principles and guidelines for programme activities established by the Executive Board in its efforts to reach the most disadvantaged in order to bring about a major improvement in child survival and child development, taking special advantage of developments in primary health care techniques and communications,

Noting the recommendations of the International Conference on Population, 1984, and the Mexico Declaration on Population and Development, which stated, *inter alia,* that those developments have the potential to achieve a virtual revolution in child survival,

Acutely aware that the present global situation adversely affects vulnerable groups, such as children, and therefore makes the need for those efforts all the more critical,

1. *Commends* the policies and activities of the United Nations Children's Fund;

2. *Endorses* the conclusions and recommendations contained in the report of the Executive Board of the United Nations Children's Fund on its 1984 session;

3. *Urges* the Executive Director of the United Nations Children's Fund, within the context of the basic services and primary health care approach for children in the delivery of programmes, to continue and intensify his efforts on the basis of recent developments in the social and biological sciences that present a new opportunity to bring about a virtual revolution in child survival and child development, at a low cost and in a relatively short time, in accordance with the relevant decisions of the Executive Board of the Fund and in co-operation with other relevant bodies and organizations, in particular the World Health Organization;

4. *Notes with satisfaction* the important efforts made by the Executive Director of the Fund to respond to the present critical emergency situation of children and mothers in Africa and urges him to continue his efforts in this respect, as well as to continue to implement child survival and child development activities generally in Africa in accordance with the decisions of the Executive Board of the Fund;

5. *Reaffirms* the goals of the International Development Strategy for the Third United Nations Development Decade with reference to children, in particular the goals of ensuring children's immunization against major diseases by 1990 and of reducing the infant mortality rate to less than 50 per 1,000 live births in all countries by the year 2000, and notes the crucial role of the child survival and child development revolution in meeting those goals;

6. *Reaffirms* the role of the Fund as the lead agency in the United Nations system responsible for co-ordinating the follow-up activities of the International Year of the Child related to the goals and objectives concerning children set forth in the International Development Strategy;

7. *Commends* the Executive Director of the Fund for his continuing efforts to enlarge the resources of the Fund so that it can respond effectively to the needs of the developing countries, in continued pursuance of its mandate;

8. *Expresses its appreciation* to Governments that have responded to the needs of the Fund and expresses the hope that more States will come forward with positive responses;

9. *Appeals* to all Governments to increase their contributions so that, in the light of the current economic situation, the Fund may be able to strengthen its co-operation with developing countries and respond to the urgent needs of children in those countries.

General Assembly resolution 39/222

18 December 1984   Meeting 104   Adopted without vote

Approved by Second Committee (A/39/791) without vote, 6 December (meeting 56); draft by Vice-Chairman (A/C.2/39/L.111), based on informal consultations on 44-nation draft (A/C.2/39/L.95); agenda item 81 (g).

Meeting numbers. GA 39th session: 2nd Committee 48-53, 55, 56; plenary 104.

The 44-nation draft—by developing and Western States—which was withdrawn in favour of the Vice-Chairman's text, was identical to that text except for drafting changes.

Medium-term plan for 1983-1987

At its 1984 session,[2] the Executive Board approved the programme objectives of the UNICEF medium-term plan for 1983-1987,[5] which aimed at accelerating child survival and development activities to reduce infant and early childhood mortality and improve child development. Priority areas to achieve that goal included primary health care, clean water, sanitation, limitation of malnutrition, universal primary education, abolition of widespread illiteracy and improvement of the situation of women. The Board approved the financial objectives of the plan, which projected that UNICEF income would increase from $350 million in 1984 to $485 million in 1987, while annual expenditure would increase from $363 million to $451 million.

Policy reviews

Policy reviews on early childhood development[6] and evaluative activities in UNICEF[7] were prepared following a request by the Executive Board in 1983. The objective of the first review was to assist UNICEF to implement its child development activities with awareness of the child's development needs, including psycho-social needs. The second policy review stressed the importance of improved regular progress reporting on project implementation, especially in the economic climate of constrained resources for social development. It examined the evolution of monitoring and evaluation policies and included specific recommendations to improve evaluative capacities. The recommendations contained in both reviews were endorsed by the Executive Board.[2]

Maurice Pate Memorial Award

In February, the Executive Director recommended that for 1984 the annual Maurice Pate Memorial Award, established to commemorate the first Executive Director of UNICEF, be awarded to the International Centre for Diarrhoeal Disease Research in Bangladesh.[8] The Centre, which conducted research and training and rendered services for treatment and control of such diseases, helped to revolutionize approaches to that health problem. The Centre planned to use the $25,000 award to support its work with poor urban mothers and to train local volunteers in the use of ORS for treating diarrhoea.

UNICEF programmes by region

Programme expenditures in 1984 increased by 11 per cent for Africa and 17 per cent for the Americas compared with 1983. Programme expenditures decreased by 4 per cent for East Asia and Pakistan, by 3.5 per cent for South Central Asia and by 32 per cent for the Middle East and North Africa. There were no expenditures for Europe. The table overleaf shows 1984 expenditures and new commitments approved by the Executive Board in 1984.[2]

Africa

The critical and worsening situation facing children and their families in Africa and the need to respond to their needs quickly and effectively became the focus of UNICEF emergency assistance in 1984. An international appeal for some $50 million was launched by UNICEF to assist 21 countries: 13 seriously affected (Angola, Burkina Faso, Cape Verde, Chad, Ethiopia, Gambia, Ghana, Mali, Mauritania, Mozambique, Niger, Senegal, Zimbabwe) and 8 others (Botswana, Djibouti, Guinea, Kenya, Lesotho, Sao Tome and Principe, Sudan, Uganda). At a subsequent meeting, the appeal was raised to $67 million. UNICEF endorsed accelerated programmes in the region, and allocated $2.8 million from the Emergency Reserve Fund for Africa during the first quarter of 1984. It also earmarked $7.2 million from the Infant Mortality Reduction Fund for child survival and development actions, and approved $23.6 million in new programmes from general resources and $15 million in new "noted" projects (projects awaiting funding) for 12 countries.

The situation of children in eastern Africa remained grim in 1984, with close to 2,000 infants dying each day from a combination of diseases, severe malnutrition, lack of shelter and clothing, and neglect.

In 1984, UNICEF continued its programmes in eastern Africa[9] and carried out major primary health care (PHC) reviews in 10 countries. In Malawi, a survey on the quality of maternal and child health (MCH) services revealed that 80 per cent of the population had access to some level of health care within 8 kilometres, some 55 per cent of the children were fully immunized, 70 per cent of mothers attended pre-natal clinics and 54 per cent had skilled assistance at delivery, and 64 per cent of the children had received growth charts and were attending clinics 6.3 times per year on the average. Despite these health services, the infant mortality rate (IMR) remained high (between 130 and 159 per 1,000 live births), suggesting that IMR was related to the high prevalence of malnutrition. In Zimbabwe, the effectiveness of community health workers was reviewed, as well as essential elements of PHC, including immunization, diarrhoeal disease control, MCH and nutrition.

Training of health staff and community-based health workers, such as traditional birth attendants, continued. Training in areas related to the essential drugs programme, the control of diarrhoeal diseases, oral rehydration, and management of immunization programmes were also given much attention.

Of the $7 million that UNICEF committed to nutrition projects in eastern Africa, 63 per cent was allocated to applied nutrition projects and the remainder to nutrition education. Ethiopia and the United Republic of Tanzania received two thirds of the nutrition commitments in the region. Other assistance during the year included an allocation of $20 million (or 10.7 per cent of total UNICEF commitments in the region) to the education sector and over $44 million (or 22.5 per cent) to water supply and sanitation projects. An additional $8 million in emergency funds was also allocated to countries affected by drought to provide food, water, medical supplies, seeds and logistical support to the most vulnerable groups.

In west and central Africa,[10] a region affected during the year by natural disasters, such as drought, and civil strife, the overall situation of children continued to deteriorate. In the light of the situation, an important feature of UNICEF activities was its defensive advocacy. Support was given to all elements concerned with child welfare (nutrition, health and education) and to efforts to bring child concerns to the attention of policy-makers and donors. Ongoing programmes were redesignated to strengthen child survival elements, and funds from the Infant Mortality Reduction Fund were used to promote child survival and development activities.

During 1984, large portions of the populations in the Sahelian region continued to suffer from famine, and UNICEF immediate emergency relief included the distribution of food supplements,

1984 UNICEF EXPENDITURE AND MULTIYEAR COMMITMENTS

(as at 31 December 1984; in US dollars)

	Expenditure	Approved new commitment		Expenditure	Approved new commitment
Africa			**Americas** (cont.)		
Angola	3,303,753	—	Mexico	1,122,237	—
Benin	900,025	3,154,000	Nicaragua	2,833,598	315,000
Botswana	339,826	—	Panama	46,507	—
Burkina Faso	2,392,630	—	Paraguay	258,530	—
Burundi	1,107,324	—	Peru	1,413,696	—
Cameroon	691,242	—	Saint Christopher and Nevis	891	—
Cape Verde	480,805	—	Saint Lucia	22,934	—
Central African Republic	1,714,233	2,294,000	Saint Vincent and the Grenadines	1,064	—
Chad	1,775,756	—	Regional projects	1,441,949	—
Comoros	78,048	178,000			
Congo	165,270	—	Subtotal	15,974,182	9,973,000
Djibouti	639,566	—			
Equatorial Guinea	71,005	374,165	**East Asia and Pakistan**		
Ethiopia	12,642,122	—	Bangladesh	13,130,075	—
Gambia	167,618	—	Burma	5,277,307	—
Ghana	1,512,605	—	China	5,158,611	50,000,000
Guinea	954,632	—	Democratic Kampuchea	3,056,328	2,490,000
Guinea-Bissau	556,652	600,000	Indonesia	11,428,114	—
Ivory Coast	326,697	—	Kampuchean relief	1,278,078	—
Kenya	1,625,881	—	Lao People's Democratic		
Lesotho	196,602	—	Republic	922,100	—
Liberia	387,986	—	Malaysia	255,295	—
Madagascar	915,728	—	Pacific islands	442,870	—
Malawi	910,458	5,724,000	Pakistan	10,034,190	—
Mali	1,786,488	—	Papua New Guinea	84,311	—
Mauritania	499,235	—	Philippines	3,565,516	—
Mauritius	105,169	—	Republic of Korea	551,389	—
Mozambique	3,044,917	—	Thailand	3,314,062	—
Niger	1,722,827	—	Viet Nam	5,289,718	—
Nigeria	5,316,233	—	Regional projects	117,719	250,000
Rwanda	924,459	—			
Sao Tome and Principe	47,710	—	Subtotal	63,905,683	52,740,000
Senegal	1,548,737	—			
Seychelles	59,695	124,000	**South Central Asia**		
Sierra Leone	622,615	—	Afghanistan	1,543,010	—
Somalia	3,185,324	5,035,000	Bhutan	1,703,860	—
Swaziland	304,184	594,000	India	31,001,586	—
Togo	226,012	3,533,000	Maldives	250,472	—
Tunisia	—	—	Mongolia	14,394	—
Uganda	5,363,451	—	Nepal	5,170,848	—
United Republic of Tanzania	8,623,149	—	Sri Lanka	2,579,618	—
Zaire	1,518,349	—			
Zambia	352,678	1,477,000	Subtotal	42,263,788	—
Zimbabwe	1,268,092	—			
Regional projects	1,938,401	500,000	**Middle East and North Africa**		
			Algeria	135,785	358,000
Subtotal	72,314,189	23,587,165	Bahrain	471,145	—
			Democratic Yemen	644,823	—
Americas			Egypt	4,015,840	13,371,000
			Iran	24,010	—
Antigua and Barbuda	26,847	—	Jordan	389,330	—
Argentina	58,000	—	Lebanon	9,085,700	—
Barbados	3,400	—	Lebanon rehabilitation	6,066,223	—
Belize	59,055	—	Morocco	1,628,323	—
Bolivia	2,341,057	3,000,000	Oman	403,600	—
Brazil	1,095,584	2,671,000	Sudan	6,232,692	—
Chile	83,388	—	Syrian Arab Republic	453,079	—
Colombia	1,763,990	—	Tunisia	413,889	—
Costa Rica	33,077	—	Turkey	148,817	—
Cuba	40,952	—	Yemen	1,999,669	—
Dominica	28,347	—	Palestine children and mothers	724,969	—
Dominican Republic	256,118	1,405,000	Regional projects	141,469	1,950,000
Eastern Caribbean	—	1,500,000			
Ecuador	565,443	—	Subtotal	32,979,363	15,679,000
El Salvador	348,952	328,000			
Grenada	29,534	—	**Interregional**	—	25,000
Guatemala	486,911	—			
Guyana	65,342	—	Savings (cancellation)	—	(50,399)
Haiti	1,153,878	—			
Honduras	337,069	616,000	Total	227,437,205	101,953,766
Jamaica	55,832	138,000			

NOTE: Approved new commitments include the following to cover over-expenditure incurred in previous commitments: Equatorial Guinea, $17,165.

SOURCES: A/40/5/Add.2, E/1984/19.

improvement of water supplies, distribution of medicines and the extension of inoculations to protect the health of enfeebled children. For example, UNICEF diverted $1.2 million from its regular country programme to provide Mali with basic drugs, vaccines and food supplements, train health workers and help transform schools into training centres for coping with changes in the ecosystem. It provided funds to Mauritania for food distribution in the community feeding centres, logistical support for medical teams and material to help combat epidemics and diarrhoeal diseases. It also supplied Chad with seeds and agricultural inputs, provided paramedical and hygiene training, helped in digging wells, and distributed food, medical and other supplies. In wartorn Angola, where the situation of children worsened during 1984 (the IMR reached 500 per 1,000 live births in certain areas), UNICEF assistance helped alleviate serious shortages of medical supplies and treatment.

On 31 October, UNICEF held in New York a special meeting on the situation of African mothers and children resulting from drought and the global recession. The UNICEF Executive Director, who had invited representatives from Chad, Ethiopia and Mozambique to address the meeting and provide first-hand accounts of the situation and relief efforts in their countries, pointed out that the silent emergency in Africa was taking the lives of 4.5 million children a year (12,000 daily). The underlying causes were projected to continue throughout the 1980s. Of emergency needs totalling some $67 million in 13 African countries, UNICEF had already channelled over $21 million—including some $11 million from donor Governments—to help meet those needs. Most available resources were already committed and additional funds were urgently needed to carry forward planned commitments beyond 1984.

Americas

In 1984, UNICEF continued its basic services programmes in Latin American and Caribbean countries,[11] a region struggling against the consequences of one of the most severe economic crises—rising unemployment and a sharp fall in family income, deterioration of living conditions among poor people and their children, increasing malnutrition and disease, heightened social tensions, and growing political instability.

UNICEF assistance centred on: PHC programmes (in Bolivia, Brazil, Colombia, Dominica, Ecuador, Haiti, Jamaica, Peru, and Saint Vincent and the Grenadines); child survival projects (immunization, control of diarrhoeal diseases through ORT, breast-feeding and appropriate weaning, monitoring child growth and development, control of acute respiratory infections and high-risk pregnancy, and perinatal problems) in Central America and Panama; immunization against five diseases (diphtheria, poliomyelitis, tetanus, pertussis and measles) in Belize, Colombia, Costa Rica, the Dominican Republic, El Salvador, Mexico, Nicaragua, Panama and Peru. It also supported national programmes for ORT in Brazil, Colombia, Haiti and Jamaica; breast-feeding in Bolivia, Brazil, Peru and Central America; growth monitoring and early childhood development in Bolivia, Brazil, Colombia, Costa Rica, Cuba and Peru; abandoned and street children in Brazil, Colombia, Ecuador and Mexico; economic activities for women in Bolivia, Brazil, Colombia, Costa Rica, Ecuador, Mexico and Peru; and, through community involvement, urban basic services in low-income areas in Argentina, Brazil, Colombia, Ecuador, Haiti, Jamaica, Peru and Central America.

Asia

In East Asia, Pakistan and China,[12] UNICEF continued to concentrate its programmes on less privileged areas, through community involvement and participation by Governments and other agencies. Promotion of the child survival and development strategy resulted in increased interest and generated many innovative activities. Other developments were the expansion of area-based projects, increased emphasis on the need to reach the poor, more systematic implementation and improved monitoring and evaluation activities. Despite the growth of the region's economy, the food situation—and hence malnutrition, mainly among the poor—improved little because of the rapid regional population growth and a series of natural calamities.

Programmes on child survival and development and PHC were implemented in several countries: Burma, in 229 townships out of a total of 314; Indonesia, in the country's 67,000 villages; the Philippines, where health structure was reorganized to strengthen PHC at the national level; and Thailand, in 73 per cent of the villages and in the primary school curriculum. Growth monitoring in the countries of the Association of South-East Asian Nations and the Republic of Korea increased during the year and, in Pakistan, it became part of the district-level programming. Bangladesh, Burma, Indonesia, Pakistan, the Philippines, the Republic of Korea and Thailand reported advances in nation-wide ORT programmes, but the need to promote the use of ORS still remained in many countries.

Implementation of national legislation based on the 1981 International Code of Marketing of Breast-milk Substitutes[13] was promising. In Bangladesh, Indonesia, Papua New Guinea, the Philippines, the Republic of Korea and Thailand, informal national codes or guidelines incorporating some of the International Code's provisions were developed. In Viet Nam, the Government controlled the marketing and distribution of breast-milk substitutes. In Fiji and Pakistan, the International Code was recommended for adoption but was awaiting government decisions. In Singapore, a voluntary code was in effect, and in Malaysia, one was being prepared.

Other UNICEF programmes during the year dealt with family nutrition improvement, water supply and environmental sanitation, urban basic services, early childhood development and women's activities. Immunization programmes increased in Burma and Pakistan, and most countries reported high coverage rates.

China, which was going through a period of social and economic transition, made a policy commitment to child health and welfare, but large areas remained in great need: over 100 million people lagged far behind the level of social progress enjoyed by the majority, and socio-economic improvements and health and education services were limited among the 56 minority populations, numbering 70 million people. The China country programme, one of the five largest UNICEF programmes, counted major achievements in 1984 in spite of constraints: vaccine production increased by some 20 per cent and immunization reached a population of 150 million in five provinces; a network linking MCH activities with local public health and medical schools to meet child health needs was expanded to reach 30 counties inhabited by 25 million people; the Child Development Centre of China conducted 31 research projects and six training courses for 720 people, and produced booklets, slides and films on child nutrition, prevention of diseases and child psychology.

In South Central Asia,[14] although some 10,000 children continued to die each day, the quality of child life was progressing. UNICEF's role in the region had evolved from simply providing relief assistance to working in collaboration with those concerned with development issues. This shift was reflected in the form of increased UNICEF financial support for training, education and communication, which were designed to promote self-reliance and the use of appropriate technology.

The year marked a turning-point regarding UNICEF's role in the region. India and UNICEF collaborated in preparing a reshaped approach to child development in the country, to be reflected, if approved by the Executive Board in 1985, in the 1985-1989 programme. UNICEF initiated plans for a more effective development partnership with Nepal and, in Sri Lanka, a new country programme was introduced, marking the beginning of a national movement in favour of child development.

UNICEF co-operation in India aimed at helping it to achieve the objectives set for the decade, such as reducing infant, child and maternal mortality and morbidity; increasing literacy and non-formal learning for out-of-school disadvantaged children, especially girls; extending services for development

of the young; and increasing the availability of basic services—health, nutrition, water supply and sanitation. Immunization was expanded in the region and, as a result, India was set for a massive countrywide immunization programme aiming at universal coverage by 1990.

In Sri Lanka, the immunization programme showed positive results. The incidence of polio and pertussis declined by two thirds between 1978 and 1983 and the reduction in diphtheria and neo-natal tetanus was even more marked. This trend continued in 1984 with the introduction of measles vaccine. National immunization coverage was planned for 1985.

Sectoral programmes, such as formal and non-formal education, health, nutrition, water supply, environmental sanitation, prevention of childhood disability and support for destitute children, were co-ordinated in the region. Although co-ordination between government ministries needed to be improved, there was a conscious effort in nearly all the countries to bring isolated resources to bear on child development. For example, the Children's Secretariat in Sri Lanka accelerated action on behalf of children. In India, the Ministry of Social Welfare played an important co-ordinating role in establishing the plan of operations for 1985-1989. Decentralization in Nepal, to be implemented in 1985, was aimed at combining services at the district and lower levels.

Middle East and North Africa

In 1984, political confrontations continued to dominate three major areas of the region (the Gulf, Lebanon and the western Sahara) and were increasing significantly in a fourth (south Sudan), affecting the lives of children and their families.[15] High levels of male migration from rural to urban areas and other countries in the region resulted in an increasing number of women becoming heads of household, a role for which they had not been trained. Urbanization also created new problems for women and children; the living conditions in peri-urban areas and shanty towns had a negative effect on the health of mothers and children. In addition, the downturn in the world economy, coupled with severe inflation and reduced expectations of oil revenue, affected the region since oil-rich States were no longer providing unlimited employment opportunities for workers from the poorer parts of the region and social services felt the effects of cut-backs.

In February, the UNICEF regional office was relocated provisionally from Beirut, Lebanon, to Amman, Jordan. The emergency nature of the move meant that the office had to function under very constrained circumstances, with limited staff and equipment. The Arab Gulf Programme for United

Nations Development Organizations (AGFUND), established in April 1981 and consisting of seven States (Bahrain, Iraq, Kuwait, Oman, Qatar, Saudi Arabia, United Arab Emirates), remained in 1984 the best regional supporter of UNICEF. At its October meeting, AGFUND approved a contribution of $3 million for a number of UNICEF projects, and further allocations were expected during the remainder of the fiscal year.

A regional programme strategy meeting (Amman, September) identified issues to be given priority attention during the following months, including the predominance of Islam and the Arabic language in a regional approach to child survival and development actions; the decrease in national incomes; the decline in breast-feeding; the situation of girls and women; and the potential for social marketing through the region's media.

UNICEF assistance in basic health infrastructures, including the promotion of PHC, continued despite set-backs resulting from the global recession and other factors. Bahrain and Jordan reported the commissioning and staffing of new health centres; Egypt and the Sudan, improved services through staff training and/or material inputs; and Egypt, a breakthrough with national acceptance and legitimization of traditional birth attendants as a formal part of the rural health team. The organization also provided support for water and sanitation projects (in Egypt, Jordan, Lebanon, Morocco, the Sudan and Yemen, progress was made in extending water-supply infrastructure); education programmes in Bahrain, Democratic Yemen, Morocco, the Syrian Arab Republic and Turkey; and improving the situation of girls and women in the region. A number of national women's organizations (Oman and the United Arab Emirates) and general unions of women (Democratic Yemen, Iraq and the Syrian Arab Republic) adopted the child survival and development strategy and started programming activities to promote the services of health ministries.

Responding to emergencies caused by both man-made and natural disasters, UNICEF provided assistance to Lebanon, the Sudan, Yemen (see Chapter III of this section) and Turkey. In co-operation with other United Nations agencies, it assisted in restoring water operations in Beirut and distributed emergency medical kits. In Turkey, a donation from Japan was used for educational equipment and school furniture damaged in the Erzerum earthquake of October 1983. In Yemen, UNICEF continued its assistance to the population affected by the 1982 Dhamar earthquake. In the Sudan, where there were warning signals of its being affected by the drought, steps were taken, in conjunction with the Government and other agencies, to deal with the anticipated emergency.

UNICEF programmes by sector

As in the previous six years, child health, including nutrition, accounted for the largest portion of UNICEF's expenditures in 1984. Other major programmes dealt with water supply and sanitation, social welfare services and education. The table below gives UNICEF expenditures and commitments by sector.

1984 UNICEF EXPENDITURE AND COMMITMENTS, BY MAIN FIELD OF CO-OPERATION
(in thousands of US dollars)

	1984 expenditure	Approved commitments
Child health	83,660	47,414
Water supply/sanitation	68,057	4,398
Social welfare services for children	15,732	11,337
Formal education	19,862	19,267
Non-formal education	10,645	3,857
Emergency relief	15,795	—
General	30,598	15,714
Programme support services	59,514	—
Total	303,863	101,987

SOURCE: A/40/5/Add.2.

Child welfare in urban areas

During 1984, UNICEF continued to support community-based activities in the slums and shanty towns of over 50 developing countries.[4] Birth-spacing methods by poor urban women became an urgent issue, not only on grounds of health and welfare, but because more than half the urban growth in developing countries was due to natural increase rather than rural-urban migration. Malnutrition remained one of the most serious problems among urban children; compared with the city average, food intake in slums and squatter settlements was only half to two thirds. There was a decline in breast-feeding since mothers often worked. The urban poor being directly involved in the cash economy, the global recession exacerbated their situation. For these reasons, child survival and development measures formed the core of most UNICEF-assisted PHC programmes during the year.

Asia and Latin America were the regions with the most UNICEF-assisted community-based urban services programmes. In India, UNICEF programmes reached over 20 cities and towns. In the Philippines, there were three urban projects on organizational development, leadership training and community participation; community-based health projects were being carried out in Manila, Quezon City and Davao City. In Pakistan, UNICEF helped construct 421 latrines in Karachi between 1979 and 1983; on a self-help basis and using a UNICEF design, individuals built another 1,346, including 500 during 1984.

In Latin America, UNICEF assistance in basic services included an urban community-based services programme in Haiti, which became fully operational during the year, including a water and sanitation component; the expansion of an urban PHC project in Guayaquil, Ecuador; and the launching in Kingston, Jamaica, of an urban basic services programme, funded by Canada.

In Africa, the urban PHC project in Addis Ababa, Ethiopia, became a good example of community-based urban services. Under the leadership of the local government and with the participation of 284 community organizations, a programme was in progress to reduce child mortality in half by 1988. With UNICEF collaboration, 100,000 children were provided ORT and there were plans to extend coverage to an additional 200,000.

With rapid urbanization throughout the world, the number of abandoned and street children increased. The total number of such children was estimated to be in the tens of millions; the problem was particularly acute in Latin America and some Asian and African cities. To remedy the problem, UNICEF developed programme guidelines emphasizing community-level prevention and providing alternatives to placing children in institutions; it also supported specific programmes in Brazil, Colombia, Ethiopia, Mexico, the Philippines and Central America. Another issue of concern was the problem of children and work; while the International Labour Organisation promoted conventions controlling or eliminating child labour, UNICEF favoured providing basic services to working children while taking measures against their exploitation.

Education

UNICEF activities in formal and non-formal education in 1984—excluding education in health, nutrition, sanitation and other programmes—accounted for $30.5 million, or 12.5 per cent of total programme expenditure, compared with 16 per cent in 1983. During the year, UNICEF co-operated in education programmes in 105 countries: 43 in Africa, 29 in Asia, 22 in the Americas and 11 in the Middle East and North Africa.

While UNICEF support for basic and primary education continued to focus on disadvantaged children, it was recognized that many children and women in the developing world were still lacking a basic level of general education. It was felt that this problem deserved serious attention at the national and international levels in order to reduce inefficiency and wastage in primary education; improve the quality and relevance of basic education, including developing relevant and useful forms of basic education in sub-Saharan Africa in the context of its continuing emergency; and increase the participation of disadvantaged groups, including women, in basic education.

UNICEF assisted several countries in school-related problems through better preparation of teachers (Bangladesh, Ethiopia, Nepal); improving curricula and textbooks (Djibouti, Madagascar, Malawi); providing supplies or helping the country to produce them (China, Lao People's Democratic Republic); and offering training and transport for supervisors (Bangladesh, United Republic of Tanzania). Dealing with the socio-economic roots of school drop-out proved to be more difficult; UNICEF supported projects attempting to attune schools more closely to the student's out-of-school circumstances and to involve the community in school concerns. For example, in Burundi, Ethiopia and Indonesia, non-formal education programmes were developed as a route to higher primary school grades. Other similar projects were under way in Bangladesh, Nepal, the Syrian Arab Republic and the United Republic of Tanzania.

The continuing African crisis underscored the need to make basic education more relevant. In countries where large numbers of people were struggling for survival, UNICEF supported community-based educational programmes linked to the urgent tasks of food production, soil and water conservation, raising animals, and meeting the daily necessities of life which were likely to be more effective than conventional schools.

In Indonesia, assistance was provided for small business activities to groups participating in non-formal programmes. In Thailand, Tunisia and Turkey, UNICEF assisted in a work-oriented curriculum, and helped several countries to extend adult literacy and training programmes to older children who missed out on formal education opportunities. UNICEF supported the production of primary education and literacy materials introducing child survival and development, such as a nutrition guidebook for primary teachers in Burundi, Arabic and French materials on health and nutrition for primary schools in Mauritania, and a manual on water use and sanitation for Gambian schools. It also assisted several countries with family-life education projects for women in Egypt, Ethiopia, Haiti, Nepal and the Philippines.

At its 1984 session, the Executive Board endorsed a comprehensive approach to early childhood development, noting that the programme actions to promote the psycho-social development of the young child through early childhood care and education were indispensable for the total development of the child.

Nutrition

In 1984, UNICEF co-operated in nutrition programmes in 100 countries—38 in Africa, 32 in Asia, 21 in the Americas and 9 in the Middle East and North Africa—with a total expenditure of $20.1 million, an increase of $900,000 over 1983. Its activities included expanding nutrition programmes in 27,000 villages, equipping nutrition centres and demonstration areas, providing stipends to train nutrition workers, and delivering 35,000 metric tons of food.

UNICEF's main thrust for assistance during the year was the $85.3 million UNICEF/WHO joint nutrition support programme (JNSP) financed by Italy. By the end of 1984, the entire sum had been committed to support 16 projects in 18 countries and other global activities. Three of the projects were in Asia (Burma, Nepal, Pakistan), eight in Africa (Angola, Ethiopia, Mali, Mozambique, Niger, Somalia, Sudan, United Republic of Tanzania) and five in the Americas (Haiti, Nicaragua, Peru, Eastern Caribbean—involving Dominica and Saint Vincent and the Grenadines, with the support of the Caribbean Food and Nutrition Institute), with one regional project to eradicate goitre and cretinism in Bolivia, Ecuador and Peru. An important feature of JNSP was that it addressed the nutritional status of children and mothers rather than simply their feeding. This distinction encouraged the promotion of a broader range of activities, such as ORT, immunization and the empowering of women, with a positive effect on nutrition. For this reason, most country projects contained priority elements of the child survival strategy, together with food supplementation or family food production and some form of female education. In the United Republic of Tanzania, for example, a project launched in the Iringa region at the end of 1983, with an impressive campaign to create public awareness, was well established within a year in all 167 villages of the project area and involved two thirds of all households. A similar campaign was launched in Haiti to promote the production, distribution and use of ORS and, by the end of 1984, a fivefold increase in its use was recorded. Although JNSP's resources were not meant to provide relief, assistance was nevertheless extended to Mali and the Sudan affected by severe drought.

UNICEF's other assistance during the year included national nutritional surveillance programmes in Lesotho, Madagascar and Malawi; food production for family use in Papua New Guinea, the Syrian Arab Republic, Uganda and other countries; nutrition introduction into the primary education system of Kenya; training of volunteers in Zimbabwe food centres; training courses for health personnel in Iraq, Oman and the Syrian Arab Republic; and nutrition education promotion through the media in Turkey.

Infant feeding

In 1984, UNICEF and WHO continued to help promote breast-feeding. Although studies published during the year confirmed that bottle-feeding was still largely confined to urban areas, its spread was becoming alarming. In Mauritius, for example, 84 per cent of babies born in hospitals and clinics were bottle-fed, and in Pakistan 50 per cent of the infants surveyed were wholly or partially bottle-fed. Efforts were made to introduce appropriate weaning foods at the correct age to ensure the health and sound nutritional status of the young child. New medical research findings showed that breast-milk might contain antibodies against cholera, that it afforded greater protection against diarrhoeal diseases than other feeding modes, and that it included a substance that killed a variety of parasites responsible for intestinal disorders, including amoebic dysentery.

To provide the necessary data for national policies in infant and young child feeding, some 15 countries conducted national surveys on breast-feeding and participated in regional workshops sponsored by UNICEF/WHO. Fiji, Mauritius and Zambia, which had completed their surveys, were involved with proposals for action; Argentina and Bangladesh designated government bodies to monitor infant-feeding practices; in Egypt, encouraging breast-feeding was an integral part of the country's diarrhoeal disease control programme; and in Nicaragua, breast-feeding programmes aimed at educating mothers and training health workers. UNICEF also assisted countries in preparing promotional and educational materials on breast-feeding. Slide-sets, films and posters were made in Ethiopia, Haiti, Iraq, Mexico and Thailand, short television spots were aired in the Philippines and Turkey, and a film was produced in Ghana.

Efforts were continued to strengthen the application of the 1981 International Code of Marketing of Breast-milk Substitutes.[13] By mid-year, the Code was in force in six countries and in the final stages of legislation in 16 others; it had been adopted as a voluntary measure in 7 countries and partially implemented in 24, while 24 others had draft national codes under consideration.

At the request of the Nestlé Company and the International Nestlé Boycott Committee, UNICEF facilitated final negotiations between the two parties in early 1984, leading to an agreement by the Company to abide by the Code and to the consequent lifting of the seven-year boycott against Nestlé.

Primary health care

UNICEF continued in 1984 to promote primary health care, spending a total of $63.5 million in that sector. Its assistance reached 109 countries (43 in Africa, 32 in Asia, 23 in the Americas and 11 in the Middle East and North Africa) and included grants for training health workers, technical assistance and equipment for health centres, especially in rural areas, and medicines and vaccines against tuberculosis, diphtheria, tetanus, typhoid, measles, poliomyelitis and other diseases.

Malaria, acute respiratory infections (ARI) and high neonatal mortality (death during the first month of life) were three of the most serious problems confronting PHC workers. As a result, WHO, in collaboration with UNICEF, strengthened its support for better maternal care and delivery practices, and ARI management was included in the PHC programmes in China, Sri Lanka and Central America. Development in PHC was uneven from region to region. Progress was evident in South-East Asia and the western Pacific; elsewhere in Asia, tremendous resource needs were overcome through strengthening PHC commitment and programmes at the local level. In Latin America, where the recession worsened the plight of the poor, greater interest was stirred in PHC and related programmes. In the Middle East and North Africa, there was a lack of trained manpower. Africa, menaced simultaneously by economic recession, civil strife, drought and famine, was facing the gravest problems.

With child survival measures as the leading thrust, UNICEF continued to advocate PHC actively through international conferences, workshops, meetings and publications. Major meetings in 1984 included an international seminar on health for all in Sri Lanka, an inter-country workshop in Jamaica on joint support for PHC, and a conference at Bellagio, Italy, for expanding immunization efforts. Training programmes, which were an important element in UNICEF's contribution to the development of PHC, included: courses for traditional birth attendants and other village-level workers, the introduction of PHC concepts into regular courses at health schools, refresher courses for health and community development workers, and seminars to sensitize officials and community leaders to PHC concepts. In Pakistan, for example, 2,500 traditional birth attendants were trained under a programme supported by the Canadian Committee for UNICEF and Canadian bilateral aid. In countries where large numbers of village health workers were to be trained, UNICEF concentrated its assistance on the training of trainers and supervisors.

UNICEF/WHO co-operation on essential drugs was pursued in 1984. In the United Republic of Tanzania, for example, UNICEF, with the financial assistance of Denmark, supplied essential-drug kits monthly to some 2,500 rural health centres and trained 3,500 health workers to use them. In Ethiopia, support was provided for manufacturing essential drugs and ORS. In Nepal, Royal Drugs Ltd. expanded its capacity to meet 70 per cent of the country's requirements for essential drugs. Over the 1983-1984 period, international competitive bidding and consolidation of procurement orders reduced prices for such drugs by 50 per cent, and UNICEF worked on a project offering developing countries improved means of obtaining essential drugs through UNICEF's supply division at Copenhagen, Denmark.

UNICEF finances

The financial position of UNICEF remained sound in 1984, despite the continuing effects of global economic recession and the strong United States dollar.[2] Total income was $332 million (including $24 million for the African emergency), the same as 1983. A total of 79 per cent ($263 million) came from Governments and intergovernmental organizations; 14 per cent ($47 million) from private sources, greeting card income and individual donations; and the remaining 7 per cent ($22 million) from United Nations organizations and miscellaneous sources. General resources income was $234 million, a decrease of 5 per cent compared with 1983. It was estimated that the effects of the strengthening exchange rate for the United States dollar had reduced income by $11 million.

Total expenditure in 1984 was $345 million compared with $332 million in 1983, or an increase of 4 per cent. General resources expenditure totalled $153 million.

Financial plan for 1984-1987

The UNICEF financial plan for 1984-1987, set out in the medium-term work plan, projected a 1984 income of $350 million, compared to the actual income of $332 million. The annual income projections for the following three years were $425 million, $455 million and $485 million. Projection levels on expenditure were $363 million for 1984, compared to the actual expenditure of $345 million, $398 million for 1985, $424 million for 1986 and $451 million for 1987.

In May,[2] the Executive Board approved the medium-term plan as a framework of projections, including the preparation of up to $327 million in programme commitments from general resources to be submitted to the Board in 1985. That amount was subject to the condition that estimates of income and expenditure made in the plan continued to be valid. The Board considered that the income projections were realistic. In 1983, the Board had requested the Executive Director to submit a revised format for UNICEF budget estimates more in line with the secretariat's organizational structure.[16] A new format was submitted and approved, and it was agreed that it would be used for future budget estimates.

Contributions

Contributions to UNICEF received in or pledged for 1984 to the UNICEF general resources and supplementary funds totalled $295,018,008 after a deduction of $2,889,896 in adjustments to prior years' income (see table opposite).

CONTRIBUTIONS TO UNICEF
(INCLUDING GENERAL RESOURCES AND SUPPLEMENTARY FUNDS)
(as at 31 December 1984; in US dollar equivalent)

Country or organization	Received in or pledged for 1984 Governmental	Received in or pledged for 1984 Non-governmental	Pledged for 1985 Governmental
Afghanistan	30,000	—	30,000
Algeria	142,000	307	142,000
Angola	—	—	5,000
Antigua and Barbuda	300	—	—
Australia	6,635,216	1,054,718	1,838,025
Austria	970,381	338,920	733,945
Bahamas	3,000	—	—
Bahrain	15,000	2,191	12,500
Bangladesh	7,229	1,490	8,208
Barbados	5,000	—	—
Belgium	946,156	235,284	903,226
Benin	9,031	—	—
Bhutan	3,630	—	4,170
Bolivia	6,000	—	—
Botswana	9,738	—	2,907
Brazil	175,783	6,941	—
British Virgin Islands	150	—	—
Brunei	1,000,000	—	—
Bulgaria	60,914	—	60,914
Burkina Faso	6,383	—	—
Burma	204,526	614	37,238
Burundi	1,626	—	—
Byelorussian SSR	70,225	—	64,804
Cameroon	68,493	—	63,158
Canada	19,050,917	10,951,936	9,671,533
Chile	100,000	42	70,000
China	350,000	685	400,000
Colombia	394,306	45	456,816
Congo	12,766	—	16,842
Costa Rica	34,395	10,000	35,025
Cuba	117,041	—	116,026
Cyprus	80,645	50,827	—
Czechoslovakia	82,576	—	82,576
Democratic Yemen	7,040	—	7,040
Denmark	16,658,576	4,545	4,955,309
Djibouti	2,000	—	1,000
Dominica	1,000	—	—
Dominican Republic	2,000	—	—
Ecuador	25,407	10	25,407
Egypt	82,202	—	82,202
Ethiopia	49,275	1,317	—
Fiji	1,900	—	2,000
Finland	7,165,302	58,045	5,797,101
France	4,313,574	3,381,898	3,684,211
German Democratic Republic	107,692	—	412,903
Germany, Federal Republic of	6,681,482	799,905	4,179,104
Ghana	9,600	—	—
Greece	137,000	84,141	135,000
Guatemala	45,191	—	14,694
Guinea	1,000	—	—
Guyana	4,480	—	3,140
Haiti	—	850	—
Holy See	1,000	—	1,000
Honduras	20,000	—	20,000
Hong Kong	14,450	—	14,587
Hungary	21,041	—	21,539
Iceland	8,269	—	7,858
India	1,671,362	—	1,648,805
Indonesia	536,967	258	300,000
Iran	—	—	50,000
Iraq	96,774	753	—
Ireland	446,251	636	380,000
Israel	50,000	—	50,000
Italy	33,113,865	1,335,798	14,778,325
Ivory Coast	—	164	20,000
Jamaica	4,250	—	3,125
Japan	12,497,475	4,012,396	14,200,000
Jordan	26,490	150	—
Kenya	17,687	784	16,149
Kuwait	200,000	—	200,000
Lao People's Democratic Republic	5,000	—	5,000
Lebanon	6,152,101	45,000	—
Lesotho	1,966	—	2,500
Liechtenstein	2,000	—	—
Luxembourg	32,312	76,377	13,492
Madagascar	11,006	—	5,271
Malawi	3,282	—	3,542
Malaysia	105,980	981	85,980
Maldives	3,000	50	3,000
Mali	—	80	1,000
Malta	4,579	—	—
Mauritius	3,331	—	—
Mexico	355,499	37,414	58,302
Monaco	3,304	—	3,410
Mongolia	3,529	—	3,598
Morocco	388,591	—	—
Nepal	15,815	—	5,267
Netherlands	9,892,478	2,793,805	6,309,130
New Zealand	695,416	—	—
Nicaragua	10,909	—	—
Nigeria	289,043	1,621	313,864
Norway	21,209,430	115,150	15,687,531
Oman	50,000	—	50,000
Pakistan	50,989	660	103,117
Panama	22,000	—	25,000
Papua New Guinea	—	54	—
Peru	120,000	—	120,000
Philippines	458,719	196	222,555
Poland	56,934	—	57,882
Portugal	15,000	13,886	—
Qatar	—	—	200,000
Republic of Korea	147,000	1,261	147,000
Romania	12,245	—	11,971
Rwanda	4,000	—	—
Saint Vincent and the Grenadines	750	—	—
Samoa	1,000	—	—
Saudi Arabia	1,000,000	59,338	1,000,000
Senegal	6,000	—	6,000
Sierra Leone	37,912	—	10,508
Somalia	2,331	—	—
Spain	440,000	994,958	435,650
Sri Lanka	10,066	220	12,671
Sudan	35,337	—	25,000
Suriname	—	—	2,500
Swaziland	3,672	—	3,250
Sweden	28,545,911	240,058	21,348,315
Switzerland	9,245,189	2,856,053	4,633,205
Syrian Arab Republic	—	—	32,051
Thailand	279,569	13,880	247,552
Togo	1,064	—	—
Tonga	5,900	—	—
Trinidad and Tobago	10,417	—	10,365
Tunisia	105,525	—	35,277
Turkey	93,346	5	59,422
Uganda	1,770	2	5,042
Ukrainian SSR	140,449	—	129,608
USSR	758,427	—	699,885
United Arab Emirates	—	16,286	—
United Kingdom	9,320,595	608,408	7,875,000
United Republic of Tanzania	16,748	6	16,761
United States	53,546,000	1,471,606	53,500,000
Uruguay	2,585	2,735	—
Venezuela	199,651	—	114,667
Viet Nam	6,000	—	6,000
Yemen	22,174	—	12,910
Yugoslavia	247,264	8,108	255,813
Zaire	2,000	—	—
Zambia	11,735	—	7,759
Zimbabwe	22,936	—	18,634
Subtotal	**258,861,810**	**31,693,848**	**179,707,669**

CONTRIBUTIONS TO UNICEF (Cont.)

Country or organization	Received in or pledged for 1984		Pledged for 1985
	Governmental	Non-governmental	Governmental
Intergovernmental agencies			
AGFUND	4,501,316	751,404	—
European Community	1,306,937	—	—
League of Arab States	51,473	—	—
OPEC	655,000	—	—
Subtotal	6,514,726	751,404	—
United Nations system	—	86,116	—
Adjustments to prior years' income	(1,982,022)	(907,874)	—
Total	263,394,514	31,623,494	—

SOURCES: A/40/5/Add.2, A/CONF.126/2.

Accounts

1982

In 1984,[2] the Executive Board reviewed and noted the observations and comments of the Board of Auditors and of the Advisory Committee on Administrative and Budgetary Questions (ACABQ) on the 1982 UNICEF financial report.[17] It also noted the Executive Director's comments and action taken in response to those observations.

The Board acted on the recommendation of its Committee on Administration and Finance, which met at Rome on 2 and 3 May.[18]

1983

In June 1984, following an audit of UNICEF accounts, the United Nations Board of Auditors submitted to the General Assembly the 1983 financial statements of UNICEF, including the Greeting Card Operation (GCO).[19] The Board noted the speed with which the Administration had dealt with matters brought to its attention and the efforts it had made to improve financial management and control systems. Its review indicated that, in some cases, project implementation was not satisfactory, and the review, monitoring and evaluation of projects were inadequate. The Board also noted that delegation of authority to regional and field offices for local procurement was not adequate, deliveries of supplies to projects were sometimes delayed and relevant rules on bidding procedures were not strictly followed. It recommended that the field offices be given more authority for local procurement and that efforts be made to award contracts to the lowest acceptable bidder; in the case of non-acceptance of the lowest bids, sufficient justifications for the decision should be recorded. Pointing out that, in some field offices, substantial cash balances were maintained in non-interest-bearing bank accounts, the Board recommended that significant cash balances not be retained in such accounts.

Regarding GCO, the Board noticed that there were long-outstanding receivables; procurement procedures followed in certain cases were inconsistent with the United Nations Financial Rules; there was a substantial stock of unused paper and unsold cards at every year-end; and there was a lack of internal control in physical stock-taking of inventories. It recommended that prompt action be taken by the Administration to rectify the situation. In addition, in order to reduce the volume of unsold cards, printing should be undertaken based on adequate market surveys and the margin for excess of demands be reviewed.

In its September 1984 report on audited financial statements,[20] ACABQ said it shared the Board's concern over procurement matters and urged the UNICEF Administration to pay closer attention to that process, to ensure full compliance with the applicable rules and to achieve optimum use of resources. Referring to the Board's report on cash balances maintained in non-interest-bearing accounts, ACABQ recalled that the Board had made a similar comment the previous year. While the Administration had indicated that the amounts involved totalled less than two weeks of UNICEF cash expenditures, ACABQ felt that cash management at field offices could be improved to reduce further the level of non-interest-bearing accounts. Concerning physical inventories of UNICEF property, ACABQ shared the Board's views since it considered that the maintenance of adequate control was essential if losses were to be avoided.

In May, the UNICEF Committee on Administration and Finance[18] noted that the balance of unspent commitments at the end of 1983 was, at $959 million, too high. It was pointed out that the balance consisted of $220 million for 1984-1985 budget commitments, $200 million of supplementary funds commitments and $539 million of general resources programme commitments. The relationship of outstanding general resources commitments relative to income levels had, from 1979 to 1983, remained stable at the equivalent of 26 months of future resources income. Outstanding commitments and income had both grown but the ratio between them had been constant.

The UNICEF Executive Board, in May,[2] reviewed and noted the 1983 financial report and statements. On 13 December, the General Assembly, in resolution 39/66, accepted the report, concurred with the ACABQ comments and requested the UNICEF Executive Director to take the required remedial action.

Organizational questions

Greeting Card Operation

During the 1983 GCO season (1 May 1983–30 April 1984), 113 million cards, 436,000 calendars,

241,000 packs of stationery and other items were sold in 130 countries, compared with 115 million cards, 441,000 calendars and 314,000 packs in the previous season.[21] The sales generated $48.1 million in gross revenues, compared to $46.9 million the previous year, yielding a net operational income of $14.8 million to UNICEF general resources, $3.3 million (18 per cent) lower than the 1982 season. The high exchange value of the United States dollar and high inflation in some major markets had a considerable impact on GCO income in 1983.

The UNICEF Executive Board, in May,[2] approved the work plan for the 1984 GCO season (1 May 1984–30 April 1985), in which planned card production ranged from 120 million to 140 million, expenditure from $26.8 million to $28 million and corresponding revenue projections from $44.5 million to $52.3 million. The work plan for the 1984 season had been recommended by the UNICEF Executive Director.[22] It was concluded that GCO's organizational structure had to be changed from its traditional concentration on production to a progressive and dynamic marketing and sales organization.

Headquarters arrangements

On the recommendation of the UNICEF Executive Director, the Executive Board accepted an offer from the United Nations Development Corporation (UNDC) to lease space for UNICEF headquarters in the new UNDC-III building, to be available for occupancy in late 1986 or early 1987. The new building, on East 44th Street in New York City, would be built to UNICEF requirements and would be known as UNICEF House.[2]

NGO relations

Co-operation with non-governmental organizations (NGOs) increased notably in 1984.[4] Several international NGOs working in developing countries initiated in their activities new child survival components and designed special programmes. The League of Red Cross and Red Crescent Societies, for example, launched the "Child Alive" programme, which, in co-operation with UNICEF, aimed at reducing diarrhoea-related mortality and morbidity by extending the correct use of ORT and by promoting breast-feeding and nutritional awareness. "Child Alive" activities were under way in Colombia, Honduras and Swaziland. In their joint International Youth Year/development education programme, the World Organization of the Scout Movement and the World Association of Girl Guides and Girl Scouts included messages on nutritional surveillance and ORT. In some countries, Haiti for example, national scouts were being trained in ORT.

Paediatricians and midwives' organizations endorsed child survival actions and encouraged their members to promote these actions. In co-operation with UNICEF, the International Paediatric Association

sponsored regional meetings on childhood mortality and morbidity, and the International Council of Nurses emphasized the importance of child survival measures in its PHC training programmes.

Church and religious leaders around the world promoted child survival measures. In Indonesia, Oman and the Philippines, advocacy with Muslim leaders and teachers led to support for child survival actions in their communities. Papal messages and initiatives by church leaders in Brazil, Colombia, Guatemala, India and the Philippines supported child survival and development actions. Co-operation increased between Rotary International and UNICEF to immunize all children against poliomyelitis. Rotary International announced that it would provide, for a five-year period, the polio vaccines needed for any approved city, state, country or regional immunization effort. In collaboration with UNICEF and WHO, vaccination campaigns began in Colombia, Haiti, India, Nigeria and the Sudan. Annual reports from UNICEF field offices showed an upsurge of activity with local and national NGOs and other groups, and efforts were under way to support community-based actions through bilateral funding.

Draft declaration on adoption and foster placement

In a September 1984 report with a later addendum,[23] the Secretary-General submitted to the General Assembly replies he had received from eight Governments concerning the draft Declaration on Social and Legal Principles relating to the Protection and Welfare of Children, with Special Reference to Foster Placement and Adoption Nationally and Internationally.

The draft Declaration had been prepared by a group of experts in response to a 1975 Economic and Social Council resolution,[24] and was submitted to the Council in 1979.[25] In 1982[26] and in 1983,[27] the Assembly had requested the Secretary-General to circulate the draft text to Member States to obtain their views.

GENERAL ASSEMBLY ACTION

On 13 December, the General Assembly, acting on the recommendation of the Sixth (Legal) Committee, adopted resolution 39/89 without vote.

Draft Declaration on Social and Legal Principles relating to the Protection and Welfare of Children, with Special Reference to Foster Placement and Adoption Nationally and Internationally

The General Assembly,

Recalling its resolution 36/167 of 16 December 1981, whereby it decided, *inter alia*, that appropriate measures should be taken to finalize the draft Declaration on Social and Legal Principles relating to the Protection and

Welfare of Children, with Special Reference to Foster Placement and Adoption Nationally and Internationally,

Noting, in this connection, that the work of the Commission on Human Rights on the draft Convention on the Rights of the Child is soon to be completed,

Bearing in mind the reports of the Secretary-General of 8 September 1980, 19 October 1982, 6 October 1983 and 10 September 1984, containing the views of Member States on the text of the draft Declaration,

Fully aware of the sovereign right of Governments to define their national and international policies in accordance with their legal systems as regards the protection and welfare of children, including foster placement, adoption and guardianship, as appropriate,

Bearing in mind the existence of different national legislation in the field of the protection and welfare of children,

Recognizing that it is the responsibility of Governments to determine the adequacy of their national services for children and to recognize those children whose needs are not being met by existing services,

Noting the usefulness of regional co-operation in matters regarding the well-being of children,

Recognizing that the best child welfare is good family welfare and that, when family care is unavailable or inappropriate, substitute family care should be considered, in conformity with national legislation,

Convinced that adoption of the draft Declaration will promote the well-being of children with special needs,

1. *Appeals* to Member States representing different legal systems to undertake consultations on the draft Declaration on Social and Legal Principles relating to the Protection and Welfare of Children, with Special Reference to Foster Placement and Adoption Nationally and Internationally, with a view to finding out the extent to which they would join the common endeavour of completing the work thereon;

2. *Also appeals* to the Member States that will take part in the consultations to submit, before the forty-first session of the General Assembly, a paper containing their common conclusions on the matter, including, if appropriate, their suggestions as to the procedure and forum for future work;

3. *Requests* the Secretary-General to circulate the paper referred to in paragraph 2 above to Member States with a view to obtaining their comments thereon, including their views as to the procedure and forum for future work, and to submit a report to the General Assembly at its forty-first session;

4. *Decides* to include in the provisional agenda of its forty-first session the item entitled "Draft Declaration on Social and Legal Principles relating to the Protection and Welfare of Children, with Special Reference to Foster Placement and Adoption Nationally and Internationally".

General Assembly resolution 39/89

13 December 1984   Meeting 99   Adopted without vote

Approved by Sixth Committee (A/39/782) without vote, 7 December (meeting 66); 10-nation draft (A/C.6/39/L.23/Rev.1); agenda item 134.
Sponsors: Colombia, Finland, Iceland, Norway, Qatar, Spain, Suriname, Sweden, Uruguay, Venezuela.
Meeting numbers. GA 39th session: 6th Committee 62, 64, 66; plenary 99.

REFERENCES
[1]YUN 1980, p. 503, GA res. 35/56, annex, 5 Dec. 1980. [2]E/1984/19. [3]A/39/292. [4]E/ICEF/1985/2. [5]E/ICEF/1984/3. [6]E/ICEF/1984/L.1. [7]E/ICEF/1984/L.3. [8]E/ICEF/1984/P/L.30. [9]E/ICEF/1985/5. [10]E/ICEF/1985/6. [11]E/ICEF/1985/7. [12]E/ICEF/1985/8 & Corr.1. [13]YUN 1981, p. 1419. [14]E/ICEF/1985/9 & Corr.1. [15]E/ICEF/1985/10 & Corr.1. [16]YUN 1983, p. 934. [17]*Ibid.*, p. 935. [18]E/ICEF/1984/AB/L.8/Rev.1. [19]A/39/5/Add.2. [20]A/39/510. [21]E/ICEF/1985/AB/L.5. [22]E/ICEF/1984/AB/L.6. [23]A/39/442 & Add.1. [24]YUN 1975, p. 684, ESC res. 1925(LVIII), 6 May 1975. [25]YUN 1979, p. 765. [26]YUN 1982, p. 1177, GA res. 37/115, 16 Dec. 1982. [27]YUN 1983, p. 937, GA res. 38/142, 19 Dec. 1983.

Youth

Activities during 1984 continued to focus on preparations for International Youth Year (1985) (IYY) and on co-ordinating and strengthening communication between youth and the United Nations. The Economic and Social Council, in resolution 1984/44, and the General Assembly, in resolution 39/24, called for further co-ordination in the field of youth as well as communication between the United Nations and youth and youth organizations.

The Council, in resolution 1984/71, requested the Secretary-General to strengthen the secretariat of the Economic Commission for Africa (ECA) to enable it to fulfil its mandate concerning youth, including the implementation of a regional plan of action on youth, and to take specific measures to increase the dissemination of information on youth. By resolution 39/22, the Assembly invited the organizers of international youth conferences and festivals in 1985 to report the results of those activities. The Assembly also called, in resolution 39/23, for the implementation of its previous resolutions on human rights relating to youth, particularly the right to education and to work.

In November 1984, the United Nations Postal Administration issued commemorative stamps and a souvenir card on IYY (see ADMINISTRATIVE AND BUDGETARY QUESTIONS, Chapter IV).

Integrating youth in development

In an April 1984 report on the social aspects of development (see Chapter XIII of this section), which reviewed progress since 1981 towards the social goals of the International Development Strategy for the Third United Nations Development Decade,[1] the Secretary-General recalled that the Strategy had recommended that all countries should give high priority to the mobilization and integration of youth in development.[2]

It was estimated that more than half of the population of developing countries was below 24 years of age. The number and proportion of young people continued to grow in the early 1980s and this trend would persist during the current decade. The youth group—persons 15 to 24 years old—increased on average at a rate of 2.8 per cent a year, and the recent decline of fertility in some developing regions would not affect their population structure during the 1980s. The Secretary-General noted that integrating youth in development involved government action and also a large number of private organizations, religious movements, clubs and associations, which had been particularly active in recent years in a number of developing countries.

Activities of the UN system

In accordance with a May 1983 resolution of the Economic and Social Council,[3] the Secretary-General issued a report in April 1984 on the action taken by the United Nations system and other organizations to facilitate co-ordination and information in the field of youth.[4] The report described the progress achieved at all levels to facilitate co-ordination of efforts and to implement the substantive decisions taken by the Advisory Committee for the International Youth Year. It also provided examples of approaches and views of the United Nations system and of co-operative efforts between the United Nations and NGOs, as well as an overview of co-ordination and information initiatives emanating from regional meetings devoted to IYY. The report concluded that preparations for IYY had strengthened co-ordination of youth activities at all levels.

The Joint United Nations Information Committee, which was responsible for co-ordinating information activities in the United Nations system, approved at its April 1984 session the recommendations of its task force on IYY. Among the planned activities were: an IYY "action-pack", a feature exchange service and a United Nations bibliography, as well as information focal points within co-operating organizations.[5] The Department of Public Information (DPI) was requested to act as a clearing-house in inter-agency information activities for IYY.[6]

ECONOMIC AND SOCIAL COUNCIL ACTION

On 25 May 1984, the Economic and Social Council, on the recommendation of its Second (Social) Committee, adopted resolution 1984/44 without vote.

Co-ordination and information in the field of youth

The Economic and Social Council,

Recalling its resolutions 1979/27 of 9 May 1979, 1980/25 of 2 May 1980, 1981/25 of 6 May 1981, 1982/28 of 4 May 1982 and 1983/26 of 26 May 1983 on co-ordination and information in the field of youth,

Recalling also General Assembly resolutions 34/151 of 17 December 1979, 36/28 of 13 November 1981, 37/48

of 3 December 1982 and 38/22 of 22 November 1983 on the International Youth Year: Participation, Development, Peace,

Considering that the implementation of the Specific Programme of Measures and Activities to be undertaken prior to and during the International Youth Year, of the recommendations made by the Advisory Committee for the International Youth Year and endorsed by the General Assembly in its resolution 37/48, and of the relevant recommendations of the five regional meetings devoted to the International Youth Year held in 1983 could contribute to intensifying and improving the co-ordination of the activities of the United Nations and specialized agencies relating to youth,

Convinced of the importance of giving widespread publicity to the activities of the United Nations in the field of youth, especially in the context of the preparations for the International Youth Year,

Taking note of the report of the Secretary-General on co-ordination and information in the field of youth,

1. *Endorses* the conclusions contained in the report of the Secretary-General on co-ordination and information in the field of youth;

2. *Invites* again all United Nations bodies, specialized agencies, regional commissions and other international intergovernmental organizations, as well as non-governmental organizations concerned, to consider at their regular meetings appropriate ways and means for the improvement of co-ordination and information in the field of youth in the context of the preparation for and observance of the International Youth Year;

3. *Requests* the Secretary-General to take all necessary organizational measures to ensure the success of the observance of the International Youth Year in 1985 within the United Nations system in accordance with the recommendations made by the Advisory Committee for the International Youth Year;

4. *Decides* to consider at its first regular session of 1985, on the basis of a report of the Secretary-General, the progress achieved in co-ordination and information in the field of youth.

Economic and Social Council resolution 1984/44

25 May 1984   Meeting 21   Adopted without vote

Approved by Second Committee (E/1984/92) without vote, 21 May (meeting 18); 38-nation draft (E/1984/C.2/L.3); agenda item 11.

Sponsors: Algeria, Argentina, Bangladesh, Benin, Botswana, China, Colombia, Congo, Costa Rica, Cuba, Djibouti, Ecuador, Egypt, France, Gambia, Germany, Federal Republic of, Greece, India, Indonesia, Liberia, Mexico, Morocco, Netherlands, Nigeria, Pakistan, Philippines, Qatar, Romania, Rwanda, Saint Lucia, Sierra Leone, Somalia, Sri Lanka, United States, Venezuela, Viet Nam, Yugoslavia, Zaire.

Strengthening channels of communication between youth and the United Nations

For many years, channels of communication between the United Nations and youth and youth organizations had been under review by the General Assembly. In order to improve the 1977[7] and 1981[8] guidelines on channels of communication, the IYY secretariat, within the Centre for Social Development and Humanitarian Affairs, organized a meeting of an Expert Group (Vienna, Austria, 9-13 January 1984). The Group took into account the diversity of programmes and mechanisms within the United Nations system devoted to youth matters and the relationships between Governments and non-governmental youth organizations, and made two sets of recommendations, one short-term and the other long-term.[9]

Suggested short-term actions included selected areas of concern to youth (peace and international understanding, development, employment, environment, culture and leisure) with priority given to collective communication between the United Nations and groups of youth organizations, the exchange of information through United Nations publications, such as the quarterly *Youth Information Bulletin*, the use of mass media, and the expansion of youth representation and involvement in national delegations to the General Assembly and to other relevant United Nations meetings.

Long-term recommendations centred on strengthening channels of communication at all levels. Among the suggestions were: at the national level, that national co-ordinating committees should continue their work after IYY and that DPI should encourage national-level communication with young people; and, at the regional level, that the regional commissions should encourage and support co-ordination within the United Nations system. At the international level, the Group recommended, among other things: that DPI should publish a catalogue of films and media materials of interest to youth and invite young people with skills and an interest in the media to take part in DPI's activities; that the consultative status for youth organizations should be reviewed and strengthened, and they should be encouraged to take a more active role in the work of the United Nations system; and that United Nations agencies should, when preparing school textbooks and other materials, collaborate with teachers' organizations.

The Advisory Committee for IYY, pursuant to a November 1983 Assembly resolution[10] requesting it to monitor and evaluate measures with respect to the implementation of the guidelines on channels of communication and to make recommendations for their implementation and further elaboration as a part of IYY, met in April (see below). The Committee's report was forwarded to the Assembly by the Secretary-General in June.[11]

In its report, the Committee requested the Secretary-General to obtain from youth NGOs and the Geneva Informal Meeting of International Youth Non-Governmental Organizations (usually convened three times a year) suggestions for activities regarding proposals in the Specific Programme of Measures and Activities, and to report to the General Assembly in 1985. It also invited national IYY co-ordinating committees and other similar structures to assist national youth organizations in their role as channels of communica-

tion between the United Nations and youth and youth organizations.

GENERAL ASSEMBLY ACTION

On 23 November, the General Assembly, acting on the recommendation of the Third (Social, Humanitarian and Cultural) Committee, adopted resolution 39/24 without vote.

Channels of communication between the United Nations and youth and youth organizations

The General Assembly,

Recalling its resolutions 32/135 of 16 December 1977 and 36/17 of 9 November 1981, in which it adopted guidelines for the improvement of the channels of communication between the United Nations and youth and youth organizations, and also recalling its resolution 38/26 of 22 November 1983,

Bearing in mind the importance of the existence of effective channels of communication between the United Nations and youth and youth organizations for the proper information of young people and their effective participation in the work of the United Nations and the specialized agencies at the national, regional and international levels,

Taking note of the report of the Secretary-General relating to youth,

Also taking note of the report of the Expert Group meeting on channels of communication, held at Vienna from 9 to 13 January 1984,

Further taking note of the report of the Advisory Committee for the International Youth Year on its third session, specifically of the paragraphs dealing with the channels of communication,

Taking note of resolution 22 on youth adopted on 25 November 1983 by the General Conference of the United Nations Educational, Scientific and Cultural Organization,

Convinced that effective and proper functioning of channels of communication between the United Nations and youth and youth organizations forms a basic prerequisite for active involvement of young people in the work of the United Nations,

Equally convinced that the effective participation of youth representatives from the Member States in international congresses dealing with youth issues will enhance and strengthen the current and future channels of communication and will help in understanding the problems facing youth in our contemporary world,

1. *Requests* the Secretary-General to prepare a detailed, structured and evaluative report on the implementation of the guidelines and additional guidelines for the improvement of the channels of communication, which would serve as a background paper at the fourth session of the Advisory Committee for the International Youth Year, and to submit that report to the General Assembly at its fortieth session;

2. *Calls upon* Member States, United Nations bodies, specialized agencies and other intergovernmental organizations to implement fully the guidelines relating to the channels of communication not only in their general terms, but also in concrete projects dealing with issues of importance to young people;

3. *Calls upon* the national co-ordinating committees of the International Youth Year and other similar struc-

tures to assist national youth organizations, upon their request, in carrying out their role as channels of communication between the United Nations and youth and youth organizations;

4. *Stresses* the necessity of making use, within the framework of the channels of communication, of mechanisms which have been set up by youth and youth organizations themselves at the national, regional and international levels;

5. *Decides* to take up at its fortieth session the question of the channels of communication between the United Nations and youth and youth organizations on the basis of the next report of the Advisory Committee for the International Youth Year.

General Assembly resolution 39/24

23 November 1984   Meeting 71   Adopted without vote

Approved by Third Committee (A/39/659) without vote, 13 November (meeting 37); 27-nation draft (A/C.3/39/L.11); agenda item 89.
Sponsors: Bangladesh, Belgium, Cameroon, Chile, Comoros, Costa Rica, Denmark, Dominican Republic, Ecuador, Egypt, Greece, Guatemala, Indonesia, Morocco, Netherlands, Norway, Philippines, Romania, Rwanda, Senegal, Spain, Sudan, Sweden, Uruguay, Venezuela, Yemen, Zaire.
Meeting numbers. GA 39th session: 3rd Committee 16-23, 27, 37; plenary 71.

Preparations for International Youth Year (1985)

In pursuance of a November 1983 General Assembly resolution,[12] the Secretary-General submitted to the Assembly the report[11] of the IYY Advisory Committee on its third session (Vienna, 2-11 April 1984). The Committee had been requested to submit a report with practical proposals on specific ways and means for observance, in 1985, of IYY in an appropriate organizational framework within the United Nations.

In its report, the Committee requested the Assembly to approve, within existing resources, the convening in 1985 of its fourth session with a view to recommending to the Assembly guidelines for further planning and follow-up in the field of youth. The Committee called on the United Nations system and NGOs to co-ordinate their efforts in order to make adequate preparations for the Year. It recommended that the Assembly devote some plenary meetings in 1985—to be designated as the United Nations World Conference for IYY—to policies and programmes relating to youth, and requested the Secretary-General to prepare a report surveying the implementation of specific proposals as contained in the Specific Programme of Measures and Activities to be undertaken prior to and during IYY. The Committee also suggested that the United Nations system, within existing resources, assist Governments with international events on youth-related issues, and it invited Member States, governmental organizations and NGOs to do their utmost to implement programmes leading to improvement in the situation of young people according to the goals of IYY: "Participation, Development, Peace".

By its resolution 39/22 (see below), the Assembly endorsed the Advisory Committee's recommen-

dations and requested the Secretary-General to ensure an appropriate observance of IYY within the United Nations system.

The Conference of Ministers of ECA (tenth meeting, Addis Ababa, Ethiopia, 24-28 May) recommended to the Economic and Social Council a draft resolution (see below), requesting the Secretary-General to take all necessary measures to strengthen the ECA secretariat to enable it to fulfil its mandate regarding youth, including the implementation of a regional plan of action (see also Chapter VIII of this section).

ECONOMIC AND SOCIAL COUNCIL ACTION

On 27 July 1984, the Economic and Social Council, on the recommendation of its First (Economic) Committee, adopted resolution 1984/71 without vote.

International Youth Year: Participation, Development, Peace

The Economic and Social Council,

Convinced of the importance of the implementation of the Specific Programme of Measures and Activities to be undertaken prior to and during the International Youth Year, as well as of the recommendations made by the Advisory Committee for the International Youth Year for the further implementation of that Programme, which were endorsed by the General Assembly in its resolution 37/48 of 3 December 1982,

Recognizing that the preparation for the observance of the International Youth Year will contribute to the reaffirmation of the goals of the new international economic order and to the implementation of the International Development Strategy for the Third United Nations Development Decade,

Aware that, for the International Youth Year to be successful and in order to maximize its impact and practical efficiency, adequate preparation and the widespread support of Governments, all specialized agencies, international, intergovernmental and non-governmental organizations and the public will be required,

1. *Requests* the Secretary-General to take all necessary measures to continue to strengthen the secretariat of the Economic Commission for Africa in order to enable it to fulfil the extended mandate entrusted to it in the field of youth, including the implementation of the Regional Plan of Action on Youth;

2. *Invites* the Secretary-General to use all means at his disposal, within the regular budget of the United Nations, to increase the resources allocated for the implementation of the Specific Programme of Measures and Activities to be undertaken prior to and during the International Youth Year;

3. *Requests* the Secretary-General and the secretariat of the Economic Commission for Africa to take specific measures to increase the dissemination of information on youth.

Economic and Social Council resolution 1984/71

27 July 1984   Meeting 50   Adopted without vote

Approved by First Committee (E/1984/142) without vote, 23 July (meeting 16); draft by ECA (E/1984/112), amended during informal consultations; agenda item 9.

In resolution 1984/15 of 24 May on promoting opportunities for young women, the Council recommended that the IYY Advisory Committee and the Secretary-General should, in all their reports, take special account of the needs of young women in rural and urban areas and of their problems. In a further resolution (1984/67 of 27 July) on the work programme and calendar of conferences of the Economic Commission for Latin America and the Caribbean, the Council requested the Secretary-General to make every effort to reallocate existing resources for the holding in 1985 of a regional meeting to review the implementation of the Regional Plan of Action for Latin America and the Caribbean for IYY.

GENERAL ASSEMBLY ACTION

On 23 November, the General Assembly adopted two resolutions dealing with youth and IYY, which were adopted on the recommendation of the Third Committee.

The Assembly adopted resolution 39/22 without vote.

International Youth Year: Participation, Development, Peace

The General Assembly,

Recalling its resolutions 34/151 of 17 December 1979, 35/126 of 11 December 1980, 36/28 of 13 November 1981, 37/48 of 3 December 1982 and 38/22 of 22 November 1983,

Recognizing the profound importance of the direct participation of youth in shaping the future of mankind and the valuable contribution that youth can make in the implementation of the new international economic order based on equity and justice,

Considering it necessary to disseminate among youth the ideals of peace, respect for human rights and fundamental freedoms, human solidarity and dedication to the objectives of progress and development,

Convinced of the imperative need to harness the energies, enthusiasms and creative abilities of youth to the tasks of nation-building, the struggle for self-determination and national independence, in accordance with the Charter of the United Nations, against foreign domination and occupation, and for the economic, social and cultural advancement of peoples, the implementation of the new international economic order, the preservation of world peace and the promotion of international co-operation and understanding,

Bearing in mind that 1985 is the fortieth anniversary of the United Nations,

Emphasizing again that the United Nations should pay more attention to the role of young people in the world of today and to their demands for the world of tomorrow,

Convinced that the preparation for and observance in 1985 of the International Youth Year with the motto "Participation, Development, Peace" will offer a useful and significant opportunity for drawing attention to the situation and specific needs and aspirations of youth, for increasing co-operation at all levels in dealing with youth issues, for undertaking concerted action programmes in favour of youth and for involving young people in the study and resolution of major national, regional and international problems,

Aware that, for the International Youth Year to be successful and to maximize its impact and practical efficiency, adequate preparation and the widespread support of Governments, all specialized agencies, international intergovernmental and non-governmental organizations and the public will be required,

Recalling that the activities of the International Youth Year at the international level should be primarily supportive of activities undertaken relative to regional, national and local youth issues,

Recognizing the important role of United Nations bodies, the specialized agencies and the regional commissions in promoting international co-operation in the field of youth and the necessity of strengthening their role in the effective implementation of the Specific Programme of Measures and Activities to be undertaken prior to and during the International Youth Year: Participation, Development, Peace,

Aware of the contribution which the United Nations Educational, Scientific and Cultural Organization is making to the promotion of international co-operation in the field of youth,

Noting with satisfaction the progress made in the implementation of the Specific Programme of Measures and Activities to be undertaken prior to and during the International Youth Year,

Also noting with satisfaction that many Governments have established national committees or other mechanisms to facilitate the planning, implementation and co-ordination of the activities related to the preparation for and observance of the International Youth Year,

1. *Endorses* the recommendations made by the Advisory Committee for the International Youth Year contained in the report on its third session;

2. *Decides* to devote an appropriate number of plenary meetings at its fortieth session, in 1985, to policies and programmes relating to youth and to designate these meetings as the United Nations World Conference for the International Youth Year which should take place in keeping with the procedures and practices of the General Assembly;

3. *Requests* the Secretary-General to take all measures recommended by the Advisory Committee for the International Youth Year with a view to ensuring an appropriate observance of the International Youth Year within the United Nations system;

4. *Recommends* to all Member States that they should include youth representatives in their delegations to the fortieth session of the General Assembly;

5. *Decides* that the fourth session of the Advisory Committee for the International Youth Year shall be convened, within existing resources, at Vienna, from 25 March to 3 April 1985 with a view to working out, on the basis of a draft prepared by the Secretary-General, guidelines for further planning and suitable follow-up in the field of youth which will be transmitted for approval to the General Assembly at its fortieth session;

6. *Stresses again* the importance of active and direct participation of youth organizations in the activities organized at the local, national, regional and international levels for the preparation for and observance of the International Youth Year;

7. *Invites* all international governmental and non-governmental organizations that have planned specific activities devoted to the International Youth Year, as well as the organizers of international youth conferences and

festivals in 1985, to be inspired, in the process of preparing and implementing those activities, by the motto of the International Youth Year: "Participation, Development, Peace" and by the provisions of the Specific Programme of Measures and Activities to be undertaken prior to and during the International Youth Year endorsed by the General Assembly;

8. *Also invites* the organizers of international youth conferences and festivals in 1985 to inform the General Assembly at its fortieth session, through the Secretary-General, of the results of those activities and the documents adopted;

9. *Decides* to include in the provisional agenda of its fortieth session the item entitled "International Youth Year: Participation, Development, Peace" and to grant it high priority.

General Assembly resolution 39/22

23 November 1984   Meeting 71   Adopted without vote

Approved by Third Committee (A/39/655) without vote, 13 November (meeting 37); 105-nation draft (A/C.3/39/L.6), orally revised; agenda item 85.

Sponsors: Algeria, Angola, Antigua and Barbuda, Argentina, Austria, Bangladesh, Barbados, Benin, Bhutan, Bolivia, Botswana, Brunei Darussalam, Burkina Faso, Cameroon, Central African Republic, Chad, Chile, China, Colombia, Comoros, Congo, Costa Rica, Cuba, Cyprus, Djibouti, Democratic Yemen, Dominica, Dominican Republic, Ecuador, El Salvador, Equatorial Guinea, Ethiopia, Gambia, Germany, Federal Republic of, Greece, Guatemala, Guinea, Guinea-Bissau, Guyana, Haiti, Honduras, India, Indonesia, Iran, Iraq, Italy, Ivory Coast, Jamaica, Japan, Jordan, Kenya, Lebanon, Lesotho, Liberia, Libyan Arab Jamahiriya, Madagascar, Malawi, Malaysia, Mali, Malta, Mauritania, Mauritius, Mexico, Morocco, Mozambique, Nepal, Netherlands, Nicaragua, Niger, Nigeria, Oman, Pakistan, Panama, Peru, Philippines, Qatar, Romania, Rwanda, Saint Lucia, Sao Tome and Principe, Senegal, Sierra Leone, Singapore, Somalia, Spain, Sri Lanka, Sudan, Suriname, Syrian Arab Republic, Thailand, Togo, Trinidad and Tobago, Turkey, Uganda, United Arab Emirates, United Republic of Tanzania, United States, Uruguay, Venezuela, Viet Nam, Yemen, Yugoslavia, Zaire, Zambia, Zimbabwe.

Financial implications. 5th Committee, A/39/682; S-G, A/C.3/39/L.15 & Add.1, A/C.5/39/30.

Meeting numbers. GA 39th session: 3rd Committee 16-23, 27, 37; 5th Committee 32; plenary 71.

The Assembly adopted resolution 39/23 without vote.

Efforts and measures for securing the implementation and the enjoyment by youth of human rights, particularly the right to education and to work

The General Assembly,

Recalling its resolutions 36/29 of 13 November 1981, 37/49 of 3 December 1982 and 38/23 of 22 November 1983, in which it, *inter alia,* recognized the need to adopt appropriate measures for securing the implementation and the enjoyment by youth of human rights, particularly the right to education and to work,

Recalling also its resolution 34/151 of 17 December 1979, by which it decided to designate 1985 as International Youth Year: Participation, Development, Peace,

Convinced that it is necessary to ensure full enjoyment by youth of the rights stipulated in the Universal Declaration of Human Rights, the International Covenant on Economic, Social and Cultural Rights and the International Covenant on Civil and Political Rights, with special regard for the right to education and to work,

Aware of the fact that insufficient education and the unemployment of young people limit their ability to participate in the development process, and, in this regard, emphasizing the importance of secondary and higher education for young people, as well as access for them

to appropriate technical and vocational guidance and training programmes,

Expressing its serious interest in the success of the forthcoming International Youth Year which should, *inter alia,* promote increasing participation of young people in the socio-economic life of their country,

1. *Calls upon* all States, all governmental and non-governmental organizations and the interested bodies of the United Nations and specialized agencies to pay continuous attention to the implementation of General Assembly resolutions 36/29, 37/49 and 38/23 relating to efforts and measures aimed at the promotion of human rights and their enjoyment by youth, particularly the right to education and vocational training and to work, with a view to resolving the problem of unemployment among youth;

2. *Requests* the Advisory Committee for the International Youth Year to pay, in its activities, full attention to resolutions 36/29, 37/49 and 38/23 and to all relevant international human rights instruments, particularly in elaborating guidelines for further planning and suitable follow-up in the field of youth;

3. *Invites* national co-ordinating committees or other organs of co-ordination for the International Youth Year: Participation, Development, Peace to give appropriate priority in the activities to be undertaken during the Year to the implementation and the enjoyment by youth of human rights, particularly the right to education and to work;

4. *Requests* the Secretary-General to pay adequate attention, in his report surveying the implementation of the Specific Programme of Measures and Activities to be undertaken prior to and during the International Youth Year, to the enjoyment by youth of human rights, particularly to the right to education and to work.

General Assembly resolution 39/23

23 November 1984   Meeting 71   Adopted without vote

Approved by Third Committee (A/39/655) without vote, 13 November (meeting 37); 19-nation draft (A/C.3/39/L.12); agenda item 85.

Sponsors: Afghanistan, Algeria, Angola, Bulgaria, Byelorussian SSR, Congo, Cuba, Czechoslovakia, Democratic Yemen, Ethiopia, German Democratic Republic, Lao People's Democratic Republic, Mongolia, Mozambique, Nicaragua, Nigeria, Syrian Arab Republic, Venezuela, Viet Nam.

Meeting numbers. GA 39th session: 3rd Committee 16-23, 27, 37; plenary 71.

In resolution 39/25 on the question of aging (see below), the Assembly requested the Secretary-General to continue promoting, in co-operation with national committees, joint activities as they related to intergenerational matters, especially during IYY. The Assembly, in resolution 39/72 A on the *apartheid* policies of South Africa, recommended that, in connection with the observance of IYY in 1985, Governments and organizations give special attention to the role of youth and students in the struggle against *apartheid* and effectively observe the anniversary of the Soweto uprising on 16 June 1985; the Assembly's action had been suggested by the Special Committee against *Apartheid.*[13]

REFERENCES

[1]YUN 1980, p. 503, GA res. 35/56, annex, 5 Dec. 1980. [2]A/39/171-E/1984/54. [3]YUN 1983, p. 940, ESC res. 1983/26, 26 May 1983. [4]E/1984/40 & Corr.1. [5]A/AC.198/77. [6]ACC/1984/15. [7]YUN 1977, p. 801, GA res. 32/135, annex,

16 Dec. 1977. (8)YUN 1981, p. 1018, GA res. 36/17, annex, 9 Nov. 1981. (9)*Youth: Identifying Measures for Strengthening Channels of Communication between the United Nations and Youth and Youth Organizations* (ST/ESA/167), Sales No. E.85.IV.9. (10)YUN 1983, p. 941, GA res. 38/26, 22 Nov. 1983. (11)A/39/262. (12)YUN 1983, p. 943, GA res. 38/22, 22 Nov. 1983. (13)A/39/22.

Aging persons

Activities during 1984 relating to aging persons—people aged 60 and over—centred on follow-up actions to implement the 1982 Vienna International Plan of Action on Aging. In resolution 39/25, the General Assembly called on Governments to consider the changing age structure of the population in their economic and social development plans and to contribute to the United Nations Trust Fund for Aging. It also requested the Secretary-General to continue promoting joint activities on aging and youth, especially during IYY (see p. 929).

Implementation of the Plan of Action

Report of the Secretary-General. In October 1984, the Secretary-General submitted a report[1] on the question of aging to the General Assembly, prepared in pursuance of its November request[2] that efforts be continued to implement the Vienna International Plan of Action on Aging adopted in 1982 by the World Assembly on Aging.[3]

During the year, the Secretary-General continued his assistance to national committees on aging, some of which had held national conferences to review the Plan of Action within the context of the economic, social and cultural circumstances of their country. Since the adoption of the Plan, the international network for information exchange on aging had been strengthened, enabling it to become a significant instrument for information exchange. Membership in the network expanded to over 60 organizations representing every region of the world. In addition, the United Nations strengthened its own information exchange activities: the periodical *Bulletin on Aging* was issued quarterly in English and French and its circulation increased, while *The Aging Periodical* (to be issued annually) was launched to provide scholarly information to policy-makers, planners, researchers, human service practitioners and researchers.

Co-operation within the United Nations system and other intergovernmental organizations also continued. The Centre for Social Development and Humanitarian Affairs of the Department of International Economic and Social Affairs, identified as the focal point for the question of aging, undertook various activities, such as information exchange, the assessment review and appraisal of the Plan of Action and technical co-operation. Together with organizations responsible for international population assistance, the United Nations Fund for Population Activities continued its financial assistance to the Centre to carry out activities related to the aging of populations. The United Nations also co-operated with intergovernmental organizations in exchanging information, knowledge and experience.

The Secretary-General reported that NGOs were playing a major role in implementing the Plan and two NGO committees on aging (one in New York and the other in Vienna) had been particularly active. NGOs had also convened numerous conferences, symposia and meetings on specific aspects of the Plan at the national, regional and international levels. The question of aging was included in international events sponsored by the United Nations, such as the 1984 International Conference on Population (see p. 714), International Youth Year (1985) (see p. 929), the World Conference to Review and Appraise the Achievements of the United Nations Decade for Women (1985) (see p. 889) and the Seventh United Nations Congress on the Prevention of Crime and the Treatment of Offenders (1985) (see p. 698).

On the question of elderly women, the Commission on the Status of Women, at its 1984 session, recommended to the Economic and Social Council the adoption of a draft, which the Council on 24 May adopted as resolution 1984/13. The Council requested the Secretary-General to prepare a report on the status and situation of elderly women in their societies, to be presented to the Commission in 1986 with a view to recommending necessary action relating to their plight throughout the world (see Chapter XIX of this section).

Regarding the question of youth, the Secretary-General transmitted to the IYY secretariat the Plan of Action on Aging, in order to bring the recommendations and conclusions of the World Assembly on Aging to the attention of national planning committees concerned with developing ideas for IYY.

As also requested by the Assembly in 1983,[2] the Secretary-General brought the question of the aging of populations to the attention of United Nations bodies responsible for the preparation of the International Conference on Population in order for this question to be considered by the Conference itself.

Action by the Conference on Population. The International Conference on Population[4] (Mexico City, 6-14 August) urged Governments to reaffirm their commitment to implementing the Vienna Plan of Action. It recommended that further efforts be made to analyse the issue of aging, particularly its implications for overall development, social services, medical care and other related fields. On the basis of such data, Governments were urged to secure the welfare and safety of older people, with particular attention to the situation and needs of older women. Governments and international agencies were requested to increase their efforts to improve care for the aged within the family unit, and to view the aging sector of the population not merely as a dependent group, but in terms of the active contribution that older persons had already made and could still make to the economic, social and cultural life of their families and community.

The Assembly, in resolution 39/228, endorsed the recommendations of the Conference.

UN Trust Fund

The first Conference for the Development of the United Nations Trust Fund for Aging met at Vienna on 9 March 1984 to establish an advisory group to support and strengthen the Fund. The group was to follow up Conference recommendations for stimulating interest in and support for the Fund and to assure a consistent flow of resources.

According to the Secretary-General's October report,[(1)] requests for assistance from the Fund—established in pursuance of a 1980 General Assembly resolution[(5)] to provide funds for the preparation of the 1982 World Assembly and then used to meet the increasing needs of the aging in developing countries—exceeded the $500,000 in programmable resources for 1984. Despite the Secretary-General's appeals and promotional activities, voluntary contributions to the Fund during the year were minimal. Contributions in 1984 amounted to $39,110 and during 1983 to $46,102. The balance of available resources as at 31 December 1984 was $493,051.

GENERAL ASSEMBLY ACTION

On 23 November, the General Assembly, on the recommendation of the Third Committee, adopted resolution 39/25 without vote.

Question of aging

The General Assembly,

Reaffirming its resolution 38/27 of 22 November 1983, in which it called upon Governments to make efforts to implement the principles and recommendations contained in the International Plan of Action on Aging in accordance with their economic, social and cultural systems and social values and changes, taking into account the circumstances of each country,

Reaffirming its resolution 37/51 of 3 December 1982, in which it requested the Secretary-General to continue to use the United Nations Trust Fund for Aging so as to assist countries, in particular developing countries and least developed countries, in formulating and implementing policies and programmes for aging in order to meet the rapidly increasing needs of older persons,

Recognizing the role played by the United Nations and the specialized agencies through their efforts in the field of aging and the need to strengthen this role, especially at the regional level, in order to ensure the implementation of the Plan of Action and the systematic and effi-

cient functioning of the technical advisory and co-ordination services of the United Nations,

Recalling recommendation 58 of the recommendations for the further implementation of the World Population Plan of Action, adopted at the International Conference on Population, 1984, which urged Governments to make further efforts to analyse the issue of aging, particularly its implications for overall development, social services, medical care and other related fields,

Reconfirming that aging is a population issue which affects development and is affected by it,

Recognizing the increasing awareness in many countries of issues related to aging and of the need to provide national authorities, at their request, with technical and financial assistance in their efforts to implement policies and programmes,

Stressing the importance of the activities of the United Nations Trust Fund for Aging towards the realization of the goals and objectives of the Plan of Action,

Acknowledging that aging is an interdisciplinary issue and that the United Nations and the specialized agencies must ensure a well co-ordinated international response to this question,

Confident that the first review of the Plan of Action, to be undertaken by the Commission for Social Development at its twenty-ninth session in 1985, will be of considerable value in view of further measures with regard to the question of aging,

Noting with satisfaction that the question of older women will be considered at the World Conference to Review and Appraise the Achievements of the United Nations Decade for Women: Equality, Development and Peace, to be held at Nairobi from 15 to 26 July 1985,

Noting that the Plan of Action recognizes the relationship between aging and youth, particularly as it relates to intergenerational matters,

Appreciating the role of non-governmental organizations in promoting international awareness of and action on the issues of aging,

1. *Takes note* of the report of the Secretary-General on the question of aging;

2. *Calls upon* Governments to consider the changing age structure of the population in their plans for economic and social development;

3. *Invites* Governments to retain or establish appropriate mechanisms at the national level to promote an effective and co-ordinated response to the implementation of the principles and the recommendations contained in the International Plan of Action on Aging;

4. *Requests* the Secretary-General to continue his efforts for the implementation of the Plan of Action at the national, regional and international levels and to continue to promote the United Nations Trust Fund for Aging so as to assist countries in formulating and implementing policies and programmes for aging;

5. *Invites* Governments to continue, and increase when possible, their contributions to the Trust Fund and calls upon Governments that have not yet done so to consider contributing to the Fund;

6. *Requests* the Secretary-General to continue to promote the exchange of information and experience in order to stimulate progress in the field of aging, to encourage the adoption of measures to respond to the economic and social implications of aging and to meet the needs of older persons;

7.   *Urges* the Secretary-General to include advisory services to developing countries that request them in technical co-operation programmes, to the extent feasible under the funding of those programmes;

8.   *Also requests* the Secretary-General to continue to promote, in co-operation with the national committees concerned, joint activities in the field of aging and youth, particularly as they relate to intergenerational matters, especially during the International Youth Year, to be observed in 1985;

9.   *Further requests* the Secretary-General to ensure a well co-ordinated system-wide response in implementing the provisions of the Plan of Action;

10.   *Urges* the United Nations Fund for Population Activities, in co-operation with all organizations responsible for international population assistance, to continue its assistance, within its mandate, in the field of aging, particularly in developing countries;

11.   *Invites* the regional commissions and specialized agencies to continue contributing to the realization of the objectives of the Plan of Action;

12.   *Invites* the non-governmental organizations concerned to join in the co-operative effort to implement the Plan of Action and accomplish its objectives;

13.   *Requests* the Secretary-General to report to the General Assembly at its fortieth session on the measures taken to implement the present resolution, taking into consideration the first review of the Plan of Action to be undertaken by the Commission for Social Development at its twenty-ninth session in 1985;

14.   *Decides* to include in the provisional agenda of its fortieth session the item entitled "Question of aging".

General Assembly resolution 39/25

23 November 1984   Meeting 71   Adopted without vote

Approved by Third Committee (A/39/660) without vote, 13 November (meeting 37); 30-nation draft (A/C.3/39/L.13); agenda item 90.

Sponsors: Austria, Bangladesh, Bolivia, Chile, China, Colombia, Costa Rica, Cyprus, Dominican Republic, Egypt, Germany, Federal Republic of, Greece, Guatemala, Jordan, Mali, Malta, Morocco, Pakistan, Philippines, Romania, Samoa, Senegal, Somalia, Spain, Sudan, Suriname, Thailand, United States, Uruguay, Venezuela.

Meeting numbers. GA 39th session: 3rd Committee 16-23, 27, 37; plenary 71.

REFERENCES
[1]A/39/147. [2]YUN 1983, p. 947, GA res. 38/27, 22 Nov. 1983. [3]YUN 1982, p. 1184. [4]*Report of the International Conference on Population, 1984, Mexico City, 6-14 August 1984* (E/CONF.76/19), Sales No. E.84.XIII.8 & corrigenda. [5]YUN 1980, p. 1019, GA res. 35/129, 11 Dec. 1980.

Chapter XXI

Refugees and displaced persons

During 1984, the Office of the United Nations High Commissioner for Refugees (UNHCR) faced the challenge of attaining durable solutions to refugee problems in the midst of seriously deteriorating situations in some parts of the world and the onset of a major emergency in Africa. In November, the High Commissioner issued a special appeal in response to a refugee crisis in four drought-stricken countries—the Central African Republic, Ethiopia, Somalia and the Sudan.

The Second International Conference on Assistance to Refugees in Africa (ICARA II) (Geneva, 9-11 July) examined some 128 projects valued at $362 million designed to help African host countries. The Conference emphasized the complementarity between refugee aid and development assistance, urging that refugee projects be integrated into the development process. The first such conference had been held in 1981.

Major assistance programmes were maintained, notably in Pakistan, which had the largest refugee population in the world, and in South-East Asia, where Indo-Chinese refugees continued to arrive. Resettlement in third countries remained the primary solution for the latter, some 68,500 of whom were resettled in 1984. In Somalia and the Sudan, care and maintenance programmes were accompanied by local integration activities until late 1984, when attention had to be diverted to emergency relief. Local integration activities were also carried out in Central America, Mexico, Uganda and Zaire.

Assistance to Palestine refugees continued as in past years under the United Nations Relief and Works Agency for Palestine Refugees in the Near East (UNRWA) (see p. 335).

At the thirty-fifth session of the Executive Committee of the UNHCR Programme (Geneva, 8-18 October), the High Commissioner reported that 42 per cent of the 1985 UNHCR budget would be devoted to durable solutions through voluntary repatriation, local integration and resettlement, adding that UNHCR would like that percentage to be much higher.

Violations of the physical safety of refugees continued. The ninth meeting of the Sub-Committee of the Whole on International Protection (Geneva, 3, 4, 11 and 15 October) discussed military and armed attacks on refugee camps.

In December, the General Assembly urged States to ensure the safety of refugees and asylum-seekers and to support the High Commissioner in pursuing durable solutions to the refugee problem (resolution 39/140); emphasized the vital importance of the complementarity of refugee aid and development assistance (39/139); and called for emergency assistance to returnees and displaced persons in Chad (39/106) and Ethiopia (39/105), as well as refugees in Djibouti (39/107), Somalia (39/104) and the Sudan (39/108) and student refugees in southern Africa (39/109).

The Assembly called on the Group of Governmental Experts on International Co-operation to Avert New Flows of Refugees to work expeditiously to complete its review of the problem (39/100). It expressed the hope that the 1985 Assembly would adopt a declaration on the human rights of individuals who were not citizens of the country in which they lived (39/103).

The International Conference on Population (Mexico City, 6-14 August 1984) invited States that had not done so to accede to the international instruments concerning refugees and urged Governments and international agencies to find durable solutions to refugee problems and work towards their elimination (see p. 716).

The 1984 Nansen Medal—awarded in honour of Fridtjof Nansen, the first League of Nations High Commissioner for Refugees—went to Captain Lewis M. Hiller of the United States merchant ship *Rose City* and two of his crew members, Jeff Kass and Gregg Turay, for their rescue of 85 Indo-Chinese refugees adrift in a storm in the South China Sea.

In November 1984, the United Nations Postal Administration issued commemorative stamps on the theme "A Future for Refugees" (see ADMINISTRATIVE AND BUDGETARY QUESTIONS, Chapter IV).

Topics related to this chapter. Middle East: Palestine refugees. Human rights: human rights of non-citizens.

Programme and finances of UNHCR

Programme policy

Executive Committee action. At its October 1984 session, the Executive Committee of the UNHCR Programme[1] considered various aspects of the refugee problem, among them international protection and the role of UNHCR in promoting durable solutions, assistance to refugees and their development. The Committee expressed satisfaction at the absence of new large-scale outflows of refugees but noted the continuing severity of refugee problems in various parts of the world, particularly in Africa, Asia and Central America, and urged the international community to intensify its efforts to address the root causes of those problems in appropriate international forums. It also urged the High Commissioner to continue pursuing durable solutions, notably voluntary repatriation, while calling on the international community to ensure that the needs of refugees were met.

The Committee welcomed the continued strengthening of the legal framework for international protection; nevertheless, it expressed concern at a deterioration in the protection situation and serious violations of the physical safety of refugees, including armed attacks, piracy and failure to rescue asylum-seekers in distress at sea.

Noting that in different parts of the world the principle of *non-refoulement*—under which asylum-seekers were not forcibly returned to countries where they faced persecution or death—had been violated, the Committee regretted the adoption of less liberal asylum practices and falling standards in the treatment of asylum-seekers. It recommended that States ensure that refugees were provided with documents establishing their identity and refugee status, and that asylum applicants whose applications could not be decided without delay be provided with provisional documentation to ensure their protection against expulsion or *refoulement*.

The Committee recommended that Governments co-operate with UNHCR in establishing appropriate processing mechanisms for the resettlement of refugees, and welcomed continuing co-operation between Governments and UNHCR in operation of the Orderly Departure Programme from Viet Nam (see p. 952); it also welcomed UNHCR initiatives to arrange meetings and discussion forums on resettlement planning.

It stressed the importance of providing development-oriented assistance to refugees and returnees in developing countries, as the best means of helping them to support themselves. UNHCR, in implementing such assistance, continued to co-operate with other United Nations organizations (see p. 941).

UNHCR also continued its co-operation with the Organization of African Unity (OAU), the Organization of American States, the Intergovernmental Committee for Migration, liberation movements, and some 300 non-governmental organizations (NGOs). The Executive Committee urged further strengthening of that co-operation.

GENERAL ASSEMBLY ACTION

Following consideration of the 1984 report of the High Commissioner,[(2)] the General Assembly, on the recommendation of the Third (Social, Hu-

manitarian and Cultural) Committee, adopted on 14 December resolution 39/140 without vote.

Report of the United Nations High Commissioner for Refugees

The General Assembly,

Having considered the report of the United Nations High Commissioner for Refugees on the activities of his Office, as well as the report of the Executive Committee of the Programme of the High Commissioner on the work of its thirty-fifth session, and having heard the statement made by the High Commissioner on 12 November 1984,

Recalling its resolution 38/121 of 16 December 1983,

Reaffirming the purely humanitarian and non-political character of the activities of the Office of the High Commissioner,

Deeply concerned that refugees and displaced persons of concern to the High Commissioner continue to face distressingly serious problems in all parts of the world,

Stressing the fundamental importance of the High Commissioner's international protection function and the need for States to co-operate with the High Commissioner in the exercise of this essential function, particularly in view of the continued and persistent violations of the basic rights of persons of concern to his Office,

Welcoming the additional accessions by States to the 1951 Convention and the 1967 Protocol relating to the Status of Refugees,

Particularly concerned that in various regions the safety and welfare of refugees and asylum-seekers continue to be seriously jeopardized on account of military or armed attacks, acts of piracy and other forms of brutality,

Emphasizing that voluntary repatriation or return remains the most desirable solution to problems of refugees and displaced persons of concern to the High Commissioner,

Emphasizing also the importance for the international community to continue to provide assistance and resettlement opportunities for those refugees for whom no other durable solution may be in sight, particularly in regions where countries of first refuge continue generously to receive refugees arriving by land or by sea,

Noting with deep appreciation the valuable support extended by many Governments to the High Commissioner in carrying out his humanitarian task,

Noting with satisfaction the positive results achieved by the Second International Conference on Assistance to Refugees in Africa, held at Geneva from 9 to 11 July 1984, as part of a continuing process of increasing international interest in the situation of refugees in Africa and support for those refugees,

Welcoming the progress made by the High Commissioner in improving the management of his Office and urging him to pursue his efforts in this direction in line with the relevant resolutions of the General Assembly and decisions of the Executive Committee of the Programme of the High Commissioner,

Taking note of the decision of the Executive Committee on the inclusion of Arabic, Chinese and Spanish among the official languages of the Executive Committee,

1. *Commends* the United Nations High Commissioner for Refugees and his staff for the dedicated and efficient manner in which they continue to discharge their responsibilities;

2. *Strongly reaffirms* the fundamental nature of the High Commissioner's function to provide international pro-

tection and the need for Governments to continue to co-operate fully with his Office in order to facilitate the effective exercise of this function, in particular by acceding to and fully implementing the relevant international and regional refugee instruments and by scrupulously observing the principles of asylum and *non-refoulement*;

3. *Condemns* all violations of the rights and safety of refugees and asylum-seekers, in particular those perpetrated through military or armed attacks against refugee camps and settlements and other forms of brutality and by the failure to rescue asylum-seekers in distress at sea;

4. *Urges* all States, in co-operation with the Office of the High Commissioner and other competent international bodies, to take all measures necessary to ensure the safety of refugees and asylum-seekers;

5. *Also urges* all States to support the High Commissioner in discharging his responsibility to pursue durable solutions to the problem of refugees and displaced persons of concern to his Office, primarily through voluntary repatriation or return, including assistance to returnees, as appropriate, or, wherever appropriate, through integration in countries of asylum or resettlement in third countries;

6. *Expresses deep appreciation* for the valuable material and humanitarian response of many receiving countries, in particular those developing countries that, despite serious economic crises and limited resources, continue to admit, on a permanent or temporary basis, large numbers of refugees and displaced persons of concern to the Office of the High Commissioner, and, reaffirming the principle of international solidarity and burden-sharing, urges the international community to assist receiving countries in order to enable them to cope with the additional burden created by their presence;

7. *Notes with satisfaction* the initiatives taken by the High Commissioner in developing the concept of development-oriented assistance to refugees and returnees, wherever appropriate, and urges him to pursue those efforts in co-operation with interested Governments, as well as with the World Bank, the United Nations Development Programme and other developmental organizations, including non-governmental organizations;

8. *Commends* all States that facilitate the attainment of durable solutions and contribute generously to the High Commissioner's programmes;

9. *Notes with appreciation* the support consistently given to the High Commissioner by agencies of the United Nations system, as well as intergovernmental and non-governmental organizations, in carrying out his humanitarian task and requests the High Commissioner to continue to co-ordinate his efforts with those agencies and organizations;

10. *Calls upon* all States to promote durable solutions and to contribute generously to the High Commissioner's humanitarian programmes in order to assist persons of concern to the High Commissioner in a spirit of international solidarity and burden-sharing.

General Assembly resolution 39/140

14 December 1984   Meeting 101   Adopted without vote

Approved by Third Committee (A/39/709) without vote, 28 November (meeting 53); 43-nation draft (A/C.3/39/L.37); agenda item 100 (a).
Sponsors: Argentina, Australia, Austria, Bangladesh, Belgium, Benin, Bolivia, Canada, Central African Republic, Comoros, Congo, Costa Rica, Cyprus, Den-

mark, Djibouti, Dominican Republic, Egypt, Finland, France, Gambia, Germany, Federal Republic of, Greece, Honduras, Iceland, Italy, Japan, Lesotho, Madagascar, New Zealand, Nicaragua, Norway, Pakistan, Philippines, Portugal, Senegal, Sierra Leone, Somalia, Sudan, Sweden, Thailand, United States, Venezuela, Zaire.
Financial implications. 5th Committee, A/39/804; S-G, A/C.3/39/L.52, A/C.5/39/63.
Meeting numbers. GA 39th session: 3rd Committee 36, 38-41, 47, 50, 53; 5th Committee 41; plenary 101.

Financial and administrative questions

In 1984, total UNHCR expenditure amounted to $444.8 million. Of that total, voluntary funds expenditure represented $444.1 million, including $346 million under General Programmes and $98.1 million under Special Programmes. Voluntary funds expenditure had increased by approximately 10 per cent over 1983, reflecting additional refugee assistance requirements, particularly in Africa and the Americas.

Total income for 1984 was $388.9 million.

Contributions

In 1984, contributions from government sources totalled some $292 million, while intergovernmental organizations provided an additional $26.7 million, mostly in food, and NGOs assisted in cash and kind valued at $5.5 million.

Appeals by the Commissioner for contributions to Special Programmes continued in response to specific needs,[3] those related, for example, to returnees to Ethiopia, Kampuchea and the Lao People's Democratic Republic, the Orderly Departure Programme from Viet Nam, the Refugee Education Account and the South-East Asia Anti-Piracy Programme.

The UNHCR Executive Committee[1] approved in October a target of $374,288,500 (not including the $10 million Emergency Fund) for 1985 General Programmes. Having noted a possible reduction in funding for those Programmes, the Committee asked that governmental and non-governmental agencies implement assistance projects in the most efficient way possible. It also took note of the considerable increase in resources devoted to durable solutions in Africa, commending the High Commissioner's efforts to promote voluntary repatriation.

The Committee reaffirmed the universal character of the refugee problem and the need for more widespread financial support for UNHCR programmes. It urged Governments to make increased contributions to the 1985 General Programmes and to make them as early as possible.

At a meeting on 16 November 1984 of the *Ad Hoc* Committee of the General Assembly for the Announcement of Voluntary Contributions to the 1985 Programme of UNHCR,[4] pledges totalling $126,653,763 were made.

CONTRIBUTIONS PAID OR PLEDGED TO UNHCR ASSISTANCE PROGRAMMES, 1984

(as at 31 December 1984; in US dollar equivalent)

State	1984 payment or pledge	State	1984 payment or pledge	State	1984 payment or pledge
Algeria	50,000	Jamaica	550	Thailand	20,000
Australia	10,381,036	Japan	43,842,680	Togo	1,064
Austria	108,907	Jordan	3,000	Tunisia	4,459
Bahamas	4,500	Kenya	576	Turkey	22,322
Bahrain	41,257	Kuwait	566,316	United Kingdom	18,764,696
Bangladesh	1,000	Lao People's Democratic Republic	6,000	United Republic of Tanzania	3,200
Barbados	500	Lebanon	10,000	United States	111,703,299
Belgium	1,552,691	Liechtenstein	20,972	Venezuela	40,000
Botswana	1,351	Luxembourg	44,037	Viet Nam	834
Brazil	25,000	Madagascar	4,348	Yugoslavia	60,000
Burma	10,000	Malawi	3,969	Zaire	1,500
Burundi	1,269	Malaysia	30,000	Zambia	5,032
Cameroon	6,383	Mexico	55,037	Zimbabwe	38,337
Canada	12,559,172	Monaco	1,047		
Chile	20,000	Morocco	10,000	Subtotal	291,934,611
China	700,000	Netherlands	7,367,581		
Colombia	18,000	New Zealand	430,392	*Intergovernmental organizations*	
Costa Rica	3,264	Norway	13,359,827		
Cyprus	6,613	Oman	716,000	European Economic Community	26,307,437
Democratic Kampuchea	500	Pakistan	3,751	United Nations Trust Fund	
Denmark	9,935,304	Panama	500	for Southern Africans	200,000
Djibouti	2,000	Philippines	6,000	United Nations Decade	
Egypt	7,302	Portugal	100,000	for Women	13,323
Finland	2,073,985	Republic of Korea	30,000	United Nations Trust Fund	
France	2,225,923	Rwanda	4,826	for Population Activities	46,526
Germany, Federal Republic of	30,722,140	San Marino	3,000	United Nations Trust Fund for	
Ghana	12,987	Saudi Arabia	4,220,526	Humanitarian Assistance to	
Greece	82,543	Senegal	3,000	Displaced Persons in Pakistan	165,362
Guyana	6,666	Singapore	5,000	UNICEF	4,965
Holy See	2,500	Spain	256,000		
Iceland	30,200	Sri Lanka	2,009	Subtotal	26,737,613
India	18,780	Sudan	2,404		
Indonesia	4,000	Swaziland	1,633	*Private sources*	5,497,291
Ireland	456,129	Sweden	11,068,359		
Israel	20,000	Switzerland	5,831,363	Total	324,169,515
Italy	2,155,263	Syrian Arab Republic	12,000		

SOURCE: A/40/5/Add.5.

Accounts of voluntary funds for 1983

The audited financial statements on the voluntary funds administered by UNHCR for the year ended 31 December 1983 showed a total expenditure of $398 million and total income of $377.8 million.

After examining the financial statements, the Board of Auditors, in its report[5] transmitted to the General Assembly in June 1984, recommended that efforts be intensified to collect long-outstanding pledges and that cash balances in the field offices be kept to the minimum possible level. Noting that in certain cases procurement was uneconomical, the Board recommended that contracts be awarded to the lowest acceptable bidders in accordance with United Nations practice. For proper monitoring of project activities, it recommended that periodic reports be obtained in time for review; financial closure of completed projects be expedited; and efforts be made to enforce the stipulations of agreements with executing agencies and operating partners and to ensure timely completion of project activities and evaluation reports.

Commenting on the Board's audit in a September report,[6] the Advisory Committee on Administrative and Budgetary Questions (ACABQ) urged that closer attention be paid to all aspects of the procurement process, both to ensure full compliance with the applicable rules and to achieve optimum use of resources.

In October,[1] the Executive Committee of the UNHCR Programme took note of the accounts and the reports of the Board of Auditors and ACABQ, and further noted with appreciation efforts to improve financial planning and control.

The General Assembly by resolution 39/66 accepted the financial report and the audit opinions of the Board, concurred with ACABQ's observations, and requested that the High Commissioner take remedial action as might be required by the Board.

REFERENCES

[1]A/39/12/Add.1. [2]A/39/12 (E/1984/61). [3]A/AC.96/641 & Corr.1. [4]A/AC.224/SR.1. [5]A/39/5/Add.5 & Add.5/Corr.1. [6]A/39/510.

Activities for refugees

Assistance

In 1984, UNHCR's primary objective remained the promotion of durable solutions for refugees, while continuing to respond to requests for emergency assistance and to pursue care and maintenance programmes (food, shelter, water, health services, education) for refugees for whom no immediate solution could be devised.[1] The High Commissioner could allocate up to $10 million annually from his Emergency Fund, providing that the amount made available for a single emergency did not exceed $4 million.

A total of $9,760,787 was obligated from the Emergency Fund during the year, with a significant part of those funds used in Africa. Some $2.4 million was used to finance assistance to Ethiopians arriving in eastern Sudan, and $3.1 million was allocated for refugees from Chad in the Central African Republic. Allocations also were made to Mozambican refugees in Swaziland ($100,000) and Zimbabwe ($954,103) and to Angolan refugees in Zaire ($1,334,310) and Zambia ($137,442). Elsewhere, $940,000 was allocated for refugees from Irian Jaya (Indonesia) in Papua New Guinea, with smaller amounts being utilized to assist displaced Lebanese in Cyprus ($64,957), Spain ($100,000) and the Syrian Arab Republic ($150,000) and within Lebanon itself ($500,000).

To facilitate planning and rapid action, UNHCR launched a series of profiles containing basic data on countries receiving large numbers of refugees. The UNHCR *Handbook for Emergencies*, published in English in 1982 and in French in 1983, was issued in Spanish. Demand for the English and French language editions remained high. A total of 119 UNHCR/WHO health kits, 30 field kits and 26 office kits were distributed, and a nutrition kit was added to the specialized emergency equipment for staff members and operational partners.

Care and maintenance programmes in 1984 amounted to approximately 59 per cent of total General Programmes expenditures, down from 65.3 per cent in 1983. The largest single programme of that type continued to be for Afghan refugees in Pakistan, for which $59.2 million was obligated. Some $48.3 million was obligated for Indo-Chinese refugees in East and South-East Asia, of which $24.3 million was for refugees in Thailand, pending a more durable solution, which in most cases was resettlement outside the region. A total of $22.7 million was allocated for Ethiopian refugees in Somalia and $20 million for activities in Central America, although significant progress towards more durable local settlement programmes was made in Costa Rica, Mexico and Nicaragua.

More than $103.4 million, or some 30 per cent of General Programmes funds, was used for voluntary repatriation, local integration in the country of first asylum or resettlement. In South-East Asia, following voluntary repatriation of 148 persons from Thailand to the Lao People's Democratic Republic early in 1984, the programme was temporarily suspended. Movements resumed in December and by the end of the year 204 persons had been repatriated, bringing to 2,603 the number voluntarily repatriated since the start of the programme in 1980. A special programme of assistance to Ethiopian returnees was almost fully implemented by the end of 1984, except for one agricultural project in Hararghe Province which, due to severe drought, was in need of support for another planting season. The project had provided some $17.1 million in food and other aid to 120,000 returnees. The voluntary repatriation of Ethiopian refugees from Djibouti continued throughout 1984, except for the period between January and April when damage to the Djibouti–Dire Dawa railway caused a suspension. In Latin America, repatriations to Argentina and Chile continued.

Expenditure on local settlement activities in 1984 amounted to some $87 million, 25 per cent of General Programmes expenditures. Local settlement projects were carried out in the Central African Republic, Ethiopia, Mexico, Somalia, Uganda and Zaire.

Some $11.8 million was spent on resettling refugees during 1984. Approximately 68,500 Indo-Chinese refugees were resettled; of those, 33,000 were Vietnamese, 26,000 Kampuchean and 9,500 Lao. An additional 29,000 Vietnamese were reunited with family members abroad under the Orderly Departure Programme from Viet Nam. Many countries admitted Indo-Chinese rescued on the high seas by vessels flying their flags. A new scheme, Rescue at Sea Resettlement Offers, was elaborated in 1984 to share more equitably the burden of resettling persons rescued at sea; it was to become operational in 1985. Meanwhile, the Disembarkation Resettlement Offers scheme, which had been in operation for a number of years, continued to ensure the resettlement of persons rescued by vessels flying flags of convenience or of countries not able to accept refugees.

At its October 1984 session,[2] the UNHCR Executive Committee stressed the importance of development-oriented assistance to refugees and returnees in developing countries and of their integration into the development process; commended the High Commissioner and concerned Governments for action taken in that direction with UNDP, the World Bank and other organizations; recommended that Governments co-operate with UNHCR in establishing mechanisms for refugee resettlement, with full regard for international protection and material assistance; and called on States to facilitate admission, especially of disabled refugees and of those in emergency situations.

UNHCR EXPENDITURE IN 1984 BY COUNTRY OR AREA*

(in thousands of US dollars)

Country or area	Local settlement	Resettlement	Voluntary repatriation	Relief† and other assistance	Total
AFRICA					
Algeria	3,534.5	—	4.2	5.0	3,543.7
Angola	5,693.1	—	12.0	345.1	6,050.2
Botswana	1,105.8	31.9	5.4	89.5	1,232.6
Burundi	858.9	0.5	15.0	100.0	974.4
Cameroon	741.9	4.1	1.9	—	747.9
Djibouti	2,651.9	7.8	472.7	175.5	3,307.9
Egypt	2,054.9	190.7	—	83.5	2,329.1
Ethiopia	7,568.0	99.6	5,380.4	376.1	13,424.1
Kenya	2,572.8	27.5	10.0	709.0	3,319.3
Lesotho	584.3	30.0	—	68.1	682.4
Nigeria	891.6	—	0.5	100.0	992.1
Rwanda	4,202.6	4.2	1.7	41.4	4,249.9
Senegal	705.9	187.9	2.6	103.1	999.5
Somalia	27,211.6	2.7	—	15,245.0	42,459.3
Sudan	35,823.6	293.8	350.0	10,823.4	47,290.8
Swaziland	1,093.4	11.4	—	180.0	1,284.8
Uganda	2,307.4	5.4	1,981.1	1,127.0	5,420.9
United Republic of Tanzania	5,215.4	—	80.0	80.7	5,376.1
Zaire	6,928.2	35.0	782.9	1,293.1	9,039.2
Zambia	2,112.8	8.1	153.6	980.7	3,255.2
Zimbabwe	177.7	—	—	2,897.6	3,075.3
Other	3,715.1	11.2	1,198.8	5,215.8	10,140.9
Follow-up on recommendations of Pan-African Conference on Refugees	—	—	—	224.2	224.2
Subtotal	117,751.4	951.8	10,452.8	40,263.8	169,419.8
AMERICAS					
Argentina	2,665.6	47.4	359.9	876.0	3,948.9
Costa Rica	1,920.0	13.0	72.7	5,566.2	7,571.9
Honduras	4,343.2	—	100.0	7,598.8	12,042.0
Mexico	656.7	40.6	575.2	8,475.4	9,747.9
Nicaragua	1,248.3	10.1	66.5	418.5	1,743.4
Peru	425.0	8.0	0.3	62.0	495.3
Other northern Latin America	3,407.5	76.1	52.9	337.2	3,873.7
Other north-western South America	602.9	289.0	44.5	499.1	1,435.5
Other southern Latin America	428.3	2.8	75.0	211.7	717.8
North America	11.7	19.6	89.7	187.9	308.9
Subtotal	15,709.2	506.6	1,436.7	24,232.8	41,885.3
EAST AND SOUTH ASIA AND OCEANIA					
Australia	—	—	5.9	—	5.9
China	4,126.0	59.2	—	11.9	4,197.1
Hong Kong	—	721.1	—	3,983.9	4,705.0
Indonesia	—	903.9	—	3,268.2	4,172.1
Lao People's Democratic Republic	129.5	0.2	630.0	—	759.7
Malaysia	1,395.2	640.0	—	5,106.8	7,142.0
Philippines	—	393.6	3.8	8,671.0	9,068.4
Thailand	—	3,042.7	35.3	28,357.3	31,435.3
Viet Nam	905.5	2,320.0	—	9.0	3,234.5
Other	575.3	537.3	1.1	11,348.9	12,462.6
Subtotal	7,131.5	8,618	676.1	60,757	77,182.6
EUROPE					
Austria	251.4	336.4	24.2	72.7	684.7
Belgium	51.9	5.3	72.7	63.1	193.0
France	346.4	61.5	236.2	31.9	676.0
Germany, Federal Republic of	223.6	2.6	54.9	565.0	846.1
Greece	615.7	234.5	—	333.3	1,183.5
Italy	418.2	1,279.6	105.2	997.5	2,800.5
Portugal	376.9	1.0	2.6	74.6	455.1
Spain	156.6	2.7	732.8	150.0	1,042.1
Turkey	59.4	709.9	—	23.6	792.9
United Kingdom	88.9	0.7	10.7	167.6	267.9
Yugoslavia	14.0	220.1	4.2	1,516.9	1,755.2
Other	187.0	75.9	128.4	352.5	743.8
Subtotal	2,790.0	2,930.2	1,371.9	4,348.7	11,440.8

Country or area MIDDLE EAST AND SOUTH-WEST ASIA	Local settlement	Resettlement	Voluntary repatriation	Relieft and other assistance	Total
Cyprus	7,006.5	5.6	—	421.8	7,433.9
Iran	7,502.0	23.5	—	149.5	7,675.0
Lebanon	119.4	7.9	—	515.0	642.3
Pakistan	1,337.8	197.6	—	84,312.6	85,848.0
Western Asia	329.8	233.1	—	231.1	794.0
Subtotal	16,295.5	467.7	—	85,630.0	102,393.2
GLOBAL AND REGIONAL	885.7	379.0	143.6	1,020.0	2,428.3
Total	160,563.3	13,853.3	14,081.1	216,252.3	404,750.0

*Not including expenditure for programme support and administration.
†Including donations in kind, such as food.
SOURCE: A/40/12.

To meet the needs of refugees, UNHCR continued to co-operate with other United Nations organizations. For example, the International Labour Organisation (ILO) promoted small-scale enterprise development and income-generating activities in refugee settlements. In Zaire, under a joint ILO/UNHCR project, 40 self-sustaining refugee co-operatives were set up in the Bas-Fleuve region. Activities included fishing, pisciculture, baking, tailoring, carpentry, shoemaking, soap-making, handicrafts, blacksmithing and marketing of agricultural produce.

The United Nations Children's Fund provided support to programmes related to emergency rehabilitation, water supply and sanitation, health care and education for refugee children. Collaboration with the United Nations Development Programme (UNDP) was strengthened by establishing joint guidelines for co-operation in situations requiring longer-term assistance to refugees.

A joint mission was organized by UNHCR and the World Bank in November 1984 to examine an income-generating project for refugee areas in Pakistan. The World Health Organization (WHO) continued to supply medicines to refugees in Africa; joint appointments of UNHCR-WHO health co-ordinators were made for refugee programmes in Pakistan and Somalia. The United Nations Fund for Population Activities co-operated with UNHCR in family planning programmes for Indo-Chinese families in Hong Kong.

The World Food Programme (WFP) continued to meet most of the basic food needs of refugees in many areas of the world.

Africa

There were about 4 million African refugees and returnees in several geographical areas. The largest concentration was in the Horn of Africa and the eastern and central parts of the Sudan, while other concentrations were to be found in central Africa (Rwanda, the southern part of the Sudan, Uganda and Zaire); in a region involving Burundi, Rwanda, the United Republic of Tanzania and Zaire; and in southern Africa. The refugee and returnee problem in West Africa most often concerned individual cases of asylum and voluntary repatriation.

An overwhelming majority of refugees were from rural areas, though the proportion of those coming from or arriving in urban and semi-urban areas was increasing. Demographically, the two main groups within the African refugee population were women and children and young adult single males.

Direct international assistance to rural refugees was usually provided in organized settlements or camps in rural areas on land made available by host Governments. Through such programmes, the essential needs for shelter, health and sanitation services, water and transport were covered. In addition, several hundred thousand refugees had spontaneously settled in rural areas of host countries.

All of the African countries that hosted refugees and returnees were at a stage of development where they had great difficulty meeting the basic needs, including infrastructural services, of their nationals. Several were classified as least developed countries. Nevertheless, as a matter of both official government policy and traditional African hospitality, refugees and returnees were most often readily accepted. Local resources, however meagre, were shared with them, and usually UNHCR and other humanitarian agencies were called in to provide additional assistance.

In 1984, UNHCR voluntary fund expenditures in Africa amounted to some $178.2 million, of which $131.6 million was obligated under General Programmes and $46.6 million under Special Programmes.

Continuing drought, particularly in the Horn of Africa and the Sudan, affected UNHCR's efforts to achieve durable solutions for refugees. In late 1984, the High Commissioner launched a special appeal for emergency relief programmes to ensure the survival of refugees in the Central African Republic, Ethiopia, Somalia and the Sudan. More than $100 million was required.

The refugee situation in the Sudan changed dramatically during the latter part of 1984. In eastern Sudan, the harvest failed in the 20 Ethiopian refugee settlements where food self-sufficiency had been expected to be attained. With WFP, UNHCR had to revert to full food aid for the 130,000 refugees in the settlements. That was coupled at the end of the year with the arrival from Ethiopia of up to 3,000 persons a day in search of food, medical care and water as well as a haven from civil disorder. In western Sudan, there was an influx of 60,000 persons from Chad to whom emergency assistance was given.

Governments, WFP and UNHCR renewed their efforts to provide a regular food-supply flow into Somalia, which continued to host a large refugee population; emergency measures, including additional food, were provided to 50,000 new refugees in the north-west and Gedo regions. In the central, south-western and western regions of Uganda, a large number of Rwandese refugees were displaced by unrest and moved into settlements such as Nakivale, Oruchinga and Kyaka. A new settlement—Kyaka II—was established for some 17,000 refugees and 22,000 head of cattle.

South African refugees continued to be assisted by UNHCR (see TRUSTEESHIP AND DECOLONIZATION, Chapter I). More than 27,500 of them continued to reside in Angola, Botswana, Lesotho, Mozambique, Swaziland, the United Republic of Tanzania, Zambia and Zimbabwe, which, with Malawi, made up the Southern African Development Co-ordination Conference (SADCC). Assistance included subsistence allowances, scholarships and the promotion of self-sufficiency, either in rural settlements or through individual income-generating activities. The southern African liberation movements recognized by OAU received further support through provision of agricultural equipment for their farms in Angola and the United Republic of Tanzania. Some 70,000 Namibian refugees in Angola, Zambia and other countries also received UNHCR assistance.

A resolution on refugees in Africa was adopted by the OAU Council of Ministers (Addis Ababa, Ethiopia, 27 February–5 March).[3] Reaffirming the need for the OAU Commission of Fifteen on Refugees to undertake missions to OAU member States overburdened by the refugee problem, and to mobilize international assistance to refugees and the host countries, the Council appealed to OAU members to enact amnesty laws ensuring the safety of those returning from exile, and decided to include an item on the root causes of refugees in Africa in the agenda of its next session. The Council called on SADCC to organize an international conference on the refugee problem in southern Africa.

At its October 1984 session,[2] the Executive Committee of the UNHCR Programme took note of the considerable increase in resources devoted by the High Commissioner to durable solutions in Africa, and in particular commended his efforts to promote voluntary repatriation.

The General Assembly, in resolution 39/8 on co-operation between the United Nations and OAU, urged Member States and regional and international organizations to continue supporting African refugee programmes and to assist host countries. The Assembly also adopted resolutions on ICARA II; refugees in Djibouti, Somalia and the Sudan; displaced persons in Chad and Ethiopia; and South African student refugees (see below).

*Second International Conference
on Assistance to Refugees in Africa*

Conference preparations. In the six months prior to ICARA II, preparations focused on completing the required documentation and mobilizing support for its objectives. Two principal documents—one providing a summary of needs,[4] the other giving background information on each affected country, a detailed description of needs and project outlines[5]—were prepared.

Responsible for the overall direction of the preparatory work was a Steering Committee composed of representatives of the Secretary-General, OAU, UNHCR and UNDP. The inclusion of UNDP underscored the special emphasis on the role of development in support of ongoing refugee programmes and in the search for longer-term solutions. The Committee was assisted by a technical team—personnel from OAU, the United Nations Secretariat, UNDP, UNHCR and the Food and Agriculture Organization of the United Nations—which visited host countries to consult with them on the nature and extent of assistance required to strengthen their capacity to cope with the refugee situation.

To mobilize support for ICARA II, the Steering Committee held several meetings with the regional groups, representatives of the United Nations system and NGOs. Committee members also visited traditional and potential donor countries.

Fourteen countries (Angola, Botswana, Burundi, Ethiopia, Kenya, Lesotho, Rwanda, Somalia, Sudan, Swaziland, Uganda, United Republic of Tanzania, Zaire, Zambia) indicated that they wished to present their needs to the Conference. The technical team identified 128 projects designed to strengthen and expand infrastructure to benefit refugees, returnees and the local population in the areas concerned.

More specifically, they would aim at developing human resources through basic education, skills training and provision of health and sanitation facilities; strengthening the agricultural base and increasing productivity; and improving transport. Their implementation would require $362.3 million over a three- to five-year period. Also submitted were proposals for additional assistance in the amount of $10.9 million to supplement the UNHCR regular programme for 1984; these proposals were made in response to the General Assembly's 1982 call for additional assistance for relief, rehabilitation and resettlement programmes.[6]

The Secretary-General, also in response to that 1982 resolution,[6] submitted in March 1984[5] a report containing a detailed description of needs, project outlines and background information on the refugee situation in Africa. Annexed was a comprehensive report by the Steering Committee, describing the refugee and returnee burden on host countries and the need for continuing and additional assistance to enable Governments to carry out relief, rehabilitation and resettlement programmes, as well as assistance required to strengthen the social and economic infrastructure of host countries. The Secretary-General observed that special emphasis was placed on the need to intensify efforts to achieve lasting solutions to existing refugee situations. Assistance programmes needed to be complemented by increased political and developmental efforts to achieve such solutions, he added. A report on the situation in each of the 14 countries seeking assistance was provided.

Six additional countries—Benin, Cameroon, the Central African Republic, Chad, Djibouti and Guinea—had signified their need for assistance; the last five were visited in September/October by the technical team which reported its findings in November.[7]

The OAU Council of Ministers, at its February/March session,[3] reaffirmed the urgent need for a concerted effort to pursue lasting solutions to the refugee problems in Africa, and urged all invited Governments to participate in ICARA II at the highest level. The Council stressed that, in order to facilitate lasting solutions, assistance for refugees must be development-oriented. It stressed the need for assistance to countries of asylum as well as to those of origin, and appealed for additional resources. It also appealed to UNDP and development agencies to incorporate assistance to refugees and returnees in their development programmes.

The UNDP Governing Council, in a decision of 29 June,[8] requested the UNDP Administrator to support the Conference and the follow-up to it (see p. 468). The Administrator established in 1984 two UNDP trust funds to assist refugees and to combat poverty and hunger in Africa.

Conference action. ICARA II was held at Geneva from 9 to 11 July,[9] attended by 107 participating States, as well as five States and some 145 governmental and non-governmental organizations in the capacity of observer (for participants and officers, see APPENDIX III). Several Governments announced support in cash, in kind or in principle towards the projects presented to the Conference. Contributions amounting to $18,531,828 were pledged to help cover the High Commissioner's programme for Africa, including relief, rehabilitation and resettlement programmes in response to the Assembly's 1982 call.[6] In addition, some $6,241,000 was committed without specification as to its allocation.

The Conference adopted a Declaration and Programme of Action by acclamation. In the Declaration, it recognized that caring for refugees was a global responsibility. It stated that, in dealing with the African refugee situation, special account must be taken of regionally relevant legal instruments, such as the Charter and resolutions of OAU and the 1969 OAU Convention Governing the Specific Aspects of Refugee Problems in Africa.[10] The Conference stated that the recommendations of the 1979 Arusha Conference on the Situation of Refugees in Africa,[11] remained important for protecting and assisting African refugees and that the 92 recommendations adopted in March 1983 at a meeting between OAU and voluntary agencies constituted a realistic approach to the refugee problem in Africa. In the Conference's view, the entry into force of the 1981 OAU Charter of Human and People's Rights[12] would contribute to reducing the number of refugees. Everything possible must be done to prevent the causes of refugee flows and resolve the problem of African refugees, the Conference stated. International co-operation to that effect must be strengthened, and States must refrain from measures aggravating refugee problems. Essential conditions for repatriation, the best means of promoting permanent solutions, should be established, either through amnesty laws or respect for the principle of *non-refoulement*. Where voluntary return was not feasible, conditions should be created for temporary settlement or integration of refugees within the country of asylum. For solutions to last, assistance to refugees must aim at their participation, productivity and durable self-reliance; should be development-oriented; and in least developed countries should take into account the needs of local people as well.

The Programme of Action covered voluntary repatriation, local settlement, infrastructural assistance, the process and structures for providing assistance, and Conference follow-up. It pointed out that further fact-finding missions, accurate data collection and feasibility studies might be necessary. The Secretary-General, in co-operation with OAU, was requested to monitor follow-up, and Governments were requested to keep him informed of any action taken relating to Conference projects.

Reporting to the General Assembly on ICARA II results and follow-up in November/December 1984,[13] as requested in the Programme of Action, the Secretary-General stated that pledges or contributions in cash or kind had been received from 27 countries—Austria, Belgium, Canada, Chile, China, Cyprus, Denmark, Finland, Federal Republic of Germany, India, Indonesia, Italy, Japan, Liechtenstein, Malaysia, Netherlands, New Zealand, Norway, Oman, Portugal, Saudi Arabia, Sweden, Switzerland, Turkey, United Kingdom, United States, Yugoslavia.

GENERAL ASSEMBLY ACTION

On 14 December, on the recommendation of the Third Committee, the General Assembly adopted without vote resolution 39/139.

Second International Conference on Assistance to Refugees in Africa

The General Assembly,

Recalling its resolutions 37/197 of 18 December 1982 and 38/120 of 16 December 1983,

Having considered the report of the Secretary-General on the Second International Conference on Assistance to Refugees in Africa, held at Geneva from 9 to 11 July 1984,

Welcoming the results obtained by the Conference, in particular the adoption of the Declaration and Programme of Action, which provide the international community with a collective strategy to achieve lasting solutions,

Gravely concerned at the persistent and serious problem of large numbers of refugees on the African continent,

Aware of the economic and social burden borne by African countries of asylum on account of the presence of these refugees and its consequences for their national development and of the heavy sacrifices made by them, despite their limited resources,

Recognizing the universal collective responsibility of sharing the urgent and overwhelming burden of the problem of African refugees through effective mobilization of resources to meet the urgent and long-term needs of the refugees and to strengthen the capacity of countries of asylum to provide adequately for the refugees while they remain in those countries, as well as to assist the countries of origin in the rehabilitation of voluntary returnees,

Emphasizing the vital importance of the complementarity between refugee aid and development assistance,

Noting with satisfaction the wide participation of Member States, specialized agencies and intergovernmental and non-governmental organizations, and the commitments and pledges made at the Conference,

1. *Expresses its appreciation* to the Secretary-General of the United Nations, the Secretary-General of the Organization of African Unity, the United Nations High Commissioner for Refugees and the Administrator of the United Nations Development Programme for their commendable effort in organizing the Second International Conference on Assistance to Refugees in Africa;

2. *Endorses* the Declaration and Programme of Action of the Second International Conference on Assistance to Refugees in Africa;

3. *Expresses its deep appreciation* to African host countries, which are the biggest donors, for their generous contribution and continuous efforts to alleviate the plight of refugees in spite of their critical economic situation;

4. *Expresses once again its appreciation* to the international community and, in particular, to all donor countries, specialized agencies, regional organizations and intergovernmental and non-governmental organizations for their support and initial response to the projects submitted to the Conference;

5. *Urges* the international community to maintain the momentum created by the Conference and to translate into reality the projects submitted as well as the principles in the Declaration and Programme of Action agreed upon by the Conference;

6. *Emphasizes* the vital importance of the complementarity of refugee aid and development assistance and of achieving durable solutions to the problems of refugees in Africa through the voluntary repatriation or local integration of refugees and the necessity of providing assistance for the strengthening of the social and economic infrastructures of African countries receiving refugees and returnees;

7. *Requests* the United Nations High Commissioner for Refugees to continue to keep the situation of refugees in Africa under constant review with a view to providing adequate humanitarian assistance for relief and expanded durable solutions;

8. *Calls upon* all pertinent organizations of the United Nations system, as well as relevant regional, intergovernmental and non-governmental organizations, to lend their support, within their respective spheres of competence, to the realization of the goals of the Conference;

9. *Requests* the Secretary-General, in accordance with the Declaration and Programme of Action, to monitor, in consultation and close co-operation with the Organization of African Unity and, in particular, the United Nations High Commissioner for Refugees and the United Nations Development Programme, the follow-up to the Conference;

10. *Also requests* the Secretary-General to report to the General Assembly at its fortieth session, through the Economic and Social Council, on the implementation of the present resolution.

General Assembly resolution 39/139

14 December 1984   Meeting 101   Adopted without vote

Approved by Third Committee (A/39/709) without vote, 26 November (meeting 50); draft by Cameroon, for African Group (A/C.3/39/L.38); agenda item 100 *(b)*.
Meeting numbers. GA 39th session: 3rd Committee 36, 38-41, 47, 50; plenary 101.

The United States and Israel declared that, while they had joined in the consensus on the text, they did not accept every provision contained in the various documents and instruments referred to in the Declaration endorsed by it. In particular, they disagreed with the 1981 OAU Charter of Human and People's Rights, which they felt was gravely flawed by its call for the elimination of zionism.

In a related action, the Assembly, in resolution 39/8 on co-operation between the United Nations and OAU, expressed appreciation to the United Nations Secretary-General, the OAU Secretary-General, the High Commissioner and the UNDP Administrator for organizing ICARA II, and invited Governments and organizations to implement the Declaration and Programme of Action.

Chad

On 9 October 1984, Chad reiterated before the General Assembly its appeal for international emergency aid to help it cope with the consequences of the exodus of population and livestock from the north, east and centre to other parts of the country, caused by civil strife and drought and deterioration of the environment.

Appeals for aid to Chad were also made by the Secretary-General, the latest on 1 November (see p. 467).

As follow-up to ICARA II (see p. 943), a technical team visited the country to help formulate infrastructural assistance programmes to cope with the refugee situation.

GENERAL ASSEMBLY ACTION

On 14 December, on the recommendation of the Third Committee, the General Assembly adopted without vote resolution 39/106.

Emergency assistance to returnees and displaced persons in Chad

The General Assembly,

Gravely concerned by the unprecedented drought which is wreaking havoc in Chad at the present time, compounding the already precarious food and health situation in that country,

Conscious that the large number of voluntary returnees and displaced persons as a result of the war and the drought in Chad poses a serious problem of integrating them into society,

Considering that, in addition to being a land-locked country and one of the least developed countries, Chad is placed in a particularly difficult situation by reason of the war and the drought,

Bearing in mind the many appeals made by the Government of Chad, in particular that made on 9 October 1984 to the General Assembly, and by humanitarian organizations regarding the gravity of the food and health situation in Chad,

Recalling the urgent appeal of the Secretary-General dated 1 November 1984 for international emergency assistance to the voluntary returnees and displaced persons in Chad afflicted by natural disasters,

1. *Endorses* the appeals made by the Government of Chad and the Secretary-General concerning emergency assistance to the voluntary returnees and displaced persons in Chad;

2. *Invites* all States and intergovernmental and non-governmental organizations to support by generous contributions the efforts being made by the Government of Chad to assist and resettle the voluntary returnees and displaced persons;

3. *Takes note with approval* of the action undertaken by the various bodies of the United Nations system and the specialized agencies with a view to mobilizing emergency humanitarian assistance to the voluntary returnees and displaced persons in Chad;

4. *Requests* the United Nations High Commissioner for Refugees and the United Nations Disaster Relief Co-ordinator to mobilize, in accordance with their respective mandates, emergency humanitarian assistance to the voluntary returnees and displaced persons in Chad;

5. *Requests* the Secretary-General, in co-operation with the United Nations Disaster Relief Co-ordinator and the United Nations High Commissioner for Refugees, to report to the General Assembly at its fortieth session on the implementation of the present resolution.

General Assembly resolution 39/106

14 December 1984   Meeting 101   Adopted without vote

Approved by Third Committee (A/39/700) without vote, 6 December (meeting 63); 37-nation draft (A/C.3/39/L.41/Rev.1); agenda item 12.

Sponsors: Burkina Faso, Cameroon, Cape Verde, Central African Republic, Chad, Chile, China, Colombia, Comoros, Democratic Kampuchea, Djibouti, Egypt, France, Gabon, Germany, Federal Republic of, Greece, Guinea, Guinea-Bissau, Haiti, Honduras, Indonesia, Italy, Ivory Coast, Japan, Mali, Niger, Nigeria, Pakistan, Saudi Arabia, Senegal, Somalia, Sudan, Thailand, Togo, United States, Vanuatu, Zaire.

Meeting numbers. GA 39th session: 3rd Committee 63; plenary 27, 101.

In resolution 39/195, the Assembly requested the Secretary-General to monitor, in close collaboration with the agencies concerned, the humanitarian needs, particularly in the area of food and health, of the people of Chad displaced by war and drought. It further requested him to mobilize special humanitarian assistance for persons who had suffered as a result of the war and drought and for the resettlement of displaced persons.

Djibouti

The High Commissioner, in a September 1984[14] report submitted to the General Assembly in accordance with its December 1983 request,[15] stated that in Djibouti the limited water supply, further diminished by the current drought, had hindered the local integration of rural refugees from Ethiopia and that voluntary repatriation had remained the most viable of the standard durable solutions. By the end of June, some 14,000 of an estimated 35,000 refugees had left Djibouti and returned to Ethiopia where they were registered in UNHCR reception centres. Meanwhile, efforts continued to improve conditions for refugees in camps in the Djibouti districts of Ali Sabieh and Dikhil. Assistance measures consisted of food distribution, construction of communal facilities, improvements in supply and storage of potable water and upgrading of sanitary conditions.

The Government, through its Office national d'assistance aux réfugiés et sinistrés (ONARS), continued to act as UNHCR's main implementing partner. Most basic food items were donated through WFP and the Catholic Relief Services. A number of voluntary agencies assisted UNHCR and ONARS with specific aspects of the assistance programme, including primary education, vocational training, language classes, adult education, building work, agricultural activities and medical care. In view of conditions in the country and the voluntary repatriation programme, it was not deemed feasible to present projects relating to local integration of refugees to ICARA II, the High Commissioner stated.

However, as follow-up to ICARA II (see p. 943), a technical team sent by the Secretary-General visited the country to help develop projects relating to the strengthening of infrastructure in areas with refugees.

GENERAL ASSEMBLY ACTION

On 14 December, on the recommendation of the Third Committee, the General Assembly adopted without vote resolution 39/107.

Humanitarian assistance to refugees in Djibouti
The General Assembly,

Recalling its resolutions 35/182 of 15 December 1980, 36/156 of 16 December 1981, 37/176 of 17 December 1982 and 38/89 of 16 December 1983 on humanitarian assistance to refugees in Djibouti,

Having heard the statement made on 12 November 1984 by the United Nations High Commissioner for Refugees,

Having considered with satisfaction reports of the United Nations High Commissioner for Refugees on humanitarian assistance to refugees in Djibouti,

Appreciating the determined and sustained efforts made by the Government of Djibouti, despite its modest economic resources and limited means, to cope with the pressing needs of the refugees,

Aware of the social and economic burden placed on the Government and people of Djibouti as a result of the presence of refugees and of the consequent impact on the development and infrastructure of the country,

Deeply concerned about the continuing plight of the refugees and displaced persons in the country, which has been aggravated by the devastating effects of the prolonged drought,

Noting with appreciation the steps taken by the Government of Djibouti, in close co-operation with the High Commissioner, to implement adequate, appropriate and lasting solutions in respect of the refugees in Djibouti,

Also noting with appreciation the concern and unremitting efforts of the Office of the United Nations High Commissioner for Refugees, the United Nations Development Programme, the United Nations Children's Fund, the World Health Organization, the World Food Programme, the Food and Agriculture Organization of the United Nations, the intergovernmental and non-governmental organizations and the voluntary agencies which have worked closely with the Government of Djibouti in the relief and rehabilitation programme for the refugees in that country,

1. *Takes note with appreciation* of the reports of the United Nations High Commissioner for Refugees on humanitarian assistance to refugees in Djibouti and appreciates his efforts to keep their situation under constant review;

2. *Welcomes* the steps taken by the Government of Djibouti, in close co-operation with the High Commissioner, to implement adequate, appropriate and lasting solutions in respect of the refugees in Djibouti;

3. *Requests* the High Commissioner to mobilize the necessary resources to implement lasting solutions in respect of the refugees in Djibouti;

4. *Urges* the High Commissioner to continue to take the necessary measures to ensure that adequate, appropriate and lasting solutions are implemented to assist the refugees in Djibouti, in co-operation with Member States, intergovernmental and non-governmental organizations and the voluntary agencies concerned, with a view to mobilizing the necessary assistance to enable the Government of Djibouti to cope effectively with the refugee problem, which has

been particularly aggravated by the debilitating effects of the prolonged drought;

5. *Appreciates* the assistance provided thus far by Member States, the specialized agencies, intergovernmental and non-governmental organizations and voluntary agencies to the relief and rehabilitation programmes for the refugees and displaced persons in Djibouti;

6. *Calls upon* all Member States, the organizations of the United Nations system, the specialized agencies, intergovernmental and non-governmental organizations and voluntary agencies to continue to support the efforts constantly being made by the Government of Djibouti to cope with the current needs of the refugees and the other victims of drought in that country;

7. *Requests* the High Commissioner, in close co-operation with the Secretary-General, to report to the General Assembly at its fortieth session on the implementation of the present resolution.

General Assembly resolution 39/107

14 December 1984   Meeting 101   Adopted without vote

Approved by Third Committee (A/39/700) without vote, 6 December (meeting 63); 76-nation draft (A/C.3/39/L.42/Rev.1); agenda item 12.

Sponsors: Algeria, Argentina, Austria, Bahrain, Bangladesh, Benin, Botswana, Burkina Faso, Burundi, Cameroon, Cape Verde, Central African Republic, Chad, China, Comoros, Congo, Democratic Yemen, Djibouti, Egypt, Equatorial Guinea, Ethiopia, France, Gambia, Ghana, Guinea, Guinea-Bissau, Honduras, India, Indonesia, Italy, Ivory Coast, Japan, Jordan, Kenya, Kuwait, Lebanon, Lesotho, Liberia, Libyan Arab Jamahiriya, Madagascar, Malawi, Mali, Mauritania, Morocco, Niger, Nigeria, Oman, Pakistan, Panama, Philippines, Qatar, Rwanda, Sao Tome and Principe, Saudi Arabia, Senegal, Sierra Leone, Singapore, Somalia, Sri Lanka, Sudan, Swaziland, Syrian Arab Republic, Thailand, Togo, Trinidad and Tobago, Tunisia, Turkey, Uganda, United Arab Emirates, United Republic of Tanzania, United States, Yemen, Yugoslavia, Zaire, Zambia, Zimbabwe.

Meeting numbers. GA 39th session: 3rd Committee 36, 63; plenary 101.

By resolution 39/200, the Assembly appealed for financial, technical and material assistance for Djibouti.

Ethiopia

In response to a December 1983 General Assembly resolution,[16] the Secretary-General submitted a report in September 1984[17] on assistance to displaced persons in Ethiopia. He reported that the first voluntary repatriation of Ethiopian refugees in Djibouti, under the 1983 tripartite agreement between Djibouti, Ethiopia and UNHCR,[18] had occurred between September 1983 and September 1984. There had been some 14,340 registered repatriations, 6,497 persons having returned spontaneously and 7,846 under the organized repatriation programme. All registered repatriates were eligible to receive reintegration and rehabilitation assistance for one year from their date of arrival in Ethiopia. A total of $8.2 million had been budgeted for that special assistance programme, including $2.2 million for basic food provided through WFP. Fourteen focal points had been designated along the Dire Dawa–Dewele railway and at the time of their registration the returnees were able to choose their destination. A 1980 amnesty proclamation by Ethiopia had been extended until the end of 1984.

Since March 1983, a sizeable influx of people into the Ogaden had been reported, comprising a mix of returnees and refugees. Following a UNHCR fact-finding mission, the League of Red Cross Societies was completing their registration, and an emergency assistance programme had been developed. Since May 1983, there had been an influx into the Gambela/Itang area, estimated at 47,000 refugees. A $1.1-million emergency assistance programme was initiated there in November 1983 and renewed with an additional $2.8 million for the period from April to December 1984. The number of UNHCR staff in Ethiopia was increased from 15 to 38 between 1981 and 1984.

GENERAL ASSEMBLY ACTION

On 14 December 1984, on the recommendation of the Third Committee, the General Assembly adopted without vote resolution 39/105.

Assistance to displaced persons in Ethiopia

The General Assembly,

Recalling its resolutions 35/91 of 5 December 1980, 36/161 of 16 December 1981, 37/175 of 17 December 1982 and 38/91 of 16 December 1983 and Economic and Social Council resolutions 1980/54 of 24 July 1980 and 1982/2 of 27 April 1982,

Recalling also the report of the Secretary-General, prepared pursuant to Economic and Social Council resolution 1980/8 of 28 April 1980,

Taking note of the report of the Secretary-General on assistance to displaced persons in Ethiopia,

Having heard the statement made on 12 November 1984 by the United Nations High Commissioner for Refugees,

Recognizing the increasing number of voluntary returnees and refugees in Ethiopia,

Deeply concerned at the plight of displaced persons and voluntary returnees in the country, which has been aggravated by the devastating effect of the prolonged drought,

Aware of the heavy burden placed on the Government of Ethiopia in caring for displaced persons and victims of natural disasters, as well as for returnees and refugees,

1. *Commends* the efforts made so far by various organs of the United Nations and the specialized agencies in mobilizing humanitarian assistance to assist the efforts of the Government of Ethiopia;

2. *Appeals* to Member States and to international organizations and voluntary agencies to render maximum material, financial and technical assistance to the Government of Ethiopia in its efforts to provide relief and rehabilitation to displaced persons, voluntary returnees and refugees in Ethiopia;

3. *Requests* the United Nations High Commissioner for Refugees to intensify his efforts in mobilizing humanitarian assistance for the relief, rehabilitation and resettlement of voluntary returnees, refugees and displaced persons in Ethiopia;

4. *Requests* the Secretary-General, in co-operation with the High Commissioner, to apprise the Economic and Social Council, at its second regular session of 1985, of the implementation of the present resolution and to report thereon to the General Assembly at its fortieth session.

General Assembly resolution 39/105

14 December 1984   Meeting 101   Adopted without vote

Approved by Third Committee (A/39/700) without vote, 6 December (meeting 63); 67-nation draft (A/C.3/39/L.34), orally revised; agenda item 12.

Sponsors: Afghanistan, Algeria, Angola, Argentina, Austria, Bangladesh, Benin, Botswana, Bulgaria, Burkina Faso, Central African Republic, China, Comoros, Congo, Cuba, Cyprus, Czechoslovakia, Democratic Yemen, Djibouti, Egypt, Equatorial Guinea, Ethiopia, Gambia, German Democratic Republic, Ghana, Greece, Guinea, Guinea-Bissau, Guyana, Hungary, India, Iran, Italy, Ivory Coast, Japan, Kenya, Lao People's Democratic Republic, Lesotho, Liberia, Madagascar, Malawi, Mali, Mauritania, Mongolia, Morocco, Mozambique, Nicaragua, Niger, Nigeria, Pakistan, Philippines, Rwanda, Sao Tome and Principe, Senegal, Sierra Leone, Sri Lanka, Suriname, Swaziland, Togo, Trinidad and Tobago, Ukrainian SSR, USSR, Viet Nam, Yemen, Yugoslavia, Zaire, Zambia.

Meeting numbers. GA 39th session: 3rd Committee 36, 63; plenary 101.

According to amendments proposed by Somalia, later withdrawn,[19] the Assembly would have spoken of "genuine and voluntary returnees" and deleted references to "refugees".

In resolution 39/201, the Assembly requested the Secretary-General to continue mobilizing assistance for the victims of drought in Ethiopia who wished to resettle.

Somalia

In pursuance of a December 1983 Assembly resolution,[20] the High Commissioner prepared a review of the needs of refugees in Somalia. In his report, submitted to the Assembly in September 1984,[21] he stated that Somalia was attempting to cope with an estimated 700,000 refugees while facing critical economic and social problems arising from weak economic infrastructure, limited natural resources and a difficult international economic environment. The refugees were located in 36 widely scattered camps in four regions—Hiran, Gedo, the northwest and lower Shebelle. Approximately 60 per cent of the refugees were children under 15 years of age, 30 per cent women and 10 per cent men.

The search for durable solutions remained a top priority. Somalia had reaffirmed its position that voluntary repatriation remained the most appropriate long-term solution, but that in the mean time a programme of local settlement would be formulated through which the refugees would be able to attain a degree of self-sufficiency impossible in the camps. To implement the local settlement programme, a new organizational structure had been established comprising a steering committee, a technical unit and executing agencies. The steering committee was chaired by a representative of the Somali National Refugee Commission and composed of representatives of the Somali Ministry of Planning, UNDP and UNHCR. It would be supported by the technical unit consisting of a rural settlements specialist, an agronomist, a water development expert and a physical planner. The steering committee had met twice and examined two projects submitted by the Government: salt production in Tokoshi village, in the north-west, for 1,000 families, and agricultural land settlement in Furjano in the lower Shebelle region for 3,000 families. An estimated $128.3 million would be required for assistance in 1985, an increase of some $2.6 million over 1984.

In preparing for ICARA II (see p. 942), a technical team visited Somalia, as well as 13 other African countries, to help it identify projects for strengthening infrastructure in areas with refugees.

On 14 December 1984, on the recommendation of the Third Committee, the General Assembly adopted without vote resolution 39/104.

Assistance to refugees in Somalia
The General Assembly,

Recalling its resolutions 35/180 of 15 December 1980, 36/153 of 16 December 1981, 37/174 of 17 December 1982 and 38/88 of 16 December 1983 on the question of assistance to refugees in Somalia,

Having considered the report of the United Nations High Commissioner for Refugees on assistance to refugees in Somalia, in particular section IV of that report,

Taking note of the report of the Secretary-General on the Second International Conference on Assistance to Refugees in Africa, held at Geneva from 9 to 11 July 1984,

Deeply concerned that the refugee problem in Somalia has not yet been resolved,

Aware of the additional burden imposed by the new influx of refugees and the consequent urgent need for further international assistance,

Aware of serious shortfalls in the provision of food assistance, which have resulted in critical ration restrictions and extreme hardship in refugee camps in Somalia,

Recognizing from the recommendations contained in the report of the High Commissioner that there remains an urgent need for increased assistance in the provision of food, water and medicine, the strengthening of health and educational facilities in the refugee camps and the expansion of the number of self-help schemes and small-scale farming and settlement projects necessary for the promotion of self-reliance among the refugees,

Aware of the continued consequences of the social and economic burden placed on the Government and people of Somalia as a result of the continued presence of refugees and the consequent impact on national development and the infrastructure of the country,

1. *Takes note* of the report of the United Nations High Commissioner for Refugees;

2. *Expresses its appreciation* to the Secretary-General and the High Commissioner for their continued efforts to mobilize international assistance on behalf of the refugees in Somalia;

3. *Takes note with satisfaction* of the assistance rendered to refugees in Somalia by various Member States, the Office of the United Nations High Commissioner for Refugees, the World Food Programme, the United Nations Children's Fund and other concerned intergovernmental and non-governmental organizations;

4. *Appeals* to Member States, international organizations and voluntary agencies to render maximum material, financial and technical assistance to the Government of Somalia in its efforts to provide all necessary assistance to the refugees, and to fulfil the pledges undertaken at or after the Second International Conference on Assistance to Refugees in Africa to support the developmental and other essential projects which were submitted by the Government of Somalia, as a matter of urgency;

5. *Requests* the High Commissioner, in consultation with the Secretary-General, to apprise the Economic and Social Council, at its second regular session of 1985, of the refugee situation in Somalia;

6. *Also requests* the High Commissioner, in consultation with the Secretary-General, to submit to the General Assembly at its fortieth session a report on the progress achieved in the implementation of the present resolution.

General Assembly resolution 39/104

14 December 1984   Meeting 101   Adopted without vote

Approved by Third Committee (A/39/700) without vote, 6 December (meeting 63); 60-nation draft (A/C.3/39/L.32); agenda item 12.

Sponsors: Bahrain, Bangladesh, Botswana, Central African Republic, Chad, China, Colombia, Comoros, Democratic Kampuchea, Djibouti, Egypt, Gambia, Guinea, Guatemala, Guyana, Indonesia, Italy, Ivory Coast, Japan, Jordan, Kenya, Kuwait, Lebanon, Lesotho, Liberia, Madagascar, Malawi, Malaysia, Mali, Mauritania, Mauritius, Morocco, Nepal, Niger, Nigeria, Oman, Pakistan, Philippines, Qatar, Rwanda, Samoa, Saudi Arabia, Sierra Leone, Singapore, Senegal, Somalia, Sudan, Suriname, Swaziland, Syrian Arab Republic, Thailand, Togo, Trinidad and Tobago, Tunisia, Turkey, United Arab Emirates, United States, Yemen, Zaire, Zambia.

By resolution 39/205, the Assembly called for assistance to Somalia, as one of the countries in East Africa stricken by drought.

Sudan

The High Commissioner, in response to a December 1983 General Assembly resolution,[22] reported in September 1984[23] that refugees were continuing to seek asylum in the Sudan, and by the end of March had reached an estimated 699,700. Approximately 498,700 were from Ethiopia, 195,000 from Uganda, 5,000 from Zaire and 1,000 from Chad. The influx into eastern Sudan was continuing at the rate of 200 to 300 persons per day, and two new transit centres had been established for their reception and sustenance. Throughout the Sudan, more than 30 voluntary agencies were assisting refugees and in many cases complementing UNHCR resources.

The assistance programme continued to emphasize the creation of settlements in which agriculture was the main economic activity. There were 26 such settlements in eastern and 47 in southern Sudan. Progress was being made towards providing sufficient land and water for the settlements, particularly in the south. Plans were being completed by UNHCR together with ILO to implement a package of income-generating activities designed to reduce the dependence of refugees on agricultural production and the vagaries of related employment. Some 15 projects would benefit about 11,000 households and maximize the participation of female household heads. The Sudan was host to UNHCR's largest education programme for refugees; some 6,000 students were being assisted in academic, vocational and technical fields at the post-primary level. Assistance was being given to construct, upgrade or maintain eight new intermediate schools, and two refugee teacher-training programmes had been set up in the eastern region, one in English and one in Arabic.

In southern Sudan, UNHCR/UNDP co-operation aimed at integrated development for the benefit of both refugees and local inhabitants.

In addition to these assistance programmes, the Sudan presented 30 projects totalling $92.6 million to ICARA II.

GENERAL ASSEMBLY ACTION

Acting on the recommendation of the Third Committee, the General Assembly on 14 December adopted without vote resolution 39/108.

Situation of refugees in the Sudan

The General Assembly,

Recalling its resolutions 35/181 of 15 December 1980, 36/158 of 16 December 1981, 37/173 of 17 December 1982 and 38/90 of 16 December 1983 on the situation of refugees in the Sudan,

Having considered the reports of the United Nations High Commissioner for Refugees on the situation of refugees in the Sudan,

Taking note of the ever-increasing number of refugees arriving in the Sudan,

Appreciating the measures which the Government of the Sudan is taking in order to provide shelter, food, education, and health and other humanitarian services to the growing number of refugees in the Sudan,

Recognizing the heavy burden placed on the Government of the Sudan and the sacrifices it is making in caring for the refugees and the need for more international assistance to enable it to continue its efforts to provide assistance to the refugees,

Expressing its appreciation for the assistance rendered to the Sudan by Member States and intergovernmental and non-governmental organizations in support of the refugee programme,

1. *Takes note* of the report of the United Nations High Commissioner for Refugees on the progress made in the implementation of the recommendations of the inter-agency technical follow-up missions, as well as in the implementation of resolution 38/90;

2. *Commends* the measures that the Government of the Sudan is taking to provide shelter, food, education, and health and other humanitarian services to the refugees, in spite of the drought and the serious economic situation it faces;

3. *Expresses its appreciation* to the Secretary-General, the High Commissioner, donor countries and voluntary agencies for their efforts to assist the refugees in the Sudan;

4. *Recognizes* the need for development-oriented projects that would generate work opportunities and long-term livelihood for refugees and local people in affected areas, and, in this context, commends the efforts of the High Commissioner and the International Labour Office to create income-generating activities for refugees in the Sudan;

5. *Requests* the Secretary-General to mobilize the necessary financial and material assistance for the full implementation of the recommendations of the various inter-agency missions and of the projects submitted by the Government of the Sudan to the Second International Conference on Assistance to Refugees in Africa, held at Geneva from 9 to 11 July 1984;

6. *Appeals* to Member States, the appropriate organs, organizations and programmes of the United Nations, other intergovernmental and non-governmental organizations and the international financial institutions to provide the Government of the Sudan with the necessary resources for the implementation of development assistance projects in regions affected by the presence of refugees, as envisaged in the reports of the various inter-agency missions, and to strengthen its social and economic infrastructure so that essential services and facilities for refugees can be strengthened and expanded;

7. *Requests* the High Commissioner to continue co-ordination with the appropriate specialized agencies in order to consolidate and ensure the continuation of essential services to the refugees in their settlements;

8. *Requests* the Secretary-General, in consultation and co-ordination with the High Commissioner and the United Nations Development Programme, to submit to the General Assembly at its fortieth session, through the Economic and Social Council, a comprehensive report on the progress made in the implementation of the recommendations of the inter-agency technical follow-up missions and of the projects submitted by the Government of the Sudan to the Second International Conference on Assistance to Refugees in Africa, as well as on the implementation of the present resolution.

General Assembly resolution 39/108

14 December 1984   Meeting 101   Adopted without vote

Approved by Third Committee (A/39/700) without vote, 6 December (meeting 63); 78-nation draft (A/C.3/39/L.45); agenda item 12.

Sponsors: Algeria, Argentina, Bahrain, Bangladesh, Botswana, Burkina Faso, Cameroon, Canada, Cape Verde, Central African Republic, Chad, Chile, China, Comoros, Cyprus, Djibouti, Egypt, Equatorial Guinea, France, Gambia, Germany, Federal Republic of, Greece, Guinea, Guinea-Bissau, Guyana, Haiti, India, Indonesia, Iraq, Italy, Ivory Coast, Jamaica, Japan, Jordan, Kenya, Kuwait, Lebanon, Lesotho, Liberia, Madagascar, Malawi, Malaysia, Mali, Mauritania, Mauritius, Morocco, Nepal, Niger, Nigeria, Oman, Pakistan, Philippines, Qatar, Romania, Rwanda, Sao Tome and Principe, Saudi Arabia, Senegal, Sierra Leone, Singapore, Somalia, Sri Lanka, Sudan, Suriname, Swaziland, Syrian Arab Republic, Thailand, Togo, Trinidad and Tobago, Tunisia, Turkey, United Arab Emirates, United Kingdom, United States, Yemen, Zaire, Zambia, Zimbabwe.

In resolution 39/205, the Assembly urged for an assistance programme to help meet the needs of the people of the Sudan, as one of the six countries in East Africa affected by drought.

Southern African student refugees

Pursuant to a December 1983 General Assembly request,[24] the High Commissioner submitted in September 1984 a report[25] on assistance to student refugees in southern Africa between 1 July 1983 and 30 June 1984—in Botswana, Lesotho, Swaziland, Zambia and Zimbabwe.

An average of 20 refugee students were arriving monthly in Botswana from South Africa and Namibia; 25 South African and seven Namibian students were enrolled in institutions of higher education in Botswana, and 15 South African and 17 Namibian students were enrolled in secondary schools. Some 11,500 refugees, mainly South Africans, of school age were in Lesotho, about 1,300 of whom were registered with UNHCR, and received assistance. Among the 7,000 refugees in Swaziland, 210 South African students were attending educational institutions. In Zambia, 5,008 Namibians and 272 South Africans received educational assistance from UNHCR. Zimbabwe recorded the arrival of 152 South African student refugees (see TRUSTEESHIP AND DECOLONIZATION, Chapter I).

The High Commissioner noted that all of the projects to alleviate the burden imposed on asylum countries by the presence of student refugees had been successfully completed. Projects being financed by UNHCR or in co-operation with UNHCR in the period under review totalled $4.2 million.

GENERAL ASSEMBLY ACTION

On 14 December 1984, on the recommendation of the Third Committee, the General Assembly adopted without vote resolution 39/109.

Assistance to student refugees in southern Africa

The General Assembly,

Recalling its resolution 38/95 of 16 December 1983, in which it, *inter alia,* requested the Secretary-General, in co-operation with the United Nations High Commissioner for Refugees, to continue to organize and implement an effective programme of educational and other appropriate assistance for student refugees from Namibia and South Africa who have been granted asylum in Botswana, Lesotho, Swaziland and Zambia,

Having considered the report of the High Commissioner on the assistance programme to student refugees from South Africa and Namibia,

Noting with appreciation that some of the projects recommended in the report on assistance to student refugees in southern Africa have been successfully completed,

Noting with concern the continued influx into Botswana, Lesotho, Swaziland and Zambia of student refugees from South Africa, as well as from Namibia,

Convinced that the discriminatory policies and repressive measures being applied in South Africa and Namibia have led and continue to lead to a further exodus of student refugees from those countries,

Conscious of the burden placed on the limited financial, material and administrative resources of the host countries by the increasing number of student refugees,

Appreciating the efforts of the host countries to deal with their student refugee populations, with the assistance of the international community,

1. *Endorses* the assessments and recommendations contained in the report of the United Nations High Commissioner for Refugees and commends him for his efforts to mobilize resources and organize the programme of assistance for student refugees in the host countries of southern Africa;

2. *Expresses its appreciation* to the Governments of Botswana, Lesotho, Swaziland and Zambia for granting asylum and making educational and other facilities available to the student refugees, in spite of the pressure which the continuing influx of those refugees exerts on facilities in their countries;

3. *Also expresses its appreciation* to the Governments of Botswana, Lesotho, Swaziland and Zambia for the co-operation which they have extended to the High Commissioner on matters concerning the welfare of these refugees;

4. *Notes with appreciation* the financial and material support provided for the student refugees by Member States, the Office of the United Nations High Commissioner for Refugees, other bodies of the United Nations system and intergovernmental and non-governmental organizations;

5. *Requests* the High Commissioner, in co-operation with the Secretary-General, to continue to organize and implement an effective programme of educational and other appropriate assistance for student refugees from Namibia and South Africa who have been granted asylum in Botswana, Lesotho, Swaziland and Zambia;

6. *Urges* all Member States and intergovernmental and non-governmental organizations to continue contributing generously to the assistance programme for student refugees, through financial support of the regular programmes of the High Commissioner and of the projects and programmes, including unfunded projects, which were submitted to the Second International Conference on Assistance to Refugees in Africa, held at Geneva from 9 to 11 July 1984;

7. *Also urges* all Member States and all intergovernmental and non-governmental organizations to assist the countries of asylum materially and otherwise to enable them to continue to discharge their humanitarian obligations towards refugees;

8. *Appeals* to the Office of the United Nations High Commissioner for Refugees, the United Nations Development Programme and the United Nations Educational, Scientific and Cultural Organization, as well as other international and non-governmental organizations, to continue providing humanitarian and development assistance to expedite the settlement of student refugees from South Africa who have been granted asylum in Botswana, Lesotho, Swaziland and Zambia;

9. *Calls upon* agencies and programmes of the United Nations system to continue co-operating with the Secretary-General and the High Commissioner in the implementation of humanitarian programmes of assistance for the student refugees in southern Africa;

10. *Requests* the High Commissioner, in co-operation with the Secretary-General, to continue to keep the matter under review, to apprise the Economic and Social Council, at its second regular session of 1985, of the current status of the programmes and to report to the General Assembly at its fortieth session on the implementation of the present resolution.

General Assembly resolution 39/109

14 December 1984   Meeting 101   Adopted without vote

Approved by Third Committee (A/39/700) without vote, 6 December (meeting 64); 42-nation draft (A/C.3/39/L.54); agenda item 12.

Sponsors: Algeria, Angola, Bahamas, Botswana, Burkina Faso, Burundi, Cameroon, China, Congo, Djibouti, Egypt, Ethiopia, Gambia, Ghana, Guinea-Bissau, Indonesia, Ivory Coast, Kenya, Liberia, Lesotho, Madagascar, Malawi, Mali, Morocco, Mozambique, Nigeria, Philippines, Senegal, Sierra Leone, Singapore, Somalia, Sudan, Suriname, Swaziland, Togo, Trinidad and Tobago, Uganda, United Republic of Tanzania, Yugoslavia, Zaire, Zambia, Zimbabwe.

Meeting numbers. GA 39th session: 3rd Committee 61, 64; plenary 101.

The Americas and Europe

UNHCR obligations in the Americas and Europe totalled $57.4 million in 1984, of which $54.9 million was under General Programmes and $2.5 million under Special Programmes.[1]

The Americas

During 1984, voluntary repatriation movements to Argentina and Chile continued.

The number of refugees in Central America and Mexico increased only slightly, from some 330,000 to 338,000, about 103,200 of whom were assisted by UNHCR. Efforts to integrate refugees in rural areas were pursued in Belize, Costa Rica, Honduras, Mexico, Nicaragua and Panama. Measures aimed at urban integration were undertaken in Costa Rica, the Dominican Republic and Panama.

In Honduras, some 19,500 Salvadorian and 500 Guatemalan refugees continued to receive assistance in camps near the western border, notably in Colomoncagua, Mesa Grande and El Tesoro. Honduras reversed a decision to transfer those refugees from the border area to the northern part of the country, requiring that UNHCR care and maintenance assistance continue. Approximately 15,500 Nicaraguan refugees of Indian origin continued to receive local integration assistance. Some 3,700 other Nicaraguan refugees were benefiting from UNHCR care and maintenance assistance in two small villages in the area of Danli. It was expected that most of the refugees would become self-sufficient in regard to food requirements in 1985.

In Mexico, nearly 26,500 Guatemalan refugees continued to receive care and maintenance despite a difficult logistical situation. During the latter part of 1984, Mexico and UNHCR began to establish local settlements for some 16,500 Guatemalan refugees.

At its October 1984 session,[2] the Executive Committee of the UNHCR Programme noted the emergence of new prospects for durable solutions in Central America and Mexico through local settlement and voluntary repatriation and requested the High Commissioner and States concerned to continue exploring and promoting such solutions.

Europe

The flow of asylum-seekers into Western Europe continued to increase in 1984, particularly from developing countries and certain countries in Eastern Europe. The number of asylum-seekers totalled some 103,500, compared to about 100,000 the previous year. The countries receiving the most asylum-seekers continued to be the Federal Republic of Germany and France; the influx into the former almost doubled to 35,300 and that into the latter increased marginally to 15,900. Sweden was third, taking some 14,000 persons. In relation to its population, Switzerland again received the highest percentage of refugees in Europe.

An increasing reluctance on the part of many European Governments to accept refugees and persons in refugee-like situations was noted. Sometimes, restrictive measures were taken to curb the flow. To discourage economic migrants from utilizing the asylum procedure, Governments applied such deterrents as prohibition from working and reduction of social benefits while applications were being examined. Preoccupied with domestic economic difficulties and the increasing burden of asylum-

seekers, certain Governments were unwilling to maintain their traditionally generous admission criteria. That trend coincided with a decrease in admission of refugees by the traditional resettlement countries. As a result, refugees awaiting resettlement became more apparent in first-asylum countries— Austria, Greece, Italy, Turkey and Yugoslavia.

A contact group of government, UNHCR and NGO representatives, established following the September 1983 seminar on the integration of refugees in Europe,[26] met twice in 1984 to follow up on the seminar's recommendations. The group made proposals for a legal and institutional framework for refugee integration, including mobilizing public opinion and promoting the employment and self-employment of refugees. It suggested that UNHCR prepare a note on significant developments in refugee integration in each country.

At its October 1984 session,[2] the Executive Committee noted with deep regret that restrictive practices were being followed with respect to the granting of asylum, the determination of refugee status and the treatment of asylum-seekers and refugees. It expressed satisfaction that despite those trends States were continuing to grant asylum to large numbers of refugees and to ensure that they were treated in accordance with international humanitarian standards.

East and South Asia and Oceania

By the end of 1984, the number of Indo-Chinese refugees in camps and centres in asylum countries in East and South Asia and Oceania stood at 160,217, of whom 36,117 were boat people. That represented the lowest number of registered refugees in the region since 1977. The largest refugee population was in Thailand, which hosted 82,094 Lao, 41,619 Kampucheans and 4,726 Vietnamese. Other countries and territories providing temporary asylum to significant numbers of refugees included Hong Kong, Indonesia, Japan, Macau, Malaysia, the Philippines and Singapore. In addition, two refugee processing centres, at Bataan in the Philippines and Galang in Indonesia, were providing temporary accommodation to nearly 16,000 Indo-Chinese who had been accepted for resettlement and were in transit. There were also some 276,000 Indo-Chinese refugees in China and an estimated 21,000 receiving UNHCR assistance in Viet Nam.

In China, the planned phasing-out of assistance to the 276,000 Indo-Chinese refugees settled on State farms in various provinces continued; at the end of 1984, only some 56,000 refugees were still receiving assistance. Some 1,200 Kampucheans, who were considered to be self-sufficient, chose to remain in the Lao People's Democratic Republic, following repatriation of the majority of Kampuchean refugees; some 21,000 UNHCR-assisted Kampuchean refugees in Viet Nam had not reached self-sufficiency.

Assistance to refugees in the East Malaysian State of Sabah aimed at socio-economic integration through the improvement of housing, construction of schools and further development of counselling services to deal with refugee needs. Following the arrival in Papua New Guinea of some 10,000 refugees from the province of Irian Jaya, Indonesia, UNHCR launched an emergency programme in camps along the border, providing food, water, shelter, medicines and domestic supplies.

During the year, $71.6 million was obligated for assistance to refugees in East and South Asia and Oceania under General Programmes and $10.2 million under Special Programmes. Of that, some $53.2 million was used for Indo-Chinese refugees.

In October,[2] the High Commissioner told the Executive Committee that there had been little progress in voluntary repatriation in South-East Asia. He had reached agreement with Thailand on the basic conditions for repatriation, but obstacles still existed to any major organized repatriation to Kampuchea and, although repatriation to the Lao People's Democratic Republic had been going on for some time, it had recently encountered obstacles. Viet Nam had informed him that its situation would not currently permit the return of significant numbers of refugees, but that individual applications would be considered on a case-by-case basis. He was encouraged by the success of the Orderly Departure Programme from Viet Nam and by the conclusion of a new arrangement with Thailand to extend the Anti-Piracy Programme for another year. He hoped that UNHCR appeals, made jointly with the International Maritime Organization to shipowners and masters not to turn a blind eye when they came across a refugee boat in distress, would continue to be heard.

The Executive Committee[2] welcomed the continuing co-operation between Governments and UNHCR concerning the operation of the Orderly Departure Programme.

In an October report on the situation in Kampuchea,[27] the Secretary-General said that during the past five years assistance programmes had channelled a substantial amount of aid to the Kampuchean people. The Kampucheans who had sought refuge along the Thai-Kampuchean border and those in the Khao-I-Dang UNHCR holding centre remained dependent on assistance. The year had again been one of much difficulty for the United Nations Border Relief Operation, mainly as a result of armed border incidents.

During the year, the Secretary-General received a number of communications related to incidents on the common borders of Democratic Kampuchea, Thailand and Viet Nam, which also dealt with the Indo-Chinese refugee problem (see p. 214).

Middle East and South-West Asia

In 1984, total voluntary funds expenditure in the Middle East and South-West Asia was $104.3 million, of which $68.7 million was obligated under General Programmes and $35.5 million under Special Programmes.

An estimated 2.3 million Afghans in Pakistan represented the largest concentration of refugees in the world. UNHCR shifted its emphasis in 1984 from care and maintenance assistance towards self-help and self-reliance, including projects to provide training and employment. Training projects were being funded by UNHCR and implemented by ILO and the Federal Republic of Germany in Baluchistan and the North-West Frontier province. A UNHCR–World Bank project to provide employment and income for refugees as well as the local population was also being implemented in those areas. Relocation by Pakistan of part of the refugee population from the North-West Frontier to the Punjab progressed slowly; by the end of 1984, approximately 90,000 refugees were registered at Kot Chandana in Mianwali district. A new site was developed in nearby Darratang, which was to accommodate an additional 15,000 refugees.

The number of Afghan refugees in Iran was estimated at 1.8 million, of whom more than 50 per cent were living in Khorasan and Sistan-Baluchistan provinces. In October, a UNHCR office was established at Teheran. During 1984, $7.5 million was obligated in support of programmes implemented by the Council for Afghan Refugees in the areas of health, nutrition, water and sanitation, infrastructure, household and personal equipment, transport, agriculture, training and self-help activities.

UNHCR continued to provide emergency assistance to some 100,000 families uprooted in Lebanon. During the first part of 1984, $500,000 was allocated for the purchase and transport of basic relief supplies. Despite precarious circumstances, the UNHCR regional office in Beirut continued to provide assistance to some 2,900 refugees.

In the Syrian Arab Republic, UNHCR provided relief items for Lebanese and Palestinians not registered with UNRWA who had taken refuge in that country and were residing in the Sitti Zeinab camp.

In Cyprus, UNHCR continued to co-ordinate aid to persons displaced as a result of the 1974 events[28] (see p. 251). It also assisted some 1,750 Ethiopian refugees of Eritrean origin residing in the Al Khaukha camp on the Red Sea coast of Yemen.

Refugee protection

During 1984, the exercise of the High Commissioner's international protection functions encountered serious difficulties in different areas of the world due to the absence of readily available and adequate durable solutions. Violations of the physical safety of refugees continued; refugees suffered injury and death through military or armed attacks on refugee camps, abduction and pirate attacks at sea.

Acts of piracy continued against asylum-seekers in the South China Sea, although there was an encouraging decline in the percentage of boats attacked. Of the boats arriving in Thailand and Malaysia, 34 per cent were attacked in 1984 compared with 43 per cent in 1983. However, the level of violence in such attacks remained high; during 1984, 130 abductions were reported, 110 women were known to have been sexually assaulted, and there were 59 known deaths. Under the Anti-Piracy Programme established by UNHCR and Thailand,[29] which was extended for a third year through the co-operation of a number of Governments, countermeasures included sea and air patrols, follow-up investigation and prosecution of suspects, and nation-wide registration of fishing boats.

A disquieting development was a tendency on the part of several States to refuse or withdraw asylum for some refugees in order to maintain good relations with their countries of origin which were seeking to have them returned or expelled. That occurred, for example, when refugees had to leave their countries of asylum, where some had lawfully resided for a number of years, due to the conclusion of security agreements between their country of origin and neighbouring countries. When expulsion measures were adopted in such cases, UNHCR was usually given a very short period within which to secure admission for those affected to another country.

Another emerging problem was the steady buildup in the number of persons in holding centres in several countries for whom no durable solution had been found. Some had been waiting in camps for several years. Unless appropriate solutions were found, there might be adverse consequences for asylum, not to mention the suffering of the persons concerned. Some countries had adopted or maintained a blanket detention policy under which all "illegal" or "excludable" entrants were automatically detained even if their identity and the *bona fide* character of their asylum claim had been established. A few countries kept asylum-seekers in detention to deter further arrivals. A major problem encountered by UNHCR in a number of countries was lack of access to asylum-seekers in detention, who in the main were not informed of UNHCR availability to help them.

At its October 1984 session,[2] the Executive Committee of the UNHCR Programme noted that the High Commissioner's protection function had become increasingly complex and difficult, that special problems had arisen due to the changing nature of refugee movements, that the principle of *nonrefoulement* had been violated in various parts of the world, and that restrictive practices were being followed in regard to asylum, refugee status and refugee treatment. The Committee expressed satisfaction that despite those trends States continued to grant asylum to large numbers of refugees, and stressed the importance of UNHCR being granted access to asylum applicants and refugees. The Committee also took note of the discussions at the ninth meeting of the Sub-Committee of the Whole on International Protection (Geneva, 3, 4, 11 and 15 October)[30] concerning military and armed attacks on refugee camps, and requested the Chairman to continue consultations on prohibiting such attacks. The Sub-Committee considered draft conclusions on military attacks against refugee camps in southern Africa and elsewhere, but was not able to reach agreement on the text.

On the basis of conclusions of the Sub-Committee, the Executive Committee strongly recommended that the Rescue at Sea Resettlement Offers scheme proposed by the High Commissioner, in consultation with interested Governments, be implemented on a trial basis and that additional resettlement places be urgently provided, and recognized the need for continued support for the Disembarkation Resettlement Offers scheme, under which resettlement places were made available for asylum-seekers rescued by ships of open registry or of States which were unable to accept refugees for resettlement.

Also based on the Sub-Committee's conclusions, the Executive Committee recommended that asylum applicants whose applications could not be decided without delay be provided with provisional documentation sufficient to protect them against expulsion or *refoulement* until a decision was made; it also recommended that States which had not done so undertake registration and documentation programmes.

In resolution 39/140, the General Assembly strongly reaffirmed the fundamental nature of the High Commissioner's function to protect refugees and the need for Governments to continue to co-operate with his Office, in particular by scrupulously observing the principles of asylum and *non-refoulement*.

International instruments

As at 31 December 1984, the 1951 Convention relating to the Status of Refugees[31] and the 1967 Protocol[32] had been ratified or acceded to by 95 and 94 States, respectively, as a result of the 1984 accession to them by Haiti.[33]

The General Assembly, in resolution 39/140, reaffirmed the need for Governments to accede to and implement fully international and regional refugee instruments.

REFERENCES

[1]A/40/12. [2]A/39/12/Add.1. [3]A/39/207. [4]A/CONF.125/1. [5]A/CONF.125/2. [6]YUN 1982, p. 1203, GA res. 37/197, 18 Dec. 1982. [7]A/CONF.125/2/Add.1. [8]E/1984/20 (dec. 1984/18). [9]A/39/402. [10]YUN 1969, p. 470. [11]YUN 1979, p. 916. [12]YUN 1981, p. 942. [13]A/39/402/Add.1,2. [14]A/39/444. [15]YUN 1983, p. 958, GA res. 38/89, 16 Dec. 1983. [16]*Ibid.*, p. 959, GA res. 38/91, 16 Dec. 1983. [17]A/39/446. [18]YUN

1983, p. 957. [19]A/C.3/39/L.47. [20]YUN 1983, p. 960, GA res. 38/88, 16 Dec. 1983. [21]A/39/443. [22]YUN 1983, p. 961, GA res. 38/90, 16 Dec. 1983. [23]A/39/445. [24]YUN 1983, p. 961, GA res. 38/95, 16 Dec. 1983. [25]A/39/447. [26]YUN 1983, p. 963. [27]A/39/576. [28]YUN 1974, p. 256. [29]YUN 1982, p. 1217. [30]A/AC.96/649 & Add.1. [31]YUN 1951, p. 520. [32]YUN 1967, p. 769. [33]*Multilateral Treaties Deposited with the Secretary-General: Status as at 31 December 1984* (ST/LEG/SER.E/3), Sales No. E.85.V.4.

International co-operation to avert new refugee flows

The Group of Governmental Experts on International Co-operation to Avert New Flows of Refugees, established by the General Assembly in 1981[1] to review the problem and develop recommendations, held its third and fourth sessions in 1984 (New York, 26 March–6 April and 11-22 June).[2] The Group considered the background and dimension of the problem and an analysis of its mandate, including questions relating to terms, and began examining the circumstances causing new massive flows of refugees. The Group requested a renewal of its mandate, adding that it would require two 2-week sessions in 1985. It reiterated the necessity of having all experts present at its future sessions.

GENERAL ASSEMBLY ACTION

On 14 December 1984, on the recommendation of the Special Political Committee, the General Assembly adopted without vote resolution 39/100.

International co-operation to avert new flows of refugees

The General Assembly,

Reaffirming its resolutions 36/148 of 16 December 1981, 37/121 of 16 December 1982 and 38/84 of 15 December 1983 on international co-operation to avert new flows of refugees,

Having examined the report of the Group of Governmental Experts on International Co-operation to Avert New Flows of Refugees,

Considering the urgency, magnitude and complexity of the task before the Group of Governmental Experts,

Welcoming the fact that experts coming from least developed countries were enabled to participate in the 1984 sessions of the Group,

Recognizing the necessity of having all the experts participate in the future sessions of the Group,

1. *Welcomes* the report of the Group of Governmental Experts on International Co-operation to Avert New Flows of Refugees, including its recommendations, as a further constructive step in the fulfilment of its mandate;

2. *Reaffirms and extends* the mandate of the Group of Governmental Experts as defined in General Assembly resolutions 36/148 and 37/121;

3. *Calls upon* the Secretary-General, without prejudice to the rule contained in resolution 36/148, to continue to assist, as far as possible and by way of exception, the experts coming from least developed countries, appointed by the Secretary-General, to participate fully in the work of the Group of Governmental Experts, in order to fulfil its mandate;

4. *Requests* the Secretary-General to prepare a compilation of the comments and suggestions he may receive from Member States on this item;

5. *Calls upon* the Group of Governmental Experts to work expeditiously on the fulfilment of its mandate in two sessions of two weeks' duration each during 1985 and to make every effort to conclude its comprehensive review of the problem in all its aspects;

6. *Requests* the Group of Governmental Experts to submit a report on its work in time for consideration by the General Assembly at its fortieth session;

7. *Decides* to include in the provisional agenda of its fortieth session the item entitled "International co-operation to avert new flows of refugees".

General Assembly resolution 39/100

14 December 1984   Meeting 100   Adopted without vote

Approved by SPC (A/39/621) without vote, 23 October (meeting 11); 38-nation draft (A/SPC/39/L.4), orally revised; agenda item 76.

Sponsors: Australia, Austria, Bangladesh, Brunei Darussalam, Cameroon, Canada, Chad, Comoros, Costa Rica, Denmark, Djibouti, Egypt, Germany, Federal Republic of, Honduras, Iceland, Indonesia, Ireland, Italy, Japan, Jordan, Lebanon, Lesotho, Luxembourg, Malaysia, Mali, Norway, Pakistan, Philippines, Rwanda, Samoa, Senegal, Sierra Leone, Singapore, Somalia, Spain, Sudan, Thailand, Togo.

Financial implications. 5th Committee, A/39/664; S-G, A/C.5/39/31, A/SPC/39/L.6.

Meeting numbers. GA 39th session: SPC 8-11; 5th Committee 26; plenary 100.

The United States hoped that the Group would be able to formulate practical proposals to help avoid in future the suffering currently experienced by millions of refugees; it stated that, because of the urgency of the refugee problem, it had not opposed an increase in the assessed portion of the United Nations budget for that purpose.

In resolution 39/18 on the universal realization of the right of peoples to self-determination, the Assembly deplored the plight of the millions of refugees and displaced persons who had been uprooted by military intervention and acts of repression, discrimination, exploitation and maltreatment, and reaffirmed their right to return to their homes voluntarily in safety and honour. In resolution 39/117 on human rights and mass exoduses, the Assembly invited Governments to intensify their co-operation in world-wide efforts to address the problem of mass exoduses of refugees and displaced persons.

REFERENCES

[1]YUN 1981, p. 1053, GA res. 36/148, 16 Dec. 1981. [2]A/39/327 & Corr.1.

Chapter XXII

Drugs of abuse

During 1984, drug abuse continued to threaten a large segment of society and to undermine economic and social order in most parts of the world. The unprecedented dimensions of the danger to societies had led the Governments concerned to launch similarly unparalleled counter-offensives against traffickers.

The Secretary-General, in his 1984 report on the work of the Organization (p. 3), noted that the growing problem of narcotic drugs had become a major international anxiety, and that efforts were needed to arrest the traffic in and use of drugs, which had appalling effect on both individuals and societies. Steps had been taken to improve co-ordination within the United Nations system in that regard.

The General Assembly, in December, adopted a Declaration on the Control of Drug Trafficking and Drug Abuse, stating that the eradication of trafficking in narcotic drugs was the collective responsibility of all States and calling for efforts to combat the grave threat the drug abuse situation posed to societies (resolution 39/142). The Assembly also requested that the Commission on Narcotic Drugs begin preparing in 1985 a draft convention against such illicit traffic (39/141), and recommended preparation of specific technical and economic co-operation programmes for the countries most seriously affected (39/143).

Acting on the recommendations of the Commission (eighth special session, Vienna, Austria, 6-10 February), the Economic and Social Council, in May, recommended that all Governments combat cannabis abuse (resolution 1984/22), called for urgent regulation of the demand and supply of opiates for medical and scientific needs (1984/21), and urged the World Health Organization (WHO) to review certain amphetamine-like drugs for international control (1984/23).

The International Narcotics Control Board—holding two sessions at Vienna (thirty-fifth session, 14-25 May; thirty-sixth session, 8-25 October)—discussed the international drug control system for narcotic drugs, psychotropic substances and precursor materials; reported on the demand and supply of opiates for medical and scientific needs; and analysed the world situation by region and country.

The Narcotics Laboratory Section of the United Nations Division of Narcotic Drugs continued to assist national narcotics laboratories and to collect and analyse drug samples, and the United Nations Fund for Drug Abuse Control (UNFDAC) initiated a large coca control programme in South America and expanded its assistance to Asian countries.

International control

INCB report. The International Narcotics Control Board (INCB), in its 1984 annual report,[1] discussed the international control system involving the exchanges of import/export authorization documents and collection and analysis of data by the Board on the use and movement of narcotic drugs or psychotropic substances.

The Board reported that a large number of Governments had responded favourably to its March 1984 request for copies of the official forms used for exporting/importing narcotic drugs under international control, in an effort to counter the threat to the control system posed by forged or falsified import certificates.

The Board's annual technical reports—containing information submitted by Governments and INCB analyses of data—contributed to verifying whether Governments were adequately applying the provisions of the 1961 Single Convention on Narcotic Drugs and its 1972 Protocol (see below). The reports provided estimated opium production and licit requirements of narcotic drugs;[2] statistics on narcotic drugs, accompanied by an analysis of the major trends in the licit movement of such drugs;[3] and a comparative statement of estimates and statistics.[4]

Information provided to INCB by both parties and non-parties to the 1971 Convention on Psychotropic Substances (see below), on assessments of legitimate needs and quarterly trade data for such substances under international control, helped bring to light cases of attempted diversions.

The Board also noted the need to monitor the movement of precursors, essential chemicals and other substances not falling under the 1961 and 1971 Conventions that could be used in the illicit manufacture of drugs, with a view to preventing their availability for illicit use.

JIU report. By a November note,[5] the Secretary-General forwarded to the General Assembly a report of the Joint Inspection Unit (JIU) on drug abuse control activities in the United Nations system. Noting that the Assembly's past appeals for greater activity in drug control had not been followed up adequately among the agencies and organizations in the system, JIU recommended that the specialized agencies develop specific drug control programmes for consideration by their member Governments, and suggested that drug abuse control projects in developing countries should have specific conditions which would require Governments to enforce the purpose and goal of the projects.

Implementation of the
International Drug Abuse Control Strategy

Activities of the Commission on Narcotic Drugs. In 1984, the Commission on Narcotic Drugs[6] met in pursuance of a December 1983 General Assembly request[7] as a task force to review, monitor and co-ordinate the implementation of the Assembly's 1981 International Drug Abuse Control Strategy[8] and the five-year programme of action (1982-1986). It considered two reports of the Secretary-General concerning activities for the second and the third years of the programme of action—one summarizing the 1983 activities[9] and the other proposing projects for 1984.[10]

The activities under the programme aimed, among other things, at: reducing excessive stocks of licit opiate raw materials; developing and promoting effective drug law enforcement; promoting scientific research; promoting demand reduction measures; and processing relevant information.

On 9 February,[11] the Commission approved, in principle, the 1984 programme of action proposed by the Secretary-General, to be implemented to the extent possible within resources available under the United Nations regular budget, or from extrabudgetary voluntarily provided resources.

Report of the Secretary-General. In addition to an October note on action taken by the Commission on the 1984 programme of action,[12] the Secretary-General submitted to the Assembly, in November, an annual report on international co-operation in drug abuse control,[13] describing the relevant 1984 activities of 12 agencies and units within the United Nations system. The Secretary-General reported that the seventh *ad hoc* inter-agency meeting on co-ordination in matters of international drug abuse control (Geneva, 3-5 September), convened by the United Nations Division of Narcotic Drugs, noted the designation of the Under-Secretary-General for Political and General Assembly Affairs as the focal point of the three Secretariat units primarily responsible for the drug control programme—the Division of Narcotic Drugs, INCB and UNFDAC.

Various seminars, expert meetings and training workshops were organized during the year, and meetings were held, as in previous years, of the Sub-Commission on Illicit Drug Traffic and Related Matters in the Near and Middle East, and the Opera-

tional Heads of National Narcotics Law Enforcement Agencies, Far East Region (HONLEA), as well as inter-agency meetings on co-ordination of drug abuse control.

Other units or agencies reporting their activities were: the Centre for Social Development and Humanitarian Affairs, the United Nations Social Defence Research Institute, UNIDO, UNDP, ILO, FAO, UNESCO, WHO and UPU.

UN Fund for Drug Abuse Control

During 1984, UNFDAC supported more than 50 projects, including 37 projects in 22 countries, initiating large-scale coca control programmes in Bolivia, Colombia and Peru and expanding its assistance to Asian countries.[14] Programme expenditures for 1984 were estimated at $9.9 million.

CONTRIBUTIONS TO THE UNITED NATIONS FUND
FOR DRUG ABUSE CONTROL, 1984 AND 1985
(as at 31 December 1984; in US dollar equivalent)

Country or Territory	1984 payment	1985 pledge
Australia	138,195	126,050
Austria	78,011	69,767
Barbados	250	—
Belgium	17,515	—
Brazil	10,000	—
Cameroon	2,379	2,128
Canada	241,723	—
Chile	5,000	5,000
Cyprus	300	—
Denmark	14,433	13,455
Ecuador	—	2,500
Egypt	1,000	1,000
France	186,273	159,575
Germany, Federal Republic of	1,476,461	728,477
Greece	2,000	—
Hong Kong	12,791	—
Iceland	2,000	2,000
India	7,000	10,000
Indonesia	2,000	2,000
Ireland	5,000	—
Israel	4,764	—
Italy	802,368	*
Jamaica	303	235
Kenya	3,971	3,660
Madagascar	—	2,000
Malaysia	—	8,500
Malta	215	—
Mexico	659	—
New Zealand	23,652	—
Norway	728,576	677,966
Pakistan	—	1,754
Panama	1,235	2,470
Philippines	2,967	1,000
Saudi Arabia	340,000	50,000
Spain	—	36,235
Sweden	557,081	914,286
Switzerland	34,523	36,000
Turkey	9,991	15,570
United Kingdom	377,070	—
United States	1,400,000	—
Venezuela	2,000	—
Yugoslavia	—	6,000
Total	6,491,706	2,877,628

SOURCE: Accounts for the 12-month period of the biennium 1984-1985 ended 31 December 1984—Schedules of individual trust funds.

*In 1983, Italy pledged $40,880,530 to be used over a five-year period for agreed projects.

In 1984, 35 States and one Territory contributed some $6.5 million to UNFDAC and 26 countries pledged $2.9 million for 1985 (see table above).

In December, the General Assembly, by resolution 39/143 (see below), urged Member States to contribute to UNFDAC.

UN Narcotics Laboratory

The Narcotics Laboratory Section of the United Nations Division of Narcotic Drugs[15] continued to assist national narcotics laboratories by selecting/procuring basic equipment and reference books, and providing reference samples of drugs under international control. It continued to collect and analyse seized samples of traditional drugs such as heroin, cocaine and cannabis, while developing methods to identify and analyse substances newly brought under international control. The Section also produced and distributed some 450 low-cost, portable drug-identification kits to law enforcement authorities and to narcotics laboratories in 44 countries.

With financial support from UNFDAC, the Division began developing a microform/microfiche sub-collection in order to provide easier access to the ever-expanding reference collection, and the Section provided training in drug identification and analysis to 19 fellows from 13 countries.

Drug abuse

INCB, in its 1984 report,[1] observed that very few countries remained unaffected by drug abuse, which posed health hazards to individuals and threatened not only the economies and legal institutions but also the very security of some States. Authorities in many countries were placing new stress on measures to prevent abuse as well as to treat and rehabilitate abusers, and steps were being taken to advance epidemiological research to identify causes, patterns and extent of abuse. INCB cautioned against loosening legal and other restrictions in the case of so-called soft drugs, asserting that such action led to an escalation of drug abuse and of trafficking to meet the increased demand.

In a January background note[16] to the Commission on Narcotic Drugs, the Secretary-General stated that multiple drug abuse, often with alcohol, was becoming predominant. Cannabis appeared to be the most widely abused drug worldwide, and a relatively new and dangerous combination of coca paste and cannabis had been identified. The continued spread of heroin abuse was a significant trend in Western Europe, the Near and Middle East, Asia and the Far East, North America and Oceania. Cocaine abuse continued to increase in the Americas and Europe, with smoking of cocaine base reported for the first time in the latter. Abuse of amphetamines and similar substances increased in all regions and, in some countries, abuse by injection reached serious proportions. The abuse of sedative hypnotics, barbiturates and benzodiazepines, often used with alcohol or opiates, contributed to an increase in drug-related emergencies and deaths.

Youth remained the predominantly affected age group; while the majority of drug abusers continued to be men, there was an increasing tendency for women to abuse drugs. Impairment of health, personal and social dysfunction, traffic and other accidents, violence and crime remained the most frequent problems reportedly associated with drug abuse.

The Economic and Social Council, by resolution 1984/23 of 24 May on the scheduling of amphetamine-like drugs (see below), urged WHO to review those substances known for the most serious social and health consequences, and to submit its findings to the Commission in 1985.

Cannabis

INCB[1] again reaffirmed in 1984 that non-medical consumption of cannabis was illegal under the 1961 Convention.

ECONOMIC AND SOCIAL COUNCIL ACTION

On 24 May, on the recommendation of its Second (Social) Committee, the Economic and Social Council adopted resolution 1984/22 without vote.

The cannabis problem

The Economic and Social Council,

Recalling its resolution 1933(LVIII) of 6 May 1975,

Bearing in mind that the Single Convention on Narcotic Drugs, 1961, requires, *inter alia,* that the use and possession of all the substances listed in Schedule I should be confined exclusively to medical and scientific purposes,

Bearing in mind also that the Convention recommends, for the substances listed in Schedule IV, including cannabis and cannabis resin, application of all the special control measures which the contracting parties have deemed necessary in the light of the particularly dangerous properties of those substances,

Recognizing that knowledge concerning the harm that the use of cannabis and cannabis resin can cause to the human organism, especially to the brain, the lungs and cell structures, is considerably greater today than it was a few years ago,

Noting with great concern that the International Narcotics Control Board, in its two most recent annual reports, has emphasized that the abuse, illicit cultivation and trafficking of cannabis and cannabis resin are increasing in a majority of regions of the world,

Aware that in many regions of the world cannabis and cannabis resin obviously play an important role in the spread of drug abuse and in the illicit drug traffic, particularly among young persons,

1. *Recommends* that all Governments should combat systematically the abuse of cannabis and cannabis resin

and intensify national and international efforts to fight the illicit cultivation of, and traffic in, those narcotic drugs;

2. *Recommends also* that all Governments that have not yet done so should consider all appropriate measures needed to confine the cultivation and the licit use of cannabis products to medical and scientific research, in accordance with article 2, paragraph 5 *(b)*, of the Single Convention on Narcotic Drugs, 1961;

3. *Recommends further* that scientific research, especially long-term investigations into the effects of cannabis abuse on the human organism, should be continued and accelerated;

4. *Recommends,* in addition, that all Governments should maintain or adopt appropriate preventive measures concerning the hazardous consequences of cannabis abuse;

5. *Requests* the Secretary-General to inform all Governments of the present resolution, and to invite them to take action with a view to its effective implementation, in accordance with the pertinent provisions of the Single Convention on Narcotic Drugs, 1961.

Economic and Social Council resolution 1984/22

24 May 1984   Meeting 19   Adopted without vote

Approved by Second Committee (E/1984/86) without vote, 3 May (meeting 3); draft by Commission on Narcotic Drugs (E/1984/13); agenda item 13.

Supply and demand

Narcotic raw materials for licit use

In 1984, INCB[1] reported that over the past decade global demand for opiates had stabilized and was likely to remain at the current level over the next four or five years. The production of raw materials (opium or poppy straw), which for many years had continued to exceed demand, had been reduced, especially in India and Turkey and also in Australia and France, and had, for the time being, been brought approximately in line with demand. However, the existence of substantial raw material stocks, mainly in India and Turkey, remained a serious problem.

In implementation of a 1984 Economic and Social Council request (resolution 1984/21, see below), INCB asked 34 of the countries most directly concerned to propose specific measures to bring about a balance and a reduction in stocks of licit opiate raw materials. Most of them considered that reducing cultivation was the most effective way to obtain a balance, and that improving techniques for assessing demand would help producing countries in decision-making. There was wide support for a suggestion that surplus stocks of raw materials should be converted into codeine preparations for developing countries.

ECONOMIC AND SOCIAL COUNCIL ACTION

On the recommendation of its Second Committee, the Economic and Social Council, on 24 May, adopted resolution 1984/21 without vote.

Demand and supply of opiates for medical and scientific needs

The Economic and Social Council,

Recalling its resolutions 1979/8 of 9 May 1979, 1980/20 of 30 April 1980, 1981/8 of 6 May 1981, 1982/12 of 30 April 1982 and 1983/3 of 24 May 1983, as well as Commission on Narcotic Drugs resolution 1(XXIX) of 11 February 1981 entitled "Strategy and policies for drug control",

Having considered the report of the International Narcotics Control Board for 1983, on the demand and supply of opiates for medical and scientific needs,

Noting with concern the apprehension of the International Narcotics Control Board that a return to overproduction is likely and that the possibility of an increase in the already excessive stocks cannot be excluded,

Further noting with concern that the traditional supplier countries continue to hold large accumulated stocks of opiate raw materials which constitute heavy financial and other burdens for them,

Bearing in mind the urgent need to liquidate the accumulated stocks held by the traditional supplier countries with a view to achieving a lasting world-wide balance between demand and supply of opiates for medical and scientific purposes,

Taking into account paragraph 55 of the report of the International Narcotics Control Board for 1983,

1. *Urges* the Governments of those countries that have not already done so to take urgent and effective steps to implement the above-mentioned resolutions;

2. *Requests* the International Narcotics Control Board to devise and take, in accordance with the Single Convention on Narcotic Drugs, 1961, appropriate measures with a view to promoting and monitoring the urgent implementation of the above-mentioned resolutions;

3. *Further requests* the International Narcotics Control Board, in consultation with the producing and the consuming countries and the concerned United Nations bodies, to assist in the further development of effective ways of ensuring a balance in supply and demand and of reducing excessive stocks of licit opiate raw materials, included as activity A.1 to be undertaken by the Secretary-General, during the biennium 1984-1985, under the basic five-year programme of action of the International Drug Abuse Control Strategy, adopted by the General Assembly in its resolution 36/168 of 16 December 1981;

4. *Requests* the Secretary-General to transmit the present resolution to all Governments for their consideration and implementation.

Economic and Social Council resolution 1984/21

24 May 1984   Meeting 19   Adopted without vote

Approved by Second Committee (E/1984/86) without vote, 3 May (meeting 3); draft by Commission on Narcotic Drugs (E/1984/13); agenda item 13.

Illicit traffic

By a letter dated 14 August 1984[17] addressed to the Secretary-General, Bolivia, Colombia, Ecuador, Nicaragua, Panama, Peru and Venezuela transmitted the text of the Quito Declaration against Traffic in Narcotic Drugs, signed by them at Quito, Ecuador, on 11 August. By the Declaration, they called on the competent international organizations to consider establishing an international or regional fund to assist developing countries affected by traffic in narcotic drugs—a crime against humanity—with a view to combating underlying causes and providing them with means to control such unlawful activities.

On 2 October,[18] the Secretary-General received from Argentina, Bolivia, Brazil, Colombia, Ecuador, Peru and Venezuela the text of the New York Declaration against Drug Trafficking and the Illicit Use of Drugs, adopted by Foreign Ministers of those States on 1 October. They urged the United Nations to convene a special conference with a view to adopting an international plan of action against drug trafficking, declaring drug trafficking to be a crime against humanity, and considering the establishment of an international fund to assist less developed countries combat trafficking.

Bolivia also informed the Secretary-General by a letter of 15 August[19] that it had declared its Chapare tropical region in Cochabamba a military zone with a view to combating illicit cocaine production and traffic.

GENERAL ASSEMBLY ACTION

On 14 December, on the recommendation of the Third (Social, Humanitarian and Cultural) Committee, the General Assembly adopted resolution 39/142 without vote.

Declaration on the Control of Drug Trafficking and Drug Abuse

The General Assembly,

Recalling its resolutions 33/168 of 20 December 1978, 35/195 of 15 December 1980, 36/132 of 14 December 1981, 36/168 of 16 December 1981, 37/168 of 17 December 1982, 37/198 of 18 December 1982, 38/93, 38/98 and 38/122 of 16 December 1983 and other relevant provisions,

Recognizing the concern that prevails in the international community about the problem of the illegal production of, illicit trafficking in and abuse of drugs,

Adopts the Declaration set forth in the annex to the present resolution.

ANNEX
Declaration on the Control of Drug Trafficking and Drug Abuse

The General Assembly,

Bearing in mind that the purposes and principles of the Charter of the United Nations reaffirm faith in the dignity and worth of the human person and promote social progress and better standards of life in larger freedom and international co-operation in solving problems of an economic, social, cultural or humanitarian character,

Considering that Member States have undertaken in the Universal Declaration of Human Rights to promote social progress and better standards of life for the peoples of the world,

Considering that the international community has expressed grave concern at the fact that trafficking in narcotics and drug abuse constitute an obstacle to the physical and moral well-being of peoples and of youth in particular,

Desiring to heighten the awareness of the international community of the urgency of preventing and punishing the illicit demand for, abuse of and illicit production of and traffic in drugs,

Considering that the Quito Declaration against Traffic in Narcotic Drugs of 11 August 1984 and the New York Declaration against Drug Trafficking and the Illicit Use of Drugs of 1 October 1984 recognize the international nature of this problem and emphasize that it should be solved with the firm support of the entire international community,

Considering that the Commission on Narcotic Drugs, the International Narcotics Control Board and the United Nations Fund for Drug Abuse Control have made valuable contributions to the control and elimination of drug trafficking and drug abuse,

Recognizing that existing international instruments, including the Single Convention on Narcotic Drugs of 1961, as amended by the 1972 Protocol Amending the Single Convention on Narcotic Drugs of 1961, and the Convention on Psychotropic Substances of 1971, have created a legal framework for combating trafficking in narcotic drugs and drug abuse in their specialized fields,

Declares that:

1. Drug trafficking and drug abuse are extremely serious problems which, owing to their magnitude, scope and widespread pernicious effects, have become an international criminal activity demanding urgent attention and maximum priority.

2. The illegal production of, illicit demand for, abuse of and illicit trafficking in drugs impede economic and social progress, constitute a grave threat to the security and development of many countries and peoples and should be combated by all moral, legal and institutional means, at the national, regional and international levels.

3. The eradication of trafficking in narcotic drugs is the collective responsibility of all States, especially those affected by problems relating to illicit production, trafficking or abuse.

4. States Members shall utilize the legal instruments against the illicit production of and demand for, abuse of and illicit traffic in drugs and adopt additional measures to counter new manifestations of this shameful and heinous crime.

5. States Members undertake to intensify efforts and to co-ordinate strategies aimed at the control and eradication of the complex problem of drug trafficking and drug abuse through programmes including economic, social and cultural alternatives.

General Assembly resolution 39/142

14 December 1984   Meeting 101   Adopted without vote

Approved by Third Committee (A/39/710) without vote, 28 November (meeting 53); 35-nation draft (A/C.3/39/L.31/Rev.1); agenda item 101.

Sponsors: Argentina, Bolivia, Brazil, Chile, Colombia, Costa Rica, Cuba, Dominican Republic, Ecuador, El Salvador, Germany, Federal Republic of, Guatemala, Guyana, Haiti, Honduras, India, Indonesia, Italy, Ivory Coast, Malaysia, Mexico, Morocco, Nigeria, Pakistan, Panama, Peru, Philippines, Singapore, Suriname, Thailand, Turkey, United States, Uruguay, Venezuela, Yugoslavia.

Meeting numbers. GA 39th session: 3rd Committee 41-44, 47, 53; plenary 101.

Drug law enforcement

INCB report. INCB observed in its 1984 report[1] that the development of new and more comprehensive co-operation among countries— including new extradition agreements or tightening of legislation—had contributed to more rapid and comprehensive investigations, leading to larger numbers of arrests and to the detection and seizure of traffickers' immense financial and other assets. The Board agreed with Governments that drug trafficking could constitute a crime against mankind, and suggested that they adopt a universal declaration for intensified concerted action against illicit drug activities. The Board also noted that UNFDAC was expanding its resources and increasing support, in many developing countries, for measures to fight the illicit traffic.

Reports of the Secretary-General. In a January 1984 background note[16] to the Commission on Narcotic Drugs, the Secretary-General reported on recent trends in illicit traffic in psychotropic substances and narcotic drugs, including increased smuggling of wholesale quantities and changes in trafficking techniques. Based on information provided by Governments and other sources, and focusing on developments mainly in 1982, the note pointed out that traffickers were becoming better organized and more sophisticated in their smuggling and more devious in managing the profits and proceeds from the illicit activities. A growing number of States had increased the maximum penalties for serious drug-related offences, developed legislation for the forfeiture of profits and proceeds of drug crimes, and adopted other relevant measures.

The Secretary-General reported to the General Assembly in October,[20] in response to its December 1983 request,[21] on activities carried out in the context of the international campaign against traffic in drugs. The report focused on co-ordination mechanisms for drug law enforcement, measures to alleviate the special problems of transit States and efforts to convene an interregional meeting of heads of national drug law enforcement agencies.

The Secretary-General observed that two subsidiary bodies of the Commission—the Sub-Commission on Illicit Drug Traffic and Related Matters in the Near and Middle East, and the annual meetings of HONLEA—served as co-ordination mechanisms for drug law enforcement at the regional level. Other regional arrangements included the South American Agreement on Narcotic Drugs and Psychotropic Substances, the Pan-Arab Bureau for Narcotic Affairs of the League of Arab States, and the Co-operation Group to Combat Drug Abuse and Illicit Trafficking in Drugs of the Council of Europe (Pompidou Group). In Africa, seminars were organized in 1984 for drug control and law enforcement professionals from French-speaking States (Ivory Coast, April) and English-speaking States (Egypt, December).

Efforts to alleviate the special problems of transit States included publication of quarterly summaries of reports on illicit transactions, and improving communications for drug-control law enforcement, especially in the Near and Middle East, Asia and the Pacific, and the Caribbean.

Consultations, which had begun in 1983,[22] continued during 1984 on plans to convene an interregional meeting of heads of national drug law enforcement agencies in 1986.

Action by the Commission on Narcotic Drugs. At its 1984 special session, the Commission on Narcotic Drugs, by a 9 February resolution on the international campaign against the traffic in drugs,[23] requested Member States to adopt legislative and administrative measures to enable drug law enforcement agencies to collect and exchange information on drug trafficking groups and operations, and to identify measures for the tracing and forfeiture of the profits of drug crimes.

GENERAL ASSEMBLY ACTION

On the recommendation of the Third Committee, the Assembly adopted resolution 39/143 without vote on 14 December.

International campaign against traffic in drugs

The General Assembly,

Recalling its resolutions 35/195 of 15 December 1980, 36/168 of 16 December 1981, in which it adopted the International Drug Abuse Control Strategy, 37/168 of 17 December 1982, 37/198 of 18 December 1982, 38/98 and 38/122 of 16 December 1983 and other relevant general provisions,

Recalling also its resolutions 36/132 of 14 December 1981 and 38/93 of 16 December 1983, in which it specifically acknowledged the economic and technical constraints impeding many developing countries from combating the illegal production of and illicit traffic in drugs and drug abuse,

Noting the concern expressed by the Secretary-General in his report on the work of the Organization, in which he recognized the need for greater efforts to reduce the traffic in and illicit use of drugs,

Taking note of the Quito Declaration against Traffic in Narcotic Drugs of 11 August 1984 and the New York Declaration against Drug Trafficking and the Illicit Use of Drugs of 1 October 1984 signed by a number of Latin American countries, in which drug trafficking was considered to be a crime against humanity and integrated, effective and urgent regional and international action was demanded, to be supported by the resources necessary for successfully overcoming the problem,

Considering the activities of the Commission on Narcotic Drugs and the International Narcotics Control Board,

Appreciating the action being taken by the United Nations Fund for Drug Abuse Control in providing financial resources and support for integrated development programmes, including the replacement of illicit crops in affected areas,

Reaffirming the need to improve and maintain regional and interregional co-operation and co-ordination, particularly in law enforcement, in order to eliminate drug trafficking and drug abuse, and noting the growing interest in regional and interregional co-ordination,

Concerned that, despite the significant national efforts deployed for this purpose, including those of a number of Latin American and Caribbean and Asian countries, the illicit traffic in narcotic drugs and psychotropic substances has increased noticeably,

Aware of the serious impact on the life and health of peoples and on the stability of democratic institutions resulting from the illicit production, marketing, distribution and use of drugs,

Recognizing that, to root out this evil, integrated action is required for simultaneously reducing and controlling illicit demand, production, distribution and marketing,

Aware that action to eliminate the illegal cultivation of and traffic in drugs must be accompanied by economic and social development programmes for the affected areas,

Bearing in mind the desirability of programming activities for replacing illegal crops in such a manner as to conserve the environment and improve the quality of life of the social sectors concerned,

Recognizing the dilemma of transit States which are seriously affected, both domestically and internationally, by drug trafficking, stimulated by demand for and production and use of illicit drugs and psychotropic substances in other countries,

Aware of the need to mobilize a co-ordinated strategy at the national, regional and international levels, which would cover countries with illegal users and producers and countries used for transit in the world-wide distribution and marketing circuit, in order to eliminate drug trafficking and drug abuse,

Recognizing the importance of ratifying and acceding to the international drug control treaties,

1. *Takes note* of the report of the Secretary-General;
2. *Reiterates* that urgent attention and highest priority should be given to the struggle against the illicit production of, demand for, use of and traffic in drugs;
3. *Calls upon* Member States that have not yet done so to ratify the international drug control treaties and, in the meantime, to make serious efforts to comply with the provisions thereof;
4. *Reiterates* the importance of integrated action, co-ordinated at the regional and international levels, and, for this purpose, requests the Secretary-General and the Commission on Narcotic Drugs to step up efforts and initiatives designed to establish, on a continuing basis, co-ordinating machinery for law enforcement in regions where this does not yet exist;
5. *Recommends* that the highest priority be given to the preparation of specific technical and economic co-operation programmes for the countries most affected by the illicit production of and traffic in drugs and drug abuse;
6. *Also recommends* that appropriate priority be given to the adoption of measures designed to solve the specific problems of transit States through joint regional and interregional efforts;

7. *Urges* Member States with available resources and experience to increase their contributions for combating the illegal production of and illicit traffic in drugs and drug abuse, in particular in the countries most affected and where the problem is most serious;
8. *Encourages* Member States to contribute or to continue contributing to the United Nations Fund for Drug Abuse Control so as to enable it to increase its support of drug abuse control programmes;
9. *Requests* the Economic and Social Council, through the Commission on Narcotic Drugs, to consider the legal, institutional and social elements relevant to all aspects of combating drug trafficking, including the possibility of convening a specialized conference;
10. *Requests* the Secretary-General to ensure that appropriate steps are taken to implement paragraph 5 *(c)* of resolution 37/198 and that a meeting of heads of national drug law enforcement agencies is convened in 1986;
11. *Also requests* the Secretary-General to make the necessary arrangements for holding, within the framework of advisory services, interregional seminars to study the experience gained by the United Nations system, in particular by the United Nations Fund for Drug Abuse Control, and by Member States in integrated rural development programmes for replacing illegal crops;
12. *Calls upon* the specialized agencies and all other relevant bodies of the United Nations system to participate actively in the implementation of the present resolution;
13. *Requests* the Secretary-General to report to the General Assembly at its fortieth session on the implementation of the present resolution;
14. *Decides* to include in the provisional agenda of its fortieth session the item entitled "International campaign against traffic in drugs".

General Assembly resolution 39/143

14 December 1984   Meeting 101   Adopted without vote

Approved by Third Committee (A/39/710) without vote, 28 November (meeting 53); 35-nation draft (A/C.3/39/L.33/Rev.1); agenda item 101.

Sponsors: Argentina, Australia, Bahamas, Bolivia, Brazil, Brunei Darussalam, Central African Republic, Colombia, Costa Rica, Cuba, Dominican Republic, Ecuador, El Salvador, Finland, Germany, Federal Republic of, Greece, Guatemala, Honduras, Indonesia, Jamaica, Malaysia, Mexico, Morocco, Nicaragua, Norway, Panama, Paraguay, Peru, Philippines, Singapore, Sweden, Thailand, Trinidad and Tobago, Uruguay, Venezuela.

Financial implications. 5th Committee, A/39/768; S-G, A/C.3/39/L.35, A/C.5/39/66.

Meeting numbers. GA 39th session: 3rd Committee 41-44, 47, 53; 5th Committee 43; plenary 101.

In related action, the Assembly, by resolution 39/112, invited the Seventh United Nations Congress on the Prevention of Crime and Treatment of Offenders to pay particular attention to the question of illicit drug trafficking (see also Chapter XIII of this section).

Proposed draft convention against illicit drug traffic

GENERAL ASSEMBLY ACTION

On the recommendation of the Third Committee, the Assembly, on 14 December, adopted resolution 39/141 without vote.

Draft Convention against Traffic in Narcotic Drugs and Psychotropic Substances and Related Activities

The General Assembly,

Recalling its resolutions 33/168 of 20 December 1978, 35/195 of 15 December 1980, 36/132 of 14 December 1981, 36/168 of 16 December 1981, 37/168 of 17 December 1982, 37/198 of 18 December 1982, 38/93 and 38/122 of 16 December 1983 and other relevant provisions,

Aware of the dangers posed by the illegal production of drugs, illicit demand, illicit drug traffic and drug abuse and of the need to pay renewed attention to these problems and to their pernicious effects,

Concerned at the increasing damage which the illicit drug traffic causes to public health, the economic and social development of peoples, and young people in particular,

Bearing in mind the Quito Declaration against Traffic in Narcotic Drugs of 11 August 1984 and the New York Declaration against Drug Trafficking and the Illicit Use of Drugs of 1 October 1984, in which profound alarm was expressed at the seriousness of the problem,

Recognizing the valuable contribution made by existing international legal instruments in their specialized areas, including the Single Convention on Narcotic Drugs of 1961, as amended by the 1972 Protocol Amending the Single Convention on Narcotic Drugs of 1961, and the Convention on Psychotropic Substances of 1971,

Convinced that the wide scope of the illicit traffic in narcotic drugs and its consequences make it necessary to prepare a convention which considers the various aspects of the problem as a whole and, in particular, those not envisaged in existing international instruments,

Commending the important work of the Commission on Narcotic Drugs, the United Nations Fund for Drug Abuse Control and the International Narcotics Control Board,

1.   *Reiterates* that the struggle against the illegal production and demand and the illicit use and traffic in drugs deserves urgent treatment of the highest priority;

2.   *Requests* the Economic and Social Council, taking into consideration Article 62, paragraph 3, and Article 66, paragraph 1, of the Charter of the United Nations and Council resolution 9(I) of 16 February 1946, to request the Commission on Narcotic Drugs to initiate at its thirty-first session, to be held in February 1985, as a matter of priority, the preparation of a draft convention against illicit traffic in narcotic drugs which considers the various aspects of the problem as a whole and, in particular, those not envisaged in existing international instruments, and, to that end, to transmit to it the draft Convention annexed to the present resolution as a working paper;

3.   *Requests* the Secretary-General to propose to the Commission on Narcotic Drugs that it adjust the agenda of its thirty-first session, as approved by the Economic and Social Council in its decision 1983/115 of 24 May 1983, to enable the Commission to initiate the preparation of the draft convention referred to in paragraph 2 above;

4.   *Requests* the Commission on Narcotic Drugs to report to the Economic and Social Council, if possible at its first regular session of 1985, on the results achieved in this respect;

5.   *Requests* the Secretary-General to report to the General Assembly at its fortieth session on the implementation of the present resolution.

ANNEX
Draft Convention against Traffic in Narcotic Drugs and Psychotropic Substances and Related Activities

Preamble

The States Parties to the present Convention,

Concerned that illicit traffic in and use of narcotic drugs and psychotropic substances transcend the sphere of the physical and moral well-being of mankind and are detrimental to the identity and integration of peoples, since they constitute a factor of dependence and corruption which undermines their spiritual, cultural, social and economic values, and *aware* that such problems must be dealt with within the framework of international co-operation and global geopolitics, since drugs are goods used to weaken the legitimate economies of the countries and to undermine their sovereignty, and that such practices are impeding development, especially in the countries of the Andean region, *agree* to declare illicit traffic in narcotic drugs and psychotropic substances, the fundamental means of promoting illicit use of such substances, which use is inflicting serious harm on the youth of the world, to be a grave crime against humanity under international law, having regard to the following considerations:

1.   Whereas illicit traffic in and use of such substances are detrimental to the integrity and identity of our peoples since they undermine their spiritual, historical and social values, and, as a result of technical advances in the communications media, unprecedented expansion in untoward cross-cultural influences, increase in organized crime and other factors, have reached proportions too great to be dealt with through the isolated demands and actions of States,

2.   Whereas there is clear evidence that illicit trafficking is closely linked to the designs and actions of some aimed at subverting the legal order and social peace in our countries in pursuit of their despicable commercial aims, and that it constitutes a factor of dependence for developing peoples and impedes economic integration in keeping with their common interests,

3.   Whereas it is clearly established that illicit trafficking operates by corrupting the political and administrative structures of producing and consuming countries and undermines the security and defence of peoples by sapping their military strength and affecting their sovereignty,

4.   Whereas there is a need for international legislation that would provide a basis for effective action to combat illicit trafficking in and use of narcotic drugs and psychotropic substances beyond national boundaries, and for punishing those responsible wherever they may be,

5.   Whereas the volume, magnitude and extent of illicit trafficking and use represent a challenge to society as a whole and constitute activities threatening the very existence and future development of human beings and especially affect youth, a key factor for the development of the peoples of the world,

6.   Whereas drug addiction is detrimental to health, one of the basic assets and inalienable rights of every human being, and whereas without individual health there is no public health, a fact which in turn bears upon and determines the economic development of peoples,

7. Bearing in mind that the repeated use of narcotic drugs and psychotropic substances affects the individual and that, through its biological, psychological and social effects, damages the personality and creates problems for the family, society and the State,

8. Whereas the illicit use of narcotic drugs and psychotropic substances is taking a very serious and often irreversible toll on youth, which is the noblest part of the human resources of the world's peoples, and weakens their capacity for cultural and material progress,

Have agreed as follows:

Article 1
Definitions

For the purposes of the present Convention:

(a) Trafficking shall mean the preparation, production, extraction, cultivation, preservation, acquisition, distribution, financing, organization and management, transport, supply and/or storing of any of the substances, or their raw materials, referred to in the present Convention, except those enumerated for medical or scientific use in the 1972 Protocol Amending the Single Convention on Narcotic Drugs of 1961, and in the Convention on Psychotropic Substances of 1971;

(b) Narcotic drugs and psychotropic substances shall mean the substances, preparations and proprietary drugs listed in the schedules to the Single Convention on Narcotic Drugs of 1961, as amended by the 1972 Protocol, and the Convention on Psychotropic Substances of 1971, and such others as may, as determined by the World Health Organization, produce a state of dependence, stimulation or depression of the central nervous system, result in hallucinations or disturbances in motor function or thinking, behaviour, perception or mood, or the use of which may produce effects similar to those produced by any of the substances referred to above.

Article 2
Nature of the crime

Trafficking in narcotic drugs or psychotropic substances is a grave international crime against humanity. The States Parties to the present Convention undertake to prevent and suppress it.

Article 3
Illicit activities

The following shall be deemed illicit activities: trafficking, distribution, supply, manufacture, elaboration, refining, processing, extraction, preparation, production, cultivation, preservation, transport and storage and the management, organization, financing or facilitating of the traffic in any of the substances or their raw materials referred to in the present Convention.

Article 4
Aggravating circumstance

It shall be deemed an aggravating circumstance if an individual responsible for such activities performs a public function of any kind.

Article 5
Character of the crime

The illicit activities enumerated in the present Convention shall not be considered as political crimes for the purpose of extradition.

Article 6
Imprescriptibility of the crimes

1. The crimes enumerated in the present Convention shall be imprescriptible. Irrespective of the date on which they were committed, they shall be investigated, and individuals against whom there exists sufficient evidence of having committed such crimes shall be sought, arrested, charged and, if found guilty, punished.

2. The States Parties undertake to adopt, in accordance with their respective laws, any legislative or other measures as may be necessary to ensure that statutory or other limitations shall not apply to the prosecution or punishment, as determined by law or otherwise, of the crimes referred to in article 3 and part A, paragraph 2, of article 10 of the present Convention, and that, where they exist, such statutory limitations shall be abolished.

Article 7
Duties of the States Parties

The States Parties undertake to adopt the legislative measures necessary to ensure implementation of the provisions of the present Convention and, in particular, to provide for stringent criminal penalties against individuals responsible for the activities referred to herein.

Article 8
Duties of international organizations

Any State Party or competent international organization may seek to have the relevant bodies of the United Nations or of other regional organizations take such action as they deem appropriate, in accordance with the international instruments governing them, to prevent and suppress the illicit activities enumerated in the present Convention.

Article 9
International co-operation

1. The States Parties shall co-operate on a bilateral and multilateral basis to prevent and suppress the illicit activities enumerated in the present Convention and shall take all necessary measures towards that end.

2. Accordingly, they shall:

(a) Ensure that, at the national level, there is co-ordination of preventive and repressive action against illicit trafficking in narcotic drugs and psychotropic substances. They may assign responsibility for such co-ordination to an appropriate agency;

(b) Provide mutual assistance in combating illicit trafficking and co-operate with each other in identifying, arresting and taking legal action against those suspected of engaging in such illicit activities and their accomplices or abettors and also in seizing and destroying such substances;

(c) Co-operate closely with each other and with competent international organizations of which they are members in a co-ordinated effort to combat illicit trafficking, particularly by collecting information and documents relevant to investigation with the aim of facilitating the prosecution of the persons referred to in the preceding paragraph, and exchange such information;

(d) See to it that international co-operation between the relevant agencies is expeditiously carried out;

(e) Ensure that writs for judicial action are transmitted between countries directly and expeditiously to the organs designated by the States Parties. This provision shall not prevent any State Party from exercising its right to require that such writs be transmitted to it through the diplomatic channel or from Government to Government;

(f) Provide information on illicit activities within their territories that involve narcotic drugs and psychotropic substances, including information on the cultivation, production and manufacture of, trafficking in and use of such substances;

(g) Refrain from enacting legislative provisions or taking measures of any other kind which might be prejudicial to the international obligations which they have assumed with respect to the identification, arrest, extradition and punishment of individuals guilty of the crimes enumerated in the present Convention.

Article 10
Penal provisions
A

1. Each of the crimes enumerated in the present Convention, whether committed by one individual or by several acting in collusion in different countries, shall be considered a distinct offence.

2. Participation or association in the commission of any such crime, conspiracy, instigation or the attempt to commit any such crime, and preparatory actions for such crimes, shall be considered offences.

3. Convictions obtained abroad in respect of such crimes shall be taken into account in determining whether the accused is a habitual offender.

4. Crimes committed by both nationals and aliens shall be tried by the State Party in whose territory the crime was committed, or by the State Party in whose territory the offender is present if extradition is not authorized under the law of the State Party to which a request for extradition is made and if the offender has not yet been tried and sentenced for one of the crimes enumerated in the present Convention.

B

1. Each of the crimes enumerated in article 3 and part A, paragraph 2, of the present article shall be deemed to be included among the extraditable offences covered by any extradition treaty which has been or may hereafter be concluded between the States Parties.

2. If a State Party which makes extradition contingent on the existence of a treaty receives a request for extradition from another State Party with which it has no treaty, it may, should it so choose, consider the present Convention as the necessary legal basis for extradition in respect of the crimes enumerated in article 3 and in part A, paragraph 2, of the present article. Extradition shall be subject to any other conditions laid down by the law of the State Party to which the application is made.

3. States Parties which do not make extradition contingent on the existence of a treaty shall recognize the crimes enumerated in article 3 and in part A, paragraph 2, of the present article as extraditable offences as between them, subject to any conditions laid down by the law of the State Party to which the application for extradition is made.

4. The provisions of the present article shall not affect the principle that the crimes in question must be prosecuted and punished in accordance with the national law of each State Party.

Article 11
Courts having jurisdiction in such cases

Anyone involved in any of the activities enumerated in the present Convention may be tried by a competent tribunal in any of the States in whose territory an act or acts to which the present Convention applies was or were committed, or by such international criminal tribunal as may have jurisdiction under the applicable legal rules.

Article 12
Assistance fund

A fund shall be established to assist developing countries affected by the illicit traffic in narcotic drugs and psychotropic substances with a view to combating and overcoming the causes of those phenomena and providing them with adequate means of combating such illicit activities. The fund shall be constituted by contributions from States which are Parties to the present Convention on the basis of the method of assessment used by the United Nations and by voluntary contributions.

Article 13
Governing Board

The fund shall be administered by a Governing Board composed of an equal number of representatives from each of the States Parties.

Article 14
Control

The States Parties agree to entrust the task of overseeing the activities and obligations set out in the present Convention to the Commission on Narcotic Drugs and the International Narcotics Control Board of the Economic and Social Council of the United Nations.

Article 15
Settlement of disputes

Disputes relating to the interpretation, application or fulfilment of the present Convention shall be submitted to the International Court of Justice at the request of one of the States Parties to the dispute.

Article 16
Signature or accession

The present Convention shall be open for signature or accession by all States, whether they are Members or non-members of the United Nations, without limitation as to time; it shall be subject to ratification and the respective instruments shall be deposited with the Secretary-General of the United Nations.

Article 17
Entry into force

The present Convention shall enter into force on the tenth day following the date on which the twentieth instrument of ratification or accession is deposited.

Article 18
Duration

The present Convention shall remain in effect for a period of fifty years following its entry into force.

General Assembly resolution 39/141

14 December 1984   Meeting 101   Adopted without vote

Approved by Third Committee (A/39/710) without vote, 28 November (meeting 53); 24-nation draft (A/C.3/39/L.30/Rev.2); agenda item 101.

Sponsors: Argentina, Bahamas, Bolivia, Canada, Central African Republic, Chile, Colombia, Costa Rica, Dominican Republic, Ecuador, El Salvador, Guatemala,

Guinea, Guyana, Haiti, Honduras, Malaysia, Morocco, Panama, Peru, Philippines, United States, Uruguay, Venezuela.
Meeting numbers. GA 39th session: 3rd Committee 41-44, 47, 53; plenary 101.

Conventions

As at the end of 1984, 115 States were parties to the 1961 Single Convention on Narcotic Drugs, with Botswana acceding to it during the year; the number of parties to the Convention as amended by the 25 March 1972 Protocol rose to 78, with Belgium and Botswana adhering; and 78 States were parties to the 1971 Convention on Psychotropic Substances, with Botswana and the Ivory Coast acceding in 1984.[24]

INCB, in its 1984 report,[1] called on parties to the 1961 and 1971 Conventions to review existing extradition agreements and the need for new arrangements, adding that the 1961 Convention as amended could, in certain circumstances, serve in lieu of an extradition treaty.

The Commission on Narcotic Drugs, at its 1984 special session, considered a note by the Secretary-General[25] on a review of the questionnaire completed by States parties when fulfilling the annual reports requirement of these Conventions. It concluded that it would be premature and counter-productive to review the questionnaire until the form of data that would be compatible with a computerized retrieval and dissemination system had been more clearly established.

On 14 December, the General Assembly, by resolution 39/143 (see above), called on Member States that had not done so to ratify the international drug control treaties and, until that time, to endeavour to abide by them.

1961 Single Convention on Narcotic Drugs

In May 1984, the Economic and Social Council, on the recommendation of the Commission on Narcotic Drugs, adopted resolution 1984/22 on the cannabis problem (see above), calling for measures to confine cannabis cultivation and use to medical and scientific purposes in accordance with the provisions of the 1961 Single Convention on Narcotic Drugs.

The Commission decided by consensus on 6 February[26] to include alfentanil in Schedule I of the 1961 Convention, based on a recommendation by WHO,[27] which had examined a proposal to that effect by Belgium.

1971 Convention on Psychotropic Substances

In its 1984 report,[1] INCB stated that data provided voluntarily by States—both parties to the 1971 Convention and non-parties—had enabled it to assist effectively in international control of psychotropic substances.

Scheduling of psychotropic substances

The Commission on Narcotic Drugs, in 1984, discussed the advisability, as recommended by WHO, of scheduling (listing) 33 benzodiazepines under Schedule IV—one of four categories of international control under the 1971 Convention. As a result of votes on each substance—including roll-call votes at the request of the United States on alprazolam and diazepam—all 33 substances were included in Schedule IV.[28]

The Commission recommended that the Economic and Social Council urge WHO to review for scheduling those amphetamine-like drugs for which data had been collected and which represented the most serious social and health consequences.

While deciding to include pentazocine in Schedule III of the 1971 Convention,[29] the Commission requested WHO to examine further the case for scheduling similar substances (opioid agonists and antagonists) under the 1961 Convention, taking into account the argument that they were more similar to those controlled under the latter Convention.[30]

ECONOMIC AND SOCIAL COUNCIL ACTION

On 24 May, on the recommendation of its Second Committee, the Economic and Social Council adopted resolution 1984/23 without vote.

Review for scheduling of the amphetamine-like drugs

The Economic and Social Council,

Recalling Commission on Narcotic Drugs resolution 4(XXX) of 16 February 1983,

Noting with concern the serious health and social problems posed by amphetamine-like drugs in some countries,

Noting also with concern the growing traffic in and abuse of amphetamine-like drugs in some countries not currently subject to international control,

Aware that many of those substances have limited or no recognized therapeutic use,

Recognizing that the Secretary-General has recently obtained information from many States with respect to those substances, in response to his request,

1. *Urges* the World Health Organization to select any of those amphetamine-like drugs for which data have been collected and which represent the most serious social and health consequences, to review those substances immediately, in accordance with Commission on Narcotic Drugs resolution 2(S-VII) of 8 February 1982 and consistent with the principles governing the new review procedures of the World Health Organization, and to make its findings available to the Commission at its thirty-first session;

2. *Requests* the Secretary-General to analyse the information recently obtained by him, in accordance with all relevant provisions of Commission on Narcotic Drugs resolution 2(S-VII), to prepare a report on the basis of that analysis, and to transmit that report, together with the report of the World Health Organi-

zation, to parties to the Single Convention on Narcotic Drugs, 1961, and the 1971 Convention on Psychotropic Substances and to members of the Commission not later than two months prior to the beginning of the thirty-first session of the Commission.

Economic and Social Council resolution 1984/23

24 May 1984　　　　　Meeting 19　　　　　Adopted without vote

Approved by Second Committee (E/1984/86) without vote, 3 May (meeting 3); draft by Commission on Narcotic Drugs (E/1984/13); agenda item 13.

Guidelines for exemptions

On 9 February 1984,[31] the Commission approved guidelines for its use, as well as for use by national authorities and WHO, for exempting various types of preparations from certain control measures under the provisions of the 1971 Convention. The guidelines set out, among other things, that a preparation containing a psychotropic substance in association with another such substance, a narcotic drug or a psychoactive substance not under international control with known abuse potential should not be exempted, unless compounded in a way that presented a negligible risk of abuse. A preparation with a psychotropic substance in injectable dosage form was also excluded from exemption.

Organizational questions

Commission on Narcotic Drugs

Periodicity of Commission sessions

The Commission on Narcotic Drugs, at its 1984 special session, examined how best to respond to certain treaty-based or annual functions in view of the 1983 Economic and Social Council recommendation[32] that the Commission should adhere to the established biennial cycle of meetings. The Commission, at its 1982 special session,[33] had requested authorization to meet annually in a regular session of no fewer than eight working days, asserting that it had found it necessary to meet annually in regular and special sessions since 1946 (except for 1967 and 1972).

The Commission had before it a January 1984 note by the Secretary-General,[34] outlining certain treaty-based or other functions that might require action by the Commission on an annual basis, along with alternative means of fulfilling such functions.

By a decision of 9 February,[35] the Commission decided to defer further discussion of the question until its 1985 regular session.

Report of the Commission

ECONOMIC AND SOCIAL COUNCIL ACTION

On 24 May, the Economic and Social Council, on the recommendation of its Second Committee, adopted decision 1984/128 without vote.

Report of the Commission on Narcotic Drugs

At its 19th plenary meeting, on 24 May 1984, the Council took note of the report of the Commission on Narcotic Drugs on its eighth special session.

Economic and Social Council decision 1984/128

Adopted without vote

Approved by Second Committee (E/1984/86) without vote, 3 May (meeting 3); draft by Commission on Narcotic Drugs (E/1984/13); agenda item 13.

International Narcotics Control Board

ECONOMIC AND SOCIAL COUNCIL ACTION

In 1984, the Economic and Social Council had before it the 1983 report of INCB.[36] Acting on the recommendation of its Second Committee, the Council, on 24 May, adopted decision 1984/127 without vote.

Report of the International Narcotics Control Board

At its 19th plenary meeting, on 24 May 1984, the Council took note of the report of the International Narcotics Control Board for 1983.

Economic and Social Council decision 1984/127

Adopted without vote

Approved by Second Committee (E/1984/86) without vote, 3 May (meeting 3); draft by Commission on Narcotic Drugs (E/1984/13); agenda item 13.

REFERENCES

[1]Report of the International Narcotics Control Board for 1984 (E/INCB/1984/1), Sales No. E.84.XI.4. [2]Estimated World Requirements of Narcotic Drugs in 1985 and Supplements Nos. 1-12 (E/INCB/1984/2 & Supp.1-12), Sales Nos. E/F/S.84.XI.5 & Supp.1-12. [3]Statistics on Narcotic Drugs for 1983 Furnished by Governments in accordance with the International Treaties and Maximum Levels of Opium Stock (E/INCB/1984/3), Sales No. E/F/S.84.XI.6. [4]Comparative Statement of Estimates and Statistics on Narcotic Drugs for 1983 Furnished by Governments in accordance with the International Treaties (E/INCB/1984/5), Sales No. E/F/S.84.XI.8. [5]A/39/646. [6]E/1984/13. [7]YUN 1983, p. 969, GA res. 38/98, 16 Dec. 1983. [8]YUN 1981, p. 1058, GA res. 36/168, 16 Dec. 1981. [9]E/CN.7/1984/10. [10]E/CN.7/1984/6. [11]E/1984/13 (dec. 1(S-VIII)). [12]A/39/577. [13]A/39/193. [14]E/1985/23. [15]E/CN.7/1985/11. [16]E/CN.7/1984/2. [17]A/39/407. [18]A/39/551 & Corr.1,2. [19]A/39/421. [20]A/39/194. [21]YUN 1983, p. 974, GA res. 38/122, 16 Dec. 1983. [22]Ibid., p. 975. [23]E/1984/13 (res. 3(S-VIII)). [24]Multilateral Treaties Deposited with the Secretary-General: Status as at 31 December 1984 (ST/LEG/SER.E/3), Sales No. E.85.V.4. [25]E/CN.7/1984/5. [26]E/1984/13 (dec. 3(S-VIII)). [27]E/CN.7/1984/3. [28]E/1984/13 (dec. 5(S-VIII)–37(S-VIII)). [29]Ibid. (dec. 4(S-VIII)). [30]Ibid. (res. 2(S-VIII)). [31]Ibid. (res. 1(S-VIII)). [32]YUN 1983, p. 1004, ESC dec. 1983/184, sect. IV, 29 July 1983. [33]YUN 1982, p. 1231. [34]E/CN.7/1984/7. [35]E/1984/13 (dec. 2(S-VIII)). [36]Report of the International Narcotics Control Board for 1983 (E/INCB/1983/1), Sales No. E.83.XI.6.

OTHER PUBLICATIONS

Bulletin on Narcotics, vol. XXXVI, Nos. 1-4 (quarterly). Estimated World Requirements of Narcotic Drugs in 1984 and Supplements Nos. 1-12 (E/INCB/1983/2 & Supp.1-12), Sales Nos. E/F/S.84.XI.2 & Supp.1-12. Statistics on Narcotic Drugs for 1984 (E/INCB/1985/3), Sales No. E/F/S.85.XI.3. Statistics on Psychotropic Substances for 1984 (E/INCB/1985/4), Sales No. E/F/S.85.XI.4. Comparative Statement of Estimates and Statistics on Narcotic Drugs for 1984 Furnished by Governments in accordance with the International Treaties (E/INCB/1985/5), Sales No. E/F/S.85.XI.5.

Chapter XXIII

Statistics

In 1984, the Statistical Office of the United Nations continued to collect and publish a wide range of statistical data, including those on international trade, industry, transport, energy, national accounts and population.

The office also continued its work on development of standards and methods for improving national statistics and statistical systems, and published a number of technical reports on methods in various fields of statistics. Substantive support for technical co-operation to developing countries was provided on behalf of the Department of Technical Co-operation for Development for the improvement of national statistics and statistical data processing capability. The office continued to promote the co-ordination of international statistical activities among international organizations and provided statistical services to the United Nations Secretariat and intergovernmental expert bodies.

The Secretary-General issued a number of reports on statistical activities, for consideration by the Statistical Commission at its 1985 session. The Commission, which meets biennially, did not meet in 1984.

UN statistical bodies

ACC Sub-Committee

The Sub-Committee on Statistical Activities of the Administrative Committee on Co-ordination (eighteenth session, Rome, Italy, 30 April–4 May 1984)[1] analysed the relevant work carried out by organizations and agencies of the United Nations system and identified the need for reports or future approaches in such areas as energy, environment, price, service, tourism and migration, trade and transport, local area and social statistics. It also considered revision of the System of National Accounts, harmonization of economic classifications, the Living Standards Measurement Study, the National Household Survey Capability Programme and the Statistical Computing Project (see also below).

In reviewing the data dissemination policy within the United Nations system, the Sub-Committee agreed that the Statistical Office should clarify and extend, where necessary, the guidelines for data exchange and dissemination in machine-readable form.

It also recommended that its nineteenth session be held at Madrid, Spain, from 24 to 28 June 1985.

The Sub-Committee's Technical Working Group on Statistical Data Bases (Geneva, 13 April) discussed the experiences and possibilities for inter-agency connection over communication facilities, data catalogues, and the use of microcomputers to support data base management systems.

Statistical Commission

1985 Agenda

Taking into account a view expressed at the 1983 session of the Statistical Commission, the Secretary-General, by a December 1984 note,[2] proposed inclusion in the Commission's 1985 agenda[3] of a sub-item entitled "System of Balances of the National Economy", under an item on national accounts and balances.

Economic statistics

Energy and environment statistics

A September 1984 report of the Secretary-General on energy and environment statistics[4] outlined the current work programmes and future plans of the Statistical Office.

Among other things, the report stated that parts of the first phase of the three-phase work programme on new and renewable sources of energy—assessing current and planned statistical activities on the topic in countries, regional commissions, specialized agencies and other international organizations—had been completed. The Statistical Office continued its methodological work on guidelines for statistics concerning fresh water, human settlements and energy, focusing on delimitation of the environmental aspects of human settlements and energy and on the assessment of national and international statistical work in those areas.

In an October report on mineral resources statistics,[5] prepared in response to a 1983 Economic and Social Council resolution,[6] the Secretary-General reviewed the steps taken over the preceding 10 years in fostering international comparability of data on reserves, production and consumption of mineral resources, and discussed the 1983 recommendations of the group of experts on the standardization of definitions and terminology for statistics on mineral production and consumption and their implications for the work programme of the Statistical Office.

National accounts and balances

An October 1984 report of the Secretary-General on progress made in revising the System of National Accounts (SNA)[7] contained a summary of the SNA review since 1975, a schedule of meetings organized by the Intersecretariat Working Group on National Accounts and by the regional commissions, and a review of the consolidated work programme of the Intersecretariat Working Group members for the 1990 revision of SNA.

Progress made in establishing links between SNA and the System of Balances of the National Economy (MPS) was described in a September report of the Secretary-General.[8] It discussed, among other things, the results of experimental illustrative calculations of gross domestic product and net material product of selected centrally planned and market economies, as well as work by the Statistical Office in improving and elaborating the conceptual framework of SNA and MPS comparisons.

In addition, the Secretary-General transmitted, by a December note,[9] a report prepared by the Council for Mutual Economic Assistance, summarizing the main points in the draft basic methodological provisions for the compilation of MPS (see also under "1985 Agenda" above).

Price statistics

Phase IV of the International Comparison Project—involving comparisons in price statistics, used for assessing the relative economic development of countries—was completed in 1984, while planning for phase V for 1985 continued.

An October 1984 report on the topic[10] discussed, among other things, the procedures used and results obtained in phase IV, organization and implementation of phase V, development of the overall international price statistics programme, and relevant manuals and publications issued or under preparation.

International economic classifications

The Secretary-General submitted in October 1984 a progress report on harmonization of international economic classifications,[11] containing an outline of work on the Integrated System of Classifications of Activities and Products and information on the current situation and future plans with regard to the Harmonized Commodity Description and Coding System of the Customs Co-operation Council. The report also described drafts of: the part of the proposed revision of the International Standard Industrial Classification of All Economic Activities covering activities producing transportable goods; the proposed combined trade/production goods classification; and the third revision of the Standard International Trade Classification.

Social and demographic statistics

Social indicators

In a November 1984 report on the future direction of work on social indicators,[12] the Secretary-General reviewed some implications for future work of selected major developments and trends in national and international work on relevant statistical issues. The report discussed the development and/or use of: integrated or co-ordinated basic statistics and related methodology; automated data bases and dissemination techniques; social indicators on special population groups; and social indicators as general measures of development and well-being.

Annexed to the report were the conclusions and recommendations of technical meetings concerned with social indicators. Among the meetings in 1984 were the Expert Consultation on a System of Socio-Economic Indicators for African Planners (Addis Ababa, Ethiopia, 23-27 January), convened by the Economic Commission for Africa; the Working Party on the Framework for the Integration of Social and Demographic Statistics of the Conference of European Statisticians (eighth session, Geneva, 30 January–3 February); and the Expert Group on Development of Statistics on Disabled Persons (Vienna, Austria, 2-6 April), convened by the Statistical Office and the United Nations Centre for Social Development and Humanitarian Affairs.

More detailed information on current national and international work on social indicators and the integration of social, demographic and related statistics was provided in an October report of the Secretary-General.[13]

Population and housing censuses

Proposals concerning the 1990 World Population and Housing Census Programme, scheduled to be carried out during 1985-1994, were contained in a November 1984 report of the Secretary-General.[14]

The report included an overview of the 1980 Programme—implemented during 1975-1984 and covering over 95 per cent of the world's population in 191 countries or areas—as well as the emerging issues related to census-taking. It also discussed the implications for the 1990 Programme of two recent developments relating to the economic characteristics of the population: the new concepts and standards concerning statistics of the economically active population, employment, unemployment and underemployment, adopted by the International Labour Organisation in 1982; and the planned revisions pertaining to major standard classifications of industry, occupation and status in employment. Information was also provided on a range of proposed activities relevant to the 1990 Programme, related census work of the regional commissions and a tentative calendar of preparatory activities.

National Household Survey Capability Programme

An October 1984 report of the Secretary-General reviewed the prospects for, or progress made in, implementing the National Household Survey Capability Programme,[15] a technical co-operation project bringing together national donors and international agencies to assist developing countries in producing socio-economic and demographic statistics needed for their development plans.

Living Standards Measurement Study

The World Bank, in a July 1984 report,[16] updated information on progress and activities of its Living Standards Measurement Study (LSMS), aimed primarily at identifying ways to monitor changes in living standards. The report, among other things, pointed to recent trends towards a more explicit focus on operational considerations and a stronger emphasis on using LSMS data for behavioural analysis.

Other statistical activities

Technical co-operation

Information on the technical co-operation programmes in statistics during 1980-1984 of the United Nations system and of other bilateral or multilateral agencies, updating a 1983 report on the topic,[17] was summarized in a December 1984 report of the Secretary-General.[18] The estimated 1984 expenditure in that regard by the United Nations system stood at $35.9 million, as against $30.6 million in 1983; similar expenditure by other multilateral agencies totalled $2.7 million in 1984, and $3.5 million in 1983.

In addition to current training activities, the report dealt with emerging issues in statistical data processing, involving, among other things, the advent of microcomputer systems.

In a September report,[19] the Secretary-General discussed the problems faced by the statistically least developed countries, such as staff shortages and a lack of statistical planning and co-ordination, high costs of data collection, delays in data processing, and inadequacy of statistical training and of data analysis and utilization.

Publication policy

In a November 1984 report on publication policies of international statistical agencies,[20] prepared at the 1983 request of the Statistical Commission,[21] the Secretary-General stated that the Statistical Office currently produced 12 publications which were issued at least annually; eight recurrent publications which were issued every few years as directories, supplements or compendia; and other methodological studies and international standards as warranted by its work programme.

The report contained a summary of existing practices, a review of objectives and constraints and proposals for future developments.

In a related matter, the Secretary-General discussed, in a September report,[22] the dissemination of international statistics to users, and described proposals for improving user services and assessing the potential users.

Also in 1984, the Secretary-General submitted two reports on statistical activities of the United Nations system and other international organizations—an October report covering future plans,[23] and a December report containing an overall review for the period 1982 to mid-1984.[24]

REFERENCES

[1]ACC/1984/14. [2]E/CN.3/1985/21. [3]E/CN.3/1985/1. [4]E/CN.3/1985/10. [5]E/CN.3/1985/9 & Corr.1. [6]YUN 1983, p. 665, ESC res. 1983/53, 28 July 1983. [7]E/CN.3/1985/5. [8]E/CN.3/1985/6. [9]E/CN.3/1985/22. [10]E/CN.3/1985/8 & Corr.1. [11]E/CN.3/1985/7. [12]E/CN.3/1985/3. [13]E/CN.3/1985/11. [14]E/CN.3/1985/12. [15]E/CN.3/1985/14. [16]E/CN.3/1985/15. [17]YUN 1983, p. 981. [18]E/CN.3/1985/13. [19]E/CN.3/1985/16. [20]E/CN.3/1985/4. [21]YUN 1983, p. 982. [22]E/CN.3/1985/2. [23]E/CN.3/1985/19. [24]E/CN.3/1985/18.

PUBLICATIONS

Compiling Social Indicators on the Situation of Women: A Technical Report (ST/ESA/STAT/SER.F/32), Sales No. E.84.XVII.2. *Improving Concepts and Methods for Statistics and Indicators on the Situation of Women* (ST/ESA/STAT/SER.F/33), Sales No. E.84.XVII.3. *Handbook of Vital Statistics Systems and Methods*, vol. II: *Review of National Practices* (ST/ESA/STAT/SER.F/35), Sales No. E.84.XVII.11. *A Framework for the Development of Environment Statistics* (ST/ESA/STAT/SER.M/78), Sales No. E.84.XVII.12. *Statistical Yearbook 1983-1984* (ST/ESA/STAT/SER.S/10), Sales No. E/F.85.XVII.1. *World Statistics in Brief (United Nations Statistical Pocketbook)* (1984 data) (ST/ESA/STAT/SER.V/10), Sales No. E.86.XVII.8. *Energy Statistics Yearbook 1984* (ST/ESA/STAT/SER.J/28), Sales No. E/F.86.XVII.2. *Energy Balances and Electricity Profiles (1984)* (ST/ESA/STAT/SER.W/3), Sales No. E.86.XVII.14. *National Accounts Statistics: Main Aggregates and Detailed Tables 1984* (ST/ESA/STAT/SER.X/8), Sales No. E.86.XVII.26. *National Accounts Statistics: Analysis of Main Aggregates, 1983/84* (ST/ESA/STAT/SER.X/5), Sales No. E.86.XVII.4. *International Trade Statistics Yearbook, 1984*, vols. I and II (ST/ESA/STAT/SER.G/33 and Add.1), Sales No. E/F.86.XVII.7, vols. I and II. *Industrial Statistics Yearbook 1984*, vol. I: *General Industrial Statistics* (ESA/STAT/SER.P/23), Sales No. E/F.86.XVII.18; vol. II: *Commodity Production Data* (ST/ESA/STAT/SER.P/23), Sales No. E/F.86.XVII.19. *Construction Statistics Yearbook 1984* (ST/ESA/STAT/SER.U/13), Sales No. E.86.XVII.20. *Demographic Yearbook, 1984* (ST/ESA/STAT/SER.R/14), Sales No. E/F.85.XIII.1. *Population and Vital Statistics Report 1984*—data available 1 January, 1 April, 1 July, 1 October 1984 (ST/ESA/STAT/SER.A/148-151), vol. XXXVI. *Population and Vital Statistics Report, 1984 Special Supplement*, Sales No. E/F.84.XIII.2. *Compendium of Human Settlements Statistics 1983* (ST/ESA/STAT/SER.N/4), Sales No. E/F.84.XVII.5. *Monthly Bulletin of Statistics*, vol. XXXVIII, Nos. 1-12. *Commodity Trade Statistics 1984*, Statistical Papers, Series D.

Chapter XXIV

Institutional arrangements

Harmonization and co-ordination of programme activities of the United Nations system continued to be pursued in 1984 by the Administrative Committee on Co-ordination (ACC) and the Committee for Programme and Co-ordination (CPC). In its 1983/84 report, ACC noted that the executive heads of the system fully shared the Secretary-General's concern that the value of multilateral diplomacy was being questioned and that international institutions were all too often not being fully utilized. Recent developments, ACC observed, had indicated increasing scepticism and criticism of particular organizations and of the system as a whole. The executive heads were determined to meet this challenge constructively and remained committed to improving further the efficiency of their organizations, individually and collectively, so that the United Nations might continue to make an invaluable contribution to solving the problems confronting the world community.

During the year, in addition to a review of various aspects of the 1984-1989 medium-term plan, a cross-organizational programme analysis in human settlements was undertaken, as was an analysis of the mandates of the system and problems addressed in economic and technical co-operation among developing countries. Efforts were also made to co-ordinate relief activities for Africa.

The General Assembly reviewed progress made in restructuring the economic and social sectors of the United Nations system, initiated in 1977. Restructuring activities in 1984 focused on the revitalization of the Economic and Social Council with respect to its calendar of meetings, reports submitted to it and meetings of its subsidiary bodies; and on the formulation of a biennial work programme for the Second (Economic and Financial) Committee, which the Assembly set forth in resolution 39/217. The functioning of the regional commissions and of the Office of Secretariat Services for Economic and Social Matters (OSSECS) was also analysed.

Topics related to this chapter. Regional economic and social activities: strengthening of regional commissions. United Nations programmes: programme planning; administrative and budgetary co-ordination.

Co-ordination in the UN system

ACC activities

In 1984, ACC discussed inter-agency collaboration and co-ordination in a number of areas, among them development and international economic co-operation (see p. 387), the review and appraisal of implementation of the International Development Strategy for the Third United Nations Development Decade (the 1980s) (see p. 392), operational activities in support of the least developed countries (see p. 414), and efforts to alleviate the critical economic situation in Africa (see p. 467). ACC examined cross-organizational programme analyses (see below) and joint planning of complementary programmes, and reviewed progress in sectors previously selected for such planning—health care; aging; energy information systems; and research and training in energy assessment, planning and utilization.

Also discussed were integrated approaches in respect of interrelationships between resources, environment, people and development (see p. 406), rural development (see p. 410), nutrition, as it referred in particular to Africa (see p. 467), water resources development (see p. 648), implementation of the Nairobi Programme of Action for the Development and Utilization of New and Renewable Sources of Energy (see p. 659), environment (see p. 745), information systems (see p. 1182), and disarmament and development. Activities in support of international conferences (on population, crime prevention, women), years (of youth, peace, shelter for the homeless) and decades (of disabled persons) were also reviewed.

As to management and institutional policy issues, ACC considered such personnel and general administrative questions as remuneration of staff in the Professional and higher categories, and the pension and post adjustment systems. It also reviewed harmonization of budgetary presentations, including a system-wide classification of objects of expenditure and a recommended format, accounting and financial reporting, arrangements for payment of staff salaries and allowances, cash management and general financial systems (use of central files for administrative data, insurance and procurement arrangements, common positions on support costs for technical co-operation and other activities).

ACC continued to rationalize its work and to improve the efficiency of its machinery, keeping it to a minimum without impairing its function, and meeting specific requirements of intergovernmental bodies through such *ad hoc* arrangements as consultations and working group meetings. Economy measures had also been achieved in documentation. ACC expressed concern, however, over the increasing number both of decisions of intergovernmental bodies calling for inter-agency consultations or meetings, and of requests from bodies outside the system for meetings with United Nations organizations and for inputs into their work.

ACC described the foregoing activities in annual overview reports for 1983/84[1] and 1984/85.[2] It adopted 22 decisions in 1984—12 at its first regular session (London, 16-18 April), 1 at an extraordinary session (Geneva, 3 and 4 July) and 9 at its second regular session (New York, 22 and 23 October). (For details, refer to SUBJECT INDEX or the relevant chapter.)

ACC held an organizational session in New York (15-17 February). Its principal subsidiary bodies met during the year as follows:

Consultative Committee on Administrative Questions (CCAQ) (Personnel and General Administrative Questions) (sixtieth session, Paris, 27 February–16 March; sixty-first session, New York, 25 June–13 July; special session, Geneva, 1-3 October); CCAQ (Financial and Budgetary Questions) (sixtieth session, Vienna, Austria, 12-16 March; sixty-first session, New York, 10-14 September); Consultative Committee on Substantive Questions (CCSQ) (Operational Activities) (first regular session, Geneva, 20-23 March; second regular session, New York, 3-6 December); CCSQ (Programme Matters) (first regular session, Geneva, 26-30 March; second regular session, New York, 4-9 October); Organizational Committee (Geneva, 3-5 April; New York, 10-12 October).

ACC bodies on specific subjects met as follows:

Task Force on Science and Technology for Development, fifth session, Rome, 17-19 January; *Ad Hoc* Task Force on the International Conference on Population, third meeting, New York, 30 and 31 January; *ad hoc* inter-agency meeting on the cross-organizational programme analysis on economic and technical co-operation for development, New York, 6 and 7 February, and on human settlements activities of the United Nations system, New York, 8-10 February; Panel on Monitoring and Evaluation of the Task Force on Rural Development, third session, Rome, 20 and 21 February; Task Force on Rural Development, twelfth meeting, Rome, 22-24 February; Sub-Committee on Nutrition and its Advisory Group, tenth session, Rome, 5-9 March; second inter-agency meeting on the preparations for the World Conference to Review and Appraise the Achievements of the United Nations Decade for Women (1985), Vienna, 8 and 9 March; Steering Committee, Advisory Committee for the Co-ordination of Information Systems, Geneva, 23 March; third *ad hoc* inter-agency consultation on International Youth Year, Vienna, 29 and 30 March; Joint United Nations Information Committee (JUNIC), eleventh session, Paris, 3-6 April; third inter-agency consultation on the follow-up of the Substantial New Programme of Action for the 1980s for the Least Developed Countries, Geneva, 9 and 10 April; *ad hoc* meeting of focal points within the United Nations system on the relationship between disarmament and development, New York, 10 April; Inter-Agency Group on New and Renewable Sources of Energy, third session, New York, 18 and 19 April and 2-4 May; Sub-Committee on Statistical Activities, eighteenth session, Rome, 30 April–4 May; second inter-agency meeting on the United Nations Decade of Disabled Persons, Vienna, 3 and 4 September; Advisory Committee for the Co-ordination of Information Systems, second session, Geneva, 24-26 September; inter-agency meeting on outer space activities, Geneva, 1-3 October; *Ad Hoc* Inter-Agency Working Group on Demographic Estimates and Projections, New York, 15-17 October; Intersecretariat Group for Water Resources, fifth session, Vienna, 29 October–2 November; Task Force on Long-Term Development Objectives, thirteenth session, Geneva, 28-30 November (in June, a technical energy group met for its sixth session at Vienna, and a technical working group for its twelfth, at Geneva).

Report for 1983/84

On 29 May, CPC[3] commended ACC on the quality of its 1983/84 annual overview report[1] and endorsed its conclusions. CPC recommended continued efforts in joint planning, and publication, in connection with the commemoration of the fortieth anniversary of the United Nations (see p. 382), of the overview of the objectives and plans of the organizations of the United Nations system, to include a short introductory critique of the system's strengths and weaknesses. Further work on the abstract of the overview, which CPC had requested in 1983,[4] was not to be pursued; accordingly, the Secretary-General informed the Economic and Social Council, by a note of 14 June,[5] that an abstract was not being submitted.

CPC also recommended that documents forming part of ACC decisions but not appearing in the documents list annexed to the report should be made available to Member States. It requested the Secretary-General to continue his efforts to rationalize the work of ACC and to streamline its subsidiary machinery.

ECONOMIC AND SOCIAL COUNCIL ACTION

In July, acting without vote on the recommendation of its Third (Programme and Co-ordination) Committee, the Economic and Social Council adopted decision 1984/176.

**Reports considered by the
Economic and Social Council in connection with
the question of international co-operation and
co-ordination within the United Nations system**

At its 49th plenary meeting, on 26 July 1984, the
Council:

(a)   Took note of the following documents:

(i)   Report of the Joint Inspection Unit entitled "United
      Nations system co-operation in developing evalu-
      ation by Governments" and the comments of the
      Administrative Committee on Co-ordination
      thereon;

(ii) Letter dated 6 February 1984 from the Director-
      General of the United Nations Educational, Scien-
      tific and Cultural Organization to the Secretary-
      General;

(iii) Annual overview report of the Administrative Com-
      mittee on Co-ordination for 1983/84;

(iv) Report of the Administrative Committee on Co-
      ordination on expenditures of the United Nations
      system in relation to programmes;

(v)   Note by the Secretary-General on the overview
      of the objectives and plans of the organizations
      of the United Nations system;

(vi) Note by the Secretary-General concerning the
      progress report of the World Health Organiza-
      tion on the Global Strategy for Health for All by
      the Year 2000;

(b)   Took note of the reports of the Secretary-General
on the analysis of the mandates of, and problems addressed
by, the United Nations system in economic and technical co-operation among developing countries and on the
exchange of information on banned hazardous chemicals and unsafe pharmaceutical products and decided
to transmit those reports to the General Assembly.

Economic and Social Council decision 1984/176

Adopted without vote

Approved by Third Committee (E/1984/150) without vote, 23 July (meeting 15); oral
proposal by Chairman; agenda item 20.

CPC activities

In 1984, CPC met in New York for an organizational meeting on 22 March and for its twenty-fourth
session from 23 April to 1 June.[3]

At that session, CPC discussed both the programme performance for the 1982-1983 biennium
and proposed revisions to the 1984-1989 medium-
term plan, to incorporate legislative mandates formulated since adoption of the plan in 1982[6] (see
ADMINISTRATIVE AND BUDGETARY QUESTIONS,
Chapter II).

Aspects of the medium-term plan and programme
budget considered by CPC included: the expeditious
submission of documentation to CPC and the Advisory Committee on Administrative and Budgetary
Questions (ACABQ) during budget preparation (see
p. 1142); a new system of priority-setting in the plan
and programme budget proposals (see p. 1139); cross-
sectional programme analysis of the 1984-1985 programme budget (see p. 1141); decentralization of
activities to the regional commissions (see p. 602);
the United Nations Industrial Development Or-

ganization (UNIDO) 1984-1985 work programme
(see p. 564); progress in implementing the 1983
General Assembly resolutions on the Transport and
Communications Decade in Africa[7] and on the
Industrial Development Decade for Africa[8] (see
pp. 606 and 610); and institutional and financial
arrangements for the Information Systems Unit of
the Department of International Economic and Social Affairs (DIESA) (see p. 409).

In the area of programme evaluation, CPC considered several reports: by the Secretary-General
on the 1983 evaluation of UNIDO-executed technical
co-operation activities in manufactures funded by
the United Nations Development Programme (see
p. 570) and on the activities of JUNIC; and by the
Joint Inspection Unit (JIU) on the functioning of
the Department of Technical Co-operation for Development (see p. 456). It reviewed a possible timetable for in-depth and triennial evaluation studies for
1986-1992 and examined the feasibility of linking
the themes of such studies with those of cross-
organizational programme analyses, as well as ways
of improving the documents dissemination system
(see p. 1177).

CPC examined cross-organizational analyses of
two United Nations programmes, and, in addition
to making recommendations concerning future analyses, decided on the programme to be analysed
in 1986 (see below). As a follow-up to the 1983 analysis in marine affairs, CPC considered a preliminary
report by the International Maritime Organization
and the United Nations Conference on Trade and
Development (UNCTAD) on joint activities in maritime transport (see p. 650).

Finally, CPC considered the question of improved
secretariat support services to it (see below).

ECONOMIC AND SOCIAL COUNCIL ACTION

Acting without vote on the recommendation of
its Third Committee, the Economic and Social
Council adopted resolution 1984/61 A on 26 July
1984.

**Report of the Committee
for Programme and Co-ordination on the work of
its twenty-fourth session**

The Economic and Social Council,

Having considered the report of the Committee for Programme and Co-ordination on the work of its twenty-
fourth session,

I

1.   *Takes note with appreciation* of the report of the Committee for Programme and Co-ordination on the work
of its twenty-fourth session and endorses the conclusions
and recommendations contained therein;

2.   *Emphasizes* the importance of the programming
and co-ordination functions carried out by the Committee
and stresses the need for timely and full implementation
of intergovernmental mandates concerning the submission

of reports to the Committee by the organizations, organs and bodies of the United Nations system;

II

Proposed revisions to the medium-term plan for the period 1984-1989 to incorporate the programme implications of the resolutions and decisions adopted by intergovernmental organs or international conferences

1. *Endorses* the conclusions and recommendations of the Committee for Programme and Co-ordination concerning the proposed revisions to the medium-term plan for the period 1984-1989 to incorporate the programme implications of the resolutions and decisions adopted by intergovernmental organs or international conferences;

2. *Reiterates* that the medium-term plan should continue to serve as the framework for future biennial programme budgets;

3. *Requests* the Secretary-General, when preparing the future proposed revisions to the medium-term plan, to make every effort:

(a) To identify in the revisions the specific paragraphs of new legislative mandates on which the proposed revisions are based;

(b) To apply fully the methodology adopted by the General Assembly in resolution 34/224 of 20 December 1979 on medium-term planning in the United Nations, particularly in so far as it concerns the participation of sectoral and regional intergovernmental bodies in the review of medium-term plan proposals;

III

Operation of the new system for setting priorities

Requests the Secretary-General to redouble his efforts to ensure that, in future, the provisions of the relevant General Assembly resolutions, including resolutions 36/228 of 18 December 1981, 37/234 of 21 December 1982 and 38/227 of 20 December 1983, will be implemented more systematically;

IV

Programme performance for the biennium 1982-1983

Requests the Secretary-General to implement fully the recommendations of the Committee for Programme and Co-ordination concerning programme performance for the biennium 1982-1983 when preparing the programme performance report for the biennium 1984-1985;

V

Evaluation of the United Nations Development Programme-financed technical co-operation activities of the United Nations Industrial Development Organization in the field of manufactures

1. *Takes note with appreciation* of the implementation of those recommendations cited in paragraph 79 of the report of the Secretary-General on the evaluation of the United Nations Development Programme-financed technical co-operation activities of the United Nations Industrial Development Organization in the field of manufactures which the Programme and the Organization had stated were under implementation before the finalization of the staff evaluation report;

2. *Takes note* of decision 84/15 of 29 June 1984 of the Governing Council of the United Nations Development Programme;

3. *Invites* the Governing Council of the United Nations Development Programme and the Industrial Development Board of the United Nations Industrial Development Organization:

(a) To ensure that the above-mentioned recommendations will continue to be implemented systematically and that follow-up will be pursued actively;

(b) To adopt and implement the recommendations referred to in paragraph 81 of the report of the Secretary-General;

(c) To give careful consideration to the recommendations referred to in paragraphs 82 and 84 to 87 of the report of the Secretary-General;

(d) To request their secretariats to report to them on the recommendations referred to in paragraphs 83 and 87 of the report of the Secretary-General;

(e) To request their secretariats to continue efforts to improve their evaluation methodology;

(f) To study regularly the means likely to strengthen further the effectiveness and impact of technical co-operation activities in the manufactures sector;

4. *Invites* the Governing Council of the United Nations Development Programme and the Industrial Development Board and its Permanent Committee to include this question in the agenda of their next sessions;

5. *Requests* the Secretary-General to report to the Economic and Social Council at its second regular session of 1987, through the Committee for Programme and Co-ordination at its twenty-seventh session, on the implementation of and follow-up to the above-mentioned recommendations;

6. *Invites* Member States to give careful consideration to the recommendations referred to in paragraphs 80 and 82 of the report of the Secretary-General;

VI

Cross-organizational programme analyses

1. *Welcomes* the improvements in the recent cross-organizational programme analyses, in particular the cross-organizational programme analysis of the activities of the United Nations system in human settlements;

2. *Invites* all organizations, organs and bodies of the United Nations system carefully to review and follow up the cross-organizational programme analyses in their respective sectors;

3. *Requests* the Secretary-General to ensure that future cross-organizational programme analyses, in particular the analysis of economic and technical co-operation among developing countries, will provide a critical analysis of gaps in coverage of the activities mandated and of questions of priorities, as well as of overlaps and co-ordination, taking into consideration problems which may exist in defining the relative competences of the United Nations Development Programme and the United Nations Conference on Trade and Development or in co-ordination between the activities of the two organizational units;

A. Cross-organizational programme analysis
of the activities of the
United Nations system in human settlements

4. *Invites* the Commission on Human Settlements, at its eighth session in 1985, to give due consideration to the cross-organizational programme analysis of the activities of the United Nations system in human settlements, as well as to the assessment and recommendations of the Committee for Programme and Co-ordination;

5. *Invites* the Commission on Human Settlements, with the assistance of the United Nations Centre for Human Settlements (Habitat), to exercise vigorously its co-ordination role;

B. Mandates of, and problems addressed by,
the United Nations system in economic and technical
co-operation among developing countries

6. *Requests* the Secretary-General to refine further the
criteria, proposed in his report on the question, for identifying
activities to be included in the analysis of the mandates
of, and problems addressed by, the United Nations system in economic and technical co-operation among developing countries;

7. *Recommends* that the cross-organizational programme
analysis of economic and technical co-operation among
developing countries should contain a critical analytical assessment of the role of the United Nations system
and the relationship between its activities and the mandates it has been given, including the difficulties encountered;

VII

*Measures to improve secretariat support for the
Committee for Programme and Co-ordination*

1. *Regrets* that no concrete proposals were submitted
to the Committee for Programme and Co-ordination at
its twenty-fourth session;

2. *Reiterates* the recommendation of the Committee
that the consultations referred to in the statement made
by the Under-Secretary-General for Administration and
Management before the Committee at its twenty-fourth
session should be held with the widest possible participation of Member States;

3. *Re-emphasizes* that the programme planning and
evaluation functions of the Secretariat are an essential
element of General Assembly resolution 32/197 of 20 December 1977;

4. *Recommends* that the proposals referred to in paragraph
1 of the present section should take into account the integrity of the programming and co-ordinating functions
of the Committee, as reflected in its mandate;

5. *Requests* the Secretary-General, in his report to be
submitted to the General Assembly pursuant to section
II of its resolution 38/227 A, to take into account the views
expressed by Member States at the twenty-fourth session of the Committee and at the second regular session
of 1984 of the Council;

VIII

*Preparation of the documentation for the proposed
programme budget for the biennium 1986-1987*

Requests the Secretary-General to ensure that the arrangements set out in his report on the preparation of
the documentation for the proposed programme budget
for the biennium 1986-1987 will be followed.

Economic and Social Council resolution 1984/61 A

26 July 1984   Meeting 49   Adopted without vote

Approved by Third Committee (E/1984/150) without vote, 23 July (meeting 15); 4-
nation draft (E/1984/C.3/L.6, part A), orally revised; agenda item 20.
Sponsors: Indonesia, Netherlands, Pakistan, Yugoslavia.

Also on 26 July, the Council, by resolution 1984/62,
requested CPC to study in depth the JIU report on
reporting to the Council, taking into account Member
States' views and the Secretary-General's preliminary
comments, and to submit proposals on the report
to the Council in 1985 (see under "Economic and
Social Council" below).

Report of the Secretary-General. In a November
1984 report on the restructuring of the economic

and social sectors of the United Nations system,[9]
the Secretary-General stated that the experimental phase of programme planning and programme
budgeting work, which had largely been concluded,
indicated that these processes as day-to-day management tools needed to be strengthened. Several aspects
of the interactions between CPC and sectoral and
regional bodies needed to be further clarified and
the evaluation function further strengthened.

The Secretary-General's report was taken note
of by the General Assembly in decision 39/437.

Secretariat services

On 15 and 16 May, CPC considered a statement
by the Under-Secretary-General for Administration and Management concerning measures taken
to improve secretariat support for CPC, in which
he informed the Committee that an inquiry was
under way, with consultations scheduled for June.
CPC recommended that proposals for integrating
planning and budgeting functions, to make possible a more exhaustive analysis, should be considered at the consultations. The consultations should
have the widest possible participation and should
attach due importance to the Assembly's 1977 resolution on restructuring the economic and social sectors
of the United Nations system[10] and its 1983 resolution on programme planning.[11] Proposals by the
Secretary-General should take account of the integrity of the programming and co-ordinating functions
of CPC.

ECONOMIC AND SOCIAL COUNCIL ACTION

By section VII of resolution 1984/61 A, the Economic and Social Council regretted that no proposals
to improve secretariat support services for CPC had
been submitted. It reiterated the CPC recommendation that the June consultations be held with the
widest possible participation of Member States and
re-emphasized that the programme planning and
evaluation functions of the Secretariat were an essential element of the 1977 Assembly resolution on
restructuring.[10] The Council recommended that
proposals should take account of the integrity of
the programming and co-ordinating functions of
CPC, as reflected in its mandate, and asked that the
Secretary-General's report on the subject, to be submitted pursuant to the December 1983 Assembly
resolution,[11] take account of the views expressed
by Member States at the 1984 CPC and Council (July)
sessions.

Organization of work

ECONOMIC AND SOCIAL COUNCIL ACTION

Acting without vote on the recommendation of
its Third Committee, the Economic and Social Council
adopted resolution 1984/61 C on 26 July 1984.

Twenty-fifth and twenty-sixth sessions of the Committee for Programme and Co-ordination

The Economic and Social Council

Recommends that the twenty-fifth and twenty-sixth sessions of the Committee for Programme and Co-ordination should each be of five weeks' duration, on an experimental basis, in order to allow the Committee adequate time for the discussion, *inter alia*, of the proposed programme budget for the biennium 1986-1987.

Economic and Social Council resolution 1984/61 C

26 July 1984   Meeting 49   Adopted without vote

Approved by Third Committee (E/1984/150) without vote, 23 July (meeting 15); 4-nation draft (E/1984/C.3/L.6, part C); agenda item 20.
Sponsors: Indonesia, Netherlands, Pakistan, Yugoslavia.
Financial implications. S-G, E/1984/C.3/L.12.

Following adoption of the resolution, the United States stated its understanding that the financial implications of the resolution would be included in the consolidated statement of conference-servicing requirements to be presented to the General Assembly at its 1984 session.

Joint Meetings of CPC and ACC

As it had decided in July 1983,[12] the Economic and Social Council reviewed the functioning of the Joint Meetings of CPC and ACC at its February 1984 organizational session. The Council had before it a Secretariat note[13] reproducing a 1983 ACC statement and CPC recommendations[14] on the topic, as well as the General Assembly's December request[15] regarding the application of its 1976 decision to pay out of United Nations funds the travel and subsistence expenses of one representative of each Member State represented on CPC.[16]

ECONOMIC AND SOCIAL COUNCIL ACTION

On 10 February 1984, the Economic and Social Council adopted resolution 1984/1 without vote.

Review of the functioning of the Joint Meetings of the Committee for Programme and Co-ordination and the Administrative Committee on Co-ordination

The Economic and Social Council,

Recalling its decision 1983/173 of 28 July 1983, by which it decided to review, at its organizational session for 1984, the functioning of the Joint Meetings of the Committee for Programme and Co-ordination and the Administrative Committee on Co-ordination,

Having considered the comments made in this regard by the Committee for Programme and Co-ordination and the Administrative Committee on Co-ordination,

Having considered also, in accordance with the request made by the General Assembly in its resolution 38/227 B of 20 December 1983, the question of and application of paragraph 12 of General Assembly resolution 31/93 of 14 December 1976,

1. *Decides* that the Joint Meetings of the Committee for Programme and Co-ordination and the Administrative Committee on Co-ordination shall be held at Geneva on 2 and 3 July 1984;

2. *Decides also* to review at its organizational session for 1985 the functioning of the Joint Meetings;

3. *Recommends* the Committee for Programme and Co-ordination and the Administrative Committee on Co-ordination to discuss at their next Joint Meetings the topic of the implementation of the International Development Strategy for the Third United Nations Development Decade with system-wide implications, and with special emphasis on Africa, by the organs, organizations and bodies of the United Nations system;

4. *Endorses* the conclusions and recommendations of the Committee for Programme and Co-ordination, as approved by the General Assembly in its resolution 38/227 B;

5. *Decides* to recommend to the General Assembly the continuation of the current application of paragraph 12 of Assembly resolution 31/93.

Economic and Social Council resolution 1984/1

10 February 1984   Meeting 2   Adopted without vote

Draft by President for Bureau (E/1984/L.14 & Corr.1), orally revised following informal consultations; agenda item 2.

Activities of the Joint Meetings. Pursuant to that decision, CPC and ACC held the nineteenth in their series of Joint Meetings at Geneva on 2 and 3 July 1984.[17] The topics discussed included implementation of the International Development Strategy for the Third United Nations Development Decade, with special emphasis on Africa (see p. 394); economic and technical co-operation among developing countries (see p. 401); and the functioning of the Meetings, including the agenda for 1985.

The Joint Meetings noted that, as a follow-up to the previous year's discussion on their functioning, a number of procedural improvements were being implemented. There was general agreement that the improved quality of documentation had led to a more meaningful discussion at the current Meetings, notably the ACC report on system-wide support to economic and technical co-operation among developing countries. Nevertheless, considerable dissatisfaction remained with the Meetings' functioning. It was thus agreed that the format of the proceedings needed further improvement to allow for real dialogue instead of a series of prepared statements, and that discussion should focus on problems and action-oriented solutions.

ECONOMIC AND SOCIAL COUNCIL ACTION

Acting without vote on the recommendation of its Third Committee, the Economic and Social Council adopted resolution 1984/61 B on 26 July 1984.

Joint Meetings of the Committee for Programme and Co-ordination and the Administrative Committee on Co-ordination

The Economic and Social Council

1. *Takes note* of the report of the Chairmen of the Committee for Programme and Co-ordination and the Administrative Committee on Co-ordination on the nineteenth series of Joint Meetings of the two Committees, devoted to the implementation of the International Development

Strategy for the Third United Nations Development Decade, with special emphasis on Africa, and to economic and technical co-operation among developing countries;

2. *Notes* the improvements made in the preparation of the Joint Meeting;

3. *Welcomes* the summing-up by the Secretary-General at the Joint Meeting;

4. *Notes,* however, that further progress could be made, particularly in achieving a real dialogue between the two bodies;

5. *Stresses* that the Joint Meetings should highlight the problems and difficulties faced by the specialized agencies;

6. *Recommends* in this context that:

(a) The Administrative Committee on Co-ordination should prepare for the Committee for Programme and Co-ordination a background paper on the subjects chosen for discussion at the twentieth series of Joint Meetings, that the background paper should be problem- and action-oriented, and that it should include problems faced by organizations in the field of interorganizational co-ordination;

(b) Interventions at the Joint Meetings should enable participants to focus on the problems and their solutions and to improve the dialogue between the Committee for Programme and Co-ordination and the Administrative Committee on Co-ordination.

Economic and Social Council resolution 1984/61 B

26 July 1984	Meeting 49	Adopted without vote

Approved by Third Committee (E/1984/150) without vote, 23 July (meeting 15); 4-nation draft (E/1984/C.3/L.6, part B); agenda item 20.
Sponsors: Indonesia, Netherlands, Pakistan, Yugoslavia.

Cross-organizational programme analyses

In its annual report for 1984/85,[2] ACC stated that, in 1984, two cross-organizational programme analyses were reviewed by CPC, as well as by ACC through CCSQ (Programme Matters). One was on United Nations activities in human settlements (see p. 782) and the other was undertaken in preparation for the 1985 review of economic and technical co-operation among developing countries in the medium-term plans of the United Nations system (see p. 400).

As to future cross-organizational programme analyses, CPC recommended that they should provide a basis for making specific recommendations to intergovernmental bodies and secretariats of the United Nations system, particularly on gaps in coverage, overlaps, priorities and co-ordination.

Following an ACC proposal for one of two activities—either economic and social policy research and analysis, or transport—as the subject of analysis in 1986,[18] CPC decided on the first, for which it requested the Secretariat to prepare a preliminary report on the scope and general approach to be followed; that report was discussed by ACC in October.

ECONOMIC AND SOCIAL COUNCIL ACTION

By section VI of resolution 1984/61 A, the Economic and Social Council welcomed the improvements in the recent cross-organizational programme analyses and invited all organizations, organs and bodies of the United Nations system carefully to review and follow up such analyses in their respective sectors. It requested the Secretary-General to ensure that future analyses provided a critical analysis of gaps in the coverage of mandated activities and of questions of priorities, as well as of overlaps and co-ordination.

Medium-term plans

In accordance with its 1983 decision to review on a biennial basis, starting in 1985, one or more major sectors in the medium-term plans of the organizations of the United Nations system,[19] the Economic and Social Council, by decision 1984/101 of 10 February, decided to review, on a cross-organizational basis, the question of women and development at its first regular session of 1985, and, at its second, the activities of the United Nations system in economic and technical co-operation among developing countries (see above).

In preparation for the review of women and development, a draft report was considered by the relevant machinery of ACC in October. Based on those discussions a second draft would be circulated to organizations early in 1985.

REFERENCES

[1]E/1984/66. [2]E/1985/57. [3]A/39/38 & Corr.1,2 & Add.1. [4]YUN 1983, p. 985. [5]E/1984/87. [6]YUN 1982, p. 1430, GA res. 37/234, 21 Dec. 1982. [7]YUN 1983, p. 629, GA res. 38/150, 19 Dec. 1983. [8]*Ibid.*, p. 580, GA res. 38/192, 20 Dec. 1983. [9]A/39/476. [10]YUN 1977, p. 438, GA res. 32/197, 20 Dec. 1977. [11]YUN 1983, p. 1165, GA res. 38/227 A, 20 Dec. 1983. [12]*Ibid.,* p. 988, ESC dec. 1983/173, 28 July 1983. [13]E/1984/L.12. [14]YUN 1983, p. 989. [15]*Ibid.,* p. 987, GA res. 38/227 B, 20 Dec. 1983. [16]YUN 1976, p. 888, GA res. 31/93, 14 Dec. 1976. [17]E/1984/119. [18]E/AC.51/1984/3. [19]YUN 1983, p. 990, ESC res. 1983/78, 29 July 1983.

Economic and Social Council

Proposed organizational change

The President of the Economic and Social Council, in response to a 1983 Council request,[1] orally reported on 26 July 1984 on his consultations with delegations concerning revitalization of the Council. It had repeatedly been stressed at the consultations, the President stated, that true revitalization, leading to progress on substantive issues on the Council's agenda, required first and foremost political will on the part of Member States.

Proposals put forward included focusing the Council's work on a few major themes of interest to all regions and on problems of a cross-sectoral or interdisciplinary nature, and giving increased attention to the social dimension of development. To avoid overloading the agenda, procedures should be adopted to allow more time for policy discussion of central issues, to reduce routine activities and to avoid adoption of repetitive resolutions.

As to the Council's co-ordination function, the need for a more integrated approach to United Nations activities in economic and social co-operation had been emphasized. Despite general support for more dialogue between Council members and executive heads, it had been suggested that dialogue should be limited to points made by the executive heads and to co-ordination problems requiring Council attention.

Whereas the general debate was regarded by some as a basic function of the Council, others preferred that it be abolished and replaced by substantive discussion of major agenda items, and still others that it should concentrate on specific themes, with a time-limit prescribed for statements. Interest was expressed in more informal exchange of views and in the desirability of formulating appropriate conclusions on the debate.

A study had been proposed of alternative formats for Council meetings in conjunction with a discussion of convening subject-oriented or special sessions of the Council devoted to specific issues of special concern to the international community.

ECONOMIC AND SOCIAL COUNCIL ACTION

Following the President's report, the Economic and Social Council adopted decision 1984/177.

Revitalization of the Economic and Social Council

At its 49th plenary meeting, on 26 July 1984, the Council took note of the oral report made by the President on the consultations he had held with delegations, in pursuance of Council decision 1983/181 of 29 July 1983, on the question of the revitalization of the Council.

Economic and Social Council decision 1984/177

Adopted without vote

Oral proposal by President; agenda item 5.

In connection with the President's oral report on the Council's revitalization, Mexico introduced a draft decision on alternative formats for Council meetings.[2] By the decision, the Council would bear in mind the President's statement that a renewed examination of alternatives had been recommended, as follows: the current format—an organizational session and two regular sessions, the first in New York in the spring and the second at Geneva in the summer; the same format, with the second session to take place also in New York; or one annual session of longer duration, to be convened either in New York or at Geneva, or to alternate between the two. The Council would request the Secretary-General to report on the practical implications of these alternatives for its consideration in 1985.

Pakistan said it did not see the usefulness of the proposed report because it would not come to grips with basic issues; the only way to achieve progress was to hold consultations leading to a consensus. It therefore moved that no decision be taken on the draft. The motion was adopted by a roll-call vote of 26 to 8, with 15 abstentions.

Explanations by Indonesia, Malaysia, Saint Lucia, Thailand and Yugoslavia of their affirmative votes, and by Algeria of its abstention, were to the effect that consultations on the draft had not been adequate.

Report of the Secretary-General. In a November 1984 report on the restructuring of the economic and social sectors of the United Nations system,[3] the Secretary-General described progress made by the Economic and Social Council in revitalizing its work for the effective discharge of its responsibilities. Following a 1982 resolution,[4] by which the Council had decided to identify items for priority consideration and to focus attention on selected major policy issues, items identified so far—operational activities (1983 and every three years thereafter), and the critical economic situation in Africa (1984)—were those allocated to its second regular session; it was therefore suggested that the practice be extended for items allocated to the first session. Efforts to enhance the usefulness of the general debate by formulating conclusions and recommendations had not been successful and should be pursued. Beyond the Council decision to convene, if necessary, special sessions to deal with specific issues, nothing further had resulted from Council or Assembly discussions on implementing the Assembly's recommendation that subject-oriented special sessions or periodic meetings of the Council, at the ministerial level, be convened.[5]

To carry out its co-ordination responsibilities, the Council decided in February to conduct a cross-organizational review in 1985 of two major sectors in the medium-term plans of the United Nations system (see above). At its second regular session of 1984, it introduced arrangements for an exchange of views between Council members and executive heads, following the latter's statements in plenary meeting. An additional step suggested to improve co-ordination was for the Council, at its annual organizational session, to identify for consideration a limited number of specific issues.

While no agreement had been reached on the question of the universal membership of the Council, its rules of procedure had permitted many States not Council members to co-sponsor draft proposals submitted to it. The format adopted for the Council's informal consultations for arriving at a consensus on draft proposals had encouraged active participation by States not Council members, a participation that had increased from 49 in 1982 to 67 in 1984.

As to the Assembly's recommendation that the Council assist in the preparation of the work of the

Assembly, the Council, in decision 1984/182, suggested a biennial work programme for the Assembly's Second Committee, taking into account its own biennial work programme.

Reporting procedures

By a note of May 1984,[6] the Secretary-General transmitted to the Assembly and the Council a report prepared by JIU on the subject of reporting to the Council. The report sought to highlight the problem of relations between the Secretariat and intergovernmental organs and to suggest ways to reduce difficulties preventing effective co-operation between them. JIU examined documents distributed to the Council, selected for their importance with respect to three essential functions performed by the United Nations and to which the Council contributed significantly: defining policies, co-ordinating plans and programmes in terms of content and procedures; and planning and programming of economic, social and human rights programmes.

The selected documents examined were: an issue of the *World Economic Survey*, the Committee for Development Planning (CDP) report, and other reports on world economic problems submitted mainly by organizations within the system, but also from without, which formed the basis for the Council's general debate; and the annual reports of ACC, CPC, and the CPC/ACC Joint Meetings. JIU used the example of the Committee on Natural Resources (CNR) to illustrate difficulties encountered by the Council's subsidiary bodies in contributing to its planning and programming function due to inadequate documentation.

To assist the Council to define policies through the integration of economic and social data on the world economic situation discussed at the general debate and the resultant agreed conclusions, JIU recommended that: the list and content of dossiers on specific issues for debate be established in advance; documentation guidelines with regard to maximum length, summaries and recommendations be reissued; and the format of the general debate, including formulation of conclusions, be revised, as well as the role and conditions of operation of CDP to enable the Council to use its reports.

To enhance the Council's co-ordination function, intergovernmental bodies, through CPC, should use non-secretariat experts to examine problems of system-wide co-ordination of programmes, activities and cross-organizational programme analyses.

To improve planning and programming, JIU recommended that reports of the Council's subsidiary bodies should devote a section to examining the content of all United Nations programmes in the sector concerning them at least every two years; and, on a regular basis, a section to examining the programmes of all organizations in the system in the same sector, including examination of draft medium-term plans, draft programme budgets, and other reports and analyses. All documents for the planning, programming and evaluation cycle should be distributed promptly, and a calendar for such distribution should be drawn up. Other measures concerned the improvement and wider distribution of the relevant instruments and rules and regulations; recourse to outside expertise by CPC, the Council and the Assembly; and instructions for formulating recommendations and defining procedures concerning decision-making on recommendations.

JIU concluded that revising documentation submitted to the Council would improve dialogue between the Secretariat and intergovernmental organs and increase the system's effectiveness in the economic and social fields.

Commenting on the JIU report, the Secretary-General noted[7] that, while its wide-ranging recommendations needed further examination, he would take up several points to facilitate Council discussion of the report. Although he recognized the important contribution made by outside experts to the Organization and emphasized the complementarity of their role and the Secretariat's, he asserted that the Secretariat was fully capable of making critical assessments and action-oriented recommendations when called for by legislative mandates, and possessed the requisite objectivity and professional capacity to respond to the needs of intergovernmental bodies.

On the JIU perception of a crisis in the Council's functioning, the Secretary-General drew attention to the Council's continuous efforts since 1952 to improve its working methods. The situation could not be regarded as peculiar to the Council, for it was in part a reflection of problems confronting international economic relations and multilateral co-operation.

While stressing the difficulty in reaching agreed recommendations in the general debate, given the range and complexity of the issues addressed and the diversity of interests involved, the Secretary-General concurred with the desirability of such recommendations, which the Secretariat was prepared to present if so required. He agreed that many documents issued for the debate had no direct bearing on the world economic situation. He concurred that it was necessary to ensure timely availability of documentation and to improve the quality of the *World Economic Survey*, although not that it should be reduced to a set of policy recommendations with supporting commentary on arguments for and against alternative courses of action. He confirmed that cross-organizational programme analyses had so far resulted in few substantive recommendations and that the Joint Meetings had not served their intended purposes.

Referring to the organization and financing of outside expertise by transferring part of the credits for consultants currently assigned to the Secretariat, the Secretary-General stated that, as chief administrative officer of the United Nations, he was responsible for entering into contractual arrangements on behalf of the Organization. He would, of course, respond to Assembly or Council requests for specific consultants on a priority basis. As to deficiencies in programming and co-ordination, as illustrated by the CNR report, the Secretary-General commented that improving documentation might be a necessary but not a sufficient condition for more effective governmental decision-making: the committees themselves must be willing to exercise their mandates in that area.

Finally, the Secretary-General stated that recommendations relating to the improvement of various planning, programming and evaluation instruments, the formulation of recommendations, and a production and distribution calendar for documentation required careful consideration by the Secretariat units concerned, as well as by the Programming, Planning and Budgeting Board.

ECONOMIC AND SOCIAL COUNCIL ACTION

On 26 July 1984, acting on the recommendation of its Third Committee, the Economic and Social Council adopted resolution 1984/62 without vote.

Report of the Joint Inspection Unit on reporting to the Economic and Social Council

The Economic and Social Council,

Having considered the report of the Joint Inspection Unit entitled "Reporting to the Economic and Social Council" and the comments of the Secretary-General thereon,

1. *Takes note with appreciation* of the report of the Joint Inspection Unit and the preliminary comments of the Secretary-General thereon;

2. *Recognizes* the importance of the issues covered in the report;

3. *Requests* the Secretary-General to finalize his comments on the report;

4. *Requests* the Committee for Programme and Co-ordination, at its twenty-fifth session, to study in depth the report of the Joint Inspection Unit, in accordance with its mandate, taking into account the views expressed by Member States and the comments made by the Secretary-General, and to submit its proposals on the report to the Economic and Social Council at its second regular session of 1985 for full consideration.

Economic and Social Council resolution 1984/62

26 July 1984   Meeting 49   Adopted without vote

Approved by Third Committee (E/1984/150) without vote, 23 July (meeting 15); 9-nation draft (E/1984/C.3/L.10); agenda item 20.

Sponsors: Austria, Canada, Denmark, Finland, France, Germany, Federal Republic of, Netherlands, Norway, Sweden.

GENERAL ASSEMBLY ACTION

By decision 39/437, the General Assembly took note of the JIU report and of the Secretary-General's comments thereon.

Co-operation with other organizations

Non-governmental organizations

The Committee on Non-Governmental Organizations (NGOs) met three times in 1984: in New York from 30 January to 3 February in special session,[8] and on 1 and 9 May;[9] and at Geneva on 6 July.[10]

At the special session, the Committee reviewed applications from NGOs for consultative status with the Council or for a reclassification of their status. One was recommended for category II consultative status, 13 for the Roster, one was reclassified from category II to category I and three from the Roster to category II. No decision was reached on 17 other applications. Another four were not considered, three of them on the applicant's request.

As stated in its report, the Committee also reviewed quadrennial reports submitted by 26 NGOs in categories I and II on their United Nations–related activities during 1978-1981. It took note of 23 of these and postponed consideration of the remaining three, pending, in one case, receipt of additional information, and, in another, clarification that the reporting NGO's activities were in line with relevant Council resolutions. Of the NGOs which failed to submit reports, the Committee was informed that two had been dissolved; four others were recommended to the Council for suspension and ultimately for the withdrawal of their consultative status if they failed to submit their reports in 1984.

In May and July, the Committee heard requests from NGOs with consultative status to address the Council or its committees in connection with items on the Council's agenda. Three organizations in category I were recommended to be heard at the Council's May session, and eight in the same category at its July session. The Council received statements from eight NGOs[11] concerning specific areas of its work.

ECONOMIC AND SOCIAL COUNCIL ACTION

In May, acting on recommendations of the Committee on NGOs, the Economic and Social Council adopted decision 1984/113, section I by roll-call vote and sections II and III without vote.

Non-governmental organizations

I

Report of the Committee on Non-Governmental Organizations on its special session

At its 10th plenary meeting, on 9 May 1984, the Council decided:

(a) To take note of the report of the Committee on Non-Governmental Organizations on its 1984 special session, with the exception of the recommendation for the reclassification from the Roster to category II of the International Police Association;

(b) Taking into account the concern expressed by members of the Council on the link between the International Police Association and *apartheid* South Africa and having in mind its resolution 1982/16 of 4 May 1982, not to approve the reclassification to category II of the International Police Association;

(c) In accordance with the relevant provisions of resolution 1296(XLIV) of 23 May 1968, to invite the Committee on Non-Governmental Organizations to reconsider the current status of the International Police Association, bearing in mind Council resolution 1982/16;

(d) To consider further the current status of the International Police Association with a view to taking a final decision at its first regular session of 1985.

II
Applications for consultative status
and requests for reclassification received
from non-governmental organizations

At the same meeting, the Council further decided:

(a) To grant the following non-governmental organizations consultative status:

Category II
Asociación Interamericana Presupuesto Público;

Roster
Asian Pacific Youth Forum, The (APYF);
Association of Geoscientists for International Development;
Continental Africa Chamber of Commerce (CACC);
International Advertising Association (IAA);
International Centre of Sociological, Penal and Penitentiary Research and Studies;
International Committee on Public Relations in Rehabilitation (ICPRR);
International Confederation of Ex-Prisoners of War;
International Narcotic Enforcement Officers Association, Inc. (INEOA);
International Public Policy Institute;
National Indian Youth Council, The;
Regional Studies Association (RSA);
Union of Technical Assistance for Motor Vehicle and Road Traffic (UNATAC);
Water Supply Improvement Association;

(b) To reclassify Soroptimist International from category II to category I consultative status and the International Abolitionist Federation and OISCA— International (Organization for Industrial, Spiritual and Cultural Advancement—International) from the Roster to category II.

III
Suspension of non-governmental organizations
in consultative status with the Council

Also at the same meeting, the Council, regretting that four non-governmental organizations in category II consultative status, namely, the Federation of Arab Economists, the Inter-American Federation of Public Relations Associations, the International Federation of Landscape Architects and the World Council of Management, had failed to submit quadrennial reports pursuant to the provisions of Council resolution 1296(XLIV), decided to suspend those organizations, and also decided that, if the quadrennial reports were not received from them in 1984, it would withdraw their consultative status.

Economic and Social Council decision 1984/113

Sect. I, 45-1-4 (roll-call vote); II & III, without vote

Section I—24-nation draft (E/1984/L.20), orally revised; sections II and III—drafts by Committee on NGOs (E/1984/29), section II orally amended by President; agenda item 7.

Sponsors: Algeria, Bolivia, Congo, Cuba, Cyprus, Ecuador, Gambia, Guyana, Indonesia, Malaysia, Mali, Mexico, Nicaragua, Nigeria, Pakistan, Saint Lucia, Sierra Leone, Somalia, Thailand, Uganda, USSR, Yugoslavia, Zaire, Zambia.
Meeting numbers. ESC 5-7, 10, 11.

Roll-call vote in Council as follows:

In favour: Algeria, Argentina, Austria, Botswana, Brazil, Bulgaria, Canada, China, Colombia, Congo, Costa Rica, Djibouti, Ecuador, Finland, German Democratic Republic, Greece, Indonesia, Japan, Lebanon, Liberia, Luxembourg, Malaysia, Mali, Mexico, Netherlands, New Zealand, Pakistan, Papua New Guinea, Poland, Romania, Rwanda, Saint Lucia, Saudi Arabia, Sierra Leone, Somalia, Suriname, Swaziland, Sweden, Thailand, Tunisia, Uganda, USSR, Venezuela, Yugoslavia, Zaire.
Against: United States.
Abstaining: France, Germany, Federal Republic of, Portugal, United Kingdom.

Before its adoption, the President amended paragraph (b) of section II of the draft to delete the International Police Association (IPA) from among the NGOs recommended for reclassification from the Roster to category II.

In explanation of vote on section I of the decision, the United States said it was unfortunate that the sponsors had preferred to sacrifice the moral authority of a consensus decision for the sake of slogans. If the Council meant to establish criteria based on human rights violations, as paragraph (b) seemed to suggest, a universal application of such criteria would be required, which could lead to a paralysing politicization of the Committee's work.

France regretted the failure to reach a compromise, since there was no disagreement on substance. The implied link between IPA and the _apartheid_ régime did not reflect the true situation. Moreover, paragraph (b) went beyond the 1982 Council resolution on NGO activities,[12] making the granting of consultative status conditional on an NGO having no members in South Africa. Such a condition was contrary to the principle of universality of the United Nations.

Saying its abstention was due to the wording of paragraphs (b) to (d), the United Kingdom said it could not accept their implication that the application for reclassification of an NGO with members in South Africa would be turned down. Section I had set a precedent for the treatment of NGOs, which the Council might come to regret.

Canada hoped that procedures for dealing with NGOs with involvement in South Africa could be finalized so that the Committee could continue to work by consensus. While regretting the lack of consensus in this instance, Japan fully shared the feeling of Council members concerning the misleading information provided by IPA. Finland and Sweden supported further Committee consideration of IPA's application but felt that the decision went beyond what they would have liked to see in a procedural text. Given the substantial contribution made by NGOs to the work of the United Nations, the Netherlands felt it important that the forthcoming Committee deliberations should not be prejudiced.

The number of NGOs in consultative status with the Council rose to 712 during 1984.[13] They were divided into three groups: category I, organizations representative of major population segments in a large number of countries, involved with the economic and social life of the areas they represented; category II, international organizations having special competence in a few of the Council's areas of activity; and organizations on the Roster, considered able to make occasional and useful contributions to the Council's work. (For list of NGOs in consultative status as at 31 December 1983, see YUN 1983, p. 992.)

Intergovernmental organizations

Intergovernmental Bureau for Informatics

ECONOMIC AND SOCIAL COUNCIL ACTION

In July, the Economic and Social Council adopted decision 1984/158 without vote.

Participation of the Intergovernmental Bureau for Informatics in the work of the Economic and Social Council

At its 30th plenary meeting, on 10 July 1984, the Council, having considered the application of the Intergovernmental Bureau for Informatics, decided, in accordance with rule 79 of the rules of procedure of the Council, that the Intergovernmental Bureau for Informatics might participate, on a continuing basis, without the right to vote, in the deliberations of the Council on questions within the scope of the activities of that organization.

Economic and Social Council decision 1984/158

Adopted without vote

Draft by President, for Bureau (E/1984/L.35); agenda item 2.

Other organizational matters

Work programme for 1984-1985

At its 1984 organizational session, held in New York from 7 to 10 and 21 February and on 16 March, the Economic and Social Council considered the draft basic programme of work for 1984-1985, submitted by the Secretary-General.[14] It also considered a draft decision on the provisional agenda of its first and second regular sessions, including questions for inclusion in its work programme for 1985.[15] Following consideration of both documents, the Council, on 10 February, adopted decision 1984/101 without vote.

By that decision, the Council approved the basic work programme and provisional agenda for the first and second regular sessions of 1984, and allocated items to its sessional committees and plenary meetings. It decided, among other things: to give priority consideration, at its second regular session, to the critical economic situation in Africa, and at its first regular session, to consider the question of the second priority issue; to have a sessional working group review, also at the first session, the draft guidelines on consumer protection; to consider progress in implementing its July 1983 resolution on the promotion of interregional economic and technical co-

operation among developing countries;[16] to review recurrent and other documents requested under existing legislative authority to determine whether they should be issued at longer intervals or discontinued as redundant; and to transmit directly to the General Assembly the annual reports of the Council of the United Nations University, the Trade and Development Board and the Human Rights Committee, and to consider in 1984 rescheduling the Board and Committee meetings.

The Council took note of a list of questions for inclusion in its 1985 work programme and decided, in accordance with its resolutions of 1982[4] and 1983,[17] to review, on a cross-organizational basis, during its first 1985 regular session, the question of women and development, and, during the second, the activities of the United Nations system in economic and technical co-operation among developing countries.

The Council held its first regular session in New York from 1 to 25 May, and its second regular session at Geneva from 4 to 27 July. The Second (Social) Committee met at the first session, and the Sessional Working Group of Governmental Experts on the Implementation of the International Covenant on Economic, Social and Cultural Rights met prior to and at that session. The First (Economic) Committee and the Third (Programme and Co-ordination) Committee met at the second session.

Meeting numbers. ESC 1, 2.

Agenda of 1984 sessions

On 7 February 1984, the Economic and Social Council adopted the provisional agenda for its February/March organizational session, which contained six items together with background information on each.[18] The provisional annotated agenda for the first regular session listing 15 items[19]—approved on 10 February by decision 1984/101—together with the proposed schedule of work, as revised,[20] was adopted on 1 May.[21]

On 25 May, the Council had before it a provisional agenda for its second regular session, containing 24 items and a suggested organization of work,[22] which it approved after adding an item entitled "Elections and nominations" and orally revising the work organization (see below). The agenda was adopted at the opening of the session, on 4 July,[23] based on an annotated provisional agenda.[24] (For the agenda lists, see APPENDIX IV.)

ECONOMIC AND SOCIAL COUNCIL ACTION

In May, the Economic and Social Council adopted without vote decision 1984/157.

Provisional agenda and organization of work for the second regular session of 1984 of the Council

At its 22nd plenary meeting, on 25 May 1984, the Council approved the draft provisional agenda for the second regular session of 1984, and the proposed organization of work for that session, as orally revised.

Economic and Social Council decision 1984/157

Adopted without vote

Draft provisional agenda and suggested organization of work (E/1984/L.31), orally revised by President; agenda item 15.

Meetings of subsidiary bodies

ECONOMIC AND SOCIAL COUNCIL ACTION

In February, the Economic and Social Council adopted without vote decision 1984/104.

Review of the cycle of meetings of subsidiary bodies of the Economic and Social Council

At its 2nd plenary meeting, on 10 February 1984, the Council decided, pursuant to General Assembly decision 38/429 of 19 December 1983, and Council resolution 1768(LIV) of 18 May 1973, to request its subsidiary bodies that currently meet on an annual basis to consider adopting, on an experimental basis, a biennial cycle of meetings, and to report thereon to the Council in 1984.

Economic and Social Council decision 1984/104

Adopted without vote

Draft by President, for Bureau (E/1984/L.14 & Corr.1); agenda item 2.

Following adoption of the decision, France—referring to existing authorization for CDP, the Commission on Human Rights and its Sub-Commission, and the regional commissions to meet in annual session—said it was the European Economic Community's understanding that the decision in no way prejudiced any decisions that might be taken by those bodies on the periodicity of their meetings. The United States associated itself with that remark. For Tunisia, the decision would lighten the work-load of the Council and the General Assembly by reducing the number of reports submitted to them for consideration.

Limitation of documentation

In 1984, the Secretariat reported in April[25] and June[26] on the state of preparedness of documentation for the Economic and Social Council's first and second regular sessions. The reports were submitted in keeping with 1979 Council resolutions[27] on the limitation of documents and their circulation in all working languages six weeks before the opening of the Council sessions and those of its subsidiary bodies.

The reports noted that, to allow time for clearances and editing, documentation should have been submitted for the first session by 21 February and circulated by 20 March, and, for the second, by 25 April and circulated by 23 May. A table on the status of documentation annexed to each report showed the documents that failed to make the circulation date; explanations for the delay were to be provided by the responsible offices.

Financial implications of resolutions and decisions

In a July 1984 report,[28] the Secretary-General submitted a summary of estimates of programme budget implications of resolutions and decisions adopted by the Economic and Social Council in 1984. The estimated costs for 1984-1985, excluding those for conference servicing ($3,608,500), totalled $1,321,500. This figure was subject to change in the light of a review by the General Assembly to determine how much of the costs might be absorbed within appropriations.

ECONOMIC AND SOCIAL COUNCIL ACTION

In July, following consideration of the Secretary-General's report and acting without vote on an oral proposal by its President, the Economic and Social Council adopted decision 1984/189.

Summary of estimates of programme budget implications of resolutions and decisions adopted by the Economic and Social Council during its first and second regular sessions of 1984

At its 50th plenary meeting, on 27 July 1984, the Council took note of the report of the Secretary-General containing the summary of estimates of programme budget implications of resolutions and decisions adopted by the Council during its first and second regular sessions of 1984.

Economic and Social Council decision 1984/189

Adopted without vote

Oral proposal by President.

GENERAL ASSEMBLY ACTION

On the recommendation of the Fifth (Administrative and Budgetary) Committee, the General Assembly approved a net addition of $794,000 to the 1984-1985 budget to cover a number of 1984 Economic and Social Council actions having financial implications. This amount—of which $517,000 related to 1984 and $277,000 to 1985—was approved by the Fifth Committee, on 27 November 1984, by 77 votes to 2, with 7 abstentions, based on a recommendation by ACABQ[29] reducing (by $101,600) the amount ($895,600) requested by the Secretary-General in a report revising his initial submission for the budget as a whole.[30]

Related conference-servicing requirements were dealt with separately (see p. 1175).

During consideration of the revised estimates and ACABQ recommendations, the United Kingdom questioned the need for what it regarded as still a considerable sum for the Seventh (1985) United Nations Congress on the Prevention of Crime and the Treatment of Offenders. The United Kingdom questioned the increase in expert consultants invited to the Congress, from the original 5 provided for in the budget to 25, and the attendance of so many Department of Public Information staff at considerable financial cost. The United States, which had requested the vote, considered the additional appropriation excessive and could not support it.

Meeting number. GA 39th session: 5th Committee 35.

Report for 1984

The work of the Economic and Social Council at its organizational and two regular sessions in 1984 was summarized in its annual report to the General Assembly.[31] Parts of the report were considered by the plenary Assembly, others by the Second, Third, Fourth and Fifth Committees.

GENERAL ASSEMBLY ACTION

In December, the General Assembly adopted two decisions on the report: 39/449, taking note of those chapters that had been allocated to the Fifth Committee; and 39/453, of those assigned to the plenary Assembly.

Decision 39/449 was adopted without vote, following consideration of the Committee's recommendation.

Report of the Economic and Social Council

At its 105th plenary meeting, on 18 December 1984, the General Assembly, on the recommendation of the Fifth Committee, took note of chapters I, III (part I, sect. B, and part II, sect. F), V (sect. C), VI (sect. C), VIII and IX (part I, sects. C, F, G, I and Q, and part II, sects. F and G) of the report of the Economic and Social Council.

General Assembly decision 39/449

Adopted without vote

Approved by Fifth Committee (A/39/847) without objection, 15 December (meeting 53); agenda item 12.

Decision 39/453 was also adopted without vote, following an oral proposal by the Assembly President.

Report of the Economic and Social Council

At its 105th plenary meeting, on 18 December 1984, the General Assembly took note of chapters I, II, VIII and IX (part I, sects. A, B and P, and part II, sects. A to E) of the report of the Economic and Social Council.

General Assembly decision 39/453

Adopted without vote

Oral proposal by President; agenda item 12.

Also in December, acting without vote on the recommendation of its Second Committee, the Assembly adopted decision 39/445.

Documents relating to the report of the Economic and Social Council

At its 104th plenary meeting, on 18 December 1984, the General Assembly, on the recommendation of the Second Committee, took note of the following reports:

(a) Report of the Secretary-General on the world population situation in 1983;

(b) Report of the Secretary-General entitled "Transport and Communications Decade in Africa: implementation of General Assembly resolution 38/150";

(c) Report of the Secretary-General on the Transport and Communications Decade in Africa;

(d) Report of the Secretary-General on special measures for the social and economic development of Africa in the 1980s;

(e) Report of the Secretary-General on permanent sovereignty over national resources in the occupied Palestinian and other Arab territories.

General Assembly decision 39/445

Adopted without vote

Approved by Second Committee (A/39/789/Add.2) without vote, 14 December (meeting 60); oral proposal by Chairman; agenda item 12.

REFERENCES

[1]YUN 1983, p. 991, ESC dec. 1983/181, 29 July 1983. [2]E/1984/L.39. [3]A/39/476. [4]YUN 1982, p. 1241, ESC res. 1982/50, 28 July 1982. [5]YUN 1977, p. 438, GA res. 32/197, 20 Dec. 1977. [6]A/39/281-E/1984/81 & Corr.1 & Add.1. [7]A/39/281/Add.2-E/1984/81/Add.2. [8]E/1984/29. [9]E/1984/80 & Add.1. [10]E/1984/131. [11]E/1984/NGO/1-8. [12]YUN 1982, p. 304, ESC res. 1982/16, 4 May 1982. [13]E/1984/INF/7. [14]E/1984/1 & Add.1. [15]E/1984/L.14 & Corr.1. [16]YUN 1983, p. 418, ESC res. 1983/66, 29 July 1983. [17]*Ibid.*, p. 990, ESC res. 1983/78, 29 July 1983. [18]E/1984/2. [19]E/1984/30. [20]E/1984/L.17. [21]E/1984/73. [22]E/1984/L.31. [23]E/1984/128. [24]E/1984/100. [25]E/1984/L.16/Rev.1. [26]E/1984/L.32. [27]YUN 1979, pp. 1217 & 1218, ESC res. 1979/1 & 1979/69, 9 Feb. & 2 Aug. 1979. [28]E/1984/152 & Corr.1. [29]A/39/7/Add.6. [30]A/C.5/39/25. [31]A/39/3.

PUBLICATIONS

Index to Proceedings of the Economic and Social Council, Organizational session, First regular session, Second regular session—1984 (ST/LIB/SER.B/E.61), Sales No. E.85.I.12. *Resolutions and Decisions of the Economic and Social Council*, 1984: organizational session (New York, 7-10 and 21 February and 16 March); first regular session (New York, 1-25 May); second regular session (Geneva, 4-27 July), E/1984/84 & Add.1.

Organizational structure

In addition to a review of the structure and functioning of the Department of Technical Co-operation for Development (see p. 456), and of the question of strengthening the regional commissions (see p. 602) and revitalizing the Economic and Social Council (see p. 976), other aspects of the ongoing process of restructuring the economic and social sectors of the United Nations system, initiated with the adoption in 1977 of a General Assembly resolution on the subject,[1] were considered in 1984. These concerned the organization of work of the Assembly's Second Committee, as well as restructuring issues relating to DIESA and OSSECS (see below).

In his November 1984 report on restructuring,[2] the Secretary-General noted improvements in planning and programming; in the co-ordination of operational activities for development at the field level, and of certain secretariat support services at Headquarters and in the regions; and in the functioning of central intergovernmental bodies, particularly the Economic and Social Council, and of the intersecretariat co-ordination machinery. There was an urgent need, however, for Member Governments, with Secretariat assistance, to take such measures as were necessary for the Assembly to play the central role in the economic and social sectors of the United Nations system envisaged for it in the 1977 resolution.

In that context, the Secretary-General urged that special consideration be given to: the continued streamlining of the Economic and Social Council for a more effective functioning, particularly in co-ordination responsibilities; strengthening the role of other intergovernmental negotiating forums, including UNCTAD, ensuring their close interaction with the Council and the Assembly; increasing the efficiency of secretariat support services by enhanced complementarity of work of their constituent units; overcoming compartmentalization of research activities, on the one hand, and technical co-operation activities on the other, and improving their quality and relevance; strengthening regional structures; improving interagency co-ordination; and flexibility and adaptability of policies and procedures governing operational activities for development to take account of the changing requirements of developing countries.

ECONOMIC AND SOCIAL COUNCIL ACTION

In July, having considered several reports relating to the restructuring of the economic and social sectors of the United Nations system, the Economic and Social Council adopted decision 1984/178 without vote.

Reports considered by the Economic and Social Council in connection with the question of the restructuring of the economic and social sectors of the United Nations system, including the revitalization of the Council

At its 49th plenary meeting, on 26 July 1984, the Council took note of the following reports:

(a) Report of the Joint Inspection Unit entitled "United Nations Department of Technical Co-operation for Development" and the comments of the Secretary-General thereon;

(b) Report of the Joint Inspection Unit entitled "United Nations Department of International Economic and Social Affairs" and the comments of the Secretary-General thereon;

(c) Report of the Joint Inspection Unit entitled "Office of Secretariat Services for Economic and Social Matters" and the comments of the Secretary-General thereon;

(d) Report of the Secretary-General on the further implementation of General Assembly resolution 37/214 of 20 December 1982.

Economic and Social Council decision 1984/178

Adopted without vote

Draft orally proposed by President; agenda item 6.

GENERAL ASSEMBLY ACTION

In accordance with a 1982 decision,[3] the General Assembly had before it a note by the Secretariat[4] containing a draft resolution on implementation of section II of the annex to the 1977 Assembly resolution.[1] In December, acting without vote on the recommendation of the Second Committee, the Assembly adopted decision 39/436.

Implementation of section II of the annex to General Assembly resolution 32/197 on the restructuring of the economic and social sectors of the United Nations system

At its 104th plenary meeting, on 18 December 1984, the General Assembly, on the recommendation of the Second Committee, decided to refer to its forty-second session for consideration the draft resolution entitled "Implementation of section II of the annex to General Assembly resolution 32/197 on the restructuring of the economic and social sectors of the United Nations system".

General Assembly decision 39/436

Adopted without vote

Approved by Second Committee (A/39/790/Add.8) without vote, 14 December (meeting 61); oral proposal by Vice-Chairman; agenda item 80 (h).

General Assembly

In his November report,[2] the Secretary-General summarized the progress made in strengthening the effectiveness of the General Assembly as the principal forum for policy-making and harmonizing international efforts to resolve economic, social and related problems.

One of the most comprehensive actions by the Assembly in that area was its adoption of the International Development Strategy for the Third United Nations Development Decade[5] as the policy framework for formulating and implementing the work programmes and medium-term plans of the United Nations system. To allow the Assembly to monitor follow-up action to its policy recommendations, such mechanisms as the annual review and comprehensive triennial policy review of operational activities for development were instituted.

The Assembly also adopted several major programmes of international action (in new and renewable sources of energy, and science and technology; for the least developed countries, the advancement of women, the aging and the disabled), established committees to assist it in guiding such activities, and acted on the outcome of major international conferences, such as the sixth session of UNCTAD (1983). It adopted resolutions covering a wide range of international issues and concerns, from food and agriculture to various aspects of the social situation.

A number of constraints continued to exist, however, including the failure to launch the global negotiations on international economic co-operation for development called for by the Assembly in 1979[6] (see also p. 390). Deliberations in the Committee of the Whole had highlighted the difficulty of reaching agreement on a proper balance between the central role of the Assembly and the sectoral role of other United Nations negotiating forums.

Second Committee

The Secretary-General observed in his November report on restructuring[2] that consideration of the biennial programme of work of the Second Committee at the 1984 General Assembly session could provide an opportunity to review the formulation and clustering of agenda items in the economic and social area. Referring to the further rationalization of the decision-making process in the Second and Third Committees, he suggested that the goal should be a more systematic effort to identify priority issues. The distribution of work between the two Committees should be given further attention, with the Second Committee concentrating on economic policy issues, and the Third, on social policy issues. Arrangements for consultations between the Bureaux of the two Committees could be usefully instituted to this end.

ECONOMIC AND SOCIAL COUNCIL ACTION

Pursuant to an Assembly request of December 1983,[7] the Economic and Social Council formulated recommendations for a biennial programme of work for the Assembly's Second Committee, which were annexed to decision 1984/182, adopted without vote in July.

Biennial programme of work for the Second Committee of the General Assembly

At its 50th plenary meeting, on 27 July 1984, the Council, pursuant to General Assembly decision 38/429 of 19 December 1983, decided:

(a) To recommend to the General Assembly the consideration of the suggestions relating to the biennial programme of work for the Second Committee of the General Assembly as contained in the annex to the present decision;

(b) To request the Secretary-General to prepare accordingly proposals for a draft biennial programme of work for the Second Committee of the General Assembly and to submit it to the Assembly at its thirty-ninth session.

ANNEX
Suggestions relating to the biennial programme of work for the Second Committee of the General Assembly

1. The Second Committee of the General Assembly, in drawing up its biennial programmes of work, should endeavour to adopt, to the extent possible, a biennial cycle of consideration of reports submitted to it, with the exception of those reports which are specifically to be considered annually, once every three years or more, or on an *ad hoc* basis.

2. To this end, the Second Committee should consider all reports of standing intergovernmental bodies on a biennial basis, except the reports of the Economic and Social Council, the Trade and Development Board and the United Nations Development Programme. In alternate years, when those reports are not considered directly by the General Assembly, the Economic and Social Council should consider and take action on them and, where appropriate, submit its recommendations to the Second Committee. In respect of those reports, the General Assembly, in those years, will act only on the recommendations of the Council.

3. The Second Committee should also consider, in principle, all recurrent Secretariat reports on a biennial basis, except the report of the Director-General for Development and International Economic Co-operation on operational activities for development and all those reports which are specifically to be considered once every three years or more. The cycle of submission of Secretariat reports should henceforth conform to the biennial programme of work of the Second Committee.

4. Future requests for Secretariat reports to be submitted to the Second Committee should be in conformity with the biennial programme of work.

5. Intergovernmental bodies reporting to the Second Committee are further requested to consider adopting a biennial cycle of meetings in conformity with the biennial programme of work of the Second Committee.

6. The Second Committee should accordingly draw up its biennial programme of work with the following proposed breakdown and should review it periodically thereafter:

(a) Annual consideration:
(i) General debate;
(ii) Development and international economic co-operation;
(iii) Report of the Economic and Social Council;
(iv) Trade and development;
(v) Operational activities for development: report of the Director-General for Development and International Economic Co-operation;
(vi) Report of the Governing Council of the United Nations Development Programme;

(b) Biennial consideration in odd years:
(i) Environment;
(ii) Human settlements;
(iii) Science and technology for development;
(iv) Economic and technical co-operation among developing countries;
(v) Implementation of the Substantial New Programme of Action for the 1980s for the Least Developed Countries;
(vi) Effective mobilization and integration of women in development;
(vii) United Nations Institute for Training and Research;
(viii) United Nations University;
(ix) Technical co-operation activities undertaken by the Secretary-General;
(x) Role of the public sector in promoting the economic development of developing countries;
(xi) Special programmes of economic assistance (first cluster of countries to be identified later);

(c) Biennial consideration in even years:
(i) Industrialization;
(ii) Food problems;
(iii) New and renewable sources of energy;
(iv) Development of the energy resources of developing countries;
(v) Office of the United Nations Disaster Relief Co-ordinator;
(vi) World Food Programme;

(vii)   United Nations Capital Development Fund;
(viii) United Nations Fund for Population Activities;
(ix)   United Nations Volunteers programme;
(x)   United Nations Children's Fund;
(xi)   Implementation of the medium-term and long-term recovery and rehabilitation programme in the Sudano-Sahelian region;
(xii)   Special programmes of economic assistance (second cluster of countries to be identified later);
(d)   Consideration as required or at longer intervals:
(i)   Review and appraisal of the International Development Strategy for the Third United Nations Development Decade;
(ii)   Charter of Economic Rights and Duties of States;
(iii)   Immediate measures in favour of the developing countries;
(iv)   Restructuring of the economic and social sectors of the United Nations system;*
(v)   United Nations Special Fund;
(vi)   United Nations Revolving Fund for Natural Resources Exploration;
(vii)   United Nations Special Fund for Land-locked Developing Countries;
(viii) Unified approach to development analysis and planning;
(ix)   Long-term trends in economic development;
(x)   Role of qualified national personnel in the social and economic development of developing countries.

---

*The Second Committee should consider this item every three years, and the cycle of its consideration should correspond to that of the proposed medium-term plan by the General Assembly.

Economic and Social Council decision 1984/182

Adopted without vote

Draft by President (E/1984/L.40), orally revised following informal consultations; agenda item 6.
Meeting numbers. ESC 49, 50.

Before adoption of the decision, Mexico stated that the Group of 77 developing countries felt that the question of the Second Committee's programme of work was a delicate matter, affecting the division of functions among main United Nations organs. The Group, therefore, supported the draft text on the understanding that the decision was a temporary one, to be superseded by a final decision that should be reached through detailed analysis and wide-ranging consultations, and reserved the right to propose amendments when the Assembly considered the Council recommendations.

GENERAL ASSEMBLY ACTION

Acting without vote on the recommendation of the Second Committee, the General Assembly adopted resolution 39/217 on 18 December 1984.

Biennial programme of work for the Second Committee

The General Assembly,

Recalling its decision 38/429 of 19 December 1983, in which it decided to adopt, beginning at its fortieth ses-

sion, a biennial programme of work for the Second Committee, apart from its general debate,

Taking note of Economic and Social Council decision 1984/182 of 27 July 1984, in which it recommended to the General Assembly for its consideration a number of suggestions relating to the biennial programme of work for the Second Committee, contained in the annex to that decision,

1. *Decides* that the Second Committee, in drawing up its biennial programmes of work, should:

(a) Endeavour to adopt a biennial cycle of consideration of reports submitted to it, with the exception of those reports which are specifically mandated to be considered annually, once every three years or more, or on an *ad hoc* basis;

(b) Consider all reports of standing intergovernmental bodies on a biennial basis, except the reports of the Economic and Social Council, the Trade and Development Board and the Governing Council of the United Nations Development Programme;

(c) Consider, in principle, all recurrent Secretariat reports on a biennial basis, except the report of the Director-General for Development and International Economic Co-operation on operational activities for development;

2. *Decides* to approve, in principle, annex I to the present resolution as the basis for the formulation of the biennial programme of work for the Second Committee and to review it periodically;

3. *Decides* that all requests for Secretariat reports to be submitted to the Second Committee should henceforth conform to the biennial programme of work, except where the urgency of the subject-matter requires otherwise;

4. *Requests* intergovernmental bodies reporting to the Second Committee to adjust their cycle of meetings to conform to the biennial programme of work;

5. *Requests* the Secretary-General to submit to the Second Committee for consideration and approval each year a proposed biennial programme of work, taking into account relevant resolutions and decisions of the General Assembly of that year;

6. *Requests* the Economic and Social Council, in discharging its responsibilities in preparing the work of the General Assembly in the economic, social and related fields, to take fully into account the approved programme of work for the Second Committee of the General Assembly in formulating its own biennial programme of work and in this context:

(a) To concentrate, in its consideration of reports of intergovernmental bodies submitted through it to the General Assembly, on the co-ordination aspect of the work of those bodies in conformity with the relevant provisions of the Charter of the United Nations;

(b) To consider undertaking an in-depth review of the reports of intergovernmental bodies which the General Assembly does not consider directly in a given year and to submit substantive recommendations thereon to the Assembly for consideration and action;

(c) To consider reviewing those reports of intergovernmental bodies which the General Assembly considers directly in a given year but not to consider draft proposals on them, except specific recommendations contained in the reports which require action by the Council and proposals that concern matters relating to the co-ordination aspect of the work of those bodies;

(d) To transmit in some cases, as it deems appropriate, certain reports directly to the General Assembly without debate;

7. *Decides* to approve the biennial programme of work for the Second Committee for 1985-1986 contained in annex II to the present resolution.

ANNEX I
Programme of work for the Second Committee
A. *Annual consideration*
1. General debate
2. Development and international economic co-operation
3. Report of the Economic and Social Council
4. Report of the Trade and Development Board
5. Report of the Director-General for Development and International Economic Co-operation on operational activities for development of the United Nations system
6. Report of the Governing Council of the United Nations Development Programme

B. *Biennial consideration in odd years*
1. Environment
2. Human settlements
3. Science and technology for development
4. Economic and technical co-operation among developing countries
5. Implementation of the Substantial New Programme of Action for the 1980s for the Least Developed Countries
6. Effective mobilization and integration of women in development
7. Technical co-operation activities undertaken by the Secretary-General
8. United Nations Capital Development Fund
9. United Nations Volunteers programme
10. Special programmes of economic assistance*

C. *Biennial consideration in even years*
1. Industrialization
2. Food problems
3. New and renewable sources of energy
4. Development of the energy resources of developing countries
5. Office of the United Nations Disaster Relief Coordinator
6. World Food Programme
7. United Nations Fund for Population Activities
8. United Nations Children's Fund
9. United Nations Institute for Training and Research
10. United Nations University
11. Implementation of the medium-term and long-term recovery and rehabilitation programme in the Sudano-Sahelian region
12. Special programmes of economic assistance*

D. *Consideration as required or at longer intervals*
1. Review and appraisal of the International Development Strategy for the Third United Nations Development Decade
2. Charter of Economic Rights and Duties of States
3. Restructuring of the economic and social sectors of the United Nations system†
4. United Nations Special Fund

5. United Nations Revolving Fund for Natural Resources Exploration
6. United Nations Special Fund for Land-locked Developing Countries
7. Unified approach to development analysis and planning
8. Long-term trends in economic development
9. Role of qualified national personnel in the social and economic development of developing countries
10. Role of the public sector in promoting the economic development of developing countries

ANNEX II
Biennial programme of work for the Second Committee for 1985-1986‡
1985
Item 1. *Report of the Economic and Social Council*§
  (a) *Permanent sovereignty over national resources in the occupied Palestinian and other Arab territories*
  Documentation
    Report of the Secretary-General on permanent sovereignty over national resources in the occupied Palestinian and other Arab territories
  (b) *Assistance to the Palestinian people*
  Documentation
    Report of the Secretary-General on assistance to the Palestinian people
    Report of the Secretary-General on economic development projects in the occupied Palestinian territories
  (c) *Transport and Communications Decade in Africa*
  Documentation
    Report of the Secretary-General on the Transport and Communications Decade in Africa
  (d) *Critical situation of food and agriculture in Africa*
  Documentation
    Report of the Secretary-General on the critical situation of food and agriculture in Africa
  (e) *Industrial Development Decade for Africa*
  Documentation
    Report of the Secretary-General on the Industrial Development Decade for Africa
  (f) *Countries stricken by desertification and drought*
  Documentation
    Report of the Secretary-General on countries stricken by desertification and drought
  (g) *Target for World Food Programme pledges for the period 1987-1988*
  (h) *Code of conduct on transnational corporations*
  Documentation
    Report of the Commission on Transnational Corporations on its reconvened special session
  (i) *World Tourism Organization*
  Documentation
    Report of the Secretary-General of the World Tourism Organization on the implementation of the Manila Declaration and the Acapulco Document on World Tourism

Item 2. *Development and international economic co-operation*||
  Documentation
    Report of the Secretary-General on international co-operation in the fields of money, finance, debt and resource flows, including development assistance and trade, with special attention to the interests of developing countries

(a)   *International Development Strategy for the Third United Nations Development Decade*

(b)   *Charter of Economic Rights and Duties of States*
Documentation
  Report of the *Ad Hoc* Committee of the Whole to Review the Implementation of the Charter of Economic Rights and Duties of States

(c)   *Trade and development*
Documentation
  Report of the Trade and Development Board
  Report of the Secretary-General on the development aspects of the reverse transfer of technology
  Report of the Secretary-General on economic measures as a means of political and economic coercion against developing countries

(d)   *Science and technology for development*
Documentation
  Report of the Intergovernmental Committee on Science and Technology for Development

(e)   *Economic and technical co-operation among developing countries*
Documentation
  Report of the High-level Committee on the Review of Technical Co-operation among Developing Countries
  Report of the Secretary-General on activities of the United Nations system in support of economic co-operation among developing countries

(f)   *Environment*
Documentation
  Report of the Governing Council of the United Nations Environment Programme
  Report of the Governing Council of the United Nations Environment Programme on the implementation of the Plan of Action to Combat Desertification
  Report of the Governing Council of the United Nations Environment Programme on the implementation of the Plan of Action to Combat Desertification in the Sudano-Sahelian region
  Note by the Secretary-General on international conventions and protocols in the field of the environment
  Report of the Secretary-General on remnants of war

(g)   *Human settlements*
Documentation
  Report of the Commission on Human Settlements
  Report of the Secretary-General on the living conditions of the Palestinian people in the occupied Palestinian territories
  Report of the Secretary-General on the co-ordination of human settlements programmes within the United Nations system

(h)   *Effective mobilization and integration of women in development*
Documentation
  Report of the Secretary-General on the world survey on the role of women in overall development

(i)   *Implementation of the Substantial New Programme of Action for the 1980s for the Least Developed Countries*
Documentation
  Report of the Secretary-General on the implementation of the Substantial New Programme of Action

(j)   *New international human order: moral aspects of development*
Documentation
  Report of the Secretary-General in pursuance of General Assembly resolution 38/170

(k)   *Long-term trends in economic development*
Documentation
  Report of the Secretary-General on the overall socio-economic perspective of the world economy to the year 2000

(l)   *Immediate measures in favour of the developing countries*
Documentation
  Report of the Secretary-General on immediate measures in favour of developing countries

(m)   *New and renewable sources of energy¶*
Documentation
  Report of the Secretary-General on the implementation of the Nairobi Programme of Action for the Development and Utilization of New and Renewable Sources of Energy

(n)   *Development of the energy resources of developing countries¶*
Documentation
  Report of the Secretary-General on the development of the energy resources of developing countries

Item 3. *Operational activities for development*
(a)   *Operational activities of the United Nations system*
Documentation
  Report of the Director-General for Development and International Economic Co-operation on the operational activities of the United Nations system
  Report of the Secretary-General on the role of qualified national personnel in the social and economic development of developing countries

(b)   *United Nations Development Programme*
Documentation
  Relevant chapters of the report of the Governing Council of the United Nations Development Programme

(c)   *United Nations Capital Development Fund*
Documentation
  Relevant chapter of the report of the Governing Council of the United Nations Development Programme

(d)   *United Nations technical co-operation activities*
Documentation
  Report of the Secretary-General on United Nations technical co-operation activities
  Relevant chapter of the report of the Governing Council of the United Nations Development Programme

(e)   *United Nations Volunteers programme*
Documentation
  Relevant chapters of the report of the Governing Council of the United Nations Development Programme

(f) *Liquidation of the United Nations Emergency Operation Trust Fund and allocation of the remaining balance*

Item 4. *United Nations Institute for Training and Research*¶
Documentation
  Report of the Secretary-General on the future programmes and needs of the United Nations Institute for Training and Research

Item 5. *Special programmes of economic assistance*
Documentation
  Reports of the Secretary-General on individual countries
  Report of the Secretary-General presenting summary reports on countries with no separate individual reports in that year

1986**

Item 1. *Report of the Economic and Social Council*
(a) *Population and development*
Documentation
  Report of the Secretary-General on action taken on the recommendations of the International Conference on Population for the further implementation of the World Population Plan of Action
(b) *Transport and Communications Decade for Asia and the Pacific, 1985-1994*
Documentation
  Report of the Secretary-General on the Transport and Communications Decade for Asia and the Pacific, 1985-1994
(c) *Confidence-building in international economic relations*
Documentation
  Report of the Secretary-General on confidence-building in international economic relations
(d) *Protection against products harmful to health and the environment*
Documentation
  Report of the Secretary-General on protection against products harmful to health and the environment

Item 2. *Development and international economic co-operation*††
(a) *Trade and development*
Documentation
  Report of the Trade and Development Board
  Report of the Secretary-General on special measures in favour of island developing countries
(b) *Industrialization*
Documentation
  Report of the Industrial Development Board
  Report of the Secretary-General on the Industrial Development Decade for Africa
(c) *Food problems*
Documentation
  Report of the World Food Council
  ⸙ Report of the Secretary-General on the situation of food and agriculture in Africa
(d) *New and renewable sources of energy*
Documentation
  Report of the Committee on the Development and Utilization of New and Renewable Sources of Energy

(e) *Development of the energy resources of developing countries*
Documentation
  Report of the Secretary-General on the development of the energy resources of developing countries

Item 3. *Operational activities for development*
(a) *Operational activities of the United Nations system*
Documentation
  Report of the Director-General for Development and International Economic Co-operation on a comprehensive policy review of the operational activities of the United Nations system
(b) *United Nations Development Programme*
Documentation
  Relevant chapters of the report of the Governing Council of the United Nations Development Programme
(c) *United Nations Fund for Population Activities*
Documentation
  Relevant chapters of the report of the Governing Council of the United Nations Development Programme
  Note by the Secretary-General transmitting the report of the Executive Director of the United Nations Fund for Population Activities on the United Nations Population Award and Trust Fund
(d) *United Nations Children's Fund*
Documentation
  Relevant chapter of the report of the Economic and Social Council
(e) *World Food Programme*

Item 4. *Training and research*
(a) *United Nations Institute for Training and Research*
Documentation
  Report of the Executive Director of the United Nations Institute for Training and Research
(b) *United Nations University*
Documentation
  Report of the Council of the United Nations University
(c) *Unified approach to development analysis and planning*
Documentation
  Report of the Secretary-General on a unified approach to development analysis and planning

Item 5. *Special economic and disaster relief assistance*
(a) *Office of the United Nations Disaster Relief Co-ordinator*
Documentation
  Report of the Secretary-General on the Office of the United Nations Disaster Relief Coordinator
(b) *Special programmes of economic assistance*
Documentation
  Reports of the Secretary-General on individual countries
  Report of the Secretary-General presenting summary reports on countries with no separate individual reports in that year
(c) *Implementation of the medium-term and long-term recovery and rehabilitation programme in the Sudano-Sahelian region*

Documentation

Report of the Secretary-General on the implementation of the medium-term and long-term recovery and rehabilitation programme in the Sudano-Sahelian region

---

*Upon a request of the General Assembly that a special programme of economic assistance be organized for a specific country, the Secretary-General arranges for a mission to that country and submits an individual report to the Assembly at its following session. Thereafter, the periodicity of review missions and individual reports is at the discretion of the country concerned. As a general rule, individual reports would be submitted every two years on the basis of a review mission. In alternate years, reporting to the Assembly is based on information provided by the Government concerned, which is included in a report covering a number of countries.

†The Second Committee should consider this item every three years, and the cycle of its consideration should correspond to that of the proposed medium-term plan by the General Assembly.

‡The Second Committee will, in accordance with established practice and in pursuance of General Assembly decision 38/429, hold a general debate each year at the beginning of its work.

§The list of questions and documentation under this item is only indicative of requests for reports from the General Assembly. The list will be finalized only after the Economic and Social Council completes its work each year.

‖Under this item the Second Committee will also have before it the reports of the Industrial Development Board and the World Food Council. The Committee may wish to decide not to consider draft proposals on these reports, except specific proposals requiring action by the General Assembly contained in the reports of these bodies or in the report of the Economic and Social Council.

¶Sub-items 2 (m) and (n) and item 4 are included, as an exception, for 1985 in the light of requests contained in resolutions 39/173, 39/176 and 39/177 for reports of the Secretary-General.

**The programme of work and documentation list for 1986 will be updated in 1985, taking into account relevant decisions of the General Assembly at its fortieth session.

††Under this item the Second Committee will also have before it the reports of the Intergovernmental Committee on Science and Technology for Development and the Commission on Human Settlements. The Second Committee may wish to decide not to consider draft proposals on these reports, except specific recommendations requiring action by the General Assembly contained in the reports of these bodies or in the report of the Economic and Social Council.

General Assembly resolution 39/217

18 December 1984   Meeting 104   Adopted without vote

Approved by Second Committee (A/39/790/Add.8) without vote, 14 December (meeting 61); draft by Vice-Chairman based on informal consultations (A/C.2/39/L.129/Rev.1), orally revised, and orally amended by Egypt for Group of 77; agenda item 80 (h).

Before the Second Committee approved the draft resolution, Egypt, on behalf of the Group of 77 developing countries, orally amended section D of annex I to delete an item, namely,

"Immediate measures in favour of developing countries".

Secretariat

Department of International Economic and Social Affairs

In 1984, the Economic and Social Council had before it a JIU report on DIESA. Submitted in August 1983,[8] along with the Secretary-General's comments issued in November,[9] the report was prepared in connection with implementation of the 1977 General Assembly resolution on restructuring.[1]

The Council took note of the report and comments on 26 July 1984, in decision 1984/178.

Office of Secretariat Services for Economic and Social Matters

In April 1984, the Secretary-General transmitted to the Economic and Social Council and the General Assembly a report by JIU on OSSECS,[10] a separate organizational entity created to provide integrated technical secretariat services to CPC, the Council, the Assembly, *ad hoc* conferences and intersecretariat co-ordination machinery. One of a series of JIU reports prepared in connection with implementation of the 1977 Assembly resolution on restructuring,[1] the report sought to analyse the performance by OSSECS of its functions, its relationships with other organizations of the United Nations system and its contribution to the system's economic and social work.

JIU recommended that the Secretary-General consider extending OSSECS technical services to other Assembly Committees, in addition to the Second and Third, and to some special conferences outside the economic and social sectors. Before making final changes to draft papers, OSSECS should communicate to their authors all proposed modifications. The Secretariat's Administrative Management Service should examine the question of inter-departmental distribution of editorial responsibility and advise the Secretary-General accordingly. Terms of reference for OSSECS should be issued by the Secretary-General without delay. The responsibility of OSSECS and of the Department of Conference Services for servicing informal meetings, especially those related to the Council and the Second Committee, should be accepted as legitimate grounds for requests for budgetary resources.

Commenting on the report,[11] the Secretary-General noted that extending technical secretariat services to additional committees and special conferences implied substantial organizational changes within the Secretariat; nevertheless, consideration could be given to bodies within the purview of OSSECS. In the Secretary-General's opinion, the recommended review of the distribution of editorial services needed further consideration, since the current situation was satisfactory. He would take fully into account the Assembly's overall review of the implementation of its 1977 resolution in drawing up the OSSECS terms of reference. As to increased requirements for secretariat services for informal consultations, the Secretary-General pointed out that it was in keeping with a 1978 Assembly request.[12] He believed that informal consultations should be regarded as an integral part of the proceedings of intergovernmental bodies concerned with economic and social matters.

The JIU report and comments of the Secretary-General were taken note of by the Economic and Social Council in decision 1984/178.

GENERAL ASSEMBLY ACTION

In December, the General Assembly adopted decision 39/437 without vote.

Restructuring of the economic and social sectors of the United Nations system

At its 104th plenary meeting, on 18 December 1984, the General Assembly, on the recommendation of the Second Committee, took note of the following documents:

(a) Note by the Secretary-General transmitting the report of the Joint Inspection Unit entitled "Office of Secretariat Services for Economic and Social Matters" and the comments of the Secretary-General thereon;

(b) Report of the Secretary-General on the further implementation of General Assembly resolution 37/214;

(c) Note by the Secretary-General transmitting the report of the Joint Inspection Unit entitled "Reporting to the Economic and Social Council" and comments of the Secretary-General thereon;

(d) Report of the Secretary-General submitted pursuant to General Assembly decision 37/442 of 20 December 1982, on the further implementation of Assembly resolution 32/197.

General Assembly decision 39/437

Adopted without vote

Approved by Second Committee (A/39/790/Add.8) without vote, 14 December (meeting 61); oral proposal by Chairman; agenda item 80 *(h)*.

REFERENCES

[1]YUN 1977, p. 438, GA res. 32/197, 20 Dec. 1977. [2]A/39/476. [3]YUN 1982, p. 1255, GA dec. 37/442, 20 Dec. 1982. [4]A/C.2/39/L.5. [5]YUN 1980, p. 503, GA res. 35/56, annex, 5 Dec. 1980. [6]YUN 1979, p. 468, GA res. 34/138, 14 Dec. 1979. [7]YUN 1983, p. 1008, GA dec. 38/429, 19 Dec. 1983. [8]*Ibid.*, p. 1008. [9]*Ibid.*, p. 1009. [10]A/39/94-E/1984/60. [11]A/39/94/Add.1-E/1984/60/Add.1. [12]YUN 1978, p. 1049, GA dec. 33/417, 14 Dec. 1978.

Trusteeship and decolonization

General questions relating to colonial countries

During 1984, the General Assembly's Special Committee on the Situation with regard to the Implementation of the Declaration on the Granting of Independence to Colonial Countries and Peoples (Committee on colonial countries) continued to address the implementation of the Assembly's 1960 Declaration. It considered the action of international organizations and action impeding implementation by foreign economic and military interests.

In addition to the general question of decolonization, the Committee examined situations in the following individual Territories: Trust Territory of the Pacific Islands (see next chapter); Namibia (see Chapter III of this section); Falkland Islands (Malvinas), East Timor, Western Sahara, American Samoa, Anguilla, Bermuda, British Virgin Islands, Cayman Islands, Cocos (Keeling) Islands, Gibraltar, Guam, Montserrat, Pitcairn, St. Helena, Tokelau, Turks and Caicos Islands, United States Virgin Islands (see Chapter IV of this section).

In July, the Economic and Social Council adopted resolution 1984/55, in which it reaffirmed the need for assistance by the United Nations system to the peoples of the colonial Territories and their national liberation movements and deplored the collaboration of the International Monetary Fund (IMF) with South Africa.

Acting on recommendations by the Committee on colonial countries, the General Assembly took action in December on several general aspects of the subject. By resolution 39/93 and decision 39/420, it endorsed a programme of activities for the twenty-fifth anniversary in 1985 of the 1960 Declaration and, by resolution 39/161 B, associated this event with the United Nations fortieth anniversary (1985). By resolution 39/91, the Assembly called for implementation of the Declaration and by resolution 39/43 for the assistance of the specialized agencies and the international institutions associated with the United Nations. By resolution 39/42, it condemned activities of foreign economic and other interests impeding the Declaration's implementation and by decision 39/412

condemned military activities in colonial Territories which denied peoples their right to self-determination and independence and which were detrimental to their interests.

By resolution 39/92 on the dissemination of information on decolonization, the Assembly requested the Secretary-General to publicize the work of the United Nations on decolonization. Resolution 39/45 included an invitation to States to make offers of study and training facilities to the inhabitants of Non-Self-Governing Territories (NSGTs). In resolution 39/41, the Assembly requested the administering Powers to transmit information as prescribed in the United Nations Charter as well as information on political and constitutional developments in the Territories concerned.

Topics related to this chapter. Africa: South Africa and *apartheid*. Namibia. Other colonial Territories.

The 1960 Declaration on colonial countries

Committee on colonial countries

During the year, the Committee on colonial countries considered various aspects of the implementation of the 1960 Declaration on the Granting of Independence to Colonial Countries and Peoples.[1] Meeting in New York, the 25-member Committee held two sessions—from 13 February to 9 May and from 7 to 24 August—and also held an extra-sessional meeting on 25 October.[2] Recommendations for action by the Committee were made by its subsidiary bodies, the Sub-Committee on Petitions, Information and Assistance and the Sub-Committee on Small Territories, which met between 8 March and 10 August and between 9 May and 22 August, respectively.

Action was taken by the Committee on the implementation of the Declaration by international organizations, on foreign interests and military bases impeding implementation of the Declaration in NSGTs, on dissemination of information on decolonization and of reports on the Territories supplied by their administering Powers and by visiting missions of the Committee, and on the twenty-fifth (1985) anniversary of the Declaration.

The President of the General Assembly received a letter dated 30 October[3] from Papua New Guinea asking to become a member of the Committee. After he informed the Assembly that he had received several communications from Member States expressing a similar desire, the Assembly agreed to the President's suggestion that he should hold further consultations with regional groups with a view to making an early appointment.

Twenty-fifth anniversary (1985)

Action by Committee on colonial countries. In preparation for the twenty-fifth anniversary in 1985 of the adoption of the 1960 Declaration on colonial countries, the Chairman of the Committee consulted with Ministers of Information of the non-aligned countries, with the Council of Ministers of the Organization of African Unity (OAU) and with the United Nations Council for Namibia. A suggested programme of activities was then made available for comments to the Committee, the administering Powers and a number of intergovernmental bodies, including the Preparatory Committee for the Commemoration of the Fortieth Anniversary of the United Nations (see PO-LITICAL AND SECURITY QUESTIONS, Chapter XI). In August, the Committee on colonial countries decided that any further suggestions should be submitted by 30 October. It prepared a revised draft programme of activities, endorsed by a majority of Committee members, and submitted it to the Assembly for consideration.

Other views on the programme were expressed by several States. On 13 August, Sweden suggested that an extraordinary session of the Committee proposed for 1985 be held at Headquarters and that seminars should not be linked to the twenty-fifth anniversary but should be viewed as a follow-up of a seminar held with non-governmental organizations (NGOs) on dissemination of information on decolonization (Vienna, Austria, 21-23 February 1984).[4] In a letter of 5 September, the United Kingdom stressed that the decolonization process was almost at an end and that, although this deserved to be marked by the United Nations, resources should not be devoted to commemorating past events, however significant, but to solving problems. Australia, in a letter dated 10 September, stated that decolonization had been one of the most important achievements of the United Nations and that the twenty-fifth anniversary

should be celebrated. It pointed out, however, that, except for Namibia, the list of remaining small Territories required less, not more, activity and intervention, and that the Committee should therefore hold a special meeting at Headquarters without an ambitious programme of meetings elsewhere. In a letter of 23 October, Venezuela suggested that a historical compendium be prepared to record the achievements of the United Nations concerning each Territory which had been considered by the Organization with regard to decolonization.

GENERAL ASSEMBLY ACTION

On 14 December, the General Assembly adopted by recorded vote resolution 39/93 on the basis of a draft by the Committee on colonial countries.

Programme of Activities in Observance of the Twenty-fifth Anniversary of the Declaration on the Granting of Independence to Colonial Countries and Peoples

The General Assembly,

Having considered the relevant chapter of the report of the Special Committee on the Situation with regard to the Implementation of the Declaration on the Granting of Independence to Colonial Countries and Peoples,

Bearing in mind that the year 1985 will mark the fortieth anniversary of the establishment of the United Nations, as well as the twenty-fifth anniversary of the Declaration on the Granting of Independence to Colonial Countries and Peoples,

Emphasizing the importance of the occasion to evaluate the progress achieved during the period in the process of decolonization, in particular in the implementation of the Declaration during the past twenty-five years, as well as the role played by the United Nations and its system of organizations in that regard, and to formulate specific measures for the elimination of the remaining vestiges of colonialism in all its forms and manifestations in various areas of the world,

1. *Approves* the relevant chapter of the report of the Special Committee on the Situation with regard to the Implementation of the Declaration on the Granting of Independence to Colonial Countries and Peoples and endorses the Programme of Activities in Observance of the Twenty-fifth Anniversary of the Declaration on the Granting of Independence to Colonial Countries and Peoples set out in the annex to the present resolution;

2. *Commends* the Programme, for appropriate action, to all States, the United Nations bodies concerned, the specialized agencies and other organizations of the United Nations system and the non-governmental organizations active in the field of decolonization;

3. *Requests* the Special Committee, in connection with the observance of the twenty-fifth anniversary of the Declaration, to co-operate and work closely with the Preparatory Committee for the Fortieth Anniversary of the United Nations;

4. *Requests* the Secretary-General to assist in the implementation of the present resolution and, in particular, to make adequate resources available for undertaking the measures envisaged in the Programme;

5. *Requests* the Special Committee to report to the General Assembly at its fortieth session on the implementation of the present resolution.

ANNEX
Programme of Activities in Observance of the Twenty-fifth Anniversary of the Declaration on the Granting of Independence to Colonial Countries and Peoples

1. The commemoration of the twenty-fifth anniversary of the Declaration on the Granting of Independence to Colonial Countries and Peoples would be an appropriate occasion to evaluate the progress achieved during the past twenty-five years in the implementation of the Declaration, as well as the role played by the United Nations and its system of organizations in that regard, and to formulate specific measures for the elimination of the remaining vestiges of colonialism in all its forms and manifestations in various areas of the world. To that end, the following special programme of activities is envisaged.

A. Activities at the international level

Commemorative meeting of the General Assembly

2. The General Assembly shall hold a special commemorative meeting in observance of the twenty-fifth anniversary of the Declaration, it being understood that the specific modalities and procedures for the commemoration would be the subject of subsequent consultations between the President of the Assembly and the Chairman of the Special Committee on the Situation with regard to the Implementation of the Declaration on the Granting of Independence to Colonial Countries and Peoples.

3. The meeting shall be held on Friday, 13 December 1985, or alternatively, in October 1985 in conjunction with ceremonies planned for the celebration of the fortieth anniversary of the United Nations and the proclamation of 1986 as International Year of Peace, in the light of the presence at United Nations Headquarters of a number of heads of State or Government.

Extraordinary session of the Special Committee

4. The Special Committee shall organize an extraordinary session away from Headquarters in 1985, as appropriate.

Special declaration/final document to be adopted by the General Assembly

5. The Special Committee shall prepare in 1985 the draft text of a special declaration/final document with a view to facilitating the full and speedy implementation of the Declaration on the Granting of Independence to Colonial Countries and Peoples, for submission to the General Assembly at its fortieth session.

Seminars to be held by the Special Committee

6. The Special Committee shall hold in 1985 two regional seminars on the subject of decolonization.

7. The Special Committee shall organize, in close consultation with the Department of Public Information of the Secretariat, a seminar on dissemination of information on decolonization and on the struggle of the peoples of southern Africa and their national liberation movements, to be held at United Nations Headquarters in close co-operation with the Special Committee against *Apartheid*, the United Nations Council for Namibia, the Organization of African Unity and the national liberation movements, with the participation of press agencies, newspapers and other mass communication media.

Activities by the specialized agencies and other organizations of the United Nations system, other international organizations and the non-governmental organizations concerned

8. The organizations concerned are requested to undertake various activities in commemoration of the anniversary during 1985. These activities may include the preparation of special publications and studies and the holding of exhibits, seminars and symposia. An account of the activities undertaken should be given the widest possible publicity.

9. The organizations concerned are requested to draw up concrete programmes of assistance to the peoples of colonial Territories and the national liberation movements, as well as to the refugees from Territories under colonial domination. In particular, they are requested to launch new projects for assisting the Namibian people and seek additional funds in support of such projects.

Dissemination of information on decolonization

10. The Secretary-General is requested to take concrete measures through all the media at his disposal to give widespread and intensified publicity to the situation in the Territories concerned and to the work of the United Nations in the field of decolonization. In particular, the Department of Public Information, the Department of Political Affairs, Trusteeship and Decolonization and the Office of the United Nations Commissioner for Namibia are requested, in consultation with the Special Committee:

(a) To prepare special publications devoted to the twenty-fifth anniversary of the Declaration, including special issues of *Decolonization, Objective: Justice*, the *Namibia Bulletin* and the *United Nations and Decolonization*;

(b) To produce a special film on the theme of decolonization and to hold public screenings of the film, as well as other films concerning the process of decolonization;

(c) To prepare and distribute to national radio and television stations audio-visual materials on decolonization;

(d) To hold exhibitions of photographs and publications related to decolonization, both at United Nations Headquarters and at various United Nations information centres;

(e) To organize special briefings of non-governmental organizations on the subject of decolonization.

Other activities

11. The motto "Decolonization, Freedom, Independence" shall mark the anniversary.

12. The Secretary-General is requested:

(a) To arrange for a special postal cancellation and the issuance of a special cachet, through the United Nations Postal Administration;

(b) To issue a commemorative medal marking the anniversary, to be conferred upon eminent personalities by the Special Committee;

(c) To publicize the foregoing through the appropriate media.

B.   Activities at the regional level

13.   Intergovernmental regional organizations are requested, in co-operation with the United Nations, to intensify their activities designed to help eliminate the last vestiges of colonialism and, to that end, to increase their collaboration with one another. They may also hold commemorative meetings and seminars, prepare special studies on various aspects of colonial questions and adopt measures to increase moral and material assistance to the peoples concerned.

C.   Activities at the national level

14.   Special messages may be issued on the occasion of the anniversary by heads of State or Government and other high-ranking officials, as well as by representatives of political movements, religious organizations, trade unions and other national organizations.

15.   Governments are requested to establish, in co-operation with national United Nations associations, national committees for the commemoration of the anniversary to plan and co-ordinate various activities to be undertaken in 1985 within the context of the twenty-fifth anniversary of the Declaration and the fortieth anniversary of the United Nations, such as publicizing the work of the United Nations on decolonization through, *inter alia*, publications, educational programmes in schools and universities, special studies, seminars and radio-television programmes, including the widest possible dissemination in their national languages of the Declaration and the various resolutions and decisions of the United Nations on decolonization; the conferring of national awards or special scholarships for outstanding studies or essays on colonial questions; and the issuance of a commemorative postage stamp and other activities. In particular, Governments are requested to prepare special educational materials on the subject of decolonization for dissemination through schools, universities and other educational institutions, including information on past achievements and the roles played by the national liberation movements, the Organization of African Unity and the United Nations.

16.   In undertaking the above activities, particular attention shall be devoted to the various manifestations of colonialism, including racial discrimination and *apartheid*, activities of foreign economic and other interests impeding the implementation of the Declaration on the Granting of Independence to Colonial Countries and Peoples and military activities and arrangements by colonial Powers in Territories under their administration impeding the implementation of the Declaration.

General Assembly resolution 39/93

14 December 1984   Meeting 100   137-2-7 (recorded vote)

Draft by Committee on colonial countries (A/39/23); agenda item 18.

Recorded vote in Assembly as follows:

In favour: Afghanistan, Albania, Algeria, Angola, Argentina, Australia, Austria, Bahamas, Bahrain, Bangladesh, Barbados, Belize, Benin, Bhutan, Bolivia, Botswana, Brazil, Brunei Darussalam, Bulgaria, Burkina Faso, Burma, Burundi, Byelorussian SSR, Cameroon, Cape Verde, Chad, Chile, China, Colombia, Congo, Costa Rica, Cuba, Cyprus, Czechoslovakia, Democratic Kampuchea, Democratic Yemen, Denmark, Djibouti, Dominican Republic, Ecuador, Egypt, El Salvador, Equatorial Guinea, Ethiopia, Fiji, Finland, Gabon, Gambia, German Democratic Republic, Ghana, Greece, Guatemala, Guinea, Guinea-Bissau, Guyana, Haiti, Honduras, Hungary, Iceland, India, Indonesia, Iran, Iraq, Ireland, Ivory Coast, Jamaica, Japan, Jordan, Kenya, Kuwait, Lao People's Democratic Republic, Lebanon, Lesotho, Liberia, Libyan Arab Jamahiriya, Madagascar, Malawi, Malaysia, Maldives, Mali, Malta, Mauritania, Mauritius, Mexico, Mongolia, Morocco, Mozambique, Nepal, New Zealand, Nicaragua, Niger, Nigeria, Norway, Oman, Pakistan, Panama, Papua New Guinea, Peru, Philippines, Poland, Portugal, Qatar, Romania,

Rwanda, Samoa, Sao Tome and Principe, Saudi Arabia, Senegal, Seychelles, Sierra Leone, Singapore, Somalia, Spain, Sri Lanka, Sudan, Suriname, Sweden, Syrian Arab Republic, Thailand, Togo, Trinidad and Tobago, Tunisia, Turkey, Uganda, Ukrainian SSR, USSR, United Arab Emirates, United Republic of Tanzania, Uruguay, Vanuatu, Venezuela, Viet Nam, Yemen, Yugoslavia, Zaire, Zambia, Zimbabwe.

Against: United Kingdom, United States.

Abstaining: Belgium, Canada, France, Germany, Federal Republic of, Italy, Luxembourg, Netherlands.

A number of States explained their votes. The United Kingdom felt that expenditure for famine relief in Africa for colonial peoples would be better than the activities proposed.

Sweden, also speaking for Denmark, Finland, Iceland and Norway, had reservations regarding the additional expenditures that the proposed large meetings away from Headquarters would involve. Speaking similarly, Australia said the United Nations should consider how it might arrive at viable permanent solutions for the remaining small Territories, rather than seeking to develop ambitious plans for the continuation of the Special Committee's work. Canada also had reservations about the financial implications, while the Netherlands felt that the resources for the anniversary observance should be found within the regular budget.

Japan commended the authors on avoiding unnecessary elements in the resolution that it said had appeared in previous ones on decolonization, but could not support some activities in the annex; it was particularly concerned that organs of the Assembly should observe a 1976 resolution[5] stating that they might hold sessions away from Headquarters only when host Governments agreed to pay the additional costs.

The Assembly took two further actions concerning the twenty-fifth anniversary.

On 14 December, it adopted without vote decision 39/420 as orally proposed by its President.

Activities in observance of the twenty-fifth anniversary of the Declaration on the Granting of Independence to Colonial Countries and Peoples

At its 100th plenary meeting, on 14 December 1984, the General Assembly adopted the recommendations contained in chapter II, paragraph 10, of the report of the Special Committee on the Situation with regard to the Implementation of the Declaration on the Granting of Independence to Colonial Countries and Peoples.

General Assembly decision 39/420

Adopted without vote

Oral proposal by President; recommendations by Committee on colonial countries (A/39/23); agenda item 18.

Chapter II, paragraph 10, of the Committee's report contained further specific recommendations for activities to be undertaken in observance of the anniversary.

Before the decision was adopted, the Chairman of the Committee pointed out that no Assembly action needed to be taken on the compendium suggested by Venezuela (see above), and referred to in the Committee's report, since the Committee had agreed that a study might be undertaken in the future in another context.

On 17 December, the Assembly, in preparing for the fortieth anniversary of the United Nations to be commemorated in 1985, adopted by recorded vote resolution 39/161 B also dealing with the anniversary of the 1960 Declaration.

The General Assembly,

Taking note of the report of the Preparatory Committee for the Fortieth Anniversary of the United Nations,[6] established in connection with the observance in 1985 of the fortieth anniversary of the United Nations,

Noting that the year 1985 will also mark the twenty-fifth anniversary of the adoption of the historic Declaration on the Granting of Independence to Colonial Countries and Peoples and noting the important role that the United Nations plays in its implementation,

Decides that the events commemorating the fortieth anniversary of the United Nations should reflect in an appropriate manner the observance of the twenty-fifth anniversary, also in 1985, of the Declaration on the Granting of Independence to Colonial Countries and Peoples with a view to strengthening international commitment to the full achievement of decolonization.

General Assembly resolution 39/161 B

17 December 1984   Meeting 103   143-1-2 (recorded vote)

Draft by India (A/39/L.45); agenda item 40.

Recorded vote in Assembly as follows:

In favour: Afghanistan, Albania, Algeria, Angola, Argentina, Australia, Austria, Bahamas, Bahrain, Bangladesh, Barbados, Belgium, Benin, Bhutan, Bolivia, Botswana, Brazil, Brunei Darussalam, Bulgaria, Burkina Faso, Burma, Burundi, Byelorussian SSR, Cameroon, Canada, Cape Verde, Chad, Chile, China, Colombia, Congo, Costa Rica, Cuba, Cyprus, Czechoslovakia, Democratic Kampuchea, Democratic Yemen, Denmark, Djibouti, Dominican Republic, Ecuador, Egypt, El Salvador, Equatorial Guinea, Ethiopia, Fiji, Finland, Gabon, Gambia, German Democratic Republic, Germany, Federal Republic of, Ghana, Greece, Guatemala, Guinea, Guinea-Bissau, Guyana, Haiti, Honduras, Hungary, Iceland, India, Indonesia, Iran, Iraq, Ireland, Italy, Ivory Coast, Jamaica, Japan, Jordan, Kenya, Kuwait, Lao People's Democratic Republic, Lebanon, Lesotho, Liberia, Libyan Arab Jamahiriya, Luxembourg, Madagascar, Malawi, Malaysia, Maldives, Mali, Malta, Mauritania, Mauritius, Mexico, Mongolia, Morocco, Mozambique, Nepal, Netherlands, New Zealand, Nicaragua, Niger, Nigeria, Norway, Oman, Pakistan, Panama, Papua New Guinea, Paraguay, Peru, Philippines, Poland, Portugal, Qatar, Romania, Rwanda, Saint Lucia, Samoa, Sao Tome and Principe, Saudi Arabia, Senegal, Sierra Leone, Singapore, Somalia, Spain, Sri Lanka, Sudan, Suriname, Swaziland, Sweden, Syrian Arab Republic, Thailand, Togo, Trinidad and Tobago, Tunisia, Turkey, Uganda, USSR, United Arab Emirates, United Republic of Tanzania, Uruguay, Vanuatu, Venezuela, Viet Nam, Yemen, Yugoslavia, Zaire, Zambia, Zimbabwe.

Against: United States.

Abstaining: France, United Kingdom.

The United States explained that, since the 1960 Declaration made no reference to the principle of self-determination, it had not supported its adoption; for that reason, it could not support the current resolution.

Implementation of the Declaration

GENERAL ASSEMBLY ACTION

On 14 December 1984, the General Assembly again called for the implementation of its 1960

Declaration when it adopted by recorded vote resolution 39/91.

Implementation of the Declaration on the Granting of Independence to Colonial Countries and Peoples

The General Assembly,

Having examined the report of the Special Committee on the Situation with regard to the Implementation of the Declaration on the Granting of Independence to Colonial Countries and Peoples,

Recalling its resolutions 1514(XV) of 14 December 1960, containing the Declaration on the Granting of Independence to Colonial Countries and Peoples, 2621(XXV) of 12 October 1970, containing the programme of action for the full implementation of the Declaration, and 35/118 of 11 December 1980, the annex to which contains the Plan of Action for the Full Implementation of the Declaration,

Recalling all its previous resolutions concerning the implementation of the Declaration, in particular resolution 38/54 of 7 December 1983, as well as the relevant resolutions of the Security Council,

Recalling the relevant provisions of the Bangkok Declaration and Programme of Action on Namibia, adopted by the United Nations Council for Namibia on 25 May 1984 at its extraordinary plenary meetings held at Bangkok,

Condemning the continued colonialist and racist repression of millions of Africans, particularly in Namibia, by the Government of South Africa through its persistent, illegal occupation of the international Territory and its intransigent attitude towards all efforts being made to bring about an internationally acceptable solution to the situation obtaining in the Territory,

Deeply conscious of the urgent need to take all necessary measures to eliminate forthwith the remaining vestiges of colonialism, particularly in respect of Namibia where desperate attempts by South Africa to perpetuate its illegal occupation have brought untold suffering and bloodshed to the people,

Strongly condemning the policies of those States which, in defiance of the relevant resolutions of the United Nations, have continued to collaborate with the Government of South Africa in its domination of the people of Namibia,

Conscious that the success of the national liberation struggle and the resultant international situation have provided the international community with a unique opportunity to make a decisive contribution towards the total elimination of colonialism in all its forms and manifestations in Africa,

Welcoming the accession to independence by Brunei Darussalam on 1 January 1984 and its admission to membership in the United Nations on 21 September 1984,

Noting with satisfaction the work accomplished by the Special Committee with a view to securing the effective and complete implementation of the Declaration and the other relevant resolutions of the United Nations,

Noting also with satisfaction the co-operation and active participation of the administering Powers concerned in the relevant work of the Special Committee, as well as the continued readiness of the Governments concerned to receive United Nations visiting missions in the Territories under their administration,

Reiterating its conviction that the total eradication of racial discrimination, *apartheid* and violations of the basic human rights of the peoples of colonial Territories will be achieved most expeditiously by the faithful and complete implementation of the Declaration, particularly in Namibia, and by the speediest possible complete elimination of the presence of the illegal occupying régime therefrom,

Keenly aware of the pressing needs of the newly independent and emerging States for assistance from the United Nations and its system of organizations in the economic, social and other fields,

1. *Reaffirms* its resolutions 1514(XV), 2621(XXV) and 38/54 and all other resolutions on decolonization and calls upon the administering Powers, in accordance with those resolutions, to take all necessary steps to enable the dependent peoples of the Territories concerned to exercise fully and without further delay their inalienable right to self-determination and independence;

2. *Affirms once again* that the continuation of colonialism in all its forms and manifestations—including racism, *apartheid*, the exploitation by foreign and other interests of economic and human resources and the waging of colonial wars to suppress national liberation movements—is incompatible with the Charter of the United Nations, the Universal Declaration of Human Rights and the Declaration on the Granting of Independence to Colonial Countries and Peoples and poses a serious threat to international peace and security;

3. *Reaffirms its determination* to take all necessary steps with a view to the complete and speedy eradication of colonialism and to the faithful and strict observance by all States of the relevant provisions of the Charter, the Declaration on the Granting of Independence to Colonial Countries and Peoples and the guiding principles of the Universal Declaration of Human Rights;

4. *Affirms once again* its recognition of the legitimacy of the struggle of the peoples under colonial and alien domination to exercise their right to self-determination and independence by all the necessary means at their disposal;

5. *Approves* the report of the Special Committee on the Situation with regard to the Implementation of the Declaration on the Granting of Independence to Colonial Countries and Peoples covering its work during 1984, including the programme of work envisaged for 1985;

6. *Calls upon* all States, in particular the administering Powers, and the specialized agencies and other organizations of the United Nations system to give effect to the recommendations contained in the report of the Special Committee for the speedy implementation of the Declaration and the other relevant resolutions of the United Nations;

7. *Condemns* the continuing activities of foreign economic and other interests which are impeding the implementation of the Declaration with respect to the colonial Territories, particularly Namibia;

8. *Strongly condemns* all collaboration, particularly in the nuclear and military fields, with the Government of South Africa and calls upon the States concerned to cease forthwith all such collaboration;

9. *Requests* all States, directly and through their action in the specialized agencies and other organizations of the United Nations system, to withhold assistance of any kind from the Government of South Africa until

the inalienable right of the people of Namibia to self-determination and independence within a united and integrated Namibia, including Walvis Bay, has been restored, and to refrain from taking any action which might imply recognition of the legitimacy of the illegal occupation of Namibia by that régime;

10. *Calls upon* the colonial Powers to withdraw immediately and unconditionally their military bases and installations from colonial Territories, to refrain from establishing new ones and not to involve those Territories in any offensive acts or interference against other States;

11. *Urges* all States, directly and through their action in the specialized agencies and other organizations of the United Nations system, to provide all moral and material assistance to the oppressed people of Namibia and, in respect of the other Territories, requests the administering Powers, in consultation with the Governments of the Territories under their administration, to take steps to enlist and make effective use of all possible assistance, on both a bilateral and a multilateral basis, in the strengthening of the economies of those Territories;

12. *Requests* the Special Committee to continue to seek suitable means for the immediate and full implementation of General Assembly resolution 1514(XV) in all Territories that have not yet attained independence and, in particular:

(a) To formulate specific proposals for the elimination of the remaining manifestations of colonialism and to report thereon to the General Assembly at its fortieth session;

(b) To make concrete suggestions which could assist the Security Council in considering appropriate measures under the Charter with regard to developments in colonial Territories that are likely to threaten international peace and security;

(c) To continue to examine the compliance of Member States with the Declaration and with other relevant resolutions on decolonization, particularly those relating to Namibia;

(d) To continue to pay particular attention to the small Territories, including the sending of visiting missions to them, as appropriate, and to recommend to the General Assembly the most suitable steps to be taken to enable the populations of those Territories to exercise their right to self-determination, freedom and independence;

(e) To take all necessary steps to enlist world-wide support among Governments, as well as national and international organizations having a special interest in decolonization, for the achievement of the objectives of the Declaration and the implementation of the relevant resolutions of the United Nations, particularly as concerns the oppressed people of Namibia;

13. *Calls upon* the administering Powers to continue to co-operate with the Special Committee in the discharge of its mandate and, in particular, to permit the access of visiting missions to the Territories to secure first-hand information and ascertain the wishes and aspirations of their inhabitants;

14. *Requests* the Secretary-General and the specialized agencies and other organizations of the United Nations system to provide or continue to provide to the newly independent and emerging States all possible assistance in the economic, social and other fields;

15.   *Requests* the Secretary-General to provide the Special Committee with the facilities and services required for the implementation of the present resolution, as well as of the various resolutions and decisions on decolonization adopted by the General Assembly and the Special Committee.

General Assembly resolution 39/91

14 December 1984   Meeting 100   138-2-6 (recorded vote)

26-nation draft (A/39/L.17 & Corr.1 & Add.1); agenda item 18.
Sponsors: Afghanistan, Algeria, Byelorussian SSR, Congo, Cuba, Cyprus, Czechoslovakia, Ethiopia, Guyana, India, Lao People's Democratic Republic, Libyan Arab Jamahiriya, Madagascar, Mali, Mongolia, Papua New Guinea, Sierra Leone, Syrian Arab Republic, Trinidad and Tobago, Tunisia, Ukrainian SSR, United Republic of Tanzania, Venezuela, Viet Nam, Yugoslavia, Zambia.
Financial implications. ACABQ, A/39/7/Add.14; 5th Committee, A/39/825; S-G, A/C.5/39/80 & Add.1.
Meeting numbers. GA 39th session: 5th Committee 49; plenary 85-87, 100.

Recorded vote in Assembly as follows:

In favour: Afghanistan, Albania, Algeria, Angola, Argentina, Australia, Austria, Bahamas, Bahrain, Bangladesh, Barbados, Belize, Benin, Bhutan, Bolivia, Botswana, Brazil, Brunei Darussalam, Bulgaria, Burkina Faso, Burma, Burundi, Byelorussian SSR, Cameroon, Cape Verde, Chad, Chile, China, Colombia, Congo, Costa Rica, Cuba, Cyprus, Czechoslovakia, Democratic Kampuchea, Democratic Yemen, Denmark, Djibouti, Dominican Republic, Ecuador, Egypt, El Salvador, Equatorial Guinea, Ethiopia, Fiji, Finland, Gabon, Gambia, German Democratic Republic, Ghana, Greece, Guatemala, Guinea, Guinea-Bissau, Guyana, Haiti, Honduras, Hungary, Iceland, India, Indonesia, Iran, Iraq, Ireland, Ivory Coast, Jamaica, Japan, Jordan, Kenya, Kuwait, Lao People's Democratic Republic, Lebanon, Lesotho, Liberia, Libyan Arab Jamahiriya, Madagascar, Malawi, Malaysia, Maldives, Mali, Malta, Mauritania, Mauritius, Mexico, Mongolia, Morocco, Mozambique, Nepal, Netherlands, New Zealand, Nicaragua, Niger, Nigeria, Norway, Oman, Pakistan, Panama, Papua New Guinea, Peru, Philippines, Poland, Portugal, Qatar, Romania, Rwanda, Samoa, Sao Tome and Principe, Saudi Arabia, Senegal, Seychelles, Sierra Leone, Singapore, Somalia, Spain, Sri Lanka, Sudan, Suriname, Sweden, Syrian Arab Republic, Thailand, Togo, Trinidad and Tobago, Tunisia, Turkey, Uganda, Ukrainian SSR, USSR, United Arab Emirates, United Republic of Tanzania, Uruguay, Vanuatu, Venezuela, Viet Nam, Yemen, Yugoslavia, Zaire, Zambia, Zimbabwe.

Against: United Kingdom, United States.

Abstaining: Belgium, Canada, France, Germany, Federal Republic of, Italy, Luxembourg.

Explaining its vote, the United Kingdom pointed out that the text was primarily concerned with *apartheid* and Namibia and said nothing about the situation in the remaining British dependent Territories although these made up about half of the Committee's agenda; scant account had been taken of the aspirations and interests of the Governments and peoples of those Territories.

Sweden, speaking on behalf of the five Nordic countries, said the text contained formulations which they did not support; paragraph 4 was contrary to the principle that the United Nations should always encourage only peaceful solutions and paragraph 10 was too categorical, a point shared by Turkey. Australia believed that the Organization should seek peaceful solutions, and— together with Canada—could not accept endorsement of armed struggle, nor did it feel that NSGTs posed a serious threat to international peace and security. Canada also did not agree with the unconditional call for the withdrawal of military bases from colonial Territories.

Japan had reservations regarding paragraphs 4, 5, 6 and 10, and interpreted paragraph 5 as condemning only those foreign economic activities which in fact were impeding self-determination.

The Netherlands had reservations on paragraphs 2, 4, 7, 8 and 10.

In resolution 39/155, the Assembly again urged States to speed the implementation of the 1960 Declaration.

Implementation by international organizations

In response to requests of the General Assembly for implementation of its 1960 Declaration, including a December 1983 resolution,[7] United Nations specialized agencies and other related bodies continued providing assistance to peoples of colonial countries and their national liberation movements. In accordance with the 1983 resolution, a 1984 report[8] by the Secretary-General summarized the replies of United Nations bodies on action taken. (See Chapter III of this section for action taken regarding Namibia.)

During 1984, the International Labour Organisation (ILO) Conference Committee on *Apartheid* endorsed a proposed international conference on an oil embargo against South Africa. Its Committee on Discrimination reviewed its expanded technical co-operation programme and the actions taken against *apartheid* by Governments and by workers' and employers' organizations. In May, ILO organized a tripartite conference at Lusaka, Zambia, to review its experience on assistance programmes. Pilot vocational centres were established for South Africans and a further programme in vocational training was launched in co-operation with India. Other ILO programmes aimed at creating employment to help front-line and neighbouring States reduce their economic and social dependence on South Africa.

The Food and Agriculture Organization of the United Nations (FAO) undertook activities to enable refugee communities administered by national liberation movements to become self-sufficient in food and to develop agricultural skills and leadership.

During the year, the United Nations Educational, Scientific and Cultural Organization (UNESCO) continued to consult with national liberation movements to implement the 1960 Declaration, including projects to provide educational training. It supported a seminar held in November at the Education Centre of the Solomon Mahlangu Freedom College at Mazimbu, United Republic of Tanzania, served as executing agency for United Nations Development Programme (UNDP) projects giving school materials and laboratory and sports equipment to the educational centres of South African liberation movements and paid their support staff. It published the English edition of a book on human rights recourse procedures and an analysis of South African school history textbooks entitled *History in*

Black and White. UNESCO also took part in a meeting of experts in Beijing, China, from 15 to 25 November that chose the studies to be undertaken on the causes of racism and *apartheid* and organized a conference on tolerance in Paris on 21 March inaugurating public conferences to mark the International Day for the Elimination of Racial Discrimination and focusing on popular culture as a factor of inter-cultural understanding using reggae music as an example.

The World Health Organization continued to provide medical supplies, drugs and fellowships to national liberation movements, to refugees in Africa and to Lesotho and Swaziland.

In 1984, the Universal Postal Union provided one fellowship to each of six Caribbean countries—Antigua and Barbuda, Dominica, Grenada, Saint Christopher and Nevis, Saint Lucia, and Saint Vincent and the Grenadines—and to one NSGT—Anguilla—for a subregional course for supervisors that it organized at Kingston, Jamaica, from 16 April to 15 June. Other activities in the Caribbean included a mission on postal management questions, which visited Saint Vincent and the Grenadines from 1 July to 3 August, and one fellowship for Grenada for a course in the Netherlands from 15 October to 16 December in the operation of postal services. Other activities for newly independent countries included two fellowships for a course on mail-routing at Ndola, Zambia, fellowships for participation in courses for postal instructors at Blantyre, Malawi, and at Nairobi, Kenya, in postal statistics at Nairobi, in postal management at Rugby, United Kingdom, and in post-office savings at Dar es Salaam, United Republic of Tanzania. Other such postal training fellowships were financed by UNDP during the year.

The International Maritime Organization (IMO) continued assistance to newly independent countries and to peoples fighting for their independence in Africa under its 1974 co-operation agreement with OAU, consulting on possible provision of maritime training to African refugees. It invited national liberation movements to attend IMO meetings and conferences as observers.

The World Intellectual Property Organization (WIPO) continued discussions with OAU on assistance to colonial peoples in Africa and their national liberation movements, and offered two fellowships for each movement. It also invited newly independent countries and emerging States to propose candidates for training in 1984; Angola, Vanuatu and Zimbabwe proposed 22 candidates and were awarded eight fellowships in industrial property and copyright. In September, WIPO organized and financed, jointly with Portugal, a seminar on industrial property systems for Portuguese-speaking African countries, attended by two officials from Angola, two from Guinea-Bissau, three from Mozambique and one from Sao Tome and Principe. During the year, fellowships in the WIPO training programme were awarded to top candidates from five front-line States: Angola, Mozambique, United Republic of Tanzania, Zambia and Zimbabwe.

The International Fund for Agricultural Development (IFAD) pointed out that it could assist only developing States that were members of IFAD; therefore, none had been assisted in relation to the implementation of the 1960 Declaration.

The United Nations Conference on Trade and Development (UNCTAD) set up a special economic unit on assistance to the Palestinian people. In September 1984, the Trade and Development Board, in pursuance of UNCTAD resolution 147(VI),[9] urged the Administrator of UNDP to provide resources to the UNCTAD Secretary-General to enable him to carry out his mandate relating to the oppressed people of South Africa (see p. 168).

UNDP reported that its role was limited to providing development assistance to peoples living in asylum in neighbouring countries and geared to obtaining self-sufficiency and to training for future responsible participation when conditions were right for their return. This included support for educational projects executed by UNESCO and food production and training projects carried out by FAO (see above).

The Office of the United Nations High Commissioner for Refugees (UNHCR) continued assisting South African refugees in health, education, local integration and resettlement. In Angola, $617,500 was committed to assist 9,000 South African refugees in the urban areas of Luanda and Benguele and in Malange province for a vocational training centre and to develop agricultural production at a farm run by ANC and to improve its transport capacity.

In Botswana, 212 registered South African refugees were assisted through various income-generating projects and 130 South Africans who arrived in late 1984 were given supplementary assistance while efforts were made to find durable solutions. A further 33 South Africans, who found employment in education, administration, catering, hairdressing, skilled trades, finance and law, were provided with work permits, and 24 South Africans, including nine dependants, were resettled in the United States.

In Lesotho, during the year, some 160 South Africans who had no other source of income were given assistance for their daily needs. An ILO project, to develop small enterprises for refugees, set up 18 businesses, creating jobs for 70 people based on loans of some $72,000, and another

21 South Africans were assisted with resettlement in other African countries, Australia, Canada and the United States.

At the end of December 1984, there were 419 South African refugees in Mozambique who were provided with supplementary aid, including food and medical treatment, and some 90 South Africans were also assisted with Portuguese language training. In Zimbabwe, where there were 440 South African refugees, some 90 received supplementary aid.

In 1984, $71,300 was allocated to equip a vocational training institute in the United Republic of Tanzania in the Dakawa Development Centre and farm run by ANC, some $80,000 was granted to PAC to clear a farm and procure farm equipment, and $97,000 was used for both organizations for transportation, tents, bedding and emergency food for about 200 South African refugees. In Zambia, UNHCR gave $140,000 to ANC for the purchase of farm equipment, livestock, animal feed and veterinary drugs for its farm near Lusaka.

UNHCR committed an additional $211,000 for educational assistance to 191 South African students in eight countries of asylum, and it continued its close co-operation with the liberation movements recognized by OAU and the United Nations whose representatives attended the October 1984 session of the Executive Committee of the High Commissioner's Programme as observers.

The World Food Programme reported that, as at 31 December 1984, it had committed for liberation movement refugees and displaced persons a total of $75.9 million for 27 projects, of which six were still current.

In accordance with a July 1983 request of the Economic and Social Council,[10] its President and the Chairman of the Committee on colonial countries continued consultations[11] on co-ordinating the activities of United Nations bodies in implementing the 1960 Declaration. The two presiding officers noted that many organizations had co-operated closely with front-line States and hoped that they would continue to intensify their efforts for the extension of assistance, adding that measures to withhold assistance from South Africa continued to be in force. They also drew attention to the forthcoming Second International Conference on Assistance to Refugees in Africa which was to consider their relief and resettlement (see p. 942).

Further to the same Council request,[10] consultations were held between the Council's President and the Chairman of the Special Committee against *Apartheid*. Attention was paid to the aggression against the front-line States by the Pretoria régime, and its refusal to comply with United Nations decisions, with the Committee Chairman

emphasizing that national liberation movements should be provided with sufficient assistance to isolate *apartheid* South Africa. The Chairman also drew attention to the application of the International Police Association (IPA) to the Committee on Non-Governmental Organizations for reclassification of its consultative status from the Roster to category II; IPA had not, however, informed the Committee that it had accepted the South African Police Association as a member. The Chairman requested that the consultative status of IPA be suspended. The Council took note of the link between IPA and *apartheid* South Africa and decided not to approve its reclassification and to consider its status in 1985 (see p. 979).

ECONOMIC AND SOCIAL COUNCIL ACTION

On 25 July, the Economic and Social Council adopted by roll-call vote resolution 1984/55 as recommended by its Third (Programme and Co-ordination) Committee.

Implementation of the Declaration on the Granting of Independence to Colonial Countries and Peoples by the specialized agencies and the international institutions associated with the United Nations

The Economic and Social Council,

Having examined the report of the Secretary-General and the report of the President of the Economic and Social Council concerning the question of the implementation of the Declaration on the Granting of Independence to Colonial Countries and Peoples by the specialized agencies and the international institutions associated with the United Nations,

Having heard the statements of the Chairman of the Special Committee on the Situation with regard to the Implementation of the Declaration on the Granting of Independence to Colonial Countries and Peoples and the representative of the Chairman of the Special Committee against *Apartheid,*

Recalling General Assembly resolution 1514(XV) of 14 December 1960, containing the Declaration on the Granting of Independence to Colonial Countries and Peoples, and all other resolutions adopted by United Nations bodies on this subject, including in particular Assembly resolution 38/51 of 7 December 1983 and Council resolution 1983/42 of 25 July 1983,

Reaffirming the responsibility of the specialized agencies and other organizations within the United Nations system to take all effective measures, within their respective spheres of competence, to ensure the full and speedy implementation of the Declaration on the Granting of Independence to Colonial Countries and Peoples and other relevant resolutions of United Nations bodies,

Noting with deep concern that the situation in southern Africa continues to present a serious threat to peace and security as a result of South Africa's intensified and ruthless repression, its policy and practice of *apartheid* and other gross violations of the human rights of the peoples in Namibia and South Africa and its armed aggression and military, political and economic destabilization directed against independent States in the region,

Deeply conscious of the continuing critical need of the people of Namibia and their national liberation movement, the South West Africa People's Organization, for concrete assistance from the specialized agencies and the international institutions associated with the United Nations in their struggle for liberation from the illegal occupation of their country by the racist minority régime in South Africa,

Deeply concerned that, while progress has been maintained through the continuing efforts of the United Nations High Commissioner for Refugees in the extension of assistance to refugees from southern Africa, the action taken thus far by the organizations and agencies concerned in the provision of assistance generally to the people of Namibia is still far from adequate to meet their urgent and growing needs,

Gravely concerned at the continued collaboration of the International Monetary Fund with the Government of South Africa, in disregard of relevant General Assembly resolutions,

Noting with satisfaction the continuing efforts of the United Nations Development Programme in the extension of assistance to the national liberation movements concerned, and commending the initiative taken by that organization in establishing channels for closer, periodic contacts and consultations between the specialized agencies and United Nations institutions and the Organization of African Unity and the national liberation movements in the formulation of assistance programmes,

Noting further the communiqué issued by the Summit Meeting of the heads of State and Government of the Front-line States and leaders of liberation movements, held at Arusha, United Republic of Tanzania, on 29 April 1984,[12]

Bearing in mind the Bangkok Declaration and Programme of Action adopted by the United Nations Council for Namibia at its 424th meeting, held at Bangkok on 25 May 1984,

1. *Takes note* of the report of the President of the Economic and Social Council and endorses the observations and suggestions contained therein;

2. *Reaffirms* that the recognition by the General Assembly, the Security Council and other United Nations organs of the legitimacy of the struggle of colonial peoples to exercise their right to self-determination and independence entails, as a corollary, the extension by the United Nations system of organizations of all the necessary moral and material assistance to the peoples of the colonial Territories and their national liberation movements;

3. *Expresses its appreciation* to those specialized agencies and organizations within the United Nations system which have continued to co-operate in varying degrees with the United Nations and the Organization of African Unity in the implementation of the Declaration on the Granting of Independence to Colonial Countries and Peoples and other relevant resolutions of United Nations bodies, and urges all the specialized agencies and other organizations within the United Nations system to accelerate the full and speedy implementation of the relevant provisions of those resolutions;

4. *Requests* the specialized agencies and other organizations within the United Nations system, in the light of the intensification of the liberation struggle in Namibia, to do everything possible as a matter of urgency to render increased assistance to the people of Namibia,

in consultation with the Organization of African Unity and the United Nations Council for Namibia, in particular in connection with the Nationhood Programme for Namibia;

5. *Also requests* the specialized agencies and other organizations within the United Nations system to continue to take, in accordance with the relevant resolutions of the General Assembly and the Security Council, all necessary measures to withhold any financial, economic, technical or other assistance to the Government of South Africa until that Government restores to the people of Namibia their inalienable right to self-determination and independence, and to refrain from taking any action which might imply recognition of, or support for, the illegal occupation of Namibia by that régime;

6. *Further requests* the specialized agencies and other organizations within the United Nations system, in accordance with the relevant resolutions of the General Assembly and the Security Council on the *apartheid* policy of the Government of South Africa, to intensify their support for the oppressed people of South Africa and to take such measures as will totally isolate the *apartheid* régime and mobilize world public opinion against *apartheid*;

7. *Condemns* the latest attempts being made by the Government of South Africa to circumvent the implementation of the United Nations plan for the independence of Namibia, approved by the Security Council in its resolution 435(1978) of 29 September 1978;

8. *Deeply deplores* the persistent collaboration of the International Monetary Fund with the Government of South Africa, in disregard of repeated General Assembly resolutions to the contrary, and urgently calls upon the Fund to put an end to such collaboration;

9. *Recommends* that a separate item on assistance to national liberation movements recognized by the Organization of African Unity should be included in the agenda of future high-level meetings of the General Secretariat of the Organization of African Unity and the secretariats of the United Nations and other organizations within the United Nations system, with a view to strengthening further the existing measures for co-ordination of action to ensure the best use of available resources for assistance to the peoples of the colonial Territories;

10. *Notes with satisfaction* the inclusion of Namibia, represented by the United Nations Council for Namibia, in the membership of various agencies and organizations within the United Nations system and urges those which have not yet granted full membership to the United Nations Council for Namibia to do so without delay;

11. *Notes with satisfaction also* the arrangements made by several specialized agencies and United Nations institutions which enable representatives of the national liberation movements recognized by the Organization of African Unity to participate fully as observers in proceedings relating to matters concerning their respective countries, and calls upon those international institutions which have not yet done so to follow that example and make the necessary arrangements without delay, including arrangements to defray the costs of the participation of those representatives;

12. *Recommends* that all States should intensify their efforts in the specialized agencies and other organizations within the United Nations system of which they

are members to ensure the full and effective implementation of the Declaration on the Granting of Independence to Colonial Countries and Peoples and other relevant resolutions of United Nations bodies;

13. *Urges* those specialized agencies and organizations within the United Nations system which have not already done so to include in the agenda of the regular meetings of their governing bodies a separate item on the progress made by those organizations in their implementation of the Declaration on the Granting of Independence to Colonial Countries and Peoples and other relevant resolutions of United Nations bodies;

14. *Also urges* the executive heads of the specialized agencies and other organizations within the United Nations system to formulate, with the active cooperation of the Organization of African Unity, and to submit, as a matter of priority, to their governing and legislative organs concrete proposals for the full implementation of the relevant United Nations decisions;

15. *Draws the attention* of the Special Committee on the Situation with regard to the Implementation of the Declaration on the Granting of Independence to Colonial Countries and Peoples to the present resolution and to the discussions on the subject at the second regular session of 1984 of the Economic and Social Council;

16. *Requests* the President of the Economic and Social Council to continue consultations on these matters with the Chairman of the Special Committee on the Situation with regard to the Implementation of the Declaration on the Granting of Independence to Colonial Countries and Peoples and the Chairman of the Special Committee against *Apartheid* and to report thereon to the Council;

17. *Requests* the Secretary-General to follow the implementation of the present resolution and to report thereon to the Council at its second regular session of 1985;

18. *Decides* to keep these questions under continuous review.

Economic and Social Council resolution 1984/55

25 July 1984   Meeting 48   36-1-11 (roll-call vote)

Approved by Third Committee (E/1984/137) by roll-call vote (24-1-11), 13 July (meeting 6); 15-nation draft (E/1984/C.3/L.3), orally revised; agenda item 22.
Sponsors: Algeria, Bangladesh, China, Congo, Indonesia, Malaysia, Pakistan, Papua New Guinea, Saint Lucia, Sierra Leone, Sri Lanka, Thailand, Tunisia, Uganda, Yugoslavia.

Roll-call vote in Council as follows:

In favour: Algeria, Argentina, Benin, Brazil, Bulgaria, China, Congo, Costa Rica, Djibouti, Finland, German Democratic Republic, Guyana, Indonesia, Lebanon, Malaysia, Mexico, Pakistan, Papua New Guinea, Poland, Qatar, Romania, Rwanda, Saint Lucia, Saudi Arabia, Sierra Leone, Somalia, Sri Lanka, Suriname, Sweden, Thailand, Tunisia, Uganda, USSR, Venezuela, Yugoslavia, Zaire.

Against: United States.

Abstaining: Austria, Canada, France, Germany, Federal Republic of, Greece, Japan, Luxembourg, Netherlands, New Zealand, Portugal, United Kingdom.

Before the draft was approved by the Third Committee, separate votes were taken on the eighth preambular paragraph and on paragraph 8; both were approved by 21 to 3, with 11 abstentions, with the latter being a roll-call vote. Roll-call votes were also taken in the Council on the same paragraphs, both of which were adopted by 33 to 2, with 12 abstentions.

Explaining its vote, the United Kingdom said it abhorred the system of *apartheid* and, although it endorsed much of the text, there were parts concerning the standing of IMF in the contested paragraphs which it could not support. Portugal, stressing that it opposed *apartheid* and supported United Nations action to hasten the independence of the peoples of southern Africa, said it could not support the text's discriminatory references. Luxembourg, speaking for the member States of the European Community (EC), said they remained firmly against *apartheid* and for early implementation of the 1978 Security Council resolution on the United Nations plan for the independence of Namibia;[13] they commended the specialized agencies for their assistance to refugees from South Africa and Namibia, but felt that the text, particularly the two paragraphs in question, was at variance with their views. Speaking in like manner, New Zealand was concerned over the wording concerning IMF which it said must be free to act according to its mandate. Austria saw the text as a challenge to the autonomy of IMF.

The United States believed that the criticism of IMF was symptomatic of attempts being encouraged by countries playing no constructive part in the specialized agencies to introduce extraneous political issues; although supporting UNHCR's programmes for Namibian and South African refugees, it could not accept the South West Africa People's Organization (SWAPO) as exclusively representing the Namibian people or as specifically deserving agency support.

Poland, speaking also for Bulgaria, the Byelorussian SSR, Czechoslovakia, the German Democratic Republic, Hungary, Mongolia, the Ukrainian SSR and the USSR, would have liked to have seen a condemnation of the western nations' continued assistance to South Africa, a call for them to desist and a denunciation of the plunder by Western transnational corporations of Namibia's wealth.

Action by the Committee on colonial countries. The Committee on colonial countries continued in August 1984 to consider the role of the specialized agencies and other United Nations bodies in implementing the 1960 Declaration, in accordance with the Assembly's 1983 request.[14] On 22 August, the Committee adopted a resolution[15] which became the basis for a draft recommended to the Assembly.

GENERAL ASSEMBLY ACTION

On 5 December, acting on the recommendation of the Fourth Committee, the General

Assembly adopted by recorded vote resolution 39/43 which was based on the text by the Committee on colonial countries.

Implementation of the Declaration on the Granting of Independence to Colonial Countries and Peoples by the specialized agencies and the international institutions associated with the United Nations

The General Assembly,

Having examined the item entitled "Implementation of the Declaration on the Granting of Independence to Colonial Countries and Peoples by the specialized agencies and the international institutions associated with the United Nations",

Recalling the Declaration on the Granting of Independence to Colonial Countries and Peoples, contained in its resolution 1514(XV) of 14 December 1960, and the Plan of Action for the Full Implementation of the Declaration, contained in the annex to its resolution 35/118 of 11 December 1980, as well as all other relevant resolutions adopted by the General Assembly on this subject, in particular resolutions 38/51 of 7 December 1983 on the item and 38/36 of 1 December 1983 on the question of Namibia,

Having examined the reports submitted on the item by the Secretary-General, the Economic and Social Council and the Special Committee on the Situation with regard to the Implementation of the Declaration on the Granting of Independence to Colonial Countries and Peoples,

Taking into account the relevant provisions of the Paris Declaration on Namibia and the Programme of Action on Namibia, adopted at the International Conference in Support of the Struggle of the Namibian People for Independence, and of the Bangkok Declaration and Programme of Action on Namibia, adopted by the United Nations Council for Namibia on 25 May 1984 at its extraordinary plenary meetings held at Bangkok,

Bearing in mind the relevant provisions of the Political Declaration adopted by the Seventh Conference of Heads of State or Government of Non-Aligned Countries, held at New Delhi from 7 to 12 March 1983, and other documents of the Co-ordinating Bureau of the Non-Aligned Countries,

Noting the Final Communiqué of the Summit Meeting of Front-line States, held at Arusha, United Republic of Tanzania, on 29 April 1984,[12]

Aware that the struggle of the people of Namibia for self-determination and independence is in its crucial stage and has sharply intensified as a consequence of the stepped-up aggression of the illegal colonialist régime of Pretoria against the people of the Territory and the increased general support rendered to that régime by certain Western countries, coupled with efforts to deprive the Namibian people of their hard-won victories in the liberation struggle, and that it is therefore incumbent upon the entire international community decisively to intensify concerted action in support of the people of Namibia and their sole and authentic representative, the South West Africa People's Organization, for the attainment of their goal,

Concerned that the policy of "constructive engagement" with the *apartheid* régime of South Africa, linked with the economic and military collaboration maintained by some Western States and Israel with Pretoria, has only encouraged and strengthened the racist régime in its continued illegal occupation and massive militarization and exploitation of Namibia in violation of the relevant resolutions and decisions of the United Nations,

Gravely concerned at the continued imperialist and neo-colonialist attempts to delay the attainment of independence by Namibia, as well as South Africa's aggressive policy to destabilize independent States in southern Africa, in particular the front-line States,

Deeply conscious of the continuing critical need of the Namibian people and their national liberation movement, the South West Africa People's Organization, and of the peoples of other colonial Territories for concrete assistance from the specialized agencies and other organizations of the United Nations system in their struggle for liberation from colonial rule and in their efforts to achieve and consolidate their national independence,

Reaffirming the responsibility of the specialized agencies and other organizations of the United Nations system to take all the necessary measures, within their respective spheres of competence, to ensure the full and speedy implementation of the Declaration on the Granting of Independence to Colonial Countries and Peoples and other relevant resolutions of the United Nations, particularly those relating to the provision of moral and material assistance, on a priority basis, to the peoples of the colonial Territories and their national liberation movements,

Deeply concerned that, although there has been progress in the extension of assistance to refugees from Namibia, the action taken hitherto by the organizations concerned in providing assistance to the people of the Territory through their national liberation movement, the South West Africa People's Organization, still remains inadequate to meet the urgent and growing needs of the Namibian people,

Expressing its confident hope that closer contacts and consultations between the specialized agencies and other organizations of the United Nations system and the Organization of African Unity and the national liberation movement concerned will help to overcome procedural and other difficulties which have impeded or delayed the implementation of some assistance programmes,

Recalling its resolution 38/36 C of 1 December 1983, requesting all specialized agencies and other organizations and institutions of the United Nations system to grant full membership to Namibia, represented by the United Nations Council for Namibia as the legal Administering Authority for Namibia,

Expressing its appreciation to the General Secretariat of the Organization of African Unity for the continued co-operation and assistance extended by it to the specialized agencies and other organizations of the United Nations system in connection with the implementation of the relevant resolutions of the United Nations,

Expressing its appreciation also to the Governments of the front-line States for the steadfast support extended to the people of Namibia and their national liberation movement, the South West Africa People's Organization, in their just and legitimate struggle for the attainment of freedom and independence, despite increased armed attacks by the forces of the racist régime of South Africa, and aware of the particular needs of those Governments for assistance in that connection,

Noting the continued efforts of the United Nations Development Programme in the extension of assistance to the national liberation movements and commending its initiative in establishing channels for closer periodic contacts and consultations between the specialized agencies and other organizations of the United Nations system and the Organization of African Unity and the national liberation movements in the formulation of assistance programmes,

Commending the continued substantial contribution of the United Nations Educational, Scientific and Cultural Organization to the implementation of the Declaration on the Granting of Independence to Colonial Countries and Peoples and the effective support it provides to the national liberation movements in educating the populations of colonial Territories concerning self-determination and independence,

Noting also the support given by the specialized agencies and other organizations of the United Nations system to the implementation of the Nationhood Programme for Namibia, in accordance with General Assembly resolution 32/9 A of 4 November 1977,

Deploring the continued links with and assistance rendered to South Africa by certain specialized agencies in the financial, economic, technical and other fields, in contravention of the relevant resolutions of the United Nations,

Gravely concerned at the continued collaboration between the International Monetary Fund and the Government of South Africa in disregard of relevant General Assembly resolutions, in particular resolution 37/2 of 21 October 1982,

Bearing in mind the importance of the activities of non-governmental organizations aimed at putting an end to the assistance which is still being rendered to South Africa by some specialized agencies and taking into account the consultations held by the Special Committee with non-governmental organizations and the relevant conclusions and recommendations on the Seminar with Non-Governmental Organizations Based in Europe on Dissemination of Information on Decolonization, held at Vienna from 21 to 23 February 1984,

Mindful of the necessity of keeping under continuous review the activities of the specialized agencies and other organizations of the United Nations system in the implementation of the various United Nations decisions relating to decolonization,

1. *Approves* the chapter of the report of the Special Committee on the Situation with regard to the Implementation of the Declaration on the Granting of Independence to Colonial Countries and Peoples relating to the question;

2. *Reaffirms* that the specialized agencies and other organizations and institutions of the United Nations system should continue to be guided by the relevant resolutions of the United Nations in their efforts to contribute, within their spheres of competence, to the full and speedy implementation of the Declaration on the Granting of Independence to Colonial Countries and Peoples, contained in General Assembly resolution 1514(XV);

3. *Reaffirms also* that the recognition by the General Assembly, the Security Council and other United Nations organs of the legitimacy of the struggle of colonial peoples to exercise their right to self-determination and independence entails, as a corollary, the extension by the specialized agencies and other organizations of the United Nations system of all the necessary moral and material assistance to those peoples and their national liberation movements;

4. *Expresses its appreciation* to those specialized agencies and other organizations of the United Nations system which have continued to co-operate in varying degrees with the United Nations and the Organization of African Unity in the implementation of the Declaration and other relevant resolutions of the United Nations, and urges all specialized agencies and other organizations of the United Nations system to accelerate the full and speedy implementation of the relevant provisions of those resolutions;

5. *Expresses its concern* that the assistance extended thus far by certain specialized agencies and other organizations of the United Nations system to the colonial peoples, particularly the people of Namibia and their national liberation movement, the South West Africa People's Organization, is far from adequate in relation to the actual needs of the peoples concerned;

6. *Requests* all specialized agencies and other organizations and bodies of the United Nations system, in accordance with the relevant resolutions of the General Assembly and the Security Council, to take all necessary measures to withhold from the racist régime of South Africa any form of co-operation and assistance in the financial, economic, technical and other fields and to discontinue all support to that régime until the people of Namibia have exercised fully their inalienable right to self-determination, freedom and national independence in a united Namibia and until the inhuman system of *apartheid* has been totally eradicated;

7. *Reiterates its conviction* that the specialized agencies and other organizations and bodies of the United Nations system should refrain from taking any action which might imply recognition of, or support for, the legitimacy of the domination of the Territory by the racist régime of South Africa;

8. *Regrets* that, notwithstanding the repeated assurances by the representative of the World Bank to the effect that the Bank has terminated business relations with the South African régime, the World Bank and also the International Monetary Fund continue to maintain links with the racist régime of Pretoria, as exemplified by the continued membership of South Africa in both agencies, and expresses the view that the two agencies should put an end to all links with the racist régime;

9. *Strongly condemns* the persistent collaboration between the International Monetary Fund and South Africa, in disregard of repeated resolutions to the contrary by the General Assembly, particularly the granting of a loan of $1.1 billion to South Africa in November 1982 in defiance of General Assembly resolution 37/2, and calls upon the International Monetary Fund to rescind the loan, to put an end to such collaboration and not to grant any new loans to the racist régime of South Africa;

10. *Commends* those non-governmental organizations which, by their activities, as exemplified by the co-operation between the Center for International Policy and the United Nations Council for Namibia, are helping to inform public opinion and mobilize it against the assistance rendered by the International Monetary Fund to South Africa, and calls upon all non-governmental organizations to redouble their efforts in this respect;

11. *Once again urges* the executive heads of the World Bank and the International Monetary Fund to draw the

particular attention of their governing bodies to the present resolution, with a view to formulating specific programmes beneficial to the peoples of the colonial Territories, particularly Namibia;

12.   *Requests* the specialized agencies and other organizations of the United Nations system to render or continue to render, as a matter of urgency, all possible moral and material assistance to the colonial peoples struggling for liberation from colonial rule, bearing in mind that such assistance should not only meet their immediate needs but also create conditions for development after they have exercised their right to self-determination and independence;

13.   *Once again requests* the specialized agencies and other organizations of the United Nations system to continue to provide all moral and material assistance to the newly independent and emerging States;

14.   *Reiterates its recommendation* that the specialized agencies and other organizations of the United Nations system should initiate or broaden contacts and co-operation with the colonial peoples and their national liberation movements directly or, where appropriate, through the Organization of African Unity, and review and introduce greater flexibility in their procedures with respect to the formulation and preparation of assistance programmes and projects so as to be able to extend the necessary assistance without delay to help the colonial peoples and their national liberation movements in their struggle to exercise their inalienable right to self-determination and independence in accordance with General Assembly resolution 1514(XV);

15.   *Notes with satisfaction* that the South West Africa People's Organization continues to be the beneficiary of a number of programmes established within the framework of the United Nations Institute for Namibia at Lusaka and that the United Nations Council for Namibia, in co-operation with the South West Africa People's Organization, continues to represent the people of Namibia at meetings of the specialized agencies and other organizations and institutions of the United Nations system, and urges those agencies and organizations to increase their assistance to the South West Africa People's Organization, as well as to the United Nations Institute for Namibia and the Nationhood Programme for Namibia;

16.   *Recommends* that a separate item on assistance to national liberation movements recognized by the Organization of African Unity should be included in the agenda of future high-level meetings between the General Secretariat of the Organization of African Unity and the secretariats of the United Nations and other organizations of the United Nations system, with a view to strengthening further the existing measures of co-ordination of action to ensure the best use of available resources for assistance to the peoples of the colonial Territories;

17.   *Urges* the specialized agencies and other organizations of the United Nations system that have not already done so to include in the agenda of the regular meetings of their governing bodies a separate item on the progress they have made in the implementation of the Declaration and the other relevant resolutions of the United Nations;

18.   *Notes with satisfaction* the arrangements made by several specialized agencies and other organizations of the United Nations system which enable representatives of the national liberation movements recognized by the Organization of African Unity to participate fully as observers in the proceedings relating to matters concerning their respective countries, and calls upon those agencies and organizations that have not yet done so to follow this example and to make the necessary arrangements without delay;

19.   *Notes with satisfaction* the inclusion of Namibia, represented by the United Nations Council for Namibia, in the membership of various specialized agencies and other organizations of the United Nations system, and urges those agencies and organizations that have not so far granted full membership to the United Nations Council for Namibia to do so without delay;

20.   *Urges* the specialized agencies and other organizations and institutions of the United Nations system to extend, as a matter of priority, substantial material assistance to the Governments of the front-line States in order to enable them to support more effectively the struggle of the people of Namibia for freedom and independence and to resist the violation of their territorial integrity by the armed forces of the racist régime of South Africa directly or, as in Angola and Mozambique, through puppet traitor groups in the service of Pretoria;

21.   *Urges* the specialized agencies and other organizations and institutions of the United Nations system to assist in accelerating progress in all sectors of the national life of the small Territories, particularly in the development of their economies;

22.   *Recommends* that all Governments should intensify their efforts in the specialized agencies and other organizations of the United Nations system of which they are members to ensure the full and effective implementation of the Declaration and other relevant resolutions of the United Nations and, in that connection, that they should accord priority to the question of providing assistance on an emergency basis to the peoples of the colonial Territories and their national liberation movements;

23.   *Reiterates its proposal*, under article III of the Agreement between the United Nations and the International Monetary Fund, for the urgent inclusion in the agenda of the Board of Governors of the Fund of an item dealing with the relationship between the Fund and South Africa and further reiterates its proposal that, in pursuance of article II of the Agreement, the relevant organs of the United Nations should participate in any meeting of the Board of Governors called by the Fund for the purpose of discussing the item, and urges the Fund to discuss its relationship with South Africa at its annual meeting, in compliance with the above-mentioned Agreement;

24.   *Draws the attention* of the specialized agencies and other organizations of the United Nations system to the Plan of Action for the Full Implementation of the Declaration on the Granting of Independence to Colonial Countries and Peoples, contained in the annex to General Assembly resolution 35/118, in particular to those provisions calling upon the agencies and organizations to render all possible moral and material assistance to the peoples of the colonial Territories and their national liberation movements;

25.   *Urges* the executive heads of the specialized agencies and other organizations of the United Nations system, having regard to the provisions of paragraphs 14 and 24 above, to formulate, with the active co-operation

of the Organization of African Unity where appropriate, and to submit, as a matter of priority, to their governing and legislative organs concrete proposals for the full implementation of the relevant United Nations decisions, in particular specific programmes of assistance to the peoples of the colonial Territories and their national liberation movements;

26. *Requests* the Secretary-General to continue to assist the specialized agencies and other organizations of the United Nations system in working out appropriate measures for implementing the relevant resolutions of the United Nations and to prepare for submission to the relevant bodies, with the assistance of those agencies and organizations, a report on the action taken in implementation of the relevant resolutions, including the present resolution, since the circulation of his previous report;

27. *Requests* the Economic and Social Council to continue to consider, in consultation with the Special Committee on the Situation with regard to the Implementation of the Declaration on the Granting of Independence to Colonial Countries and Peoples, appropriate measures for the co-ordination of the policies and activities of the specialized agencies and other organizations of the United Nations system in implementing the relevant resolutions of the General Assembly;

28. *Requests* all specialized agencies and other organizations of the United Nations system to mark, in their respective fields of operation, the twenty-fifth anniversary of the adoption of the Declaration on the Granting of Independence to Colonial Countries and Peoples and to report to the Secretary-General on the measures taken;

29. *Requests* the Special Committee to continue to examine this question and to report thereon to the General Assembly at its fortieth session.

General Assembly resolution 39/43

5 December 1984   Meeting 87   119-3-22 (recorded vote)

Approved by Fourth Committee (A/39/690 & Corr.1) by recorded vote (116-3-23), 13 November (meeting 19); draft by Committee on colonial countries (A/39/23); amended by Cameroon, for African Group (A/C.4/39/L.11) and by United States (A/C.4/39/L.8); agenda items 12 and 105.
Meeting numbers. GA 39th session: 4th Committee 12-19; plenary 87.

Recorded vote in Assembly as follows:

In favour: Afghanistan, Albania, Algeria, Angola, Argentina, Bahrain, Bangladesh, Barbados, Belize, Benin, Bhutan, Bolivia, Botswana, Brazil, Brunei Darussalam, Bulgaria, Burkina Faso, Burma, Burundi, Byelorussian SSR, Cameroon, Cape Verde, Central African Republic, Chad, Chile, China, Colombia, Congo, Costa Rica, Cuba, Cyprus, Czechoslovakia, Democratic Kampuchea, Democratic Yemen, Djibouti, Dominican Republic, Ecuador, Egypt, El Salvador, Equatorial Guinea, Ethiopia, Fiji, Gabon, Gambia, German Democratic Republic, Ghana, Greece, Guinea, Guinea-Bissau, Guyana, Haiti, Honduras, Hungary, India, Indonesia, Iran, Iraq, Jamaica, Jordan, Kenya, Kuwait, Lao People's Democratic Republic, Lebanon, Liberia, Libyan Arab Jamahiriya, Madagascar, Malaysia, Maldives, Mali, Malta, Mauritania, Mauritius, Mexico, Mongolia, Morocco, Mozambique, Nepal, Nicaragua, Niger, Nigeria, Oman, Pakistan, Panama, Papua New Guinea, Peru, Philippines, Poland, Qatar, Romania, Rwanda, Samoa, Sao Tome and Principe, Saudi Arabia, Senegal, Seychelles, Sierra Leone, Singapore, Sri Lanka, Sudan, Suriname, Syrian Arab Republic, Thailand, Togo, Trinidad and Tobago, Tunisia, Turkey, Uganda, Ukrainian SSR, USSR, United Arab Emirates, United Republic of Tanzania, Uruguay, Venezuela, Viet Nam, Yemen, Yugoslavia, Zaire, Zambia, Zimbabwe.

Against: Israel, United Kingdom, United States.

Abstaining: Australia, Austria, Belgium, Canada, Denmark, Finland, France, Germany, Federal Republic of, Iceland, Ireland, Italy, Ivory Coast, Japan, Lesotho, Luxembourg, Malawi, Netherlands, New Zealand, Norway, Portugal, Spain, Sweden.

Before approving the draft as a whole, the Fourth Committee approved several amendments

by recorded vote. The United States proposed deleting from the seventh preambular paragraph, after "certain Western countries", the phrase "especially the United States of America and Israel", and deleting from paragraph 10, after "public opinion", the phrase "in the United States of America and elsewhere". The first amendment was approved by 62 votes to 50, with 20 abstentions, and the second by 64 to 39, with 28 abstentions.

An amendment by Cameroon, on behalf of the Group of African States,[16] would have inserted a new eighth preambular paragraph to have the Assembly express concern that the policy of constructive engagement with the *apartheid* régime of South Africa adopted by a certain Member State had further encouraged and strengthened the racist régime in its continued illegal occupation and massive militarization and exploitation of Namibia. The amendment was subsequently withdrawn by the sponsors and a new one introduced to add the eighth preambular paragraph of the adopted text. That amendment was approved by 90 votes to 28, with 20 abstentions.

A number of States explained their positions. The United States said that specific mention of any country in connection with a recommendation to mobilize public opinion constituted direct interference in its internal affairs and that no delegation could seriously maintain that the United States was blocking a solution to the Namibian crisis since, at times, persuasion and patient diplomacy were the best ways to proceed. The United Kingdom opposed the amendment concerning constructive engagement which, it said, raised new hopes for the independence of Namibia; it also objected to selective references to specific States, as did Israel which pointed out that most if not all countries in the United Nations had dealings of some kind with South Africa. Other States which regretted the inclusion of selective references to particular Member States were: Argentina, Australia, Canada, Chile, Dominican Republic, Ecuador, France, Federal Republic of Germany, Greece, Ireland, Italy, Japan, Netherlands, New Zealand, Norway on behalf of the five Nordic States, Togo, Turkey and Uruguay.

Canada said decisions of IMF and the World Bank had to be based on their mandates as autonomous institutions and not on political considerations, a view shared by the United Kingdom and the Federal Republic of Germany which regretted that the text questioned South Africa's right to membership in those bodies and did not give due consideration to their statutes. The Netherlands also felt that such criticism was not acceptable. Ireland took the same position while expressing agreement with the draft's general thrust. New Zealand spoke in similar vein, but also supported provisions for assistance to the people of NSGTs, which it encouraged in the case of Tokelau.

Japan agreed that international organizations should be encouraged to help colonial countries in accordance with their specific functions. Italy said the Assembly should not give the specialized agencies instructions, while France, stressing its support of the universality and independence of the specialized agencies, opposed criticisms of the World Bank and IMF. Norway, speaking for the five Nordic countries, supported increased assistance to peoples struggling for self-determination where, it said, the international agencies had an important role, and regretted that some paragraphs were irrelevant and others overlooked the statutes and universal character of the agencies. Australia also objected to questioning the independence of the agencies and to including paragraphs unrelated to the subject of the draft. Botswana had reservations on the paragraphs referring to IMF, while Chile and the Dominican Republic regretted the criticism levelled at the financial institutions.

France considered the issues raised by Cameroon on constructive engagement out of place in the text, while Colombia regretted their selective character.

Foreign interests impeding implementation of the Declaration

In 1984, the Committee on colonial countries and the General Assembly reaffirmed their concern that the activities of foreign economic, financial and other interests operating in the colonial Territories, particularly in southern Africa, obstructed the political independence of the indigenous populations.

On 21 August, the Committee adopted a resolution[(17)] on the activities of foreign interests which became the basis of a draft resolution recommended to the Assembly.

GENERAL ASSEMBLY ACTION

On 5 December, acting on the recommendation of the Fourth Committee, the General Assembly adopted by recorded vote resolution 39/42.

Activities of foreign economic and other interests which are impeding the implementation of the Declaration on the Granting of Independence to Colonial Countries and Peoples in Namibia and in all other Territories under colonial domination and efforts to eliminate colonialism, *apartheid* and racial discrimination in southern Africa

The General Assembly,

Having considered the item entitled "Activities of foreign economic and other interests which are impeding the implementation of the Declaration on the Granting of Independence to Colonial Countries and Peoples in Namibia and in all other Territories under colonial domination and efforts to eliminate colonialism, *apartheid* and racial discrimination in southern Africa",

Having examined the chapter of the report of the Special Committee on the Situation with regard to the Implementation of the Declaration on the Granting of Independence to Colonial Countries and Peoples relating to the item,

Taking into consideration the relevant chapters of the report of the United Nations Council for Namibia,

Recalling its resolutions 1514(XV) of 14 December 1960, containing the Declaration on the Granting of Independence to Colonial Countries and Peoples, 2621(XXV) of 12 October 1970, containing the programme of action for the full implementation of the Declaration, and 35/118 of 11 December 1980, the annex to which contains the Plan of Action for the Full Implementation of the Declaration, as well as all other resolutions of the United Nations relating to the item,

Reaffirming the solemn obligation of the administering Powers under the Charter of the United Nations to promote the political, economic, social and educational advancement of the inhabitants of the Territories under their administration and to protect the human and natural resources of those Territories against abuses,

Taking into account the relevant provisions of the Paris Declaration on Namibia and the Programme of Action on Namibia, adopted at the International Conference in Support of the Struggle of the Namibian People for Independence,

Reaffirming that any economic or other activity which impedes the implementation of the Declaration on the Granting of Independence to Colonial Countries and Peoples and obstructs efforts aimed at the elimination of colonialism, *apartheid* and racial discrimination in southern Africa and other colonial Territories is in direct violation of the rights of the inhabitants and of the principles of the Charter and all relevant resolutions of the United Nations,

Reaffirming that the natural resources of all Territories under colonial and racist domination are the heritage of the peoples of those Territories and that the exploitation and depletion of those resources by foreign economic interests, in particular in Namibia, in association with the occupying régime of South Africa, constitute a direct violation of the rights of the peoples and of the principles of the Charter and all relevant resolutions of the United Nations,

Bearing in mind the relevant provisions of the Economic Declaration and other documents of the Seventh Conference of Heads of State or Government of Non-Aligned Countries, held at New Delhi from 7 to 12 March 1983,

Taking into account the relevant provisions of the Bangkok Declaration and Programme of Action on Namibia, adopted by the United Nations Council for Namibia on 25 May 1984 at its extraordinary plenary meetings held at Bangkok, and the conclusions and recommendations of the Seminar on the Activities of Foreign Economic Interests in the Exploitation of Namibia's Natural and Human Resources, organized by the Council at Ljubljana, Yugoslavia, from 16 to 20 April 1984,

Noting with profound concern that the colonial Powers and certain States, through their activities in the colonial Territories, have continued to disregard United Nations decisions relating to the item and that they have failed to implement, in particular, the relevant provisions of General Assembly resolutions 2621(XXV) of 12 October 1970 and 38/50 of 7 December 1983, by which the Assembly called upon the colonial Powers and those

Governments that had not yet done so to take legislative, administrative or other measures in respect of their nationals and the bodies corporate under their jurisdiction that own and operate enterprises in colonial Territories, particularly in Africa, which are detrimental to the interests of the inhabitants of those Territories, in order to put an end to such enterprises and to prevent new investments that run counter to the interests of the inhabitants of those Territories,

Condemning the intensified activities of those foreign economic, financial and other interests which continue to exploit the natural and human resources of the colonial Territories and to accumulate and repatriate huge profits to the detriment of the interests of the inhabitants, particularly in the case of Namibia, thereby impeding the realization by the peoples of the Territories of their legitimate aspirations for self-determination and independence,

Strongly condemning the support which the racist minority régime of South Africa continues to receive from those foreign economic, financial and other interests which are collaborating with the régime in the exploitation of the natural and human resources of the international Territory of Namibia, in the further entrenchment of its illegal racist domination over the Territory and in the strengthening of its system of *apartheid*,

Strongly condemning the investment of foreign capital in the production of uranium and the collaboration by certain Western States and other States with the racist minority régime of South Africa in the nuclear field which, by providing that régime with nuclear equipment and technology, enable it to develop nuclear and military capabilities and to become a nuclear Power, thereby promoting South Africa's continued illegal occupation of Namibia,

Reaffirming that the natural resources of Namibia, including its marine resources, are the inviolable heritage of the Namibian people and that the exploitation of those resources by foreign economic interests under the protection of the illegal colonial administration, in violation of the Charter, of the relevant resolutions of the General Assembly and the Security Council and of Decree No. 1 for the Protection of the Natural Resources of Namibia, enacted by the United Nations Council for Namibia on 27 September 1974, and in disregard of the advisory opinion of the International Court of Justice of 21 June 1971, is illegal, contributes to the maintenance of the illegal occupation régime and is a grave threat to the integrity and prosperity of an independent Namibia,

Concerned about the conditions in other colonial Territories, including certain Territories in the Caribbean and the Pacific Ocean regions, where foreign economic, financial and other interests continue to deprive the indigenous populations of their rights over the wealth of their countries, and where the inhabitants of those Territories continue to suffer from a loss of land ownership as a result of the failure of the administering Powers concerned to restrict the sale of land to foreigners, despite the repeated appeals of the General Assembly,

Conscious of the continuing need to mobilize world public opinion against the involvement of foreign economic, financial and other interests in the exploitation of natural and human resources, which impedes the independence of colonial Territories and the elimination of racism, particularly in southern Africa,

1. *Reaffirms* the inalienable right of the peoples of dependent Territories to self-determination and independence and to the enjoyment of the natural resources of their Territories, as well as their right to dispose of those resources in their best interests;

2. *Reiterates* that any administering or occupying Power that deprives the colonial peoples of the exercise of their legitimate rights over their natural resources or subordinates the rights and interests of those peoples to foreign economic and financial interests violates the solemn obligations it has assumed under the Charter of the United Nations;

3. *Reaffirms* that, by their depletive exploitation of natural resources, the continued accumulation and repatriation of huge profits and the use of those profits for the enrichment of foreign settlers and the perpetuation of colonial domination and racial discrimination in the Territories, the activities of foreign economic, financial and other interests operating at present in the colonial Territories, particularly in southern Africa, constitute a major obstacle to political independence and racial equality, as well as to the enjoyment of the natural resources of those Territories by the indigenous inhabitants;

4. *Condemns* the activities of foreign economic and other interests in the colonial Territories impeding the implementation of the Declaration on the Granting of Independence to Colonial Countries and Peoples, contained in General Assembly resolution 1514(XV), and the efforts to eliminate colonialism, *apartheid* and racial discrimination;

5. *Condemns* the policies of Governments that continue to support or collaborate with those foreign economic and other interests engaged in exploiting the natural and human resources of the Territories, including, in particular, illegally exploiting Namibia's marine resources, violating the political, economic and social rights and interests of the indigenous peoples and thus obstructing the full and speedy implementation of the Declaration in respect of those Territories;

6. *Strongly condemns* the collusion of the Governments of certain Western States and other States with the racist minority régime of South Africa in the nuclear field and calls upon those and all other Governments to refrain from supplying that régime, directly or indirectly, with installations that might enable it to produce uranium, plutonium and other nuclear materials, reactors or military equipment;

7. *Requests* the Special Committee on the Situation with regard to the Implementation of the Declaration on the Granting of Independence to Colonial Countries and Peoples to continue to monitor closely the situation in the remaining colonial Territories so as to ensure that all economic activities in those Territories are aimed at strengthening and diversifying their economies in the interests of the indigenous peoples and their speedy accession to independence and, in that connection, requests the administering Powers concerned to ensure that the peoples of the Territories under their administration are not exploited for political, military and other purposes detrimental to their interests;

8. *Strongly condemns* those Western States and all other States, as well as the transnational corporations, which continue their investments in, and supply of armaments and oil and nuclear technology to, the racist régime of South Africa, thus buttressing it and aggravating the threat to world peace;

9. *Calls upon* all States, in particular certain Western States, to take urgent, effective measures to terminate all collaboration with the racist régime of South Africa in the political, diplomatic, economic, trade, military and nuclear fields and to refrain from entering into other relations with that régime in violation of the relevant resolutions of the United Nations and of the Organization of African Unity;

10. *Calls once again upon* all Governments that have not yet done so to take legislative, administrative or other measures in respect of their nationals and the bodies corporate under their jurisdiction that own and operate enterprises in colonial Territories, particularly in Africa, which are detrimental to the interests of the inhabitants of those Territories, in order to put an end to such enterprises and to prevent new investments that run counter to the interests of the inhabitants of those Territories;

11. *Calls upon* all States to terminate, or cause to have terminated, any investments in Namibia or loans to the racist minority régime of South Africa and to refrain from any agreements or measures to promote trade or other economic relations with that régime;

12. *Requests* all States that have not yet done so to take effective measures to end the supply of funds and other forms of assistance, including military supplies and equipment, to the racist minority régime of South Africa, which uses such assistance to repress the people of Namibia and their national liberation movement;

13. *Strongly condemns* South Africa for its continued exploitation and plundering of the natural resources of Namibia, in complete disregard of the legitimate interests of the Namibian people, for the creation in the Territory of an economic structure dependent essentially upon its mineral resources and for its illegal extension of the territorial sea and its proclamation of an economic zone off the coast of Namibia;

14. *Declares* that all activities of foreign economic interests in Namibia are illegal under international law and that consequently South Africa and all the foreign economic interests operating in Namibia are liable to pay damages to the future lawful Government of an independent Namibia;

15. *Calls upon* those oil-producing and oil-exporting countries that have not yet done so to take effective measures against the oil companies concerned so as to terminate the supply of crude oil and petroleum products to the racist régime of South Africa;

16. *Reiterates* that the exploitation and plundering of the marine and other natural resources of Namibia by South African and other foreign economic interests, including the activities of those transnational corporations which are engaged in the exploitation and export of the Territory's uranium ores and other resources, in violation of the relevant resolutions of the General Assembly and the Security Council and of Decree No. 1 for the Protection of the Natural Resources of Namibia, are illegal, contribute to the maintenance of the illegal occupation régime and are a grave threat to the integrity and prosperity of an independent Namibia;

17. *Condemns* the plunder of Namibian uranium and calls upon the Governments of all States, particularly those whose nationals and corporations are involved in the mining or enrichment of, or traffic in, Namibian uranium, to take all appropriate measures in compliance with the provisions of Decree No. 1 for the Protection of the Natural Resources of Namibia, including

the practice of requiring negative certificates of origin, to prohibit and prevent State-owned and other corporations, together with their subsidiaries, from dealing in Namibian uranium and from engaging in uranium prospecting activities in Namibia;

18. *Requests* all States to take legislative, administrative and other measures, as appropriate, in order effectively to isolate South Africa politically, economically, militarily and culturally, in accordance with General Assembly resolutions ES-8/2 of 14 September 1981, 36/121 B of 10 December 1981, 37/233 A of 20 December 1982 and 38/36 A of 1 December 1983;

19. *Calls once again upon* all States to discontinue all economic, financial and trade relations with the racist minority régime of South Africa concerning Namibia and to refrain from entering into any relations with South Africa, purporting to act on behalf of or concerning Namibia, which may lend support to its continued illegal occupation of that Territory;

20. *Invites* all Governments and organizations of the United Nations system, having regard to the relevant provisions of the Declaration on the Establishment of a New International Economic Order, contained in General Assembly resolution 3201(S-VI) of 1 May 1974, and of the Charter of Economic Rights and Duties of States, contained in Assembly resolution 3281(XXIX) of 12 December 1974, to ensure, in particular, that the permanent sovereignty of the colonial Territories over their natural resources is fully respected and safeguarded;

21. *Calls upon* the administering Powers to abolish all discriminatory and unjust wage systems and working conditions prevailing in the Territories under their administration and to apply in each Territory a uniform system of wages to all the inhabitants without any discrimination;

22. *Requests* the Secretary-General to undertake, through the Department of Public Information of the Secretariat, a sustained and broad campaign with a view to informing world public opinion of the facts concerning the pillaging of natural resources in colonial Territories and the exploitation of their indigenous populations by foreign monopolies and, in respect of Namibia, the support they render to the racist minority régime of South Africa;

23. *Appeals* to all non-governmental organizations to continue their campaign to mobilize international public opinion for the enforcement of economic and other sanctions against the Pretoria régime;

24. *Requests* the Special Committee to continue to examine this question and to report thereon to the General Assembly at its fortieth session.

General Assembly resolution 39/42

5 December 1984   Meeting 87   121-2-22 (recorded vote)

Approved by Fourth Committee (A/39/663) by recorded vote (112-4-23), 26 October (meeting 11); draft by Committee on colonial countries (A/39/23); agenda item 104.

Meeting numbers. GA 39th session: 4th Committee 2-11; plenary 87.

Recorded vote in Assembly as follows:

In favour: Afghanistan, Albania, Algeria, Angola, Argentina, Australia, Bahrain, Bangladesh, Barbados, Belize, Benin, Bhutan, Bolivia, Botswana, Brazil, Brunei Darussalam, Bulgaria, Burkina Faso, Burma, Burundi, Byelorussian SSR, Cameroon, Cape Verde, Central African Republic, Chad, Chile, China, Colombia, Congo, Costa Rica, Cuba, Cyprus, Czechoslovakia, Democratic Kampuchea, Democratic Yemen, Djibouti, Dominican Republic, Ecuador, Egypt, El Salvador,

Equatorial Guinea, Ethiopia, Fiji, Gabon, Gambia, German Democratic Republic, Ghana, Guinea, Guinea-Bissau, Guyana, Haiti, Honduras, Hungary, India, Indonesia, Iran, Iraq, Ivory Coast, Jamaica, Jordan, Kenya, Kuwait, Lao People's Democratic Republic, Lebanon, Liberia, Libyan Arab Jamahiriya, Madagascar, Malaysia, Maldives, Mali, Malta, Mauritania, Mauritius, Mexico, Mongolia, Morocco, Nepal, New Zealand, Nicaragua, Niger, Nigeria, Oman, Pakistan, Panama, Papua New Guinea, Peru, Philippines, Poland, Qatar, Romania, Rwanda, Samoa, Sao Tome and Principe, Saudi Arabia, Senegal, Seychelles, Sierra Leone, Singapore, Somalia, Sri Lanka, Sudan, Suriname, Syrian Arab Republic, Thailand, Togo, Trinidad and Tobago, Tunisia, Turkey, Uganda, Ukrainian SSR, USSR, United Arab Emirates, United Republic of Tanzania, Uruguay, Venezuela, Viet Nam, Yemen, Yugoslavia, Zaire, Zimbabwe.

Against: United Kingdom, United States.

Abstaining: Austria, Belgium, Canada, Denmark, Finland, France, Germany, Federal Republic of, Greece, Iceland, Ireland, Israel, Italy, Japan, Lesotho, Luxembourg, Malawi, Mozambique, Netherlands, Norway, Portugal, Spain, Sweden.

In explanation of vote, a number of States said they could not accept the assumption that foreign economic interests always had detrimental effects on NSGTs. Ireland said that carefully promoted development was an important factor in preparing Territories for independence. Italy felt that the facts showed the useful role NSGTs could play in the right circumstances. The Federal Republic of Germany said that the draft failed to distinguish between harmful activities and those which might contribute to development. Japan spoke similarly and pointed out that Namibia, which had been under illegal occupation for many years, was a special case. France believed that there were situations where natural resources were exploited without regard for the people, due mainly to the unbalanced relations between developing and industrialized countries. Norway also noted that foreign activities could be essential to industrialization and employment, especially in smaller dependent Territories.

Sweden said that some paragraphs of the text caused the Nordic countries difficulties, specifically those concerning the division of competence between the main United Nations organs. Denmark spoke in like manner. Norway felt that some elements in the draft fell within the competence of the Security Council.

Sweden also said the Nordic countries could not accept the formulation in paragraph 14 on the idea that all foreign economic interests in Namibia were illegal under international law. Canada shared that view, as did the Netherlands which said that, having recognized the competence of the Council for Namibia to issue Decree No. 1 for the protection of Namibia's natural resources and favouring selective sanctions against South Africa, it rejected the termination of all ties and shared the view that all foreign economic interests in NSGTs were not predatory; it also regretted the accusations levelled at administering Powers by countries which did not distinguish between the situation in Namibia and in other Territories.

Chad, Malawi, the Netherlands, Senegal and Turkey objected to the continued selective criticism of Western countries.

Canada said it was time to re-examine assumptions and to focus on such basic issues as the impact of transnational corporations, which it believed could be beneficial for development and technology transfer; it felt the Fourth Committee might become irrelevant and even hinder decolonization if it condemned them categorically, and that ending all economic and diplomatic relations with South Africa was not a means of advancing the cause of Namibia's independence. Austria did not believe the resolution took sufficient account of the concerns of the smaller Territories.

Belgium, expressing support for efforts to end the illegal occupation of Namibia, had reservations on that part of the draft which applied to other NSGTs since it supported the view that foreign investment had contributed to their development. Australia agreed and noted a contradiction with calls made in other resolutions for their further economic development. New Zealand also shared these views and supported upholding the principle that foreign economic interests should not impede the political and economic development or self-determination of NSGTs. Fiji added that such interests could make a useful contribution with regard to technology, skills and job opportunities; it was for the inhabitants of the dependent Territories to decide whether such interests were impeding them. Chile spoke in like vein and noted that sometimes the people of the Territories themselves requested such help, as was the case in Anguilla.

Malawi opposed activities that deliberately blocked Namibian independence and the abolition of *apartheid.*

During its consideration of the topic, the Fourth Committee heard statements by J. A. González-González, a newspaperman, and Wilma E. Reverón of the Oficina de Información Internacional para la Independencia de Puerto Rico, whose requests for hearings[18] had been approved by the Committee.

Military bases in colonial countries

Action by the Committee on colonial countries. Further to a December 1983 request of the General Assembly,[19] the Committee on colonial countries continued to consider in 1984 military activities and bases in colonial Territories, approving a decision on the subject on 21 August.[20] The Committee recommended a draft decision based on that text to the Assembly.

GENERAL ASSEMBLY ACTION

General Assembly decision 39/412, as recommended by the Fourth Committee, was adopted by the General Assembly by recorded vote in December.

Military activities and arrangements by colonial Powers in Territories under their administration which might be impeding the implementation of the Declaration on the Granting of Independence to Colonial Countries and Peoples

At its 87th plenary meeting, on 5 December 1984, the General Assembly, on the recommendation of the Fourth Committee, adopted the following text:

"1. The General Assembly, having considered the chapter of the report of the Special Committee on the Situation with regard to the Implementation of the Declaration on the Granting of Independence to Colonial Countries and Peoples relating to an item on the Special Committee's agenda entitled 'Military activities and arrangements by colonial Powers in Territories under their administration which might be impeding the implementation of the Declaration on the Granting of Independence to Colonial Countries and Peoples', and recalling its decision 38/419 of 7 December 1983 on this subject, deplores the fact that the colonial Powers concerned have taken no steps to implement the requests repeatedly addressed to them by the Assembly, most recently in paragraph 10 of its resolution 38/54 of 7 December 1983, to withdraw immediately and unconditionally their military bases and installations from colonial Territories and to refrain from establishing new ones.

"2. The General Assembly, in recalling its resolution 1514(XV) and all other relevant United Nations resolutions and decisions relating to military bases and installations in colonial and Non-Self-Governing Territories, reaffirms its strong conviction that the presence of military bases and installations in the Territories concerned could constitute a major obstacle to the implementation of the Declaration on the Granting of Independence to Colonial Countries and Peoples and that it is the responsibility of the administering Powers concerned in that regard to ensure that the existence of such bases and installations does not hinder the populations of the Territories from exercising their right to self-determination and independence in conformity with the purposes and principles of the Charter of the United Nations. Furthermore, aware of the presence of military bases and installations of the administering Powers concerned and of other countries in those Territories, the Assembly urges the administering Powers concerned to continue to take all necessary measures not to involve those Territories in any offensive acts or interference against other States and to comply fully with the purposes and principles of the Charter, the Declaration on the Granting of Independence to Colonial Countries and Peoples and the resolutions and decisions of the United Nations relating to military activities and arrangements by colonial Powers in Territories under their administration.

"3. The General Assembly deplores the fact that South Africa and the colonial Powers continue to engage in activities and dispositions of a military character and to establish and maintain bases and other military installations in Namibia and other colonial Territories in violation of the purposes and principles of the Charter and of Assembly resolution 1514(XV).

"4. The General Assembly condemns all military activities and arrangements in colonial Territories which deny the peoples concerned their right to self-determination and independence.

"5. The General Assembly notes that, in southern Africa in general and in and around Namibia in particular, a critical situation continues to prevail as a result of South Africa's continued illegal occupation of the Territory. The illegal occupying régime has resorted to desperate measures in order to suppress by force the legitimate aspirations of the people and maintain its control over the Territory. In its escalating war against the people of Namibia and their national liberation movement, the South West Africa People's Organization, struggling for freedom and independence, the régime has repeatedly committed acts of armed aggression against the neighbouring independent African countries, particularly Angola, which have caused extensive loss of human lives and destruction of the economic infrastructure.

"6. The General Assembly, noting that in Namibia, the South African Government has continued to expand its network of military bases and carried out a massive buildup of its military forces, condemns any continuing co-operation of certain Western States and other States with South Africa in supplying it with arms and military equipment as well as technology, including technology and equipment in the nuclear field capable of being utilized for military purposes. The Assembly condemns South Africa for its ever increasing and large-scale military buildup in Namibia, its introduction of compulsory military service for Namibians, its forced recruitment and training of Namibians for tribal armies and its recruitment of mercenaries and other foreign agents in order to carry out its policies of internal repression and its military attacks against independent African States. In this connection, the Assembly calls upon all States to co-operate in taking effective measures to prevent the recruitment, training and transit of mercenaries for service in Namibia. The Assembly is particularly mindful in that regard of the relevant resolutions of the Organization of African Unity, the Political Declaration adopted by the Seventh Conference of Heads of State or Government of Non-Aligned Countries, held at New Delhi from 7 to 12 March 1983, the Final Communiqué of the Summit Meeting of Front-line States, held at Arusha, United Republic of Tanzania, on 29 April 1984, the Final Communiqué of the Regional Symposium on South Africa's Illegal Occupation of Namibia: The Threat to International Peace and Security, held at Arusha, United Republic of Tanzania, from 2 to 5 April 1984, the relevant provisions of the Declaration adopted by the International Conference on the Alliance between South Africa and Israel, held at Vienna from 11 to 13 July 1983, and the relevant decisions adopted by the Fourth Islamic Summit Conference, held at Casablanca (Morocco) from 16 to 19 January 1984.

"7. The General Assembly, accordingly, demands the immediate cessation of the war of oppression waged by the racist minority régime against the people of Namibia and their national liberation movement, as well as the urgent dismantling of all military bases in the Territory. Reaffirming the legitimacy of the struggle of the people of Namibia to achieve their freedom and independence, the Assembly appeals to all States to render sustained and increased moral and political support, as well as financial, military and other material assistance, to the South West Africa People's Organization to enable it to intensify its struggle for the liberation of Namibia.

"8. The General Assembly condemns any continued military collaboration and support which certain Western States and other States render to the Government of South Africa and calls upon all States to cease such collaboration and support to that Government, particularly the sale of weapons and other *matériel*, which increases its capacity to wage wars against neighbouring African States. In particular, the Assembly calls upon all Governments to comply strictly with the provisions of Security Council resolution 418(1977) of 4 November 1977, by which the Council, acting under Chapter VII of the Charter, decided to apply specific sanctions against South Africa. In this connection, the Assembly draws particular attention to the relevant provisions of its resolution 38/36 of 1 December 1983, the Paris Declaration on Namibia and the Programme of Action on Namibia, and the Bangkok Declaration and Programme of Action on Namibia adopted by the United Nations Council for Namibia on 25 May 1984 at its extraordinary plenary meetings held at Bangkok.

"9. The General Assembly considers that the acquisition of nuclear weapons capability by the racist régime of South Africa, with its infamous record of violence and aggression, constitutes a further effort on its part to terrorize and intimidate independent States in the region into submission while also posing a threat to all mankind. The continuing assistance rendered to the South African régime by certain Western States and other States in the military and nuclear fields belies their stated opposition to the racist practice of the South African régime and makes them willing partners of its hegemonistic and criminal policies. The Assembly accordingly condemns the continued nuclear co-operation by certain Western States and other States with South Africa. It calls upon the States concerned to end all such co-operation and, in particular, to halt the supply to South Africa of equipment, technology, nuclear materials and related training, which increases its nuclear capability.

"10. The General Assembly, noting that the militarization of Namibia has led to the forced conscription of Namibians, to a greatly intensified flow of refugees and to a tragic disorganization of the family life of the Namibian people, strongly condemns the forcible and wholesale displacement of Namibians from their homes for military and political purposes and the introduction of compulsory military service for Namibians and declares that all measures by the illegal occupation régime to enforce military conscription in Namibia are null and void. In this connection, the Assembly urges all Governments, the specialized agencies and other intergovernmental organizations to provide increased material assistance to the thousands of refugees who have been forced by the *apartheid* régime's oppressive policies in Namibia and South Africa to flee into the neighbouring front-line States.

"11. The General Assembly recalls its resolution ES-8/2 of 14 September 1981, by which it strongly urged States to cease forthwith, individually and collectively, all dealings with South Africa in order totally to isolate it politically, economically, militarily and culturally.

"12. The General Assembly strongly deprecates the establishment and maintenance by colonial Powers and their allies of military bases and other installations in the colonial Territories under their administration which impede the implementation of the Declaration on the Granting of Independence to Colonial Countries and Peoples and which are incompatible with the purposes and principles of the Charter of the United Nations and of Assembly resolution 1514(XV).

"13. The General Assembly reiterates its condemnation of all military activities and arrangements by colonial Powers in Territories under their administration which are detrimental to the interests and rights of the colonial peoples concerned, especially their right to self-determination and independence. The Assembly once again calls upon the colonial Powers concerned to terminate such activities and eliminate such military bases in compliance with its relevant resolutions and in particular with paragraph 9 of the Plan of Action for the Full Implementation of the Declaration on the Granting of Independence to Colonial Countries and Peoples, contained in the annex to its resolution 35/118 of 11 December 1980.

"14. The General Assembly deprecates the continued alienation of land in colonial Territories for military installations. While it has been argued that the servicing of such installations creates employment, nevertheless, the large-scale utilization of local economic and manpower resources for this purpose diverts resources which could be more beneficially utilized in promoting the economic development of the Territories concerned and is thus contrary to the interests of their populations.

"15. The General Assembly requests the Secretary-General to continue, through the Department of Public Information of the Secretariat, an intensified campaign of publicity with a view to informing world public opinion of the facts concerning the military activities and arrangements in colonial Territories which are impeding the implementation of the Declaration on the Granting of Independence to Colonial Countries and Peoples, contained in Assembly resolution 1514(XV).

"16. The General Assembly requests the Special Committee to continue its consideration of the item and to report thereon to the Assembly at its fortieth session."

General Assembly decision 39/412

5 December 1984   Meeting 87   118-10-15 (recorded vote)

Approved by Fourth Committee (A/39/663) by recorded vote (115-11-15), 26 October (meeting 11); draft by Committee on colonial countries (A/39/23), amended by United States (A/C.4/39/L.2); agenda item 104.

Meeting numbers. GA 39th session: 4th Committee 2-11; plenary 87.

Recorded vote in Assembly as follows:

In favour: Afghanistan, Albania, Algeria, Angola, Argentina, Bahrain, Bangladesh, Barbados, Belize, Benin, Bhutan, Bolivia, Botswana, Brazil, Brunei Darussalam, Bulgaria, Burkina Faso, Burma, Burundi, Byelorussian SSR, Cameroon, Cape Verde, Central African Republic, Chad, China, Colombia, Congo, Costa Rica, Cuba, Cyprus, Czechoslovakia, Democratic Kampuchea, Democratic Yemen, Djibouti, Dominican Republic, Ecuador, Egypt, El Salvador, Equatorial Guinea, Ethiopia, Fiji, Gabon, Gambia, German Democratic Republic, Ghana, Guinea, Guinea-Bissau, Guyana, Haiti, Honduras, Hungary, India, Indonesia, Iran, Iraq, Ivory Coast, Jamaica, Jordan, Kenya, Kuwait, Lao People's Democratic Republic, Lebanon, Lesotho, Liberia, Libyan Arab Jamahiriya, Madagascar, Malaysia, Maldives, Mali, Malta, Mauritania, Mauritius, Mexico, Mongolia, Nepal, Nicaragua, Niger, Nigeria, Oman, Pakistan, Panama, Papua New Guinea, Peru, Philippines, Poland, Qatar, Romania, Rwanda, Samoa, Sao Tome and Principe, Saudi Arabia, Senegal, Seychelles, Sierra Leone, Singapore, Somalia, Sri Lanka, Sudan, Suriname, Syrian Arab Republic, Thailand, Togo, Trinidad and Tobago, Tunisia, Turkey, Uganda, Ukrainian SSR, USSR, United Arab Emirates, United Republic of Tanzania, Uruguay, Venezuela, Viet Nam, Yemen, Yugoslavia, Zaire, Zambia, Zimbabwe.

Against: Belgium, Canada, France, Germany, Federal Republic of, Italy, Japan, Luxembourg, Netherlands, United Kingdom, United States.

Abstaining: Australia, Austria, Denmark, Finland, Greece, Iceland, Ireland, Israel, Malawi, Mozambique,[a] New Zealand, Norway, Portugal, Spain, Sweden.

[a]Later advised the Secretariat that it had intended to vote in favour.

Before action was taken on the draft decision as a whole in the Fourth Committee, the United States submitted amendments to delete from the first sentence of paragraph 8 and from the penultimate sentence of paragraph 9, after "and other States", the phrase "in particular the United States of America and Israel". Both amendments were approved by recorded vote: the first by 62 to 47, with 24 abstentions, and the second by 62 to 47, with 25 abstentions.

Speaking in explanation of vote, a number of States expressed concern over voting on a draft dealing with a subject that was not among the items assigned to the Fourth Committee. These States included Canada, France, the Federal Republic of Germany, and Ireland on behalf of the EC members. Australia and New Zealand also shared this view, with Australia saying that there were no military facilities nor plans for any in the Cocos (Keeling) Islands and New Zealand making the same point with regard to Tokelau.

Several States stressed their objections to selective references to specific States, among them Australia, Barbados, Ireland for the EC members, Israel, Jamaica, Oman, Papua New Guinea, Senegal and Zaire. The United States said that acceptance of its amendments marked a turning away from name-calling. Ireland, for the EC members, added that the draft contained misleading language. Israel agreed and pointed out that most if not all of the States represented in the Committee had dealings with South Africa. Malawi agreed and added that singling out two of them would create a credibility gap that would not expedite a satisfactory solution; it opposed military activities designed to intimidate, but was convinced that mere condemnation was not enough. Greece felt the decision was not worded in a balanced way, although it maintained its position on the negative impact that military activities could have on speedy independence.

Although against selective references, Zaire favoured naming those responsible for prolonging the illegal occupation of Namibia and the policy of *apartheid* and for making South Africa the dominant military power in Africa. Chad was also in favour of condemning the countries which maintained relations with South Africa. Oman said it abstained on the United States amendments because of its friendly relations with that country, but that did not change its position on Israel. The Sudan said there was close military collaboration between Israel and South Africa.

The Dominican Republic felt the references to specific countries were not sufficiently balanced. Turkey supported the principles in the draft, even though it believed paragraphs 2, 4, 12, 13 and 14 could have been more balanced, and despite its reservations about the references to a particular

group of States. Uruguay doubted the relevance of the text to the item on the agenda.

Botswana said that, although it supported an arms embargo against South Africa and condemned nuclear collaboration and any military exchanges, it could not support or implement economic sanctions or an oil embargo against South Africa because the destabilization of the front-line States and the obstruction of Namibian independence by South Africa had left Botswana no trade routes which did not involve South Africa.

Viet Nam thought "could" should have been deleted from paragraph 2 since a number of reports of the Committee and the debate demonstrated that military activities constituted an obstacle to decolonization and a threat to international peace and security, and it felt "to continue" in the same paragraph was misleading and that the Assembly should urge the administering Powers concerned to take all necessary measures not to involve those Territories in any offensive acts.

In further action on 5 December, the Assembly, in resolutions 39/32 on Guam and 39/33 on Bermuda (see Chapter IV of this section), reaffirmed that the administering Powers must ensure that military bases and installations did not hinder the population of the Territories from exercising their right to self-determination and independence. On 14 December, in resolution 39/91 (see above), the Assembly called on the colonial Powers to withdraw their military bases and installations from colonial Territories, to refrain from establishing new ones and not to involve those Territories in any offensive acts or interference against other States.

Information dissemination

The Committee on colonial countries considered dissemination of information on decolonization at four meetings between 26 April and 20 August, approving the recommendations put forward by its Sub-Committee on Petitions, Information and Assistance,[2] including recommendations concerning Namibia (see Chapter III of this section).

The Sub-Committee gave details of consultations with OAU and representatives of the national liberation movements concerning implementation of a 1980 Assembly resolution[21] to which was annexed a plan of action for implementing the 1960 Declaration. Progress made in carrying the plan into effect was also considered, with the Sub-Committee reiterating a recommendation that the Secretariat be requested to prepare a survey of activities taken for submission to the Sub-Committee in 1985. The Sub-Committee recommended intensified efforts by the United Nations Department of Political Affairs, Trusteeship and Decolonization and the Department of Public Information (DPI) to increase and widen dissemination of information on decolonization. Other recommendations included: denouncing attempts by the United States and certain Western countries, as well as South Africa and Israel, and their mass media to misrepresent national liberation movements as terrorists; preparation of studies on atrocities committed by the *apartheid* régime in occupied Namibia and subversion by South Africa against its neighbours, on Puerto Rico, on the importance of decolonization in promoting world peace, and on military bases in colonial countries; strengthening co-operation with the pool of non-aligned press agencies; providing press releases in both English and French; producing new visual material on the most vital problems of decolonization; providing feedback reports from United Nations information centres; and obtaining wider coverage by the mass media, particularly in Western Europe and the Americas, which received limited coverage. Both Departments were called on to increase their speaking engagements at North American universities on the subject of decolonization, with particular emphasis on Namibia.

The General Assembly, in decision 39/412 (see above), requested the Secretary-General to continue, through DPI, an intensified campaign to inform world public opinion of the facts concerning military activities in colonial Territories which were impeding the implementation of the 1960 Declaration.

GENERAL ASSEMBLY ACTION

On 14 December, the General Assembly adopted resolution 39/92 by recorded vote.

Dissemination of information on decolonization

The General Assembly,

Having examined the chapter of the report of the Special Committee on the Situation with regard to the Implementation of the Declaration on the Granting of Independence to Colonial Countries and Peoples relating to the dissemination of information on decolonization and publicity for the work of the United Nations in the field of decolonization,

Recalling its resolution 1514(XV) of 14 December 1960, containing the Declaration on the Granting of Independence to Colonial Countries and Peoples, and all other resolutions and decisions of the United Nations concerning the dissemination of information on decolonization, in particular General Assembly resolution 38/55 of 7 December 1983,

Reiterating the importance of publicity as an instrument for furthering the aims and purposes of the Declaration and mindful of the continuing pressing need to take all possible steps to acquaint world public opinion with all aspects of the problems of decolonization with a view to assisting effectively the peoples of the colonial Territories to achieve self-determination, freedom and independence,

Aware of the increasingly important role being played in the widespread dissemination of relevant information by a number of non-governmental organizations having a special interest in decolonization, and noting with satisfaction the intensified efforts of the Special Committee in enlisting the support of those organizations in that regard,

1. *Approves* the chapter of the report of the Special Committee on the Situation with regard to the Implementation of the Declaration on the Granting of Independence to Colonial Countries and Peoples relating to the dissemination of information on decolonization and publicity for the work of the United Nations in the field of decolonization;

2. *Reaffirms* the importance of effecting the widest possible dissemination of information on the evils and dangers of colonialism, on the determined efforts of the colonial peoples to achieve self-determination, freedom and independence and on the assistance being provided by the international community towards the elimination of the remaining vestiges of colonialism in all its forms;

3. *Requests* the Secretary-General, having regard to the suggestions of the Special Committee, to continue to take concrete measures through all the media at his disposal, including publications, radio and television, to give widespread and continuous publicity to the work of the United Nations in the field of decolonization, and, *inter alia:*

(*a*) To continue, in consultation with the Special Committee, to collect, prepare and disseminate basic material, studies and articles relating to the problems of decolonization and, in particular, to continue to publish the periodical *Objective: Justice* and other publications, special articles and studies, including the *Decolonization* series, and to select from them appropriate material for wider dissemination by means of reprints in various languages;

(*b*) To seek the full co-operation of the administering Powers concerned in the discharge of the tasks referred to above;

(*c*) To intensify the activities of all United Nations information centres, particularly those located in Western Europe and the Americas;

(*d*) To maintain a close working relationship with the Organization of African Unity by holding periodic consultations and by systematically exchanging relevant information with that organization;

(*e*) To enlist, with the close co-operation of United Nations information centres, the support of non-governmental organizations having a special interest in decolonization in the dissemination of the relevant information;

(*f*) To ensure the availability of the necessary facilities and services in this regard;

(*g*) To report to the Special Committee on the measures taken in implementation of the present resolution;

4. *Requests* all States, in particular the administering Powers, the specialized agencies and other organizations of the United Nations system and non-governmental organizations having a special interest in decolonization to undertake or intensify, in co-operation with the Secretary-General and within their respective spheres of competence, the large-scale dissemination of the information referred to in paragraph 2 above;

5. *Requests* the Special Committee to follow the implementation of the present resolution and report thereon to the General Assembly at its fortieth session.

General Assembly resolution 39/92

14 December 1984   Meeting 100   139-2-6 (recorded vote)

27-nation draft (A/39/L.18 & Add.1); agenda item 18.

Sponsors: Afghanistan, Algeria, Congo, Cuba, Cyprus, Czechoslovakia, Ethiopia, German Democratic Republic, Guyana, Hungary, India, Lao People's Democratic Republic, Libyan Arab Jamahiriya, Madagascar, Mali, Mongolia, Papua New Guinea, Romania, Sierra Leone, Syrian Arab Republic, Trinidad and Tobago, Tunisia, United Republic of Tanzania, Venezuela, Viet Nam, Yugoslavia, Zambia.

Financial implications. ACABQ, A/39/7/Add.14; 5th Committee, A/39/825; S-G, A/C.5/39/80 & Add.1.

Meeting numbers. GA 39th session: 5th Committee 49; plenary 85-87, 100.

Recorded vote in Assembly as follows:

In favour: Afghanistan, Albania, Algeria, Angola, Argentina, Australia, Austria, Bahamas, Bahrain, Bangladesh, Barbados, Belize, Benin, Bhutan, Bolivia, Botswana, Brazil, Brunei Darussalam, Bulgaria, Burkina Faso, Burma, Burundi, Byelorussian SSR, Cameroon, Canada, Cape Verde, Chad, Chile, China, Colombia, Congo, Costa Rica, Cuba, Cyprus, Czechoslovakia, Democratic Kampuchea, Democratic Yemen, Denmark, Djibouti, Dominican Republic, Ecuador, Egypt, El Salvador, Equatorial Guinea, Ethiopia, Fiji, Finland, Gabon, Gambia, German Democratic Republic, Ghana, Greece, Guatemala, Guinea, Guinea-Bissau, Guyana, Haiti, Honduras, Hungary, Iceland, India, Indonesia, Iran, Iraq, Ireland, Ivory Coast, Jamaica, Japan, Jordan, Kenya, Kuwait, Lao People's Democratic Republic, Lebanon, Lesotho, Liberia, Libyan Arab Jamahiriya, Madagascar, Malawi, Malaysia, Maldives, Mali, Malta, Mauritania, Mauritius, Mexico, Mongolia, Morocco, Mozambique, Nepal, New Zealand, Nicaragua, Niger, Nigeria, Norway, Oman, Pakistan, Panama, Papua New Guinea, Paraguay, Peru, Philippines, Poland, Portugal, Qatar, Romania, Rwanda, Samoa, Sao Tome and Principe, Saudi Arabia, Senegal, Seychelles, Sierra Leone, Singapore, Somalia, Spain, Sri Lanka, Sudan, Suriname, Sweden, Syrian Arab Republic, Thailand, Togo, Trinidad and Tobago, Tunisia, Turkey, Uganda, Ukrainian SSR, USSR, United Arab Emirates, United Republic of Tanzania, Uruguay, Vanuatu, Venezuela, Viet Nam, Yemen, Yugoslavia, Zaire, Zambia, Zimbabwe.

Against: United Kingdom, United States.

Abstaining: Belgium, France, Germany, Federal Republic of, Italy, Luxembourg, Netherlands.

Speaking in explanation of vote, the United Kingdom supported publicity to promote awareness of the right to self-determination, but questioned the necessity of a separate resolution on the topic when the United Nations had adequate machinery to deal with information, much of the proposed work was contentious and unnecessary, and information should be decreased as colonialism diminished.

A number of States expressed reservations on elements contained in the report of the Committee on colonial countries. Italy said the draft resolution implied approval of that report which contained unjustified criticism of countries and groups of countries and references to questions not included in the Committee's mandate. The Netherlands, speaking in similar vein, regretted that some of the recommendations sought to make the interests of the peoples of the dependent Territories subservient to a defamation campaign against one group of countries.

Japan also had reservations on the draft's endorsement of the Committee's report, as did Sweden, speaking for the Nordic States, which said their votes should not be seen as approving references to the study on Puerto Rico which was not on the list of NSGTs approved by the Assembly. Australia shared that view. Canada said that the Committee should not involve itself in domestic matters or matters concerning strategic Trust Territories, citing Palau as an example of

the latter; it also rejected the notion of restricting freedom of the press for foreign correspondents in South Africa, did not accept that there was a campaign to depict national liberation movements as terrorists and said there was no link between Western Governments and the mass media. Ireland also had reservations on some Committee recommendations.

Week of Solidarity with peoples of Namibia and all other colonial Territories

The Week of Solidarity with the Peoples of Namibia and All Other Colonial Territories, as well as those in South Africa, Fighting for Freedom, Independence and Human Rights was observed by a series of United Nations activities from 25 to 31 May 1984.

The activities proposed by the Committee on colonial countries[2] were undertaken by DPI at Headquarters and United Nations information centres. These events included an exhibition of photographs and publications, screening of films, distribution of audio-visual materials, briefing of NGOs, press releases, and a *UN Chronicle* report on the activities.

As proposed by the Committee, on 25 May at Bangkok, Thailand, the Committee, the Special Committee against *Apartheid* and the United Nations Council for Namibia held a joint special meeting in observance of Africa Liberation Day and the Week of Solidarity. The Chairman of the Committee on colonial countries appealed to all States and organizations of the United Nations system to mobilize maximum support for the peoples of southern Africa struggling for freedom.

Role of NGOs

The Sub-Committee on Petitions, Information and Assistance of the Committee on colonial countries noted in 1984 that a considerable number of NGOs played an important role by disseminating information on decolonization, monitoring the activities of foreign interests, and providing assistance to the colonial people and their national liberation movements.[2]

Adopting the recommendations of the Sub-Committee, the Committee on colonial countries urged NGOs to distribute accurate information and disseminate basic documentation such as the Constitution of SWAPO and the Freedom Charter of ANC to counteract campaigns depicting national liberation movements as terrorist organizations; urged DPI and the United Nations information centres to provide clear information to NGOs and the public at large; and expressed support for events arranged by NGOs such as the conference organized by the Non-Governmental

Organizations Sub-Committee on Racism, Racial Discrimination, *Apartheid* and Decolonization to mark the one hundredth year of the colonization of Namibia (Geneva, 2-5 July 1984) and the conference for peace in southern Africa initiated by the International Committee against *Apartheid*, Racism and Colonialism in Southern Africa and organized by the Anti-*Apartheid* Movement of the Federal Republic of Germany (Bonn, 12-14 October). It decided to strengthen its links with NGOs and co-operate with them to consider methods to bring about the embodiment of the principles of decolonization in all levels of educational systems, particularly those of the colonial Powers and Territories, and to request the Secretariat to establish regional lists of NGOs active in decolonization.

Puerto Rico

During 1984, the Committee on colonial countries reviewed the list of Territories to which the 1960 Declaration[1] applied and considered a separate item based on its August 1982 decision[22] concerning Puerto Rico.

At meetings held on 22 and 23 August, the Committee heard the representatives of 32 organizations, mainly from Puerto Rico. By a resolution of 24 August,[23] adopted by 11 votes to 2, with 9 abstentions, the Committee reaffirmed the inalienable right of peoples to self-determination and the applicability of the principles of the 1960 Declaration to Puerto Rico, expressed hope that its people might exercise without hindrance that right and requested the Rapporteur to report to the Committee on the implementation of its resolutions on Puerto Rico. That same day, the resolution was transmitted to the United States.

On 30 April, Cuba addressed a letter[24] to the Chairman of the Committee asking him to hold consultations with the United States as the administering Power of Puerto Rico so that an observer mission could visit the Territory to observe military manoeuvres on the island of Vieques, which it said might constitute an obstacle to the implementation of the Declaration.

REFERENCES

[1]YUN 1960, p. 49, GA res. 1514(XV), 14 Dec. 1960. [2]A/39/23. [3]A/39/723. [4]A/AC.109/L.1499 & Add.1. [5]YUN 1976, p. 908, GA res. 31/140, 17 Dec. 1976. [6]A/39/49. [7]YUN 1983, p. 1017, GA res. 38/51, 7 Dec. 1983. [8]A/39/293 & Add.1-3. [9]YUN 1983, p. 160. [10]*Ibid.*, p. 1017, ESC res. 1983/42, 25 July 1983. [11]E/1984/123. [12]A/AC.115/L.611. [13]YUN 1978, p. 915, SC res. 435(1978), 29 Sep. 1978. [14]YUN 1983, p. 1017, GA res. 38/51, 7 Dec. 1983. [15]A/39/23 (A/AC.109/797). [16]A/C.4/39/10. [17]A/39/23 (A/AC.109/795). [18]A/C.4/39/7 & Add.1. [19]YUN 1983, p. 1025, GA dec. 38/419, 7 Dec. 1983. [20]A/39/23 (A/AC.109/796). [21]YUN 1980, p. 1057, GA res. 35/118, 11 Dec. 1980. [22]YUN 1982, p. 1275. [23]A/39/23 (A/AC.109/798). [24]A/AC.109/771.

Other general questions concerning NSGTs

Fellowships and scholarships

In a report to the General Assembly covering 1 October 1983 to 30 September 1984,[1] the Secretary-General stated that the following 35 States had offered to make scholarships and fellowships available to persons from NSGTs for secondary, vocational and post-graduate studies: Austria, Brazil, Bulgaria, Byelorussian SSR, Cyprus, Czechoslovakia, Egypt, German Democratic Republic, Federal Republic of Germany, Ghana, Greece, Hungary, India, Iran, Israel, Italy, Libyan Arab Jamahiriya, Malawi, Malta, Mexico, New Zealand, Pakistan, Philippines, Poland, Romania, Sri Lanka, Syrian Arab Republic, Tunisia, Turkey, Uganda, Ukrainian SSR, USSR, United Arab Emirates, United States, Yugoslavia. Information about these offers was included in the twenty-fourth edition of the handbook *Study Abroad* (1983/84, 1984/85, 1985/86), published by UNESCO.

During the period, 91 students requested information and application forms from the Secretariat; those from Namibian students were forwarded to the Office of the United Nations Commissioner for Namibia and those from students in other NSGTs were transmitted to the offering States for consideration and to the administering Powers for information. A number of offering States also received requests directly, and applicants wishing to study in Ghana, Poland, the USSR and the United States applied directly to those Governments.

Several offering States informed the Secretary-General of new developments in their facilities: Austria had a new training project for students from Namibia; Czechoslovakia offered 20 scholarships to students from NSGTs, but none had been used during the 1983/84 and 1984/85 academic years; Greece no longer provided undergraduate scholarships; Italy would provide 10 scholarships for professional training to students from southern Africa with the selection and course priorities to be decided in consultation with the United Nations Secretariat; New Zealand provided budgetary support for 121 Tokelauans to study in New Zealand; Poland granted five scholarships for Trust Territory candidates for the 1984/85 year; and 135 students from NSGTs studied in higher and specialized secondary educational institutions in the USSR, the Ukrainian SSR and the Byelorussian SSR during 1984.

GENERAL ASSEMBLY ACTION

Following the recommendation of the Fourth Committee, the General Assembly adopted without vote resolution 39/45 on 5 December.

Offers by Member States of study and training facilities for inhabitants of Non-Self-Governing Territories

The General Assembly,

Recalling its resolution 38/53 of 7 December 1983,

Having examined the report of the Secretary-General on offers by Member States of study and training facilities for inhabitants of Non-Self-Governing Territories, prepared pursuant to General Assembly resolution 845(IX) of 22 November 1954,

Considering that more scholarships should be made available to the inhabitants of Non-Self-Governing Territories in all parts of the world and that steps should be taken to encourage applications from students in those Territories,

1. *Takes note* of the report of the Secretary-General;

2. *Expresses its appreciation* to those Member States that have made scholarships available to the inhabitants of Non-Self-Governing Territories;

3. *Invites* all States to make or continue to make generous offers of study and training facilities to the inhabitants of those Territories that have not yet attained self-government or independence and, wherever possible, to provide travel funds to prospective students;

4. *Urges* the administering Powers to take effective measures to ensure the widespread and continuous dissemination in the Territories under their administration of information relating to offers of study and training facilities made by States and to provide all the necessary facilities to enable students to avail themselves of such offers;

5. *Requests* the Secretary-General to report to the General Assembly at its fortieth session on the implementation of the present resolution;

6. *Draws the attention* of the Special Committee on the Situation with regard to the Implementation of the Declaration on the Granting of Independence to Colonial Countries and Peoples to the present resolution.

General Assembly resolution 39/45

5 December 1984   Meeting 87   Adopted without vote

Approved by Fourth Committee (A/39/678) without objection, 12 November (meeting 18); 36-nation draft (A/C.4/39/L.6); agenda item 107.

Sponsors: Angola, Australia, Bangladesh, Barbados, Bulgaria, Colombia, Cuba, Cyprus, Czechoslovakia, Egypt, Fiji, Guyana, India, Israel, Jamaica, Japan, Kenya, Madagascar, New Zealand, Nigeria, Pakistan, Papua New Guinea, Philippines, Samoa, Sierra Leone, Singapore, Syrian Arab Republic, Togo, Trinidad and Tobago, Turkey, United Republic of Tanzania, United States, Vanuatu, Venezuela, Yugoslavia, Zambia.

Meeting numbers. GA 39th session: 4th Committee 12-18; plenary 87.

Information to the United Nations

States responsible for the administration of Territories which had not attained full self-government continued to transmit regularly to the Secretary-General information on their economic, social and educational conditions under the terms of Article 73 *e* in Chapter XI of the Charter of the United Nations and in accordance with several General Assembly resolutions. In the most recent such resolution of December 1983,[2] the Assembly requested the fullest possible information on political and constitutional

developments. In a September 1984 report to the Assembly,[3] the Secretary-General stated that he had received information with respect to the following NSGTs:

Australia: Cocos (Keeling) Islands

New Zealand: Tokelau

United Kingdom: Anguilla, Bermuda, British Virgin Islands, Cayman Islands, Falkland Islands (Malvinas), Gibraltar, Montserrat, Pitcairn, St. Helena, Turks and Caicos Islands

United States: American Samoa, Guam, United States Virgin Islands

On 12 March,[4] Portugal informed the Secretary-General that it had nothing to add to the information provided in a 1979 note which stated that conditions in East Timor had prevented it from assuming its responsibilities for the Territory's administration.[5]

With respect to Western Sahara, the Secretary-General noted in his report[3] that Spain had informed him in 1976 that, with the termination of its presence in the Territory, it considered itself exempt from any international responsibility in connection with the Territory's administration.[6]

GENERAL ASSEMBLY ACTION

On 5 December, the General Assembly adopted by recorded vote resolution 39/41 on the recommendation of the Fourth Committee.

Information from Non-Self-Governing Territories transmitted under Article 73 *e* of the Charter of the United Nations

The General Assembly,

Having examined the chapter of the report of the Special Committee on the Situation with regard to the Implementation of the Declaration on the Granting of Independence to Colonial Countries and Peoples relating to the information from Non-Self-Governing Territories transmitted under Article 73 *e* of the Charter of the United Nations and the action taken by the Committee in respect of that information,

Having also examined the report of the Secretary-General on the question,

Recalling its resolution 1970(XVIII) of 16 December 1963, in which it requested the Special Committee to study the information transmitted to the Secretary-General in accordance with Article 73 *e* of the Charter and to take such information fully into account in examining the situation with regard to the implementation of the Declaration on the Granting of Independence to Colonial Countries and Peoples, contained in General Assembly resolution 1514(XV) of 14 December 1960,

Recalling also its resolution 38/49 of 7 December 1983, in which it requested the Special Committee to continue to discharge the functions entrusted to it under resolution 1970(XVIII),

1. *Approves* the chapter of the report of the Special Committee on the Situation with regard to the Im-

plementation of the Declaration on the Granting of Independence to Colonial Countries and Peoples relating to the information from Non-Self-Governing Territories transmitted under Article 73 *e* of the Charter of the United Nations;

2. *Reaffirms* that, in the absence of a decision by the General Assembly itself that a Non-Self-Governing Territory has attained a full measure of self-government under the terms of Chapter XI of the Charter, the administering Power concerned should continue to transmit information under Article 73 *e* of the Charter with respect to that Territory;

3. *Requests* the administering Powers concerned to transmit, or continue to transmit, to the Secretary-General the information prescribed in Article 73 *e* of the Charter, as well as the fullest possible information on political and constitutional developments in the Territories concerned, within a maximum period of six months following the expiration of the administrative year in those Territories;

4. *Requests* the Special Committee to continue to discharge the functions entrusted to it under General Assembly resolution 1970(XVIII), in accordance with established procedures, and to report thereon to the Assembly at its fortieth session.

General Assembly resolution 39/41

5 December 1984   Meeting 87   142-0-3 (recorded vote)

Approved by Fourth Committee (A/39/676) by recorded vote (130-0-3), 12 November (meeting 18); draft by Committee on colonial countries (A/39/23); agenda item 103.

Meeting numbers. GA 39th session: 4th Committee 12-18; plenary 87.

Recorded vote in Assembly as follows:

In favour: Afghanistan, Albania, Algeria, Angola, Argentina, Australia, Austria, Bahrain, Bangladesh, Barbados, Belgium, Belize, Benin, Bhutan, Bolivia, Botswana, Brazil, Brunei Darussalam, Bulgaria, Burkina Faso, Burma, Burundi, Byelorussian SSR, Cameroon, Canada, Cape Verde, Central African Republic, Chad, Chile, China, Colombia, Congo, Costa Rica, Cuba, Cyprus, Czechoslovakia, Democratic Kampuchea, Democratic Yemen, Denmark, Djibouti, Dominican Republic, Ecuador, Egypt, El Salvador, Equatorial Guinea, Ethiopia, Fiji, Finland, Gabon, German Democratic Republic, Germany, Federal Republic of, Ghana, Greece, Guinea, Guinea-Bissau, Guyana, Haiti, Honduras, Hungary, Iceland, India, Indonesia, Iran, Iraq, Ireland, Israel, Italy, Ivory Coast, Jamaica, Japan, Jordan, Kenya, Kuwait, Lao People's Democratic Republic, Lebanon, Lesotho, Liberia, Libyan Arab Jamahiriya, Luxembourg, Madagascar, Malawi, Malaysia, Maldives, Mali, Malta, Mauritania, Mauritius, Mexico, Mongolia, Morocco, Mozambique, Nepal, Netherlands, New Zealand, Nicaragua, Niger, Nigeria, Norway, Oman, Pakistan, Panama, Papua New Guinea, Paraguay, Peru, Philippines, Poland, Portugal, Qatar, Romania, Rwanda, Samoa, Sao Tome and Principe, Saudi Arabia, Senegal, Seychelles, Sierra Leone, Singapore, Somalia, Spain, Sri Lanka, Sudan, Suriname, Sweden, Syrian Arab Republic, Thailand, Togo, Trinidad and Tobago, Tunisia, Turkey, Uganda, Ukrainian SSR, USSR, United Arab Emirates, United Republic of Tanzania, Uruguay, Venezuela, Viet Nam, Yemen, Yugoslavia, Zaire, Zambia, Zimbabwe.

Against: None.

Abstaining: France, United Kingdom, United States.

In explanation of vote, the United Kingdom said the draft resolution implied that it was for the Assembly to decide when an NSGT had attained a full measure of self-government, whereas it thought such decisions were best left to to the administering Power and the local Government.

Visiting missions

In August, the Committee on colonial countries adopted a resolution on the question of sending visiting missions to Territories,[7] stressing the need to continue to dispatch periodic missions to facilitate the full implementation of the 1960 Declaration,[8] calling on the administering Powers concerned to continue to co-operate with the United Nations by permitting visiting missions access to Territories under their administration and requesting its Chairman to continue consultations with those Powers regarding such missions.

In resolution 39/91 of 14 December (see above), the General Assembly called on the administering Powers to continue to co-operate with the Committee in the discharge of its mandate and, in particular, to permit the access of visiting missions to the Territories to secure first-hand information and ascertain the wishes of their inhabitants.

The question of sending visiting missions to other Territories was also dealt with by the Assembly in individual resolutions on these Territories (see Chapter IV of this section).

REFERENCES

[1]A/39/541 & Corr.1 & Add.1,2. [2]YUN 1983, p. 1031, GA res. 38/49, 7 Dec. 1983. [3]A/39/519. [4]A/39/136. [5]YUN 1979, p. 1117. [6]YUN 1976, p. 738. [7]A/39/23 (A/AC.109/789 & Corr.1). [8]YUN 1960, p. 49, GA res. 1514(XV), 14 Dec. 1960.

Chapter II

International Trusteeship System

On behalf of the Security Council, the Trusteeship Council continued during 1984 to supervise the one Trust Territory remaining under the International Trusteeship System—the Trust Territory of the Pacific Islands, a strategic territory administered by the United States.

The Trusteeship Council considered the Administering Authority's annual report, heard 12 petitioners and examined 15 written petitions and 12 communications regarding the Territory.

The Council held its fifty-first session at United Nations Headquarters from 14 May to 18 July; of its five members (China, France, USSR, United Kingdom, United States), China did not participate.

Trust Territory of the Pacific Islands

Conditions in the Territory

The Trust Territory of the Pacific Islands, designated as a strategic area and administered by the United States under an Agreement approved by the Security Council in 1947,[1] comprised three archipelagos of more than 2,100 islands and atolls scattered over an area of some 7.8 million square kilometres of the western Pacific Ocean, north of the Equator. The Territory, known collectively as Micronesia, had a population of some 133,000.[2]

There were four administrative entities within the Territory—the Federated States of Micronesia, the Marshall Islands, the Northern Mariana Islands and Palau. As a result of referendums, each had its own constitution and popularly elected legislature and executive head.

Trusteeship Council action. The Trusteeship Council at its 1984 session adopted its report[3] to the Security Council after considering the annual report for the year ending 30 September 1983, submitted by the United States as Administering Authority for the Trust Territory. The Trusteeship Council's report, covering the period 29 November 1983–18 July 1984, contained conclusions and recommendations on such questions as war-related damage claims; political, economic, social and educational advancement; and the plebiscites and constitutional development and progress towards self-government and independence.

The conclusions and recommendations, based on the Council's discussions, were annexed to a report on conditions in the Trust Territory,[4] prepared by a Drafting Committee (France and the United Kingdom); on 14 June, the Council adopted them before adopting its own report[3] by 3 votes to 1.

In explanation of its negative vote, the USSR felt that the conclusions and recommendations were inconsistent with the interests of the people of the Territory and reflected solely the views of the three Western members, all of which were colonial Powers; they omitted the paramount conclusion—the Micronesians remained politically fragmented and had not been prepared for genuine independence but for annexation to the United States, which was transforming the Territory into a military-strategic base. The USSR had expressed similar views in a 27 March note verbale to the Secretary-General.[5]

The United Kingdom pointed out that the conclusions and recommendations were critical of the United States and therefore the idea that they reflected the view of the Western Powers was not true. It would be unreasonable to call on the Administering Authority to preserve the unity of the Territory when the people themselves did not wish to remain a single entity.

Action by the Committee on colonial countries. The General Assembly's Special Committee on the Situation with regard to the Implementation of the Declaration on the Granting of Independence to Colonial Countries and Peoples (Committee on colonial countries) considered the Trust Territory at meetings held between 7 and 24 August[6] and adopted conclusions and recommendations on the Territory made by its Sub-Committee on Small Territories. The Committee recommended to the Assembly a draft resolution to have it, *inter alia*, call on the United States to ensure its representation at Committee meetings and affirm its strong conviction that the presence of military bases and installations in the Territory could constitute a major obstacle to implementing the 1960 Declaration on the Granting of Independence to Colonial Countries and Peoples.[7] The Assembly would have recognized that it was ultimately for the people of the Territory to decide their political destiny and called on the Administering Authority not to impede the Territory's unity or the rights of the people in accordance with the Declaration. (See also below.)

General Assembly consideration. Consideration of the topic was referred to the Fourth Committee. On 12 November, its Chairman suggested, based on consultations with his counterpart of the Committee on colonial countries and concerned delegations, that no action be taken on the draft resolution. That suggestion was adopted without objection.[8]

Self-determination and independence

Trusteeship Council action. The Trusteeship Council[3] reaffirmed the inalienable rights of the people of Micronesia to self-determination, including the right to independence, in accordance with the Charter of the United Nations and the Trusteeship Agreement. It reiterated that free association was an option that was not incompatible with that Agreement, provided that the populations concerned had freely accepted it. The Council hoped that in the near future the Administering Authority would take up the matter of termination of the Agreement both with the Trusteeship Council and the Security Council, in accordance with Article 83 of the Charter.

The Trusteeship Council took note of the reports of the 1983 visiting missions which had observed the plebiscites in the Federated States of Micronesia and the Marshall Islands[9] (see below). It endorsed the missions' conclusions that, despite some administrative shortcomings, both plebiscites were run by the constitutional Governments so as to ensure the free and fair expression of the wishes of the people.

Action by the Committee on colonial countries. The Committee on colonial countries[6] reaffirmed the inalienable right of the people of the Trust Territory to self-determination and independence in accordance with the Charter and the 1960 Declaration. It reaffirmed the importance of ensuring that the people freely exercised that right and that the obligations of the Administering Authority were duly discharged.

The Committee reiterated that such factors as territorial size, geographical location, size of population and limited natural resources should in no way delay the speedy implementation of the Declaration. It regretted the repeated refusal of the Authority to co-operate with the Committee by declining to participate in its meetings. It reiterated that it was an obligation of the Authority to create such conditions in the Territory as would enable its people to exercise freely, with full knowledge of the possible options and without interference, their right to self-determination. The Committee regretted that there was no co-operation between it and the Trusteeship Council in relation to the Territory and reiterated its readiness to engage in such co-operation.

Recalling previous appeals to the Authority that the people of Micronesia be given the fullest opportunity to educate themselves about the options open to them in exercise of their right to self-determination, the Committee felt that such programmes should be extended and reinforced. It recognized that it was ultimately for the people to decide their political destiny and called on the Authority not to impede the unity of the Territory or the people's rights until those rights were implemented. It urged the Authority to ensure that the early termination of the Trusteeship Agreement was done in strict conformity with the Charter.

The Committee reaffirmed that military installations in the Territory should not hinder the population from exercising its rights. It also regretted that the High Commissioner maintained the power to suspend certain legislation.

Politics and government

Trusteeship Council action. The Trusteeship Council[3] considered the political advancement of the Territory in conjunction with its self-determination and independence (see above). The Council also noted with satisfaction that the Territory had continued to expand its international relations. It urged that priority continue to be given to promoting closer contact with countries of the region, not only in the economic field, but also at the political, educational and cultural level.

Action by the Committee on colonial countries. Noting that reports on the Territory were a matter of which the Security Council was currently seized, the Committee invited the attention of the relevant organs of the United Nations to Article 83 of the Charter, under which the Security Council was to exercise all United Nations functions relating to strategic areas, including approval of the terms of the trusteeship agreements and of their alteration or amendment and, *inter alia*, was to avail itself of the assistance of the Trusteeship Council to perform those functions under the Trusteeship System relating to political, economic, social and educational matters in the strategic areas. The Chairman of the Committee on colonial countries drew particular attention to the above when he transmitted the Committee's conclusions and recommendations to the President of the Security Council on 24 August.[10]

Economic conditions

Trusteeship Council action. While noting that responsibility for development lay primarily with the four constitutional Governments, the Trusteeship Council[3] regretted that the concept of drawing up an overall development programme for the Territory as a whole had not made more headway. In particular it regretted the disparities in levels of development between different areas and instances of duplication, which were likely to discourage potential investors. It urged the Administering Authority to play a constructive role by promoting procedures for consultation among the various authorities concerned.

Noting that the economic section of the Authority's report too often favoured mere compilation of information, the Council called for future reports to indicate guiding principles applied in economic policy, the objectives envisaged, the criteria of choice and the order of priorities. It also noted the inadequacy of statistical information submitted and requested that the next report contain such information.

In regard to public finance, the Council noted that the constitutional Governments' budgetary allocation for operations had increased by 7.5 per cent and that the grant for infrastructural improvement had almost doubled. It reiterated concern that certain federal programmes had been reduced or discontinued by the United States. It hoped Palau's request for rescheduling of funds would be reconsidered and approved in the near future.

Concerning international trade, the Council noted with satisfaction that duty-free entry into the United States would be allowed for products exported by the Territory. Noting that the Territory remained largely dependent on the outside world, even for basic necessities, the Council hoped plans for reduction of that dependence would be drawn up. It also hoped for the establishment of a customs union.

Regarding agriculture, the Council recommended that a study be undertaken to determine the types of production and farming that would enable Micronesians to use comparative advantages with a view to increasing exports and reducing dependence on imports. Development of marine resources should also be a priority goal.

The Council welcomed the establishment of new companies in the Territory but reiterated concern at the inadequate industrial development, reaffirming that priority should be given to establishing small-scale local industry. It regarded the construction industry as a key to Micronesia's economic development.

Another key to development was the telecommunication system. It hoped the system would be operational throughout the Territory as soon as possible. It also hoped that the Territory would soon have a road network serving main urban areas and a minimum network in the outer islands, and that air services between Micronesia and the outside world would be increased.

Emphasizing the importance of tourism in the development of the Territory's economy, the Council said it should however be gradual so that small and fragile economies, social structures, environment and cultural conditions were not overwhelmed.

The Council expressed satisfaction that in many cases land leased in the Northern Mariana Islands for contingency military purposes had been leased back to its original owners for a nominal fee for continued civilian use.

Action by the Committee on colonial countries. The Committee on colonial countries[6] noted that the Territory was still, to a large extent, economically and financially dependent on the Administering Authority and that structural imbalances in the economy appeared not to have been reduced. It said the Authority should increase its economic assistance so that the people could achieve economic independence to the greatest extent possible and reduce the structural imbalances. It noted that the budgetary allocation for operations of the local authorities and the grant for infrastructural improvement had increased and recalled the Authority's obligation relating to economic development.

It urged the Authority to continue safeguarding, in co-operation with the local authorities, the right of the people of Micronesia to own and dispose freely of the natural resources and to establish and maintain control of their future development. It reaffirmed that the rights of the people over a 200-mile exclusive maritime zone should be respected and that they should receive all benefits deriving from it.

Social conditions

Noting that responsibility for health care had been devolved to the constitutional Governments, the Trusteeship Council[3] urged the Administering Authority to establish a co-ordinating mechanism to continue the work of the Office of Health Services after termination of the Trusteeship Agreement. It noted with satisfaction that the Authority continued to give priority to developing hospital services throughout the Territory, while expressing concern over the reported inadequacy of health care in some regions.

The Council expressed concern at the continued incidence of cholera. It appreciated the efforts made to eradicate the disease, urged increased attention to improving sanitation facilities and disinfecting water supplies and noted with satisfaction that although 165 cases had been reported since 1983 there had been no deaths.

The Council stressed the importance of continuing efforts in family planning. It noted with concern that severe budget cut-backs in federal programmes for training of health care professionals was likely to have a negative impact in Micronesia and said every effort should be made to find funding. It urged the Authority to give urgent attention to the financial problems of the Marshall Islands regarding the cost of medical referrals.

While noting the Authority's view that employment policies were best left to the local Governments, the Council considered it the Authority's responsibility to assist in and contribute to the reduction of employment. It urged priority for a co-ordinated employment policy and facilitation of free movement of labour. The Council noted that community development projects continued to prove successful and applauded work in promoting self-reliance in the local population.

Education

Regarding education, the Trusteeship Council[3] recognized that a shortage of skilled teachers was still a major problem and hoped the Territorial Teacher Training Program would be extended at least until termination of the Trusteeship Agreement. It was concerned at set-backs faced by the Marshall Islands in education and urged the Authority to respond positively to requests for assistance. It noted with concern that many elementary school facilities remained inadequate.

Since termination of the Agreement was near, the Council urged that more resources be devoted to teaching English and asked that steps be taken to enable learning of other languages. It noted with pleasure the establishment of the Northern Marianas College, aimed at providing the skills essential to development in Micronesia. It urged the Authority and Governments of the Territory to see that those receiving vocational training or higher education at government expense were obliged for a specific period after graduation to offer their services to the State or a government agency. It welcomed the wide range of vocational training provided by federal agencies.

Claims

The Trusteeship Council[3] noted that payment of $24.3 million in war claims was subject to the provisions of a United States Public Law being met. It hoped that disbursement of these funds would not be delayed based on legal technicalities and that the United States Administration and the Congress would ensure that the money was released before termination of the Agreement.

Radioactive waste management

Despite the absence of any evidence that nuclear wastes had been dumped in the waters of the Territory, the Trusteeship Council[3] nevertheless recognized that the matter could be one of serious concern to the inhabitants, who looked to the Authority to defend their interests in the matter. It noted that studies on the environmental impact of any dumping were under way and that if plans were to be made to continue a nuclear-waste storage facility there would be opportunities to conduct scientific studies and consult with all interested parties.

Compensation for Bikini and Enewetak populations

The Trusteeship Council[3] took note of the substantial sums of money the Administering Authority had paid to Bikini Islanders for damages inflicted on their atoll by nuclear tests. While recognizing that no amount of financial assistance could adequately compensate for loss of their homeland, the Council nevertheless recognized that the Authority had accepted liability and had been generous. It also noted the financial provisions made under the compact of free association in regard to the Marshall Islands.

The Council reiterated its concern that the people of Bikini and Enewetak and their dependants, who had suffered as a result of the nuclear tests, should continue to receive adequate medical care, even after the Agreement's termination. The Council welcomed the Authority's undertaking to keep it informed of the results of radiological tests on Bikini and asked the Authority to continue to eliminate the radiation risks to which the inhabitants of the Marshall Islands might be exposed.

Visiting missions

In 1983, visiting missions had been sent by the Trusteeship Council to the Federated States of Micronesia and Marshall Islands to observe plebiscites there.[9] The aim was to see that the voting public understood the issues involved in the plebiscites and that they had been carried out in accordance with the regulations which ensured the secrecy of the vote and the accuracy of the counting. Both missions had concluded that the voters had approved the compact of free association in plebiscites that had been run so as to ensure the free and fair expression of the wishes of the people.

Trusteeship Council action. The Trusteeship Council on 29 May 1984 adopted resolutions 2177(LI) and 2178(LI), both by vote.

Report of the United Nations Visiting Mission to observe the plebiscite in the Federated States of Micronesia, Trust Territory of the Pacific Islands, June 1983

The Trusteeship Council,

Having examined at its fifty-first session the report of the United Nations Visiting Mission, dispatched at the invitation of the Administering Authority and pursuant to its resolution 2174(S-XV) of 20 December 1982, to observe the plebiscite in the Federated States of Micronesia, Trust Territory of the Pacific Islands,

1. *Takes note* of the report of the Visiting Mission;

2. *Expresses its appreciation* of the work accomplished by the Visiting Mission on its behalf.

Trusteeship Council resolution 2177(LI)

Trusteeship Council resolution 2177(LI)

29 May 1984   Meeting 1576   3-1

Draft by France and United Kingdom (T/L.1241 and Corr.1); agenda item 7.

Report of the United Nations Visiting Mission to observe the plebiscite in the Marshall Islands, Trust Territory of the Pacific Islands, September 1983

The Trusteeship Council,

Having examined at its fifty-first session the report of the United Nations Visiting Mission, dispatched at the invitation of the Administering Authority and pursuant to its resolution 2174(S-XV) of 20 December 1982, to observe the plebiscite in the Marshall Islands, Trust Territory of the Pacific Islands,

1. *Takes note* of the report of the Visiting Mission;
2. *Expresses its appreciation* of the work accomplished by the Visiting Mission on its behalf.

Trusteeship Council resolution 2178(LI)

29 May 1984   Meeting 1576   3-1

Draft by France and United Kingdom (T/L.1242 and Corr.1); agenda item 8.

The USSR, which voted negatively, said that United States actions regarding Micronesia, which were aimed at dividing the Territory and imposing on its various parts a commonwealth and free association, were illegal and contrary to the Charter, the Trusteeship Agreement and the 1960 Declaration on colonial countries. Changes in the status of a strategic Trust Territory could be made only by the Security Council. The USSR rejected the conclusions of the missions as a smoke-screen for the political show organized by the Administering Authority to seize the Territory illegally.

Hearings

Between 16 and 22 May 1984, the Trusteeship Council heard 12 petitioners who were concerned mainly with the future status of the Trust Territory, its political, economic and social conditions, the question of compensation to victims of atomic tests and radiation and the scale of payments for land leased on Kwajalein Atoll by the Administering Authority for missile tests. The petitioners were: Mayor Tomaki Juda and Jonathan M. Weisgall, on behalf of the people of Bikini; Julian Riklon from Rongelap Atoll, Marshall Islands; Senator Carl Heine from Jaluit Atoll, Marshall Islands; Senator Ataji Balos of Kwajalein Atoll Corporation; David Anderson, a lawyer appearing on behalf of the people of Enewetak; Father William Wood, Focus on Micronesia Coalition; Glenn Alcalay for the United States Pacific Network; Susanne R. Roff, Minority Rights Group (New York), Inc.; Harold Matthew, Mayor of Utirik Atoll, Marshall Islands; and Edward Temengil and Roman Bedor of Palau.

Meeting numbers. TC 1566-1569, 1571.

On 30 October and 2 November, the General Assembly's Fourth Committee heard statements by Elizabeth Bounds, National Council of the Churches of Christ in the United States; Vincent McGee, Minority Rights Group; Susanne R. Roff and Jonathan M. Weisgall.

Meeting numbers. GA 39th session: 4th Committee 12, 13.

In the Fourth Committee, the United States said the question of Micronesia was expressly reserved to the Security Council and the Trusteeship Council and appearance of petitioners in the Fourth Committee would be a departure from established practice and from Article 83 of the Charter. Australia, and Sweden, on behalf of the five Nordic countries, held similar views.

Petitions, communications and observations

The Trusteeship Council on 22 May took decisions on 12 written communications and 15 written petitions. It drew the attention of the petitioners to the observations of the Administering Authority where applicable.

Responding to a September 1983 letter from Senator Peter Sugiyama of Palau, the United States, in a 22 February 1984 letter to the President of the Trusteeship Council, stated that it had no intention of submitting the compact of free association for Palau[11] to the United States Congress until Palau had completed its own approval process.

Meeting number. TC 1570.

REFERENCES

[1]YUN 1946-47, p. 398. [2]T/L.1240 & Add.1. [3]S/16738. [4]T/L.1243/Rev.1. [5]A/39/156-S/16441 (T/1862). [6]A/39/23. [7]YUN 1960, p. 49, GA res. 1514(XV), 14 Dec. 1960. [8]A/39/696. [9]YUN 1983, p. 1035. [10]S/16721. [11]YUN 1983, p. 1034.

Other aspects of the International Trusteeship System

Fellowships and scholarships

Under a scholarship programme, launched by the General Assembly in 1952,[1] 11 Member States had in the past made scholarships available for students from Trust Territories: Czechoslovakia, Hungary, Indonesia, Italy, Mexico, Pakistan, Philippines, Poland, Tunisia, USSR, Yugoslavia. In a May 1984 report to the Trusteeship Council,[2] the Secretary-General stated that he had asked for up-to-date information, receiving a reply from one offering State, the USSR, which said that currently no inhabitant from the Trust Territory of the Pacific Islands was studying in the USSR.

In the Council, the USSR said it regretted that the report omitted details of scholarships and fellowships offered by Member States to the Territory's inhabitants, pointing out that the last such description had appeared more than 16 years previously. The USSR had information that many offers never reached the inhabitants or that they had been so hemmed in by obstacles that they had found it impossible to take advantage of them.

The United States said Micronesians were involved in a number of foreign training programmes, mostly in the Pacific, and scholarships most in demand were those where the language of instruction was English. Local Governments handled all international scholarships; information about scholarships offered by the USSR had been made available to Micronesians through those Governments. It was up to the students to decide whether they wanted to apply for them.

On 24 May, the Council took note of the report without objection.[3]

Meeting number. TC 1575.

Information dissemination

A report by the Secretary-General covering 1 May 1983 to 30 April 1984[4] described activities by the United Nations Department of Public Information (DPI) in distributing United Nations documents, official records and informational materials throughout the Trust Territory. Such information was distributed directly and through its information centres, primarily the United Nations Information Centre (UNIC) in Tokyo. In March, an information officer from that Centre visited the Territory to review arrangements for efficient dissemination, confirming that the offices and libraries of each place he visited were receiving the materials. Video cassettes were found to be a new and effective means of disseminating information, since all educational institutions in Micronesia had video cassette players. United Nations radio programmes were often used in Palau and Yap. The UNIC at Washington, D.C., continued to distribute Council documents and other United Nations material to the United States Congress, Departments of State and the Interior, non-governmental organizations and information media.

Speaking in the Council, the USSR said the Administering Authority had not explained in its annual report how it fulfilled its responsibility for disseminating information. The Micronesians had commented on the lack of information and the report failed to mention whether DPI had corrected that regrettable state of affairs.

The United States said all documents received by the regional Governments were disseminated; none were blocked or controlled under any pretext.

On 24 May, the Council took note of the Secretary-General's report without objection.[3]

Meeting number. TC 1575.

Trusteeship Council

The Trusteeship Council held its fifty-first session in New York from 14 May to 18 July, adopting its agenda[5] on 14 May and its report to the Security Council[3] on 18 July.

Meeting numbers. TC 1564, 1580.

Co-operation with the Committee on colonial countries

At its 1984 session,[3] the Trusteeship Council again considered the attainment of self-government or independence by the Trust Territory and co-operation with the Committee on colonial countries.

During the discussion of the item in the Council, the USSR said the Administering Authority's report was silent on the implementation of the 1960 Declaration on the Granting of Independence to Colonial Countries and Peoples.[6] The Authority's claim that it was accountable only to the Trusteeship Council and the Security Council was incorrect. The Territory fell within the framework of the Declaration, since the Micronesians had not attained independence, and the Authority's and the Trusteeship Council's refusal to co-operate with the Committee on colonial countries was in defiance of the General Assembly and generally counter-productive to decolonization.

The United States said Article 83 of the Charter, reserving jurisdiction over the Territory to the Security Council rather than the Assembly, was quite definite; the Committee on colonial countries and the Assembly had no jurisdiction with respect to the Territory. France and the United Kingdom agreed with that interpretation of Article 83.

Meeting numbers. TC 1577, 1579.

Co-operation with CERD and the Decade against racial discrimination

Co-operation with the Committee on the Elimination of Racial Discrimination (CERD) and the Decade for Action to Combat Racism and Racial Discrimination was again considered by the Trusteeship Council in 1984.[3]

During the discussion in the Council, the USSR said since CERD made recommendations on petitions, the Council was expected to transmit such petitions to CERD, which should also receive reports concerning legislative, judicial, administrative and other measures directly related to the International Convention on the Elimination of All Forms of Racial Discrimination;[7] the Council had material of that nature which should be submitted. The USSR said it had been established during the current Council session that instances of racial discrimination had taken place in the Territory and one petitioner had made material available attesting to a policy of racial discrimination, particularly regarding wages. A CERD representative should be invited to attend the current Council session.

The United Kingdom said it had witnessed no racial discrimination during two visits to Micronesia; however, the question of wages could be examined as a possible example of racial discrimination. Concerning co-operation with CERD, the United Kingdom referred to Article 83 of the Charter on the general question of jurisdiction; the United States subscribed to those views, adding that the one case of alleged wage discrimination was currently under litigation in a Court in the Northern Mariana Islands and copies of the subsequent judgement would be made available.

The representative of the Government of the Federated States of Micronesia said it had not complained about racial discrimination because

it had never experienced it; in the preceding four years of constitutional government the question of racial discrimination had never arisen.

On 29 May, the Council took note, without objection, of the statements.[3]

Meeting number. TC 1576.

REFERENCES

[1]YUN 1951, p. 788, GA res. 557(VI), 18 Jan. 1952. [2]T/1867. [3]S/16738. [4]T/1866. [5]T/1864 & Add.1. [6]YUN 1960, p. 49, GA res. 1514(XV), 14 Dec. 1960. [7]YUN 1965, p. 440, GA res. 2106 A (XX), annex, 21 Dec. 1965.

Chapter III

Namibia

The United Nations continued in 1984 to work for the independence of Namibia, the largest Territory remaining under colonial rule. As the legal Administering Authority for Namibia until its independence, the United Nations Council for Namibia monitored the situation there and participated in formulating United Nations policy on the Territory. At extraordinary plenary meetings at Bangkok, Thailand, the Council adopted in May its Bangkok Declaration and Programme of Action, outlining its policies.

In its 1984 annual report to the General Assembly, the Council reviewed the political and military situation, foreign investment in the Territory, the exploitation of its natural resources, and social conditions and the labour situation under the continued illegal occupation of the South African administration. It said that South Africa was attempting to maintain control of Namibia through the establishment of a puppet institution, the so-called Multi-Party Conference (MPC). Furthermore, South Africa continued to insist on the withdrawal of Cuban forces from Angola before acting on independence plans. Independence talks between the South West Africa People's Organization (SWAPO), the South African Administrator-General of Namibia and an MPC delegation took place at Lusaka, Zambia, in May, and at Mindelo, Cape Verde, in July, the first direct encounter between South Africa and SWAPO since 1981, but the conferences ended without agreement on key issues. According to the Council, the talks failed because MPC members refused to support the independence plan endorsed by the Security Council in 1978 and insisted on linking independence to extraneous issues such as the Cuban withdrawal from Angola.

Cuba and Angola, in a joint declaration issued in March, stated their intention to initiate the gradual removal of Cuban forces from Angola as soon as certain conditions had been met, including South Africa's withdrawal of its forces from Angola and implementation of the independence plan.

The General Assembly, in resolution 39/50 A, condemned South Africa for attempting to circumvent the United Nations plan for Namibia by promoting an internal settlement through MPC, and for sabotaging the independence talks held in 1984 by insisting on the "linkage" pre-condition. It urged the Security Council to fulfil United Nations responsibility over Namibia and ensure that the Organization's independence plan was not undermined.

In resolution 39/50 B, the Assembly again called for the plan's implementation, as endorsed by the Council in 1978, and demanded that South Africa and the United States desist from their attempts to establish linkage.

The Council for Namibia viewed with concern the increased assistance given by major Western countries and Israel to South Africa in the economic and financial areas, and said such help was a hostile act against the Namibian people. It reported that certain Western States, in disregard of United Nations resolutions, continued to maintain their wide-ranging economic interests in Namibia. Their unwillingness to prevent those activities had contributed to the illegal exploitation of the Territory's natural and human resources. Foreign economic interests were attracted to Namibia because of the high profitability made possible by the abundance of cheap, enslaved labour. Such interests, particularly South African– and Western-based transnational corporations, continued to exploit the natural resources without reinvesting much of the profit in the Territory. The Council, having sought information and advice about initiating legal proceedings in domestic courts of countries whose nationals and companies were involved, reiterated its resolve to end the plunder through such means as legal action. The Assembly declared that the activities of foreign economic interests in Namibia were illegal under international law and demanded that transnational corporations refrain from activities there.

In co-operation with the United Nations Department of Public Information, the Council disseminated information on Namibia in order to mobilize world public opinion in support of independence. As part of the publicity campaign, it organized seminars and missions, issued publications and broadcast materials, maintained contacts with non-governmental organizations and held observances. The Assembly, in resolution 39/50 D, called for United Nations and other action to promote international public opinion in support of Namibia. By resolution 39/50 C, it decided on the work programme of the Council.

Namibians outside their country continued to receive assistance from various United Nations programmes, financed primarily by the Fund for Namibia. In 1984, the Fund spent $7.5 million, while voluntary contributions by States totalled $4.4 million. Funding was also provided from the regular United Nations budget, the United Nations Development Programme (UNDP) and specialized agencies. The Fund consisted of three main programmes—the Nationhood Programme for Namibia, which financed training programmes and surveys of the economic and social sectors in preparation for independence; the United Nations Institute for Namibia, involved with research, training and planning activities; and educational, social and relief assistance to Namibians, which emphasized their immediate needs and welfare. In resolution 39/50 E, the Assembly appealed for increased contributions to the Fund and urged United Nations organizations to implement projects approved by the Council and to allocate funds for them.

Topics related to this chapter. Africa: South Africa and *apartheid;* Angola–South Africa armed incidents and South African occupation of Angola. Human rights: human rights violations, South Africa and Namibia. General questions relating to colonial countries. Refugees and displaced persons: Africa.

Namibia question

Activities of the UN Council for Namibia. The United Nations Council for Namibia, a policy-making organ of the United Nations and the legal Administering Authority for the Territory until independence under the role mandated by the General Assembly in 1967,[1] continued its work in 1984. It reported to the Assembly in November on developments concerning Namibia and on Council activities from 1 September 1983 to 31 August 1984.[2] Later 1984 activities were described in its 1985 report.[3] As in previous years, the Council participated in the work of other United Nations bodies whenever they dealt with the question of Namibia and related matters: it co-operated with the Organization of African Unity (OAU) and the Movement of Non-Aligned Countries; dispatched consultation missions to various countries; organized seminars and regional symposia on Namibia in order to mobilize further international public opinion in support of the Territory's independence; and co-operated with non-governmental organizations (NGOs) in efforts to expose the illegal occupation of Namibia by South Africa and to mobilize international public opinion. The Council continued to consult with the South West Africa People's Organization (SWAPO), recognized by the Assembly as the sole and authentic representative of the Namibian people.

Acting as the representative of Namibia, the Council continued to serve as a full member of UNCTAD, UNIDO, the Executive Committee of the Programme of UNHCR, IAEA, ILO, FAO, UNESCO and ITU, and was an associate member in WHO.

During 1984, the Council was represented at other conferences and meetings, including: Greater London Council ceremony to declare Greater London an anti-*apartheid* zone (London, 9-11 January); ninth meeting of the States Parties to the International Convention on the Elimination of All Forms of Racial Discrimination[4] (New York, 20 January); seminar with NGOs based in Europe, organized by the Special Committee on the Situation with regard to the Implementation of the Declaration on the Granting of Independence to Colonial Countries and Peoples (Committee on colonial countries) (Vienna, Austria, 21-23 February); Preparatory Commission for the International Sea-Bed Authority and for the International Tribunal for the Law of the Sea (Kingston, Jamaica, 19 March–13 April, Geneva, 8-10 August and 13 August–5 September); congressional briefing on United States policy and the war in southern Africa (Washington, D.C., 25 April); North American Regional Conference for Action against *Apartheid* (New York, 18-21 June); International NGO Conference for the Independence of Namibia and the Eradication of *Apartheid* (Geneva, 2-5 July); Conference of Arab Solidarity with the Struggle for Liberation in Southern Africa (Tunis, Tunisia, 7-9 August); Committee on the Elimination of Racial Discrimination (Geneva, 7-15 August); seminar on the Legal Status of the *Apartheid* Régime in South Africa and Other Legal Aspects of the Struggle against *Apartheid* (Lagos, Nigeria, 13-16 August); meeting to observe the International Day of Solidarity with South African Political Prisoners (11 October); meeting of the Council of the International Centre for Public Enterprises in Developing Countries (Ljubljana, Yugoslavia, 25-27 October); and special meeting to commemorate the International Day of Solidarity with the Palestinian People (New York, 29 November).

On 25 May, the Council held its annual meeting in observance of Africa Liberation Day and of the twenty-first anniversary of the founding of OAU. The Council also commemorated Namibia Day on 26 August, and the Week of Solidarity with the People of Namibia and Their Liberation Movement, SWAPO, on 27 October. As in previous years, the Council participated as observer in meetings of the OAU Assembly of Heads of State and Government and the OAU Council of Ministers.

The Council continued to organize and participate in various seminars and conferences, among them a regional symposium on South Africa's Illegal Occupation of Namibia: The Threat to International Peace and Security (Arusha, United Republic of Tanzania, 2-5 April). It made recommendations at the international, regional and national levels, and called for comprehensive mandatory sanctions against South Africa.

The Seminar on the Efforts by the International Community to End South Africa's Illegal Occupation of Namibia (Montreal, Canada, 23-27 July) considered South Africa's refusal to implement the 1978 United Nations plan for Namibia's independence endorsed in Security Council resolution 435(1978).[5] The seminar called for sanctions should South Africa fail to implement the independence plan and for an immediate Council meeting to take urgent action. It urged the international community to increase all kinds of support to SWAPO and recommended future action for the Council for Namibia.

As part of the Week of Solidarity with the People of Namibia, the Council organized a symposium on A Century of Heroic Struggle by the Namibian People against Colonialism (New York, 31 October–2 November). The symposium recommended measures for the Council and called on the international community, in particular the peoples of countries that were allies of South Africa, especially the United States and members of the European Economic Community (EEC), to pressure their Governments and South Africa to end the illegal occupation of Namibia through the implementation of the United Nations plan. The participants condemned the United States policy of "linkage" of the issues of Namibia's independence and the withdrawal of Cuban forces from Angola, and called on it to close its so-called Liaison Office at Windhoek in Namibia.

Seminars were also held on exploitation of Namibia's natural and human resources (see below) and on the protection of Namibia's natural resources (see below).

Bangkok Declaration and Programme of Action. The Council for Namibia, at the conclusion of its 1984 extraordinary plenary meetings (Bangkok, 21-25 May), adopted by acclamation the Bangkok Declaration and Programme of Action on Namibia. On 31 May,[6] the Council's President transmitted the texts to the Secretary-General. Australia, Belgium, Botswana, Chile, Finland and Turkey, while joining the consensus, expressed reservations or made clarifications concerning certain references therein. At the Bangkok meetings, the Council reviewed the situation in the context of the continued illegal occupation by South Africa and its implications for international peace and security, analysed the causes for the delay in implementing the 1978 United Nations plan for independence,[5] and examined measures to increase support for the independence struggle of the Namibians led by SWAPO, their sole and authentic representative, and to assist the frontline States in resisting South Africa's acts of aggression and destabilization.

The Council expressed the hope that its meetings in Asia would cause the Governments and peoples of that continent, and the entire international community, to redouble their efforts to achieve Namibia's liberation from colonial and racist oc-

cupation. The Council took note of recent United Nations action, as well as a resolution on Namibia adopted by the OAU Council of Ministers at its fortieth session (Addis Ababa, Ethiopia, 27 February–5 March 1984)[7] (see below, under "Communications"), and welcomed the Final Communiqué of the Summit Meeting of Front-line States (Arusha, 29 April).[8] It reaffirmed the inalienable right of the Namibian people to self-determination and independence in a united Namibia, that South Africa's occupation constituted an act of aggression against the people in terms of the Definition of Aggression adopted by the General Assembly in 1974,[9] and that the Namibian people in the exercise of their right of self-defence were entitled to use all means at their disposal, including armed struggle, to repel South Africa. The Council reaffirmed its solidarity with, and support for, SWAPO and commended it for continuing the struggle on all fronts, including the armed struggle. It called on States to give political, moral, material, military and financial support to SWAPO, and on United Nations bodies to provide assistance to the Namibian people through SWAPO.

In the light of the current critical situation resulting from South Africa's continued occupation, its defiance of United Nations resolutions, its manœuvres to subvert the United Nations independence plan, the encouragement it received from Western countries, its increasing military strength, rendered more dangerous by its nuclear weapons capability, and its aggression against African States, the Council called for action from the United Nations, States and intergovernmental organizations. The Council would consult with Governments, NGOs and other support groups because it deemed it important to maintain contacts with those Member States whose position on Namibia did not conform with that of the Council, with a view to convincing them of the need to comply with United Nations resolutions and to cease collaboration with South Africa and to pressure it to expedite Namibia's independence; it was incumbent upon all States and the international community to compel South Africa to comply with United Nations resolutions. In regard to follow-up action, the Council would maintain regular diplomatic contacts with countries visited by its missions.

The Council reaffirmed that Namibia's accession to independence must be with its Territory intact, including Walvis Bay and the offshore islands, and it called on the Security Council to counter any South African dismemberment attempts.

Condemning South Africa for its repression of the Namibian people, its *apartheid* policy and other human rights violations (see p. 784 *et seq.*), the Council demanded an end to those policies. It demanded the unconditional release of all Namibian political prisoners (see p. 155) and denounced South Africa for its military buildup in Namibia, its introduction of compulsory military service for Namibians, and its recruitment of mercenaries.

The support of front-line States for the Namibian cause continued to be of paramount importance in bringing independence, in the Council's view, and it called on the international community to render financial, material, military and political support to those States. The Council also reaffirmed its support for the Southern African Development Co-ordination Conference (SADCC) and called on States to assist it in its efforts to promote regional economic co-operation and development and to reduce the economic dependence of countries in the area on South Africa.

Stating that the United Nations plan for Namibia approved by the Security Council[5] remained the only basis for a peaceful settlement of the Namibia question, the Council reaffirmed the need to implement it without modification, qualification or pre-condition and that Namibia remained a decolonization issue and should be resolved in accordance with the 1960 Declaration on the Granting of Independence to Colonial Countries and Peoples.[10] Any attempt to portray the question as part of an East-West confrontation, or to link it with other extraneous considerations, was in defiance of the international community. The Council rejected attempts by the United States and South Africa to establish a linkage between the independence of Namibia and extraneous issues, in particular the withdrawal of Cuban forces from Angola (see p. 180).

The Council also condemned South Africa's attempts to circumvent the United Nations plan for Namibia by promoting an internal settlement through the so-called MPC. Such attempts, immediately following the decision to establish a so-called state council to draw up a "constitution", again made clear that South Africa had no intention of complying with the United Nations plan and sought instead to consolidate its illegitimate hold on the Territory through the installation of puppet political institutions. According to the Council, there were only two parties to the conflict, namely the people of Namibia, led by SWAPO, and South Africa. The Council called on all States and the international community not to recognize any effort to impose any such illegal arrangements.

It urged the Security Council to act decisively to ensure the full implementation of resolution 435(1978),[5] the only acceptable basis for peaceful settlement of the question. It commended the Secretary-General for his efforts in pursuing Security Council and General Assembly resolutions and urged him to intensify those efforts. The Council said that, as the representative of Namibia in United Nations organizations, it would make proposals within the respective spheres of competence of those bodies to promote the interests of the Namibian people. It called on NGOs to intensify international action

in support of the liberation struggle and to increase support to SWAPO.

In addition, the Council stated its position in regard to States' relations with South Africa (see p. 136), the exploitation of Namibian natural resources (see below), the relations of the International Monetary Fund (IMF) with South Africa (see p. 150), the imposition of mandatory sanctions against South Africa to ensure its compliance with United Nations resolutions (see p. 138), tightening the existing arms embargo against South Africa (see p. 142), assistance to the United Nations Fund for Namibia (see below), and mobilization of public opinion (see below).

Missions. In accordance with a 1983 General Assembly resolution,[11] the Council for Namibia sent consultation missions to Western Europe, Latin America and the Asia-Pacific region, covering the following countries and organizations:[2] the Netherlands, Belgium, Luxembourg, the European Parliament and the Commission of the European Communities from 16 to 31 January; Japan, New Zealand and Australia from 12 to 24 March; and Trinidad and Tobago and Argentina from 7 to 16 April. The purpose of those missions was to promote the implementation of United Nations resolutions on Namibia and to mobilize international support for its independence. Meanwhile, another mission—to France, the Netherlands, the Federal Republic of Germany and the United Kingdom from 24 April to 12 May—sought legal advice from lawyers on the possibilities of instituting legal proceedings in the domestic courts to ensure compliance with Decree No. 1 for the Protection of the Natural Resources of Namibia (see below).[12] In addition, the Council sent a mission to New Delhi, India, to consult with the Chairperson of the Movement of Non-Aligned Countries from 16 to 18 May on developments in Namibia and the role the Movement could play to mobilize support for the Namibian cause.

The missions urged the Governments, pending the imposition by the Security Council of comprehensive mandatory sanctions against South Africa, to apply sanctions unilaterally and collectively.

During the visit to the Netherlands, its Government said it opposed extraneous pre-conditions to implementing the United Nations independence plan, and declared its willingness to co-operate in implementing Decree No. 1 to the extent possible under its law. With regard to exploiting Namibian uranium by foreign economic interests, the Netherlands maintained that no uranium from Namibia was being imported for use in nuclear plants in the Netherlands. Regarding sanctions, it said it had taken such measures as imposing strict visa requirements for South African nationals seeking entry into the Netherlands and abrogating a cultural agreement with that country.

In Belgium, the mission expressed concern over the presence there of a South African military attaché. Belgium maintained that it had no military co-operation with South Africa and that his presence had no particular significance; it still had some trading links with South Africa through private enterprise, but no Belgian enterprise or bank had financial interests in Namibia. Regarding Decree No. 1, it said that although the matter raised questions under international law, in practical terms Belgium adhered to its provisions; no Belgian State-owned or private company was engaged in exploiting Namibia's natural resources.

Luxembourg told the mission it rejected South Africa's attempts to impose an internal settlement in Namibia outside the framework of resolution 435(1978). Luxembourg believed that the Western contact group—Canada, France, the Federal Republic of Germany, the United Kingdom and the United States, which were attempting to negotiate with South Africa on the implementation of the independence plan—could help solve the remaining difficulties. It also rejected the linkage issue.

In Brussels, the mission raised objections to a resolution adopted by the European Parliament in January 1983[13] on the need for development aid for Namibia.

The mission to Japan was informed of the Government's continued support for the United Nations plan, and that it welcomed recent diplomatic initiatives towards solving the problems in southern Africa through dialogue. Regarding the proposed United Nations Transition Assistance Group (UNTAG) to be established under resolution 435(1978), Japan said it would consider making voluntary contributions and providing personnel to the civilian component of UNTAG; in 1975, it had drawn the attention of Japanese companies to Decree No. 1.

New Zealand reiterated its rejection of any linkage and maintained that the United Nations plan should be executed without pre-conditions. It hoped that diplomatic initiatives would contribute to easing tensions in the area. Following the consultations, New Zealand, for the first time, issued a statement jointly with the mission.

Australia also reaffirmed its support of the plan, rejected any linkage, and hoped that the initiatives would contribute to peace and security in the region.

The mission to Trinidad and Tobago was told that the Government would recognize the Namibian travel documents issued by the Council in its capacity as the legal Administering Authority for Namibia until independence. Trinidad and Tobago said it did not trade with South Africa, although there was a possibility of some illegal trade, which would be investigated. As for imposing economic sanctions, it was willing to raise the question at the next meeting of the Ministers of Trade of the African, Caribbean and Pacific (ACP) States to obtain the concurrence of the Caribbean countries to observe an economic boycott.

Argentina declared that resolution 435(1978) was the only basis for a negotiated settlement of the question and rejected any extraneous pre-conditions.

Communications. In 1984, a number of countries and organizations sent letters to the Secretary-General concerning Namibia. Angola, Cuba, South Africa, and SWAPO (whose communications were forwarded by Zimbabwe) addressed the immediate situation in the Territory; several organizations or conferences outlined their policy on Namibia, particularly the implementation of the United Nations plan for independence; and the United Kingdom disputed a statement made in the Special Committee against *Apartheid*.

On 5 January,[14] the President of SWAPO, responding to a proposal by Angola of 31 December 1983[15] that the Secretary-General consult with SWAPO and South Africa on a date for a cease-fire in Namibia, agreed with that proposal and suggested that the Secretary-General immediately convene a meeting between the two sides to discuss the final details of the cease-fire, in accordance with the provisions of Security Council resolution 435(1978).[5]

Angola and Cuba, in a joint declaration issued at Havana on 19 March 1984,[16] said they would initiate a gradual withdrawal of Cuban forces from Angola when certain requirements were met, including the implementation of resolution 435(1978) and the withdrawal of South African troops from Namibia (see p. 181). Referring to the joint declaration on 26 March,[17] South Africa said the statement contradicted the February Lusaka agreement on military disengagement in southern Africa (see p. 179), and added that it remained prepared to seek a peaceful settlement to the Namibia question based on resolution 435(1978) within the framework of the understanding reached with the Western contact group; the remaining issue was Cuban withdrawal from Angola, on the understanding that they would not be replaced by other hostile forces.

In a 13 August statement,[18] SWAPO reaffirmed its readiness to cease armed struggle in Namibia if South Africa agreed to a specified time frame, with a fixed date for commencing implementation of resolution 435(1978); SWAPO would not agree to a South African–controlled transitional process, but it remained ready for direct, constructive high-level contacts with South Africa. On 6 September,[19] South Africa said that SWAPO's letter was simply a repetition of the organization's position that the resolution must be implemented without an agreement on Cuban withdrawal; that withdrawal was not a subject on which SWAPO had any say, but was a matter which rested with Angola and was under discussion. Angola, on 17 November,[20] said it had held talks with the United States and South Africa on Namibia's independence and the cessation of South Africa's aggression. Angola had outlined its position on a future agreement—that it would be guaranteed by the Security Council and would provide for United Nations troops monitoring the South African withdrawal from Namibia, to be followed by the Cuban withdrawal over a three-year period. Referring to Angola's letter on 23 November,[21] South Africa said it insisted on an agreement providing for the Cuban withdrawal from Angola parallel with the reduction of South African forces in Namibia. South Africa enclosed its proposals to achieve independence for Namibia based on resolution 435(1978), including a 12-week timetable for the total removal of Cuban forces.

On 20 December,[22] South Africa forwarded a letter from the Secretary of the "Multi-Party Conference of South West Africa/Namibia" (MPC) to the President of the General Assembly, explaining that MPC came into being on 12 November 1983 at Windhoek when delegates from six Namibian parties came together to speak for the people of the Territory, rejecting claims of other States, including South Africa, the Western contact group, and the Eastern European countries, to speak for Namibians; MPC rejected the General Assembly's designating SWAPO—which had been invited to join a forthcoming conference—as the sole and authentic representative of the Namibian people.

Among organizations presenting views on Namibia, EEC put forward its policy as contained in a declaration adopted on 28 February at its Ministerial Meeting on European Political Cooperation, and forwarded by France on 2 March.[23] The members welcomed the recent agreement on disengagement in southern Angola (see below) and the understanding between South Africa and Mozambique (see p. 184), hoped that those developments would contribute to mutual confidence and would facilitate the implementation of resolution 435(1978), and expressed readiness to assist in developing a free and independent Namibia.

Morocco forwarded the final communiqué of the Fourth Islamic Summit Conference (Casablanca, Morocco, 16-19 January) to the Secretary-General on 13 March.[24] The Conference recognized the legitimacy of the liberation struggle of the peoples of South Africa and Namibia, through all means at their disposal, including armed struggle, rejected the linkage question established by South Africa, denounced the dilatory tactics of some members of the Western contact group, and requested it to accelerate its proceedings so that Namibia could become independent by the end of 1984.

On 18 April,[7] Upper Volta transmitted the resolutions adopted at the fortieth ordinary session of the OAU Council of Ministers (Addis Ababa, 27 February–5 March). In one resolution, the Ministers condemned South Africa's use of Namibia as a springboard for aggression against African States, condemned its attempts to impose institutions on the Namibians as well as its propping up puppet

political alliances to legitimize an internal settlement, welcomed the Security Council's 1983 condemnation of linkage,[25] and called for sanctions against South Africa to compel it to accede to Namibia's independence.

The Chairman of the Special Committee against *Apartheid* transmitted on 11 August[26] the declaration and resolutions adopted by the Conference of Arab Solidarity with the Struggle for Liberation in Southern Africa (Tunis, 7-9 August), in which it condemned the manœuvres of South Africa to sabotage the implementation of the United Nations independence plan and rejected the linkage question.

India forwarded on 8 October[27] the final communiqué adopted by the Meeting of Ministers for Foreign Affairs and Heads of Delegations of the Non-Aligned Countries to the 1984 General Assembly session (New York, 1-5 October), in which they condemned South Africa for its militarization of Namibia and its use as a springboard for aggression, denounced it and the United States for insisting on the linkage pre-condition, and condemned South Africa's attempts to set up puppet political institutions and impose an internal settlement.

By a letter of 16 October,[28] the Sudan forwarded the resolutions adopted by the seventy-second Inter-Parliamentary Conference (Geneva, 29 September), including one in which it called for the implementation of resolution 435(1978), condemned the killing of civilians in Namibia by South Africa's security forces, and blamed South Africa for the failure of its talks with SWAPO at Mindelo and Lusaka, aimed at bringing about a cease-fire and Namibia's independence.

Djibouti forwarded, on 10 January 1985,[29] resolutions adopted by the twentieth ordinary session of the Assembly of Heads of State and Government of OAU (Addis Ababa, 12-15 November 1984), including one on Namibia, in which they condemned South Africa for its obstruction of the United Nations plan, rejected the linkage question, encouraged SWAPO to intensify its struggle, and expressed support for the United Nations Secretary-General in his efforts to expedite independence.

The United Kingdom, on 2 July,[30] referred to a statement made in the Special Committee against *Apartheid* concerning its alleged support for linkage, and affirmed that there had been no change in the Government's position on Namibia; it remained committed to the implementation of resolution 435(1978).

Secretary-General's report. In response to two December 1983 General Assembly resolutions on Namibia, one on the situation in Namibia resulting from South Africa's occupation[31] and the other[32] on implementing Security Council resolution 435(1978),[5] the Secretary-General, in a report of 19 September,[33] forwarded replies he had received from Governments on implementation of those resolutions. By the 1983 action, the Assembly had, *inter alia*, called on States to support SWAPO and the front-line States and assist Namibian refugees; to isolate South Africa; and to reject any attempt to link the independence of Namibia with extraneous issues. The report contained replies from 15 Governments which described developments in their relations with South Africa.

Action by Committee on colonial countries. The Committee on colonial countries, in a 20 August decision[34] (see also p. 137), stated that South Africa was responsible for the critical situation in and around Namibia, and that its delaying tactics to prevent the implementation of resolution 435(1978), its military buildup in Namibia and its aggression against Namibians made it more urgent that the United Nations reassert its legal responsibility for Namibia. The Committee rejected all manoeuvres by South Africa to bring about sham independence in Namibia under fraudulent schemes, and condemned attempts to circumvent the United Nations plan by promoting an internal settlement through the so-called MPC. The Committee reiterated that a political solution must be based on the termination of South Africa's illegal occupation, withdrawal of its forces and the free exercise by the people of self-determination, in accordance with the 1960 Declaration on colonial countries.[10]

In its view, the issue remained one of decolonization, and was not part of an East-West confrontation. Therefore, the Committee rejected United States and South African attempts to link the question with the withdrawal of Cuban forces from Angola. Condemning South Africa's attempts to destroy SWAPO, the Committee expressed support for it as the representative of the Namibian people and recommended that the Security Council act against any dilatoriness by South Africa aimed at impeding independence and that it impose sanctions against that country.

In a resolution of 22 August,[35] the Committee requested all United Nations bodies to withhold from South Africa any form of co-operation or assistance until the people of Namibia had exercised their right to self-determination, freedom and national independence in a united Namibia.

Action by the Commission on Human Rights. The Commission on Human Rights, in a 28 February resolution on violations of human rights in southern Africa,[36] reaffirmed the right of the Namibian people to self-determination and independence, in accordance with Security Council decisions, and condemned South Africa for its oppression and the militarization of Namibia. In another 28 February resolution,[37] the Commission expressed abhorrence of the violation of human rights in Namibia and renewed its request to South Africa to allow an Expert Group to investigate the living conditions in Namibian prisons and the treatment of

prisoners. In a third resolution of the same date,[38] the Commission called on Governments to take measures, in respect of their nationals and bodies corporate under their jurisdiction that owned and operated enterprises in Namibia, with a view to stopping their trading, manufacturing and investing activities there. (See p. 852.)

ECONOMIC AND SOCIAL COUNCIL ACTION

In resolution 1984/55, the Economic and Social Council requested United Nations organizations to withhold all assistance to South Africa until it restored independence and self-determination to the Namibian people, and to refrain from any action which might imply recognition of, or support for, the occupation of Namibia. The Council condemned attempts by South Africa to circumvent the implementation of Security Council resolution 435(1978).[5] It noted with satisfaction the inclusion of Namibia, represented by the Council for Namibia, as a member of various United Nations organizations and urged those which had not granted it membership to do so.

In resolution 1984/53, the Council called on home countries of transnational corporations to prevent new investments and bring about a withdrawal of existing ones in Namibia and South Africa.

GENERAL ASSEMBLY ACTION

Five 1984 General Assembly resolutions (39/50 A-E) dealt with Namibia; two of these (39/50 A and B) concerned the situation there.

On 12 December, the Assembly adopted resolution 39/50 A by recorded vote.

Situation in Namibia resulting from the illegal occupation of the Territory by South Africa

The General Assembly,

Having examined the report of the United Nations Council for Namibia and the relevant chapters of the report of the Special Committee on the Situation with regard to the Implementation of the Declaration on the Granting of Independence to Colonial Countries and Peoples,

Recalling its resolution 1514(XV) of 14 December 1960, containing the Declaration on the Granting of Independence to Colonial Countries and Peoples,

Recalling, in particular, its resolutions 2145(XXI) of 27 October 1966 and 2248(S-V) of 19 May 1967 and subsequent resolutions of the General Assembly and the Security Council relating to Namibia, as well as the advisory opinion of the International Court of Justice of 21 June 1971, delivered in response to the request addressed to it by the Security Council in its resolution 284(1970) of 29 July 1970,

Recalling also its resolutions 3111(XXVIII) of 12 December 1973 and 31/146 and 31/152 of 20 December 1976, by which it, *inter alia*, recognized the South West Africa People's Organization as the sole and authentic representative of the Namibian people and granted observer status to it,

Recalling further its resolutions ES-8/2 of 14 September 1981 and 36/121 B of 10 December 1981, by which it called upon States to cease forthwith, individually and collectively, all dealings with South Africa in order totally to isolate it politically, economically, militarily and culturally,

Taking note of Security Council resolutions 532(1983) of 31 May 1983 and 539(1983) of 28 October 1983,

Noting also the Final Communiqué of the Commonwealth Heads of Government Meeting, held at New Delhi from 23 to 29 November 1983, the resolution on Namibia adopted by the Council of Ministers of the Organization of African Unity at its fortieth ordinary session, held at Addis Ababa from 27 February to 5 March 1984, the Final Communiqué of the Summit Meeting of the Frontline States, held at Arusha, United Republic of Tanzania, on 29 April 1984,[8] the Bangkok Declaration and Programme of Action on Namibia, adopted by the United Nations Council for Namibia on 25 May 1984 at its extraordinary plenary meetings held at Bangkok, the resolution on Namibia adopted by the Organization of African Unity Co-ordinating Committee for the Liberation of Africa at its forty-second session, held at Dar es Salaam from 30 August to 1 September 1984, and the Final Communiqué of the Meeting of Ministers and Heads of Delegation of the Non-Aligned Countries to the thirty-ninth session of the General Assembly, held in New York from 1 to 5 October 1984,

Welcoming the resolution on relations between the European Economic Community and Namibia adopted by the European Parliament on 22 May 1984,

Strongly reiterating that the continuing illegal and colonial occupation of Namibia by South Africa, in defiance of repeated General Assembly and Security Council resolutions, constitutes an act of aggression against the Namibian people and a challenge to the authority of the United Nations, which has direct responsibility for Namibia until independence,

Stressing the solemn responsibility of the international community to take all possible measures in support of the Namibian people in their liberation struggle under the leadership of their sole and authentic representative, the South West Africa People's Organization,

Reaffirming its full support for the armed struggle of the Namibian people, under the leadership of the South West Africa People's Organization, to achieve self-determination, freedom and national independence in a united Namibia, and recognizing that 1984 marks the one hundredth year of heroic struggle of the Namibian people against colonial occupation,

Indignant at South Africa's refusal to comply with repeated resolutions of the Security Council, in particular resolutions 385(1976) of 30 January 1976, 435(1978) of 29 September 1978, 439(1978) of 13 November 1978, 532(1983) of 31 May 1983 and 539(1983) of 28 October 1983, and at its manœuvres aimed at perpetuating its brutal colonial domination and exploitation of the Namibian people,

Deploring South Africa's intransigent stand and insistence on new pre-conditions and its demands for concessions from the South West Africa People's Organization which led to the failure of the Namibian independence talks held in 1984 at Lusaka and Mindelo,

Commending the front-line States and the South West Africa People's Organization for the statesmanlike and constructive attitude which they have displayed in the efforts aimed at implementing Security Council resolution 435(1978),

Strongly condemning the racist régime of South Africa for developing a nuclear capability for military and aggressive purposes,

Deeply concerned at the increasing militarization of Namibia, the forced conscription of Namibians, the creation of tribal armies and the use of mercenaries for the repression of the Namibian people and for carrying out aggression against neighbouring States,

Noting with grave concern that, as a result of the Security Council's failure on 31 August 1981, on account of the veto of the United States of America, to exercise effectively its responsibilities, unprovoked armed aggression against Angola continues and parts of southern Angola are still under occupation by South African troops,

Expressing its strong condemnation of South Africa's continuing acts of aggression against independent African States, particularly Angola, which have caused extensive loss of human life and destruction of economic infrastructures,

Reaffirming that the resources of Namibia are the inviolable heritage of the Namibian people and that the exploitation of those resources by foreign economic interests under the protection of the illegal South African colonial régime, in violation of the Charter of the United Nations, of the relevant resolutions of the General Assembly and the Security Council and of Decree No. 1 for the Protection of the Natural Resources of Namibia, enacted by the United Nations Council for Namibia on 27 September 1974, and in disregard of the advisory opinion of the International Court of Justice of 21 June 1971, is illegal and encourages the occupation régime to be even more intransigent and defiant,

Deeply deploring the continued collaboration with South Africa of certain Western States, in particular the United States of America, as well as that of Israel, in the political, military, economic and nuclear fields, in disregard of the relevant resolutions of the General Assembly and the Security Council,

Deeply concerned at the continued assistance rendered to the racist Pretoria régime by certain international organizations and institutions, in particular the International Monetary Fund, in disregard of the relevant resolutions of the General Assembly,

Indignant at the continuing arbitrary imprisonment and detention of leaders, members and supporters of the South West Africa People's Organization, the killing of Namibian patriots and other acts of brutality, including the wanton beating, torture and murder of innocent Namibians, and other inhuman measures by the illegal occupation régime designed to intimidate the Namibian people and to destroy their determination to fulfil their legitimate aspirations for self-determination, freedom and national independence in a united Namibia,

Noting with grave concern that the Security Council has been prevented from taking effective action against South Africa in the discharge of its responsibilities under Chapter VII of the Charter on account of the vetoes cast by one or more of the Western permanent members of the Security Council,

Commending the efforts of the United Nations Council for Namibia in the discharge of the responsibilities entrusted to it under the relevant resolutions of the General Assembly as the legal Administering Authority for Namibia until independence,

1. *Approves* the report of the United Nations Council for Namibia;

2. *Takes special note* of the Bangkok Declaration and Programme of Action on Namibia;

3. *Takes note* of the debate on the question of Namibia held in the Security Council from 20 to 28 October 1983, culminating in the adoption of resolution 539(1983), by which the Council rejected South Africa's insistence on linking the independence of Namibia to irrelevant and extraneous issues as incompatible with Council resolution 435(1978) and declared that the independence of Namibia could not be held hostage to the resolution of issues that were alien to resolution 435(1978);

4. *Further takes note* of Security Council resolution 539(1983) by which the Council decided, in the event of continued obstruction by South Africa, to consider the adoption of appropriate measures under the Charter of the United Nations;

5. *Reaffirms* the inalienable right of the people of Namibia to self-determination, freedom and national independence in a united Namibia, in accordance with the Charter of the United Nations and as recognized in General Assembly resolutions 1514(XV) and 2145(XXI) and in subsequent resolutions of the Assembly relating to Namibia, as well as the legitimacy of their struggle by all the means at their disposal, including armed struggle, against the illegal occupation of their territory by South Africa;

6. *Reiterates* that, in accordance with its resolution 2145(XXI), Namibia is the direct responsibility of the United Nations until genuine self-determination and national independence are achieved in the Territory and, for this purpose, reaffirms the mandate given to the United Nations Council for Namibia as the legal Administering Authority for Namibia until independence under resolution 2248(S-V) and subsequent resolutions of the General Assembly;

7. *Reaffirms* that the South West Africa People's Organization, the national liberation movement of Namibia, is the sole and authentic representative of the Namibian people;

8. *Further reaffirms* that the genuine independence of Namibia can be achieved only with the direct and full participation of the South West Africa People's Organization in all efforts to implement resolutions of the United Nations relating to Namibia;

9. *Strongly condemns* the South African régime for its continued illegal occupation of Namibia in defiance of the resolutions of the United Nations relating to Namibia;

10. *Declares* that South Africa's illegal occupation of Namibia constitutes an act of aggression against the Namibian people in terms of the Definition of Aggression contained in General Assembly resolution 3314(XXIX) of 14 December 1974 and supports the armed struggle of the Namibian people, under the leadership of the South West Africa People's Organization, to repel South Africa's aggression and to achieve self-determination, freedom and national independence in a united Namibia;

11. *Reaffirms* that Security Council resolution 435(1978) remains the only acceptable basis for a peaceful settlement of the Namibian question and calls once again for its immediate and unconditional implementation;

12. *Urges* the Security Council to act decisively in fulfilment of the direct responsibility of the United Nations over Namibia and to take, without further delay, appropriate action to ensure that the United Nations plan, as contained in Security Council resolution 435(1978), is not undermined or modified in any way and that it is fully respected and implemented;

13. *Reiterates its conviction* that South Africa's continued illegal occupation of Namibia, its defiance of United Nations resolutions, its brutal repression of the Namibian people, its acts of destabilization and aggression against independent African States and its policies of *apartheid* constitute a threat to international peace and security;

14. *Expresses its dismay* at the failure to date of the Security Council to discharge effectively its responsibilities for the maintenance of international peace and security, owing to the opposition of its Western permanent members;

15. *Declares* that comprehensive mandatory sanctions under Chapter VII of the Charter of the United Nations are the only effective measures to ensure South Africa's compliance with the resolutions and decisions of the United Nations;

16. *Denounces* all fraudulent constitutional and political schemes through which the illegal racist régime of South Africa may attempt to perpetuate its colonial domination of Namibia and, in particular, calls upon the international community, especially all Member States, to continue to refrain from according any recognition or extending any co-operation to any régime which the illegal South African administration may impose upon the Namibian people in disregard of Security Council resolutions 385(1976), 435(1978), 439(1978), 532(1983) and 539(1983) and of other relevant resolutions of the General Assembly and the Council;

17. *Condemns* South Africa for its continued attempts to circumvent the United Nations plan for Namibia by promoting an internal settlement through the so-called "Multi-Party Conference" and declares that such attempts by the racist régime, immediately following the decision to establish a so-called State Council with the object of drawing up a "Constitution", once again make clear that Pretoria has no intention of complying with the letter and spirit of the United Nations plan and seeks, instead, to consolidate its illegitimate hold on the Territory through the installation of puppet political institutions subservient to its own interests;

18. *Reaffirms* that all such manœuvres are fraudulent and null and void and that they must be rejected categorically by all States as called for in the relevant resolutions of the General Assembly and the Security Council;

19. *Reiterates* that there are only two parties to the conflict in Namibia, namely, the people of Namibia, led by their sole and authentic representative, the South West Africa People's Organization, on the one hand, and the illegal occupation régime of South Africa, on the other;

20. *Further reiterates* that all efforts must be deployed to counter any sinister manœuvres aimed at circumventing the United Nations and undermining its primary responsibility for the decolonization of Namibia;

21. *Firmly rejects and condemns* the persistent attempts by the United States of America and South Africa to establish a "linkage" or "parallelism" between the independence of Namibia and any extraneous and irrelevant issues, in particular the withdrawal of Cuban forces from Angola, and emphasizes unequivocally that all such attempts are designed to delay the decolonization process in Namibia and that they constitute interference in the internal affairs of Angola;

22. *Expresses its appreciation* to the front-line States and the South West Africa People's Organization for their statesmanlike and constructive attitude in the efforts aimed at implementing Security Council resolution 435(1978);

23. *Reaffirms its conviction* that the solidarity and support of the front-line States for the Namibian cause continues to be a factor of paramount importance in the efforts to bring genuine independence to the Territory;

24. *Strongly urges* the international community to increase, as a matter of urgency, financial, material, military and political support to the front-line States so as to enable them to resolve their own economic difficulties, which are largely a consequence of Pretoria's policies of aggression and subversion, and to defend themselves better against South Africa's persistent attempts to destabilize them;

25. *Commends* the South West Africa People's Organization for its continued intensification of the struggle on all fronts, including the armed struggle, and for its commitment to embrace all Namibian patriots in an effort to strengthen further the national unity so as to ensure the territorial integrity and sovereignty of a united Namibia, and welcomes the consolidation of unity in action by the patriotic forces in Namibia under the leadership of the South West Africa People's Organization, during the critical phase of their struggle for national and social liberation;

26. *Reaffirms its solidarity* with, and support for, the South West Africa People's Organization, the sole and authentic representative of the Namibian people, and pays tribute to that organization for sacrifices it has made in the field of battle and also for the spirit of statesmanship, co-operation and far-sightedness it has displayed in the political and diplomatic arena despite the most extreme provocations on the part of the racist Pretoria régime;

27. *Welcomes* the release of Andimba Toivo ya Toivo, Secretary-General of the South West Africa People's Organization, and other leaders of that organization and considers it a victory for the international campaign;

28. *Declares* that all so-called laws and proclamations issued by the illegal occupation régime in Namibia are illegal, null and void;

29. *Calls upon* Member States and the specialized agencies and other organizations of the United Nations system to render sustained and increased support as well as material, financial, military and other assistance to the South West Africa People's Organization so as to enable it to intensify its struggle for the liberation of Namibia;

30. *Urges* all Governments and the specialized agencies and other intergovernmental organizations to provide increased material assistance to the thousands of Namibian refugees who have been forced by the *apartheid* régime's oppressive policies to flee Namibia, especially into the neighbouring front-line States;

31. *Solemnly reaffirms* that Namibia's accession to independence must be with its territorial integrity intact, including Walvis Bay and the offshore islands, and reiterates that, in accordance with the resolutions of the United Nations, in particular Security Council resolution 432(1978) of 27 July 1978 and General Assembly resolutions S-9/2 of 3 May 1978 and 35/227 A of 6 March 1981, any attempt by South Africa to annex them is, therefore, illegal, null and void;

32. *Calls upon* the Security Council to declare categorically that Walvis Bay is an integral part of Namibia and that the question should not be left as a matter for negotiation between an independent Namibia and South Africa;

33. *Strongly condemns* South Africa for obstructing the implementation of United Nations resolutions, in particular Security Council resolutions 385(1976), 435(1978), 439(1978), 532(1983) and 539(1983), and for its manœuvres, in contravention of those resolutions, designed to consolidate its colonial and neo-colonial interests at the expense of the legitimate aspirations of the Namibian people for genuine self-determination, freedom and national independence in a united Namibia;

34. *Condemns* racist South Africa for sabotaging the Namibian independence talks held in 1984 at Lusaka and Mindelo by insisting on the notorious "linkage" precondition and introducing new insidious subterfuge as alternatives to Security Council resolution 435(1978);

35. *Condemns and rejects* the puppet "Multi-Party Conference" as the latest in a series of political stratagems through which Pretoria attempts to impose a neo-colonial settlement in Namibia;

36. *Strongly urges* the Security Council to act decisively against any dilatory manœuvres and fraudulent schemes of the illegal occupation régime aimed at frustrating the legitimate struggle of the Namibian people, under the leadership of the South West Africa People's Organization, for self-determination and national liberation;

37. *Condemns* the increased assistance rendered by the major Western countries and Israel to South Africa in the political, economic, financial and particularly the military and nuclear fields, expresses its conviction that this assistance constitutes a hostile action against the people of Namibia and the front-line States since it is bound to strengthen further the aggressive military machine of the racist régime, and therefore demands that such assistance be immediately terminated;

38. *Denounces* the establishment of the so-called Liaison Office of the United States Government at Windhoek in direct violation of relevant resolutions and decisions of the General Assembly and the Security Council, in particular Council resolutions 283(1970) of 29 July 1970 and 301(1971) of 20 October 1971, and in total disregard of the advisory opinion of the International Court of Justice of 21 June 1971, and calls for its immediate closure and withdrawal;

39. *Calls once again upon* all Governments, especially those which have close links with South Africa, to support, in co-operation with the United Nations Council for Namibia, the actions of the United Nations to defend the national rights of the Namibian people until independence;

40. *Strongly condemns* South Africa for its military build-up in Namibia, its introduction of compulsory military service for Namibians, its recruitment and training of Namibians for tribal armies, its use of mercenaries to suppress the Namibian people and to carry out its military attacks against independent African States, its threats and acts of subversion and aggression against those States and the forcible displacement of Namibians from their homes;

41. *Strongly condemns* South Africa for its recent imposition of military conscription of all Namibian males between seventeen and fifty-five years of age into the occupying colonial army, in yet another sinister attempt to suppress the national liberation struggle of the Namibian people and to force Namibians to kill one another, and declares that all measures taken by racist South Africa by which the illegal occupation régime attempts to enforce military conscription in Namibia are illegal, null and void;

42. *Condemns* the racist régime of South Africa for its use of the territory of Namibia as a staging ground from which to launch acts of subversion, destabilization and aggression against neighbouring African States;

43. *Strongly condemns* South Africa, in particular for its persistent acts of subversion and aggression against Angola, including continued occupation of parts of Angolan territory in gross violation of its sovereignty, and calls upon South Africa to cease all acts of aggression against Angola and withdraw immediately and unconditionally all its troops from that country;

44. *Condemns* the continuing military and nuclear collaboration on the part of certain Western States and Israel with the racist régime of South Africa, in violation of the arms embargo imposed against South Africa under Security Council resolution 418(1977) of 4 November 1977;

45. *Declares* that such collaboration encourages the Pretoria régime in its defiance of the international community and obstructs efforts to eliminate *apartheid* and bring South Africa's illegal occupation of Namibia to an end and calls for immediate cessation of such collaboration;

46. *Calls upon* the Security Council to adopt the necessary measures to tighten the arms embargo imposed against South Africa under Council resolution 418(1977) and to ensure strict compliance with the embargo by all States;

47. *Further calls upon* the Security Council to implement, as a matter of urgency, the recommendations contained in the report of the Security Council Committee established in pursuance of resolution 421(1977);

48. *Expresses its grave concern* at the acquisition of nuclear weapons capability by the racist régime of South Africa and declares that such acquisition constitutes a threat to peace and security in Africa while posing a danger to all mankind;

49. *Strongly condemns* the collusion between South Africa, Israel and certain Western States, particularly the United States of America, in the nuclear field and calls upon France and all other States to refrain from supplying the racist minority régime of South Africa, directly or indirectly, with installations that might enable it to produce uranium, plutonium or other nuclear materials, reactors or military equipment;

50. *Reiterates its call* upon all States to take legislative and other appropriate measures to prevent the recruitment, training and transit of mercenaries for service in Namibia;

51. *Strongly condemns* the illegal occupation régime of South Africa for its massive repression of the people of Namibia and their liberation movement, the South West Africa People's Organization, in an attempt to intimidate and terrorize them into submission;

52. *Demands once again* that South Africa immediately release all Namibian political prisoners, including all those imprisoned or detained under the so-called internal security laws, martial law or any other arbitrary measures, whether such Namibians have been charged or tried or are being held without charge in Namibia or South Africa;

53. *Demands* that South Africa account for all "disappeared" Namibians and release any who are still alive and declares that South Africa shall be liable to compensate the victims, their families and the future lawful Government of an independent Namibia for the losses sustained;

54. *Reaffirms* that the natural resources of Namibia are the inviolable heritage of the Namibian people and expresses its deep concern at the rapid depletion of the natural resources of the Territory, particularly its uranium deposits, as a result of their reckless plunder by South Africa and certain Western and other foreign economic interests, in violation of the pertinent resolutions of the General Assembly and of the Security Council, of the advisory opinion of the International Court of Justice of 21 June 1971 and of Decree No. 1 for the Protection of the Natural Resources of Namibia;

55. *Strongly condemns* the activities of all foreign economic interests operating in Namibia which are illegally exploiting the resources of the Territory and demands that transnational corporations engaged in such exploitation comply with all the relevant resolutions and decisions of the United Nations by immediately refraining from any new investment or any other activity in Namibia, by withdrawing from the Territory and by putting an end to their co-operation with the illegal South African administration;

56. *Declares* that all activities of foreign economic interests in Namibia are illegal under international law and that all the foreign economic interests operating in Namibia are liable to pay damages to the future lawful Government of an independent Namibia;

57. *Requests once again* all Member States, particularly those States whose corporations are engaged in the exploitation of Namibian resources, to take all appropriate measures, including legislation and enforcement action, to ensure the full application of, and compliance by all corporations and individuals within their jurisdiction with, the provisions of Decree No. 1 for the Protection of the Natural Resources of Namibia;

58. *Declares* that, by their depletive exploitation of natural resources and continued accumulation and repatriation of huge profits, the foreign economic, financial and other interests operating in Namibia constitute a major obstacle to its independence;

59. *Calls upon* the Governments of all States, particularly those whose corporations are involved in the mining and processing of Namibian uranium, to take all appropriate measures in compliance with United Nations resolutions and decisions and Decree No. 1 for the Protection of the Natural Resources of Namibia, including the practice of requiring negative certificates of origin, to prohibit State-owned and other corporations, together with their subsidiaries, from dealing in Namibian uranium and from engaging in any uranium-prospecting activities in Namibia;

60. *Urges* the United Nations Council for Namibia, in its capacity as the legal Administering Authority for Namibia until independence, to consider the promulgation of additional decrees and other legislation in order to protect and promote the interest of the people of Namibia and to implement effectively such legislation;

61. *Requests* the Governments of the Federal Republic of Germany, the Netherlands and the United Kingdom of Great Britain and Northern Ireland, which operate the Urenco uranium-enrichment plant, to have Namibian uranium specifically excluded from the Treaty of Almelo, which regulates the activities of Urenco;

62. *Calls upon* all specialized agencies, in particular the International Monetary Fund, to terminate all collaboration with and assistance to the racist régime of South Africa, since such assistance serves to augment the military capability of the Pretoria régime thus enabling it not only to continue the brutal repression in Namibia and South

Africa itself, but also to commit blatant aggression against independent neighbouring States;

63. *Reiterates its request* to all States, pending the imposition of mandatory sanctions against South Africa, to take legislative, administrative and other measures unilaterally and collectively, as appropriate, in order to effectively to isolate South Africa politically, economically, militarily and culturally, in accordance with General Assembly resolutions ES-8/2 and 36/121 B, and 37/233 A of 20 December 1982;

64. *Requests* the United Nations Council for Namibia, in implementation of paragraph 15 of General Assembly resolution ES-8/2 and of the relevant provisions of Assembly resolutions 36/121 B and 37/233 A, to continue to monitor the boycott of South Africa and to submit to the Assembly at its fortieth session a comprehensive report on all contacts between Member States and South Africa, containing an analysis of the information received from Member States and other sources on the continuing political, economic, financial and other relations of States and their economic and other interest groups with South Africa and of measures taken by States to terminate all dealings with the racist régime of South Africa;

65. *Requests* all States to co-operate fully with the United Nations Council for Namibia in the fulfilment of its task concerning the implementation of General Assembly resolutions ES-8/2, 36/121 B and 37/233 A and to report to the Secretary-General by the fortieth session of the Assembly on the measures taken by them in the implementation of those resolutions;

66. *Declares* that the liberation struggle in Namibia is a conflict of an international character in terms of article 1, paragraph 4, of Additional Protocol I to the Geneva Conventions of 12 August 1949 and, in this regard, demands that the Conventions and Additional Protocol I be applied by South Africa, and in particular that all captured freedom fighters be accorded prisoner-of-war status as called for by the Geneva Convention relative to the Treatment of Prisoners of War and Additional Protocol thereto;

67. *Declares* that South Africa's defiance of the United Nations, its illegal occupation of the Territory of Namibia, its war of repression against the Namibian people, its persistent acts of aggression against independent African States, its policies of *apartheid* and its development of nuclear weapons constitute a serious threat to international peace and security;

68. *Strongly urges* the Security Council, in the light of the serious threat to international peace and security posed by South Africa, to respond positively to the overwhelming demand of the international community by immediately imposing comprehensive mandatory sanctions against that country, as provided for in Chapter VII of the Charter of the United Nations;

69. *Requests* the Secretary-General to report to the General Assembly at its fortieth session on the implementation of the present resolution.

General Assembly resolution 39/50 A

12 December 1984   Meeting 97   128-0-25 (recorded vote)

Draft by Council for Namibia (A/39/24); agenda item 29.

Financial implications. ACABQ, A/39/7/Add.13 & Corr.1; 5th Committee, A/39/813; S-G, A/39/C.5/70 & Corr.1 & Add.1.

Meeting numbers. GA 39th session: 4th Committee 15, 19; 5th Committee 46; plenary 78-84, 86, 94, 97.

Recorded vote in Assembly as follows:

In favour: Afghanistan, Albania, Algeria, Angola, Antigua and Barbuda, Argentina, Bahamas, Bahrain, Bangladesh, Barbados, Belize, Benin, Bhutan, Bolivia, Botswana, Brazil, Brunei Darussalam, Bulgaria, Burkina Faso, Burma, Burundi, Byelorussian SSR, Cameroon, Cape Verde, Central African Republic, Chad, China, Colombia, Comoros, Congo, Costa Rica, Cuba, Cyprus, Czechoslovakia, Democratic Kampuchea, Democratic Yemen, Djibouti, Dominica, Dominican Republic, Ecuador, Egypt, El Salvador, Equatorial Guinea, Ethiopia, Fiji, Gabon, Gambia, German Democratic Republic, Ghana, Greece, Guatemala, Guinea, Guinea-Bissau, Guyana, Haiti, Honduras, Hungary, India, Indonesia, Iran, Iraq, Jamaica, Jordan, Kenya, Kuwait, Lao People's Democratic Republic, Lebanon, Lesotho, Liberia, Libyan Arab Jamahiriya, Madagascar, Malaysia, Maldives, Mali, Malta, Mauritania, Mexico, Mongolia, Morocco, Mozambique, Nepal, Nicaragua, Niger, Nigeria, Oman, Pakistan, Panama, Papua New Guinea, Peru, Philippines, Poland, Qatar, Romania, Rwanda, Saint Lucia, Saint Vincent and the Grenadines, Samoa, Sao Tome and Principe, Saudi Arabia, Senegal, Seychelles, Sierra Leone, Singapore, Somalia, Sri Lanka, Sudan, Suriname, Swaziland, Syrian Arab Republic, Thailand, Togo, Trinidad and Tobago, Tunisia, Turkey, Uganda, Ukrainian SSR, USSR, United Arab Emirates, United Republic of Tanzania, Uruguay, Vanuatu, Venezuela, Viet Nam, Yemen, Yugoslavia, Zaire, Zambia, Zimbabwe.

Against: None.

Abstaining: Australia, Austria, Belgium, Canada, Denmark, Finland, France, Germany, Federal Republic of, Grenada, Iceland, Ireland, Italy, Ivory Coast, Japan, Luxembourg, Malawi, Netherlands, New Zealand, Norway, Paraguay, Portugal, Spain, Sweden, United Kingdom, United States.

Also on 12 December, the Assembly adopted resolution 39/50 B by recorded vote.

Implementation of Security Council resolution 435(1978)

The General Assembly,

Indignant at South Africa's refusal to comply with Security Council resolutions 385(1976) of 30 January 1976, 431(1978) of 27 July 1978, 435(1978) of 29 September 1978, 439(1978) of 13 November 1978, 532(1983) of 31 May 1983 and 539(1983) of 28 October 1983 and at its manoeuvres aimed at gaining international recognition for illegitimate groups which it has installed in Namibia, and which are subservient to Pretoria's interests, in order to maintain its policies of domination and exploitation of the people and natural resources of Namibia,

Reaffirming the imperative need to proceed without any further delay with the implementation of Security Council resolution 435(1978), which, together with Council resolution 385(1976), is the only basis for a peaceful settlement of the question of Namibia,

Condemning the attempts by South Africa and the United States of America to continue to deny the Namibian people their inalienable right to self-determination and independence by linking the independence of Namibia with totally irrelevant and extraneous issues,

Reaffirming that the Cuban forces are in Angola by a sovereign act of the Government of Angola, in accordance with the provisions of the Charter of the United Nations, and that the attempts to link their presence in that country with Namibia's independence constitute interference in the internal affairs of Angola,

Reaffirming that the only parties to the conflict in Namibia are, on the one hand, the Namibian people represented by the South West Africa People's Organization, their sole and authentic representative, and, on the other, the racist régime of South Africa, which illegally occupies Namibia,

Recalling its request to the Security Council, in the light of the serious threat to international peace and security posed by South Africa, to respond positively to the overwhelming demand of the international community by immediately imposing comprehensive mandatory sanctions against that country as provided for in Chapter VII of the Charter,

Recalling its call upon all States, in view of the threat to international peace and security posed by South Africa, to impose comprehensive mandatory sanctions against that country in accordance with the provisions of the Charter,

Taking note of the further reports of the Secretary-General dated 19 May 1983, 29 August 1983 and 29 December 1983 concerning the implementation of Security Council resolutions 435(1978) and 439(1978) on the question of Namibia,

1. *Strongly condemns* South Africa for obstructing the implementation of Security Council resolutions 385(1976), 435(1978), 439(1978), 532(1983) and 539(1983) and for its manœuvres, in contravention of those resolutions, designed to consolidate its colonial and neo-colonial interests at the expense of the legitimate aspirations of the Namibian people for genuine self-determination, freedom and national independence in a united Namibia;

2. *Reaffirms* the direct responsibility of the United Nations for Namibia pending its achievement of genuine self-determination and national independence;

3. *Reiterates* that Security Council resolution 435(1978), in which the Council endorsed the United Nations plan for the independence of Namibia, is the only basis for a peaceful settlement of the question of Namibia and demands its immediate and unconditional implementation without qualification, modification or amendment or the introduction of extraneous and irrelevant issues such as "linkage", "parallelism" or "reciprocity" insisted upon by the United States of America and South Africa;

4. *Strongly condemns* racist South Africa for sabotaging the Namibian independence talks held in 1984 at Lusaka and Mindelo by insisting on the notorious "linkage" pre-condition and introducing new insidious subterfuge as alternatives to Security Council resolution 435(1978);

5. *Condemns* the continuing attempts by racist South Africa to set up puppet political institutions and impose an "internal settlement" in Namibia, in defiance of United Nations resolutions and decisions, and, in this context, condemns and rejects the puppet "Multi-Party Conference" as the latest in a series of political stratagems through which Pretoria attempts to impose a neo-colonial settlement in Namibia;

6. *Emphasizes once again* that the only parties to the conflict in Namibia are, on the one hand, the Namibian people represented by the South West Africa People's Organization, their sole and authentic representative, and, on the other, the racist régime of South Africa, which illegally occupies Namibia;

7. *Demands* that South Africa urgently comply fully and unconditionally with the resolutions of the Security Council, in particular resolutions 385(1976) and 435(1978) and subsequent resolutions of the Council relating to Namibia;

8. *Firmly rejects and condemns* the persistent attempts by the United States of America and South Africa to establish a linkage or parallelism between the independence of Namibia and any extraneous and irrelevant issues, in particular the presence of Cuban forces in Angola, and emphasizes unequivocally that all such attempts are designed to delay the decolonization process in Namibia and that they constitute interference in the internal affairs of Angola;

9. *Demands* that racist South Africa and the United States Administration desist from their reprehensible positions in order to allow Namibia to attain its long overdue independence;

10. *Calls upon* all States to condemn and reject any attempt to link the independence of Namibia with extraneous and irrelevant issues;

11. *Expresses its dismay* at the fact that the Security Council has been prevented by its three Western permanent members from adopting effective measures against South Africa in the discharge of its responsibilities for the maintenance of international peace and security, and considers that comprehensive and mandatory sanctions under Chapter VII of the Charter of the United Nations would ensure South Africa's compliance with the decisions of the United Nations;

12. *Requests* the Security Council to exercise its authority with regard to the implementation of its resolutions 385(1976), 435(1978), 532(1983) and 539(1983) so as to bring about the independence of Namibia without further delay, and to act decisively against any dilatory manœuvres and fraudulent schemes of the South African administration in Namibia aimed at frustrating the legitimate struggle of the Namibian people for independence;

13. *Urges* the Security Council to impose comprehensive mandatory sanctions against the racist régime of South Africa under Chapter VII of the Charter, in order to ensure the total cessation of all co-operation with that régime, particularly in the military and nuclear fields, by Governments, corporations, institutions and individuals;

14. *Requests* the Secretary-General to report to the General Assembly at its fortieth session on the implementation of the present resolution.

General Assembly resolution 39/50 B

12 December 1984   Meeting 97   129-0-25 (recorded vote)

Draft by Council for Namibia (A/39/24); agenda item 29.

Financial implications. ACABQ, A/39/7/Add.13 & Corr.1; 5th Committee, A/39/813; S-G, A/39/C.5/70 & Add.1 & Corr.1.

Meeting numbers. GA 39th session: 4th Committee 15, 19; 5th Committee 46; plenary 78-84, 86, 94, 97.

Recorded vote in Assembly as follows:

In favour: Afghanistan, Albania, Algeria, Angola, Antigua and Barbuda, Argentina, Bahamas, Bahrain, Bangladesh, Barbados, Belize, Benin, Bhutan, Bolivia, Botswana, Brazil, Brunei Darussalam, Bulgaria, Burkina Faso, Burma, Burundi, Byelorussian SSR, Cameroon, Cape Verde, Central African Republic, Chad, Chile, China, Colombia, Comoros, Congo, Costa Rica, Cuba, Cyprus, Czechoslovakia, Democratic Kampuchea, Democratic Yemen, Djibouti, Dominica, Dominican Republic, Ecuador, Egypt, El Salvador, Equatorial Guinea, Ethiopia, Fiji, Gabon, Gambia, German Democratic Republic, Ghana, Greece, Guatemala, Guinea, Guinea-Bissau, Guyana, Haiti, Honduras, Hungary, India, Indonesia, Iran, Iraq, Jamaica, Jordan, Kenya, Kuwait, Lao People's Democratic Republic, Lebanon, Lesotho, Liberia, Libyan Arab Jamahiriya, Madagascar, Malaysia, Maldives, Mali, Malta, Mauritania, Mexico, Mongolia, Morocco, Mozambique, Nepal, Nicaragua, Niger, Nigeria, Oman, Pakistan, Panama, Papua New Guinea, Peru, Philippines, Poland, Qatar, Romania, Rwanda, Saint Lucia, Saint Vincent and the Grenadines, Samoa, Sao Tome and Principe, Saudi Arabia, Senegal, Seychelles, Sierra Leone, Singapore, Somalia, Sri Lanka, Sudan, Suriname, Swaziland, Syrian Arab Republic, Thailand, Togo, Trinidad and Tobago, Tunisia, Turkey, Uganda, Ukrainian SSR, USSR, United Arab Emirates, United Republic of Tanzania, Uruguay, Vanuatu, Venezuela, Viet Nam, Yemen, Yugoslavia, Zaire, Zambia, Zimbabwe.

Against: None.

Abstaining: Australia, Austria, Belgium, Canada, Denmark, Finland, France, Germany, Federal Republic of, Grenada, Iceland, Ireland, Italy, Ivory Coast, Japan, Luxembourg, Malawi, Netherlands, New Zealand, Norway, Paraguay, Portugal, Spain, Sweden, United Kingdom, United States.

After the drafts recommended by the Council for Namibia were introduced, the United States, stating that direct and inaccurate references to particular Member States in the texts were contrary to the principles of civility and fairness, put forward amendments to a number of paragraphs of the two texts which were rejected by separate recorded votes.

Prior to the votes, the Assembly had decided, as suggested by Guyana, that, to be adopted, the amendments would require a two-thirds majority, since under Article 18 of the Charter of the United Nations they were considered an important question.

Under the proposed amendments to resolution 39/50 A, changes would have been made to five paragraphs. In the seventeenth preambular paragraph, the reference to the United States veto would have been deleted (the vote was 55 to 65, with 25 abstentions); similarly, in the twentieth preambular paragraph, the references to the United States and Israel would have been omitted (57 to 63, with 22 abstentions). By the proposed amendment to paragraph 21, the Assembly would have rejected attempts by South Africa to establish linkage between Namibia and extraneous issues, rather than attempts by South Africa and the United States to do so (56 to 60, with 29 abstentions). Paragraph 38, by which the Assembly denounced the establishment of a liaison office of the United States in Windhoek, would have been omitted (45 to 65, with 32 abstentions). Finally, the mention of Israel in paragraph 49 would also have been deleted (54 to 66, with 23 abstentions).

The United States also proposed amendments to resolution 39/50 B, by which mention of it would have been removed. The proposed change to the third preambular paragraph was rejected by a vote of 58 in favour, 60 against and 30 abstentions. The change to paragraph 3 was rejected by 53 to 67, with 27 abstentions; the proposal on paragraph 8 was defeated by 55 to 62, with 30 abstentions; and the proposal on paragraph 9 was rejected by 59 to 54, with 30 abstentions.

Countries explained their general reservations on the five resolutions on Namibia (39/50 A-E); in addition, some made specific comments on certain provisions of the five texts.

Most of those expressing reservations objected to the selective or arbitrary singling out of certain States or groups of States for condemnation. Argentina, Australia, Austria, Burma, the Central African Republic, Chad, Chile, Colombia, Denmark (for the five Nordic countries), Honduras, Ireland (for the EEC countries), Japan, Liberia, Malawi, the Netherlands, Peru, Portugal, Senegal, Sri Lanka, Turkey and Vanuatu made such statements. Chad, for example, did not think that condemnation by name would facilitate a solution and believed it would be judicious not to discourage those States which, like the United States, were approaching South Africa

in order to induce it to grant independence to Namibia. Liberia considered those paragraphs arbitrarily singling out a few countries for exposure, criticism and condemnation, while deliberately shielding others which were co-operating with South Africa, to be divisive and self-defeating. Senegal favoured most of the proposed amendments because it believed that objectivity and credibility required that condemnations be total rather than selective and that the texts would remain valid in the absence of selectivity. The Bahamas felt that name-calling was sometimes necessary, but repetitious and inconsistent references tended to compromise the balance of the texts and their possible future efficacy.

Brazil, Portugal, Senegal and Vanuatu had objections to some of the language in the texts. Brazil said that certain paragraphs used language which could not be considered as a positive contribution to the objective of achieving Namibia's independence. Ireland (for the EEC countries), Liberia, Malta and Vanuatu regretted that the drafters had not attempted to achieve a consensus. Vanuatu added that independence could be achieved with the support of a broad international constituency.

Reservations were expressed by Austria, Chile and Denmark (for the Nordic countries) about the Assembly making recommendations on measures that fell within the competence of the Security Council. In that regard, several countries raised objections to the Assembly's request that States, pending the imposition of mandatory sanctions against South Africa, take such measures to isolate it. Lesotho had difficulties with those paragraphs which invoked Chapter VII of the United Nations Charter, dealing with action with respect to threats to and breaches of the peace, and acts of aggression. Because of its geographical predicament and its belief in the policy of contact and dialogue, Malawi was unable to support the policy of isolating South Africa and sanctions against it; similarly, Swaziland said it had reservations on economic sanctions. Mozambique supported the imposition of sanctions, but it was not in a position to do so itself. The Netherlands did not agree with the call for the total isolation of South Africa because such measures would run counter to the objective of seeking international agreement on Namibia's independence. Belgium, too, was against breaking off all relations.

Australia, Austria, Belgium, Denmark (for the Nordic countries), Ireland (for the EEC) and the Netherlands objected to the references to SWAPO as the sole and authentic representative of the Namibian people since that organization had not been so elected. According to Austria, the Assembly should not prejudge the free and democratic political expression of the Namibian people.

Australia, Belgium, Denmark (for the Nordic countries), Ireland (for the EEC), the Netherlands and Swaziland did not accept armed struggle as a means to independence. The Nordic countries opposed endorsing armed struggle since they supported peaceful solutions to international problems; for the same reason, they could not support calls for military assistance to SWAPO. Australia, Chile and the Netherlands were opposed to excluding South Africa from international organizations to pressure it to accept Namibia's independence. Australia pointed out that it was through such membership that South Africa was confronted with the international opposition to its unacceptable policies in relation to *apartheid* and Namibia. Chile believed the mention of technical financial bodies was counter to their constitutional autonomies, which were based on purely technical considerations.

Concerns about the financial implications of the resolutions were expressed by Denmark (for the Nordic countries), the Federal Republic of Germany and Ireland (for the EEC).

Canada, France, the Federal Republic of Germany, the United Kingdom and the United States—the Western contact group—said they abstained on all five resolutions (39/50 A-E) because they might be involved in future negotiations concerning implementation of resolution 435(1978)[5] and did not want to prejudge the outcome of any such negotiations.

Ireland (for the EEC) said the texts did not take fully into consideration efforts which the Ten had supported, such as those of the Secretary-General, aimed at bringing about a solution to the question in accordance with resolution 435(1978). Malta said that its positive votes on the texts did not imply that it was in full accord with every provision, particularly resolution 39/50 A.

Several other countries mentioned reservations regarding specific paragraphs in resolution 39/50 A.

In regard to the seventeenth preambular paragraph, the United States said it was objectionable that the argument was made that, as a result of its veto to defeat sanctions against South Africa, armed aggression against Angola continued; that the United States was the direct cause of that aggression was not true; also, successful efforts undertaken by the United States to achieve an end to the South African intervention were ignored. The United States also disagreed with paragraph 38 by which the Assembly denounced the establishment of the liaison office at Windhoek since that office was opened as a direct result of the Angola–South Africa Lusaka agreements so that United States representatives could participate in the Joint Monitoring Commission at the request of the parties in order to facilitate the withdrawal of South African troops from southern Angola (see p. 184); the office was in no way accredited to the South African Government or to the authorities in Namibia and was entirely consistent with United Nations resolutions.

Angola opposed all the United States amendments, particularly that in paragraph 38 of resolution 39/50 A, as it rejected the allegation that there was any kind of understanding with the United States to establish the so-called liaison office.

The Bahamas expressed reservations about the seventeenth preambular paragraph because it called into question the Security Council's rules and procedures; its vote against the amendment to paragraph 38 was determined by its belief that until Namibia achieved independence no foreign Government should establish any representative office in that country, particularly since Namibia was being administered by the Council for Namibia.

Chile objected to bringing to the Assembly, in respect of the Namibia question, accusations that would be better placed in the context of the East-West conflict to be debated in other forums; a case in point was paragraph 14, which it said was selective with regard to the general responsibility that Security Council members bore for the maintenance of international peace and security. Reservations were expressed by Turkey about references to the Western countries in the seventeenth, twentieth and twenty-third preambular paragraphs and in paragraphs 14, 21 and 49.

Among those expressing specific reservations about provisions of resolution 39/50 B, Belgium said that it could not accept the unjustified attacks on the United States and the criticism directed at other Western members of the Security Council. Similarly, Turkey disapproved of the mention by name of a Western country and all the countries of that region in the third preambular paragraph and in operative paragraphs 3, 9 and 11. The Netherlands said that the exercise by the Namibians of their right to self-determination and independence should not be impeded because of the situation in a neighbouring country; that independence remained the essential and primary responsibility of the United Nations which must take precedence over other considerations.

Earlier, on 3 September, the Assembly, which had decided to consider the Namibia question directly in plenary meetings, decided that hearings of concerned organizations would be held in the Fourth Committee.

By a letter of 2 October to the Chairman of the Fourth Committee,[39] the representative of Amnesty International at the United Nations requested such a hearing. The Committee granted that request and heard the representative's statement on 13 November.[40]

The Assembly took related action in resolution 39/17, by which it called for the implementation of the declarations and programmes of action on Namibia adopted by international conferences on the question, reaffirmed its condemnation of South

Africa's illegal occupation, condemned its oppression of the Namibian people and the militarization of Namibia, condemned its attempts to dismember the Territory, demanded the implementation of the 1981 Assembly resolution calling on States to adopt sanctions against South Africa,[41] and urged States and organizations to support the Namibians, through SWAPO, in their struggle to gain independence.

In resolution 39/21, the Assembly encouraged the Council for Namibia in its endeavours towards eliminating *apartheid* from the Territory and attaining independence for the Namibian people. The Assembly, in resolution 39/91, requested States to withhold all assistance from South Africa until the Namibian people achieved independence, within a united Namibia including Walvis Bay, and to refrain from actions which might imply recognition of the legitimacy of that régime's occupation of Namibia. States were urged to provide moral and material assistance to the Namibian people.

Work programme of the UN Council for Namibia

On 12 December, the General Assembly adopted resolution 39/50 C by recorded vote.

Programme of work of the United Nations Council for Namibia

The General Assembly,

Having examined the report of the United Nations Council for Namibia,

Reaffirming that Namibia is the direct responsibility of the United Nations and that the Namibian people must be enabled to attain self-determination and independence in a united Namibia,

Recalling its resolution 2248(S-V) of 19 May 1967, by which it established the United Nations Council for Namibia as the legal Administering Authority for Namibia until independence,

Taking into consideration the Bangkok Declaration and Programme of Action on Namibia, adopted by the United Nations Council for Namibia on 25 May 1984 at its extraordinary plenary meetings held at Bangkok,

Convinced of the need for continued consultations with the South West Africa People's Organization in the formulation and implementation of the programme of work of the United Nations Council for Namibia, as well as in any matter of interest to the Namibian people,

Deeply conscious of the urgent and continuing need to press for the termination of South Africa's illegal occupation of Namibia and to put an end to its repression of the Namibian people and its exploitation of the natural resources of the Territory,

1. *Approves* the report of the United Nations Council for Namibia, including the recommendations contained therein, and decides to make adequate financial provision for their implementation;

2. *Expresses its strong support* for the efforts of the United Nations Council for Namibia in the discharge of the responsibilities entrusted to it both as the legal Administering Authority for Namibia and as a policy-making organ of the United Nations;

3. *Requests* all Member States to co-operate fully with the United Nations Council for Namibia in the discharge

of the mandate entrusted to it under the provisions of General Assembly resolution 2248(S-V) and subsequent resolutions of the Assembly;

4. *Decides* that the United Nations Council for Namibia, in the discharge of its responsibilities as the legal Administering Authority for Namibia until independence, shall:

(a) Continue to mobilize international support in order to press for the speedy withdrawal of the illegal South African administration from Namibia in accordance with the resolutions of the United Nations relating to Namibia;

(b) Counter the policies of South Africa against the Namibian people and against the United Nations, as well as against the United Nations Council for Namibia as the legal Administering Authority for Namibia;

(c) Denounce and seek the rejection by all States of all fraudulent constitutional or political schemes through which South Africa may attempt to perpetuate its presence in Namibia;

(d) Ensure non-recognition of any administration or entity installed at Windhoek not issuing from free elections in Namibia conducted under the supervision and control of the United Nations, in accordance with the relevant resolutions of the Security Council, in particular resolution 439(1978) of 13 November 1978;

(e) Undertake a concerted effort to counter the attempts to establish linkage or parallelism between the independence of Namibia and extraneous issues such as the withdrawal of Cuban forces from Angola;

5. *Decides further* that, in pursuance of the aforementioned objectives, the United Nations Council for Namibia shall:

(a) Consult Governments in order to further the implementation of United Nations resolutions on the question of Namibia and to mobilize support for the cause of Namibia;

(b) Represent Namibia in United Nations conferences and intergovernmental and non-governmental organizations, bodies and conferences to ensure that the rights and interests of Namibia shall be adequately protected;

6. *Decides* that Namibia, represented by the United Nations Council for Namibia, shall participate as a full member in all conferences and meetings organized by the United Nations to which all States or, in the case of regional conferences and meetings, all African States are invited;

7. *Requests* all committees and other subsidiary bodies of the General Assembly and of the Economic and Social Council to continue to invite a representative of the United Nations Council for Namibia to participate whenever the rights and interests of Namibians are discussed, and to consult closely with the Council before submitting any draft resolution which may involve the rights and interests of Namibians;

8. *Reiterates its request* to all specialized agencies and other organizations and institutions of the United Nations system to grant full membership to Namibia, represented by the United Nations Council for Namibia, so that the Council may participate as the legal Administering Authority for Namibia in the work of those agencies, organizations and institutions;

9. *Reiterates its request* to all specialized agencies and other organizations of the United Nations system that have not yet done so to grant a waiver of the assessment of Namibia during the period in which it is represented by the United Nations Council for Namibia;

10. *Again requests* all intergovernmental organizations, bodies and conferences to ensure that the rights and interests of Namibia are protected and to invite Namibia, represented by the United Nations Council for Namibia, to participate as a full member whenever such rights and interests are involved;

11. *Requests* the United Nations Council for Namibia, in its capacity as the legal Administering Authority for Namibia, to accede to any international conventions as it may deem appropriate;

12. *Takes note* of the final communiqués issued by the regional symposia and seminars organized by the United Nations Council for Namibia in 1984;

13. *Requests* the United Nations Council for Namibia to promote and secure the implementation of the Bangkok Programme of Action on Namibia;

14. *Decides* that the United Nations Council for Namibia shall:

(a) Consult regularly with the leadership of the South West Africa People's Organization by inviting them to New York and by sending high-level missions to the headquarters of that organization, as it deems appropriate, in order to review the progress of the liberation struggle in Namibia;

(b) Review the progress of the liberation struggle in Namibia in its political, military and social aspects and prepare periodic reports related thereto;

(c) Consider the compliance of Member States with the relevant United Nations resolutions relating to Namibia, taking into account the advisory opinion of the International Court of Justice of 21 June 1971;

(d) Consider the activities of foreign economic interests operating in Namibia with a view to recommending appropriate policies to the General Assembly in order to counter the support which those foreign economic interests give to the illegal South African administration in Namibia;

(e) Continue to examine the exploitation of and trade in Namibian uranium by foreign economic interests and report on its findings to the General Assembly at its fortieth session;

(f) Notify the Governments of States whose corporations, whether public or private, operate in Namibia of the illegality of such operations;

(g) Send missions of consultation to Governments of States whose corporations have investments in Namibia in order to review with them all possible action to discourage the continuation of such investments;

(h) Contact administering and managing bodies of corporations, tanker companies and other shipping interests involved in the illicit transportation and/or supply of petroleum and petroleum products to South Africa and Namibia;

(i) Contact specialized agencies and other international institutions associated with the United Nations, in particular the International Monetary Fund, with a view to protecting Namibia's interests;

(j) Draw the attention of the specialized agencies to Decree No. 1 for the Protection of the Natural Resources of Namibia, enacted by the United Nations Council for Namibia on 27 September 1974;

(k) Take all measures to ensure compliance with the provisions of Decree No. 1 for the Protection of the Natural Resources of Namibia, including consideration of the institution of legal proceedings in the domestic courts of States and other appropriate bodies;

(l) Conduct hearings, seminars and workshops in order to obtain relevant information on all aspects of the situation in and relating to Namibia, in particular, the exploitation of the people and resources of Namibia by South African and other foreign interests, and to expose such activities;

(m) Organize regional symposia on the situation in Namibia with a view to intensifying active support for the Namibian cause;

(n) Prepare and publish reports on the political, economic, military, legal and social situation in and relating to Namibia;

(o) Secure the territorial integrity of Namibia as a unitary State, including Walvis Bay and the offshore islands of Namibia;

15. *Decides* to make adequate financial provision in the section of the programme budget of the United Nations relating to the United Nations Council for Namibia to finance the office of the South West Africa People's Organization in New York in order to ensure appropriate representation of the people of Namibia at the United Nations through the South West Africa People's Organization;

16. *Decides* to continue to defray the expenses of representatives of the South West Africa People's Organization, whenever the United Nations Council for Namibia so decides;

17. *Requests* the United Nations Council for Namibia to continue to consult with the South West Africa People's Organization in the formulation and implementation of its programme of work, as well as in any matter of interest to the Namibian people;

18. *Requests* the United Nations Council for Namibia to facilitate the participation of the liberation movements, recognized by the Organization of African Unity, in meetings of the Council away from Headquarters, whenever such participation is deemed necessary;

19. *Requests* the United Nations Council for Namibia, in the discharge of its responsibilities as the legal Administering Authority for Namibia, to hold a series of plenary meetings in Western Europe during 1985 and to recommend appropriate action to the General Assembly in the light of South Africa's refusal to implement Security Council resolution 435(1978) of 29 September 1978;

20. *Requests* the Secretary-General to defray the cost of the plenary meetings of the United Nations Council for Namibia and to provide the necessary staff and services for them;

21. *Decides* that, in order to expedite training of the personnel required for an independent Namibia, qualified Namibians should be given opportunities to develop further their skills in the work of the United Nations Secretariat and the specialized agencies and other organizations of the United Nations system, and authorizes the United Nations Council for Namibia, in consultation with the South West Africa People's Organization, to take, on an urgent basis, necessary action towards that end;

22. *Requests* the Secretary-General, in consultation with the President of the United Nations Council for Namibia, to review the requirements of personnel and facilities of all units which service the Council so that the Council may fully and effectively discharge all tasks and functions arising out of its mandate;

23. *Requests* the Secretary-General to provide the Office of the United Nations Commissioner for Namibia with

the necessary resources in order for it to strengthen, under the guidance of the United Nations Council for Namibia, the assistance programmes and services for Namibians, the implementation of Decree No. 1 for the Protection of the Natural Resources of Namibia, the preparation of economic and legal studies and the existing activities of dissemination of information undertaken by the Office.

General Assembly resolution 39/50 C

12 December 1984   Meeting 97   148-0-7 (recorded vote)

Draft by Council for Namibia (A/39/24); agenda item 29.
Financial implications. ACABQ, A/39/7/Add.13 & Corr.1; 5th Committee, A/39/813; S-G, A/39/C.5/39/70 & Add.1 & Corr.1.
Meeting numbers. GA 39th session: 4th Committee 15, 19; 5th Committee 46; plenary 78-84, 86, 94, 97.

Recorded vote in Assembly as follows:

In favour: Afghanistan, Albania, Algeria, Angola, Antigua and Barbuda, Argentina, Australia, Austria, Bahamas, Bahrain, Bangladesh, Barbados, Belgium, Belize, Benin, Bhutan, Bolivia, Botswana, Brazil, Brunei Darussalam, Bulgaria, Burkina Faso, Burma, Burundi, Byelorussian SSR, Cameroon, Cape Verde, Central African Republic, Chad, Chile, China, Colombia, Comoros, Congo, Costa Rica, Cuba, Cyprus, Czechoslovakia, Democratic Kampuchea, Democratic Yemen, Denmark, Djibouti, Dominica, Dominican Republic, Ecuador, Egypt, El Salvador, Equatorial Guinea, Ethiopia, Fiji, Finland, Gabon, Gambia, German Democratic Republic, Ghana, Greece, Guatemala, Guinea, Guinea-Bissau, Guyana, Haiti, Honduras, Hungary, Iceland, India, Indonesia, Iran, Iraq, Ireland, Italy, Ivory Coast, Jamaica, Japan, Jordan, Kenya, Kuwait, Lao People's Democratic Republic, Lebanon, Lesotho, Liberia, Libyan Arab Jamahiriya, Luxembourg, Madagascar, Malawi, Malaysia, Maldives, Mali, Malta, Mauritania, Mauritius, Mexico, Mongolia, Morocco, Mozambique, Nepal, Netherlands, New Zealand, Nicaragua, Niger, Nigeria, Norway, Oman, Pakistan, Panama, Papua New Guinea, Peru, Philippines, Poland, Portugal, Qatar, Romania, Rwanda, Saint Lucia, Saint Vincent and the Grenadines, Samoa, Sao Tome and Principe, Saudi Arabia, Senegal, Seychelles, Sierra Leone, Singapore, Somalia, Spain, Sri Lanka, Sudan, Suriname, Swaziland, Sweden, Syrian Arab Republic, Thailand, Togo, Trinidad and Tobago, Tunisia, Turkey, Uganda, Ukrainian SSR, USSR, United Arab Emirates, United Republic of Tanzania, Uruguay, Vanuatu, Venezuela, Viet Nam, Yemen, Yugoslavia, Zaire, Zambia, Zimbabwe.
Against: None.
Abstaining: Canada, France, Germany, Federal Republic of, Grenada, Paraguay, United Kingdom, United States.

In explanation of vote, Japan said that its positive vote should not be construed as support for all paragraphs; as in previous years, it had reservations on parts of the Council's report. For the Netherlands, the request to the Council, in paragraph 19, to hold 1985 meetings away from Headquarters would require considerable additional cost in return for a questionable benefit; furthermore, it did not agree that the Council must enjoy the same rights in international organizations as those reserved for States. Belgium also had strong reservations on the financial implications of the resolution.

Information dissemination

In 1984, the Council for Namibia continued its activities aimed at disseminating information to Governments, organizations and directly to the public in order to mobilize world public opinion in support of independence for Namibia.[2] In these efforts, the Council acted through its Standing Committee III which co-operated with the Department of Public Information (DPI) of the Secretariat and with NGOs supporting the Namibian cause and opposing *apartheid*, and disseminated information to leading opinion makers, the media,

political and academic institutions and cultural organizations.

The Council organized publicity for its symposia, seminars and missions (see above). Press releases were disseminated to the press, delegations and NGOs at Headquarters and to United Nations information centres (UNICs) around the world, and material was provided to the pool of non-aligned news agencies. On the occasion of Namibia Day (26 August) and the Week of Solidarity with the People of Namibia and Their Liberation Movement, SWAPO (week of 29 October), coverage was provided in press releases, radio and television, and by a special photographic exhibit at Headquarters. For those two events, most UNICs issued press releases and organized activities such as screenings of United Nations films, lectures and round-tables on the United Nations role in the liberation of Namibia, press conferences and television interviews. Pamphlets were issued on the military situation in Namibia and on social conditions there. A series of six 15-minute radio programmes (in English, French and Spanish), entitled *Namibia: Update*, and three programmes of the feature series *Perspective* dealing exclusively with Namibia were produced.

The Department continued to give film, television and photo coverage of the Council's activities to news syndicators. It also distributed 25 television news packages and filmed 260 metres of archival material. Some 140 copies of the films *Free Namibia* and *Namibia: A Trust Betrayed* were distributed through UNICs and the Office of the Commissioner for Namibia. DPI organized five journalists' encounters in advance of the Council's symposia, seminars and extraordinary plenary meetings. The encounters—discussions between a panel of the Council and 15 journalists and broadcasters approved by the Council, as well as some local and foreign-based journalists—focused on specific aspects of the Namibia question and on the role of the media in generating greater public awareness of the Namibian cause and promoting the implementation of United Nations resolutions on the issue. The President of the Council addressed the Inter-Regional Mass Media Leaders' Round-table on the Problems of Southern Africa (Arusha, 26-28 March), which was attended by approximately 30 media leaders.

As part of its co-operation with NGOs to intensify the efforts of the international community to bring about Namibia's independence, the Council made financial contributions to seven such organizations for their publicity campaigns. DPI held several briefings on developments in Namibia for non-governmental and other organizations.

The Office of the Commissioner for Namibia served as an additional source of information and assisted the Council in many activities, including publication and distribution of United Nations and other materials on Namibia. It prepared the *Namibia Bulletin*, a quarterly review and analysis of events relating to Namibia issued in English, French, German and Spanish, and *Namibia in the News*, a weekly newsletter. The Office also gave briefings to support groups on the Council's activities. At the Asia and Pacific Mass Media Leaders' Round Table (Shanghai, China, 30 April–3 May), the Commissioner discussed Namibia and southern Africa. UNICs at Copenhagen, Brussels, Dar es Salaam, Paris and Vienna arranged for press conferences when the Commissioner visited the respective countries.

In its Bangkok Declaration and Programme of Action, the Council emphasized the importance of action by local authorities, trade unions, religious bodies, academic institutions, mass media, solidarity movements and other NGOs, as well as individuals, in mobilizing public opinion, particularly in Western countries, in support of the Namibian liberation struggle. The Council stated it would intensify efforts to mobilize international public opinion and to expose the intransigence of the South African régime and its flouting of United Nations resolutions. The Council appealed to NGOs to increase awareness of their national communities regarding the exploitation of Namibian resources by foreign economic interests (see below), and to insist that they withdraw from Namibia. NGOs were urged to campaign in their countries in support of sanctions in order to isolate South Africa. The Council appealed to the media to intensify the dissemination of information on Namibia's struggle for independence and said DPI should try to reach a wider audience, particularly in countries where information was lacking or available in distorted form.

The Committee on colonial countries, in a decision of 20 August,[34] repeated its request that the Secretary-General, in view of the publicity campaign by South Africa to gain support for its occupation of Namibia, intensify his efforts, through all available media, to mobilize world public opinion against South Africa's policy on Namibia and, in particular, to increase dissemination of information on the liberation struggle. The Committee also emphasized the importance of action by all in mobilizing Governments and public opinion, particularly in the Western countries.

GENERAL ASSEMBLY ACTION

On 12 December, the General Assembly adopted resolution 39/50 D by recorded vote.

Dissemination of information and mobilization of international public opinion in support of Namibia

The General Assembly,

Having examined the report of the United Nations Council for Namibia and the relevant chapters of the report of the Special Committee on the Situation with regard to the Implementation of the Declaration on the Granting of Independence to Colonial Countries and Peoples,

Recalling its resolutions 2145(XXI) of 27 October 1966, 2248(S-V) of 19 May 1967 and 38/36 A to E of 1 December 1983, as well as all other resolutions of the General Assembly and the Security Council relating to Namibia,

Taking into consideration the Paris Declaration on Namibia and the report of the Committee of the Whole and the Programme of Action on Namibia,

Taking into consideration the Bangkok Declaration and Programme of Action on Namibia, adopted by the United Nations Council for Namibia on 25 May 1984 at its extraordinary plenary meetings held at Bangkok,

Taking into consideration also the conclusions and recommendations adopted at the Regional Symposium in Support of the Namibian Cause in Latin America, held at San José from 16 to 19 August 1983, the Regional Symposium on South Africa's Illegal Occupation of Namibia: The Threat to International Peace and Security, held at Arusha, United Republic of Tanzania, from 2 to 5 April 1984,[42] the Seminar on the Activities of Foreign Economic Interests in the Exploitation of Namibia's Natural and Human Resources, held at Ljubljana, Yugoslavia, from 16 to 20 April 1984, the Seminar on the Efforts by the International Community to End South Africa's Illegal Occupation of Namibia, held at Montreal, Canada, from 23 to 27 July 1984, and the Regional Symposium on International Efforts to Implement Decree No. 1 for the Protection of the Natural Resources of Namibia, held at Geneva from 27 to 31 August 1984,[43]

Deploring the continued assistance rendered by Israel and certain Western States, especially the United States of America, to South Africa in the political, economic, military and cultural fields and expressing its conviction that this assistance should be exposed by the United Nations Council for Namibia by all means available to it,

Stressing the urgent need to mobilize international public opinion on a continuous basis with a view to assisting effectively the people of Namibia in the achievement of self-determination, freedom and independence in a united Namibia and, in particular, to intensify the world-wide and continuous dissemination of information on the struggle for liberation being waged by the people of Namibia under the leadership of the South West Africa People's Organization, their sole and authentic representative,

Recognizing the important role that non-governmental organizations are playing in the dissemination of information on Namibia and in the mobilization of international public opinion in support of the Namibian cause,

Reiterating the importance of publicity as an instrument for furthering the mandate given by the General Assembly to the United Nations Council for Namibia and mindful of the pressing need for the Department of Public Information of the Secretariat to intensify its efforts to acquaint world public opinion with all aspects of the question of Namibia, in accordance with policy guidelines formulated by the Council,

1. *Requests* the United Nations Council for Namibia, in pursuance of its international campaign in support of the struggle of the Namibian people for independence, to continue to consider ways and means of increasing the dissemination of information relating to Namibia;

2. *Requests* the Secretary-General to ensure that the Department of Public Information of the Secretariat, in all its activities of dissemination of information on the

question of Namibia, follows the policy guidelines laid down by the United Nations Council for Namibia as the legal Administering Authority for Namibia;

3. *Requests* the Secretary-General to direct the Department of Public Information, in addition to its responsibilities relating to southern Africa, to assist, as a matter of priority, the United Nations Council for Namibia in the implementation of its programme of dissemination of information in order that the United Nations may intensify its efforts to generate publicity and disseminate information with a view to mobilizing public support for the independence of Namibia, particularly in the Western States;

4. *Requests* the United Nations Council for Namibia to continue to organize journalists' encounters prior to the activities of the Council during 1985, in order to mobilize further international public support for the just struggle of the Namibian people under the leadership of the South West Africa People's Organization, their sole and authentic representative;

5. *Decides* to intensify its international campaign in support of the cause of Namibia and to expose and denounce the collusion of the United States of America, certain other Western countries and Israel with the South African racists and, to this end, requests the United Nations Council for Namibia to include in its programme of dissemination of information for 1985 the following activities:

(a) Preparation and dissemination of publications on the political, economic, military and social consequences of the illegal occupation of Namibia by South Africa, as well as on legal matters, on the question of the territorial integrity of Namibia and on contacts between Member States and South Africa;

(b) Production and dissemination of radio programmes in the English, French, German and Spanish languages designed to draw the attention of world public opinion to the current situation in and around Namibia;

(c) Production of material for publicity through radio and television broadcasts;

(d) Placement of advertisements in newspapers and magazines;

(e) Production of films, film-strips and slide sets on Namibia;

(f) Production and dissemination of posters;

(g) Full utilization of the resources related to press releases, press conferences and press briefings in order to maintain a constant flow of information to the public on all aspects of the question of Namibia;

(h) Production and dissemination of a comprehensive economic map of Namibia;

(i) Production and dissemination of booklets on the activities of the Council;

(j) Preparation and wide dissemination of a booklet containing resolutions of the General Assembly and the Security Council relating to Namibia, together with relevant portions of Assembly resolutions on the activities of foreign economic interests in Namibia and on military activities in Namibia;

(k) Publicity for and distribution of an indexed reference book on transnational corporations which plunder the natural and human resources of Namibia, and on the profits extracted from the Territory;

(l) Preparation and dissemination of a booklet based on a study on the implementation of Decree No. 1 for the Protection of the Natural Resources of Namibia, enacted by the Council on 27 September 1974;

(m) Acquisition of books, pamphlets and other materials relating to Namibia for further dissemination;

6. *Requests* the United Nations Council for Namibia to organize an international conference at United Nations Headquarters in 1985 with the participation of prominent personalities, parliamentarians, scholars, support groups and others from all parts of the world, in order to mobilize and strengthen further international support for the just cause and heroic struggle of the Namibian people, led by their sole and authentic representative, the South West Africa People's Organization;

7. *Requests* the Secretary-General to allocate, in consultation with the United Nations Council for Namibia, sales numbers to publications on Namibia selected by the Council;

8. *Requests* the Secretary-General to provide the United Nations Council for Namibia with the work programme of the Department of Public Information for the year 1985 covering the activities of dissemination of information on Namibia, followed by periodic reports on the programmes undertaken, including details of expenses incurred;

9. *Requests* the Secretary-General to group under a single heading, in the section of the proposed programme budget of the United Nations for the biennium 1986-1987 relating to the Department of Public Information, all the activities of the Department relating to the dissemination of information on Namibia, and to direct the Department of Public Information to present to the United Nations Council for Namibia a detailed report on the utilization of the allocated funds;

10. *Requests* the Secretary-General to direct the Department of Public Information to disseminate the list of prisoners in Namibia;

11. *Requests* the Secretary-General to direct the Department of Public Information to give the widest possible publicity and to disseminate information on the commemoration of a century of heroic struggle of the Namibian people against colonial occupation;

12. *Requests* Member States to broadcast programmes on their national radio and television networks and to publish material in their official news media, informing their populations about the situation in and around Namibia and the obligation of Governments and peoples to assist in the struggle of Namibia for independence;

13. *Requests* the United Nations Council for Namibia, in co-operation with the Department of Public Information and the Department of Conference Services of the Secretariat, to continue to inform and provide information material to leading opinion makers, media leaders, academic institutions, trade unions, cultural organizations, support groups and other concerned persons and non-governmental organizations about the objectives and functions of the United Nations Council for Namibia and the struggle of the Namibian people under the leadership of the South West Africa People's Organization and also to hold consultations with, and seek the co-operation of, those personalities and institutions by inviting them on special occasions to participate in the deliberations of the Council, and to continue to establish for this purpose a regular and expeditious pattern of distribution of information material to political parties, universities, libraries, churches, students, teachers,

professional associations and others falling into the general categories enumerated above;

14. *Requests* all Member States to commemorate and publicize Namibia Day and to issue special postage stamps for the occasion;

15. *Requests* the Secretary-General to direct the United Nations Postal Administration to issue a special postage stamp on Namibia by the end of 1985 in commemoration of Namibia Day;

16. *Calls upon* the United Nations Council for Namibia to enlist the support of non-governmental organizations in its efforts to mobilize international public opinion in support of the liberation struggle of the Namibian people and of their sole and authentic representative, the South West Africa People's Organization;

17. *Requests* the United Nations Council for Namibia to prepare, update and continually disseminate lists of non-governmental organizations from all over the world, in particular those in the major Western countries, in order to ensure better co-operation and co-ordination among non-governmental organizations working in support of the Namibian cause and against *apartheid*;

18. *Requests* those non-governmental organizations and support groups that are actively engaged in supporting the struggle of the Namibian people under the leadership of the South West Africa People's Organization, their sole and authentic representative, to continue to intensify, in co-operation with the United Nations Council for Namibia, international action in support of the liberation struggle of the Namibian people, including assistance to the Council in the monitoring of the boycott of South Africa called for in General Assembly resolution ES-8/2 of 14 September 1981;

19. *Decides* to allocate the sum of $300,000 to be used by the United Nations Council for Namibia for its programme of co-operation with non-governmental organizations, including support to conferences in solidarity with Namibia arranged by those organizations, dissemination of conclusions of such conferences and support to such other activities as will promote the cause of the liberation struggle of the Namibian people, subject to decisions of the Council in each individual case taken in consultation with the South West Africa People's Organization.

General Assembly resolution 39/50 D

12 December 1984   Meeting 97   130-0-24 (recorded vote)

Draft by Council for Namibia (A/39/24); agenda item 29.

Financial implications. ACABQ, A/39/7/Add.13 & Corr.1; Fifth Committee, A/39/813; S-G, A/39/C.5/39/70 & Corr.1 & Add.1.

Meeting numbers. GA 39th session: 4th Committee 15, 19; 5th Committee 46; plenary 78-84, 86, 94, 97.

Recorded vote in Assembly as follows:

In favour: Afghanistan, Albania, Algeria, Angola, Antigua and Barbuda, Argentina, Bahamas, Bahrain, Bangladesh, Barbados, Belize, Benin, Bhutan, Bolivia, Botswana, Brazil, Brunei Darussalam, Bulgaria, Burkina Faso, Burma, Burundi, Byelorussian SSR, Cameroon, Cape Verde, Central African Republic, Chad, Chile, China, Colombia, Comoros, Congo, Costa Rica, Cuba, Cyprus, Czechoslovakia, Democratic Kampuchea, Democratic Yemen, Djibouti, Dominica, Dominican Republic, Ecuador, Egypt, El Salvador, Equatorial Guinea, Ethiopia, Fiji, Gabon, Gambia, German Democratic Republic, Ghana, Greece, Guatemala, Guinea, Guinea-Bissau, Guyana, Haiti, Honduras, Hungary, India, Indonesia, Iran, Iraq, Jamaica, Jordan, Kenya, Kuwait, Lao People's Democratic Republic, Lebanon, Lesotho, Liberia, Libyan Arab Jamahiriya, Madagascar, Malawi, Malaysia, Maldives, Mali, Malta, Mauritania, Mexico, Mongolia, Morocco, Mozambique, Nepal, Nicaragua, Niger, Nigeria, Oman, Pakistan, Panama, Papua New Guinea, Peru, Philippines, Poland, Qatar, Romania, Rwanda, Saint Lucia, Saint Vincent and the Grenadines, Samoa, Sao Tome and Principe, Saudi Arabia, Senegal, Seychelles, Sierra Leone, Singapore, Somalia, Sri Lanka, Sudan, Suriname, Swaziland, Syrian Arab Republic, Thailand, Togo, Trinidad and Tobago, Tunisia, Turkey, Uganda, Ukrainian SSR, USSR, United Arab Emirates, United Republic of Tanzania, Uruguay, Vanuatu, Venezuela, Viet Nam, Yemen, Yugoslavia, Zaire, Zambia, Zimbabwe.

Against: None.

Abstaining: Australia, Austria, Belgium, Canada, Denmark, Finland, France, Germany, Federal Republic of, Grenada, Iceland, Ireland, Italy, Ivory Coast, Japan, Luxembourg, Netherlands, New Zealand, Norway, Paraguay, Portugal, Spain, Sweden, United Kingdom, United States.

The United States proposed amending the sixth preambular paragraph and paragraph 5 to delete references to itself and Israel. Both amendments were rejected: by votes of 52 in favour to 66 against, with 26 abstentions, and 61 to 63, with 21 abstentions, respectively.

Before the votes, the Assembly had decided that the amendments were important questions and would therefore need a two-thirds majority for adoption (see p. 1040).

Explaining its vote on the text as a whole, Belgium said that the volume of the programme of information dissemination and mobilization was excessive, and that it contained points of view that Belgium did not share. Japan stressed that information to be disseminated must be accurate and fair; it supported close co-operation and co-ordination between the Council for Namibia and DPI so that the latter's facilities would be utilized effectively. Turkey had reservations about the mention of a specific country and group of countries. The Bahamas felt that the language of paragraph 5 failed to show any correlation between the objective thought and the methods to be employed.

UN Commissioner for Namibia

Activities of the Commissioner

The Office of the Commissioner for Namibia continued in 1984 to collect and analyse information on Namibia, including related information on internal political, economic and legal developments in South Africa.[2] The Commissioner, through his offices at Headquarters; Gaborone, Botswana; Luanda, Angola; and Lusaka, Zambia; acted to protect Namibian interests by issuing travel documents through the Council for Namibia and by attempts to implement the 1974 Decree No. 1 for the Protection of the Natural Resources of Namibia, banning extraction of those resources without the Council's consent[12] (see below). From 1 September 1983 to 31 August 1984, the offices issued 1,472 new and renewed travel and identity documents in Africa, 29 in North America and 16 in Western Europe.

As part of its activities to implement Decree No. 1, the Office arranged briefings for NGOs and educational institutions. In March, a representative addressed the John Jay College of Criminal Justice of the City University of New York on Namibia and the Decree's implementation. Pursuant to a 1982 General Assembly resolution,[44] the Office was preparing a reference book on transnational corporations operating or investing in Namibia, to identify foreign commercial and investment practices there and the extent of their exploitation of Namibian resources. It continued work on studies on assistance needs of the front-line States and on economic planning in an independent Namibia. A study analysing the demographic structure and socio-economic characteristics of the Namibian population, including size estimates and growth projections, was completed in May. Concerning the legal situation, the Office prepared: a review of "legislation" promulgated by the illegal administration in Namibia in 1983; a booklet on labour legislation and labour conditions; and a draft booklet on the administration's attempts to devise new "constitutions" from 1968 to 1983.

The Office continued to administer assistance programmes under the United Nations Fund for Namibia (see below), executing 11 projects and preparing project proposals for the Fund's Committee. The Commissioner and his staff met with the SWAPO Co-ordinating Committee on the Nationhood Programme in Lusaka in April 1984 to review the assistance programme for Namibians.

The Luanda Office, which became operational in 1983, served as liaison between the New York Office and SWAPO's provisional headquarters at Luanda. In 1984, the Luanda Office was responsible for 31 projects and was involved in preparing others in consultation with SWAPO and the executing agencies concerned. It facilitated the work of a consultant responsible for a training programme for Namibian broadcasters and assisted in placing Namibians in training programmes in various countries. It also facilitated the travel and participation of SWAPO officials in international meetings and concluded negotiations with Angola regarding the issuance of Council for Namibia travel documents.

The Lusaka Office operated as an administrative office for assistance programmes under the Fund for Namibia, and as a centre for political and information activities in the region. It was responsible for 26 projects, providing support for executing agencies and consultants. From September 1983 to August 1984, several consultancies were completed and three project seminars were held to review draft consultancy reports. Some 63 students completed their training in Zambia, which included labour administration, teacher training and video and cinematography; others continued their training in radio broadcasting, railway operations, soil surveying, labour administration and teacher training.

Implementation of assistance programmes was the main concern of the Gaborone Office, which also continued to monitor developments in southern Africa. It maintained contact with Botswana, SWAPO, UNDP and UNHCR concerning aid to Namibian refugees, particularly at the Dukwe

settlement, and also assisted in placing Namibians in educational institutions.

Appointment of the Commissioner

On 14 December,[45] the Secretary-General proposed to the General Assembly that it extend the appointment of Brajesh Chandra Mishra as United Nations Commissioner for Namibia for one year beginning on 1 January 1985; he had served in that capacity since 1 April 1982.[46]

GENERAL ASSEMBLY ACTION

On the Secretary-General's recommendation, the General Assembly adopted decision 39/325 without vote.

Appointment of the United Nations Commissioner for Namibia

At its 105th plenary meeting, on 18 December 1984, the General Assembly, on the proposal of the Secretary-General, appointed Mr. Brajesh Chandra Mishra as United Nations Commissioner for Namibia for a further one-year term beginning on 1 January 1985.

General Assembly decision 39/325

18 December 1984   Meeting 105   Adopted without vote

Proposal by Secretary-General (A/39/832); agenda item 17 *(j)*.

Political and military aspects

The Council for Namibia continued in 1984 to monitor the political and military aspects of Namibia. The Council's Standing Committee II, in two April reports, reviewed political developments[47] and the military situation.[48] In addition, the Secretariat of the Committee on colonial countries issued a July working paper on military activities and arrangements in Namibia impeding its independence[49] and another in August which described political developments in Namibia from August 1983 to May 1984.[50]

In its annual report,[2] the Council said that South Africa sought to entrench its occupation through militarization of Namibia, brutalization of Namibians, and detention and assassination of SWAPO members and supporters. Refusing to co-operate in the 1978 United Nations independence plan for Namibia, South Africa continued to impose on the Namibian people puppet institutions in contravention of that plan. Following the collapse in 1983 of two internal settlements proposed by South Africa,[51] a third scheme, known as the Multi-Party Conference (MPC), was sponsored by South Africa as an "internal alternative to SWAPO".

On 16 February, Angola and South Africa held high-level talks at Lusaka, and agreed to set up a joint military commission to monitor the disengagement of forces in southern Angola. Subsequently, the United States established a mission in Windhoek to help monitor the disengagement. On 19 March, Cuba and Angola stated their intention to initiate the gradual withdrawal of Cuban forces from Angola as soon as South Africa had withdrawn from Angolan territory, resolution 435(1978)[5] had been implemented, South African aggression against Angola had ceased, and Western aid to counter-revolutionary organizations, such as the União Nacional para a Independência Total de Angola (UNITA), was cut off (see also p. 1031). In April and May, the Prime Minister of South Africa reiterated that his Government would not change its demand for the Cuban withdrawal before granting independence to Namibia. Independence talks between SWAPO, the South African Administrator-General of Namibia and a delegation of MPC took place at Lusaka from 10 to 13 May, the first direct encounter between South Africa and SWAPO since the failure of pre-implementation meetings in Geneva in January 1981.[52] The Lusaka conference ended without agreement on key issues. On 27 June, the Prime Minister said in South African Parliament that his country remained committed to resolution 435(1978), but added that Cuban withdrawal from Angola was an absolute prerequisite.

According to the Council, the Lusaka talks failed because MPC refused to call for the implementation of resolution 435(1978) and insisted on linking Namibian independence to extraneous issues.

South African forces in Namibia were estimated at 100,000, stationed at approximately 85 to 90 bases. During preparations for attacks against Angola, additional troops were moved into the Territory. On 28 March, South Africa announced a 21.4 per cent increase in military spending for 1984. For the planned 1984/85 budget, the increase would bring military spending to $3 billion out of the total budget of $20.7 billion. *The Windhoek Advertiser* reported on 23 October that South Africa had made its Defence Act applicable to Namibia, thus imposing conscription into the South African army on all Namibian males between 17 and 55 years of age.

The People's Liberation Army of Namibia (PLAN) continued to mount attacks against South African military installations in Namibia, resulting in the régime's loss of arms and military aircraft. The combat zone covered nearly half of the Territory.

The Council reported that South Africa's nuclear capability had been enhanced and accelerated by the collaboration extended by certain Western States, particularly the United States, and by Israel, through assistance in uranium extraction and processing, the supply of nuclear equipment, and the transfer of technology. The Council quoted press reports stating that in 1984 Israel and South Africa established a ministerial committee to work out an agreement by which South Africa would be supplied with technology for nuclear armaments. (See also p. 140.)

In 1984, South Africa selectively released political prisoners, especially those who had caught the attention of the international community, but detained others. Following its release in March 1983 of Andimba Toivo ya Toivo, the founder of SWAPO, who had been imprisoned for 16 years, South Africa released in May 1984 another 15 SWAPO members who were serving jail sentences and 54 detainees. South Africa admitted it was holding 146 others at the Mariental prison near Windhoek. In June, South Africa detained for a few days 37 prominent leaders and supporters of SWAPO as well as two white lawyers who had supported that organization. Most of them would be tried for violating the Prohibition and Notification of Meetings Act of 1981. There were also numerous cases of "disappearances" and torture of civilian detainees under interrogation.

In its Bangkok Declaration and Programme of Action, the Council denounced South Africa for its illegal occupation, its increasing and large-scale military buildup in Namibia, its use of Namibian territory as a staging ground for launching armed aggression against neighbouring States, its introduction of compulsory military service for Namibians, its forced recruitment and training of Namibians for tribal armies and its use of mercenaries to carry out internal repression and external aggression. The Council called on States to prevent the recruitment, training and transit of mercenaries for service in Namibia.

The Committee on colonial countries, on 20 August,[34] condemned South Africa for the same reasons and called on States to take the same action. As the Council had done, it condemned military and other collaboration between South Africa and certain Western and other States. On 21 August,[53] the Committee on colonial countries, again condemning South Africa for those reasons, deplored that it engaged in military activities and maintained bases in Namibia, and that, in its war against the Namibians, it committed aggression against neighbouring countries. The Committee appealed to States to render moral, political, financial, military and other support to SWAPO to enable it to intensify its struggle for Namibian independence. It stated that the militarization of Namibia had led to forced conscription and to a flow of refugees. The Committee condemned the displacement of Namibians from their homes.

SECURITY COUNCIL ACTION

In resolution 546(1984) of 6 January adopted after Angola complained of South Africa's aggression, the Security Council condemned South Africa for its bombing, as well as its continuing occupation of parts of Angola, and for its use of Namibia as a springboard for perpetrating the attacks.

GENERAL ASSEMBLY ACTION

The General Assembly, in decision 39/412, deplored South Africa's military activities and its maintaining military bases in Namibia, and condemned it for its military buildup, the compulsory military service for Namibans, the forced recruitment for tribal armies and the use of mercenaries—calling on States to prevent their use and to provide all kinds of support to SWAPO. It demanded the dismantling of all those military bases and condemned the forcible displacement of Namibians from their homes for military and political purposes. Compulsory military conscription was declared null and void.

By resolution 39/42, the Assembly requested States to end all assistance, including military supplies, to South Africa, which used such assistance to repress the Namibians.

In resolution 39/50 A, it denounced all fraudulent constitutional and political schemes through which South Africa might attempt to perpetuate its colonial domination, condemned its attempts through MPC to circumvent the United Nations independence plan, and declared such manœuvres null and void. The Assembly welcomed the release of SWAPO leaders as a victory for the international campaign. It declared that all laws proclaimed by South Africa in Namibia were illegal. With regard to the military situation, the Assembly condemned South Africa for the military buildup in Namibia, the imposition of compulsory military service there, the recruitment of Namibians for tribal armies, the use of mercenaries, the forcible displacement of Namibians from their homes, and its use of Namibian territory as a staging ground for launching aggression against neighbouring States. States were called upon to prevent the recruitment, training and transit of mercenaries for service in Namibia. The Assembly called on all specialized agencies to terminate collaboration with South Africa, since such assistance augmented the military capability of South Africa, thus enabling it to continue repression in Namibia and South Africa and to commit aggression against neighbouring States.

In resolution 39/50 B, the Assembly condemned South Africa's attempts to set up puppet political institutions and impose an "internal settlement" in Namibia, in defiance of the United Nations, and, in that context, rejected the puppet MPC as the latest in a series of political stratagems aimed at imposing a neo-colonial settlement in Namibia.

The Assembly, in resolution 39/50 C, decided that the Council for Namibia would denounce and seek rejection by States of fraudulent schemes by which South Africa might attempt to perpetuate its presence in Namibia; it would ensure nonrecognition of any administration installed at Windhoek not issuing from free elections in Namibia conducted in accordance with Security Council resolutions, and counter attempts to link the independence of Namibia and extraneous is-

sues such as the withdrawal of Cuban forces from Angola.

REFERENCES

[1]YUN 1967, p. 709, GA res. 2248(S-V), sect. II, 19 May 1967. [2]A/39/24. [3]A/40/24. [4]YUN 1965, p. 440, GA res. 2106 A (XX), annex, 21 Dec. 1965. [5]YUN 1978, p. 915, SC res. 435(1978), 29 Sept. 1978. [6]A/39/286-S/16601. [7]A/39/207. [8]A/AC.115/L.611. [9]YUN 1974, p. 846, GA res. 3314(XXIX), 14 Dec. 1974. [10]YUN 1960, p. 49, GA res. 1514(XXV), 14 Dec. 1960. [11]YUN 1983, p. 1069, GA res. 38/36 C, 1 Dec. 1983. [12]YUN 1974, p. 152. [13]YUN 1983, p. 1077. [14]S/16256. [15]YUN 1983, p. 174. [16]A/39/138-S/16427. [17]A/39/151-S/16434. [18]S/16725. [19]S/16735. [20]A/39/688-S/16838. [21]A/39/689-S/16839. [22]A/40/56-S/16869. [23]S/16389. [24]A/39/131-S/16414 & Corr.1. [25]YUN 1983, p. 1055, SC res. 539(1983), 28 Oct. 1983. [26]A/39/450-S/16726. [27]A/39/560-S/16773. [28]A/39/590 & Corr.1. [29]A/40/87. [30]A/39/336. [31]YUN 1983, p. 1061, GA res. 38/36 A, 1 Dec. 1983. [32]*Ibid.*, p. 1066, GA res. 38/36 B, 1 Dec. 1983. [33]A/39/508. [34]A/39/23 (dec. A/AC.109/794). [35]*Ibid.* (res. A/AC.109/797). [36]E/1984/14 (res. 1984/4). [37]*Ibid.* (res. 1984/5). [38]*Ibid.* (res. 1984/6). [39]A/C.4/39/4. [40]A/39/675. [41]YUN 1981, p. 1153, GA res. ES-8/2, 14 Sept. 1981. [42]A/AC.131/116. [43]A/AC.131/138. [44]YUN 1982, p. 1314, GA res. 37/233 E, 20 Dec. 1982. [45]A/39/832. [46]YUN 1982, p. 1310, GA dec. 36/325, 29 Mar. 1982. [47]A/AC.131/114. [48]A/AC.131/119. [49]A/AC.109/781. [50]A/AC.109/784. [51]YUN 1983, p. 1060. [52]YUN 1981, p. 1128. [53]A/39/23 (dec. A/AC.109/796).

Economic and social conditions

Foreign investment

The Council for Namibia, in its Bangkok Declaration and Programme of Action on Namibia included in its 1984 annual report to the General Assembly,[1] viewed with concern the increased assistance rendered by major Western countries and Israel to South Africa in several areas, including economic and financial areas, and stated that such assistance constituted a hostile act against the Namibian people and the front-line States. The Council demanded that an immediate end be put to such assistance and called on the international community to intensify efforts for South Africa's complete isolation.

The Council's Standing Committee II, in an April report on the activities of foreign economic interests operating in Namibia,[2] described recent international action against such interests and stated that the campaign against economic cooperation with South Africa had grown rapidly. The campaign had sought the support of church, university and community groups in promoting action by stockholders in favour of disinvestment in South African interests, as well as boycotts of community banks and other firms doing business with South Africa. Most observers, the Council said, felt that disinvestment had proved a particularly effective way to organize church and university groups. In disregard of the international campaign and of United Nations resolutions against South Africa and other foreign economic interests operating illegally in Namibia, certain Western nations continued to maintain wide-ranging economic interests in Namibia and South Africa. The unwillingness on the part of those countries to prevent the activities of transnational corporations (TNCs) and their subsidiaries operating in Namibia had contributed to the illegal exploitation of the Territory's natural and human resources (see below), it said.

The mining and agricultural sectors (see below) provided the major portion of Namibia's gross domestic product (GDP). Namibia's commercial and manufacturing sectors produced 10 to 15 per cent of GDP. All sectors were completely dominated by South Africa and other foreign economic interests. The manufacturing sector comprised fewer than 300 enterprises, accounted for under 5 per cent of GDP and employed 10 per cent of the workforce. The South African presence in the manufacturing and commercial sectors was strong, and foreign interests held direct and indirect interests, mainly in mining, but also in such areas as property, building, drilling, freight services, insurance and banking and trade. Financing was mainly generated in South Africa. Decades of foreign economic investment in Namibia and the magnitude of profits had encouraged South Africa's intransigence with regard to Namibia's independence. By their operations in Namibia, TNCs supported South Africa, thereby reinforcing and perpetuating its occupation of Namibia. South Africa did not require TNCs in Namibia to reinvest any part of their profits in the Territory for development purposes. The bulk of profits were repatriated to foreign shareholders, resulting in a huge gap between the Territory's GDP, the total value of goods and services produced, and gross national product (GNP), the total value of products after foreign payments were made.

In an August working paper on Namibia,[3] the secretariat of the Committee on colonial countries stated that the economic distortions created in Namibia by years of colonial domination, by the ravages of South African and other foreign economic interests and by South Africa's war of attrition against the people had left the Territory's economy in a state of near collapse. The Territory's rich resources were exclusively controlled by South Africa and other foreign economic interests. Some studies showed that as much as 60 per cent of Namibia's GDP was appropriated as company profits before taxes. As a result, Namibia continued to suffer an economic decline—recent GDP figures showed negative growth rates while administrative expenditures by the illegal administration of the Territory continued to increase. In the Territory's 1983/84 budget, 75 per cent of total funds were allotted for administrative expenditures which included the military and police.

The secretariat, in another working paper on Namibia,[4] gave an overview of the Namibian economy and the activities of foreign economic interests in the Territory. Stating that South Africa's economic grip on Namibia was a stranglehold, the secretariat noted that South Africa owned the rail-transport system, the airline and the communication network, it supplied the Territory's oil and coal, and most of the civil servants were South Africans. Two thirds of the Territory's imports originated in South Africa and nearly half of its imports from other countries were routed through that country. As in previous years, Namibia had to borrow to balance its 1983/84 budget. The borrowing rate equalled 15 per cent of its GDP; if the trend continued, Namibia's external debt would, by 1987, equal its GDP, making it one of the most indebted countries in the world. Capital outflow to South Africa amounted to about 20 per cent of its GDP and nearly a third of its 1983/84 budget. The disparities between social expenditure for blacks and whites continued; for example, the white minority, which comprised 7 per cent of the population, received over 50 per cent of the 1983 drought aid.

The secretariat said that foreign economic interests, which were lured to Namibia because of unusually high profits made possible by abundant cheap, enslaved labour under South Africa's *apartheid* system, conducted their operations under licences issued by South Africa.

In order to obtain information on the exploitation of the Namibian people and resources by South Africa and other foreign economic interests and to expose such activities, the Council for Namibia conducted the Seminar on the Activities of Foreign Economic Interests in the Exploitation of Namibia's Natural and Human Resources (Ljubljana, 16-20 April).[1] The seminar was also intended to mobilize international public opinion in support of United Nations demands that foreign economic, financial and other interests operating in Namibia refrain from new investments or activities there, withdraw from the Territory and end their co-operation with the South African administration.

Among its recommendations, the seminar said the Council should commission an investigation into the role of the mineral resources of South Africa and Namibia in the economies of the importing countries and the part played by TNCs in exploiting those resources. The Council was urged to stimulate further research on strategic shipping links with Namibia, compile legislation from countries which adhered to the oil embargo and publish a list of tankers and oil companies which had been involved in shipping oil to Namibia and South Africa. It also recommended that action be taken in national courts of certain States which permitted their TNCs to plunder Namibia's natural resources. Governments, specialized agencies, trade unions and other organizations were urged to expand their support to the National Union of Namibian Workers so that it might resist the growing exploitation of labour by South Africa and the TNCs.

Japan, in a note verbale of 13 September to the President of the Council,[5] protested the seminar's recommendation that the Council urge Japan to stop the purchase of Namibian uranium by Japanese companies. Japan said it had published in the official Japanese trade bulletin its recognition of Decree No. 1 for the Protection of the Natural Resources of Namibia, adopted by the Council in 1974 to prevent the exploitation of Namibia's resources;[6] since then, there had been no official record of Namibian uranium having been imported into Japan (see also p. 1031).

On 20 August[7] and again on 21 August,[8] the Committee on colonial countries also took action on foreign investment in Namibia. The Committee condemned South African and other foreign economic interests exploiting and plundering the Territory's human and natural resources. It reaffirmed that all such resources were the heritage of the people, and condemned South Africa's exploitation, including its extension of the territorial sea, its proclamation of an economic zone off the coast of Namibia and its exploitation of marine resources. It demanded that States whose TNCs were operating in Namibia comply with United Nations resolutions, withdraw all investments from Namibia and end co-operation between those TNCs and the South African administration.

The Committee also called on States to terminate any investments in Namibia or loans to South Africa and to refrain from promoting trade or other economic relations with that country. It declared that all activities of foreign economic interests in Namibia were illegal and that South Africa and those interests were liable to pay damages to its future lawful Government.

In December, the General Assembly also took action on foreign economic interests in Namibia. In resolution 39/42, it called on States to terminate any investments in Namibia or loans to South Africa and to refrain from promoting trade or economic relations with it. The Assembly also declared the activities of such interests illegal and that they were liable for damages to the future Namibian Government. In resolution 39/50 C, the Assembly decided on the work programme of the Council for Namibia, which included: considering policies to counter the support which foreign economic interests gave to the South African administration; notifying States whose corporations operated in Namibia of their illegality; sending missions to consult those Governments to discourage the continuation of investments; contacting international organizations with a view to pro

tecting Namibia's interests, and drawing their attention to Decree No. 1 to protect its natural resources;[6] ensuring compliance with the Decree, including consideration of legal proceedings in domestic courts of States and other appropriate bodies; and conducting hearings, seminars and workshops to obtain information on the exploitation of the Namibian people and resources and to expose such activities.

Natural resources

Activities of the Council for Namibia. The Council for Namibia, in its annual report,[1] described the exploitation of Namibia's natural resources by foreign economic interests, and, as requested by the Assembly in 1983,[9] recommended policies to counter their support to the illegal South African administration. The Council based its findings on the April report of its Standing Committee II.[2] According to the Council, Western-based TNCs and other interests continued to exploit, in collaboration with South Africa, the natural resources, despite repeated United Nations resolutions and the Council's 1974 Decree No. 1 for the Protection of the Natural Resources of Namibia,[6] banning the exploitation of those resources without the Council's permission. Namibia's rich natural resources (including uranium, diamonds, copper, lead, zinc, aluminium, silver, gold, pyrite, tin, vanadium, tungsten, manganese, coal, iron, platinum and other metals, as well as agricultural and fishery products) were controlled by South Africa and other foreign economic and financial interests, thereby causing an unbalanced and precarious economic structure.

Although mining constituted almost half of the Territory's total GDP, it employed only 10 per cent of the labour force. Commercial agriculture provided a lucrative income for some 5,000 white farmers who produced more than 95 per cent of the marketed agricultural output. Subsistence agriculture constituted virtually the only economic activity for the indigenous population and its share of the total marketed agricultural output was 2.5 per cent. The agricultural sector contributed about 14 per cent to the GDP and 20 per cent to exports. In the past, Namibia's fish resources were economically significant, but exploitation by South African and other foreign economic interests had seriously depleted those resources, resulting in the loss of several thousand jobs.

The gap between Namibia's GDP and GNP indicated the extent of exploitation. Over 60 per cent of Namibia's GDP was appropriated as company profits before taxes. Foreign economic interests involved in exploiting Namibia's resources included some of the world's largest corporations and financial institutions from South Africa, Western Europe and North America—all licensed by South

Africa. They were attracted to Namibia because of the unusually high profits made possible by South Africa's *apartheid* system, which provided abundant cheap labour.

In the mining sector, which contributed almost half of the GDP and nearly 90 per cent of exports, four corporations—two mostly South African owned, one United States owned and another mostly British owned—accounted for about 95 per cent of mineral production and exports and held approximately 80 per cent of the Territory's mineral assets. Diamond production and exports were controlled by South Africa through the Diamond Board of Namibia and marketed through the De Beers Central Selling Organization, which buffered market fluctuations through stockpiling and selective sales. A wide range of base metals and other precious metals made up 20 per cent of the total output of the mining sector.

For more than a decade, Namibia's reserves of uranium, estimated to be among the largest in the world, had attracted foreign mining interests. South Africa, in particular, sought to maintain its control over the Territory's uranium deposits. The only active uranium mine in Namibia was operated by a consortium of Western and South African firms incorporated in 1970, Rössing Uranium, Ltd. United States companies were prospecting for uranium.

In the agricultural sector, white farmers owned and managed the most important commercially oriented agricultural activities, namely, cattle raising, dairy farming and the production of caracul pelts (a valuable type of sheep's fleece), producing over 97 per cent of the total marketed agricultural output. The main market for beef was South Africa with its Meat Board setting quotas for Namibian exports. The fishing industry was also controlled by South Africa.

The Council, in its Bangkok Declaration and Programme of Action adopted on 25 May, reaffirmed that the natural, including marine, resources of Namibia were the inviolable heritage of its people, and in that regard, underscored the importance of implementing Decree No. 1. It said that the rapid depletion of the resources, as a result of their illegal plunder by South Africa and other foreign economic interests, was a threat to the integrity and prosperity of an independent Namibia. Calling on corporations to terminate such activities, the Council urged Governments to ensure the cessation of those activities and any new investments in Namibia by corporations under their jurisdiction, as well as their compliance with the Decree. The Council reiterated its resolve to ensure compliance, including by initiating legal proceedings in domestic courts. It reaffirmed that foreign economic interests which were illegally exploiting Namibia's resources were liable to pay reparations to an independent Namibia. Condemning the exploitation of Namibia's resources, including uranium, it reiterated its request to the Federal Republic of Germany, the Netherlands and the United Kingdom, which operated the Urenco uranium-enrichment plant at Almelo, the Netherlands, to have Namibian uranium specifically excluded from the 1970 Treaty of Almelo, which regulated Urenco's activities. The Council urged Governments, particularly of those Western States and Israel whose corporations were involved in mining and processing Namibian uranium, to take measures, including requiring negative certificates of origin, to prohibit State-owned and other corporations from dealing in Namibian uranium and from engaging in uranium prospecting in Namibia. The Council stated its intention to consider the feasibility, in the exercise of its rights under the United Nations Convention on the Law of the Sea,[10] of proclaiming an exclusive economic zone for Namibia.

Council's mission to Western Europe. In 1984, the Council sent a mission to France, the Netherlands, the Federal Republic of Germany and the United Kingdom (24 April to 12 May), in pursuance of the General Assembly's 1983 decision[9] that it should take all measures to ensure compliance with Decree No. 1 on protecting Namibia's natural resources,[6] including consideration of legal proceedings in the domestic courts of States and other appropriate bodies. The mission held discussions with NGOs and other groups on ways of implementing the Decree. It sought legal advice on the possibility of the Council's instituting legal proceedings in national courts against TNCs and other business concerns importing or dealing with Namibian goods incompatible with the Decree. It sought clarification on three issues: the legal status in those countries of the United Nations resolutions on Namibia; persons or organizations competent to bring legal action in those countries; and possible procedures for instituting legal action. In July, the mission made recommendations to the Council for action.[1]

In France, the mission was informed that the resolutions did not have juridical value under French law, except for those of the Security Council relating to maintenance of peace. It was suggested that indirect enforcement of the Decree could be achieved by bringing it within the purview of international instruments of human rights, or through corporate action. The Netherlands had recognized both the Decree and the competence of the Council to enact it. In the Federal Republic of Germany and the United Kingdom, the Decree could not be enforced by the courts since an Assembly resolution was not considered binding. In its recommendations to the Council, the mission strongly advised that the Council clarify the relationship between the Decree and relevant resolutions of the Security Council so as to enhance its effectiveness and enforceability in those countries whose Governments regarded it as a mere recommmendation of the Assembly.

Concerning the issue of who was competent to bring legal action, lawyers said that in France legal standing could be given to the Council, the United Nations Commissioner for Namibia, NGOs with United Nations consultative status, anyone who advocated the principles of human rights, SWAPO and/or Namibians residing in France. In the Federal Republic of Germany, only the Council, acting on behalf of the United Nations, would have legal standing in its courts. In the Netherlands, such standing would be accorded to either the Council or the Commissioner. In the United Kingdom, there could be reasonable grounds for satisfying the courts that the Council had legal standing, but it was advisable for the United Nations itself and the Council to be joint plaintiffs. The mission said that the suggestion that the Council consider initiating legal proceedings by bodies or persons other than the Council, and without using the Decree as the basis of the proceedings, should be examined, bearing in mind that such a course of action might be interpreted as compromising the legal standing of the Council and/or that of the Decree.

To commence legal action, French lawyers suggested that an investigation be conducted to ascertain what actions stood the best chances of success with regard to the involvement of French corporations engaged in the illegal exploitation of Namibian resources. In the Netherlands, the recommended preliminary procedural step was to obtain from scholars of international law a written opinion on all the issues involved in the implementation of the Decree in that country. The lawyers in the Federal Republic of Germany considered that action could be initiated in the European Court in Luxembourg, which considered alleged illegal acts by corporations in EEC countries, against those buying Namibian uranium or arranging contracts for delivery. Lawyers in the United Kingdom suggested that legal Counsel draft the documentation in order to commence the proceedings, whether in the form of writ or summons or petition, depending on the nature of the proceedings. Possible defendants would include companies in the United Kingdom involved in exploring, exploiting or exporting Namibian natural resources, or companies which imported or distributed such resources.

The mission recommended that any legal action envisaged by the Council for Namibia be brought first in the courts of the Netherlands, since it had recognized the Council and its competence to enact the Decree. Such legal action should initially focus on the exploitation of Namibian uranium. As for the suggestion that legal proceedings be initiated by bodies or persons other than the Council without using the Decree as the basis for such proceedings, this might be interpreted as admission of a certain weakness in the legal standing of the Council and the Decree. The Council called for frequent con-

tact with NGOs in the countries it visited. It recommended that the Office of the United Nations Commissioner for Namibia prepare a compendium of all existing reports and studies on the implementation of the Decree.

Symposium on implementation of Decree No. 1. The Council organized the Symposium on International Efforts to Implement Decree No. 1 for the Protection of the Natural Resources of Namibia (Geneva, 27-31 August) to consider ways of instituting legal proceedings in the domestic courts of States and other appropriate bodies in order to ensure compliance with the Council's 1974 Decree.[6] Attended by 13 Member States, 40 participants from NGOs and trade unions, as well as lawyers and parliamentarians, the Symposium came to a number of conclusions and made recommendations to the Council.[1]

The Symposium recommended, among other things, that the Council and the Commissioner institute legal proceedings in the Netherlands as soon as possible, and prepare similar action in other countries known to be involved in mining, transporting, processing or receiving Namibian minerals, paying particular attention to Belgium—a Council member. They were also urged to: notify Governments whose national corporations defied the Decree and United Nations resolutions; request States to promote the Decree's implementation; notify each corporation violating it of their intention to institute legal proceedings; consider recommending that the Security Council or the General Assembly request another advisory opinion from the International Court of Justice on what measures the Security Council should apply to States refusing to comply with its resolutions and the Decree; and engage experts in those Western States whose corporations were exploiting the resources to compile a list for publication.

The Symposium also recommended that the Council establish a register of profits earned by corporations through their Namibia operations, and to publicize the Decree with the help of public relations experts. It was urged to ensure Namibia's territorial integrity by countering South Africa's claims to the Orange River, Walvis Bay and the offshore islands, and to proclaim an exclusive economic zone for Namibia under the Law of the Sea Convention.[10] The Council was also called on to assist trade unions trying to prevent transportation of natural resources originating in Namibia, and to publish a list of tankers and oil companies involved in shipping oil to it.

Activities of the Committee on colonial countries. The secretariat of the Committee on colonial countries, in an August working paper on activities of foreign economic and other interests in Namibia,[4] reported findings similar to those of the Council for Namibia. It named some corporations based in Western Europe which operated or invested in Namibia, and noted that they included two of the ten largest mining corporations of the Western world (both of the United Kingdom); two of the largest international banking companies (of the United Kingdom and the Federal Republic of Germany); and two of the seven largest Western petroleum companies (one of the United Kingdom and the other a multinational corporation mostly Dutch and British owned). The United States was involved as part owner of mining concerns operating in Namibia. Other North American corporations were involved in the oil and caracul industries. Since 1980, the trend in the activities of foreign economic interests operating in the Namibian mineral sector had been towards maintaining the existing level of direct foreign investment without any appreciable expansion, and staking mining claims and prospecting. A few companies had pulled out of the Territory during that period, resulting in a corresponding increase in South African ownership of Namibian mines and other economic activities.

Action by Committee on colonial countries. On 21 August,[8] the Committee on colonial countries condemned South Africa for plundering Namibia's natural resources, for creating an economic structure there dependent on its mineral resources, and for its illegal extension of the territorial sea and proclamation of an economic zone off Namibia's coast. It reiterated that such exploitation by South African and other foreign interests was illegal and contributed to maintaining the occupation régime. The Committee condemned the plunder of Namibian uranium and called on States to comply with Decree No. 1 to prevent corporations from dealing in and prospecting for it.

On 20 August,[7] the Committee demanded that foreign exploitation cease and reaffirmed that the natural resources were the inviolable heritage of the Namibians. Noting with concern their rapid depletion as a result of the illegal plunder, the Committee considered it a grave threat to an independent Namibia. It demanded that those States whose TNCs operated in Namibia under the illegal administration of South Africa comply with United Nations resolutions by immediately withdrawing all investments from Namibia.

GENERAL ASSEMBLY ACTION

In resolution 39/42, the General Assembly condemned the Governments supporting foreign interests exploiting the resources of the colonial Territories, particularly Namibia's marine resources. It called on States to stop investing in Namibia. South Africa was condemned for its plunder, for creating an economic structure in Namibia dependent on its minerals and for the illegal extension of the territorial sea and proclaiming the economic coastal zone. The Assembly declared that all activities of foreign economic interests in Namibia were illegal and that consequently they and South Africa were liable to pay damages to the future lawful Government. States were called on to comply with Decree No. 1, including the requirement of negative certificates of origin, to prevent corporations from dealing in Namibian uranium and from prospecting.

States were also called on to refrain from relations with South Africa and to cease economic and trade relations with it which might support its occupation of Namibia. The Assembly requested the Secretary-General to expose the pillaging of natural resources in colonial Territories by foreign monopolies and, in respect of Namibia, the support they rendered to South Africa.

The Assembly took similar action in resolution 39/50 A, reaffirming that the resources were the inviolable heritage of the people and declaring the illegality of the activities of foreign economic interests. It expressed concern at the rapid depletion of the natural resources, particularly uranium, as a result of plunder by South Africa and certain Western and other foreign interests, in violation of United Nations decisions. Governments were again called on to prohibit corporations from dealing in Namibian uranium. The Assembly requested the Federal Republic of Germany, the Netherlands and the United Kingdom to have uranium specifically excluded from the Treaty of Almelo, which regulated activities of the Urenco uranium-processing plant. The Assembly demanded that TNCs engaged in exploitation withdraw from the Territory and end co-operation with the South African administration and Member States were requested to ensure compliance with Decree No. 1. The Assembly declared that by their exploitation, the interests were obstructing Namibia's independence.

The Assembly, in resolution 39/50 C on the work programme of the Council for Namibia, decided that it would continue to examine the exploitation of and trade in Namibian uranium by foreign interests, draw the attention of the specialized agencies to Decree No. 1, and take measures to ensure compliance with it, including consideration of instituting legal proceeding in States' domestic courts and other bodies. By resolution 39/50 D, the Assembly requested the Council to include in its 1985 activities distribution of a book on TNCs plundering Namibian resources and on the profits extracted, and a booklet on implementation of the Decree.

Social conditions and exploitation of labour

The Council for Namibia, in its 1984 annual report,[1] as well as its Standing Committee II, in April[2] and July[11] reports, reviewed the social conditions and exploitation of labour in the Territory.

The secretariat of the Committee on colonial countries also described that exploitation in an August working paper on Namibia.[3] The Council noted that in Namibia, as in South Africa, the division of the population into ethnic groups (bantus) was the principal means by which the régime sought to perpetuate white power, prevent unity among black Namibians and maintain a pool of cheap labour. The African population had been forced into the poverty-stricken "homelands" or "bantustans". The educational system imposed in Namibia was designed to perpetuate white supremacy, with education for blacks based on the premise that they were to be trained for subservient jobs. Educational facilities for black children were non-existent in some areas and mediocre at best in others. According to available information, $1,500 per year was spent on educating each white child, seven times more than the allocation for each black and "coloured" (mixed race) child.

The health sector was also characterized by gross inequities, with health services for the black majority either rudimentary or virtually non-existent while those available to whites were comparable to that of the best of any country. Many diseases associated with malnutrition resulting from abject poverty and overcrowded living conditions were common among blacks, but almost unknown among whites. Housing was governed by discriminatory laws, and that provided for black Namibians was exceptionally poor. Temporary and makeshift camps and shanties were a prominent feature of black townships, where living conditions were cramped with minimal facilities.

South Africa continued to apply its repressive laws aimed at thwarting the legitimate national liberation struggle of the Namibian people, giving the South African police and occupation forces power to carry out mass arrests, to ban organizations and publications, to detain or deport Namibians without trial, to ban meetings, and to restrict the movement of opposition leaders. The security forces conducted arrests, intimidation, detention, incarceration and murder. Expropriation, war and repression had forced thousands of Namibians to flee to Angola and Zambia. According to 1984 figures compiled by UNHCR, there were some 70,000 Namibian refugees in Angola and 4,500 in Zambia, which had created emergency needs in agriculture, health, education and housing. Namibians in Angola were frequently a target of South African forces based in Namibia who crossed the border into Angola to harass the refugees, operating under the pretext that the camps were SWAPO bases.

In Namibia, the labour force was divided racially; *apartheid* existed in the conditions of work, wages earned, the right to organize in trade unions and the types of jobs available. The system provided a captive cheap labour force for the white economy. The total black work force was estimated at 500,000, of whom 240,000 were engaged in subsistence agriculture. Of the remainder, about 56,500 worked on commercial farms, 28,000 in mining, 7,500 in the fishing industry, 28,500 in the secondary and 148,000 in the tertiary sectors, and 75,000 in domestic service. Almost half of the non-agricultural labour force excluding whites (about 110,000) were migrant workers on short-term contracts and were mainly from the north. The estimated unemployment level for 1984 was 25 per cent, which did not take into account the agricultural sector where unemployment was exacerbated by the 1983 drought.

Cosmetic changes in racist labour laws introduced by South Africa to placate the labour force and to improve its image abroad had not changed the status of black workers. The requirements of the registration laws for black trade unions had made it almost impossible for them to function, thereby forcing the National Union of Namibian Workers, a country-wide organization affiliated with SWAPO, to operate underground since 1980. Laws prohibited trade unions from pursuing political objectives and the administration had frequently banned union activity.

In the Bangkok Declaration and Programme of Action, the Council urged Governments, specialized agencies and other organizations to provide material assistance to the Namibian refugees who had been forced to flee into neighbouring States.

REFERENCES

[1]A/39/24. [2]A/AC.131/115. [3]A/AC.109/784. [4]A/AC.109/782. [5]A/39/489. [6]YUN 1974, p. 152. [7]A/39/23 (dec. A/AC.109/794). [8]*Ibid.* (res. A/AC.109/795). [9]YUN 1983, p. 1069, GA res. 38/36 C, 1 Dec. 1983. [10]YUN 1982, p. 181. [11]A/AC.131/130.

International assistance

The Council for Namibia, in its Bangkok Declaration and Programme of Action, included in its 1984 annual report,[1] stated that, at the current critical stage in the struggle of the Namibian people for independence, all-round support to SWAPO must be urgently intensified. It urged all States and United Nations bodies to increase political, moral, material, military and financial assistance to SWAPO in that struggle, as well as material assistance to Namibian refugees forced to flee into neighbouring countries. United Nations organizations were urged to give priority to assisting Namibians through SWAPO.

The Council believed that the front-line States' support for the Namibian cause continued to be important in efforts to achieve independence. It deemed it necessary that the international community urgently increase financial, material, military and political support to those States so as to enable them to resolve their own economic difficulties and to defend themselves against South Africa's destabilizing attempts. Reaffirming support for SADCC, it called on States to assist SADCC in promoting regional economic co-operation and development and to reduce the economic dependence of countries on South Africa. NGOs were urged to intensify, in co-operation with the Council, international action in support of the liberation struggle and to increase their support to SWAPO.

The Committee on colonial countries also called for support for the Namibian people. On 20 August,[2] it paid particular tribute to the front-line States for their commitment and assistance to the Namibians and SWAPO. It also called on the international community to increase all kinds of support to those States and to assist SADCC. It also urged States and United Nations organizations to support all assistance programmes organized by the Council to benefit the Namibians.

On 22 August,[3] the Committee expressed concern that assistance extended so far by United Nations organizations to the colonial peoples, particularly the Namibian people and SWAPO, was inadequate. It noted with satisfaction that SWAPO continued to benefit from programmes established within the framework of the United Nations Institute for Namibia (see p. 1061). It urged the organizations to increase assistance to SWAPO, as well as to the Institute and the Nationhood Programme for Namibia (see p. 1060) and to extend material assistance to the front-line States.

In 1982[4] and 1983,[5] the General Assembly had requested the Secretary-General to develop a comprehensive programme of assistance to the States in question to enable them to become self-reliant. In 1983, he had reported that the basic elements of such a programme were available in the national development plans of those States and in the SADCC programmes, and concluded that since those programmes reflected the judgements of the Governments concerned, additional international assistance to ensure their implementation would be the most realistic approach.[6] On 15 October 1984,[7] the Secretary-General stated that as the Governments concerned had not indicated any change in their positions, his 1983 suggestion continued to be the most appropriate response.

The Assembly, in resolution 39/43, expressed concern that assistance extended by United Nations organizations to the colonial peoples, particularly the Namibians and SWAPO, was far from adequate. It called on United Nations organizations to increase assistance to SWAPO, the Institute for Namibia and the Nationhood Programme, and to extend material aid to the front-line States so that they could sup-

port Namibia's struggle and defend themselves against South Africa. In resolution 39/50 E, the Assembly decided that the Council would continue to formulate assistance policies and co-ordinate assistance for Namibia provided by United Nations organizations.

UN Fund for Namibia

Activities of the Fund

The United Nations Fund for Namibia, financed mainly by voluntary contributions, continued to serve in 1984 as the main vehicle through which the Council for Namibia channelled assistance to the Territory. The Council was trustee for the Fund, which became operative in 1972.[8] As the Council reported in 1984,[1] the Fund's activities were divided into three main programmes: the United Nations Institute for Namibia (see below); the Nationhood Programme for Namibia (see below); and educational, social and relief assistance to Namibians. Expenditures in 1984 from the Fund in the three programmes were: $3,563,147 for the Institute; $1,770,055 for the Nationhood Programme; and $2,188,569 for educational, social and relief assistance.

The first two programmes were set up with particular reference towards future independence, whereas the third programme, which provided individual scholarships under the administration of the Commissioner's Office, emphasized the immediate needs and welfare of Namibians. Financed by the Fund's General Account, it provided assistance for health and medical care, nutrition and social welfare, books and periodicals for Namibian refugee camps and SWAPO offices, and assistance to Namibian representatives at international meetings. During the period from 1 July 1983 to 30 June 1984, 51 new scholarships were approved and 52 students completed their courses. As of 1 July 1984, a total of 124 awards were being used in various fields of study in 11 countries. Vocational training was provided in the following fields: law enforcement, radio broadcasting, cinematography, video techniques, land use for agriculture, journalism and communications, and clerical and transport services. A list of allocations from the General Account and a brief description of the activities under the programme were provided in an April report of the Commissioner for Namibia.[9]

In its Bangkok Declaration and Programme of Action, the Council expressed appreciation to Governments and United Nations organizations that had contributed to the Fund and appealed to them to contribute or to increase their contributions.

GENERAL ASSEMBLY ACTION

On 12 December, the General Assembly adopted resolution 39/50 E by recorded vote.

United Nations Fund for Namibia

The General Assembly,

Having examined the parts of the report of the United Nations Council for Namibia relating to the United Nations Fund for Namibia,

Recalling its resolution 2679(XXV) of 9 December 1970, by which it established the United Nations Fund for Namibia,

Recalling also its resolution 3112(XXVIII) of 12 December 1973, by which it appointed the United Nations Council for Namibia trustee of the United Nations Fund for Namibia,

Recalling its resolution 31/153 of 20 December 1976, by which it decided to launch the Nationhood Programme for Namibia,

Recalling further its resolution 34/92 A of 12 December 1979, by which it approved the Charter of the United Nations Institute for Namibia, and its resolution 37/233 E of 20 December 1982, by which it approved amendments to the Charter,

1. *Takes note* of the relevant parts of the report of the United Nations Council for Namibia;

2. *Decides* that the United Nations Council for Namibia shall:

(a) Continue to formulate policies of assistance to Namibians and co-ordinate assistance for Namibia provided by the specialized agencies and other organizations and institutions of the United Nations system;

(b) Continue to act as trustee of the United Nations Fund for Namibia, and, in this capacity, administer and manage the Fund;

(c) Continue to provide broad guidelines and formulate principles and policies for the United Nations Institute for Namibia;

(d) Continue to co-ordinate, plan and direct the Nationhood Programme for Namibia in consultation with the South West Africa People's Organization, with the aim of consolidating all measures of assistance by the specialized agencies and other organizations and institutions of the United Nations system into a comprehensive assistance programme;

(e) Continue to consult with the South West Africa People's Organization in the formulation and implementation of assistance programmes for Namibians;

(f) Report to the General Assembly at its fortieth session on the programmes and activities undertaken through the United Nations Fund for Namibia;

3. *Decides* that the United Nations Fund for Namibia, which comprises the General Account, the United Nations Institute for Namibia Account and the Nationhood Programme Account, shall be the primary source of assistance to Namibians;

4. *Expresses its appreciation* to all States, specialized agencies and other organizations of the United Nations system, governmental and non-governmental organizations and individuals that have made contributions to the United Nations Fund for Namibia to support the activities under the General Account, the activities of the United Nations Institute for Namibia and the Nationhood Programme for Namibia and calls upon them to increase their assistance to Namibians through those channels;

5. *Decides* to allocate as a temporary measure to the United Nations Fund for Namibia the sum of $1 million from the regular budget of the United Nations for 1985;

6. *Requests* the Secretary-General and the President of the United Nations Council for Namibia to intensify appeals to Governments, intergovernmental and non-governmental organizations and individuals for more generous voluntary contributions to the General Account, the Nationhood Programme Account and the United Nations Institute for Namibia Account of the United Nations Fund for Namibia in view of the increased activities undertaken through the Fund, and, in this connection, emphasizes the need for contributions in order to increase the number of scholarships awarded to Namibians under the United Nations Fund for Namibia;

7. *Invites* Governments to appeal once more to their national organizations and institutions for voluntary contributions to the United Nations Fund for Namibia;

8. *Requests* the Office of the United Nations Commissioner for Namibia, in order to mobilize additional resources, to formulate, in consultation with the South West Africa People's Organization, a programme of assistance to the Namibian people to be undertaken by means of projects co-financed by Governments and non-governmental organizations;

9. *Requests* the specialized agencies and other organizations and institutions of the United Nations system, in the light of the urgent need to strengthen the programme of assistance to the Namibian people, to make every effort to expedite the execution of Nationhood Programme for Namibia projects and other projects in favour of Namibians on the basis of procedures which will reflect the role of the United Nations Council for Namibia as the legal Administering Authority for Namibia;

10. *Expresses its appreciation* to those specialized agencies and other organizations and institutions of the United Nations system that have contributed to the Nationhood Programme for Namibia and calls upon them to continue their participation in the Programme by:

(a) Implementing projects approved by the United Nations Council for Namibia;

(b) Planning and initiating new project proposals in co-operation with, and at the request of, the Council;

(c) Allocating funds from their own financial resources for the implementation of the projects approved by the Council;

11. *Emphasizes* the need for Namibians to gain practical on-the-job experience in various countries, and appeals to all Governments to make generous contributions to the United Nations Fund for Namibia to enable Namibians trained under various programmes to be placed in administrations and institutions in diverse countries, particularly in Africa;

12. *Expresses its appreciation* to the United Nations Development Programme for its contribution to the financing and administration of the Nationhood Programme for Namibia and the financing of the United Nations Institute for Namibia and calls upon it to continue to allocate, at the request of the United Nations Council for Namibia, funds from the indicative planning figure for Namibia for the implementation of the projects within the Nationhood Programme and for the United Nations Institute for Namibia;

13. *Calls upon* the United Nations Development Programme to raise the indicative planning figure for Namibia;

14. *Expresses its appreciation* for the assistance provided by the United Nations Children's Fund, the Office of the United Nations High Commissioner for Refugees and the World Food Programme to Namibian refugees and requests them to expand their assistance in order to provide for the basic needs of the refugees;

15. *Expresses its appreciation* to those specialized agencies and other organizations of the United Nations system which have waived agency support costs in respect of projects in favour of Namibians, financed from the United Nations Fund for Namibia and other sources, and urges those that have not yet done so to take appropriate steps in this regard;

16. *Notes with appreciation* that agreement has been reached between the United Nations Development Programme and the organizations of the United Nations system to reduce overhead charges to 3.5 per cent for certain types of project costs financed from the United Nations Fund for Namibia;

17. *Decides* that Namibians shall continue to be eligible for assistance through the United Nations Educational and Training Programme for Southern Africa and the United Nations Trust Fund for South Africa;

18. *Commends* the progress made in the implementation of the pre-independence components of the Nationhood Programme for Namibia and requests the United Nations Council for Namibia to elaborate and consider policies and contingency plans regarding the transitional and post-independence phases of the Programme;

19. *Commends* the United Nations Institute for Namibia for the effectiveness of its training programmes for Namibians and its research activities on Namibia, which contribute substantially to the struggle for freedom of the Namibian people and to the establishment of an independent State of Namibia;

20. *Urges* the specialized agencies and other organizations and institutions of the United Nations system to co-operate closely with the United Nations Institute for Namibia in strengthening its programme of activities;

21. *Requests* the United Nations Council for Namibia, through the United Nations Institute for Namibia, to finalize and publish at an early date a comprehensive reference book on Namibia covering all aspects of the question of Namibia as considered by the United Nations since its inception, in accordance with an outline to be prepared by the Council;

22. *Requests* the United Nations Council for Namibia, in consultation with the Office of the United Nations Commissioner for Namibia, to finalize and publish at an early date a demographic study of the Namibian population and a study of its educational needs;

23. *Requests* the United Nations Institute for Namibia to complete the preparation, in co-operation with the South West Africa People's Organization, the Office of the United Nations Commissioner for Namibia and the United Nations Development Programme, of a comprehensive document on all aspects of economic planning in an independent Namibia, and requests the Secretary-General to continue to provide substantive support through the Office of the Commissioner for the preparation of that document;

24. *Requests* the Secretary-General to continue to provide the Office of the United Nations Commissioner for Namibia with the necessary resources for the performance of the responsibilities entrusted to it by the United Nations Council for Namibia as the co-ordinating authority

for the implementation of the Nationhood Programme for Namibia, as well as other assistance programmes.

General Assembly resolution 39/50 E

12 December 1984   Meeting 97   149-0-5 (recorded vote)

Draft by Council for Namibia (A/39/24); agenda item 29.
Financial implications. ACABQ, A/39/7/Add.13 & Corr.1; 5th Committee, A/39/813; S-G, A/39/C.5/39/70 & Add.1 & Corr.1.
Meeting numbers. GA 39th session: 4th Committee 15, 19; 5th Committee 46; plenary 78-84, 86, 94, 97.

Recorded vote in Assembly as follows:

In favour: Afghanistan, Albania, Algeria, Angola, Antigua and Barbuda, Argentina, Australia, Austria, Bahamas, Bahrain, Bangladesh, Barbados, Belgium, Belize, Benin, Bhutan, Bolivia, Botswana, Brazil, Brunei Darussalam, Bulgaria, Burkina Faso, Burma, Burundi, Byelorussian SSR, Cameroon, Cape Verde, Central African Republic, Chad, Chile, China, Colombia, Comoros, Congo, Costa Rica, Cuba, Cyprus, Czechoslovakia, Democratic Kampuchea, Democratic Yemen, Denmark, Djibouti, Dominica, Dominican Republic, Ecuador, Egypt, El Salvador, Equatorial Guinea, Ethiopia, Fiji, Finland, Gabon, Gambia, German Democratic Republic, Ghana, Greece, Grenada, Guatemala, Guinea, Guinea-Bissau, Guyana, Haiti, Honduras, Hungary, Iceland, India, Indonesia, Iran, Iraq, Ireland, Italy, Ivory Coast, Jamaica, Japan, Jordan, Kenya, Kuwait, Lao People's Democratic Republic, Lebanon, Lesotho, Liberia, Libyan Arab Jamahiriya, Luxembourg, Madagascar, Malawi, Malaysia, Maldives, Mali, Malta, Mauritania, Mauritius, Mexico, Mongolia, Morocco, Mozambique, Nepal, Netherlands, New Zealand, Nicaragua, Niger, Norway, Oman, Pakistan, Panama, Papua New Guinea, Paraguay, Peru, Philippines, Poland, Portugal, Qatar, Romania, Rwanda, Saint Lucia, Saint Vincent and the Grenadines, Samoa, Sao Tome and Principe, Saudi Arabia, Senegal, Seychelles, Sierra Leone, Singapore, Somalia, Spain, Sri Lanka, Sudan, Suriname, Swaziland, Sweden, Syrian Arab Republic, Thailand, Togo, Trinidad and Tobago, Tunisia, Turkey, Uganda, Ukrainian SSR, USSR, United Arab Emirates, United Republic of Tanzania, Uruguay, Vanuatu, Venezuela, Viet Nam, Yemen, Yugoslavia, Zaire, Zambia, Zimbabwe.

Against: None.

Abstaining: Canada, France, Germany, Federal Republic of, United Kingdom, United States.

In explanation of vote, Japan said that its affirmative vote should not be construed as support for all paragraphs; in regard to the increase in the budget appropriations, Japan, while recognizing and appreciating the role that the United Nations Fund for Namibia was playing, recalled that it was established as a voluntary fund and expressed reservations regarding paragraph 5, which allocated $1 million from the regular budget.

Financing of the Fund

In 1984, 41 States made a total contribution of $4,397,313 to the United Nations Fund for Namibia (see table). In addition to voluntary contributions, the Fund was financed by the United Nations regular budget ($1 million for 1984 as authorized by the General Assembly in 1983[10]) and UNDP assistance for projects. For that purpose, UNDP had established an indicative planning figure (IPF) for Namibia ($7,750,000 for 1982-1986).

The Council for Namibia organized several fund-raising missions in 1984: to Denmark, Norway, Finland and Sweden (11 to 18 April); Japan (28 and 29 May); and Austria, the Federal Republic of Germany, the Netherlands, Belgium, EEC, Italy and France (13 to 22 June).[1] Those Governments recognized the need to prepare the Namibian people for independence and expressed their continuing support for the Council's assistance programmes.

By resolution 39/50 E, the General Assembly called for increased assistance to Namibians through the Fund, and decided to allocate $1 million from the 1985 regular United Nations budget. It requested the Secretary-General and the President of the Council to appeal for more contributions in view of the Fund's increased activities and the need for more scholarships. Governments were invited to appeal to their national organizations for voluntary contributions.

CONTRIBUTIONS TO THE UN FUND FOR NAMIBIA, 1984

(as at 31 December 1984)

Amount (in US dollar equivalent)

Country	General Account	Nationhood Programme	Institute for Namibia
Afghanistan	—	—	500
Australia	65,219	—	—
Austria	15,500	—	—
Bahamas	1,000	—	—
Bangladesh	15,000	—	—
Barbados	500	—	—
Cameroon	2,519	—	—
Canada	—	—	153,363
China	30,000	—	—
Cyprus	196	196	—
Denmark	—	95,932	435,054
Egypt	—	—	—
Finland	62,002	442,870	259,619
France	39,429	—	104,058
Germany, Federal Republic of	—	—	75,680
Greece	4,500	—	5,500
Guyana	16,000	—	—
Iceland	2,000	—	—
India	2,000	2,000	4,000
Indonesia	4,000	—	—
Ireland	6,069	6,069	6,069
Italy	25,981	—	—
Japan	10,000	—	210,000
Kuwait	4,000	—	1,000
Mexico	5,000	—	—
Netherlands	50,847	—	101,695
New Zealand	3,321	—	—
Norway	—	256,115	311,148
Pakistan	3,000	—	—
Panama	1,000	—	—
Republic of Korea	—	—	7,000
Swaziland	777	—	—
Sweden	379,747	—	500,801
Thailand	—	—	1,000
Togo	172	—	172
Trinidad and Tobago	1,493	—	—
Tunisia	824	—	206
Turkey	5,406	—	976
United States	—	—	621,986
Venezuela	4,000	—	2,000
Zimbabwe	30,802	—	—
Total	792,304	803,182	2,801,827

SOURCE: Accounts for the 12-month period of the biennium 1984-1985 ended 31 December 1984. Schedules of Individual Trust Funds.

Nationhood Programme

The Nationhood Programme for Namibia, launched by the General Assembly in 1976 to help the Territory prepare for independence,[11] continued in 1984 to finance training programmes and surveys of the Namibian economic and social sectors. The Council for Namibia[1] reported that during 1983 and the first half of 1984, a new group of students commenced training in the administration of public enterprises, English language, fisheries management

and fish processing, labour administration, electricity supply, water supply, pilot training, nursing, shoemaking and leatherwork, and teacher education. In-service training began in truck maintenance, mining and railways operations, and labour administration, and continued in statistics, mining and land use for agriculture. A group of disabled Namibians began six-month training courses in various technical areas. Training continued in geology and mining, maritime economics and management, aircraft maintenance and traffic control, and development planning.

The United Nations Vocational Training Centre for Namibia in Angola, which became operational in 1983,[12] could not be staffed by internationally recruited supervisors at the level envisaged because of the situation in the area where the Centre was located. Its Governing Board held its fifth meeting in Angola in May 1984, and took measures to ensure continuous adequate staffing.

All of the surveys envisaged since the inception of the Programme were either completed or were expected to be completed by the end of 1984. Final reports on transport, health, land use, human settlements development, labour legislation and transnational corporations had been distributed to the Council. The reports on civil aviation, telecommunications and a draft harbour survey had been finalized and awaited distribution. Draft reports on agrarian reform, land suitability, protection of food supplies, agricultural education, public administration systems, the criminal justice system and energy supply had been prepared and awaited further discussion.

In resolution 1984/55, the Economic and Social Council requested United Nations organizations to increase assistance to the Namibian people in consultation with OAU and the Council for Namibia, particularly concerning the Nationhood Programme.

The General Assembly, in resolution 38/50 E, decided that the Council for Namibia would continue to act as trustee of the Fund, and in that capacity, administer and manage it. The Assembly requested United Nations organizations to expedite Nationhood Programme projects and others in favour of Namibians based on procedures reflecting the Council's role as the legal Administering Authority for Namibia. The organizations were urged to continue participating in the Programme by implementing projects, initiating new project proposals, and allocating funds from their own financial resources for projects approved by the Council. In that regard, the Assembly urged UNDP to continue to allocate funds from the IPF for Namibia for the projects. The Assembly commended the progress made in implementing pre-independence components of the Programme and requested the Council to elaborate policies and contingency plans for transitional and post-independence phases.

UN Institute for Namibia

Inaugurated in 1976 at Lusaka,[13] the United Nations Institute for Namibia continued in 1984 to develop human resources in anticipation of Namibia's independence.[1] Open to all persons of Namibian origin who met the requirements of the Institute's 16-member Senate, the Institute held training courses and undertook applied research in various sectors. The Senate, which reported annually to the Council for Namibia, operated on an average annual budget of $4 million financed through the Fund for Namibia. Financial assistance was also provided by UNDP and UNHCR. In 1984, the enrolment totaled 457 students, of whom 183 were new. The curriculum was expanded to include a teacher-training upgrading programme, a special programme for magistrates, a secretarial programme, courses in English, statistics and mathematics. In March, the fifth group of students (92 in 1984) graduated from the Institute with diplomas in management and development studies, thus bringing the total number of graduates to 374.

The Institute's research programme was intended to make available basic documentation for policy formulation by the future Government of an independent Namibia. Studies had been completed and published on human resources requirements, constitutional options, agrarian reform, a language policy for Namibia, a legal system, agricultural economics and a health survey. Studies were under way on development strategy options, the mining industry, an administrative system, trade policy options, monetary policy options, wages and income policy options, the caracul industry and others. The Institute continued its work on a Handbook on Namibia covering various aspects of the question as considered by the United Nations since its inception, and on a comprehensive study on economic planning in an independent Namibia.

In 1984, the Institute's Namibian Extension Unit, which administered an education programme for Namibians whose access to formal education was limited, served some 40,000 Namibian adults and youths in Angola and Zambia.

In resolution 39/59 E, the General Assembly decided that the Council would continue to provide broad guidelines and formulate principles and policies for the Institute. It called on UNDP to continue allocating funds from the IPF for Namibia for the Institute's projects. The Assembly requested the Institute to complete the document on economic planning in an independent Namibia, and requested the Secretary-General to continue providing support for its preparation.

Other UN assistance

UN Educational and Training Programme. In an October 1984 report to the General Assembly,[14] the Secretary-General stated that for the 1983/84 academic year, the United Nations Educational and Training Programme for Southern Africa (see p. 190) granted 32 new scholarship awards to Namibians and extended 17. The scholarships did not include awards financed by the United Nations Fund for Namibia.

UNDP assistance. In 1984, UNDP continued to provide assistance to SWAPO through four ongoing projects—three in education and one in health—for a total value of $882,617, according to the UNDP Administrator's March 1985 report on assistance to national liberation movements recognized by OAU.[15] The educational projects, all executed by UNESCO, included two aimed at strengthening SWAPO's Namibia Education Centres—the movement's own primary and secondary school system—in its settlements at Kwanza Sul, Angola, and Nyango, Zambia. UNDP assistance went towards the salaries of five Zambian mathematics and science teachers, and living allowances for 48 Namibian teachers at the two settlements. Assistance was also provided to meet the living allowances of support personnel. The third educational project was training for women's role in development, for which courses were organized in teaching, development of co-operatives, nutrition, home economics and handicrafts.

The fourth project was strengthening basic health services, including training, in the two SWAPO settlements, with WHO acting as executing agency. According to the UNDP Administrator, the agency had not been punctual in paying the allowances for the three Namibian doctors and 69 paramedical personnel working in settlements, or in processing fellowship forms for SWAPO candidates.

In response to a 1983 UNDP Governing Council decision,[16] the UNDP Administrator submitted a progress report[17] to the 1984 Council on support costs of projects financed from the United Nations Fund for Namibia (see above). In accordance with the Administrator's recommendation, the Council adopted a 19 June decision[18] by which it expressed appreciation to him and the executing agencies for action taken to treat part of project costs as expenditures against government cash counterpart contributions, took note of agencies' views and those of the Commissioner for Namibia on granting total waiver of such support costs, and noted that the Commissioner intended to continue discussions with agencies with a view to obtaining full waiver.

UNCTAD activities. In 1983, UNCTAD VI, by resolution 147(VI)[19] had urged the UNCTAD Secretary-General to co-operate with the Institute for Namibia, through the provision of technical expertise, in preparing a document on economic planning in an independent Namibia. In response, the UNCTAD secretariat approached UNDP to secure the resources, but funds were not available, according to a June 1984 report by the United Nations

Secretary-General.[20] On 21 September,[21] the Trade and Development Board requested the UNCTAD Secretary-General to implement the 1983 resolution, and urged the UNDP Administrator to provide adequate resources.

Agency assistance. The Secretary-General, in a June 1984 report to the General Assembly,[20] transmitted information from the specialized agencies and other United Nations organizations on their assistance to colonial countries (see p. 999), including aid to Namibians. Updated information was included in a 1985 report.[22] Some agencies, including FAO and ILO, provided aid through the Nationhood Programme for Namibia. FAO conducted workshops on nutrition and agriculture, provided supplies for a day-care centre, and assisted in agricultural surveys and related policy options. WHO provided training, fellowships, drugs and medical equipment. UNHCR provided $4.3 million for Namibian refugees in Angola for projects including purchase of medicines, basic relief items, vehicles and agricultural goods; an addition to a vocational training centre; construction of a rehabilitation centre for handicapped refugees and school facilities; construction materials for a self-help housing plan and the upgrading of roads;

parts to repair vehicles; and scholarships to 386 Namibians at the lower secondary and vocational levels. UNESCO provided training for teachers at all levels, school materials and audio-visual equipment for centres managed by SWAPO.

ECONOMIC AND SOCIAL COUNCIL ACTION

In resolution 1984/55, the Economic and Social Council requested United Nations organizations, in the light of the liberation struggle in Namibia, to do everything possible to increase assistance to the Namibian people, in consultation with OAU and the Council for Namibia, in particular in connection with the Nationhood Programme.

REFERENCES

[1]A/39/24. [2]A/39/23 (dec. A/AC.109/794). [3]*Ibid.* (res. A/AC.109/797). [4]YUN 1982, p. 1300, GA res. 37/233 A, 20 Dec. 1982. [5]YUN 1983, p. 1061, GA res. 38/36 A, 1 Dec. 1983. [6]*Ibid.*, p. 1076. [7]A/39/582. [8]YUN 1972, p. 616. [9]A/AC.131/113. [10]YUN 1983, p. 1077, GA res. 38/36 E, 1 Dec. 1983. [11]YUN 1976, p. 791, GA res. 31/153, 20 Dec. 1976. [12]YUN 1983, p. 1080. [13]YUN 1976, p. 779. [14]A/39/351. [15]DP/1985/17. [16]YUN 1983, p. 1082. [17]DP/1984/14/Add.1. [18]E/1984/20 (dec. 84/13). [19]YUN 1983, p. 1082. [20]A/39/293 & Add.1-3. [21]A/39/15, vol. II (res. 304(XXIX)). [22]A/40/318 & Add.1.

Chapter IV

Other colonial Territories

Conflicts in Western Sahara and East Timor and the sovereignty dispute between Argentina and the United Kingdom over the Falkland Islands (Malvinas) continued to be considered in 1984 by the General Assembly and its Special Committee on the Situation with regard to the Implementation of the Declaration on the Granting of Independence to Colonial Countries and Peoples (Committee on colonial countries).

The Assembly, in resolution 39/40, reaffirming that the Western Sahara question was related to decolonization, again requested Morocco and the Frente Popular para la Liberación de Saguia el-Hamra y de Río de Oro to undertake direct negotiations for a cease-fire and a self-determination referendum among the people of Western Sahara, under the auspices of the United Nations and the Organization of African Unity. By decision 39/402, it decided to consider the East Timor question in 1985. Meanwhile, the human rights situations in both Western Sahara (see p. 811) and East Timor (see p. 808) were also examined in 1984.

In resolution 39/6, the Assembly again requested Argentina and the United Kingdom to resume negotiations for a peaceful solution to their sovereignty dispute and other differences over the Falkland Islands (Malvinas); it also requested the Secretary-General to continue his good offices mission.

The Assembly adopted resolutions on American Samoa (39/31), Guam (39/32) and the United States Virgin Islands (39/38), under United States administration, and on Bermuda (39/33), the British Virgin Islands (39/34), the Cayman Islands (39/35), Montserrat (39/36) and the Turks and Caicos Islands (39/37), under United Kingdom administration.

A United Nations mission visited Anguilla in 1984, and the Assembly, in resolution 39/39, called on the United Kingdom as the administering Power to intensify its programmes of political education and development assistance in Anguilla. The Assembly noted in resolution 39/30 that another visiting mission had observed an act of self-determination in the Cocos (Keeling) Islands by which a substantial majority of the people voted for integration with Australia. In decision 39/410, it welcomed an agreement by Spain and the United Kingdom to implement their 1980 Lisbon Declaration on Gibraltar by February 1985, in-

cluding equality of rights, freedom of movement, and negotiation of differences.

It called on the United Kingdom in decision 39/409 to safeguard the interests of the people of Pitcairn, and declared in decisions 39/408 and 39/411 that the possibility of sending visiting missions to Tokelau and St. Helena should be kept under review.

Background information on developments in most of the Territories was prepared for the Committee on colonial countries by the United Nations Secretariat. The Committee, and usually its Sub-Committee on Small Territories, considered the situation in each Territory, and made recommendations which were taken up mainly by the Assembly's Fourth Committee.

Topics related to this chapter. General questions relating to colonial countries: information to the United Nations; visiting missions.

Falkland Islands (Malvinas)

Communications (January-August). Letters concerning the question of the Falkland Islands (Malvinas) were sent by Argentina, Brazil and the United Kingdom to the President of the Security Council and the Secretary-General between January and August 1984.

Argentina, on 9 January,[1] transmitted a press release issued on 3 January noting that the day marked the 151st anniversary of what it called the occupation of the Malvinas by the United Kingdom, and underscoring Argentina's desire that the Malvinas, South Georgia and the South Sandwich Islands be restored to its jurisdiction. Argentina also reiterated its readiness to open the negotiations which the General Assembly had recommended in November 1983.[2]

On 10 February,[3] Argentina charged that British aircraft had committed acts of provocation against Argentine fishing vessels, outside a so-called protection zone arbitrarily established by the United Kingdom; on 6 November 1983, a Royal Air Force plane had twice overflown the *Api IV*, and on 24 December, two British aircraft had twice overflown the *Atilio Malvagni*.

On 23 July,[4] Argentina stated that it had met with the United Kingdom (Berne, Switzerland, 18 and 19 July) in the presence of representatives of

Brazil, and had reaffirmed its right of sovereignty over the Malvinas, South Georgia and the South Sandwich Islands; according to the letter, the United Kingdom would not enter into negotiations on the sovereignty issue.

On 27 July,[5] Brazil transmitted a joint communiqué issued by Brazil and Switzerland following the Berne meeting stating that Argentina had reaffirmed it was necessary to establish machinery to discuss the sovereignty question, while the United Kingdom was not prepared to discuss the matter but had advanced several proposals which it said might lend themselves to negotiation; Argentina had replied that it was not prepared to go into those points if the sovereignty question could not be examined.

Referring to the 23 July letter from Argentina, the United Kingdom on 2 August[6] declared that the best way to establish more normal relations with Argentina was to discuss practical issues such as resuming commercial relations, restoring air services, and a visit by Argentine next-of-kin to graves on the Falkland Islands, but Argentina was not prepared to negotiate on that basis.

Action by the Committee on colonial countries. The Committee on colonial countries considered the Falkland Islands (Malvinas) question on 16 and 20 August, hearing statements by the United Kingdom as the administering Power, by representatives of the Falklands Legislative Council, by Argentina and by Committee members. On 20 August,[7] the Committee urged the two States to resume negotiations, reiterating its support for a renewed good offices mission by the Secretary-General based on 1982[8] and 1983[2] Assembly resolutions and deciding to keep the question under review, subject to Assembly directives.

Report of the Secretary-General. The Secretary-General, in pursuance of the 1983 Assembly resolution,[2] submitted a report in October 1984 on the question.[9] He said that he had had extensive exchanges with Argentina and the United Kingdom, including meetings with the President of Argentina and the Prime Minister of the United Kingdom as well as their Foreign Ministers. Though the Berne talks (see above) had not achieved the desired progress and it had not yet proven possible to implement the 1983 Assembly resolution, he continued to believe that dialogue and confidence-building measures could help both countries to restore normalcy in the South Atlantic. He stood ready to assist the parties in that process.

Communications (October-December). By a letter of 8 October,[10] India forwarded the final communiqué adopted by the Meeting of Foreign Ministers and Heads of Delegation of Non-Aligned Countries to the 1984 General Assembly (New York, 1-5 October) in which they reiterated

support for the return of the Malvinas to Argentina, for the resumption of negotiations with the participation of the Secretary-General, and for due regard to the interests of the population of the islands.

On 4 December,[11] Argentina transmitted a resolution on the Malvinas question adopted by the Organization of American States (OAS) on 17 November, expressing support for Assembly resolutions requesting the two States to resume negotiations and the Secretary-General to continue his good offices mission and also expressing concern over the lack of progress in complying with those resolutions.

GENERAL ASSEMBLY ACTION

On 1 November, the General Assembly adopted resolution 39/6 by recorded vote.

Question of the Falkland Islands (Malvinas)
The General Assembly,

Having considered the question of the Falkland Islands (Malvinas) and having received the report of the Secretary-General,

Recalling its resolutions 1514(XV) of 14 December 1960, 2065(XX) of 16 December 1965, 3160(XXVIII) of 14 December 1973, 31/49 of 1 December 1976, 37/9 of 4 November 1982 and 38/12 of 16 November 1983, together with Security Council resolutions 502(1982) of 3 April 1982 and 505(1982) of 26 May 1982,

Reaffirming the principles of the Charter of the United Nations on the non-use of force or the threat of force in international relations and the obligation of States to settle their international disputes by peaceful means and recalling that, in this respect, the General Assembly has repeatedly requested the Governments of Argentina and the United Kingdom of Great Britain and Northern Ireland to resume negotiations in order to find as soon as possible a peaceful, just and definitive solution to the sovereignty dispute relating to the question of the Falkland Islands (Malvinas),

Observing with concern that, in spite of the time which has elapsed since the adoption of resolution 2065(XX), the prolonged dispute has not yet been resolved,

Aware of the interest of the international community in the settlement by the Governments of Argentina and the United Kingdom of all their differences, in accordance with the United Nations ideals of peace and friendship among peoples,

Taking note of the communiqué issued by the representatives of the Government of Switzerland and the Government of Brazil at Berne on 20 July 1984,

Reaffirming the need for the parties to take due account of the interests of the population of the Falkland Islands (Malvinas) in accordance with the provisions of General Assembly resolutions 2065(XX), 3160(XXVIII), 37/9 and 38/12,

1. *Reiterates its request* to the Governments of Argentina and the United Kingdom of Great Britain and Northern Ireland to resume negotiations in order to find as soon as possible a peaceful solution to the sovereignty dispute and their remaining differences relating to the question of the Falkland Islands (Malvinas);

2. *Requests* the Secretary-General to continue his renewed mission of good offices in order to assist the parties in complying with the request made in paragraph 1 above, and to take the necessary measures to that end;

3. *Requests* the Secretary-General to submit to the General Assembly at its fortieth session a report on the progress made in the implementation of the present resolution;

4. *Decides* to include in the provisional agenda of its fortieth session the item entitled "Question of the Falkland Islands (Malvinas)".

General Assembly resolution 39/6

1 November 1984   Meeting 46   89-9-54 (recorded vote)

20-nation draft (A/39/L.8); agenda item 26.
Sponsors: Argentina, Bolivia, Brazil, Chile, Colombia, Costa Rica, Cuba, Dominican Republic, Ecuador, El Salvador, Guatemala, Haiti, Honduras, Mexico, Nicaragua, Panama, Paraguay, Peru, Uruguay, Venezuela.
Meeting numbers. GA 39th session: plenary 44-46.

Recorded vote in Assembly as follows:

In favour: Afghanistan, Albania, Algeria, Angola, Argentina, Austria, Barbados, Benin, Bolivia, Botswana, Brazil, Bulgaria, Burkina Faso, Burundi, Byelorussian SSR, Cape Verde, Central African Republic, Chile, China, Colombia, Comoros, Congo, Costa Rica, Cuba, Cyprus, Czechoslovakia, Democratic Kampuchea, Democratic Yemen, Djibouti, Dominican Republic, Ecuador, El Salvador, Equatorial Guinea, Ethiopia, Gabon, German Democratic Republic, Ghana, Guatemala, Guinea, Guinea-Bissau, Guyana, Haiti, Honduras, Hungary, India, Indonesia, Iran, Iraq, Ivory Coast, Japan, Lao People's Democratic Republic, Libyan Arab Jamahiriya, Madagascar, Malaysia, Mali, Malta, Mauritania, Mexico, Mongolia, Morocco, Nicaragua, Nigeria, Pakistan, Panama, Paraguay, Peru, Philippines, Poland, Romania, Rwanda, Somalia, Spain, Suriname, Syrian Arab Republic, Togo, Tunisia, Uganda, Ukrainian SSR, USSR, United Republic of Tanzania, United States, Uruguay, Venezuela, Viet Nam, Yemen, Yugoslavia, Zaire, Zambia, Zimbabwe.
Against: Belize, Dominica, Grenada, Malawi, New Zealand, Oman, Solomon Islands, Sri Lanka, United Kingdom.
Abstaining: Antigua and Barbuda, Australia, Bahamas, Bahrain, Bangladesh, Belgium, Bhutan, Brunei Darussalam, Burma, Cameroon, Canada, Chad, Denmark, Egypt, Fiji, Finland, France, Germany, Federal Republic of, Greece, Iceland, Ireland, Israel, Italy, Jamaica, Jordan, Kenya, Kuwait, Lebanon, Lesotho, Liberia, Luxembourg, Maldives, Mauritius, Nepal, Netherlands, Norway, Papua New Guinea, Portugal, Qatar, Saint Lucia, Saint Vincent and the Grenadines, Samoa, Saudi Arabia, Senegal, Sierra Leone, Singapore, Sudan, Swaziland, Sweden, Thailand, Trinidad and Tobago, Turkey, United Arab Emirates, Vanuatu.

The United Kingdom, Belize, Malawi and New Zealand explained their opposition to the resolution. The United Kingdom said the policy of the current Argentine Government on sovereignty and self-determination did not differ from its predecessors. The text was full of references to negotiations about sovereignty, it said, and, moreover, insinuated that the wishes of the population of the Falkland Islands might be open to negotiation. However, the principle of self-determination applied in the case of the Falklands just as in other cases; the islanders had a Government that they had chosen and had the right to choose for themselves in the future. Belize was not convinced that the text contained elements conducive to a just and lasting solution. Malawi held that the text did not reconcile the two elements in dispute—sovereignty and self-determination. New Zealand opposed the resolution because it believed it did not adequately acknowledge the right of the Falklanders to a say in their future.

Among those that abstained, France was not convinced that the United Nations provided the best framework for the necessary negotiations. The

Netherlands felt that the draft contained references prejudging the outcome of the proposed negotiations. A lack of balance of essential elements of the problem in the text was discerned by Belgium. Australia, Chad, Norway and Saint Lucia felt that the interests of the islanders were not adequately served by the text. Greece said its vote was to enhance the appeal that the parties should resume negotiations. The Federal Republic of Germany spoke similarly, adding that the resolution contained several controversial elements. Turkey regretted that a consensus text had not been formulated. The Maldives said that the resolution did not give adequate emphasis to finding a negotiated settlement. Sweden felt it did not explicitly endorse or even refer to the fundamental principle of self-determination. Egypt hoped the two States involved would resume negotiations as soon as possible.

Although it saw the sovereignty of Argentina over the Malvinas as legitimate, Viet Nam said it hoped the parties would resume their talks. Similarly, Mongolia, while sympathizing with Argentina, voted for the resolution in the hope of a peaceful solution.

Earlier, on 31 October, the Assembly adopted without vote decision 39/404. The following petitioners had requested hearings[12] and made statements before the Fourth Committee on 30 October:[13] Lionel G. Blake and John E. Cheek, members of the Falkland Islands Legislative Council, and Alexander Jacob Betts and Susan Coutts de Maciello, natives of the Falkland Islands (Malvinas).

Question of the Falkland Islands (Malvinas)

At its 44th plenary meeting, on 31 October 1984, the General Assembly took note of the report of the Fourth Committee.

General Assembly decision 39/404

Adopted without vote

Oral proposal by President; agenda item 26.
Meeting numbers. GA 38th session: 4th Committee 3, 5, 7, 11-12; plenary 44.

REFERENCES

(1)A/39/72 & Corr.1. (2)YUN 1983, p. 1085, GA res. 38/12, 16 Nov. 1983. (3)S/16336. (4)A/39/359. (5)A/39/364. (6)A/39/373. (7)A/39/23 (A/AC.109/793). (8)YUN 1982, p. 1347, GA res. 37/9, 4 Nov. 1982. (9)A/39/589. (10)A/39/560-S/16773. (11)A/39/765. (12)A/C.4/39/3 & Add.1,2. (13)A/39/615.

East Timor

Communications. Three notes verbales on the question of East Timor were addressed to either the Secretary-General or the Secretariat in 1984.

On 12 March,[1] Portugal stated that it had nothing to add to information it had provided in 1979, as required by Article 73 *e* of the Charter of the United Nations.

On 3 July,[2] Sao Tome and Principe transmitted a statement of 26 January by the Frente Revolucionária de Timor Leste Independente (FRETILIN) on FRETILIN counter-attacks against what were said to be invasions by Indonesian forces; a 16 February letter from the Indonesian-appointed Apostolic Administrator of East Timor on the suffering of the population in several areas from sickness, hunger, lack of liberty and persecution; an appeal by Indonesian bishops for an end to the war; and two press articles—one by the Agence France Presse correspondent in Jakarta, Indonesia, on starvation caused by disruption of food production by military operations, the other by the Lisbon, Portugal, correspondent for major British and Australian newspapers on an Indonesian troop sweep across East Timor.

On 24 September,[3] Mozambique transmitted excerpts from a 14 July letter by a Catholic priest concerning events resulting from what was said to be the presence of Indonesian forces in East Timor between January and June and an interview with the former papal administrator of East Timor, published in *Newsweek* international of 3 September.

Report of the Secretary-General. On 25 July 1984, the Secretary-General submitted a progress report to the General Assembly on his efforts to promote a comprehensive settlement of the East Timor problem.[4] The report should have been submitted in 1983, but was not because he did not consider it opportune at that time.[5] In September 1983, the Assembly had deferred consideration of the topic until 1984.[6] The Secretary-General said that he or Under-Secretary-General Rafeeuddin Ahmed had held consultations with the Foreign Minister of Indonesia and the Prime Minister and Foreign Minister of Portugal; in addition, a Secretariat team had been formed to explore possible approaches to a settlement. The Secretary-General had requested Indonesia to facilitate the activities of such humanitarian organizations as the United Nations Children's Fund (UNICEF) and the International Committee of the Red Cross (ICRC) in East Timor. A UNICEF nutrition, primary health care and community development operation had covered 33 villages, with a population of 45,000, and ICRC was carrying out a family reunion/repatriation programme to Australia and Portugal. He said he would continue to try to improve the situation of the people of East Timor, which remained one of his primary concerns, reiterating his readiness to assist in trying to achieve a comprehensive settlement of the problem.

Action by the Committee on colonial countries. The Committee on colonial countries considered the East Timor question on 13 and 20 August 1984,[7] examining the military, human rights and food situations as well as economic, social and educational conditions.

The Committee, after hearing statements by Portugal as the administering Power, Indonesia, Mozambique, Sao Tome and Principe, FRETILIN, Amnesty International and the International League for Human Rights, decided to continue consideration of the question in 1985, subject to Assembly directives.

GENERAL ASSEMBLY ACTION

On 21 September 1984, the Assembly adopted decision 39/402 by which it decided to include the East Timor question in its provisional 1985 agenda (see p. 375). It took this action after the General Committee had recommended that the item be deferred.[8]

REFERENCES
[1]A/39/136. [2]A/39/345-S/16668. [3]S/16759. [4]A/39/361. [5]YUN 1983, p. 1086. [6]YUN 1983, p. 392, GA dec. 38/402, 23 Sep. 1983. [7]A/39/23. [8]A/39/250.

Western Sahara

Action by the Committee on colonial countries. Developments relating to the Western Sahara question were considered by the Committee on colonial countries on 17 August 1984,[1] with the Committee hearing statements by a representative of the Frente Popular para la Liberación de Saguia el-Hamra y de Río de Oro (POLISARIO Front), Cuba, Iran, Mali and Sweden. It decided to continue consideration of the question in 1985, subject to General Assembly directives.

Co-operation with OAU. The Secretary-General, in response to a 1983 Assembly resolution,[2] submitted to that body a 6 November report on the Western Sahara conflict.[3] The Assembly had urged him to co-operate with the Organization of African Unity (OAU) and its Implementation Committee on Western Sahara in organizing a referendum on self-determination in the Territory.

The Secretary-General stated that on 6 March he had informed the OAU Secretary-General that he remained ready to assist and co-operate with OAU and, on 25 July, had requested information on OAU activities related to the question. Replying on 22 October, the OAU secretariat stated that the Implementation Committee had met (Addis Ababa, Ethiopia, 21 and 22 September 1983) but had adjourned in view of the difficulties for the parties to the conflict to negotiate directly to establish a cease-fire; the Committee had not been convened since then. On 21 November,[4] the Secretary-General added that in a communication of that day OAU stated that the Saharan Arab Democratic Republic (SADR) had resumed its seat as an OAU member during its twentieth session (Addis Ababa, 12-15 November), resulting in Morocco withdrawing from OAU and Zaire suspending its participation.

By a 21 November letter,[5] the United Republic of Tanzania transmitted to the Secretary-General the report of the Implementation Committee which had been adopted at the November OAU meeting.

The Committee pointed out that by OAU resolution AHG/Res.104(XIX) of 1983,[6] it had been required to report on the conduct of the referendum on self-determination, but due to Morocco's refusal to negotiate on a cease-fire to create the conditions for a peaceful and fair referendum it had not been organized.

GENERAL ASSEMBLY ACTION

On 5 December, on the recommendation of the Fourth Committee, the General Assembly adopted resolution 39/40 by recorded vote.

Question of Western Sahara

The General Assembly,

Having considered in depth the question of Western Sahara,

Recalling the inalienable right of all peoples to self-determination and independence in accordance with the principles set forth in the Charter of the United Nations and in General Assembly resolution 1514(XV) of 14 December 1960, containing the Declaration on the Granting of Independence to Colonial Countries and Peoples,

Recalling its resolution 38/40 of 7 December 1983 on the question of Western Sahara,

Having considered the relevant chapter of the report of the Special Committee on the Situation with regard to the Implementation of the Declaration on the Granting of Independence to Colonial Countries and Peoples,

Taking note of the report of the Implementation Committee of the Organization of African Unity on Western Sahara,

Recalling resolution AHG/Res.104(XIX) on Western Sahara, adopted by the Assembly of Heads of State and Government of the Organization of African Unity at its nineteenth ordinary session, held at Addis Ababa from 6 to 12 June 1983,

1. *Reaffirms* that the question of Western Sahara is a question of decolonization which remains to be completed on the basis of the exercise by the people of Western Sahara of their inalienable right to self-determination and independence;

2. *Reaffirms* that the solution of the question of Western Sahara lies in the implementation of resolution AHG/Res.104(XIX) of the Assembly of Heads of State and Government of the Organization of African Unity, which establishes ways and means for a just and definitive political solution to the Western Sahara conflict;

3. *Requests*, to that end, the parties to the conflict, the Kingdom of Morocco and the Frente Popular para la Liberación de Saguia el-Hamra y de Río de Oro, to undertake direct negotiations with a view to bringing about a cease-fire to create the necessary conditions for a peaceful and fair referendum for self-determination of the people of Western Sahara, a referendum without any administrative or military constraints, under the auspices of the Organization of African Unity and the United Nations;

4. *Welcomes* the efforts of the Organization of African Unity and its Implementation Committee with a view to promoting a just and definitive solution to the question of Western Sahara in accordance with the resolutions and decisions of that organization and the United Nations on the question;

5. *Reaffirms* the determination of the United Nations to co-operate fully with the Organization of African Unity with a view to implementing the relevant decisions of that organization, in particular resolution AHG/Res.104(XIX);

6. *Requests* the Special Committee on the Situation with regard to the Implementation of the Declaration on the Granting of Independence to Colonial Countries and Peoples to continue to consider the situation in Western Sahara as a matter of priority and to report thereon to the General Assembly at its fortieth session;

7. *Invites* the Secretary-General of the Organization of African Unity to keep the Secretary-General of the United Nations informed of the progress achieved in the implementation of the decisions of the Organization of African Unity relating to Western Sahara;

8. *Invites* the Secretary-General to follow the situation in Western Sahara closely with a view to the implementation of the present resolution and to report to the General Assembly at its fortieth session.

General Assembly resolution 39/40

5 December 1984   Meeting 87   90-0-42 (recorded vote)

Approved by Fourth Committee (A/39/696) by roll-call vote (90-1-45), 28 November (meeting 24); 41-nation draft (A/C.4/39/L.13); agenda item 18.

Sponsors: Afghanistan, Algeria, Angola, Benin, Belize, Bolivia, Botswana, Burkina Faso, Burundi, Cape Verde, Congo, Costa Rica, Cuba, Cyprus, Democratic Yemen, Ethiopia, Ghana, Guinea-Bissau, Guyana, Iran, Lao People's Democratic Republic, Lesotho, Madagascar, Malawi, Mali, Mauritania, Mexico, Mozambique, Nicaragua, Panama, Rwanda, Sao Tome and Principe, Senegal, Seychelles, Togo, Uganda, Vanuatu, Viet Nam, Yugoslavia, Zambia, Zimbabwe.

Meeting numbers. GA 39th session: 4th Committee 7, 20-24; plenary 87.

Recorded vote in Assembly as follows:

In favour: Afghanistan, Albania, Algeria, Angola, Argentina, Australia, Austria, Barbados, Belize, Benin, Botswana, Brazil, Bulgaria, Burkina Faso, Burundi, Byelorussian SSR, Cameroon, Cape Verde, Central African Republic, Chad, Colombia, Congo, Costa Rica, Cuba, Cyprus, Czechoslovakia, Democratic Yemen, Dominican Republic, Ecuador, Egypt, Ethiopia, Fiji, Finland, Gambia, German Democratic Republic, Ghana, Greece, Guinea-Bissau, Guyana, Haiti, Hungary, India, Iran, Jamaica, Kenya, Lao People's Democratic Republic, Lesotho, Liberia, Madagascar, Malawi, Mali, Malta, Mauritania, Mauritius, Mexico, Mongolia, Mozambique, New Zealand, Nicaragua, Niger, Nigeria, Panama, Papua New Guinea, Peru, Poland, Rwanda, Sao Tome and Principe, Senegal, Seychelles, Sierra Leone, Spain, Suriname, Sweden, Syrian Arab Republic, Togo, Trinidad and Tobago, Tunisia, Uganda, Ukrainian SSR, USSR, United Republic of Tanzania, Uruguay, Vanuatu, Venezuela, Viet Nam, Yugoslavia, Zambia, Zimbabwe.

Against: None.

Abstaining: Bangladesh, Belgium, Brunei Darussalam, Burma, Canada, Chile, China, Denmark, El Salvador, France, Gabon, Germany, Federal Republic of, Honduras, Iceland, Indonesia, Ireland, Israel, Italy, Ivory Coast, Japan, Jordan, Luxembourg, Malaysia, Maldives, Nepal, Netherlands, Norway, Pakistan, Paraguay, Philippines, Portugal, Samoa, Saudi Arabia, Singapore, Somalia, Sri Lanka, Sudan, Thailand, Turkey, United Kingdom, United States, Zaire.

Morocco also submitted a draft resolution,[7] to which amendments were offered by Sao Tome and Principe, Burkina Faso, and Algeria, Madagascar and Mozambique. By that text, the Assembly would have requested the Secretary-General to pursue consideration of the question, lend his good offices to the speedy attainment of a cease-fire and organize a referendum on self-determination. Subsequently, Morocco withdrew the draft, and stated that it would not participate in voting on a draft which, it said, disregarded all the efforts made and retained only one condition—the most controversial—which had not been retained by the OAU Implementation Committee, namely, direct negotiations between Morocco and the so-called Liberation Front.

Several States explained their abstentions. The United States regretted that it had not been possible to bridge the positions put forward in the two drafts, while China felt it would be useful to African unity if patient negotiations rather than confrontation could settle the problem. Gabon declared that its vote reflected its concern for a peaceful solution. The Sudan did not like the inclusion of certain language in the text. Honduras, which voted for the text in the Committee, abstained in plenary because several African countries had abstained in the Committee or had not participated in the vote.

On 23 November, the Assembly in resolution 39/17 reabffirmed the 1981 and 1983 OAU resolutions on organizing a referendum.

During its consideration of the question, the Fourth Committee heard the following petitioners:[8] Thomas Jallaud, President, Association des amis de la République arabe sahraouie démocratique; Ahmed Rachid, Secretary-General, Mouvement des originaires du Sahara; Breika Zerouali, for the deputies of the Saharan provinces, Laayoune; Dakhil Khalil, Parti de l'Union nationale sahraouie, Laayoune; Malika M'barka Zaraiali, Union des femmes du Sahara marocaines, Laayoune; Rachid Douihi, Secretary-General, Front de libération et de l'unité; Hamdati Chbihanna Maalainine, President, Association des anciens membres de l'armée de libération marocaine dans les provinces sahariennes Es-Smara (Morocco); Leili Mohamed Salem, Association des parents des séquestrés de Tindouf Oued-ed-dahab (Morocco); Biadillah Mohamed Cheikh, Secretary-General, Front de libération du Sahara (Morocco); Taquiollah Maalainine, on behalf of those elected by the communes and occupational chambers, Laayoune (Morocco); Ali Habib Kentaoui, deputy representative of POLISARIO in New York; and Mohamed Maalainine, Assemblée sahraouie, Laayoune (*Jema'a*).

It was orally pointed out to the Fourth Committee that the draft which became resolution 39/40 would have financial implications because it required United Nations co-operation in implementing the OAU resolution which called for a joint United Nations–OAU peace-keeping force in Western Sahara. As the Secretary-General was currently not in a position to prepare estimates of those financial implications, he intended, subject to the concurrence of the Advisory Committee on Administrative and Budgetary Questions, to incur such expenditures as might be necessary under unforeseen and extraordinary expenses.

Other action. A call for the OAU resolutions, particularly that of 1983, to be implemented immediately was also made by the Movement of Non-Aligned Countries (New York, 1-5 October).[9]

REFERENCES

[1]A/39/23. [2]YUN 1983, p. 1087, GA res. 38/40, 7 Dec. 1983. [3]A/39/634. [4]A/39/634/Add.1. [5]A/39/680. [6]YUN 1983, p. 1087. [7]A/C.4/39/L.14/Rev.1. [8]A/C.4/39/2 & Add.2,3 & Add.3/Corr.1 & Add.5-10 & Add.12 & Add.12/Corr.1. [9]A/39/560-S/16773.

Other Territories

American Samoa

GENERAL ASSEMBLY ACTION

On 5 December 1984, on the recommendation of the Fourth Committee, the General Assembly adopted without vote resolution 39/31.

Question of American Samoa
The General Assembly,

Having considered the question of American Samoa,

Having examined the relevant chapters of the report of the Special Committee on the Situation with regard to the Implementation of the Declaration on the Granting of Independence to Colonial Countries and Peoples,

Recalling its resolution 1514(XV) of 14 December 1960, containing the Declaration on the Granting of Independence to Colonial Countries and Peoples, and all other resolutions and decisions of the United Nations relating to American Samoa, including in particular its resolution 38/41 of 7 December 1983,

Taking into account the statement of the representative of the administering Power relating to American Samoa,

Conscious of the need to promote progress towards the full implementation of the Declaration in respect of American Samoa,

Noting with appreciation the continued participation of the administering Power in the work of the Special Committee in regard to American Samoa, thereby enabling it to conduct a more informed and meaningful examination of the situation in the Territory,

Reiterating the view that it remains the obligation of the administering Power to carry out a thorough programme of political education so as to ensure that the people of American Samoa are made fully aware of their inalienable right to self-determination and independence in accordance with General Assembly resolution 1514(XV),

Noting that the first five-year economic development plan for the Territory, implemented by the Development Planning Office of the Government of American Samoa, is due to expire at the end of 1984,

Aware of the special circumstances of the geographical location and economic conditions of American Samoa and stressing the necessity of diversifying the economy of the Territory as a matter of priority in order to reduce its dependence on fluctuating market conditions,

Mindful that United Nations visiting missions provide an effective means of ascertaining the situation in the small Territories and expressing its satisfaction at the willingness of the administering Power to receive visiting missions in the Territories under its administration,

1. *Approves* the chapter of the report of the Special Committee on the Situation with regard to the Implementation of the Declaration on the Granting of Independence to Colonial Countries and Peoples relating to American Samoa;

2. *Reaffirms* the inalienable right of the people of American Samoa to self-determination and independence in conformity with the Declaration on the Granting of Independence to Colonial Countries and Peoples, contained in General Assembly resolution 1514(XV);

3. *Reiterates* the view that such factors as territorial size, geographical location, size of population and limited natural resources should in no way delay the speedy exercise by the people of the Territory of their inalienable right to self-determination and independence in conformity with the Declaration contained in General Assembly resolution 1514(XV), which fully applies to American Samoa;

4. *Calls upon* the Government of the United States of America, as the administering Power, to take all necessary steps, taking into account the freely expressed wishes of the people of American Samoa, to expedite the process of decolonization of the Territory in accordance with the relevant provisions of the Charter of the United Nations and the Declaration;

5. *Reaffirms* that it is the responsibility of the administering Power to carry out a thorough programme of political education so as to ensure that the people of American Samoa are kept fully aware of their inalienable right to self-determination and independence;

6. *Takes note* of the fact that a constitutional convention was held in American Samoa and that the convention adopted, on 16 February 1984, a revised draft constitution for the Territory, which was transmitted to the Congress of the United States;

7. *Reaffirms* the responsibility of the administering Power, under the Charter, for the economic and social development of the Territory;

8. *Calls upon* the administering Power to intensify its efforts to strengthen and diversify the economy of American Samoa in order to reduce its heavy dependence on economic and financial support from the United States and to create employment opportunities for the people of the Territory;

9. *Urges* the administering Power, in co-operation with the territorial Government, to strengthen and extend the responsibilities of the Development Planning Office following the expiration of the five-year development plan at the end of 1984;

10. *Urges* the administering Power to continue to facilitate close relations and co-operation between the peoples of the Territory and the neighbouring island communities and between the territorial Government and the regional institutions in order to enhance further the economic welfare of the people of American Samoa;

11. *Urges* the administering Power, in co-operation with the territorial Government, to safeguard the inalienable right of the people of the Territory to the enjoyment of their natural resources by taking effective measures to ensure their right to own and dispose of those resources and to establish and maintain control of their future development;

12. *Considers* that the possibility of sending a further visiting mission to American Samoa should be kept under review;

13. *Requests* the Special Committee to continue the examination of this question at its next session, including the dispatch of a further visiting mission to American Samoa, in consultation with the administering Power, taking into account, in particular, the wishes of the people of the Territory, and to report thereon to the General Assembly at its fortieth session.

General Assembly resolution 39/31

5 December 1984   Meeting 87   Adopted without vote

Approved by Fourth Committee (A/39/696) without objection, 12 November (meeting 18); draft by Committee on colonial countries (A/39/23); agenda item 18.
Financial implications. S-G, A/C.4/39/L.4.
Meeting numbers. GA 39th session: 4th Committee 12-18; plenary 87.

The draft was recommended by the Committee on colonial countries on 7 August,[1] following its approval of the conclusions and recommendations of its Sub-Committee on Small Territories.

Anguilla

On 2 May,[2] the United Kingdom invited the Committee on colonial countries to send a visiting mission to Anguilla in September.

The mission, which visited the Territory from 11 to 16 September, submitted its report to the Committee in October.[3] The report provided information on the constitutional and political developments as well as economic, social and educational conditions in the Territory, outlined the mission's activities and gave its conclusions and recommendations. Annexed to the report were memoranda presented to the mission by the Anguilla National Alliance and the Anguilla Democratic Party.

The mission recommended that the administering Power, with the territorial Government, continue to develop the economy of Anguilla, in particular, to promote the tourist industry, including improvement of airport facilities; develop the fishing industry; facilitate the establishment of light industry; encourage development of agriculture; and improve roads and communications, water and electrical systems. It also recommended the construction of a new hospital and improvement of health services; expansion of secondary, technical and vocational training facilities; and development of the mass media and communication system. Noting that the Anguillan people had freely expressed their views, the mission said it was confident that their practical approach would enable them to exercise freely their right to self-determination in accordance with the Declaration on the Granting of Independence to Colonial Countries and Peoples.[4]

GENERAL ASSEMBLY ACTION

The General Assembly, on the recommendation of the Fourth Committee, adopted resolution 39/39 without vote on 5 December.

Question of Anguilla

The General Assembly,

Having considered the question of Anguilla,

Having examined the relevant chapters of the report of the Special Committee on the Situation with regard to the Implementation of the Declaration on the Granting of Independence to Colonial Countries and Peoples,

Recalling its resolution 1514(XV) of 14 December 1960, containing the Declaration on the Granting of Independence to Colonial Countries and Peoples,

Having examined the report of the United Nations Visiting Mission dispatched to Anguilla in September 1984 at the invitation of the United Kingdom of Great Britain and Northern Ireland, as the administering Power,

Having heard the statement of the Chairman of the Visiting Mission,

Having heard the statement of the representative of the administering Power,

Welcoming the co-operation of the administering Power with regard to the work of the Special Committee relating to the Territories under United Kingdom administration and its readiness to permit access by United Nations visiting missions to those Territories,

Aware of the special problems facing the Territory by virtue of its location, small size, limited resources and lack of infrastructure,

Reiterating the view that such factors as territorial size, geographical location, size of population and limited natural resources should in no way delay the implementation of the Declaration contained in General Assembly resolution 1514(XV), which fully applies to Anguilla,

1. *Approves* the chapter of the report of the Special Committee on the Situation with regard to the Implementation of the Declaration on the Granting of Independence to Colonial Countries and Peoples relating to Anguilla;

2. *Approves also* the report of the United Nations Visiting Mission to Anguilla in 1984;

3. *Reaffirms* the inalienable right of the people of Anguilla to self-determination and independence in accordance with the Declaration on the Granting of Independence to Colonial Countries and Peoples, contained in General Assembly resolution 1514(XV);

4. *Expresses its appreciation* to the administering Power and to the Government of Anguilla for the close co-operation and assistance extended to the Mission;

5. *Urges* the administering Power, in co-operation with the Government of Anguilla, to expand the programmes of political education so as to improve the awareness of the people of the Territory of the options available to them in the exercise of their right to self-determination and independence, in accordance with the Charter of the United Nations and the Declaration;

6. *Expresses the view* that measures to promote the economic and social development of Anguilla are an essential element in the process of self-determination and, in that connection, calls upon the administering Power, in close co-operation with the territorial Government, to continue to intensify and diversify its programmes of development assistance to Anguilla;

7. *Requests* the administering Power, in the light of the observations, conclusions and recommendations of the Visiting Mission, to continue to enlist the assistance of the specialized agencies and other organizations of the United Nations system, as well as other regional and international bodies, in the development and strengthening of the economy of the Territory;

8. *Further requests* the administering Power to facilitate the participation of the Territory as an associate member of various organizations of the United Nations system, as well as other regional and international bodies;

9. *Considers* that the possibility of sending a further visiting mission to Anguilla at an appropriate time should be kept under review;

10. *Requests* the Special Committee to continue the examination of this question at its next session, including the possible dispatch of a visiting mission to Anguilla at an appropriate time and in consultation with the administering Power, and to report thereon to the General Assembly at its fortieth session.

General Assembly resolution 39/39

5 December 1984   Meeting 87   Adopted without vote

Approved by Fourth Committee (A/39/696) without objection, 12 November (meeting 18); draft by Committee on colonial countries (A/39/23); agenda item 18.
Financial implications. S-G, A/C.4/39/L.4.
Meeting numbers. GA 39th session: 4th Committee 12-18; plenary 87.

The Committee on colonial countries recommended the draft to the Assembly on 25 October.[1]

Bermuda

GENERAL ASSEMBLY ACTION

On 5 December, following the recommendation of the Fourth Committee, the General Assembly adopted without vote resolution 39/33.

Question of Bermuda

The General Assembly,

Having considered the question of Bermuda,

Having examined the relevant chapters of the report of the Special Committee on the Situation with regard to the Implementation of the Declaration on the Granting of Independence to Colonial Countries and Peoples,

Recalling its resolution 1514(XV) of 14 December 1960, containing the Declaration on the Granting of Independence to Colonial Countries and Peoples, and all other resolutions and decisions of the United Nations relating to Bermuda, including in particular its resolution 38/43 of 7 December 1983,

Taking into account the statement of the representative of the administering Power relating to the Territory, in which he said that his Government would fully respect the wishes of the people of Bermuda in determining the future constitutional status of the Territory,

Conscious of the need to ensure the full and speedy implementation of the Declaration in respect of the Territory,

Welcoming the continued co-operation of the administering Power in the work of the Special Committee in regard to Bermuda, which contributes to informed consideration of conditions in the Territory, with a view to accelerating the process of decolonization for the purpose of the full implementation of the Declaration,

Recalling all relevant resolutions of the United Nations relating to military bases and installations in colonial and Non-Self-Governing Territories, and aware of the presence of military bases and installations of the administering Power and other countries in Bermuda,

Noting that the economy of the Territory continues to be based on revenue generated from tourism and the registration of foreign companies, which creates a heavy dependence on those activities,

Noting also that Bermuda has been somewhat isolated from its Caribbean neighbours,

Aware of the special circumstances of the geographical location and economic conditions of the Territory and bearing in mind the necessity of diversifying and strengthening further its economy as a matter of priority in order to promote economic stability,

Mindful that United Nations visiting missions provide an effective means of ascertaining the situation in the small Territories, acquiring first-hand information on the situation prevailing in those Territories and ascertaining the views of the peoples concerning their future political status,

1. *Approves* the chapter of the report of the Special Committee on the Situation with regard to the Implementation of the Declaration on the Granting of Independence to Colonial Countries and Peoples relating to Bermuda;

2. *Reaffirms* the inalienable right of the people of Bermuda to self-determination and independence in conformity with the Declaration on the Granting of Independence to Colonial Countries and Peoples, contained in General Assembly resolution 1514(XV);

3. *Reiterates* the view that such factors as territorial size, geographical location, size of population and limited natural resources should in no way delay the speedy exercise by the people of the Territory of their inalienable right to self-determination and independence, in conformity with the Declaration contained in General Assembly resolution 1514(XV), which fully applies to Bermuda;

4. *Urges* the United Kingdom of Great Britain and Northern Ireland, as the administering Power, taking into account the freely expressed will and desire of the people of Bermuda, to continue to take all necessary steps to ensure the full and speedy implementation of General Assembly resolution 1514(XV);

5. *Reiterates* that it is the obligation of the administering Power to create such conditions in the Territory as will enable the people of Bermuda to exercise freely and without interference their inalienable right to self-determination and independence in accordance with General Assembly resolution 1514(XV) and, in that con-

nection, reaffirms the importance of fostering an awareness among the people of Bermuda of the possibilities open to them in the exercise of that right;

6. *Reaffirms* that, in accordance with the relevant provisions of the Charter of the United Nations and the Declaration contained in General Assembly resolution 1514(XV), it is ultimately for the people of Bermuda themselves to decide on their future political status;

7. *Reaffirms its strong conviction* that the presence of military bases and installations in the Territory could constitute a major obstacle to the implementation of the Declaration and that it is the responsibility of the administering Power to ensure that the existence of such bases and installations does not hinder the population of the Territory from exercising its right to self-determination and independence in conformity with the purposes and principles of the Charter of the United Nations;

8. *Urges* the administering Power to continue to take all necessary measures not to involve the Territory in any offensive acts or interference directed against other States and to comply fully with the purposes and principles of the Charter, the Declaration and the resolutions and decisions of the General Assembly relating to military activities and arrangements by colonial Powers in Territories under their administration;

9. *Welcomes* the recent exchanges and visits undertaken by the territorial Government with its Caribbean neighbours and recommends that further regional contacts be pursued;

10. *Urges once again* the administering Power, in co-operation with the territorial Government, to continue to take all effective measures to guarantee the right of the people of Bermuda to own and dispose of their natural resources and to establish and maintain control of their future development;

11. *Strongly urges* the administering Power, in consultation with the Government of Bermuda, to make every effort to diversify the economy of Bermuda, including increased efforts to promote agriculture, fisheries and the manufacturing sector, which will benefit the people of the Territory;

12. *Welcomes* the role being played in the Territory by the United Nations Development Programme in providing assistance in the fields of agriculture, forestry and fisheries and urges the specialized agencies and all other organizations of the United Nations system to continue to pay special attention to the development needs of Bermuda;

13. *Reiterates its call* upon the administering Power, in co-operation with the local authorities, to continue to expedite the process of "bermudianization" in the Territory and, in that connection, urges that particular attention be paid to greater localization of the managerial, executive and professional positions of the public service and the private sector;

14. *Calls upon* the Government of the United Kingdom of Great Britain and Northern Ireland to receive a visiting mission in the Territory at an appropriate time;

15. *Requests* the Special Committee to continue the examination of this question at its next session, including the possible dispatch of a visiting mission to Bermuda at an appropriate time and in consultation with the administering Power, and to report thereon to the General Assembly at its fortieth session.

General Assembly resolution 39/33

5 December 1984   Meeting 87   Adopted without vote

Approved by Fourth Committee (A/39/696) without objection, 12 November (meeting 18); draft by Committee on colonial countries (A/39/23); agenda item 18.
Financial implications. S-G, A/C.4/39/L.4.
Meeting numbers. GA 39th session: 4th Committee 12-18; plenary 87.

The Committee on colonial countries recommended the draft on 20 August, following its approval of the conclusions and recommendations of its Sub-Committee on Small Territories.[1] The Committee had considered the Territory's property development, tourism, financial, constitutional and political developments, economic, social and educational conditions, and military installations, activities and arrangements.

British Virgin Islands

GENERAL ASSEMBLY ACTION

The General Assembly, on the recommendation of the Fourth Committee, adopted without vote resolution 39/34 on 5 December.

Question of the British Virgin Islands

The General Assembly,

Having considered the question of the British Virgin Islands,

Having examined the relevant chapters of the report of the Special Committee on the Situation with regard to the Implementation of the Declaration on the Granting of Independence to Colonial Countries and Peoples,

Recalling its resolution 1514(XV) of 14 December 1960, containing the Declaration on the Granting of Independence to Colonial Countries and Peoples, and all other resolutions and decisions of the United Nations relating to the British Virgin Islands, including in particular its resolution 38/44 of 7 December 1983,

Taking into account the statement of the representative of the administering Power relating to the Territory, in which he said that his Government would fully respect the wishes of the people of the British Virgin Islands in determining the future political status of the Territory,

Conscious of the need to ensure the full and speedy implementation of the Declaration in respect of the Territory,

Noting with appreciation the continued active participation of the administering Power in the work of the Special Committee in regard to the British Virgin Islands, thereby enabling it to conduct a more informed and meaningful examination of the situation in the Territory, with a view to accelerating the process of decolonization for the purpose of the full implementation of the Declaration,

Reaffirming the responsibility of the administering Power for the economic and social development of the Territory,

Taking note of the fact that the economy of the Territory has continued to grow, particularly in the real estate, construction, tourist and banking industries, although at a slower pace, due to the world recession,

Aware of the special circumstances of the geographical location and economic conditions of the Territory and bearing in mind the necessity of diversifying and strengthening further its economy as a matter of priority in order to promote economic stability,

Recalling the recommendation of the United Nations visiting mission dispatched to the British Virgin Islands in 1976 that the administering Power should facilitate the participation of the Territory as an associate member in various organizations of the United Nations system as part of the overall strategy of accelerating the decolonization process,

Mindful that United Nations visiting missions provide an effective means of ascertaining the situation in the small Territories and expressing its satisfaction at the willingness of the administering Power to receive visiting missions in the Territories under its administration,

1.   *Approves* the chapter of the report of the Special Committee on the Situation with regard to the Implementation of the Declaration on the Granting of Independence to Colonial Countries and Peoples relating to the British Virgin Islands;

2.   *Reaffirms* the inalienable right of the people of the British Virgin Islands to self-determination and independence in conformity with the Declaration on the Granting of Independence to Colonial Countries and Peoples, contained in General Assembly resolution 1514(XV);

3.   *Reiterates* the view that such factors as territorial size, geographical location, size of population and limited natural resources should in no way delay the speedy exercise by the people of the Territory of their inalienable right to self-determination and independence in conformity with the Declaration contained in General Assembly resolution 1514(XV), which fully applies to the British Virgin Islands;

4.   *Reiterates* that it is the responsibility of the United Kingdom of Great Britain and Northern Ireland, as the administering Power, to create such conditions in the Territory as will enable the people of the British Virgin Islands to exercise freely and without interference their inalienable right to self-determination and independence in accordance with General Assembly resolution 1514(XV), as well as all other relevant resolutions of the Assembly;

5.   *Reaffirms* that it is ultimately for the people of the British Virgin Islands themselves to determine their future political status in accordance with the relevant provisions of the Charter of the United Nations and the Declaration, takes note of the general elections held in the Territory on 11 November 1983 and reaffirms the importance of fostering an awareness among the people of the Territory of the possibilities open to them in the exercise of their right to self-determination;

6.   *Notes* the continuing commitment of the territorial Government to the goal of economic diversification, particularly in the areas of agriculture, fisheries and small industries, and reiterates its call upon the administering Power, in consultation with the local authorities, to intensify its efforts in this regard;

7.   *Urges* the administering Power, in co-operation with the territorial Government, to safeguard the inalienable right of the people of the British Virgin Islands to the enjoyment of their natural resources by taking effective measures to ensure their right to own and dispose of those resources and to establish and maintain control of their future development;

8.   *Urges* the specialized agencies and other organizations of the United Nations system, as well as regional institutions such as the Caribbean Development Bank,

to take or intensify measures to accelerate progress in the social and economic life of the British Virgin Islands and, in that regard, notes with appreciation the contribution which the United Nations Development Programme continues to make to the development of the Territory;

9. *Notes with satisfaction* the admission of the British Virgin Islands as an associate member of the United Nations Educational, Scientific and Cultural Organization, the Economic Commission for Latin America and the Caribbean and its subsidiary body, the Caribbean Development and Co-operation Committee, as well as of various other international and regional organizations, and calls upon the administering Power to facilitate further the participation of the British Virgin Islands in those organizations;

10. *Considers* that the possibility of sending a further visiting mission to the British Virgin Islands at an appropriate time should be kept under review;

11. *Requests* the Special Committee to continue the examination of this question at its next session, including the possible dispatch of a visiting mission to the British Virgin Islands at an appropriate time and in consultation with the administering Power, and to report thereon to the General Assembly at its fortieth session.

General Assembly resolution 39/34

5 December 1984   Meeting 87   Adopted without vote

Approved by Fourth Committee (A/39/696) without objection, 12 November (meeting 18); draft by Committee on colonial countries (A/39/23); agenda item 18.
Financial implications. S-G, A/C.4/39/L.4.
Meeting numbers. GA 39th session: 4th Committee 12-18; plenary 87.

The draft was recommended by the Committee on colonial countries on 20 August, following its endorsement of the conclusions and recommendations of its Sub-Committee on Small Territories.[1] The Committee had taken up constitutional and political developments and economic, social and educational conditions.

Cayman Islands

GENERAL ASSEMBLY ACTION

The General Assembly, on the recommendation of the Fourth Committee, adopted without vote resolution 39/35 on 5 December.

Question of the Cayman Islands

The General Assembly,

Having considered the question of the Cayman Islands,

Having examined the relevant chapters of the report of the Special Committee on the Situation with regard to the Implementation of the Declaration on the Granting of Independence to Colonial Countries and Peoples,

Recalling its resolution 1514(XV) of 14 December 1960, containing the Declaration on the Granting of Independence to Colonial Countries and Peoples, and all other resolutions and decisions of the United Nations relating to the Cayman Islands, including in particular its resolution 38/45 of 7 December 1983,

Noting the statement of the representative of the administering Power relating to the Territory, in which he said that his Government would fully respect the wishes of the people of the Cayman Islands in determining the future political status of the Territory,

Conscious of the need to ensure the full and speedy implementation of the Declaration in respect of the Territory,

Noting that although the main sectors of the economy of the Cayman Islands, specifically tourism, international finance and real estate, continued to sustain some degree of growth during the period under review, they have shown signs of being affected by the world recession,

Aware of the special circumstances of the geographical location and economic conditions of the Territory and bearing in mind the necessity of diversifying and strengthening further its economy as a matter of priority in order to promote economic stability,

Mindful that United Nations visiting missions provide an effective means of ascertaining the situation in the small Territories and expressing its satisfaction at the willingness of the administering Power to receive visiting missions in the Territories under its administration,

1. *Approves* the chapter of the report of the Special Committee on the Situation with regard to the Implementation of the Declaration on the Granting of Independence to Colonial Countries and Peoples relating to the Cayman Islands;

2. *Reaffirms* the inalienable right of the people of the Cayman Islands to self-determination and independence in conformity with the Declaration on the Granting of Independence to Colonial Countries and Peoples, contained in General Assembly resolution 1514(XV);

3. *Reiterates* the view that such factors as territorial size, geographical location, size of population and limited natural resources should in no way delay the speedy exercise by the people of the Territory of their inalienable right to self-determination and independence in conformity with the Declaration contained in General Assembly resolution 1514(XV), which fully applies to the Cayman Islands;

4. *Notes with appreciation* the participation of the United Kingdom of Great Britain and Northern Ireland, as the administering Power, in the work of the Special Committee in regard to the Cayman Islands, thereby enabling it to conduct a more informed and meaningful examination of the situation in the Territory, with a view to accelerating the process of decolonization for the purpose of the full implementation of the Declaration;

5. *Reiterates* that it is the responsibility of the administering Power to create such conditions in the Cayman Islands as will enable the people of the Territory to exercise freely and without interference their inalienable right to self-determination and independence in accordance with General Assembly resolution 1514(XV), as well as all other relevant resolutions of the Assembly;

6. *Reaffirms* that it is ultimately for the people of the Cayman Islands themselves to determine their future political status in accordance with the relevant provisions of the Charter of the United Nations and the Declaration and reaffirms the importance of fostering an awareness among the people of the Territory of the possibilities open to them in the exercise of their right to self-determination;

7. *Reaffirms* the responsibility of the administering Power for the economic and social development of the Territory and urges it, in co-operation with the territorial Government, to render continuing support, to the fullest extent possible, to the development of programmes of economic diversification that will benefit the people of the Territory;

8. *Urges* the administering Power, in co-operation with the territorial Government, to safeguard the inalienable right of the people of the Territory to the enjoyment of their natural resources by taking effective measures to ensure their right to own and dispose of those resources and to establish and maintain control of their future development and, in that connection, to continue its efforts to persuade the Government of the United States of America to relax its ban on the importation of turtle products from the Cayman Islands;

9. *Calls upon* the specialized agencies and other organizations of the United Nations system, as well as regional institutions such as the Caribbean Development Bank, to continue to take all necessary measures to accelerate progress in the social and economic life of the Cayman Islands and, in that respect, notes with appreciation the continued contribution of the United Nations Development Programme to the development of the Territory;

10. *Considers* that the possibility of sending a further visiting mission to the Cayman Islands at an appropriate time should be kept under review;

11. *Requests* the Special Committee to continue the examination of this question at its next session, including the possible dispatch of a visiting mission to the Cayman Islands at an appropriate time and in consultation with the administering Power, and to report thereon to the General Assembly at its fortieth session.

General Assembly resolution 39/35

5 December 1984   Meeting 87   Adopted without vote

Approved by Fourth Committee (A/39/696) without objection, 12 November (meeting 18); draft by Committee on colonial countries (A/39/23); agenda item 18.
Financial implications. S-G, A/C.4/39/L.4.
Meeting numbers. GA 39th session: 4th Committee 12-18; plenary 87.

The draft was recommended by the Committee on colonial countries on 7 August, following its endorsement of the conclusions and recommendations of its Sub-Committee on Small Territories.[1] The Committee had considered financial developments, property development, mariculture and the oil industry as well as constitutional and political developments and economic, social and educational conditions in the Cayman Islands.

Cocos (Keeling) Islands

GENERAL ASSEMBLY ACTION

On 5 December, following the recommendation of the Fourth Committee, the General Assembly adopted without vote resolution 39/30.

Question of the Cocos (Keeling) Islands

The General Assembly,

Having considered the question of the Cocos (Keeling) Islands,

Having heard the statements of the representatives of Australia,

Having heard the statement of the Chairman of the Cocos (Keeling) Islands Council,

Recalling its resolutions 1514(XV) of 14 December 1960, containing the Declaration on the Granting of Independence to Colonial Countries and Peoples, and 1541(XV) of 15 December 1960,

Recalling also its decision 38/412 of 7 December 1983, by which it noted, *inter alia*, that the administering Power had discussed with the representatives of the Cocos (Keeling) Islands community the question of holding an act of self-determination to determine their future political status, and its decision 38/420 of 7 December 1983, by which it authorized the Secretary-General to appoint and dispatch a United Nations mission to visit the Cocos (Keeling) Islands in 1984 and requested him to submit to the General Assembly at its thirty-ninth session a report on the findings of the mission,

Having heard the statement of the Chairman of the United Nations Visiting Mission dispatched to the Cocos (Keeling) Islands in April 1984 pursuant to General Assembly decision 38/420 and having considered the report of the Visiting Mission,

Noting with appreciation the active participation of the administering Power in the work of the Special Committee on the Situation with regard to the Implementation of the Declaration on the Granting of Independence to Colonial Countries and Peoples in regard to the Cocos (Keeling) Islands and the co-operation it has extended to the Committee, including the receiving of visiting missions to the Territory in 1974 and 1980,

1. *Notes with satisfaction* the observations and recommendations of the United Nations Visiting Mission to Observe the Act of Self-Determination in the Cocos (Keeling) Islands, 1984;

2. *Takes note* that the people of the Cocos (Keeling) Islands voted by a substantial majority for integration with Australia;

3. *Endorses* the view of the Visiting Mission that, in so doing, the people of the Territory have exercised their right to self-determination in accordance with the principles of the Charter of the United Nations and the Declaration on the Granting of Independence to Colonial Countries and Peoples, contained in General Assembly resolution 1514(XV);

4. *Considers it appropriate* that, in view of the decision of the people of the Cocos (Keeling) Islands, the transmission of information in respect of the Cocos (Keeling) Islands under Article 73 *e* of the Charter should cease;

5. *Takes note* of the actions taken by the Government of Australia to transfer ownership of land to the Cocos (Keeling) Islands community and to extend relevant legislation to the community so that it may enjoy the same benefits as those available to the Australian community at large, as well as the Government's assurances that the unique cultural identity, heritage and traditions of the Cocos community will be preserved;

6. *Expresses its appreciation* to the Government of Australia, as the administering Power concerned, and to the Cocos (Keeling) Islands Council for the co-operation extended to the United Nations;

7. *Expresses its appreciation* to the Special Committee on the Situation with regard to the Implementation of the Declaration on the Granting of Independence to Colonial Countries and Peoples for the work it has accomplished, in close co-operation with the administering Power, in respect of the Territory.

General Assembly resolution 39/30

5 December 1984   Meeting 87   Adopted without vote

Approved by Fourth Committee (A/39/696) without objection, 7 November (meeting 15); 21-nation draft (A/C.4/39/L.3); agenda item 18.
Sponsors: Bahamas, Denmark, Egypt, Fiji, Indonesia, Ivory Coast, Japan, Mali, New Zealand, Papua New Guinea, Philippines, Samoa, Sierra Leone, Singapore, Solomon Islands, Sweden, Trinidad and Tobago, United Republic of Tanzania, Vanuatu, Venezuela, Yugoslavia.
Meeting numbers. GA 39th session: 4th Committee 12-18; plenary 87.

On 9 August,[5] Australia informed the Secretary-General that it had organized an act of self-determination in the Territory on 6 April to enable the people to determine their future political status. A total of 261 votes were cast in a plebiscite, of which 229 were in favour of integration with Australia, 21 in favour of free association with Australia and 9 in favour of independence. There were 2 informal votes. The decision was acceptable to the Australian Government.

On 24 August,[1] the Chairman informed the Committee on colonial countries that the visiting mission, authorized by the Assembly to visit the islands,[6] had observed the plebiscite. In its report,[7] the mission stated that the vote had been carried out in a free and fair manner, that the people had requested the United Nations to guarantee that ownership of the land would be transferred to them in perpetuity, and that Australia had given assurances that title to the land would be transferred to the people within three months. The mission recommended that the role of the Cocos (Keeling) Islands Council and the Management Committee of the Co-operative Society should be extended.

Gibraltar

GENERAL ASSEMBLY ACTION

In December, on the recommendation of the Fourth Committee, the General Assembly adopted without vote decision 39/410.

Question of Gibraltar

At its 87th plenary meeting, on 5 December 1984, the General Assembly, on the recommendation of the Fourth Committee, adopted the following text as representing the consensus of the members of the Assembly:

"The General Assembly, noting that the Governments of Spain and the United Kingdom of Great Britain and Northern Ireland signed a Declaration on 10 April 1980 at Lisbon, intending, in accordance with the relevant resolutions of the United Nations, to resolve the problem of Gibraltar, agreeing to that end to start negotiations aimed at overcoming all the differences between them on Gibraltar, agreeing also to the re-establishment of direct communications in the region, the Government of Spain having decided to suspend the application of the measures at present in force, and both Governments agreeing to base future co-operation on reciprocity and full equality of rights, noting that both Governments agreed on 8 January 1982 in London to fix the date of 20 April 1982 for the full implementation of the Lisbon Declaration, including the initiation of negotiations and the simultaneous re-establishment of direct communications in the region, and noting that, when it was subsequently agreed to postpone these arrangements, both Governments expressed their determination to keep alive the process initiated by the Lisbon Declaration of April 1980 and their intention to set a new date for its implementation, welcomes the fact that both Governments agreed on 27 November 1984 at Brussels, in a joint statement, to apply by not later than 15 February 1985 the Lisbon Declaration in all its parts, and urges both Governments to make possible the initiation of the negotiations as envisaged in the consensus adopted by the Assembly on 14 December 1973, with the object of reaching a lasting solution to the problem of Gibraltar in the light of the relevant resolutions of the Assembly and in the spirit of the Charter of the United Nations."

General Assembly decision 39/410

Adopted without vote

Approved by Fourth Committee (A/39/696 (Part I)) without objection, 12 November (meeting 18); draft consensus by Chairman (A/C.4/39/L.7); agenda item 18.
Meeting numbers. GA 39th session: 4th Committee 12-18; plenary 87.

In the Assembly, an amendment by Spain and the United Kingdom was adopted without a vote. The amendment inserted the phrase, "welcomes the fact that both Governments agreed on 27 November 1984 at Brussels, in a joint statement[8] [see below], to apply by not later than 15 February 1985 the Lisbon Declaration in all its parts, and".

On 4 December,[8] Spain and the United Kingdom transmitted to the Secretary-General a joint communiqué issued after a meeting by their Foreign Ministers (Brussels, Belgium, 27 November). The Ministers had agreed on the way in which their Governments would apply the 1980 Lisbon Declaration.[9] That would involve simultaneously, the communiqué stated, equality and reciprocity of rights for Spaniards in Gibraltar and Gibraltarians in Spain; free movement of persons, vehicles and goods between Gibraltar and the neighbouring territory; and establishment of a process to negotiate differences. Moreover, Spain would allow safe and effective air communications; and meetings of working groups would be reviewed periodically by the Spanish and British Foreign Ministers.

Taking into account the continuing discussions, the Committee on colonial countries had decided on 20 August[1] to continue considering the item at its 1985 session, subject to any Assembly directives. The Committee had examined political developments and economic, social and educational conditions in Gibraltar.

Guam

GENERAL ASSEMBLY ACTION

The General Assembly, on the recommendation of the Fourth Committee, adopted without vote resolution 39/32 on 5 December.

Question of Guam

The General Assembly,

Having considered the question of Guam,

Having examined the relevant chapters of the report of the Special Committee on the Situation with regard to the Implementation of the Declaration on the Granting of Independence to Colonial Countries and Peoples,

Recalling its resolution 1514(XV) of 14 December 1960, containing the Declaration on the Granting of Independence to Colonial Countries and Peoples, and all other resolutions and decisions of the United Nations relating to Guam, including in particular its resolution 38/42 of 7 December 1983,

Having heard the statement of the representative of the administering Power relating to Guam,

Noting with appreciation the continued active participation of the administering Power in the work of the Special Committee in regard to Guam, thereby enabling it to conduct a more informed and meaningful examination of the situation in the Territory with a view to accelerating the process of decolonization towards the full and speedy implementation of the Declaration,

Noting that a referendum on political status was organized in the Territory, the final phase of which was held on 4 September 1982,

Recalling all relevant resolutions of the United Nations relating to military bases and installations in colonial and Non-Self-Governing Territories and aware of the presence of military bases and installations of the administering Power in Guam,

Aware of the special circumstances of the geographical location and economic conditions of Guam and the necessity of diversifying the economy of the Territory as a matter of priority and noting the great potential for diversification and development offered by commercial fishing, agriculture and development of the transportation industry,

Mindful that United Nations visiting missions provide an effective means of ascertaining the situation in the small Territories and expressing its satisfaction at the willingness of the administering Power to receive visiting missions in the Territories under its administration,

1. *Approves* the chapter of the report of the Special Committee on the Situation with regard to the Implementation of the Declaration on the Granting of Independence to Colonial Countries and Peoples relating to Guam;

2. *Reaffirms* the inalienable right of the people of Guam to self-determination and independence in conformity with the Declaration on the Granting of Independence to Colonial Countries and Peoples, contained in General Assembly resolution 1514(XV);

3. *Reaffirms its conviction* that such factors as territorial size, geographical location, size of population and limited natural resources should in no way delay the speedy exercise by the people of the Territory of their inalienable right to self-determination and independence in conformity with the Declaration contained in General Assembly resolution 1514(XV), which fully applies to Guam;

4. *Takes note* of the fact that in the referendum on political status, the final phase of which was held on 4 September 1982, 75 per cent of the participants voted for Commonwealth status in association with the United States of America, and of the statement by the ad-

ministering Power that the Congress of the United States has requested the Guamanian Status Commission to draft legislation establishing Guam as a Commonwealth of the United States and to submit it to the Congress for approval;

5. *Calls upon* the administering Power, in co-operation with the territorial Government, to expedite the process of decolonization strictly in accordance with the expressed wishes of the people of the Territory;

6. *Reaffirms its strong conviction* that the presence of military bases and installations in the Territory could constitute a major obstacle to the implementation of the Declaration and that it is the responsibility of the administering Power to ensure that the existence of such bases and installations does not hinder the population of the Territory from exercising its right to self-determination and independence in conformity with the purposes and principles of the Charter of the United Nations;

7. *Urges* the administering Power to continue to take all necessary measures not to involve the Territory in any offensive acts or interference directed against other States and to comply fully with the purposes and principles of the Charter, the Declaration and the resolutions and decisions of the General Assembly relating to military activities and arrangements by colonial Powers in Territories under their administration;

8. *Reaffirms* the responsibility of the administering Power, under the Charter, for the economic and social development of Guam and calls upon the administering Power to take all necessary steps to strengthen and diversify the economy of the Territory, with a view to reducing the Territory's economic dependence on the administering Power;

9. *Reiterates* the view that one obstacle to economic development, particularly in the agricultural sector, stems from the fact that large tracts of land are held by the federal authorities and calls upon the administering Power, in co-operation with the local authorities, to continue the transfer of land to the people of the Territory;

10. *Reiterates its call* upon the administering Power, in co-operation with the territorial Government, to take measures aimed at removing constraints to growth in the areas of commercial fishing, agriculture and the transportation industry and to ensure their development to the fullest extent;

11. *Urges* the administering Power, in co-operation with the territorial Government, to continue to take effective measures to safeguard and guarantee the right of the people of Guam to their natural resources and to establish and maintain control over their future development and requests the administering Power to take all necessary steps to protect the property rights of the people of the Territory;

12. *Takes note* of the steps taken by the administering Power to develop and promote the language and culture of the Chamorro people, who are the indigenous population of the Territory, and reaffirms the importance of further efforts in that field;

13. *Considers* that the possibility of sending a further visiting mission to Guam at an appropriate time should be kept under review;

14. *Requests* the Special Committee to continue the examination of this question at its next session, including the possible dispatch of a further visiting mission

to Guam at an appropriate time and in consultation with the administering Power, and to report thereon to the General Assembly at its fortieth session.

General Assembly resolution 39/32

5 December 1984   Meeting 87   Adopted without vote

Approved by Fourth Committee (A/39/696) without objection, 12 November (meeting 18); draft by Committee on colonial countries (A/39/23); agenda item 18.
Financial implications. S-G, A/C.4/39/L.4.
Meeting numbers. GA 39th session: 4th Committee 12-18; plenary 87.

The Committee on colonial countries recommended the draft on 24 August,[1] following its approval of the conclusions and recommendations of its Sub-Committee on Small Territories. The Committee had considered the military installations, activities and arrangements on Guam and its economic, social and educational conditions and constitutional and political developments.

Montserrat

GENERAL ASSEMBLY ACTION

On 5 December, following the recommendation of the Fourth Committee, the General Assembly adopted without vote resolution 39/36.

Question of Montserrat

The General Assembly,

Having considered the question of Montserrat,

Having examined the relevant chapters of the report of the Special Committee on the Situation with regard to the Implementation of the Declaration on the Granting of Independence to Colonial Countries and Peoples,

Recalling its resolution 1514(XV) of 14 December 1960, containing the Declaration on the Granting of Independence to Colonial Countries and Peoples, and all other resolutions and decisions of the United Nations relating to Montserrat, including in particular its resolution 38/46 of 7 December 1983,

Noting the statement of the representative of the administering Power relating to the Territory, in which he said that his Government would respect the wishes of the people of Montserrat in determining the future political status of the Territory,

Noting the statement of the Government of Montserrat that independence was inevitable and desirable and that the Government would work towards that end,

Reaffirming the responsibility of the administering Power for the economic and social development of the Territory,

Noting with concern that during the period under review the general slowdown in the world economy also affected Montserrat, particularly in its vital sectors, such as tourism, construction, agriculture and manufacturing,

Welcoming the establishment of a Civil Service Training Centre by the Government of Montserrat and noting that the review of the organization and training needs of the civil service was expected to be completed in 1984,

Welcoming the contribution to the development of the Territory by the United Nations Development Programme and those specialized agencies and other organizations of the United Nations system operating in Montserrat and noting in particular the increase envisaged by the Programme for the period 1982-1986,

Aware of the special problems facing the Territory by virtue of its isolation, small size, limited resources and lack of infrastructure,

Recalling the dispatch, in 1975 and 1982, of United Nations visiting missions to the Territory,

Mindful that visiting missions provide an effective means of ascertaining the situation in the small Territories,

1. *Approves* the chapter of the report of the Special Committee on the Situation with regard to the Implementation of the Declaration on the Granting of Independence to Colonial Countries and Peoples relating to Montserrat;

2. *Reaffirms* the inalienable right of the people of Montserrat to self-determination and independence in conformity with the Declaration on the Granting of Independence to Colonial Countries and Peoples, contained in General Assembly resolution 1514(XV);

3. *Reiterates* the view that such factors as territorial size, geographical location, size of population and limited natural resources should in no way delay the speedy exercise by the people of the Territory of their inalienable right to self-determination and independence in conformity with the Declaration contained in General Assembly resolution 1514(XV), which fully applies to Montserrat;

4. *Notes with appreciation* the continued participation of the United Kingdom of Great Britain and Northern Ireland, as the administering Power, in the work of the Special Committee in regard to Montserrat, thereby enabling it to conduct a more informed and meaningful examination of the situation in the Territory with a view to accelerating the process of decolonization for the purpose of the full implementation of the Declaration;

5. *Reiterates* that it is the responsibility of the administering Power to create such conditions in Montserrat as will enable its people to exercise freely and without interference, from a well-informed standpoint as to the available options, their inalienable right to self-determination and independence in accordance with General Assembly resolution 1514(XV), as well as all other relevant resolutions of the Assembly;

6. *Reaffirms* that it is ultimately for the people of Montserrat themselves to determine their future political status in accordance with the relevant provisions of the Charter of the United Nations and the Declaration and reiterates its call upon the administering Power, in co-operation with the territorial Government, to launch programmes of political education so that the people of Montserrat will be fully informed of the options available to them in the exercise of their right to self-determination and independence;

7. *Calls upon* the administering Power, in co-operation with the territorial Government, to continue to strengthen the economy and to increase its assistance to programmes of diversification in order to promote the economic and financial viability of the Territory;

8. *Urges* the administering Power to take the necessary measures, in co-operation with the territorial Government, to restore sustained and balanced growth to the economy of the Territory and to intensify its assistance in the development of all sectors thereof, which will benefit the people of the Territory, and expresses the hope that Montserrat's non-budgetary grant-in-aid status can be maintained;

9. *Also urges* the administering Power, in co-operation with the territorial Government, to take effective measures to safeguard, guarantee and ensure the rights of the people of Montserrat to own and dispose of their natural resources and to establish and maintain control of their future development;

10. *Further urges* the administering Power, in co-operation with the territorial Government, to continue to provide the assistance necessary for the localization of the civil service at all levels, particularly the senior levels;

11. *Takes note* of the continued participation of the Territory in the work of the Caribbean Group for Co-operation and Economic Development, as well as such regional organizations as the Caribbean Community and the Caribbean Development Bank, and calls upon the organizations of the United Nations system, as well as donor Governments and regional organizations, to intensify their efforts to accelerate progress in the economic and social life of the Territory;

12. *Considers* that the possibility of sending a further visiting mission to Montserrat at an appropriate time should be kept under review;

13. *Requests* the Special Committee to continue the examination of this question at its next session, including the possible dispatch of a further visiting mission to Montserrat at an appropriate time and in consultation with the administering Power, and to report thereon to the General Assembly at its fortieth session.

General Assembly resolution 39/36

5 December 1984   Meeting 87   Adopted without vote

Approved by Fourth Committee (A/39/696) without objection, 12 November (meeting 18); draft by Committee on colonial countries (A/39/23); agenda item 18.
Financial implications. S-G, A/C.4/39/L.4.
Meeting numbers. GA 39th session: 4th Committee 12-18; plenary 87.

The Committee on colonial countries recommended the draft on 20 August,[1] following its endorsement of the conclusions and recommendations of its Sub-Committee on Small Territories. The Committee had considered constitutional and political developments and economic, social and educational conditions in Montserrat.

Pitcairn

GENERAL ASSEMBLY ACTION

In December, the General Assembly, on the recommendation of the Fourth Committee, adopted without vote decision 39/409.

Question of Pitcairn

At its 87th plenary meeting, on 5 December 1984, the General Assembly, on the recommendation of the Fourth Committee, adopted the following text as representing the consensus of the members of the Assembly:

"The General Assembly, having examined the relevant chapter of the report of the Special Committee on the Situation with regard to the Implementation of the Declaration on the Granting of Independence to Colonial Countries and Peoples, takes note of the statement of the representative of the United Kingdom of Great Britain and Northern Ireland affirming the policy of his Government to respect the wishes

of the people of Pitcairn when it considers the future constitutional arrangements for the Territory and to give further encouragement to the people of Pitcairn to pursue the way of life that they themselves have chosen and that best suits their own particular circumstances. The Assembly calls once again upon the administering Power to continue to take the necessary measures to safeguard the interests of the people of Pitcairn. The Assembly requests the Special Committee to continue to examine the question at its next session and to report thereon to the Assembly at its fortieth session."

General Assembly decision 39/409

Adopted without vote

Approved by Fourth Committee (A/39/696) without objection, 12 November (meeting 18); draft consensus by Committee on colonial countries (A/39/23); agenda item 18.
Meeting numbers. GA 39th session: 4th Committee 12-18; plenary 87.

The draft was recommended by the Committee on colonial countries on 20 August,[1] following adoption of the draft consensus submitted by the Sub-Committee on Small Territories. The Committee had considered the constitutional and political developments and economic, social and educational conditions on Pitcairn.

St. Helena

GENERAL ASSEMBLY ACTION

In December, on the recommendation of the Fourth Committee, the General Assembly adopted by recorded vote decision 39/411.

Question of St. Helena

At its 87th plenary meeting, on 5 December 1984, the General Assembly, on the recommendation of the Fourth Committee, having examined the relevant chapters of the report of the Special Committee on the Situation with regard to the Implementation of the Declaration on the Granting of Independence to Colonial Countries and Peoples and having heard the statement of the representative of the United Kingdom of Great Britain and Northern Ireland, as the administering Power, reaffirmed the inalienable right of the people of St. Helena to self-determination and independence in conformity with the Declaration on the Granting of Independence to Colonial Countries and Peoples, contained in Assembly resolution 1514(XV) of 14 December 1960. The Assembly noted the commitment of the Government of the United Kingdom to respect the wishes of the people of the Territory in relation to their future political status and, in that regard, urged the administering Power, in consultation with the legislative Council, and other representatives of the people of St. Helena, to continue to take all necessary steps to ensure the speedy implementation of the Declaration in respect of this Territory and in that connection reaffirmed the importance of promoting an awareness among the people of St. Helena of the possibilities open to them in the exercise of their right to self-determination. The Assembly expressed the hope that the administering Power would continue to implement infrastructure and community development projects aimed at improving the general welfare of the community and to encourage local initiative and enterprise, particularly in the areas of forestry and the handicrafts industry. The Assembly noted the willingness of the administering Power to revitalize the fishing industry of the Territory. The Assembly reaffirmed that continued development assistance from the administering Power, together with any assistance that the international community might be able to provide, constituted an important means of developing the economic potential of the Territory and of enhancing the capacity of its people to realize fully the goals set forth in the relevant provisions of the Charter of the United Nations. The Assembly noted with concern the presence of a military base on the dependency of Ascension Island and, in that regard, recalled all the relevant United Nations resolutions and decisions concerning military bases and installations in colonial and Non-Self-Governing Territories. Noting the positive attitude of the administering Power with respect to the question of receiving United Nations visiting missions in the Territories under its administration, the Assembly considered that the possibility of dispatching such a mission to St. Helena at an appropriate time should be kept under review. The Assembly requested the Special Committee to continue to examine the question at its next session, including the possible dispatch of a visiting mission to St. Helena, at an appropriate time and in consultation with the administering Power, and to report thereon to the Assembly at its fortieth session.

General Assembly decision 39/411

5 December 1984   Meeting 87   119-2-24 (recorded vote)

Approved by Fourth Committee (A/39/696) by recorded vote (111-3-26), 12 November (meeting 18); draft by Committee on colonial countries (A/39/23); agenda item 18.
Financial implications. S-G, A/C.4/39/L.4.
Meeting numbers. GA 39th session: 4th Committee 12-18; plenary 87.

Recorded vote in Assembly as follows:

In favour: Afghanistan, Albania, Algeria, Angola, Argentina, Bahrain, Bangladesh, Barbados, Benin, Bhutan, Bolivia, Botswana, Brazil, Brunei Darussalam, Bulgaria, Burkina Faso, Burma, Burundi, Byelorussian SSR, Cameroon, Cape Verde, Central African Republic, Chad, China, Colombia, Congo, Costa Rica, Cuba, Cyprus, Czechoslovakia, Democratic Kampuchea, Democratic Yemen, Djibouti, Dominican Republic, Ecuador, Egypt, El Salvador, Equatorial Guinea, Ethiopia, Gabon, Gambia, German Democratic Republic, Ghana, Guinea, Guinea-Bissau, Guyana, Haiti, Honduras, Hungary, India, Indonesia, Iran, Iraq, Ivory Coast, Jamaica, Jordan, Kenya, Kuwait, Lao People's Democratic Republic, Lebanon, Lesotho, Liberia, Libyan Arab Jamahiriya, Madagascar, Malawi, Malaysia, Maldives, Mali, Malta, Mauritania, Mauritius, Mexico, Mongolia, Mozambique, Nepal, Nicaragua, Niger, Nigeria, Oman, Pakistan, Panama, Papua New Guinea, Paraguay, Peru, Philippines, Poland, Qatar, Romania, Rwanda, Sao Tome and Principe, Saudi Arabia, Senegal, Seychelles, Sierra Leone, Singapore, Somalia, Spain, Sri Lanka, Sudan, Suriname, Syrian Arab Republic, Thailand, Togo, Trinidad and Tobago, Tunisia, Uganda, Ukrainian SSR, USSR, United Arab Emirates, United Republic of Tanzania, Uruguay, Vanuatu, Venezuela, Viet Nam, Yemen, Yugoslavia, Zaire, Zambia, Zimbabwe.
Against: United Kingdom, United States.
Abstaining: Australia, Austria, Belgium, Belize, Canada, Denmark, Finland, France, Germany, Federal Republic of, Greece, Iceland, Ireland, Israel, Italy, Japan, Luxembourg, Netherlands, New Zealand, Norway, Portugal, Samoa, Sweden, Turkey.

The Committee on colonial countries recommended the draft on 24 August,[1] after endorsing the conclusions and recommendations of its Sub-Committee on Small Territories. The Committee had considered St. Helena's constitutional arrangements, its economic, social and educational conditions, and its dependencies—Tristan da Cunha and Ascension Island.

Prior to approving the draft as a whole, the Fourth Committee, in a separate vote requested by the United Kingdom, approved the sixth sentence—which referred to a military base on Ascension Island—by 61 to 33, with 36 abstentions.

The United Kingdom felt that references to that island were not appropriate since the text was meant to address the problems of the inhabitants of St. Helena and that it was unclear how an airbase on Ascension, an isolated piece of rock inhabited by migratory birds, green turtles, Atlantic seals and temporary contract employees, could affect St. Helena's population. Sweden, speaking for the Nordic countries, declared they shared the view that the Assembly's 1960 Declaration on colonial countries[4] did not cover Ascension Island.

Tokelau

GENERAL ASSEMBLY ACTION

In December, on the recommendation of the Fourth Committee, the General Assembly adopted without vote decision 39/408.

Question of Tokelau

At its 87th plenary meeting, on 5 December 1984, the General Assembly, on the recommendation of the Fourth Committee, adopted the following text as representing the consensus of the members of the Assembly:

"The General Assembly, having examined the relevant chapters of the report of the Special Committee on the Situation with regard to the Implementation of the Declaration on the Granting of Independence to Colonial Countries and Peoples and having heard the statement of the representative of New Zealand with regard to Tokelau, notes with appreciation the willingness of the administering Power to maintain its close co-operation with the United Nations in the exercise of its responsibility towards Tokelau. The Assembly reaffirms the inalienable right of the people of Tokelau to self-determination and independence in conformity with the Declaration on the Granting of Independence to Colonial Countries and Peoples, contained in Assembly resolution 1514(XV) of 14 December 1960, and reaffirms further that it is the responsibility of the administering Power to keep the people of Tokelau fully informed of that right. In this regard, the Assembly notes that the people of the Territory have expressed the view that, at the present time, they do not wish to review the nature of the existing relationship between Tokelau and New Zealand. The Assembly welcomes the assurances of the administering Power that it will continue to be guided solely by the wishes of the people of Tokelau as to the future status of the Territory and notes that the administering Power has assured the people of Tokelau of its continuing assistance in the event that they should desire to change their status. The Assembly calls upon the administering Power to continue its programme of political education within the context of its efforts to ensure the preservation of the identity and cultural heritage of the people of Tokelau. The Assembly notes with satisfaction that the administering Power is making a compilation of all laws and regulations applying to the Territory, including traditional laws, and urges the administering Power to expedite this process as well as the translation of the laws and regulations into Tokelauan. The Assembly is of the opinion that the administering Power should continue to inform the Tokelauan people of the consideration of their Territory by the United Nations. The Assembly recognizes that the political and economic development of Tokelau is an important element in the process of self-determination. In this connection, the Assembly notes with satisfaction that the General *Fono* (Council) of Tokelau is assuming greater authority in local political, economic and financial affairs. The Assembly notes further the continuing efforts of the administering Power to promote the economic development of the Territory and the measures it has taken to safeguard and guarantee the rights of the people of Tokelau to all their natural resources and the benefits derived therefrom. In this connection, the Assembly notes with satisfaction the conclusion, in September 1983, of a fisheries access agreement with the American Tunaboat Association covering the combined economic zones of the Cook Islands, Niue, Tokelau, Tuvalu and the State of Western Samoa. The Assembly notes that the Treaty of Toke-hega, between New Zealand and the United States of America, which delimits the maritime boundary between Tokelau and American Samoa, entered into force on 3 September 1983. The Assembly is of the opinion that the administering Power should continue to expand its programme of budgetary support and development aid to the Territory. The Assembly notes with appreciation the continuing efforts of the administering Power to make improvements in the fields of public health, public works and education. The Assembly reiterates its expression of appreciation to the specialized agencies and other organizations of the United Nations system, as well as to the regional organizations, for their assistance to Tokelau and calls upon them to continue providing assistance to the Territory. Mindful that United Nations visiting missions provide an effective means of ascertaining the situation in the small Territories, the Assembly considers that the possibility of sending a further visiting mission to the Territory at an appropriate time should be kept under review, taking into account, in particular, the wishes of the people of Tokelau. The Assembly requests the Special Committee to continue to examine the question at its next session, including the possible dispatch of a further visiting mission to Tokelau, at an appropriate time and in consultation with the administering Power, and to report thereon to the Assembly at its fortieth session."

General Assembly decision 39/408

Adopted without vote

Approved by Fourth Committee (A/39/696) without objection, 12 November (meeting 18); draft consensus by Committee on colonial countries (A/39/23); agenda item 18.

Financial implications. S-G, A/C.4/39/L.4.

Meeting numbers. GA 39th session: 4th Committee 12-18; plenary 87.

The draft was recommended by the Committee on colonial countries on 20 August,[(1)] following approval of a draft consensus submitted by its Sub-Committee on Small Territories. The Committee had considered constitutional and political developments, and economic, social and educational conditions in Tokelau.

Turks and Caicos Islands

GENERAL ASSEMBLY ACTION

On 7 December, on the recommendation of the Fourth Committee, the General Assembly adopted without vote resolution 39/37.

Question of the Turks and Caicos Islands

The General Assembly,

Having considered the question of the Turks and Caicos Islands,

Having examined the relevant chapters of the report of the Special Committee on the Situation with regard to the Implementation of the Declaration on the Granting of Independence to Colonial Countries and Peoples,

Recalling its resolution 1514(XV) of 14 December 1960, containing the Declaration on the Granting of Independence to Colonial Countries and Peoples, and all other resolutions and decisions of the United Nations relating to the Turks and Caicos Islands, including in particular its resolution 38/47 of 7 December 1983,

Taking into account the statement of the representative of the administering Power relating to the Territory, in which he said that his Government would fully respect the wishes of the people of the Turks and Caicos Islands in determining the future constitutional status of the Territory, and bearing in mind the importance of fostering an awareness among the people of the Territory of the possibilities open to them,

Conscious of the need to ensure the full and speedy implementation of the Declaration in respect of the Territory,

Noting with appreciation the participation of the administering Power in the work of the Special Committee, thereby enabling it to conduct a more informed and meaningful examination of the situation in the Territory,

Aware of the special circumstances of the geographical location and economic conditions of the Territory and bearing in mind the necessity of diversifying and strengthening further its economy as a matter of priority in order to promote economic stability and to develop a wider economic base for the Territory,

Recalling its strong conviction that military bases and installations must not hinder the populations of the Non-Self-Governing Territories from exercising their right to self-determination and independence in conformity with the purposes and principles of the Charter and the relevant resolutions of the United Nations,

Noting the statement of the administering Power that an experimental farm has been set up on North Caicos to study agricultural techniques,

Mindful that United Nations visiting missions provide an effective means of ascertaining the situation in the small Territories and expressing its satisfaction at the willingness of the administering Power to receive visiting missions in the Territories under its administration,

1. *Approves* the chapter of the report of the Special Committee on the Situation with regard to the Implementation of the Declaration on the Granting of Indepen-

dence to Colonial Countries and Peoples relating to the Turks and Caicos Islands;

2. *Reaffirms* the inalienable right of the people of the Turks and Caicos Islands to self-determination and independence in conformity with the Declaration on the Granting of Independence to Colonial Countries and Peoples, contained in General Assembly resolution 1514(XV);

3. *Reiterates* the view that such factors as territorial size, geographical location, size of population and limited natural resources should in no way delay the speedy exercise by the people of the Territory of their inalienable right to self-determination and independence in conformity with the Declaration contained in General Assembly resolution 1514(XV), which fully applies to the Turks and Caicos Islands;

4. *Reiterates* that it is the obligation of the United Kingdom of Great Britain and Northern Ireland, as the administering Power, to create such conditions in the Territory as will enable the people of the Turks and Caicos Islands to exercise freely and without interference their inalienable right to self-determination and independence in accordance with General Assembly resolution 1514(XV), as well as all other relevant resolutions of the Assembly;

5. *Reaffirms* that it is the responsibility of the administering Power under the Charter of the United Nations to develop its dependent Territories economically and socially and urges the administering Power, in consultation with the territorial Government, to take the necessary measures to promote the economic and social development of the Turks and Caicos Islands and, in particular, to intensify and expand its programme of assistance in order to accelerate the development of the economic and social infrastructure of the Territory;

6. *Emphasizes* that greater attention should be paid to diversification of the economy, particularly in the promotion of agriculture and fisheries, which will benefit the people of the Territory;

7. *Recalls* that it is the responsibility of the administering Power, in accordance with the wishes of the people of the Turks and Caicos Islands, to safeguard, guarantee and ensure the inalienable right of the people to the enjoyment of their natural resources by taking effective measures to guarantee their right to own and dispose of those resources and to establish and maintain control of their future development;

8. *Takes note* of the statement of the administering Power to the effect that the military facility in the Turks and Caicos Islands has been closed and that the territorial Government now has complete control over the disposition of the land vacated by the base;

9. *Urges* the specialized agencies and other organizations of the United Nations system, as well as such regional institutions as the Caribbean Development Bank, to continue to pay special attention to the development needs of the Turks and Caicos Islands and welcomes the continuing contribution of the United Nations Development Programme;

10. *Requests* the administering Power, in consultation with the territorial Government, to continue to provide the assistance necessary for the training of qualified local personnel in the skills essential to the development of economic and social sectors of the Territory;

11. *Considers* that the possibility of sending a further visiting mission to the Turks and Caicos Islands at an appropriate time should be kept under review;

12. *Requests* the Special Committee to continue the examination of this question at its next session, including the possible dispatch of a further visiting mission to the Turks and Caicos Islands at an appropriate time and in consultation with the administering Power, and to report thereon to the General Assembly at its fortieth session.

General Assembly resolution 39/37

5 December 1984   Meeting 87   Adopted without vote

Approved by Fourth Committee (A/39/696) without objection, 12 November (meeting 18); draft by Committee on colonial countries (A/39/23); agenda item 18.
Financial implications. S-G, A/C.4/39/L.4.
Meeting numbers. GA 39th session: 4th Committee 12-18; plenary 87.

The draft resolution was recommended by the Committee on colonial countries on 20 August,[1] following endorsement of the conclusions and recommendations of the Sub-Committee on Small Territories. The Committee had considered military installations, activities and arrangements; the role of foreign capital and major development activities; constitutional and political developments; and economic, social and educational conditions in the islands.

On 11 May 1984,[10] the United Kingdom had invited the Committee on colonial countries to send a visiting mission to the Turks and Caicos Islands to observe the 29 May general election in the Territory.

United States Virgin Islands

GENERAL ASSEMBLY ACTION

On 5 December, on the recommendation of the Fourth Committee, the General Assembly adopted without vote resolution 39/38.

Question of the United States Virgin Islands
The General Assembly,

Having considered the question of the United States Virgin Islands,

Having examined the relevant chapters of the report of the Special Committee on the Situation with regard to the Implementation of the Declaration on the Granting of Independence to Colonial Countries and Peoples,

Recalling its resolution 1514(XV) of 14 December 1960, containing the Declaration on the Granting of Independence to Colonial Countries and Peoples, and all other resolutions and decisions of the United Nations relating to the United States Virgin Islands, including in particular its resolution 38/48 of 7 December 1983,

Noting with appreciation the continued participation of the United States of America, as the administering Power, in the work of the Special Committee in regard to the United States Virgin Islands, thereby enabling it to conduct a more informed and meaningful examination of the situation in the Territory, and expressing its satisfaction at the willingness of the administering Power to receive visiting missions in the Territories under its administration,

Welcoming the participation of a representative of the territorial Government in the work of the Special Committee,

Having heard the statement of the representative of the administering Power relating to the United States Virgin Islands,

Noting that the territorial Government has undertaken to intensify its efforts to expand and diversify the economy and further noting the growth in the manufacturing, construction and tourism sectors and in per capita income, as well as the relatively low unemployment rate in the Territory,

Noting that the territorial Government is encouraging the growth of agriculture and to that end recently purchased 804 hectares of land on St. Croix for agricultural development, home ownership and the construction of a vocational school,

Reiterating the view that the participation of Territories as associate members in organizations of the United Nations system is a part of the overall strategy of accelerating the decolonization process,

Aware that in 1967 the administering Power transferred possession of its former naval base on St. Thomas to the territorial Government while retaining the right to reoccupy it, and that it maintains a radar and sonar calibration station and an underwater tracking range off the west coast of St. Croix,

1. *Approves* the chapter of the report of the Special Committee on the Situation with regard to the Implementation of the Declaration on the Granting of Independence to Colonial Countries and Peoples relating to the United States Virgin Islands;

2. *Reaffirms* the inalienable right of the people of the United States Virgin Islands to self-determination and independence in conformity with the Declaration on the Granting of Independence to Colonial Countries and Peoples, contained in General Assembly resolution 1514(XV);

3. *Reiterates* the view that such factors as territorial size, geographical location, size of population and limited natural resources should in no way delay the speedy exercise by the people of the Territory of their inalienable right to self-determination and independence in conformity with the Declaration contained in General Assembly resolution 1514(XV), which fully applies to the United States Virgin Islands;

4. *Reiterates* that it is the responsibility of the administering Power to create such conditions in the United States Virgin Islands as will enable the people of the Territory to exercise freely and without interference their inalienable right to self-determination and independence in conformity with General Assembly resolution 1514(XV);

5. *Calls upon* the administering Power, taking into account the wish of the people of the United States Virgin Islands, to take all necessary steps to expedite the process of decolonization in accordance with the relevant provisions of the Charter of the United Nations and the Declaration, as well as all other relevant resolutions and decisions of the General Assembly;

6. *Notes* that the Senate of the United States Virgin Islands has established a Select Committee to ascertain the views of the people of the Territory on their future status and to make recommendations in that regard to the Legislature and further notes that public hearings are being held throughout the Territory;

7. *Reaffirms* the responsibility of the administering Power under the Charter for the economic and social development of the Territory;

8. *Urges* the administering Power, in co-operation with the territorial Government, to strengthen the economy of the Territory by taking additional measures of diversification in all fields and developing an adequate infra-structure with a view to reducing its economic dependence on the administering Power;

9. *Notes with satisfaction* the recent admission of the United States Virgin Islands as an associate member of the Economic Commission for Latin America and the Caribbean and its subsidiary body, the Caribbean Development and Co-operation Committee, and calls upon the administering Power to facilitate the participation of the Territory in other organizations of the United Nations system;

10. *Urges* the administering Power, in co-operation with the Government of the United States Virgin Islands, to safeguard the inalienable right of the people of the Territory to the enjoyment of their natural resources by taking effective measures to guarantee their right to own and dispose of those resources and to establish and maintain control of their future development;

11. *Also urges* the administering Power, in co-operation with the territorial Government, to continue to improve social conditions and to pay particular attention to overcoming problems of public housing, health care, education and crime and, in that connection, notes that further efforts are necessary to revitalize the health care programme, to improve crime prevention, to discourage juvenile delinquency and to expand and upgrade school facilities;

12. *Further urges* the administering Power to continue to take all necessary measures to comply fully with the purposes and principles of the Charter, the Declaration and the relevant resolutions and decisions of the General Assembly relating to military activities and arrangements by colonial Powers in Territories under their administration;

13. *Considers* that the possibility of sending a further visiting mission to the United States Virgin Islands at an appropriate time should be kept under review;

14. *Requests* the Special Committee to continue the examination of this question at its next session, including the possible dispatch of a further visiting mission to the United States Virgin Islands at an appropriate time and in consultation with the administering Power, and to report thereon to the General Assembly at its fortieth session.

General Assembly resolution 39/38

5 December 1984   Meeting 87   Adopted without vote

Approved by Fourth Committee (A/39/696) without objection, 12 November (meeting 18); draft by Committee on colonial countries (A/39/23); agenda item 18.
Financial implications. S-G, A/C.4/39/L.4.
Meeting numbers. GA 39th session: 4th Committee 12-18; plenary 87.

The draft was recommended by the Committee on colonial countries on 24 August,[1] following its endorsement of the conclusions and recommendations of the Sub-Committee on Small Territories. The Committee had considered the military installations, arrangements and activities, constitutional and political developments, and economic, social and educational conditions in the islands.

REFERENCES

[1]A/39/23. [2]A/AC.109/772. [3]A/AC.109/799. [4]YUN 1960, p. 49, GA res. 1514(XV), 14 Dec. 1960. [5]A/39/401. [6]YUN 1983, p. 1094, GA dec. 38/420, 7 Dec. 1983. [7]A/39/494. [8]A/39/732. [9]YUN 1980, p. 1082. [10]A/AC.109/774.

Legal questions

International Court of Justice

In 1984, the International Court of Justice continued to deal with three contentious cases. A fourth dispute was referred to it in April. In addition, it received two requests—one for the revision of a 1982 Judgment and the other for an advisory opinion.

Three Judges were re-elected and two others were elected to the Court for terms beginning in February 1985 (see APPENDIX III).

Judicial work of the Court

In 1984, the Court or its Chamber—meeting at The Hague, Netherlands—considered contentious cases concerning the continental shelf delimitation (Tunisia/Libyan Arab Jamahiriya, Libyan Arab Jamahiriya/Malta), delimitation of the maritime boundary (Canada/United States), a frontier dispute (Burkina Faso/Mali), and responsibility for military and paramilitary activities in and against Nicaragua (Nicaragua v. United States). In addition, it received a request for an advisory opinion concerning a judgement of the United Nations Administrative Tribunal.

Continental shelf delimitation between Tunisia and the Libyan Arab Jamahiriya

On 27 July 1984, Tunisia, invoking the discovery of a new fact, submitted to the Court[1] an Application for the revision and the interpretation of the Judgment given by the Court on 24 February 1982[2] in the case concerning the delimitation of the continental shelf between it and the Libyan Arab Jamahiriya.

Pursuant to the Rules of Court, the Vice-President fixed a time-limit, expiring on 15 October 1984, within which the Libyan Arab Jamahiriya presented written observations on the Tunisian Application, in particular its admissibility.

Continental shelf delimitation between the Libyan Arab Jamahiriya and Malta

In view of the objections raised by the Libyan Arab Jamahiriya and Malta to Italy's 1983 request for intervention in the continental shelf delimita-tion case between the Libyan Arab Jamahiriya and Malta,[3] the Court held public sittings in 1984 during which speeches were made on behalf of Italy and the original two parties concerned. Italy indicated that its object in intervening was to enable it to participate in the proceedings to defend its rights over certain areas claimed by the parties.

On 21 March 1984, the Court delivered at a public sitting a Judgment,[4] whose operative paragraph read as follows:

> *The Court,*
> By eleven votes to five,
> *Finds* that the Application of the Italian Republic, filed in the Registry of the Court on 24 October 1983, for permission to intervene under Article 62 of the Statute of the Court, cannot be granted.
>
> In favour: President Elias; Judges Lachs, Morozov, Nagendra Singh, Ruda, El-Khani, de Lacharrière, Mbaye, Bedjaoui; Judges *ad hoc* Jiménez de Aréchaga and Castañeda.
>
> Against: Vice-President Sette Câmara; Judges Oda, Ago, Schwebel and Sir Robert Jennings.

Judges Morozov, Nagendra Singh and Mbaye and Judge *ad hoc* Jiménez de Aréchaga appended separate opinions to the Judgment. Vice-President Sette Câmara and Judges Oda, Ago, Schwebel and Sir Robert Jennings appended dissenting opinions.

After the decision, the proceedings continued. On 21 March, the President made an Order[5] fixing 12 July 1984 as the time-limit for the filing of Replies by the Libyan Arab Jamahiriya and Malta, both States having expressed the wish to submit a further pleading as provided in their Special Agreement of 1976, which had requested the Court to indicate the principles and rules applicable to delimitation of the continental shelf between the parties and the practical method for their application. The parties each filed their Replies within the time-limit.

Following the resignation for health reasons of Judge *ad hoc* Jorge Castañeda, Malta appointed N. Valticos as its new Judge *ad hoc*.

Public sittings were held between 26 November and 14 December 1984.[6]

Maritime boundary delimitation between Canada and the United States

The five-member Chamber of the Court continued in 1984 to consider the question, submitted in 1981 by Canada and the United States,[7] concerning the course of the maritime boundary dividing the continental shelf and fisheries zones in the Gulf of Maine area.

By an Order of 30 March 1984,[8] the Chamber, acceding to a request made by the parties in accordance with their Special Agreement, signed on 29 March 1979 and in force from 20 November 1981, appointed a technical expert to assist it, particularly in preparing the description of the maritime boundary and the charts required.

Between 2 April and 11 May, the Chamber heard, at 26 public sittings, oral arguments presented on behalf of the parties.

On 12 October, the Chamber delivered its Judgment[9] at a public sitting. The operative part of the Judgment read as follows:

The Chamber,
By four votes to one,
Decides

That the course of the single maritime boundary that divides the continental shelf and the exclusive fisheries zones of Canada and the United States of America in the area referred to in the Special Agreement concluded by those two States on 29 March 1979 shall be defined by geodetic lines connecting the points with the following co-ordinates:

	Latitude North	*Longitude West*
A	44° 11′ 12″	67° 16′ 46″
B	42° 53′ 14″	67° 44′ 35″
C	42° 31′ 08″	67° 28′ 05″
D	40° 27′ 05″	65° 41′ 59″

In favour: President Ago; Judges Mosler, Schwebel; Judge *ad hoc* Cohen.
Against: Judge Gros.

Judge Schwebel appended a separate opinion to the Judgment and Judge Gros appended a dissenting opinion.

Frontier dispute between Burkina Faso and Mali

In 1984, the Court remained seized of the question of the delimitation of part of the land frontier between Burkina Faso (formerly the Upper Volta, as renamed on 6 August 1984, see p. 373) and Mali—which had been referred to it on 14 October 1983.[3]

Military and paramilitary activities in and against Nicaragua

On 9 April 1984,[1] Nicaragua filed an Application instituting proceedings against the United States, accompanied by a request for the indica-

tion of provisional measures, in respect of a dispute concerning responsibility for military and paramilitary activities in and against Nicaragua. (See also p. 206.)

On 13 April, the United States informed the Court that it was appointing an agent for the case, while indicating its conviction that the Court was without jurisdiction to deal with the Application and was *a fortiori* without jurisdiction to indicate the provisional measures requested by Nicaragua.

Having held public sittings on 25 and 27 April to hear the oral observations of both parties, the Court, at a public sitting on 10 May, delivered an Order[10] indicating such measures. The operative provisions of the Order read as follows:

The Court,
A. Unanimously,

Rejects the request made by the United States of America that the proceedings on the Application filed by the Republic of Nicaragua on 9 April 1984, and on the request filed the same day by the Republic of Nicaragua for the indication of provisional measures, be terminated by the removal of the case from the list;

B. *Indicates*, pending its final decision in the proceedings instituted on 9 April 1984 by the Republic of Nicaragua against the United States of America, the following provisional measures:

1. Unanimously,

The United States of America should immediately cease and refrain from any action restricting, blocking or endangering access to or from Nicaraguan ports, and, in particular, the laying of mines.

2. By fourteen votes to one,

The right to sovereignty and to political independence possessed by the Republic of Nicaragua, like any other State of the region or or of the world, should be fully respected and should not in any way be jeopardized by any military and paramilitary activities which are prohibited by the principles of international law, in particular the principle that States should refrain in their international relations from the threat or use of force against the territorial integrity or the political independence of any State, and the principle concerning the duty not to intervene in matters within the domestic jurisdiction of a State, principles embodied in the United Nations Charter and the Charter of the Organization of American States.

In favour: President Elias; Vice-President Sette Câmara; Judges Lachs, Morozov, Nagendra Singh, Ruda, Mosler, Oda, Ago, El-Khani, Sir Robert Jennings, de Lacharrière, Mbaye, Bedjaoui.
Against: Judge Schwebel.

3. Unanimously,

The Governments of the United States of America and the Republic of Nicaragua should each of them ensure that no action of any kind is taken which might aggravate or extend the dispute submitted to the Court.

4. Unanimously,

The Governments of the United States of America and the Republic of Nicaragua should each of them ensure that no action is taken which might prejudice the rights of the other Party in respect of the carrying out of whatever decision the Court may render in the case;

    C. Unanimously,

Decides further that, until the Court delivers its final judgment in the present case, it will keep the matters covered by this Order continuously under review;

    D. Unanimously,

Decides that the written proceedings shall first be addressed to the questions of the jurisdiction of the Court to entertain the dispute and of the admissibility of the Application;

And reserves the fixing of the time-limits for the said written proceedings, and the subsequent procedure, for further decision.

Judges Mosler and Sir Robert Jennings appended a joint separate opinion to the Order and Judge Schwebel appended a dissenting opinion.

In accordance with Article 41, paragraph 2, of the Statute of the Court, the Registrar immediately notified the parties and the Security Council of the indication of those measures.[11]

By an Order of 14 May,[12] the President of the Court fixed the following time-limits for the filing of pleadings addressed to the questions of jurisdiction and admissibility: 30 June for the Memorial of Nicaragua, and 17 August for the Counter-Memorial of the United States. The pleadings were filed within the prescribed time-limits.

On 15 August,[6] El Salvador filed a Declaration of Intervention in the case under Article 63 of the Statute, asserting that the Court had no jurisdiction to entertain Nicaragua's Application. Having regard to the written observations submitted by the parties on that Declaration, the Court made an Order on 4 October[13] whose operative provisions read as follows:

The Court,

(i) By nine votes to six,

Decides not to hold a hearing on the Declaration of Intervention of the Republic of El Salvador.

    In favour: President Elias; Vice-President Sette Câmara; Judges Lachs, Morozov, Nagendra Singh, Oda, El-Khani, Mbaye, Bedjaoui.

    Against: Judges Ruda, Mosler, Ago, Schwebel, Sir Robert Jennings, de Lacharrière.

(ii) By fourteen votes to one,

Decides that the Declaration of Intervention of the Republic of El Salvador is inadmissible inasmuch as it relates to the current phase of the proceedings brought by Nicaragua against the United States of America.

    In favour: President Elias; Vice-President Sette Câmara; Judges Lachs, Morozov, Nagendra Singh, Ruda, Mosler, Oda, Ago, El-Khani, Sir Robert Jennings, de Lacharrière, Mbaye, Bedjaoui.

    Against: Judge Schwebel.

From 8 to 18 October,[6] the Court held 10 public sittings during which speeches were made on behalf of Nicaragua and the United States on the questions of jurisdiction and admissibility. The Judge *ad hoc* appointed by Nicaragua, C.-A. Colliard, participated in the Court's work from that stage of the proceedings.

At a public sitting held on 26 November, the Court delivered its Judgment,[14] whose operative provisions read as follows:

The Court,

(1) *(a) finds*, by eleven votes to five, that it has jurisdiction to entertain the Application filed by the Republic of Nicaragua on 9 April 1984, on the basis of Article 36, paragraphs 2 and 5, of the Statute of the Court;

    In favour: President Elias; Vice-President Sette Câmara; Judges Lachs, Morozov, Nagendra Singh, Ruda, El-Khani, de Lacharrière, Mbaye, Bedjaoui; Judge *ad hoc* Colliard.

    Against: Judges Mosler, Oda, Ago, Schwebel and Sir Robert Jennings.

(b) finds, by fourteen votes to two, that it has jurisdiction to entertain the Application filed by the Republic of Nicaragua on 9 April 1984, in so far as that Application relates to a dispute concerning the interpretation or application of the Treaty of Friendship, Commerce and Navigation between the United States of America and the Republic of Nicaragua signed at Managua on 21 January 1956, on the basis of Article XXIV of that Treaty;

    In favour: President Elias; Vice-President Sette Câmara; Judges Lachs, Morozov, Nagendra Singh, Mosler, Oda, Ago, El-Khani, Sir Robert Jennings, de Lacharrière, Mbaye, Bedjaoui; Judge *ad hoc* Colliard.

    Against: Judges Ruda and Schwebel.

(c) finds, by fifteen votes to one, that it has jurisdiction to entertain the case;

    In favour: President Elias; Vice-President Sette Câmara; Judges Lachs, Morozov, Nagendra Singh, Ruda, Mosler, Oda, Ago, El-Khani, Sir Robert Jennings, de Lacharrière, Mbaye, Bedjaoui; Judge *ad hoc* Colliard.

    Against: Judge Schwebel.

(2) *finds*, unanimously, that the said Application is admissible.

Judges Nagendra Singh, Ruda, Mosler, Oda, Ago and Sir Robert Jennings appended separate opinions to the Judgment. Judge Schwebel appended a dissenting opinion.

Review of a judgement by the UN Administrative Tribunal

On 10 September 1984,[6] the Court received a request for an advisory opinion, from the General Assembly's Committee on Applications for Review of Administrative Tribunal Judgements, in respect of Judgement No. 333,[15] delivered at Geneva on 8 June by the Tribunal in the case of Yakimetz v. the Secretary-

General, involving the staff member's request for further employment after the expiry of his contract with the Organization.

The Committee's decision to request the Court's opinion, under article 11 of the Tribunal's statute, was made on 23 August at the request of the interested party.

By Judgement No. 333, the Tribunal had determined that Vladimir Victorovich Yakimetz, during the period of his service with the United Nations, was on a five-year fixed-term contract under secondment from the USSR Government, which could not be modified without the consent of all three parties (the United Nations, the USSR Government and Mr. Yakimetz); and that no tacit agreement existed between Mr. Yakimetz and the United Nations between 10 February 1983 (when he resigned from the service of the USSR Government, after seeking asylum in the United States the previous day) and 26 December 1983 (when his contract expired) changing the character of their relationship. The Tribunal questioned his suitability as an international civil servant under the existing circumstances, and concluded that Mr. Yakimetz's pleas, including those for monetary relief, could not be sustained.

By an Order of 13 September,[16] the Court's President fixed 14 December as the time-limit for submission of written statements by the United Nations and its Member States; by an Order of 30 November,[17] the time-limit was extended to 28 February 1985.

Organizational questions

Reports of the Court

The 1984 activities of the International Court of Justice were contained in two reports to the General Assembly, covering the periods 1 August 1983 to 31 July 1984[18] and 1 August 1984 to 31 July 1985.[19]

GENERAL ASSEMBLY ACTION

In December, the General Assembly, on an oral proposal by its President, adopted decision 39/414 without vote.

Report of the International Court of Justice

At its 94th plenary meeting, on 11 December 1984, the General Assembly took note of the report of the International Court of Justice.[18]

General Assembly decision 39/414

Adopted without vote

Oral proposal by President; agenda item 13.

REFERENCES

[1]*International Court of Justice Yearbook 1983-1984*, No. 38, I.C.J. Sales No. 502. [2]YUN 1982, p. 1365. [3]YUN 1983, p. 1103. [4]*Case concerning the Continental Shelf* (Libyan Arab Jamahiriya/Malta), *Judgment of 21 March 1984*, I.C.J. Sales No. 496. [5]*Ibid.*, *Order of 21 March 1984*, I.C.J. Sales No. 497. [6]*International Court of Justice Yearbook 1984-1985*, No. 39, I.C.J. Sales No. 514. [7]YUN 1981, p. 1202. [8]*Case concerning Delimitation of the Maritime Boundary in the Gulf of Maine Area* (Canada/United States of America), *Order of 30 March 1984*, I.C.J. Sales No. 498. [9]*Ibid.*, *Judgment of 12 October 1984*, I.C.J. Sales No. 505. [10]*Case concerning Military and Paramilitary Activities in and against Nicaragua* (Nicaragua v. United States of America), *Order of 10 May 1984*, I.C.J. Sales No. 499. [11]S/16564. [12]*Case concerning Military and Paramilitary Activities in and against Nicaragua* (Nicaragua v. United States of America), *Order of 14 May 1984*, I.C.J. Sales No. 500. [13]*Ibid.*, *Order of 4 October 1984*, I.C.J. Sales No. 504. [14]*Ibid.*, *Judgment of 26 November 1984*, I.C.J. Sales No. 506. [15]AT/DEC/333. [16]*Application for Review of Judgement No. 333 of the United Nations Administrative Tribunal* (Request for advisory opinion), *Order of 13 September 1984*, I.C.J. Sales No. 503. [17]*Ibid.*, *Order of 30 November 1984*, I.C.J. Sales No. 507. [18]A/39/4. [19]A/40/4.

OTHER PUBLICATIONS

International Court of Justice: Reports of Judgments, Advisory Opinions and Orders, Index 1984, I.C.J. Sales No. 509. *Bibliography of the International Court of Justice*, No. 38, *1984*, I.C.J. Sales No. 510.

Chapter II

Legal aspects of international political relations

In 1984, the United Nations continued working towards effective legal measures for promoting friendly relations among States. The General Assembly, in December, called for continuation of work towards the legal codification of: non-use of force in international relations (resolution 39/81), offences against the peace and security of mankind (39/80) and an international convention against mercenary activities (39/84). It also requested the Secretary-General to prepare a draft handbook on the peaceful settlement of disputes between States (39/79), decided to begin identifying good-neighbourliness between them (39/78), and recommended that work continue on draft articles on the non-navigational use of international watercourses (39/85).

Topic related to this chapter. International peace and security.

Peaceful settlement of disputes between States

As in previous years, the question of peaceful settlement of disputes between States was considered by the General Assembly and its Special Committee on the Charter of the United Nations and on the Strengthening of the Role of the Organization. In December 1984, the Assembly requested the Secretary-General to prepare a draft handbook on the topic for consideration by the Committee in 1985.

Special Committee consideration. The Special Committee, at its April 1984 session,[1] continued work on the peaceful settlement of disputes, as called for by the Assembly in December 1983.[2] This was one of three main questions considered by the Committee, the others being proposals on rationalizing the existing procedures of the United Nations and ways to maintain international peace and security (see p. 1100).

An open-ended Working Group of the Committee held six meetings on the question between 6 and 11 April, at three of which it considered a 1983 proposal by Nigeria, the Philippines and Romania[3] for the creation of a United Nations permanent commission on good offices, mediation and conciliation for the settlement of disputes and the prevention of conflicts among States. The proposal was later submitted to the Assembly's Sixth (Legal) Committee as a working paper.[4]

The Working Group also discussed a proposed handbook on dispute settlement—focusing on the approach and the contents, and on the manner of preparation—based on a preliminary draft outline,[5] prepared by the Secretary-General at the Assembly's 1983 request,[2] and working papers submitted by France in 1981[6] and 1984.[7] The Committee concluded that the Assembly should request the Secretary-General to prepare a draft handbook, based on the outline it had agreed on during the session, and to report to the Committee in 1985 on the progress of work.

GENERAL ASSEMBLY ACTION

On 13 December, the General Assembly, on the recommendation of the Sixth Committee, adopted resolution 39/79 without vote.

Peaceful settlement of disputes between States

The General Assembly,

Having examined the item entitled "Peaceful settlement of disputes between States",

Recalling its resolution 37/10 of 15 November 1982, by which it approved the Manila Declaration on the Peaceful Settlement of International Disputes, annexed thereto,

Recalling also its resolution 38/131 of 19 December 1983,

Deeply concerned at the continuation of conflict situations and the emergence of new sources of disputes and tension in international life, and especially at the growing tendency to resort to force or the threat of force and to intervention in internal affairs, and at the escalation of the arms race, which gravely endanger the independence and security of States as well as international peace and security,

Taking into account the need to exert the utmost effort in order to settle any situations and disputes between States exclusively by peaceful means and to avoid any military action and hostilities against other States, which can only make more difficult the solution of existing problems,

Considering that the question of the peaceful settlement of disputes should represent one of the central concerns for States and for the United Nations, and that efforts for strengthening the process of peaceful settlement of disputes should be continued,

Taking note of the working papers on the establishment of a commission on good offices, mediation and conciliation for the settlement of disputes and the prevention of conflicts among States, submitted to the General Assembly by Nigeria, the Philippines and Romania,

Taking into account the elaboration by the Special Committee on the Charter of the United Nations and on the Strengthening of the Role of the Organization of the outline for a handbook on the peaceful settlement of disputes between States and the conclusions thereon,

1. *Again urges* all States to observe and promote in good faith the provisions of the Manila Declaration on the Peaceful Settlement of International Disputes in the settlement of their international disputes;

2. *Stresses* the need to continue efforts to strengthen the process of the peaceful settlement of disputes through the progressive development and codification of international law and through enhancing the effectiveness of the United Nations in this field;

3. *Requests* the Special Committee on the Charter of the United Nations and on the Strengthening of the Role of the Organization, during its session in 1985, to continue its work on the question of the peaceful settlement of disputes between States and, in this context:

(a) To continue the consideration of the proposal contained in the above-mentioned working papers;

(b) To examine the report of the Secretary-General on the progress of work on the draft handbook on the peaceful settlement of disputes between States;

4. *Requests* the Secretary-General to prepare, on the basis of the outline elaborated by the Special Committee and in the light of the views expressed in the course of the discussions in the Sixth Committee and in the Special Committee, a draft handbook on the peaceful settlement of disputes between States, and to report to the Special Committee at its session in 1985 on the progress of work, before submitting to it the draft handbook in its final form, with a view to its approval at a later stage;

5. *Decides* to include in the provisional agenda of its fortieth session the item entitled "Peaceful settlement of disputes between States".

General Assembly resolution 39/79

13 December 1984   Meeting 99   Adopted without vote

Approved by Sixth Committee (A/39/774) without vote, 6 December (meeting 64); 31-nation draft (A/C.6/39/L.7); agenda item 124.

Sponsors: Australia, Bolivia, Chile, Costa Rica, Cyprus, Dominican Republic, Egypt, Ethiopia, Guatemala, Guinea, Guyana, Indonesia, Madagascar, Mali, Mexico, Morocco, Nigeria, Panama, Philippines, Romania, Rwanda, Senegal, Singapore, Sudan, Suriname, Togo, Uganda, Uruguay, Yugoslavia, Zaire, Zambia.

Meeting numbers. GA 39th session: 6th Committee 23-31, 64; plenary 99.

In explanation of position, the USSR expressed its opposition to the proposed commission, asserting that the idea ran counter to the Charter of the United Nations and would undermine the prerogatives of the Security Council; however, it had not objected to the adoption of the text which it considered to be procedural in nature.

Good-neighbourliness between States

The General Assembly, in December 1984, decided to start identifying and clarifying the elements of good-neighbourliness between States.

In connection with the Assembly's agenda item on the subject, the Libyan Arab Jamahiriya and Morocco addressed a letter on 15 October to the Secretary-General,[8] transmitting the text of a treaty, signed by them on 13 August, establishing a union between the two States to be called the Arab-African Union.

On the recommendation of the Sixth Committee, the General Assembly, on 13 December 1984, adopted resolution 39/78 without vote.

Development and strengthening of good-neighbourliness between States

The General Assembly,

Bearing in mind the determination of the peoples of the United Nations, as expressed in the Charter of the United Nations, to practise tolerance and live together in peace with one another as good neighbours,

Recalling the Declaration on Principles of International Law concerning Friendly Relations and Co-operation among States in accordance with the Charter of the United Nations, approved by its resolution 2625(XXV) of 24 October 1970,

Recalling its resolutions 1236(XII) of 14 December 1957, 1301(XIII) of 10 December 1958, 2129(XX) of 21 December 1965, 34/99 of 14 December 1979, 36/101 of 9 December 1981, 37/117 of 16 December 1982 and 38/126 of 19 December 1983,

Bearing in mind that, owing to geographic proximity and to other relevant reasons, there are particularly favourable opportunities for co-operation and mutual advantage between neighbouring countries, in many fields and various forms, and that the development of such co-operation may have a positive influence on international relations as a whole,

Considering that the great changes of a political, economic and social nature, as well as the scientific and technological progress which has taken place in the world and led to unprecedented interdependence of nations, have given new dimensions to good-neighbourliness in the conduct of States and increased the need to develop and strengthen it,

Taking into account the working paper concerning the development and strengthening of good-neighbourliness between States, as well as the written replies sent by States and international organizations on the content of good-neighbourliness and on ways and means to enhance it[9] and the views expressed by States on this subject in the General Assembly,

Recalling its opinion that it is necessary to continue to examine the question of good-neighbourliness in order to strengthen and develop its content, as well as ways and modalities to enhance its effectiveness, and that the results of this examination could be included, at an appropriate time, in a suitable international document,

1. *Reaffirms* that good-neighbourliness fully conforms with the purposes of the United Nations and shall be founded upon the strict observance of the principles of the Charter of the United Nations and of the Declaration on Principles of International Law concerning Friendly Relations and Co-operation among States in accordance with the Charter of the United Nations, and so presupposes the rejection of any acts seeking to establish zones of influence or domination;

2. *Calls once again upon* States, in the interest of the maintenance of international peace and security, to develop good-neighbourly relations, acting on the basis of these principles;

3. *Reaffirms* that the generalization of the long practice of good-neighbourliness and of principles and rules pertaining to it is likely to strengthen friendly relations

and co-operation among States in accordance with the Charter;

4. *Deems it appropriate*, on the basis of the working paper concerning the development and strengthening of good-neighbourliness between States mentioned above, as well as of other proposals and ideas which have been or will be submitted by States, and the replies and views of States and international organizations, to start clarifying and formulating the elements of good-neighbourliness as part of a process of elaboration of a suitable international document on the subject;

5. *Decides* to proceed with the task of identifying and clarifying the elements of good-neighbourliness within the framework of a working group or other appropriate organ of the Sixth Committee as may be decided upon by the Committee when organizing its work at the fortieth session of the General Assembly;

6. *Invites once again* Governments, United Nations bodies and programmes and the specialized agencies, within their respective fields of competence, to communicate to the Secretary-General their views and suggestions or, if they deem it appropriate, to update the replies already given by them, on the content of good-neighbourliness and ways and means to strengthen it;

7. *Requests* the Secretary-General to submit to the General Assembly at its fortieth session a report containing the replies received in accordance with paragraph 6 above;

8. *Decides* to include in the provisional agenda of its fortieth session the item entitled "Development and strengthening of good-neighbourliness between States".

General Assembly resolution 39/78

13 December 1984   Meeting 99   Adopted without vote

Approved by Sixth Committee (A/39/773) without vote, 3 December (meeting 61); 37-nation draft (A/C.6/39/L.14); agenda item 123.
Sponsors: Bangladesh, Bolivia, Burundi, Congo, Costa Rica, France, Guinea, Guinea-Bissau, Guyana, Indonesia, Iraq, Kenya, Liberia, Madagascar, Mali, Mauritania, Morocco, Mozambique, Niger, Nigeria, Panama, Philippines, Portugal, Romania, Rwanda, Sao Tome and Principe, Senegal, Singapore, Spain, Sri Lanka, Sudan, Suriname, Tunisia, Turkey, Uganda, Yugoslavia, Zambia.
Meeting numbers. GA 39th session: 6th Committee 20-23, 61; plenary 99.

In explanation of position, the Netherlands said the working paper by Romania addressed a wide range of topics, some of which were being dealt with in other forums; care should be taken, therefore, not to duplicate such work, and the option of a working group suggested in paragraph 5 should not be pursued. If the elements of good-neighbourliness had to be formulated, the task should be assigned to the Special Committee on the Charter of the United Nations and on the Strengthening of the Role of the Organization.

Non-use of force in international relations

In December 1984, the General Assembly renewed its previous requests to the Special Committee on Enhancing the Effectiveness of the Principle of Non-Use of Force in International Relations to continue its work towards drafting a world treaty on that principle.

Special Committee consideration. The Special Committee—established in 1977[10] to consider, among other things, proposals and suggestions with the goal of drafting a world treaty on the non-use of force in international relations—met at United Nations Headquarters from 21 February to 16 March 1984.[11]

As in the previous year, the 35-member Committee had before it a draft world treaty on the non-use of force, submitted in 1976 by the USSR;[12] a 1979 working paper by Belgium, France, the Federal Republic of Germany, Italy and the United Kingdom;[13] and a 1981 revised working paper from 10 non-aligned countries (Benin, Cyprus, Egypt, India, Iraq, Morocco, Nepal, Nicaragua, Senegal, Uganda).[14] Also before the Committee was an informal paper by the Chairman of the Committee's 1982 session, grouping together the suggestions made in the Committee,[15] and a document[16] containing comments submitted by two States in reply to a renewed Assembly invitation in December 1983 for States' observations.[17]

An open-ended Working Group, re-established by the Committee in 1984, held 15 meetings between 28 February and 9 March. On 7 March, the Chairman suggested compiling the proposals officially made, so as to help the delegations to see the existing differences and the areas of possible agreement. His suggestion, and an informal paper he subsequently circulated, met with varying response.

Similarly, differing views were expressed on the progress of work, or lack thereof, in the Committee, and suggestions were made on the future course of action, including a view that the Committee be disbanded.

On 16 March, the Committee approved the Group's report as well as its own. Since the Committee had not completed its work, it generally recognized the desirability of further considering the question before it.

GENERAL ASSEMBLY ACTION

For its consideration of the item, the General Assembly's Sixth Committee had before it the report of the Special Committee on its 1984 session,[11] along with an August report[18] of the Secretary-General containing observations received from six States on the drafting of a world treaty. The Secretary-General also submitted to the Sixth Committee, at the request of Austria and France, a letter from them dated 19/21 September[19] calling for early ratification of an amendment on the non-use of force against civil aircraft to the 1944 Convention on International Civil Aviation, as adopted by the Assembly of the International Civil Aviation Organization on 10 May 1984 at an extraordinary session; the text of the amendment was annexed to the letter (see also PART TWO, Chapter X).

On the recommendation of the Sixth Committee, the Assembly, on 13 December 1984, adopted resolution 39/81 by recorded vote.

Report of the Special Committee on Enhancing the Effectiveness of the Principle of Non-Use of Force in International Relations

The General Assembly,

Recalling its resolution 31/9 of 8 November 1976, in which it invited Member States to examine further the draft World Treaty on the Non-Use of Force in International Relations, as well as other proposals made during the consideration of this item,

Recalling also its resolution 32/150 of 19 December 1977, by which it established the Special Committee on Enhancing the Effectiveness of the Principle of Non-Use of Force in International Relations,

Recalling, in particular, its resolutions 33/96 of 16 December 1978, 34/13 of 9 November 1979, 35/50 of 4 December 1980, 36/31 of 13 November 1981, 37/105 of 16 December 1982 and 38/133 of 19 December 1983, in which it decided that the Special Committee should continue its work,

Taking note of the statements made by the Chairmen of the Special Committee at its sessions in 1983 and 1984, based on the informal working paper presented by the Chairman of the Special Committee at its session in 1982,

Having considered the report of the Special Committee on the work of the session it held in 1984,

Taking into account that the Special Committee has not completed the mandate entrusted to it,

Reaffirming the need for effectiveness in the universal application of the principle of non-use of force in international relations and for assistance by the United Nations in this endeavour,

Expressing the hope that the Special Committee will, on the basis of the proposals before it, complete the mandate entrusted to it as soon as possible,

1. *Takes note* of the report of the Special Committee on Enhancing the Effectiveness of the Principle of Non-Use of Force in International Relations;

2. *Decides* that the Special Committee shall continue its work with the goal of drafting, at the earliest possible date, a world treaty on the non-use of force in international relations as well as the peaceful settlement of disputes or such other recommendations as the Committee deems appropriate;

3. *Requests* the Special Committee, in order to ensure progress in its work, to speed up at its session in 1985 the elaboration of the formulas of the working paper containing the main elements of the principle of non-use of force in international relations, taking duly into account the proposals submitted to it and the efforts undertaken at its sessions in 1982, 1983 and 1984;

4. *Invites* Governments to communicate their comments or suggestions or to bring them up to date, in accordance with General Assembly resolution 31/9;

5. *Requests* the Special Committee to be mindful of the importance of reaching general agreement whenever it has significance for the outcome of its work;

6. *Decides* that the Special Committee shall accept the participation of observers of Member States, including participation in the meetings of its working group;

7. *Requests* the Special Committee to concentrate its work in the framework of its working group;

8. *Requests* the Secretary-General to provide the Special Committee with the necessary facilities and services;

9. *Invites* the Special Committee to submit a report on its work to the General Assembly at its fortieth session;

10. *Decides* to include in the provisional agenda of its fortieth session the item entitled "Report of the Special Committee on Enhancing the Effectiveness of the Principle of Non-Use of Force in International Relations".

General Assembly resolution 39/81

13 December 1984   Meeting 99   111-15-10 (recorded vote)

Approved by Sixth Committee (A/39/776) by recorded vote (80-16-11), 28 November (meeting 58); 31-nation draft (A/C.6/39/L.9); agenda item 126.

Sponsors: Afghanistan, Angola, Benin, Bulgaria, Byelorussian SSR, Cuba, Cyprus, Czechoslovakia, Democratic Yemen, Ecuador, Egypt, Ethiopia, German Democratic Republic, Hungary, India, Iraq, Lao People's Democratic Republic, Libyan Arab Jamahiriya, Madagascar, Mali, Mongolia, Mozambique, Nicaragua, Poland, Romania, Syrian Arab Republic, Uganda, Ukrainian SSR, USSR, Venezuela, Viet Nam.

Financial implications. 5th Committee, A/39/734; S-G, A/C.5/39/68, A/C.6/39/L.11.

Meeting numbers. GA 39th session: 5th Committee 41; 6th Committee 12-19, 58, 64; plenary 99.

Recorded vote in Assembly as follows:

In favour: Afghanistan, Algeria, Angola, Argentina, Bahamas, Bahrain, Bangladesh, Barbados, Benin, Bhutan, Bolivia, Botswana, Brunei Darussalam, Bulgaria, Burkina Faso, Burma, Burundi, Byelorussian SSR, Cameroon, Cape Verde, Chad, Chile, China, Colombia, Congo, Costa Rica, Cuba, Cyprus, Czechoslovakia, Democratic Yemen, Djibouti, Dominican Republic, Ecuador, Egypt, El Salvador, Ethiopia, Fiji, Finland, Gabon, German Democratic Republic, Ghana, Greece, Guatemala, Guinea, Guyana, Haiti, Honduras, Hungary, India, Indonesia, Iran, Iraq, Jamaica, Jordan, Kenya, Kuwait, Lao People's Democratic Republic, Lebanon, Lesotho, Liberia, Libyan Arab Jamahiriya, Madagascar, Malawi, Malaysia, Maldives, Mali, Mauritania, Mauritius, Mexico, Mongolia, Morocco, Mozambique, Nepal, Nicaragua, Niger, Nigeria, Oman, Pakistan, Panama, Papua New Guinea, Peru, Philippines, Poland, Qatar, Romania, Rwanda, Sao Tome and Principe, Saudi Arabia, Senegal, Sierra Leone, Singapore, Somalia, Sri Lanka, Sudan, Suriname, Syrian Arab Republic, Thailand, Togo, Trinidad and Tobago, Tunisia, Uganda, Ukrainian SSR, USSR, United Arab Emirates, Uruguay, Venezuela, Viet Nam, Yemen, Yugoslavia, Zaire, Zambia.

Against: Belgium, Canada, Denmark, France, Iceland, Israel, Italy, Japan, Luxembourg, Netherlands, Norway, Portugal, Spain, United Kingdom, United States.

Abstaining: Australia, Austria, Brazil, Germany, Federal Republic of, Ireland, Ivory Coast, New Zealand, Paraguay, Sweden, Turkey.

In explanation of vote, Australia, the Netherlands and Spain felt that the best way of enhancing the principle of non-use of force in international relations, already enshrined in the United Nations Charter, was not by elaborating a world treaty but by improving the existing mechanisms such as the system of collective security. The Netherlands added that its negative vote was because paragraph 2 stated that the drafting of such a treaty was the *raison d'être* of the Special Committee. Australia felt that the Committee's very existence would come under question if no progress was achieved in the future.

Argentina, Brazil and Mexico hoped that, in the future, extraneous factors such as political issues and activities being addressed in other forums would not hinder the work of the Special Committee. Along with Brazil, Kenya felt the Committee needed a clear mandate to make progress.

Draft Code of Offences against peace and security

The General Assembly, in December 1984, requested the International Law Commission (ILC) to continue work on the draft Code of Offences against the Peace and Security of Mankind by elaborating an introduction as well as a list of offences. Prepared by ILC in 1954[20] in response to a 1947 Assembly request,[21] the draft Code defined offences which were crimes under international law and for which the responsible individual was to be punished. In 1982,[22] ILC had resumed work on the topic pursuant to a 1981 Assembly invitation.[23]

ILC consideration. The Commission, at its 1984 session,[24] considered the second report submitted by its Special Rapporteur on the topic, Doudou Thiam (Senegal).[25] In the report, he observed that while all offences against the peace and security of mankind were international crimes, the reverse was not necessarily true; and that the ILC objective was to prepare a code of offences against the peace and security of mankind and not an international penal code.

After considering a list of acts to be classified as offences suggested by the Special Rapporteur, ILC agreed to focus on the criminal liability of individuals and to begin drawing up a provisional list of offences, while bearing in mind the drafting of an introduction summarizing the general principles of relevant international criminal law. In addition to the offences covered in the 1954 Code, there was a general trend in ILC in favour of including colonialism, *apartheid*, acts causing serious damage to the human environment and economic aggression. At the same time, it considered that such phenomena as the taking of hostages, violence against persons enjoying diplomatic privileges and immunities, and the hijacking of aircraft should be approached from the angle of international terrorism; and that it would be desirable also to take account of the work of the *Ad Hoc* Committee on the Drafting of an International Convention against the Recruitment, Use, Financing and Training of Mercenaries (see below). ILC also discussed the appropriateness of including specific provisions on the use of atomic weapons in the draft Code, and agreed to consider the matter in greater depth in the light of any views expressed in the General Assembly. These conclusions were contained in paragraph 65 of the ILC report to the Assembly.[24]

GENERAL ASSEMBLY ACTION

The Secretary-General submitted to the General Assembly comments received from 10 Member States[26] in response to a December 1983 Assembly request.[27]

On 13 December 1984, the Assembly, on the recommendation of the Sixth Committee, adopted resolution 39/80 by recorded vote.

Draft Code of Offences against the Peace and Security of Mankind

The General Assembly,

Mindful of Article 13, paragraph 1 *a*, of the Charter of the United Nations, which provides that the General Assembly shall initiate studies and make recommendations for the purpose of encouraging the progressive development of international law and its codification,

Recalling its resolution 177(II) of 21 November 1947, by which it directed the International Law Commission to prepare a draft code of offences against the peace and security of mankind,

Having considered the draft Code of Offences against the Peace and Security of Mankind prepared by the International Law Commission and submitted to the General Assembly in 1954,

Recalling its belief that the elaboration of a code of offences against the peace and security of mankind could contribute to strengthening international peace and security and thus to promoting and implementing the purposes and principles set forth in the Charter of the United Nations,

Recalling also its resolution 36/106 of 10 December 1981, in which it invited the International Law Commission to resume its work with a view to elaborating the draft Code and to examine it with the required priority in order to review it, taking into account the results achieved by the process of the progressive development of international law,

Bearing in mind that the International Law Commission should fulfil its task on the basis of the early elaboration of draft articles,

Having considered chapter II of the report of the International Law Commission on the work of its thirty-sixth session, in particular paragraph 65 of the report, containing the Commission's conclusions,

Taking note of the report of the Secretary-General,

Taking into account the views expressed during the debate on this item at the current session,

Recognizing the importance and the urgency of the subject,

1. *Requests* the International Law Commission to continue its work on the elaboration of the draft Code of Offences against the Peace and Security of Mankind by elaborating an introduction as well as a list of the offences, taking into account the progress made at its thirty-sixth session, as well as the views expressed during the thirty-ninth session of the General Assembly;

2. *Requests* the Secretary-General to seek the views of Member States and intergovernmental organizations regarding the conclusions contained in paragraph 65 of the report of the International Law Commission and to include them in a report to be submitted to the General Assembly at its fortieth session with a view to adopting, at the appropriate time, the necessary decision thereon;

3. *Decides* to include in the provisional agenda of its fortieth session the item entitled "Draft Code of Offences against the Peace and Security of Mankind", to be considered in conjunction with the consideration of the report of the International Law Commission.

General Assembly resolution 39/80

13 December 1984   Meeting 99   122-0-15 (recorded vote)

Approved by Sixth Committee (A/39/775) by recorded vote (96-0-16), 5 December (meeting 63); 30-nation draft (A/C.6/39/L.21); agenda item 125.

Sponsors: Algeria, Angola, Benin, Bolivia, Congo, Cuba, Cyprus, Egypt, Gabon, German Democratic Republic, Iran, Ivory Coast, Kenya, Lao People's Democratic Republic, Mali, Mauritania, Mongolia, Morocco, Nigeria, Philippines, Poland, Rwanda, Sao Tome and Principe, Senegal, Sudan, Thailand, Togo, Tunisia, Viet Nam, Zaire.

Meeting numbers. GA 39th session: 6th Committee 47-49, 63; plenary 99.

Recorded vote in Assembly as follows:

In favour: Afghanistan, Algeria, Angola, Argentina, Australia, Austria, Bahamas, Bahrain, Bangladesh, Barbados, Benin, Bhutan, Bolivia, Botswana, Brazil, Brunei Darussalam, Bulgaria, Burkina Faso, Burundi, Byelorussian SSR, Cameroon, Cape

Verde, Chad, Chile, China, Colombia, Congo, Costa Rica, Cuba, Cyprus, Czechoslovakia, Democratic Kampuchea, Democratic Yemen, Denmark, Djibouti, Dominican Republic, Ecuador, Egypt, El Salvador, Ethiopia, Fiji, Finland, Gabon, German Democratic Republic, Ghana, Greece, Guatemala, Guinea, Guyana, Haiti, Honduras, Hungary, Iceland, India, Indonesia, Iran, Iraq, Ireland, Ivory Coast, Jamaica, Jordan, Kenya, Kuwait, Lao People's Democratic Republic, Lebanon, Lesotho, Liberia, Libyan Arab Jamahiriya, Madagascar, Malawi, Malaysia, Maldives, Mali, Mauritania, Mauritius, Mexico, Mongolia, Morocco, Mozambique, Nepal, New Zealand, Nicaragua, Niger, Nigeria, Norway, Oman, Pakistan, Panama, Papua New Guinea, Paraguay, Peru, Philippines, Poland, Qatar, Romania, Rwanda, Sao Tome and Principe, Saudi Arabia, Senegal, Sierra Leone, Singapore, Somalia, Sri Lanka, Sudan, Suriname, Sweden, Syrian Arab Republic, Thailand, Togo, Trinidad and Tobago, Tunisia, Uganda, Ukrainian SSR, USSR, United Arab Emirates, Uruguay, Venezuela, Viet Nam, Yemen, Yugoslavia, Zaire, Zambia.

Against: None.

Abstaining: Belgium, Burma, Canada, France, Germany, Federal Republic of, Israel, Italy, Japan, Luxembourg, Netherlands, Portugal, Spain, Turkey, United Kingdom, United States.

Several States explained their abstentions. The United Kingdom said it had abstained out of regard for the African sponsors which attached particular political importance to the item. Similarly, the United States deferred to the good intentions of the sponsors. France abstained out of consideration for ILC and to safeguard the consensus necessary for its continued work. Italy, a sponsor of the draft resolution on the ILC report (see Chapter VII of this section), felt it would be inconsistent to support a text which sought to alter the Commission's work programme and priorities.

Most delegations that explained their vote questioned the wisdom of keeping the subject separate from the agenda item on the ILC report. France and Israel observed that the topic had already been entrusted to ILC. Keeping the topic as a separate item, the United Kingdom felt, put political pressure on the Commission. The United States thought the approach had a subversive effect on that body and on the long-term prospects for the codification and progressive development of international law; further, it considered it imprudent to have ILC continue work on the Code, and pushing the draft resolution to a vote was irresponsible. The Federal Republic of Germany added that separate treatment of the item could jeopardize the consensus achieved on the work of ILC.

Similar points were made by Australia and Norway (on behalf also of Denmark, Finland, Iceland and Sweden), which, nevertheless, voted in favour of the text. Ireland, while supporting the Code's elaboration, did not favour separate treatment of the topic; it also preferred that the draft resolution did not refer to the early elaboration of the draft articles, as it felt that ILC required sufficient time to produce an authoritative text.

Reservations were expressed by a number of States—among them, the Nordic countries—about paragraph 3. Australia would have voted against that paragraph, had a vote been taken. The Federal Republic of Germany and Israel said ILC did not require detailed instructions from the Sixth Committee. The United Kingdom, which had difficulties also with the sixth and last preambu-

lar paragraphs, said paragraphs 1 and 3 gave the impression that the Sixth Committee lacked confidence in ILC's ability to carry out its mandate.

France feared that ILC would lose its credibility as a juridical body if it took up such issues as nuclear weapons as part of the Code.

Draft convention against mercenaries

In December 1984, the General Assembly decided that its *Ad Hoc* Committee on the Drafting of an International Convention against the Recruitment, Use, Financing and Training of Mercenaries should continue its work towards that goal, with a view to completing its mandate in 1985.

Work of the Committee against mercenaries. The *Ad Hoc* Committee held its fourth session at United Nations Headquarters from 30 July to 24 August 1984,[28] in pursuance of a December 1983 Assembly resolution.[29]

The Committee re-established two Working Groups: Group A to deal with issues of definition and the convention's scope, and Group B to deal with all other issues relevant to the future convention. In addition to the documents considered at its 1983 session,[30] the *Ad Hoc* Committee had before it a working paper submitted later that year by Mexico to the Assembly's Sixth Committee,[31] and a topical summary of the Sixth Committee's 1983 discussion on the question,[32] as prepared by the Secretary-General at the Assembly's request.[29]

The 1984 report of the *Ad Hoc* Committee incorporated the reports of its Working Groups and a document prepared by the Committee's Bureau to serve as a consolidated negotiating basis for facilitating further work. In addition to definitions and the obligations of States, Group A considered the question of the characterization of offences to be covered and State responsibility, discussed a document submitted by its Chairman on a draft structure for the provisions under discussion, and produced 12 draft articles. Group B, which produced 13 draft articles, considered such questions as jurisdiction and extradition, preventive measures, status of mercenaries, damage reparation and dispute settlement, as well as a machinery for enhancing the effectiveness of the convention and a saving clause concerning the application of relevant existing international instruments.

The Committee—established in 1980[33] with envisaged membership of 35 Member States—continued to have one vacancy in 1984 (see APPENDIX III).

In the course of 1984, the Secretary-General received a series of letters with requests that they be circulated under the agenda item on mercenaries. These letters included the situations in Afghanistan (see p. 224) and in Central America (see p. 195).

ghanistan (see p. 224) and in Central America (see p. 195).

GENERAL ASSEMBLY ACTION

On 13 December 1984, the General Assembly, on the recommendation of the Sixth Committee, adopted resolution 39/84 without vote.

Drafting of an international convention against the recruitment, use, financing and training of mercenaries

The General Assembly,

Bearing in mind the need for strict observance of the principles of sovereign equality, political independence, territorial integrity of States and self-determination of peoples, enshrined in the Charter of the United Nations and developed in the Declaration on Principles of International Law concerning Friendly Relations and Co-operation among States in accordance with the Charter of the United Nations,

Recalling its resolutions, particularly resolutions 2395(XXIII) of 29 November 1968, 2465(XXIII) of 20 December 1968, 2548(XXIV) of 11 December 1969, 2708(XXV) of 14 December 1970 and 3103(XXVIII) of 12 December 1973, and its resolution 1514(XV) of 14 December 1960, as well as Security Council resolutions 405(1977) of 14 April 1977, 419(1977) of 24 November 1977, 496(1981) of 15 December 1981 and 507(1982) of 28 May 1982, in which the United Nations denounced the practice of using mercenaries, in particular against developing countries and national liberation movements,

Recalling in particular its resolution 38/137 of 19 December 1983, by which it renewed the mandate of the *Ad Hoc* Committee on the Drafting of an International Convention against the Recruitment, Use, Financing and Training of Mercenaries,

Having considered the report of the *Ad Hoc* Committee on its fourth session,

Recognizing that the activities of mercenaries are contrary to fundamental principles of international law, such as non-interference in the internal affairs of States, territorial integrity and independence, and seriously impede the process of self-determination of peoples struggling against colonialism, racism and *apartheid* and all forms of foreign domination,

Bearing in mind the pernicious impact that the activities of mercenaries have on international peace and security,

Considering that the progressive development and codification of the rules of international law on mercenaries would contribute immensely to the implementation of the purposes and principles of the Charter,

Taking account of the fact that, although the *Ad Hoc* Committee has made some progress, it has not yet fulfilled its mandate,

Reaffirming the need for the elaboration, at the earliest possible date, of an international convention against the recruitment, use, financing and training of mercenaries,

1. *Takes note* of the report of the *Ad Hoc* Committee on the Drafting of an International Convention against the Recruitment, Use, Financing and Training of Mercenaries and the progress made by the *Ad Hoc* Committee, especially during its fourth session;

2. *Decides* to renew the mandate of the *Ad Hoc* Committee to enable it to continue its work on the drafting of an international convention against the recruitment, use, financing and training of mercenaries;

3. *Requests* the *Ad Hoc* Committee, in the fulfilment of its mandate, to use the draft articles contained in chapter IV of its report, entitled "Consolidated Negotiating Basis of a convention against the recruitment, use, financing and training of mercenaries", as a basis for future negotiation on the text of the proposed international convention;

4. *Invites* the *Ad Hoc* Committee to take into account the suggestions and proposals of Member States submitted to the Secretary-General on the subject and the views and comments expressed at the thirty-ninth session of the General Assembly during the debate in the Sixth Committee devoted to the consideration of the report of the *Ad Hoc* Committee;

5. *Decides* that the *Ad Hoc* Committee shall accept the participation of observers of Member States, including participation in the meetings of its working groups;

6. *Requests* the Secretary-General to make available to the *Ad Hoc* Committee at its fifth session a topical summary of the discussions which took place in the Sixth Committee during the thirty-ninth session of the General Assembly and any up-to-date and relevant documentation on the subject;

7. *Also requests* the Secretary-General to provide the *Ad Hoc* Committee with any assistance and facilities it may require for the performance of its work;

8. *Decides* that the *Ad Hoc* Committee shall hold its fifth session for four weeks, from 8 April to 3 May 1985;

9. *Requests* the *Ad Hoc* Committee to make every effort to complete its mandate at its fifth session and to submit a draft convention to the General Assembly at its fortieth session;

10. *Decides* to include in the provisional agenda of its fortieth session the item entitled "Report of the *Ad Hoc* Committee on the Drafting of an International Convention against the Recruitment, Use, Financing and Training of Mercenaries".

General Assembly resolution 39/84

13 December 1984   Meeting 99   Adopted without vote

Approved by Sixth Committee (A/39/777) by consensus, 6 December (meeting 64); 49-nation draft (A/C.6/39/L.13), orally revised; agenda item 129.

Sponsors: Afghanistan, Algeria, Angola, Bangladesh, Barbados, Benin, Burkina Faso, Burundi, Cameroon, Congo, Cuba, Cyprus, Egypt, Ethiopia, German Democratic Republic, Ghana, Guyana, India, Iraq, Kenya, Lao People's Democratic Republic, Lesotho, Libyan Arab Jamahiriya, Madagascar, Malawi, Malaysia, Mali, Mauritania, Mexico, Mongolia, Morocco, Mozambique, Nicaragua, Niger, Nigeria, Romania, Senegal, Suriname, Syrian Arab Republic, Togo, Trinidad and Tobago, Tunisia, Turkey, Uganda, Ukrainian SSR, Viet Nam, Yugoslavia, Zaire, Zambia.

Financial implications. 5th Committee, A/39/817; S-G, A/C.5/39/78, A/C.6/39/L.17.

Meeting numbers. GA 39th session: 5th Committee 45; 6th Committee 49-57, 64; plenary 99.

In explanation of position, Ireland (on behalf of the 10 States members of the European Community (EC)), Denmark (on behalf of the five Nordic States) and Japan felt that the wording of the fifth preambular paragraph was far-reaching: the misdeeds of private individuals acting in a personal capacity could not be imputed to States or regarded as breaches of international law. The United States said its participation in the consensus did not mean agreement with that paragraph. Concurring with the United States that paragraph 9 should not be interpreted as imposing a rigid time-limit for the completion of the Committee's mandate, the EC members asserted that a draft convention should not be submitted until all outstanding issues had been solved, and that the Committee must continue to work on the basis of consensus.

Draft articles on non-navigational uses of international watercourses

The International Law Commission, at its 1984 session,[24] continued work on the law of the non-navigational uses of international watercourses, as recommended by the General Assembly in December 1983,[34] by taking up the second report by its Special Rapporteur, Jens Evensen (Norway).[35]

The report—the fifth on the topic, including those prepared by two predecessors to the current Special Rapporteur—contained a tentative draft of a convention, revised on the basis of debates in ILC and the Assembly's Sixth Committee on the 1983 draft.[36] The Special Rapporteur observed in the report that the political aspect of the drafting task could not be underestimated if the convention was to be broadly acceptable to the international community.

The 1984 draft consisted of 41 articles contained in six chapters: two new articles added to the 1983 text concerned the status of international watercourses, their waters, constructions, etc. in armed conflicts; and obligations under general, regional or bilateral agreements or arrangements. As suggested by the Special Rapporteur, ILC, at its 1984 session, focused its discussion on the nine articles comprising the first two chapters—an introduction, and general principles, rights and duties of watercourse States—and subsequently referred them to its Drafting Committee for further consideration. Owing to lack of time, however, the Committee was unable to do so at the 1984 session.

In its 1984 resolution (39/85) on the work of ILC, the Assembly recommended that, taking into account government comments, ILC should continue work on the topic.

REFERENCES

[1]A/39/33. [2]YUN 1983, p. 1106, GA res. 38/131, 19 Dec. 1983. [3]*Ibid.*, p. 1106. [4]A/C.6/39/L.2. [5]A/AC.182/L.36. [6]A/AC.182/L.24. [7]A/AC.182/L.37. [8]A/C.6/39/4. [9]YUN 1983, p. 1107. [10]YUN 1977, p. 118, GA res. 32/150, 19 Dec. 1977. [11]A/39/41. [12]YUN 1976, p. 105. [13]YUN 1979, p. 153. [14]YUN 1981, p. 1204. [15]YUN 1982, p. 1374. [16]A/AC.193/6 & Add.1. [17]YUN 1983, p. 1109, GA res. 38/133, 19 Dec. 1983. [18]A/39/440. [19]A/C.6/39/3. [20]YUN 1954, p. 411. [21]YUN 1947-48, p. 215, GA res. 177(II), 21 Nov. 1947. [22]YUN 1982, p. 1375. [23]YUN 1981, p. 1214, GA res. 36/106, 10 Dec. 1981. [24]A/39/10. [25]A/CN.4/377 & Corr.1. [26]A/39/439 & Add.1-5. [27]YUN 1983, p. 1110, GA res. 38/132, 19 Dec. 1983. [28]A/39/43 & Corr.1. [29]YUN 1983, p. 1112, GA res. 38/137, 19 Dec. 1983. [30]*Ibid.*, p. 1111. [31]*Ibid.*, p. 1112. [32]A/AC.207/L.19. [33]YUN 1980, p. 1145, GA res. 35/48, 4 Dec. 1980. [34]YUN 1983, p. 1139, GA res. 38/138, 19 Dec. 1983. [35]A/CN.4/381. [36]YUN 1983, p. 1115.

Chapter III

States and international law

Protecting diplomats and consular missions continued to be a major concern for the United Nations, which received, throughout 1984, reports of incidents threatening their security and safety. In December, the General Assembly condemned, by resolution 39/83, acts of violence against diplomatic and consular missions and representatives, and urged States to ensure their security.

The International Law Commission (ILC) (see p. 1117) continued preparing draft articles with a view to elaborating legal instruments on the status of the diplomatic courier and the diplomatic bag not accompanied by courier, jurisdictional immunities of States and their property, international liability for injurious consequences arising from acts not prohibited by international law, and State responsibility for internationally wrongful acts.

In the past 40 years, more had been done by the United Nations in codifying international law than in all the previous years of history, the Secretary-General pointed out (see p. 4).

Topics related to this chapter. International organizations and international law: host country relations. Other legal questions: International Law Commission.

Diplomatic relations

Protection of diplomats

As at 31 December 1984, the number of parties to the various international instruments relating to the protection of diplomats and to diplomatic and consular relations[1] was as follows: 142 States were parties to the 1961 Vienna Convention on Diplomatic Relations,[2] 41 States were parties to the Optional Protocol concerning acquisition of nationality,[3] and 52 States were parties to the Optional Protocol concerning the compulsory settlement of disputes,[3] the Netherlands having acceded to the three instruments in 1984.

With Liberia acceding in 1984, the 1963 Vienna Convention on Consular Relations[4] had 109 parties; 32 States were parties to the Optional Protocol concerning the acquisition of nationality;[5] and 40 States were parties to the Optional Protocol on compulsory dispute settlement.[5]

The 1973 Convention on the Prevention and Punishment of Crimes against Internationally Protected Persons, including Diplomatic Agents,[6] had 61 States parties, Greece and Jamaica having adhered in 1984.

Report of the Secretary-General. Following a December 1983 request of the General Assembly,[7] the Secretary-General submitted in September 1984 a report, with later addenda,[8] containing information from States on serious violations of the protection, security and safety of diplomatic and consular missions and representatives, and on actions taken to bring offenders to justice.

Austria reported a June 1984 car-bombing near the Turkish Embassy in Vienna, which killed a Turkish diplomat. Referring to attacks in May and July 1983 against Turkish representatives,[9] Belgium said the perpetrators were being sought, as were those responsible for a May 1983 bombing of a Greek travel agency in Brussels.

Burma reported an October 1983 bombing attack in Rangoon (see p. 213), during a visit by the President of the Republic of Korea, resulting in a number of people being killed and injured. Burma stated that the perpetrators, acting on the order of the Democratic People's Republic of Korea, had been sentenced. The latter said the allegations were groundless and quoted evidence showing, in its view, that the incident had been staged by the Republic of Korea.

Greece provided information on several 1983 and 1984 incidents. In 1983 were the January theft of a Syrian Embassy diplomatic pouch; the June placing of explosive devices at the Iraqi Embassy; and the gunning down of a Jordanian Embassy employee and killing of a United States sailor in November. The 1984 incidents were: the killing of the British Cultural Attaché and thwarting of an attempted assassination of the Israeli Chargé d'affaires, in March; and an attempt on the life of a United States soldier in April. Greece also reported that the culprits in the 1982 seizure of the Nigerian Embassy and Consulate in Athens had been convicted.

Jordan updated information on October 1983 assassination attempts against its Ambassadors to India and Italy, and the killings in November 1983 of two officers of its Athens Embassy and a Madrid Embassy officer in December. Jordan also reported that in April 1984 its Embassy in the Libyan Arab Jamahiriya had been set afire and looted. The Netherlands reported two 1983 incidents—windows of the Consulate-General of El Salvador at The Hague broken in March, and an attempt to set fire to the chancery of the Iranian Embassy at The Hague in September. It also presented information concerning a January 1984 break-in at the Surinamese Embassy at The Hague by a group of people who were subsequently charged.

The USSR recounted incidents during 1983 in various countries: in the United States, attacks on the San Francisco USSR Consul in June and Consulate in September, and several acts against its Mission to the United Nations and USSR employees of the Secretariat, in February and March; in Japan, attacks with explosives against Consulates in Osaka (May) and Sapporo (September); and in France, an armed attack in April on the Marseilles Consulate. In 1984 the incidents were: the February bombing of the residential complex of its New York Mission; the May arrest of an attaché of the USSR Washington Embassy; a March attack on a Tokyo Embassy official; in the Federal Republic of Germany, aggressive acts against the USSR Bonn Embassy and its Hamburg Consulate in June and July, and the July detention of a vehicle carrying a diplomatic bag at Helmstad.

Other 1984 incidents were reported by: Cyprus, the October car-bombing of the Israeli Embassy in Nicosia, also reported by Israel; and France, the February assassination of the Ambassador of the United Arab Emirates to France and the March shooting of the United States Consul-General at Strasbourg.

Equatorial Guinea, Finland, Kiribati, Lesotho and Suriname informed the Secretary-General that they had no incidents to report.

The Secretary-General's report also contained a report on the state of ratification of and accession to the instruments relevant to the protection, security and safety of diplomatic and consular missions and representatives, and the views of eight States (Australia, Austria, Egypt, Finland, France, Israel, Sweden, USSR) on measures needed to enhance the protection of diplomatic missions and representatives.

Communications. By a letter of 17 April 1984 to the Secretary-General,[10] the Libyan Arab Jamahiriya reported that its diplomatic mission in London had been surrounded that day by the British authorities, and that other incidents involving the British police had taken place, such as the detention of several of its diplomats and a correspondent, and the breaking into of the Libyan Arab College and residences of Libyan students in London.

That version of events was disputed on 18 April by the United Kingdom,[11] which stated that its police wished to search the mission with the permission of the authorities of the Libyan Arab Jamahiriya after shots fired from it had killed a policewoman and injured 10 people. It also said that no Libyan was currently under arrest as a result of the incident and that no attempt had been made to force entry into the school or students' homes.

GENERAL ASSEMBLY ACTION

On 13 December 1984, the General Assembly adopted without vote resolution 39/83, as recommended by the Sixth (Legal) Committee.

Consideration of effective measures to enhance the protection, security and safety of diplomatic and consular missions and representatives

The General Assembly,

Having considered the report of the Secretary-General,

Emphasizing the important role of diplomatic and consular missions and representatives, as well as of missions and representatives to international intergovernmental organizations and officials of such organizations, in the maintenance of international peace and the promotion of friendly relations among States and also the need for enhancing global understanding thereof,

Emphasizing also the duty of States to take all appropriate steps, as required by international law:

(*a*) To protect the premises of diplomatic and consular missions, as well as of missions to international intergovernmental organizations,

(*b*) To prevent any attacks on diplomatic and consular representatives, as well as on representatives to international intergovernmental organizations and officials of such organizations,

(*c*) To apprehend the offenders and to bring them to justice,

Deeply concerned about the continued large number of failures to respect the inviolability of diplomatic and consular missions and representatives, and about the serious threat presented by such violations to the maintenance of normal and peaceful international relations, which are necessary for co-operation among States,

Expressing its sympathy for the victims of illegal acts against diplomatic and consular representatives and missions, as well as against representatives and missions to international intergovernmental organizations and officials of such organizations,

Convinced that respect for the principles and rules of international law governing diplomatic and consular relations, in particular those aimed at ensuring the inviolability of diplomatic and consular missions and representatives, is a basic prerequisite for the normal conduct of relations among States and for the fulfilment of the purposes and principles of the Charter of the United Nations,

Noting that only a small number of States have so far, in response to the call by the General Assembly at its thirty-fifth, thirty-sixth, thirty-seventh and thirty-eighth sessions, become parties to the relevant conventions concerning the inviolability of diplomatic and consular missions and representatives,

Convinced that the reporting procedures established under General Assembly resolution 35/168 of 15 December 1980 and further elaborated in Assembly resolutions 36/33 of 13 November 1981, 37/108 of 16 December 1982 and 38/136 of 19 December 1983 are important steps in the efforts to enhance the protection, security and safety of diplomatic and consular missions and representatives,

Desiring to maintain and further strengthen those reporting procedures,

1. *Takes note* of the report of the Secretary-General;

2. *Strongly condemns* acts of violence against diplomatic and consular missions and representatives, as well as against missions and representatives to international

intergovernmental organizations and officials of such organizations;

3. *Emphasizes* the importance of enhanced awareness throughout the world of the necessity of ensuring the protection, security and safety of such missions, representatives and officials, as well as of the role of the United Nations in this regard;

4. *Urges* States to observe and to implement the principles and rules of international law governing diplomatic and consular relations and, in particular, to take all necessary measures in conformity with their international obligations to ensure effectively the protection, security and safety of all diplomatic and consular missions and representatives officially present in territory under their jurisdiction, including practicable measures to prohibit in their territories illegal activities of persons, groups and organizations that encourage, instigate, organize or engage in the perpetration of acts against the security and safety of such missions and representatives;

5. *Recommends* that States should co-operate closely through, *inter alia*, contacts between the diplomatic and consular missions and the receiving State, with regard to practical measures designed to enhance the protection, security and safety of diplomatic and consular missions and representatives and with regard to exchange of information on the circumstances of all serious violations thereof;

6. *Calls upon* States that have not yet done so to consider becoming parties to the instruments relevant to the protection, security and safety of diplomatic and consular missions and representatives;

7. *Calls upon* States, in cases where a dispute arises in connection with a violation of the principles and rules of international law concerning the inviolability of diplomatic and consular missions and representatives, to make use of the means for peaceful settlement of disputes, including the good offices of the Secretary-General;

8. *Requests*:

   (a) All States to report to the Secretary-General as promptly as possible serious violations of the protection, security and safety of diplomatic and consular missions and representatives;

   (b) The State in which the violation took place—and, to the extent applicable, the State where the alleged offender is present—to report as promptly as possible on measures taken to bring the offender to justice and eventually to communicate, in accordance with its laws, the final outcome of the proceedings against the offender, and on measures adopted with a view to preventing a repetition of such violations;

9. *Requests* the Secretary-General to circulate to all States, upon receipt, the reports received by him pursuant to paragraph 8 above, unless the reporting State requests otherwise;

10. *Requests* the Secretary-General to invite States to inform him of their views with respect to any measures needed to enhance the protection, security and safety of diplomatic and consular missions and representatives;

11. *Also requests* the Secretary-General, when a serious violation has been reported pursuant to paragraph 8 *(a)* above, to draw the attention, when appropriate, of the States directly concerned to the reporting procedures provided for in paragraph 8 above;

12. *Further requests* the Secretary-General to submit to the General Assembly at its fortieth session a report on the state of ratification of, and accessions to, the instruments referred to in paragraph 6 above, as well as the reports received and views expressed pursuant to paragraphs 8 and 10 above, and invites him to submit any views he may wish to express on these matters;

13. *Decides* to include in the provisional agenda of its fortieth session the item entitled "Consideration of effective measures to enhance the protection, security and safety of diplomatic and consular missions and representatives: report of the Secretary-General".

General Assembly resolution 39/83

13 December 1984   Meeting 99   Adopted without vote

Approved by Sixth Committee (A/39/722) without vote, 23 November (meeting 55); 17-nation draft (A/C.6/39/L.8); agenda item 128.

Sponsors: Argentina, Australia, Austria, Canada, Denmark, Ecuador, Finland, Germany, Federal Republic of, Iceland, Japan, Nigeria, Norway, Philippines, Sierra Leone, Sweden, Turkey, Uruguay.

Meeting numbers. GA 39th session: 6th Committee 8-13, 55; plenary 99.

Status of diplomatic bags and couriers

In response to a December 1983 Assembly request,[12] ILC, at its 1984 session,[13] continued preparing draft articles on the status of the diplomatic courier and the diplomatic bag not accompanied by courier, with a view to elaborating a legal instrument on the topic.

The Special Rapporteur, Alexander Yankov (Bulgaria), in presenting his fifth report,[14] noted that ILC had at its disposal at the current session the complete set of draft articles on the topic. The fifth report was essentially a progress report intended to establish a linkage between the work accomplished and future work; it sought to ascertain the extent to which the draft articles coincided with the views arising from the Sixth Committee's 1983 debate and from the new materials provided by Governments or obtained from research by the Secretariat's Codification Division. Information received from 18 Governments on national laws, regulations, administrative acts and recommended practices relating to the topic was also provided to ILC.[15]

The Special Rapporteur also submitted addenda to his fourth (1983) report,[16] containing the text of, and explanations to, draft articles 20 to 42.

The Commission resumed its discussion of draft articles 20 to 23 (on inviolability and immunity from jurisdiction) and considered draft articles 24 to 35 (on various categories of exemption and status), referring all those articles to its Drafting Committee. It also commenced discussion, and decided to resume consideration in 1985, of draft articles 36 to 42: inviolability of the diplomatic bag (article 36), exemption from customs and other inspection (article 37), exemption from customs duties and all dues and taxes (article 38), protective measures in circumstances preventing the delivery of the diplomatic bag (article 39), obligations of the transit State in case of *force majeure* or fortuitous event (article 40), non-recognition of States or Governments or absence of diplomatic or consular relations (article 41) and relation to other conventions and international agreements (article 42).

On the recommendation of the Drafting Committee, ILC provisionally adopted in 1984 draft articles and commentaries concerning the diplomatic courier's nationality (article 9), functions (article 10), end of the functions (article 11), the courier declared *persona non grata* or not acceptable (article 12), facilities (article 13), entry into the territory of the receiving State or the transit State (article 14), freedom of movement (article 15), personal protection and inviolability (article 16), inviolability of temporary accommodation (article 17), exemption from personal examination, customs duties and inspection (article 19) and exemption from dues and taxes (article 20), as well as an amendment to draft article 8 (appointment of the courier) and its modified commentary.

The articles provisionally adopted in 1984, along with those previously adopted, were transmitted to the Assembly by the Secretary-General in August.[17]

REFERENCES

[1]*Mutilateral Treaties Deposited with the Secretary-General: Status as at 31 December 1984* (ST/LEG/SER.E/3), Sales No. E.85.V.4. [2]YUN 1961, p. 512. [3]*Ibid.*, p. 516. [4]YUN 1963, p. 510. [5]*Ibid.*, p. 512. [6]YUN 1973, p. 775, GA res. 3166(XXVIII), annex, 14 Dec. 1973. [7]YUN 1983, p. 1117, GA res. 38/136, 19 Dec. 1983. [8]A/39/456 & Add.1-4. [9]YUN 1983, p. 1116. [10]A/39/186. [11]A/39/188. [12]YUN 1983, p. 1139, GA res. 38/138, 19 Dec. 1983. [13]A/39/10. [14]A/CN.4/382. [15]A/CN.4/379 & Add.1. [16]YUN 1983, p. 1118. [17]A/39/412.

State immunities, liability and responsibility

In response to a December 1983 General Assembly recommendation,[1] ILC, at its 1984 session,[2] continued drafting articles on three aspects of international law concerning States: jurisdictional immunities of States and their property, international liability for injurious consequences arising out of acts not prohibited by international law, and State responsibility for internationally wrongful acts.

In resolution 39/85, adopted in December, the Assembly recommended that, taking into account government comments, ILC should continue its work on those topics.

Draft articles on State immunities

In 1984, ILC continued preparing draft articles on the jurisdictional immunities of States and their property. Its work, detailed in its report,[2] was based on a sixth report by the Special Rapporteur, Sompong Sucharitkul (Thailand),[3] containing five draft articles for part III (which comprised articles 11 to 20, concerning exceptions to State immunity). The five draft articles covered patents, trade marks and other intellectual properties (article 16), fiscal liabilities and customs duties (article 17), share-holdings and membership of bodies corporate (article 18), ships employed in commercial service (article 19) and arbitration (article 20).

While the Commission did not conclude its deliberations on article 19 or take up article 20, due to lack of time, it adopted provisionally, on the recommendations of its Drafting Committee, draft articles and commentaries on contracts of employment (article 13) and personal injuries and damage to property (article 14)—both of which had been revised in 1983[4]—and articles 16 to 18. The texts were transmitted to the Assembly in August by the Secretary-General.[5]

On draft article 19, some ILC members asserted that it would put in a disadvantageous position the maritime transport and trade of developing countries, which were basically controlled by Governments and hence not always motivated by profit-making. Others considered it unfair in the context of international shipping to expect a private merchant ship to deal or compete with a governmental one while the latter enjoyed complete immunity from jurisdiction. A number of members preferred the draft article to use more general terms than rely heavily on Anglo-American systems of law and particularly admiralty law. Based on the discussion, the Special Rapporteur subsequently submitted to the Drafting Committee a revised version of the draft article.

Draft articles on State liability

ILC at its 1984 session continued work on international liability for injurious consequences arising out of acts not prohibited by international law. It had before it the fourth (1983) report[6] of the Special Rapporteur, Robert Q. Quentin-Baxter (New Zealand), as well as his fifth (1984) report.[7] The latter report presented, and commented on, draft articles 1 to 5, which covered general provisions that corresponded broadly to the first section of the schematic outline prepared in 1982.[8]

Also before ILC was a survey of State practice[9] prepared by the Secretariat in response to the Commission's 1983 request,[6] and a report[10] containing the replies received, as at 9 February 1984, to a 1983 questionnaire, prepared by the Special Rapporteur with the Secretariat's assistance and addressed to 16 selected United Nations and other organizations to ascertain whether obligations which States owed each other and discharged as members of international organizations might fulfil or replace some procedures indicated in the topic's schematic outline as previously prepared.[6] Those responding were the International Narcotics Control Board, IAEA, FAO, WHO and the Organisation for Economic Co-operation and Development.

Although significant differences of opinion and emphasis remained, there was almost unanimous agreement in ILC that its work on the question should continue, and that the topic was correctly centred on the need to avoid—or to minimize and, if necessary, repair—transboundary loss or injury arising as a physical consequence of an activity within the territory or control of another State. Many stressed the difficulty and novelty of the topic, but concluded that challenges must be met—if only because scientific progress could not be stopped and because traditional rules of international responsibility for wrongful acts were no longer responsive to all the international community's needs.

Based on the discussion, the Commission, rather than sending the proposed draft articles to its Drafting Committee, invited the Special Rapporteur to continue his research and to prepare draft articles which could be considered together with draft articles 1 to 5.

Draft articles on State responsibility

In 1984, ILC continued preparing draft articles on State responsibility for internationally wrongful acts, and had before it a fifth report by the Special Rapporteur, Willem Riphagen (Netherlands),[11] containing 12 new draft articles (articles 5 to 16) to follow four others (articles 1 to 4) provisionally adopted in 1983[6] for part II, on the content, forms and degrees of State responsibility. (Article 4 had been provisionally adopted in 1983 as article 5.) The new drafts, based on previous reports and discussions, were meant to replace all earlier draft articles proposed for part II, and dealt with the legal consequences of international crimes, including aggression.

In discussing the drafts, several Commission members commented that the new submission marked a major breakthrough in considering part II and that it should enable ILC to progress in the drafting of articles within a measurable time-scale. The Commission referred to the Drafting Committee draft articles 5 and 6, dealing with definitions and certain rights of an "injured" State.

REFERENCES

[1]YUN 1983, p. 1139, GA res. 38/138, 19 Dec. 1983. [2]A/39/10. [3]A/CN.4/376 & Add.1,2. [4]YUN 1983, p. 1119. [5]A/39/412. [6]YUN 1983, p. 1120. [7]A/CN.4/383. [8]YUN 1982, p. 1384. [9]A/CN.4/384. [10]A/CN.4/378. [11]A/CN.4/380 & Corr.1.

Chapter IV

International organizations and international law

In 1984, the United Nations remained concerned with strengthening its role in maintaining international peace and security, and the General Assembly requested the Special Committee on the Charter of the United Nations and on the Strengthening of the Role of the Organization to devote more time to considering that question (resolution 39/88 A).

The Assembly, having considered the annual report of the Committee on Relations with the Host Country, urged the host country, the United States, to continue ensuring the security of diplomatic missions and their personnel (resolution 39/87). The Assembly again called on States which hosted international organizations or conferences to accord to specified national liberation movements the facilities, privileges and immunities necessary for their functioning (resolution 39/76).

The Assembly once more deferred consideration of an item on the implementation of United Nations resolutions, until it resumed its thirty-ninth session in 1985 (decision 39/456), and of draft standard rules of procedure for United Nations conferences, until its fortieth (1985) session (decision 39/419).

Topics related to this chapter. International peace and security. Legal aspects of international political relations.

Strengthening the role of the United Nations

In 1984, the Special Committee on the Charter of the United Nations and on the Strengthening of the Role of the Organization discussed, but did not conclude consideration of, the question of maintaining international peace and security in all its aspects in order to strengthen the role of the United Nations, in particular the Security Council, and to enable it to discharge fully its responsibilities under the Charter.

Report of the Secretary-General for 1983/84

The Secretary-General, in his annual report to the General Assembly on the work of the Organization (p. 3), stressed the importance of preserving and strengthening the United Nations as a centre for harmonizing the actions of nations, and

pointed out that general acceptance of Charter principles as rules to be lived by at all times by Governments was still far away.

Noting, among other things, that the non-implementation and proliferation of resolutions had had debilitating effects on the Organization's efforts in promoting peace and economic co-operation, the Secretary-General stressed the need to reaffirm Charter obligations and for all States to work towards striking a balance between national and international interests in order to make the United Nations work better.

Activities of the Special Committee

The 47-member Special Committee on the Charter of the United Nations and on the Strengthening of the Role of the Organization, meeting in New York from 2 to 27 April 1984,[1] resumed its consideration of Member States' proposals on rationalizing the existing procedures of the United Nations and adopted agreed conclusions towards that end. Those conclusions were subsequently approved by the Assembly in resolution 39/88 B (see p. 376). In addition, the Committee continued considering the peaceful settlement of disputes (see p. 1087) and ways to maintain international peace and security (see also p. 114).

Taking up the latter topic under an extended mandate given by the Assembly in 1983,[2] an open-ended Working Group of the Committee held 13 meetings between 11 and 23 April, devoting the first six to discussing how to proceed with its work. It also considered a working paper—submitted by Belgium, the Federal Republic of Germany, Italy, Japan, New Zealand and Spain—on prevention and removal of threats to the peace and of situations which might lead to international friction or give rise to a dispute,[3] containing suggested points for discussion and proposals for enhancing the functions of the United Nations organs for preventing international conflicts, particularly those of the Security Council and the Secretary-General, and the strengthening of co-operation between the organs.

GENERAL ASSEMBLY ACTION

During its consideration of the question, the General Assembly had before it an August 1984 report by the Secretary-General,[4] containing the comments submitted by Suriname in response to a 1983 Assembly invitation[2] for States' observations on strengthening the United Nations role in the maintenance of international peace and security and on related proposals.

On 13 December, the Assembly, on the recommendation of the Sixth (Legal) Committee, adopted, under the agenda item on the report of the Special Committee, resolution 39/88 A without vote.

The General Assembly,

Reaffirming its support for the purposes and principles set forth in the Charter of the United Nations,

Recalling its resolutions 686(VII) of 5 December 1952, 992(X) of 21 November 1955, 2285(XXII) of 5 December 1967, 2552(XXIV) of 12 December 1969, 2697(XXV) of 11 December 1970, 2968(XXVII) of 14 December 1972 and 3349(XXIX) of 17 December 1974,

Recalling also its resolutions 2925(XXVII) of 27 November 1972, 3073(XXVIII) of 30 November 1973 and 3282(XXIX) of 12 December 1974 on the strengthening of the role of the United Nations,

Recalling especially its resolution 3499(XXX) of 15 December 1975, by which it established the Special Committee on the Charter of the United Nations and on the Strengthening of the Role of the Organization, and its resolutions 31/28 of 29 November 1976, 32/45 of 8 December 1977, 33/94 of 16 December 1978, 34/147 of 17 December 1979, 35/164 of 15 December 1980, 36/122 of 11 December 1981, 37/114 of 16 December 1982 and 38/141 of 19 December 1983,

Taking note of the reports of the Secretary-General on the work of the Organization submitted to the General Assembly at its thirty-seventh and thirty-ninth sessions as well as of the views and comments expressed on them by Member States,

Having considered the report of the Special Committee on the Charter of the United Nations and on the Strengthening of the Role of the Organization on the work of the session it held in 1984,

Taking into account the elaboration by the Special Committee of the outline for a handbook on the peaceful settlement of disputes between States and the conclusions thereon,

Noting the importance that pre-session consultations among the members of the Special Committee and other interested States may have in facilitating the fulfilment of its task,

Conscious of the fact that the year 1985 marks the fortieth anniversary of the United Nations,

Considering that the Special Committee has not yet fulfilled the mandate entrusted to it,

1. *Takes note* of the report of the Special Committee on the Charter of the United Nations and on the Strengthening of the Role of the Organization;

2. *Decides* that the Special Committee shall convene its next session from 4 to 29 March 1985;

3. *Requests* the Special Committee at its session in 1985:

(a) To accord priority by devoting more time to the question of the maintenance of international peace and security in all its aspects in order to strengthen the role of the United Nations, in particular the Security Council, and to enable it to discharge fully its responsibilities under the Charter in this field; this necessitates the examination, *inter alia,* of the prevention and removal of threats to the peace and of situations which may lead to international friction or give rise to a dispute; the Special Committee will work on all questions with the aim of submitting its conclusions to the General Assembly, in accordance with paragraph 5 below, for the adoption of such recommendations as the Assembly deems appropriate; in doing so, the Special Committee should continue its work on the working paper on the prevention and removal of threats to the peace and of situations which may lead to international friction or give rise to a dispute or any revision thereof, as well as other proposals which might be made;

(b) To continue its work on the question of the peaceful settlement of disputes between States and, in this context:

(i) To continue consideration of the proposal contained in the working papers on the establishment of a commission on good offices, mediation and conciliation;

(ii) To examine the report of the Secretary-General on the progress of work on the draft handbook on the peaceful settlement of disputes between States;

4. *Requests* the Special Committee to keep the question of the rationalization of the procedures of the United Nations under review and to revert to its work on this topic when it deems appropriate;

5. *Also requests* the Special Committee to be mindful of the importance of reaching general agreement whenever that has significance for the outcome of its work;

6. *Urges* members of the Special Committee to participate fully in its work in fulfilment of the mandate entrusted to it;

7. *Decides* that the Special Committee shall accept the participation of observers of Member States, including in the meetings of its working groups;

8. *Invites* Governments to submit or to bring up to date, if they deem it necessary, their observations and proposals, in accordance with General Assembly resolution 3499(XXX);

9. *Requests* the Secretary-General to render all assistance to the Special Committee;

10. *Requests* the Secretary-General to prepare, on the basis of the outline elaborated by the Special Committee and in the light of the views expressed in the course of the discussions in the Sixth Committee and in the Special Committee, a draft handbook on the peaceful settlement of disputes between States, and to report to the Special Committee at its session in 1985 on the progress of work, before submitting to it the draft handbook in its final form, with a view to its approval at a later stage;

11. *Requests* the Special Committee to submit a report on its work to the General Assembly at its fortieth session;

12. *Decides* to include in the provisional agenda of its fortieth session the item entitled "Report of the Special Committee on the Charter of the United Nations and on the Strengthening of the Role of the Organization".

General Assembly resolution 39/88 A

13 December 1984   Meeting 99   Adopted without vote

Approved by Sixth Committee (A/39/781 & Corr.1) without vote, 6 December (meeting 64); 35-nation draft (A/C.6/39/L.18 & Corr.1), orally revised; agenda item 133.

Sponsors: Argentina, Australia, Belgium, Bolivia, Brazil, Brunei Darussalam, Chile, Congo, Cyprus, Egypt, Germany, Federal Republic of, Indonesia, Italy, Ivory Coast, Japan, Kenya, Malaysia, Mexico, New Zealand, Nigeria, Papua New Guinea, Paraguay, Philippines, Romania, Rwanda, Samoa, Sao Tome and Principe, Senegal, Singapore, Spain, Thailand, Venezuela, Yugoslavia, Zaire, Zambia.

Financial implications. 5th Committee, A/39/818; S-G, A/C.5/39/79, A/C.6/39/L.20.

Meeting numbers. GA 39th session: 5th Committee 45; 6th Committee 23-31, 64; plenary 99.

Another draft, sponsored by Iran and the Libyan Arab Jamahiriya,[5] was not acted on.

The Sixth Committee acted first on the 35-nation draft, on the proposal (adopted by 73 votes to 23, with 26 abstentions) of Belgium, the Federal Republic of Germany, Italy, Japan, New Zealand and Spain. The Committee took no action on the two-nation draft as a result of a proposal by France and the United Kingdom that the Committee, under rule 131 of the Assembly's rules of procedure, decide not to vote on a second draft on the same question; that proposal was adopted by 46 votes to 36, with 39 abstentions. The Libyan Arab Jamahiriya said that the proposal was designed to subvert the democratic character of United Nations proceedings and that such tactics would lead to paralysis and a new kind of veto. The Syrian Arab Republic stated that the proposal was a procedural manœuvre to prevent a vote on the two-nation draft; if there was general opposition to that draft, it should be expressed through a democratic vote. Iran also spoke against the motion. Egypt abstained in that action, stating that the Sixth Committee was not the right place to discuss the content of the two-nation text.

The two-Power draft would have had the Assembly request the Special Committee to examine what the text's sponsors termed the adverse effects of the voting method in the Security Council, taking into account, among other things, the need to restrict the use of the unanimity rule (the right of veto) with respect to questions relating to the rights of peoples struggling for self-determination and liberation, and the fact that maintaining international peace and security was the common responsibility of all Member States.

Implementation of UN resolutions

GENERAL ASSEMBLY ACTION

The General Assembly—which, in December 1983,[6] had retained on its agenda an item on implementation of United Nations resolutions for consideration at its resumed thirty-eighth session—adopted decision 38/459 on an oral proposal by its President at the closing of that session in September 1984.

Implementation of the resolutions of the United Nations

At its 106th plenary meeting, on 17 September 1984, the General Assembly decided to include in the draft agenda of its thirty-ninth session the item entitled "Implementation of the resolutions of the United Nations".

General Assembly decision 38/459

Adopted without vote

Oral proposal by President; agenda item 42.

By decision 39/456 of 18 December, the Assembly decided to resume its thirty-ninth session, at a date to be announced, for the sole purpose of considering 13 items, one of which was the implementation of United Nations resolutions (see p. 374).

REFERENCES

[1]A/39/33. [2]YUN 1983, p. 1122, GA res. 38/141, 19 Dec. 1983. [3]A/AC.182/L.38. [4]A/39/441. [5]A/C.6/39/L.4. [6]YUN 1983, p. 391, GA dec. 38/456, 20 Dec. 1983.

Host country relations

Throughout 1984, the Committee on Relations with the Host Country continued its efforts to resolve with the United States, the host country, questions of common concern to the United Nations diplomatic community and to help improve the community's relations with New York City's local population.

Consideration by the Committee on host country relations. The 15-member Committee on Relations with the Host Country met seven times in 1984,[1] in pursuance of a December 1983 General Assembly request,[2] and considered various aspects of relations between the Headquarters diplomatic community and the United States. Summaries of communications by Member States on the security of their missions were contained in the Committee's report to the Assembly.[1]

In February, the USSR complained that three explosives, thrown into its Riverdale (New York City) residential complex by what it called the terrorist organization "Jewish Direct Action", had destroyed one car and seriously damaged two others. The United States condemned the attack and stated that an intensive investigation was being carried out by the Federal Bureau of Investigation and the New York City Police Department under the auspices of the Joint Terrorist Task Force; further, it pointed out that it had placed additional security coverage at USSR diplomatic locations.

In October, the Libyan Arab Jamahiriya, recalling similar protests in January 1984 and June 1983,[3] complained to the Committee of restrictions imposed on the use of its residential property in Englewood, New Jersey, and on the movement of its mission members (limited to the five boroughs of New York City); it asked the Committee to negotiate elimination of harassment of missions based on political factors and to request the Secretary-General to arbitrate. The United States replied that its actions had not been based on reciprocity or political considerations but on certain events which were breaches of diplomatic norms; no country waived its right to maintain public order or diminish its capability to protect its citizens. It added that no delegate had the right to reside anywhere in the United States; a residence in the proximity of the United Nations seemed appropriate and for this purpose the five New York City boroughs were more than adequate.

The Committee discussed at four meetings the implications of the most recent United States legislation pertinent to the United Nations diplomatic community: its 1983 Foreign Missions Amendments Act, by which, beginning on 1 February 1984, the head of a mission was required to notify the United States Department of State of the lapse or termination of liability insurance coverage held on motor vehicles, vessels and aircraft owned by the mission, its members or their families; when any such person not covered by liability insurance was found negligent on, or was legally liable for, injury or damage, the State Department would impose a surcharge on the mission amounting to the unsatisfied portion of the judgement or an estimated amount of damage incurred by the victim.

At meetings in February, April and June, the Committee heard the views of States on the question. The USSR called the new legislation a departure from the Agreement between the United Nations and the United States of America regarding the Headquarters of the United Nations[4] and the 1961 Vienna Convention on Diplomatic Relations, adding that the insurance problem could be dealt with adequately without jeopardizing the missions' diplomatic status, rights and privileges. Bulgaria shared that view. France and Honduras regretted that no consultations had taken place before the legislation was enacted. The United States, observing that some 20,000 diplomatic vehicles in the country fell under different state-mandated laws, spoke of the merit of a unified approach for safeguarding mandatory insurance requirements; needless to say, the Headquarters Agreement and the 1961 Vienna Convention continued to govern privileges and immunities accorded to United Nations missions.

Subsequently, in July, the United States notified all missions that a programme had been developed to meet the liability insurance needs of the diplomatic community, and that the federal Government, instead of state authorities, would henceforth issue all diplomatic motor vehicle registrations and licence plates. Under the new arrangement, special justification was required for missions to use more than five official cars,

and the State Department's Office of Foreign Missions would keep the record of proof of vehicle ownership.

The Committee, in co-operation with the United Nations Secretariat and the United States Mission to the United Nations, organized two talks in 1984: one, in February, on immunities of diplomats in United States court proceedings, and the other, in May, concerning the parking situation in New York City. A contact group, subsequently established to seek practical solutions relating to the first topic, met twice and submitted questions to the host country on the possibility of gathering admissible evidence from a diplomat outside formal court proceedings.

Other matters considered by the Committee included immigration and customs procedures at New York airports, the possibility of establishing a commissary at Headquarters for diplomats and staff, the feasibility of medical insurance for the diplomatic community, and the public image of that community in the host city.

By recommendations approved on 18 November, the Committee, among other things, urged the host country to prevent, and punish, acts violating the security of missions and the safety of their personnel. It also expressed hope that its contact group would contribute to establishing procedures for prosecuting law-breakers, and agreed that adherence to the Headquarters Agreement was indispensable to ensure normal functioning of the United Nations and missions. The Committee appealed to the host country to review diplomatic parking measures and to consult with the Committee on them. It urged intensified efforts to acquaint the people of New York City with the importance of the functions of diplomatic missions.

GENERAL ASSEMBLY ACTION

On 13 December 1984, the General Assembly, on the recommendation of the Sixth Committee, adopted resolution 39/87 without vote.

Report of the Committee on Relations with the Host Country

The General Assembly,

Having considered the report of the Committee on Relations with the Host Country,

Recalling Article 105 of the Charter of the United Nations, the Convention on the Privileges and Immunities of the United Nations and the Agreement between the United Nations and the United States of America regarding the Headquarters of the United Nations,

Recalling further that the problems related to the privileges and immunities of all missions accredited to the United Nations, the security of the missions and the safety of their personnel are of great importance and concern to Member States, as well as the primary responsibility of the host country,

Noting with deep concern the continued acts violating the security and the safety of the personnel of those missions accredited to the United Nations,

Recognizing that effective measures should continue to be taken by the competent authorities of the host country, in particular to prevent any acts violating the security of missions and the safety of their personnel,

1. *Endorses* the recommendations of the Committee on Relations with the Host Country contained in paragraph 58 of its report;

2. *Strongly condemns* any terrorist and criminal acts violating the security of missions accredited to the United Nations and the safety of their personnel;

3. *Urges* the host country to continue to take all necessary measures to ensure effectively the protection, security and safety of the missions accredited to the United Nations and their personnel, including practicable measures to prohibit illegal activities of persons, groups and organizations that encourage, instigate, organize or engage in the perpetration of acts and activities against the security and safety of such missions and representatives;

4. *Reiterates* that adherence of all Member States to the Agreement between the United Nations and the United States of America regarding the Headquarters of the United Nations and to other relevant agreements is an indispensable condition for the normal functioning of the Organization and permanent missions in New York and underlines the necessity for avoiding any action not consistent with obligations in accordance with the Agreement and international law;

5. *Calls upon* all countries, especially the host country, to build up public awareness by explaining, through all available means, the importance of the role played by the United Nations and all missions accredited to it in the strengthening of international peace and security;

6. *Requests* the Secretary-General to remain actively engaged in all aspects of the relations of the United Nations with the host country and to continue to stress the importance of effective measures to avoid acts of terrorism and violence against the missions and their personnel;

7. *Requests* the Committee on Relations with the Host Country to continue its work, in conformity with General Assembly resolution 2819(XXVI) of 15 December 1971;

8. *Decides* to include in the provisional agenda of its fortieth session the item entitled "Report of the Committee on Relations with the Host Country".

General Assembly resolution 39/87

13 December 1984   Meeting 99   Adopted without vote

Approved by Sixth Committee (A/39/780) by consensus, 6 December (meeting 64); draft by Cyprus (A/C.6/39/L.22); agenda item 132.

Meeting numbers. GA 39th session: 6th Committee 58, 59, 61, 64; plenary 99.

REFERENCES

[1]A/39/26 & Corr.1. [2]YUN 1983, p. 1125, GA res. 38/140, 19 Dec. 1983. [3]*Ibid.*, p. 1124. [4]YUN 1947-48, p. 199, GA res. 169(II), 31 Oct. 1947.

Observer status of national liberation movements in international organizations

The Secretary-General submitted a report in September 1984,[1] containing comments received from seven Governments (Argentina, Byelorussian SSR, Hungary, Mexico, Sri Lanka, Ukrainian SSR, USSR) on their implementation of a 1982 General Assembly resolution concerning the observer status of national liberation movements recognized by the Organization of African Unity and/or by the League of Arab States.[2] In 1980,[3] and again in 1982,[2] the Assembly had called on States to accord to the movements in question the facilities, privileges and immunities necessary to perform their functions, in accordance with the provisions of the 1975 Vienna Convention on the Representation of States in Their Relations with International Organizations of a Universal Character.[4]

GENERAL ASSEMBLY ACTION

On 13 December 1984, the General Assembly, on the recommendation of the Sixth Committee, adopted resolution 39/76 by recorded vote.

Observer status of national liberation movements recognized by the Organization of African Unity and/or by the League of Arab States

The General Assembly,

Recalling its resolutions 35/167 of 15 December 1980 and 37/104 of 16 December 1982,

Recalling also its resolutions 3237(XXIX) of 22 November 1974, 3280(XXIX) of 10 December 1974 and 31/152 of 20 December 1976,

Taking note of the report of the Secretary-General,

Bearing in mind the resolution of the United Nations Conference on the Representation of States in Their Relations with International Organizations relating to the observer status of national liberation movements recognized by the Organization of African Unity and/or by the League of Arab States,

Noting that the Vienna Convention on the Representation of States in Their Relations with International Organizations of a Universal Character, of 14 March 1975, regulates only the representation of States in their relations with international organizations,

Taking into account the continued and uninterrupted current practice of inviting the above-mentioned national liberation movements to participate as observers in the sessions of the General Assembly, specialized agencies and other organizations of the United Nations system and in the work of the conferences held under the auspices of such international organizations,

Convinced that the participation of the national liberation movements referred to above in the work of international organizations helps to strengthen international peace and co-operation,

Desirous of ensuring the effective participation of the above-mentioned national liberation movements as observers in the work of international organizations and of regulating, to that end, their status and the facilities, privileges and immunities necessary for the performance of their functions,

1. *Urges* all States that have not done so, in particular those which are hosts to international organizations or to conferences convened by, or held under the auspices of, international organizations of a universal character, to consider as soon as possible the question of ratifying, or acceding to, the Vienna Convention on the Representation of States in Their Relations with International Organizations of a Universal Character;

2. *Calls once more upon* the States concerned to accord to the delegations of the national liberation movements recognized by the Organization of African Unity and/or by the League of Arab States, and accorded observer status by international organizations, the facilities, privileges and immunities necessary for the performance of their functions in accordance with the provisions of the Vienna Convention on the Representation of States in Their Relations with International Organizations of a Universal Character;

3. *Requests* the Secretary-General to report to the General Assembly at its forty-first session on the implementation of the present resolution.

General Assembly resolution 39/76

13 December 1984   Meeting 99   106-10-21 (recorded vote)

Approved by Sixth Committee (A/39/771) by vote (92-10-17), 7 December (meeting 65); 27-nation draft (A/C.6/39/L.25); agenda item 121.

Sponsors: Algeria, Angola, Bahrain, Benin, Burkina Faso, Cuba, Democratic Yemen, Iraq, Kuwait, Lebanon, Libyan Arab Jamahiriya, Mali, Mauritania, Mozambique, Nicaragua, Niger, Nigeria, Qatar, Saudi Arabia, Sudan, Syrian Arab Republic, Tunisia, Uganda, United Arab Emirates, Yemen, Yugoslavia, Zambia.

Meeting numbers. GA 39th session: 6th Committee 31-33, 65; plenary 99.

Recorded vote in Assembly as follows:

In favour: Afghanistan, Albania, Algeria, Angola, Argentina, Bahamas, Bahrain, Bangladesh, Barbados, Benin, Bhutan, Bolivia, Botswana, Brazil, Brunei Darussalam, Bulgaria, Burkina Faso, Burundi, Byelorussian SSR, Cameroon, Cape Verde, Chad, Chile, China, Congo, Cuba, Cyprus, Czechoslovakia, Democratic Kampuchea, Democratic Yemen, Djibouti, Dominican Republic, Ecuador, Egypt, El Salvador, Ethiopia, Gabon, German Democratic Republic, Ghana, Greece, Guinea, Guyana, Hungary, India, Indonesia, Iran, Iraq, Ivory Coast, Jamaica, Jordan, Kenya, Kuwait, Lao People's Democratic Republic, Lebanon, Lesotho, Liberia, Libyan Arab Jamahiriya, Madagascar, Malawi, Malaysia, Maldives, Mali, Mauritania, Mauritius, Mexico, Mongolia, Morocco, Mozambique, Nepal, Nicaragua, Niger, Nigeria, Oman, Pakistan, Panama, Papua New Guinea, Peru, Philippines, Poland, Qatar, Romania, Rwanda, Sao Tome and Principe, Saudi Arabia, Senegal, Sierra Leone, Singapore, Somalia, Sri Lanka, Sudan, Syrian Arab Republic, Thailand, Togo, Trinidad and Tobago, Tunisia, Turkey, Uganda, Ukrainian SSR, USSR, United Arab Emirates, Venezuela, Viet Nam, Yemen, Yugoslavia, Zaire, Zambia.

Against: Belgium, Canada, France, Germany, Federal Republic of, Israel, Italy, Luxembourg, Netherlands, United Kingdom, United States.

Abstaining: Australia, Austria, Burma, Colombia, Costa Rica, Denmark, Fiji, Finland, Guatemala, Haiti, Honduras, Iceland, Ireland, Japan, New Zealand, Norway, Paraguay, Portugal, Spain, Sweden, Uruguay.

The vote in the Sixth Committee was requested by Israel.

In explanation of vote, Israel and the United Kingdom observed that the 1975 Convention, whose entry into force required ratification or accession by 35 States, had 26 signatories to date, including only a few of the sponsors of the draft resolution and none of the principal host States of United Nations bodies.

Israel went on to question the draft's legal value, since, it said, States not parties to a convention, which was not in force, were being asked to apply that instrument to an entity possessing none of the attributes of a State, and the Secretary-General was being requested to follow up the implementation of an inapplicable resolution. In a similar vein, Belgium, France and the United Kingdom believed that paragraph 1 did not reflect established law and that the Convention was applicable only to States. Japan and the United States similarly objected to the paragraph. France and Belgium said the Convention's scope of application could not be enlarged by an Assembly resolution. Further, Belgium, Canada and the United Kingdom considered it unwarranted to accord to representatives of national liberation movements privileges and immunities on the same footing as those of States. The Netherlands, while not opposed in principle to granting certain privileges and immunities to those movements having observer status, felt that such status did not carry the right to the same privileges and immunities granted to representatives of States. Japan and the United States considered paragraph 2 to have no legal basis.

Belgium and Italy—both hosts to international organizations—pointed out that they were not party to the Convention; they, and the United Kingdom, especially objected to the reference to host countries. Kenya said attempts had been made to give the impression that the States which had not become parties to the Convention were opposed to the granting of privileges and immunities to the liberation movements; that was not the case with Kenya, which was host to a number of international organizations.

The United States felt that texts of the kind in question weakened the authority of resolutions on widely accepted conventions, urging States that had not done so to accede to them. The United Kingdom felt it would be undesirable for the Committee to take up the question in future.

REFERENCES
(1)A/39/437. (2)YUN 1982, p. 1393, GA res. 37/104, 16 Dec. 1982. (3)YUN 1980, p. 1156, GA res. 35/167, 15 Dec. 1980. (4)YUN 1975, p. 880.

Draft standard rules of procedure for conferences

The General Assembly, which had asked the Secretary-General in 1980[1] to propose draft standard rules of procedure for special conferences of the United Nations, had deferred consideration of the topic since his first report, issued in 1981.[2]

In a November 1984 report,[3] submitted in pursuance of a December 1983 General Assembly request,[4] the Secretary-General stated that he had received no comments from either Governments or international organizations and had no changes to propose in the draft texts he had submitted in 1983.[5]

GENERAL ASSEMBLY ACTION

The Assembly, in December, on the recommendation of the Sixth Committee, adopted decision 39/419 without vote.

Draft standard rules of procedure for United Nations conferences

At its 99th plenary meeting, on 13 December 1984, the General Assembly, on the recommendation of the Sixth Committee:

(a) Decided to defer until its fortieth session consideration of the reports of the Secretary-General on draft standard rules of procedure for United Nations conferences;

(b) Again invited Governments and the international organizations concerned to communicate to the Secretary-General, by 1 May 1985, their observations on the above-mentioned reports;

(c) Decided to request the Secretary-General to submit to the General Assembly at its fortieth session a report on draft standard rules of procedure for United Nations conferences.

General Assembly decision 39/419

Adopted without vote

Approved by Sixth Committee (A/39/785) by consensus, 6 December (meeting 64); draft by Chairman (A/C.6/39/L.24); agenda item 137.

REFERENCES

(1)YUN 1980, p. 1225, GA res. 35/10 C, 3 Nov. 1980. (2)YUN 1981, p. 1370. (3)A/C.6/39/6. (4)YUN 1983, p. 1126, GA dec. 38/427, 19 Dec. 1983. (5)*Ibid.*, p. 1126.

Chapter V

Treaties and agreements

In 1984, the General Assembly decided by resolution 39/86 that the United Nations Conference on the Law of Treaties between States and International Organizations or between International Organizations should be held at Vienna, Austria, from 18 February to 21 March 1986.

Work reviewing the multilateral treaty-making process was completed in 1984, and the Assembly, in resolution 39/90, recommended to States which were considering initiating such a treaty to give attention to the procedures set forth by the Working Group established to review that process.

The Agreement Governing the Activities of States on the Moon and Other Celestial Bodies entered into force in July 1984 (see p. 106)

Review of the multilateral treaty-making process

The Working Group on the Review of the Multilateral Treaty-making Process, first established by the General Assembly in 1981[1] to determine whether current treaty-making methods were as efficient, economical and effective as they could be, completed its review and on 23 November 1984 adopted a final document on the subject.[2] The Group, established in 1984 by the Sixth (Legal) Committee pursuant to a December 1983 Assembly decision,[3] held 13 meetings between 27 September and 23 November,[4] basing its work on a compilation by its Chairman of ideas, suggestions and proposals submitted by members of the Group during its 1982[5] and 1983[6] sessions.

The final document adopted by the Group listed questions to be taken into account by a State wishing to initiate a multilateral treaty, including whether such a treaty was the best means for achieving the intended objective; the extent to which the subject of the proposed treaty was already regulated by international law through treaties and State practice; and the extent of the international community's interest. It also set out drafting and adoption procedures and suggested the preparation of a handbook on multilateral treaty-making.

GENERAL ASSEMBLY ACTION

On 13 December 1984, on the recommendation of the Sixth Committee, the General Assembly adopted by recorded vote resolution 39/90.

Review of the multilateral treaty-making process

The General Assembly,

Bearing in mind that multilateral treaties are an important means of ensuring co-operation among States and an important primary source of international law,

Conscious, therefore, that the process of elaboration of multilateral treaties, directed towards the progressive development of international law and its codification, forms an important part of the work of the United Nations and of the international community in general,

Aware of the responsibility which active involvement in the process of multilateral treaty-making places on Governments,

Convinced that optimum use should be made of the finite resources available for the elaboration of multilateral treaties,

Conscious of the desirability of consolidating and disseminating information on the procedures followed by the United Nations in the preparation and formulation of the text of multilateral treaties,

Taking into account that in certain important and specialized areas interested parties have developed methods of negotiation of proven and continued value,

Bearing in mind the important contribution of the International Law Commission to the preparation of multilateral treaties during the past thirty-six years,

Aware that the Asian-African Legal Consultative Committee has been reviewing certain aspects of multilateral treaty-making,

Having taken note of the report of the Secretary-General on the review of the multilateral treaty-making process submitted to the General Assembly at its thirty-fifth session and of the views of Governments and of the International Law Commission contained in the addenda thereto,

Having taken note also of the subsequent reports of the Secretary-General submitted to the General Assembly at its thirty-sixth and thirty-seventh sessions and of the replies and observations made by Governments and international organizations,

Having considered the statements made at the current session during the debate in the Sixth Committee,

Noting that the Working Group on the Review of the Multilateral Treaty-making Process, first established in accordance with General Assembly resolution 36/112 of 10 December 1981, concluded its mandate, and taking note of the report of the Working Group, together with its final document on the review of the multilateral treaty-making process,

1. *Expresses its appreciation* to the Working Group on the Review of the Multilateral Treaty-making Process for the completion of its mandate and for its final document;

2. *Requests* the Secretary-General to circulate to all States Members the final document of the Working Group on the Review of the Multilateral Treaty-making Process;

3.   *Recommends* to all States which are considering the initiation of a multilateral treaty within the framework of the United Nations to give consideration to the procedures set out in the final document of the Working Group on the Review of the Multilateral Treaty-making Process;

4.   *Also requests* the Secretary-General to prepare, for information and possible use by Governments, a handbook on multilateral treaty-making as described in paragraph 18 of the final document of the Working Group on the Review of the Multilateral Treaty-making Process, to be made available within two years;

5.   *Further requests* the Secretary-General:

(a)   To examine, together with the specialized and related agencies, and other international organizations exercising depositary functions, the feasibility and financial implications of consolidating, in a similar way to the volumes entitled *Multilateral Treaties Deposited with the Secretary-General*, the information regarding depositary functions performed by these international organizations;

(b)   To hold consultations on the feasibility and financial implications of publishing, at regular intervals, consolidated information regarding depositary functions performed by Governments;

(c)   To examine the regulations in force for giving effect to Article 102 of the Charter of the United Nations, with a view to their possible updating;

(d)   To invite the specialized and related agencies, and other international organizations in consultative status with the United Nations, to communicate to the Secretary-General information regarding their respective treaty-making activities; and to report thereon to the Sixth Committee;

6.   *Reiterates its request* to the Secretary-General to continue to prepare for publication as soon as possible new editions of the *Handbook of Final Clauses* and the *Summary of the Practice of the Secretary-General as Depositary of Multilateral Agreements*, taking into account relevant developments and practices in that respect.

General Assembly resolution 39/90

13 December 1984   Meeting 99   125-0-12 (recorded vote)

Approved by Sixth Committee (A/39/783) by vote (111-0-13), 6 December (meeting 64); 2-nation draft (A/C.6/39/L.16/Rev.2); agenda item 135.

Sponsors: Australia, Thailand.

Meeting numbers. GA 39th session: 6th Committee 59, 60, 64; plenary 99.

Recorded vote in Assembly as follows:

In favour: Algeria, Angola, Argentina, Australia, Austria, Bahamas, Bahrain, Bangladesh, Barbados, Belgium, Benin, Bhutan, Bolivia, Botswana, Brazil, Brunei Darussalam, Burkina Faso, Burma, Burundi, Cameroon, Canada, Cape Verde, Chad, Chile, China, Colombia, Congo, Costa Rica, Cyprus, Democratic Kampuchea, Democratic Yemen, Denmark, Djibouti, Dominican Republic, Ecuador, Egypt, El Salvador, Ethiopia, Fiji, Finland, France, Gabon, Germany, Federal Republic of, Ghana, Greece, Guatemala, Guinea, Guyana, Haiti, Honduras, Iceland, India, Indonesia, Iran, Iraq, Ireland, Israel, Italy, Ivory Coast, Jamaica, Japan, Jordan, Kenya, Kuwait, Lebanon, Lesotho, Liberia, Libyan Arab Jamahiriya, Luxembourg, Madagascar, Malawi, Malaysia, Maldives, Mali, Mauritania, Mauritius, Mexico, Morocco, Mozambique, Nepal, Netherlands, New Zealand, Nicaragua, Niger, Nigeria, Norway, Oman, Pakistan, Panama, Papua New Guinea, Paraguay, Peru, Philippines, Portugal, Qatar, Romania, Rwanda, Sao Tome and Principe, Saudi Arabia, Senegal, Sierra Leone, Singapore, Somalia, Spain, Sri Lanka, Sudan, Suriname, Sweden, Syrian Arab Republic, Thailand, Togo, Trinidad and Tobago, Tunisia, Turkey, Uganda, United Arab Emirates, United Kingdom, United States, Uruguay, Venezuela, Viet Nam, Yemen, Yugoslavia, Zaire, Zambia.

Against: None.

Abstaining: Afghanistan, Bulgaria, Byelorussian SSR, Cuba, Czechoslovakia, German Democratic Republic, Hungary, Lao People's Democratic Republic, Mongolia, Poland, Ukrainian SSR, USSR.

The USSR explained that it had abstained because the so-called "final document" had never been submitted to Governments for their reaction or properly discussed in the Sixth Committee and because it could be used to justify the positions of those countries which were opposed to the progressive development of international law.

The United States pointed out that the negotiations leading up to the draft resolution had been conducted on the understanding that a consensus would be reached; to prey on the willingness of others to attain general agreement and make concessions and then request a vote at the last minute was to negotiate in bad faith.

Treaties involving international organizations

In pursuance of a December 1983 General Assembly resolution,[7] the Secretary-General invited States and international intergovernmental organizations that had not done so to submit their comments on final draft articles, adopted by the International Law Commission in 1982,[8] on the law of treaties between States and international organizations or between such organizations, In a September 1984 report,[9] he stated that two additional Governments and one United Nations specialized agency had replied. As at 10 September, a total of 15 Governments, seven agencies and organizations within the United Nations system and two other international intergovernmental organizations had submitted their views.

GENERAL ASSEMBLY ACTION

On 13 December, on the recommendation of the Sixth Committee, the General Assembly adopted without vote resolution 39/86.

United Nations Conference on the Law of Treaties between States and International Organizations or between International Organizations

The General Assembly,

Recalling its resolution 37/112 of 16 December 1982, by which it decided that an international convention should be concluded on the basis of the draft articles on the law of treaties between States and international organizations or between international organizations, adopted by the International Law Commission at its thirty-fourth session,

Recalling also its resolution 38/139 of 19 December 1983, by which it decided that the appropriate forum for the final consideration of the draft articles should be a conference of plenipotentiaries to be convened not earlier than 1985 and agreed to decide at its thirty-ninth session upon the question of the date and place for the convening of the United Nations Conference on the Law of Treaties between States and International Organizations or between International Organizations, as well as upon the question of participation in the Conference,

Having received the report of the Secretary-General, which contains comments and observations submitted by States and principal international intergovernmental organizations, in accordance with General Assembly resolution 38/139,

Recognizing the importance of achieving a successful conclusion of the work of the Conference through the promotion of general agreement,

Bearing in mind the relationship between the law of treaties between States and the subject-matter to be dealt with by the Conference,

Noting with appreciation that an invitation has been extended by the Government of Austria to hold the Conference at Vienna,

1. *Decides* that the United Nations Conference on the Law of Treaties between States and International Organizations or between International Organizations shall be held at Vienna from 18 February to 21 March 1986;

2. *Requests* the Secretary-General to invite:

(*a*) All States to participate in the Conference;

(*b*) Namibia, represented by the United Nations Council for Namibia, to participate in the Conference, in accordance with paragraph 6 of General Assembly resolution 37/233 C of 20 December 1982;

(*c*) Representatives of organizations that have received a standing invitation from the General Assembly to participate in the sessions and the work of all international conferences convened under its auspices in the capacity of observers to participate in the Conference in that capacity, in accordance with General Assembly resolutions 3237(XXIX) of 22 November 1974 and 31/152 of 20 December 1976;

(*d*) Representatives of the national liberation movements recognized in its region by the Organization of African Unity to participate in the Conference as observers, in accordance with General Assembly resolution 3280(XXIX) of 10 December 1974;

(*e*) Representatives of international intergovernmental organizations that have traditionally been invited to participate as observers at legal codification conferences convened under the auspices of the United Nations to participate in the Conference in a capacity to be considered during the consultations referred to in paragraph 8 below and to be decided upon by the General Assembly at its fortieth session;

3. *Invites* the participants referred to in paragraph 2 above to include as far as possible among their representatives experts competent in the field to be considered;

4. *Decides* that the languages of the Conference shall be the official and working languages of the General Assembly, its committees and its sub-committees;

5. *Refers* to the Conference, as the basic proposal for its consideration, the draft articles on the law of treaties between States and international organizations or between international organizations adopted by the International Law Commission at its thirty-fourth session;

6. *Requests* the Secretary-General to submit to the Conference all relevant documentation and recommendations relating to the rules of procedure and methods of work, taking into account the importance of promoting general agreement on the final results of the work of the Conference, and to arrange for the necessary staff, facilities and services which it will require, including the provision of summary records;

7. *Also requests* the Secretary-General to arrange for the presence at the Conference, as an expert, of the International Law Commission's Special Rapporteur on the question of treaties concluded between States and international organizations or between two or more international organizations;

8. *Appeals* to participants in the Conference to organize consultations, primarily on the organization and methods of work of the Conference, including rules of procedure, and on major issues of substance, including final clauses and settlement of disputes, prior to the convening of the Conference in order to facilitate a successful conclusion of its work through the promotion of general agreement;

9. *Decides* to include in the provisional agenda of its fortieth session an item entitled "Preparation for the United Nations Conference on the Law of Treaties between States and International Organizations or between International Organizations".

General Assembly resolution 39/86

13 December 1984   Meeting 99   Adopted without vote

Approved by Sixth Committee (A/39/779 & Corr.1) by consensus, 7 December (meeting 65); 47-nation draft (A/C.6/39/L.27); agenda item 131.

Sponsors: Algeria, Angola, Argentina, Australia, Austria, Bahrain, Bangladesh, Barbados, Cape Verde, Chile, Colombia, Cyprus, Ecuador, Egypt, Germany, Federal Republic of, Ghana, Guatemala, Guyana, Honduras, India, Iraq, Kenya, Kuwait, Libyan Arab Jamahiriya, Madagascar, Mauritania, Mozambique, Oman, Panama, Paraguay, Peru, Philippines, Qatar, Samoa, Sao Tome and Principe, Saudi Arabia, Sierra Leone, Somalia, Sri Lanka, Sudan, Suriname, Swaziland, Syrian Arab Republic, Thailand, United Arab Emirates, Yemen, Zambia.

Financial implications. S-G, A/C.6/39/L.28.

Meeting numbers. GA 39th session: 6th Committee 31-33, 65; plenary 99.

In explanation of position, the United Kingdom stressed that Conference costs should be kept to a minimum. The USSR pointed out that it had proposed the Sixth Committee draft the convention in question, which would have saved the United Nations some $3 million; the programme budget implications should be duly considered by the Fifth Committee. The United States endorsed the observations of the USSR and the United Kingdom. Israel felt the Sixth Committee could have undertaken the work to be done by the Conference. France, in the light of its traditional position concerning the Council for Namibia and its legal capacity to represent Namibia, expressed reservations concerning the invitation to that body to take part in the Conference.

Registration and publication of treaties by the United Nations

During 1984, some 670 international agreements and 407 subsequent actions were received by the Secretariat for registration or filing and recording. In addition, there were 233 registrations of formalities concerning agreements for which the Secretary-General performs depositary functions.

The texts of international agreements registered or filed and recorded are published in the United Nations *Treaty Series* in the original languages, with translations into English and French where necessary. In 1984, the following volumes of the *Treaty Series* covering treaties registered or filed and recorded in 1975, 1976 and 1977 were issued:

976, 980, 985, 991, 992, 993, 996, 1006, 1008, 1010, 1011, 1012, 1013, 1014, 1015, 1016, 1018, 1019, 1020, 1021, 1022, 1023, 1025, 1026, 1028, 1029, 1030, 1031, 1033, 1034, 1035, 1036, 1037, 1038, 1039, 1041, 1042, 1043, 1045, 1046, 1048, 1049, 1054, 1055, 1058, 1061, 1062.

Multilateral treaties

New multilateral treaties
concluded under United Nations auspices

The following treaties, concluded under United Nations auspices, were deposited with the Secretary-General during 1984:[10]

International Tropical Timber Agreement, 1983, concluded at Geneva on 18 November 1983
International Sugar Agreement, 1984, concluded at Geneva on 5 July 1984
Protocol to the 1979 Convention on Long-Range Transboundary Air Pollution on Long-Term Financing of the Co-operative Programme for Monitoring and Evaluation of the Long-Range Transmission of Air Pollutants in Europe (EMEP), done at Geneva on 28 September 1984
Regulation No. 61: Uniform provisions concerning the approval of commercial vehicles with regard to their external projections forward of the cab's rear panel; Regulation No. 62: Uniform provisions concerning the approval of power-driven vehicles with two wheels with regard to their protection against unauthorized use, both annexed to the *Agreement concerning the Adoption of Uniform Conditions of Approval and Reciprocal Recognition of Approval for Motor Vehicle Equipment and Parts*, done at Geneva on 20 March 1958

Multilateral treaties
deposited with the Secretary-General

The number of multilateral treaties for which the Secretary-General performed depositary functions stood at 677 at the end of 1984. During the year, 112 signatures were affixed to treaties for which the Secretary-General performed depositary functions and 230 instruments of ratification, accession, acceptance and approval or notifications were transmitted to him. In addition, the Secretary-General received 164 communications from States expressing observations or declarations and reservations made by certain States at the time of signature, raitifcation or accession.

The following multilateral treaties,[10] in respect of which the Secretary-General acts as depositary, came into force during 1984:

Agreement Governing the Activities of States on the Moon and Other Celestial Bodies, adopted by the General Assembly on 5 December 1979
International Agreement on Jute and Jute Products, 1982, concluded at Geneva on 1 October 1982
Regulation No. 60: Uniform provisions concerning the approval of two-wheeled motor cycles and mopeds with regard to driver-operated controls including the identification of controls, tell-tales and indicators; Regulation No. 61: Uniform provisions concerning the approval of commercial vehicles with regard to their external projections forward of the cab's rear panel; Regulation No. 62: Uniform provisions concerning the approval of power-driven vehicles with two wheels with regard to their protection against unauthorized use, all annexed to the *Agreement concerning the Adoption of Uniform Conditions of Approval and Reciprocal Recognition of Approval for Motor Vehicle Equipment and Parts*, done at Geneva on 20 March 1958
Amendments to the Convention on the International Maritime Organization relating to the institutionalization of the Committee on Technical Co-operation in the Convention, adopted by the Assembly of the International Maritime Organization in resolution A.400(X) of 17 November 1977
Amendments to articles 17, 18, 20 and 51 of the Convention on the International Maritime Organization, adopted by the Assembly of the International Maritime Organization in resolution A.450(XI) of 15 November 1979

REFERENCES

[1]YUN 1981, p. 1247, GA res. 36/112, 10 Dec. 1981. [2]A/C.6/39/8. [3]YUN 1983, p. 1127, GA dec. 38/425, 19 Dec. 1983. [4]A/C.6/39/L.12. [5]YUN 1982, p. 1395. [6]YUN 1983, p. 1127. [7]*Ibid.*, p. 1128, GA res. 38/139, 19 Dec. 1983. [8]YUN 1982, p. 1396. [9]A/39/491. [10]*Multilateral Treaties Deposited with the Secretary-General: Status as at 31 December 1984* (ST/LEG/SER.E/3), Sales No. E.85.V.4.

OTHER PUBLICATIONS

United Nations Juridicial Yearbook 1981 (ST/LEG/SER.C/19), Sales No. E.84.V.1. *Statement of Treaties and International Agreements*, registered or filed and recorded with the Secretariat during 1984, ST/LEG/SER.A/443-454 (monthly); *Statement of Treaties and International Agreements*, registered or filed and recorded with the Secretariat, *Cumulative Index No. 12* (vols. 751-800), I: Treaties Nos. 10762 to 11405 (registered); II: Treaties Nos. 658 to 664 (filed and recorded).

Chapter VI

International economic law

In 1984, the United Nations Commission on International Trade Law (UNCITRAL) and the General Assembly's Sixth (Legal) Committee continued to deal with legal aspects of international economic relations.

The Assembly, by resolution 39/82, recommended that UNCITRAL continue its work on the topics in its work programme and reaffirmed the importance of training and assistance in international trade law, particularly for developing countries. The United Nations Institute for Training and Research completed an analytical study on the progressive development of the principles and norms of international law relating to the new international economic order, and the Assembly, by resolution 39/75, urged States to submit their comments on the study, including proposals for further action.

Topics related to this chapter. Development policy and international economic co-operation: economic rights and duties of States. Industrial development: industrial co-operation contracts.

General aspects

Report of UNCITRAL

At its seventeenth session, held in New York from 25 June to 10 July 1984,[1] UNCITRAL considered legal aspects of international commercial arbitration, international payments, liability of operators of transport terminals, co-ordination of trade law activities, and training and assistance, as well as various legal aspects of the new international economic order.

The 1984 report of UNCITRAL was considered and taken note of by the Trade and Development Board of the United Nations Conference on Trade and Development (UNCTAD) on 14 September[2]—an action which the Secretary-General reported to the General Assembly in October.[3]

GENERAL ASSEMBLY ACTION

By resolution 39/82, adopted without vote on 13 December, the Assembly, on the recommendation of the Sixth Committee, also took note of the UNCITRAL report.

Report of the United Nations Commission on International Trade Law

The General Assembly,

Having considered the report of the United Nations Commission on International Trade Law on the work of its seventeenth session,

Recalling that the object of the Commission is the promotion of the progressive harmonization and unification of international trade law,

Recalling, in this regard, its resolution 2205(XXI) of 17 December 1966, as well as all its other resolutions relating to the work of the Commission,

Recalling also its resolutions 3201(S-VI) and 3202(S-VI) of 1 May 1974, 3281(XXIX) of 12 December 1974 and 3362(S-VII) of 16 September 1975,

Reaffirming its conviction that the progressive harmonization and unification of international trade law, in reducing or removing legal obstacles to the flow of international trade, especially those affecting the developing countries, would significantly contribute to universal economic co-operation among all States on a basis of equality, equity and common interest and to the elimination of discrimination in international trade and, thereby, to the well-being of all peoples,

Having regard for the need to take into account the different social and legal systems in harmonizing and unifying the rules of international trade law,

Stressing the value of participation by States at all levels of economic development, including developing countries, in the process of harmonizing and unifying rules of international trade law,

1. *Takes note with appreciation* of the report of the United Nations Commission on International Trade Law on the work of its seventeenth session;

2. *Commends* the Commission for the progress made in its work, in particular towards the preparation of a draft convention on international bills of exchange and international promissory notes, a model law on international commercial arbitration, a legal guide on drawing up international contracts for the construction of industrial works and a legal guide on electronic funds transfers, and for having reached decisions by consensus;

3. *Calls upon* the Commission, in particular its Working Group on the New International Economic Order, to continue to take account of the relevant provisions of the resolutions concerning the new international economic order, as adopted by the General Assembly at its sixth and seventh special sessions;

4. *Notes* that the Commission has assigned to its Working Group on International Contract Practices the task of preparing uniform legal rules on the liability of operators of transport terminals, and that the Commission has placed in its programme of work as a priority item the topic of legal implications of automatic data processing to the flow of international trade;

5. *Reaffirms* the mandate of the Commission, as the core legal body within the United Nations system in the field of international trade law, to co-ordinate legal activities in this field in order to avoid duplication of effort and to promote efficiency, consistency and coherence in the unification and harmonization of international trade law, and, in this connection, recommends that the Commission should continue to maintain close co-operation with the other international organs and organizations, including regional organizations, active in the field of international trade law;

6. *Reaffirms also* the importance, in particular for the developing countries, of the work of the Commission concerned with training and assistance in the field of international trade law and the desirability for it to sponsor symposia and seminars, in particular those organized on a regional basis, to promote such training and assistance, and, in this connection:

(*a*) Expresses its appreciation to those Governments, regional organizations and institutions that have collaborated with the secretariat of the Commission in organizing regional seminars and symposia in the field of international trade law;

(*b*) Welcomes the additional initiatives being undertaken by the Commission and its secretariat to collaborate with other organizations and institutions in the organization of regional seminars;

(*c*) Invites Governments, international organizations and institutions to assist the secretariat of the Commission in financing and organizing regional seminars and symposia, in particular in developing countries;

(*d*) Invites Governments, relevant United Nations organs, organizations, institutions and individuals to make voluntary contributions to allow the resumption of the programme of the Commission for the award of fellowships on a regular basis to candidates from developing countries to enable them to participate in such symposia and seminars;

7. *Recommends* that the Commission should continue its work on the topics included in its programme of work;

8. *Reaffirms* the important role of the International Trade Law Branch of the Office of Legal Affairs of the Secretariat, as the substantive secretariat of the Commission, in assisting in the implementation of the work programme of the Commission and expresses the hope that the same high quality of the work of the Secretariat will be maintained for the future.

General Assembly resolution 39/82

13 December 1984　　　　Meeting 99　　　　Adopted without vote

Approved by Sixth Committee (A/39/698) by consensus, 14 November (meeting 46); 30-nation draft (A/C.6/39/L.5); agenda item 127.

Sponsors: Argentina, Australia, Austria, Belgium, Brazil, Canada, Chile, Cyprus, Egypt, Finland, France, Germany, Federal Republic of, Greece, Hungary, Italy, Jamaica, Japan, Kenya, Morocco, Netherlands, Nigeria, Pakistan, Philippines, Senegal, Singapore, Spain, Sweden, Thailand, Turkey, Yugoslavia.

Meeting numbers. GA 39th session: 6th Committee 3-7, 46; plenary 99.

REFERENCES

[1]A/39/17. [2]A/39/15, vol. II. [3]A/C.6/39/L.3.

PUBLICATION

United Nations Commission on International Trade Law Yearbook, vol. XV: *1984* (A/CN.9/SER.A/1984), Sales No. E.86.V.2.

International trade law

In 1984, UNCITRAL continued its consideration of a draft model law on international commercial arbitration and the draft Conventions on international bills of exchange and promissory notes and on international cheques. It adopted the Arabic and Chinese versions of its 1976 Arbitration Rules and considered the progress made in preparing a legal guide on electronic funds transfers.

The Commission also continued its co-ordination of trade law activities, promoted training and assistance, and held symposia and seminars on international trade law.

Unification of trade law

International commercial arbitration

Draft model law

In 1981,[1] UNCITRAL had requested its Working Group on International Contract Practices to prepare a draft model law on international commercial arbitration for use in modernizing and harmonizing related national laws and practices. The Group, which began work on the project in 1982,[2] held its seventh session in New York from 6 to 17 February 1984,[3] and completed its work by adopting the text of a draft model law, after a drafting group had established corresponding language versions in the six languages of UNCITRAL.

UNCITRAL, at its June/July 1984 session,[4] took note of the Working Group's reports on its sixth[5] and seventh sessions, and expressed appreciation to it for having completed its task. The Commission requested the Secretary-General to transmit the draft text to all Governments and interested international organizations for their comments, to be submitted no later than 30 November 1984, and asked its secretariat to submit to its 1985 session a commentary on the draft text, which it would consider in the light of those comments, with a view to finalizing and adopting a model law.

In resolution 39/82, the Assembly commended UNCITRAL for the progress made on the draft model law and recommended that it continue its work.

Arbitration Rules

In 1984,[4] UNCITRAL noted that its Arbitration Rules[6]—for optional use in *ad hoc* arbitration relating to international trade—had been reviewed, before their adoption in 1976, by a drafting group only in the official languages of UNCITRAL pertaining at that time (English, French, Russian, Spanish). Subsequently, translations into Arabic and Chinese—which had become official languages of the General Assembly—were prepared but needed to be revised, especially the legal terminology. At its 1984 session, the Commission had before it the revised texts which had been prepared by its secretariat with the assistance of experts. Regarding the Arabic version, it was noted that minor changes were still needed, a task which was entrusted to an *ad hoc* working party of States using that language.

On 6 July, the Commission adopted the Arabic, as modified by the working party, and the Chinese texts of the UNCITRAL Arbitration Rules.

International payments

Draft Conventions on international bills of exchange and promissory notes and on international cheques

As it had decided in 1983,[5] UNCITRAL took up in 1984[4] the major controversial and other issues contained in written comments from Governments and international organizations concerning draft Conventions on international bills of exchange and promissory notes (mainly credit instruments) and on international cheques (mainly payment instruments). The texts of the draft Conventions—adopted by UNCITRAL's Working Group on International Negotiable Instruments in 1981[7]—had been sent for comments in 1982 and the deadline for such views extended until September 1983.[8]

At its 1984 session, UNCITRAL had before it a report of the Secretary-General containing an analytical compilation of the comments by Governments and international organizations,[9] a secretariat note identifying the major controversial and other issues inferred from those comments[10] and a secretariat note setting forth a summary of the comments of two States which were received after the first note had been prepared.[11] Opinions on the draft Conventions were divided on whether further work on negotiable instruments was justified.

In view of the significant degree of support for the unification of negotiable instruments law along lines earlier agreed to by UNCITRAL, it agreed that further work was justified. It decided that such work should concentrate on the draft Convention on international bills of exchange and promissory notes, and that work on the draft Convention on international cheques should be postponed until work on the former draft had been concluded.

UNCITRAL considered the manner in which future work on the draft Convention on international bills of exchange and promissory notes might be undertaken and decided that preparatory work was to be undertaken by a working group. It noted that

the Arabic version of the draft was inadequate, particularly the legal terminology, and that it had to be revised.

On 5 and 6 July, the Commission requested the Working Group on International Negotiable Instruments to revise the draft Convention in the light of decisions and discussion at UNCITRAL's 1984 session and to submit a progress report in 1985.

In resolution 39/82, the Assembly commended the Commission for the progress made towards the preparation of the draft Convention and recommended that it continue working on that item.

Electronic funds transfers

In 1984,[4] the UNCITRAL secretariat and its Study Group on International Payments—a consultative body consisting of representatives of banking and trade institutions—continued preparing a legal guide on electronic funds transfers to identify the legal issues, describe the various approaches, point out the advantages and disadvantages of each approach and suggest alternative solutions. At its 1984 session, UNCITRAL had before it a report of the Secretary-General[12] containing several draft chapters of the guide, which laid the basis for the development of an international common understanding of the legal issues involved. The Commission noted that it would be premature to formulate uniform legal rules governing electronic funds transfers before an international common understanding on the subject had been reached.

The secretariat informed UNCITRAL that an additional chapter on finality of honour of a funds transfer instruction, currently under preparation, and a list of legal issues to be considered in electronic funds transfer systems would be submitted to the Commission in 1985. It suggested that the work already completed might be submitted to Governments and interested international organizations for their comments. UNCITRAL instructed the secretariat to complete its work on the topic, which was to be considered by the Commission in 1985.

In resolution 39/82, the General Assembly commended UNCITRAL for the progress made towards preparing the legal guide, recommending that it continue work on that subject.

Liability of operators of transport terminals

In 1984, the Commission[4] had before it a report of the Secretary-General[13] on the liability of operators of transport terminals which it had requested in 1983.[14] Annexed to the report was the preliminary draft Convention adopted in 1983 by the International Institute for the Unification of Private Law (UNIDROIT).

The Commission requested its Working Group on International Contract Practices to consider approaches to be adopted on issues arising from the liability of operators of transport terminals and to proceed with the drafting of uniform rules on the subject. It further decided that the Group should base its work on the Secretary-General's report and consider issues not dealt with in the UNIDROIT preliminary draft Convention as well as any other relevant issues.

UNCTAD informed UNCITRAL that it would participate in the Working Group. In view of UNCTAD's expertise in maritime and multimodal transport, port operations and other aspects of containerization, and its relevance to issues concerning the proposed uniform rules, the Commission welcomed that co-operation.

Co-ordination of trade law activities

During 1984, UNCITRAL[4] continued its coordination of trade law activities. It took note of the Secretary-General's report[15] on current activities of international organizations related to the unification and harmonization of international trade law. It noted the Asian-African Legal Consultative Committee's recommendation that Asian-African Governments should ratify or adhere to the 1978 United Nations Convention on the Carriage of Goods by Sea (the Hamburg Rules)[16] and the 1980 United Nations Convention on Contracts for the International Sale of Goods.[17] The Committee reported that the UNCITRAL Arbitration Rules (see above) were used by the regional arbitration centres at Cairo (Egypt) and Kuala Lumpur (Malaysia) with some modifications.

Among other things, the Commission noted UNCTAD's co-operation regarding legal implications of automatic data processing. The observer from the Hague Conference on Private International Law indicated that the Diplomatic Conference to consider the draft Convention on the Law Applicable to Contracts for the International Sale of Goods would be held in October 1985 and that all States were invited. Concerning the 1983 revision of the Uniform Customs and Practice for Documentary Credits, UNCITRAL adopted on 6 July a decision commending the use of that revision, as from 1 October 1984, in transactions involving the establishment of a documentary credit. On current activities of international organizations in barter and barter-like transactions, the Commission decided to await a report, being prepared by its secretariat, before deciding whether further steps should be undertaken.

UNCITRAL also had before it a report[18] of the Secretary-General describing several legal problems arising out of the use of automatic data processing in international trade. As suggested in the report, UNCITRAL decided to place the matter on its work programme as a priority item.

Training and assistance

During the year, the UNCITRAL secretariat continued to promote training and assistance and to publicize the work of UNCITRAL.[19] Symposia and seminars on international trade law were held in collaboration with other organizations.

Meetings held in 1984 included: a regional symposium on international commercial arbitration organized by the Asian-African Legal Consultative Committee and hosted by the Indian Council of Arbitration (New Delhi, March); a regional symposium, organized by the Chamber of Commerce of Bogotá (Colombia, June), dealing with the 1980 United Nations Convention on Contracts for the International Sale of Goods,[17] the model law on international commercial arbitration, the Hamburg Rules, the draft legal guide on drawing up international contracts for the construction of industrial works, and the relevance of UNCITRAL's work to the Andean region; and an Asian-Pacific regional trade law seminar on the unification and harmonization of international trade law and practices, conducted by the Attorney-General's Department of Australia (Canberra, November).

The Commission[4] suggested that in future efforts be made to organize symposia and seminars in Africa in order to disseminate in that region information on UNCITRAL activities.

In resolution 39/82, the Assembly reaffirmed the importance of training and assistance in international trade law, particularly for developing countries, and invited Governments, United Nations bodies and individuals to help finance and organize seminars.

REFERENCES

[1]YUN 1981, p. 1253. [2]YUN 1982, p. 1401. [3]A/CN.9/246. [4]A/39/17. [5]YUN 1983, p. 1133. [6]YUN 1976, p. 823. [7]YUN 1981, p. 1254. [8]YUN 1982, p. 1402. [9]A/CN.9/248. [10]A/CN.9/249. [11]A/CN.9/249/Add.1. [12]A/CN.9/250 & Add.1-4. [13]A/CN.9/252. [14]YUN 1983, p. 1134. [15]A/CN.9/255. [16]YUN 1978, p. 956. [17]YUN 1980, p. 1131. [18]A/CN.9/254. [19]A/CN.9/256.

Legal aspects of the new international economic order

In 1984, legal aspects of the new international economic order (NIEO) continued to be dealt with by UNCITRAL[1] and the General Assembly's Sixth Committee, while other aspects were considered by other United Nations bodies (see p. 395). As requested by the Assembly in 1983, the United Nations Institute for Training and

Research (UNITAR) submitted the third and final phase of an analytical study on the progressive development of the principles and norms of international law relating to NIEO. In December, the Assembly, by resolution 39/75, urged States to submit their views on that study no later than 30 June 1985.

UNCITRAL Working Group action. The UNCITRAL Working Group on the New International Economic Order (fifth session, New York, 23 January–3 February 1984) continued drafting a legal guide on drawing up contracts for the supply and construction of industrial works (see p. 575).

UNITAR study. In response to a December 1983 Assembly resolution,[2] the Secretary-General submitted to that body in October 1984 a report[3] which included the third and final phase of an analytical study by UNITAR on the progressive development of the principles and norms of international law relating to NIEO—a study requested by the Assembly in 1980.[4] One addendum gave information received from Cuba on the topic, while the other contained annexes outlining and summarizing the study's third phase.

The first phase of the study—a compendium of topics or issues of the principles and norms of international law relating to NIEO—had been forwarded to the Assembly in 1981.[5] The second phase, submitted in 1982, dealt with analytical papers on three principles: preferential treatment for developing countries, stabilization of their export earnings, and permanent sovereignty over natural resources.[6] In 1983, UNITAR, with the assistance of an expert panel engaged to carry out the last phase, had completed analytical papers on: every State's right to benefit from science and technology, entitlement of developing countries to development assistance, and the common heritage of mankind. An analytical paper on the principle of participatory equality of developing countries in international economic relations had also been submitted to the Assembly but required revisions, and the expert panel had recommended that, in view of the task's complexity, UNITAR should submit its completed study in 1984 or, more realistically, in 1985. In order to complete the tasks, the Assembly had extended UNITAR's mandate.[2]

In the third phase of its study, UNITAR analysed the seven principles listed above, as well as an additional principle on freedom of choice of economic system, which UNITAR felt deserved inclusion. The study analysed, among other things, the integration of those eight principles into the general framework of international law and examined the legal scope of their content, concentrating on salient legal issues.

UNITAR concluded in its report[3] that the evaluation made in the study was warranted in international law where, in the absence of legislative power, there was no possibility of instant creation of norms of general international law, except for the far-fetched hypothesis of a treaty to be adopted simultaneously by the whole international community. The principles which had been discussed—and the NIEO to which they gave legal expression—were considered as necessary preconditions for the creation of an international economic environment favourable to the development of the less developed countries and could thus be viewed as collectively constituting for those countries a "right to development", parallel, on the economic level, to self-determination on the political plane.

To further the progressive development of the principles and norms, UNITAR recommended building on what had already been accepted as law and, through the United Nations process of progressive development of international law, clarifying the areas of shade, with the hope that the process of progressive development and elaboration of those principles and norms would favour a widening consensus over them, thus contributing to consolidating their legal status. It further recommended that consideration be given to continuing action of progressive development by means of an intergovernmental working group within the framework of the Assembly's Sixth Committee or that the task be entrusted to a commission with appropriate machinery and expert resources.

GENERAL ASSEMBLY ACTION

On 13 December, the General Assembly adopted by recorded vote resolution 39/75, as recommended by the Sixth Committee.

Progressive development of the principles and norms of international law relating to the new international economic order

The General Assembly,

Bearing in mind that, in accordance with the Charter of the United Nations, the General Assembly is called upon to initiate studies and make recommendations for the purpose of encouraging the progressive development of international law and its codification,

Recalling its resolutions 3201(S-VI) and 3202(S-VI) of 1 May 1974, containing the Declaration and the Programme of Action on the Establishment of a New International Economic Order, 3281(XXIX) of 12 December 1974, containing the Charter of Economic Rights and Duties of States, 3362(S-VII) of 16 September 1975 on development and international economic co-operation and 35/56 of 5 December 1980, the annex to which contains the International Development Strategy for the Third United Nations Development Decade,

Recalling its resolutions 34/150 of 17 December 1979 and 35/166 of 15 December 1980, entitled "Consolidation and progressive development of the principles and norms of international economic law relating in particular to the legal aspects of the new international economic order", and its resolutions 36/107 of 10 December 1981, 37/103 of 16 December 1982 and 38/128 of 19 December 1983, entitled "Progressive development of the principles and norms of international law relating to the new international economic order",

Recognizing the need for a systematic and progressive development of the principles and norms of international law relating to the new international economic order,

1. *Expresses its appreciation* to the United Nations Institute for Training and Research for the completion of the analytical study on the progressive development of the principles and norms of international law relating to the new international economic order;

2. *Urges* Member States to submit, not later than 30 June 1985, their views and comments on the study, including proposals concerning further action and procedures to be adopted within the framework of the Sixth Committee with regard to the consideration of the analytical study;

3. *Decides* to include in the provisional agenda of its fortieth session the item entitled "Progressive development of the principles and norms of international law relating to the new international economic order".

General Assembly resolution 39/75

13 December 1984   Meeting 99   120-0-17 (recorded vote)

Approved by Sixth Committee (A/39/770 & Corr.1) by vote (92-0-16), 5 December (meeting 63); 16-nation draft (A/C.6/39/L.19); agenda item 120.

Sponsors: Egypt, India, Kenya, Malaysia, Mexico, Morocco, Nigeria, Pakistan, Philippines, Romania, Senegal, Thailand, Tunisia, Venezuela, Zaire, Zambia.

Meeting numbers. GA 39th session: 6th Committee 50, 55-58, 63; plenary 99.

Recorded vote in Assembly as follows:

In favour: Afghanistan, Algeria, Angola, Argentina, Austria, Bahamas, Bahrain, Bangladesh, Barbados, Benin, Bhutan, Bolivia, Botswana, Brazil, Brunei Darussalam, Bulgaria, Burkina Faso, Burma, Burundi, Byelorussian SSR, Cameroon, Cape Verde, Chad, Chile, China, Colombia, Congo, Costa Rica, Cuba, Cyprus, Czechoslovakia, Democratic Kampuchea, Democratic Yemen, Djibouti, Dominican Republic, Ecuador, Egypt, El Salvador, Ethiopia, Fiji, Finland, Gabon, German Democratic Republic, Ghana, Greece, Guatemala, Guinea, Guyana, Haiti, Honduras, Hungary, India, Indonesia, Iran, Iraq, Ivory Coast, Jamaica, Jordan, Kenya, Kuwait, Lao People's Democratic Republic, Lebanon, Lesotho, Liberia, Libyan Arab Jamahiriya, Luxembourg, Madagascar, Malawi, Malaysia, Maldives, Mali, Mauritania, Mauritius, Mexico, Mongolia, Morocco, Mozambique, Nepal, Netherlands, Nicaragua, Niger, Nigeria, Oman, Pakistan, Panama, Papua New Guinea, Paraguay, Peru, Philippines, Poland, Qatar, Romania, Rwanda, Sao Tome and Principe, Saudi Arabia, Senegal, Sierra Leone, Singapore, Somalia, Spain, Sri Lanka, Sudan, Suriname, Syrian Arab Republic, Thailand, Togo, Trinidad and Tobago, Tunisia, Turkey, Uganda, Ukrainian SSR, USSR, United Arab Emirates, Uruguay, Venezuela, Viet Nam, Yemen, Yugoslavia, Zaire, Zambia.

Against: None.

Abstaining: Australia, Belgium, Canada, Denmark, France, Germany, Federal Republic of, Iceland, Ireland, Israel, Italy, Japan, New Zealand, Norway, Portugal, Sweden, United Kingdom, United States.

In explanation of vote, the United States said it could not accept some of the text's preambular provisions referring to the need for a systematic and progressive development of the principles and norms of international law relating to NIEO.

Argentina and Chile, which had abstained on similar texts in previous years because of their objection to UNITAR's classifying Antarctica under the heading of the common heritage of mankind, maintained those earlier objections.

Spain felt that the deadline for the submission of views (30 June 1985) should have been later; its vote did not prejudge its position with regard to the further action referred to in paragraph 2. Poland doubted that UNITAR was the best body for conducting the study, but was convinced that the development of international law relating to NIEO would contribute to its promotion.

REFERENCES

[1]A/39/17. [2]YUN 1983, p. 1137, GA res. 38/128, 19 Dec. 1983. [3]A/39/504 & Add.1,2. [4]YUN 1980, p. 532, GA res. 35/166, 15 Dec. 1980. [5]YUN 1981, p. 1261. [6]YUN 1982, p. 1403.

Chapter VII

Other legal questions

In 1984, the International Law Commission (ILC) held its thirty-sixth session at Geneva from 7 May to 27 July, continuing work on the progressive development and codification of international law and maintaining co-operation with several juridical bodies. By resolution 39/85, the General Assembly recommended that ILC continue work on all the topics in its current programme.

The International Law Seminar held its twentieth session at Geneva. Other seminars and training courses were offered in 1984 as part of the United Nations Programme of Assistance in the Teaching, Study, Dissemination and Wider Appreciation of International Law.

By resolution 39/47, the Assembly requested the Secretary-General to continue promoting co-operation between the United Nations and the Asian-African Legal Consultative Committee.

International Law Commission

ILC work programme

The 1984 ILC session (Geneva, 7 May–27 July)[1] was devoted mainly to considering draft articles on the following aspects of international law: jurisdictional immunities of States and their property (see p. 1098); State responsibility (see p. 1099); status of the diplomatic courier and the diplomatic bag not accompanied by courier (see p. 1097); non-navigational uses of international watercourses (see p. 1094); and international liability for injurious consequences arising out of acts not prohibited by international law (see p. 1098). It also continued work on elaborating the draft Code of Offences against the Peace and Security of Mankind, which it had prepared in 1954 (see p. 1090).

The Commission decided to continue, in 1985, work on all the topics on its current programme, bearing in mind the desirability of achieving maximum progress in preparing draft articles on topics in the remaining two years of the Commission's current five-year term of membership. The Commission felt that it might be able to complete, before the term concluded in 1986, a first reading of draft articles on two topics—status of the diplomatic courier and the diplomatic bag not accompanied by diplomatic courier, and jurisdictional immunities of States and their property—with a possibility of giving similar treatment to parts two

and three of the draft articles on State responsibility.

The Secretary-General, in August,[2] transmitted to the General Assembly the draft articles which had been provisionally adopted by ILC in 1984 on the status of diplomatic couriers and bags, and on jurisdictional immunities of States and their property.

Throughout 1984, ILC continued to co-operate with several other juridical bodies, namely the Inter-American Juridical Committee, the Asian-African Legal Consultative Committee (see below), the European Committee on Legal Co-operation and the Arab Commission for International Law. Such co-operation included ILC representation at meetings of those bodies or their sending observers to the ILC session.

The Commission also considered the desirability of dividing its annual session into two parts, alternating between Geneva and New York, but concluded that it was not in a position to suggest any change in the current practice of one annual session.

GENERAL ASSEMBLY ACTION

On the recommendation of the Sixth (Legal) Committee, the General Assembly, on 13 December 1984, adopted resolution 39/85 without vote.

Report of the International Law Commission
The General Assembly,

Having considered the report of the International Law Commission on the work of its thirty-sixth session,

Emphasizing the need for the progressive development of international law and its codification in order to make it a more effective means of implementing the purposes and principles set forth in the Charter of the United Nations and in the Declaration on Principles of International Law concerning Friendly Relations and Co-operation among States in accordance with the Charter of the United Nations and to give increasing importance to its role in relations among States,

Recognizing the importance of referring legal and drafting questions to the Sixth Committee, including topics which might be submitted to the International Law Commission, and of enabling the Sixth Committee and the Commission further to enhance their contributions to the progressive development of international law and its codification,

Recalling the need to keep under review those topics of international law which, given their new or renewed interest for the contemporary international community, may be suitable for progressive development and codification of international law and therefore may be included in the future programme of work of the International Law Commission,

1. *Takes note* of the report of the International Law Commission on the work of its thirty-sixth session;

2. *Expresses its appreciation* to the International Law Commission for the work accomplished at that session;

3. *Recommends* that, taking into account the comments of Governments, whether in writing or expressed orally in debates in the General Assembly, the International Law Commission should continue its work on all the topics in its current programme;

4. *Expresses its satisfaction* with the conclusions and intentions of the International Law Commission concerning its procedures and methods of work, as reflected in paragraphs 385 to 397 of its report;

5. *Reaffirms* its previous decisions concerning the increased role of the Codification Division of the Office of Legal Affairs of the Secretariat and those concerning the documentation of the International Law Commission;

6. *Appeals* to Governments and, as appropriate, to international organizations to respond as fully and expeditiously as possible to the requests of the International Law Commission for comments, observations and replies to questionnaires and for materials on topics in its programme of work;

7. *Reaffirms its wish* that the International Law Commission continue to enhance its co-operation with intergovernmental legal bodies whose work is of interest for the progressive development of international law and its codification;

8. *Expresses the wish* that seminars will continue to be held in conjunction with sessions of the International Law Commission and that an increasing number of participants from developing countries will be given the opportunity to attend those seminars;

9. *Requests* the Secretary-General to forward to the International Law Commission, for its attention, the records of the debate on the report of the Commission at the thirty-ninth session of the General Assembly and to prepare and distribute a topical summary of the debate.

General Assembly resolution 39/85

13 December 1984   Meeting 99   Adopted without vote

Approved by Sixth Committee (A/39/778/Rev.1) by consensus, 7 December (meeting 65); 76-nation draft (A/C.6/39/L.26); agenda item 130.

Sponsors: Algeria, Angola, Argentina, Australia, Austria, Bahrain, Barbados, Belgium, Benin, Brazil, Bulgaria, Canada, Cape Verde, Chile, China, Colombia, Cyprus, Ecuador, Egypt, France, German Democratic Republic, Germany, Federal Republic of, Ghana, Greece, Guatemala, Guyana, Honduras, India, Iraq, Italy, Japan, Kenya, Kuwait, Lebanon, Libyan Arab Jamahiriya, Madagascar, Mauritania, Mongolia, Morocco, Mozambique, New Zealand, Niger, Nigeria, Norway, Oman, Pakistan, Panama, Paraguay, Peru, Philippines, Qatar, Romania, Samoa, Sao Tome and Principe, Saudi Arabia, Sierra Leone, Somalia, Spain, Sri Lanka, Sudan, Suriname, Swaziland, Syrian Arab Republic, Thailand, Togo, Trinidad and Tobago, Tunisia, Uganda, United Arab Emirates, United Kingdom, United States, Venezuela, Yemen, Yugoslavia, Zaire, Zambia.

Meeting numbers. GA 39th session: 6th Committee 33-47, 65; plenary 99.

UN Programme for the teaching and study of international law

International Law Seminar

In accordance with a December 1983 General Assembly wish,[3] the twentieth session of the International Law Seminar—for advanced students and junior professors or government officials dealing with international law—was held at Geneva from 4 to 22 June, with 24 participants, all of different nationality and mostly from developing countries.[1] In addition, three holders of fellowships from the United Nations Institute for Training and Research (UNITAR) and three observers were admitted to the Seminar. Participants followed the work of the 1984 ILC session and heard lectures given by its members and by others. As in the past, none of the costs of the Seminar fell on the United Nations. Austria, Denmark, Finland and the Federal Republic of Germany made fellowships available to participants from developing countries. Fellowships were awarded to 15 participants in 1984. Since the beginning of the Seminar in 1965,[4] fellowships have been awarded to 213 of the total of 447 participants, representing 108 nationalities.

Other activities

A number of training courses were offered in 1984 as part of the United Nations Programme of Assistance in the Teaching, Study, Dissemination and Wider Appreciation of International Law. Under the annual joint United Nations/UNITAR fellowship programme, conducted by UNITAR,[5] 18 middle-grade government legal officers and young international legal experts took courses at The Hague Academy of International Law (Netherlands) and attended seminars organized by UNITAR (2 July–10 August). Several fellows also received practical training at legal offices of the United Nations and related organizations.

Other activities, offered or co-sponsored by UNITAR, included a practical course in drafting treaties, resolutions and other international instruments (New York, 9-13 and 18 April), a briefing on developments in international humanitarian law (Geneva, 18 and 20 June), and a regional training and refresher course in international law for Africa (Yaoundé, Cameroon, 12-24 November).

The Secretary-General reported[6] that, during 1984, $95,246 had been voluntarily contributed to the Hamilton Shirley Amerasinghe Memorial Fellowship, established in 1981[7] for study and research in the law of the sea.

Co-operation between the United Nations and the Asian-African Legal Consultative Committee

In pursuance of a December 1983 General Assembly resolution,[8] the Secretary-General submitted to that body in 1984 a report[9] on co-operation between the United Nations and the Asian-African Legal Consultative Committee—an organization to which the Assembly had accorded permanent observer status in 1980.[10]

On 10 December 1984, the General Assembly adopted resolution 39/47 without vote.

Co-operation between the United Nations and the Asian-African Legal Consultative Committee

The General Asssembly,

Recalling its resolutions 36/38 of 18 November 1981, 37/8 of 29 October 1982 and 38/37 of 5 December 1983,

Having considered the report of the Secretary-General on co-operation between the United Nations and the Asian-African Legal Consultative Committee,

Having heard the statement of the Secretary-General of the Asian-African Legal Consultative Committee on the continuing close and effective co-operation between the two organizations,

1. *Takes note with appreciation* of the report of the Secretary-General;

2. *Notes with satisfaction* the progress achieved towards strengthening the existing co-operation between the United Nations and the Asian-African Legal Consultative Committee;

3. *Commends* the Asian-African Legal Consultative Committee for orienting its programme to strengthen its supportive role to the work of the United Nations in wider areas, as called for by the General Assembly in its resolution 36/38;

4. *Requests* the Secretary-General to continue to take steps to promote co-operation between the United Nations and the Asian-African Legal Consultative Committee in the field of progressive development and codification of international law and other areas of common interest;

5. *Requests* the Secretary-General to submit to the General Assembly at its fortieth session a report on co-operation between the United Nations and the Asian-African Legal Consultative Committee;

6. *Decides* to include in the provisional agenda of its fortieth session the item entitled "Co-operation between the United Nations and the Asian-African Legal Consultative Committee".

General Assembly resolution 39/47

10 December 1984   Meeting 93   Adopted without vote

27-nation draft (A/39/L.34 and Add.1); agenda item 30.

Sponsors: Australia, Bangladesh, Cyprus, Egypt, India, Indonesia, Iraq, Japan, Jordan, Kenya, Libyan Arab Jamahiriya, Mongolia, Nepal, New Zealand, Nigeria, Oman, Pakistan, Philippines, Senegal, Sierra Leone, Somalia, Sri Lanka, Sudan, Syrian Arab Republic, Thailand, Turkey, Uganda.

REFERENCES

[1]A/39/10. [2]A/39/412. [3]YUN 1983, p. 1139, GA res. 38/138, 19 Dec. 1983. [4]YUN 1965, p. 624. [5]A/41/14. [6]A/40/893. [7]YUN 1981, p. 139. [8]YUN 1983, p. 1142, GA res. 38/37, 5 Dec. 1983. [9]A/39/565. [10]YUN 1980, p. 469, GA res. 35/2, 13 Oct. 1980.

PUBLICATIONS

Yearbook of the International Law Commission 1984, vol. I: *Summary Records of the Meetings of the Thirty-sixth Session, 7 May–27 July 1984* (A/CN.4/SER.A/1984), Sales No. E.85.V.6; vol. II *Part One: Documents of the Thirty-sixth Session & Part Two: Report of the Commission to the General Assembly on the Work of its Thirty-sixth Session* (A/CN.4/SER.A/1984/Add.1, Parts 1, 2), Sales No. E.85.V.7 (Parts 1, 2).

Administrative and budgetary questions

Chapter I

United Nations financing

A number of actions were taken by the General Assembly in 1984 on various aspects of United Nations financing.

With the short-term deficit of the United Nations expected to amount to $356 million by the end of 1984, the General Assembly again appealed to States to pay their assessed contributions promptly (resolution 39/239 B). Concerned also about the impact of inflation and monetary instability on the Organization's regular budget, the Secretary-General was asked to prepare a study on the problem (resolution 39/240).

The Assembly also took several decisions on the 1984-1985 programme budget. It increased budget appropriations by $24.4 million, raising the amount appropriated for the two-year period to $1.6 billion (resolution 39/237 A) and increased income estimates, other than income from Member States, by $17.5 million, to $301.4 million (39/237 B). The Assembly also specified the amounts to be obtained to finance appropriations during the second year of the biennium (39/237 C).

Regarding budget contributions, the Assembly established the rates for the Organization's newest members (39/247 A) but deferred action on adjusting the assessments of all Members until 1985 (decision 39/456).

In view of the growth of United Nations activities, the Assembly requested the Secretary-General to carry out a review of the Secretariat's Internal Audit Division to determine whether its resources were adequate to handle its increased responsibilities (decision 39/416).

UN budget

Budget for 1984-1985

Appropriations

In December 1984, the General Assembly approved a $24,391,400 increase in the United Nations

programme budget for 1984-1985, raising appropriations for the biennium to $1,611,551,200.

This increase over the initial level approved by the Assembly in December 1983[1] resulted from a number of additional expenditures authorized by the Assembly at its 1984 session. The most sizeable of these were $5.2 million to expand conference facilities at Bangkok for the Economic and Social Commission for Asia and the Pacific (ESCAP), $5 million for the Industrial Development Decade for Africa (1980-1990), $4.2 million for conference-servicing costs of additional meetings scheduled for 1985 ($2.2 million for Headquarters and $2 million for Vienna), $4.1 million for activities relating to the Namibia question (including $1 million for public information), $3.2 million for conference facilities at Addis Ababa for the Economic Commission for Africa (ECA), $1.5 million for the United Nations Institute for Training and Research (UNITAR), $1.5 million to improve the United Nations communications system, $1.4 million for the Transport and Communications Decade in Africa (1978-1988), $1.4 million for Senior Industrial Development Field Advisers (SIDFAs), and $1.1 million for Chinese language verbatim reporting services for the Assembly and Security Council.

The increase would have been higher but for savings resulting from more favourable foreign exchange rates and lower inflation rates than had been assumed when the budget was initially approved in 1983. According to calculations by the Secretary-General in his first budget performance report for the biennium, submitted to the Fifth (Administrative and Budgetary) Committee in December 1984,[2] the strengthening of the United States dollar, the currency in which the budget was expressed, would net the United Nations some $45.7 million in 1984-1985 by lowering the cost of its expenditures in non-dollar currencies. At the same time, an estimated $2.6 million would be saved thanks to lower-than-anticipated inflation.

An analysis of the Secretary-General's report by the Advisory Committee on Administrative and Budgetary Questions (ACABQ),[3] also issued in December 1984, showed that the net savings from inflation were due to lower costs at United Nations offices other than New York, offsetting a projected $20 million net increase at Headquarters. Major factors in the increase were an $8 million salary raise for General Service staff, a $4.1 million rise in the post adjustment (cost-of-living) component of Professional staff salaries, $3.6 million in higher common staff costs (fringe benefits), and $3.1 million in cost increases for common services.

Another increase cited in the Secretary-General's report was a $22.4 million rise in common staff costs, due to such factors as a higher pension contribution and increased insurance costs. In the other direction, a higher-than-expected staff vacancy rate would save an estimated $9.8 million.

On the recommendation of ACABQ, the Fifth Committee approved on 15 December the figures contained in the performance report, including a $9,158,700 decrease in appropriations. This was the net effect of all budget changes not due to specific Assembly action during its 1984 session. The results of the recorded vote were 70 to 9 (Bulgaria, Byelorussian SSR, Czechoslovakia, German Democratic Republic, Hungary, Mongolia, Ukrainian SSR, USSR, United States), with 12 abstentions.

Fifth Committee voting on other revised budget estimates submitted by the Secretary-General and exceeding $1 million apiece was as follows: ECA conference facilities, $3,231,400 gross ($3,215,100 net of staff assessment), 83 to 3, with 13 abstentions (recorded vote), 16 October; ESCAP conference facilities, $5,213,200 gross ($5,200,400 net), 104 to 11, with 8 abstentions (recorded vote), 30 November; communications system, $1,537,000 gross ($1,497,400 net), 75 to 8, with 14 abstentions (recorded vote), 11 December; and conference servicing, $5,150,000 gross ($4,250,000 net), 70 to 21 (recorded vote), 15 December. The additional $1,251,400 for Chinese language services was approved without vote on 11 October.

Fifth Committee voting on the programme budget implications of draft resolutions subsequently approved by the Assembly was as follows for totals exceeding $1 million: Namibia question, $4,123,100 gross ($4,097,000 net), 92 to 8, with 8 abstentions (recorded vote), 11 December; UNITAR, $1,500,000, 60 to 15, with 17 abstentions (recorded vote), 13 December; SIDFAs, $1,373,500 gross ($1,135,000 net), 71 to 17, with 11 abstentions (recorded vote), 15 December; Industrial Development Decade for Africa, $5 million, 71 to 18, with 10 abstentions (recorded vote), 15 December; and Transport and Communications Decade in Africa, $1,439,600, 73 to 17, with 9 abstentions (recorded vote), 15 December.

The budget increases approved by the Assembly in 1984 provided for 29 additional established posts in the Secretariat, of which 18 were for a new Chinese Verbatim Unit in the Department of Conference Services.

The United Nations Controller informed the Fifth Committee on 17 December that the revised budget represented a 0.55 per cent increase over the initial level, in real terms. As the initial appropriation had recorded a 0.9 per cent real growth over the 1982-1983 budget,[4] total real growth amounted to 1.5 per cent over the previous biennium. (Real growth calculations exclude cost increases due to foreign exchange fluctuations and inflation, as well as costs that do not recur from year to year.)

GENERAL ASSEMBLY ACTION

On the recommendation of the Fifth Committee, the Assembly on 18 December 1984 adopted by recorded vote resolution 39/237 A, revising the 1984-1985 appropriations.

Revised budget appropriations for the biennium 1984-1985

The General Assembly

Resolves that for the biennium 1984-1985 the amount of $US 1,587,159,800 appropriated by its resolution 38/236 A of 20 December 1983 shall be increased by $US 24,391,400 as follows:

Section	Amount appropriated by resolution 38/236 A	Increase or (decrease)	Revised appropriation
		(US dollars)	
PART I. *Overall policy-making, direction and co-ordination*			
1. Overall policy-making, direction and co-ordination	39,960,500	212,900	40,173,400
Total, PART I	39,960,500	212,900	40,173,400
PART II. *Political and Security Council affairs; peace-keeping activities*			
2A. Political and Security Council affairs, peace-keeping activities	81,866,700	401,200	82,267,900
2B. Department for Disarmament Affairs	8,893,000	423,500	9,316,500
Total, PART II	90,759,700	824,700	91,584,400
PART III. *Political affairs, trusteeship and decolonization*			
3. Political affairs, trusteeship and decolonization	23,052,300	5,644,200	28,696,500
Total, PART III	23,052,300	5,644,200	28,696,500
PART IV. *Economic, social and humanitarian activities*			
4. Policy-making organs (economic and social activities)	3,823,700	112,300	3,936,000
5A. Office of the Director-General for Development and International Economic Co-operation	3,655,600	116,600	3,772,200
5B. Centre for Science and Technology for Development	3,872,500	122,700	3,995,200

Section	Amount appropriated by resolution 38/236 A	Increase or (decrease)	Revised appropriation
	(US dollars)		
5C. Regional Commissions Liaison Office	597,400	23,500	620,900
6. Department of International Economic and Social Affairs	48,900,000	1,156,800	50,056,800
7. Department of Technical Co-operation for Development	17,493,700	606,700	18,100,400
8. Office of Secretariat Services for Economic and Social Matters	3,774,800	151,800	3,926,600
9. Transnational corporations	9,608,200	175,300	9,783,500
10. Economic Commission for Europe	25,109,300	(2,324,500)	22,784,800
11. Economic and Social Commission for Asia and the Pacific	34,818,600	179,400	34,998,000
12. Economic Commission for Latin America and the Caribbean	46,929,700	(3,719,400)	43,210,300
13. Economic Commission for Africa	46,312,300	45,800	46,358,100
14. Economic Commission for Western Asia	26,408,600	894,200	27,302,800
15. United Nations Conference on Trade and Development	56,459,000	(4,881,500)	51,577,500
16. International Trade Centre	8,627,100	(734,800)	7,892,300
17. United Nations Industrial Development Organization	72,149,500	2,173,800	74,323,300
18. United Nations Environment Programme	10,761,100	(784,800)	9,976,300
19. United Nations Centre for Human Settlements (Habitat)	9,429,000	(612,100)	8,816,900
20. International drug control	5,808,900	(357,300)	5,451,600
21. Office of the United Nations High Commissioner for Refugees	30,025,000	(1,540,600)	28,484,400
22. Office of the United Nations Disaster Relief Co-ordinator	5,236,400	(442,400)	4,794,000
23. Human rights	10,247,700	62,300	10,310,000
24. Regular programme of technical co-operation	32,910,900	22,000	32,932,900
Total, PART IV	512,959,000	(9,554,200)	503,404,800
PART V. *International justice and law*			
25. International Court of Justice	9,048,600	1,100	9,049,700
26. Legal activities	14,750,600	290,100	15,040,700
Total, PART V	23,799,200	291,200	24,090,400
PART VI. *Public information*			
27. Public information	71,649,400	(1,478,800)	70,170,600
Total, PART VI	71,649,400	(1,478,800)	70,170,600
PART VII. *Common support services*			
28. Administration and management	304,707,200	(1,250,700)	303,456,500
29. Conference and library services	266,012,300	591,400	266,603,700
Total, PART VII	570,719,500	(659,300)	570,060,200
PART VIII. *Special expenses*			
30. United Nations bond issue	16,769,100	—	16,769,100
Total, PART VIII	16,769,100	—	16,769,100
PART IX. *Staff assessment*			
31. Staff assessment	224,869,600	19,866,000	244,735,600
Total, PART IX	224,869,600	19,866,000	244,735,600
PART X. *Capital expenditures*			
32. Construction, alteration, improvement and major maintenance of premises	12,621,500	7,744,700	20,366,200
Total, PART X	12,621,500	7,744,700	20,366,200

Section	Amount appropriated by resolution 38/236 A	Increase or (decrease)	Revised appropriation
	(US dollars)		
PART XI. *Special grants*			
33. Special grant to the United Nations Institute for Training and Research	—	1,500,000	1,500,000
Total, PART XI	—	1,500,000	1,500,000
GRAND TOTAL	1,587,159,800	24,391,400	1,611,551,200

General Assembly resolution 39/237 A

18 December 1984   Meeting 105   124-17-6 (recorded vote)

Approved by Fifth Committee (A/39/839) by recorded vote (87-16-7), 17 December (meeting 55); agenda item 109.

Meeting numbers. GA 39th session: 5th Committee 8, 9, 12, 13, 15, 18, 22, 25-28, 32, 34-36, 39-41, 43-47, 49-55; plenary 105.

Recorded vote in Assembly as follows:

In favour: Algeria, Angola, Antigua and Barbuda, Argentina, Austria, Bahamas, Bahrain, Bangladesh, Barbados, Benin, Bhutan, Bolivia, Botswana, Brazil, Brunei Darussalam, Burkina Faso, Burma, Burundi, Cameroon, Cape Verde, Central African Republic, Chad, Chile, China, Colombia, Congo, Costa Rica, Cuba, Cyprus, Democratic Kampuchea, Democratic Yemen, Denmark, Djibouti, Dominican Republic, Ecuador, Egypt, El Salvador, Equatorial Guinea, Ethiopia, Fiji, Finland, Gabon, Gambia, Ghana, Greece, Guatemala, Guinea, Guinea-Bissau, Guyana, Haiti, Honduras, Iceland, India, Indonesia, Iran, Iraq, Ireland, Ivory Coast, Jamaica, Jordan, Kenya, Kuwait, Lebanon, Lesotho, Liberia, Libyan Arab Jamahiriya, Madagascar, Malawi, Malaysia, Maldives, Mali, Malta, Mauritania, Mauritius, Mexico, Morocco, Mozambique, Nepal, Nicaragua, Niger, Nigeria, Norway, Oman, Pakistan, Panama, Papua New Guinea, Paraguay, Peru, Philippines, Portugal, Qatar, Rwanda, Saint Christopher and Nevis, Saint Lucia, Samoa, Sao Tome and Principe, Saudi Arabia, Senegal, Sierra Leone, Singapore, Somalia, Spain, Sri Lanka, Sudan, Suriname, Swaziland, Sweden, Syrian Arab Republic, Thailand, Togo, Trinidad and Tobago, Tunisia, Turkey, Uganda, United Arab Emirates, United Republic of Tanzania, Uruguay, Vanuatu, Venezuela, Yemen, Yugoslavia, Zaire, Zambia, Zimbabwe.

Against: Belgium, Bulgaria, Byelorussian SSR, Czechoslovakia, German Democratic Republic, Germany, Federal Republic of, Hungary, Israel, Japan, Luxembourg, Mongolia, Netherlands, Poland, Ukrainian SSR, USSR, United Kingdom, United States.

Abstaining: Australia, Canada, France, Italy, New Zealand, Romania.

Several of the States voting against the revised appropriations objected to the budget growth resulting from Assembly approval of additional expenditures.

Among them, Belgium said its support for zero budget growth meant that it would have to curtail voluntary contributions. The Federal Republic of Germany, noting that it had abstained when the initial budget was approved in 1983, described the revised budget as no longer reasonable. Japan remarked that the Secretary-General's financial implications statements had failed to reveal determined efforts to absorb costs through savings or redeployment. The Netherlands said its increasingly strong position on budget restraint stemmed from a concern for sound and prudent management. The USSR, urging redeployment rather than budget increases, said additional funds should be appropriated only for the essential tasks of maintaining international peace and security, promoting disarmament and averting world war. The United Kingdom also stressed the need for financing new or expanded programmes by redeploying existing resources, improving efficiency and curtailing obsolete activities. The United States, saying the financing system offered little incentive to limit budget growth, felt that neither Member States nor the Secretariat had shown much fiscal responsibility; it particularly objected to the construction projects at Addis Ababa and Bangkok, which it called costly status symbols, and to subsidies for the voluntarily financed UNITAR and United Nations Institute for Disarmament Research.

Canada, abstaining in the vote, voiced concern at the increasing unwillingness of States to share United Nations financing, together with an unrestrained enthusiasm for new and expanded activities. France urged better Secretariat control over expenditure growth, particularly operational costs, coupled with further efforts on salary policy and the regular-budget financing of activities that should be funded voluntarily. Italy cited a need for rigid financial discipline at a time when States had to contain their national budgets because of persistent economic difficulties.

While acknowledging efforts to limit expenditures, Spain was discouraged that appropriations had proved inadequate before the end of the budget biennium's first year.

Voting for the appropriations, Austria thought the increase modest and said far more was being spent elsewhere for far less noble causes; whether the money was being spent to further the Organization's goals and to obtain the best value from it was another issue, however. Cameroon did not see how a modest increase could be avoided when negotiations within the United Nations had become more difficult and time-consuming. Cuba, while supporting the concerns of those favouring financial soundness, said it firmly opposed the intentions of those wanting budget cuts in order to limit the United Nations role.

Egypt thought Member States had shown responsibility by curtailing many programmes and avoiding many requests for valid activities in recognition of financial constraints. Ireland said the United Nations should have sufficient funds to perform its functions, while at the same time it welcomed efforts to redeploy funds and set priorities.

Nigeria believed that financial responsibility could be improved if States showed political will for multilateral co-operation. In the view of Pakistan, preoccupation with budgetary restraint should not reduce the Organization's capacity to implement programmes effectively, especially those important to developing countries. Sweden, on behalf of the Nordic States, endorsed the idea of rational redeployment of resources to make room for new and urgent activities, but believed that Member States were getting reasonably good value for their investment in the United Nations. Tunisia thought the Secretariat had made commendable efforts to eliminate waste.

Income sources

Revised income estimates under the United Nations programme budget for 1984-1985, covering income other than that derived from assessments of Member States, were approved by the General Assembly in December 1984 in the amount of $301,439,100. This was $17,546,300 above the total approved when the Assembly acted on the initial estimates in December 1983.[5]

According to the Secretary-General's December 1984 budget performance report[2] and the analysis of that report by ACABQ,[3] the main factor responsible for the increase was a technical one: the consolidation into base salaries of a portion of the post adjustment (cost-of-living component) paid to Professional staff, as approved by the Assembly in resolution 39/27 of 30 November 1984. This adjustment had no appreciable effect on the net budget or on take-home pay. At the same time, the estimate of income from revenue-producing activities was decreased by $1.6 million, due mainly to reduced sales by the gift and souvenir shops at United Nations Headquarters.

GENERAL ASSEMBLY ACTION

On the recommendation of the Fifth Committee, the Assembly on 18 December 1984 adopted by recorded vote resolution 39/237 B, revising the 1984-1985 income estimates.

Revised income estimates for the biennium 1984-1985

The General Assembly

Resolves that for the biennium 1984-1985 the estimates of income of $US 283,892,800 approved by its resolution 38/236 B of 20 December 1983 shall be increased by $US 17,546,300 as follows:

Income section	Amount appropriated by resolution 38/236 B	Increase or (decrease)	Revised appropriation
		(US dollars)	
PART I. *Income from staff assessment*			
1. Income from staff assessment	226,751,400	20,144,900	246,896,300
Total, PART I	226,751,400	20,144,900	246,896,300
PART II. *Other income*			
2. General income	36,639,300	(1,021,500)	35,617,800
3. Revenue-producing activities	20,502,100	(1,577,100)	18,925,000
Total, PART II	57,141,400	(2,598,600)	54,542,800
GRAND TOTAL	283,892,800	17,546,300	301,439,100

General Assembly resolution 39/237 B

18 December 1984   Meeting 105   126-11-10 (recorded vote)

Approved by Fifth Committee (A/39/839) by recorded vote (85-11-11), 17 December (meeting 55); agenda item 109.

Recorded vote in Assembly as follows:

In favour: Algeria, Angola, Antigua and Barbuda, Argentina, Austria, Bahamas, Bahrain, Bangladesh, Barbados, Benin, Bhutan, Bolivia, Botswana, Brazil, Brunei Darussalam, Burkina Faso, Burma, Burundi, Cameroon, Canada, Cape Verde, Central African Republic, Chad, Chile, China, Colombia, Congo, Costa Rica, Cuba, Cyprus, Democratic Kampuchea, Democratic Yemen, Denmark, Djibouti, Dominican Republic, Ecuador, Egypt, El Salvador, Equatorial Guinea, Ethiopia,

Fiji, Finland, Gabon, Gambia, Ghana, Greece, Guatemala, Guinea, Guinea-Bissau, Guyana, Haiti, Honduras, Iceland, India, Indonesia, Iran, Iraq, Ireland, Ivory Coast, Jamaica, Jordan, Kenya, Kuwait, Lebanon, Lesotho, Liberia, Libyan Arab Jamahiriya, Madagascar, Malawi, Malaysia, Maldives, Mali, Malta, Mauritania, Mauritius, Mexico, Morocco, Mozambique, Nepal, Nicaragua, Niger, Nigeria, Norway, Oman, Pakistan, Panama, Papua New Guinea, Paraguay, Peru, Philippines, Portugal, Qatar, Romania, Rwanda, Saint Christopher and Nevis, Saint Lucia, Samoa, Sao Tome and Principe, Saudi Arabia, Senegal, Sierra Leone, Singapore, Somalia, Spain, Sri Lanka, Sudan, Suriname, Swaziland, Sweden, Syrian Arab Republic, Thailand, Togo, Trinidad and Tobago, Tunisia, Turkey, Uganda, United Arab Emirates, United Republic of Tanzania, Uruguay, Vanuatu, Venezuela, Yemen, Yugoslavia, Zaire, Zambia, Zimbabwe.

Against: Bulgaria, Byelorussian SSR, Czechoslovakia, German Democratic Republic, Hungary, Israel, Mongolia, Poland, Ukrainian SSR, USSR, United States.

Abstaining: Australia, Belgium, France, Germany, Federal Republic of, Italy, Japan, Luxembourg, Netherlands, New Zealand, United Kingdom.

Explaining its negative vote, the United States objected to the addition of seven posts to the Headquarters garage administration staff, chargeable to revenue-producing activities (see also p. 1178).

Financing 1985 appropriations

GENERAL ASSEMBLY ACTION

On the recommendation of the Fifth Committee, the General Assembly on 18 December 1984 adopted by recorded vote resolution 39/237 C, specifying the amounts to be obtained from each major income source in order to finance appropriations during the second year of the 1984-1985 biennium. Member States were to be assessed $658,500,126.

Financing of appropriations for the year 1985

The General Assembly

Resolves that for the year 1985:

1. Budget appropriations in a total amount of $US 817,971,300 consisting of $US 793,579,900, being half of the appropriations initially approved for the biennium 1984-1985 by General Assembly resolution 38/236 A of 20 December 1983, plus $US 24,391,400, being the increase in appropriations approved during the thirty-ninth session by resolution A above, shall be financed in accordance with regulations 5.1 and 5.2 of the Financial Regulations of the United Nations as follows:

(*a*) $25,972,100, consisting of $28,570,700, being half of the estimated income other than staff assessment income approved for the biennium 1984-1985 by resolution 38/236 B of 20 December 1983 less $2,598,600, being the decrease in estimated income other than from staff assessment approved by resolution B above;

(*b*) $93,162 being contributions of new Member States for 1983 and 1984;

(*c*) $791,906,038 being the assessment on Member States in accordance with General Assembly resolution 37/125 A of 17 December 1982 on the scale of assessments for the years 1983, 1984 and 1985;

2. There shall be set off against the assessment on Member States, in accordance with the provisions of General Assembly resolution 973(X) of 15 December 1955, their respective share in the Tax Equalization Fund in the total amount of $US 133,499,074 consisting of:

(*a*) $113,375,700 being half of the estimated staff assessment income approved by resolution 38/236 B;

(*b*) Plus $20,144,900 being the estimated increase in income from staff assessment approved by resolution B above;

(*c*) Less $51,660 being the decrease in actual income from staff assessment compared to the revised estimates for the biennium 1982-1983, approved by General Assembly resolution 38/226 B of 20 December 1983;

(*d*) Plus $30,134 representing additional income from staff assessment in respect of adjustments for prior financial periods.

General Assembly resolution 39/237 C

18 December 1984   Meeting 105   122-16-7 (recorded vote)

Approved by Fifth Committee (A/39/839) by recorded vote (86-14-8), 17 December (meeting 55); agenda item 109.

Recorded vote in Assembly as follows:

In favour: Algeria, Angola, Antigua and Barbuda, Argentina, Austria, Bahamas, Bahrain, Bangladesh, Barbados, Benin, Bhutan, Bolivia, Botswana, Brazil, Brunei Darussalam, Burkina Faso, Burma, Burundi, Cameroon, Cape Verde, Central African Republic, Chad, Chile, China, Colombia, Congo, Costa Rica, Cuba, Cyprus, Democratic Kampuchea, Democratic Yemen, Denmark, Djibouti, Dominican Republic, Ecuador, Egypt, El Salvador, Equatorial Guinea, Fiji, Finland, Gabon, Gambia, Ghana, Greece, Guatemala, Guinea, Guinea-Bissau, Guyana, Haiti, Honduras, Iceland, India, Indonesia, Iran, Iraq, Ireland, Israel, Ivory Coast, Jamaica, Jordan, Kenya, Kuwait, Lebanon, Lesotho, Liberia, Libyan Arab Jamahiriya, Madagascar, Malawi, Malaysia, Maldives, Mali, Malta, Mauritania, Mauritius, Mexico, Morocco, Mozambique, Nepal, Nicaragua, Niger, Nigeria, Norway, Oman, Pakistan, Panama, Papua New Guinea, Paraguay, Peru, Philippines, Portugal, Qatar, Rwanda, Saint Christopher and Nevis, Saint Lucia, Samoa, Sao Tome and Principe, Saudi Arabia, Senegal, Sierra Leone, Singapore, Somalia, Sri Lanka, Sudan, Suriname, Swaziland, Sweden, Thailand, Togo, Trinidad and Tobago, Tunisia, Turkey, Uganda, United Arab Emirates, United Republic of Tanzania, Uruguay, Vanuatu, Venezuela, Yemen, Yugoslavia, Zaire, Zambia, Zimbabwe.

Against: Belgium, Bulgaria, Byelorussian SSR, Czechoslovakia, German Democratic Republic, Germany, Federal Republic of, Hungary, Japan, Luxembourg, Mongolia, Netherlands, Poland, Ukrainian SSR, USSR, United Kingdom, United States.

Abstaining: Australia, Canada, France, Italy, New Zealand, Romania, Spain.

Report of ACABQ

The Advisory Committee on Administrative and Budgetary Questions reported to the General Assembly in September[6] on its activities during the second and third quarters of 1984, during which time it had held meetings in New York, Geneva, Addis Ababa (Ethiopia) and Bangkok (Thailand) to discuss problems and make recommendations pertaining to the programme budget for the 1984-1985 biennium. Also, having examined programme budget performance for 1982-1983 and the question of unliquidated obligations and proposed transfers among budget sections, ACABQ said it believed that the current method of estimating requirements and forecasting expenditure needed refining.

In addition to recommending several interim parking measures for the Headquarters garage, the Committee concurred in requests by the Secretary-General to enter into commitments in connection with Chinese language services and with leasing satellite telecommunications capacity for peacekeeping and emergency relief activities (see Chapter IV of this section, under "UN premises", "Documents" and "Computerized and other information systems and communications"). It also authorized commitments to implement human rights activities approved by the Economic and Social Council earlier in 1984, and for rental subsidies until completion of residential buildings at Baghdad, Iraq, for staff of the Economic Commission for Western Asia.

GENERAL ASSEMBLY ACTION

Acting without vote on the recommendation of the Fifth Committee, the General Assembly adopted resolution 39/236, section I, on 18 December 1984.

First report of the Advisory Committee on Administrative and Budgetary Questions
[*The General Assembly*]

Takes note with appreciation of the first report of the Advisory Committee on Administrative and Budgetary Questions;

. . .

General Assembly resolution 39/236, section I

18 December 1984   Meeting 105   Adopted without vote

Approved by Fifth Committee (A/39/839) without objection, 11 October (meeting 9); oral proposal by Chairman; agenda item 109.
Meeting numbers. GA 39th session: 5th Committee 8, 9; plenary 105.

REFERENCES
[1]YUN 1983, p. 1150, GA res. 38/236 A, 20 Dec. 1983. [2]A/C.5/39/88. [3]A/39/7/Add.15. [4]YUN 1983, p. 1156. [5]*Ibid.*, p. 1152, GA res. 38/236 B, 20 Dec. 1983. [6]A/39/7.

Budget contributions

The General Assembly's Committee on Contributions continued in 1984 its study of ways to make the assessments of Member States towards the United Nations budget reflect more closely their capacity to pay. On the Fifth Committee's recommendation, the Assembly, by decision 39/456 of 18 December, put off action on the Contribution Committee's recommendations until its resumed session in 1985, to allow time for continued efforts at agreement on a resolution. In resolution 39/247 A of the same date, the Assembly fixed rates for the two newest Members, Brunei Darussalam and Saint Christopher and Nevis.

Action by the Committee on Contributions. The Committee on Contributions held its forty-fourth session in New York from 4 to 29 June 1984. In its report to the Assembly,[1] it described its further exploratory work in response to the Assembly's 1981 request[2] for a thorough study of alternative methods to assess the real capacity of Member States to pay.

The Committee concentrated on possible variants of the current methodology for assessing the national income of Members as a prime determinant of their capacity to pay. Specifically, it examined the use of economic and social indicators and ways of taking account of the effects of inflation and foreign exchange rate conversion.

The Committee selected 10 economic and social indicators, and tested them for their effects on assessment rates. The indicators pertained to each State's economic development, educational development, health, external debt and international monetary reserves and changes in terms of trade. Had these data been used, the Committee found, most developed countries would have had lower rates and most developing countries, higher ones. Given those results, and the fact that statistical data were often not comparable between States, the Committee decided not to propose that the indicators be used. Instead, it proposed to examine the matter further, studying other indicators, trying different weights and norms, and exploring new methods.

The results of its study of possible adjustments for inflation and foreign exchange rate changes were equally inconclusive.

The Committee made three recommendations affecting components of the current assessment methodology: to maintain the 10-year statistical base period, by which national income data for each State were averaged over the most recent decade so as to lessen the effects of short-term economic fluctuations; to raise from $2,100 to $2,200 the per capita income limit, below which States were entitled to reduced assessments; and to apply a new formula for avoiding excessive variations of individual assessment rates between two successive scales. The formula combined percentage and percentage-point limits on a sliding scale, so that, for example, a State paying at the minimum rate of 0.01 per cent would not have its rate raised by more than one point (to 0.02), while the limit for a State paying 5 per cent or more could be raised by no more than 5 per cent or 75 points, whichever was smaller.

In response to the Assembly's 1981 request[2] for guidelines on presentation and collection of uniform and comparable data by Member States, the Committee generally endorsed guidelines already followed by the United Nations Statistical Office in soliciting statistical data from States.

GENERAL ASSEMBLY CONSIDERATION

The Fifth Committee discussed the recommendations of the Committee on Contributions in October 1984 and again in December. However, it was unable to reach agreement on a draft resolution by the time the Assembly concluded the first part of its 1984 session. Neither of two drafts submitted in December, one on behalf of the Member States which were members of the Group of 77 developing countries and the other by 27 Eastern European and Western States, was acceptable to the entire Committee.

The first draft,[3] submitted by Egypt on behalf of the Group of 77, would have had the Assembly approve the three recommendations of the Committee on Contributions, but with modifications more favourable to the smallest contributors and States with the lowest per capita income. Specifically, for States paying shares of less than 1 per cent each, scale-to-scale variations would be limited more than the Committee had recommended. Further, in addition to raising the upper limit of the low per capita income allowance formula as recommended by the Committee, the maximum relief gradient for such States would be raised from 85 to 90 per cent, thereby authorizing a greater reduction from regular assessment rates.

The draft added two further elements to the Committee's recommendations: that assessment calculations should include indicators reflecting the serious world economic and financial situation, particularly the high external debts of developing countries; and that all of the least developed countries be assessed at the floor level (0.01 per cent). It further specified that redistribution of the relief burden (the cost that others would have to bear as a result of the reduced rates for the poorest and smallest States) must not fall on developing countries.

The draft would have had the Committee on Contributions study two matters: what the scale of assessments for 1983-1985 would have looked like if the Committee's current recommendations on limiting scale-to-scale variations had been in effect, and whether relief for low per capita income States might be modified by assigning a relief gradient (percentage reduction) on the basis of gross domestic product.

The sponsors accepted an oral amendment by Poland to amend this draft by expanding projected relief for debtor developing countries to include others facing high debt levels.

The second draft resolution,[4] introduced by Denmark, was ultimately sponsored also by Australia, Austria, Belgium, Bulgaria, the Byelorussian SSR, Canada, Czechoslovakia, Finland, France, the German Democratic Republic, the Federal Republic of Germany, Hungary, Iceland, Ireland, Italy, Japan, Mongolia, the Netherlands, New Zealand, Norway, Portugal, Spain, Sweden, the Ukrainian SSR, the USSR, the United Kingdom and the United States.

This draft would have had the Assembly accept without change the three recommendations of the Committee on Contributions, with maximum reductions for low per capita income States remaining at 85 per cent. With regard to the least developed countries, it would specify that their rates should not exceed their current level.

Japan orally proposed an amendment to the second draft favouring rate reductions for developing countries in light of their severe economic and financial situation, particularly as regards the ratio of export earnings to debt servicing, as well as in cases where national revenue depended primarily on the export of one or a few products or where per capita income had fallen below the $2,200 limit for the first time. However, Japan later withdrew its amendment and became a sponsor of the draft.

Canada, supported by Austria and Sweden, orally proposed that the Assembly simply request the Committee on Contributions to take the two drafts into account in preparing the next scale of assessments. The Fifth Committee Chairman agreed with an interpretation by Cuba that the Canadian proposal be regarded as a third draft resolution to be taken up after the first two. Canada then moved adjournment of the meeting, and the Committee accepted this proposal by 56 votes to 50.

Following further consideration in an informal working group, the Chairman informed the Committee that the group had considered two possibilities: adoption of the Canadian proposal or postponement of a decision on the scale of assessments until a resumed Assembly session in 1985. He suggested that, if postponement was agreed to, work should continue in January in an informal working group chaired by himself, in which any interested United Nations Member could participate. The Committee, acting without vote on 18 December, recommended postponement until the resumed session. The Assembly, before suspending its session later that day, included the item in the list of topics for consideration at the resumed session (decision 39/456).

Budget contributions of new Members

GENERAL ASSEMBLY ACTION

On the recommendation of the Committee on Contributions and the Fifth Committee, the General Assembly, by resolution 39/247 A of 18 December 1984 adopted without vote, fixed the assessment rates of Brunei Darussalam, admitted to the United Nations in September 1984 (see p. 371), and Saint Christopher and Nevis, admitted in September 1983.[5]

Scale of assessments for the apportionment of the expenses of the United Nations

The General Assembly

Resolves that:

1. The rates of assessment for the following States, admitted to membership in the United Nations on 23 September 1983 and on 21 September 1984, respectively, shall be as follows:

Member State	Per cent
Saint Christopher and Nevis	0.01
Brunei Darussalam	0.03

For 1983, 1984 and 1985, these rates shall be added to the scale of assessments established under General Assembly resolution 37/125 A of 17 December 1982;

2. For the year of their admission, Saint Christopher and Nevis and Brunei Darussalam shall contribute at

the rate of one ninth of 0.01 and 0.03 per cent, respectively, such contributions to be taken into account as miscellaneous income under regulation 5.2 (c) of the Financial Regulations of the United Nations;

3. For the years 1984 and 1985, Saint Christopher and Nevis shall contribute at the rate of 0.01 per cent and for the year 1985 Brunei Darussalam shall contribute 0.03 per cent; such contribution for 1984 by Saint Christopher and Nevis also to be taken into account as miscellaneous income under regulation 5.2 (c) of the Financial Regulations of the United Nations;

4. The contributions of Saint Christopher and Nevis for 1983 and 1984 and Brunei Darussalam for 1984 shall be applied to the same basis of assessment as for other Member States, except that, in the case of appropriations or apportionments approved under General Assembly resolutions 37/38 A of 30 November 1982 and 38/35 A of 1 December 1983 for the financing of the United Nations Disengagement Observer Force, and resolutions 37/127 A of 17 December 1982 and 38/38 A of 5 December 1983 for the financing of the United Nations Interim Force in Lebanon, the contributions of those States, as determined by the group of contributors to which they may be assigned by the Assembly, shall be calculated in proportion to the calendar year;

5. The advances of Saint Christopher and Nevis and Brunei Darussalam to the Working Capital Fund, under regulation 5.8 of the Financial Regulations of the United Nations, shall be calculated by the application of the rates of assessment of 0.01 and 0.03 per cent, respectively, to the authorized level of the Fund, such advances to be added to the Fund pending the incorporation of the new Members' rates of assessment in a 100 per cent scale.

General Assembly resolution 39/247 A

18 December 1984   Meeting 105   Adopted without vote

Approved by Fifth Committee (A/39/844) without vote, 18 December (meeting 56); draft recommended by Committee on Contributions (A/39/11 and Corr.1); agenda item 115.

Meeting numbers. GA 39th session: 5th Committee 4-11, 13, 14, 51, 53, 55, 56; plenary 105.

Budget contributions in 1984

Of the $847.9 million in contributions for the United Nations regular budget payable as at 1 January 1984, $681.7 million had been collected from Member States by 31 December, leaving $166.2 million outstanding[6] (see table, "Status of contributions to the UN regular budget"). Of the amount payable, net assessments for 1984, due early in the year, totalled $677.8 million; the remaining $170.1 million related to previous years. In addition, seven non-member States were assessed a total of $2.3 million for their share of United Nations activities in which they participated[7] (see table, "Assessment of non-member States for 1984 expenses of UN activities in which they participated"). Budget assessments of Members and non-members were in accordance with scales for 1983-1985 approved by the General Assembly in 1982.[8]

The continuing shortfall in collections was

among matters dealt with by the Secretary-General in a report to the Assembly on the Organization's financial situation (see below).

At the resumption of the Assembly's 1983 session on 26 June 1984, the Secretary-General, in a letter of that date,[9] informed the Assembly President that seven Members—Chad, Comoros, El Salvador, Equatorial Guinea, Grenada, Mauritania and South Africa—were more than two years in arrears in the payment of their budget contributions. By 17 September,[10] Equatorial Guinea, Grenada and Mauritania had made payments bringing their arrears below the two-year limit.

When the Assembly opened its regular 1984 session on 18 September, the Secretary-General reported[11] that only El Salvador and South Africa were more than two years in arrears. On 20 September,[12] he reported that El Salvador had paid enough to reduce its arrears below the two-year limit. Consequently, South Africa alone remained in arrears throughout 1984; it would have had to pay $17,910,970 to remove itself from that category.

This information was conveyed by the President to the Assembly, which took note of it at both its resumed and regular sessions in 1984, without adopting a formal decision.

Under Article 19 of the Charter of the United Nations, a Member in arrears to the extent of contributions due for the preceding two full years shall have no vote in the Assembly, but the Assembly can permit such a Member to vote if it is satisfied that failure to pay was due to conditions beyond the State's control.

Meeting numbers. GA 38th session: plenary 105, 106. GA 39th session: plenary 1, 3.

ASSESSMENT OF NON-MEMBER STATES FOR 1984 EXPENSES OF UN ACTIVITIES IN WHICH THEY PARTICIPATED

(amounts in US dollars)

Non-member State	Rate of assessment	Amount
Democratic People's Republic of Korea	0.05	54,893
Holy See	0.01	13,794
Liechtenstein	0.01	10,857
Republic of Korea	0.18	291,074
San Marino	0.01	2,302
Switzerland	1.10	1,905,628
Tonga	0.01	1,991
Total		2,280,539

NOTE: Activities, conferences and subsidiary bodies for which non-member States were assessed were: International Court of Justice, ESCAP, ECE, international drug control, UNCTAD, UNIDO, 1984 International Conference on Population, UNEP, transnational corporations, UNHCR, Second International Conference on Assistance to Refugees in Africa (1984), Committee on the Development and Utilization of New and Renewable Sources of Energy, Preparatory Commission for the International Sea-Bed Authority and for the International Tribunal for the Law of the Sea, Intergovernmental Committee on Science and Technology for Development, World Food Council and Committee on the Peaceful Uses of Outer Space.

SOURCE: ST/ADM/SER.B/279.

STATUS OF CONTRIBUTIONS TO THE UN REGULAR BUDGET

(amounts in US dollars)

Member State	1983-1985 scale of assessments (per cent)	Collections in 1984	Contributions outstanding as at 31 Dec. 1984	Net assessment for 1985
Afghanistan	0.01	123,803	—	65,814
Albania	0.01	150,000	9,803	65,814
Algeria	0.13	844,591	—	855,587
Angola	0.01	72,797	157,077	65,814
Antigua and Barbuda	0.01	75,000	50,600	65,814
Argentina	0.71	370,000	4,542,037	4,672,821
Australia	1.57	10,200,062	—	10,332,858
Austria	0.75	4,872,640	—	4,936,078
Bahamas	0.01	64,969	—	65,814
Bahrain	0.01	64,969	—	65,814
Bangladesh	0.03	194,905	—	197,443
Barbados	0.01	47,063	32,323	65,814
Belgium	1.28	7,065,716	1,281,111	8,424,240
Belize	0.01	64,969	—	65,814
Benin	0.01	58,834	124,138	65,814
Bhutan	0.01	64,969	—	65,814
Bolivia	0.01	—	175,738	65,814
Botswana	0.01	64,969	—	65,814
Brazil	1.39	4,685,438	16,596,022	9,148,199
Brunei Darussalam*	0.03	—	—	197,443
Bulgaria	0.18	1,126,000	768,357	1,184,659
Burkina Faso	0.01	—	122,902	65,814
Burma	0.01	64,969	—	65,814
Burundi	0.01	10,869	173,383	65,814
Byelorussian SSR	0.36	2,292,331	1,897,478	2,369,317
Cameroon	0.01	105,870	84,062	65,814
Canada	3.08	20,010,313	—	20,270,827
Cape Verde	0.01	51,206	123,803	65,814
Central African Republic	0.01	44,828	147,502	65,814
Chad	0.01	58,814	197,521	65,814
Chile	0.07	454,780	—	460,701
China	0.88	5,643,448	4,252,876	5,791,666
Colombia	0.11	714,654	—	723,958
Comoros	0.01	75,494	184,252	65,814
Congo	0.01	95,015	8,716	65,814
Costa Rica	0.02	238,389	52,467	131,629
Cuba	0.09	716,277	611,182	592,329
Cyprus	0.01	64,969	—	65,814
Czechoslovakia	0.76	4,873,886	2,418,958	5,001,893
Democratic Kampuchea	0.01	60,684	182,282	65,814
Democratic Yemen	0.01	64,969	—	65,814
Denmark	0.75	4,872,640	—	4,936,078
Djibouti	0.01	—	175,009	65,814
Dominica	0.01	73,904	95,640	65,814
Dominican Republic	0.03	267,177	194,905	197,443
Ecuador	0.02	211,654	40,383	131,629
Egypt	0.07	454,780	—	460,701
El Salvador	0.01	60,727	197,976	65,814
Equatorial Guinea	0.01	43,380	188,515	65,814
Ethiopia	0.01	64,969	—	65,814
Fiji	0.01	64,969	—	65,814
Finland	0.48	3,118,490	—	3,159,090
France	6.51	42,294,525	4,357,157	42,845,156
Gabon	0.02	123,344	199,677	131,629
Gambia	0.01	—	154,366	65,814
German Democratic Republic	1.39	8,663,981	3,409,651	9,148,199
Germany, Federal Republic of	8.54	55,483,141	—	56,205,474
Ghana	0.02	129,937	—	131,629
Greece	0.40	2,598,741	—	2,632,575
Grenada	0.01	141,066	118,077	65,814
Guatemala	0.02	—	129,937	131,629
Guinea	0.01	66,180	—	65,814
Guinea-Bissau	0.01	61,130	180,250	65,814
Guyana	0.01	172,250	17,009	65,814
Haiti	0.01	—	165,623	65,814
Honduras	0.01	122,645	—	65,814
Hungary	0.23	1,519,275	1,481,040	1,513,731
Iceland	0.03	194,905	—	197,443
India	0.36	2,628,867	47,662	2,369,317
Indonesia	0.13	844,591	—	855,587
Iran	0.58	4,695,645	3,683,971	3,817,234
Iraq	0.12	1,553,818	—	789,772
Ireland	0.18	1,169,434	—	1,184,659
Israel	0.23	1,522,633	2,836,060	1,513,731
Italy	3.74	24,298,237	—	24,614,576
Ivory Coast	0.03	113,636	281,672	197,443
Jamaica	0.02	120,872	9,065	131,629
Japan	10.32	67,047,543	—	67,920,430
Jordan	0.01	64,969	—	65,814
Kenya	0.01	136,420	—	65,814
Kuwait	0.25	1,624,214	—	1,645,360
Lao People's Democratic Republic	0.01	—	123,803	65,814
Lebanon	0.02	28,000	101,937	131,629
Lesotho	0.01	64,969	—	65,814
Liberia	0.01	10,148	101,877	65,814
Libyan Arab Jamahiriya	0.26	—	3,218,887	1,711,173
Luxembourg	0.06	389,811	—	394,887
Madagascar	0.01	66,685	103,130	65,814
Malawi	0.01	64,969	—	65,814
Malaysia	0.09	584,717	—	592,329
Maldives	0.01	60,449	78,597	65,814
Mali	0.01	102,230	84,492	65,814
Malta	0.01	64,969	—	65,814
Mauritania	0.01	91,502	160,777	65,814
Mauritius	0.01	123,803	—	65,814
Mexico	0.88	5,717,232	—	5,791,666
Mongolia	0.01	63,292	59,349	65,814
Morocco	0.05	324,843	—	329,072
Mozambique	0.01	64,969	—	65,814
Nepal	0.01	64,969	—	65,814
Netherlands	1.78	11,571,822	—	11,714,958
New Zealand	0.26	1,689,182	—	1,711,173
Nicaragua	0.01	—	181,252	65,814
Niger	0.01	119,650	80,007	65,814
Nigeria	0.19	20,900	1,343,347	1,250,473
Norway	0.51	3,313,395	—	3,356,533
Oman	0.01	64,969	—	65,814
Pakistan	0.06	370,119	19,692	394,887
Panama	0.02	129,937	—	131,629
Papua New Guinea	0.01	64,969	—	65,814
Paraguay	0.01	55,098	182,282	65,814
Peru	0.07	171,346	1,093,969	460,701
Philippines	0.09	463,983	329,004	592,329
Poland	0.72	10,270,000	12,595,401	4,738,636
Portugal	0.18	1,169,434	—	1,184,659
Qatar	0.03	194,905	—	197,443
Romania	0.19	520,000	2,894,983	1,250,473
Rwanda	0.01	64,969	—	65,814
Saint Christopher and Nevis†	0.01	—	—	65,814
Saint Lucia	0.01	—	185,252	65,814
Saint Vincent and the Grenadines	0.01	64,969	—	65,814
Samoa	0.01	—	199,090	65,814
Sao Tome and Principe	0.01	—	64,969	65,814
Saudi Arabia	0.86	5,587,294	—	5,660,037
Senegal	0.01	64,969	—	65,814
Seychelles	0.01	64,969	—	65,814
Sierra Leone	0.01	58,929	81,825	65,814
Singapore	0.09	584,717	—	592,329
Solomon Islands	0.01	64,969	—	65,814
Somalia	0.01	—	67,512	65,814
South Africa	0.41	—	21,786,114	2,698,390
Spain	1.93	12,538,929	—	12,702,174
Sri Lanka	0.01	64,969	—	65,814
Sudan	0.01	—	64,969	65,814
Suriname	0.01	—	64,969	65,814
Swaziland	0.01	39,364	27,800	65,814

STATUS OF CONTRIBUTIONS *(cont.)*

Member State	1983-1985 scale of assessments (per cent)	Collections in 1984	Contributions outstanding as at 31 Dec. 1984	Net assessment for 1985
Sweden	1.32	8,575,848	—	8,687,498
Syrian Arab Republic	0.03	—	389,415	197,443
Thailand	0.08	519,749	—	526,515
Togo	0.01	—	150,966	65,814
Trinidad and Tobago	0.03	194,905	—	197,443
Tunisia	0.03	194,905	—	197,443
Turkey	0.32	1,169,623	2,575,546	2,111,667
Uganda	0.01	59,334	64,969	65,814
Ukrainian SSR	1.32	8,405,217	6,078,124	8,687,498
USSR	10.54	67,114,385	42,534,050	69,368,348
United Arab Emirates	0.16	—	1,039,497	1,053,030
United Kingdom	4.67	30,340,312	—	30,735,312
United Republic of Tanzania	0.01	—	140,237	67,912
United States	25.00	206,450,981	11,503,803	197,897,350
Uruguay	0.04	453,135	283,875	263,258
Vanuatu	0.01	64,969	—	65,814
Venezuela	0.55	4,108,991	396,793	3,619,791
Viet Nam	0.02	10,000	237,607	131,629
Yemen	0.01	112,107	17,696	65,814
Yugoslavia	0.46	3,935,259	3,018,278	3,027,461
Zaire	0.01	10,000	248,023	65,814
Zambia	0.01	64,969	—	65,814
Zimbabwe	0.02	129,937	117,670	131,629
Total	100.04	681,669,087	166,250,070	691,776,091

*The 1984 assessment of Brunei Darussalam, admitted to the United Nations in 1984, was fixed in December 1984 at $21,656 (one ninth of the regular rate).
†The 1983 assessment of Saint Christopher and Nevis, admitted to the United Nations in 1983, was fixed in December 1984 at $6,537 (one ninth of the regular rate), and its 1984 assessment was set at $64,969 (the full rate).
SOURCE: ST/ADM/SER.B/275, ST/ADM/SER.B/276 & Corr.1.

REFERENCES

[1]A/39/11 & Corr.1. [2]YUN 1981, p. 1292, GA res. 36/231 A, 18 Dec. 1981. [3]A/C.5/39/L.18. [4]A/C.5/39/L.26. [5]YUN 1983, p. 388, GA res. 38/1, 23 Sep. 1983. [6]ST/ADM/SER.B/276 & Corr.1. [7]ST/ADM/SER.B/279. [8]YUN 1982, p. 1418, GA res. 37/125 A, 17 Dec. 1982. [9]A/38/822. [10]A/38/822/Add.1. [11]A/39/498. [12]A/39/498/Add.1.

Financial situation

Amounts collected from Member States in 1984 in payment of their assessed contributions were insufficient to meet the Organization's cash need, the Secretary-General informed the General Assembly in a 9 October report[1] on the United Nations financial situation requested by the Assembly in December 1983.[2] It had therefore been necessary in September 1984 to borrow temporarily from the account for peace-keeping activities in order to meet obligations under the regular budget, as normal reserve funds—the Working Capital Fund and the United Nations Special Account—had been depleted.

The Secretary-General ascribed the problem mainly to delays in payment. By the end of September, he stated, only 53 Members, or 33.8 per cent of the membership, had paid their contribution in full, despite the requirement of the Finan-

cial Regulations of the United Nations that they be paid within 30 days after each State was notified of its assessment. Including partial payments, only 47.7 per cent of total assessments had been paid by then, the lowest proportion since 1978. He urged Members to settle their accounts expeditiously and appealed for further efforts to ensure early and full payment. If the situation did not improve during 1985, revisions to the Financial Regulations would have to be considered.

The report added that cash balances had increased by $25.8 million since 1981 as a result of the Assembly's 1981 decision[3] to suspend financial regulations requiring unspent appropriations to be returned to Members. In addition, $624,897 had been placed in the Special Account, representing half the proceeds from the 1982 United Nations postage stamps on nature conservation, in accordance with Assembly decisions of 1980[4] and 1983.[5]

The short-term deficit of the United Nations, another measure of its financial difficulties, would rise by an estimated $12.8 million during 1984, to a projected total of $356 million, the Secretary-General reported (see cumulative table below). Of the increase, $13.3 million related to withholdings by certain Members of their share for peace-keeping operations to which they had political and legal objections. The $93.2 million deficit in the regular budget, a part of this total, included an estimated $3.5 million in withholdings for 1984.

In its report to the Assembly on this subject, also issued in October 1984,[6] ACABQ said it shared the Secretary-General's concerns and thought that further examination of issues he and ACABQ had raised in 1981 reports to the Assembly[7] would provide a useful basis for considering measures to alleviate the financial situation.

The Negotiating Committee on the Financial Emergency of the United Nations, established by the Assembly in 1975,[8] did not meet in 1984.

GENERAL ASSEMBLY ACTION

A renewed appeal to Members for prompt payment of assessments was contained in resolution 39/239 B, adopted by the Assembly without vote on 18 December 1984, on the Fifth Committee's recommendation.

Financial situation of the United Nations

The General Assembly,

Having considered the report of the Secretary-General on the analysis of the financial situation of the United Nations,

Recalling its resolutions 3049 A (XXVII) of 19 December 1972, 3538(XXX) of 17 December 1975, 32/104 of 14 December 1977, 35/113 of 10 December 1980, 36/116 B of 10 December 1981, 37/13 of 16 November 1982 and 38/228 B of 20 December 1983,

Mindful of the report of the Negotiating Committee on the Financial Emergency of the United Nations and of the views expressed by Member States thereon in the Fifth Committee at the thirty-second session of the General Assembly,

Reiterating earlier appeals to Member States, without prejudice to their position of principle, to make voluntary contributions to the Special Account referred to in annex IV of the report of the Secretary-General on the analysis of the financial situation of the United Nations,

Noting with concern that the short-term deficit of the Organization is expected to exceed $356 million as at 31 December 1984,

Concerned at the increasingly precarious financial situation of peace-keeping operations and, in particular, its adverse impact on developing-country troop contributors,

Noting also with concern that delays and partial payment of assessed contributions continue to create serious cash-flow problems for the Organization,

Considering the possibility that for many Member States administrative considerations, including a calendar difference between the national fiscal year and that of the Organization, may be responsible for the delay in the payment of assessed contributions,

Taking note of the views expressed in the Fifth Committee,

1. *Reaffirms* its commitment to seek a comprehensive and generally acceptable solution to the financial problems of the United Nations, based on the principle of collective financial responsibility of Member States and in strict compliance with the Charter of the United Nations;

2. *Urges* all Member States to meet their financial obligations;

3. *Renews its appeal* to all Member States to make their best efforts to overcome constraints to the prompt payment early each year of full assessed contributions and of advances to the Working Capital Fund;

4. *Expresses its appreciation* to all Member States which pay their assessed contributions in full within thirty days of the receipt of the Secretary-General's communication, in accordance with regulation 5.4 of the Financial Regulations of the United Nations;

5. *Requests* the Secretary-General, in addition to his official communications to the permanent representatives of Member States, to approach, as and when appropriate, the Governments of Member States for the purpose of encouraging expeditious payment in full of assessed contributions, in compliance with regulation 5.4 of the Financial Regulations of the United Nations;

6. *Invites* Member States also to provide, in response to the Secretary-General's official communication and consistent with regulation 5.4 of the Financial Regulations of the United Nations, information regarding their expected pattern of payments, in order to facilitate the financial planning by the Secretary-General;

7. *Requests* the Negotiating Committee on the Financial Emergency of the United Nations to keep the financial situation of the Organization under review and to report, as and when appropriate, to the General Assembly;

8. *Requests* the Secretary-General to submit to the General Assembly at its fortieth session detailed information relating to the extent, rate of increase and composition of the deficit of the Organization, the pattern of payments of Member States, the cash-flow situation and voluntary contributions received from Member States and other sources pursuant to Assembly resolutions 2053 A (XX) of 15 December 1965 and 3049 A (XXVII) of 19 December 1972;

9. *Decides* to include in the provisional agenda of its fortieth session the item entitled "Financial emergency of the United Nations".

General Assembly resolution 39/239 B

18 December 1984   Meeting 105   Adopted without vote

Approved by Fifth Committee (A/39/841 & Corr.1) without vote, 14 December (meeting 51); 10-nation draft (A/C.5/39/L.23), orally revised; agenda item 111.

Sponsors: Bangladesh, Canada, Denmark, Finland, Ireland, Nigeria, Norway, Pakistan, Sweden, Trinidad and Tobago.

Meeting numbers. GA 39th session: 5th Committee 33, 40, 43, 46, 51; plenary 105.

The United Kingdom observed that the word "so-called" preceding the words "short-term deficit" in the fifth preambular paragraph of the 10-nation draft introduced by Sweden was imprecise; it was intended to qualify "short term" rather than "deficit". The United Kingdom's suggestion that it be deleted was supported by Sweden and Bangladesh on behalf of the sponsors, and the text, as amended, was approved without vote.

CUMULATIVE WITHHOLDINGS OF ASSESSED CONTRIBUTIONS
BY MEMBER STATES
*(estimated as at end of 1984 financial periods;
in thousands of US dollars)*

Member State	Regular budget*	UNEF/ UNDOF†	UNIFIL‡
Albania	9.8	21.6	18.8
Algeria	—	—	222.6
Benin	—	10.6	9.1
Bulgaria	663.9	27.5	303.4
Byelorussian SSR	1,344.0	624.1	3,640.0
China	4,252.6	—	—
Cuba	—	—	196.6
Czechoslovakia	1,888.6	397.7	7,658.1
Democratic Kampuchea	70.6	21.6	—
Democratic Yemen	—	5.7	9.1
France	4,357.1	—	—
German Democratic Republic	3,265.1	1,223.7	12,968.3
Hungary	1,079.7	—	568.5
Iraq	—	108.5	208.4
Israel	9.0	—	—
Lao People's Democratic Republic	—	—	9.1
Libyan Arab Jamahiriya	—	223.9	418.5
Mongolia	55.9	8.8	18.9
Poland	2,679.1	—	10,630.3
Romania	918.0	—	—
South Africa	21,786.1	3,001.3	3,931.9
Syrian Arab Republic	—	31.2	52.1
Ukrainian SSR	5,977.1	2,329.0	13,541.9
USSR	41,435.2	20,772.3	124,909.5
United States	3,371.7	—	—
Viet Nam	11.3	18.8	51.2
Yemen	—	10.2	9.1
Total	93,174.8	28,836.5	179,375.4

*Estimated withholdings from the regular budget, projected to 31 December 1984, consisted of $44,501,100 relating to the 1961 United Nations bond issue, $19,572,100 relating to the regular programme of technical assistance, and $29,101,600 relating to other budget items.

†Estimated withholdings relating to the second United Nations Emergency Force (UNEF II) from its inception in 1973 to the completion of its liquidation and from the inception of UNDOF in 1974 to 30 November 1984.

‡Estimated withholdings from the inception of UNIFIL on 19 March 1978 to 18 October 1984.

SOURCE: A/C.5/39/10.

The USSR said the major reasons for the financial emergency were the inclusion in the budget of expenses contrary to the Charter, the imposition on all Members of costs incurred by Israel's aggression, and the high growth of overall expenditures. The bond issue and technical assistance expenditures should be removed from the regular budget and financed through voluntary contributions, and budgetary expenditures in general should be reduced and subjected to strict financial control.

Along with this text, the Assembly adopted resolution 39/239 A, by which it authorized a United Nations postage stamp on the social and economic crisis in Africa, with half of the revenue to go to the United Nations Special Account (see Chapter IV of this section).

Effects of currency instability and inflation

In a report of 20 November 1984,[9] the Secretary-General reviewed the interplay of various economic factors that appeared to be at the roots of inflation and exchange rate movements, and analysed their impact on the real domestic cost of Member States' assessed contributions as well as their effect on the United Nations budget by expenditure category. The report was submitted in response to a 1982 Assembly request[10] for preparation of a more penetrating and detailed study of the impact of inflation and monetary instability on the budget than the one submitted to the 1982 session.[11]

The report observed that there seemed to be no consensus on the nature of inflation or its precise causes, but two features that had characterized it in recent years were its accelerating pace and its transmission across international borders through trade—the most likely vehicle—as well as through other international economic linkages. Exchange-rate volatility was of particular relevance to inflation, movements in the value of the United States dollar *vis-à-vis* other currencies assuming special importance. The impact of inflation and monetary instability on the "burden" of sharing in the budget was examined within the framework of a theoretical analysis describing the various stages in the investigation of those phenomena and their relation to the real economic growth of the contributing countries.

Conceptually, the Secretary-General concluded, it was possible to pinpoint one or more factors contributing to inflation and trace their impact on the economy. However, it was exceedingly difficult to measure each factor's contribution to a given rate of inflation, or to determine the weights of domestic factors as opposed to those of an international origin; hence the difficulty of drawing conclusions on specific causes of inflation. Based on the assumptions used, the Secretary-General concluded that the precise causes of monetary instability which are reflected in sharp fluctuations in exchange rates, and their effect on the burden of financing mandated requirements expressed in one or a few national currency units, might be difficult to identify with any precision.

Irrespective of the impact of inflation and exchange rate fluctuations on domestic price movements in the various duty stations and wherever else the United Nations spent its money, the general drift of prices would affect the local cost of mandated goods and services. In addition, exchange rate fluctuations among the currencies the United Nations used might have a direct bearing on the total dollar cost of those outlays. The United Nations budget contained several expenditure categories, each affected in different ways by inflation and exchange rate fluctuations. Mandated purchases of goods and services other than those contracted for at pre-specified rates and adjustment mechanisms were directly affected by price fluctuations at the place where the money was spent.

Regardless of the origin of inflation and monetary instability, cost changes were eventually reflected in the dollar magnitude of the budget. Inflationary forces and exchange rate fluctuations affected budget expenditures, though not necessarily fully and immediately, and the rates of inflation and exchange rate fluctuations reported in the statistics issued by the countries in which the various duty stations were located were not appropriate indicators of the impact of price and exchange rate changes on the budget. Some expenditures were subjected to cost increases when new contracts were negotiated; others were buffered by threshold criteria (costs linked to escalation clauses or automatic cost-of-living adjustment provisions), minimum costing periods, incomplete transmission of fluctuations, and other factors.

Annexed to the report were a summary table indicating the rates of exchange and inflation reported in programme budget performance reports for the last four bienniums for four major duty stations (New York, Geneva, Nairobi and Vienna), and two graphs: one showing the cumulative impact of inflation on local currency expenditures at each of the four locations, and the other the annual fluctuations in the value of the local currencies of the last three locations in relation to the dollar.

GENERAL ASSEMBLY ACTION

By resolution 39/240, adopted by the General Assembly on the recommendation of the Fifth Committee, the Secretary-General was requested to prepare for it in 1985 another detailed study on the impact of inflation and monetary instability on the United Nations budget, taking into account the views expressed by Member States at its 1984 session.

Impact of inflation and monetary instability on the regular budget of the United Nations

The General Assembly,

Recalling its resolutions 36/230 of 18 December 1981 and 37/130 of 17 December 1982,

Deeply concerned at the increased cost of the goods and services associated with the operation of the United Nations and the United Nations system as a whole as a result of the persistence of inflation and monetary instability in those developed countries in which the United Nations makes its main expenditures,

Convinced that many Member States are not responsible for the losses that the budget of the United Nations experiences as a result of the monetary phenomena referred to in the preceding paragraph,

Stressing that, in order to cover the substantial losses caused by inflation and monetary instability, there is a need for a continuing review of procedures that could help to meet the above-mentioned budget costs in the most appropriate way,

Having considered the report of the Secretary-General on the impact of inflation and monetary instability on the regular budget of the United Nations,

Convinced of the need to analyse more thoroughly all aspects of the increased costs of the goods and services associated with the operations of the United Nations,

1. *Takes note* of the report of the Secretary-General on the impact of inflation and monetary instability on the regular budget of the United Nations;

2. *Requests* the Secretary-General to prepare a more penetrating, extensive and detailed study on the impact of inflation and monetary instability on the regular budget of the United Nations, as was requested in General Assembly resolution 37/130, taking very duly into consideration the content of the preambular paragraphs of Assembly resolutions 36/230, 37/130 and the present resolution, together with the opinions expressed by Member States during the debates on this item at the thirty-ninth session of the Assembly, and to submit it to the Assembly at its fortieth session;

3. *Also requests* that the above-mentioned study include:

(a) The amounts which, over the last four bienniums, have resulted from inflation and monetary instability in the developed countries where United Nations organizations have their headquarters;

(b) A comparison between real, net and growth increases and increases due to inflation during the last four bienniums.

General Assembly resolution 39/240

18 December 1984   Meeting 105   83-25-23 (recorded vote)

Approved by Fifth Committee (A/39/842) by recorded vote (43-23-11), 15 December (meeting 52); 6-nation draft (A/C.5/39/L.22); agenda item 112 (b).

Sponsors: Cuba, Guinea-Bissau, Iran, Libyan Arab Jamahiriya, Mexico, Nicaragua.

Meeting numbers. GA 39th session: 5th Committee 33, 42, 44, 46, 51-53; plenary 105.

Recorded vote in Assembly as follows:

In favour: Afghanistan, Algeria, Angola, Antigua and Barbuda, Argentina, Bahrain, Benin, Bolivia, Brazil, Bulgaria, Burkina Faso, Burma, Burundi, Byelorussian SSR, Cape Verde, Central African Republic, Chad, Colombia, Congo, Costa Rica, Cuba, Czechoslovakia, Democratic Yemen, Djibouti, Ecuador, El Salvador, Ethiopia, Fiji, Gabon, Gambia, German Democratic Republic, Guatemala, Guinea-Bissau, Guyana, Hungary, Iran, Jordan, Kenya, Kuwait, Lao People's Democratic Republic, Lebanon, Lesotho, Liberia, Libyan Arab Jamahiriya, Madagascar, Malawi, Mali, Malta, Mauritius, Mexico, Mongolia, Mozambique, Nicaragua, Niger, Nigeria, Panama, Paraguay, Peru, Poland, Qatar, Romania, Rwanda, Sao Tome and Principe, Saudi Arabia, Senegal, Sierra Leone, Sri Lanka, Sudan, Syrian Arab Republic, Togo, Uganda, Ukrainian SSR, USSR, United Arab Emirates, Uruguay, Vanuatu, Venezuela, Viet Nam, Yemen, Yugoslavia, Zaire, Zambia, Zimbabwe.

Against: Australia, Austria, Belgium, Canada, Denmark, Egypt, Finland, France, Germany, Federal Republic of, Greece, Iceland, Ireland, Israel, Italy, Japan, Luxembourg, Netherlands, New Zealand, Norway, Portugal, Spain, Sweden, Turkey, United Kingdom, United States.

Abstaining: Bahamas, Bangladesh, Barbados, Bhutan, Botswana, Cameroon, Chile, Ghana, India, Ivory Coast, Jamaica, Maldives, Mauritania, Nepal, Pakistan, Papua New Guinea, Saint Lucia, Samoa, Singapore, Suriname, Swaziland, Tunisia, United Republic of Tanzania.

The United States contended that the average inflation rate over the past decade for the developed countries in which the United Nations incurred its main expenditures had been five times less than for the developing countries in which it incurred substantial expenditures, and the resolution was thus based on false assertions; moreover, the proposed study would waste valuable resources and the time should instead be used to study the real economic problems impeding development and growth. Egypt also made the point that inflation in the developed countries had for several years been lower than at other duty stations.

Cuba, on the other hand, said the inflation in developing countries where the United Nations had duty stations had been imported from the developed countries. The USSR was in agreement that budget growth in the United Nations system was attributable largely to inflation in the various host countries and that not all Member States were responsible for the increased costs resulting therefrom.

Canada, as well as Ireland speaking on behalf of the 10 member countries of the European Community, said the text was clearly politically, not financially, motivated. It suggested, Ireland said, that the developed countries alone were to blame for inflation and monetary instability and should compensate other countries accordingly. Resources should not be wasted on a pointless study, especially when inflation was slowing down world-wide.

Austria could not see what was meant by paragraph 3, and said that a preambular paragraph seemed to suggest that Austria experienced persistent monetary instability; the text was unclear, was based on false assumptions and analyses and called for a study which was beyond the capacity of the Office of Financial Services. While Cameroon believed the new study was necessary, it also found some of the preambular paragraphs problematic: it had not been proved that the Assembly was "convinced" that many Member States were not responsible for losses from inflation and monetary instability, it said, nor that there was "a need for a continuing review" of procedures that could help meet budget costs.

REFERENCES

[1]A/C.5/39/10 & Corr.1. [2]YUN 1983, p. 1161, GA res. 38/228 B, 20 Dec. 1983. [3]YUN 1981, p. 1298, GA res. 36/116 B, 10 Dec. 1981. [4]YUN 1980, p. 1220, GA res. 35/113, 10 Dec. 1980. [5]YUN 1983, p. 1211, GA res. 38/228 A, 20 Dec. 1983. [6]A/39/622. [7]YUN 1981, p. 1295-96. [8]YUN 1975, p. 957, 3535(XXX), 17 Dec. 1975. [9]A/C.5/39/44. [10]YUN 1982, p. 1426, GA res. 37/130, 17 Dec. 1982. [11]*Ibid.*, p. 1425.

Accounts and auditing

Accounts for 1983

The 1983 accounts and financial statements of the United Nations and nine voluntarily financed United Nations development and humanitarian assistance programmes were accepted by the General Assembly at its 1984 session, along with the audit opinions on those programmes by the United Nations Board of Auditors. The Assembly also concurred with the observations of ACABQ on the subject. These actions were incorporated into resolution 39/66, adopted without vote on 13 December 1984, as recommended by the Fifth Committee.

Financial reports and audited financial statements and reports of the Board of Auditors

The General Assembly,

Having considered the financial reports and audited financial statements for the period ended 31 December 1983 of the United Nations, the United Nations Development Programme, the United Nations Children's Fund, the United Nations Relief and Works Agency for Palestine Refugees in the Near East, the United Nations Institute for Training and Research, the voluntary funds administered by the United Nations High Commissioner for Refugees, the Fund of the United Nations Environment Programme, the United Nations Fund for Population Activities, the United Nations Habitat and Human Settlements Foundation and the United Nations Industrial Development Fund, the audit opinions of the Board of Auditors and the report of the Advisory Committee on Administrative and Budgetary Questions,

Taking into account the views expressed by delegations during the debate in the Fifth Committee, particularly in support of measures for the sound financial management and control of the United Nations family of organizations,

1. *Accepts* the financial reports and audited financial statements and the audit opinions of the Board of Auditors;

2. *Concurs* with the observations and comments made by the Advisory Committee on Administrative and Budgetary Questions in its report;

3. *Requests* the Board of Auditors and the Advisory Committee on Administrative and Budgetary Questions to continue to give greater attention to areas regarding which they have made observations and comments;

4. *Further requests* the executive heads of the organizations and programmes concerned within the United Nations system to take such remedial action in areas falling within their competence as may be required by the observations and comments made by the Board of Auditors in its reports;

5. *Renews its invitation* to the governing bodies of the organizations concerned to consider each year at their regular sessions the remedial action taken by the respective executive heads in response to the observations and comments made by the Board of Auditors in its reports.

General Assembly resolution 39/66

13 December 1984   Meeting 98   Adopted without vote

Approved by Fifth Committee (A/39/618) without vote, 19 October (meeting 14); draft by Chairman (A/C.5/39/L.3), amended by Philippines (A/C.5/39/L.4) and by Ireland (A/C.5/39/L.5), orally revised); agenda item 108.
Meeting numbers. GA 39th session: 5th Committee, 3-7, 13, 14; plenary 98.

The draft, proposed by the Fifth Committee Chairman, incorporated two amendments approved in Committee without objection. The first was the addition by the Philippines of a phrase to the second preambular paragraph taking into account delegations' views "particularly in support of measures for the sound financial management and control of the United Nations family of organizations". The second was an amendment by Ireland adding paragraph 5, which it further orally revised to "renew its invitation to" rather than "invite" governing bodies to consider remedial action.

The Secretary-General transmitted to the Board of Auditors on 31 March 1984 his financial report on the accounts for the United Nations (including the International Trade Centre (ITC) jointly sponsored by the United Nations Conference on Trade and Development and the General Agreement on Tariffs and Trade, and the United Nations University (UNU))[1] for the 1982-1983 biennium. It included a statement of income and expenditure as shown in the table below (in millions of United States dollars):

Account	Income	Expenditure
General Fund	1,469.6	1,462.4
Other General Fund–related activities	15.1	—
Peace-keeping missions	529.6	470.8
Technical co-operation activities	606.5	608.4
General trust funds	146.2	119.4
Special accounts for programme support costs	88.6	88.5

SOURCE: A/39/5 and Corr.1.

The Board of Auditors made recommendations and observations on various aspects of the financial management of the United Nations for the biennium and on the following programmes or organs for the year ended 31 December 1983, on which financial reports and audited financial statements[2] had also been submitted to the Assembly (see the headings "Accounts for 1983" in the chapters of this book pertaining to individual programmes): United Nations Development Programme (UNDP); United Nations Children's Fund

(UNICEF); United Nations Relief and Works Agency for Palestine Refugees in the Near East (UNRWA); United Nations Institute for Training and Research (UNITAR); voluntary funds administered by the United Nations High Commissioner for Refugees; Fund of the United Nations Environment Programme (UNEP); United Nations Fund for Population Activities; United Nations Habitat and Human Settlements Foundation; and United Nations Industrial Development Fund (of UNIDO).

The Board's report on the United Nations was transmitted to the Assembly on 18 June;[1] its reports on other programmes and organs were included in the financial reports of those programmes.[2] In its review, the Board had concentrated on cash management, budgetary control, trust funds, the procurement system, including control over expendable and revenue-producing activities, and internal audit. ACABQ commented on the Board's recommendations in its report of 20 September[3] before they were reviewed by the Fifth Committee. Among the Board's findings, and comments thereon by ACABQ, were the following.

Some submissions of budgetary proposals to the Budget Division were tardy; others did not conform to the prescribed format, or contained significant errors. ACABQ said it intended to return to the question of a full determination of the validity of unliquidated obligations, on which the Board recommended regular and thorough reviews, when it examined modalities for estimating requirements and forecasting expenditures.

The cost of some non-recurrent maintenance at Geneva had been incorrectly charged to the current maintenance account. Some undelivered purchases were charged against the wrong biennial appropriations; ACABQ noted that the administration had already issued instructions to discontinue that practice. Trust fund expenditure control was inadequate and closure of inactive funds unduly delayed.

The Board commented on procurement practices at the United Nations, ITC, UNICEF, UNRWA and UNHCR. Procurement systems and procedures at Headquarters and Geneva needed improvement, as did inventory-record maintenance. Established procedures should be followed in conducting inventories; regulations relating to contracts and purchases were not adequately applied at Geneva, and there was need for better contract arrangements for equipment-and-services-supply for projects at the Office of the United Nations Disaster Relief Co-ordinator. Procedures for reporting losses and writing off property should be reviewed and guidelines set up. The automated purchase and payment system required refinement, although it was doubtful that its full im-

plementation would be achieved. ACABQ shared the Board's concern regarding inventories, write-off procedures and procurement practices and urged that administrations pay closer attention to all aspects of the procurement process.

The success of measures to control travel costs would depend on the co-operation of officers authorized to approve their own travel plans; and the Economic and Social Commission for Asia and the Pacific should enter into contractual arrangements with a travel agent.

A weakness persisted in implementing and monitoring technical co-operation projects; reporting on and evaluating fellowship programmes should be enhanced; and budgetary control for UNIDO's project expenditures should be made more effective and project implementation improved through timely project inputs. ACABQ felt that the Board's observations on technical co-operation activities could be brought to the attention of the UNDP Governing Council.

Concerning computer operations, inter-agency co-ordination procedures related to electronic data processing (EDP) facilities and resources needed to be harmonized and developed, and a formal monitoring process established to ensure compliance with security, quality control and performance standards of the New York Computing Service. Guidelines should be drawn up to establish a formal and consistent basis for EDP planning and budget formulation procedures. ACABQ agreed with the Board that compliance with the standards set by the Electronic Data Processing and Information Systems Division should be monitored.

Internal Audit Division coverage needed to be improved (see below), and collection of assessed contributions required further efforts.

ACABQ had no comments on the Board's reports on the financial statements of UNU, UNITAR, the UNEP Fund or UNIDO.

Accounts and financial statements for 1984 relating to the above organs and programmes, other than the United Nations, the UNEP Fund and the Habitat and Human Settlements Foundation, were submitted to the Assembly in 1985.[4]

Auditing practices

In its 1984 report to the General Assembly, contained in the financial report and audited financial statements on the United Nations for the 1982-1983 biennium,[1] the Board of Auditors reported on its review of the Internal Audit Division, describing the Division's new responsibilities relating to the audit of programme performance, including determining the validity of submissions, the effectiveness of monitoring procedures, the accuracy of data and the reliability of results. It concluded that, particularly in the light of the growth of United Nations activities, Division resources were inadequate to handle effectively the additional responsibilities. It recommended a review of the Division's resources and measures taken to correct deficiencies, as well as a review of its training programme. ACABQ[3] considered that the reviews recommended by the Board should be undertaken without delay and their results reflected in the proposed 1986-1987 budget.

GENERAL ASSEMBLY ACTION

A decision with the effect of endorsing ACABQ's recommendations was proposed in the Fifth Committee by Canada, which revised its text and orally edited the revision, changing the original request for a report to be submitted to the Assembly at its 1985 session to one to be submitted in the context of the proposed programme budget for the biennium 1986-1987. The Committee approved the text without vote, and the Assembly adopted it in the same manner as decision 39/416 in December 1984.

Internal Audit Division

At its 98th plenary meeting, on 13 December 1984, the General Assembly, on the recommendation of the Fifth Committee, recognized the continuing and invaluable contribution of the Internal Audit Division of the Secretariat in ensuring that internal controls were operating effectively and decided to request the Secretary-General to conduct a review of the Internal Audit Division as recommended by the Board of Auditors, taking into account, *inter alia*:

(*a*) Staff qualifications;

(*b*) The adequacy of audit coverage of United Nations programmes, particularly in offices away from Headquarters, in the light of the decentralization of accounting functions;

(*c*) The need for training in order to keep abreast of contemporary audit practices and techniques;

and to report thereon in the context of the proposed programme budget for the biennium 1986-1987.

General Assembly decision 39/416

Adopted without vote

Approved by Fifth Committee (A/39/618) without vote, 24 October (meeting 16); draft by Canada (A/C.5/39/L.7/Rev.1), orally revised; agenda item 108.
Meeting numbers. GA 39th session: 5th Committee 3-7, 15, 16; plenary 98.

REFERENCES

[1]A/39/5 and Corr.1, vols. I-III. [2]A/39/5/Add.1-4, A/39/5/Add.5 & Corr.1, A/39/5/Add.6 & 7, A/39/5/Add.8 & Corr.1, A/39/5/Add.9. [3]A/39/510. [4]A/40/5/Add.1-5, 7 & 9.

Chapter II

United Nations programmes

Further action was taken in 1984 to improve United Nations programme planning, budgeting and evaluation. The Committee for Programme and Co-ordination (CPC) reported progress in joint planning on human settlements, nutrition and rural development. CPC's recommendations and conclusions, taken at its twenty-fourth annual session, were endorsed by the Economic and Social Council in resolution 1984/61 A. The General Assembly, by resolution 39/238 on programme planning, adopted addenda and revisions proposed by the Secretary-General to the medium-term plan for 1984-1989.

A timetable for intergovernmental review of in-depth and triennial evaluation studies scheduled for 1986-1992 was accepted by the Assembly, also by resolution 39/238, as were other aspects of programme planning. The complete text of regulations governing programme planning, programme aspects of the budget, monitoring of programme implementation and evaluation methods was issued by the Secretary-General in September 1984.

The Joint Inspection Unit (JIU) presented 15 reports, most of which evaluated specific United Nations programmes, and the Assembly, in resolution 39/242, requested JIU to concentrate its work programme on areas of greatest importance within the system, and renewed its invitation to United Nations organs to bear in mind specific decisions on JIU recommendations for effective follow-up.

The annual report on administrative and budgetary co-ordination in the United Nations system, prepared by the Advisory Committee on Administrative and Budgetary Questions (ACABQ), focused in 1984 on budgetary practices of the specialized agencies and of the International Atomic Energy Agency (IAEA). The Assembly, in resolution 39/241, concurred with ACABQ's observations and recommendations.

Topics related to this chapter. Development policy and international economic co-operation: economic co-operation among developing countries—co-ordination in the United Nations system; rural development. Operational activities for development: interagency co-operation—programme evaluation; technical co-operation through UNDP—UNDP programme planning and execution; other technical co-operation—Department of Technical Co-operation for Development. Institutional arrangements: co-ordination in the United Nations system. United Nations financing.

Programme planning

Aspects of the programme planning and budgeting process in the United Nations Secretariat, including the medium-term plan for 1984-1989 and programme monitoring and evaluation, were the subject in 1984 of recommendations by CPC and the General Assembly.

CPC, in a report on the work of its 1984 session,[1] noted that the progress achieved in joint planning since the adoption of a 1977 Assembly resolution on the restructuring of the economic and social sectors of the United Nations system[2] had been slow but, nevertheless, satisfactory. The Committee expressed appreciation for such achievements as the cross-organizational programme analysis on human settlements (see p. 782) which would serve as a basis for joint planning. Other examples of areas where joint planning had been successful were nutrition, monitored by the Sub-Committee on Nutrition of the Administrative Committee on Co-ordination (ACC) (see p. 735), and rural development, dealt with by the ACC Task Force on Rural Development (see p. 410). CPC also pointed out that prior consultations on work programmes, particularly those which took place before programme proposals were completed, provided a useful tool for joint planning and gave it the opportunity to take into account comments made on proposed activities by organizations of the United Nations system.

Joint planning of the United Nations organizations was a subject of the ACC annual overview report for 1983-1984 and a CPC recommendation (see p. 971).

ECONOMIC AND SOCIAL COUNCIL ACTION

In section I of resolution 1984/61 A, the Economic and Social Council endorsed the conclusions and recommendations in the CPC report and emphasized the importance of the Committee's programming and co-ordination functions. The Council stressed the need for timely and full implementation of intergovernmental mandates concerning the submission of reports to CPC by the United Nations organizations, organs and bodies.

On 18 December, following the recommendation of the Fifth (Administrative and Budgetary) Committee, the General Assembly adopted without vote resolution 39/238.

Programme planning

The General Assembly,

Recalling its resolutions 32/197 of 20 December 1977, 33/118 of 19 December 1978, 34/224 of 20 December 1979, 35/9 of 3 November 1980, 36/228 of 18 December 1981, 37/234 of 21 December 1982 and 38/227 of 20 December 1983,

Having considered the report of the Committee for Programme and Co-ordination on the work of its twenty-fourth session,

Having considered the proposed revisions to the medium-term plan for the period 1984-1989 and the report of the Secretary-General on the strengthening of the capacity of the United Nations evaluation units and systems,

Having considered the report of the Secretary-General on the medium-term plan for financial, common and conference services,

Taking note of Economic and Social Council resolution 1984/61 of 26 July 1984,

Noting also the views expressed by the Main Committees of the General Assembly on the revision of various chapters of the medium-term plan,

1. *Takes note with satisfaction* of the report of the Committee for Programme and Co-ordination on the work of its twenty-fourth session;

2. *Adopts* the revisions to the medium-term plan contained in the report of the Secretary-General, as modified by the recommendations contained in chapter X, paragraphs 305 to 323, of the report of the Committee for Programme and Co-ordination and approved by the Economic and Social Council in its resolution 1984/61 A;

3. *Approves* the conclusions and other recommendations of the Committee for Programme and Co-ordination contained in chapter X of its report and the decisions of the Economic and Social Council contained in its resolution 1984/61;

4. *Endorses* the proposals by the Secretary-General in paragraphs 18 and 19 of his report on the strengthening of the capacity of the United Nations evaluation units and systems;

5. *Also endorses* the medium-term plan for financial, common and conference services and the views thereon expressed by the Advisory Committee on Administrative and Budgetary Questions.

General Assembly resolution 39/238

18 December 1984   Meeting 105   Adopted without vote

Approved by Fifth Committee (A/39/840) without vote, 14 December (meeting 51); draft by Cameroon (A/C.5/39/L.21), orally revised; agenda item 110.

Meeting numbers. GA 39th session: 5th Committee 16, 17, 29, 35, 36, 50, 51, 53, 54; plenary 105.

Explaining its position before the Committee took action, the Byelorussian SSR said while CPC had made some recommendations for rationalizing the Organization's work and improving programmes, it could have made more substantial proposals for strengthening co-ordination within the system and eliminating ineffective programmes. One of the main reasons for introducing the new system of programme planning and budgeting had been to enable managers to provide intergovernmental bodies with timely analyses of all aspects of activities and of the resources available. The system having been in place for 10 years, Member States were justified in asking the Administration to ensure that programme managers released funds for new activities by cutting out obsolete or secondary programme elements.

Indonesia and the United States voiced reservations on certain aspects of the medium-term plan.

In other action concerning programme planning, the Assembly, by decision 39/456, decided to resume its thirty-ninth session to consider a number of agenda items, including programme planning, thereby postponing action on a draft decision introduced by Cameroon[3] which would have changed "sections" to "section" in paragraph 7 *(c)* (iii) of its 1983 resolution on programme planning[4] concerning one of the guidelines for statements to be provided by the Secretary-General on programme implications of draft resolutions.

The Fifth Committee adopted on 15 December 1984 a motion by Egypt for closure of debate on the draft decision, by a recorded vote of 63 to 22, with 7 abstentions.

Speaking against the motion, the United States, which had requested the vote, said that Egypt's request to close the debate before the Committee had heard the opinion of the Legal Counsel confirmed the suspicion that what was being sought was probably not in accordance with the legal rules of the Assembly. Whether or not the wording of the 1983 resolution was a mistake, it should remain; if some were unhappy with it, they should make new proposals. The use of the singular "section" implied a substantive difference; as the decision would actually change the wording of a previous resolution, a legal opinion on it should be sought. Following adoption of the decision, the United States expressed the view that in the light of the vote, the 1983 resolution could no longer be considered to have been adopted by consensus.

Appealing to the United States not to press for a vote, Egypt said that the Committee had been assured by the Under-Secretary-General for Administration and Management that the word "sections" was a typographical error.

Given those assurances, Sweden felt that there was no need for a decision on the matter; in interpreting and applying the 1983 resolution, the Secretariat would follow the wording of the agreed text.

Italy asked whether the decision would mean that when the Secretary-General was requested to undertake specific activities within existing resources, he was limited to the resources of the relevant budget section and was prevented from using those of other sections; if that was the case, Italy would be even more strongly in favour of the decision.

Speaking as Chairman of CPC, Cameroon said the real issue was that if a resolution contained an error, it should be corrected. The substantive issues arising from the 1983 resolution could be discussed by the Assembly in 1985.

Priority setting

In accordance with recommendations for a new system of setting priorities made by CPC in 1981[5] and endorsed by the General Assembly the same year,[6] the Secretary-General submitted in February 1984 to the Assembly's Fifth Committee a report[7] on operating the new system and the experience gained with it in formulating and reviewing the medium-term plan and the programme budget. The report also provided an overview of the institutional aspects of priority setting.

The Secretary-General stated that in spite of efforts made at the Secretariat and intergovernmental levels, setting priorities in the manner envisaged proved difficult in the context of the medium-term plan for 1984-1989. However, priorities were sucessfully set in substantive areas in the proposed 1984-1985 programme budget. It was too early to draw clear conclusions about the effect of such designations on implementing the work programme proposed in the narrative of the programme budget or on the adjustment of that work programme by the incorporation of supplementary activities mandated by intergovernmental bodies.

As a consequence, the operation of the new system of setting priorities would be kept under review. For the time being, however, no changes were suggested in the concept of priority setting or in the programme planning regulations adopted by the Assembly in 1982.[8]

Following consideration of the report, CPC stated that it shared the Secretary-General's view that it was too early to draw clear conclusions concerning the effect of priority setting and that, while no changes were suggested for the time being, its operation would be kept under review. The system had not yet been fully implemented by some intergovernmental bodies and Secretariat services, and there was still no system for submitting Secretariat proposals on priorities to intergovernmental bodies. CPC therefore requested the Secretariat to ensure that the relevant Assembly resolutions on programme planning and priority setting[9] would be implemented more systematically.

ECONOMIC AND SOCIAL COUNCIL ACTION

In section III of resolution 1984/61 A, the Economic and Social Council requested the Secretary-General to redouble his efforts to ensure that in future the relevant Assembly resolutions would be implemented more systematically.

Regulations for programme planning and evaluation

In September 1984, the Secretary-General issued the complete text of regulations governing programme planning, the programme aspects of the budget, the monitoring of programme implementation and methods of evaluation,[10] as adopted by the General Assembly in 1982,[8] and the rules formulated by him for implementing those regulations. The Secretary-General had been asked by the Assembly in December 1983[4] to issue the regulations, taking into account the CPC recommendations of May of that year.[11]

Financial rules of UN

The Secretary-General, in an October 1984 report,[12] issued revisions to the United Nations Financial Rules required as a result of the restructuring of the economic and social sectors of the United Nations under a 1977 General Assembly resolution.[2] The revisions were made in the light of the new programme planning and budgeting regulations and procedures, and covered definitions, budget estimates, the form of the proposed programme budget, publication of the approved programme budget, submission of supplementary programme budget proposals, internal audit, and resolutions involving expenditures.

The Chairman of ACABQ, in an oral report before the General Assembly's Fifth Committee[13] noted that ACABQ had received the Secretary-General's report and had discussed it with the Controller on 23 October. The corrigendum to the report reflected ACABQ's suggestions with regard to a number of points which had required clarification.

GENERAL ASSEMBLY ACTION

By decision 39/456, the General Assembly suspended its thirty-ninth session until a date to be announced, when it would further consider programme planning, among other agenda items. The Fifth Committee had recommended to the Assembly on 17 December that it adopt a draft decision taking note of the revisions to the Financial Rules promulgated by the Secretary-General.

Meeting number. GA 39th session: 5th Committee 54.

Medium-term plan (1984-1989)

Experience gained in applying the new system for setting priorities in the medium-term plan for 1984-1989 was reviewed in a February 1984 report by the Secretary-General (see above).[7] He stated that as it was too early to draw conclusions about the effect of the new system on implementation of the work programme, consequently, it would be kept under review.

The medium-term plan, adopted by the General Assembly in 1982,[14] covered the entire range of United Nations activities, both global and regional. It described those activities in major programmes or chapters covering a broad sectoral area, which themselves were broken down into programmes and subprogrammes.[15] In 1983,[4] an additional chapter had been added to the original 24. In 1984, the Secretary-General submitted four more chapters, which were approved by the Assembly in its resolution 39/238 on programme planning, as were the revisions proposed by the Secretary-General to existing chapters or programmes.

Medium-term plan revisions

In a March 1984 report,[16] the Secretary-General proposed revisions to the medium-term plan, incorporating new developments and making necessary adjustments so that the plan could provide a framework for the proposed programme budgets for 1986-1987 and 1988-1989. The revisions pertained to entire programmes or individual subprogrammes and also included textual revisions. No significant revision was required in ten of the major programmes.

After reviewing the proposed revisions, CPC drew several conclusions.[1] It agreed that the revisions reflected fairly and comprehensively all new mandates having programme implications for the next biennial budgets. The 15 major programmes for which revisions had been proposed were appropriate, although there were two other major programmes where CPC thought some amendments were called for and accordingly proposed changes. CPC generally agreed on the interpretation of the new legislative mandates. It noted that some revisions were not the result of the adoption of new mandates but due to the lack of anticipated extrabudgetary resources or to a disproportionately high rate of staff vacancies in some of the regional commissions.

Turning to methodological considerations, CPC felt that the link between medium-term plan and programme budget needed careful interpretation. It pointed out that some of the proposed programme revisions stemmed from decisions that had been approved within the context of the 1984-1985 programme budget. It recognized that time constraints might necessitate such procedure, but reiterated that the medium-term plan should continue to serve as the framework for future biennial budgets.

To improve future revisions, CPC suggested that further efforts be made to identify the specific paragraphs of new legislative mandates on which the proposed revisions were based, and to apply more systematically the methodology for medium-term planning adopted by the General Assembly in 1979,[17] particularly with regard to the participation of sectoral and regional intergovernmental bodies.

CPC recommended that the Assembly adopt the proposed revisions with modifications specified by CPC for each programme and subprogramme.

ECONOMIC AND SOCIAL COUNCIL ACTION

In July 1984, the Economic and Social Council adopted without vote decision 1984/172.

Proposed revisions to the medium-term plan for the period 1984-1989

At its 48th plenary meeting, on 25 July 1984, the Council decided to endorse the conclusions and recommendations of the Committee for Programme and Co-ordination with regard to the proposed revisions to the medium-term plan for the period 1984-1989, as contained in the report of the Committee on the work of its twenty-fourth session.

Economic and Social Council decision 1984/172

Adopted without vote

Approved by Third Committee (E/1984/136) without vote, 12 July (meeting 5); oral proposal by Chairman; agenda item 21).

In section II of resolution 1984/61 A, the Council endorsed CPC conclusions and recommendations regarding the proposed revisions to the medium-term plan to incorporate the programme implications of resolutions and decisions adopted by intergovernmental organs or international conferences. The Council reiterated that the plan should continue to serve as the framework for future programme budgets. It requested the Secretary-General, when preparing future revisions, to identify the specific paragraphs of new legislative mandates on which the proposed revisions were based and to apply the methodology for medium-term planning adopted by the Assembly in 1979.[17]

GENERAL ASSEMBLY ACTION

In a note of 13 December 1984,[18] the Fifth Committee Chairman summarized replies received in response to his letters[19] of 20 November to the other Main Committees of the General Assembly asking for their views on the proposed revisions in the relevant chapters of the medium-term plan. In doing so, the Chairman followed the CPC recommendation endorsed by the Assembly in 1981,[6] that each chapter be submitted to the appropriate Main Committee before the plan as a whole was adopted by the Assembly.

The First, Special Political and Third Committees had no comments. The Second Committee, on 6 December 1984[20] recommended adoption of the revisions of the relevant chapters. The Fourth Committee Chairman stated that the attention of the Committee members had been drawn to the letter. The Sixth Committee said there were no further views it wished to express on chapter III (International justice and law) of the medium-term plan, concerning the work of the United Nations Commission on International Trade Law (UNCITRAL).[21]

Following the recommendation of the Fifth Committee, the Assembly in resolution 39/238 approved the Secretary-General's proposed revisions to the medium-term plan as modified by the CPC recommendations and approved by the Economic and Social Council.

Addenda to medium-term plan

The Secretary-General submitted to the General Assembly in 1984 an addendum to the medium-term plan for 1984-1989 on chapters 26 to 30,[22] covering financial services, personnel management services, general services and other management and technical support services, and conference and library services.

The addendum was considered ACABQ in November.[23] While agreeing that the major programmes discussed in those chapters should correspond to main organizational units, ACABQ believed nevertheless that both presentation and substance of the proposals could have been considerably refined. In its opinion, the subdivisions within each chapter corresponded too closely to the subunits of each main organizational unit; the existence of those subunits seemed to have been a major factor in deciding whether certain subprogrammes should be identified separately. Such a compartmentalized approach had resulted in some activities appearing as subprogrammes which did not warrant that designation, it stated. Furthermore, this approach did not facilitate the examination of activities that cut across organizational units, nor did it help in presenting a consolidated picture of those activities.

ACABQ believed that subsequent medium-term plans for servicing activities should be more general, and that the Secretariat should define the responsibilities and themes of each major organizational unit, analyse the related problems and outline corrective activities and strategies. It stated that the amount of detail contained in the proposals and the subdivision of programmes were excessive.

Among other observations, ACABQ noted that several of the proposed activities were listed as continuing, but some of a continuing nature were listed as activities proposed for the plan period mainly because the Secretary-General planned to enhance or reorient them. ACABQ believed that a clearer differentiation should be made between new and continuing activities, including those being reoriented or reinforced. It was also of the opinion that a more concise description of continuing activities should be incorporated into future plans.

With regard to computer and other technological innovations, to which numerous references were made throughout the Secretary-General's proposals, the Advisory Committee requested additional information on the totality of those innovations both in the plan for common services and that for conference and library services, and on the schedule for implementing them. ACABQ also commented

on each of the programmes and subprogrammes as proposed by the Secretary-General.

The Assembly, in resolution 39/238, endorsed the medium-term plan for financial, common and conference services and the views expressed by ACABQ.

Another addendum covering the programme on marine affairs and a subprogramme in the area of social development and humanitarian affairs, both adopted by the Assembly in December 1983,[4] was issued by the Secretary-General in March 1984.[24]

REFERENCES

[1]A/39/38. [2]YUN 1977, p. 438, GA res. 32/197, 20 Dec. 1977. [3]A/C.5/39/L.28. [4]YUN 1983, p. 1165, GA res. 38/227 A, 20 Dec. 1983. [5]YUN 1981, p. 1305. [6]*Ibid.*, p. 1308, GA res. 36/228 A, 18 Dec. 1981. [7]A/C.5/39/1 & Corr.1. [8]YUN 1982, p. 1430, GA res. 37/234, 21 Dec. 1982. [9]YUN 1981, p. 1308, GA res. 36/228 A, 18 Dec. 1981; YUN 1982, p. 1430, GA res. 37/234, 21 Dec. 1982; YUN 1983, p. 1165, GA res. 38/227 A, 20 Dec. 1983. [10]ST/SGB/204. [11]YUN 1983, p. 1167. [12]A/C.5/39/21 & Corr.1. [13]A/39/7 & Add.1-16, Annex. [14]YUN 1982, p. 1430, GA res. 37/234, 21 Dec. 1982. [15]*Ibid.*, p. 1433. [16]A/39/6 & Corr.1. [17]YUN 1979, p. 1200, GA res. 34/224, 20 Dec. 1979. [18]A/C.5/39/99. [19]A/C.1/39/8; A/SPC/39/L.32; A/C.2/39/13; A/C.3/39/10; A/C.4/39/L.15. [20]A/C.2/39/L.119. [21]A/C.6/39/7. [22]A/37/6/Add.2. [23]A/39/667. [24]A/37/6/Add.1.

Programme budgeting

Cross-sectional programme analysis of the 1984-1985 budget

In May 1984,[1] the Secretary-General submitted to CPC a cross-sectional programme analysis using the population programme as an example. An analysis had been requested by CPC in 1983 for its consideration in 1984 of the 1984-1985 programme budget.

Following consideration of the Secretary-General's report, CPC, at its 1984 session,[2] concluded that his analysis made it possible to grasp the way in which an activity was covered in the budget, as well as to identify gaps, shortcomings and overlappings. The Committee further concluded that cross-sectional programme analyses could usefully complement cross-organizational analyses, but that some aspects of the methodology required clarification; for example, the basis on which programmes would be chosen for analysis was not clear. CPC recommended that the Secretary-General submit on an *ad hoc* basis cross-sectional analyses of certain programmes which it would choose or which presented specific problems.

A possible linkage between in-depth evaluation and cross-organizational programme analyses was examined in a February note by the Secretary-General (see p. 1143).

Programme performance report (1982-1983)

In April 1984,[3] the Secretary-General submitted to the General Assembly a programme performance report for 1982-1983, examining departures from programmed commitments in terms of causes of reformulations, postponements, terminations and additions, and in terms of organizational units. Those results, he stated, would be utilized in preparing the 1986-1987 programme budget.

The volume of postponements and terminations was greater than expected, the primary cause for that being that the United Nations budget consisted of two very different sources of financing—the predictable regular budget and extrabudgetary resources which could only be estimated at the time of budget preparation. The mixture of funding also presented difficulties in programming and performance reporting.

The Secretary-General noted that a Central Monitoring Unit had been established under the authority of the Programme Planning and Budgeting Board (PPBB). In the year to come, the Unit would establish procedures: to reinforce monitoring capacities in individual organizations and set up a methodology for periodic performance reporting; to establish mechanisms for an independent central check of output production; and to hold consultations on significant departures from programmed commitments. In addition, the financial rules were being changed to incorporate a programme audit function into the responsibilities of the Internal Audit Division.

Upon consideration of the report, CPC recommended that steps be taken to improve the methodology of programme performance reports, especially by expanding their scope so as to include the greatest possible number of administrative units and all categories of activities and by improving the system of rating implementation. It also recommended that programme elements and outputs with more than 50 per cent financing from extrabudgetary resources be separately identified; outputs designated as highest priority have an implementation rate close to 100 per cent; urgent steps be taken to alleviate the vacancy situation in several units, which was adversely affecting programme implementation; and a review of submissions to intergovernmental bodies of integrated management instruments (the medium-term plan, programme budget, programme performance and evaluation reports) be undertaken to bring about closer harmonization.

By section IV of resolution 1984/61 A, the Economic and Social Council requested the Secretary-General to implement those recommendations when preparing the programme performance report for 1984-1985.

The General Assembly, in resolution 39/238 on programme planning, approved CPC's conclusions and recommendations.

Programme budget documentation

In April 1984,[4] the Secretary-General submitted to the General Assembly through CPC a report on preparation of proposed programme budget documentation, as requested by the Economic and Social Council in July 1983.[5] He stated that work had begun on the drafting of instructions for preparing budget submissions by heads of offices and departments; in that connection, a small task force had been established within the Secretariat. The possibility of an instruction manual was considered. It was expected that the instructions would be reviewed by PPBB and prepared for issuance by 31 May to give programme managers time to prepare budget proposals and adhere to a deadline of 31 October for submissions.

Improvement of budget submissions would expedite their review by the Office of Financial Services of the Department of Administration and Management and, where applicable, the Office for Programme Planning and Co-ordination of the Department of International Economic and Social Affairs. The central review would be streamlined to remedy shortcomings identified by the Secretary-General in 1983.[6] The preliminary analysis of submissions was to be completed by the end of December 1984; by that date, preliminary decisions would be taken by PPBB on all sections of the budget based on a review of summary sheets prepared by the Office of Financial Services or, in the case of economic and social sections, prepared jointly with the Office for Programme Planning and Co-ordination. PPBB would take final decisions starting in January 1985.

Other improvements were contemplated to facilitate the task of the central reviewing units and to expedite budget preparation. Such improvements included direct inputting of data by submitting offices with access to computer terminals and compilation during the last quarter of 1984 of all data necessary to produce a revalued base. That would require daily updating of the 1984-1985 budget formulation file to reflect action taken by the Assembly at its 1984 regular session in respect of revised estimates and statements of programme, financial and administrative implications.

Those initiatives should be viewed as part of an ongoing process of management improvement, the report concluded; solutions identified in 1983 by the Secretary-General[6] either had already been devised or were being pursued.

CPC expressed satisfaction with the Secretary-General's efforts to improve the budget preparation process and ensure timely submission of budget documentation; however, it added, there was a need for those efforts to result in substantial improvements in presenting budget proposals for 1986-1987. It suggested that the Secretariat include submission dates with each fascicle.[2]

While commenting favourably on the Secretariat's intention to prepare an instruction manual, the Committee felt that the manual should reflect the budgetary procedures established by the Assembly and other intergovernmental bodies. CPC requested the Secretary-General to ensure that the arrangements indicated in his report would be followed and that special attention would be paid to regulation 4.7 of the Regulations Governing Programme Planning, the Programme Aspects of the Budget, the Monitoring of Implementation and the Methods of Evaluation. The regulation stipulated that heads of departments and offices should submit programme proposals and budget estimates as prescribed by the Secretary-General; that PPBB review submissions and report to the Secretary-General, who would decide on programme content and resource allocation; and that work programmes submitted by programme managers to specialized intergovernmental organs contain programme elements and output specifications identical to those in the programme portion of the proposed budget. The Secretary-General would then provide CPC and ACABQ with copies of the proposed budget by the end of April of the year preceding the budgetary period.

In section VIII of resolution 1984/61 A, the Economic and Social Council requested the Secretary-General to ensure that the arrangements set out in his report would be followed. The Assembly, in resolution 39/238, approved CPC's conclusions and recommendations and the Council decision in resolution 1984/61.

REFERENCES

(1)E/AC.51/1984/CRP.1. (2)A/39/38. (3)A/39/173 & Corr.1 & Add.1. (4)E/AC.51/1984/10. (5)YUN 1983, p. 1169, ESC res. 1983/51, 28 July 1983. (6)*Ibid.*, p. 1169.

Programme evaluation

Possibilities for further action to strengthen Secretariat machinery for evaluating the efficiency and impact of United Nations programmes and activities were examined in 1984 by CPC, JIU and the General Assembly.

The text of regulations and rules governing programme planning, programme aspects of the budget, programme implementation and the methods of evaluation were issued by the Secretary-General in September 1984 (see p. 1139).

Questions related to evaluation were considered by CPC at its 1984 session in the following areas: the United Nations Development Programme-financed technical co-operation activities of the United Nations Industrial Development Organization in the field of manufactures (see p. 570); JIU report on the United Nations Department of Technical Co-operation for Development (p. 456); report on the programme and activities of the Joint United Nations Information Committee (p. 367); and a tentative timetable for intergovernmental review of in-depth and triennial evaluation studies scheduled for 1986 to 1992 (see below).

The Economic and Social Council, by decision 1984/176, took note of a 1983 JIU report on United Nations system co-operation in developing evaluation by Governments and the ACC comments thereon.[1] In September 1984, the Secretary-General reported on implementation of JIU's recommendations (see p. 433).

Strengthening of UN evaluation units

In response to a December 1983 General Assembly resolution,[2] the Secretary-General in a November 1984 report[3] reviewed the possibilities of strengthening United Nations evaluation units and systems. He stated that six units had examined their 1984-1985 staffing tables to identify posts which could be redeployed for evaluation work. The units were the Office for Programme Planning and Co-ordination of the Department of International Economic and Social Affairs; the Economic and Social Commission for Asia and the Pacific; the Economic Commission for Latin America and the Caribbean; the Economic Commission for Africa; the Centre for Human Settlements (Habitat); and the United Nations Conference on Trade and Development. They indicated that although executive heads and programme managers recognized the importance of strengthening programme evaluation, the scarcity of resources was a limiting factor.

In view of the situation, the Secretary-General said he would propose permanent solutions for strengthening the evaluation functions in those units in his proposed programme budget for 1986-1987. Meanwhile, he would try to reallocate resources for evaluation from savings in other sections of the 1984-1985 budget.

The Secretary-General's proposals were endorsed by the General Assembly in resolution 39/238.

Intergovernmental review of in-depth and triennial evaluation studies

In a February 1984 note,[4] the Secretary-General submitted a timetable for intergovernmental review of in-depth and triennial evaluation studies scheduled for 1986 to 1992, as proposed in 1983.[5] At its 1984 session, CPC recommended acceptance of the timetable.[6]

In his note, the Secretary-General also examined a possible linkage between themes of in-depth evaluation studies and of cross-organizational programme analyses, which were both ways of looking at United

Nations programmes. However, while the latter were designed to give an overview of all the activities within a programme or subject area currently under way or to be undertaken in the forthcoming budget period by agencies and organizations throughout the system, evaluation studies requested by CPC only covered activities of units and bodies within the United Nations proper. Also, an evaluation focused on completed activities or those well under way to assess their impact and aimed at improving planning, design and implementation of individual programmes; a cross-organizational analysis, on the other hand, looked at projected activities and its aim was to improve co-ordination among organizations in a given area. Based on those differences, the Secretary-General concluded, a direct linkage between both types of analyses would be unfeasible, though certain aspects could be harmonized. He suggested that the Committee approve the principle that they be designed to provide complementary information and that, to the extent possible, the data bases assembled for them be compatible.

Expressing disagreement with the Secretary-General's proposal that direct linkage between in-depth evaluation and cross-organizational analyses would be unfeasible, CPC reconfirmed its recommendation that the relationship should be complementary; that linkage should be maintained by scheduling evaluations and analyses of the same or related topics as close as practicable to each other; and that each should make use of the information generated by the other.

In view of the requirement that all programmes in the medium-term plan be reviewed within the six-year plan period, CPC recommended that other types of evaluation be considered to supplement the in-depth evaluation. In particular, the broadening of scope should be envisaged through employing the following kinds of programme review: self-evaluation by the Administration Management Service of the Department of Administration and Management; external evaluation, such as that undertaken by JIU; and evaluations undertaken by Governments.

The Assembly, in resolution 39/238, approved CPC's conclusions and recommendations.

Joint Inspection Unit

Fifteen reports, most of which evaluated specific programmes of the United Nations and the United Nations system, were submitted during 1984 by JIU.

Two of the reports covered organizational units: the Office of Secretariat Services for Economic and Social Matters[7] (see p. 990) and the International Maritime Organization.[8] Thirteen reports were studies of activities—co-operation between and management of libraries of the United Nations system (see p. 1185);[9] the International Labour Organisation (ILO) social security major pro-

gramme;[10] recruitment policy and its application in ILO;[11] publications policy and practice in the United Nations system (see p. 367);[12] reporting to the Economic and Social Council (see p. 978);[13] personnel problems in the World Food Programme (see p. 674);[14] the impact of the International Atomic Energy Agency's technical co-operation on the nuclear energy development programmes of member States;[15] common services of United Nations organizations at the Vienna international centre (see p. 1181);[16] competitive examinations in the United Nations (see p. 1154);[17] staff costs and some aspects of utilization of human and financial resources in the United Nations Secretariat (see p. 1154);[18] United Nations technical co-operation in Central America and the Caribbean (see p. 636);[19] role of the Office of the United Nations High Commissioner for Refugees in South-East Asia (circulated in 1985);[20] and drug abuse control activities in the United Nations system (see p. 955).[21]

In addition, JIU sent to the Director-General of the United Nations Educational, Scientific and Cultural Organization (UNESCO) in July a note containing the results of a management review of the Joint Nordic–UNESCO Project in Africa. The note was sent to UNESCO for action and to the other participating organizations of JIU for information.

Circulated in 1984 was a 1983 JIU report on the Office for Projects Execution of the United Nations Development Programme (UNDP) (see p. 441), transmitted to the General Assembly by the Secretary-General in February 1984.[22]

The activities of JIU from 1 July 1983 to 30 June 1984 were described in its sixteenth report to the General Assembly.[23] The rest of the year was covered in its 1984-1985 report.[24]

The work programme of JIU for 1984 was transmitted to the General Assembly by a February note of the Secretary-General.[25] In its 1984 report, JIU pointed out that its 1984 work programme included a study concerning the structure of the field representation of United Nations organs, requested by the Assembly in 1983.[26] The study would be presented to the 1985 Assembly.

The widest possible contacts continued to be maintained by JIU. Inspectors held informal meetings in January 1984 with representatives of the group of Western European and other States and the Latin American group; JIU considered those meetings useful as they enabled it to obtain a sense of how its work was viewed by Member States. In March, it arranged a three-day informal interagency evaluation meeting attended by evaluation specialists and representatives from 25 organizations; among other topics, the meeting discussed national evaluation efforts, the impact of evaluation on management decision-making and policy formulation, and built-in self-evaluation. In May, JIU met with ACABQ at

Geneva to discuss the development of several JIU reports. JIU also maintained contact with the International Civil Service Commission, the Panel of External Auditors and the management and audit services of several secretariats.

In accordance with procedures established by the General Assembly in 1977,[27] the Secretary-General provided information in a September 1984 report[28] on the status of implementation of 1983 JIU recommendations on the following matters: contribution of the United Nations system to the conservation and management of Latin American cultural and natural heritage (see p. 638); United Nations system co-operation in developing evaluation by Governments (see p. 433); activities of the United Nations Sudano-Sahelian Office (see p. 510); progress of regional programmes in the conservation of African wildlife (p. 617); UNDP field offices (see p. 453); and reports on the United Nations Department of Technical Co-operation for Development (see p. 456), the United Nations Department of International Economic and Social Affairs (see p. 990), and the United Nations Relief and Works Agency for Palestine Refugees in the Near East (see p. 337).

During a brief discussion of the JIU reports at CPC's 1984 session, several delegations expressed the view that the reports were not receiving adequate consideration by CPC.[6] The Committee decided that in future, programming aspects of JIU reports would be reviewed even without the written comments of the Secretary-General and that it would select at its organizational meeting each year the JIU reports to be examined at its regular session.

GENERAL ASSEMBLY ACTION

On 18 December, on the recommendation of the Fifth Committee, the General Assembly adopted without vote resolution 39/242.

Joint Inspection Unit
The General Assembly,

I

Annual Report

Having considered the report of the Joint Inspection Unit on its activities during the period 1 July 1983 to 30 June 1984, the work programme of the Unit for 1984 and the report of the Secretary-General on the implementation of the recommendations of the Unit,

Recalling the fundamental role of the Joint Inspection Unit in the independent investigation and evaluation of activities undertaken by organizations for efficiency of services, proper use of funds and improved management and methods to achieve greater coordination between organizations,

Recalling further its resolution 38/229 of 20 December 1983,

1. *Takes note with appreciation* of the annual report of the Joint Inspection Unit and the report of the

Secretary-General on the implementation of the recommendations of the Unit;

2. *Renews its invitation* to United Nations organs to bear in mind, when considering reports of the Joint Inspection Unit, the importance of specific, clear decisions on the recommendations contained in the Unit's reports for effective follow-up action by the Unit;

3. *Requests* the Joint Inspection Unit, when preparing its annual programme of work, to concentrate, to the greatest extent possible, on those areas which are of greatest importance and relevance within the United Nations system;

4. *Invites* the Joint Inspection Unit to include in its annual report to the General Assembly on its programme of work, the basis for the selection of each study;

5. *Requests* the Secretary-General to ensure that the reports of the Joint Inspection Unit, together with the comments of the Secretary-General thereon, are provided on a regular basis to the appropriate subsidiary organs of the General Assembly for review;

II

Publications Policy and Practice in the United Nations System

Having considered the report of the Joint Inspection Unit on publications policy and practice in the United Nations system, the related comments of the Secretary-General and the Administrative Committee on Co-ordination and the related report of the Advisory Committee on Administrative and Budgetary Questions,

1. *Concurs* with the recommendations and observations of the Advisory Committee on Administrative and Budgetary Questions contained in its report;

2. *Requests* the Secretary-General to implement these recommendations accordingly;

III

Co-operation between and Management of Libraries of the United Nations System

Having considered the report of the Joint Inspection Unit on co-operation between and management of libraries of the United Nations system, the related comments of the Secretary-General and the Administrative Committee on Co-ordination and the related report of the Advisory Committee on Administrative and Budgetary Questions,

Taking into account the views expressed during the debate in the Fifth Committee,

1. *Concurs* with the recommendations and observations of the Advisory Committee on Administrative and Budgetary Questions contained in its report;

2. *Requests* the Secretary-General to implement these recommendations accordingly;

IV

Common Services of United Nations Organizations at the Vienna International Centre

Having considered the report of the Joint Inspection Unit on common services of United Nations organizations at the Vienna International Centre, the related comments of the Secretary-General and the related report of the Advisory Committee on Administrative and Budgetary Questions,

1. *Concurs* with the recommendations and observations of the Advisory Committee on Administrative and Budgetary Questions contained in its report;

2. *Requests* the Secretary-General to submit to the General Assembly at its fortieth session a further report setting out his proposals to give effect to those recommendations.

General Assembly resolution 39/242

18 December 1984   Meeting 105   Adopted without vote

Approved by Fifth Committee (A/39/843) without vote, 15 December (meeting 53);
draft by Bahamas (A/C.5/39/L.25, also relating to agenda item 112), orally revised;
agenda item 113.
Meeting numbers. GA 39th session: 5th Committee 26, 31, 35, 38, 44, 53; plenary 105.

REFERENCES

[1]YUN 1983, p. 453. [2]YUN 1983, p. 1165, GA res. 38/227 A, 20 Dec. 1983. [3]A/C.5/39/45 & Corr.1. [4]E/AC.51/1984/2. [5]YUN 1983, p. 1171. [6]A/39/38. [7]A/39/94-E/1984/60. [8]JIU/REP/84/4. [9]A/39/299. [10]JIU/REP/84/2. [11]JIU/REP/84/3. [12]A/39/239. [13]A/39/281-E/1984/81 & Add.1. [14]JIU/REP/1984/8. [15]JIU/REP/1984/9. [16]A/39/520. [17]A/39/483. [18]A/39/522 & Corr.1. [19]E/1985/3. [20]A/40/135. [21]A/39/646. [22]A/39/80 & Add.1. [23]A/39/34. [24]A/40/34. [25]A/39/87. [26]YUN 1983, p. 442, GA res. 38/171, 19 Dec. 1983. [27]YUN 1977, p. 1053, GA res. 32/199, 21 Dec. 1977. [28]A/39/145 & Corr.1.

Administrative and budgetary co-ordination in the UN system

In its annual report to the General Assembly on administrative and budgetary co-ordination in the United Nations system, submitted in October 1984,[1] ACABQ reviewed bugeting practices of the specialized agencies and the International Atomic Energy Agency (IAEA). Discussions covered such questions as inflation, exchange rates, categories of budget increase, personnel lapse factors and distributed costs.

While many similarities existed in the ways the agencies prepared their budgets, ACABQ observed that there were differences resulting from a variety of factors such as the size of an agency, the frequency with which its legislative body met, and the nature of its programme. Of prime importance, ACABQ believed, was co-ordination among the agencies with a view to harmonizing their budgeting practices. Progress had been made, particularly concerning the adoption of biennial budgeting, synchronization of budget cycles, and the development of a common budget structure, including comparable prefatory material.

GENERAL ASSEMBLY ACTION

On 18 December, on the recommendation of the Fifth Committee, the General Assembly adopted without vote resolution 39/241.

Administrative and budgetary co-ordination of the United Nations with the specialized agencies and the International Atomic Energy Agency

The General Assembly

1. *Takes note of* the report of the Advisory Committee on Administrative and Budgetary Questions on the administrative and budgetary co-ordination of the United Nations with the specialized agencies and the International Atomic Energy Agency;

2. *Concurs* with the comments and recommendations of the Advisory Committee as contained in its report;

3. *Refers* to the organizations concerned the report of the Advisory Committee as well as the comments and observations made in the course of its consideration in the Fifth Committee;

4. *Requests* the Secretary-General to refer to the executive heads of the organizations of the United Nations system, through the Administrative Committee on Co-ordination, matters arising from the report of the Advisory Committee and from the related debate in the Fifth Committee that call for their attention and necessary action;

5. *Transmits* the report of the Advisory Committee to the Board of Auditors, the Panel of External Auditors, the Committee for Programme and Co-ordination, the International Civil Service Commission and the Joint Inspection Unit for their information.

General Assembly resolution 39/241

18 December 1984   Meeting 105   Adopted without vote

Approved by Fifth Committee (A/39/842) without vote, 15 December (meeting 52);
draft by Chairman (A/C.5/39/L.30); agenda item 112.
Meeting numbers. GA 39th session: 5th Committee 33, 42-44, 46, 51-53; plenary 105.

Expenditure in relation to programmes

The seventeenth ACC report on expenditures of the United Nations system in relation to programmes was presented to the Economic and Social Council in July 1984.[2] The report was based on interorganization classification of programmes developed by ACC in consultation with individual Governments and other interested parties. In tables, it showed expenditures of regular budget and extrabudgetary funds for 1982-1983 and estimated expenditures of those funds for 1984-1985.

The Economic and Social Council took note of the report in decision 1984/176.

REFERENCES
[1]A/39/592. [2]E/1984/70.

Chapter III

United Nations officials

Staff in organizations of the United Nations system belonging to the common system of salaries and fringe benefits of the international civil service totalled 50,544 as at 31 December 1984, according to figures compiled for the inter-agency Administrative Committee on Co-ordination (ACC). This total consisted of 26,251 in the United Nations Secretariat and the balance in specialized agencies and other related intergovernmental organizations. The common system encompassed the entire United Nations system except for international financial institutions headquartered at Washington, D.C.

Of the total in the system, 21,346, or 42 per cent, were stationed at the organizations' headquarters, 20,688, or 40 per cent, were at other established offices, and 8,510, or 16 per cent, were project staff, working on technical co-operation and other operational activities in the field. By category, 18,875 were Professionals and 31,669 were in the General Service or related categories.

As in previous years, the General Assembly acted on issues affecting working conditions, salaries and benefits, guided by advice from the International Civil Service Commission (ICSC), which in turn consulted the participating intergovernmental organizations. In 1984, ICSC held its nineteenth and twentieth sessions, from 5 to 23 March in Paris, and from 5 to 27 July in New York.

By resolutions 39/27 and 39/69, the Assembly adopted a number of changes in the United Nations salary system with effect from 1 January 1985 for staff in the Professional and higher categories. It requested ICSC to re-examine, and recommend to the Assembly in 1985, a desirable margin between the net remuneration (net base salary and post adjustment) of the United Nations and that of the best-paid national civil service and its effect on the operation of the post adjustment system; and to suspend implementation of the post adjustment increase for New York, while ensuring equivalence of purchasing power at all duty stations. The Assembly also ruled on consolidation of post adjustment into net base salaries, rates of staff assessment, and separation payments.

After examining the United Nations pension system, the Assembly adopted changes in the pensionable remuneration for the Professional and higher categories and approved amendments to the Regulations of the United Nations Joint Staff Pension Fund and to its pension adjustment system, with a view to improving the Fund's actuarial balance (resolution

39/246). The action followed recommendations of the United Nations Joint Staff Pension Board, ICSC and the Advisory Committee on Administrative and Budgetary Questions (ACABQ).

By resolution 39/245 on the composition of the Secretariat, the Assembly expressed concern over the lack of progress regarding unrepresented and underrepresented Member States; the recruitment, career development and promotion of women; and the achievement of a balanced and equitable geographical distribution of staff. It supported the Secretary-General's decision to designate, on a temporary basis, a Co-ordinator for the Improvement of the Status of Women in the Secretariat, and requested the Secretary-General to: review the system of competitive examinations in the United Nations, pursue work on the design and implementation of a career development system, strengthen various appeals machinery and examine the feasibility of setting up an office of Ombudsman. The Assembly urged the Secretary-General to give priority to reporting and follow-up of cases of arrest, detention and other matters related to the safety of international civil servants (resolution 39/244).

In 1984, the United Nations Administrative Tribunal delivered 21 judgements with respect to claims arising under labour contracts. The Assembly decided to defer consideration, until 1985, of the feasibility of establishing a single administrative tribunal for the entire common system (decision 39/450), and conditions of service and compensation for non-Secretariat officials (resolution 39/236, section V). It requested the Secretary-General to provide, in future, details on all exceptions to the rules on standards of accommodation for air travel (resolution 39/236, section VII) and to continue to assure maximum restraint in the travel of United Nations officials to attend Assembly sessions (section VIII).

Personnel management

In 1984, the General Assembly acted on personnel management questions based on information provided by the Secretary-General and by bodies such as ICSC, ACABQ and the Joint Inspection Unit (JIU). Written comments were submitted to the Fifth (Administrative and Budgetary) Committee by the representatives of staff in the United Nations system—the staff unions and associations of the United Nations Secretariat, the Co-ordinating Committee for Independent Staff Unions and Associations of the United Nations System (CCISUA) and the Federation of International Civil Servants' Associations (FICSA). These questions concerned management improvement, staff composition, career development, personnel policies, Staff Rules, field staff, and privileges and immunities.

The 1984 ICSC report[1] to the Assembly covered various aspects of conditions of service, including salaries, post adjustment and other benefits; human resources planning; and recruitment, promotion and training.

GENERAL ASSEMBLY ACTION

On 13 December 1984, the General Assembly, on the recommendation of the Fifth Committee, adopted without vote resolution 39/69. Specific issues raised in the resolution are discussed throughout this chapter.

United Nations common system: report of the International Civil Service Commission (chaps. IV-IX)

The General Assembly,

Having considered the remaining chapters of the report of the International Civil Service Commission,

Reaffirming that, in the exercise of its functions, the Commission shall be guided by the principle which aims at the development of a single unified international civil service through the application of common personnel standards and arrangements,

Noting the progress made by the Commission in the regulation and co-ordination of the conditions of service of the United Nations common system,

Noting also the implementation of recommendations and decisions of the Commission by the organizations of the common system, as requested in General Assembly resolutions 36/233 of 18 December 1981 and 38/232 of 20 December 1983,

I

1.   *Notes* the survey of best prevailing conditions of service for the General Service and related categories in New York conducted by the International Civil Service Commission under article 12 of its statute;

2.   *Notes also* that the Commission has approved a methodology for surveys of best prevailing conditions of service for locally recruited staff at non-headquarters duty stations which is to be applied from 1985 onwards;

3.   *Requests* the Commission to keep under review the implementation of the methodology for surveys of best prevailing conditions of service for locally recruited staff at non-headquarters duty stations and to re-examine, where necessary, the technical aspects of the methodology in the light of experience;

II

1.   *Decides* that, with effect from 1 January 1985, for all staff in the Professional and higher categories, separation payments (commutation of accrued annual leave, repatriation grant, death grant and termination indemnities) should continue to be based on the scale which has been

in effect since 1 January 1981, subject to the current adjustment procedure approved by the General Assembly and to the revised scale of staff assessment set out in annex V to the report of the International Civil Service Commission;

2.   *Requests* the Commission, in conformity with article 10 of its statute, to review the practices of the organizations of the United Nations common system as regards long service steps for staff in the Professional category, to examine ways in which uniformity on this question may be established within the common system and to report thereon to the General Assembly at its fortieth session;

III

1.   *Notes* the progress made by the International Civil Service Commission in the establishment of job classification standards;

2.   *Takes note* of the recommendations made by the Commission to the organizations of the United Nations common system on the use of selection interviews, on the role of selection mechanisms and processes and on promotion policy, and requests the Secretary-General, taking into account the views expressed by Member States, to report to the General Assembly at its forty-first session on the action taken on these recommendations in the United Nations Secretariat;

3.   *Notes* the intention of the Commission to pursue its work on the development of training policies by elaborating an approach to the evaluation of training programmes;

4.   *Requests* the Commission to report to the General Assembly at its fortieth session on the use of competitive examinations for both selection and promotion;

IV

Approves the amendments to the Staff Regulations of the United Nations, with effect from 1 January 1985, as set forth in the annex to the present resolution, to replace the present schedules of net and gross salaries, post adjustment amounts, and the scales of staff assessment.

ANNEX
Amendments to the Staff Regulations of the United Nations

Regulation 3.3

Replace paragraph *(b)* (i) by the following text:

"*(b)* (i) The assessment shall be calculated at the following rates for staff whose salary rates are set forth in paragraphs 1 and 3 of annex I to the present Regulations:

	Assessment (per cent)	
Total assessable payments (US dollars)	Staff member with a dependent spouse or a dependent child	Staff member with neither a dependent spouse nor a dependent child
First $16,000 per year	14.7	19.2
Next $4,000 per year	31.0	36.0
Next $4,000 per year	34.0	39.0
Next $4,000 per year	37.0	42.0
Next $5,000 per year	39.0	44.2
Next $5,000 per year	42.0	47.2
Next $5,000 per year	44.0	49.4
Next $6,000 per year	47.0	52.1
Next $6,000 per year	50.0	55.0
Next $6,000 per year	52.0	57.0
Next $7,000 per year	53.5	58.1
Next $7,000 per year	55.0	59.4
Next $7,000 per year	56.0	60.4
Next $8,000 per year	57.0	62.1
Next $10,000 per year	59.0	64.5
Next $10,000 per year	60.5	66.5
Next $10,000 per year	62.0	68.5
Remaining assessable payments	63.5	71.0"

SALARY SCALES FOR THE PROFESSIONAL AND HIGHER CATEGORIES SHOWING ANNUAL GROSS SALARIES AND THE NET EQUIVALENTS AFTER APPLICATION OF STAFF ASSESSMENT

(in US dollars; effective 1 January 1985)

D = Rate applicable to staff members with a dependent spouse or child; S = Rate applicable to staff members with no dependent spouse or child.

Level	I	II	III	IV	V	VI	VII	VIII	IX	X	XI	XII	XIII
Under-Secretary-General (USG)													
Gross	121,046.00												
Net D	64,534.95												
Net S	58,294.47												
Assistant Secretary-General (ASG)													
Gross	107,089.00												
Net D	59,203.09												
Net S	53,865.76												
Director (D-2)													
Gross		85,671.00	88,102.00	90,606.00									
Net D		50,441.42	51,486.76	52,551.63									
Net S		46,300.21	47,221.57	48,156.28									
Principal Officer (D-1)													
Gross	69,840.00	72,044.00	74,220.00	76,440.00	78,660.00	80,843.00	82,996.00						
Net D	43,461.09	44,452.67	45,431.91	46,416.70	47,393.37	48,353.88	49,286.77						
Net S	40,042.12	40,936.75	41,820.23	42,707.33	43,586.34	44,450.80	45,282.51						
Senior Officer (P-5)													
Gross	60,816.00	62,578.00	64,298.00	65,966.00	67,655.00	69,358.00	71,084.00	72,800.00	74,528.00	76,266.00			
Net D	39,289.74	40,111.89	40,911.51	41,687.05	42,472.50	43,244.07	44,020.98	44,792.89	45,570.57	46,339.97			
Net S	36,282.94	37,023.29	37,743.81	38,442.63	39,150.38	39,846.32	40,547.27	41,243.70	41,945.34	42,638.27			
First Officer (P-4)													
Gross	47,315.00	48,833.00	50,433.00	52,033.00	53,665.00	55,216.00	56,815.00	58,416.00	60,096.00	61,825.00	63,518.00	65,151.00	
Net D	32,605.00	33,409.31	34,214.67	35,014.45	35,830.41	36,601.51	37,369.44	38,137.50	38,944.13	39,761.48	40,549.06	41,308.32	
Net S	30,274.93	31,001.84	31,727.01	32,446.81	33,181.17	33,874.73	34,562.66	35,250.72	35,973.32	36,707.55	37,417.22	38,101.37	
Second Officer (P-3)													
Gross	37,613.00	38,980.00	40,329.00	41,639.00	42,983.00	44,431.00	45,878.00	47,295.00	48,586.00	49,910.00	51,278.00	52,623.00	53,997.00
Net D	27,293.59	28,066.89	28,822.48	29,555.58	30,308.70	31,076.59	31,843.32	32,594.45	33,278.80	33,952.76	34,636.94	35,309.72	35,996.52
Net S	25,473.71	26,173.96	26,856.69	27,519.10	28,199.60	28,893.59	29,586.55	30,265.39	30,883.90	31,491.28	32,107.05	32,712.55	33,330.67
Associate Officer (P-2)													
Gross	29,815.00	30,878.00	31,930.00	32,987.00	34,105.00	35,215.00	36,336.00	37,439.00	38,575.00	39,731.00	40,868.00		
Net D	22,675.43	23,323.45	23,965.42	24,609.84	25,259.16	25,902.80	26,552.83	27,192.90	27,839.77	28,487.43	29,124.27		
Net S	21,261.03	21,853.80	22,441.05	23,030.54	23,621.68	24,207.61	24,799.37	25,382.05	25,968.74	26,553.95	27,129.38		
Assistant Officer (P-1)													
Gross	22,315.00	23,257.00	24,220.00	25,194.00	26,184.00	27,173.00	28,191.00	29,182.00	30,156.00	31,098.00			
Net D	17,935.98	18,557.38	19,186.72	19,800.49	20,423.97	21,047.12	21,684.23	22,289.18	22,883.22	23,457.56			
Net S	16,900.22	17,474.55	18,055.71	18,620.77	19,194.77	19,768.46	20,354.32	20,907.70	21,451.10	21,976.48			

Steps

SCHEDULES OF POST ADJUSTMENTS (AMOUNT PER INDEX POINT)

(in US dollars; effective 1 January 1985)

D = Rate applicable to staff members with a dependent spouse or child; S = Rate applicable to staff members with no dependent spouse or child.

(i) Additions (where cost of living is higher than at the base)

Level		I	II	III	IV	V	VI	VII	VIII	IX	X	XI	XII	XIII
Under-Secretary-General (USG)	D	532.19												
	S	480.73												
Assistant Secretary-General (ASG)	D	488.36												
	S	444.33												
Director (D-2)	D	406.81	415.70	424.52	433.32									
	S	373.72	381.57	389.35	397.08									
Principal Officer (D-1)	D	370.99	377.17	382.93	389.09	394.90	401.21	407.19						
	S	341.81	347.33	352.49	358.00	363.18	368.83	374.11						
Senior Officer (P-5)	D	341.73	346.73	351.46	356.29	361.88	366.33	371.99	377.26	382.46	387.31			
	S	315.57	320.03	324.25	328.56	333.57	337.54	342.63	347.36	352.04	356.37			
First Officer (P-4)	D	286.82	293.19	299.60	305.57	312.76	318.02	323.30	328.59	334.12	341.35	348.15	354.70	
	S	266.32	272.06	277.82	283.16	289.64	294.33	299.02	303.72	308.63	315.14	321.26	327.16	
Second Officer (P-3)	D	240.91	247.85	253.97	259.78	266.34	272.91	279.83	286.44	291.98	297.15	302.68	307.86	313.84
	S	224.85	231.13	236.65	241.88	247.81	253.74	259.99	265.97	270.97	275.61	280.57	285.21	290.59
Associate Officer (P-2)	D	200.14	206.22	211.49	217.22	222.87	228.58	234.27	239.57	245.26	250.96	256.25		
	S	187.66	193.23	198.04	203.28	208.42	213.62	218.80	223.61	228.78	233.93	238.70		
Assistant Officer (P-1)	D	159.75	165.14	170.46	175.84	181.21	186.56	192.30	196.90	201.93	206.99			
	S	150.53	155.50	160.41	165.37	170.31	175.22	180.51	184.70	189.29	193.92			

(ii) Deductions (where cost of living is lower than at the base)

Level		I	II	III	IV	V	VI	VII	VIII	IX	X	XI	XII	XIII
Under-Secretary-General (USG)	D	515.99												
	S	466.10												
Assistant Secretary-General (ASG)	D	473.62												
	S	430.92												
Director (D-2)	D	394.53	403.10	411.66	420.29									
	S	362.44	370.01	377.55	385.14									
Principal Officer (D-1)	D	347.50	355.36	363.18	371.04	378.85	386.42	393.75						
	S	320.16	327.25	334.31	341.39	348.42	355.23	361.76						
Senior Officer (P-5)	D	314.23	320.78	327.13	333.25	339.55	345.56	351.81	357.97	364.17	370.28			
	S	290.18	296.08	301.80	307.32	312.99	318.41	324.05	329.60	335.20	340.70			
First Officer (P-4)	D	260.83	267.27	273.71	280.11	286.64	292.71	298.73	304.75	311.07	317.64	324.12	330.31	
	S	242.19	248.01	253.81	259.57	265.45	270.90	276.29	281.68	287.34	293.25	299.09	304.66	
Second Officer (P-3)	D	218.35	224.53	230.57	236.44	242.46	248.60	254.74	260.75	266.22	271.62	277.09	282.47	287.96
	S	203.79	209.38	214.85	220.15	225.58	231.14	236.68	242.12	247.06	251.92	256.85	261.69	266.63
Associate Officer (P-2)	D	181.20	186.58	191.71	196.87	202.07	207.21	212.42	217.54	222.71	227.89	232.99		
	S	169.90	174.83	179.52	184.24	188.97	193.65	198.39	203.05	207.74	212.42	217.03		
Assistant Officer (P-1)	D	143.42	148.37	153.37	158.35	163.31	168.26	173.37	178.09	182.92	187.65			
	S	135.14	139.71	144.32	148.91	153.48	158.04	162.73	167.05	171.48	175.80			

Annex I to the Staff Regulations

Salary scales and related provisions

1. In paragraph 1, the salary figures for an Under-Secretary-General and an Assistant Secretary-General shall read $US 121,046 and $US 107,089, respectively.

2. Replace the tables at the end of annex I by the [tables on pgs. 1149 and 1150]:

General Assembly resolution 39/69

13 December 1984   Meeting 98   Adopted without vote

Approved by Fifth Committee (A/39/718/Add.1) without vote, 11 December (meeting 45); draft by Vice-Chairman (A/C.5/39/L.16), based on informal consultations; agenda item 117.
Meeting numbers. GA 39th session: 5th Committee 16, 17, 19, 21, 24-30, 34, 36, 37, 44, 45; plenary 98.

In related action, the Assembly requested the Secretary-General to improve the recruitment policy and procedures (resolution 39/245), and addressed staff questions of the Economic Commission for Western Africa (39/243).

Management improvement programme

Measures to achieve improved efficiency and effectiveness of the Secretariat through a management improvement programme were the focus of a December 1984 report[2] of the Secretary-General to the General Assembly. Introduced in the autumn of 1984 on the basis of June recommendations of a high-level Secretariat advisory group on administrative reform, the programme sought to minimize duplication of effort, clarify the lines of authority and responsibility, reduce administrative complexity, strengthen cost-control mechanisms, and develop the professional and managerial capability of staff members (see p. 1156). Some of the measures initiated included the establishment of a staff incentive programme, a temporary suspension of staff recruitment, and strengthening of personnel management; in addition, a number of initiatives were taken at the departmental level.

GENERAL ASSEMBLY ACTION

On 18 December 1984, on the recommendation of the Fifth Committee, the General Assembly adopted section XVI of resolution 39/236 without vote.

Management improvement programme

[The General Assembly . . .]

Takes note of the report of the Secretary-General on the management improvement programme;

General Assembly resolution 39/236, section XVI

18 December 1984   Meeting 105   Adopted without vote

Approved by Fifth Committee (A/39/839) without objection, 14 December (meeting 51); oral proposal by Chairman; agenda item 109.

International Civil Service Commission

ICSC statute

Following a December 1983 Assembly request,[3] ICSC discussed, in March 1984,[1] a proposal to amend its statute by removing a provision that required a member leaving the Commission to wait three years before working in a United Nations organization that accepted the statute. The Commission informed the Secretary-General, in his capacity as ACC Chairman, that it considered it inappropriate to express its views on an issue dealing directly with its members. With regard to the procedure envisaged in 1983[4] for amending its statute, ICSC felt that prior consultations with all of the current contracting parties would help avoid a deadlock.

In September,[5] the Secretary-General presented the results of his consultations with ICSC and the member organizations of the United Nations common system; the latter did not favour the proposed amendment, asserting that the restriction in question guaranteed ICSC members' independence and impartiality.

GENERAL ASSEMBLY ACTION

In December 1984, the General Assembly, on the recommendation of the Fifth Committee, adopted decision 39/417 without vote.

Statute of the International Civil Service Commission

At its 98th plenary meeting, on 13 December 1984, the General Assembly, on the recommendation of the Fifth Committee, took note of the report of the Secretary-General on the statute of the International Civil Service Commission.

General Assembly decision 39/417

Adopted without vote

Approved by Fifth Committee (A/39/718/Add.1) without objection, 11 December (meeting 45); oral proposal by Chairman; agenda item 117.

Revised ICSC budget estimates

Reporting on the revised estimates for the ICSC programme budget for 1984-1985 relating to an ongoing three-phase project to computerize the ICSC administrative data base,[6] the Secretary-General noted that provisions had already been made for the first phase of the project, covering the computerization of data on the daily subsistence allowance. Based on the recommendations of the ACC Consultative Committee on Administrative Questions (CCAQ), the Secretary-General requested an additional appropriation of $51,500 for the remaining two phases (post adjustment and rental subsidy, and classification of duty stations). In view of expected savings in the future resulting from computerization, ACABQ did not object to the requested appropriation.[7]

Staff composition

In a September 1984 report to the Assembly,[8] the Secretary-General presented statistical data on the composition of the United Nations Secretariat staff as at 30 June, including information on nationalities, sex and type of appointment (contract).

The staff with appointments for a year or more totalled 15,861, including 11,263 paid from the regular budget, and 4,598 from extrabudgetary resources; of the total, 3,090 held posts subject to geographical distribution, and 984 were in posts with special language requirements (mainly interpreters and translators).

The report stated that 15 out of the 158 Member States did not have their nationals represented in posts subject to geographical distribution: Albania, Bahrain, Djibouti, Gabon, Guinea-Bissau, Kuwait, Maldives, Mongolia, Papua New Guinea, Qatar, Saint Christopher and Nevis, Saint Lucia, Sao Tome and Principe, Solomon Islands, Vanuatu. The "geographical" posts excluded personnel such as those with appointments of less than one year, in the General Service and in posts with special language requirements.

Twenty-four Members, one fewer than in 1983, were underrepresented, in the sense that the number of their nationals was less than the lower limit of their desirable ranges of representation, calculated according to a formula based largely on budget contributions. During the year covered, 225 appointments had been made to geographical posts, of which 46 were of unrepresented or underrepresented Members, 138 were of those within range, and 40 were of overrepresented States. It was noted, however, that those appointments excluded those resulting from the competitive examinations held in 1983 in a number of mostly underrepresented Member States, whose successful candidates were to be appointed in 1984.

In response to Assembly resolutions of 1980[9] and 1982,[10] reaffirming the need for increased representation of developing countries in senior and policy-making posts, the Secretary-General provided two sets of information on the distribution of staff: at levels D-1 and above according to four groups of Member States, and at levels D-2 and above, by region and nationality.

In another September report,[11] the Secretary-General submitted to the Assembly a list of Secretariat staff members as of 30 June 1984. In November, the Secretariat informed the Assembly of the evolution, between 1980 and 1984, of the desirable ranges of Member States.[12]

The question of a unified personnel structure was again raised by the Secretariat staff representatives,[13] who called on the Assembly to request a feasibility study of such a structure incorporating a more uniform system of salaries and allowances, unified career development, and a more streamlined personnel administration.

GENERAL ASSEMBLY ACTION

On 18 December 1984, the General Assembly, on the recommendation of the Fifth Committee, adopted resolution 39/245 without vote. The issues raised in the resolution are discussed throughout this chapter.

Composition of the Secretariat

The General Assembly,

I

Recalling its previous resolutions on personnel policy and in particular resolutions 33/143 of 20 December 1978, 35/210 of 17 December 1980, 37/235 of 21 December 1982 and 38/231 of 20 December 1983,

Bearing in mind Article 101, paragraph 3, of the Charter of the United Nations which states that "The paramount consideration in the employment of the staff and in the determination of the conditions of service shall be the necessity of securing the highest standards of efficiency, competence and integrity. Due regard shall be paid to the importance of recruiting the staff on as wide a geographical basis as possible",

Taking note of the reports of the Secretary-General on the composition of the Secretariat, on personnel policies and on the status of the linguistic skills of United Nations staff,

Having considered the report of the Joint Inspection Unit on competitive examinations in the United Nations and the related comments of the Secretary-General,

Concerned by the lack of progress towards meeting the goals and objectives established with respect to:

(a) The situation of unrepresented and underrepresented Member States,

(b) The recruitment, career development and promotion of women,

(c) The achievement of a balanced and equitable geographical distribution of staff throughout the Secretariat,

1. *Reaffirms* the principles embodied in its resolutions 33/143, 35/210, 37/235 and 38/231;

2. *Requests* the Secretary-General to make special efforts to pursue an active recruitment policy in order to accelerate recruitment from unrepresented Member States and to increase the number of staff recruited from underrepresented Member States and from Member States below the mid-point of their desirable ranges, to the extent possible towards their mid-point, and further to report to the General Assembly at its fortieth session on the results of these efforts to achieve a balanced and equitable geographical distribution of staff throughout the Secretariat;

3. *Requests* the Secretary-General to take all necessary measures in order to ensure that the recruitment procedures are completed with all due speed within a reasonable time frame, bearing in mind the need for the co-operation of the substantive departments and offices with the Office of Personnel Services of the Secretariat, and that all candidates are duly notified of the result of their applications;

4. *Further requests* the Secretary-General to continue to increase the representation of developing countries in senior and policy-formulating posts, while safeguarding the principle of equitable geographical distribution in accordance with the relevant resolutions of the General Assembly;

5. *Takes note* of the decision of the Secretary-General to designate, on a temporary basis, a senior official with the title of Co-ordinator for the Improvement of the Status of Women in the Secretariat of the United Nations, to review the situation of women in the Secretariat and to make proposals for its improvement, in the framework

of the report of the Secretary-General to be submitted to the General Assembly at its fortieth session, requests that the Co-ordinator function within the Office of Personnel Services, requests further that the Office of Personnel Services ensure that the Co-ordinator is provided with all necessary assistance for the effective carrying out of all tasks assigned to the Co-ordinator and notes that the Office of Personnel Services will continue to be responsible for the implementation of General Assembly directives and the Secretary-General's policies in personnel matters, for the formulation and application of personnel policy and for the recruitment and administration of all staff;

6. *Requests* the Secretary-General:

(a) To implement recommendations 1, 2 and 3 of the report of the Joint Inspection Unit to the extent possible and in such a manner that implementation will not adversely affect the flexibility of personnel policy;

(b) To ensure to the extent possible that the creation of new posts in budgets include a reasonable proportion of P-1 and P-2 posts;

(c) To conduct an overall review of the system of competitive examinations in the United Nations, including the consequences of the proposed expansion of the competitive examinations to the P-3 level and, taking into account the recommendations of the report of the Joint Inspection Unit on the subject, to submit his views in this regard to the General Assembly at its fortieth session;

(d) To pursue his work programme on the design and implementation of a career development system, taking into account staff serving on different types of contracts, and to report thereon to the General Assembly at its fortieth session;

(e) To strengthen the various appeals machinery, with a view to eliminating the backlog of cases;

(f) To report to the General Assembly at its fortieth session on the feasibility of establishing an office of Ombudsman;

(g) To implement recommendation 7 of the Joint Inspection Unit with a view to facilitating an in-depth consideration of the matter of appointment of staff in the General Service category by the General Assembly at its fortieth session;

(h) To study ways and means of applying the population factor and to report to the General Assembly at its fortieth session, taking into account the views expressed by Member States at its thirty-ninth session;

7. *Reiterates its request* to the Secretary-General to strengthen the role and emphasize the authority of the Office of Personnel Services in recruitment and other personnel matters throughout the Secretariat and to report to the General Assembly at its fortieth session on measures taken to this effect;

8. *Invites* legislative bodies of all organizations of the United Nations system to examine as soon as possible the situation with regard to the implementation of the principle of equitable geographical distribution in their respective secretariats and to take measures, where appropriate, with the aim of securing its implementation throughout the system, within the framework of Article 101, paragraph 3, of the Charter of the United Nations and the relevant provisions of the constitutional instruments of the other organizations;

II

Recalling its decision with respect to the education grant referred to in section III, paragraph 3 *(a)*, of its resolution 38/232 of 20 December 1983,

Taking note of the report of the Secretary-General on amendments to the Staff Regulations of the United Nations,

Approves the amendments to the Staff Regulations of the United Nations with effect from 1 January 1984, as set forth in the annex to the present resolution, to give effect to its decision with respect to the education grant.

ANNEX
Amendments to the Staff Regulations of the United Nations
Regulation 3.2
In the first paragraph, replace the third sentence by the following text:
"The amount of the grant per scholastic year for each child shall be 75 per cent of the first $6,000 of admissible educational expenses, up to a maximum grant of $4,500."
In the third paragraph, replace the second sentence by the following text:
"The amount of this grant per year for each disabled child shall be equal to 100 per cent of the educational expenses actually incurred, up to a maximum of $6,000."

General Assembly resolution 39/245

18 December 1984   Meeting 105   Adopted without vote

Approved by Fifth Committee (A/39/845) without vote, 17 December (meeting 54); draft by Chairman (A/C.5/39/L.32 & Corr.1), orally revised and orally amended by Morocco; agenda item 116 *(a)* and *(c)*.

Meeting numbers. GA 39th session: 5th Committee 14, 15, 17-30, 38, 40, 42, 44, 46, 48, 49, 53-55; plenary 105.

The United Kingdom and the United States expressed concern about the Committee's preoccupation with geographical distribution, at the expense of efficiency and competence, and hoped that the Secretary-General would be left free to fulfil his tasks in accordance with the Charter and the principles of good management. Canada, Nigeria and Pakistan also stressed the importance of applying Article 101, paragraph 3, of the Charter through a balanced recruitment of staff. Egypt and Spain added that balance should be struck between competence and geographical distribution. Bangladesh and China hoped that paragraph 6 *(h)* would be implemented in the context of section II of Assembly resolution 35/210 of 1980. India shared the views of China and Pakistan, and Kuwait hoped serious attention would be paid to section I, paragraph 2.

Spain and the United States regretted the deletion from paragraph 6 *(e)*, as a result of Morocco's oral amendment, of reference to the conciliation and mediation functions of the appeals machinery.

In other action, the Assembly requested ICSC to report in 1985 on the use of competitive examinations for staff selection/promotion (resolution 39/69, section III), and adopted a recommendation of the Committee on Information to increase representation of underrepresented countries in the Department of Public Information (resolution 39/98 A, annex).

Recruitment policy

In 1984, ICSC[1] reviewed various aspects of recruitment policy selection mechanisms and recommended, among other things: the use of formal examinations, to be further standardized on an inter-agency basis, in recruiting personnel for language-related posts; standardizing examinations for several other categories of personnel; and improving the testing of Professional staff for language proficiency. It requested the United Nations to present in 1985 an evaluation of the effectiveness of competitive examinations in selecting junior professionals, as well as in promoting the staff in the General Service to the Professional category (see p. 1156).

In a September report on personnel policies,[14] submitted in response to 1982[10] and 1983[15] Assembly resolutions, the Secretary-General described action taken to meet the 1983-1984 recruitment targets, including efforts, as a temporary measure, to earmark 40 per cent of all posts at the P-3 and higher levels for the nationals of inadequately represented countries. He also discussed the scope and results of external competitive examinations held in 1982 and 1983; reported that six Member States were participating in such examinations in 1984; and described the difficulties involved, such as the decreasing availability of vacancies at the P-1/P-2 levels for the placement of successful candidates. The Secretary-General stressed that eliminating imbalances in geographical distribution required special additional measures, such as widening the use of competitive examinations and extending that system, on a trial basis, to posts at the P-3 level.

In recommending the use of external national competitive examinations for recruitment at P-1/P-2 levels and extending it in a modified form for the P-3 level, JIU in September[16] proposed procedures for preparing a list of successful candidates, emphasized the need to re-establish a normal pyramid of Professional grades through creation of a substantial proportion of P-1/P-2 posts, and suggested the possibility of extending the examination system to several United Nations programmes and agencies.

Commenting on the JIU recommendations, the Secretary-General[17] discussed some problems in their implementation as well as measures envisaged or taken to improve the recruitment procedures.

In another September report,[18] JIU concluded that the Secretariat currently had sufficient human resources; it recommended that within the next two budget periods there should be neither establishment of new posts nor transfer of staff from extrabudgetary to budgetary financing, and that the Assembly should consider redeploying existing staff by eliminating ineffective activities and examining staff requirements. In its comments on the report, ACC[19] noted with concern that the JIU attempt to consider the substance of ICSC-recommended personnel policies could undermine the Commission's authority and create a confusion of responsibilities with regard to the United Nations common sys-

tem. The Secretary-General[20] refuted as baseless the assertions regarding the so-called persisting inefficiency of the Secretariat. (See also p. 1159.) In his annual report on the work of the Organization (p. 3), he said he had directed that there should be a temporary suspension of recruitment; by an administrative instruction issued in September, he announced a six-month suspension of external recruitment to posts found vacant on or after 14 September 1984, as an initial step in effecting management improvement and cost reduction throughout the Secretariat.

The staff representatives[13] were of the view that long-range planning—involving greater co-ordination among Member States, recruitment officers, examination and public information specialists—was needed in recruiting qualified candidates from unrepresented and underrepresented countries.

Status of women in the Secretariat

Pursuant to a December 1983 Assembly request,[15] the Secretary-General reported, in September 1984,[8] that the percentage of female staff against the total Secretariat staff in geographical posts had risen in the year ended 30 June 1984 from 22.3 to 22.6 per cent; a comparison of the number of female staff in geographical and language posts in 1974 and in 1984 showed the percentage increase from 16 to 22.6 for the former category and from 31.4 to 33.6 for the latter. He stated in another report[14] that, despite reminders to Member States of the Secretariat's interest in identifying women candidates, only 10 per cent of those nominated by Governments for the candidates roster had been women. In the course of the year, major women's and other professional organizations were contacted for assistance in identifying women candidates.

In December,[21] the Secretary-General informed the Fifth Committee of the details concerning the appointment at the Assistant Secretary-General level, on an experimental basis beginning in early 1985 for a period not exceeding one year, of a Co-ordinator for the Improvement of the Status of Women in the Secretariat of the United Nations. The Co-ordinator—whose post, supporting staff and travel were to be financed out of savings in 1985—was entrusted to review the situation, in consultation with the Assistant Secretary-General for Personnel Services, and prepare a comprehensive plan of action with specific strategies to improve the status of women in the Secretariat.

The General Assembly, in resolution 39/245, took note of the Secretary-General's designation of the Co-ordinator and requested the Office of Personnel Services to assist him.

The Secretariat staff representatives,[13] recalling a 1978 Assembly resolution[22] setting at 25 per cent the target for the proportion of women holding geographical posts in 1982, stated that 75 per cent of women in those posts were at the junior levels (P-1 to P-3), the same percentage distribution as in 1974; that only 16 per cent of Professionals recruited were women; that only 6 out of the 103 staff members recruited above the P-3 level in the year ending in June 1984 were women; and that the current recruitment policy was inadequate to correct the imbalance. The staff representatives hoped that the appointment of a Co-ordinator with a sufficiently broad mandate could help bring about a significant improvement.

ECONOMIC AND SOCIAL COUNCIL ACTION

On 24 May 1984, the Economic and Social Council, on the recommendation of its Second (Social) Committee, adopted resolution 1984/11 without vote.

Equal opportunity for women employed in the United Nations system

The Economic and Social Council,

Bearing in mind the long-standing commitment of the United Nations to the equal rights of women and men as expressed in the Preamble to the Charter of the United Nations and in the Convention on the Elimination of All Forms of Discrimination against Women and, in particular, Article 8 of the Charter of the United Nations on the eligibility of men and women to participate in any capacity and under conditions of equality in the work of the Organization,

Concerned by the lack of progress towards increasing the proportion of women in the Secretariat, in particular the failure to reach by 1982 the target of 25 per cent of the total number of women in posts subject to geographical distribution which was set by the General Assembly in section III of resolution 33/143 of 20 December 1978,

Keeping in mind that the 25 per cent target should not be viewed as a limit on the number of women employed, and paying particular attention to those areas of the United Nations system where compliance with General Assembly resolution 33/143 has lagged,

Reaffirming section III of General Assembly resolution 33/143, section V of Assembly resolution 35/210 of 17 December 1980 and Assembly resolutions 37/235 B of 21 December 1982 and 38/231 of 20 December 1983, as well as resolution 24 of the World Conference of the United Nations Decade for Women: Equality, Development and Peace, in which the Conference, *inter alia*, called upon the Secretary-General and the heads of the specialized agencies and other United Nations bodies to end all forms of discrimination based upon sex in the recruitment, promotion and training of women and to increase the proportion of women employed, particularly at the senior levels,

1. *Requests* the Secretary-General to implement the relevant recommendations of the General Assembly and the Joint Inspection Unit and, in particular, to promote the recruitment and hiring of women in Secretariat Professional posts at middle and high levels, whether as permanent, temporary or fixed-term appointees, or as experts or consultants;

2. *Calls upon* Member States to include the names of qualified women in lists of candidates nominated for appointment to advertised United Nations posts;

3. *Requests* the Commission on the Status of Women to consider at its thirty-first session strategies for the achievement of equal employment opportunities for women in the United Nations system on the basis of the reports prepared by the Joint Inspection Unit on the status of women in the Professional category and above and of any other relevant reports;

4. *Requests* the Secretary-General to invite, through the Administrative Committee on Co-ordination, organizations within the United Nations system to provide information to the Commission on the Status of Women at its thirty-first session on measures taken and results achieved in pursuit of equal opportunity for women within their organizations.

Economic and Social Council resolution 1984/11

24 May 1984   Meeting 19   Adopted without vote

Approved by Second Committee (E/1984/93) without vote, 10 May (meeting 9); draft by Commission on women (E/1984/15), orally corrected by Secretariat; agenda item 12.

Also on 24 May, and on the Second Committee's recommendation, the Council adopted resolution 1984/12 without vote.

Concerns of women within the United Nations system

The Economic and Social Council,

Recalling the terms of reference of the Commission on the Status of Women set forth in Economic and Social Council resolution 48(IV) of 29 March 1947,

Noting that, in the programme budget for the biennium 1984-1985, women are listed as only one of several specific population groups that are disadvantaged,

Reaffirming the central but not exclusive role of the Commission on the Status of Women within the United Nations in considering matters relating to the achievement of the objectives of the United Nations Decade for Women: Equality, Development and Peace,

Reaffirming that within the United Nations system the Branch for the Advancement of Women of the Centre for Social Development and Humanitarian Affairs of the Department of International Economic and Social Affairs of the Secretariat remains the focal point for co-ordination, consultation, promotion and advice on matters relevant to women,

Recognizing that planning for, as well as monitoring of, efforts is essential to advancing the status of women within the United Nations system,

Recognizing also the efforts made by the specialized agencies to integrate women into their ongoing programmes, especially into the establishment of cross-sectoral mechanisms,

Concerned about the need to strengthen and go beyond the present integrated reporting system,

Deeply concerned that international efforts on behalf of women should keep pace with the heightened national efforts to concentrate on more effective national machineries and resources to ensure the integration of women into all stages of planning, monitoring and development activities,

1. *Requests* the Secretary-General to examine the ways in which the needs and concerns of women can be integrated into all planning and programme activities of the United Nations system and the implications of so doing, and to report the findings of such an examination to the Commission on the Status of Women at its thirty-first session;

2. *Also requests* the Secretary-General to provide in the programme budget for the biennium 1986-1987 and the revised medium-term plan for the period 1984-1989 for a special financial component, within existing over-all budgetary resources, that will reflect the need for on-going analysis of the impact of programmes on the advancement of women;

3. *Recommends* the General Assembly to request the specialized agencies to ensure continued co-operation and co-ordination with the Commission on the Status of Women beyond the World Conference to Review and Appraise the Achievements of the United Nations Decade for Women: Equality, Development and Peace, to be held in 1985, in order to achieve the goals of the Decade;

4. *Requests* the Secretary-General to report to the Commission on the Status of Women at each session on all significant developments pertaining to the advancement of women within the United Nations system that have occurred since the previous session.

Economic and Social Council resolution 1984/12

24 May 1984   Meeting 19   Adopted without vote

Approved by Second Committee (E/1984/93) without vote, 10 May (meeting 9); draft by Commission on women (E/1984/15); agenda item 12.

In related action, the Assembly requested the Secretary-General to regularize the senior women's programme officers posts at the regional commissions (resolution 39/127) (see p. 1172).

Career development

In 1984, ICSC[1] examined the promotion policies of United Nations organizations and recommended that they: announce all vacancies open for internal advancement and give full regard to internal candidates; develop criteria for promotion to supervisory and managerial positions; and adopt procedures providing for supervisors' presence at meetings of promotion bodies. Other recommendations included the scope of "personal promotions" given in recognition of exceptional merit and situations, importance of seniority in addition to merit and competence, and a need to develop strict criteria for accelerated promotions. In all other cases, the recommended minimum time-in-grade requirements were: five years for promotions to D-1 and P-5, two years to P-2 and three years for all other levels.

With regard to the use of competitive examinations in promoting General Service staff to the Professional (G to P) category, ICSC, anticipating its examination of the issue in 1985, requested the United Nations to evaluate its experience with that selection method, and CCAQ to provide details on G-to-P promotion policies and practices. JIU[16] observed that the examinations had brought to light questions going beyond the movement from one category to another and dealing with the entire concept of a General Service staff policy. The Secretary-General[14] noted that 137 staff had been promoted through the four examinations since 1979, and that the fifth G-to-P examination was to be completed in September 1984.

The Secretary-General reported in October[23] on his efforts to establish a comprehensive career development system for all categories of Secretariat staff, aimed at the rational use and training of human resources for the efficient functioning of the Organization. The system envisaged the use of computerized inventories of skills, and covered, among other things, career paths, performance evaluation, assignment and promotion, mobility and rotation, counselling and training, and dissemination of information on vacancies and career opportunities. A task force had been set up in the Office of Personnel Services in 1984, and the system was expected to become operational in two years. The Secretary-General stated that should the Assembly approve his proposals, additional appropriations of $302,800 would be required for 1985. ACABQ[24] agreed to that amount, pending a review of resource requirements in the 1986-1987 proposed programme budget.

The Secretariat staff representatives[13] urged the Fifth Committee to endorse the Secretary-General's proposal, calling it an important first step in modernizing and rationalizing personnel management.

Other aspects of career development, including occupational and language training (see p. 1157), were discussed in a September report of the Secretary-General on personnel policies.[14]

The staff representatives[13] expressed concern at the declining availability of junior Professional posts for promotion, a trend which could severely curtail the career prospects of General Service staff; they also felt that a career development plan should address the particular needs of the General Service and field staff. CCISUA[25] also called for a common career development system for all categories.

In December, the General Assembly requested the Secretary-General to report on the action taken on various aspects of promotion and selection policies and practices (resolution 39/69, section III), and on the design and implementation of a career development system (resolution 39/245, section I).

Job classification

Continuing its effort to develop job classification standards for various occupational groups throughout the international civil service, ICSC considered in 1984 progress made in applying a three-tiered system of job classification standards, which it had formulated in 1980.[26] After assessing the application to project posts of the system's Tier I, or the Master Standard, ICSC requested that a supplement be presented in 1985, when it would promulgate the Tier II grade-level standard, retaining the P-1 level, for financial management specialists, and urged the organizations to develop jointly the relevant quantitative indicators for its consideration that year.

With regard to classification standards for the General Service and related categories at Vienna,

Austria, and Addis Ababa, Ethiopia, ICSC welcomed the initiative taken by the organizations with established offices at Vienna to start consultations developing common classification standards before the 1986 salary survey, and requested information on the Joint Committee on Job Classification established at that duty station; it heard an oral report by a similar Joint Committee at Addis Ababa on its plans to begin the job-description process.

In its comments, CCISUA[25] stressed that, as progress on job classification proceeded, the need for a system-wide approach to human resources development became more essential.

In December, the General Assembly noted the progress made by ICSC in establishing job classification standards (resolution 39/69, section III).

Training

Affirming that management should determine staff training needs in the context of human resources planning, ICSC[1] requested the organizations of the common system to report in 1985 on their methods of identifying such needs and on the feasibility of following ICSC guidelines on the topic. It stressed that the assessment of training needs should be linked to overall organizational objectives and that the cost-effectiveness of training activities should be demonstrated. It asked for a progress report by its secretariat in 1985 on developing training policies and on the prospects of expanding inter-agency co-operation in training. The Secretariat staff representatives,[13] stressing the importance of proper training and counselling, said the Training and Examinations Service lacked the resources needed to update staff skills.

In a September report on the linguistic skills of United Nations staff,[27] submitted in response to a December 1983 Assembly request,[28] the Secretary-General noted that the financial and other incentives as currently offered to encourage the broader use of the official languages had not fully met their objectives; an analysis of alternative incentives revealed disadvantages, thus providing no justification for changing the current system.

Staff representation

In his September report on personnel questions,[14] the Secretary-General stated that the Staff-Management Co-ordination Committee (SMCC) had drafted administrative instructions on the establishment of panels on discrimination and other grievances and on outside activities, and that, on its recommendation, privileged confidential files at Headquarters and elsewhere had been abolished. SMCC also participated in the discussions on various questions of human resources planning and development.

In the view of the staff representatives,[13] however, a series of problems in staff-management

relations pointed to the need for stronger Assembly action to ensure full implementation of the Staff Rules and Regulations and to prevent possible abuses of administrative authority resulting from the decentralization of functions.

Field staff

In March 1984, ICSC[1] considered a report of its tripartite Working Group on the Classification of Duty Stations according to Conditions of Life and Work, composed of representatives of the Commission, CCAQ and staff. The Commission made recommendations on matters including travel and shipping entitlements, and the 18-month home leave provision, and decided to establish two levels of financial incentives to become effective, respectively, on 1 July 1984 and 1 January 1985, and to review them every three years. With regard to duty stations with prevailing hazardous conditions, ICSC authorized its Chairman to take exceptional measures such as temporary reclassification of their status and provision of additional entitlements. In July, ICSC commenced a study of salary and allowances and other conditions of work of the Field Service category.

In their written comments, the Secretariat staff representatives[13] stated that it had become increasingly difficult to attract and maintain qualified field staff because of limited promotion and career development opportunities, both during field assignment and upon returning to Headquarters. They felt that greater attention should be paid to health facilities, and suggested the establishment of a Secretariat-wide revolving fund to facilitate the provision of housing in difficult duty stations and of an educational assistance programme for the children of locally recruited staff. CCISUA[25] urged ICSC to undertake a more detailed and long-range study, with emphasis on staff serving far from designated duty stations and on the provision of housing.

In December, the General Assembly requested ICSC to keep under review its methodology for surveys of best prevailing conditions of service for locally recruited staff at non-headquarters duty stations (resolution 39/69, section I).

Staff rules of the United Nations

In August 1984, the Secretary-General submitted an annual report containing the full text of provisional staff rules, and amendments[29] made to them since the previous report in 1983.[30] The changes concerned, among other things, salaries and related allowances (see p. 1162), appointment and promotion, special and home leave, travel and removal expenses, and the composition of the Joint Disciplinary Committee.

In a September addendum to his report,[31] the Secretary-General reviewed, in response to a December 1983 Assembly request,[32] amendments to two rules concerning staff/management relations, as proposed in 1983 by the USSR.[30] The Secretary-General said he intended to maintain the text of staff rule 108.1, subparagraph *(d)*, which granted staff representatives the right to participate in an advisory capacity in resolving issues of personnel policies; the USSR had proposed deleting from it the phrase "and other personnel policies", which it felt could be interpreted as giving staff representatives powers that ran counter to the Secretary-General's role as chief administrative officer. Regarding the proposal to delete subparagraph 108.2 *(c)*, the Secretary-General said he intended to amend the text by deleting the phrase "if made with the concurrence of the staff representatives," so as to avoid the misleading impression that he required their concurrence in issuing instructions or directives.

In order to reflect in the Staff Regulations the provisions of a December 1983 Assembly resolution[28] concerning the education grant for eligible staff members and the reimbursement rate for disabled children, the Secretary-General[33] proposed to make corresponding amendments to regulation 3.2 and consequential amendments to the Staff Rules (see p. 1162).

GENERAL ASSEMBLY ACTION

In December 1984, the General Assembly, on the recommendation of the Fifth Committee, adopted decision 39/451 without vote.

Amendments to the Staff Rules

At its 105th plenary meeting, on 18 December 1984, the General Assembly, on the recommendation of the Fifth Committee, took note of the reports of the Secretary-General on the amendments to the Staff Rules.

General Assembly decision 39/451

Adopted without vote

Approved by Fifth Committee (A/39/845) without vote, 17 December (meeting 55); oral proposal by Chairman; agenda item 116 *(c)*.
Meeting numbers. GA 39th session: 5th Committee 14, 15, 17-30, 38, 40, 42, 44, 46, 48, 49, 53-55; plenary 105.

Privileges and immunities of the international civil service

In October 1984, the Secretary-General submitted his annual report,[34] on behalf of ACC, on measures to safeguard staff security and encourage respect for the privileges and immunities of United Nations officials. He stated that 84 cases of arrest and detention of officials in 28 countries or territories had been reported during the year ended 31 August 1984. In all but 10 of those new cases, either the organizations concerned were able to exercise their right of functional protection or the officials were released.

As regards long-standing cases, the Secretary-General intended to give priority in 1985 to nine cases of detention in four countries or areas. He added that a number of SMCC recommendations had been implemented and that an interdepartmental advisory committee had been established to advise him on cases which could not be resolved at the local level; a United Nations Security Co-ordinator had been designated as a focal point for the reporting of arrest and detention cases. The particulars, provided by the organizations concerned regarding the 10 new cases, were attached to the report.

In presenting information available as at 30 September on the arrests, imprisonments, disappearances and deaths of staff members, the United Nations staff representatives[13] asserted that in all instances the Governments in question had failed to inform the United Nations of the charges or to facilitate the determination of the applicability of the provisions of the Convention on the Privileges and Immunities of the United Nations.[35] The staff representatives suggested that special representatives be sent to duty stations where staff members were imprisoned, that information be updated quarterly rather than annually, and that the possibility of raising claims in the International Court of Justice might be considered. In their view, United Nations funds should not be used in countries that continued to violate the Charter. FICSA[36] suggested that the Secretary-General, as ACC Chairman, should report on how the different organizations of the common system complied with the Assembly resolutions on the subject. It requested the Assembly to urge them to provide residential protection of the staff in high-crime field duty stations.

GENERAL ASSEMBLY ACTION

On 18 December 1984, the General Assembly, on the recommendation of the Fifth Committee, adopted resolution 39/244 without vote.

Respect for the privileges and immunities of officials of the United Nations and the specialized agencies and related organizations

The General Assembly,

Recalling its resolutions 35/212 of 17 December 1980, 36/232 of 18 December 1981, 37/236 of 21 December 1982 and 38/230 of 20 December 1983,

Recalling that, under Article 105 of the Charter of the United Nations, officials of the Organization shall enjoy in the territory of each of its Member States such privileges and immunities as are necessary for the independent exercise of their functions in connection with the Organization, which is indispensable for the proper discharge of their duties,

Recalling the obligation of the staff in the conduct of their duty to observe fully the laws and regulations of Member States,

1. *Takes note with concern* of the report submitted to the General Assembly by the Secretary-General on behalf of the Administrative Committee on Co-ordination, which shows a continuing neglect of the observance of the principles related to respect for the privileges and immunities of officials of the United Nations and the specialized agencies and related organizations;

2. *Reaffirms* the above-mentioned resolutions;

3. *Welcomes* the measures already taken by the Secretary-General in furtherance of the safety and security of international civil servants, as outlined in paragraph 7 of his report;

4. *Calls upon* the Secretary-General, as chief administrative officer of the Organization, to continue personally to act as the focal point in promoting and ensuring the observance of the privileges and immunities of officials of the United Nations and the specialized agencies and related organizations by using all such means as are available to him;

5. *Urges* the Secretary-General to give priority, through the United Nations Security Co-ordinator and the other special representatives, to the reporting and prompt follow-up of cases of arrest, detention and other possible matters relating to the security of officials of the United Nations and the specialized agencies and related organizations;

6. *Calls upon* the staff of the United Nations and of the specialized agencies and related organizations to comply with the obligations arising from the Staff Regulations of the United Nations, in particular regulation 1.8, and from the equivalent provisions governing the staff of the other agencies;

7. *Requests* the Secretary-General, as Chairman of the Administrative Committee on Co-ordination, to review and appraise the measures already taken to enhance the safety and protection of international civil servants and to modify them where necessary;

8. *Invites* the Secretary-General, as Chairman of the Administrative Committee on Co-ordination, to suggest in his next annual report to the General Assembly further steps designed to alleviate the present situation.

General Assembly resolution 39/244

18 December 1984   Meeting 105   Adopted without vote

Approved by Fifth Committee (A/39/845) without vote, 15 December (meeting 53); 17-nation draft (A/C.5/39/L.24), orally revised; agenda item 116 *(b)*.

Sponsors: Australia, Bahamas, Barbados, Belgium, Canada, Denmark, Finland, Germany, Federal Republic of, Iceland, Ireland, Netherlands, New Zealand, Norway, Sierra Leone, Spain, Sweden, Tunisia.

Meeting numbers. GA 39th session: 5th Committee 14, 15, 17-30, 38, 40, 42, 44, 46, 48, 49, 53; plenary 105.

In resolution 39/99 I, the Assembly called on Israel to release the employees of the United Nations Relief and Works Agency for Palestine Refugees in the Near East.

REFERENCES

[1]A/39/30 & Corr.1,2. [2]A/C.5/39/83. [3]YUN 1983, p. 1177, GA dec. 38/451, 20 Dec. 1983. [4]*Ibid.*, p. 1178. [5]A/C.5/39/13. [6]A/C.5/39/22. [7]A/39/7/Add.4. [8]A/39/453. [9]YUN 1980, p. 1164, GA res. 35/210, 17 Dec. 1980. [10]YUN 1982, p. 1449, GA res. 37/235 A, 21 Dec. 1982. [11]A/C.5/39/L.2. [12]A/C.5/39/CRP.3. [13]A/C.5/39/23. [14]A/C.5/39/9. [15]YUN 1983, p. 1180, GA res. 38/231, 20 Dec. 1983. [16]A/39/483. [17]A/39/483/Add.1 & Add.1/Corr.1. [18]A/39/522 & Corr.1. [19]A/39/522/Add.1. [20]A/39/522/Add.2. [21]A/C.5/39/CRP.4. [22]YUN 1978, p. 988, GA res. 33/143, 20 Dec. 1978. [23]A/C.5/39/11. [24]A/39/7/Add.5. [25]A/C.5/39/27. [26]YUN 1980, p. 1169. [27]A/C.5/39/6 & Corr.1. [28]YUN 1983, p. 1175, GA res. 38/232, 20 Dec. 1983. [29]A/C.5/39/4 & Corr.1. [30]YUN 1983, p. 1184. [31]A/C.5/39/4/Add.1. [32]YUN 1983, p. 1184, GA dec. 38/450, 20 Dec. 1983. [33]A/C.5/39/2. [34]A/C.5/39/17. [35]YUN 1946-47, p. 100, GA res. 22 A (I), annex, 13 Feb. 1946. [36]A/C.5/39/18.

Staff costs

Salaries and allowances

Salaries

As in previous years, ICSC reported in 1984 on the margin between the remuneration of the United States federal civil service and that of the Professional staff of the United Nations system.[1] It based its calculations for the period from 1 October 1983 on two methodologies: the traditional one using net base salaries only, and a new one, agreed in 1983,[2] comparing all benefits except expatriate benefits. The average net remuneration of international staff was 17 per cent above that of the United States civil service, the comparator service, up from a 16.5 per cent difference for the previous 12 months. This calculation of the pay margin between the United Nations staff and that of a comparator representing the best-paying national service took into account net salaries (which correspond to after-tax salaries in national services) and post adjustment payable to United Nations staff based in New York, adjusted for the cost-of-living differential between New York and Washington, D.C.

The Commission noted factors that had influenced the margin figure. One was a 4 per cent increase in United States federal civil service gross salaries effective 1 January 1984, or three months later than the traditional date of October each year; another was the ICSC decision to correct the post adjustment index for New York. Those factors had also affected the margin based on total compensation, indicating United Nations salaries were 10.6 per cent above those of the United States civil service. In accordance with a 1983 General Assembly resolution,[3] ICSC decided that in future the margin would be calculated on the basis of total non-expatriate benefits applicable to both sides. It noted, however, that being a continuously evolving process, the new methodology would be further reviewed and refined. With regard to the level of remuneration, the Commission decided that for the time being there was no justification for any increase in the levels for the Professional and higher categories.

On the question of salary scales, ICSC recommended to the Assembly that an additional step be introduced for long service at levels P.1 to P.5, and recommended to executive heads that the same action be taken at those duty stations where the salary scales of General Service and other locally-recruited categories did not contain longevity steps. Such steps, it suggested, should be pensionable and should take effect as of 1 January 1985.

ICSC conclusions drew comments from a number of United Nations bodies and staff organizations. After assessing remuneration of Professional and higher categories, JIU recommended[4] that the Assembly should not increase salaries at its 1984 session, but should request ICSC to reconsider the question, report on the results in 1986 and develop further methodology for the compensation comparison between the United Nations and United States civil services. JIU also recommended that the Assembly request all organs dealing with the determination of salaries and post adjustment (see below) to observe strictly the Noblemaire Principle (whereby salaries in the Professional and higher categories were based on the best-paid national civil service) and relevant Assembly decisions. In its comments on the JIU conclusions, ACC proposed[5] that the part of the report dealing with remuneration be referred to ICSC, before its consideration by the Assembly, particularly because it contained errors of substance and detail. Earlier, at its extraordinary July session,[6] ACC had reiterated its 1982 recommendation[7] for an increase in the salaries of staff in the Professional and higher categories.

Concern over the ICSC conclusions regarding the basis and level of remuneration was expressed by FICSA,[8] which stated that it would ask the Commission to take up the matter again in 1985 with a view to acting on the Federation's long-standing request for a 10 per cent adjustment in Professional base salaries. FICSA also felt that ICSC's recommendation to grant one additional long-service step was not adequate and therefore it intended to request an early review of the issue. CCISUA,[9] on the other hand, informed the Fifth Committee that it had no recommendation in respect of the proper level of Professional remuneration but that it hoped to contribute some in 1985.

The Assembly, by section IV of resolution 39/69, approved amendments to the Staff Regulations, effective 1 January 1985, affecting salaries, post adjustment amounts and the scales of staff assessment.

Post adjustment

Matters relating to post adjustment were high on the agenda of ICSC's March and July sessions,[1] the latter one acting on the findings of the Commission's Advisory Committee on Post Adjustment Questions (ACPAQ), which held its ninth session at Geneva from 7 to 23 May. ICSC agreed on the need to consolidate 20 points of post adjustment into net base salary with effect from 1 January 1985 and recommended the resulting gross salary scales and amounts of post adjustment per index point to the General Assembly. It also recommended that modified rates of staff assessment for staff in the Professional and higher categories take effect from 1 January 1985. In assessing ways of eliminating all major consolidation-related costs, ICSC suggested that the Assembly once again request Member States that had not done so to exempt their nationals from income taxation so that the Taxation Equalization Fund could be abolished.

After discussing ACPAQ's recommendations pertaining to the cost-of-living surveys in major duty stations, ICSC agreed that the anomalies in the post adjustment index for New York must be corrected through a 9.6 per cent increase, bringing it to the level of 170.86. In other actions, the Commission decided that the adjusted index for New York should be used for determining post adjustment classifications of all duty stations effective 1 August 1984; approved cost-of-living relativities between New York and the other six headquarters duty stations and Washington, D.C.; noted the recommended procedure for cost-of-living surveys at field duty stations; and agreed that adjustments of four and one multiplier points to the post adjustment classifications of Geneva and Vienna, respectively, should cease to be made with effect from 1 August 1984. The overall financial implications of ICSC's decisions for the United Nations common system amounted to $2,833,800 for 1984; $6,454,600 for 1985; and $2,048,000 for 1986. The Commission also approved a number of special measures for cases of abrupt and substantial devaluation and high inflation.

In a July 1984 decision on personnel matters,[6] ACC welcomed ACPAQ's recommendation to correct the understated post adjustment index in New York and urged its immediate and full application. ACPAQ's conclusions were also endorsed by CCISUA, which urged that the relevant ICSC decision be respected.[9]

GENERAL ASSEMBLY ACTION

Acting on the recommendation of the Fifth Committee, the General Assembly adopted on 30 November resolution 39/27 without vote.

United Nations common system: report of the International Civil Service Commission (chap. III)

The General Assembly,

Having considered chapter III of the report of the International Civil Service Commission for the year 1984,

Having received the report of the Joint Inspection Unit on staff costs and some aspects of utilization of human and financial resources in the United Nations Secretariat and the comments thereon of the Administrative Committee on Co-ordination,

Noting the Commission's consideration of the basis and level of remuneration of the Professional and higher categories as requested in section II of General Assembly resolution 37/126 of 17 December 1982,

Reaffirming that the Noblemaire Principle is the basis for the determination of the level of remuneration for staff in the Professional and higher categories in New York, the base city for the post adjustment system, and in other duty stations,

Recalling that, in previous resolutions, the General Assembly took note of the levels of the margin, ranging from 9.3 per cent to 18.2 per cent, reported by the Commission between the net remuneration of the United Nations in New York and that of the comparator service, at present the United States federal civil service,

Recalling further its resolution 31/141 B of 17 December 1976, in which it decided that at any time that the Commission considered corrective action was necessary it should either recommend such action to the General Assembly or, if urgent conservatory action was necessary between sessions of the Assembly to prevent an undue widening of the margin of United Nations remuneration over that of the comparator civil service, take appropriate measures itself within the operation of the post adjustment system,

Noting with concern that the margin between the net remuneration of the United Nations and that of the comparator civil service would widen to the order of 24 per cent following the Commission's decision to increase the post adjustment index at the base city, New York, by 9.6 per cent, which decision led to an increase of one class of post adjustment in New York in August 1984 and would entail a further class in December 1984,

1. *Considers* that a margin of 24 per cent is too high in relation to past levels of the margin and, consequently, requests the International Civil Service Commission to:

(a) Re-examine, in the light of the views expressed in the Fifth Committee at the current session, what would constitute a desirable margin between the net remuneration of the United Nations in New York and that of the comparator civil service and its effect on the operation of the post adjustment system;

(b) Submit its recommendations to the General Assembly at its fortieth session on:

(i) A specific range for the net remuneration margin, together with a concise summary of the methodology applied in calculating that margin, taking into account that, on average, the margin in the past has been within a reasonable range of 15 per cent;

(ii) The technical measures which would be applied by the Commission to ensure that the post adjustment system operates within the framework of the defined margin range;

(c) Take the necessary measures to suspend implementation of the increase in post adjustment for New York envisaged for December 1984, pending receipt by the General Assembly at its fortieth session, and action thereon, of the Commission's recommendations regarding the margin and other measures referred to in subparagraphs *(a)* and *(b)* above; and take whatever related measures are required in respect of the post adjustment levels at other duty stations to ensure equivalence of purchasing power as soon as possible at all duty stations in relation to the level of net remuneration in New York;

2. *Decides* that:

(a) The International Civil Service Commission should continue to report the margins in respect of both total compensation comparisons and net remuneration comparisons of the United Nations system and the comparator civil service;

(b) In determining the total compensation margin, the Commission should consider all relevant factors in the two services including, *inter alia*, the differences in annual leave, taking into account the views expressed in the Fifth Committee;

3. *Decides* to refer to the International Civil Service Commission the report of the Joint Inspection Unit, the related comments of the Administrative Committee on Co-ordination, and the views of Member States and requests the Commission to report thereon to the General Assembly at its fortieth session;

4. *Decides* that 20 points of post adjustment shall be consolidated into the base salaries of the Professional and higher categories with effect from 1 January 1985, in conformity with the recommendation of the Commission in paragraph 137 of its report, thereby establishing the salary scales (gross and net), post adjustment schedules and scales of staff assessment set forth in annexes III, IV and V to the report of the Commission and the corrigendum thereto, and that the base of the post adjustment system shall be changed from New York at 100 as at October 1977 to New York at 100 as at December 1979;

5. *Renews* its earlier request, made in resolution 239 C (III) of 18 November 1948, to Member States that have not done so to take necessary action to exempt their nationals employed by the United Nations from national income taxation with respect to their salaries and emoluments paid to them by the United Nations, which could result in the abolition of the Tax Equalization Fund.

General Assembly resolution 39/27

30 November 1984   Meeting 81   Adopted without vote

Approved by Fifth Committee (A/39/718) without vote, 29 November (meeting 37); draft by Vice-Chairman (A/C.5/39/L.10), following informal consultations; agenda item 117.

Financial implications. ACABQ, A/39/7/Add.4; S-G, A/C.5/39/26.

Meeting numbers. GA 39th session: 5th Committee 16, 17, 19, 21, 24-30, 34, 36, 37; plenary 81.

A draft resolution[10] sponsored by the USSR and the United States was not pressed to a vote. It would have had the Assembly revoke ICSC's decision to increase the New York post adjustment index and instruct the Commission to eliminate unjustified over-payments at duty stations with a higher level of post adjustment than the results of the latest cost-of-living survey could justify.

Emoluments of top-echelon officials

The question of emoluments of top-echelon officials, last reviewed by the General Assembly in 1980,[11] was considered in 1984 by ACABQ,[12] which submitted its recommendations to the Assembly. As revised, the Secretary-General's net salary stood at $85,000 with dependants and at $74,621 without them ($163,300 gross). ACABQ also recommended that 20 points of post adjustment be consolidated into the base salaries of the Administrator of the United Nations Development Programme and the Director-General for Development and International Economic Co-operation, the resulting net salary increasing to $78,430 and $69,334, with and without dependants ($159,115 gross). With regard to pensionable remuneration of those two officials, ACABQ recommended that, should the Assembly approve the scale for the Professional and higher categories proposed by ICSC (see p. 1163), pensionable remuneration for them be established at $143,400 as of 1 January 1985. It believed that the recommendations need not give rise to additional appropriations for 1984-1985.

GENERAL ASSEMBLY ACTION

Acting on the recommendation of the Fifth Committee, the General Assembly adopted, on 18 December 1984, section XVII of resolution 39/236, without vote.

Emoluments of the Secretary-General, the Director-General for Development and International Economic Co-operation and the Administrator of the United Nations Development Programme

[The General Assembly . . .]

Having considered the report of the Advisory Committee on Administrative and Budgetary Questions on the emoluments of the Secretary-General, the Director-General for Development and International Economic Co-operation and the Administrator of the United Nations Development Programme,

1. *Concurs* with the recommendation of the Advisory Committee on Administrative and Budgetary Questions concerning the emoluments of the Secretary-General, contained in paragraph 10 of its report;

2. *Also concurs* with the recommendations of the Advisory Committee concerning the emoluments, including the level of pensionable remuneration, of the Director-General for Development and International Economic Co-operation and the Administrator of the United Nations Development Programme, contained in paragraphs 11 and 13 of its report;

3. *Approves* the amendment to the Staff Regulations of the United Nations, with effect from 1 January 1985, as set forth in the annex to the present resolution.

ANNEX
Amendment to the Staff Regulations of the United Nations

Annex 1
Salary scales and related provisions
In paragraph 1, the salary figure for the Administrator of the United Nations Development Programme and

the Director-General for Development and International Economic Co-operation shall read $US 159,115.

General Assembly resolution 39/236, section XVII

18 December 1984   Meeting 105   Adopted without vote

Approved by Fifth Committee (A/39/839) without objection, 15 December (meeting 52); draft by ACABQ (A/39/7/Add.16); agenda item 109.

Allowances

Education grant

Following a December 1983 General Assembly decision[3] to increase the maximum of the education grant payable to international civil service staff serving outside their home country, the Secretary-General proposed in March 1984[13] corresponding amendments to the Staff Regulations. He noted that the relevant provisions of the 1983 Assembly resolution had been implemented through administrative instructions, and consequential amendments would be made to the Staff Rules.

In the view of the staff representatives,[14] the current eligibility requirements for education benefits gave rise to the impression of unequal treatment. Factors such as the availability of adequate public educational facilities and the economic need of parents should be taken into account, and the category or nationality of the staff member concerned should not preclude assistance.

GENERAL ASSEMBLY ACTION

As proposed by the Secretary-General, the General Assembly, in section II of resolution 39/245, approved the amendments to the Staff Regulations to give effect, from 1 January 1984, to its 1983 decision on the education grant.[3]

Other allowances

On receiving comments from United Nations organizations and staff representatives with regard to the establishment, in 1983, of a methodology for non-resident's allowance and the granting, on a trial basis, of a rental subsidy to staff with non-resident status,[15] ICSC decided to continue the trial scheme and re-examine in 1985 the question of rental subsidy for internationally recruited staff in the General Service category. CCISUA,[9] in its comments on the problem of non-resident General Service staff, expressed the hope that ICSC would address the matter and find an equitable formula for applying the rental subsidy scheme to this group of staff. With regard to dependency allowances for General Service staff, CCISUA stressed that equalization of the children's allowance for all staff categories and the issue of educational assistance for staff not eligible for the education grant should receive priority attention.

Acting on the question of separation payments, the General Assembly decided in resolution 39/69 that commutation of accrued annual leave, repatriation grant, death grant and termination indemnities should continue to be based on the scale in effect since 1981.[16]

Pensions

During 1984, the United Nations Joint Staff Pension Fund, providing retirement, death, disability and related benefits for staff upon cessation of their services with the United Nations, increased from $3,115,548,779 to $3,500,632,266, with the number of its participants reaching 53,204. Investment income during the year amounted to $334,556,580 ($330,706,767 net). From that amount, the Fund paid $314,546,040 in benefits, including 7,571 retirement benefits amounting to $166,232,793. In addition, it paid 7,514 early and deferred retirement benefits, 2,578 widows' and widowers' benefits, 4,199 children's benefits, 477 disability benefits and 39 secondary dependants' benefits. In the course of the year, it also paid 3,596 lump-sum withdrawal and other settlements.

In considering the United Nations pension system, the General Assembly focused in 1984 on two major aspects: the Fund's actuarial situation and the pensionable remuneration for the Professional and higher categories. The Assembly acted on the basis of information and recommendations submitted by the United Nations Joint Staff Pension Board, ICSC and ACABQ.

The 21-member Pension Board, charged with administering the Fund, held its thirty-second (special) session in March in Paris and the thirty-third session in August at Vienna. In its annual report to the Assembly,[17] the Board outlined measures to improve the Fund's actuarial balance which, as at 1 January, showed a shortfall equal to 4.04 per cent of pensionable remuneration, based on the valuation as of 31 December 1982. The Board proposed an amendment to the Fund's Regulations concerning an increase in the level of pensionable remuneration for the Professional and higher categories, as of 1 October 1984, recommended by ICSC, and examined questions related to the management of its investments. It also studied the effect of marriage and its dissolution on benefits from the Fund.

Recommendations on the appropriate level of pensionable remuneration were presented by ICSC,[1] after it had examined various aspects of the problem in response to a December 1983 Assembly request.[18] Its conclusions were drawn from a comparison of United Nations and United States pensions within the framework of total compensation comparisons. In its calculations, the Commission took into account a seven-year difference between the average length of service in the United States federal civil service (27 years) and that applicable to the United Nations (20 years), and, on the other hand, a higher level for United Nations net remuneration than United States net salaries, to allow, *inter alia,* for the expatriate nature of United Nations service. Account was also taken of the mandatory age of separation in the United States federal civil service which was quantified as an additional benefit for 2.4 years of service.

ICSC concluded that the appropriate step differential for pensionable remuneration amounts would be 4.0, 3.5, 3.5, 3.0, 3.0, 3.0 and 3.0 per cent of step I for grades P-1 through D-2, respectively. It recommended to the Assembly a scale of pensionable remuneration to be implemented for staff in grades P-1 through Under-Secretary-General with effect from 1 January 1985 and proposed a scheme for applying the new scale to staff with various pensionable remuneration levels, times of appointment and other variables. The Commission drew the Assembly's attention to the fact that under the proposed method for determining pensionable remuneration amounts, the scale of staff assessment would not have any direct bearing on the level of those amounts. It also suggested that the current dual mechanism—the weighted average of post adjustments and the consumer price index— for adjusting pensionable remuneration amounts between comprehensive reviews should continue to be used with some modifications, and recommended increasing, as of 1 October 1984, the levels of pensionable remuneration for those in the Professional and higher categories.

ICSC's conclusions were reiterated in an October report of ACABQ,[19] which concurred with a number of the Pension Board's recommendations concerning: measures to improve the actuarial balance of the Fund, including increasing the interest rate used to calculate the amount of lump-sum commutation; a new unisex mortality table reflecting longer life expectancies; re-examination of early retirement provisions; imposition of a ceiling on the highest level of pensions; and a reduction of cost-of-living adjustments. ACABQ agreed with the Board that the existing survivor benefits should be not be disturbed and that the lump sum should not be paid in net equivalent terms, suggestions that had been made by the Assembly in December 1983.[18]

The United Nations pension system, particularly the question of pensionable remuneration, was the subject of two ACC actions. At its July (extraordinary) session,[6] the Committee urged the Assembly to take steps aimed at restoring the Fund's actuarial balance through an increase in the rate of combined organization/staff contributions to 24 per cent. To preserve the acquired rights of the staff, no retroactive measures reducing benefits should be taken. Pensionable remuneration had to be seen together with the benefits to be provided, and both had to be approached in terms of total compensation, which was the only sound basis for comparison with the United States federal civil service. That approach required more thorough studies, as well as harmonization in determining the level of pensionable remuneration by ICSC and the nature and level of benefits by the Fund. In a statement to the Assembly, approved at its October session,[20] ACC said the package of measures proposed by the Pension Board, if accepted in their entirety, would virtually eliminate the deficit of the Fund's actuarial balance. With regard to the scale of pensionable remuneration recommended by ICSC, ACC felt that it preserved the acquired rights and conditions of service, while taking into account the concerns of Member States. ACC also believed that the adjustment in pensionable remuneration due on 1 October 1984 should be implemented throughout the system.

FICSA, in its comments,[8] recommended that the Assembly decide to apply the 5.4 per cent adjustment to Professional pensionable remuneration due on 1 October 1984 and that ICSC pursue its studies concerning a new approach for determining that remuneration. It stressed the need to protect fully the acquired rights of serving staff and to study in depth the actuarial impact of the proposed remuneration scale. Support for the new methodology of calculating pensionable remuneration levels was also expressed by CCISUA.[9] In connection with a December 1983 Assembly decision to defer any increase in pensionable remuneration due in 1984,[18] CCISUA expressed concern over a procedure which appeared to jeopardize acquired rights. It felt that in future any such changes should be referred to the appropriate bodies for consultation, in this case the Pension Board.

GENERAL ASSEMBLY ACTION

Acting on the recommendation of the Fifth Committee, the General Assembly adopted, on 18 December, resolution 39/246 without vote.

Report of the United Nations Joint Staff Pension Board

The General Assembly,

Recalling its resolution 38/233 of 20 December 1983,

Having considered the report of the United Nations Joint Staff Pension Board for 1984 to the General Assembly and to the member organizations of the United Nations Joint Staff Pension Fund, chapter II of the report of the International Civil Service Commission and the related report of the Advisory Committee on Administrative and Budgetary Questions,

I

Actuarial situation of the United Nations Joint Staff Pension Fund

Recalling that in resolution 38/233 it indicated that a co-operative effort by member organizations, participants and beneficiaries is required if the actuarial imbalance is to be reduced or eliminated, thereby securing an adequate level of benefits under the United Nations Joint Staff Pension Fund,

Noting the proposals made by the United Nations Joint Staff Pension Board in response to the request addressed to it in section II of General Assembly resolution 38/233,

1. *Approves* the following measures which will result in an improvement of the actuarial balance of the United Nations Joint Staff Pension Fund:

(*a*) For participants taking early retirement between the ages of 55 and 60 after 25 years or more but less than 30 years of contributory service, the reduction factor shall be increased from 2 per cent for every year below age 60 to 3 per cent for service performed as from 1 January 1985;

(*b*) The periodicity of adjustment of benefits in payment for changes in the cost of living shall be reduced from twice a year to once a year, subject to the modalities set out in annex X to the report of the United Nations Joint Staff Pension Board;

(*c*) On the first occasion after 1 January 1985 when a benefit in payment is to be adjusted for a change in the cost of living, the adjustment shall be reduced by 1.5 percentage points, except as specified in paragraph 4 of the present section;

(*d*) In the case of participants to whom the two-track adjustment system is applicable, the adjusted amount of the United States dollar benefit, when converted into local currency, shall be limited to 120 per cent of the adjusted local currency benefit, subject to the transitional measures described in annex X to the report of the Pension Board;

(*e*) The periodic benefits of participants who separate from service on or after 31 December 1984 shall be paid at the end of the month to which they relate;

(*f*) Organizations' monthly contributions to the Fund should be remitted during the first two working days of the month following the month to which they relate;

(*g*) The interest rate used for the purpose of lump-sum commutation shall be raised from 4.5 to 6.5 per cent as stated in paragraph 20 of the report of the Pension Board;

2. *Defers* action on the question of changing the statutory age of separation;

3. *Amends*, with effect from 1 January 1985 and without retroactive effect, article 29 (*b*) (ii) of the Regulations of the United Nations Joint Staff Pension Fund, as set out in the annex to the present resolution;

4. *Approves*, with effect from 1 January 1985 and without retroactive effect, the changes in the system of adjusting benefits in payment, set out in annex X to the report of the United Nations Joint Staff Pension

Board, except that the one-time reduction of the cost-of-living adjustment by 1.5 percentage points shall not apply to the minimum benefits under the Regulations of the Fund and the benefits under sections E and F of the pension adjustment system;

5. *Requests* the United Nations Joint Staff Pension Board, with the assistance of the Committee of Actuaries, to review the method of calculating the lump-sum commutation of benefits using a uniform discount rate and to make recommendations thereon to the General Assembly at its fortieth session;

6. *Requests* the Pension Board to keep under review the question of the determination of the lump sum in net equivalent terms;

7. *Further requests* the Pension Board to re-examine the question of the imposition of a ceiling on the highest levels of pensions and to make recommendations thereon, and also on the imposition of a ceiling on the amount that may be paid to a participant by way of lump-sum commutation of part of his periodic benefit, to the General Assembly at its fortieth session;

8. *Requests* the Pension Board to re-examine the operation of the two-track pension adjustment system in countries where the adjusted United States dollar amount, when converted into local currency, yields a larger benefit in local currency units than the adjusted local currency amount and to report to the General Assembly at its fortieth session on further limiting the resultant excess benefits;

9. *Requests* the Pension Board, in the light of the results of the actuarial valuation of the Fund as at 31 December 1984, to consider additional measures, with a view to avoiding, if possible, further increases in the rate of contribution of member organizations and participants to the Fund, and to report thereon to the General Assembly at its fortieth session;

10. *Requests* the Pension Board to consider measures for the fair and equitable treatment of all participants, whatever their dates of entry into contributory service or of separation, and to submit such consequential amendments to the Regulations of the Fund and to the pension adjustment system as may be required;

II
Pensionable remuneration for the Professional and higher categories

Recalling section III of its resolution 38/233,

Having considered chapter II, section B, of the report of the International Civil Service Commission and section III.B of the report of the United Nations Joint Staff Pension Board,

1. *Decides* that the upward adjustment by 5.4 per cent of the scale of pensionable remuneration for the Professional and higher categories, which became due as of 1 October 1984 on the basis of article 54 (*b*) of the Regulations of the United Nations Joint Staff Pension Fund but the implementation of which had been deferred in accordance with section III, paragraph 4, of resolution 38/233, shall be implemented and shall be applicable during the three-month period from 1 October to 31 December 1984;

2. *Approves*, for implementation with effect from 1 January 1985 for all staff members in the Professional and higher categories in the member organizations of the Fund, the scale of pensionable remuneration

which was recommended by the International Civil Service Commission and which is reproduced in the appendix to the annex to the present resolution, and amends the first sentence of article 54 (*b*) of the Regulations of the Fund, as set forth in the said annex;

3. *Requests* the United Nations Joint Staff Pension Board to consider, taking into account, *inter alia*, the legal aspects of the question, any compensatory or interim measures regarding participants whose pensionable remuneration has been higher than it will be as of 1 January 1985, and to make appropriate recommendations to the General Assembly at its fortieth session, it being understood that such recommendations will also address the question of the equality of treatment of participants retiring on different dates, and that such measures as will be approved by the Assembly would, if necessary, be applicable with effect from 1 January 1985;

4. *Notes* from paragraph 53 of the report of the International Civil Service Commission that no interim adjustment of the scale is contemplated in 1985;

5. *Requests* the International Civil Service Commission, in co-operation with the United Nations Joint Staff Pension Board, to re-examine the procedure for adjustment of pensionable remuneration in between comprehensive reviews, taking into account the views expressed in the Fifth Committee, and to report thereon to the General Assembly at its fortieth session, and in the mean time suspends the operation of the adjustment procedure in article 54 (*b*) of the Regulations of the United Nations Joint Staff Pension Fund and defers until its fortieth session further consideration of the recommendation of the Pension Board regarding amendment of the said article;

6. *Requests* the International Civil Service Commission, in co-operation with the United Nations Joint Staff Pension Board, taking into account the views expressed in the Fifth Committee, to review the methodology for the determination of pensionable remuneration for the Professional and higher categories and for monitoring the level of pensionable remuneration, and to submit a report thereon to the General Assembly at its fortieth session, so that the Assembly could consider whether it would be appropriate to request the Commission to propose a new scale of pensionable remuneration to its forty-first session;

7. *Invites* all member organizations of the United Nations Joint Staff Pension Fund to take the necessary measures to implement the provisions of paragraphs 1, 2 and 5 above;

III
Non-resident's allowance

Recalling section IV, paragraph 2, of its resolution 38/232 of 20 December 1983,

Amends, with effect from 1 January 1985 and without retroactive effect, article 54 (*a*), of the Regulations of the United Nations Joint Staff Pension Fund, as set forth in the annex to the present resolution;

IV
Exclusion from participation under Article 21 (*a*) of the Regulations of the United Nations Joint Staff Pension Fund

Recalling section VI of its resolution 37/131 of 17 December 1982,

Notes that junior professional officers and associate experts who are participants in a national pension scheme may be excluded under the terms of their appointment from participation in the United Nations Joint Staff Pension Fund in accordance with the provisions of article 21 *(a)* of the Regulations of the Fund;

V
Special index for pensioners

Decides that the procedures applicable to existing pensioners as set out in section C, paragraph *(d)*, of annex X to the report of the United Nations Joint Staff Pension Board to the General Assembly at its thirty-seventh session shall be amended so that no retroactive adjustment will be made for the period between the date entitlement began and 31 December 1984, but the reduced local currency amount will become effective from 1 January 1985;

VI
Emergency Fund

Authorizes the United Nations Joint Staff Pension Board to supplement the voluntary contributions to the Emergency Fund, for a further period of one year, by an amount not exceeding $100,000;

VII
Administrative expenses

Approves expenses, chargeable directly to the United Nations Joint Staff Pension Fund, totalling $7,440,800 (net) for 1985 and additional expenses of $6,500 (net) for 1984 for the administration of the Fund;

VIII
Biennial budget

1. *Decides* that the estimates of administrative expenses of the United Nations Joint Staff Pension Fund shall be prepared on a biennial basis beginning with the biennium 1986-1987;

2. *Amends* article 15 *(b)* of the Regulations of the United Nations Joint Staff Pension Fund, without retroactive effect, as set forth in the annex to the present resolution;

IX
Composition of the United Nations Joint Staff Pension Board

Requests the United Nations Joint Staff Pension Board, taking into account the views expressed in the Fifth Committee, to review its composition and to submit recommendations thereon to the General Assembly at its fortieth session.

ANNEX
Amendments to the Regulations of the United Nations Joint Staff Pension Fund

Article 15
Administrative expenses

(a) Expenses incurred by the Board in the administration of these Regulations shall be met by the Fund.

(b) Biennial estimates of the expenses to be incurred under *(a)* above shall be submitted to the General Assembly for approval during the year immediately preceding the biennium to which the said estimates relate. Supplementary estimates may similarly be submitted in the first and/or the second year of the biennium to which the budget relates.

(c) Expenses incurred in the administration of these Regulations by a member organization shall be met by that organization.

Article 29
Early retirement benefit

(a) An early retirement benefit shall be payable to a participant whose age on separation is at least 55 but less than 60 and whose contributory service was five years or longer.

(b) The benefit shall be payable at the standard annual rate for a retirement benefit, reduced for each year or part thereof by which the age of the participant on separation was less than 60, at the rate of:

(i)   if the contributory service of the participant was 30 years or longer, 1 per cent a year, or

(ii)   if the contributory service of the participant was 25 years or longer but less than 30 years, 2 per cent a year in respect of the period of contributory service performed before 1 January 1985, and 3 per cent a year in respect of the period of such service performed as from 1 January 1985, or

(iii) if the contributory service of the participant was less than 25 years, 6 per cent a year.

(c) The benefit may be commuted by the participant into a lump sum to the extent specified in article 28 *(f)* for a retirement benefit.

Article 54
Pensionable remuneration

(a) In the case of participants in the General Service and other locally-recruited categories, pensionable remuneration shall be the equivalent in dollars of the sum of:

(i)   The participant's gross salary,

(ii)   Any language allowance payable to him, and

(iii) In the case of a participant who became entitled to a pensionable non-resident's allowance prior to 1 September 1983, and for as long as he continues to be entitled thereto, the amount of such allowance.

(b) In the case of participants in the Professional and higher categories, the pensionable remuneration effective 1 January 1985 shall be that set out in the appendix hereto.*

---

*This sentence replaces the first sentence of the existing article 54 *(b)*. The operation of the remaining provisions of that article is suspended pursuant to paragraph 5 of section II of the present resolution.

Appendix
Scale of pensionable remuneration for the Professional and higher categories
(United States dollars)

Grade						Steps							
	I	II	III	IV	V	VI	VII	VIII	IX	X	XI	XII	XIII
Under-Secretary-General (USG)	115,700												
Assistant Secretary-General (ASG)	103,900												
Director (D-2)	84,800	87,300	89,900	92,400									
Principal Officer (D-1)	74,500	76,700	79,000	81,200	83,400	85,700	87,900						
Senior Officer (P-5)	66,100	68,100	70,100	72,000	74,000	76,000	78,000	80,000	82,000	83,900			
First Officer (P-4)	53,300	54,900	56,500	58,100	59,700	61,300	62,900	64,500	66,100	67,700	69,300	70,900	
Second Officer (P-3)	43,800	45,300	46,900	48,400	49,900	51,500	53,000	54,500	56,100	57,600	59,100	60,700	62,200
Associate Officer (P-2)	35,500	36,700	38,000	39,200	40,500	41,700	43,000	44,200	45,400	46,700	47,900		
Assistant Officer (P-1)	27,500	28,600	29,700	30,000	31,900	33,000	34,100	35,200	36,300	37,400			

General Assembly resolution 39/246

18 December 1984   Meeting 105   Adopted without vote

Approved by Fifth Committee (A/39/846) without vote, 14 December (meeting 51); draft by Vice-Chairman (A/C.5/39/L.20), following informal consultations; agenda item 118.

Meeting numbers. GA 39th session: 5th Committee 19, 23, 25, 27-30, 32, 51; plenary 105.

Explaining its position, Belgium pointed out, in relation to paragraphs 5 and 6 of section II, that adjustments of benefits were not justified at the base of the system, i.e. New York, since they ought to be made in the light of comparison with the national civil service. The USSR was not entirely satisfied with the text, saying that the proposed measures would not fully eliminate the Fund's actuarial imbalance and that the pensions of Secretariat staff would continue to exceed a reasonable level under the Noblemaire Principle. It also hoped that the Pension Board would demonstrate political astuteness in implementing the text's requests relating to measures aimed at avoiding increases in the rate of contribution to the Fund and regarding the composition of the Board.

Pension Fund investments

The market value of Pension Fund investments stood at $3,727,447,000 as at 31 December 1984, compared to $3,519,891,000 a year earlier. After deduction of investment management costs of $3,849,813, net investment income during 1984 amounted to $330,706,767.

Investment return for the year ending 31 March 1984 was 13.01 per cent, according to a report of the Secretary-General on the Fund's investments, submitted to the Fifth Committee in September.[21] Over the preceding 34 years, the total book value of the portfolio had risen from $13 million to $3,167 million, a compound increase of 17.5 per cent a year. The report attributed that increase to contributions by participants and member organizations, reinvested investment income and net realized capital gains, less benefit payments and investment expenses. For the year up to 31 March, equities (stocks) provided the best total investment return at 15.7 per cent, followed by real estate at 13.3 per cent, short-term investments at 13.1 per cent and bonds at 8.7 per cent. Bonds constituted 39 per cent of the Fund's portfolio, the same as a year earlier, while equities decreased from 52 to 48 per cent.

In accordance with General Assembly requests, special emphasis was given to identifying more investment opportunities in developing countries, resulting in a 15 per cent increase in development-related investments, which reached $636 million on 30 June 1984, as compared with $554 million a year before. In Africa, for example, those investments had increased to $69.5 million from $52.6 million. The combined investments in developing countries as at 30 June represented 20.1 per cent of the total Fund.

The Pension Board, in its annual report to the Assembly,[17] noted that, as at 31 March, $1,884 million, or 55 per cent, of the Fund's long-term investments were allocated to markets outside the United States. The Fund was invested in 44 countries, including 23 developing countries. Substantial investments had been made through international and regional development institutions. For reasons of currency and geographic diversification, funds had been invested in 20 different currencies (other than the United States dollar) and in 19 equity markets, including 5 in developing countries. Noting that the inflation-adjusted rate of return over the past 24 years had been 1.5 per cent compared with the current actuarial assumption of 3 per cent, the Board did not expect that the real rate of return would exceed 3 per cent a year or that the increase in the rate would, on its own, eliminate the existing imbalance.

GENERAL ASSEMBLY ACTION

In December, acting on a recommendation of the Fifth Committee, the General Assembly adopted decision 39/452 without vote.

Investments of the United Nations Joint Staff Pension Fund

At its 105th plenary meeting, on 18 December 1984, the General Assembly, on the recommendation of the Fifth Committee, took note of the report of the Secretary-General on the investments of the United Nations Joint Staff Pension Fund.

General Assembly decision 39/452

Adopted without vote

Approved by Fifth Committee (A/39/846) without objection, 14 December (meeting 51); oral proposal by Chairman; agenda item 118.

REFERENCES

[1]A/39/30 & Corr.1,2. [2]YUN 1983, p. 1187. [3]*Ibid.*, p. 1175, GA res. 38/232, 20 Dec. 1983. [4]A/39/522 & Corr.1. [5]A/39/522/Add.1. [6]ACC/1984/DEC/13. [7]YUN 1982, p. 1472. [8]A/C.5/39/18. [9]A/C.5/39/27. [10]A/C.5/39/L.8. [11]YUN 1980, p. 1177, GA res. 35/217, sect. XVII, 17 Dec. 1980. [12]A/39/7/Add.16. [13]A/C.5/39/2. [14]A/C.5/39/23. [15]YUN 1983, p. 1189. [16]YUN 1981, p. 1342. [17]A/39/9 & Corr.1. [18]YUN 1983, p. 1190, GA res. 38/233, 20 Dec. 1983. [19]A/39/608. [20]ACC/1984/DEC/14-22 (dec. 1984/19). [21]A/C.5/39/15 & Corr.1.

UN Administrative Tribunal

Activities of the Tribunal

In 1984, the United Nations Administrative Tribunal met in annual plenary session in New York on 1 November, and held two panel sessions—2 May to 8 June (Geneva) and 8 October to 2 November (New York). As in previous years, it submitted a note to the General Assembly outlining its activities for the year.[1]

The Tribunal delivered 21 judgements during the year in cases brought by staff members against the Secretary-General or the executive heads of other organizations in the United Nations system with respect to claims arising under labour contracts of the international civil service. It also considered the question of harmonizing its statute, rules and practices with those of the ILO Administrative Tribunal (see below), the other of the two existing common system tribunals.

The Assembly's Committee on Applications for Review of Administrative Tribunal Judgements held its twenty-third and twenty-fourth sessions in New York, on 9 January and from 21 to 28 August, respectively.

Feasibility of establishing a single tribunal

Following a November 1983 Assembly request,[2] the Secretary-General submitted in September 1984 a report on the feasibility of establishing a single administrative tribunal for the entire common system.[3] He commented on the proposed reforms designed to improve and/or harmonize the proceedings of the two tribunals, covering such issues as jurisdiction, proceedings, procedures, remedies, review of judgements and co-operation between the tribunals. Annexed to the report was a set of existing texts of, and proposed revisions to, the two tribunals' statutes and rules, and a draft resolution by which the Assembly could adopt the proposed changes and accomplish a number of other reforms. The proposals had been prepared by the United Nations Secretariat with the assistance of legal advisers and comments from ILO, the International Telecommunication Union and FICSA; the decisions of the United Nations Joint Staff Pension Board were also taken into consideration.

The Board noted in its report[4] that the amendments recommended by the Secretary-General had possible bearing on appeals against its decisions, review of Tribunal judgements in Pension Fund cases, and the requesting of advisory opinions; the Board proposed to amend its Regulations to include the review procedure provided for in the Tribunal's statute.

GENERAL ASSEMBLY ACTION

In December 1984, the General Assembly, on the recommendation of the Fifth Committee, adopted decision 39/450 without vote.

Feasibility of establishing a single administrative tribunal

At its 105th plenary meeting, on 18 December 1984, the General Assembly, on the recommendation of the Fifth Committee, decided:

(a) To defer consideration of the report of the Secretary-General on the feasibility of establishing a single administrative tribunal until its fortieth session;

(b) To consider at its fortieth session how to proceed with the examination of this matter at that session.

General Assembly decision 39/450

Adopted without vote

Approved by Fifth Committee (A/39/842) without vote, 15 December (meeting 52); draft by Chairman (A/C.5/39/L.31), orally amended by USSR; agenda item 112 *(c)*. *Meeting numbers.* GA 39th session: 5th Committee 33, 42-44, 46, 51, 52; plenary 105.

Before approving the draft, the Committee agreed to an oral amendment by the USSR to delete a request for Member States comments, by 30 June 1985, to the Secretary-General's 1984 report.

Proposed office of Ombudsman

In their written comments to the Fifth Committee, the staff representatives[5] made a number of proposals aimed at reforming the current machinery for the administration of justice in the Secretariat, suggesting that an office of Ombudsman be established at Headquarters and at other duty stations; the Ombudsman, who would be solely responsible and accountable to the General Assembly, should be elected by the International Court of Justice (ICJ) from among eminent jurists, diplomats or former senior international civil servants recommended by the Joint Advisory Committee—a committee composed of representatives of the staff and of the Secretary-General to advise him on personnel policies and general questions of staff welfare.

The staff representatives also proposed that an office for the administration of justice be created within the Executive Office of the Secretary-General.

In December, the General Assembly requested the Secretary-General to strengthen the various appeals machinery, and to report in 1985 on the feasibility of establishing an office of Ombudsman (resolution 39/245).

REFERENCES

[1]A/INF/39/5. [2]YUN 1983, p. 1198, GA dec. 38/409, 25 Nov. 1983. [3]A/C.5/39/7 & Corr.1. [4]A/39/9 & Corr.1. [5]A/C.5/39/23.

Travel

In an annual report, presented in October, on the savings achieved through utilization of economy and other air fares,[1] the Secretary-General informed the General Assembly that an estimated $449,000 had been saved during the year ended 30 June 1984, as a result of cost-saving measures taken in pursuance of a 1977 Assembly decision[2] that limited the first-class travel of United Nations officials.

On 18 December 1984, the General Assembly, on the recommendation of the Fifth Committee, adopted section VII of resolution 39/236 without vote.

First-class travel

[The General Assembly . . .]

1. *Takes note* of the report of the Secretary-General on first-class travel;

2. *Decides* that the reports on this subject should in future be entitled "Standards of accommodation for air travel";

3. *Requests* the Secretary-General, in preparing future annual reports on this subject, to include details of, resultant additional costs of, and reasons for all exceptions made to the rules on standards of accommodation for air travel established pursuant to General Assembly resolution 32/198 of 21 December 1977, as amended by resolutions 35/217, section X, of 17 December 1980 and 37/237, section III, of 21 December 1982;

. . .

General Assembly resolution 39/236, section VII

18 December 1984   Meeting 105   Adopted without vote

Approved by Fifth Committee (A/39/839) without objection, 3 December (meeting 40); draft by United Kingdom (A/C.5/39/L.13); agenda item 109. *Meeting numbers.* GA 39th session: 5th Committee 27, 28, 40; plenary 105.

Staff travel to General Assembly sessions

On behalf of the Secretary-General, the Under-Secretary-General for Administration and Management orally reported to the Fifth Committee in November 1984 that the Secretary-General, in response to a December 1983 Assembly resolution,[3] had informed all heads of departments and offices outside Headquarters of the need to limit the travel of staff to attend Assembly sessions; in September, the Secretary-General introduced new procedures by which the prior approval of his Office was required for all travel of staff to attend meetings and conferences.

At the request of the United States, the Secretariat submitted to the Fifth Committee in December[4] a breakdown and brief explanation of all staff travel to attend the 1984 regular session of the Assembly: 38 staff members had travelled to New York for this purpose from overseas United Nations offices, two of them making two trips each.

On the recommendation of the Fifth Committee, the General Assembly adopted, on 18 December 1984, section VIII of resolution 39/236 without vote.

Travel of United Nations officials to attend sessions of the General Assembly

[The General Assembly . . .]

1. *Takes note* of the oral report of the Secretary-General on the question of travel by United Nations officials to attend sessions of the General Assembly;

2. *Requests* the Secretary-General to continue to assure that the maximum restraint be exercised concerning such travel;

3. *Decides* to keep the matter under periodic review;

. . .

General Assembly resolution 39/236, section VIII

18 December 1984   Meeting 105   Adopted without vote

Approved by Fifth Committee (A/39/839) without objection, 5 December (meeting 43); oral proposal by Poland; agenda item 109.
Meeting numbers. GA 39th session: 5th Committee 28, 43; plenary 105.

REFERENCES

[1]A/C.5/39/16. [2]YUN 1977, p. 1004, GA res. 32/198, 21 Dec. 1977. [3]YUN 1983, p. 1199, GA res. 38/234, sect. XVI, 20 Dec. 1983. [4]A/C.5/39/L.14.

Other UN officials

Conditions of service

In September 1984, ACABQ[1] presented its recommendations regarding allowances for the Chairman and Vice-Chairman of ICSC and members of ICJ, following its examination of the Secretary-General's 1983 report on conditions of service and compensation for officials other than Secretariat officials.[2] The Assembly, in December 1983,[3] had deferred consideration of that report until 1984.

ACABQ concurred with the Secretary-General's proposals to raise the special allowance payable to the ICSC Chairman from $5,000 to $8,000 per year; and to approve an installation grant, an education grant and a death benefit to both the Chairman and Vice-Chairman. However, it recommended against introducing a $2,000 special annual allowance for the ICSC Vice-Chairman, a distinction in compensation to both officials according to dependency status, and a relocation allowance.

With regard to ICJ members, ACABQ recommended that the special annual allowance payable to the Court President be set at $15,000 as of 1 January 1985 with a corresponding adjustment to $94 per day (up to a maximum of $9,400 per year) for the special daily allowance paid to the Vice-President when acting as President. The Committee agreed that the President and members of the Court who had taken up residence at The Hague should be reimbursed $4,500 maximum per child per school year for the actual cost of their education in addition to one related travel per year to The Hague from the place of scholastic attendance when outside the Netherlands. It also recommended a death benefit scheme for ICJ members, and lump-sum payments, upon completion of service and relocation outside the Netherlands, for those judges who had maintained, on a continuous basis, a *bona fide* primary residence at The Hague for a specified number of years.

GENERAL ASSEMBLY ACTION

On 18 December 1984, the General Assembly adopted, without vote, section V of resolution 39/236, on the recommendation of the Fifth Committee.

Conditions of service and compensation for officials other than Secretariat officials

[*The General Assembly . . .*]

Decides to defer consideration of the question of conditions of service and compensation for officials other than Secretariat officials until its fortieth session;

. . .

General Assembly resolution 39/236, section V

18 December 1984   Meeting 105   Adopted without vote

Approved by Fifth Committee (A/39/839) without objection, 15 December (meeting 52); oral proposal by Chairman; agenda item 109.
Meeting numbers. GA 39th session: 5th Committee 15, 52; plenary 105.

On compensation in the event of disabilities attributable to service with the United Nations, and health insurance for members of commissions, committees and similar bodies, the Secretary-General[4] proposed, in November, to increase, with effect from 1 January 1985, the fixed amounts payable in the event of death, injury or illness, respectively, from $100,000 to $130,000, $50,000 to $65,000, and $100,000 to $130,000; he also proposed that the scale of compensation be reviewed again in 1988. The Secretary-General considered the current arrangements for health insurance to be appropriate, given the modest cost of the insurance coverage to the members, its ready availability and its optional character.

ACABQ[5] supported the Secretary-General's recommendations.

GENERAL ASSEMBLY ACTION

On 18 December 1984, the General Assembly, on the recommendation of the Fifth Committee, adopted section X of resolution 39/236 without vote.

Compensation in the event of death, injury or illness attributable to service with the United Nations and health insurance for members of commissions, committees and similar bodies

[*The General Assembly . . .*]

1. *Takes note* of the note by the Secretary-General on compensation in the event of death, injury or illness attributable to service with the United Nations and health insurance for members of commissions, committees and similar bodies;

2. *Approves* the proposals of the Secretary-General, as contained in paragraph 6 of his note;

. . .

General Assembly resolution 39/236, section X

18 December 1984   Meeting 105   Adopted without vote

Approved by Fifth Committee (A/39/839) without objection, 27 November (meeting 35); oral proposal by Chairman; agenda item 109.

Experts and consultants

In a November report,[6] submitted in response to a 1982 Assembly request,[7] on the United Nations use of consultants and participants in *ad hoc* expert groups in 1982-1983, the Secretary-General said a total of $15,580,100 covered the remuneration and cost of related travel of 2,361 individuals and 48 institutions engaged as consultants, while an additional $3,215,100 covered 1,677 payments of travel expenses of 1,527 participants in *ad hoc* expert groups. Of a total of 210 contracts issued during the period to 165 former staff members as consultants, 134 were for 100 individuals over 60 years of age. The majority of consultant services related to special analytical studies (60.5 per cent), followed by advisory services (9.4 per cent) and programme implementation (8.2 per cent). In accordance with the guideline requiring the selection of outside expertise from as wide and representative a number of countries as possible, nationals of 124 Member States, including 75 developing countries, had been engaged as consultants, and those of 127 Member States, including 95 developing countries, had been invited to participate in *ad hoc* groups.

In December, ACABQ[8] stressed that only in exceptional circumstances should departures occur from the interim measure instituted by the Assembly in 1982[7] that excluded former staff members who were beneficiaries of the United Nations Joint Staff Pension Fund from receiving emoluments exceeding $12,000 from the United Nations in any one calendar year; it requested the Secretary-General to report in future on exceptions to that and another requirement that consultancy agreements should be short term in nature.

GENERAL ASSEMBLY ACTION

On the recommendation of the Fifth Committee, the General Assembly, on 18 December 1984, adopted section XII of resolution 39/236 without vote.

Use of experts, consultants and participants in *ad hoc* expert groups

[*The General Assembly . . .*]

Taking note of the report of the Secretary-General on the use of consultants and participants in *ad hoc* expert groups in the United Nations in 1982-1983 and of the related report of the Advisory Committee on Administrative and Budgetary Questions,

1. *Requests* the Secretary-General to report to the General Assembly at its forty-first session on the use of consultants and participants in *ad hoc* expert groups for the biennium 1984-1985 and, in preparing his report, to take into account the comments of the Advisory Committee on Administrative and Budgetary Questions and the views of Member States expressed in the course of the debate in the Fifth Committee;

2. *Confirms* the interim measure instituted by section VIII, paragraph 3, of its resolution 37/237 of 21 December 1982 and decides to review the situation at its fortieth session in the light of additional information to be provided by the Secretary-General on former staff members of any organ, organization or body of the United Nations system in receipt of a pension benefit from the United Nations Joint Staff Pension Fund who are engaged by the Secretary-General in any capacity;

. . .

General Assembly resolution 39/236, section XII

18 December 1984   Meeting 105   Adopted without vote

Approved by Fifth Committee (A/39/839) without vote, 15 December (meeting 53); draft by Chairman (A/C.5/39/L.29), orally amended by Belgium; agenda item 109.

Meeting numbers. GA 39th session: 5th Committee 43, 52, 53; plenary 105.

The text incorporated oral amendments by Belgium to include the word "experts" in the title, and to decide, in paragraph 2, to review the situation in 1985, rather than to continue the 1982 interim measure as suggested in the original draft.

REFERENCES

[1]A/39/7/Add.1. [2]YUN 1983, p. 1199. [3]*Ibid.*, GA res. 38/234, sect. XVII, 20 Dec. 1983. [4]A/C.5/39/36. [5]A/39/7 & Add.1-16. [6]A/C.5/39/19. [7]YUN 1982, p. 1489, GA res. 37/237, sect. VIII, 21 Dec. 1982. [8]A/39/7/Add.9.

Questions relating to regional commissions

In October 1984,[1] the Secretary-General informed the General Assembly that the permanent redeployment of regular budget resources for continuing senior women's programme officers posts at the regional commissions could jeopardize the overall work programme, and that, while temporary arrangements could continue in 1985, he intended to seek the regularizing of the staffing situation. In 1983,[2] the Assembly had urged the Secretary-General to continue those posts within the commissions' regular budget.

GENERAL ASSEMBLY ACTION

On 14 December 1984, the Assembly, on the recommendation of the Third (Social, Humanitarian and Cultural) Committee, adopted resolution 39/127 by recorded vote.

Senior women's programme officers posts at the regional commissions

The General Assembly,

Recalling its resolutions 33/188 of 29 January 1979, 35/137 of 11 December 1980 and 37/62 of 3 December 1982 and, in particular, its view that the appointment of senior women's programme officers at the regional commissions represents a valuable contribution to the implementation of the goals of the United Nations Decade for Women: Equality, Development and Peace,

Recalling also its resolution 38/106 of 16 December 1983, in particular the reference to the question of senior women's programme officers posts at the regional commissions contained in paragraphs 2 and 3 of that resolution,

Reaffirming that questions concerning women should be approached and dealt with as an integral part of overall policies and programmes in the field of social and economic development,

Convinced that further efforts are needed to ensure the maintenance and continuation, at the appropriate level, of posts assigned to women's programmes at the regional commissions,

Recognizing that these posts are integral to the successful outcome of national and regional programmes for women,

1. *Takes due note* of the report of the Secretary-General on the situation of senior women's programme officers posts at the regional commissions;

2. *Takes note* of the decision of the Secretary-General to continue posts through temporary arrangements during 1985;

3. *Expresses deep concern* that there has been a lack of progress in regularizing senior women's programme officers posts at the regional commissions and that work with respect to women's programmes is thereby seriously impeded;

4. *Stresses* that the appointment of senior women's programme officers at the regional commissions represents a valuable contribution to the implementation of the goals of the United Nations Decade for Women: Equality, Development and Peace, and beyond;

5. *Requests* the Secretary-General, in consultation with the executive secretaries of the five regional commissions, to reassess all individual work programmes, with a view to incorporating women's concerns at all levels in the overall programme of work of each Commission;

6. *Also requests* the Secretary-General, in consultation with the executive secretaries of the five regional commissions, to allocate sufficient budgetary resources to staff, including, where possible, by redeployment, within the context of the 1986-1987 programme budget, in order to regularize all temporary and permanent senior women's programme officers posts at the regional commissions before the end of the Decade, so as to allow the integration of policies and programmes concerning women;

7. *Further requests* the Secretary-General to report to the General Assembly at its fortieth session on measures taken in implementation of paragraph 5 above.

General Assembly resolution 39/127

14 December 1984   Meeting 101   135-1-8 (recorded vote)

Approved by Third Committee (A/39/702) by recorded vote (124-1-10), 26 November (meeting 50); 17-nation draft (A/C.3/39/L.28); agenda item 93.

Sponsors: Australia, Bahamas, Barbados, Bolivia, Cameroon, Canada, Colombia, Costa Rica, Guyana, India, Ivory Coast, Jamaica, Kenya, Norway, Philippines, Trinidad and Tobago, United Kingdom.

Meeting numbers. GA 39th session: 3rd Committee 23-33, 42, 47, 50; plenary 101.

Recorded vote in Assembly as follows:

In favour: Afghanistan, Algeria, Angola, Argentina, Australia, Austria, Bahamas, Bahrain, Bangladesh, Barbados, Belgium, Belize, Benin, Bhutan, Bolivia, Botswana, Brazil, Brunei Darussalam, Burkina Faso, Burma, Burundi, Cameroon, Canada, Cape Verde, Central African Republic, Chad, Chile, China, Colombia, Congo, Costa Rica, Cuba, Cyprus, Democratic Kampuchea, Democratic Yemen, Denmark, Djibouti, Dominican Republic, Ecuador, Egypt, El Salvador, Equatorial Guinea, Ethiopia, Fiji, Finland, France, Gabon, Gambia, Germany, Federal Republic of, Ghana, Greece, Guatemala, Guinea, Guyana, Haiti, Honduras, Iceland, India, Indonesia, Iran, Iraq, Ireland, Italy, Ivory Coast, Jamaica, Japan, Jordan, Kenya, Kuwait, Lao People's Democratic Republic, Lebanon, Lesotho, Liberia, Libyan Arab Jamahiriya, Luxembourg, Madagascar, Malawi, Maldives, Mali, Malta, Mauritania, Mauritius, Mexico, Morocco, Mozambique, Nepal, Netherlands, New Zealand, Nicaragua, Niger, Nigeria, Norway, Oman, Pakistan, Panama, Papua New Guinea, Paraguay, Peru, Philippines, Portugal, Qatar, Romania, Rwanda, Saint Vincent and the Grenadines, Samoa, Sao Tome and Principe, Senegal, Seychelles, Sierra Leone, Singapore, Somalia, Spain, Sri Lanka, Sudan, Suriname, Swaziland, Sweden, Syrian Arab Republic, Thailand, Togo, Trinidad and Tobago, Tunisia, Turkey, Uganda, United Arab Emirates, United Kingdom, United Republic of Tanzania, Uruguay, Vanuatu, Venezuela, Viet Nam, Yemen, Yugoslavia, Zaire, Zambia.

Against: United States.

Abstaining: Bulgaria, Byelorussian SSR, Czechoslovakia, Hungary, Israel, Poland, Ukrainian SSR, USSR.

The United States, which had asked for the vote, opposed creating new positions, as against redeployment. Similarly, the USSR felt that, under paragraph 6, financial implications could arise in the 1987-1988 programme budget. While sharing that concern, Canada believed that better staffing arrangements at regional commissions would result in more efficient use of resources. Morocco felt the text could help the position of women at the commissions. The Budget Division Director stated that should financial implications arise, they would be presented to the Assembly in the 1987-1988 budget.

REFERENCES

[1]A/39/569/Add.1. [2]YUN 1983, p. 912, GA res. 38/106, 16 Dec. 1983.

Chapter IV

Other administrative and management questions

In 1984, the General Assembly took a number of actions related to United Nations administration and management. It continued to foster the rational use of conference resources and to pursue the possibility of shortening sessions (resolution 39/68 B), and to seek improvement in the pattern of conferences (39/68 C) and in the control and limitation of documents (39/68 D). The Assembly authorized meetings of subsidiary organs during its 1984 session (decision 39/403) and approved the revised calendar of meetings for 1985 (39/68 A). It also took action on the catering operation (39/67) and parking facilities at United Nations Headquarters (39/236, section II), on the United Nations Office at Nairobi, Kenya (39/236, sections XIII-XV), and on the management of support services shared by the various entities of the United Nations system at the Vienna International Centre, Austria (39/242, section IV).

The Assembly set the United Nations share of the costs of the Advisory Committee for the Co-ordination of Information Systems for 1984-1985 (39/236, section IX) and approved the 1985 budget for the International Computing Centre (39/236, section VI). In December, the Fifth (Administrative and Budgetary) Committee approved an additional net amount of $1,497,400 for 1984-1985 to improve the United Nations communications system.

To strengthen the role of United Nations libraries in information systems, the Assembly requested implementation of recommendations to improve the functioning of those libraries (39/242, section III).

In connection with the activities of the United Nations Postal Administration, the Assembly called for a special postage stamp issue to sensitize the international community to the social and economic crisis in Africa (39/239 A).

Topics related to this chapter. Institutional machinery. Institutional arrangements.

Conferences and meetings

In 1984, the 22-member Committee on Conferences held in New York an organizational meeting on 9 March and its substantive session from 30 April to 4 May and from 20 August to 5 September. Its work centred on the calendar of conferences, control and limitation of documentation,

effective use of conference resources, proposals for conference services in the medium-term plan for 1984-1989 and special conferences. The Committee also adopted guidelines for its review of proposals for conferences and meetings involving exceptions to General Assembly resolutions and decisions, as well as administrative and financial implications.

The Committee's report[1] contained four draft resolutions on the main aspects of its work, which the Assembly adopted as resolutions 39/68 A-D (see below).

Calendar of meetings

In keeping with a General Assembly request of November 1983,[2] the Committee on Conferences in 1984 discussed a Secretariat note containing the proposed additions and changes to the existing provisions of a 1976 Assembly resolution governing conferences and meetings of United Nations bodies.[3]

The Committee continued its efforts to reduce the conference resources allocated to those bodies found to have used less than 75 per cent of their meeting resources during 1980-1982. Thus in April 1984, the Committee Chairman issued a reminder to the 10 bodies that had not replied to his July 1983 letter suggesting the possibility of such a reduction. In May, after examining the 13 replies received,[4] the Committee agreed that the bodies concerned should be urged to ensure that their requests for conference services corresponded accurately to their requirements, to utilize rationally the services provided, to consider reducing formal meetings by increasing the use of informal consultations, and to provide for such consultations, drafting committees and report preparation in their programmes of work.

The Committee recommended a draft resolution on each of these two topics for Assembly action.

GENERAL ASSEMBLY ACTION

On 13 December 1984, the General Assembly, acting on recommendations of the Fifth Committee, adopted two resolutions. Resolution 39/68 C was adopted without vote.

Pattern of conferences

The General Assembly,

Recalling its resolution 38/32 C of 25 November 1983,

Having considered the report of the Committee on Conferences on its efforts to implement that resolution,

Requests the Committee on Conferences to undertake an in-depth study of all existing provisions relating to the pattern of conferences, taking into account all the modifications proposed during the thirty-eighth session of the General Assembly, with a view to reporting to the Assembly at its fortieth session.

General Assembly resolution 39/68 C

13 December 1984   Meeting 98   Adopted without vote

Approved by Fifth Committee (A/39/730) without vote, 16 November (meeting 29); draft by Committee on Conferences (A/39/32); agenda item 114.
Meeting numbers. GA 39th session: 5th Committee 6, 11-15, 18, 27, 29; plenary 98.

Resolution 39/68 B was adopted without vote.

Shortening of sessions or adoption of a biennial cycle for sessions of United Nations organs

The General Assembly,

Reaffirming its resolutions 32/71, section IV, and 32/72 of 9 December 1977, 33/55, section II, of 14 December 1978, 35/10 A of 3 November 1980, 36/117 A, section I, of 10 December 1981 and 38/32 D of 25 November 1983,

Emphasizing the continued need for maximum efficiency in the provision of conference services,

1. *Takes note with appreciation* of the efforts made by the Committee on Conferences to improve utilization of conference-servicing resources in consultation with the officers of those organs which have in recent years utilized 75 per cent or less of the conference resources made available to them;

2. *Urges* subsidiary organs of the General Assembly to make further efforts, on the basis, *inter alia*, of current statistical data, to ensure that their requests for conference services correspond accurately to their requirements and that the services provided to them are utilized rationally and efficiently;

3. *Further urges* those organs, when submitting requests for conference services, to make due provision for meetings when no interpretation services are required, such as informal consultations and periods allocated to drafting, to the extent that such needs might be anticipated on the basis of past practice, and to consider an appropriate reduction in the number of formal meetings to allow the balance of time to be utilized for informal meetings and/or consultations;

4. *Recommends* that the bureaux of those organs monitor their utilization of the conference-servicing resources allocated to them with a view to including in their reports to the General Assembly an analytical survey of their utilization of those resources;

5. *Reaffirms* that in drawing up future calendars of conferences and meetings, the document-processing capacity of the Secretariat and the reporting schedules of subsidiary organs of the General Assembly should be taken into account;

6. *Requests* those organs also to discuss at their organizational sessions the possibility of meeting on a biennial basis;

7. *Invites* the Secretary-General to determine, in the course of 1985, the extent to which subsidiary organs of the General Assembly, through both formal and informal meetings and/or consultations, utilize the conference services they have requested, with a view to achieving the most effective utilization of conference resources;

8. *Invites* the Committee on Conferences to continue its examination of this question and to make a further report to the General Assembly at its fortieth session.

General Assembly resolution 39/68 B

13 December 1984   Meeting 98   Adopted without vote

Approved by Fifth Committee (A/39/730) without vote, 16 November (meeting 29); draft by Committee on Conferences (A/39/32), amended by Vice-Chairman (A/C.5/39/L.9/Rev.1) following consultations; agenda item 114.
Meeting numbers. GA 39th session: 5th Committee 6, 11-15, 18, 27, 29; plenary 98.

The original text differed from that adopted in that the first preambular paragraph did not mention Assembly resolution 33/55, section II, of 14 December 1978, and the second referred to maximum economy in the effective use of conference-servicing resources; paragraph 4 would have had the Assembly recommend that each organ make one member of its bureau responsible for the rational use of such resources; paragraph 5 was not part of the original text; paragraph 6 would have had the Assembly request inclusion in reports to it of an analytical statement on the utilization of resources, with an explanation for any under-utilization; and the last phrase in paragraph 7 had read "with a view to the future redeployment of unused resources".

Calendar for 1984

Two inter-sessional departures from the calendar of conferences for 1984 involving financial implications were approved by the Committee on Conferences in accordance with its 1974 mandate,[5] as redefined in 1977,[6] to act on behalf of the General Assembly with respect to such departures. One was a change of dates of the resumed session of the Committee on the Review and Appraisal of the Implementation of the International Development Strategy for the Third United Nations Development Decade (the 1980s) (see p. 392), which was approved on the understanding that services would be provided on an "as available" basis. The second was a one-day extension of the Fourth General Conference of the United Nations Industrial Development Organization (UNIDO) (see p. 558).

By letters of 14 and 18 September and 1 and 15 October,[7] the Committee Chairman informed the Assembly President that requests to meet in New York during the 1984 regular session of the Assembly had been received from a number of its subsidiary organs. The Chairman asked that the meetings be authorized as requested, on the understanding that they would be accommodated as facilities and services became available so as not to affect Assembly activities adversely.

The Economic and Social Council, by decisions 1984/102, 1984/103, 1984/105 and 1984/110, also authorized changes to the calendar of meetings for 1984 in respect of four of its subsidiary bodies.

GENERAL ASSEMBLY ACTION

The General Assembly adopted decision 39/403 without vote.

Meetings of subsidiary organs during the thirty-ninth session

At its 3rd, 27th and 32nd plenary meetings, on 21 September and 9 and 17 October 1984, the General Assembly, on the recommendations of the Committee on Conferences and of the General Committee, decided that the following subsidiary organs should be authorized to hold meetings during the thirty-ninth session:

(a) *Ad Hoc* Committee on the Drafting of an International Convention against *Apartheid* in Sports;

(b) *Ad Hoc* Committee on the Indian Ocean;

(c) Advisory Committee on the United Nations Educational and Training Programme for Southern Africa;

(d) Committee of Trustees of the United Nations Trust Fund for South Africa;

(e) Committee on Applications for Review of Administrative Tribunal Judgements;

(f) Committee on Relations with the Host Country;

(g) Committee on the Exercise of the Inalienable Rights of the Palestinian People;

(h) Preparatory Committee for the Fortieth Anniversary of the United Nations;

(i) Special Committee against *Apartheid;*

(j) Special Committee on the Situation with regard to the Implementation of the Declaration on the Granting of Independence to Colonial Countries and Peoples;

(k) United Nations Council for Namibia;

(l) Working Group on the Financing of the United Nations Relief and Works Agency for Palestine Refugees in the Near East.

General Assembly decision 39/403

Adopted without vote

Approved by General Committee (A/39/250 & Add.2), 19 September and 9 October (meetings 1, 2, 4); proposals by Committee on Conferences (A/39/482 & Add.1-3); agenda item 8.

Calendar for 1985

During its August/September 1984 meetings, the Committee on Conferences recommended for General Assembly adoption a draft revised calendar of conferences and meetings of United Nations bodies for 1985. The revised calendar, drawn up as at 31 August 1984 and annexed to the Committee's report,[1] incorporated the change made by Economic and Social Council decision 1984/117 with respect to the Third United Nations Regional Cartographic Conference for the Americas.

Noting that several bodies had decided to extend or change session dates and venues or accept government offers to host sessions, the Committee agreed to issue a reminder that such decisions could be taken only by the Assembly on the Committee's recommendation, and that rescheduling of sessions should be proposed in reports to the Assembly.

GENERAL ASSEMBLY ACTION

Acting without vote on the recommendation of the Fifth Committee, the General Assembly adopted resolution 39/68 A on 13 December 1984.

Report of the Committee on Conferences

The General Assembly,

Having considered the report of the Committee on Conferences,

1. *Takes note with appreciation* of the report of the Committee on Conferences;

2. *Approves* the draft revised calendar of conferences and meetings of the United Nations for 1985 as submitted by the Committee on Conferences;

3. *Authorizes* the Committee on Conferences to make adjustments in the calendar of conferences and meetings for 1985 which may become necessary as a result of action and decisions taken by the General Assembly at its thirty-ninth session;

4. *Requests* the Secretary-General, in the interests of maximum efficiency and cost-effectiveness, to consider organizing the conference-servicing staff at the Vienna International Centre into a single conference-servicing operation;

5. *Invites* the International Atomic Energy Agency to participate in the consideration of this matter.

General Assembly resolution 39/68 A

13 December 1984   Meeting 98   Adopted without vote

Approved by Fifth Committee (A/39/730) without vote, 16 November (meeting 29); draft by Committee on Conferences (A/39/32), amended by Vice-Chairman (A/C.5/39/L.9/Rev.1) following consultations; agenda item 114.
Meeting numbers. GA 39th session: 5th Committee 6, 11-15, 18, 27, 29; plenary 98.

Amendments to the original text deleted: a paragraph by which the Assembly would have reaffirmed that, for meetings included in the calendar of conferences as approved, the Department of Conference Services at Headquarters would be responsible for servicing meetings in North and South America and in Asia, and the United Nations Office at Geneva for those in Europe, Africa and the Middle East; and "within the resources approved in the biennial budget for 1984-1985" at the end of paragraph 4. Paragraph 5 was amended to read "consideration of this matter" instead of "study of this question".

Conference and meeting services

Following consideration of the Secretary-General's consolidated statement[8] of programme budget implications of conference-servicing costs for the 1984-1985 programme budget (see Chapter I of this section), as well as of the recommendation of the Advisory Committee on Administrative and Budgetary Questions (ACABQ),[9] the Fifth Committee on 15 December 1984 approved, by recorded vote of 70 to 21, an additional appropriation totalling $4,250,000 for such costs for 1985.

The Secretary-General had requested an additional amount of $9,238,200 for 1985, in the light of the calendar of conferences as approved by the General Assembly on 13 December 1984 (see above), distributed as follows: $4,616,800 for Headquarters, $4,600,000 for the United Nations Office at Vienna and $21,400 for the United Nations

Office at Geneva. In the opinion of ACABQ, there was room for increased productivity and better preparation of documents in New York, the method of estimating conference-servicing requirements for Vienna should be refined, and, in certain cases, forecasts for documentation could be decreased without jeopardizing the work of bodies reviewing such documents. On that basis, ACABQ scaled down the request to the approved amount, to be appropriated as follows: $2,250,000 for Headquarters and $2,000,000 for Vienna.

Improvement of conference resources

In keeping with a November 1983 General Assembly request,[10] the Committee on Conferences considered a report of the Secretary-General on existing conference resources, services and facilities within the United Nations system.[11] It also examined conference room papers on Headquarters conference-servicing capacity, external conference-servicing resources, and the revised calendar of conferences and anticipated United Nations meetings for 1985, grouped by subject-matter.

A revision of the reports was suggested, to illustrate better, by quantifying and comparing the demand for and supply of conference resources, the impact of delegation demand on the physical and human resources available to the Organization. It was agreed that draft calendars of conferences and meetings should continue to be presented in traditional chronological form, but that there was value in indicating documentation requirements.

GENERAL ASSEMBLY ACTION

In resolution 39/68 A, the General Assembly requested the Secretary-General, for maximum efficiency and cost-effectiveness, to consider organizing the conference-servicing staff at the Vienna International Centre into a single conference-servicing operation. It invited the International Atomic Energy Agency (IAEA) to participate in the consideration of that matter.

Draft rules of procedure for conferences

By decision 39/419, the General Assembly deferred to its regular 1985 session consideration of the 1983[12] and 1984 (see p. 1106) reports of the Secretary-General on draft standard rules of procedure for United Nations conferences. It invited Governments to communicate to him their observations on those reports by 1 May 1985.

REFERENCES

[1]A/39/32. [2]YUN 1983, p. 1200, GA res. 38/32 C, 25 Nov. 1983. [3]YUN 1976, p. 908, GA res. 31/140, 17 Dec. 1976. [4]A/AC.172/96 & Add.1. [5]YUN 1974, p. 922, GA res. 3351(XXIX), 18 Dec. 1974. [6]YUN 1977, p. 1039, GA res. 32/72, 9 Dec. 1977. [7]A/39/482 & Add.1-3. [8]A/C.5/39/98. [9]A/39/7 & Add.1-16 (annex). [10]YUN 1983, p. 1204, GA res. 38/32 F, 25 Nov. 1983. [11]A/AC.172/100/Rev.1 & Rev.1/Corr.1. [12]YUN 1983, p. 1126.

Documents

Documents limitation

Various aspects of controlling and limiting United Nations documents were examined by the Committee on Conferences in 1984.[1] They included the feasibility of instituting an abbreviated form of summary record,[2] the causes of late issuance of documentation[3] and backlogs in publications.[4]

The Committee agreed that the samples of abbreviated summary records examined, as well as the observations made on them, should be communicated to United Nations organs entitled to summary records, with a request for their views on the form of record most appropriate for their purposes, to enable the Committee to report to the General Assembly in 1985. Identified as causes of late issuance of documentation were: failure of author departments to adhere to timetables; the low proportion of terminologists to translators (six to over 300), a proportion incompatible with the demands of the Organization's increasingly specialized activities for specialized vocabularies to be established in some languages; and the overload to which the document-processing services were subjected by the clustering of sessions with heavy documentation needs. It was agreed that author departments, United Nations organs and servicing units should abide by the relevant guidelines set forth by the Assembly in 1978[5] and 1981.[6]

The report on publication backlogs dealt with three publications: the *Yearbook of the United Nations;* the *Treaty Series;* and the *Official Records of the United Nations*, for which temporary assistance had been granted.

GENERAL ASSEMBLY ACTION

Acting without vote on the recommendation of the Fifth Committee, the General Assembly adopted resolution 39/68 D on 13 December 1984.

Control and limitation of documentation

The General Assembly,

Recalling its resolutions 2292(XXII) of 8 December 1967, 2538(XXIV) of 11 December 1969, 2732(XXV) of 16 December 1970, 31/140, section II, of 17 December 1976, 33/56, section II, of 14 December 1978, 34/50 of 23 November 1979, 36/117 of 10 December 1981, 37/14 C and D of 16 November 1982 and 38/32 E of 25

November 1983 and its decision 34/401 of 21 September, 25 October, 29 November and 12 December 1979,

1. *Takes note* of the results of the study of the feasibility of instituting an abbreviated form of summary record;

2. *Notes* that the Committee on Conferences will further examine, after consulting with the United Nations organs entitled to receive summary records, the relative suitability of summary records as now prepared and the abbreviated summary records prepared by the Secretariat on an experimental basis, with a view to reporting to the General Assembly at its fortieth session;

3. *Requests* the Secretary-General:

(a) To instruct all Secretariat units responsible for the drafting of documents to ensure that their manuscripts are delivered to the Department of Conference Services in accordance with the prescribed timetable for their submission;

(b) To circulate eight weeks before the opening of the session of each United Nations organ, including the Main Committees of the General Assembly, a report on the state of preparation at that time of all the documents in all languages required for the session;

(c) To include in that report an explanation for any delay in processing the documentation and to identify the Secretariat unit responsible for that delay;

4. *Reaffirms* that lists of all documents requested by each United Nations organ, including the Main Committees of the General Assembly, shall be submitted by the Secretary-General at the end of each session, with an indication of the date on which it will be possible to issue each document in all required languages, reflecting the time required for its preparation by both the substantive and conference-servicing units of the Secretariat.

General Assembly resolution 39/68 D

13 December 1984   Meeting 98   Adopted without vote

Approved by Fifth Committee (A/39/730) without vote, 16 November (meeting 29); draft by Committee on Conferences (A/39/32), amended by Vice-Chairman (A/C.5/39/L.9/Rev.1) following consultations; agenda item 114.
Meeting numbers. GA 39th session: 5th Committee 6, 11-15, 18, 27, 29; plenary 98.

The amendments to the original text consisted of editing changes to paragraphs 3 (b) and 4.

Meeting records

Chinese language services

In a September 1984 report,[7] the Secretary-General provided information regarding recent developments in Chinese language services for producing documentation in that language, which he indicated had not been provided on the same level as the other working languages of the General Assembly and the Security Council. Chinese had been included as a working language of those bodies in 1973.[8]

The report stated that, in 1983, in response to a 6 September complaint from China that service was inadequate, efforts were made, within available resources, to ensure the simultaneous distribution of documentation and more timely issuance of summary records in Chinese. In view of the primary importance attached to simultaneous distribution of verbatim records in all languages including Chinese, it was felt that the creation of the necessary facilities for that purpose could no longer be postponed.

The Secretary-General thus requested, and obtained, the concurrence of ACABQ[9] to enter into additional commitments in 1984 in an amount not exceeding $998,400 under the provisions of the December 1983 Assembly resolution on unforeseen and extraordinary expenses for the 1984-1985 biennium.[10] This amount provided for the nucleus of a Chinese Verbatim Unit, on a temporary basis from 1 August to 31 December; for temporary assistance equivalent to 24 posts from 1 October to 31 December; and for costs relating to the acquisition of reproduction and specialized equipment, paper, office supplies and furniture, and alterations to premises.

The Secretary-General further requested an additional $1,114,400 to provide the same temporary assistance for the 1985 Assembly session. ACABQ had no objection and accordingly recommended approval of that amount in the 1984-1985 budget.

Proposals to restructure the Chinese language service were to be made to the Assembly as part of the proposed programme budget for the 1986-1987 biennium.

Documents distribution

In response to a 1982 request by the Committee for Programme and Co-ordination (CPC),[11] the Secretary-General submitted to it in April 1984 a report[12] addressing the question of whether the distribution system for United Nations documents provided a mechanism whereby studies and reports produced by the Secretariat could effectively reach the target-users for whom, as defined in the programme budget, they were intended.

The report concluded that the system was appropriately designed for the purpose, but that additional attention could be given to ensure its more effective use. To this end the report recommended that programme managers be made fully aware of the system. They should keep their distribution lists under continuing review, and methodically update and improve them, particularly in respect of developing countries. Instructions for the preparation of the 1986-1987 programme budget estimates would require that proposals for publication of studies and reports be supported by evidence that target-users had been identified and were on a mailing list. Compliance with this requirement would be examined through the existing machinery for programme budget review, in-depth programme evaluation, and performance monitoring at the Secretariat and intergovernmental levels.

The report also mentioned that the central maintenance of departmental lists was undergoing conversion from an addressograph system to a computerized one, thus allowing for their review by user departments.

Following its consideration of the report, CPC recommended[13] that the Secretary-General make the documents dissemination system more effective, in particular by clearly identifying end-users. Efforts should be made to find alternative means of documents distribution and to follow up on the results. Criteria could be defined to assist distribution services systematically to bring different United Nations publications to end-users, particularly in developing countries.

REFERENCES

[1]A/39/32. [2]A/AC.172/97. [3]A/AC.172/98. [4]A/AC.172/99. [5]YUN 1978, p. 1051, GA res. 33/56, 14 Dec. 1978. [6]YUN 1981, p. 1364, GA res. 36/117 A, 10 Dec. 1981. [7]A/C.5/39/12. [8]YUN 1973, p. 803, GA res. 3189(XXVIII), 18 Dec. 1973. [9]A/39/7. [10]YUN 1983, p. 1153, GA res. 38/237, 20 Dec. 1983. [11]YUN 1982, p. 1502. [12]E/AC.51/1984/6. [13]A/39/38.

UN premises

Headquarters

Catering

The continuing financial deficit in the catering operation at United Nations Headquarters was taken up by the General Assembly in 1984.

GENERAL ASSEMBLY ACTION

Acting without vote on the recommendation of the Fifth Committee, the Assembly adopted resolution 39/67 on 13 December 1984.

Catering operation at United Nations Headquarters
The General Assembly,

Noting that, in spite of the Secretary-General's statement that the financial objective of the catering operation at United Nations Headquarters is a break-even result, deficits have occurred in the last two bienniums,

1. *Confirms* that the catering operation at United Nations Headquarters should be financially self-supporting to the extent possible;

2. *Requests* the Secretary-General to take steps to rectify the situation that is causing the deficit in the catering operation;

3. *Requests* the Secretary-General to report to the General Assembly at its fortieth session on the situation.

General Assembly resolution 39/67

13 December 1984   Meeting 98   Adopted without vote

Approved by Fifth Committee (A/39/618) without vote, 24 October (meeting 16); draft by United States (A/C.5/39/L.6), orally revised; agenda item 108.
Meeting numbers. GA 39th session: 5th Committee 3-7, 13, 14; plenary 98.

Explaining its position in the Fifth Committee, Iraq said that it would be unacceptable if the draft

resolution resulted in catering price increases without prior examination of the causes of the deficits referred to and without benefit of an opinion from ACABQ.

Parking

In information provided to ACABQ on parking in the United Nations garage, the Secretary-General stated that the Garage Review Board, established in 1982, had recently completed a review of all parking authorizations except those of delegates and had established procedures for future annual reviews. The measures recommended by the Board, the Secretary-General stated, adequately addressed the problem of parking for staff and other qualified users; therefore, his information dealt mainly with the parking problems of diplomatic cars.

In the light of that information, ACABQ recommended[1] the following interim measures: increasing parking spaces for delegates from 200 to 300 by immediately making available 100 additional spaces in the second level of the garage; making available, as of September 1985, an additional 100 spaces during the General Assembly's regular sessions; eliminating dead-storage parking currently held for staff reassigned to other duty stations or no longer acting in their official capacity; discontinuing the practice of allowing delegation chauffeurs to park their own vehicles in the garage when removing official delegation vehicles; for security reasons and to prevent evasion of garage admission rules, permitting the parking of delegation rented cars only if rented from a *bona fide* rental company; limiting parking privileges to one car per delegate; as of September 1985, suspending the parking privileges of any delegate in arrears of parking fees by more than three months.

These measures, ACABQ believed, should be continually monitored and evaluated. It stated that, if further remedial action were warranted, consideration could be given to other measures, including increasing the overnight parking fee or eliminating 24-hour and overnight parking, particularly during Assembly sessions.

Noting that garage revenue for 1984-1985 had been estimated at $989,900 (gross), ACABQ concurred with the Secretary-General's proposal to augment the garage administration staff as at 1 January 1985 with one additional clerk and six security officers, whose costs would total $242,600 (gross) in 1985.

GENERAL ASSEMBLY ACTION

Acting on the recommendation of the Fifth Committee, the General Assembly adopted section II of resolution 39/236 by recorded vote on 18 December 1984.

Parking in the United Nations Headquarters garage

[*The General Assembly . . .*]

Endorses the recommendations contained in paragraphs 41 to 43 of the first report of the Advisory Committee on Administrative and Budgetary Questions;

. . .

General Assembly resolution 39/236, section II

18 December 1984   Meeting 105   119-14-9 (recorded vote)

Approved by Fifth Committee (A/39/839) without objection, 11 October (meeting 9); oral proposal by Chairman; agenda item 109.

Meeting numbers. GA 39th session: 5th Committee 8, 9; plenary 105.

Recorded vote in Assembly as follows:

In favour: Algeria, Angola, Antigua and Barbuda, Argentina, Austria, Bahamas, Bahrain, Bangladesh, Barbados, Benin, Bhutan, Bolivia, Botswana, Brazil, Brunei Darussalam, Burkina Faso, Burma, Burundi, Cameroon, Cape Verde, Central African Republic, Chad, Chile, China, Colombia, Congo, Costa Rica, Cuba, Cyprus, Democratic Kampuchea, Democratic Yemen, Denmark, Djibouti, Dominican Republic, Ecuador, Egypt, El Salvador, Ethiopia, Fiji, Finland, Gabon, Gambia, Ghana, Greece, Guatemala, Guinea, Guinea-Bissau, Guyana, Honduras, Iceland, India, Indonesia, Iraq, Ireland, Ivory Coast, Jamaica, Jordan, Kenya, Kuwait, Lebanon, Lesotho, Liberia, Libyan Arab Jamahiriya, Madagascar, Malawi, Malaysia, Maldives, Mali, Malta, Mauritania, Mauritius, Mexico, Morocco, Mozambique, Nepal, Nicaragua, Niger, Nigeria, Norway, Oman, Pakistan, Panama, Papua New Guinea, Paraguay, Peru, Philippines, Qatar, Romania, Rwanda, Saint Lucia, Samoa, Sao Tome and Principe, Saudi Arabia, Senegal, Sierra Leone, Singapore, Somalia, Sri Lanka, Sudan, Suriname, Swaziland, Sweden, Syrian Arab Republic, Thailand, Togo, Trinidad and Tobago, Tunisia, Turkey, Uganda, United Arab Emirates, United Republic of Tanzania, Uruguay, Vanuatu, Venezuela, Yemen, Yugoslavia, Zaire, Zambia, Zimbabwe.

Against: Bulgaria, Byelorussian SSR, Czechoslovakia, German Democratic Republic, Germany, Federal Republic of, Hungary, Japan, Mongolia, Netherlands, Poland, Ukrainian SSR, USSR, United Kingdom, United States.

Abstaining: Australia, Belgium, Canada, France, Italy, Luxembourg, New Zealand, Portugal, Spain.

Addis Ababa

In 1984, the General Assembly considered two reports by the Secretary-General on the proposed new conference and related facilities of the Economic Commission for Africa at Addis Ababa, Ethiopia. One was submitted in 1983;[2] and the other in September 1984,[3] containing updated information, including a breakdown of the cost of the project, based on preliminary plans and recosted at 1984 prices.

Having examined the Secretary-General's proposals, ACABQ, in a related report,[4] made a series of recommendations, including approval in principle of the project, based on which the Assembly adopted section III of resolution 39/236.

(For details, see p. 619.)

Bangkok

In 1984, the General Assembly considered proposals to expand the conference facilities of the Economic and Social Commission for Asia and the Pacific (ESCAP) at Bangkok, Thailand. The facilities envisaged were deemed sufficient to meet ESCAP conference needs for some 20 years after construction. Subject to certain observations, ACABQ made a number of recommendations, which served as the basis for section XI of Assembly resolution 39/236.

(For details, see p. 627.)

Nairobi

Construction

In a November 1984 report,[5] the Secretary-General described progress made in the construction at Nairobi, Kenya, of the permanent headquarters facilities for the United Nations Environment Programme (UNEP) and the United Nations Centre for Human Settlements (Habitat), and accommodation in that complex for other United Nations offices. He stated that, with all works completed as envisaged in the tender documents plus one office block, the United Nations Office at Nairobi was officially inaugurated in May 1984. Additional works required from the contractor were completed by 30 September.

The Secretary-General annexed a summary of the status of appropriations, disbursements and obligations as at 30 September, indicating a balance of $843,562. He also itemized requirements for additional complementary equipment and external works to allow the complex to function efficiently, estimated at $415,000, which could be covered by the balance. A full-scale study was to be undertaken to determine the precise needs for maintaining the buildings and the results were to be reflected in a proposed programme budget for 1986-1987 for common services at Nairobi.

Having discussed the Secretary-General's request with UNEP representatives, ACABQ[6] was satisfied that the proposed additional requirements were essential and should be completed shortly, rather than later when costs would probably be higher.

GENERAL ASSEMBLY ACTION

Acting on the recommendation of the Fifth Committee, the General Assembly adopted section XIV of resolution 39/236 by recorded vote on 18 December 1984.

United Nations Office at Nairobi

[*The General Assembly . . .*]

Having considered the report of the Secretary-General on the United Nations Office at Nairobi and the related oral report of the Advisory Committee on Administrative and Budgetary Questions,

Approves the proposals contained in paragraph 10 of the report of the Secretary-General;

. . .

General Assembly resolution 39/236, section XIV

18 December 1984   Meeting 105   124-21-1 (recorded vote)

Approved by Fifth Committee (A/39/839) without objection, 7 December (meeting 44); oral proposal by Chairman; agenda item 109.

Recorded vote in Assembly as follows:

In favour: Algeria, Angola, Antigua and Barbuda, Argentina, Austria, Bahamas, Bahrain, Bangladesh, Barbados, Benin, Bhutan, Bolivia, Botswana, Brazil, Brunei Darussalam, Burkina Faso, Burma, Burundi, Cameroon, Cape Verde, Central African Republic, Chad, Chile, China, Colombia, Congo, Costa Rica, Cuba, Cyprus, Democratic Kampuchea, Democratic Yemen, Denmark, Djibouti, Dominican Republic, Ecuador, Egypt, El Salvador, Equatorial Guinea, Ethiopia, Fiji, Finland, Gabon, Gambia, Ghana, Greece, Guatemala, Guinea, Guinea-Bissau, Guyana,

Haiti, Honduras, Iceland, India, Indonesia, Iran, Iraq, Ireland, Israel, Ivory Coast, Jamaica, Jordan, Kenya, Kuwait, Lebanon, Lesotho, Liberia, Libyan Arab Jamahiriya, Madagascar, Malawi, Malaysia, Maldives, Mali, Malta, Mauritania, Mauritius, Mexico, Morocco, Mozambique, Nepal, Nicaragua, Niger, Nigeria, Norway, Oman, Pakistan, Panama, Paraguay, Peru, Philippines, Portugal, Qatar, Romania, Rwanda, Saint Lucia, Samoa, Sao Tome and Principe, Saudi Arabia, Senegal, Sierra Leone, Singapore, Somalia, Spain, Sri Lanka, Sudan, Suriname, Swaziland, Sweden, Syrian Arab Republic, Thailand, Togo, Trinidad and Tobago, Tunisia, Turkey, Uganda, United Arab Emirates, United Republic of Tanzania, Uruguay, Vanuatu, Venezuela, Yemen, Yugoslavia, Zaire, Zambia, Zimbabwe.

Against: Australia, Belgium, Bulgaria, Byelorussian SSR, Canada, Czechoslovakia, France, German Democratic Republic, Germany, Federal Republic of, Hungary, Italy, Japan, Luxembourg, Mongolia, Netherlands, New Zealand, Poland, Ukrainian SSR, USSR, United Kingdom, United States.

Abstaining: Papua New Guinea.

Common services

In accordance with an ACABQ recommendation on common services at the United Nations Office at Nairobi, as endorsed by the General Assembly in December 1983,[7] the Secretary-General reported in November 1984[8] on the conclusions reached with regard to rental charges to be established for users of the Office premises.

The Secretary-General stated that, following negotiations with the United Nations Children's Fund (UNICEF), the International Civil Aviation Organization (ICAO), and the United Nations Educational, Scientific and Cultural Organization (UNESCO), agreement was reached on a number of modifications in the method of calculating the rental rate. The result was that, whereas the Secretary-General had proposed an annual rental charge of $96.88 per square metre, which combined the cost of common services calculated at $54.32 and amortization charges at $42.56, the revised rate was reduced to $66 per square metre, combining the cost of services of $44.61 and amortization charges of $21.35.

The revised rate was accepted by the United Nations Environment Fund and the United Nations Human Settlements Foundation. It was expected that ICAO and UNICEF, already occupying office space in the complex, would pay the revised rate, and that UNESCO, if it moved into the premises, would do likewise. The Environment Fund would be granted remission from amortization charges for the first four and a half years of occupancy to enable it to recoup the current value of an investment of $640,000 that it had made at the time of the construction of the original building.

On these assumptions, the income estimates in the 1984-1985 budget needed to be revised from $1,295,600 to $953,900, or reduced by $341,700.

In the belief that the revised charge was not excessive and should thus be generally acceptable, ACABQ recommended approval of the proposed income reduction.[6]

GENERAL ASSEMBLY ACTION

Acting without vote on the recommendation of the Fifth Committee, the General Assembly adopted section XIII of resolution 39/236 on 18 December 1984.

Common services at the United Nations Office at Nairobi

[*The General Assembly* . . .]

Takes note of the report of the Secretary-General on common services at the United Nations Office at Nairobi;

. . .

General Assembly resolution 39/236, section XIII

18 December 1984   Meeting 105   Adopted without vote

Approved by Fifth Committee (A/39/839) without objection, 7 December (meeting 44); oral proposal by Chairman; agenda item 109.

Land grant

In a December 1984 note,[9] the Secretary-General stated that, on 21 May, in connection with the inauguration of the United Nations Office at Nairobi (see above), the Government of Kenya made an offer to grant an additional 40 acres of adjoining land to the existing 100 acres at Gigiri. The UNEP Governing Council had recommended that the General Assembly accept the offer (see p. 749), and the Secretary-General, having determined that such acceptance entailed no financial implications, made the same recommendation. If accepted, he would undertake negotiations for the formal transfer of the land to the United Nations.

GENERAL ASSEMBLY ACTION

Acting without vote on the recommendation of the Fifth Committee, the General Assembly adopted section XV of resolution 39/236 on 18 December 1984.

United Nations Office at Nairobi

[*The General Assembly* . . .]

Recalling its resolutions 32/208 of 21 December 1977, 34/233, section XI, of 20 December 1979, 35/222 of 17 December 1980, 36/235, section IX, of 18 December 1981, 37/237, section IX, of 21 December 1982 and 38/234, section XXII, of 20 December 1983, regarding the United Nations accommodation at Nairobi,

Noting the comments of the Secretary-General,

1. *Welcomes* the announcement on 21 May 1984 by the President of Kenya, Mr. Daniel arap Moi, granting the United Nations an additional 40 acres of land for the United Nations accommodation at Nairobi;

2. *Accepts with appreciation* the generous donation given by the Government of Kenya;

3. *Welcomes also* the announcement by the Government of Kenya of action to facilitate access to the accommodation by means of road improvements;

4. *Expresses its appreciation* to the Government and people of Kenya for the generous and continued hospitality they have extended to the United Nations organizations working in Kenya;

. . .

General Assembly resolution 39/236, section XV

18 December 1984   Meeting 105   Adopted without vote

Approved by Fifth Committee (A/39/839) without vote, 14 December (meeting 51); 2-nation draft (A/C.5/39/L.27); agenda item 109.
Sponsors: Egypt, Kenya.
Meeting numbers. GA 39th session: 5th Committee 44, 51; plenary 105.

Vienna

In October 1984, the Joint Inspection Unit (JIU) reported[10] on its study of the organization and management of the common support services of United Nations organizations at the Vienna International Centre. The study was undertaken pursuant to a recommendation arising from possible changes to existing common service arrangements formalized in a 1977 memorandum of understanding by the Centre occupants—the United Nations, IAEA and UNIDO—owing to the forthcoming conversion of UNIDO into a specialized agency and the subsequent transfer to the Centre of other United Nations entities. Under those arrangements, authority and responsibility for services were allocated as follows: IAEA for computer, library, printing and reproduction, medical, housing and commissary services; UNIDO for buildings management, language training and catering; and the United Nations for security and safety service, under the authority of the Director-General of the United Nations Office at Vienna.

JIU observed that, some weaknesses notwithstanding, the services functioned generally well, the costs to the user organization(s) would have been appreciably higher had services not been provided communally, and the financial benefits, knowledge and practical experience gained should be consolidated and maximized. It concluded that no change should be made to the existing common service arrangements unless it was demonstrated that a change led to more efficient and cost-effective results. The joint committees that served as co-ordinating and advisory mechanisms needed, however, to be strengthened and refined, and a series of recommendations to this end were made.

These included establishment of a joint co-ordination committee of the three organizations at the level of Chiefs of Administration, to conclude agreement on policy issues concerning financial and budgetary questions and to review costing procedures and cost-sharing patterns; representation in the common service advisory committees of all user organizations and at a high enough level to ensure implementation of recommendations; entrusting those committees with simplifying the cost-sharing keys—developed on the basis of the space occupied by an organization and the number of its staff, and in direct proportion to services received—in computer and other contested services; and an investigation as to whether the services envisaged in the 1977 memorandum of understanding and others suggested by JIU (procurement and contracting; conference; receiving, storage and inventory control; mail, pouch, visas and insurance) could be rendered on a common service basis in accordance with a set of five criteria set out in the study.

It was further recommended that the Secretary-General withhold implementation of any definitive changes in existing joint services until the new UNIDO Constitution had entered into force and, in the light of the conclusions and recommendations of the study, review changes already made. The existing UNIDO/United Nations joint conference service should continue after UNIDO assumed its new status. Current informal co-operative arrangements with some IAEA conference-servicing units should be formalized and modalities determined for pooling other IAEA conference-servicing units into a single conference structure.

Commenting on the recommendations,[11] the Secretary-General stated that he understood the recommendation directed to him as stemming from the perception of JIU that his proposal to establish separate United Nations services in the personnel, public information and legal areas prior to the change in status of UNIDO was precipitate, a view he did not share. He explained that the changes made related to internal administrative arrangements that were neither of a common service nature nor the subject of formal agreements, and that the administrative action taken with regard to personnel and information services did not prejudice consultations leading to further agreement among the three organizations to extend common services along lines compatible with their respective work programme requirements and legislative mandates.

The Secretary-General agreed with the rest of the recommendations. He stated that the question of including additional common services would receive attention during the ongoing review of the memorandum of understanding, and that he had consistently favoured unifying the conference services to achieve maximum efficiency and economy. In this connection, he affirmed United Nations readiness to assume responsibility for providing conference services for the organizations and sought the views and guidance of Member States on this question.

ACABQ[12] concurred with the JIU conclusions and recommendations. In noting the Secretary-General's observations, it supported the idea of a unified conference service and believed that responsibility for it should be assumed by the United Nations, but trusted that the merger of such services could be accomplished without adding to the existing administrative structure.

GENERAL ASSEMBLY ACTION

In section IV of its resolution 39/242, the General Assembly concurred with the recommendations and observations of ACABQ and requested the Secretary-General to set out proposals to give effect to them in a report to the Assembly in 1985.

REFERENCES

(1)A/39/7.   (2)YUN   1983,   p. 634.   (3)A/C.5/39/8.
(4)A/39/7/Add.2.   (5)A/C.5/39/61.   (6)A/39/7   and   Add.1-16
(annex).   (7)YUN 1983, p. 1208, GA res. 38/234, sect. XXI,
20 Dec. 1983.   (8)A/C.5/39/46.   (9)A/C.5/39/97.   (10)A/39/520.
(11)A/39/520/Add.1.   (12)A/39/733.

Information systems
and communications

Co-ordination of information systems

ACC activities. The Administrative Committee on Co-ordination (ACC) continued in 1984 to strengthen the co-ordination of information systems in the United Nations system through its Advisory Committee for the Co-ordination of Information Systems (ACCIS). Established in 1983,[1] ACCIS was to assist agencies to communicate with each other in the preliminary and design stages of inter-agency systems and to provide assistance in launching them. Project execution was to be entrusted to a lead agency, with common financing from participating organizations. To carry out its 1984-1985 work programme, ACCIS set up three technical panels.

At its second session, held from 24 to 26 September 1984 at Geneva,[2] ACCIS considered the work of its technical panels on a register of development activities and on computer-based communication services; the panel on data-base access met in October. ACCIS also drew up a draft programme of work and budget for the 1986-1987 biennium.

On 23 October 1984,[3] ACC approved that work programme and budget.

Register of development activities. A detailed, costed proposal for a register of development activities was drawn up by the technical panel on the subject and presented by ACCIS[2] to ACC. The register would comprehensively cover activities of the United Nations system supporting economic and social development, including activities in approved programmes and budgets, regular programmes of technical assistance funded from assessed budgets, technical assistance projects funded from extrabudgetary resources, grant-based development activities, and loans and credits. It would enable Governments to identify ongoing activities throughout the United Nations system, their subject areas and in which countries they were taking place, and rely on data that could be derived from information currently available in agencies' reporting systems.

Development of the register was envisaged in two stages: version 1 would comprise a meaningful minimum set of data elements to be derived from what was currently available in agencies' reporting systems; version 2 would add elements that were needed but not currently available and under which data from user surveys and data derived from system monitoring could be considered. Information on the register would be structured into two data bases: one to contain information on individual development activities and another on procurement/recruitment by country of origin.

The proposal included cost estimates for setting up a system based on the Programme and Project Management System of the United Nations Development Programme and operating costs for version 1 for one year. Based on available information, it was estimated that the total cost to organizations would probably be in the order of $2 million to $3 million. It was also noted that there would be no possibility of financing the project within the ACCIS budget.

On 23 October 1984,[3] ACC approved, in principle, the register's design as a basis for final consideration by a special ACCIS session. It noted that governing bodies of individual United Nations organizations might have to be apprised of costs to them for the register's implementation. ACCIS was to report to ACC on the final design, scope and implementation problems, as well as institutional arrangements and financial implications, before submitting a report on ACC's behalf to CPC in 1985.

Report of the Secretary-General. In November 1984, the Secretary-General reported[4] that, as of 30 September, total disbursements and expenditure commitments of ACCIS amounted to $350,028. Assuming an even rate of expenditure for the entire year, expenditures could amount to approximately $467,000 for 1984. Further, assuming a continuation of the current expenditure rate through 1985 and taking into account a 5.5 per cent annual inflation rate, 1985 costs might be estimated at $493,000, bringing the total estimated cost of ACCIS for 1984-1985 to $960,000. On that basis, the United Nations share (43 per cent) would be $412,600, or $139,200 in excess of the existing appropriation. The Secretary-General therefore requested an additional appropriation of $139,200 for ACCIS, on the understanding that the General Assembly would again review the matter in examining the second budget performance report in 1985.

ACABQ report. In its oral report to the Fifth Committee on 27 November 1984[5] on the request for an additional appropriation for ACCIS, ACABQ stated that, according to available information, inflation at Geneva had been lower than the initial assumed rate of 5.5 per cent and the United States dollar had been quite strong; there thus appeared less justification for the request at the Assembly's current session than there had been in 1983, when no additional appropriation had been requested.[6] Accordingly, ACABQ proposed that the revised estimates for ACCIS be approved but that no additional appropriations be authorized at the current session. If that created problems, the Secretary-General could raise the matter again in the context of the final programme budget performance report for the 1984-1985 biennium to be submitted in 1985.

GENERAL ASSEMBLY ACTION

On 18 December 1984, acting without vote on the recommendation of the Fifth Committee, the Assembly adopted section IX of resolution 39/236.

United Nations share of the costs of the Advisory Committee for the Co-ordination of Information Systems

[The General Assembly . . .]

Decides that any additional appropriation that may be required in respect of the United Nations share of the costs of the Advisory Committee for the Co-ordination of Information Systems for the biennium 1984-1985 should be reported upon in the context of the programme budget performance report to be considered by the General Assembly at its fortieth session;

. . .

General Assembly resolution 39/236, section IX

18 December 1984   Meeting 105   Adopted without vote

Approved by Fifth Committee (A/39/839) without objection, 27 November (meeting 35); oral proposal by Chairman; agenda item 109.

Other action. The United Nations continued during 1984 to operate several information systems concerned with special aspects of development. These included the Industrial and Technological Information Bank of UNIDO (see p. 583) and the International Referral System for Sources of Environmental Information of UNEP (see p. 749).

In addition, a review by the Secretary-General of the institutional and financial arrangements for the Information Systems Unit as a distinct unit within the Secretariat Library was in progress (see p. 409).

Budget of the International Computing Centre

In September 1984, the Secretary-General submitted to the Fifth Committee the 1985 budget estimates for the International Computing Centre (ICC) at Geneva,[7] as reviewed by the United Nations and 13 other participating organizations and programmes in the system which used and financed ICC services.

The United Nations share of ICC's 1985 estimated budget stood at $1,691,700 against a total of $5,691,500.

Following its review of the estimates, ACABQ[5] recommended approval of the ICC budget, with the United Nations share to be met from the resources appropriated under the 1984-1985 budget.

GENERAL ASSEMBLY ACTION

Acting without vote on the recommendation of the Fifth Committee, the General Assembly adopted section VI of resolution 39/236 on 18 December 1984.

1985 budget estimates for the International Computing Centre

[The General Assembly . . .]

Approves the 1985 budget estimates for the International Computing Centre, amounting to $5,691,500, as contained in the report of the Secretary-General;

. . .

General Assembly resolution 39/236, section VI

18 December 1984   Meeting 105   Adopted without vote

Approved by Fifth Committee (A/39/839) without objection, 13 November (meeting 26); oral proposal by Chairman; agenda item 109.

UN communications system

The United Nations communications system was the subject of a comprehensive report by the Secretary-General, submitted in November 1984[8] as a follow-up to his statement to the Fifth Committee in October 1983 that the work of the Organization necessitated considerable improvement in its communications system. The report described the existing communications network, pointed to its major deficiencies and examined opportunities for improvement and expansion.

The report contained proposals to interconnect the Organization's main offices and certain subsidiary offices with reliable multi-purpose communications circuits available 24 hours daily and dedicated exclusively to United Nations use. The network would include United Nations–owned earth stations operating on leased satellite circuits, primarily for use by peace-keeping missions. Links between the main duty stations of the United Nations would be provided by leased telecommunications circuits. The network would have the capacity to carry all teletype, facsimile and electronic data traffic generated between the duty stations connected to it, as well as a significant portion of telephone traffic. The proposals included a provision for a limited stock of communications equipment to be held in reserve against the possible establishment of new peace-keeping missions on short notice.

A multiphased programme of implementation over approximately three years (1985-1987) was envisaged, to allow an orderly integration of the improved facilities into the existing structure.

Costs for implementing the full system were estimated at $1.57 million yearly, in addition to a non-recurrent cost of $5.76 million. Of the yearly costs, $1.07 million would be covered by redeployments from various budget sections, leaving a yearly recurring amount, after full implementation of the plan, of $499,400. The portion of these costs to be covered under the regular programme budget in 1985, for which an appropriation was requested, was shown as $1.88 million ($789,000 on a recurrent basis, off-set by $536,600 from redeployments, leaving a net recurrent cost of $252,400, and a non-recurrent cost of $1.63 million).

The Secretary-General also stated that, to meet the telecommunications requirements of the United Nations peace-keeping and emergency relief activities, he had leased in July 1984, with prior ACABQ concurrence, satellite facilities from the International Telecommunications Satellite Organization for a five-year term at $200,000 yearly. The lease replaced an earlier arrangement that had been withdrawn on short notice, by which the United Nations had used, free of charge since 1976, the facilities of the experimental "Symphonie" satellite operated by a France–Federal Republic of Germany satellite consortium. No financial commitment authority was requested in respect of 1984 costs relating to the lease ($91,500 for the period from 15 July to 31 December) or the non-recurrent start-up expenses ($26,000), since they were to be absorbed within existing resources for peace-keeping activities.

Following its examination of the Secretary-General's proposals, ACABQ[9] recommended against the further expansion of the satellite network in 1986 and 1987, reducing the estimated costs of the full system in the biennium 1986-1987 by $2,350,000 (at 1984 rates) for earth stations, and by $200,000 yearly for leased facilities on a second satellite. ACABQ also recommended against the proposed procurement of reserve communications equipment, resulting in a recommended reduction in the amount of $1,580,000, of which $380,000 represented a reduction in the proposed appropriation for 1984-1985. Accordingly, ACABQ recommended that the General Assembly approve an additional appropriation of $1,497,400 in the 1984-1985 budget. It also recommended approval of the proposed redeployments between sections of the budget.

Acting on the ACABQ recommendation on 11 December 1984, the Fifth Committee approved, by a recorded vote of 75 to 8, with 14 abstentions, additional net appropriations of $1,497,400 for 1984-1985. The Committee did not concur with the Secretary-General's proposal to expand the communications satellite network.

The recorded vote had been requested by the USSR, which felt that the ACABQ recommendations still included appropriations that went beyond rational needs and would thus vote against them. The proposed expanded network would lead to the creation of a complex technical system, including satellites, not in keeping with United Nations needs. ACABQ's mandate had prevented it from examining the very principle of creating such a system. The USSR felt that the advanced high-frequency radio and telephone communica-

tions and the broad range of commercial channels available to the United Nations were sufficient to resolve all its communications problems.

Explaining its negative vote, the United States said it remained unconvinced of the need for many of the proposed expenditures. The Secretary-General's report did not provide convincing examples of how United Nations work had suffered because of inadequacies in the current communications system. Expenditures of the magnitude proposed must be carefully weighed against competing alternatives.

Communications satellite

In keeping with a recommendation by the Committee on Information as approved by the General Assembly in December 1983,[10] the Secretary-General submitted for the Committee's consideration, at its June/July 1984 session, a final report on the acquisition by the United Nations of its own communications satellite.[11] Investigation of the feasibility of such acquisition was undertaken by the International Telecommunication Union (ITU), whose assistance was requested in preparing the report.

The findings of ITU were against the acquisition on financial, regulatory, technical and political grounds. First, the projected traffic—on a complete system, a maximum of 4,519 telephone-equivalent channels in 1987, rising to 6,111 in 1996—would utilize only 31 per cent of the system's capacity in 1987 and 42 per cent by 1996. Second, two satellites would be needed for full coverage, one over the Atlantic and another over the Indian Ocean. At 1983 constant prices, those satellites and their earth system components would cost $558 million. Were this two-satellite system scaled down to a less complete, one-satellite system (over the Atlantic Ocean, covering most major United Nations locations in North and South America, Africa, the Middle East and Europe), the cost would be reduced to only $460.69 million. Presuming the imperfect yet cheaper coverage of the single-satellite system and taking account of the projected revenues from its use, the operation would still result in a yearly deficit, totalling an estimated $200.89 million by 1996. Third, since the United Nations satellite system would be competing with existing carriers, which had contractual arrangements with host countries, long negotiations would have to be entered into. Positioning the satellite in optimal orbit, given the heavy satellite traffic, would also require sensitive negotiation.

These considerations argued for two options that were less expensive, easier to co-ordinate and quicker to implement: leased space segment facilities on an as-required basis; or a backbone leased channel network, which could be defined for different services, traffic volumes and interconnection needs and could be established on conventional common carriers on commercial terms. Noting that the existing link between New York and Geneva was leased full-duplex at a yearly cost of $152,000, ITU suggested that developing similar links with other main United Nations centres and optimizing the traffic routing would perhaps only be a fraction of the cost of a United Nations–owned and operated satellite system.

In taking note of the ITU report, the Committee recommended[12] that the Secretary-General be requested to present to it in 1985 a complementary report on the acquisition of a United Nations communications satellite. The recommendation, along with the Committee's other recommendations (see p. 358), was approved by the Assembly in resolution 39/98 A.

Library management

In 1984, JIU submitted a report on a comprehensive study it had conducted of the libraries of the United Nations system,[13] using an extensive questionnaire to which 78 of those libraries had responded. The study gave an overview and summary of patterns, trends, problems and issues in the system's library operations and services. Taking into account variations in size, level of development and resources, the study also identified several weaknesses which the libraries had in common.

It was the view of JIU that the main avenue for improvement lay in co-operative actions in acquisition, in information tools, in the use of those acquired collections and tools, in greater scope of services to users, and in the progressive creation of a network of the system's libraries.

JIU submitted four recommendations. Recommendation 1 called for the establishment of an inter-library panel to meet periodically to establish a practical co-operative work programme, and report jointly to the organizations on actions taken and needed. Possible topics for the panel's consideration included common indexing vocabularies, improved standards and training for library staff, microform programmes and joint use of technologies, inter-library co-operation at local duty stations, strengthening depository library networks and closer working relationships with public libraries and international library organizations. Recommendations 2 and 3 concerned management improvement efforts and the introduction of new technology that could be undertaken by the individual libraries of the United Nations system. Recommendation 4 dealt exclusively with problems related to the library services at Geneva, calling for their streamlining and modernization.

In his comments on the JIU report, the Secretary-General[14] agreed with most of the recommendations, indicating possible steps that could be taken to implement them, but also drawing attention to their financial implications. He believed that the new mechanism to be established for improving co-operative activities among libraries should be integrated in the ACC framework. It should have a few realistic goals to be achieved within a specific time-frame, a priority being an agreement on the application of international rules and standards to facilitate development of common bibliographic control over United Nations documentation.

The Secretary-General generally endorsed the recommendations on management improvement and on the use of new technology. He also agreed that most of the problems mentioned with respect to library services at Geneva existed in varying degrees, and suggested that JIU might wish to undertake further studies into two important questions in this regard: space requirements and staffing, and grading of the library personnel.

In general, ACC[15] felt that establishing an inter-agency panel could be a first step towards implementing library co-operation. The panel could consider measures to improve compatibility among computerized operations and encourage co-operative ventures to apply new techniques and promote information interchange. In that connection, the Food and Agriculture Organization of the United Nations felt that informal *ad hoc* consultations to deal with specific needs and problems as they arose appeared more cost-effective and practical than an inter-library panel. It was accepted that co-operation among the libraries to set up new management standards and test the fast-growing technologies could only be beneficial to the whole system. It was mentioned, however, that in a period of budgetary constraints, it would be more reasonable to set limited goals to be achieved in a short period than to try to embrace the whole range of problems at the same time.

While concurring with JIU on the need for system-wide library co-operation, ACABQ[16] noted the hesitation of the Secretary-General and ACC concerning the organizational and financial implications of the proposed inter-library panel. It therefore recommended that ACC be invited to review the proposal further to determine whether or not such an approach would best achieve the intended objective. Should ACC decide to establish the panel, ACABQ recommended that the terms of reference be defined clearly and suggested that *ad hoc* meetings every three or four years might be sufficient. As to the problems at Geneva, ACABQ hoped that prompt action would be taken by the Secretary-General. It would consider any recommendations in that regard or other proposals to improve management or introduce technological innovations in the context of the proposed programme budget for the biennium 1986-1987.

GENERAL ASSEMBLY ACTION

In section III of resolution 39/242, the General Assembly, having considered the JIU report and related comments, and taking account of the views expressed during the debate in the Fifth Committee, concurred with ACABQ's recommendations and requested the Secretary-General to implement them.

During discussion of the JIU report in the Fifth Committee, the Ukrainian SSR drew attention to the additional appropriations entailed by the proposed inter-library panel and said that it shared the view of ACABQ that the proposal be given further consideration. Also sharing that view was the United States, which observed that the central issue was that the libraries were not meeting user requirements and that greater effort was needed to identify and service the real information needs of the United Nations system. Canada supported establishing such a panel provided it was granted a mandate to encourage substantive results, notably a realistic, comprehensive plan of action; a background paper should be prepared outlining proposed terms of reference, objectives and a schedule of meetings. As to the introduction of new technology, user requirements should first be identified and the costs weighed against projected benefits.

REFERENCES

[1]YUN 1983, p. 1208. [2]ACC/1984/23. [3]ACC/1984/DEC/14-22 (dec. 1984/17). [4]A/C.5/39/35. [5]A/39/7 & Add.1-16 (annex). [6]YUN 1983, p. 1209. [7]A/C.5/39/14. [8]A/C.5/39/39. [9]A/39/7/Add.12. [10]YUN 1983, p. 366, GA res. 38/82 B, 15 Dec. 1983. [11]A/AC.198/73. [12]A/39/21. [13]A/39/299. [14]A/39/299/Add.1. [15]A/39/299/Add.2 & Add.2/Corr.1. [16]A/39/603.

UN Postal Administration

In 1984, gross revenue of the United Nations Postal Administration from the sale of philatelic items at United Nations Headquarters and at overseas offices totalled nearly $5 million. Revenue from the sale of stamps for philatelic purposes was retained by the United Nations; revenue from stamps used for postage from Headquarters was retained by the United States Postal Service under an agreement between the United Nations and the United States Government. Similarly, revenue from stamps used for postage from the United Nations Office at Geneva and from the Vienna International Centre was retained by the Swiss and Austrian postal authorities, respectively, in accordance with agreements between the Organization and the Swiss and Austrian Governments.

Six commemorative stamp issues and two souvenir cards were released during the year.

The first issue, on the subject of the "International Conference on Population, 1984", was released on 3 February in denominations of 20 and 40 United States cents, 1.20 Swiss francs (SwF) and 7 Austrian schillings (S). A souvenir card was issued on the same day.

The second issue, on the theme of "World Food Day, 1984", was released on 15 March in denominations of 20 and 40 cents, SwF 0.50 and 0.80, and S 4.50 and 6.

The third issue, commemorating "World Heritage—UNESCO", was released on 18 April in denominations of 20 and 50 cents, SwF 0.50 and 0.70, and S 3.50 and 15.

The fourth issue, of 29 May, was on the theme of "A Future for Refugees". Denominations were in 20 and 50 cents, SwF 0.35 and 1.50, and S 4.50 and 8.50.

On 21 September, a group of 16 stamps was issued in the commemorative "Flag Series"—the fifth group in that series, in denominations of 20 cents each. This was the fifth commemorative issue.

The sixth and final issue, on the theme "International Youth Year" (1985), was released on 15 November in denominations of 20 and 35 cents, SwF 1.20 and S 3.50 and 6.50. A souvenir card was also released on that date.

The number of first-day covers serviced for the various issues in 1984 was:

International Conference on Population	304,015
World Food Day, 1984	465,789
World Heritage—UNESCO	470,379
A Future for Refugees	471,444
Flag Series	1,914,972
International Youth Year	387,757

Issue of special postage stamps

Pursuant to a General Assembly resolution of December 1983,[1] the Secretary-General submitted a financial report on the project to issue special postage stamps,[2] which formed part of an analysis of the financial situation of the United Nations (see Chapter I of this section).

The Secretary-General stated that the final gross proceeds from the special postage stamp issue on the conservation and protection of nature, on sale from November 1982 until November 1983,[3] amounted to $1,956,461 which, after deducting $706,666 for expenses, yielded a net revenue of $1,249,795. As stipulated by the 1983 Assembly resolution,[1] one half of the net revenue had been allocated to UNEP to contribute to financing projects promoting the conservation and protection of nature and endangered species; the other half had been placed in the United Nations Special Account.

The Executive Director of UNEP was to submit a report to the UNEP Governing Council on the results of the projects financed from the special issue.

GENERAL ASSEMBLY ACTION

Acting without vote on the recommendation of the Fifth Committee, the General Assembly adopted resolution 39/239 A on 18 December 1984.

Issue of special postage stamps

The General Assembly,

Having considered the report of the Secretary-General on the analysis of the financial situation of the United Nations,

Recalling its resolutions 35/113 of 10 December 1980, 36/116 B of 10 December 1981, 37/13 of 16 November 1982 and 38/228 A of 20 December 1983,

Noting with concern that the deficit of the Organization is projected to increase to $356 million by 31 December 1984,

Mindful of the necessity to place the finances of the Organization on a sound footing,

Taking note of the relevant statements of Member States in the Fifth Committee on this item,

Noting with appreciation the implementation of the postage stamps project as envisaged in resolution 35/113, the utilization of half of its sale proceeds for the promotion of the noble cause of conservation and protection of nature and endangered species and the allocation of the remaining half to the United Nations Special Account,

Bearing in mind that, pending comprehensive settlement of the differences which have given rise to the financial emergency of the Organization, partial or interim steps could enhance the liquidity of the Organization and alleviate its financial difficulties to some extent,

1. *Invites* the Secretary-General to take appropriate measures to issue special postage stamps on the critical social and economic crisis in Africa with a view to sensitizing the international community to the problems in Africa;

2. *Decides* that:

(a) One half of the revenues so earned shall be earmarked for the implementation of objectives as detailed in the Declaration on the Critical Economic Situation in Africa adopted by the General Assembly on 3 December 1984;

(b) The remaining revenues shall be placed in a special account;

3. *Further decides* that the provisions of regulations 5.2 and 7.1 of the Financial Regulations of the United Nations shall not apply to the sale proceeds of the above-mentioned postage stamps;

4. *Requests* the Secretary-General to give appropriate publicity to the above-mentioned postage stamps, with the aim of mobilizing the support of all States, intergovernmental and non-governmental organizations and the philatelic community;

5. *Further requests* the Secretary-General to submit to the General Assembly at its fortieth session a progress report on the status of the project on the issue of special postage stamps.

General Assembly resolution 39/239 A

18 December 1984   Meeting 105   Adopted without vote

Approved by Fifth Committee (A/39/841 & Corr.1) without vote, 14 December (meeting 51); 27-nation draft (A/C.5/39/L.19); agenda item 111.

Sponsors: Algeria, Bangladesh, Burundi, Chile, Costa Rica, Dominican Republic, Egypt, Honduras, India, Indonesia, Libyan Arab Jamahiriya, Malaysia, Mali, Morocco, Nigeria, Oman, Pakistan, Paraguay, Philippines, Saint Lucia, Saudi Arabia, Sweden, Thailand, Trinidad and Tobago, Tunisia, Turkey, Yugoslavia.

Meeting numbers. GA 39th session: 5th Committee 33, 40, 43, 46, 51; plenary 105.

REFERENCES

[1]YUN 1983, p. 1211, GA res. 38/228 A, 20 Dec. 1983. [2]A/C.5/39/10. [3]YUN 1983, p. 1211.

PART TWO

Intergovernmental organizations
related to the United Nations

Chapter I

International Atomic Energy Agency (IAEA)

In 1984, the International Atomic Energy Agency (IAEA) continued its activities to accelerate and enlarge the contributions of atomic energy to peace, health and prosperity throughout the world and to ensure that the assistance provided was not used for military purposes. Continued emphasis was placed on safeguards, the safety of nuclear power stations, nuclear fuel-cycle services and the management of nuclear wastes, and on the provision of technical assistance to member States, particularly the developing countries.

At the end of 1984, the Treaty on the Non-Proliferation of Nuclear Weapons[a] (Non-Proliferation Treaty (NPT)) had 122 non-nuclear-weapon States parties and 98 per cent of the world's nuclear facilities outside the nuclear-weapon States were under IAEA safeguards. Trends in the Agency's safeguards programme were towards greater effectiveness through structural and management changes, improvements in safeguards implementation, increased manpower for inspections and new instruments and equipment. During the year, negotiations were concluded between the Agency and the USSR for an agreement relating to its offer to place some of its peaceful nuclear installations under IAEA safeguards.

The Agency's efforts to help strengthen nuclear safety and radiation protection included three new initiatives: a scheme to make available to member States radiation protection advisory teams to assist in defining long-term technical co-operation projects in radiation protection; extension of IAEA's radiation protection service to include provision of technical advice to member States on establishing national radiation protection services; and an international nuclear safety advisory group, composed of individuals of high standing from the industrial, research and regulatory sectors, to consider current nuclear safety issues without involving itself in regulatory matters or the development of safety standards.

The IAEA Nuclear Safety Standards (NUSS) programme continued to progress; emphasis shifted towards promoting implementation of NUSS documents. During 1984, the Agency's regulations for the safe transport of radioactive materials were updated and revision of its recommended regulations was completed and published in the safety series.

During the year, IAEA continued to assist in preparations for the United Nations Conference for the Promotion of International Co-operation in the Peaceful Uses of Nuclear Energy, originally scheduled for 1986 (see ECONOMIC AND SOCIAL QUESTIONS, Chapter X).

China became a member of IAEA on 1 January 1984 bringing the number of member States to 112, including virtually all States with significant nuclear programmes.

The twenty-eighth session of the IAEA General Conference was held at Vienna, Austria, from 24 to 28 September. The Conference decided, among other things: to demand that South Africa submit its nuclear installations and facilities to IAEA inspection, and to call on member States to end nuclear co-operation with South Africa, in particular the transfer of fissionable material and technology to it, and to stop purchases of Namibian uranium; to demand that Israel undertake not to carry out further attacks on nuclear facilities in Iraq or other countries; and to request the IAEA Director General to assist in securing financing for nuclear power projects in developing countries, in particular the least developed.

To mark the twentieth anniversary of co-operation between IAEA and the Food and Agriculture Organization of the United Nations (FAO) in promoting world food production, the FAO Director-General addressed the opening meeting of the General Conference.

The Board of Governors met four times during 1984, in February, June, July/August and September at Vienna.

Agency safeguards responsibilities

As at 31 December 1984, 122 non-nuclear-weapon States and three nuclear-weapon States (USSR, United Kingdom, United States) had ratified or acceded to NPT. Safeguards agreements with IAEA, concluded under article III of the Treaty, had entered into force for 78 non-nuclear-weapon States parties. Fourteen of those agreements had also been concluded pursuant to the Treaty for the Prohibition of Nuclear Weapons in Latin America (Treaty of Tlatelolco). In addition, safeguards agreements were in force with two States pursuant to the

[a]YUN 1968, p. 17, GA res. 2373(XXII), annex, 12 June 1968.

Tlatelolco Treaty only. Negotiations were concluded to place some peaceful nuclear installations in the USSR under IAEA safeguards—it was expected that the agreement would enter into force in 1985. Similar agreements were in force with France (1981), the United Kingdom (1978) and the United States (1980).

Agency safeguards were applied under other agreements in 10 non-nuclear-weapon States not party to either NPT or the Tlatelolco Treaty but which have significant nuclear activities—Argentina, Brazil, Chile, Cuba, the Democratic People's Republic of Korea, India, Israel, Pakistan, South Africa and Spain—as well as in Viet Nam (which is a party to NPT).

At the end of 1984, safeguards applied by IAEA in non-nuclear-weapon States covered material in 165 power reactors, 174 research reactors and critical assemblies, 6 conversion, 38 fuel fabrication, 6 reprocessing and 4 enrichment plants, and in some 480 other installations.

Technical assistance

During 1984, more than 80 countries received IAEA technical assistance in the form of expert services, equipment and/or training. A total of 825 fellows carried out individual field studies and 850 persons participated in 51 group training courses. Technical assistance provided by IAEA in 1984 exceeded $32 million, some 22 per cent higher than in 1983.

The Agency served as executing agency for 23 projects in 19 countries and two regions financed by the United Nations Development Programme (UNDP); in three additional countries the IAEA provided UNDP-financed assistance in an associated agency capacity. Ten projects were completed during the year and four new ones approved.

In 1984, income to the IAEA Technical Assistance and Co-operation Fund, derived from voluntary contributions of member States and additional income, rose to over $22 million, 15.5 per cent more than in 1983. Extrabudgetary funds totalled $9.1 million, a decrease from the exceptionally high level attained in 1983. UNDP and in-kind resources at the Agency's disposal amounted to $2.5 million and $2.1 million respectively; their shares of the total available resources declined for the third consecutive year.

Programme emphasis varied from region to region in 1984, with agriculture the leading field for Africa, Latin America and the programme as a whole. Industry and hydrology ranked first in Asia and the Pacific, nuclear engineering and technology in Europe, and general atomic energy development in the Middle East.

An important development in 1984 was the increase to about 46 per cent in the share of nationals from developing countries serving on Agency-assisted projects. Of 51 training courses conducted during the year, 31 were held in developing countries.

Agency staff carried out 378 assignments in 1984; support was provided to 770 ongoing projects by 108 technical officers.

Nuclear power

At the end of 1984, 345 nuclear power plants with a total capacity of some 220,000 megawatts (electrical) accounted for around 13 per cent of the world's electricity-generating capacity. The record of operating nuclear power plants continued to be excellent; 3,470 reactor years had accumulated without any significant spread of radioactivity to the environment or any radiation-induced fatality.

The Agency continued to assist developing member States to introduce nuclear-powered electricity-generating plants with planning surveys, feasibility studies, and development of manpower and infrastructure. It also continued preparing a series of guidebooks on, for example, energy and nuclear power planning for developing countries, expansion planning for electrical generating systems, engineering and science education for nuclear power, industrial support for nuclear power, nuclear power project management, quality assurance programme auditing, operation of nuclear power plants in weak grids, qualification of nuclear power plant operations personnel, and nuclear power plant instrumentation and control.

In 1984, six interregional training courses, three of which focused on special aspects of nuclear power plant safety, were attended by about 200 participants from developing countries.

IAEA continued to develop its energy data bank and to collect and disseminate information on nuclear technology and the technical aspects of nuclear power plants. A computerized power-reactor information system containing nuclear power plant operating-experience data provided by member States since 1971, was expanded and used to analyse the technical performance of operating nuclear power plants.

Environment

During 1984, IAEA continued to attach importance to its waste management programme. A senior advisory group met in October to review the programme and make recommendations regarding its work in handling, treatment, storage and conditioning of radioactive wastes; decontamination and decommissioning of nuclear facilities; underground disposal of radioactive wastes; and environmental and radiological safety aspects of waste management.

In the area of handling and treatment of radioactive waste, an advisory group reviewed techniques and practices for the handling, transportation and storage of low- and intermediate-level waste prior to treatment. A code of practice on the management of radioactive waste from nuclear power plants was finalized and a safety guide on the design of radioactive waste management systems for nuclear power plants was completed.

A seminar on site investigation techniques and assessment methods for the underground disposal of radioactive wastes was held (Sofia, Bulgaria, February) and work was begun on a code of practice for management of wastes from the mining and milling of uranium and thorium ores and on a paper on standards and criteria for the underground disposal of high-level wastes.

Work continued on various environmental aspects of disposal of radioactive waste at sea. Revision of a document defining radioactive material unsuitable for dumping at sea neared completion.

Among material published in 1984 relating to environmental aspects of nuclear energy were: the proceedings of the 1983 International Conference on Radioactive Waste Management,[b] an IAEA/World Health Organization (WHO) booklet on nuclear power, the environment and man, the fifteenth annual edition of waste management research abstracts, three technical reports reviewing the technology of waste handling and treatment, five reports containing guidance on the safe underground disposal and sea-dumping of radioactive waste, and technical documents on the behaviour of radium in waterways and aquifers and on sediments and pollution in waterways.

Nuclear safety

At the end of 1984, with only five documents in the NUSS series of safety codes and guides for nuclear power plants to be completed, the programme's emphasis shifted towards revising the documents, preparing guidance manuals for their use, and promoting their implementation by means of training courses, seminars and visits by experts to member States.

The operational safety review teams (OSART) programme, established in 1983, sent review teams to the Philippines and Yugoslavia. The team which visited the Philippines was the first to review a nuclear power plant prior to its going into operation, the emphasis being on the adequacy of preparations for safe operation. OSART reviews were expected not only to enhance nuclear safety for specific plants, but also to contribute to the exchange of information between OSART members, observers and regulatory and operating organizations of the visited countries. They also provided insights with respect to updating the Agency's technical assistance programmes.

Under the Agency's radiological safety programme, work focused on elaborating guidelines for implementing the system of dose limitation set forth in the revised Basic Safety Standards for Radiation Protection; guidelines were elaborated for the design of radiation protection systems and for occupational monitoring, and work started on formulating principles for operational radiation protection activities. In co-operation with WHO, a symposium was organized on the assessment of radioactive contamination in man. Work on two technical reports on protection of workers in nuclear installations was completed.

By the end of the year, 17 countries had joined the Agency's incident reporting system which collected and disseminated information on significant incidents at nuclear power plants; however, incident reports were received from 20 countries. Two technical meetings were held, one to improve the system and another—organized in co-operation with the Nuclear Energy Agency of the Organisation for Economic Co-operation and Development—to evaluate significant incidents.

The Agency initiated a scheme for making available to member States the services of radiation protection advisory teams to assist in defining long-term technical co-operation projects in radiation protection; China and Iraq were the first countries visited. Missions visited Kenya, the Sudan, the United Republic of Tanzania and Zambia to advise on the establishment of national radiation protection services.

Advisory services continued throughout the year to member States with developing nuclear programmes. Teams visited four countries to advise on nuclear power plant siting, licensing and safety analysis and other nuclear power plant safety matters. Advice was provided to several member States on the safety of research reactors.

Safety information was disseminated worldwide through publications and was also provided in a number of interregional, regional and in-country training courses: 65 technical co-operation projects concerning radiation protection were handled and 13 missions visited developing member States; fellowships in radiation protection were arranged for 43 persons from developing countries; a training course on physical protection of nuclear facilities and materials was held at Madrid, Spain, and attended by 18 participants from seven member States; a revised version of the Agency's regulations for the safe

bYUN 1983, p. 1216.

transport of radioactive materials was completed; and guidelines on mutual emergency assistance arrangements were published.

Nuclear information

The International Nuclear Information System, with 73 participating countries and 14 international organizations, in 1984 enlarged its bibliographic data base on nuclear literature to some 888,000 items.

Life sciences

In co-operation with WHO and several other international organizations, IAEA continued in 1984 to promote the use of nuclear techniques in medicine, biology and health-related environmental research and improvement of the accuracy of radiation dosimetry, with emphasis on the needs of developing member States.

A symposium was held on high-dose dosimetry (Vienna, October). Seminars for the Asia and Pacific region dealt with quality control in radioimmunoassay (Bangkok, Thailand, December) and tissue banking of radiation-sterilized grafts for clinical use (Quezon City, Philippines, May). The IAEA/WHO Secondary Standard Dosimetry Laboratories (SSDLs) network advisory group met to discuss the status and future of the network (Vienna, November); another advisory group dealt with immunodiagnosis of parasitic infections using nuclear techniques (Vienna, May).

In 1984, China and Indonesia each nominated a dosimetry laboratory for membership in the IAEA/WHO network of SSDLs, bringing the number of member laboratories to 48.

Twenty-two co-ordinated research programmes were carried out during 1984. These included: maintenance plans for nuclear laboratories; quality control procedures for nuclear medicine instruments; data processing for internal quality control of radioimmunoassay; nuclear medicine procedures for the diagnosis and management of thyroid disorders; radioimmunoassay of thyroid-related hormones; application of nuclear-related techniques in occupational health; nuclear and other techniques to measure human daily dietary intakes of nutritionally important trace elements; radiation sterilization practices for local medical supplies (Africa and Middle East); radiation sterilization practices for tissue grafts (Asia and the Pacific); chromosomal aberration analysis in radiation protection; nuclear techniques for detecting parasitic antigens in body fluids; nuclear techniques for diagnosis of tropical parasitic diseases in Asian countries; development of nuclear and related techniques for monitoring malaria vectors; irradiation and radioisotopic techniques for developing defined vaccines for schistosomiasis; possible use of high-LET (linear energy transfer) radiation in cancer therapy; improvement of cancer therapy by combining conventional radiation and physical or chemical means; radiation treatment of sewage sludge for safe reutilization; and hair mineral analysis in assessing environmental mineral pollutants.

Training provided by the Agency included: a workshop on maintenance of nuclear instruments in Malaysia for participants from Asia and the Pacific; a workshop on radioimmunoassay in Mexico; an interregional training course and study tour on nuclear medicine in the USSR; a training course for radiotherapy technologists in Japan for participants from South-East Asia; and a training course on dosimetry in Brazil.

An IAEA/WHO technical co-operation project on the use of brachytherapy in treating cancer of the cervix, begun in Egypt in 1983, continued; a second training/demonstration course in November was attended by 31 participants.

Physical sciences and laboratories

IAEA's role in co-ordinating the international effort in controlled fusion continued through the International Tokamak Reactor (INTOR) Workshop, in which scientists from the major fusion laboratories of the European Atomic Energy Community, Japan, the USSR and the United States participated. Work on optimization of the INTOR design and cost/benefit/risk analysis of design alternatives also continued during 1984.

A UNDP-supported project on industrial applications of isotopes and radiation technology in Asia and the Pacific continued towards its goal of introducing these technologies in radiation processing for vulcanization of natural latex, curing surface coatings of wood products and cross-linking of products, as well as nucleonic control systems in the paper, steel and mineral industries, non-destructive testing and tracer technology.

In 1984, renewed emphasis was placed on programmes for the application of nuclear techniques to mineral exploration and exploitation. Work continued on the development of new radiopharmaceutical products and on isotope production by use of accelerators and research reactors.

Within the isotope hydrology programme, IAEA supported 37 technical co-operation projects in 29 countries, some of which were undertaken in co-operation with other United Nations organizations; the projects involved the use of isotope techniques in solving hydrological problems in water resource development, including the problem of sedimentation and sediment transport.

Two co-ordinated research programmes on isotope hydrology continued—one in the Far East, financed by Australia, and the other in Latin America, financed by the Federal Republic of Germany. A second co-ordinated research programme was launched in Latin America on the use of isotopic and geochemical techniques in geothermal exploration; at the end of the year, eight countries were participating in the programme, financed by Italy.

A regional training course for hydrologists and hydrogeologists (Arusha, United Republic of Tanzania, November) studied the potential use and scope of isotope techniques for various hydrological problems encountered in water development activities. Two regional seminars were held in Latin America during the year—one in Mexico on isotopic and geochemical techniques in geothermics and the other in Argentina on isotope hydrology.

The Agency continued to provide nuclear data services to member States. In the course of 1984, some 1,600 nuclear data reports, 60,000 sets of numerical data and more than 500 data processing computer codes were distributed to scientists on request.

Within the framework of the transfer of nuclear data technology to developing member States, IAEA held a four-week workshop on nuclear model computer codes at the International Centre for Theoretical Physics, Trieste, Italy. It continued to provide equipment, fellowships and experts for an interregional project on nuclear data techniques and instrumentation designed specifically for the training of nuclear scientists in developing countries and, at IAEA headquarters, five fellows received training in nuclear data compilation and computer processing techniques.

In 1984, the Centre celebrated its twentieth anniversary with a commemorative meeting on plasma physics, which was the subject of the first course held at the Centre in 1964. The Centre, a joint undertaking with UNESCO, continued research and training-for-research in plasma and nuclear physics, non-conventional energy, elementary particle physics and fundamental theory, applications of physics in biology, geology, and medicine, physics and development, and mathematics. It organized in June and July a workshop on high-energy physics and cosmology which attracted 88 scientists, 53 of them from developing countries. During the same period, 130 scientists took part in the eighth Trieste conference on particle physics.

The IAEA Laboratory at Seibersdorf, Austria, provided support services for the Agency's food and agriculture, life sciences, physical sciences and safeguards programmes. During 1984, agricultural work emphasized fertilizer utilization, residues left by agrochemicals, mutation breeding, and the sterile-male technique for insect control. Medical programmes included studies on trace elements in human hair and animal bone. A new medical applications and dosimetry laboratory was commissioned at Seibersdorf as the central reference for a growing network of dosimetry laboratories in member States. The Safeguards Analytical Laboratory, also at Seibersdorf, analysed nuclear fuel-cycle samples collected by IAEA safeguards inspectors.

The International Laboratory of Marine Radioactivity in Monaco, with the co-operation of the United Nations Environment Programme and the United Nations Educational, Scientific and Cultural Organization (UNESCO), conducted studies in the occurrence, distribution and behaviour of radio-nuclides and other pollutants in the Mediterranean Sea and the Pacific, Atlantic and Indian Oceans. Research activities related to the disposal of radioactive wastes in the oceans were established with several countries.

Food and agriculture

Under a joint programme with FAO, the Agency continued to help developing member States to improve their agriculture and food production through the application of isotopes, ionizing radiation and related techniques. Support was given to over 130 technical co-operation projects in 54 developing countries. Some 400 agricultural institutes and laboratories in 67 member States took part in 35 co-ordinated research programmes, for several of which extrabudgetary support was received from the Federal Republic of Germany, Italy and Sweden.

Work continued on insect control, particularly of the Mediterranean fruit fly in Egypt and Peru and the tsetse fly in Nigeria. Other projects were designed to improve crop and livestock production.

Secretariat

As at the end of 1984, 1,861 staff members were employed by IAEA. Of these, 684—drawn from 76 countries—were in the Professional and higher categories and 1,177 were in the General Service and Maintenance and Operatives Service categories.

Budget

The IAEA General Conference in September 1984 adopted a regular budget of $95,025,000 for 1985. The target for voluntary contributions to finance the Agency's technical assistance and co-operation programme for 1985 was set at $26 million.

Annex I.   MEMBERSHIP OF THE INTERNATIONAL
ATOMIC ENERGY AGENCY AND CONTRIBUTIONS

(Membership as at 31 December 1984; contributions as assessed for 1984 and 1985)

MEMBER	CONTRIBUTION FOR 1984 Percentage	CONTRIBUTION FOR 1984 Net amount (in US dollars)	CONTRIBUTION FOR 1985 Percentage	CONTRIBUTION FOR 1985 Net amount (in US dollars)	MEMBER	CONTRIBUTION FOR 1984 Percentage	CONTRIBUTION FOR 1984 Net amount (in US dollars)	CONTRIBUTION FOR 1985 Percentage	CONTRIBUTION FOR 1985 Net amount (in US dollars)
Afghanistan	0.00720	6,396	0.00717	6,260	Liberia	0.00720	6,396	0.00717	6,260
Albania	0.00720	6,396	0.00717	6,260	Libyan Arab Jamahiriya	0.26883	238,682	0.26922	235,137
Algeria	0.08571	76,096	0.08510	74,328	Liechtenstein	0.01034	9,179	0.01035	9,044
Argentina	0.48445	430,122	0.47511	414,960	Luxembourg	0.06204	55,081	0.06213	54,263
Australia	1.62330	1,441,264	1.60497	1,401,782	Madagascar	0.00720	6,396	0.00717	6,260
Austria	0.77546	688,501	0.76624	669,239	Malaysia	0.05990	53,183	0.05949	51,959
Bangladesh	0.02293	20,359	0.02284	19,951	Mali	0.00720	6,396	0.00717	6,260
Belgium	1.32346	1,175,044	1.31504	1,148,557	Mauritius	0.00720	6,396	0.00717	6,260
Bolivia	0.00720	6,396	0.00717	6,260	Mexico	0.59364	527,071	0.58346	509,597
Brazil	0.91427	811,740	0.89515	781,823	Monaco	0.01034	9,179	0.01035	9,044
Bulgaria	0.12019	106,709	0.11937	104,261	Mongolia	0.00720	6,396	0.00717	6,260
Burma	0.00751	6,671	0.00748	6,535	Morocco	0.03410	30,271	0.03388	29,591
Byelorussian SSR	0.37222	330,481	0.37277	325,576	Namibia*	—	—	—	—
Cameroon	0.00720	6,396	0.00717	6,260	Netherlands	1.84043	1,634,042	1.82242	1,591,700
Canada	3.19490	2,836,625	3.15817	2,758,345	New Zealand	0.26883	238,682	0.26922	235,137
Chile	0.05028	44,644	0.05002	43,692	Nicaragua	0.00720	6,396	0.00717	6,260
China	0.77187	685,310	0.76464	667,836	Niger	0.00720	6,396	0.00717	6,260
Colombia	0.07648	67,900	0.07603	66,404	Nigeria	0.12461	110,636	0.12371	108,052
Costa Rica	0.01356	12,039	0.01347	11,767	Norway	0.52731	468,181	0.51773	452,186
Cuba	0.06145	54,556	0.06106	53,332	Pakistan	0.04393	39,002	0.04372	38,186
Cyprus	0.00720	6,396	0.00717	6,260	Panama	0.01356	12,039	0.01347	11,767
Czechoslovakia	0.78580	697,680	0.77660	678,283	Paraguay	0.00720	6,396	0.00717	6,260
Democratic Kampuchea	0.00720	6,396	0.00717	6,260	Peru	0.04719	41,898	0.04688	40,946
Democratic People's Republic of Korea	0.03448	30,614	0.03427	29,934	Philippines	0.06454	57,303	0.06421	56,079
Denmark	0.77546	688,501	0.76624	669,239	Poland	0.58216	516,877	0.57428	501,578
Dominican Republic	0.01992	17,681	0.01978	17,273	Portugal	0.12058	107,053	0.11977	104,605
Ecuador	0.01356	12,039	0.01347	11,767	Qatar	0.03102	27,539	0.03106	27,132
Egypt	0.04912	43,615	0.04885	42,663	Republic of Korea	0.11864	105,336	0.11780	102,888
El Salvador	0.00720	6,396	0.00717	6,260	Romania	0.13273	117,844	0.13197	115,260
Ethiopia	0.00720	6,396	0.00717	6,260	Saudi Arabia	0.88920	789,483	0.88014	768,719
Finland	0.49630	440,642	0.48667	425,055	Senegal	0.00720	6,396	0.00717	6,260
France	6.74135	5,985,372	6.66840	5,824,177	Sierra Leone	0.00720	6,396	0.00717	6,260
Gabon	0.02068	18,359	0.02071	18,088	Singapore	0.05874	52,154	0.05831	50,930
German Democratic Republic	1.43719	1,276,023	1.41858	1,238,992	South Africa	0.28066	249,183	0.27261	238,101
Germany, Federal Republic of	8.84026	7,848,916	8.74968	7,641,971	Spain	1.99553	1,771,746	1.97774	1,727,357
Ghana	0.01426	12,658	0.01418	12,386	Sri Lanka	0.00751	6,671	0.00748	6,535
Greece	0.26696	237,019	0.25882	226,073	Sudan	0.00742	6,585	0.00738	6,449
Guatemala	0.01387	12,314	0.01379	12,042	Sweden	1.36481	1,211,763	1.34611	1,175,689
Haiti	0.00720	6,396	0.00717	6,260	Switzerland	1.13734	1,009,802	1.12865	985,768
Holy See	0.01034	9,179	0.01035	9,044	Syrian Arab Republic	0.01992	17,681	0.01978	17,273
Hungary	0.17850	158,486	0.17788	155,358	Thailand	0.05509	48,913	0.05476	47,825
Iceland	0.03102	27,539	0.03106	27,132	Tunisia	0.01992	17,681	0.01978	17,273
India	0.27672	245,686	0.27569	240,790	Turkey	0.21496	190,851	0.21353	186,499
Indonesia	0.09035	80,215	0.08982	78,447	Uganda	0.00720	6,396	0.00717	6,260
Iran	0.38856	344,988	0.37966	331,594	Ukrainian SSR	1.36481	1,211,763	1.34611	1,175,689
Iraq	0.07819	69,424	0.07762	67,792	USSR	10.90816	9,684,921	10.79990	9,432,635
Ireland	0.18611	165,242	0.18638	162,786	United Arab Emirates	0.16543	146,880	0.16567	144,699
Israel	0.23781	211,140	0.23816	208,006	United Kingdom	4.83888	4,296,248	4.78385	4,178,215
Italy	3.87731	3,442,506	3.83122	3,346,189	United Republic of Tanzania	0.00720	6,396	0.00717	6,260
Ivory Coast	0.01992	17,681	0.01978	17,273	United States	25.84873	22,950,050	25.88663	22,609,380
Jamaica	0.01377	12,228	0.01369	11,956	Uruguay	0.02774	24,628	0.02757	24,084
Japan	10.68070	9,482,961	10.57210	9,233,670	Venezuela	0.36228	321,654	0.35341	308,667
Jordan	0.00720	6,396	0.00717	6,260	Viet Nam	0.01503	13,344	0.01497	13,072
Kenya	0.00720	6,396	0.00717	6,260	Yugoslavia	0.30586	271,559	0.29745	259,797
Kuwait	0.25849	229,500	0.25887	226,094	Zaire	0.00742	6,585	0.00738	6,449
Lebanon	0.01387	12,314	0.01379	12,042	Zambia	0.00720	6,396	0.00717	6,260
					Total	100.00000	89,471,310	100.00000	87,340,000

*United Nations organizations were requested by the General Assembly in resolution 36/121 D of 10 December 1981 "to grant a waiver of the assessment of Namibia during the period in which it is represented by the United Nations Council for Namibia".

Annex II.   OFFICERS AND OFFICES OF THE INTERNATIONAL ATOMIC ENERGY AGENCY

BOARD OF GOVERNORS

For period October 1984-September 1985)

OFFICERS

Chairman: Mohamed El-Taher Shash (Egypt).

Vice-Chairmen: John R. Kelso (Australia), Georg Sitzlack (German Democratic Republic).

MEMBERS

Argentina, Australia, Austria, Belgium, Brazil, Canada, Chile, China, Cuba, Ecuador, Egypt, France, German Democratic Republic, Germany, Federal Republic of, Greece, Hungary, India, Indonesia, Iraq, Italy, Ivory Coast, Japan, Jordan, Malaysia, Morocco, Nigeria, Norway, Peru, Philippines, Syrian Arab Republic, Tunisia, USSR, United Kingdom, United States, Yugoslavia.

MAIN COMMITTEES OF THE BOARD OF GOVERNORS

ADMINISTRATIVE AND BUDGETARY COMMITTEE

Participation in the Administrative and Budgetary Committee is open to all members of the Board of Governors.

TECHNICAL ASSISTANCE COMMITTEE

Participation in the Technical Assistance Committee is open to all members of the Board of Governors.

SCIENTIFIC ADVISORY COMMITTEE

K. Beckurts (Federal Republic of Germany), D. Beninson (Argentina), A. Bennini (Algeria), Floyd L. Culler (United States), H. Dunster (United Kingdom), G. Fernández de la Garza (Mexico), L. Gutiérrez Jodra (Spain), J. Jennekens (Canada), Malu wa Kalenga (Zaire), J. Minczewski (Poland), H. Murata (Japan), R. Ramanna (India), I. Ursu (Romania), A. A. Vasiliev (USSR), G. Vendryes (France).

SENIOR SECRETARIAT OFFICERS

Director General: Hans Blix.

Deputy Director General for Safeguards: Peter Tempus.

Deputy Director General for Nuclear Energy and Safety: Leonard Konstantinov.

Deputy Director General for Administration: Nelson F. Sievering, Jr.

Deputy Director General for Technical Co-operation: Carlos Vélez Ocón.

Deputy Director General for Research and Isotopes: Maurizio Zifferero.

HEADQUARTERS AND OTHER OFFICE

HEADQUARTERS

International Atomic Energy Agency
Vienna International Centre
Wagramerstrasse 5, P.O. Box 100
A-1400 Vienna, Austria

Cable address: INATOM VIENNA

Telephone: (222) 2360-1270

Telex: 1-12645

LIAISON OFFICE

International Atomic Energy Agency
Liaison Office at the United Nations
United Nations Headquarters, Room DC1-1155
New York, N.Y. 10017, United States

Telephone: (212) 963-6010, 963-6011

Chapter II

International Labour Organisation (ILO)

During 1984, the International Labour Organisation (ILO) continued activities in its six major programme areas: promotion of policies to create employment and satisfy basic human needs; development of human resources; improvement of working and living conditions and environment; promoting social security; strengthening of industrial relations and tripartite (government/employer/worker) co-operation; and the advancement of human rights in the social and labour fields. The main instruments of action continued to be standard-setting, technical co-operation activities, research and publishing.

The ILO membership reached 151 with the admission of Solomon Islands on 28 May.

Meetings

The seventieth session of the International Labour Conference, held at Geneva from 6 to 26 June 1984, was attended by some 1,850 delegates and advisers from 139 countries. The Conference had before it the annual report of the ILO Governing Body, the report of the Director-General, focusing on international labour standards, and the twentieth special report on the effect of *apartheid* on labour and employment in South Africa.

The Conference adopted an International Labour Recommendation on employment policy. A general discussion was held on the ILO International Programme for the Improvement of Working Conditions and Environment (PIACT) (see below). Following first discussions on occupational health services and revision of the Convention concerning Statistics of Wages and Hours of Work, 1938, the Conference adopted resolutions by which it decided to place these questions on the agenda of its 1985 session. Other resolutions concerned productivity improvement and aid to the least developed countries.

The Conference elected members of the ILO Governing Body for the three-year term 1984-1987.

In accordance with usual practice, a tripartite Conference committee examined the application by member States of ILO Conventions and Recommendations, and reviewed the application of ILO standards concerning the reduction of hours of work, weekly rest and holidays with pay.

A special sitting of the Conference was addressed by President Luis Alberto Monge of Costa Rica.

The Fourth Tripartite Technical Meeting for Mines Other than Coal Mines (Geneva, 11-20 January) adopted conclusions on industrial relations and occupational safety and health, and resolutions concerning job creation, working time and multinational enterprises.

A Tripartite Conference on *Apartheid* (Lusaka, Zambia, 4-8 May) adopted conclusions on intensification of international action against *apartheid* in all fields and, in particular, recommended the strengthening of the economies of the front-line and neighbouring States in order to reduce their dependence on South Africa. The Tripartite Conference's conclusions and the twentieth special report by the ILO Director-General on the application of the 1964 Declaration concerning the Policy of *Apartheid* in South Africa (updated in 1981[a]) were considered in June by the ILO Conference Committee on *Apartheid*, which adopted a number of recommendations for strengthening ILO activities and those of its members in the struggle against *apartheid*.

At its twenty-fourth session (Geneva, 20-28 September), the Joint Maritime Commission adopted resolutions on safety, working conditions, social security, health protection and medical care for the world's seafarers.

Two sets of conclusions, on employment and income security and on occupational safety and health, were adopted by the eleventh session of the Textiles Committee (Geneva, 10-18 October). The Committee also adopted resolutions on multinational enterprises, free trade zones in textiles, technological change, equal pay for equal work, migrant workers, and youth and children in the textiles industry.

The first session of the Joint Committee for Postal and Telecommunications Services (Geneva, 27 November–5 December) adopted conclusions on methods of wage determination and safety and health. Resolutions were adopted on working hours, freedom of association, technological change, women and workers with family responsibilities, and youth unemployment.

At its first session (Geneva, 5-13 December), the Food and Drink Industries Committee adopted conclusions on the social effects of technological developments in the industry and on occupational safety and health. By its resolutions, the Commit-

[a]YUN 1981, p. 179.

tee urged Governments to give priority to achieving food self-sufficiency, and called for new forms of work organization to enable workers of both sexes to realize their full potential.

Working environment

Approved by the ILO Governing Body in 1976, PIACT continued to encourage member States to set definite objectives for improving working conditions and the working environment. It used all the means of action at ILO's disposal, including standard-setting, studies and research, tripartite meetings, technical co-operation and the dissemination of information. In June, the ILO Conference evaluated PIACT and adopted a resolution noting that the programme enjoyed the full support of Governments, employers and workers, as well as conclusions which set out an ambitious agenda for action at the national and international levels.

A number of technical co-operation activities were designed to assist member States in establishing policies for the improvement of working conditions and environment through the organization of tripartite national seminars or multidisciplinary team missions. Others sought to strengthen existing structures, systems, procedures and technical capabilities, or establish new ones where appropriate. A multidisciplinary team visited Portugal; national tripartite conferences or seminars were organized in the Ivory Coast, Peru and the Philippines and a needs assessment mission visited Nigeria. A technical advisory mission visited Bolivia to assist in preparing a project aimed at strengthening the institutional machinery for programme development and a similar project begun in Indonesia in 1982 was completed and plans for a second phase made.

Training activities were increased and tripartite seminars and symposia were organized in Indonesia, the Philippines and Thailand. An innovative consultancy and training programme was organized for the benefit of small-scale enterprises in Asia, and training materials suitable for the needs of various target groups were developed.

Information dissemination activities were strengthened. The Clearing-house for the Dissemination of Information on Conditions of Work published two issues of *Conditions of Work: A Cumulative Digest*, a biannual publication containing fact sheets on specific technical subjects, annotated bibliographies, listings of forthcoming meetings and information on research in progress in different countries.

Collaboration with the World Health Organization (WHO) and other United Nations agencies in occupational safety and health continued,

and included participation in the United Nations Environment Programme/WHO/ILO International Programme on Chemical Safety, as well as close co-operation with the International Atomic Energy Agency and WHO in protecting workers against ionizing radiation.

In 1984, the International Occupational Safety and Health Information Centre added two new centres to its network of national centres, bringing the total to 48.

World Employment Programme

The World Employment Programme (WEP) was launched in 1969 to assist Governments to promote an increase in employment and income, alleviate poverty and satisfy basic needs. The Declaration of Principles and Programme of Action, adopted by the 1976 World Employment Conference and endorsed by the 1979 International Labour Conference, reinforced WEP's central role in the world-wide attack on unemployment and poverty. A major event under WEP was the adoption in June by the International Labour Conference of the Employment Policy (Supplementary Provisions) Recommendation, 1984.

WEP continued to account for approximately one third of ILO's total technical co-operation activities, mainly in special works programmes, manpower and employment planning, labour market information, technology, rural development, women, refugees and population. Advisory missions at the country and regional levels remained important elements of WEP. Much of this work was carried out by WEP regional employment teams in Africa, southern Africa, Asia and Latin America.

Field activities

During 1984, ILO spent more than $83 million on technical co-operation activities (about 11.9 per cent less than in 1983) to promote employment, develop human resources and social institutions, and improve living and working conditions.

Most of this expenditure ($38.1 million) continued to be financed by the United Nations Development Programme (UNDP). The ILO regular programme provided $8.4 million, while expenditure funded from multi-bilateral arrangements and other special programmes was $32.4 million. Activities financed by the United Nations Fund for Population Activities (UNFPA) accounted for $4.4 million.

A breakdown of expenditure on technical co-operation by field of activity and source of funds, and by country, territory, region or organization, is shown in the following tables.

ASSISTANCE IN 1984 BY ACTIVITY AND SOURCE OF FUNDS
(Excluding programme support costs; in thousands of US dollars)

Activity	Regular budget	UNDP	Trust funds (including UNFPA)	Total
Training	2,184	20,640	8,294	31,118
Employment and development	1,965	9,308	15,785	27,058
Sectoral activities	469	4,169	6,337	10,975
Workers' activities	1,074	84	1,911	3,069
Industrial relations and labour administration	846	1,084	949	2,879
Working conditions and environment	405	1,865	467	2,737
Social security	213	723	323	1,259
Regional and other services	—	—	917	917
Employers' activities	456	—	378	834
Labour information and statistics	420	198	22	640
Promotion of equality	249	—	373	622
Personnel, budget and finance, internal administration	—	22	506	528
Programming and management	—	—	330	330
International labour standards	149	—	123	272
International Institute for Labour Studies	1	54	78	133
Total	8,431	38,147	36,793	83,371

COUNTRIES, TERRITORIES, REGIONS AND ORGANIZATIONS AIDED BY ILO IN 1984

EXPENDITURES ON AID GIVEN BY SOURCE OF FUNDS
(in US dollars)

COUNTRY, TERRITORY OR OTHER	No. of experts provided	No. of fellowships awarded	ILO regular programme	UNDP*	UNFPA	Trust funds	Total
Afghanistan	1	—	—	18,000	—	—	18,000
Algeria	13	9	—	1,372,000	—	27,000	1,399,000
Angola	5	41	—	875,000	—	—	875,000
Antigua	—	—	33,000	134,000	—	—	167,000
Argentina	1	36	39,000	175,000	—	—	214,000
Bahamas	5	—	—	77,000	—	75,000	152,000
Bahrain	3	9	8,000	171,000	—	—	179,000
Bangladesh	27	10	36,000	1,552,000	68,000	959,000	2,615,000
Barbados	1	1	16,000	—	—	—	16,000
Belgium	—	1	—	—	—	—	—
Belize	—	—	7,000	—	—	—	7,000
Benin	14	10	8,000	999,000	—	237,000	1,244,000
Bermuda	2	—	15,000	—	—	—	15,000
Bhutan	—	—	—	6,000	—	—	6,000
Bolivia	1	10	29,000	43,000	(4,000)	—	68,000
Botswana	15	5	7,000	143,000	—	668,000	818,000
Brazil	16	84	24,000	907,000	—	17,000	948,000
British Virgin Islands	1	—	—	—	—	7,000	7,000
Bulgaria	—	12	8,000	12,000	—	—	20,000
Burkina Faso	9	11	11,000	424,000	—	434,000	869,000
Burma	17	14	12,000	1,244,000	—	141,000	1,397,000
Burundi	17	11	41,000	838,000	—	765,000	1,644,000
Cameroon	15	11	3,000	476,000	138,000	232,000	849,000
Cape Verde	10	7	16,000	312,000	—	562,000	890,000
Caribbean islands	—	—	134,000	66,000	—	—	200,000
Cayman Islands	—	3	—	32,000	—	—	32,000
Central African Republic	5	12	—	365,000	—	—	365,000
Chad	6	53	3,000	152,000	—	—	155,000
Chile	—	11	15,000	43,000	—	—	58,000
China	6	15	37,000	—	—	—	37,000
Colombia	2	24	54,000	252,000	—	23,000	329,000
Comoros	1	2	29,000	—	—	—	29,000
Congo	14	35	83,000	861,000	—	107,000	1,051,000
Costa Rica	4	16	36,000	90,000	—	157,000	283,000
Cuba	1	3	1,000	—	—	—	1,000
Cyprus	5	5	19,000	78,000	—	—	97,000
Democratic Yemen	12	17	6,000	78,000	62,000	657,000	803,000
Djibouti	4	5	72,000	188,000	—	—	260,000
Dominica	1	—	1,000	(4,000)	—	185,000	182,000
Dominican Republic	4	15	27,000	214,000	—	—	241,000
Ecuador	1	89	54,000	258,000	—	1,000	313,000
Egypt	32	23	28,000	297,000	41,000	909,000	1,275,000
El Salvador	—	6	—	—	—	—	—
Equatorial Guinea	5	2	—	96,000	—	—	96,000
Ethiopia	25	17	104,000	868,000	—	316,000	1,288,000
Fiji	11	8	17,000	—	165,000	326,000	508,000
France	—	8	—	—	—	—	—
Gabon	9	6	—	282,000	—	125,000	407,000

COUNTRY, TERRITORY OR OTHER	No. of experts provided	No. of fellowships awarded	ILO regular programme	UNDP*	UNFPA	Trust funds	Total
				EXPENDITURES ON AID GIVEN BY SOURCE OF FUNDS (in US dollars)			
Gambia	9	6	27,000	208,000	—	294,000	529,000
Ghana	2	5	14,000	—	—	152,000	166,000
Greece	1	24	13,000	—	—	66,000	79,000
Grenada	1	1	10,000	—	—	—	10,000
Guatemala	1	5	1,000	31,000	166,000	—	198,000
Guinea	2	10	—	66,000	17,000	—	83,000
Guinea-Bissau	9	8	1,000	416,000	—	75,000	492,000
Guyana	—	—	3,000	—	—	—	3,000
Haiti	11	6	124,000	725,000	—	152,000	1,001,000
Honduras	5	13	18,000	407,000	—	9,000	434,000
Hong Kong	—	2	12,000	6,000	—	—	18,000
Hungary	—	2	3,000	—	—	—	3,000
India	15	37	168,000	498,000	238,000	359,000	1,263,000
Indonesia	24	23	49,000	1,873,000	—	347,000	2,269,000
Iran	6	12	—	969,000	—	—	969,000
Iraq	15	9	4,000	236,000	—	803,000	1,043,000
Israel	—	—	15,000	—	—	—	15,000
Italy	—	172	—	—	—	—	—
Ivory Coast	11	11	7,000	30,000	—	511,000	548,000
Jamaica	1	1	15,000	—	—	—	15,000
Japan	—	2	—	—	—	—	—
Jordan	3	10	4,000	171,000	44,000	—	219,000
Kenya	10	17	39,000	436,000	—	448,000	923,000
Kiribati	—	—	—	6,000	15,000	—	21,000
Kuwait	1	1	—	58,000	—	—	58,000
Lao People's Democratic Republic	9	3	—	743,000	—	153,000	896,000
Lesotho	7	11	—	69,000	—	456,000	525,000
Liberia	1	9	23,000	5,000	—	(3,000)	25,000
Libyan Arab Jamahiriya	6	40	—	387,000	—	11,000	398,000
Madagascar	6	18	10,000	150,000	—	100,000	260,000
Malawi	10	2	15,000	367,000	—	2,000	384,000
Malaysia	3	43	3,000	121,000	3,000	20,000	147,000
Maldives	2	1	—	419,000	—	—	419,000
Mali	7	19	24,000	70,000	141,000	381,000	616,000
Malta	—	1	1,000	—	—	—	1,000
Mauritania	10	10	38,000	503,000	—	85,000	626,000
Mauritius	1	2	49,000	45,000	—	2,000	96,000
Mexico	7	11	13,000	414,000	—	75,000	502,000
Mongolia	—	—	—	(2,000)	—	—	(2,000)
Morocco	—	12	1,000	1,000	—	28,000	30,000
Mozambique	3	16	21,000	105,000	—	165,000	291,000
Namibia	4	—	—	581,000	—	363,000	944,000
National liberation movements†	—	28	102,000	4,000	—	201,000	307,000
Nepal	21	21	59,000	830,000	90,000	1,004,000	1,983,000
Netherlands Antilles	3	—	1,000	147,000	—	—	148,000
New Caledonia	—	—	—	—	—	(3,000)	(3,000)
Nicaragua	3	5	16,000	8,000	5,000	268,000	297,000
Niger	12	18	12,000	368,000	—	231,000	611,000
Nigeria	13	9	1,000	812,000	—	—	813,000
Niue	—	—	—	(1,000)	—	—	(1,000)
Oman	—	1	—	—	—	—	—
Pakistan	18	35	80,000	789,000	54,000	748,000	1,671,000
Panama	5	7	13,000	222,000	—	50,000	285,000
Papua New Guinea	5	2	43,000	2,000	—	46,000	91,000
Paraguay	3	10	47,000	101,000	—	148,000	296,000
Peru	13	18	63,000	52,000	1,000	78,000	194,000
Philippines	4	14	79,000	41,000	—	159,000	279,000
Poland	—	5	—	29,000	—	—	29,000
Portugal	2	68	72,000	359,000	—	—	431,000
Republic of Korea	—	4	7,000	—	—	—	7,000
Romania	—	3	3,000	—	—	—	3,000
Rwanda	4	1	26,000	95,000	—	903,000	1,024,000
Saint Christopher and Nevis	2	—	—	40,000	—	—	40,000
Saint Lucia	1	1	—	14,000	—	—	14,000
Saint Vincent and the Grenadines	1	2	4,000	33,000	—	—	37,000
Samoa	—	—	9,000	—	—	—	9,000
Sao Tome and Principe	2	6	8,000	21,000	—	—	29,000
Saudi Arabia	3	3	4,000	42,000	—	—	46,000
Senegal	15	39	19,000	516,000	—	526,000	1,061,000
Sierra Leone	1	1	2,000	—	42,000	117,000	161,000
Singapore	—	2	8,000	—	—	—	8,000
Solomon Islands	2	—	—	(2,000)	—	—	(2,000)
Somalia	9	15	15,000	403,000	206,000	236,000	860,000
Spain	—	42	17,000	—	—	—	17,000
Sri Lanka	7	12	13,000	486,000	64,000	127,000	690,000
Sudan	18	28	46,000	490,000	143,000	863,000	1,542,000
Suriname	1	2	—	58,000	—	—	58,000
Swaziland	2	4	7,000	73,000	—	15,000	95,000

EXPENDITURES ON AID GIVEN BY SOURCE OF FUNDS
(in US dollars)

COUNTRY, TERRITORY OR OTHER	No. of experts provided	No. of fellowships awarded	ILO regular programme	UNDP*	UNFPA	Trust funds	Total
Syrian Arab Republic	4	12	18,000	51,000	131,000	—	200,000
Thailand	24	30	55,000	961,000	—	396,000	1,412,000
Togo	8	6	8,000	465,000	—	143,000	616,000
Tonga	—	1	2,000	8,000	—	—	10,000
Trinidad and Tobago	1	1	—	107,000	—	22,000	129,000
Trust Territory of the Pacific Islands	—	—	2,000	—	—	—	2,000
Tunisia	4	7	25,000	58,000	—	—	83,000
Turkey	1	12	78,000	46,000	—	—	124,000
Uganda	15	4	111,000	871,000	—	26,000	1,008,000
United Arab Emirates	1	—	1,000	38,000	—	—	39,000
United Republic of Tanzania	12	42	56,000	302,000	—	1,282,000	1,640,000
Uruguay	1	8	7,000	1,000	—	—	8,000
Vanuatu	1	1	—	7,000	—	—	7,000
Venezuela	1	12	24,000	91,000	—	—	115,000
Viet Nam	—	2	—	—	—	—	—
Yemen	—	—	9,000	—	—	—	9,000
Zaire	8	33	8,000	425,000	—	87,000	520,000
Zambia	11	12	40,000	—	61,000	236,000	337,000
Zimbabwe	11	13	102,000	366,000	—	(7,000)	461,000
Occupied Arab territories	—	25	—	—	—	—	—
Geneva headquarters	4	3	—	—	—	—	—
Subtotal	801	1,862	3,080,000	33,937,000	1,891,000	19,886,000	58,794,000
INTERCOUNTRY REGIONAL PROJECTS							
Africa	62	—	1,140,000	1,016,000	440,000	3,622,000	6,218,000
Asia	50	—	1,438,000	1,369,000	510,000	2,002,000	5,319,000
Europe	2	—	42,000	269,000	—	—	311,000
Latin America and the Caribbean	32	—	1,748,000	176,000	239,000	1,252,000	3,415,000
Arab States in the Middle East	6	—	187,000	77,000	267,000	187,000	718,000
Subtotal	152	—	4,555,000	2,907,000	1,456,000	7,063,000	15,981,000
INTERREGIONAL PROJECTS	67	—	796,000	1,303,000	1,062,000	5,438,000	8,599,000
Total	1,020	1,862	8,431,000	38,147,000	4,409,000	32,387,000	83,374,000

NOTE: Figures in parentheses indicate negative adjustments to figures previously reported.

*Includes projects for which ILO acted as executing and associated agency.

†Liberation movements of South Africa.

Educational activities

The International Institute for Labour Studies at Geneva, an ILO centre for advanced labour and social studies, held its nineteenth annual international internship course on active labour policy development from 25 April to 6 June 1984 in English. Twenty-four participants from 18 countries in Africa, the Americas, Asia and Europe attended the course which focused on: processes of economic and social change; demographic, employment and related aspects of development; comparative industrial relations; and the role of ILO in formulating and implementing labour and social policy.

The Fourth Tripartite International Course on Labour-Management Relations in the Petroleum Industry (Geneva, 2-19 October), organized by the Institute, was attended by some 30 participants from Governments, employers' organizations and trade unions from petroleum-producing countries and those in which refining was a major industry. The general theme was the respective roles

of Government, employers, trade unions and workers in labour-management relations in the context of the petroleum industry. Specifically, the topics covered were: the economic structure and environment of the industry; the structure of employers' and workers' organizations, including questions of recognition, workers' representation and participation in decision-making within the enterprise; collective bargaining; dispute resolution and grievance adjustment; working conditions; and in-plant labour-management relations.

The Institute also organized a number of seminars or meetings, including a tripartite national seminar in Israel on employment and unemployment problems and a meeting in Hungary for some 25 participants from European labour courts and related institutions.

During 1984, the ILO International Centre for Advanced Technical and Vocational Training at Turin, Italy, organized 68 courses and seminars, attended by 1,387 participants from 124 countries, and granted fellowships or financed study tours for 486 individuals. There was increased demand for the training of trainers and managers, particularly in the energy, co-operatives and transport sectors, and in workers' education. Management courses and seminars represented almost a third of the Centre's total activity. Seminars and workshops implemented either partly or wholly in the field included: training of technicians in job analysis and classification, and training trainers in road maintenance (Africa); training of trainers for supervisory development, and audio-visual aids technology (Asia); management training for industrial co-operatives, and training of trainers (Europe); and small enterprise development in the non-informal rural sector, and training of trainers (Latin America).

Publications

ILO's published research covered a wide range of topical social and labour questions. New volumes issued in 1984 included: *Clandestine Employment: The Situation in the Industrialised Market Economy Countries; Financing Social Security: The Options; Income Distribution and Economic Development: An Analytical Survey; Into the Twenty-first Century: The Development of Social Security; Managing Construction Projects: A Guide to Processes and Procedures; Profession: Journalist—A Study on the Working Conditions of Journalists; The Reduction of Working Time: Scope and Implications in Industrialised Market Economies; Safety in the Use of Asbestos: An ILO code of Practice; The Trade Union Situation and Industrial Relations in Norway; The Trade Union Situation and Industrial Relations in Hungary; and Voluntary Arbitration of Interest Disputes: A Practical Guide.*

The first volume of *World Labour Report*, surveying the main labour issues in the world, was published, and the forty-fourth (1984) issue of the *Year Book of Labour Statistics* appeared. Regular periodicals and technical series continued to be published, including the bimonthly *International Labour Review*, the quarterly *Social and Labour Bulletin* and the biannual *Legislative Series*.

Secretariat

As at 31 December 1984, the total number of full-time staff under permanent, fixed-term and short-term appointments at ILO headquarters and elsewhere was 2,870. Of these, 1,399 were in the Professional and higher categories (drawn from 116 nationalities) and 1,471 were in the General Service or Maintenance categories. Of the Professional staff, 614 were assigned to technical co-operation projects.

Budget

The International Labour Conference in June 1983 adopted a budget of $254.7 million for 1984-1985.

MAIN CATEGORIES OF EXPENDITURE IN 1984

	Amount (in US dollars)
Staff costs	68,368,373
Operational activities	8,410,164
General operating expenses	6,767,221
Fellowships, grants and contributions	6,539,838
Travel on official business	4,047,703
Contractual services	2,514,796
Acquisition and improvement of premises	2,239,619
Supplies and materials	811,712
Joint activities within the UN system	764,701
Acquisition of furniture and equipment	540,840
Total	101,004,967

Annex I. MEMBERSHIP OF THE INTERNATIONAL LABOUR ORGANISATION AND CONTRIBUTIONS

(Membership as at 31 December 1984; contributions as assessed for 1985)

MEMBER	CONTRIBUTION Percentage	Gross amount (in US dollars)	MEMBER	CONTRIBUTION Percentage	Gross amount (in US dollars)	MEMBER	CONTRIBUTION Percentage	Gross amount (in US dollars)
Afghanistan	0.01	12,737	Burkina Faso	0.01	12,737	Democratic Kampuchea	0.01	12,737
Algeria	0.13	165,584	Burma	0.01	12,737	Democratic Yemen	0.01	12,737
Angola	0.01	12,737	Burundi	0.01	12,737	Denmark	0.74	942,553
Antigua and Barbuda	0.01	12,737	Byelorussian SSR	0.36	458,539	Djibouti	0.01	12,737
Argentina	0.70	891,604	Cameroon	0.01	12,737	Dominican Republic	0.03	38,212
Australia	1.56	1,987,003	Canada	3.05	3,884,846	Dominica	0.01	12,737
Austria	0.74	942,553	Cape Verde	0.01	12,737	Ecuador	0.02	25,475
Bahamas	0.01	12,737	Central African Republic	0.01	12,737	Egypt	0.07	89,160
Bahrain	0.01	12,737	Chad	0.01	12,737	El Salvador	0.01	12,737
Bangladesh	0.03	38,212	Chile	0.07	89,160	Equatorial Guinea	0.01	12,737
Barbados	0.01	12,737	China	0.87	1,108,137	Ethiopia	0.01	12,737
Belgium	1.27	1,617,625	Colombia	0.11	140,109	Fiji	0.01	12,737
Belize	0.01	12,737	Comoros	0.01	12,737	Finland	0.48	611,386
Benin	0.01	12,737	Congo	0.01	12,737	France	6.46	8,228,231
Bolivia	0.01	12,737	Costa Rica	0.02	25,475	Gabon	0.02	25,475
Botswana	0.01	12,737	Cuba	0.09	114,635	German Democratic Republic	1.38	1,757,734
Brazil	1.38	1,757,734	Cyprus	0.01	12,737			
Bulgaria	0.18	229,270	Czechoslovakia	0.75	955,290			

| MEMBER | CONTRIBUTION | | MEMBER | CONTRIBUTION | | MEMBER | CONTRIBUTION | |
	Percent-age	Gross amount (in US dollars)		Percent-age	Gross amount (in US dollars)		Percent-age	Gross amount (in US dollars)
Germany, Federal Republic of	8.47	10,788,409	Malaysia	0.09	114,635	Singapore	0.09	114,635
Ghana	0.02	25,475	Mali	0.01	12,737	Solomon Islands*	—	—
Greece	0.40	509,488	Malta	0.01	12,737	Somalia	0.01	12,737
Grenada	0.01	12,737	Mauritania	0.01	12,737	Spain	1.91	2,432,805
Guatemala	0.02	25,475	Mauritius	0.01	12,737	Sri Lanka	0.01	12,737
Guinea	0.01	12,737	Mexico	0.87	1,108,137	Sudan	0.01	12,737
Guinea-Bissau	0.01	12,737	Mongolia	0.01	12,737	Suriname	0.01	12,737
Guyana	0.01	12,737	Morocco	0.05	63,686	Swaziland	0.01	12,737
Haiti	0.01	12,737	Mozambique	0.01	12,737	Sweden	1.31	1,668,573
Honduras	0.01	12,737	Namibia	0.01	12,737	Switzerland	1.09	1,388,355
Hungary	0.23	292,956	Nepal	0.01	12,737	Syrian Arab Republic	0.03	38,212
Iceland	0.03	38,212	Netherlands	1.76	2,241,747	Thailand	0.08	101,898
India	0.36	458,539	New Zealand	0.26	331,167	Togo	0.01	12,737
Indonesia	0.13	165,584	Nicaragua	0.01	12,737	Trinidad and Tobago	0.03	38,212
Iran	0.57	726,021	Niger	0.01	12,737	Tunisia	0.03	38,212
Iraq	0.12	152,846	Nigeria	0.19	242,007	Turkey	0.32	407,590
Ireland	0.18	229,270	Norway	0.50	636,860	Uganda	0.01	12,737
Israel	0.23	292,956	Pakistan	0.06	76,423	Ukrainian SSR	1.31	1,668,573
Italy	3.71	4,725,501	Panama	0.02	25,475	USSR	10.45	13,310,374
Ivory Coast	0.03	38,212	Papua New Guinea	0.01	12,737	United Arab Emirates	0.16	203,795
Jamaica	0.02	25,475	Paraguay	0.01	12,737	United Kingdom	4.63	5,897,324
Japan	10.23	13,030,156	Peru	0.07	89,160	United Republic of Tanzania	0.01	12,737
Jordan	0.01	12,737	Philippines	0.09	114,635	United States	25.00	31,843,000
Kenya	0.01	12,737	Poland	0.71	904,341	Uruguay	0.04	50,949
Kuwait	0.25	318,430	Portugal	0.18	229,270	Venezuela	0.54	687,809
Lao People's Democratic Republic	0.01	12,737	Qatar	0.03	38,212	Viet Nam	0.02	25,475
			Romania	0.19	242,007	Yemen	0.01	12,737
Lebanon	0.02	25,475	Rwanda	0.01	12,737	Yugoslavia	0.46	585,911
Lesotho	0.01	12,737	Saint Lucia	0.01	12,737	Zaire	0.01	12,737
Liberia	0.01	12,737	San Marino	0.01	12,737	Zambia	0.01	12,737
Libyan Arab Jamahiriya	0.26	331,167	Sao Tome and Principe	0.01	12,737	Zimbabwe	0.02	25,475
Luxembourg	0.06	76,423	Saudi Arabia	0.85	1,082,662			
Madagascar	0.01	12,737	Senegal	0.01	12,737			
Malawi	0.01	12,737	Seychelles	0.01	12,737			
			Sierra Leone	0.01	12,737	Total	100.00	127,372,000

*Became a member on 28 May 1984, after the assessments for 1985 had been established.

Annex II. OFFICERS AND OFFICES OF THE INTERNATIONAL LABOUR ORGANISATION
(As at 31 December 1984)

MEMBERSHIP OF THE GOVERNING BODY OF THE INTERNATIONAL LABOUR OFFICE

Chairman: B. G. Deshmukh (India).
Vice-Chairmen: Jean-Jacques Oechslin (France), Employers' Group; Gerd Muhr (Federal Republic of Germany), Workers' Group.

REGULAR MEMBERS

Government members
Algeria, Angola, Argentina, Brazil,* Burkina Faso, Canada, China,* Ethiopia, Finland, France,* Germany, Federal Republic of,* Ghana, Hungary, India,* Indonesia, Iraq, Italy,* Jamaica, Japan,* Mongolia, Nicaragua, Pakistan, Ukrainian SSR, USSR,* United Kingdom,* United States,* Venezuela, Zimbabwe.

Employers' members
J. Escobar Padrón (Colombia), Daniel J. Flunder (United Kingdom), Henri Georget (Niger), A. Katz (United States), Wolf-Dieter Lindner (Federal Republic of Germany), Marwan Nasr (Lebanon), Jean-Jacques Oechslin (France), Tom D. Owuor (Kenya), Aurelio Periquet (Philippines), Najib Said (Tunisia), Naval H. Tata (India), Johan von Holten (Sweden), Fernando Yllanes Ramos (Mexico), Koh Yoshino (Japan).

Workers' members
N. Adiko (Ivory Coast), Youcef Briki (Algeria), Irving Brown (United States), Shirley Carr (Canada), J. J. Delpino (Venezuela), Cliff O. Dolan (Australia), A. Graham (United Kingdom), Kanti Mehta (India), A. M. Mire (Somalia), Gerd Muhr (Fed-

eral Republic of Germany), Alfonso Sánchez Madariaga (Mexico), A. M. Soubbotine (USSR), John Svenningsen (Denmark), Yoshikazu Tanaka (Japan).

DEPUTY MEMBERS

Government deputy members
Australia, Austria, Benin, Bolivia, Botswana, Burundi, Cuba, Cyprus, Czechoslovakia, Djibouti, Iran, Libyan Arab Jamahiriya, Mexico, Norway, Sao Tome and Principe, Spain, Thailand, Yugoslavia.

Employers' deputy members
Agil Al-Jassem (Kuwait), Sidney B. Chambers (Jamaica), Albert Deschamps (Canada), F. Díaz Garaycoa (Ecuador), A. Gharbaoui (Morocco), C. Hak (Netherlands), N. Kouadio (Ivory Coast), J. M. Lacasa Aso (Spain), Munga-wa-Nyasa (Zaire), G. C. Okogwu (Nigeria), J. W. Rowe (New Zealand), J. Santos Neves Filho (Brazil), Lucia Sasso-Mazzufferi (Italy), Fanuel C. Sumbwe (Zambia).

Workers' deputy members
R. A. Baldassini (Argentina), Marc Blondel (France), A. Chiroma (Nigeria), V. David (Malaysia), M. Diop (Senegal), Heribert Maier (Austria), Democrito T. Mendoza (Philippines), A. Mohamed (Niger), Agus Sudono (Indonesia), Jozsef Timmer (Hungary), Raffaele Vanni (Italy), Frank Walcott (Barbados), Wang Jiachong (China), Newstead L. Zimba (Zambia).

*Member holding a non-elective seat as a State of chief industrial importance.

SENIOR OFFICIALS OF THE INTERNATIONAL LABOUR OFFICE

Director-General: Francis Blanchard.
Deputy Directors-General: Bertil Bolin, Surendra K. Jain, David P. Taylor.

Assistant Directors-General: Vladimir G. Chkounaev, Fuyao Jin, Elimane Kane, Shigeru Nakatani, Franz von Mutius, Francis Wolf.

HEADQUARTERS, REGIONAL, LIAISON AND OTHER OFFICES

HEADQUARTERS

International Labour Office
4 Route des Morillons
1211 Geneva 22, Switzerland
Cable address: INTERLAB GENEVA
Telephone: (022) 99 61 11
Telex: 22271

REGIONAL OFFICES

International Labour Organisation Regional
Office for Africa
P.O. Box 2788
Addis Ababa, Ethiopia
Cable address: INTERLAB ADDISABABA

International Labour Organisation Regional
Office for the Americas
Apartado Postal 3638
Lima 1, Peru
Cable address: INTERLAB LIMA

International Labour Organisation Regional
Office for Asia and the Pacific
P.O. Box 1759
Bangkok 2, Thailand
Cable address: INTERLAB BANGKOK

International Labour Organisation Regional
Office for Europe
1211 Geneva 22, Switzerland
Cable address: INTERLAB GENEVA

LIAISON OFFICES

International Labour Organisation Liaison
Office with the European Communities and
the Benelux
40 Rue Aimé Smekens
B-1040 Brussels, Belgium

International Labour Organisation Liaison
Office with the United Nations
300 East 44th Street, 18th floor
New York, N.Y. 10017, United States

International Labour Organisation Liaison
Office with the United Nations Economic
Commission for Latin America
Correo Central 2353
Santiago, Chile

OTHER OFFICES

International Labour Organisation Office
01-Boîte Postale 3960
Abidjan 01, Ivory Coast

International Labour Organisation Office
Boîte Postale 226
Alger-Gare, Algeria

International Labour Organisation Office
P.K. 407
Ankara, Turkey

International Labour Organisation Office
Boîte Postale 683
101-Antananarivo, Madagascar

OTHER OFFICES *(cont.)*

International Labour Organisation Office
Boîte Postale 114-5096
Beirut, Lebanon

International Labour Organisation Office
Hohenzollernstrasse 21
D-5300 Bonn 2, Federal Republic of Germany

International Labour Organisation Office
Caixa Postal 041401-403
70312-Brasilia DF, Brazil

International Labour Organisation Office
Avenida Julio A. Roca 620 (3o piso)
1067 Buenos Aires, Argentina

International Labour Organisation Office
9 Taha Hussein Street
11561 Zamalek
Cairo, Egypt

International Labour Organisation Office
P.O. Box 1505
Colombo, Sri Lanka

International Labour Organisation Office
Boîte Postale 414
Dakar, Senegal

International Labour Organisation Office
P.O. Box 9212
Dar es Salaam, United Republic of Tanzania

International Labour Organisation Office
P.O. Box 2061
Dhaka, Bangladesh

International Labour Organisation Office
P.O. Box 1047
Islamabad, Pakistan

International Labour Organisation Office
P.O. Box 75
Jakarta 10001, Indonesia

International Labour Organisation Office
Boîte Postale 7248
Kinshasa 1, Zaire

International Labour Organisation Office
P.O. Box 20275 SAFAT
Kuwait, Kuwait

International Labour Organisation Office
P.O. Box 2331
Lagos, Nigeria

International Labour Organisation Office
96/98 Marsham Street
London SW1P 4LY, England

International Labour Organisation Office
P.O. Box 32181
Lusaka, Zambia

International Labour Organisation Office
P.O. Box 7587 ADC/MIA
Metro Manila, Philippines

OTHER OFFICES *(cont.)*

International Labour Organisation Office
Apartado Postal 12-992
Mexico 03000 D.F., Mexico

International Labour Organisation Office
Petrovka 15, Apt. 23
Moscow 103 031, USSR

International Labour Organisation Office
7 Sardar Patel Marg
New Delhi 110021 India

International Labour Organisation Office
Fuller Building, Suite 202
79 Albert Street
Ottawa K1P 5E7, Ontario, Canada

International Labour Organisation Office
205 Boulevard Saint-Germain
F-75340 Paris Cedex 07, France

International Labour Organisation Office
P.O. Box 1201
Port of Spain, Trinidad

International Labour Organisation Office
Villa Aldobrandini
Via Panisperna 28
I-00184 Rome, Italy

International Labour Organisation Office
Apartado Postal 10170, Correo Central
1000 San José, Costa Rica

International Labour Organisation Office
P.O. Box 1546
Government Buildings
Suva, Fiji

International Labour Organisation Office
5th floor, Nippon Press Center Building
2-1, Uchisaiwai-cho 2-Chome
Chiyoda-Ku
Tokyo 100, Japan

International Labour Organisation Office
1750 New York Avenue, N.W., Suite 330
Washington, D.C. 20006, United States

International Labour Organisation Office
Boîte Postale 13
Yaoundé, Cameroon

International Labour Organisation Office for Iran
1211 Geneva 22, Switzerland

INSTITUTE

International Institute for Labour Studies
4 Route des Morillons
1211 Geneva 22, Switzerland

TRAINING CENTRES

Jobs and Skills Programme for Africa
(JASPA)
P.O. Box 2532
Addis Ababa, Ethiopia

TRAINING CENTRES *(cont.)*

Asian Regional Project for Strengthening
    Labour/Manpower Administration (ARPLA)
c/o ILO Regional Office for Asia
    and the Pacific
P.O. Box 1759
Bangkok 2, Thailand

Asian Regional Team for Employment
    Promotion (ARTEP)
P.O. Box 2-146
Bangkok 2, Thailand

Asian and Pacific Regional Skill Development
    Programme (APSDEP)
P.O. Box 1423
Islamabad, Pakistan

TRAINING CENTRES *(cont.)*

Inter-American Labour Administration Centre
    (CIAT)
Apartado Postal 3638
Lima 1, Peru

Inter-American Centre of Research and
    Documentation on Vocational Training
    (CINTERFOR)
Casilla de Correo 1761
Montevideo, Uruguay

African Regional Labour Administration
    Centre (ARLAC)
P.O. Box 59672
Nairobi, Kenya

TRAINING CENTRES *(cont.)*

Regional Employment Programme for Latin
    America and the Caribbean (PREALC)
Casilla de Correo 618
Santiago, Chile

International Centre for Advanced Technical
    and Vocational Training
Via Ventimiglia 201
I-10127 Turin, Italy

African Regional Labour Administration
    Centre (CRADAT)
Boîte Postale 1055
Yaoundé, Cameroon

Chapter III

Food and Agriculture Organization of the United Nations (FAO)

The 49-member Council of the Food and Agriculture Organization of the United Nations (FAO), the organization's governing body between biennial meetings of the FAO Conference, held its eighty-sixth session at Rome, Italy, from 19 to 30 November 1984. The Council expressed grave concern at the extremely serious food situation in Africa, particularly in Ethiopia and countries south of the Sahara, and urged Governments and international organizations to assist those countries in preventing the death of those most threatened by food shortages and in rehabilitating their agricultural and livestock sectors.

The Council also expressed concern over the destruction and depletion of the world's forests and the consequent harm to the environment and agricultural production. It noted that the Ninth World Forestry Congress would be held in Mexico in 1985 and declared 1985 the International Year of the Forest.

During 1984, FAO held conferences in each of its five regions to enable member nations to assess problems specific to their regions and to identify priorities for the next biennium. The conferences also promoted co-operation among countries and reviewed FAO's performance within each region.

At the Conference for the Near East (Aden, Democratic Yemen, 11-15 March); representatives of 26 nations discussed education and training for agricultural and rural development, regional agricultural price policies, agricultural investment strategies, development of agro-industries, and prospects for regional co-operation.

The Conference for Asia and the Pacific (Islamabad, Pakistan, 24 April-3 May), attended by representatives from 21 member countries and three observer nations and by observers from 15 international organizations, discussed training for agricultural and rural development, agricultural price policies, development of renewable energy sources, and the performance of selected FAO regional commissions.

The Conference for Africa (Harare, Zimbabwe, 16-25 July), attended by representatives from 41 nations, discussed training for agricultural and rural development, agricultural pricing policies, monitoring the implementation of the 1980 Lagos Plan of Action for the economic development of Africa,[a] follow-up to the 1979 World Conference on Agrarian Reform and Rural Development

(WCARRD),[b] irrigation development, implementation of the Pan-African Rinderpest Campaign, and development and transfer of food and agricultural technology. The Conference approved the Harare Declaration, a regional call to action, and adopted a resolution expressing concern about continuing acute food shortages in Africa and appealing to the international community for additional food aid and support for agricultural development.

The Conference for Latin America and the Caribbean (Buenos Aires, Argentina, 6-15 August), attended by representatives from 29 countries, including 16 Ministers of Agriculture, discussed education and training for rural development, agricultural pricing policies, food security and follow-up to WCARRD. The Conference adopted the Buenos Aires Declaration, which emphasized the close relationship between the financial problems of the region and the deterioration of the food situation. The Declaration also asked developed countries to remove protectionist measures which restricted the development of Latin American agricultural trade, requested countries to redouble efforts to reach international agreement on tropical products, particularly sugar and bananas, and condemned the use of food as a political weapon.

The Conference for Europe (Reykjavik, Iceland, 17-21 September), attended by representatives of 27 countries, discussed research in support of agricultural policies, protection of European forest resources and follow-up to WCARRD. The Conference requested countries to promote public awareness of the importance of forests and called for legislation to strengthen long-term forest protection.

During 1984, membership of FAO remained unchanged at 156 countries.

World food and agricultural situation

In 1984, global food production increased by 4 per cent over 1983, with cereal production rising between 9 and 10 per cent, boosting estimated supplies at the beginning of the 1984/85 season to an all-time record level. However, in the course of the year the worst drought of the century reached its peak and well over 30 million people in 21 African countries were directly threatened by starvation.

[a]YUN 1980, p. 548.
[b]YUN 1979, p. 500.

Agricultural output of developing countries increased by 2.9 per cent in 1984, less than the average annual growth of 3.6 per cent of the preceding five years but above the population growth of about 2 per cent. In Asia, the combined increase of 1983 and 1984 was between 9 and 10 per cent. Latin America and the Near East had more favourable weather and production recovered somewhat. Some recovery in food and agricultural production was also recorded in Africa, which was due mainly to improved production in the coastal countries of western Africa. Many countries in southern and eastern Africa were afflicted by drought, with Chad, Ethiopia, Mali, Mauritania, Mozambique, the Niger and the Sudan having the most acute food supply problems.

In developed countries, food and agricultural production rose between 5 and 5.5 per cent. Much of the increase was a consequence of the North American recovery from the sharp decline of 1983. Western Europe also had exceptionally good harvests of cereals and some progress was made in the USSR and Eastern Europe. Crop production in the south-west Pacific fell a little from the very good results of 1983.

Funding

FAO funds come from three main sources: contributions by member nations, national trust funds and the United Nations Development Programme (UNDP).

The regular programme, financed by members according to a scale of contributions set by the FAO Conference, supports field work and enables FAO to advise Governments, to provide a neutral forum for discussing issues related to food and agriculture and to provide the international farming community with information.

The FAO field programme is supported by UNDP and funds provided in trust mainly by individual countries or international financing institutions. In the early 1970s, UNDP provided well over 80 per cent of the funding for field programme expenditures but the amount of UNDP support available for development activities had decreased sharply. The main sources of alternative funding in 1984 were trust funds provided through the FAO Government Co-operative Programme. The trust funds allowed one nation to assist another directly, while enabling both countries to benefit from FAO expertise and technical backstopping for field projects. In 1984, trust funds provided $135 million in extrabudgetary funding for FAO field projects and UNDP provided $117 million.

Activities in 1984

Agricultural development. In order to help developing countries create the necessary framework for agricultural development, FAO collected, analysed and disseminated information, advised Governments on policy and planning, promoted consultations and co-operation among member countries, and provided technical assistance.

On 1 January 1984, FAO inaugurated the Research and Technology Development Division to promote individual and co-operative research efforts among member nations, provide technical assistance for remote sensing applications, co-ordinate environment and energy activities, and foster dissemination of information on research and technology related to agriculture, forestry and fisheries.

The International Information System for the Agricultural Sciences and Technology (AGRIS) entered its tenth year of operation. During the year, the number of participating centres reached 131 and the number of entries in the AGRIS data base passed the 1 million mark.

The FAO field programme in agricultural planning included a record 106 projects. Of these, 67 were in planning assistance and 12 in training. Another 27 technical assistance projects had a major planning component. Review and planning missions on agricultural research were organized for Burundi, Chad, Democratic Yemen, Egypt, Iraq, Liberia, Mali, Mauritania, Mozambique, Nigeria, Panama and Uganda. At the regional level, research directors and project managers from nine African countries participated in a workshop on agricultural research management at Morogoro, United Republic of Tanzania. Co-operative research efforts were organized among the member nations of the Great Lake Economic Community (Burundi, Rwanda, Zaire) and among those of the Gambian River Basin Development Organization (Gambia, Guinea, Guinea-Bissau, Senegal).

Rural development. In accordance with the Programme of Action of the 1979 WCARRD, FAO continued to support national policies to alleviate rural poverty and to promote rural development. During the year, WCARRD follow-up missions visited Mozambique and Sri Lanka, bringing to 16 the number of countries which had requested such help since 1979; missions to Colombia, Costa Rica and Uganda were scheduled for 1985. In addition, in-depth studies on alleviating rural poverty were conducted in Bangladesh, Cameroon, Democratic Yemen, Ecuador, Ethiopia, Indonesia, Nicaragua, the Republic of Korea and Sri Lanka. Another important part of WCARRD follow-up was direct technical assistance to member countries; in 1984, FAO provided technical support to 116 rural development field projects in 68 countries.

Food security. At the ninth session of the FAO Committee on World Food Security in April 1984, the Director-General proposed the development of a World Food Security Compact—a long-term framework for the establishment of a fully effective world food security system. The aim of the Compact would be to consolidate into an authoritative charter the consensus that already existed in a variety of texts. Adherence to it would not involve legally or financially binding obligations, but a moral commitment from Governments, non-governmental organizations and public figures.

Throughout the year, the FAO Global Information and Early Warning System continued to monitor changes in the balance of food supply and demand. In view of the precarious food situation in many African countries, the System paid special attention to that region and provided up-to-date information for the three 1984 reports of the FAO/World Food Programme (WFP) Task Force on Africa.

The FAO Food Security Assistance Scheme, which helped to build up national food security systems, including grain reserves, storage facilities and distribution capabilities, organized missions to 14 African countries during 1984 to help identify food security training needs.

In August 1984, FAO approved a project to assist in establishing a subregional food security system for the Andean Pact countries (Bolivia, Colombia, Ecuador, Peru, Venezuela). The project would help to assess the food security situation, compile a list of projects to contribute to food security, and formulate a plan for a subregional early warning system.

Country projects with food security planning components were started in Bhutan, Costa Rica, Nepal and Rwanda. An FAO mission helped Yemen prepare a policy to improve food security through increased cereal production. Switzerland agreed to provide $2 million for a food security project for Bangladesh.

Women in agriculture. FAO was committed to supporting rural women in its programmes and projects at all stages and in all disciplines. Although women were responsible for growing more than half of the food produced in developing countries and for processing an even larger proportion of it, comparatively little agricultural assistance had been directed towards them. FAO's assistance priorities included strengthening rural women's organizations and improving women's access to training, inputs, services and credit. A working group on women in development was established to monitor progress and advise the Director-General accordingly.

A government consultation on the role of women in food production and food security in the African region (Harare, 10-13 July), which brought together delegates from 38 countries, effectively linked so-called women's issues to the basic issues of food production and food security. Similar meetings were held in the Near East and in Latin America during the year.

In 1984, the theme of FAO's World Food Day (16 October) was women in agriculture.

Land and water management. During 1984, FAO helped countries to assess the potential of land and water resources, and to promote their development on a sound environmental basis.

An important event in soil resource assessment was the publication of a study on the potential of land in the developing world to meet the food needs of future populations. The study, covering 117 countries, prompted the implementation of national follow-ups in Kenya, Malaysia, the Philippines and Thailand. Prepared with the support of the United Nations Fund for Population Activities and in collaboration with the International Institute for Applied Systems Analysis, the study revealed that large areas of land in the developing world would have insufficient potential to feed their populations if traditional farming methods continued. No fewer than 64 countries—29 of them in Africa—would be unable to feed their projected populations from their own land resources. Most, however, would be able to feed their people if they could raise the level of farming or slow down the rate of population growth.

FAO estimated that between 5 and 7 million hectares of good land were lost to agricultural use annually through soil degradation. Consequently, the number of requests from member countries for assistance in erosion and desertification control and in reclaiming degraded lands continued to increase.

In Brazil, an FAO/UNDP project helped to build a nation-wide soil and water conservation programme, a basic part of which was the promotion of exchanges of expertise in soil conservation techniques between Brazil and other developing countries.

The first phase of a regional project on soil conservation in Africa—funded by Norway—assessed erosion problems in 31 countries.

In view of the continued depletion and degradation of forest resources in the developing countries, especially in the tropics, renewed efforts in inventory and monitoring of forest lands were needed. FAO's activities in this area included helping a regional training centre at Dehra Dun, India, to disseminate forest inventory techniques and publishing a manual on land evaluation for forestry uses. In addition, a regional study on improving techniques for assessing and mapping desertification hazards in North Africa and the Near East was completed with financial assistance from the United Nations Environment Programme.

Crops. In 1984, over 450 FAO projects to improve crop and grassland production were in operation. Cereals, rice and food legumes, which supplied more than half of the world's total calories, continued to be a primary focus. Improvement of indigenous grains such as sorghum and millet became increasingly important, as developing countries, particularly those in Africa, strove to reduce their dependence on imported cereals. In Kenya, a project to improve sorghum production resulted in yield increases of up to 300 per cent. During the year, on-farm demonstrations of improved cropping methods for maize, sorghum, millet and wheat were held in Burkina Faso, Burundi, Cape Verde, Ghana, the Niger, Rwanda and Zambia.

FAO's work in rice—the staple food of more than half of the world's population—concentrated on developing village production systems in Africa. In Mauritania, under an FAO-supported project, villagers pooled their resources by combining one-hectare plots and jointly purchasing a large tractor. Irrigation ditches, which had occupied 15 per cent of the total crop area and allowed more than half the water to drain away, were replaced by buried plastic pipe, thus increasing the efficiency of both land and water use; yield had been more than doubled. In areas of Guinea-Bissau and Senegal, water-buffaloes were introduced for lowland rice cultivation and for transport.

In 1984, FAO formulated 22 projects to improve seed production and helped strengthen national seed services in 12 countries. National training courses were held in 15 countries for over 300 participants. At the regional level, training courses on improving seed production, processing, quality control and distribution were held in Latin America and the Caribbean (Brazil); Africa (Cameroon); Asia and the Pacific (Indonesia); and the Near East (Egypt and Tunisia). In addition, 16 countries were assisted in improving seed quality control and a videotape course on seed testing was completed. The FAO Seed Laboratory distributed more than 20,000 seed samples to over 90 countries for use in breeding experiments.

To breed new high-yielding varieties of crops, a wide variety of samples, including primitive strains and wild species, was needed. Through the International Board for Plant Genetic Resources (IBPGR)—jointly sponsored by FAO, UNDP and the World Bank—FAO helped to collect, evaluate, document and conserve samples. In 1984, IBPGR concluded its first decade of activity, during which hundreds of collecting missions had been mounted and a world-wide network of over 60 plant gene banks had been established.

FAO continued to assist countries to increase food production through the judicious use of mineral fertilizers and organic sources of plant nutrients. In 1984, projects were under way in 18 countries; since the start of the FAO Fertilizer Programme in 1961, more than 3.5 million farmers had been trained in efficient fertilizer use.

Most of FAO's 123 horticultural projects in 1984 concentrated on improving fruit and vegetable production by small-scale farmers to help guarantee family supplies of nutritious foods. However, some projects also demonstrated how horticultural products could be cultivated as cash crops. In Africa, a series of projects was funded to develop more productive varieties of traditional vegetables, including amaranth, okra and taro, which, although grown widely, had been neglected in development plans because of their low yield.

FAO's plant protection activities fell into three broad categories: development of disease-resistant crop varieties; promotion of efficient and environmentally sound use of chemical pesticides; and expansion of integrated pest control systems. In Latin America, where banana and plantain production suffered heavy losses as a result of a fungus, FAO provided emergency training to national extension workers in identification and quarantine techniques in Bolivia, Colombia, Ecuador, Peru and Venezuela. In Africa, where cassava crops suffered 30 to 80 per cent losses due to mealy-bug and green spider mite infestation, a regional project helped train national plant protection workers in Nigeria to propagate and spread a tiny wasp which preyed on the mealy-bug. Twenty-two other African countries requested similar assistance.

Livestock. In 1984, FAO was involved in over 200 projects to improve animal production: 58 projects on fodder improvement were under way and another 18 were formulated in a total of 64 countries. Drought in Africa led to an increase in the number of requests for both emergency and long-term aid to the animal feed sector. FAO missions visited Botswana, Chad, Ethiopia, Lesotho, Senegal, Swaziland, Zambia and Zimbabwe to evaluate feed resources and formulate proposals for assistance projects. Plans were also finalized for a comprehensive animal-feed security programme to begin in 1985, with special emphasis on the drought-prone countries of Africa.

To assist in the conservation of animal genetic resources, the Netherlands agreed in November to fund a five-year programme to maintain liquid nitrogen units for the cryogenic storage of such resources in Egypt, Ethiopia, Rwanda, Somalia, the United Republic of Tanzania and Zaire.

Fisheries. At the World Conference on Fisheries Management and Development (Rome, 27 June–6 July), representatives from 147 countries and over 60 international organizations discussed the problems and potential of world fisheries as a vital source of food, employment and income. In particular, they focused on the difficulties faced by developing and developed countries in adjusting to the new legal régime of the oceans, as embodied in the 1982 United Nations Convention on the Law of the Sea.[c] The Conference endorsed a global strategy and five special action programmes to promote the rational development of fisheries, including aquaculture.

A large part of FAO's activities in fishery development concentrated on improving the capabilities of small-scale fisheries, which, although they supplied more than 40 per cent of the world's food-fish, had received little development assistance. Projects were under way in the Congo River Basin to improve fishing and fish processing techniques; in India's Bay of Bengal to introduce inboard diesel engines for fishing craft; in Rwanda to train people in night fishing; and in Somalia to train fishermen to use sails in conjunction with motors.

Forestry. In 1984, FAO was involved in projects to increase fuelwood production in all regions of the developing world. In Cape Verde, forestry development was being promoted in naturally treeless areas to control erosion and help capture atmospheric humidity and return it to the soil; in the Peruvian sierra, a project supported by the Netherlands was helping to re-establish depleted forest resources; in Papua New Guinea, mangrove tree development was being combined with crocodile raising; and in Senegal, trees were being planted for fuelwood, enrichment of soil nutrients and erosion control.

Special relief operations. While most of FAO's assistance to agricultural development was of a medium- or long-term nature, emergency and rehabilitation assistance was available through the Office for Special Relief Operations, which, throughout 1984, continued to serve as the focal point for the FAO/WFP Task Force on Africa. Of its more than 70 projects in operation during the year, over a third focused on the drought-stricken countries of Africa.

World Food Programme. In 1984, WFP provided $1.1 billion in assistance to developing countries. Since beginning operations in 1963, it had provided over $7.5 billion worth of food to almost 250 million people.

During the year, WFP committed more than $575 million of food aid to agricultural and rural development projects, which included land reclamation, irrigation systems and better farming systems. Labourers received food rations for their work and projects took place during periods when no other work was available. The availability of food aid also helped Governments widen their development programmes. Substantial assistance ($325 million in 1984) was also provided to poor rural populations most likely to be malnourished, especially mothers, infants and young children. Such projects usually also incorporated activities to improve social and economic well-being, including nutrition education and health care.

In 1984, WFP also supplied more than $200 million in assistance to emergency operations, both from its own resources and from the International Emergency Food Reserve. Over half of this went to sub-Saharan Africa, where drought and civil strife had led to severe malnutrition and starvation. Other major operations supplied flood victims in Bangladesh and refugees in Pakistan. During the year, WFP also bought, shipped or monitored the movement of 500,000 tonnes of aid on behalf of bilateral donors.

Secretariat

At the end of 1984, the number of staff employed by FAO at its headquarters was 3,331, of whom 1,145 were in the Professional and higher categories. Field project personnel working in 122 countries numbered 1,288 in the Professional and higher categories and 658 in the General Service category. Regional office, joint division and country representation staff numbered 242 in the Professional and higher categories and 668 in the General Service category. Of the 315 associate experts working with FAO, 264 were in the field, 13 in regional and country offices and 38 at headquarters. In addition, WFP employed 105 Professional and higher category staff and 159 General Service personnel at headquarters and 185 staff in the field.

Budget

The November 1983 session of the FAO Conference approved a budget of some $421 million for 1984-1985.

Annex I. MEMBERSHIP OF THE FOOD AND AGRICULTURE ORGANIZATION AND CONTRIBUTIONS

(Membership as at 31 December 1984; contributions as assessed for 1984 and 1985)

MEMBER	CONTRIBUTION Percentage	CONTRIBUTION Net amount (in US dollars)	MEMBER	CONTRIBUTION Percentage	CONTRIBUTION Net amount (in US dollars)	MEMBER	CONTRIBUTION Percentage	CONTRIBUTION Net amount (in US dollars)
Afghanistan	0.01	19,729	Bangladesh	0.04	78,916	Burkina Faso	0.01	19,729
Albania	0.01	19,729	Barbados	0.01	19,729	Burma	0.01	19,729
Algeria	0.16	315,664	Belgium	1.55	3,057,995	Burundi	0.01	19,729
Angola	0.01	19,729	Belize	0.01	19,729	Cameroon	0.01	19,729
Antigua and Barbuda	0.01	19,729	Benin	0.01	19,729	Canada	3.72	7,339,188
Argentina	0.86	1,696,694	Bhutan	0.01	19,729	Cape Verde	0.01	19,729
Australia	1.90	3,748,510	Bolivia	0.01	19,729	Central African Republic	0.01	19,729
Austria	0.91	1,795,339	Botswana	0.01	19,729	Chad	0.01	19,729
Bahamas	0.01	19,729	Brazil	1.68	3,314,472	Chile	0.08	157,832
Bahrain	0.01	19,729	Bulgaria	0.22	434,038	China	1.06	2,091,274

MEMBER	CONTRIBUTION Percent-age	Net amount (in US dollars)	MEMBER	CONTRIBUTION Percent-age	Net amount (in US dollars)	MEMBER	CONTRIBUTION Percent-age	Net amount (in US dollars)
Colombia	0.13	256,477	Ivory Coast	0.04	78,916	Rwanda	0.01	19,729
Comoros	0.01	19,729	Jamaica	0.02	39,458	Saint Christopher and		
Congo	0.01	19,729	Japan	12.46	24,582,334	Nevis	0.01	19,729
Costa Rica	0.02	39,458	Jordan	0.01	19,729	Saint Lucia	0.01	19,729
Cuba	0.11	217,019	Kenya	0.01	19,729	Saint Vincent and the		
Cyprus	0.01	19,729	Kuwait	0.30	591,870	Grenadines	0.01	19,729
Czechoslovakia	0.92	1,815,068	Lao People's Democratic			Samoa	0.01	19,729
Democratic Kampuchea	0.01	19,729	Republic	0.01	19,729	Sao Tome and Principe	0.01	19,729
Democratic People's			Lebanon	0.02	39,458	Saudi Arabia	1.04	2,051,816
Republic of Korea	0.06	118,374	Lesotho	0.01	19,729	Senegal	0.01	19,729
Democratic Yemen	0.01	19,729	Liberia	0.01	19,729	Seychelles	0.01	19,729
Denmark	0.91	1,795,339	Libyan Arab Jamahiriya	0.31	611,599	Sierra Leone	0.01	19,729
Djibouti	0.01	19,729	Luxembourg	0.07	138,103	Somalia	0.01	19,729
Dominica	0.01	19,729	Madagascar	0.01	19,729	Spain	2.33	4,596,857
Dominican Republic	0.04	78,916	Malawi	0.01	19,729	Sri Lanka	0.01	19,729
Ecuador	0.02	39,458	Malaysia	0.11	217,019	Sudan	0.01	19,729
Egypt	0.08	157,832	Maldives	0.01	19,729	Suriname	0.01	19,729
El Salvador	0.01	19,729	Mali	0.01	19,729	Swaziland	0.01	19,729
Equatorial Guinea	0.01	19,729	Malta	0.01	19,729	Sweden	1.59	3,136,911
Ethiopia	0.01	19,729	Mauritania	0.01	19,729	Switzerland	1.33	2,623,957
Fiji	0.01	19,729	Mauritius	0.01	19,729	Syrian Arab Republic	0.04	78,916
Finland	0.58	1,144,282	Mexico	1.06	2,091,274	Thailand	0.10	197,290
France	7.86	15,506,994	Mongolia	0.01	19,729	Togo	0.01	19,729
Gabon	0.02	39,458	Morocco	0.06	118,374	Tonga	0.01	19,729
Gambia	0.01	19,729	Mozambique	0.01	19,729	Trinidad and Tobago	0.04	78,916
Germany, Federal			Namibia	0.01	19,729	Tunisia	0.04	78,916
Republic of	10.31	20,340,599	Nepal	0.01	19,729	Turkey	0.39	769,431
Ghana	0.02	39,458	Netherlands	2.15	4,241,735	Uganda	0.01	19,729
Greece	0.48	946,992	New Zealand	0.31	611,599	United Arab Emirates	0.19	374,851
Grenada	0.01	19,729	Nicaragua	0.01	19,729	United Kingdom	5.64	11,127,156
Guatemala	0.02	39,458	Niger	0.01	19,729	United Republic of		
Guinea	0.01	19,729	Nigeria	0.23	453,767	Tanzania	0.01	19,729
Guinea-Bissau	0.01	19,729	Norway	0.62	1,223,198	United States	25.00	49,972,500
Guyana	0.01	19,729	Oman	0.01	19,729	Uruguay	0.05	98,645
Haiti	0.01	19,729	Pakistan	0.07	138,103	Vanuatu	0.01	19,729
Honduras	0.01	19,729	Panama	0.02	39,458	Venezuela	0.66	1,302,114
Hungary	0.28	552,412	Papua New Guinea	0.01	19,729	Viet Nam	0.02	39,458
Iceland	0.04	78,916	Paraguay	0.01	19,729	Yemen	0.01	19,729
India	0.43	848,347	Peru	0.08	157,832	Yugoslavia	0.56	1,104,824
Indonesia	0.16	315,664	Philippines	0.11	217,019	Zaire	0.01	19,729
Iran	0.70	1,381,030	Poland	0.87	1,716,423	Zambia	0.01	19,729
Iraq	0.15	295,935	Portugal	0.22	434,038	Zimbabwe	0.02	39,458
Ireland	0.22	434,038	Qatar	0.04	78,916			
Israel	0.28	552,412	Republic of Korea	0.22	434,038	Total	100.0	197,940,000*
Italy	4.52	8,917,508	Romania	0.23	453,767			

*The total sum for the 1984-1985 biennium was $395,880,000.

Annex II.   MEMBERS OF THE COUNCIL OF THE FOOD AND AGRICULTURE ORGANIZATION

Holding office until 31 December 1984: Burkina Faso, Cape Verde, Ecuador, Egypt, Ethiopia, France, India, Italy, Lesotho, New Zealand, Norway, Pakistan, Philippines, Saudi Arabia, Sudan, United Kingdom.

Holding office until conclusion of twenty-third session of the FAO Conference, November 1985: Argentina, Bangladesh, Benin, China, Cyprus, Germany, Federal Republic of, Indonesia, Iraq, Japan, Malawi, Malaysia, Panama, Rwanda, Spain, Thailand, Venezuela.

Holding office until 31 December 1986: Austria, Brazil, Bulgaria, Canada, Colombia, Congo, Cuba, Czechoslovakia, Democratic Yemen, Lebanon, Mexico, Sao Tome and Principe, Sierra Leone, Trinidad and Tobago, Tunisia, Uganda, United States.

Annex III.   OFFICERS AND OFFICES OF THE FOOD AND AGRICULTURE ORGANIZATION

OFFICERS

OFFICE OF THE DIRECTOR-GENERAL
Director-General: Edouard Saouma.
Deputy Director-General: Edward M. West.
Executive Director, World Food Programme: James Charles Ingram.

DEPARTMENTS
Assistant Director-General, Administration and Finance Department: Dean K. Crowther.
Assistant Director-General, Agriculture Department: D. F. R. Bommer.
Assistant Director-General, Development Department: R. S. Lignon.
Assistant Director-General, Forestry Department: M. A. Flores Rodas.
Assistant Director-General, Department of General Affairs and Information: P. Savary.

Assistant Director-General, Economic and Social Department: N. Islam.
Assistant Director-General, Fisheries Department: J. E. Carroz.

REGIONAL REPRESENTATIVES OF THE DIRECTOR-GENERAL
Assistant Director-General and Regional Representative for Africa: J. A. C. Davies.
Assistant Director-General and Regional Representative for Asia and the Pacific: S. S. Puri.
Assistant Director-General and Regional Representative for Latin America and the Caribbean: M. E. Jalil.
Assistant Director-General and Regional Representative for the Near East: S. Jum'a.
Regional Representative for Europe: A. Bozzini.

HEADQUARTERS AND REGIONAL OFFICES

HEADQUARTERS

Food and Agriculture Organization
Via delle Terme di Caracalla
Rome 00100, Italy
  Cable address: FOODAGRI ROME
  Telephone: 57971
  Telex: 610181

REGIONAL AND OTHER OFFICES

Food and Agriculture Organization Regional
  Office for Africa
United Nations Agency Building
North Maxwell Road
P.O. Box 1628
Accra, Ghana

REGIONAL AND OTHER OFFICES *(cont.)*

Food and Agriculture Organization Regional
  Office for Asia and the Pacific
Maliwan Mansion
Phra Atit Road
Bangkok 10200, Thailand

Food and Agriculture Organization Regional
  Office for the Near East
Via delle Terme di Caracalla
Rome 00100, Italy

Food and Agriculture Organization Regional
  Office for Europe
Via delle Terme di Caracalla
Rome 00100, Italy

REGIONAL AND OTHER OFFICES *(cont.)*

Food and Agriculture Organization Regional
  Office for Latin America and the Caribbean
Avenida Providencia 871
Casilla de Correo 10095
Santiago, Chile

Food and Agriculture Organization Liaison
  Office with the United Nations
United Nations Headquarters, Room DC1-1125
New York, N.Y. 10017, United States

Food and Agriculture Organization Liaison
  Office for North America
1001 22nd Street, N.W., Suite 300
Washington, D.C. 20437, United States

Chapter IV

United Nations Educational, Scientific and Cultural Organization (UNESCO)

During 1984, the United Nations Educational, Scientific and Cultural Organization (UNESCO) continued a broad range of activities by promoting collaboration among nations through education, natural and social sciences, culture and communication.

Following the withdrawal of the United States from the organization on 31 December 1984, the membership of UNESCO decreased to 160; the associate membership went down to two after the British Eastern Caribbean Group ceased to be a member on 31 December.

Education

The 1984 UNESCO education programmes continued to focus on education for development. UNESCO, which originated literacy drives, had some of its achievements neutralized by the world's population growth. Among its education programmes were: the democratization of education; out-of-school and lifelong education for all; the formulation of educational policies; and improved financing and administration of educational institutions.

In its fight against illiteracy, UNESCO assisted literacy programmes outside formal education systems for adults, as well as girls, women and groups or sectors of the population that encountered difficulties in exercising their right to education. It assisted member States at the national level and promoted regional and international co-operation for educational purposes: training educational personnel, mainly at the primary and special education levels; and promoting technical, vocational and adult education, integrated rural development and educational participation of the elderly.

An intergovernmental regional committee (Mexico City, 5-9 November) reviewed efforts of member States and adopted a regional plan of action for the eradication of illiteracy by the year 2000, a minimum schooling of 8 to 10 years and an improvement in the quality of education in Latin America and the Caribbean.

Seminars, workshops and meetings were held during the year in Asia, Africa, Latin America and the Arab States for the improvement of rural teaching and the use of technology. Others, which took place in Argentina, China, Guatemala, Malawi, Mali and Zaire, dealt with agricultural education, vocational training activities, the adaptation of curricula to meet rural development needs, and upgraded teaching.

Other efforts by UNESCO to develop co-operation with member States in education included: promoting the equality of educational opportunities for girls and women in Cape Verde, India, Peru and the Syrian Arab Republic; special education programmes in Africa; educational programmes for liberation movements and Palestinian refugees; and studies to meet the needs of migrant workers and their families.

UNESCO contributed in 1984 to the formulation and application of education policies and the strengthening of national capacities for educational planning, management, administration and economics. The thirty-ninth session of the International Conference on Education (Geneva, 16-25 October), with more than 500 participants, discussed the relationship between education for all and the new scientific and technological environment. It highlighted the importance of science and technology education as a means of equal opportunity in some societies and examined aspects of the repercussion of informatics on education.

UNESCO continued its technical and financial assistance to the five regional and subregional networks of educational innovation for development (Africa, Asia and the Pacific, Arab States, South and South-East Europe, and the Caribbean), which organized over 100 meetings and workshops to exchange experiences.

Other activities dealt with the interaction between education and society: education and culture; education and communication; education and science and technology; education and the work market; and education and sports. The role of higher education, particularly its training and research functions, was discussed. Financial and technical support was provided for studies on national languages and mother tongues, including those of ethnic minorities, as a means of educational teaching and cultural exchange. Regional meetings in Latin America and the Caribbean considered strategies for using the media to improve and develop educational services to disadvantaged sectors of the population and to promote education for peace and the respect of human rights.

UNESCO also provided technical assistance to: member States to strengthen national infrastructures and launch projects on science and technology education; the Association of African Universities for studies on the potential of higher education institutions and research centres in Africa; and the

Regional Institute on Higher Education and Development in Asia for the implementation of research projects and the development of informational resources.

The fifth regional conference of Arab education ministers and those responsible for economic planning, rescheduled for 1984, was postponed to 1986.

During 1984, UNESCO participated in over 300 national, regional and subregional education projects with financial assistance from the United Nations Development Programme (UNDP), the United Nations Fund for Population Activities (UNFPA), the World Bank, regional banks and funds-in-trust.

Natural sciences

In 1984, UNESCO continued to assist member States to use the resources of science and technology for development. It initiated a new programme to set up an international system of regional networks for training, research and information exchange in science and technology policy management.

In co-operation with the International Council of Scientific Unions, UNESCO provided research training to some 3,000 scientists from developing countries.

The International Geological Correlation Programme pursued its undertaking of geological science projects and, in co-operation with 116 countries, implemented 48 such projects in 1984.

The International Hydrological Programme entered its third phase (1984-1989). Thirty post-graduate courses in hydrology and water resources were sponsored, mainly for participants from developing countries, and several seminars, training courses and workshops were offered.

In the ecological sciences, the eighth session of the International Co-ordinating Council of the Man and the Biosphere programme drew up a plan of action for biosphere reserves from 1985 to 1989. Other activities for the assessment of natural hazards of geological origin, such as earthquakes, volcanic eruptions and landslides, were characterized by regional operational projects, and a study for an international early-warning system for volcanic eruptions was prepared.

In the marine sciences, some 400 specialists were helped to improve their scientific skills and research through participation in 30 training courses, meetings and seminars, and through fellowships and travel grants. Scientific reports and publications, designed to stimulate research in areas such as the mangrove ecosystem, coral reefs, pollution research, and coastal zone management in the Indian Ocean region, were published. Several developing countries were also assisted in strengthening their marine science infrastructure through national and regional extrabudgetary projects.

In addition to its regular programme activities, UNESCO assisted member States in the execution of over 100 science and technology projects financed from extrabudgetary funds. Other extrabudgetary activities contributed to the development of science and technology through science training for research, technical application and information exchange.

Social sciences

During 1984, UNESCO continued to support the development of social sciences at various levels: at the national level, by strengthening research, training and documentation capacities within disciplines and in interdisciplinal work; at the regional level, by expanding networks of co-operation; and at the international level, by reinforcing co-operation with the scientific community through governmental and non-governmental organizations and professional associations over a wide range of activities, including scientific exchanges of data, an international journal, publications and scholars.

Philosophical and interdisciplinary activities were also carried out in several areas: the unity of man in the perspective of neurophysiology; behavioural neurosciences and cognitive science; goals of development; varieties of development planning; ethical dimensions of peace; and philosophical aspects of human rights.

Concerning population activities, technical assistance was provided to 35 national projects in communication training, research and planning. Co-operation was sought with regional broadcasting organizations, such as the Asia Pacific Institute for Broadcasting Development, the Arab States Broadcasting Union and the Asociación Interamericana de Radiodifusión. Other projects dealt with migration and its socio-economic effects, and the interrelationships between population, resources, environment and development.

Activities for and concerning youth aimed at: encouraging research about young people in different parts of the world; promoting the dissemination and exchange of information; and assisting with the drafting of policies and the implementation of programmes to increase youth's participation in social life. UNESCO co-operated also with member States and youth organizations to promote sports, mainly in rural areas, to expand voluntary work among young people and to examine the circumstances which led young people to become socially deprived.

On the question of *apartheid*, UNESCO organized meetings at Dakar, Senegal, for specialists from scientific, religious and cultural communities. On 21 March 1984, a public lecture was held at UNESCO headquarters on the occasion of the International Day for the Elimination of Racial Discrimination. UNESCO also assisted national liberation movements recognized by the Organization of African Unity in social sciences training.

The organization continued to analyse human rights violations and the conditions for peace. Research activities centred on: human rights in different cultural and religious traditions; ways of improving the human rights of disadvantaged social groups; and technological and scientific progress and human rights. Legal, sociological, historical and philosophical studies were undertaken to elucidate the concept of peoples' rights, as were training sessions, publications and studies to promote human rights teaching.

UNESCO's status of women programmes included research on women's participation in political and public life and the effects of socio-economic change within their societies. The 1984 publication *Women in the Villages, Men in the Towns* dealt with the situation of rural women left as heads of household because of male migration. It included case-studies on Bangladesh, India, the Philippines, the Republic of Korea and Thailand.

Culture

In 1984, UNESCO continued its international campaigns for the protection of cultural and natural heritage. The 29 campaigns approved by the UN-ESCO General Conference were either being conducted or in preparation and, by the end of the year, $12.5 million had been raised. New campaigns were launched to safeguard in Yemen the historic city of Sana'a, and in Democratic Yemen the monuments and sites of Wadi Hadramawt and the walled city of Shibam.

The World Heritage Committee (eighth session, Buenos Aires, Argentina, 29 October–2 November), established under the 1972 International Convention concerning the Protection of the World Cultural and Natural Heritage, added 23 sites to the World Heritage List, raising the number to 186 cultural and natural properties in 48 countries protected by the Convention, which had 86 States parties as at 31 December 1984. Efforts continued to promote public awareness of the Convention's objectives and to encourage contributions to the World Heritage Fund, which provided assistance for training activities and restoration work on World Heritage sites.

Other activities during 1984 included: studies on African, Latin American, Caribbean, Arab, Asian, European and Arctic culture; the printing of the *General History of Africa* in Arabic, English, French, Portuguese and Spanish; the revision of *The History of the Scientific and Cultural Development of Mankind*, dealing with various world cultures and their development; the preparation of travelling exhibits and art albums; a seminar in Finland on the theoretical and methodological aspects of cultural development with UNESCO's financial assistance; studies in Latin America on cultural activities to motivate local populations in support of development; consultant missions to regional and international economic co-operation bodies to emphasize the importance of the cultural dimension in

economic development strategies; a meeting of specialists at Bogotá, Colombia, for the planning and administration of cultural activities in Latin America and the Caribbean; a regional training workshop at New Delhi, India, for the administration of cultural activities in Asia and the Pacific; and studies for the training of cultural personnel in Asia and the Pacific and in East Africa.

Regarding international cultural co-operation, studies were carried out on co-operation between industrialized and developing countries and on measures likely to foster in international cultural exchanges a more balanced participation by developing countries or countries whose languages were not widely known. In Europe, five projects on problems related to cultural development were launched in the framework of studies conducted under the aegis of national commissions with the support of UNESCO.

In the field of artistic creativity, an international survey on art in society was undertaken. A series of music rostra, to promote high-quality works and performances in co-operation with broadcasting organizations, were organized in Africa, Asia and Europe with the assistance of the International Music Council. An international meeting of experts on the preservation and development of crafts in the contemporary world was held in co-operation with the World Crafts Council at Rio de Janeiro, Brazil. A film workshop on the art of depicting the real-life situation of rural dwellers was held at Luxor, Egypt.

Communications

During 1984, UNESCO continued to promote a free flow and wider and better-balanced dissemination of information, primarily by reinforcing communication systems in developing countries and training communication personnel. It also dealt with the role of communication in society, emphasizing new technologies and formulating national policies and plans.

Consultations on the programme "The right to communicate" and seminars on the international flow of information were held. Plurality in communication, the "watch-dog" role of the press, media education and the media's contribution to worldwide security and peace were also studied. The publication *Many Voices, One World*, originally issued as a hardback in 1980, was printed in English and French in 1984 as a paperback and widely distributed.

The Intergovernmental Council of the International Programme for the Development of Communication (IPDC) (fifth session, Paris, 3-9 May) approved 32 projects from developing countries for full or partial funding. Other projects were recommended by the Council for funding through funds-in-trust or other similar arrangements. Since January 1982, over $5.6

million had been provided for communication development and some $5 million pledged in the form of expert and fellowship assistance.

Development of communication infrastructures continued to be one of IPDC's major objectives and funds-in-trust provided the largest source of finance.

The Council approved the establishment of a biennial IPDC-UNESCO Prize for Rural Communication to reward innovative activities of exceptional merit undertaken by individuals or groups working in a private capacity to improve communication in rural communities through such media as local newspapers, radio and television programmes, printing equipment and films.

Other activities in 1984 included: national and regional training; the development of human and physical resources in a particular region through greater use of accumulated experience and research on the use of local skills and materials; the expansion of news agencies and exchange systems; and making available to smaller agencies modern computer-based techniques in news editing and dispatching. With the increased interest in preserving the national heritage in sound and images, a new programme initiated activities in the development of film and sound archives and in training specialists in film and tape preservation techniques.

A programme in Latin America for the co-publishing of books was expanded and several children's books were published with print-runs ranging from 30,000 to 100,000 copies per title. The cycle of regional monitoring groups on follow-up action to the 1982 UNESCO World Congress on Books[a] continued and recommendations were adopted at 1984 meetings held in Europe and the Arab States for measures to be taken at the national, regional and international levels to implement the Congress's resolutions. Training was provided to some 200 book specialists, with national and subregional courses held in Africa, the Arab States, Asia and the Pacific, and Europe. In addition, an annotated bibliography of books for linguistically retarded children was produced.

General Information Programme

In 1984, the UNESCO General Information Programme provided assistance at the national, regional and international levels for the development and promotion of information systems in scientific and technological information, documentation, libraries and archives.

The Programme emphasized: the improvement of access to information through modern technologies, standardization and interconnection of information systems; and required infrastructures, policies and training for the processing and dissemination of specialized information. It also aimed at strengthening national capabilities for

handling information through the development of national information systems.

Technical assistance

Participation Programme

Allocations approved by the Director-General for 1984-1985 under the UNESCO Participation Programme, through which member States and organizations participate in technical assistance activities, amounted to $14,712,904.

The amounts (in United States dollars) by sector and by region were as follows:

Sector	Allocation
Education	3,731,553
Culture	3,696,968
Natural sciences	2,669,280
Social sciences	1,483,354
General Information Programme	1,366,030
Communication	858,064
Training abroad and national commissions	736,447
Programme support	171,208
Total	**14,712,904**

Region	
Africa	4,279,291
Latin America and the Caribbean	2,822,564
Asia and the Pacific	2,376,004
Europe	2,259,640
Arab States	1,502,835
Interregional	1,472,570
Total	**14,712,904**

SOURCE: UNESCO 1984-1985: report of the Director-General.

Extrabudgetary programmes

Expenditure incurred in 1984 in respect of projects for which UNESCO served as executing agency, financed by UNDP, UNFPA and other extrabudgetary sources, totalled $96.8 million as shown below:

Source	Amount (in thousands of US dollars)
UNDP	36,382
UNFPA	5,863
Other United Nations sources	5,405
World Bank technical assistance	2,474
Regional banks and funds	1,952
Self-benefiting funds	26,717
Donated funds	9,246
Associate experts	2,324
Special accounts and voluntary contributions	6,418
Total	**96,781**

Sector	
Education	36,587
Natural sciences	23,212
Culture	23,137
Communication	6,114
General Information Programme	3,430
Social and human sciences	2,681
Other	1,620
Total	**96,781**

[a]YUN 1982, p. 1535.

Region	Amount (in thousands of US dollars)
Arab States	35,126
Africa	25,074
Asia and the Pacific	16,990
Latin America and the Caribbean	8,950
Interregional and global	7,683
Europe	2,958
Total	96,781

Secretariat

As at 31 December 1984, the number of full-time staff employed by UNESCO on permanent, fixed-term and short-term appointments was 3,382 drawn from 134 nationalities. Of these, 1,344 were in the Professional or higher categories and 2,038 were in the General Service and Maintenance Worker categories.

Of the Professional staff, 436 were serving in the field, as were 465 General Service and Maintenance Worker staff.

Budget

The 1983 session of the UNESCO General Conference had approved a budget of $374,410,000 for 1984-1985. Donations amounting to $453,246 were added, bringing the total budget for the biennium to $374,863,246. Amounts allocated (in thousands of United States dollars) are shown in the table below:

UNESCO REGULAR BUDGET

	Amount
Programme operations and services	255,498
Programme support services	50,852
Common services	33,255
General administrative services	32,517
General policy and direction	24,182
Appropriation reserve	19,859
Capital expenditure	4,845
Negative provision for currency fluctuation	(46,145)
Total	374,863

Annex I. MEMBERSHIP OF THE UNITED NATIONS EDUCATIONAL, SCIENTIFIC AND CULTURAL ORGANIZATION AND CONTRIBUTIONS

(Membership as at 31 December 1984; annual contributions as assessed for 1984 and 1985)

MEMBER	CONTRIBUTION Percentage	CONTRIBUTION Amount (in US dollars)	MEMBER	CONTRIBUTION Percentage	CONTRIBUTION Amount (in US dollars)	MEMBER	CONTRIBUTION Percentage	CONTRIBUTION Amount (in US dollars)
Afghanistan	0.01	17,235	Democratic Yemen	0.01	17,235	Kuwait	0.25	430,875
Albania	0.01	17,235	Denmark	0.74	1,275,390	Lao People's Democratic		
Algeria	0.13	224,055	Dominica	0.01	17,235	Republic	0.01	17,235
Angola	0.01	17,235	Dominican Republic	0.03	51,705	Lebanon	0.02	34,470
Antigua and Barbuda	0.01	17,235	Ecuador	0.02	34,470	Lesotho	0.01	17,235
Argentina	0.70	1,206,450	Egypt	0.07	120,645	Liberia	0.01	17,235
Australia	1.55	2,671,425	El Salvador	0.01	17,235	Libyan Arab Jamahiriya	0.26	448,110
Austria	0.74	1,275,390	Equatorial Guinea	0.01	17,235	Luxembourg	0.06	103,410
Bahamas	0.01	17,235	Ethiopia	0.01	17,235	Madagascar	0.01	17,235
Bahrain	0.01	17,235	Fiji	0.01	17,235	Malawi	0.01	17,235
Bangladesh	0.03	51,705	Finland	0.47	810,045	Malaysia	0.09	155,115
Barbados	0.01	17,235	France	6.43	11,082,105	Maldives	0.01	17,235
Belgium	1.26	2,171,610	Gabon	0.02	34,470	Mali	0.01	17,235
Belize	0.01	17,235	Gambia	0.01	17,235	Malta	0.01	17,235
Benin	0.01	17,235	German Democratic			Mauritania	0.01	17,235
Bhutan	0.01	17,235	Republic	1.37	2,361,195	Mauritius	0.01	17,235
Bolivia	0.01	17,235	Germany, Federal			Mexico	0.87	1,499,445
Botswana	0.01	17,235	Republic of	8.44	14,546,340	Monaco	0.01	17,235
Brazil	1.37	2,361,195	Ghana	0.02	34,470	Mongolia	0.01	17,235
Bulgaria	0.18	310,230	Greece	0.39	672,165	Morocco	0.05	86,175
Burkina Faso	0.01	17,235	Grenada	0.01	17,235	Mozambique	0.01	17,235
Burma	0.01	17,235	Guatemala	0.02	34,470	Namibia*	—	—
Burundi	0.01	17,235	Guinea	0.01	17,235	Nepal	0.01	17,235
Byelorussian SSR	0.36	620,460	Guinea-Bissau	0.01	17,235	Netherlands	1.76	3,033,360
Cameroon	0.01	17,235	Guyana	0.01	17,235	New Zealand	0.26	448,110
Canada	3.04	5,239,440	Haiti	0.01	17,235	Nicaragua	0.01	17,235
Cape Verde	0.01	17,235	Honduras	0.01	17,235	Niger	0.01	17,235
Central African Republic	0.01	17,235	Hungary	0.23	396,405	Nigeria	0.19	327,465
Chad	0.01	17,235	Iceland	0.03	51,705	Norway	0.50	861,750
Chile	0.07	120,645	India	0.36	620,460	Oman	0.01	17,235
China	0.87	1,499,445	Indonesia	0.13	224,055	Pakistan	0.06	103,410
Colombia	0.11	189,585	Iran	0.57	982,395	Panama	0.02	34,470
Comoros	0.01	17,235	Iraq	0.12	206,820	Papua New Guinea	0.01	17,235
Congo	0.01	17,235	Ireland	0.18	310,230	Paraguay	0.01	17,235
Costa Rica	0.02	34,470	Israel	0.23	396,405	Peru	0.07	120,645
Cuba	0.09	155,115	Italy	3.69	6,359,715	Philippines	0.09	155,115
Cyprus	0.01	17,235	Ivory Coast	0.03	51,705	Poland	0.71	1,223,685
Czechoslovakia	0.75	1,292,625	Jamaica	0.02	34,470	Portugal	0.18	310,230
Democratic Kampuchea	0.01	17,235	Japan	10.19	17,562,465	Qatar	0.03	51,705
Democratic People's			Jordan	0.01	17,235	Republic of Korea	0.18	310,230
Republic of Korea	0.05	86,175	Kenya	0.01	17,235	Romania	0.19	327,465

MEMBER	CONTRIBUTION		MEMBER	CONTRIBUTION		MEMBER	CONTRIBUTION	
	Percent-age	Amount (in US dollars)		Percent-age	Amount (in US dollars)		Percent-age	Amount (in US dollars)
Rwanda	0.01	17,235	Swaziland	0.01	17,235	Venezuela	0.54	930,690
Saint Christopher and			Sweden	1.30	2,240,550	Viet Nam	0.02	34,470
Nevis	0.01	17,235	Switzerland	1.09	1,878,615	Yemen	0.01	17,235
Saint Lucia	0.01	17,235	Syrian Arab Republic	0.03	51,705	Yugoslavia	0.45	775,575
Saint Vincent and the			Thailand	0.08	137,880	Zaire	0.01	17,235
Grenadines	0.01	17,235	Togo	0.01	17,235	Zambia	0.01	17,235
Samoa	0.01	17,235	Tonga	0.01	17,235	Zimbabwe	0.02	34,470
San Marino	0.01	17,235	Trinidad and Tobago	0.03	51,705			
Sao Tome and Principe	0.01	17,235	Tunisia	0.03	51,705	Total‡	100.02	172,384,470
Saudi Arabia	0.85	1,464,975	Turkey	0.31	534,285			
Senegal	0.01	17,235	Uganda	0.01	17,235	ASSOCIATE		
Seychelles	0.01	17,235	Ukrainian SSR	1.30	2,240,550	MEMBER		
Sierra Leone	0.01	17,235	USSR	10.41	17,941,635			
Singapore	0.09	155,115	United Arab Emirates	0.16	275,760	British Eastern		
Somalia	0.01	17,235	United Kingdom	4.61	7,945,335	Caribbean Group§	0.01	17,235
Spain	1.91	3,291,885	United Republic of			British Virgin Islands	0.01	17,235
Sri Lanka	0.01	17,235	Tanzania	0.01	17,235	Netherlands Antilles	0.01	17,235
Sudan	0.01	17,235	United States†	25.00	43,087,500			
Suriname	0.01	17,235	Uruguay	0.04	68,940	Total	0.03	51,705

*Assessment remained suspended in 1984.

†Withdrew from UNESCO on 31 December 1984.

‡Includes contributions assessed for Fiji and Saint Christopher and Nevis, admitted as members after assessments for 1984-1985 had been established.

§Saint Christopher and Nevis having become a full member, the British Eastern Caribbean Group ceased to be an associate member effective 31 December 1984.

Annex II. OFFICERS AND OFFICES OF THE UNITED NATIONS
EDUCATIONAL, SCIENTIFIC AND CULTURAL ORGANIZATION

(As at 31 December 1984)

MEMBERS OF THE EXECUTIVE BOARD

Chairman: Patrick K. Seddoh (Ghana).

Vice-Chairmen: Jean B. S. Gerard (United States), Mamadi Keita (Guinea), Mahmoud Messadi (Tunisia), Ladislav Smid (Czechoslovakia), José Israel Vargas (Brazil), Yang Bozhen (China).

Members: Eid Abdo (Syrian Arab Republic), José Luis Abellán (Spain), Camille Aboussouan (Lebanon), Daniel Arango (Colombia), Jacqueline Baudrier (France), Alphonse Blagué (Central African Republic), Mário Cabral (Guinea-Bissau), Estrella Z. de Carazo (Costa Rica), Ian Christie Clark (Canada), Dimitri Cosmadopoulos (Greece), Buyantyn Dashtseren (Mongolia), William A. Dodd (United Kingdom), Georges-Henri Dumont (Belgium), Dmitri V. Ermolenko (USSR), Pierre Foulani (Niger), Jean B. S. Gerard (United States), Carmen Guerrero-Nakpil (Philippines), Alfredo Guevara (Cuba), Abdul Aziz Hussein (Kuwait), Attiya Inayatullah (Pakistan), Andri Isaksson (Iceland), Osman Sid Ahmed Ismail (Sudan), Ben Kufakunesu Jambga (Zimbabwe), Takaaki Kagawa (Japan), Triloki Nath Kaul (India), Mamadi Keita (Guinea), A. Majeed Khan (Bangladesh), Donald M. Kusenha (United Republic of Tanzania), Jean-Félix Loung (Cameroon), Edward Victor Luckhoo (Guyana), Ivo Margan (Yugoslavia), Mahmoud Messadi (Tunisia), Karl Moersch (Federal Republic of Germany), Musa Justice Nsibande (Swaziland), A. Bola Olaniyan (Nigeria), Luis Manuel Peñalver (Venezuela), Demodetdo Y. Pendje (Zaire), Jean Ping (Gabon), Gian Franco Pompei (Italy), Abdellatif Rahal (Algeria), Guy A. Rajaonson (Madagascar), Jesús Reyes Heroles (Mexico), Hubert de Ronceray (Haiti), Saeed Abdullah Salman (United Arab Emirates), Patrick K. Seddoh (Ghana), Ladislav Smid (Czechoslovakia), Kaw Swasdi Panich (Thailand), Gleb N. Tsvetkov (Ukrainian SSR), José Israel Vargas (Brazil), Hector L. Wynter (Jamaica), Yang Bozhen (China).

PRINCIPAL OFFICERS OF THE SECRETARIAT

Director-General: Amadou Mahtar M'Bow.

Assistant Director-General, Director of the Executive Office: Chikh Békri.

Assistant Directors-General: Gérard Bolla, John Borema Kaboré, Abdul-Razzak Kaddoura, Jean Knapp, Henri Lopes, Makaminan Makagiansar, Zala Lusibu N'Kanza, George Saddler, Sema Tanguiane, Tien-Chang Young.

HEADQUARTERS AND OTHER OFFICE

HEADQUARTERS
UNESCO House
7 Place de Fontenoy
75700 Paris, France
Cable address: UNESCO PARIS
Telephone: 568-10-00
Telex: 204461

NEW YORK OFFICE
United Nations Educational, Scientific and
Cultural Organization
2 United Nations Plaza
New York, N.Y. 10017, United States
Cable Address: UNESCORG NEWYORK
Telephone: (212) 963-5995

Chapter V

World Health Organization (WHO)

The thirty-seventh World Health Assembly, which met at Geneva from 7 to 17 May 1984, reviewed the first progress report on the implementation of strategies towards achieving health for all by the year 2000, in conformity with the plan of action approved in 1982.[a] The report indicated that the political will to achieve health for all existed in most countries and that many had already formulated health policies, strategies and plans. The Assembly urged member States to accelerate their action, especially the reorientation of health systems towards primary health care, and to strengthen further the managerial capacity of those systems. It also called for support by the World Health Organization (WHO) to be intensive and target-oriented.

Concern that pharmaceuticals should be cost-effective as well as acceptably safe was reflected in an Assembly resolution requesting the Director-General to convene in 1985 a conference of experts on the rational use of drugs and the role of marketing practices.

The organization's financial position, infant and young child nutrition, prevention of xerophthalmia and intensified co-operation with member States affected by natural and man-made disasters were among other issues dealt with by the Assembly.

Four countries became members of WHO during 1984—Antigua and Barbuda on 12 March, the Cook Islands on 9 May, Kiribati on 26 July and Saint Christopher and Nevis on 3 December—which brought its membership to 165 and one associate member.

Co-ordination with other organizations

During 1984, WHO continued its collaboration with bilateral agencies, funding agencies within the United Nations system, the World Bank, regional banks and other institutions to mobilize resources for health for all. Activities included the fourth meeting of the Committee of the Health Resources Group for Primary Health Care (Geneva, November) and the first overall review and appraisal of the implementation of the International Development Strategy for the Third United Nations Development Decade (see also p. 391). WHO also responded to the appeal of the United Nations to deal urgently with socio-economic problems facing sub-Saharan Africa by establishing an emergency standing committee in the regional office for Africa.

Research promotion and development

Following its 1983 decision to concentrate on broad health research policy issues instead of reviewing specific technical programmes, the Advisory Committee on Medical Research (ACMR) established, in co-operation with its regional committees, three sub-committees, to deal with health research strategy for health for all, health manpower research, and the transfer of health technology to developing countries. ACMR also decided to involve national medical research councils whenever feasible.

With regard to drugs in use or in an advanced stage of development, work at various collaborating centres had resulted in a new antimalarial drug effective against strains of *plasmodium falciparum* resistant to chloroquine and other drugs, and another promising compound for the control of filariasis was undergoing field tests.

Primary health care

The Declaration of Alma-Ata (USSR, 1978)[b] set forth the eight elements of primary health care through which the goal of health for all by the year 2000 was to be achieved. Activities of WHO during 1984 in respect of these elements are set out below, followed by a ninth section on other health concerns.

Health education

Efforts by countries to inform and educate people to promote healthy life-styles and practices encouraging self-reliance were supported by WHO at country, regional and global levels through an exchange of experiences, technical co-operation, training, research and dissemination of information.

In South-East Asia, a workshop on integration of public information and education for health examined strategies and suggested plans to strengthen them. At another workshop supported by WHO, the first Caribbean strategy and plan of action for community participation was adopted. The first symposium on smoking and health in southern Europe led to the creation of the Mediterranean Committee on Health Promotion and Smoking Control, and an inter-country meeting at Riyadh, Saudi Arabia, formulated guidelines

aYUN 1982, p. 1538.
bYUN 1978, p. 1107.

on the integration of health education within primary health care and on collaboration between the ministries of health and education.

The 1984 slogan for World Health Day, "Children's health—tomorrow's wealth", was used to convey the message that children were a priceless resource and that any nation which neglected them (and their health) did so at its peril. Many countries used the slogan to promote related health education and information activities. In Europe, a system linking government departments, universities, research and training centres and experts in a network for the exchange of education technology and information was established. Similar networks were also considered in the Americas and the Western Pacific.

A draft manual on health education in primary health care for use by health workers was circulated for review and field-testing to WHO member States, collaborating institutions and technical experts.

Food and nutrition

Food and nutrition projects, supported by the WHO/UNICEF Joint Nutrition Support Programme and funded by Italy, were launched in eight countries in Asia, Africa and the Caribbean. A joint UNICEF/UNDP/IFAD programme, aided by the Belgian Third World Survival Fund, was implemented in Kenya and Uganda. Nutrition education began in four African countries; health systems research on nutrition was the subject of projects in seven African countries, and research on breast-feeding was supported in five others.

A Central American health plan, adopted in Costa Rica in March, identified food and nutrition as a priority area, and the regional office, in collaboration with the Institute of Nutrition of Central America and Panama, formulated project proposals for submission to donors. Several countries of the Western Pacific participated in infant and young child nutrition studies and national nutrition surveys.

Safe water and basic sanitation

Progress reports on the implementation of the objectives of the International Drinking Water Supply and Sanitation Decade (1981-1990) were received from some 80 member States and territories representing three quarters of the developing world's population. In co-operation with UNDP, the World Bank and other agencies, WHO reviewed the mobilization of external resources for improving water supplies and sanitation in the Decade.

An agreement for strengthening human resources in Central America, the Dominican Republic and Panama was concluded with the Inter-American Development Bank and the Agency for Technical Co-operation (Gesellschaft für Technische Zusammenarbeit) of the Federal Republic of Germany. The Pan American Centre for Sanitary Engineering and Environmental Sciences organized an international seminar at Brasilia, Brazil, on water system losses. Fifty participants from 10 countries in the Americas developed strategies for prevention of wastage and drew up an agreement on inter-country co-operation through a network of centres. In the Eastern Mediterranean region, WHO decided to establish in Jordan a regional centre for environmental health activities aimed at developing human resources and disseminating technical information. The Arab Gulf Programme for United Nations Development Organizations approved a $1 million funding to meet the cost of fellowships, equipment and personnel for the centre.

Maternal and child health, including family planning

WHO provided in 1984 technical and managerial support to some 90 countries to improve their health care services for mothers and children. To strengthen national managerial capabilities, WHO and UNFPA jointly initiated workshops for national programme managers and WHO/UNFPA country staff to improve programme formulation, problem-solving and evaluation skills. Two workshops were held during the year: one for English-speaking countries of Africa and the other for countries of the European and Eastern Mediterranean regions.

Several countries initiated studies on perinatal, infant, early childhood and maternal mortality and morbidity to identify priority areas for action and develop appropriate preventive measures. A regional meeting in the Americas on infant mortality and primary health-care strategies (Mexico, May) highlighted the advances made in reducing infant and child mortality and the relationship between those advances and the implementation of such strategies.

An international task force worked closely with WHO collaborating centres, research institutes in developing countries and interested non-governmental organizations (NGOs). Research activities included: evaluation of equipment and methods for home deliveries; development of birth-weight surrogates; evaluation and quality control of supplies and equipment for use in maternal and child health programmes—including family planning—in health systems based on primary health; appraisal of various means of temperature control in relation to the new-born; and evaluation of environments in which deliveries and care of the new-born take place.

As part of its participation in preparations for the International Youth Year (1985), WHO convened in June a study group on young people and health for all by the year 2000 to review adolescent and youth health and health-related issues, and to analyse health systems on the basis of their relevance, resources and service gaps in the specific needs of that age group.

Immunization against major infectious diseases

During 1984, improvements in immunization services and coverage were made in all regions. Reductions in the incidence of diseases— diphtheria, pertussis, tetanus, measles, poliomyelitis and tuberculosis—covered by the Expanded Programme on Immunization (EPI) were also reported. In the Americas, all countries had set national coverage targets for immunization against these diseases; in its health-for-all strategy, the European region specified that by the year 2000 those diseases would have been eliminated.

WHO supported immunization services in member States through the implementation of a five-point action programme: promotion of EPI within primary health care; development of human resources; mobilization and investment of financial resources; continuous monitoring and evaluation to increase the programme's effectiveness; and research. Training of health workers in immunization continued to be a priority, with a shift from training of managers using materials developed at the global level to training of middle- and peripheral-level health workers, often in national languages, using materials adapted for national use.

Further development of the "cold-chain" monitor and of solar-powered refrigeration was notable, as well as the evaluation of sterilizable plastic syringes and pressure-cooker sterilizers for use in rural health centres. Vaccine availability and the cold-chain situation generally improved during the year.

The Bellagio Conference (Italy, March), co-sponsored by UNDP, UNICEF, WHO and the World Bank and supported by the United States Rockefeller Foundation, created a child-survival task force to reduce childhood morbidity and mortality through the acceleration of key primary health-care activities. Support concentrated on Colombia, India and Senegal.

Prevention and control of locally endemic diseases

Locally endemic diseases continued to affect a large number of people in developing countries where diarrhoeal diseases, acute respiratory infections and EPI-covered diseases were major causes of death and illness among young chil-

dren. WHO reported that, with recent advances in technology for diagnosis and treatment, the control and prevention of malaria, tuberculosis and parasitic and tropical diseases (such as schistosomiasis, leprosy and filariasis) had improved, and member States were taking further steps to strengthen that element of primary health care.

Progress was made in *diarrhoeal disease control*. WHO provided technical co-operation to member States for the development of national plans, training of managerial and supervisory personnel and programme evaluation. By the end of 1984, 88 developing countries had operation plans for controlling diarrhoeal diseases and 62 of them had begun implementing their plans. In collaboration with UNICEF, WHO also supported countries in the local production and supply of oral rehydration salts.

Health systems research and clinical studies on *acute respiratory infections* were being carried out in over 20 countries in all WHO regions, mainly to test the feasibility of a standard plan for case management at the primary health-care level. A working group on case management in developing countries evaluated methods of diagnosis and treatment in children, identifying those most suitable for rural areas and recommending training materials.

Brazil and the Republic of Korea joined other countries participating in the evaluation of the effectiveness of the Bacillus Calmette-Guérin vaccination against *tuberculosis* in infants and young children. The first national prevalence survey in the Philippines was completed in April. A global survey of mycobacterial resistance to antituberculosis drugs was started with WHO collaborating centres in bacteriology of tuberculosis to determine regional and global levels of initial and acquired drug resistance.

Leprosy remained a major public health problem in many developing countries. WHO activities concentrated mainly on research and development, including clinical trials with multidrug therapy, training and promoting community involvement, and integration of leprosy control services into primary health care.

Little change was reported in the world *malaria* situation. Information on a number of cases in the preceding 10 years was published, together with a map of the distribution of chloroquine-resistant *plasmodium falciparum*, in the *World Health Statistics Quarterly*. Member States continued searching for effective means to implement malaria control strategies within primary health care and for new and simpler technologies, and WHO provided technical support in programme planning and evaluation, training and research and promoted inter-country co-operation. The report of the Study Group on Malaria Control as Part of Primary Health Care was published.

Progress in *vector biology and control* included: the development of impregnated bed-nets for malaria mosquito control in the African and Western Pacific regions and simple tsetse-fly traps in West Africa; the elimination of larval habitats of filariasis vectors in southern India; and a large-scale trial of control of *aedes aegypti* vectors of dengue and dengue haemorrhagic fever, employing students and schoolteachers with other volunteers, in Thailand. Field trials of new insecticides against *anopheles* vectors of malaria were carried out in Indonesia, and against *simulium* vectors under the Onchocerciasis Control Programme in West Africa.

Treatment of common diseases and injuries

In several countries, the health care delivery infrastructure needed strengthening to provide treatment of common diseases and injuries. In collaboration with WHO, member States searched for simple technologies and practical approaches to prevent and control common non-communicable diseases and promote oral health, mental health, and health of workers and of the elderly. To further those aims, WHO supported information exchange among countries, training, transfer of technology, research—especially on appropriate technology—and dissemination of information. A guide on managing services for the disabled in the community was prepared to improve the competence of health and community workers in this field.

WHO supported training activities in rehabilitation at national and inter-country levels. Financial resources were provided by the Norwegian Red Cross, the Norwegian Agency for International Development and the Swedish International Development Authority for inter-country and global activities. Member States, mainly in South-East Asia and the Western Pacific, strengthened their *eye care services* within primary health care.

There was an increase in 1984 of non-communicable diseases—particularly *cancer* and *cardiovascular diseases*—among adult populations in both developed and developing countries. Many countries took steps to accelerate health activities aimed at prevention through changes in life-styles and behaviour, early detection and treatment, and promotion of self-care. WHO further supported research, training and exchange of experience in technology. An estimate of the effects of 12 major cancers on the five continents was published in the 1984 *Bulletin of the World Health Organization*. Guiding principles for the formulation of national cancer programmes in developing countries, prepared by WHO, were used to identify priorities in

a number of countries, including India and Sri Lanka.

A WHO expert committee on prevention and control of cardiovascular diseases in the community, convened in December, reviewed health problems such as hypertension (including cerebrovascular stroke), coronary heart disease, and rheumatic fever/rheumatic heart disease.

Essential drugs

WHO reported that many countries had accelerated actions towards the development of drug legislation, policies and implementation plans along the lines of the Action Programme on Essential Drugs and Vaccines. A review of progress in five regions showed that some 90 member States had established a list of essential drugs, 36 were in various stages of establishing or implementing measures in accordance with the Action Programme, and another 27 were developing national policies. Most countries already implementing essential drug programmes were making good progress with or without international collaboration. WHO assistance included the formulation of national plans and programmes, drug legislation, training, exchange of experience and dissemination of information, procurement and production of essential drugs, and quality control. Inter-country co-operation and co-ordination at the international level was particularly promoted.

A four-day international conference on essential drugs in primary health care, sponsored by UNICEF, WHO, the United States Agency for International Development and member companies in the International Federation of Pharmaceutical Manufacturers Associations, held at the Harvard University School of Public Health (Boston, United States, April 1984), attracted over 160 participants, including 60 from developing countries. The purpose of the conference was to develop problem-oriented teaching and training material for use in public-health schools.

Opportunities for promoting consolidated procurement within individual countries, as well as among groups of countries through pool procurement schemes, were explored in Africa, the Americas and the Western Pacific. In Central America and Panama, high priority was placed on promoting and developing national and sub-regional programmes, and a revolving fund for the joint procurement of essential drugs, based on studies undertaken by the Pan American Health Organization and the Central American Bank, was in the process of being established.

Other health concerns

WHO also supported member States in developing health policies for the *care of the elderly* as an integral part of primary health care. The role of

NGOs and voluntary organizations in this area was promoted. An NGO/WHO collaborating group on aging provided manuals for community workers on self-care and health promotion, suitably adapted to particular regional and cultural groups.

Field trials of various models of primary health-care delivery to underserved working people in agriculture and small industries were made in several countries, including Burkina Faso, Chile, China, Egypt, Nigeria, the Republic of Korea, the Sudan, Thailand, the United Republic of Tanzania and Zimbabwe. Countries exchanged experiences through regional workshops in the Americas and South-East Asia.

Regarding *mental health*, a major study on the epidemiology of schizophrenia and related disorders was completed in 13 geographically defined areas in Colombia, Czechoslovakia, Denmark, India, Ireland, Japan, Nigeria, the USSR, the United Kingdom and the United States. This was the first investigation of the incidence of this group of disorders in which uniform instruments and research techniques were employed, allowing direct comparisons of areas in different countries. The findings provided a basis for long-term forecasts of treatment needed and for the planning of appropriate services, as well as clues to aetiologically oriented research.

Neuro-epidemiological studies co-ordinated by WHO in China, Ecuador and Nigeria were completed, providing information for programmes for the prevention and control of neurological disorders and for application, after suitable adaptation, in Chile, India, Italy, Peru, Senegal, Tunisia and Venezuela. A related training programme included seminars co-sponsored by WHO at Quito, Ecuador, and Bombay, India.

Responding to an alarming global increase in *drug abuse*—particularly cocaine—WHO launched a project to study the adverse health consequences of cocaine and coca-paste smoking. In that con-text, an advisory group (Bogotá, Colombia, September) reviewed the methodology of problem assessment and treatment approaches.

Secretariat

As at 31 December 1984, the total number of full-time staff employed by WHO stood at 4,449 on permanent and fixed-term contracts. Of these, 1,454 staff members, drawn from 122 nationalities, were in the Professional and higher categories and 2,995 were in the General Service category. Of the total number of staff, 122 were in posts financed by UNDP, UNEP, UNFDAC and UNFPA.

Budget

The thirty-sixth (1983) World Health Assembly had approved a working budget of $520,100,000 for 1984-1985.[c]

INTEGRATED INTERNATIONAL HEALTH PROGRAMME OBLIGATIONS BY SOURCE OF FINANCING FOR THE TWO-YEAR PERIOD 1984-1985

Source	Amount (in US dollars)
Regular budget	520,100,000
Pan American Health Organization	139,095,000
International Agency for Research on Cancer	20,960,000
Other sources	
Voluntary Fund for Health Promotion	95,490,900
Tropical Diseases Research	64,136,000
Onchocerciasis Control Programme	41,000,000
Sasakawa Health Trust Fund	6,499,700
United Nations sources	
UNICEF	60,000
UNDP	36,718,100
UNEP	965,000
UNFDAC	596,200
UNFPA	39,332,500
UNHCR	142,000
Trust funds	14,739,900
Special Account for Servicing Costs	10,295,700
Total	990,131,000

[c]YUN 1983, p. 1250.

SERVICES AND CO-OPERATION EXTENDED BY WHO IN THE TWO-YEAR PERIOD 1984-1985, BY REGION AND COUNTRY OR TERRITORY
(in US dollars)

	Regular budget	Other sources	Total		Regular budget	Other sources	Total
Africa				*Africa* (cont.)			
Angola	1,399,400	—	1,399,400	Equatorial Guinea	824,600	479,000	1,303,600
Benin	986,300	—	986,300	Ethiopia	2,831,300	1,500,000	4,331,300
Botswana	684,300	15,200	699,500	Gabon	750,000	636,000	1,386,000
Burkina Faso	1,363,100	2,590,400	3,953,500	Gambia	869,500	300,000	1,169,500
Burundi	1,237,500	143,700	1,381,200	Ghana	981,700	—	981,700
Cameroon	807,300	—	807,300	Guinea	1,346,400	730,000	2,076,400
Cape Verde	888,800	—	888,800	Guinea-Bissau	999,600	730,000	1,729,600
Central African Republic	1,158,200	741,900	1,900,100	Ivory Coast	789,700	—	789,700
Chad	1,245,000	—	1,245,000	Kenya	1,161,900	—	1,161,900
Comoros	1,319,800	—	1,319,800	Lesotho	944,800	—	944,800
Congo	853,200	366,500	1,219,700	Liberia	1,120,200	—	1,120,200

	Regular budget	Other sources	Total		Regular budget	Other sources	Total
Africa (cont.)				*South-East Asia* (cont.)			
Madagascar	869,900	1,583,000	2,452,900	Maldives	770,500	45,000	815,500
Malawi	927,900	1,372,200	2,300,100	Mongolia	1,491,100	270,000	1,761,100
Mali	1,332,100	20,500	1,352,600	Nepal	4,492,000	414,300	4,906,300
Mauritania	1,051,400	198,000	1,249,400	Sri Lanka	3,264,000	190,400	3,454,400
Mauritius	400,600	—	400,600	Thailand	3,824,000	10,900	3,834,900
Mozambique	1,325,200	2,542,300	3,867,500				
Namibia	547,500	—	547,500	Inter-country programmes	11,351,300	4,902,300	16,253,600
Niger	1,334,500	313,000	1,647,500				
Nigeria	2,471,400	—	2,471,400	Subtotal	54,666,300	18,859,300	73,525,600
Réunion	67,400	—	67,400				
Rwanda	1,464,200	—	1,464,200	*Europe*			
St. Helena	58,500	—	58,500	Albania	33,100	—	33,100
Sao Tome and Principe	541,800	600,000	1,141,800	Algeria	396,000	2,137,500	2,533,500
Senegal	911,000	—	911,000	Austria	24,800	—	24,800
Seychelles	455,400	—	455,400	Belgium	20,600	—	20,600
Sierra Leone	920,900	—	920,900	Bulgaria	92,400	—	92,400
Swaziland	586,700	211,100	797,800	Czechoslovakia	24,800	—	24,800
Togo	928,900	—	928,900	Denmark	20,600	—	20,600
Uganda	1,283,900	—	1,283,900	Finland	20,600	—	20,600
United Republic of Tanzania	1,373,600	—	1,373,600	France	27,600	—	27,600
Zaire	1,741,600	—	1,741,600	German Democratic Republic	30,400	—	30,400
Zambia	1,408,000	785,000	2,193,000	Germany, Federal Republic of	27,600	—	27,600
Zimbabwe	1,669,000	—	1,669,000	Greece	30,400	—	30,400
				Hungary	36,000	—	36,000
Inter-country programmes	27,660,700	46,563,900	74,224,600	Iceland	20,600	—	20,600
				Ireland	24,800	—	24,800
Subtotal	75,894,700	62,421,700	138,316,400	Italy	30,400	—	30,400
				Luxembourg	15,100	—	15,100
The Americas				Malta	24,800	—	24,800
Argentina	1,271,200	957,600	2,228,800	Monaco	3,000	—	3,000
Bahamas	360,000	317,000	677,000	Morocco	462,000	1,823,000	2,285,000
Barbados	86,400	481,900	568,300	Netherlands	24,800	—	24,800
Belize	471,300	43,200	514,500	Norway	20,600	—	20,600
Bolivia	358,100	2,094,000	2,452,100	Poland	45,600	—	45,600
Brazil	1,407,600	13,142,900	14,550,500	Portugal	72,000	206,800	278,800
Canada	45,000	45,000	90,000	Romania	45,600	—	45,600
Chile	783,500	856,200	1,639,700	San Marino	3,000	—	3,000
Colombia	1,230,700	1,831,700	3,062,400	Spain	30,400	—	30,400
Costa Rica	741,800	964,700	1,706,500	Sweden	20,600	—	20,600
Cuba	777,200	739,000	1,516,200	Switzerland	20,600	—	20,600
Dominica	—	173,400	173,400	Turkey	525,800	201,300	727,100
Dominican Republic	526,600	1,323,000	1,849,600	USSR	60,700	—	60,700
Ecuador	1,733,800	724,200	2,458,000	United Kingdom	27,600	—	27,600
El Salvador	984,200	715,900	1,700,100	Yugoslavia	37,200	—	37,200
French Guiana	—	52,900	52,900				
Grenada	—	110,500	110,500	Inter-country programmes	18,869,700	7,901,700	26,771,400
Guatemala	737,900	1,334,800	2,072,700				
Guyana	973,800	1,644,100	2,617,900	Subtotal	21,169,800	12,270,300	33,440,100
Haiti	990,800	23,500	1,014,300				
Honduras	688,200	1,256,600	1,944,800	*Eastern Mediterranean*			
Jamaica	783,400	907,400	1,690,800	Afghanistan	4,534,100	1,307,600	5,841,700
Mexico	829,200	4,186,400	5,015,600	Bahrain	139,500	31,700	171,200
Netherlands Antilles	65,600	21,100	86,700	Cyprus	568,000	—	568,000
Nicaragua	508,000	748,700	1,256,700	Democratic Yemen	3,313,000	1,941,900	5,254,900
Panama	876,700	217,900	1,094,600	Djibouti	708,300	120,000	828,300
Paraguay	287,600	1,543,400	1,831,000	Egypt	1,898,600	390,800	2,289,400
Peru	605,500	1,905,200	2,510,700	Iran	469,000	—	469,000
Saint Lucia	—	110,500	110,500	Iraq	687,300	187,900	875,200
Saint Vincent and the Grenadines	—	110,500	110,500	Israel	453,000	—	453,000
Suriname	337,900	649,500	987,400	Jordan	1,140,900	1,642,600	2,783,500
Trinidad and Tobago	807,300	506,200	1,313,500	Kuwait	126,400	107,400	233,800
United States	417,500	340,400	757,900	Lebanon	1,140,000	206,600	1,346,600
Uruguay	489,400	492,400	981,800	Libyan Arab Jamahiriya	109,000	2,036,300	2,145,300
Venezuela	854,500	3,115,800	3,970,300	Oman	864,600	1,163,200	2,027,800
West Indies	553,500	557,300	1,110,800	Pakistan	2,930,300	270,200	3,200,500
				Qatar	64,000	67,800	131,800
Inter-country programmes	21,990,400	90,745,300	112,735,700	Saudi Arabia	165,700	5,637,000	5,802,700
				Somalia	4,167,600	759,500	4,927,100
Subtotal	43,574,600	134,990,100	178,564,700	Sudan	3,138,600	538,500	3,677,100
				Syrian Arab Republic	1,749,400	—	1,749,400
South-East Asia				Tunisia	1,700,000	182,500	1,882,500
Bangladesh	6,348,000	277,500	6,625,500	United Arab Emirates	55,300	104,000	159,300
Bhutan	642,000	413,300	1,055,300	Yemen	3,180,100	8,491,500	11,671,600
Burma	4,123,000	5,376,300	9,499,300				
Democratic People's Republic of Korea	1,327,400	—	1,327,400	Inter-country programmes	14,843,000	3,119,300	17,962,300
India	9,920,000	6,525,400	16,445,400				
Indonesia	7,113,000	433,900	7,546,900	Subtotal	48,145,700	28,306,300	76,452,000

Western Pacific	Regular budget	Other sources	Total	Western Pacific (cont.)	Regular budget	Other sources	Total
American Samoa	115,000	—	115,000	Philippines	1,758,400	100,000	1,858,400
Australia	100,000	—	100,000	Republic of Korea	1,544,300	—	1,544,300
China	4,242,800	1,142,800	5,385,600	Samoa	824,700	155,100	979,800
Cook Islands	452,300	96,100	548,400	Singapore	552,000	292,800	844,800
Democratic Kampuchea	500,000	—	500,000	Solomon Islands	849,700	457,000	1,306,700
Fiji	1,004,900	—	1,004,900	Tokelau	20,000	—	20,000
French Polynesia	70,000	—	70,000	Tonga	824,300	137,700	962,000
Guam	80,000	—	80,000	Trust Territory of the Pacific Islands	672,300	36,500	708,800
Hong Kong	110,000	—	110,000	Tuvalu	75,000	—	75,000
Japan	100,000	—	100,000	Vanuatu	904,800	400,000	1,304,800
Kiribati	622,300	207,400	829,700	Viet Nam	3,751,400	57,400	3,808,800
Lao People's Democratic Republic	1,430,000	433,000	1,863,000	Inter-country programmes	14,483,000	6,409,300	20,892,300
Macau	50,000	—	50,000				
Malaysia	1,159,100	—	1,159,100	Subtotal	38,620,100	10,888,800	49,508,900
New Zealand	60,000	—	60,000	Total	282,071,200	267,736,500	549,807,700
Niue	58,000	—	58,000				
Papua New Guinea	2,205,800	963,700	3,169,500				

ASSISTANCE RENDERED BY WHO IN 1984-1985, BY SECTOR AND REGION
(in US dollars)

	REGION							
SECTOR	Global and interregional activities	Africa	The Americas	South-East Asia	Europe	Eastern Mediter-ranean	Western Pacific	Total
Direction, co-ordination and management	35,095,100	7,285,400	2,820,300	2,183,500	5,947,400	3,341,000	4,265,900	60,938,600
Health system infrastructure	21,302,500	46,755,100	21,800,100	28,380,100	7,774,500	23,726,000	20,487,700	170,226,000
Health science and technology—health promotion and care	24,195,300	15,089,400	9,497,500	15,635,300	6,930,900	10,640,400	9,587,900	91,576,700
Health science and technology—disease prevention and control	27,480,200	11,431,600	9,584,900	10,174,900	1,792,900	11,131,200	6,930,000	78,525,700
Programme support	70,456,900	13,348,500	7,131,200	4,935,200	13,137,300	4,970,400	4,853,500	118,833,000
Total	178,530,000	93,910,000	50,834,000	61,309,000	35,583,000	53,809,000	46,125,000	520,100,000

Annex I.   MEMBERSHIP OF THE WORLD HEALTH ORGANIZATION AND CONTRIBUTIONS
(Membership as at 31 December 1984; contributions as assessed for 1984-1985)

MEMBER	CONTRIBUTION Percent-age	CONTRIBUTION Amount* (in US dollars)	MEMBER	CONTRIBUTION Percent-age	CONTRIBUTION Amount* (in US dollars)	MEMBER	CONTRIBUTION Percent-age	CONTRIBUTION Amount* (in US dollars)
Afghanistan	0.01	47,020	Bolivia	0.01	47,020	Colombia	0.11	517,270
Albania	0.01	47,020	Botswana	0.01	47,020	Comoros	0.01	47,020
Algeria	0.13	611,320	Brazil	1.36	6,395,270	Congo	0.01	76,020
Angola	0.01	47,020	Bulgaria	0.18	846,440	Cook Islands	(0.01)†	(31,347)†
Antigua and Barbuda	(0.01)†	(31,347)†	Burkina Faso	0.01	47,020	Costa Rica	0.02	94,050
Argentina	0.70	3,291,680	Burma	0.01	47,020	Cuba	0.09	423,220
Australia	1.54	7,241,700	Burundi	0.01	47,020	Cyprus	0.01	47,020
Austria	0.74	3,479,780	Byelorussian SSR	0.35	1,645,840	Czechoslovakia	0.75	3,526,800
Bahamas	0.01	47,020	Cameroon	0.01	47,020	Democratic Kampuchea	0.01	47,020
Bahrain	0.01	47,020	Canada	3.02	14,241,250	Democratic People's Republic of Korea	0.05	235,120
Bangladesh	0.03	141,080	Cape Verde	0.01	47,020	Democratic Yemen	0.01	52,020
Barbados	0.01	47,020	Central African Republic	0.01	47,020	Denmark	0.74	3,479,780
Belgium	1.26	5,925,030	Chad	0.01	47,020	Djibouti	0.01	47,020
Benin	0.01	47,020	Chile	0.07	329,170	Dominica	0.01	47,020
Bhutan	0.01	47,020	China	0.86	4,044,070			

MEMBER	CONTRIBUTION Percentage	Amount* (in US dollars)	MEMBER	CONTRIBUTION Percentage	Amount* (in US dollars)	MEMBER	CONTRIBUTION Percentage	Amount* (in US dollars)
Dominican Republic	0.03	141,080	Liberia	0.01	47,020	Saudi Arabia	0.84	3,950,020
Ecuador	0.02	94,050	Libyan Arab Jamahiriya	0.25	1,175,600	Senegal	0.01	47,020
Egypt	0.07	329,170	Luxembourg	0.06	282,150	Seychelles	0.01	47,020
El Salvador	0.01	47,020	Madagascar	0.01	47,020	Sierra Leone	0.01	47,020
Equatorial Guinea	0.01	47,020	Malawi	0.01	47,020	Singapore	0.09	423,220
Ethiopia	0.01	47,020	Malaysia	0.09	423,220	Solomon Islands	0.01	47,020
Fiji	0.01	47,020	Maldives	0.01	47,020	Somalia	0.01	47,020
Finland	0.47	2,210,130	Mali	0.01	47,020	South Africa	0.40	1,880,940
France	6.39	30,998,330	Malta	0.01	47,020	Spain	1.90	8,934,560
Gabon	0.02	94,050	Mauritania	0.01	47,020	Sri Lanka	0.01	47,020
Gambia	0.01	47,020	Mauritius	0.01	47,020	Sudan	0.01	47,020
German Democratic Republic	1.36	6,395,270	Mexico	0.86	4,044,070	Suriname	0.01	47,020
Germany, Federal Republic of	8.39	39,453,130	Monaco	0.01	47,020	Swaziland	0.01	47,020
			Mongolia	0.01	47,020	Sweden	1.30	6,113,120
Ghana	0.02	94,050	Morocco	0.05	235,120	Switzerland	1.08	5,078,590
Greece	0.39	1,833,940	Mozambique	0.01	47,020	Syrian Arab Republic	0.03	141,080
Grenada	0.01	47,020	Nepal	0.01	47,020	Thailand	0.08	376,190
Guatemala	0.02	94,050	Netherlands	1.75	8,229,200	Togo	0.01	47,020
Guinea	0.01	47,020	New Zealand	0.25	1,175,600	Tonga	0.01	47,020
Guinea-Bissau	0.01	47,020	Nicaragua	0.01	47,020	Trinidad and Tobago	0.03	141,080
Guyana	0.01	47,020	Niger	0.01	47,020	Tunisia	0.03	141,080
Haiti	0.01	47,020	Nigeria	0.19	893,460	Turkey	0.31	1,457,750
Honduras	0.01	47,020	Norway	0.50	2,351,200	Uganda	0.01	47,020
Hungary	0.22	1,034,530	Oman	0.01	47,020	Ukrainian SSR	1.30	6,113,120
Iceland	0.03	141,080	Pakistan	0.06	282,150	USSR	10.35	48,669,840
India	0.35	1,645,840	Panama	0.02	94,050	United Arab Emirates	0.16	752,390
Indonesia	0.13	611,320	Papua New Guinea	0.01	47,020	United Kingdom	4.59	21,584,010
Iran	0.57	2,680,370	Paraguay	0.01	47,020	United Republic of Tanzania	0.01	47,020
Iraq	0.12	564,290	Peru	0.07	329,170	United States	25.00	122,291,980
Ireland	0.18	846,440	Philippines	0.09	423,220	Uruguay	0.04	188,100
Israel	0.22	1,034,530	Poland	0.71	3,338,710	Vanuatu	0.01	47,020
Italy	3.67	17,257,810	Portugal	0.18	846,440	Venezuela	0.54	2,539,300
Ivory Coast	0.03	141,080	Qatar	0.03	141,080	Viet Nam	0.02	94,050
Jamaica	0.02	94,050	Republic of Korea	0.18	846,440	Yemen	0.01	47,020
Japan	10.14	47,682,340	Romania	0.19	893,460	Yugoslavia	0.45	2,116,080
Jordan	0.01	47,020	Rwanda	0.01	47,020	Zaire	0.01	47,020
Kenya	0.01	47,020	Saint Christopher and Nevis	(0.01)†	(23,510)†	Zambia	0.01	47,020
Kiribati	(0.01)†	(31,347)†	Saint Lucia	0.01	47,020	Zimbabwe	0.02	94,050
Kuwait	0.24	1,128,580	Saint Vincent and the Grenadines	(0.01)†	(47,020)†			
Lao People's Democratic Republic	0.01	47,020	Samoa	0.01	47,020	ASSOCIATE MEMBER		
Lebanon	0.02	94,050	San Marino	0.01	47,020	Namibia	0.01	47,020
Lesotho	0.01	47,020	Sao Tome and Principe	0.01	47,020	Total	100.00	475,995,900

*Adjusted to take into account the actual amounts paid to staff as reimbursement for taxes levied by member countries on the WHO emoluments of their nationals.

†The figures shown in parentheses, and not included in the totals, represent the assessments on countries that became members in 1983 or 1984, but were not included in the total assessments for the 1984-1985 budget.

Annex II.   OFFICERS AND OFFICES OF THE WORLD HEALTH ORGANIZATION
(As at 31 December 1984)

OFFICERS OF THE THIRTY-SEVENTH WORLD HEALTH ASSEMBLY

President: Dr. G. Soberon Acevedo (Mexico).
Vice Presidents: Dr. S. H. Alwash (Iraq), P. D. Boussoukou-Boumba (Congo), Dr. A. Grech (Malta), Dr. M. Shamsul Haq (Bangladesh), M. P. To Vadek (Papua New Guinea).
Chairman, Committee A: Dr. K. Al-Ajlouni (Jordan).
Chairman, Committee B: Dr. N. Rosdahl (Denmark).

MEMBERS OF THE EXECUTIVE BOARD*

Chairman: Professor J. Roux (France).
Vice-Chairmen: Professor B. Jazbi (Pakistan), Dr. A. Khalid Bin Sahan (Malaysia), Dr. G. Tadesse (Ethiopia).
Rapporteurs: Professor A. Lafontaine (Belgium), Dr. Elizabeth S. M. Quamina (Trinidad and Tobago).

Members were designated by: Argentina, Belgium, Chile, China, Djibouti, Egypt, Equatorial Guinea, Ethiopia, France, Ghana, Guinea, Hungary, Iceland, Indonesia, Iraq, Ivory Coast, Kenya, Nepal, Pakistan, Panama, Republic of Korea, Syrian Arab Republic, Thailand, Trinidad and Tobago, USSR, United Kingdom, United States, Venezuela, Zimbabwe.

*The Board consists of 31 persons designated by as many member States which have been elected for such purpose by WHO.

SENIOR OFFICERS OF THE SECRETARIAT

Director-General: Dr. Halfdan Mahler.

Deputy Director-General: Dr. T. Adeoye Lambo.
Assistant Directors-General: Warren W. Furth, Dr. J. Hamon, Dr. S. K. Litvinov,
   Dr. Lu Rushan, Dr. F. Partow, Dr. David Tejada-de-Rivero.
Director, Regional Office for Africa: Dr. G. L. Monekosso.

Director, Regional Office for the Americas (Pan American Sanitary Bureau): Dr.
   C. Guerra de Macedo.
Director, Regional Office for South-East Asia: Dr. U Ko Ko.
Director, Regional Office for Europe: Dr. J. E. Asvall.
Director, Regional Office for the Eastern Mediterranean: Dr. Hussein A. Gezairy.
Director, Regional Office for the Western Pacific: Dr. Hiroshi Nakajima.

HEADQUARTERS AND OTHER OFFICES

HEADQUARTERS
World Health Organization
Avenue Appia
1211 Geneva 27, Switzerland
   Cable address: UNISANTE GENEVA
   Telephone: 91 21 11
   Telex: 27821

LIAISON OFFICE WITH THE
   UNITED NATIONS
World Health Organization
New York, N.Y. 10017, United States
   Cable address: UNISANTE NEWYORK
   Telephone: (212) 963-6004, 963-6005
   Telex: 234292

REGIONAL OFFICE FOR THE EASTERN
   MEDITERRANEAN
World Health Organization
P.O. Box 1517
Alexandria, Egypt
   Cable address: UNISANTE ALEXANDRIA
   Telephone: 802318, 807843
   Telex: 54028

REGIONAL OFFICE FOR AFRICA
World Health Organization
P.O. Box No. 6
Brazzaville, Congo
   Cable address: UNISANTE BRAZZAVILLE
   Telephone: 81 38 60-65
   Telex: 5217, 6004

REGIONAL OFFICE FOR EUROPE
World Health Organization
8 Scherfigsvej
DK-2100 Copenhagen O, Denmark
   Cable address: UNISANTE COPENHAGEN
   Telephone: 29 01 11
   Telex: 15348

REGIONAL OFFICE FOR THE WESTERN
   PACIFIC
World Health Organization
P.O. Box 2932
12115 Manila, Philippines
   Cable address: UNISANTE MANILA
   Telephone: 59 20 41, 59 37 21
   Telex: 27652, 40365, 63620

REGIONAL OFFICE FOR SOUTH-EAST ASIA
World Health Organization
World Health House
Indraprastha Estate, Mahatma Gandhi Road
New Delhi 110002, India
   Cable address: WHO NEWDELHI
   Telephone: 27 01 81 88
   Telex: 312241, 312195

REGIONAL OFFICE FOR THE AMERICAS/
   PAN AMERICAN SANITARY BUREAU
World Health Organization
525 23rd Street, N.W.
Washington, D.C. 20037, United States
   Cable address: OFSANPAN WASHINGTON
   Telephone: (202) 861-3200
   Telex: 248338, 440057, 64152

Chapter VI

International Bank for Reconstruction and Development (World Bank)

During the fiscal year 1 July 1983 to 30 June 1984, the International Bank for Reconstruction and Development (World Bank) and its affiliate, the International Development Association (IDA), continued to help developing countries to raise their standards of living by channelling financial resources to them from developed countries.

Lending commitments by the Bank, credit approvals from IDA, and investment commitments by a second affiliate, the International Finance Corporation (IFC), amounted to $16,220 million—up $898 million from the previous fiscal year.

Membership in the Bank rose to 148 in 1984, with the admission of Saint Christopher and Nevis (15 August) and Mozambique (24 September).

Lending operations

In the fiscal year ending 30 June 1984, the World Bank made 129 loans amounting to $11,949.2 million to 43 countries, an increase of $813 million over fiscal year 1983. This brought the cumulative total of loan commitments by the Bank since its inception in 1946 to $101,565.4 million.

The following table summarizes World Bank lending in fiscal 1984 by region or country and by purpose.

WORLD BANK LOANS APPROVED BY REGION/COUNTRY AND PURPOSE
1 JULY 1983–30 JUNE 1984
(in millions of US dollars)

REGION/COUNTRY	Agriculture and rural development	Development finance companies	Education	Energy	Industry	Non-project	Population, health and nutrition	Small-scale enterprises	Technical assistance	Telecommunications	Transportation	Urbanization	Water supply and sewerage	Total
Eastern Africa														
Botswana	—	12.3	—	—	—	—	11.0	—	—	—	—	—	22.0	45.3
Kenya	—	—	—	95.0	—	—	—	—	—	—	50.0	—	—	145.0
Malawi	—	—	—	—	—	—	—	—	—	—	18.0	—	—	18.0
Mauritius	—	—	—	—	—	40.0	—	—	5.0	—	15.2	—	—	60.2
Swaziland	—	—	—	5.6	—	—	—	—	—	—	—	—	—	5.6
Zambia	—	—	—	—	75.0	—	—	—	—	—	—	—	—	75.0
Zimbabwe	13.1	—	—	—	—	—	—	—	—	—	40.0	43.0	—	96.1
Subtotal	13.1	12.3	—	100.6	75.0	40.0	11.0	—	5.0	—	123.2	43.0	22.0	445.2
Western Africa														
Cameroon	21.5	—	—	—	—	—	—	—	—	—	—	—	—	21.5
Ivory Coast	—	—	—	—	—	250.7	—	—	—	—	—	—	—	250.7
Nigeria	372.0	—	—	25.00	—	—	—	41.0	—	—	—	—	—	438.0
Subtotal	393.5	—	—	25.0	—	250.7	—	41.0	—	—	—	—	—	710.2
East Asia and Pacific														
China	—	105.0	45.3	245.7	—	—	—	—	—	—	220.0	—	—	616.0
Indonesia	233.2	—	106.3	210.0	—	—	204.6	—	—	—	240.0	39.3	—	1,033.4
Malaysia	—	—	—	70.0	—	—	—	—	—	—	—	—	—	70.0
Papua New Guinea	—	—	49.3	—	—	—	—	—	—	—	—	—	—	49.3
Philippines	30.7	—	—	—	—	—	—	—	—	—	102.0	50.5	—	183.2
Republic of Korea	—	—	100.0	—	—	300.0	—	—	—	—	230.0	60.0	78.5	768.5
Thailand	85.0	—	—	59.1	—	—	—	—	8.5	—	—	—	—	152.6
Subtotal	348.9	105.0	300.9	584.8	—	300.0	204.6	—	8.5	—	792.0	149.8	78.5	2,873.0
South Asia														
India	—	—	—	987.1	203.6	—	—	—	—	—	530.7	—	—	1,721.4
Pakistan	—	50.0	—	81.5	—	—	—	—	—	—	—	—	—	131.5
Sri Lanka	12.1	—	—	—	—	—	—	—	—	—	—	—	—	12.1
Subtotal	12.1	50.0	—	1,068.6	203.6	—	—	—	—	—	530.7	—	—	1,865.00

REGION/COUNTRY	Agriculture and rural development	Development finance companies	Education	Energy	Industry	Non-project	Population, health and nutrition	Small-scale enterprises	Technical assistance	Telecommunications	Transportation	Urbanization	Water supply and sewerage	Total
Europe, the Middle East and North Africa														
Algeria	—	—	—	—	—	—	—	—	—	128.0	—	—	290.0	418.0
Cyprus	27.0	—	—	—	—	—	—	—	—	—	—	—	16.8	43.8
Egypt	—	395.0	—	59.0	—	—	—	—	—	—	—	—	4.0	458.00
Hungary	30.0	110.0	—	90.0	8.8	—	—	—	—	—	—	—	—	238.8
Jordan	—	—	40.0	30.0	—	—	—	—	—	—	—	30.0	30.0	130.0
Morocco	115.4	—	—	—	150.4	—	—	—	—	—	—	—	—	265.8
Oman	—	—	15.0	—	—	—	—	—	—	—	—	—	—	15.0
Portugal	7.4	—	30.5	—	34.7	—	—	—	—	—	—	—	—	72.6
Syrian Arab Republic	—	—	—	—	—	—	—	—	—	—	—	—	30.0	30.0
Tunisia	—	—	—	38.7	13.4	—	—	—	—	—	—	33.0	50.0	135.1
Turkey	187.5	—	36.8	—	7.6	376.0	—	—	—	—	186.4	—	—	794.3
Yugoslavia	90.0	70.0	—	181.0	—	—	—	—	—	—	110.0	—	—	451.0
Subtotal	457.3	575.0	122.3	398.7	214.9	376.0	—	—	—	128.0	296.4	63.0	420.8	3,052.4
Latin America and the Caribbean														
Barbados	—	—	3.0	—	—	—	—	—	—	—	11.0	—	—	14.0
Brazil	398.7	—	60.0	473.4	—	—	57.5	352.0	—	—	210.0	52.7	—	1,604.3
Colombia	50.0	—	—	364.6	9.5	—	—	—	—	—	—	40.0	—	464.1
Dominican Republic	—	—	—	—	—	—	—	—	—	—	3.8	—	—	3.8
Guatemala	—	20.0	—	—	—	—	—	—	—	30.0	—	—	—	50.0
Honduras	—	—	—	—	—	—	—	—	—	—	—	—	19.6	19.6
Jamaica	15.1	—	—	—	—	—	—	—	4.5	—	—	16.0	9.0	44.6
Mexico	300.0	—	—	—	—	—	—	—	—	—	276.3	—	—	576.3
Panama	9.0	—	—	—	—	60.2	—	—	5.0	—	—	—	—	74.2
Paraguay	25.0	—	5.0	—	—	—	—	—	—	—	—	—	—	30.0
Peru	40.0	—	—	—	—	—	—	—	—	—	—	82.5	—	122.5
Subtotal	837.8	20.0	68.0	838.0	9.5	60.2	57.5	352.0	9.5	30.0	501.1	191.2	28.6	3,003.4
Total	2,062.7	762.3	491.2	3,015.7	503.0	1,026.9	68.5	597.6	14.5	166.5	2,243.4	447.0	549.9	11,949.2
NUMBER OF LOANS	26	9	12	22	7	5	2	3	3	3	17	10	10	129

Agriculture and rural development

The Bank continued its commitment to agriculture and rural development, making 26 loans in fiscal 1984 amounting to $2,062.7 million in 20 countries. Brazil received $398.7 million, of which $303 million was to support a general agricultural-investment credit line, as well as a revolving fund to rediscount pre-financing credits for exporters of agricultural and agro-industrial products. Nigeria received $372 million, of which $250 million was to provide approximately 60 per cent of an estimated 2 million tons of fertilizer needed for 1984 and 1985. Of $233.2 million provided to Indonesia, $89 million went to strengthen irrigation services of eight island provinces and $79.2 million to develop some 12,400 hectares of sugar-cane, expected to produce 50,000 tons of sugar a year.

Development finance companies

The Bank made nine loans totalling $762.3 million in fiscal 1984 to assist development finance companies in seven countries. The larger borrowers were Egypt ($395 million to help expand small and medium-sized industries and manufactured exports and improve the construction industry), Hungary ($110 million to support governmental programmes for industrial restructuring and export promotion and to strengthen the development-banking role of the National Bank of Hungary), and China ($105 million to assist the China Investment Bank to finance investment loans for small and medium-sized industrial projects in need of foreign exchange).

Education

During fiscal 1984, the Bank granted 12 loans totalling $491.2 million for education projects in 11 countries. Indonesia received $106.3 million for middle-level agricultural manpower training and to provide basic education and training in employment-oriented skills to some 800,000 illiterates and school drop-outs. The Republic of Korea received $100 million to upgrade the country's science and technology education. Papua New Guinea received $49.3 million to expand and improve schools, to upgrade teacher training and to provide textbooks and other teaching materials with a view to increasing the number of secondary-school graduates.

Energy

Twenty-two energy projects—in oil, gas, coal and power—were assisted in 16 countries during fiscal 1984 at a total cost of $3,015.7 million.

Five loans totalling $987.1 million were made to India, of which $300.8 million was to help meet electricity demand in the eastern region by the addition of 1,000 megawatts to the thermal power-generating capacity of the Farakka thermal power plant in West Bengal. Brazil received two loans amounting to $473.4 million, of which $250.6 million was to expand and modernize power-distribution systems in five less-developed states in the north-eastern and north-western regions and in the low-income metropolitan areas of Rio de Janeiro and São Paulo. Colombia received $364.6 million, of which $164.5 million was for the construction of facilities needed to provide safe and reliable water supply to the Antioquia region by 1990, and to finance hydropower infrastructure. Of two loans totalling $245.7 million to China, $145.4 million was to provide additional generating capacity and energy to the Yunnan power grid, to introduce modern technology in the construction of dams, tunnels and underground powerhouses, and to provide technical assistance and staff training.

Industry

The Bank made seven loans to eight countries for the industrial sector, amounting to $503 million during fiscal 1984. The largest loans included $203.6 million to India for the construction of a fertilizer plant; $150.4 million to Morocco to support implementation of the first phase of its industrial and trade policy-adjustment programme, aimed principally at introducing structural changes in a system of incentives to eliminate bias against export production and to lower manufacturing costs; and $75 million to Zambia to finance the first phase of a five-year programme to modernize the Zambia Consolidated Copper Mines Limited.

Non-project

Five non-project loans totalling $1,026.9 million were made to five countries during the fiscal year, all in support of programmes for the structural adjustment of national economies. Turkey received $376 million, the fifth in a series of loans to finance essential imports. A $300-million loan to the Republic of Korea was for structural reforms in industry, energy and public-sector efficiency. The Ivory Coast received $250.7 million to promote sustainable growth and increase public savings.

Smaller loans to two other countries were for import financing and to help accelerate production of export goods by the private sector.

Population, health and nutrition

Two loans amounting to $68.5 million were made to two countries in fiscal 1984. Brazil received $57.5 million to provide São Paulo with a basic health-care system emphasizing preventive care, and to support a study programme designed to help the Government to formulate policy and implement medium-term plans for the health sector. Botswana received $11 million to make health and family-planning services more accessible, better focused and more cost effective.

Small-scale enterprises

Three loans totalling $597.6 million were made to three countries for small-scale enterprises during the fiscal year. Brazil received $352 million to expand its manufactured exports by liberalizing imports and increasing the availability of foreign exchange. A $204.6-million loan to Indonesia was to assist in financing small-enterprise projects nationwide in nearly all economic sectors. Nigeria received $41 million to initiate a programme to provide technical advice, training and credit to small- and medium-scale enterprises.

Technical assistance

During fiscal 1984, three countries received loans for technical assistance amounting to $14.5 million. Mauritius and Panama each received $5 million to assist government structural-adjustment programmes. A $4.5-million loan went to Jamaica to provide consultants, training and equipment in support of its administrative reform programme.

The largest element of technical assistance continued to be that financed under the lending programme, particularly as a component of loans for other purposes. Some 90 per cent of loans included technical assistance components. These totalled $1,093.2 million in 203 operations, compared with $1,275.3 million in 219 operations in fiscal 1983. Among the larger amounts of such components were $41.4 million in an energy loan to India, $35 million in a highway loan to Indonesia, $32 million in a power loan to Kenya and $26.9 million in a railway loan to Zimbabwe.

The Bank continued to serve as executing agency for projects financed by the United Nations Development Programme (UNDP). At the end of fiscal 1984, the number of projects in progress stood at 115—down from 127 the previous year—while 26 new projects, involving commitments of $12.3 million, were approved during the year, compared to 33 projects with commitments of $33.1 million in 1983. Among the largest new UNDP-financed projects were a coal pre-investment study in Colombia, the third phase of a planning project in the Sudan, an energy assessment in Paraguay and the first of four seminars in energy policy for the Bank's members from sub-Saharan Africa.

The Bank's technical co-operation was extended to capital-surplus developing countries in Europe, the Middle East and North Africa, on a reimbursable basis when the annual programme exceeded a staff-year of Bank input, and on a non-reimbursable basis in response to *ad hoc* requests for programmes. In fiscal 1984, about 32 staff-years of reimbursable technical assistance were provided by the Bank, some 90 per cent of it to Saudi Arabia. Non-reimbursable technical assistance was provided to Kuwait in the form of a general economic review and assistance in manpower planning.

Telecommunications

Three loans amounting to $166.5 million were made to three countries in fiscal 1984. Algeria received $128 million for the expansion of a telecommunication network and provision of related equipment, technical assistance and training. Guatemala received $30 million for the installation of more than 100,000 lines of local-exchange equipment in urban areas to improve telecommunication services.

Transportation

Seventeen loans totalling $2,243.4 million were made to 15 countries during fiscal 1984 to help develop their transportation systems. India received $530.7 million for the modernization of Indian Railways and construction of a new container and bulk-freight port near Bombay to accommodate projected growth in marine freight through 1993. A $276.3-million loan to Mexico went to road reconstruction (trunk-roads) and maintenance (rural roads) and upgrading of industrial port installations. Indonesia received $240 million for the restoration and upgrading of its road network and bridges, and improvement of highway planning and management. Other loans were for highway and railroad construction and improvement, to include equipment, technical assistance and training.

Urbanization

In fiscal 1984, 10 countries received 10 loans amounting to $447 million to aid the urban poor. Peru received $82.5 million to support the transfer of urban administration from national to local government and improve high-priority infrastructure and services. A $60-million loan went to the Republic of Korea to promote economic development in the Jeonju region, currently the poorest in the country. Brazil received $52.7 million to provide 287 towns in the State of Parana with infrastructure and public and social services.

Water supply and sewerage

The Bank made 10 loans totalling $549.9 million in fiscal 1984 for water supply and sewerage projects in 10 countries. Algeria received $290 million to increase water supply and distribution in the Greater Algiers area. A $78.5-million loan was made to the Republic of Korea to provide water supply services to 13 cities and 24 towns, and for pilot sub-projects in leak detection and in the use of microcomputers for water utilities. Tunisia received $50 million to improve water supply in rural areas.

Economic Development Institute

Fiscal 1984 was a year of transition for the Economic Development Institute (EDI)—designed to train senior officials of the Bank's developing member countries in economic management and investment—as preparations began for a new five-year plan for fiscal 1985 through 1989. The plan defined new objectives and instruments to achieve them.

The year was also one of experimentation with newly designed courses and seminars, while core training activities continued. A total of 72 courses and seminars were held—19 in the United States (18 at Washington, D.C., and 1 in New York) and 53 in other countries; participants totalled 2,400. New courses introduced were on such topics as technical and vocational education (Washington, D.C.); energy assessment and planning, co-sponsored by UNDP (New York); port projects (China); railway projects and policies (Kenya); and planning, financing and managing city growth (Thailand).

In anticipation of the new plan, EDI increased to eight the number of policy seminars for high-level officials. Topics included development management, management of agricultural research, rural health care, industrial policy (three seminars), energy policy, and railway management. At Washington, D.C., the seventh annual seminar on world development issues, co-sponsored by the United Nations Institute for Training and Research, was held for diplomats assigned to United Nations Headquarters.

Other seminars were for trainers of training institutions in developing countries. During fiscal 1984, 39 such institutions acted as partners for EDI activities—3 in Africa; 18 in Asia; 9 in Europe, the Middle East and North Africa; and 9 in Latin America and the Caribbean. EDI also mounted, jointly with other aid agencies, its first broad review mission of a training institution, namely the Eastern and Southern African Management Institute at Arusha, United Republic of Tanzania.

A Training Materials Policy Committee was created to set and administer standards in the production of training material. During fiscal 1984, material produced included 30 course notes, 14 project case-studies and 20 exercises, as well as the first computerized policy-simulation model. Work was completed on eight new multimedia modules in a series of 16 planned on water supply and sanitation. A number of revisions or translations of EDI books were published.

New EDI financial partners in fiscal 1984 included the Australian Development Assistance Bureau, the Gulbenkian Foundation of Portugal, the Organization of American States, and the Statistical, Economic and Social Research and Training Centre for Islamic Countries of the Organization of the Islamic Conference.

Co-financing

Despite difficult market conditions affecting the availability of private and export-credit funds, the flow of funds to developing countries continued to be maintained through co-financing with the World Bank. The Bank's contribution during fiscal 1984 amounted to over $4.6 billion. A meeting with 25 credit and insurance agencies (Washington, D.C., November 1983) reviewed co-financing policies and procedures. As a result, a set of suggested measures to increase export credit for priority purposes and to help secure the best possible terms was under consideration. A key objective of the Bank's co-financing efforts was to help reinstate a net inflow of commercial funds on long maturities appropriate for development finance. Through the B-loan pilot programme, nine such loans amounting to $1.1 billion were processed during the fiscal year, including two B-loans for Paraguay and Hungary totalling $502 million, to be signed early in fiscal 1985.

Special Assistance Programme

The Special Assistance Programme, approved in fiscal 1983,[a] was intended to strengthen the World Bank's ability to assist developing countries to adjust to the current economic environment. The Programme's major elements included: expansion in lending for high-priority operations that supported structural adjustment, policy changes, production for export, fuller use of existing capacity and maintenance of crucial infrastructure; accelerated disbursements under existing and new commitments to ensure timely implementation of high-priority projects; expanded advisory services on the design and implementation of appropriate policies; and efforts aimed at enlisting similar action from other donors.

In March 1984, the Executive Directors met to assess the progress achieved during calendar year 1983. They agreed that progress had been accomplished towards meeting the Programme's objectives, although it was too soon to assess its impact. A further assessment of the Programme, covering operations through June 1984, was to be made later in calendar year 1984.

Financing activities

During fiscal 1984, the World Bank borrowed the equivalent of $9,831 million: $2,418.1 million in United States dollars, $2,299.7 million in Swiss francs, $1,838.3 million in Deutsche mark, $1,700.2 million in Japanese yen, $828.4 million in Netherlands guilders, $421 million in pounds sterling, $101.3 million in Lybian dinars, $68.3 million in European currency units, $57.1 million in Canadian dollars, $40.8 million in Austrian schillings, $39.8 million in Belgian francs and $18 million in Luxembourg francs.

Of the 94 medium- and long-term borrowing operations conducted by the Bank, 71 were public issues or private placements throughout the world, which accounted for $6,502 million, or 66 per cent of the total amount of funds borrowed. The other 23 issues, totalling $2,072 million or 21 per cent of the funds raised, were placed with official sources: the Bank's member Governments, central banks and government institutions. Short-term borrowings outstanding as at 30 June amounted to $2,749 million.

As at 30 June 1984, the Bank's outstanding obligations totalled $45,029 million—an increase of $5,622 million over fiscal 1983—denominated in 20 different currencies.

During fiscal 1984, the Bank continued to engage in currency swaps[b] as a means of increasing its access to low nominal-cost currencies. It executed 44 currency-swap transactions aggregating $1,299 million ($893 million into Swiss francs, $306 million into Deutsche mark, $59 million into Netherlands guilders and $41 million into Austrian schillings), compared with $1,731 million in fiscal 1983.

Capitalization

For the fiscal year ending 30 June 1984, the value of the World Bank's capital stock was expressed on the basis of special drawing rights (SDRs) in terms of the United States dollar as computed by the International Monetary Fund on 30 June. On that date, the value of the SDR was set at $1.03121.

The subscribed capital of the Bank, as at 30 June, totalled SDR 54,315 million, an increase of over SDR 5,500 million from fiscal 1983.

Income, expenditures and reserves

The World Bank's gross revenues, generated primarily from loans and investments, increased by $422 million, or 10 per cent, to a total of $4,655 million in fiscal 1984. Net income was $600 million, a decrease of $152 million compared with fiscal 1983. The 20 per cent decrease was anticipated, since the previous year's net income had resulted primarily from high rates of return on the Bank's liquidity.

Expenses totalled $4,022 million, an increase of 16 per cent from the previous fiscal year. Administrative costs amounted to $330 million, up by $8 million.

The General Reserve of the Bank amounted to $3,450 million at the end of fiscal 1984.

[a]YUN 1983, p. 1259.
[b]*Ibid.*

Secretariat

As at 30 June 1984, the staff of the World Bank numbered 5,697, of whom 2,855 were in the Professional or higher categories, drawn from 110 nationalities.

STATEMENT OF INCOME AND EXPENSES
(for the fiscal year ended 30 June 1984)

Income	Amount (in thousands of US dollars)
Income from investments*	1,399,022
Income from loans	
Interest	2,961,922
Commitment charges	239,828
Front-end fees	33,964
Other income†	19,786
Total income	4,654,522

Expenses	Amount (in thousands of US dollars)
Administrative expenses‡	329,959
Interest on borrowings	3,638,395
Bond issuance and other financial expenses	54,129
Contributions to special programmes	32,000
Total expenses	4,054,483
Net income	600,039

*Includes net losses of $44,516,000 resulting from sales of investments.

†Includes net gains of $18,043,000 resulting from repurchases of obligations of the Bank prior to maturity.

‡All administrative expenses of the Bank and IDA and a portion of those of IFC are paid by the Bank. The administrative expenses are net of a management fee of $249,225,000 charged to IDA and of a service and support fee of $3,050,000 charged to IFC.

Annex I.   MEMBERS OF THE WORLD BANK, SUBSCRIPTIONS AND VOTING POWER

(As at 30 June 1984)

MEMBER	SUBSCRIPTION Amount (in SDRs)	Percentage of total	VOTING POWER Number of votes	Percentage of total	MEMBER	SUBSCRIPTION Amount (in SDRs)	Percentage of total	VOTING POWER Number of votes	Percentage of total
Afghanistan	30,000	0.06	550	0.09	Germany, Federal Republic of	3,434,700	6.32	34,597	5.97
Algeria	475,500	0.88	5,005	0.86	Ghana	85,600	0.16	1,106	0.19
Antigua and Barbuda	2,000	*	270	0.05	Greece	94,500	0.17	1,195	0.21
Argentina	583,100	1.07	6,081	1.05	Grenada	1,700	*	267	0.05
Australia	1,273,700	2.35	12,987	2.24	Guatemala	16,700	0.03	417	0.07
Austria	546,900	1.01	5,719	0.99	Guinea†	20,000	0.04	450	0.08
Bahamas	17,100	0.03	421	0.07	Guinea-Bissau	2,700	*	277	0.05
Bahrain	56,600	0.10	816	0.14	Guyana†	57,900	0.11	829	0.14
Bangladesh†	124,200	0.23	1,492	0.26	Haiti†	17,400	0.03	424	0.07
Barbados	51,900	0.10	769	0.13	Honduras†	8,400	0.02	334	0.06
Belgium	1,241,800	2.29	12,668	2.19	Hungary	204,200	0.38	2,292	0.40
Belize	3,900	0.01	289	0.05	Iceland	68,000	0.13	930	0.16
Benin	10,000	0.02	350	0.06	India	2,300,600	4.23	23,252	4.01
Bhutan†	900	*	259	0.04	Indonesia	777,700	1.43	8,027	1.38
Bolivia	26,400	0.05	514	0.09	Iran	158,000	0.29	1,830	0.32
Botswana	33,100	0.06	581	0.10	Iraq	95,600	0.18	1,206	0.21
Brazil	1,070,600	1.97	10,956	1.89	Ireland	270,100	0.50	2,951	0.51
Burma†	59,100	0.11	841	0.15	Israel	110,800	0.20	1,358	0.23
Burundi	15,000	0.03	400	0.07	Italy	1,984,200	3.65	20,092	3.47
Cameroon	20,000	0.04	450	0.08	Ivory Coast	58,400	0.11	834	0.14
Canada	1,843,800	3.39	18,688	3.22	Jamaica	44,600	0.08	696	0.12
Cape Verde	1,600	*	266	0.05	Japan	3,420,600	6.30	34,456	5.94
Central African Republic	10,000	0.02	350	0.06	Jordan	23,300	0.04	483	0.08
Chad	10,000	0.02	350	0.06	Kenya	55,000	0.10	800	0.14
Chile	124,000	0.23	1,490	0.26	Kuwait	645,100	1.19	6,701	1.16
China	2,348,200	4.32	23,732	4.09	Lao People's Democratic				
Colombia	117,500	0.22	1,425	0.25	Republic	10,000	0.02	350	0.06
Comoros	1,600	*	266	0.05	Lebanon	9,000	0.02	340	0.06
Congo	10,000	0.02	350	0.06	Lesotho	36,200	0.07	612	0.11
Costa Rica	13,100	0.02	381	0.07	Liberia	21,300	0.04	463	0.08
Cyprus	78,800	0.15	1,038	0.18	Libyan Arab Jamahiriya	195,100	0.36	2,201	0.38
Democratic Kampuchea	21,400	0.04	464	0.08	Luxembourg	77,000	0.14	1,020	0.18
Democratic Yemen	33,600	0.06	586	0.10	Madagascar	21,900	0.04	469	0.08
Denmark	513,600	0.95	5,386	0.93	Malawi†	15,000	0.03	400	0.07
Djibouti	3,100	0.01	281	0.05	Malaysia	425,000	0.78	4,500	0.78
Dominica	1,600	*	266	0.05	Maldives	26,200	0.05	512	0.09
Dominican Republic	58,900	0.11	839	0.14	Mali	17,300	0.03	423	0.07
Ecuador	36,800	0.07	618	0.11	Malta	16,300	0.03	413	0.07
Egypt	344,400	0.63	3,694	0.64	Mauritania	10,000	0.02	350	0.06
El Salvador†	12,000	0.02	370	0.06	Mauritius†	22,100	0.04	471	0.08
Equatorial Guinea	6,400	0.01	314	0.05	Mexico	636,000	1.17	6,610	1.14
Ethiopia	53,300	0.10	783	0.14	Morocco	261,200	0.48	2,862	0.49
Fiji	45,300	0.08	703	0.12	Nepal	53,300	0.10	783	0.14
Finland	339,200	0.62	3,642	0.63	Netherlands	1,511,700	2.78	15,367	2.65
France	2,891,400	5.32	29,164	5.03	New Zealand	301,900	0.56	3,269	0.56
Gabon	12,000	0.02	370	0.06	Nicaragua	9,100	0.02	341	0.06
Gambia	5,300	0.01	303	0.05	Niger†	10,000	0.02	350	0.06

MEMBER	SUBSCRIPTION		VOTING POWER		MEMBER	SUBSCRIPTION		VOTING POWER	
	Amount (in SDRs)	Percent-age of total	Number of votes	Percent-age of total		Amount (in SDRs)	Percent-age of total	Number of votes	Percent-age of total
Nigeria	294,100	0.54	3,191	0.55	Sudan	60,000	0.11	850	0.15
Norway†	241,000	0.44	2,660	0.46	Suriname	16,200	0.03	412	0.07
Oman	19,200	0.04	442	0.08	Swaziland	44,000	0.08	690	0.12
Pakistan†	251,900	0.46	2,769	0.48	Sweden	736,700	1.36	7,617	1.31
Panama	21,600	0.04	466	0.08	Syrian Arab Republic	123,300	0.23	1,483	0.26
Papua New Guinea	24,600	0.05	496	0.09	Thailand	311,100	0.57	3,361	0.58
Paraguay	38,600	0.07	636	0.11	Togo	15,000	0.03	400	0.07
Peru	93,800	0.17	1,188	0.20	Trinidad and Tobago	66,700	0.12	917	0.16
Philippines	359,800	0.66	3,848	0.66	Tunisia	37,300	0.07	623	0.11
Portugal	132,400	0.24	1,574	0.27	Turkey	340,800	0.63	3,658	0.63
Qatar†	32,700	0.06	577	0.10	Uganda	33,300	0.06	583	0.10
Republic of Korea	294,700	0.54	3,197	0.55	United Arab Emirates†	98,000	0.18	1,230	0.21
Romania	200,100	0.37	2,251	0.39	United Kingdom	3,537,600	6.51	35,626	6.15
Rwanda†	17,400	0.03	424	0.07	United Republic of Tanzania†	35,000	0.06	600	0.10
Saint Lucia	2,900	0.01	279	0.05	United States	11,105,000	20.45	111,300	19.20
Saint Vincent and the Grenadines	1,300	*	263	0.05	Upper Volta‡	10,000	0.02	350	0.06
Samoa	1,700	*	267	0.05	Uruguay	41,100	0.08	661	0.11
Sao Tome and Principe	1,400	*	264	0.05	Vanuatu	32,300	0.06	573	0.10
Saudi Arabia	1,121,200	2.06	11,462	1.98	Venezuela	756,000	1.39	7,810	1.35
Senegal	36,200	0.07	612	0.11	Viet Nam	54,300	0.10	793	0.14
Seychelles	1,100	*	261	0.05	Yemen	45,500	0.08	705	0.12
Sierra Leone	15,000	0.03	400	0.07	Yugoslavia†	150,900	0.28	1,759	0.30
Singapore	32,000	0.06	570	0.10	Zaire†	96,000	0.18	1,210	0.21
Solomon Islands†	1,700	*	267	0.05	Zambia†	115,100	0.21	1,401	0.24
Somalia	18,900	0.03	439	0.08	Zimbabwe	84,700	0.15	1,067	0.18
South Africa	346,300	0.64	3,713	0.64					
Spain	455,100	0.84	4,801	0.83	Total	54,315,400	100.00§	579,654	100.00§
Sri Lanka†	96,100	0.18	1,211	0.21					

NOTE: Saint Christopher and Nevis, and Mozambique became members on 15 August and 24 September, respectively.

*Less than 0.005 per cent.

†Amounts aggregating the equivalent of $58,667,000, in current United States dollars, had been received from members on account of increases in subscriptions, which were in process of completion: Bangladesh $6,188,000, Bhutan $7,000, Burma $2,854,000, El Salvador $253,000, Guinea $250,000, Guyana $252,000, Haiti $1,344,000, Honduras $311,000, Malawi $211,000, Mauritius $187,000, Niger $40,000, Norway $6,915,000, Pakistan $18,735,000, Qatar $3,470,000, Rwanda $1,383,000, Solomon Islands $106,000, Sri Lanka $5,442,000, United Arab Emirates $1,082,000, United Republic of Tanzania $130,000, Yugoslavia $959,000, Zaire $3,813,000 and Zambia $4,735,000.

‡Changed its name to Burkina Faso on 6 August 1984

§May differ from the sum of the individual percentages because of rounding.

Annex II.   EXECUTIVE DIRECTORS AND ALTERNATES OF THE WORLD BANK
(As at 30 June 1984)

Appointed Director	Appointed Alternate	Casting the vote of
James B. Burnham	Hugh W. Foster	United States
Nigel L. Wicks	Richard Manning	United Kingdom
Reinhard Münzberg	Michael von Harpe*	Federal Republic of Germany
Kenji Yamaguchi	Toshihiro Yamakawa	Japan
Bruno de Maulde	Francis Mayer	France

Elected Director	Elected Alternate	Casting the votes of
Said E. El-Naggar (Egypt)	Mohammad Al-Shawi (Saudi Arabia)	Bahrain, Egypt, Iraq, Jordan, Kuwait, Lebanon, Maldives, Oman, Pakistan, Qatar, Saudi Arabia, Syrian Arab Republic, United Arab Emirates, Yemen
H. N. Ray (India)	Gholam Kibria (Bangladesh)	Bangladesh, Bhutan, India, Sri Lanka
Morris Miller (Canada)	George L. Reid (Barbados)	Bahamas, Barbados, Belize, Canada, Dominica, Grenada, Guyana, Ireland, Jamaica, Saint Lucia, Saint Vincent and the Grenadines
Jacques de Groote (Belgium)	Herbert A. Lust (Austria)	Austria, Belgium, Hungary, Luxembourg, Turkey
Xu Naijiong (China)	Fei Lizhi (China)	China
Giorgio Ragazzi (Italy)	Rodrigo M. Guimarães (Portugal)	Greece, Italy, Portugal
Patricio Ayala-González (Mexico)	Roberto Mayorga-Cortés (Nicaragua)	Costa Rica, El Salvador, Guatemala, Honduras, Mexico, Nicaragua, Panama, Spain, Suriname, Venezuela
Ferdinand van Dam (Netherlands)	Riza Sapunxhiu (Yugoslavia)	Cyprus, Israel, Netherlands, Romania, Yugoslavia
Ronald H. Dean (Australia)	You Kwang Park (Republic of Korea)	Australia, New Zealand, Papua New Guinea, Republic of Korea, Samoa, Solomon Islands, Vanuatu
Pekka Korpinen (Finland)	Per Taxell (Sweden)	Denmark, Finland, Iceland, Norway, Sweden
Phaichitr Uathavikul (Thailand)	Nibhat Bhukkanasut (Thailand)	Burma, Fiji, Indonesia, Lao People's Democratic Republic, Malaysia, Nepal, Singapore, Thailand, Viet Nam

Elected Director	Elected Alternate	Casting the votes of
Antonio V. Romuáldez (Philippines)	Héctor Echeverri (Colombia)	Brazil, Colombia, Dominican Republic, Ecuador, Haiti, Philippines
Mourad Benachenhou (Algeria)	Salem Mohamed Omeish (Libyan Arab Jamahiriya)	Afghanistan, Algeria, Democratic Yemen, Ghana, Iran, Libyan Arab Jamahiriya, Morocco, Tunisia
William Smith (Liberia)	Astère Girukwigomba (Burundi)	Botswana, Burundi, Ethiopia, Gambia, Guinea, Kenya, Lesotho, Liberia, Malawi, Nigeria, Seychelles, Sierra Leone, Sudan, Swaziland, Trinidad and Tobago, Uganda, United Republic of Tanzania, Zambia, Zimbabwe
Eduardo Zalduendo (Argentina)	Pedro O. Montórfano (Paraguay)	Argentina, Bolivia, Chile, Paraguay, Peru, Uruguay
Nicéphore Soglo (Benin)	André Milongo (Congo)	Benin, Cameroon, Cape Verde, Central African Republic, Chad, Comoros, Congo, Djibouti, Equatorial Guinea, Gabon, Guinea-Bissau, Ivory Coast, Madagascar, Mali, Mauritania, Mauritius, Niger, Rwanda, Sao Tome and Principe, Senegal, Somalia, Togo, Upper Volta,† Zaire

NOTE: Democratic Kampuchea and South Africa did not participate in the 1982 regular election of Executive Directors. Antigua and Barbuda, and Malta became members after that election.

*Appointment effective 1 July 1984.

†Changed its name to Burkina Faso on 6 August 1984.

Annex III.   PRINCIPAL OFFICERS AND OFFICES OF THE WORLD BANK
(As at 1 July 1984)

PRINCIPAL OFFICERS*

President: A. W. Clausen.
Senior Vice-President, Finance: Moeen A. Qureshi.
Senior Vice-President, Operations: Ernest Stern.
Vice-President: Warren C. Baum.
Vice-President, External Relations: Munir P. Benjenk.†
Vice-President, Energy and Industry: Jean-Loup Dherse.
Vice-President, Pension Fund: K. Georg Gabriel.
Vice-President and Controller: Hans C. Hittmair.
Regional Vice-President, South Asia: W. David Hopper.
Vice-President, Operations Policy: S. Shahid Husain.
Regional Vice-President, Eastern Africa: Edward V. K. Jaycox.
Director-General, Operations Evaluation: Shiv S. Kapur.

Regional Vice-President, East Asia and Pacific: Attila Karaosmanoglu.
Regional Vice-President, Latin America and the Caribbean: A. David Knox.
Vice-President, Economics and Research: Anne O. Krueger.
Vice-President, Co-financing: Teruyuki Ohuchi.
Vice-President, Personnel and Administration: Martijn J. W. M. Paijmans.
Vice-President and Treasurer: Eugene H. Rotberg.
Vice-President and General Counsel: Ibrahim F. I. Shihata.
Vice-President and Secretary: Timothy T. Thahane.
Regional Vice-President, Western Africa: Wilfried P. Thalwitz.
Regional Vice-President, Europe, Middle East and North Africa: Willi A. Wapenhans.
Vice-President, Financial Policy, Planning and Budgeting: D. Joseph Wood.

*The World Bank and IDA had the same officers and staff.

†Retired on 30 June 1984.

HEADQUARTERS AND OTHER OFFICES

HEADQUARTERS
The World Bank
1818 H Street, N.W.
Washington, D.C. 20433, United States
Cable address: INTBAFRAD WASHINGTONDC
Telephone: (202) 477-1234
Telex: RCA 248423 WORLDBK,
Telex: WUI 64145 WORLDBANK

NEW YORK OFFICE
The World Bank Mission to the United Nations
747 Third Avenue, 26th floor
New York, N.Y. 10017, United States
Cable address: INTBAFRAD NEWYORK
Telephone: (212) 963-6008

EUROPEAN OFFICE
The World Bank
66 Avenue d'Iéna
75116 Paris, France
Cable address: INTBAFRAD PARIS
Telephone: (1) 4 723-54-21
Telex: 620628

LONDON OFFICE
The World Bank
New Zealand House, 15th floor, Haymarket
London SW1 Y4TE, England
Cable address: INTBAFRAD LONDON
Telephone: (01) 930-8511
Telex: 919462

GENEVA OFFICE
The World Bank
ITC Building
54 Rue de Montbrillant
(P. O. Box 104)
1211 Geneva 20 CIC, Switzerland
Telephone: (22) 33 21 20
Telex: 28883

TOKYO OFFICE
The World Bank
Kokusai Building, Room 916
1-1 Marunouchi 3-chome, Chiyoda-ku
Tokyo 100, Japan
Cable address: INTBAFRAD TOKYO
Telephone: (03) 214-5001, 5002
Telex: 26838

REGIONAL MISSION IN EASTERN AFRICA
The World Bank
Reinsurance Plaza, 5th and 6th floors
Taifa Road
(P. O. Box 30577)
Nairobi, Kenya
Cable address: INTBAFRAD NAIROBI
Telephone: (254-2) 338868, 24391
Telex: 22022

REGIONAL MISSION IN WESTERN AFRICA
The World Bank
Immeuble Shell, 64 Avenue Lamblin
(Boîte Postale 1850)
Abidjan 01, Ivory Coast
Cable address: INTBAFRAD ABIDJAN
Telephone: (225) 44 22 27, 32 90 06, 44 20 38
Telex: 28132

REGIONAL MISSION IN THAILAND
The World Bank
Udom Vidhya Building, 956 Rama IV Road
Sala Daeng
Bangkok 5, Thailand
Cable address: INTBAFRAD BANGKOK
Telephone: (66-2) 235-5300-8
Telex: 82817

Chapter VII

International Finance Corporation (IFC)

The International Finance Corporation (IFC) was established in 1956 as an affiliate of the International Bank for Reconstruction and Development (World Bank) to provide the financing and investment expertise particularly suited to attracting private sector investors in developing countries. IFC also attracts funds for promising ventures in developing countries from international capital markets by syndicating loans and by underwritings and standby financing. It is one of the few international organizations which can provide risk capital as well as long-term loans without government guarantees.

During the fiscal year ending 30 June 1984, IFC investment operations and technical assistance efforts reflected the difficult economic conditions encountered by many private firms in the developing countries. The prolonged recession kept many private investors from undertaking large industrial projects in those countries, where much of the investment demand was for consolidating and improving productivity in existing industrial facilities. The IFC Board of Directors approved 62 projects totalling $696 million in fiscal 1984; of those, 34 were to expand, modernize or restructure existing businesses.

A total of $632 million was approved for loans made in line with prevailing commercial rates and for a bonding guarantee. The typical loan was for seven years with a grace period of three years. Although the majority of loans continued to be denominated in United States dollars, $121.1 million was in other major currencies, including Deutsche mark, French francs, Japanese yen, Pounds sterling and Swiss francs.

The Corporation's co-financing efforts, which became more important in light of economic uncertainties in many countries, continued to attract commercial financing for private sector project financing through the syndication of its loans. During the 1984 fiscal year, some 75 institutions signed a record $415 million worth of participations in IFC loans. In response to the economic situation, the Corporation also expanded its operations in a relatively new area—the physical and financial restructuring of existing firms which faced temporary financial difficulties but were otherwise sound. Ten such efforts were undertaken; four resulted in new investment opportunities, and in the others, IFC arranged the corporate restructuring without investing funds of its own. In addition, IFC helped create a bonding facility for construction firms operating outside their own countries, helped establish a secondary mortgage market institution and provided financing for a region-ally oriented venture capital company. For the first time, it participated as a co-lead manager in a major equity underwriting for a diversified, closed-end investment company.

The estimated total cost of approved projects was $2,473 million, which meant that for every dollar invested by IFC, others invested $5—about the same as during the previous year. Projects were located in 37 countries, in three of which—Barbados, the Gambia and Ghana—IFC had not previously invested and in four of which it had not undertaken investments during the prior three years . Nineteen investments were in Africa, 18 in Asia, 19 in Latin America and the Caribbean, and 6 in the Middle East/European region.

Of the total 62 ventures financed, most were in manufacturing. IFC provided technical assistance and financing for six chemical plants, five basic construction material manufacturers and five pulp, paper and timber firms. Agribusiness projects continued to figure prominently in IFC activities, with nine ventures financed in as many countries. Of the other investments, eight were in fuel and non-fuel minerals and 13 were in a wide variety of financial institutions, including two leasing companies and three venture capital companies. The Corporation also invested in three hotels. Of the projects approved, 33 were wholly privately-owned enterprises and 29 were mixed government/private enterprises.

In sub-Saharan Africa, 16 projects, four more than during the previous year, were approved. They had an estimated total cost of $342 million of which IFC expected to provide $137 million, about double the amount invested in the region the previous year. A prime IFC objective, especially in that region, continued to be expansion of assistance to resource development projects, particularly agriculture; of the total number of projects, 36 were in resource development. Another central objective of IFC was increased support to ventures in low-income countries; 24 projects were in countries with a per capita annual income of $805 or less.

Operating income for fiscal 1984 rose to $151.1 million up from $137.4 million in fiscal 1983. Interest and dividend income equalled $134.1 million. Equity sales of $11.6 million included $7.4 million of capital gains. While most firms continued to service their obligations and pay dividends throughout the year, a combination of the lack of foreign exchange and the continuing economic recession forced some companies into arrears. Net income of $26.3 million, compared to $23 million in the previous year, was added to accumulated earnings and brought that total to $230.1 million.

Membership in IFC increased to 125 countries, with the admission of the Gambia.

IFC COMMITMENTS BY TYPE OF BUSINESS
(as at 30 June 1984)

Sector	Amount (in millions of US dollars)
Guarantee facility	150.00
Energy and mining	146.57
Cement and construction materials	74.66
Chemicals and petrochemicals	73.80
Pulp, paper and timber	66.42
Manufacturing	42.04
Capital markets	40.38
Automotive/vehicles	26.40
Foods and agribusiness	24.35
Textiles	20.05
Development financing	13.59
Iron and steel	12.13
Tourism	5.25

IFC INVESTMENTS
(1 July 1983–30 June 1984)

Recipient	Sector	Amount (in thousands of US dollars)
Argentina	Chemicals and petrochemicals	25,000
	Textiles	9,500
	Pulp, paper and timber	7,500
	Foods and agribusiness	650
Barbados	Capital markets	300
Brazil	Chemicals and petrochemicals	30,800
	Energy and mining	20,000
	Pulp and paper and timber	10,000
	Iron and steel	400
Colombia	Textiles	6,750
Congo	Pulp, paper and timber	1,500
Ecuador	Cement and construction materials	60
Egypt	Manufacturing	8,000
Gambia	Tourism	2,980
Ghana	Energy and mining	60,000
India	Automotive/vehicles	22,000
	Iron and steel	11,730
	Cement and construction materials	9,960
Indonesia	Capital markets	7,060
Ivory Coast	Foods and agribusiness	1,300
Jordan	Cement and construction materials	740
Kenya	Pulp, paper and timber	47,150
Liberia	Development finance	150
Malaysia	Capital markets	1,000
Mexico	Chemicals and petrochemicals	18,000
	Automotive/vehicles	4,400
	Foods and agribusiness	2,770
Nepal	Energy and Mining	3,000
Nigeria	Manufacturing	4,900
Pakistan	Energy and Mining	14,830
	Cement and construction materials	6,000
	Capital markets	4,510
Paraguay	Tourism	270
Peru	Energy and mining	9,240
Portugal	Development finance	12,480
	Tourism	2,000
Republic of Korea	Capital markets	21,800
	Cement and construction materials	9,000
	Manufacturing	3,530
	Pulp, paper and timber	270
Rwanda	Foods and agribusiness	300
Senegal	Foods and agribusiness	3,150
Sri Lanka	Capital markets	90

Recipient	Sector	Amount (in thousands of US dollars)
Thailand	Cement and construction materials	48,900
	Foods and agribusiness	7,820
	Capital markets	1,000
Trinidad and Tobago	Capital markets	660
Tunisia	Capital markets	570
	Energy and mining	410
Turkey	Guarantee facility	150,000*
Uganda	Foods and agribusiness	2,500
	Development finance	380
United Republic of Tanzania	Foods and agribusiness	3,850
Yugoslavia	Energy and mining	39,500
	Manufacturing	25,200
Zaire	Development finance	580
Zambia	Textiles	3,800
	Foods and agribusiness	2,010
Zimbabwe	Capital markets	2,340
Regional Asia	Capital markets	1,050
Total		695,640†

*Contractor bonding facility.
†Includes bonding facility.

Financial operations

IFC's total operating income in fiscal 1984 was $151.1 million. After administrative expenses and financial charges on borrowings, income from operations amounted to almost $57.3 million. Net income was $26.3 million.

STATEMENT OF INCOME AND EXPENDITURE
(for fiscal year ending 30 June 1984)

Income	Amount (in thousands of US dollars)
Income from obligations of Governments	1,683
Income from loan and equity investments	
Interest	123,689
Dividends and profit participations	10,774
Realized gain on equity sales	7,390
Commitment charges	5,483
Commissions	2,235
Other operating income	(125)
Total income	151,129
Expenditure	
Charges on borrowings	48,835
Administrative expenses*	45,017
Total expenditure	93,852
Income from operations	57,277
Provision for losses	(30,954)
Net income—transferred to accumulated earnings	26,323

*The World Bank charges IFC an annual service and support fee which for the year ending 30 June 1984 was fixed at $3,050,000.

Capital and accumulated earnings

The net income of $26.3 million was allocated to accumulated earnings, bringing the total to $230.1 million as at 30 June 1984. Paid-in capital and accumulated earnings totalled $774.3 million, up from $747.6 million the previous year.

Secretariat

As at 30 June 1984, IFC staff numbered 412, drawn from 68 countries.

Annex I.   MEMBERS OF THE INTERNATIONAL FINANCE
CORPORATION, SUBSCRIPTIONS AND VOTING POWER
(As at 30 June 1984)

MEMBER	SUBSCRIPTION Amount (in thousands of US dollars)	SUBSCRIPTION Percentage of total	VOTING POWER Number of votes	VOTING POWER Percentage of total	MEMBER	SUBSCRIPTION Amount (in thousands of US dollars)	SUBSCRIPTION Percentage of total	VOTING POWER Number of votes	VOTING POWER Percentage of total
Afghanistan	111	0.02	361	0.06	Malawi	368	0.07	618	0.11
Argentina	9,821	1.80	10,071	1.75	Malaysia	3,921	0.72	4,171	0.72
Australia	12,191	2.24	12,441	2.16	Maldives	4	*	254	0.04
Austria	5,085	0.93	5,335	0.93	Mali	116	0.02	366	0.06
Bangladesh	2,328	0.43	2,578	0.45	Mauritania	55	0.01	305	0.05
Barbados	93	0.02	343	0.06	Mauritius	429	0.08	679	0.12
Belgium	13,723	2.52	13,973	2.43	Mexico	6,004	1.10	6,254	1.09
Belize	26	*	276	0.05	Morocco	2,328	0.43	2,578	0.45
Bolivia	490	0.09	740	0.13	Nepal	306	0.06	556	0.10
Botswana	29	0.01	279	0.05	Netherlands	14,458	2.66	14,708	2.56
Brazil	10,169	1.87	10,419	1.81	New Zealand	923	0.17	1,173	0.20
Burma	666	0.12	916	0.16	Nicaragua	184	0.03	434	0.08
Burundi	100	0.02	350	0.06	Niger	67	0.01	317	0.06
Cameroon	490	0.09	740	0.13	Nigeria	5,575	1.02	5,825	1.01
Canada	20,952	3.85	21,202	3.68	Norway	4,533	0.83	4,783	0.83
Chile	2,328	0.43	2,578	0.45	Oman	306	0.06	556	0.10
China	4,154	0.76	4,404	0.77	Pakistan	4,411	0.81	4,661	0.81
Colombia	2,083	0.38	2,333	0.41	Panama	344	0.06	594	0.10
Congo	67	0.01	317	0.06	Papua New Guinea	490	0.09	740	0.13
Costa Rica	245	0.05	495	0.09	Paraguay	123	0.02	373	0.06
Cyprus	551	0.10	801	0.14	Peru	1,777	0.33	2,027	0.35
Denmark	4,779	0.88	5,029	0.87	Philippines	3,247	0.60	3,497	0.61
Djibouti	21	*	271	0.05	Portugal	2,144	0.39	2,394	0.42
Dominica	11	*	261	0.05	Republic of Korea	2,450	0.45	2,700	0.47
Dominican Republic	306	0.06	556	0.10	Rwanda	306	0.06	556	0.10
Ecuador	674	0.12	924	0.16	Saint Lucia	19	*	269	0.05
Egypt	3,124	0.57	3,374	0.59	Samoa	9	*	259	0.05
El Salvador	11	*	261	0.05	Saudi Arabia	9,251	1.70	9,501	1.65
Ethiopia	33	0.01	283	0.05	Senegal	707	0.13	957	0.17
Fiji	74	0.01	324	0.06	Seychelles	7	*	257	0.04
Finland	4,043	0.74	4,293	0.75	Sierra Leone	83	0.02	333	0.06
France	29,528	5.43	29,778	5.17	Singapore	177	0.03	427	0.07
Gabon	429	0.08	679	0.12	Solomon Islands	11	*	261	0.05
Gambia	35	0.01	285	0.05	Somalia	83	0.02	333	0.06
Germany, Federal Republic of	33,204	6.10	33,454	5.81	South Africa	4,108	0.75	4,358	0.76
Ghana	1,306	0.24	1,556	0.27	Spain	6,004	1.10	6,254	1.09
Greece	1,777	0.33	2,027	0.35	Sri Lanka	1,838	0.34	2,088	0.36
Grenada	21	*	271	0.05	Sudan	111	0.02	361	0.06
Guatemala	306	0.06	556	0.10	Swaziland	184	0.03	434	0.08
Guinea	134	0.02	384	0.07	Sweden	6,923	1.27	7,173	1.25
Guinea-Bissau	18	*	268	0.05	Syrian Arab Republic	72	0.01	322	0.06
Guyana	368	0.07	618	0.11	Thailand	2,818	0.52	3,068	0.53
Haiti	306	0.06	556	0.10	Togo	368	0.07	618	0.11
Honduras	184	0.03	434	0.08	Trinidad and Tobago	1,059	0.19	1,309	0.23
Iceland	11	*	261	0.05	Tunisia	919	0.17	1,169	0.20
India	19,788	3.64	20,038	3.48	Turkey	3,063	0.56	3,313	0.58
Indonesia	7,351	1.35	7,601	1.32	Uganda	735	0.14	985	0.17
Iran	372	0.07	622	0.11	United Arab Emirates	1,838	0.34	2,088	0.36
Iraq	67	0.01	317	0.06	United Kingdom	37,900	6.96	38,150	6.63
Ireland	332	0.06	582	0.10	United Republic of Tanzania	724	0.13	974	0.17
Israel	550	0.10	800	0.14	United States	146,661	26.95	146,911	25.53
Italy	19,114	3.51	19,364	3.36	Upper Volta‡	245	0.05	495	0.09
Ivory Coast	913	0.17	1,163	0.20	Uruguay	919	0.17	1,169	0.20
Jamaica	1,103	0.20	1,353	0.24	Vanuatu	25	*	275	0.05
Japan	25,546	4.69	25,796	4.48	Venezuela	7,106	1.31	7,356	1.28
Jordan	429	0.08	679	0.12	Viet Nam	166	0.03	416	0.07
Kenya	1,041	0.19	1,291	0.22	Yemen	184	0.03	434	0.08
Kuwait	4,533	0.83	4,783	0.83	Yugoslavia	2,879	0.53	3,129	0.54
Lebanon	50	0.01	300	0.05	Zaire	1,929	0.35	2,179	0.38
Lesotho	18	*	268	0.05	Zambia	1,286	0.24	1,536	0.27
Liberia	83	0.02	333	0.06	Zimbabwe	546	0.10	796	0.14
Libyan Arab Jamahiriya	55	0.01	305	0.05					
Luxembourg	551	0.10	801	0.14	Total	544,238	100.00†	575,488	100.00†
Madagascar	111	0.02	361	0.06					

*Less than 0.005 per cent.
†May differ from the sum of the individual percentages because of rounding.
‡Upper Volta changed its name to Burkina Faso on 6 August 1984.

Annex II.   EXECUTIVE DIRECTORS AND ALTERNATES
OF THE INTERNATIONAL FINANCE CORPORATION
(As at 1 July 1984)

Appointed Director	*Appointed Alternate*	*Casting the vote of*
James B. Burnham	Hugh W. Foster	United States
Nigel L. Wicks	Richard Manning	United Kingdom
Reinhard Münzberg	Michael von Harpe	Federal Republic of Germany
Bruno de Maulde	Francis Mayer	France
Kenji Yamaguchi	Toshihiro Yamakawa	Japan

Elected Director	*Elected Alternate*	*Casting the votes of*
Said E. El-Naggar (Egypt)	Mohammed Al-Shawi (Saudi Arabia)	Egypt, Iraq, Jordan, Kuwait, Lebanon, Maldives, Oman, Pakistan, Saudi Arabia, Syrian Arab Republic, United Arab Emirates, Yemen
Morris Miller (Canada)	George L. Reid (Barbados)	Barbados, Belize, Canada, Dominica, Grenada, Guyana, Ireland, Jamaica, Saint Lucia
H. N. Ray (India)	Gholam Kibria (Bangladesh)	Bangladesh, India, Sri Lanka
Giorgio Ragazzi (Italy)	Rodrigo M. Guimarães (Portugal)	Greece, Italy, Portugal
Jacques de Groote (Belgium)	Herbert A. Lust (Austria)	Austria, Belgium, Luxembourg, Turkey
Patricio Ayala-González (Mexico)	Roberto Mayorga-Cortés (Nicaragua)	Costa Rica, El Salvador, Guatemala, Honduras, Mexico, Nicaragua, Panama, Spain, Venezuela
Pekka Korpinen (Finland)	Per Taxell (Sweden)	Denmark, Finland, Iceland, Norway, Sweden
Ferdinand van Dam (Netherlands)	Riza Sapunxhiu (Yugoslavia)	Cyprus, Israel, Netherlands, Yugoslavia
Antonio V. Romuáldez (Philippines)	Héctor Echeverri (Colombia)	Brazil, Colombia, Dominican Republic, Ecuador, Haiti, Philippines
Ronald H. Dean (Australia)	You Kwang Park (Republic of Korea)	Australia, New Zealand, Papua New Guinea, Republic of Korea, Samoa, Solomon Islands, Vanuatu
Phaichitr Uathavikul (Thailand)	Nibhat Bhukkanasut (Thailand)	Burma, Fiji, Indonesia, Malaysia, Nepal, Singapore, Thailand, Viet Nam
Eduardo Zalduendo (Argentina)	Pedro O. Montórfano (Paraguay)	Argentina, Bolivia, Chile, Paraguay, Peru, Uruguay
William Smith (Liberia)	Astère Girukwigomba (Burundi)	Botswana, Burundi, Ethiopia, Gambia, Guinea, Kenya, Lesotho, Liberia, Malawi, Nigeria, Seychelles, Sierra Leone, Sudan, Swaziland, Trinidad and Tobago, Uganda, United Republic of Tanzania, Zambia, Zimbabwe
Nicéphore Soglo (Benin)	André Milongo (Congo)	Cameroon, Congo, Djibouti, Gabon, Guinea-Bissau, Ivory Coast, Madagascar, Mali, Mauritania, Mauritius, Niger, Rwanda, Senegal, Somalia, Togo, Upper Volta*, Zaire
Mourad Benachenhou (Algeria)	Salem Mohamed Omeish (Libyan Arab Jamahiriya)	Afghanistan, Ghana, Iran, Libyan Arab Jamahiriya, Morocco, Tunisia
Xu Naijiong (China)	Fei Lizhi (China)	China

NOTE: South Africa did not participate in the regular election of Executive Directors.
*Upper Volta changed its name to Burkina Faso on 6 August 1984.

Annex III.   PRINCIPAL OFFICERS AND OFFICES
OF THE INTERNATIONAL FINANCE CORPORATION
(As at 1 July 1984)

PRINCIPAL OFFICERS

President: A. W. Clausen.*
Executive Vice-President: Hans A. Wuttke.
Vice President, Finance and Planning: K. Georg Gabriel.
 Director, Financial Management and Planning: Richard H. Frank.
 Director, Management Systems and Accounting: Roswitha J. Klement-Francis
Vice-President, Asia, Europe and Middle East: Judhvir Parmar.
 Director, Department of Investments, Asia: Torstein Stephansen.
 Director, Department of Investments, Europe and Middle East: Douglas Gustafson.
Vice-President, Latin America and the Caribbean: Jose M. Ruisanchez.
 Director, Department of Investments, Latin America and Caribbean I: Giovanni Vacchelli.
 Director, Department of Investments, Latin America and Caribbean II: Daniel F. Adams.
Vice-President, Africa: Sven K. Riskaer.
 Director, Department of Investments, Africa I: Gunter H. Kreuter.
 Director, Department of Investments, Africa II: M. Azam K. Alizai.

Vice-President and General Counsel: Jose E. Camacho.
 Deputy General Counsel: Walter F. Norris.
 Director, Capital Markets Department: David Gill.
 Deputy Director, Capital Markets Department: Wilfried E. Kaffenberger.
 Director, Syndications: Rolf Th. Lundberg.
Vice-President, Engineering and Technical Assistance: Makarand V. Dehejia.
 Deputy Director: David B. Minch (Acting).
Director-General, Operations Evaluation: Shiv S. Kapur.*
Secretary: Timothy T. Thahane.*
 Economic Adviser and Director, Development Department: Richard W. Richardson.
 Director, Compensation Department: R. A. Clarke.*
 Director, Administrative Services Department: William J. Cosgrove.*
 Director, Personnel Management Department: Anthony P. Williams.*
 Director, Internal Auditing Department: Lawrence N. Rapley.*
 Director, Planning and Budgeting Department: Shinji Asanuma.*
 Chief, Information Office: Carl T. Bell.

Special Representative, Middle East: Cherif Hassan.
Special Representative, Far East: Naokado Nishihara.
Special Representative, Europe: Hans Pollan.
Regional Mission in East Asia: Vijay K. Chaudhry.
Regional Mission in Eastern Africa: V. S. Raghavan.

Regional Mission in India: Athishdam Tharmaratnam.
Regional Mission in Indonesia: Peter L. F. Edmonds
Regional Mission in Western Africa: Jean-Olivier Fraisse.
Special Advisor: James M. Kearns.

*Held the same position in the World Bank.

HEADQUARTERS AND OTHER OFFICES

HEADQUARTERS
International Finance Corporation
1818 H Street, N. W.
Washington, D. C. 20433, United States
  Cable address: CORINTFIN
  WASHINGTONDC
  Telephone: (202) 477-1234
  Telex: ITT 440098, RCA 248423, WU 64145

NEW YORK OFFICE
International Finance Corporation
747 Third Avenue, 26th floor
New York, N. Y. 10017, United States
  Cable address: CORINTFIN NEWYORK
  Telephone: (212) 963-6008

EUROPEAN OFFICE
International Finance Corporation
New Zealand House, 15th floor
Haymarket, London SW1 Y4TE, England
  Cable address: CORINTFIN LONDON
  Telephone: (01) 930-8741
  Telex: 851-919462

PARIS OFFICE
International Finance Corporation
66 Avenue d'léna
75116 Paris, France
  Cable address: CORINTFIN PARIS
  Telephone: (1) 4 723-54-21
  Telex: 842-620628

TOKYO OFFICE
International Finance Corporation
5-1 Nibancho, Chiyoda-ku
Tokyo 102, Japan
  Cable address: SPCORINTFIN TOKYO
  Telephone: (03) 261-3626
  Telex: 781-26554

REGIONAL MISSION IN EAST ASIA
World Bank Group
Central Bank of the Philippines
Manila, Philippines
  Cable address: CORINTFIN MANILA
  Telephone: 59-99-35
  Telex: 742-40541

REGIONAL MISSION IN EASTERN AFRICA
International Finance Corporation
Reinsurance Plaza, 5th Floor
Taifa Road
(P. O. Box 30577)
Nairobi, Kenya
  Cable address: CORINTFIN NAIROBI
  Telephone: 24726
  Telex: 963-22022

REGIONAL MISSION IN INDIA
International Finance Corporation
55 Lodi Estate
(P. O. Box 416)
New Delhi 110003 India
  Cable address: CORINTFIN NEWDELHI
  Telephone: 617241
  Telex: 953-313150

REGIONAL MISSION IN INDONESIA
International Finance Corporation
Jl. Rasuna Said, Kav. B-10
Suite 301
(P. O. Box 324/JKT)
Kuningan, Jakarta 12940
Indonesia
  Cable address: CORINTFIN JAKARTA
  Telephone: 516089
  Telex: 796-44456

REGIONAL MISSION IN THE MIDDLE EAST
International Finance Corporation
3 Elbergas Street, Garden City
Cairo, Egypt
  Cable address: IFCAI CAIRO
  Telephone: 982914
  Telex: 927-93110

REGIONAL MISSION IN WESTERN AFRICA
International Finance Corporation
Immeuble Alpha 2000, Rue Gourgas
01-P. O. Box 1748
Abidjan-01, Ivory Coast
  Cable address: CORINTFIN ABIDJAN
  Telephone: 32-65-97, 33-11-51
  Telex: 969-23533

Chapter VIII

International Development Association (IDA)

The International Development Association (IDA) was established in 1960 as an affiliate of the International Bank for Reconstruction and Development (World Bank) to provide assistance for the same purposes as the Bank, but primarily in the poorer developing countries and on easier terms. Though legally and financially distinct from the Bank, IDA shares the same staff.

During the fiscal year 1984 (1 July 1983 to 30 June 1984), IDA continued to promote economic development, concentrating on countries with an annual per capita gross national product of less than $806 (in 1982 dollars). Over 50 countries were eligible under that criterion.

The funds lent by IDA—called credits to distinguish them from World Bank loans—come mostly from three sources: subscriptions in convertible currencies from members; general replenishments from IDA's more industrialized and developed members; and transfers from the Bank's net earnings. IDA credits are repayable over 50 years without interest, except for a service charge of 0.75 per cent on disbursed and 0.5 per cent on undisbursed balances to cover administrative costs; there is a grace period of 10 years before repayment begins.

Unlike the Bank, which may lend to public and private entities with government guarantees, IDA lends only to Governments. In the case of revenue-producing projects, IDA credits are re-lent by the Governments on terms reflecting the local cost of capital. Therefore, IDA terms assist Governments to finance economic development without distorting the local credit structure.

At the end of fiscal 1984, IDA's resources amounted to $30,872 million.

The bulk of IDA funds for lending is provided by its Part I (richer) member countries and several Part II (developing) countries under a series of replenishment agreements.

Negotiations for the seventh replenishment of resources to provide IDA with funds for fiscal 1985-1987 were launched when the IDA Deputies (representatives of 33 donor countries) met at Washington, D.C., in November 1982.[a] They met four times in fiscal 1984 to discuss burden-sharing and implementation arrangements for replenishment, including conditions of effectiveness, method of payment and voting rights. The meetings were held in Tokyo (19-21 July 1983), Washington, D.C. (24 September 1983 and 12-14 January 1984), and Paris (9-10 December 1983).

At their final meeting in January, the Deputies reaffirmed their support for IDA and its activities. At that meeting, the United States reiterated its decision to contribute to IDA a maximum of $2.25 billion ($750 million a year) and to limit its share to 25 per cent. All other donors repeated the concern they had expressed at an earlier meeting in Paris that the United States position on its contribution would result in limiting the seventh replenishment to $9 billion, an amount they felt was inadequate in view of the needs of the poorest countries for development assistance. They suggested that, in order to reach a conclusive outcome and prevent a hiatus in IDA's commitment authority as of 1 July 1984, agreement should be reached on a replenishment size to which all donors could subscribe.

On 24 May 1984, the Bank's Executive Directors approved reports recommending that the Board of Governors authorize a seventh replenishment of IDA resources for the period fiscal 1985-1987 in the amount of $9 billion. They also provided IDA with a mandate to raise additional resources to close the gap between the $9 billion agreed upon and the level of $12 billion, which most donors considered the minimum level of resources required by IDA for its 1985-1987 programme.

Although fiscal year 1984 should have been the first year of lending under the seventh replenishment, the delay in the United States contribution to the sixth replenishment (two instalments totalling $1,190 million were received during fiscal 1984) made it impossible. To augment inadequate lending resources, donors other than the United States provided special contributions totalling $1,844 million to either a Fiscal Year 1984 Account or a Special Fund.[b] Seventeen countries contributed $1,241 million to the Fiscal Year 1984 Account during fiscal 1984 and four pledged $85 million to be paid early fiscal 1985. Six countries provided contributions totalling $413 million to the Special Fund in fiscal 1984 and another was expected to contribute $73 million in early fiscal 1985. Another four countries, whose special contributions amounted to $32 million, had not indicated as of 30 June 1984 the account to which they would contribute.

Membership of IDA rose to 132 in 1984 after the admission of Mozambique on 24 September.

[a]YUN 1983, p. 1269.
[b]YUN 1983, p. 1269.

Lending operations (credits)

By 30 June 1984, IDA had made cumulative net commitments totalling $33,653.9 million. Commitments in fiscal 1984 amounted to $3,575 million, of which $1,835.6 million went to seven countries in South Asia and $741.4 million to 16 countries and the region of Eastern Africa. India was the largest borrower during the year with nine credits amounting to $1,001 million, followed by China with five credits of $423.5 million and Bangladesh with 10 credits totalling $393.1 million.

The following table summarizes IDA lending in fiscal 1984 by region or country and by purpose.

IDA CREDITS APPROVED BY REGION/COUNTRY AND PURPOSE
1 JULY 1983–30 JUNE 1984
(including IDA share of joint Bank/IDA operations; in millions of US dollars)

REGION/COUNTRY	Agriculture and rural development	Development finance companies	Education	Energy	Industry	Non-project	Population, health and nutrition	Small-scale enterprises	Technical assistance	Transportation	Urbanization	Water supply and sewerage	Total
Eastern Africa													
Burundi	—	—	—	—	—	—	—	—	5.1	—	—	—	5.1
Comoros	5.0	—	—	—	—	—	2.8	—	—	—	—	—	7.8
Djibouti	—	—	—	6.0	—	—	—	—	—	—	—	—	6.0
Ethiopia	35.0	—	—	—	—	—	—	—	—	70.0	—	—	105.0
Kenya	—	—	—	24.5	—	—	—	—	—	40.0	—	—	64.5
Lesotho	—	—	—	—	—	—	—	—	—	15.2	—	—	15.2
Madagascar	17.8	—	—	—	—	—	—	—	—	—	12.8	—	30.6
Malawi	—	—	—	—	—	55.0	—	—	1.5	26.9	—	—	83.4
Rwanda	—	—	—	9.0	—	—	—	—	—	—	—	—	9.0
Somalia	13.5	—	—	18.0	—	—	—	—	—	—	—	—	31.5
Sudan	60.0	—	15.4	—	—	—	—	—	—	16.0	—	—	91.4
Uganda	—	—	—	—	—	50.0	—	—	15.0	58.0	—	—	123.0
United Republic of Tanzania	—	—	—	35.0	—	—	—	—	—	—	—	—	35.0
Zaire	—	36.0	—	4.5	—	—	—	—	—	26.0	—	—	66.5
Zambia	22.4	—	—	—	—	—	—	—	—	—	—	—	22.4
Eastern Africa Region	—	—	—	45.0	—	—	—	—	—	—	—	—	45.0
Subtotal	153.7	36.0	15.4	142.0	—	105.0	2.8	—	21.6	252.1	12.8	—	741.4
Western Africa													
Benin	5.4	—	—	18.0	—	—	—	—	—	12.0	—	—	35.4
Equatorial Guinea	—	—	—	—	—	—	—	—	6.0	—	—	—	6.0
Gambia	9.4	—	—	—	—	—	—	—	—	—	11.5	—	20.9
Ghana	25.0	—	—	—	6.9	76.0	—	—	17.1	—	—	—	125.0
Guinea	—	—	—	8.0	—	—	—	—	—	28.0	10.7	—	46.7
Guinea-Bissau	—	—	—	—	—	—	—	—	—	8.0	—	—	8.0
Liberia	6.7	—	—	—	—	—	—	—	—	11.4	—	—	18.1
Mali	25.9	—	9.5	—	7.6	—	16.7	—	—	—	—	10.9	70.6
Mauritania	—	—	—	—	—	—	—	—	—	8.1	—	—	8.1
Niger	—	—	—	—	—	—	—	—	—	11.7	—	—	11.7
Senegal	16.1	—	—	—	—	—	—	—	11.0	29.0	6.0	—	62.1
Sierra Leone	21.5	—	—	—	—	—	—	—	—	—	—	—	21.5
Upper Volta*	—	—	—	—	7.4	—	—	—	—	—	—	—	7.4
Western Africa Region	—	—	—	30.0	—	—	—	—	—	—	—	—	30.0
Subtotal	110.0	—	9.5	56.0	21.9	76.0	16.7	—	53.9	88.4	28.2	10.9	471.5
East Asia and Pacific													
China	150.0	70.0	108.5	—	—	—	85.0	—	10.0	—	—	—	423.5
Solomon Islands	3.5	—	—	—	—	—	—	—	—	—	—	—	3.5
Vanuatu	2.0	—	—	—	—	—	—	—	—	—	—	—	2.0
Subtotal	155.5	70.0	108.5	—	—	—	85.0	—	10.0	—	—	—	429.0
South Asia													
Bangladesh	94.1	45.0	36.0	23.0	—	170.0	—	—	25.0	—	—	—	393.1
Bhutan	5.5	—	—	—	—	—	—	—	3.0	—	—	—	8.5
Burma	25.0	—	—	—	29.7	—	—	—	—	—	—	—	54.7
India	715.0	—	—	143.0	—	—	70.0	—	—	—	—	73.0	1,001.0
Nepal	18.0	—	12.8	118.0	—	—	—	—	—	—	—	—	148.8
Pakistan	67.5	50.0	—	—	—	—	—	50.0	7.0	—	—	—	174.5
Sri Lanka	30.0	—	—	—	—	—	—	25.0	—	—	—	—	55.0
Subtotal	955.1	95.0	48.8	284.0	29.7	170.0	70.0	75.0	35.0	—	—	73.0	1,835.6

REGION/COUNTRY	Agriculture and rural development	Development finance companies	Education	Energy	Industry	Non-project	Population, health and nutrition	Small-scale enterprises	Technical assistance	Transportation	Urbanization	Water supply and sewerage	Total
Europe, the Middle East and North Africa													
Democratic Yemen	—	—	10.4	—	—	—	—	—	—	—	—	7.0	17.4
Yemen	8.0	—	10.0	13.0	—	—	—	—	—	13.0	12.0	—	56.0
Subtotal	8.0	—	20.4	13.0	—	—	—	—	—	13.0	12.0	7.0	73.4
Latin America and the Caribbean													
Haiti	19.1	—	—	—	—	—	—	—	—	—	—	—	19.1
St. Vincent and the Grenadines	—	—	—	5.0	—	—	—	—	—	—	—	—	5.0
Subtotal	19.1	—	—	5.0	—	—	—	—	—	—	—	—	24.1
Total	1,401.4	201.0	202.6	500.0	51.6	351.0	174.5	75.0	120.5	353.5	53.0	90.9	3,575
NUMBER OF CREDITS	36	4	8	16	4	5	4	2	12	14	5	3	113

*Changed its name to Burkina Faso on 6 August 1984.

Agriculture and rural development

In fiscal 1984, as in previous years, credits for agriculture and rural development accounted for the largest portion of IDA lending in fiscal 1984. Thirty-six credits totalling $1,401.4 million were committed in 25 countries.

Of credits totalling $715 million made to India, one of $172 million went to construct or modernize 29 irrigation projects, creating some 241,000 hectares of additional irrigated area and improving the water supply for existing irrigation. China received two credits amounting to $150 million, of which $100 million funded the planting and replanting of 40,000 hectares of rubber in the Guangdong province, the planting of windbreaks in typhoon-prone areas, the modernization of transport and agricultural machinery and the upgrading of timber-processing facilities.

Other credits were committed to agricultural research and development, agro-industry, irrigation and drainage, fisheries, forestry, livestock, training and technical assistance.

Development finance companies

IDA made four credits in fiscal 1984 totalling $201 million to development finance companies in four countries.

A credit of $70 million went to China to develop further the China Investment Bank, an institution providing investment loans for small and medium-sized industries. The South Asia region received $95 million to upgrade textile industries in Bangladesh and support five participating financial institutions in Pakistan which provided investment loans to medium- and large-sized industries. A $36-million credit was made to Zaire to support the capital-investment requirements of sub-projects approved by the Société Financière de Développement in the agricultural, transportation, industrial and agro-industrial sectors.

Education

Seven countries received eight credits totalling $202.6 million for educational projects during fiscal 1984.

China received $108.5 million, of which $85 million went to improve the quality of skilled technical manpower by supplying facilities and equipment to the television university system and to 17 post-secondary-level polytechnic institutions. A $36-million credit was made to Bangladesh to increase its technical manpower by improving education programmes and training at engineering colleges and polytechnics.

Other purposes for which credits were committed included projects to improve access to, and quality of, primary and secondary education, technical and vocational training, and educational materials, and to increase the number of schools.

Energy

Fifteen countries or regions received credits totalling $500 million for energy-related projects.

India received $143 million to increase the power-generating capacity in Madhya Pradesh state and the western region of India by 500 megawatts. A credit of $107 million was made to Nepal to build a hydroelectric power plant with a power-generating capacity of 69 megawatts. The United Republic of Tanzania was granted a credit of $35 million to increase its electricity-generating capacity by building a water intake at the Mtera reservoir and a system-control centre at Dar es Salaam, to upgrade power-system plants, and to initiate a four-year management-training programme.

Other credits went for strengthening the management of national petroleum industries, geothermal energy and hydroelectric development, evaluation of hydrocarbon potential, and technical assistance and training.

Industry

Four countries received credits totalling $51.6 million for industrial development projects in fiscal 1984.

Burma received a credit of $29.7 million to redress the structural imbalance of its fabric-finishing capacity by constructing a new plant and phasing out inefficient finishing capacities, reorganizing its Textile Industries Corporation, and upgrading its management-information and control systems. A credit of $7.6 million went to Mali for various improvements aimed at reducing the country's dependence on petroleum imports through development of other energy sources and investments to rehabilitate the Office du Niger, a parastatal enterprise operating the largest irrigation network in West Africa. Upper Volta received a $7.4-million credit to attract private foreign investors for developing the Perkoa zinc-silver deposit.

Other countries received credits for technical and economic feasibility studies of the mining and petroleum industries.

Non-project

IDA made five credits amounting to $351 million to four countries in the non-project sector during the fiscal year.

Bangladesh received two credits totalling $170 million to finance general imports and support on-going projects in irrigation, rehabilitation of the fertilizer industry, developing the Chittagong port and rural electrification. A $76-million credit was made to Ghana for the rehabilitation of traditional export industries (cocoa, timber and gold mining) through provision of spare parts, equipment and materials and the improvement of port facilities. Malawi received $55 million to diversify exports, encourage import substitution, adjust incentives, improve the public sector's financial performance and strengthen policy-making capability. A $50-million credit went to Uganda to finance high-priority imports, support policy and institutional reforms and generate resources for the Government's budget.

Population, health and nutrition

During fiscal 1984, four countries received credits amounting to $174.5 million for projects in population, health and nutrition.

China received $85 million for health improvement projects and for upgrading teaching and research programmes of the country's 13 core medical schools. A $70-million credit went to India towards its integrated health and family-welfare programme to be implemented throughout India by the year 2000. Mali received $16.7 million to improve the effectiveness of primary health-care services in one of the poorest areas of the country and to strengthen health-support systems at the national level. A $2.8-million credit was made to the Comoros to develop a programme to slow population growth and strengthen basic health and family-planning services.

Small-scale enterprises

Two countries received credits totalling $75 million for small-scale enterprises.

A $50-million credit went to Pakistan to promote investments in small-scale industries and modernize existing ones. Sri Lanka received $25 million in technical assistance and credit to finance imported equipment to increase the output, efficiency and employment of industrial enterprises.

Technical assistance

Credits totalling $120.5 million were awarded to 12 countries for technical assistance in fiscal 1984.

Bangladesh received $25 million for technical assistance in pre-investment planning, engineering studies and the formulation of economic policies and plans. Ghana was awarded $17.1 million to assist the Government in implementing export policy and institutional reforms, build local capability through staff training, and ensure management capacity of cocoa, timber and gold mining organizations. Another $15 million went to Uganda to strengthen the country's decision-making, planning, project-preparation and implementation capabilities and to transfer skills to Ugandans through training.

Other credits were made for technical assistance in training, education, equipment, agricultural reforms, export development and investment, and tourism promotion.

Transportation

Fourteen credits totalling $353.5 million went to 13 countries for transportation projects during fiscal 1984.

Ethiopia received $70 million for a road project to promote agricultural and industrial production by improving access to productive areas, upgrade social services to the rural population and provide better access to drought-prone areas. A $58-million credit went to build a third highway, improve road maintenance, train road-maintenance personnel, develop the local construction industry and improve traffic-safety regulations in Uganda. Kenya received $40 million to help finance a highway project. Credits approved for other countries went for construction or improvement of roads, railway systems and ports, technical assistance, equipment and training.

Urbanization

Five countries received credits amounting to $53 million for urban development during fiscal 1984.

Madagascar received $12.8 million to assist two municipalities in tax collection, financial management and institution building, to expand production of local building materials and to finance a programme to improve living conditions. A $12-million credit was made to Yemen to provide affordable infrastructure services to the low-income population of Hodeidah and to strengthen the Government's capacity to plan, design and execute urban-development programmes.

Credits were also awarded for land development, upgrading settlements, equipment, technical assistance and training.

Water supply and sewerage

Of three credits totalling $90.9 million for water supply and sewerage, $73 million went to India to expand facilities to provide safe drinking-water to some 3.3 million people of Tamil Nadu state and to improve sanitation facilities. A $10.9-million credit to Mali went to upgrade living and sanitary conditions in the western part of the country, and to provide technical assistance, equipment and training.

Democratic Yemen received $7 million to begin construction of a long-term water-supply plan, carry out water-supply studies and provide technical assistance and training.

Secretariat

The principal officers, staff, headquarters and other offices of IDA are the same as those of the World Bank (see pp. 1234 and 1236).

STATEMENT OF INCOME AND EXPENSES
(for the fiscal year ended 30 June 1984)

	Amount (in thousands of US dollars)
Income	
Income from development credits:	
Service charges	139,712
Commitment charges	19,320
From investments	17,779
Total income	176,811
Expenses	
Management fee to World Bank	249,225
Operating loss (income less expenses)	(72,414)
Translation adjustments for fiscal year	1,556
Net loss	(70,858)

Annex I.   MEMBERS OF THE INTERNATIONAL DEVELOPMENT ASSOCIATION, SUBSCRIPTIONS, VOTING POWER AND SUPPLEMENTARY RESOURCES

(As at 30 June 1984)

MEMBER	TOTAL SUBSCRIPTIONS AND SUPPLEMENTARY RESOURCES (in thousands of US dollars)		VOTING POWER		MEMBER	TOTAL SUBSCRIPTIONS AND SUPPLEMENTARY RESOURCES (in thousands of US dollars)		VOTING POWER	
	Amount (in current US dollars)	Percentage of total	Number of votes	Percentage of total		Amount (in current US dollars)	Percentage of total	Number of votes	Percentage of total
Part I countries					*Part II countries*				
Australia	586,368	2.01	69,115	1.44	Afghanistan	1,175	0.01	13,557	0.28
Austria	199,309	0.68	29,657	0.62	Algeria	4,553	0.02	18,481	0.39
Belgium	385,817	1.32	58,076	1.21	Argentina	45,998	0.15	81,053	1.69
Canada	1,460,017	5.00	165,730	3.45	Bangladesh	6,044	0.02	29,522	0.62
Denmark	276,019	0.95	45,928	0.96	Belize	208	*	540	0.01
Finland	144,252	0.49	25,939	0.54	Benin	524	*	600	0.01
France	1,316,808	4.51	179,648	3.74	Bhutan	52	*	510	0.01
Germany, Federal					Bolivia	1,154	0.01	13,748	0.29
Republic of	3,413,426	11.70	342,586	7.14	Botswana	181	*	10,487	0.22
Iceland	2,408	0.01	10,658	0.22	Brazil	60,227	0.21	81,496	1.70
Ireland	32,034	0.11	13,702	0.29	Burma	2,306	0.01	17,284	0.36
Italy	778,337	2.67	123,671	2.58	Burundi	868	*	12,667	0.26
Japan	4,065,230	13.93	338,756	7.06	Cameroon	1,117	0.01	7,771	0.16
Kuwait	508,535	1.74	54,021	1.13	Cape Verde	84	*	516	0.01
Luxembourg	13,003	0.04	11,397	0.24	Central African				
Netherlands	755,243	2.59	96,098	2.00	Republic	558	*	9,720	0.20
New Zealand	29,230	0.10	13,410	0.28	Chad	544	*	2,093	0.04
Norway	270,841	0.93	42,759	0.89	Chile	3,854	0.01	17,113	0.36
South Africa	45,520	0.16	15,065	0.31	China	33,981	0.12	91,311	1.90
Sweden	806,549	2.76	114,958	2.40	Colombia	9,231	0.03	23,784	0.50
United Arab Emirates	136,464	0.47	15,942	0.33	Comoros	89	*	5,774	0.12
United Kingdom	2,950,842	10.11	336,440	7.01	Congo	553	*	6,685	0.14
United States	9,643,966	33.04	937,355	19.54	Costa Rica	224	*	7,844	0.16
					Cyprus	863	*	12,667	0.26
Subtotal	27,820,218	95.32	3,040,911	63.38	Democratic				
					Kampuchea	1,117	0.01	7,826	0.16
					Democratic Yemen	1,348	0.01	10,591	0.22

MEMBER	TOTAL SUBSCRIPTIONS AND SUPPLEMENTARY RESOURCES (in thousands of US dollars)		VOTING POWER	
	Amount (in current US dollars)	Percentage of total	Number of votes	Percentage of total
Part II countries (cont.)				
Djibouti	170	*	532	0.01
Dominica	86	*	3,186	0.07
Dominican Republic	534	*	11,379	0.24
Ecuador	883	*	12,273	0.26
Egypt	5,789	0.02	28,424	0.59
El Salvador	358	*	6,244	0.13
Equatorial Guinea	348	*	1,967	0.04
Ethiopia	602	*	11,727	0.24
Fiji	609	*	2,130	0.04
Gabon	548	*	2,093	0.04
Gambia	301	*	10,644	0.22
Ghana	2,577	0.01	15,362	0.32
Greece	5,298	0.02	19,656	0.41
Grenada	104	*	10,186	0.21
Guatemala	465	*	11,367	0.24
Guinea	1,165	0.01	13,557	0.28
Guinea-Bissau	147	*	528	0.01
Guyana	920	*	12,859	0.27
Haiti	884	*	12,667	0.26
Honduras	350	*	10,982	0.23
India	50,604	0.17	157,108	3.27
Indonesia	12,472	0.04	50,392	1.05
Iran	5,817	0.02	15,455	0.32
Iraq	867	*	9,407	0.20
Israel	2,390	0.01	9,386	0.20
Ivory Coast	1,117	0.01	7,771	0.16
Jordan	392	*	10,982	0.23
Kenya	1,906	0.01	16,021	0.33
Lao People's Democratic Republic	550	*	11,723	0.24
Lebanon	501	*	8,562	0.18
Lesotho	181	*	10,487	0.22
Liberia	884	*	12,667	0.26
Libyan Arab Jamahiriya	1,136	0.01	7,771	0.16
Madagascar	1,059	0.01	702	0.01
Malawi	862	*	12,667	0.26
Malaysia	2,929	0.01	19,079	0.40
Maldives	34	*	10,008	0.21
Mali	980	*	12,307	0.26
Mauritania	560	*	6,685	0.14
Mauritius	1,001	0.01	13,055	0.27
Mexico	13,529	0.05	21,392	0.45
Morocco	3,966	0.01	22,789	0.47
Nepal	570	*	11,723	0.24
Nicaragua	416	*	10,896	0.23
Niger	563	*	11,578	0.24
Nigeria	3,735	0.01	4,057	0.08
Oman	372	*	10,985	0.23
Pakistan	11,618	0.04	46,750	0.97
Panama	26	*	5,657	0.12
Papua New Guinea	988	*	13,050	0.27
Paraguay	342	*	8,124	0.17
Peru	1,856	0.01	854	0.02
Philippines	5,664	0.02	16,583	0.35
Republic of Korea	4,519	0.02	14,959	0.31
Rwanda	878	*	12,667	0.26
Saint Lucia	173	*	10,445	0.22
Saint Vincent and the Grenadines	73	*	514	0.01
Samoa	100	*	7,537	0.16
Sao Tome and Principe	73	*	514	0.01
Saudi Arabia	903,880	3.09	106,443	2.22
Senegal	1,892	0.01	16,021	0.33
Sierra Leone	853	*	12,667	0.26
Solomon Islands	96	*	518	0.01
Somalia	844	*	10,506	0.22
Spain	66,418	0.23	57,788	1.20
Sri Lanka	3,382	0.01	20,940	0.44
Sudan	1,140	0.01	12,684	0.26
Swaziland	361	*	11,073	0.23
Syrian Arab Republic	1,068	0.01	7,651	0.16
Thailand	3,496	0.01	20,940	0.44
Togo	856	*	12,667	0.26
Trinidad and Tobago	1,416	0.01	770	0.02
Tunisia	1,645	0.01	2,793	0.06
Turkey	6,394	0.02	23,450	0.49
Uganda	1,833	0.01	16,021	0.33
United Republic of Tanzania	1,884	0.01	16,021	0.33
Upper Volta†	558	*	9,720	0.20
Vanuatu	198	*	538	0.01
Viet Nam	1,651	0.01	8,889	0.19
Yemen	495	*	11,468	0.24
Yugoslavia	20,527	0.07	29,446	0.61
Zaire	3,290	0.01	12,164	0.25
Zambia	3,008	0.01	19,730	0.41
Zimbabwe	4,364	0.01	1,324	0.03
Subtotal	1,366,243	4.68	1,756,944	36.62
Total	29,186,461	100.00‡	4,797,855	100.00‡

NOTE: Mozambique became a member on 24 September.

*Less than 0.005 per cent.

†Upper Volta changed its name to Burkina Faso on 6 August 1984.

‡May differ from the sum of the individual percentages because of rounding.

Annex II. EXECUTIVE DIRECTORS AND ALTERNATES OF THE INTERNATIONAL DEVELOPMENT ASSOCIATION (As at 30 June 1984)

Appointed Director	Appointed Alternate	Casting the vote of
James B. Burnham	Hugh W. Foster	United States
Reinhard Münzberg	Michael von Harpe	Germany, Federal Republic of
Kenji Yamaguchi	Toshihiro Yamakawa	Japan
Nigel L. Wicks	Richard Manning	United Kingdom
Bruno de Maulde	Francis Mayer	France

Elected Director	Elected Alternate	Casting the votes of
Said E. El-Naggar (Egypt)	Mohammad Al-Shawi (Saudi Arabia)	Egypt, Iraq, Jordan, Kuwait, Lebanon, Maldives, Oman, Pakistan, Saudi Arabia, Syrian Arab Republic, United Arab Emirates, Yemen
Pekka Korpinen (Finland)	Per Taxell (Sweden)	Denmark, Finland, Iceland, Norway, Sweden
Morris Miller (Canada)	George L. Reid (Barbados)	Belize, Canada, Dominica, Grenada, Guyana, Ireland, Saint Lucia, Saint Vincent and the Grenadines

Elected Director	Elected Alternate	Casting the votes of
H. N. Ray (India)	Gholam Kibria (Bangladesh)	Bangladesh, Bhutan, India, Sri Lanka
William Smith (Liberia)	Astère Girukwigomba (Burundi)	Botswana, Burundi, Ethiopia, Gambia, Guinea, Kenya, Lesotho, Liberia, Malawi, Nigeria, Sierra Leone, Sudan, Swaziland, Trinidad and Tobago, Uganda, United Republic of Tanzania, Zambia, Zimbabwe
Nicéphore Soglo (Benin)	André Milongo (Congo)	Benin, Cameroon, Cape Verde, Central African Republic, Chad, Comoros, Congo, Djibouti, Equatorial Guinea, Gabon, Guinea-Bissau, Ivory Coast, Madagascar, Mali, Mauritania, Mauritius, Niger, Rwanda, Sao Tome and Principe, Senegal, Somalia, Togo, Upper Volta*, Zaire
Antonio V. Romuáldez (Philippines)	Héctor Echeverri (Colombia)	Brazil, Colombia, Dominican Republic, Ecuador, Haiti, Philippines
Ferdinand van Dam (Netherlands)	Riza Sapunxhiu (Yugoslavia)	Cyprus, Israel, Netherlands, Yugoslavia
Giorgio Ragazzi (Italy)	Rodrigo M. Guimarães (Portugal)	Greece, Italy
Phaichitr Uathavikul (Thailand)	Nibhat Bhukkanasut (Thailand)	Burma, Fiji, Indonesia, Lao People's Democratic Republic, Malaysia, Nepal, Thailand, Viet Nam
Patricio Ayala-González (Mexico)	Roberto Mayorga-Cortés (Nicaragua)	Costa Rica, El Salvador, Guatemala, Honduras, Mexico, Nicaragua, Panama, Spain
Jacques de Groote (Belgium)	Herbert A. Lust (Austria)	Austria, Belgium, Luxembourg, Turkey
Eduardo Zalduendo (Argentina)	Pedro O. Montórfano (Paraguay)	Argentina, Bolivia, Chile, Paraguay, Peru
Ronald H. Dean (Australia)	You Kwang Park (Republic of Korea)	Australia, New Zealand, Papua New Guinea, Republic of Korea, Samoa, Solomon Islands, Vanuatu
Mourad Benachenhou (Algeria)	Salem Mohamed Omeish (Libyan Arab Jamahiriya)	Afghanistan, Algeria, Democratic Yemen, Ghana, Iran, Libyan Arab Jamahiriya, Morocco, Tunisia
Xu Naijiong (China)	Fei Lizhi (China)	China

NOTE: Democratic Kampuchea and South Africa did not participate in the 1982 regular election of Executive Directors. Antigua and Barbuda, and Malta, became members after that election.

*Changed its name to Burkina Faso in August 1984.

Annex III.   HEADQUARTERS AND OTHER OFFICES

HEADQUARTERS
International Development Association
1818 H Street, N.W.
Washington, D.C. 20433, United States
   Cable address: INDEVAS WASHINGTONDC
   Telephone: (202) 477-1234
   Telex: RCA 248423 INDEVAS
         WUI 64145 INDEVAS

NEW YORK OFFICE
International Development Association
747 Third Avenue, 26th floor
New York, N.Y. 10017, United States
   Cable address: INDEVAS NEWYORK
   Telephone: (212) 963-6008

EUROPEAN OFFICE
International Development Association
66 Avenue d'Iéna
75116 Paris, France
   Cable address: INDEVAS PARIS
   Telephone: (1) (4) 723-54-21
   Telex: 620628

LONDON OFFICE
International Development Association
New Zealand House, 15th floor, Haymarket
London SW1 Y4TE, England
   Cable address: INDEVAS LONDON
   Telephone: (01) 930-8511
   Telex: 919462

GENEVA OFFICE
International Development Association
ITC Building
54 Rue de Montbrillant
(P.O. Box 104)
1211 Geneva 20 CIC, Switzerland
   Telephone: 33 21 20
   Telex: 28883

TOKYO OFFICE
International Development Association
Kokusai Building, Room 916
1-1 Marunouchi 3-chome, Chiyoda-ku
Tokyo 100, Japan
   Cable address: INDEVAS TOKYO
   Telephone: (03) 214-5001, 5002
   Telex: 26838

REGIONAL MISSION IN EASTERN AFRICA
International Development Association
Reinsurance Plaza, 5th and 6th floors
Taifa Road
(P.O. Box 30577)
Nairobi, Kenya
   Cable address: INDEVAS NAIROBI
   Telephone: (254-2) 338868, 24391
   Telex: 22022

REGIONAL MISSION IN WESTERN AFRICA
International Development Association
Immeuble Shell, 64 Avenue Lamblin
(Boîte Postale 1850)
Abidjan 01, Ivory Coast
   Cable address: INDEVAS ABIDJAN
   Telephone: (225) 44-22-27, 32-90-06, 44-20-38
   Telex: 3533

REGIONAL MISSION IN THAILAND
International Development Association
Udom Vidhya Building, 956 Rama IV Road
Sala Daeng
Bangkok 5, Thailand
   Cable address: INDEVAS BANGKOK
   Telephone: 235-9115-9
   Telex: 82817

Chapter IX

International Monetary Fund (IMF)

After years marked by global recession, stagnating world trade and debt crises, 1984 marked the beginning of recovery both in industrial and developing nations. The degree of recovery, however, varied from country to country.

The improving world economic situation was reflected in the fact that member countries of the International Monetary Fund (IMF) made less use of the Fund's financial resources than in 1983. Total purchases—measured in special drawing rights (SDRs), the unit of account of IMF—amounted to SDR 7.3 billion, a decrease of 42.2 per cent from 12.6 billion in the previous year. Nevertheless, the 1984 drawings were the third highest in IMF history.

The Fund's financial resources were made available through various policies and facilities, which differed mainly in respect of members' balance of payments difficulty and the degree of conditionality attached to them. Conditionality requirements, which linked financial assistance to the adoption of economic adjustment policies by members and aimed at achieving a viable balance of payments position, were less rigorous for purchases in the first credit tranche (under which a member may draw up to 25 per cent of its quota). Drawings in the first credit tranche required only that members made reasonable efforts to overcome their external payments imbalances.

Purchases in the upper credit tranches, which were generally under stand-by or extended arrangements, required substantial justification and were subject to performance criteria and phasing (that is, made available in instalments). Extended arrangements provided financial assistance to meet balance-of-payments deficits for longer periods and in larger amounts than under credit tranches; they incorporated a wider range of policies and included economic and financial measures geared to a medium-term adjustment of structural imbalances in production, trade and prices.

Accompanying the reduction in credit use during 1984 was an acceleration of a trend by members towards making a larger proportion of drawings under highly conditional facilities. About 89 per cent of drawings in 1984—SDR 3.1 billion and 3.3 billion respectively—were under stand-by arrangements (typically made over a one-year period), or under the extended facility (usually made over three years), which indicated strenuous economic adjustment efforts in member countries using Fund resources. The largest adjustments in 1984 were made by seven major borrowers—Argentina, Brazil, Indonesia, Mexico, the Philippines, the Republic of Korea and Venezuela. At the end of the year, 33 stand-by and extended arrangements were in effect between the Fund and its members, totalling SDR 14.8 billion.

In addition to tranche policies, IMF's special facilities assisted members with balance-of-payments difficulties identifiable by specific economic criteria. The compensatory financing facility assisted members with deficits arising from shortfalls in export receipts that were short term and largely beyond their control. The buffer stock financing facility supported members' contributions to international buffer stocks concerned with commodity price stabilization. Drawings in 1984 under the compensatory financing facility totalled SDR 0.8 billion, while those under the buffer stock financing facility totalled SDR 2.1 million, drawings under both facilities accounted for 11 per cent of total 1984 drawings, compared with nearly 25 per cent in 1983.

IMF liquidity

The Fund's liquidity position was again reviewed in February 1984 by its Executive Board, resulting in an increase in members' quotas by a third to SDR 89,236.3 million (about $90 billion). Borrowing arrangements were put into place with the Saudi Arabian Monetary Agency, the Bank for International Settlements, Japan, and the National Bank of Belgium.

Following a February 1984 decision of the Executive Board that IMF should aim at reducing its SDR holdings to approximately SDR 4 billion by the end of May 1985, the Fund made more use of SDR relative to currencies available in the operational budget for transfers.

Access to IMF resources

The Fund's policy of enlarged access to its resources enabled it to provide supplementary financing to members whose balance of payments deficits were large in relation to their quotas and which needed resources in larger amounts and for longer periods than were available under the regular credit tranches. The IMF Executive Board reviewed the enlarged access policy on 16 November 1984 and decided to continue it in 1985 with access limits adjusted slightly downward as follows. Access would be subject to annual limits of 95 or 115 per cent of quota (previously 102 or 125 per cent), three-year limits of 280 or 345 per cent of quota (previously 306 or 375 per cent), and cumulative limits of 408 or 450 per cent of quota (previously 408 or 500 per cent), depending on the seriousness of a member's balance-of-payments need and the strength of its adjustment effort. However, in exceptional circumstances, arrangements could be approved for amounts above those limits. The enlarged access policy and revised access limits were to be revised in 1985.

Exchange rate policies

During 1984, IMF strengthened its surveillance over the exchange rate policies of both industrial and developing countries. At the June 1984 economic summit in London, the leaders of the seven major industrial countries expressed their intent to co-operate with the Fund in its surveillance of exchange rates. The Fund's function in that regard was to ensure that its members' exchange rate policies were guided by principles adopted in 1977[a] enjoining members to avoid manipulating exchange rates or the international monetary system. The 1977 agreement also obliged members to collaborate with IMF and other members in promoting a stable system of exchange rates.

In March 1984, the Executive Board conducted both its biennial review of the 1977 agreement and its annual review of the implementation of surveillance. It concluded that no revision of the principles and procedures set out in 1977 was necessary, but called for more active implementation. A further point noted during the 1984 surveillance review was that many of the international economic difficulties of recent years had been associated with pronounced swings in exchange rates between major industrial countries and with the repercussions of the prevailing low levels of economic activity and high interest rates in those countries on the rest of the world. The Board concluded that it was incumbent on the Fund to form a view on domestic policies needed to foster the smooth working of the system and to attempt to persuade its members to follow such policies.

Publications

Publications issued by the IMF in 1984 included the *Annual Report of the Executive Board*, the *Annual Report on Exchange Arrangements and Exchange Restrictions*, *International Financial Statistics*, *Balance of Payments Statistics* (monthly and *Yearbook*), *Government Finance Statistics Yearbook*, and *Direction of Trade Statistics* (monthly, *Yearbook* and biannual supplement). Periodicals included *Staff Papers*, *Finance and Development* (published jointly with the World Bank), and the *IMF Survey* (published 23 times a year). Also published were a series of papers on wide-ranging subjects of interest to the international financial community, explanatory pamphlets on the workings of

the Fund, books on monetary and fiscal issues and seminar volumes.

Membership

Membership of the Fund rose to 148 in 1984 with the admission of Saint Christopher and Nevis on 15 August and Mozambique on 24 September.

Secretariat

As at 31 December 1984, IMF staff numbered 1,750, drawn from more than 100 countries.

[a]YUN 1977, p. 1126.

DRAWINGS AND REPURCHASES IN 1984
(in millions of SDRs)

	Drawings	Repurchases
World	8,105.0	2,294.7
Industrial countries	28.5	—
New Zealand	28.5	—
Developing countries	8,076.5	—
Oil exporting countries	67.5	3.6
Indonesia	—	3.6
Iraq	67.5	—
Non-oil developing countries	8,009.0*	2,291.9*
Africa	1,225.9*	552.8*
Burundi	—	4.8
Cameroon	7.0	—
Central African Republic	6.5	6.3
Chad	3.2	2.7
Comoros	0.3	—
Congo	2.5	—
Djibouti	0.6	—
Equatorial Guinea	—	6.1
Ethiopia	4.2	25.2
Gabon	7.0	1.8
Gambia	2.6	1.9
Ghana	213.6	4.0
Guinea-Bissau	1.9	0.4
Ivory Coast	41.4	27.7
Kenya	46.2	58.0
Liberia	35.5	19.6
Madagascar	41.4	23.5
Malawi	37.8	20.4
Mali	24.0	3.2
Mauritania	—	9.0
Mauritius	24.8	31.5
Morocco	180.0	47.5
Niger	14.4	—
Sao Tome and Principe	0.9	—
Senegal	31.5	14.5
Sierra Leone	19.0	8.3
Somalia	—	2.9
Sudan	45.5	31.6
Swaziland	—	—
Togo	18.0	5.2
Uganda	21.0	37.7
United Republic of Tanzania	—	24.4
Zaire	158.0	54.0
Zambia	147.5	71.3
Zimbabwe	89.9	9.4
Asia	1,340.6*	905.0*
Bangladesh	—	58.0
Burma	—	6.1
India	600.0	133.0
Lao People's Democratic Republic	1.3	4.7
Malaysia	—	52.2
Maldives	0.5	—
Nepal	—	5.2
Pakistan	—	51.6
Papua New Guinea	—	28.3

	Drawings	Repurchases
Asia (cont.)		
Philippines	85.0	221.3
Republic of Korea	619.3	261.5
Samoa	3.4	0.8
Solomon Islands	—	0.2
Sri Lanka	31.2	22.7
Thailand	—	59.3
Europe	1,366.1*	614.9
Cyprus	—	2.3
Hungary	463.9	—
Portugal	217.2	—
Romania	183.6	132.5
Turkey	168.8	210.8
Yugoslavia	332.7	269.3
Middle East	87.5	—
Democratic Yemen	3.9	—
Egypt	30.4	—
Israel	34.8	—
Jordan	7.2	—
Syrian Arab Republic	11.2	—
Western hemisphere	3,989.0*	218.5*
Barbados	7.8	—
Belize	1.2	—
Bolivia	—	20.3
Brazil	1,744.2	—
Chile	216.0	—
Colombia	258.6	—
Costa Rica	—	24.3
Dominica	1.5	1.8
Dominican Republic	7.4	9.5
Ecuador	50.8	—
El Salvador	—	5.4
Grenada	—	0.9
Guatemala	27.0	—
Guyana	—	1.0
Haiti	14.0	—
Honduras	4.2	1.6
Jamaica	109.2	58.3
Mexico	1,294.5	—
Nicaragua	4.3	4.3
Panama	108.7	7.5
Peru	125.9	82.7
Saint Christopher and Nevis	1.0	—
Saint Lucia	—	0.5
Saint Vincent and the Grenadines	0.4	0.5
Suriname	3.0	—
Uruguay	9.5	—

*Differs from sum of individual figures because of rounding.
SOURCE: *International Financial Statistics Yearbook, 1985.*

CURRENCIES DRAWN AND REPURCHASES BY CURRENCY OF REPURCHASE IN 1984
(in millions of SDRs)

	Currencies drawn	Repurchases by currency of repurchase
World	8,105.0	2,294.7
Industrial countries	3,964.6*	1,608.1*
Australian dollars	27.0	—
Austrian schillings	10.2	22.2
Belgian francs	15.0	19.2
Canadian dollars	7.8	36.0
Danish kroner	—	13.7
Deutsche mark	294.6	160.3
Finnish markkaa	—	5.8
French francs	—	54.5
Irish pounds	7.5	6.4
Italian lire	108.2	69.8
Japanese yen	363.9	120.0
Netherlands guilders	69.3	54.5
Norwegian kroner	30.7	24.3
Pounds sterling	55.0	89.3
Spanish pesetas	—	11.7
Swedish kronor	10.0	5.7
United States dollars	2,965.5	914.8
Developing countries		
Oil-exporting countries	765.5	124.0*
Algerian dinars	—	6.9
Kuwaiti dinars	64.2	13.8
Qatar riyals	1.2	—
Rials Omani	3.5	0.9
Saudi Arabian riyals	689.6	82.0
United Arab Emirates dirhams	7.0	1.7
Venezuelan bolívares	—	18.8
Non-oil developing countries	110.4	24.4
Africa	1.0	0.7
Botswana pula	1.0	—
Tunisian dinars	—	0.7
Asia	103.0	9.5*
Chinese yuan	99.0	6.2
Singapore dollars	4.0	3.4
Europe	2.4	5.1*
Greek drachmas	—	4.8
Maltese liri	2.4	0.4
Western hemisphere	4.0	9.1*
Colombian pesos	—	3.5
Trinidad and Tobago dollars	4.0	5.6
SDRs	3,264.5	538.1

*Differs from sum of individual figures because of rounding.
SOURCE: *International Financial Statistics Yearbook, 1985.*

Annex I. MEMBERSHIP OF THE INTERNATIONAL MONETARY FUND, QUOTAS AND VOTING POWER
(As at 18 March 1985)

MEMBER	QUOTA Amount (in millions of SDRs)	General and SDR Departments percentage of total*	VOTING POWER Number of votes†	General and SDR Departments percentage of total	MEMBER	QUOTA Amount (in millions of SDRs)	General and SDR Departments percentage of total*	VOTING POWER Number of votes†	General and SDR Departments percentage of total
Afghanistan	86.70	0.10	1,117	0.12	Belgium	2,080.40	2.33	21,054	2.26
Algeria	623.10	0.70	6,481	0.70	Belize	9.50	0.01	345	0.04
Antigua and Barbuda	5.00	0.01	300	0.03	Benin	31.30	0.04	563	0.06
Argentina	1,113.00	1.25	11,380	1.22	Bhutan	2.50	0.002	275	0.03
Australia	1,619.20	1.81	16,442	1.77	Bolivia	90.70	0.10	1,157	0.12
Austria	775.60	0.87	8,006	0.86	Botswana	22.10	0.02	471	0.05
Bahamas	66.40	0.07	914	0.10	Brazil	1,461.30	1.64	14,863	1.60
Bahrain	48.90	0.05	739	0.08	Burkina Faso	31.60	0.04	566	0.06
Bangladesh	287.50	0.32	3,125	0.34	Burma	137.00	0.15	1,620	0.17
Barbados	34.10	0.04	591	0.06	Burundi	42.70	0.05	677	0.07

MEMBER	QUOTA Amount (in millions of SDRs)	QUOTA General and SDR Departments percentage of total*	VOTING POWER Number of votes†	VOTING POWER General and SDR Departments percentage of total	MEMBER	QUOTA Amount (in millions of SDRs)	QUOTA General and SDR Departments percentage of total*	VOTING POWER Number of votes†	VOTING POWER General and SDR Departments percentage of total
Cameroon	92.7	0.10	1,177	0.13	Mauritius	53.60	0.06	786	0.08
Canada	2,941.00	3.29	29,660	3.19	Mexico	1,165.50	1.31	11,905	1.28
Cape Verde	4.50	0.01	295	0.03	Morocco	306.60	0.34	3,316	0.36
Central African Republic	30.40	0.03	554	0.06	Mozambique	61.00	0.07	860	0.09
Chad	30.60	0.03	556	0.06	Nepal	37.30	0.04	623	0.07
Chile	440.50	0.49	4,655	0.50	Netherlands	2,264.80	2.54	22,898	2.46
China	2,390.90	2.68	24,159	2.60	New Zealand	461.60	0.52	4,866	0.52
Colombia	394.20	0.44	4,192	0.45	Nicaragua	68.20	0.08	932	0.10
Comoros	4.50	0.01	295	0.03	Niger	33.70	0.04	587	0.06
Congo	37.30	0.04	623	0.07	Nigeria	849.50	0.95	8,745	0.94
Costa Rica	84.10	0.09	1,091	0.12	Norway	699.00	0.78	7,240	0.78
Cyprus	69.70	0.08	947	0.10	Oman	63.10	0.07	881	0.09
Democratic Kampuchea	25.00	0.03	500	0.05	Pakistan	546.30	0.61	5,713	0.61
Democratic Yemen	77.20	0.09	1,022	0.11	Panama	102.20	0.11	1,272	0.14
Denmark	711.00	0.80	7,360	0.79	Papua New Guinea	65.90	0.07	909	0.10
Djibouti	8.00	0.01	330	0.04	Paraguay	48.40	0.05	734	0.08
Dominica	4.00	0.004	290	0.03	Peru	330.90	0.37	3,559	0.38
Dominican Republic	112.10	0.13	1,371	0.15	Philippines	440.40	0.49	4,654	0.50
Ecuador	150.70	0.17	1,757	0.19	Portugal	376.60	0.42	4,016	0.43
Egypt	463.40	0.52	4,884	0.53	Qatar	114.90	0.13	1,399	0.15
El Salvador	89.00	0.10	1,140	0.12	Republic of Korea	462.80	0.52	4,878	0.52
Equatorial Guinea	18.40	0.02	434	0.05	Romania	523.40	0.59	5,484	0.59
Ethiopia	70.60	0.08	956	0.10	Rwanda	43.80	0.05	688	0.07
Fiji	36.50	0.04	615	0.07	Saint Christopher and Nevis	4.50	0.01	295	0.03
Finland	574.90	0.64	5,999	0.65	Saint Lucia	7.50	0.01	325	0.03
France	4,482.80	5.02	45,078	4.85	Saint Vincent and the Grenadines	4.00	0.004	290	0.03
Gabon	73.10	0.08	981	0.11	Samoa	6.00	0.01	310	0.03
Gambia	17.10	0.02	421	0.05	Sao Tome and Principe	4.00	0.004	290	0.03
Germany, Federal Republic of	5,403.70	6.05	54,287	5.84	Saudi Arabia	3,202.40	3.59	32,274	3.47
Ghana	204.50	0.23	2,295	0.25	Senegal	85.10	0.10	1,101	0.12
Greece	399.90	0.45	4,249	0.46	Seychelles	3.00	0.003	280	0.03
Grenada	6.00	0.01	310	0.03	Sierra Leone	57.90	0.06	829	0.09
Guatemala	108.00	0.12	1,330	0.14	Singapore	92.40	0.10	1,174	0.13
Guinea	57.90	0.06	829	0.09	Solomon Islands	5.00	0.01	300	0.03
Guinea-Bissau	7.50	0.01	325	0.03	Somalia	44.20	0.05	692	0.07
Guyana	49.20	0.06	742	0.08	South Africa	915.70	1.03	9,407	1.01
Haiti	44.10	0.05	691	0.07	Spain	1,286.00	1.44	13,110	1.41
Honduras	67.80	0.08	928	0.10	Sri Lanka	223.10	0.25	2,481	0.27
Hungary	530.70	0.59	5,557	0.60	Sudan	169.70	0.19	1,947	0.21
Iceland	59.60	0.07	846	0.09	Suriname	49.30	0.06	743	0.08
India	2,207.70	2.47	22,327	2.40	Swaziland	24.70	0.03	497	0.05
Indonesia	1,009.70	1.13	10,347	1.11	Sweden	1,064.30	1.19	10,893	1.17
Iran	660.00	0.74	6,850	0.74	Syrian Arab Republic	139.10	0.16	1,641	0.18
Iraq	504.00	0.56	5,290	0.57	Thailand	386.60	0.43	4,116	0.44
Ireland	343.40	0.38	3,684	0.40	Togo	38.40	0.04	634	0.07
Israel	446.60	0.50	4,716	0.51	Trinidad and Tobago	170.10	0.19	1,951	0.21
Italy	2,909.10	3.26	29,341	3.15	Tunisia	138.20	0.15	1,632	0.18
Ivory Coast	165.50	0.19	1,905	0.20	Turkey	429.10	0.48	4,541	0.49
Jamaica	145.50	0.16	1,705	0.18	Uganda	99.60	0.11	1,246	0.13
Japan	4,223.30	4.73	42,483	4.57	United Arab Emirates	202.60	0.23	2,276	0.24
Jordan	73.90	0.08	989	0.11	United Kingdom	6,194.00	6.94	62,190	6.69
Kenya	142.00	0.16	1,670	0.18	United Republic of Tanzania	107.00	0.12	1,320	0.14
Kuwait	635.30	0.71	6,603	0.71	United States	17,918.30	20.06	179,433	19.29
Lao People's Democratic Republic	29.30	0.03	543	0.06	Uruguay	163.80	0.18	1,888	0.20
Lebanon	78.70	0.09	1,037	0.11	Vanuatu	9.00	0.01	340	0.04
Lesotho	15.10	0.02	401	0.04	Venezuela	1,371.50	1.54	13,965	1.50
Liberia	71.30	0.08	963	0.10	Viet Nam	176.80	0.20	2,018	0.22
Libyan Arab Jamahiriya	515.70	0.58	5,407	0.58	Yemen	43.30	0.05	683	0.07
Luxembourg	77.00	0.09	1,020	0.11	Yugoslavia	613.00	0.69	6,380	0.69
Madagascar	66.40	0.07	914	0.10	Zaire	291.00	0.33	3,160	0.34
Malawi	37.20	0.04	622	0.07	Zambia	270.30	0.30	2,953	0.32
Malaysia	550.60	0.62	5,756	0.62	Zimbabwe	191.00	0.21	2,160	0.23
Maldives	2.00	0.002	270	0.03					
Mali	50.80	0.06	758	0.08	Total	89,301.8	100.00‡	930,018	100.00‡
Malta	45.10	0.05	701	0.08					
Mauritania	33.90	0.04	589	0.06					

*All members were participants in the SDR Department.

†Voting power varies on certain matters pertaining to the General Department with use of the Fund's resources in that Department, which comprised four accounts: the General Resources Account, the Borrowed Resources Suspense Account, the Special Disbursement Account and the Investment Account.

‡May differ from the sum of the individual percentages because of rounding.

Annex II. EXECUTIVE DIRECTORS AND ALTERNATES OF THE INTERNATIONAL MONETARY FUND
(As at 31 December 1984)

Appointed Director	*Appointed Alternate*	*Casting the vote of*
Charles H. Dallara	Mary K. Bush	United States
Nigel L. Wicks	T. A. Clark	United Kingdom
Guenter Grosche	Bernd Goos	Federal Republic of Germany
Bruno de Maulde	Xavier Blandin	France
Hirotake Fujino	Masahiro Sugita	Japan
Yusuf A. Nimatallah	Jobarah E. Suraisry	Saudi Arabia

Elected Director	*Elected Alternate*	*Casting the votes of*
Pedro Pérez (Spain)	Guillermo Ortiz (Mexico)	Costa Rica, El Salvador, Guatemala, Honduras, Mexico, Nicaragua, Spain, Venezuela
J. J. Polak (Netherlands)	J. de Beaufort Wijnholds (Netherlands)	Cyprus, Israel, Netherlands, Romania, Yugoslavia
Jacques de Groote (Belgium)	Heinrich G. Schneider (Austria)	Austria, Belgium, Hungary, Luxembourg, Turkey
Robert K. Joyce (Canada)	Luke Leonard (Ireland)	Antigua and Barbuda, Bahamas, Barbados, Belize, Canada, Dominica, Grenada, Ireland, Jamaica, Saint Christopher and Nevis, Saint Lucia, Saint Vincent and the Grenadines
Salvatore Zecchini (Italy)	Nikolaos Coumbis (Greece)	Greece, Italy, Malta, Portugal
Mohamed Finaish (Libyan Arab Jamahiriya)	Tariq Alhaimus (Iraq)	Bahrain, Democratic Yemen, Iraq, Jordan, Kuwait, Lebanon, Libyan Arab Jamahiriya, Maldives, Oman, Pakistan, Qatar, Somalia, Syrian Arab Republic, United Arab Emirates, Yemen
C. R. Rye (Australia)	Antonio V. Romuáldez (Philippines)	Australia, New Zealand, Papua New Guinea, Philippines, Republic of Korea, Samoa, Seychelles, Solomon Islands, Vanuatu
Hans Lundström (Sweden)	Henrik Fugmann (Denmark)	Denmark, Finland, Iceland, Norway, Sweden
Arjun K. Sengupta (India)	A. S. Jayawardena (Sri Lanka)	Bangladesh, Bhutan, India, Sri Lanka
Alexandre Kafka (Brazil)	Hernando Arias (Panama)	Brazil, Colombia, Dominican Republic, Ecuador, Guyana, Haiti, Panama, Suriname, Trinidad and Tobago
E. I. M. Mtei (United Republic of Tanzania)	Ahmed Abdallah (Kenya)	Botswana, Burundi, Ethiopia, Gambia, Guinea, Kenya, Lesotho, Liberia, Malawi, Mozambique, Nigeria, Sierra Leone, Sudan, Swaziland, Uganda, United Republic of Tanzania, Zambia, Zimbabwe
J. E. Ismael (Indonesia)	Jaafar Ahmad (Malaysia)	Burma, Fiji, Indonesia, Lao People's Democratic Republic, Malaysia, Nepal, Singapore, Thailand, Viet Nam
Zhang Zicun (China)	Wang Enshao (China)	China
Fernando L. Nebbia (Argentina)	Brian Jensen (Peru)	Argentina, Bolivia, Chile, Paraguay, Peru, Uruguay
Ghassem Salehkhou (Iran)	Omar Kabbaj (Morocco)	Afghanistan, Algeria, Ghana, Iran, Morocco, Tunisia
Abderrahmane Alfidja (Niger)	wa Bilenga Tshishimbi (Zaire)	Benin, Burkina Faso, Cameroon, Cape Verde, Central African Republic, Chad, Comoros, Congo, Djibouti, Equatorial Guinea, Gabon, Guinea-Bissau, Ivory Coast, Madagascar, Mali, Mauritania, Mauritius, Niger, Rwanda, Sao Tome and Principe, Senegal, Togo, Zaire

NOTE: Democratic Kampuchea, Egypt and South Africa did not participate in the regular election of Executive Directors.

Annex III. PRINCIPAL OFFICERS AND OFFICES OF THE INTERNATIONAL MONETARY FUND
(As at 31 December 1984)

PRINCIPAL OFFICERS

Managing Director: Jacques de Larosière.
Deputy Managing Director: Richard D. Erb.
Counsellor: Walter O. Habermeier.*
Economic Counsellor: William C. Hood.*
Counsellor: L. A. Whittome.*
Director, Administration Department: Roland Tenconi.
Director, African Department: Alassane D. Ouattara.
Director, Asian Department: Tun Thin.
Director, Central Banking Department: J. B. Zulu.
Director, European Department: L. A. Whittome.
Director, Exchange and Trade Relations Department: C. David Finch.
Director, External Relations Department: Azizali F. Mohammed.
Director, Fiscal Affairs Department: Vito Tanzi.

Director, IMF Institute: Gérard M. Teyssier.
Director, Legal Department: George Nicoletopoulos.
Director, Middle Eastern Department: A. Shakour Shaalan.
Director, Research Department: William C. Hood.
Secretary, Secretary's Department: Leo Van Houtven.
Treasurer, Treasurer's Department: Walter O. Habermeier.
Director, Western Hemisphere Department: Eduardo Wiesner.
Director, Bureau of Computing Services: Warren N. Minami.
Director, Bureau of Language Services: Andrew J. Beith.
Director, Bureau of Statistics: Werner Dannemann.
Director, Office in Europe (Paris): Aldo Guetta.
Director, Office in Geneva: Carlos A. Sansón.
Internal Auditor: Peter A. Whipple.
Special Representative to the United Nations: Jan-Maarten Zegers.

*Alphabetical listing.

HEADQUARTERS AND OTHER OFFICES

HEADQUARTERS

International Monetary Fund
700 19th Street N.W.
Washington, D.C. 20431, United States
  Cable address: INTERFUND WASHINGTONDC
  Telephone: (202) 623-7000
  Telex: (RCA)248331 IMF UR, (ITT) 440040 UI,
    (TRT)197677 FUND UT
    (MCI)64111 INTERFUND UW

OTHER OFFICES

International Monetary Fund
European Office
64-66 Avenue d'Iéna
75116 Paris, France
  Cable address: INTERFUND PARIS
  Telephone: (1) 4 723-54-21
  Telex: 610712 INTERFUND PARIS

International Monetary Fund
58, Rue de Moillebeau
1209 Geneva, Switzerland
  Cable address: INTERFUND GENEVA
  Telephone: 34-30-00
  Telex: 23503 IMF CH

International Monetary Fund Office
United Nations Headquarters, Room DC1-1146
New York, N.Y. 10017, United States
  Telephone: (212) 963-6009

Chapter X

International Civil Aviation Organization (ICAO)

The International Civil Aviation Organization (ICAO) estimated total traffic of the world's scheduled airlines to be over 157 billion tonne-kilometres during 1984, an increase of 8 per cent over 1983. The airlines carried over 830 million passengers at a load factor of 65 per cent, 1 percentage point above 1983. Air freight increased by 13 per cent to almost 39 billion tonne-kilometres, the highest annual increase during the past decade. Airmail traffic amounted to over 4 billion tonne-kilometres, an increase of 7 per cent, higher than the average rate of increase in 10 years.

In 1984, the ICAO Council held three regular sessions and also convened an extraordinary session to consider an amendment to the Convention on International Civil Aviation (Chicago, United States, 1944) following the 1983 destruction of a Korean Air Lines civil aircraft (for further details, see below, under "Legal matters").

During 1984, membership of ICAO rose to 153 with the admission of Tonga on 2 December.

Activities in 1984

Air navigation

During 1984, ICAO's efforts in air navigation continued to be directed towards updating and implementing ICAO Specifications, guidance material and Regional Plans. The Specifications consisted of International Standards and Recommended Practices contained in 17 technical annexes to the Chicago Convention, and of Procedures for Air Navigation Services (PANS) contained in three PANS documents. Regional Plans set forth air navigation facilities and services required for international air navigation in the nine ICAO regions.

During the year, the Specifications in six annexes and in one PANS document were amended. Amendments were also made to Regional Plans.

Seven air navigation meetings were held in 1984. They covered a wide range of subjects and recommended changes to ICAO Specifications. To promote their uniform application, ICAO made available guidance material—new and revised technical manuals and ICAO circulars—to assist States in establishing and maintaining up-to-date and effective aeronautical infrastructures.

ICAO regional offices assisted States to implement Regional Plans and, in addition, experts were sent to advise on installing new facilities and services and on operating existing ones.

Special attention was given to: aircraft airworthiness and operation; environmental protection; accident investigation and prevention; aerodromes; air traffic control; aeronautical charts, communications, information services and meteorology; helicopter operations; personnel licensing and training; search and rescue; aviation medicine and security; and transport of dangerous goods.

Air transport

ICAO continued its programmes of economic studies, collecting and publishing air transport statistics, promoting greater facilitation in international air transport and preparing for the Third Air Transport Conference (scheduled for October/November 1985). Air transport meetings convened during the year included three meetings of expert panels, four regional workshops and one facilitation area meeting.

Panel meetings considered guidelines on route facility cost accounting and cost allocation (Montreal, Canada, February/March and December) and international air transport fares and rates (Montreal, October). Workshops were held on international fares and rates (Nairobi, Kenya, October/November), statistics (Bangkok, Thailand, November) and airport and route facility economics (Dakar, Senegal, April; Panama, June). The facilitation meeting discussed problems in the Middle East area (Riyadh, Saudi Arabia, November).

ICAO publications in 1984 included a document on international signs to provide guidance to persons at airports, the regular series of digests of civil aviation statistics, the yearbook on world civil aviation statistics, policy and guidance material on international air transport regulation and tariffs, a new edition of the manual on the ICAO statistics programme, a manual of airport and air navigation facility tariffs, a study of regional differences in fares, rates and costs for international air transport for 1982 and a survey of international air transport fares and rates in 1983.

During the year, ICAO continued to co-operate closely with other international organizations such as the International Air Transport Association, the Airport Associations Co-ordinating Council, the Customs Co-operation Council, the World Tourism Organization and the Universal Postal Union. It also continued to provide secretariat services to three independent regional civil aviation bodies—the African Civil Aviation Commission, the European Civil Aviation Conference and the Latin American Civil Aviation Commission.

Following a 1982 conference to amend the 1956 Danish and Icelandic joint financing agreements for air navigation services in Greenland and the Faeroe Islands, the two agreements as amended were provisionally applied from 1 January 1983. By the end of 1984, the protocols of amendment had been accepted by 10 countries.

Legal matters

Early in the year, the ICAO Council considered the final report of the ICAO Secretary-General on the investigation carried out in accordance with a Council resolution of September 1983 following the destruction of a Korean Air Lines civil aircraft earlier that month.[a] On 6 March, it condemned the use of armed force which resulted in the destruction of the airliner and urged all contracting States to co-operate fully in examining and adopting an amendment to the Chicago Convention and in improving measures for preventing a recurrence of this type of tragedy.

At its extraordinary session at Montreal from 24 April to 10 May 1984, the ICAO Assembly unanimously adopted an amendment (article 3 *bis*), embodied in a Protocol, to the Chicago Convention which reaffirmed the principle that every State must refrain from resorting to the use of weapons against civil aircraft in flight. The amendment was to enter into force after ratification by two thirds of ICAO's members. By the end of the year, two States had ratified the Protocol.

As requested by the Council in December 1983, a sub-committee of the Legal Committee met at Montreal from 25 September to 3 October 1984 to consider the preparation of a draft instrument on the interception of civil aircraft. The sub-committee concluded that this item should be considered only after the entry into force of the amendment to the Chicago Convention and the completion of the work of the Air Navigation Commission and the Council on the review of ICAO Standards, Recommended Practices and guidance material on the subject of the interception of civil aircraft. On 16 November, the Council considered the report of the sub-committee and requested the Secretary-General to prepare a preliminary study of appropriate action to be submitted to the Council in March 1985.

The Committee on Unlawful Interference with International Civil Aviation and Its Facilities held three meetings during the year. It reviewed proposals for the amendment of Specifications on security—safeguarding international aviation against acts of unlawful interference. As a result of the Committee's recommendations, the ICAO Council adopted on 30 November an amendment differentiating between the requirements for the carriage of weapons on board aircraft by law enforcement officers and authorized persons and the requirements for the transportation of weapons in other cases. The Committee also considered improving the current system of obtaining and analysing information from States concerned in incidents of unlawful interference.

The following conventions and protocols on international air law concluded under ICAO auspices were ratified or adhered to during 1984:

Convention on Offences and Certain Other Acts Committed on Board Aircraft (Tokyo, 1963)
Bahrain, Czechoslovakia, Haiti, Nauru

Convention for the Suppression of Unlawful Seizure of Aircraft (The Hague, 1970)
Bahrain, Guinea, Haiti, Monaco, Nauru

Convention for the Suppression of Unlawful Acts against the Safety of Civil Aviation (Montreal, 1971)
Bahrain, Guinea, Haiti, Monaco, Nauru

Additional Protocol No. 1 to Amend the Convention for the Unification of Certain Rules relating to International Carriage by Air signed at Warsaw on 12 October 1929 (Montreal, 1975) (not in force)
United Kingdom

Additional Protocol No. 2 to Amend the Convention for the Unification of Certain Rules relating to International Carriage by Air signed at Warsaw on 12 October 1929, as amended by the Protocol done at The Hague on 28 September 1955 (Montreal, 1975) (not in force)
United Kingdom

Additional Protocol No. 3 to Amend the Convention for the Unification of Certain Rules relating to International Carriage by Air signed at Warsaw on 12 October 1929, as amended by the Protocols done at The Hague on 28 September 1955 and at Guatemala City on 8 March 1971 (Montreal, 1975) (not in force)
United Kingdom

Montreal Protocol No. 4 to Amend the Convention for the Unification of Certain Rules relating to International Carriage by Air signed at Warsaw on 12 October 1929, as amended by the Protocol done at The Hague on 28 September 1955 (Montreal, 1975) (not in force)
United Kingdom

Technical assistance

During 1984, ICAO provided technical assistance to 93 States; in 54 of these, there were resident missions consisting of one or more experts. In addition to resident expertise, assistance was provided in the form of equipment, fellowships and scholarships and through short missions by experts.

Eight new large-scale projects, each costing more than $500,000, for which ICAO was to be the

[a]YUN 1983, p. 1284.

executing agency, were approved by the Administrator of the United Nations Development Programme (UNDP). Three large-scale projects were financed under trust fund assistance.

ICAO employed 589 experts from 49 countries during all or part of 1984, 349 on assignments under UNDP and 250 on trust fund projects (including 11 under the associate experts programme). There were also 27 United Nations Volunteers. The number of experts in the field at the end of 1984 was 331 as compared with 373 at the end of 1983.

A total of 1,106 fellowships were awarded in 1984 (as compared with 985 in 1983), of which 1,042 were implemented.

Equipment purchases and sub-contracts were a substantial proportion of the technical assistance programme in 1984. Thirty-nine Governments or organizations had registered with ICAO under the Civil Aviation Purchasing Service. The total sum committed to equipment under technical assistance during the year amounted to $10.5 million.

The following countries and Territories were aided:

Africa: Angola, Benin, Botswana, Cameroon, Cape Verde, Chad, Equatorial Guinea, Ethiopia, Gabon, Ghana, Guinea, Guinea-Bissau, Ivory Coast, Kenya, Lesotho, Liberia, Madagascar, Malawi, Mali, Mauritania, Mauritius, Mozambique, Niger, Nigeria, Rwanda, Senegal, Seychelles, Sierra Leone, Swaziland, Togo, Uganda, United Republic of Tanzania, Zaire, Zambia, Zimbabwe.

Americas: Antigua and Barbuda, Argentina, Bahamas, Bolivia, Brazil, Cayman Islands, Chile, Colombia, Ecuador, Guatemala, Haiti, Honduras, Netherlands Antilles, Panama, Peru, Saint Lucia, Suriname, Trinidad and Tobago, Turks and Caicos Islands, Uruguay, Venezuela.

Asia/Pacific: Afghanistan, Bangladesh, Brunei Darussalam, Burma, China, Democratic People's Republic of Korea, Hong Kong, India, Indonesia, Lao People's Democratic Republic, Malaysia, Maldives,

Nepal, Pakistan, Philippines, Republic of Korea, Samoa, Singapore, Sri Lanka, Thailand, Tonga, Viet Nam.

Europe, Mediterranean and Middle East: Algeria, Democratic Yemen, Djibouti, Egypt, Iraq, Jordan, Kuwait, Lebanon, Libyan Arab Jamahiriya, Morocco, Oman, Poland, Qatar, Saudi Arabia, Somalia, Sudan, Syrian Arab Republic, Yemen.

Included in the above were the following, aided during the year under trust fund arrangements: Argentina, Bolivia, Brunei Darussalam, Cape Verde, Iraq, Ivory Coast, Jordan, Libyan Arab Jamahiriya, Morocco, Nigeria, Peru, Saudi Arabia, Suriname, Trinidad and Tobago, Venezuela, Yemen.

Secretariat

As at 31 December 1984, the total number of staff members employed in the ICAO secretariat stood at 861: 308 in the Professional and higher categories drawn from 71 nationalities, and 553 in the General Service and related categories. In addition, 212 persons were employed in regional offices and 159 in the Professional category served as technical experts on UNDP projects in the field.

Budget

The revised appropriations for the 1984 financial year totalled $32,889,000. Modifications were approved by the ICAO Council and are reflected below (in United States dollars):

	Appropriations	Revised appropriations	Actual obligations
Meetings	450,000	400,000	399,206
Secretariat	27,112,000	27,062,000	27,061,400
General services	4,132,000	3,955,000	3,895,861
Equipment	593,000	817,000	816,864
Other budgetary provisions	132,000	35,000	34,866
Contingencies	2,776,000	620,000	—
Total	35,195,000	32,889,000	32,208,197

Annex I.   MEMBERSHIP OF THE INTERNATIONAL CIVIL AVIATION ORGANIZATION AND CONTRIBUTIONS

(Membership as at 31 December 1984; contributions as assessed for 1984)

MEMBER	Percentage	Net amount (in US dollars)	MEMBER	Percentage	Net amount (in US dollars)	MEMBER	Percentage	Net amount (in US dollars)
Afghanistan	0.06	17,017	Belgium	1.16	328,999	Cape Verde	0.06	17,017
Algeria	0.17	48,215	Benin	0.06	17,017	Central African Republic	0.06	17,017
Angola	0.06	17,017	Bolivia	0.06	17,017	Chad	0.06	17,017
Antigua and Barbuda	0.06	17,017	Botswana	0.06	17,017	Chile	0.15	42,543
Argentina	0.70	198,534	Brazil	1.53	433,939	China	0.56	158,827
Australia	1.64	465,137	Bulgaria	0.14	39,707	Colombia	0.21	59,560
Austria	0.59	167,336	Burkina Faso	0.06	17,017	Congo	0.06	17,017
Bahamas	0.06	17,017	Burma	0.06	17,017	Costa Rica	0.06	17,017
Bahrain	0.06	17,017	Burundi	0.06	17,017	Cuba	0.10	28,362
Bangladesh	0.06	17,017	Cameroon	0.06	17,017	Cyprus	0.06	17,017
Barbados	0.06	17,017	Canada	2.93	831,007	Czechoslovakia	0.56	158,827

MEMBER	CONTRIBUTION Percent-age	CONTRIBUTION Net amount (in US dollars)	MEMBER	CONTRIBUTION Percent-age	CONTRIBUTION Net amount (in US dollars)	MEMBER	CONTRIBUTION Percent-age	CONTRIBUTION Net amount (in US dollars)
Democratic Kampuchea	0.06	17,017	Kiribati	0.06	17,017	Saint Lucia	0.06	17,017
Democratic People's Republic of Korea	0.06	17,017	Kuwait	0.33	93,595	Saint Vincent and the Grenadines	0.06	17,017
Democratic Yemen	0.06	17,017	Lao People's Democratic Republic	0.06	17,017	Sao Tome and Principe	0.06	17,017
Denmark	0.65	184,353	Lebanon	0.17	48,215	Saudi Arabia	0.64	181,517
Djibouti	0.06	17,017	Lesotho	0.06	17,017	Senegal	0.06	17,017
Dominican Republic	0.06	17,017	Liberia	0.06	17,017	Seychelles	0.06	17,017
Ecuador	0.06	17,017	Libyan Arab Jamahiriya	0.23	65,233	Sierra Leone	0.06	17,017
Egypt	0.16	45,379	Luxembourg	0.06	17,017	Singapore	0.59	167,336
El Salvador	0.06	17,017	Madagascar	0.06	17,017	Somalia	0.06	17,017
Equatorial Guinea	0.06	17,017	Malawi	0.06	17,017	South Africa	0.56	158,827
Ethiopia	0.06	17,017	Malaysia	0.18	51,052	Spain	1.92	544,550
Fiji	0.06	17,017	Maldives	0.06	17,017	Sri Lanka	0.06	17,017
Finland	0.42	119,120	Mali	0.06	17,017	Sudan	0.06	17,017
France	5.97	1,693,211	Malta	0.06	17,017	Suriname	0.06	17,017
Gabon	0.06	17,017	Mauritania	0.06	17,017	Swaziland	0.06	17,017
Gambia	0.06	17,017	Mauritius	0.06	17,017	Sweden	1.12	317,654
Germany, Federal Republic of	7.08	2,008,030	Mexico	0.94	266,603	Switzerland	1.20	340,344
Ghana	0.06	17,017	Monaco	0.06	17,017	Syrian Arab Republic	0.07	19,853
Greece	0.47	133,301	Morocco	0.10	28,362	Thailand	0.30	85,086
Grenada	0.06	17,017	Mozambique	0.06	17,017	Togo	0.06	17,017
Guatemala	0.06	17,017	Nauru	0.06	17,017	Tonga*	—	—
Guinea	0.06	17,017	Nepal	0.06	17,017	Trinidad and Tobago	0.08	22,690
Guinea-Bissau	0.06	17,017	Netherlands	1.93	547,387	Tunisia	0.06	17,017
Guyana	0.06	17,017	New Zealand	0.35	99,267	Turkey	0.28	79,414
Haiti	0.06	17,017	Nicaragua	0.06	17,017	Uganda	0.06	17,017
Honduras	0.06	17,017	Niger	0.06	17,017	USSR	9.70	2,751,114
Hungary	0.16	45,379	Nigeria	0.23	65,233	United Arab Emirates	0.18	51,052
Iceland	0.06	17,017	Norway	0.48	136,138	United Kingdom	5.13	1,454,971
India	0.52	147,482	Oman	0.06	17,017	United Republic of Tanzania	0.06	17,017
Indonesia	0.31	87,922	Pakistan	0.26	73,741	United States	25.00	7,090,500
Iran	0.45	127,629	Panama	0.06	17,017	Uruguay	0.06	17,017
Iraq	0.19	53,888	Papua New Guinea	0.06	17,017	Vanuatu	0.06	17,017
Ireland	0.19	53,888	Paraguay	0.06	17,017	Venezuela	0.62	175,844
Israel	0.33	93,595	Peru	0.11	31,198	Viet Nam	0.06	17,017
Italy	3.21	910,420	Philippines	0.28	79,414	Yemen	0.06	17,017
Ivory Coast	0.06	17,017	Poland	0.49	138,974	Yugoslavia	0.46	130,465
Jamaica	0.06	17,017	Portugal	0.25	70,905	Zaire	0.06	17,017
Japan	9.03	2,561,089	Qatar	0.06	17,017	Zambia	0.06	17,017
Jordan	0.12	34,034	Republic of Korea	0.59	167,336	Zimbabwe	0.06	17,017
Kenya	0.06	17,017	Romania	0.19	53,888	Total†	100.06	28,379,001
			Rwanda	0.06	17,017			

*Tonga became a contracting State of ICAO on 2 December 1984.

†Includes assessment for Saint Vincent and the Grenadines, which became a contracting State after current assessment rates were set.

Annex II.   OFFICERS AND OFFICES OF THE INTERNATIONAL CIVIL AVIATION ORGANIZATION

(As at 31 December 1984)

ICAO COUNCIL

OFFICERS
President: Assad Kotaite (Lebanon).
First Vice-President: J.-P. Ghuysen (France).
Second Vice-President: K. B. Ganesan (India).
Third Vice-President: Lt.-Col. A. Alvarado (Guatemala).
Secretary: Yves Lambert (France).

MEMBERS
Algeria, Argentina, Australia, Belgium, Brazil, Canada, China, Colombia, Czecho-slovakia, Egypt, France, Germany, Federal Republic of, Guatemala, India, Indonesia, Iraq, Italy, Jamaica, Japan, Kenya, Lebanon, Madagascar, Mexico, Nigeria, Norway, Pakistan, Senegal, Spain, USSR, United Kingdom, United Republic of Tanzania, United States, Venezuela.

PRINCIPAL OFFICERS OF THE SECRETARIAT

Secretary-General: Yves Lambert.
Director, Air Navigation Bureau: D. W. Freer.
Director, Air Transport Bureau: R. A. Bickley.

Director, Legal Bureau: B. S. Gidwani.
Director, Technical Assistance Bureau: M. J. Challons.
Chief, Public Information Office: Eugene Sochor.

OFFICES

HEADQUARTERS

International Civil Aviation Organization
1000 Sherbrooke Street West, Suite 400
Montreal, Quebec, Canada H3A 2R2
    Cable address: ICAO MONTREAL
    Telephone: (514) 285-8219
    Telex: 05-24513

REGIONAL OFFICES

International Civil Aviation Organization
African Office
Boîte Postale 2356
Dakar, Senegal
    Cable address: ICAOREP DAKAR
    Telephone: 21-42-13, 22-47-86
    Telex: 3348 ICAO SG

International Civil Aviation Organization
Eastern African Office
P.O. Box 46 294
Nairobi, Kenya
    Cable address: ICAOREP NAIROBI
    Telephone: 333 930
    Telex: 22068 UNITERRA (FOR ICAO)

International Civil Aviation Organization
North American and Caribbean Office
Apartado Postal 5-377
Mexico 5, D.F., Mexico
    Cable address: ICAOREP MEXICO
    Telephone: 250-32-11
    Telex: 1777598 ICAO ME

International Civil Aviation Organization
South American Office
Apartado 4127
Lima 100, Peru
    Cable address: ICAOREP LIMA
    Telephone: 51-5414, 51-5325, 51-5497
    Telex: 25689 PE ICAO

International Civil Aviation Organization
European Office
3 *bis*, Villa Emile-Bergerat
92522 Neuilly-sur-Seine (Cedex)
France
    Cable address: ICAOREP PARIS
    Telephone: 745-13-28
    Telex: 610075 ECAC (FOR ICAOREP)

International Civil Aviation Organization
Asia and Pacific Office
P.O. Box 614
Bangkok, Thailand
    Cable address: ICAOREP BANGKOK
    Telephone: 281-5366, 281-5571, 281-0138
    Telex: 87969 ICAOBKK TH

International Civil Aviation Organization
Middle East Office
16 Hassan Sabri
Zamalek
Cairo, Egypt
    Cable address: ICAOREP CAIRO
    Telephone: 698163, 698344, 698463, 698532
    Telex: 92459 ICAOR UN

Chapter XI

Universal Postal Union (UPU)

The Universal Postal Union (UPU), established at Berne, Switzerland, in 1874 for the exchange of postal services between nations, is one of the oldest international intergovernmental organizations. It promotes the organization and improvement of postal services, plays an important role in the development of international collaboration and participates, at the request of its members, in various forms of postal technical assistance.

In 1984, the membership of UPU rose to 167 following the admission of Solomon Islands (4 May) and Kiribati (14 August) and the confirmation by the Congress of the expulsion of South Africa.

Activities of UPU organs

Universal Postal Congress

The Universal Postal Congress, composed of all member States, is the supreme legislative authority of UPU and usually meets every five years. The nineteenth session of the Congress was held at Hamburg, Federal Republic of Germany, from 18 June to 27 July 1984, and the next was scheduled to meet at Washington, D.C., in 1989.

The 1984 Congress revised the Acts of the Union on the basis of proposals submitted by member States, the Executive Council and the Consultative Council for Postal Studies. It also considered the work accomplished during the preceding five years and set the framework and scope of future work.

In addition to its legislative and regulatory functions, the Congress dealt with the Union's finances, the work programmes of its permanent bodies, technical co-operation, and election of the senior officers of the International Bureau and members of the Executive and Consultative Councils. It also decided to replace the name "UPU Day" (celebrated on 9 October every year) by "World Post Day".

Because of communications-market development, the Congress discussed changes in the postal system, which resulted in the Declaration of Hamburg, stressing that UPU must "actively participate in strengthening the international postal service as a whole and in improving the standard and speed of international mail circulation and postal exchanges". It also relaxed the existing provisions to permit the introduction of new services between Congresses.

On technical co-operation, the Congress decided that means should be found for improving and developing the postal services, particularly in the least developed countries, and drew up the general framework of UPU activities for 1985-1989.

Executive Council

At its 1984 session, held at Berne from 27 February to 8 March, the 40-member Executive Council—which carries the work of UPU between sessions of the Congress by maintaining close contact with postal administrations, exercising control over the International Bureau, promoting technical assistance and working with the United Nations and other organizations—considered administrative matters, completed the tasks referred to it by the 1979 Congress and finalized the proposals and documents to be submitted to the 1984 Congress.

The new Executive Council, elected by the 1984 Congress, held an organizational meeting on 23 July during the Congress.

Consultative Council for Postal Studies

The 35-member Consultative Council for Postal Studies pursued in 1984 its studies of various technical, economic and operational problems affecting postal administrations of UPU member States, and examined teaching and training difficulties in newly independent and developing countries.

The new Council, elected by the 1984 Congress, held an organizational meeting on 24 July during the Congress. At its annual meeting held at Berne from 29 October to 2 November, the Council adopted the work programme approved by the Congress and assigned to its committees studies to be undertaken during 1984-1989. Pursuant to a 1982 decision, the Council decided to prepare for publication the fifth edition of the *Multilingual Vocabulary of the International Postal Service*. It also dealt with technical co-operation, international high-speed mail and computers in the postal service.

International Bureau

Under the general supervision of the Government of the Swiss Confederation, the International Bureau—the secretariat of UPU—continued to serve the postal administrations of member States as an organ for liaison, information and consultation.

During 1984, the Bureau was responsible for collecting, co-ordinating, publishing and disseminating international postal service information. At the request of postal administrations, it also conducted inquiries and acted as a clearing-house for settling certain accounts between them. In addition, the Bureau considered requests for amendments to the Acts of the Union, gave notice of changes adopted and took part in the preparatory work for the 1984 Congress.

The Congress elected Adwaldo Cardoso Botto de Barros and Félix Cicéron as Director-General and Deputy Director-General of the Bureau, respectively, to take office on 1 January 1985.

As at 31 December 1984, the number of staff members employed by the UPU secretariat stood at 138: 57 in the Professional and higher categories (drawn from 46 countries) and 81 in the General Service category. Also, 15 officials were employed in the Arabic, English, Portuguese, Russian and Spanish translation services.

Technical co-operation

In 1984, UPU technical co-operation was financed mainly by the United Nations Development Programme (UNDP), with expenditures amounting to some $1.6 million.

Assistance was also provided through the UPU Special Fund (voluntary contributions in cash and kind from member States) and the regular budget. Total expenditures from these two sources in 1984 amounted to approximately $878,000. In addition, postal administrations provided assistance on a bilateral basis.

Training of postal instructors continued to be given priority. Several training courses were organized in France, the United Kingdom and other regional training centres. Other courses were held in various developing countries.

Thirty-two national and regional projects concerning postal services were carried out under UNDP. Forty-six expert missions were undertaken and 272 fellowships were awarded (two thirds for study courses). Several projects received assistance in the form of equipment. The projects dealt with all main branches of postal service, including national or regional vocational training centres.

The Special Fund and the regular budget funded missions by experts and consultants, scholarships for training, instruction materials and equipment. During 1984, 36 consultants carried out technical missions in 44 postal administrations and 157 fellowships were granted for training courses and technical meetings.

In addition, the Special Fund programme included a contribution by Belgium to continue a project to assist the drought-stricken Sahelian region of Africa. Other technical assistance activities, such as fellowships and training courses, were also offered by several countries during the year.

UPU continued its programme of technical assistance subject to payment, under which member States could finance assistance themselves by funds on deposit.

Budget

Since 1981, under UPU's self-financing system, contributions are payable in advance by member States on the basis of the following year's budget. At its 1984 session, the Executive Council approved a budget of 22,961,300 Swiss francs for 1985 (see table).

Income	*Amount (in Swiss francs)*
Contributions from member States	20,022,000
Taken from reserve funds	990,000
Contribution allocated by UNDP for support of technical co-operation projects	959,200
Sale of publications	227,000
Other	763,100
Total	22,961,300*
Expenditure	
Staff	17,937,700
General expenses	5,023,600
Total	22,961,300*

*Equal to $10,986,268 on the basis of 2.09 Swiss francs = $US 1.00.

Each member State of UPU chooses its class of contribution, on a scale of 1 to 50 units. For 1984, the Executive Council fixed the amount of the contributory unit at 18,800 Swiss francs on the basis of a total of 1,067 units. The following table gives assessments in Swiss francs by class of contribution:

	ASSESSMENTS	
CLASS OF CONTRIBUTION	*Swiss francs*	*US dollar equivalent**
50 units	940,000	449,760
25 units	470,000	224,880
20 units	376,000	179,904
15 units	282,000	134,928
10 units	188,000	89,952
5 units	94,000	44,976
3 units	56,400	26,985
1 unit	18,800	8,995

*Calculated on the basis of 2.09 Swiss francs = $US 1.00.

Three new assessment classes of contribution (applicable on 1 January 1986) were added by the 1984 Congress: 40, 35 and 0.5 units. The last class is reserved for the least developed countries listed by the United Nations and for other countries designated by the Executive Council.

Annex I.   MEMBERSHIP OF THE UNIVERSAL POSTAL UNION AND CLASS OF CONTRIBUTION

(Membership as at 31 December 1984; contributions as assessed for 1985)

Member	Class of contri-bution;* no. of units	Member	Class of contri-bution;* no. of units	Member	Class of contri-bution;* no. of units	Member	Class of contri-bution;* no. of units	Member	Class of contri-bution;* no. of units	Member	Class of contri-bution;* no. of units
Afghanistan	1	Comoros	1	Germany, Federal Republic of	50	Lebanon	1	Papua New Guinea	1	Syrian Arab Republic	1
Albania	1	Congo	1	Ghana	3	Lesotho	1	Paraguay	1	Thailand	3
Algeria	5	Costa Rica	1	Greece	3	Liberia	1	Peru	3	Togo	1
Angola	1	Cuba	3	Grenada	1	Libyan Arab Jamahiriya	5	Philippines	1	Tonga	1
Argentina	20	Cyprus	1	Guatemala	3	Liechtenstein	1	Poland	10	Trinidad and Tobago	1
Australia	25	Czecho-slovakia	10	Guinea	1	Luxembourg	3	Portugal	5	Tunisia	5
Austria	5	Democratic Kampuchea	1	Guinea-Bissau	1	Madagascar	3	Qatar	5	Turkey	5
Bahamas	1	Democratic People's Republic of Korea	5	Guyana	1	Malawi	1	Republic of Korea	1	Tuvalu	1
Bahrain	1			Haiti	3	Malaysia	3	Romania	5	Uganda	1
Bangladesh	15	Democratic Yemen	1	Honduras	1	Maldives	1	Rwanda	1	Ukrainian SSR	10
Barbados	1	Denmark	10	Hungary	10	Mali	1	Saint Lucia	1	USSR	25
Belgium	15	Djibouti	1	Iceland	1	Malta	1	Saint Vincent and the Grenadines	1	United Arab Emirates	1
Belize	1	Dominica	1	India	25	Mauritania	1	San Marino	1	United Kingdom	50
Benin	1	Dominican Republic	3	Indonesia	10	Mauritius	1	Sao Tome and Principe	1	United Kingdom Overseas Territories	5
Bhutan	1	Ecuador	3	Iran	5	Mexico	15	Saudi Arabia	25	United Republic of Tanzania	1
Bolivia	1	Egypt	15	Iraq	5	Monaco	1	Senegal	1	United States	50
Botswana	1	El Salvador	1	Ireland	10	Mongolia	1	Seychelles	1	Uruguay	3
Brazil	25	Equatorial Guinea	3	Israel	3	Morocco	5	Sierra Leone	1	Vanuatu	1
Bulgaria	3	Ethiopia	1	Italy	25	Mozambique	1	Singapore	1	Vatican	1
Burkina Faso	1	Fiji	1	Ivory Coast	3	Nauru	1	Solomon Islands	1	Venezuela	3
Burma	3	Finland	10	Jamaica	1	Nepal	3	Somalia	1	Viet Nam	1
Burundi	1	France	50	Japan	50	Netherlands	15	Spain	25	Yemen	1
Byelorussian SSR	3	Gabon	1	Jordan	1	Netherlands Antilles	1	Sri Lanka	5	Yugoslavia	5
Cameroon	1	Gambia	1	Kenya	3	New Zealand	20	Sudan	1	Zaire	3
Canada	50	German Democratic Republic	15	Kiribati	1	Nicaragua	1	Suriname	1	Zambia	3
Cape Verde	1			Kuwait	10	Niger	1	Swaziland	1	Zimbabwe	3
Central African Republic	1			Lao People's Democratic Republic	1	Nigeria	10	Sweden	15		
Chad	1					Norway	10	Switzerland	15		
Chile	5					Oman	1				
China	50					Pakistan	15				
Colombia	3					Panama	1				

NOTE: The UPU official nomenclature differs from that of the United Nations.
*For amount of contributions from members, see table under BUDGET above.

ANNEX II.   ORGANS, OFFICERS AND OFFICE OF THE UNIVERSAL POSTAL UNION

EXECUTIVE COUNCIL

(Held office until the nineteenth (1984) Universal Postal Congress)

Chairman: Brazil.
Vice-Chairmen: China, Liberia, Spain, USSR.
Secretary-General: Mohamed I. Sobhi, Director-General of the International Bureau.
Members: Algeria, Argentina, Bangladesh, Barbados, Brazil, Canada, Chile, China, Cuba, Czechoslovakia, Denmark, Egypt, France, Gabon, Germany, Federal Repub-lic of, Guinea, Honduras, India, Iraq, Ireland, Ivory Coast, Jordan, Kenya, Liberia, Libyan Arab Jamahiriya, Malaysia, Mali, Mexico, Mongolia, Saudi Arabia, Sene-gal, Spain, Sri Lanka, Sudan, Syrian Arab Republic, Thailand, USSR, United Kingdom, United States, Yugoslavia.

(Elected to hold office until the twentieth (1989) Universal Postal Congress)

Chairman: Germany, Federal Republic of.
Vice-Chairmen: Benin, Jordan, Mexico, USSR.
Secretary-General: Adwaldo Cardoso Botto de Barros, Director-General of the In-ternational Bureau.
Members: Algeria, Australia, Belgium, Benin, Brazil, Cameroon, Chile, Colombia, Egypt, Ethiopia, France, Gabon, Germany, Federal Republic of, Honduras, Hun-gary, India, Iraq, Ireland, Ivory Coast, Japan, Jordan, Lebanon, Madagascar, Mex-ico, New Zealand, Nigeria, Norway, Pakistan, Peru, Poland, Portugal, Romania, Saudi Arabia, Senegal, Switzerland, Thailand, USSR, United States, Uruguay, Zambia.

CONSULTATIVE COUNCIL FOR POSTAL STUDIES

(Held office until the nineteenth (1984) Universal Postal Congress)

Chairman: United Kingdom.
Vice-Chairman: Tunisia.
Secretary-General: Mohamed I. Sobhi, Director-General of the International Bureau.
Members: Algeria, Argentina, Australia, Austria, Bangladesh, Belgium, Brazil, Cameroon, China, Colombia, Egypt, France, German Democratic Republic, Germany, Federal Republic of, India, Indonesia, Iraq, Italy, Japan, Mexico, Morocco, Netherlands, New Zealand, Nigeria, Pakistan, Poland, Romania, Spain, Sweden, Switzerland, Thailand, Tunisia, USSR, United Kingdom, United States.

(Elected to hold office until the twentieth (1989) Universal Postal Congress)

Chairman: Tunisia.
Vice-Chairman: Canada.
Secretary-General: Adwaldo Cardoso Botto de Barros, Director-General of the International Bureau.
Members: Algeria, Argentina, Australia, Austria, Bangladesh, Belgium, Brazil, Canada, China, Cuba, Egypt, Finland, France, Germany, Federal Republic of, India, Indonesia, Italy, Japan, Kenya, Morocco, Netherlands, New Zealand, Pakistan, Spain, Sri Lanka, Sudan, Switzerland, Thailand, Tunisia, USSR, United Kingdom, United Republic of Tanzania, United States, Yugoslavia, Zimbabwe.

INTERNATIONAL BUREAU

OFFICERS

Director-General: Mohamed I. Sobhi.
Deputy Director-General a.i.: Félix Cicéron.
Assistant Directors-General: Félix Cicéron, Abdel Kader Baghdadi, El Mostafa Gharbi.
Assistant Director-General a.i.: Sven Backström.

HEADQUARTERS

Bureau international de l'Union postale universelle
Weltpoststrasse 4
Berne, Switzerland
  Postal address: Union postale universelle
  Case postale
  3000 Berne 15 (Suisse)
  Cable address: UPU BERNE
  Telephone: (031) 43 22 11
  Telex: 32 842 UPU CH

Chapter XII

International Telecommunication Union (ITU)

During 1984, membership of the International Telecommunication Union (ITU) rose to 160 with the admission of Namibia (represented by the United Nations Council for Namibia) on 25 January and Brunei Darussalam on 19 November.

Administrative Council

The thirty-ninth session of the Administrative Council of ITU was held from 2 to 19 April 1984 at ITU headquarters, Geneva. It reviewed administrative matters, approved a revised schedule of conferences, and drew up the agenda for the first (1986) session of the Regional Administrative Radio Conference for broadcasting in the frequency band 1605-1705 kilohertz in Region 2 (the Americas and Greenland). The Council also strengthened ITU's regional presence in technical co-operation activities and reviewed its computer facilities concerning radio frequency spectrum management and administrative radio conferences.

Administrative radio conferences

The first session of the World Administrative Radio Conference for the planning of the HF (high frequency) bands allocated to the Broadcasting Service was held at Geneva from 10 January to 11 February 1984. It adopted a technical report to the second (1987) session and five resolutions to improve the planning and use of HF broadcasting bands.

The second session of the Regional Administrative Conference for the planning of VHF (very high frequency) sound broadcasting in Region 1 (Africa and Europe) and certain countries in Region 3 (Asia and Australasia), held at Geneva from 29 October to 7 December, adopted a regional agreement incorporating a plan for FM (frequency modulation) sound broadcasting stations in the frequency band 87.5-108 megahertz.

International consultative committees

In 1984, the International Radio Consultative Committee (CCIR) made important progress in system standards for fixed-satellite service systems and terrestrial radio relay systems, particularly in digital transmission, and on the hypothetical reference path in the Integrated Services Digital Network (ISDN) reference connection. New recommendations were drafted on land-mobile and maritime-mobile systems, with particular progress

on cellular radio systems, radio paging and the future global maritime distress and safety system.

The CCIR Conference Preparatory Meeting (Geneva, 25 June–20 July) prepared technical guidelines for the 1985 World Administrative Radio Conference (WARC) on the use of the geostationary satellite orbit and the planning of the space services using it.

The International Telegraph and Telephone Consultative Committee (CCITT) eighth plenary assembly (Malaga-Torremolinos, Spain, 8-19 October) approved a large number of recommendations to appear in the CCITT book to be published in 1985. Topics covered in the principal study groups included: transmission systems; telephone operation and quality, data transmission on the public-switched telephone and public data networks; digital networks; switching and signalling; maintenance and protection; and general tariff principles. Special study groups produced manuals and case-studies of particular interest to developing countries on subjects such as: general network planning; primary sources of energy; rural telecommunications; regional satellite communications; transition from analogue to digital telecommunication networks; effects of inflation on telecommunications organizations; allocation of scarce resources and application of information technology; and socio-economic implications of teleprocessing.

International Frequency Registration Board

During the year, the International Frequency Registration Board (IFRB) continued to implement the decisions taken at the 1979 WARC, including a review of the Master International Frequency Register (MIFR), activities related to computer analysis and the search for replacement frequencies, conversion and transfer of MIFR resulting from revision of the International Frequency List, and conversion of MIFR to a new method of designating emissions.

IFRB's other activities were follow-up actions to the 1981 Regional Administrative MF (medium frequency) Broadcasting Conference (Region 2) and the first (1982) session of the Regional Administrative Conference for FM sound broadcasting in the VHF band (Region 1 and certain countries in Region 3) and preparation for and participation in the second (1984) session; organization of international monitoring programmes;

preparation for administrative radio conferences and the 1985 WARC; and examination of frequency matters.

Technical co-operation

In 1984, ITU continued its activities of technical co-operation in conformity with the 1982 ITU Plenipotentiary Conference[a] (Nairobi, Kenya) which made a provision in the Nairobi Convention—which entered into force on 1 January 1984—to strengthen ITU's role in promoting and providing supportive action in addition to its regulatory, standardization and co-ordination activities.

The slowing down of activities financed by the United Nations Development Programme (UNDP) increased during 1984. However, towards year's end, resources available to UNDP began to level out and even to show a slight upturn, giving promise of additional funds to be carried forward and become available during the rest of the programming cycle until the end of 1986.

Under ITU programmes of technical co-operation in developing countries, 477 expert missions were carried out, 629 fellows were trained abroad and equipment valued at $4,044,819 was delivered for various field projects. The total cost of this assistance amounted to $23,558,312.

The following countries and territories were aided:

Africa: Angola, Benin, Burundi, Cameroon, Central African Republic, Chad, Congo, Djibouti, Egypt, Equatorial Guinea, Ethiopia, Gambia, Ivory Coast, Lesotho, Mauritania, Morocco, Mozambique, Namibia, Nigeria, Rwanda, Senegal, Somalia, Sudan, Swaziland, Tunisia, Uganda, Zaire, Zimbabwe.

The Americas: Argentina, Brazil, Cuba, Ecuador, Guatemala, Haiti, Honduras, Nicaragua, Panama, Peru, Saint Christopher and Nevis, Trinidad and Tobago, Uruguay.

Asia and the Pacific: Afghanistan, Bangladesh, Bhutan, Burma, China, India, Indonesia, Iran, Lao People's Democratic Republic, Malaysia, Mongolia, Nepal, Pakistan, Papua New Guinea, Philippines, Republic of Korea, Samoa, Singapore, Sri Lanka, Tokelau, Tonga.

Europe and the Middle East: Albania, Bulgaria, Cyprus, Czechoslovakia, Democratic Yemen, Greece, Hungary, Jordan, Kuwait, Oman, Qatar, Romania, Saudi Arabia, Turkey, United Arab Emirates, Yemen.

The main objectives of ITU technical co-operation continued to be: promoting development of regional telecommunications networks in Africa, the Americas, Asia, the Pacific, the Middle East and the Mediterranean Basin; strengthening telecommunication technical and administrative services in developing countries; and vocational training.

ITU continued to promote development of regional telecommunication networks and their in-tegration into the world-wide telecommunication system, in accordance with objectives established by the World Plan Committee and regional plan committees.

The Pan-African Telecommunications (PANAFTEL) Network progressed at interconnecting countries without transit beyond the continent. Most of the network was installed during the year, with the exception of the subregion of Central Africa.

In 1984, other ITU activities included: the search for solutions to interface problems; the study of trunk routes in the Kagera River Basin (United Republic of Tanzania); participation in acceptance tests for several links; and specific technical proposals, such as the synchronization of central frequency generators. ITU also encouraged administrations to sign mutual operational agreements aiming at facilitating the use of PANAFTEL's installations and continued its study and implementation of subregional routing plans for telephony and telex.

By the end of 1984, 18 countries had begun to develop their national plan for the improvement of maintenance based on the existing general strategy and the manual issued in 1983.[b]

In the Americas, several projects were under way to strengthen national telecommunication technical and administrative services, notably in Bermuda—advice on a draft of a new telecommunications act; Brazil—advice on technology transfer and procurement of high-technology equipment; Cuba—assistance to the Central Telecommunications Laboratory; Haiti—preparation of development plans; Panama—assistance in installing a new maritime radio system; Peru—support with outside plant planning, design and engineering, and contract management; and Uruguay—introduction of data communication services.

Together with the Asia-Pacific Telecommunity, ITU prepared a work programme for implementation in 1985, and assisted the least developed countries of the region in developing rural networks, improving maintenance standards and upgrading telecommunication services. Under a UNDP/ITU regional project on development, operation and maintenance, South Pacific countries were assisted in planning new telecommunication facilities and implementing development projects. Another South Pacific project provided training in radio frequency monitoring and management.

Activities continued in the Middle East and Mediterranean Basin to develop the regional network, under the 1978 master plan. This included: enhancing technical capabilities in transmission switching, traffic, network planning, maintenance, management and ISDN networks; assisting in the

[a]YUN 1982, p. 1575.
[b]YUN 1983, p. 1293.

implementation of projects in the master plan; enhancing capabilities of Arab regional organizations; and co-ordinating the international terrestrial and satellite networks regionally.

In co-operation with GULFVISION, ITU continued its study of radio propagation in the Gulf area, enabling the countries of the region to make the best use of the allocated bands for television and sound/FM broadcasting services. The main objective of the European regional project was to provide countries concerned with a more effective international telecommunications infrastructure. In Albania, a project was under way to develop national links and two international links—to Greece and Italy. Other projects in Europe and the Middle East were devoted to the development and strengthening of administration and to training.

Training activities

By year's end, 190 training packages were available through the ITU sharing system for training and a comprehensive basic course in teletraffic engineering was designed. Under the course development in telecommunications project, 56 course developers from eight countries had completed their training and 40 more had started.

Publications

Publications issued by ITU in either trilingual or separate English, French and Spanish editions during 1984 included:

> *Report on the Activities of the Union, 1983*
> *Financial Operating Report for 1983*
> *Twenty-third Report by the International Telecommunication Union on Telecommunication and the Peaceful Uses of Outer Space*, Information Booklet No. 32
> *Final Acts of the Regional Administrative Radio Conference for the Planning of the Broadcasting-Satellite Service, Region 2* (Geneva, 1983)
> *List of International Telephone Routes*, 24th ed., 1984
> *Table of International Telex Relations and Traffic*, 1984
> *Yearbook of Common Carrier Telecommunication Statistics*, 11th ed., 1984
> *List of Coast Stations*, vol. I, 10th ed., 1984
> *List of Ship Stations*, 24th ed., 1984, and Supplement Nos. 1-3
> *Map of Coast Stations open to Public Correspondence*, 11th ed., 1984
> *Catalogue of Telecommunication Training Opportunities*, Publication No. 2, 1984
> *Documents of the CCIR XVth Plenary Assembly*, Geneva, 1982: vol. I, Add.; vol. VIII, Add.; vol. XIV.2
> *Study of Financial and Accounting Problems related to the Effects of Inflation on Telecommunications Authorities* (GAS 5/6)
> *Study of Management Information System for Telecommunications Authorities and Appropriate Application of the Information Technology* (GAS 5/7)
> *Optimum Allocation and Use of Scarce Resources in Order to Meet Telecommunication Needs in Urban or Rural Areas of a Country* (GAS 5/8)
> *Determination of the Economic Impact of New Services on Telecommunication Undertakings* (GAS 5/9)

> *Preliminary Assessment of the Socio-economic Implications of Teleprocessing for National Economies at Different Stages of Development* (GAS 5/10)
> *Plan Book for Europe and the Mediterranean Basin* (Nicosia, 1983)
> *General Plan for the Development of the Regional Telecommunication Network in Africa* (Libreville, 1983)
> *Economic and Technical Aspects of the Transition from Analogue to Digital Telecommunication Networks* (GAS 9)
> *Case Study on an Urban Network* (GAS 9)
> *Economic and Technical Impact of Implementing a Regional Satellite Network* (GAS 8)
> *Optical Fibres for Telecommunications*
> *Quality of Service, Network Management and Network Maintenance*

Secretariat

As at 31 December 1984, the total staff of ITU numbered 709 officials (excluding staff on short-term contracts). Of these, nine were elected officials, 564 had permanent contracts and 136 had fixed-term contracts; 53 nationalities were represented in posts subject to geographical distribution.

Budget

The following budget for 1984 was adopted by the Administrative Council in 1983:

	Amount (in Swiss francs)
Income	
Contribution by members and private operating agencies	93,554,000
Contribution by UNDP for technical co-operation administrative expenses	9,987,000
Sales of publications	8,205,000
Miscellaneous	85,000
Total	111,831,000
Expenditures	
Administrative Council	789,000
Common headquarters expenditure	73,221,000
Miscellaneous	85,000
Conferences and meetings	17,544,000
Other expenses	2,000,000
Total general expenses	93,639,000
Technical co-operation	9,987,000
Publications	8,205,000
Total	111,831,000

Each member of ITU chooses the class of contribution in which it wishes to be included and pays in advance its annual contributory share to the budget on the basis of the budgetary provision. In accordance with the 1982 International Telecommunication Convention, new classes of contribution were chosen by ITU members with effect from 1 January 1984. The classes of contribution for 1985 for members are listed in ANNEX I below.

As at the end of 1984, the total of units for members was 393. The contributory unit for 1984 was 209,000 Swiss francs; the contributory unit for 1985 was to be 221,400 Swiss francs.

Annex I. MEMBERSHIP OF THE INTERNATIONAL TELECOMMUNICATION UNION AND CONTRIBUTIONS

(Membership as at 31 December 1984; contributions as assessed for 1985)

MEMBER	Class of contribution; no. of units	In Swiss francs*
Afghanistan	1/8	27,675
Albania	1/4	55,350
Algeria	1	221,400
Angola	1/4	55,350
Argentina	3	664,200
Australia	18	3,985,200
Austria	1	221,400
Bahamas	1/2	110,700
Bahrain	1/2	110,700
Bangladesh	1/8	27,675
Barbados	1/4	55,350
Belgium	5	1,107,000
Belize	1/8	27,675
Benin	1/4	55,350
Bolivia	1/4	55,350
Botswana	1/2	110,700
Brazil	3	664,200
Brunei Darussalam	1/2	110,700
Bulgaria	1	221,400
Burkina Faso	1/8	27,675
Burma	1/2	110,700
Burundi	1/8	27,675
Byelorussian SSR	1/2	110,700
Cameroon	1/2	110,700
Canada	18	3,985,200
Cape Verde	1/8	27,675
Central African Republic	1/8	27,675
Chad	1/8	27,675
Chile	1	221,400
China	10	2,214,000
Colombia	1	221,400
Comoros	1/8	27,675
Congo	1/2	110,700
Costa Rica	1/4	55,350
Cuba	1/2	110,700
Cyprus	1/4	55,350
Czechoslovakia	2	442,800
Democratic Kampuchea	1/2	110,700
Democratic People's Republic of Korea	1/4	55,350
Democratic Yemen	1/8	27,675
Denmark	5	1,107,000
Djibouti	1/8	27,675
Dominican Republic	1/2	110,700
Ecuador	1/2	110,700
Egypt	1	221,400
El Salvador	1/4	55,350
Equatorial Guinea	1/8	27,675
Ethiopia	1/8	27,675
Fiji	1/4	55,350
Finland	5	1,107,000
France	30	6,642,000
Gabon	1/2	110,700
Gambia	1/8	27,675
German Democratic Republic	3	664,200
Germany, Federal Republic of	30	6,642,000
Ghana	1/4	55,350
Greece	1	221,400
Grenada	1/8	27,675
Guatemala	1/4	55,350
Guinea	1/8	27,675
Guinea-Bissau	1/8	27,675
Guyana	1/4	55,350
Haiti	1/8	27,675
Honduras	1/4	55,350
Hungary	1	221,400
Iceland	1/4	55,350
India	10	2,214,000
Indonesia	1	221,400
Iran	1	221,400
Iraq	1/4	55,350
Ireland	2	442,800
Israel	1	221,400
Italy	10	2,214,000
Ivory Coast	1	221,400
Jamaica	1/4	55,350
Japan	30	6,642,000
Jordan	1/2	110,700
Kenya	1/4	55,350
Kuwait	1	221,400
Lao People's Democratic Republic	1/2	110,700
Lebanon	1/4	55,350
Lesotho	1/8	27,675
Liberia	1/4	55,350
Libyan Arab Jamahiriya	1 1/2	332,100
Liechtenstein	1/2	110,700
Luxembourg	1/2	110,700
Madagascar	1/4	55,350
Malawi	1/8	27,675
Malaysia	3	664,200
Maldives	1/8	27,675
Mali	1/8	27,675
Malta	1/4	55,350
Mauritania	1/4	55,350
Mauritius	1/4	55,350
Mexico	1	221,400
Monaco	1/4	55,350
Mongolia	1/4	55,350
Morocco	1	221,400
Mozambique	1/4	55,350
Namibia†	—	—
Nauru	1/8	27,675
Nepal	1/8	27,675
Netherlands	10	2,214,000
New Zealand	2	442,800
Nicaragua	1/2	110,700
Niger	1/8	27,675
Nigeria	2	442,800
Norway	5	1,107,000
Oman	1/2	110,700
Pakistan	2	442,800
Panama	1/2	110,700
Papua New Guinea	1/2	110,700
Paraguay	1/2	110,700
Peru	1/4	55,350
Philippines	1	221,400
Poland	2	442,800
Portugal	1	221,400
Qatar	1/2	110,700
Republic of Korea	1	221,400
Romania	1/2	110,700
Rwanda	1/8	27,675
Saint Vincent and the Grenadines	1/8	27,675
San Marino	1/4	55,350
Sao Tome and Principe	1/8	27,675
Saudi Arabia	10	2,214,000
Senegal	1	221,400
Sierra Leone	1/8	27,675
Singapore	1	221,400
Somalia	1/8	27,675
South Africa	1	221,400
Spain	3	664,200
Sri Lanka	1/2	110,700
Sudan	1/8	27,675
Suriname	1/4	55,350
Swaziland	1/4	55,350
Sweden	10	2,214,000
Switzerland	10	2,214,000
Syrian Arab Republic	1/2	110,700
Thailand	1 1/2	332,100
Togo	1/4	55,350
Tonga	1/8	27,675
Trinidad and Tobago	1	221,400
Tunisia	1	221,400
Turkey	1	221,400
Uganda	1/8	27,675
Ukrainian SSR	1	221,400
USSR	30	6,642,000
United Arab Emirates	1	221,400
United Kingdom	30	6,642,000
United Republic of Tanzania	1/8	27,675
United States	30	6,642,000
Uruguay	1/2	110,700
Vatican City State	1/4	55,350
Venezuela	2	442,800
Viet Nam	1/2	110,700
Yemen	1/4	55,350
Yugoslavia	1	221,400
Zaire	1/2	110,700
Zambia	1/4	55,350
Zimbabwe	1/2	110,700
Total	393	87,010,200

NOTE: The ITU nomenclature differs from that of the United Nations.

*For the equivalent amounts in United States dollars, the rate of exchange that was to be applicable on 1 January 1985 was 2.58 Swiss francs = $US 1.00.

†Exempt from payment until it accedes to independence.

Annex II. OFFICERS AND OFFICES OF THE INTERNATIONAL TELECOMMUNICATION UNION

ADMINISTRATIVE COUNCIL, INTERNATIONAL FREQUENCY REGISTRATION BOARD AND PRINCIPAL OFFICERS

PRINCIPAL OFFICERS OF THE UNION
Secretary-General: Richard E. Butler.
Deputy Secretary-General: Jean Jipguep.

ITU ADMINISTRATIVE COUNCIL
Algeria *(Chairman)*, Argentina, Australia, Benin, Brazil, Cameroon, Canada, China, Colombia, Egypt, Ethiopia, France, German Democratic Republic, Germany, Federal Republic of, India, Indonesia, Italy, Japan, Kenya, Kuwait, Lebanon, Mexico, Morocco, Nigeria, Pakistan, Peru, Philippines *(Vice-Chairman)*, Romania, Saudi Arabia, Senegal, Spain, Sweden, Switzerland, Thailand, USSR, United Kingdom, United Republic of Tanzania, United States, Venezuela, Yugoslavia, Zambia.

INTERNATIONAL FREQUENCY REGISTRATION BOARD
Chairman: Abderrazak Berrada (Morocco).
Vice-Chairman: Gary C. Brooks (Canada).
Members: William H. Bellchambers (United Kingdom), Petr S. Kurakov (USSR), Yoshitaka Kurihara (Japan).

OFFICERS OF THE INTERNATIONAL CONSULTATIVE COMMITTEES
Director, International Radio Consultative Committee (CCIR): Richard C. Kirby (United States).
Director, International Telegraph and Telephone Consultative Committee (CCITT): Theodor Irmer (Federal Republic of Germany).

HEADQUARTERS

General Secretariat of the International Telecommunication Union
Place des Nations
1211 Geneva 20, Switzerland
  Cable address: BURINTERNA GENEVA
  Telephone: (22) 99 51 11
  Telex: 421000 UIT CH
  Telefax: (Groups 2 and 3) (22) 33 72 56

Chapter XIII

World Meteorological Organization (WMO)

With the admission of Brunei on 26 December, the membership of the World Meteorological Organization (WMO) rose to 158 in 1984—153 States and five territories.

WMO carried out its 1984 work in accordance with the programme and budget adopted for 1984-1987 by the Ninth (1983) World Meteorological Congress, the highest body of WMO, which meets at least once every four years.

The 36-member Executive Council (known as the Executive Committee until 1983[a]), which supervises implementation of Congress resolutions and regulations, held its thirty-sixth session at Geneva from 6 to 23 June 1984.

The twenty-ninth annual International Meteorological Organization Prize, commemorating the non-governmental organization which preceded WMO, was awarded to Thomas F. Malone (United States) for outstanding contributions to the development of international meteorology, leadership in atmospheric sciences and collaboration in meteorology.

Activities in 1984

World Weather Watch

The World Weather Watch (WWW), the basic programme of WMO, continued to provide in 1984 the observational data and processed information required by member States for operational and research purposes. Its essential elements were: the Global Observing System (GOS), which obtained observational data; the Global Data-processing System (GDPS), which provided for processing, storage and retrieval of observational data and made available processed information; and the Global Telecommunication System (GTS), which offered telecommunication facilities and arrangements for rapid and reliable collection, exchange and distribution of observational data and processed information.

The activities of GOS continued under its two sub-systems—one surface-based and the other space-based. The surface-based sub-system provided conventional basic data from regional synoptic networks, other observational networks of stations on land and at sea, and aircraft meteorological observations required for operation and research. In the space-based sub-system, meteorological satellites in near-polar orbiting and geostationary systems took direct observations and provided data collection and dissemination. GOS also provided member States with both quantitative information derived from instrument measurements, such as atmospheric pressure, humidity, air temperature and wind velocity, and qualitative information aimed at describing phenomena by providing information on the state of the sky, forms of clouds and types of precipitation.

Meteorological satellite systems operated by member States and the European Space Agency continued to provide valuable information. Progress was achieved in developing observation systems involving new technology to improve global coverage of observational data, especially from oceans and data-sparse areas. Two important elements for improving GOS—the Aircraft to Satellite Data Relay System for automatic meteorological observations from wide-bodied commercial aircraft and the Automated Shipboard Aerological Programme for upper-air observations from merchant ships and drifting buoy systems—were expected to be operational by 1985-1986.

To assist member States in providing meteorological services required for the socio-economic development of their countries, upgrading to high-quality observations and products was achieved during 1984 on GOS, GDPS and GTS. Steps were taken within GDPS to make available numerical weather prediction and other products to enable countries to provide extended and improved services for various applications of meteorology and operational hydrology. Further improvement in the operation of GTS was achieved through the upgrading of circuits, making them capable of high-speed data transmission, the use of multiplexed channels and the progressive automation of centres for handling increased volumes of traffic.

Ocean affairs

In 1984, WMO continued to promote marine meteorological services over high seas and coastal areas and the application of marine climatological information for planning marine activities. The Commission for Marine Meteorology (CMM) (ninth session, Geneva, 1-12 October) adopted several resolutions and recommendations relating to the Marine Meteorology Programme, and approved its work programme for the four-year inter-sessional period. As the demand for marine meteorological information increased, CMM acted on several issues, including means of improving data coverage of the

[a]YUN 1983, p. 1297.

world's oceans using the latest advances in marine telecommunications, satellite systems and automation techniques. To this end, the Commission approved a plan for a WMO Wave Programme and suggested the establishment of a guide to applications of marine climatology. It also recommended that workshops and seminars on the intercalibration of conventional and remotely sensed marine data be continued, and proposed the creation of a digital sea-ice data bank.

In addition to marine activities co-ordinated by CMM, other ocean-related activities were carried out by the Integrated Global Ocean Services System, a joint WMO/Intergovernmental Oceanographic Commission programme. WMO's support for the meteorological component of the investigation of the phenomenon known as "El Niño" was also continued.

Aviation

At its June session, the Executive Council recommended that the activities of the Aviation Meteorology Programme be expanded and strengthened. In this connection, a revision of WMO Technical Regulations, where they applied to international aviation services, was undertaken in view of their relevance to the World Area Forecast System. Other activities were also being carried out within the Aeronautical Meteorology Programme, in close co-operation with the International Civil Aviation Organization, to assist member States with the aeronautical meteorological services required to ensure the safety, efficiency and economy of air navigation. The WMO Commission for Aeronautical Meteorology recommended the development of work and specific studies aimed at improving forecasting accuracy in respect of meteorological parameters affecting the safety and economy of air navigation.

World Climate Programme

During 1984, the objectives of the World Climate Programme (WCP), which was accorded a high priority by the Ninth (1983) Congress,[b] continued to aid nations in applying climate information to human activities, to improve the knowledge of climate processes and to develop the capability to foresee changes of climate which might affect human activities. Responsibilities within WCP are divided between the World Climate Applications Programme (WCAP), the World Climate Data Programme (WCDP), the World Climate Impact Studies Programme (WCIP) and the World Climate Research Programme (WCRP).

Activities within WCAP included a Technical Conference on Urban Climatology and Its Applications with Special Regard to Tropical Areas (Mexico City, 26-30 November 1984), with 95 participants. Progress was made towards a WMO/WHO/UNEP Symposium

on Climate and Human Health to be held at Leningrad, USSR, in 1985.

WCDP activities included data requirements and data exchange; assistance to countries for the improvement of climate data management systems/services; transfer of technology in climate data processing; information on climate observing stations, data sets and data sources; climate system monitoring (CSM); international co-ordination; and world weather records. At a meeting (Niamey, Niger, 3-7 December) which reviewed climate data management in Africa, deficiencies were identified and remedial action requiring national and international support suggested. Progress was made by an expert meeting (Offenbach, Federal Republic of Germany, July) to define the structure and format for the compilation and preparation of the World Climate Data Information Referral Service catalogue of published data sets. A CSM scientific review meeting (Geneva, 19-23 November), supported by UNEP, developed the first "prototype" CSM review.

The main activity within WCIP, carried out by UNEP in collaboration with WMO, focused on the impact of climate variations on national food systems, assessment of the impact of man's activities on climate (especially increased atmospheric carbon dioxide) and the methodology of climate impact assessments.

WCRP work, conducted jointly by WMO and the International Council of Scientific Unions to determine the extent of climate predictability and of man's influence on climate, included studies on cloud climatology and radiation, ocean-atmosphere interaction and ocean processes, and ozone concentration trends.

Research and development

The Research and Development Programme continued to focus on weather prediction, tropical meteorology, environmental pollution monitoring and weather modification research. The responsibility for promoting and co-ordinating these research activities lay with the WMO Commission for Atmospheric Sciences (CAS).

In 1984, progress was achieved in the implementation of expanded programmes approved by the Ninth Congress concerning short- and medium-range weather prediction research and long-range forecasting research. As requested by the Congress, a Steering Group on Numerical Experimentation was established within CAS (first session, Geneva, 19-21 November) to review, promote and co-ordinate weather prediction research based on data from the First GARP Global Experiment (also known as the Global Weather Experiment) and other Global Atmospheric Research Programme (GARP) experiments and improve operational weather forecast-

[b]*Ibid.*, p. 1298.

ing models and techniques. A WMO workshop on limited-area numerical weather prediction (NWP) models for computers of limited power was held (Erice, Italy, 1-14 October) to discuss the needs of developing countries in implementing NWP systems. At a symposium (Norrköping, Sweden, 3-7 September), experts exchanged experiences and technical information on mesoscale phenomena and their observation and forecasting, as well as economic benefits and user requirements. A CAS Working Group on Long-range Weather Forecasting Research (first session, Geneva, 2-6 April) met to discuss the development of the Programme on Long-range Forecasting Research (PLRF) established by the Ninth Congress and, at another meeting of experts on ocean-atmosphere interaction relevant to long-range weather forecasting (Geneva, 14-16 November), proposals for the development of this aspect of PLRF were formulated.

Efforts were made during the year to implement the WMO Tropical Meteorology Programme (TMP). The CAS Working Group (Geneva, April) reviewed the progress achieved in implementing 12 ongoing specific priority projects within TMP and provided guidance on their implementation. In the monsoon component, a detailed implementation plan was developed by the Steering Committee (Kuala Lumpur, Malaysia, December) for studies of the South-East Asian winter monsoons. Under the semi-arid zone meteorological/tropical drought component, progress was achieved in implementing the long-term project on research and monitoring of the moisture budget in the Sahel, with an activity centre at Niamey.

Under the Environmental Pollution Monitoring and Research Programme, further progress was achieved in the implementation of the Background Air Pollution Monitoring Network (BAPMoN). IAEA laboratories in Vienna and Monaco collaborated in analysing aerosol and precipitation samples from over 50 stations. A panel of experts (Garmisch-Partenkirchen, Federal Republic of Germany, 30 April–4 May) discussed BAPMoN activities, long-range transport of air pollution, integrated monitoring and exchange of pollutants between the atmosphere and the oceans and impact-level air pollution aspects. Other activities included a course on background air pollution measurements (Budapest, Hungary), a seminar on BAPMoN operational functions and on interpretation of data (Kuala Lumpur, October) and the issuance and preparation of publications.

WMO also continued its collaboration in projects on long-range transmission of air pollutants in Europe, mainly through operational Meteorological Synthesizing Centres (MSCs) in Moscow and Oslo, Norway; expert meetings were held in May and November to discuss technical aspects of the intercomparison of routine model calculations used by these two MSCs.

A two-year joint WMO/UNEP/UNESCO pilot project on integrated monitoring—supported by the national meteorological and forest services—was launched during the year in the Torres del Paine National Park (Patagonia, Chile). Air-sea material interchange on the pollutant modification of ocean-related processes—especially those pertinent to climate—was provided by the WMO-led Working Group on the Interchange of Pollutants between the Atmosphere and the Oceans (INTERPOLL). At the request of the Group of Experts on the Scientific Aspects of Marine Pollution (Vienna, 26-30 March), an *ad hoc* expert group was created within INTERPOLL to prepare a report on atmospheric transport of pollutants into the Mediterranean region. Progress was also achieved in the Mediterranean in developing computational models to assess the transport of heavy metals into the sea via the atmosphere. An expert meeting (Spain, December) elaborated an experimental programme aimed at direct (aircraft and ground-based) measuring of the composition of the atmosphere and assessing long-range transport of trace elements from the Atlantic Ocean to the Mediterranean Sea. This experiment will also contribute to the study of long-range transport of air pollutants in Europe and to verifying the vertical and horizontal gradient of selected pollutants in the vicinity of existing BAPMoN baseline stations.

The long-term objectives of the Weather Modification Programme approved by the Ninth Congress were to encourage research activities and to facilitate the exchange of information on weather modification operations and research. As a result, technical papers were issued in 1984 and information was made available to member States, as well as to the United Nations and other international organizations. Among other activities, WMO organized a meeting of experts on the evaluation of hail suppression experiments (Nalchik, USSR, September) and provided information on the status of weather modification to the review conference of the parties to the Convention on the Prohibition of Military or Any Other Hostile Use of Environmental Modification Techniques.[c]

Hydrology and water resources development

The Hydrology and Water Resources Programme—composed of the Operational Hydrology Programme, applications and services to water resources, and co-operation with water-related programmes of other international organizations—was re-established by the Ninth Congress as a major programme for the period 1984-1987 to promote world-wide co-operation in the evaluation of water resources and to assist in their development through the co-ordination of hydrological networks and services.

The Commission for Hydrology—which meets every four years—held its seventh session at Geneva

[c]YUN 1976, p. 45, GA res. 31/72, annex, 10 Dec. 1976.

(August/September 1984) to review the work accomplished during the inter-sessional period 1980-1984.

In 1984, the second phase of the Hydrological Operational Multi-purpose Subprogramme (HOMS) was launched. It was to provide an international and systematic framework for the integration of techniques for data collection and processing. In co-operation with UNDP, WMO organized workshops on river basin simulation (Madras, India, September) and planning and implementation of HOMS in Asia and the South-West Pacific (Bangkok, Thailand, October), and a meeting of representatives of HOMS national reference centres on standardization of HOMS data-processing systems (Geneva, December).

Technical support to other WMO programmes, such as the Tropical Cyclone Programme and the World Climate Programme, continued to be provided. In addition, co-operation with water-related programmes of other international organizations was maintained, in particular with the International Hydrological Programme of UNESCO.

Education and training

The main activities of the Education and Training Programme in 1984 were the awarding of fellowships, strengthening of regional meteorological training centres, organization and co-sponsorship of courses, seminars and workshops, preparation of training publications and other training aids, surveys of training needs, provision of advice and information on education and training, and collaboration with other organizations.

The WMO Executive Council's Panel of Experts on Education and Training (eleventh session, Algeria, 27 February–2 March) reviewed proposals for programme development, with special attention to problems experienced at the WMO Regional Meteorological Training Centres.

Twenty-seven training events organized or co-sponsored by WMO during 1984 covered: tropical meteorology and tropical storm forecasting (United States); Global Telecommunication System operation for North and West Africa (Algeria); hydrological forecasting (United States); operational applications of agrometeorology in semi-arid zones (Italy); limited-area NWP models for computers of limited power and use of NWP products (Italy); BAP-MoN operational functions and interpretation of data (Malaysia); combined use of data from the space-based and ground-based GOS sub-systems (Nepal); teaching methods and techniques for instructors (Italy); instruction for instrument specialists (Argentina); utilization of satellite data and radar meteorology (Mozambique); marine meteorological services (Colombia, Costa Rica, Uruguay); intercalibration of conventional and remotely sensed sea surface temperature data (United States);

agrometeorology (Belgium, USSR); water resources technology in developing countries (United Kingdom); meteorology (Costa Rica); practical use of NWP (United Kingdom); background air pollution monitoring (Hungary); practical techniques for regionalizing and transferring hydrological variables (United Kingdom); disaster prevention and preparedness (Mauritius); satellite applications to flood forecast, control and preparedness (Italy); operational meteorology (Brazil); use of hydrometeorological instruments (Colombia); climatology (Argentina); Integrated Global Ocean Services System operation and data management (Argentina); and operational and applied hydrology (Switzerland).

Over 650 participants, mainly from developing countries, participated in WMO training events and 271 fellowships were awarded and commenced during the year. Financial assistance was also provided to 82 participants in various WMO-supported training events.

Technical co-operation

In 1984, under the WMO technical co-operation programme, assistance was provided to 116 countries through UNDP, the Voluntary Co-operation Programme (VCP), trust-fund arrangements and the WMO regular budget.

Under UNDP, assistance in meteorological and hydrological services development and for personnel training was provided to 88 countries in 1984 at an estimated value of $11.8 million, compared with $11.3 million in 1983. Under UNDP sectoral support in meteorology and operational hydrology, missions were undertaken to 29 countries for the formulation of new projects.

Under VCP, assistance was provided mainly to the GOS element of WWW and to the establishment or updating of automatic picture transmission/weather facsimile and upper-air stations. Fellowships for training meteorological personnel were also awarded. The value of assistance provided under VCP in 1984 amounted to approximately $5.2 million, compared with some $4.9 million in 1983.

Thirty-three fellowships were awarded from WMO's regular budget and financial support was given for participation in group training, technical conferences and study tours. Under the technical co-operation programme, 582 fellows received meteorological or hydrological training during the year: 267 under UNDP, 218 under VCP, 76 under the regular budget and 21 under trust funds. Under the associate expert programme, six young professionals with limited experience worked in association with, and under the guidance of, senior experts. Thirteen United Nations volunteers served in WMO-executed projects during the year—six in Yemen, two each in Botswana and Qatar, and one each in the Gambia, Paraguay and Sierra Leone.

Secretariat

As at 31 December 1984, the total number of full-time staff employed by WMO (excluding 63 professionals on technical assistance projects) on permanent and fixed-term contracts stood at 296. Of these, 134 were in the Professional and higher categories (drawn from 48 nationalities) and 162 in the General Service and related categories.

Budget

The year 1984 was the first year of the ninth financial period (1984-1987), for which the Ninth (1983) Congress had established a maximum expenditure of $77.5 million. It had authorized additional expenditures of no more than $1 million to provide for circumstances such as losses resulting from currency exchange rate changes or urgent unforeseen programme activities.

The regular budget for 1984 amounted to $18,750,000; the budget for technical co-operation activities, financed from overhead allocations and other extrabudgetary sources, amounted to an additional $2,545,300.

At its June 1984 session, the Executive Council approved the following regular budget for 1985.

	Amount (in US dollars)
Income	
Contributions	19,480,000
Total	19,480,000
Expenditure	
Policy-making organs	478,400
Executive management	892,900
Scientific and technical programmes	
World Weather Watch	2,840,100
World Climate Programme	2,343,900
Education and training	1,484,500
Regional programme	1,319,900
Research and development	1,309,900
Hydrology and water resources	899,000
Overall co-ordination	248,600
Technical co-operation activities	209,400
Programme supporting activities	3,865,300
Administration and common services	3,117,900
Other budgetary provisions	470,200
Total	19,480,000

Annex I. MEMBERSHIP OF THE WORLD METEOROLOGICAL ORGANIZATION AND CONTRIBUTIONS

(Membership as at 31 December 1984; contributions as assessed for 1985)

MEMBER	CONTRIBUTION Percentage	Net amount (in US dollars)	MEMBER	CONTRIBUTION Percentage	Net amount (in US dollars)	MEMBER	CONTRIBUTION Percentage	Net amount (in US dollars)
Afghanistan	0.04	7,708	Cyprus	0.04	7,708	Indonesia	0.51	98,277
Albania	0.04	7,708	Czechoslovakia	0.90	173,430	Iran	0.45	86,715
Algeria	0.10	19,270	Democratic Kampuchea	0.04	7,708	Iraq	0.09	17,343
Angola	0.07	13,489	Democratic People's			Ireland	0.25	48,175
Argentina	1.18	227,386	Republic			Israel	0.26	50,102
Australia	1.73	333,371	of Korea	0.08	15,416	Italy	2.59	499,093
Austria	0.62	119,474	Democratic Yemen	0.04	7,708	Ivory Coast	0.08	15,416
Bahamas	0.04	7,708	Denmark	0.72	138,744	Jamaica	0.08	15,416
Bahrain	0.04	7,708	Djibouti	0.04	7,708	Japan	4.45	857,515
Bangladesh	0.04	7,708	Dominica	0.04	7,708	Jordan	0.04	7,708
Barbados	0.04	7,708	Dominican Republic	0.08	15,416	Kenya	0.04	7,708
Belgium	1.26	242,802	Ecuador	0.08	15,416	Kuwait	0.17	32,759
Belize	0.04	7,708	Egypt	0.35	67,445	Lao People's Democratic		
Benin	0.04	7,708	El Salvador	0.04	7,708	Republic	0.04	7,708
Bolivia	0.12	23,124	Ethiopia	0.04	7,708	Lebanon	0.08	15,416
Botswana	0.04	7,708	Fiji	0.04	7,708	Lesotho	0.04	7,708
Brazil	1.35	260,145	Finland	0.52	100,204	Liberia	0.04	7,708
Brunei	0.03	5,781	France	5.08	978,916	Libyan Arab Jamahiriya	0.14	26,978
Bulgaria	0.31	59,737	Gabon	0.04	7,708	Luxembourg	0.09	17,343
Burkina Faso	0.04	7,708	Gambia	0.04	7,708	Madagascar	0.04	7,708
Burma	0.10	19,270	German Democratic			Malawi	0.04	7,708
Burundi	0.04	7,708	Republic	1.38	265,926	Malaysia	0.30	57,810
Byelorussian SSR	0.47	90,569	Germany, Federal			Maldives	0.04	7,708
Cameroon	0.04	7,708	Republic of	5.81	1,119,587	Mali	0.04	7,708
Canada	2.72	524,144	Ghana	0.10	19,270	Malta	0.04	7,708
Cape Verde	0.04	7,708	Greece	0.31	59,737	Mauritania	0.04	7,708
Central African Republic	0.04	7,708	Guatemala	0.08	15,416	Mauritius	0.04	7,708
Chad	0.04	7,708	Guinea	0.04	7,708	Mexico	0.86	165,722
Chile	0.29	55,883	Guinea-Bissau	0.04	7,708	Mongolia	0.04	7,708
China	3.09	595,443	Guyana	0.04	7,708	Morocco	0.15	28,905
Colombia	0.26	50,102	Haiti	0.04	7,708	Mozambique	0.07	13,489
Comoros	0.04	7,708	Honduras	0.04	7,708	Nepal	0.04	7,708
Congo	0.04	7,708	Hungary	0.46	88,642	Netherlands	1.28	246,656
Costa Rica	0.08	15,416	Iceland	0.08	15,416	New Zealand	0.48	92,496
Cuba	0.22	42,394	India	1.46	281,342	Nicaragua	0.04	7,708

MEMBER	CONTRIBUTION Percent-age	Net amount (in US dollars)	MEMBER	CONTRIBUTION Percent-age	Net amount (in US dollars)	MEMBER	CONTRIBUTION Percent-age	Net amount (in US dollars)
Niger	0.04	7,708	Seychelles	0.04	7,708	USSR	10.31	1,986,737
Nigeria	0.25	48,175	Sierra Leone	0.04	7,708	United Kingdom	5.42	1,044,434
Norway	0.61	117,547	Singapore	0.09	17,343	United Republic of Tanzania	0.04	7,708
Oman	0.04	7,708	Somalia	0.04	7,708	United States	24.45	4,711,515
Pakistan	0.18	34,686	South Africa*	0.71	136,817	Uruguay	0.23	44,321
Panama	0.08	15,416	Spain	1.41	271,707	Vanuatu	0.04	7,708
Papua New Guinea	0.04	7,708	Sri Lanka	0.12	23,124	Venezuela	0.54	104,058
Paraguay	0.04	7,708	Sudan	0.09	17,343	Viet Nam	0.08	15,416
Peru	0.26	50,102	Suriname	0.04	7,708	Yemen	0.04	7,708
Philippines	0.33	63,591	Swaziland	0.04	7,708	Yugoslavia	0.52	100,204
Poland	1.16	223,532	Sweden	1.37	263,999	Zaire	0.10	19,270
Portugal	0.25	48,175	Switzerland	1.15	221,605	Zambia	0.07	13,489
Qatar	0.08	15,416	Syrian Arab Republic	0.14	26,978	Zimbabwe	0.04	7,708
Republic of Korea	0.18	34,686	Thailand	0.26	50,102			
Romania	0.36	69,372	Togo	0.04	7,708	British Caribbean Territories	0.04	7,708
Rwanda	0.04	7,708	Trinidad and Tobago	0.08	15,416	French Polynesia	0.04	7,708
Saint Lucia	0.04	7,708	Tunisia	0.08	15,416	Hong Kong	0.04	7,708
Sao Tome and Principe	0.04	7,708	Turkey	0.48	92,496	Netherlands Antilles	0.04	7,708
Saudi Arabia	0.34	65,518	Uganda	0.04	7,708	New Caledonia	0.04	7,708
Senegal	0.04	7,708	Ukrainian SSR	1.54	296,758	Total	100.03	19,275,781

*Suspended by the Seventh (1975) WMO Congress from exercising the rights and privileges of a member.

Annex II.   OFFICERS AND OFFICE OF THE WORLD METEOROLOGICAL ORGANIZATION

MEMBERS OF THE WMO EXECUTIVE COUNCIL

President: R. L. Kintanar (Philippines).
First Vice-President: Ju. A. Izrael (USSR).
Second Vice-President: Zou Jingmeng (China).
Third Vice-President: J. P. Bruce (Canada).
Members (one seat vacant): S. P. Adhikary (Nepal), S. Aguilar Anguiano* (Mexico), L.-K. Ahialegbezdi (Togo), S. Alaimo (Argentina), M. A. Badran (Egypt), A. Bensari (Morocco), C. E. Berridge (British Caribbean Territories), C. M. Contreras Viñals (Spain) (acting), S. K. Das (India), Workineh Degefu* (Ethiopia), J. Djig-

benou (Ivory Coast), H. Gonzáles Pacheco (Peru) (acting), J. González-Montoto (Cuba), C. A. Grezzi* (Uruguay), R. E. Hallgren (United States), J. T. Houghton (United Kingdom) (acting), E. J. Jatila (Finland), S. A. A. Kazmi* (Pakistan), J. P. N. Labrousse (France), U. B. Lifiga (United Republic of Tanzania) (acting), G. Mankedi (Congo), L. A. Mendes Victor* (Portugal) (acting), A. Nania (Italy), C. Padilha (Brazil), V. Richter (Czechoslovakia), R. M. Romaih (Saudi Arabia), M. Seck (Senegal), V. A. Simango (Zambia), S. Suyehiro (Japan), Ho Tong Yuen* (Malaysia), J. W. Zillman (Australia).

NOTE: The Executive Council is composed of four elected officers, the six Presidents of the regional associations (indicated by an asterisk), who are *ex-officio* members, and 26 elected members. Members serve in their personal capacities, not as representatives of Governments.

SENIOR MEMBERS OF THE WMO SECRETARIAT

Secretary-General: G. O. P. Obasi.
Deputy Secretary-General: D. K. Smith.
Director, Scientific and Technical Programmes: R. Czelnai.
Director, World Weather Watch Department: G. K. Weiss.
Director, Research and Development Department: A. Zaitsev.
Director, Hydrology and Water Resources Department: J. Nemec.
Director, Technical Co-operation Department: G. Gosset.
Director, Education and Training Department: M. J. Connaughton.
Director, Administration Department: J. K. Murithi.

Director, Languages, Publications and Conferences Department: A. W. Kabakibo.
Director, World Climate Programme Department: T. D. Potter.
Director, World Climate Research Programme: P. Morel.
Regional Director for Africa: S. Chacowry.
Regional Director for the Americas: I. G. Meira-Filho.
Regional Director for Asia and the South-West Pacific: K. Rajendram.
Special Assistant to the Secretary-General: A. K. Elamly.
Executive Assistant to the Secretary-General: J. B. L. Breslin.

PRESIDENTS OF REGIONAL ASSOCIATIONS AND TECHNICAL COMMISSIONS

REGIONAL ASSOCIATIONS

I.   Africa: Workineh Degefu (Ethiopia).
II.   Asia: S. A. A. Kazmi (Pakistan).
III.   South America: C. A. Grezzi (Uruguay).

IV.   North and Central America: S. Aguilar Anguiano (Mexico).
V.   South-West Pacific: Ho Tong Yuen (Malaysia).
VI.   Europe: L. A. Mendes Victor (Portugal) (acting).

TECHNICAL COMMISSIONS

Aeronautical Meteorology: J. Kastelein (Netherlands).
Agricultural Meteorology: M. N. Gerbier (France).
Atmospheric Sciences: F. Mesinger (Yugoslavia).
Basic Systems: J. R. Neilon (United States).

Climatology: J. L. Rasmussen (United States).
Hydrology: O. Starosolszky (Hungary).
Instruments and Methods of Observation: S. Huovila (Finland).
Marine Meteorology: F. Gérard (France).

HEADQUARTERS

World Meteorological Organization
41, Avenue Giuseppe-Motta
Case Postale No. 5
1211 Geneva 20, Switzerland
  Cable address: METEOMOND GENEVA
  Telephone: 34 64 00
  Telex: 23260

Chapter XIV

International Maritime Organization (IMO)

During 1984, several legal instruments adopted under the auspices of the International Maritime Organization (IMO) entered into force, while various new measures were adopted.

Following the entry into force on 10 November 1984 of the 1979 amendments to the IMO Convention, membership of the IMO Council increased from 24 to 32 member States.

As at 31 December 1984, IMO membership stood at 127 and one associate member. New members admitted during the year were Viet Nam (12 June) and Brunei Darussalam (31 December).

Activities in 1984

Safe containers

Amendments to the International Convention for Safe Containers, 1972, which were adopted in June 1983, entered into force on 1 January 1984. The amendments dealt with container examinations and testing procedures.

Training

The International Convention on Standards of Training, Certification and Watchkeeping for Seafarers, 1978, entered into force on 28 April 1984. The Convention established minimum standards of training, certification and watchkeeping for masters, officers and crew members.

Liability and compensation

The International Conference on Liability and Compensation for Damage in Connection with the Carriage of certain Substances by Sea, which was held at IMO headquarters (30 April–25 May 1984), adopted amendments to the International Convention on Civil Liability for Oil Pollution Damage, 1969, and the International Convention on the Establishment of an International Fund for Compensation for Oil Pollution Damage, 1971. As a result, liability limits of both instruments were increased substantially.

A proposed convention on liability and compensation for damage caused by hazardous and noxious substances was to be studied further by IMO.

Facilitation

The 1973 amendments to the Convention on Facilitation of International Maritime Traffic, 1965, entered into force on 2 June 1984. These amendments would enable any future changes to be implemented much faster than previously.

Search and rescue

The conditions for entry into force of the the International Convention on Maritime Search and Rescue, 1979, were fulfilled on 21 June 1984. The Convention was to enter into force on 22 June 1985.

Safety of life at sea

Amendments to the International Convention for the Safety of Life at Sea, 1974 (SOLAS Convention), entered into force on 1 September 1984. These amendments had been adopted by the IMO Maritime Safety Committee in 1981.

Prevention of pollution

Amendments to the International Convention for the Prevention of Pollution from Ships, 1973, as modified by the 1978 Protocol which entered into force in 1983 (MARPOL 73/78),[a] were adopted by the Marine Environment Protection Committee on 7 September 1984. The amendments, affecting regulations designed to combat pollution by oil, were to enter into force on 7 January 1986.

A seminar on reception facilities for shipborne wastes was held at IMO headquarters (30-31 August 1984) to assist compliance with measures contained in the Convention and Protocol.

IMO Convention

The 1977 and 1979 amendments to the IMO Convention entered into force on 10 November 1984. The main effect of the 1977 amendments was to institutionalize the Technical Co-operation Committee by making reference to it throughout the Convention, while the 1979 amendments increased the size of the IMO Council from 24 to 32 member States.

International Conventions

IMO performed depositary and related functions in respect of the following international conventions and other treaty instruments almost all of which were adopted under its auspices:

International Convention for the Safety of Life at Sea, 1948, 1960

International Convention for the Safety of Life at Sea, 1974 and the 1978 Protocol relating thereto (replacing and superseding the 1948 and 1960 instruments)

International Convention for the Prevention of Pollution of the Sea by Oil, 1954, as amended in 1962 and 1969

---

[a]YUN 1983, p. 1303.

International Convention for the Prevention of Pollution from Ships, 1973, and the 1978 Protocol relating thereto (replacing and superseding the 1954 instrument)

Convention on Facilitation of International Maritime Traffic, 1965, as amended in 1973

International Convention on Load Lines, 1966

International Convention on Tonnage Measurement of Ships, 1969

International Convention Relating to Intervention on the High Seas in Cases of Oil Pollution Casualties, 1969

Protocol Relating to Intervention on the High Seas in Cases of Pollution by Substances Other Than Oil, 1973

International Convention on Civil Liability for Oil Pollution Damage, 1969

Protocol of 1976 to the International Convention on Civil Liability for Oil Pollution Damage, 1969

Protocol of 1984 to amend the International Convention on Civil Liability for Oil Pollution Damage, 1969

Convention on Limitation of Liability for Maritime Claims, 1976

International Convention on the Establishment of an International Fund for Compensation for Oil Pollution Damage, 1971

Protocol of 1976 to the International Convention on the Establishment of an International Fund for Compensation for Oil Pollution Damage, 1971

Protocol of 1984 to amend the International Convention on the Establishment of an International Fund for Compensation for Oil Pollution Damage, 1971

Convention Relating to Civil Liability in the Field of Maritime Carriage of Nuclear Materials, 1971

Special Trade Passenger Ships Agreement, 1971

Protocol on Space Requirements for Special Trade Passenger Ships, 1973

Convention on the International Regulations for Preventing Collisions at Sea, 1972, as amended in 1981

International Convention for Safe Containers, 1972, as amended in 1981

Athens Convention Relating to the Carriage of Passengers and Their Luggage by Sea, 1974

Protocol to the Athens Convention Relating to the Carriage of Passengers and Their Luggage by Sea, 1974

Convention on the International Maritime Satellite Organization, 1976

Operating Agreement on the International Maritime Satellite Organization, 1976

Torremolinos International Convention for the Safety of Fishing Vessels, 1977

International Convention on Standards of Training, Certification and Watchkeeping for Seafarers, 1978

International Convention on Maritime Search and Rescue, 1979

Convention on the Prevention of Marine Pollution by Dumping of Wastes and Other Matter, 1972

World Maritime Day

The theme for World Maritime Day (27 September 1984) was Global co-operation for the training of maritime personnel. On that day, the International Maritime Prize, awarded annually for the most significant contribution to the work and objectives of IMO, was awarded to Hjalmar R. Bardarson of Iceland.

In his World Maritime Day message, the IMO Secretary-General announced the launching of an appeal to raise $25 million for the World Maritime University, established at Malmö, Sweden, in 1983.[b]

Publications

Among publications issued by IMO during 1984 were: amendment No. 5 to *Ships' Routeing*; the *Code for Special Purpose Ships; Resolutions and other decisions of the thirteenth IMO Assembly* (November 1983); the amended *IMO Convention*; amendments Nos. 21-83 and 21-84 to the *International Maritime Dangerous Goods Code*; amendments to the *Medical First Aid Guide for use in Accidents involving Dangerous Goods*; and a supplement to *Facilities in Ports for the Reception of Oily Wastes*.

Secretariat

As at 31 December 1984, the IMO secretariat employed 270 full-time staff members (excluding those on technical assistance projects). Of these, 90 were in the Professional and higher categories and 180 were in the General Service and related categories. There were 30 Professional and 8 General Service staff employed on technical assistance projects.

Budget

In November 1983, the IMO Assembly had adopted a budget of $25.8 million for the 1984-1985 biennium ($12.6 million for 1984 and $13.2 million for 1985).

[b]*Ibid.*

Annex I.   MEMBERSHIP OF THE INTERNATIONAL MARITIME ORGANIZATION AND CONTRIBUTIONS

(Membership as at 31 December 1984; contributions as assessed for 1984)

MEMBER	CONTRIBUTION Percentage of total	Net amount (in US dollars)	MEMBER	CONTRIBUTION Percentage of total	Net amount (in US dollars)	MEMBER	CONTRIBUTION Percentage of total	Net amount (in US dollars)
Algeria	0.36	37,783	Austria	0.12	12,214	Barbados	0.04	4,623
Angola	0.05	4,811	Bahamas	0.21	22,823	Belgium	0.64	68,165
Argentina	0.63	67,398	Bahrain	0.02	2,296	Benin	0.02	2,296
Australia	0.59	62,263	Bangladesh	0.11	11,556	Brazil	1.42	150,941

MEMBER	CONTRIBUTION Percentage of total	Net amount (in US dollars)	MEMBER	CONTRIBUTION Percentage of total	Net amount (in US dollars)	MEMBER	CONTRIBUTION Percentage of total	Net amount (in US dollars)
Brunei Darussalam*	—	—	Hungary	0.07	7,638	Republic of Korea	1.46	155,295
Bulgaria	0.34	36,002	Iceland	0.06	6,849	Romania	0.58	61,721
Burma	0.05	5,162	India	1.46	155,398	Saint Lucia	0.02	2,296
Cameroon	0.02	2,296	Indonesia	0.48	51,391	Saint Vincent and the		
Canada	0.97	102,989	Iran	0.48	51,588	Grenadines	0.04	4,530
Cape Verde	0.02	2,296	Iraq	0.40	42,280	Saudi Arabia	1.25	133,614
Chile	0.16	17,147	Ireland	0.10	10,940	Senegal	0.02	2,296
China	2.00	212,736	Israel	0.21	21,879	Seychelles	0.02	2,296
Colombia	0.13	14,126	Italy	2.42	258,282	Sierra Leone	0.02	2,296
Congo	0.02	2,296	Ivory Coast	0.06	6,263	Singapore	1.60	169,887
Costa Rica	0.02	2,296	Jamaica	0.02	2,296	Somalia	0.02	2,296
Cuba	0.27	28,226	Japan	9.67	1,029,890	Spain	1.79	190,690
Cyprus	0.78	83,464	Jordan	0.02	2,296	Sri Lanka	0.11	11,556
Czechoslovakia	0.13	13,854	Kenya	0.02	2,296	Sudan	0.05	4,858
Democratic Kampuchea	0.02	2,296	Kuwait	0.61	65,398	Suriname	0.02	2,296
Democratic Yemen	0.02	2,296	Lebanon	0.13	13,407	Sweden	0.90	95,312
Denmark	1.21	129,351	Liberia	14.88	1,585,193	Switzerland	0.21	22,421
Djibouti	0.02	2,296	Libyan Arab Jamahiriya	0.29	30,718	Syrian Arab		
Dominica	0.02	2,296	Madagascar	0.04	4,459	Republic	0.02	2,296
Dominican Republic	0.02	2,296	Malaysia	0.38	40,265	Thailand	0.18	18,998
Ecuador	0.11	11,744	Maldives	0.07	6,942	Togo	0.04	3,897
Egypt	0.20	21,246	Malta	0.22	23,900	Trinidad and Tobago	0.02	2,296
El Salvador	0.02	2,296	Mauritania	0.02	2,296	Tunisia	0.08	8,980
Equatorial Guinea	0.02	2,296	Mauritius	0.02	2,296	Turkey	0.65	68,663
Ethiopia	0.02	2,296	Mexico	0.41	44,092	USSR	6.11	650,371
Fiji	0.02	2,296	Morocco	0.11	11,931	United Arab Emirates	0.12	12,767
Finland	0.61	64,775	Mozambique	0.02	2,296	United Kingdom	4.43	471,570
France	2.54	270,146	Nepal	0.02	2,296	United Republic of		
Gabon	0.04	4,483	Netherlands	1.23	130,610	Tanzania	0.04	4,038
Gambia	0.02	2,296	New Zealand	0.15	15,423	United States	4.96	528,783
German Democratic			Nicaragua	0.02	2,296	Uruguay	0.07	7,739
Republic	0.45	48,186	Nigeria	0.16	16,585	Venezuela	0.30	32,334
Germany, Federal			Norway	4.32	459,964	Viet Nam†	—	4,479
Republic of	1.88	200,557	Oman	0.02	2,296	Yemen	0.02	2,296
Ghana	0.08	8,605	Pakistan	0.18	18,716	Yugoslavia	0.65	69,202
Greece	8.33	887,383	Panama	7.65	814,630	Zaire	0.05	4,811
Guatemala	0.02	2,296	Papua New Guinea	0.02	2,296			
Guinea	0.02	2,296	Peru	0.23	24,010	ASSOCIATE MEMBER		
Guinea-Bissau	0.02	2,296	Philippines	0.71	75,142	Hong Kong	0.49	52,086
Guyana	0.02	2,296	Poland	0.90	95,880			
Haiti	0.02	2,296	Portugal	0.35	37,525	Total	100.0	10,658,279
Honduras	0.07	7,856	Qatar	0.09	10,034			

*Became a member on 31 December 1984.

†Became a member on 12 June 1984.

Annex II. OFFICERS AND OFFICES OF THE INTERNATIONAL MARITIME ORGANIZATION
(As at 31 December 1984)

IMO COUNCIL AND MARITIME SAFETY COMMITTEE

IMO COUNCIL

Chairman: W. A. O'Neill (Canada).

Members: Algeria, Argentina, Bangladesh, Brazil, Bulgaria, Canada, Chile, China, Cuba, Egypt, France, Gabon, Germany, Federal Republic of, Ghana, Greece, India, Indonesia, Italy, Japan, Kuwait, Lebanon, Liberia, Morocco, Nigeria, Netherlands, Norway, Saudi Arabia, Spain, Trinidad and Tobago, USSR, United Kingdom, United States.

MARITIME SAFETY COMMITTEE

Chairman: E. Jansen (Norway)

Membership in the Maritime Safety Committee is open to all member States.

OFFICERS AND OFFICES

PRINCIPAL OFFICERS OF IMO SECRETARIAT

Secretary-General: Chandrika Prasad Srivastava.

Assistant Secretary-General: T. A. Mensah.

Secretary, Maritime Safety Committee: Y. Sasamura.

HEADQUARTERS

International Maritime Organization
4 Albert Embankment
London, SE1 7SR, England
  Cable address: INTERMAR LONDON
  Telephone: 01-735-7611
  Telex: 23588

Chapter XV

World Intellectual Property Organization (WIPO)

During 1984, membership of the World Intellectual Property Organization (WIPO) rose to 109 with the admission of Cyprus, New Zealand, Rwanda and Venezuela. Berne Union membership increased to 76 as a result of the accession of Rwanda to the Berne Convention for the Protection of Literary and Artistic Works. Barbados, China, Rwanda and the Sudan acceded to the Paris Convention for the Protection of Industrial Property, bringing membership of the Paris Union to 96.

Sixteen intergovernmental Unions in the two main areas of intellectual property were administered by WIPO in 1984. They were founded on the multilateral treaties, conventions and agreements listed below in order of adoption:

Industrial property: Paris Convention for the Protection of Industrial Property; Madrid Agreement for the Repression of False or Deceptive Indications of Source on Goods; Madrid Agreement concerning the International Registration of Marks; The Hague Agreement concerning the International Deposit of Industrial Designs; Nice Agreement concerning the International Classification of Goods and Services for the Purpose of the Registration of Marks; Lisbon Agreement for the Protection of Appellations of Origin and Their International Registration; Locarno Agreement establishing an International Classification for Industrial Designs; Patent Co-operation Treaty (PCT); International Patent Classification (IPC) Agreement; Trade Mark Registration Treaty; Budapest Treaty on the International Recognition of the Deposit of Micro-organisms for the Purposes of Patent Procedure; Nairobi Treaty on the Protection of the Olympic Symbol.

Copyright and neighbouring rights: Berne Convention for the Protection of Literary and Artistic Works; Rome Convention for the Protection of Performers, Producers of Phonograms and Broadcasting Organizations; Geneva Convention for the Protection of Producers of Phonograms against Unauthorized Duplication of Their Phonograms; Brussels Convention relating to the Distribution of Programme-Carrying Signals Transmitted by Satellite.

At the fifteenth series of meetings, held at Geneva in September 1984, the governing bodies of WIPO and the Unions administered by it approved reports on activities, and the Co-ordination Committee decided to nominate Arpad Bogsch for reappointment by the WIPO General Assembly at its 1985 session for a six-year term as Director General of WIPO.

Activities in 1984

Development co-operation activities

Two WIPO permanent programmes, supervised by intergovernmental permanent committees, provided the framework for development co-operation relating to industrial property and to copyright and neighbouring rights.

Regarding development co-operation relating to industrial property, WIPO organized the following meetings: a training course on industrial property for developing countries of Asia and the Pacific (Colombo, Sri Lanka), seminars on the role of industrial property in technological and economic development (Dhaka, Bangladesh; Islamabad and Karachi, Pakistan), a seminar on patent licensing in industry (Jakarta, Indonesia), a trade mark seminar (Beijing, China), a workshop on the law of intellectual property (Maseru, Lesotho), a seminar on industrial property for Portuguese-speaking African countries (Lisbon, Portugal), a seminar on the use of trade marks and patents in trade and industry (Singapore), a seminar on the use of industrial property for trade and industry (Port Moresby, Papua New Guinea), a seminar for industrial property agents and lawyers (Nairobi, Kenya), a workshop on patent drafting and patent agency (Kuala Lumpur, Malaysia), a seminar on trade marks (Hanoi, Viet Nam), a course on patent classification and documentation (San José, Costa Rica), a meeting of the heads of industrial property offices of the countries of the Central American isthmus, and a course on office organization and management (Panama), a meeting of industrial property directors from Argentina, Chile, Paraguay and Uruguay (Montevideo, Uruguay), a training course on trade marks for the Andean countries (Caracas, Venezuela), a regional meeting on industrial property for Latin America and the Caribbean (Bogotá, Colombia), and a seminar on industrial property for the member States of the Co-operation Council for the Arab States of the Gulf (Riyadh, Saudi Arabia).

Medals and prizes for inventors were awarded by WIPO at exhibitions and competitions held in Bulgaria, China, Egypt, France, the Federal Republic of Germany, Japan, the Philippines, the Republic of Korea, Switzerland and the USSR.

In continuation of a programme initiated in 1975, 270 state-of-the-art search reports on technology disclosed in patent documents and related literature were furnished to developing countries, free of charge, under agreements concluded between WIPO and contributing industrial property offices in developed countries. Most of the reports were prepared by the Federal Republic of Germany (103), Austria (57), the German Democratic Republic (38), Sweden (25) and Australia (15).

Development co-operation activities in copyright and neighbouring rights included the convening, by WIPO, of a subregional course (Manila, Philippines), a specialized training course (Montevideo), a specialized training course on the administration of those rights (Zurich, Switzerland) and a general introductory course (London). In addition, a regional committee of experts on means of implementation in the Arab States of model provisions on intellectual property aspects of protection of expressions of folklore, convened by WIPO and the United Nations Educational, Scientific and Cultural Organization (UNESCO), met at Doha, Qatar.

Within the framework of the WIPO training programmes in industrial property and in copyright, training courses were organized also at Geneva, The Hague, Madrid, Moscow, Munich, Rio de Janeiro, Stockholm and Strasbourg. The training programmes in both areas continued to grow, with 216 fellowships granted in 1984 to nationals of 76 developing countries.

WIPO also co-operated during 1984 with Governments of 69 developing countries and with eight intergovernmental organizations in their development projects relating to intellectual property, by assisting in the preparation of legislation, or establishment or modernization of national or regional institutions, including patent documentation and information services.

Industrial property

The fourth session of the Diplomatic Conference on the Revision of the Paris Convention took place at Geneva from 27 February to 23 March 1984. It recommended to the Paris Union Assembly that it reconvene the Conference as soon as it found prospects for positive results and asked the Assembly to consider setting up machinery for consultations designed to prepare, in substance, the Conference's next session. The Assembly, at an extraordinary session (24-28 September), decided that the machinery would consist of consultative meetings, the first to take place in June 1985. The object of the Convention's revision was to introduce special provisions to meet developing countries' needs more effectively and to incorporate new provisions giving full recognition to inventors' certificates, a form of protection of inventions existing in some socialist countries.

Work continued on keeping up to date IPC and other classifications relating to industrial designs or registration of trade marks and service marks; the fourth edition of the *International Patent Classification* was published in nine volumes in June 1984. As in the past, WIPO assisted the International Patent Documentation Centre and remained on its Supervisory Board. Efforts continued towards early conclusion of the Computerized Administration of Patent Documents Reclassified According to IPC.

At the end of 1984, 39 States were party to PCT. During the year, 5,733 international applications were filed. Thirty issues of the *PCT Gazette* were published in 1984, containing information on 5,012 published international applications.

Meetings were convened of a Committee of Experts on the Grace Period for Public Disclosure of an Invention Before Filing an Application (Geneva) and of a Working Group on Technical Questions relating to the Legal Protection of Computer Software (Canberra, Australia); the WIPO *Joint Inventive Activity Guide* was published.

Publications on industrial property included those on industrial property statistics and on industrial property laws and treaties, the monthly review *Industrial Property* and several guides on related activities.

Copyright and neighbouring rights

In 1984, meetings were convened, jointly with ILO, UNESCO or both, on questions of copyright and neighbouring rights: a discussion meeting on the possible contents of copyright legislation concerning employee authors (Geneva), a group of experts on the international protection of expressions of folklore by intellectual property (Paris), a group of experts on unauthorized private copying of recordings, broadcasts and printed matter (Geneva), a group of experts on the rental of phonograms and videograms (Paris), and a group of consultants on the advisability of setting up an international register of audiovisual works (Geneva).

Publications on copyright included copyright laws and treaties, a *Guide de la Convention de Madrid sur la double imposition* and the monthly periodical *Copyright*.

Secretariat

As at 31 December 1984, WIPO employed 252 full-time staff members. Of those, 89 were in the Professional and higher categories (drawn from 38 member States); 163 were in the General Service category. In addition, 71 experts were employed on development co-operation projects during the year.

Budget

The principal sources of the WIPO budget—approximately 86 million Swiss francs for the 1984-

1985 biennium—are ordinary and special contributions from member States and income derived from international registration services.

Ordinary contributions are paid on the basis of a class-and-unit system by members of the Paris, Berne, Nice, Locarno and IPC Unions and by WIPO member States that do not belong to any of the Unions.

States members of those five Unions are placed in seven classes (I to VII) to determine the amounts of their ordinary contributions. Other WIPO member States are placed in three classes (A, B or C) for the same purpose. States in Class I or A pay the highest contributions of their group and those in Class VII or C the lowest. The class in which a State is placed is decided solely by the State. The rights of each State are the same, irrespective of class chosen.

The contribution class for each member State of WIPO and of the Paris or Berne Unions, together with the amount of the ordinary contribution of each State, is given in Annex I below (the class indicated for the Paris Union also applies to the Nice, Locarno and IPC Unions). Members of the Paris or Berne Unions do not pay separate contributions to WIPO; the Unions themselves contribute towards the costs of WIPO's International Bureau and programme of legal-technical assistance.

The amounts of ordinary contributions for 1984 and 1985 are given in the table below.

Income and expenditure

Summary figures for income and expenditure for 1984-1985 are as follows:

	In thousands of Swiss francs	Equivalent in thousands of US dollars*
Income		
Contributions	40,065	19,170
Income from registration services	40,908	19,573
Publications and miscellaneous	8,416	4,027
Total	89,389	42,770
Expenditure		
Staff	55,449	26,531
Publications	4,538	2,171
Buildings†	9,759	4,669
Travel	2,732	1,307
Meetings	1,179	564
Other	13,093	6,265
Total	86,750	41,507

*At the United Nations rate of exchange for December 1985: 2.09 Swiss francs = $US 1.00.

†Includes maintenance, rental and amortization of the building loan.

CONTRIBUTION SCALES FOR 1985

(2.50 Swiss francs = $US 1.00: United Nations rate as at 31 December 1984)

	In Swiss francs	Equivalent in US dollars			In Swiss francs	Equivalent in US dollars
WIPO*				II	†	†
Class				III	10,764	4,306
A	75,000	30,000		IV	7,176	2,870
B	22,500	9,000		V	3,589	1,436
C	7,500	3,000		VI	2,153	861
PARIS UNION				VII	†	†
Class				**BERNE UNION**		
I	509,791	203,916		*Class*		
II	†	†		I	296,970	118,788
III	305,874	122,350		II	237,576	95,030
IV	203,917	81,567		III	178,182	71,273
V	101,959	40,784		IV	118,789	47,516
VI	61,175	24,470		V	59,395	23,758
VII	20,392	8,157		VI	35,636	14,254
NICE UNION				VII	11,879	4,752
Class				**IPC UNION**		
I	46,301	18,520		*Class*		
II	†	†		I	242,479	96,992
III	27,781	11,112		II	†	†
IV	18,521	7,408		III	145,488	58,195
V	9,259	3,704		IV	96,991	38,796
VI	5,556	2,222		V	†	†
VII	1,853	741		VI	29,097	11,639
LOCARNO UNION				VII	9,699	3,880
Class						
I	17,941	7,176		Total	2,921,183	1,168,473

NOTE: There were no contributions to the PCT Union for 1985.

*The amounts indicated are payable by those States members of WIPO which are not members of any of the Unions (see Annex I).

†No State currently belonged to this class.

Annex I. MEMBERSHIP OF THE WORLD INTELLECTUAL PROPERTY ORGANIZATION AND UNIONS ADMINISTERED TO WHICH CONTRIBUTIONS ARE PAYABLE
(As at 31 December 1984; ordinary contributions payable in 1985)

STATE OR OTHER	MEMBER						CLASS W	CLASS P	CLASS B	CONTRIBUTION In Swiss francs	Equivalent in US dollars*
Algeria	W	P	—	N	—	—	—	VI	—	66,731	26,692
Argentina	W	P	B	—	—	—	—	VI	VI	96,811	38,724
Australia	W	P	B	N	—	IPC	—	III	III	657,325	262,930
Austria	W	P	B	N	—	IPC	—	IV	VI	355,065	142,027
Bahamas	W	P	B	—	—	—	—	VII	VII	32,271	12,908
Barbados	W	P	B	—	—	—	—	—	VII	11,879	4,752
Belgium	W	P	B	N	—	IPC	—	III	III	657,325	262,930
Benin	W	P	B	N	—	—	—	VII	VII	34,124	13,650
Brazil	W	P	B	—	—	IPC	—	IV	IV	419,697	167,879
Bulgaria	W	P	B	—	—	—	—	VI	VI	96,811	38,724
Burkina Faso	W	P	B	—	—	—	—	VII	VII	32,271	12,908
Burundi	W	P	—	—	—	—	—	VII	—	20,392	8,157
Byelorussian SSR	W	—	—	—	—	—	C	—	—	7,500	3,000
Cameroon	W	P	B	—	—	—	—	VII	VI	56,028	22,411
Canada	W	P	B	—	—	—	—	III	III	484,056	193,622
Central African Republic	W	P	B	—	—	—	—	VII	VII	32,271	12,908
Chad	W	P	B	—	—	—	—	VII	VII	32,271	12,908
Chile	W	—	B	—	—	—	—	—	VI	35,636	14,254
China	W	P	—	—	—	—	B	—	—	22,500	9,000
Colombia	W	—	—	—	—	—	C	—	—	7,500	3,000
Congo	W	P	B	—	—	—	—	VII	VII	32,271	12,908
Costa Rica	W	—	B	—	—	—	—	—	VII	11,879	4,752
Cuba	W	P	—	—	—	—	—	VI	—	61,175	24,470
Cyprus	W	P	B	—	—	—	—	VII	VII	32,271	12,908
Czechoslovakia	W	P	B	N	LO	IPC	—	IV	IV	445,394	178,158
Democratic People's Republic of Korea	W	P	—	—	—	—	—	VII	—	20,392	8,157
Denmark	W	P	B	N	LO	IPC	—	IV	IV	445,394	178,158
Dominican Republic	—	P	—	—	—	—	—	VI	—	61,175	24,470
Egypt	W	P	B	—	—	IPC	—	VI	VII	102,151	40,860
El Salvador	W	—	—	—	—	—	C	—	—	7,500	3,000
Fiji	W	—	B	—	—	—	—	—	VII	11,879	4,752
Finland	W	P	B	N	LO	IPC	—	IV	IV	445,394	178,158
France	W	P	B	N	LO	IPC	—	I	I	1,113,482	445,393
Gabon	W	P	B	—	—	—	—	VII	VII	32,271	12,908
Gambia	W	—	—	—	—	—	C	—	—	7,500	3,000
German Democratic Republic	W	P	B	N	LO	IPC	—	III	V	549,302	219,721
Germany, Federal Republic of	W	P	B	N	—	IPC	—	I	I	1,095,541	438,217
Ghana	W	P	—	—	—	—	—	VII	—	20,392	8,157
Greece	W	P	B	—	—	—	—	V	VI	137,595	55,038
Guatemala	W	—	—	—	—	—	C	—	—	7,500	3,000
Guinea	W	P	B	—	—	—	—	VII	VII	32,271	12,908
Haiti	W	P	—	—	—	—	—	VII	—	20,392	8,157
Holy See	W	P	B	—	—	—	—	VII	VII	32,271	12,908
Honduras	W	—	—	—	—	—	C	—	—	7,500	3,000
Hungary	W	P	B	N	LO	—	—	V	VI	150,443	60,177
Iceland	—	P	B	—	—	—	—	VII	VII	32,271	12,908
India	W	—	B	—	—	—	—	—	IV	118,789	47,516
Indonesia	W	P	—	—	—	—	—	VI	—	61,175	24,470
Iran	—	P	—	—	—	—	—	VI	—	61,175	24,470
Iraq	W	P	—	—	—	—	—	VI	—	61,175	24,470
Ireland	W	P	B	N	LO	IPC	—	IV	IV	445,394	178,158
Israel	W	P	B	N	—	IPC	—	VI	VI	131,464	52,586
Italy	W	P	B	N	LO	IPC	—	III	III	668,089	267,236
Ivory Coast	W	P	B	—	—	—	—	VII	VI	56,028	22,411
Jamaica	W	—	—	—	—	—	C	—	—	7,500	3,000
Japan	W	P	B	—	—	IPC	—	I	II	989,846	395,938
Jordan	W	P	—	—	—	—	—	VII	—	20,392	8,157
Kenya	W	P	—	—	—	—	—	VI	—	61,175	24,470
Lebanon	—	P	B	N	—	—	—	VI	VI	102,367	40,947
Libyan Arab Jamahiriya	W	P	B	—	—	—	—	VI	VI	96,811	38,724
Liechtenstein	W	P	B	N	—	—	—	VII	VII	34,124	13,650
Luxembourg	W	P	B	N	—	IPC	—	VII	VII	43,823	17,529
Madagascar	—	P	B	—	—	—	—	VII	VI	56,028	22,411
Malawi	W	P	—	—	—	—	—	VII	—	20,392	8,157
Mali	W	P	B	—	—	—	—	VII	VII	32,271	12,908
Malta	W	P	B	—	—	—	—	VII	VII	32,271	12,908
Mauritania	W	P	B	—	—	—	—	VII	VII	32,271	12,908
Mauritius	W	P	—	—	—	—	—	VII	—	20,392	8,157
Mexico	W	P	B	—	—	—	—	IV	IV	322,706	129,083
Monaco	W	P	B	N	—	IPC	—	VII	VII	43,823	17,529
Mongolia	W	—	—	—	—	—	C	—	—	7,500	3,000
Morocco	W	P	B	N	—	—	—	VI	VI	102,367	40,947
Netherlands	W	P	B	N	LO	IPC	—	III	III	668,089	267,236
New Zealand	W	P	B	—	—	—	—	V	V	161,354	64,542

STATE OR OTHER	MEMBER						CLASS			CONTRIBUTION	
							W	P	B	In Swiss francs	Equivalent in US dollars*
Niger	W	P	B	—	—	—	—	VII	VII	32,271	12,908
Nigeria	—	P	—	—	—	—	—	VI	—	61,175	24,470
Norway	W	P	B	N	LO	IPC	—	IV	IV	445,394	178,158
Pakistan	W	—	B	—	—	—	—	—	VI	35,636	14,254
Panama	W	—	—	—	—	—	C	—	—	7,500	3,000
Peru	W	—	—	—	—	—	C	—	—	7,500	3,000
Philippines	W	P	B	—	—	—	—	VI	VI	96,811	38,724
Poland	W	P	B	—	—	—	—	V	VI	137,595	55,038
Portugal	W	P	B	N	—	IPC	—	IV	V	378,824	151,530
Qatar	W	—	—	—	—	—	B	—	—	22,500	9,000
Republic of Korea	W	P	—	—	—	—	—	—	VI	61,175	24,470
Romania	W	P	B	—	—	—	—	V	VI	137,595	55,038
Rwanda	W	P	B	—	—	—	—	VII	VII	32,271	12,908
San Marino	—	P	—	—	—	—	—	VI	—	61,175	24,470
Saudi Arabia	W	—	—	—	—	—	A	—	—	75,000	30,000
Senegal	W	P	B	—	—	—	—	VII	VI	56,028	22,411
Somalia	W	—	—	—	—	—	C	—	—	7,500	3,000
South Africa	W	P	B	—	—	—	—	IV	IV	322,706	129,082
Spain	W	P	B	N	LO	IPC	—	IV	II	564,181	225,672
Sri Lanka	W	P	B	—	—	—	—	VII	VII	32,271	12,908
Sudan	W	P	—	—	—	—	—	VII	—	20,392	8,157
Suriname	W	P	B	N	—	IPC	—	VII	VII	43,823	17,529
Sweden	W	P	B	N	LO	IPC	—	III	III	668,089	267,236
Switzerland	W	P	B	N	LO	IPC	—	III	III	668,089	267,236
Syrian Arab Republic	—	P	—	—	—	—	—	VI	—	61,175	24,470
Thailand	—	—	B	—	—	—	—	—	VII	11,879	4,752
Togo	W	P	B	—	—	—	—	VII	VII	32,271	12,908
Trinidad and Tobago	—	P	—	—	—	—	—	VI	—	61,175	24,470
Tunisia	W	P	B	N	—	—	—	VI	VI	102,367	40,947
Turkey	W	P	B	—	—	—	—	VI	VI	96,811	38,724
Uganda	W	P	—	—	—	—	—	VII	—	20,392	8,157
Ukrainian SSR	W	—	—	—	—	—	C	—	—	7,500	3,000
USSR	W	P	—	N	LO	IPC	—	I	—	816,512	326,606
United Arab Emirates	W	—	—	—	—	—	B	—	—	22,500	9,000
United Kingdom	W	P	B	N	—	IPC	—	I	I	1,095,541	438,217
United Republic of Tanzania	W	P	—	—	—	—	—	VII	—	20,392	8,157
United States	W	P	—	N	—	IPC	—	I	—	798,571	319,428
Uruguay	W	P	B	—	—	—	—	VII	VII	32,271	12,908
Venezuela	W	—	B	—	—	—	—	—	V	59,395	23,758
Viet Nam	W	P	—	—	—	—	—	VII	—	20,392	8,157
Yemen	W	—	—	—	—	—	C	—	—	7,500	3,000
Yugoslavia	W	P	B	N	LO	—	—	VI	VI	104,520	41,808
Zaire	W	P	B	—	—	—	—	VI	VI	96,811	38,724
Zambia	W	P	—	—	—	—	—	VII	—	20,392	8,157
Zimbabwe	W	P	B	—	—	—	—	VII	VII	32,271	12,908
Total	109	96	76	32	15	27				20,029,000	8,011,600

NOTE: Membership in WIPO is indicated by "W"; in the Paris Union by "P"; in the Berne Union by "B"; in the Nice Union by "N"; in the Locarno Union by "LO"; in the Strasbourg (IPC) Union by "IPC". The class indicated for the Paris Union applies equally to the Nice, Locarno and IPC Unions.

*Calculated on the basis of the United Nations rate of exchange for December 1984: 2.50 Swiss francs = $US 1.00.

Annex II. OFFICERS AND OFFICES OF THE WORLD INTELLECTUAL PROPERTY ORGANIZATION
(As at 31 December 1984)

CO-ORDINATION COMMITTEE

OFFICERS
Chairman: Carlos Fernandez Ballesteros (Uruguay).
First Vice-Chairman: Iana Markova (Bulgaria).
Second Vice-Chairman: José Mota Maia (Portugal).

MEMBERS
Algeria, Argentina, Australia, Austria, Benin, Brazil, Bulgaria, Canada, Chile, China, Colombia, Congo, Costa Rica, Czechoslovakia, Egypt, France, German Democratic Republic, Germany, Federal Republic of, Hungary, India, Italy, Ivory Coast, Japan, Lebanon, Mexico, Mongolia, Morocco, Netherlands, Norway, Poland, Portugal, Senegal, Sudan, Switzerland, Tunisia, Turkey, USSR, United Kingdom, United Republic of Tanzania, United States, Uruguay, Viet Nam, Yugoslavia, Zaire, Zambia.

SENIOR OFFICERS OF THE INTERNATIONAL BUREAU

Director General: Arpad Bogsch.
Deputy Directors General: Klaus Pfanner, Marino Porzio, Lev Kostikov.
Director, Public Information and Copyright Department: Claude Masouyé.
Director, Copyright Law Division: Gyorgy Boytha.
Director, Developing Countries Division (Copyright): Shahid Alikhan.
Director, Public Information Division: Roger Harben.
Director, Development Co-operation and External Relations Bureau for Asia and the Pacific: Laksmanathan Kadirgamar.
Director, Industrial Property Division: Ludwig Baeumer.

Director, Classifications and Patent Information Division: Paul Claus.
Director, Patent Co-operation Treaty Division: François Curchod.
Director, Administrative Division: Thomas Keefer.
Legal Counsel: Gust Ledakis.
Director, Development Co-operation and External Relations Bureau for Latin America and the Caribbean: Enrique Pareja.
Director, Development Co-operation and External Relations Bureau for Africa and Western Asia: Ibrahima Thiam.

HEADQUARTERS AND OTHER OFFICE

HEADQUARTERS
World Intellectual Property Organization
34 Chemin des Colombettes
1211 Geneva 20, Switzerland
  Cable address: WIPO Geneva *or* OMPI Genève
  Telephone: 999111
  Telex: 22376 OMPI CH

LIAISON OFFICE WITH THE UNITED NATIONS IN NEW YORK
World Intellectual Property Organization
2 United Nations Plaza, Room 560
New York, N.Y. 10017, United States
  Telephone: (212) 963-6813
  Telex: 420544 UNH UI

Chapter XVI

International Fund for Agricultural Development (IFAD)

The International Fund for Agricultural Development (IFAD) completed its seventh year of operations in 1984, during which it continued to provide concessional-term resources for agricultural development in developing countries, emphasizing self-sufficiency and self-reliance. Through IFAD loans, small farmers, labourers, artisans, fishermen and herdsmen benefited from the strengthening of existing local organizations, the promotion of new farm groups and the use of village associations. Following the approval of loans in 1984 to six countries not previously covered, IFAD had provided loans to nearly all low-income and low-middle-income countries.

The IFAD Executive Board, which met three times in 1984 (in April, September and December), approved 25 projects and 26 technical assistance grants. At the eighth session of the Governing Council (Paris, 22-26 October), Idriss Jazairy of Algeria was unanimously appointed second President of IFAD for a period of three years, effective 19 November 1984. In addition, the Governing Council approved an administrative budget of $26.6 million for 1985—an increase of $1.8 million over 1984.

Membership of IFAD remained at 139 countries in 1984. Of these, 20 were in Category I (developed countries), 12 in Category II (oil-exporting developing countries) and 107 in Category III (other developing countries).

Since 1979, approved loans have been denominated in special drawing rights (SDRs), an international unit of account. Dollar figures in this chapter are based on the SDR/United States dollar conversion rate at 31 December 1984 (SDR 1 = $US 0.980205). However, approximate amounts in United States dollars for loans approved since 1979 have been based on the SDR/United States dollar exchange rate at the time of loan negotiations.

With the approval of 25 additional projects in 1984, total assistance provided by the Fund to 84 member countries since 1978 amounted to SDR 1,765.4 million ($2,058 million), of which SDR 1,685.4 million ($1,968 million) was provided for 160 projects and SDR 80 million ($90 million) for technical assistance grants.

Of the 160 loans granted since 1978, 57 were for projects in Africa, 44 in Asia, 31 in Latin America and the Caribbean, and 28 in the Near East and North Africa. Most loans (67.6 per cent) were made on highly concessional terms, with a service charge of 1 per cent per annum, a 50-year maturity period and a 10-year grace period. Another 26.5 per cent of the loans were made available on intermediate terms (at 4 per cent, 20 years maturity and a five-year grace period) and the remaining 5.9 per cent on ordinary terms (8 per cent, 15-18 years maturity and a three-year grace period).

Resources

The Fund's resource situation worsened during 1984, forcing it to reduce its operations. Several first replenishment contributions remained outstanding at the end of 1984. Contributions pledged by Category I and II members towards the first replenishment amounted to $1,050 million at the valuation date, 11 December 1980. As a result of fluctuating exchange rates, these pledges totalled $913,083,000 at 31 December 1984; payments towards them by Category I and II countries amounted to $849,137,612. Payments by Category III countries as at 31 December 1984 totalled $30,952,765 against pledges of $31,643,499.

Considerable attention was given to the second replenishment of IFAD's resources in 1984. Members of the consultation on the second replenishment agreed on the period (1985-1987) and the approximate level of replenishment, but a decision on the relative share of the two major donor groups (Categories I and II) had not been reached by the end of the year. In a resolution adopted in October, the IFAD Governing Council requested that consultations be continued and encouraged member countries to make advance contributions. As at 31 December 1984, advance payments of $2.5 million had been received from 15 Category III members towards the second replenishment.

Investments

Investment of the Fund's liquid assets, which totalled $574.5 million at the end of 1984, continued to be restricted to obligations (bonds) issued or fully guaranteed by Governments and to time deposits with major banks. Of these assets, $15.8 million was held on demand deposit, $296.6 million was held on deposit with or in obligations issued by commercial banks, and $262.1 million was in bonds and similar securities issued or guaranteed by member Governments. While the maximum maturity for any of these investments was five years, the average length of investment was 15 months. The Fund had a total of $182.2 million (31.7 per cent of its total liquid assets) deposited with banks of developing countries or in bonds or similar securities issued by their Governments and international development institutions.

In 1984, interest rates in the United States remained relatively high, while the rates of other major currencies were somewhat stable. The average rate of return on the Fund's investments in 1984 was about 11.06 per cent, compared to 11 per cent in 1983.

Activities in 1984

During 1984, IFAD approved 25 new loans totalling SDR 192.8 million ($196 million) and technical assistance grants of SDR 13.9 million ($14.2 million), bringing the total financial assistance provided that year to SDR 206.7 million ($210.2 million), a 22 per cent reduction from the 1983 level.

The tables below indicate the project loans and technical assistance grants approved during 1984.

In addition to its activities to identify investment and technical assistance projects, IFAD organized special programming missions to analyse in depth the overall socio-economic environment of selected countries. In 1984, it launched two such missions—to Guatemala and Democratic Yemen. These two countries were selected on the basis of their broad regional representation and low per capita income.

Of the 25 projects approved in 1984, 14 were initiated by IFAD and 11 by co-operating institutions; the share of IFAD's contribution in total investment declined from an average of 31 per cent in 1980-1981 to 24 per cent in 1984, reflecting the Fund's effectiveness in its resource mobilization effort.

IFAD continued also to mobilize resources from other external donors, as evidenced by the agreements it signed with two member countries in 1984. Under one of them, signed in May with the Government of Belgium for the Survival Fund for the Third World, IFAD acted as the focal point in the execution of the IFAD/WHO/UNICEF/UNDP joint programme for the Fund. The Fund, established in October 1983, aimed at increasing food production and improving health and nutrition of the rural poor in regions with the highest mortality rates. The launching of the first project—for farmers' groups and community support in Kenya—began in 1984. Activities were also intensified to ensure an early start of projects in Ethiopia, Somalia and Uganda and to commence the preparation of a medium-term programme of assistance (1985-1986) of $60 million, jointly set up

by the participating agencies and approved by the Belgian Council of Ministers. Under the second agreement, approved in December, the Government of the Netherlands was to reimburse IFAD some $15 million against amounts disbursed under loans to six countries for seven projects.

Income and expenditure

Total revenue for 1984 was $73.6 million, mainly from investments but including $8.4 million from interest and service charges on loans. Total expenses for the year amounted to $18.7 million compared with a budget of $24 million. The excess of revenue over expenses for the year was $54.9 million.

Secretariat

As at 31 December 1984, the secretariat of IFAD totalled 165, of whom 71 were executive or technical staff (Professional category and above) drawn from 42 countries and 94 were support staff (General Service category).

TECHNICAL ASSISTANCE GRANTS

Recipient	Amount (in thousands of US dollars)
CGIAR*-supported international centres	
International Centre for Agricultural Research in the Dry Areas, Aleppo, Syrian Arab Republic	1,500
International Institute for Tropical Agriculture, Ibadan, Nigeria	1,300
International Potato Centre, Lima, Peru	500
International Food Policy Research Institute, Washington, D.C.	200
Centro Internacional de Agricultura Tropical, Cali, Colombia	1,000
International Livestock Centre for Africa, Addis Ababa, Ethiopia	500
International Rice Research Institute, Los Baños, Philippines	1,300
West African Rice Development Association, Monrovia, Liberia	200
Subtotal	6,500
Other agricultural research centres	
Scientific, Technical and Research Commission of OAU, Ouagadougou, Burkina Faso	1,000
Arab Centre for the Study of Arid Zones and Dry Lands, Damascus, Syrian Arab Republic	850
Centro Agronómico Tropical de Investigación y Enseñanza, Turrialba, Costa Rica	850
International Centre for Insect Physiology and Ecology, Nairobi, Kenya	900
Subtotal	3,600
Other technical assistance grants	
Foundation for the Simon Bolivar Agricultural Experimental College, Caracas, Venezuela	1,200
Scientific, Technical and Research Commission of OAU, Ouagadougou, Burkina Faso	1,450
Subtotal	2,650
Total	12,750

*Consultative Group on International Agricultural Research.

PROJECT LOANS APPROVED AND TECHNICAL
ASSISTANCE GRANTED DURING 1984

Country	Purpose	Loan Amount (in millions of SDRs)	Loan Amount* (in millions of US dollars)	Technical assistance Amount* (in thousands of US dollars)
Bangladesh	Grameen Bank	23.60	23.60	—
Bolivia	Cotagaita-San Juan del Oro agricultural development	11.35	12.00	—
Central African Republic	Ombella Mpoko rural development	3.15	3.30	—
China	Rural credit	24.25	25.00	—
	Guangdong freshwater fish culture	—	—	200
Comoros	Rural services	3.15	3.30	—
Cyprus	Smallholder sheep and goat production‡	4.65	4.90	—
Djibouti	Artisanal fisheries development	—	—	100
Dominican Republic	South-western region small farmers' credit and food development	—	—	150
Egypt	Fayoum agricultural development†	10.10	10.20	—
El Salvador	Agricultural credit†	5.05	5.00	—
Gambia	Agricultural development	4.75	5.00	—
Guatemala	Generation and transfer of agricultural technology and seed production†	4.95	5.00	—
Guyana	East bank Essequibo small farmers' development	—	—	105
Indonesia	Smallholder cattle development	—	—	150
Ivory Coast	Artisanal fisheries development in the Aby Lagoon†	2.70	2.85	—
Liberia	Bong County agricultural development	5.50	5.80	—
Malawi	Kasungu agricultural development	13.65	13.60	—
Morocco	Abda Plain development	—	—	130
Pakistan	Gujranwala agricultural development	8.65	8.60	—
Paraguay	Agricultural credit‡	7.10	7.00	—
Rwanda	Birunga maize	3.75	3.80	—
Sao Tome and Principe	Artisanal fisheries	2.10	2.13	—
Sierra Leone	Agricultural sector support	5.10	5.40	—
Solomon Islands	Agricultural development	1.45	1.50	—
Somalia	North-west region agricultural development	7.05	7.00	—
	Livestock health services	—	—	67
Sudan	Stock route	5.95	6.00	—
	Northern Agricultural Production Corporation	—	—	300
Turkey	Agricultural extension and applied research‡	9.70	10.00	—
Uganda	Agricultural development	14.60	14.50	—
United Republic of Tanzania	Southern highlands smallholder foodcrop programme	—	—	190
Yemen	Central highlands agricultural development	3.90	4.00	—
Zaire	Lulua agricultural development	6.55	6.50	—
	Upper Shaba mining area agricultural development	—	—	90
Total		192.75	195.98	1,482

*Dollar equivalent based on SDR/United States dollar exchange rate at the time of loan negotiations.

NOTE: Loans are on highly concessional terms except for those marked †, which are on intermediate terms, and ‡, which are on ordinary terms.

Annex I. MEMBERSHIP OF THE INTERNATIONAL FUND FOR AGRICULTURAL DEVELOPMENT AND CONTRIBUTIONS PLEDGED AND PAID
(As at 31 December 1984)

MEMBER	INITIAL CONTRIBUTIONS (in US dollar equivalents) Pledged	Paid	FIRST REPLENISHMENT CONTRIBUTIONS (in US dollar equivalents) Pledged	Paid	MEMBER	INITIAL CONTRIBUTIONS (in US dollar equivalents) Pledged	Paid	FIRST REPLENISHMENT CONTRIBUTIONS (in US dollar equivalents) Pledged	Paid
Category I					*Category I* (cont.)				
Australia	6,611,570	6,611,570	7,409,091	7,409,091	New Zealand	952,381	952,381	992,286	992,286
Austria	4,800,000	4,800,000	3,374,830	3,374,830	Norway	14,301,430	14,301,430	19,949,147	19,949,147
Belgium	8,926,443	8,926,443	7,375,396	7,375,396	Spain	2,000,000	2,000,000	2,000,000	2,000,000
Canada	25,000,000	25,000,000	31,818,182	31,818,182	Sweden	12,763,596	12,763,596	16,457,270	16,457,270
Denmark	7,500,000	7,500,000	5,328,597	5,328,597	Switzerland	8,494,208	8,494,208	10,980,695	10,980,695
Finland	1,837,672	1,837,672	3,675,345	3,675,345	United Kingdom	20,809,248	20,809,248	14,914,598	14,914,598
France	13,267,430	13,267,430	23,875,130	23,875,130	United States	200,000,000	200,000,000	180,000,000	180,000,000
Germany, Federal Republic of	55,000,000	55,000,000	37,085,714	37,085,714	Subtotal	494,405,618	494,405,618	483,083,279	483,083,279
Ireland	658,960	658,960	631,213	631,213					
Italy	25,000,000	25,000,000	38,700,000	38,700,000	*Category II*				
Japan	55,000,000	55,000,000	50,638,768	50,638,768	Algeria	10,000,000	10,000,000	15,580,000	15,580,000
Luxembourg	313,666	313,666	206,595	206,595	Gabon	500,000	500,000	801,000	801,000
Netherlands	31,169,014	31,169,014	27,670,422	27,670,422	Indonesia	1,250,000	1,250,000	1,909,000	1,909,000

MEMBER	INITIAL CONTRIBUTIONS (in US dollar equivalents)		FIRST REPLENISHMENT CONTRIBUTIONS (in US dollar equivalents)	
	Pledged	Paid	Pledged	Paid
Category II (cont.)				
Iran	124,750,000	41,583,333	—	—
Iraq	20,000,000	20,000,000	31,099,000	31,099,000
Kuwait	36,000,000	36,000,000	56,041,000	56,041,000
Libyan Arab Jamahiriya	20,000,000	20,000,000	—	—
Nigeria	26,000,000	26,000,000	40,459,000	26,857,333
Qatar	9,000,000	9,000,000	13,980,000	13,980,000
Saudi Arabia	105,500,000	105,500,000	155,618,000	155,618,000
United Arab Emirates	16,500,000	16,500,000	25,680,000	25,680,000
Venezuela	66,000,000	66,000,000	38,489,000	38,489,000
Subtotal	435,500,000	352,333,333	379,656,000	366,054,333
Category III				
Afghanistan	8,696	8,696	—	—
Angola*	—	—	—	—
Argentina	134	134	900,000	900,000
Bangladesh	288,462	288,462	669,269	669,269
Barbados	1,000	1,000	—	—
Belize	—	—	—	—
Benin	10,000	10,000	10,000	10,000
Bhutan	—	—	1,000	1,000
Bolivia	—	—	50,000	—
Botswana	—	—	15,000	15,000
Brazil	—	—	9,521,987	9,521,987
Burkina Faso	10,000	10,000	—	—
Burundi	—	—	79,885	—
Cameroon	50,000	50,000	41,702	41,702
Cape Verde	1,000	1,000	—	—
Central African Republic	2,081	2,081	6,255	6,255
Chad	—	—	—	—
Chile	50,000	50,000	—	—
China	814,286	814,286	1,300,000	1,300,000
Colombia	—	—	—	—
Comoros	20,851	10,426	—	—
Congo	—	—	98,737	98,737
Costa Rica	—	—	—	—
Cuba	—	—	94,536	94,536
Cyprus	25,000	25,000	12,000	12,000
Democratic Yemen	—	—	50,000	50,000
Djibouti	—	—	3,000	3,000
Dominica	—	—	10,987	10,987
Dominican Republic	25,000	25,000	—	—
Ecuador	25,047	25,047	50,946	50,946
Egypt	94,488	94,488	141,732	141,732
El Salvador	40,000	40,000	—	—
Equatorial Guinea	—	—	—	—
Ethiopia	23,623	23,623	23,623	—
Fiji	10,000	10,000	10,000	10,000
Gambia	—	—	—	—
Ghana	100,000	100,000	—	—
Greece	150,000	150,000	200,000	200,000
Grenada	—	—	—	—
Guatemala	—	—	—	—
Guinea	992,851	992,851	60,000	—
Guinea-Bissau	—	—	10,000	10,000
Guyana	—	—	30,000	30,000
Haiti	16,470	16,470	13,530	13,530
Honduras	25,000	25,000	50,000	50,000
India	5,000,000	5,000,000	6,500,000	6,500,000
Israel	150,000	150,000	150,000	—
Ivory Coast	—	—	—	—
Jamaica	4,274	4,274	15,000	15,000
Jordan	30,000	30,000	75,000	75,000
Kenya	523,526	523,526	841,406	841,406

MEMBER	INITIAL CONTRIBUTIONS (in US dollar equivalents)		FIRST REPLENISHMENT CONTRIBUTIONS (in US dollar equivalents)	
	Pledged	Paid	Pledged	Paid
Category III (cont.)				
Lao People's Democratic Republic	10,000	10,000	—	—
Lebanon	—	—	25,000	25,000
Lesotho	15,000	15,000	50,000	50,000
Liberia	10,000	10,000	10,000	10,000
Madagascar	—	—	—	—
Malawi	5,000	5,000	18,365	18,365
Maldives	—	—	—	—
Mali	—	—	10,000	10,000
Malta	—	—	—	—
Mauritania	—	—	—	—
Mauritius	—	—	—	—
Mexico	5,000,000	5,000,000	6,503,166	6,503,166
Morocco	226,395	226,395	90,558	90,558
Mozambique	27,298	27,298	81,893	81,893
Nepal	5,000	5,000	5,000	5,000
Nicaragua	28,571	28,571	—	—
Niger	31,217	31,217	31,217	31,217
Oman	—	—	75,000	75,000
Pakistan	825,309	825,309	1,121,297	1,121,297
Panama	—	—	25,000	25,000
Papua New Guinea	20,000	20,000	—	—
Paraguay	—	—	—	—
Peru	—	—	60,000	60,000
Philippines	250,000	250,000	250,000	50,000
Portugal	—	—	—	—
Republic of Korea	163,182	163,182	283,274	283,274
Romania	391,339	391,339	—	—
Rwanda	—	—	14,499	14,499
Saint Lucia	—	—	—	—
Saint Vincent and the Grenadines*	—	—	—	—
Samoa	10,000	10,000	—	—
Sao Tome and Principe	—	—	—	—
Senegal	10,000	10,000	10,425	10,425
Seychelles	5,000	1,667	—	—
Sierra Leone	18,296	18,296	18,430	18,430
Solomon Islands	—	—	10,000	10,000
Somalia	10,000	10,000	—	—
Sri Lanka	795,662	795,662	1,000,000	1,000,000
Sudan	10,000	10,000	10,000	10,000
Suriname	—	—	—	—
Swaziland	—	—	8,980	8,980
Syrian Arab Republic	127,226	127,226	127,226	—
Thailand	100,000	100,000	100,000	100,000
Togo	6,244	6,244	3,122	3,122
Tonga	—	—	—	—
Tunisia	57,870	57,870	300,000	300,000
Turkey	8,917	8,917	22,639	22,639
Uganda	385	385	59,615	59,615
United Republic of Tanzania	16,575	16,575	38,941	38,941
Uruguay	—	—	—	—
Viet Nam	47,214	47,214	—	—
Yemen	50,000	50,000	—	—
Yugoslavia	25,502	25,502	151,570	151,570
Zaire	30,000	6,053	—	—
Zambia	27,863	27,863	92,687	92,687
Zimbabwe	—	—	—	—
Subtotal	16,856,854	16,819,149	31,643,499	30,952,765
Total	946,762,472	863,558,100	894,382,778	880,090,377
Special contributions				
OPEC Fund	—	—	20,000,000	20,000,000
Others	101,157	101,157	—	—

NOTE: According to article 4, section 2 (c), of the Agreement establishing IFAD, members' initial contributions are payable in cash or promissory notes, either in a single sum or in three annual instalments. Contributions have been translated on the basis of International Monetary Fund exchange rates as at 31 December 1984.

*Had not completed the required membership formalities.

Annex II.   OFFICERS AND OFFICES OF THE
             INTERNATIONAL FUND FOR AGRICULTURAL DEVELOPMENT
             (As at 31 December 1984)

EXECUTIVE BOARD

Chairman: Idriss Jazairy.

MEMBERS

Category I: Belgium, Denmark, Germany, Federal Republic of, Italy, Japan, United States. *Alternates:* Canada, Finland, France, Netherlands, United Kingdom.

Category II: Algeria, Iraq, Kuwait, Nigeria, Saudi Arabia, Venezuela. *Alternates:* Gabon, Indonesia, Iran, Libyan Arab Jamahiriya, Qatar, United Arab Emirates.

Category III: Brazil, Cameroon, Kenya, Mexico, Pakistan, Philippines. *Alternates:* Colombia, Cuba, Egypt, Ghana, India, Sri Lanka.

SENIOR SECRETARIAT OFFICERS

President: Idriss Jazairy.
Vice-President: Donald S. Brown.
Assistant President, Head of Economic and Planning Department: Vacant.
Assistant President, Head of Project Management Department: Moise Mensah.
Assistant President, Head of General Affairs Department: Vacant.

Controller, Financial Services Division: Desmond Saldanha.
Treasurer, Financial Services Division: My Huynh Cong.
Chief, Personnel Services Division: Alan Prien.
Director, Legal Services Division: Mohammed Nawaz.

HEADQUARTERS AND OTHER OFFICE

HEADQUARTERS
International Fund for Agricultural Development
107 Via del Serafico
00142 Rome, Italy
  Cable address: IFAD ROME
  Telephone: 54591
  Telex: 614160, 614162

ACTING LIAISON OFFICE WITH THE UNITED NATIONS IN NEW YORK
International Fund for Agricultural Development
Room S-2955
United Nations Headquarters
New York, N.Y. 10017, United States
  Telephone: (212) 963-4245, 4246, 4248

Chapter XVII

Interim Commission for the International Trade Organization (ICITO) and the General Agreement on Tariffs and Trade (GATT)

The United Nations Conference on Trade and Employment, held at Havana, Cuba, between November 1947 and March 1948, drew up a charter for an International Trade Organization (ITO) and established an Interim Commission for the International Trade Organization (ICITO). Since the charter itself was never accepted, ITO was not established. However, while drawing up the charter, the Preparatory Committee's members negotiated on tariffs among themselves, and also drew up the General Agreement on Tariffs and Trade (GATT). The Agreement—a multilateral treaty embodying reciprocal rights and obligations—is the only multilateral instrument that lays down agreed rules for international trade. It entered into force on 1 January 1948 with 23 contracting parties. Since then, ICITO has provided the GATT secretariat.

As at the end of 1984, the number of contracting parties to GATT stood at 90. One other country, Tunisia, had acceded provisionally. The contracting parties conducted about 85 per cent of all international trade while 31 other countries applied the rules of GATT.

Multilateral trade negotiations

The multilateral work programme pursued within GATT during 1984 had two distinct strands—the continuation of work resulting from the conclusion of the Tokyo Round of multilateral trade negotiations in 1979,[a] and the work programme set out by the 1982 GATT Ministerial Meeting.[b]

Implementation of the Tokyo Round agreements

The agreements of the Tokyo Round, the seventh "round" of multilateral trade negotiations in the 37-year history of GATT, provided an improved framework for the conduct of world trade and were adopted as an integral part of the rules of GATT.

Tariff negotiations during the Tokyo Round resulted in agreement on import duty reductions to be effected in eight annual cuts by the industrialized countries. On 1 January 1984, the fifth of such cuts was made, and several countries agreed to accelerate their remaining cuts to some degree, especially with regard to products of interest to developing countries.

In 1984, the GATT Committee on Tariff Concessions continued compiling tariff schedules in looseleaf form to allow an easier reference to changes made during rounds of tariff negotiations. It also considered procedures for renegotiating tariff schedules following GATT's decision at its 1982 ministerial session to adopt the Harmonized Commodity Description and Coding System developed by the Customs Co-operation Council at Brussels, Belgium. The Harmonized System, which would facilitate the analysis of trade statistics and monitor and protect the value of tariff concessions, was to be implemented in January 1987.

During the year, the Committee on Subsidies and Countervailing Measures continued to oversee the implementation of a code on the topic, which provided a mechanism for international surveillance and dispute settlement and for ensuring that the use of subsidies by any signatory did not harm the trading interests of others. It continued to consider panel reports on complaints by the United States on alleged subsidies by the European Community (EC) on exports of wheat flour and pasta products and by EC concerning a section of a 1984 United States Trade and Tariff Act relating to the wine industry.

The Committee on Anti-Dumping Practices continued to examine national laws and legislation and studied an EC request for conciliation concerning an anti-dumping investigation by Canada on electric generators from Italy.

The Government Procurement Committee examined laws, procedures and regulations and made further progress in renegotiating the Agreement on Government Procurement. The Committee adopted a dispute panel report on a United States complaint against EC practices in relation to the exclusion of value added tax from the contract price of government purchases in EC member States.

The International Meat Council met twice in 1984 to discuss the bovine meat market situation and outlook. The 26 signatories to the Arrangement regarding Bovine Meat—one of two multilateral agreements relating to trade in agricultural products negotiated during the Tokyo Round (the other covered dairy products)—accounted for some 90 per cent

[a]YUN 1979, p. 1328.
[b]YUN 1982, p. 1598.

of the world's exports of fresh, chilled and frozen beef and veal (excluding intra-EC trade), or about 60 per cent of both world imports and production.

The International Dairy Products Council, which supervised the International Dairy Arrangement, met in late 1984 to consider problems raised by EC's decision to sell public stocks of butter at prices which, because of the product's age, would be below the agreed minimum.

Work also continued during the year in committees overseeing the agreements on trade in civil aircraft, technical barriers to trade, import licensing and customs valuation. The Committee on Customs Valuation in 1984 adopted decisions dealing with interest charges in the customs valuation of imported goods and with the valuation of carrier media bearing software for data processing equipment.

Ministerial work programme

In 1984, GATT continued to implement the multilateral work programme set out by the 1982 GATT Ministerial Meeting. The ministerial declaration had called for efforts to achieve a comprehensive understanding on safeguards—the right of GATT contracting parties to impose temporary trade restrictions on imports which seriously injured a domestic industry or threatened to do so. Consultations held during the year, revealed some convergence of views on several issues relating to safeguards; in November, the contracting parties decided that the work on safeguards should be continued with a view to its rapid completion.

The Committee on Trade in Agriculture, established by the Ministerial Meeting, continued to examine trade measures in its member countries, focusing on measures affecting market access and supplies, the General Agreement's operation with respect to agricultural subsidies and measures maintained under exceptions or derogations from GATT. In November, the contracting parties adopted the Committee recommendations on elaborating a number of approaches on quantitative restrictions and related measures affecting imports, export subsidies and other forms of export assistance, including subsidized export credits, and the use of sanitary and phytosanitary regulations and other technical barriers to trade.

The Committee on Trade and Development held further consultations with, and examined the trading policies of, a number of countries in relation to Part IV of the General Agreement dealing with special treatment for developing countries. Consultations covering trade in tropical products and barriers affecting the trading prospects of the least developed countries were also continued.

Other aspects of the ministerial work programme included the examination of quantitative restrictions and other non-tariff measures in order to eliminate those not in conformity with GATT and a further

review of the adequacy and effectiveness of the Tokyo Round agreements and obstacles to their acceptance by non-signatories.

Other GATT activities

Contracting parties session

In November 1984, at a session held at the senior official level, GATT contracting parties reviewed progress made in implementing the 1982 ministerial work programme and the Tokyo Round agreements.

Council of Representatives

In 1984, the Council of Representatives, GATT's highest body between sessions of the contracting parties, held two special meetings—in May and November—to review developments in the trading system. It acted on several international trade policy issues and disputes, and four new dispute panels were set up during the year.

Consultative Group of Eighteen

At its three meetings held in 1984, the Consultative Group of Eighteen—a high-level forum for discussing problems facing international trade—reviewed progress in implementing the 1982 ministerial work programme and considered ways for moving the programme towards the stage of joint action by Governments to maintain and strengthen the trading system, including the possibility of initiating a new multilateral trade round. The Group also discussed subsidies and counter-trade questions.

Balance-of-payments restrictions

During 1984, the GATT Committee on Balance-of-Payments Import Restrictions held full consultations with Hungary, Israel, Nigeria, Portugal and the Republic of Korea whose balance-of-payments difficulties had led them to restrict imports. Consultations also took place, under a simplified procedure, with Bangladesh, India, the Philippines and Yugoslavia.

Textiles Arrangement

The Arrangement regarding International Trade in Textiles, known as the Multifibre Arrangement (MFA), regulating most of the $15 billion worth of textiles and clothing which MFA member countries in the developing world exported to those in the developed world, was extended a second time in 1981[c] until 31 July 1986. By the end of 1984, the Protocol extending the Arrangement had been accepted by 42 signatories representing 51 countries. In October 1984, the Textiles Committee, which had before it a report of the Textiles Surveillance Body, conducted its third annual review of the current extension.

[c]YUN 1981, p. 1484.

Technical assistance

In 1984, the GATT secretariat's Technical Co-operation Division organized missions to, or seminars in, the following developing countries: Brazil, Cameroon, Chile, China, Cuba, Indonesia (twice), Kenya, Macao, Panama, the Philippines, Singapore and Zimbabwe. GATT officials also participated in seminars sponsored by regional organizations.

Training programme

Two commercial policy training courses were held at Geneva in 1984. These were the fifty-seventh and fifty-eighth in a series which began in 1955 and which, by the end of 1984, had been attended by 907 officials from 112 countries and eight regional organizations. In the past, courses had been held in English and French only, but one of the two courses in 1984 was conducted in Spanish for the first time.

International Trade Centre

Established by GATT in 1964, and jointly operated by GATT and the United Nations Conference on Trade and Development since 1968, the International Trade Centre continued to provide trade information and trade promotion advisory services for developing countries. The Centre's work was directed at assisting developing countries to formulate and implement trade promotion programmes and activities and to become self-reliant. The value of its technical co-operation programme in 1984 was estimated at $15 million.

Publications

Publications issued in 1984 included the annual volumes of *GATT Activities* and *International Trade*, and the monthly newsletter *GATT Focus*. Other publications included *Textiles and Clothing in the World Economy* and *The World Market for Dairy Products*.

Secretariat

As at 31 December 1984, the GATT secretariat employed 283 staff members; of these, 119 were in the Professional and higher categories and 164 were in the General Service category. They were drawn from 38 nationalities.

Financial arrangements

Member countries of GATT contribute to the budget in accordance with a scale assessed on the basis of each country's share in the total trade of the contracting parties and associated Governments. The budget for 1984 was 51,805,000 Swiss francs. The scale of contributions for 1984 is given below. (The United Nations rate of exchange for December 1984 was SwF 2.50 = $US 1.00.)

Annex I. CONTRACTING PARTIES TO THE GENERAL AGREEMENT ON TARIFFS AND TRADE AND SCALE OF CONTRIBUTIONS FOR 1984

(As at 31 December 1984)

Contracting party	CONTRIBUTION		Contracting party	CONTRIBUTION		Contracting party	CONTRIBUTION	
	Percent-age	Net contribution (in Swiss francs)		Percent-age	Net contribution (in Swiss francs)		Percent-age	Net contribution (in Swiss francs)
Argentina	0.52	263,640	France	7.06	3,579,420	Mauritius	0.12	60,840
Australia	1.42	719,940	Gabon	0.12	60,840	Netherlands	4.37	2,215,590
Austria	1.14	577,980	Gambia	0.12	60,840	New Zealand	0.34	172,380
Bangladesh	0.12	60,840	Germany, Federal			Nicaragua	0.12	60,840
Barbados	0.12	60,840	Republic of	10.57	5,358,990	Niger	0.12	60,840
Belgium	3.37	1,708,590	Ghana	0.12	60,840	Nigeria	1.15	583,050
Belize	0.12	60,840	Greece	0.43	218,010	Norway	1.03	522,210
Benin	0.12	60,840	Guyana	0.12	60,840	Pakistan	0.24	121,680
Brazil	1.34	679,380	Haiti	0.12	60,840	Peru	0.20	101,400
Burkina Faso	0.12	60,840	Hungary	0.54	273,780	Philippines	0.42	212,940
Burma	0.12	60,840	Iceland	0.12	60,840	Poland	0.90	456,300
Burundi	0.12	60,840	India	0.62	314,340	Portugal	0.40	202,800
Cameroon	0.12	60,840	Indonesia	0.91	461,370	Republic of Korea	1.34	679,380
Canada	4.04	2,048,280	Ireland	0.56	283,920	Romania	0.75	380,250
Central African			Israel	0.45	228,150	Rwanda	0.12	60,840
Republic	0.12	60,840	Italy	5.05	2,560,350	Senegal	0.12	60,840
Chad	0.12	60,840	Ivory Coast	0.16	81,120	Sierra Leone	0.12	60,840
Chile	0.27	136,890	Jamaica	0.12	60,840	Singapore	1.03	522,210
Colombia	0.23	116,610	Japan	8.39	4,253,730	South Africa	1.12	567,840
Congo	0.12	60,840	Kenya	0.12	60,840	Spain	1.60	811,200
Cuba	0.31	157,170	Kuwait	0.70	354,900	Sri Lanka	0.12	60,840
Cyprus	0.12	60,840	Luxembourg	0.29	147,030	Suriname	0.12	60,840
Czechoslovakia	0.95	481,650	Madagascar	0.12	60,840	Sweden	1.77	897,390
Denmark	1.04	527,280	Malawi	0.12	60,840	Switzerland	1.79	907,530
Dominican			Malaysia	0.72	365,040	Thailand	0.48	243,360
Republic	0.12	60,840	Maldives	0.12	60,840	Togo	0.12	60,840
Egypt	0.32	162,240	Malta	0.12	60,840	Trinidad and		
Finland	0.85	430,950	Mauritania	0.12	60,840	Tobago	0.21	106,470

| Contracting party | CONTRIBUTION | | Contracting party | CONTRIBUTION | | Contracting party | CONTRIBUTION | |
	Percent-age	Net contribution (in Swiss francs)		Percent-age	Net contribution (in Swiss francs)		Percent-age	Net contribution (in Swiss francs)
Turkey	0.39	197,730	United States	14.59	7,397,130	Associated Governments		
Uganda	0.12	60,840	Uruguay	0.12	60,840			
United Kingdom	7.78	3,944,460	Yugoslavia	0.75	380,250	Democratic Kampuchea	0.12	60,840
United Republic of Tanzania	0.12	60,840	Zaire	0.12	60,840	Tunisia	0.18	91,260
			Zambia	0.12	60,840			
			Zimbabwe	0.12	60,840	Total	100.12	50,760,840

Annex II.   OFFICERS AND OFFICE OF THE GENERAL AGREEMENT ON TARIFFS AND TRADE

(As at 31 December 1984)

OFFICERS

OFFICERS OF THE CONTRACTING PARTIES*

Chairman of the Contracting Parties: Felipe Jaramillo (Colombia).
Vice-Chairmen of the Contracting Parties: Hortencio Brillantes (Philippines), Paavo Rantanen (Finland), Boguslaw Sosnowski (Poland).
Chairman of the Council of Representatives: Kazuo Chiba (Japan).
Chairman of the Committee on Trade and Development: Mahmoud Abdel-Bari Hamza (Egypt).

SENIOR OFFICERS OF THE SECRETARIAT
Director-General: Arthur Dunkel.
Deputy Directors-General: Madan G. Mathur, William B. Kelly.

SENIOR OFFICERS OF THE
INTERNATIONAL TRADE CENTRE UNCTAD/GATT
Executive Director: Göran Engblom.
Deputy Executive Director: Said T. Harb.

*Elected at the end of the November 1984 session, to hold office until the end of the next session.

HEADQUARTERS

GATT Secretariat
Centre William Rappard
Rue de Lausanne, 154
1211 Geneva 21, Switzerland
   Cable address: GATT GENEVA
   Telephone: 39 51 11
   Telex: 28787

Appendices

Appendix I

Roster of the United Nations

(As at 31 December 1984)

MEMBER	DATE OF ADMISSION	MEMBER	DATE OF ADMISSION	MEMBER	DATE OF ADMISSION
Afghanistan	19 Nov. 1946	Germany, Federal		Peru	31 Oct. 1945
Albania	14 Dec. 1955	Republic of	18 Sep. 1973	Philippines	24 Oct. 1945
Algeria	8 Oct. 1962	Ghana	8 Mar. 1957	Poland	24 Oct. 1945
Angola	1 Dec. 1976	Greece	25 Oct. 1945	Portugal	14 Dec. 1955
Antigua and Barbuda	11 Nov. 1981	Grenada	17 Sep. 1974	Qatar	21 Sep. 1971
Argentina	24 Oct. 1945	Guatemala	21 Nov. 1945	Romania	14 Dec. 1955
Australia	1 Nov. 1945	Guinea	12 Dec. 1958	Rwanda	18 Sep. 1962
Austria	14 Dec. 1955	Guinea-Bissau	17 Sep. 1974	Saint Christopher	
Bahamas	18 Sep. 1973	Guyana	20 Sep. 1966	and Nevis	23 Sep. 1983
Bahrain	21 Sep. 1971	Haiti	24 Oct. 1945	Saint Lucia	18 Sep. 1979
Bangladesh	17 Sep. 1974	Honduras	17 Dec. 1945	Saint Vincent and	
Barbados	9 Dec. 1966	Hungary	14 Dec. 1955	the Grenadines	16 Sep. 1980
Belgium	27 Dec. 1945	Iceland	19 Nov. 1946	Samoa	15 Dec. 1976
Belize	25 Sep. 1981	India	30 Oct. 1945	Sao Tome and	
Benin	20 Sep. 1960	Indonesia[4]	28 Sep. 1950	Principe	16 Sep. 1975
Bhutan	21 Sep. 1971	Iran (Islamic		Saudi Arabia	24 Oct. 1945
Bolivia	14 Nov. 1945	Republic of)	24 Oct. 1945	Senegal	28 Sep. 1960
Botswana	17 Oct. 1966	Iraq	21 Dec. 1945	Seychelles	21 Sep. 1976
Brazil	24 Oct. 1945	Ireland	14 Dec. 1955	Sierra Leone	27 Sep. 1961
Brunei Darussalam	21 Sep. 1984	Israel	11 May 1949	Singapore[5]	21 Sep. 1965
Bulgaria	14 Dec. 1955	Italy	14 Dec. 1955	Solomon Islands	19 Sep. 1978
Burkina Faso[1]	20 Sep. 1960	Ivory Coast	20 Sep. 1960	Somalia	20 Sep. 1960
Burma	19 Apr. 1948	Jamaica	18 Sep. 1962	South Africa	7 Nov. 1945
Burundi	18 Sep. 1962	Japan	18 Dec. 1956	Spain	14 Dec. 1955
Byelorussian Soviet		Jordan	14 Dec. 1955	Sri Lanka	14 Dec. 1955
Socialist Republic	24 Oct. 1945	Kenya	16 Dec. 1963	Sudan	12 Nov. 1956
Cameroon[2]	20 Sep. 1960	Kuwait	14 May 1963	Suriname	4 Dec. 1975
Canada	9 Nov. 1945	Lao People's		Swaziland	24 Sep. 1968
Cape Verde	16 Sep. 1975	Democratic Republic	14 Dec. 1955	Sweden	19 Nov. 1946
Central African		Lebanon	24 Oct. 1945	Syrian Arab	
Republic	20 Sep. 1960	Lesotho	17 Oct. 1966	Republic[3]	24 Oct. 1945
Chad	20 Sep. 1960	Liberia	2 Nov. 1945	Thailand	16 Dec. 1946
Chile	24 Oct. 1945	Libyan Arab		Togo	20 Sep. 1960
China	24 Oct. 1945	Jamahiriya	14 Dec. 1955	Trinidad and	
Colombia	5 Nov. 1945	Luxembourg	24 Oct. 1945	Tobago	18 Sep. 1962
Comoros	12 Nov. 1975	Madagascar	20 Sep. 1960	Tunisia	12 Nov. 1956
Congo	20 Sep. 1960	Malawi	1 Dec. 1964	Turkey	24 Oct. 1945
Costa Rica	2 Nov. 1945	Malaysia[5]	17 Sep. 1957	Uganda	25 Oct. 1962
Cuba	24 Oct. 1945	Maldives	21 Sep. 1965	Ukrainian Soviet	
Cyprus	20 Sep. 1960	Mali	28 Sep. 1960	Socialist Republic	24 Oct. 1945
Czechoslovakia	24 Oct. 1945	Malta	1 Dec. 1964	Union of Soviet	
Democratic Kampuchea	14 Dec. 1955	Mauritania	27 Oct. 1961	Socialist Republics	24 Oct. 1945
Democratic Yemen	14 Dec. 1967	Mauritius	24 Apr. 1968	United Arab Emirates	9 Dec. 1971
Denmark	24 Oct. 1945	Mexico	7 Nov. 1945	United Kingdom of	
Djibouti	20 Sep. 1977	Mongolia	27 Oct. 1961	Great Britain and	
Dominica	18 Dec. 1978	Morocco	12 Nov. 1956	Northern Ireland	24 Oct. 1945
Dominican Republic	24 Oct. 1945	Mozambique	16 Sep. 1975	United Republic	
Ecuador	21 Dec. 1945	Nepal	14 Dec. 1955	of Tanzania[6]	14 Dec. 1961
Egypt[3]	24 Oct. 1945	Netherlands	10 Dec. 1945	United States	
El Salvador	24 Oct. 1945	New Zealand	24 Oct. 1945	of America	24 Oct. 1945
Equatorial Guinea	12 Nov. 1968	Nicaragua	24 Oct. 1945	Uruguay	18 Dec. 1945
Ethiopia	13 Nov. 1945	Niger	20 Sep. 1960	Vanuatu	15 Sep. 1981
Fiji	13 Oct. 1970	Nigeria	7 Oct. 1960	Venezuela	15 Nov. 1945
Finland	14 Dec. 1955	Norway	27 Nov. 1945	Viet Nam	20 Sep. 1977
France	24 Oct. 1945	Oman	7 Oct. 1971	Yemen	30 Sep. 1947
Gabon	20 Sep. 1960	Pakistan	30 Sep. 1947	Yugoslavia	24 Oct. 1945
Gambia	21 Sep. 1965	Panama	13 Nov. 1945	Zaire	20 Sep. 1960
German Democratic		Papua New Guinea	10 Oct. 1975	Zambia	1 Dec. 1964
Republic	18 Sep. 1973	Paraguay	24 Oct. 1945	Zimbabwe	25 Aug. 1980

(footnotes on next page)

(footnotes for preceding page)

[1]The Upper Volta changed its name to Burkina Faso on 6 August 1984.

[2]The United Republic of Cameroon changed its name to Cameroon on 4 February 1984.

[3]Egypt and Syria, both of which became Members of the United Nations on 24 October 1945, joined together—following a plebiscite held in those countries on 21 February 1958—to form the United Arab Republic. On 13 October 1961, Syria, having resumed its status as an independent State, also resumed its separate membership in the United Nations; it changed its name to the Syrian Arab Republic on 14 September 1971. The United Arab Republic continued as a Member of the United Nations and reverted to the name of Egypt on 2 September 1971.

[4]By a letter of 20 January 1965, Indonesia informed the Secretary-General that it had decided to withdraw from the United Nations. By a telegram of 19 September 1966, it notified the Secretary-General of its decision to resume participation in the activities of the United Nations. On 28 September 1966, the General Assembly took note of that decision and the President invited the representatives of Indonesia to take their seats in the Assembly.

[5]On 16 September 1963, Sabah (North Borneo), Sarawak and Singapore joined with the Federation of Malaya (which became a United Nations Member on 17 September 1957) to form Malaysia. On 9 August 1965, Singapore became an independent State and on 21 September 1965 it became a Member of the United Nations.

[6]Tanganyika was admitted to the United Nations on 14 December 1961, and Zanzibar, on 16 December 1963. Following ratification, on 26 April 1964, of the Articles of Union between Tanganyika and Zanzibar, the two States became represented as a single Member: the United Republic of Tanganyika and Zanzibar; it changed its name to the United Republic of Tanzania on 1 November 1964.

Appendix II

Charter of the United Nations and Statute of the International Court of Justice

Charter of the United Nations

NOTE: The Charter of the United Nations was signed on 26 June 1945, in San Francisco, at the conclusion of the United Nations Conference on International Organization, and came into force on 24 October 1945. The Statute of the International Court of Justice is an integral part of the Charter.

Amendments to Articles 23, 27 and 61 of the Charter were adopted by the General Assembly on 17 December 1963 and came into force on 31 August 1965. A further amendment to Article 61 was adopted by the General Assembly on 20 December 1971, and came into force on 24 September 1973. An amendment to Article 109, adopted by the General Assembly on 20 December 1965, came into force on 12 June 1968.

The amendment to Article 23 enlarges the membership of the Security Council from 11 to 15. The amended Article 27 provides that decisions of the Security Council on procedural matters shall be made by an affirmative vote of nine members (formerly seven) and on all other matters by an affirmative vote of nine members (formerly seven), in-

cluding the concurring votes of the five permanent members of the Security Council.

The amendment to Article 61, which entered into force on 31 August 1965, enlarged the membership of the Economic and Social Council from 18 to 27. The subsequent amendment to that Article, which entered into force on 24 September 1973, further increased the membership of the Council from 27 to 54.

The amendment to Article 109, which relates to the first paragraph of that Article, provides that a General Conference of Member States for the purpose of reviewing the Charter may be held at a date and place to be fixed by a two-thirds vote of the members of the General Assembly and by a vote of any nine members (formerly seven) of the Security Council. Paragraph 3 of Article 109, which deals with the consideration of a possible review conference during the tenth regular session of the General Assembly, has been retained in its original form in its reference to a "vote of any seven members of the Security Council", the paragraph having been acted upon in 1955 by the General Assembly, at its tenth regular session, and by the Security Council.

WE THE PEOPLES
OF THE UNITED NATIONS
DETERMINED
to save succeeding generations from the scourge of war, which twice in our lifetime has brought untold sorrow to mankind, and
to reaffirm faith in fundamental human rights, in the dignity and worth of the human person, in the equal rights of men and women and of nations large and small, and
to establish conditions under which justice and respect for the obligations arising from treaties and other sources of international law can be maintained, and
to promote social progress and better standards of life in larger freedom,

AND FOR THESE ENDS
to practice tolerance and live together in peace with one another as good neighbours, and
to unite our strength to maintain international peace and security, and
to ensure, by the acceptance of principles and the institution of methods, that armed force shall not be used, save in the common interest, and
to employ international machinery for the promotion of the economic and social advancement of all peoples,

HAVE RESOLVED TO
COMBINE OUR EFFORTS TO
ACCOMPLISH THESE AIMS
Accordingly, our respective Governments, through representatives assembled in the city of San Francisco, who have exhibited their full powers found to be in good and due form, have agreed to the present Charter of the United Nations and do hereby establish an international organization to be known as the United Nations.

Chapter I
PURPOSES AND PRINCIPLES

Article 1
The Purposes of the United Nations are:
1. To maintain international peace and security, and to that end: to take effective collective measures for the prevention and removal of threats to the peace, and for the suppression of acts of aggression or other breaches of the peace, and to bring about by peaceful means, and in conformity with the principles of justice and international law, adjustment or settlement of international disputes or situations which might lead to a breach of the peace;
2. To develop friendly relations among nations based on respect for the principle of equal rights and self-determination of peoples, and to take other appropriate measures to strengthen universal peace;
3. To achieve international co-operation in solving international problems of an economic, social, cultural, or humanitarian character, and in promoting and encouraging respect for human rights and for fundamental freedoms for all without distinction as to race, sex, language, or religion; and
4. To be a centre for harmonizing the actions of nations in the attainment of these common ends.

Article 2
The Organization and its Members, in pursuit of the Purposes stated in Article 1, shall act in accordance with the following Principles.
1. The Organization is based on the principle of the sovereign equality of all its Members.
2. All Members, in order to ensure to all of them the rights and benefits resulting from membership, shall fulfil in good faith the obligations assumed by them in accordance with the present Charter.

3. All Members shall settle their international disputes by peaceful means in such a manner that international peace and security, and justice, are not endangered.

4. All Members shall refrain in their international relations from the threat or use of force against the territorial integrity or political independence of any state, or in any other manner inconsistent with the Purposes of the United Nations.

5. All Members shall give the United Nations every assistance in any action it takes in accordance with the present Charter, and shall refrain from giving assistance to any state against which the United Nations is taking preventive or enforcement action.

6. The Organization shall ensure that states which are not Members of the United Nations act in accordance with these Principles so far as may be necessary for the maintenance of international peace and security.

7. Nothing contained in the present Charter shall authorize the United Nations to intervene in matters which are essentially within the domestic jurisdiction of any state or shall require the Members to submit such matters to settlement under the present Charter; but this principle shall not prejudice the application of enforcement measures under Chapter VII.

Chapter II
MEMBERSHIP

Article 3

The original Members of the United Nations shall be the states which, having participated in the United Nations Conference on International Organization at San Francisco, or having previously signed the Declaration by United Nations of 1 January 1942, sign the present Charter and ratify it in accordance with Article 110.

Article 4

1. Membership in the United Nations is open to all other peace-loving states which accept the obligations contained in the present Charter and, in the judgment of the Organization, are able and willing to carry out these obligations.

2. The admission of any such state to membership in the United Nations will be effected by a decision of the General Assembly upon the recommendation of the Security Council.

Article 5

A Member of the United Nations against which preventive or enforcement action has been taken by the Security Council may be suspended from the exercise of the rights and privileges of membership by the General Assembly upon the recommendation of the Security Council. The exercise of these rights and privileges may be restored by the Security Council.

Article 6

A Member of the United Nations which has persistently violated the Principles contained in the present Charter may be expelled from the Organization by the General Assembly upon the recommendation of the Security Council.

Chapter III
ORGANS

Article 7

1. There are established as the principal organs of the United Nations: a General Assembly, a Security Council, an Economic and Social Council, a Trusteeship Council, an International Court of Justice, and a Secretariat.

2. Such subsidiary organs as may be found necessary may be established in accordance with the present Charter.

Article 8

The United Nations shall place no restrictions on the eligibility of men and women to participate in any capacity and under conditions of equality in its principal and subsidiary organs.

Chapter IV
THE GENERAL ASSEMBLY

Composition

Article 9

1. The General Assembly shall consist of all the Members of the United Nations.

2. Each Member shall have not more than five representatives in the General Assembly.

Functions and powers

Article 10

The General Assembly may discuss any questions or any matters within the scope of the present Charter or relating to the powers and functions of any organs provided for in the present Charter, and, except as provided in Article 12, may make recommendations to the Members of the United Nations or to the Security Council or to both on any such questions or matters.

Article 11

1. The General Assembly may consider the general principles of co-operation in the maintenance of international peace and security, including the principles governing disarmament and the regulation of armaments, and may make recommendations with regard to such principles to the Members or to the Security Council or to both.

2. The General Assembly may discuss any questions relating to the maintenance of international peace and security brought before it by any Member of the United Nations, or by the Security Council, or by a state which is not a Member of the United Nations in accordance with Article 35, paragraph 2, and, except as provided in Article 12, may make recommendations with regard to any such questions to the state or states concerned or to the Security Council or to both. Any such question on which action is necessary shall be referred to the Security Council by the General Assembly either before or after discussion.

3. The General Assembly may call the attention of the Security Council to situations which are likely to endanger international peace and security.

4. The powers of the General Assembly set forth in this Article shall not limit the general scope of Article 10.

Article 12

1. While the Security Council is exercising in respect of any dispute or situation the functions assigned to it in the present Charter, the General Assembly shall not make any recommendation with regard to that dispute or situation unless the Security Council so requests.

2. The Secretary-General, with the consent of the Security Council, shall notify the General Assembly at each session of any matters relative to the maintenance of international peace and security which are being dealt with by the Security Council and shall similarly notify the General Assembly, or the Members of the United Nations if the General Assembly is not in session, immediately the Security Council ceases to deal with such matters.

Article 13

1. The General Assembly shall initiate studies and make recommendations for the purpose of:
   a. promoting international co-operation in the political field and encouraging the progressive development of international law and its codification;
   b. promoting international co-operation in the economic, social, cultural, educational, and health fields, and assisting in the realization of human rights and fundamental freedoms for all without distinction as to race, sex, language, or religion.

2. The further responsibilities, functions and powers of the General Assembly with respect to matters mentioned in paragraph 1(b) above are set forth in Chapters IX and X.

Article 14

Subject to the provisions of Article 12, the General Assembly may recommend measures for the peaceful adjustment of any situation, regardless of origin, which it deems likely to impair the general welfare or friendly relations among nations, including situations resulting from a violation of the provisions of the present Charter setting forth the Purposes and Principles of the United Nations.

Article 15

1. The General Assembly shall receive and consider annual and special reports from the Security Council; these reports shall include an account of the measures that the Security Council has decided upon or taken to maintain international peace and security.

2. The General Assembly shall receive and consider reports from the other organs of the United Nations.

Article 16

The General Assembly shall perform such functions with respect to the international trusteeship system as are assigned to it under Chapters XII and XIII, including the approval of the trusteeship agreements for areas not designated as strategic.

Article 17

1. The General Assembly shall consider and approve the budget of the Organization.

2. The expenses of the Organization shall be borne by the Members as apportioned by the General Assembly.

3. The General Assembly shall consider and approve any financial and budgetary arrangements with specialized agencies referred to in Article 57 and shall examine the administrative budgets of such specialized agencies with a view to making recommendations to the agencies concerned.

Voting

Article 18

1. Each member of the General Assembly shall have one vote.

2. Decisions of the General Assembly on important questions shall be made by a two-thirds majority of the members present and voting. These questions shall include: recommendations with respect to the maintenance of international peace and security, the election of the non-permanent members of the Security Council, the election of the members of the Economic and Social Council, the election of members of the Trusteeship Council in accordance with paragraph 1(c) of Article 86, the admission of new Members to the United Nations, the suspension of the rights and privileges of membership, the expulsion of Members, questions relating to the operation of the trusteeship system, and budgetary questions.

3. Decisions on other questions, including the determination of additional categories of questions to be decided by a two-thirds majority, shall be made by a majority of the members present and voting.

Article 19

A Member of the United Nations which is in arrears in the payment of its financial contributions to the Organization shall have no vote in the General Assembly if the amount of its arrears equals or exceeds the amount of the contributions due from it for the preceding two full years. The General Assembly may, nevertheless, permit such a Member to vote if it is satisfied that the failure to pay is due to conditions beyond the control of the Member.

Procedure

Article 20

The General Assembly shall meet in regular annual sessions and in such special sessions as occasion may require. Special sessions shall be convoked by the Secretary-General at the request of the Security Council or of a majority of the Members of the United Nations.

Article 21

The General Assembly shall adopt its own rules of procedure. It shall elect its President for each session.

Article 22

The General Assembly may establish such subsidiary organs as it deems necessary for the performance of its functions.

Chapter V
THE SECURITY COUNCIL

Composition

Article 23[1]

1. The Security Council shall consist of fifteen Members of the United Nations. The Republic of China, France, the Union of Soviet Socialist Republics, the United Kingdom of Great Britain and Northern Ireland, and the United States of America shall be permanent members of the Security Council. The General Assembly shall elect ten other Members of the United Nations to be non-permanent members of the Security Council, due regard being specially paid, in the first instance to the contribution of Members of the United Nations to the maintenance of international peace and security and to the other purposes of the Organization, and also to equitable geographical distribution.

2. The non-permanent members of the Security Council shall be elected for a term of two years. In the first election of the non-permanent members after the increase of the membership of the Security Council from eleven to fifteen, two of the four additional members shall be chosen for a term of one year. A retiring member shall not be eligible for immediate re-election.

3. Each member of the Security Council shall have one representative.

Functions and powers

Article 24

1. In order to ensure prompt and effective action by the United Nations, its Members confer on the Security Council primary responsibility for the maintenance of international peace and security, and agree that in carrying out its duties under this responsibility the Security Council acts on their behalf.

2. In discharging these duties the Security Council shall act in accordance with the Purposes and Principles of the United Nations. The specific powers granted to the Security Council for the discharge of these duties are laid down in Chapters VI, VII, VIII, and XII.

3. The Security Council shall submit annual and, when necessary, special reports to the General Assembly for its consideration.

Article 25

The Members of the United Nations agree to accept and carry out the decisions of the Security Council in accordance with the present Charter.

Article 26

In order to promote the establishment and maintenance of international peace and security with the least diversion for armaments of the world's human and economic resources, the Security Council shall be responsible for formulating, with the assistance of the Military Staff Committee referred to in Article 47, plans to be submitted to the Members of the United Nations for the establishment of a system for the regulation of armaments.

---

[1]Amended text of Article 23 which came into force on 31 August 1965. (The text of Article 23 before it was amended read as follows:

1. The Security Council shall consist of eleven Members of the United Nations. The Republic of China, France, the Union of Soviet Socialist Republics, the United Kingdom of Great Britain and Northern Ireland, and the United States of America shall be permanent members of the Security Council. The General Assembly shall elect six other Members of the United Nations to be non-permanent members of the Security Council, due regard being specially paid, in the first instance to the contribution of Members of the United Nations to the maintenance of international peace and security and to the other purposes of the Organization, and also to equitable geographical distribution.

2. The non-permanent members of the Security Council shall be elected for a term of two years. In the first election of non-permanent members, however, three shall be chosen for a term of one year. A retiring member shall not be eligible for immediate re-election.

3. Each member of the Security Council shall have one representative.)

Voting

Article 27 [2]

1. Each member of the Security Council shall have one vote.

2. Decisions of the Security Council on procedural matters shall be made by an affirmative vote of nine members.

3. Decisions of the Security Council on all other matters shall be made by an affirmative vote of nine members including the concurring votes of the permanent members; provided that, in decisions under Chapter VI, and under paragraph 3 of Article 52, a party to a dispute shall abstain from voting.

Procedure

Article 28

1. The Security Council shall be so organized as to be able to function continuously. Each member of the Security Council shall for this purpose be represented at all times at the seat of the Organization.

2. The Security Council shall hold periodic meetings at which each of its members may, if it so desires, be represented by a member of the government or by some other specially designated representative.

3. The Security Council may hold meetings at such places other than the seat of the Organization as in its judgment will best facilitate its work.

Article 29

The Security Council may establish such subsidiary organs as it deems necessary for the performance of its functions.

Article 30

The Security Council shall adopt its own rules of procedure, including the method of selecting its President.

Article 31

Any Member of the United Nations which is not a member of the Security Council may participate, without vote, in the discussion of any question brought before the Security Council whenever the latter considers that the interests of that Member are specially affected.

Article 32

Any Member of the United Nations which is not a member of the Security Council or any state which is not a Member of the United Nations, if it is a party to a dispute under consideration by the Security Council, shall be invited to participate, without vote, in the discussion relating to the dispute. The Security Council shall lay down such conditions as it deems just for the participation of a state which is not a Member of the United Nations.

Chapter VI
PACIFIC SETTLEMENT OF DISPUTES

Article 33

1. The parties to any dispute, the continuance of which is likely to endanger the maintenance of international peace and security, shall, first of all, seek a solution by negotiation, enquiry, mediation, conciliation, arbitration, judicial settlement, resort to regional agencies or arrangements, or other peaceful means of their own choice.

2. The Security Council shall, when it deems necessary, call upon the parties to settle their dispute by such means.

Article 34

The Security Council may investigate any dispute or any situation which might lead to international friction or give rise to a dispute, in order to determine whether the continuance of the dispute or situation is likely to endanger the maintenance of international peace and security.

Article 35

1. Any Member of the United Nations may bring any dispute, or any situation of the nature referred to in Article 34, to the attention of the Security Council or of the General Assembly.

2. A state which is not a Member of the United Nations may bring to the attention of the Security Council or of the General Assembly any dispute to which it is a party if it accepts in advance, for the purposes of the dispute, the obligations of pacific settlement provided in the present Charter.

3. The proceedings of the General Assembly in respect of matters brought to its attention under this Article will be subject to the provisions of Articles 11 and 12.

Article 36

1. The Security Council may, at any stage of a dispute of the nature referred to in Article 33 or of a situation of like nature, recommend appropriate procedures or methods of adjustment.

2. The Security Council should take into consideration any procedures for the settlement of the dispute which have already been adopted by the parties.

3. In making recommendations under this Article the Security Council should also take into consideration that legal disputes should as a general rule be referred by the parties to the International Court of Justice in accordance with the provisions of the Statute of the Court.

Article 37

1. Should the parties to a dispute of the nature referred to in Article 33 fail to settle it by the means indicated in that Article, they shall refer it to the Security Council.

2. If the Security Council deems that the continuance of the dispute is in fact likely to endanger the maintenance of international peace and security, it shall decide whether to take action under Article 36 or to recommend such terms of settlement as it may consider appropriate.

Article 38

Without prejudice to the provisions of Articles 33 to 37, the Security Council may, if all the parties to any dispute so request, make recommendations to the parties with a view to a pacific settlement of the dispute.

Chapter VII
ACTION WITH RESPECT TO THREATS TO THE PEACE, BREACHES OF THE PEACE, AND ACTS OF AGGRESSION

Article 39

The Security Council shall determine the existence of any threat to the peace, breach of the peace, or act of aggression and shall make recommendations, or decide what measures shall be taken in accordance with Articles 41 and 42, to maintain or restore international peace and security.

Article 40

In order to prevent an aggravation of the situation, the Security Council may, before making the recommendations or deciding upon the measures provided for in Article 39, call upon the parties concerned to comply with such provisional measures as it deems necessary or desirable. Such provisional measures shall be without prejudice to the rights, claims, or position of the parties concerned. The Security Council shall duly take account of failure to comply with such provisional measures.

Article 41

The Security Council may decide what measures not involving the use of armed force are to be employed to give effect to its decisions, and it may call upon the Members of the United Nations to apply such measures. These may include complete or partial interruption of economic relations and of rail, sea, air, postal, telegraphic, radio, and other means of communication, and the severance of diplomatic relations.

---

[2]Amended text of Article 27 which came into force on 31 August 1965.
(The text of Article 27 before it was amended read as follows:

1. Each member of the Security Council shall have one vote.

2. Decisions of the Security Council on procedural matters shall be made by an affirmative vote of seven members.

3. Decisions of the Security Council on all other matters shall be made by an affirmative vote of seven members including the concurring votes of the permanent members; provided that, in decisions under Chapter VI, and under paragraph 3 of Article 52, a party to a dispute shall abstain from voting.)

Article 42

Should the Security Council consider that measures provided for in Article 41 would be inadequate or have proved to be inadequate, it may take such action by air, sea, or land forces as may be necessary to maintain or restore international peace and security. Such action may include demonstrations, blockade, and other operations by air, sea, or land forces of Members of the United Nations.

Article 43

1. All Members of the United Nations, in order to contribute to the maintenance of international peace and security, undertake to make available to the Security Council, on its call and in accordance with a special agreement or agreements, armed forces, assistance, and facilities, including rights of passage, necessary for the purpose of maintaining international peace and security.

2. Such agreement or agreements shall govern the numbers and types of forces, their degree of readiness and general location, and the nature of the facilities and assistance to be provided.

3. The agreement or agreements shall be negotiated as soon as possible on the initiative of the Security Council. They shall be concluded between the Security Council and Members or between the Security Council and groups of Members and shall be subject to ratification by the signatory states in accordance with their respective constitutional processes.

Article 44

When the Security Council has decided to use force it shall, before calling upon a Member not represented on it to provide armed forces in fulfilment of the obligations assumed under Article 43, invite that Member, if the Member so desires, to participate in the decisions of the Security Council concerning the employment of contingents of that Member's armed forces.

Article 45

In order to enable the United Nations to take urgent military measures, Members shall hold immediately available national air-force contingents for combined international enforcement action. The strength and degree of readiness of these contingents and plans for their combined action shall be determined, within the limits laid down in the special agreement or agreements referred to in Article 43, by the Security Council with the assistance of the Military Staff Committee.

Article 46

Plans for the application of armed force shall be made by the Security Council with the assistance of the Military Staff Committee.

Article 47

1. There shall be established a Military Staff Committee to advise and assist the Security Council on all questions relating to the Security Council's military requirements for the maintenance of international peace and security, the employment and command of forces placed at its disposal, the regulation of armaments, and possible disarmament.

2. The Military Staff Committee shall consist of the Chiefs of Staff of the permanent members of the Security Council or their representatives. Any Member of the United Nations not permanently represented on the Committee shall be invited by the Committee to be associated with it when the efficient discharge of the Committee's responsibilities requires the participation of that Member in its work.

3. The Military Staff Committee shall be responsible under the Security Council for the strategic direction of any armed forces placed at the disposal of the Security Council. Questions relating to the command of such forces shall be worked out subsequently.

4. The Military Staff Committee, with the authorization of the Security Council and after consultation with appropriate regional agencies, may establish regional sub-committees.

Article 48

1. The action required to carry out the decisions of the Security Council for the maintenance of international peace and security shall be taken by all the Members of the United Nations or by some of them, as the Security Council may determine.

2. Such decisions shall be carried out by the Members of the United Nations directly and through their action in the appropriate international agencies of which they are members.

Article 49

The Members of the United Nations shall join in affording mutual assistance in carrying out the measures decided upon by the Security Council.

Article 50

If preventive or enforcement measures against any state are taken by the Security Council, any other state, whether a Member of the United Nations or not, which finds itself confronted with special economic problems arising from the carrying out of those measures shall have the right to consult the Security Council with regard to a solution of those problems.

Article 51

Nothing in the present Charter shall impair the inherent right of individual or collective self-defence if an armed attack occurs against a Member of the United Nations, until the Security Council has taken measures necessary to maintain international peace and security. Measures taken by Members in the exercise of this right of self-defence shall be immediately reported to the Security Council and shall not in any way affect the authority and responsibility of the Security Council under the present Charter to take at any time such action as it deems necessary in order to maintain or restore international peace and security.

Chapter VIII
REGIONAL ARRANGEMENTS

Article 52

1. Nothing in the present Charter precludes the existence of regional arrangements or agencies for dealing with such matters relating to the maintenance of international peace and security as are appropriate for regional action, provided that such arrangements or agencies and their activities are consistent with the Purposes and Principles of the United Nations.

2. The Members of the United Nations entering into such arrangements or constituting such agencies shall make every effort to achieve pacific settlement of local disputes through such regional arrangements or by such regional agencies before referring them to the Security Council.

3. The Security Council shall encourage the development of pacific settlement of local disputes through such regional arrangements or by such regional agencies either on the initiative of the states concerned or by reference from the Security Council.

4. This Article in no way impairs the application of Articles 34 and 35.

Article 53

1. The Security Council shall, where appropriate, utilize such regional arrangements or agencies for enforcement action under its authority. But no enforcement action shall be taken under regional arrangements or by regional agencies without the authorization of the Security Council, with the exception of measures against any enemy state, as defined in paragraph 2 of this Article, provided for pursuant to Article 107 or in regional arrangements directed against renewal of aggressive policy on the part of any such state, until such time as the Organization may, on request of the Governments concerned, be charged with the responsibility for preventing further aggression by such a state.

2. The term enemy state as used in paragraph 1 of this Article applies to any state which during the Second World War has been an enemy of any signatory of the present Charter.

Article 54

The Security Council shall at all times be kept fully informed of activities undertaken or in contemplation under regional arrangements or by regional agencies for the maintenance of international peace and security.

Chapter IX
INTERNATIONAL ECONOMIC AND SOCIAL CO-OPERATION

Article 55

With a view to the creation of conditions of stability and well-being which are necessary for peaceful and friendly relations among nations based on respect for the principle of equal rights and self-determination of peoples, the United Nations shall promote:

a. higher standards of living, full employment, and conditions of economic and social progress and development;

b. solutions of international economic, social, health, and related problems; and international cultural and educational co-operation; and

c. universal respect for, and observance of, human rights and fundamental freedoms for all without distinction as to race, sex, language, or religion.

Article 56

All Members pledge themselves to take joint and separate action in co-operation with the Organization for the achievement of the purposes set forth in Article 55.

Article 57

1. The various specialized agencies, established by intergovernmental agreement and having wide international responsibilities, as defined in their basic instruments, in economic, social, cultural, educational, health, and related fields, shall be brought into relationship with the United Nations in accordance with the provisions of Article 63.

2. Such agencies thus brought into relationship with the United Nations are hereinafter referred to as specialized agencies.

Article 58

The Organization shall make recommendations for the co-ordination of the policies and activities of the specialized agencies.

Article 59

The Organization shall, where appropriate, initiate negotiations among the states concerned for the creation of any new specialized agencies required for the accomplishment of the purposes set forth in Article 55.

Article 60

Responsibility for the discharge of the functions of the Organization set forth in this Chapter shall be vested in the General Assembly and, under the authority of the General Assembly, in the Economic and Social Council, which shall have for this purpose the powers set forth in Chapter X.

Chapter X
THE ECONOMIC AND SOCIAL COUNCIL

Composition

Article 61[3]

1. The Economic and Social Council shall consist of fifty-four Members of the United Nations elected by the General Assembly.

2. Subject to the provisions of paragraph 3, eighteen members of the Economic and Social Council shall be elected each year for a term of three years. A retiring member shall be eligible for immediate re-election.

3. At the first election after the increase in the membership of the Economic and Social Council from twenty-seven to fifty-four members, in addition to the members elected in place of the nine members whose term of office expires at the end of that year, twenty-seven additional members shall be elected. Of these twenty-seven additional members, the term of office of nine members so elected shall expire at the end of one year, and of nine other members at the end of two years, in accordance with arrangements made by the General Assembly.

4. Each member of the Economic and Social Council shall have one representative.

Functions and powers

Article 62

1. The Economic and Social Council may make or initiate studies and reports with respect to international economic, social, cultural, educational, health, and related matters and may make recommendations with respect to any such matters to the General Assembly, to the Members of the United Nations, and to the specialized agencies concerned.

2. It may make recommendations for the purpose of promoting respect for, and observance of, human rights and fundamental freedoms for all.

3. It may prepare draft conventions for submission to the General Assembly, with respect to matters falling within its competence.

4. It may call, in accordance with the rules prescribed by the United Nations, international conferences on matters falling within its competence.

Article 63

1. The Economic and Social Council may enter into agreements with any of the agencies referred to in Article 57, defining the terms on which the agency concerned shall be brought into relationship with the United Nations. Such agreements shall be subject to approval by the General Assembly.

2. It may co-ordinate the activities of the specialized agencies through consultation with and recommendations to such agencies and through recommendations to the General Assembly and to the Members of the United Nations.

Article 64

1. The Economic and Social Council may take appropriate steps to obtain regular reports from the specialized agencies. It may make arrangements with the Members of the United Nations and with the specialized agencies to obtain reports on the steps taken to give effect to its own recommendations and to recommendations on matters falling within its competence made by the General Assembly.

2. It may communicate its observations on these reports to the General Assembly.

Article 65

The Economic and Social Council may furnish information to the Security Council and shall assist the Security Council upon its request.

Article 66

1. The Economic and Social Council shall perform such functions as fall within its competence in connexion with the carrying out of the recommendations of the General Assembly.

2. It may, with the approval of the General Assembly, perform services at the request of Members of the United Nations and at the request of specialized agencies.

3. It shall perform such other functions as are specified elsewhere in the present Charter or as may be assigned to it by the General Assembly.

Voting

Article 67

1. Each member of the Economic and Social Council shall have one vote.

2. Decisions of the Economic and Social Council shall be made by a majority of the members present and voting.

Procedure

Article 68

The Economic and Social Council shall set up commissions in economic and social fields and for the promotion of human rights, and such other commissions as may be required for the performance of its functions.

---

[3]Amended text of Article 61, which came into force on 24 September 1973. (The text of Article 61 as previously amended on 31 August 1965 read as follows:

1. The Economic and Social Council shall consist of twenty-seven Members of the United Nations elected by the General Assembly.

2. Subject to the provisions of paragraph 3, nine members of the Economic and Social Council shall be elected each year for a term of three years. A retiring member shall be eligible for immediate re-election.

3. At the first election after the increase in the membership of the Economic and Social Council from eighteen to twenty-seven members, in addition to the members elected in place of the six members whose term of office expires at the end of that year, nine additional members shall be elected. Of these nine additional members, the term of office of three members so elected shall expire at the end of one year, and of three other members at the end of two years, in accordance with arrangements made by the General Assembly.

4. Each member of the Economic and Social Council shall have one representative.)

Article 69

The Economic and Social Council shall invite any Member of the United Nations to participate, without vote, in its deliberations on any matter of particular concern to that Member.

Article 70

The Economic and Social Council may make arrangements for representatives of the specialized agencies to participate, without vote, in its deliberations and in those of the commissions established by it, and for its representatives to participate in the deliberations of the specialized agencies.

Article 71

The Economic and Social Council may make suitable arrangements for consultation with non-governmental organizations which are concerned with matters within its competence. Such arrangements may be made with international organizations and, where appropriate, with national organizations after consultation with the Member of the United Nations concerned.

Article 72

1. The Economic and Social Council shall adopt its own rules of procedure, including the method of selecting its President.

2. The Economic and Social Council shall meet as required in accordance with its rules, which shall include provision for the convening of meetings on the request of a majority of its members.

Chapter XI
DECLARATION REGARDING
NON-SELF-GOVERNING TERRITORIES

Article 73

Members of the United Nations which have or assume responsibilities for the administration of territories whose peoples have not yet attained a full measure of self-government recognize the principle that the interests of the inhabitants of these territories are paramount, and accept as a sacred trust the obligation to promote to the utmost, within the system of international peace and security established by the present Charter, the well-being of the inhabitants of these territories, and, to this end:

a. to ensure, with due respect for the culture of the peoples concerned, their political, economic, social, and educational advancement, their just treatment, and their protection against abuses;

b. to develop self-government, to take due account of the political aspirations of the peoples, and to assist them in the progressive development of their free political institutions, according to the particular circumstances of each territory and its peoples and their varying stages of advancement;

c. to further international peace and security;

d. to promote constructive measures of development, to encourage research, and to co-operate with one another and, when and where appropriate, with specialized international bodies with a view to the practical achievement of the social, economic, and scientific purposes set forth in this Article; and

e. to transmit regularly to the Secretary-General for information purposes, subject to such limitation as security and constitutional considerations may require, statistical and other information of a technical nature relating to economic, social, and educational conditions in the territories for which they are respectively responsible other than those territories to which Chapters XII and XIII apply.

Article 74

Members of the United Nations also agree that their policy in respect of the territories to which this Chapter applies, no less than in respect of their metropolitan areas, must be based on the general principle of good-neighbourliness, due account being taken of the interests and well-being of the rest of the world, in social, economic, and commercial matters.

Chapter XII
INTERNATIONAL TRUSTEESHIP SYSTEM

Article 75

The United Nations shall establish under its authority an international trusteeship system for the administration and supervision of such territories as may be placed thereunder by subsequent individual agreements. These territories are hereinafter referred to as trust territories.

Article 76

The basic objectives of the trusteeship system, in accordance with the Purposes of the United Nations laid down in Article 1 of the present Charter, shall be:

a. to further international peace and security;

b. to promote the political, economic, social, and educational advancement of the inhabitants of the trust territories, and their progressive development towards self-government or independence as may be appropriate to the particular circumstances of each territory and its peoples and the freely expressed wishes of the peoples concerned, and as may be provided by the terms of each trusteeship agreement;

c. to encourage respect for human rights and for fundamental freedoms for all without distinction as to race, sex, language, or religion, and to encourage recognition of the interdependence of the peoples of the world; and

d. to ensure equal treatment in social, economic, and commercial matters for all Members of the United Nations and their nationals, and also equal treatment for the latter in the administration of justice, without prejudice to the attainment of the foregoing objectives and subject to the provisions of Article 80.

Article 77

1. The trusteeship system shall apply to such territories in the following categories as may be placed thereunder by means of trusteeship agreements:

a. territories now held under mandate;

b. territories which may be detached from enemy states as a result of the Second World War; and

c. territories voluntarily placed under the system by states responsible for their administration.

2. It will be a matter for subsequent agreement as to which territories in the foregoing categories will be brought under the trusteeship system and upon what terms.

Article 78

The trusteeship system shall not apply to territories which have become Members of the United Nations, relationship among which shall be based on respect for the principle of sovereign equality.

Article 79

The terms of trusteeship for each territory to be placed under the trusteeship system, including any alteration or amendment, shall be agreed upon by the states directly concerned, including the mandatory power in the case of territories held under mandate by a Member of the United Nations, and shall be approved as provided for in Articles 83 and 85.

Article 80

1. Except as may be agreed upon in individual trusteeship agreements, made under Articles 77, 79, and 81, placing each territory under the trusteeship system, and until such agreements have been concluded, nothing in this Chapter shall be construed in or of itself to alter in any manner the rights whatsoever of any states or any peoples or the terms of existing international instruments to which Members of the United Nations may respectively be parties.

2. Paragraph 1 of this Article shall not be interpreted as giving grounds for delay or postponement of the negotiation and conclusion of agreements for placing mandated and other territories under the trusteeship system as provided for in Article 77.

Article 81

The trusteeship agreement shall in each case include the terms under which the trust territory will be administered and designate the authority which will exercise the administration of the trust territory. Such authority, hereinafter called the administering authority, may be one or more states or the Organization itself.

Article 82

There may be designated, in any trusteeship agreement, a strategic area or areas which may include part or all of the trust territory to which the agreement applies, without prejudice to any special agreement or agreements made under Article 43.

Article 83

1. All functions of the United Nations relating to strategic areas, including the approval of the terms of the trusteeship agreements and of their alteration or amendments, shall be exercised by the Security Council.

2. The basic objectives set forth in Article 76 shall be applicable to the people of each strategic area.

3. The Security Council shall, subject to the provisions of the trusteeship agreements and without prejudice to security considerations, avail itself of the assistance of the Trusteeship Council to perform those functions of the United Nations under the trusteeship system relating to political, economic, social, and educational matters in the strategic areas.

Article 84

It shall be the duty of the administering authority to ensure that the trust territory shall play its part in the maintenance of international peace and security. To this end the administering authority may make use of volunteer forces, facilities, and assistance from the trust territory in carrying out the obligations towards the Security Council undertaken in this regard by the administering authority, as well as for local defence and the maintenance of law and order within the trust territory.

Article 85

1. The functions of the United Nations with regard to trusteeship agreements for all areas not designated as strategic, including the approval of the terms of the trusteeship agreements and of their alteration or amendment, shall be exercised by the General Assembly.

2. The Trusteeship Council, operating under the authority of the General Assembly, shall assist the General Assembly in carrying out these functions.

Chapter XIII
THE TRUSTEESHIP COUNCIL

Composition

Article 86

1. The Trusteeship Council shall consist of the following Members of the United Nations:
   a. those Members administering trust territories;
   b. such of those Members mentioned by name in Article 23 as are not administering trust territories; and
   c. as many other Members elected for three-year terms by the General Assembly as may be necessary to ensure that the total number of members of the Trusteeship Council is equally divided between those Members of the United Nations which administer trust territories and those which do not.

2. Each member of the Trusteeship Council shall designate one specially qualified person to represent it therein.

Functions and powers

Article 87

The General Assembly and, under its authority, the Trusteeship Council, in carrying out their functions, may:
   a. consider reports submitted by the administering authority;
   b. accept petitions and examine them in consultation with the administering authority;
   c. provide for periodic visits to the respective trust territories at times agreed upon with the administering authority; and
   d. take these and other actions in conformity with the terms of the trusteeship agreements.

Article 88

The Trusteeship Council shall formulate a questionnaire on the political, economic, social, and educational advancement of the inhabitants of each trust territory, and the administering authority for each trust territory within the competence of the General Assembly shall make an annual report to the General Assembly upon the basis of such questionnaire.

Voting

Article 89

1. Each member of the Trusteeship Council shall have one vote.
2. Decisions of the Trusteeship Council shall be made by a majority of the members present and voting.

Procedure

Article 90

1. The Trusteeship Council shall adopt its own rules of procedure, including the method of selecting its President.
2. The Trusteeship Council shall meet as required in accordance with its rules, which shall include provision for the convening of meetings on the request of a majority of its members.

Article 91

The Trusteeship Council shall, when appropriate, avail itself of the assistance of the Economic and Social Council and of the specialized agencies in regard to matters with which they are respectively concerned.

Chapter XIV
THE INTERNATIONAL COURT OF JUSTICE

Article 92

The International Court of Justice shall be the principal judicial organ of the United Nations. It shall function in accordance with the annexed Statute, which is based upon the Statute of the Permanent Court of International Justice and forms an integral part of the present Charter.

Article 93

1. All Members of the United Nations are *ipso facto* parties to the Statute of the International Court of Justice.
2. A state which is not a Member of the United Nations may become a party to the Statute of the International Court of Justice on conditions to be determined in each case by the General Assembly upon the recommendation of the Security Council.

Article 94

1. Each Member of the United Nations undertakes to comply with the decision of the International Court of Justice in any case to which it is a party.
2. If any party to a case fails to perform the obligations incumbent upon it under a judgment rendered by the Court, the other party may have recourse to the Security Council, which may, if it deems necessary, make recommendations or decide upon measures to be taken to give effect to the judgment.

Article 95

Nothing in the present Charter shall prevent Members of the United Nations from entrusting the solution of their differences to other tribunals by virtue of agreements already in existence or which may be concluded in the future.

Article 96

1. The General Assembly or the Security Council may request the International Court of Justice to give an advisory opinion on any legal question.
2. Other organs of the United Nations and specialized agencies, which may at any time be so authorized by the General Assembly, may also request advisory opinions of the Court on legal questions arising within the scope of their activities.

Chapter XV
THE SECRETARIAT

Article 97

The Secretariat shall comprise a Secretary-General and such staff as the Organization may require. The Secretary-General shall be appointed by the General Assembly upon the recommendation of the Security Council. He shall be the chief administrative officer of the Organization.

Article 98

The Secretary-General shall act in that capacity in all meetings of the General Assembly, of the Security Council, of the Economic and Social Council, and of the Trusteeship Council, and shall perform such other functions as are entrusted to him by these organs. The Secretary-General shall make an annual report to the General Assembly on the work of the Organization.

Article 99

The Secretary-General may bring to the attention of the Security Council any matter which in his opinion may threaten the maintenance of international peace and security.

Article 100

1. In the performance of their duties the Secretary-General and the staff shall not seek or receive instructions from any government or from any other authority external to the Organization. They shall refrain from any action which might reflect on their position as international officials responsible only to the Organization.

2. Each Member of the United Nations undertakes to respect the exclusively international character of the responsibilities of the Secretary-General and the staff and not to seek to influence them in the discharge of their responsibilities.

Article 101

1. The staff shall be appointed by the Secretary-General under regulations established by the General Assembly.

2. Appropriate staffs shall be permanently assigned to the Economic and Social Council, the Trusteeship Council, and, as required, to other organs of the United Nations. These staffs shall form a part of the Secretariat.

3. The paramount consideration in the employment of the staff and in the determination of the conditions of service shall be the necessity of securing the highest standards of efficiency, competence, and integrity. Due regard shall be paid to the importance of recruiting the staff on as wide a geographical basis as possible.

Chapter XVI
MISCELLANEOUS PROVISIONS

Article 102

1. Every treaty and every international agreement entered into by any Member of the United Nations after the present Charter comes into force shall as soon as possible be registered with the Secretariat and published by it.

2. No party to any such treaty or international agreement which has not been registered in accordance with the provisions of paragraph 1 of this Article may invoke that treaty or agreement before any organ of the United Nations.

Article 103

In the event of a conflict between the obligations of the Members of the United Nations under the present Charter and their obligations under any other international agreement, their obligations under the present Charter shall prevail.

Article 104

The Organization shall enjoy in the territory of each of its Members such legal capacity as may be necessary for the exercise of its functions and the fulfilment of its purposes.

Article 105

1. The Organization shall enjoy in the territory of each of its Members such privileges and immunities as are necessary for the fulfilment of its purposes.

2. Representatives of the Members of the United Nations and officials of the Organization shall similarly enjoy such privileges and immunities as are necessary for the independent exercise of their functions in connexion with the Organization.

3. The General Assembly may make recommendations with a view to determining the details of the application of paragraphs 1 and 2 of this Article or may propose conventions to the Members of the United Nations for this purpose.

Chapter XVII
TRANSITIONAL SECURITY ARRANGEMENTS

Article 106

Pending the coming into force of such special agreements referred to in Article 43 as in the opinion of the Security Council enable it to begin the exercise of its responsibilities under Article 42, the parties to the Four-Nation Declaration, signed at Moscow, 30 October 1943, and France, shall, in accordance with the provisions of paragraph 5 of that Declaration, consult with one another and as occasion requires with other Members of the United Nations with a view to such joint action on behalf of the Organization as may be necessary for the purpose of maintaining international peace and security.

Article 107

Nothing in the present Charter shall invalidate or preclude action, in relation to any state which during the Second World War has been an enemy of any signatory to the present Charter, taken or authorized as a result of that war by the Governments having responsibility for such action.

Chapter XVIII
AMENDMENTS

Article 108

Amendments to the present Charter shall come into force for all Members of the United Nations when they have been adopted by a vote of two thirds of the members of the General Assembly and ratified in accordance with their respective constitutional processes by two thirds of the Members of the United Nations, including all the permanent members of the Security Council.

Article 109 [4]

1. A General Conference of the Members of the United Nations for the purpose of reviewing the present Charter may be held at a date and place to be fixed by a two-thirds vote of the members of the General Assembly and by a vote of any nine members of the Security Council. Each Member of the United Nations shall have one vote in the conference.

2. Any alteration of the present Charter recommended by a two-thirds vote of the conference shall take effect when ratified in accordance with their respective constitutional processes by two thirds of the Members of the United Nations including all the permanent members of the Security Council.

3. If such a conference has not been held before the tenth annual session of the General Assembly following the coming into force of the present Charter, the proposal to call such a conference shall be

---

[4] Amended text of Article 109 which came into force on 12 June 1968. (The text of Article 109 before it was amended read as follows:

1. A General Conference of the Members of the United Nations for the purpose of reviewing the present Charter may be held at a date and place to be fixed by a two-thirds vote of the members of the General Assembly and by a vote of any seven members of the Security Council. Each Member of the United Nations shall have one vote in the conference.

2. Any alteration of the present Charter recommended by a two-thirds vote of the conference shall take effect when ratified in accordance with their respective constitutional processes by two thirds of the Members of the United Nations including all the permanent members of the Security Council.

3. If such a conference has not been held before the tenth annual session of the General Assembly following the coming into force of the present Charter, the proposal to call such a conference shall be placed on the agenda of that session of the General Assembly, and the conference shall be held if so decided by a majority vote of the members of the General Assembly and by a vote of any seven members of the Security Council.)

placed on the agenda of that session of the General Assembly, and the conference shall be held if so decided by a majority vote of the members of the General Assembly and by a vote of any seven members of the Security Council.

Chapter XIX
RATIFICATION AND SIGNATURE

Article 110

1.   The present Charter shall be ratified by the signatory states in accordance with their respective constitutional processes.

2.   The ratifications shall be deposited with the Government of the United States of America, which shall notify all the signatory states of each deposit as well as the Secretary-General of the Organization when he has been appointed.

3.   The present Charter shall come into force upon the deposit of ratifications by the Republic of China, France, the Union of Soviet Socialist Republics, the United Kingdom of Great Britain and Northern Ireland, and the United States of America, and by a majority of the other signatory states. A protocol of the ratifications deposited shall thereupon be drawn up by the Government of the United States of America which shall communicate copies thereof to all the signatory states.

4.   The states signatory to the present Charter which ratify it after it has come into force will become original Members of the United Nations on the date of the deposit of their respective ratifications.

Article 111

The present Charter, of which the Chinese, French, Russian, English, and Spanish texts are equally authentic, shall remain deposited in the archives of the Government of the United States of America. Duly certified copies thereof shall be transmitted by that Government to the Governments of the other signatory states.

IN FAITH WHEREOF the representatives of the Governments of the United Nations have signed the present Charter.

DONE at the city of San Francisco the twenty-sixth day of June, one thousand nine hundred and forty-five.

Statute of the International Court of Justice

Article 1

THE INTERNATIONAL COURT OF JUSTICE established by the Charter of the United Nations as the principal judicial organ of the United Nations shall be constituted and shall function in accordance with the provisions of the present Statute.

Chapter I
ORGANIZATION OF THE COURT

Article 2

The Court shall be composed of a body of independent judges, elected regardless of their nationality from among persons of high moral character, who possess the qualifications required in their respective countries for appointment to the highest judicial offices, or are jurisconsults of recognized competence in international law.

Article 3

1.   The Court shall consist of fifteen members, no two of whom may be nationals of the same state.

2.   A person who for the purposes of membership in the Court could be regarded as a national of more than one state shall be deemed to be a national of the one in which he ordinarily exercises civil and political rights.

Article 4

1.   The members of the Court shall be elected by the General Assembly and by the Security Council from a list of persons nominated by the national groups in the Permanent Court of Arbitration, in accordance with the following provisions.

2.   In the case of Members of the United Nations not represented in the Permanent Court of Arbitration, candidates shall be nominated by national groups appointed for this purpose by their governments under the same conditions as those prescribed for members of the Permanent Court of Arbitration by Article 44 of the Convention of The Hague of 1907 for the pacific settlement of international disputes.

3.   The conditions under which a state which is a party to the present Statute but is not a Member of the United Nations may participate in electing the members of the Court shall, in the absence of a special agreement, be laid down by the General Assembly upon recommendation of the Security Council.

Article 5

1.   At least three months before the date of the election, the Secretary-General of the United Nations shall address a written request to the members of the Permanent Court of Arbitration belonging to the states which are parties to the present Statute, and to the members of the national groups appointed under Article 4, paragraph 2, inviting them to undertake, within a given time, by national groups, the nomination of persons in a position to accept the duties of a member of the Court.

2.   No group may nominate more than four persons, not more than two of whom shall be of their own nationality. In no case may the number of candidates nominated by a group be more than double the number of seats to be filled.

Article 6

Before making these nominations, each national group is recommended to consult its highest court of justice, its legal faculties and schools of law, and its national academies and national sections of international academies devoted to the study of law.

Article 7

1.   The Secretary-General shall prepare a list in alphabetical order of all the persons thus nominated. Save as provided in Article 12, paragraph 2, these shall be the only persons eligible.

2.   The Secretary-General shall submit this list to the General Assembly and to the Security Council.

Article 8

The General Assembly and the Security Council shall proceed independently of one another to elect the members of the Court.

Article 9

At every election, the electors shall bear in mind not only that the persons to be elected should individually possess the qualifications required, but also that in the body as a whole the representation of the main forms of civilization and of the principal legal systems of the world should be assured.

Article 10

1.   Those candidates who obtain an absolute majority of votes in the General Assembly and in the Security Council shall be considered as elected.

2.   Any vote of the Security Council, whether for the election of judges or for the appointment of members of the conference envisaged in Article 12, shall be taken without any distinction between permanent and non-permanent members of the Security Council.

3.   In the event of more than one national of the same state obtaining an absolute majority of the votes both of the General Assembly and of the Security Council, the eldest of these only shall be considered as elected.

Article 11

If, after the first meeting held for the purpose of the election, one or more seats remain to be filled, a second and, if necessary, a third meeting shall take place.

Article 12

1. If, after the third meeting, one or more seats still remain unfilled, a joint conference consisting of six members, three appointed by the General Assembly and three by the Security Council, may be formed at any time at the request of either the General Assembly or the Security Council, for the purpose of choosing by the vote of an absolute majority one name for each seat still vacant, to submit to the General Assembly and the Security Council for their respective acceptance.

2. If the joint conference is unanimously agreed upon any person who fulfils the required conditions, he may be included in its list, even though he was not included in the list of nominations referred to in Article 7.

3. If the joint conference is satisfied that it will not be successful in procuring an election, those members of the Court who have already been elected shall, within a period to be fixed by the Security Council, proceed to fill the vacant seats by selection from among those candidates who have obtained votes either in the General Assembly or in the Security Council.

4. In the event of an equality of votes among the judges, the eldest judge shall have a casting vote.

Article 13

1. The members of the Court shall be elected for nine years and may be re-elected; provided, however, that of the judges elected at the first election, the terms of five judges shall expire at the end of three years and the terms of five more judges shall expire at the end of six years.

2. The judges whose terms are to expire at the end of the above-mentioned initial periods of three and six years shall be chosen by lot to be drawn by the Secretary-General immediately after the first election has been completed.

3. The members of the Court shall continue to discharge their duties until their places have been filled. Though replaced, they shall finish any cases which they may have begun.

4. In the case of the resignation of a member of the Court, the resignation shall be addressed to the President of the Court for transmission to the Secretary-General. This last notification makes the place vacant.

Article 14

Vacancies shall be filled by the same method as that laid down for the first election, subject to the following provision: the Secretary-General shall, within one month of the occurrence of the vacancy, proceed to issue the invitations provided for in Article 5, and the date of the election shall be fixed by the Security Council.

Article 15

A member of the Court elected to replace a member whose term of office has not expired shall hold office for the remainder of his predecessor's term.

Article 16

1. No member of the Court may exercise any political or administrative function, or engage in any other occupation of a professional nature.

2. Any doubt on this point shall be settled by the decision of the Court.

Article 17

1. No member of the Court may act as agent, counsel, or advocate in any case.

2. No member may participate in the decision of any case in which he has previously taken part as agent, counsel, or advocate for one of the parties, or as a member of a national or international court, or of a commission of enquiry, or in any other capacity.

3. Any doubt on this point shall be settled by the decision of the Court.

Article 18

1. No member of the Court can be dismissed unless, in the unanimous opinion of the other members, he has ceased to fulfil the required conditions.

2. Formal notification thereof shall be made to the Secretary-General by the Registrar.

3. This notification makes the place vacant.

Article 19

The members of the Court, when engaged on the business of the Court, shall enjoy diplomatic privileges and immunities.

Article 20

Every member of the Court shall, before taking up his duties, make a solemn declaration in open court that he will exercise his powers impartially and conscientiously.

Article 21

1. The Court shall elect its President and Vice-President for three years; they may be re-elected.

2. The Court shall appoint its Registrar and may provide for the appointment of such other officers as may be necessary.

Article 22

1. The seat of the Court shall be established at The Hague. This, however, shall not prevent the Court from sitting and exercising its functions elsewhere whenever the Court considers it desirable.

2. The President and the Registrar shall reside at the seat of the Court.

Article 23

1. The Court shall remain permanently in session, except during the judicial vacations, the dates and duration of which shall be fixed by the Court.

2. Members of the Court are entitled to periodic leave, the dates and duration of which shall be fixed by the Court, having in mind the distance between The Hague and the home of each judge.

3. Members of the Court shall be bound, unless they are on leave or prevented from attending by illness or other serious reasons duly explained to the President, to hold themselves permanently at the disposal of the Court.

Article 24

1. If, for some special reason, a member of the Court considers that he should not take part in the decision of a particular case, he shall so inform the President.

2. If the President considers that for some special reason one of the members of the Court should not sit in a particular case, he shall give him notice accordingly.

3. If in any such case the member of the Court and the President disagree, the matter shall be settled by the decision of the Court.

Article 25

1. The full Court shall sit except when it is expressly provided otherwise in the present Statute.

2. Subject to the condition that the number of judges available to constitute the Court is not thereby reduced below eleven, the Rules of the Court may provide for allowing one or more judges, according to circumstances and in rotation, to be dispensed from sitting.

3. A quorum of nine judges shall suffice to constitute the Court.

Article 26

1. The Court may from time to time form one or more chambers, composed of three or more judges as the Court may determine, for dealing with particular categories of cases; for example, labour cases and cases relating to transit and communications.

2. The Court may at any time form a chamber for dealing with a particular case. The number of judges to constitute such a chamber shall be determined by the Court with the approval of the parties.

3. Cases shall be heard and determined by the chambers provided for in this Article if the parties so request.

Article 27

A judgment given by any of the chambers provided for in Articles 26 and 29 shall be considered as rendered by the Court.

Article 28

The chambers provided for in Articles 26 and 29 may, with the consent of the parties, sit and exercise their functions elsewhere than at The Hague.

Article 29

With a view to the speedy dispatch of business, the Court shall form annually a chamber composed of five judges which, at the request of the parties, may hear and determine cases by summary procedure. In addition, two judges shall be selected for the purpose of replacing judges who find it impossible to sit.

Article 30

1. The Court shall frame rules for carrying out its functions. In particular, it shall lay down rules of procedure.
2. The Rules of the Court may provide for assessors to sit with the Court or with any of its chambers, without the right to vote.

Article 31

1. Judges of the nationality of each of the parties shall retain their right to sit in the case before the Court.
2. If the Court includes upon the Bench a judge of the nationality of one of the parties, any other party may choose a person to sit as judge. Such person shall be chosen preferably from among those persons who have been nominated as candidates as provided in Articles 4 and 5.
3. If the Court includes upon the Bench no judge of the nationality of the parties, each of these parties may proceed to choose a judge as provided in paragraph 2 of this Article.
4. The provisions of this Article shall apply to the case of Articles 26 and 29. In such cases, the President shall request one or, if necessary, two of the members of the Court forming the chamber to give place to the members of the Court of the nationality of the parties concerned, and, failing such, or if they are unable to be present, to the judges specially chosen by the parties.
5. Should there be several parties in the same interest, they shall, for the purpose of the preceding provisions, be reckoned as one party only. Any doubt upon this point shall be settled by the decision of the Court.
6. Judges chosen as laid down in paragraphs 2, 3 and 4 of this Article shall fulfil the conditions required by Articles 2, 17 (paragraph 2), 20, and 24 of the present Statute. They shall take part in the decision on terms of complete equality with their colleagues.

Article 32

1. Each member of the Court shall receive an annual salary.
2. The President shall receive a special annual allowance.
3. The Vice-President shall receive a special allowance for every day on which he acts as President.
4. The judges chosen under Article 31, other than members of the Court, shall receive compensation for each day on which they exercise their functions.
5. These salaries, allowances, and compensation shall be fixed by the General Assembly. They may not be decreased during the term of office.
6. The salary of the Registrar shall be fixed by the General Assembly on the proposal of the Court.
7. Regulations made by the General Assembly shall fix the conditions under which retirement pensions may be given to members of the Court and to the Registrar, and the conditions under which members of the Court and the Registrar shall have their travelling expenses refunded.
8. The above salaries, allowances, and compensation shall be free of all taxation.

Article 33

The expenses of the Court shall be borne by the United Nations in such a manner as shall be decided by the General Assembly.

Chapter II
COMPETENCE OF THE COURT

Article 34

1. Only states may be parties in cases before the Court.
2. The Court, subject to and in conformity with its Rules, may request of public international organizations information relevant to cases before it, and shall receive such information presented by such organizations on their own initiative.

3. Whenever the construction of the constituent instrument of a public international organization or of an international convention adopted thereunder is in question in a case before the Court, the Registrar shall so notify the public international organization concerned and shall communicate to it copies of all the written proceedings.

Article 35

1. The Court shall be open to the states parties to the present Statute.
2. The conditions under which the Court shall be open to other states shall, subject to the special provisions contained in treaties in force, be laid down by the Security Council, but in no case shall such conditions place the parties in a position of inequality before the Court.
3. When a state which is not a Member of the United Nations is a party to a case, the Court shall fix the amount which that party is to contribute towards the expenses of the Court. This provision shall not apply if such state is bearing a share of the expenses of the Court.

Article 36

1. The jurisdiction of the Court comprises all cases which the parties refer to it and all matters specially provided for in the Charter of the United Nations or in treaties and conventions in force.
2. The states parties to the present Statute may at any time declare that they recognize as compulsory *ipso facto* and without special agreement, in relation to any other state accepting the same obligation, the jurisdiction of the Court in all legal disputes concerning:
   a. the interpretation of a treaty;
   b. any question of international law;
   c. the existence of any fact which, if established, would constitute a breach of an international obligation;
   d. the nature or extent of the reparation to be made for the breach of an international obligation.
3. The declarations referred to above may be made unconditionally or on condition of reciprocity on the part of several or certain states, or for a certain time.
4. Such declarations shall be deposited with the Secretary-General of the United Nations, who shall transmit copies thereof to the parties to the Statute and to the Registrar of the Court.
5. Declarations made under Article 36 of the Statute of the Permanent Court of International Justice and which are still in force shall be deemed, as between the parties to the present Statute, to be acceptances of the compulsory jurisdiction of the International Court of Justice for the period which they still have to run and in accordance with their terms.
6. In the event of a dispute as to whether the Court has jurisdiction, the matter shall be settled by the decision of the Court.

Article 37

Whenever a treaty or convention in force provides for reference of a matter to a tribunal to have been instituted by the League of Nations, or to the Permanent Court of International Justice, the matter shall, as between the parties to the present Statute, be referred to the International Court of Justice.

Article 38

1. The Court, whose function is to decide in accordance with international law such disputes as are submitted to it, shall apply:
   a. international conventions, whether general or particular, establishing rules expressly recognized by the contesting states;
   b. international custom, as evidence of a general practice accepted as law;
   c. the general principles of law recognized by civilized nations;
   d. subject to the provisions of Article 59, judicial decisions and the teachings of the most highly qualified publicists of the various nations, as subsidiary means for the determination of rules of law.
2. This provision shall not prejudice the power of the Court to decide a case *ex aequo et bono*, if the parties agree thereto.

Chapter III
PROCEDURE

Article 39

1. The official languages of the Court shall be French and English. If the parties agree that the case shall be conducted in French, the

judgment shall be delivered in French. If the parties agree that the case shall be conducted in English, the judgment shall be delivered in English.

2. In the absence of an agreement as to which language shall be employed, each party may, in the pleadings, use the language which it prefers; the decision of the Court shall be given in French and English. In this case the Court shall at the same time determine which of the two texts shall be considered as authoritative.

3. The Court shall, at the request of any party, authorize a language other than French or English to be used by that party.

Article 40

1. Cases are brought before the Court, as the case may be, either by the notification of the special agreement or by a written application addressed to the Registrar. In either case the subject of the dispute and the parties shall be indicated.

2. The Registrar shall forthwith communicate the application to all concerned.

3. He shall also notify the Members of the United Nations through the Secretary-General, and also any other states entitled to appear before the Court.

Article 41

1. The Court shall have the power to indicate, if it considers that circumstances so require, any provisional measures which ought to be taken to preserve the respective rights of either party.

2. Pending the final decision, notice of the measures suggested shall forthwith be given to the parties and to the Security Council.

Article 42

1. The parties shall be represented by agents.

2. They may have the assistance of counsel or advocates before the Court.

3. The agents, counsel, and advocates of parties before the Court shall enjoy the privileges and immunities necessary to the independent exercise of their duties.

Article 43

1. The procedure shall consist of two parts: written and oral.

2. The written proceedings shall consist of the communication to the Court and to the parties of memorials, counter-memorials and, if necessary, replies; also all papers and documents in support.

3. These communications shall be made through the Registrar, in the order and within the time fixed by the Court.

4. A certified copy of every document produced by one party shall be communicated to the other party.

5. The oral proceedings shall consist of the hearing by the Court of witnesses, experts, agents, counsel, and advocates.

Article 44

1. For the service of all notices upon persons other than the agents, counsel, and advocates, the Court shall apply direct to the government of the state upon whose territory the notice has to be served.

2. The same provision shall apply whenever steps are to be taken to procure evidence on the spot.

Article 45

The hearing shall be under the control of the President or, if he is unable to preside, of the Vice-President; if neither is able to preside, the senior judge present shall preside.

Article 46

The hearing in Court shall be public, unless the Court shall decide otherwise, or unless the parties demand that the public be not admitted.

Article 47

1. Minutes shall be made at each hearing and signed by the Registrar and the President.

2. These minutes alone shall be authentic.

Article 48

The Court shall make orders for the conduct of the case, shall decide the form and time in which each party must conclude its arguments, and make all arrangements connected with the taking of evidence.

Article 49

The Court may, even before the hearing begins, call upon the agents to produce any document or to supply any explanations. Formal note shall be taken of any refusal.

Article 50

The Court may, at any time, entrust any individual, body, bureau, commission, or other organization that it may select, with the task of carrying out an enquiry or giving an expert opinion.

Article 51

During the hearing any relevant questions are to be put to the witnesses and experts under the conditions laid down by the Court in the rules of procedure referred to in Article 30.

Article 52

After the Court has received the proofs and evidence within the time specified for the purpose, it may refuse to accept any further oral or written evidence that one party may desire to present unless the other side consents.

Article 53

1. Whenever one of the parties does not appear before the Court, or fails to defend its case, the other party may call upon the Court to decide in favour of its claim.

2. The Court must, before doing so, satisfy itself, not only that it has jurisdiction in accordance with Articles 36 and 37, but also that the claim is well founded in fact and law.

Article 54

1. When, subject to the control of the Court, the agents, counsel, and advocates have completed their presentation of the case, the President shall declare the hearing closed.

2. The Court shall withdraw to consider the judgment.

3. The deliberations of the Court shall take place in private and remain secret.

Article 55

1. All questions shall be decided by a majority of the judges present.

2. In the event of an equality of votes, the President or the judge who acts in his place shall have a casting vote.

Article 56

1. The judgment shall state the reasons on which it is based.

2. It shall contain the names of the judges who have taken part in the decision.

Article 57

If the judgment does not represent in whole or in part the unanimous opinion of the judges, any judge shall be entitled to deliver a separate opinion.

Article 58

The judgment shall be signed by the President and by the Registrar. It shall be read in open court, due notice having been given to the agents.

Article 59

The decision of the Court has no binding force except between the parties and in respect of that particular case.

Article 60

The judgment is final and without appeal. In the event of dispute as to the meaning or scope of the judgment, the Court shall construe it upon the request of any party.

Article 61

1. An application for revision of a judgment may be made only when it is based upon the discovery of some fact of such a nature as to be a decisive factor, which fact was, when the judgment was given, unknown to the Court and also to the party claiming revision, always provided that such ignorance was not due to negligence.

2. The proceedings for revision shall be opened by a judgment of the Court expressly recording the existence of the new fact, recognizing

that it has such a character as to lay the case open to revision, and declaring the application admissible on this ground.

3.   The Court may require previous compliance with the terms of the judgment before it admits proceedings in revision.

4.   The application for revision must be made at latest within six months of the discovery of the new fact.

5.   No application for revision may be made after the lapse of ten years from the date of the judgment.

Article 62

1.   Should a state consider that it has an interest of a legal nature which may be affected by the decision in the case, it may submit a request to the Court to be permitted to intervene.

2.   It shall be for the Court to decide upon this request.

Article 63

1.   Whenever the construction of a convention to which states other than those concerned in the case are parties is in question, the Registrar shall notify all such states forthwith.

2.   Every state so notified has the right to intervene in the proceedings; but if it uses this right, the construction given by the judgment will be equally binding upon it.

Article 64

Unless otherwise decided by the Court, each party shall bear its own costs.

Chapter IV
ADVISORY OPINIONS

Article 65

1.   The Court may give an advisory opinion on any legal question at the request of whatever body may be authorized by or in accordance with the Charter of the United Nations to make such a request.

2.   Questions upon which the advisory opinion of the Court is asked shall be laid before the Court by means of a written request containing an exact statement of the question upon which an opinion is required, and accompanied by all documents likely to throw light upon the question.

Article 66

1.   The Registrar shall forthwith give notice of the request for an advisory opinion to all states entitled to appear before the Court.

2.   The Registrar shall also, by means of a special and direct communication, notify any state entitled to appear before the Court or international organization considered by the Court, or, should it not be

sitting, by the President, as likely to be able to furnish information on the question, that the Court will be prepared to receive, within a time limit to be fixed by the President, written statements, or to hear, at a public sitting to be held for the purpose, oral statements relating to the question.

3.   Should any such state entitled to appear before the Court have failed to receive the special communication referred to in paragraph 2 of this Article, such state may express a desire to submit a written statement or to be heard; and the Court will decide.

4.   States and organizations having presented written or oral statements or both shall be permitted to comment on the statements made by other states or organizations in the form, to the extent, and within the time limits which the Court, or, should it not be sitting, the President, shall decide in each particular case. Accordingly, the Registrar shall in due time communicate any such written statements to states and organizations having submitted similar statements.

Article 67

The Court shall deliver its advisory opinions in open court, notice having been given to the Secretary-General and to the representatives of Members of the United Nations, of other states and of international organizations immediately concerned.

Article 68

In the exercise of its advisory functions the Court shall further be guided by the provisions of the present Statute which apply in contentious cases to the extent to which it recognizes them to be applicable.

Chapter V
AMENDMENT

Article 69

Amendments to the present Statute shall be effected by the same procedure as is provided by the Charter of the United Nations for amendments to that Charter, subject however to any provisions which the General Assembly upon recommendation of the Security Council may adopt concerning the participation of states which are parties to the present Statute but are not Members of the United Nations.

Article 70

The Court shall have power to propose such amendments to the present Statute as it may deem necessary, through written communications to the Secretary-General, for consideration in conformity with the provisions of Article 69.

Appendix III

Structure of the United Nations

General Assembly

The General Assembly is composed of all the Members of the United Nations.

SESSIONS
Resumed thirty-eighth session: 26 June and 17 September 1984.
Thirty-ninth session:[1] 18 September–18 December 1984 (suspended).

OFFICERS
Resumed thirty-eighth session
President: Jorge Enrique Illueca (Panama).
Vice-Presidents: Algeria, Belgium, Bhutan, Burundi, Canada, China, Czechoslovakia, France, Guyana, Lebanon, Liberia, Nepal, Pakistan, Sierra Leone, Singapore, Sudan, Swaziland, USSR, United Kingdom, United States, Venezuela.

Thirty-ninth session
President: Paul John Firmino Lusaka (Zambia).[a]
Vice-Presidents:[b] Bahrain, Bangladesh, Bolivia, Bulgaria, Chad, China, Cuba, Cyprus, Djibouti, France, Ghana, Guatemala, Iceland, Italy, Malaysia, Morocco, Togo, USSR, United Kingdom, United States, Yemen.

[a]Elected on 18 September 1984 (decision 39/302).
[b]Elected on 18 September 1984 (decision 39/304).

The Assembly has four types of committees: (1) Main Committees; (2) procedural committees; (3) standing committees; (4) subsidiary and *ad hoc* bodies. In addition, it convenes conferences to deal with specific subjects.

Main Committees

Seven Main Committees have been established as follows:

Political and Security Committee (disarmament and related international security questions) (First Committee)
Special Political Committee
Economic and Financial Committee (Second Committee)
Social, Humanitarian and Cultural Committee (Third Committee)
Trusteeship Committee (including Non-Self-Governing Territories) (Fourth Committee)
Administrative and Budgetary Committee (Fifth Committee)
Legal Committee (Sixth Committee)

The General Assembly may constitute other committees, on which all Members of the United Nations have the right to be represented.

OFFICERS OF THE MAIN COMMITTEES

Thirty-ninth session[a]

[a]Chairmen elected by the Main Committees; announced by the Assembly President on 18 September 1984 (decision 39/303).

First Committee
Chairman: Celso Antônio de Souza e Silva (Brazil).
Vice-Chairmen: Milos Vejvoda (Czechoslovakia), Henning Wegener (Federal Republic of Germany).
Rapporteur: Ngaré Kessely (Chad).

Special Political Committee
Chairman: Alpha Ibrahima Diallo (Guinea).
Vice-Chairmen: Hussain Bin Ali Bin Abdullatif (Oman), Giovanni Jannuzzi (Italy).
Rapporteur: Jorge Eduardo Chen-Charpentier (Mexico).

Second Committee
Chairman: Bryce Harland (New Zealand).
Vice-Chairmen: Enrique J. de la Torre (Argentina), Habib M. Kaabachi (Tunisia).
Rapporteur: Ahmed Alawi Al-Haddad (Democratic Yemen).

Third Committee
Chairman: Ali Abdi Madar (Somalia).
Vice-Chairmen: Elsa Boccheciampe de Crovati (Venezuela), Rosalinda V. Tirona (Philippines).
Rapporteur: Grzegorz Polowczyk (Poland).

Fourth Committee
Chairman: Renagi Renagi Lohia (Papua New Guinea).
Vice-Chairmen: Mohamed Kamel Amr (Egypt), Jiri Pulz (Czechoslovakia).
Rapporteur: Demetrio Infante (Chile).

Fifth Committee
Chairman: Ernest Besley Maycock (Barbados).
Vice-Chairmen: Mihail Bushev (Bulgaria), Otto Ditz (Austria).
Rapporteur: Ali Achraf Mojtahed (Iran).

Sixth Committee
Chairman: Gunter Goerner (German Democratic Republic).
Vice-Chairmen: Rajab A. Azzarouk (Libyan Arab Jamahiriya), Moritaka Hayashi (Japan).
Rapporteur: Mehmet Guney (Turkey).

Procedural committees

General Committee
The General Committee consists of the President of the General Assembly, as Chairman, the 21 Vice-Presidents and the chairmen of the seven Main Committees.

Credentials Committee
The Credentials Committee consists of nine members appointed by the General Assembly on the proposal of the President.

Thirty-ninth session
Bhutan *(Chairman),* China, Cuba, Equatorial Guinea, Italy, Ivory Coast, Paraguay, USSR, United States.[a]

[a]Appointed on 18 September 1984 (decision 39/301).

Standing committees

The two standing committees consist of experts appointed in their individual capacity for three-year terms.

[1]The thirty-ninth session of the General Assembly resumed in 1985 from 9 to 12 April and on 16 September.

Advisory Committee on Administrative and Budgetary Questions

Members:

To serve until 31 December 1984: Enrique Ferrer Vieyra (Argentina); Virginia C. Housholder (United States); I. V. Khalevinski (USSR); Rachid Lahlou (Morocco); Carl C. Pedersen (Canada).

To serve until 31 December 1985: Traian Chebeleu (Romania); Mohamed Malloum Fall (Mauritania); Mohammad Samir Mansouri (Syrian Arab Republic); C. S. M. Mselle, *Chairman* (United Republic of Tanzania); Christopher R. Thomas (Trinidad and Tobago).

To serve until 31 December 1986: Henrik Amneus (Sweden); Ma Longde (China); Andrew Robin Murray (United Kingdom); Samuel Pinheiro-Guimarães (Brazil); Banbit A. Roy (India); Yukio Takasu (Japan).

On 13 December 1984 (decision 39/317), the General Assembly appointed the following five members for a three-year term beginning on 1 January 1985 to fill the vacancies occurring on 31 December 1984: Even Fontaine-Ortiz (Cuba), Jobst Holborn (Federal Republic of Germany), Virginia C. Housholder (United States), I. V. Khalevinski (USSR), Rachid Lahlou (Morocco).

Committee on Contributions

Members:

To serve until 31 December 1984: Syed Amjad Ali, *Chairman* (Pakistan); Javier Castillo Ayala (Mexico); A. S. Chistyakov (USSR); Wilfried Koschorreck (Federal Republic of Germany); Yang Hushan (China); Philippe Zeller (France).

To serve until 31 December 1985: Andrzej Abraszewski (Poland); Nobutoshi Akao (Japan);[a] Mohammed Sadiq Al-Mahdi (Iraq); Hamed Arabi El-Houderi (Libyan Arab Jamahiriya); Richard Vognild Hennes (United States); Zoran Lazarevic (Yugoslavia).

To serve until 31 December 1986: Marco Antônio Diniz Brandão (Brazil); Leoncio Fernández Maroto (Spain); Lance Louis E. Joseph (Australia); Atilio Norberto Molteni, *Vice-Chairman* (Argentina); Aluseye D. Oduyemi (Nigeria); Omar Sirry (Egypt).

[a]Resigned on 23 November 1984; Yasuo Noguchi (Japan) was appointed by the General Assembly on 13 December (decision 39/318) for a one-year term beginning on 1 January 1985 to fill the resultant vacancy.

On 13 December 1984 (decision 39/318), the General Assembly appointed the following six members for a three-year term beginning on 1 January 1985 to fill the vacancies occurring on 31 December 1984: Syed Amjad Ali (Pakistan), Ernesto Battisti (Italy), Javier Castillo Ayala (Mexico), A. S. Chistyakov (USSR), Dominique Souchet (France), Wang Liansheng (China).

Subsidiary, *ad hoc* and related bodies

The following subsidiary, *ad hoc* and related bodies were in existence or functioning in 1984, or were established during the General Assembly's thirty-ninth session, held from 18 September to 18 December 1984. (For other related bodies, see p. 1336.)

Ad Hoc Committee of the General Assembly for the Announcement of Voluntary Contributions to the 1985

Programme of the United Nations High Commissioner for Refugees

As soon as practicable after the opening of each regular session of the General Assembly, an *ad hoc* committee of the whole of the Assembly meets, under the chairmanship of the President of the session, to enable Governments to announce pledges of voluntary contributions to the programme of UNHCR for the following year. Also invited to announce their pledges are States which are members of specialized agencies but not Members of the United Nations. In 1984, the *Ad Hoc* Committee met on 16 November.

Ad Hoc Committee of the General Assembly for the Announcement of Voluntary Contributions to the United Nations

Relief and Works Agency for Palestine Refugees in the Near East

As soon as practicable after the opening of each regular session of the General Assembly, an *ad hoc* committee of the whole of the Assembly meets, under the chairmanship of the President of the session, to enable Governments to announce pledges of voluntary contributions to the programme of UNRWA for the following year. Also invited to announce their pledges are States which are members of specialized agencies

but not Members of the United Nations. In 1984, the *Ad Hoc* Committee met on 19 November.

Ad Hoc Committee of the International Conference on Kampuchea

The *Ad Hoc* Committee of the International Conference on Kampuchea held six meetings between 9 January and 17 September 1984, at United Nations Headquarters.

Members: Belgium, Japan, Malaysia, Nepal, Nigeria, Peru, Senegal, Sri Lanka, Sudan, Thailand.

Chairman: Massamba Sarré (Senegal).
Vice-Chairman: Edmonde Dever (Belgium).
Rapporteur: Zain Azraai (Malaysia).

Ad Hoc Committee of the Whole to Review the Implementation of the Charter of Economic Rights and Duties of States

On 17 December 1984, the General Assembly established an *Ad Hoc* Committee of the Whole to Review the Implementation of the Charter of Economic Rights and Duties of States.[2] The Committee, which was to meet in 1985, was to undertake a thorough review of the Charter's implementation in order to identify actions for its implementation that would lead to lasting solutions to developing countries' economic problems.

Ad Hoc Committee on the Drafting of an International Convention against *Apartheid* in Sports

The *Ad Hoc* Committee on the Drafting of an International Convention against *Apartheid* in Sports, which was to consist of 25 members, had a membership of 24 in 1984. It held two meetings during the year, at United Nations Headquarters, on 27 January and 15 October.

Members: Algeria, Barbados, Canada, Congo, German Democratic Republic, Ghana, Guinea, Haiti, Hungary, India, Indonesia, Jamaica, Malaysia, Nepal, Nigeria, Peru, Philippines, Somalia, Sudan, Syrian Arab Republic, Trinidad and Tobago, Ukrainian SSR, United Republic of Tanzania, Yugoslavia.

Chairman: Ernest Besley Maycock (Barbados).
Vice-Chairmen: Keshav Raj Jha (Nepal), Shani O. Lweno (United Republic of Tanzania), Janos Matus (Hungary).
Rapporteur: Earl Alexander Carr (Jamaica).

Ad Hoc Committee on the Drafting of an International Convention against the Recruitment, Use, Financing and Training of Mercenaries

The *Ad Hoc* Committee on the Drafting of an International Convention against the Recruitment, Use, Financing and Training of Mercenaries, which was to be composed of 35 members, had a membership of 34 in 1984. It held its fourth session at United Nations Headquarters from 30 July to 24 August.

Members: Algeria, Angola, Bangladesh, Barbados, Benin,[a] Bulgaria, Canada, Cuba,[b] Democratic Yemen, Ethiopia, France, German Democratic Republic, Germany, Federal Republic of, Guyana,[a] India, Italy, Jamaica, Japan, Mongolia, Portugal, Senegal,[b] Seychelles, Spain, Suriname, Togo, Turkey, Ukrainian SSR, USSR, United Kingdom, United States, Uruguay, Yugoslavia, Zaire, Zambia.

[a]Benin withdrew on 31 December 1984 in accordance with a schedule of rotation agreed on by the Group of African States; Guyana resigned on 26 July. On 18 December (decision 39/327), the General Assembly confirmed the appointment by its President of Nigeria and Haiti, effective 1 January 1985, to fill the resultant vacancies.
[b]Appointed by the President of the General Assembly's thirty-eighth session to replace the Bahamas and Nigeria, respectively, taking into account the schedules of rotation agreed on by the Groups of Latin American and African States, as communicated to the Secretary-General on 28 June 1984.

Chairman: Harley S. L. Moseley (Barbados).
Vice-Chairmen: Ramdane Lamamra (Algeria), B. I. Tarasyuk (Ukrainian SSR), Tullio Treves (Italy).
Rapporteur: Moritaka Hayashi (Japan).

---

[2]YUN 1974, p. 403, GA res. 3281(XXIX), 12 Dec. 1974.

Ad Hoc Committee on the Implementation of the Collective Security Provisions of the Charter of the United Nations

The *Ad Hoc* Committee on the Implementation of the Collective Security Provisions of the Charter of the United Nations, established in 1983, had not been constituted by the end of 1984. On 17 December, the General Assembly requested its President to undertake consultations with the regional groups to appoint 54 Member States to constitute the Committee's membership on the basis of equitable geographical representation and including the permanent members of the Security Council.

Ad Hoc Committee on the Indian Ocean

In 1984, the membership of the *Ad Hoc* Committee on the Indian Ocean rose from 47 to 48, pursuant to a 1979 General Assembly decision to enlarge it.[3]

The Committee, continuing the preparatory work for the Conference on the Indian Ocean (to be convened no later than 1988 at Colombo, Sri Lanka), held three sessions during the year—from 12 to 23 March, from 9 to 20 July and from 20 to 31 August—with an additional meeting on 21 November, all at United Nations Headquarters.

Members: Australia, Bangladesh, Bulgaria, Canada, China, Democratic Yemen, Djibouti, Egypt, Ethiopia, France, German Democratic Republic, Germany, Federal Republic of, Greece, India, Indonesia, Iran, Iraq, Italy, Japan, Kenya, Liberia, Madagascar, Malaysia, Maldives, Mauritius, Mozambique, Netherlands, Norway, Oman, Pakistan, Panama, Poland, Romania, Seychelles, Singapore, Somalia, Sri Lanka, Sudan, Thailand, Uganda,[a] USSR, United Arab Emirates, United Kingdom, United Republic of Tanzania, United States, Yemen, Yugoslavia, Zambia.

Sweden, a major maritime user of the Indian Ocean, continued to participate in the meetings as an observer.

[a]Appointed by the President of the General Assembly's thirty-eighth session, on the basis of a Committee recommendation, as stated in his communication of 26 July 1984 to the Secretary-General.

Chairman: S. W. Arthur de Silva (Sri Lanka) (until 9 July), Nissanka Wijewardane (Sri Lanka) (from 9 July).
Vice-Chairmen: Susan Jennifer Boyd (Australia); Manuel dos Santos (Mozambique); Izhar Ibrahim (Indonesia); Siegfried Kahn (German Democratic Republic) (until 31 August), Wilhelm Grundmann (German Democratic Republic) (from 31 August).
Rapporteur: André Tahindro (Madagascar).

Ad Hoc Committee on the World Disarmament Conference

The 40-member *Ad Hoc* Committee on the World Disarmament Conference held two sessions in 1984, at United Nations Headquarters: the first from 2 to 5 April; and the second from 2 to 6 July.

Members: Algeria, Argentina, Austria, Belgium, Brazil, Bulgaria, Burundi, Canada, Chile, Colombia, Czechoslovakia, Egypt, Ethiopia, Hungary, India, Indonesia, Iran, Italy, Japan, Lebanon, Liberia, Mexico, Mongolia, Morocco, Netherlands, Nigeria, Pakistan, Peru, Philippines, Poland, Romania, Spain, Sri Lanka, Sweden, Tunisia, Turkey, Venezuela, Yugoslavia, Zaire, Zambia.

The USSR participated in the work of the *Ad Hoc* Committee, while China, France, the United Kingdom and the United States maintained contact with it through its Chairman, pursuant to a 1973 General Assembly resolution.[4]

Chairman: S. W. Arthur de Silva (Sri Lanka) (until 2 July), Nissanka Wijewardane (Sri Lanka) (from 2 July).
Vice-Chairmen:[a] Ryszard Krystosik (Poland).
Rapporteur: Arturo Laclaustra (Spain).

[a]Two posts remained vacant.

WORKING GROUP
Members: Burundi, Egypt, Hungary, India, Iran, Italy, Mexico, Peru, Poland, Spain *(Chairman)*, Sri Lanka.

Advisory Committee for the International Youth Year

The 24-member Advisory Committee for the International Youth Year held its third session at Vienna, Austria, from 2 to 11 April 1984.

Members: Algeria, Chile, Costa Rica, Democratic Yemen, Germany, Federal Republic of, Guatemala, Guinea, Indonesia, Ireland, Jamaica, Japan, Lebanon, Morocco, Mozambique, Netherlands, Nigeria, Norway, Poland, Romania, Rwanda, Sri Lanka, USSR, United States, Venezuela.

Chairman: Nicu Ceauscescu (Romania).
Vice-Chairmen: Lasisi Araoye (Nigeria), Edmund Bartlett (Jamaica), Mr. Soenaryo (Indonesia).
Rapporteur: Manfred Gerwinat (Federal Republic of Germany).

Advisory Committee on the United Nations Educational and Training Programme for Southern Africa

Members: Byelorussian SSR, Canada, Denmark, India, Japan, Liberia, Nigeria, Norway, United Republic of Tanzania, United States, Venezuela, Zaire, Zambia.

Chairman: Tom Eric Vraalsen (Norway).
Vice-Chairman: Love Kunda M'tesa (Zambia).

Advisory Committee on the United Nations Programme of Assistance in the Teaching, Study, Dissemination and Wider Appreciation of International Law

The Advisory Committee on the United Nations Programme of Assistance in the Teaching, Study, Dissemination and Wider Appreciation of International Law held its nineteenth session on 11 December 1984 at United Nations Headquarters.

Members (until 31 December 1987):[a] Barbados, Cyprus, France, Ghana, Libyan Arab Jamahiriya, Netherlands, Romania, Sierra Leone, Syrian Arab Republic, Turkey, USSR, United Kingdom, Venezuela.

[a]Nominated by the General Assembly President and appointed by the Assembly on 20 November and 5 December 1984 (decision 39/308).

Chairman: Yaw Konadu-Yiadom (Ghana).

Board of Auditors

The Board of Auditors consists of three members appointed by the General Assembly for three-year terms.

Members:
To serve until 30 June 1985: Auditor-General of Ghana.
To serve until 30 June 1986: Senior President of the Audit Office of Belgium.
To serve until 30 June 1987: Chairman of the Commission of Audit of the Philippines.

On 13 December 1984 (decision 39/319), the General Assembly reappointed the Auditor-General of Ghana for a three-year term beginning on 1 July 1985.

Collective Measures Committee

Established in 1950 under the General Assembly's "Uniting for Peace" resolution,[5] the Collective Measures Committee reported three times to the Assembly. In noting the third report, to its ninth (1954) session, the Assembly directed the Committee to remain in a position to pursue such further studies as it may deem desirable to strengthen the capability of the United Nations to maintain peace and to report to the Security Council and to the Assembly as appropriate.[6]

Members: Australia, Belgium, Brazil, Burma, Canada, Egypt, France, Mexico, Philippines, Turkey, United Kingdom, United States, Venezuela, Yugoslavia.

Commission on Human Settlements

The Commission on Human Settlements reports to the General Assembly through the Economic and Social Council.

[3]YUN 1979, p. 67, res. 34/80 B, 11 Dec. 1979.
[4]YUN 1973, p. 18, res. 3183(XXVIII), 18 Dec. 1973.
[5]YUN 1950, p. 194, res. 377(V), part A, para. 11, 3 Nov. 1950.
[6]YUN 1954, p. 23, res. 809(IX), 4 Nov. 1954.

For details of the Commission's membership and session in 1984, see p. 1333.

Committee for Programme and Co-ordination

The Committee for Programme and Co-ordination is the main subsidiary organ of the Economic and Social Council and of the General Assembly for planning, programming and co-ordination; it reports to both.

For details of the Committee's membership and session in 1984, see p. 1334.

Committee for the United Nations Population Award

The Committee for the United Nations Population Award is composed of: *(a)* 10 representatives of United Nations Member States elected by the Economic and Social Council for a three-year period, with due regard for equitable geographical representation and the need to include Member States that had made contributions for the Award; *(b)* the Secretary-General and the UNFPA Executive Director, to serve *ex officio;* and *(c)* five individuals eminent for their significant contributions to population-related activities, selected by the Committee, to serve as honorary members in an advisory capacity for a renewable three-year term.

In 1984, the Committee held eight meetings between 18 January and 27 July 1984, at United Nations Headquarters.

Members (until 31 December 1985): Australia, Bangladesh, Burundi, China, Colombia, Egypt, Japan, Mexico, Tunisia, Yugoslavia.
Ex-officio members: The Secretary-General and the UNFPA Executive Director.
Honorary members (until 31 December 1985): Kenneth K. S. Dadzie, Nobusuke Kishi, Alva Myrdal, Raúl Prebisch, Robert E. Turner III.[a]

[a]Selected by the Committee on 6 February 1984 to replace Theodore W. Schultz, who had resigned in 1983.

Chairman: Anwarul Karim Chowdhury (Bangladesh).

Committee of Trustees of the United Nations Trust Fund for South Africa
Members: Chile, Morocco, Nigeria, Pakistan, Sweden.

Chairman: Anders Ferm (Sweden).
Vice-Chairman: Joseph N. Garba (Nigeria).

Committee on Applications for Review of Administrative Tribunal Judgements

In 1984, the Committee on Applications for Review of Administrative Tribunal Judgements held two sessions, at United Nations Headquarters: its twenty-third on 9 January; and its twenty-fourth from 20 to 28 August.

Members (until 17 September 1984) (based on the composition of the General Committee at the General Assembly's thirty-eighth session): Algeria, Belgium, Bhutan, Burundi, Canada, China, Colombia, Czechoslovakia, France, German Democratic Republic, Guyana, Japan, Lebanon, Liberia, Libyan Arab Jamahiriya, Nepal, Norway, Pakistan, Panama, Sierra Leone, Singapore, Sudan, Swaziland, Thailand, Tunisia, USSR, United Kingdom, United States, Venezuela.

Twenty-third session
Chairman: Taieb Slim (Tunisia).
Rapporteur: Franklin D. Berman (United Kingdom).

Twenty-fourth session
Chairman: Elies Gastli (Tunisia).
Rapporteur: David M. Edwards (United Kingdom).

Members (from 18 September 1984) (based on the composition of the General Committee at the General Assembly's thirty-ninth session): Bahrain, Bangladesh, Barbados, Bolivia, Brazil, Bulgaria, Chad, China, Cuba, Cyprus, Djibouti, France, German Democratic Republic, Ghana, Guatemala, Guinea, Iceland, Italy, Malaysia, Morocco, New Zealand, Papua New Guinea, Somalia, Togo, USSR, United Kingdom, United States, Yemen, Zambia.

Committee on Arrangements for a Conference for the Purpose of Reviewing the Charter

All Members of the United Nations are members of the Committee on Arrangements for a Conference for the Purpose of Reviewing the Charter. The Committee, established in 1955, last met in 1967, following which the General Assembly decided to keep it in being.[7]

Committee on Conferences

The Committee on Conferences consists of 22 Member States appointed by the President of the General Assembly on the basis of equitable geographical balance, to serve for a three-year term.

Members (until 31 December 1986):[a] Algeria, Austria, Bahamas, Bulgaria, Byelorussian SSR, Chile, Cyprus, France, Germany, Federal Republic of, Honduras, Indonesia, Italy, Japan, Kenya, Mexico, Nigeria, Senegal, Sri Lanka, Tunisia, USSR, United Kingdom, United States.

[a]Appointed on 1 March 1984.

Chairman: Michael George Okeyo (Kenya).
Vice-Chairmen: Mihail Bushev (Bulgaria), Patricio Damm (Chile), Bernard A. B. Goonetilleke (Sri Lanka).
Rapporteur: Wilfried Almoslechner (Austria).

Committee on Information

In 1984, the 67-member Committee on Information held, at United Nations Headquarters, an organizational session on 19 March and its sixth session from 18 June to 6 July and on 6 September.

Members: Algeria, Argentina, Bangladesh, Belgium, Benin, Brazil, Bulgaria, Burundi, Chile, Colombia, Congo, Costa Rica, Cuba, Cyprus, Denmark, Ecuador, Egypt, El Salvador, Ethiopia, Finland, France, German Democratic Republic, Germany, Federal Republic of, Ghana, Greece, Guatemala, Guinea, Guyana, India, Indonesia, Italy, Ivory Coast, Japan, Jordan, Kenya, Lebanon, Mongolia, Morocco, Netherlands, Niger, Nigeria, Pakistan, Peru, Philippines, Poland, Portugal, Romania, Singapore, Somalia, Spain, Sri Lanka, Sudan, Syrian Arab Republic, Togo, Trinidad and Tobago, Tunisia, Turkey, Ukrainian SSR, USSR, United Kingdom, United Republic of Tanzania, United States, Venezuela, Viet Nam, Yemen, Yugoslavia, Zaire.

Chairman: Luis Moreno-Salcedo (Philippines).
Vice-Chairmen: Miguel A. Albornoz (Ecuador), Rachid Lahlou (Morocco), Willi Schlegel (German Democratic Republic).
Rapporteur: Uta-Maria Mayer-Schalburg (Federal Republic of Germany).

On 14 December 1984, the General Assembly increased the Committee's membership from 67 to 69 and appointed China and Mexico as new members.

Committee on Relations with the Host Country
Members: Bulgaria, Canada, China, Costa Rica, Cyprus, France, Honduras, Iraq, Ivory Coast, Mali, Senegal, Spain, USSR, United Kingdom, United States (host country).

Chairman: Constantine Moushoutas (Cyprus).
Vice-Chairmen: Bulgaria, Canada, Ivory Coast.
Rapporteur: Emilia Castro de Barish (Costa Rica).

Committee on the Development and Utilization of New and Renewable Sources of Energy

The Committee on the Development and Utilization of New and Renewable Sources of Energy, open to the participation of all States as full members, held its second session at United Nations Headquarters from 23 April to 4 May 1984.

Chairman: Awad Mohamed Elhassan (Sudan).
Vice-Chairmen: Mihail Bushev (Bulgaria), George Papadatos (Greece), Faruq S. Ziada (Iraq).
Rapporteur: Ellen Osthoff Ferreira de Barros (Brazil).

---

[7]YUN 1967, p. 291, res. 2285(XXII), 5 Dec. 1967.

Committee on the Exercise of the Inalienable Rights of the Palestinian People
Members: Afghanistan, Cuba, Cyprus, German Democratic Republic, Guinea, Guyana, Hungary, India, Indonesia, Lao People's Democratic Republic, Madagascar, Malaysia, Mali, Malta, Nigeria, Pakistan, Romania, Senegal, Sierra Leone, Tunisia, Turkey, Ukrainian SSR, Yugoslavia.

Chairman: Massamba Sarré (Senegal).
Vice-Chairmen: Raúl Roa Kouri (Cuba) (until 18 September), Oscar Oramas Oliva (Cuba) (from 18 September); Mohammad Farid Zarif (Afghanistan).
Rapporteur: Victor J. Gauci (Malta).

WORKING GROUP
Members: Afghanistan, Cuba, German Democratic Republic, Guinea, Guyana, India, Malta *(Chairman)*, Pakistan, Senegal, Tunisia, Turkey, Ukrainian SSR; Palestine Liberation Organization.

Committee on the Peaceful Uses of Outer Space
The 53-member Committee on the Peaceful Uses of Outer Space held its twenty-seventh session at Vienna, Austria, from 12 to 21 June 1984.

Members: Albania, Argentina, Australia, Austria, Belgium, Benin, Brazil, Bulgaria, Cameroon, Canada, Chad, Chile, China, Colombia, Czechoslovakia, Ecuador, Egypt, France, German Democratic Republic, Germany, Federal Republic of, Hungary, India, Indonesia, Iran, Iraq, Italy, Japan, Kenya, Lebanon, Mexico, Mongolia, Morocco, Netherlands, Niger, Nigeria, Pakistan, Philippines, Poland,[a] Romania, Sierra Leone, Sudan, Sweden, Syrian Arab Republic, Turkey,[a] USSR, United Kingdom, United States, Upper Volta, Uruguay, Venezuela, Viet Nam, Yugoslavia.

[a]Replaced Spain and Greece, respectively, in accordance with a three-year system of rotation agreed on by the Group of Western European and Other States.

Chairman: Peter Jankowitsch (Austria).
Vice-Chairman: Teodor Marinescu (Romania).
Rapporteur: Henrique Rodrigues Valle (Brazil).

LEGAL SUB-COMMITTEE
The Legal Sub-Committee, a committee of the whole, held its twenty-third session at Geneva from 19 March to 6 April 1984.

Chairman: Ludek Handl (Czechoslovakia).

SCIENTIFIC AND TECHNICAL SUB-COMMITTEE
The Scientific and Technical Sub-Committee, a committee of the whole, held its twenty-first session at United Nations Headquarters from 13 to 24 February 1984.

Chairman: J. H. Carver (Australia).

Committee on the Review and Appraisal of the Implementation of the International Development Strategy for the Third United Nations Development Decade
The Committee on the Review and Appraisal of the Implementation of the International Development Strategy for the Third United Nations Development Decade, open to the participation of all States as full members, held its first session at United Nations Headquarters from 7 to 25 May and from 10 to 18 September 1984.

Chairman: Kenneth K. S. Dadzie (Ghana).
Vice-Chairmen: Oscar R. de Rojas (Venezuela), Per Jodahl (Sweden), Konstantin Kolev (Bulgaria).
Rapporteur: Yousif Gewaily (Qatar).

Disarmament Commission
In 1984, the Disarmament Commission, composed of all the Members of the United Nations, held a series of meetings between 7 May and 1 June and organizational meetings on 3 and 5 December, all at United Nations Headquarters.

Chairman: James Victor Gbeho (Ghana).
Vice-Chairmen: Argentina, Bahamas, German Democratic Republic, Germany, Federal Republic of, Greece, Nepal, Pakistan, Sudan.
Rapporteur: S. N. Martynov (Byelorussian SSR).

High-level Committee on the Review of Technical Co-operation among Developing Countries
The High-level Committee on the Review of Technical Co-operation among Developing Countries, composed of all States participating in UNDP, did not meet in 1984.

Intergovernmental Committee on Science and Technology for Development
The Intergovernmental Committee on Science and Technology for Development, open to the participation of all States as full members, held its sixth session at United Nations Headquarters from 29 May to 8 June 1984.

Chairman: Klaus Stubenrauch (German Democratic Republic).
Vice-Chairmen: Carlos Abeledo (Argentina), Lars Anell (Sweden), Mazhar Qurashi (Pakistan).
Rapporteur: José S. Figueiredo Ramos (Cape Verde).

ADVISORY COMMITTEE ON SCIENCE AND TECHNOLOGY FOR DEVELOPMENT
The 28-member Advisory Committee on Science and Technology for Development held its fourth session at United Nations Headquarters from 14 to 21 February 1984.

Members:
To serve until 31 December 1984: Sadak Ben Jamaa, *Vice-Chairman* (Tunisia); Just Faaland (Norway); Edmundo Flores (Mexico); Peter Gacii (Kenya); Dennis Irvine (Jamaica); Lu Jing-ting (China); Loretta Makasiar-Sicat (Philippines); Rodney W. Nichols (United States); V. I. Popkov (USSR); Hamida Radouane (Algeria); Bachtiar Rifai (Indonesia); Leopold Schmetterer (Austria); Adnan Shihab-Eldin (Kuwait); Klaus Stubenrauch, *Vice-Chairman* (German Democratic Republic). *To serve until 31 December 1986:* Oscar Aguero Wood (Chile); Umberto Colombo, *Chairman* (Italy); Etienne Cracco (Belgium); Djibril Fall (Senegal); Essam El Din Galal (Egypt); Henri Hogbe-Nlend, *Rapporteur* (Cameroon); Mumtaz Ali Kazi, *Vice-Chairman* (Pakistan); Lydia Makhubu (Swaziland); James Mullin (Canada); Tiberiu Muresan (Romania); Keichi Oshima (Japan); Francisco R. Sagasti (Peru); M. S. Swaminathan (India); José Israel Vargas, *Vice-Chairman* (Brazil).

On 2 June 1984, the Intergovernmental Committee appointed the following members of the Advisory Committee for a three-year term beginning on 1 January 1985 to fill the vacancies occurring on 31 December 1984: Lars Anell (Sweden), Ang How-Ghee (Singapore), Saleh Abdulrahman Athel (Saudi Arabia), Sadak Ben Jamaa (Tunisia), I. D. Ivanov (USSR), Ernst Keller (Switzerland), Stefen Kwiatkowski (Poland), Manlio D. Martinez (Honduras), Abdou Dioffo Moumouni (Niger), V. Nyathi (Zimbabwe), Sanga Sabhasri (Thailand), Yannis Tsividis (Greece), Lawrence A. Wilson (Trinidad and Tobago), Xu Zhaoxiang (China).

Interim Committee of the General Assembly
The Interim Committee of the General Assembly, on which each Member of the United Nations has the right to appoint one representative, was originally established by the Assembly in 1947 to function between the Assembly's regular sessions. It was re-established in 1948 for a further year and in 1949[8] for an indefinite period. The Committee has not met since 1961.[9]

International Civil Service Commission
The International Civil Service Commission consists of 15 members who serve in their personal capacity as individuals of recognized competence in public administration or related fields, particularly in personnel management. They are appointed by the General Assembly, with due regard for equitable geographical distribution, for four-year terms.

[8]YUN 1948-49, p. 411, res. 295(IV), 21 Nov. 1949.
[9]YUN 1961, p. 705.

The Commission held two sessions in 1984: its nineteenth in Paris from 5 to 23 March; and its twentieth at United Nations Headquarters from 5 to 27 July.

Members:
To serve until 31 December 1984: Syed Amjad Ali (Pakistan); Michael O. Ani (Nigeria); V. V. Tsybukov (USSR); M. A. Vellodi (India); Halima Embarek Warzazi (Morocco).
To serve until 31 December 1985: Michel Auchère (France); Ralph Enckell (Finland); Masao Kanazawa (Japan); Helmut Kitschenberg (Federal Republic of Germany); Antônio Fonseca Pimentel (Brazil).
To serve until 31 December 1986: Richard M. Akwei, *Chairman* (Ghana); Gastón de Prat Gay, *Vice-Chairman* (Argentina);[a] Moulaye El Hassen (Mauritania); Dayton W. Hull (United States); Jiri Nosek (Czechoslovakia).

[a]Resigned on 15 August 1984; Carlos S. Vegega (Argentina) was appointed by the General Assembly on 13 December (decision 39/322) to fill the resultant vacancy, beginning on 1 January 1985. By the same decision, the Assembly designated him Vice-Chairman for the same term.

On 13 December 1984 (decision 39/322), the General Assembly appointed the following members for a four-year term beginning on 1 January 1985 to fill the vacancies occurring on 31 December 1984: Syed Amjad Ali (Pakistan), Michael O. Ani (Nigeria), Omar Sirry (Egypt), V. V. Tsybukov (USSR), M. A. Vellodi (India).

ADVISORY COMMITTEE ON
POST ADJUSTMENT QUESTIONS
The Advisory Committee on Post Adjustment Questions consists of six members, of whom five are chosen from the geographical regions of Africa, Asia, Latin America, Eastern Europe, and Western Europe and other States; and one, from ICSC, who serves *ex officio* as Chairman. Members are appointed by the ICSC Chairman to serve for four-year terms.
The Advisory Committee held its ninth session at Geneva from 7 to 23 May 1984.

Members:
To serve until 31 December 1984: G. K. Nair (Malaysia).
To serve until 31 December 1985: Nana Wereko Ampem II (also known as Emmanuel Noi Omaboe) (Ghana).
To serve until 31 December 1986: Carmen McFarlane (Jamaica); Hugues Picard (France).
To serve until 31 December 1987: A. F. Revenko (USSR).[a]
Ex-officio member: Jiri Nosek, *Chairman* (Czechoslovakia).

[a]Reappointed in March 1984.

International Law Commission
The International Law Commission consists of 34 persons of recognized competence in international law, elected by the General Assembly to serve in their individual capacity for a five-year term. Vacancies occurring within the five-year period are filled by the Commission.
The Commission held its thirty-sixth session at Geneva from 7 May to 27 July 1984.

Members (until 31 December 1986): Richard Osuolale A. Akinjide (Nigeria); Riyadh Mahmoud Sami Al-Qaysi (Iraq); Balanda Mikuin Leliel (Zaire); Julio Barboza, *Second Vice-Chairman* (Argentina); Boutros Boutros-Ghali (Egypt); Carlos Calero Rodrigues (Brazil); Jorge Castañeda (Mexico); Leonardo Díaz-González (Venezuela); Khalafalla El Rasheed Mohamed-Ahmed (Sudan); Jens Evensen, *Rapporteur* (Norway);[a] Constantin Flitan (Romania); Laurel B. Francis (Jamaica); Jorge Enrique Illueca (Panama); Andreas J. Jacovides (Cyprus); Satya Pal Jagota (India); Abdul G. Koroma (Sierra Leone); José Manuel Lacleta Muñoz (Spain); Ahmed Mahiou (Algeria); Chafic Malek (Lebanon); Stephen C. McCaffrey (United States); Ni Zhengyu (China);[a] Frank X. J. C. Njenga (Kenya); Motoo Ogiso (Japan); Syed Sharifuddin Pirzada (Pakistan); Robert Q. Quentin-Baxter (New Zealand);[b] Edilbert Razafindralambo (Madagascar); Paul Reuter (France); Willem Riphagen (Netherlands); Sir Ian Sinclair (United Kingdom); Constantin A. Stavropoulos (Greece);[b] Sompong Sucharitkul, *First Vice-Chairman* (Thailand); Doudou Thiam (Senegal); N. A. Ushakov (USSR); Alexander Yankov, *Chairman* (Bulgaria).

[a]Elected to the International Court of Justice on 7 November 1984; the resultant vacancies were not filled in 1984.
[b]Died on 25 September and 5 November 1984, respectively; the resultant vacancies were not filled in 1984.

Investments Committee
The Investments Committee consists of nine members appointed by the Secretary-General, after consultation with the United Nations Joint Staff Pension Board and ACABQ, subject to confirmation by the General Assembly. Members serve for three-year terms.

Members:
To serve until 31 December 1984: Jean Guyot; George Johnston; Michiya Matsukawa.
To serve until 31 December 1985: Aloysio de Andrade Faria; Braj Kumar Nehru, *Chairman;* Stanislaw Raczkowski.
To serve until 31 December 1986: David Montagu; Yves Oltramare; Emmanuel Noi Omaboe (also known as Nana Wereko Ampem II).

In addition, during 1984, Ahmed Abdullatif and Juergen Reimnitz served in an *ad hoc* consultative capacity.

On 13 December 1984 (decision 39/320), the General Assembly confirmed the appointment by the Secretary-General of Jean Guyot, George Johnston and Michiya Matsukawa as members for a three-year term beginning on 1 January 1985.

Joint Advisory Group on the International Trade Centre UNCTAD/GATT
The Joint Advisory Group was established in accordance with an agreement between UNCTAD and GATT with effect from 1 January 1968, the date on which their joint sponsorship of the International Trade Centre commenced.
Participation in the Group is open to all States members of UNCTAD and to all Contracting Parties to GATT.
The Group held its seventeenth session at Geneva from 9 to 16 April 1984.

Chairman: A. K. H. Morshed (Bangladesh).
Vice-Chairmen: V. Petrov (USSR), Rasmus Rasmusson (Sweden).
Rapporteur: E. J. Mbaga (United Republic of Tanzania).

TECHNICAL COMMITTEE
The Technical Committee of the Joint Advisory Group, which is open to the participation of experts, as well as officials responsible for national trade promotion activities, from any country represented in the Group, reviews the Centre's work programme and organizational structure and reports to the Group.
In 1984, for the second year of a two-year experiment, meetings of the Committee and the Group were combined in a single meeting—the Group's seventeenth session.

Joint Inspection Unit
The Joint Inspection Unit consists of not more than 11 Inspectors appointed by the General Assembly from candidates nominated by Member States following appropriate consultations, including consultations with the President of the Economic and Social Council and with the Chairman of ACC. The Inspectors, chosen for their special experience in national or international administrative and financial matters, with due regard for equitable geographical distribution and reasonable rotation, serve in their personal capacity for five-year terms.

Members:
To serve until 31 December 1985: Maurice Bertrand (France); Alfred Nathaniel Forde, *Chairman* (Barbados); Moustapha Ould Khalifa (Mauritania); Earl D. Sohm (United States); Miljenko Vukovic (Yugoslavia).
To serve until 31 December 1987: Mark E. Allen (United Kingdom);[a] A. S. Efimov (USSR); Toman Hutagalung (Indonesia);[b] Mohamed Salah Eldin Ibrahim, *Vice-Chairman* (Egypt); Nasser Kaddour (Syrian Arab Republic); Norman Williams (Panama).

[a]Resigned with effect from 21 September 1984; on that day (decision 39/305 A), the General Assembly appointed Siegfried Schumm (Federal Republic of Germany) to fill the resultant vacancy.
[b]Died on 19 December 1984; the resultant vacancy was not filled during 1984.

On 18 December 1984 (decision 39/305 B), the General Assembly appointed the following members for a five-year term beginning on 1 January 1986 to fill the vacancies occurring on 31 December 1985: Enrique Ferrer Vieyra (Argentina), Alain Gourdon (France), Richard Vognild Hennes (United States), Ivan Kojic (Yugoslavia), Kabongo Tunsala (Zaire).

Negotiating Committee on the Financial Emergency of the United Nations

Established in 1975 by the General Assembly[10] to consist of 54 Member States appointed by its President on the basis of equitable geographical balance, the Negotiating Committee on the Financial Emergency of the United Nations has a membership of 48. It has not met since 1976.[11]

Members: Argentina, Austria, Bangladesh, Bolivia, Burkina Faso, Canada, Chad, Colombia, Cuba, Ecuador, Egypt, Finland, France, Gabon, German Democratic Republic, Germany, Federal Republic of, Ghana, Greece, Grenada, India, Indonesia, Iran, Ireland, Italy, Jamaica, Japan, Jordan, Kenya, Kuwait, Libyan Arab Jamahiriya, Malawi, Mexico, Morocco, Nigeria, Pakistan, Philippines, Poland, Spain, Sudan, Swaziland, Sweden, Trinidad and Tobago, Tunisia, Turkey, USSR, United Kingdom, United States, Venezuela.

Office of the United Nations High Commissioner for Refugees (UNHCR)

EXECUTIVE COMMITTEE OF THE HIGH COMMISSIONER'S PROGRAMME

The Executive Committee held the first part of its thirty-fifth session at Geneva from 8 to 18 October 1984.

Members: Algeria, Argentina, Australia, Austria, Belgium, Brazil, Canada, China, Colombia, Denmark, Finland, France, Germany, Federal Republic of, Greece, Holy See, Iran, Israel, Italy, Japan, Lebanon, Lesotho, Madagascar, Morocco, Netherlands, Nicaragua, Nigeria, Norway, Sudan, Sweden, Switzerland, Thailand, Tunisia, Turkey, Uganda, United Kingdom, United Republic of Tanzania, United States, Venezuela, Yugoslavia, Zaire; Namibia (represented by the United Nations Council for Namibia).

Chairman: F. Mebazaa (Tunisia).
Vice-Chairman: K. Chiba (Japan).
Rapporteur: I. Uusitalo (Finland).

United Nations High Commissioner for Refugees: Poul Hartling.
Deputy High Commissioner: William Richard Smyser.

SUB-COMMITTEE OF THE WHOLE ON INTERNATIONAL PROTECTION

The Sub-Committee of the Whole on International Protection held its ninth meeting at Geneva on 3, 4, 11 and 15 October 1984.

Chairman: Hans V. Ewerlof (Sweden).

SUB-COMMITTEE ON ADMINISTRATIVE AND FINANCIAL MATTERS

The Sub-Committee on Administrative and Financial Matters, which is composed of all members of the Executive Committee, held its fourth meeting at Geneva concurrently with the ninth meeting of the Sub-Committee of the Whole on International Protection.

Chairman: F. Mebazaa (Tunisia).

Panel for Inquiry and Conciliation

The Panel for Inquiry and Conciliation was created by the General Assembly in 1949[12] to consist of qualified persons, designated by United Nations Member States, each to serve for a term of five years. Information concerning the Panel's composition had from time to time been communicated to the Assembly and the Security Council; the last consolidated list was issued by the Secretary-General in a note of 20 January 1961.

Panel of External Auditors

The Panel of External Auditors consists of the members of the United Nations Board of Auditors and the appointed external auditors of the specialized agencies and IAEA.

Panel of Military Experts

The General Assembly's "Uniting for Peace" resolution[13] called for the appointment of military experts to be available, on request, to United Nations Member States wishing to obtain technical advice on the organization, training and equipment of elements within their national armed forces which could be made available, in accordance with national constitutional processes, for service as a unit or units of the United Nations upon the recommendation of the Security Council or the Assembly.

Preparatory Committee for the Fortieth Anniversary of the United Nations

The Preparatory Committee for the Fortieth Anniversary of the United Nations (to be observed in 1985), consisting of the members of the General Committee at the General Assembly's thirty-eighth (1983) session and open to the participation of all Member States on an equal basis, held five meetings between 31 May and 14 December 1984.

Chairman:[a] Jorge Enrique Illueca (Panama).

[a]The remaining officers had not been elected at the end of 1984.

On 17 December 1984, the General Assembly decided that the Preparatory Committee should continue to function in 1985 under the chairmanship of the President of the Assembly's thirty-ninth (1984) session.

Preparatory Committee for the International Conference on the Relationship between Disarmament and Development

On 17 December 1984, the General Assembly established a Preparatory Committee for the International Conference on the Relationship between Disarmament and Development (scheduled for 1986) to formulate and submit to the Assembly at its fortieth (1985) session recommendations concerning the arrangements for the Conference. The Committee, to be composed of 54 members appointed by the Assembly President, was not constituted in 1984.

Preparatory Committee for the United Nations Conference for the Promotion of International Co-operation in the Peaceful Uses of Nuclear Energy

In 1984, the Preparatory Committee for the United Nations Conference for the Promotion of International Co-operation in the Peaceful Uses of Nuclear Energy (rescheduled for 1987), which was to be composed of 70 Member States and, on an equal footing, other Member States which might express interest in participating in the Committee's work, had a membership of 66. It held its fifth session at United Nations Headquarters from 25 June to 6 July.

Members: Algeria, Argentina, Australia, Austria, Belgium, Brazil, Bulgaria, Byelorussian SSR, Cameroon, Canada, Chile, China, Colombia, Costa Rica, Cuba, Czechoslovakia, Denmark, Ecuador, Egypt, Finland, France, German Democratic Republic, Germany, Federal Republic of, Ghana, Greece, Guatemala, Hungary, India, Indonesia, Iran, Iraq, Ireland, Italy, Ivory Coast, Japan, Libyan Arab Jamahiriya, Malaysia, Mauritania, Mexico, Morocco, Netherlands, Niger, Nigeria, Norway, Pakistan, Peru, Philippines, Poland, Romania, Saudi Arabia, Senegal, Spain, Sri Lanka, Sweden, Syrian Arab Republic, Thailand, Turkey, Ukrainian SSR, USSR, United Arab Emirates, United Kingdom, United States, Uruguay, Venezuela, Yugoslavia, Zaire.

Chairman: Novak Pribicevic (Yugoslavia).
Vice-Chairmen: F. K. A. Allotey (Ghana); Juan Carlos Beltramino (Argentina); Essam El-Din Hawas (Egypt); Zdenek Kamis (Czechoslo-

[10]YUN 1975, p. 957, res. 3538(XXX), 17 Dec. 1975.
[11]YUN 1976, pp. 889 and 1064.
[12]YUN 1948-49, p. 416, res. 268 D (III), 28 Apr. 1949.
[13]YUN 1950, p. 194, res. 377(V), part A, para. 10, 3 Nov. 1950.

vakia); Suror Merza Mahmoud (Iraq); Johan Nordenfelt (Sweden); Frans J. A. Terwisscha van Scheltinga (Netherlands); Jorge Voto Bernales (Peru).
Rapporteur: Enny Soeprapto (Indonesia).

Special Committee against *Apartheid*

The Special Committee against *Apartheid* has a membership of 18. Additional members remained to be appointed by the end of 1984 in pursuance of a 1979 General Assembly request[14] to increase that number.

Members: Algeria, German Democratic Republic, Ghana, Guinea, Haiti, Hungary, India, Indonesia, Malaysia, Nepal, Nigeria, Peru, Philippines, Somalia, Sudan, Syrian Arab Republic, Trinidad and Tobago, Ukrainian SSR.

Chairman: Joseph N. Garba (Nigeria).
Vice-Chairmen: Uddhav Deo Bhatt (Nepal), V. A. Kravets (Ukrainian SSR).
Rapporteur: Gervais Charles (Haiti).

SUB-COMMITTEE ON PETITIONS AND INFORMATION
Members: Algeria *(Chairman)*, German Democratic Republic, Nepal, Somalia, Trinidad and Tobago.

SUB-COMMITTEE ON THE IMPLEMENTATION
OF UNITED NATIONS RESOLUTIONS
AND COLLABORATION WITH SOUTH AFRICA
Members: Ghana *(Chairman)*, Hungary, India, Peru, Sudan.

Special Committee on Enhancing the Effectiveness of the Principle of Non-Use of Force in International Relations

The 35-member Special Committee on Enhancing the Effectiveness of the Principle of Non-Use of Force in International Relations held a series of meetings at United Nations Headquarters between 21 February and 16 March 1984.

Members: Argentina,[a] Belgium, Benin, Brazil,[a] Bulgaria, Chile,[a] Cuba,[b] Cyprus, Ecuador,[b] Egypt, Finland, France, Germany, Federal Republic of, Greece, Guinea, Hungary, India, Iraq, Italy, Japan, Mexico,[b] Mongolia, Morocco, Nepal, Poland, Romania, Senegal, Somalia, Spain, Togo, Turkey, Uganda, USSR, United Kingdom, United States.

[a]Withdrew from membership with effect from 31 December 1984, as stated in a letter of 10 December to the Secretary-General from the Chairman of the Latin American Group. On 18 December (decision 39/326), the General Assembly confirmed the appointment by its President of Nicaragua, Panama and Peru, effective 1 January 1985, to fill the resultant vacancies.
[b]Replaced Nicaragua, Panama and Peru, in accordance with a system of rotation agreed upon by the Latin American States when the Special Committee was constituted.

Chairman: Ryszard Krystosik (Poland).
Vice-Chairmen: Domingo S. Cullen (Argentina), Ahmed Amin Fathalla (Egypt), P. Sreenivasa Rao (India).
Rapporteur: Agustín Font (Spain).

Special Committee on Peace-keeping Operations

The 33-member Special Committee on Peace-keeping Operations did not meet in 1984.

Members: Afghanistan, Algeria, Argentina, Australia, Austria, Canada, Denmark, Egypt, El Salvador, Ethiopia, France, German Democratic Republic, Guatemala, Hungary, India, Iraq, Italy, Japan, Mauritania, Mexico, Netherlands, Nigeria, Pakistan, Poland, Romania, Sierra Leone, Spain, Thailand, USSR, United Kingdom, United States, Venezuela, Yugoslavia.

WORKING GROUP
Members: Argentina, Canada, Egypt, France, Hungary, India, Japan, Mexico, Nigeria, Pakistan, USSR, United Kingdom, United States.

Special Committee on the Charter of the United Nations and on the Strengthening of the Role of the Organization

The 47-member Special Committee on the Charter of the United Nations and on the Strengthening of the Role of the Organization held a series of meetings at United Nations Headquarters between 2 and 27 April 1984.

Members: Algeria, Argentina, Barbados, Belgium, Brazil, China, Colombia, Congo, Cyprus, Czechoslovakia, Ecuador, Egypt, El Salvador, Finland, France, German Democratic Republic, Germany, Federal Republic of, Ghana, Greece, Guyana, India, Indonesia, Iran, Iraq, Italy, Japan, Kenya, Liberia, Mexico, Nepal, New Zealand, Nigeria, Pakistan, Philippines, Poland, Romania, Rwanda, Sierra Leone, Spain, Tunisia, Turkey, USSR, United Kingdom, United States, Venezuela, Yugoslavia, Zambia.

Chairman: Bengt H. G. A. Broms (Finland).
Vice-Chairmen: Yasin A. Aena (Iraq), Carlos Bernal (Mexico), Ramdane Lamamra (Algeria).
Rapporteur: Jiri Pavlovsky (Czechoslovakia).

Special Committee on the Situation with regard to the Implementation of the Declaration on the Granting of Independence to Colonial Countries and Peoples

Members: Afghanistan, Australia, Bulgaria, Chile, China, Congo, Cuba, Czechoslovakia, Ethiopia, Fiji, India, Indonesia, Iran, Iraq, Ivory Coast, Mali, Sierra Leone, Sweden, Syrian Arab Republic, Trinidad and Tobago, Tunisia, USSR, United Republic of Tanzania, Venezuela, Yugoslavia.

Chairman: Abdul G. Koroma (Sierra Leone).
Vice-Chairmen: Jan Lundvik (Sweden), Jiri Pulz (Czechoslovakia), Raúl Roa Kouri (Cuba).
Rapporteur: Mohamed Farouk Adhami (Syrian Arab Republic).

SUB-COMMITTEE ON PETITIONS,
INFORMATION AND ASSISTANCE
Members: Afghanistan, Bulgaria, Congo, Cuba, Czechoslovakia *(Chairman)*, Indonesia, Iran, Iraq, Mali, Sierra Leone, Sweden, Syrian Arab Republic, Tunisia, United Republic of Tanzania.

SUB-COMMITTEE ON SMALL TERRITORIES
Members: Afghanistan, Australia *(Rapporteur)*, Bulgaria, Chile, Cuba, Czechoslovakia, Ethiopia, Fiji, India, Indonesia, Iran, Iraq, Ivory Coast, Mali, Sweden, Trinidad and Tobago, Tunisia *(Chairman)*,[a] United Republic of Tanzania, Venezuela, Yugoslavia.

[a]Became a member on 9 May 1984, as agreed by the Special Committee.

WORKING GROUP
In 1984, the Working Group of the Special Committee, which functions as a steering committee, consisted of: Congo, Iran; the five officers of the Special Committee; and the Chairman and the Rapporteur of the Sub-Committee on Small Territories.

Special Committee to Investigate Israeli Practices Affecting the Human Rights of the Population of the Occupied Territories
Members: Senegal, Sri Lanka *(Chairman)*, Yugoslavia.

Special Committee to Select the Winners of the United Nations Human Rights Prize

The Special Committee to Select the Winners of the United Nations Human Rights Prize was established pursuant to a 1966 resolution of the General Assembly[15] recommending that a prize or prizes in the field of human rights be awarded not more often than at five-year intervals. Prizes were awarded for the third time on 11 December 1978.[16]

Members: The President of the General Assembly, the President of the Economic and Social Council, the Chairman of the Commission on Human Rights, the Chairman of the Commission on the Status of Women and the Chairman of the Sub-Commission on Prevention of Discrimination and Protection of Minorities.

---

[14]YUN 1979, p. 201, res. 34/93 R, 17 Dec. 1979.
[15]YUN 1966, p. 458, res. 2217 A (XXI), annex, 19 Dec. 1966.
[16]YUN 1978, p. 721.

United Nations Administrative Tribunal

Members:

To serve until 31 December 1984: Luis María de Posadas Montero (Uruguay); Endre Ustor, *President* (Hungary).

To serve until 31 December 1985: Mutuale Tshikankie (Zaire); Roger Pinto (France); Samarendranath Sen, *First Vice-President* (India).

To serve until 31 December 1986: Arnold Wilfred Geoffrey Kean, *Second Vice-President* (United Kingdom); Herbert K. Reis (United States).

On 13 December 1984 (decision 39/321), the General Assembly appointed Luis María de Posadas Montero (Uruguay) and Endre Ustor (Hungary) for a three-year term beginning on 1 January 1985 to fill the vacancies occurring on 31 December 1984.

United Nations Capital Development Fund

The United Nations Capital Development Fund was set up as an organ of the General Assembly to function as an autonomous organization within the United Nations framework, with the control of its policies and operations to be exercised by a 24-member Executive Board elected by the Assembly from Members of the United Nations or members of the specialized agencies or of IAEA. The chief executive officer of the Fund, the Managing Director, exercises his functions under the general direction of the Executive Board, which reports to the Assembly through the Economic and Social Council.

EXECUTIVE BOARD

The UNDP Governing Council (p. 1337) acts as the Executive Board of the Fund—and the UNDP Administrator as its Managing Director—in conformity with measures the General Assembly adopted provisionally in 1967[17] and reconfirmed yearly until 1980.[18] In 1981 the Assembly decided that UNDP continue to provide the Fund with, among other things, all headquarters administrative support services;[19] the Fund thus continued to operate under the same arrangements, which remained unchanged in 1984.

Managing Director: F. Bradford Morse (UNDP Administrator).

United Nations Children's Fund (UNICEF)

EXECUTIVE BOARD

The Executive Board of UNICEF (p. 1337) reports to the Economic and Social Council and, as appropriate, to the General Assembly.

United Nations Commission on International Trade Law (UNCITRAL)

The United Nations Commission on International Trade Law consists of 36 members elected by the General Assembly, in accordance with a formula providing equitable geographical representation and adequate representation of the principal economic and legal systems of the world. Members serve for six-year terms.

The Commission held its seventeenth session at United Nations Headquarters from 25 June to 10 July 1984.

Members:

To serve until the day preceding the Commission's regular annual session in 1986: Cuba, Cyprus, Czechoslovakia, Germany, Federal Republic of, Guatemala, Hungary, India, Iraq, Italy, Kenya, Peru, Philippines, Senegal, Sierra Leone, Spain, Trinidad and Tobago, Uganda, United States, Yugoslavia.

To serve until the day preceding the Commission's regular annual session in 1989: Algeria, Australia, Austria, Brazil, Central African Republic, China, Egypt, France, German Democratic Republic, Japan, Mexico, Nigeria, Singapore, Sweden, USSR, United Kingdom, United Republic of Tanzania.

Chairman: Ivan Szasz (Hungary).

Vice-Chairmen: Jorge Barrera Graf (Mexico), R. K. Dixit (India), Peter Kihara Mathanjuki (Kenya).

Rapporteur: M. Olivencia Ruiz (Spain).

WORKING GROUP ON
INTERNATIONAL CONTRACT PRACTICES

The Working Group on International Contract Practices, which is composed of all States members of UNCITRAL, held two sessions in

1984: its seventh at United Nations Headquarters from 6 to 17 February; and its eighth at Vienna, Austria, from 3 to 13 December.

Chairman: Ivan Szasz (Hungary) (seventh session), Michael Joachim Bonell (Italy) (eighth session).

Rapporteur: James C. Droushiotis (Cyprus) (seventh session), K. Venkatramiah (India) (eighth session).

WORKING GROUP ON
INTERNATIONAL NEGOTIABLE INSTRUMENTS

The Working Group on International Negotiable Instruments, reconstituted by UNCITRAL on 6 July 1984 with an enlarged membership, did not meet during 1984.

Members: Australia, Cuba, Czechoslovakia, Egypt, France, India, Japan, Mexico, Nigeria, Sierra Leone, Spain, USSR, United Kingdom, United States.

WORKING GROUP ON THE
NEW INTERNATIONAL ECONOMIC ORDER

The Working Group on the New International Economic Order, composed of all States members of UNCITRAL, held two sessions in 1984: its fifth at United Nations Headquarters from 23 January to 3 February; and its sixth at Vienna, Austria, from 10 to 20 September.

Chairman: Leif Sevon (Finland).[a]

Rapporteur: Peter Kihara Mathanjuki (Kenya) (fifth session), Jelena Vilus (Yugoslavia) (sixth session).

[a]Elected in his personal capacity.

United Nations Conciliation Commission for Palestine

Members: France, Turkey, United States.

United Nations Conference on Trade and Development (UNCTAD)

Members of UNCTAD are Members of the United Nations or members of the specialized agencies or of IAEA.

TRADE AND DEVELOPMENT BOARD

The Trade and Development Board is a permanent organ of UNCTAD. Its membership is drawn from the following list of UNCTAD members.

Part A. Afghanistan, Algeria, Angola, Bahrain, Bangladesh, Benin, Bhutan, Botswana, Brunei Darussalam,[a] Burkina Faso, Burma, Burundi, Cameroon, Cape Verde, Central African Republic, Chad, China, Comoros, Congo, Democratic Kampuchea, Democratic People's Republic of Korea, Democratic Yemen, Djibouti, Egypt, Equatorial Guinea, Ethiopia, Fiji, Gabon, Gambia, Ghana, Guinea, Guinea-Bissau, India, Indonesia, Iran, Iraq, Israel, Ivory Coast, Jordan, Kenya, Kuwait, Lao People's Democratic Republic, Lebanon, Lesotho, Liberia, Libyan Arab Jamahiriya, Madagascar, Malawi, Malaysia, Maldives, Mali, Mauritania, Mauritius, Mongolia, Morocco, Mozambique, Nepal, Niger, Nigeria, Oman, Pakistan, Papua New Guinea, Philippines, Qatar, Republic of Korea, Rwanda, Samoa, Sao Tome and Principe, Saudi Arabia, Senegal, Seychelles, Sierra Leone, Singapore, Solomon Islands, Somalia, South Africa, Sri Lanka, Sudan, Swaziland, Syrian Arab Republic, Thailand, Togo, Tonga, Tunisia, Uganda, United Arab Emirates, United Republic of Tanzania, Vanuatu, Viet Nam, Yemen, Yugoslavia, Zaire, Zambia, Zimbabwe; Namibia.

Part B. Australia, Austria, Belgium, Canada, Cyprus, Denmark, Finland, France, Germany, Federal Republic of, Greece, Holy See, Iceland, Ireland, Italy, Japan, Liechtenstein, Luxembourg, Malta, Monaco, Netherlands, New Zealand, Norway, Portugal, San Marino, Spain, Sweden, Switzerland, Turkey, United Kingdom, United States.

Part C. Antigua and Barbuda, Argentina, Bahamas, Barbados, Belize, Bolivia, Brazil, Chile, Colombia, Costa Rica, Cuba, Dominica, Dominican Republic, Ecuador, El Salvador, Grenada, Guatemala, Guyana,

---

[17]YUN 1967, p. 372, res. 2321(XXII), 15 Dec. 1967.
[18]YUN 1980, p. 607, dec. 35/422, 5 Dec. 1980.
[19]YUN 1981, p. 469, res. 36/196, 17 Dec. 1981.

Haiti, Honduras, Jamaica, Mexico, Nicaragua, Panama, Paraguay, Peru, Saint Christopher and Nevis,[b] Saint Lucia, Saint Vincent and the Grenadines, Suriname, Trinidad and Tobago, Uruguay, Venezuela.
Part D. Albania, Bulgaria, Byelorussian SSR, Czechoslovakia, German Democratic Republic, Hungary, Poland, Romania, Ukrainian SSR, USSR.

[a]Became a Member of the United Nations and, *ipso facto*, of UNCTAD on 21 September 1984, after the sixth (1983) session of the Conference. On 27 September 1984, the Board decided that it should be associated with the countries listed in Part A for the purpose of elections, pending approval by the Conference at its seventh (1987) session.
[b]Became a member of UNCTAD after the sixth (1983) session of the Conference. By decision of the Board, it was subsequently included in Part C for the purpose of elections, pending approval by the Conference at its seventh (1987) session.

BOARD MEMBERS AND SESSIONS
The membership of the Board is open to all UNCTAD members. Those wishing to become members of the Board communicate their intention to the Secretary-General of UNCTAD for transmittal to the Board President, who announces the membership on the basis of such notifications.
The Board held the following sessions in 1984, at Geneva: its twenty-eighth from 26 March to 6 April; its thirteenth special session from 2 to 6 April; and its twenty-ninth session from 10 to 27 September.

Members: Afghanistan, Algeria, Angola, Argentina, Australia, Austria, Bahrain, Bangladesh, Barbados, Belgium, Benin, Bolivia, Brazil, Bulgaria, Burkina Faso,[a] Burma, Burundi, Byelorussian SSR, Cameroon, Canada, Central African Republic, Chad, Chile, China, Colombia, Congo, Costa Rica, Cuba, Cyprus, Czechoslovakia, Democratic People's Republic of Korea, Democratic Yemen, Denmark, Dominican Republic, Ecuador, Egypt, El Salvador, Ethiopia, Finland, France, Gabon, German Democratic Republic, Germany, Federal Republic of, Ghana, Greece, Grenada, Guatemala, Guinea, Guyana, Haiti, Honduras, Hungary, India, Indonesia, Iran, Iraq, Ireland, Israel, Italy, Ivory Coast, Jamaica, Japan, Jordan, Kenya, Kuwait, Lebanon, Liberia, Libyan Arab Jamahiriya, Liechtenstein, Luxembourg, Madagascar, Malaysia, Mali, Malta, Mauritania, Mauritius, Mexico, Mongolia, Morocco, Nepal, Netherlands, New Zealand, Nicaragua, Nigeria, Norway, Oman, Pakistan, Panama, Papua New Guinea, Peru, Philippines, Poland, Portugal, Qatar, Republic of Korea, Romania, Saudi Arabia, Senegal, Sierra Leone, Singapore, Somalia, Spain, Sri Lanka, Sudan, Suriname, Sweden, Switzerland, Syrian Arab Republic, Thailand, Togo, Trinidad and Tobago, Tunisia, Turkey, Uganda, Ukrainian SSR, USSR, United Arab Emirates, United Kingdom, United Republic of Tanzania, United States, Uruguay, Venezuela, Viet Nam, Yemen, Yugoslavia, Zaire, Zambia.

[a]The Upper Volta changed its name to Burkina Faso on 6 August 1984.

OFFICERS (BUREAU) OF THE BOARD
Twenty-eighth and thirteenth special sessions
President: G. Reisch (Austria).
Vice-Presidents: Mario Alemán (Ecuador), Ivan Anastassov (Bulgaria), A. de la Serna (Spain), B. Ould-Rouis (Algeria), Bogdan Sosnowski (Poland), G. Streeb (United States), Gustavo Adolfo Vargas (Nicaragua), K. Vidas (Yugoslavia), J. Warin (France), D. Yong (Cameroon).
Rapporteur: E. A. Manalo (Philippines).

Twenty-ninth session
President: Mansur Ahmad (Pakistan).
Vice-Presidents: Ghaleb Z. Barakat (Jordan), Gerald P. Carmen (United States), M. I. El Deeb (Sudan), Hans V. Ewerlof (Sweden), C. Gaedt (German Democratic Republic), Francis Mahon Hayes (Ireland), R. Makarov (USSR), J. M. Maldonado Muñoz (Honduras), R. Peña Alfaro (Mexico), S. E. Quarm (Ghana).
Rapporteur: J. Oestreich (Federal Republic of Germany).

SUBSIDIARY ORGANS OF THE
TRADE AND DEVELOPMENT BOARD
The main committees of the Board are open to the participation of all interested UNCTAD members, on the understanding that those wishing to attend a particular session of one or more of the main committees communicate their intention to the Secretary-General of UNCTAD during the preceding regular session of the Board. On the basis of such notifications, the Board determines the membership of the main committees.

COMMITTEE ON COMMODITIES
The Committee on Commodities did not meet in 1984.

Members: Algeria, Argentina, Australia, Austria, Bahrain, Bangladesh, Belgium, Bolivia, Brazil, Bulgaria, Burkina Faso, Burma, Burundi, Cameroon, Canada, Central African Republic, Chad, Chile, China, Colombia, Costa Rica, Cuba, Czechoslovakia, Democratic People's Republic of Korea, Democratic Yemen, Denmark, Dominican Republic, Ecuador, Egypt, El Salvador, Ethiopia, Finland, France, Gabon, German Democratic Republic, Germany, Federal Republic of, Ghana, Greece, Guatemala, Guinea, Haiti, Honduras, Hungary, India, Indonesia, Iran, Iraq, Ireland, Israel, Italy, Ivory Coast, Jamaica, Japan, Jordan, Kenya, Kuwait, Liberia, Libyan Arab Jamahiriya, Madagascar, Malaysia, Malta, Mauritius, Mexico, Morocco, Netherlands, New Zealand, Nicaragua, Nigeria, Norway, Pakistan, Panama, Peru, Philippines, Poland, Qatar, Republic of Korea, Romania, Rwanda, Saudi Arabia, Senegal, Somalia, Spain, Sri Lanka, Sudan, Sweden, Switzerland, Syrian Arab Republic, Thailand, Togo, Trinidad and Tobago, Tunisia, Turkey, Uganda, USSR, United Kingdom, United Republic of Tanzania, United States, Uruguay, Venezuela, Viet Nam, Yemen, Yugoslavia, Zaire.

COMMITTEE ON TUNGSTEN
The Committee on Tungsten held its sixteenth session at Geneva from 10 to 14 December 1984.

Members: Argentina, Australia, Austria, Belgium, Bolivia, Brazil, Canada, China, Cyprus, France, Gabon, Germany, Federal Republic of, Italy, Japan, Mexico, Netherlands, Peru, Poland, Portugal, Republic of Korea, Romania, Rwanda, Spain, Sweden, Thailand, Turkey, USSR, United Kingdom, United States.

Chairman: F. Laschinger (Canada).
Vice-Chairman/Rapporteur: J. Harris (United Kingdom).

PERMANENT GROUP ON SYNTHETICS AND SUBSTITUTES
The Permanent Group on Synthetics and Substitutes did not meet in 1984.

Members: Argentina, Brazil, Canada, Chad, Egypt, France, Germany, Federal Republic of, Indonesia, Italy, Japan, Malaysia, Mexico, Netherlands, Nigeria, Philippines, Poland, Senegal, Sri Lanka, Sudan, Uganda, USSR, United Kingdom, United States, Viet Nam.

PERMANENT SUB-COMMITTEE ON COMMODITIES
The Permanent Sub-Committee on Commodities, whose membership is identical to that of the Committee on Commodities, did not meet in 1984.

COMMITTEE ON ECONOMIC CO-OPERATION
AMONG DEVELOPING COUNTRIES
The Committee on Economic Co-operation among Developing Countries did not meet in 1984.

Members: Algeria, Argentina, Australia, Austria, Bahrain, Bangladesh, Belgium, Benin, Brazil, Bulgaria, Burma, Cameroon, Canada, Central African Republic, Chile, China, Colombia, Costa Rica, Cuba, Czechoslovakia, Democratic People's Republic of Korea, Democratic Yemen, Denmark, Dominican Republic, Ecuador, Egypt, El Salvador, Ethiopia, Finland, France, Gabon, German Democratic Republic, Germany, Federal Republic of, Ghana, Greece, Guatemala, Guyana, Haiti, Honduras, Hungary, India, Indonesia, Iran, Iraq, Ireland, Israel, Italy, Ivory Coast, Jamaica, Japan, Jordan, Kenya, Kuwait, Lebanon, Liberia, Libyan Arab Jamahiriya, Madagascar, Malaysia, Malta, Mauritius, Mexico, Morocco, Netherlands, New Zealand, Nicaragua, Nigeria, Norway, Oman, Pakistan, Panama, Peru, Philippines, Poland, Qatar, Republic of Korea, Romania, Saudi Arabia, Senegal, Singapore, Somalia, Spain, Sri Lanka, Sudan, Suriname, Sweden, Switzerland, Syrian Arab Republic, Thailand, Togo, Trinidad and Tobago,

Tunisia, Turkey, Uganda, USSR, United Arab Emirates, United Kingdom, United Republic of Tanzania, United States, Uruguay, Venezuela, Viet Nam, Yemen, Yugoslavia, Zaire, Zambia.

COMMITTEE ON INVISIBLES AND FINANCING RELATED TO TRADE

The Committee on Invisibles and Financing related to Trade did not meet in 1984.

Members: Algeria, Argentina, Australia, Austria, Bahrain, Bangladesh, Belgium, Bolivia, Brazil, Bulgaria, Burkina Faso, Burundi, Cameroon, Canada, Central African Republic, Chad, Chile, China, Colombia, Costa Rica, Cuba, Czechoslovakia, Democratic People's Republic of Korea, Democratic Yemen, Denmark, Dominican Republic, Ecuador, Egypt, El Salvador, Ethiopia, Finland, France, German Democratic Republic, Germany, Federal Republic of, Ghana, Greece, Guatemala, Guinea, Honduras, Hungary, India, Indonesia, Iran, Iraq, Ireland, Israel, Italy, Ivory Coast, Jamaica, Japan, Jordan, Kenya, Kuwait, Lebanon, Liberia, Libyan Arab Jamahiriya, Madagascar, Malaysia, Mali, Malta, Mexico, Morocco, Netherlands, New Zealand, Nicaragua, Nigeria, Norway, Pakistan, Panama, Peru, Philippines, Poland, Qatar, Republic of Korea, Romania, Saudi Arabia, Senegal, Somalia, Spain, Sri Lanka, Sudan, Sweden, Switzerland, Syrian Arab Republic, Thailand, Trinidad and Tobago, Tunisia, Turkey, Uganda, USSR, United Kingdom, United Republic of Tanzania, United States, Uruguay, Venezuela, Viet Nam, Yemen, Yugoslavia, Zaire, Zimbabwe.

COMMITTEE ON MANUFACTURES

The Committee on Manufactures did not meet in 1984.

Members: Algeria, Argentina, Australia, Austria, Bahrain, Bangladesh, Belgium, Bolivia, Brazil, Bulgaria, Burkina Faso, Cameroon, Canada, Central African Republic, Chile, China, Colombia, Costa Rica, Cuba, Czechoslovakia, Democratic People's Republic of Korea, Democratic Yemen, Denmark, Dominican Republic, Ecuador, Egypt, El Salvador, Ethiopia, Finland, France, German Democratic Republic, Germany, Federal Republic of, Ghana, Greece, Guatemala, Haiti, Honduras, Hungary, India, Indonesia, Iran, Iraq, Ireland, Israel, Italy, Ivory Coast, Jamaica, Japan, Jordan, Kenya, Kuwait, Liberia, Libyan Arab Jamahiriya, Madagascar, Malaysia, Mali, Malta, Mauritius, Mexico, Morocco, Netherlands, New Zealand, Nicaragua, Nigeria, Norway, Pakistan, Panama, Peru, Philippines, Poland, Qatar, Republic of Korea, Romania, Saudi Arabia, Senegal, Singapore, Somalia, Spain, Sri Lanka, Sudan, Sweden, Switzerland, Syrian Arab Republic, Thailand, Trinidad and Tobago, Tunisia, Turkey, USSR, United Kingdom, United Republic of Tanzania, United States, Uruguay, Venezuela, Viet Nam, Yemen, Yugoslavia, Zaire.

COMMITTEE ON SHIPPING

The Committee on Shipping held its eleventh session at Geneva from 19 to 30 November 1984.

Members: Algeria, Argentina, Australia, Bahrain, Bangladesh, Belgium, Benin, Bolivia, Brazil, Bulgaria, Burkina Faso, Cameroon, Canada, Central African Republic, Chile, China, Colombia, Costa Rica, Cuba, Cyprus, Czechoslovakia, Democratic People's Republic of Korea, Democratic Yemen, Denmark, Dominican Republic, Ecuador, Egypt, El Salvador, Ethiopia, Finland, France, Gabon, German Democratic Republic, Germany, Federal Republic of, Ghana, Greece, Guatemala, Guinea, Honduras, Hungary, India, Indonesia, Iran, Iraq, Israel, Italy, Ivory Coast, Jamaica, Japan, Jordan, Kenya, Kuwait, Lebanon, Liberia, Libyan Arab Jamahiriya, Madagascar, Malaysia, Malta, Mauritius, Mexico, Morocco, Netherlands, New Zealand, Nicaragua, Nigeria, Norway, Pakistan, Panama, Peru, Philippines, Poland, Portugal, Qatar, Republic of Korea, Romania, Saudi Arabia, Senegal, Somalia, Spain, Sri Lanka, Sudan, Sweden, Switzerland, Syrian Arab Republic, Thailand, Trinidad and Tobago, Tunisia, Turkey, Uganda, USSR, United Arab Emirates,[a] United Kingdom, United Republic of Tanzania, United States, Uruguay, Venezuela, Viet Nam, Yemen, Yugoslavia, Zaire.

[a]Declared elected by the Trade and Development Board on 26 March 1984, raising the Committee's membership to 100.

Chairman: Leif Asbjorn Nygaard (Norway).

Vice-Chairmen: Karl Distler (German Democratic Republic), I. G. Lochhead (Canada), Georges A. Mathas (Gabon), Andros A. Nicolaides (Cyprus), Ibrahima Sy (Senegal).
Rapporteur: Sergio Cerda (Argentina).

WORKING GROUP ON INTERNATIONAL SHIPPING LEGISLATION

The Working Group on International Shipping Legislation, whose membership is identical to that of the Committee on Shipping, held its tenth session at Geneva from 24 September to 5 October 1984.

Chairman: B. I. Kraseev (USSR).
Vice-Chairmen: M. Baha el-Din Nosrah (Egypt), E. Chavez Gutierrez (Mexico), Claude Douay (France), R. A. Frewin (United Kingdom), Rifaat Izzat Rifaat (Iraq).
Rapporteur: A. Tahiri (Morocco).

COMMITTEE ON TRANSFER OF TECHNOLOGY

In 1984, the Committee on Transfer of Technology held, at Geneva, its first special session from 13 to 22 February and its fifth session from 3 to 20 December.

Members: Algeria, Argentina, Australia, Austria, Bahrain, Bangladesh,[a] Belgium, Bolivia, Brazil, Bulgaria, Burkina Faso,[b] Cameroon, Canada, Chile, China, Colombia, Costa Rica, Cuba, Czechoslovakia, Democratic People's Republic of Korea, Democratic Yemen, Denmark, Ecuador, Egypt, El Salvador, Ethiopia, Finland, France, German Democratic Republic, Germany, Federal Republic of, Ghana, Greece, Guatemala, Haiti, Honduras, Hungary, India, Indonesia, Iran, Iraq, Ireland, Israel, Italy, Ivory Coast, Jamaica, Japan, Jordan, Kenya, Kuwait, Liberia, Libyan Arab Jamahiriya, Madagascar, Malaysia, Malta, Mauritius, Mexico, Morocco, Netherlands, New Zealand, Nicaragua, Nigeria, Norway, Pakistan, Panama, Peru, Philippines, Poland, Qatar, Republic of Korea, Romania, Saudi Arabia, Senegal, Sierra Leone, Somalia, Spain, Sri Lanka, Sudan, Sweden, Switzerland, Syrian Arab Republic, Thailand, Trinidad and Tobago, Tunisia, Turkey, USSR, United Arab Emirates, United Kingdom, United Republic of Tanzania, United States, Venezuela, Viet Nam, Yemen, Yugoslavia, Zaire.

[a]Declared elected by the Trade and Development Board on 10 September 1984, raising the Committee's membership to 94.
[b]The Upper Volta changed its name to Burkina Faso on 6 August 1984.

First special session
Chairman: Mohamed Baha-Eldin Fayez (Egypt).
Vice-Chairmen: A. Akopyan (USSR), Jean de Breucker (Belgium), Hugo Suárez (Venezuela), K. V. Swaminathan (India), Kwasi Yeboah-Konadu (Ghana).
Rapporteur: Walter Goode (Australia).

Fifth session
Chairman: Roberto Villambrosa (Argentina).
Vice-Chairmen: Peter Balas (Hungary), Christian Faber-Rad (Denmark), Nestor Fomekong (Cameroon), Ilija Jankovic (Yugoslavia), Juan Lopez de Chicheri (Spain).
Rapporteur: Djismun Kasri (Indonesia).

SPECIAL COMMITTEE ON PREFERENCES

The Special Committee on Preferences, which is open to the participation of all UNCTAD members, held its twelfth session at Geneva from 24 April to 4 May 1984.

Chairman: E.-A. Hörig (Federal Republic of Germany).
Vice-Chairmen: P. Baev (Bulgaria), Inga Magistad (Norway), M. Porto (Brazil), M. Sbihi (Morocco), A. Veselinovic (Yugoslavia).
Rapporteur: R. Peña Alfaro (Mexico).

United Nations Council for Namibia

Members: Algeria, Angola, Australia, Bangladesh, Belgium, Botswana, Bulgaria, Burundi, Cameroon, Chile, China, Colombia, Cyprus, Egypt, Finland, Guyana, Haiti, India, Indonesia, Liberia, Mexico, Nigeria, Pakistan, Poland, Romania, Senegal, Turkey, USSR, Venezuela, Yugoslavia, Zambia.

President: Paul John Firmino Lusaka (Zambia).

Vice-Presidents: Ignac Golob (Yugoslavia), A. Coskun Kirca (Turkey), Natarajan Krishnan (India), Mohamed Sahnoun (Algeria),[a] Noel G. Sinclair (Guyana).

[a]Replaced on 29 October 1984 by Hocine Djoudi (Algeria).

United Nations Commissioner for Namibia: Brajesh Chandra Mishra.[a]

[a]Reappointed by the General Assembly on 18 December 1984 (decision 39/325) for a one-year term beginning on 1 January 1985.

COMMITTEE ON THE UNITED NATIONS FUND FOR NAMIBIA

Members: Australia, Finland, India, Nigeria, Romania, Senegal, Turkey, Venezuela *(Vice-Chairman/Rapporteur)*, Yugoslavia, Zambia; the President of the Council *(ex-officio Chairman)*.

STANDING COMMITTEE I

Members: Algeria, Cameroon *(Chairman)*, China, Colombia, Finland, Haiti, Indonesia, Nigeria, Poland, Senegal, Turkey *(Vice-Chairman)*, USSR, Venezuela, Zambia.

STANDING COMMITTEE II

Members: Angola, Australia, Bangladesh, Botswana, Bulgaria, Chile, Colombia, Cyprus, Finland, Guyana, Liberia (Vice-Chairman), Mexico, Pakistan *(Chairman)*, Romania, Zambia.

STANDING COMMITTEE III

Members: Algeria, Angola, Australia, Belgium, Bulgaria *(Chairman)*, Burundi, Colombia, Cyprus, Egypt, India, Mexico *(Vice-Chairman)*, Nigeria, Pakistan, Romania, Venezuela, Yugoslavia, Zambia.

STEERING COMMITTEE

In 1984, the Steering Committee consisted of the Council's President and five Vice-Presidents, the chairmen of its three standing committees and the Vice-Chairman/Rapporteur of the Committee on the United Nations Fund for Namibia.

United Nations Development Fund for Women (UNIFEM)

On 14 December 1984, the General Assembly decided that the activities of the Voluntary Fund for the United Nations Decade for Women be continued through establishment of the United Nations Development Fund for Women, which was to be a separate entity in autonomous association with UNDP. The UNDP Administrator was to be accountable for the management and operations of the Fund and was to report annually to the UNDP Governing Council, the Assembly and the Commission on the Status of Women.

The Director of the Fund, to have the authority to conduct all matters related to its mandate, was to be appointed by the UNDP Administrator.

CONSULTATIVE COMMITTEE

A Consultative Committee to advise the UNDP Administrator on all policy matters affecting the Fund's activities was to be composed of five Member States designated by the Assembly President with due regard for the financing of the Fund from voluntary contributions and to equitable geographical distribution. Each State member of the Committee, to serve for a three-year term, was to designate a person with expertise in development co-operation activities, including those benefiting women.

As at the end of 1984, the Committee remained to be constituted.

United Nations Development Programme (UNDP)

GOVERNING COUNCIL

The Governing Council of UNDP (p. 1337) reports to the Economic and Social Council and through it to the General Assembly.

United Nations Environment Programme (UNEP)

GOVERNING COUNCIL

The Governing Council of UNEP consists of 58 members elected by the General Assembly for three-year terms.

Seats on the Governing Council are allocated as follows: 16 to African States, 13 to Asian States, 6 to Eastern European States, 10 to Latin American States, and 13 to Western European and other States.

The Governing Council, which reports to the Assembly through the

Economic and Social Council, held its twelfth session at Nairobi, Kenya, from 16 to 29 May 1984.

Members:

To serve until 31 December 1984: Afghanistan, Botswana, Burundi, Byelorussian SSR, Canada, Colombia, Greece, Guinea, India, Jamaica, Mexico, Morocco, Oman, Poland, Senegal, Spain, Thailand, United Kingdom, United Republic of Tanzania, Uruguay.

To serve until 31 December 1985: Argentina, Australia, Cameroon, Chile, China, Finland, France, Hungary, Indonesia, Italy, Ivory Coast, Lesotho, Nigeria, Papua New Guinea, Peru, Philippines, Saudi Arabia, Uganda, Yugoslavia.

To serve until 31 December 1986: Algeria, Austria, Belgium, Brazil, Germany, Federal Republic of, Haiti, Japan, Kuwait, Malaysia, Nepal, Norway, Rwanda, Sudan, Togo, Ukrainian SSR, USSR, United States, Venezuela, Zaire.

President: A. Al Agib (Sudan).
Vice-Presidents: Abdulbar A. Al-Gain (Saudi Arabia), J. A. de Medicis (Brazil), G. Woschnagg (Austria).
Rapporteur: J. Janczak (Poland).

Executive Director of UNEP: Mostafa Kamal Tolba.[a]
Deputy Executive Director: Joseph C. Wheeler.

[a]Elected by the General Assembly on 10 December 1984 (decision 39/314) for a further four-year term beginning on 1 January 1985.

On 10 December 1984 (decision 39/310), the General Assembly elected the following 20 members for a three-year term beginning on 1 January 1985 to fill the vacancies occurring on 31 December 1984: Botswana, Bulgaria, Canada, Colombia, Ghana, India, Jamaica, Jordan, Kenya, Libyan Arab Jamahiriya, Malta, Mexico, Niger, Oman, Panama, Poland, Sri Lanka, Tunisia, Turkey, United Kingdom.

INTERGOVERNMENTAL INTER-SESSIONAL
PREPARATORY COMMITTEE ON THE ENVIRONMENTAL
PERSPECTIVE TO THE YEAR 2000 AND BEYOND

At its May 1984 session, the UNEP Governing Council established a 30-member Intergovernmental Inter-sessional Preparatory Committee, as approved by the General Assembly in December 1983,[20] to assist the Council in preparing the Environmental Perspective to the Year 2000 and Beyond.

Seats on the Committee were allocated as follows: eight to African States, seven to Asian States, three to Eastern European States, five to Latin American States, and seven to Western European and other States.

The Committee, which reports to the Governing Council, held its first session at Nairobi, Kenya, on 28 and 29 May 1984.

Members: Algeria, Argentina, Austria, Bangladesh, Botswana, Brazil, Cameroon, Canada, Chile, China, Denmark, Germany, Federal Republic of, Greece, India, Indonesia, Ivory Coast, Jamaica, Japan, Kenya, Malawi, Malaysia, Mexico, Morocco, Netherlands, Poland, Saudi Arabia, Senegal, Switzerland, Ukrainian SSR, USSR.

Chairman: Mourad Bencheikh (Algeria).
Vice-Chairmen: J. Richard Gaechter (Switzerland), Carlos Negri (Chile), Kishan K. S. Rana (India).
Rapporteur: Y. Bogayevsky (Ukrainian SSR).

SPECIAL COMMISSION ON THE ENVIRONMENTAL
PERSPECTIVE TO THE YEAR 2000 AND BEYOND

A Special Commission, also known as the World Commission on Environment and Development, was formally established on 15 May 1984, in pursuance of a December 1983 General Assembly decision.[21] In close co-operation with the Intergovernmental Inter-sessional Preparatory Committee (see above), the Commission was to prepare a report on environment and the global *problématique* to the year 2000 and

---

[20]YUN 1983, p. 771, res. 38/161, 19 Dec. 1983.
[21]*Ibid.*

beyond, including proposed strategies for sustainable development. Its report would be considered by the UNEP Governing Council, for transmission to the Assembly and for use in the preparation, for adoption by the Assembly, of the Environmental Perspective to the Year 2000 and Beyond.

The Commission was to be composed of 22 members, 14 from developing countries and 8 from developed countries, serving in their individual capacity, selected by the Commission's Chairman and Vice-Chairman.

In 1984, the Commission held, at Geneva, an organizational session on 15 and 16 May and an inaugural meeting from 1 to 3 October.

Members:[a] Susanna Agnelli (Italy); Saleh Abdulrahman Al-Athel (Saudi Arabia); Gro Harlem Brundtland, *Chairman* (Norway);[b] Bernard T. G. Chidzero (Zimbabwe); Pablo Gonsalez Casanova (Mexico); Volker Hauff (Federal Republic of Germany); Mansour Khalid, *Vice-Chairman* (Sudan);[b] Istvan Lang (Hungary); Margarita Marino de Botero (Colombia); Saburo Okita (Japan); Shridath S. Ramphal (Guyana); William D. Ruckelshaus (United States); Mohamed Sahnoun (Algeria); Emil Salim (Indonesia); Bukar Shaib (Nigeria); Nagendra Singh (India).

[a]The remaining six members had not been selected by the end of 1984.
[b]Appointed by the Secretary-General in December 1983 and January 1984, respectively.

United Nations Financing System for Science and Technology for Development

The United Nations Financing System for Science and Technology for Development finances, at the request of Governments, a broad range of activities intended to strengthen the endogenous scientific and technological capacities of developing countries. Its policy-making body is the Intergovernmental Committee on Science and Technology for Development (p. 1315) and the overall supervision of its management is entrusted to the UNDP Administrator, who was to be accountable to an Executive Board responsible for the System's operation and conduct. The Administrator, in consultation with the Director-General for Development and International Economic Co-operation, reports annually to the Intergovernmental Committee.

On 17 December 1984, the General Assembly decided to continue the existing operating procedures of the Financing System.

EXECUTIVE BOARD

The Executive Board was to be composed of 21 directors elected by the Intergovernmental Committee on Science and Technology for Development for three-year terms, one third to be drawn from developed countries and two thirds from developing countries reflecting an appropriate balance between donors and recipients.

The Board had not been constituted by the end of 1984.

United Nations Fund for Population Activities (UNFPA)

The United Nations Fund for Population Activities, a subsidiary organ of the General Assembly, plays a leading role within the United Nations system in promoting population programmes and in providing assistance to developing countries at their request in dealing with their population problems. It operates under the overall policy guidance of the Economic and Social Council and under the financial and administrative policy guidance of the Governing Council of UNDP.

Executive Director: Rafael M. Salas.
Deputy Executive Director: Heino E. Wittrin.

United Nations Industrial Development Organization (UNIDO)

The Fourth General Conference of UNIDO was held at Vienna, Austria, from 2 to 19 August 1984. Participating were the following 139 States and the United Nations Council for Namibia:

Afghanistan, Albania, Algeria, Angola, Argentina, Australia, Austria, Bahrain, Bangladesh, Barbados, Belgium, Benin, Bhutan, Bolivia, Botswana, Brazil, Brunei, Bulgaria, Burkina Faso, Burundi, Byelorussian SSR, Cameroon, Canada, Cape Verde, Central African Republic, Chad, Chile, China, Colombia, Comoros, Congo, Cuba, Cyprus, Czechoslovakia, Democratic People's Republic of Korea, Democratic Yemen, Denmark, Djibouti, Dominican Republic, Ecuador, Egypt, Equatorial Guinea, Ethiopia, Finland, France, Gabon, Gambia, German Democratic Republic, Germany, Federal Republic of, Ghana, Greece, Guatemala, Guinea, Guinea-

Bissau, Guyana, Haiti, Holy See, Hungary, India, Indonesia, Iran, Iraq, Ireland, Israel, Italy, Ivory Coast, Jamaica, Japan, Jordan, Kenya, Kuwait, Lebanon, Lesotho, Liberia, Libyan Arab Jamahiriya, Liechtenstein, Luxembourg, Madagascar, Malawi, Malaysia, Maldives, Mali, Malta, Mauritania, Mauritius, Mexico, Mongolia, Morocco, Mozambique, Nepal, Netherlands, New Zealand, Nicaragua, Niger, Nigeria, Norway, Oman, Pakistan, Panama, Peru, Philippines, Poland, Portugal, Qatar, Republic of Korea, Romania, Rwanda, Samoa, Sao Tome and Principe, Saudi Arabia, Senegal, Sierra Leone, Somalia, Spain, Sri Lanka, Sudan, Sweden, Switzerland, Syrian Arab Republic, Thailand, Togo, Trinidad and Tobago, Tunisia, Turkey, Uganda, Ukrainian SSR, USSR, United Arab Emirates, United Kingdom, United Republic of Tanzania, United States, Uruguay, Venezuela, Viet Nam, Yemen, Yugoslavia, Zaire, Zambia, Zimbabwe.

President: Gerrit Willem van Barneveld Kooy (Netherlands).
Vice-Presidents: Canada, China, Cuba, Mexico, Pakistan, Poland, Saudi Arabia, USSR, Zambia.
Rapporteur-General: A. K. Tiberondwa (Uganda).

Chairmen of committees:
  Committee I: Juan Carlos Beltramino (Argentina).
  Committee II: E. Ivan (Hungary).
  Drafting Committee: I. S. Chadha (India).
  Credentials Committee: A. K. Tiberondwa (Uganda).

INDUSTRIAL DEVELOPMENT BOARD

The Industrial Development Board, the principal organ of UNIDO, consists of 45 States elected by the General Assembly, on the basis of equitable geographical distribution, to serve for three-year terms. States eligible for election to the Board are those which are Members of the United Nations or members of the specialized agencies or of IAEA.

The Board reports annually to the Assembly through the Economic and Social Council.

The Board's membership is drawn from the following four groups of States:

List A. 18 of the following States: Afghanistan, Algeria, Angola, Bahrain, Bangladesh, Benin, Bhutan, Botswana, Brunei Darussalam,[a] Burkina Faso, Burma, Burundi, Cameroon, Cape Verde, Central African Republic, Chad, China, Comoros, Congo, Democratic Kampuchea, Democratic People's Republic of Korea, Democratic Yemen, Djibouti, Egypt, Equatorial Guinea, Ethiopia, Fiji, Gabon, Gambia, Ghana, Guinea, Guinea-Bissau, India, Indonesia, Iran, Iraq, Israel, Ivory Coast, Jordan, Kenya, Kuwait, Lao People's Democratic Republic, Lebanon, Lesotho, Liberia, Libyan Arab Jamahiriya, Madagascar, Malawi, Malaysia, Maldives, Mali, Mauritania, Mauritius, Mongolia, Morocco, Mozambique, Nepal, Niger, Nigeria, Oman, Pakistan, Papua New Guinea, Philippines, Qatar, Republic of Korea, Rwanda, Sao Tome and Principe, Saudi Arabia, Senegal, Seychelles, Sierra Leone, Singapore, Solomon Islands, Somalia, South Africa, Sri Lanka, Sudan, Swaziland, Syrian Arab Republic, Thailand, Togo, Tunisia, Uganda, United Arab Emirates, United Republic of Tanzania, Vanuatu, Viet Nam, Yemen, Yugoslavia, Zaire, Zambia, Zimbabwe.
List B. 15 of the following States: Australia, Austria, Belgium, Canada, Cyprus, Denmark, Finland, France, Germany, Federal Republic of, Greece, Iceland, Ireland, Italy, Japan, Liechtenstein, Luxembourg, Malta, Monaco, Netherlands, New Zealand, Norway, Portugal, Spain, Sweden, Switzerland, Turkey, United Kingdom, United States.
List C. 7 of the following States: Antigua and Barbuda, Argentina, Bahamas, Barbados, Belize, Bolivia, Brazil, Chile, Colombia, Costa Rica, Cuba, Dominica, Dominican Republic, Ecuador, El Salvador, Grenada, Guatemala, Guyana, Haiti, Honduras, Jamaica, Mexico, Nicaragua, Panama, Paraguay, Peru, Saint Christopher and Nevis, Saint Lucia, Saint Vincent and the Grenadines, Suriname, Trinidad and Tobago, Uruguay, Venezuela.
List D. 5 of the following States: Albania, Bulgaria, Byelorussian SSR, Czechoslovakia, German Democratic Republic, Hungary, Poland, Romania, Ukrainian SSR, USSR.

[a]Included in list A by a General Assembly resolution of 18 December 1984.

The Industrial Development Board held its eighteenth session at Vienna from 2 to 19 May 1984.

BOARD MEMBERS

To serve until 31 December 1984: Australia, China, Germany, Federal Republic of, Iraq, Lesotho, Liberia, Malaysia, Mexico, Panama, Sierra Leone, Spain, Turkey, Ukrainian SSR, United Kingdom, Venezuela.

To serve until 31 December 1985: Austria, Belgium, Bulgaria, Chad, Chile, Finland, Indonesia, Italy, Libyan Arab Jamahiriya, Peru, Rwanda, Sudan, Switzerland, Uganda, USSR.

To serve until 31 December 1986: Argentina, Brazil, Democratic Yemen, France, Ghana, Hungary, India, Japan, Malawi, Netherlands, Norway, Pakistan, Romania, United Arab Emirates, United States.

President: Adolfo R. Taylhardat (Venezuela).
Vice-Presidents: M. I. B. El Deeb (Sudan), S. K. Singh (India), T. Somjen (Hungary).
Rapporteur: B. R. Hemenway (United States).

Executive Director of UNIDO: Abd-El Rahman Khane.[a]
Deputy Executive Director: Philippe Jacques Farlan Carré.

[a] Reappointed by the Secretary-General for a further two-year term ending on 31 December 1986, or the date on which the Director-General of UNIDO (as a new specialized agency) assumed office, whichever was earlier; reappointment confirmed by the General Assembly on 10 December 1984 (decision 39/315).

On 10 December 1984 (decision 39/309), the General Assembly elected the following 15 members of the Industrial Development Board for a three-year term beginning on 1 January 1985 to fill the vacancies occurring on 31 December 1984: Australia, China, Czechoslovakia, Ecuador, Germany, Federal Republic of, Iraq, Ivory Coast, Lesotho, Mexico, Philippines, Sierra Leone, Spain, Turkey, United Kingdom, Venezuela.

PERMANENT COMMITTEE

The Permanent Committee has the same membership as the Industrial Development Board and normally meets twice a year. In 1984, however, the Committee held only one session, its twenty-first, from 19 to 23 November at Vienna.

Chairman: Adolfo R. Taylhardat (Venezuela).
Vice-Chairmen: M. I. B. El Deeb (Sudan), S. K. Singh (India), T. Somjen (Hungary).
Rapporteur: D. A. Vernon (United States).

United Nations Institute for Disarmament Research (UNIDIR)

BOARD OF TRUSTEES

The Secretary-General's Advisory Board on Disarmament Studies, composed in 1984 of 23 eminent persons selected on the basis of their personal expertise and taking into account the principle of equitable geographical representation, functions as the Board of Trustees of UNIDIR; the Director of UNIDIR reports to the General Assembly and, since the Assembly's approval of the statute of UNIDIR on 17 December 1984, is an *ex-officio* member of the Advisory Board when it acts as the Board of Trustees.

Members: Oluyemi Adeniji (Nigeria); Hadj Benabdelkader Azzout, *Chairman* (Algeria); Rolf Björnerstedt (Sweden);[a] O. N. Bykov (USSR); James E. Dougherty (United States); Omran El-Shafei (Egypt); Constantin Ene (Romania); Edgar Faure (France); Alfonso García Robles (Mexico); Ignac Golob (Yugoslavia); A. C. Shahul Hameed (Sri Lanka); Carlos Lechuga Hevia (Cuba);[b] Liang Yufan (China); Sir Ronald Mason (United Kingdom); Akira Matsui (Japan); William Eteki Mboumoua (Cameroon); Manfred Mueller (German Democratic Republic); Carlos Ortiz de Rozas (Argentina); Maharajakrishna K. Rasgotra (India); Friedrich Ruth (Federal Republic of Germany); Agha Shahi (Pakistan); Tadeusz Strulak (Poland); Oscar Vaernö (Norway).

[a] Appointed on 16 February 1984.
[b] Appointed on 23 August 1984 to replace José A. Tabares del Real (Cuba).

Director of UNIDIR: Liviu Bota.

United Nations Institute for Training and Research (UNITAR)

The Executive Director of UNITAR, in consultation with the Board of Trustees of the Institute, reports through the Secretary-General to the General Assembly and, as appropriate, to the Economic and Social Council and other United Nations bodies.

BOARD OF TRUSTEES

The Board of Trustees of UNITAR is composed of: *(a)* not less than 11 and not more than 30 members, which may include one or more officials of the United Nations Secretariat, appointed on a broad geographical basis by the Secretary-General, in consultation with the Presidents of the General Assembly and the Economic and Social Council; and *(b)* four *ex-officio* members.

The Board held two sessions in 1984, at United Nations Headquarters: its twenty-second from 19 to 23 March, and a special session from 17 to 19 December.

Members (until 30 June 1984):
To serve until 30 June 1984: Siméon Aké (Ivory Coast); William H. Barton, *Chairman* (Canada); Adhemar M. A. d'Alcantara (Belgium); Roberto E. Guyer (Argentina); K. Natwar-Singh (India); Shizuo Saito (Japan); Joel Segall (United States); Rüdiger von Wechmar (Federal Republic of Germany).
To serve until 30 June 1985: Ole Algard (Norway); Stephane Hessel (France); Johan Kaufmann (Netherlands); Porfirio Muñoz-Ledo (Mexico); Olara Otunnu (Uganda); José Luis Pardos (Spain); Taieb Slim, *Vice-Chairman* (Tunisia); Anders I. Thunborg (Sweden); B. S. Vaganov (USSR).
To serve until 30 June 1986: Margaret Joan Anstee (Secretariat); Mohamed Omar Madani (Saudi Arabia); Donald O. Mills (Jamaica); Pei Monong (China); Agha Shahi (Pakistan); Ali A. Treiki (Libyan Arab Jamahiriya); Victor Umbricht (Switzerland); Anton Vratusa (Yugoslavia).

The Secretary-General appointed the following 10 members of the Board for terms beginning on 1 July 1984 and expiring on 30 June of the year indicated: 1986—William H. Barton (Canada), Roberto E. Guyer (Argentina), Shizuo Saito (Japan); 1987—Siméon Aké (Ivory Coast), Adhemar M. A. d'Alcantara (Belgium), Alan L. Keyes (United States), Umberto La Rocca (Italy), K. Natwar-Singh (India), Klaus Törnudd (Finland), Rüdiger von Wechmar (Federal Republic of Germany).

As recommended by the Board at its December 1984 special session, the Secretary-General decided that, as from 1985, the terms of all Board members were to expire on 31 December instead of 30 June.

Members (from 1 July 1984):
To serve until 31 December 1985: Ole Algard (Norway); Stephane Hessel (France); Johan Kaufmann (Netherlands); Porfirio Muñoz-Ledo (Mexico); Olara Otunnu (Uganda); José Luis Pardos (Spain); Taieb Slim, *Vice-Chairman* (Tunisia); Anders I. Thunborg (Sweden); B. S. Vaganov (USSR).
To serve until 31 December 1986: Margaret Joan Anstee (Secretariat); William H. Barton, *Chairman* (Canada); Roberto E. Guyer (Argentina); Mohamed Omar Madani (Saudi Arabia); Donald O. Mills (Jamaica); Pei Monong (China); Shizuo Saito (Japan); Agha Shahi (Pakistan); Ali A. Treiki (Libyan Arab Jamahiriya); Victor Umbricht (Switzerland); Anton Vratusa (Yugoslavia).
To serve until 31 December 1987: Siméon Aké (Ivory Coast); Adhemar M. A. d'Alcantara (Belgium); Alan L. Keyes (United States); Umberto La Rocca (Italy); K. Natwar-Singh (India); Klaus Törnudd (Finland); Rüdiger von Wechmar (Federal Republic of Germany).

Ex-officio members: The Secretary-General, the President of the General Assembly, the President of the Economic and Social Council and the Executive Director of UNITAR.

Executive Director of UNITAR: Michel Doo Kingué.

United Nations Joint Staff Pension Board

The United Nations Joint Staff Pension Board is composed of 21 members, as follows:

Six appointed by the United Nations Staff Pension Committee (two from members elected by the General Assembly, two from those appointed by the Secretary-General, two from those elected by participants).
Fifteen appointed by Staff Pension Committees of other member organizations of the United Nations Joint Staff Pension Fund, as fol-

lows: two each by WHO, FAO, UNESCO; and one each by ILO, ICAO, IAEA, WMO, IMO, ITU, ICITO/GATT, WIPO, IFAD.

In 1984, the Board held two sessions: its thirty-second (special) in Paris from 21 to 28 March; and its thirty-third at Vienna, Austria, from 8 to 17 August.

Members:
United Nations
  Representing the General Assembly: Representatives: Mario Majoli (Italy);[a] Sol Kuttner (United States). Alternates: Eduardo César Añón Noceti (Uruguay); Jobst Holborn, *Rapporteur, thirty-third session* (Federal Republic of Germany);[b] Michael George Okeyo (Kenya); Yukio Takasu, *Rapporteur, thirty-second session* (Japan).
  Representing the Secretary-General: Representatives: J. Richard Foran (Canada); Louis-Pascal Nègre (Mali). Alternates: Paul C. Szasz (United States); Raymond Gieri (United States); V. Elissejev (USSR);[c] Matias de la Mota (Spain);[c] Clayton C. Timbrell (United States).[d]
  Representing the Participants: Representative: Susanna H. Johnston (United States); Rosa María Vicien-Milburn (Argentina). Alternates: Bruce C. Hillis (Canada); Gualtiero Fulcheri (Italy); Sergio Zampetti (Italy); Anders Tholle (Denmark).
International Labour Organisation
  Representing the Participants: Representative: Edmond Ryser (Switzerland). Alternates: B. Debbas (Lebanon); E. Denti (Italy); M. Voirin (France); Gerald F. Starr (Canada).[d]
World Health Organization
  Representing the Governing Body: Representative: Dr. Arnold Sauter, *Chairman, thirty-second session* (Switzerland). Alternates: Dr. N. A. Perrone (Argentina);[c] Sung Woo Lee (Republic of Korea);[c] Dr. I. Kone (Ivory Coast);[c] Basharat Jazbi (Pakistan);[c] Dr. D. N. Regmi (Nepal).[c]
  Representing the Participants: Representative: Ram L. Rai (India). Alternates: Dr. Alain Vessereau (France); Vincent Bambinelli (United States); Dr. D. Ray (India);[d] D. Payne (United Kingdom);[d] Dr. H. Schmidtkunz (Federal Republic of Germany).[d]
Food and Agriculture Organization of the United Nations
  Representing the Executive Head: Representative: Mohsen Bel Hadj Amor (Tunisia). Alternate: Maria Grazia Iuri (Italy).
  Representing the Participants: Representative: Aurelio Marcucci, *First Vice-Chairman, thirty-second session* (Italy). Alternate: Massimo Arrigo (Italy).
United Nations Educational, Scientific and Cultural Organization
  Representing the Governing Body: Representative: Gollerkery Vishvanath Rao, *First Vice-Chairman, thirty-third session* (India). Alternates: J. Q. Cleland (Ghana);[c] A. Boudjelti (Algeria);[d] I. de Freitas (Brazil).[d]
  Representing the Participants: Representative: Witold Zyss (Israel). Alternates: Robert Brouard (Mauritius); Erwin S. Solomon (United States).
International Civil Aviation Organization
  Representing the Governing Body: Representatives: Alan R. Boyd (Canada);[a] G. Birch (Australia).[d] Alternate: O. Ogunbiyi (Nigeria).[c]
International Atomic Energy Agency
  Representing the Governing Body: Representative: M. Ugalde (Chile). Alternates: J. A. Lozada, Jr. (Philippines);[c] P. Dartois (Belgium);[c] S. Nitzsche (German Democratic Republic).[c]
World Meteorological Organization
  Representing the Governing Body: Representative: Bernhard Ziese (Federal Republic of Germany).
International Maritime Organization
  Representing the Executive Head: Representatives: Denis G. Aitken, *Second Vice-Chairman, thirty-second session* (United Kingdom);[a] Marcel Landey (Canada).[d] Alternate: Kaare Stangeland (Norway).[d]
International Telecommunication Union
  Representing the Participants: Representative: Jacques Bacaly (France). Alternate: Liliane Jeanmonod (France).
Interim Commission for the International Trade Organization/General Agreement on Tariffs and Trade
  Representing the Executive Head: Representative: Cyril F. Johnson (United Kingdom).
World Intellectual Property Organization
  Representing the Executive Head: Representatives: Dirk Jan Goossen (Netherlands);[c] Thomas A. J. Keefer (Canada).[d]

International Fund for Agricultural Development
  Representing the Executive Head: Representative: Tor Myrvang (Norway).

[a]Alternate, thirty-second session; representative, thirty-third session.
[b]Representative, thirty-second session; alternate, thirty-third session.
[c]Accredited to the thirty-third session.
[d]Accredited to the thirty-second session.

STANDING COMMITTEE OF THE PENSION BOARD
Members (elected at the Board's thirty-third session):

United Nations (Group I)
  Representing the General Assembly: Representative: Mario Majoli. Alternates: Sol Kuttner, Michael George Okeyo, Jobst Holborn, Yukio Takasu, Eduardo César Añón Noceti.
  Representing the Secretary-General: Representative: J. Richard Foran. Alternates: Louis-Pascal Nègre, Paul C. Szasz, Raymond Gieri, V. Elissejev, Matias de la Mota.
  Representing the Participants: Representative: Susanna H. Johnston. Alternates: Rosa María Vicien-Milburn, Bruce C. Hillis, Gualtiero Fulcheri, Sergio Zampetti, Anders Tholle.
Specialized agencies (Group II)
  Representing the Governing Body: Representative: Dr. Arnold Sauter (WHO). Alternates: Dr. N. A. Perrone (WHO), Sung Woo Lee (WHO), Dr. I. Kone (WHO), Basharat Jazbi (WHO), Dr. D. N. Regmi (WHO).
  Representing the Executive Head: Representative: Denis G. Aitken (IMO). Alternates: Michel Bardoux (ITU), Dieter Goethel (IAEA), M. Fellague (WMO).
  Representing the Participants: Representative: Edmond Ryser (ILO). Alternates: E. Denti (ILO), M. Voirin (ILO), B. Debbas (ILO), M. Copin (ILO), A. Bonnin (ILO).
Specialized agencies (Group III)
  Representing the Governing Body: Representative: Gollerkery Vishvanath Rao (UNESCO). Alternate: J. Q. Cleland (UNESCO).
  Representing the Executive Head: Representative: Shelton E. Jayasekera (ICAO). Alternates: Tor Myrvang (IFAD), Cyril F. Johnson (ICITO), Thomas A. J. Keefer (WIPO).
  Representing the Participants: Representative: Aurelio Marcucci (FAO). Alternates: Massimo Arrigo (FAO), C. Cherubini (FAO), E. Paardekooper (FAO), P. J. Myers (FAO), M. Palmieri (FAO).

COMMITTEE OF ACTUARIES
  The Committee of Actuaries consists of five members, each representing one of the five geographical regions of the United Nations.

Members: Ajibola O. Ogunshola (Nigeria), *Region I* (African States); Kunio Takeuchi (Japan), *Region II* (Asian States); E. M. Chetyrkin (USSR), *Region III* (Eastern European States); Dr. Gonzalo Arroba (Ecuador), *Region IV* (Latin American States); Robert J. Myers (United States), *Region V* (Western European and other States).

United Nations Relief and Works Agency for Palestine Refugees in the Near East (UNRWA)

ADVISORY COMMISSION OF UNRWA
  The Advisory Commission of UNRWA met at Vienna, Austria, on 30 August 1984.

Members: Belgium, Egypt, France, Japan, Jordan *(Chairman)*, Lebanon, Syrian Arab Republic, Turkey, United Kingdom, United States.

WORKING GROUP ON THE FINANCING OF UNRWA
Members: France, Ghana *(Vice-Chairman)*, Japan, Lebanon, Norway *(Rapporteur)*, Trinidad and Tobago, Turkey *(Chairman)*, United Kingdom, United States.

Commissioner-General of UNRWA: Olof Rydbeck.
Deputy Commissioner-General: Alan J. Brown.

United Nations Scientific Advisory Committee
  Established by the General Assembly in 1954 as a seven-member advisory committee on the International Conference on the Peaceful Uses of Atomic Energy (1955), the United Nations Scientific Advisory Committee was so renamed and its mandate revised by the Assembly in

1958,[22] retaining its original composition. The Committee has not met since 1956.[23]

Members: Brazil, Canada, France, India, USSR, United Kingdom, United States.

United Nations Scientific Committee on the Effects of Atomic Radiation

The 20-member United Nations Scientific Committee on the Effects of Atomic Radiation held its thirty-third session at Vienna, Austria, from 25 to 29 June 1984.

Members: Argentina, Australia, Belgium, Brazil, Canada, Czechoslovakia, Egypt, France, Germany, Federal Republic of, India, Indonesia, Japan, Mexico, Peru, Poland, Sudan, Sweden, USSR, United Kingdom, United States.

Chairman: D. Beninson (Argentina).
Vice-Chairman: T. Kumatori (Japan).
Rapporteur: A. Hidayatalla (Sudan).

United Nations Special Fund
(to provide emergency relief and development assistance)

BOARD OF GOVERNORS
The activities of the United Nations Special Fund were suspended, *ad interim*, in 1978 by the General Assembly, which assumed the functions of the Board of Governors of the Fund. In 1981,[24] the Assembly decided to continue performing those functions, within the context of its consideration of the item on development and international economic cooperation, pending consideration of the question in 1983. However, no action was taken in 1983 or 1984.

United Nations Special Fund for Land-locked Developing Countries

The General Assembly established the United Nations Special Fund for Land-locked Developing Countries in 1975[25] and approved its statute in 1976.[26] The Special Fund was to operate as an organ of the Assembly, with its policies and procedures to be formulated by a Board of Governors.

The chief executive officer of the Special Fund, the Executive Director, to be appointed by the Secretary-General subject to the confirmation of the Assembly, was to discharge his functions under the guidance and supervision of the Board of Governors and an Executive Committee, if established.

Pending appointment of the Executive Director, the Administrator of UNDP, in close collaboration with the Secretary-General of UNCTAD, manages the Fund.

BOARD OF GOVERNORS
A 36-member Board of Governors of the United Nations Special Fund for Land-locked Developing Countries was to be elected by the General Assembly from among Members of the United Nations or members of the specialized agencies or of IAEA, keeping in view the need for a balanced representation of the beneficiary land-locked developing countries and their transit neighbours, on the one hand, and potential donor countries on the other.

Members were to serve three-year terms, except that at the first election the terms of one third of the members were to be for one year and those of a further third for two years.

The Board was to report annually to the Assembly through the Economic and Social Council.

On 10 December 1984 (decision 39/313), the Assembly deferred election of the Board to its fortieth (1985) session.

United Nations Staff Pension Committee
The United Nations Staff Pension Committee consists of three members elected by the General Assembly, three appointed by the Secretary-General and three elected by the participants in the United Nations Joint Staff Pension Fund. The term of office of the elected members is three years, or until the election of their successors.

Members:
Elected by Assembly (to serve until 31 December 1985): *Members:* Sol Kuttner *(Chairman)*, Mario Majoli, Michael George Okeyo. *Alternates:*

Eduardo César Añón Noceti, Jobst Holborn, Yukio Takasu.
Appointed by Secretary-General (to serve until further notice): *Members:* J. Richard Foran, Louis-Pascal Nègre, Clayton C. Timbrell.[a] *Alternates:* Raymond Gieri, V. Elissejev, Paul C. Szasz,[b] Matias de la Mota.[c]
Elected by Participants (to serve until 31 December 1985): *Members:* Susanna H. Johnston, Rosa María Vicien-Milburn,[d] Bruce C. Hillis. *Alternates:* Gualtiero Fulcheri, Sergio Zampetti, Anders Tholle.

[a]Retired effective 7 July 1984.
[b]Member effective 18 July 1984.
[c]Appointed effective 18 July 1984.
[d]Resigned effective 1 November 1984.

United Nations University

COUNCIL OF THE UNITED NATIONS UNIVERSITY
The Council of the United Nations University, the governing board of the University, consists of: *(a)* 24 members appointed jointly by the Secretary-General and the Director-General of UNESCO, in consultation with the agencies and programmes concerned including UNITAR, who serve in their personal capacity for six-year terms; *(b)* the Secretary-General, the Director-General of UNESCO and the Executive Director of UNITAR, who are *ex-officio* members; and *(c)* the Rector of the University, who is normally appointed for a five-year term.

In 1984, the Council held two sessions: its twenty-third from 1 to 6 July at Oxford, United Kingdom; and its twenty-fourth from 10 to 14 December at Tokyo, Japan.

Members:
To serve until 2 May 1986:[a] Ungku Abdul Aziz (Malaysia); Elise M. Boulding (United States); Satish Chandra, *Vice-Chairman* (India); Donald E. U. Ekong (Nigeria);[b] André Louis Jaumotte (Belgium); Reimut Jochimsen (Federal Republic of Germany); F. S. C. P. Kalpage (Sri Lanka); Sir John Kendrew, *Chairman* (United Kingdom); Shizuo Saito (Japan); Charles Valy Tuho (Ivory Coast); Víctor Luis Urquidi, *Vice-Chairman* (Mexico).
To serve until 2 May 1989: Bakr Abdullah Bakr (Saudi Arabia); Bashir Bakri (Sudan), Marie-Thérèse Basse (Senegal); André Blanc-Lapierre (France); Jozsef Bognar (Hungary);[b] Mercedes B. Concepción, *Vice-Chairman* (Philippines); Walter Joseph Kamba (Zimbabwe); Maria de Lourdes Pintasilgo, *Vice-Chairman* (Portugal); Y. M. Primakov (USSR); Alberto Wagner de Reyna (Peru); Zhao Dihua (China).
Ex-officio members: The Secretary-General, the Director-General of UNESCO and the Executive Director of UNITAR.
Rector of the United Nations University: Mr. Soedjatmoko.

[a]Daniel Adzei Bekoe (Ghana), Dennis H. Irvine (Guyana) and Karl Eric Knutsson (Sweden) resigned as of April, June and 26 January 1984, respectively; two of the resultant vacancies remained unfilled in 1984.
[b]Appointed in July and March 1984, respectively.

The Council maintained four standing committees during 1984: the Committee on Finance and Budget; the Committee on Institutional and Programmatic Development; the Committee on Statutes, Rules and Guidelines; and the Committee on the Report of the Council.

United Nations Voluntary Fund for Victims of Torture

BOARD OF TRUSTEES
The Board of Trustees to advise the Secretary-General in his administration of the United Nations Voluntary Fund for Victims of Torture consists of five members with wide experience in the field of human rights, appointed in their personal capacity by the Secretary-General with due regard for equitable geographical distribution and in consultation with their Governments.

The Board held its third session from 27 to 29 August 1984 at Geneva.

Members (to serve until 31 December 1985): Hans Danelius, *Chairman* (Sweden); Elizabeth Odio Benito (Costa Rica); Waleed M. Sadi (Jor-

---

[22]YUN 1958, p. 31, res. 1344(XIII), 13 Dec. 1958.
[23]YUN 1956, p. 108.
[24]YUN 1981, p. 418, dec. 36/424, 4 Dec. 1981.
[25]YUN 1975, p. 387, res. 3504(XXX), 15 Dec. 1975.
[26]YUN 1976, p. 356, res. 31/177, annex, 21 Dec. 1976.

dan); Ivan Tosevski (Yugoslavia);[a] Amos Wako (Kenya).

[a]Appointed in August 1984.

World Food Council

The World Food Council, at the ministerial or plenipotentiary level, functions as an organ of the United Nations and reports to the General Assembly through the Economic and Social Council. It consists of 36 members, nominated by the Economic and Social Council and elected by the Assembly according to the following pattern: nine members from African States, eight from Asian States, seven from Latin American States, four from socialist States of Eastern Europe and eight from Western European and other States. Members serve for three-year terms.

During 1984, the World Food Council held its tenth session at Addis Ababa, Ethiopia, from 11 to 15 June. It was preceded by a preparatory meeting held at Rome, Italy, from 30 April to 3 May.

Members:
To serve until 31 December 1984: Botswana, Canada, China, Colombia, Gambia, Greece, India, Mexico, Thailand, United Republic of Tanzania, United States, Yugoslavia.
To serve until 31 December 1985: Australia, Bangladesh, Ecuador, Ethiopia, German Democratic Republic, Germany, Federal Republic of, Ghana, Nicaragua, Nigeria, USSR, United Arab Emirates, Venezuela.
To serve until 31 December 1986: Argentina, Burundi, Central African Republic, Chile, Finland, France, Hungary, Iraq, Italy, Japan, Morocco, Pakistan.

President: Eugene F. Whelan (Canada).
Vice-Presidents: Pedro Antonio Blandón (Nicaragua), Karl Friedrich Gebhardt (German Democratic Republic), A. G. Mahmud (Bangladesh), Saihou Sabally (Gambia).
Rapporteur: Reaz Rahman (Bangladesh).

Executive Director: Maurice J. Williams.
Deputy Executive Director: Diogo A. N. de Gaspar.

On 23 May 1984 (decision 1984/156), the Economic and Social Council nominated the following 13 States, 12 of which were to be elected by the General Assembly, for a three-year term beginning on 1 January 1985 to fill the vacancies occurring on 31 December 1984: Brazil, Bulgaria, Canada, Colombia, China, Ivory Coast, Kenya, Mexico, Sri Lanka, Thailand, Turkey, United States, Zambia. All but Colombia were elected by the Assembly on 10 December 1984 (decision 39/311).

Conferences

International Conference on Population

The International Conference on Population was held at Mexico City from 6 to 14 August 1984. Participating were the following 146 States and the United Nations Council for Namibia:

Afghanistan, Albania, Algeria, Angola, Antigua and Barbuda, Argentina, Australia, Austria, Bahamas, Bangladesh, Barbados, Belgium, Belize, Benin, Bhutan, Bolivia, Botswana, Brazil, Bulgaria, Burkina Faso, Burma, Burundi, Byelorussian SSR, Cameroon, Canada, Cape Verde, Central African Republic, Chad, Chile, China, Colombia, Comoros, Congo, Costa Rica, Cuba, Cyprus, Czechoslovakia, Democratic Kampuchea, Democratic People's Republic of Korea, Democratic Yemen, Denmark, Dominica, Dominican Republic, Ecuador, Egypt, El Salvador, Ethiopia, Finland, France, Gabon, Gambia, German Democratic Republic, Germany, Federal Republic of, Ghana, Greece, Grenada, Guatemala, Guinea, Guinea-Bissau, Guyana, Haiti, Holy See, Honduras, Hungary, India, Indonesia, Iran, Iraq, Ireland, Israel, Italy, Ivory Coast, Jamaica, Japan, Jordan, Kenya, Kuwait, Lebanon, Lesotho, Liberia, Madagascar, Malawi, Malaysia, Maldives, Mali, Malta, Mauritania, Mauritius, Mexico, Morocco, Mozambique, Nepal, Netherlands, New Zealand, Nicaragua, Niger, Nigeria, Norway, Pakistan, Panama, Papua New Guinea, Paraguay, Peru, Philippines, Poland, Portugal, Republic of Korea, Romania, Rwanda, Saint Christopher and Nevis, Saint Lucia, Saint Vincent and the Grenadines, Samoa, Sao Tome and Principe, Saudi Arabia, Senegal, Sierra Leone, Somalia, Spain, Sri Lanka, Sudan, Suriname, Swaziland, Sweden, Switzerland, Thailand, Togo, Tonga, Trinidad and Tobago, Tunisia, Turkey, Uganda, Ukrainian SSR, USSR, United Arab Emirates, United Kingdom, United Republic of Tanzania, United States,

Uruguay, Venezuela, Viet Nam, Yemen, Yugoslavia, Zaire, Zambia, Zimbabwe.

President: Manuel Bartlett Diaz (Mexico).
Vice-Presidents for co-ordination: M. Shamsul Haq (Bangladesh), Dirk Jan van de Kaa (Netherlands).
Vice-Presidents: Austria, Brazil, Bulgaria, Burundi, Cameroon, China, Cuba, France, India, Iraq, Italy, Japan, Malaysia, Pakistan, Peru, Saint Vincent and the Grenadines, Senegal, Sierra Leone, Spain, Sri Lanka, Sudan, Sweden, Tunisia, USSR, United Republic of Tanzania, Zambia.
Rapporteur-General: Andras Klinger (Hungary).

Presiding Officers of committees:
Main Committee: Frederick Sai (Ghana).
Credentials Committee: Sam Odaka (Uganda).

Second International Conference on Assistance to Refugees in Africa

The Second International Conference on Assistance to Refugees in Africa was held at Geneva from 9 to 11 July 1984. Participating were the following 107 States:

Afghanistan, Algeria, Angola, Argentina, Australia, Austria, Bahrain, Bangladesh, Belgium, Benin, Botswana, Brazil, Burundi, Cameroon, Canada, Central African Republic, Chad, Chile, China, Colombia, Congo, Costa Rica, Cyprus, Democratic Kampuchea, Democratic Yemen, Denmark, Djibouti, Dominican Republic, Ecuador, Egypt, Ethiopia, Finland, France, Gabon, Germany, Federal Republic of, Ghana, Greece, Guinea, Haiti, Holy See, Iceland, India, Indonesia, Iran, Iraq, Ireland, Israel, Italy, Ivory Coast, Jamaica, Japan, Jordan, Kenya, Kuwait, Lebanon, Lesotho, Liberia, Luxembourg, Madagascar, Malawi, Malaysia, Morocco, Mozambique, Netherlands, New Zealand, Nicaragua, Niger, Nigeria, Norway, Oman, Pakistan, Panama, Peru, Philippines, Portugal, Qatar, Republic of Korea, Rwanda, San Marino, Saudi Arabia, Senegal, Sierra Leone, Singapore, Somalia, Spain, Sri Lanka, Sudan, Swaziland, Sweden, Switzerland, Syrian Arab Republic, Thailand, Togo, Trinidad and Tobago, Tunisia, Turkey, Uganda, United Kingdom, United Republic of Tanzania, United States, Venezuela, Viet Nam, Yemen, Yugoslavia, Zaire, Zambia, Zimbabwe.

President: Leo Tindemans (Belgium).
Vice-Presidents: Ibrahim Gambari (Nigeria), Ali Kaiser Morshed (Bangladesh), Paulo Nogueira Batista (Brazil).

United Nations Conference on Conditions for Registration of Ships

The first part of the United Nations Conference on Conditions for Registration of Ships was held at Geneva from 16 July to 3 August 1984. Participating were the following 92 States:

Algeria, Argentina, Australia, Austria, Bahamas, Belgium, Bolivia, Brazil, Bulgaria, Byelorussian SSR, Cameroon, Canada, Chile, China, Colombia, Congo, Cuba, Cyprus, Czechoslovakia, Democratic Yemen, Denmark, Ecuador, Egypt, El Salvador, Ethiopia, Finland, France, Gabon, Gambia, German Democratic Republic, Germany, Federal Republic of, Ghana, Greece, Haiti, Hungary, India, Indonesia, Iran, Iraq, Ireland, Israel, Italy, Ivory Coast, Jamaica, Japan, Jordan, Kuwait, Lebanon, Liberia, Libyan Arab Jamahiriya, Madagascar, Malaysia, Malta, Mauritius, Mexico, Morocco, Netherlands, New Zealand, Nicaragua, Nigeria, Norway, Oman, Pakistan, Panama, Peru, Philippines, Poland, Portugal, Republic of Korea, Senegal, Singapore, Somalia, Spain, Sri Lanka, Sudan, Sweden, Switzerland, Thailand, Trinidad and Tobago, Tunisia, Turkey, Ukrainian SSR, USSR, United Kingdom, United Republic of Tanzania, United States, Uruguay, Vanuatu, Venezuela, Yemen, Yugoslavia, Zaire.

President: Lamine Fadika (Ivory Coast).
Vice-Presidents: Australia, Bolivia, China, Czechoslovakia, Egypt, France, Indonesia, Japan, Lebanon, Liberia, Norway, Peru, USSR, United States.
Rapporteur: Arturo Hotton-Risler (Argentina).

Chairmen of committees:
General Committee: Lamine Fadika (Ivory Coast).
First Committee: Krzysztof Dabrowski (Poland).
Second Committee: Rudi Okken (Netherlands).
Drafting Committee: Yashwant Sinha (India).
Credentials Committee: G. A. Mathas (Gabon).

Security Council

The Security Council consists of 15 Member States of the United Nations, in accordance with the provisions of Article 23 of the United Nations Charter as amended in 1965.

MEMBERS

Permanent members: China, France, USSR, United Kingdom, United States.

Non-permanent members: Burkina Faso, Egypt, India, Malta, Netherlands, Nicaragua, Pakistan, Peru, Ukrainian SSR, Zimbabwe.

On 22 October and 18 December 1984 (decision 39/323), the General Assembly elected Australia, Denmark, Madagascar, Thailand, and Trinidad and Tobago for a two-year term beginning on 1 January 1985, to replace Malta, the Netherlands, Nicaragua, Pakistan and Zimbabwe, whose terms of office were to expire on 31 December 1984.

PRESIDENTS

The presidency of the Council rotates monthly, according to the English alphabetical listing of its member States. The following served as Presidents during 1984:

Month	Member	Representative
January	Nicaragua	Francisco Javier Chamorro Mora
February	Pakistan	S. Shah Nawaz
March	Peru	Javier Arias Stella
April	Ukrainian SSR	V. A. Kravets
May	USSR	O. A. Troyanovsky
June	United Kingdom	Sir John Adam Thomson
July	United States	Jeane J. Kirkpatrick
August	Upper Volta[a]	Léandre Bassolé
September	Zimbabwe	Elleck Kufakunesu Mashingaidze
October	Burkina Faso[a]	Basile Laetare Guissou
		Léandre Bassolé
November	China	Ling Qing
December	Egypt	Ahmed Tawfik Khalil

[a]On 6 August 1984, the Upper Volta became Burkina Faso and therefore changed its position in the Council's alphabetical rotation.

Collective Measures Committee

The Collective Measures Committee (p. 1313) reports to both the General Assembly and the Security Council.

Military Staff Committee

The Military Staff Committee consists of the chiefs of staff of the permanent members of the Security Council or their representatives. It met fortnightly throughout 1984; the first meeting was held on 12 January and the last on 21 December.

Standing committees

Each of the two standing committees of the Security Council is composed of representatives of all Council members:

Committee of Experts (to examine the provisional rules of procedure of the Council and any other matters entrusted to it by the Council)
Committee on the Admission of New Members

In addition, the Council maintains an *ad hoc* Committee on Council Meetings Away from Headquarters.

Ad hoc bodies

Ad Hoc Committee established under resolution 507(1982)
Members: France *(Chairman),* Guyana,[a] Jordan,[a] Uganda.[a]

[a]Not Council members in 1984.

Ad Hoc Sub-Committee on Namibia
The *Ad Hoc* Sub-Committee on Namibia consists of all the members of the Security Council. It did not meet in 1984.

Committee of Experts established by the Security Council at its 1506th meeting
(on the question of micro-States)
The Committee of Experts consists of all the members of the Security Council. The chairmanship is rotated monthly in the English alphabetical order of the member States.
The Committee did not meet in 1984.

Committee on the Exercise of the Inalienable Rights of the Palestinian People
The Committee (p. 1315) reports to the General Assembly, which has also drawn the attention of the Security Council to the need for urgent action on the recommendations of the Committee.

Security Council Commission established under resolution 446(1979)
(to examine the situation relating to settlements in the Arab territories occupied since 1967, including Jerusalem)
Members:[a] Bolivia, Portugal *(Chairman),* Zambia.

[a]Not Council members in 1984.

Security Council Committee established by resolution 421(1977) concerning the question of South Africa
The Committee consists of all the members of the Security Council.

Special Committee against *Apartheid*
The Special Committee against *Apartheid* (p. 1318) reports to both the General Assembly and, as appropriate, to the Security Council.

PEACE-KEEPING OPERATIONS AND SPECIAL MISSIONS

United Nations Truce Supervision Organization (UNTSO)
Chief of Staff: Lieutenant-General Emmanuel Alexander Erskine.

United Nations Disengagement Observer Force (UNDOF)
Force Commander: Major-General Carl-Gustav Stahl.

United Nations Interim Force in Lebanon (UNIFIL)
Force Commander: Lieutenant-General William Callaghan.

United Nations Peace-keeping Force in Cyprus (UNFICYP)
Special Representative of the Secretary-General in Cyprus: Hugo J. Gobbi.
Force Commander: Major-General Günther G. Greindl.

United Nations Military Observer Group in India and Pakistan (UNMOGIP)
Chief Military Observer: Brigadier-General Thor A. Johnsen.

United Nations Transition Assistance Group (UNTAG)
Authorized by the Security Council in 1978,[27] the United Nations Transition Assistance Group had not been emplaced in Namibia by the end of 1984.

Special Representative of the Secretary-General: Martti Ahtisaari.
Commander-designate: Lieutenant-General Dewan Prem Chand.

---

[27]YUN 1978, p. 915, res. 435(1978), 29 Sep. 1978.

Economic and Social Council

The Economic and Social Council consists of 54 Member States of the United Nations, elected by the General Assembly, each for a three-year term, in accordance with the provisions of Article 61 of the United Nations Charter as amended in 1965 and 1973.

MEMBERS
To serve until 31 December 1984: Austria, Benin, Brazil, Colombia, France, Germany, Federal Republic of, Greece, Japan, Liberia, Mali, Pakistan, Portugal, Qatar, Romania, Saint Lucia, Swaziland, Tunisia, Venezuela.
To serve until 31 December 1985: Algeria, Botswana, Bulgaria, Congo, Djibouti, Ecuador, German Democratic Republic, Lebanon, Luxembourg, Malaysia, Mexico, Netherlands, New Zealand, Saudi Arabia, Sierra Leone, Suriname, Thailand, United States.
To serve until 31 December 1986: Argentina, Canada, China, Costa Rica, Finland, Guyana,[a] Indonesia, Papua New Guinea, Poland, Rwanda, Somalia, Sri Lanka, Sweden, Uganda, USSR, United Kingdom, Yugoslavia, Zaire.

[a]Elected on 26 June 1984 (decision 38/307).

On 22 October 1984 (decision 39/306), the General Assembly elected the following 18 States for a three-year term beginning on 1 January 1985 to fill the vacancies occurring on 31 December 1984: Bangladesh, Brazil, Colombia, France, Germany, Federal Republic of, Guinea, Haiti, Iceland, India, Japan, Morocco, Nigeria, Romania, Senegal, Spain, Turkey, Venezuela, Zimbabwe.

SESSIONS
Organizational session for 1984: United Nations Headquarters, 7-10 and 21 February and 16 March.
First regular session of 1984: United Nations Headquarters, 1-25 May.
Second regular session of 1984: Geneva, 4-27 July.

OFFICERS
President: Karl Fischer (Austria).
Vice-Presidents: Mohamed Bouyoucef (Algeria), Tomohiko Kobayashi (Japan), Wlodzimierz Natorf (Poland), Donatus St. Aimée (Saint Lucia).

Subsidiary and other related organs

SUBSIDIARY ORGANS
In addition to three regular sessional committees, the Economic and Social Council may, at each session, set up other committees or working groups, of the whole or of limited membership, and refer to them any items on the agenda for study and report.
Other subsidiary organs reporting to the Council consist of functional commissions, regional commissions, standing committees, expert bodies and *ad hoc* bodies.
The inter-agency Administrative Committee on Co-ordination also reports to the Council.

Sessional bodies

SESSIONAL COMMITTEES
Each of the sessional committees of the Economic and Social Council consists of the 54 members of the Council.

First (Economic) Committee. Chairman: Tomohiko Kobayashi (Japan). *Vice-Chairmen:* Stoyan Bakalov (Bulgaria), Ana Maria Sampaio-Fernandes (Brazil).
Second (Social) Committee. Chairman: Mohamed Bouyoucef (Algeria). *Vice-Chairmen:* Shireen Moiz (Pakistan), Fanny Umaña (Colombia).
Third (Programme and Co-ordination) Committee. Chairman: Wlodzimierz Natorf (Poland). *Vice-Chairmen:* Margaret H. Ford (Canada), Désiré Nkounkou (Congo).

SESSIONAL WORKING GROUP OF GOVERNMENTAL EXPERTS ON THE IMPLEMENTATION OF THE INTERNATIONAL COVENANT ON ECONOMIC, SOCIAL AND CULTURAL RIGHTS
The Sessional Working Group of Governmental Experts on the Implementation of the International Covenant on Economic, Social and Cultural Rights, which was to consist of 15 members elected by the Council from among the States parties to the Covenant, met at United Nations Headquarters from 16 April to 4 May 1984.

Members:
To serve until 31 December 1984: Bulgaria, Ecuador, Jordan, Libyan Arab Jamahiriya, Spain.
To serve until 31 December 1985:[a] France, Kenya, Peru, USSR.
To serve until 31 December 1986:[b] Denmark, German Democratic Republic, Japan, Tunisia.

[a]One seat allocated to a member from Asian States remained unfilled in 1984.
[b]One seat allocated to a member from Latin American States remained unfilled in 1984.

Chairman: Michael Urban Bendix (Denmark).
Vice-Chairmen: Sharif G. Alkalbash (Libyan Arab Jamahiriya), Farouk Kasrawi (Jordan), Kalin Mitrev (Bulgaria).
Rapporteur: Carlos Játiva (Ecuador).

On 23 May 1984 (decision 1984/156), the Economic and Social Council elected Bulgaria and Spain for a three-year term beginning on 1 January 1985 to fill two of the five vacancies occurring on 31 December 1984. No further elections were held in 1984 to fill the remaining seats, allocated to one member each from African, Asian and Latin American States.
On 24 May 1984 (decision 1984/122), the Council decided that the Group's 1985 Bureau be constituted as follows: Chairman—Eastern European States; Vice-Chairmen—Asian States, Latin American States, Western European and other States; Rapporteur—African States.

Functional commissions and subsidiaries

Commission for Social Development
The Commission for Social Development consists of 32 members, elected for four-year terms by the Economic and Social Council according to a specific pattern of equitable geographical distribution.
The Commission did not meet in 1984.

Members:
To serve until 31 December 1984: Chile, Italy, Madagascar, Panama, Philippines, Poland, Sudan, Sweden, Thailand, Turkey.
To serve until 31 December 1986: Argentina, Austria, Byelorussian SSR, Central African Republic, Cyprus, Ecuador, Finland, Ghana, India, Liberia, Togo.
To serve until 31 December 1987: Canada, El Salvador, France, Haiti, Kenya, Malaysia, Mongolia, Morocco, Romania, USSR, United States.

On 23 May 1984 (decision 1984/156), the Economic and Social Council elected the following members for a four-year term beginning on 1 January 1985 to fill 8 of the 10 vacancies occurring on 31 December 1984: Chile, Denmark, Italy, Netherlands, Panama, Poland, Thailand, Zimbabwe. No further elections were held in 1984 to fill the remaining seats, allocated to one member each from African and Asian States.

Commission on Human Rights
The Commission on Human Rights consists of 43 members, elected for three-year terms by the Economic and Social Council according to a specific pattern of equitable geographical distribution.
The Commission held its fortieth session at Geneva from 6 February to 16 March 1984.

Members:

To serve until 31 December 1984: Argentina, Bulgaria, Canada, China, Cuba, Gambia, Germany, Federal Republic of, Italy, Japan, Pakistan, Rwanda, Togo, United Kingdom, Uruguay, Zimbabwe.

To serve until 31 December 1985: Bangladesh, Colombia, Costa Rica, Cyprus, Finland, India, Ireland, Libyan Arab Jamahiriya, Mozambique, Netherlands, Nicaragua, Ukrainian SSR, USSR, United Republic of Tanzania.

To serve until 31 December 1986: Brazil, Cameroon, France, German Democratic Republic, Jordan, Kenya, Mauritania, Mexico, Philippines, Senegal, Spain, Syrian Arab Republic, United States, Yugoslavia.

Chairman: Peter H. Kooijmans (Netherlands).

Vice-Chairmen: Ghaleb Z. Barakat (Jordan), Roberto Bianchi (Argentina), Todor Dichev (Bulgaria).

Rapporteur: Murade Isaac Murargy (Mozambique).

On 23 May 1984 (decision 1984/156), the Economic and Social Council elected the following 15 members for a three-year term beginning on 1 January 1985 to fill the vacancies occurring on 31 December 1984: Argentina, Australia, Austria, Bulgaria, China, Congo, Gambia, Germany, Federal Republic of, Japan, Lesotho, Liberia, Peru, Sri Lanka, United Kingdom, Venezuela.

AD HOC WORKING GROUP OF EXPERTS
(established by Commission on Human Rights resolution 2(XXIII) of 6 March 1967)

Members: Balanda Mikuin Leliel (Zaire); Annan Arkyin Cato, *Chairman/Rapporteur* (Ghana); Humberto Díaz-Casanueva (Chile); Felix Ermacora (Austria); Branimir M. Jankovic, *Vice-Chairman* (Yugoslavia); Mulka Govinda Reddy (India).

GROUP OF THREE ESTABLISHED UNDER THE INTERNATIONAL CONVENTION ON THE SUPPRESSION AND PUNISHMENT OF THE CRIME OF *APARTHEID*

The Group of Three held its seventh session at Geneva from 30 January to 3 February 1984.

Members: Bulgaria, Mexico, Syrian Arab Republic.

Chairman/Rapporteur: Vicente Montemayor Cantú (Mexico).

SUB-COMMISSION ON PREVENTION OF DISCRIMINATION AND PROTECTION OF MINORITIES

The Sub-Commission consists of 26 members elected by the Commission on Human Rights from candidates nominated by Member States of the United Nations, in accordance with a scheme to ensure equitable geographical distribution. Members serve in their individual capacity as experts, rather than as governmental representatives, each for a three-year term.

The Sub-Commission held its thirty-seventh session at Geneva from 6 to 31 August 1984.

Members (until March 1987):[a] Miguel Alfonso Martínez (Cuba); Awn Shawkat Al Khasawneh (Jordan); Murlidhar Chandrakant Bhandare, *Vice-Chairman* (India); Marc Bossuyt (Belgium); Abu Sayeed Chowdhury (Bangladesh); Erica-Irene A. Daes (Greece); Driss Dahak (Morocco); Jules Deschênes (Canada); George Dove-Edwin (Nigeria); Enzo Giustozzi (Argentina); Gu Yijie (China); Aidiid Abdillahi Ilkahanaf (Somalia); Louis Joinet, *Vice-Chairman* (France); Ahmed Mohamed Khalifa (Egypt); Antonio Martínez Báez (Mexico); Dumitru Mazilu (Romania); Chama L. C. Mubanga-Chipoya (Zambia); John P. Roche (United States); Kwesi B. S. Simpson (Ghana); V. N. Sofinsky (USSR); Masayuki Takemoto (Japan); Ivan Tosevski, *Chairman* (Yugoslavia); Antonio Jose Uribe Portocarrero (Colombia); Rodrigo Valdez Baquero (Ecuador); Benjamin Charles George Whitaker (United Kingdom); Fisseha Yimer, *Vice-Chairman* (Ethiopia).

[a] Elected on 13 March 1984.

Rapporteur: Leandro Despouy (Argentina).

Working Group
(established by resolution 2(XXIV) of 16 August 1971 of the Sub-Commission on Prevention of Discrimination and Protection of Minorities pursuant to Economic and Social Council resolution 1503(XLVIII))

The Working Group on Communications concerning human rights held its thirteenth session at Geneva from 23 July to 3 August 1984.

Members: Murlidhar Chandrakant Bhandare (India); Marc Bossuyt (Belgium); Antonio Martínez Báez (Mexico), V. N. Sofinsky, *Chairman/Rapporteur* (USSR); Fisseha Yimer (Ethiopia).

Working Group
(established on 21 August 1974 by resolution 11(XXVII) of the Sub-Commission on Prevention of Discrimination and Protection of Minorities)

The Working Group on Slavery held its tenth session at Geneva from 30 July to 3 August 1984.

Members: Abu Sayeed Chowdhury, *Chairman/Rapporteur* (Bangladesh); Jules Deschênes (Canada); Dumitru Mazilu (Romania); Chama L. C. Mubanga-Chipoya (Zambia); Rodrigo Valdez Baquero (Ecuador).

Working Group on Detention

On 7 August 1984, the Sub-Commission on Prevention of Discrimination and Protection of Minorities established a Working Group on Detention, which met at Geneva between 13 and 21 August.

Members: Miguel Alfonso Martínez (Cuba); Murlidhar Chandrakant Bhandare (India); Driss Dahak (Morocco); Dumitru Mazilu (Romania); John P. Roche, *Chairman/Rapporteur* (United States).

Working Group on Indigenous Populations

The Working Group on Indigenous Populations held its third session at Geneva from 30 July to 2 August and on 6 August 1984.

Members: Erica-Irene A. Daes, *Chairman/Rapporteur* (Greece); Enzo Giustozzi (Argentina); Gu Yijie (China); Aidiid Abdillahi Ilkahanaf (Somalia); Ivan Tosevski (Yugoslavia).

WORKING GROUP OF GOVERNMENTAL EXPERTS ON THE RIGHT TO DEVELOPMENT

The Working Group of Governmental Experts on the Right to Development held two sessions in 1984, at Geneva: its eighth from 24 September to 5 October; and its ninth from 3 to 14 December.

Members: Luís Aguirre Gallardo (Panama); Juan Alvarez Vita (Peru); Peter L. Berger (United States); D. V. Bykov (USSR); K. L. Dalal, *Vice-Chairman* (India);[a] Paul J. I. M. de Waart (Netherlands); Georges Gautier, *Rapporteur* (France); Riyadh Aziz Hadi (Iraq); Julio Heredia Pérez, *Vice-Chairman* (Cuba); Irina Kolarova (Bulgaria);[a] Fatma Z. Ksentini (Algeria); Ahmed Saker (Syrian Arab Republic); Alioune Sène, *Chairman* (Senegal); Kongit Sinegiorgis (Ethiopia); Danilo Turk, *Vice-Chairman* (Yugoslavia).

[a] Replaced, respectively, Viswanathan Ramachandran (India) and Henryk J. Sokalski (Poland), who had resigned.

WORKING GROUP ON ENFORCED OR INVOLUNTARY DISAPPEARANCES

During 1984, the mandate of the Working Group on Enforced or Involuntary Disappearances was extended for one year by a Commission on Human Rights resolution of 6 March, as approved by the Economic and Social Council on 24 May (decision 1984/135).

The Working Group held three sessions in 1984: its thirteenth at United Nations Headquarters from 4 to 8 June; its fourteenth at San José, Costa Rica, from 3 to 11 October; and its fifteenth at Geneva from 5 to 14 December.

Members: Jonas Kwami Dotse Foli (Ghana); Agha Hilaly (Pakistan); Ivan Tosevski, *Chairman/Rapporteur* (Yugoslavia); Toine F. van Dongen (Netherlands);[a] Luis Alberto Varela Quirós (Costa Rica).

[a] Replaced Viscount Colville of Culross (United Kingdom), who had resigned.

WORKING GROUPS
*(to study situations revealing a consistent
pattern of gross violations of human rights)*

*Working Group established by Commission on
Human Rights decision 1983/110 of 28 February 1983:*
Members: Todor Dichev (Bulgaria);[a] Minoru Endo (Japan);[a] Francis
Mahon Hayes (Ireland); E. E. E. Mtango, *Chairman/Rapporteur*
(United Republic of Tanzania); Luis Solá Vila (Cuba).

[a]Replaced, respectively, Borislav Konstantinov (Bulgaria) and Sadako Ogata
(Japan), who were unable to attend the Group's 1984 meetings.

*Working Group established by Commission on
Human Rights decision 1984/114 of 6 March 1984:*
Members: Ghaleb Z. Barakat (Jordan), Roberto Bianchi (Argentina),
Todor Dichev (Bulgaria), Francis Mahon Hayes (Ireland), E. E. E.
Mtango (United Republic of Tanzania).

WORKING GROUPS (OPEN-ENDED)

*Working Group established by Commission on
Human Rights resolution 1983/52 of 10 March 1983
(to draft a convention on the rights of the child):*
Chairman/Rapporteur: Adam Lopatka (Poland).

*Working Group established by Commission on
Human Rights resolution 1983/48 of 9 March 1983
(to draft a convention against torture and other
cruel, inhuman or degrading treatment or punishment):*
Chairman/Rapporteur: Jan Herman Burgers (Netherlands).

Commission on Narcotic Drugs

The Commission on Narcotic Drugs consists of 40 members, elected
for four-year terms by the Economic and Social Council from among
the Members of the United Nations and members of the specialized
agencies and the parties to the Single Convention on Narcotic Drugs,
1961, with due regard for the adequate representation of *(a)* countries
which are important producers of opium or coca leaves, *(b)* countries
which are important in the manufacture of narcotic drugs, and *(c)* countries in which drug addiction or the illicit traffic in narcotic drugs constitutes an important problem, as well as taking into account the principle of equitable geographical distribution.

The Commission held its eighth special session at Vienna, Austria,
from 6 to 10 February 1984.

Members:
To serve until 31 December 1985: Argentina, Australia, Austria, Ba-
hamas, Belgium, Bulgaria, Hungary, India, Ivory Coast, Japan, Malay-
sia, Mexico, Nigeria, Panama, Republic of Korea, Senegal, Turkey,
USSR, United Kingdom, Zaire.
To serve until 31 December 1987: Algeria, Brazil, Canada, Colombia,
Finland, France, German Democratic Republic, Germany, Federal
Republic of, Greece, Iran, Italy, Madagascar, Morocco, Netherlands,
Pakistan, Peru, Sri Lanka, Thailand, United States, Yugoslavia.

Chairman: Istvan Bayer (Hungary).
First Vice-Chairman: Maurice Randrianame (Madagascar).
Second Vice-Chairman: Mairaj Husain (Pakistan).
Rapporteur: Ben J. A. Huyghe-Braeckmans (Belgium).

SUB-COMMISSION ON ILLICIT DRUG TRAFFIC AND
RELATED MATTERS IN THE NEAR AND MIDDLE EAST

During 1984, the Sub-Commission held two sessions, at Vienna, Austria: its seventeenth on 2 February, and its eighteenth from 1 to 3
October.

Members: Afghanistan, Iran, Pakistan, Sweden, Turkey.

Chairman: Erdem Erner (Turkey).
Vice-Chairman: Mairaj Husain (Pakistan).

MEETING OF OPERATIONAL HEADS
OF NATIONAL NARCOTICS LAW ENFORCEMENT
AGENCIES, FAR EAST REGION (HONLEA)

A meeting to co-ordinate regional activities against illicit drug traffic,
convened annually in one of the region's capitals, is open to any country or territory in the region approved by the Commission, as well as
to observers from the Association of South-East Asian Nations, the
Colombo Plan Bureau, the Customs Co-operation Council, the International Criminal Police Organization and the International Narcotics
Control Board. Any interested Government outside the region may be
invited by the Secretary-General to send an observer at its own expense.

The eleventh meeting of HONLEA was held at Bangkok, Thailand,
from 26 to 30 November 1984.

Commission on the Status of Women

The Commission on the Status of Women consists of 32 members,
elected for four-year terms by the Economic and Social Council according to a specific pattern of equitable geographical distribution.

The Commission was designated by the Council as the preparatory
body for the World Conference to Review and Appraise the Achievements of the United Nations Decade for Women (p. 1336), scheduled
for 1985.

The Commission held its thirtieth session at Vienna, Austria, from
15 to 25 February 1984.

Members:
To serve until 31 December 1984: Canada, Egypt, India, Italy, Japan,
Spain, Sudan, Trinidad and Tobago, Ukrainian SSR, Venezuela, Zaire.
To serve until 31 December 1986: Australia, Czechoslovakia, Indonesia,
Kenya, Liberia, Mexico, Philippines, Sierra Leone, USSR, United King-
dom, United States.
To serve until 31 December 1987: China, Cuba, Denmark, Ecuador, Ger-
man Democratic Republic, Germany, Federal Republic of, Nicaragua,
Pakistan, Togo, Zambia.

Chairman: Rosario G. Manalo (Philippines).
Vice-Chairmen: Lombe Chibesakunda (Zambia), Dagmar Molkova
(Czechoslovakia), Luzmila Rodríguez de Troya (Ecuador).
Rapporteur: Kathleen Joan Taperell (Australia).

On 23 May 1984 (decision 1984/156), the Economic and Social Council elected the following 11 members for a four-year term beginning
on 1 January 1985 to fill the vacancies occurring on 31 December 1984:
Brazil, Byelorussian SSR, Canada, France, Greece, India, Japan,
Mauritius, Sudan, Tunisia, Venezuela.

Population Commission

The Population Commission consists of 27 members, elected for four-
year terms by the Economic and Social Council according to a specific
pattern of equitable geographical distribution.

The Commission was designated by the Council as the Preparatory
Committee for the International Conference on Population (p. 1336).

The Commission held its twenty-second session at United Nations
Headquarters from 18 to 20 January 1984.

Members:
To serve until 31 December 1984: Greece, Honduras, Hungary, Nether-
lands, Norway, Peru, Rwanda, Thailand, Zaire.
To serve until 31 December 1985: Bolivia, China, Japan, Mexico, Sudan,
USSR, United Kingdom, United States, Zambia.
To serve until 31 December 1987: Bulgaria, Costa Rica, Egypt, France,
India, Malaysia, Nigeria, Sweden, Togo.

Chairman: Dirk Jan van de Kaa (Netherlands).
Vice-Chairmen: Noor Laily Dato Abu Bakar (Malaysia), Aziz Elbendary
(Egypt), Victor Hugo Morgan (Costa Rica).
Rapporteur: Andras Klinger (Hungary).

On 23 May 1984 (decision 1984/156), the Economic and Social Council elected the following nine members for a four-year term beginning
on 1 January 1985 to fill the vacancies occurring on 31 December 1984:
Brazil, Cameroon, Colombia, Germany, Federal Republic of, Mauritius,
Netherlands, Thailand, Turkey, Ukrainian SSR.

Statistical Commission

The Statistical Commission consists of 24 members, elected for four-year terms by the Economic and Social Council according to a specific pattern of equitable geographical distribution.

The Commission did not meet in 1984.

Members:

To serve until 31 December 1984: Australia, Brazil, Finland, Japan, Malaysia, Mexico, Ukrainian SSR, United Kingdom.

To serve until 31 December 1985: Argentina, France, Ireland, Libyan Arab Jamahiriya, Nigeria, Spain, Togo, USSR.

To serve until 31 December 1987: Bulgaria, China, Cuba, Czechoslovakia, Ghana, Kenya, Pakistan, United States.

On 23 May 1984 (decision 1984/156), the Economic and Social Council elected the following eight members for a four-year term beginning on 1 January 1985 to fill the vacancies occurring on 31 December 1984: Brazil, Finland, India, Japan, Mexico, New Zealand, Ukrainian SSR, United Kingdom.

WORKING GROUP ON INTERNATIONAL
STATISTICAL PROGRAMMES AND CO-ORDINATION

The Working Group consists of the Bureau of the Statistical Commission; the representatives to the Commission of the two major contributors to the United Nations budget, unless these are already represented in the Bureau; and one representative to the Commission from a developing country from among members of each of the following: ECA, ECLAC and ESCAP, unless these are also already represented in the Bureau. Members serve two-year terms.

The Working Group did not meet in 1984.

Regional commissions

Economic and Social Commission for Asia and the Pacific (ESCAP)

The Economic and Social Commission for Asia and the Pacific held its fortieth session at Tokyo, Japan, from 17 to 27 April 1984.

Members: Afghanistan, Australia, Bangladesh, Bhutan, Burma, China, Democratic Kampuchea, Fiji, France, India, Indonesia, Iran, Japan, Lao People's Democratic Republic, Malaysia, Maldives, Mongolia, Nauru, Nepal, Netherlands, New Zealand, Pakistan, Papua New Guinea, Philippines, Republic of Korea, Samoa, Singapore, Solomon Islands, Sri Lanka, Thailand, Tonga, USSR, United Kingdom, United States, Vanuatu,[a] Viet Nam.

Associate members: Brunei,[b] Cook Islands, Guam, Hong Kong, Kiribati, Niue, Trust Territory of the Pacific Islands, Tuvalu.

Switzerland, not a Member of the United Nations, participates in a consultative capacity in the work of the Commission.

[a]Became a full member on 17 February 1984.
[b]Retained associate membership in 1984 although admitted to the United Nations as Brunei Darussalam on 21 September.

Chairman: Shintaro Abe (Japan).

Vice-Chairmen: Mohammad Taghi Banki (Iran), Tserenpiliin Gombosuren (Mongolia), Mr. Hartarto (Indonesia), William Hayden (Australia), Damrong Lathapipat (Thailand), Chung-Oh Lee (Republic of Korea), M. H. M. Naina Marikar (Sri Lanka), Sela Molisa (Vanuatu), Masahiro Nishibori (Japan), Qian Qichen (China), Mafizur Rahman (Bangladesh), Karl Stack (Papua New Guinea).

Following are the main subsidiary and related bodies of the Commission:

Advisory body: Advisory Committee of Permanent Representatives and Other Representatives Designated by Members of the Commission.

Legislative bodies: Committee on Agricultural Development; Committee on Development Planning; Committee on Industry, Technology, Human Settlements and the Environment; Committee on Natural Resources; Committee on Population; Committee on Shipping, and Transport and Communications; Committee on Social Development; Committee on Statistics; Committee on Trade.

Regional institutions: Regional Centre for Technology Transfer; Regional Co-ordination Centre for Research and Development of Coarse Grains, Pulses, Roots and Tuber Crops in the Humid Tropics of Asia and the Pacific; Regional Mineral Resources Development Centre; Regional Network for Agricultural Machinery; Statistical Institute for Asia and the Pacific.

Related intergovernmental bodies: Asian and Pacific Development Centre; Committee for Co-ordination of Joint Prospecting for Mineral Resources in Asian Offshore Areas; Committee for Co-ordination of Joint Prospecting for Mineral Resources in South Pacific Offshore Areas; Interim Committee for Co-ordination of Investigations of the Lower Mekong Basin; Typhoon Committee.

Intergovernmental meeting convened by ESCAP: Special Body on Land-locked Countries.

Economic Commission for Africa (ECA)

The Economic Commission for Africa meets in annual session at the ministerial level known as the Conference of Ministers.

The Commission held its nineteenth session (tenth meeting of the Conference of Ministers) at Addis Ababa, Ethiopia, from 24 to 28 May 1984.

Members: Algeria, Angola, Benin, Botswana, Burundi, Cameroon, Cape Verde, Central African Republic, Chad, Comoros, Congo, Djibouti, Egypt, Equatorial Guinea, Ethiopia, Gabon, Gambia, Ghana, Guinea, Guinea-Bissau, Ivory Coast, Kenya, Lesotho, Liberia, Libyan Arab Jamahiriya, Madagascar, Malawi, Mali, Mauritania, Mauritius, Morocco, Mozambique, Niger, Nigeria, Rwanda, Sao Tome and Principe, Senegal, Seychelles, Sierra Leone, Somalia, South Africa,[a] Sudan, Swaziland, Togo, Tunisia, Uganda, United Republic of Tanzania, Upper Volta, Zaire, Zambia, Zimbabwe.

Switzerland, not a Member of the United Nations, participates in a consultative capacity in the work of the Commission.

[a]On 30 July 1963, the Economic and Social Council decided that South Africa should not take part in the work of ECA until conditions for constructive co-operation had been restored by a change in South Africa's racial policy (YUN 1963, p. 274, res. 974 D IV (XXXVII)).

Chairman: Mulumba Lukoji (Zaire).
First Vice-Chairman: Mohammed Wafik Hosni (Egypt).
Second Vice-Chairman: Ahmed Mohamed Ag Hamany (Mali).
Rapporteur: Stephen A. Echakara (Kenya).

The Commission has established the following principal legislative organs:

Conference of Ministers; sectoral ministerial conferences, each assisted by an appropriate committee of technical officials; Council of Ministers of each Multinational Programming and Operational Centre, assisted by its committee of officials.

The Commission has also established the following subsidiary bodies:

Joint Conference of African Planners, Statisticians and Demographers, and Technical Preparatory Committee of the Whole (two standing technical bodies); Governing Council, African Institute for Economic Development and Planning; Institut de formation et de recherche démographiques; Intergovernmental Committee of Experts for Science and Technology Development; Joint Intergovernmental Regional Committee on Human Settlements and Environment; Regional Institute for Population Studies.

Economic Commission for Europe (ECE)

The Economic Commission for Europe held its thirty-ninth session at Geneva from 3 to 14 April 1984.

Members: Albania, Austria, Belgium, Bulgaria, Byelorussian SSR, Canada, Cyprus, Czechoslovakia, Denmark, Finland, France, German Democratic Republic, Germany, Federal Republic of, Greece, Hungary, Iceland, Ireland, Italy, Luxembourg, Malta, Netherlands, Norway, Poland, Portugal, Romania, Spain, Sweden, Switzerland, Turkey, Ukrainian SSR, USSR, United Kingdom, United States, Yugoslavia.

The Holy See, Liechtenstein and San Marino, which are not Members of the United Nations, participate in a consultative capacity in the work of the Commission.

Chairman: Luben Gotsev (Bulgaria).
Vice-Chairman: Athanasios Petropoulos (Greece).
Rapporteurs: Anders Aslund (Sweden), Jan Bielawski (Poland).

Following are the principal subsidiary bodies of the Commission: Chemical Industry Committee; Coal Committee; Committee on Agricultural Problems; Committee on Electric Power; Committee on Gas; Committee on Housing, Building and Planning; Committee on the Development of Trade; Committee on Water Problems; Conference of European Statisticians; Inland Transport Committee; Senior Advisers to ECE Governments on Environmental Problems; Senior Advisers to ECE Governments on Science and Technology; Senior Economic Advisers to ECE Governments; Steel Committee; Timber Committee.

Other subsidiary bodies are: Senior Advisers to ECE Governments on Energy; Working Party on Engineering Industries and Automation.

Ad hoc meetings of experts are convened for sectors of activity not dealt with by these principal bodies.

Economic Commission for Latin America and the Caribbean (ECLAC)

The Economic Commission for Latin America held its twentieth session at Lima, Peru, from 29 March to 6 April 1984.

The Economic and Social Council changed the Commission's name to Economic Commission for Latin America and the Caribbean on 27 July.

Members: Antigua and Barbuda, Argentina *(First Vice-Chairman)*, Bahamas, Barbados, Belize, Bolivia, Brazil, Canada, Chile, Colombia, Costa Rica, Cuba, Dominica, Dominican Republic, Ecuador, El Salvador, France, Grenada, Guatemala, Guyana, Haiti, Honduras, Jamaica, Mexico, Netherlands, Nicaragua *(Third Vice-Chairman)*, Panama, Paraguay, Peru *(Chairman)*, Portugal,[a] Saint Christopher and Nevis, Saint Lucia, Saint Vincent and the Grenadines, Spain *(Rapporteur)*, Suriname, Trinidad and Tobago *(Second Vice-Chairman)*, United Kingdom, United States, Uruguay, Venezuela.
Associate members: British Virgin Islands,[b] Montserrat, Netherlands Antilles, United States Virgin Islands.[b]

Switzerland, not a Member of the United Nations, participates in a consultative capacity in the work of the Commission.

[a]Became a member on 27 July 1984.
[b]Became associate members on 6 April 1984.

The Commission has established the following principal subsidiary bodies:
Caribbean Development and Co-operation Committee; Central American Economic Co-operation Committee and its Inter-agency Committee; Committee of High-level Government Experts; Committee of the Whole; Technical Committee, Latin American Institute for Economic and Social Planning; Trade Committee.

The Latin American Demographic Centre forms part of the ECLAC system as an autonomous institution.

Economic Commission for Western Asia (ECWA)

The Economic Commission for Western Asia held its eleventh session at Baghdad, Iraq, from 22 to 26 April 1984.

Members: Bahrain, Democratic Yemen, Egypt, Iraq, Jordan, Kuwait, Lebanon, Oman, Qatar, Saudi Arabia, Syrian Arab Republic, United Arab Emirates, Yemen; Palestine Liberation Organization.

Chairman: Haidar Abu Bakr Al-Attas (Democratic Yemen).
Vice-Chairmen: Muhammad Al-Khadim Al-Wajih (Yemen), Jamal Al-Surani (Palestine Liberation Organization).
Rapporteur: Mohammed Wafik Hosni (Egypt).

The Commission's one main subsidiary organ, the Standing Committee for the Programme, composed of all ECWA members, was designated by the Economic and Social Council on 27 July 1984 as the Technical Committee.

Standing committees

Commission on Human Settlements

The Commission on Human Settlements consists of 58 members elected by the Economic and Social Council for three-year terms according to a specific pattern of equitable geographical distribution; it reports to the General Assembly through the Council.

In the framework of its regular sessions, the Commission is the United Nations intergovernmental body responsible for organizing the International Year of Shelter for the Homeless (1987).

The Commission held its seventh session at Libreville, Gabon, from 30 April to 11 May 1984.

Members:
To serve until 31 December 1984: Bangladesh, Bolivia, Byelorussian SSR, Chile, Cyprus, El Salvador, Germany, Federal Republic of, Greece, India, Italy, Jordan, Kenya, Liberia, Morocco, New Zealand, Romania, Sri Lanka, Sudan, Zimbabwe.
To serve until 31 December 1985: Algeria, Canada, Colombia, Cuba, France, German Democratic Republic, Hungary, Indonesia, Lebanon, Libyan Arab Jamahiriya, Malaysia, Netherlands, Nigeria, Norway, Papua New Guinea, Peru, Sierra Leone, Sweden, Uganda.
To serve until 31 December 1986: Bulgaria, Central African Republic, Finland, Gabon, Ghana, Guinea, Haiti, Honduras, Iraq, Japan, Nicaragua, Pakistan, Philippines, Rwanda, Spain, Turkey, USSR, United Republic of Tanzania, United States, Venezuela.

Chairman: General Ba Oumar (Gabon).
Vice-Chairmen: Ramesh Chandra (India), John J. Howley (United States), Jorge Mora-Brugere (Chile).
Rapporteur: Y. N. Sokolov (USSR).

On 23 May 1984 (decision 1984/156), the Economic and Social Council elected the following for a three-year term beginning on 1 January 1985 to fill 16 of the 19 vacancies occurring on 31 December 1984: Bangladesh, Botswana, Burundi, Chile, Cyprus, Germany, Federal Republic of, Greece, India, Jamaica, Jordan, Kenya, Lesotho, Mexico, Sri Lanka, Tunisia, Ukrainian SSR. No further elections were held in 1984 to fill the remaining seats, allocated to one member from Eastern European States and two members from Western European and other States.

Commission on Transnational Corporations

The Commission on Transnational Corporations consists of 48 members, elected from all States for three-year terms by the Economic and Social Council according to a specific pattern of geographical distribution.

In 1984, the Commission reconvened its special session, open to the participation of all States, from 9 to 13 January and from 11 to 29 June, and held its tenth session from 17 to 27 April, both at United Nations Headquarters.

Members:
To serve until 31 December 1984: Algeria, Canada, Congo, Ghana, India, Iran, Italy, Jamaica, Pakistan, Peru, Republic of Korea, Swaziland, Turkey, Ukrainian SSR, Venezuela, Yugoslavia.
To serve until 31 December 1985: Bahamas, Brazil, Central African Republic, Cuba, Cyprus, Indonesia, Kenya, Mexico, Netherlands, Nigeria, Norway, Thailand, Uganda, USSR, United Kingdom, United States.
To serve until 31 December 1986: Bangladesh, China, Colombia, Costa Rica, Czechoslovakia, Egypt, France, German Democratic Republic, Germany, Federal Republic of, Guinea, Japan, Morocco, Philippines, Switzerland, Togo, Trinidad and Tobago.
Expert advisers (through the tenth session): Michael A. Ajomo (Nigeria), Friedrich Dribbusch (Federal Republic of Germany),[a] Wim Kok (Netherlands),[a] Elias J. Mashasi (United Republic of Tanzania),[a] Charles Albert Michalet (France),[a] Zuhayr Mikdashi (Lebanon),[a] Carlos Omar Navarro Carrasco (Venezuela), Jones Santos Neves (Brazil), Mario Joel Ramos da Silva (Portugal), Bogdan Sosnowski (Poland), David Sycip (Philippines),[a] Louis von Planta (Switzerland), Branko Vukmir (Yugoslavia), Nat Weinberg (United States),[a] Ralph A. Weller (United States), Eduardo White (Argentina).[a]

[a]Reappointed by the Commission on 25 April 1984 to serve for a further two years, up to and including the twelfth (1986) session. Appointed on the same date for the

same term were: Thomas J. Bata (Canada), Celso Lafer (Brazil), Luis Enrique Marius (Uruguay/Italy), Alassane Dramane Ouattara (Upper Volta), Brian Price (United Kingdom), John Bower Rhodes (United States), Teng Weizao (China), V. P. Trepelkov (USSR).

Reconvened special session (January)
Chairman: Sergio González-Gálvez (Mexico).
Vice-Chairmen: Horst Heininger (German Democratic Republic), Jürgen Kühn (Federal Republic of Germany), Nitish Kumar Sengupta (India).
Rapporteur: Raouf A. Saad (Egypt).

Tenth session
Chairman: Philippe Levy (Switzerland).
Vice-Chairmen: V. I. Philippov (Ukrainian SSR), Ahmed Rhazaoui (Morocco), Ransford Smith (Jamaica).
Rapporteur: Irtiza Husain (Pakistan).

Reconvened special session (June)
Chairman: Miguel Marín-Bosch (Mexico).
Vice-Chairmen: Irtiza Husain (Pakistan), Jürgen Kühn (Federal Republic of Germany), Wolfgang Sproete (German Democratic Republic).
Rapporteur: Raouf A. Saad (Egypt).

On 23 May 1984 (decision 1984/156), the Economic and Social Council elected the following 16 members for a three-year term beginning on 1 January 1985 to fill the vacancies occurring on 31 December 1984: Algeria, Argentina, Bulgaria, Cameroon, Canada, Ghana, India, Iraq, Italy, Jamaica, Mauritius, Pakistan, Republic of Korea, Turkey, Ukrainian SSR, Venezuela.

INTERGOVERNMENTAL WORKING GROUP
OF EXPERTS ON INTERNATIONAL
STANDARDS OF ACCOUNTING AND REPORTING
The Intergovernmental Working Group of Experts on International Standards of Accounting and Reporting (p. 1336) reports to the Commission on Transnational Corporations.

Committee for Programme and Co-ordination
The Committee for Programme and Co-ordination is the main subsidiary organ of the Economic and Social Council and of the General Assembly for planning, programming and co-ordination and reports directly to both. It consists of 21 members nominated by the Council and elected by the Assembly for three-year terms according to a specific pattern of equitable geographical distribution.
During 1984, the Committee held, at United Nations Headquarters, an organizational meeting on 22 March and its twenty-fourth session from 23 April to 1 June.

Members:
To serve until 31 December 1984: Germany, Federal Republic of, Netherlands, Pakistan, Romania, Trinidad and Tobago, United Kingdom, Yugoslavia.
To serve until 31 December 1985: Argentina, Chile, Ethiopia, France, Nigeria, USSR, United States.
To serve until 31 December 1986: Brazil, Cameroon, Egypt, India, Indonesia, Japan, Liberia.

Chairman: Tommo Monthe (Cameroon).
Vice-Chairmen: Jan Berteling (Netherlands), Soemadi D. M. Brotodiningrat (Indonesia), Miodrag Cabric (Yugoslavia).
Rapporteur: Roberto Gomes de Matos Jaguaribe (Brazil).

On 23 May 1984 (decision 1984/156) and (with respect to the Byelorussian SSR and Yugoslavia) on 26 July (decision 1984/180), the Economic and Social Council nominated the following 10 Member States of the United Nations, 7 of which were to be elected by the General Assembly, for a three-year term beginning on 1 January 1985 to fill the vacancies occurring on 31 December 1984: Bangladesh, Bolivia, Byelorussian SSR, Germany, Federal Republic of, Iraq, Netherlands, Sri Lanka, Trinidad and Tobago, United Kingdom, Yugoslavia. All but Bolivia, Iraq and Sri Lanka were elected by the Assembly on 10 December 1984 (decision 39/312).

Committee on Natural Resources
The Committee on Natural Resources consists of 54 members, elected by the Economic and Social Council for four-year terms in accordance with the geographical distribution of seats in the Council.
The Committee did not meet in 1984.

Members:
To serve until 31 December 1984:[a] Bangladesh, Belgium, Botswana, Brazil, Canada, Colombia, Dominican Republic, Greece, Guinea, India, Jamaica, Japan, Kenya, Morocco, Niger, Paraguay, Peru, Sierra Leone, Sudan, Ukrainian SSR, USSR, United Kingdom, Uruguay, Venezuela, Zaire.
To serve until 31 December 1986:[b] Algeria, Australia, Bolivia, Burkina Faso, Central African Republic, Czechoslovakia, Denmark, France, German Democratic Republic, Germany, Federal Republic of, Hungary,[c] Italy, Liberia, Mexico, Norway, Pakistan, Philippines, Spain, Thailand, Turkey, Uganda, United States, Yugoslavia, Zimbabwe.

[a]Two seats allocated to members from Asian States remained unfilled in 1984.
[b]Three seats allocated to members from Asian States remained unfilled in 1984.
[c]Elected on 23 May 1984 (decision 1984/156).

On 23 May 1984 (decision 1984/156), the Economic and Social Council elected the following for a four-year term beginning on 1 January 1985 to fill 24 of the 27 vacancies occurring on 31 December 1984: Bangladesh, Botswana, Brazil, Burundi, Canada, Chile, China, Colombia, Ecuador, Egypt, Ghana, Greece, India, Japan, Kenya, Libyan Arab Jamahiriya, Malaysia, Morocco, Netherlands, Sudan, Ukrainian SSR, USSR, Uruguay, Venezuela. No further elections were held in 1984 to fill the remaining seats, allocated to two members from Latin American States and one member from Western European and other States.

Committee on Negotiations with Intergovernmental Agencies
The Committee on Negotiations with Intergovernmental Agencies was originally established by the Economic and Social Council in 1946.
In 1983,[28] the Council authorized its President, in consultation with the Chairmen of the regional groups, to appoint the members of the Committee from among the States members of the Council, in pursuance of a General Assembly request[29] that the Council arrange for the negotiation with UNIDO of an agreement to constitute it as a specialized agency.
The members remained to be appointed as of the end of 1984.

Committee on Non-Governmental Organizations
The Committee on Non-Governmental Organizations consists of 19 members, elected by the Economic and Social Council for a four-year term according to a specific pattern of equitable geographical representation.
In 1984, the Committee met at United Nations Headquarters between 30 January and 3 February and at Geneva on 6 July.

Members (until 31 December 1986): Chile, Costa Rica, Cuba, Cyprus, France, Ghana, India, Kenya, Libyan Arab Jamahiriya, Nicaragua, Nigeria, Pakistan, Rwanda, Sweden, Thailand, USSR, United Kingdom, United States, Yugoslavia.

Chairman: Emilia Castro de Barish (Costa Rica).
Vice-Chairman: Rose Adhiambo Arungu-Olende (Kenya).
Rapporteur: Jean-Marc Rochereau de La Sablière (France).

Expert bodies

Ad Hoc Group of Experts on International Co-operation in Tax Matters
The membership of the *Ad Hoc* Group of Experts on International Co-operation in Tax Matters—to consist of 25 members drawn from 15 developing and 10 developed countries, appointed by the Secretary-General to serve in their individual capacity—remained at 24 in 1984, with one member from a developing country still to be appointed.
The *Ad Hoc* Group, which normally meets biennially, did not meet in 1984.

Members: Maurice Hugh Collins (United Kingdom), Jean François Court (France), Ton Dekker (Netherlands), Francisco O. N. Dornelles (Brazil), Hussein M. El Baroudy (Egypt), Mordecai S. Feinberg (United

[28]YUN 1983, p. 585, dec. 1983/105, 4 Feb. 1983.
[29]YUN 1979, p. 622, res. 34/96, 13 Dec. 1979.

States), José Ramón Fernández Pérez (Spain), Antonio H. Figueroa (Argentina), Mayer Gabay (Israel), R. R. Khosla (India), Marwan Koudsi (Syrian Arab Republic), Felipe Lamarca (Chile), Daniel Luthi (Switzerland), Mohamed Medaghri-Alaoui (Morocco), Thomas Menck (Federal Republic of Germany), Canute R. Miller (Jamaica), Muhammad Wasim Mirza (Pakistan), Alberto Navarro Rodríguez (Mexico), Isaac O. Oni (Nigeria), Alfred Philipp (Austria), Rainer Söderholm (Finland), Sikuan Sutanto (Indonesia),[a] Tetsuo Takikawa (Japan), André Titty (Cameroon).

[a]Appointed on 14 November 1984 to replace Sutadi Sukarya (Indonesia).

Committee for Development Planning

The Committee for Development Planning is composed of 24 experts representing different planning systems. They are appointed by the Economic and Social Council, on nomination by the Secretary-General, to serve in their personal capacity for a term of three years.

In 1984, the Committee held two sessions: its twentieth from 17 to 21 May at United Nations Headquarters, and the first part of its twenty-first from 19 to 21 November at Geneva.

Members (until 31 December 1986):[a] Ismail-Sabri Abdalla (Egypt); Abdlatif Y. Al-Hamad (Kuwait); Gerassimos D. Arsenis (Greece); Sir Kenneth Berrill (United Kingdom); Bernard Chidzero (Zimbabwe); Jean-Pierre Cot (France); Hernando de Soto (Peru); Celso Furtado (Brazil); Armin Gutowski (Federal Republic of Germany); Gerald K. Helleiner (Canada); Huan Xiang (China); Shinichi Ichimura (Japan); V. N. Kirichenko (USSR); Robert S. McNamara (United States); Joseph Elenga Ngamporo (Congo); G. O. Nwankwo (Nigeria); Goran Ohlin, *Rapporteur* (Sweden); Jozef Pajestka, *Vice-Chairman* (Poland); I. G. Patel (India); Shridath S. Ramphal, *Chairman* (Guyana); Luis A. Rojo (Spain); Mohammad Sadli (Indonesia); Rehman Sobhan (Bangladesh); Janez Stanovnic (Yugoslavia).

[a]Appointed on 16 March 1984 (decision 1984/108) and (with respect to Sir Kenneth Berrill (United Kingdom)) on 2 May (decision 1984/156).

Committee of Experts on the Transport of Dangerous Goods

The Committee of Experts on the Transport of Dangerous Goods is composed of experts from countries interested in the international transport of dangerous goods. The experts are made available by their Governments at the request of the Secretary-General. The membership, to be increased to 15 in accordance with a 1975 resolution of the Economic and Social Council,[30] remained at 13 in 1984.

The Committee held its thirteenth session at Geneva from 3 to 12 December 1984.

Members: Canada, France, Germany, Federal Republic of, Iran,[a] Iraq,[a] Italy, Japan, Norway, Poland, Thailand,[a] USSR, United Kingdom, United States.

[a]Inactive member.

Chairman: A. I. Roberts (United States).

The Committee may alter, as required, the composition of its subsidiary bodies. In addition, any Committee member may participate in the work of and vote in those bodies provided such member notify the United Nations Secretariat of the intention to do so.

GROUP OF EXPERTS ON EXPLOSIVES

The Group of Experts on Explosives held its twenty-fourth session at Geneva from 6 to 10 August 1984.

Chairman: R. R. Watson (United Kingdom).

GROUP OF RAPPORTEURS OF THE COMMITTEE OF
EXPERTS ON THE TRANSPORT OF DANGEROUS GOODS

In 1984, the Group of Rapporteurs of the Committee of Experts on the Transport of Dangerous Goods held two sessions, at Geneva: its thirty-first from 12 to 16 March, and its thirty-second from 13 to 17 August.

Chairman: J. Engeland (Federal Republic of Germany).
Vice-Chairman: L. Grainger (United Kingdom) (Vice-Chairman, thirty-first session; co-Chairman, thirty-second session).

Committee on Crime Prevention and Control

The Committee on Crime Prevention and Control consists of 27 members elected for four-year terms by the Economic and Social Council, according to a specific pattern of equitable geographical representation, from among experts nominated by Member States.

The Committee held its eighth session at Vienna, Austria, from 21 to 30 March 1984.

Members:
To serve until 31 December 1984: A. Adeyemi (Nigeria); Anthony John Edward Brennan (United Kingdom); Ronald L. Gainer (United States); Jozsef Godony (Hungary); Aura Guerra de Villaláz (Panama); Ds. Hudioro (Indonesia); Abdul Meguid Ibrahim Kharbit (Kuwait); Mawik-Ndi-Muyeng (Zaire); Juan Manuel Mayorca (Venezuela); Albert Metzger, *Rapporteur* (Sierra Leone); Gioacchino Polimeni (Italy); Abdel Aziz Abdalla Shiddo (Sudan); Ramananda Prasad Singh (Nepal).
To serve until 31 December 1986: André Bissonnette (Canada); S. V. Borodin (USSR);[a] Dusan Cotic, *Vice-Chairman* (Yugoslavia); Ahmed Mohamed Khalifa (Egypt); Robert Linke (Austria); Manuel López-Rey y Arrojo, *Chairman* (Bolivia); Charles Alfred Lunn (Barbados); Jorge Arturo Montero-Castro (Costa Rica); Mphanza Patrick Mvunga (Zambia); Amadou Racine Ba (Mauritania); Simone Andrée Rozes, *Vice-Chairman* (France); Yoshio Suzuki, *Vice-Chairman* (Japan); Mervyn Patrick Wijesinha (Sri Lanka); Wu Han (China).

[a]Resigned on 17 April 1984; replaced by A. Y. Kudryavtsev (USSR), who was elected on 23 May (decision 1984/156).

On 23 May 1984 (decision 1984/156) and (with respect to Aura Guerra de Villaláz (Panama) and Miguel A. Sánchez Méndez (Colombia)) on 26 July (decision 1984/180), the Economic and Social Council elected the following 13 members for a four-year term beginning on 1 January 1985 to fill the vacancies occurring on 31 December 1984: Mohamed Aboulashi (Morocco), David Faulkner (United Kingdom), Ronald L. Gainer (United States), Jozsef Godony (Hungary), Aura Guerra de Villaláz (Panama), A. R. Khandker (Bangladesh), Abdul Meguid Ibrahim Kharbit (Kuwait), Farouk A. Mourad (Saudi Arabia), Bertin Pandi (Central African Republic), Aregba Polo (Togo), Miguel A. Sánchez Méndez (Colombia), Abdel Aziz Abdalla Shiddo (Sudan), Bo Svensson (Sweden).

United Nations Group of Experts on Geographical Names

The United Nations Group of Experts on Geographical Names represents various geographical/linguistic divisions, of which there were 17 in 1984, as follows: Africa Central; Africa East; Africa West; Arabic; Asia East (other than China); Asia South-East and Pacific South-West; Asia South-West (other than Arabic); China; Dutch- and German-speaking; East Central and South-East Europe; India; Latin America; Norden; Romano-Hellenic; Union of Soviet Socialist Republics; United Kingdom; United States of America and Canada.

The Group of Experts held its eleventh session at Geneva from 15 to 23 October 1984.

Chairman: Dirk P. Blok (Netherlands).
Vice-Chairman: Ydelis R. Velásquez García (Cuba).
Rapporteur: Alan Rayburn (Canada).

Ad hoc bodies

Ad Hoc Committee on the Preparations for the Public Hearings on the Activities of Transnational Corporations in South Africa and Namibia

The *Ad Hoc* Committee on the Preparations for the Public Hearings on the Activities of Transnational Corporations in South Africa and Namibia, to be composed of five States, had four members in 1984.

The *Ad Hoc* Committee met at United Nations Headquarters on 31 July and 25 September 1984.

Members:[a] Bangladesh, Cuba, German Democratic Republic, Nigeria.

[a]Appointed by the President of the Economic and Social Council, as stated in his letter of 21 June 1984 to the Secretary-General.

Chairman/Rapporteur: Kennedy F. Apoe (Nigeria).

---

[30]YUN 1975, p. 734, res. 1973(LIX), 30 July 1975.

Commission on the Status of Women acting as the Preparatory Body for the World Conference to Review and Appraise the Achievements of the United Nations Decade for Women

The Commission on the Status of Women (p. 1331) acting as the Preparatory Body for the World Conference to Review and Appraise the Achievements of the United Nations Decade for Women (scheduled for 1985) held its second session at Vienna, Austria, from 27 February to 7 March 1984. The officers were the same as those at the Commission's thirtieth session.

Committee on Candidatures for Election to the International Narcotics Control Board

The Committee on Candidatures, originally established by the Economic and Social Council on 4 March 1966, was re-established by the Council on 7 February 1984 (decision 1984/107) for the purpose of selecting nominees for election to the International Narcotics Control Board for a term of office from 2 March 1985 to 1 March 1990.

The Committee met at Vienna, Austria, from 19 to 21 March 1984.

Members:[a] Argentina, Belgium, Canada, Colombia, Greece, India, Morocco, Pakistan, Peru, Thailand, USSR, United Kingdom, United States.

[a]Elected on 10 February 1984.

Chairman: S. Chutasmit (Thailand).

Intergovernmental Working Group of Experts on International Standards of Accounting and Reporting

The Intergovernmental Working Group of Experts on International Standards of Accounting and Reporting, which reports to the Commission on Transnational Corporations (p. 1333), consists of 34 members, elected for three-year terms by the Economic and Social Council according to a specific pattern of equitable geographical distribution. Each State elected appoints an expert with appropriate experience in accounting and reporting.

The Group held its second session at United Nations Headquarters from 12 to 23 March 1984.

Members:
To serve until 31 December 1984:[a] Argentina, Brazil, Canada, China, Egypt, France, Grenada, Liberia, Netherlands, Nigeria, Norway, Pakistan, Philippines, Spain, Swaziland, Zaire.
To serve until 31 December 1985:[b] Algeria, Cyprus, Ecuador, Germany, Federal Republic of, India, Italy, Japan, Morocco, Panama, Saint Lucia, Tunisia, Uganda, United Kingdom, United States.

[a]One seat allocated to a member from Eastern European States remained unfilled in 1984.
[b]The seats allocated to one member from Asian States and two members from Eastern European States remained unfilled in 1984.

Chairman: Pieter A. Wessel (Netherlands).
Vice-Chairmen: Mohamed Adel El-Safty (Egypt), Irtiza Husain (Pakistan).
Rapporteur: R. S. Gupta (India).

On 23 May 1984 (decision 1984/156) and (with respect to Swaziland) on 26 July (decision 1984/180), the Economic and Social Council elected the following for a three-year term beginning on 1 January 1985 to fill 13 of the 17 vacancies occurring on 31 December 1984: Barbados, Brazil, Canada, China, Egypt, France, Malaysia, Norway, Pakistan, Spain, Swaziland, Switzerland, Zaire. No further elections were held in 1984 to fill the remaining seats allocated to two members from African States, one member from Eastern European States and one member from Latin American States.

Preparatory Committee for the International Conference on Population

The Population Commission (p. 1331) was designated by the Economic and Social Council as the Preparatory Committee for the International Conference on Population (p. 1327).

The Preparatory Committee, open to the participation of all States, held its only session at United Nations Headquarters from 23 to 27 January and from 12 to 17 March 1984.

Chairman: Gerónimo Martínez (Mexico).

Vice-Chairmen: Pavel Grecu (Romania), R. P. Kapoor (India), Frederick Sai (Ghana).
Rapporteur: Ewald Brouwers (Netherlands).

Administrative Committee on Co-ordination

The Administrative Committee on Co-ordination held four sessions in 1984: an organizational session at United Nations Headquarters from 15 to 17 February; its first in London from 16 to 18 April; an extraordinary session at Geneva on 3 and 4 July; and its second at United Nations Headquarters on 22 and 23 October.

The membership of ACC, under the chairmanship of the Secretary-General of the United Nations, also includes the executive heads of ILO, FAO, UNESCO, WHO, the World Bank, IMF, ICAO, UPU, ITU, WMO, IMO, WIPO, IFAD, IAEA and the secretariat of the Contracting Parties to GATT.

Also taking part in the work of ACC are the United Nations Director-General for Development and International Economic Co-operation; the Under-Secretaries-General for International Economic and Social Affairs, for Administration, Finance and Management, for Technical Co-operation for Development, and for Legal Affairs; and the executive heads of UNCTAD, UNDP, UNEP, UNFPA, UNHCR, UNICEF, UNIDO, UNITAR, UNRWA and WFP.

ACC has established subsidiary bodies on organizational, administrative and substantive questions.

Other related bodies

Intergovernmental Committee on Science and Technology for Development

The Intergovernmental Committee on Science and Technology for Development (p. 1315) reports annually to the General Assembly through the Economic and Social Council.

International Research and Training Institute for the Advancement of Women (INSTRAW)

The International Research and Training Institute for the Advancement of Women, a body of the United Nations financed through voluntary contributions, functions under the authority of a Board of Trustees.

BOARD OF TRUSTEES

The Board of Trustees of INSTRAW is composed of a President appointed by the Secretary-General; 10 members serving in their individual capacity, appointed by the Economic and Social Council on the nomination of the Secretary-General; and *ex-officio* members. Members serve for three-year terms, with a maximum of two terms.

The Board, which reports annually to the Council, held its fourth session at Santo Domingo, Dominican Republic, from 23 to 28 January 1984.

Members (until 30 June 1984):
To serve until 30 June 1984: Marcelle Devaud, *Vice-President* (France); Aziza Hussein (Egypt); Nobuko Takahashi (Japan).
To serve until 30 June 1985: Gulzar Bano (Pakistan); Ester Boserup (Denmark); Vilma Espín de Castro, *Vice-President* (Cuba); Vida Tomsic (Yugoslavia).
To serve until 30 June 1986: Helen Arnopoulos Stamiris (Greece); Suad Ibrahim Eissa, *Rapporteur* (Sudan); María Lavalle Urbina (Mexico).

On 23 May 1984 (decision 1984/156), the Economic and Social Council appointed Daniela Colombo (Italy), Zhor Lazrak (Morocco) and Achie Sudiarti Luhulima (Indonesia) for a three-year term beginning on 1 July 1984 to fill the vacancies occurring on 30 June.

Members (from 1 July 1984):
To serve until 30 June 1985: Gulzar Bano (Pakistan), Ester Boserup (Denmark), Vilma Espín de Castro (Cuba), Vida Tomsic (Yugoslavia).
To serve until 30 June 1986: Helen Arnopoulos Stamiris (Greece), Suad Ibrahim Eissa (Sudan), María Lavalle Urbina (Mexico).
To serve until 30 June 1987: Daniela Colombo (Italy), Zhor Lazrak (Morocco), Achie Sudiarti Luhulima (Indonesia).

President: Delphine Tsanga (Cameroon).
Ex-officio members: The representative of the Secretary-General, the Director of the Institute and the directors of the centres and programmes for women of the regional commissions.

Director of the Institute: Dunja Pastizzi-Ferencic.

Office of the United Nations High Commissioner for Refugees (UNHCR)

The United Nations High Commissioner for Refugees (p. 1317) reports annually to the General Assembly through the Economic and Social Council.

United Nations Capital Development Fund

EXECUTIVE BOARD

The Executive Board of the United Nations Capital Development Fund (p. 1319) reports annually to the General Assembly through the Economic and Social Council.

United Nations Children's Fund (UNICEF)

EXECUTIVE BOARD

The UNICEF Executive Board consists of 41 members elected by the Economic and Social Council from Member States of the United Nations or members of the specialized agencies or of IAEA, for three-year terms.

In 1984, the Executive Board held a series of meetings between 24 April and 4 May at Rome, Italy, and (with its composition as of 1 August) organizational meetings on 8 and 14 June at United Nations Headquarters.

Members (until 31 July 1984):
To serve until 31 July 1984: Austria, German Democratic Republic, India, Ivory Coast, Pakistan, Sweden, Switzerland, Togo, United Arab Emirates, Venezuela.
To serve until 31 July 1985: Algeria, Bahrain, Bangladesh, Central African Republic, Chad, Chile, France, Hungary, Italy, Japan, Madagascar, Mexico, Nepal, Netherlands, Panama, Somalia, Swaziland, USSR, United Kingdom, United States, Upper Volta.
To serve until 31 July 1986: Australia, Canada, China, Colombia, Cuba, Finland, Germany, Federal Republic of, Lesotho, Thailand, Yugoslavia.

Chairman: Dr. Haydee Martínez de Osorio (Venezuela).
First Vice-Chairman: Umberto La Rocca (Italy).
Second Vice-Chairman: Mihaly Simai (Hungary).
Third Vice-Chairman: Atsu-Koffi Amega (Togo).
Fourth Vice-Chairman: Richard Manning (Australia).

On 23 May 1984 (decision 1984/156), the Economic and Social Council elected the following 10 members for a three-year term beginning on 1 August 1984 to fill the vacancies occurring on 31 July: Belgium, Benin, Bhutan, Denmark, India, Indonesia, Niger, Romania, Switzerland, Venezuela.

Members (from 1 August 1984):
To serve until 31 July 1985: Algeria, Bahrain, Bangladesh, Central African Republic, Chad, Chile, France, Hungary, Italy, Japan, Madagascar, Mexico, Nepal, Netherlands, Panama, Somalia, Swaziland, USSR, United Kingdom, United States, Upper Volta.
To serve until 31 July 1986: Australia, Canada, China, Colombia, Cuba, Finland, Germany, Federal Republic of, Lesotho, Thailand, Yugoslavia.
To serve until 31 July 1987: Belgium, Benin, Bhutan, Denmark, India, Indonesia, Niger, Romania, Switzerland, Venezuela.

Chairman: Richard Manning (Australia).
First Vice-Chairman: Jassim Buallay (Bahrain).
Second Vice-Chairman: Mihaly Simai (Hungary).
Third Vice-Chairman: Bernadette Palle (Upper Volta).
Fourth Vice-Chairman: Martti Ahtisaari (Finland).

Executive Director of UNICEF: James P. Grant.

COMMITTEE ON ADMINISTRATION AND FINANCE

The Committee on Administration and Finance is a committee of the whole of the UNICEF Executive Board.

Chairman: Jassim Buallay (Bahrain) (until 31 July), Hisami Kurokochi (Japan) (from 1 August).
Vice-Chairman: Hisami Kurokochi (Japan) (until 31 July), A. P. Maruping (Lesotho) (from 1 August).

PROGRAMME COMMITTEE

The Programme Committee is a committee of the whole of the UNICEF Executive Board.

Chairman: Anwarul Karim Chowdhury (Bangladesh).
Vice-Chairman: Ngaré Kessely (Chad) (until 31 July), Gabriel Restrepo (Colombia) (from 1 August).

UNICEF/WHO Joint Committee on Health Policy

The UNICEF/WHO Joint Committee on Health Policy consists of: six members of the UNICEF Executive Board, among whom are the chairmen of the Executive Board and the Programme Committee who serve *ex officio;* and six members of the WHO Executive Board.

The Joint Committee, which meets biennially, did not meet in 1984.

United Nations Conference on Trade and Development (UNCTAD)

TRADE AND DEVELOPMENT BOARD

The Trade and Development Board (p. 1319) reports to UNCTAD; it also reports annually to the General Assembly through the Economic and Social Council.

United Nations Development Programme (UNDP)

GOVERNING COUNCIL

The Governing Council of UNDP consists of 48 members, elected by the Economic and Social Council from Member States of the United Nations or members of the specialized agencies or of IAEA. Twenty-seven seats are allocated to developing countries as follows: 11 to African countries, 9 to Asian countries and Yugoslavia, and 7 to Latin American countries. Twenty-one seats are allocated to economically more advanced countries as follows: 17 to Western European and other countries, and 4 to Eastern European countries. The term of office is three years, one third of the members being elected each year.

During 1984, the Governing Council held an organizational meeting at United Nations Headquarters on 22 and 23 February and its thirty-first session at Geneva from 4 to 30 June.

Members:
To serve until 31 December 1984: Austria, Barbados, Bhutan, China, Ecuador, Fiji, Italy, Japan, Mali, Mexico, Spain, Tunisia, USSR, United Kingdom, United States, Zambia.
To serve until 31 December 1985: Australia, Belgium, Brazil, Canada, Central African Republic, Chad, Denmark, Finland, France, German Democratic Republic, Lesotho, Mauritania, Nepal, Philippines, United Republic of Tanzania, Yugoslavia.
To serve until 31 December 1986: Argentina, Bahrain, Bangladesh, Ethiopia, Gambia, Germany, Federal Republic of, Hungary, India, Jamaica, Netherlands, Norway, Poland, Switzerland, Togo, Turkey, Venezuela.

President: Leandro I. Verceles (Philippines) (until 4 June), Hortencio J. Brillantes (Philippines) (from 4 June).
First Vice-President: Jacques G. Van Hellenberg Hubar (Netherlands).
Second Vice-President: Miguel A. Albornoz (Ecuador) (until 20 June), Graciela Vasquez-Diaz (Mexico) (from 20 June).
Third Vice-President: Ahmed Ould Sid'Ahmed (Mauritania) (until 20 June), Thabo Makeka (Lesotho) (from 20 June).
Fourth Vice-President: Janusz Czamarski (Poland).

On 23 May 1984 (decision 1984/156), the Economic and Social Council elected the following 16 members for a three-year term beginning on 1 January 1985 to fill the vacancies occurring on 31 December 1984: Austria, Benin, Chile, China, Cuba, Italy, Japan, Mexico, Pakistan, Saudi Arabia, Swaziland, Sweden, Tunisia, USSR, United Kingdom, United States.

Administrator of UNDP: F. Bradford Morse.
Associate Administrator: G. Arthur Brown.

BUDGETARY AND FINANCE COMMITTEE

The Budgetary and Finance Committee, a committee of the whole, held a series of meetings at Geneva between 4 and 29 June 1984.

Chairman: Jacques G. Van Hellenberg Hubar (Netherlands).
Rapporteur: Miguel Angel Ortega-Nalda (Mexico).

COMMITTEE OF THE WHOLE

In accordance with its 1983 decision,[31] the Governing Council resolved itself into a Committee of the Whole and held meetings between 4 and 8 June 1984 to consider matters related to programme management. The President of the Governing Council acted as presiding officer.

United Nations Environment Programme (UNEP)

GOVERNING COUNCIL

The Governing Council of UNEP (p. 1322) reports to the General Assembly through the Economic and Social Council.

United Nations Industrial Development Organization (UNIDO)

INDUSTRIAL DEVELOPMENT BOARD

The Industrial Development Board (p. 1323), the principal organ of UNIDO, reports annually to the General Assembly through the Economic and Social Council.

United Nations Institute for Training and Research (UNITAR)

The Executive Director of UNITAR (p. 1324) reports to the General Assembly and, as appropriate, to the Economic and Social Council.

United Nations Research Institute for Social Development (UNRISD)

BOARD OF DIRECTORS

The Board of Directors of UNRISD reports to the Economic and Social Council through the Commission for Social Development.

The Board consists of:

The Chairman, appointed by the Secretary-General: Paul-Marc Henry (France);[a]

Seven members, nominated by the Commission for Social Development and confirmed by the Economic and Social Council (to serve until 30 June 1985): Gustavo Esteva (Mexico), Paul-Marc Henry (France),[a] Vera Nyitrai (Hungary), Achola Pala Okeyo (Kenya), K. N. Raj (India), Eugene B. Skolnikoff (United States); (to serve until 30 June 1987): Ulf Hannerz (Sweden);

Eight other members, as follows: a representative of the Secretary-General, the Director of the Latin American Institute for Economic and Social Planning, the Director of the Asian and Pacific Development Centre, the Director of the African Institute for Economic Development and Planning, the Executive Secretary of ECWA, the Director of UNRISD *(ex officio)*, and the representatives of two of the following specialized agencies appointed as members and observers in annual rotation: ILO and FAO (observers); UNESCO and WHO (members).

[a]Appointed Chairman on 25 March 1984; no nomination was made in 1984 to fill the resultant vacancy in the membership.

Director of the Institute: Enrique Oteiza.[a]

[a]Succeeded Solon Barraclough with effect from 15 January 1984.

United Nations Special Fund

BOARD OF GOVERNORS

The Board of Governors of the United Nations Special Fund (p. 1326) reports annually to the General Assembly through the Economic and Social Council.

United Nations Special Fund for Land-locked Developing Countries

BOARD OF GOVERNORS

A Board of Governors of the United Nations Special Fund for Land-locked Developing Countries (p. 1326), when constituted, was to report to the General Assembly through the Economic and Social Council.

United Nations University

COUNCIL OF THE UNITED NATIONS UNIVERSITY

The Council of the United Nations University (p. 1326), the governing board of the University, reports annually to the General Assembly, to the Economic and Social Council and to the UNESCO Executive Board through the Secretary-General and the UNESCO Director-General.

World Food Council

The World Food Council (p. 1327), an organ of the United Nations at the ministerial or plenipotentiary level, reports to the General Assembly through the Economic and Social Council.

World Food Programme

COMMITTEE ON FOOD AID POLICIES AND PROGRAMMES

The Committee on Food Aid Policies and Programmes, the governing body of WFP, consists of 30 members, of which 15 are elected by the Economic and Social Council and 15 by the FAO Council, from Member States of the United Nations or from members of FAO. Members serve for three-year terms.

The Committee reports annually to the Economic and Social Council, the FAO Council and the World Food Council.

The Committee held two sessions during 1984, at Rome, Italy: its seventeenth from 28 May to 8 June; and its eighteenth from 29 October to 7 November.

Members:
To serve until 31 December 1984:
  Elected by Economic and Social Council: Belgium, Finland, Japan, Pakistan, Somalia.
  Elected by FAO Council: Brazil, Congo, Mali, Netherlands, Thailand.
To serve until 31 December 1985:
  Elected by Economic and Social Council: Colombia *(Chairman)*, Mexico, Sweden, United Kingdom *(First Vice-Chairman, eighteenth session)*, Upper Volta.[a]
  Elected by FAO Council: Cuba, France, Germany, Federal Republic of, Nigeria, Zambia.
To serve until 31 December 1986:
  Elected by Economic and Social Council: Egypt *(Second Vice-Chairman)*, Hungary, India, Italy, Norway.
  Elected by FAO Council: Australia, Bangladesh, Canada *(First Vice-Chairman, seventeenth session)*, Saudi Arabia, United States.

[a]The Upper Volta changed its name to Burkina Faso on 6 August 1984.

On 23 May 1984 (decision 1984/156), the Economic and Social Council elected Belgium, Denmark, Japan, Lesotho and Pakistan; and, on 28 November, the FAO Council elected Brazil, Congo, Kenya, Netherlands and Thailand, all for a three-year term beginning on 1 January 1985 to fill the vacancies occurring on 31 December 1984.

Executive Director of WFP: James Charles Ingram.
Deputy Executive Director: Salahuddin Ahmed.

---

[31]YUN 1983, p. 1365.

Trusteeship Council

Article 86 of the United Nations Charter lays down that the Trusteeship Council shall consist of the following:

Members of the United Nations administering Trust Territories;
Permanent members of the Security Council which do not administer Trust Territories;

As many other members elected for a three-year term by the General Assembly as will ensure that the membership of the Council is equally divided between United Nations Members which administer Trust Territories and those which do not.[a]

[a]During 1984, only one Member of the United Nations was an administering member of the Trusteeship Council, while four permanent members of the Security Council

continued as non-administering members. Therefore, the parity called for by Article 86 of the Charter was not maintained.

MEMBERS
Member administering a Trust Territory: United States.
Non-administering members: China, France, USSR, United Kingdom.

SESSION
Fifty-first session: United Nations Headquarters, 14 May–18 July 1984.

OFFICERS
President: Laurent Rapin (France).
Vice-President: John W. D. Margetson (United Kingdom).

International Court of Justice

Judges of the Court

The International Court of Justice consists of 15 Judges elected for nine-year terms by the General Assembly and the Security Council, each voting independently.

The following were the Judges of the Court serving in 1984, listed in the order of precedence:

Judge	Country of nationality	End of term[a]
Taslim Olawale Elias, *President*	Nigeria	1985
José Sette Câmara, *Vice-President*	Brazil	1988
Manfred Lachs	Poland	1985
Platon D. Morozov	USSR	1988
Nagendra Singh	India	1991
José María Ruda	Argentina	1991
Hermann Mosler	Federal Republic of Germany	1985
Shigeru Oda	Japan	1985
Roberto Ago	Italy	1988
Abdallah Fikri El-Khani	Syrian Arab Republic	1985
Stephen M. Schwebel	United States	1988
Sir Robert Y. Jennings	United Kingdom	1991
Guy Ladreit de Lacharrière	France	1991
Kéba Mbaye	Senegal	1991
Mohammed Bedjaoui	Algeria	1988

[a]Term expires on 5 February of the year indicated.

Registrar: Santiago Torres Bernárdez.
Deputy Registrar: Alain Pillepich (until 10 April 1984), Eduardo Valencia-Ospina (from 11 April).

On 7 November 1984, elections were held in both the General Assembly (decision 39/307) and the Security Council to fill the vacancies occurring on 6 February 1985 with the expiration of the terms of office of the following Judges: Taslim Olawale Elias (Nigeria), Manfred Lachs (Poland), Hermann Mosler (Federal Republic of Germany), Shigeru Oda (Japan), Abdallah Fikri El-Khani (Syrian Arab Republic).

The following Judges were elected for a term of office ending on 5 February 1994: Taslim Olawale Elias (Nigeria), Jens Evensen (Norway), Manfred Lachs (Poland), Ni Zhengyu (China), Shigeru Oda (Japan).

Chamber formed in the case concerning *Delimitation of the maritime boundary in the Gulf of Maine area (Canada/United States of America)*
Members: Roberto Ago *(President)*, André Gros,[a] Hermann Mosler, Stephen M. Schwebel.
Ad hoc member: Maxwell Cohen.[b]

[a]Member of the Court whose term of office expired on 5 February 1982, but who continued to sit as a member of the Chamber in accordance with Article 13, paragraph 3, of the Statute.
[b]As the Court noted in its Order constituting the Chamber, one of the members of the Court elected to the Chamber gave place to the Judge *ad hoc* chosen by one of the parties (Canada) in accordance with Article 31, paragraph 4, of the Statute.

The Chamber sat until 12 October 1984, when it delivered its Judgment.

Chamber of Summary Procedure
(as constituted by the Court on 23 January 1984)
Members: Taslim Olawale Elias *(ex officio)*, José Sette Câmara *(ex officio)*, Nagendra Singh, Abdallah Fikri El-Khani, Guy Ladreit de Lacharrière.
Substitute members: Kéba Mbaye, Mohammed Bedjaoui.

Parties to the Court's Statute

All Members of the United Nations are *ipso facto* parties to the Statute of the International Court of Justice. Also parties to it are the following non-members: Liechtenstein, San Marino, Switzerland.

States accepting the compulsory jurisdiction of the Court

Declarations made by the following States accepting the Court's compulsory jurisdiction (or made under the Statute of the Permanent Court of International Justice and deemed to be an acceptance of the jurisdiction of the International Court) were in force at the end of 1984:

Australia, Austria, Barbados, Belgium, Botswana, Canada, Colombia, Costa Rica, Democratic Kampuchea, Denmark, Dominican Republic, Egypt, El Salvador, Finland, Gambia, Haiti, Honduras, India, Israel, Japan, Kenya, Liberia, Liechtenstein, Luxembourg, Malawi, Malta, Mauritius, Mexico, Netherlands, New Zealand, Nicaragua, Nigeria, Norway, Pakistan, Panama, Philippines, Portugal, Somalia, Sudan, Swaziland, Sweden, Switzerland, Togo, Uganda, United Kingdom, United States, Uruguay.

United Nations organs and specialized and related agencies authorized to request advisory opinions from the Court
Authorized by the United Nations Charter to request opinions on any legal question: General Assembly, Security Council.
Authorized by the General Assembly in accordance with the Charter to request opinions on legal questions arising within the scope of their activities: Economic and Social Council, Trusteeship Council, Interim Committee of the General Assembly, Committee on Applications for Review of Administrative Tribunal Judgements, ILO, FAO, UNESCO, WHO, World Bank, IFC, IDA, IMF, ICAO, ITU, WMO, IMO, WIPO, IFAD, IAEA.

Committees of the Court

BUDGETARY AND ADMINISTRATIVE COMMITTEE
Members: Taslim Olawale Elias *(ex officio)*, José Sette Câmara *(ex officio)*, Manfred Lachs, Nagendra Singh, Stephen M. Schwebel.

COMMITTEE ON RELATIONS
Members: Platon D. Morozov, Guy Ladreit de Lacharrière, Kéba Mbaye.

LIBRARY COMMITTEE
Members: José María Ruda, Hermann Mosler, Shigeru Oda, Sir Robert Y. Jennings.

RULES COMMITTEE
Members: Manfred Lachs, Platon D. Morozov, José María Ruda, Hermann Mosler, Shigeru Oda, Roberto Ago, Sir Robert Y. Jennings.

Other United Nations-related bodies

The following bodies are not subsidiary to any principal organ of the United Nations but were established by an international treaty instrument or arrangement sponsored by the United Nations and are thus related to the Organization and its work. These bodies, often referred to as "treaty organs", are serviced by the United Nations Secretariat and may be financed in part or wholly from the Organization's regular budget, as authorized by the General Assembly, to which most of them report annually.

Committee on the Elimination of Discrimination against Women
The Committee on the Elimination of Discrimination against Women was established under the Convention on the Elimination of All Forms of Discrimination against Women.[32] It consists of 23 experts elected by the States parties to the Convention to serve in their personal capacity, with due regard for equitable geographical distribution and for representation of the different forms of civilization and principal legal systems. Members serve for four-year terms.

The Committee, which reports annually to the General Assembly through the Economic and Social Council, held its third session at United Nations Headquarters from 26 March to 6 April 1984.

Members:

To serve until 15 April 1984: Desirée P. Bernard, *Rapporteur* (Guyana); Marie Caron, *Vice-Chairman* (Canada); Graciela Escudero-Moscoso (Ecuador); Aída González Martínez (Mexico); Vanda Lamm (Hungary); Maria Margarida de Rego da Costa Salema Moura Ribeiro (Portugal); Nguyen Ngoc Dung (Viet Nam); Johan Nordenfelt (Sweden); Edith Oeser (German Democratic Republic); Lia Patiño de Martínez (Panama); Esther Véliz Díaz de Villalvilla (Cuba).

To serve until 15 April 1986: A. P. Biryukova (USSR); Irene R. Cortes (Philippines); Farida Abou El-Fetouh (Egypt); Guan Minqian (China); Luvsandanzangyn Ider, *Chairman* (Mongolia); Zagorka Ilic, *Vice-Chairman* (Yugoslavia); Vinitha Jayasinghe (Sri Lanka); Raquel Macedo de Sheppard (Uruguay); Landrada Mukayiranga, *Vice-Chairman* (Rwanda); Vesselina Peytcheva (Bulgaria); Maria Regent-Lechowicz (Poland); Lucy Smith (Norway).

On 9 April 1984, the States parties to the Convention elected the following 11 members for a four-year term beginning on 16 April 1984 to fill the vacancies occurring on 15 April: Desirée P. Bernard (Guyana), Marie Caron (Canada), Elizabeth Evatt (Australia), Aída González Martínez (Mexico), Chryssanthi Laiou-Antoniou (Greece), Alma Montenegro de Fletcher (Panama), Maria Margarida de Rego da Costa Salema Moura Ribeiro (Portugal), Edith Oeser (German Democratic Republic), Kongit Sinegiorgis (Ethiopia), Esther Véliz Díaz de Villalvilla (Cuba), Margareta Wadstein (Sweden).

Committee on the Elimination of Racial Discrimination
The Committee on the Elimination of Racial Discrimination was established under the International Convention on the Elimination of All Forms of Racial Discrimination.[33] It consists of 18 experts elected by the States parties to the Convention to serve in their personal capacity, with due regard for equitable geographical distribution and for representation of the different forms of civilization and principal legal systems. Members serve for four-year terms.

The Committee, which reports annually to the General Assembly through the Secretary-General, held two sessions in 1984: its twenty-ninth at United Nations Headquarters from 5 to 23 March; and its thirtieth at Geneva from 6 to 24 August.

Members:

To serve until 19 January 1986: Jean-Marie Apiou (Upper Volta[a]); Dimitrios J. Evrigenis (Greece);[b] Oladapo Olusola Fafowora (Nigeria); Abdel Moneim M. Ghoneim (Egypt); George O. Lamptey, *Vice-Chairman* (Ghana); Karl Josef Partsch, *Rapporteur* (Federal Republic of Germany); Agha Shahi (Pakistan); Michael E. Sherifis, *Vice-Chairman* (Cyprus); Luis Valencia Rodríguez, *Chairman* (Ecuador).

To serve until 19 January 1988:[c] Nikola Cicanovic (Yugoslavia); John J. Cremona (Malta); Nicolás de Pierola y Balta (Peru); Matey Karasimeonov, *Vice-Chairman* (Bulgaria); Kjell Oberg (Sweden);

Shanti Sadiq Ali (India); Song Shuhua (China); G. B. Starushenko (USSR); Mario Jorge Yutzis (Argentina).

[a]The Upper Volta changed its name to Burkina Faso on 6 August 1984.
[b]Resigned by a letter of 10 August 1984; the appointment of Emmanuel Roucounas (Greece) was approved by the Committee on 13 August to fill the resultant vacancy.
[c]Elected on 20 January 1984.

Conference on Disarmament
The Conference on Disarmament,[a] the multilateral negotiating forum on disarmament, reports annually to the General Assembly and is serviced by the United Nations Secretariat. It was composed of 40 members in 1984.

The Conference met at Geneva in 1984 from 7 February to 27 April and from 12 June to 31 August.

[a]Pursuant to a 1983 decision of the Committee on Disarmament (YUN 1983, p. 13), the Committee became the Conference on Disarmament on 7 February 1984.

Members: Algeria, Argentina, Australia, Belgium, Brazil, Bulgaria, Burma, Canada, China, Cuba, Czechoslovakia, Egypt, Ethiopia, France, German Democratic Republic, Germany, Federal Republic of, Hungary, India, Indonesia, Iran, Italy, Japan, Kenya, Mexico, Mongolia, Morocco, Netherlands, Nigeria, Pakistan, Peru, Poland, Romania, Sri Lanka, Sweden, USSR, United Kingdom, United States, Venezuela, Yugoslavia, Zaire.

The presidency, which rotates in English alphabetical order among the members, was held by the following in 1984: February, Poland; March, Romania; April and the recess between the first and second parts of the 1984 session, Sri Lanka; June, Sweden; July, USSR; August and the recess until the 1985 session, United Kingdom.

Human Rights Committee
The Human Rights Committee was established under the International Covenant on Civil and Political Rights.[34] It consists of 18 experts elected by the States parties to the Covenant to serve in their personal capacity for four-year terms.

The Committee, which reports annually to the General Assembly through the Economic and Social Council, held three sessions in 1984: its twenty-first at United Nations Headquarters from 26 March to 13 April; and its twenty-second and twenty-third at Geneva from 9 to 27 July and from 22 October to 9 November, respectively.

Members:

To serve until 31 December 1984: Andrés Aguilar (Venezuela); Mohammed Abdullah Ahmed Al Douri (Iraq); Gisèle Côté-Harper (Canada); Felix Ermacora (Austria); Sir Vincent Evans (United Kingdom); Vladimir Hanga (Romania); Andreas V. Mavrommatis, *Chairman* (Cyprus); A. P. Movchan (USSR); Alejandro Serrano Caldera (Nicaragua).[a]

To serve until 31 December 1986: Néjib Bouziri, *Vice-Chairman* (Tunisia); Joseph A. L. Cooray (Sri Lanka); Vojin Dimitrijevic (Yugoslavia); Roger Errera (France); Bernhard Graefrath, *Vice-Chairman* (German Democratic Republic); Birame Ndiaye (Senegal); Torkel Opsahl, *Rapporteur* (Norway); Julio Prado Vallejo, *Vice-Chairman* (Ecuador); Christian Tomuschat (Federal Republic of Germany).

[a]Elected on 24 February 1984 to fill the vacancy created by the death in 1983 of Leonte Herdocia Ortega (Nicaragua).

On 14 September 1984, the States parties to the Covenant elected the following nine members for a four-year term beginning on 1 January 1985 to fill the vacancies occurring on 31 December 1984: Andrés Aguilar (Venezuela), Rosalyn Higgins (United Kingdom), Rajsoomer Lallah (Mauritius), Andreas V. Mavrommatis (Cyprus), A. P. Movchan

---

[32]YUN 1979, p. 898, GA res. 34/180, annex, article 17, 18 Dec. 1979.
[33]YUN 1965, p. 443, GA res. 2106 A (XX), annex, article 8, 21 Dec. 1965.
[34]YUN 1966, p. 427, GA res. 2200 A (XXI), annex, part IV, 16 Dec. 1966.

(USSR), Fausto Pocar (Italy), Alejandro Serrano Caldera (Nicaragua), S. Amos Wako (Kenya), Adam Zielinski (Poland).

International Narcotics Control Board (INCB)

The International Narcotics Control Board, established under the Single Convention on Narcotic Drugs, 1961, as amended by the 1972 Protocol, consists of 13 members, elected by the Economic and Social Council for five-year terms, 3 from candidates nominated by WHO and 10 from candidates nominated by Members of the United Nations and parties to the Single Convention.

The Board held two sessions in 1984, at Vienna, Austria: its thirty-fifth from 14 to 25 May; and its thirty-sixth from 8 to 25 October.

Members:
To serve until 1 March 1985: Dr. Bela Bolcs (Hungary); Dr. John C. Ebie (Nigeria);[a] Dr. Diego Garcés-Giraldo (Colombia); Dr. Mohsen Kchouk (Tunisia); Dr. Victorio V. Olguín, *President* (Argentina); Jasjit Singh, *Rapporteur* (India).
To serve until 1 March 1987: Dr. Ramón de la Fuente Muñiz (Mexico);[a] Betty C. Gough, *First Vice-President* (United States); Dr. Sukru Kaymakcalan, *Second Vice-President* (Turkey);[a,b] Paul Reuter (France); Dr. Bror Anders Rexed (Sweden); Adolf-Heinrich von Arnim (Federal Republic of Germany); Sir Edward Williams (Australia).

[a]Elected from candidates nominated by WHO.
[b]Died on 22 July 1984; the vacancy remained unfilled in 1984.

On 23 May 1984 (decision 1984/156), the Economic and Social Council elected the following six members for a five-year term beginning on 2 March 1985 to fill the vacancies occurring on 1 March: Sahibzada Raoof Ali Khan (Pakistan), Dr. Cai Zhi-ji (China), Dr. John C. Ebie (Nigeria) (elected from candidates nominated by WHO), Dr. Diego Garcés-Giraldo (Colombia), Ben J. A. Huyghe-Braeckmans (Belgium), Dr. Mohsen Kchouk (Tunisia).

Preparatory Commission for the International Sea-Bed Authority and for the International Tribunal for the Law of the Sea

The Preparatory Commission for the International Sea-Bed Authority and for the International Tribunal for the Law of the Sea, established by the Third United Nations Conference on the Law of the Sea, consists of the States which have signed or acceded to the United Nations Convention on the Law of the Sea, which numbered 155 as at 31 December 1984, as well as the Cook Islands, the European Economic Community, Namibia (represented by the United Nations Council for Namibia) and Niue.

In 1984, the Commission held its second session at Kingston, Jamaica, from 19 March to 13 April and meetings at Geneva between 13 August and 5 September.

Members: Afghanistan, Algeria, Angola, Antigua and Barbuda, Argentina, Australia, Austria, Bahamas, Bahrain, Bangladesh, Barbados, Belgium, Belize, Benin, Bhutan, Bolivia, Botswana, Brazil, Brunei Darussalam, Bulgaria, Burma, Burundi, Byelorussian SSR, Cameroon, Canada, Cape Verde, Central African Republic, Chad, Chile, China, Colombia, Comoros, Congo, Cook Islands, Costa Rica, Cuba, Cyprus, Czechoslovakia, Democratic Kampuchea, Democratic People's Republic of Korea, Democratic Yemen, Denmark, Djibouti, Dominica, Dominican Republic, Egypt, El Salvador, Equatorial Guinea, Ethiopia, European Economic Community, Fiji, Finland, France, Gabon, Gambia, German Democratic Republic, Ghana, Greece, Grenada, Guatemala, Guinea, Guinea-Bissau, Guyana, Haiti, Honduras, Hungary, Iceland, India, Indonesia, Iran, Iraq, Ireland, Italy, Ivory Coast, Jamaica, Japan, Kenya, Kuwait, Lao People's Democratic Republic, Lebanon, Lesotho, Liberia, Libyan Arab Jamahiriya, Liechtenstein, Luxembourg, Madagascar, Malawi, Malaysia, Maldives, Mali, Malta, Mauritania, Mauritius, Mexico, Monaco, Mongolia, Morocco, Mozambique, Namibia (United Nations Council for), Nauru, Nepal, Netherlands, New Zealand, Nicaragua, Niger, Nigeria, Niue, Norway, Oman, Pakistan, Panama, Papua New Guinea, Paraguay, Philippines, Poland, Portugal, Qatar, Republic of Korea, Romania, Rwanda, Saint Christopher and Nevis, Saint Lucia, Saint Vincent and the Grenadines, Samoa, Sao Tome and Principe, Saudi Arabia, Senegal, Seychelles, Sierra Leone, Singapore, Solomon Islands, Somalia, South Africa, Spain, Sri Lanka, Sudan, Suriname, Swaziland, Sweden, Switzerland, Thailand, Togo, Trinidad and Tobago, Tunisia, Tuvalu, Uganda, Ukrainian SSR, USSR, United Arab Emirates, United Republic of Tanzania, Upper Volta,[a] Uruguay, Vanuatu, Viet Nam, Yemen, Yugoslavia, Zaire, Zambia, Zimbabwe.

[a]The Upper Volta changed its name to Burkina Faso on 6 August 1984.

Chairman: Joseph S. Warioba (United Republic of Tanzania).
Vice-Chairmen: Algeria, Australia, Brazil, Cameroon, Chile, China, France, India, Iraq, Japan, Liberia, Nigeria, Sri Lanka, USSR.
Rapporteur-General: Kenneth O. Rattray (Jamaica).

CREDENTIALS COMMITTEE
Members: Austria, China, Colombia, Costa Rica, Hungary, Ireland, Ivory Coast, Japan, Somalia.
Chairman: Karl Wolf (Austria).

GENERAL COMMITTEE
The General Committee consists of the Commission's Chairman, the 14 Vice-Chairmen, the Rapporteur-General and the 20 officers of the four Special Commissions.

SPECIAL COMMISSIONS
The four Special Commissions are each composed of all the members of the Commission.

Special Commission 1 (on the problem of land-based producers)
Chairman: Hasjim Djalal (Indonesia).
Vice-Chairmen: Austria, Cuba, Romania, Zambia.

Special Commission 2 (on the Enterprise)
Chairman: Lennox Ballah (Trinidad and Tobago).
Vice-Chairmen: Canada, Mongolia, Senegal, Yugoslavia.

Special Commission 3 (on the mining code)
Chairman: Hans H. M. Sondaal (Netherlands).
Vice-Chairmen: Gabon, Mexico, Pakistan, Poland.

Special Commission 4 (on the International Tribunal for the Law of the Sea)
Chairman: Gunter Goerner (German Democratic Republic).
Vice-Chairmen: Colombia, Greece, Philippines, Sudan.

Principal members of the United Nations Secretariat

(as at 31 December 1984)

Secretariat

The Secretary-General: Javier Pérez de Cuéllar

Executive Office of the Secretary-General
Under-Secretary-General, Chef de Cabinet: Virendra Dayal

Office of the Director-General for Development and International Economic Co-operation
Director-General: Jean L. Ripert

Office of the Under-Secretaries-General for Special Political Affairs
Under-Secretaries-General: Diego Cordovez, Brian E. Urquhart
Assistant Secretaries-General: Fou-Tchin Liu, George L. Sherry

Office for Special Political Questions
Under-Secretary-General, Co-ordinator, Special Economic Assistance Programmes: Abdulrahim Abby Farah

**Office of the Under-Secretary-General for
Political and General Assembly Affairs**
Under-Secretary-General: William B. Buffum
Assistant Secretary-General, in charge of preparations for the fortieth anniversary of the United Nations: Robert G. Muller

Office of Secretariat Services for Economic and Social Matters
Assistant Secretary-General: Sotirios Mousouris

Office for Field Operational and External Support Activities
Assistant Secretary-General: James O. C. Jonah

Office of Legal Affairs
Under-Secretary-General, the Legal Counsel: Carl-August Fleischhauer

Department of Political and Security Council Affairs
Under-Secretary-General: Viacheslav A. Ustinov
Assistant Secretary-General, Centre against Apartheid: Enuga S. Reddy

Department of Political Affairs, Trusteeship and Decolonization
Under-Secretary-General: Rafeeuddin Ahmed

Department for Disarmament Affairs
Under-Secretary-General: Jan Martenson

Department of International Economic and Social Affairs
Under-Secretary-General: Shuaib Uthman Yolah
Assistant Secretary-General for Development Research and Policy Analysis: P. N. Dhar
Assistant Secretary-General for Programme Planning and Co-ordination: Peter Hansen
Assistant Secretary-General for Social Development and Humanitarian Affairs: Leticia R. Shahani
Assistant Secretary-General for Special Assignments: Vladimir S. Pozharski

Department of Technical Co-operation for Development
Under-Secretary-General: Bi Jilong
Assistant Secretary-General: Margaret Joan Anstee

Economic Commission for Europe
Under-Secretary-General, Executive Secretary: Klaus Aksel Sahlgren

Economic and Social Commission for Asia and the Pacific
Under-Secretary-General, Executive Secretary: Shah A. M. S. Kibria

Economic Commission for Latin America and the Caribbean
Under-Secretary-General, Executive Secretary: Enrique V. Iglesias

Economic Commission for Africa
Under-Secretary-General, Executive Secretary: Adebayo Adedeji

Economic Commission for Western Asia
Under-Secretary-General, Executive Secretary: Mohamed Said Al-Attar

Centre for Science and Technology for Development
Assistant Secretary-General, Executive Director: Amilcar F. Ferrari

United Nations Centre for Human Settlements
Under-Secretary-General, Executive Director: Arcot Ramachandran
Assistant Secretary-General, Deputy Administrator: Sumihiro Kuyama

United Nations Centre on Transnational Corporations
Assistant Secretary-General, Executive Director: Sidney Dell

Department of Administration and Management
Under-Secretary-General: Patricio Ruedas

OFFICE OF FINANCIAL SERVICES
Assistant Secretary-General: J. Richard Foran

OFFICE OF PERSONNEL SERVICES
Assistant Secretary-General: Louis-Pascal Nègre

OFFICE OF GENERAL SERVICES
Assistant Secretary-General: Alice Weil

Department of Conference Services
Under-Secretary-General for Conference Services and Special Assignments: Eugeniusz Wyzner

Department of Public Information
Under-Secretary-General: Yasushi Akashi

United Nations Office at Geneva
Under-Secretary-General, Director-General of the United Nations Office at Geneva: Erik Suy
Assistant Secretary-General, Personal Representative of the Secretary-General, Secretary-General of the Conference on Disarmament: Rikhi Jaipal

Centre for Human Rights
Assistant Secretary-General: Kurt Herndl

United Nations Office at Vienna
Under-Secretary-General, Director-General of the United Nations Office at Vienna: Mowaffak Allaf

International Court of Justice Registry
Assistant Secretary-General, Registrar: Santiago Torres Bernárdez

Secretariats of subsidiary organs, special representatives and other related bodies

**Office of the Special Representative of the Secretary-General
for Emergency Operations in Ethiopia**
Special Representative of the Secretary-General: Kurt Jansson (Finland)

**Office of the Special Representative of
the Secretary-General for Namibia**
Under-Secretary-General, Special Representative of the Secretary-General: Martti Ahtisaari

Office of the United Nations Disaster Relief Co-ordinator
Under-Secretary-General, Disaster Relief Co-ordinator: M'Hamed Essaafi

**Office of the Special Representative of the Secretary-General for
Co-ordinating Kampuchean Humanitarian Assistance Programmes**
Under-Secretary-General, Senior Advisor to the Secretary-General: Sir Robert Jackson
Assistant Secretary-General, Special Representative of the Secretary-General: Tatsuro Kunugi

**Office of the Special Representative of the Secretary-General
for Humanitarian Affairs in South-East Asia**
Under-Secretary-General, Special Representative of the Secretary-General: Rafeeuddin Ahmed

Office of the United Nations High Commissioner for Refugees
Under-Secretary-General, High Commissioner: Poul Hartling
Assistant Secretary-General, Deputy High Commissioner: William Richard Smyser

**United Nations Conference for the Promotion of International
Co-operation in the Peaceful Uses of Nuclear Energy**
Assistant Secretary-General, Secretary-General of the Conference: Amrik S. Mehta

**Office of the Special Representative of the Secretary-General
for the Law of the Sea**
Assistant Secretary-General, Special Representative of the Secretary-General: Satya N. Nandan

Office of the Co-ordinator of United Nations Assistance for the Reconstruction and Development of Lebanon
Assistant Secretary-General, Co-ordinator: Iqbal A. Akhund

Office of the United Nations Commissioner for Namibia
Assistant Secretary-General, Commissioner for Namibia: Brajesh Chandra Mishra

International Trade Centre UNCTAD/GATT
Assistant Secretary-General, Executive Director: Goran M. Engblom

United Nations Children's Fund
Under-Secretary-General, Executive Director: James P. Grant
Assistant Secretary-General, Deputy Executive Director, Operations: Karl-Eric Knutsson
Assistant Secretary-General, Deputy Executive Director, Programmes: Richard Jolly
Assistant Secretary-General, Deputy Executive Director for External Relations: Varindra T. Vittachi

United Nations Conference on Trade and Development
Under-Secretary-General, Secretary-General of the Conference: Gamani Corea
Assistant Secretaries-General, Deputy Secretaries-General of the Conference: Alister McIntyre, Johannes Pronk

United Nations Development Programme
Administrator: F. Bradford Morse
Associate Administrator: G. Arthur Brown
Assistant Administrator, Bureau for Finance and Administration: Pierre Vinde
Assistant Administrator, Bureau for Special Activities: Paul Thyness
Assistant Administrator and Director, Bureau for Programme Policy and Evaluation: Horst P. Wiesebach
Executive Director, United Nations Fund for Population Activities: Rafael M. Salas
Deputy Executive Director, United Nations Fund for Population Activities: Heino E. Wittrin
Assistant Executive Director, United Nations Fund for Population Activities: Nafis I. Sadik
Assistant Administrator and Regional Director, Regional Bureau for Africa: Pierre-Claver Damiba
Assistant Administrator and Regional Director, Regional Bureau for Arab States: Mustapha Zaanouni
Assistant Administrator and Regional Director, Regional Bureau for Asia and the Pacific: Andrew J. Joseph
Assistant Administrator and Regional Director, Regional Bureau for Latin America: Hugo Navajas-Mogro
Assistant Administrator and Director, European Office, Geneva: Pierre Bourgois

United Nations Disengagement Observer Force
Assistant Secretary-General, Force Commander: Major-General Carl-Gustav Stahl

United Nations Environment Programme
Under-Secretary-General, Executive Director: Mostafa Kamal Tolba
Assistant Secretary-General, Deputy Executive Director: Joseph Wheeler
Assistant Secretary-General, Assistant Executive Director, Office of the Environment Programme: Gennady N. Golubev
Assistant Secretary-General, Assistant Executive Director, Office of the Environment Fund and Administration: Rudolf Schmidt

United Nations Fund for Drug Abuse Control
Assistant Secretary-General, Executive Director: Giuseppe di Gennaro

United Nations Industrial Development Organization
Under-Secretary-General, Executive Director: Abd-El Rahman Khane
Assistant Secretary-General, Deputy Executive Director: Philippe Jacques Farlan Carré

United Nations Institute for Training and Research
Under-Secretary-General, Executive Director: Michel Doo Kingué

United Nations Interim Force in Lebanon
Assistant Secretary-General, Force Commander: Lieutenant-General William Callaghan

United Nations Peace-keeping Force in Cyprus
Assistant Secretary-General, Force Commander: Major-General Günther G. Greindl
Assistant Secretary-General, Special Representative of the Secretary-General: Hugo J. Gobbi

United Nations Relief and Works Agency for Palestine Refugees in the Near East
Under-Secretary-General, Commissioner-General: Olof Rydbeck

United Nations Truce Supervision Organization
Assistant Secretary-General, Chief of Staff: Lieutenant-General Emmanuel Alexander Erskine

United Nations University
Under-Secretary-General, Rector: Mr. Soedjatmoko

World Food Council
Assistant Secretary-General, Executive Director: Maurice J. Williams

---

On 31 December 1984, the total number of staff of the United Nations holding permanent, probationary and fixed-term appointments with service or expected service of a year or more was 26,723. Of these, 8,818 were in the Professional and higher categories and 17,905 were in the General Service, Manual Worker and Field Service categories.

Of the same total, 24,496 were regular staff serving at Headquarters or other established offices and 2,227 were assigned as project personnel to technical co-operation projects. In addition, UNRWA had some 17,000 local area staff.

Appendix IV

Agenda of United Nations principal organs in 1984

This appendix lists the items on the agenda of the General Assembly, the Security Council, the Economic and Social Council and the Trusteeship Council during 1984. For the Assembly and the Economic and Social Council, the column headed "Allocation" indicates the assignment of each item to plenary meetings or committees.

Agenda item titles have been shortened by omitting mention of reports following the subject of the item. Thus, "Question of Cyprus: report of the Secretary-General" has been shortened to "Question of Cyprus". Where the subject-matter of the item is not apparent from its title, the subject is identified in square brackets; this is not part of the title.

General Assembly

Agenda items considered at the resumed thirty-eighth session
(26 June and 17 September 1984)

Item No.	Title	Allocation
2.	Minute of silent prayer or meditation.	Plenary
15.	Elections to fill vacancies in principal organs:	
	(b) Election of one member of the Economic and Social Council.	Plenary
38.	Launching of global negotiations on international economic co-operation for development.	Plenary
40.	Observance of the quincentenary of the discovery of America.	Plenary
41.	Question of Cyprus.	Plenary
42.	Implementation of the resolutions of the United Nations.	Plenary
115.	Scale of assessments for the apportionment of the expenses of the United Nations.	[1]
138.	Consequences of the prolongation of the armed conflict between Iran and Iraq.	Plenary

Agenda of the thirty-ninth session
(first part, 18 September–18 December 1984)

Item No.	Title	Allocation
1.	Opening of the session by the Chairman of the delegation of Panama.	Plenary
2.	Minute of silent prayer or meditation.	Plenary
3.	Credentials of representatives to the thirty-ninth session of the General Assembly:	
	(a) Appointment of the members of the Credentials Committee;	Plenary
	(b) Report of the Credentials Committee.	Plenary
4.	Election of the President of the General Assembly.	Plenary
5.	Election of the officers of the Main Committees.	Plenary
6.	Election of the Vice-Presidents of the General Assembly.	Plenary
7.	Notification by the Secretary-General under Article 12, paragraph 2, of the Charter of the United Nations.	Plenary
8.	Adoption of the agenda and organization of work.	Plenary
9.	General debate.	Plenary
10.	Report of the Secretary-General on the work of the Organization.	Plenary
11.	Report of the Security Council.	Plenary
12.	Report of the Economic and Social Council.	Plenary, 2nd, 3rd, 4th, 5th
13.	Report of the International Court of Justice.	Plenary
14.	Report of the International Atomic Energy Agency.	Plenary
15.	Elections to fill vacancies in principal organs:	
	(a) Election of five non-permanent members of the Security Council;	Plenary
	(b) Election of eighteen members of the Economic and Social Council;	Plenary
	(c) Election of five members of the International Court of Justice.	Plenary
16.	Elections to fill vacancies in subsidiary organs and other elections:	
	(a) Election of fifteen members of the Industrial Development Board;	Plenary

---

[1]Allocated to the Fifth Committee at the first part of the session in 1983 but considered only in plenary meetings at the resumed session.

Item No.	Title	Allocation
(b)	Election of twenty members of the Governing Council of the United Nations Environment Programme;	Plenary
(c)	Election of twelve members of the World Food Council;	Plenary
(d)	Election of seven members of the Committee for Programme and Co-ordination;	Plenary
(e)	Election of the members of the Board of Governors of the United Nations Special Fund for Land-locked Developing Countries;	Plenary
(f)	Election of the Executive Director of the United Nations Environment Programme.	Plenary
17.	Appointments to fill vacancies in subsidiary organs and other appointments:	
(a)	Appointment of members of the Advisory Committee on Administrative and Budgetary Questions;	5th
(b)	Appointment of members of the Committee on Contributions;	5th
(c)	Appointment of a member of the Board of Auditors;	5th
(d)	Confirmation of the appointment of members of the Investments Committee;	5th
(e)	Appointment of members of the United Nations Administrative Tribunal;	5th
(f)	International Civil Service Commission:	5th
	(i) Appointment of members of the Commission;	
	(ii) Designation of the Vice-Chairman of the Commission;	
(g)	Appointment of members of the Joint Inspection Unit;	Plenary
(h)	Confirmation of the appointment of the Executive Director of the United Nations Industrial Development Organization;	Plenary
(i)	Confirmation of the appointment of the Secretary-General of the United Nations Conference on Trade and Development;	Plenary
(j)	Appointment of the United Nations Commissioner for Namibia;	Plenary
(k)	Confirmation of the appointment of the Executive Director of the United Nations Special Fund for Land-locked Developing Countries.	Plenary
18.	Implementation of the Declaration on the Granting of Independence to Colonial Countries and Peoples.	Plenary, 4th
19.	Admission of new Members to the United Nations.	Plenary
20.	The situation in Kampuchea.	Plenary
21.	Co-operation between the United Nations and the Organization of the Islamic Conference.	Plenary
22.	Co-operation between the United Nations and the Organization of African Unity.	Plenary
23.	Co-operation between the United Nations and the League of Arab States.	Plenary
24.	Armed Israeli aggression against the Iraqi nuclear installations and its grave consequences for the established international system concerning the peaceful uses of nuclear energy, the non-proliferation of nuclear weapons and international peace and security.	Plenary
25.	The situation in Central America: threats to international peace and security and peace initiatives.	Plenary
26.	Question of the Falkland Islands (Malvinas).	Plenary, 4th[2]
27.	Question of the Comorian island of Mayotte.	Plenary
28.	The situation in Afghanistan and its implications for international peace and security.	Plenary
29.	Question of Namibia.	Plenary, 4th[2]
30.	Co-operation between the United Nations and the Asian-African Legal Consultative Committee.	Plenary
31.	Policies of *apartheid* of the Government of South Africa.	Plenary, SPC[2]
32.	International Year of Peace.	Plenary
33.	Question of Palestine.	Plenary
34.	Law of the sea.	Plenary
35.	United Nations Conference for the Promotion of International Co-operation in the Peaceful Uses of Nuclear Energy.	Plenary
36.	The situation in the Middle East.	Plenary
37.	Question of peace, stability and co-operation in South-East Asia.	Plenary
38.	Launching of global negotiations on international economic co-operation for development.	Plenary
39.	Question of equitable representation on and increase in the membership of the Security Council.	Plenary
40.	Commemoration of the fortieth anniversary of the United Nations in 1985.	Plenary
41.	Observance of the quincentenary of the discovery of America.	Plenary
42.	Question of Cyprus.	[3]
43.	Implementation of the resolutions of the United Nations.	Plenary
44.	Consequences of the prolongation of the armed conflict between Iran and Iraq.	Plenary
45.	Implementation of General Assembly resolution 38/61 concerning the signature and ratification of Additional Protocol I of the Treaty for the Prohibition of Nuclear Weapons in Latin America (Treaty of Tlatelolco).	1st

---

[2]Hearings of organizations.

[3]On 21 September 1984, the General Assembly adopted the General Committee's recommendation that the allocation of item 42 be deferred until an appropriate time in the future.

Item No.	*Title*	*Allocation*
	(a) Implementation of the Declaration on the Strengthening of International Security;	1st
	(b) Implementation of the Declaration on the Preparation of Societies for Life in Peace.	1st
69.	Implementation of the collective security provisions of the Charter of the United Nations for the maintenance of international peace and security.	1st
70.	Effects of atomic radiation.	SPC
71.	Report of the Special Committee to Investigate Israeli Practices Affecting the Human Rights of the Population of the Occupied Territories.	SPC
72.	International co-operation in the peaceful uses of outer space:	
	(a) Report of the Committee on the Peaceful Uses of Outer Space;	SPC
	(b) Implementation of the recommendations of the Second United Nations Conference on the Exploration and Peaceful Uses of Outer Space.	SPC
73.	Comprehensive review of the whole question of peace-keeping operations in all their aspects.	SPC
74.	Questions relating to information.	SPC
75.	United Nations Relief and Works Agency for Palestine Refugees in the Near East.	SPC
76.	International co-operation to avert new flows of refugees.	SPC
77.	Israel's decision to build a canal linking the Mediterranean Sea to the Dead Sea.	SPC
78.	Question of the Malagasy islands of Glorieuses, Juan de Nova, Europa and Bassas da India.	SPC
79.	Question of the composition of the relevant organs of the United Nations.	SPC
80.	Development and international economic co-operation:	
	(a) International Development Strategy for the Third United Nations Development Decade;	2nd
	(b) Review of the implementation of the Charter of Economic Rights and Duties of States;	Plenary,[4] 2nd
	(c) Trade and development;	2nd
	(d) Industrialization;	2nd
	(e) Science and technology for development;	2nd
	(f) Food problems;	2nd
	(g) Economic and technical co-operation among developing countries;	2nd
	(h) Restructuring of the economic and social sectors of the United Nations system;	2nd
	(i) Environment;	2nd
	(j) Human settlements;	2nd
	(k) Effective mobilization and integration of women in development;	2nd
	(l) United Nations Special Fund;	2nd
	(m) New and renewable sources of energy;	2nd
	(n) Implementation of the Substantial New Programme of Action for the 1980s for the Least Developed Countries;	2nd
	(o) Immediate measures in favour of the developing countries;	2nd
	(p) Development of the energy resources of developing countries.	2nd
81.	Operational activities for development:	
	(a) Operational activities of the United Nations system;	2nd
	(b) United Nations Development Programme;	2nd
	(c) United Nations Capital Development Fund;	2nd
	(d) United Nations Fund for Population Activities;	2nd
	(e) United Nations Volunteers programme;	2nd
	(f) United Nations Special Fund for Land-locked Developing Countries;	2nd
	(g) United Nations Children's Fund;	2nd
	(h) World Food Programme;	2nd
	(i) Technical co-operation activities undertaken by the Secretary-General;	2nd
	(j) Liquidation of the United Nations Emergency Operation Trust Fund and allocation of the remaining balance.	2nd
82.	Training and research:	
	(a) United Nations Institute for Training and Research;	2nd
	(b) United Nations University.	2nd
83.	Special economic and disaster relief assistance:	
	(a) Office of the United Nations Disaster Relief Co-ordinator;	2nd
	(b) Special programmes of economic assistance;	2nd
	(c) Implementation of the medium-term and long-term recovery and rehabilitation programme in the Sudano-Sahelian region.	2nd
84.	Adverse consequences for the enjoyment of human rights of political, military, economic and other forms of assistance given to the racist and colonialist régime of South Africa.	3rd
85.	International Youth Year: Participation, Development, Peace.	3rd
86.	Implementation of the Programme of Action for the Second Decade to Combat Racism and Racial Discrimination.	3rd
87.	Importance of the universal realization of the right of peoples to self-determination and of the speedy granting of independence to colonial countries and peoples for the effective guarantee and observance of human rights.	3rd

---

[4]Commemoration of the tenth anniversary of the adoption of the Charter of Economic Rights and Duties of States.

Item No.	Title	Allocation
88.	Elimination of all forms of racial discrimination:	
	(a) Report of the Committee on the Elimination of Racial Discrimination;	3rd
	(b) Status of the International Convention on the Elimination of All Forms of Racial Discrimination;	3rd
	(c) Status of the International Convention on the Suppression and Punishment of the Crime of Apartheid.	3rd
89.	Policies and programmes relating to youth.	3rd
90.	Question of aging.	3rd
91.	Implementation of the World Programme of Action concerning Disabled Persons.	3rd
92.	International Research and Training Institute for the Advancement of Women.	3rd
93.	United Nations Decade for Women: Equality, Development and Peace:	
	(a) Implementation of the Programme of Action for the Second Half of the United Nations Decade for Women;	3rd
	(b) Preparations for the World Conference to Review and Appraise the Achievements of the United Nations Decade for Women;	3rd
	(c) Voluntary Fund for the United Nations Decade for Women.	3rd
94.	Elimination of all forms of discrimination against women:	
	(a) Report of the Committee on the Elimination of Discrimination against Women;	3rd
	(b) Status of the Convention on the Elimination of All Forms of Discrimination against Women.	3rd
95.	Elimination of all forms of religious intolerance.	3rd
96.	Human rights and scientific and technological developments.	3rd
97.	Question of a convention on the rights of the child.	3rd
98.	International Covenants on Human Rights:	
	(a) Report of the Human Rights Committee;	3rd
	(b) Status of the International Covenant on Economic, Social and Cultural Rights, the International Covenant on Civil and Political Rights and the Optional Protocol to the International Covenant on Civil and Political Rights;	3rd
	(c) Elaboration of a second optional protocol to the International Covenant on Civil and Political Rights, aiming at the abolition of the death penalty.	3rd
99.	Torture and other cruel, inhuman or degrading treatment or punishment.	3rd
100.	Office of the United Nations High Commissioner for Refugees:	
	(a) Report of the High Commissioner;	3rd
	(b) Assistance to refugees in Africa.	3rd
101.	International campaign against traffic in drugs.	3rd
102.	Alternative approaches and ways and means within the United Nations system for improving the effective enjoyment of human rights and fundamental freedoms:	
	(a) Implementation of General Assembly resolution 38/124;	3rd
	(b) National institutions for the protection and promotion of human rights.	3rd
103.	Information from Non-Self-Governing Territories transmitted under Article 73 *e* of the Charter of the United Nations.	4th
104.	Activities of foreign economic and other interests which are impeding the implementation of the Declaration on the Granting of Independence to Colonial Countries and Peoples in Namibia and in all other Territories under colonial domination and efforts to eliminate colonialism, *apartheid* and racial discrimination in southern Africa.	4th
105.	Implementation of the Declaration on the Granting of Independence to Colonial Countries and Peoples by the specialized agencies and the international institutions associated with the United Nations.	4th
106.	United Nations Educational and Training Programme for Southern Africa.	4th
107.	Offers by Member States of study and training facilities for inhabitants of Non-Self-Governing Territories.	4th
108.	Financial reports and audited financial statements, and reports of the Board of Auditors:	
	(a) United Nations;	5th
	(b) United Nations Development Programme;	5th
	(c) United Nations Children's Fund;	5th
	(d) United Nations Relief and Works Agency for Palestine Refugees in the Near East;	5th
	(e) United Nations Institute for Training and Research;	5th
	(f) Voluntary funds administered by the United Nations High Commissioner for Refugees;	5th
	(g) Fund of the United Nations Environment Programme;	5th
	(h) United Nations Fund for Population Activities;	5th
	(i) United Nations Habitat and Human Settlements Foundation;	5th
	(j) United Nations Industrial Development Fund.	5th
109.	Programme budget for the biennium 1984-1985.	5th
110.	Programme planning.	5th
111.	Financial emergency of the United Nations.	5th
112.	Administrative and budgetary co-ordination of the United Nations with the specialized agencies and the International Atomic Energy Agency:	
	(a) Report of the Advisory Committee on Administrative and Budgetary Questions;	5th
	(b) Impact of inflation and monetary instability on the regular budget of the United Nations;	5th
	(c) Feasibility of establishing a single administrative tribunal.	5th

Item No.	*Title*	*Allocation*
113.	Joint Inspection Unit.	5th
114.	Pattern of conferences.	5th
115.	Scale of assessments for the apportionment of the expenses of the United Nations.	5th
116.	Personnel questions:	
	(a) Composition of the Secretariat;	5th
	(b) Respect for the privileges and immunities of officials of the United Nations and the specialized agencies and related organizations;	5th
	(c) Other personnel questions.	5th
117.	United Nations common system.	5th
118.	United Nations pension system.	5th
119.	Financing of the United Nations peace-keeping forces in the Middle East:	
	(a) United Nations Disengagement Observer Force;	5th
	(b) United Nations Interim Force in Lebanon.	5th
120.	Progressive development of the principles and norms of international law relating to the new international economic order.	6th
121.	Observer status of national liberation movements recognized by the Organization of African Unity and/or by the League of Arab States.	6th
122.	Status of the Protocols Additional to the Geneva Conventions of 1949 and relating to the protection of victims of armed conflicts.	6th
123.	Development and strengthening of good-neighbourliness between States.	6th
124.	Peaceful settlement of disputes between States.	6th
125.	Draft Code of Offences against the Peace and Security of Mankind.	6th
126.	Report of the Special Committee on Enhancing the Effectiveness of the Principle of Non-Use of Force in International Relations.	6th
127.	Report of the United Nations Commission on International Trade Law on the work of its seventeenth session.	6th
128.	Consideration of effective measures to enhance the protection, security and safety of diplomatic and consular missions and representatives.	6th
129.	Report of the *Ad Hoc* Committee on the Drafting of an International Convention against the Recruitment, Use, Financing and Training of Mercenaries.	6th
130.	Report of the International Law Commission on the work of its thirty-sixth session.	6th
131.	United Nations Conference on the Law of Treaties between States and International Organizations or between International Organizations.	6th
132.	Report of the Committee on Relations with the Host Country.	6th
133.	Report of the Special Committee on the Charter of the United Nations and on the Strengthening of the Role of the Organization.	6th
134.	Draft Declaration on Social and Legal Principles relating to the Protection and Welfare of Children, with Special Reference to Foster Placement and Adoption Nationally and Internationally.	6th
135.	Review of the multilateral treaty-making process.	6th
136.	Draft Body of Principles for the Protection of All Persons under Any Form of Detention or Imprisonment.	6th
137.	Draft standard rules of procedure for United Nations conferences.	6th
138.	Right of peoples to peace.	Plenary
139.	Critical economic situation in Africa.	Plenary
140.	Celebration of the one-hundred-and-fiftieth anniversary of the emancipation of slaves in the British Empire.	Plenary
141.	Countries stricken by desertification and drought.	2nd
142.	Use of outer space exclusively for peaceful purposes for the benefit of mankind.	1st
143.	Inadmissibility of the policy of State terrorism and any actions by States aimed at undermining the socio-political system in other sovereign States.	1st

Security Council

Agenda items considered during 1984[5]

Item No.	*Title*
1.	Complaint by Angola against South Africa.
2.	The question of South Africa.
3.	Letter dated 3 February 1984 from the Chargé d'affaires a.i. of the Permanent Mission of Nicaragua to the United Nations addressed to the President of the Security Council (complaint against Honduras).

[5]Numbers indicate the order in which items were taken up in 1984.

Item
No.   *Title*

4. The situation in the Middle East.

5. Admission of new Members.

6. Letter dated 18 March 1984 from the Permanent Representative of the Sudan to the United Nations addressed to the President of the Security Council (complaint against the Libyan Arab Jamahiriya).

7. Letter dated 22 March 1984 from the Chargé d'affaires a.i. of the Permanent Mission of the Libyan Arab Jamahiriya to the United Nations addressed to the President of the Security Council (complaint against the United States).

8. The situation between Iran and Iraq.

9. Letter dated 29 March 1984 from the Permanent Representative of Nicaragua to the United Nations addressed to the President of the Security Council (complaint against the United States).

10. The situation in Cyprus.

11. Letter dated 21 May 1984 from the representatives of Bahrain, Kuwait, Oman, Qatar, Saudi Arabia and the United Arab Emirates addressed to the President of the Security Council (complaint against Iran).

12. Letter dated 4 September 1984 from the Chargé d'affaires a.i. of the Permanent Mission of Nicaragua to the United Nations addressed to the President of the Security Council (complaint against the United States).

13. Letter dated 3 October 1984 from the Permanent Representative of the Lao People's Democratic Republic to the United Nations addressed to the President of the Security Council (complaint against Thailand).

14. Election of five members of the International Court of Justice.

15. Letter dated 9 November 1984 from the Permanent Representative of Nicaragua to the United Nations addressed to the President of the Security Council (complaint against the United States).

Economic and Social Council

Agenda of the organizational session for 1984
(7-10 and 21 February and 16 March 1984)

Item No.	Title	Allocation
1.	Election of the Bureau.	Plenary
2.	Adoption of the agenda and other organizational matters.	Plenary
3.	Basic programme of work of the Council for 1984 and 1985.	Plenary
4.	Reconvened special session of the Committee on Transnational Corporations.	Plenary
5.	Elections to subsidiary bodies of the Council and confirmation of representatives on the functional commissions and on the Sessional Working Group of Governmental Experts on the Implementation of the International Covenant on Economic, Social and Cultural Rights.	Plenary
6.	Provisional agenda for the first regular session of 1984 and organizational matters.	Plenary

Agenda of the first regular session of 1984
(1-25 May 1984)

Item No.	Title	Allocation
1.	Adoption of the agenda and other organizational matters.	Plenary
2.	Second Decade to Combat Racism and Racial Discrimination.	Plenary
3.	Implementation of the International Covenant on Economic, Social and Cultural Rights.	6
4.	Convention on the Elimination of All Forms of Discrimination against Women.	Plenary
5.	International Covenant on Civil and Political Rights.	Plenary
6.	Population questions.	Plenary
7.	Non-governmental organizations.	Plenary
8.	Cartography.	Plenary
9.	International co-operation in tax matters.	Plenary
10.	Human rights.	2nd
11.	Social development.	2nd
12.	Activities for the advancement of women; United Nations Decade for Women: Equality, Development and Peace.	2nd
13.	Narcotic drugs.	2nd

6Allocated to the Sessional Working Group of Governmental Experts on the Implementation of the International Covenant on Economic, Social and Cultural Rights.

Item No.	*Title*	*Allocation*
14.	Elections and nominations.	Plenary
15.	Consideration of the provisional agenda for the second regular session of 1984.	Plenary

Agenda of the second regular session of 1984
(4-27 July 1984)

Item No.	*Title*	*Allocation*
1.	Opening of the session.	Plenary
2.	Adoption of the agenda and other organizational matters.	Plenary
3.	General discussion of international economic and social policy, including regional and sectoral developments.	Plenary
4.	Critical economic situation in Africa.	Plenary
5.	Review and appraisal of the implementation of the International Development Strategy for the Third United Nations Development Decade.	Plenary
6.	Restructuring of the economic and social sectors of the United Nations system, including revitalization of the Economic and Social Council.	Plenary
7.	Report of the United Nations High Commissioner for Refugees.	Plenary
8.	Permanent sovereignty over national resources in the occupied Palestinian and other Arab territories.	Plenary
9.	Regional co-operation.	1st
10.	Transnational corporations.	1st
11.	Food problems.	1st
12.	Review and analysis of agrarian reform and rural development.	1st
13.	Industrial development co-operation.	1st
14.	International co-operation on the environment.	1st
15.	International co-operation in the field of human settlements.	1st
16.	Science and technology for development.	1st
17.	Development and utilization of new and renewable sources of energy.	1st
18.	Special economic, humanitarian and disaster relief assistance.	3rd
19.	Operational activities for development.	3rd
20.	International co-operation and co-ordination within the United Nations system.	3rd
21.	Proposed revisions to the medium-term plan for the period 1984-1989.	3rd
22.	Implementation of the Declaration on the Granting of Independence to Colonial Countries and Peoples by the specialized agencies and the international institutions associated with the United Nations.	3rd
23.	Trade and development.	Plenary
24.	United Nations University.	Plenary
25.	Elections and nominations.	Plenary

Trusteeship Council

Agenda of the fifty-first session
(14 May-18 July 1984)

Item No.	*Title*
1.	Adoption of the agenda.
2.	Report of the Secretary-General on credentials.
3.	Election of the President and the Vice-President.
4.	Form and style of future reports of the Trusteeship Council to the Security Council.
5.	Examination of the annual report of the Administering Authority for the year ended 30 September 1983: Trust Territory of the Pacific Islands.
6.	Examination of petitions listed in the annex to the agenda.
7.	Report of the United Nations Visiting Mission to observe the plebiscite in the Federated States of Micronesia, Trust Territory of the Pacific Islands, June 1983.
8.	Report of the United Nations Visiting Mission to observe the plebiscite in the Marshall Islands, Trust Territory of the Pacific Islands, September 1983.
9.	Offers by Member States of study and training facilities for inhabitants of Trust Territories.

Appendix V

United Nations Information Centres and Services

(As at 31 December 1984)

ACCRA. United Nations Information Centre
Liberia and Maxwell Roads
(P.O. Box 2339)
Accra, Ghana
Serving: Ghana, Sierra Leone

ADDIS ABABA. United Nations Information
Service, Economic Commission for Africa
Africa Hall
(P.O. Box 3001)
Addis Ababa, Ethiopia
Serving: Ethiopia

ALGIERS. United Nations Information Centre
19 Avenue Chahid El Ouali Mustapha Sayed
Algiers, Algeria
Serving: Algeria

ANKARA. United Nations Information Centre
197 Ataturk Bulvari
(P.K. 407)
Ankara, Turkey
Serving: Turkey

ANTANANARIVO. United Nations Information
Centre
22 Rue Rainitovo
Antsahavola
(Boîte Postale 1348)
Antananarivo, Madagascar
Serving: Madagascar

ASUNCION. United Nations Information
Centre
Casilla de Correo 1107
Asunción, Paraguay
Serving: Paraguay

ATHENS. United Nations Information Centre
36 Amalia Avenue
GR-105, 58 Athens, Greece
Serving: Cyprus, Greece, Israel

BAGHDAD. United Nations Information Serv-
ice, Economic Commission for Western Asia
Amiriya, Airport Street
(P.O. Box 27)
Baghdad, Iraq
Serving: Iraq

BANGKOK. United Nations Information Serv-
ice, Economic and Social Commission for
Asia and the Pacific
United Nations Building
Rajdamnern Avenue
Bangkok 10200, Thailand
Serving: Democratic Kampuchea, Hong
Kong, Lao People's Democratic Republic,
Malaysia, Singapore, Thailand, Viet Nam

BEIRUT. United Nations Information Centre
Apt. No. 1, Fakhoury Building
Montée Bain Militaire, Ardati Street
(P.O. Box 4656)
Beirut, Lebanon
Serving: Jordan, Kuwait, Lebanon, Syrian
Arab Republic

BELGRADE. United Nations Information Centre
Svetozara Markovica 58
(P.O. Box 157)
Belgrade, Yugoslavia YU-11001
Serving: Albania, Yugoslavia

BOGOTA. United Nations Information Centre
Calle 61 No. 13-23 (piso 5)
(Apartado Aéreo 058964)
Bogotá 2, Colombia
Serving: Colombia, Ecuador, Venezuela

BRAZZAVILLE. United Nations Information
Centre
Boîte Postale 465
Brazzaville, Congo
Serving: Congo

BRUSSELS. United Nations Information Centre
108 Rue d'Arlon
1040 Brussels, Belgium
Serving: Belgium, Luxembourg, Netherlands; liaison with European Economic Community

BUCHAREST. United Nations Information Centre
16 Aurel Vlaicu Street
(P.O. Box 1-701)
Bucharest, Romania
Serving: Romania

BUENOS AIRES. United Nations Information
Centre
Junín 1940 (1er piso)
1113 Buenos Aires, Argentina
Serving: Argentina, Uruguay

BUJUMBURA. United Nations Information
Centre
Avenue de la Poste 7
Place de l'Indépendance
(Boîte Postale 2160)
Bujumbura, Burundi
Serving: Burundi

CAIRO. United Nations Information Centre
1 Osiris Street
Tagher Building (Garden City)
(Boîte Postale 262)
Cairo, Egypt
Serving: Egypt, Saudi Arabia, Yemen

COLOMBO. United Nations Information Centre
202-204 Bauddhaloka Mawatha
(P.O. Box 1505)
Colombo, Sri Lanka
Serving: Maldives, Sri Lanka

COPENHAGEN. United Nations Information
Centre
37 H. C. Andersen Boulevard
DK-1553 Copenhagen V, Denmark
Serving: Denmark, Finland, Iceland, Norway,
Sweden

DAKAR. United Nations Information Centre
9 Allée Robert Delmas
(Boîte Postale 154)
Dakar, Senegal
Serving: Cape Verde, Gambia, Guinea,
Guinea-Bissau, Ivory Coast, Mauritania, Senegal

DAR ES SALAAM. United Nations Information
Centre
Samora Machel Avenue
Matasalamat Building (1st floor)
(P.O. Box 9224)
Dar es Salaam, United Republic of Tanzania
Serving: United Republic of Tanzania

DHAKA. United Nations Information Centre
House 12, Road 6
Dhanmondi
(G.P.O. Box 3658)
Dhaka, Bangladesh
Serving: Bangladesh

GENEVA. United Nations Information Service,
United Nations Office at Geneva
Palais des Nations
1211 Geneva 10, Switzerland
Serving: Bulgaria, Hungary, Poland, Spain,
Switzerland

HARARE. United Nations Information Centre
Lenbern House, Moffat Street/Union Avenue
(P.O. Box 4408)
Harare, Zimbabwe
Serving: Zimbabwe

ISLAMABAD. United Nations Information Centre
House No. 26
88th Street, Ramna 6/3
(P.O. Box 1107)
Islamabad, Pakistan
Serving: Pakistan

KABUL. United Nations Information Centre
Shah Mahmoud Ghazi Watt
(P.O. Box 5)
Kabul, Afghanistan
Serving: Afghanistan

KATHMANDU. United Nations Information Centre
P.O. Box 107
Lazimpat
Kathmandu, Nepal
  Serving: Nepal

KHARTOUM. United Nations Information Centre
Al Qasr Avenue, Street No. 15
Block 3, House No. 3
Khartoum East
(P.O. Box 1992)
Khartoum, Sudan
  Serving: Somalia, Sudan

KINSHASA. United Nations Information Centre
Bâtiment Deuxième République
Boulevard du 30 Juin
(Boîte Postale 7248)
Kinshasa, Zaire
  Serving: Zaire

LAGOS. United Nations Information Centre
17 Kingsway Road, Ikoyi
(P.O. Box 1068)
Lagos, Nigeria
  Serving: Nigeria

LA PAZ. United Nations Information Centre
Avenida Arce No. 2529
Edificio Santa Isabel
Bloque C (2º mezzanine)
(Apartado Postal 686)
La Paz, Bolivia
  Serving: Bolivia

LIMA. United Nations Information Centre
Mariscal Blas Cerdeña 450
San Isidro
(Apartado Postal 11199)
Lima, Peru
  Serving: Peru

LISBON. United Nations Information Centre
Rua Latino Coelho No. 1
Edificio Aviz, Bloco A-1, 10º
1000 Lisbon, Portugal
  Serving: Portugal

LOME. United Nations Information Centre
107 Boulevard Circulaire
(Boîte Postale 911)
Lomé, Togo
  Serving: Benin, Togo

LONDON. United Nations Information Centre
Ship House
20 Buckingham Gate
London, SW1E 6LB, England
  Serving: Ireland, United Kingdom

LUSAKA. United Nations Information Centre
P.O. Box 32905
Lusaka, Zambia
  Serving: Botswana, Malawi, Namibia,
  Swaziland, Zambia

MANAGUA. United Nations Information Centre
De Plaza España, 2 cuadras abajo
Bolonia
(Apartado Postal 3260)
Managua, Nicaragua
  Serving: Nicaragua

MANAMA. United Nations Information Centre
King Faisal Road, Gufool
(P.O. Box 26004)
Manama, Bahrain
  Serving: Bahrain, Qatar, United Arab
  Emirates

MANILA. United Nations Information Centre
NEDA Building (ground floor)
106 Amorsolo Street
Legaspi Village, Makati
(P.O. Box 7285 (ADC), MIA Road, Pasay City)
Metro Manila, Philippines
  Serving: Philippines

MASERU. United Nations Information Centre
Corner Kingsway and Hilton Roads
  opposite Sanlam Centre
(P.O. Box 301)
Maseru, 100 Lesotho
  Serving: Lesotho

MEXICO CITY. United Nations Information
  Centre
Presidente Masaryk 29 (7º piso)
11570 México, D.F., Mexico
  Serving: Cuba, Dominican Republic,
  Mexico

MONROVIA. United Nations Information
  Centre
LBDI Building
Tubman Boulevard
(P.O. Box 274)
Monrovia, Liberia
  Serving: Liberia

MOSCOW. United Nations Information Centre
4/16 Ulitsa Lunacharskogo
Moscow 121002, USSR
  Serving: Byelorussian SSR, Ukrainian
  SSR, USSR

NAIROBI. United Nations Information Centre
Electricity House
Harambee Avenue
(P.O. Box 30218)
Nairobi, Kenya
  Serving: Kenya, Seychelles, Uganda

NEW DELHI. United Nations Information
  Centre
55 Lodi Estate
New Delhi 110 003, India
  Serving: Bhutan, India

OUAGADOUGOU. United Nations Information
  Centre
218 Rue de la Gare
(Boîte Postale 135)
Ouagadougou, Burkina Faso
  Serving: Burkina Faso, Chad, Mali, Niger

PANAMA CITY. United Nations Information
  Centre
Urbanización Obarrio
Calle 54 y Avenida Tercera Sur, No. 17
(P.O. Box 6-9083 El Dorado)
Panama City, Panama
  Serving: Panama

PARIS. United Nations Information Centre
4 et 6 Avenue de Saxe
75700 Paris, France
  Serving: France

PORT MORESBY. United Nations Information
  Centre
Credit House (third floor)
Musgrave Street, Ela Beach
(P.O. Box 472)
Port Moresby, Papua New Guinea
  Serving: Papua New Guinea, Solomon
  Islands

PORT OF SPAIN. United Nations Information
  Centre
15 Keate Street
(P.O. Box 130)
Port of Spain, Trinidad
  Serving: Antigua and Barbuda, Bahamas,
  Barbados, Belize, Dominica, Grenada, Guyana,
  Jamaica, Netherlands Antilles, Saint Christopher
  and Nevis, Saint Lucia, Saint Vincent and the
  Grenadines, Suriname, Trinidad and Tobago

PRAGUE. United Nations Information Centre
Panska 5
11000 Prague 1, Czechoslovakia
  Serving: Czechoslovakia, German Democratic Republic

RABAT. United Nations Information Centre
Angle Charia Moulay Hassan et Zankat Assafi
(Casier ONU)
Rabat-Chellah, Morocco
  Serving: Morocco

RANGOON. United Nations Information Centre
28A Manawhari Road
(P.O. Box 230)
Rangoon, Burma
  Serving: Burma

RIO DE JANEIRO. United Nations Information
  Centre
Rua Cruz Lima 19, Grupo 201
22230 Rio de Janeiro, Brazil RJ
  Serving: Brazil

ROME. United Nations Information Centre
Palazzetto Venezia
Piazza San Marco 50
Rome, Italy
  Serving: Holy See, Italy, Malta

SAN SALVADOR. United Nations Information
  Centre
Edificio Escalón (2º piso)
Paseo General Escalón y 87 Avenida Norte
Colonia Escalón
(Apartado Postal 2157)
San Salvador, El Salvador
  Serving: Costa Rica, El Salvador, Guatemala,
  Honduras

SANTIAGO. United Nations Information Service,
  Economic Commission for Latin America and
  the Caribbean
Edificio Naciones Unidas
Avenida Dag Hammarskjold
(Casilla 179-D)
Santiago, Chile
  Serving: Chile

SYDNEY. United Nations Information Centre
National Mutual Centre
44 Market Street (16th floor)
(P.O. Box 4045, Sydney 2001, N.S.W.)
Sydney 2000, N.S.W., Australia

Serving: Australia, Fiji, Kiribati, Nauru, New Zealand, Samoa, Tonga, Tuvalu, Vanuatu

TEHERAN. United Nations Information Centre
Avenue Gandhi, 43 Street No. 3
(P.O. Box 1555)
Teheran, Iran

Serving: Iran

TOKYO. United Nations Information Centre
Shin Aoyama Building Nishikan (22nd floor)
1-1 Minami Aoyama 1-chome, Minato-ku
Tokyo 107, Japan

Serving: Japan, Trust Territory of the Pacific Islands

TRIPOLI. United Nations Information Centre
Zawia Street
(P.O. Box 286)
Tripoli, Libyan Arab Jamahiriya

Serving: Libyan Arab Jamahiriya

TUNIS. United Nations Information Centre
61 Boulevard Bab-Benat
(Boîte Postale 863)
Tunis, Tunisia

Serving: Tunisia

VIENNA. United Nations Information Service, United Nations Office at Vienna
Vienna International Centre
Wagramer Strasse 5
(P.O. Box 500, A-1400 Vienna)
A-1220 Vienna, Austria

Serving: Austria, Federal Republic of Germany

WASHINGTON, D.C. United Nations Information Centre
1889 F Street, N.W.
Washington, D.C. 20006, United States

Serving: United States

YAOUNDE. United Nations Information Centre
Immeuble Kamden
Rue Joseph Clerc
(Boîte Postale 836)
Yaoundé, Cameroon

Serving: Cameroon, Central African Republic, Gabon

Indexes

Using the subject index

The subject index to the *Yearbook of the United Nations 1984* is designed to assist the reader to find information on specific subjects. The designations employed and the presentation of entries in the index do not imply the expression of any opinion by the Department of Public Information of the United Nations. The subject index contains four types of entries:

Subject terms, including geographical names, are in bold face and, in most cases, are based on the subject descriptors used in the United Nations Bibliographical Information System (UNBIS), published in the *UNBIS Thesaurus* (United Nations Publication: Sales No. E.85.I.20). In order to minimize subentries, the index lists broad and narrow terms in their separate alphabetical positions; for example, "human rights", "racial discrimination" and "right to development". Subjects pertaining to the United Nations or the system as a whole, such as "contributions (UN)", "finances (UN)" and "staff (UN/UN system)", are indexed separately, with cross-references under "United Nations".

NAMES of organizations and subsidiary bodies, conferences, United Nations Secretariat departments and offices, programmes, and special decades and observances, are given in full in capitals and small capitals and are alphabetized in either of two ways: (1) Names of bodies, units and programmes that are part of the United Nations, names of subsidiary bodies of specialized agencies and of their affiliated institutions, and titles of special decades and observances, are indexed under their key word: APARTHEID, SPEC. CT. AGAINST; DEVELOPMENT DECADE, 3RD UN; LAW OF THE SEA, 3RD UN CF. ON THE; MARITIME DAY, WORLD; TECHNICAL CO-OPERATION FOR DEVELOPMENT, DEPARTMENT OF. (2) Names of specialized agencies and of non–United Nations organizations are alphabetized under the first word of their title: INTER-AMERICAN CS. ON HUMAN RIGHTS; WORLD METEOROLOGICAL ORGANIZATION.

Names of publications are italicized, with only those receiving relatively extensive treatment in *Yearbook* articles, such as *Development Forum* and the *World Economic Survey 1984*, being listed.

Cross-references are not given to entries in close proximity; for example, there is a cross-reference to "economic development" under "development" but not "development assistance".

Bodies/subjects/topics are listed only when substantive information is given.

Entries are alphabetized word by word. Examples: **human rights**; HUMAN RIGHTS, CS. ON; **humanitarian assistance**.

Within most entries, the organization, body or unit dealing with the subject is indicated (by abbreviation or short title) in parentheses, preceded or followed by the appropriate page number(s). Boldface numbers refer to resolution or decision texts. Thus, the entry

cardiovascular diseases, 1223 (WHO)

indicates that WHO activities relating to cardiovascular diseases are described on the page cited. The entry

Bermuda: 1070-72 (Colonial Countries Ct., 1072; GA, **1070-72**); information to UN, 1018

indicates that information on Bermuda appears on pages 1070 to 1072, and that, on this topic, the activities of the Special Committee on the Situation with regard to the Implementation of the Declaration on the Granting of Independence to Colonial Countries and Peoples are described on page 1072; the text of one or more General Assembly resolution(s)/decision(s) is on pages 1070-1072; and related information can be found on page 1018.

Abbreviations

In addition to the abbreviations contained in the list on pp. xiv-xv, the subject index uses the following:

CD	Conference on Disarmament (formerly Committee on Disarmament)
cf(s).	conference(s)
cl(s).	council(s)
cs(s).	commission(s)
ct(s).	committee(s)
DC	Disarmament Commission
DG	Director-General
mtg(s).	meeting(s)
sess.	session
SCPDPM	Sub-Commission on Prevention of Discrimination and Protection of Minorities of the Commission of Human Rights
spec.	special
UNCLS	United Nations Conference on the Law of the Sea
UNJSPB	United Nations Joint Staff Pension Board

Subject index

Page numbers in boldface type indicate resolutions and decisions

disarmament *(cont.)*
conventional weapons; deterrence; nuclear disarmament; nuclear-weapon-free zones; nuclear weapons; outer space: arms race; radiological weapons; weapons of mass destruction; zones of peace

DISARMAMENT, AD HOC WORKING GROUP ON THE COMPREHENSIVE PROGRAMME OF, 12

DISARMAMENT, CT. ON (CD), *see* Disarmament, Cf. on

DISARMAMENT, CF. ON (CT. ON DISARMAMENT), 6 (SG), 13-15 (GA, **13-14**, 14, **17**); *ad hoc* bodies, re-establishment, 13, **14** (GA); members/structure, 13, 1340; participation in, 13, **15** (GA)

DISARMAMENT AFFAIRS, UN DEPARTMENT FOR (SECRETARIAT): & Disarmament Week, 90; Under-SG, 1342; & World Disarmament Campaign, 86 (CPC), 87 (SG)

DISARMAMENT AND DEVELOPMENT, GROUP OF GOVERNMENTAL EXPERTS ON RELATIONSHIP BETWEEN: *1981* study, 83,

DISARMAMENT AND DEVELOPMENT, INTERNATIONAL CF. ON RELATIONSHIP BETWEEN *(1986)*, 83-84 (DC Working Group IV, 83; GA, **83-84**, 84); Preparatory Ct., 1317; venue, 84, **84** (GA)

DISARMAMENT CAMPAIGN, WORLD: implementation, 86-90 (Advisory Board, 87, 92; CPC, 86; GA, **87-88**, 88; SG, 87-88); financing, 89-90 (GA, **89-90**, 90; SG, 89); Pledging Cf., 89; Voluntary Trust Fund, 89
& mass media role, **362** (GA), 364 (Information Ct.)
regional/institutional arrangements, 87 (SG), **87-88**, 88 (GA)

DISARMAMENT CS. (DC), 15-16, **16**, **17** (GA); Ct. of the Whole, establishment, 15; members/officers, 1315

DISARMAMENT CF., AD HOC CT. ON THE WORLD, 85; members/officers, 1313; Working Group, members, 1313

DISARMAMENT CF., WORLD, 85-86 (*Ad Hoc* Ct., 85-86; GA, **86**, 86)

DISARMAMENT DECADE, 2ND: Declaration of the 1980s, implementation, *1985* review, 20, **20** (GA)

DISARMAMENT IN EUROPE, CF. ON CONFIDENCE- AND SECURITY-BUILDING MEASURES AND, 116 (GA)

DISARMAMENT RESEARCH, UN INSTITUTE FOR (UNIDIR), 92-96; Board of Trustees, 93, 1324 (members); Director, 1324; Statute, 93-96 (ACABQ, 93; GA, **93-95**, 95-96), 93-95 *(text)*

DISARMAMENT STUDIES, ADVISORY BOARD ON, 91-92; as UNIDIR Board of Trustees, 93

DISARMAMENT WEEK: mass media role, **362**, 364 (GA/Information Ct.); observance, 90-91 (GA, **90-91**, 91; SG, 90); NGO Forum, 90

DISASTER INFORMATION DATA BASE SYSTEM/DISASTER INFORMATION SYSTEM, 501

DISASTER PREPAREDNESS AND PREVENTION PROJECT, PAN-CARIBBEAN, 521

disaster preparedness and prevention, *see under* disasters

disaster relief, *see under* disasters

DISASTER RELIEF ASSISTANCE, UN TRUST FUNDS FOR, 505-6; contributions, 505, 505-6 *(table)*; expenditures, **344** *(table)*, 505

DISASTER RELIEF CO-ORDINATOR, OFFICE OF THE UN (UNDRO), 500-6; (ESC, **502-3**, 503; GA, **464**, 503, **503-4**; SG, 505); appropriations, UN budget *(1984-1985)*, 505, **1123**; financing, Trust Funds, 505-6 (ESC, **503**; GA, **504**); missions, 500; publications, 501; Under-SG (Co-ordinator), 1342

disasters, 500-22; aid delivery, draft convention, 504-5, **505** (SG/SG); & co-ordination in UN system, 506-7 (SG); mobile units, 500; OAU/UN co-operation, **193** (GA); preparedness/prevention, 520-22; public information, 500-1; relief assistance, **193** (GA), 501-2 *(list)*, 507-20; satellite applications, 501; technical assistance, 520; & UNICEF, 919; *see also country names* and regional entries; drought-stricken areas; earthquakes; floods; typhoons

discrimination, *see* indigenous population; minorities; nazism/fascism; racial discrimination

DISCRIMINATION AND PROTECTION OF MINORITIES, SUB-CS. ON PREVENTION OF (SCPDPM): calendar of mtgs., 843; members/sess., 1330; report, **947** (ESC); Working Groups, members, 1330; work organization/programme, review, 842-43 (ESC, **842**; SCPDPM, 843; Working Group, 842-43)

diseases, 731; prevention/control, 732 (WHO), 913 (UNICEF), 552-53 (WHO); research/training, 1194 (IAEA/WHO); treatment, 1223 (WHO); water-borne, 755 (Egypt/UNEP); *see also* immunization; *names of diseases; and under* children

DISENGAGEMENT OBSERVER FORCE, UN (UNDOF), 304-5 (SC, **305**, 305; SG, 304-5); Commander, 1328, 1343; composition, 305; contributions, 306, **307** (GA/SG), 308-9 *(table)*; financing, 305-9 (ACABQ/SG, 306; GA, **306-7**, 307-8); suspension of financial regulations, 306, **308** (GA); troop contributors' reimbursement, **314**, 314-15 (GA); & UNTSO, 305; *see also* Golan Heights; Syrian Arab Republic

disputes, peaceful settlement of, 1087-88 (Charter Ct., 1087; GA, **1087-88**, 1088); proposed handbook, 1087, **1088** (GA/SG/Spec. Ct.); *see also* international relations: non-use of force

Djibouti: economic assistance, 479-80 (GA, **480**, 480; SG, 479); emergency drought aid, 512 (communication), **513-14** (ESC), **515** (GA); investment programme, 480; refugee assistance, 945-46 (GA, **945**; SG, 946; UNHCR, 945); tripartite repatriation agreement *(1983)*, 946; *see also* East Africa, drought-stricken areas; Ethiopia

documentation (UN), 1176-78; distribution, 1177-78 (CPC/SG); language services, 1122 (ACABQ/GA), 1177 (SG); limitation, 1176-77 (Ct. on Cfs., 1176; GA, **1176-77**, 1177); *see also under* ESC; UNIDO

Dominican Republic: industrial project, 574 (SIS)

DOSIMETRY LABORATORIES, SECONDARY STANDARD, 1194 (IAEA/WHO)

dosimetry radiation, 1194 (IAEA)

drinking water: & children's diseases, 731 (UNICEF/WHO); regional activities, 649 (UNEP); sanitation, 919 *(table)*; *see also* sewerage; water supply

DRINKING WATER SUPPLY AND SANITATION DECADE, INTERNATIONAL *(1981-1990)*, implementation, 648 (ACC Group), 649 (UNEP/WHO); & participation of women, 901 (INSTRAW); WHO projects, 1221

drought: impact on foreign trade, 756 (UNCTAD study); Scientific Round-Table, 507-8; & UNIDO IV, 561; *see also country names*; desertification; East Africa; Sudano-Sahelian region; *and entries under* Sahel

Drought Control in the Sahel, Permanent Inter-State Ct. on, *see* Sahel, Permanent Inter-State Ct. on Drought Control

drug abuse, 957-58; international control, 955-57 (INCB, 955; JIU, 955-56; Narcotic Drugs Cs./SG, 956); co-ordination, 956 (*ad hoc* inter-agency mtg.; GA, **961**); WHO project, 1224; *see also* narcotic drugs; psychotropic substances

DRUG ABUSE CONTROL, UN FUND FOR (UNFDAC), 956-57, **961** (GA); contributions, 956 *(table)*; Executive Director, 1343

DRUG ABUSE CONTROL STRATEGY, INTERNATIONAL: implementation, 956 (Narcotic Drugs Cs./SG)

DRUG TRAFFIC AND RELATED MATTERS IN NEAR AND MIDDLE EAST, SUB-COMMISSION ON ILLICIT, 956, 960; members/officers, 1331

DRUG TRAFFICKING AND DRUG ABUSE, DECLARATION ON CONTROL OF, 959 *(text)*

DRUG TRAFFICKING AND ILLICIT USE OF DRUGS, NEW YORK DECLARATION AGAINST, 959

drugs: of abuse, multiple, 732, 957; essential, production, 587 (UNIDO), 732 (WHO); UNFDAC/UNIDO project, 584; WHO activities, 1223; *see also* primary health care; psychotropic substances *and under* narcotic drugs

DRUGS AND VACCINES, ACTION PROGRAMME ON ESSENTIAL, 1223 (WHO)

EARTHQUAKE PREPAREDNESS, BALKAN REGIONAL SEMINAR ON, 501

EARTHQUAKE RISK REDUCTION, INTERNATIONAL GOVERNMENTAL CT. FOR: establishment, 521

earthquakes, 501 (UNDRO), 521 (UNDRO/UNCHS), 919 (UNICEF) *see also* Yemen

Earthwatch, *see under* Environmental Monitoring System, Global

East Africa: development credits, 1243 (IDA); emergency disaster assistance, 512-13 (SG), **514-15**, 515 (GA); food production, 466 (FAO/SG); intergovernmental body, proposed, 512; regional seas programme (UNEP), 766

EAST AFRICAN COMMUNITY: division of assets/liabilities *(1983* Arusha Accord), 494

Kenya: drought aid, 512 (SG), **515** (GA); natural resources exploration, 646 (UNRFNRE)

Kiribati: admission to UPU, 666, WHO, 1220; inclusion in LDC list, consideration, 416-17, **417** (ESC)

Korea, Republic of, *see* Republic of Korea

Korean question, 213-14 (communications, 214; UN Command, 213); Rangoon bombing attack, 213-14 (communications)

Kuwait, *see under* Iran-Iraq conflict

labour: educational activities, 1202-3 (ILO); publications, 1203; seminars, 1202; *see also* employment; International Labour Organisation; trade unions; technical/vocational training; working conditions

LABOUR-MANAGEMENT RELATIONS IN THE PETROLEUM INDUSTRY, 4TH TRIPARTITE CF. (ILO), 1202

LABOUR STUDIES, INTERNATIONAL INSTITUTE FOR (ILO), 1200 *(table)*, 1203

Lagos Plan of Action, *see* Africa, Lagos Plan of Action for the Implementation of the Monrovia Strategy *(1980)*

land-locked developing countries, 417-22 (GA, **419-20**, 420; UNCTAD, 417-19); & Commodities Fund, 420, **420** (GA); transit/transport situation, 418-19 (*Ad Hoc* Expert Group/UNCTAD); & UNCHS, 776; *see also* Zaire

LAND-LOCKED DEVELOPING COUNTRIES, AD HOC GROUP OF EXPERTS TO STUDY WAYS AND MEANS OF IMPROVING TRANSIT-TRANSPORT INFRASTRUCTURES AND SERVICES FOR: report, 418-19 (GA, **420**; TDB, 419)

LAND-LOCKED DEVELOPING COUNTRIES, UN SPECIAL FUND FOR, 420-22 (GA, **421**, 421), 1338; Board of Governors, election deferred, **422** (GA), 1326; contributions, 420 (UNDP), 421 *(table)*; Executive Director, confirmation, 421-22, **422** (GA/SG); project expenditures, 421

land management, 1209 (FAO); UNCHS projects, 775; *see also* soil conservation

land-mines, *see* material remnants of war

language services (UN): Arabic, ECWA staff, **642, 642** (ESC/GA); Chinese, 1122, 1125, 1177 (ACABQ/GA/SG); French, use of in DPI, **361** (GA); & UNCITRAL Arbitration Rules, 1112-13; *see also* conferences/meetings (UN); documentation (UN); staff (UN/UN system): language staff

Lao People's Democratic Republic: dispute with Thailand, 221-23 (communications, 221-22, 223; SC, 222-23); refugees in, 951 (UNHCR); *see also under* Kampuchea situation

Latin America: biotechnology network, 588 (UNIDO/UNDP/UNESCO); child welfare, 919-20 (UNICEF); communications, 351-52 (IPDC), 1217 (UNESCO); cultural/natural heritage, protection, 638 (SG/JIU), 764 (JIU/UNEP Cl.); culture, 1216 (UNESCO); debt crisis, 544 (communications), 634 (ECLAC), 636 (Cartagena Consensus/ECLAC); development assistance, 674 (WFP); development

policy/co-operation, 634-35 (ECLAC/ILPES); economic/social trends, 405 (DIESA/TDB reports), **406** (ESC), 634; economic crisis in, 389 (communications), 633 (ECLAC); education, 1214 (UNESCO); energy, 637 (ECLAC); environment, 638 (ECLAC/UNEP), 747 (UNEP Cl.); environmental training, 771 (UNEP); export promotion, 534 (ITC); food/agriculture, 588 (UNIDO/FAO), 637 (ECLAC/FAO), 668 (WFC), 675 (WFP) 1207, 1210 (FAO); industrial development, 637 (ECLAC/UNIDO), 581 (UNIDO), industrial property, 1278 (WIPO); international trade/finance, 533, 635 (ECLAC); natural resources, 637 (ECLAC); political and security questions, 557-74; population, 638 (ECLAC), 721 (UNFPA); pre-disaster planning, 521 (UNDRO/ECLAC); science and technology, 637 (ECLAC/Vienna Programme), 685 (UNFSSTD); SIDFA Programme, 573; social/cultural development, 637-38 (ECLAC); statistics, 638 (ECLAC); technical co-operation, 436 (UNDP/ECLAC), 636 (CELADE/ECLAC/ILPES), 1217 (UNESCO); & TNCs (ECLAC/Centre); transport, 636 (ECLAC); volunteer programme, 457 (UNV); natural/water resources, 637, 645 (ECLAC/UNRFNRE); *see also* Americas; Caribbean region; Central America; Economic Cs. for Latin America and the Caribbean; human rights violations; *and country names*

Latin America, Treaty for the Prohibition of Nuclear Weapons in, *see* Nuclear Weapons in Latin America, Treaty for the Prohibition of (Treaty of Tlatelolco, *1967*)

LATIN AMERICA AND THE CARIBBEAN, EXTERNAL TRADE DATA BANK, 638 (ECLAC)

LATIN AMERICA AND THE CARIBBEAN, FAO CF. FOR, 1207; Buenos Aires Declaration, 1207; Quito Declaration *(1984)*, 389

LATIN AMERICA AND THE CARIBBEAN, 3RD REGIONAL INTERGOVERNMENTAL MEETING ON THE ENVIRONMENT, 747 (UNEP Cl.)

LATIN AMERICA ECONOMIC SYSTEM: Santo Domingo Pledge, 635

LATIN AMERICAN DEMOGRAPHIC CENTRE (CELADE), 636, 638 (ECLAC/UNFPA)

LATIN AMERICAN ECONOMIC CF., 635; Declaration/Action Plan, 389, 635

LATIN AMERICAN ENERGY ORGANIZATION, 635 (Quito Declaration); & UNIDO, 661

LATIN AMERICAN INSTITUTE FOR ECONOMIC AND SOCIAL PLANNING (ILPES): Technical Sub-Ct., 635; & TNCs, 596 (ECLAC/Centre)

LATIN AMERICAN INTEGRATION ASSOCIATION (ALADI), 636

LATIN AMERICAN MINING AGENCY: articles of association, 637

law, *see* adoption law; international law; international trade law

law of the sea, 108-13

Amerasinghe Fellowship, 112 (SG); contributions, 1118 (SG)

co-operation in, 109-10 (ACC)

medium-term plan *(1984-1989)*, **306** (GA)

publication programme, 111

SG, Office of Spec. Representative: functions, 111-12

see also exclusive economic zone; land-locked states; marine affairs; territorial sea; *and under* sea; sea-bed

LAW OF THE SEA, INTERNATIONAL TRIBUNAL FOR, 110; draft procedural rules, 111; establishment, 111 (Spec. Cs.); proposed site, 111, 112

LAW OF THE SEA, OFFICE OF THE SPEC. REPRESENTATIVE OF THE SG FOR, 111-12 (GA, 112, **113**); SG/Assistant SG, 1342

LAW OF THE SEA, PREPARATORY CS. FOR THE INTERNATIONAL SEA-BED AUTHORITY FOR, 110-11 (GA, **113**); Credentials/General Cts., 1341 (officers); *1985* mtgs. programme, **306** (GA); members/officers, 1341; Spec. Css., 110-11, 1341 (members/officers); staffing, 110

LAW OF THE SEA, 3RD UN CF. ON THE, 108, **112** (GA)

LAW OF THE SEA, UN CONVENTION ON THE *(1982)*, 4 (SG), 108-13 (ACC, 109-10; GA, 110, **112-13**; SG, 108-9); implementation, 111-12, **306** (GA/SG); legislative history, 111; ratifications/signatures, 108, **112** (GA)

Law of the Sea Bulletin, 111, 112

LEAGUE OF ARAB STATES: co-operation with UN, implementation of *1983* Tunis recommendations, **378-80**, 380 (GA), 378 (SG); food/agriculture, joint mtg., 378, **379** (GA); participation in SC 289, 296, 298, 378 (Lebanon/Iran-Iraq/Middle East); UNEP co-operation, 747

LEAGUE OF RED CROSS SOCIETIES: & WMO cts. (typhoons/cyclones), 520-21

least developed countries, 412-17; assistance, 414 (UNCTAD), 415 (UNDP), **416** (GA); co-ordinator of assistance, appointment, 415; drought/food problems, 413 (SG); economic situation/prospects, 413 (SG); export promotion, 414 (UNCTAD), 534 (ITC); human settlements, 776; identification, 413, 416-17; industrial development, 415 (UNIDO), 559, 561 (UNIDO IV), 576 (IDB); inter-agency consultations, 414 (ACC); ODA targets, 413 (DAC/UNCTAD); postal services development, 666 (UPU); publication, 414; spec. measures, 415 (UNCTAD); & trade preferences, 531 (Spec. Ct.); & UNCDF projects, 461; *see also under* Africa: least developed countries; economic assistance; island developing countries; land-locked developing countries

LEAST DEVELOPED COUNTRIES, INTER-GOVERNMENTAL GROUP ON (UNCTAD), 414 (ACC), **415** (GA)

LEAST DEVELOPED COUNTRIES, 2ND MTG. OF MULTILATERAL AND BILATERAL FINANCIAL AND TECHNICAL ASSISTANCE INSTITUTIONS WITH REPRESENTATIVES OF (UNCTAD), 414, **416** (GA); 3rd Mtg. *(1985)*, 414

LEAST DEVELOPED COUNTRIES, SPEC. MEASURES FUND FOR THE (UNDP), 413 (SG); contributions/expenditures, 414, 415, 435 (UNDP)

LEAST DEVELOPED COUNTRIES, SUBSTANTIAL NEW PROGRAMME OF ACTION FOR THE 1980S: country review mtgs., 413-14 (SG), 414 (UNDP/World Bank), **416** (GA); implementation, 413-16 (ACC, 414; CDP,

primary health care *(cont.)*
  see also children; diseases; health; nutrition; *and under* drugs
PRIMARY HEALTH CARE, CT. OF THE HEALTH RESOURCES GROUP FOR: 4th mtg., 1220
prisoners
  alternatives to prison/social resettlement, 711, **711** (ESC/SG)
  Standard Minimum Rules for treatment of *(1955)*: implementation, 704-8 (ESC, 704, **705-7**; GA, 707, **707-8**; SG, 704); *see also* detainees; extradition of Ziad Abu Eain; human rights in emergency situations; summary executions; territories occupied by Israel; torture and other cruel treatment; women; youth
prisoners of war, *see under* Geneva Conventions
privileges and immunities, 1158, **1158-59** (FICSA/SG/GA)
PRIVILEGES AND IMMUNITIES OF THE UNITED NATIONS, CONVENTION ON, 1158
Programme and Co-ordination, Ct. for, *see* Co-ordination, Ct. for Programme and
programme planning, UN, 1137-46
  budgeting: cross-sectional programme analysis, 1141 (CPC/SG); documentation, 1142-43 (CPC/SG, 1142-43; ESC, **974**, 1143; GA, **1138**, 1143); performance report *(1982-1983)*, 1142 (CPC/SG, 1142; ESC, **973**, 1142; GA, **1138**, 1142)
  co-ordination, 1137-38 (CPC, 1137; ESC, **972-73**, 1137; GA, **1138**, 1138-39)
  evaluation, 1143-46; inter-governmental reviews, **1138**, 1143-44 (GA/ASG); strengthening UN units, **1138**, 1143 (GA/CPC/SG); *see also* Joint Inspection Unit
  medium-term plan *(1984-1989)*, 1139-41; addenda, 1141 (ACABQ/SG); revisions, 1140-41 (CPC, 1140; ESC, **973**, **1140**, 1140; GA, **1138**, 1140-41; SG, 1140)
  priority setting, 1139 (CPC/SG, 1139; ESC, **973**, 1139)
  rules/regulations, 1139 (SG)
  & UN financial rules, **374**, 1139 (ACABQ/GA/SG)
  see also co-ordination in UN system; work programme (UN)
prostitution: conventions, 843-44 (Working Group/SCPDPM); *see also* slavery/slavery-like practices; *and under* women
protectionism, *see under* international trade
psychotropic substances, 957 (SG); guidelines for exemptions, 966 (Narcotic Drugs Cs.); scheduling, 965, **965-66** (ESC/Narcotic Drugs Cs.); traffic in, draft convention, 961, **962-65**
PSYCHOTROPIC SUBSTANCES, *1971* CONVENTION: implementation, 955, 965 (INCB); States parties, 965
public accounting, *see* accounts (UN) *and entries following* audit/auditing
public administration and finance, 408-9 (DTCD/Experts' Mtg.), 455 (DTCD); co-ordination of activities, 409; *1984-1985* programme budget, 409; *see also* taxation
PUBLIC ADMINISTRATION AND FINANCE, UN PROGRAMME IN, 7TH MTG. OF EXPERTS ON, 409, **409** (ESC/SG)

public information (UN system), 356-63 (GA, **356-63**; Information Ct., 356); co-ordination in UN system, 366-67 (CPC/Information Ct./SG, 367; GA, **353**, **357**, 367; JUNIC, 366); & Palestine question, 274-75 (GA, **274**, 274-75; Palestinian Rights Ct., 274); UNEP Desertification Campaign, 749; *see also Development Forum*; Disarmament Campaign, World; new world information and communication order; news agencies; radio broadcasting; television broadcasting; *Yearbook of the United Nations*; *and under* apartheid, information *and other topics*
PUBLIC INFORMATION, DEPARTMENT OF (DPI) (Secretariat), 363-66 (Information Ct.); evaluation, 365-66 (Information Ct./SG); liaison services, **362** (GA); official languages, 364 (Information Ct.); staff, geographical distribution, 363; Under-SG, 1342; *see also* Information Centres (UN); Radio and Visual Services Division; television broadcasting
Puerto Rico, 1017 (Colonial Countries Ct.)

racial discrimination/racism, elimination of: measures to combat, 788-89 (ESC, **788-89**, 789; Human Rights Cs., 788); spec. study *(1976)*, proposed update, 785; studies, proposed publication, 788, **791** (CERD/GA); *see also apartheid*; discrimination; minorities
RACIAL DISCRIMINATION, CT. ON THE ELIMINATION OF (CERD), 789-90, **790-91** (GA); co-operation with TC, 790, **791** (GA), 1025-26; members/officers, 1340
RACIAL DISCRIMINATION, 1ST DECADE FOR ACTION TO COMBAT RACISM AND *(1973-1983)*: implementation, 784 (Human Rights Cs./SG), **785** (ESC)
RACIAL DISCRIMINATION, INTERNATIONAL CONVENTION ON THE ELIMINATION OF ALL FORMS OF *(1965)*: accessions/ratifications, 789, **789** (GA/SG); implementation, 789-92 (CERD, 789-90; communication, 789; GA, **790-91**, 791-92); reporting obligations, 790 (CERD) violations, CERD competence, 790
RACIAL DISCRIMINATION, INTERNATIONAL DAY FOR THE ELIMINATION OF, 1000, 1215 (UNESCO)
RACIAL DISCRIMINATION, 2ND DECADE FOR ACTION TO COMBAT RACISM AND *(1983-1993)*: Action Programme, implementation, 784-88 (CERD/SCPDPM, 787; ESC, **785-86**, 786-87; GA, **787-88**, 788; Human Rights Cs., 784; SG, 785); activities *(1985-1989)*, SG draft plan, 785, **785-86** (ESC); UNESCO/DPI action, 785
radiation: dosimetry, 1194 (IAEA/WHO); effects of, 368-69 (GA, **369**; UNSCEAR, 368); protection/emergency planning, 1193-94 (IAEA; symposium, 1193 (IAEA/WHO)
RADIATION, UN SCIENTIFIC CT. ON THE EFFECTS OF ATOMIC (UNSCEAR), 368, **369** (GA); members/officers, 1326
RADIATION PROTECTION, BASIC SAFETY STANDARDS FOR (IAEA/ILO/WHO), 1193

radioactive waste management, 663, 1192-93 (IAEA); IAEA/WHO annual, 1193; *see also* marine environment; oceans; sea-bed mining; Pacific Islands Trust Territory (Micronesia)
RADIOACTIVE WASTE MANAGEMENT, INTERNATIONAL CF. ON *(1983)*, 1193
RADIO AND TELEVISION ORGANIZATIONS OF AFRICA, UNION OF NATIONAL: co-operation with DPI, 364 (Information Ct.)
RADIO AND VISUAL SERVICES DIVISION (DPI), 361 (GA), 364 (Information Ct./SG)
radio broadcasting, 361 (GA); administrative cfs., 1264; consultative cts., 1264; frequency allocation, 1264-65 (ITU); 1264-65 (IFRB); regional organizations, 1215 (UNESCO); short wave networks, 361 (GA), 364 (Information Ct./SG)
RADIO CF., WORLD ADMINISTRATIVE (WARC), 1264 (ITU); *1979* Cf., implementation, 1264-65 (IFRB); *1985* Cf., preparations, 1264 (CCIR); scientific/technical criteria for, 103 (COPUOS)
RADIO CONSULTATIVE CT., INTERNATIONAL (CCIR), 1264 (ITU): Preparatory Meeting, *1985* WARC, 1264
radiological weapons, 62-63, **63** (CD/GA)
RADIOLOGICAL WEAPONS, *Ad Hoc* Ct. (CD): establishment, 13, 62, **63** (CD/GA)
railways: European network, draft, 630 (ECE); World Bank loans, 1232
raw materials: processing, 580 (UNIDO Cf.); *see also* natural resources
Reactor Workshop, International Tokamak (INTOR), *see under* nuclear fusion
Red Cross, International Ct. of the, *see* International Ct. of the Red Cross
Red Cross Societies, League of, *see* League of Red Cross Societies
Red Sea: mining of, 109 (SG); regional seas programme (UNEP), 747, 766
refugees/displaced persons, 4 (SG), 716 (Population Cf.), 935-54
  assistance, 939-41 (UNHCR); development-oriented, 936, **937**, 939 (Executive Ct./GA); General/Spec. Programmes, 937; expenditures by country/area, 940-41 *(table)*
  asylum-seekers/&non-refoulement, 936, **937** (Executive Ct./GA), 943 (ICARA II), 953 (UNHCR); & sea rescue, 939
  care/maintenance programmes: expenditures, 939; health programmes, 941 (UNDP/UNICEF); medicines/family planning, 941 (UNFPA/WHO)
  commemorative stamp, 538, 935
  Handbook for Emergencies, 939
  international co-operation to avert new flows of, 966, **966** (Experts Group/GA)
  international instruments, accessions/ratifications, **936-37**, 953 (GA)
  Nansen Medal, award, 935
  programme policy, 935-37 (Executive Ct., 935-36; GA, **936-37**)
  protection, 953-54 (UNHCR); anti-piracy programme, 952, 953; military/armed attacks on refugee camps, 954 (Sub-Ct.); strengthening, 936, **937** (Executive Ct./GA)
  resettlement, 939; mechanisms, 936, 939 (Executive Ct.)
  voluntary repatriation/integration, **937**, 939 (GA/UNHCR)

Working Group/ESC/SG); *see also under*
South Africa
TRADE UNIONS, WORLD FEDERATION OF,
859
traffic safety, *see under* road transport
training and research: diplomacy, 737
(UNITAR); energy, 737 (UNITAR/Italy); environment, 770-71; human settlements,
779; international law, 737 (UNITAR); ILO
world cf. on, proposed, 560 (UNIDO Cf.);
population, 737 (UNITAR); public administration, 599 (TNCs Centre); scholarships, southern Africa, 190, **191** (GA);
trade & development, 572 (UNIDO); &
UNU, 740-41; *see also* fellowships;
human resources; vocational training;
and country names
TRAINING AND RESEARCH, UN INSTITUTE
FOR (UNITAR), 736-40; accounts *(1983)*,
738 (ACABQ/Auditors' Board, 738; GA
1134); Board of Trustees, 736-37, **737**
(GA); contributions, **738**, 738 (GA), 738
(table); Executive Director, 1338, 1343;
income/expenditures, 738; long-term
financing, 739-40 (ACABQ, 740; Board of
Trustees/SG, 739; GA, **739-40**, 740); pub-
lications/study, 737 (SG)
TRAINMAR, interregional maritime
programme, 554 (Ct. on Ship-
ping/UNCTAD)
transboundary air pollution, *see* air pollution
transboundary water pollution, *see under*
water problems
TRANSFER OF KNOWLEDGE THROUGH EX-
PATRIATE NATIONALS, 460-461 (UNC-
TAD/UNDP)
transfer of technology, *see* technology
transfer
Transition Assistance Group, UN, *see under*
Namibia question
Transkei, 151 *(Apartheid* Ct.)
transnational corporations (TNCs),
591-600
accounting and reporting standards, 594
(Intergovernmental Experts Group/Cs.)
bilateral/international/regional arrangements, 593-94 (Centre, 593; Cs., 594)
code of conduct (draft), 591-93 (Cs., 591;
ESC, **591-92**; GA, **593**, 593)
definition, 593 (Centre/Cs.)
& development, 597-98 (Centre/Cs.)
& environmental aspects, 769 (UNEP
Centre)
information system, 595-96 (Centre/Cs.)
& new world information/communication
order, 355
public hearings on southern Africa activities, **148-49** (ESC), 149 (*Ad Hoc*
Ct./GA), 595 (Centre/ESC)
& regional css., joint units, 596
register of profits, proposed, 1054 (Symposium on Decree No. 1)
research programmes, 596-97 (Cs./SG)
technical co-operation, 598-99 (Cs.);
financing, 599
toxic substances, revised list, 596
(Centre)
transborder data flows, 598 (Centre/Cs.)
see also under colonial countries;
Namibia; South Africa; *and under*
regional entries
TRANSNATIONAL CORPORATIONS, CS. ON,
591; agenda, *(1985)*, **599-600** (ESC); cycle

of meetings, proposed change, 600
(ESC); co-operation with Information Ct.,
598; Intergovernmental Working Group,
594, 1334; members/officers, 1333-34;
participation of expert advisers, 592
(ESC, 592, **592**; GA, **593**, 593; SG, 592);
reconvened spec. sess., officers, 1334
TRANSNATIONAL CORPORATIONS, UN
CENTRE ON (Secretariat), 594-99
(Cs./SG, 595); Executive Director, 594;
Trust Fund, contributions, 599
TRANSNATIONAL CORPORATIONS IN SOUTH
AFRICA AND NAMIBIA, *AD HOC* CT. ON
THE PREPARATIONS FOR THE PUBLIC
HEARINGS ON THE ACTIVITIES OF, 149,
149 (GA), 1335 (members/chairman)
transport, 550-56, 630-31 (ECE), 636
(ECLAC), 640-41 (ECWA), 623-25
(ESCAP); customs transit for goods
transport international routier (TIR)/Con-
vention, *1975*, 555, **555-56** (ESC); IDA
credits, 1243-44 *(table)*, 1245; and land-
locked developing countries, 418-19;
statistics, ECE Experts Group, 631; terminals, operator liability, 559-60 (SG/UN-
CITRAL); & UNCHS programme, 775;
World Bank loans, 1229-30 *(table)*, 1232;
see also Africa, Transport and Communications Decade in; air transport; Asia
and Pacific, proposed transport and
communications decade; dangerous
goods; inland transport; maritime transport; multimodal transport; ports; railways; roads; shipping; space transportation
transport of dangerous goods, 554-55;
explosives, draft manual, 554-55 (Expert
Group); UN Recommendations, 554 (Expert Ct.)
TRANSPORT OF DANGEROUS GOODS, CT.
OF EXPERTS ON, 554-55, 1335 (mem-
bers/officers); Explosives, Group of Experts, 555, 1335 (chairman); Group of
Rapporteurs, 554, 1335 (officers)
TRANSPORT OF LIQUID HYDROCARBONS IN
BULK, GROUP OF EXPERTS ON INTER-
NATIONAL SEA, 553
treaties, 1107-10; & international organiza-
tions, draft convention, 1108-9 (GA,
1109; ILC, 1108); registration/publication,
1109-10; *see also* multilateral treaties;
States
TREATIES BETWEEN STATES AND INTERNA-
TIONAL ORGANIZATIONS OR BETWEEN
INTERNATIONAL ORGANIZATIONS, UN
CF. ON THE LAW OF *(1986)*, 1108-9;
dates/location, 1108, **1108-9** (GA); par-
ticipants, **1108** (GA)
Treaty Series (UN), 1109-10; backlog, 1176
(Ct. on Cfs.)
TREES, YEAR OF, FOR SOUTH ASIA *(1988)*,
626-27
TROPICAL CYCLONE PROGRAMME (WMO),
1272; *see also under* cyclones
TROPICAL DISEASES, SPECIAL
PROGRAMME FOR RESEARCH AND
TRAINING (WHO), 731
tropical forests: co-operation, 763 (FAO);
management, 762-63 (UNEP);
research/training, 763
tropical timber, 534 (ITC), 539 (UNCTAD)
TROPICAL TIMBER AGREEMENT, INTERNA-
TIONAL *(1983)*: ratifications/signatures,
539, 763 (UNEP)

TROPICAL TIMBER CL., PREPARATORY CT.
FOR THE INTERNATIONAL: Cl./Organiza-
tion, proposed establishment, 539
TRUCE SUPERVISION ORGANIZATION, UN
(UNTSO), 303; Chief of Staff, 303, 1328;
& Observer Group Beirut, 303; & Observer Group Lebanon, 303
**Trust Territory of the Pacific Islands
(Micronesia)**, 1020-24 (Colonial Countries Ct./TC, 1020; GA, 1021); claims,
1023 (TC); economic conditions, 1021-22
(Colonial Countries Ct./TC); education,
1023 (TC); fellowships/scholarships, 1024-
25 (SG/TC); hearings/petitions, 1024 (TC);
information dissemination, 912 (TC/SG);
military bases/installations, 1020
(Colonial Countries Ct.); politics/govern-
ment, 1021 (Colonial Countries Ct./TC);
radioactive waste management, 1023
(TC); self-determination, 1021 (Colonial
Countries Ct./TC); social conditions,
1022-23 (TC); visiting missions, reports,
1023, **1023-24** (TC); *see also* Marshall Islands; Micronesia, Federated States;
Northern Mariana Islands; Palau
TRUSTEESHIP AND DECOLONIZATION,
OFFICE OF POLITICAL AFFAIRS AND
(Secretariat): Under-SG, 1332
TRUSTEESHIP CL. (TC), 1020, 1025-26,
1338-39; Administering Authority, 1020;
agenda, 1351-52 *(list)*; & CERD, 1025-26;
& Colonial Countries Ct., 1025; mem-
bers/officers/sess., 1339
Trusteeship System, International,
1020-26
trypanosomiasis, 731 (WHO)
tuberculosis, 1222 (WHO)
tungsten, 540 (UNCTAD); exploration, 646;
market situation, working group established, 540; publication, 540
TUNGSTEN, CT. ON (TDB), 540; mem-
bers/officers, 1320
Tunisia: & GATT, provisional accession,
1289; & Libyan Arab Jamahiriya, continental shelf dispute, 1083 (ICJ)
Turkey, industrial training, 572 (UNIDO);
see also Cyprus
Turks and Caicos Islands, 1080-81, 1081
(Colonial Countries Ct./GA); general election, 1081; information to UN, 1018
Tuvalu: inclusion in LDC list, consideration,
416-17, **417** (ESC)
TYPHOON CT., 520, 627 (ESCAP/WMO)
TYPHOON OPERATIONAL EXPERIMENT:
evaluation, 520

Uganda: drought aid, 512 (SG), **514-15**
(GA); economic assistance, 494-95 (GA,
494-95, 495; SG/UNCTAD/UNDP, 494-
95); human rights assistance, 848
(Human Rights Cs./SG)
Union of Socialist Soviet Republics
(USSR): acceptance of IAEA safeguards,
663 (IAEA DG)
United Kingdom: NSGT information to
UN, 1018; *see also* Falkland Islands
(Malvinas); Gibraltar
UNITED NATIONS
anniversary (40th, *1985*), preparations: 3
(SG), 382-84 (ESC, **382-83**; GA, **383**,
383-84, 384; Preparatory Ct., 382);
DPI, **360**, 384 (GA); Under-SG for

Index of names

Page numbers in bold-face type indicate resolutions and decisions

Index of resolutions and decisions

[a]Adopted on 10 February to approve the basic programme of work of the Economic and Social Council for 1984 and 1985.

How to obtain previous volumes of the *Yearbook*

Volumes of the *Yearbook of the United Nations* published previously may be obtained in many bookstores throughout the world and also from the Sales Section, United Nations, New York, N. Y. 10017, or from United Nations Publications, Palais des Nations, 1211 Geneva 10, Switzerland. Volumes listed below with an asterisk (*) are special reprints of editions out of print.

Yearbook of the United Nations, 1983
Vol. 37. Sales No. E.86.I.1 $85.

Yearbook of the United Nations, 1982
Vol. 36. Sales No. E.85.I.1 $75.

Yearbook of the United Nations, 1981
Vol. 35. Sales No. E.84.I.1 $75.

Yearbook of the United Nations, 1980
Vol. 34. Sales No. E.83.I.1 $72.

Yearbook of the United Nations, 1979
Vol. 33. Sales No. E.82.I.1 $72.

Yearbook of the United Nations, 1978
Vol. 32. Sales No. E.80.I.1 $60.

Yearbook of the United Nations, 1977
Vol. 31. Sales No. E.79.I.1 $50.

Yearbook of the United Nations, 1976
Vol. 30. Sales No. E.78.I.1 $42.

Yearbook of the United Nations, 1975
Vol. 29. Sales No. E.77.I.1 $35.

Yearbook of the United Nations, 1974
Vol. 28. Sales No. E.76.I.1 $35.

Yearbook of the United Nations, 1973
Vol. 27. Sales No. E.75.I.1 $35.

Yearbook of the United Nations, 1972
Vol. 26. Sales No. E.74.I.1 $35.

Yearbook of the United Nations, 1971
Vol. 25. Sales No. E.73.I.1 $35.

Yearbook of the United Nations, 1970*
Vol. 24. Sales No. E.72.I.1 $35.

Yearbook of the United Nations, 1969
Vol. 23. Sales No. E.71.I.1 $35.

Yearbook of the United Nations, 1968
Vol. 22. Sales No. E.70.I.1 $35.

Yearbook of the United Nations, 1967
Vol. 21. Sales No. E.68.I.1 $35.

Yearbook of the United Nations, 1966*
Vol. 20. Sales No. E.67.I.1 $50.

Yearbook of the United Nations, 1965*
Vol. 19. Sales No. 66.I.1 $50.

Yearbook of the United Nations, 1964*
Vol. 18. Sales No. 65.I.1 $58.

Yearbook of the United Nations, 1963
Vol. 17. Sales No. 64.I.1 $35.

Yearbook of the United Nations, 1962
Vol. 16. Sales No. 63.I.1 $35.

Yearbook of the United Nations, 1961
Vol. 15. Sales No. 62.I.1 $35.

Yearbook of the United Nations, 1960
Vol. 14. Sales No. 61.I.1 $35.

Yearbook of the United Nations, 1959*
Vol. 13. Sales No. 60.I.1 $58.

Yearbook of the United Nations, 1958
Vol. 12. Sales No. 59.I.1 $35.

Yearbook of the United Nations, 1957*
Vol. 11. Sales No. 58.I.1 $58.

Yearbook Volumes 1-36 (1946-1982) are now also available in microfiche at the cost of $US 1,382.00 for silver halide or $US 1,209.25 for diazo duplication. Orders for microfiche sets should be sent either to the Sales Section, United Nations, New York, N. Y. 10017, or to United Nations Publications, Palais des Nations, 1211 Geneva 10, Switzerland.

Yearbook of the United Nations, 1984

Volume 38   Sales No. E.87.I.1

Compiled by the Yearbook Section of the Department of Public Information, United Nations, New York. Although the *Yearbook* is based on official sources, it is not an official record.

Chief Editor: James A. Beresford Lubin.

Senior Editors/Writers: Hiroko Kimura, Christine B. Koerner.

Editors/Writers: Elizabeth G. Baldwin, Eliane Freeman, Kathryn Gordon, Donald Paneth, Juanita J. B. Phelan, Alexander Taukatch.

Contributing Editors/Writers: J. Kendrick Anderson, Frank Barabas, Keith Beavan.

Copy Editor: Alison M. Koppelman.

Indexer: Elaine P. Adams.

Editorial Assistants/Production Staff/Typesetters: Sunita Chabra, Georgina Kettles, Minnie N. Roque, Joyce B. Rosenblum, Leonard M. Simon.

NOTES

NOTES

NOTES

NOTES

NOTES

NOTES

NOTES